Map Locator

Russia
74
68
Finland
Est.
Latvia
Belarus
70
Ukraine
99
Mongolia
78
80
Beijing-Tianjin
80
81
N. Korea
82
Uzbekistan
Kyr.
Geo.
Turkey
Turkmen.
Taj.
Shanghai
80
S. Korea
Seoul
81
Japan
Tokyo-Yokohama
83
Syria
Iraq
Iran
Afghanistan
98
China
84
108
102
Pakistan
96
Nepal
92
Osaka-Nagoya
83
Egypt
Saudi Arabia
Oman
India
Bang.
86
85
Taiwan
ASIA
77
95
Myanmar
Laos
94
Hong Kong
87
100
Yemen
Sudan
Thai-land
88
Manila
88
CENTRAL PACIFIC OCEAN
136
Cam.
Vietnam
Philippines
90
Somalia
Ethiopia
Sri Lanka
Cent Afr. Rep.
118
Malaysia
Uganda
Kenya
Singapore
89
Dem. Rep. of the Congo
Indonesia
91
89
Tanzania
128
Papua New Guinea
89
119
E.Timor
Malawi
Zambia
125
134
Fiji
137
Zimb.
Mozambique
Madagascar
125
Mauritius and Réunion
130
137
New Caledonia
Botswana
122
124
Witwatersrand
Brisbane
134
South Africa
124
Cape Region
124
Perth
130
131
133
Sydney
134
135
Auckland
135
AUSTRALIA
127
Melbourne
132
132
Wellington
135
New Zealand

Central Europe
Sweden
Lith.
Denmark
Rus.
U.K.
52
Poland
Neth.
Berlin
42
Germany
54
Belgium
56
Lux.
58
Paris
30
Czech Rep.
Slovakia
60
Vienna
51
Austria
Hungary
France
Switzerland
Rom.
Slovakia
64
62
Croatia
Bos. and Herz.
Monaco
62
Italy
Yugoslavia (Serb. & Mont.)
Spain
FYROM
Alb.

Europe
Norway
Sweden
Finland
31
40
Saint Petersburg
69
31
Helsinki
39
Russia
Oslo
38
Est.
33
Copenhagen
39
Stockholm
39
Moscow
69
Latvia
Den.
Lith.
Ire.
34
U.K.
42
32
72
36
Belarus
London
30
Neth.
Poland
44
Belg.
Germany
Ukraine
Czech.
France
Switz.
Hun.
Mol.
Aus.
Budapest
51
Romania
Georgia
46
Cro.
Istanbul
103
Lisbon
47
Port.
Italy
Bos.
Yugo. (S.M.)
Bul.
50
Spain
Madrid
47
Barcelona
47
65
Vatican City
65
FYROM
Turkey
Alb.
Greece
112
112
112
Athens
49
48
104
Syria
Cyprus
Leb.
105
Malta
48
Morocco
Isr.
Algeria
Tunisia
113
Jor.
Libya
Egypt
Saudi Arabia

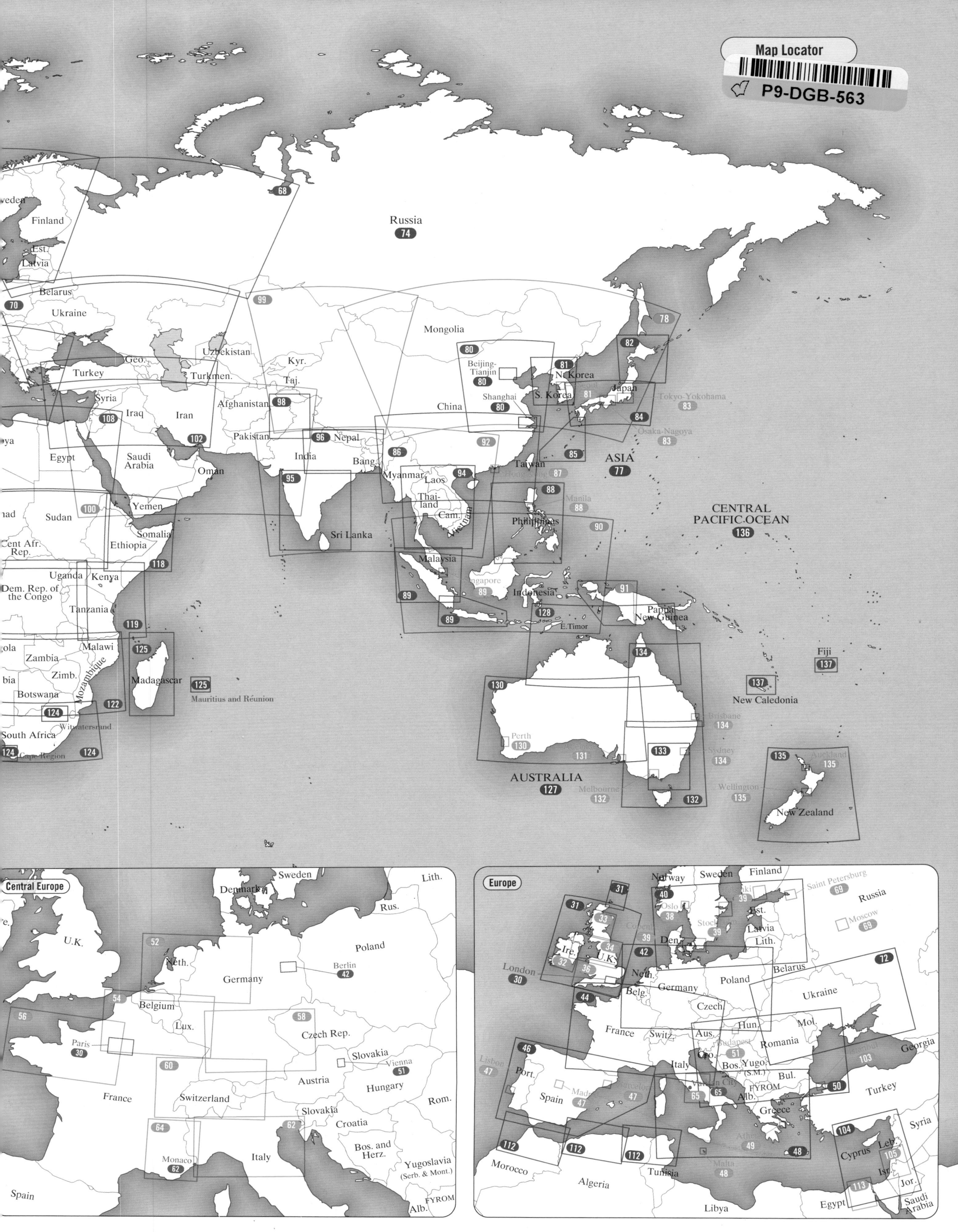

HAMMOND
WORLD
ATLAS

> " **What I love is near at hand,**
> **Always, in earth and air.**"

Theodore Roethke
The Far Field, 1964

HAMMOND
WORLD ATLAS

HAMMOND World Atlas Corporation
Mapmakers for the 21st Century

15°

20°

25°

30°

35°

40°

45°

50°

55°

60°

Publisher	Hammond World Atlas Corporation
Chairman	Andreas Langenscheidt
President	Stuart Dolgins
Director of Cartography	Vera Benson
Director Sales Administration	Charles L. Koch
Director Database Resources	Theophrastos E. Giouvanos
Cartography	Sudha Govindaraju Janice Hulik Walter H. Jones Jr. Sharon Lightner Harry E. Morin Andrew J. Murphy James Padykula Thomas J. Scheffer
Media and Production	Susan Miskewitz John A. DiGiorgio
Technology	Barry A. Moraller
Cover Design	Yang Zhao
Map Text Blocks	Helmut Vieser; Klartext Journalistenbüro, Stuttgart
Map Layout Graphics	Dipl.-Ing. (FH) Jörg Radtke

Thematic Section

Conception and Editorial Supervision	Dr. Eva Maria Brugger
Writers	Dr. Joachim Born, Technische Universität Dresden Dr. Eva Maria Brugger, Heidelberg Prof. Dr. Eckart Ehlers, Universität Bonn Dr. Horst Eichler, Universität Heidelberg Dr. Gernot Gruber, Wiesbaden Prof. Uwe Jäschke, Hochschule für Technik und Wirtschaft Dresden Wolfhard Keimer, Dossenheim Prof. Dr. Wilhelm Lauer & Daud Rafiqpoor, Universität Bonn Prof. Dr. Franz-Dieter Miotke, Garbsen Prof. Dr. Stefan Rahmsdorf, Institut für Klimafolgenforschung Potsdam Prof. Dr. Theo Sundermeier, Universität Heidelberg
Layout and Composition	Matthias Hugo; Hugo Grafische Formgebung, Köln
Informational Graphics	Matthias Hugo; Hugo Grafische Formgebung, Köln Joachim Knappe, Hamburg
Cartography	Dipl.-Ing. (FH) Jörg Radtke Dipl.-Ing. (FH) Manuela Lipp Erika Korbien

Satellite Section

Conception and Design Supervision	Dipl.-Geogr. Ellen Astor
Consultation and Photo Procurement	Dr. Lothar Beckel; GEOSPACE, Salzburg
Layout and Composition	Sigrid Hecker / doppelpack, Mannheim

Translation

German to English	John S. Southard
Editorial Assistance	Michael Venhoff Ellen Astor
Technology	Sigrid Hecker Jörg Radtke
Author of Thematic and Satellite Sections	Bibliographisches Institut & F. A. Brockhaus AG

Hammond World Atlas
Fourth Edition

Library of Congress
Cataloging-in-Publication Data

Hammond World Atlas Corporation.
  Hammond world atlas. - 4th ed.
    p. cm.
  Relief shown by shading and gradient tints.
  Includes statistic tables and index.
    ISBN 0-8437-1836-6
    1. Atlases.
    I. Title: World Atlas
    II. Title.
  G1021. H2665   2000
  912--dc21   2002068882

Introduction

Throughout the ages, humankind has been driven by a need to explore. From early on in our history, we recorded our explorations and marked our place in the world through the creation of maps. Although the art and science of cartography have evolved enormously, our sense of wonder at the world around us remains constant. Today, our need to know, and our demand for the latest information and sophisticated cartography, are satisfied with the help of computer technology that enables us to portray our planet with more accuracy, precision, and visual power than ever before.

The work you are holding in your hands is the definitive atlas for our new century. It describes a world of breathtaking beauty and heartbreaking devastation. A world that exists as a benefit to mankind and endures in spite of us. A world of contrasts. A world of mysteries. As you leaf through the evocative maps and fascinating text in this Fourth Edition of the *Hammond World Atlas* you'll experience the excitement of exploration for yourself, of the world and of this book – the culmination of years of painstaking and dedicated labor.

At the heart of the atlas is the outstanding digital cartography that has become synonymous with the Hammond name. In the physical map section realistic computer simulated relief, enhanced with naturalistic coloration, gives a vivid, 3-dimensional impression of the forms and landscapes of the earth. Hypsometric tints for land elevations, and bathymetric tints to depict ocean depths, are used to dramatic effect in the world map section. The map image practically leaps off the page while the clear typography of the nomenclature makes places and other features easy to identify.

If the maps are the heart of the atlas, then the extensive collection of front matter that will capture your imagination is the soul. The maps will help you find your place in the world, while the thematic text and satellite images that precede them will draw you into the planet's mysteries, wonders, and ills. Filled with intellectually stimulating information and compelling photography and graphics, the text in the thematic section guides you through funda-mentals of geography and natural science and will enhance your awareness of the interrelatedness of the earth and all the living things that share its space.

The opulent satellite photography is nothing short of spectacular and further illustrates the concepts presented in the thematic text. Each of these photos, taken from the perspective of space, is accompanied by technical information and description that satisfies the intellectual curiosity of the reader. They offer a greater understanding of the technologies that allow us to explore the world in ways our ancestors never imagined.

You may have picked up this book for its utility – just to look up a place and continue on with your day. You may want to refer to it for research, study, or business. If so, the clear organization and the comprehensive index will make it easy for you to quickly find what you need. Nevertheless, when the human need to explore stirs within you, we invite you to take the time to sit back and let the beauty of the atlas inspire you on a fascinating journey of the intellect and the imagination. We are confident you will find it a rewarding experience.

The Publisher

Table of Contents

Map Locator
Title
Attribution
Introduction
Contents
Map and Photo Credits

Satellite Section

Thematic Section

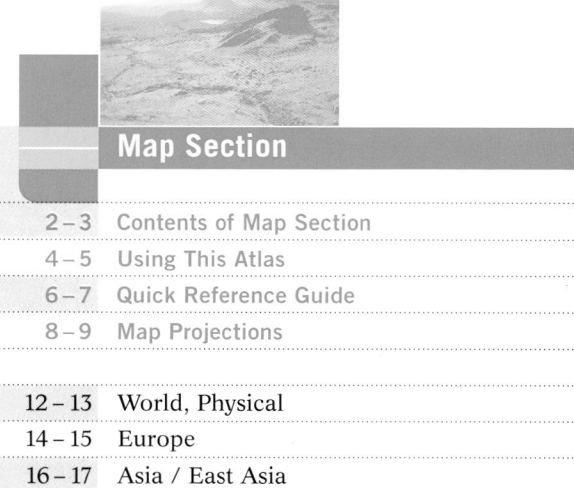

Map Section

Map and Photo Credits

Thematic Section

The Universe – Our Place in Space

"The works of incredible grandeur are as glorious as on the First Day"

Lifting our gaze upward from the earth, we look into space, but we call what we see the sky. Hung there, so it seems, are all the lights that shine upon us – the warming sun during the day, the cool moon, and the twinkling stars at night.
Ages passed before we humans abandoned the concept of an existence beneath an all-encompassing protective sky and dared to venture, intellectually at first, then through experiment, and finally in concrete steps, into the vastness of space, into the world of worlds, into the universe.

A Grain of Sand in the Desert

How can we comprehend a phenomenon like the universe, something we cannot grasp because it is too large, too small, or too far away? Modern science relies on precise observation linked with proven principles to form explanatory hypotheses. If such hypotheses stand up to all theoretical and practical attempts to refute them, they are regarded as true, and we incorporate them into our fund of knowledge.

Applying this method, we have learned that our earth is like a grain of sand in the desert in comparison to the universe. We have also come to realize that earth is not the center of the universe – indeed, that the universe has no center at all. Does that mean that the earth could as easily be somewhere else? In another solar system, another star system, or another galaxy? Theoretically, the answer is yes, but whether there would then be life on earth, or even human beings, is another question altogether.

Ordinarily, being somewhere else means being in a different place and a different environment. Modern cosmology tells us that place or position in the universe is generally inconsequential but that environment is crucial. And the heavenly bodies nearest the earth show that this must be true. Although very different from one another, the moon and our neighboring planets Venus and Mars have one thing in common which distinguishes them from the earth: As far as we know, they are devoid of life.

Galaxies – Structures of the Universe

Aside from the moon, our constant, though changeable companion, the most prominent features of the nighttime sky are stars and a nebulous, luminous band known as the Milky Way. Despite all appearances, this band of light we perceive is a system of stars to which the sun – one of millions upon millions of stars – also belongs, and with it the earth and we ourselves.

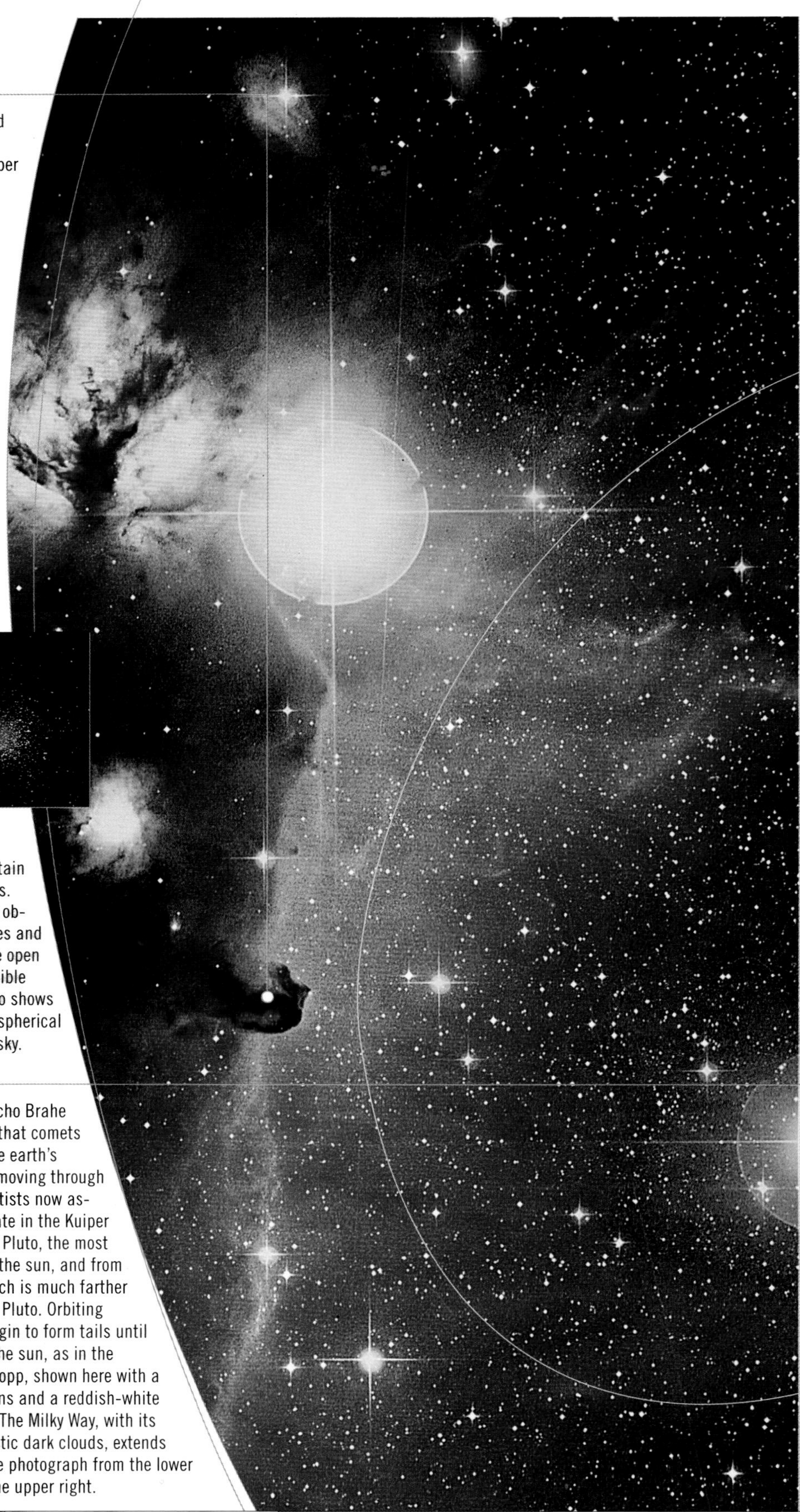

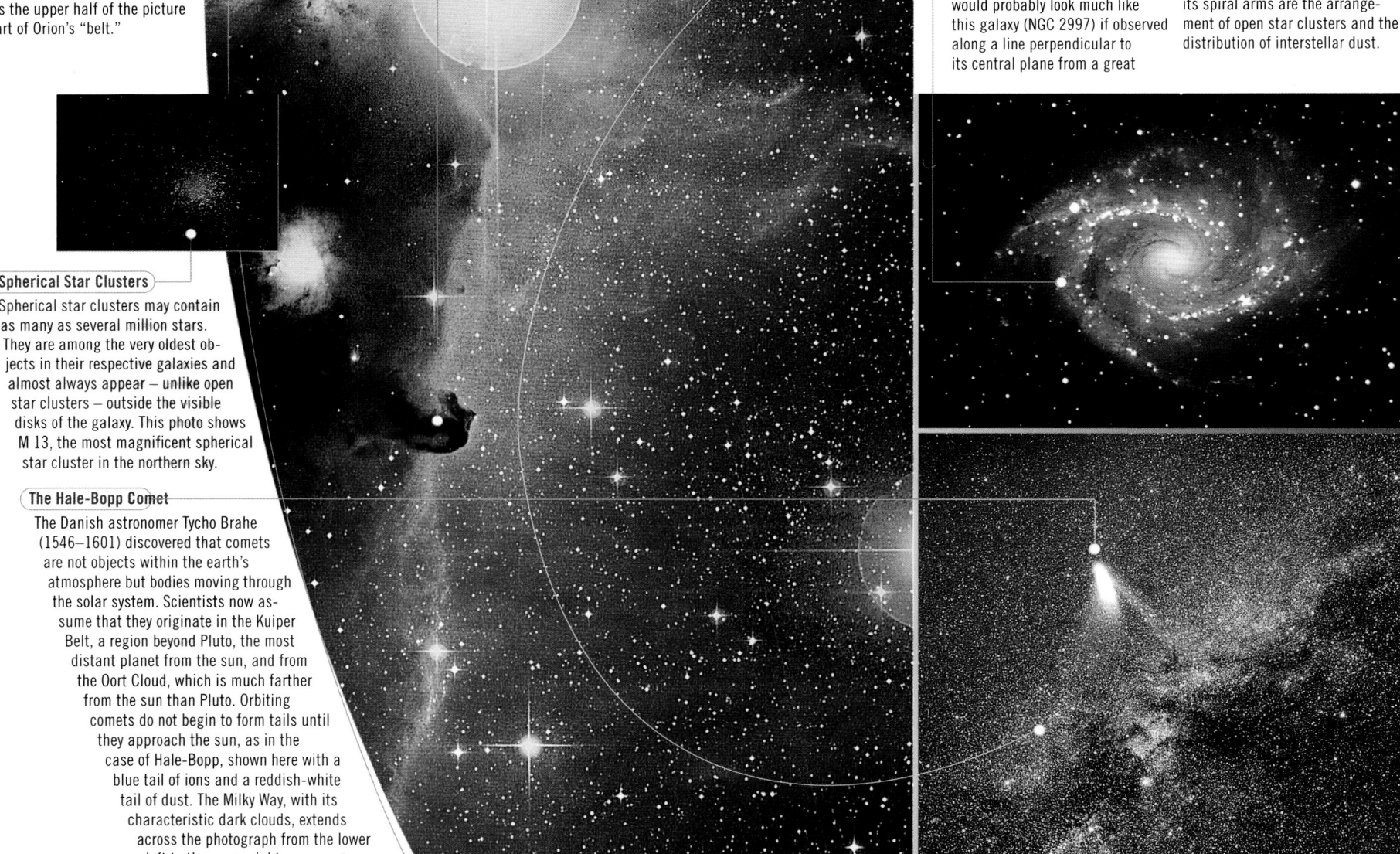

Horsehead Nebula

Named for its shape, a horsehead nebula is an extension of a huge, dark cloud of dust (seen in the upper left-hand portion of the picture) that has expanded in such a way that light from any star positioned behind it cannot penetrate it. The dark cloud covers a nebula that emits reddish light. The only stars visible in the vicinity of the dark cloud are those located in front of it. The reflective nebula of the dust cloud is visible on the left above the "horse's head," where a foreground star (which cannot be seen because it is swallowed up by the light coming from behind it) shines against the wall of dust from the front. The bright star that dominates the upper half of the picture is part of Orion's "belt."

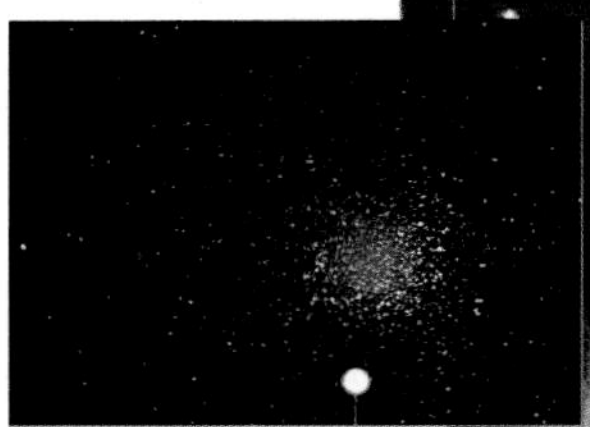

Spherical Star Clusters

Spherical star clusters may contain as many as several million stars. They are among the very oldest objects in their respective galaxies and almost always appear – unlike open star clusters – outside the visible disks of the galaxy. This photo shows M 13, the most magnificent spherical star cluster in the northern sky.

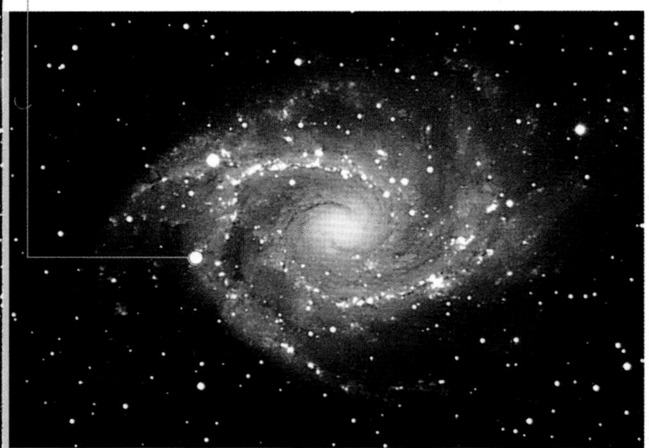

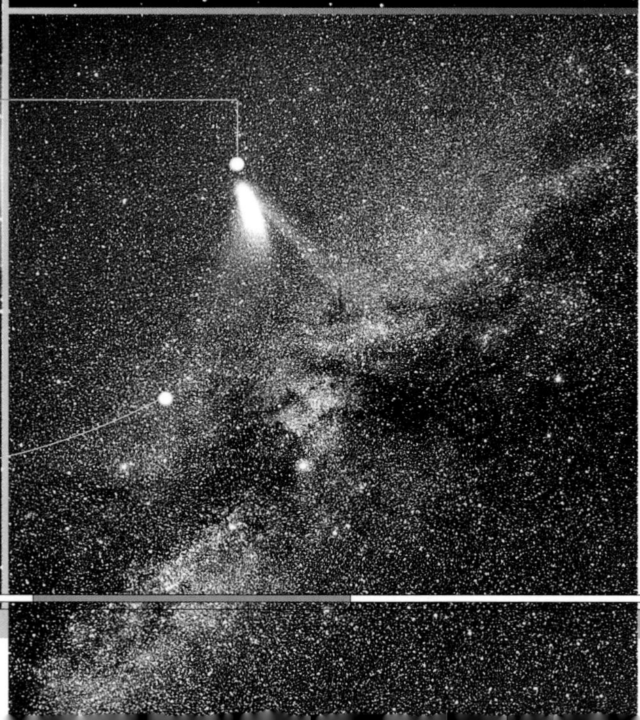

The Hale-Bopp Comet

The Danish astronomer Tycho Brahe (1546–1601) discovered that comets are not objects within the earth's atmosphere but bodies moving through the solar system. Scientists now assume that they originate in the Kuiper Belt, a region beyond Pluto, the most distant planet from the sun, and from the Oort Cloud, which is much farther from the sun than Pluto. Orbiting comets do not begin to form tails until they approach the sun, as in the case of Hale-Bopp, shown here with a blue tail of ions and a reddish-white tail of dust. The Milky Way, with its characteristic dark clouds, extends across the photograph from the lower left to the upper right.

Spiral Galaxy

Our home galaxy, the Milky Way, would probably look much like this galaxy (NGC 2997) if observed along a line perpendicular to its central plane from a great distance. Easily recognizable in its spiral arms are the arrangement of open star clusters and the distribution of interstellar dust.

The idea that the earth and the sun are a part of the Milky Way seems somewhat more plausible if we consider that the band of the Milky Way encircles the earth completely with roughly the same intensity of light at all points. Yet it would be wrong to conclude from this observation that we are located at the center. The sun is actually far from the middle and much nearer to the edge of the system. The insight that the earth is a part of the Milky Way, the luminous band of stars we perceive, leads us to a second, valid conclusion, however: that the stars are very far apart, separated by distances much greater than that between the earth and the sun. The star closest to us, Proxima Centauri, is seven thousand times farther from the sun than Pluto, its most distant planet, which is visible to us only through a telescope.

The universe comprises a multitude of star systems of different types and sizes, generally referred to as galaxies. Astronomers estimate that there are between several hundred billion and several trillion such galaxies. The spiral galaxy closest to earth is 2.2 million light years away. Depending upon their type and size, galaxies may consist of as few as a billion or as many as a trillion stars. Not all of these are single stars but may appear as double or multiple stellar systems and star clusters. We use the term galaxy to distinguish our home star system from all others.

The structural principle of larger objects composed of several or many similar smaller objects can be applied with respect to galaxies to derive the existence of both smaller and larger objects.

Galaxies form galactic groups and galactic clusters which may contain as many as several thousand individual galaxies, and several dozen galactic clusters may form a supercluster. Superclusters are immense cosmic structures, some of which measure more than a million light years across and are separated by equally large voids. A million light years is the distance light travels in one million years (moving at a speed of about 300,000 kilometers per second). Our galaxy and the Andromeda Galaxy are the largest members of a galactic cluster known as the Local Group.

Some stars – including our sun – have their own solar planet systems. Astronomers have determined that there are other planet systems in the Milky Way besides our solar system.

Stars and Interstellar Matter

Galactic matter appears not only in highly condensed form as stars but also as finely distributed particles in clouds of dust and gas which are observed through a telescope as luminous nebulas. There is a very close relationship between this kind of matter, which scientists refer to as interstellar matter because it is distributed between stars, and the early and late phases – the birth and death – in the development of stars. Stars form in and from interstellar matter. The greater their initial mass, the shorter their lifespans and the more forceful and violent their deaths, which often occur in explosions involving the release of huge quantities of gas and dust.

All of the stars we have observed and named as individual objects belong to the Milky Way system. To facilitate their location in the sky, ancient observers of the heavens assigned the visible stars to certain prominent celestial constellations. Since 1933, astronomers have defined constellations as specific rectangular sectors on the celestial sphere, which is divided into eighty-eight such areas.

We notice three things immediately when we gaze at the nighttime sky: that all stars twinkle, that some are brighter than others, and that they appear in different colors ranging from bluish or whitish to reddish-yellow. The twinkling effect is not produced by the stars themselves but by turbulence in the earth's atmosphere, while perceived differences in brightness depend upon the

relative distance of stars from the earth and on such factors as a star's size and temperature. The color of a star is also a function of its temperature and the direction in which it is moving – toward or away from the observer. Stars are categorized within light and spectral classes on the basis of these characteristics.

The fact that stars seem to hang motionless in the sky has to do with their great distance from us. They actually move through space at tremendous speeds, and their positions in the heavens change accordingly over the course of millennia. The constellation we know as the Big Dipper looked much different 100,000 years ago than it does now, and its shape will have changed again in another 100,000 years. Many stars classified as "changeable" exhibit changes in brightness over periods of several days or less, some of them, the novas or supernovas, as a result of massive explosions.

During the greater part of their lives, stars emit energy generated by nuclear fusion in their interiors at temperatures of up to several million degrees Fahrenheit.

The Unity of Nature

We are moved emotionally by the beauty of the heavens. By observing and measuring celestial bodies, we gain insight into the nature of the universe. Through thousands of years of increasingly precise observation of planets, stars, solar systems, and galaxies, we have learned that the laws of nature discovered on earth apply to the universe as well, and this principle has become very useful in the exploration of space. It was the basis for the heuristic hypothesis that the information we obtain about outer space can be explained with the aid of laws of nature discovered on earth – scientific explanation of the universe would be impossible otherwise. This is the theory of the unity of nature.

Particularly useful aids to our study of space are the laws of mechanics, the theory of gravitation, and the laws

of nuclear physics, particularly as they apply to spectral analysis. The currently accepted theory of gravitation is Einstein's General Theory of Relativity. The nature of atoms and their interaction both with one another and with electromagnetic radiation are described by various quantum theories, most notably the theory of quantum mechanics.

By applying the laws of mechanics and the theory of gravitation, we have succeeded in computing the movement of objects in the universe – both man-made and natural objects, from spacecraft to galaxies. The use of spectral analysis in combination with quantum theory has enabled us to explain cosmic structures, from elementary particles to atoms and molecules, and to describe the structures of such bodies as stars, stellar systems, and superclusters. Our capacity to describe and explain covers a broad spectrum of phenomena, beginning with the Big Bang, the earliest phase in the history of the universe, and extending practically to the origin of life on earth. We know that our solar system is five billion years old and that the Milky Way has existed for twelve billion years in a universe that is now fourteen billion years old. And we have learned that the universe and space itself have been expanding since the very first moment of their existence.

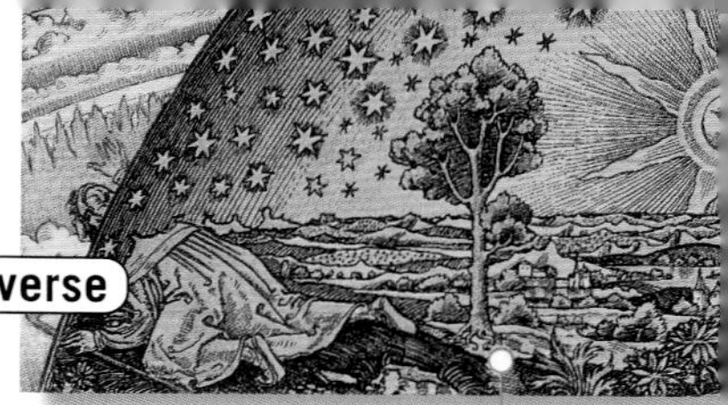

Gazing into the Universe
Breaking away from the medieval concept of the self-enclosed world, represented as an attempt to gaze beyond the sphere of the fixed stars by a late-nineteenth-century artist painting in the style of the period around 1520.

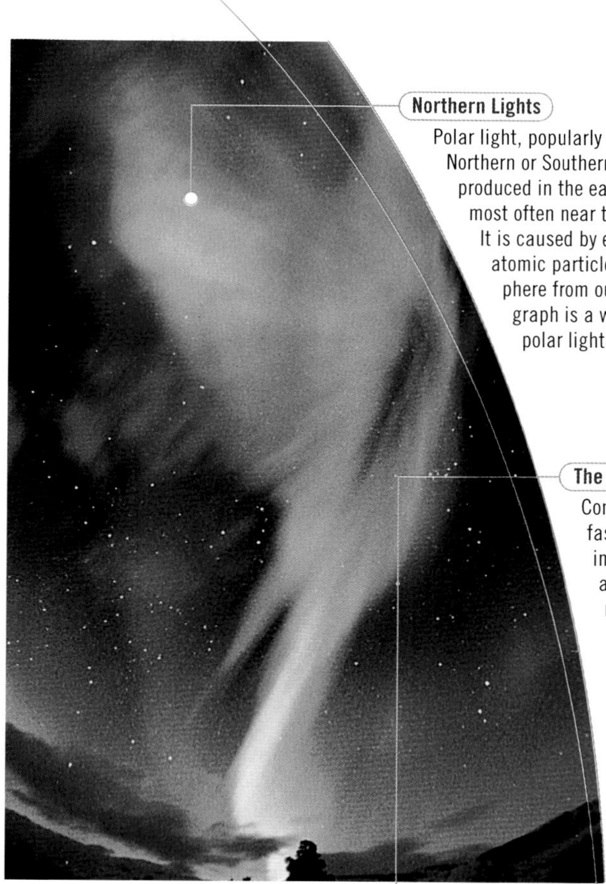

Northern Lights
Polar light, popularly known as the Northern or Southern Lights, is produced in the earth's atmosphere, most often near the polar circles. It is caused by electrically charged atomic particles entering the atmosphere from outer space. The photograph is a wide-angle exposure of a polar light display taken in Norway.

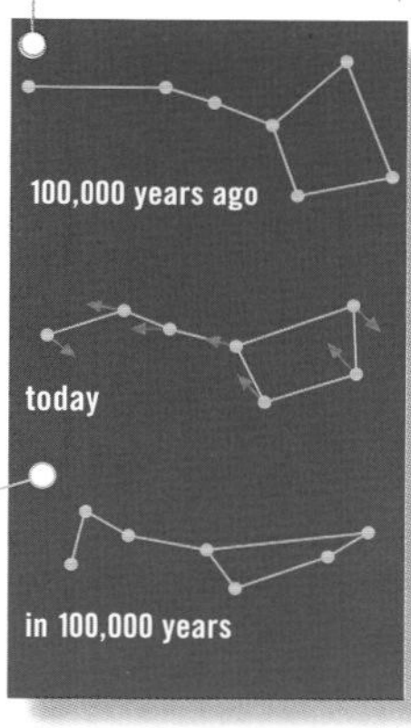

The Big Dipper
Constellations have been a source of fascination to mankind since time immemorial. It was their beauty that attracted Caroline Herschel to astronomy. Although stellar constellations appear fixed and unchangeable to us, they actually do change over long periods of time. The illustration shows how the Big Dipper probably looked 100,000 years ago, how we see it today, and how it can be expected to appear 100,000 years from now.

100,000 years ago

today

in 100,000 years

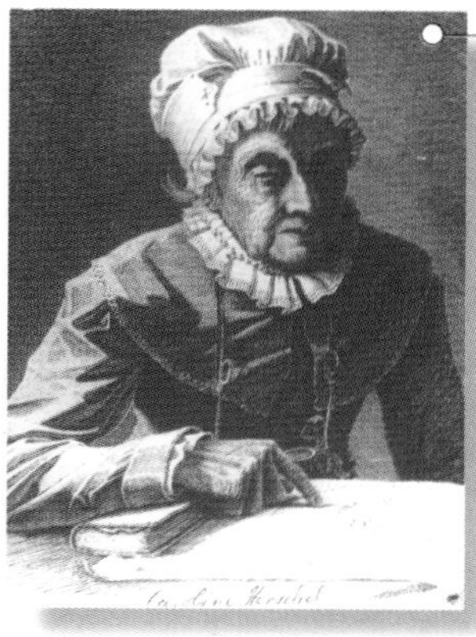

Caroline Herschel
"The object is a comet," she noted in her diary with respect to a new object she had discovered in the sky the night before. The astronomer Caroline Herschel (1750–1848) discovered several other comets during her lifetime. Her contribution helped shape the view of the world accepted by modern astronomers. She was awarded the Gold Medal of the London Astronomical Society in 1828.

The Solar System

Our Home Star and Its Orbiting Planets

The sun is just one star among billions in our galaxy, the Milky Way. The solar system comprises the nine large planets (and their moons), Mercury, Venus, Earth (one moon), Mars (2), Jupiter (16), Saturn (17), Uranus (15), Neptune (8), and Pluto (1) as well as numerous other smaller objects, such as comets, meteorites, and asteroids. Most asteroids are less than 100 km in diameter, and nearly all of their paths pass between Mars and Jupiter. Unlike the stars, the planets, their moons, and the small celestial bodies emit no light and are visible to us only because they are illuminated by the sun.

Seen through a telescope, the planets appear as disks of various sizes. Images transmitted from spacecraft provide information about their surface features. The planets move along elliptical orbits on planes which deviate only slightly from that of the earth's orbit (e.g. 7°, Pluto 17°, Uranus nearly 0°). Puzzled by apparent reversals of direction, ancient and medieval observers were unable to explain the motions of the planets as seen from the earth.

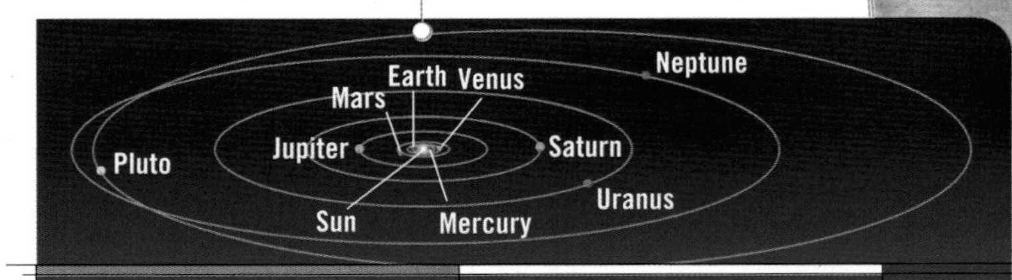

Key Data: The Sun	
Diameter:	1,392,000 km
Mass:	333,000 x earth mass
Mean density:	1.409 g/ccm
Distance from earth:	149.6 mill. km
Time of light travel sun−earth:	8 min 20 s

Key Data: The Moon	
Distance earth−moon:	384,403 km
Mass:	0.0123 x earth mass
Mean density:	3.341 g/ccm
Daytime temp.:	265 °F
Nighttime temp.:	−240 °F

	Mass (x earth mass)	Density (g/ccm)
Mercury	0.055	5.43
Venus	0.815	5.24
Earth	1.000	5.52
Mars	0.107	3.93
Jupiter	318.0	1.33
Saturn	95.1	0.70
Uranus	14.4	1.30
Neptune	17.2	1.76
Pluto	0.002	1.7

Sizes and Distances

Because the inner, "earthlike" planets Mercury, Venus, Earth, and Mars are composed of metals and rock (rock planets), they are relatively dense. The outer, Jovian planets – Jupiter, Saturn, Uranus, Neptune – and Pluto consist primarily of gases (including hydrogen, helium, and methane) and frozen water. The asteroid belt lies between the inner and outer planets. The distribution of light and heavy matter took place during the infancy of the solar system, as lighter materials condensed in the colder outer regions of the system. With the exception of Pluto, all of the other planets (known as giant planets) are considerably larger than the earth. The diameter of Jupiter is eleven times greater than that of the earth, that of Saturn almost ten times greater. The sun's diameter is ten times larger than Jupiter's. A comparison of the masses of the objects in the solar system reveals even more marked differences. Added together, the masses of all nine planets amount to only 13% of the sun's mass, and Jupiter alone accounts for 70% of that total. Relative sizes and distances can be illustrated on the basis of the following example: The distance between the sun and Pluto is 5.9 billion kilometers. If the sun had a diameter of one meter, Pluto would measure two millimeters across, and the distance between the two would be four kilometers.

Born of a Cloud of Dust

Some five billion years ago, a cloud of interstellar dust began to condense, a reaction perhaps triggered by a nearby supernova. As gravitational forces increased, the core of the cloud grew increasingly dense, while the concentration of mass in the center accelerated the system's rotation. Gradually, a flat disk formed, from which the planets later emerged. Temperatures at the center of the disk approached eighteen million degrees F, generating nuclear fusion of the hydrogen atoms. The sun began to radiate. At its core, 655 million tons of hydrogen are converted into 650 million tons of helium every second, while five million tons of matter were transformed into energy. Five billion years from now, when its nuclear energy has been consumed, the sun will enter its final phase, at which point it will turn first into a red giant and later into a white dwarf.

The Earth's Reliable Heater

The sun produces temperatures of up to 27 million degrees F at its core. Pressure at that point is 200 billion times that recorded on the earth's surface. The visible surface of the sun is called the photosphere. It is about 400 km thick and has a mean temperature of 9,900 degrees F. Sunspots form where magnetic-field lines break through the surface. Granules (giant bubbles) measuring about 1,500 km in diameter form on the upper surface of the photosphere and bubble upward. Flames of gas (protuberances) shoot forth from the outer layer (the chromosphere), reaching heights up to tens of thousands of kilometers. The outer atmosphere of the sun (the corona) has very low density and temperatures around 1.8 million degrees F. It extends beyond the photosphere to heights equivalent to several times the radius of the sun.

The Inner Planets

Mercury, the second-smallest planet after to Pluto, is closest to the sun. Humans could not possibly survive its surface temperatures of 780°F during the day and –325°F during the night. The atmosphere (helium, argon) above the moonlike, cratered landscape is extremely thin.

The surface of Venus is not visible from the earth. Thick clouds of carbon dioxide (96%), nitrogen (3%), and trace amounts of water vapor and other gases reflect 65% of the sun's rays, making Venus the third brightest object in the sky, after the sun and the moon. The greenhouse effect caused by its mantle of gases raises the surface temperatures of the planet's craters and lava fields (80%) to temperatures in the range of 850°F. There is no liquid water, and there are no rivers or oceans, only a few dunes.

The distance between the earth and the sun is favorable to life as we know it, and temperatures are neither too high nor too low.

People long assumed that there could be some form of life on Mars – intelligent or at least primitive life. The pattern of lines on the planet's surface thought to be a network of irrigation canals proved to be an optical illusion however, although valleys marked by meanders do suggest that rivers must have flowed through them at one time. The cold crater landscapes of the "Red Planet" (with lows at the poles approaching 300°F) are marked by rocky deserts. The largest shield volcano on Mars is 700 km wide, 25 km high and presumably several hundred million years old.

Predictable Relationships

The planets travel in elliptical orbits on planes which, unlike those of comet orbits, are "tilted" only slightly off the earth's orbital plane. The inner planets, Mercury, Venus, the earth, and Mars, are closest to the sun and receive more warming solar radiation than the distant outer planets, which are accordingly much colder.

Middleweight 2

Seen through a telescope, Uranus appears as a blue-green disk without visible surface features. It was not until 1986 that Voyager 2 provided a more detailed picture, revealing cloud structures, the presence of a magnetic field, and ten previously undiscovered moons. The planet's greater density indicates a composition containing metals heavier than those on Saturn. Its atmosphere consists primarily of hydrogen and helium.

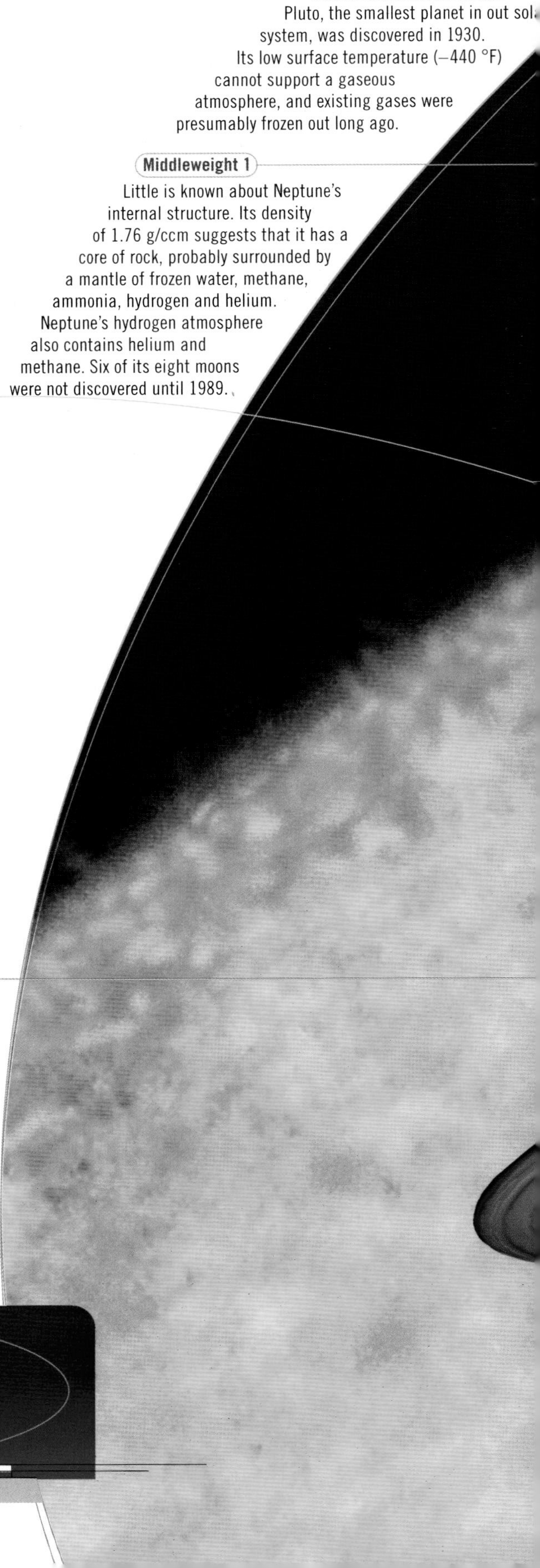

The Smallest of the Group

Pluto, the smallest planet in out solar system, was discovered in 1930. Its low surface temperature (−440 °F) cannot support a gaseous atmosphere, and existing gases were presumably frozen out long ago.

Middleweight 1

Little is known about Neptune's internal structure. Its density of 1.76 g/ccm suggests that it has a core of rock, probably surrounded by a mantle of frozen water, methane, ammonia, hydrogen and helium. Neptune's hydrogen atmosphere also contains helium and methane. Six of its eight moons were not discovered until 1989.

Earth Venus

Mars

Neptune

Pluto

Jupiter

Saturn

Sun Mercury

Uranus

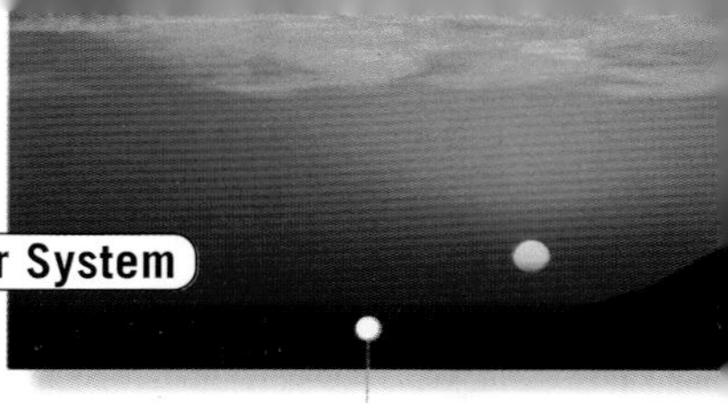

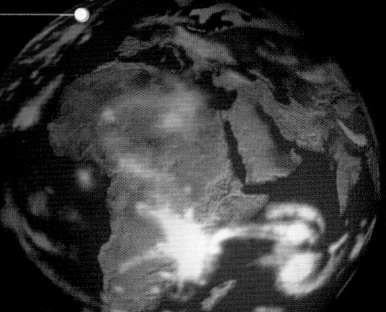

Our Moon

When Astronauts Armstrong and Aldrin took their first steps on the moon on July 21, 1969, they fulfilled an age-old human dream. Since then, plans have been in the making for a manned mission to Mars. Although that goal has yet to be achieved, a number of unmanned spacecraft have explored the depths of space as far away as Neptune.

The Blue Planet

The view from the porthole of a spacecraft shows how lost our planet is in space. Compared with the giant planets or the sun, it seems infinitely small. If mankind is to survive, we must manage our resources wisely. Viewed from outer space, our planet appears predominantly blue.

A Glaring Ball of Fire

Only when the sun is just above the horizon can we gaze at it without protecting our eyes. From this position, sunlight travels farther through the atmosphere, and the energy-laden blue rays are largely filtered out. Looking directly at the sun at midday without protection causes irreparable damage to the retina.

Giant Twins

The rings of Saturn and several of Jupiter's moons are clearly visible through even a small telescope. The giant planets Jupiter and Saturn are so large that the earth is dwarfed in comparison. Like other giant planets, Jupiter also has a system of rings, although it is not as prominent as that of Saturn. Both planets have many moons and are encircled by bands of clouds. Their atmospheres consist of hydrogen, helium and minute admixtures of methane and ammonia. Towards the interior, these gases pass through transitions from gaseous to liquid (on the planet's surface) to solid states (at their cores). The two giants have strong magnetic fields. Io, the innermost planet of Jupiter, became famous through images sent back to earth by Voyager, which provided the first opportunity to observe extraterrestrial volcanic activity. Fountains of lava expelled at speeds of up to 1,000 m/s traveled as high as 300 m above the surrounding areas covered with multi-colored lava and frozen sulfur-dioxide. No older impact craters have been identified.

Mars

Venus

Mercury

Earth

Planet Earth

... and it truly does move!

If we could look from a great distance at the supposedly firm and motionless ground on which we normally stand, we would see that it is anything but motionless. Our Earth is a dynamic celestial body which rotates on its own axis and revolves around the sun. The very point at which we stand moves along a complicated orbit through space.

Dancing on a Volcano

An entirely different kind of motion involving shifts in the positions of points on Earth relative to one another ordinarily takes place unnoticed and so slowly that extraordinarily precise instruments are required to prove that it occurs at all. Yet a time-lapse film in which 10 million years are compressed into a single second would provide striking evidence of how much the Earth's appearance has changed since prehistoric times and become the planet we know today. The key terms used to describe this process are "continental drift" and "plate tectonics." The only effects of these changes we perceive directly are the – often disastrous – earthquakes and seaquakes, frequently followed by massive tidal waves, that frequently accompany movements of the large plates in the uppermost layers of the Earth's crust.

Like our perceptions of the positions and movements of objects in the sky, much of what we experience on Earth – the alternation of day and night, the changing seasons – is caused by the motion of the Earth. The alternation of day and night would seem easy enough to explain: The Earth turns completely around its own axis every 24 hours, and thus every place on Earth experiences a sunrise and a sunset. But wait! There are regions on Earth in which the sun doesn't rise for months and doesn't set

again until more months have passed: the polar zones within the Arctic and Antarctic Circles. These periods of time are referred to as polar nights and polar days.

The cause of both – and for the changing seasons everywhere on Earth – is the fact that the Earth's rotational axis is inclined 23.5 degrees to the plane of the Earth's orbit around the sun. Because the angle of the Earth's axis does not change as it revolves around the sun – its northern extension always points towards the North Star – one hemisphere is always closer to the sun: the northern hemisphere during the northern summer and the southern hemisphere during the northern winter. Only at the spring and fall equinoxes, when days and nights are equally long, are the northern and southern hemispheres exposed to the same intensity of solar radiation.

Moon – Calendar – Clock

The Earth has a constant companion on its journey around the sun – the moon. The movements of the Earth and the moon are the basis for our reckoning of time, the rhythm of our clocks, and our calendar system. The corresponding units of time are days, months, and years – the interval between one arrival of the sun at its zenith and the next; the period between full moons, and the length of time it takes the Earth to complete a full revolution around the sun. Precise astronomical observations are required to measure the lengths of these periods. Ancient astronomers discovered that neither a revolution of the Earth around the sun nor of the moon around the Earth equated to a full number of revolutions of the Earth around its

own axis. There are approximately 365 ½ days in a year and about 29 ½ days in a (lunar) month. That is what makes designing a precise, reliable calendar such a difficult matter. Sophisticated correction systems are required to keep the calendar in step with the movements of the celestial bodies. Depending upon the system in use, these systems involve the addition of additional days or months to the calendar at regular intervals (in leap years, for example).

- Upper mantle
- Lower mantle
- Continental crust
- Oceanic crust
- Outer core
- Inner core

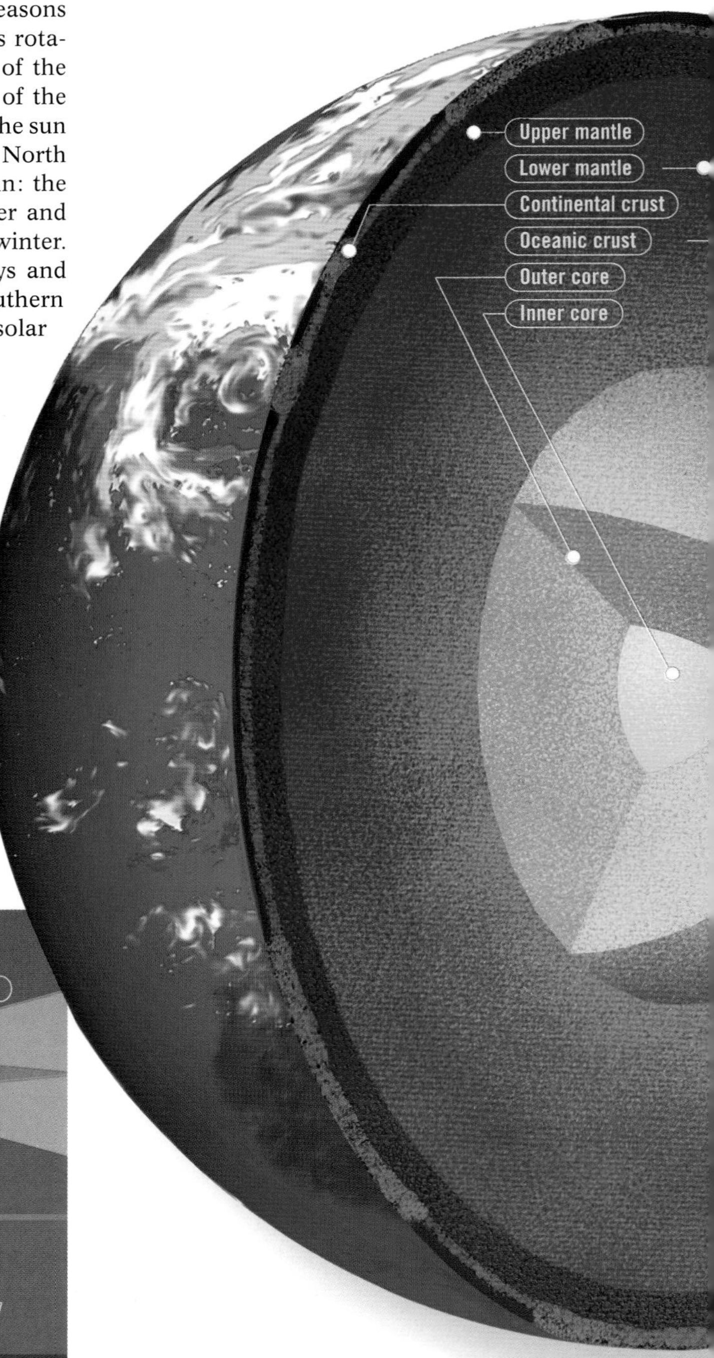

Light and Shadow

During a solar eclipse, the moon passes between the Earth and the sun, whereas a lunar eclipse occurs when the moon moves through the shadow cast by the Earth and thus grows dark. Depending upon their relative positions the sun and the moon may totally or only partially obscured. We can observe a total eclipse of the sun from a place at which the moon's umbra falls. During a total lunar eclipse, the moon is encompassed entirely within the Earth's umbra.

Solar eclipse

Lunar eclipse

Magnetosphere

- Dayside melting
- Plasmasphere
- Melting with Earth's magnetic field
- Plasma layer
- Magnetopause
- Plasmoid
- Van Allen Radiation Belt
- Ring current
- Solar wind magnetic field

Solar wind

Front impact wave

Solar wind magnetic field

Erde

Solar wind

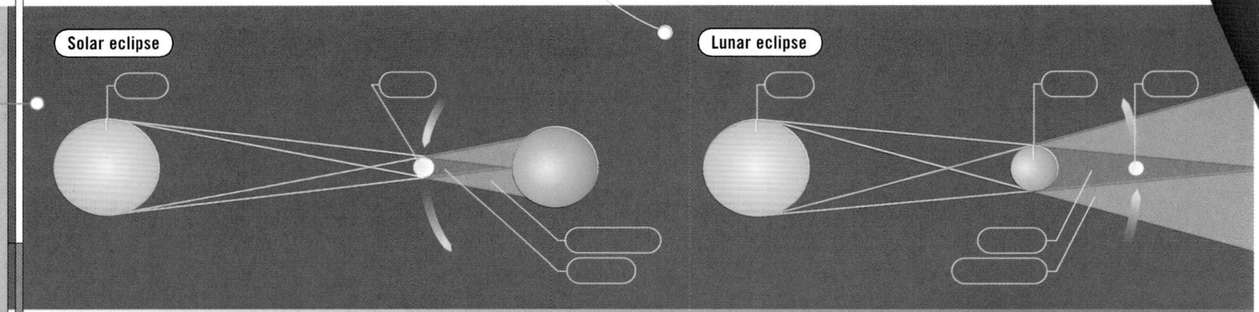

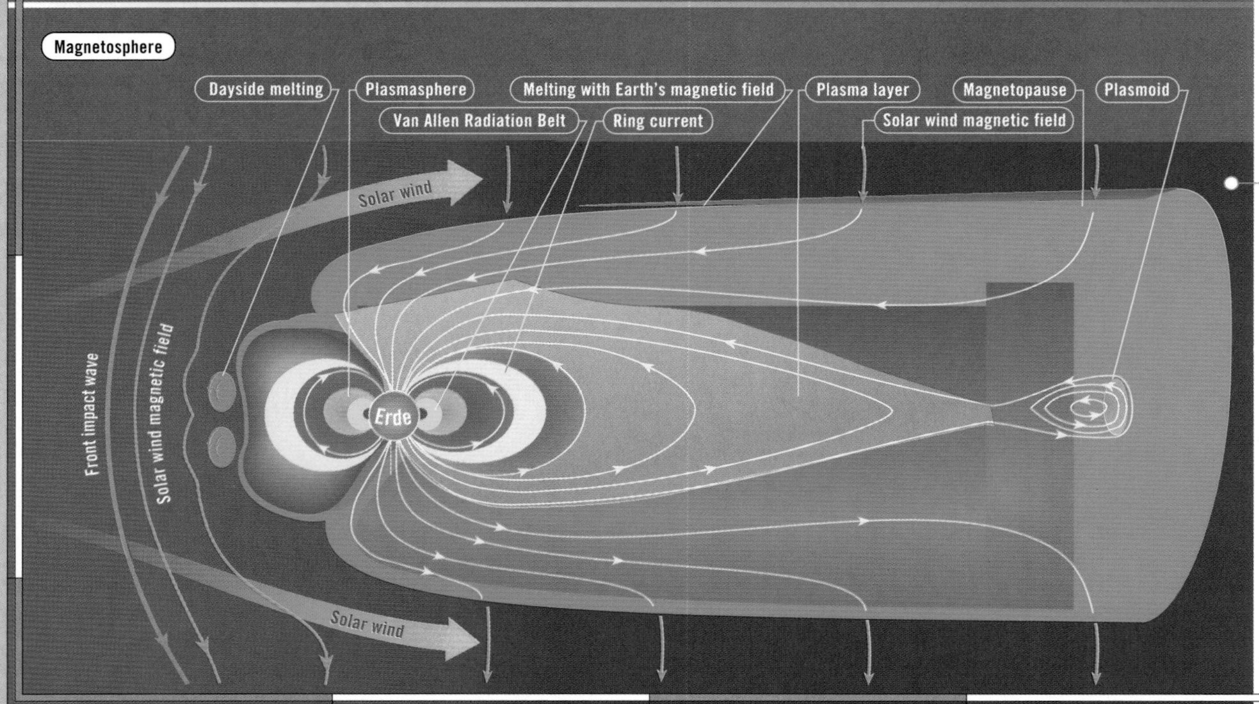

An Invisible Cloak

Generated within the Earth's core, the Earth magnetic field is shaped and limited by solar wind, a stream of electrically charged particles emitted by the sun. The space it encloses is known as the magnetosphere. On the side of the Earth facing the sun, the magnetosphere extends to a distance equivalent to between 10 and 20 Earth radii. On the opposite side of the Earth, it pulls a tail measuring some 1,000 Earth radii in length. In the Van Allen radiation belt, electrically charged particles captured from cosmic radiation by the magnetosphere move back and forth between the Earth's magnetic poles. The term "plasma" denotes a gas consisting of positively and negatively charged particles, whose charges offset one another. Plasmoids are lumps of plasma that are cut off and catapulted from the tail of the magnetosphere.

Occasional corrections to clock time are required, usually in late June and/or late December, for a different reason: the irregular rotation of the Earth. This irregularity was not discovered until the 1930s, following the invention of quarz clocks that were more exact than the Earth's own rotation. These smaller corrections involve the addition of leap seconds.

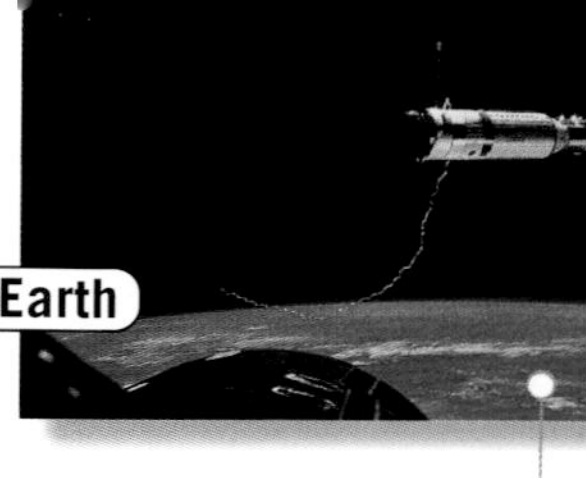

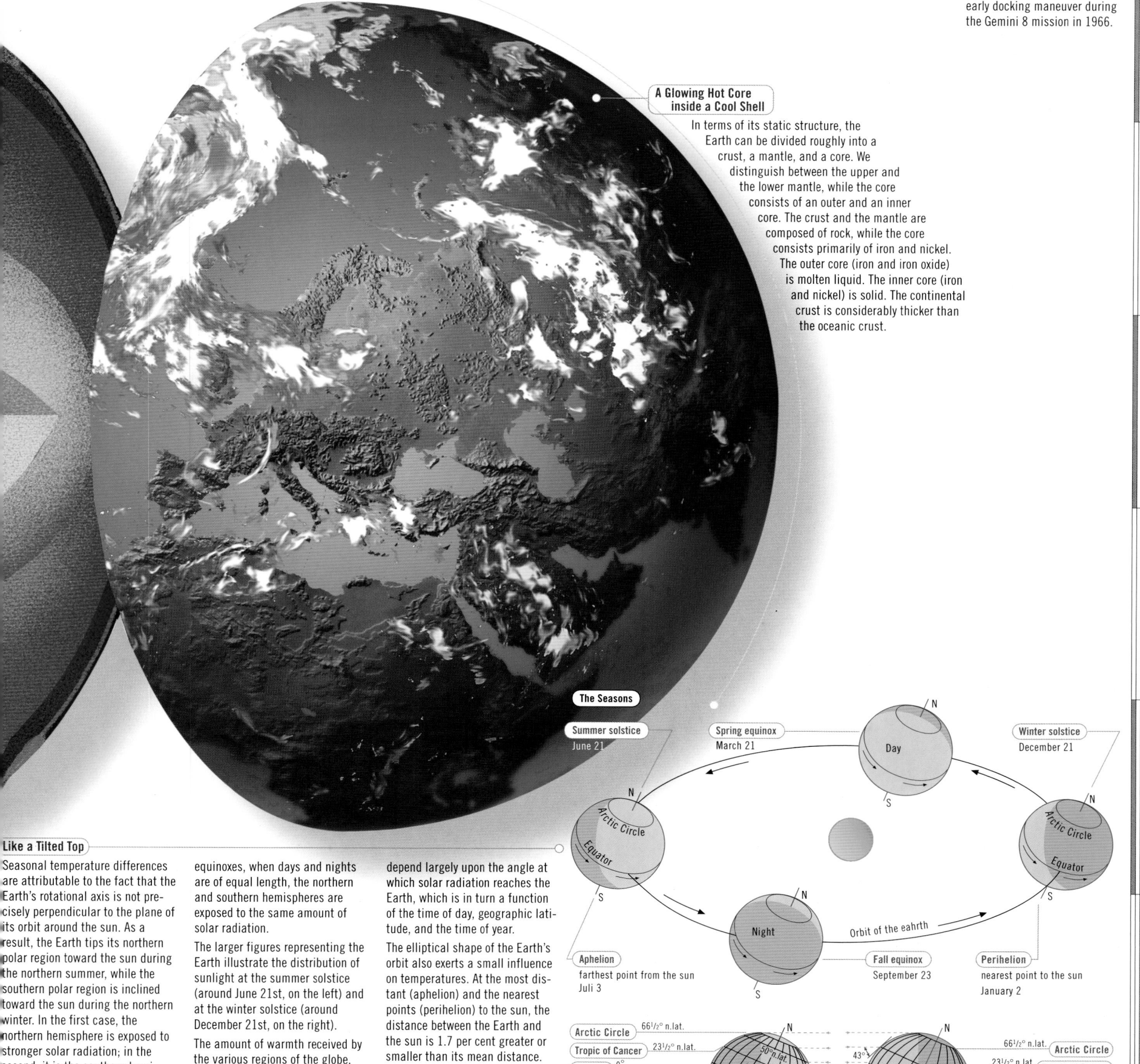

The Earth Seen from Space

Although mankind has long been aware that the Earth is an object in space, like the sun and the moon, people did not truly appreciate that fact until the age of space exploration began in the early sixties. The image shows an early docking maneuver during the Gemini 8 mission in 1966.

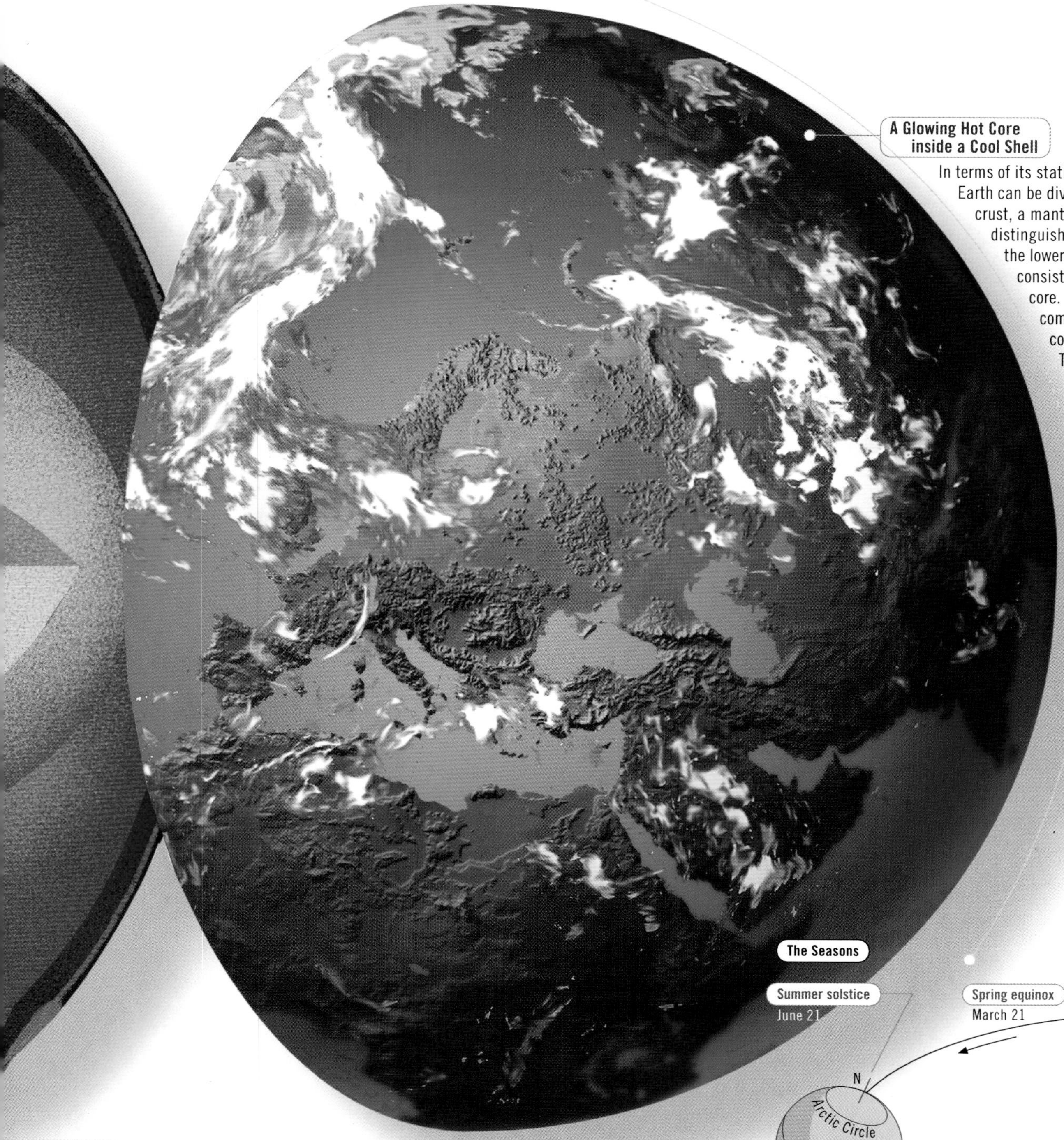

A Glowing Hot Core inside a Cool Shell

In terms of its static structure, the Earth can be divided roughly into a crust, a mantle, and a core. We distinguish between the upper and the lower mantle, while the core consists of an outer and an inner core. The crust and the mantle are composed of rock, while the core consists primarily of iron and nickel. The outer core (iron and iron oxide) is molten liquid. The inner core (iron and nickel) is solid. The continental crust is considerably thicker than the oceanic crust.

The Seasons

Summer solstice
June 21

Spring equinox
March 21

Day

Winter solstice
December 21

N

Arctic Circle

Equator

S

N

S

Arctic Circle

Equator

N

S

Aphelion
farthest point from the sun
Juli 3

Night

N

S

Fall equinox
September 23

Orbit of the eahrth

Perihelion
nearest point to the sun
January 2

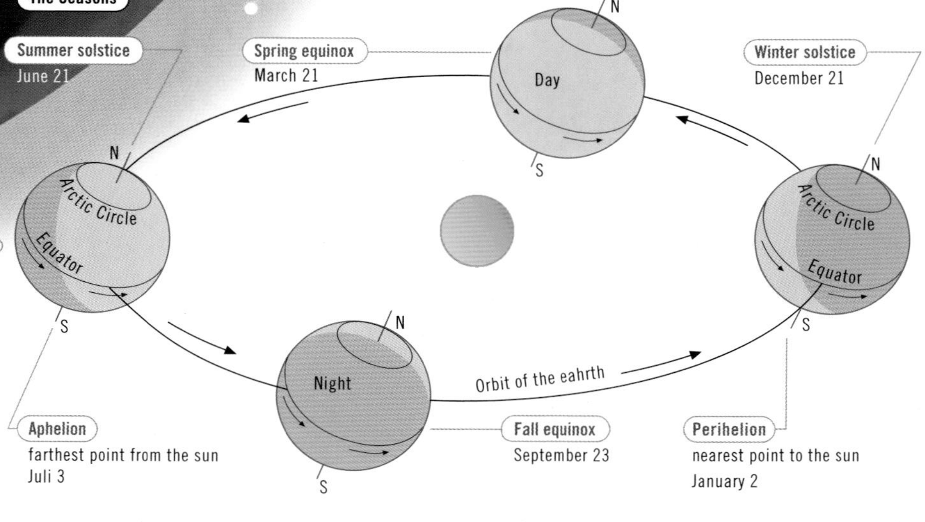

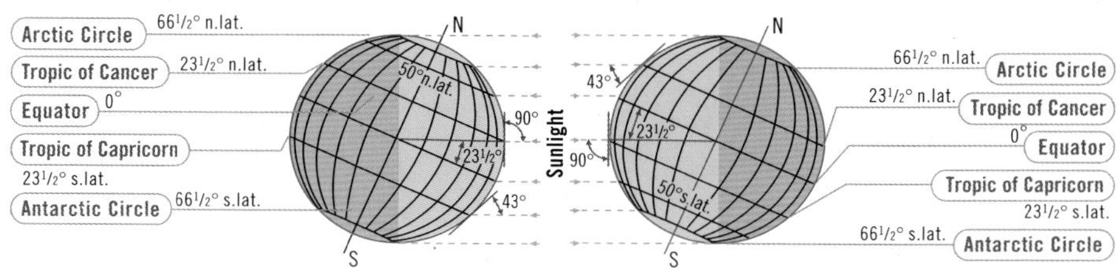

Like a Tilted Top

Seasonal temperature differences are attributable to the fact that the Earth's rotational axis is not precisely perpendicular to the plane of its orbit around the sun. As a result, the Earth tips its northern polar region toward the sun during the northern summer, while the southern polar region is inclined toward the sun during the northern winter. In the first case, the northern hemisphere is exposed to stronger solar radiation; in the second, it is the southern hemisphere that is bathed in warmer sunlight. At the spring and autumn

equinoxes, when days and nights are of equal length, the northern and southern hemispheres are exposed to the same amount of solar radiation.

The larger figures representing the Earth illustrate the distribution of sunlight at the summer solstice (around June 21st, on the left) and at the winter solstice (around December 21st, on the right).

The amount of warmth received by the various regions of the globe, and thus the temperature characteristics of the four seasons,

depend largely upon the angle at which solar radiation reaches the Earth, which is in turn a function of the time of day, geographic latitude, and the time of year.

The elliptical shape of the Earth's orbit also exerts a small influence on temperatures. At the most distant (aphelion) and the nearest points (perihelion) to the sun, the distance between the Earth and the sun is 1.7 per cent greater or smaller than its mean distance. Thus at these points, solar radiation is also nearly 3.5 per cent stronger or weaker, respectively.

Arctic Circle	66$\frac{1}{2}$° n.lat.
Tropic of Cancer	23$\frac{1}{2}$° n.lat.
Equator	0°
Tropic of Capricorn	23$\frac{1}{2}$° s.lat.
Antarctic Circle	66$\frac{1}{2}$° s.lat.

N

50° n.lat.

90°

23$\frac{1}{2}$°

43°

S

Sunlight

N

43°

23$\frac{1}{2}$°

90°

50° s.lat.

S

66$\frac{1}{2}$° n.lat.	Arctic Circle
23$\frac{1}{2}$° n.lat.	Tropic of Cancer
0°	Equator
23$\frac{1}{2}$° s.lat.	Tropic of Capricorn
66$\frac{1}{2}$° s.lat.	Antarctic Circle

Drifting Lithospheric Plates

The Evolution of Continents and Oceans

Meteorologist Alfred Wegener first presented his hypothesis of continental drift at a geologists' conference in Frankfurt in 1912. He later published a detailed discussion of his theory of continental division and drift in his book Die Entstehung der Kontinente und Ozeane (The Origins of Continents and Oceans, 1915), showing evidence of astounding similarities between geological structures, rock, fossils, and fossilized climatic evidence on both sides of the Atlantic.

Seams in the Earth

Geologist Eduard Sueß had previously postulated the existence of a huge Paleozoic continent (Gondwana). Based upon the same concept, Wegener now reconstructed a supercontinent called Pangaea, which originally encompassed all of the Earth's land masses and later broke apart. His bold ideas were almost unanimously rejected by geologists, and it was not until 50 years later that studies based on new research methods confirmed his work.

Plate Tectonics, the New View of the Earth

The lithosphere consists of about twelve large plates and a number of smaller ones, all of which drift over the upper crust of the Earth. In the course of geological history, they have collided, drifted past one another, separated, and broken up into new plate segments. Beneath the continents, they are between 80 and 120 km thick, but they are much thinner under the oceans (30–70 km). The largest plate (the Pacific Plate) measures 12,000 km in diameter. Given its expansive horizontal dimensions, the lithosphere is very thin. Plates move at speeds ranging from one to 18 cm per year. Where their edges collide or overlap, the earth quakes, forming mountain ranges, faults, and volcanoes. Plates drifting apart create oceanic trenches, continental margins, and mid-oceanic ridges.

Beneath the lithosphere is the asthenosphere which in its upper region where it meets the lithosphere, is semi-plastic and near the melting point, and thus acts as a lubricant over which the plates can glide. The underlying crust is solid but not completely rigid. Slow movement is possible there under the influence of high temperatures and pressure.

Hot Currents Move Segments of the Earth's Crust

Convection currents in the mantle set the plates in motion. When one plate begins to drift, the others are moved as well. Some 500 million years ago, the continents were distributed widely over the surface of the Earth. But they later converged to form the supercontinent Pangaea. The remainder of the globe was covered by the superocean Panthalassa, which continued to expand into Pangaea north of the equator. The east-west arm of the sea (Tethys) eventually split the great land mass apart, forming Laurasia and Gondwana.

These two continents also broke apart as time passed. The present-day distribution of land and sea is only a momentary state. India has already joined Eurasia, and Africa is approaching it. "Panta rhei" (everything is in flux), declared the Greek philosopher Heraclitus with reference to this perpetual process of growth, change, and decline.

Scientists began exploring the ocean floor with the aid of sonar in 1945. The mid-oceanic ridges were discovered, along with such phenomena as seafloor spreading and subduction, the underthrusting of heavy oceanic plates beneath lighter continental plates. More recently, measurements of magnetic anomalies and radiometric rock dating techniques have shed new light on the processes involved in plate tectonics.

Disappearing Crust

When one oceanic plate slides beneath another in a process known as subduction, oceanic trenches and island chains are formed. Steeper subduction produces straighter trenches and island chains. Abrupt subduction triggers earthquakes at depths of up to 700 km. The underlying plate becomes soft and begins to melt. Cracks form in the overriding plate; parts break away and are thrust downward. The movement of the sinking plate may be blocked, forming bulges which in turn raise previously sunken volcanic islands to the surface again. Lighter oceanic sediments are not carried deep into the Earth's crust. They accumulate along with rock from the volcanic chain in deep-sea trenches, some of which are more than 10,000 meters deep. Deformed, partially folded, and thrust above the ocean surface at certain points, this chaotic mass (mélange) builds an accretionary prism that can form a chain of islands off the main volcanic chain. Volcanoes are formed by rising granodoritic magma above the area where the sinking plate begins to melt. Interarc basins, in which spread zones sink or are forced apart, are created behind the main chain. This opens channels through which lava flows to the surface.

Hot Spots and Wandering Volcanoes

In the lower crust, 2,900 m below the Earth's surface, matter along the boundary to the outer core is heated so intensely that basalt magma plumes are forced upward through the lower and upper crust. At the surface, shield volcanoes are formed above these hot spots (Hawaii is a good example). New volcanoes are created wherever oceanic crust drifts over the stationary hot spots. The extinct volcanoes in a thus created island chain are eroded and gradually submerge. Hot spots are also found beneath continents.

Building New Crust

Hot streams of magma in the crust underneath mid-oceanic ridges thrust the relatively thin oceanic plate upward, breaking it apart. Basalt lava emerges beneath the sea and closes the fissures in the crust. On both sides of the fault line, the crust drifts in the direction of the subduction zone where it is melted deep inside the Earth. Since plates drift at different speeds, transform faults emerge along the ridge. Larger volcanic islands (Iceland is an example) form at certain points. Mid-oceanic ridges can reach elevations of over 3,000 m. Oceanic crust in ocean basins is no more than 160 million years old. Only recently discovered, black smokers are hydrothermal vents – hot springs on the seafloor. They release water containing hydrogen sulphide at temperatures of over 630 °F, from which sulphide minerals precipitate in the cold water at the bottom of the ocean.

High Mountain Ranges at the Edges of Continental Plates

Deep-ocean trenches, accretionary prisms, and marginal trenches filled with sediment also form where oceanic plates subduct beneath continental plates. The continental crust is folded, broken apart, and raised in some places. Intrusions of granite magma occur, often forming magma chambers from which magma is extruded and frequently rises to the surface. High mountain chains (orogenes) topped by shield volcanoes are created at these points. Plate segments drift apart in the spread

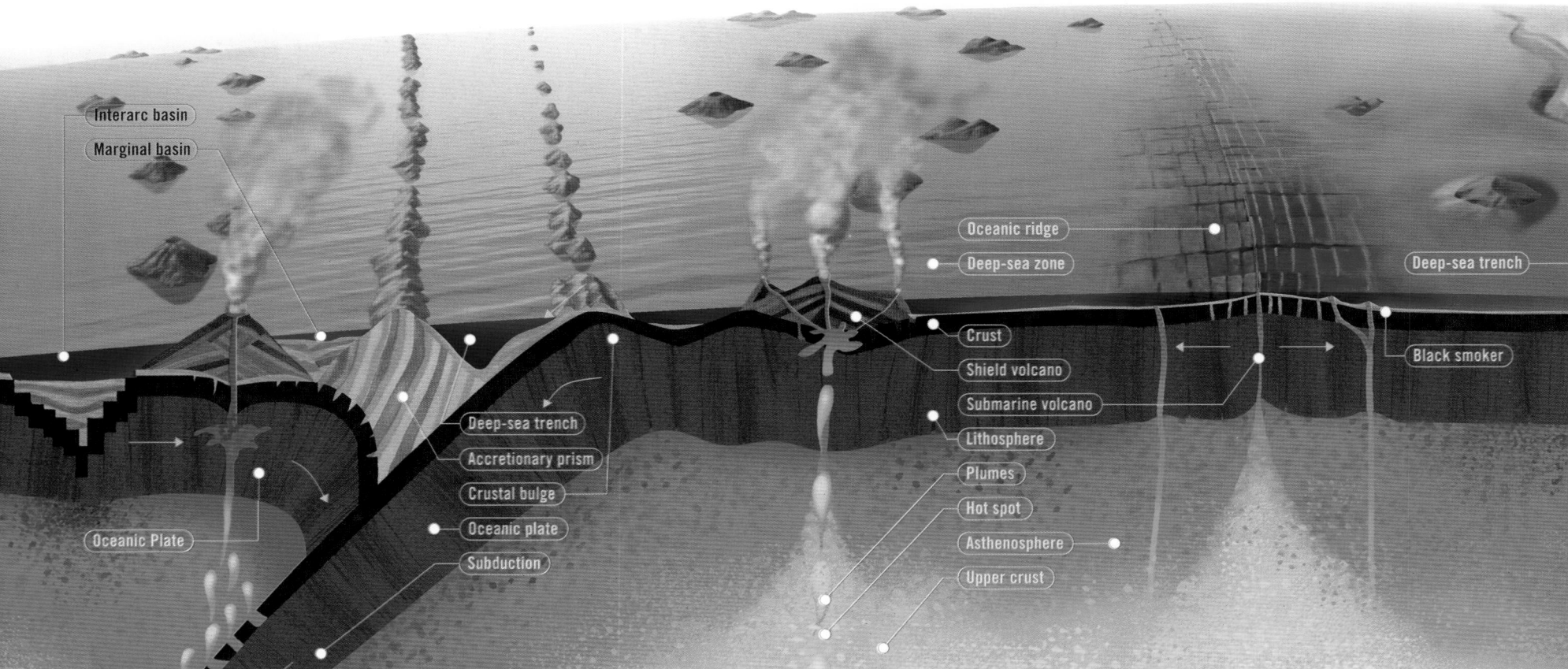

Interarc basin
Marginal basin
Oceanic ridge
Deep-sea zone
Deep-sea trench
Crust
Shield volcano
Submarine volcano
Lithosphere
Plumes
Hot spot
Asthenosphere
Upper crust
Deep-sea trench
Accretionary prism
Crustal bulge
Oceanic plate
Subduction
Oceanic Plate
Black smoker

Plates Drifting Past Each Other in California

Along the San Andreas Fault in California, the Pacific Plate (right-hand side of the illustration), which forms the edge of the North American continent, is pushed horizontally against the North American Plate (on the left) towards the viewer – that is, to the northwest. Along the fault line, both plates are slightly elevated and heavily scarred by erosion.

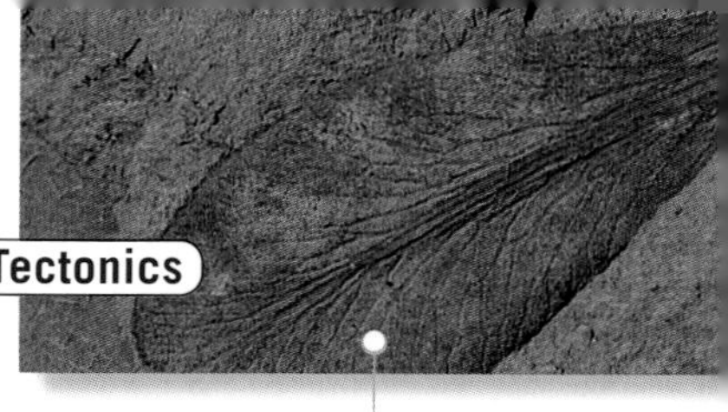

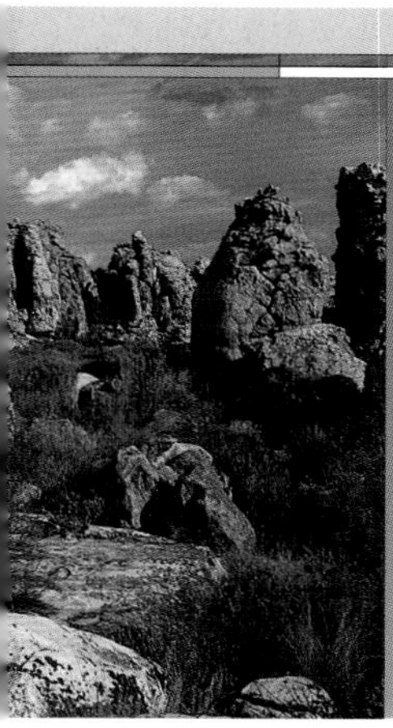

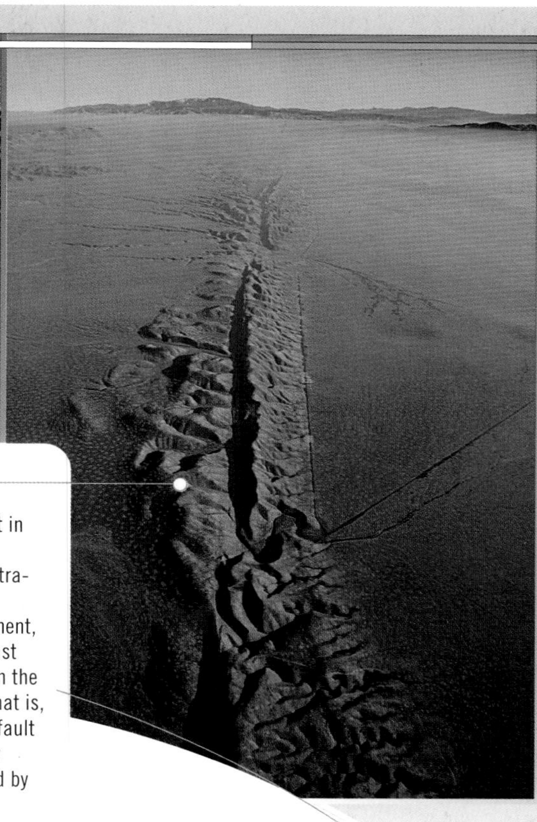

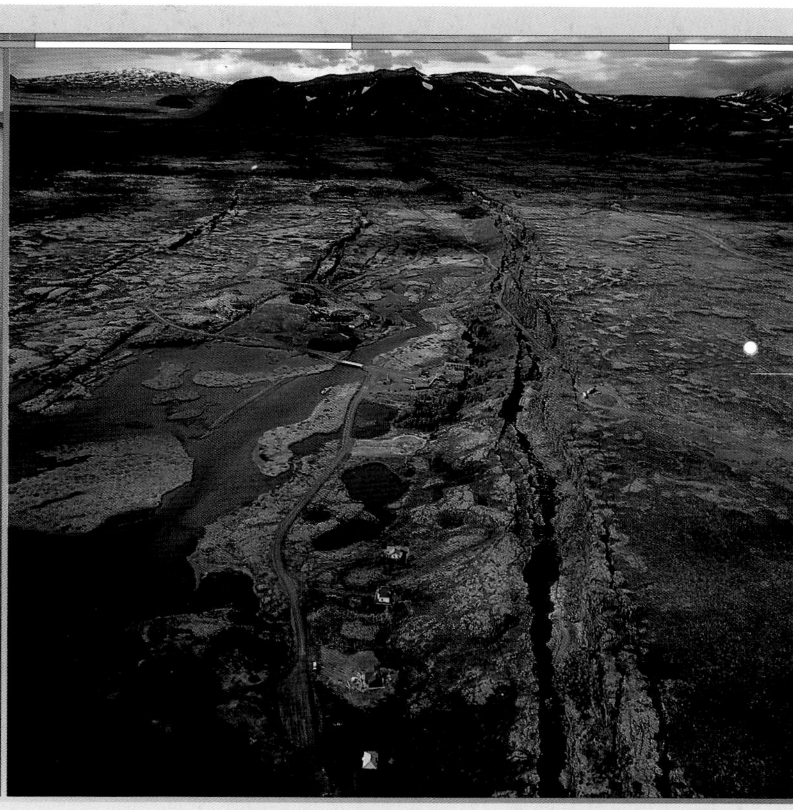

Prehistoric Evidence

A fossilized leaf of glossopteris, a tree-shaped fern that flourished in cool to temperate regions of Gondwana near the poles from the Carboniferous to the Jurassic. Its distribution is further evidence of the existence of the ancient continent as a contiguous land mass.

Plates Drifting Apart in Iceland

The Mid-Atlantic Ridge rises from the sea in Iceland. The North American Plate drifts toward the west, the Eurasian Plate toward the east. A young, still active volcanic zone runs through the middle of the island. The photo shows the Thingvellir Plain at the edge of the Almannagjá Gorge.

zones in the interior of the continent, producing rift valleys. Magma rises at the rift lines, forming basalt floors and volcanoes. These basalt floors often reach massive and expansive proportions.

Young Oceans, Old Shields

Oceanic rifts eventually grow so wide that new crust is formed by magma rising from below. This marks the birth of a new ocean. The rift often fills with fresh water (e.g. the lakes of East Africa), which is later mixed with inflowing seawater. The collision of two continental plates may lead to

subduction when the rock is too light to penetrate into the heavier material of the upper crust. This causes overthrusting, which creates formations up to 80 km thick (as in the Himalayas). The continental plates have grown larger over the course of geological history. Only in the continental plates have crust segments (shields) several million years old survived as the only remaining evidence of the Earth's early history.

Continents in Motion

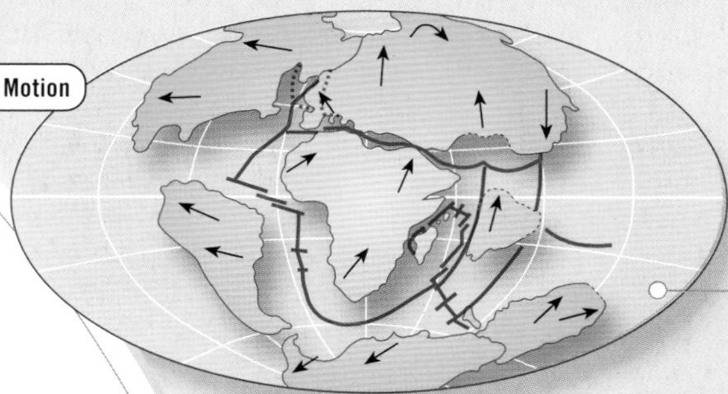

End of the Cretaceous
65 million years ago

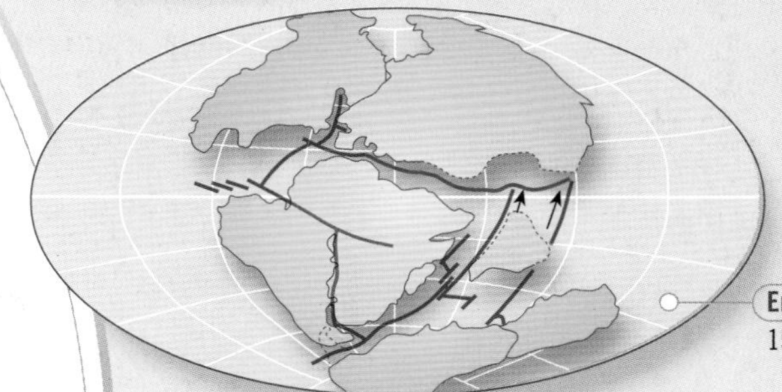

End of the Jurassic
150 million years ago

LAURASIA

GONDWANA

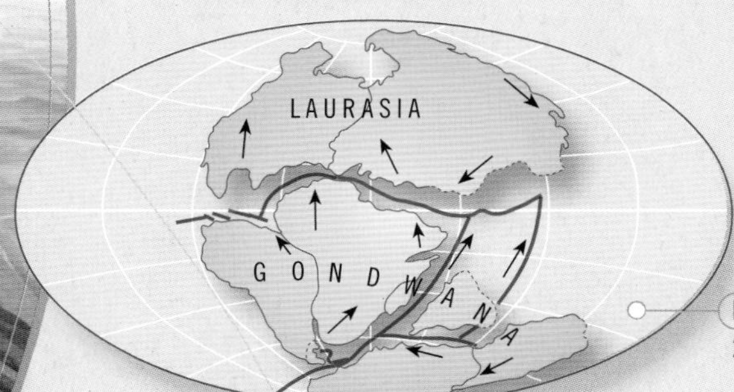

End of the Triassic
220 million years ago

PANGAEA

TETHYS

End of the Paleozoic
250 million years ago

High mountain ranges

Foothills

Coastal plain

Basalt floor

Stratovolcano

Granite

Fault tectonics

Magma chamber

Continental plate

Deep earthquake

Melt zone

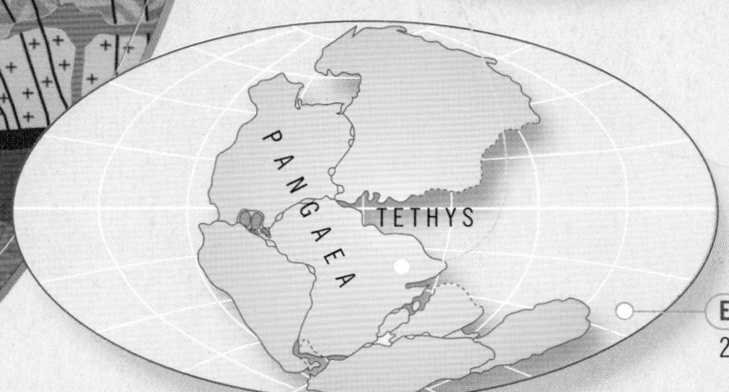

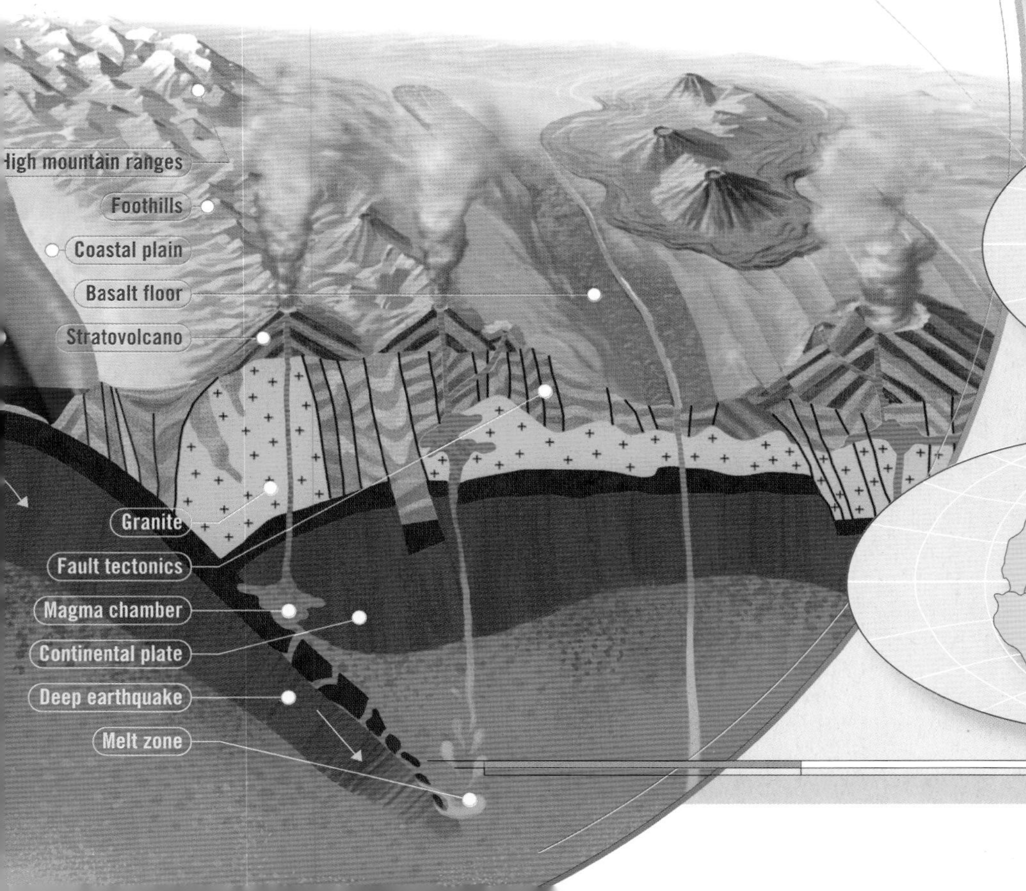

Earthquakes – Danger from the Depths

When the ground begins to shake beneath our feet

Well into the Middle Ages, earthquakes were regarded as the work of mythical, supernatural beings or signs of the wrath of God. The quake that destroyed Lisbon in cataclysmic waves of fire and flooding on November 1, 1775 caused many people to wonder about the validity of prevailing philosophical systems. Could anyone still look upon our world as the "best of all possible worlds," as a planet governed by reliable natural laws? And why had Lisbon, of all places, a city of churches and monasteries devoted to piety, been singled out by God for such terrible punishment? That earthquake marked the beginning of the science of seismology. The Portuguese minister Pombal had reports compiled by observers all over the country. The British engineer John Michell computed the speed of the shock waves. Questions were raised about the origin and the causes of the quake.

The Restless Earth

Although we rarely notice it, the Earth's crust is constantly moving. The oceans and atmosphere are subject to patterns of natural motion, and so are the seemingly fixed landmasses of the continents, though their movements are so slow that we do not perceive them. Much more obvious – and dangerous – are the brief (lasting less than a minute), abrupt, and rapid shifts of larger segments of crust caused by tensions inside the Earth. The amplitude of these movements of ground may amount to as much as several decimeters. The energy released in the process spreads in the form of elastic waves through the Earth's interior: longitudinal and transverse waves. Longitudinal waves (also known as P or primary waves) move faster and arrive at a given distant point sooner than transverse waves (S or secondary waves). The slowest but most highly energized waves are surface waves (L and Rayleigh waves).

The source of an earthquake, known as the focus or hypocenter, may be near the surface or deep within the Earth's crust. Based upon its distance from the epicenter, the point of greatest surface movement, seismologists distinguish between shallow, intermediate, and deep-focus earthquakes. At depths below 720 km, rock is so soft and malleable that no abrupt shifts occur.

On average, 10,000 earthquakes classified as grade 4 or higher on the Richter Scale are recorded annually. Between 10 and 15 of these cause significant damage. In 1999, more than 22,000 people died as a result of earthquakes, while the average death toll for the preceding years is about 10,000. Some 15 percent of the Earth's land area is subject to severe earthquake activity. Another 40 percent is classified as virtually risk-free.

Measuring Earthquake Energy and Effects

Earthquakes are registered and recorded in seismograms using highly sensitive measuring instruments known as seismographs. The direction, distance, and energy of an earthquake can be derived from the data in the seismogram, i. e. the amplitude of the waves generated by an earthquake. Energy is expressed as magnitude, which is computed on the basis of ground amplitude, wave duration, and a calibration function. Earthquakes are classified on the Richter Scale of Earthquake Magnitude according to the maximum amplitude measured at a distance of 100 km from the epicenter. Magnitude values range from zero to between 7.7 and 8.6, but the scale has no upper limit.

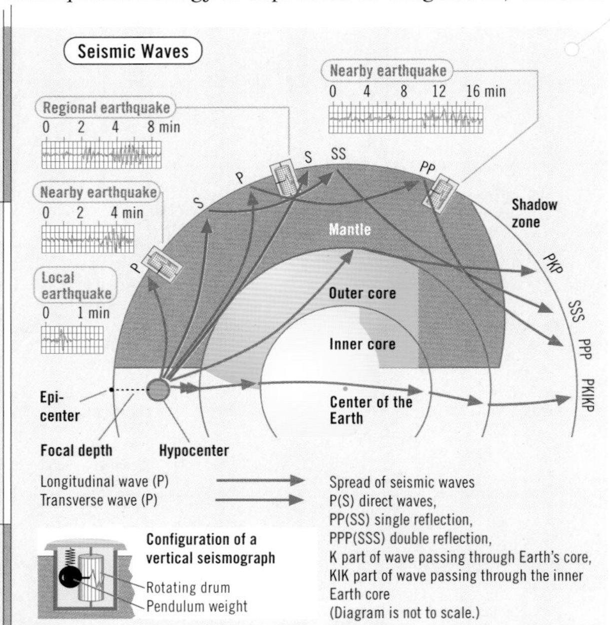

California Awaits "The Big One"

The United States Geological Survey (USGS) estimates the probability of a major earthquake in northern California by the year 2020 at 70 per cent. USGS experts anticipate a seismic event comparable to the San Francisco earthquake of 1906, which measured 8.3 on the Richter Scale and laid much of the city to waste, causing numerous fires and killing some 2,000 people. The quake in Northridge near Los Angeles in 1994 took 60 human lives, and total damage was valued at $ 30–40 billion (a U.S. record). The American West Coast is one of the most severely endangered regions in the world. The Pacific Plate thrusts against the North American Plate along several fault lines, the best known of which is the San Andreas fault. These movements are not gradual and consistent but abrupt and violent, and they are responsible for a seemingly endless series of earthquakes. Some 7,800 earthquakes are registered in California each year, although most of them can only be detected by sensitive seismographic instruments.

Seismic Waves Explore the Earth's Interior

Physical bores are mere pinpricks in the Earth's crust (at about 13 km, the deepest bore ever made reached a depth equivalent to only about 0.2 per cent of the Earth's radius). We learn a great deal more about the structure of the Earth's interior from seismic waves that penetrate to the core and beyond. This method is the basis for the shell model of the Earth, with a crust (50–70 km thick beneath the continents, 5–10 km thick below the oceans), a mantle (2,900 km thick, divided in two by a transition zone), and a core (outer core to a depth of 5,200 km, inner core to a depth of 6,371 km). Correlations between wave speeds and experimental findings generate conclusions about the density, the temperature, and the chemical and mineral composition of the different zones.

Are Earthquakes Predictable?

People in ancient China observed unusual behavior in animals immediately preceding earthquake events, although they realized this only later. Today, even seismologists disagree about whether the location, time, and magnitude of an earthquake can be predicted. Researchers have been trying to identify reliable signs for decades. Using automatic recording devices, they systematically measure changes in specific characteristics – temperature, chemical composition, gas concentration (radon) and electrical groundwater resistance, groundwater levels and spring behavior, movements at fault lines, and deformations of the Earth's surface. All of these phenomena can – but do not necessarily – indicate impending earthquake activity.

Crisis Management – Emergency Disaster Aid

In industrialized countries threatened by earthquakes, such as Japan, the U. S. (especially California), and Italy, plans have been made for responses to natural disasters. Kindergarten and school children in Japan and California learn rules for behavior when danger threatens. Public emergency disaster exercises are conducted on a broad basis in Japan. Plans are modified in response to experience gained in such emergencies. California has established a network of decentralized emergency aid stations staffed and equipped to meet specific local needs. The central Japanese authority failed to respond adequately during the Kobe earthquake.

Earthquake-Proof Construction – Only an Illusion?

The first building designed to resist earthquake shock was erected by American architect Frank Lloyd Wright in Tokyo between 1916 and 1922. It survived the earthquake of 1923 virtually undamaged. In the years since, architects have employed special methods of stable or flexible construction at locations in Japan, California, and other

---

Seismic Waves

Nearby earthquake
0   4   8   12   16 min

Regional earthquake
0   2   4   8 min

Nearby earthquake
0   2   4 min

Local earthquake
0   1 min

Mantle

Outer core

Inner core

Shadow zone

Epicenter

Center of the Earth

Focal depth   Hypocenter

Longitudinal wave (P)
Transverse wave (P)

Spread of seismic waves
P(S) direct waves,
PP(SS) single reflection,
PPP(SSS) double reflection,
K part of wave passing through Earth's core,
KIK part of wave passing through the inner Earth core
(Diagram is not to scale.)

Configuration of a vertical seismograph
Rotating drum
Pendulum weight

Earthquake Epicenters and Plate Boundaries

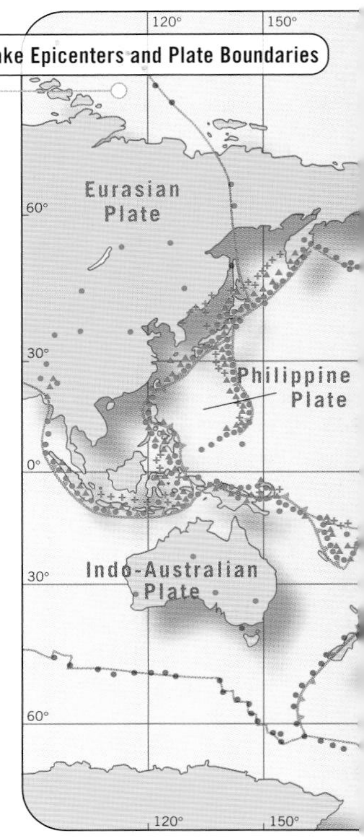

Zones of Critical Seismic Activity

Ninety per cent of all earthquakes are caused by seismic activity (volcanism and collapsing hollow areas in the Earth account for the remainder). Thus the theory of plate tectonics has given rise to new insights into the causes and distribution of earthquakes. As this map of epicenters shows, seismic activity is most intense along plate margins. The Circum-Pacific Belt coincides primarily with subduction zones (these incline toward the continental interiors, which explains the locations of deep-focus earthquakes), while the Mediterranean-Transasian Belt is aligned with converging continental plates. Weaker earthquakes originate at the edges of plates moving away from another near mid-oceanic ridges.

Eurasian Plate

Philippine Plate

Indo-Australian Plate

Where the Ball Rolls – the First Seismograph

The first device used to register earthquake activity was invented in China in the first century AD. The pot-bellied vessel is adorned with eight dragon figures, each facing a crouching toad positioned on the base below. When a tremor occurs, the pendulum inside begins to swing. The mouth of the dragon on the side opposite the direction of the shock wave opens and drops a ball into the mouth of the toad beneath it. This was believed to indicate the direction of the earthquake.

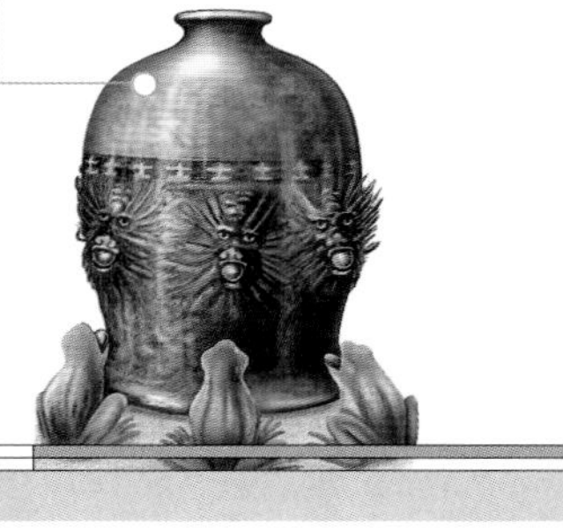

An Earthquake Exposes Weaknesses in Japanese Society

The quake that shook the Japanese industrial and port city of Kobe in the early morning of January 17, 1995 lasted no more than a few seconds. More than 20,000 buildings were heavily damaged or destroyed; 6,432 people were killed, and 350,000 lost their homes. The supports beneath 500 m of the Hanshin Highway collapsed, and the supposedly earthquake-proof elevated road crashed to the ground. The multi-story buildings nearby remained undamaged. The seemingly well-organized disaster aid and rescue system was largely ineffective.

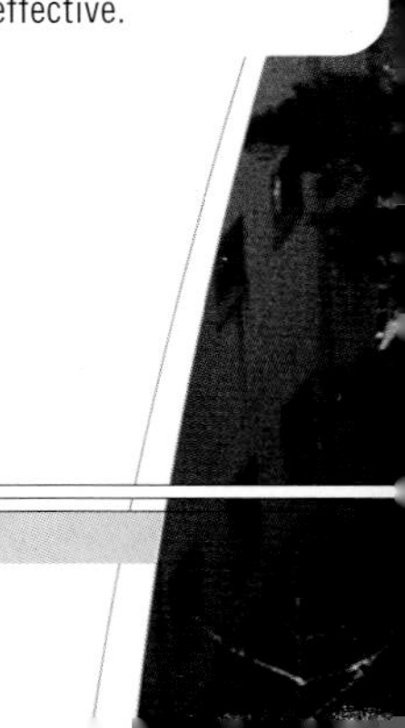

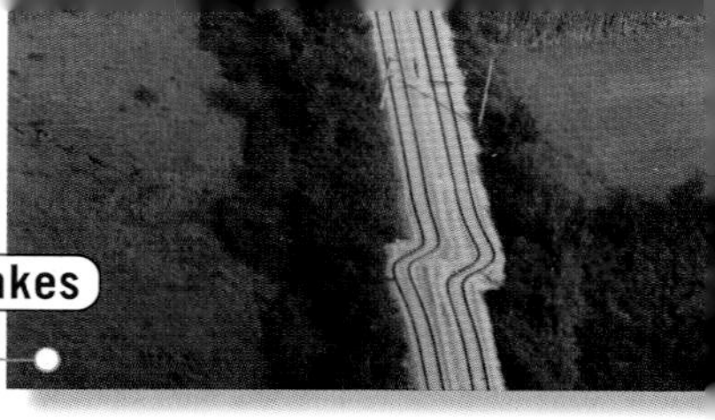

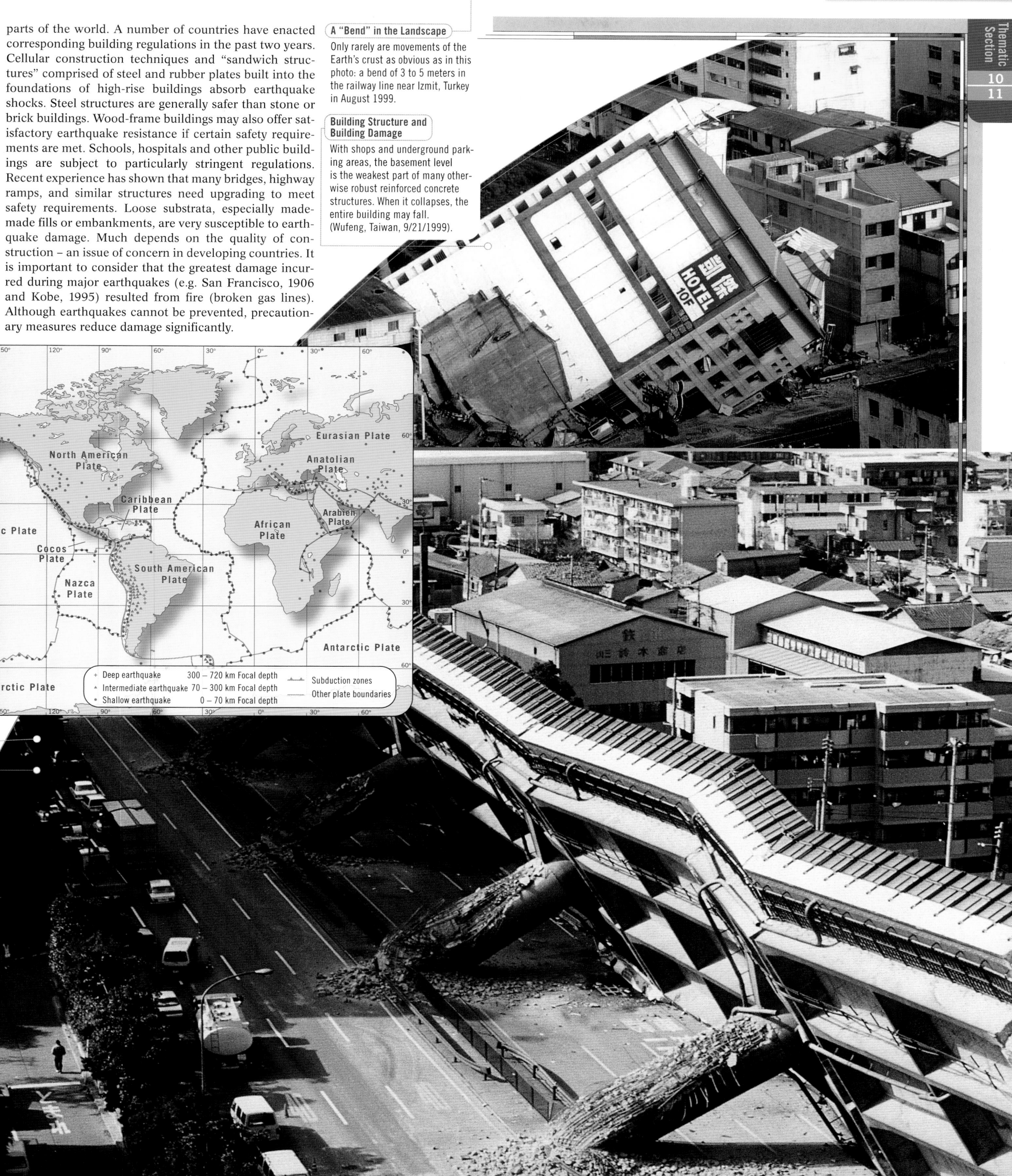

parts of the world. A number of countries have enacted corresponding building regulations in the past two years. Cellular construction techniques and "sandwich structures" comprised of steel and rubber plates built into the foundations of high-rise buildings absorb earthquake shocks. Steel structures are generally safer than stone or brick buildings. Wood-frame buildings may also offer satisfactory earthquake resistance if certain safety requirements are met. Schools, hospitals and other public buildings are subject to particularly stringent regulations. Recent experience has shown that many bridges, highway ramps, and similar structures need upgrading to meet safety requirements. Loose substrata, especially made-made fills or embankments, are very susceptible to earthquake damage. Much depends on the quality of construction – an issue of concern in developing countries. It is important to consider that the greatest damage incurred during major earthquakes (e.g. San Francisco, 1906 and Kobe, 1995) resulted from fire (broken gas lines). Although earthquakes cannot be prevented, precautionary measures reduce damage significantly.

A "Bend" in the Landscape

Only rarely are movements of the Earth's crust as obvious as in this photo: a bend of 3 to 5 meters in the railway line near Izmit, Turkey in August 1999.

Building Structure and Building Damage

With shops and underground parking areas, the basement level is the weakest part of many otherwise robust reinforced concrete structures. When it collapses, the entire building may fall. (Wufeng, Taiwan, 9/21/1999).

Eurasian Plate

North American Plate

Anatolian Plate

Caribbean Plate

African Plate

Arabien Plate

...ic Plate

Cocos Plate

South American Plate

Nazca Plate

...arctic Plate

Antarctic Plate

+ Deep earthquake   300 – 720 km Focal depth
▲ Intermediate earthquake 70 – 300 km Focal depth   —— Subduction zones
• Shallow earthquake   0 – 70 km Focal depth   —— Other plate boundaries

HOTEL 10F

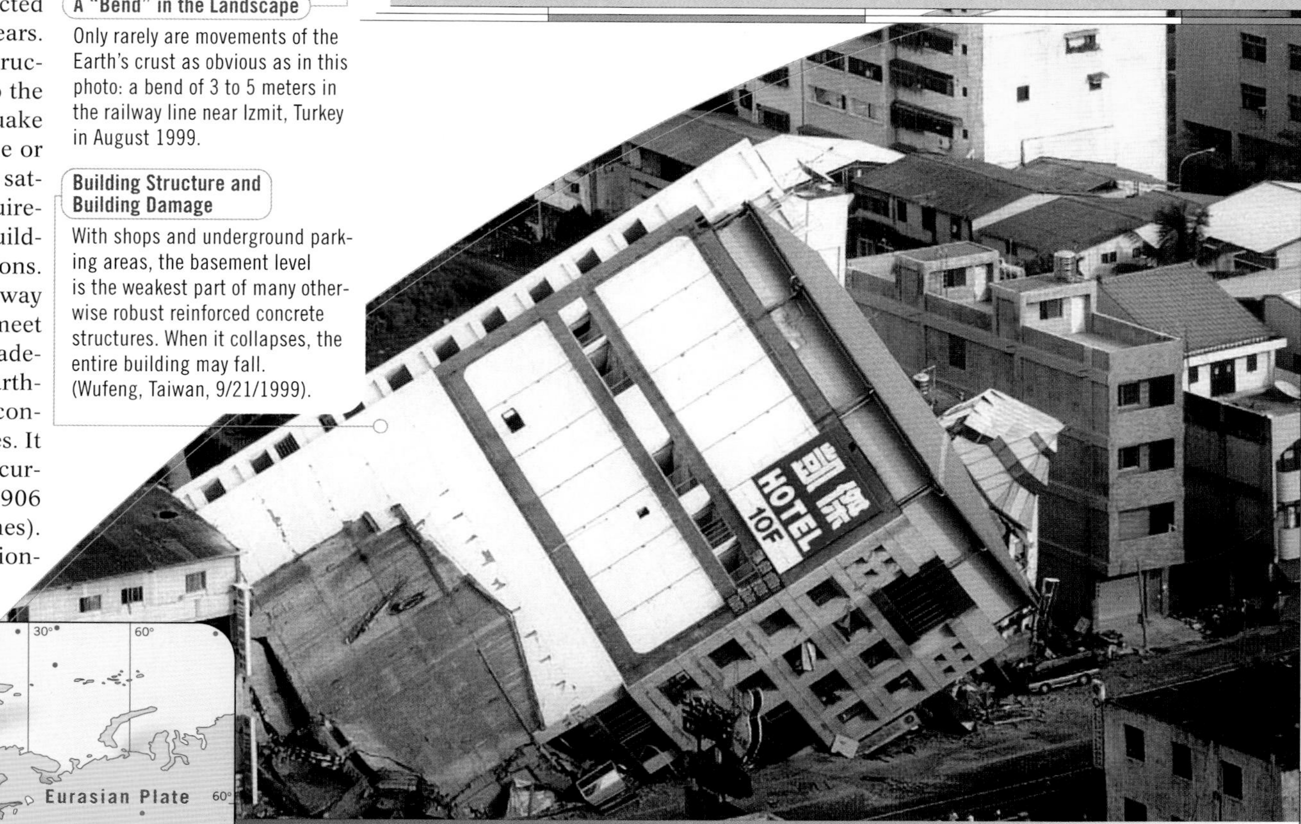

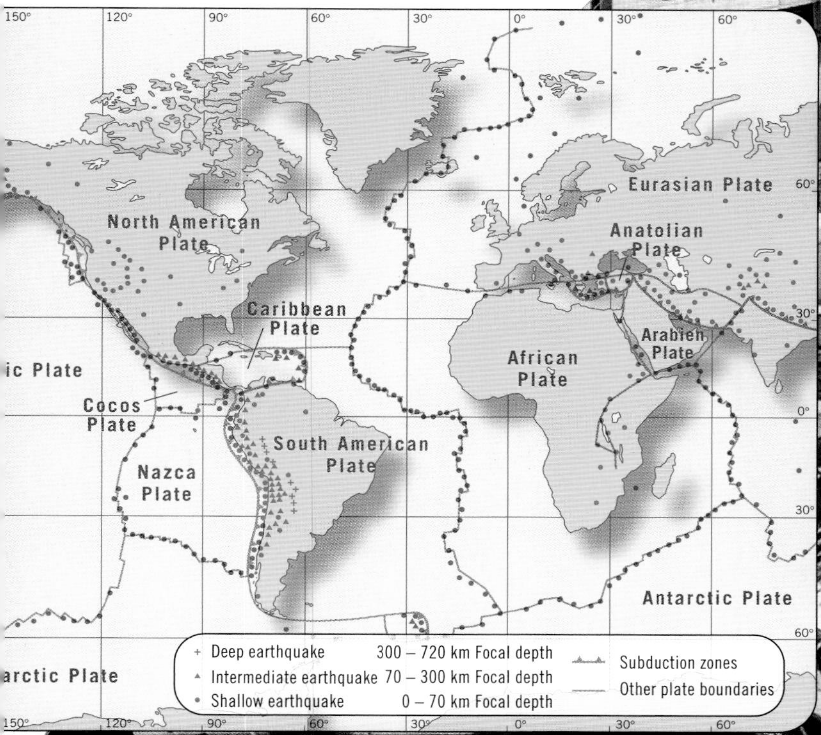

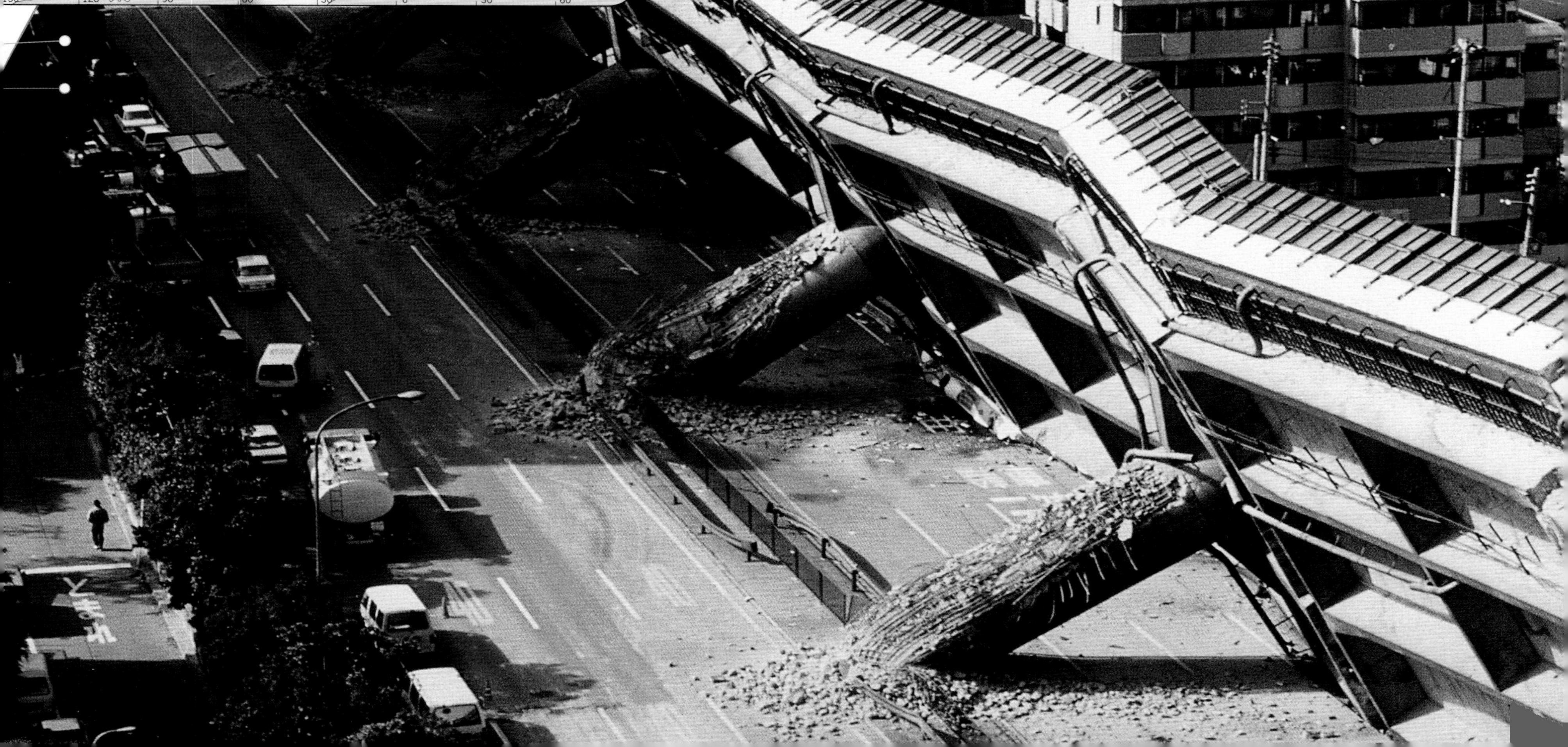

Volcanism – Unbridled Forces from the Earth's Interior

Fertile Soil – Ever-Present Danger

In the early morning hours of August 27, 1883, the small volcanic island of Krakatoa in the Sundra Strait was shaken by violent explosions which virtually blew the island paradise apart. The enormous bang was heard more than 5,000 km away, and atmospheric pressure rose by 1.45 millibars in Tokyo. Massive tremors that triggered tsunamis traveling at the speed of an airliner battered the coastlines of Java and Sumatra. Roughly 36,000 people lost their lives as a direct result of the eruptions. And this was by no means the worst volcanic disaster in history. Eruptions on the Indonesian island of Sumbawa in 1815 ejected more than 180 cubic km of lava and ash (compared to only 20 cubic km on Krakatoa). The volcano, the tidal waves, and the famine that followed were responsible for some 90,000 deaths. Dust in the atmosphere darkened the sky for weeks.

A Bubbling Inferno Beneath Us

The solid crust that floats on the hot molten rock of the upper mantle is actually very thin. Continental crust attains a maximum thickness of 70 km, while oceanic

An Eruption in Hawaii

An eruption of Kilauea in Hawaii begins with a fountain of lava lasting several hours. Escaping gas catapults the red-hot molten mass hundreds of meters into the air.

"Rushing Stream"

This is the literal translation of the Islandic word for geyser (geysir). Rainwater seeping into the hot volcanic underground is heated and ejected – often at regular intervals – through fissures in the rock. (photo: geysers in the Rotorua region of New Zealand). The process is a part of the waning phase of volcanic activity.

Volcanic Breakthrough in a Glacier

In 1996, the volcano beneath the Vatnajökull Glacier in Iceland melted a hole in the ice cap, sending clouds of ash as high as 4,000 m into the air. The lava eruptions that followed were accompanied by severe earthquakes.

Aa and Pahoehoe Lava

A skin forms on the surface of the thin, red-hot pahoehoe lava as it flows. Once it has cooled and solidified, the lava may look much like lengths of intertwining twisted ropes or strings.

A Volcanic Blessing

Geothermal energy is a readily available alternative energy source in volcanically active regions like Italy, Iceland, and New Zealand.

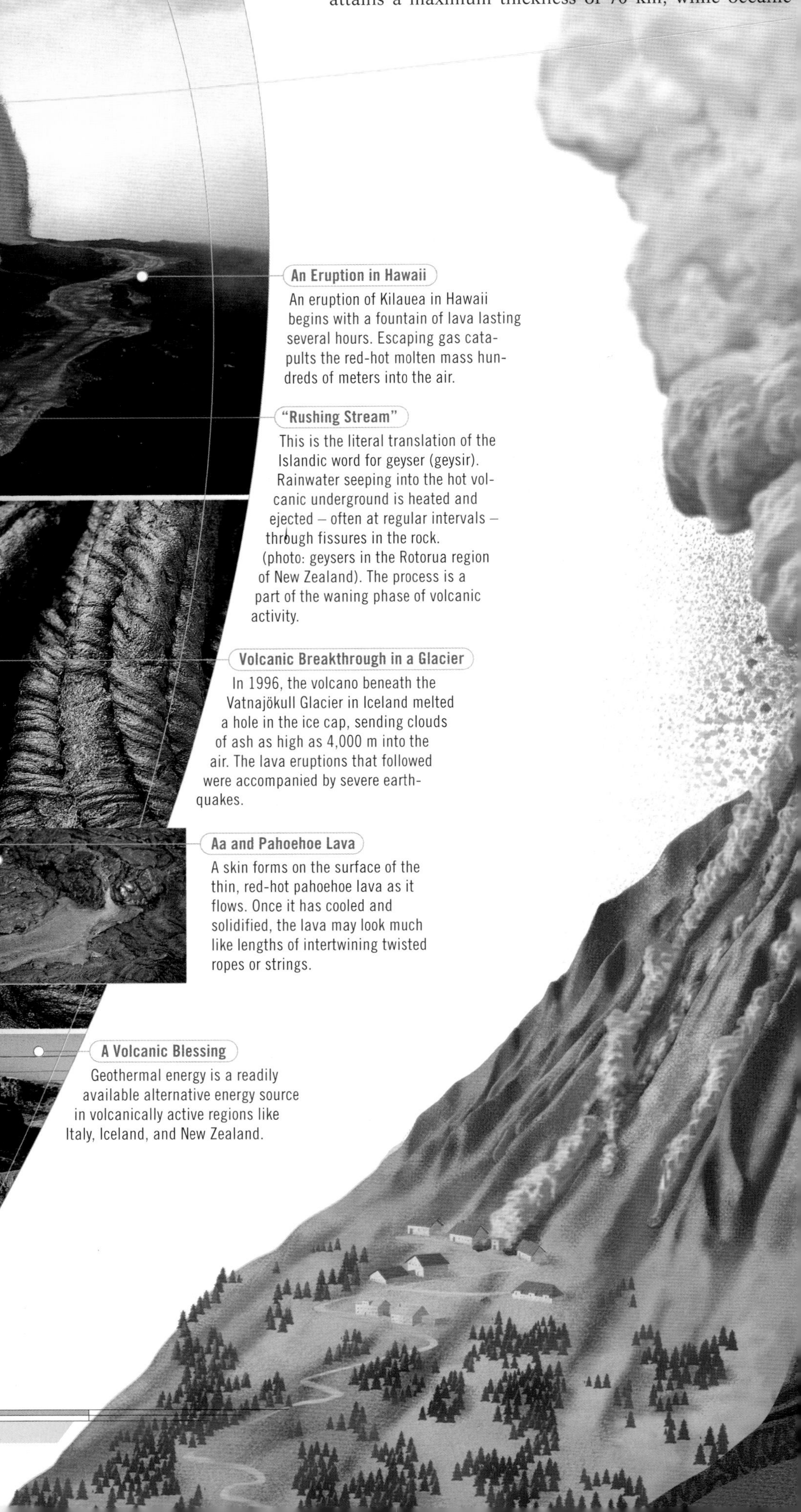

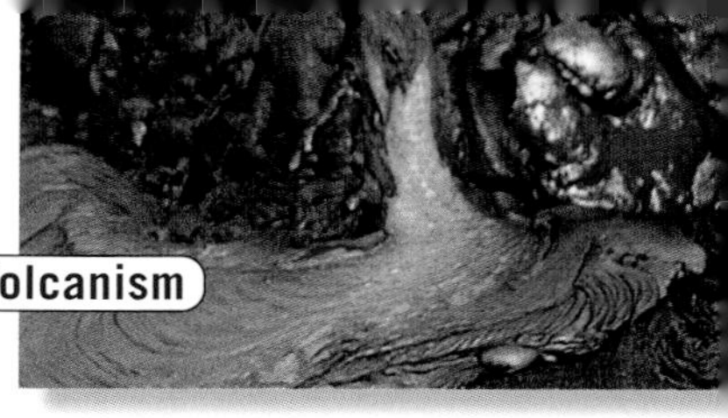

crust is ordinarily between 5 and 10 km thick. (Imagine an orange measuring 12 cm in diameter with a peel only 0.3 mm thick!). And thus it is no wonder that the Earth's thin crust is extremely fragile. Molten rock accumulates in large magma chambers beneath the surface and rises where faults or openings develop. Magma that emerges at the surface is called lava.

Harmless and Dangerous Volcanoes

The flow characteristics of lava depend on its chemical composition and gas content. Thin, basaltic lava (50 % SiO2) of the kind that erupts from Kilauea (Hawaii) is often ejected in towering fountains which then flow smoothly from the crater. Andesitic magma rich in silicic acid (60 % SiO2) is catapulted from volcanic Mount Saint Helens to heights of several kilometers. Gases escape easily from thin magma, whereas thick, highly gaseous magma builds up high pressures that are released suddenly and explosively near the surface, where outside pressure decreases rapidly. At these points, lava shoots from the volcano like champagne from a shaken bottle. Basaltic lava forms relatively flat (12 degrees) shield volcanoes like those in Hawaii, or basalt floors (Dekkan, India). Acidic lava tends to erupt violently, although it may also flow quietly down volcanic slopes. Alternating deposits of lava and tuff form cone-shaped stratovolcanoes with slopes as steep as 30 degrees. The most famous volcano of this type is Fujiama in Japan. When underground pressure has no means of escape, domes of lava form, raising the overlying layers and the Earth's surface above. The destructive power of explosive eruptions makes living in these areas extremely dangerous. The worst outbreak of this kind occurred at the Montagne Pelée on the island of Martinique in 1902. Extremely hot air (1,440° F) loaded with ash enveloped the nearby city of Saint-Pierre in a red-hot cloud, killing 29,000 people. The only survivor was found at the island prison.

Volcanoes – Gigantic Dirt Canons

Volcanic eruptions also hurl huge blocks of rock (bombs) far into the surrounding countryside. Fine particles are shot up to 10 km into the atmosphere, where they may circulate around the Earth for years. Bombs, lapilli (fragments measuring from two to 64 mm), and fine ash fall to the ground, forming volcanic tuff. Fragments that have not cooled sufficiently fuse into clinkers. Rock baked from larger masses becomes volcanic breccia. Storms among the high clouds above the volcano bring heavy rains, often causing massive mudflows that obliterate everything in their paths to the valleys below.

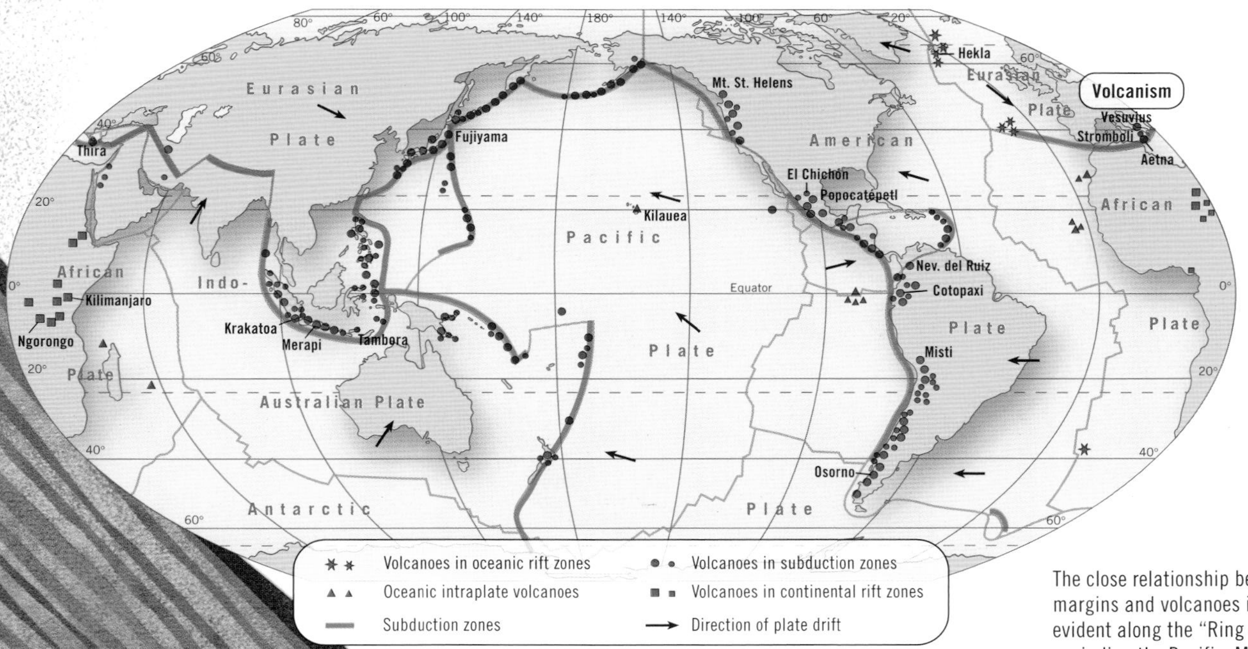

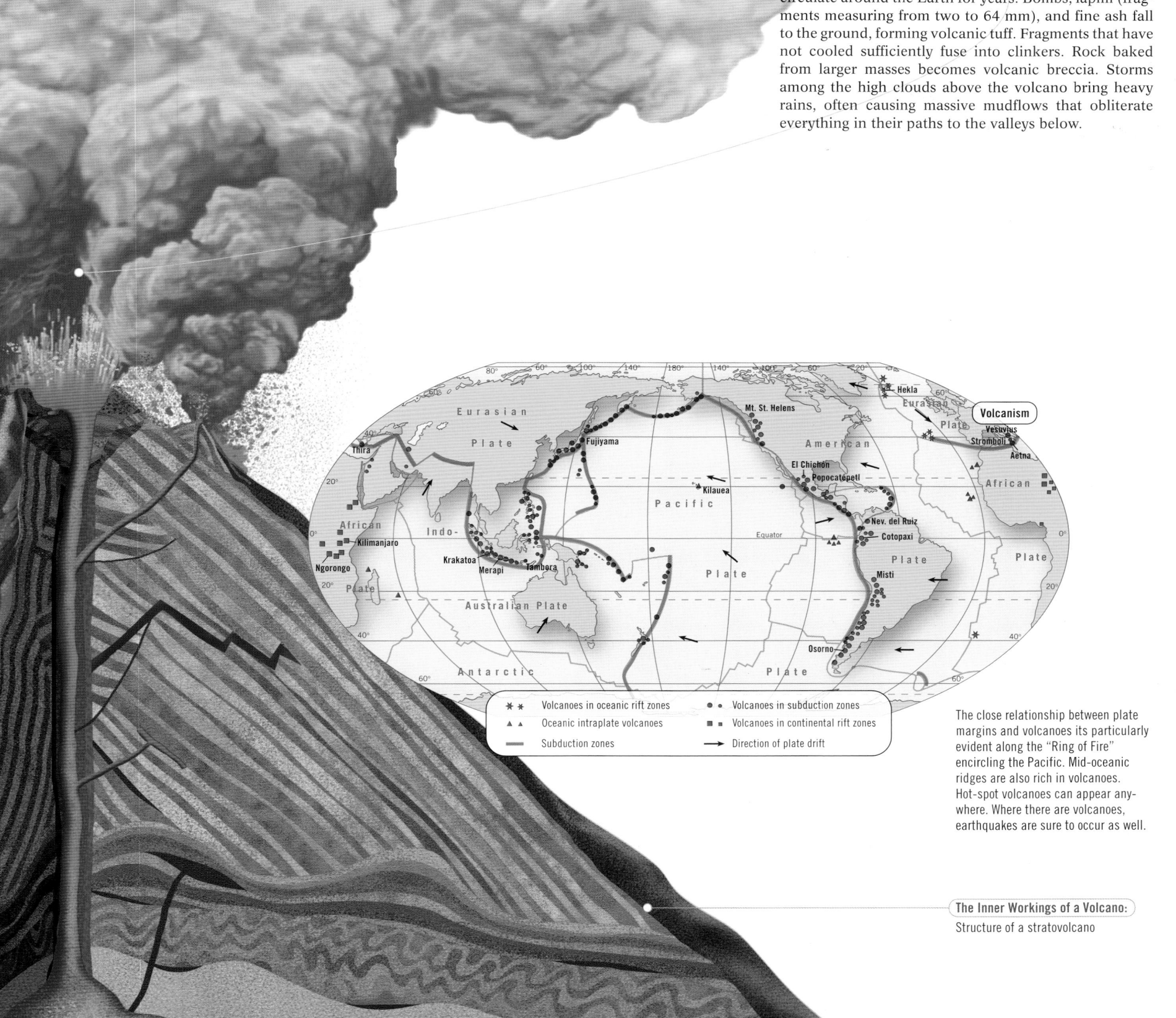

The close relationship between plate margins and volcanoes its particularly evident along the "Ring of Fire" encircling the Pacific. Mid-oceanic ridges are also rich in volcanoes. Hot-spot volcanoes can appear anywhere. Where there are volcanoes, earthquakes are sure to occur as well.

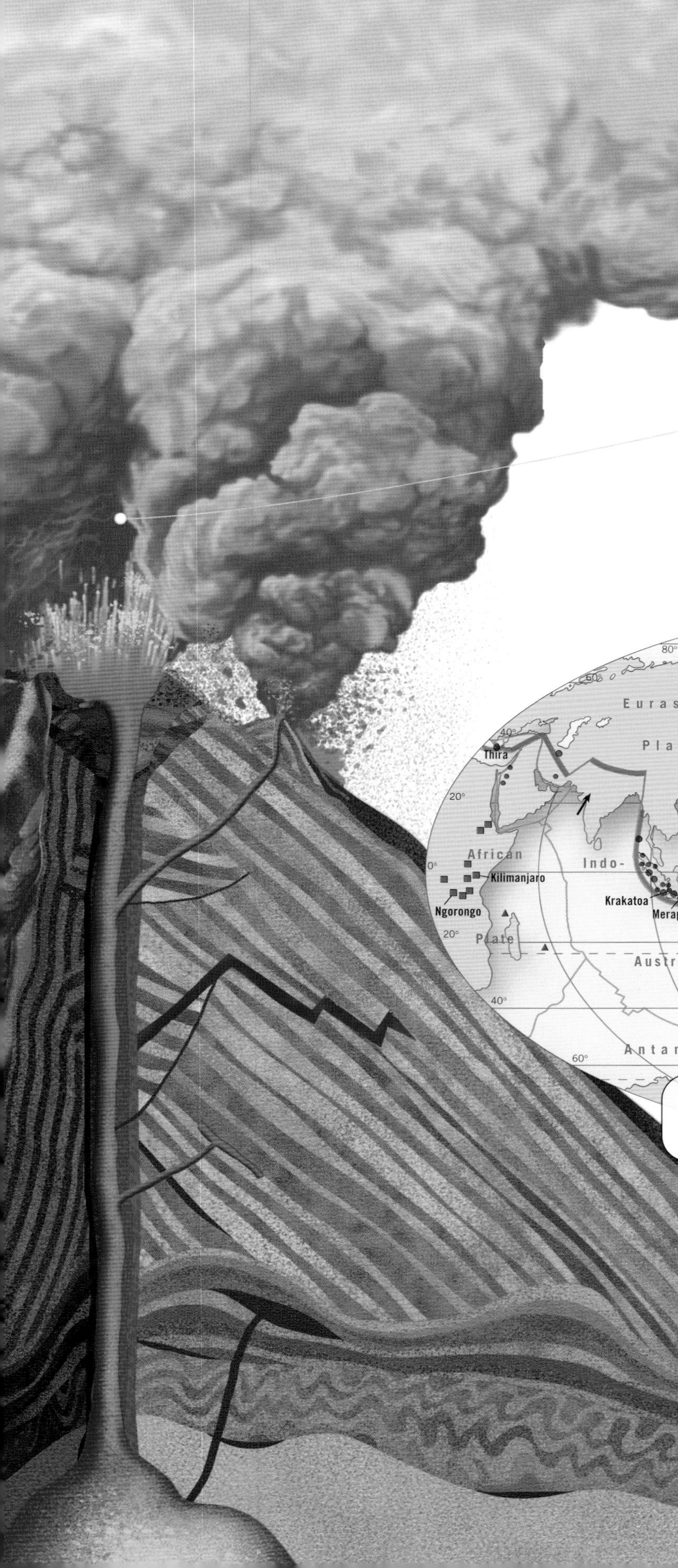

The Inner Workings of a Volcano:
Structure of a stratovolcano

Water Molds the Landscape

Water's Journey from the Sea to the Mountains and Back

Life came to Earth with water, which entered the cloud of gas that surrounds our planet in the form of gas released from molten magma. The cooling process produced the first rains, and the seas began to form. In the protective watery environment and under the influence of rising oxygen concentrations, life burst forth explosively several hundred million years ago. We come from water, and we need water to live. The human body is 70 percent water. Although we can live for weeks without food, we would die within days without water. More than half of the human race suffers from a shortage of clean drinking water. Eighty percent of the diseases responsible for millions of deaths every year are carried by water. Water is an essential, life-giving substance that is unequally distributed. Some people die of thirst, while others drown.

High into the Atmosphere and back to Earth. The Water Cycle

How does water find its way back to the sea? Raindrops falling to earth have several ways of returning to the bodies of water from which they came. They may evaporate, flow over the surface, or seep into the earth, emerging again later through springs. Water that remains on the surface reaches the sea in a matter of weeks. Yet water held captive in a freshwater lake can take years to return to the ocean. Water that falls as snow and turns to ice in cold regions of the Earth like the Antarctic, may not return to the sea for hundreds of thousands of years. Once there, it is ready to embark upon another long journey. Many water molecules take refuge at safe ocean depths, however, thus escaping the routine of constant travel.

The water cycle begins with the evaporation of liquid water, most of which takes place on the ocean surface. At a temperature of 77 °F, this process consumes 583 calories per gram of water. Molecules of water vapor transport this kinetic energy over long distances. The water condenses again only after a journey of hours or even days through the air. At this point, raindrops are formed during the transition from the gaseous to the liquid state, and evaporation heat is released again. That is how warmth from the Caribbean, for example, travels via the Gulf Stream to Norway. When raindrops freeze (changing from liquid to solid), 79.4 calories are released per gram of water. Thus, as strange as it may seem, the freezing process generates heat. Molecules move more slowly in ice than in liquid water.

Water Shapes Mountains and Valleys by Day and by Night

With rare exceptions, water flows downhill toward the sea, quickly forming drainage lines on the surface. As the kinetic energy of water rushing downhill tears away material and carries it away, long cuts form in the earth – the valleys of streams and rivers. Naturally, elevated ridges are left standing between these valleys. The product is a relief of mountains and valleys. Depending upon elevation and slope, mountains of different heights are created and cut apart by water and/or ice (glaciers). The higher the mountain range, the steeper the forms carved by the water.

A Steady Drip Hollows the Stone

Water is the most important element in the weathering process that shapes rock – just as it is when automobiles succumb to rust (corrosion). Limestone is one of the most highly soluble types of rock, and large caves and other karsts are often found in limestone formations. Apart from its corrosive effect, moving water also works mechanically to hasten the process of rock destruction.

The effects of wind, water, and salt have combined to undercut a coastal rock formation on the island of Lanzarote.

Crashing waves strike steep coastal formations with incredible force (one cubic meter of water weighs roughly a ton), wielding sand and pebbles as abrasive weapons. Although these forces are weaker in rivers, a substantial amount of material is eroded and carried away from riverbeds and banks over the course of time. Deep, V-shaped valleys and gorges offer striking evidence of the destructive power of water. Bank and bed erosion caused by flowing water forms valleys in a multitude of different shapes.

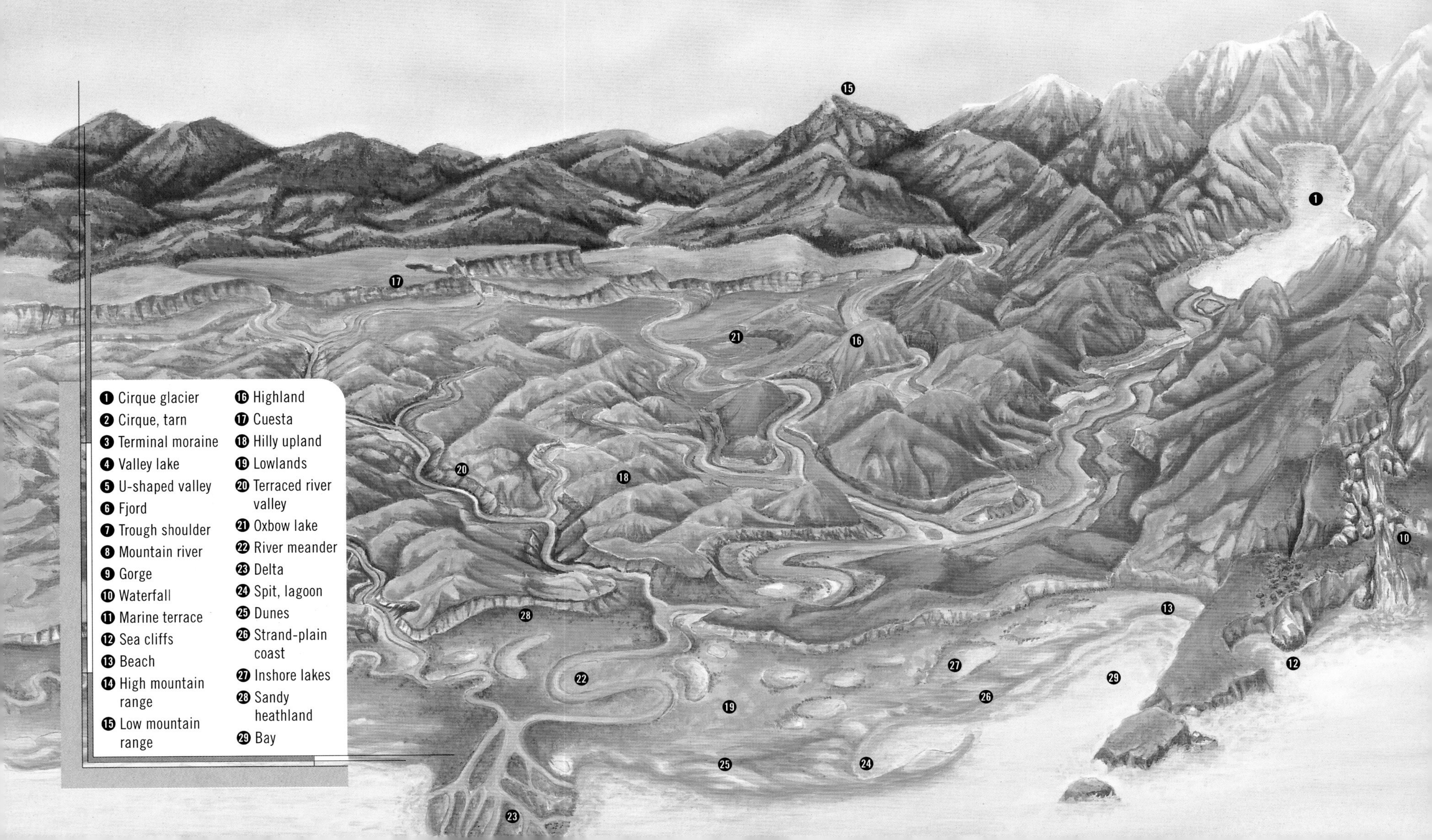

❶ Cirque glacier
❷ Cirque, tarn
❸ Terminal moraine
❹ Valley lake
❺ U-shaped valley
❻ Fjord
❼ Trough shoulder
❽ Mountain river
❾ Gorge
❿ Waterfall
⓫ Marine terrace
⓬ Sea cliffs
⓭ Beach
⓮ High mountain range
⓯ Low mountain range
⓰ Highland
⓱ Cuesta
⓲ Hilly upland
⓳ Lowlands
⓴ Terraced river valley
㉑ Oxbow lake
㉒ River meander
㉓ Delta
㉔ Spit, lagoon
㉕ Dunes
㉖ Strand-plain coast
㉗ Inshore lakes
㉘ Sandy heathland
㉙ Bay

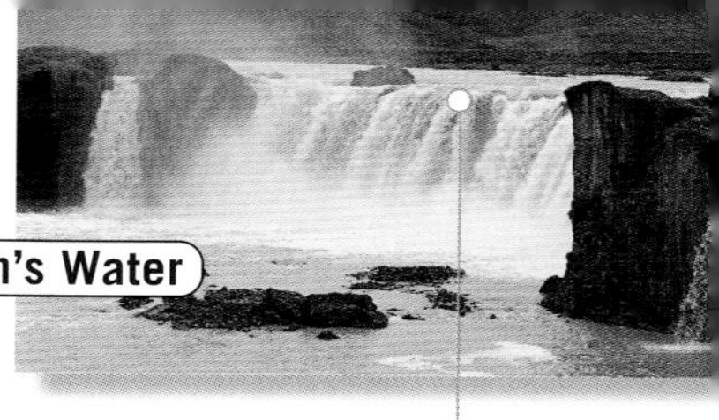

Glacial ice has even greater erosive power. The high pressure exerted by the ice causes severe erosion (detersion, exaration) even at low flow speeds. Blocks of stone the size of a house may be torn away and carried downward. This is how deep U-shaped valleys are formed. The eroded material is deposited in glacial moraines. Water and ice cover three-quarters of the Earth's surface. Although the total quantity of water on earth – some 1.4 billion square km – is almost impossible to imagine, this immense treasure is of little use to us, as 96.5 per cent of it is salty. Methods developed for desalinating seawater are too costly for most countries. And it is hardly practical to tow icebergs from the Antarctic to the arid regions of the world. We may expect future water shortages to reach life-threatening proportions in many places on Earth.

No Escape from Water

Although water is in short supply in many parts of the world, thousands die or lose their homes in water-related disasters every year. Floods, typhoons, and tsunamis ravage broad stretches of land. Melting snow and torrential rains cause rivers to swell and overflow their banks in low-lying areas. Dykes often do not hold or are simply not high enough.

When the ground freezes during the winter and is covered by a thick blanket of snow, it takes only a brief interlude of warm temperatures accompanied by heavy rainfall to melt the snow and cause severe flooding in the valleys. The frozen soil prevents water from seeping into the ground and accelerates the speed of surface runoff.

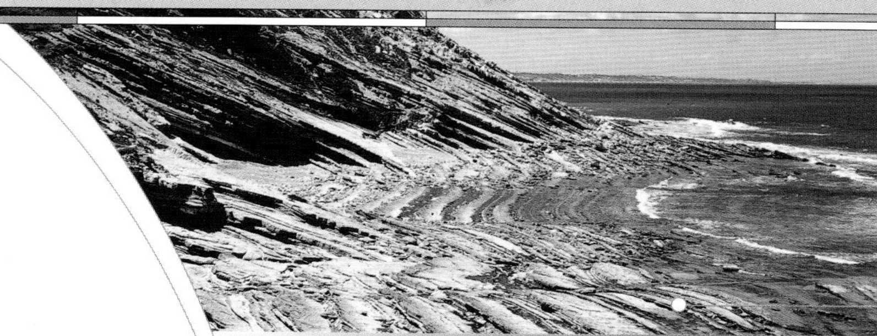

Spectacle of Nature

A thundering waterfall crashes over a steep drop in Iceland. The energy of flowing water, which mankind has not yet begun to exploit significantly, is a powerful force that here continues to erode the step in the terrain.

Planed and Leveled

The surf along the Basque coast near Saint-Jean-de-Luz has worn a flat abrasion plate in the terraced slopes of the Pyrenees.

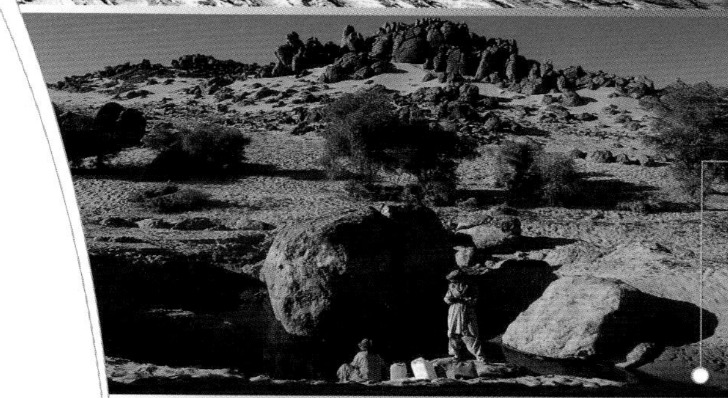

Source of Life

Water is extremely scarce in deserts. Knowledge of the few, often hidden sources of water is crucial to survival in these extremely arid regions. Surface springs like this one in the Aïr Massif (Niger) are rare, and water must often be drawn from wells or water holes dug in the sands of dry riverbeds.

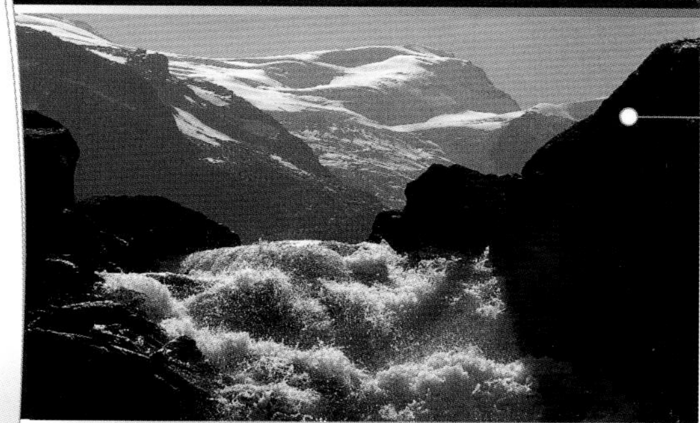

Unbridled Force

Water from melting snow and ice flows to the sea. In steep terrain, the milky glacial melt rushes unhindered to the valleys below. The fine sand dispersed in the water consists of rock material ground away under massive glacial pressure. In mountainous regions, the force of flowing water is strong enough to move even large blocks of stone.

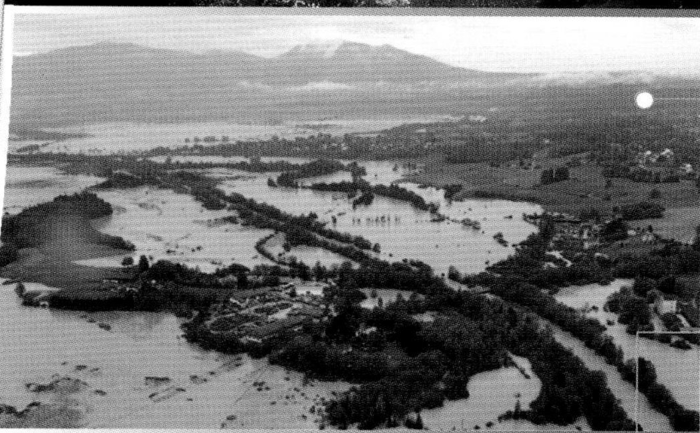

Floods

When the snows melt in spring or rains are especially heavy in summer, flooding often occurs on the coastal plains and alpine piedmont regions of Europe.

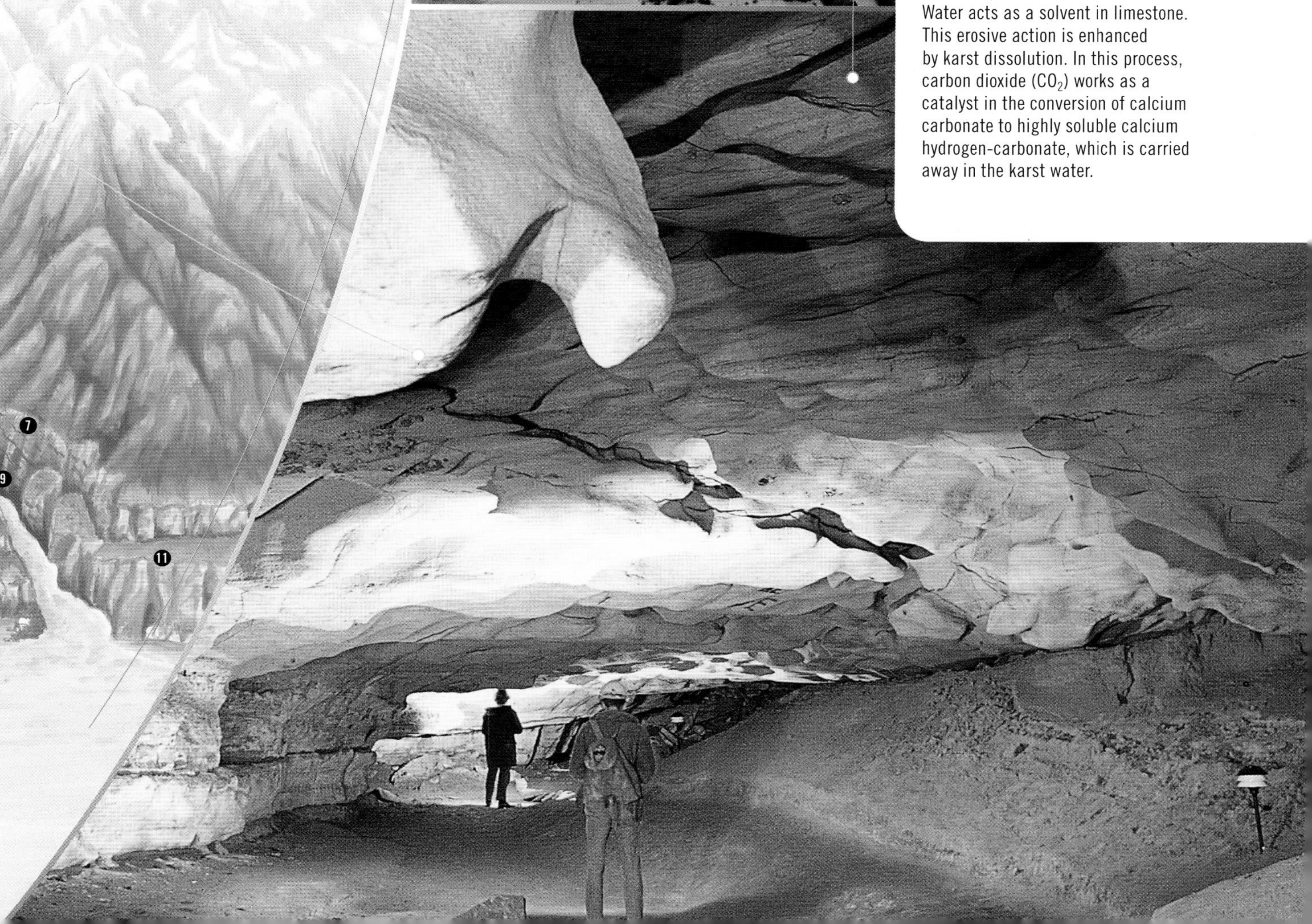

In the Underworld

Underground erosion creates caves (photo: Wyandotte Cave, Indiana). Water acts as a solvent in limestone. This erosive action is enhanced by karst dissolution. In this process, carbon dioxide (CO_2) works as a catalyst in the conversion of calcium carbonate to highly soluble calcium hydrogen-carbonate, which is carried away in the karst water.

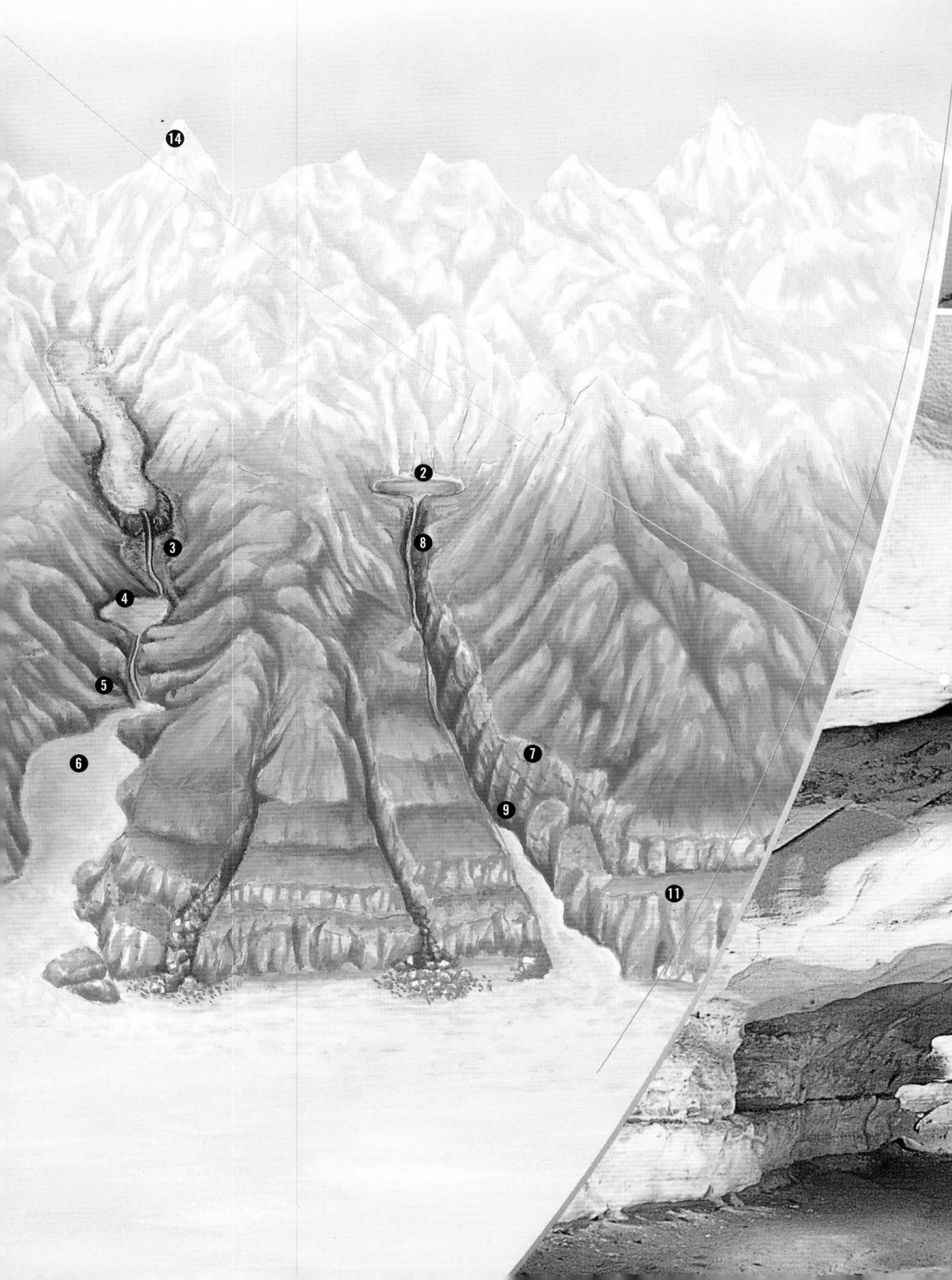

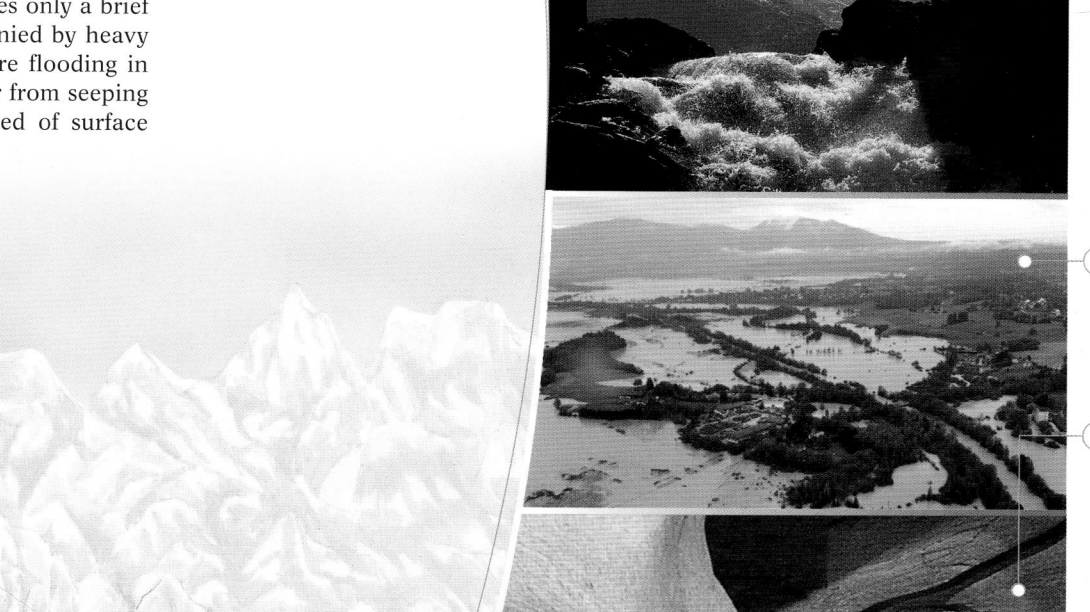

Natural Disasters – Human Catastrophes

Does Mankind Pose a Challenge to Nature?

The media provide news about a terrible natural disaster somewhere in the world virtually every day. Our television screens show us images of devastation and often of the dramatic events themselves as they unfold. Sober assessments of underlying causes are often overshadowed in the public mind by such sensational reports.

Yet there are several questions we cannot ignore: "To what extent are we humans at fault?" Is mankind inevitably doomed to destruction, or can we find a way to avert it?

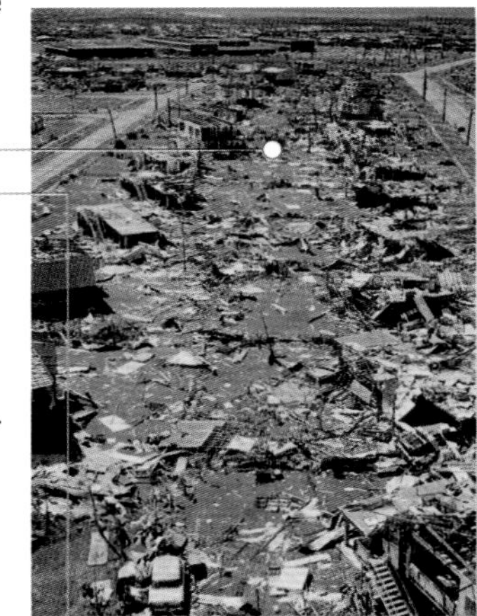

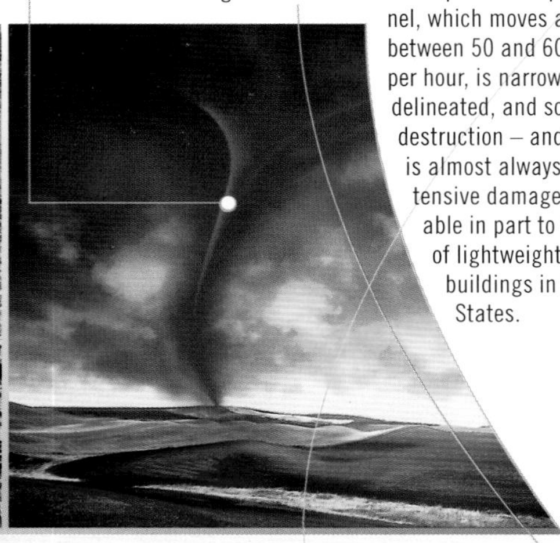

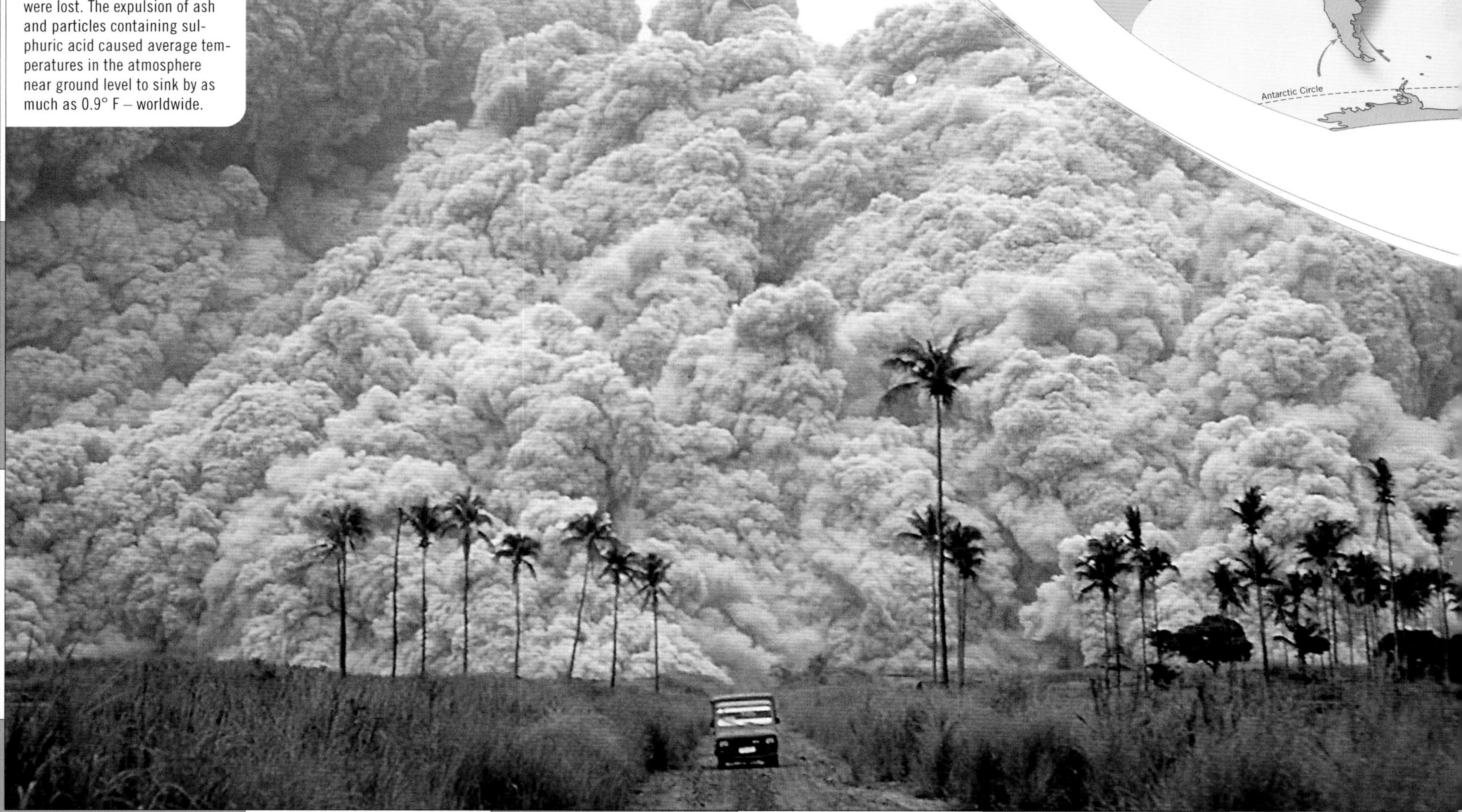

Disasters Mark the Course of the Earth's History

The history of the Earth teaches us that catastrophic events have always played a role in global and regional developments and have even impacted on the evolution of living organisms. Yet from our somewhat short-sighted present-day perspective, we tend to overlook the length of time involved in these processes. Experts continue to debate the question of whether the mass extinction of life forms some 65 million years ago was caused by a collision with an extraterrestrial body, a severe outbreak of volcanic activity, or other geological, perhaps tectonic events. Most agree, however, that the extinction of the dinosaurs (along with many other forms of animal life) paved the way for the development of mammals and thus ultimately for the origin of Homo sapiens. But when we speak of natural disasters, we are usually thinking of events that affect human beings directly.

A Devastating Christmas Present

On Christmas Day of 1974, Tropical Storm Tracy battered the city of Darwin in northern Australia. With average wind speeds of 140 kilometers per hour and gusts peaking at 260 kilometers per hour, the storm completely destroyed more than 5,000 of the 8,000 lightweight houses built on stilts. Forty-nine people died, and property damage amounted to 3 billion Australian dollars. Of Darwin's 45,000 inhabitants, 25,000 were evacuated by air, while 10,000 people fled the city by car toward the south. This was the greatest natural disaster in Australia's history.

Flight from the Inferno

In early April 1991, Pinatubo, a volcano on the Philippine island of Luzon, erupted again for the first time in human memory. In June, the mountain collapsed and lost 300 meters of elevation. Red-hot clouds spread like avalanches, covering distances of as much as 20 km. Ten cubic km of ash, gas, and other erupted matter were catapulted into the stratosphere to heights of up to 40 km. Torrential rains generated by a tropical storm turned the accumulated ash into massive streams of mud. More than 200,000 people fled the looming catastrophe; 400 lives were lost. The expulsion of ash and particles containing sulphuric acid caused average temperatures in the atmosphere near ground level to sink by as much as 0.9° F – worldwide.

Tornadoes – Dangerous Twisters

The narrow funnel of a tornado dips threateningly earthward. The air rising inside the funnel rotates at speeds that accelerate to a maximum of 200 kilometers per hour toward the inside. The suction force generated inside the funnel rips buildings apart and bursts lungs and blood vessels in human victims. Objects carried away become dangerous projectiles; dust and water are hurled high into the atmosphere. The path of the funnel, which moves at speeds between 50 and 60 kilometers per hour, is narrow and clearly delineated, and so is its wake of destruction – and destruction is almost always total. The extensive damage is attributable in part to the prevalence of lightweight, wood-frame buildings in the United States.

Cyclones

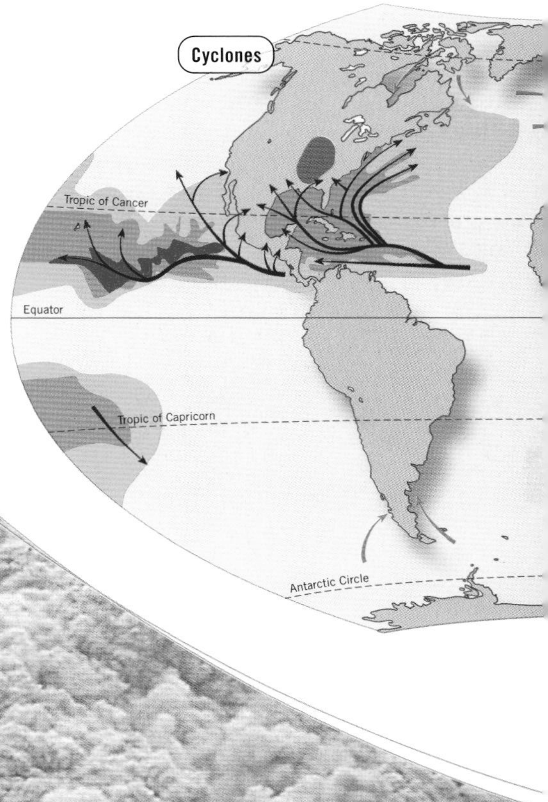

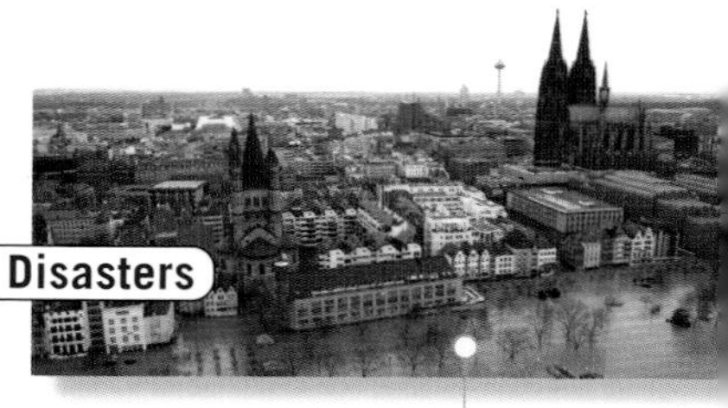

The Earth's Vast Destructive Potential

The "restless Earth" poses many dangers. Earthquakes and volcanic eruptions are concentrated in certain regions. While it is impossible to prevent such events from occurring, precautions can be taken against their consequences. The number of severe earthquakes (measuring 7.0 or above on the Richter Scale) did not increase worldwide during the twentieth century. Yet the toll in human lives and property damage has risen steadily, due to increasing population and building density, to the spread of settlements into endangered areas people once avoided, to the increasing value of property and goods (concentrated primarily in metropolitan areas) that has accompanied the rise in living standards, and to the increased susceptibility of modern societies and technologies to damage. Explosive population growth is another significant factor. The Kobe earthquake (1995) clearly showed seismic activity affects not only developing countries but often industrialized nations as well. And much the same applies to volcanism. We find ourselves in the midst of a heated debate about the dangers posed by the Earth's atmosphere and waters. Is the number of incidents rising? Are they growing in severity? And what or who is to blame – nature or mankind? A closely related issue is the question of mankind's impact on climate. Hurricanes are not the only destructive climatic phenomenon. Extended periods of heavy rain or snow storms; hail, ice, droughts; heat waves and periods of extreme cold; forest, bush, and prairie fires caused by lightning; avalanches, fog and smog all leave destruction in their wake. Excessive precipitation causes floods, landslips, and mudslides.

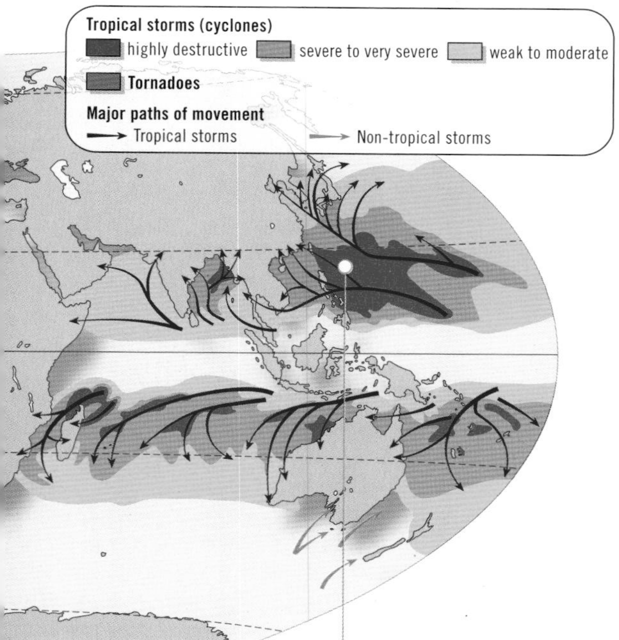

Stormy Times

The most dangerous storms originate in the Tropics: hurricanes along the coasts of Central and North America, typhoons over the waters off East and Southeast Asia, and cyclones in the Bay of Bengal (Bangladesh). They often wander for days over the sea in a westerly direction, only to turn suddenly north or south just before landfall. Their low pressure areas measure between 300 and 1,000 km in diameter. The center (known as the eye) of such storms is virtually cloudless and calm. It is encircled by a spiral of clouds that rotates at speeds up to 400 kilometers per hour. Torrential rain falls from massive cloud formations towering to heights of more than 15,000 meters. Storms that reach land wreak tremendous destruction, to which tidal waves also contribute, but then quickly lose intensity and dissipate. Hurricane Andrew caused $ 30 billion in damage. In Bangladesh, more than 300,000 people lost their lives in flooding caused by cyclones in 1970. The energy bundled in such storms is equivalent to that of several atomic bombs.

The tornadoes that occur frequently in the Midwestern United States are born when warm, moist air from the Gulf of Mexico is overlayered by dry, cool air from the Rocky Mountains or the Arctic. The temperature differential (between 36° and 54°F) generates incredibly high wind speeds. An average of 750 tornadoes are registered in the U.S. every year. They have costs the lives of hundreds of people – despite the well-organized warning system.

Tropical storms (cyclones)
- highly destructive
- severe to very severe
- weak to moderate
- Tornadoes

Major paths of movement
→ Tropical storms   → Non-tropical storms

Dangerous Tropical Storms

Tropical storms originate over waters with surface temperatures of at least 48°F in northern and southern latitudes between 5° and 30° during the late summer and early fall. A mass of moist, warm air with towering formations of cumulonimbus clouds gathers above the water. Condensation of the water vapor releases huge amounts of heat energy which accelerate the movement of rising air and the speed of the whirling mass of clouds. Tropical storms are generated by wavelike disruptions along the edge of the subtropical high-pressure belt or by the intrusion of low-pressure centers from the west-wind zone into the tropical circulation belt. Due to defrection caused by the Earth's rotation (Coriolis effect), storms spin clockwise in the southern hemisphere and counterclockwise in the northern hemisphere. Cyclonic storms do not occur near the equator, as the Coriolis effect is too weak to accelerate the rotating masses of air.

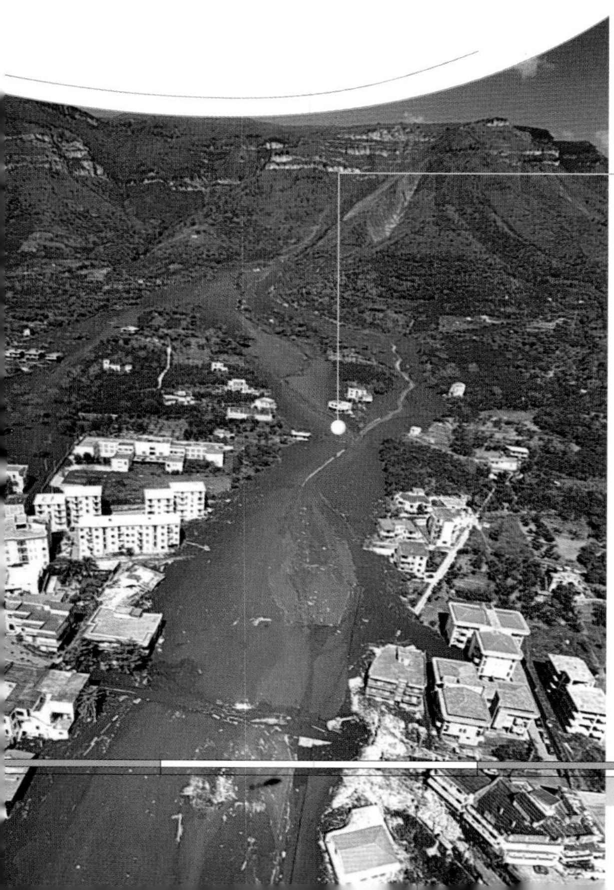

When the Earth Slides Away

Saturation of debris or "soft," porous rock on mountain slopes or hillsides by heavy, sustained rainfall or melting snow can cause extensive landslips or mudslides. When these huge masses of mud and debris are carried into the valleys below, the descending wave cuts a broad path of destruction through the landscape. Mudslides of this kind occur often in the Apennines (photo taken near Sarno, east of Mt. Vesuvius), especially in areas where slopes have been stripped of vegetation through deforestation or overgrazing.

Those Who Look for Trouble ...
The map divides the eastern and southeastern coasts of the United States into 58 numbered sections (each 80 km wide). Based on long-term observation, it is possible to estimate the probability of hurricane activity in a given year as a percentage value. The number of "normal" hurricanes (wind speeds higher than 33 meters per second) is entered in the inner row of boxes; "major" hurricanes (56 meters per second and higher) are listed in the outer row, which has several large gaps. Hurricane activity is most frequent in August and September.

Year in, Year out ...
Floods caused by high water on the Rhine (photo: Cologne) and its tributaries are practically a regular occurrence. Data gathered at water-level measuring stations enable authorities to issue advance warnings and initiate evacuation procedures. Dykes and ad hoc precautionary measures (such as mobile protective walls) can help prevent some but by no means all flood damage. Flooding in 1993 and 1995 caused total property damage estimated at five billion dollars.

Hurricane distribution

CANADA
UNITED STATES OF AMERICA
BAHAMAS
CUBA
Lake Superior
Lake Ontario
Lake Erie
All hurricanes
Major hurricanes

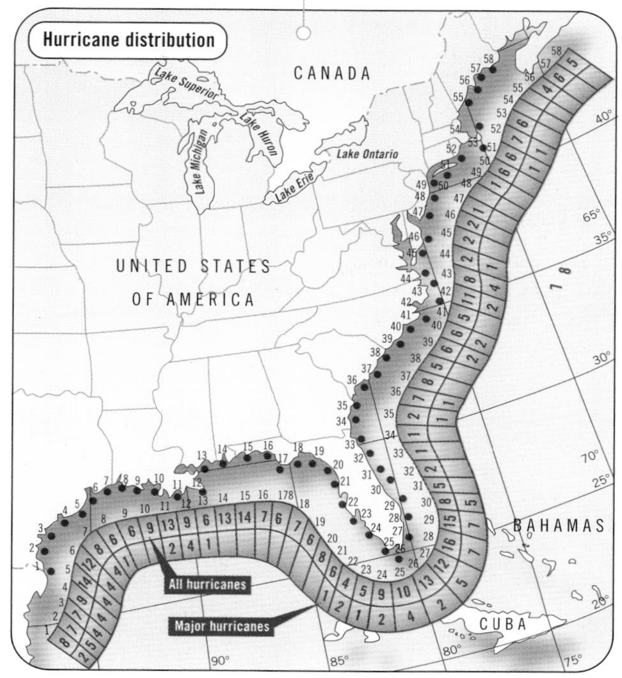

The Great Flood Yet to Come?

High water is ordinarily caused by unusually long periods of heavy precipitation or by rapid melting of winter snows. Repeated reports of catastrophic flooding evoke the impression that these disastrous events are becoming more frequent. Are they a by-product of global climatic changes that are reflected in increasingly heavy precipitation in Central Europe and the American Midwest? Catastrophic floods have occurred often in the past, as high-water marks show, but they had less far-reaching consequences, as agriculture and housing development were much less extensive than they are today. Various human interventions in the balance of nature have accelerated runoff activity and increased the danger of flooding. Prime examples are deforestation, ground-surface sealing (roads, housing developments, etc.), soil compaction (resulting from machine plowing and the conversion of meadowlands to fields), riverbed constriction with dams and dykes, river straightening, and the draining of wetlands (along the Mississippi, Missouri, and Red Rivers, for example), in combination with ground settlement and rising riverbed levels caused by accumulating silt deposits. Awakened from their lethargy by the increasing frequency and impact of floods, experts and regulatory authorities have instituted renaturation programs for river areas. Efforts to restore natural flood plains (retention areas) often encounter stiff opposition from local farmers, however.

Oceans and Marine Circulation Systems

The Global Climate Pump

Seen from space, the Earth is truly a blue planet, as more than two-thirds of its surface is covered by water. No other planet in our solar system has liquid water or the life it supports. The Earth's oceans are in constant motion, as water travels in powerful currents across them and circulate between the seafloor and the surface. Our seas are stirred by eddies and gyres and moved by winds and tidal forces. Visible waves on the surface are complemented by invisible ones in the ocean depths. The dynamics of the oceans have a significant impact on our planet's climate.

Driving Forces

Three different forces prevent the seas from ever coming to rest. The first is the gravitational pull of the Moon and (to a lesser extent) the Sun, which creates tidal action beneath which the Earth passes as it rotates. As a result, the seas shift in a twelve-hour (and in some places 24-hour) rhythm within their basins, rising and falling along their coasts (tidal action). Twice each month, the Moon, the Sun, and the Earth align with one another, causing particularly strong tidal action (spring and neap tides).

The second force that moves the seas is wind. It propels the major ocean surface currents, such as the Gulf and Brazil Currents in the Atlantic and the Kuroshio and Humboldt Currents in the Pacific. Highly characteristic, constant circulation patterns are sustained by prevailing winds – the trade winds in the subtropics and the West Wind Drift in the temperate zones – which are ultimately caused by the spheroid form and rotation of the Earth. Winds affect only the surface of the seas, and thus wind-driven circulation is restricted for the most part to the top 200 meters of water. However, the average depth of the world's oceans is about 4,000 meters, and their deepest

point (the Mariana Trench in the northwestern Pacific) is more than 11,000 meters below the surface.

The third driving force results from differences in seawater density. Water density depends upon temperature and salt content (which ranges between 3.4 % and 3.6 % in most marine waters), and thus this motion is referred to as thermohaline circulation (from the Greek word háls, for salt). The densest, heaviest water tends to sink and is found most commonly in the European North Atlantic and near the Antarctic. The sinking masses of heavier water circulate around the Earth in the depths of the oceans, while warm surface water flows into the sinking regions. In this way, all of the water in all of the oceans on the globe circulates between the seafloor and the surface and is enriched with oxygen. On average, the journey of a single water molecule from the North Atlantic to the depths of the Pacific takes about a thousand years.

The rotation of the Earth (in the form of deflection caused by the Coriolis force) plays an important role in the dynamics of marine circulation systems, causing much stronger currents along the western rims of ocean basins.

The Effects of Climate

The uppermost two meters of the ocean can store as much heat as the entire atmosphere, since water has a very high heat-retention capacity. This storage capacity works like a buffer that partially evens out seasonal temperature fluctuations. The range of these fluctuations is therefore much narrower in coastal maritime climates than in continental inland areas. The average difference between summer and winter temperatures on the East Coast of the United States is about 60 °F, but increases to 105 °F in Edmonton, Canada. In addition, ocean currents transport stored solar heat over tremendous distances, normally from the tropics to the poles. In this way, they help to narrow temperature gaps caused by the unequal distribution of solar radiation on earth.

The Atlantic is unique in that heat is transported through its waters by thermohaline circulation from the southern hemisphere to regions off the coasts of Europe. There, this warmth ascends into the air, which is carried by prevailing westerly winds to the European mainland. Europeans are familiar with the mild winter temperatures brought by westerly winds from time to time. This Atlantic central heating system raises the average annual air temperature in northwestern Europe by more than 9° F (5° C) – an effect that was instrumental in the development of agriculture and the rise of northern European cultures.

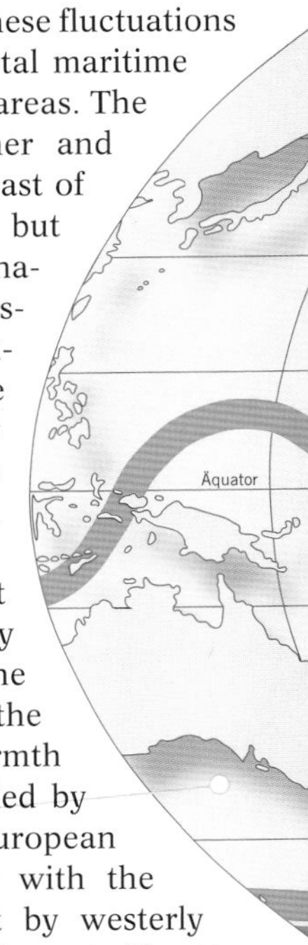

El Niño, the Christ Child

The interaction of marine currents, waves, and trade winds in the Pacific tropics produces a natural climatic fluctuation known as El Niño – Southern Oscillation (ENSO). At intervals of between three and seven years, the trade winds dissipate, the cold, nutrient-rich Humboldt current slows, and unusually warm water accumulates off the Pacific coast of South America. The people of the region have named this phenomenon El Niño after the Christ Child, because the coastal waters ordinarily grow warmer around Christmas. El Niño generates waves beneath the surface of the ocean which travel across the entire Pacific along the Equator. They are reflected at its western edge and return to the east, where their arrival marks the beginning of the end of the warm phase. The reverse phase of this fluctuation – unusually cold temperatures in the eastern Pacific – is called La Niña. Occurrences of El-Niño cause massive fish death

The El Niño Phenomenon
A satellite image showing the unusual warming pattern. The white zone represents high-temperature associated with the highest surface elevation, ranging between 14 and 32 cm above the average level. The ocean surface in the purple zone is lower, and the red zones indicate unusually high heat retention.

10 NOV 97

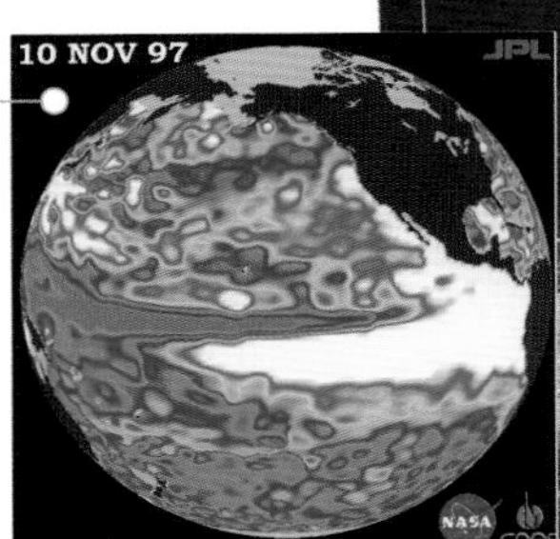

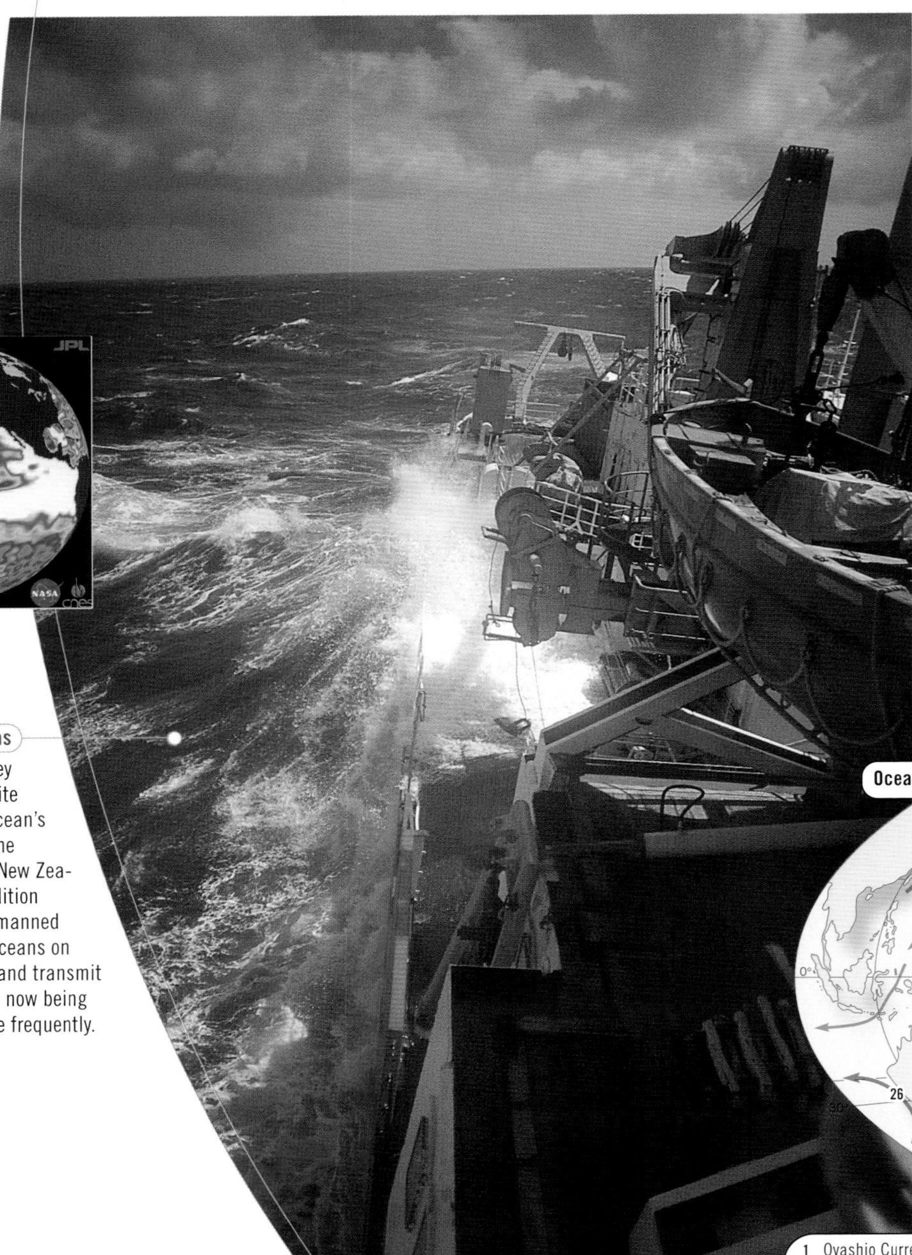

Research Vessel in Heavy Seas
Ships are still needed to survey marine currents, since satellite imagery captures only the ocean's surface. The photo shows the "Rapuhia", a vessel from New Zealand on a scientific expedition in the South Pacific. Unmanned probes that cross the oceans on programmed courses and transmit data to satellites are now being used more and more frequently.

Ocean Currents

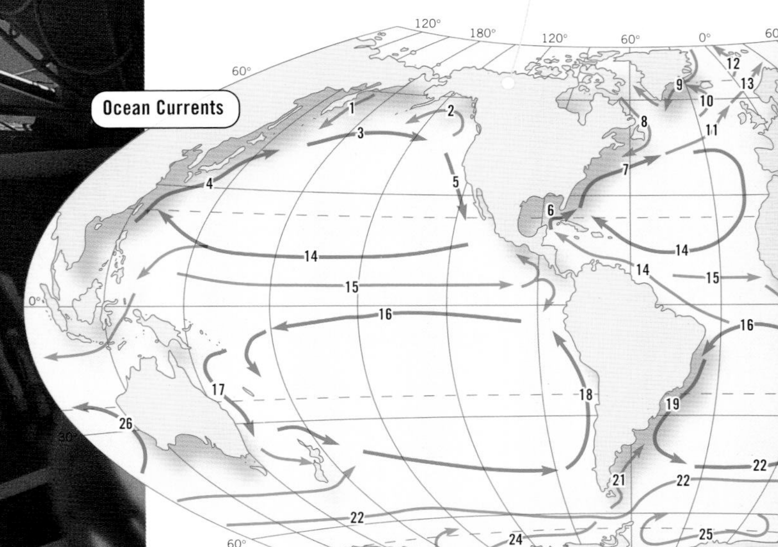

1 Oyashio Current	6 Florida Current	11 North Atlantic Current	16 South Equatorial
2 Alaska Current	7 Gulf Stream	12 North Cape Current	17 East Australian
3 North Pacific Current	8 Labrador Current	13 Norwegian Current	18 Humboldt Curre
4 Kuroshio	9 East Greenland Current	14 North Equatorial Current	19 Brazil Current
5 California Current	10 Irminger Current	15 Equatorial countercurrents	20 Benguela Curre

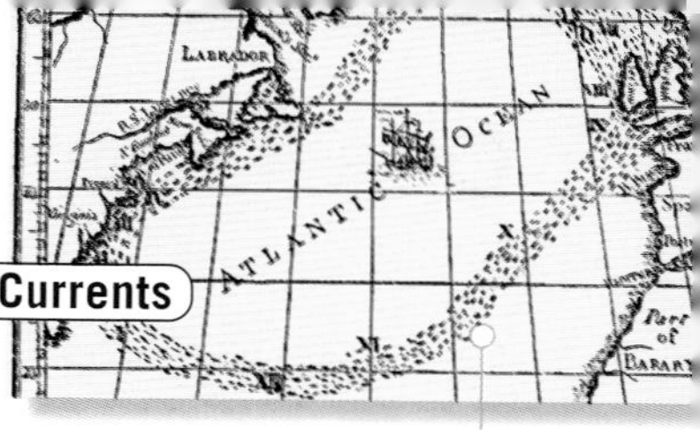

The Oceanic Climate Pump

	Surface currents
	Intermediate-depth currents
	Seafloor currents
	Sinking zones

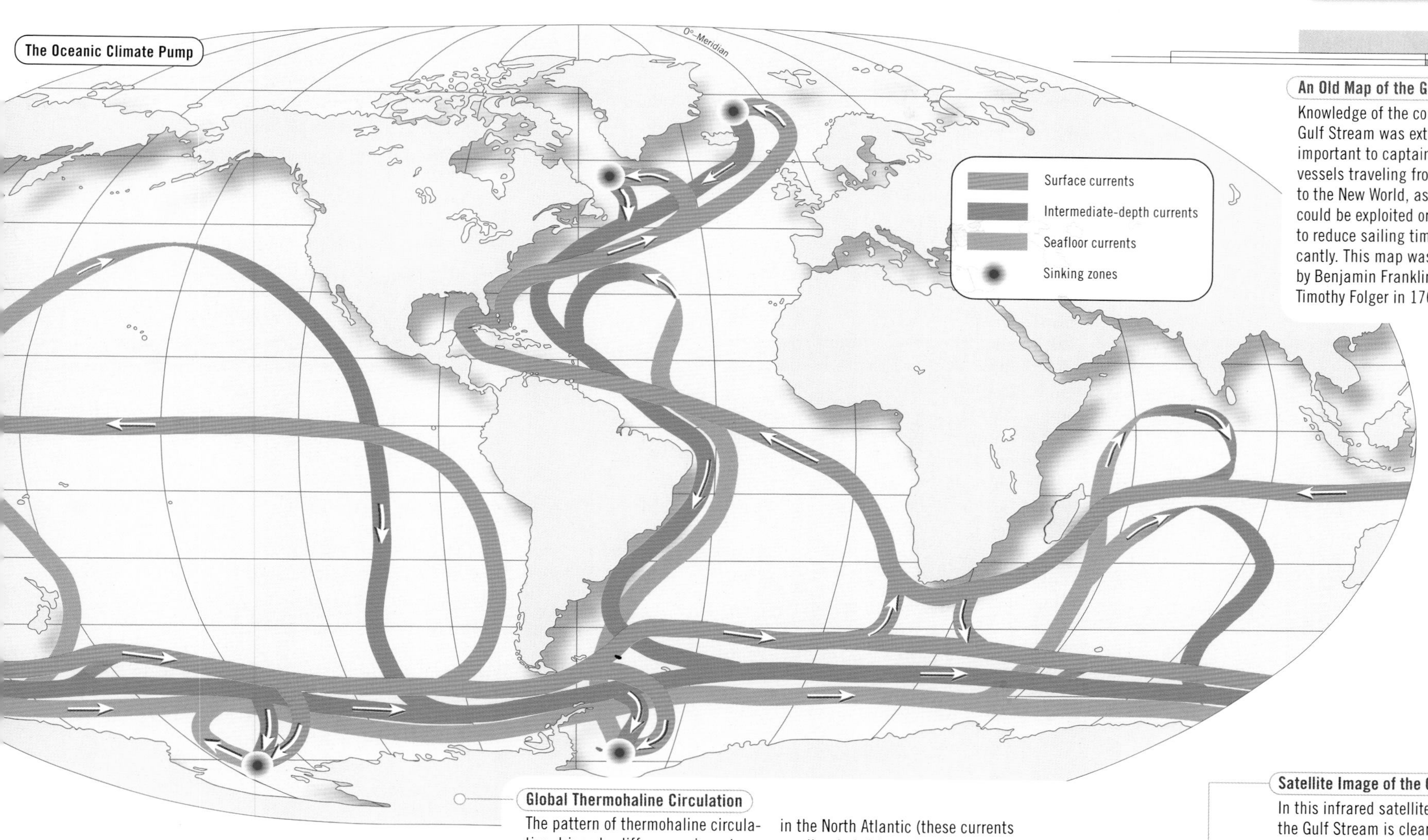

An Old Map of the Gulf Stream

Knowledge of the course of the Gulf Stream was extremely important to captains of ocean vessels traveling from Europe to the New World, as the current could be exploited or avoided to reduce sailing times significantly. This map was compiled by Benjamin Franklin and Timothy Folger in 1769.

off the coasts of Peru and Ecuador and are responsible for weather extremes all over the globe. Today, they can be predicted several months in advance on the basis of computer simulations. If farmers respond in time, crop failures can be avoided for the most part.

Currents of Life

Ocean currents circulate vast quantities of nutrients and trace substances and supply oxygen to the depths of the sea. Thus they are essential to marine life. Without currents, the oceans of the Earth would be nearly dead. The rich fishing grounds off the coast of Peru are fed by the Humboldt Current, and thermohaline circulation promotes especially vigorous algae growth in the North Atlantic. Currents also carry carbon dioxide into the depths of the sea, thus helping rid the atmosphere of man-made emissions that contribute to global warming.

Global Thermohaline Circulation

The pattern of thermohaline circulation driven by differences in water density spans the Earth like a gigantic conveyor belt. Thus warm water near the surface of the Atlantic flows northward from the southern tip of Africa through the Benguela Current, the Gulf Stream, and the North Atlantic Current into the sinking regions in the North Atlantic (these currents overlie wind-driven circulation patterns). From there, it flows as cold water at a depth of two to three kilometers back to the south. In the process, 1015 Watts of thermal energy are transported into the North Atlantic region – the equivalent of the output of 500,000 large power plants.

Satellite Image of the Gulf Stream

In this infrared satellite image, the Gulf Stream is clearly identifiable as a warm (black and red) band. It veers from the North American coast off Cape Hatteras and breaks apart, forming meanders and gyres. Its warm water flows with the North Atlantic Stream to regions off the coasts of northern Europe.

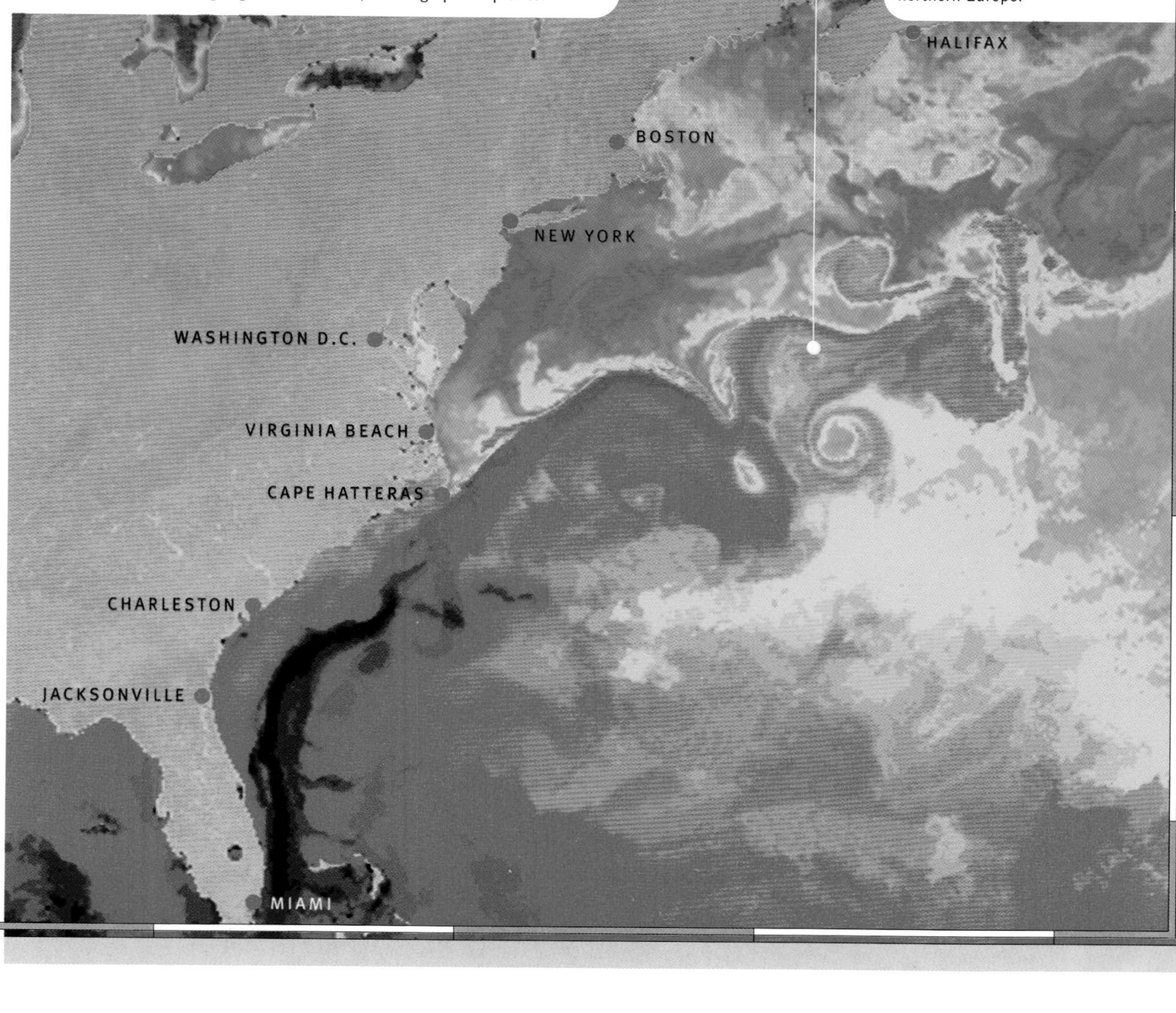

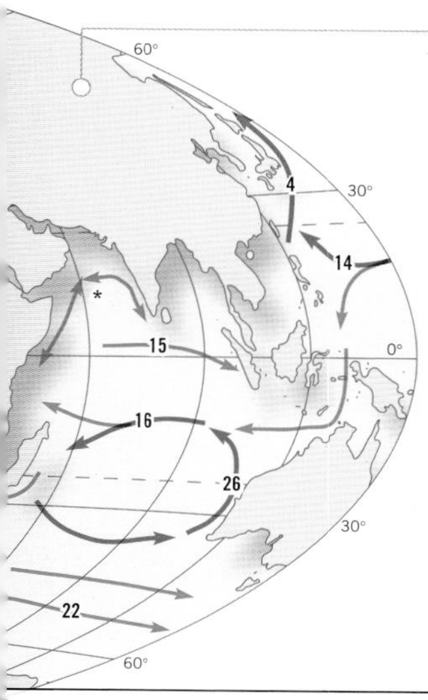

Surface Currents

Ocean currents which flow near the surface are largely wind-driven but may also be propelled by differences in seawater density. The prevailing trade and west winds are responsible for the largest subtropical gyre, along the western edge of which the strong boundary currents (including the Gulf Stream, the Kuroshio and the Brazil Current) flow toward the poles.

HALIFAX

BOSTON

NEW YORK

WASHINGTON D.C.

VIRGINIA BEACH

CAPE HATTERAS

CHARLESTON

JACKSONVILLE

MIAMI

kland Current	**25** Wedell Gyre
tarctic Circum-	**26** West Australien Current
ar Current	→ Major subtropical gyres
ulhas Current	→ Strong Currents
ss-Sea Gyre	* Direction depends upon the season

The Earth's Ice – A Remnant of the Ice Age

Is Ice on Earth Melting or is a New Ice Age Coming?

Many people today are concerned that global warming will eventually melt all of the Earth's ice. Were this to happen, the sea level would rise as much as 70 meters. Coastal cities like New York, London, and Hamburg would be flooded completely. Many low-lying areas and countless islands would be submerged.

On the other hand, the warming process could also produce heavier precipitation in the polar regions, adding to the existing Antarctic ice sheet. Yet the danger could come from another quarter. Oceanic warming could affect ocean currents. The Gulf Stream, our warm water heating system, could disperse, and the climate in the North Atlantic region would become much colder. Those who think in terms of geological time know that a new ice age will come sooner or later, as many warm periods lasted hardly longer than the Holocene, our own post-glacial era.

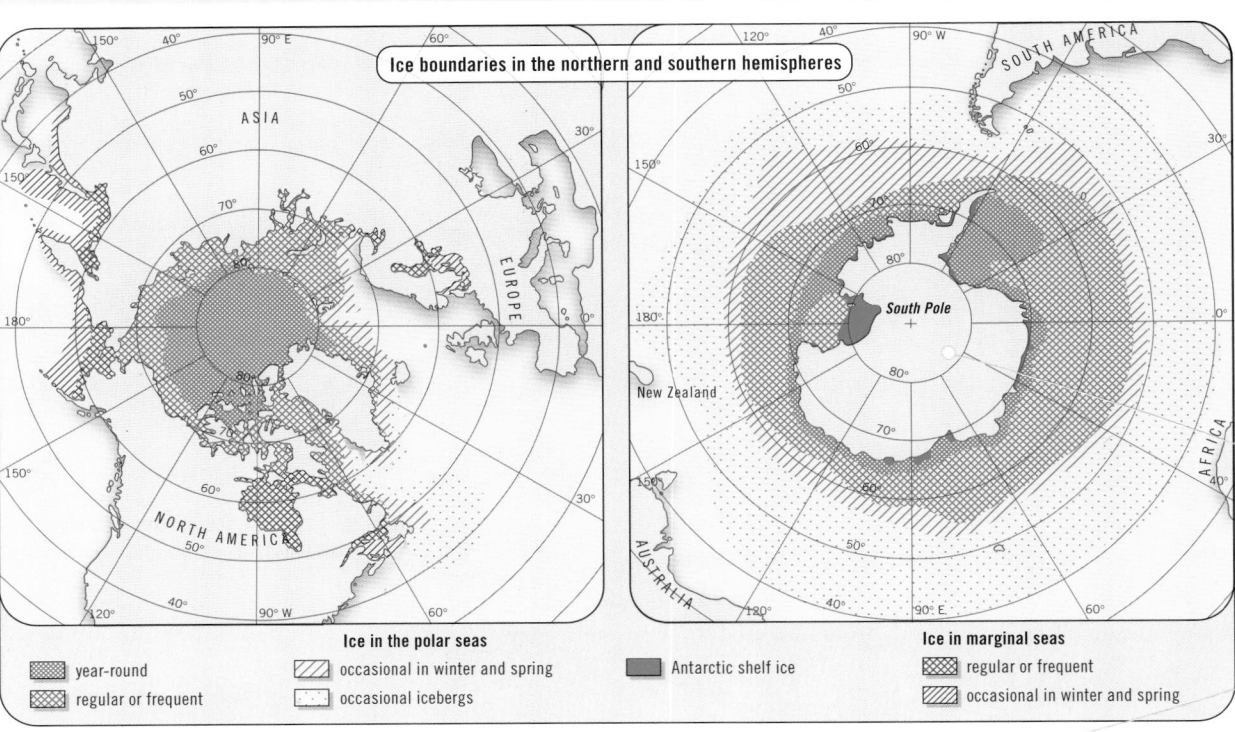

Ice boundaries in the northern and southern hemispheres

Ice in the polar seas		
year-round	occasional in winter and spring	
regular or frequent	occasional icebergs	

Ice in marginal seas	
Antarctic shelf ice	regular or frequent
	occasional in winter and spring

From Snow to Glacial Ice

Dry, fresh snow (density: 0.01–0.04 g/ccm) is 90 % air. Delicate ice crystals in snowflakes soon break down; the snow settles, melts to a certain degree, and freezes again (regelation). Developing grains of ice form firn snow (0.55 g/ccm), which contains 50 % air, and then firn ice (0.84 g/ccm), in which air bubbles account for only 30 % of total mass. The final phase is glacial ice (0.90 g/ccm), which is impermeable to air and water. Pure ice has a density of 0.917 g/ccm. In the Alps, ice grains measuring up to eight centimeters in diameter form after several years, while grains of ice at the South Pole can take 200 years to reach a diameter of one centimeter.

Ice Shapes the Topography

Although ice moves more slowly than flowing water, it exerts tremendous pressure on the underlying rock (100 to 5000 tons per square meter). Pressure and motion grind the rock away (detersion) and form roches moutonnées with flat ice-facing slopes and steeply inclined back sides. Rock fragments carried by the flow cut grooves in the smoothly ground rock, which later make it possible to trace the direction of glacial movement. V-shaped valleys carved by flowing water before the formation of ice are reshaped into U-shaped valleys. Rock debris broken away by the ice is transported to the edge of the ice flow, where it is melted out and deposited in terminal moraines. Unlike flowing water, ice is capable of moving huge boulders, which are left as erratics in the landscape after the ice recedes.

Flowing Glaciers

In contrast to rigid sea ice, glacial ice is granulated and becomes malleable and flowable under pressure. Regelation plays an important role in this process. The much colder ice in the Antarctic glides only as rigid block formations.

The Water Vapor – Ice – Water Cycle

Water evaporates from the warm oceans and rises with air currents into the high mountain regions. At these ice-cold elevations, it forms small ice crystals that fall to the ground as snow, even during the summer. This snow turns to ice, which then flows downward toward warmer areas, actually reaching the sea in some places. Icebergs are calved as inland ice slides into the sea. This cycle is driven by solar energy.

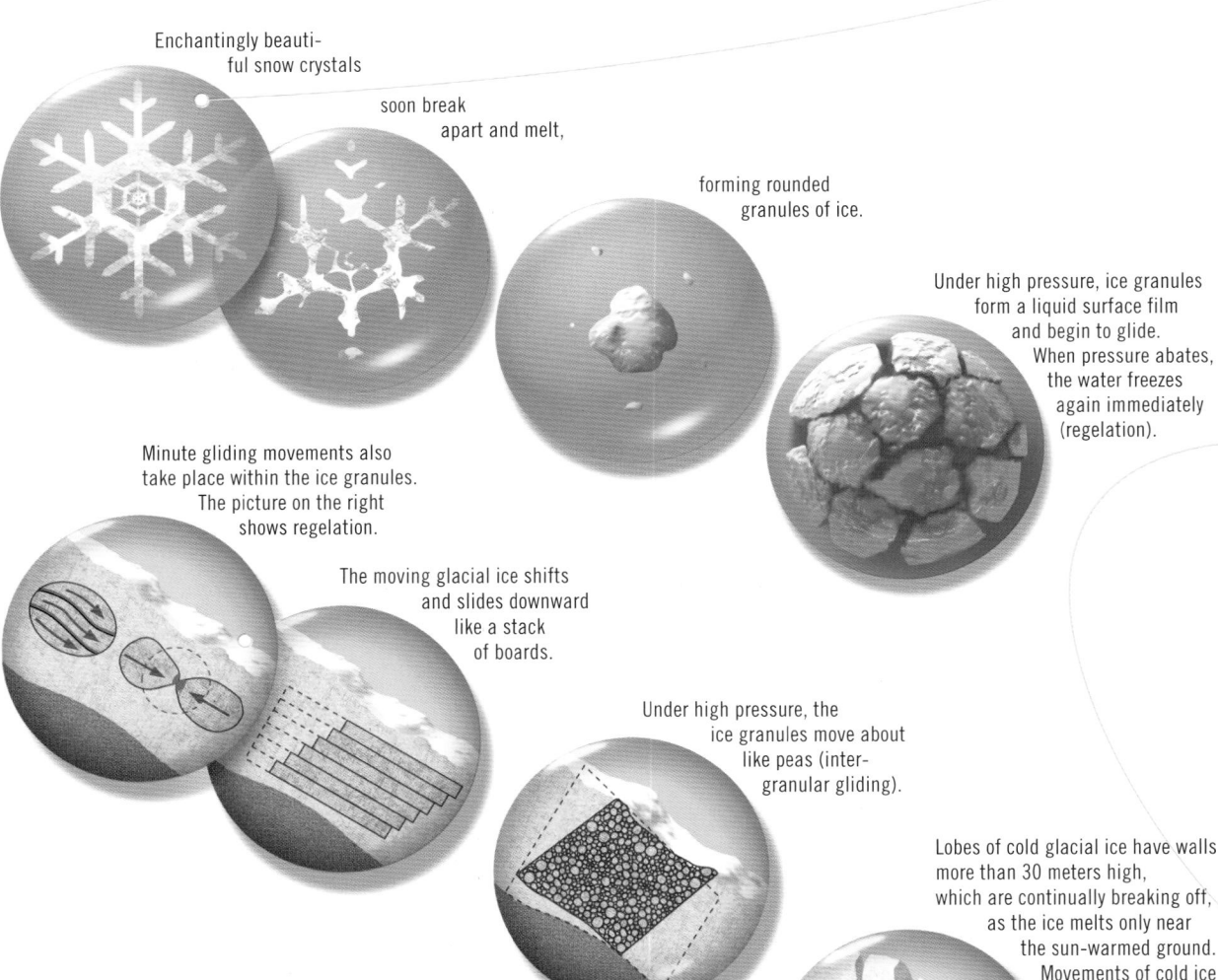

Enchantingly beautiful snow crystals

soon break apart and melt,

forming rounded granules of ice.

Under high pressure, ice granules form a liquid surface film and begin to glide. When pressure abates, the water freezes again immediately (regelation).

Minute gliding movements also take place within the ice granules. The picture on the right shows regelation.

The moving glacial ice shifts and slides downward like a stack of boards.

Under high pressure, the ice granules move about like peas (inter-granular gliding).

Lobes of cold glacial ice have walls more than 30 meters high, which are continually breaking off, as the ice melts only near the sun-warmed ground. Movements of cold ice are abrupt but cause only minor glacial erosion.

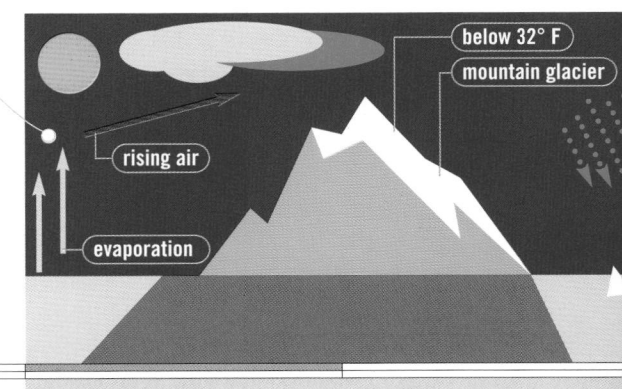

below 32° F
mountain glacier
rising air
evaporation

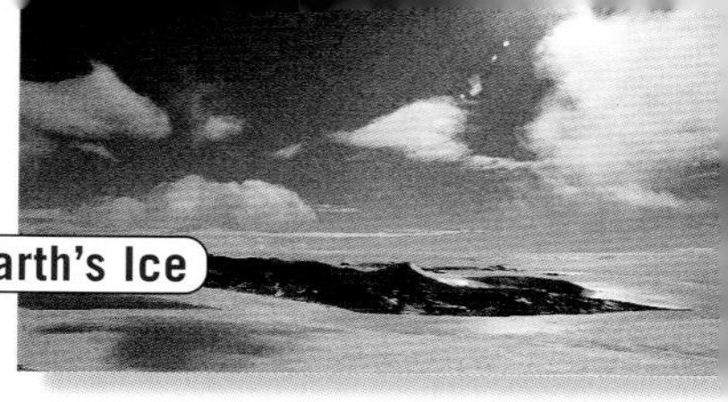

The Earth's Frozen Caps

The lower boundary of permanent ice in the mountains depends largely on the climate. The ice line lies at about 2,600 m on the northern face of the Alps, 4,800 m at the Equator, and over 6,000 m in dry subtropical regions, such as Tibet. Snow descends quickly to the valleys in avalanches from very steep terrain but forms glacial ice wherever it can accumulate.

The rocky summits of many of the world's highest mountains are hidden from view by ice caps. On steep slopes, the ice breaks apart, forming deep crevasses. Concealed by a covering of snow, these pose a particular danger to mountain climbers. Ice avalanches are common on extremely steep inclines.

There are hundreds of glaciers in northwestern Canada and Alaska. The Malaspina Glacier in Alaska, the longest valley glacier in the world, is 115 km long. Glaciers are numerous in the Rocky Mountains of the United States and the Andes in South America.

When Islands Merge with the Mainland

Global sea levels fall as increasing amounts of water are captured in ice. During the last ice age, the sea level was 135 meters lower than it is today. Many areas now far below the ocean's surface were once dry land. A land bridge across the Bering Strait connected Asia with North America. England was not an island, and coral isles rose as small mountains from the sea. During warm periods, the ice melts and sea levels begin to rise again. The Antarctic ice sheet (12.6 million square km) has presumably existed for some 20 million years. Sea ice in the Arctic (2 million square km) is only three centimeters thick and tends to melt and regelate quickly. The massive Greenland ice sheet (1.7 million square km) is relatively stable.

When Water Freezes, Everything Changes

Liquid water assumes a solid state at temperatures below 32° F. Average temperatures remain below the freezing point the year round in the polar regions and in the high mountain areas above the snow line. The polar caps are exposed to insufficient warming solar radiation, and the thin air in the alpine regions grows increasingly colder at higher elevations. Temperatures fall by up to 1.8° F per 100 meters of elevation. At heights of 5,000 meters and above, mountain slopes are covered constantly with ice and snow, even in hot, tropical inland areas. In the coldest regions of the world, the ground is frozen permanently (permafrost), though not beneath the inland ice sheets.

Ice Sheets Cover Entire Continents

During glacial periods ice may bury entire mountain ranges and expand far into the surrounding landscape. In North America, the Laurentide Ice Sheet, which once covered Canada and northern parts of the United States, covered a total area of more than 13 million square km. Today, only two parts of the world remain covered by enormous inland ice sheets: Greenland and the Antarctic. Ice in the Antarctic is some 4,800 meters thick in some places. If the 30 million cubic km of ice in the Antarctic were distributed among five million people, each of them would receive a ton of ice every minute for ten years. The same quantity of ice would cover all the dry land on earth with a layer 180 meters thick.

Snow

Inland ice sheet

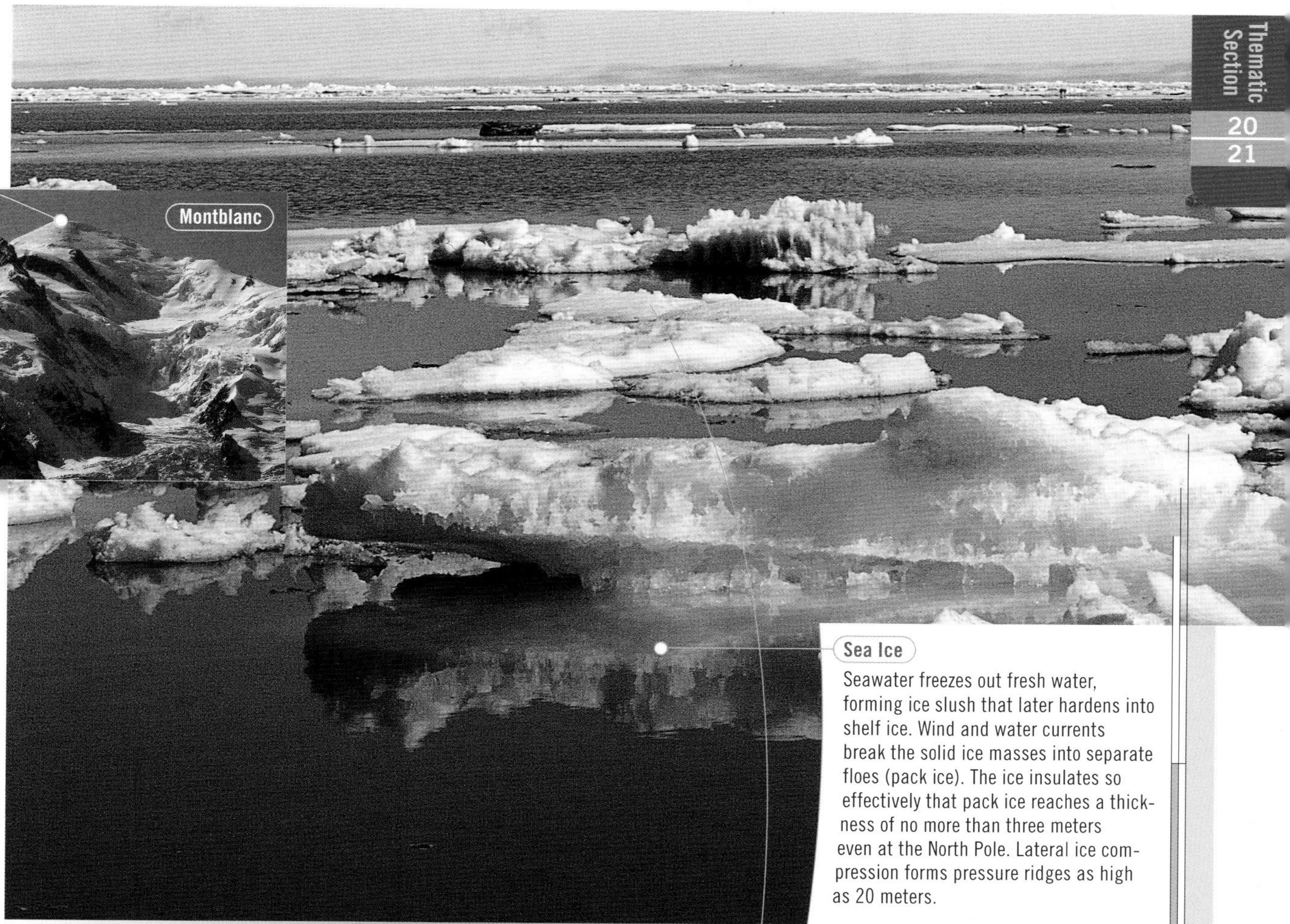

Montblanc

Sea Ice

Seawater freezes out fresh water, forming ice slush that later hardens into shelf ice. Wind and water currents break the solid ice masses into separate floes (pack ice). The ice insulates so effectively that pack ice reaches a thickness of no more than three meters even at the North Pole. Lateral ice compression forms pressure ridges as high as 20 meters.

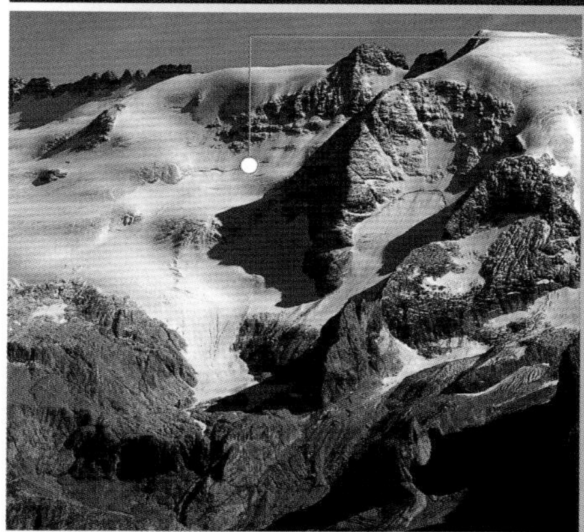

Eternal Snow

The snow line becomes visible in the summer, when snow at lower mountain elevations melts completely. Above the snow line, precipitation falls almost exclusively in the form of snow, and more snow falls than melts in the course of the year. This surplus of snow turns to glacial ice. In the late fall, the snow line begins its gradual descent to lower elevations (temporary snow line).

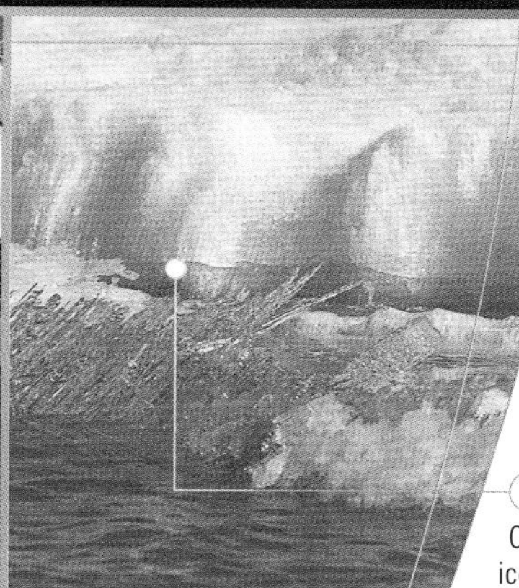

Solid Ice

Column-shaped ice crystals give sheets of ice on fresh-water lakes considerable strength. These crystals grow downward from the surface. Rigid lake ice is inflexible and very strong. Depending upon its thickness, it can support skaters or even large cargo aircraft.

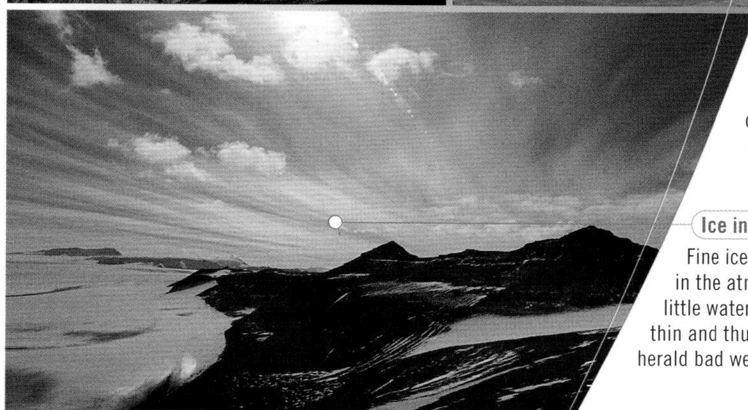

Ice in the Sky (Cirrus Clouds)

Fine ice crystals form from water vapor high in the atmosphere. Since cold air contains very little water, these clouds of ice crystals are very thin and thus transparent. Cirrus clouds often herald bad weather.

Ice-Cold Ground

Water contained in soil is completely frozen in permafrost regions. When the upper layer of ground thaws in the summer and liquid surface water seeps into fissures in the ground, it freezes immediately and seals the hollow spaces. (photo from an underground tunnel).

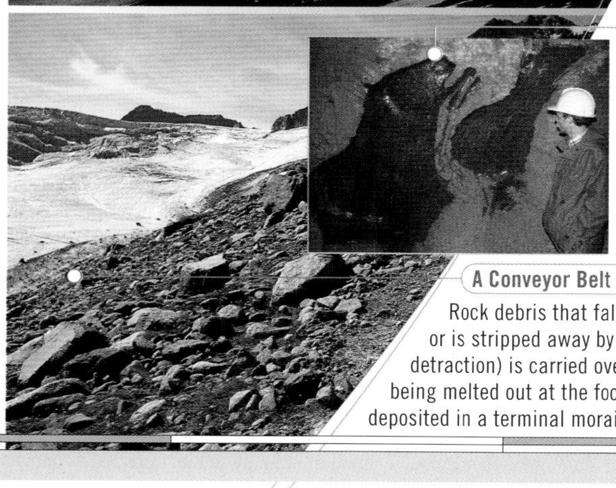

A Conveyor Belt of Ice

Rock debris that falls from mountain slopes or is stripped away by glacial ice (exaration, detraction) is carried over long distances before being melted out at the foot of the glacier and deposited in a terminal moraine.

Global Climate Zones

Stable or Constantly in Flux?

Today's climate patterns are certain to change. Just 5,000 years ago, average summer temperatures in North America were 36.5 degrees higher than today, and deciduous forests stood where conifers thrive today. The state of New Hampshire was covered by an ice sheet as recently as 18,000 years ago.
Core samples from the Greenland Ice Sheet show how abruptly climate can change. Scientists studying samples from a lake in southern Italy recently learned that local vegetation changed from dense forest to sparse steppe growth and back again within only 200 years about 75,000 years ago. The discovery came as a surprise to the many people who believed that the natural phenomenon of climate is constant over extended periods of time.

The Varying Intensity of Solar Heat

During the ice ages, plants, animals, and human beings were forced out of vast areas of the northern hemisphere. Life did not return to these regions until temperatures rose again and the ice gradually receded. We still do not know precisely what caused these drastic climatic changes, although experts agree that solar radiation is a crucial determinant of climate. Our planet is close enough to the sun to benefit from its warmth, yet far enough away that our atmosphere does not evaporate. The parallel rays of the sun strike the earth at a ninety-degree angle at the equator but reach the poles at a much flatter angle. Differences in pressure resulting from this unequal distribution of solar energy generate massive air currents. The influx of solar energy also differs from point to point depending upon the season and time of day, and this affects local weather as well. This results in part from the fact that the Earth's axis is not perpendicular to the plane of its orbit around the sun but is instead inclined at an angle of 23.5 degrees. The effects of this tilt are particularly noticeable in the polar regions (polar days and nights).

Global Respiration

Masses of air warmed in the tropics rise and drift into cooler northern or southern regions, while colder polar air flows toward the Equator. This general pattern of atmospheric circulation is a blessing that balances extremes in different climate zones. Yet a number of other factors also contribute to climate differences: elevation, topography, the distribution of land and seas, and cold or warm ocean currents. The macroclimates of specific climate zones can be broken down into mesoclimates (local weather patterns) and microclimates nearest the Earth's surface.

Weather activity takes place primarily in the troposphere, which lies beneath the stratosphere and extends to an altitude of about 13 km. The composition of our atmosphere is remarkably constant. Dry air is composed of nitrogen (78% by volume), oxygen (21%) and small amounts of argon (0.9%), carbon dioxide (0.03%), neon, helium, and other gases. It can also contain up to 4% water vapor. Terrestrial organisms have adapted to this mixture of gases. When oxygen concentration falls below 20% (at high altitudes or in poorly ventilated rooms, for example), we feel the unpleasant effects immediately.

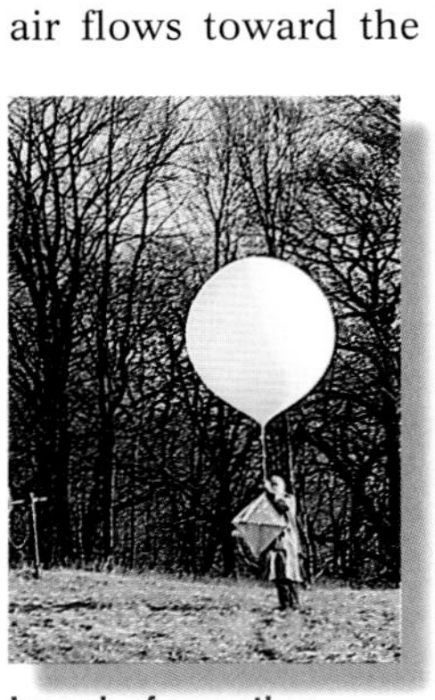

Launch of a weather balloon equipped with a radio sensor that transmits readings from high altitudes. Special balloons rise to altitudes of 35 km. Satellites send back data and images from as high as 36,000 km above the earth.

Weather, Weather Patterns, and Climate

A look at the formations and movements of clouds in the sky tells us a great deal about local weather at any given moment. Average prevailing weather conditions at a specific location represent general weather patterns. Prevailing weather patterns that persist over long periods of time make up the climate of a particular region.

Adaptation – Creating Our Own Microclimates

Human beings depend on weather and climate more than any other living organisms. It is no coincidence that most ancient cultures had weather gods – Zeus in ancient Greece and Thor, the god of thunder in the Germanic world are just two examples. Yet unlike other living beings, humans possess the ability to protect themselves against extreme weather.

Humans have little difficulty coping with conditions in the warmer climate zones, as they adapt easily to high temperatures (due perhaps to their origin in the African savannahs). But to survive in the cold regions of the Earth, man had to gain command of fire, develop appropriate clothing, and learn to build tolerable microclimates – tents made of hides, igloos built with blocks of snow, wooden houses or urban housing developments.

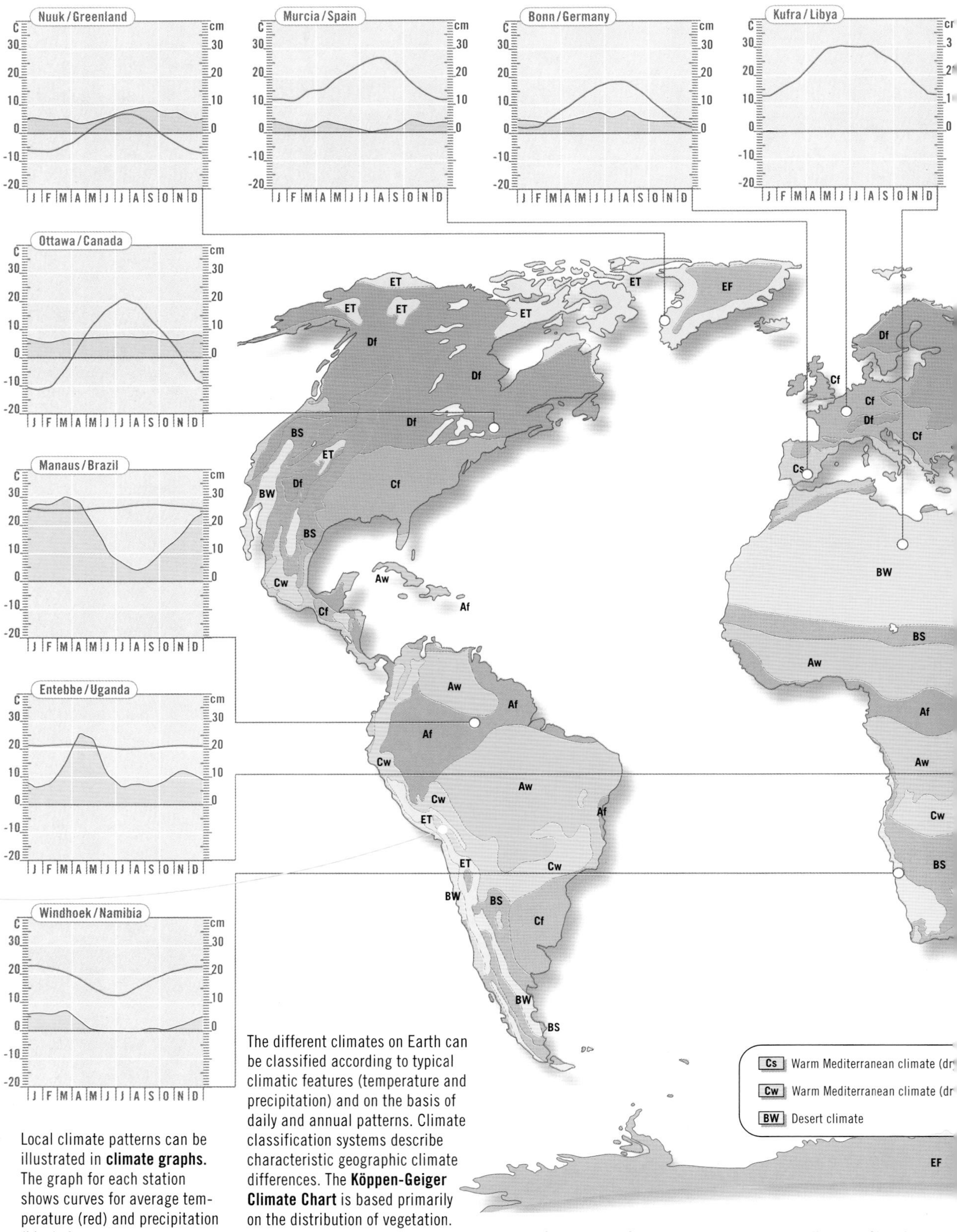

Local climate patterns can be illustrated in **climate graphs**. The graph for each station shows curves for average temperature (red) and precipitation (blue). A temperature curve that lies above the precipitation curve indicates arid conditions, while the reverse is an indicator of humidity.

The different climates on Earth can be classified according to typical climatic features (temperature and precipitation) and on the basis of daily and annual patterns. Climate classification systems describe characteristic geographic climate differences. The **Köppen-Geiger Climate Chart** is based primarily on the distribution of vegetation. Since climate conditions are among the most important factors affecting plant growth, vegetation is a good indicator of climate at a given location.

A simplified version of Köppen-Geiger's classification scheme distinguishes among tropical wet-dry and arid climates (A), desert and steppe climates (B), humid temperate climates (C), cold dry continental climates (D) and tundra and snow-and-ice climates (E).

Cs	Warm Mediterranean climate (dr
Cw	Warm Mediterranean climate (dr
BW	Desert climate

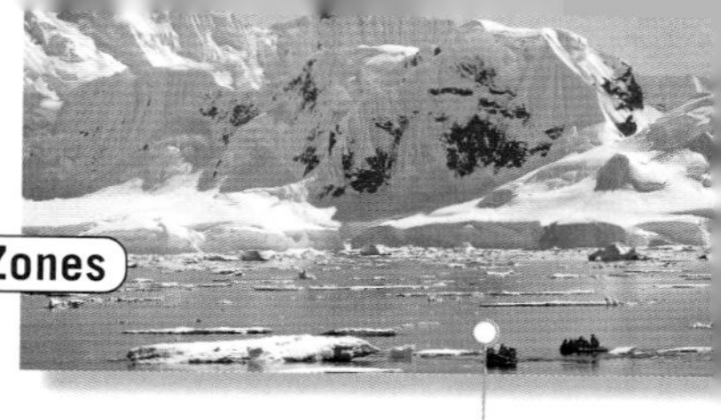

Alpine Elevation Zones

Mountain climates grow increasingly inhospitable at higher altitudes. Temperatures fall, and the air becomes moister and stormier. Vegetation is also distributed in belts at different elevations depending upon local climate conditions. The upper vegetation boundary borders on a zone of debris, snow, and ice near the summit (photo taken near Haines, Alaska). The ground is covered by snow for longer periods at higher elevations, thus shortening vegetation periods during which photosynthesis is possible. This basic heat deficit is offset somewhat by solar radiation, which is filtered only slightly by the thin atmosphere (as mountain climbers learn when they experience their first severe case of ultra-violet sunburn). Not only are air and ground temperatures lower at high altitudes, atmospheric pressure falls as well, reducing the supply of life-giving oxygen, carbon dioxide and water vapor in the air. The unfavorable conditions in the high mountain regions restrict species diversity. Summer temperatures are a crucial factor. The tree line is highest where summer solar radiation is most intense. Although plants in polar and alpine regions have much in common, they also exhibit major differences, as these climates are subject to different annual climatic shifts to which living organisms must adjust accordingly.

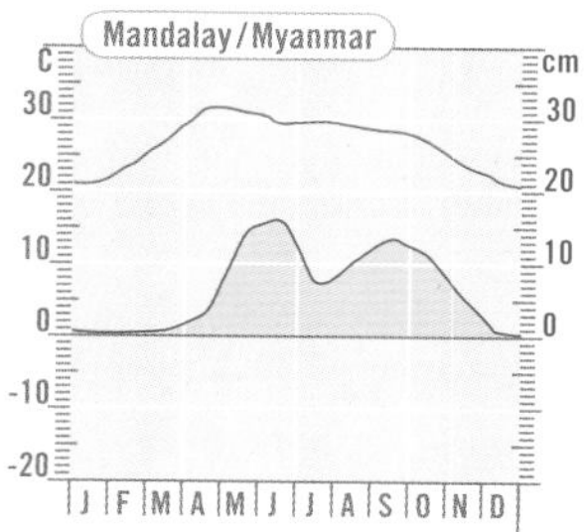

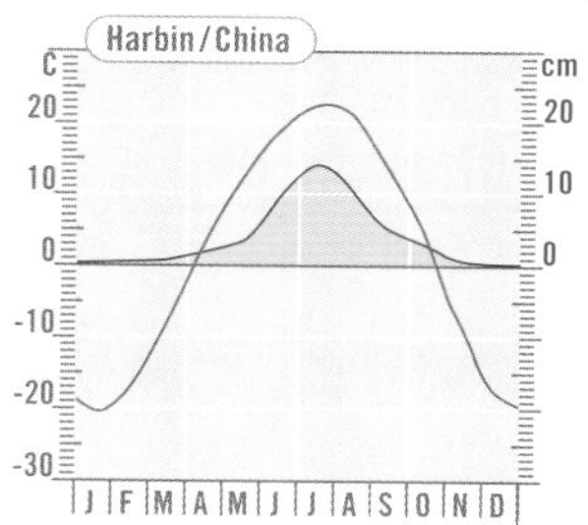

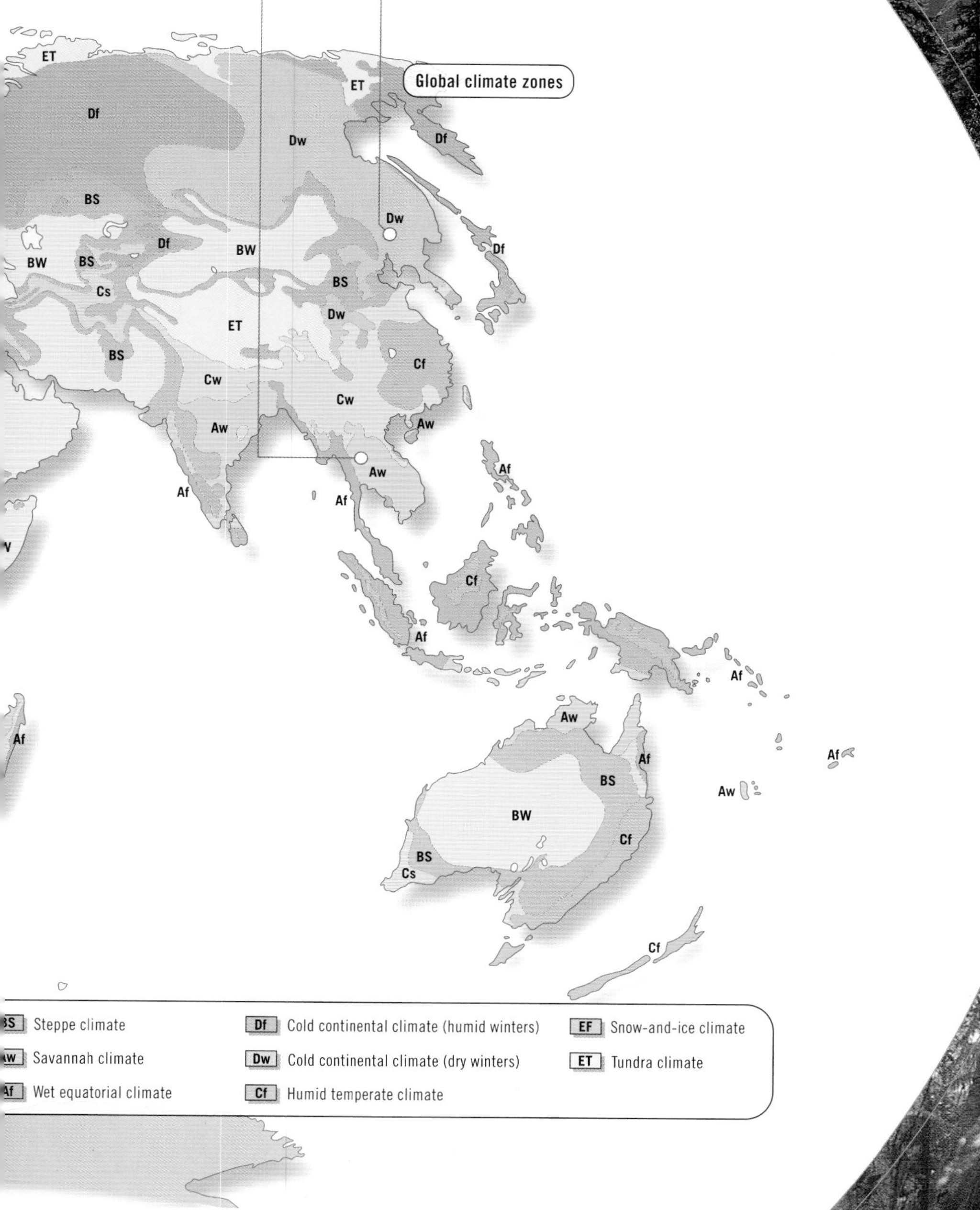

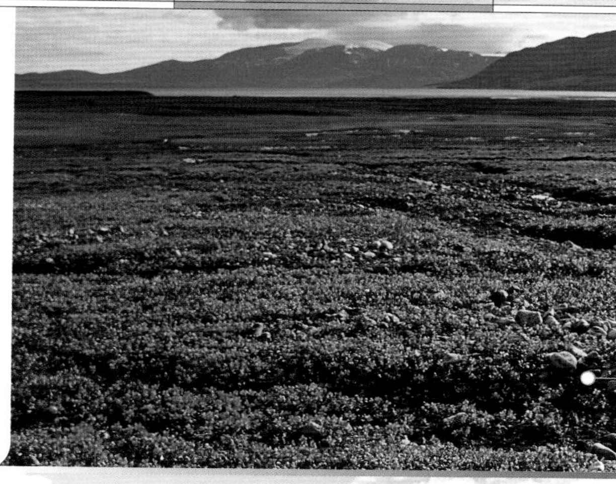

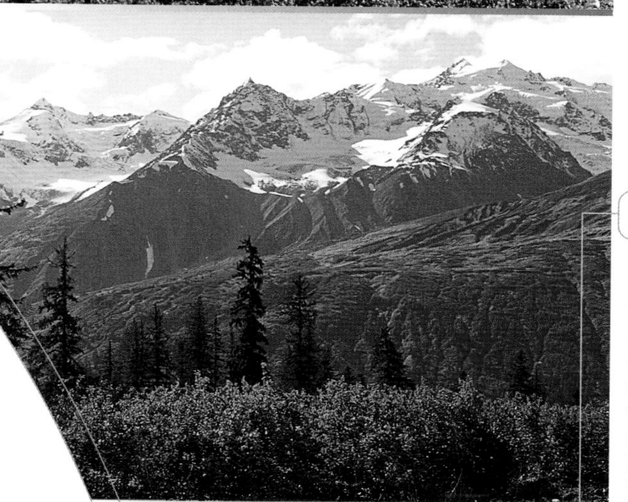

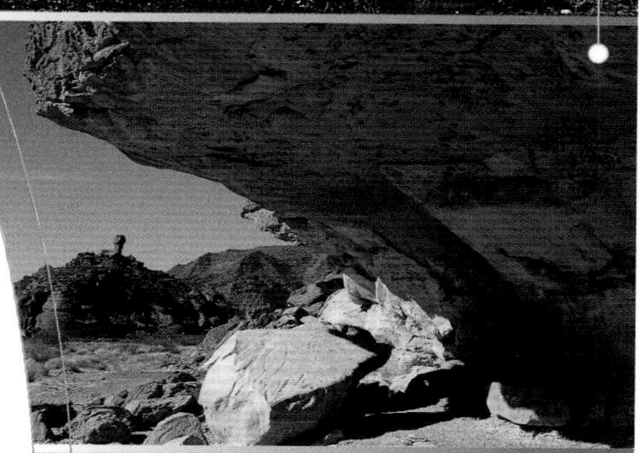

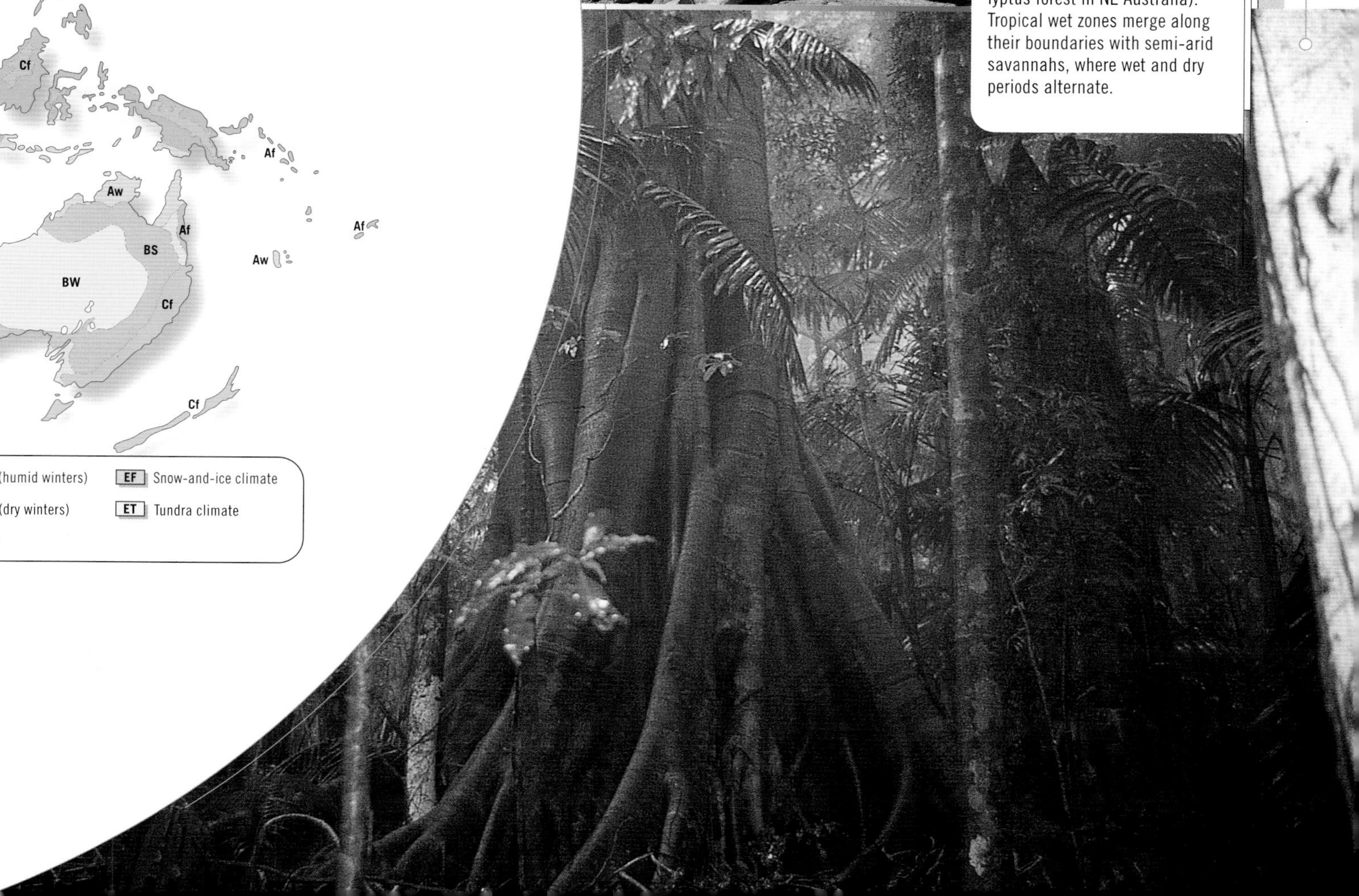

Virtually Lifeless Regions of Snow and Ice

The polar regions are not only cold, they are among the most arid areas on Earth. The capacity of air to retain water vapor diminishes as it grows colder. Thus the high Antarctic Plateau is drier than the Sahara. Human beings living here consume an average of six liters of water per day (photo: Paradise Bay, Antarctica).

Tundra Climate in the Arctic North

With average annual temperatures of about 5° F, only the uppermost layer of permafrost thaws for a few months during the summer, allowing for a vegetation period of between 30 and 90 days. The photo shows a summer carpet of alpine Veronica on Ellesmere Island.

Hot, Arid Deserts with Little Vegetation

Most of the world's hot, arid zones (with less than 200 mm of precipitation per year) are found in the interiors of large continents (photo: Libyan Desert) or along the margins of cold ocean currents, where very little moisture is taken up by moving masses of air. Rainfall is also extremely sparse in trade wind belts with prevailing high pressure and on the leeward slopes of high mountain ranges.

Hot Days in the Tropics

Daily temperature fluctuations in the tropics are greater than seasonal ones. It is always hot in the lowlands. Temperatures fall only slightly during rainy periods, although humidity rises to extreme levels, creating a paradise for lush plants growth (photo: eucalyptus forest in NE Australia). Tropical wet zones merge along their boundaries with semi-arid savannahs, where wet and dry periods alternate.

Mandalay/Myanmar

Harbin/China

Global climate zones

BS Steppe climate	**Df** Cold continental climate (humid winters)	**EF** Snow-and-ice climate
Aw Savannah climate	**Dw** Cold continental climate (dry winters)	**ET** Tundra climate
Af Wet equatorial climate	**Cf** Humid temperate climate	

The Changing Global Climate

... and Mankind's Role in the Process

The history of the Earth's climate is one of changes, some gradual, others rapid and dramatic. Periods of relative stability and calm like the Holocene, which began some 10,000 years ago, are the exception rather than the rule. Yet it was precisely this climatic stability that allowed human civilization to develop. Today, the extent of human intervention in climatic processes is increasing. Are we merely a minor disruptive factor in the interplay of these powerful forces of nature, or does mankind pose a serious threat to the global climatic balance?

Variations in the Earth's Orbit

Some 20,000 years ago, at the peak of the last ice age, substantial portions of North America and northern Europe were covered by sheets of ice several thousand meters thick. This ice extended deep into the North American continent to the region now covered by the Great Lakes. The land south of the ice was arctic steppe, much like today's tundra regions. On the basis of bore samples taken from deposits thousands and even millions of years old, from layers of sediment on the ocean floor or from continental ice in Antarctica and Greenland, for example, it has been possible to reconstruct temperature patterns and many other characteristics of past climate. For at least two million years, the Earth's climate has been governed by relatively regular cycles. Ice ages lasting roughly 100,000 years have alternated with warm periods usually about 10,000 years long. These cycles are caused by subtle shifts in the Earth's orbit around the sun and in the inclination of the Earth's axis. These changes, known as Milankovitch variations, affect the seasonal and geographic distribution of solar radiation – although the total amount of radiation that reaches the Earth remains constant. It is not entirely clear why the Earth's climate reacts so dramatically to these changing radiation patterns. One crucial factor is apparently the intensity of summer sunlight over the continents of the northern hemisphere, for when the snows of the past winter do not melt completely, large sheets of ice begin to form. They reflect solar radiation and thus lead to further cooling. Our understanding of Milankovitch variations suggests that the Holocene is an unusually long warm phase, which would mean that a new ice age is not to be expected for several tens of thousands of years.

Abrupt Climatic Shifts

Scientists have learned only fairly recently that the last ice age was marked by a series of very abrupt and drastic changes in climate. In the course of these so-called Dansgaard-Oeschger Events (of which more than 20 are known to have occurred during the last ice age), average temperatures in the North Atlantic region rose rapidly – within only a few years – by between 11 and 14 °F. These unusually warm periods lasted several hundreds or thousands of years. Their effects were felt around the globe – even in the Antarctic. Evidently, sudden shifts in the course of marine currents played a significant role in these sudden climatic changes.

Even the Holocene, the current, relatively stable warm period, has not been free of climatic changes. Some 5,500 years ago, the Sahara was transformed from a landscape of swamps, lakes and areas of vegetation inhabited by many large animals and human beings into the desert we know today. In all likelihood, this process was set in motion by a shift in the Earth's orbit which triggered a fatal chain of events: a gradual decrease in rainfall resulting in diminished plant growth which led in turn to further reduction in precipitation.

The Radiation Budget

The Earth's temperature is regulated by a simple radiation budget. On average, the energy received from the sun is equal to the energy radiated by the Earth into space. If too much energy is received, temperatures rise and the Earth radiates more heat until balance is restored. If the Earth had no atmosphere, its average temperature would be somewhere near 0 °F. The atmosphere inhibits thermal radiation from the Earth's surface,

Frozen Lake, 1830
From the fifteenth to the eighteenth century, temperatures in Europe were 1.8 to 3.6 °F cooler than today. This cool period is known as the "Little Ice Age". Lake Constance froze over completely about every 20 years during that period but only once during the twentieth century (1963). Inhabitants of the alpine regions often experienced failed harvests and famine during the "Little Ice Age". This View of Frozen Lake Constance was painted by the local artist Nicolaus Hug in 1830.

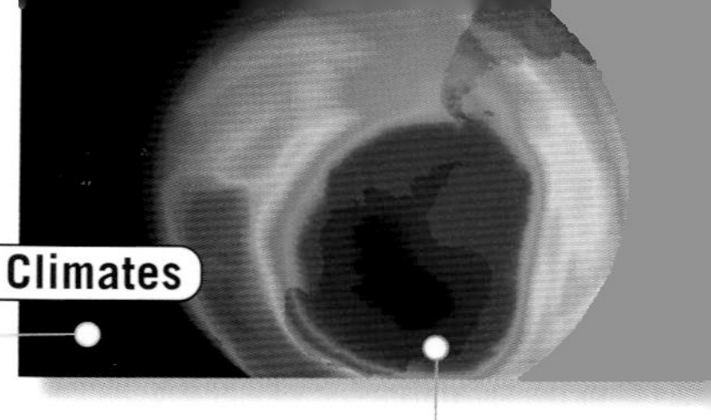

primarily due to the insulating effect of water vapor and carbon dioxide, the so-called greenhouse gases. Consequently, the Earth's surface warms until the radiation balance is restored at today's average temperature of about 59°F. It is this natural greenhouse effect that makes our planet inhabitable. Changes in the composition of the atmosphere or in the surface area of reflective ice and cloud masses can affect the radiation budget and thus raise or lower temperatures.

The Human Factor

Human impact on the global climate dates back to the Middle Ages, when people began clearing forests to make room for farmland, thereby increasing carbon dioxide levels in the atmosphere and creating lighter areas of surface that reflect more sunlight. But it was not until the Industrial Revolution in the first half of the nineteenth century that mankind developed the means to disrupt the delicate radiation balance significantly. The leading cause of these man-made changes is the use of fossil fuels – coal, petroleum, and natural gas. The fossil fuel we burn in a single year took roughly a million years to accumulate. The carbon contained in these materials oxidizes during combustion and is released into the air as carbon dioxide (CO_2). About half of it remains in the atmosphere, while the remainder is absorbed by the oceans and the biosphere. Since the beginning of the

Industrial Age, the carbon-dioxide concentration in the atmosphere has risen from 280 parts per million (ppm) to 360 ppm, and the greenhouse effect has grown stronger accordingly. Other gases released in the course of human activities intensify the greenhouse effect even further. Examples are methane and fluorocarbons, which are also responsible for the ozone hole.

Concentrations of greenhouse gases in the atmosphere have risen in recent years, raising average global temperatures by about 1.25°F – over both land and sea. Mountain glaciers are melting all over the world (total glacier volume in the Alps has already decreased by half). Artic Ice has become almost 40 per cent thinner over the past 30 years.

Using sophisticated pattern-recognition techniques, climatologists have attempted to determine the extent to which these trends are actually attributable to anthropogenic emissions and to identify other possible causes (such as fluctuations in the sun). Their findings indicate that, at the very least, the accelerated warming trend observed since 1970 is largely a man-made phenomenon.

Scientists warned as early as the late nineteenth century on the basis of simple computations that increasing concentrations of carbon dioxide in the atmosphere would lead to global warming. Today, the world's climate can be simulated with the aid of powerful computers, which make it possible both to reconstruct past climate patterns and to project scenarios for the future. If concentrations of greenhouse gases in the atmosphere continue to rise at the current pace, we can expect global temperatures to rise by between 2.7 and 9.9 degrees F over the next hundred years. Should this happen, the earth will be warmer than it has been at any time during the past 100,000 years. One consequence would be a rise in sea level of between 20 and 90 centimeters, which would persist for centuries even if the warming trend were halted. Warming would also lead to changes in precipitation patterns and thus possibly to drought and flooding, endangering many existing ecosystems in the process. Low-lying coastal regions would be threatened by flooding caused by storms, and several island nations in the Pacific would disappear beneath the sea.

In an effort to slow the process of global warming, most of the nations participating in the international conference in Kyōto, Japan in 1997 signed a Climate Treaty that obliges industrial nations to reduce emissions of greenhouse gases to five per cent below 1990 levels by the year 2012. The treaty is not yet in force, as only a few nations have ratified it, and it represents, at best, only a first small step toward effective climate protection.

Global warming trends, 1976–1999

Quelle: NCDC

in degrees Fahrenheit per century

14°F 17.6°F 21.2°F 24.8°F 28.4°F 32°F 35.6°F 39.2°F 42.8°F 46.4°F 50°F

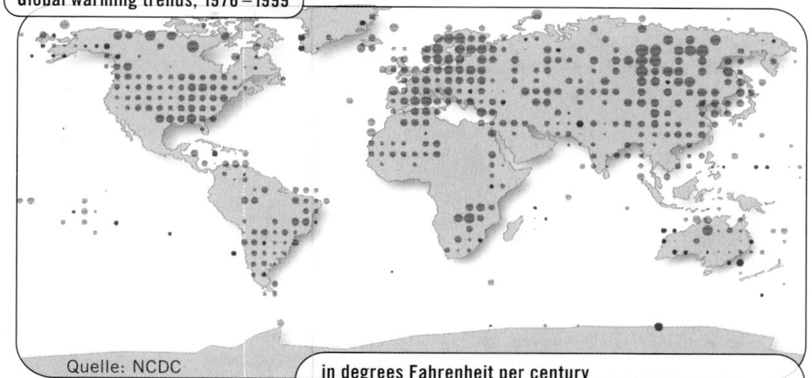

Red dots on the map mark regions that have grown warmer. Blue dots show those that have cooled. Insufficient data is available for the remaining areas.

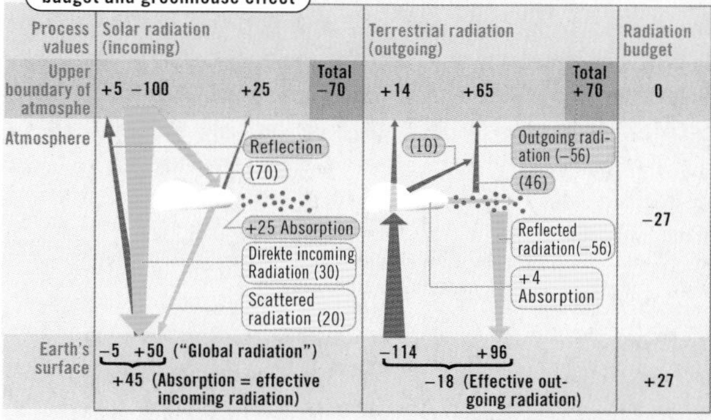

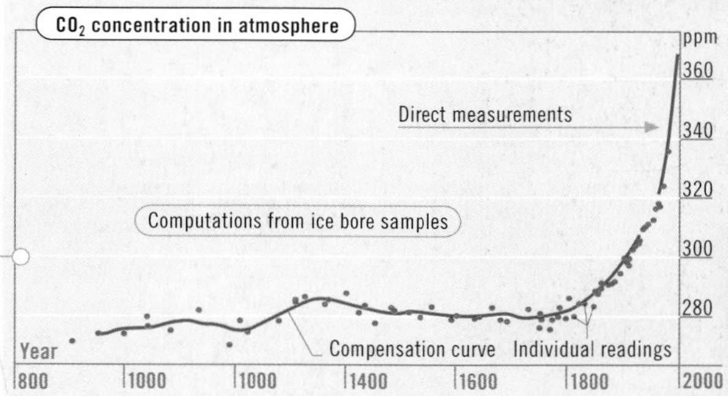

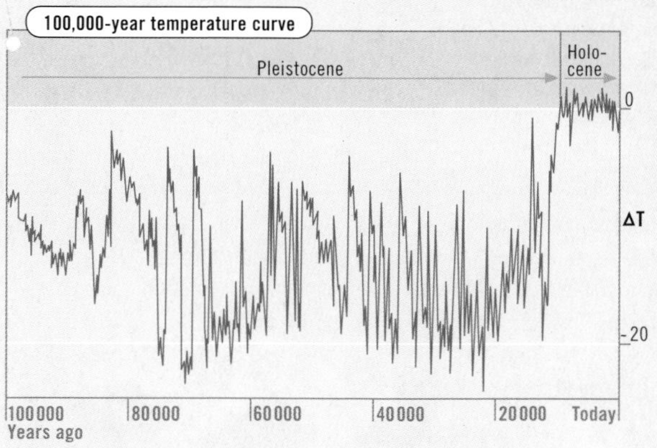

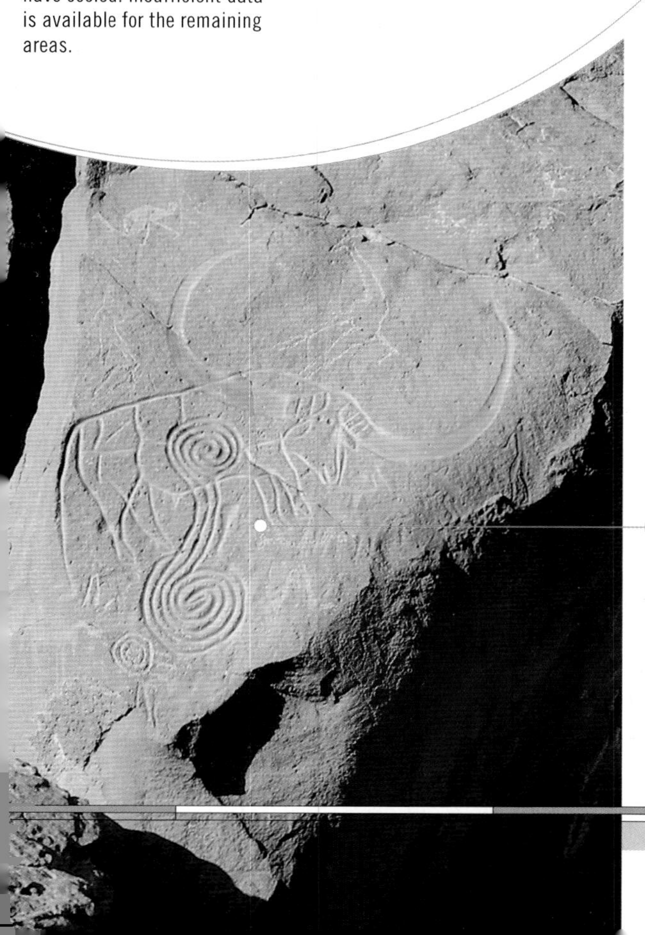

Saharan Rock Painting

Until about 6,000 years ago, the Sahara was much greener than it is today. A large number of rock drawings offer evidence of a much moister climate. The buffalo Homoioceras antiquus (Oued Djerat, Tassili n'Ajjer, Algeria) became extinct during the early Holocene.

Alarming Rise

Analyses of air bubbles in Antarctic ice and measurements taken at Mauna Loa (Hawaii) since 1957 tell us a great deal about carbon-dioxide concentration in the atmosphere: about 280 ppm during warm periods like the Holocene, 200 ppm during the ice ages, and more than 360 ppm today, thanks to our emissions.

The Radiation Budget and the Greenhouse Effect

Assuming a value of 100 % for the amount of solar radiation that actually effects the global radiation budget (342.5 Watts per square meter), only 45 % (on long-term, global average) actually reaches the Earth's surface. The remainder is absorbed or scattered. The total reflective capacity of the earth (including the atmosphere and clouds) is referred to as the Earth's albedo, and amounts to 30 % on a yearly average. The effective heat radiated by the Earth's surface is 18 %. This equates to the difference between 114 % – the value which would be expected if the Earth had no atmosphere – and 96 % – for radiation reflected back by the atmosphere (the greenhouse effect). The difference between incoming solar radiation and outgoing terrestrial radiation (27 %) at the surface is offset by heat currents.

Threatening Hole

In 1985, British researchers discovered a hole in the ozone layer of the upper atmosphere – our shield against dangerous cosmic radiation. One of the causes identified was the release of industrially produced fluorocarbons, such as those used in spray cans, into the atmosphere. The Montreal Protocol of 1987 called for a global ban on these gases, to be achieved in a step-by-step process. They are hardly used at all today, and scientists now predict that the ozone hole will gradually close over the next several decades. It will probably take more than 100 years to restore the ozone layer completely, however.

budget and greenhouse effect

CO_2 concentration in atmosphere

100,000-year temperature curve

0 = Average Holocene temperature

Climate Curves for the Last 100,000 Years from Greenland Ice

This climate curve from Greenland shows the consistently warm climate of the past 10,000 years, the Holocene period. During the preceding 100,000 ice-age years, the climate was not only much colder but also subject to sudden fluctuations.

Vegetation – The Earth's Botanical Cloak

Plant and Human Life – A Reassessment

According to the Book of Genesis, God created plants on the third day, calling upon the Earth to "bring forth grass, the herb yielding seed … and the tree yielding fruit … and God saw that it was good." (Genesis 1:11). Mankind arrived on the scene soon afterward. By current reckoning, human beings have since destroyed about 30 % of the original 62 million square kilometers of forest on Earth, transformed much of our planet's vast grasslands into arid wastelands (desertification) through overcultivation, and altered the character of natural vegetation in many regions of the world. We have intervened in natural patterns of growth and distribution, manipulated genetic makeup through breeding experiments, and replaced local flora with secondary growth over wide areas. Yet despite this massive human intervention in the plant kingdom, more than 99 % of the Earth's biomass – about 1.8 trillion tons of organic material (300 tons for every living human being) – is vegetable matter.

The Foundation of Human and Animal Life

In his famous "Canticle of the Sun," Saint Francis of Assisi spoke of "… Earth, our Mother, who feeds us in her sovereignty and produces various fruits and colored flowers and herbs." The words of Saint Francis reflect an uncomplicated view of nature and an implicit recognition of the close and vital cosmic relationship between all living organisms (the biosphere) and the Earth's inorganic crust (the lithosphere), a mystery that was not solved by modern biological science until many years later. Biologists, ecologists and biochemists agree that animal, and thus of course human life could not exist in its present form without the Earth's botanical cloak.

Plants as Chemical Factories and Nutrient Pumps

The leaves of plants contain chlorophyll (the pigment that makes them green), which they use to convert water taken up by their roots and carbon dioxide (CO_2) absorbed from the air into glucose (sugar) with the aid of light (solar energy) captured on their surfaces in a complicated process known as photosynthesis. Through their roots, which in some plants (wheat, for example) form networks of microscopically fine fibrous tendrils with combined lengths of up to several hundred kilometers, they absorb a wide variety of elements essential to all life on Earth from the soil. These they process along with the glucose into organic matter, referred to collectively as biomass (the dry weight of organic matter).

Through this process, a number of elements essential to many physiological processes, such as iron, phosphorus, calcium, magnesium, nitrogen, and sulfur, are incorporated into biomass and passed along through the food chain to herbivorous animal organisms and ultimately to carnivores (including humans as well, regardless of whether they actually eat meat or not, since the consumption of animal protein is virtually unavoidable for modern consumers).

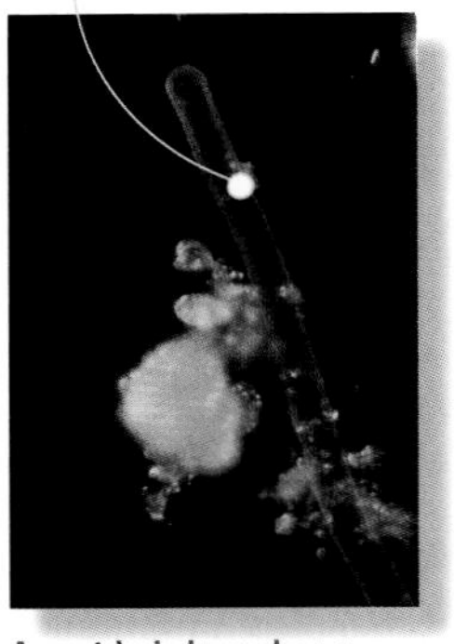

A root hair launches a biochemical attack on a calcite mineral: the first stage in the transition from mineral to chemical substance.

In this way, the massive global nutrient pump of natural vegetation extracts more than two cubic kilometers per year – roughly six billion tons – of minerals and substances of all kinds from the Earth's crust and makes them available as sustenance to animals and human beings (approximately one ton for every living human being on Earth).

Soil-Building Vegetation

Vegetable biomass consumed by animal organisms is returned to the eternal mineral cycle as feces or in the bodies of dead organisms themselves. Unconsumed biomass is also remineralized when humus is formed through the decomposition of fallen leaves and dead plants. Mineral replacement resulting from biochemical and physical root activity, on the one hand, and the accumulation of biomass, on the other, are important soil-building processes which work within an ecological network in collaboration with such non-biological factors as the warmth and moisture of vegetation in a specific region.

Trees – Unsung "Environmental Helpers"

Trees are the largest forms of plant life. A deciduous tree between 15 and 20 meters high generates three million liters of oxygen annually (four times as much as a single human being needs in a year) through the process of photosynthesis. In one year, the same tree also filters as much as 7,000 kg of dust from the air with its foliage and extracts up to 7,000 liters of water from the soil through its root system, thus contributing significantly to the prevention of soil erosion – a problem that can assume catastrophic proportions in deforested areas. For every human being on Earth today, there are about 500 trees at work providing these important environmental services.

How Do the Little Flowers Grow, and How Do Plants Give Us Food?

The preceding description shows how very important the plant kingdom is. In light of the crucial role plants play in our lives, it is shocking to realize how little we know about them. Most people in the industrialized countries of the world can name at least 20 different makes of car but not nearly as many kinds of plants! Yet botanists have now identified more than 360,000 varieties, of which about 180,000 are blossoming plants.

It is not the species of so-called "higher plants" classified into families of trees, shrubs, flowers, and grasses that are so difficult to identify with certainty. The real difficulty and suspense begins with the attempt to establish clear scientific distinctions among the varieties of "lower plant organisms" or microflora: fungi, the various species of algae, lichens as symbiotic communities of fungi and algae, and even the types of bacteria that are classified as forms of plant life – the "little beasties" discovered and described by Antonie van Leewenhoek (1632–1723) with the aid of his home-made microscope.

Although between 10,000 and 50,000 edible varieties of plants are available for human consumption, only about 150 to 200 species (between 0.3 and 2 %) are actually used for nutritional purposes. Over 75 % of all energy consumed by human beings in the form of vegetable matter comes from only about ten crop plants (between 0.002 and 0.1 % of all edible species of plants).

The Earth's Coat of Brightly Colored Stripes

Plants have no means of locomotion, and thus the characteristics they exhibit as indicator plants at the present stage of evolutionary development are always evidence of their adaptation to prevailing conditions in their local environments (known as habitat conditions). These include such features as water-retention organs (in cactuses or agaves in arid regions), shallow, broad root systems (like those of the birch tree) in permafrost regions where soil thaws only for a few months during the summer, or a thick coat of hair as protection against evaporation in alpine regions (edelweiss is an example). Thus we understand why belts of vegetation corresponding generally to the Earth's climatic zones, communities of plants known by botanists as vegetation zones, cover the Earth like a brightly-colored striped coat. And the same explanation applies to the typical vegetation patterns in mountainous regions that reflect the increasing lack of heat at progressively higher elevations, a phenomenon described with specific reference to South America by Alexander von Humboldt as early as the late eighteenth century.

(2) Tundra Vegetation

With average annual temperatures normally below 5° F, permafrost soil thaws only briefly to a depth of a few centimeters in the summer. With a growth period of 30–90 days, this type of vegetation, which forms a continuous belt only in the northern hemisphere, is characterized by an extraordinary abundance of lichens (in the Arctic north) and treeless, summer-green, flower-covered meadows (in the subpolar south).

(11) Alpine Vegetation

The most impressive alpine vegetation is found in the Andes (see photographs). Here the hierarchy of vegetation levels, from the tropical rain forest to the Paramo to the high tropical grasslands (moist puna) and the frost-prone, high, cold puna at elevations of about 5,000 m, where grass is sparse but lichens are plentiful, reflect the effects of diminishing warmth at progressively higher elevations.

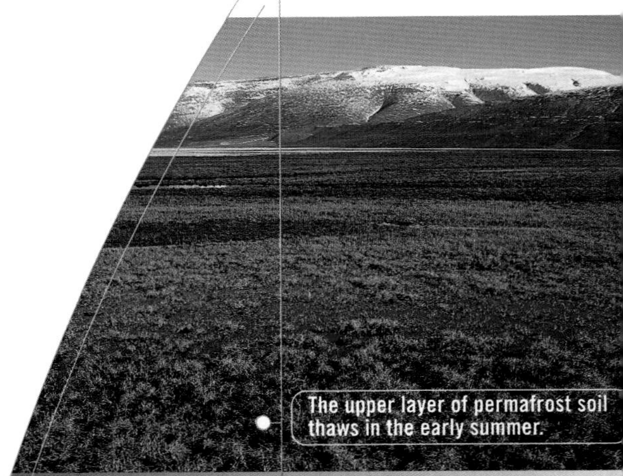

The upper layer of permafrost soil thaws in the early summer.

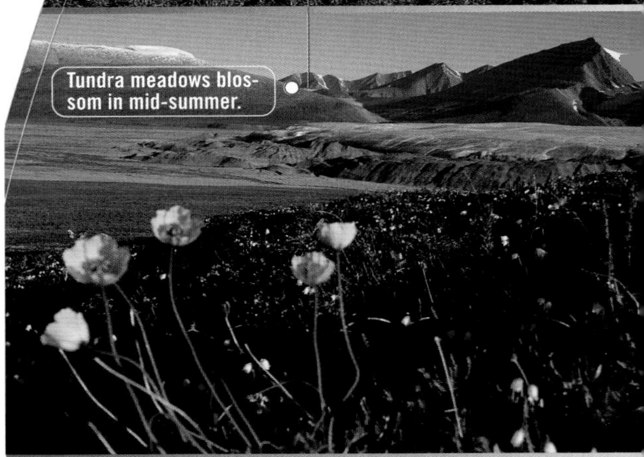

Tundra meadows blossom in mid-summer.

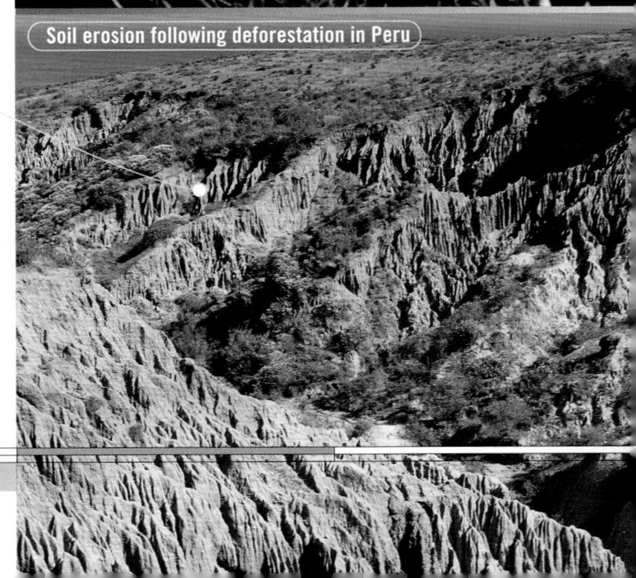

Soil erosion following deforestation in Peru

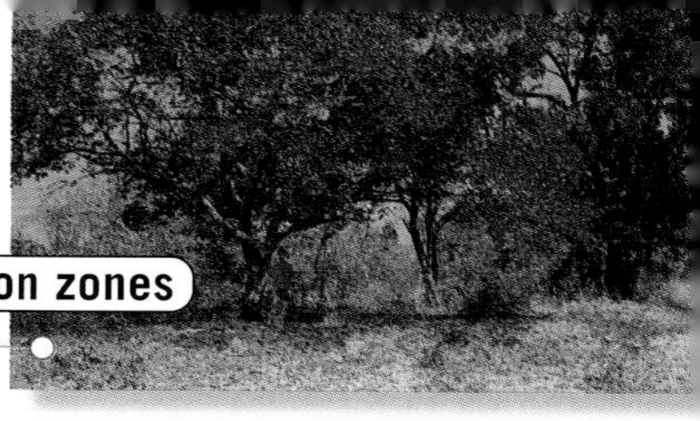

(5) Tropical deciduous forest

Despite annual precipitation often exceeding 1,000 mm, these forests of long-trunked trees that turn fully green only near their tops during the summer rainy season have a relatively short growth period, as water is scarce during the rest of the year (photo: Caprivi, Namibia). The monsoon forests of southern and Southeast Asia represent a special form of this class of vegetation.

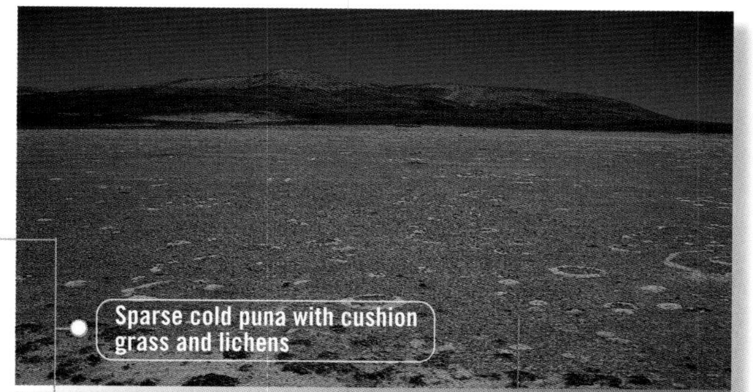

Sparse cold puna with cushion grass and lichens

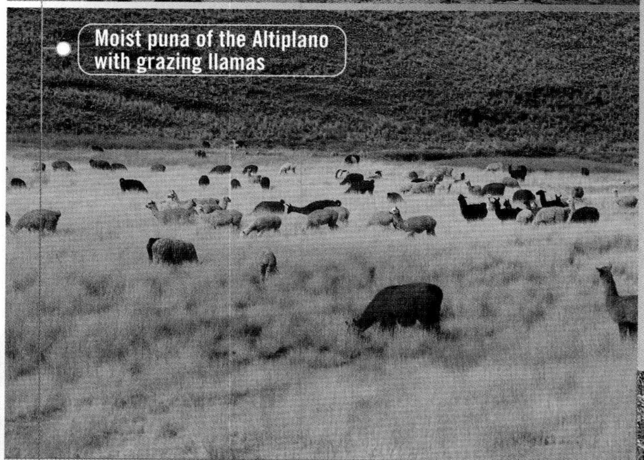

Moist puna of the Altiplano with grazing llamas

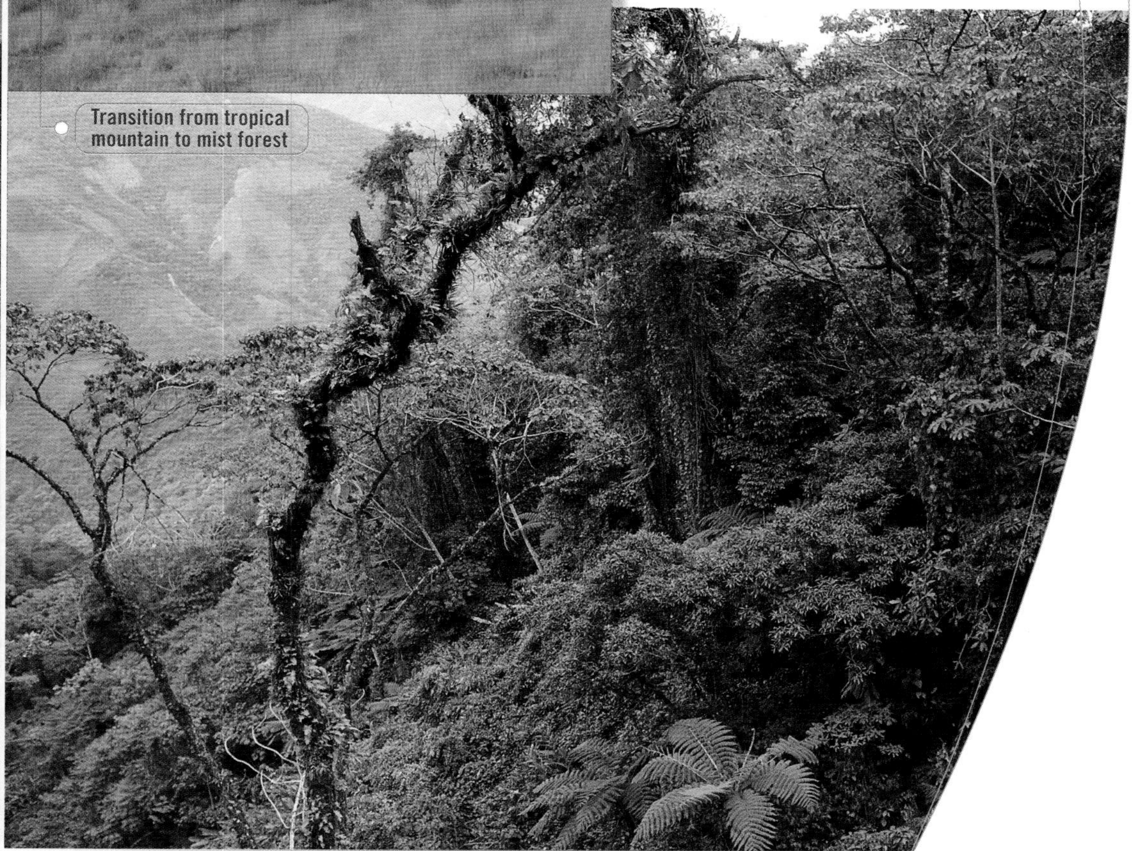

Transition from tropical mountain to mist forest

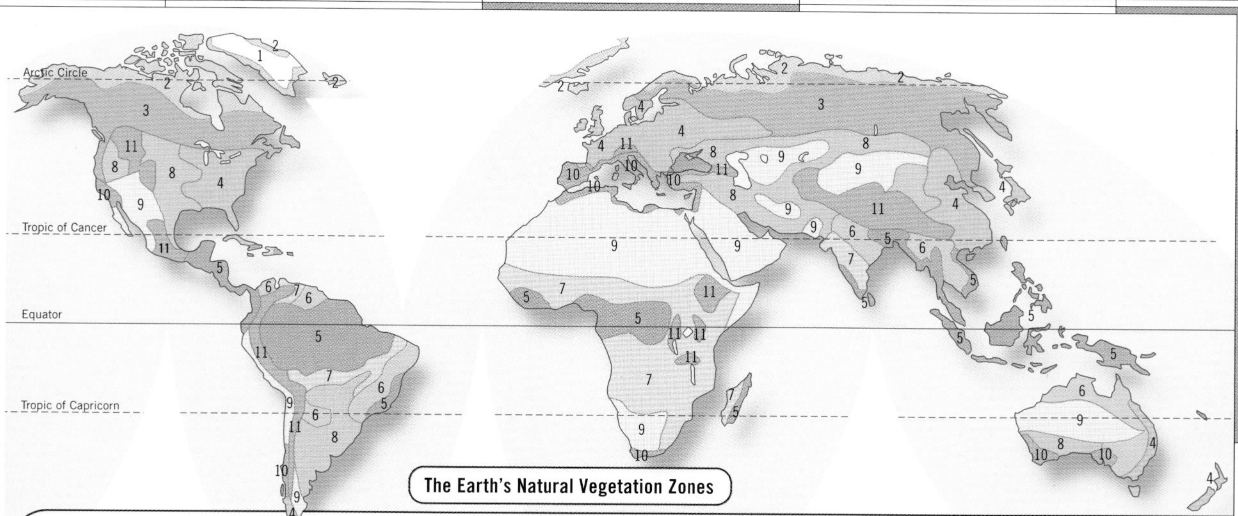

The Earth's Natural Vegetation Zones

1	Permanent ice cover	7	Tropical savanna and grassland
2	Polar barrens and Tundra	8	Subtropical grassland and steppe
3	Boreal forest, Taiga	9	Desert and semi-arid desert
4	Temperate forest and cultivated land	10	Mediterranean vegetation, sclerophyllous plants
5	Tropical rain forest	11	Alpine vegetation
6	Tropical deciduous forest		

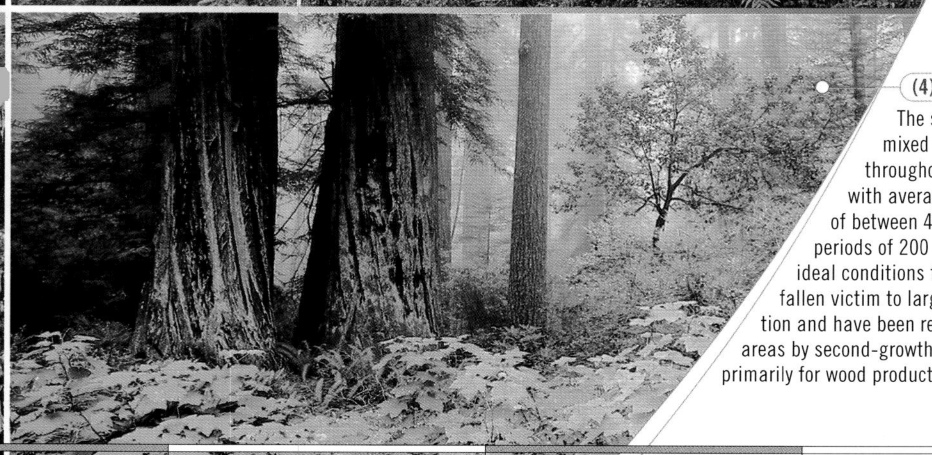

(4) Forests of the Temperate Zone

The summer-green deciduous and mixed forests that once prevailed throughout this climate zone, which with average annual temperatures of between 43 and 54°F and growth periods of 200 days or longer offers ideal conditions for agriculture, have fallen victim to large-scale deforestation and have been replaced in isolated areas by second-growth forests used primarily for wood production.

(3) Taiga – the Northern Continental Vegetation Belt

Average annual temperatures in these regions covered by boreal evergreen and summer-green coniferous forests comprising only a few species, which span the globe only in the permafrost regions of the northern hemisphere, range near 32°F. Covering some 20 million square km (about 13% of the Earth's dry land), they represent the world's largest forest formation.

(5) Tropical Rain Forest

In the tropics, where rain falls the year round and annual precipitation often exceeds 2,000 mm, temperatures determine the character of forests. Multi-tiered, evergreen equatorial rain forest – a habitat for a wide range of species – is predominant in low-lying areas with mean annual temperatures of 72–82°F. Mountain forests with fewer species are prevalent at elevations over 1,000 m and average temperatures of 57–72°F. Mist forests characterized by beard lichens, epiphytes, and tree ferns predominate only at elevations of over 2,000 m and at average temperatures of only 40–57°F. Together, these three forest types occupy a total area of about 12.5 million square km (approximately 8% of the dry land on Earth). They are seriously endangered, particularly at lower elevations, by logging operations and large-scale deforestation. The most common natural form of vegetation along the tropical coasts are mangrove forests, although they have now been almost totally destroyed.

(7) Savannas – Maximum Landscape Diversity

Savannas are generally thought of as expansive tropical grasslands (like the Serengeti). Actually, they display a number of different faces. Although grass is the dominant ground cover in all savanna landscapes, the spectrum of plant formations encompasses dry, thorny shrub vegetation, flourishing bush growth, densely wooded areas, and even true forests (such as the gallery forests along riverbanks or the Mopane and Miombo woodlands of southern Africa). Common to all types of savannas are summer rainy seasons and the absence of a thermal winter.

(8) Steppes – Non-Tropical Grasslands Under the Plow

Where grasslands once stretched to the horizon in climates with dry summers and often extremely cold winters (on the North American prairies or the black-earth regions of southern Russia), human beings have replaced the natural vegetation of the dry, short-grass and moister, long-grass steppes with vast grain fields. In many places, such industrial-scale farming operations have contributed to soil deterioration by clearing the way for wind and water erosion.

(9) Desert Vegetation

Vegetation in deserts and semi-arid regions (where climates are only slightly more favorable), is ideally adapted to the extreme conditions of their environments (scarcity of water, heat, nocturnal or winter frost, sand storms, etc.). Higher forms of plant life have developed appropriate survival tools: water-retaining organs, leaf coverings that inhibit evaporation, suspension of metabolic activity during extremely dry periods ("latent life") or disproportionately large (relative to above-ground biomass) underground plant organs (primarily roots). Microflora – ordinarily overlooked by human beings – is represented in abundance on the surface in the form of algae, fungi, and blankets of lichens that can even be seen in satellite images.

(10) Mediterranean Vegetation

The original natural vegetation of the Mediterranean regions, which are classified as subtropical climate zones with wet winters, was evergreen sclerophyllous forest (holm oak forests in the actual Mediterranean region). Extreme overuse by humans has caused much of this original vegetation to be replaced by meager second-growth formations such as broad-leaved shrubs and small trees (matorral, chaparral or maquis) and even poorer scrubland vegetation (garrigue).

Biodiversity – Geodiversity – Ecodiversity

Species Diversity – the Earth's Living Treasure

Why is the survival of every species so important? What prompted the authors of the Old Testament to emphasize species diversity in the story of Noah, whom God commanded to bring "of every living thing of all flesh, two of every sort . . . into the ark . . . to keep them alive?" Biological diversity is an essential aspect of life on earth. Research on biological diversity will play an important role in the future of mankind as a basis for advances in the fields of nutrition, medical care, and even tourism.

The Number of Species – an Unsolved Puzzle

The study of biodiversity involves identification and analysis of the structural diversity of communities of living organisms. The process of identifying all species of plants and animals is far from complete. About 1.7 million species have been identified thus far, yet we can only speculate as to the actual number of species on earth, drawing conclusions based on analogy. Scientists assume the existence of some 20 million species. New ones are being discovered every day.

Geodiversity – A New Concept

The term "geodiversity" refers to the wide range of geographic factors and combinations of influences that have emerged in the course of the Earth's history. It is the product of interaction between the atmosphere, the lithosphere, the pedosphere (dry land) and the hydrosphere. It determines local conditions in the biosphere (flora and fauna) and the anthroposphere (human beings). Climate and its component elements (solar radiation, temperature, precipitation, humidity, evaporation, wind) are the most important determinants of species distribution in different regions of the world. Patterns of distribution are also shaped by topography, the configuration of land masses, their position with respect to the oceans of the world, and ocean surface temperatures. Developments in the Earth's history, including the evolution of living species, have contributed significantly to present patterns of species diversity.

One important factor is floral migration, a process that has taken place in the recent geological past (mostly during periods of transition between ice ages and warm periods) along mountain ranges aligned with meridians. Thus Antarctic floras have long since moved into the tropics along the Andes in South America. Non-tropical plant species have invaded the tropical regions along routes parallel to the mountain chains of Southeast Asia, enriching local flora significantly. Mountain ranges oriented along lines of latitude (the Alps, the Pyreneans, and the Himalayas) have blocked these migrations.

Diversity – a Regional View

The limited species diversity of subpolar tundra and boreal coniferous forest regions is attributable to unfavorable geographic conditions (freezing temperatures, long periods of snow cover, short annual growth periods). Diversity is similarly restricted in tropical and subtropical deserts, where high levels of solar radiation and a consistently negative radiation balance result in wide fluctuations in daily and seasonal temperatures and extreme aridity, creating a hostile living environment for flora and fauna, not to mention Homo sapiens. In the Sahara, mountain ranges (Hoggar, Tibesti, Aïr) rise up from surroundings virtually devoid of vegetation as climatically and geographically favorable zones for plant growth. Inland deserts (Atacama, Libyan Desert, Tanezrouft, Ténéré, Rub al-Chali), which receive only ephemeral precipitation at very irregular intervals, exhibit an absolute minimum of diversity. The same can be said of the subpolar regions around the Antarctic and Greenland ice sheets and the Tibetan Plateau, with its cold desert.

Generally speaking, species diversity increases from the poles to the Equator. Maximum diversity – more than 5,000 species per 10,000 square km – is found in the tropical rain and mountain forests of South America, Africa, Asia, and the Indo-Malaysian Archipelago, where tropical temperatures prevail year round and precipitation is heavy and non-seasonal. In tropical inland areas, a high degree of biodiversity is possible only in combination with maximum geodiversity. This applies in particular to tropical mountain regions where, within very small areas, topographic variations (elevation, exposure, slope steepness), mountain/valley winds, an enormous evaporation potential and high levels of latent evaporation heat, differing degrees of condensation and fog at mountain forest roofs (mist and cloud forests) favor plant diversity (Choco region in Costa Rica, eastern and western roofs of the Andes in Ecuador and

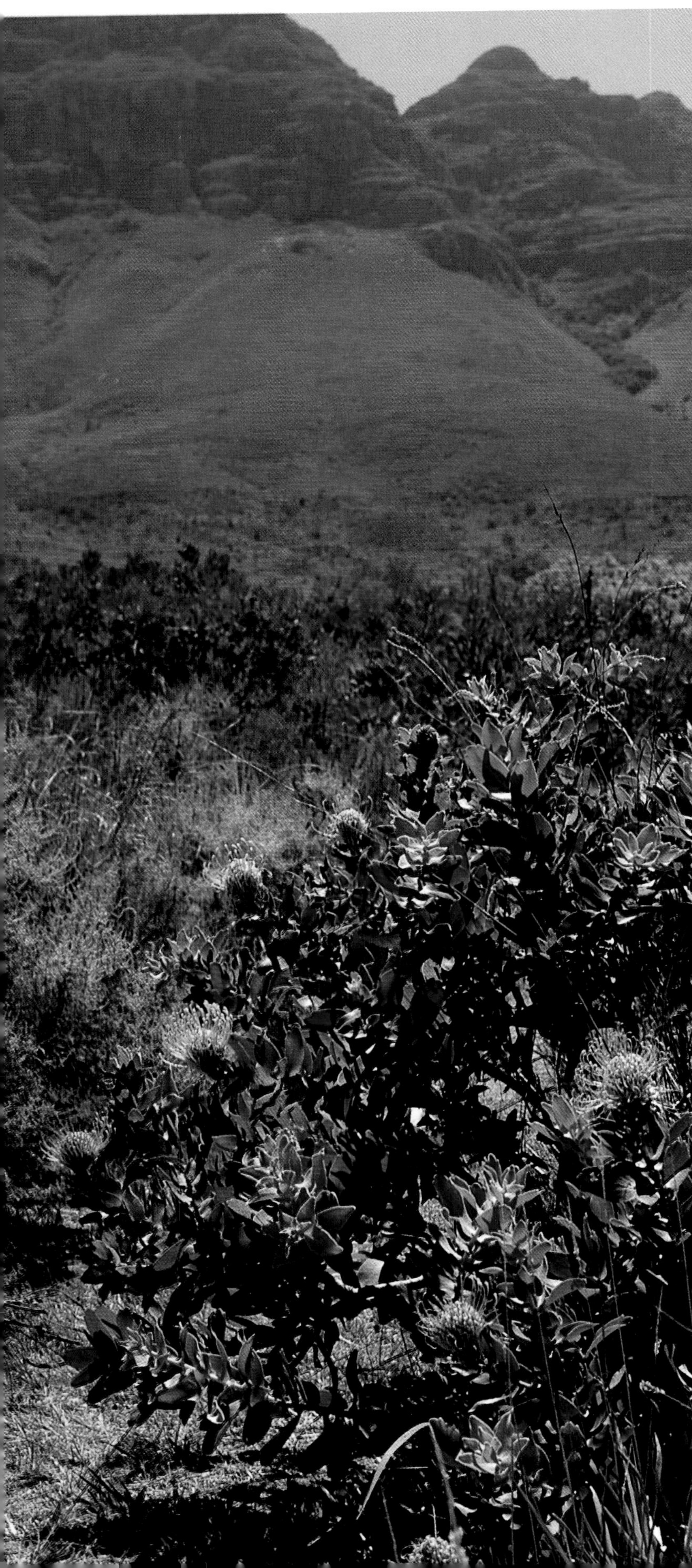

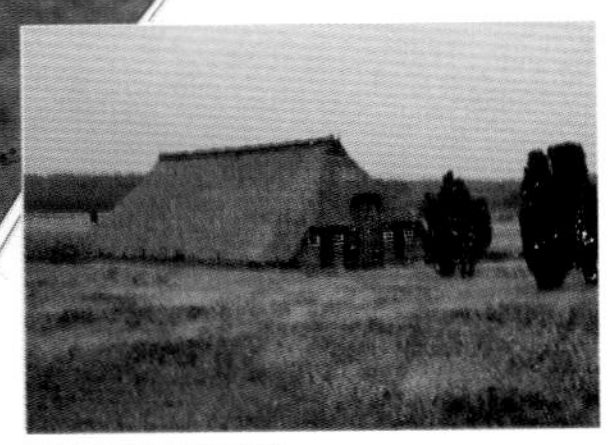

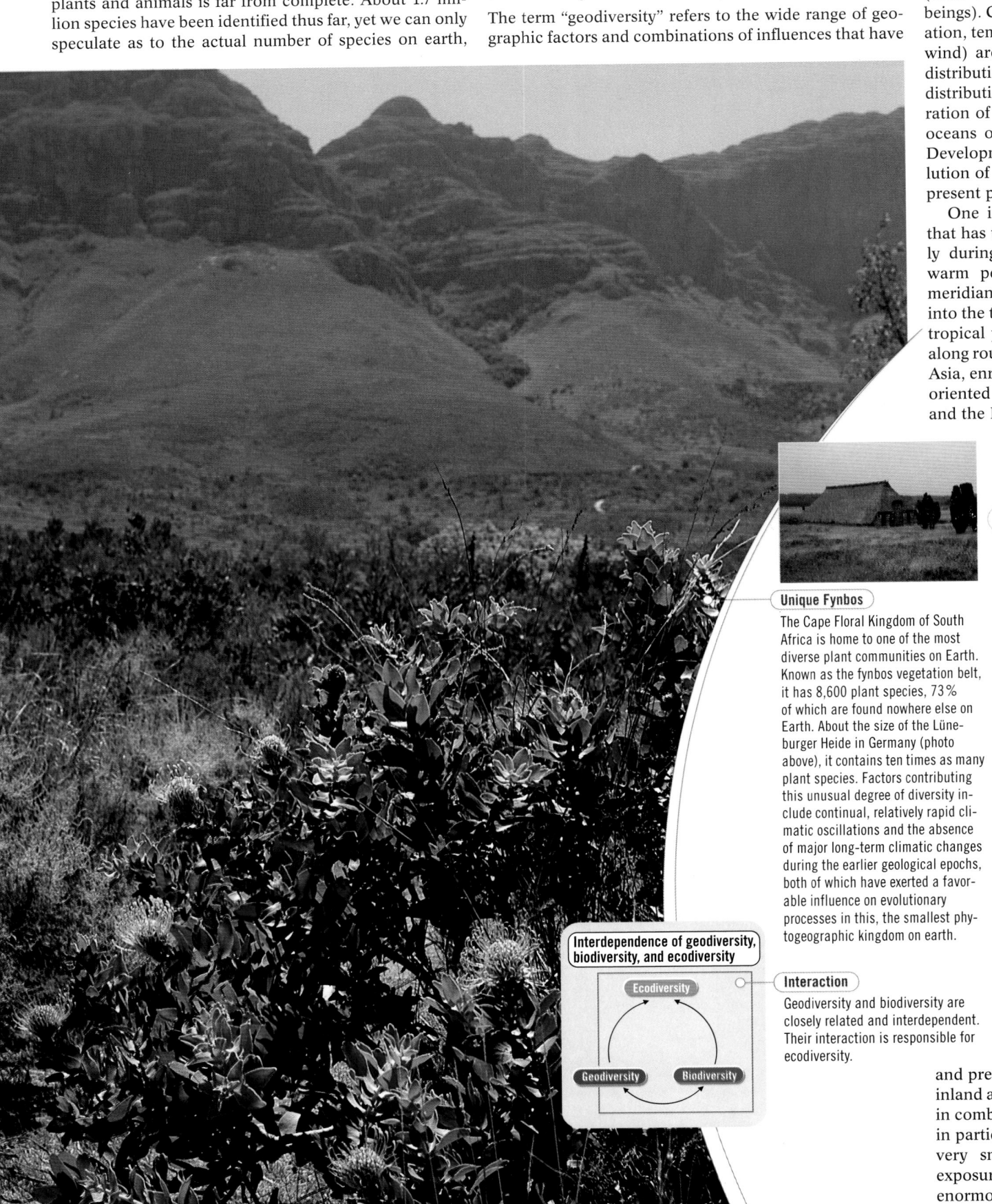

Unique Fynbos

The Cape Floral Kingdom of South Africa is home to one of the most diverse plant communities on Earth. Known as the fynbos vegetation belt, it has 8,600 plant species, 73% of which are found nowhere else on Earth. About the size of the Lüneburger Heide in Germany (photo above), it contains ten times as many plant species. Factors contributing this unusual degree of diversity include continual, relatively rapid climatic oscillations and the absence of major long-term climatic changes during the earlier geological epochs, both of which have exerted a favorable influence on evolutionary processes in this, the smallest phytogeographic kingdom on earth.

Interdependence of geodiversity, biodiversity, and ecodiversity

- Ecodiversity
- Geodiversity
- Biodiversity

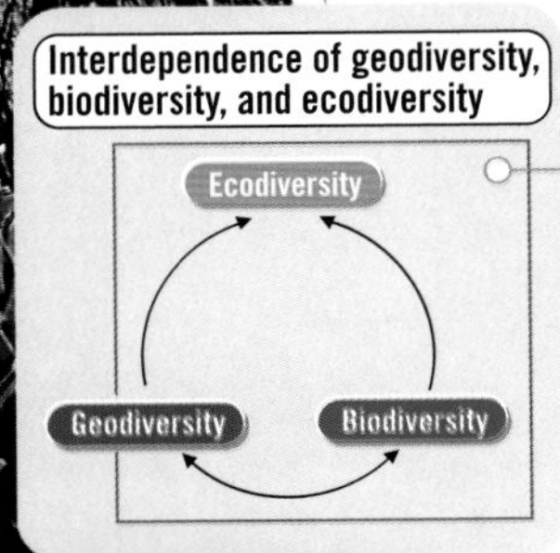

Interaction

Geodiversity and biodiversity are closely related and interdependent. Their interaction is responsible for ecodiversity.

Colombia, northeastern Brazil, eastern Himalayas/Yunnan, northern Borneo and New Guinea).

In Southeast Asia, plant diversity is supported by the monsoon-like character of the inner-tropical west wind circulation pattern, with maximum water-vapor accumulation over the warmest ocean basin of the Indo-Malaysian Archipelago. Similar conditions prevail off the western coast of Colombia and in the Gulf of Guinea.

Tropical trade wind currents blowing inland into the coastal mountain regions of the tropical-subtropical eastern continental margins (eastern Brazil, Middle America, northeastern Australia, Madagascar) also favor high levels of species diversity. In contrast, the divergent trade wind currents on the western sides of the continents tend to cause extreme aridity, although they also give impetus to the cold ocean currents. The result is a constant layer of fog over the cold ocean water, accompanied by local land/sea wind systems along the coasts. In the humid-air deserts ("fog oases"), this fog, combined with the cold ocean current, encourages the development of highly diverse flora, such as the Loma vegetation on the western coast of South America.

The subtropical regions with winter rainy seasons assume a unique status resulting from seasonal alternation of climatic factors (including most importantly rainfall) typical of tropical temperate zones. In the rainier mountainous countries, winter rains alternating with summer convection precipitation in combination with long thermal vegetation periods produce substantial phytodiversity, particularly at middle elevations, and create favorable living conditions for human beings (European Mediterranean region, Middle East, California, central Chile, the Cape Provinces of South Africa, and southwestern Australia).

Areas with high and low vascular-plant diversity are separated by transition zones. In the northern hemisphere, zones of diversity tend to run parallel to lines of latitude, much like the large landscape belts. In the southern hemisphere, they tend to align – depending upon the position and orientation of mountain ranges – concentrically in the direction of the major atmospheric currents and in response to lee/luff effects (Australia, southern Africa) or along north-south axes (South America).

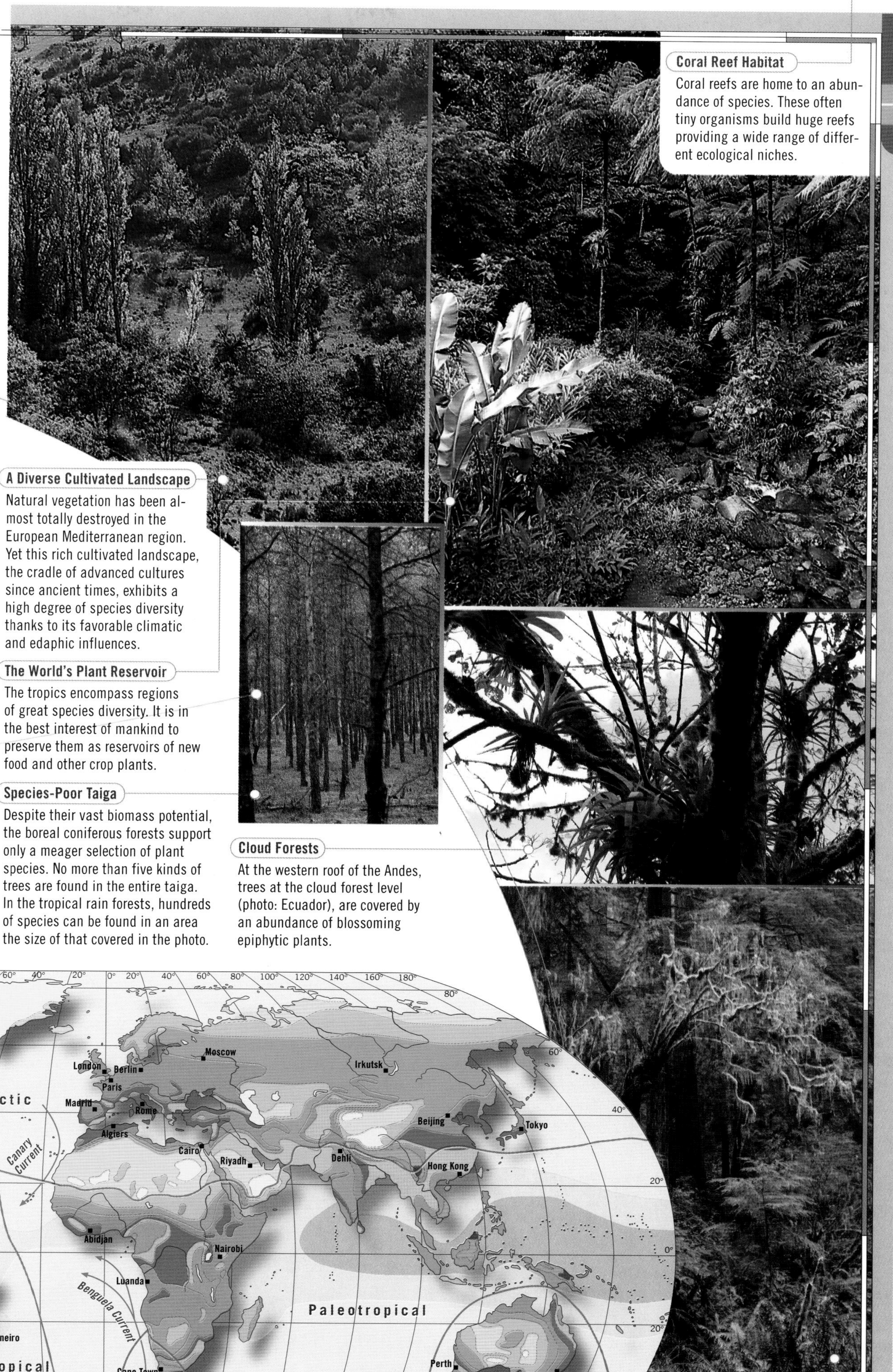

Coral Reef Habitat
Coral reefs are home to an abundance of species. These often tiny organisms build huge reefs providing a wide range of different ecological niches.

A Diverse Cultivated Landscape
Natural vegetation has been almost totally destroyed in the European Mediterranean region. Yet this rich cultivated landscape, the cradle of advanced cultures since ancient times, exhibits a high degree of species diversity thanks to its favorable climatic and edaphic influences.

The World's Plant Reservoir
The tropics encompass regions of great species diversity. It is in the best interest of mankind to preserve them as reservoirs of new food and other crop plants.

Species-Poor Taiga
Despite their vast biomass potential, the boreal coniferous forests support only a meager selection of plant species. No more than five kinds of trees are found in the entire taiga. In the tropical rain forests, hundreds of species can be found in an area the size of that covered in the photo.

Cloud Forests
At the western roof of the Andes, trees at the cloud forest level (photo: Ecuador), are covered by an abundance of blossoming epiphytic plants.

Moist Coastal Forests
Kept moist by frequent coastal fog, the mountains along the coast of northern California are densely forested. The characteristic giant redwoods (Sequoia sempervirens) are joined here by other conifers (Douglas firs, etc.) and deciduous species.

Biodiversity

Holarctic

Paleotropical

Neotropical

Paleotropical

Capensis

Australian

Antarctic

California Current
Canary Current
Humboldt Current
Benguela Current

Vancouver · Montreal · Denver · New York · San Francisco · London · Berlin · Paris · Madrid · Rome · Moscow · Irkutsk · Beijing · Tokyo · Mexico · Algiers · Cairo · Riyadh · Dehli · Hong Kong · Bogota · Manaus · Abidjan · Nairobi · Lima · Luanda · Rio de Janeiro · Santiago · Buenos Aires · Cape Town · Perth · Sydney

Zones of diversity: Number of species per 10,000 square km

DZ 1 (< 100)	DZ 4 (500 – 1000)	DZ 7 (2000 – 3000)	DZ 10 (> 5000)	**Water surface temperature**
DZ 2 (100 – 200)	DZ 5 (1000 – 1500)	DZ 8 (3000 – 4000)		> 29° C
DZ 3 (200 – 500)	DZ 6 (1500 – 2000)	DZ 9 (4000 – 5000)	cold current	> 27° C

C a p e n s i s Regions of abundant flora

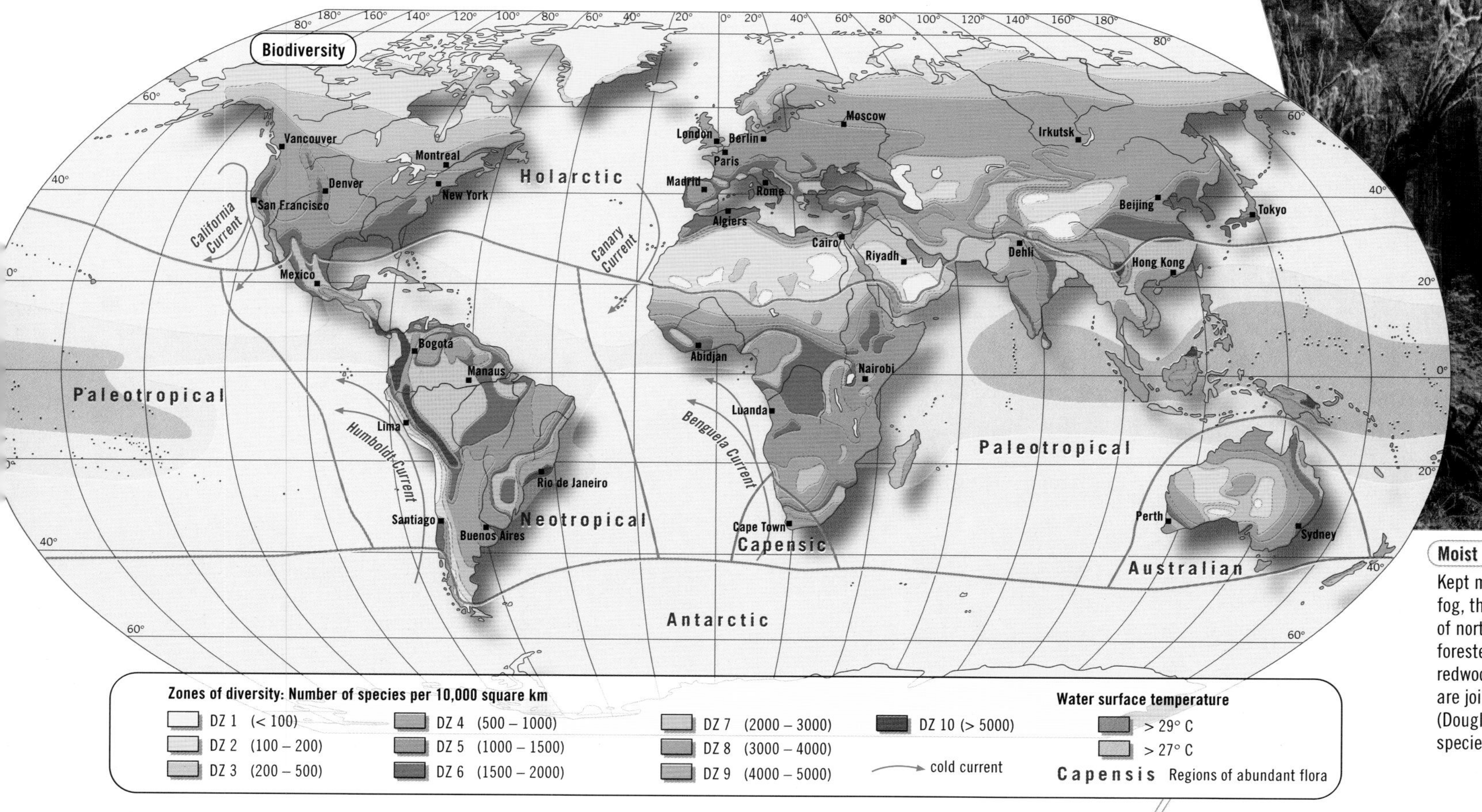

Deserts and Desertification

Are We Turning the Earth into a Desert?

Public attention was first drawn to the endangered African Sahel region by the catastrophic drought and famine of 1968–1973. Steadily dwindling harvest yields and widespread livestock death cost the lives of 100,000–200,000 people. Nomads and farmers sought refuge in cities or less arid regions in the south, many of them never to return. Since then, the percentage of nomadic people among the total population of Mauritania has fallen from 70 % to 25 %. Other drought-endangered areas of the world have experienced similar fates. The UN has officially recognized the problem of "desertification," and programs have been devoted to solving it, most recently within the framework of the Agenda 21 resolution passed at the 1992 Earth Summit in Rio de Janeiro.

What is Desertification?

Desertification is a process involving natural and man-made influences by which land is transformed into desert. It affects all dry regions on Earth – not only existing deserts but especially steppes and dry savannas that could easily become or be turned into deserts. More than one-third of the dry land on our planet, and nearly a billion of its people, are threatened by desertification. The most severely endangered countries are among the poorest in the world. Between ten and fourteen million acres of farm and grazing land are lost to desertification every year.

A Constant Water Shortage

Regions with dry climates have fragile ecosystems and are thus naturally endangered. Precipitation is not only meager but seasonal as well. In tropical regions with both dry and rainy seasons, dry winters alternate with wet summers, and precipitation levels vary significantly. Dry or wet periods often last for several years. These factors influence the make-up of plant communities, determine plant survival strategies, and affect the production of vegetable biomass. Satellite images show that the southern boundary of the Sahara may drift northward or southward depending upon precipitation. Yet it is not true that the Sahara is steadily and progressively expanding. The climate in this region has not changed significantly since northern Africa began to turn arid over 4,000 years ago. The crucial factor is mankind's disruptive intervention in the delicate equilibrium of nature. Accordingly, desert-like conditions do not expand along broad fronts but tend instead to develop in spots.

Progressive Environmental Destruction

Failure to adapt land-use practices to natural circumstances in farming and grazing operations can have devastating consequences. Thus in the Sahel region, for example, the boundary of sustainable rain-fed farming (minimum precipitation of 500 mm per year in marginal tropical regions with summer rains and 300 mm in subtropical areas with winter wet seasons) was pushed into the desert during the extended humid period from 1950 to 1967 – up to 200 km in the Sahel region and 100 km in northwestern Africa. In the process, much natural vegetation, which, although sparse, was well adapted to changing moisture conditions, was thinned or eliminated entirely, causing extensive, irreparable damage. The grass cover was stripped away, and bushes and trees were cut for firewood. The destruction of vegetation accelerates the rate of evaporation; soil grows drier and is subject to wind or water erosion. Where topsoil is completely stripped away, impermeable crusts of rock may be exposed, the soil water budget can be permanently affected, and the groundwater level may sink. Sand carried away by winds may accumulate in dunes. Sandstorms originating in the Sahel and the Sahara have been known to carry material as far away as the Caribbean and South America.

Intensive farming in the Sahel region went hand in hand with shorter fallow periods (fertilizers are ordinarily not used). Nomads who had used these fields as grazing areas were forced to move to inferior land, particularly since political boundaries have made wide-ranging migration more difficult or even impossible. Deep wells were drilled in many places to secure an adequate water supply for nomads and farmers – but this, too, produced negative effects. Herds grew larger, and the groundwater level sank even further.

Where precipitation is insufficient to support cultivation, farmers must irrigate, as they have done for thousands of years in the Valleys of the Nile, the Tigris and Euphrates, and the Indus, which are fed by heavy precipitation in the mountain along their upper reaches, and along the rivers that empty into the Aral Sea in the piedmont region of Central Asia or the Tarim Basin. Due to the high evaporation rate in dry regions, however, irrigation tends to cause excessive soil salinity, as examples from ancient history show. Damage of this kind has been much more severe in recent times, however (e.g. in Pakistan and the Al-Wadi al-Jadid in Egypt).

A Global Problem

Desertification is actually a by-product of the twentieth-century population explosion brought about in part by significant improvements in medical care. Farmers and nomads rank low in the political and economic ladders of developing countries. Since colonial times, governments have consistently encouraged or decreed market-oriented production (e.g. cotton, peanuts, meat) in order to increase tax and export revenues and ensure an adequate food supply for politically significant urban populations. Increasing economic globalization and requirements imposed by the World Bank and the International Monetary Fund have put rural populations under tremendous pressure to adapt. Worldwide, desertification is responsible for production shortfalls valued at 40 billion dollars per year – more than the combined gross national products of all of the countries of the Sahel region, from Senegal to Somalia. Desertification not only jeopardizes the fulfillment of basic human needs – nutrition, health, and education – it also contributes to the spread of poverty, the dissolution of social bonds, political

Desert

Areas in danger of desertification
- acutely endangered
- seriously endangered
- moderately endang

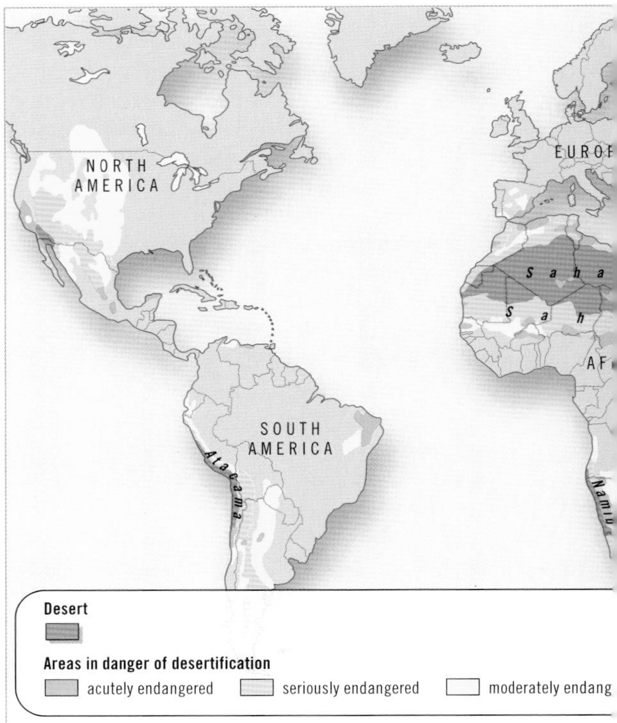

First presented at the 1977 UN Conference in Nairobi, the World Desertification Map shows that areas immediately adjacent to existing deserts are often in less danger of desertification than somewhat moister region, where the burden of cultivation and population density is greater.

Fluctuations in annual precipitation levels recorded at various measuring stations in the western Sahel region between 1901 and 1990, entered as percentage deviations from the long-term average. Older records also document similar alternating periods of precipitation deficit (1820-40) and surplus (1870-95), as do variations in the shoreline of Lake Chad.

Bread or Salt

Given sufficient water, the desert can be brought to bloom. But desert soil must be irrigated with great care, ensuring that it is well flushed in order to avoid salt accumulation. Numerous cases of excessive, irreversible soil salination have been recorded in Libya, for example, where extensive grain fields were laid out and irrigated (with long-armed rotary sprinklers) using water drawn from "fossil" reserves formed deep in the earth during wetter geological periods in the past.

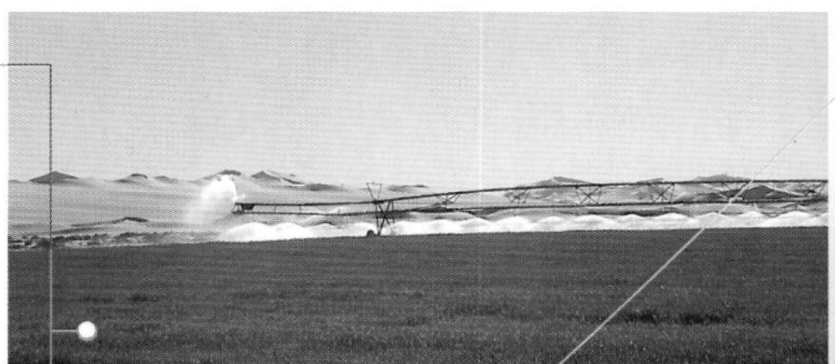

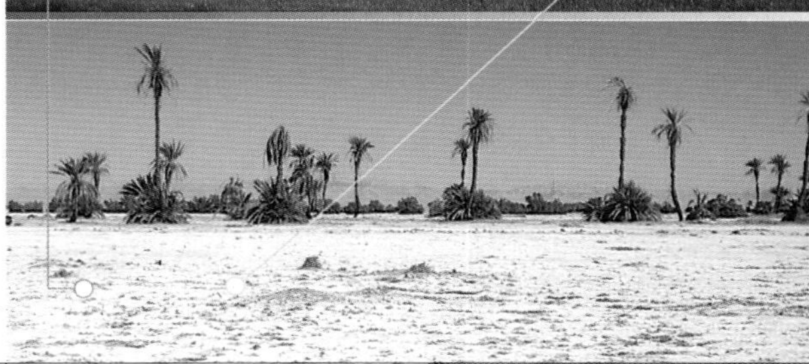

The Power of Water

Where the protective cover of vegetation in dry regions has been thinned or stripped away entirely through cultivation or grazing, brief but often very heavy rains wreak havoc on the exposed soil. Rapid runoff cuts grooves, troughs, and deep gorges in the ground, as can be seen in this photo taken in the Sierra Madre del Sur, Mexico. Badland formations of this kind are especially prevalent in areas with soft sediments.

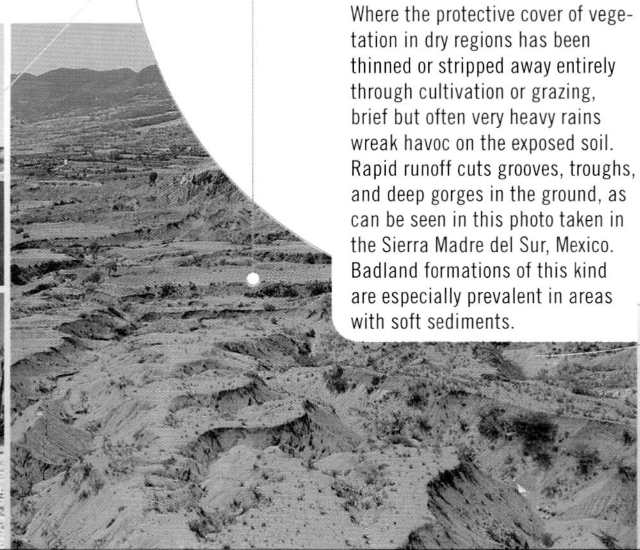

Dying of Thirst

During extended periods of drought – this photo was taken in the degraded dry Kaokoveld savanna (Namibia) in the early 1980s – water becomes so scarce that many animals die of thirst.

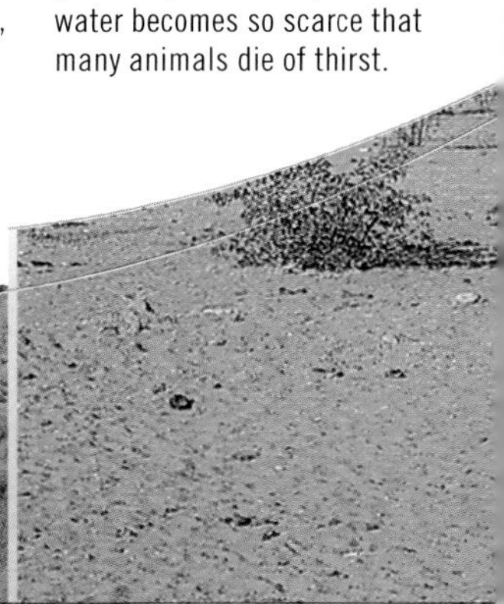

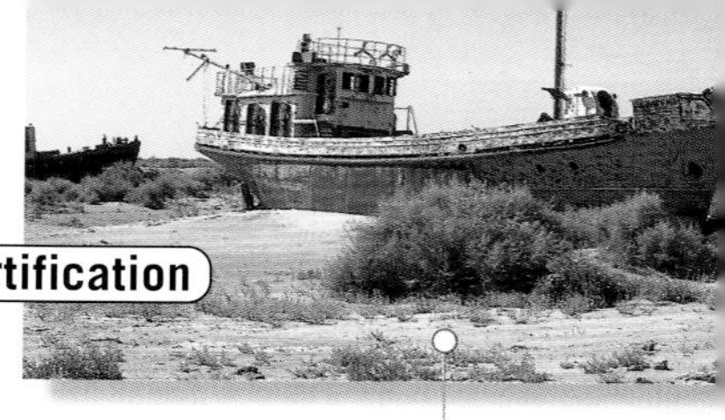

instability, and armed conflicts fueled by competition for dwindling resources. Soon, 100 million people will have joined the worldwide exodus from rural regions into the cities. The effects of this wave of migration will ultimately be felt in North America and Europe as well.

Desertification is not a new phenomenon. The ancient Romans destroyed their "granary" on the Tunisian steppe through overuse (Bedouin immigrants from Arabia reclaimed the land for grazing, and it eventually recovered, only to be converted to farmland again under French colonial rule, which hastened the process of degradation through desertification). Dust storms and soil erosion on the U.S. Great Plains ("Dust Bowl") between 1930 and 1935 (affecting 650,000 farmers and 400,000 square km of land) offered striking proof that industrialized countries are not immune to desertification. But poor countries lack the resources to overcome these problems on their own. International aid is needed, especially in light of the fact that desertification poses not only social and economic dangers but environmental ones as well. If vegetation disappears from the dry regions, huge quantities of greenhouse gases (carbon dioxide, methane), now being absorbed by plants will be released into the atmosphere – 30 times the amount of CO_2 currently emitted every year.

Can Desertification Be Stopped?

Counteractive measures need time to take effect. Once an understanding of ecological relationships is achieved, the local population must be educated and encouraged to adapt farming and grazing practices to the environment. The use of alternative forms of energy can be helpful. Other effective measures include the planting of drought-resistant crop plants, the use of appropriate agricultural methods and technologies (e.g. dams to protect against erosion, terracing, the planting of trees), and accelerated development in the non-agrarian sector.

The Aral Sea Drama

The use of water from rivers feeding the Aral Sea for irrigation caused the sea to shrink from 68,000 to 39,500 square km between 1960 and 1991. Salinity also rose to alarming levels (up to 30%), decimating the fish population. Many fishing boats were left high and dry. Salt and dust (75 million tons per year), along with accumulated toxic residues (pesticides, herbicides, fertilizers) are carried from the old seabed by winds and deposited on the surrounding fields (cotton, rice, etc.). These substances contaminate the groundwater and have led to a substantial rise in the incidence of disease, birth defects, and infant death.

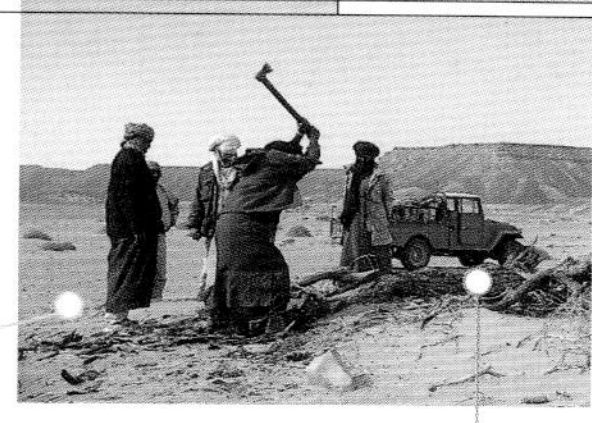

The Last Tree

In the absence of environmentally sounder energy alternatives (such as solar energy or biogas), the inhabitants of the Sahel zone, where wood is extremely scarce (photo: Tuareg tribespeople in Niger) must rely on firewood to prepare their daily meals. This results in the loss of as many as 200 savanna trees per family per year.

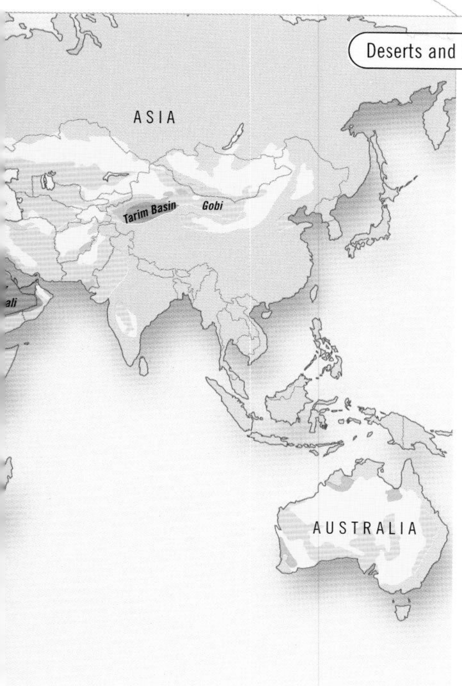

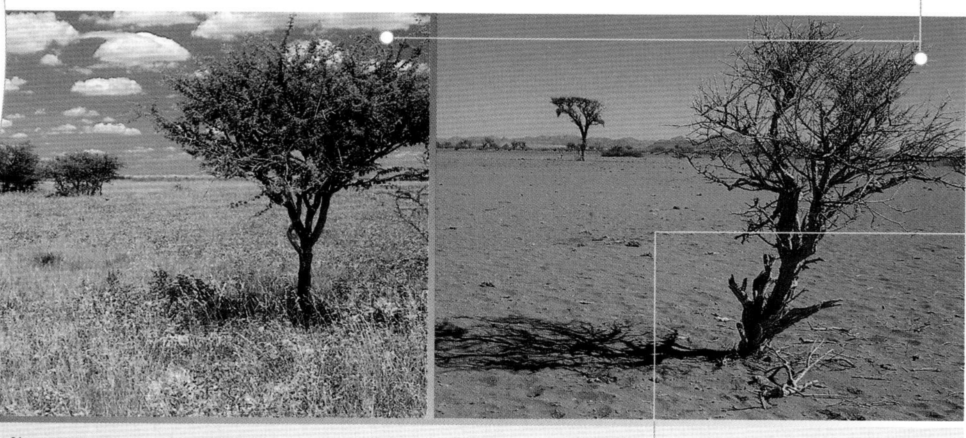

Degradation

The grass cover in the savanna is often so heavily damaged by overuse that it cannot regenerate even during the rainy season and thus leaves the bare soil exposed (left: intact or only slightly damaged savanna; right: degraded savanna). Only trees with deep roots that reach the groundwater aquifer – Acacias, for the most part – can survive.

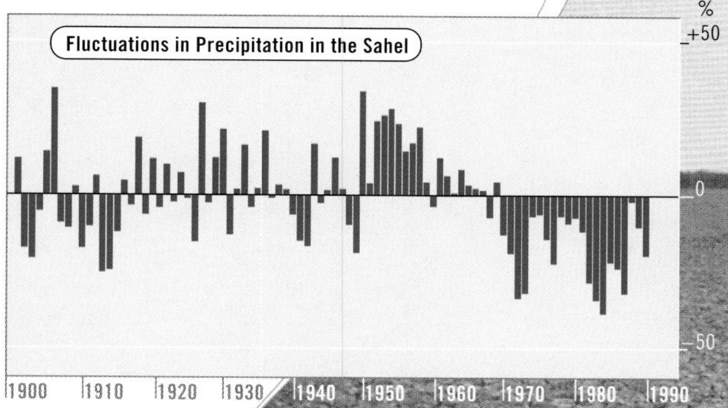

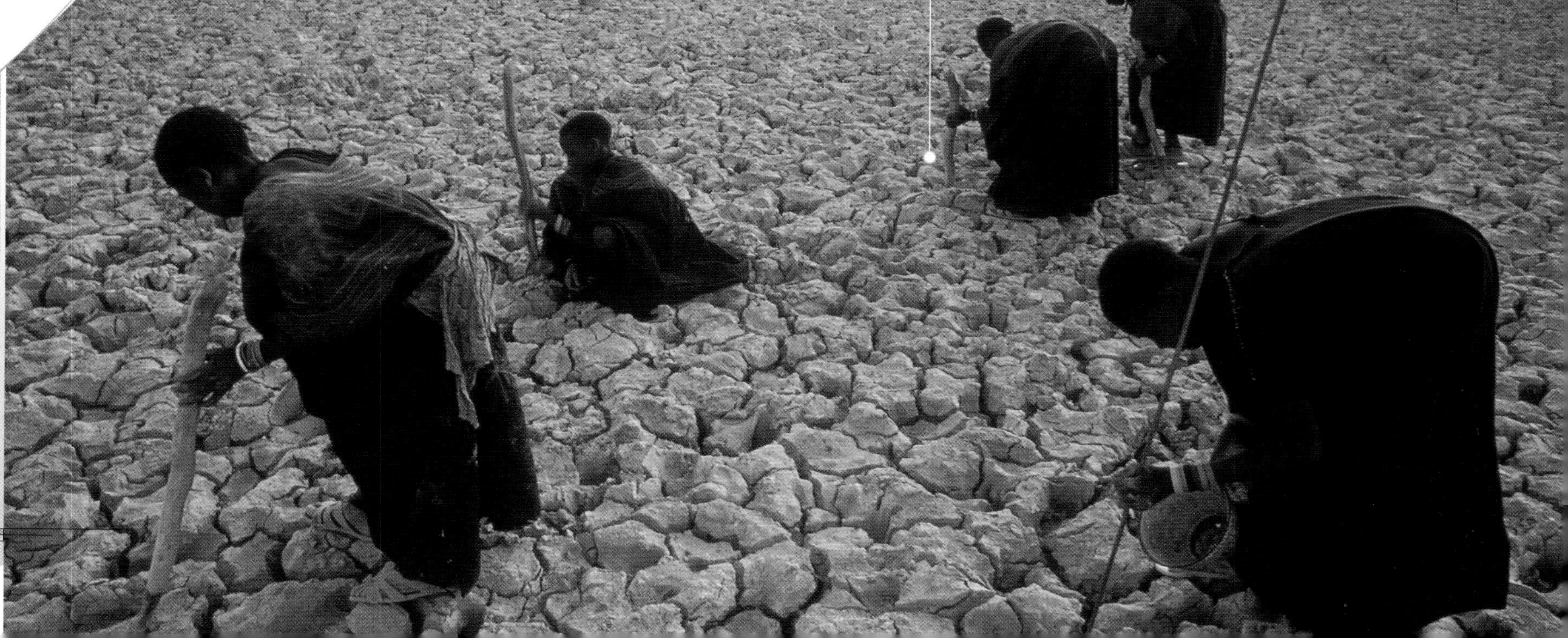

Driven by Hunger

After several years of drought, the ground in the Sahel region along the southern rim of the Sahara is severely desiccated and covered by a network of deep cracks. Desperately searching for nourishment, these women use long poles to loosen the hard clumps of soil in the hope of finding edible plants and roots beneath them.

Deserts and Desertification

ASIA

Tarim Basin Gobi

AUSTRALIA

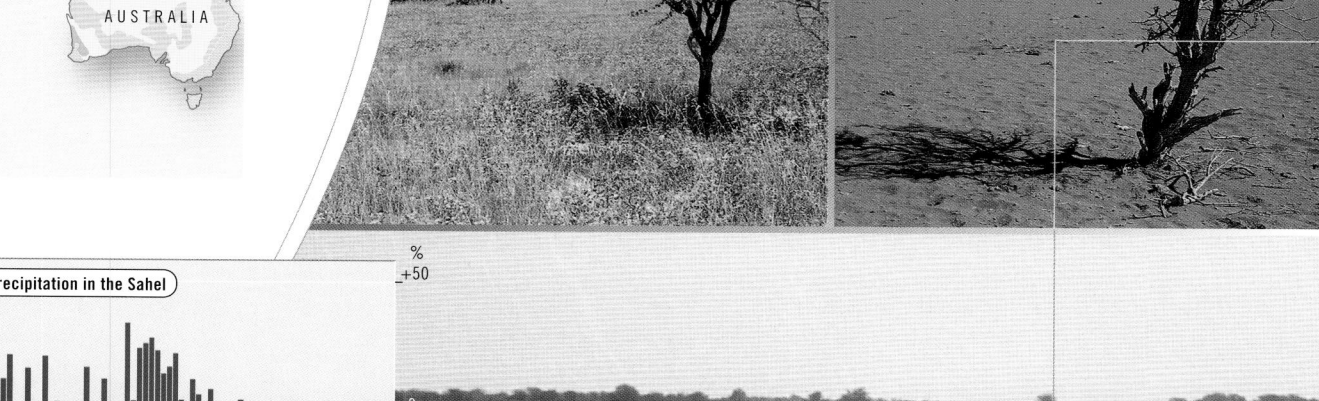

Fluctuations in Precipitation in the Sahel

%
+50

0

-50

|1900 |1910 |1920 |1930 |1940 |1950 |1960 |1970 |1980 |1990

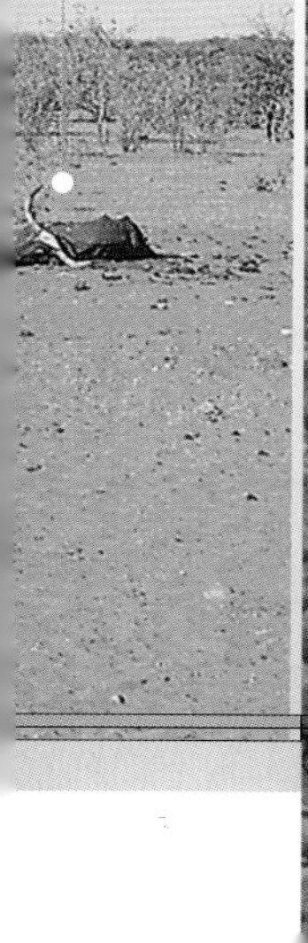

Worldwide Protection for Natural Treasures through UNESCO

Will Our Natural Heritage Be Preserved for the Next Generation?

World Natural Heritage sites are chosen for their uniqueness and outstanding universal value. Thus the goal of the UNESCO World Heritage Convention is to identify the most outstanding examples of significant natural ecosystems and landscapes and the most important geological and paleontological sites from among the many applications received. Yet some countries fear that increasing publicity will increase the pressure of tourism on already fragile landscapes and have refrained from submitting applications.

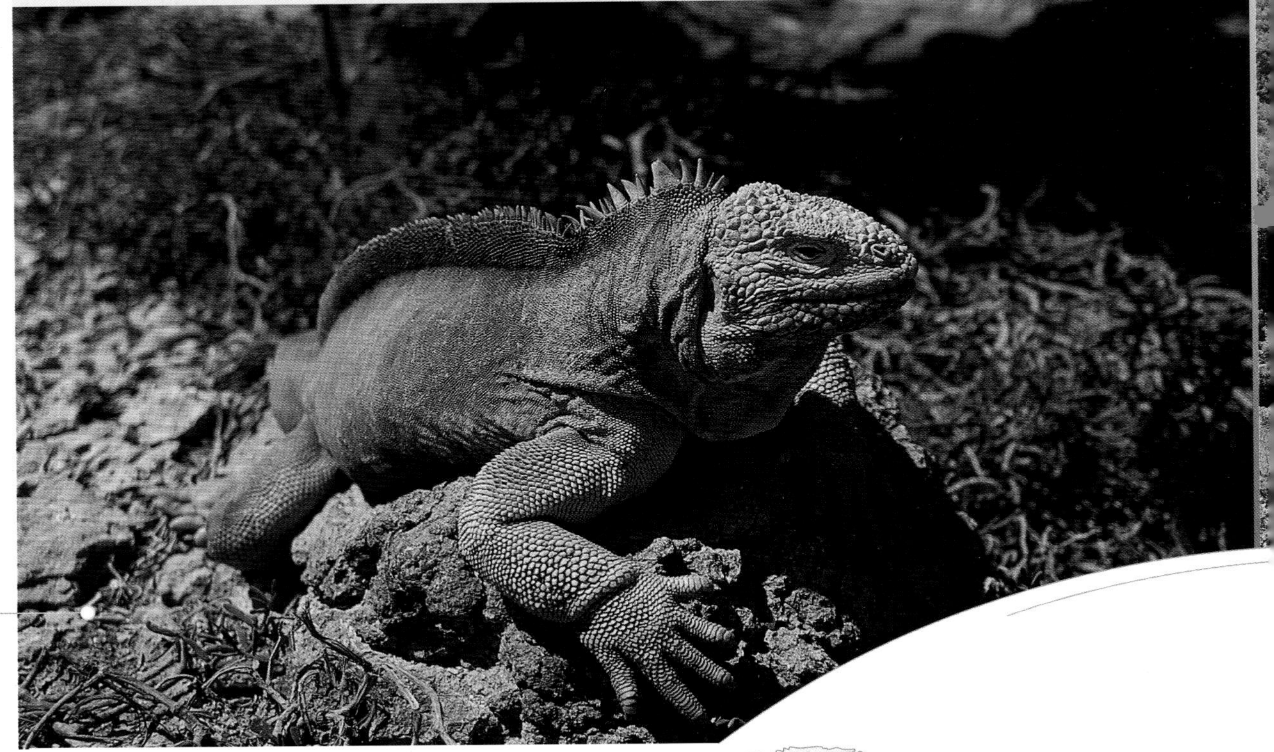

The Threat Posed by Mankind

Environmental pollution, resource depletion, population pressure! Can we truly hope to pass the heritage entrusted to us on to succeeding generations? The Convention focuses particular attention on "endangered natural heritage sites," and thus the last remaining Australian rain forests have been saved from destruction. In other cases, however, such as that of the Srebarna Danube wetlands, rescue efforts almost came too late.

Does Conservation Make Sense in Our Time?

The static concept of conservation was long the dominant guiding principle in our thinking about protecting nature. We know today that all natural systems are highly dynamic. The Agenda 21 program passed at the UN Earth Summit Conference in Rio Janeiro strongly emphasized the concept of "sustainable use and development" as a guideline for thought and action.

Home of Pele, Goddess of Fire

Kilauea is one of **Hawaii's two active volcanoes (106).** From deep in the Earth's upper mantle, the mountain brings liquid lava to the surface, where it emerges at a temperature of 2,160° F and spreads rapidly (at a speed of up to 40 km per hour) into the surrounding countryside.

Los Glaciares

The **Moreno Glacier (30)** flows eastward from the continental Patagonian ice sheet into Lago Argentino. The irregular advances of its broad tongue (more than two km wide) cause occasional flooding.

A Window on Evolution

The **Galapagos Islands (25)** were formed by a group of shield volcanoes whose peaks rise from the depth of the Pacific on both sides of the Equator. The land iguana belongs to the large group of endemic species.

Sinter Terraces

Yellowstone National Park (8) encompasses a caldera with a diameter of 79 km surrounded by high peaks in the Rocky Mountains. These sinter terraces were formed by hot springs, remnants of volcanic activity dating back 600,000 years.

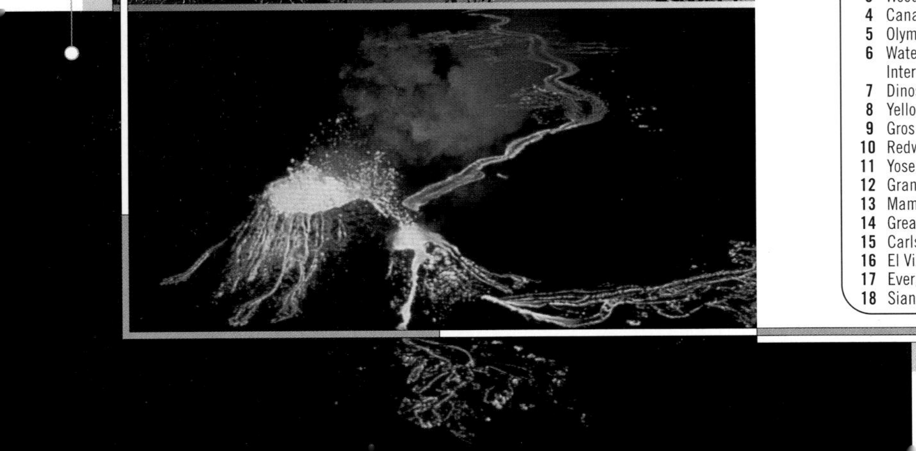

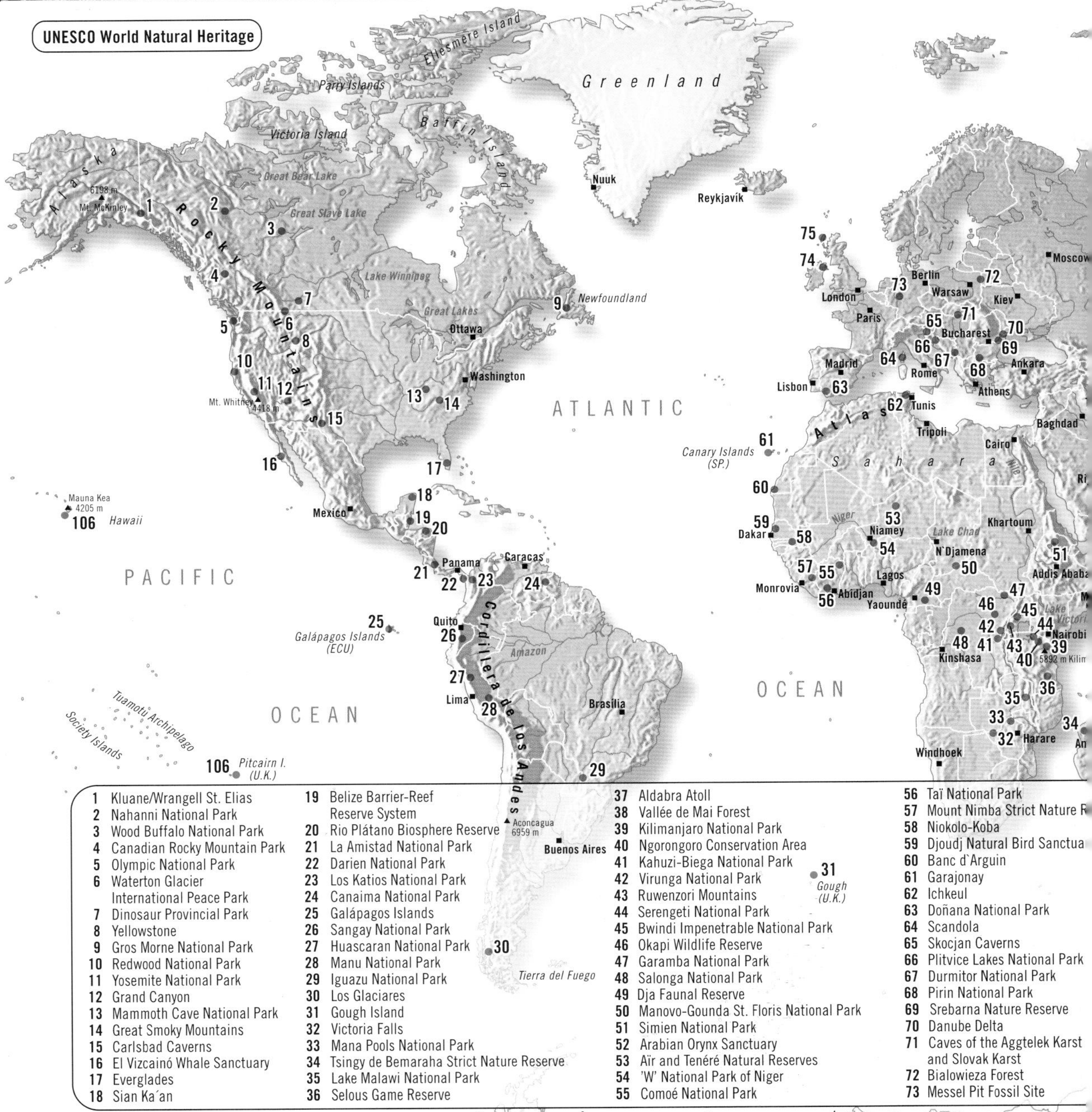
UNESCO World Natural Heritage
Greenland
Ellesmere Island
Parry Islands
Victoria Island
Baffin Island
Great Bear Lake
Great Slave Lake
Alaska
Rocky Mountains
Lake Winnipeg
Great Lakes
Newfoundland
Nuuk
Reykjavik
Ottawa
Washington
Mexico
Mt. Whitney
Mauna Kea 4205 m
Hawaii
ATLANTIC
PACIFIC
OCEAN
Galápagos Islands (ECU)
Tuamotu Archipelago
Society Islands
Pitcairn I. (U.K.)
Panama
Caracas
Quito
Lima
Amazon
Cordillera de los Andes
Brasilia
Aconcagua 6959 m
Buenos Aires
Tierra del Fuego
Gough (U.K.)
Canary Islands (SP.)
London
Paris
Berlin
Warsaw
Kiev
Moscow
Madrid
Lisbon
Rome
Bucharest
Ankara
Athens
Tunis
Tripoli
Cairo
Baghdad
Atlas
Sahara
Dakar
Niamey
Lake Chad
N'Djamena
Khartoum
Addis Ababa
Monrovia
Abidjan
Lagos
Yaoundé
Kinshasa
Nairobi
Harare
Windhoek
1 Kluane/Wrangell St. Elias
2 Nahanni National Park
3 Wood Buffalo National Park
4 Canadian Rocky Mountain Park
5 Olympic National Park
6 Waterton Glacier International Peace Park
7 Dinosaur Provincial Park
8 Yellowstone
9 Gros Morne National Park
10 Redwood National Park
11 Yosemite National Park
12 Grand Canyon
13 Mammoth Cave National Park
14 Great Smoky Mountains
15 Carlsbad Caverns
16 El Vizcaíno Whale Sanctuary
17 Everglades
18 Sian Ka'an
19 Belize Barrier-Reef Reserve System
20 Rio Plátano Biosphere Reserve
21 La Amistad National Park
22 Darien National Park
23 Los Katios National Park
24 Canaima National Park
25 Galápagos Islands
26 Sangay National Park
27 Huascaran National Park
28 Manu National Park
29 Iguazu National Park
30 Los Glaciares
31 Gough Island
32 Victoria Falls
33 Mana Pools National Park
34 Tsingy de Bemaraha Strict Nature Reserve
35 Lake Malawi National Park
36 Selous Game Reserve
37 Aldabra Atoll
38 Vallée de Mai Forest
39 Kilimanjaro National Park
40 Ngorongoro Conservation Area
41 Kahuzi-Biega National Park
42 Virunga National Park
43 Ruwenzori Mountains
44 Serengeti National Park
45 Bwindi Impenetrable National Park
46 Okapi Wildlife Reserve
47 Garamba National Park
48 Salonga National Park
49 Dja Faunal Reserve
50 Manovo-Gounda St. Floris National Park
51 Simien National Park
52 Arabian Oryx Sanctuary
53 Aïr and Ténéré Natural Reserves
54 'W' National Park of Niger
55 Comoé National Park
56 Taï National Park
57 Mount Nimba Strict Nature R
58 Niokolo-Koba
59 Djoudj Natural Bird Sanctua
60 Banc d'Arguin
61 Garajonay
62 Ichkeul
63 Doñana National Park
64 Scandola
65 Skocjan Caverns
66 Plitvice Lakes National Park
67 Durmitor National Park
68 Pirin National Park
69 Srebarna Nature Reserve
70 Danube Delta
71 Caves of the Aggtelek Karst and Slovak Karst
72 Bialowieza Forest
73 Messel Pit Fossil Site

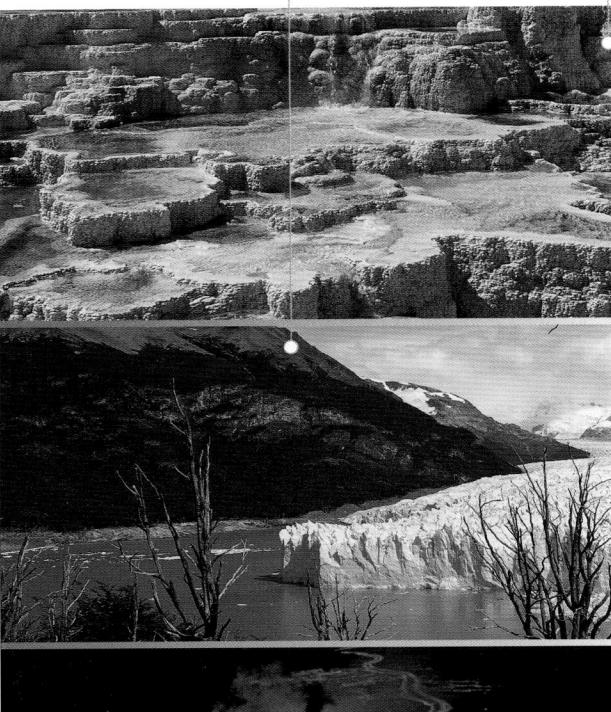

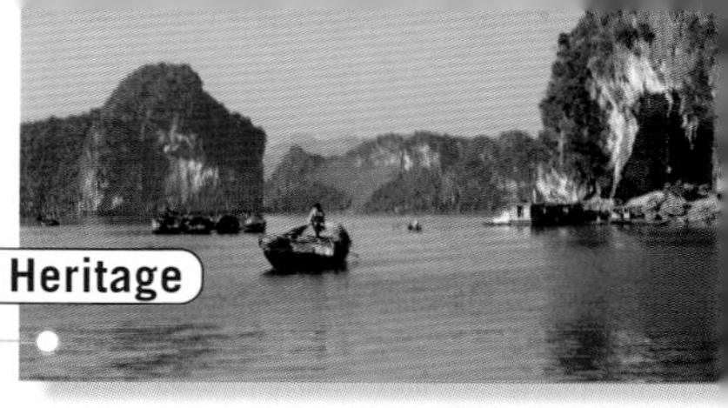

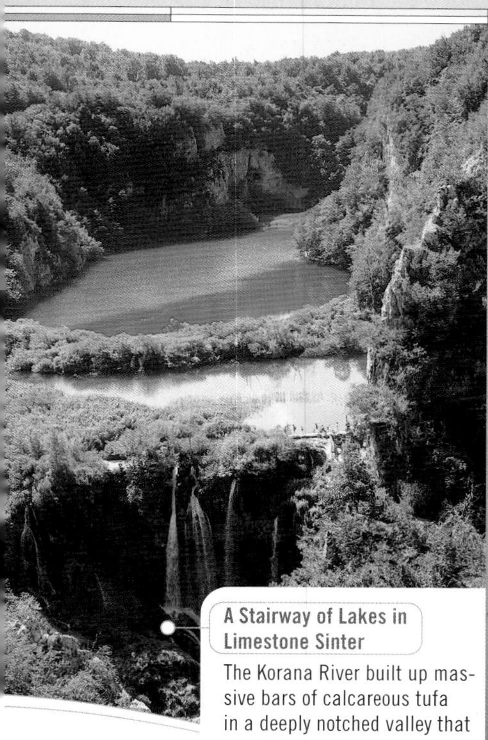

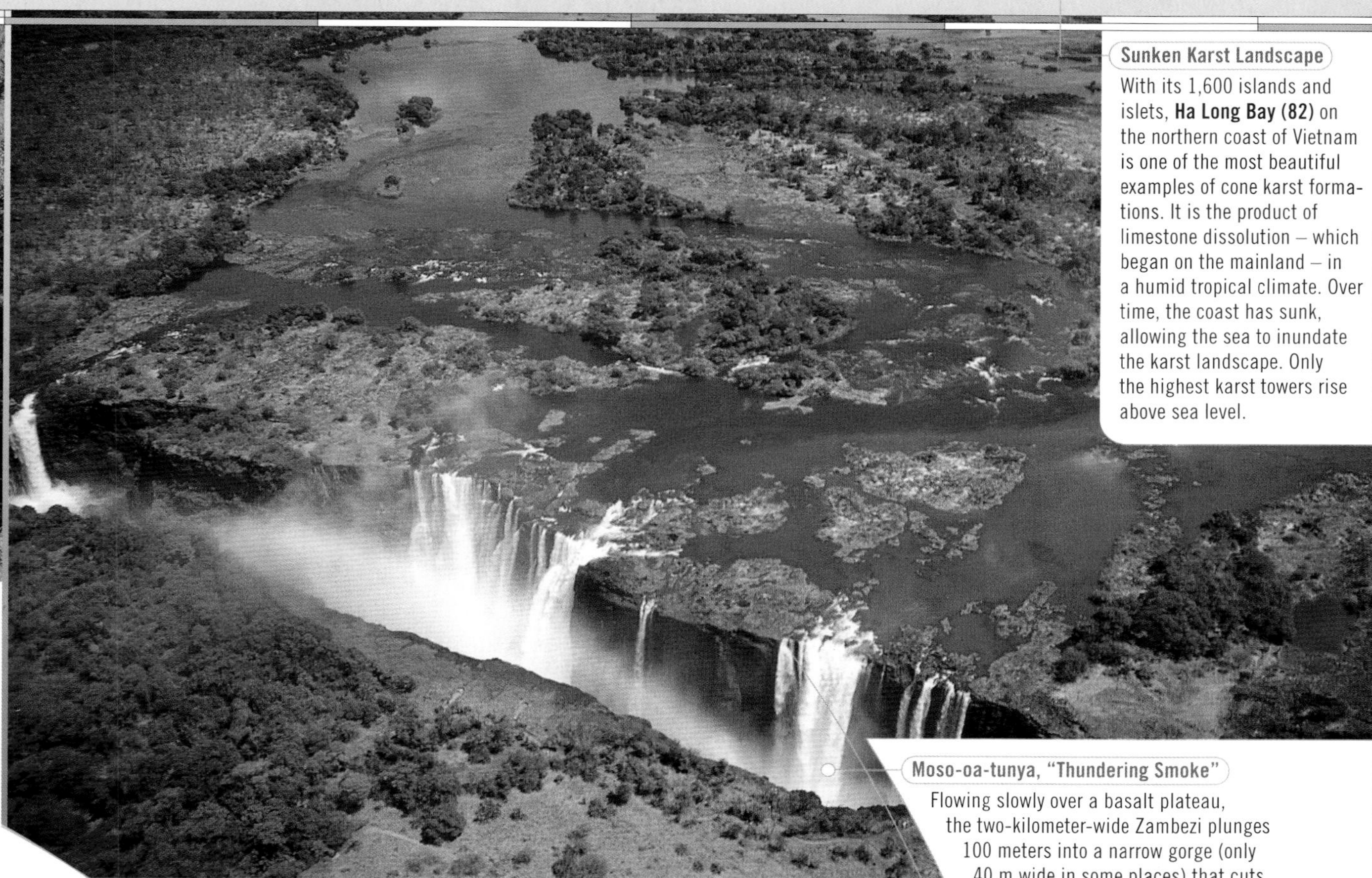

Sunken Karst Landscape

With its 1,600 islands and islets, **Ha Long Bay (82)** on the northern coast of Vietnam is one of the most beautiful examples of cone karst formations. It is the product of limestone dissolution — which began on the mainland — in a humid tropical climate. Over time, the coast has sunk, allowing the sea to inundate the karst landscape. Only the highest karst towers rise above sea level.

A Stairway of Lakes in Limestone Sinter

The Korana River built up massive bars of calcareous tufa in a deeply notched valley that cuts through the Croatian karst landscape, forming the **Plitvice Lakes (66)**, a stairway of 16 small and larger lakes covering a distance of 7 km. Some of the many waterfalls that spill over the sinter barriers are nearly 80 m high.

Moso-oa-tunya, "Thundering Smoke"

Flowing slowly over a basalt plateau, the two-kilometer-wide Zambezi plunges 100 meters into a narrow gorge (only 40 m wide in some places) that cuts straight across its course. The broad water curtain of the **Victoria Falls (32)** is transformed into clouds of spray and fine mist that promote rich plant growth.

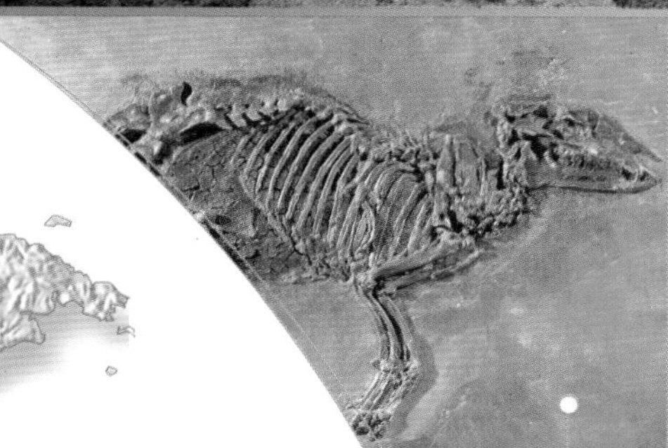

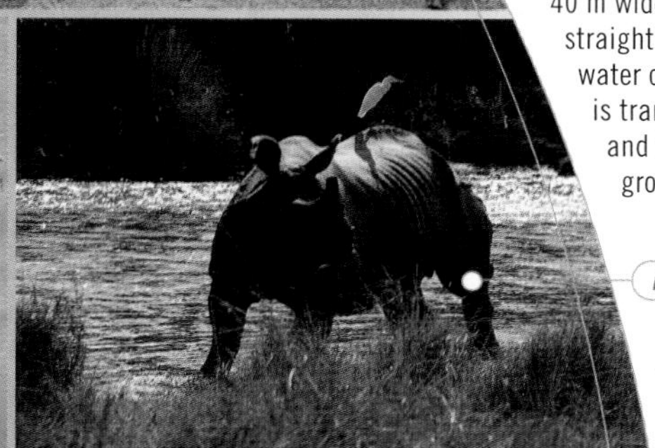

A Refuge for Rhinos

Chitwan National Park (90) in the wet lowlands of Nepal is a refuge (protected by the military) for 400 Indian Rhinos.

A Tiny Horse from a Warmer Era

Numerous fossils from the Eocene have been recovered from the oil shale layers of the **Messel Pit (73)** near Darmstadt, among them this well-preserved skeleton of the prehistoric horse Propalaeotherium parvulum. Fossil evidence of flora and fauna indicate a subtropical to tropical climate in the region some 40 to 50 million years ago.

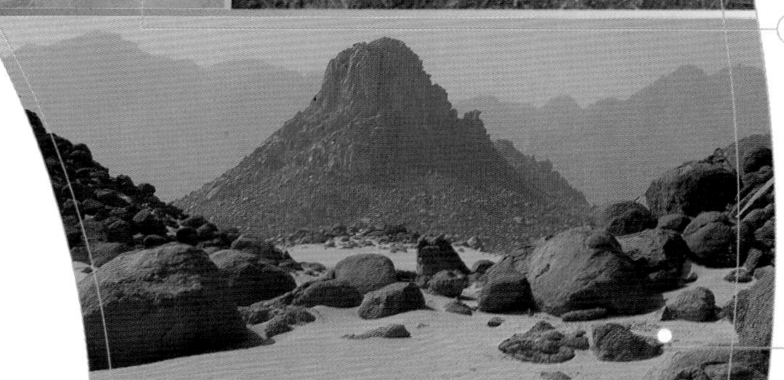

Endangered Desert Landscape

The **Aïr and Ténéré Natural Reserves (53)** comprise two different natural landscapes. The sandstone base of the Aïr desert mountain range is riddled with plutonic ring intrusions (photo: Adrar Chiriet). To the east is the Ténéré, a desolate region through which the Tuareg have traditionally driven their camel caravans, bearing salt from Bilma and Fachi to distant markets.

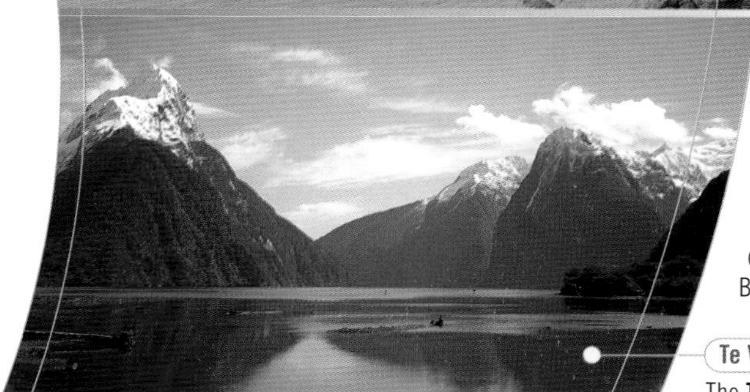

Te Wahipounamu

The **Te Wahipounamu Fiordland (103)** on the western coast of New Zealand's South Island encompasses untouched stretches of coast, 28 mountains with peaks above 3,000 m, and glaciers that descend below the tree line.

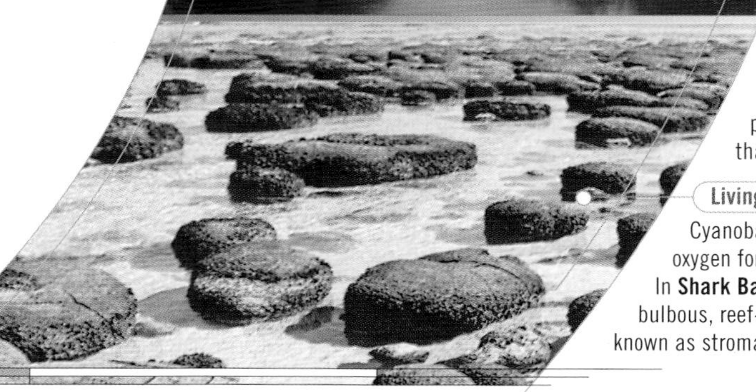

Living Fossils

Cyanobacteria have been producing oxygen for at least 2.3 billion years. In **Shark Bay (105),** they are still forming bulbous, reef-like limestone deposits known as stromatolites today.

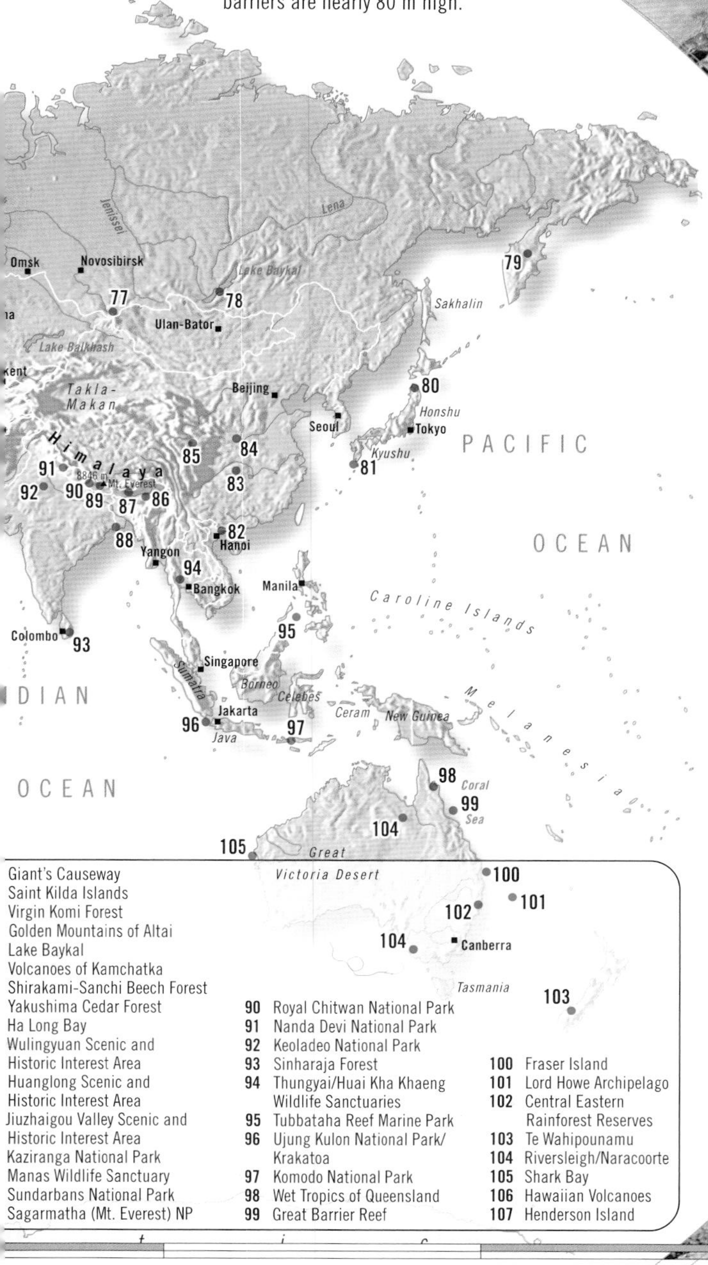

Early Human Development and Migration

Advancing to the Ends of the World

At least twice in the course of human history, our ancestors, hominids of the genus Homo, set out from Africa to conquer the world. Why did they abandon their familiar, warm, tropical homeland in the African savanna for an unknown and distant world full of surprises, challenges, and dangers – and new opportunities? Were they forced to move – 1.8 million years ago – by population pressure, changes in climate, vegetation, or fauna, or was it curiosity and the urge to explore that drove them. Although the first sedentary communities did not appear until after the end of the last ice age 10,000 years ago, individuals are unlikely to have traveled far from their homes even long before then. Human migrations over long distances presumably took place over extended periods of time.

When Apes Came Down from the Trees – It all began with an upright posture

The earliest phase of human evolution and migration began during a period of environmental change along the East African Rift. About six million years ago, the rain forest began to give way to expanding tree savannas, forcing tree-dwelling primates to adopt an upright posture in order to facilitate travel over greater distances. Remains of Australopithecines, hominids which first appeared about four million years ago (example: Lucy), show jawbone modifications indicating adaptation to a diet no longer comprised of soft fruit and leaves of rain forest plants but primarily of harder seeds, roots, grass, and nuts found in the savannas. An upright posture enhanced mobility. Bones of Australopithecines about 3.5 million years old have been found from Ethiopia to South Africa and in

Chad. A period of global cooling about 2.5 million years ago caused increasing aridity accompanied by changes in flora and fauna, intensifying the selective influence of the environment. The first hominids of the genus Homo (Homo habilis, Homo rudolfensis) appeared at this point. They used simple stone tools (such as scrapers) to process the harder foodstuffs and butcher animals (slain game or carrion?). The use of tools made them less dependent on their environment.

The shift to a carnivorous diet evidently favored brain development. About two million years ago, hominids with larger, more robust skeletons began to appear in Africa. The brains of these hominids were larger, more humanoid in structure, and thus indicative of higher intelligence. Homo erectus (known as Homo ergaster in its earliest form) had arrived.

Quest for Fire – Early migration from Africa

Barely 100,000 years after the period marked by the oldest finds in Africa (at Lake Turkana, 1.9 million years BC), Homo erectus had already occupied new lands in western, eastern, and southeastern Asia, presumably favoring familiar, warm biotopes (savannas or steppes) at first. The oldest remains of non-African hominids were discovered in Java (Mojokerto), China (Longgupo), Georgia (Dmanisi, all circa 1.8 million BC), and Palestine (Ubaidiya, 1.4 million BC). More recent evidence has been found in India, Vietnam, and Japan. Artifacts 800,000 years old unearthed on Flores and Timor suggest the use of boats. The dating of tools found in Europe (Andalusia, 1.6 – 1.8 million BC) is disputed. Did these ancestors migrate across the Strait of Gibraltar?

Homo erectus later advanced across the high mountain ranges of Eurasia into much cooler and more humid climes. This required a command of fire (oldest evidence discovered in Africa dating to 1 – 1,5 million BC). Fire provided warmth and light, helped keep animal predators at bay, made cooking possible, and served a social function (campfires as central gathering places). Only a few of the bone and wooden implements used alongside stone tools have survived (among them wooden lances about 400,000 years old found in Schöningen in the German state of Lower Saxony).

The oldest reliable evidence of the presence of humans in Europe (at least one million years ago) con-

Global expansion of modern human populations

probable original homeland of modern humans — regions covered by ice circa 18,000 BC — Global migration of Homo sapiens (sapiens)

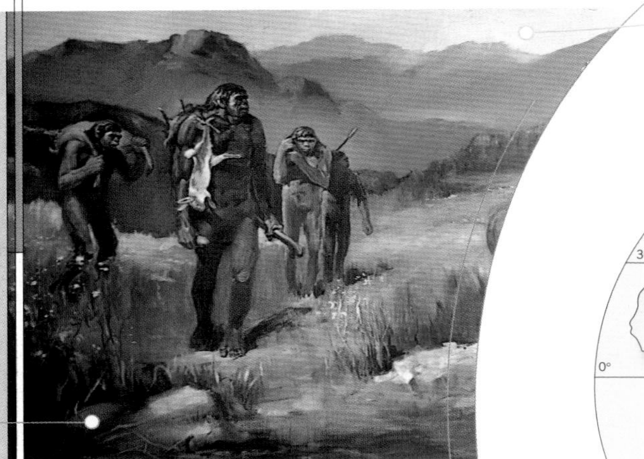

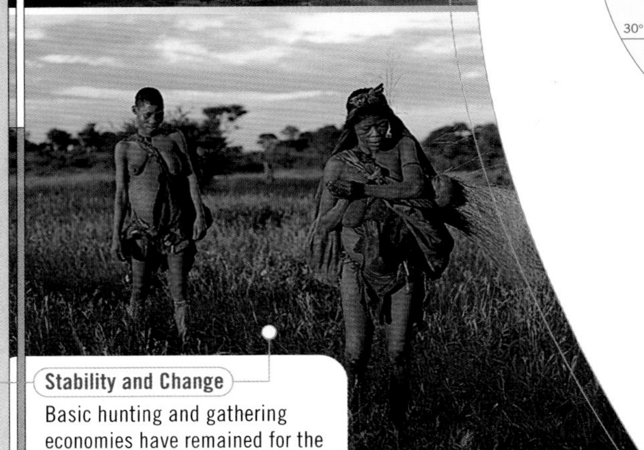

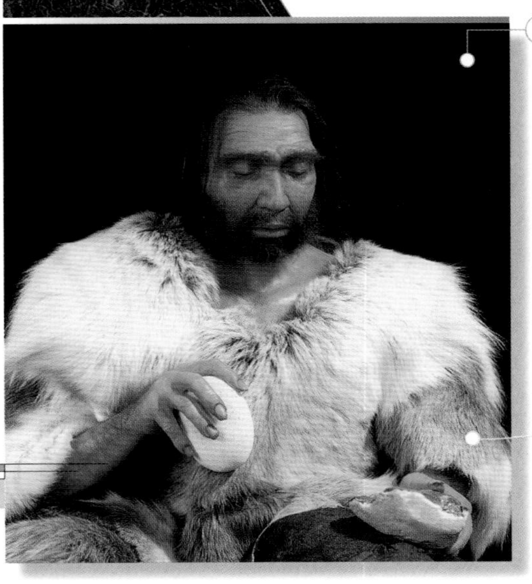

The Unjustly Maligned Neanderthal
Once considered hardly more than a "wild animal," Neanderthal Man is now regarded as an intelligent human species that adapted successfully to an inhospitable ice-age climate – either as a direct ancestor of modern Homo sapiens in accordance with the multi-regional model (parallel, independent development of modern human beings in different regions) or as an evolutionary offshoot that culminated in a dead end.

sists only of isolated artifacts (found near Nice and in the Rhine Valley). The oldest bones were found in Spain (Atepuerca, 780,000 BC). The finds uncovered in Mauer near Heidelberg (600,000 BC) and Bilzingsleben (400,000 BC) are much more recent. They have been classified along with other fossil remains as evidence of a species distinct from the humans of eastern Asia (true Homo erectus) known as Homo heidelbergensis. In general, European settlement patterns, especially in higher latitudes, reflect the influence of climatic changes associated with ice ages, which continually shifted the boundaries of inhabitable regions. It was never extremely cold south of the Alps, however. Changes in sea level impacted on settlement all over the world. During cold periods, continental shelf margins were dry and could be settled and traveled by human migrants.

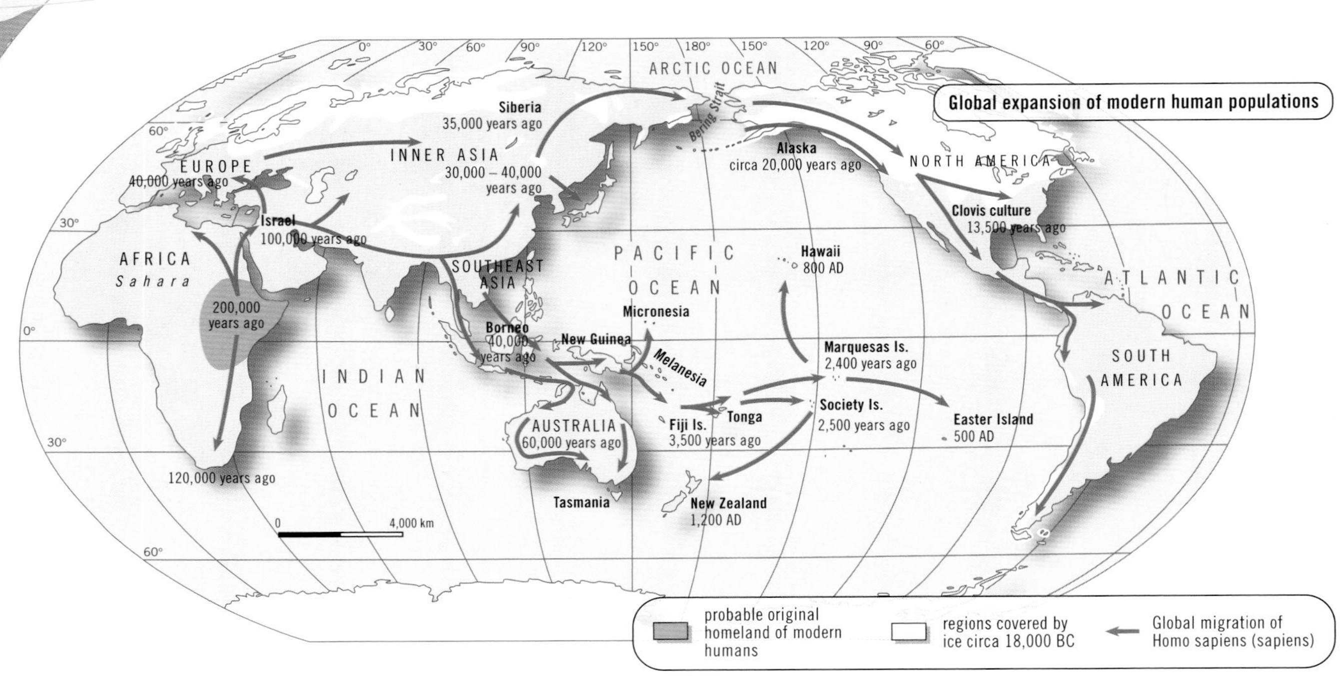

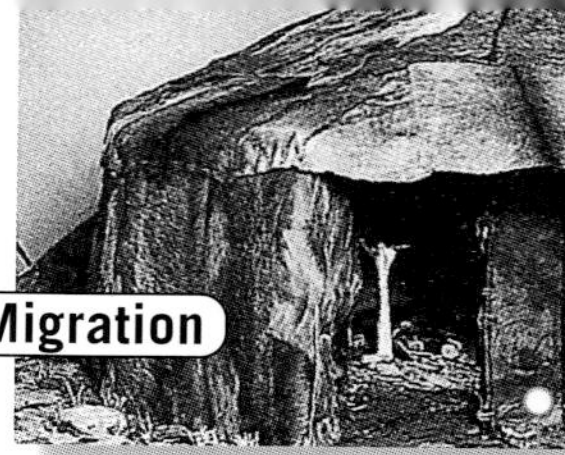

The Evolution of Homo Sapiens –
Are we all Africans by descent?

Archaic Homo sapiens emerged from Homo erectus or Homo heidelbergensis in all regions of the world. This phase of evolution probably began in Africa about 600,000 years ago and in Europe around 400,000 BC.

This early human form survived longest – until about 40,000 BC – in Southeast Asia. In Europe, primarily north of the Alps, a distinct form associated with the cold periods of the Pleistocene emerged from the late archaic Homo sapiens: the Neanderthal. The "classical" Neanderthal emerged from early Neanderthals after some 200,000 years, at the beginning of the last ice age, roughly 90,000 years ago. The sturdy, stocky build typical of the late Neanderthal presumably reflects adaptation to the cold climate of the period. Neanderthal populations appeared all over Europe, from the Iberian Peninsula to Central Asia (Uzbekistan) and did not die out until about 30,000 years ago. They advanced into western Asia about 80,000 BC. Long regarded as a direct ancestor of modern man, the Neanderthal is now seen as an evolutionary dead end, since fossil remains exhibiting the anatomical features of modern Homo sapiens (sapiens) found in Africa have been dated to about 200,000 BC, and it is only there that the evolutionary process can be traced in an unbroken line.

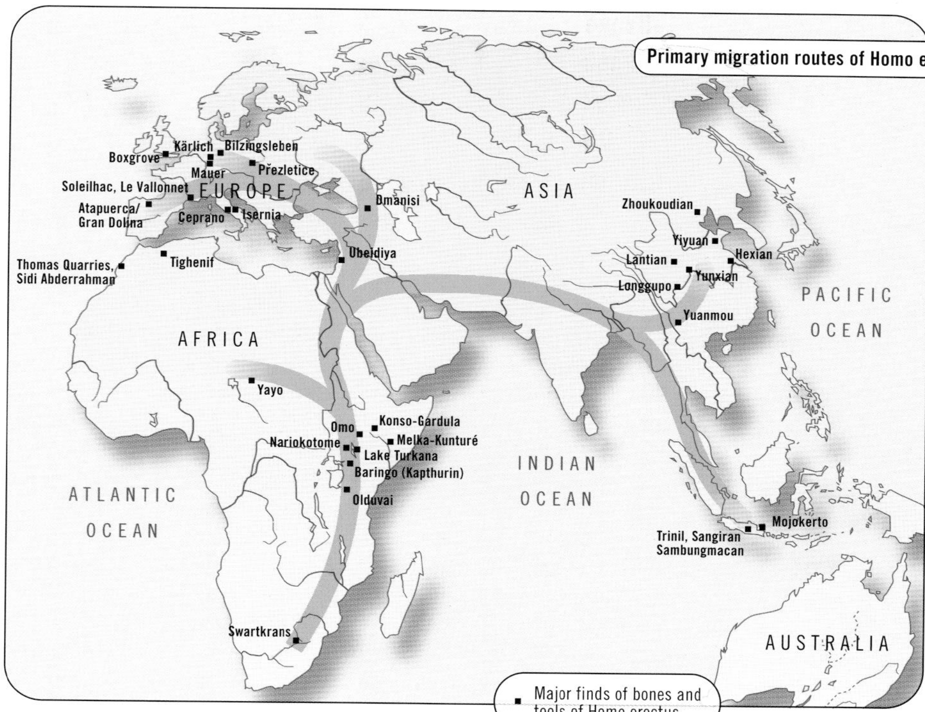

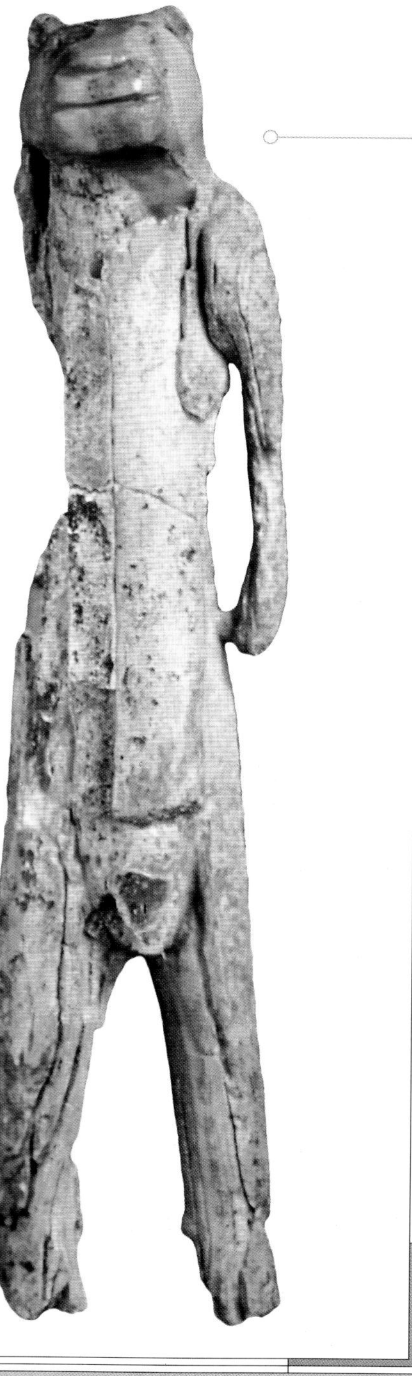

Out of Africa – Modern humans conquer the earth

As recently as 100,000 BC, modern man (as defined in anatomical terms) first appeared in western Asia, where he lived alongside Neanderthal groups for another 30,000 years. He was also a contemporary of the Neanderthal in Europe for 10,000 years, before emerging as the dominant species (Cro-Magnon People) 40,000 years ago. Isolated intermingling of the two types may have occurred.
Archaeological evidence of human settlements in Southeast Asia is dated to 40,000 BC, although humans must have arrived there much earlier, as they are known to have traveled by sea on boats or rafts to Australia more than 60,000 years ago.

Settlement in Oceania

After the settlement of New Guinea, the Bismarck Archipelago, and the Solomon Islands by forebears of the Papuans during the last ice age, Oceania – like the islands of Indonesia – witnessed an influx of Austronesian-speaking immigrants from Indochina, whose agrarian culture is identified by Lapita ceramics. The Austronesians who remained in Melanesia intermingled with the original dark-skinned population (Melanesians), and their language spread beyond the island of New Guinea. Other (light-skinned) Austronesians, who were experienced seafarers, soon moved with their food plants and domesticated animals to the islands of Polynesia. They continued to move eastward, reaching the Fiji Islands about 1,500 BC, Tonga in 1,400 BC, Samoa in 1,100 B.C, and the Society Islands in 500 BC, proceeding from there to Tahiti, Easter Island, Hawaii and New Zealand. Western Micronesia was probably settled by migrants from Indonesia or the Philippines as recently as 2,000 years ago, the remaining Micronesian islands from the south and east and the New Hebrides beginning about 1,300 BC (the Carolines were settled last, during the 3rd century AD).

The First Americans

The first humans to arrive on the American continent were anatomically modern. More than 20,000 years ago, people from hunting societies in northeastern Asia trekked over the land bridge across today's Bering Strait into the predominantly ice-free territory of Alaska.

Primary migration routes of Homo erectus

Major finds of bones and tools of Homo erectus

Protection against Cold and Rain

Reconstruction of a house from the last phase of the Late Stone Age: walls and roof (wood) are covered with horse hides; inside, a mammoth thigh bone supports a roasting spit next to the fire place.

The "Lion King"

People living during the ice age more than 30,000 years ago regarded the lion not only as a dangerous enemy and a hunting rival but also as a symbol of strength and superiority. Does this ivory (female) human-lion figure discovered in Lonetal indicate belief in a magical unity of animal and human beings?

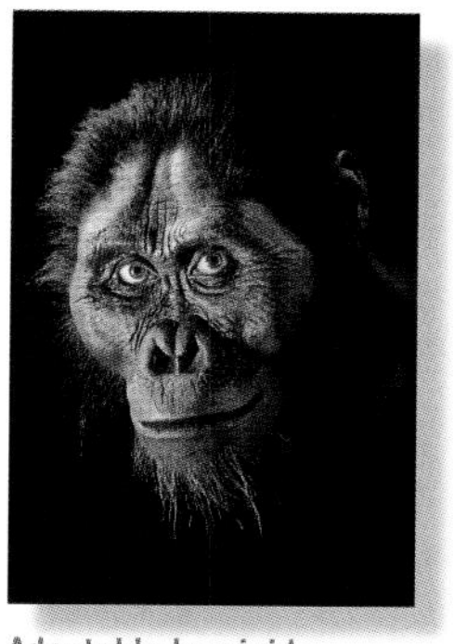

Adaptable hominid: Although the cranium of Australopithecus afarensis was no larger than that of contemporary chimpanzees, this hominid traveled on two legs through the savanna.

Following the movements of game animals (mammoth, bison, reindeer), they advanced into the continental interior along an ice-free corridor between the glacial ice of the Cordilleras and the Laurentide Ice Sheet. These Paleo-Indian peoples then spread rapidly over the American continents, advancing as far as Brazil, Patagonia and Chile. Since the Monte Verde archeological site (southern Chile) is about 14,000 years old, migration into North America must have begun much earlier than the oldest finds uncovered in the region (artifacts of the Clovis Culture, named for its characteristic arrow and spear heads, from about 13,500 BC) would indicate. Was there a pre-Clovian culture whose people lived from plants and small animals and used different, more rudimentary implements? Evidence of human settlement in the Amazon Basin near the end of the last ice age points to the existence of such a culture. The significance of much older finds in South America (dating as far back as 40,000 BC) remains in dispute, however. Presumably, human populations initially spread along the coasts.

Three distinct waves of migration have been identified on the basis of linguistic and genetic evidence. The last wave brought the ancestors of the Eskimos (Inuit) to the northern regions of Canada and Greenland some 4,000 years ago. Well adapted to their arctic environment, they survived the "little ice age" that began in the 13th century BC and put an end to Viking settlements in Greenland.

Evolutionary Model: "Out of Africa"

Modern Europeans	Modern Africans	Modern East Asians	Modern Australians
Cro-Magnon			
Neanderthal (archaic Homo sapiens)	Klasies people (modern Homo sapiens)	Dali people (archaic Homo sapiens)	Ngandong (archaic Homo sapiens/ late Homo erectus)
Ante-Neanderthal	African Homo erectus	East Asian Homo erectus	Indonesian Homo erectus

Exploration of the Earth's Surface

A Grand European Triumph?

The European seafarers of the 15th and 16th centuries were celebrated as great discoverers. And that they were, at least from the European perspective. Reports of their travels were circulated and analyzed by cartographers, and their knowledge was widely disseminated (with some valuable insights kept secret) thanks to the newly invented printing process. Yet other explorers had achieved great seafaring accomplishments long before. Perhaps the most ambitious adventure of all times was the settlement of Polynesia by Austronesians from Southeast Asia. The boldest of their advances took place in the 1st millennium BC and brought human settlements to Hawaii and Easter Island.

Ancient Discoveries

Egyptians are known to have voyaged to Punt (presumably Somalia) as early as 2,200 BC. Queen Hatshepsut sponsored a sea expedition to Punt in the 15th century BC. Phoenicians are believed to have circumnavigated the African continent under the flag of the Egyptian Pharaoh in the early 6th century BC. In the 5th century BC, Herodotus compiled a map of the known world on the basis of his own knowledge and accounts of voyages of exploration. The Greek seafarer Pytheas of Massalia (Marseilles) sailed the coasts of western and northern Europe in about 330 BC, and is thought to have reached Arctic drift ice.

The Arabs expanded the geographic knowledge amassed by the Greeks. In the Middle Ages, they had compiled the most detailed knowledge about Africa, western and southern Asia. The overland journeys of Ibn Battutah (14th century) took him to Timbuktu and China.

The Chinese first ventured to the shores of the Persian Gulf in the 5th century. Chinese naval exploration flourished in the 10th century and reached its zenith in the expeditions of Zheng He to East Africa in the 15th century. The European Age of Discovery began – after some forerunners like Marco Polo – with the great sea voyages of the 15th and 16th centuries. Under the leadership of Henry the Navigator, the Portuguese initially took the lead in ocean-going exploration, but were soon rivaled by the Spanish. Their goal was to eliminate Arab middlemen from the spice trade. Arab merchants had traveled as far as Southeast Asia, spreading the religion of Islam on their commercial crusades into these distant regions.

Who Discovered America?

Humans first set foot on the North American continent at least 20,000 years ago. Migrating over the land bridge between Alaska and northeastern Siberia across what is now the Bering Strait, they eventually settled the entire continent. The hunting societies on both sides of the Bering Strait remained in contact. The Vikings made a number of visits to the eastern coast of North America beginning in the 10th century AD, but their explorations had no lasting impact on early American or European societies. The arrival of Christopher Columbus had much more far-reaching consequences. The map of the known world grew larger. Europeans conquered the "New World." Native Americans were subjugated and their populations decimated in the centuries that followed.

"Show me Adam's will!"

This angry outburst by French King Francis I is indicative of the reactions of the English, Dutch, and Italians, who were compelled to look on passively while Spain and Portugal divided the world up between them, at first in the Treaty of Tordesillas in 1494 and later in the Treaty of Saragossa (1529). The nations of Europe did everything in their power to secure their share of the treasures of the "newly discovered" lands. The quest for northeast and northwest passages, short trade routes through Arctic waters to Asia, began under the English flag (Caboto) in the late 15th century.

"Replenish the earth, and subdue it!"

The "discovered" peoples might surely have posed the question of Adam's will with better reason. Why did the Europeans become the leading discoverers and conquerors? Why didn't the Aztecs or the Incas invade Spain? Why didn't the Chinese become a true sea power? A number of cultural, political, and technological factors combined to enable the Europeans to answer the biblical call to action. They were driven not only by hunger for power, gold, and riches, but also by missionary zeal and a curiosity about foreign lands that was alien to such cultures as the Chinese of the Middle Kingdom, for example.

By 1600, knowledge of geography had expanded immensely – as a by-product of exploration, so to speak. Scientific interest played an important role in the voyages of the last great seafaring explorer James Cook, and the continental explorations of Alexander von Humboldt, which also focused on vertical aspects of topography, were devoted exclusively to scientific inquiry.

The Wonders of the Distant Orient

Members of the Polo family traveled as merchants and trade representatives to China long before the age of European expansion. Printed in many European languages, Marco Polo's Il Milione, an account of his travels, was the most important source of information about Asia in the medieval world and is known to have influenced Columbus.

Objective Achieved

Only 28 years after the death of Henry the Navigator, Vasco da Gama discovered the sea route to India and weighed anchor off the Indian coast after a ten-month journey around Africa. He returned to Lisbon with a rich cargo of spices and jewels but with only a third of his original crew.

Prototype of an Explorer's Vessel

After the first voyages of discovery in small, agile caravels fitted with a triangular sail in the style of Arab dhows, explorers saw the need for larger ships capable of transporting troops, horses, cannons, and provisions. The new vessels were modeled after Nordic ships and powered by a square sail.

In the Name of the Cross

Portuguese seafarers placed stone pillars bearing emblems (photo from Cape Cross in Namibia) as a sign of conquest and a symbol of missionary intent.

History of Western Exploration

■ 5th century BC (Herodotus)	□ circa 16
■ 2nd century BC (Ptolemy)	□ circa 18
■ circa 1,100 AD (Adam of Bremen)	□ circa 19
□ 15th century (known boundaries of the Arab world after the great Asian explorations)	■ 20th cen

Map labels: Quebec, Tropic of Cancer, Culiacán, Guanahani, PACIFIC OCEAN, Cartagena, Cumaná, Bogotá, Equator, Lima, Cuzco, Tropic of Capricorn, Coquimbo, Antarctic Circle

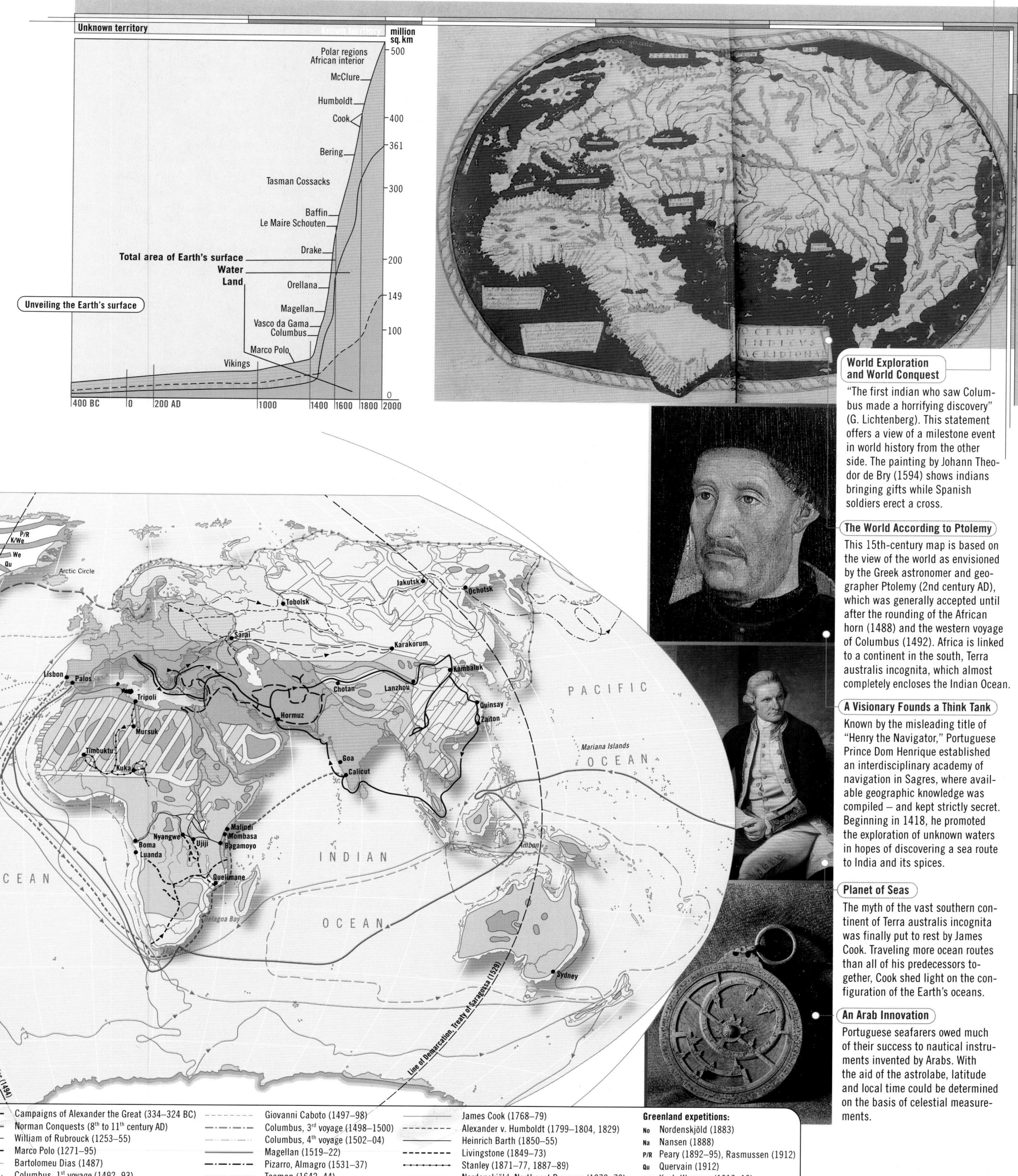

Unknown territory / Known territory

million sq. km

Polar regions
African interior — 500
McClure
Humboldt — 400
Cook
Bering — 361
Tasman Cossacks — 300
Baffin
Le Maire Schouten — 200
Drake
Total area of Earth's surface
Water
Land
Orellana — 149
Magellan — 100
Vasco da Gama
Columbus
Marco Polo
Vikings — 0

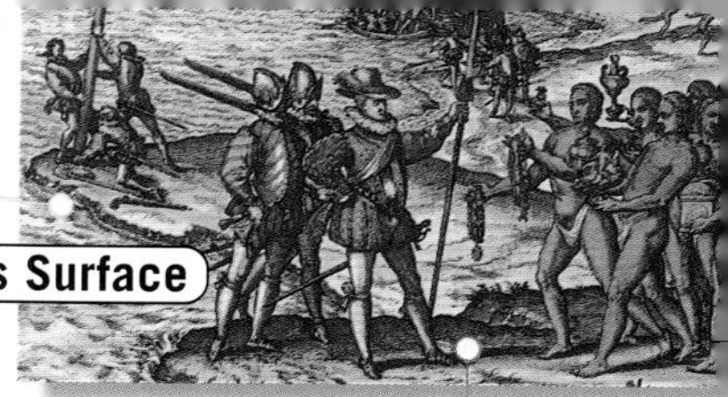

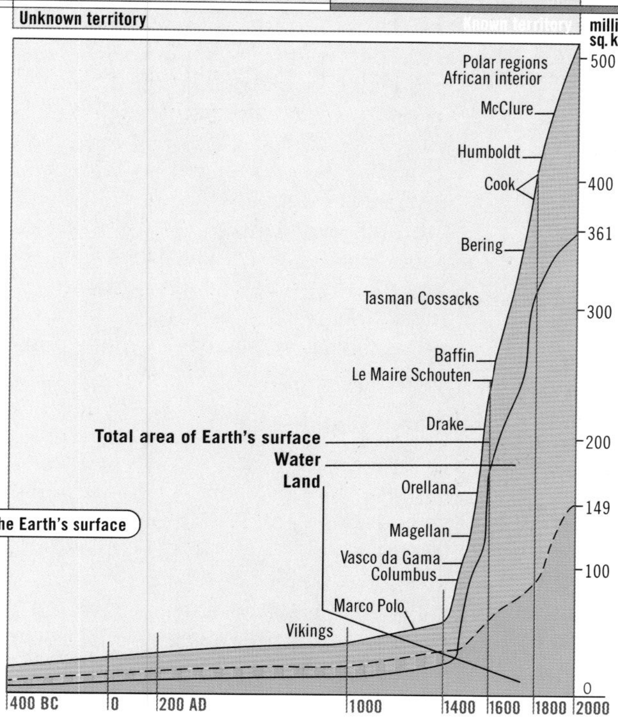

Unveiling the Earth's surface

400 BC   0   200 AD   1000   1400 1600 1800 2000

World Exploration and World Conquest

"The first indian who saw Columbus made a horrifying discovery" (G. Lichtenberg). This statement offers a view of a milestone event in world history from the other side. The painting by Johann Theodor de Bry (1594) shows indians bringing gifts while Spanish soldiers erect a cross.

The World According to Ptolemy

This 15th-century map is based on the view of the world as envisioned by the Greek astronomer and geographer Ptolemy (2nd century AD), which was generally accepted until after the rounding of the African horn (1488) and the western voyage of Columbus (1492). Africa is linked to a continent in the south, Terra australis incognita, which almost completely encloses the Indian Ocean.

A Visionary Founds a Think Tank

Known by the misleading title of "Henry the Navigator," Portuguese Prince Dom Henrique established an interdisciplinary academy of navigation in Sagres, where available geographic knowledge was compiled — and kept strictly secret. Beginning in 1418, he promoted the exploration of unknown waters in hopes of discovering a sea route to India and its spices.

Planet of Seas

The myth of the vast southern continent of Terra australis incognita was finally put to rest by James Cook. Traveling more ocean routes than all of his predecessors together, Cook shed light on the configuration of the Earth's oceans.

An Arab Innovation

Portuguese seafarers owed much of their success to nautical instruments invented by Arabs. With the aid of the astrolabe, latitude and local time could be determined on the basis of celestial measurements.

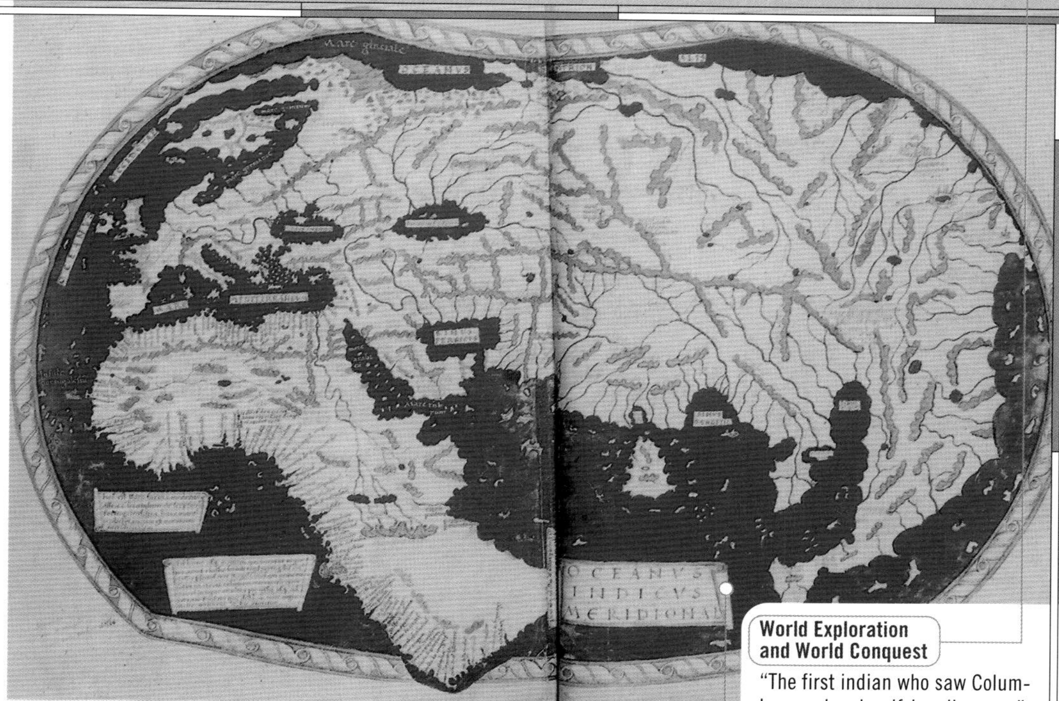

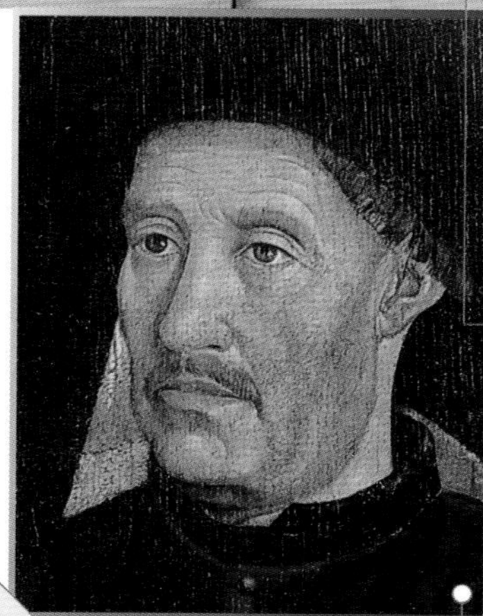

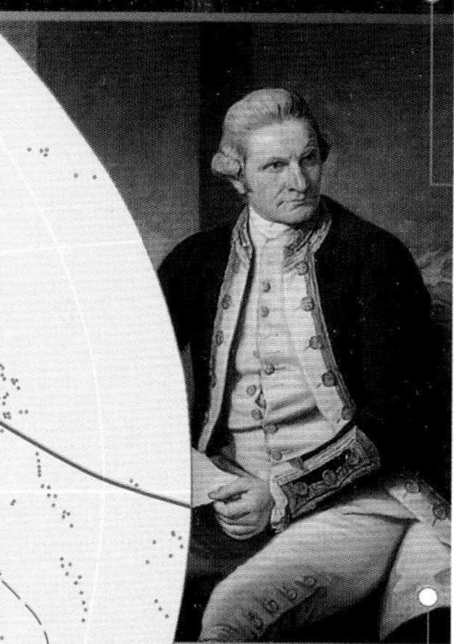

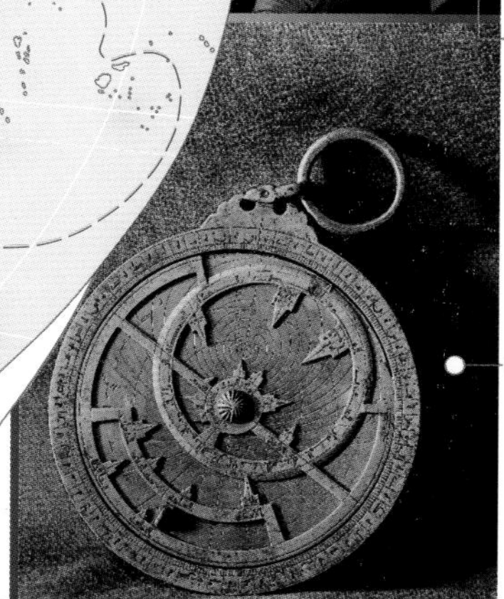

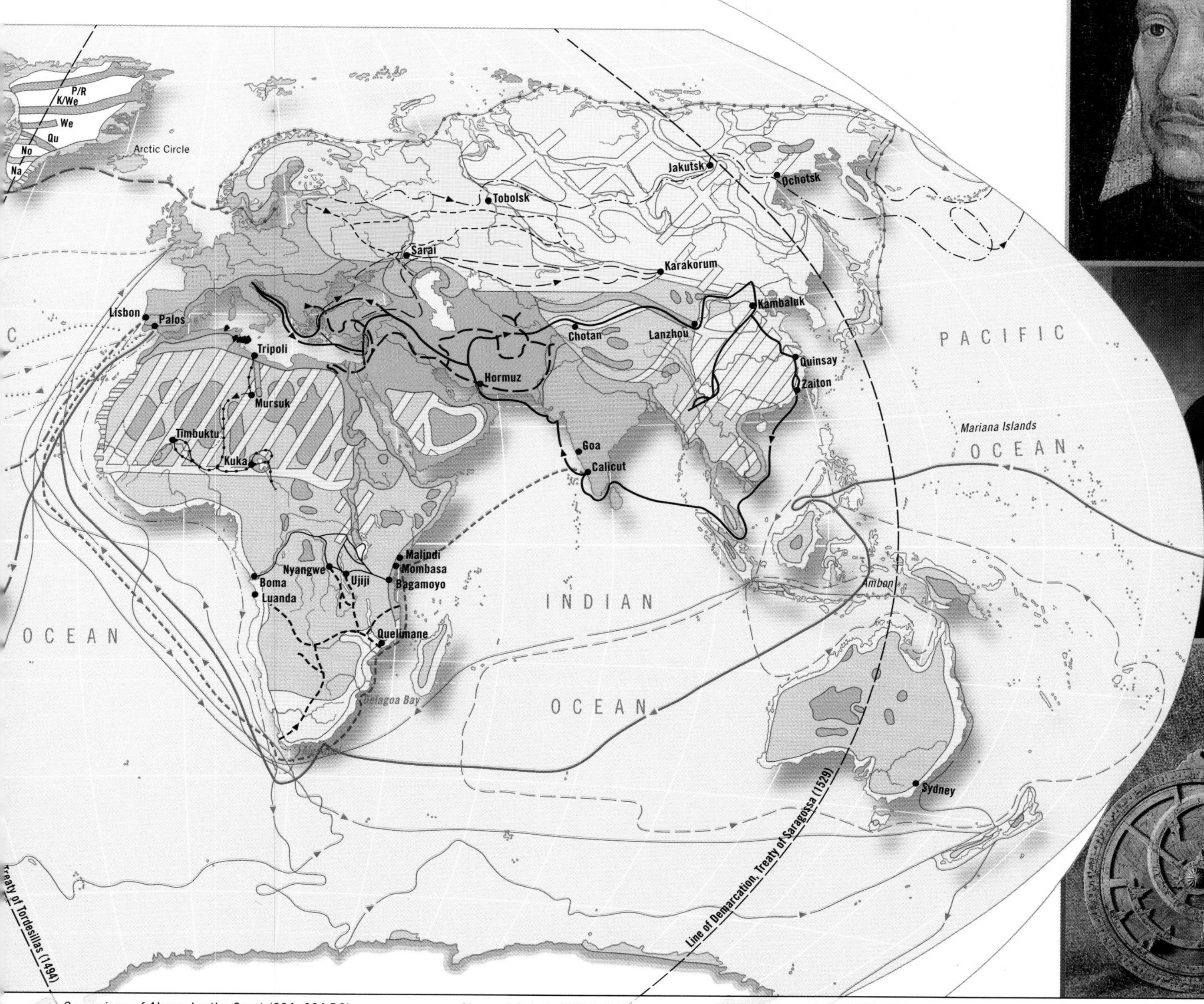

--- Campaigns of Alexander the Great (334–324 BC)
--- Norman Conquests (8th to 11th century AD)
--- William of Rubrouck (1253–55)
--- Marco Polo (1271–95)
--- Bartolomeu Dias (1487)
--- Columbus, 1st voyage (1492–93)
--- Vasco da Gama (1497–98)

--- Giovanni Caboto (1497–98)
--- Columbus, 3rd voyage (1498–1500)
--- Columbus, 4th voyage (1502–04)
--- Magellan (1519–22)
--- Pizarro, Almagro (1531–37)
--- Tasman (1642–44)
--- Bering (1728–43)

--- James Cook (1768–79)
--- Alexander v. Humboldt (1799–1804, 1829)
--- Heinrich Barth (1850–55)
--- Livingstone (1849–73)
--- Stanley (1871–77, 1887–89)
--- Nordenskjöld, Northeast Passage (1878–79)
--- Amundsen, Northwest Passage (1903–06)

Greenland expeditions:
No   Nordenskjöld (1883)
Na   Nansen (1888)
P/R Peary (1892–95), Rasmussen (1912)
Qu   Quervain (1912)
K/We Koch-Wegener (1912–13)
We   Wegener (1930)

The Dynamic Global Population

Explosion versus Stagnation

The world's population is constantly growing. When Christ was born, some 300 million people lived on Earth. By the time Columbus discovered America, the number had risen to 500 million. In 1969, the first human to set foot on the moon looked back at a world with a population of 3.5 billion. The number has since grown to six billion and continues to rise at a rate of about 80 million every year.

Battling the "Black Death"
The flagellants sought to ward off the Plague, which was regarded as God's wrath judgment, through penance and self-mortification. The Plague epidemic that broke out in Genoa and Marseille in 1347 and eventually spread throughout Europe took the lives of more than 20 million people (one-third of the total population) from southern Italy to northern England and Scandinavia between 1348 and 1352.

A Demographic Time Bomb
Populations continue to grow at a virtually unbroken pace in many countries. Masses of humanity fill the streets of Bombay, India and many other major cities.

Phases of Growth

Population growth has proceeded slowly but steadily since the Neolithic revolution, when human communities first adopted a sedentary lifestyle some 12,000 years ago. Growth accelerated rapidly after the Industrial Revolution, which began in Europe around 1800. Industrialization led to significant improvements in living standards, nutrition, medical care, and disease prevention and thus unleashed a veritable population explosion. The Demographic Transition Model reflects the interdependence of birth and mortality rates as a crucial parameter of population growth. As a rule, the later a country enters the third phase, the more significant – although shorter – the period of explosive growth will be.

Global Developments

Comparisons in time and place support this statement. England, birthplace of the Industrial Revolution in the waning 18th century (Malthus published his pessimistic treatise on the Principle of Population in 1803), did not achieve balance between birth and death rates until nearly 200 years later, whereas it took Japan only 40 to 50 years to do so. Today, many countries in Asia and especially in Africa are in the midst of demographic transition. Apparently growing without end, their populations double about every 25 years (Great Britain every 423 years; Austria every 2,310 years; Japan every 318 years!). Yet demographers expect that global population growth will slow to a standstill in the mid-21st century at a level of between ten and twelve billion people.

Possible Growth Scenarios

To an increasing extent, global population is concentrated in the developing nations today. In 1950, only about two-thirds of the estimated 2.5 billion people on Earth were inhabitants of these countries. By the mid-21st century, this figure will have risen to 88 % of a total world population of about ten billion. Rapid growth in these regions contrasts with stagnation or extremely slow growth in the industrialized countries. Both of these tendencies pose grave dangers to human societies.

Unbridled growth in Latin America, Asia, and especially Africa not only exacerbates the social and economic disparities between north and south, it also has a severe impact on the environment in the form of uncon-

Planting, sedentary lifestyle

| 12000 | 9000 | 8000 | 7000 | 6000 |

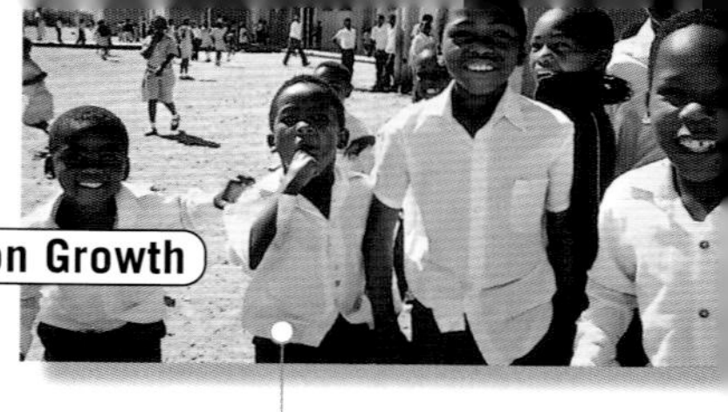

World population in 1999 – Growth and projection

	Population in millions	Birth rate per thousand	Death rate per thousand	Natural growth per cent	Population doubling (in years at current growth rate)	Projected population in 2025 (millions)	Age distribution <15	>65
World	5 982	23	9	1.4	49	8 054	31	7
Africa	771	39	14	2.5	28	1 290	43	3
North America	303	14	8	0.6	119	374	21	13
Latin America	512	24	6	1.8	38	709	33	5
Australia – Oceania	30	18	7	1.1	64	41	26	10
Asia	3 637	23	8	1.5	46	4 923	32	6
Europe	728	10	11	−0.1	–	718	18	14
Examples of extremes:								
Dem. Rep. Congo	50.5	48	16	3.2	22	105.7	48	3
Austria	8.1	10	10	0.0	2 310	8.1	17	15
Germany	82.0	10	10	−0.1	–	79.9	16	16

trolled exploitation of available land, diminishing water reserves, deforestation, and desertification. The consequences include famine, waves of refugee migration, the expansion of slums in major urban centers, increasing poverty, and the spread of disease. The devastating effects of the AIDS epidemic on societies in Africa and other parts of the world speak much louder than words.

Yet stagnation and decline (populations in several industrialized nations such as Germany and Austria are currently shrinking) pose serious problems as well. As populations dwindle, they also tend to grow older, and both trends will have a lasting impact on many areas of life – the labor market and social security systems, education and housing, public health service, commerce and transportation, to name only a few.

Limits and Dangers: Quantitative and Qualitative Population Growth

Exploding populations in some places, stagnating or declining populations in others. This disparity in a world that is becoming more closely interconnected in time and space every day poses a significant problem in itself. The situation is made worse by severe inequalities in the distribution and use of limited natural resources. The question of the Earth's ability to accommodate its inhabitants can no longer be answered simply in terms of its potential to produce food but must also be examined in the light of environmental factors. It is not necessarily the sheer numbers of people that threaten the equilibrium of System Earth. More often than not, it is the rich (we ourselves!) who jeopardize the balance through our irresponsible and insatiable urge to consume in order to satisfy what we regard as essential needs!

Demographic Transition

Birth rate
Death rate
Growth rate

Time

| Phase 1 Stable growth | Phase 2 High growth | Phase 3 Transition | Phase 4 Decreasing growth | Phase 5 Negligible growth |

Declining birth rates

Lives births per woman

■ 1950–1955
▨ 1998

	Africa	Asia	Europe	Latin America	North America	Australia–Oceania
1950–1955	6.6	5.9	2.6	5.9	3.5	3.8
1998	5.6	2.8	1.4	3.0	2.0	2.4

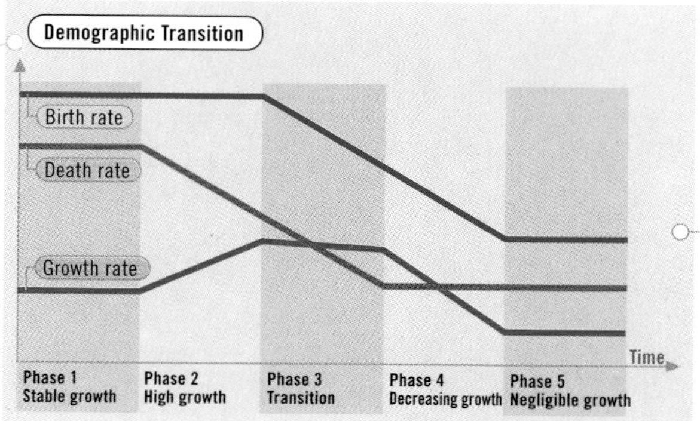

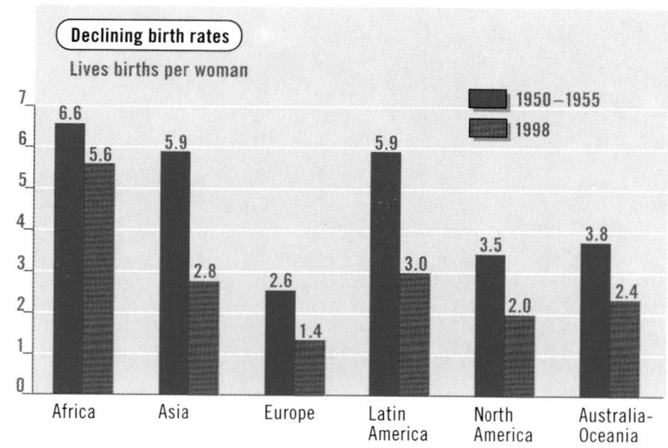

Future Fathers

With a growth rate of 2.3 % per annum (1990-98) South Africa is by no means the fastest-growing country on the African continent (that honor goes to Niger, with 3.9%). These school children in Johannesburg will probably be parents themselves in 15 years.

Unstoppable Growth?

The length of time it takes the global population to increase by one billion people has become increasingly shorter over the course of history. The one-billion mark was reached in 1804, and the total reached two million 123 years later. Successive billions were added at intervals of 33, 14, and 13 years, respectively. Only twelve years later – in October 1999 – world population reached six billion.

Changing Growth Rates

Demographic transition from an agrarian to an industrial society follows a predictable pattern. State 1 is characterized by high birth and death rates, with natural growth (the difference between the two) remaining relatively low. In State 2, death rates fall, birth rates remain stable, and the growth rate rises accordingly. In State 3, birth rates begin to fall as well. State 4 marks the transition from rapid to slow growth. In State 5, birth, death, and growth rates stabilize at a low level.

World population in billions

6

5

4

World population development

3

Vaccines

Asia

2

Artificial fertilizers

Americas

1

Industrial Revolution

Africa

Australia-Oceania

Europe

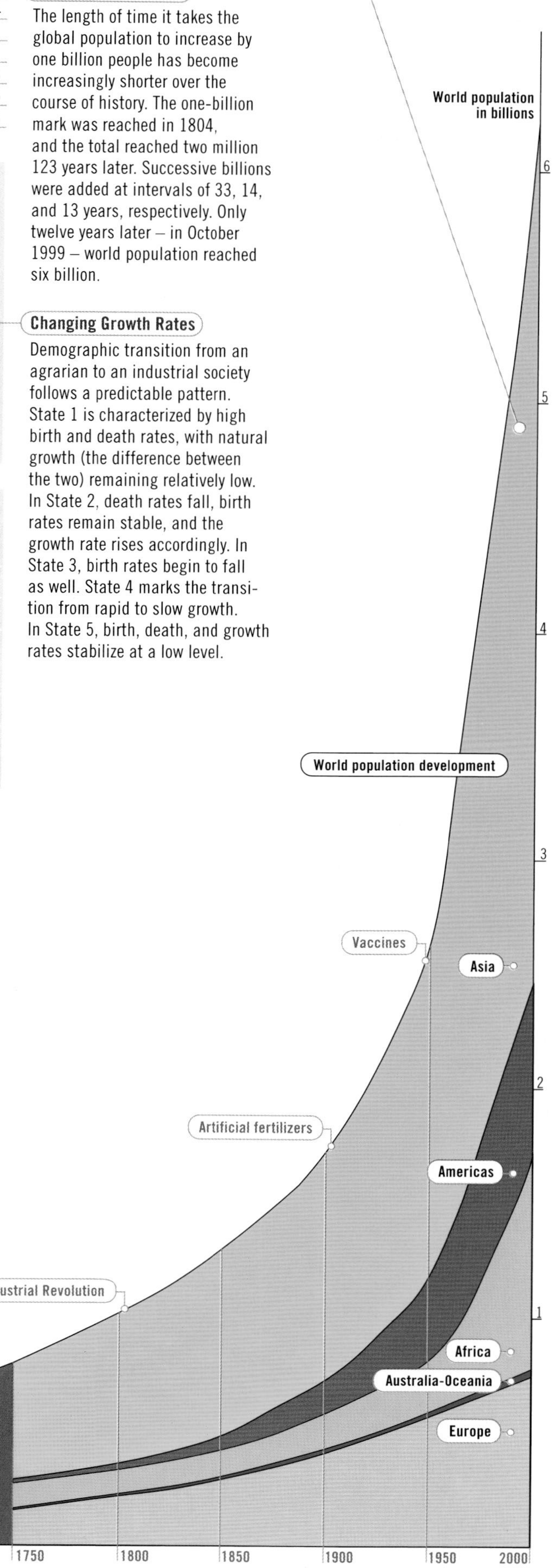

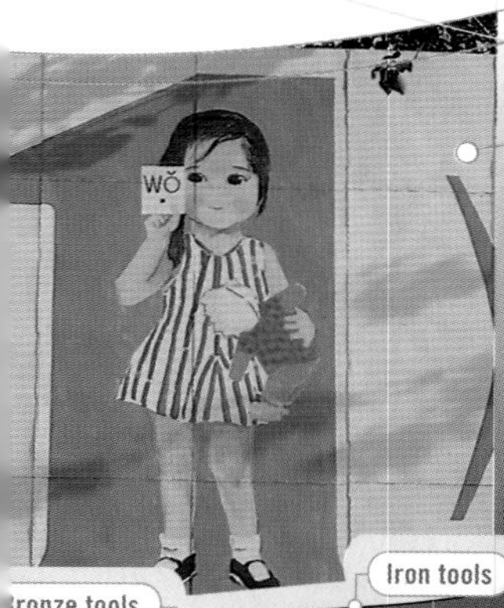

Restricted Growth

Billboards in China (photo: Beijing) appeal for acceptance of the single-child-family rule prescribed by Chinese law.

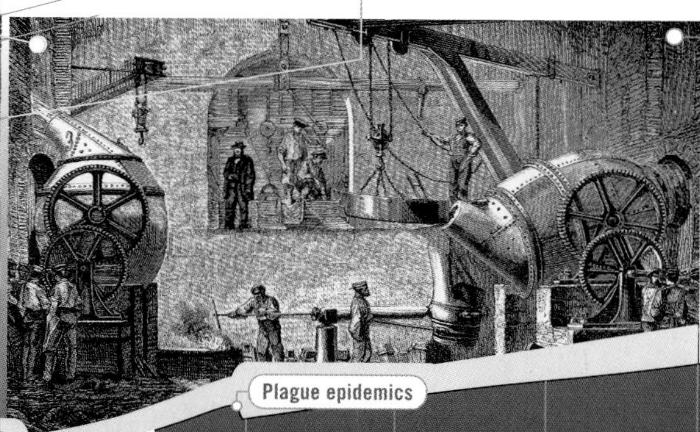

Steel Boiler, 1886

Rapid population growth began with the Industrial Revolution.

WÖ

Plague epidemics

Iron tools

Bronze tools

| 3000 | 2000 | 1000 | 0 | 1450 | 1500 | 1550 | 1600 | 1650 | 1700 | 1750 | 1800 | 1850 | 1900 | 1950 | 2000 |

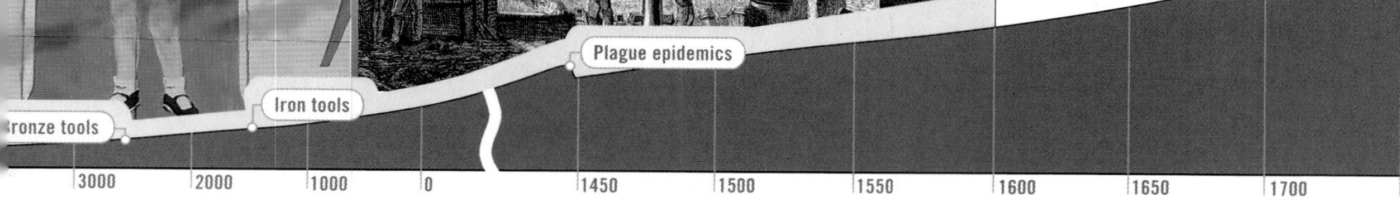

Human Migration

A Global View of Shifting Populations

The history of humanity is a history of migration – and has been since the first humans appeared on Earth. Immigrants and emigrants – invading hordes and war refugees – mass migrations: all of these terms describe aspects of a complex problem that is of crucial global importance today.

Causes of Popular Migration

In addition to the natural causes of many major population movements (floods, soil degradation, desertification, etc.), people have tended to migrate primarily for ideological and economic reasons. Aside from the many unfortunate cases of involuntary migration (banishment, deportation, flight from persecution, slavery, etc.), economic push-and-pull factors are among the most common causes of large-scale migration. Overpopulation, a shortage of work, and the corresponding economic and social misery that accompany these phenomena are and always have been important "push" factors contributing to regional migration and emigration. On the other hand, prosperity and an abundance of jobs in other countries attract workers and economic refugees, as "pull" factors, with the promise of better living conditions and opportunities for social advancement. A review of the economic and social history of the modern era clearly shows that political developments in many areas of the world have been shaped by major population movements – from the mass displacement of African slaves to the emigration of Europeans (primarily for economic or political reasons) to the New World, Australia, New Zealand, and South Africa. In the roughly one hundred years between 1830 to 1928, nearly six million Germans emigrated, about 90% of them to the U.S., the remainder to Canada, Brazil, Australia, Argentina, South Africa, and Asia.

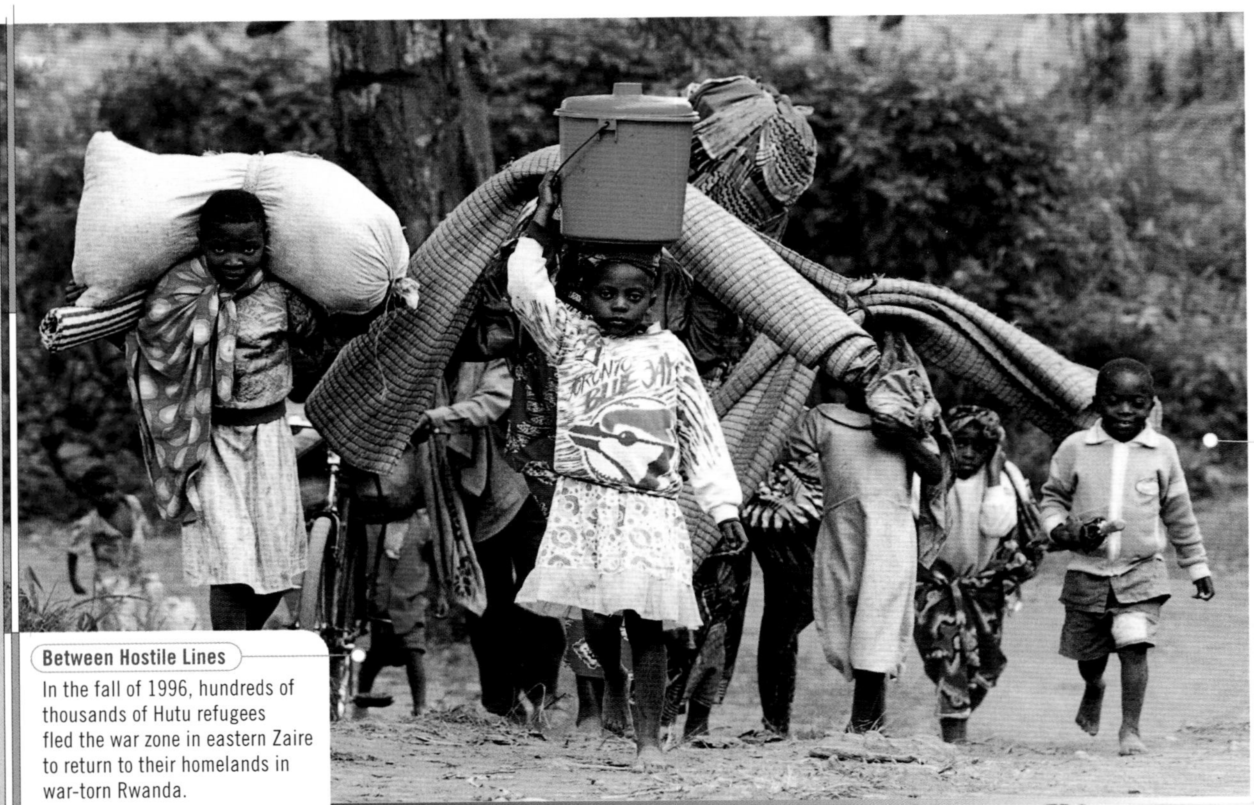

Between Hostile Lines
In the fall of 1996, hundreds of thousands of Hutu refugees fled the war zone in eastern Zaire to return to their homelands in war-torn Rwanda.

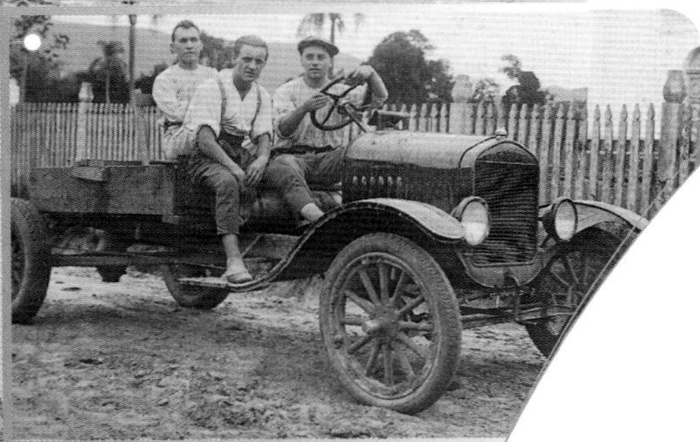

Skills Wanted Abroad
Young emigrants from Germany in Brazil (1925): automotive knowledge and skills provide the basis for a new start.

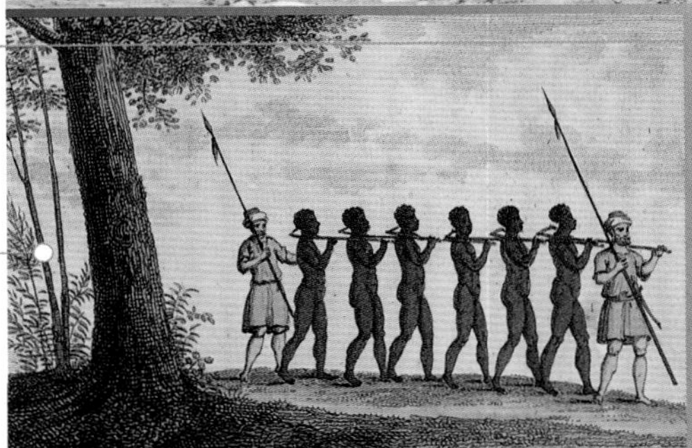

Involuntary Exile
African captives were often chained together with their hands bound to a pole during their journey into slavery.

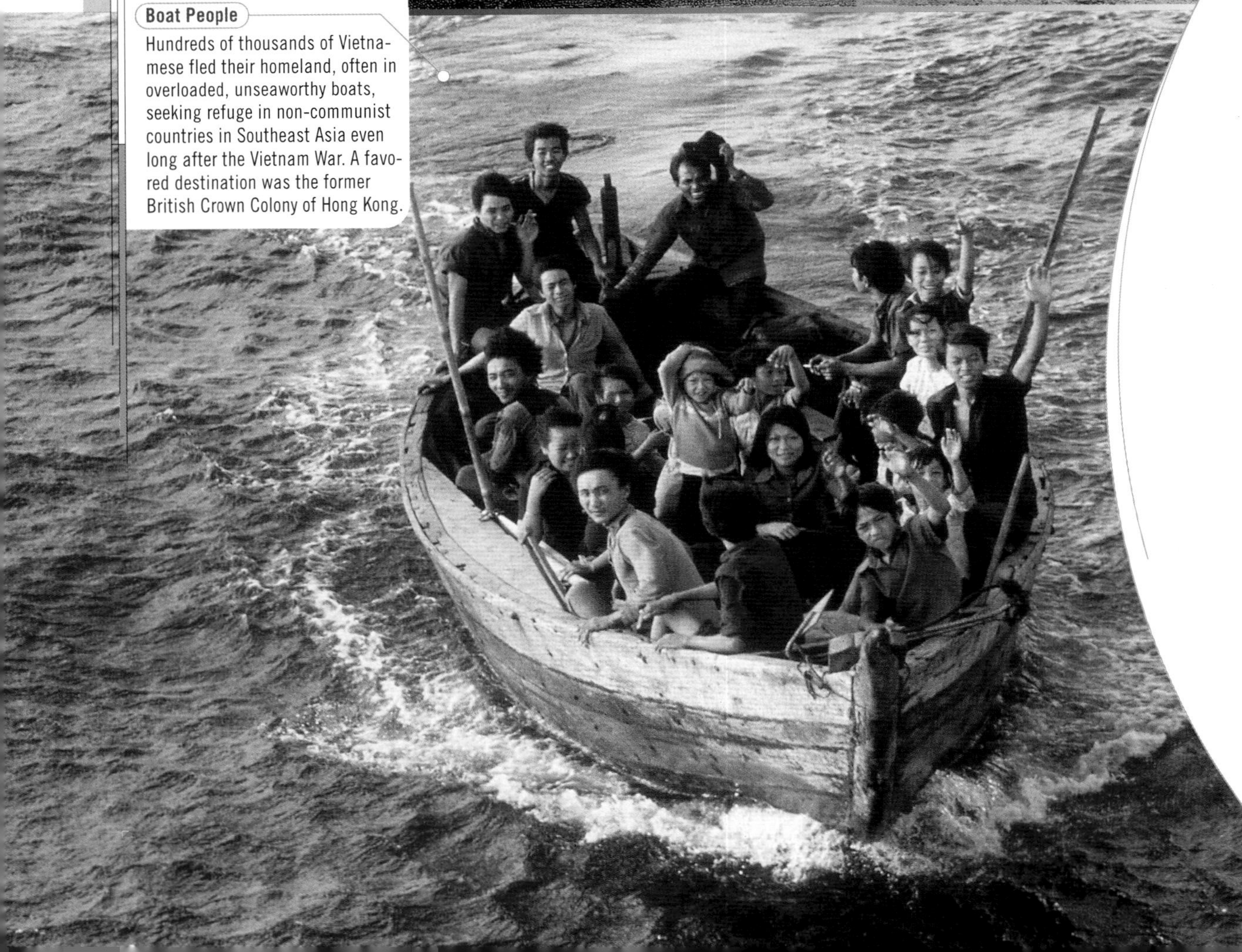

Boat People
Hundreds of thousands of Vietnamese fled their homeland, often in overloaded, unseaworthy boats, seeking refuge in non-communist countries in Southeast Asia even long after the Vietnam War. A favored destination was the former British Crown Colony of Hong Kong.

16th and 17th c.	Spanish and Portuguese
17th and 18th c.	Slave trade
18th and 19th c.	North American continental migr
18th and 20th c.	Europeans to overseas regions

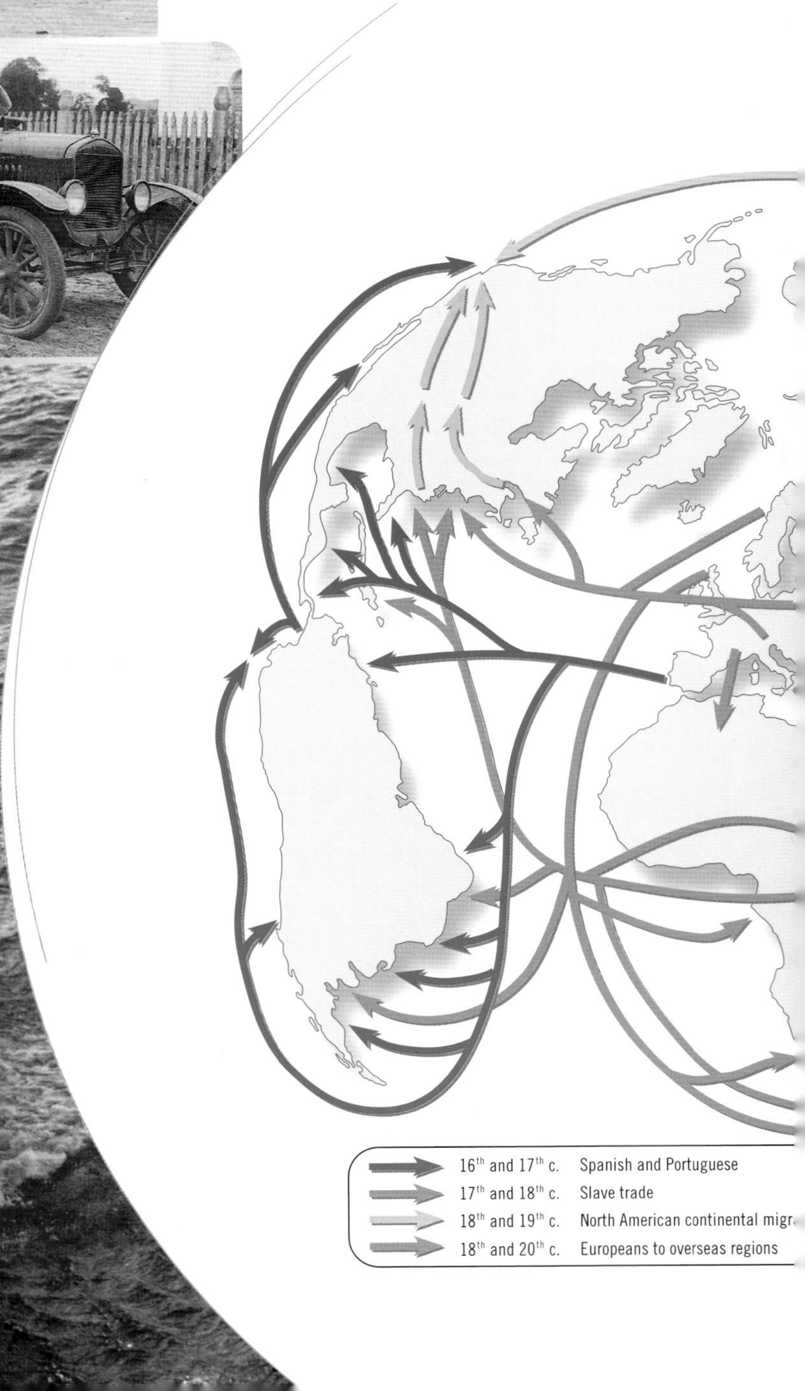

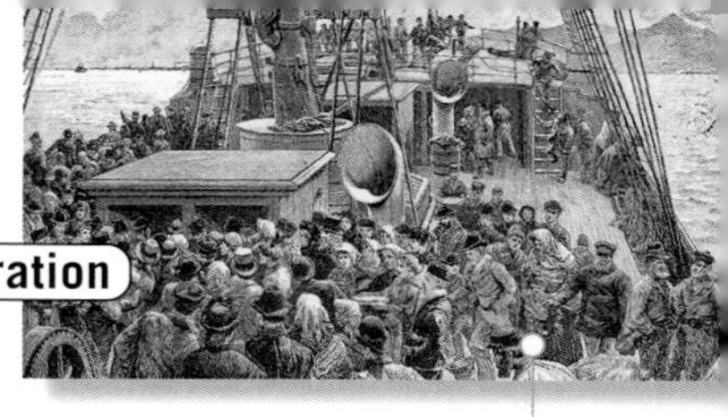

Streams of Refugees

Probably the most frequent cause of often involuntary mass migrations is war. In addition to the two World Wars, a number of more recent local wars and hostilities have caused huge groups of refugees to leave their homelands in Africa (Congo, Rwanda, the Guineas), Afghanistan, and the Middle East (where unsolved political and military conflicts between Israelis and Palestinians and problems involving Kurdish populations have persisted for decades). Striking evidence that religious and ideological differences as well as ethnic hostilities can lead to major refugee migrations can be found in the Balkan states, Southeast Asia (Christian-Moslem antagonism), and the Indian subcontinent (conflicts between Moslems and Hindus).

Environmental refugees are people who have been compelled to move away from their familiar homelands due to degradation of their natural environments and the resulting deterioration or loss of traditional foundations of life. Water shortages and water pollution, soil erosion, deforestation, desertification, and changes affecting the diversity of animal and plant species are forcing increasing numbers of people, especially in the "Third World," to abandon their native lands.

Economic refugees are prompted to leave their native lands in search of better living conditions – primarily in western industrialized countries – by worsening social and, above all, economic imbalances of regional or global proportions. Noteworthy examples include the immigration of Mexicans into the U.S., the growing stream of eastern European migrants into central and western Europe, and the rising number of Africans and Asians smuggled illegally by organized gangs into the Member States of the European Union.

Labor migration in Islamic regions

from AFRICA, ASIA

to EUROPE

from INDIA, PAKISTAN, BANGLADESH

from THAILAND, INDONESIA, PHILIPPINES

Estimated numbers of migrant workers (c. 1995)

< 20,000

20,000 – 100,000

100,000 – 300,000

300,000 – 1 Mio.

> 2 Mio.

adapted from F. Ibrahim, 1997

Major migration streams of the past 500 years

19th c.	Indians
19th and 20th c.	Russians into Asia
19th and 20th c.	Chinese (and Japanese) to overseas regions

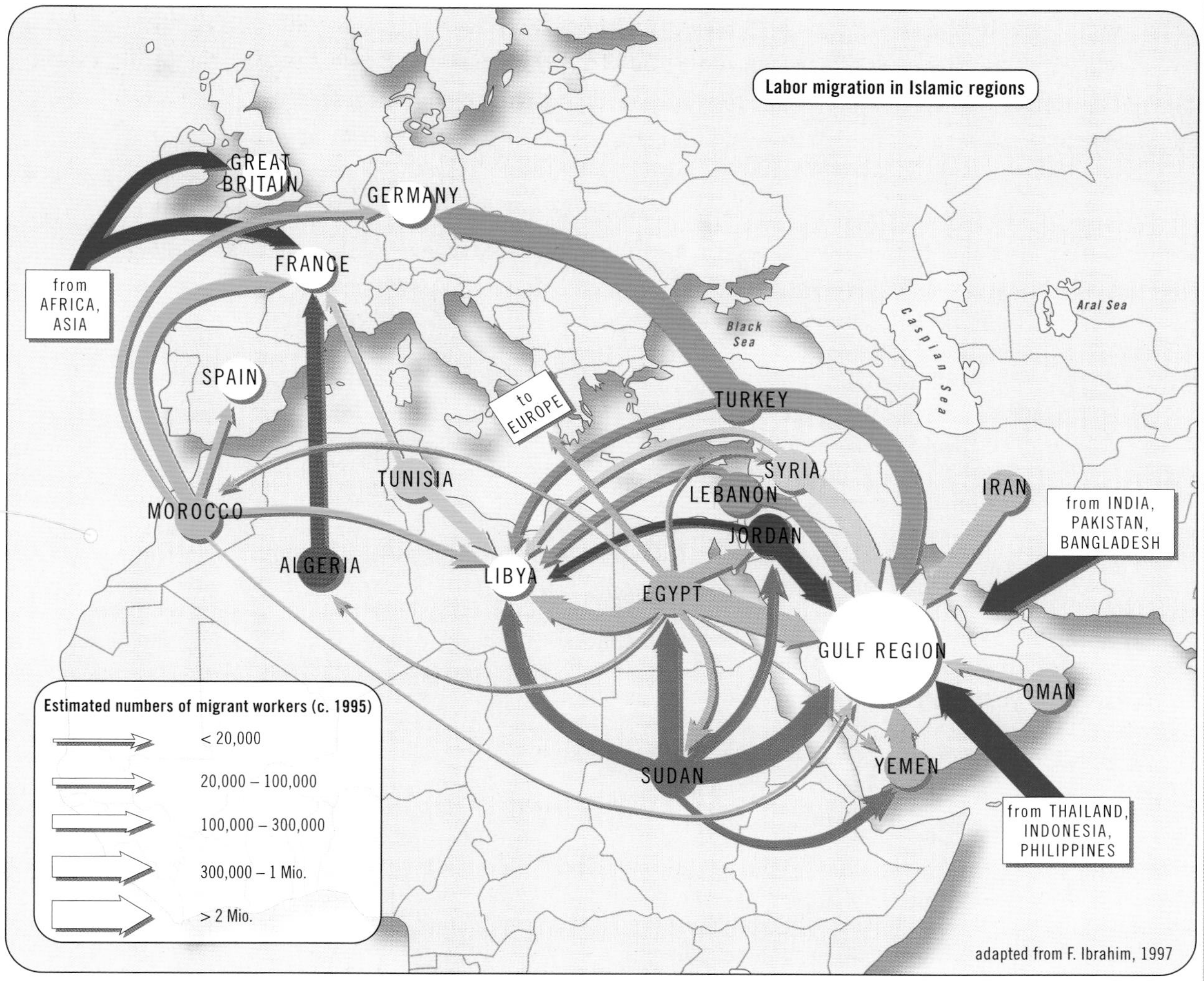

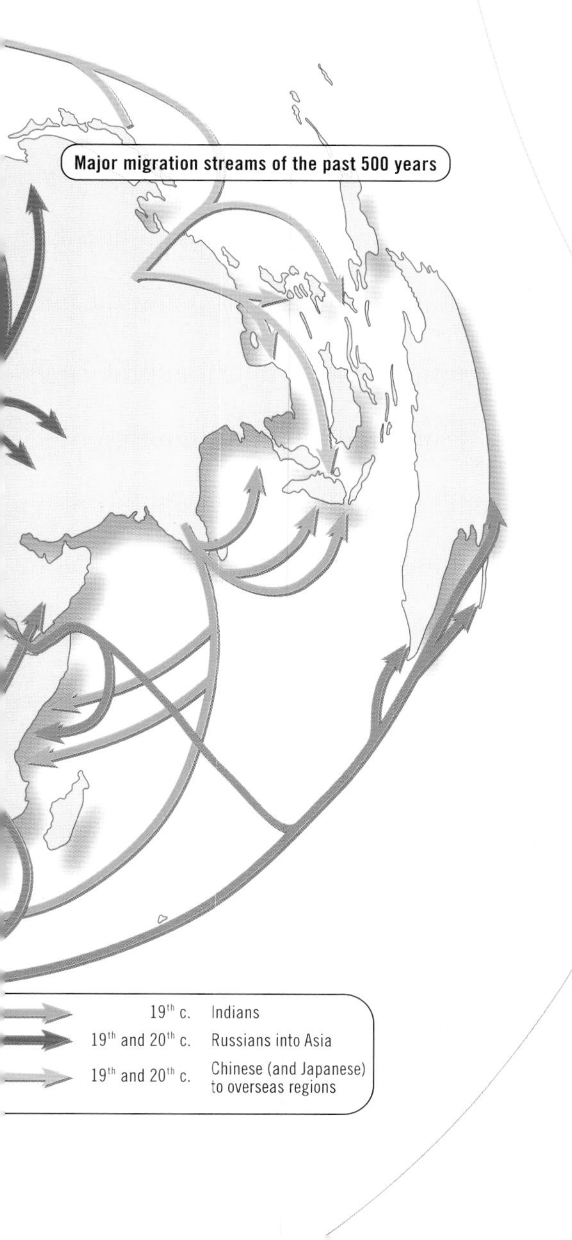

Effects of disasters on world population, 1969–1993				
Type of disaster	No. of persons		Death toll	No. of events
	affected	homeless		
Drought and famine	57,906,000	23,000	74,000	438
Floods	47,850,000	3,178,000	12,000	1,366
Tropical storms	9,417,000	1,066,000	29,000	1,551
Earthquakes	1,765,000	224,000	22,000	640
Landslides	132,000	107,000	1,600	218
Volcanic eruptions	95,000	13,000	1,000	98
Technical accidents	53,000	8,400	600	310
Fire	33,000	88,000	3,300	583

On an Emigrant Ship

During the 19th century, thousands of Irish emigrants embarked on a quest for a better life in the New World, the majority of them fleeing during the Irish potato famine of 1845–50. This 1884 woodcut shows passengers on an emigrant ship being called to breakfast by a bell.

Labor Migration

Unlike the many and diverse groups of more or less involuntary migrants, migrants who leave their homelands in search of work ordinarily do so voluntarily on the basis of personal considerations. Two examples may serve to illustrate this phenomenon.

In North America, migrant workers are needed primarily as unskilled harvest laborers in the agricultural sector. Most of these people come from the south – from Mexico or the Caribbean. According to official estimates, there were approximately 8.5 million Mexicans living and working in the U.S. in 2001, about three million of them illegally. In most cases, these migrant workers have been smuggled into the country by organized gangs. Over the years, specific migration patterns have taken shape in the United States. A significant number of migrant laborers work as fruit pickers in Florida during the winter before moving north to the New England states to help harvest tomatoes, potatoes, and apples in the summer. A second stream of migrant workers moves from Texas into the Midwest or to the West Coast in search of jobs picking fruit, vegetables, sugar beets, or cotton. A third current flows northward along the West Coast from southern California to Washington, working during the fruit and vegetable harvests.

Migrant workers often contribute significantly to the maintenance of living standards and even to increasing prosperity, as the example of the small oil-producing countries along the Persian Gulf clearly shows. Not only do "guest laborers" account for up to 80% of their populations, social institutions and economic sectors – public services, schools, universities, hospitals, private households, national and municipal administrations, the construction business and to a certain extent even the oil industry itself – depend heavily upon foreign workers and could hardly function without them.

Prospects

Environmental catastrophes, rapid population growth, and economic stagnation in some regions; sluggish population growth accompanied by strong economic expansion in others; political disputes and regional conflicts, civil wars, and famines – all of these factors will continue to cause large-scale popular migrations and waves of refugees in the 21st century. In a global economy, hardly a single country will be spared the consequences of these developments.

Global Linguistic Diversity

One World – Thousands of Languages

Depending upon the criteria applied in distinguishing them, between 2,500 and 6,500 languages are spoken on Earth. These widely diverging figures reflect both the difficulty involved in differentiating with certainty between a dialect and a language and our lack of knowledge about many languages spoken by very small groups in regions such as the Amazon Basin, New Guinea, and the African interior.

European languages account for only a small portion of the total. Somewhere between 70 and 165 different tongues are spoken on the continent. More languages (nearly 750!) are spoken in Papua New Guinea than in any other single country in the world. Only very few countries are completely unilingual (Iceland is one). Most countries are home to speakers of several or many different tongues and their variants. A number of languages die out every year, and discoveries of new languages are rare even today.

Europoid		Afric
French	Indian	Bushman (San)	Massai
Indo-European		Khoisan	Nilo-Saharan

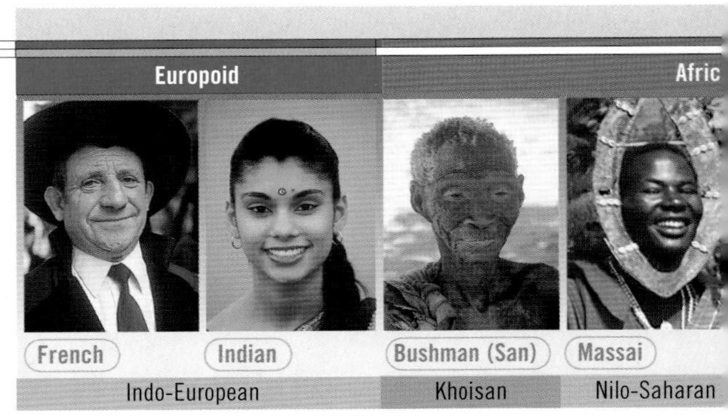

Dead Languages – Living Legacies

Some languages die out with their last speakers, while others are preserved as funds of knowledge, taught in schools (classical Arabic), used only in religious contexts (Old Hebrew), or studied as fixed points of historical reference in linguistics (Sanskrit). Still others serve as a source of new scientific terminology (Greek, Latin) or retain their vitality as literary languages (classical Chinese).

English – A Dominant World Language

Languages are affected by globalization as well. English has become the dominant language worldwide, although it ranks far behind Chinese in terms of numbers of native speakers. In sports and culture, in the high-tech world of computers and telecommunication, in the realm of travel and leisure activities, in scientific discourse and business correspondence, English has attained a degree of appeal, prestige, and influence that is unrivalled by any other language at the global level. International organizations exert considerable influence on language policy in support of other tongues. At the UN, for example, Arabic, Chinese, French, Russian, and Spanish join English as official languages. The European Union has even awarded official status to the national languages of all its member states.

Ethnic Revival – Grass Roots Resistance

The emancipation movements of the sixties and seventies led to a reassessment of the importance of language within the context of ethnic revival. Emphasis suddenly shifted from "utility" and "suitability" in a global sense to concern for linguistic diversity. "Minority" languages and tongues spoken in now independent former colonies were recognized as worthy of equal status and treatment. Languages which for centuries had been preserved and passed from one generation to the next only in oral form were systematically analyzed and described, transposed into a standardized written form, and documented in learning and reference materials such as textbooks, teachers' guides, dictionaries, and grammars (examples include Faeroese, a Germanic island language, and Swahili, the lingua franca in Africa). Bilingual or trilingual traffic and street signs, multilingual billboards, and enhanced media presence now offer striking visible and audible evidence of the new status of many once-neglected languages.

Writing Systems – Keys to Language

Human beings have employed a wide range of different writing systems to present natural, spoken language in visual form for more than three millennia. People of the ancient Egyptian, Inuit, and Maya cultures developed various forms of hieroglyphics, the Sumerians created a cuneiform system, while people of other civilizations established systems comprised of signs for words or syllables. Most forms of writing employed today make use of letters or symbols representing specific sounds. The writing systems now used in Europe and North America derive from the Phoenician alphabet developed in the 10th century BC, which also provided the basis for both the Arabic and Hebrew writing systems. Linguists have identified four major groups of alphabets: Greek (Latin, Coptic, Cyrillic, Armenian, Georgian), Semitic (Arabic, Hebrew, Ethiopian), Indian (Devanagari, Bengali, Tibetan, Burman, Thai, Khmer), and East Asian (Chinese, Japanese, Korean).

Every human has a language, but not everyone has command of its written form. Illiteracy is actually quite widespread and is particularly prevalent in the Third World. In Haiti, for example, 55 % of the population cannot read or write. Illiterates account for 40 % of the population of the Central African Republic, and 62 % of all Yemenese are unable to read a newspaper or write even a short note. Even the rich industrialized countries of the world face the problem of illiteracy, with up to 5 % of their inhabitants unable to read or express themselves in written form and thus virtually excluded from the mainstream of cultural and economic life.

Languages of the World

Indo-European languages
1 Indo-Aryan
2 Iranian
3 Armenian
4 Greek
5 Albanian
6 Slavic
7 Baltic
8 Germanic
9 Romance
10 Celtic

Hamito-Semitic languages
11 Semitic
12 Berber
13 Cushitic
14 Chadic

Uralic languages
15 Finno-Ugric
16 Samoyedic

Altaic languages
17 Turkic
18 Mongolian
19 Tungusic-Manchurian
20 Korean

Paleoasiatic languages
21 Chuchic-Koryakan
22 other Paleoasiastic (incl. Ainu)
23 Japanese

Sino-Tibetan languages
24 Sin-Tai languages
25 Tibeto-Burman languages

Austroasiatic languages
26 Mon-Khmer
27 Munda

Austronesian languages
28 Indonesian
29 Polynesian
30 Micronesian
31 Melanesian
32 Papuan
33 Andamese
34 Burushaski
35 Caucasian
36 Basque

Niger-Congo languages
37 Bantu
38 Benue-Congo & Kwa
39 Mande
40 Kordofan

41 Nilo-Saharan (incl. Kanuri)
42 Khoisan
43 Australian (Aborigine)
44 Eskimo-Aleut
45 Amerindian
46 South American Indian
Uto-Aztecan
Mayan
Misumalpan
Quechua and Aymaran
Tupi-Guarani
Araucanian

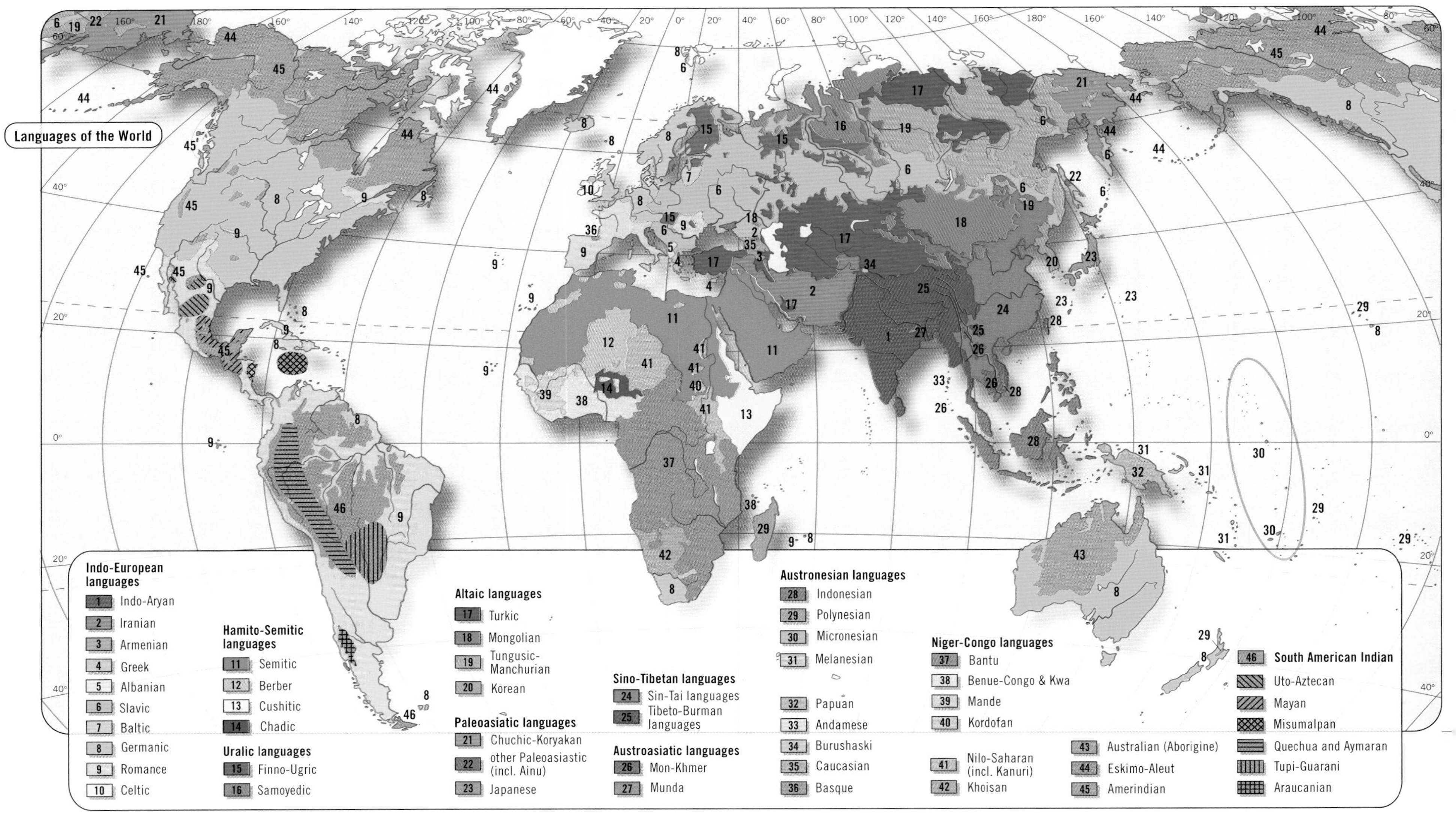

East Asian		Arctic	Amerindian			Oceanian		Australian
Pygmy	Chinese	Tibetan	Inuit	Maya	Yanomami	Polynesian	Melanesian	Australian
Niger-Kordofan	Sino-Tibetan		Eskimo-Aleut	Amerindian		Austronesian		Australian

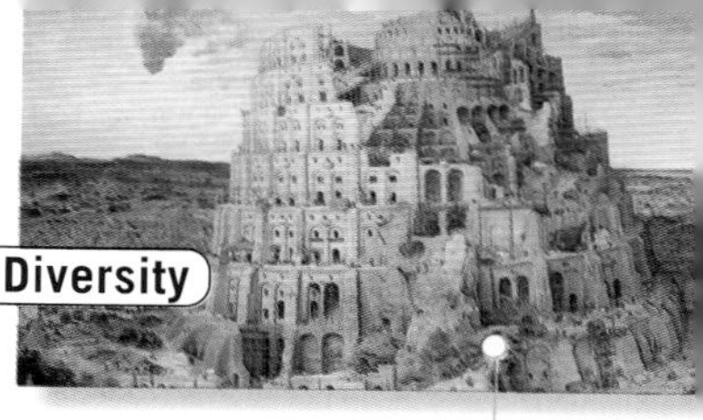

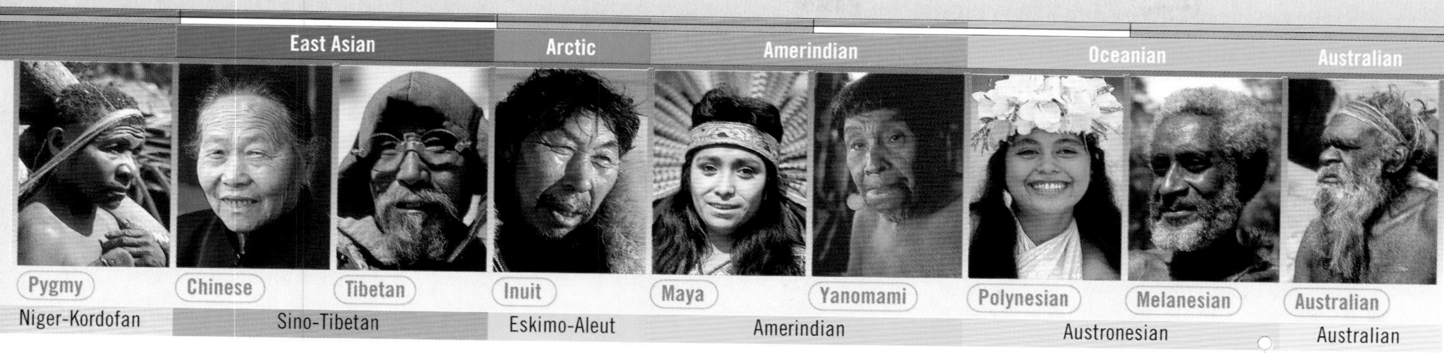

Linguistic Diversity – a Curse?
Did all humans originally speak a single language? The idea (no longer accepted) is expressed in the biblical story of the Tower of Babylon (painting by Pieter Bruegel the Elder, 1563), in which linguistic diversity is described as God's punishment for human pride and greed for power.

Linguistic Exchange – The Foreign Element

All languages have changed over the course of centuries. Apart from natural, organic evolution, languages are influenced significantly by contact among speakers of different linguistic communities – conquerors and conquered peoples, neighboring linguistic groups, etc. In this way, languages enrich one another with "foreign material" (adopted and adapted words and forms). These phenomena are referred to by historical linguistics as strata: Substrates are traces of the language of a conquered or exterminated people left behind in the language of the victors (e.g. remnants of Celtic in the Romance languages). Superstrata are elements introduced by a conquering group into the language of a subjugated people but which do not displace the original language (e.g. Franconian influences on French). Adstrata are linguistic influences which do not reflect hierarchical relationships (e.g. contacts between speakers of Germanic and Romance languages along linguistic boundaries).

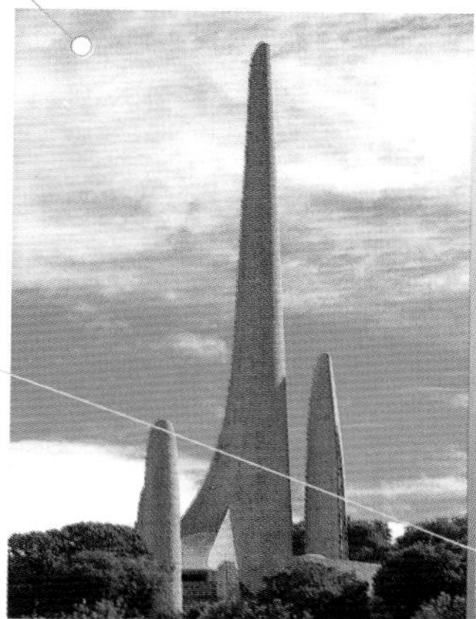

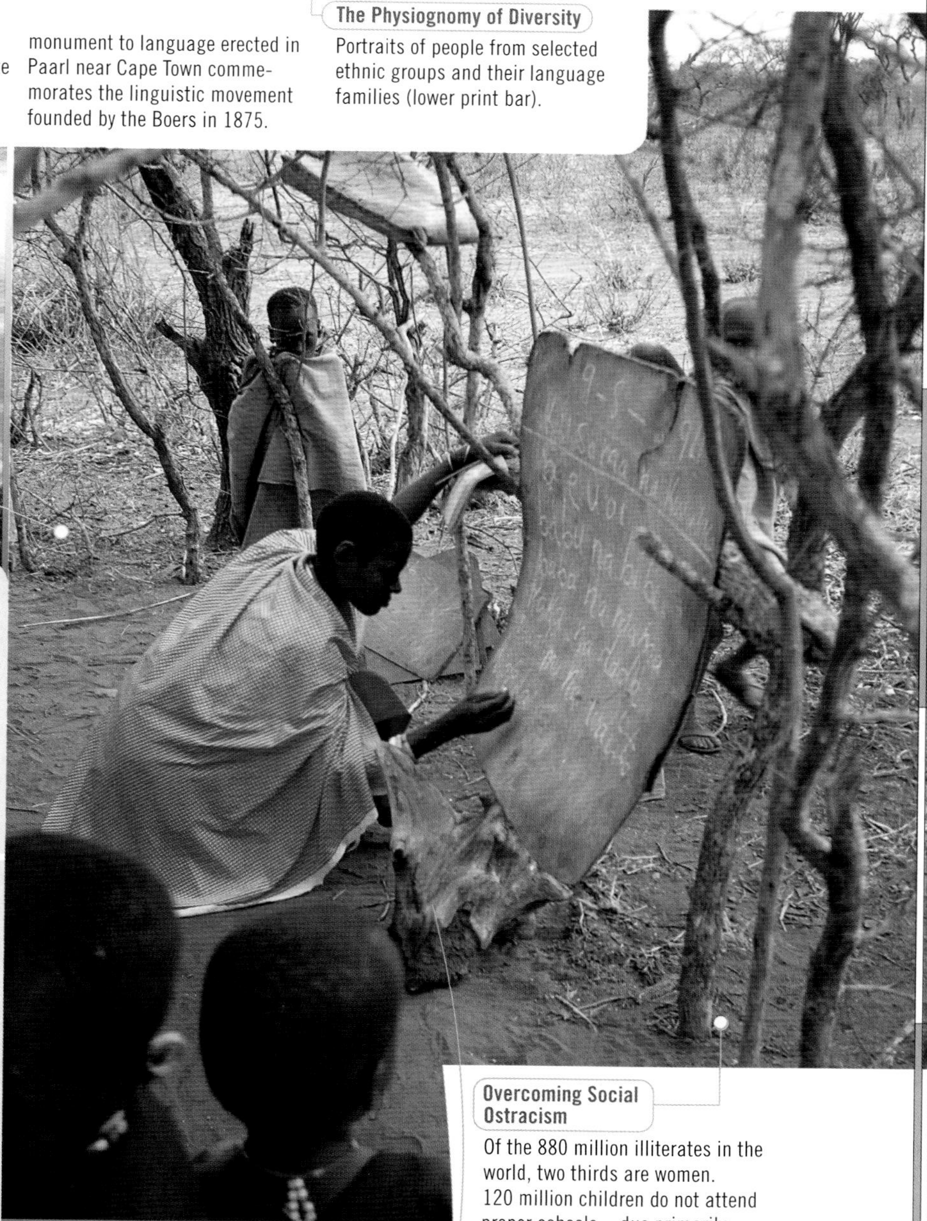

The Birth of New Languages: Pidgin and Creole forms

Pidgin and Creole languages are the products of a special form of linguistic interaction which takes place primarily when speakers of different native tongues communicate with each other. Such languages have developed through trading activity and in economies significantly influenced by slavery in the New World, Africa, Southeast Asia, and Oceania. Pidgin languages are characterized by markedly simplified structures that facilitate communication but are found in neither of the original native languages involved. Pidgin languages that become established and are passed on to succeeding generations are known as Creoles. Many Creole languages have been standardized and adopted as official national languages (in Haiti, Mauritius, and the Seychelles, for example) and thus contribute to local or national identity.

The Future of Languages

Though many have predicted the eventual demise of linguistic diversity, languages have proven astonishingly resilient. Even today, there are those who hope and believe that globalization will result in the establishment of English as the worldwide medium for communication. Yet efforts have also been undertaken to have the right to speak one's native language firmly anchored in international human rights conventions. Slowly but surely, people are beginning to realize that linguistic diversity has the capacity to enrich humanity and is not, as the Bible suggests, God's punishment for human pride, vanity, and greed. In the age of technology, languages that remain open to progress and capable of integrating it into their dynamic systems will survive and ensure the preservation of linguistic diversity in the 21st century.

A Monument to Language
A prime example of a literary language developed through deliberate effort is Afrikaans, which is spoken in South Africa. The unique monument to language erected in Paarl near Cape Town commemorates the linguistic movement founded by the Boers in 1875.

The Physiognomy of Diversity
Portraits of people from selected ethnic groups and their language families (lower print bar).

Geographic distribution of languages on Earth

- 32% Asia
- 3% Europe
- 15% America
- 19.5% Australia & Oceania
- 30.5% Africa

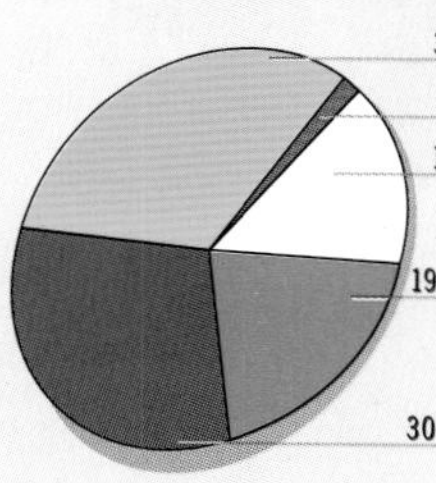

Most widely spoken languages by number of speakers
as native and second language

millions	
940	Chinese
475	English
395	Hindi
375	Spanish
300	Russian
215	Arabic
200	Bengali
185	Portuguese
155	Malayan-Indonesian
125	Japanese
122	French
118	German
100	Urdu

Overcoming Social Ostracism
Of the 880 million illiterates in the world, two thirds are women. 120 million children do not attend proper schools – due primarily to a lack of money. The photo shows a Massai "bush school" in East Africa.

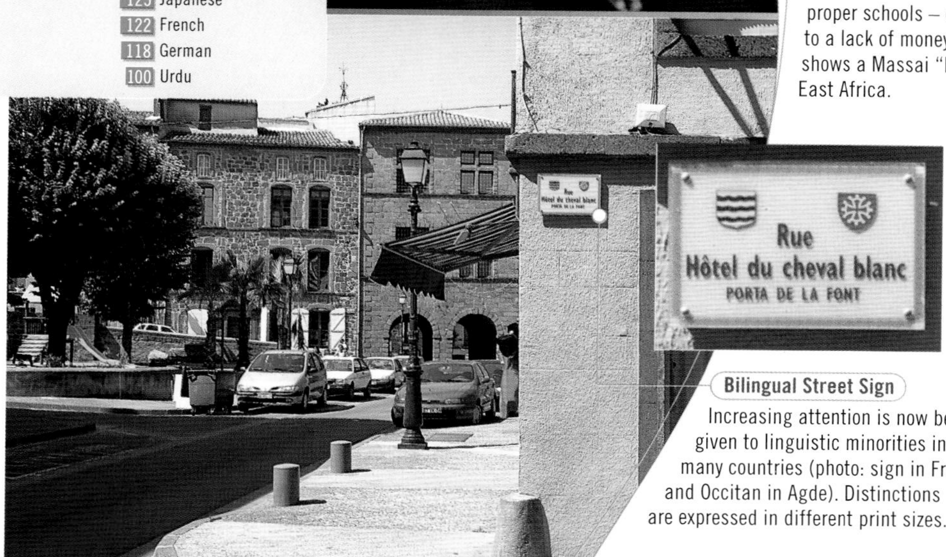

Bilingual Street Sign
Increasing attention is now being given to linguistic minorities in many countries (photo: sign in French and Occitan in Agde). Distinctions are expressed in different print sizes.

Rue
Hôtel du cheval blanc
PORTA DE LA FONT

Religions of the World

One Divine Power? Many Concepts of Divinity

Religion is an expression of human responses to the experience of divinity in ritual and doctrine. It appears in different forms in different cultures and at different times, and though distinct from other manifestations of culture, it both reflects and shapes them at the same time. Religion is always community-oriented and always involves standards of ethics, although these may differ significantly from one set of beliefs and principles to another. Religion takes public form in rituals and pilgrimages, at specific places, and in the teachings of religious leaders. Religious faith informs and molds the lives of those who share it.

A Ubiquitous Phenomenon

All human societies since prehistoric times have embraced religious beliefs of some kind. We distinguish between two basic types of religion. The first is known as "primary religion." The origin and basis for all religions, it is still clearly evident today in "tribal religions" (frequently, though imprecisely and even inaccurately referred to as "natural" or "animistic" religions). These systems of belief have primarily local or regional relevance and generally govern communal life in small societies. They provide guidance and support at critical points in life – birth, puberty, marriage, death and mourning – through "rites of passage." Events marking seasonal transitions, such as planting and harvest or the winter and summer solstices, are also celebrated in rituals and serve as fixed points of reference for communal life, much like Christmas and Easter in western societies.

The second group, "secondary religions," comprises systems of belief and ritual which can be traced to the teachings or activities of founders, reformers, and charismatic leaders. They include the five major religions of the world: Judaism, Christianity, Islam, Buddhism, and Hinduism. They all pose the question of truth, which plays no role at all in primary religions, whose "natural" legitimacy is grounded in the specific societies that embrace them. Many secondary religions have sacred scriptures, which contain the basic tenets of ethics, faith, and behavior to which their adherents subscribe. Because they claim possession of universal truth, they tend to assume a missionary character, and their founders are the central focus of teaching and devotion. Buddhism, Christianity, and Islam are prime examples of this tendency. As they spread throughout the world, these secondary religions have had to come to grips with primary religions. In the process, they have adopted and adapted existing sacred rituals, places and

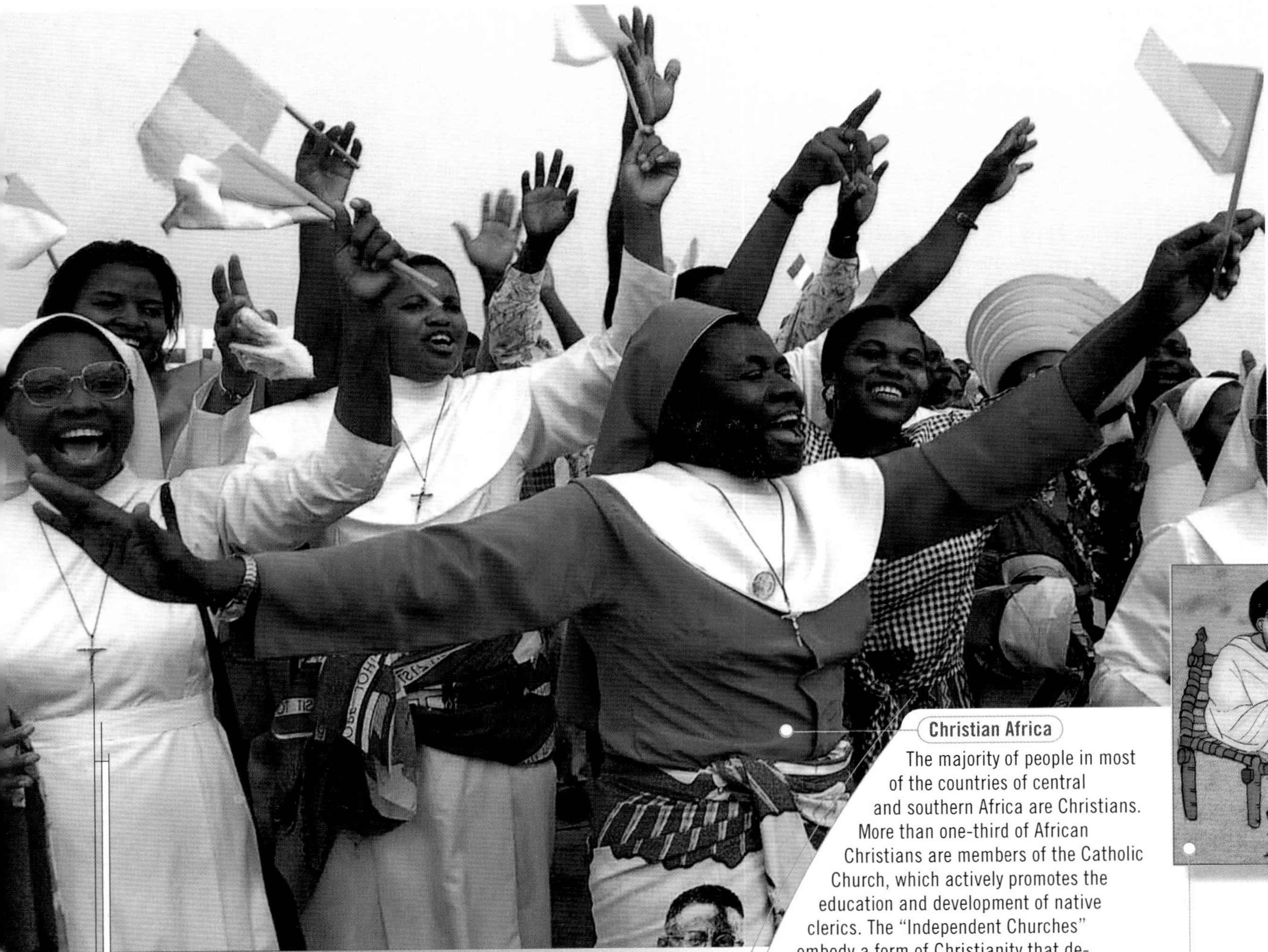

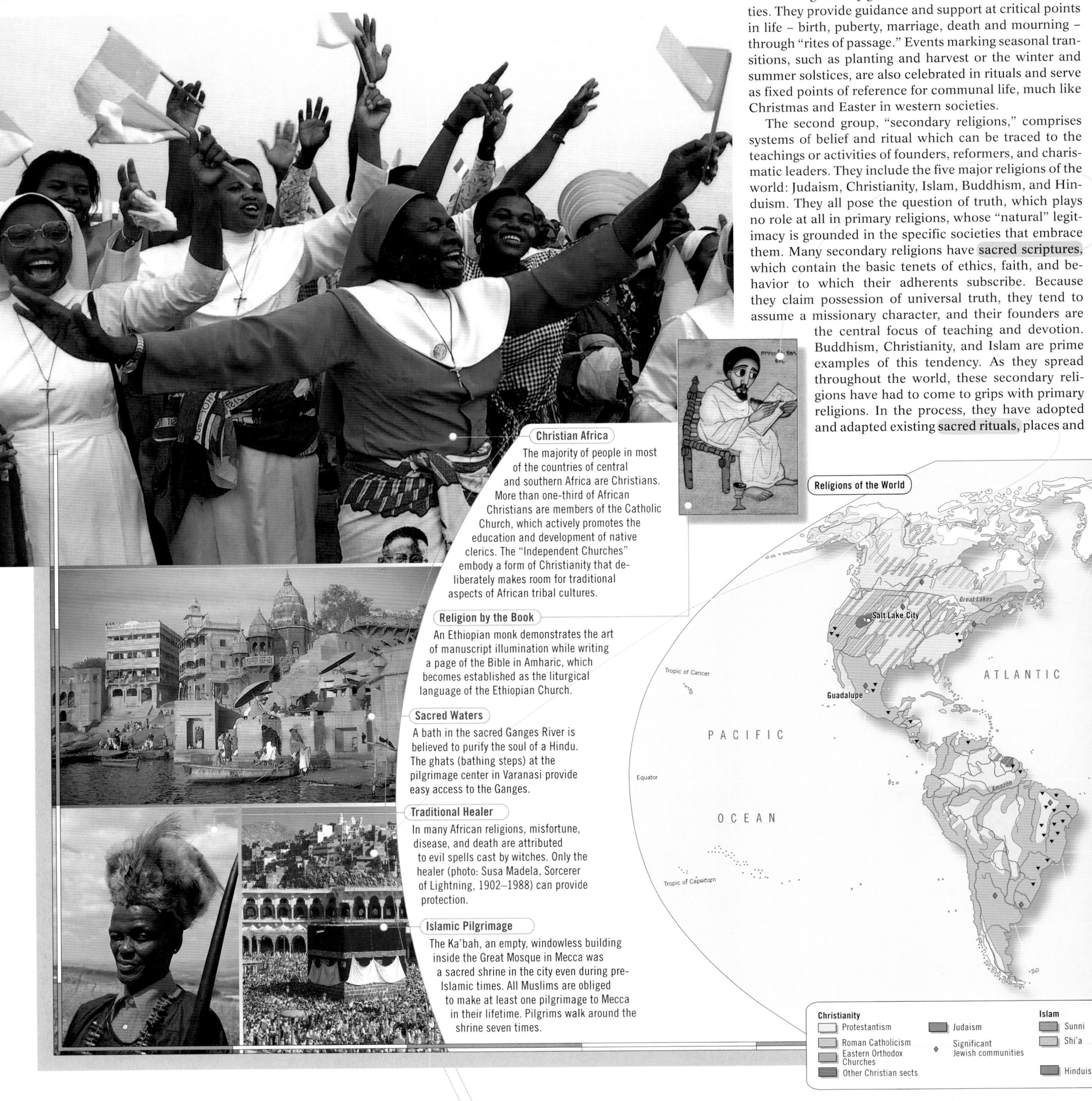

Christian Africa

The majority of people in most of the countries of central and southern Africa are Christians. More than one-third of African Christians are members of the Catholic Church, which actively promotes the education and development of native clerics. The "Independent Churches" embody a form of Christianity that deliberately makes room for traditional aspects of African tribal cultures.

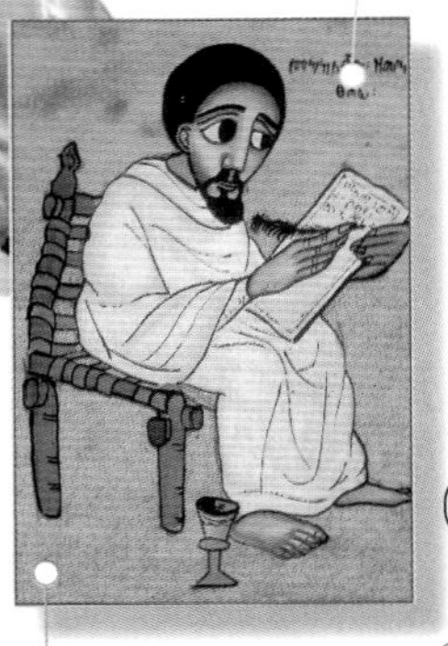

Religion by the Book

An Ethiopian monk demonstrates the art of manuscript illumination while writing a page of the Bible in Amharic, which becomes established as the liturgical language of the Ethiopian Church.

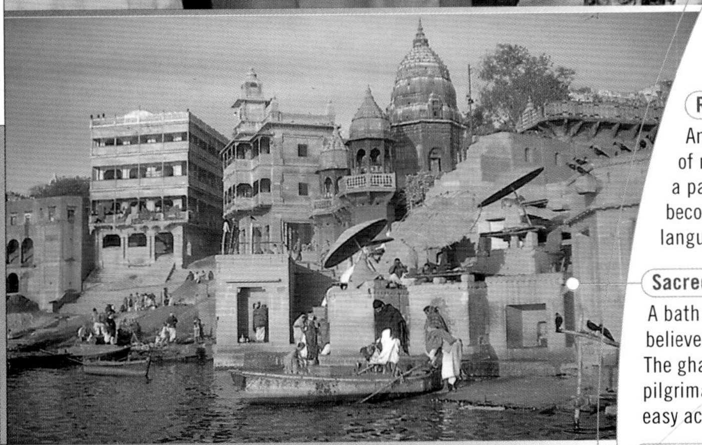

Sacred Waters

A bath in the sacred Ganges River is believed to purify the soul of a Hindu. The ghats (bathing steps) at the pilgrimage center in Varanasi provide easy access to the Ganges.

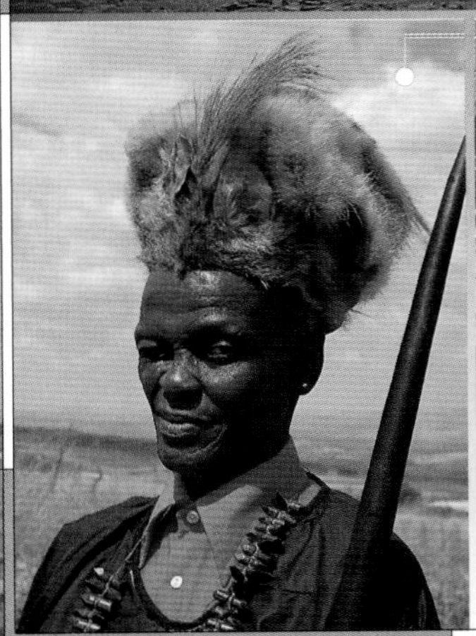

Traditional Healer

In many African religions, misfortune, disease, and death are attributed to evil spells cast by witches. Only the healer (photo: Susa Madela, Sorcerer of Lightning, 1902–1988) can provide protection.

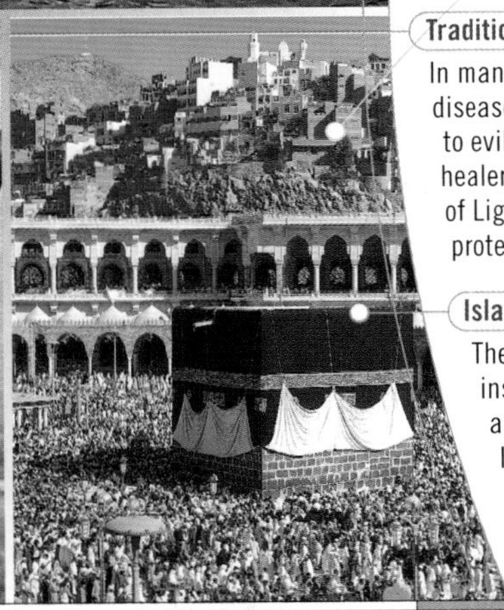

Islamic Pilgrimage

The Ka'bah, an empty, windowless building inside the Great Mosque in Mecca was a sacred shrine in the city even during pre-Islamic times. All Muslims are obliged to make at least one pilgrimage to Mecca in their lifetime. Pilgrims walk around the shrine seven times.

Religions of the World

ATLANTIC

PACIFIC OCEAN

Tropic of Cancer
Equator
Tropic of Capricorn

Great Lakes
Salt Lake City
Guadalupe
Amazon

Christianity		Islam	
Protestantism	Judaism	Sunni	
Roman Catholicism	Significant Jewish communities	Shi'a	
Eastern Orthodox Churches			
Other Christian sects		Hinduism	

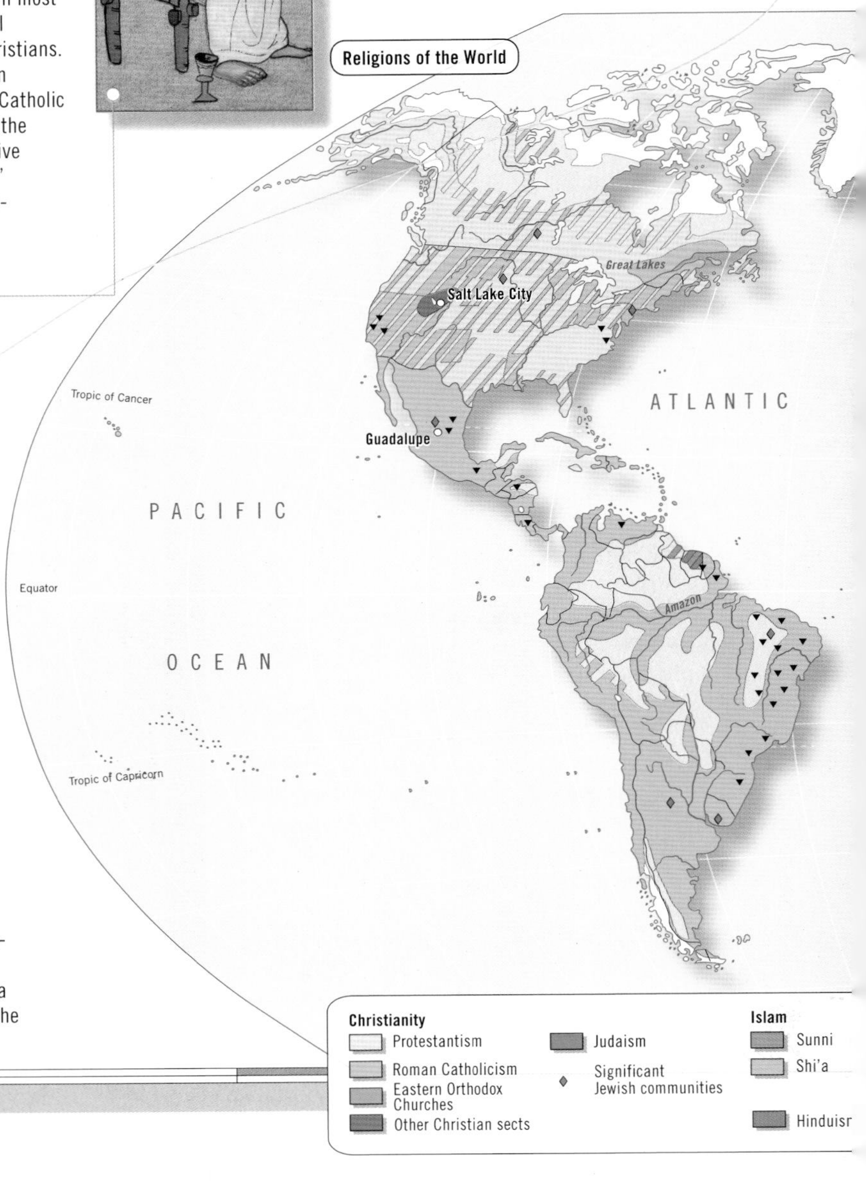

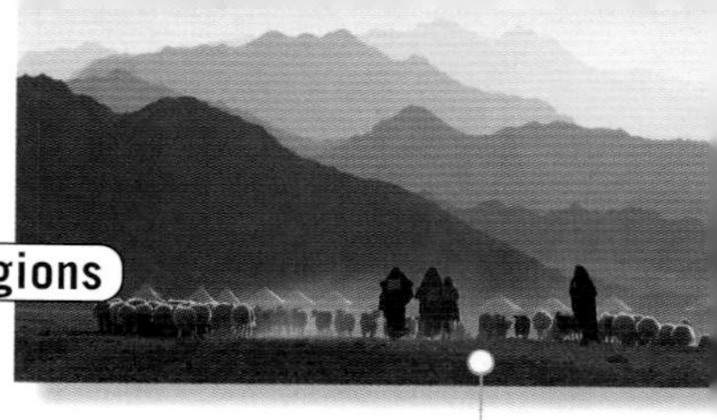

times, reinterpreting them and casting out whatever elements could not be reconciled with their teachings. Buddhism developed into Mahayana Buddhism in China, for example, in response to regional influences. Christianity split into an eastern (Orthodox) branch under the influence of the religions of Greece and Asia Minor and a western (Roman) form of Catholicism oriented toward the more dogmatic Roman religions. Islam adopted pre-Islamic and existing Judaic and Christian elements, as the life of Mohammed clearly shows.

When the great religions face a loss of vitality and begin to abandon their original doctrines under the influence of progressive enlightenment, modern patterns of thought, and the pressure of political systems, reformers appear, new sects are founded, and fundamentalist revival movements take shape, as we witness all over the world today. This tendency is reflected in new religious movements and sects in Japan (Tenrykyo and others), the United States (Mormons, Children of God, etc.), Latin America (Umbanda, voodoo cults), India (neo-Hinduism), and Africa (Kimbanguism, Aladura churches, etc.) as well as the emphatically pious New-Age religions.

Religion – a Source of Conflict?

All religions strive to control the lives of their members, and thus they play an important role in public life. Radical, often fundamentalist religious movements also seek to exert political influence, although they often expose themselves to manipulation by political forces as well. In view of the dangers all societies face in today's world, religions would do well to remember their humanitarian function and support the growth of a system of ethics that will enable human beings to live together in peace.

Religions of the World

Religions	Date of origin	Sacred scriptures	Number of adherents	% of world population
Christianity	30 AD	Bible	2 bn	33 % – increasing in the Third World
Islam	622 AD	Koran	1.3 bn	20 % – increasing
Hinduism and neo-Hinduism	c. 1,500 BC	Vedas, Upanishads	900 mil.	15 % – stagnant
Atheists and agnostics	–	–	900 mil.	15 % – decreasing
Buddhism	c. 530 BC	Tipitaka	360 mil.	6 % – stagnant
Chinese Religious Complex (ancestor and nature worship, Taoism, Confucianism*)	c. 1,500 BC	–	230 mil.	5 %
Tribal religions	prehistoric	Oral tradition	91 mil.	2 %
Yoruba religions: voodoo cults, Umbanda, etc.	?	–	30 mil.	< 1 %
New religious movements (Caodaism, Soka-Gakkai, Ananda Marge, etc.)	19th/20th c.	–	30 mil.	< 1 %
Sikhism	1500 AD	Adi Granth	18 mil.	< 1 %
Judaism	Babylonian exile (587 – 538 BC)	Torah, Talmud	15 mil.	< 1 %
Shamanism	prehistoric	Oral tradition	12 mil.	< 1 %
Spiritism*	after 1800	–	10 mil.	< 1 %
Baha'i	1863 AD	The Most Holy Book	4 mil.	< 1 %
Shintō	6th c. AD	Kojiki, Nihongi, Fudoki	4 mil.	< 1 %
Jainism	6th/5th c. BC	Extensive canon in Prakrit literature	3 mil.	< 1 %
Parsiism	500 – 250 BC	Avesta	150,000	< 1 %

* not a religion in the strict sense

The Desert – Origin of all Great Religions

The Israelites were nomads, like these shepherds on the Sinai Peninsula. They are believed to have worshiped protector gods and local divinities originally. Every tribe had its own god, to whom access was gained through the tribal elders ("fathers").

Harmony and Peace

Meditation is an important religious exercise for Buddhists, as it relieves the heart of suffering and the mind of ignorance. The simple saffron-colored robe symbolizes simplicity and self-denial; the fig tree recalls the bodhi tree beneath which Buddha achieved enlightenment.

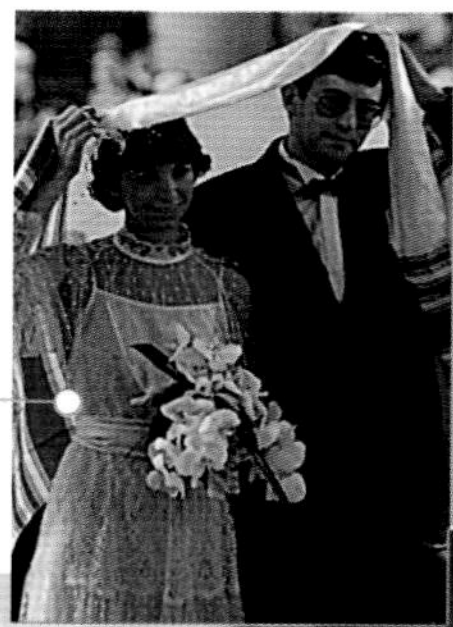

Jewish Marriage Rites

Bride and groom cover their heads with a tallit (prayer cloak) during the marriage ceremony.

Northern and southern Buddhism
Lamaistic Buddhism

Chinese Religious Complex (Confucianism, Taoism)

Shinto

Tribal religions, Shamanism

▼ ▾ New religious movements

○ Religious shrines and sites

Unpopulated areas

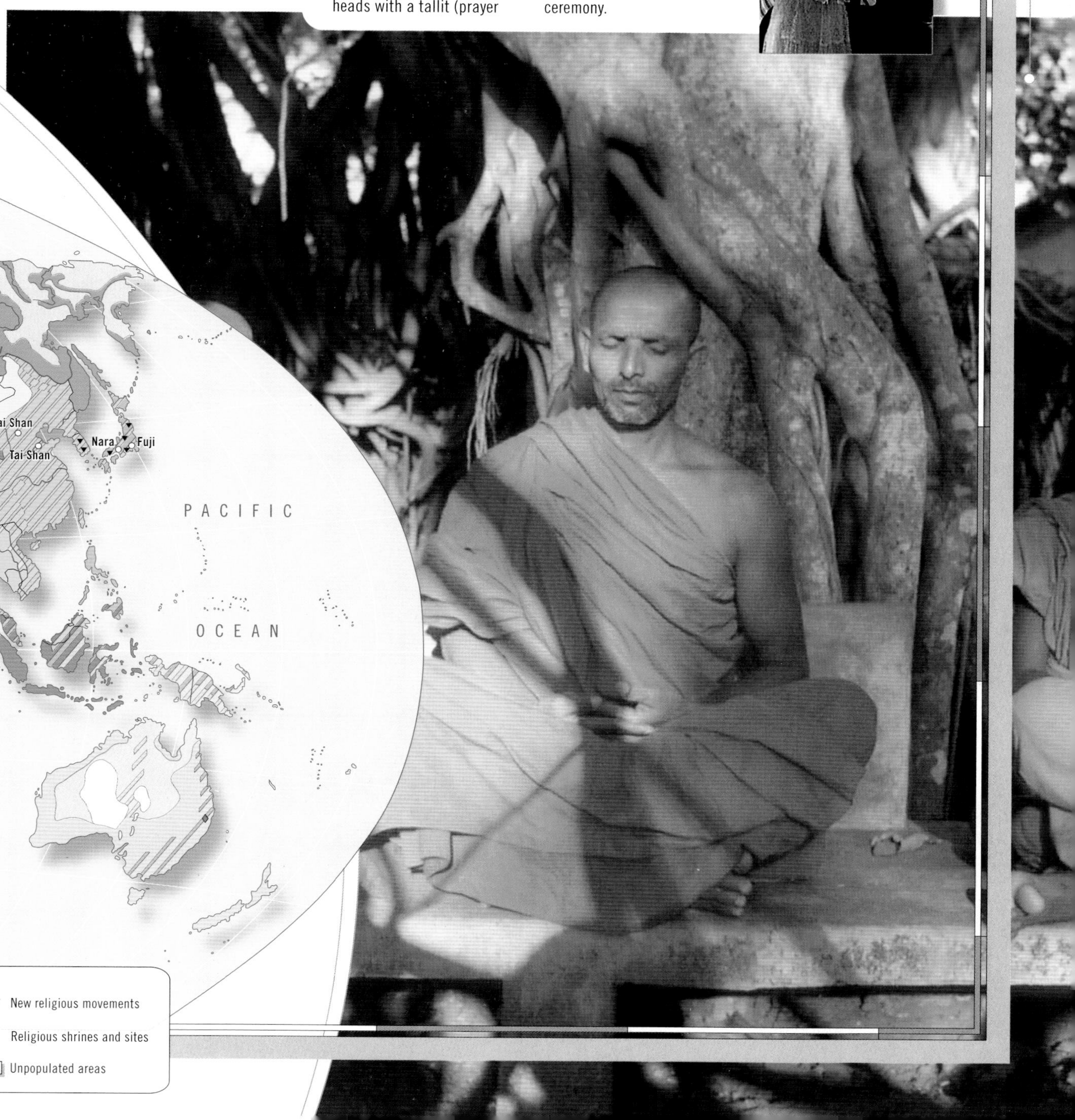

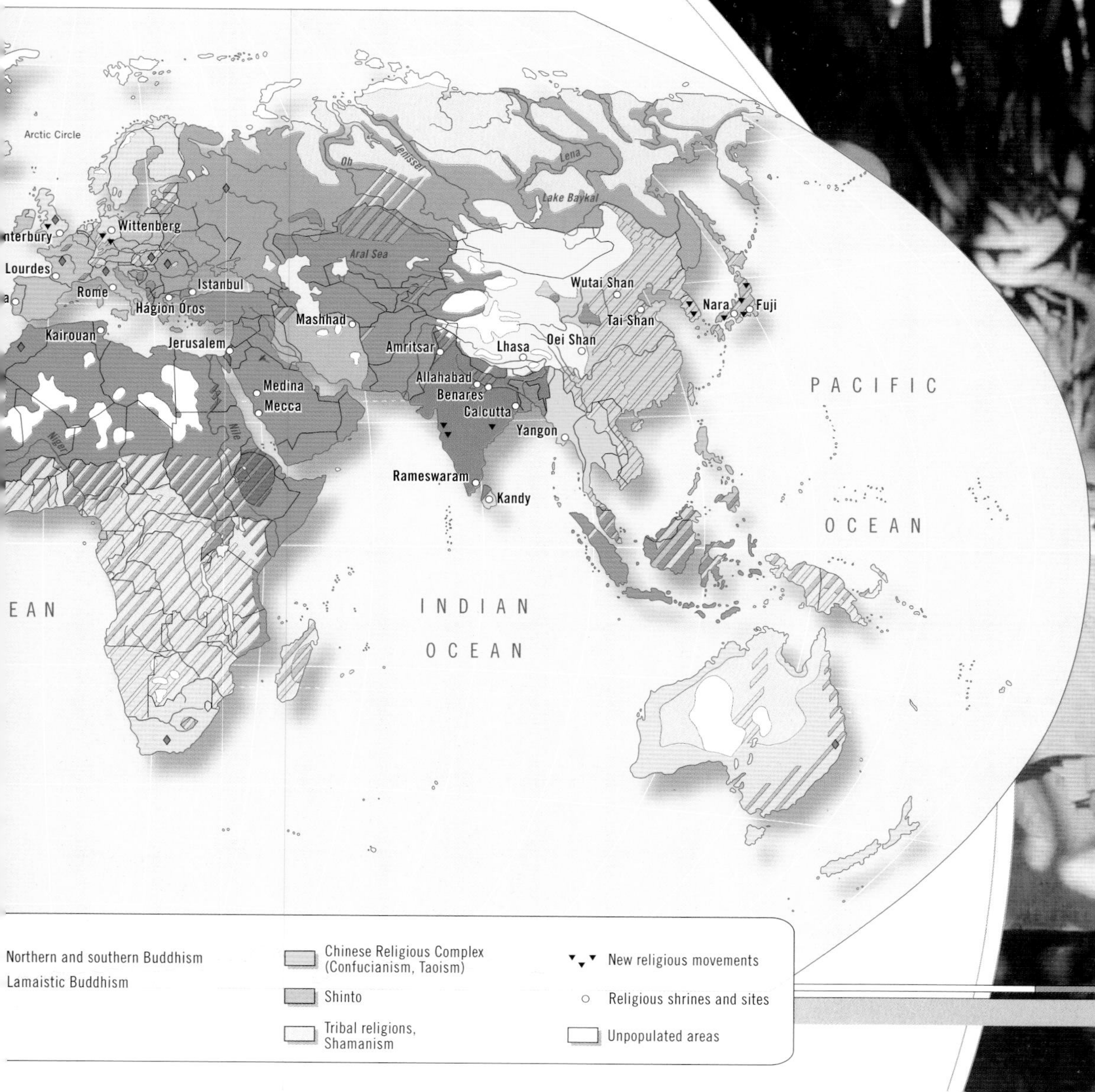

UNESCO Protects the World Cultural Heritage

What is Recognition as a World Cultural Heritage Site Worth?

What does the Roman Amphitheater at Sabratha in Libya have in common with the Inca monuments of Machu Picchu in Peru, the necropolis at Thebes in Egypt with the Great Wall of China, the orthodox monastery at Rila in Bulgaria with Ayers Rock in Australia? They are all legacies of past cultures and irreplaceable treasures that belong to the global community.

The World Heritage Convention?

The Convention on Preservation of the World Cultural and Natural Heritage was passed at the UNESCO General Assembly meeting of 1972. It has since been signed by 167 nations. Signatory countries accept the obligation to protect and preserve sites, recognized as part of the World Heritage, that lie within their borders.

The underlying principle is that sites of unique and universal value – be they architectural monuments, urban districts, or cultivated landscapes – should be recognized as the common heritage of all people on Earth and afforded international protection. The value of such objects may be aesthetic, historical, or scientific in nature.

The World Heritage Committee is composed of delegates from 21 countries selected to represent all of the major cultural regions of the world. The committee convenes once each year to choose new sites for the World Heritage List from applications submitted by participating countries. The list currently contains 721 sites, of which 554 are identified as cultural legacies, 144 as natural heritage sites, and 23 as a combination of both. The Committee also makes decisions on the use of funds contributed by the signatory countries.

Differing Attitudes about the World Heritage List

As a matter of prestige, many countries are eager to have as many sites as possible entered in the list. Others regard recognition as more of a burden than an honor, as they fear a loss of control over their own national treasures.

Prehistoric Hunters

Prehistoric hunters in central North America killed game animals by driving them over high cliffs. (Photo: **Head Smashed-in Bison Jump (2)** in Alberta)

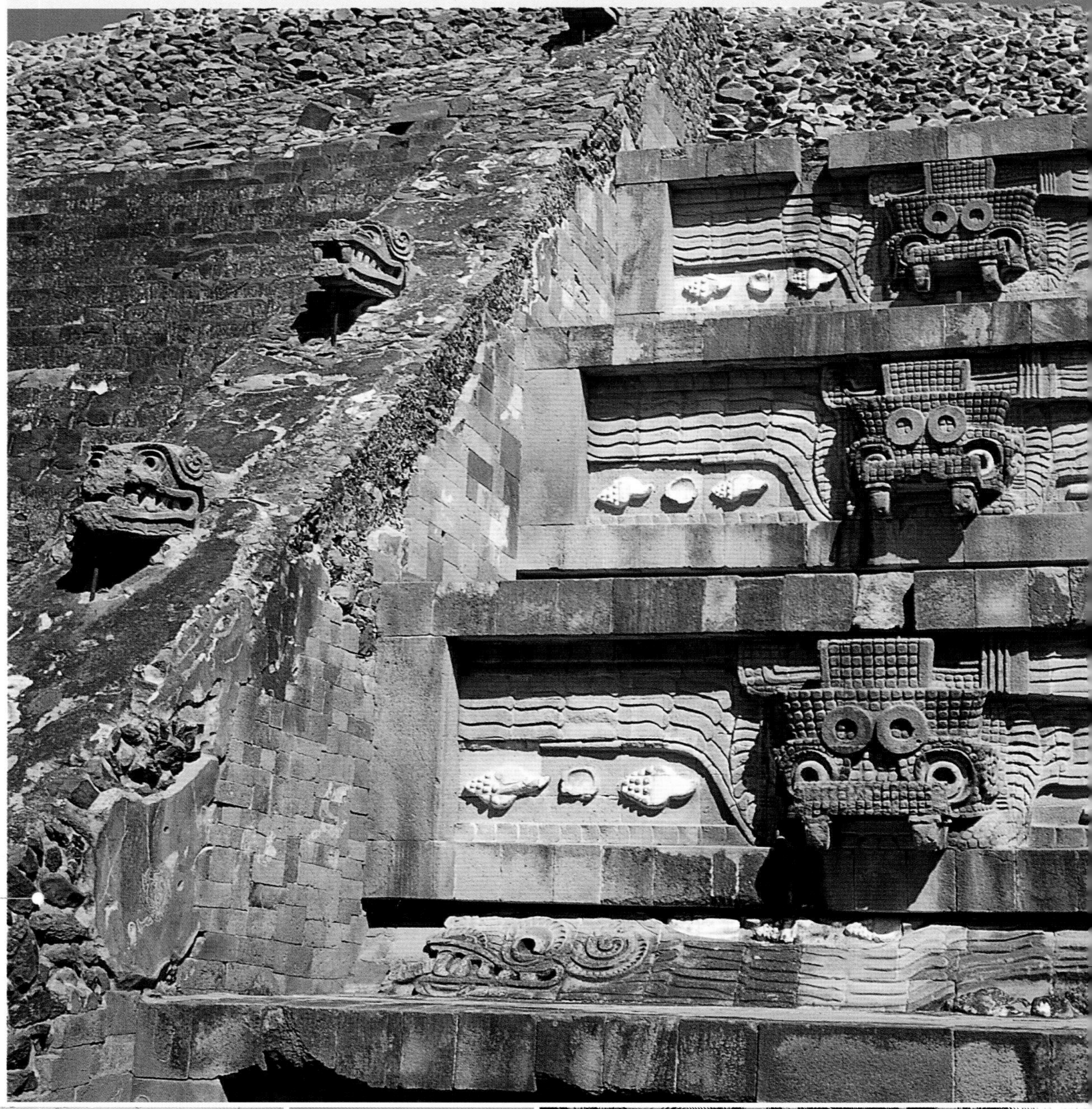

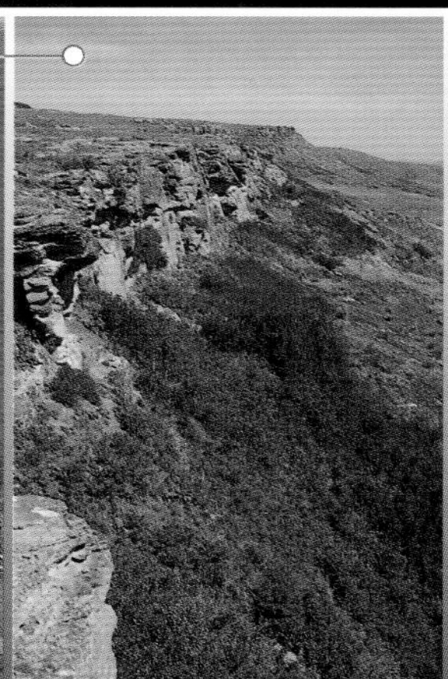

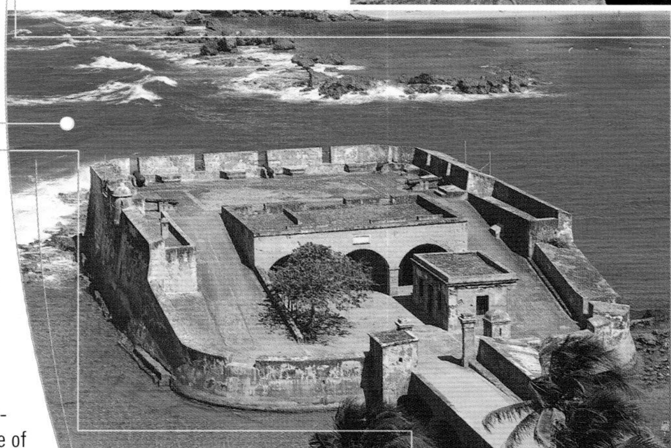

Impregnable Bastion

The fortress (16th c.) and old town of **San Juan (38)** in Puerto Rico were dominated by the massive Castillo de San Felipe del Morro. The photo shows the fortified tip of the peninsula.

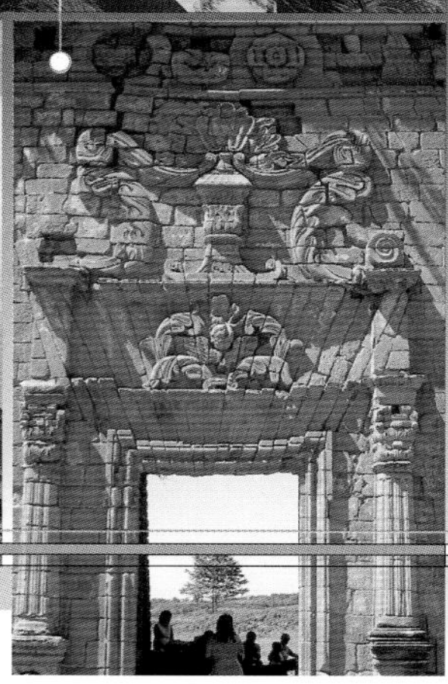

Model States

A by-product of missionary work among the Guaranís, the **Jesuit Reductions (68)** were self-governing agricultural communities that survived for 160 years. (Photo: Church portal in Trinidad, Paraguay)

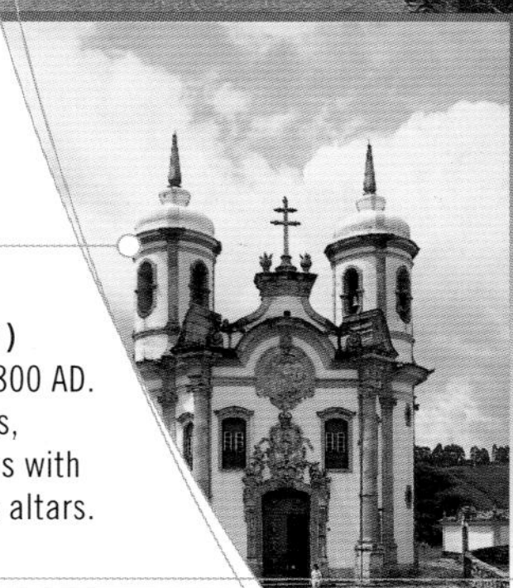

Unique Regional Baroque

A unique form of late baroque architecture emerged in the diamond and gold mining province of Minas Gerais in the 18th century. One of the most beautiful churches in **Ouro Preto (70)** is São Francisco de Assis, designed by Aleijadinho and completed in 1794.

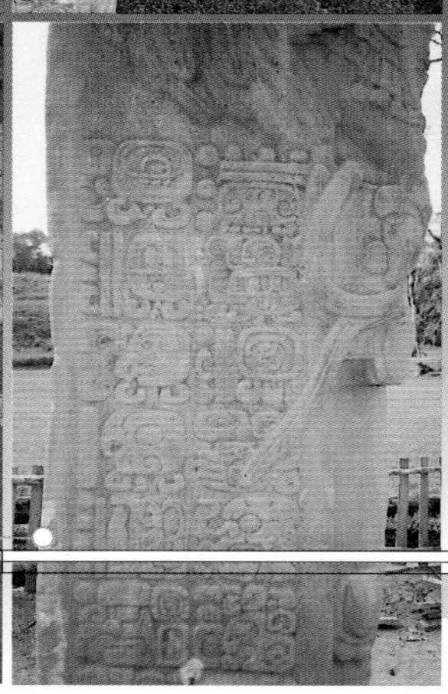

Zoomorphic Altars

The Mayan city of **Quiriguá (41)** flourished between 500 and 800 AD. Hewn from sandstone blocks, the mythical animal figures with hieroglyphs were used as altars.

City of the Gods

Relief panels on the steps of the Quetzalcoatl Pyramid exhibit the heads of the Feathered Serpent and the god of rain or thunder. Temples erected on stepped pyramids in the ceremonial district of **Teotihuacán (22)** line both sides of the Avenue of the Dead for a distance of 2 km.

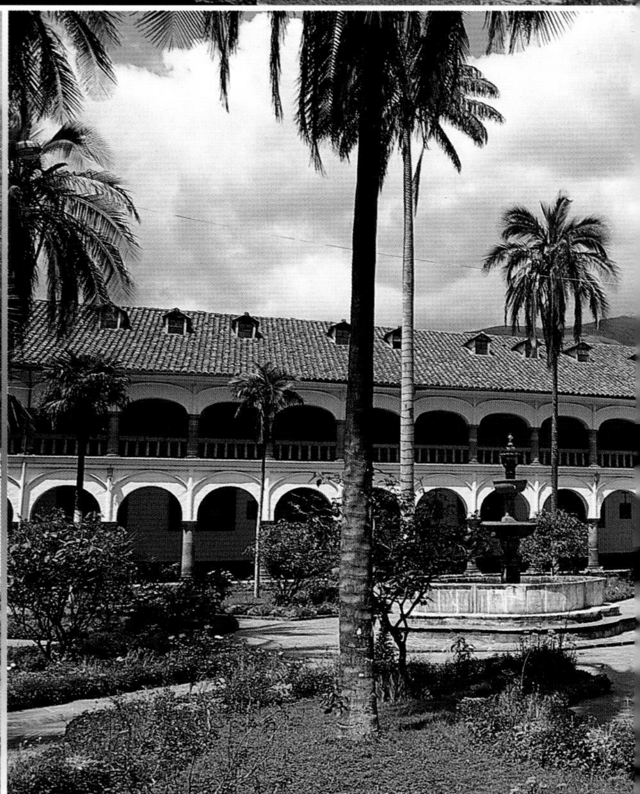

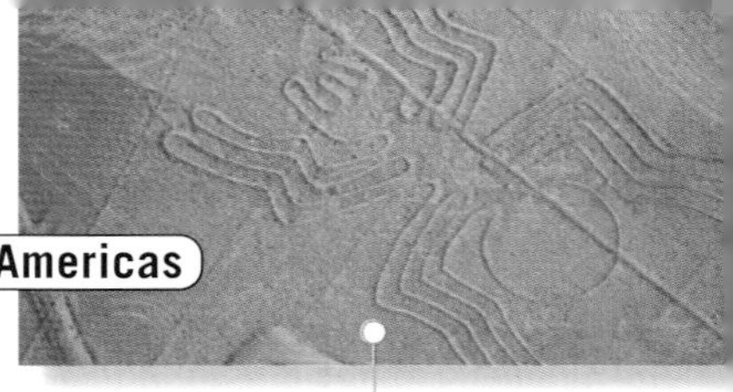

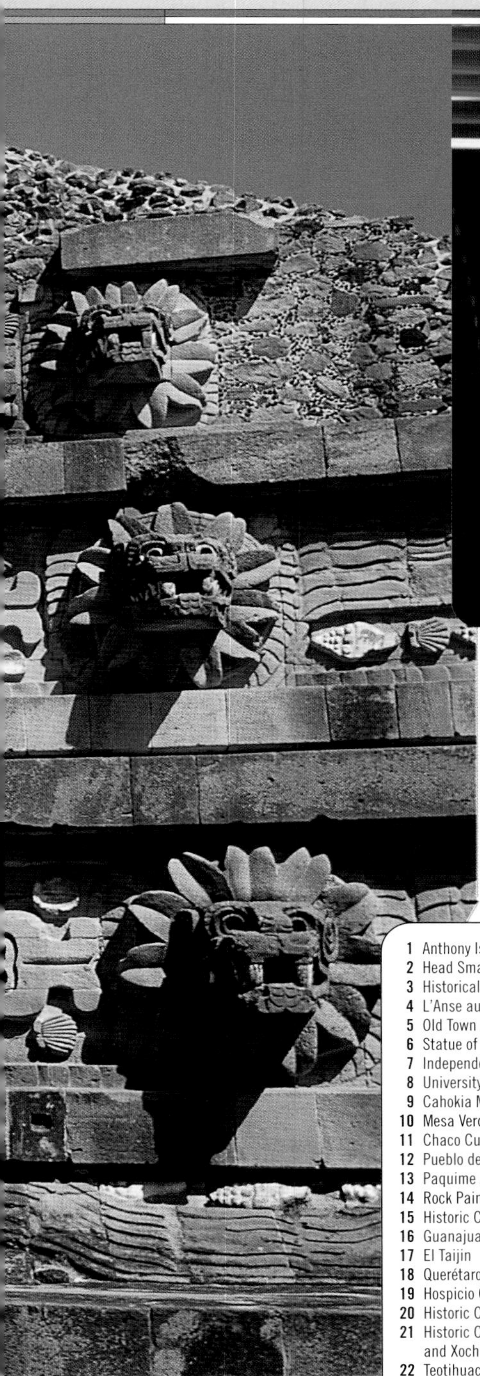

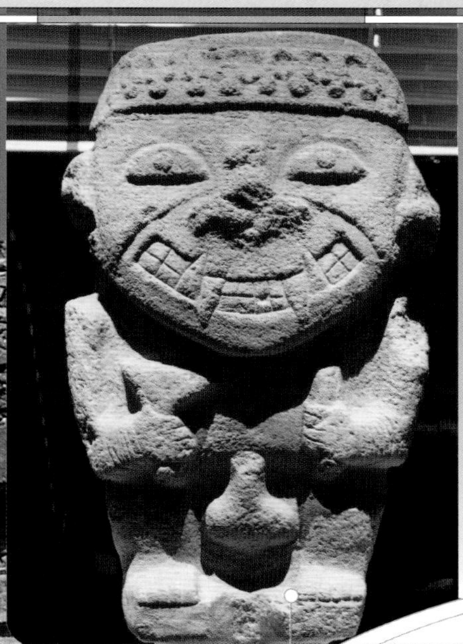

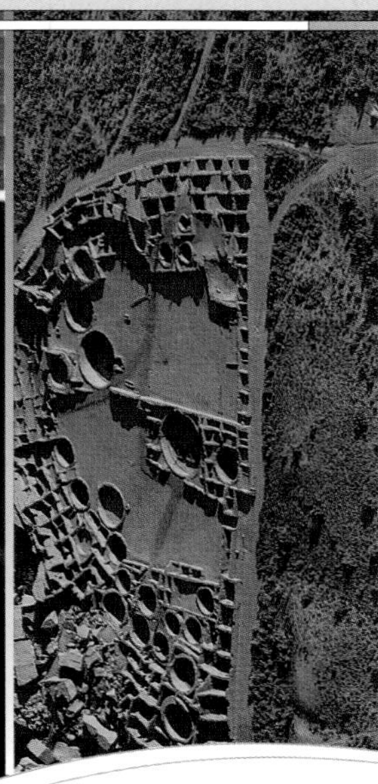

Art from the Air

On the coastal plain of Peru, the Nasca culture (200–600 AD) left behind **geoglyphs (61)** recognizable only from the air. This spider figure is 46 m long. The meaning and purpose of these ground figures remain an archeological puzzle.

Ancient Indian Housing Complex

Up to four stories high, the semi-circular housing complex of Pueblo Bonito built by the Anasazi Indians in what is now **Chaco National Park (11)** was occupied from 920 to 1120 AD. It comprised 800 living spaces and underground storage areas ("kivas"). Chaco Canyon was the hub of an extensive trading network and presumably a religious center in the 13th century.

Stone Sentry

During the cultural bloom of **San Agustín (5)** (100–1000 AD), artists produced about 400 stone sculptures (mostly hybrid human-jaguar figures), each more than four meters tall. They stood at the entrances of burial chambers and temples.

UNESCO World Cultural Heritage in the Americas

1 Anthony Island
2 Head Smashed-In Bison Jump
3 Historical Quebec
4 L'Anse aux Meadows
5 Old Town of Lunenburg
6 Statue of Liberty
7 Independence Hall, Philadelphia
8 University of Virginia, Charlottesville
9 Cahokia Mounds Historic Site
10 Mesa Verde National Park
11 Chaco Culture National Historical Park
12 Pueblo de Taos
13 Paquime Archeological Zone
14 Rock Paintings, Sierra de San Francisco
15 Historic Center of Zacatecas
16 Guanajuato
17 El Tajin
18 Querétaro
19 Hospicio Cabanas, Guadalajara
20 Historic Center of Morelia
21 Historic Center of Mexico City and Xochimilco
22 Teotihuacán
23 Xochicalco
24 Monasteries on the Slopes of Popocatépetl
25 Old Town of Puebla
26 Oaxaca and Monte Albán
27 Tlacotalpan
28 Palenque
29 Campeche
30 Uxmal
31 Chichén Itzá
32 Viñales Valley
33 Old City of Havana
34 Trinidad
35 San Pedro de la Roca Fortress
36 Haiti National Historical Park
37 Colonial City of Santo Domingo
38 Fortress and National Historic Site, San Juan
39 Brimstone Hill Fort

40 Tikal National Park
41 Quiriguá
42 Copán
43 Antigua Guatemala
44 Joya de Ceren
45 Historic District of Panama
46 Portobelo-San Lorenzo Fortifications
47 Colonial Cartagena
48 Willemstad
49 Coro
50 Santa Cruz de Mompox
51 Tierradentro National Archeological Park
52 San Agustín Archeological Park
53 Old City of Quito
54 Old City of Cuenca
55 Río Abiseo National Park
56 Chan Chan Archeological Zone
57 Chavin Archeological Site
58 Old City of Lima
59 Machu Picchu Historic Sanctuary
60 Cuzco
61 Lines and Geoglyphs of Nasca
62 Jesuit Missions of the Chiquitos
63 Samaipata Fortress
64 Historic City of Sucre
65 Potosí
66 Easter Island (NP Rapa Nui)
67 Colonia del Sacramento
68 Jesuit Mission of the Guaranís (Argentina, Brazil, Paraguay)
69 Sanctuary of Bom Jesus do Congonhas
70 Old City of Ouro Preto
71 Old City of Diamantina
72 Brasília
73 Old City of Salvador
74 Old City of Olinda
75 Serra da Capivara National Park
76 Old City of São Luís

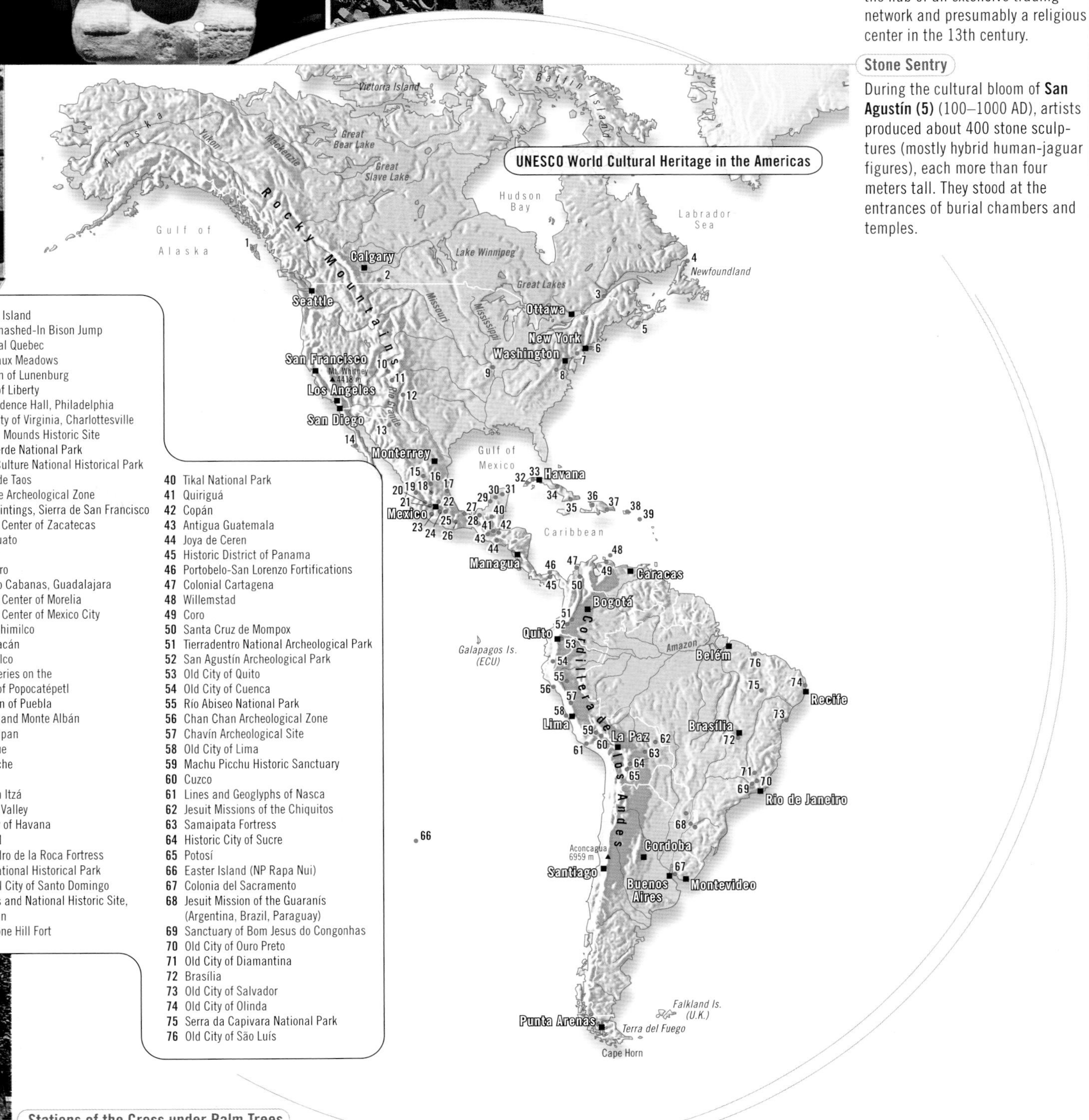

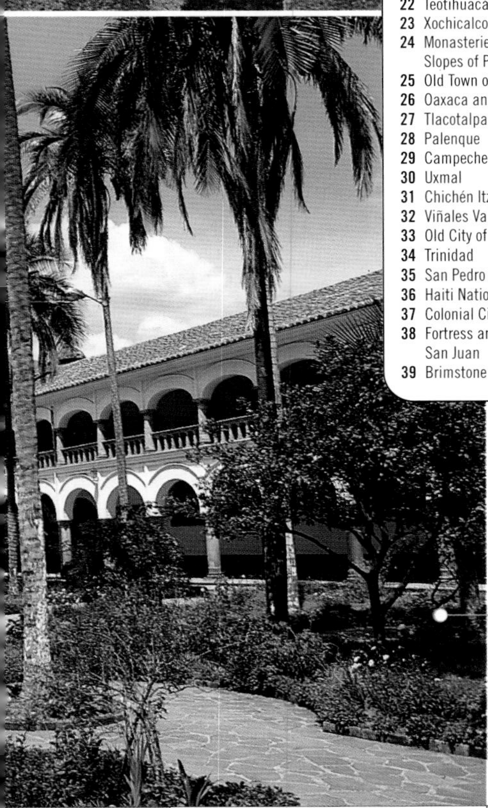

Stations of the Cross under Palm Trees

The Old City of Quito (53), the oldest capital in South America (founded in 1534), has retained its colonial flavor. The stations of the cross at the monastery of La Merced are arranged on two stories and overlook a fountain.

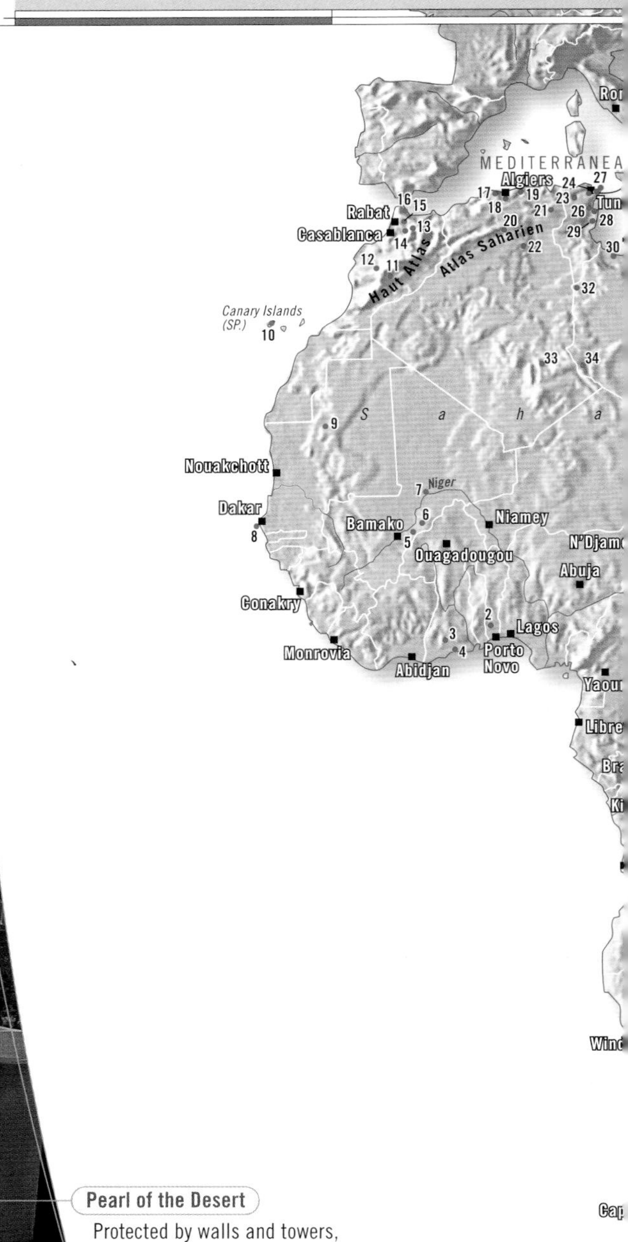

Criteria for Inclusion in the World Heritage List

A World Heritage Site must not only be authentic and intact, it must also be of outstanding universal value, as demonstrated by fulfillment of at least one of the following criteria:

• The site represents a unique artistic accomplishment, a masterpiece of human creative genius.

• The site has had a significant influence, over a span of time or within a cultural area of the world, on developments in architecture, monumental arts, town planning or landscape design.

• The site bears a unique or at least exceptional testimony to a cultural tradition or to a civilization which is living or which has disappeared.

• The site is an outstanding example of a type of building or architectural ensemble or landscape which illustrates a significant state in human history.

• The site is an outstanding example of a traditional human settlement or land use which is representative of a culture (or cultures), especially when it has become vulnerable under the impact of irreversible change.

• The site is directly or tangibly associated with events or living traditions, with ideas, or with beliefs, with artistic, or literary works of outstanding universal significance (this criterion should justify inclusion in the list only in exceptional circumstances and in conjunction with other criteria).

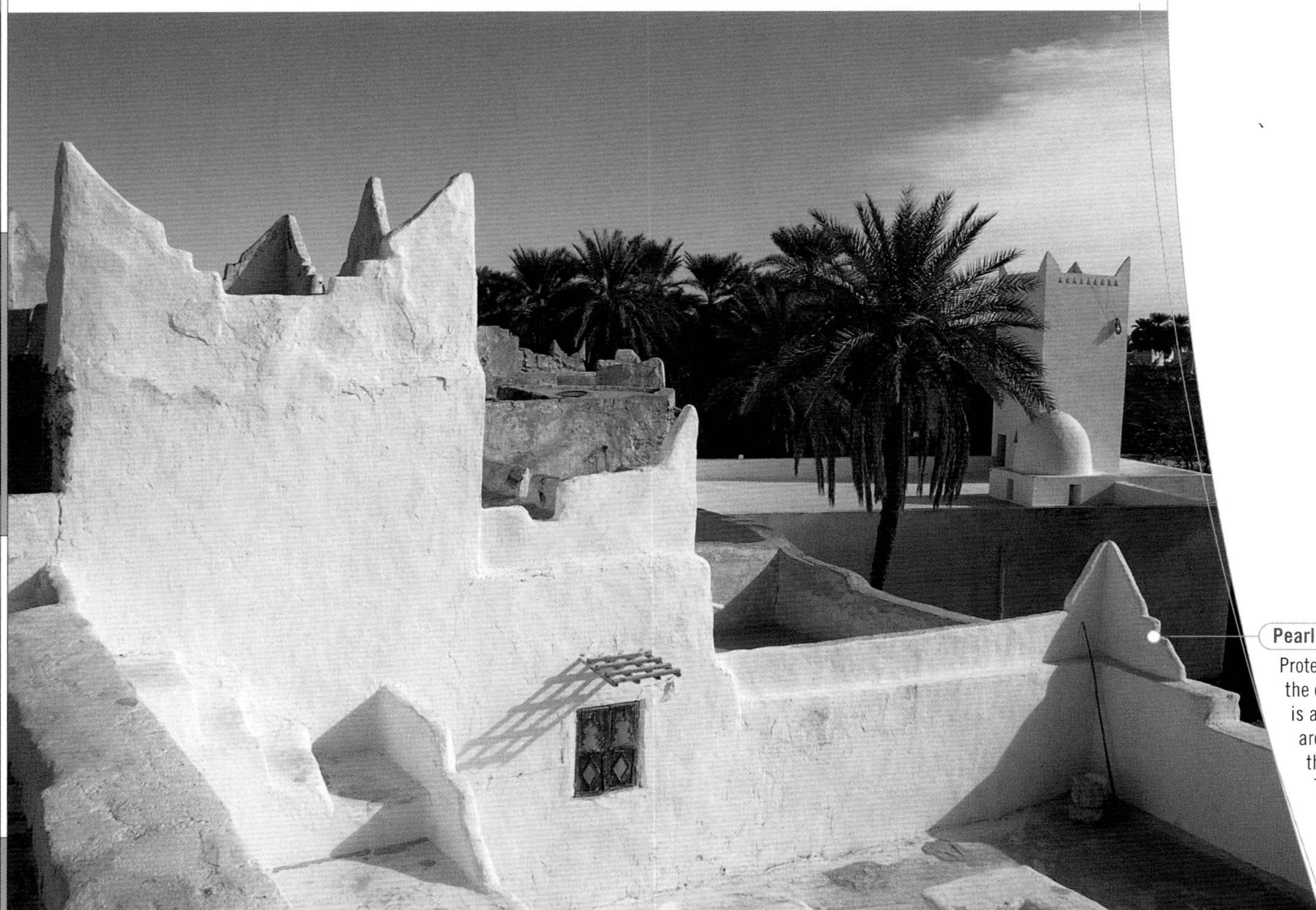

Pearl of the Desert

Protected by walls and towers, the city of **Ghadames (32)** is a masterpiece of Saharan architecture located along one of the trans-Sahara caravan routes. The three-story houses are connected by terraces — the women's realm.

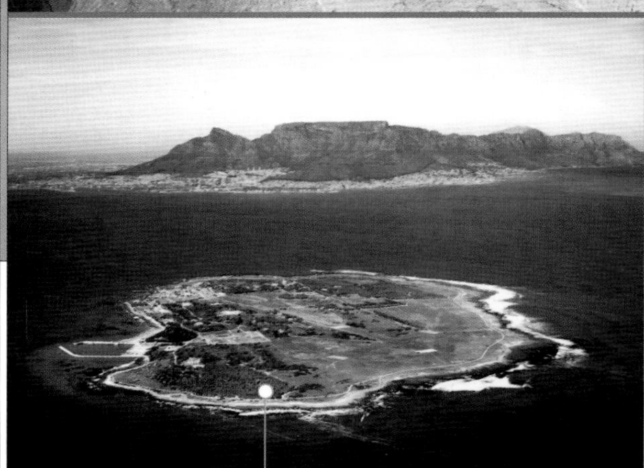

Triumph of Will

From the 17th century until 1996, **Robben Island (86),** located eight miles from Cape Town, was used as a whaling station, a camp for lepers and the mentally ill, a military base (World War II), and a penitentiary. Nelson Mandela was confined to the maximum security wing of the prison for 18 years and forced to work in the limestone quarry. The island is now an outdoor museum of human rights and one of the most popular tourist attractions on the Cape.

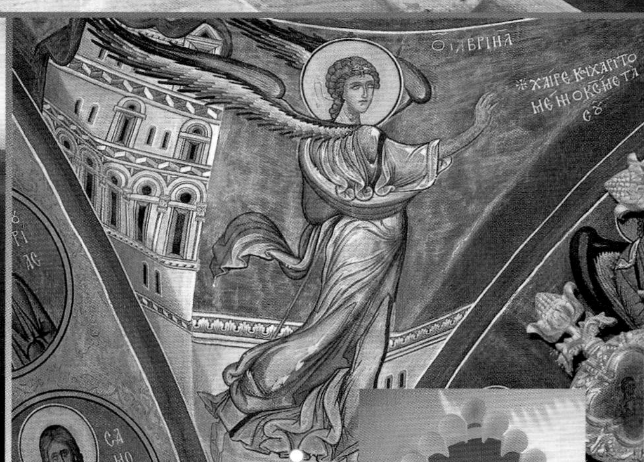

Treasures of Byzantine Art

Nowhere else are so many outstanding examples of Byzantine painting concentrated in a single region than in the **Troodos Mountains (42)** of Cyprus. The Archangel of Lagoudera (1192) is a particularly elegant work.

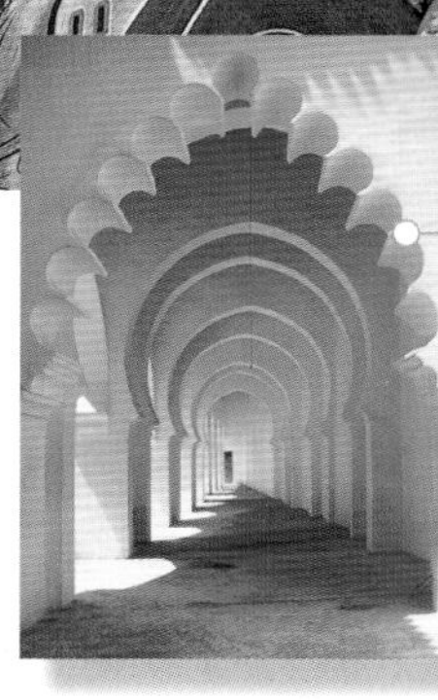

Puristic Islam

The Kutubiya Mosque (built between 1157 and 1197) is located in the pentagonal Medina of **Marrakesh (12).** The early purism of the Almohad Dynasty is evident in the emphatic formal simplicity of the horseshoe arches in the prayer hall.

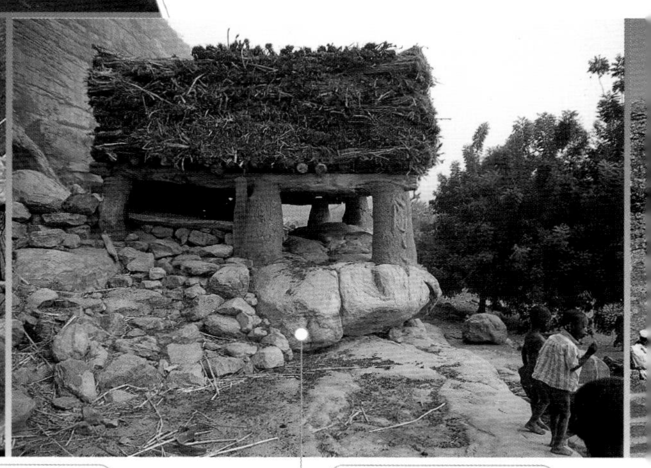

Dogon Religious Shrines

The **Cliffs of Bandiagara (6)** in Mali/Burkina Faso are home to the Dogons. Their rich cultural tradition is based upon a complex mythology of creation. Dogon shrines are built among the cliffs. The photo shows the house of the Hogon, the village religious leader.

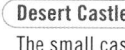

Desert Castle

The small castle of **Quseir Amra (69)** east of Amman, which dates from the Umayyad Dynasty (c. 715) features a splendidly furnished audience hall and luxurious baths.

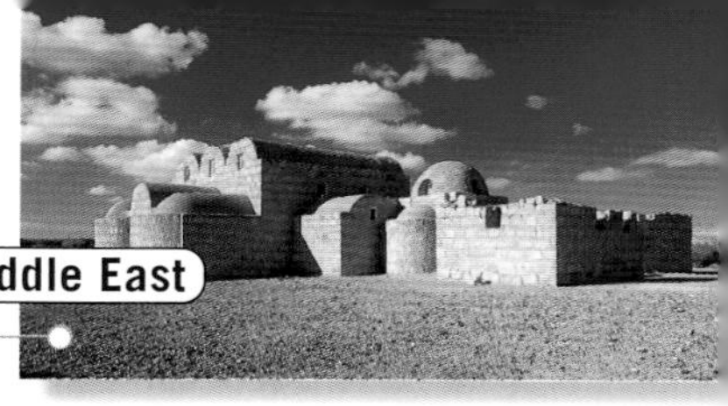

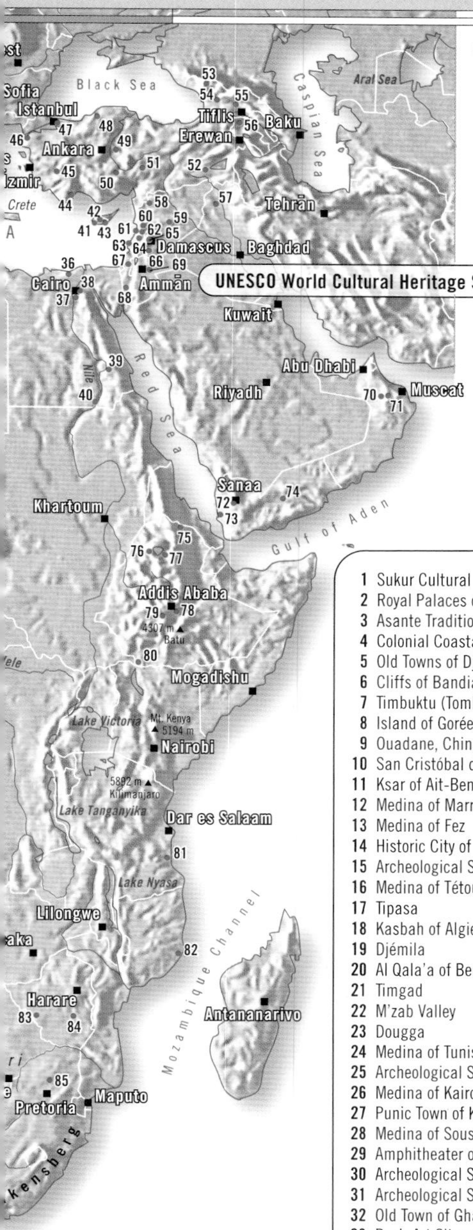

UNESCO World Cultural Heritage Sites in Africa and the Middle East

1 Sukur Cultural Landscape
2 Royal Palaces of Abomey
3 Asante Traditional Buildings
4 Colonial Coastal Forts
5 Old Towns of Djenné
6 Cliffs of Bandiagara
7 Timbuktu (Tombouctou)
8 Island of Gorée
9 Ouadane, Chinguetti, Tichitt and Oualata
10 San Cristóbal de La Laguna
11 Ksar of Aït-Ben-Haddou
12 Medina of Marrakesh
13 Medina of Fez
14 Historic City of Meknes
15 Archeological Site of Volubilis
16 Medina of Tétouan
17 Tipasa
18 Kasbah of Algiers
19 Djémila
20 Al Qala'a of Beni Hammad
21 Timgad
22 M'zab Valley
23 Dougga
24 Medina of Tunis
25 Archeological Site of Carthage
26 Medina of Kairouan
27 Punic Town of Kerkuane
28 Medina of Sousse
29 Amphitheater of El Jem
30 Archeological Site of Sabratha
31 Archeological Site of Leptis Magna
32 Old Town of Ghadames
33 Rock-Art Sites of Tassili n'Ajjer
34 Rock-Art Sites of Tadrart Acacus
35 Archeological Site of Cyrene
36 Abu Mena
37 Memphis and its Necropolis and Pyramids
38 Islamic Cairo
39 Ancient Thebes (Luxor)
40 Nubian Monuments from Abu Simbel to Philae

41 Paphos
42 Painted Churches in the Troodos Region
43 Neolithic Settlement of Choirokoitia
44 Xanthos-Letoon
45 Hieropolis-Pamukkale
46 Archeological Site of Troy
47 Historic Areas of Istanbul
48 City of Safranbolu
49 Hattusha
50 Göreme National Park and the Rock Sites of Cappadocia
51 Great Mosque and Hospital of Divriği
52 Nemrut Dağ
53 Mountain Villages in Svaneti
54 Bagrati Cathedral and Gelati Monastery
55 Historic Churches of Mtskheta
56 Monasteries of Haghbat and Sanahin
57 Hatra
58 Ancient City of Aleppo
59 Site of Palmyra
60 Quadi Qadisha and the Forest of the Cedars of God
61 Byblos
62 Baalbek
63 Tyre
64 Anjar
65 Ancient City of Damascus
66 Ancient City of Bosra
67 Old City of Jerusalem and its Walls
68 Petra
69 Quseir Amra
70 Fort of Bahla
71 Archeological Sites of Bat, Al-Khutm and Al-Ayn
72 Old City of Sanaa
73 Medina of Zabid
74 Old Walled City of Shibam
75 Aksum
76 Fasil Ghebbi, Gondar Region
77 Rock-hewn Churches of Lalibela
78 Lower Awash Valley
79 Tiya
80 Lower Omo Valley
81 Ruins of Kilwa Kisiwani and Songo Mnara
82 Island of Mozambique
83 Khami Ruins
84 Great Zimbabwe
85 Fossil Hominid Sites of Sterkfontein, Swartkrans and Kromdraai
86 Robben Island

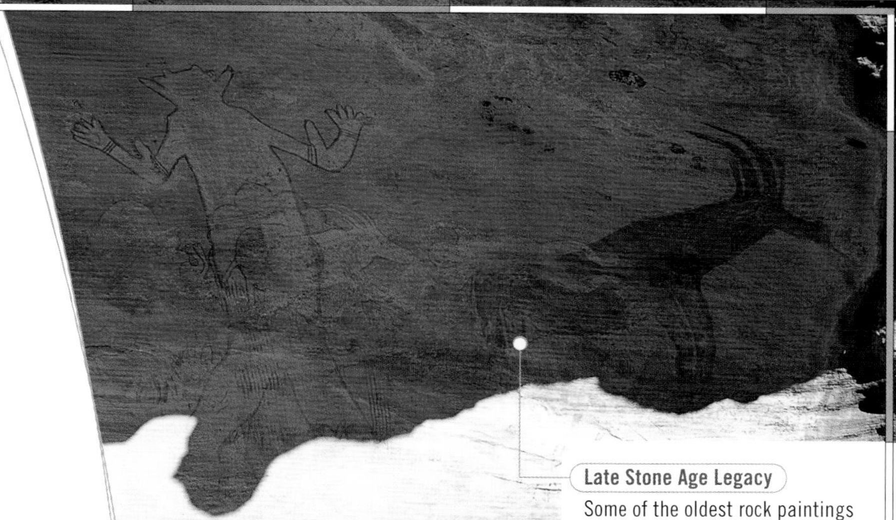

Late Stone Age Legacy

Some of the oldest rock paintings in the central Sahara are monumental works of static art. A prime example is the mysterious "Rain God Fresco" of Sefar in the **Tassili n'Ajjer (33)**.

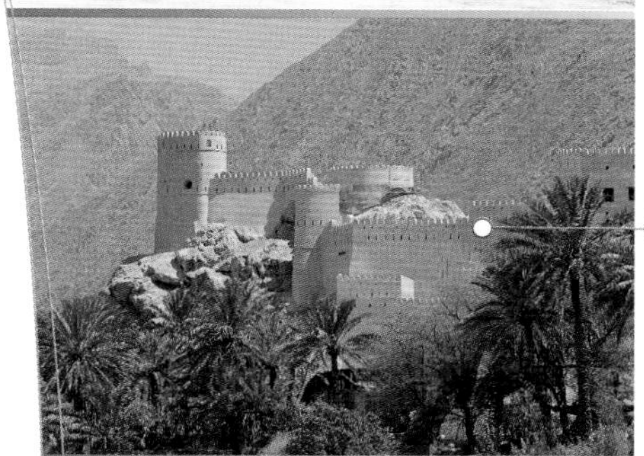

Loam Fortress

Built primarily of loam and straw, the fortress of **Bahla (70)** has towers as high as 50 m. Parts of the complex date back to pre-Islamic times. Bahla was the capital of the Sultanate of Oman at several different points in history.

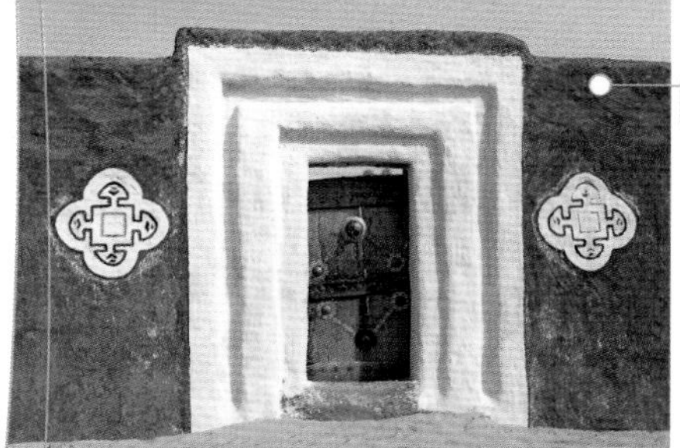

City in Ruins with a Living Artistic Tradition

A dying city today, the former trading metropolis of **Oualata (9)** on the southern edge of the Sahara is still regarded as a center of Islamic scholarship. Some of the stone buildings covered with red loam are adorned with highly symbolic ornaments.

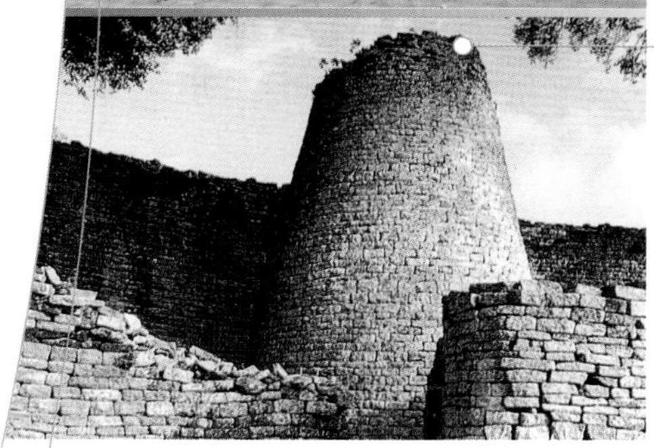

Ancient Granite Seat of Kings

The largest stone architectural complex produced by black African cultures is **Great Zimbabwe (84)**, which means "houses of stone." Built of granite blocks fitted precisely without mortared joints, the massive ring of walls bears witness to the might of the Shona Kings of the 15th century. The solid, cone-shaped stone tower resembles the grain silos used by Shona farmers.

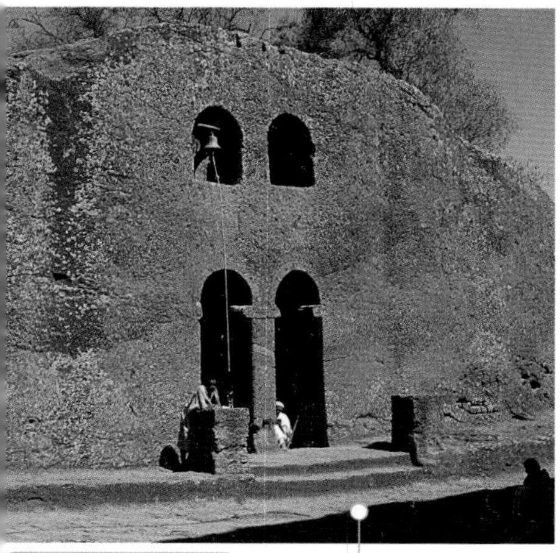

Brilliant Architecture

The **Rock Churches of Lalibela (77)** were hewn from the exposed red tuff of the Ethiopian Plateau around 1200 AD. As imitations of existing architecture, they exhibit influences from the Byzantine and ancient Aksum civilizations.

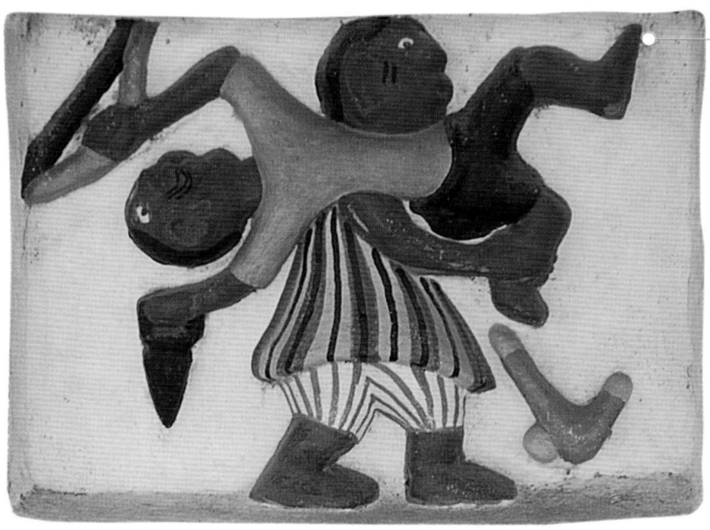

Victorious Amazons

The kingdom of Dahomey rose to affluence and power (supported by a well-trained professional army) in the 17th century. The bas-relief on the walls of the **Royal Palace of Abomey (2)** commemorates the Amazon Corps.

To What Extent Is the World Cultural Heritage Endangered? The "Red List"

In addition to the World Heritage List, the World Heritage Committee maintains a list of endangered sites – properties in need of special attention and preservation efforts. The purpose of this list is to make both governments and the pubic aware of the natural and anthropogenic dangers to which World Heritage Sites are exposed.

The list of endangered properties currently contains 27 World Heritage Sites, among them the Natural and Cultural Region of Kotor (Yugoslavia), which was shaken by an earthquake in 1979, the Royal Palace of Abomey (Benin), which suffered serious hurricane damage in 1985, the sacred temples of Timbuktu (Mali), which are beset by the destructive forces of the desert, and the monuments of Hampi (India), which are threatened by road and bridge construction.

The World Heritage Committee collaborates with individual governments in preparing an action plan for endangered sites. It provides financial support and monitors the progress of work, which usually takes considerable time. Some countries seek the Committee's help for their problems, while others tend to resent such intervention. One of the few sites that has been restored and deleted from the list is Dubrovnik (Croatia).

UNESCO World Cultural Heritage from Asia to Australia

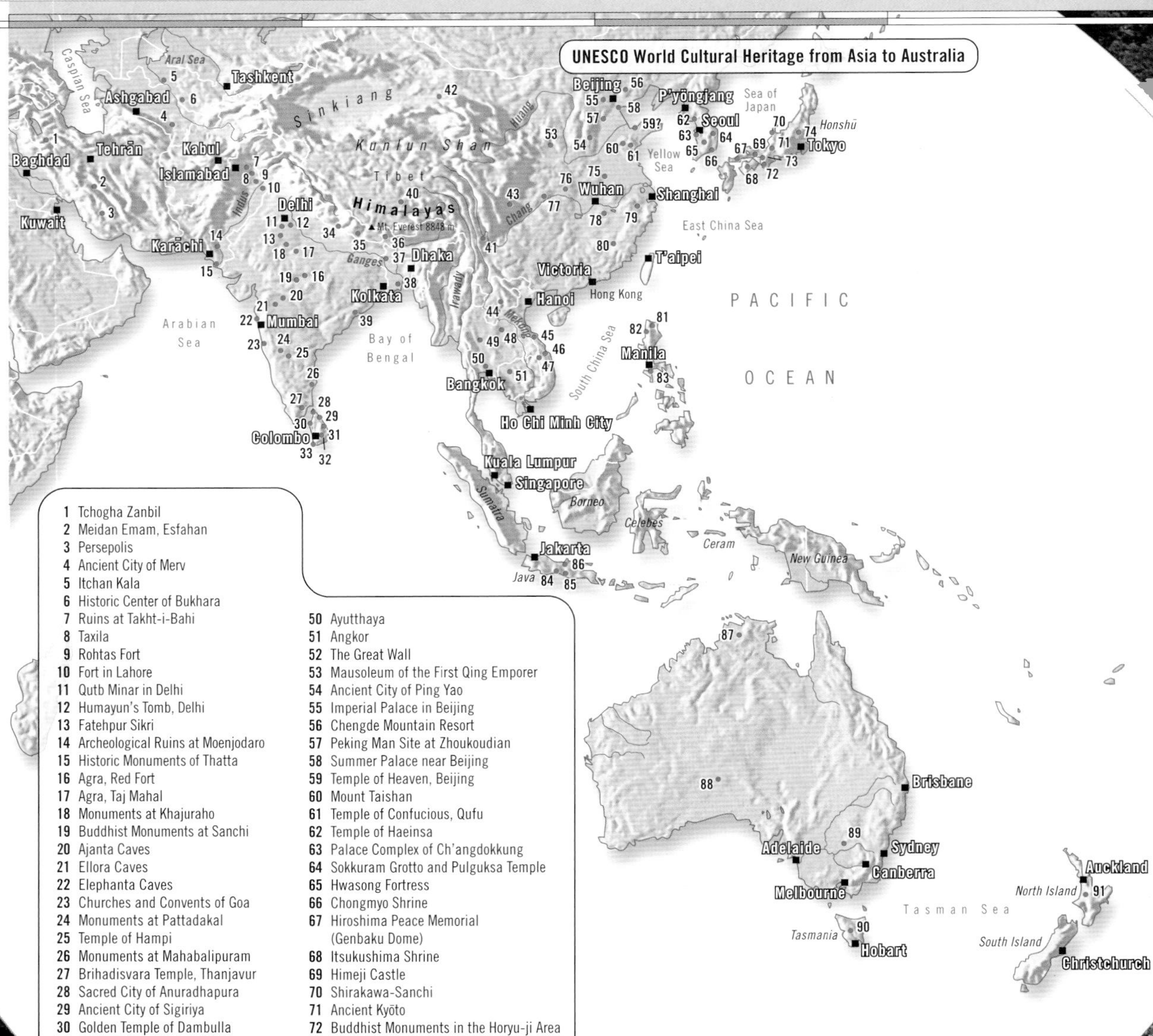

1 Tchogha Zanbil
2 Meidan Emam, Esfahan
3 Persepolis
4 Ancient City of Merv
5 Itchan Kala
6 Historic Center of Bukhara
7 Ruins at Takht-i-Bahi
8 Taxila
9 Rohtas Fort
10 Fort in Lahore
11 Qutb Minar in Delhi
12 Humayun's Tomb, Delhi
13 Fatehpur Sikri
14 Archeological Ruins at Moenjodaro
15 Historic Monuments of Thatta
16 Agra, Red Fort
17 Agra, Taj Mahal
18 Monuments at Khajuraho
19 Buddhist Monuments at Sanchi
20 Ajanta Caves
21 Ellora Caves
22 Elephanta Caves
23 Churches and Convents of Goa
24 Monuments at Pattadakal
25 Temple of Hampi
26 Monuments at Mahabalipuram
27 Brihadisvara Temple, Thanjavur
28 Sacred City of Anuradhapura
29 Ancient City of Sigiriya
30 Golden Temple of Dambulla
31 Ancient City of Polonnaruwa
32 Sacred City of Kandy
33 Old Town of Galle
34 Lumbini
35 Valley of Kathmandu
36 Darjeeling Himalayan Railway
37 Paharpur
38 Historic Mosque City of Bagerhat
39 Sun Temple of Konarak
40 Potala Palace in Lhasa
41 Old Town of Lijiang
42 Mogao Caves
43 Mt. Emei Scenic Area and Giant Buddha of Leshan
44 Luang Prabang
45 Hue
46 Hoi An Ancient Town
47 My Son Sanctuary
48 Ban Chiang
49 Sukhothai

50 Ayutthaya
51 Angkor
52 The Great Wall
53 Mausoleum of the First Qing Emperor
54 Ancient City of Ping Yao
55 Imperial Palace in Beijing
56 Chengde Mountain Resort
57 Peking Man Site at Zhoukoudian
58 Summer Palace near Beijing
59 Temple of Heaven, Beijing
60 Mount Taishan
61 Temple of Confucious, Qufu
62 Temple of Haeinsa
63 Palace Complex of Ch'angdokkung
64 Sokkuram Grotto and Pulguksa Temple
65 Hwasong Fortress
66 Chongmyo Shrine
67 Hiroshima Peace Memorial (Genbaku Dome)
68 Itsukushima Shrine
69 Himeji Castle
70 Shirakawa-Sanchi
71 Ancient Kyōto
72 Buddhist Monuments in the Horyu-ji Area
73 Ancient Nara
74 Shrines and Temples of Nikko
75 Classical Gardens of Suzhou
76 Ancient Buildings in the Wudang Mountains
77 Dazu Rock Carvings
78 Lushan National Park
79 Mount Huangshan
80 Mount Wuyi
81 Rice Terraces of the Ifugao
82 Historic Town of Vigan
83 Baroque Churches of the Philippines
84 Borobudur Temple Compounds
85 Prambanan Temple Compounds
86 Sangiran Early Man Site
87 Kakadu National Park
88 Uluru-Kata Tjuta National Park
89 Willandra Lakes Region
90 Tasmanian Wilderness
91 Tongariro National Park

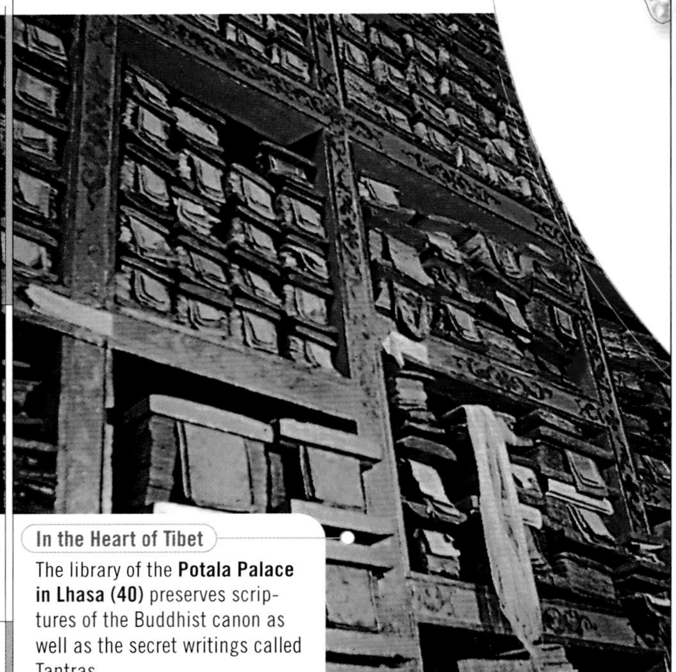

In the Heart of Tibet

The library of the **Potala Palace in Lhasa (40)** preserves scriptures of the Buddhist canon as well as the secret writings called Tantras.

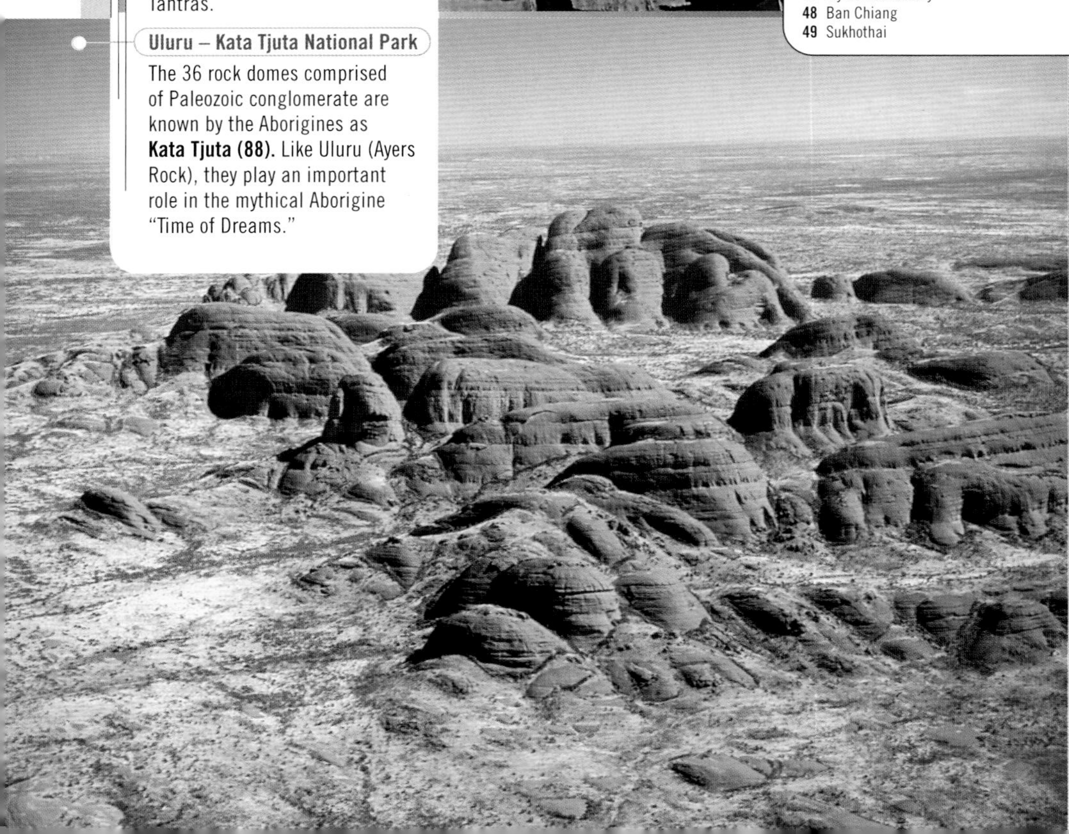

Uluru – Kata Tjuta National Park

The 36 rock domes comprised of Paleozoic conglomerate are known by the Aborigines as **Kata Tjuta (88)**. Like Uluru (Ayers Rock), they play an important role in the mythical Aborigine "Time of Dreams."

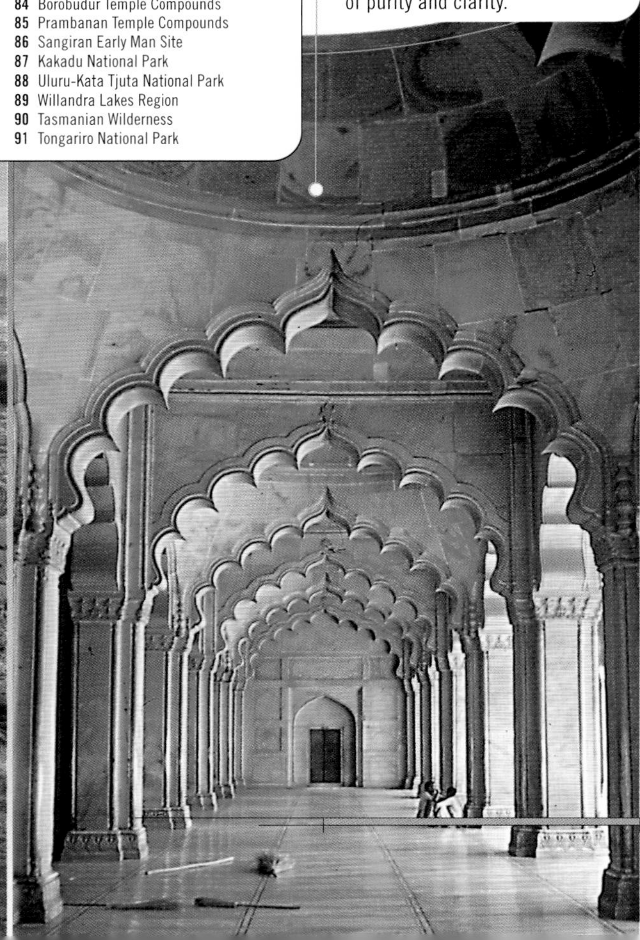

Classical Mogul Architecture

The **Red Fort (16)** of Agra comprises the Pearl Mosque (built between 1648 and 1654). The restrained decoration creates an impression of purity and clarity.

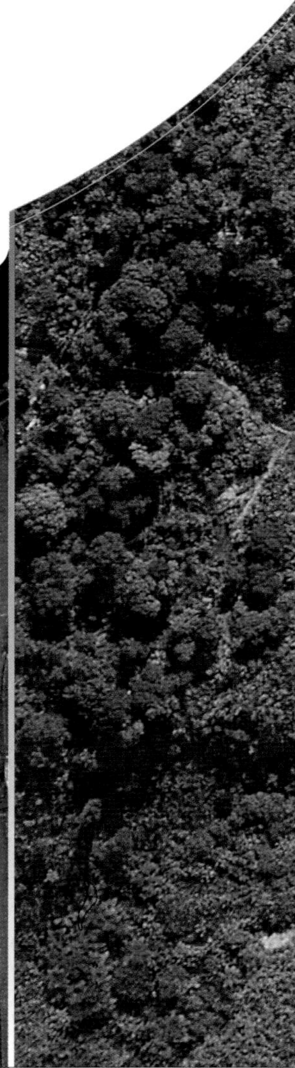

Ancient Stupa

The Dharmarajika stupa near **Taxila (8)**, originally a dome-shaped brick structure decorated with reliefs, dates to the 2nd century BC.

A Library of Wood

The repository of the **Tripitaka Koreana (62)** (13th c.) at the temple of Haeinsa near Taegu provides natural air-conditioning for the more than 81,000 wooden printing blocks, testaments of extraordinary craftsmanship.

Camels for the King

The relief on the eastern stairs of the great reception hall in **Persepolis (3)** shows Darius the Great receiving gifts.

The World's Largest Terrace System

The **Rice Terraces of the Ifugao (81)** are situated on steep mountain slopes in the northern part of the island of Luzon. Reaching heights of up to 15 meters, many of the heavy walls of stone, support terraces of only three meters wide.

Buddha Calls Upon the Earth Goddess

The sacred shrine of Wat Mahathat, containing sculptures from the 13th and 14th centuries, is located in the heart of the historic town of **Sukhothai (49)**.

Ensemble of Bay, Island, and Shrine

The island of Miyajima in the Japanese inland sea is the site of a Shinto shrine built in the 6th and 7th centuries. Pilgrims arrived from the mainland (Hiroshima) at the foot of the **Itsukushima Shrine (68)** in boats. Only 160 meters from the shore, the entrance gate is submerged at high tide.

Towering Faces

The center of the Khmer Kingdom from the 9th to the 15th century, **Angkor (51)** boasted not only an unparalleled urban architecture complemented by artificial lakes but a magnificent array of ornamentation on all exterior facades.

Measured Rhythm

The majestic roofs of the halls of the **Imperial Palace in Beijing (55)** are aligned along the main axis of the palace.

Perspectives for the World Heritage Convention

Armed conflict ranks highest among the many dangers to which the cultural heritage is exposed. The impact of industrialization and urban development is also significant. Air pollution threatens building substance, tourism detracts from the authenticity of cultural sites, and the dynamics of technical and economic progress often impair the integrity of traditional cultural treasures.

Can Tourists Save the World Cultural Heritage?

Can the goal of protecting monuments of the World Cultural Heritage be achieved without neglecting the needs of people who live near them? It is not enough merely to list the necessary protective measures. It is equally important to consider marketing issues and to respond to the wishes and expectations of visitors. This applies in particular to the cultural landscape, the youngest category of the World Heritage List. The "sustainable cultural landscape" is classified as a region in which change must take place in order to ensure that its inhabitants can continue to live normal lives. But which elements of a cultural landscape can be changed without detracting from their outstanding character, and which must be preserved unaltered? The field of possibilities is broad.

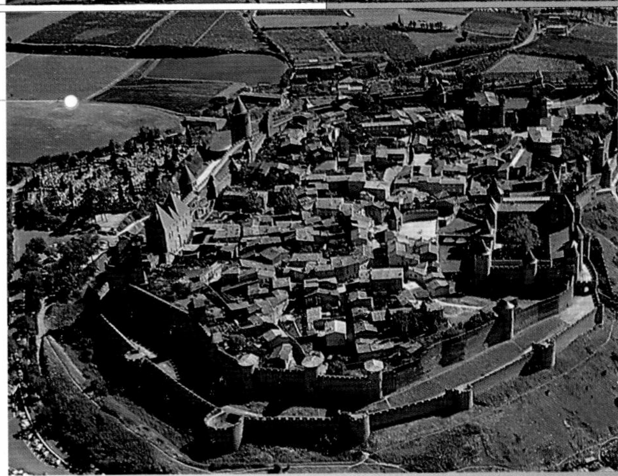

Catharist Bastion

Fortified by two rings of walls, the medieval city of **Carcassonne (38)** crowns a hill above the Aude Valley. Situated along a route from the Atlantic to the Mediterranean, its position was of strategic importance during periods of Muslim and Frankish occupation. It was captured after a long siege during the Albigensian Wars in 1209.

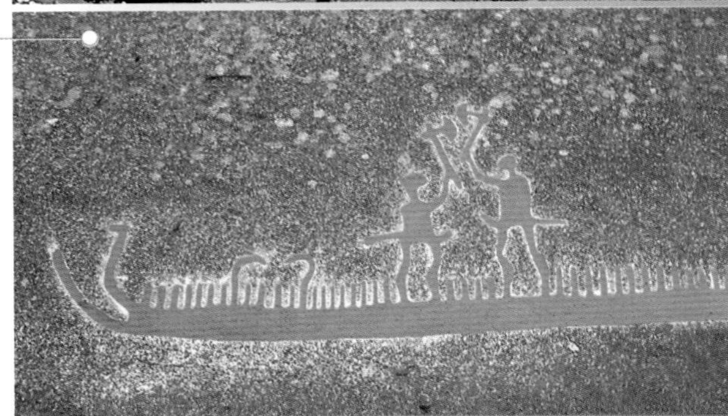

Mysterious Religious Ritual

Rock drawing of a ship and two axe-wielding warriors from the Nordic Bronze Age in **Tanum (241)**, southern Sweden.

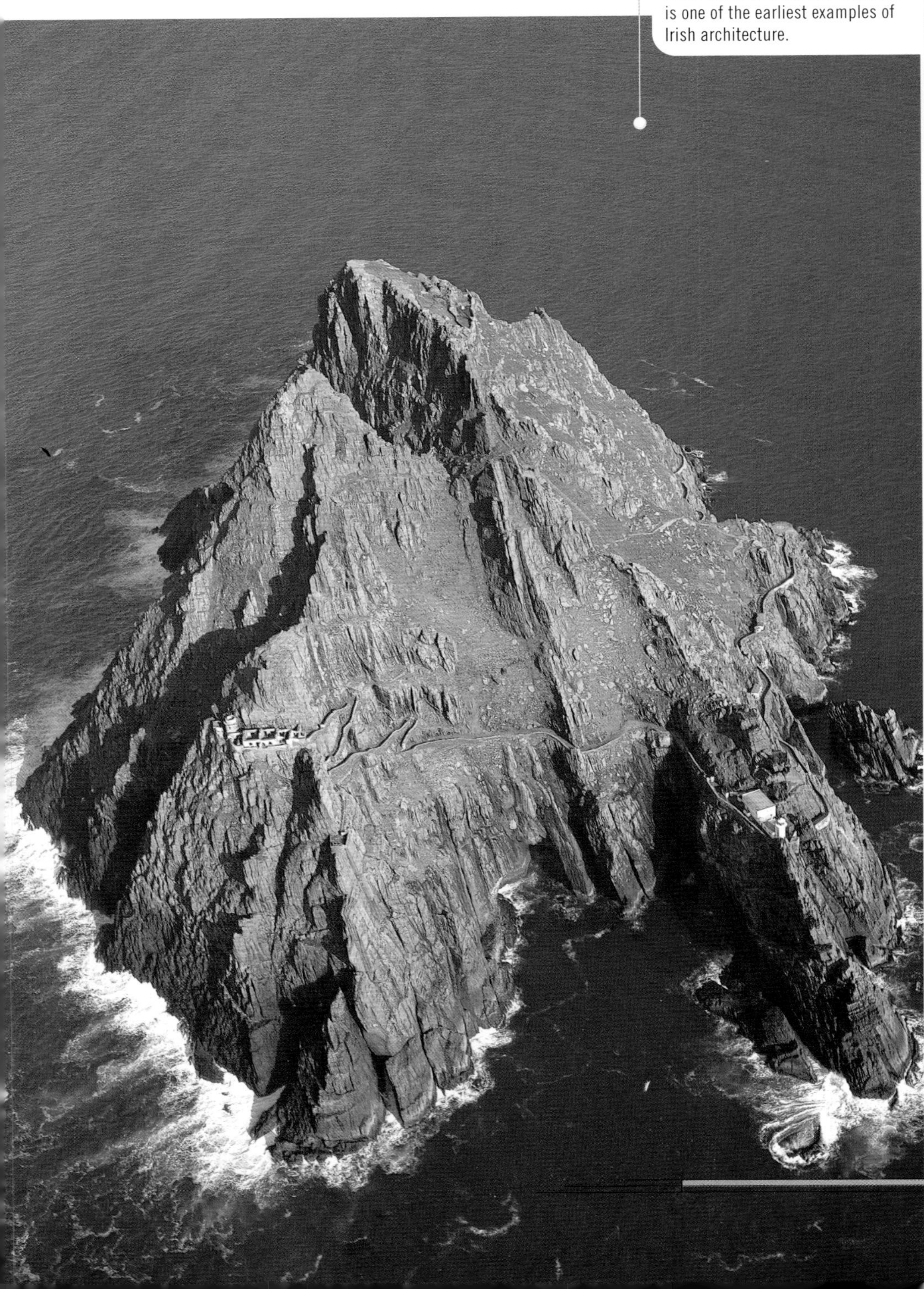

Early Christian Refuge

The rocky island of **Skellig Michael (86)** and ruins of the cloister of Saint Finan (9th c.). The structure is one of the earliest examples of Irish architecture.

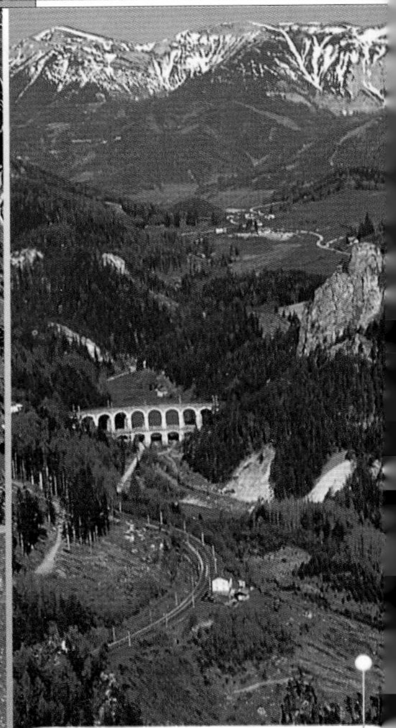

Europe's First Mountain Railway

With many tunnels and viaducts, the **Semmering Railway (121)** crosses Semmering Pass (elevation: 985 m) between Lower Austria and the Steiermark. Built between 1848 and 1854, the line is a true adhesion railway with a maximum incline of 2.5%.

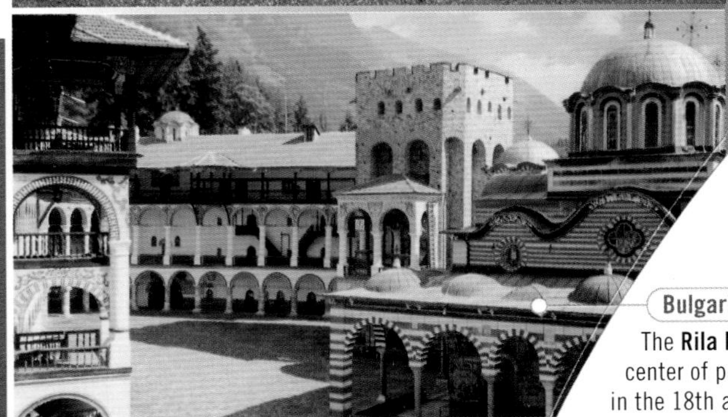

Bulgarian Renaissance Castle

The **Rila Monastery (181)** was a center of painting and literature in the 18th and 19th centuries and played an important role in the growth of a national identity. Thick, high external walls give the complex the look of a fortress.

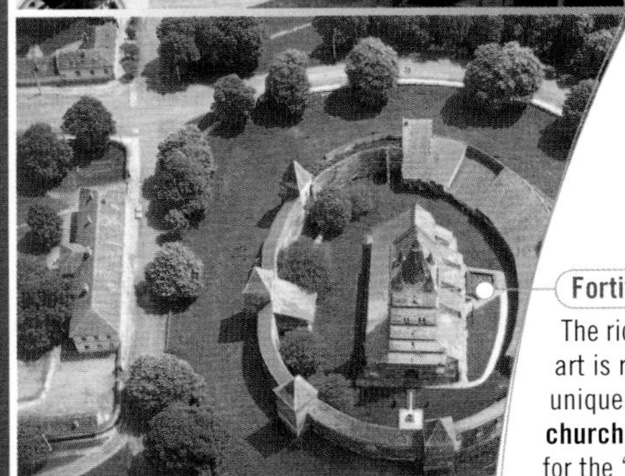

Fortified Religious Architecture

The rich heritage of Transylvanian art is represented by a number of unique churches. These **fortified churches (195)** offered protection for the "Saxons" who settled in the border region. The choir tower was the defensive core of the complex.

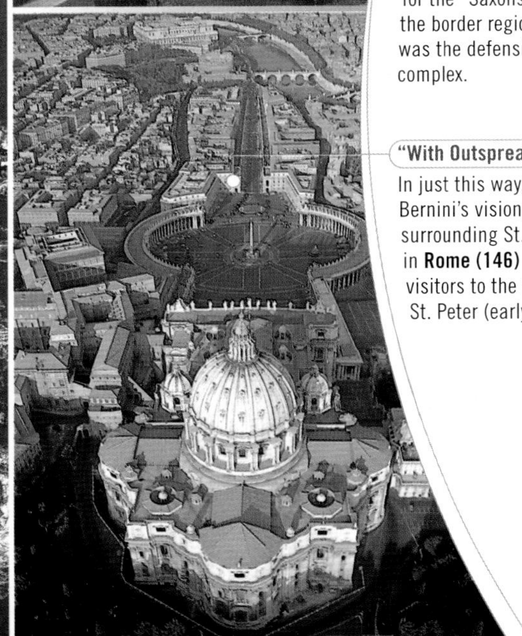

"With Outspread Arms"

In just this way, according to Bernini's vision, the collonades surrounding St. Peter's Square in **Rome (146)** were to welcome visitors to the new Basilica of St. Peter (early 17th c.).

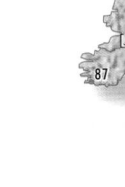

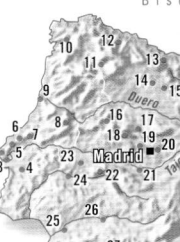

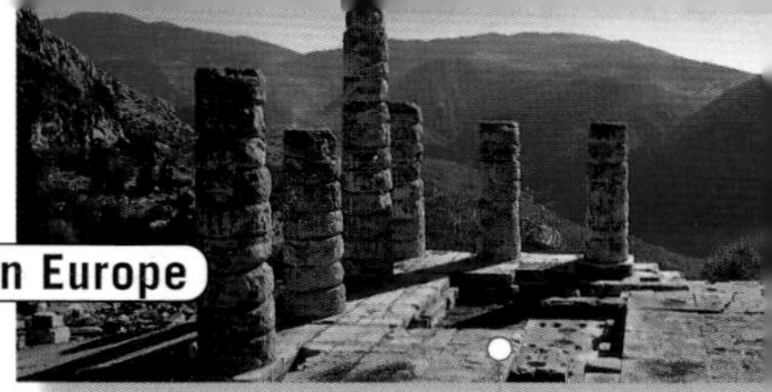

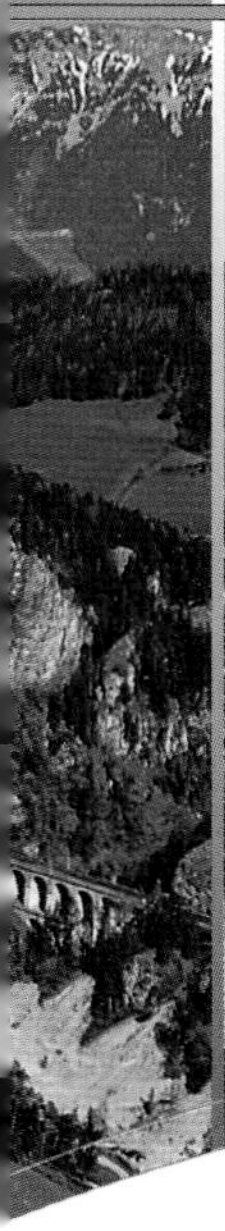

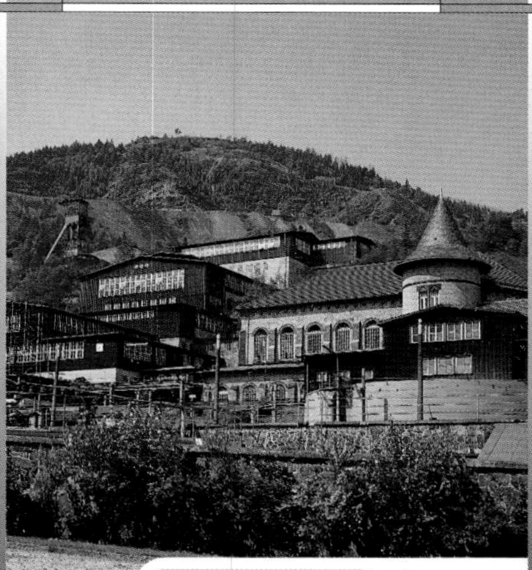

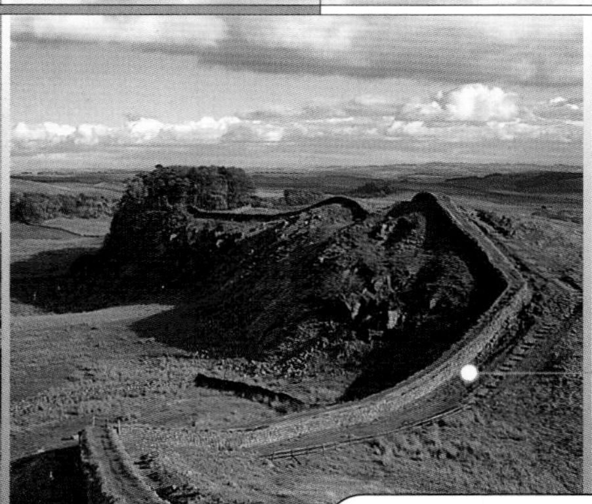

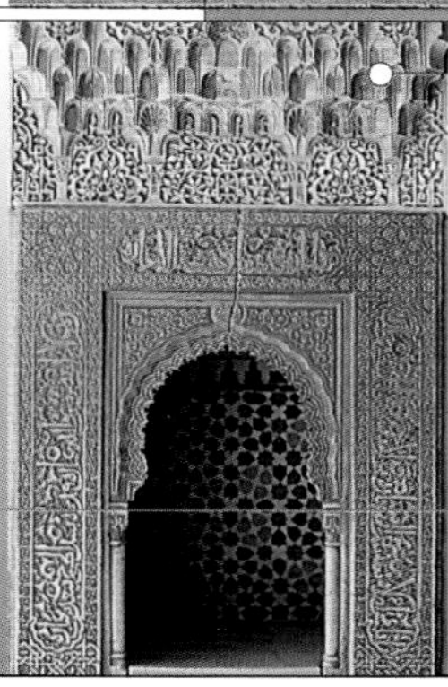

Moorish Art in Perfection

The architecture of the **Alhambra of Granada (27)** is less striking than its decorative embellishments. The intricate ornamentation of even a small niche bears witness to a tendency toward a dematerialization of objective representation.

Ancient Greek Religious Site

The Oracle of the Temple of Apollo at **Delphi (173)** was consulted by pilgrims about the prospects for success in business or political endeavors.

Northern Boundary of the Roman Empire

The borders of the empire were expanded and fortified to form a permanent defense line under Roman Emperor Hadrian.
The photo shows part of **Hadrian's Wall (82)** in northern England.

Unique Silver Mines

The **Rammelsberg Mines (108)** in the Harz Mountains is the only mine complex in the world that boasts 1,000 years of continuous operation. They were closed in 1988. A shaft from the 12th century is well preserved.

UNESCO World Cultural Heritage Sites in Europe

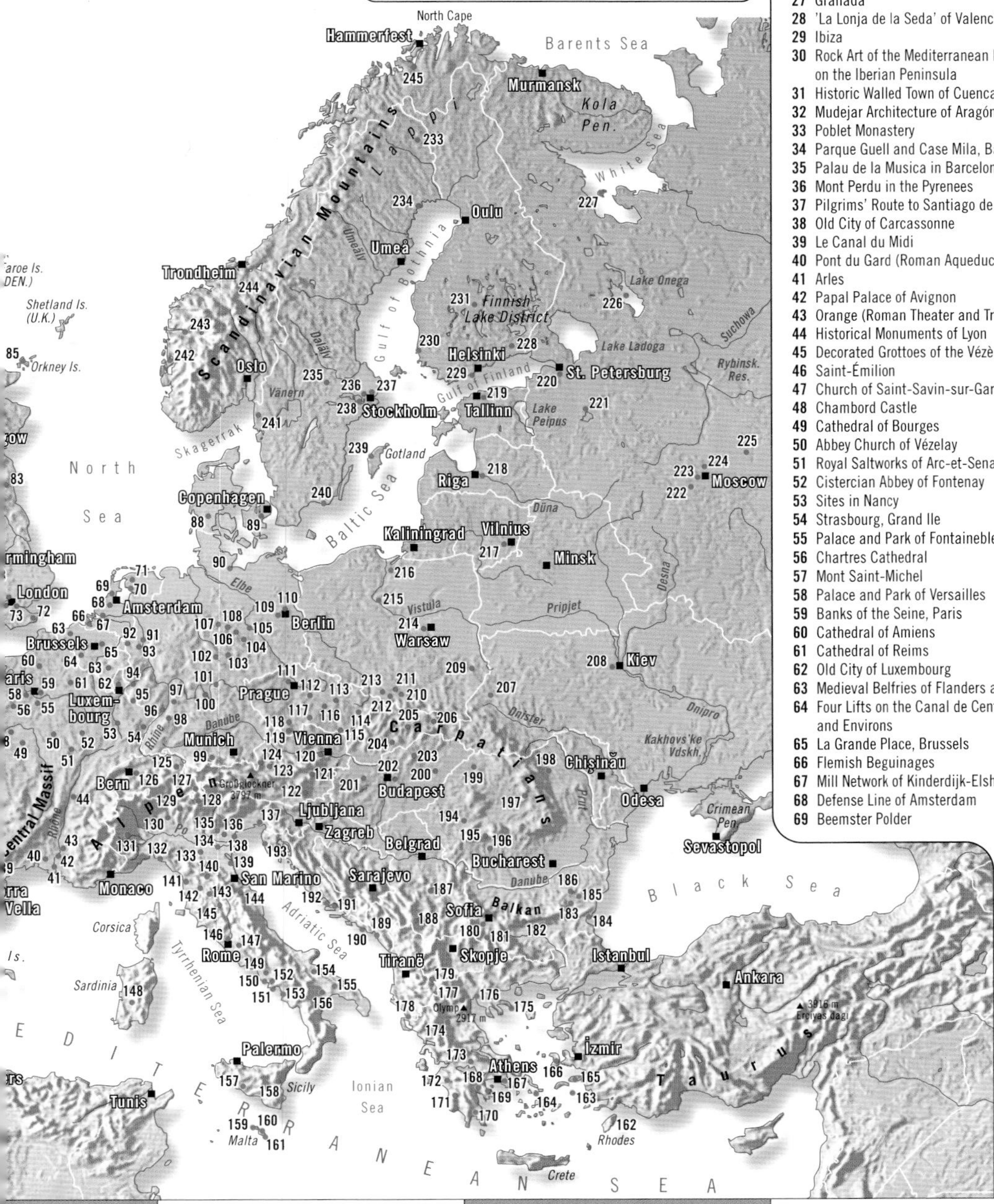

1 City Center of Angra do Heroismo, Azores (not shown on map)
2 Cultural Landscape of Sintra
3 Hieronymite Monastery and Tower of Belem
4 Historic Center of Evora
5 Alcobaca Monastery
6 Batalha Monastery
7 Convent of Christ in Tomar
8 Rock-Art Sites in the Coa Valley
9 Historic Center of Porto
10 Historic Center of Santiago de Compostela
11 Las Medulas
12 Churches of the Kingdom of the Asturias
13 Altamira Cave
14 Cathedral of Burgos
15 San Millan Yuso and Suso Monasteries
16 Old Town of Salamanca
17 Old Town of Segovia, including its aqueduct
18 Old Town of Ávila
19 El Escorial
20 Historic Precinct of Alcalá de Henares
21 Historic City of Toledo
22 Royal Monastery of Santa Maria de Guadalupe
23 Old Town of Cáceres
24 Roman Buildings in Mérida
25 Cathedral and Alcazar in Seville
26 Mosque of Córdoba
27 Granada
28 'La Lonja de la Seda' of Valencia
29 Ibiza
30 Rock Art of the Mediterranean Basin on the Iberian Peninsula
31 Historic Walled Town of Cuenca
32 Mudejar Architecture of Aragón
33 Poblet Monastery
34 Parque Guell and Case Mila, Barcelona
35 Palau de la Musica in Barcelona
36 Mont Perdu in the Pyrenees
37 Pilgrims' Route to Santiago de Compostela
38 Old City of Carcassonne
39 Le Canal du Midi
40 Pont du Gard (Roman Aqueduct)
41 Arles
42 Papal Palace of Avignon
43 Orange (Roman Theater and Triumphal Arch)
44 Historical Monuments of Lyon
45 Decorated Grottoes of the Vézère Valley
46 Saint-Émilion
47 Church of Saint-Savin-sur-Gartempe
48 Chambord Castle
49 Cathedral of Bourges
50 Abbey Church of Vézelay
51 Royal Saltworks of Arc-et-Senans
52 Cistercian Abbey of Fontenay
53 Sites in Nancy
54 Strasbourg, Grand Ile
55 Palace and Park of Fontainebleau
56 Chartres Cathedral
57 Mont Saint-Michel
58 Palace and Park of Versailles
59 Banks of the Seine, Paris
60 Cathedral of Amiens
61 Cathedral of Reims
62 Old City of Luxembourg
63 Medieval Belfries of Flanders and Wallonia
64 Four Lifts on the Canal de Centre and Environs
65 La Grande Place, Brussels
66 Flemish Beguinages
67 Net Network of Kinderdijk-Elshout
68 Defense Line of Amsterdam
69 Beemster Polder
70 Shokland and Environs
71 Steam Pump Plant in Wouda
72 Canterbury Cathedral
73 Royal Greenwich Park
74 Westminster Abbey and Church of St. Margaret, London
75 Tower of London
76 Stonehenge and Avebury
77 Bath
78 Blenheim Palace
79 Industrial Monuments in Ironbridge Valley
80 Fortifications of Edward I in Wales
81 Fountains Abbey
82 Hadrian's Wall
83 Castle and Cathedral in Durham
84 Edinburgh
85 Orkney Islands
86 Skelling Michael
87 Bend of the Boyne
88 Jelling Mounds
89 Roskilde Cathedral
90 Hanseatic City of Lübeck
91 Cologne Cathedral
92 Roman Monuments, Cathedral and Church in Trier
93 Castles in Brühl
94 Aachen Cathedral
95 Völklingen Ironworks
96 Speyer Cathedral
97 Abbey and Altenmünster of Lorsch
98 Maulbronn Monastery Complex
99 Pilgrimage Church of Wies
100 Residence in Würzburg
101 Old Town of Bamberg
102 Wartburg Castle
103 Classical Weimar
104 Luther Memorials in Eisleben and Wittenberg
105 Bauhaus Sites in Weimar and Dessau
106 Historic Sites in Quedlinburg
107 St. Mary's Cathedral and St. Michaels Church, Hildesheim
108 Mines of Rammelsberg and the Historic Town of Goslar
109 Palaces and Parks in Potsdam and Berlin
110 Museum Island, Berlin
111 Historic Center of Prague
112 Historic Center of Kutná Hora
113 Litomysl Castle
114 Gardens and Castle at Kroměříž
115 Lednice-Caltice Cultural Landscape
116 Pilgrimage Church at Zelen Hora in Žd'ár nad Sázavou
117 Historic Center of Telč
118 Holasovice Historical Village Reservation
119 Historic Center of Krumau
120 Palace and Gardens of Schönbrunn
121 Semmering Railway
122 Old City of Graz
123 Salzkammergut Cultural Landscape
124 Historic Center, City of Salzburg
125 Convent of St. Gallen
126 Old City of Bern
127 Convent of St. John at Müstair
128 Rock Drawings in Valcamonica
129 Crespi d'Adda
130 Santa Maria delle Grazie in Milan
131 Residences of the Royal House of Savoy
132 Portovenere and Cinque Terre
133 Cathedral and Piazza Grande, Modena
134 Ferrara
135 Vicenza, City of Palladio and Villas on the Veneto
136 Botanical Gardens, Padua
137 Aquileia
138 Venice
139 Early Christian Monuments and Mosaics of Ravenna
140 Historic Center of Florence
141 Piazza del Duomo, Pisa
142 Historic Center of San Gimignano
143 Historic Center of Siena
144 Historic Center of Urbino
145 Historic Center of Pienza
146 Historic Center of Rome, the Properties of the Holy See, and San Paolo Fuori le Mura
147 Villa Adriana
148 Su Nuraxi di Barumini
149 Royal Palace at Caserta
150 Historic Center of Naples
151 Costiera Amalfitana
152 Archeological Areas of Pompeii and Ercolano
153 Paestum and Certosa di Pavia
154 Castel del Monte
155 Trulli of Alberobello
156 I Sassi di Matera
157 Agrigento
158 Roman Villa of Casale
159 Megalithic Temples of Malta
160 City of Valletta
161 Hal Saflieni Hypogeum
162 Medieval City of Rhodes
163 Historical Sites, Island of Patmos
164 Island of Delos
165 Pythagoreion and Hereion of Samos
166 Monuments of Chios
167 Acropolis, Athens
168 Archeological Sites of Mycenae and Tiryns
169 Archeological Site of Epidaurus
170 Mystras
171 Temple of Apollo at Bassae
172 Archeological Site of Olympia
173 Archeological Site of Delphi
174 Meteora
175 Mount Athos
176 Monuments of Thessalonika
177 Archeological Sites of Vergina
178 Butrint
179 City and Lake of Ohrid
180 Church of Boyana
181 Monatery of Rila
182 Thracian Tomb of Kazanlak
183 Rock-hewn Churches of Ivanovo
184 Ancient City of Nessebar
185 Madara Rider
186 Thracian Tomb of Sveshtari
187 Monastery of Studenica
188 Stari Ras and Sopocani Monastery
189 Natural and Culturo-Historic Region of Kotor
190 Old City of Dubrovnik
191 Historic Complex of Split
192 Historic City of Trogir
193 Historic Center of Porec
194 Dacian Fortresses in the Orastie Mountains
195 Fortified Churches in Transylvania
196 Horezu Monastery
197 Historic Center of Sighisoara
198 Churches of Moldavia
199 Wooden Churches of Maramures
200 Hortobágy National Park
201 Benedictine Monastery of Pannonhalma
202 Budapest
203 Hollokö
204 Banska Stiavnica
205 Vlkolinec Reservation of Folk Architecture
206 Spissky Hrad and Environs
207 Historic Center of L'viv
208 Kiev
209 Old City of Zamosc
210 Wieliczka Salt Mine
211 Historic Center of Kraków
212 Kalwaria Zebrzydowska
213 Auschwitz Concentration Camp
214 Historic Center of Warsaw
215 Medieval Town of Torun
216 Malbork
217 Historic Center of Vilnius
218 Historic Center of Riga
219 Historic Center of Tallinn
220 Historic Center of St. Petersburg
221 Historic Monuments in Novgorod and Surroundings
222 Church of Anscension, Kolomenskoye
223 Kremlin and Red Square, Moscow
224 Monastery in Sergiev Possad
225 White Monuments of Vladimir and Suzdal
226 Kizhi Pogost in Lake Onega
227 Cultural and Historic Ensemble of the Solovetsky Islands
228 Verla Groundwood and Board Mill
229 Fortress of Suomenlinna
230 Old Rauma
231 Petäjävesi Old Church
232 Burial Site of Sammallahdenmäki
233 Laponian Area
234 Old City of Luleå
235 Engelsberg Ironworks
236 Skogskrykogården
237 Royal Domain of Drottningholm
238 Birka and Hovgården
239 Hanseatic Town of Visby
240 Naval Port of Karlskrona
241 Rock Carvings in Tanum
242 Bryggen, Old Hanseatic Quater of Bergen
243 Urnes Stave Church
244 Røros Mining Town
245 Rock Drawings of Alta

Map labels

North Cape
Hammerfest
Barents Sea
Murmansk
Kola Pen.
Lapland
Scandinavian Mountains
White Sea
Oulu
Umeå
Trondheim
Faroe Is. (DEN.)
Shetland Is. (U.K.)
Orkney Is.
Finnish Lake District
Lake Onega
Suchona
Helsinki
Lake Ladoga
St. Petersburg
Rybinsk. Res.
Gulf of Bothnia
Oslo
Stockholm
Gulf of Finland
Tallinn
Lake Peipus
Glåma
Vänern
Skagerrak
Gotland
Riga
Dvina
Moscow
North Sea
Copenhagen
Baltic Sea
Kaliningrad
Vilnius
Minsk
Dnipro
Birmingham
Elbe
Berlin
Warsaw
Vistula
London
Amsterdam
Brussels
Luxembourg
Prague
Kiev
Paris
Munich
Vienna
Carpathians
Desna
Pripjet
Bern
Budapest
Chisinău
Odesa
Central Massif
Ljubljana
Zagreb
Belgrad
Crimean Pen.
Sevastopol
Alps
San Marino
Sarajevo
Bucharest
Danube
Black Sea
Monaco
Corsica
Rome
Tyrrhenian Sea
Adriatic Sea
Tiranë
Sofia
Balkan
Skopje
Istanbul
Ankara
Sardinia
Palermo
Sicily
Ionian Sea
Athens
Izmir
Taurus
Tunis
Malta
Crete
Rhodes
MEDITERRANEAN SEA

Global Urbanization

From Jericho to the Global City – The City as a Human Habitat?

Jericho and urban history are inseparably intertwined. Here, in the Jordan River Valley, the roots of urban culture can be traced back to the 7th millennium BC. But evidence of early city life can also be found beneath thousands of years of accumulated rubble in other parts of the world.

In the earliest phase in the history of cities, "city-dwellers" represented only a tiny segment of the world's population (estimated at roughly 80 million around the year 1000 BC). At the dawn of the third millennium AD, after nearly nine thousand years of urban history, the majority of the six billion people on earth live in urban settlements. The number of city residents is expected to rise by nearly 100% by the year 2030, increasing from 2.9 billion (48%) in the year 2000 to about five billion (about 60%) by 2030.

What is "urban" and what is "urbanity"?

Rome, the birthplace of Caesar and Cicero, has always been regarded in the western world as the prototype of the most advanced form of human communal life. During that period it was simply called "urbs" (the city) – and clearly understood as such throughout the ancient world. Rome was the capital of a world empire, a center of art and science, of architecture, of fashion and good taste – indeed of every aspect of life in all its diversity. Thus the adjective "urban" refers to the unique and specific characteristics of the city as human living space, features embodied in ancient Rome. The term "urbanity" encompasses the idea of city life as a whole. Writing in the 18th century, English author Samuel Johnson aptly described the essence of urbanity in his famous remark about the city of London: "When a man is tired of London, he is tired of life; for there is in London all that life can afford."

The Urbanization of the Earth

The invention of the steam engine (c. 1770) revolutionized the world and especially its cities. Coal began to replace water power as the most important source of energy. Nearly everywhere (but particularly in Europe), the Industrial Revolution inundated traditional urban structures with technical innovations as societies entered the Age of Industry. Massive industrial complexes spewing filth from smokestacks laid claim to both urban space and human labor. Impoverished through overpopulation, millions of people from rural areas streamed into the rapidly ballooning cities. Between 1851 and 1901, the population of London rose from 2.5 to six million, while those of Berlin and Leipzig grew by factors of four and eight, respectively, during the same period. Country people who found no room and no means of subsistence in the overcrowded cities of Europe sought refuge in the prospering urban centers of the New World (primarily in North America) in waves of migration beginning in the mid-19th century. Working class settlements and the misery endemic to them began to shape the physiognomy of entire metropolitan areas (Manchester, Liverpool, Chicago, New York, and the Ruhr region of Germany).

In the 20th century, coal largely gave way to oil – at least in the industrialized countries of the world. The gasoline-powered automobile gained popularity rapidly, and the resulting increase in mobility was accompanied by changes in attitudes about living conditions in the urban population. New suburban developments sprang up everywhere, spreading across administrative boundaries (urban sprawl) – either invading former rural areas (suburbanization) or mixing with neighboring urban districts (to form "conurbations").

Smog is an urban environmental problem. The quality of life in densely populated metropolitan regions is often severely impaired by air pollution caused by industrial emissions and automobile exhaust – as in São Paulo (a city with over five million passenger cars).

Unreliable Statistics – Confusing Terminology

According to statistics published by the UN, there are now about 320 "urban agglomerations" (each with more than one million inhabitants) in the world. Of these, only 20 are classified on the basis of census figures for the year 1995 as "megacities" (with over 10 million inhabitants). These include the metropolitan areas of Tokyo (26.8 million), São Paulo (16.4), New York (16.3), Mexico City (15.6), Bombay (15.1), Shanghai (15.1), Los Angeles (12.4), Beijing (12.3), Kolkata (Calcutta) (11.7) and Seoul (11.6). There is no agreement among urban experts as to the precise meaning of such once commonly used terms as "city" (minimum population of 100,000 for European cities), "metropolis" (a large city with a significant central function), or "megalopolis" (urban agglomeration). Yet one thing seems clear: Global urbanization is progressing at a rapid pace – much too fast for government administrations, statisticians and urban research to follow.

The Two Faces of Development

The pattern of global urbanization mirrors the global prosperity gap between industrialized and developing countries. Urban population in the industrialized nations as a group grew at a rate of only 0.6% per year between 1995 and 2000. The figure for all developing countries for the same period was 2.9%. Demographers estimate that the statistical increase in urban population by the year 2030 will be absorbed by the urban agglomerations of the developing countries alone. This trend will result in a dramatic deterioration of urban living conditions for the latecomers, as present developments already indicate. More than half of the urban population of the developing countries now lives below the poverty line in illegal slums and hut settlements – the "favelas," "shanty towns," "squatter settlements," "barriadas," and "Bidonvilles" that have encircled existing urban structures like a constricting noose in many parts of the world. Sociologists attribute this trend to push and pull factors. Push factors such as poverty, unemployment, infrastructure deficiencies, and the generally bleak prospects of rural life turn dazzling urban behemoths into enchanting magnets that generate hopes of social and economic betterment (the pull effect). Offering ostensibly sound reasons for abandoning rural homelands, these factors have led to a general exodus from the country into the cities in the developing nations.

The Global View

At present, the urban population is growing at a rate of 2.1 per year, much faster than the total world population (1.4%). Due to climatic conditions and factors affecting transportation, the region of heaviest urban agglomeration lies within a strip of territory between 80 and 120 km wide running parallel to the coasts in the temperate zones between about 20 and 60 degrees north latitude. In other words, total urbanization of the Earth's surface is highly unlikely.

Nor has the often-cited process of economic and (in the broadest sense) cultural "globalization" eradicated the integrity and unique character of the diverse types of urban communities in the different cultural regions of

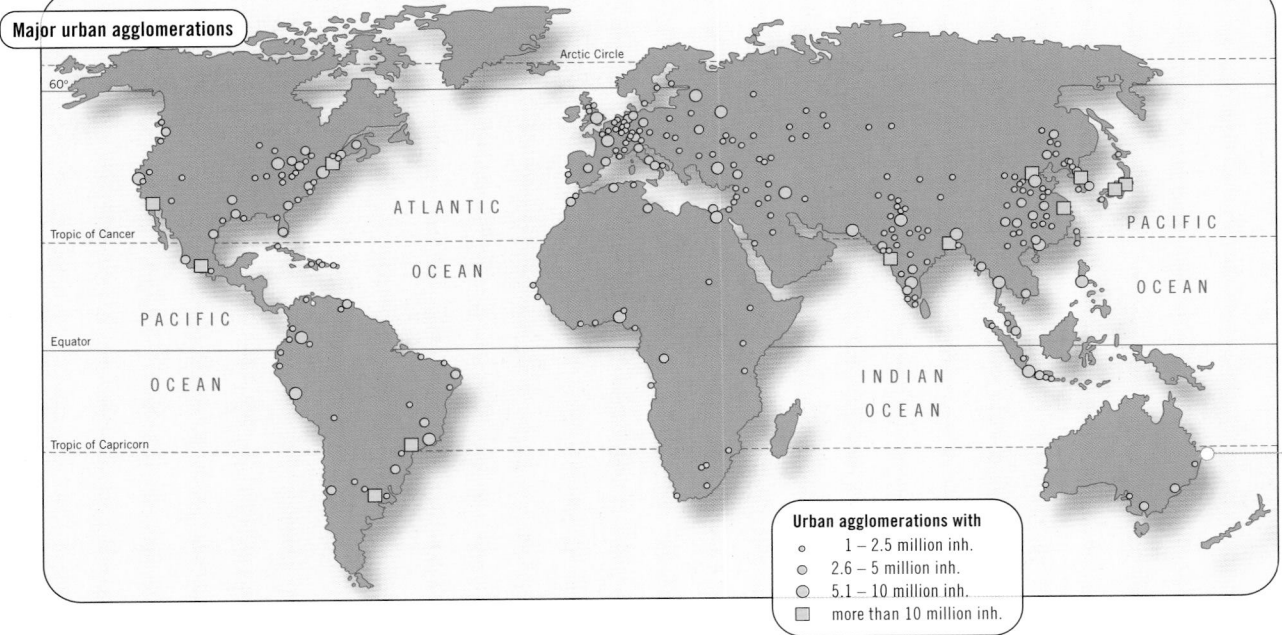

Major urban agglomerations

Arctic Circle

ATLANTIC OCEAN

PACIFIC OCEAN

INDIAN OCEAN

Tropic of Cancer

Equator

Tropic of Capricorn

Urban agglomerations with
- 1 – 2.5 million inh.
- 2.6 – 5 million inh.
- 5.1 – 10 million inh.
- more than 10 million inh.

The Dark Heart of the Continent

Satellite images of the Earth at night reveal points of light along continental coastlines – as shown in the map on the left – corresponding to major urban agglomerations. Approximately 50% of the earth's population is concentrated in regions less than 150 kilometers from the nearest coast.

Walls, a Standard Feature of Early Urban Settlements

City walls remain a typical feature of urban architecture even in our day. The photo shows the city wall in Nördlingen, Germany – built in the 14th century and still almost entirely intact today.

Traditional Cities Resist Globalization

Many cities and urban forms have retained their distinct physiognomy in spite of the current trend. One example of a type of Portuguese colonial city that has remained virtually unchanged since the 18th century is Ouro Preto in Brazil. Shibam, the "Desert Manhattan" located in the Wadi Hadhramaut (Yemen) exemplifies a form of high-rise, loam-construction typical of oriental cities, a tradition with roots in pre-Islamic times.

Global City of the Fun Society

Cities serve their surrounding regions in many ways. Situated in the Nevada desert, Las Vegas – the wide world in a pocket-sized format – is perhaps the most bizarre manifestation of the "fun city" concept.

Ersatz Walls

The politically controversial Israeli settlement of Maale Adumim stands like a fortress in the desert of Judaea in the West Bank east of Jerusalem. The compact ring of buildings serves as a substitute for a protective city wall.

Misery on the Urban Fringe

Uncontrolled immigration creates more than a planning crisis for many cities. Visible here is the sea of tin-roofed huts in the squatter town of Windhoek (Namibia). Such settlements hinder controlled growth and cause severe environmental problems (photo: legalized, sanitized developments bordered on the right by a wild hut settlement).

The City as a Magnet

Everything life has to offer can be found in the big city – and affects the surrounding countryside like a population magnet with a pull so strong that it can hardly be controlled with administrative means. An impassable fence along the border is the only defense against the lure of Hong Kong's nocturnal aura.

Life in the Vertical Dimension

The invention of reinforced concrete and the elevator, coupled with the high price of land, literally gave rise to upward growth in leaps and bounds in many cities in the early 20th century. Manhattan is a prime example. Skyscrapers, the modern temples of capitalism, now tower far above the church spires that once dominated the city profile.

the world (many of which are firmly rooted in historical tradition), despite the strong tendency toward uniformity in urban architecture. Only very few major metropolitan areas have achieved the status of "global cities," centers of international banking, global business management, international business and telecommunication, and world political power (those few include New York, London, Paris, Tokyo and the relative newcomers Río de Janeiro, Mexico City, Hong Kong, and Shanghai). These are the cities whose centers represent advanced forms of modern urban development almost everywhere in the world, although they often bear the indelible imprint of a randomly interchangeable physiognomy. Knowledgeable urban sociologists have identified in precisely these global control centers strong tendencies toward inner-urban polarization and signs of social and ethnic segregation. In the "global cities," the dominant entrepreneurial culture shaped by a profit-oriented, transnational urban aristocracy stands in stark contrast to the masses of urban fringe groups that depend upon low-paid, labor intensive jobs – a contrast much like that of the glittering facades of dream metropolises and their slum districts, whose ceaseless growth has devoured some eight million acres of valuable farmland worldwide (enough to produce food for ten million people) between 1980 and 2000.

Water as a Resource and a Source of Problems and Conflicts

"Blue Gold" – Our Most Precious Resource

During the International Hydrological Decade (IHD, 1964-1974), a global effort to assess the world's water reserves was launched under the auspices of UNESCO. Based on the results, experts now agree: There is plenty of water in the world – yet not nearly enough to satisfy the needs of the entire human race in the 21st century. According to projections presented at the World Water Conference in The Hague in March 2000, some 3.3 billion people (37% of the world's population) will be directly confronted with a shortage of water by 2025 (the number has already reached two billion), because only about 0.29% of the total water supply on earth is available as fresh water suitable for human use (for drinking, hygiene, and the production of consumer goods), while the population continues to grow at a rapid pace. In the course of the 20th century, the human population grew from 1.6 billion to 6 billion people, who now share a maximum total of 4.2 million cubic kilometers of liquid fresh water – a supply that cannot be increased significantly. Thus every new addition to the world's population reduces the amount of water available to each person on earth.

How Much Water Does a Human Being Need?

Inhabitants of temperate climate zones – North Americans, for example – need between two and three liters of water per day to satisfy their basic physical and physiological needs. People who live in hot climes require six or more liters per day. For a worker in the oil fields of Saudi Arabia, a daily ration of twelve liters of liquid is just about sufficient. If he quenches his thirst with beer, the figure of twelve liters must be multiplied by 60 (bringing the total to 720 liters), since up to 60 liters of fresh water are required to produced a single liter of beer. A scholar who stills his thirst for knowledge with three books weighing one kilogram each and places them on his bookshelf must – like the beer-drinking oil field worker – accept responsibility for the consumption of at least 750 liters of water, as it takes roughly 250 liters to produce one kilogram of paper. In light of the worldwide water shortage, the fact that between 20,000 and 30,000 liters of water are required for the production of an average passenger car should give pause for thought, especially when one considers that there are currently 750 million cars on the world's roads and that a country like China (with one-fifth of the world's population) is

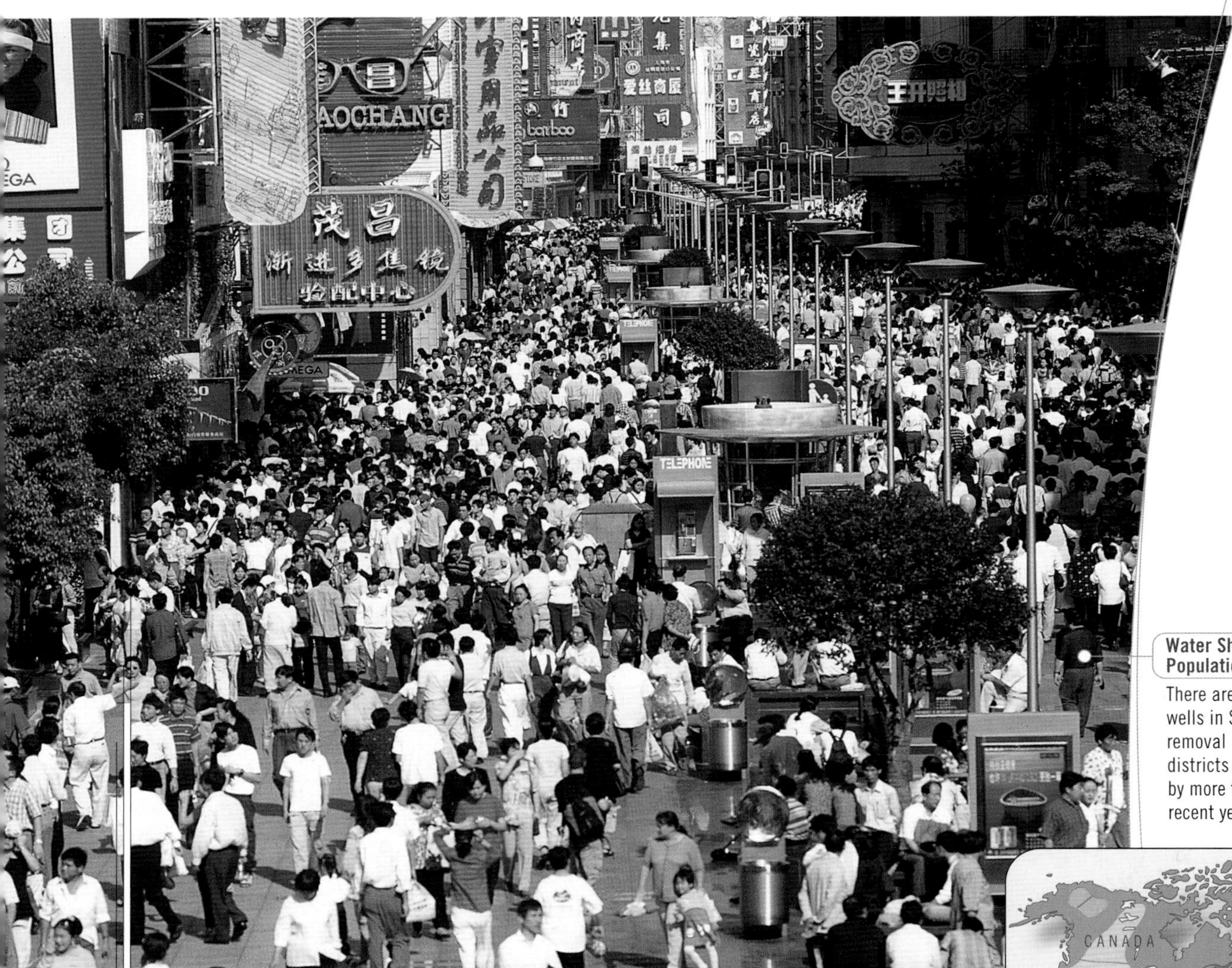

Water Shortage Caused by Population Density
There are more than 1,000 deep wells in Shanghai. Groundwater removal has caused the central districts of the city to sink by more than 13 cm annually in recent years.

Unequal Distribution
Global water resources are unfairly distributed. Only one-fourth of the world's population has access to a sufficient water supply.

World Water Resources

water surplus   increasing scarcity
sufficient supply   water shortage

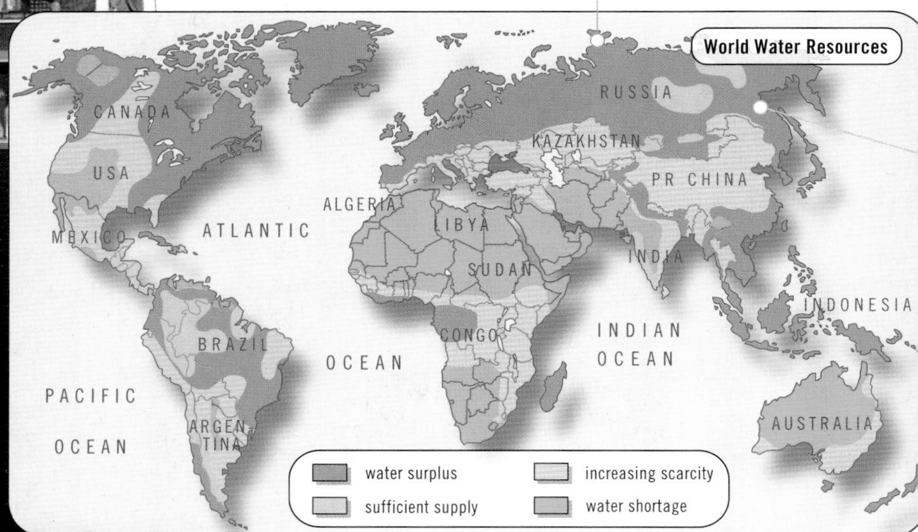

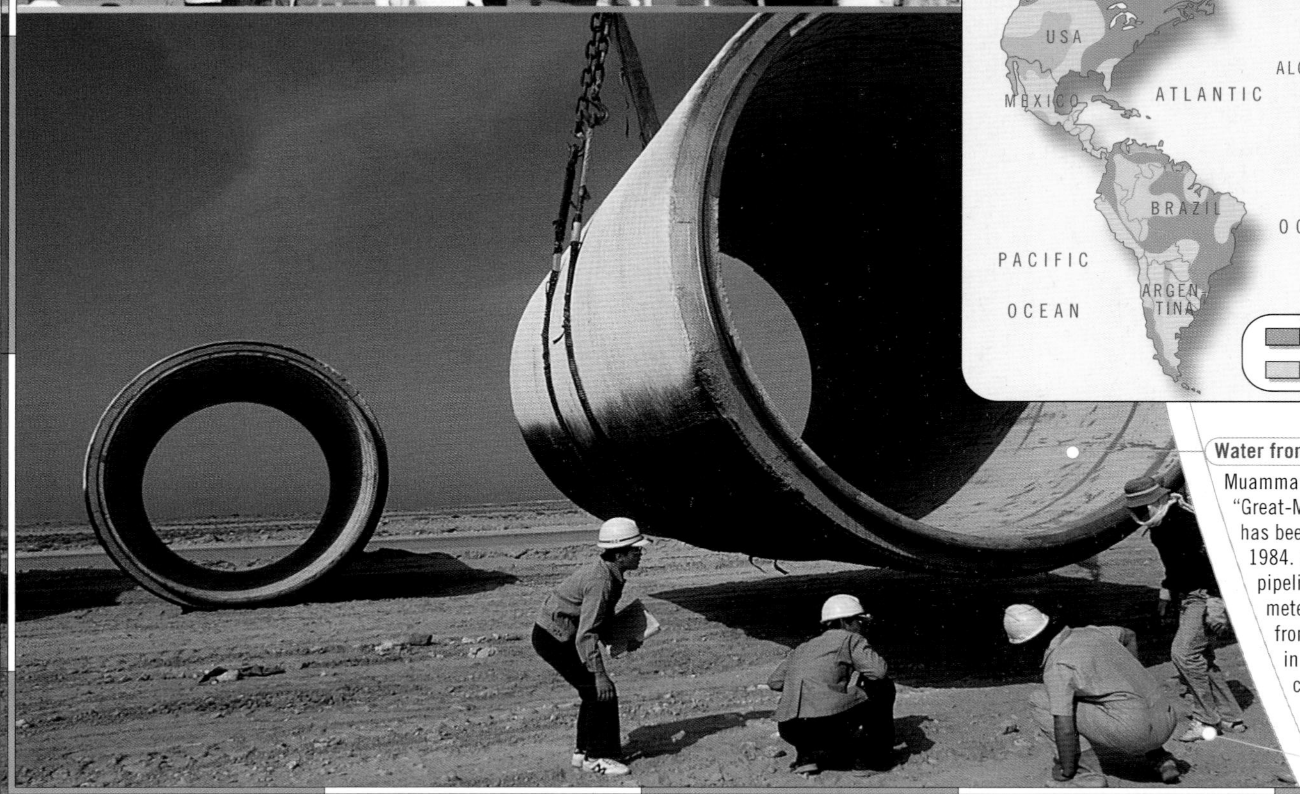

Water from the Desert
Muammar Qaddafi's mammoth "Great-Man-Made-River" project has been under construction since 1984. More than 1,000 km of pipelines with a diameter of four meters convey fossil water from depths of 400 to 1,500 m in southeastern Libya to the coastal region.

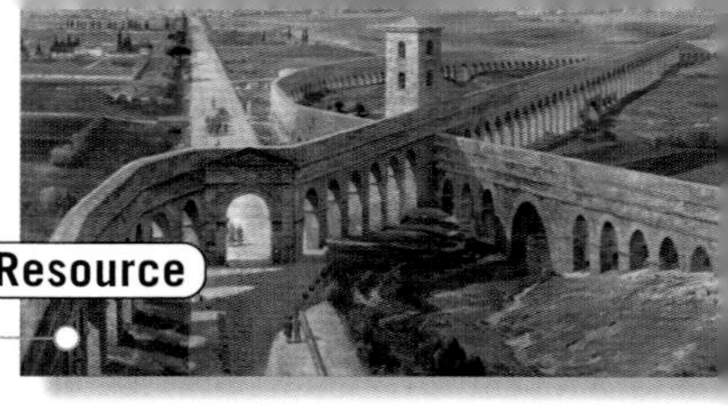

motorizing in leaps and bounds. Even more alarming is the tremendous amount of fresh water needed to ensure an adequate supply of food for the growing global population. Depending upon climate conditions, the production of one kilogram of grain requires between 1,000 and 2,000 liters of fresh water (or 1,000 to 2,000 tons of water per ton of grain). Thus our daily bread or bowl of rice – like our daily minimum ration of fresh water – is a very important factor in the calculation of per capita consumption of water, although it is seldom given sufficient consideration. The published figures for "average daily water consumption per person per day" (128 liters in Germany and about twice that amount in the U.S.) reflect only measurable household consumption and thus give a false picture of actual water use, which – particularly when viewed from a global perspective – goes far beyond daily household needs.

Who Needs and Uses How Much Water?

According to the most recent precise calculation of the global demand for fresh water (in 1990), private households, which (combined with small businesses and public consumption) account for 7.6 % of total consumption, are the smallest but most significant user group, followed in increasing size by industry (24.6 %). At 67.8 %, agriculture, in its role as the producer of food for the world, is far and away the largest consumer. In contrast to industry, which ordinarily uses water only briefly as utility or process water (which it usually returns to the water cycle as polluted waste water, however), agriculture consumes water in the production of biomass. Despite worldwide efforts to encourage economical use of water resources, the unbridled growth of the world's population is likely to make the water shortage the number-one global problem in the 21st century.

The Statistics of Scarcity

According to guidelines issued by the World Health Organization (WHO), a human being in the 21st century requires a minimum annual per capita ration of 1,000 cubic meters of fresh water (or 2,470 liters per day for food and energy production, industrial products, hygiene, education, traffic, and other purposes) to maintain a living standard appropriate in our time without endangerment to health (current per capita consumption is about 3,000 cubic meters per year in the U.S. and 1,500 cubic meters in other industrialized countries).

The water shortage is not necessarily restricted to specific climate zones. Much more important as a measure of scarcity is the quantity of renewable water resources (precipitation as well as inflowing river and groundwater) available in a given country relative to its population per year. Accordingly, countries with a fresh water supply of less than 1,000 cubic meters per person are classified as water emergency areas. Serious problems arise from water shortage where the natural supply of water falls below 1,700 – 2,000 cubic meters per person (the water stress level). Regions with renewable supplies of between 2,000 and 2,500 cubic meters and above per capita are regarded as non-critical. Africa has the largest number of water-poor countries, in which about 300 million people (one-third of the population) live under conditions of water emergency.

Reasons for Scarcity

Statistically speaking, the fresh water reserves on our "blue planet" are sufficient to serve the needs of humanity as a whole. Yet a number of factors contradict this naive statistical assessment. First of all, fresh water reserves are not equally distributed throughout the world. Nor does the presence of water in a given region necessarily mean that the other living conditions are favorable to human life. Secondly, fresh water that comes from the sky as precipitation rarely stays where it falls.

Water for Rome

Cities in the Roman Empire were supplied with water by a system of aqueducts. This painting by Zeno Diemer gives an impression of the ancient Roman water supply network.

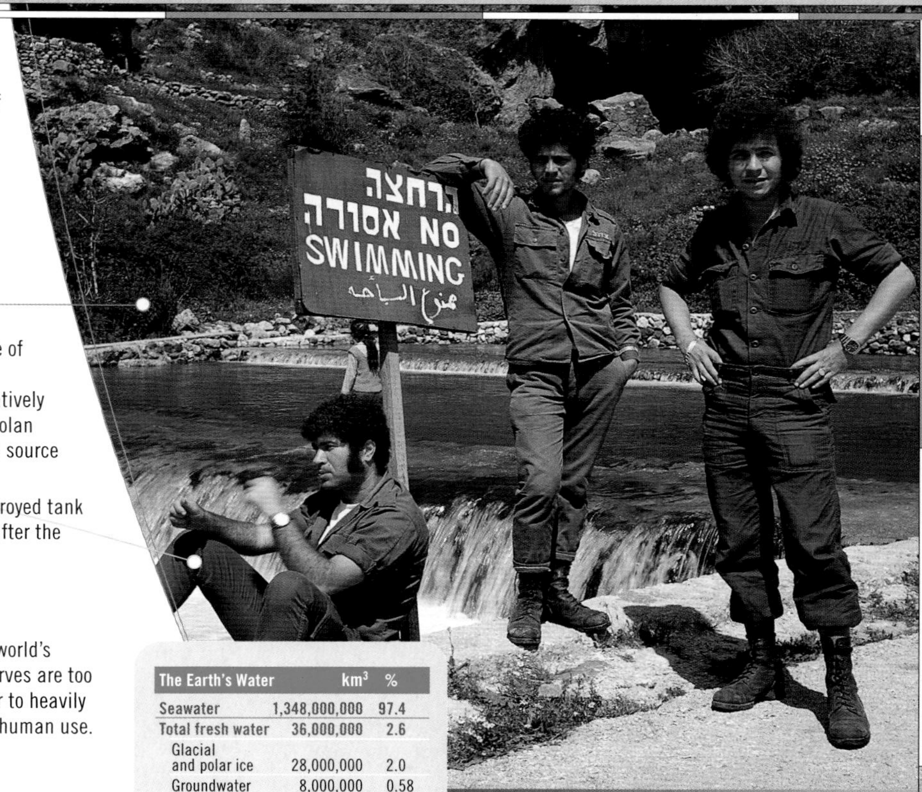

"Water War" on the Golan Heights

Israeli soldiers at the source of the Banias, a tributary of the Jordan. Blessed by relatively heavy precipitation, the Golan Heights are an important source of water for Israel.

Photo, lower right: Destroyed tank on the Golan Heights after the Six-Day War

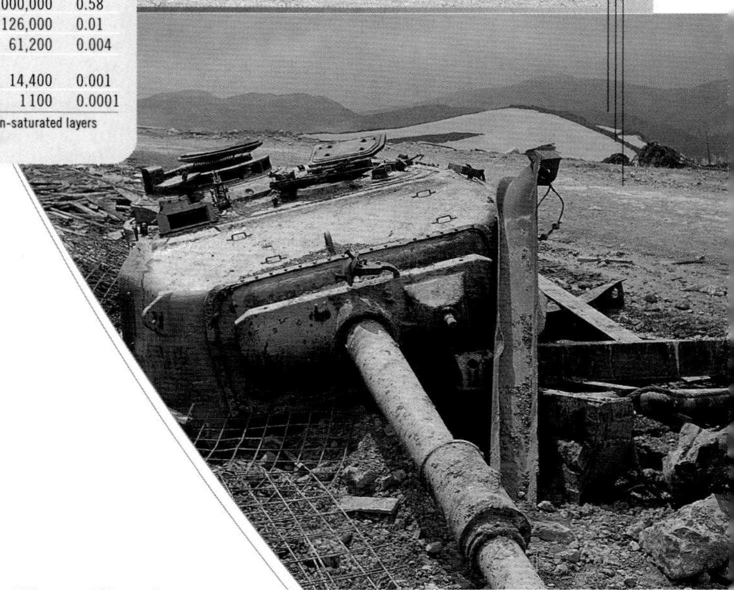

Nearly half of the world's groundwater reserves are too deep to exploit or to heavily mineralized for human use.

The Earth's Water	km³	%
Seawater	1,348,000,000	97.4
Total fresh water	36,000,000	2.6
Glacial and polar ice	28,000,000	2.0
Groundwater	8,000,000	0.58
Lakes	126,000	0.01
Soil moisture*	61,200	0.004
Atmospheric water vapor	14,400	0.001
Rivers	1 100	0.0001

* contained in the upper, non-saturated layers of soil

The nature of water – its mobility – causes it to run off, evaporate, or seep to unreachable depths in the very places it is so urgently needed by human beings and human economies. Thirdly, the global population is concentrated to an increasing degree in relatively few inhabitable regions of the Earth (about 90 % of the human race occupies four per cent of the world's dry land) and exceeds the hydrological capacity of these regions by virtue of sheer numbers alone. Finally, humans as economic beings – unlike animals and plants – tend to burden fresh water with many kinds of foreign substances (primarily chemicals) that make it unsuitable for reuse as drinking water and thus exacerbate the water shortage, particularly in densely populated urban agglomerations.

Relief Measures

Advanced cultures with large populations were forced to deal with the problem of water scarcity even in ancient times. Thus hydraulic engineering measures for the procurement and storage of scarce, life-giving water are among the oldest technical structures known to mankind. Remnants of irrigation systems from the 3rd millennium BC have been found in India, China, Yemen, and Egypt. As long ago as 1700 BC, the Babylonian King Hammurabi enacted important laws governing the use of the precious resource of water in the Code of Hammurabi.

Outstanding examples of early urban water supply systems involving technically sophisticated aqueducts are the ancient cities of Pergamum (western Anatolia) and Rome. In the 1st century AD, the Romans moved 600,000 cubic meters of water into their city daily, supplying every inhabitant with 600 liters per day. Modern water procurement systems make use of other means in addition to long-distance water conveyance via pipelines and canals (e.g. the California Aqueduct and the "Great-Man-Made-River" in Libya). Today, some 800,000 small and large dams all over the world prevent rapid water run-off, making more water available for drinking or use in farming or industrial operations than is contained in all of the rivers of the world.

Water Wars?

Experts anticipate population growth of between 30 % and 70 % in the water-poor regions of the world by the year 2025. It is highly likely that this will lead to increased competition for water, not only among cities and between agriculture and industry but between nations as well.

Forty per cent of the world's population live in regions fed by rivers that flow through more than two countries, and over 200 areas burdened by political conflict largely attributable to disputes over the use of water from such rivers clearly underscore the magnitude of the water shortage as a potential source of political conflict.

The most volatile regions of conflict over water with serious potential for armed hostilities are located along the Ganges (usage disputes between India and Bangladesh), the Tigris and Euphrates (Turkey, Syria, Iraq), the Jordan (Israel, Syria, the West Bank, Jordan), and the Nile (Egypt, Sudan, Ethiopia, Eritrea). "Real" water wars have occurred only rarely in history, but water scarcity has often been the spark that set off the powder keg of existing religious, ethnic, or territorial conflicts.

Fossil Fuels – Production and World Trade

Competition for the Earth's Energy Reserves

The recent rapid rise in prices for fuels and heating oil have reminded us how vulnerable our social and economic systems are and how dependent we are on the oil-producing countries. Our high-tech world consumes vast amounts of energy, and most industrialized countries do not have sufficient resources to cover their own needs. Cartels formed by the oil-producing countries ensure a certain degree of market stability, but they also underscore the dependence of importing countries on the suppliers of raw materials. Transnational and multinational firms operating in the raw materials markets have the power to circumvent cartel agreements more or less at will. Aside from the political and economic problems associated with fossil fuels, environmental issues are now becoming increasingly important.

The Global Oil Economy, 1999

Legend:
- Oil reserves
- Oil production
- Oil consumption
- → Main oil transport routes
- 370 / 292 Figures in million tons
- Column height in mm

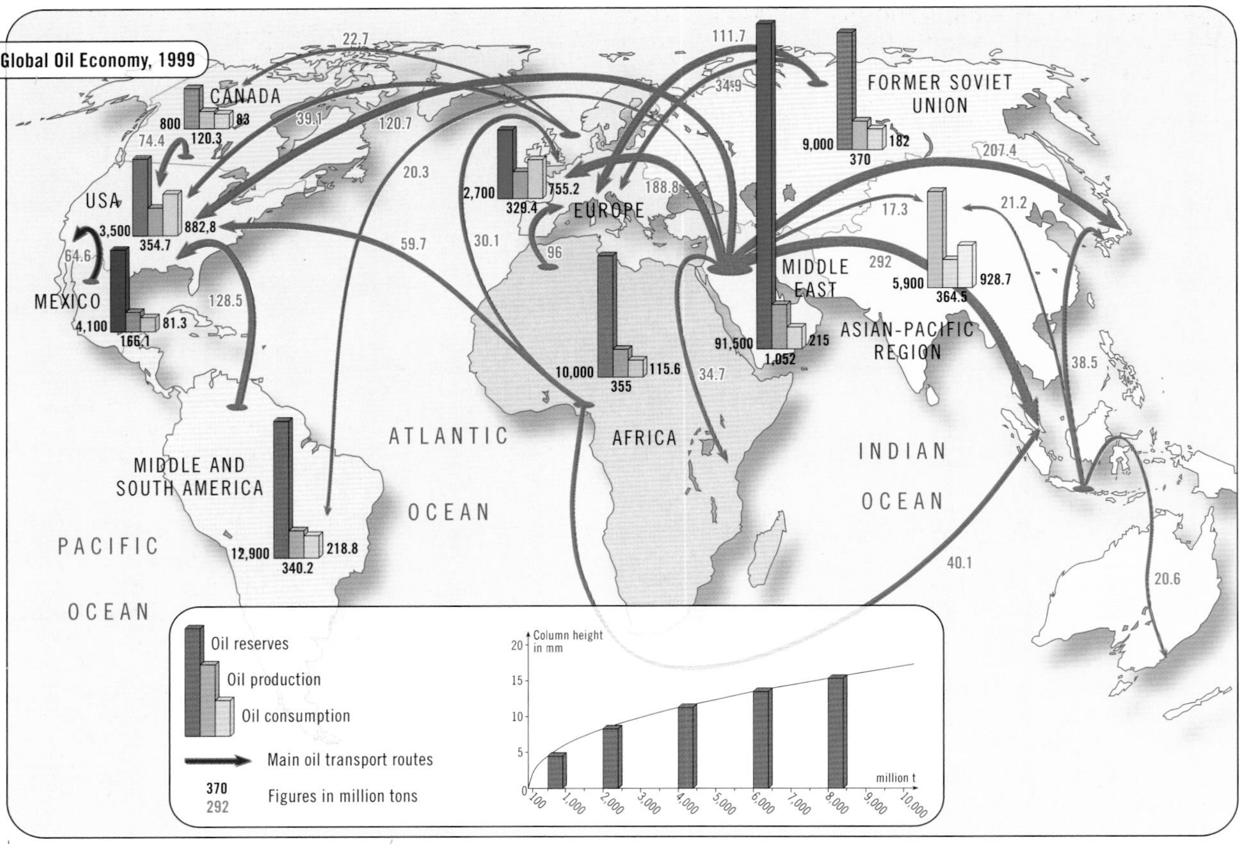

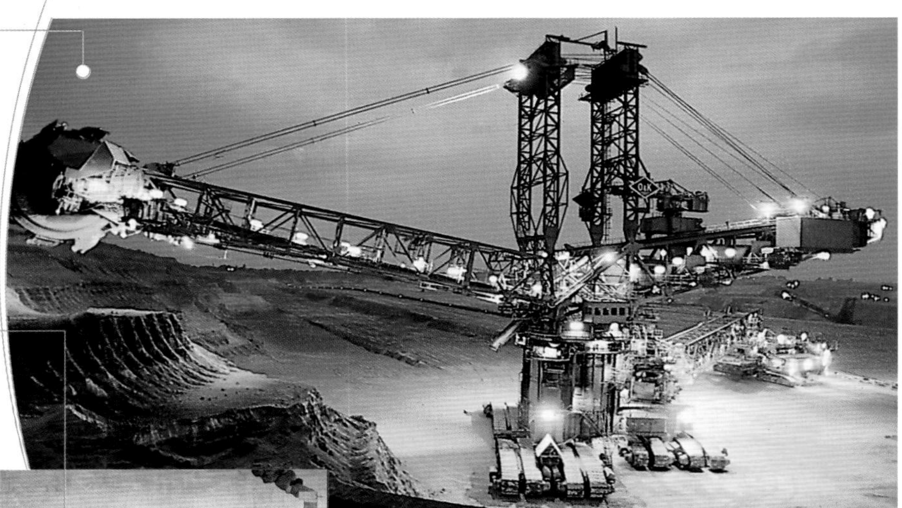

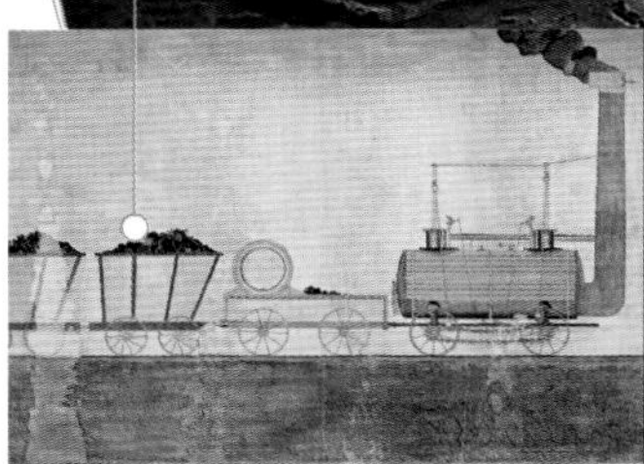

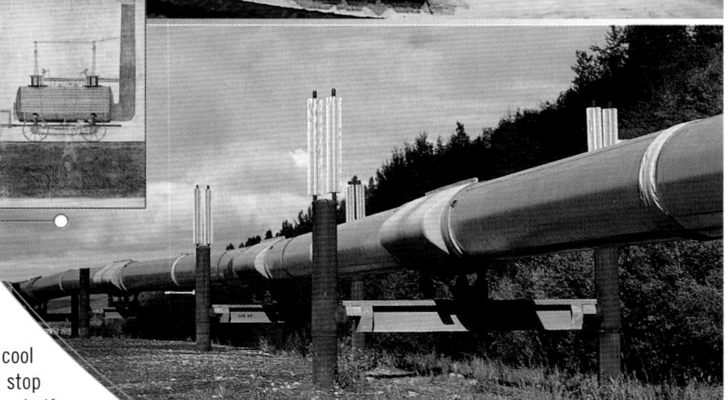

The Growing Hunger for Energy

Hunting and gathering societies met all of their energy needs with wood, a renewable source of energy. This did not change significantly during the transition to farming and animal husbandry, although wood did become scarce in heavily deforested areas. It was not until humans began processing ores to make metal implements using wood or charcoal as fuels that dependence upon renewable energy sources began to pose serious problems. Forests, which had once seemed endless, were destroyed at a pace that far outstripped their capacity to recover. Water and wind mills facilitated the processing of agricultural products and were later employed by the textile industry. The advent of industrialization and mechanized vehicles (steam locomotives) brought the need for higher-energy fossil fuels (coal). In terms of energy output, one ton of coal equated to the annual yield of two acres of forest. Electrification intensified the demand for fossil fuels and also made energy easily transportable. But this applied only to "developed countries." Around 1900, wood, wind, water, and human and animal muscle power still covered two-thirds of the world's energy needs. Only a few decades ago, wood was the only available source of heating and cooking energy for one-third of the world's population. Today, energy consumption and management prognoses must take into account the anticipated rapid rise in energy demand in the Third World.

The Underground Forest

Bituminous coal was used occasionally in ancient civilizations and to an increasing extent during the Middle Ages. Large-scale exploitation, including underground mining, did not begin until the 19th century, when coal became an indispensable source of energy. Worldwide coal production rose rapidly from twelve million tons (1820) to 1.2 billion t (1910), when 85 % of all coal produced in the world was mined in Germany, Great Britain, and the U.S.A. Although global production has stagnated in recent years (1998: 3.7 billion t) or grown only marginally, the focal points of mining activity shifted due to cost pressures. Difficult and thus expensive mining operations in the European Union (Great Britain, Germany, France) were cut back drastically in favor of cheaper coal from such countries as the U.S. The German bituminous coal-mining industry, for example, is highly subsidized, as coal costs more than $140 per ton there, while the price of imported coal is below $36. China, Australia, Colombia, South Africa, and other countries increased production, not only to cover domestic demand but for export as well. According to estimates, exploitable coal reserves amount to at least 550 billion tons of bituminous coal units, concentrated mostly in Russia, the U.S., China, Australia, and India. Due to its high water content and low energy output, brown coal is used primarily in the production of electricity and is not transported over long distances.

Petroleum, "Black Gold"

More than 140 years after the discovery of oil in Pennsylvania (1859), global economic and political developments are now more dependent than ever before on the availability of oil. This is primarily the consequence of motorization, and the rise in the use of motor vehicles to transport people and material, although petroleum is also used for heating, in power plants, and as an industrial raw material. After a modest beginning (1900: 20 million t), oil production increased dramatically following the Second World War (1950: 523 million; 1999: 4.1 billion t). Every day, nearly 10 million tons of oil are pumped from several thousand oil wells around the world. The amount of natural gas produced at the same time matches the energy value of six million tons of petroleum.

Devouring the Landscape

Brown coal deposits are usually not deep in the earth and are therefore mined almost exclusively in open pits. In the Rhenish brown-coal fields (photo), huge bucket-wheel excavators remove covering layers of sediment and mine the underlying coal. These machines can move more than 200,000 cubic meters of material a day.

Driving Force

The invention of the coal-burning steam engine launched the Industrial Revolution. The development of railroads (photo: steam locomotive built by George Stephenson, c. 1815) made it possible to transport coal, agricultural and industrial goods as well as people quickly, over long distances, and on a large scale. The loud, smoke-spewing engines gave rise to early complaints about environmental pollution.

Protection against Heat and Cold

The designers of the Alaska Pipeline (1,310 km long, 1974-77) had to find ways to protect the delicate permafrost ecosystem, in which soil thaws only near the surface in the summer and would shift if exposed to additional heat. The pipes were laid on supports above ground and equipped with automatic cooling units. But the oil entering the well-insulated pipeline at about 176° F must not cool excessively, as it would stop flowing. After four-and-a-half weeks, it arrives at the port of Valdez at about 86° F.

From Crude Oil to the Consumer

Petroleum products such as heating oil, gasoline, diesel fuel, kerosene and bitumen are produced through distillation, refining, and cracking.

Man-Made Islands

Prospecting for oil and natural gas beneath ocean floors and exploiting discovered reserves requires the use of huge platforms, which are towed to the drilling site and anchored with massive steel or concrete constructions. They must be able to withstand heavy tides and severe storms – particularly in the North Sea. The oil or gas is brought to land via pipelines or by shuttle tankers.

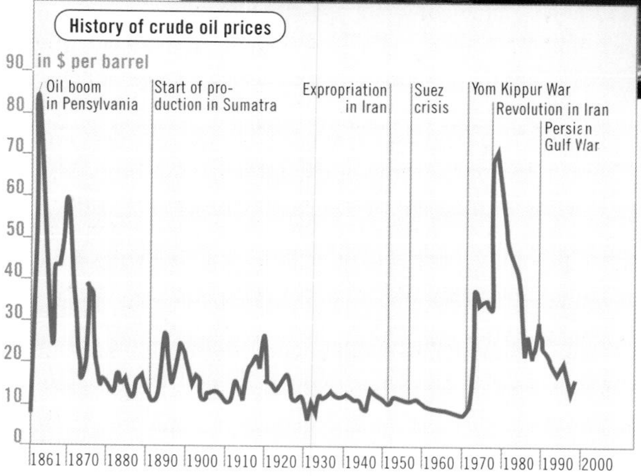

History of crude oil prices

90 in $ per barrel
80
70
60
50
40
30
20
10
0

Oil boom in Pensylvania | Start of production in Sumatra | Expropriation in Iran | Suez crisis | Yom Kippur War / Revolution in Iran / Persian Gulf War

1861 1870 1880 1890 1900 1910 1920 1930 1940 1950 1960 1970 1980 1990 2000

The present tight oil supply situation and accompanying price explosion call to mind the oil crisis of 1973, when the oil price rose 600% as the result of deliberately induced shortages in the aftermath of the Arab-Israeli War. The consequence was a worldwide economic crisis. Years before, in 1960, seven oil-exporting countries formed OPEC (Organization of Petroleum Exporting Countries, which now has eleven members), in the hope of gaining a higher share of oil revenues and exerting greater political influence as a cartel.

The end of the Oil Age predicted by the Club of Rome in 1973 did not come to pass. The sudden rise in prices made it possible to tap petroleum reserves that had previously appeared too expensive to exploit. Thanks to new fields in the North Sea and Alaska, supply rose faster than demand. The power of OPEC waned temporarily.

Natural Gas, an Increasingly Popular Fuel

The demand for natural gas has risen steadily over the past 30 to 40 years. Easily transported via pipelines, it is used to heat buildings and generate electricity. Produc-

tion is concentrated primarily in the CIS countries and the U.S. The United States, which also import natural gas from Canada and Mexico, consume more than one forth of total world production. The largest reserves are in Russia (36%), the other CIS countries, the Middle East, and Southeast Asia. More than 40% are held by the OPEC states. Germany imports nearly 80% of its natural gas (mainly from Russia, Norway, and the Netherlands).

Is an Energy Crisis Looming?

At present, 90% of the world's energy needs are covered by fossil fuels. Industrialized countries account for nearly 60% of total demand. Over the past 30 years, primary energy consumption has risen at a rate of 2% per year, although the collapse of the Eastern Bloc significantly reduced the pace of growth. Increasing motorization in the developing countries could raise the rate of increase to double that figure within the next 20 years.

Half of the energy consumed by the EU countries is imported (Germany: 60%). With only 4.5% of the world's population, the U.S. uses 25% of the annual production of primary energy. Europe (excluding the CIS countries) is not far behind at over 20%.

At present consumption levels, the known reserves of petroleum (approx. 150 billion t) would last for more than 40 years, natural gas reserves (at least 150 trillion cubic meters) for over 60 years. Moreover, new technologies favor more efficient exploitation of deposits and the discovery of new ones. This could result in a doubling of known reserves. And there are also a number of as yet untapped reserves of tar sand, oil shale, and heavy crude oil. These are expensive to exploit, however, and would

raise the price of oil accordingly. Since two thirds of the easily exploitable reserves are located in the Persian Gulf region (chiefly in Saudi Arabia), the power of OPEC is likely to increase again. The OPEC countries currently hold over 75% of known reserves and control 40% of global production. Yet the Middle East, like the oil-rich Caspian Sea region, is politically unstable, which means that disruptions of production are likely.

Protecting the Earth's Atmosphere

Two major themes have dominated discussion with regard to global energy management in recent years: the principle of sustainability and the threat – or reality – of global warming as a consequence of a man-made greenhouse effect. The joint resolution of nearly all industrialized countries (enacted 1992 without the U.S.) calling for reduction of the burning of oil, natural gas, and coal to the 1990 level by the year 2005 has born little fruit thus far. Resistance to nuclear energy (which accounts for 7.4% of primary energy worldwide) and the closing of nuclear power plants could actually result in higher CO_2 emissions due to the increased reliance of oil, gas, and coal. It is likely to take quite some time to achieve large-scale, effective use of renewable energy sources (currently 2.7% of primary energy, primarily from hydroelectric power) – photovoltaic solar cells, solar heating plants, fuel cells, wind and biomass power plants, geothermal energy, heat pumps, ocean energy (wave and tide energy, ocean warmth). It will also be necessary to seek new ways of conserving energy. Regardless of the actual size of current reserves of fossil fuels, they are ultimately limited.

Division of the Globe into Time Zones

The Stock Exchange is Always Open – Somewhere on Earth!

When we want to call someone in Europe, we need to consider the time difference in order to be sure that we don't wake up our party in the middle of the night. Business people and international airlines must be constantly alert to these time differences. Stock-market speculators are happy to know that trading is possible around the clock, as there is always a stock exchange open somewhere in the world, whether in Sydney, New York, or Frankfurt am Main.

Local Time vs. Zone Time

Long ago, local times were different virtually wherever one looked. After all, it is only natural for the noon bell to ring when the sun reaches its highest point in the sky. The time difference between two towns at the same latitude separated by only 50 km is three minutes. Before the railways were built, such discrepancies were of little significance, since travel was always slow at best. Nevertheless, local mean times were introduced toward the end of the 18th century and regarded as binding for a given center and its surrounding region – Geneva time in 1780, Berlin time in 1820, Paris time in 1826, Zurich time in 1832, Pulkow and Greenwich time in 1848, Warsaw and Bern time in 1853. North Americans, in particular, lent strong support to the plan to establish a global system for measuring time. In 1873, 71 different railroad times were still in effect here. That year, Sandford Fleming, Chief Engineer of the Canadian Pacific Railway, proposed setting up a system of 24 meridians spaced at intervals of 15 degrees – a time difference of one hour – and assigning a standard time to each. That would divide the world into 24 time zones. But where was one to start? Which meridian was to get the zero label?

Ignoring the different times in effect in the many different countries of the world, seafarers had generally agreed to go by Greenwich time. But there were also zero meridians in Ferro (now Hierro), in Venice, and in many other places as well. At the Washington conference of 1884, 27 countries agreed to establish the zero meridian at Greenwich and to divide the globe into two geographic hemispheres, the western and the eastern.

Time systems were also standardized in many other European countries in response to the increasing internationalization of travel and transport. In Germany, which was still comprised of many independent states, most of them small, the railroad system could function properly only if agreement was reached on a standard time system. This was achieved with the Reichsgesetz of 1893. France did not join the system until 1911.

Most time zones are 15 degrees wide and cover a section of the globe that lies 7.5 degrees to the east and west of one of the 24 meridians. The standard time is the same everywhere within a given time zone. In some regions, time zone boundaries do not run along lines of longitude but along national borders. This is meant to ensure that the same time applies at every location within a country. Yet , many countries are too large to be accommodated within a single time zone. The U.S. is divided into four time zones, for example.

People living in Los Angeles should call their relatives on the East Coast early in the evening in order to avoid waking them during the night. TV networks must determine the best times to broadcast programs in order to reach the largest possible number of viewers. Under certain circumstances, networks accept the need to broadcast certain programs ("breaking news") at unfavorable times. Countries spanning several time zones require a system that makes it clear which time is meant when times are announced. In the U.S. times are identified by the time zone names: Eastern, Central, Rocky Mountain, and Pacific.

Which Island Will Be the First?

As the new year 2000 approached, several island countries in the Pacific set their sights on being the first to ring in the year 2000. The Fiji Islands introduced daylight saving time, turning their clocks ahead in order to be the first to celebrate. Tonga shifted the International Date Line along the eastern edge of its territory, putting itself 13 hours ahead of Greenwich. But the island kingdom had no chance against Kiribati, with its extensive ocean territory measuring 3,870 km from west to east. The eastward protrusion of the Date Line runs along the eastern border of Kiribati. Caroline Island, the easternmost atoll, was given the name Millennium Island (14 hours ahead of Greenwich).

… and the living is easy

Daylight savings time, the practice of turning the clock ahead one hour during the summer months in the northern hemisphere, has existed in Great Britain and Ireland since 1916. In the U.S., it was reintroduced in 1967 after having been used during both World Wars as a means of conserving energy by taking advantage of daylight. The desired energy-saving effect was actually never achieved, but people enjoy having an extra hour of leisure time while the sun shines and see daylight saving time as an improvement in quality of life.

One Day Too Early

People first recognized the need for an international date line when the "Victoria," a ship from Magellan's fleet, returned to Spain after circumnavigating the globe on September 6, 1522. The entries in the ship's log were a day behind the correct date. The expedition had constantly "gained time" on its westward voyage, saving an entire day by the time it had completely circled the globe.

The First Pocket Watch

Peter Henlein is believed to have invented the spring-driven watch. Beginning in 1510, he produced a series of small, portable clocks shaped like a can – the first pocket watches.

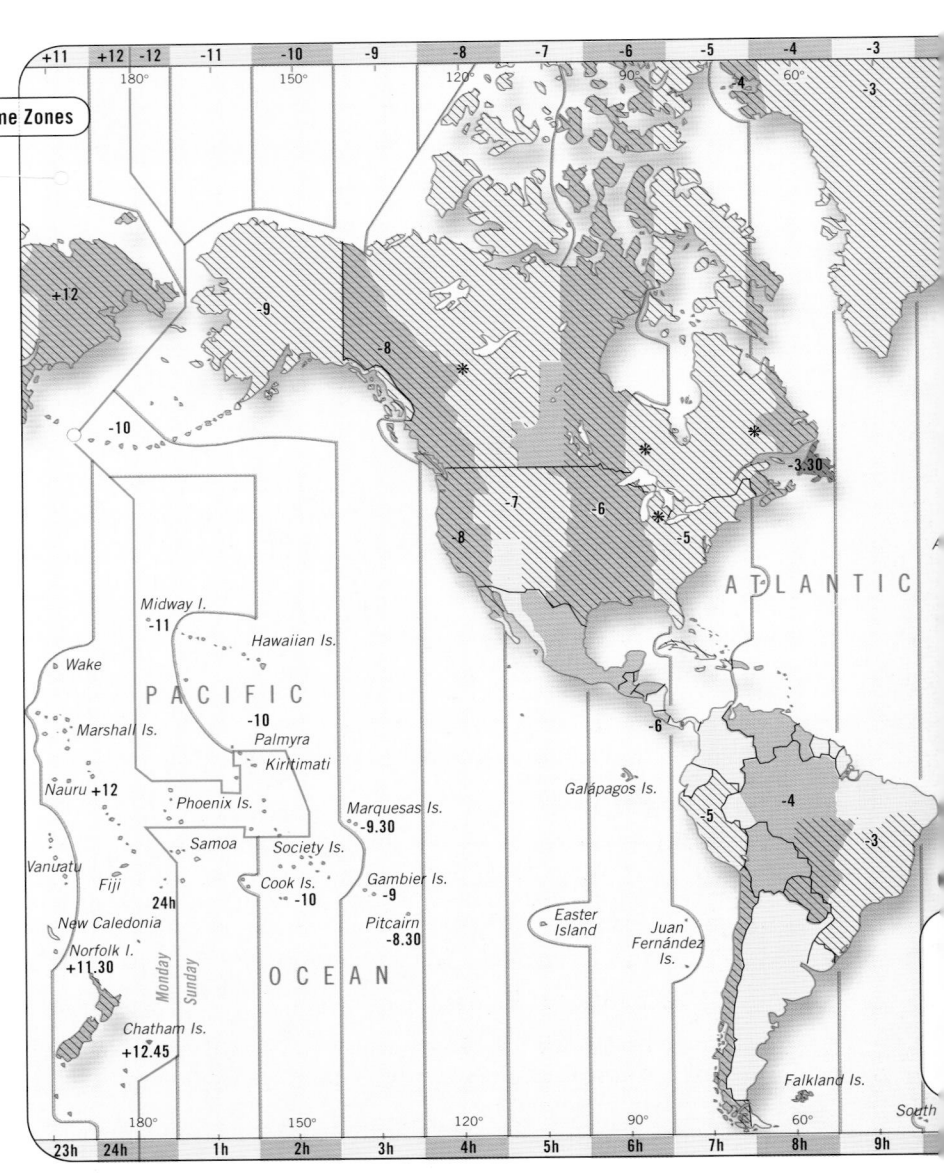

Time Zones

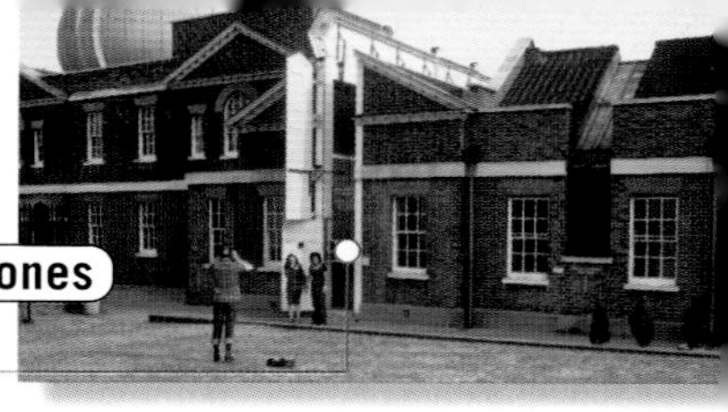

I and the Zero Meridian

The seam of our system of measuring time runs through the observatory in Greenwich (now Flamsteed House), which was established in 1675.

People who cross the International Date Line from east to west must move the calendar one day ahead. Those crossing in the reverse direction, from west to east, turn it back one day. A traveler who fails to heed this convention while circling the globe from west to east will find himself a day ahead of the local calendar upon arriving at his starting point. This happened to Phileas Fogg in Jules Verne's famous novel.

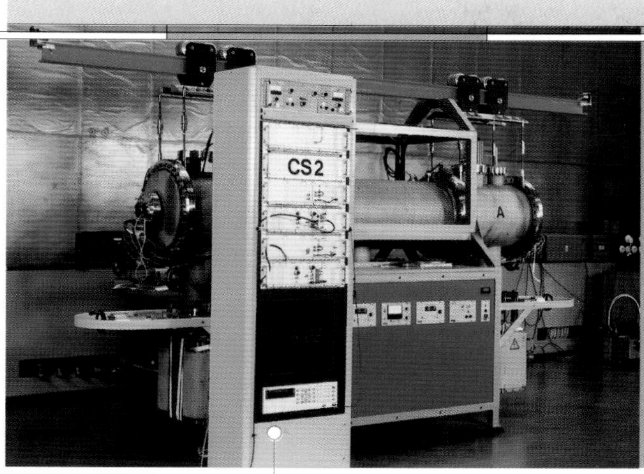

Utmost Precision

The CS 2 atomic clock at the Federal Office of Physics and Technology in Braunschweig, Germany is one of the most precise timepieces in the world. It is accurate to within a second even after two million years.

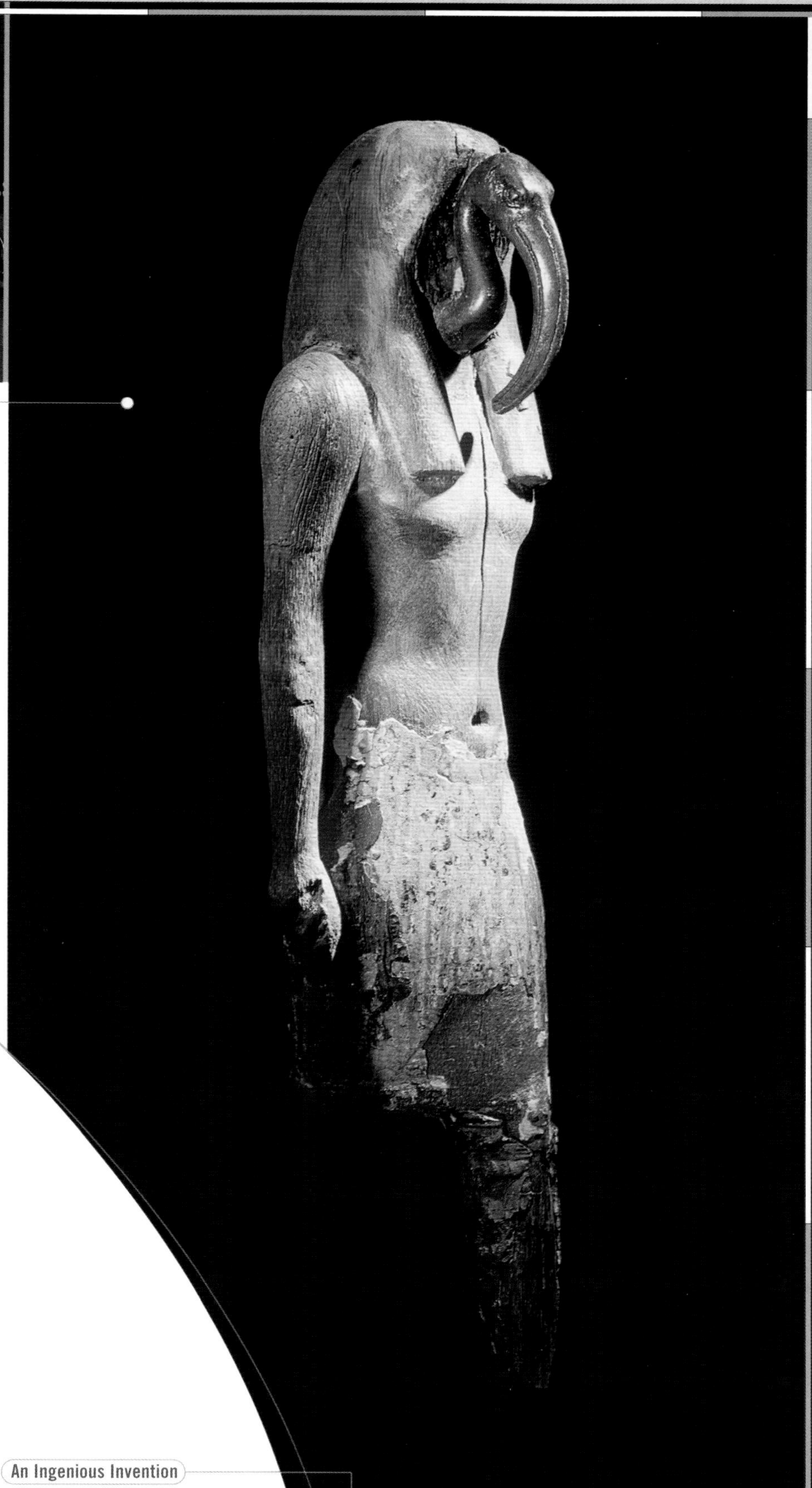

Guardian of Time

The ancient Egyptians amassed a wealth of astronomical knowledge. As early as 2750 BC, they had developed a lunar calendar and a solar calendar that divided the year into 365 days. The sciences and the calculation of time were the domain of the moon god Thot, who was often depicted as a human figure with the head of an ibis (c. 600 BC, Luxor).

International Date Line

Historical Date Line until 1845
Current International Date Line
Course until 1995

±6   Time difference from UT in hours

Regions with daylight savings time (DST), in the northern hemisphere between about April and September/October; differs widely in the southern hemisphere, between September/January and February/April

* Certain areas do not have daylight savings time

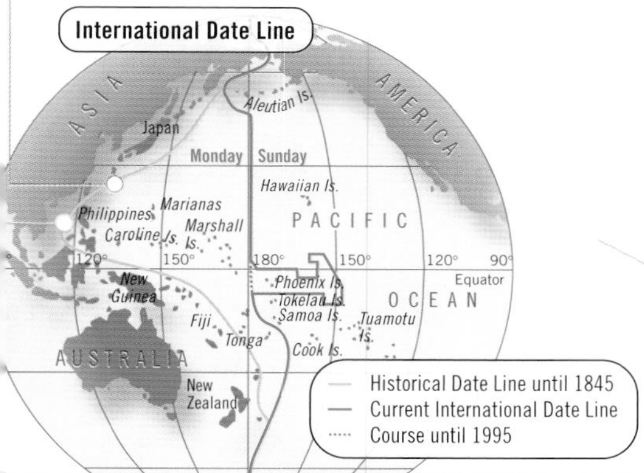

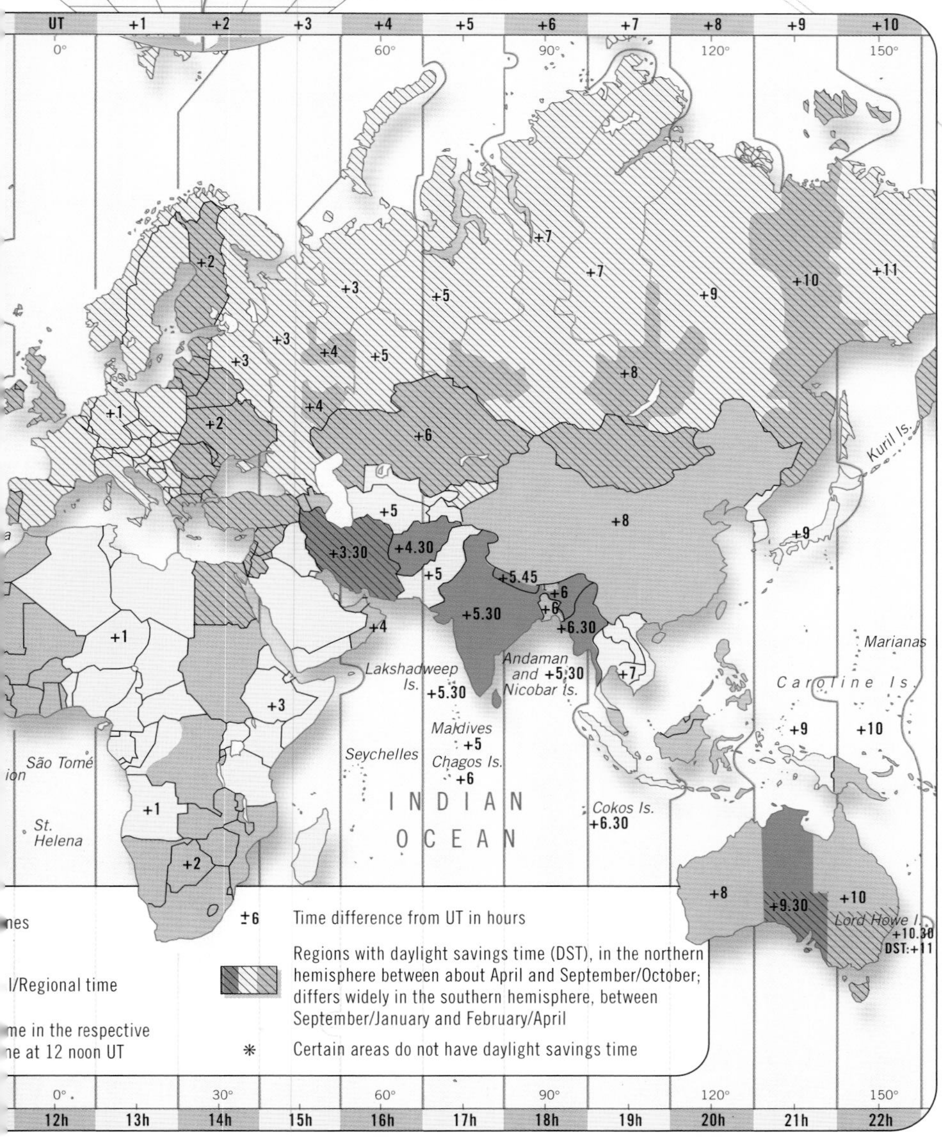

An Ingenious Invention

Portable equatorial sundial made by Johann Georg Vogler (1750), with an adjustable hour ring. The clock is positioned facing north with the aid of a compass; the plane of the hour ring is aligned with a point on the curved latitude scale that conforms to the latitude of the measurement site. In this way, the shadow-casting rod of the sundial is positioned parallel to the Earth's axis, so that its tip points to the north celestial pole and the hour ring is parallel to the earth's equator.

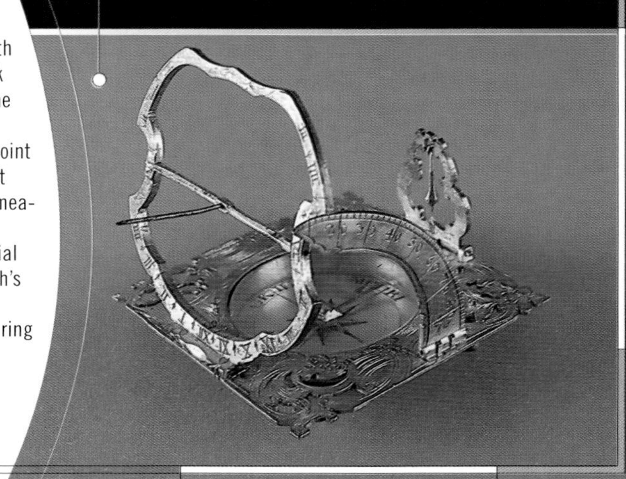

The Evolution of Cartography

Creating a Picture of the World

The first maps provided mankind with a means of creating a highly simplified, abstract image of the Earth. Long before aircraft were invented, the globe had already been depicted – from a bird's-eye view, so to speak – on a smaller, measurable scale in accordance with mathematical principles. Yet maps are never more than a reflection of social reality – of the knowledge, political visions, and religious beliefs of a given age. A map's claim to accuracy and reliability derives from the manner in which it was produced, from the degree of precision achieved by the engraver, lithographer, or draftsman, from the printer's command of his art, and from the ability of map-readers to recognize familiar aspects of their world.

Cartography

Since the mid-19th century, when the term "cartography" was first introduced, the art of map-making developed from a subdiscipline that served the needs of geodesy and geography into a science in its own right. By the early 20th century cartography had developed its own clearly defined concepts and methods.

Because of their military significance, the immense costs of making them, and the detailed nature of their contents, topographic maps remained a monopoly of the state in Europe until the latter half of the 19th century. Around the turn of the 18th to the 19th century, the nations of Europe began to establish statistical services and offices which published some of their data in topical maps intended for broad public use.

From the Disk to the Sphere

Even ancient cultures had maps of known territories showing possessions and boundaries. Excellent examples include the rock drawing of a Neolithic settlement in Çatal Hüyük dated about 6200 BC, the 3,500-year-old city map of Nippur in Babylon, and maps made by the ancient Greeks.

These early map-makers viewed the Earth as a flat disk, inhabited in the center and inaccessible at its outer edges. As knowledge increased, the disk expanded. New insights gained through the conquests of Alexander the Great and the observations of seafarers and scientists gave birth to the idea that the Earth is a sphere, for which Erastosthenes calculated a circumferences of 37,700 km (or 46,250 km, depending upon the conversion method applied) in c. 250 BC. He took his investigations a step further, projecting the three-dimensional segments of the sphere onto a flat surface and overlaying his map with a system of coordinates based upon the length and width of the Mediterranean Sea.

In the 2nd century AD, the astronomer, astrologist, and cartographer Ptolemy of Alexandria developed the first north-oriented map projection with longitudinally true lines of latitude. Ptolemy's instructions for map-making were distributed in copies, commentaries, and translations to geographers and cartographers – and along with them his globe had a circumference of only 29,000 km.

Immortalized in a Choir Loft: A wood sculpture of Claudius Ptolemaeus (Ptolemy) in the choir loft of the cathedral in Ulm (Michael Erhart, c. 1470). The publication of his Geographia in Ulm in 1482 revived the ancient concept of the shape of the world.

Mappae mundi – The Christian Image of the World

For the next several centuries, theology shaped mankind's view of the world and its representation on maps. Rome's influence waned, and the center of the new Christian world shifted to the east, to Jerusalem. Thus the maps of Christianity were oriented toward the east, and they depicted the earth once again as a flat disk. Like all works of art from this period, they proclaimed the greatness of God and the Church.

The emergence of Islam beginning in the 6th century AD posed a challenge to the dominant Christian view. Arab cartographers incorporated the ancient tradition of Ptolemy (the Earth as a sphere) into their scientific system and expanded their knowledge of the world through extensive travel and the use of astronomical instruments.

Unveiling the Earth

Maps used by seafarers and merchants were not documents of religious philosophy. Their maps were intended for practical use and were therefore as accurate as possible under the given circumstances. Portolan charts of the Mediterranean showed the coasts and major landmarks in detail, and, as studies have proven, contained only minor errors of distance.

However, maps of foreign countries and coastlines were usually kept locked away in the safes of rulers and merchants and were released for public use only after the existence of such regions had become widely known. Even Columbus lacked the most current maps on his journey of "discovery" to America. Although the Vikings had reached North America long before him, Columbus sailed westward into an "unknown" Atlantic (guided by Ptolemy's incorrect estimate of the earth's circumference) hoping to reach India. The newly discovered regions were presented on a world map made by Martin Waldseemüller as early as 1507.

Motivated by the prospect of finding new worlds beyond the horizon and by the lure of endless riches, the nations of Europe launched their campaign of worldwide exploration.

Surveying the Planet

The circumnavigation of the globe by Magellan's expedition had provided practical proof that the Earth is a sphere. Subsequent advances in science and the development of better instruments enabled cartographers to improve the accuracy and detail of their maps of the world over the course of the next several centuries. Unknown regions of the Earth were populated on maps with imaginary beings – an expression of horror vacui, the unwillingness of map-makers to reveal gaps in their knowledge to the general public. Later, they were simply entered as "white spots."

The era of cartographic precision based upon mathematical principles began in the latter half of the 18th century. In the nations of Europe, topographic surveys were carried out for military and administrative purposes, and the data obtained through these efforts serves even today as the basis for planning in modern countries.

Once it became possible to explore the Earth from space in the 20th century, the last remaining white spots disappeared from the maps of the world, and cartographers gained access to all the geographic data they could possibly need. Electronic data processing relieved map-makers of the arduous tasks of drawing and engraving maps, turning them into specialists in graphic communication.

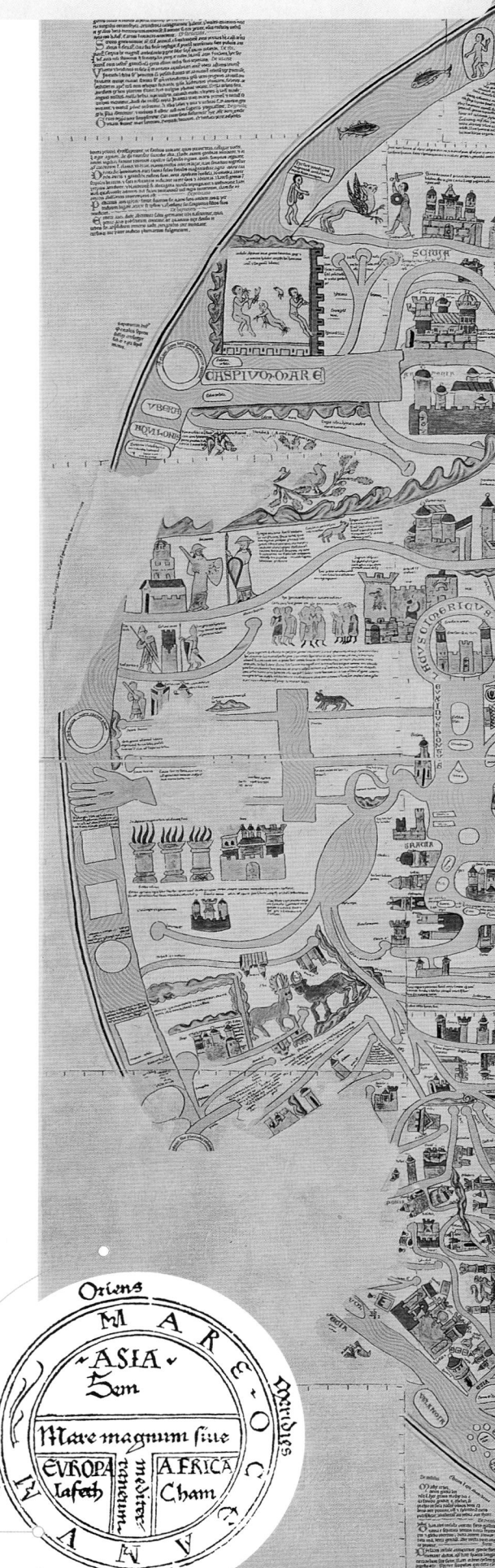

Image of the Medieval World

Produced between 1230 and 1240, the Ebstorf World Map is an example of medieval Christian cartography. Drawn in a TO configuration, it transposes the body of Christ onto the known world. Encircled by the O-shaped ocean, the Earth's landmasses are separated by the T (of the inland seas) – the symbol of Christ's death on the cross. The original map was destroyed by fire in a bombing raid on Hanover in 1943. A copy of the large map (358 x 356 cm) has survived in 30 parts.

The Schematic World

Schematic world map (TO map) by Isidor of Sevilla (1472), illustrating the Christian image of the world.

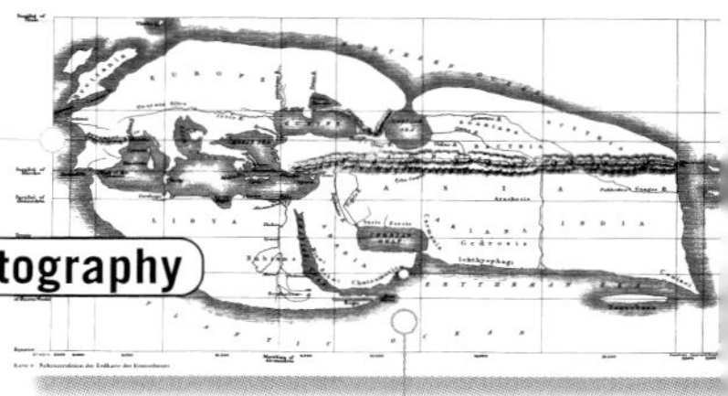

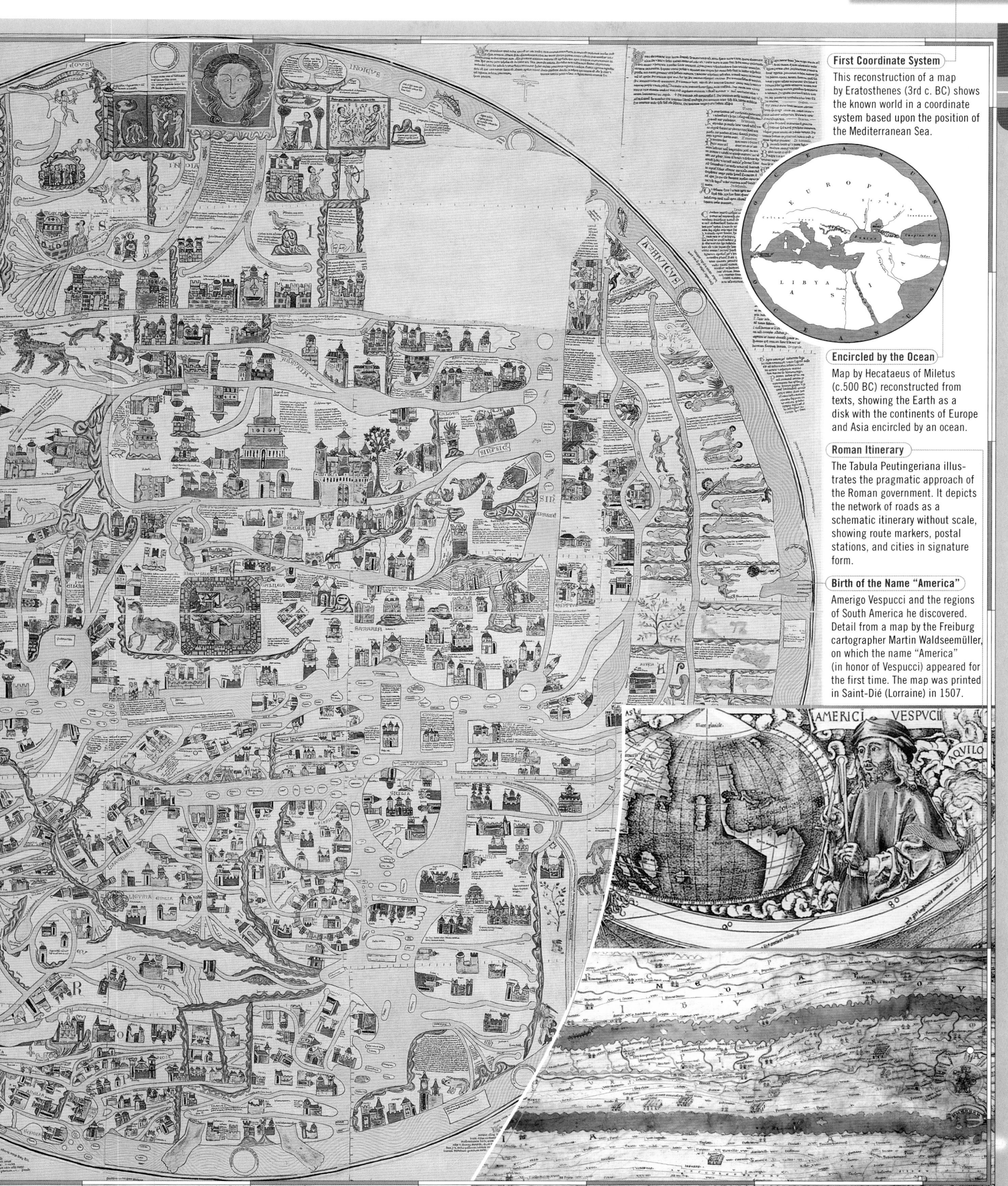

First Coordinate System

This reconstruction of a map by Eratosthenes (3rd c. BC) shows the known world in a coordinate system based upon the position of the Mediterranean Sea.

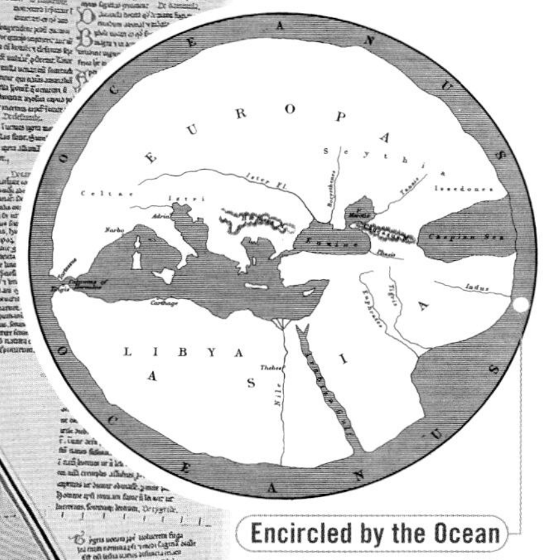

Encircled by the Ocean

Map by Hecataeus of Miletus (c.500 BC) reconstructed from texts, showing the Earth as a disk with the continents of Europe and Asia encircled by an ocean.

Roman Itinerary

The Tabula Peutingeriana illustrates the pragmatic approach of the Roman government. It depicts the network of roads as a schematic itinerary without scale, showing route markers, postal stations, and cities in signature form.

Birth of the Name "America"

Amerigo Vespucci and the regions of South America he discovered. Detail from a map by the Freiburg cartographer Martin Waldseemüller, on which the name "America" (in honor of Vespucci) appeared for the first time. The map was printed in Saint-Dié (Lorraine) in 1507.

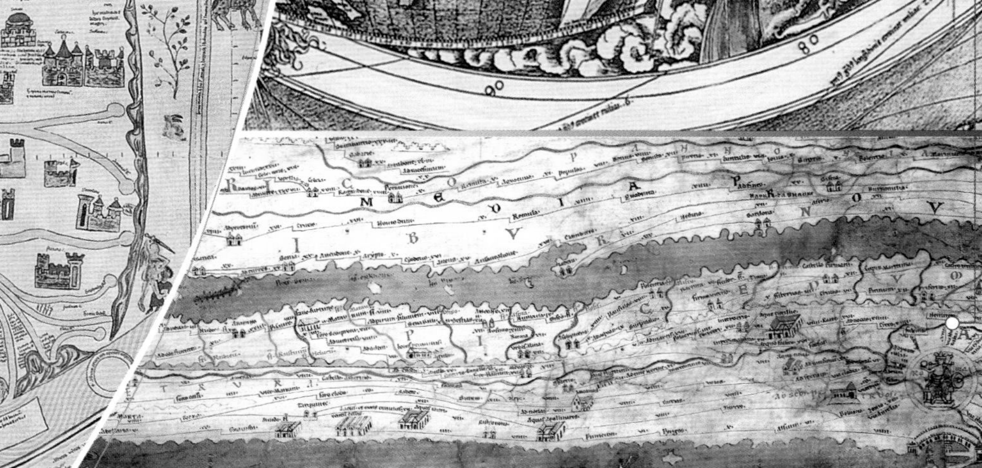

Tourism: Economics and the Environment

The Urge to Travel versus Environmental Awareness

Why do we travel, willingly accepting the costs and the risks it entails – disorientation and boredom, intestinal troubles and even malaria? Are we motivated to seek out new places less by curiosity than by the need to find ourselves? If so, the Greek philosopher Seneca reminds us that we cannot solve our problems by traveling to and fro, since "we always take ourselves along."

Aid or Exploitation

The tourist trade is the largest industry in the global economy in terms of both employees and investment volumes. The number of international tourists rose nearly 1000 % between 1960 (69 million) and 2000 (670 million). If we add those who travel within their own countries, the total number of tourists increases to about 5.3 billion. The Germans take the lead in world travel, while the French tend to stay at home and plan accordingly. The 180-km-long Mediterranean coast of the Languedoc-Roussillon region has been under development on a grand scale since 1963.

Many developing countries see tourism as a panacea for their economic problems but are often disappointed, as only a small portion of profits from the tourist trade actually flows into local economies.

A New Form of Colonialism?
Rebellion in Host Countries

People long believed that travel promotes better understanding of foreign cultures and thus contributes to inter-national peace. Yet it appears that it often has the opposite effect, as old prejudices are strengthened and new ones emerge through tourism. It has become increasingly clear since the 1970s that the influx of tourists can indeed cause grave social and environmental problems. Natural landscapes are damaged (by winter sports, for example), traditional cultural landscapes are permeated by functional architecture, long-standing customs give way to behavior patterns apparently imposed by foreign visitors. Lost local and regional cultural heritage cannot be replaced. The voices of those who are no longer willing to be marketed are growing stronger in many countries. Yet the potential positive effects of globalization through tourism should not be overlooked, as contact with tourists from abroad can provide encouragement for social and economic development.

The Hard Road to Soft Tourism

In some parts of the world, indigenous communities rely on cooperation with travel companies in the hope of generating income with innovative forms of environmental tourism without placing their own cultures and environments at risk. But to what extent is this kind of sustainable tourism really possible?

It would seem to call for a new breed of traveler. Tour organizers, airlines, and publishers of tourists' guides take an optimistic view. A number of them have joined forces in support of a code of ethics for travelers.

The Most on the Coast
Built in 1967–77 according to plans by French architect Jean Marie Balladour, La Grande-Motte, a vacation area on the coast of Languedoc near Montpellier, offers the "total beach experience."

Giddy Heights
Heliskiing in virtually unexplored terrain accessible only by helicopter. There are 43 officially recognized mountain landing sites for helicopters in Switzerland, 16 of them at elevations above 3,000 m.

Meeting of Two Worlds
Oblivious to tourist photographers, the Tuareg drive their salt caravans through the Ténéré Desert (Niger), traveling for months at a time to reach their markets in Nigeria.

Adventure tours in deserts, mountains, rainforests, in polar or other regions must be judged by the respect they show for local cultures and environments.

Satellite Section

Hurricane Floyd

From September 14 through
18, 1999, Hurricane Floyd
swept the East Coast of the
United States with heavy winds
and rains, causing extensive
flooding and storm damage. A
state of emergency was declared in ten southeastern and
mid-Atlantic states. This satellite
image provides a vivid picture of
the hurricane's vast breadth.
Future hurricanes are identified
while still in the embryonic phase
with conventional satellite imaging
techniques. Floyd was born in early
September as "Tropical Low-Pressure System Number 8" near the
Cape Verde Islands off the west
coast of Africa.

Technical data relating to the satellite images presented in this section
can be found in the small information
insets provided with each image. The
symbols in these inserts have the following meanings:

Name of satellite or imaging process — NOAA-AVHRR

Ground resolution — 1 000 m

Exposure altitude — 840 km

Date of image — Sep. 15, 1999

Remote Satellite Surveying

How Do Earth Survey Satellites Work?

Most Earth survey satellites travel around the Earth at an altitude of between 600 and 900 km in an almost circular near-polar orbit. The time it takes to complete a single orbit ranges from 90 to 120 minutes.

Depending upon the type of equipment used, satellite imaging systems scan the Earth's surface in strips varying in width from eleven to 2,000 km. Detail resolution ranges from one meter (high resolution, e.g. IKONOS) to one kilometer (medium resolution, e.g. NOAA-AVHRR weather satellites) per image pixel. The imaging sensor of some satellites can be rotated laterally or in a complete circle. This makes it possible to obtain multiple images of especially interesting regions or to produce stereoscopic images used to create digital terrain models. Image data are ordinarily transmitted by satellites to ground stations distributed around the world. Satellites also have the capacity to store image data from areas beyond the reception range of ground stations until they can be retrieved by the nearest ground receiving station.

Panoramic View of Salzburg

New perspectives for regional imaging have emerged from the combination of satellite image data with digital terrain models (DTM), which are produced either from topographic maps or stereoscopic aerial or satellite photographs. They provide elevation data on every point on the Earth's surface. Such terrain models make it possible to derive through computation a wide range of panoramic views from vertical images. They serve as the basis for virtual flights through a landscape.

The picture below is a panorama developed in this way from Landsat TM and SPOT Pan data of the Salzburg lowlands, showing the Obertrum lakes in the foreground and the regional capital of Salzburg in the center. The summits of the Hagen Mountains rise along the horizon behind the high plateau of the Tennen Mountains. Visible in the background are the Central Alps and Austria's highest peak, the Grossglockner (3,798 m).

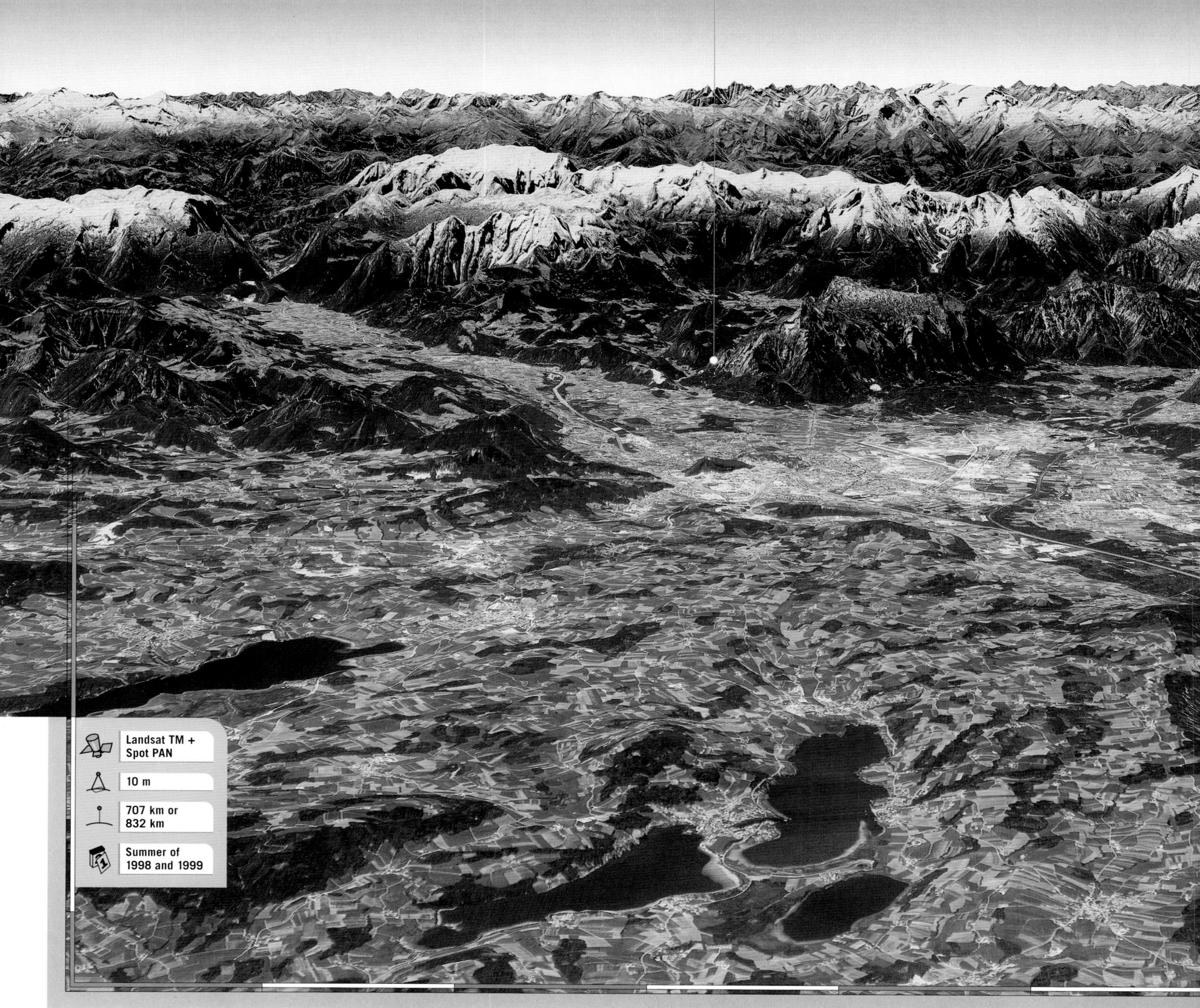

Landsat TM + Spot PAN

10 m

707 km or 832 km

Summer of 1998 and 1999

Austria

Ecuador

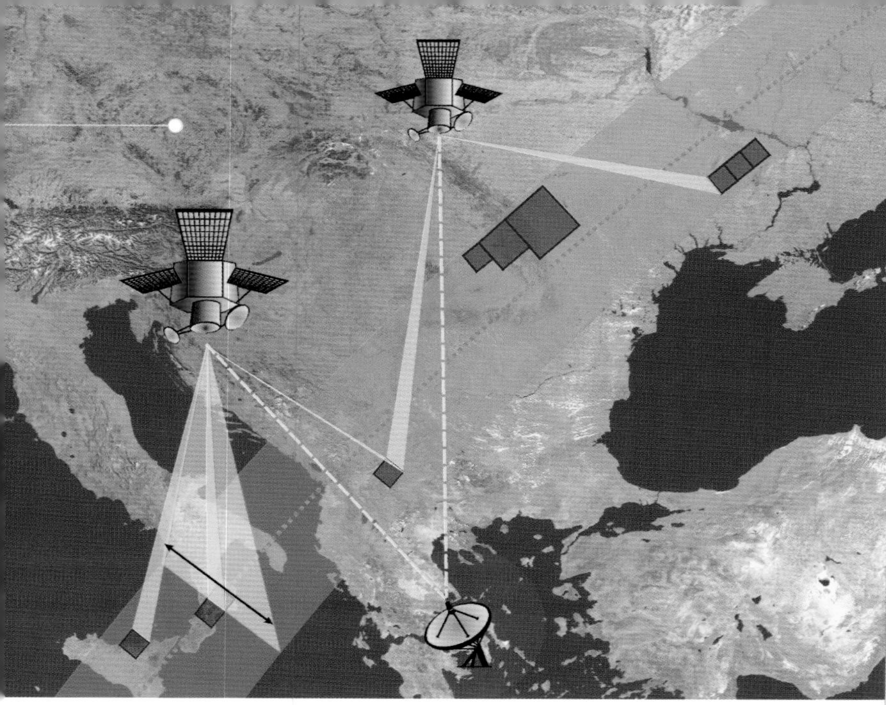

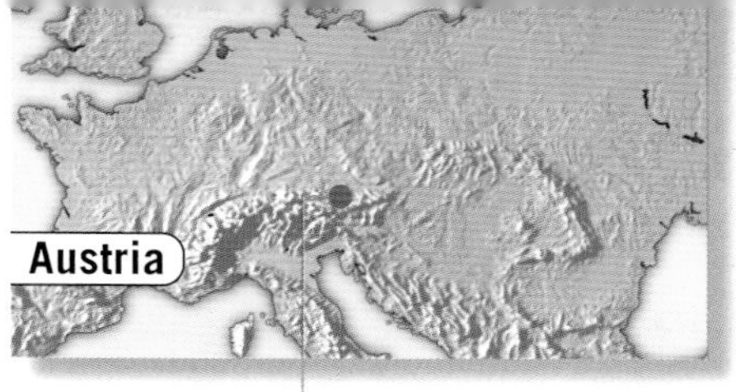

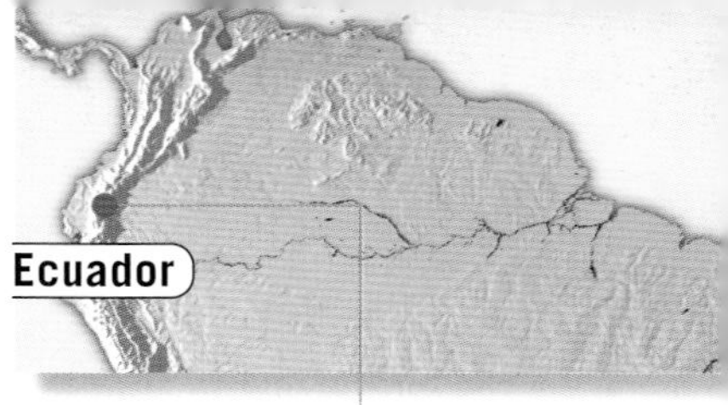

Digital Elevation Model of Cotopaxi

The Shuttle Radar Topography Mission (SRTM) achieved a new level of quality in the production of digital elevation models. In February 2000, the Space Shuttle Endeavor embarked on a mission devoted to setting up a system capable of producing a three-dimensional image of the Earth with the aid of multiple radar antennas attached to a 60-meter-long extendable mast. Using a radar interferometry technique, two radar images are taken from positions offset only slightly from one another. The differences between the two images are used to compute the elevation curves of the exposed terrain, which are then displayed on a map.

Our image shows Mount Cotopaxi in the Eastern Cordilleras of Ecuador, at 5,897 m the highest active volcano on Earth. The volcano has erupted 50 times since 1738, most recently in 1904 and 1928. The flow trenches of the cone-shaped volcano are clearly visible in the digital elevation model. As the snow line lies at an altitude of 4,000 m, the danger of mudslides in the flow trenches is great.

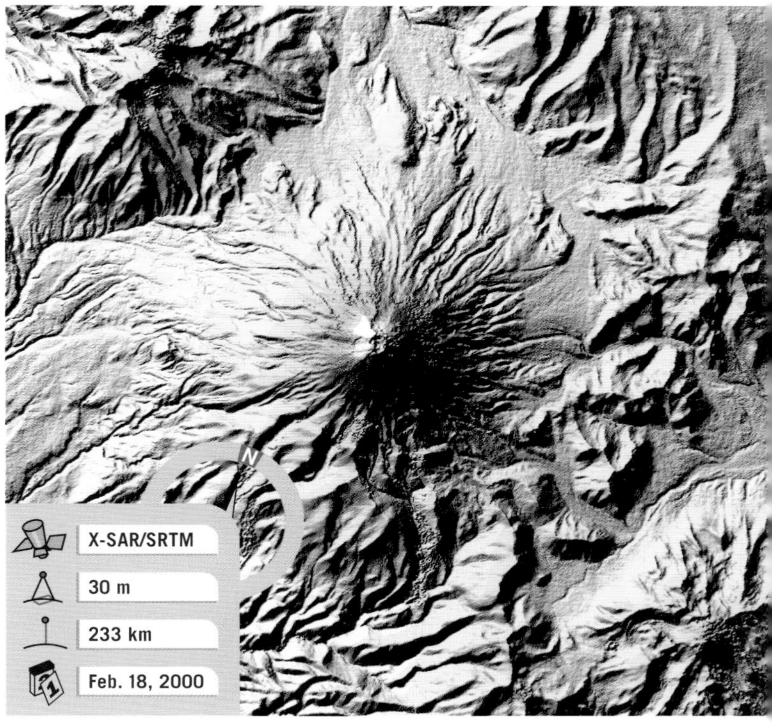

	X-SAR/SRTM
	30 m
	233 km
	Feb. 18, 2000

Source: DLR

	ERS
	25 m
	780 km
	Aug. 7, 1998

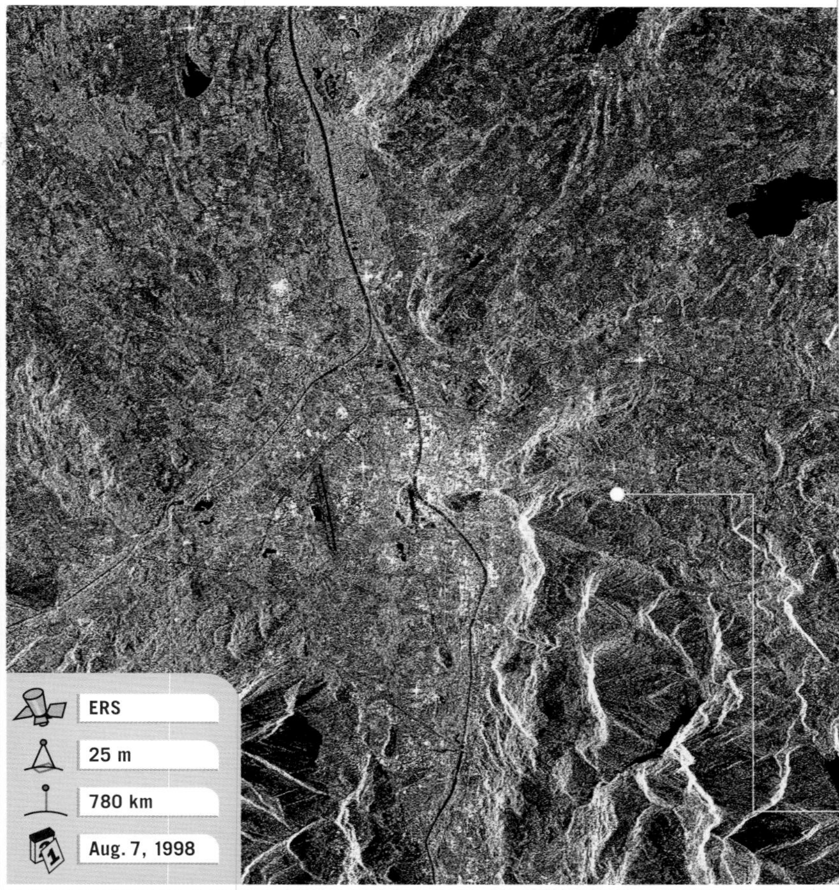

Radar Image of Salzburg

Radar image of the city of Salzburg showing parts of the Flachgau and the Tennengau. While "conventional" Earth survey satellites pick up solar radiation reflected by the Earth (passive sensing systems), many radar satellites have the capacity to emit electromagnetic impulses and measure their reflection (active sensor systems), from which "images" can be computed. The strongest reflection comes from topographic ridges. Radar images can also be obtained at night or through cloud cover.

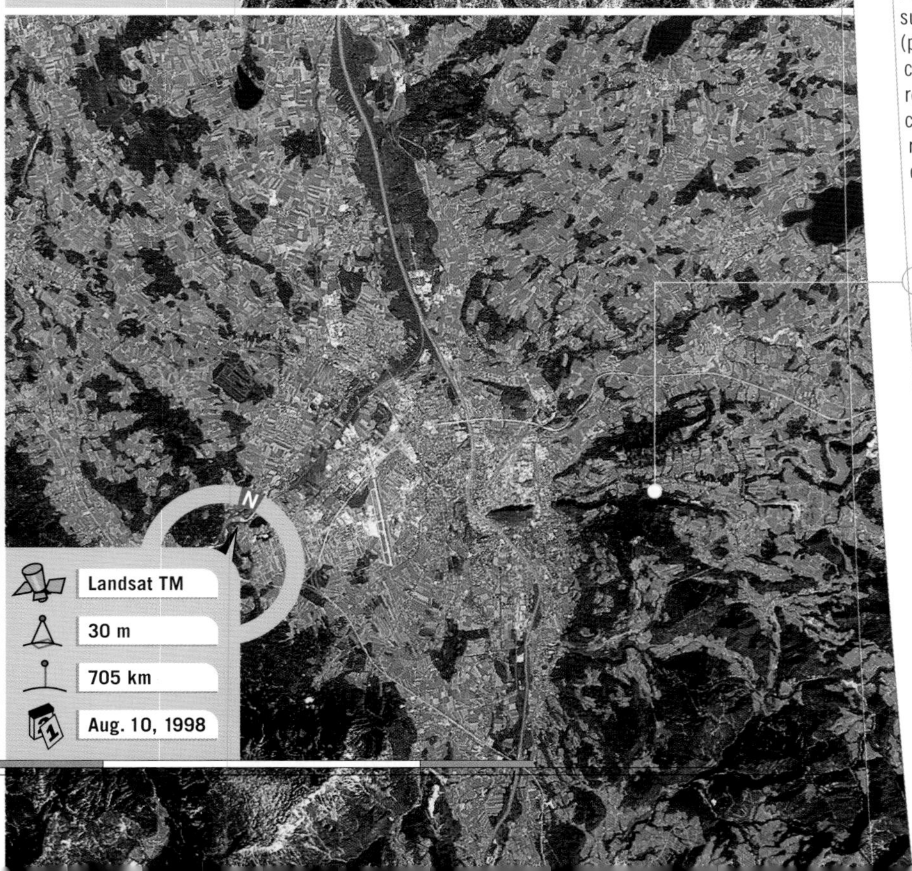

Landsat Thematic Mapper Image of Salzburg

As an example of an image produced by optical sensors, this Landsat Thematic Mapper image of Salzburg presents a much more "realistic" picture of the Earth. Optical sensors ordinarily operate in the visible, proximate infrared range. Some sensor systems produce images in the middle or thermal infrared ranges, registering in the latter the thermal radiation from the Earth's surface. The reflected radiation picked up by sensors is broken down into multiple spectral ranges (4 in SPOT, 8 in LANDSAT 7), making it possible to produce images in natural colors or in infrared or false colors (which lend themselves better to scientific analysis) from the exposures by mixing the various wavelengths. The nature of ground cover can be interpreted with the support of computer-aided imaging processes, as every surface has distinctive reflective characteristics. This facilitates recognition of water surfaces, wooded areas (deciduous, mixed, and coniferous forest), residential developments, industrial areas, etc.

	Landsat TM
	30 m
	705 km
	Aug. 10, 1998

The Earth from Space

Topographic Image

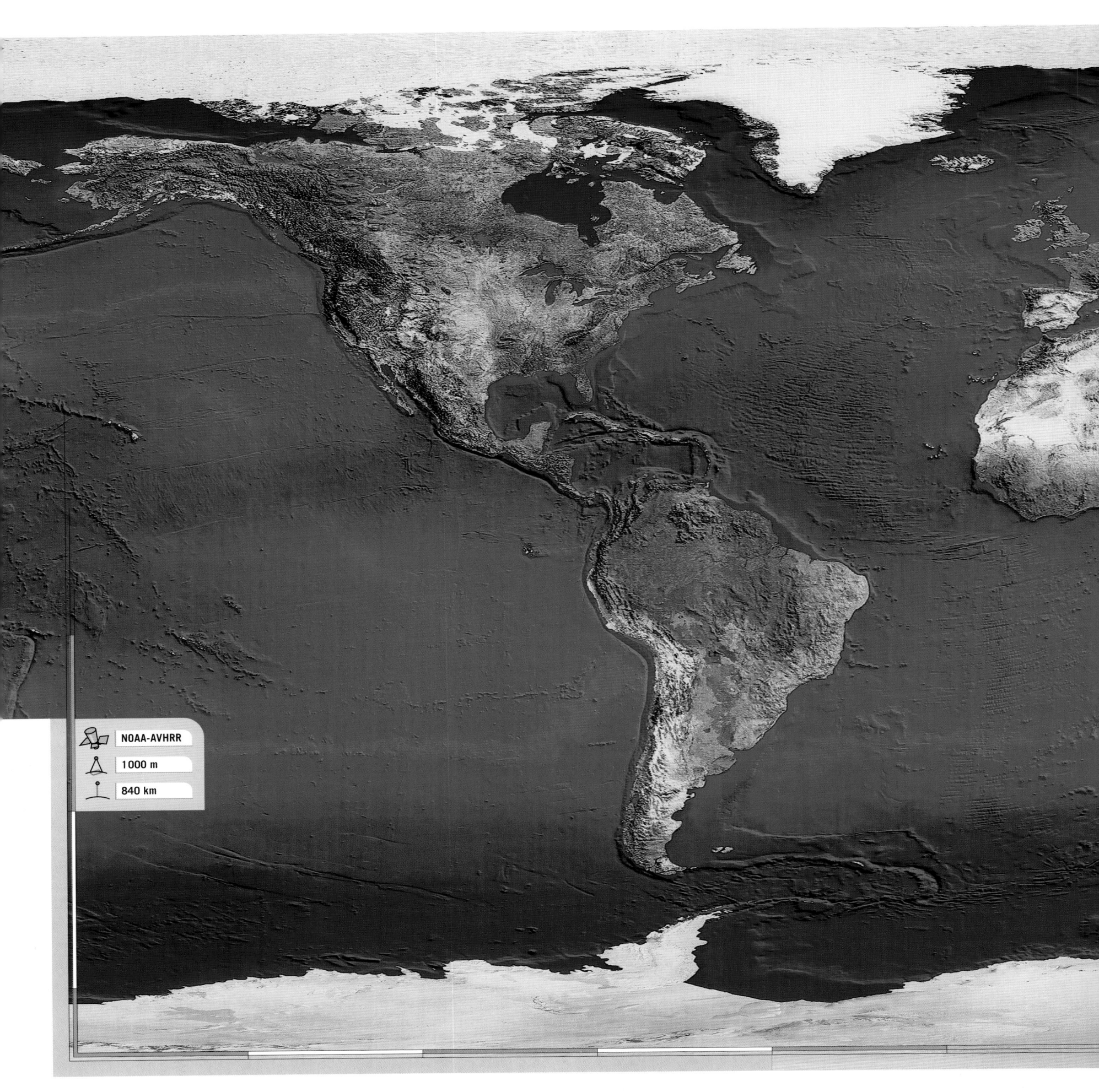

NOAA-AVHRR

1000 m

840 km

View of the Earth from Space

Several thousand images from the U.S. NOAA Satellite Series were required to compile this completely cloudless picture of the Earth.
In the projection selected for this satellite imagery map, the polar regions extend along the full length of the Equator. The continents are true to form to north and south latitudes of about 35 degrees, but distortion grows more extreme toward the poles.
This composite satellite image gives a good overview of major landscapes of the continents and their vegetation patterns. A particularly striking feature is the belt of deserts that encircles the globe.

(Copyright: GEOSPACE / World Sat International Corp. 2000)

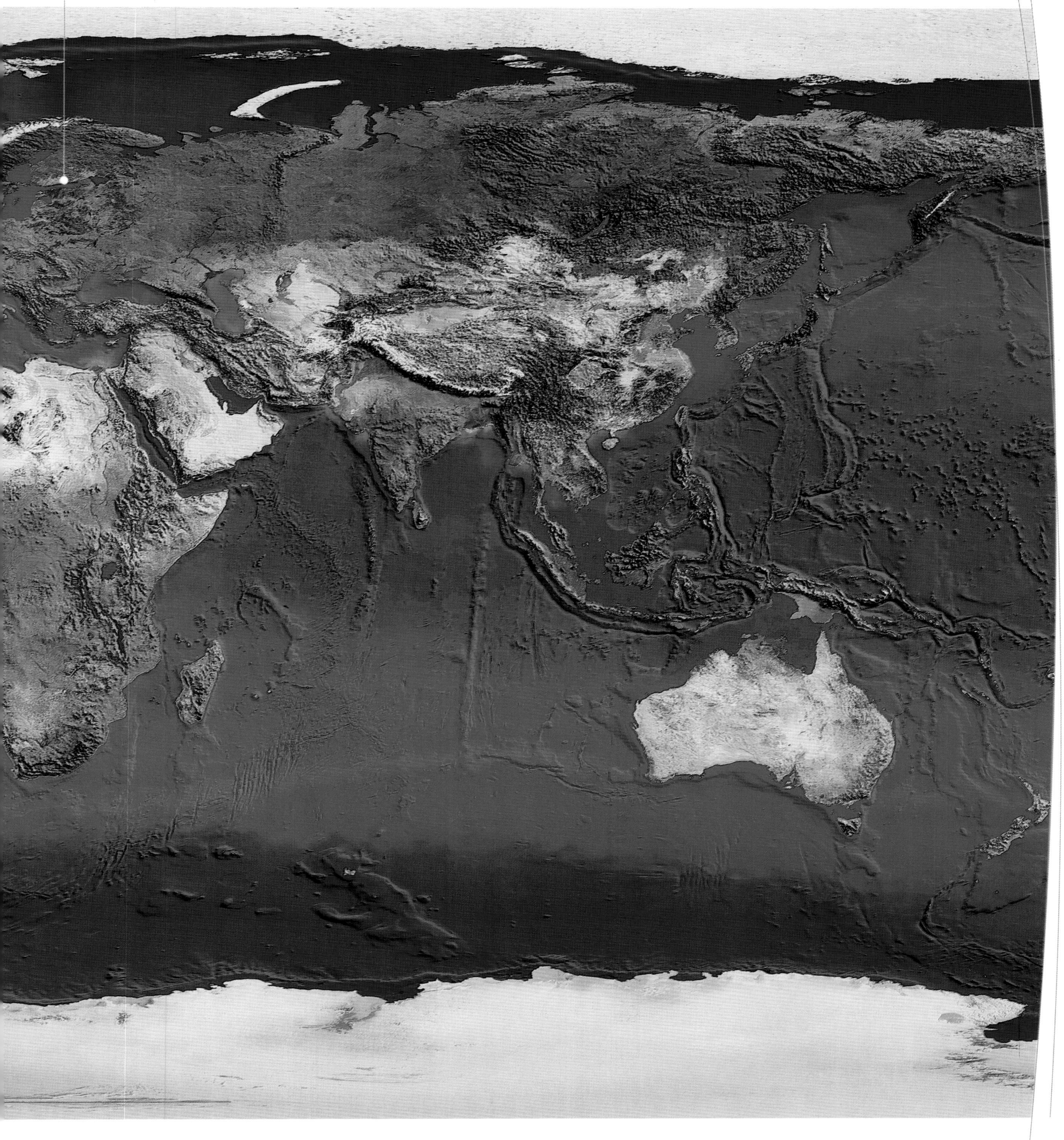

The Earth's Surface

Land and Seafloor Topography

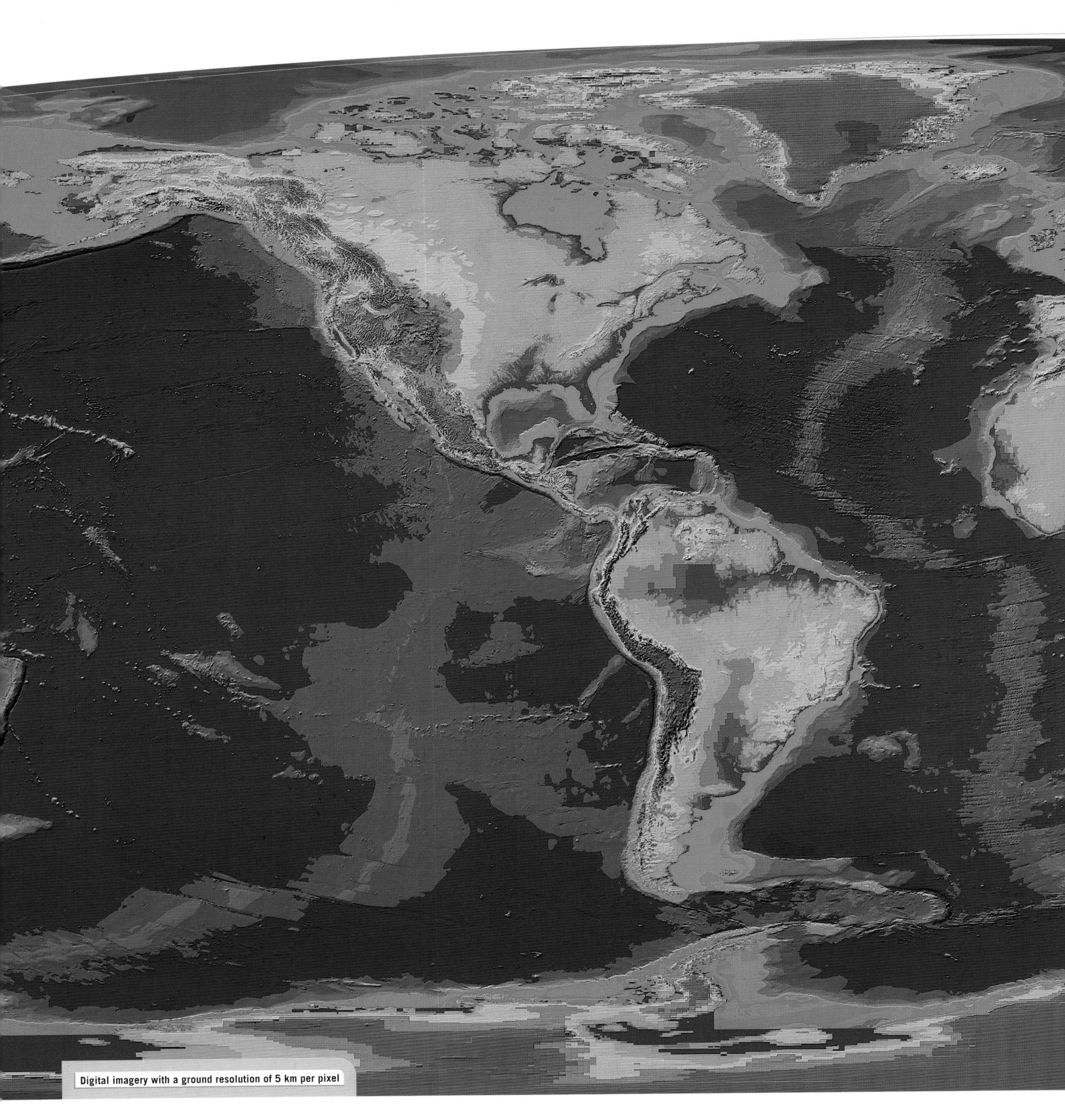

Digital imagery with a ground resolution of 5 km per pixel

The Earth's Surface

Shelf seas along the world's coastlines (light blue areas) trace the outlines of continental landmasses and highlight the topographic connections between offshore islands and their "parent" continents. The submerged oceanic ridges of the Atlantic and Indian Oceans stand out clearly as the longest continuous mountain ranges on Earth.

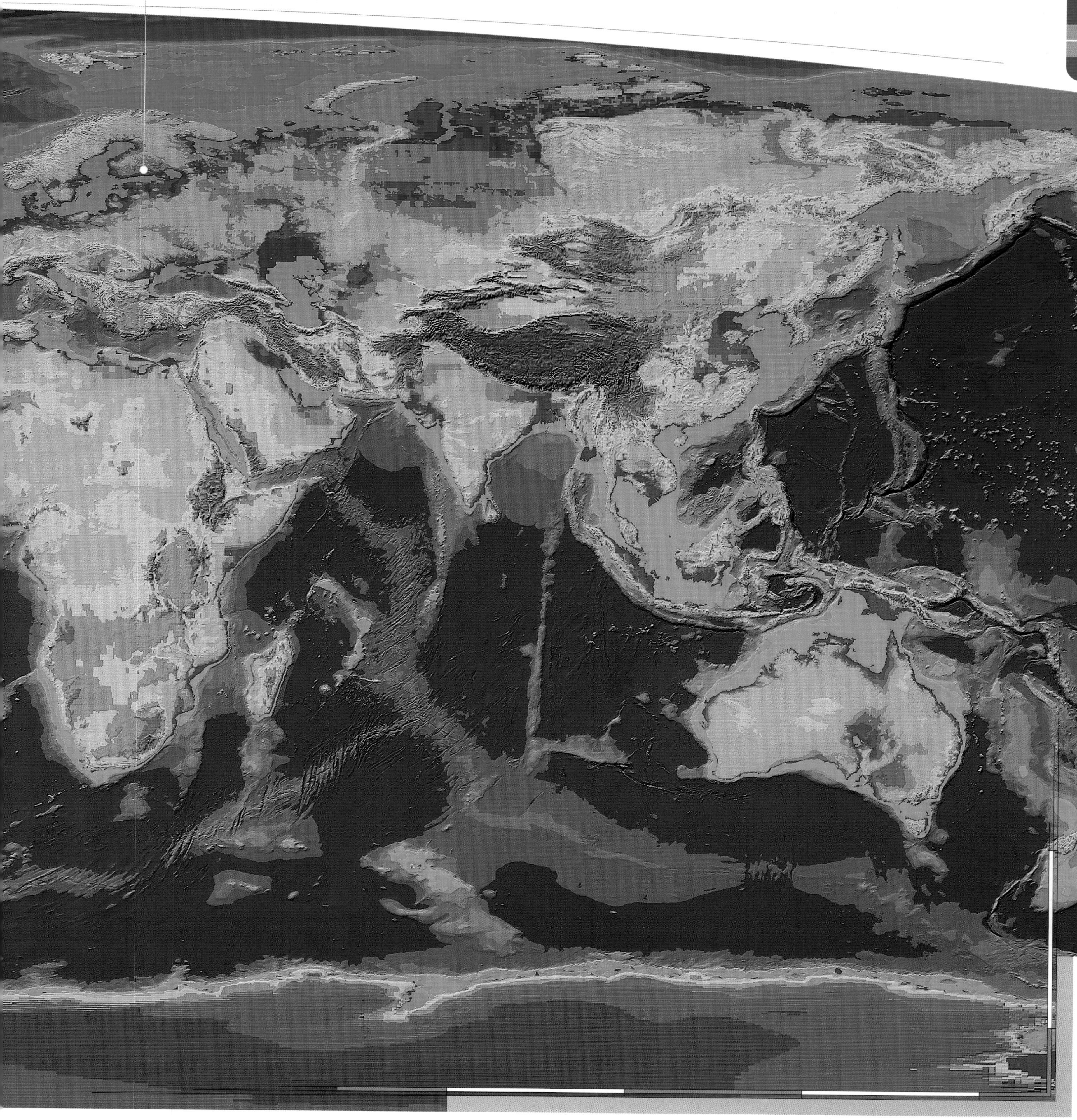

Volcanism

Living Links to the Earth's Core

Landsat TM

30 m

705 km

Aug. 20, 1986

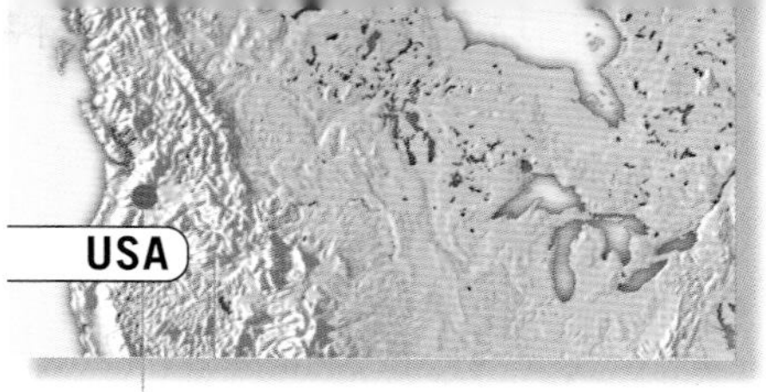

Mt. Saint Helens

One of the most spectacular natural events of the latter half of the
20th century was the eruption of Mount Saint Helens in the Cascade Range in the state of Oregon. All of the active volcanoes of North
America are located in this chain of mountains that extends from
northern California to Canada. The region without vegetation in the
center of the image is the area of volcanic devastation surrounding
the collapsed oval crater (caldera) and Spirit Lake.
Originally 2,948 m high, the mountain known by the Indians as the
"Guardian of Fire" lost about 400 m of elevation during the eruption
on May 18, 1980. Avalanches of melted snow, mud, and rock debris
rushed down two river valleys, sweeping away bridges and houses and
cutting long swaths through the forests. A massive fountain of ash
rose up to 23 km into the stratosphere from the mountain's fractured
northern flank. The shockwave knocked down all trees within miles
of the cone like matches. Sixty people died in the inferno.
Less violent eruptions occurred in 1984, 1986, 1989, and 1991.

Mount Aetna

Mount Aetna, the highest active volcano in Europe, towers
above the eastern coast of Sicily between Catania and
Taormina on the shores of the Ionian Sea.
The last major eruption of Mount Aetna (present elevation:
3,350 m) occurred in 2001 and threatened the village
of Nicolosi. This thermal image shows the pattern of temperature distribution on the surface of the powerful
volcano. Red indicates areas of high temperature; blue
represents lower surface temperatures. Temperatures are
markedly influenced by solar radiation (exposed versus
shaded surfaces). Typical of Mount Aetna are its many
parasite craters – the largest of which are clearly recognizable on the western and southeastern sides of the
volcano. Also evident are the numerous fissures and
steam springs through which magma gases are released.

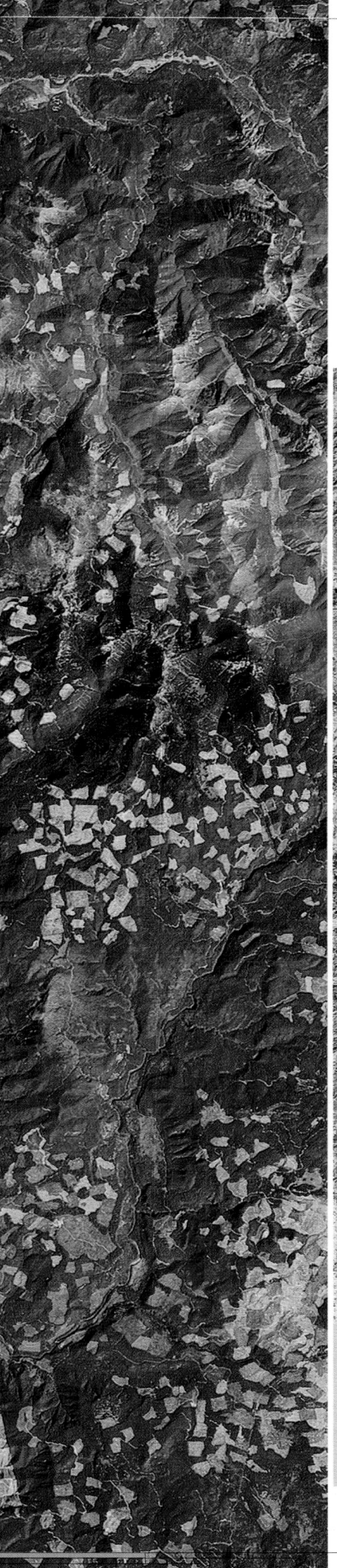

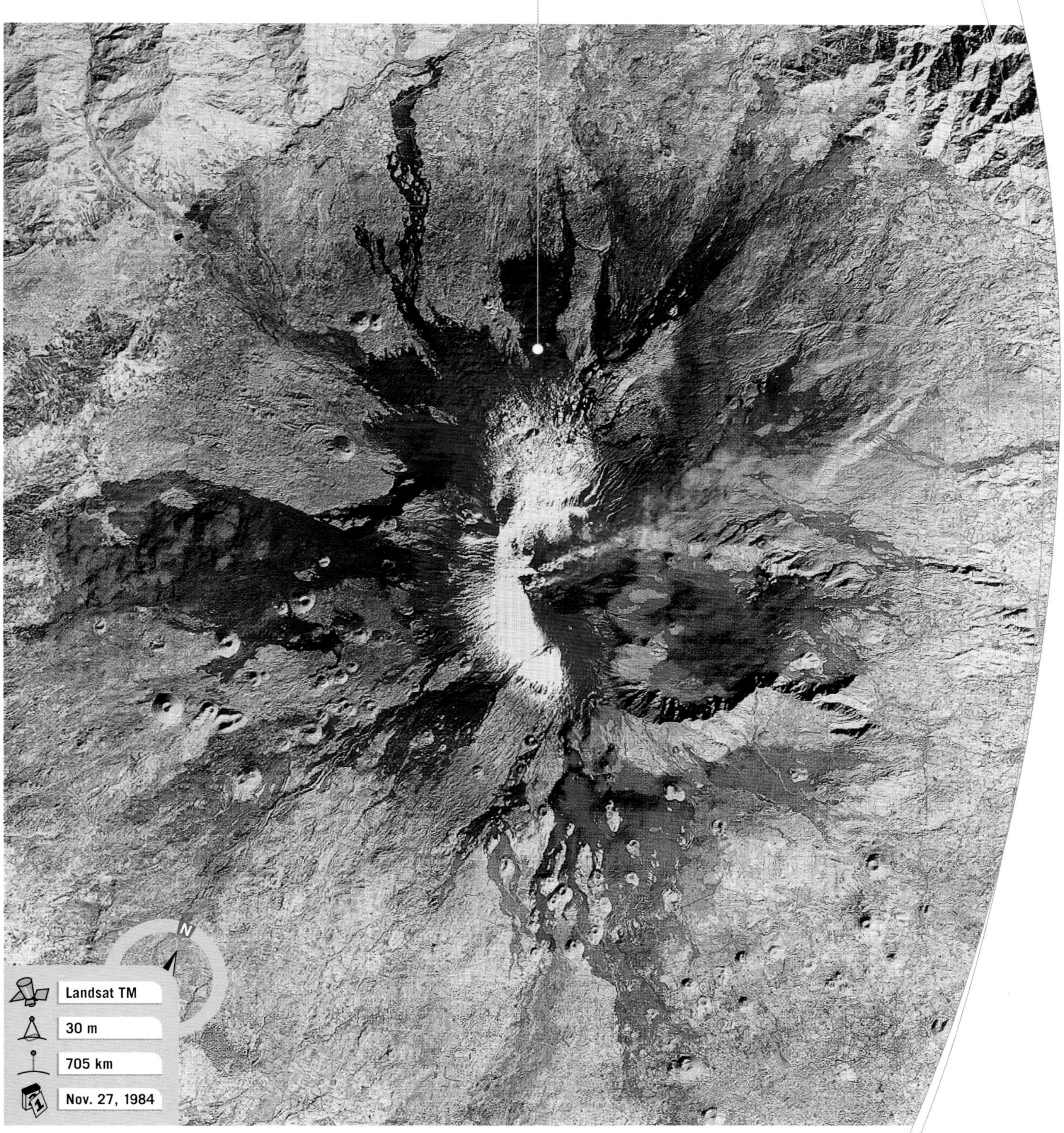

	Landsat TM
	30 m
	705 km
	Nov. 27, 1984

Meteorite Crater

Threat from Outer Space

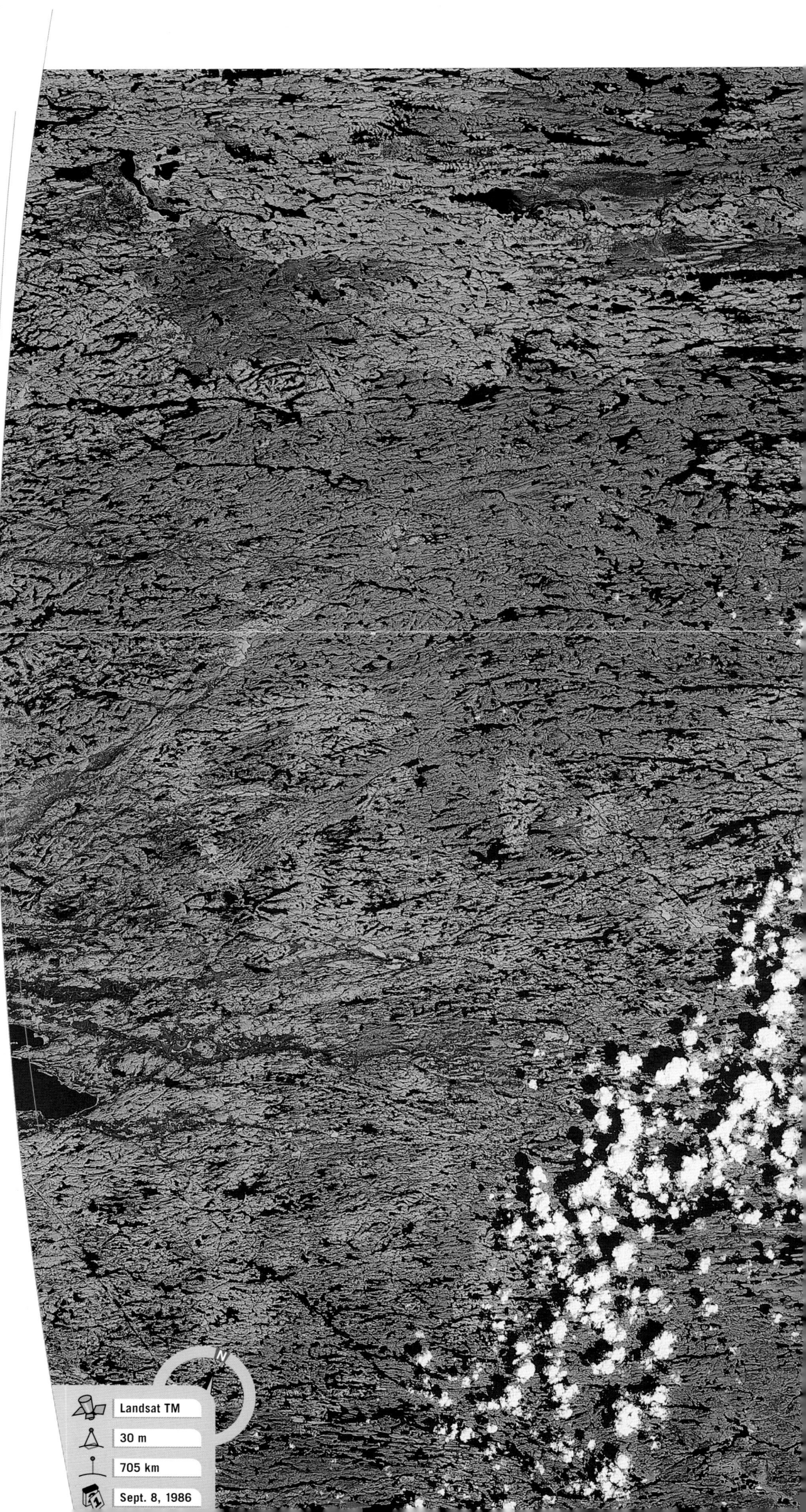

Clearwater Lake

This satellite image shows the two basins
of Clearwater Lake in the Canadian province
of Quebec. The lakebeds are the product of
an extremely rare event – the impact of "twin
meteorites" – that occurs only about once
every one million years, when two presumably
related meteorite fragments strike the earth
in succession. Complex craters formed by
impacts of large meteorites are characterized
by a central mountain formation.

The islands in the larger of the two lakes are
the visible remnants of such a central
mountain formation, left exposed after the
craters filled with water.

The impact that formed the lakes is presumed
to have occurred some 300 million years ago.

Landsat TM

30 m

705 km

Sept. 8, 1986

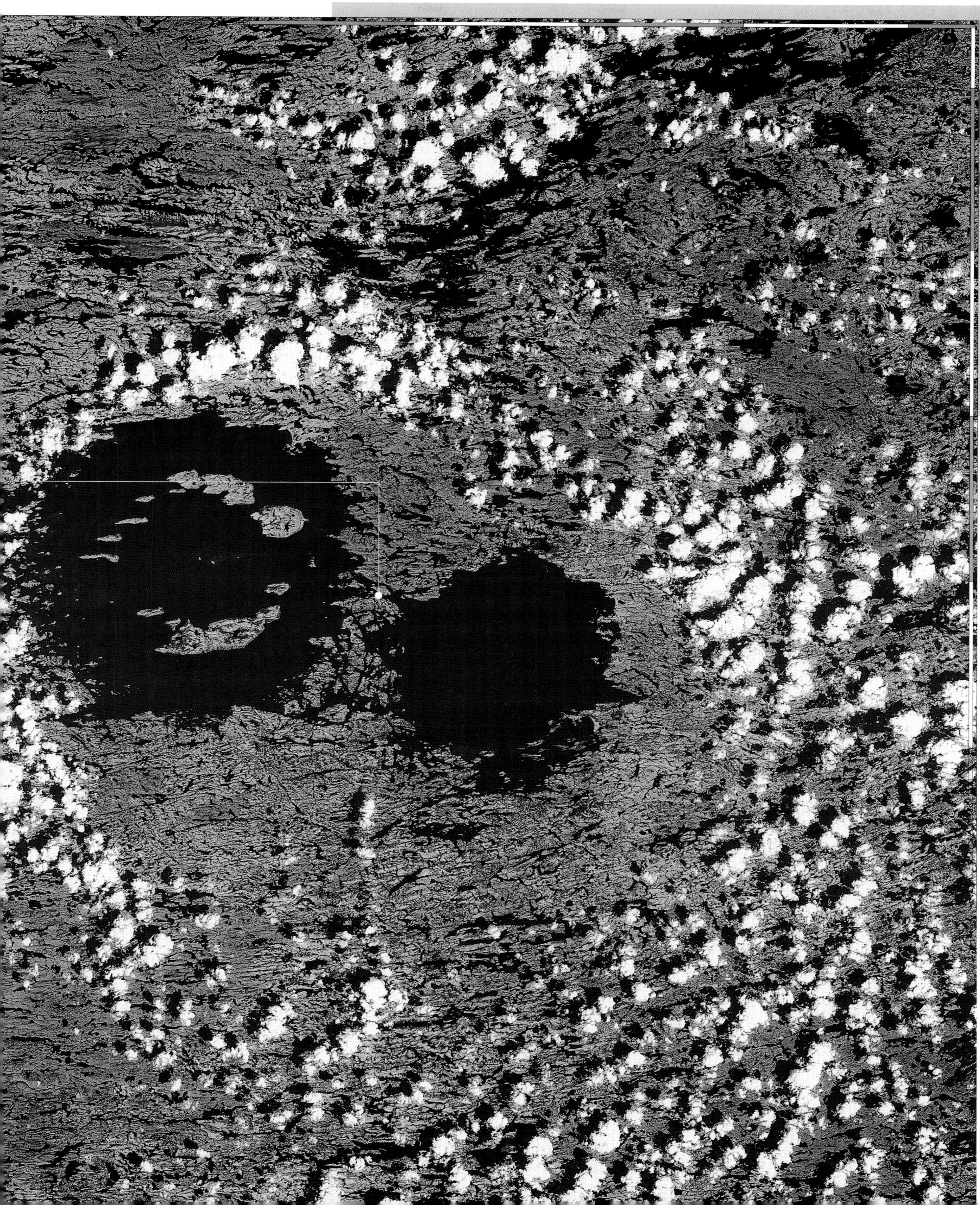

Climate

Storms and a Dangerous Christ Child

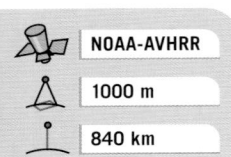

NOAA-AVHRR

1000 m

840 km

Temperature distribution
September 9, 1986

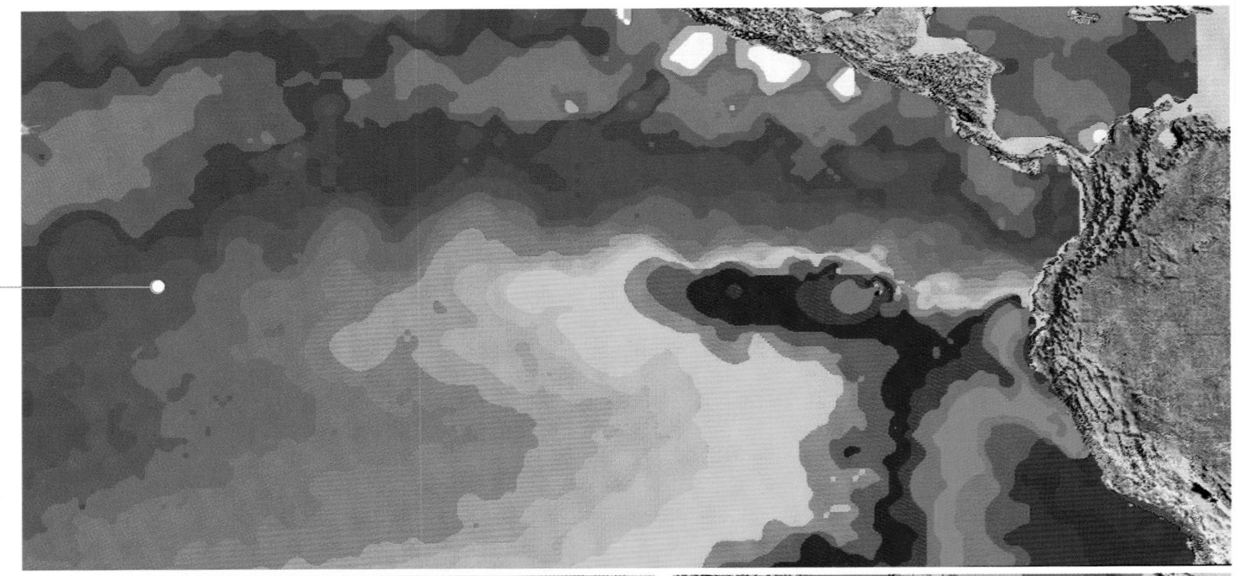

Temperature distribution
September 5, 1987

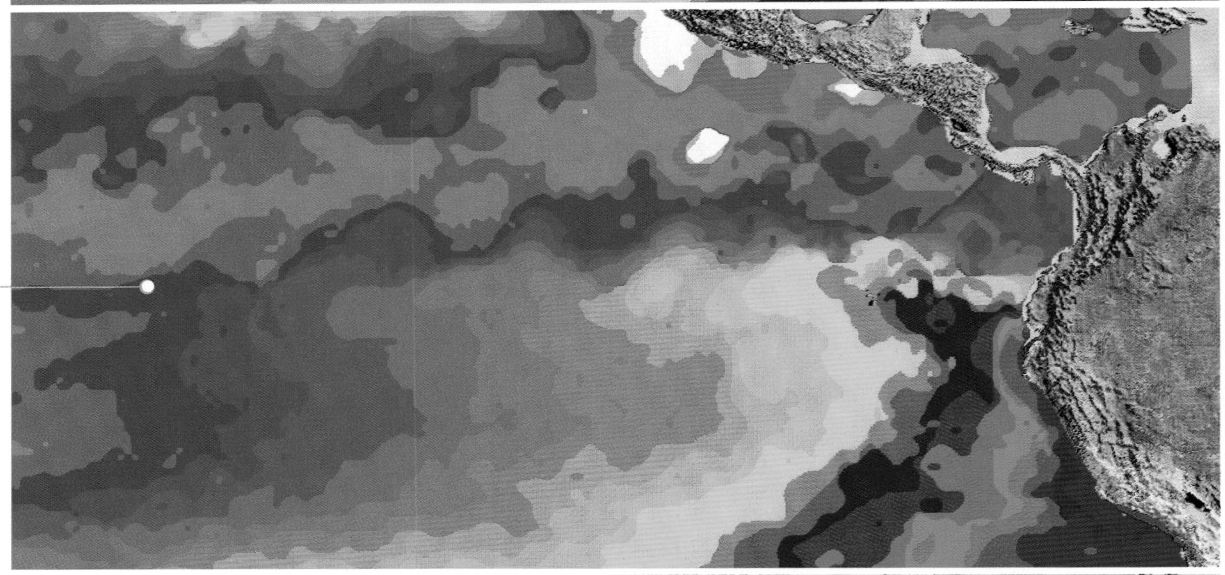

Temperature distribution
September 6, 1988

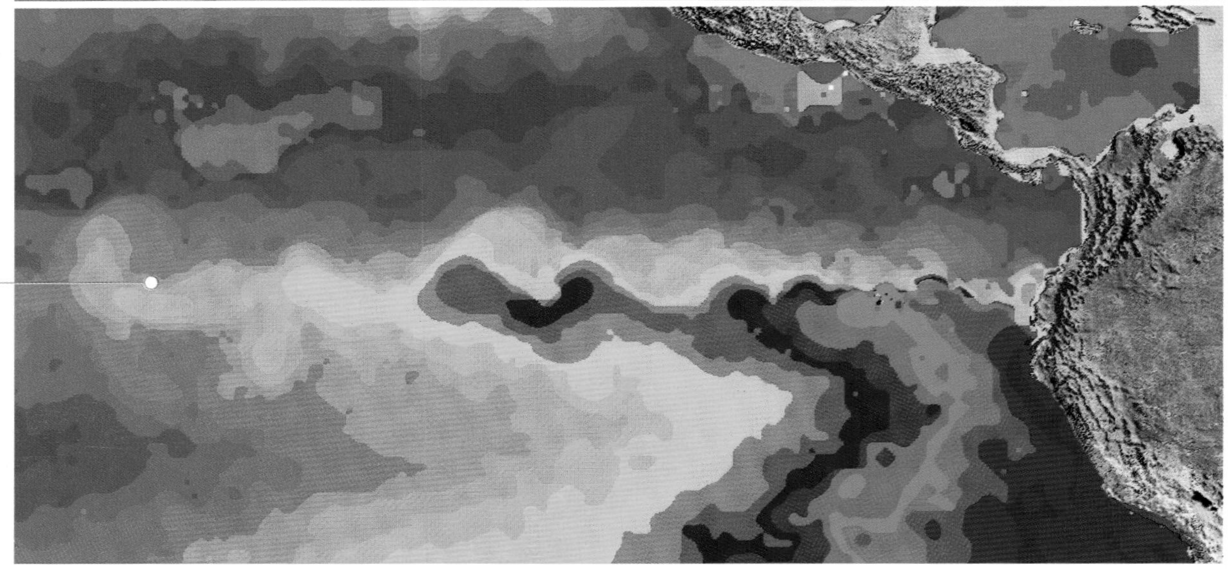

El Niño

The El Niño phenomenon appears in the Pacific around Christmas time at intervals of between four and 30 years. El Niño is Spanish for "the (Christ) Child." It is the result of extreme pressure differences between the Australo-Asiatic low-pressure and the South Pacific high-pressure systems. These differences generate strong currents of warm water moving toward the west, which in turn produce cold reverse streams at lower depths along the path of the Humboldt current. When the pressure differential changes, the warmed water begins to flow eastward again, heating the air above it. This leads to periods of heavy precipitation along the western coast of South America and corresponding droughts in large parts of Asia and Australia. One such El Niño year was registered in 1987. The phenomenon was particularly severe in 1997/98.
The thermal image of the Pacific shows masses of warm water (shades of yellow and red) approaching the South American coastline.

< 16.5 °C	21.0 – 21.5 °C	26.0 – 26.5 °C
16.5 – 17.0 °C	21.5 – 22.0 °C	26.5 – 27.0 °C
17.0 – 17.5 °C	22.0 – 22.5 °C	27.0 – 27.5 °C
17.5 – 18.0 °C	22.5 – 23.0 °C	27.5 – 28.0 °C
18.0 – 18.5 °C	23.0 – 23.5 °C	28.0 – 28.5 °C
18.5 – 19.0 °C	23.5 – 24.0 °C	28.5 – 29.0 °C
19.0 – 19.5 °C	24.0 – 24.5 °C	29.0 – 29.5 °C
19.5 – 20.0 °C	24.5 – 25.0 °C	29.5 – 30.0 °C
20.0 – 20.5 °C	25.0 – 25.5 °C	30.0 – 30.5 °C
20.5 – 21.0 °C	25.5 – 26.0 °C	> 30.5 °C

N

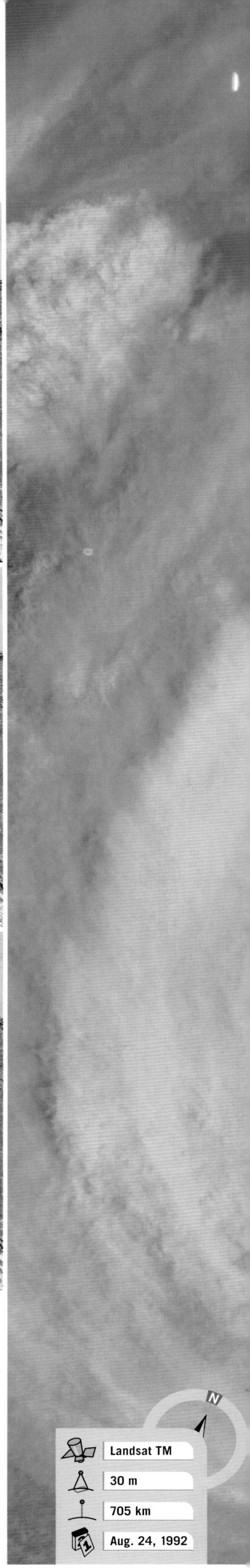

Landsat TM

30 m

705 km

Aug. 24, 1992

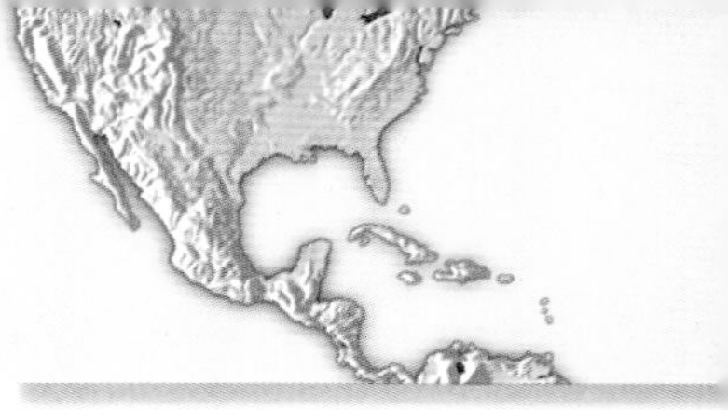

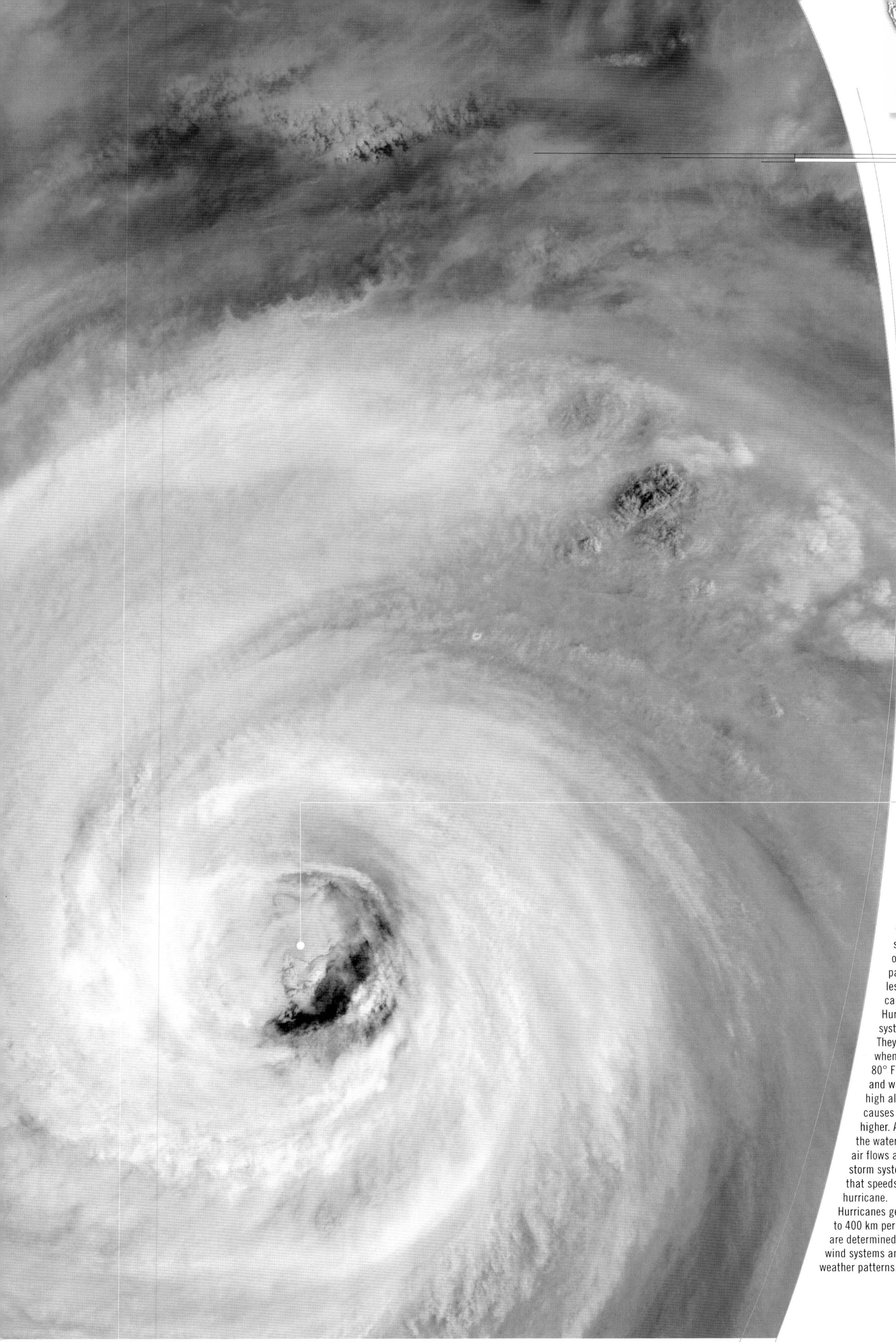

Hurricane Andrew

On August 24, 1992, Hurricane Andrew swept through the densely populated region of South Florida with peak wind speeds exceeding 270 km per hour, leaving a trail of devastation in its wake. Forty-seven people were killed, and some 350,000 lost their homes. The satellite image shows a vividly clear picture of the characteristic spiral cloud pattern and the virtually windless eye at the center of the hurricane.

Hurricanes are born as low-pressure systems formed by storm cells. They become particularly dangerous when water temperatures reach 80° F or above. Moist, warm air rises, and water vapor condenses at high altitudes, releasing heat, which causes the air column to rise even higher. Air pressure immediately above the water's surface falls, and moist air flows at an accelerated pace into the storm system — a vicious circle that speeds the development of the hurricane.

Hurricanes generate wind speeds of up to 400 km per hour. Their paths are determined by prevailing global wind systems and major regional weather patterns.

Climate   Changes in the Ozone Layer – The Ozone Hole

The large quantities of chlorofluorocarbons (CFC), used in spray dispensers and as coolants in refrigerators for example) released into the atmosphere every year produce chemical changes in the stratosphere which destroy the protective shell of the ozone layer encircling the Earth. The ozone layer absorbs some of the harmful ultraviolet B radiation emitted by the Sun and helps regulate the heat budget of the atmosphere. Ozone depletion is most severe above the southern hemisphere during the months of September and October. NASA and the Ozone Research Program of the European Union have been observing changes in the ozone layer for many years. Seasonal fluctuations are illustrated in the series of images below, which show that ozone concentrations can fall to half their normal levels in certain years.

Higher atmospheric temperatures above the Arctic (as compared to the south polar region) reduce the danger of ozone depletion, although the sequence of images shows an increase here as well. The ozone veil above the Arctic is not as thin as that in the Antarctic stratosphere. However, chemical analysis has shown that the composition of the atmosphere above the north polar regions has suffered nearly the same degree of disturbance as that above the Antarctic.

Many of the consequences of atmospheric ozone depletion for mankind are well known. The increased intensity of UV radiation causes a higher incidence of sunburn and skin cancer and a general impairment of the human immune system. High UV radiation levels also have a lasting impact on plant life.

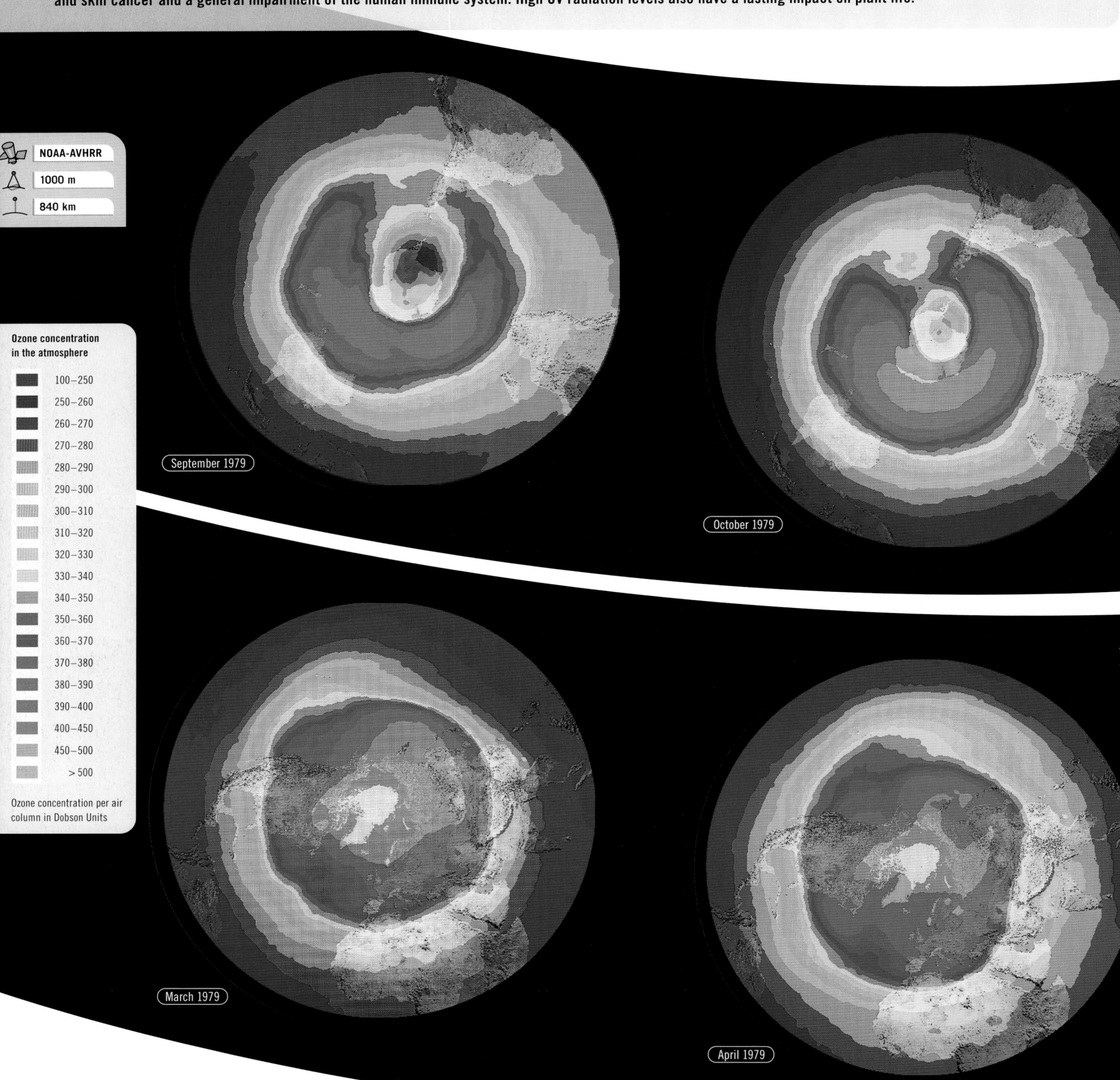

NOAA-AVHRR

1000 m

840 km

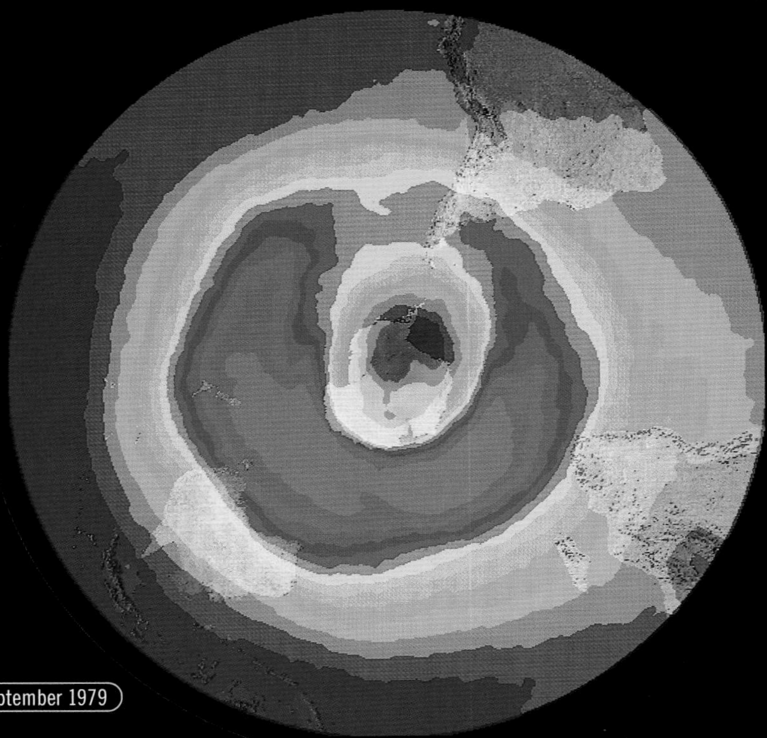

September 1979

October 1979

March 1979

April 1979

Ozone concentration in the atmosphere

- 100–250
- 250–260
- 260–270
- 270–280
- 280–290
- 290–300
- 300–310
- 310–320
- 320–330
- 330–340
- 340–350
- 350–360
- 360–370
- 370–380
- 380–390
- 390–400
- 400–450
- 450–500
- > 500

Ozone concentration per air column in Dobson Units

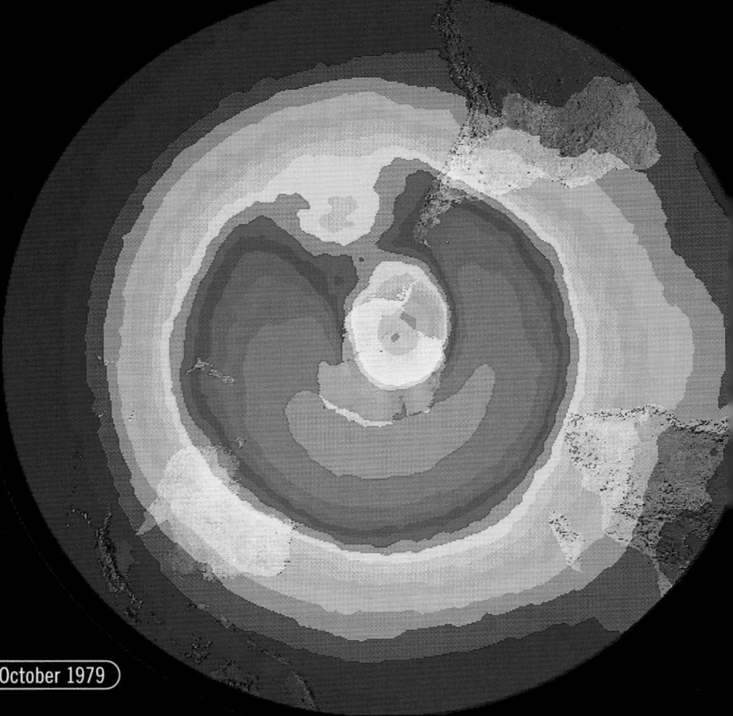

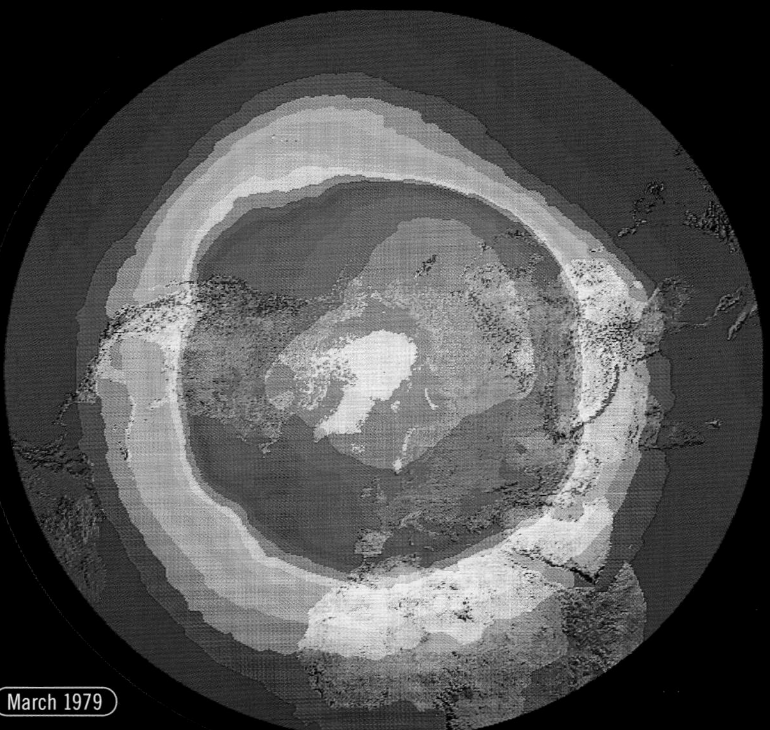

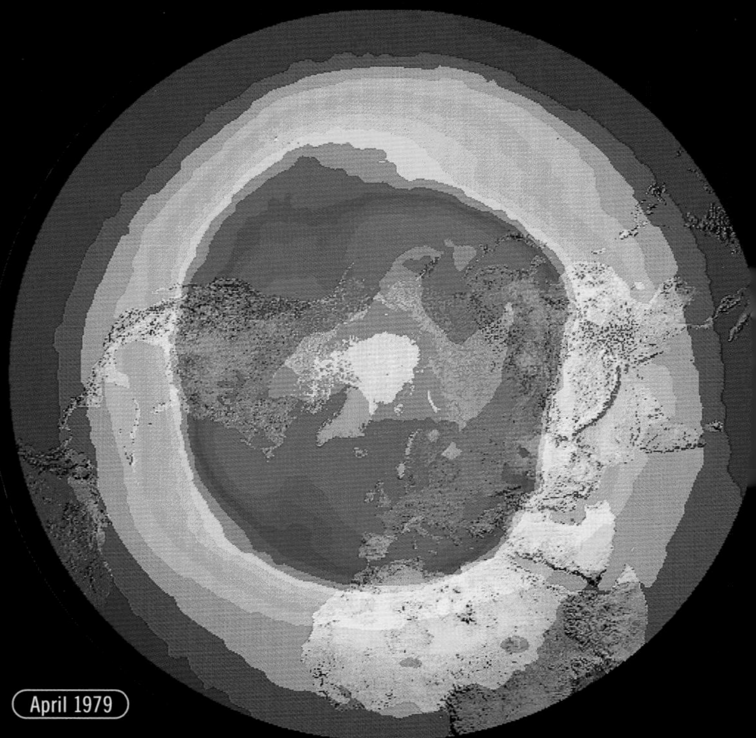

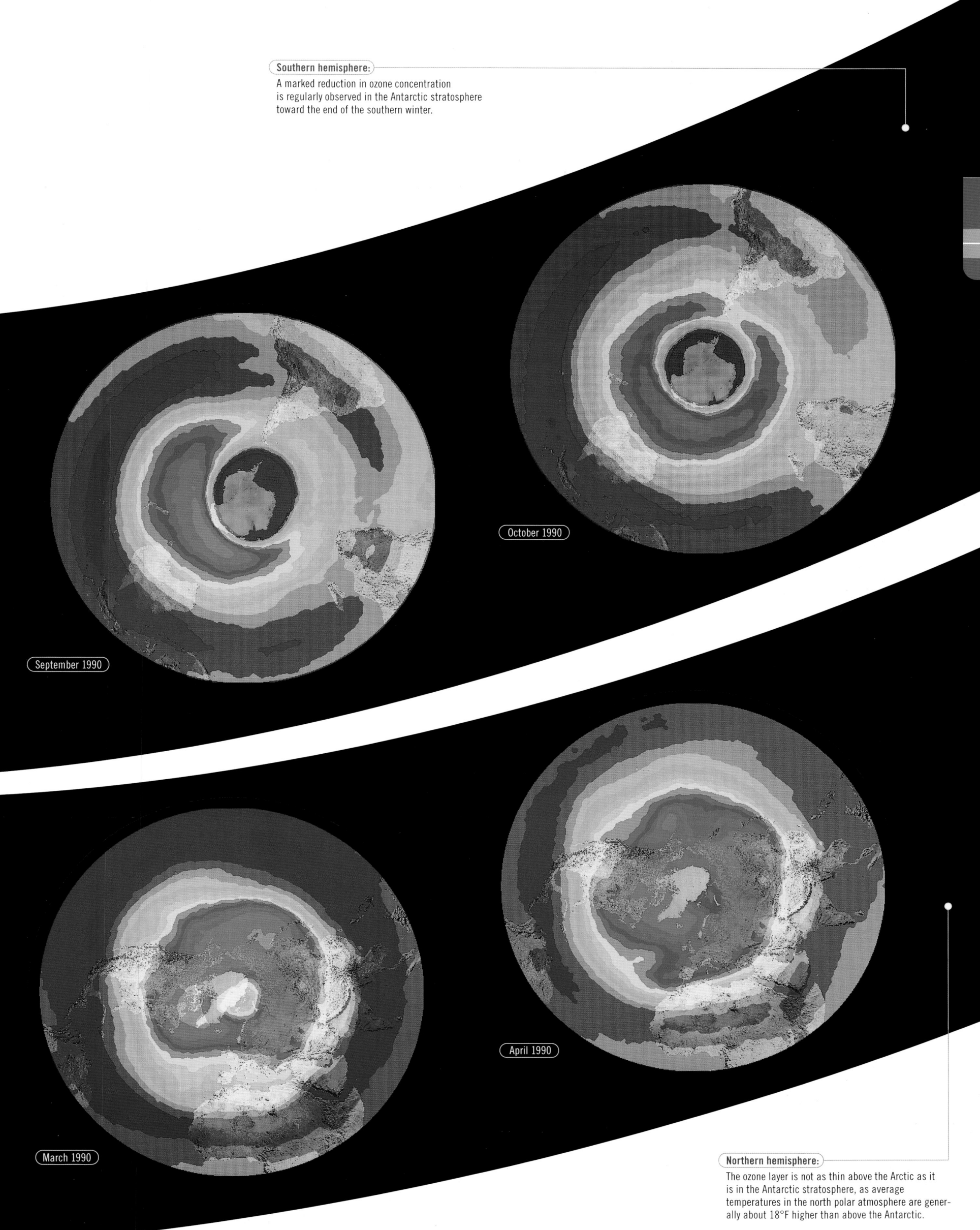

Southern hemisphere:

A marked reduction in ozone concentration
is regularly observed in the Antarctic stratosphere
toward the end of the southern winter.

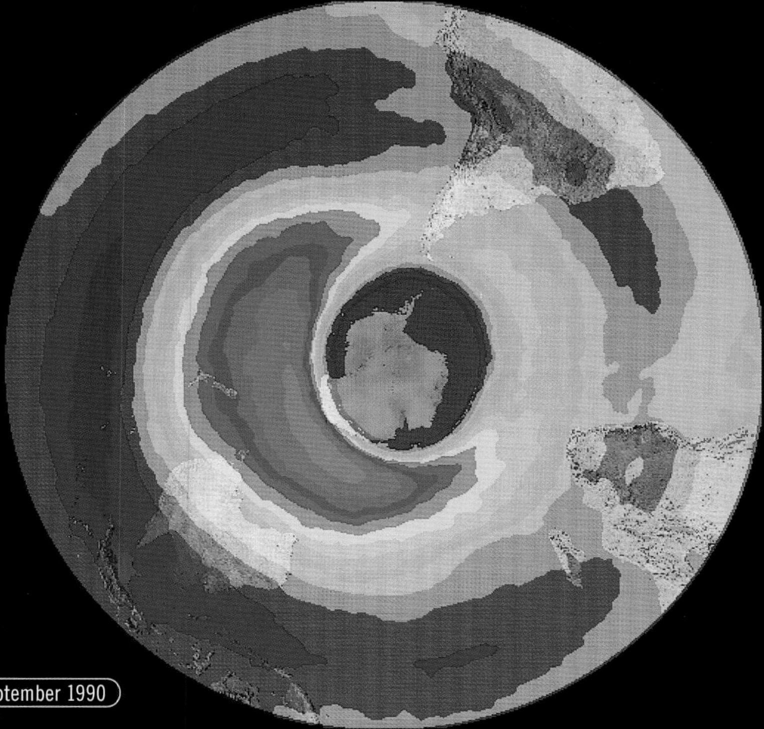

October 1990

September 1990

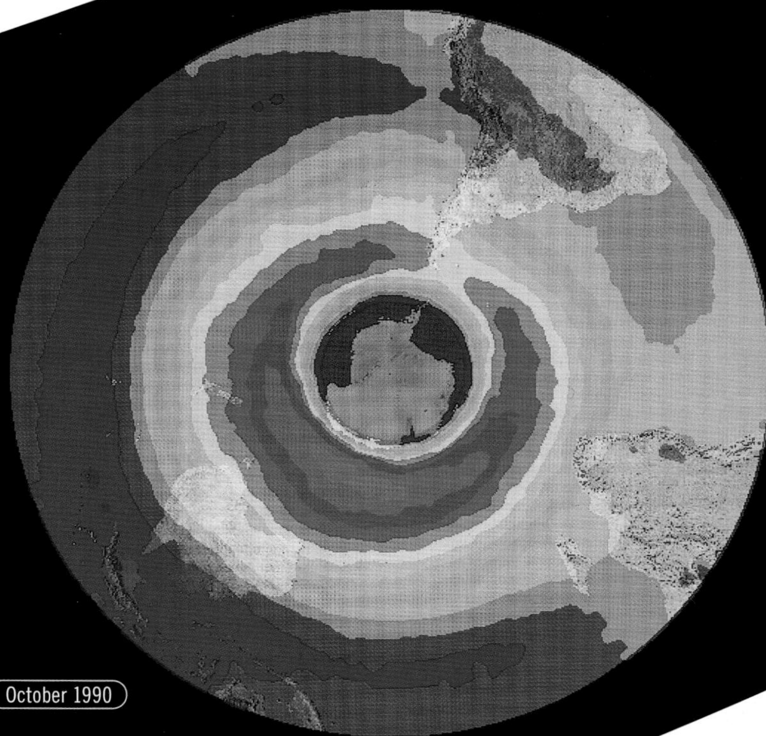

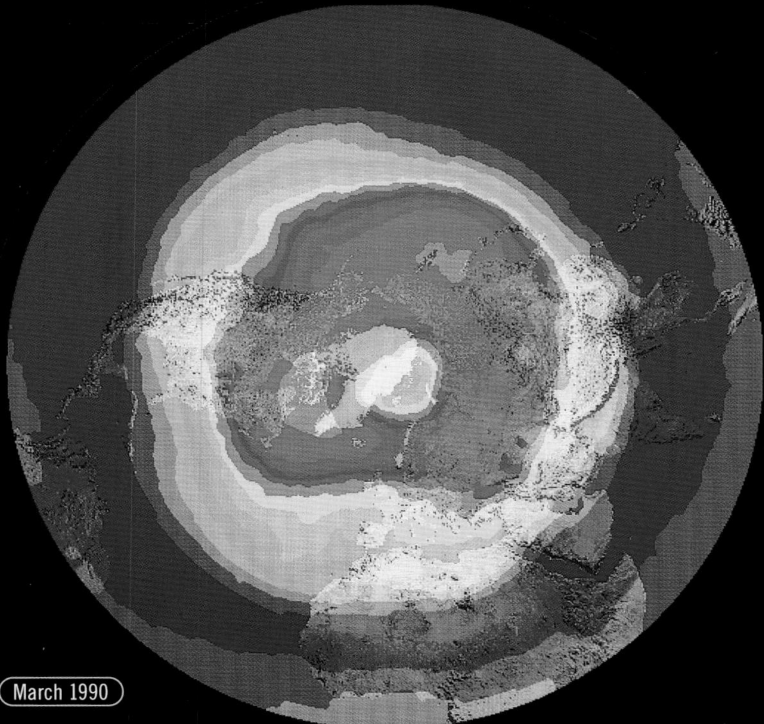

March 1990

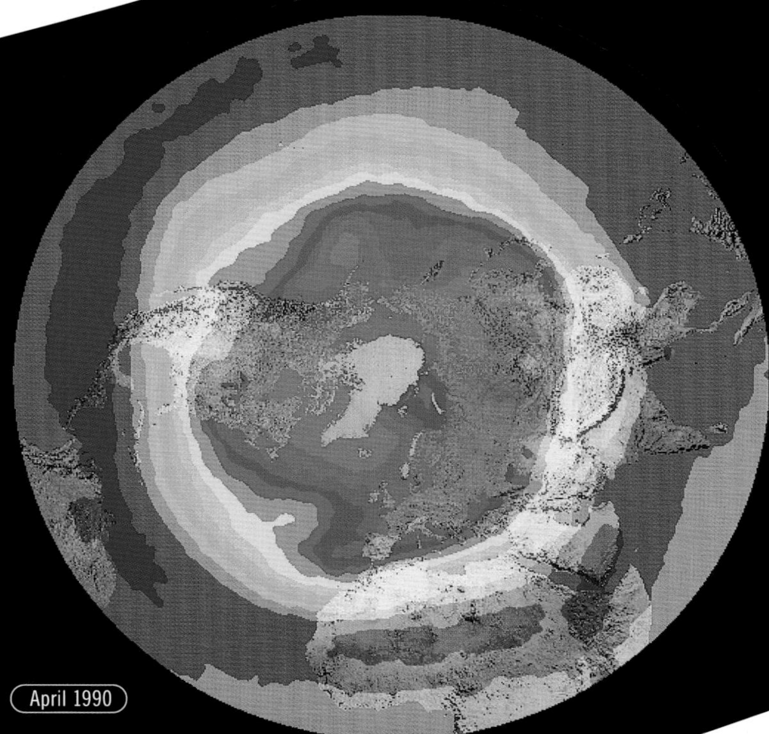

April 1990

Northern hemisphere:

The ozone layer is not as thin above the Arctic as it
is in the Antarctic stratosphere, as average
temperatures in the north polar atmosphere are generally about 18°F higher than above the Antarctic.

Bodies of Water

Rivers – Blood Vessels of a Country

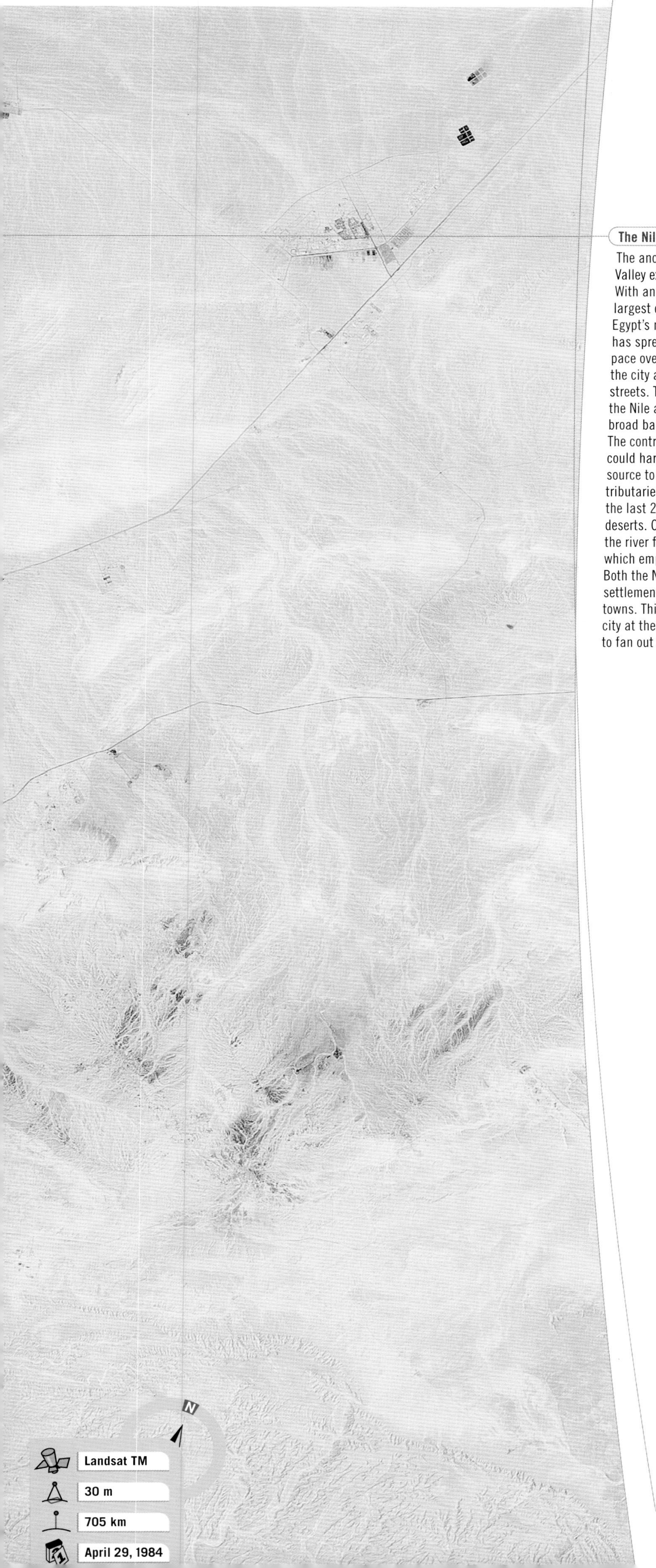

The Nile Near Cairo

The ancient Egyptian city of Cairo emerged where the Nile
Valley expands to form the Nile Delta.

With an estimated population of ten million, Cairo is the
largest city in Africa and the Arabian region. Surrounded by
Egypt's most important agricultural landscape, the city
has spread eastward into the desert at an increasingly rapid
pace over the past several decades. The nine districts of
the city are clearly delineated by their rectangular pattern of
streets. The famous pyramids of Giza are located west of
the Nile and connected to the ancient old city of Cairo by a
broad band of residential settlements.

The contrast between the uninhabited desert and the Nile Valley
could hardly be more dramatic. Measuring 6,671 km from
source to mouth, the world's second longest river flows without
tributaries in a flat-bottomed groove up to 20 km wide on
the last 2,700 km of its course between the Arabian and Nubian
deserts. Once it reaches the vast delta (24,000 sq. km),
the river forks into two branches, the Rosetta and the Damietta,
which empty into the Mediterranean Sea.

Both the Nile Valley and the Nile Delta are dotted with small
settlements positioned at regular intervals between "central"
towns. This Landsat image offers a striking picture of the
city at the point where the fertile flood plain of the river begins
to fan out into the delta.

Landsat TM

30 m

705 km

April 29, 1984

Bodies of Water

Rivers – Blood Vessels of a Country

Landsat ETM

15 m

705 km

Nov. 3, 1999

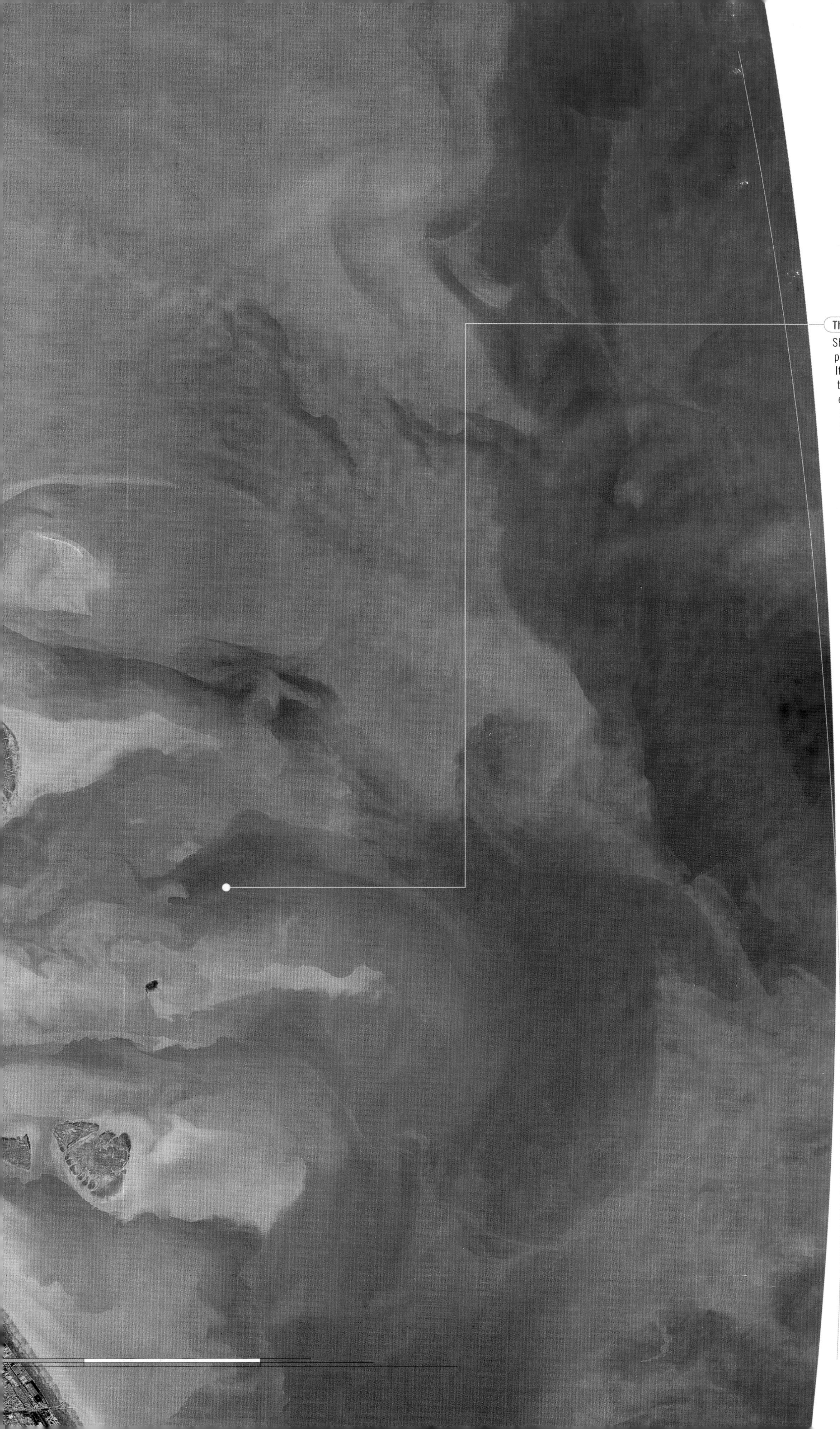

The Mouth of the Yangtze (Chang)

Shanghai is China's most important
port and its largest metropolis.
It radiates from the confluence of
the Huang River and the Yangtze
east of Tai Lake. At the turn of the
last century, the city was home
to some 12 million people, and nearly
20 million people live in greater
metropolitan Shanghai. The opening
of China to international trade
has spurred rapid growth in the city
in recent years, to which an expansive system of urban freeways
and a number of new high-rise
complexes bear witness. The amount
of developed land nearly doubled
between 1980 and 2000. In the
process, the belt of vegetation that
once encircled the city (visible
in places as spots of light-green
coloration in the satellite image)
was obliterated. Development has
been especially intensive in the
Pudong district on the right bank
of the Huang, where large areas
of the old city were demolished and
replaced by new business and
industrial centers.

Bodies of Water

Shrinking of Seas

The Dead Sea

The surface of the Dead Sea, known as Yam Ha-Melah (Salt Lake) in Hebrew, lies an average of 396 m below the level of the Mediterranean, making it the lowest-lying inland sea in the world. It is 80 km long, 18 km wide, up to 794 m deep, and covers an area of 940 sq. km. As recently as the early 1970s, the Dead Sea still consisted of two bodies of water connected by a narrow channel at the tip of the Lisan Peninsula. Increasing use of water from the sea for irrigation of fields along its tributaries, coupled with industrial potassium-mining operations in the southern basin, led to higher levels of solid salt deposits and eventually divided the sea into two separate bodies of water. The sea is fed by numerous underground springs which introduce valuable minerals and trace elements, including calcium, magnesium, silicic acid, potassium, iron, bromides, and iodine. With a salinity level of 25%, the Dead Sea is totally devoid of plant and animal life. Due to the warm climate, between two and 25 mm of water surface evaporate every day, keeping salt content high despite the influx of fresh water. Potassium, bromides, and magnesium salts are collected in the evaporation basins. The industrial facilities are clearly identified by the walls of the evaporation basins.

Located in the western part of the Jordan Rift Valley are the Judaean Heights (maximum elevation 1,014 m), a region of intensive cultivation and irrigation that slopes steeply toward the Mediterranean. The capital of Israel, Jerusalem, lies at the same latitude as the northernmost shore of the Dead Sea. The Tel Aviv-Yafo metropolitan area is visible along the coast. The Jordanian capital of Amman is located northwest of the Dead Sea along the edge of the steppe.

Landsat ETM

30 m

705 km

May 15, 1989

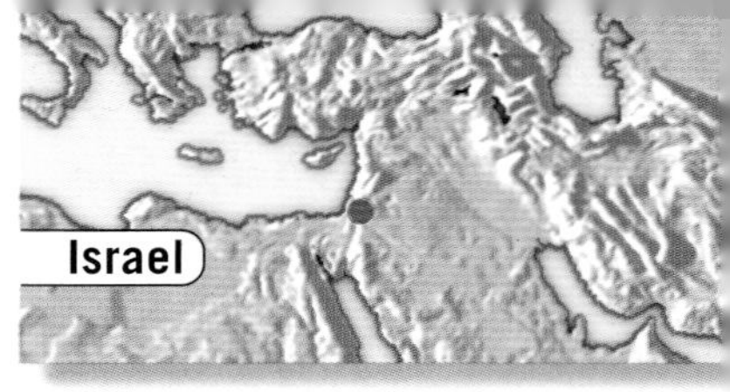

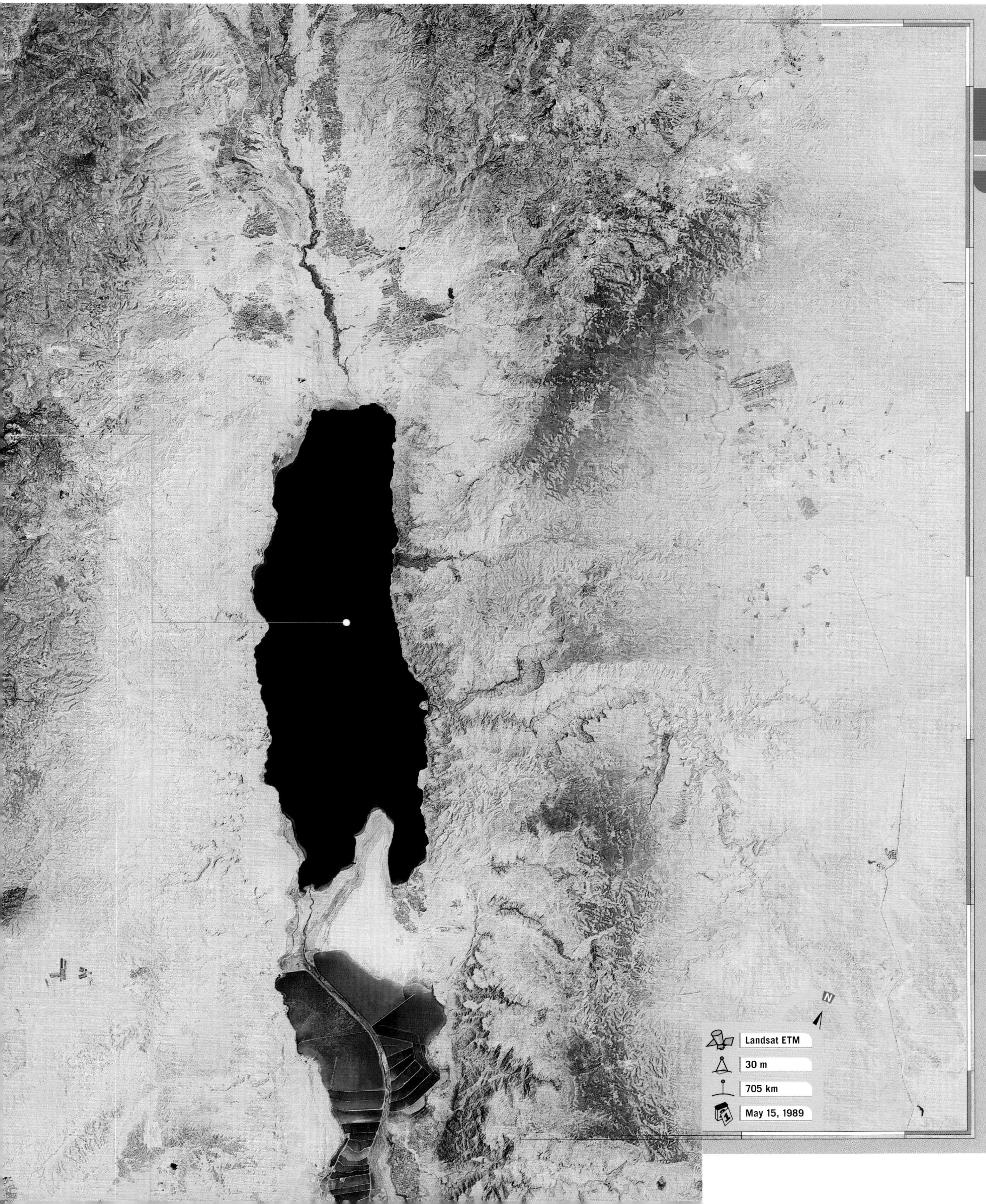

Deserts

Shifting Seas of Sand

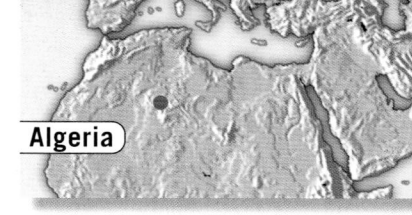

Algeria

The Sahara near Amguid in Algeria

The Sahara presents a very different face in many places. Landscapes can be distinguished on the basis of differences in surface material — exposed rock, gravel, sand, or salt clay. A large portion of the image is occupied by the debris-covered surfaces of the Hamada de Tinrhert (light gray and reddish brown areas). This bolder-strewn desert is known as Serir in Algeria. The second type of desert in the Sahara is characterized by sand sheets and dunes. A prominent feature of the landscape in this satellite image is the tongue of sand in the upper portion of the picture, with its regular pattern of star-shaped figures. Salt clay plains (bluish-turquoise coloration) are found in the broad depressions where the wadis — dry valleys through which water flows only after heavy rains — grow wider. The dark brown areas are the northern fingers of the Tassili-n-Ajjer range, with peaks as high as 1,800 m.

Landsat ETM

30 m

705 km

Winter 1987

Coastal Formations

Fjords and Skerries

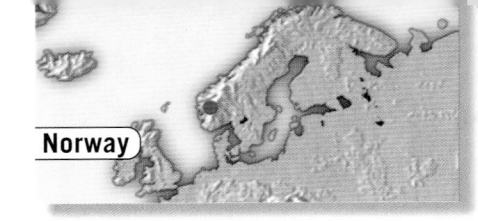

Norway

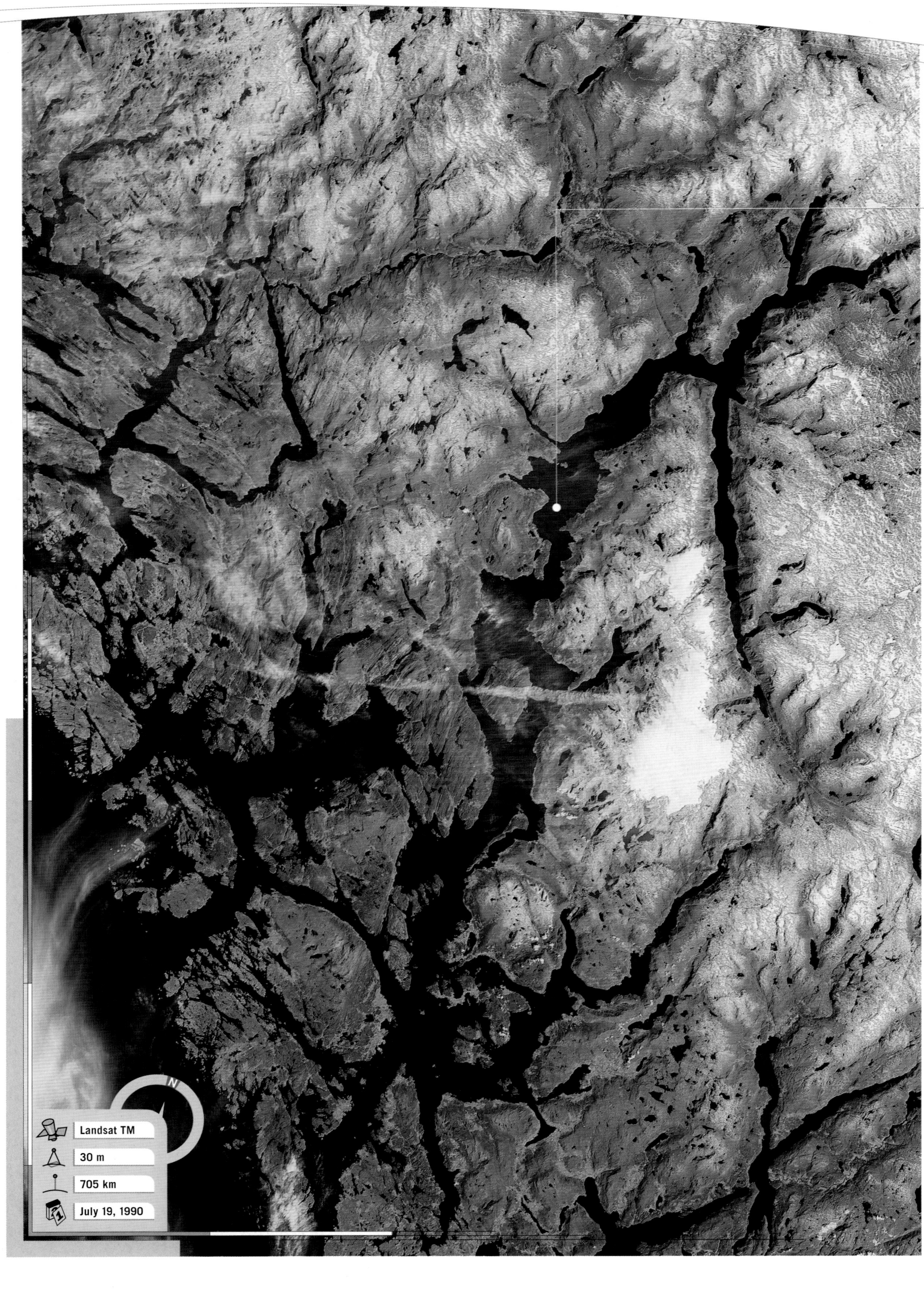

Hardangerfjorden

Framed by the Hardangerfjorden and the eastern Numedal, the snow-covered Hardangervidda in southern Norway reaches elevations of between 1,200 and 1,400 m. Covering an area of 7,500 sq. km, it is 30 times the size of the Bavarian Forest in Germany. The intricate branching network of the Hardangerfjorden extends far into the hinterland of southwestern Norway. One of the best-known fjords in the world, the Hardangerfjorden was formed during the last ice age. Huge glaciers thrust far out into the sea, pushing large volumes of debris ahead of them. When the glaciers melted, they left behind a U-shaped valley with maximum depths of more than 1,000 m, which was flooded by the sea. The debris carried by the glaciers filled the entrance to the fjord, making it relatively shallow and restricting the exchange of seawater and fresh water entering the fjord from the interior. Favored by the mild climate, large plantations of apple and cherry orchards line the shores of the Hardangerfjorden.

Landsat TM

30 m

705 km

July 19, 1990

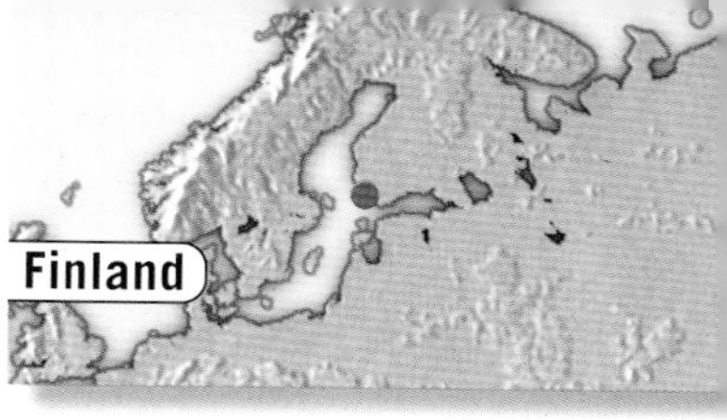

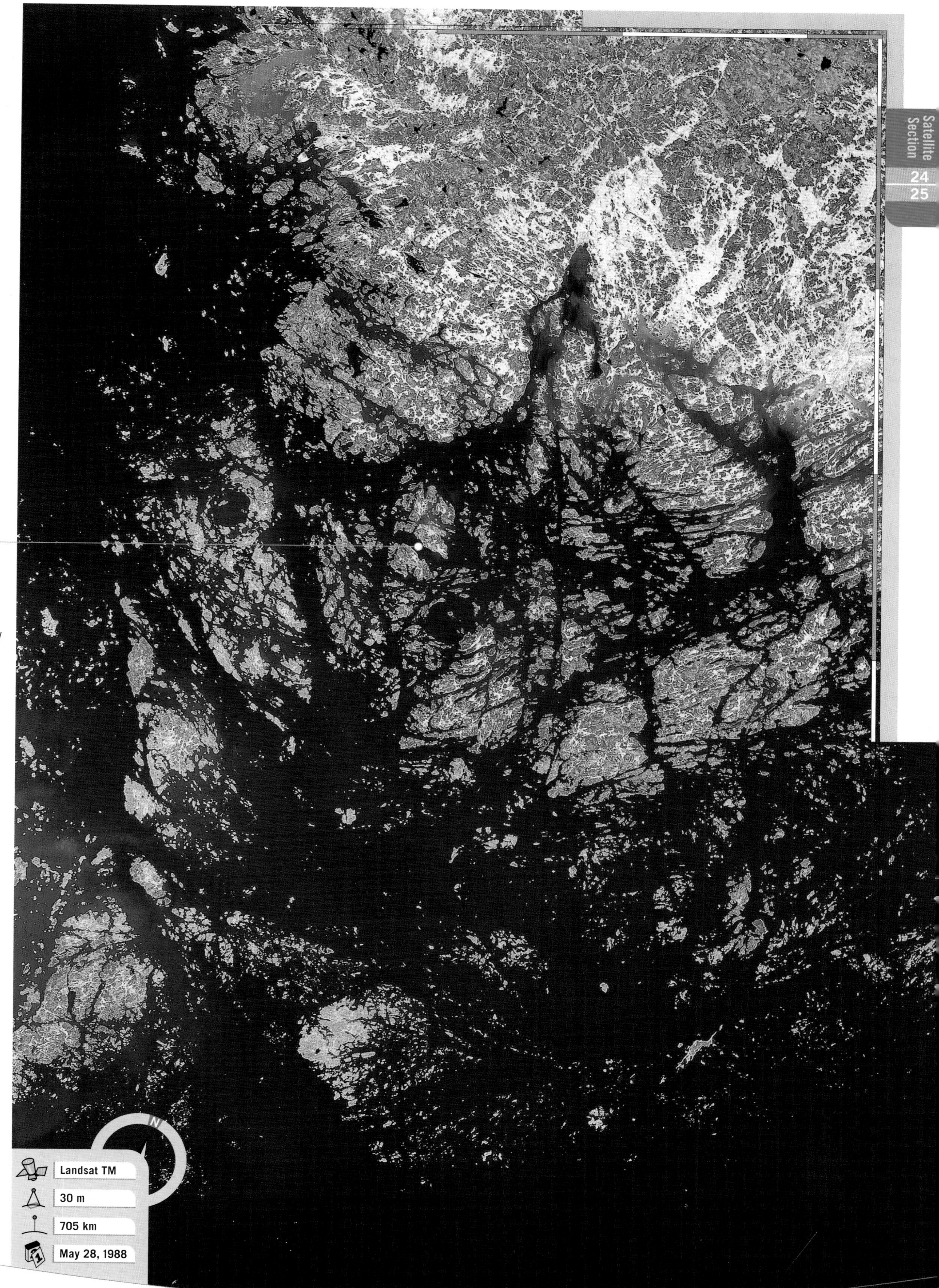

Skerry Landscape

The Åland Islands are located in the
Gulf of Bothnia between Turku
and Stockholm. The satellite image
highlights the typical features of
a skerry coast, a glacially formed
landscape of domed islets flooded by
the sea. Some of the numerous
small islands between the Åland
group and Turku are inhabited.
For generations, people have lived in
virtual isolation in the skerries.
There are very few roads, and water
routes are the most important
links to other islands and the mainland. Fishing has been the most
important source of income for centuries, although the skerry population also relies on farming, animal
husbandry, and forestry. Environmental tourism is one of the most
important sources of revenue
today.

Landsat TM

30 m

705 km

May 28, 1988

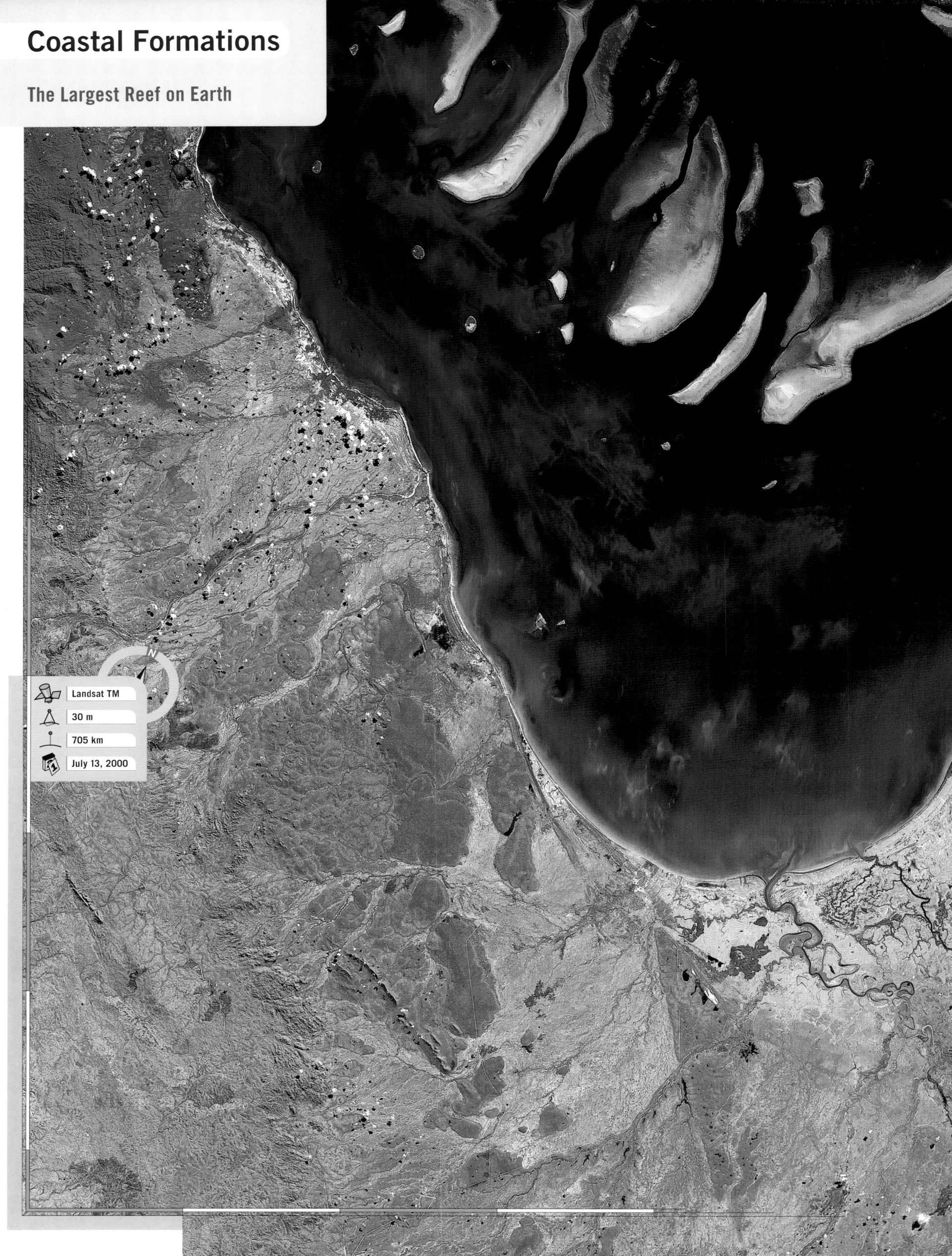

Landsat TM

30 m

705 km

July 13, 2000

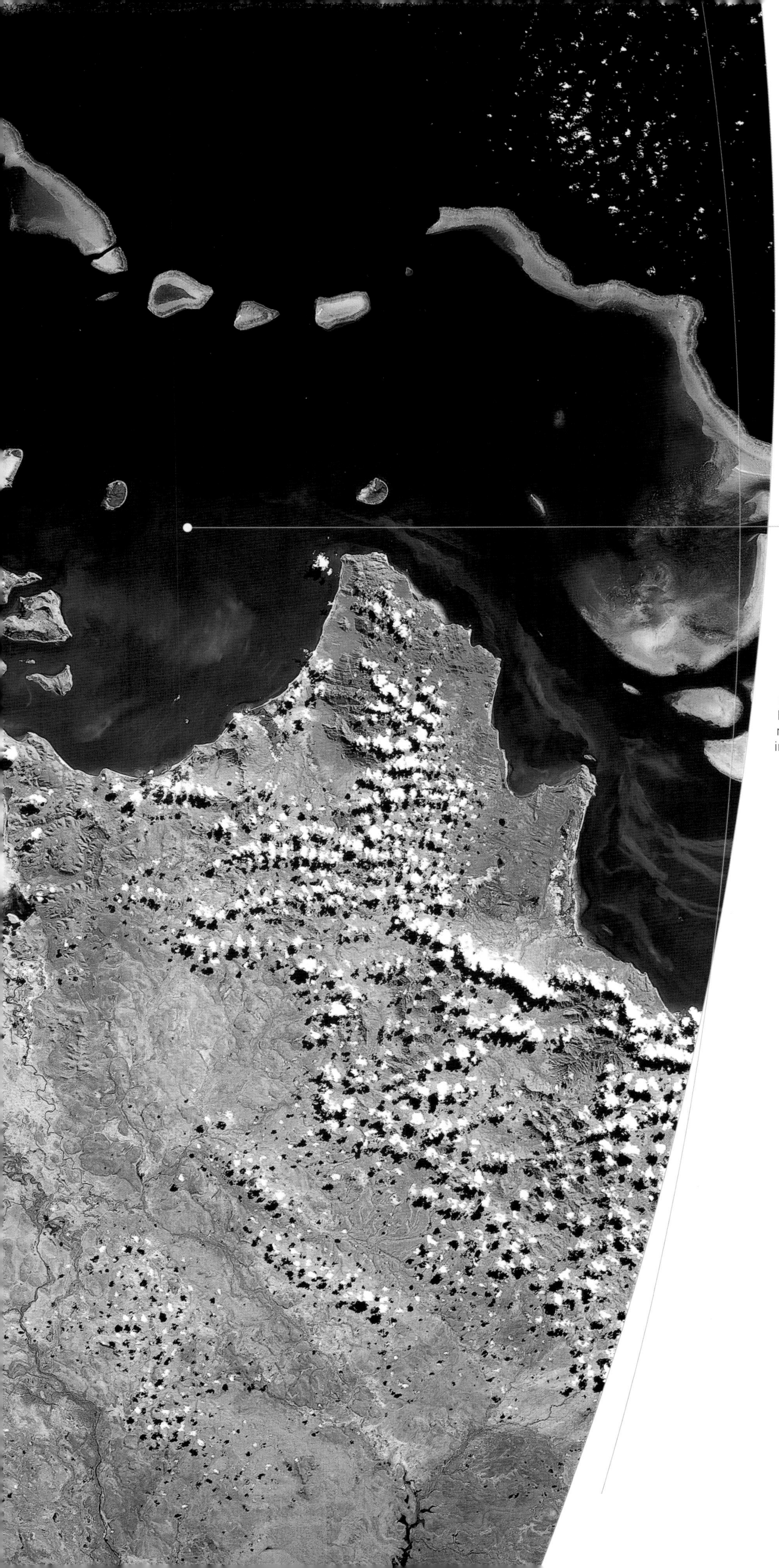

The Great Barrier Reef

The world's largest coral reef runs parallel to the coast of Australia off the shores of Queensland. This satellite image shows Princess Charlotte Bay on the southern coast of the Cape York Peninsula.

The chain of elongated, oval or circular coral reefs is discernable only from the air. Covered only by shallow waters, they appear as turquoise and light blue areas that stand out clearly against the deep blue of the open sea.

The view from the air tells us something else as well. The Great Barrier Reef is not a continuous, linear reef system but instead comprises a large number of individual reefs of different sizes distributed in a picturesque pattern in the lagoon.

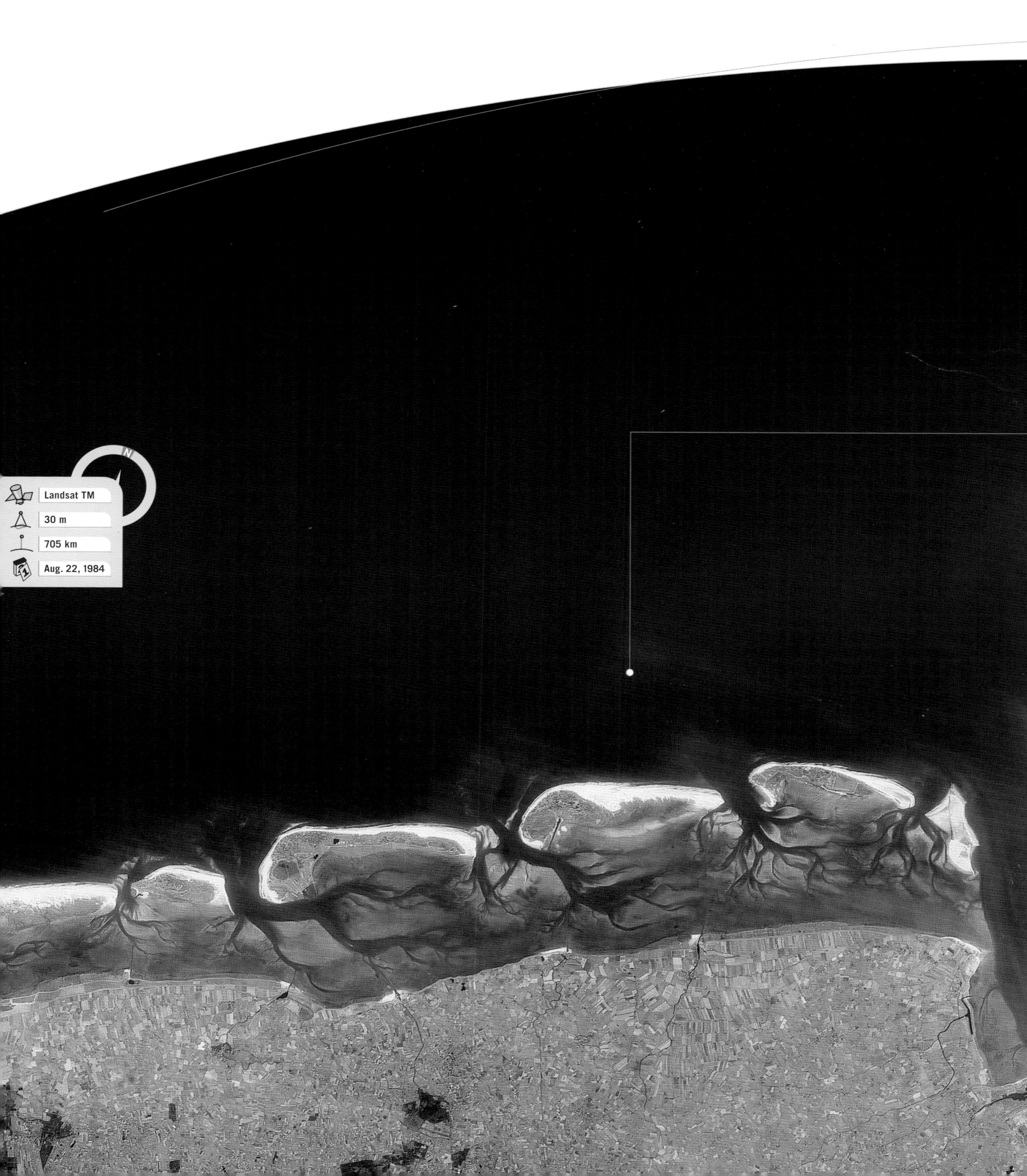

Landsat TM

30 m

705 km

Aug. 22, 1984

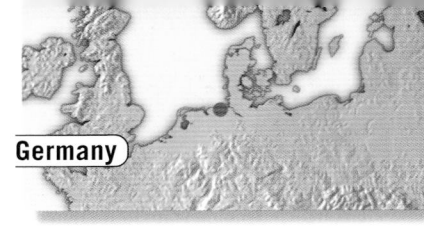

East Frisian Islands

The East Frisian Islands are massive dune islands built
on foundations of sand. The different stages in their
development are evident in this satellite image. Broad,
light-colored beaches line the northern and eastern
shores of the islands (rudimentary spits can be seen on
the eastern side of the island of Juist). Behind them
are rows of dunes — younger formations nearer the shore,
older, more heavily vegetated ones farther inland.
Situated inside the protective dune walls are marshlands
used for grazing. Frequently flooded salt meadows lie
between the beaches and the tidal flats.
The pattern of channels and flats exposed at low tide
is clearly visible in this satellite image. Rising and
falling by as much as 3 meters, the tides have cut gate-
ways to depths of up to 20 meters between the islands.
The tides are also responsible for the formation of arc
and sickle ripples. A reddish tinge identifies the ecologi-
cally significant areas of salt meadow and tidal mud
flats. The area known as the "Niedersächsisches Wattenmeer" was declared a National Park in 1986 in order
to preserve this sensitive biosphere.

Hamburg

The satellite image shows the Elbe River as a complex network
of waterways that wind through the city of Hamburg.
Clearly visible are the extensive, branching docklands of Hamburg Harbor, one of Europe's largest and commercially most
significant seaports.
The harbor and its facilities account for about 10% of the total
area of Hamburg. The characteristic finger-shaped configuration of the tidal harbor results from the dredging of artificial
harbor basins to allow ships to dock directly in front of the
city's warehouses. Germany's largest international harbor has
always been a gateway for movement of goods to and from
Europe. Once primarily a transfer point for bulk and piece goods,
Hamburg Harbor has since developed into a major logistics
center.

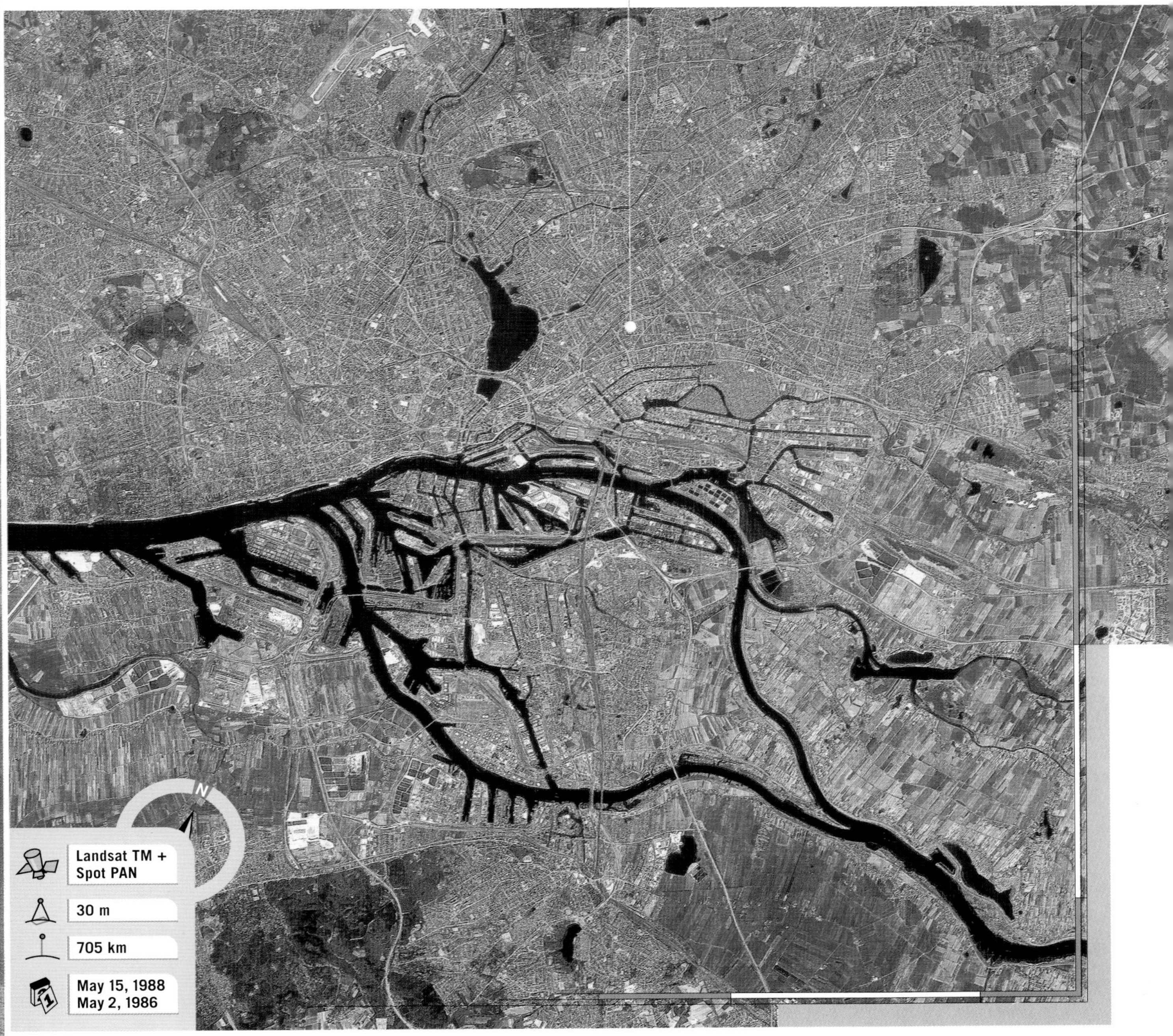

Landsat TM +
Spot PAN

30 m

705 km

May 15, 1988
May 2, 1986

Continental Divides

Natural Boundaries

Europe – Africa

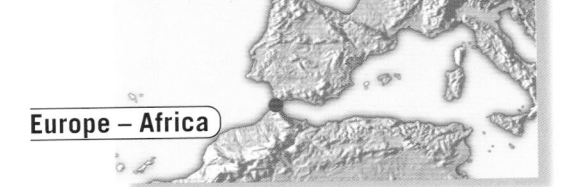

Gibraltar

Roughly 60 km long, the Strait of Gibraltar narrows from west to east, separating Spain and Morocco by only 15 km at its narrowest point.
Over the course of history, it has served as both a link between the continents of Europe and Africa and a gateway between the New and Old Worlds.
Its strategic importance has made the Strait of Gibraltar a source of ceaseless political strife.

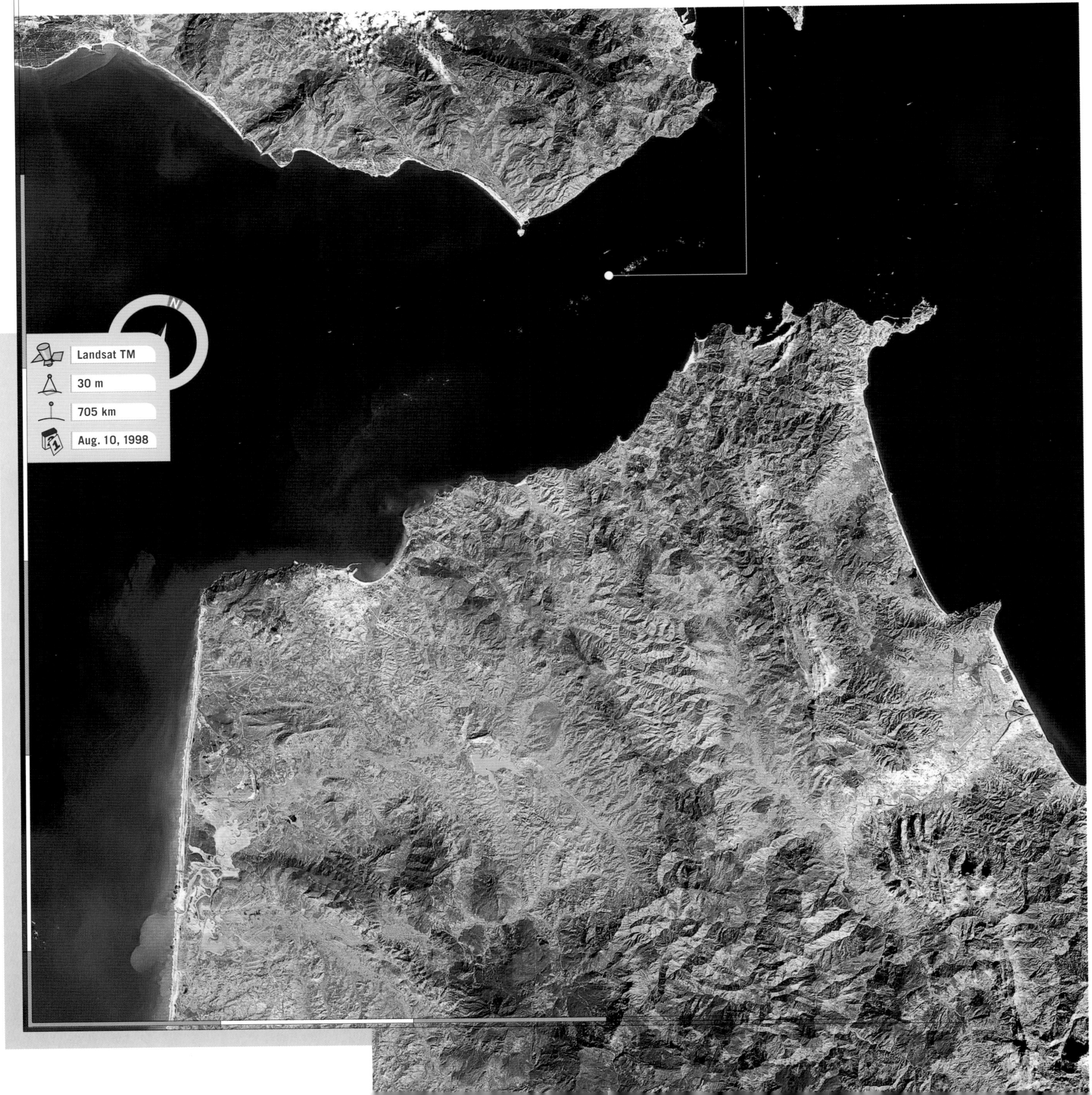

N
Landsat TM
30 m
705 km
Aug. 10, 1998

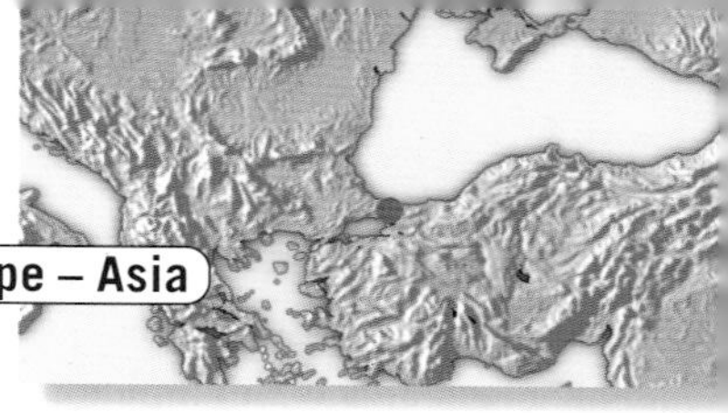

Bosporus

Measuring 31 km in length and between 660 and 3,000 m in width, the Bosporus, a narrow strait between Europe and Asia, connects the Black Sea with the Sea of Marmara. It is a flooded river valley that sank during the Würm (Wisconsin) glacial stage and eventually formed a strait linking the two seas.

The city of Istanbul sits astride the Bosporus. Like every metropolis, it is a mosaic of many different districts, each with its own distinctive character. The city center itself is divided into three parts, for which water is both a barrier and a connecting link: the Golden Horn, an arm of the sea that separates the old, formerly Greek-Byzantine Istanbul from the modern Beyoglu, and the Bosporus, which separates the European and Asian parts of the city. Although Turkey's capital was moved to Ankara in 1923, Istanbul remains the country's most important commercial and cultural center.

Suspension bridges built in 1973 and 1988 connect the European and Asian halves of the city.

Landsat ETM

15 m

705 km

Oct. 4, 1999

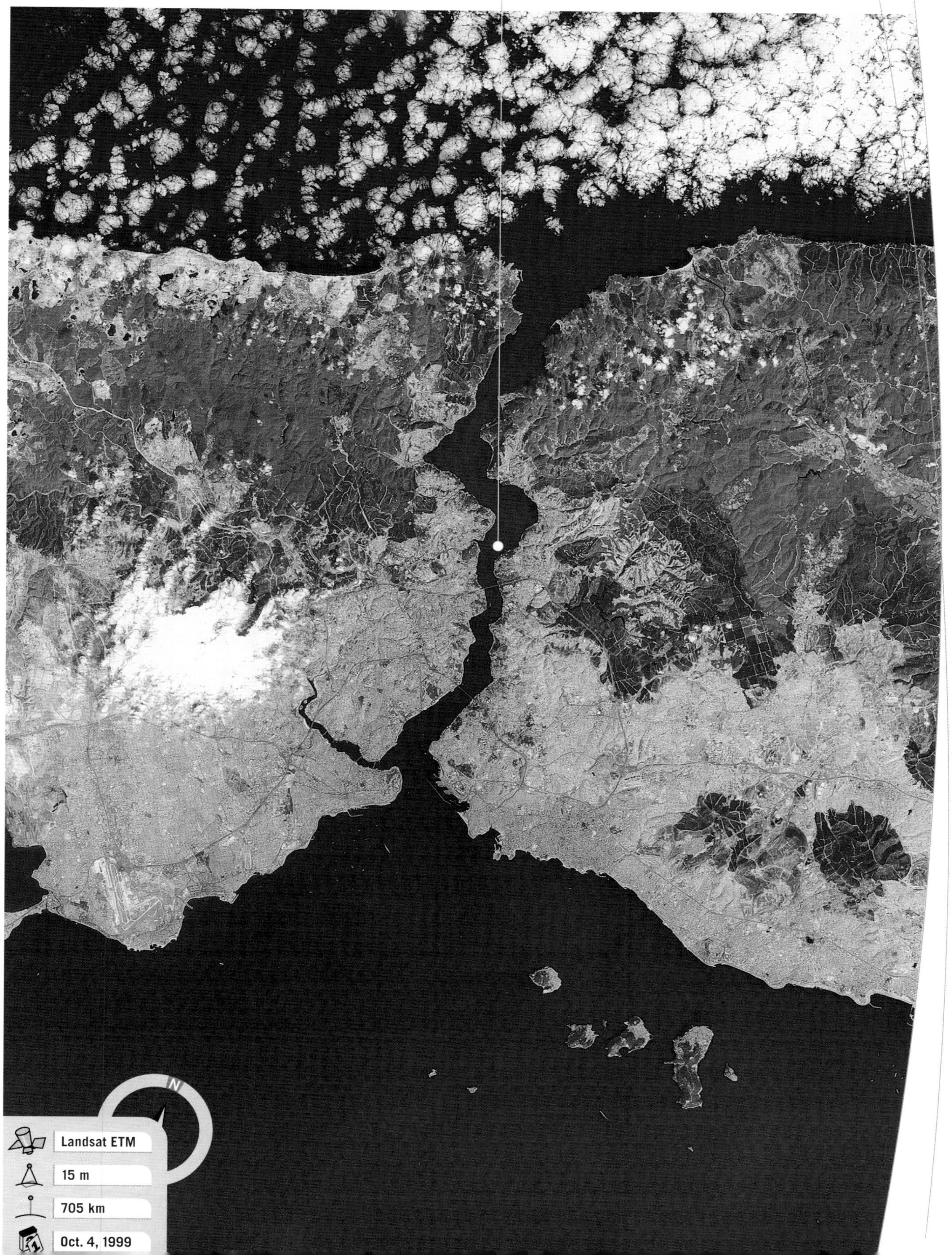

Vegetation and Land Use

Carving New Settlements from the Rainforest

Rio Paraná

In 1975, Brazil and Paraguay began constructing the world's largest dam for the Itaipú hydroelectric power plant. Itaipú means "singing stone" in the Guaraní Indian language. Since 1982, the Rio Paraná has backed up over a length of 180 km, forming a huge lake that covers an area of 1,460 sq. km. before entering a long (60 km) canyon near the city of Foz do Iguaçu. Dam projects of this magnitude have a significant impact on the environment.

The power plant went into operation at full capacity in May 1991 and now provides much of the electricity consumed in Brazil. Paraguay, which covered half of the roughly 30-million-dollar construction bill, does not need that much electrical power. The country sells 98% of its energy share to its powerful neighbor. Experts fear that silt accumulation resulting from extensive deforestation operations along the upper reaches of the river will shorten the life of the power plant.

Clearly visible in the satellite image is the sharp boundary between heavily cultivated deforested areas and the remaining virgin rain forest, which is now protected as a national park.

Landsat TM

30 m

705 km

June 25, 1987

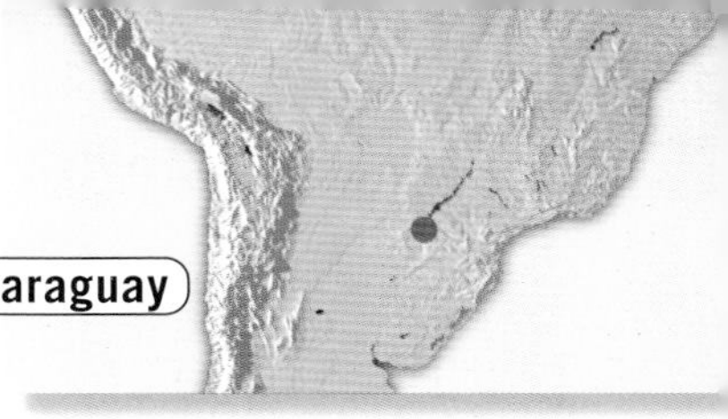

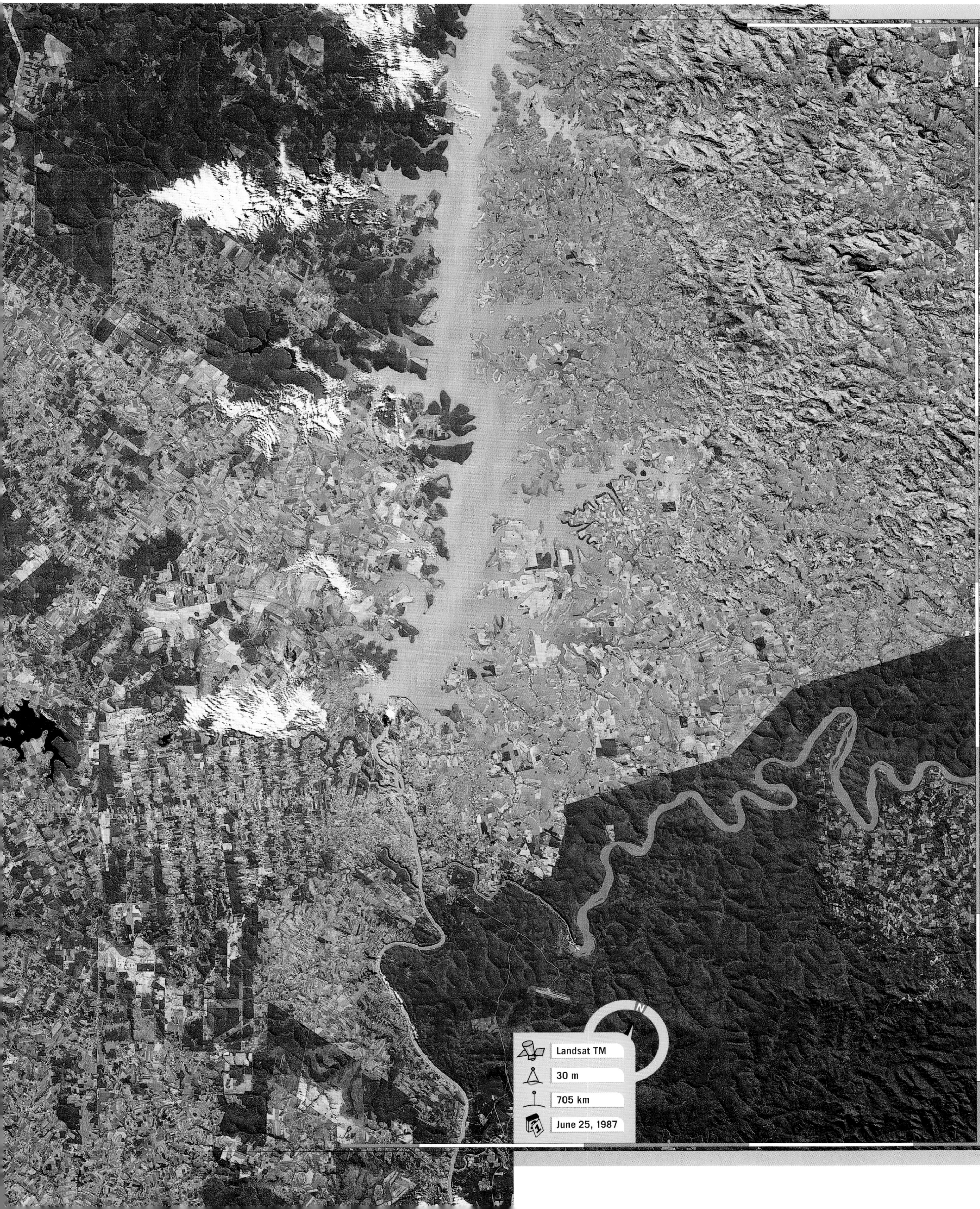

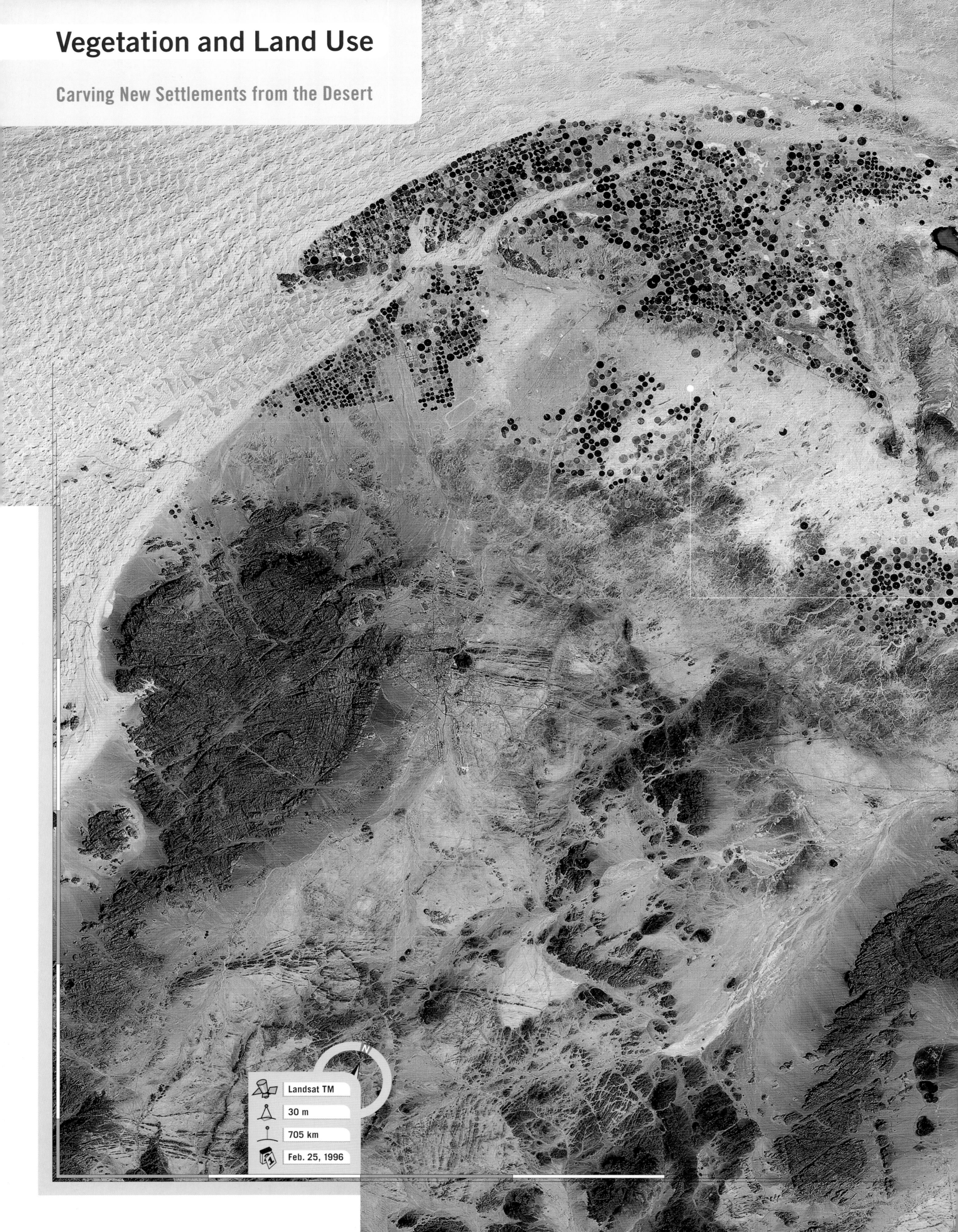

Vegetation and Land Use

Carving New Settlements from the Desert

Landsat TM

30 m

705 km

Feb. 25, 1996

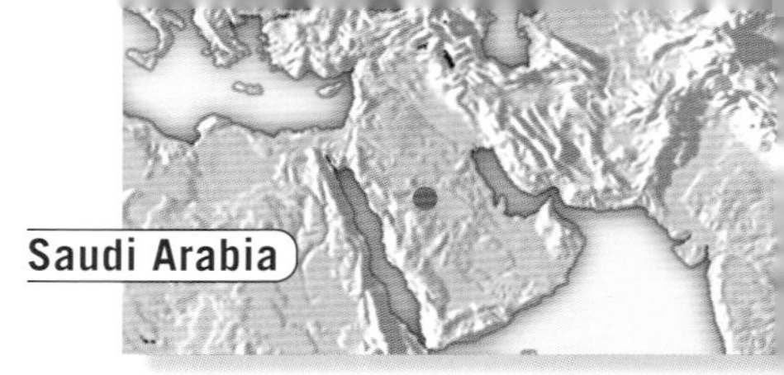

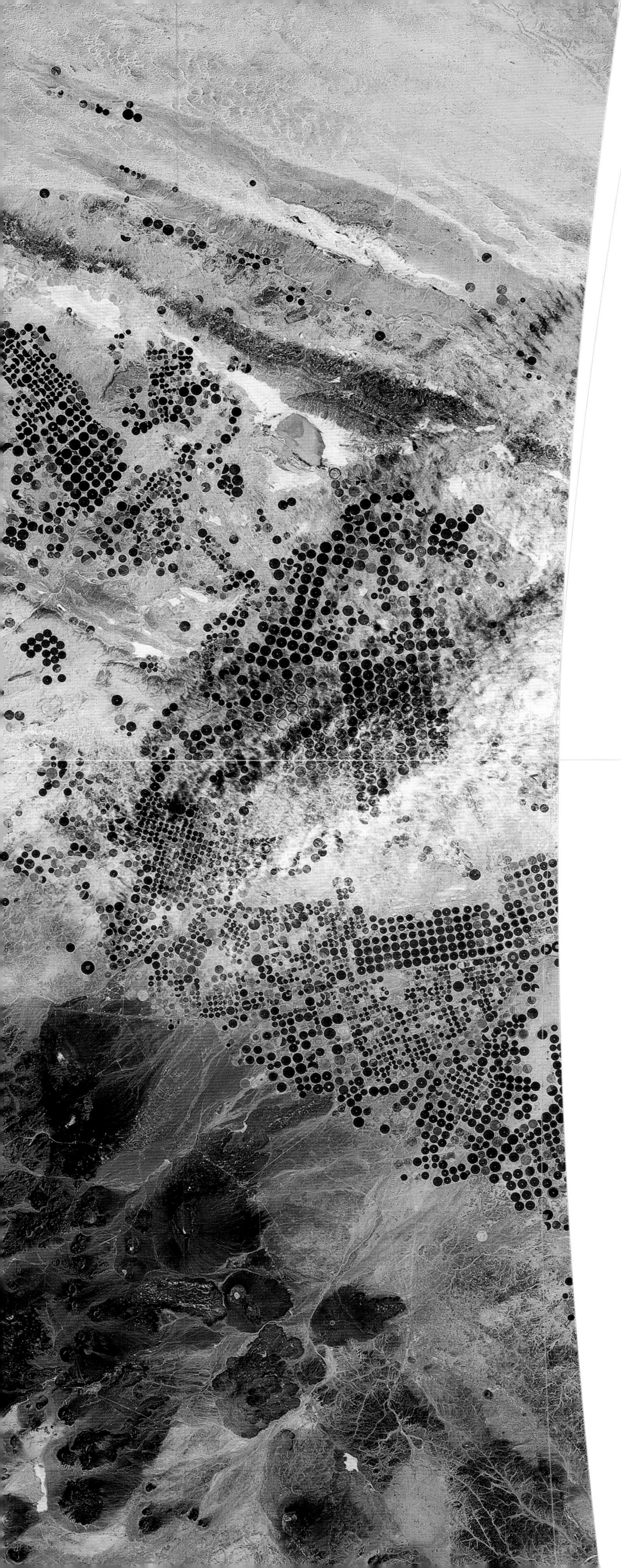

Saudi Arabia – Hā'il

Expansive plateaus irregularly interspersed with ranges of mountains and inselbergs characterize the topography of the Central Arabian Highlands. In the north, the crystalline highlands extend to the edge of the sand desert of An Nafūd. Circular patches are distributed like confetti over the yellow sand of the Wadi Ha'il – small areas of cultivation in the midst of the arid desert, irrigated with rotating sprinkler systems fed to a certain extent with fossil water. Conveyed by pumps and pipelines, the water is distributed for specified periods of time in fine veils of rain. This process enables farmers to fertilize their fields efficiently by adding plant nutrients to the water. Excessive irrigation creates swampy soil conditions, which make the fields difficult to tend. Evaporation rates are extremely high in the hot, arid regions of Saudi Arabia, and changing wind patterns can lead to unequal distribution of water vapor.

Landsat TM

30 m

705 km

Sept. 21, 1997

China

USA

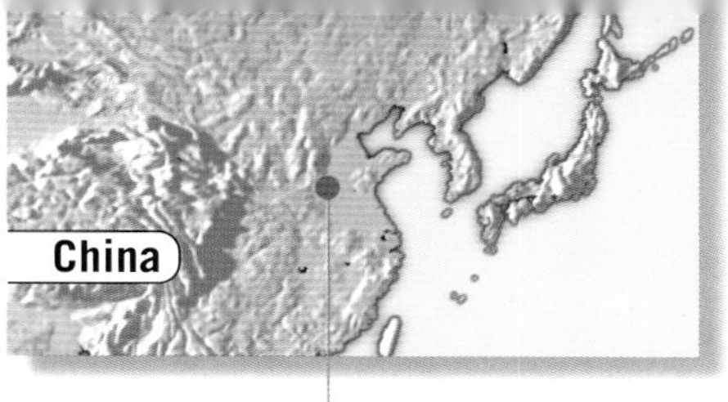

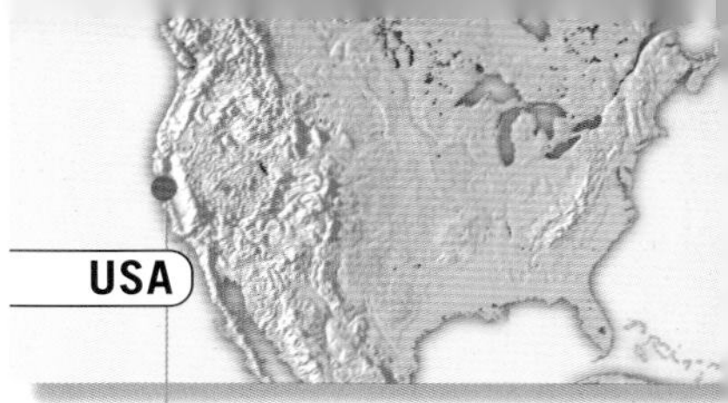

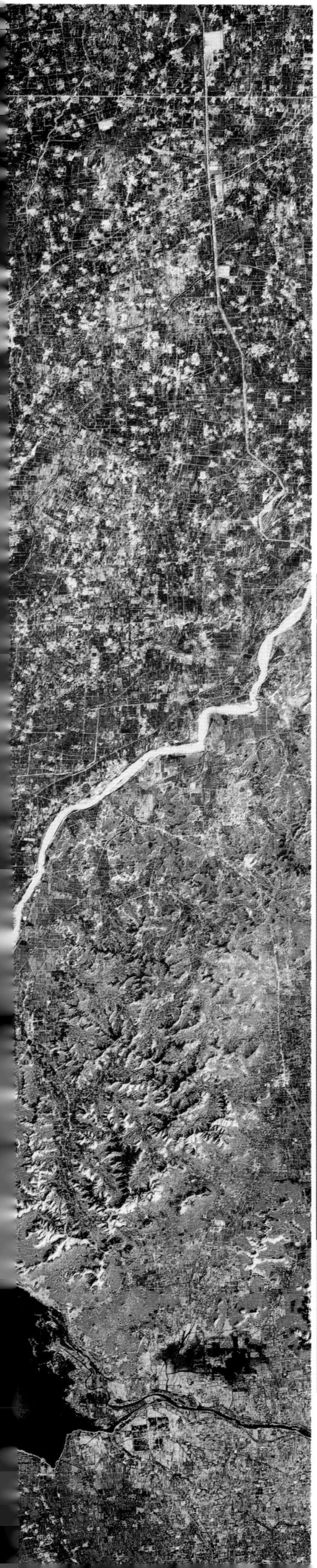

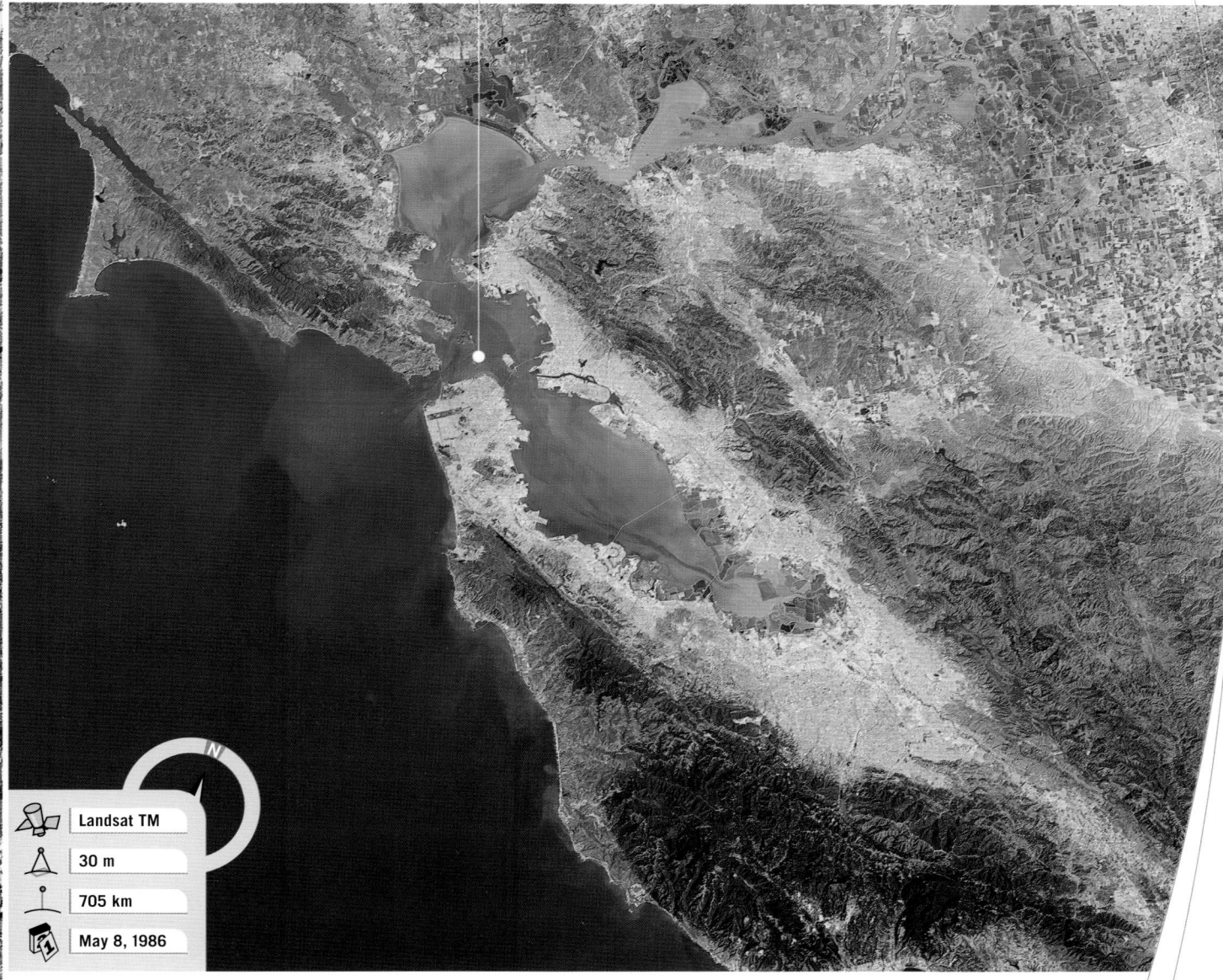

Settlement Structure in Northern China

This satellite image shows a section of the low North China Plain, where elevations range between 5 m and 50 m above sea level. The plain was formed centuries ago by frequent flooding of the Huang River and the resulting accumulation of fertile loess deposits. Extensive river regulation measures have since greatly reduced the danger of flooding. The high fertility of the region is evident in the dense, regular pattern of small rural settlements and the intensive use of land for agriculture. The most important crops in this region of northern China are wheat, corn, soybeans, peanuts, and tobacco.

San Francisco

San Francisco is famous for its location on the northern tip of the peninsula at the entrance to San Francisco Bay. The city is bordered on the west by the Pacific Ocean, on the north by the Golden Gate Strait, on the east by San Francisco Bay, and on the south by the San Bruno Mountains. The Sacramento and San Joaquin valleys open to the Bay from the northeast. Covering an area of 120 sq. km, the city encompasses Angel, Treasure and Yerba Buena islands as well as the former island prison of Alcatraz. Central San Francisco is situated on a chain of hills with elevations of up to 285 m. Cleary visible in the image is the Golden Gate, the strait (8 km long and 3 km wide) that joins the Pacific and San Francisco Bay.

Landsat TM

30 m

705 km

May 8, 1986

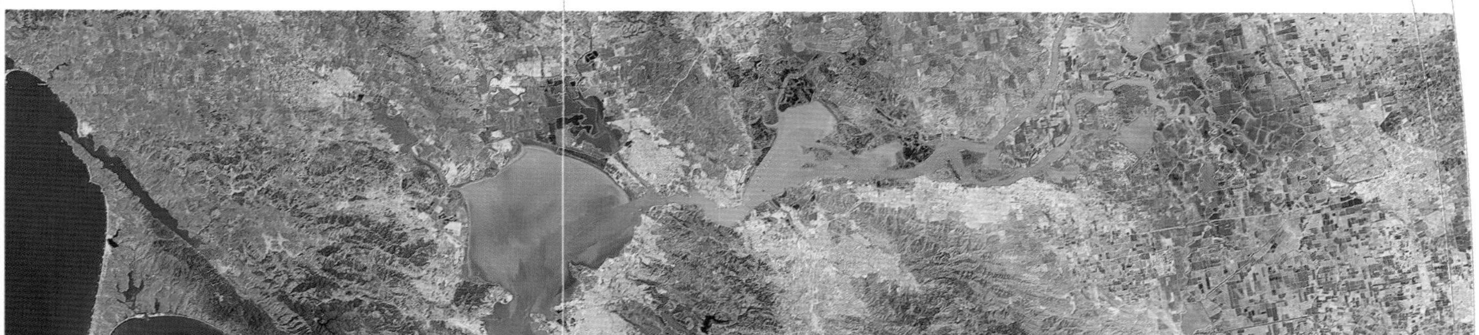

Settlement Patterns

The Metropolis

Italy

Venice

Venice was built on more than 100 small islands in the Laguna Veneta north of the Po delta. The heart of the city is St. Mark's Square, situated at the southern end of the S-shaped Canal Grande. A four-kilometer-long road and railroad bridge connects Venice to the mainland.

Venetians have lived with the threat of floods and high water for centuries. Yet flooding has grown more frequent over the past fifty years, for many different reasons. The water level in the Adriatic Sea has risen by about eight centimeters during the last one hundred years, and the city itself has sunk farther into the lagoon over the past several decades as the result of groundwater depletion on the nearby mainland.

Ikonos	
1 m	
682 km	
Sept. 15, 2000	

Ikonos

1 m

682 km

Apr. 4, 1996

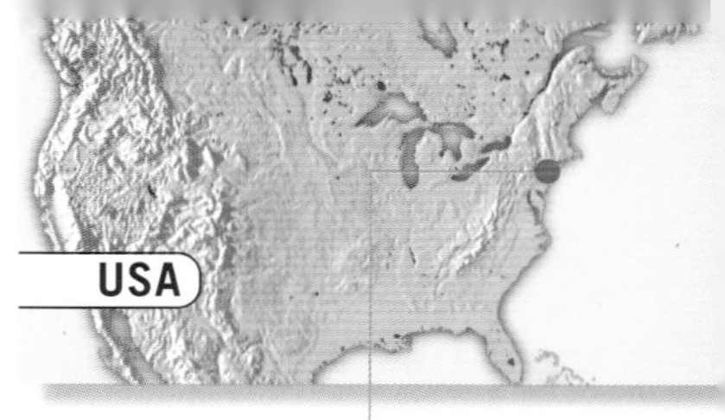

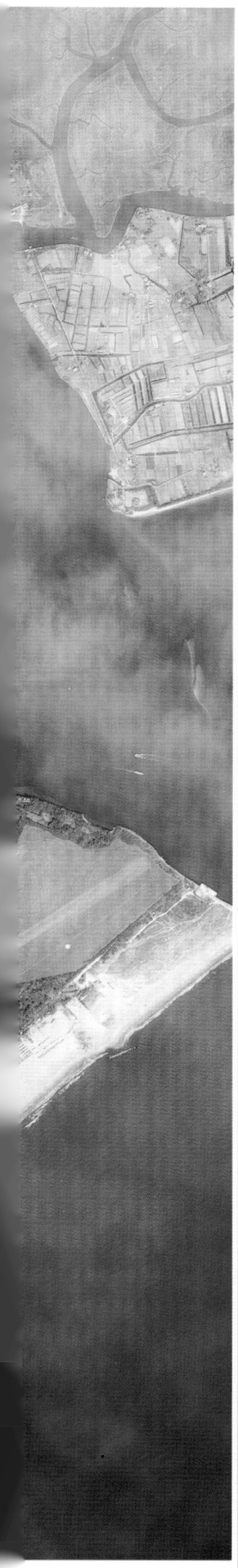

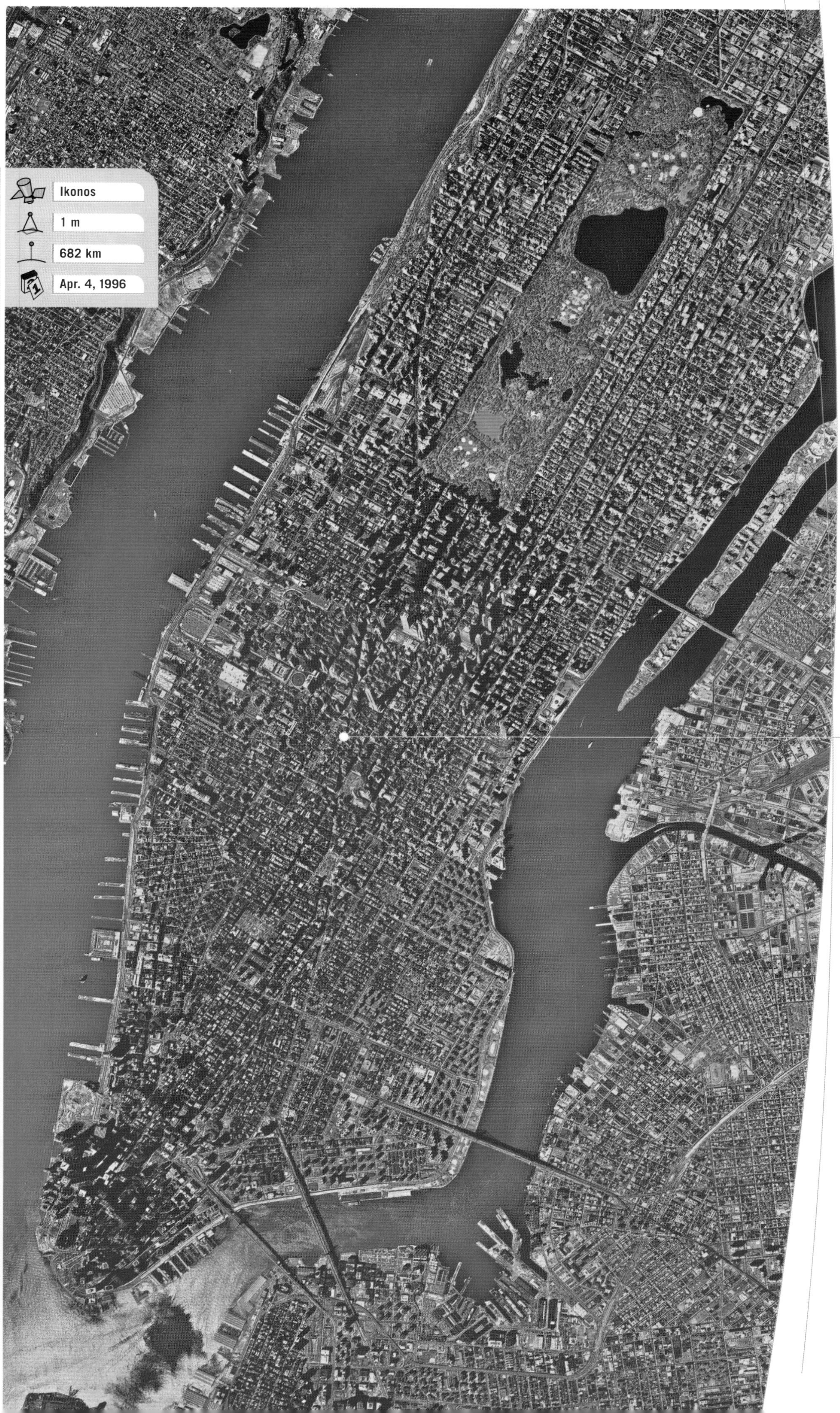

New York

From a colonial settlement
to a modern megacity: Bordered
by the Hudson, Harlem, and
East rivers, the island of Manhattan is the heart of New
York City.
With its many skyscrapers —
concentrated heavily on
the southern tip of the island
and south of Central Park —
Manhattan is the nation's commercial and financial hub
and one of the most important
cultural centers in the world.
Defying the city's checkerboard
street pattern, Broadway,
New York's most famous thor-
oughfare, presents a changing
face along its 20-km path
from one end of the island to
the other. The proportionately
large "green island" of Central
Park is clearly visible in the
middle of Manhattan. A number
of bridges connect the island
with its neighboring boroughs.

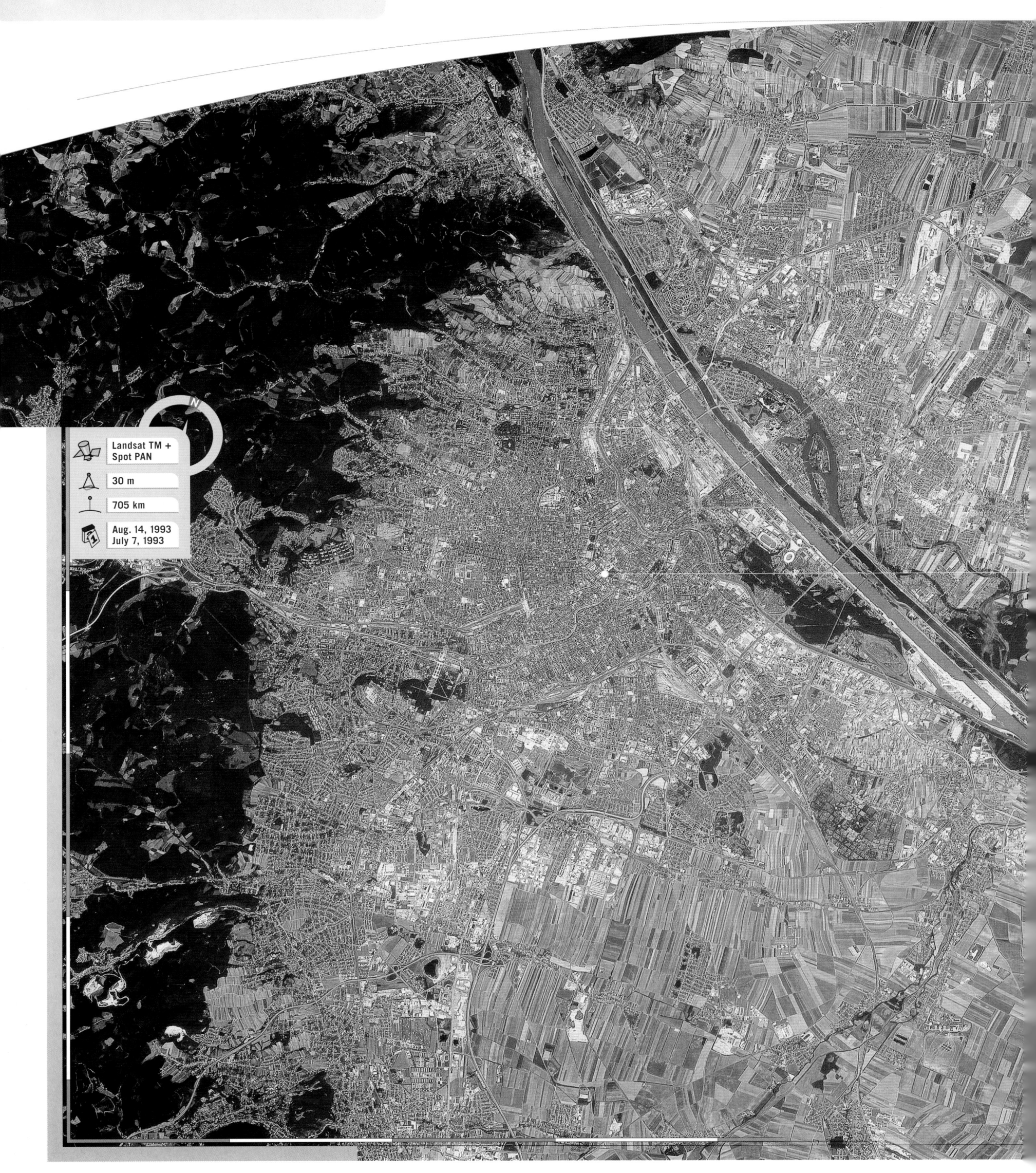

Landsat TM +
Spot PAN

30 m

705 km

Aug. 14, 1993
July 7, 1993

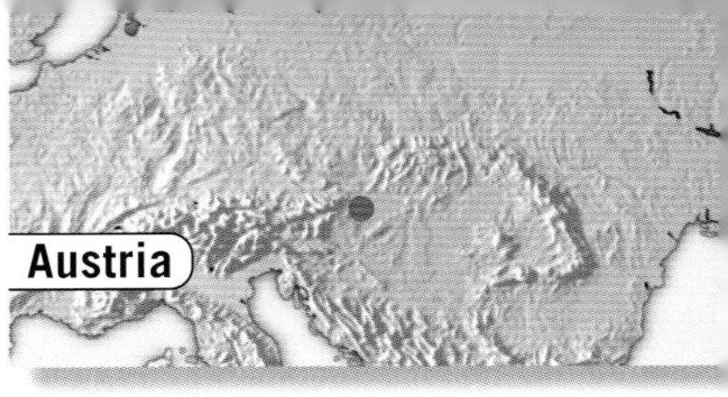

Vienna

Positioned favorably where the Alps descend to the Great Hungarian Plain at a major crossroads of traditional European trading routes from north to south, the Danube metropolis developed from a village into a world city within only few centuries.

The Danube, whose course has been artificially altered twice during the past several centuries, forms the region's natural axis. The former meanders of the Old Danube in the northern part of the satellite image serve as important urban recreation areas today.

The New Danube, which runs parallel to the river, was created in 1970 to prevent flooding. A by-product of this water-regulation measure is the Danube Island, a popular park and recreation area for the people of Vienna.

Neusiedler Lake

Despite its size — approximately 296 sq. km, including 120 sq. km of encircling reed growth, Neusiedler Lake is neither fed nor drained by a river of significant size. Its cloudy greenish-gray coloration is not caused by pollution but is a sign of the presence of billions of suspended particles that never sink entirely to the bottom of the shallow, windswept lake. The border between Austria and Hungary is vividly documented in this satellite image. The landscape in the Austrian state of Burgenland is covered by an intricate quilt of small strip parcels indicating intensive cultivation. These stand in stark contrast to the large block fields on the other side of the border — remnants of the collective farms of a bygone era.

S

40
41

	Landsat TM + Spot PAN
	30 m
	705 km
	Aug. 14, 1993 Aug. 10, 1992

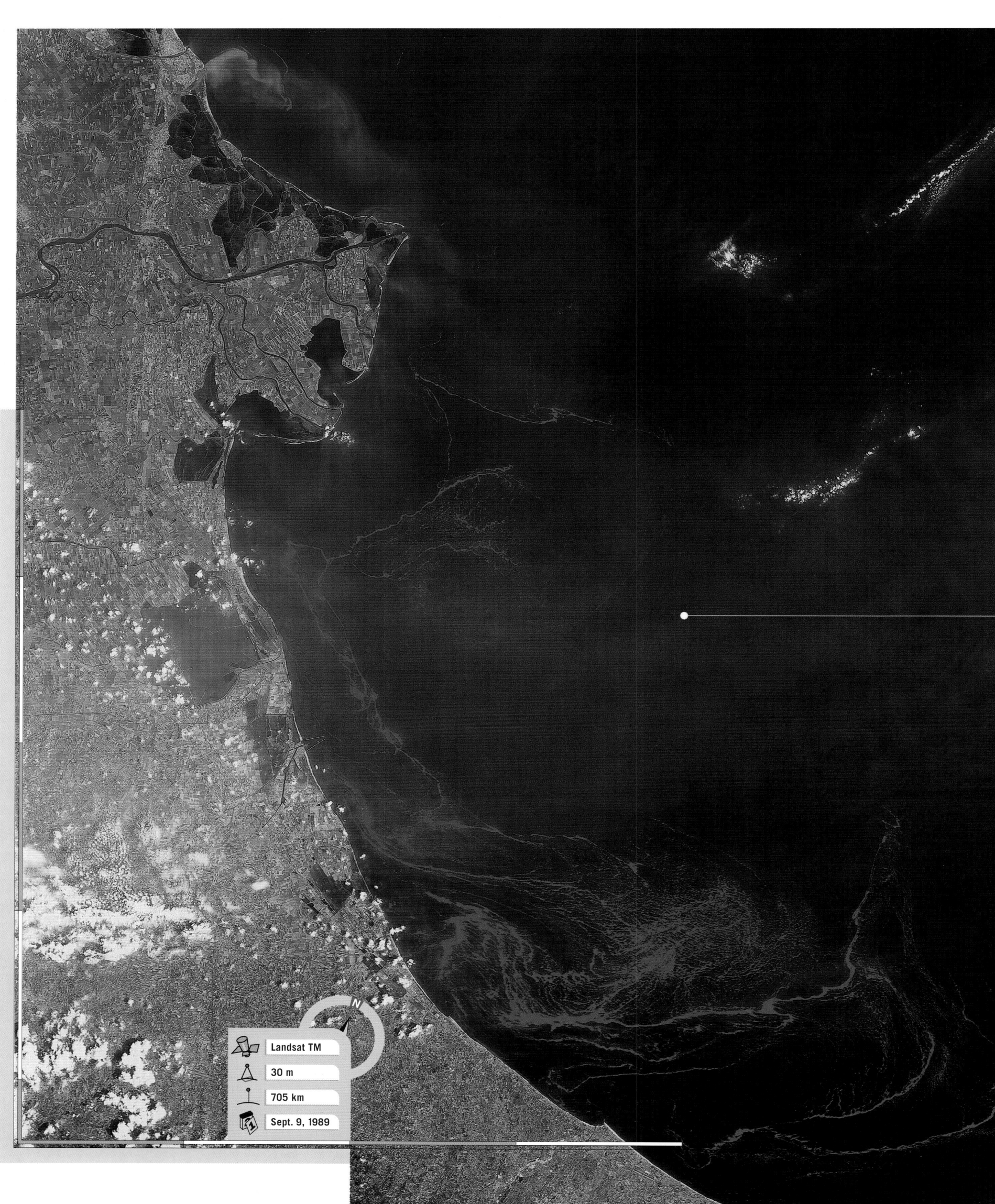

Landsat TM

30 m

705 km

Sept. 9, 1989

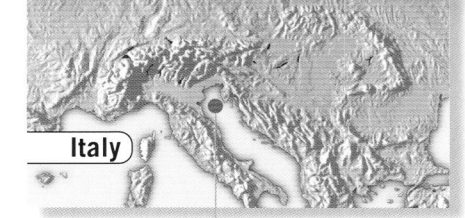

Carpet of Algae

The satellite image shows a stretch of the Italian Adriatic coastline between Chioggia in the north and Fano in the south. Particularly noticeable are the red streaks in the blue of the Adriatic Sea. Red hues indicate vegetation in the false-color image, and the streaks here represent accumulations of algae floating in the sea.

The formation of algae slime in the Mediterranean is a natural phenomenon that is intensified by long periods of good weather and placid seas. Now a common occurrence in many parts of the Mediterranean, the appearance of huge swarms of jellyfish is attributable to the influx of organic household, industrial, and agricultural waste water, which provides an abundance of nutrients for algae.

This satellite image offers impressive evidence of the expansion of the algae carpet. No other medium is capable of documenting such natural phenomena with this degree of clarity at a comparable cost.

Forest Fires on the Island of Thassos

With an area of 398 sq. km, Thassos is the second-largest island in the northern Aegean Sea and the northernmost Greek isle. The highest mountain on the rugged island is Ipsarion, which rises to an elevation of 1,203 m.

Vast areas of forest in Greece are regularly devastated by fires during the summer months. Such fires are primarily the result of dry periods that often last months at a time, although some are the work of arsonists. Disastrous forest fires on Thassos in 1985 and 1987 destroyed a large portion of the island's trees. Yet, despite the extensive damage caused by these fires, Thassos — once the most heavily forested island in Greece — has remained a green isle. The red areas visible in the southern part of the island show the regions destroyed by the fires of 1985.

Landsat TM	
30 m	
705 km	
Apr. 4, 1986	

Polar Regions

Under the Influence of Cold and Ice

Landsat TM

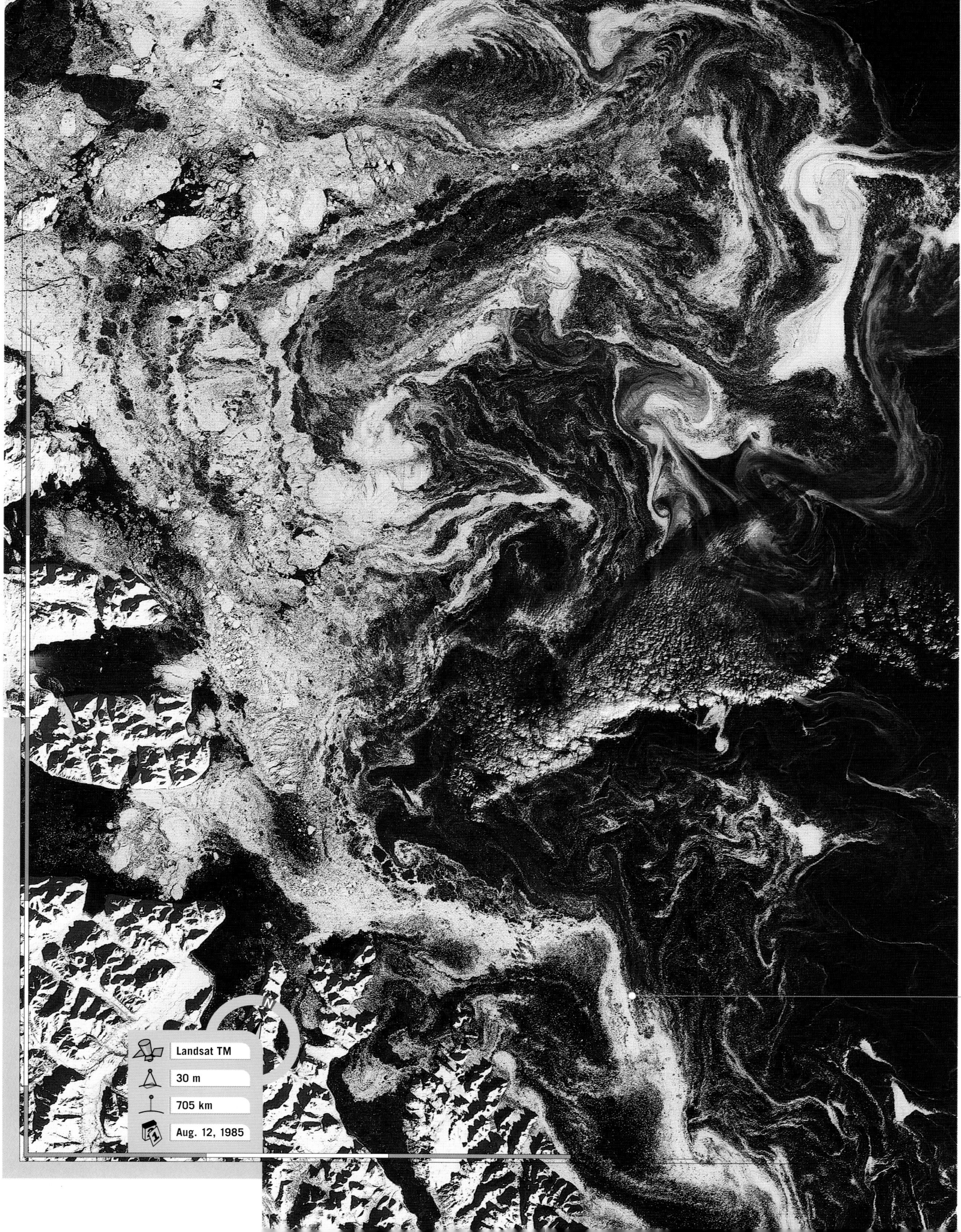

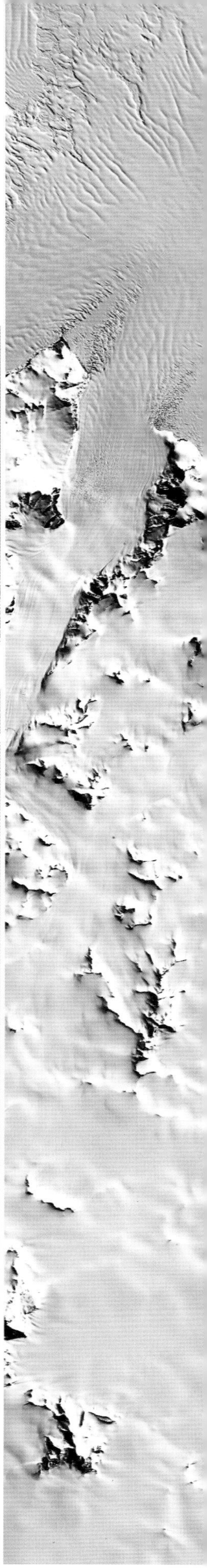

30 m

705 km

Aug. 12, 1985

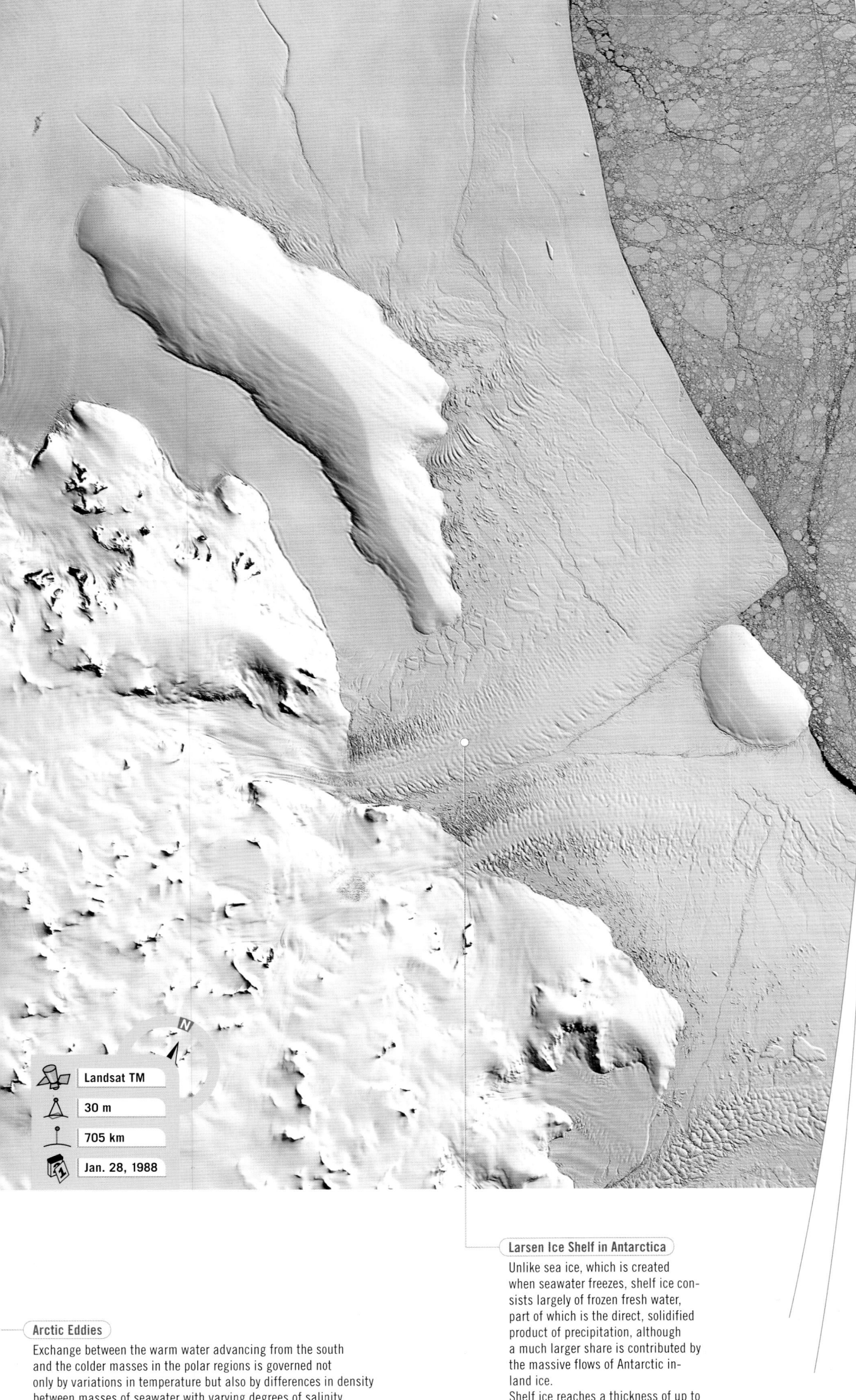

Landsat TM

30 m

705 km

Jan. 28, 1988

Larsen Ice Shelf in Antarctica

Unlike sea ice, which is created
when seawater freezes, shelf ice consists largely of frozen fresh water,
part of which is the direct, solidified
product of precipitation, although
a much larger share is contributed by
the massive flows of Antarctic inland ice.
Shelf ice reaches a thickness of up to
1,500 m at the line along which
it abuts with the Antarctic ice cap.

Arctic Eddies

Exchange between the warm water advancing from the south
and the colder masses in the polar regions is governed not
only by variations in temperature but also by differences in density
between masses of seawater with varying degrees of salinity.
The convergence of water masses with different properties — in
this case at the eastern coast of Greenland — triggers complex
interactions which in turn create marine gyres or so called eddies.

Mountain Ranges

Glacial Heights

Landsat TM	
30 m	
705 km	
Sept. 28, 1985	

The Aletsch Glacier

The Aletsch Glacier stands out strikingly against the rugged
terrain of the Bernese Alps in this satellite image. With
a length of 24.1 km (measured in 1996) and a total area of
nearly 87 sq. km (1975), it is both the longest and the
most expansive glacier of the Alps. Known as the Great Aletsch,
the main glacier flows generally southward from the junction of several other firn fields at Concordia Platz down to the
Aletsch Forest.

Mountains

Ancient Massifs

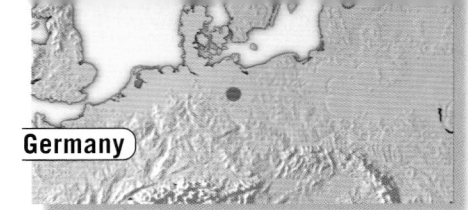

Harz

The Harz Mountain region rises like an island above the North German Plain. A very old formation, it is also the highest central mountain range in Germany north of the Main River.

The numerous different types and formations of rock make this mountain landscape an ideal laboratory for students of geological history. Thus experts refer to the Harz as "Silverland," emphasizing its broad and fascinating geographic diversity. Although its ore deposits are now nearly depleted, the richly varied landscape, with its crystal clear mountain lakes and massifs, is an El Dorado for professional and amateur geologists alike.

Rugged, canyon-like valleys are interspersed among plateaus and heaths. Parts of the Upper Harz, including Mount Brocken, its highest peak (1,141 m), have been set aside as National Park areas.

Landsat ETM

30 m

705 km

Aug. 31, 1989

Map Section

Contents

Using this Atlas
Quick Reference Guide
Map Projections
World Time Zones

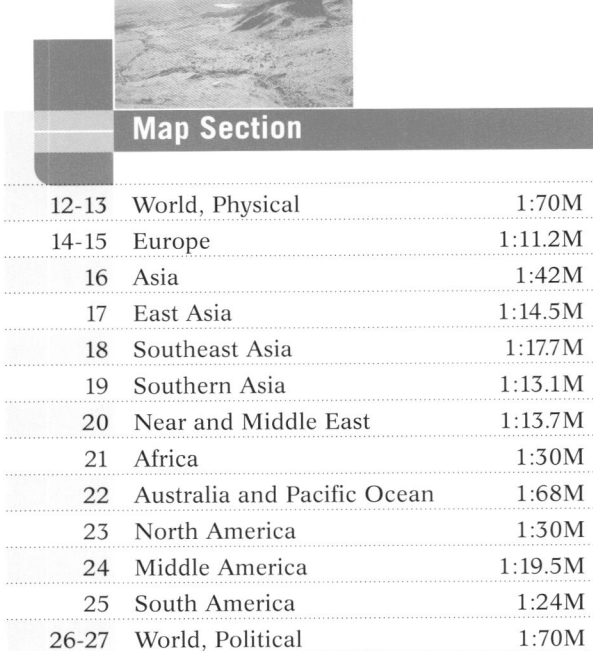

Map Section

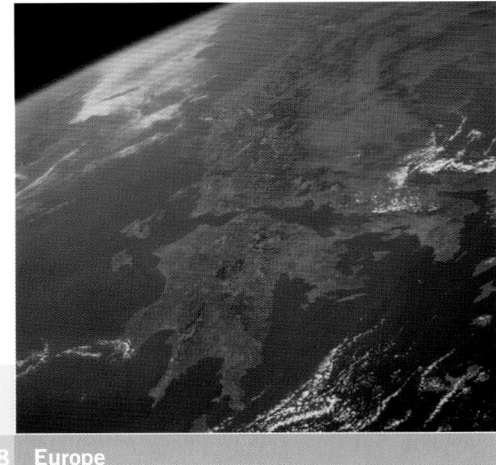

28 Europe

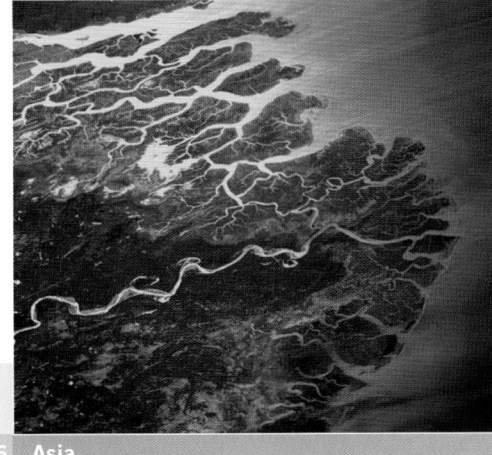

76 Asia

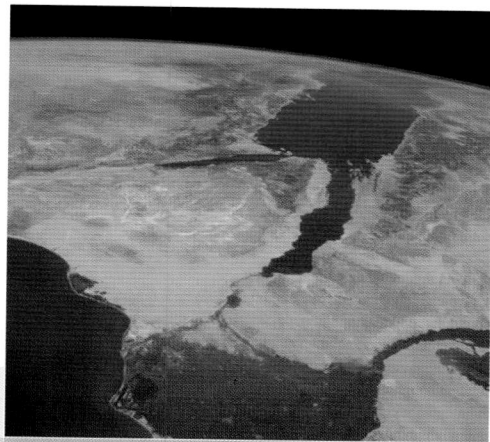

106 Africa

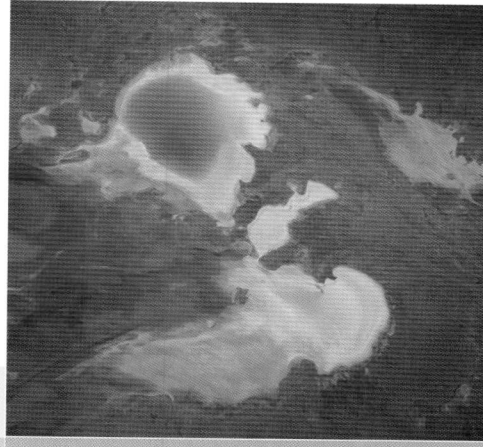

126 Australia, New Zealand and Central Pacific

138 North and Middle America

178 South America and Polar Regions

193 Statistical Tables and Index

Note: M=millions, K=thousands

Using the Map Section

The Contents and Functions of Geographic Maps

Offering a broad range of features and functions, this new Atlas of the World is not only an up-to-date reference work of superior quality but an ideal and thoroughly readable guide for virtual global exploration and armchair travel. The information provided below will help you to get the most enjoyment and benefit from its use.

Relief Maps

The relief maps of the continents – on pages 12–25 of the Map Section – provide a striking impression of the character of the entire Earth's surface, from the mountains of the continental mainlands to the depths of the ocean floor. Produced with the aid of state-of-the-art computer technology, these maps offer a vividly realistic picture of the diverse structures and forms of the global terrain.

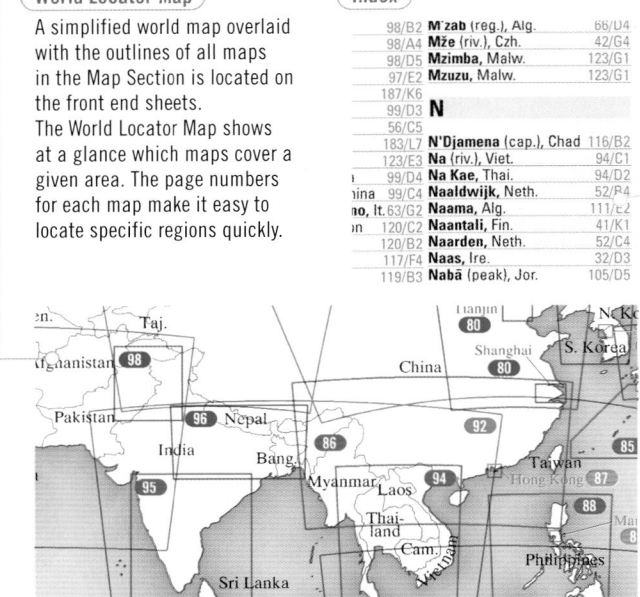

World Locator Map

A simplified world map overlaid with the outlines of all maps in the Map Section is located on the front end sheets.
The World Locator Map shows at a glance which maps cover a given area. The page numbers for each map make it easy to locate specific regions quickly.

Index

98/B2	**M'zab** (reg.), Alg.	66/D4
98/A4	**Mže** (riv.), Czh.	42/G4
98/D5	**Mzimba**, Malw.	123/G1
97/E2	**Mzuzu**, Malw.	123/G1
187/K6		
99/D3	**N**	
56/C5		
183/E4	**N'Djamena** (cap.), Chad	116/B2
123/E3	**Na** (riv.), Viet.	94/C1
99/D4	**Na Kae**, Thai.	94/D2
99/C4	**Naaldwijk**, Neth.	52/P4
no, It. 63/G2	**Naama**, Alg.	111/E2
on. 120/C2	**Naantali**, Fin.	41/K1
120/B2	**Naarden**, Neth.	52/C4
117/F4	**Naas**, Ire.	32/D3
119/B3	**Nabā** (peak), Jor.	105/D5

Geographic Maps

The detailed maps of all regions of the Earth are arranged by continent. The chapters for each of the continents are introduced with a stunning satellite image and a political map. The continental maps show each country in a different color in order to facilitate recognition of political divisions.

A variety of different symbols, line patterns, surface colors, and textures highlight distinctive features such as mountains, national parks, urban areas, forests, and deserts. These maps also provide a wealth of information on roadways and canals, geographic features, and political divisions. All of the geographic maps and the complex information they contain are the product of modern computer-assisted map development and compilation techniques.

Map Frames

The map frames contain a number of graphic features that make the atlas much easier to use. The page numbers of each map are entered in the blue chapter markers at the right-hand edge of each map. An additional locator map in the upper corner shows the position of the individual map section within a larger geographic area. The blue arrows along the four edges of each map refer by page number to the adjacent map sections and thus make it easy to find neighboring areas quickly in the atlas. The letters and numerals in the red squares positioned along the frame are search coordinates used to locate places and objects listed in the map index. In addition, integrated legends and introductory texts provide basic information about the region covered by each map.

Map Scales

A map's scale describes the relationship of any length on the map to a corresponding length on the Earth's surface. A scale of 1:3,000,000 means that one cm on the map represents 3,000,000 cm (30 km) in nature. Thus a scale of 1:1,000,000 is larger than 1:3,000,000, just as 1/1 is larger than 1/3.

Most regions are shown at a scale of either 1:3,000,000 or 1:6,000,000. Areas of particular interest are shown at 1:1,000,000. Selected densely populated areas are covered by maps with a larger scale. Whole continents and large regions are shown at a smaller scale.

Boundary and Name Policies

The atlas shows the internationally recognized national boundaries. Boundary disputes, armistice lines, and de facto boundaries are indicated by special symbols where appropriate. Generally, the names of places and geographic objects appear in the language of the respective country. Accepted conventional names are used for certain major foreign places names. Name usage also tends to vary depending upon cultural factors, however, and is subject to change over time, not least of all for political reasons. In several cases where, for example, a new name has not gained universal acceptance or the use of a traditional name persists, a second name has been entered in parentheses. Thus the selection of names is not entirely systematic and reflects important aspects of common usage.

Index to the Map Section

The index facilitates the search for a specific place in the atlas. It contains an alphabetical list of more than 110,000 names of places and geographic objects entered in the maps. The page numbers and coordinates listed for each index entry show the location of the desired place or object in the map corresponding coordinate grid. A list of the abbreviations used in the index is found on the first index page.

Map Components

A brief text provides information about the geography, history, economy, or culture of the area shown on the map.

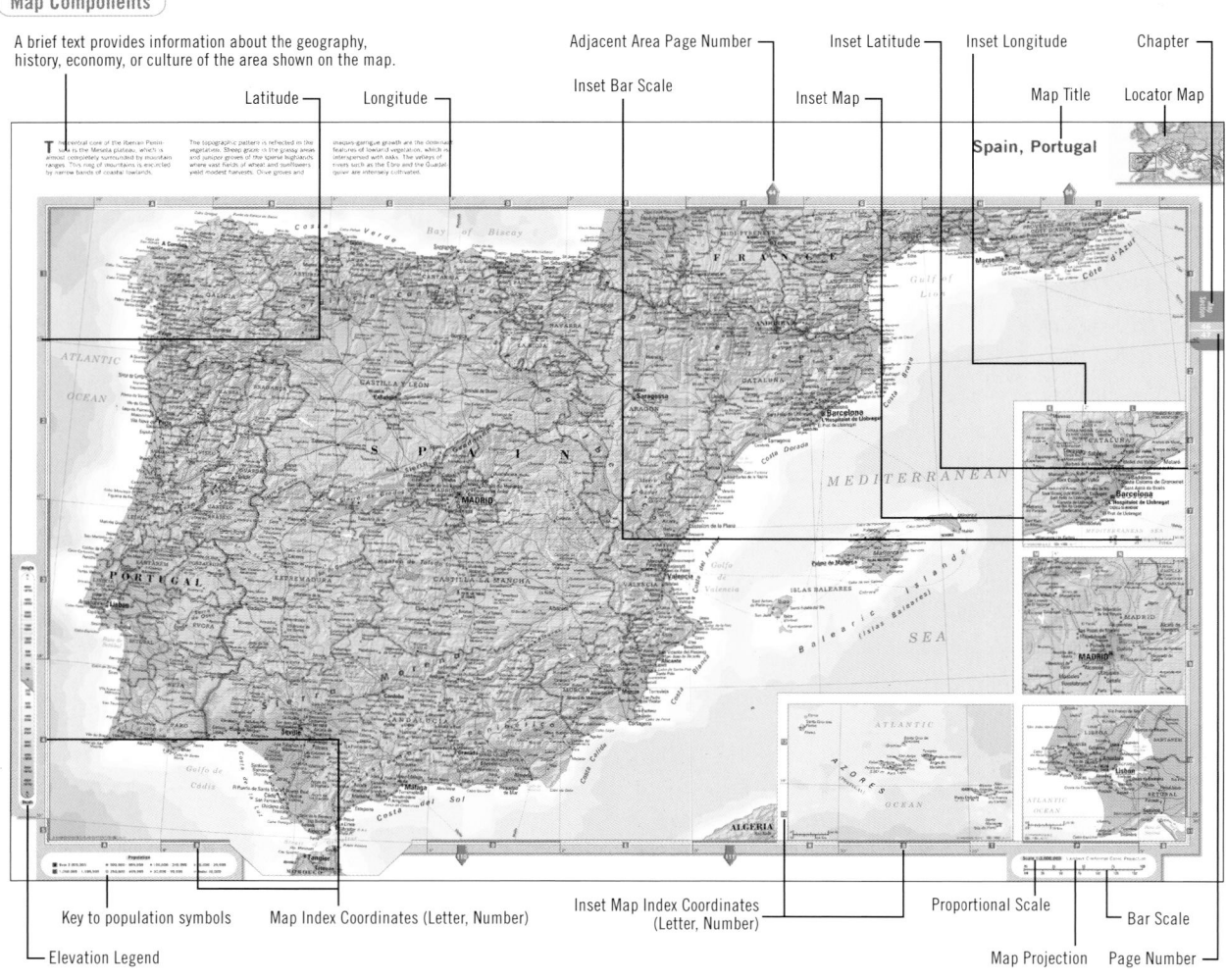

Latitude — Longitude — Adjacent Area Page Number — Inset Latitude — Inset Longitude — Chapter — Inset Bar Scale — Inset Map — Map Title — Locator Map

Spain, Portugal

Key to population symbols — Map Index Coordinates (Letter, Number) — Inset Map Index Coordinates (Letter, Number) — Proportional Scale — Bar Scale — Elevation Legend — Map Projection — Page Number

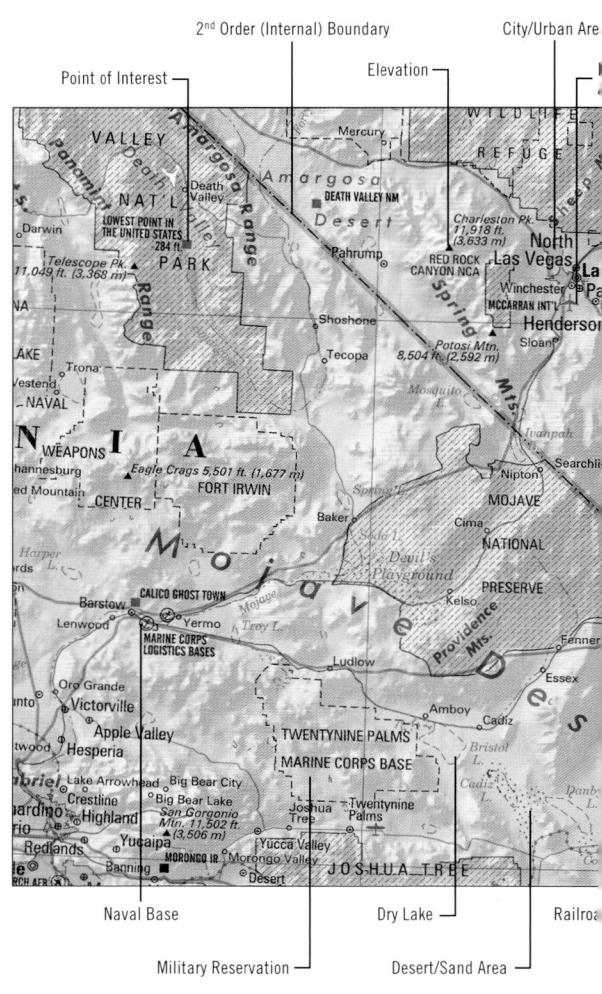

2nd Order (Internal) Boundary — City/Urban Area — Point of Interest — Elevation — Naval Base — Dry Lake — Railroad — Military Reservation — Desert/Sand Area

Map type faces

The use of different type faces helps the reader distinguish between types of map content.

Major Political Arenas

LUXEMBOURG

Internal Political Divisions

SAXONY-ANHALT

Historical Regions

Polabská Nížina

Cities and Towns

Norfolk Sumter Smyrna

Neighborhoods

BIGGIN HILL

Points of Interest

MISSION SAN BUENAVENTURA

Water Features

L. Elsinore

Capes, Points, Peaks, Passes

Cape Horn...Pt. La Jolla
Mt. Rainier

Islands, Peninsulas

Cape Breton I.

Mountain Ranges, Plateaus, Hills

Serra do Norte

Deserts, Plains, Valleys

San Fernando Valley

The spelling of geographic names conforms to the rules of the respective official language of each country. Where the official language is written in Latin characters, local spellings, including diacritical marks and modified letters, have been used. For countries with languages written in non-Latin characters, such as China, Russia or the Arabic-speaking countries, an international standard form is used, which may deviate in some cases from conventional American usage.

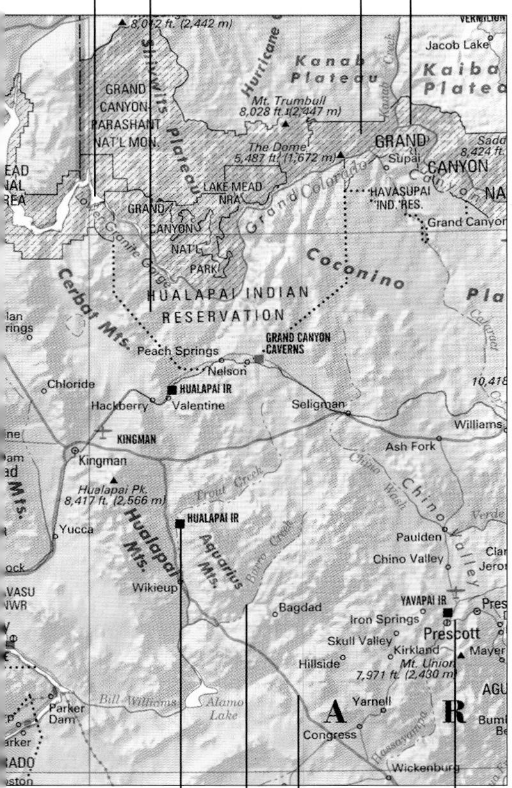

Symbols used on Maps of the World

First Order (National) Boundary

- Demarcated Land Boundary
- Demarcated Water Boundary
- Disputed Boundary
- Armistice Boundary
- De Facto Boundary
- Undefined

Second Order (Internal) Boundary

- Land/Administrative District Boundary
- Water Boundary

Third Order (Internal) Boundary

- Land/Administrative District Boundary
- Water Boundary

Cities and Towns

- Stockholm — First Order (National) Capital
- Salt Lake City — Second Order (Internal) Capital
- Manchester — Third Order (Internal) Capital
- Towns
- City District/Neighborhood
- City and Urban Area Limits

Transportation

- International Airport
- Airport
- Highways/Roads
- Railroads
- Ferries
- Tunnels (Road, Railroad)

Drainage Features

- Shoreline, River
- Intermittend River
- Canal
- Lake, Reservoir
- Intermittent Lake
- Dry Lake
- Salt Pan
- Swamp/Marsh

Other Physical Features

- ▲ Elevation
- ⨝ Pass
- ● Falls
- ✳ Rapids
- Desert/Sand Area
- Lava Flow
- Glacier/Ice Shelf

Cultural Features

- Archeological Sites, Ruins
- Dam
- 🌲 Park
- Wildlife Area
- ■ Point of Interest
- ⌣ Well
- ⊗ Air Base
- ⊘ Naval Base
- International Date Line

- Ancient Walls
- Native Reservation/Reserve
- Military/Government Reservation
- State Park/Recreation Area
- National Park/Forest/Recreation/ Wildlife Area

Elevation Legend

Height

m. ft.
6000 19700
4000 13000
2000 6500
1500 5000
1000 3300
500 1600
200 700
-0-
200 700
500 1600
1000 3300
2000 6500
3000 9800
4000 13000
5000 16400
6000 19700
m. ft.

Depth

The color tints in this bar represent both elevation of land areas and depth of the oceans. The changes between colors are labeled in meters and feet. Selective shading for the land areas highlights those regions with significant relief variations. The legend is entered next to each individual map.

Labels: Lake, National Park Area, Airport, Native Reservation, River, Native Reservation, Other Road, Principal Highway, Canal, Intermittent River

Abbreviations used in the maps

Abor. Rsv.	Aboriginal Reserve	**Fk.**	Fork	**NB**	National Battlefield	**PN**	Park National
Admin.	Administration	**For.**	Forest	**NBP**	National Battlefield Park	**Prom.**	Promontory
AFB	Air Force Base	**Ft.**	Fort	**NCA**	National Conservation Area	**Prsv.**	Preserve
Amm. Dep.	Ammunition Depot	**G.**	Gulf			**Pt.**	Point
Arch.	Archipelago	**Govt.**	Government	**NHP**	National Historical Park	**R.**	River
Aut.	Autonomous	**Gd.**	Grand	**NHS**	National Historic Site	**Rec.**	Recreation(al)
B.	Bay	**Gt.**	Great	**NL**	National Lakeshore	**Ref.**	Refuge
Bfld.	Battlefield	**Har.**	Harbor	**NM**	National Monument	**Reg.**	Region
Bk.	Brook	**Hist.**	Historic(al)	**NMEM**	National Memorial	**Rep.**	Republic
Br.	Branch	**Hts.**	Heights	**NMILP**	National Military Park	**Res.**	Reservoir, Reservation
C.	Cape	**I., Is.**	Island(s)	**No.**	Northern	**Sa.**	Sierra
Can.	Canal	**Ind. Res.**	Indian Reservation	**NP**	National Park	**Sd.**	Sound
Cap.	Capital	**Int'l**	International	**NPP**	National Park and Preserve	**So.**	Southern
C.G.	Coast Guard	**IR**	Indian Reservation			**SP**	State Park
Chan.	Channel	**Isth.**	Isthmus	**NPRSV**	National Preserve	**Spr., Sprgs.**	Spring, Springs
Co.	County	**Jct.**	Junction	**NRA**	National Recreation Area	**St.**	State
Consv.	Conservation	**L.**	Lake	**NRIV**	National River	**Sta.**	Station
Cord.	Cordillera	**Lag.**	Lagoon	**NRSV**	National Reserve	**Stm.**	Stream
Cr.	Creek	**Mem.**	Memorial	**NS**	National Seashore	**Str.**	Strait
Ctr.	Center	**Mil.**	Military	**NWR**	National Wildlife Refuge	**Terr.**	Territory
Dep.	Depot	**Mon.**	Monument	**Obl.**	Oblast	**Tun.**	Tunnel
Depr.	Depression	**Mt.**	Mount	**Occ.**	Occupied	**Twp.**	Township
Des.	Desert	**Mtn.**	Mountain	**Okr.**	Okrug	**UNDOF**	United Nations Disengagement Observer Force
Dist.	District	**Mts.**	Mountains	**Passg.**	Passage		
DMZ	Demilitarized Zone	**Nat.**	Natural	**Pen.**	Peninsula	**Val.**	Valley
Est.	Estuary	**Nat'l**	National	**Pk.**	Peak	**Vill.**	Village
Fed.	Federal	**Nav.**	Naval	**Plat.**	Plateau		

Quick Reference Guide

T his concise alphabetical reference lists continents, countries, states, territories, possessions and other major geographical areas, including the size, population and capital or chief town of each. Blue page numbers and blue alpha-numeric reference keys (which refer to the grid squares of latitude and longitude on each map) are visible at a glance. The population figures are the latest and most reliable figures obtainable.

Place	Square Miles	Square Kilometers	Population	Capital or Chief Town	Page/Index
A					
Afghanistan	250,000	647,500	27,755,775	Kabul	101/H 2
Africa	11,701,147	30,306,000	784,445,000	....	133
Alabama, U.S.	52,237	135,293	4,447,100	Montgomery	143/J 5
Alaska, U.S.	615,230	1,593,444	626,932	Juneau	142/W12
Albania	11,100	28,749	3,544,841	Tiranë	49/F 2
Alberta, Canada	255,285	661,185	3,064,200	Edmonton	140/E 3
Algeria	919,591	2,381,740	32,277,942	Algiers	111/F 3
American Samoa	77	199	68,688	Pago Pago	137/T10
Andorra	174	450	68,403	Andorra la Vella	47/F 1
Angola	481,351	1,246,700	10,593,171	Luanda	107/D 6
Anguilla, U.K.	35	91	12,446	The Valley	173/N 8
Antarctica	5,500,000	14,245,000	....	....	216
Antigua and Barbuda	170	440	67,448	St. John's	173/N 7
Argentina	1,068,296	2,766,890	37,812,817	Buenos Aires	179/B 7
Arizona, U.S.	114,006	295,276	5,130,632	Phoenix	149/F 3
Arkansas, U.S.	53,182	137,742	2,673,400	Little Rock	143/H 4
Armenia	11,506	29,800	3,330,099	Yerevan	71/H 5
Aruba, Netherlands	75	193	70,441	Oranjestad	180/D 1
Ascension Island, St. Helena	34	88	1,117	Georgetown	26/J 6
Asia	17,159,867	44,444,100	3,682,550,000	....	103
Australia	2,967,893	7,686,850	19,546,792	Canberra	153
Australian Capital Territory	938	2,430	280,132	Canberra	132/D 2
Austria	32,375	83,851	8,169,929	Vienna	45/L 3
Azerbaijan	33,436	86,600	7,798,497	Baku	71/H 4
Azores, Portugal	902	2,335	241,762	Ponta Delgada	47/R12
B					
Bahamas, The	5,382	13,939	300,529	Nassau	173/F 2
Bahrain	240	622	656,397	Manama	100/F 3
Balearic Islands, Spain	1,936	5,014	796,483	Palma	47/F 3
Bangladesh	55,598	144,000	133,376,684	Dhaka	97/G 4
Barbados	166	430	276,607	Bridgetown	173/P 8
Belarus	80,154	207,600	10,335,382	Minsk	29/G 3
Belgium	11,780	30,510	10,274,595	Brussels	42/C 3
Belize	8,865	22,960	262,999	Belmopan	176/D 2
Benin	43,483	112,620	6,787,625	Porto-Novo	141/F 4
Bermuda, U.K.	19	50	63,960	Hamilton	139/L 6
Bhutan	18,147	47,000	2,094,176	Thimphu	97/G 2
Bolivia	424,163	1,098,582	8,445,134	La Paz; Sucre	179/C 4
Bosnia & Herzegovina	19,781	51,233	3,964,388	Sarajevo	50/C 3
Botswana	231,803	600,370	1,591,232	Gaborone	107/E 7
Brazil	3,286,470	8,511,965	176,029,560	Brasília	179/D 3
British Columbia, Canada	365,946	947,800	4,095,900	Victoria	140/D 3
British Virgin Islands	59	153	13,368	Road Town	173/M7
Brunei	2,228	5,770	350,898	Bandar Seri Begawan	88/A 4
Bulgaria	42,823	110,912	7,621,337	Sofia	51/G 4
Burkina Faso	105,869	274,200	12,603,185	Ouagadougou	141/E 3
Burundi	10,745	27,830	6,373,002	Bujumbura	120/G 3
C					
California, U.S.	158,869	411,470	33,871,648	Sacramento	142/C 4
Cambodia	69,900	181,040	12,775,324	Phnom Penh	94/D 3
Cameroon	183,568	475,441	16,184,748	Yaoundé	107/D 4
Canada	3,851,787	9,976,139	31,902,268	Ottawa	166
Canary Islands, Spain	2,808	7,273	1,495,000	Las Palmas; Santa Cruz	110/A 3
Cape Verde	1,556	4,030	408,760	Praia	107/J 9
Cayman Islands, U.K.	100	259	36,273	George Town	177/F 2
Celebes, Indonesia	72,986	189,034	14,946,488	Ujung Pandang	91/E 4
Central African Republic	240,533	622,980	3,642,739	Bangui	116/C 4
Chad	495,752	1,283,998	8,997,237	N'Djamena	107/D 3
Channel Islands, U.K.	75	194	147,000	St. Helier; St. Peter Port	56/C 2
Chile	292,258	756,950	15,498,930	Santiago	179/B 6
China, People's Rep. of	3,705,386	9,596,960	1,284,303,705	Beijing	77/J 6
Christmas Island, Australia	52	135	2,771	The Settlement	27/Q 6
Cocos (Keeling) Islands, Australia	5.4	14	633	West Island	27/P 6
Colombia	439,733	1,138,910	41,008,227	Bogotá	180/C 4
Colorado, U.S.	104,100	269,618	4,301,261	Denver	142/E 4
Comoros	838	2,170	614,382	Moroni	125/G 5
Congo, Dem. Rep. of the	905,563	2,345,410	55,225,478	Kinshasa	107/E 5
Congo, Rep. of the	132,046	342,000	2,958,448	Brazzaville	120/C 3
Connecticut, U.S.	5,544	14,358	3,405,565	Hartford	161/K 4
Cook Islands, New Zealand	93	240	20,811	Avarua	137/J 6
Corsica, France	3,352	8,682	260,196	Ajaccio	48/A 1
Costa Rica	19,730	51,100	3,834,934	San José	177/F 4
Côte d'Ivoire	124,502	322,460	16,804,784	Yamoussoukro	140/D 5
Croatia	22,050	56,538	4,390,751	Zagreb	50/C 3
Cuba	42,803	110,860	11,224,321	Havana	177/F 1
Curaçao, Neth. Antilles	172	445	151,498	Willemstad	173/H 5
Cyprus	3,571	9,250	767,314	Nicosia	104/C 2
Czech Republic	30,387	78,703	10,256,760	Prague	43/H 4
D					
Delaware, U.S.	2,396	6,206	783,600	Dover	143/L 4
Denmark	16,629	43,069	5,368,854	Copenhagen	40/C 4
District of Columbia, U.S.	68	177	572,059	Washington	168/B 6
Djibouti	8,494	22,000	472,810	Djibouti	118/B 2
Dominica	290	751	70,158	Roseau	173/N 8
Dominican Republic	18,815	48,730	8,721,594	Santo Domingo	173/H 4
E					
East Timor	5,743	14,874	839,719	Dili	102/B 2
Eastern Cape, South Africa	65,858	170,616	6,665,400	Bisho	124/D 3
Ecuador	109,483	283,561	13,447,494	Quito	179/B 3
Egypt	386,650	1,001,447	70,712,345	Cairo	109/F 3
El Salvador	8,124	21,040	6,353,681	San Salvador	176/D 3
England, U.K.	50,356	130,423	49,997,100	London	31/K10
Equatorial Guinea	10,831	28,052	498,144	Malabo	120/B 2
Eritrea	46,842	121,320	4,465,651	Ásmara	107/F 3
Estonia	17,413	45,100	1,415,681	Tallinn	41/L 2
Ethiopia	435,184	1,127,127	67,673,031	Addis Ababa	107/F 4
Europe	4,066,019	10,531,000	728,887,000	....	55
F					
Falkland Islands & Dependencies, U.K.	4,699	12,170	2,895	Stanley	191M 8
Faroe Islands, Denmark	540	1,399	46,011	Tórshavn	29/D 2
Fiji	7,055	18,272	856,346	Suva	137/Y17
Finland	130,128	337,032	5,183,545	Helsinki	38/H 2
Florida, U.S.	59,928	155,214	15,982,378	Tallahassee	165/F 2
France	211,208	547,030	59,765,983	Paris	44/D 3
Free State, South Africa	49,963	129,437	2,804,600	Bloemfontein	124/D 3
French Guiana	35,135	91,000	182,333	Cayenne	182C 2
French Polynesia	1,522	3,941	257,847	Papeete	137/W15
G					
Gabon	103,347	267,670	1,233,353	Libreville	120/B 3
Gambia, The	4,363	11,300	1,455,842	Banjul	140/B 3
Gauteng, South Africa	7,241	18,760	6,847,000	Johannesburg	124/Q12
Gaza Strip	139	360	1,225,911	Gaza	104/C 4
Georgia	26,911	69,700	8,186,453	T'bilisi	71/G 4
Georgia, U.S.	58,977	152,750	4,960,951	Atlanta	143/K 5
Germany	137,803	356,910	83,251,851	Berlin	42/E 3
Ghana	92,100	238,540	20,244,154	Accra	141/E 4
Gibraltar, U.K.	2.5	6.5	27,714	Gibraltar	46/C 4
Greece	50,942	131,940	10,645,343	Athens	49/G 3
Greenland, Denmark	840,000	2,175,600	56,376	Nuuk (Godthåb)	139/N 2
Grenada	131	340	89,211	St. George's	173/N 9
Guadeloupe & Dependencies, France	687	1,779	435,739	Basse-Terre	173/N 7
Guam, U.S.	209	541	160,796	Agaña	136/D 3
Guatemala	42,042	108,889	13,314,079	Guatemala	176/D 3
Guinea	94,927	245,860	7,775,065	Conakry	140/C 4
Guinea-Bissau	13,946	36,120	1,345,479	Bissau	140/B 3
Guyana	83,000	214,970	698,209	Georgetown	181/G 3
H					
Haiti	10,714	27,750	7,063,722	Port-au-Prince	177/H 2
Hawaii, U.S.	6,459	16,729	1,211,537	Honolulu	142/S 9
Heard & McDonald Islands, Australia	159	412	....	....	216b/E
Honduras	43,277	112,087	6,560,608	Tegucigalpa	176/E 3
Hong Kong, China	402	1,040	7,303,334	Victoria	87/G 4
Howland Island, U.S.	0.6	1.6	....	....	137/H 4
Hungary	35,919	93,030	10,075,034	Budapest	50/D 2
I					
Iceland	39,768	103,000	279,384	Reykjavik	38/N 7
Idaho, U.S.	83,574	216,456	1,293,953	Boise	142/C 3
Illinois, U.S.	57,918	150,007	12,419,293	Springfield	143/J 4
India	1,269,339	3,287,588	1,045,845,226	New Delhi	92/C 3
Indiana, U.S.	36,420	94,328	6,080,485	Indianapolis	143/J 4
Indonesia	741,096	1,919,440	232,073,071	Jakarta	91/E 4
Iowa, U.S.	56,275	145,752	2,926,324	Des Moines	155/G 2
Iran	636,293	1,648,000	66,622,704	Tehran	103/H 3
Iraq	168,753	437,072	24,001,816	Baghdad	102/E 3
Ireland	27,136	70,282	3,883,159	Dublin	31/G10
Isle of Man, U.K.	227	588	73,489	Douglas	34/D 3
Israel	8,019	20,770	6,029,529	Jerusalem	104/C 3
Italy	116,305	301,230	57,715,625	Rome	67/F 2
J					
Jamaica	4,243	10,990	2,680,029	Kingston	177/G 2
Jan Mayen, Norway	144	373	....	....	29/D 1
Japan	145,882	377,835	126,974,628	Tōkyō	79/M 4
Java, Indonesia	48,842	126,500	121,352,608	Jakarta	89/E 4
Johnston Atoll, U.S.	1	2.8	327	....	137/J 3
Jordan	34,445	89,213	5,307,470	Amman	104/D 4
K					
Kansas, U.S.	82,282	213,110	2,688,418	Topeka	143/G 4
Kazakhstan	1,049,150	2,717,300	16,741,519	Aqmola	74/G 5
Kentucky, U.S.	40,411	104,665	4,041,769	Frankfort	162/E 2
Kenya	224,960	582,646	31,138,735	Nairobi	107/F 4
Kermadec Islands, New Zealand	13	33	....	....	136/G 8
Kiribati	277	717	96,335	Tarawa	136/H 5
Korea, North	46,540	120,539	22,224,195	P'yŏngyang	81/D 2
Korea, South	38,023	98,480	48,324,000	Seoul	81/D 4
Kuwait	6,880	17,820	2,111,561	Kuwait	103/F 4
KwaZulu Natal, South Africa	35,312	91,481	8,549,000	Pietermaritzburg	125/E 3
Kyrgyzstan	76,641	198,500	4,822,166	Bishkek	99/B 3
L					
Laos	91,428	236,800	5,777,180	Vientiane	94/C 2
Latvia	24,749	64,100	2,366,515	Riga	41/L 3
Lebanon	4,015	10,399	3,677,780	Beirut	104/D 3
Lesotho	11,718	30,350	2,207,954	Maseru	124/D 3
Liberia	43,000	111,370	3,288,198	Monrovia	140/C 5
Libya	679,358	1,759,537	5,368,585	Tripoli	108/C 2
Liechtenstein	62	160	32,842	Vaduz	61/F 3
Lithuania	25,174	65,200	3,601,138	Vilnius	41/K 4
Louisiana, U.S.	49,651	128,595	4,468,976	Baton Rouge	143/H 5
Luxembourg	999	2,587	448,569	Luxembourg	55/E 4
M					
Macau, Portugal	6	16	461,833	Macau	87/G 4
Macedonia (F.Y.R.O.M.)	9,781	25,333	2,054,800	Skopje	49/G 2
Madagascar	226,657	587,041	16,473,477	Antananarivo	125/H 8
Madeira Islands, Portugal	307	794	245,012	Funchal	110/A 2
Maine, U.S.	33,741	87,388	1,274,923	Augusta	158/B 3
Malawi	45,745	118,480	10,701,824	Lilongwe	107/F 6
Malaya, Malaysia	50,806	131,588	18,523,632	Kuala Lumpur	89/C 1
Malaysia	127,316	329,750	22,662,365	Kuala Lumpur	90/C 2
Maldives	116	300	320,165	Male	77/F 9
Mali	478,764	1,240,000	11,340,480	Bamako	107/B 3
Malta	124	320	397,499	Valletta	48/N 8
Manitoba, Canada	250,946	649,951	1,150,000	Winnipeg	140/F 3
Marquesas Islands, French Polynesia	405	1,049	8,064	Atuona	137/M 5
Marshall Islands	70	181	73,630	Majuro	136/G 3

Sources: CIA Factbook; U.S. Bureau of the Census, International Data Base

Place	Square Miles	Square Kilometers	Population	Capital or Chief Town	Page/Index
Martinique, France	425	1,100	422,277	Fort-de-France	173/N 8
Maryland, U.S.	12,297	31,849	5,296,486	Annapolis	143/L 4
Massachusetts, U.S.	9,241	23,934	6,349,097	Boston	143/M 3
Mauritania	397,953	1,030,700	2,828,858	Nouakchott	107/A 3
Mauritius	718	1,860	1,200,206	Port Louis	125/S15
Mayotte, France	145	375	170,879	Mamoutzou	125/H 6
Mexico	761,601	1,972,546	103,400,165	Mexico	139/G 7
Michigan, U.S.	96,705	250,465	9,938,444	Lansing	143/J 2
Micronesia, Federated States of	271	702	135,869	Palikir	136/D 4
Midway Islands, U.S.	2	5.2	453	....	136/H 2
Minnesota, U.S.	86,943	225,182	4,919,479	St. Paul	143/G 2
Mississippi, U.S.	48,286	125,060	2,844,658	Jackson	143/H 5
Missouri, U.S.	69,709	180,546	5,595,211	Jefferson City	143/H 4
Moldova	13,012	33,700	4,434,547	Chişinău	72/E 4
Monaco	0.7	1.9	31,987	....	64/D 5
Mongolia	606,163	1,569,962	2,694,432	Ulaanbaatar	78/D 2
Montana, U.S.	147,046	380,849	902,195	Helena	142/D 2
Montserrat, U.K.	39	100	8,437	Plymouth	173/N 7
Morocco	172,414	446,550	31,167,783	Rabat	110/D 2
Mozambique	309,494	801,590	19,607,519	Maputo	123/G 3
Mpumalanga, South Africa	31,581	81,816	2,838,500	Nelspruit	125/E 2
Myanmar (Burma)	261,969	678,500	42,238,224	Yangon	93/G 2
Namibia	318,694	825,418	1,820,916	Windhoek	107/D 7
Nauru	8	21	12,329	Yaren (district)	136/F 5
Nebraska, U.S.	77,358	200,358	1,711,263	Lincoln	154/D 3
Nepal	54,363	140,800	25,873,917	Kathmandu	96/D 1
Netherlands	14,413	37,330	16,067,754	The Hague; Amsterdam	52/B 5
Netherlands Antilles	371	960	214,258	Willemstad	180/D 1
Nevada, U.S.	110,567	286,367	1,998,257	Carson City	142/C 4
New Brunswick, Canada	28,355	73,440	757,100	Fredericton	158/D 2
New Caledonia & Dependencies, France	7,359	19,060	207,858	Nouméa	137/U11
Newfoundland, Canada	156,649	405,721	533,800	St. John's	141/K 3
New Hampshire, U.S.	9,283	24,044	1,235,786	Concord	161/L 3
New Jersey, U.S.	8,215	21,277	8,414,350	Trenton	168/D 3
New Mexico, U.S.	121,598	314,939	1,819,046	Santa Fe	142/E 5
New South Wales, Australia	309,498	801,600	5,731,906	Sydney	132/C 1
New York, U.S.	53,989	139,833	18,976,457	Albany	161/J 3
New Zealand	103,736	268,676	3,908,037	Wellington	161
Nicaragua	49,998	129,494	5,023,818	Managua	177/E 3
Niger	489,189	1,267,000	10,639,744	Niamey	107/C 3
Nigeria	356,668	923,770	129,934,911	Abuja	107/C 4
Niue, New Zealand	100	259	2,124	Alofi	137/J 7
Norfolk Island, Australia	13.4	34.6	2,756	Kingston	136/F 7
North America	9,355,975	24,232,000	482,992,000	....	165
North Carolina, U.S.	52,672	136,421	8,049,313	Raleigh	163/G 3
North Dakota, U.S.	70,704	183,123	642,200	Bismarck	156/D 4
Northern Cape, South Africa	140,268	363,389	763,900	Kimberley	124/C 3
Northern Ireland, U.K.	5,459	14,138	1,697,800	Belfast	31/H 9
Northern Marianas, U.S.	184	477	77,311	Saipan	136/D 3
Northern Province, South Africa	46,168	119,606	5,120,600	Pietersburg	123/F 4
Northern Territory, Australia	519,784	1,346,241	175,876	Darwin	127/C 2
North Korea	46,540	120,539	22,224,195	P'yŏngyang	81/D 2
North-West, South Africa	45,347	117,450	3,506,800	Mmabatho	124/D 2
Northwest Territories, Canada	589,315	1,526,328	40,900	Yellowknife	140/E 2
Norway	125,181	324,220	4,525,116	Oslo	38/C 3
Nova Scotia, Canada	21,425	55,491	942,700	Halifax	158/E 3
Nunavut, Canada	733,590	1,900,000	28,200	Iqaluit	141/K 2
Oceania	3,292,000	8,526,280	30,199,000	....	162
Ohio, U.S.	44,828	116,103	11,353,140	Columbus	143/K 3
Oklahoma, U.S.	69,903	181,048	3,450,654	Oklahoma City	153/E 3
Oman	82,031	212,460	2,713,462	Muscat	101/G 4
Ontario, Canada	412,580	1,068,582	11,874,400	Toronto	140/H 3
Oregon, U.S.	97,132	251,571	3,421,399	Salem	142/B 3
Orkney Islands, Scotland	376	974	19,480	Kirkwall	31/N13
Pakistan	310,403	803,944	147,663,429	Islamabad	101/H 3
Palau	177	458	19,409	Koror	136/C 4
Panama	30,193	78,200	2,882,329	Panamá	177/F 4
Papua New Guinea	178,259	461,690	5,172,033	Port Moresby	136/D 5
Paraguay	157,047	406,752	5,884,491	Asunción	188D 2
Pennsylvania, U.S.	46,058	119,291	12,281,054	Harrisburg	161/G 4
Peru	496,223	1,285,220	27,949,639	Lima	184C 3
Philippines	115,830	300,000	84,525,639	Manila	114
Pitcairn Islands, U.K.	18	47	47	Adamstown	137/N 7
Poland	120,725	312,678	38,625,478	Warsaw	43/K 2
Portugal	35,552	92,080	10,084,245	Lisbon	46/A 3
Prince Edward Island, Canada	2,184	5,657	138,500	Charlottetown	158/F 2
Puerto Rico, U.S.	3,508	9,085	3,957,988	San Juan	173/M7
Qatar	4,247	11,000	793,341	Doha	100/F 3
Québec, Canada	594,857	1,540,680	7,410,500	Québec	141/J 3
Queensland, Australia	666,872	1,727,200	2,977,813	Brisbane	134/A 3
Réunion, France	969	2,510	743,981	St-Denis	125/R15
Rhode Island, U.S.	1,231	3,189	1,048,319	Providence	161/L 4
Romania	91,699	237,500	22,317,730	Bucharest	51/F 3
Russia	6,592,735	17,075,200	144,978,573	Moscow	74/H 3
Rwanda	10,169	26,337	7,398,074	Kigali	121/G 3
Sabah, Malaysia	28,460	73,711	2,449,389	Kota Kinabalu	91/E 2
Saint Helena & Dependencies, U.K.	158	410	7,266	Jamestown	26/J 6
Saint Kitts and Nevis	104	269	38,736	Basseterre	173/N 7
Saint Lucia	239	620	160,145	Castries	173/N 8
Saint Pierre & Miquelon, France	93.5	242	6,928	Saint-Pierre	159/J 2
Saint Vincent & the Grenadines	131	340	116,394	Kingstown	173/N 8
Sakhalin, Russia	29,500	76,405	632,000	Yuzhno-Sakhalinsk	75/Q 4
Samoa	1,104	2,860	178,631	Apia	137/R 9
San Marino	23.4	60.6	27,730	San Marino	63/F 5
São Tomé and Príncipe	371	960	170,372	São Tomé	120/A 2
Sarawak, Malaysia	48,050	124,449	2,012,616	Kuching	90/D 3
Sardinia, Italy	9,301	24,090	1,648,044	Cagliari	48/A 2
Saskatchewan, Canada	251,865	652,330	1,015,800	Regina	140/F 3
Saudi Arabia	756,981	1,960,582	23,513,330	Riyadh	100/D 4
Scotland, U.K.	30,414	78,772	5,128,000	Edinburgh	31/J 8
Senegal	75,749	196,190	10,589,571	Dakar	140/B 3
Serbia and Montenegro, see Yugoslavia					
Seychelles	176	455	80,098	Victoria	27/M6
Shetland Islands, Scotland	552	1,430	22,440	Lerwick	31/N12
Sicily, Italy	9,926	25,708	5,076,700	Palermo	48/C 3
Sierra Leone	27,699	71,740	5,614,743	Freetown	140/B 4
Singapore	244	632.6	4,452,732	Singapore	89/H 6
Slovakia	18,859	48,845	5,422,366	Bratislava	43/K 4
Slovenia	7,836	20,296	1,932,917	Ljubljana	50/B 3
Society Islands, French Polynesia	677	1,753	117,703	Papeete	137/K 6
Solomon Islands	10,985	28,450	494,786	Honiara	136/E 6
Somalia	246,200	637,658	7,753,310	Mogadishu	107/G 4
South Africa	471,008	1,219,912	43,647,658	Cape Town; Pretoria	107/E 7
South America	6,879,916	17,819,000	345,782,000	....	203
South Australia, Australia	379,922	984,000	1,400,630	Adelaide	127/C 3
South Carolina, U.S.	31,189	80,779	4,012,012	Columbia	163/G 3
South Dakota, U.S.	77,121	199,744	754,844	Pierre	154/D 1
South Korea	38,023	98,480	48,324,000	Seoul	81/D 4
Spain	194,884	504,750	40,077,100	Madrid	46/C 2
Sri Lanka	25,332	65,610	19,576,783	Colombo	92/D 6
Sudan	967,494	2,505,809	37,090,298	Khartoum	107/E 3
Sumatra, Indonesia	182,811	473,481	43,259,707	Medan	89/D 3
Suriname	63,039	163,270	436,494	Paramaribo	182B 1
Svalbard, Norway	23,957	62,049	2,332	Longyearbyen	74/C 2
Swaziland	6,703	17,360	1,123,605	Mbabane; Lobamba	125/E 2
Sweden	173,731	449,964	8,876,744	Stockholm	38/E 3
Switzerland	15,943	41,292	7,301,994	Bern	60/D 4
Syria	71,498	185,180	17,155,814	Damascus	102/D 3
Tahiti, French Polynesia	402	1,041	150,707	Papeete	137/X15
Taiwan	13,892	35,980	22,548,009	T'aipei	87/J 3
Tajikistan	55,251	143,100	6,719,567	Dushanbe	74/H 6
Tanzania	364,699	945,090	37,187,939	Dar es Salaam; Dodoma	107/F 5
Tasmania, Australia	26,178	67,800	452,851	Hobart	132/C 4
Tennessee, U.S.	42,146	109,158	5,689,283	Nashville	162/D 3
Texas, U.S.	267,277	692,248	20,851,820	Austin	142/G 5
Thailand	198,455	513,998	62,354,402	Bangkok	94/C 3
Tibet, China	471,428	1,221,000	2,560,000	Lhasa	99/D 5
Togo	21,927	56,790	5,285,501	Lomé	115/F 4
Tokelau, New Zealand	3.9	10	1,445	....	137/H 5
Tonga	289	748	106,137	Nuku'alofa	137/H 7
Trinidad and Tobago	1,980	5,128	1,163,724	Port-of-Spain	173/N 9
Tristan da Cunha, St. Helena	38	98	313	Edinburgh	26/J 7
Tuamotu Archipelago, French Polynesia	266	690	15,370	Apataki	137/L 6
Tunisia	63,170	163,610	9,815,644	Tunis	111/H 2
Turkey	301,382	780,580	67,308,928	Ankara	102/C 2
Turkmenistan	188,455	488,100	4,688,963	Ashgabat	74/F 6
Turks and Caicos Islands, U.K.	166	430	18,122	Grand Turk	177/H 1
Tuvalu	10	26	11,146	Funafuti	136/G 5
Uganda	91,135	236,040	24,699,073	Kampala	107/F 4
Ukraine	233,089	603,700	48,396,470	Kiev	72/F 4
United Arab Emirates	29,182	75,581	2,445,989	Abu Dhabi	100/F 4
United Kingdom	94,525	244,820	59,778,002	London	57
United States	3,618,765	9,372,610	280,562,489	Washington, D.C.	168
Uruguay	68,039	176,220	3,386,575	Montevideo	179/D 6
Utah, U.S.	84,904	219,902	2,233,169	Salt Lake City	142/D 4
Uzbekistan	172,741	447,400	25,563,441	Tashkent	74/G 5
Vanuatu	5,699	14,760	196,178	Port-Vila	136/F 6
Vatican City	0.17	0.44	890	....	65/E 7
Venezuela	352,143	912,050	24,287,670	Caracas	181/E 3
Vermont, U.S.	9,614	24,900	608,827	Montpelier	161/K 3
Victoria, Australia	87,876	227,600	4,244,282	Melbourne	132/C 3
Vietnam	127,243	329,560	81,098,416	Hanoi	94/D 2
Virginia, U.S.	42,326	109,625	7,078,515	Richmond	163/H 2
Virgin Islands, British	59	153	21,272	Road Town	173/M7
Virgin Islands, U.S.	136	352	123,498	Charlotte Amalie	173/M7
Wake Island, U.S.	2.5	6.5	302	....	136/F 3
Wales, U.K.	8,017	20,764	2,921,100	Cardiff	31/J10
Wallis and Futuna, France	106	275	15,435	Mata Utu	136/G 6
Washington, U.S.	70,637	182,949	5,894,121	Olympia	144/D 4
West Bank	2,263	5,860	2,163,667	....	105/C 4
Western Australia, Australia	975,096	2,525,500	1,587,050	Perth	127/B 3
Western Cape, South Africa	49,943	129,386	3,620,200	Cape Town	124/C 4
Western Sahara	102,703	266,000	256,177	....	110/B 4
West Virginia, U.S.	24,231	62,758	1,808,344	Charleston	143/K 4
Wisconsin, U.S.	65,499	169,643	5,363,675	Madison	143/H 3
World	(land) 57,505,734	148,940,000	6,230,586,132		52
Wyoming, U.S.	97,818	253,349	493,782	Cheyenne	142/E 3
Yemen	203,849	527,970	18,701,257	Sanaa	100/E 5
Yugoslavia	39,517	102,350	10,656,929	Belgrade	50/E 3
Yukon Territory, Canada	186,660	483,450	29,900	Whitehorse	140/C 2
Zambia	290,583	752,610	9,959,037	Lusaka	107/E 6
Zimbabwe	150,803	390,580	11,376,676	Harare	123/F 3

Map Projections

A Difficult Problem Solved by Computers Today

A map projection is an image of the Earth or parts of the Earth on a flat plane. Every point on Earth can be identified with the aid of geographic coordinates, within a global coordinate grid, and this grid can be projected onto a flat surface. Today, computer cartography plays an important role in calculating the projection most appropriate for a particular purpose.

Basic Principles and Terms

The Earth rotates around its axis once a day. Its end points are the North and South poles; the line circling the Earth midway between the poles is the Equator. The arc from the Equator to each pole is divided into 90 degrees of latitude. The Equator itself represents 0° latitude and is divided into 360 degrees of longitude. Lines circling the globe from pole to pole which intersect with the Equator at 90-degree angles are called meridians, or great circles. The meridian passing through the Greenwich Observatory near London was chosen by international agreement as to prime meridian or 0° longitude in 1884. Meridians and lines of latitude (parallels) form the global coordinate grid, or graticule. The distance from the prime meridian to a given point to the west or east, expressed in degrees

(coordinates) is its geographic longitude. Similarly, distances north or south of the Equator represent geographic latitude. Although all meridians are equal in length, parallels become shorter as they approach the poles. Thus, while the distance between two parallels (one degree of latitude) is approximately 112 km everywhere on Earth, the distance between two meridians (one degree of longitude) varies between 112 km at the Equator and zero at the poles where the meridians converge. Each degree of longitude and latitude is divided into 60 minutes. One minute of latitude equals one nautical mile (1.85 km).

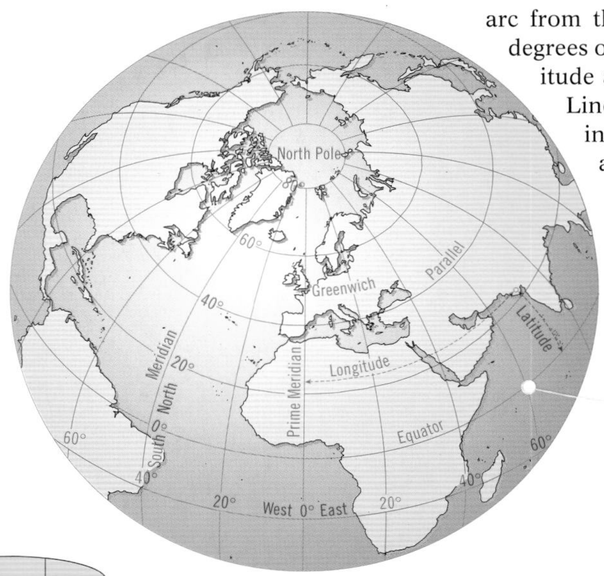

Distortion

There is only one way to represent the sphere of the Earth with absolute precision: as a globe. All attempts to project our planet's curved surface onto a plane create distortion. Depending upon the map projection selected, distortions appear in shapes and area sizes, angles or distances between points on the Earth. Only parallels or meridians (or some other set of lines) can be represented in accurate proportion. All other lines must be either

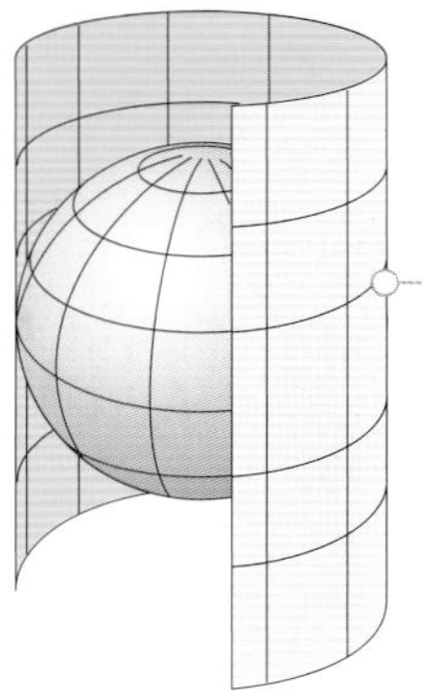

Cylindrical Projection

A cylinder of variable axis length is wrapped around the Earth. The cylinder can touch the Earth at the Equator, for example, or penetrate through the Earth, as is the case in the (conformal) Mercator projection.

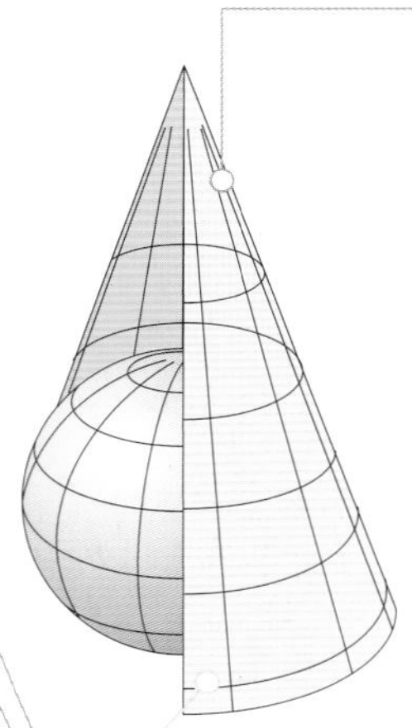

Conic Projection

This projection is produced by capping the Earth with a cone. Axis length is variable. Normally, the cone axis is aligned with an Earth axis or with the Equator. In the conic projection shown here, the cone can be made tangent to any desired parallel. One popular version of the conic projection is the Lambert Conformal Conic, in which two parallels are represented in conforming lengths.

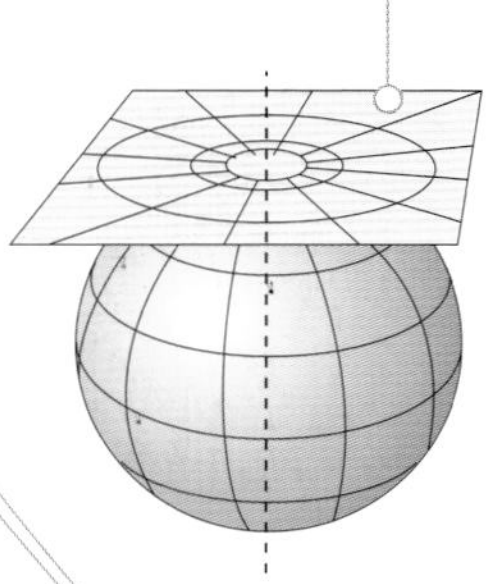

Azimuthal Projection

In azimuthal projections, the projection surface is a plane that touches the Earth at a single point. It is ordinarily used as a polar projection of the Earth — with a pole at the center of the projection. This type of projection can only show one hemisphere. Depending upon the distance from the projection axis to the Earth's axis, map projections are referred to as polar, equatorial or oblique-axis. A version frequently used for maps of continents is the Lambert Azimuthal Equal Area Projection, which shows areas with relatively little distortion of shapes.

Hammond Optimal Conformal Projection

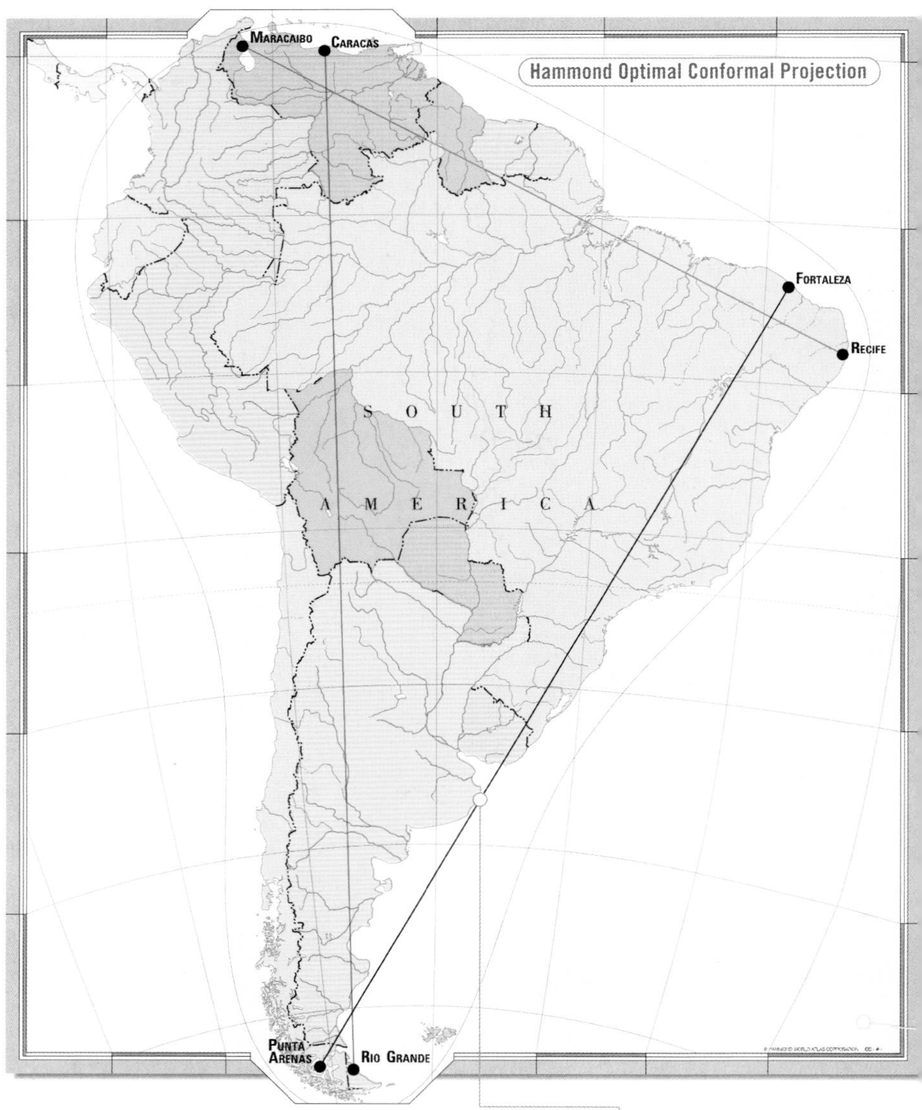

Cities	True distance	Hammond Projection	Lambert Projection
Caracas – Rio Grande	7 149 km	7 126 km	6 944 km
Maracaibo – Recife	4 560 km	4 578 km	4 533 km
Fortaleza – Punta Arenas	6 246 km	6 266 km	6 163 km

Comparison of Accuracy

The use of the Lambert Azimuthal Equal Area Projection for maps of continents produces distortions ranging from 2.3% (Europe) to 15% (Asia). The Hammond Optimal Conformal reduces these distortions by half and improves the reliability of distance measurements based on these maps.

(Robinson Projection)

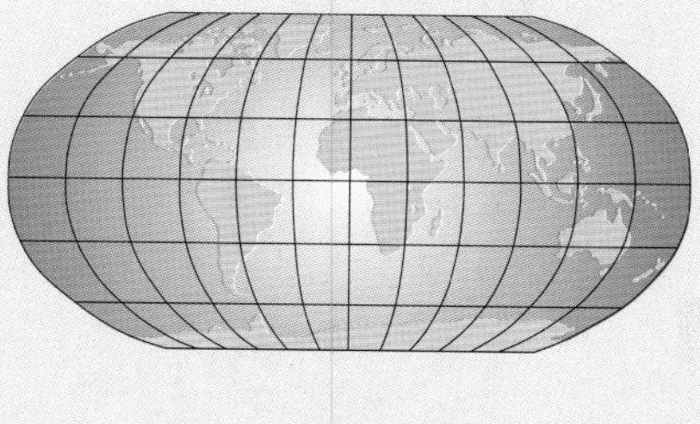

(Mercator Projection)

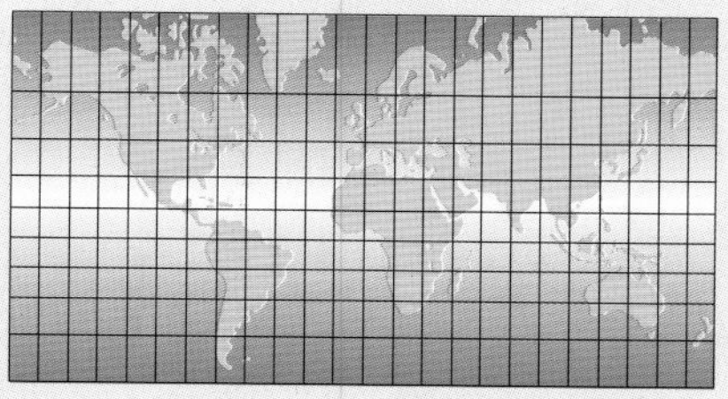

too long or too short. Accordingly, the scale on a flat map cannot be true everywhere. On world maps or very large areas, variations in scale may be extreme.

Projections: Selected Examples

The Mercator projection is a conformal, normal-axis cylindrical projection in which all meridians and parallels intersect at right angles. Because all compass directions appear as straight lines, the Mercator projection is still an important navigational tool. Moreover, every small region conforms to the shape on a globe – hence the name conformal. But because its meridians are evenly-spaced vertical lines that do not converge (unlike those on the globe), the horizontal parallels must be drawn farther apart as they approach the poles to maintain a correct relationship. Only the Equator is true to scale, and the size of areas in the higher latitudes is dramatically distorted.

The Robinson projection was used to create the two-page world map in the Map Section. It combines elements of both conformal and equal-area projections to show the whole earth with relatively true shapes and reasonably equal areas. This projection is a mediating pseudo-cylindrical representation.

The conic projection is used frequently for air navigation charts. It was used to create most of the national and regional maps in this atlas.

The Hammond Optimal Conformal projection presents an optimal view of an area by reducing shifts in scale over an entire region to the minimum degree possible. The concept underlying the Optimal Conformal projection is that, for any region on the globe, there is an ideal projection for which scale variations can be kept as small as possible. Consequently, unlike other projections, the Optimal Conformal does not use a standard formula to construct a map. Each map is a unique projection – the optimal projection for that specific area.

In practice, the cartographer first defines the map subject, then, working on a computer, draws a boundary around the region to be mapped. Next, a sophisticated software program evaluates the size and shape of the region to determine the most accurate way to project it. The results is a precise map with a minimum possible degree of distortion. All of the continent maps in this Atlas (with the exception of Antarctica) have been drawn using this projection.

Projections Compared

The following diagrams show the distortions produced by several commonly used projections. By using a simple face with familiar shapes (the Plan) as the starting point, it is easy to see the advantages and drawbacks of each. Areas or continents on a map change much like the shapes of the face in the diagram. The distortion appears not only in the features themselves, but also in the changing shapes, angles, and areas of the background grid, or graticule.

The Plan

The Plan shows the "continents" either as perfect circles or true straight lines on the Earth. They should appear that way on a "perfect" map.

Orthographic Projection (Parallel Projection)

This azimuthal view shows the "continents" on Earth as seen from space. The facial features occupy half of the Earth. Toward the edge, the eyes grow increasingly elliptical, the nose appears larger and less straight, and the mouth curves into a smile.

Mercator Projection

This cylindrical projection preserves angles exactly, but the mouth is now smiling broadly and shows extreme distortion at the map's outer edge. Typical of the rapid expansion of forms toward the outer edge is the extreme enlargement of Greenland on Mercator world maps.

Peters Projection

This equal-area cylindrical projection represents areas in their correct proportions, but it does not closely resemble the Plan. Angles, local shapes, and global relations are significantly distorted.

Gnomonic Projection

This strange-looking projection is neither conformal nor equal-area. It is a centrally positioned azimuthal projection, meaning that the center of projection lies in the center of the Earth. Although its outer regions are badly distorted, the straight mouth and precise triangle of the nose indicate a key advantage of this map: all great circles appear as straight lines. This enables the user to find the shortest path between any two points on the map simply by connecting them with a straight line.

Hammond Optimal Conformal Projection

As one can easily see, this projection minimizes inaccuracies between the angles and shapes of the Plan, yielding a near-perfect map of the given area, up to a complete hemisphere. Like all conformal maps, the Optimal projection preserves every angle exactly, but it is more successful than previous projections at spreading the inevitable curvature across the entire map. The sides of the triangle appear almost straight, although the sum of the angles is greater than 180°. Although the eyes are somewhat too large, this is the only map with eyes that appear concentric. Both mathematically and visually, it offers the best conformal map that can be made of the ideal Plan.

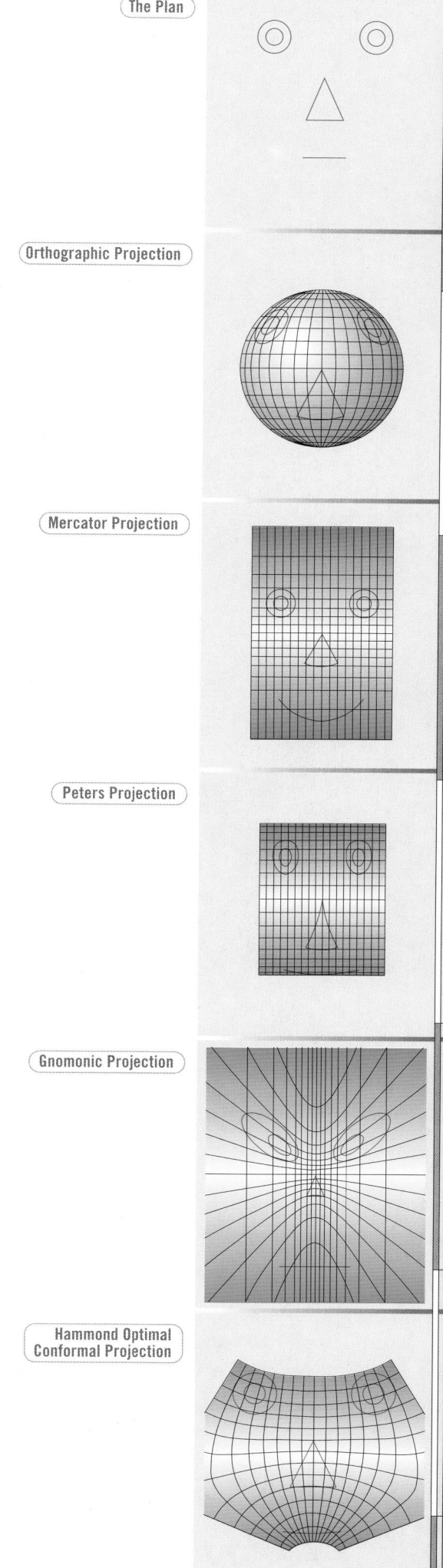

(The Plan)

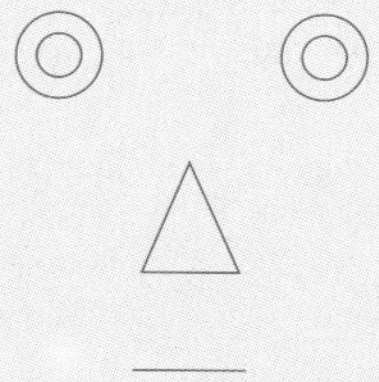

(Orthographic Projection)

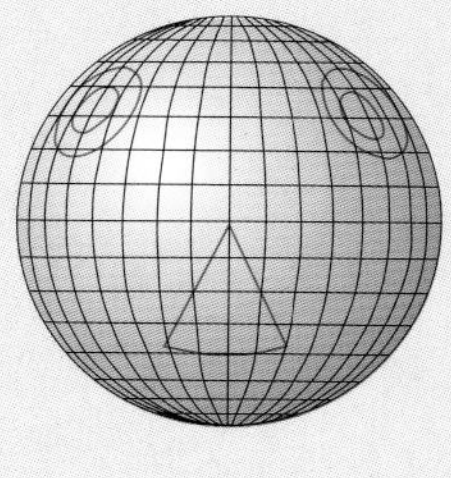

(Mercator Projection)

(Peters Projection)

(Gnomonic Projection)

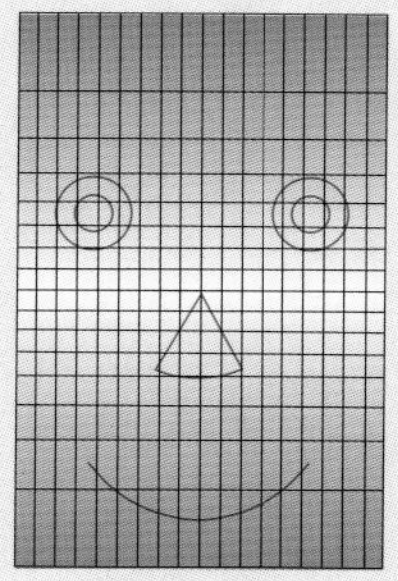

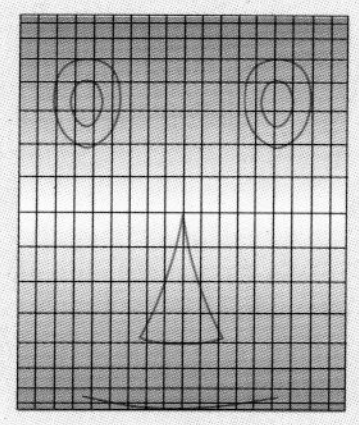

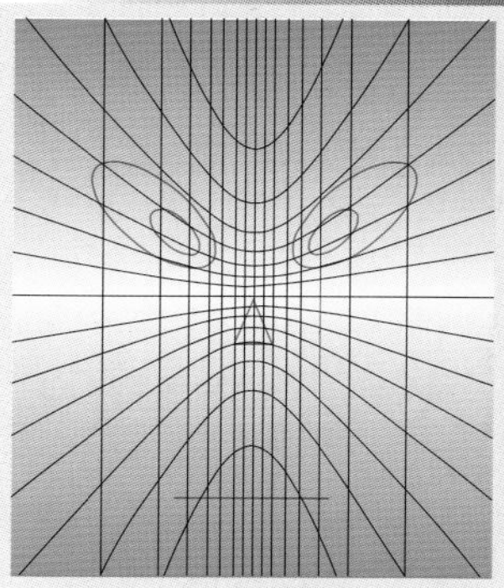

(Hammond Optimal Conformal Projection)

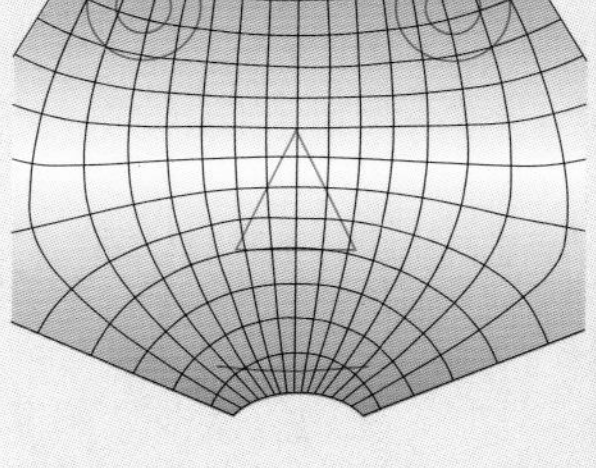

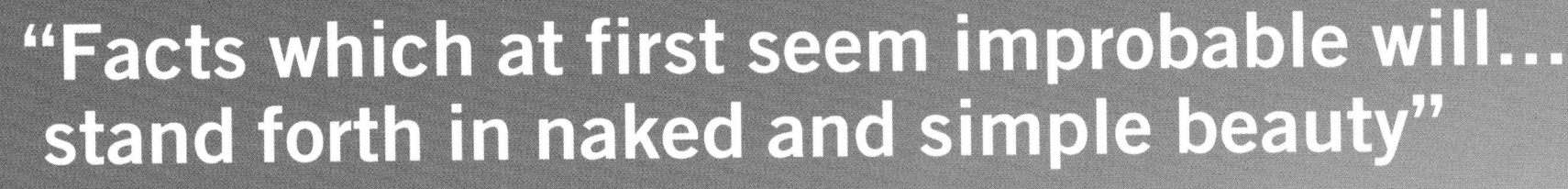

"Facts which at first seem improbable will... stand forth in naked and simple beauty"

Galileo Galilei

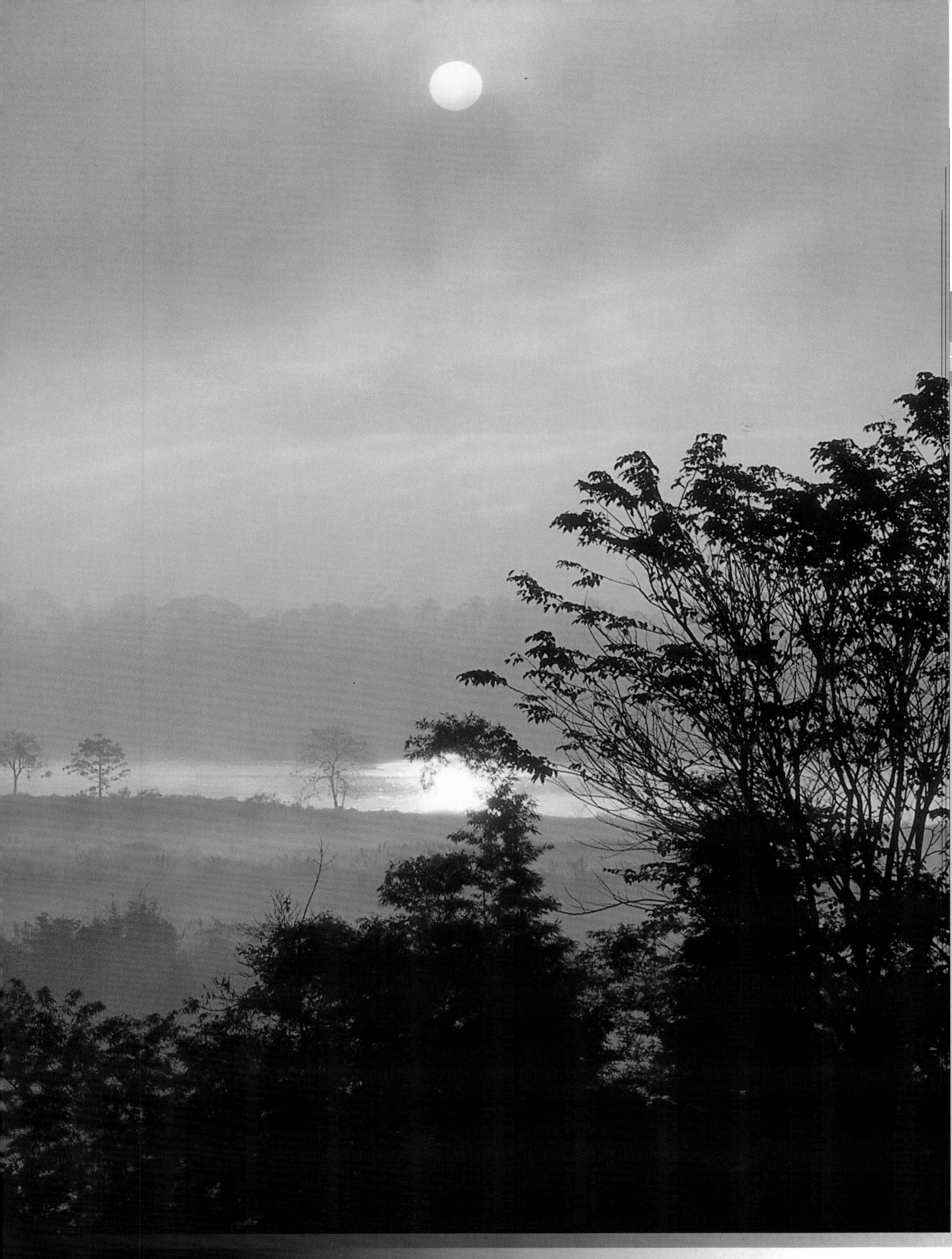

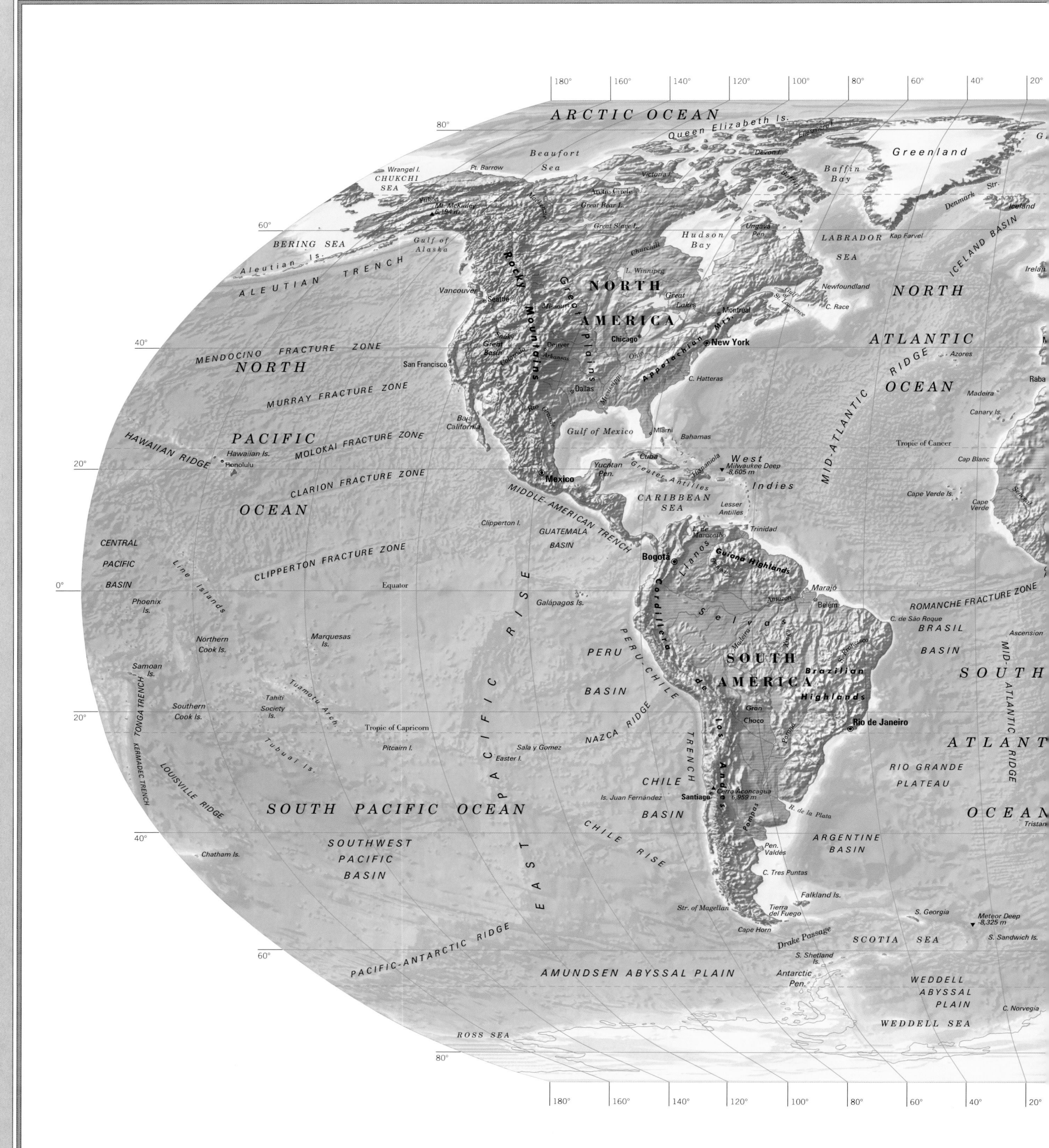

Height

m.
ft.

6000
19700

4000
13000

2000
6500

1500
5000

1000
3300

500
1600

200
700

-0-

200
700

500
1600

1000
3300

2000
6500

3000
9800

4000
13000

5000
16400

6000
19700

m.
ft.

Depth

ARCTIC OCEAN

80°

Wrangel I.
CHUKCHI
SEA

Beaufort
Sea

Pt. Barrow

Queen Elizabeth Is.

Devon I.

Greenland

Baffin
Bay

BERING SEA

60°

Aleutian Is.

Gulf of
Alaska

Mt. McKinley
6194 m.

Yukon

Victoria I.

Great Bear L.

Arctic Circle
Great Slave L.

Hudson
Bay

Ungava
Pen.

Churchill

L. Winnipeg

Denmark Str.

Iceland

LABRADOR
SEA

Kap Farvel

ICELAND BASIN

Ireland

ALEUTIAN TRENCH

Vancouver

Seattle

Rocky Mountains

Great Plains

NORTH
AMERICA

Great
Lakes

Montreal

Newfoundland

C. Race

NORTH

40°

MENDOCINO FRACTURE ZONE

NORTH

San Francisco

Great
Basin

Snake

Missouri

Denver

Arkansas

Chicago

Ohio

Appalachian Mts.

New York

ATLANTIC

Azores

MURRAY FRACTURE ZONE

Dallas

C. Hatteras

OCEAN

Madeira

PACIFIC

Baja
California

Rio Grande

Mississippi

Gulf of Mexico

Miami

Bahamas

Tropic of Cancer

Canary Is.

Cap Blanc

HAWAIIAN RIDGE

20°

Hawaiian Is.

Honolulu

MOLOKAI FRACTURE ZONE

Mexico

Yucatan
Pen.

Cuba

Greater Antilles

West
Milwaukee Deep
-8,605 m

Hispaniola

Indies

Cape Verde Is.

Cape
Verde

OCEAN

CLARION FRACTURE ZONE

CARIBBEAN
SEA

Lesser
Antilles

CENTRAL

Clipperton I.

GUATEMALA
BASIN

Trinidad

Maracaibo

ROMANCHE FRACTURE ZONE

PACIFIC

CLIPPERTON FRACTURE ZONE

Bogotá

Llanos

Guiana Highlands

BRASIL

Ascension

BASIN

0°

Line Islands

Equator

Galápagos Is.

Cordillera

Selvas

Marajó

Amazon

Belem

C. de São Roque

BASIN

MID-ATLANTIC RIDGE

Phoenix
Is.

PERU
BASIN

PERU-CHILE

SOUTH
AMERICA

Brazilian
Highlands

SOUTH

Northern
Cook Is.

Marquesas
Is.

Samoan
Is.

Tahiti
Society
Is.

Tuamotu Arch.

Pitcairn I.

Tropic of Capricorn

Sala y Gomez

Easter I.

NAZCA RIDGE

Gran
Choco

Los Andes

São Francisco

Paraná

Rio de Janeiro

ATLANTIC

Southern
Cook Is.

RIO GRANDE
PLATEAU

20°

Tubuai Is.

TONGA TRENCH

KERMADEC TRENCH

LOUISVILLE RIDGE

SOUTH PACIFIC OCEAN

EAST PACIFIC RISE

CHILE

Is. Juan Fernández

BASIN

Cerro Aconcagua
6,959 m

Santiago

Pampas

R. de la Plata

OCEAN

Tristan

ATLANTIC RIDGE

40°

Chatham Is.

SOUTHWEST
PACIFIC
BASIN

CHILE RISE

Pen.
Valdés

ARGENTINE
BASIN

C. Tres Puntas

MID-

Str. of Magellan

Tierra
del Fuego

Falkland Is.

S. Georgia

Meteor Deep
-8,325 m

Cape Horn

Drake Passage

SCOTIA
SEA

S. Sandwich Is.

60°

PACIFIC-ANTARCTIC RIDGE

AMUNDSEN ABYSSAL PLAIN

Antarctic
Pen.

S. Shetland
Is.

WEDDELL
ABYSSAL
PLAIN

C. Norvegia

ROSS SEA

80°

WEDDELL SEA

180°   160°   140°   120°   100°   80°   60°   40°   20°

Population

◉ Over 5,000,000   ◎ 500,000 - 1,999,999

◉ 2,000,000 - 4,999,999   ○ Under 500,000

World - Physical

© HAMMOND WORLD ATLAS CORPORATION

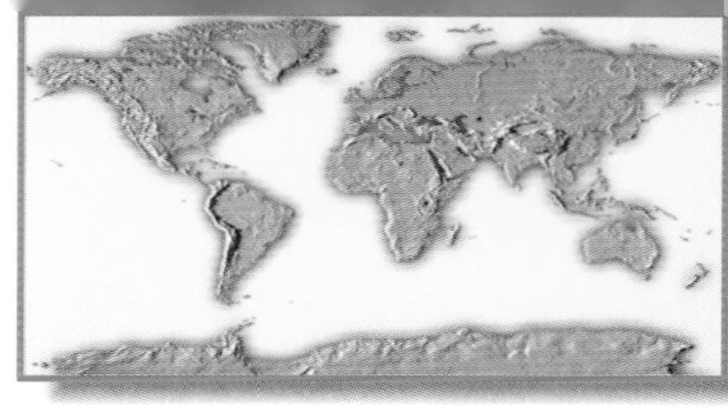

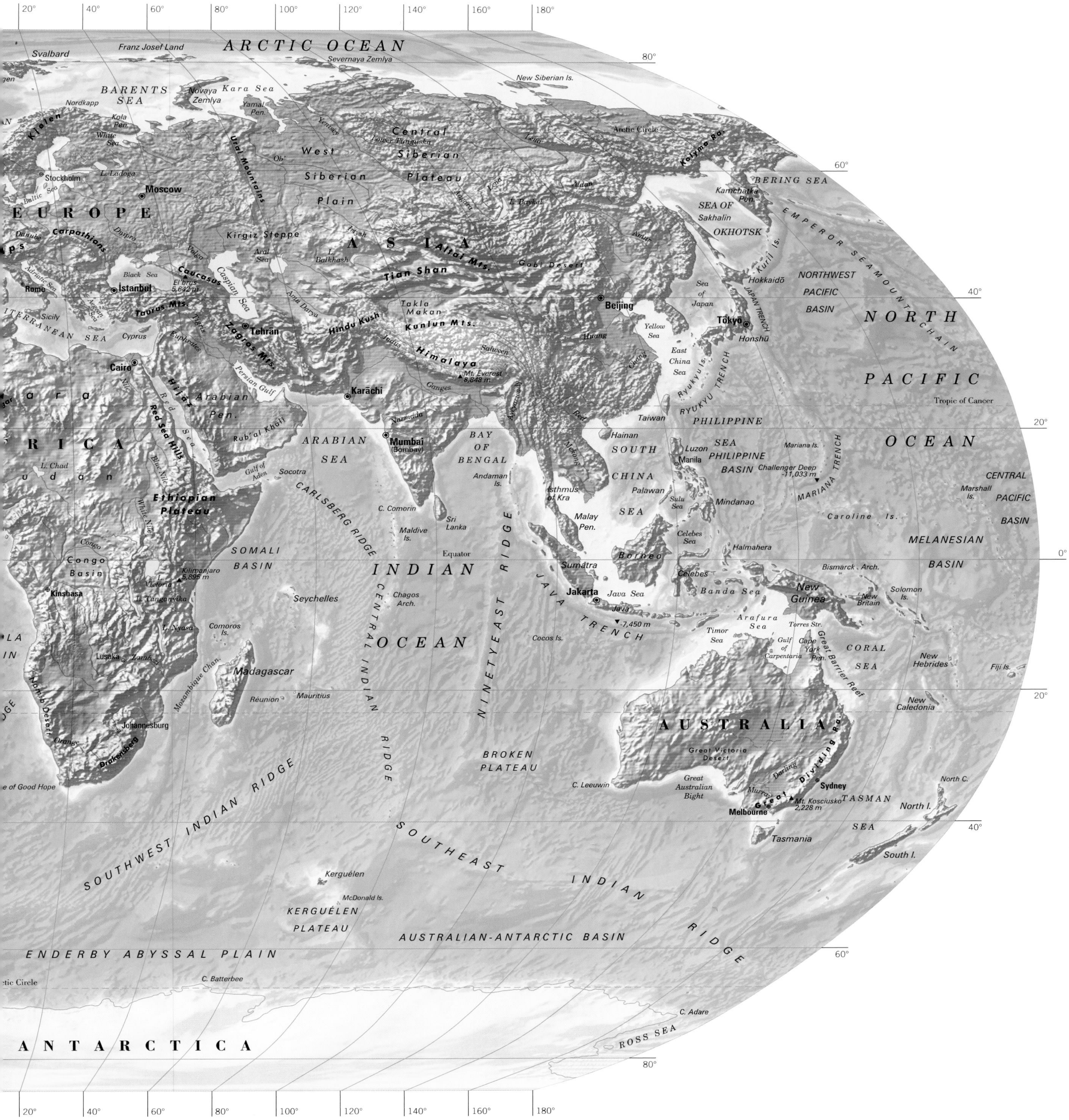

Scale 1:70,000,000 Robinson Projection

MI   600   1200   1800   2400

KM   600   1200   1800   2400   3000   3600

Europe

Height

m.
ft.
6000
19700
4000
13000
2000
6500
1500
5000
1000
3300
500
1600
200
700
-0-
200
700
500
1600
1000
3300
2000
6500
3000
9800
4000
13000
5000
16400
6000
19700

m.
ft.
Depth

NORWEGIAN
BASIN

NORWEGIAN

VORING
PLATEAU

Vesterålen

Lofoten

Reykjavik

Arctic Circle

JAN MAYEN RIDGE

S E A

Trondheim

Galdhøpiggen
2,470 m

ICELAND BASIN

Faroe Is.

HEBRIDIAN SHELF

Shetland
Is.

Bergen

Lindesnes

Vänern

Västerås

Stockholm

Vättern

ATLANTIC

ROCKALL
PLATEAU

Rockall

Hebrides

Orkney Is.

Moray Firth

NORTH

SEA

Skagerrak

Göteborg

OCEAN

ROCKALL TROUGH

Ben Nevis
1,343 m

Aberdeen

Kattegat

Glasgow

Jutland

Copenhagen

50°

PORCUPINE
BANK

Belfast

Great

Fyn

Ireland

I. of Man

Pennine Chain

Britain

Bornholm

Dublin
Irish
Sea
Liverpool

Frisian Islands

Hamburg

Weser

Elbe

Berlin

PORCUPINE ABYSSAL PLAIN

C. Clear

St. George's Chan.

Birmingham

Amsterdam

The Hague

Rhine

Leipzig

Thames

London

CELTIC
SHELF

Land's End

English Channel

Brussels

Cologne
Bonn

AREA OF OPTIMIZATION

Channel
Is.

Le Havre
Seine

Paris

BISCAY ABYSSAL
PLAIN

Nantes

Loire

Stuttgart

Danube

Vienna

Bratisl

Munich

Bay of
Biscay

Bordeaux

Garonne

Central

Lyon

Mont Blanc
4,800 m

A
L
P
S

Graz

Zag

Cabo Finisterre

Lot

Massif

Rhône

Turin

Milan

Venice

40°

Cabo de
São
Vicente

IBERIAN

ABYSSAL

PLAIN

Miño

Cordillera
Cantábrica

Bilbao

Pyrenees

Bern

Po

Genoa

Dinari

Duero

Ebro

Ligurian

Sea

Saragossa

Marseille

G. of Lion

Corsica

Apennines

Adriatic

Madrid

Barcelona

Tagus

Rome

Lisbon

Sierra Morena

Júcar

Valencia

Balearic Islands

Minorca

Sardinia

Tyrrhenian
Sea

Naples

Cabo de
São
Vicente

Ibiza

Mallorca

-3,630m

Cádiz

Cerro de Mulhacén
3,479 m

ALGERIAN PLAIN

Capo Teulada

M E D I T E R R A N E

Palermo

Str. of Gibraltar

Málaga

Mt. Etna 3,323 m

Tangier

Algiers

Rabat

Oran

Tunis

Sicily

Capo Pas

A F R I C A

Pantelleria

Malta

30°

10°

The Mediterranean Sea is a remnant of the Thethys Sea that once separated Europe and Africa. The floor of the sea between the continents was squeezed and folded to form the high mountain ranges of the Mediterranean region. North of the Alps and the Black and Caspian Seas are the old, heavily eroded central mountain ranges and lowland plains of the European continent.

50°
60°

Murmansk

Kola Pen.

Kemijoki

Arctic Circle

White Sea

Arkhange'sk

Oulu

Iijoki

Northern Dvina

Onega

othnia

Kumo

Tampere

Lake Onega

Vokaterinburg

Kama

Perm

Chelyabinsk

Ural Mountains

Lake Ladoga

A S I A

St. Petersburg

Gulf of Finland

Rybinsk Res.

Kazan'

Tallinn

Lake Peipus

L. Il'men

Volga

Nizhniy Novgorod

Kuybyshev Res.

maa

Gulf of Riga

Volga Uplands

Sámara

Kama

maa

Riga

Daugava

Moscow

Oka

Volga

50°

Vilnius

Central Russian Uplands

ropean Plain

Zhayyq (Ural)

Embi

Minsk

Khoper

Bug

Pripyat'

Desna

Don

Volgograd

Prikaspian Plain

Warsaw

Kharkiv

Volga

Astrakhan

Kiev

Dnipro

Donets

Tsimlyansk Res.

CASPIAN SEA

Vistula

San

Krakow

L'viv

Donets'k

Don

L. Urmia

Dnister

Pivdennyy Buh

Manych

Kuma

Carpathian Mts.

Prut

Sea of Azov

Kuban

40°

Great Alföld

Odesa

Krasnodar

Caucasus

Baku

Cluj-Napoca

Crimean Pen.

Tbilisi

Transylvanian Alps

Oll

Belgrade

Bucharest

Danube

BLACK SEA

Balkan Mts.

-2,211m

Aras

Sofia

Skopje

Bosporus

L. Van

Tirane

Istanbul

Ankara

A S I A

Sea of Marmara

Kizilirmak

Thessaloniki

L. Tuz

Tigris

Pindus Mts.

Aegean Sea

Lésvos

Taurus Mts.

Izmir

Evvoia

Ionian Islands

Athens

Cyclades

a

Peloponnésus

-5,150 m

Ákra Tainaron

Cyprus

Baghdad

Euphrates

Nicosia

SEA

Crete

Rhodes

Beirut

Damascus

© HAMMOND WORLD ATLAS CORPORATION

CC·A

40°

Scale 1:11,250,000 Hammond Optimal Conformal

MI   100   200   300   400
KM   100   200   300   400   500   600

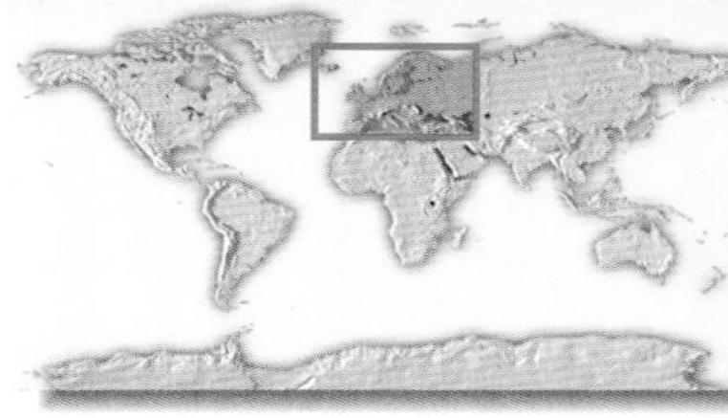

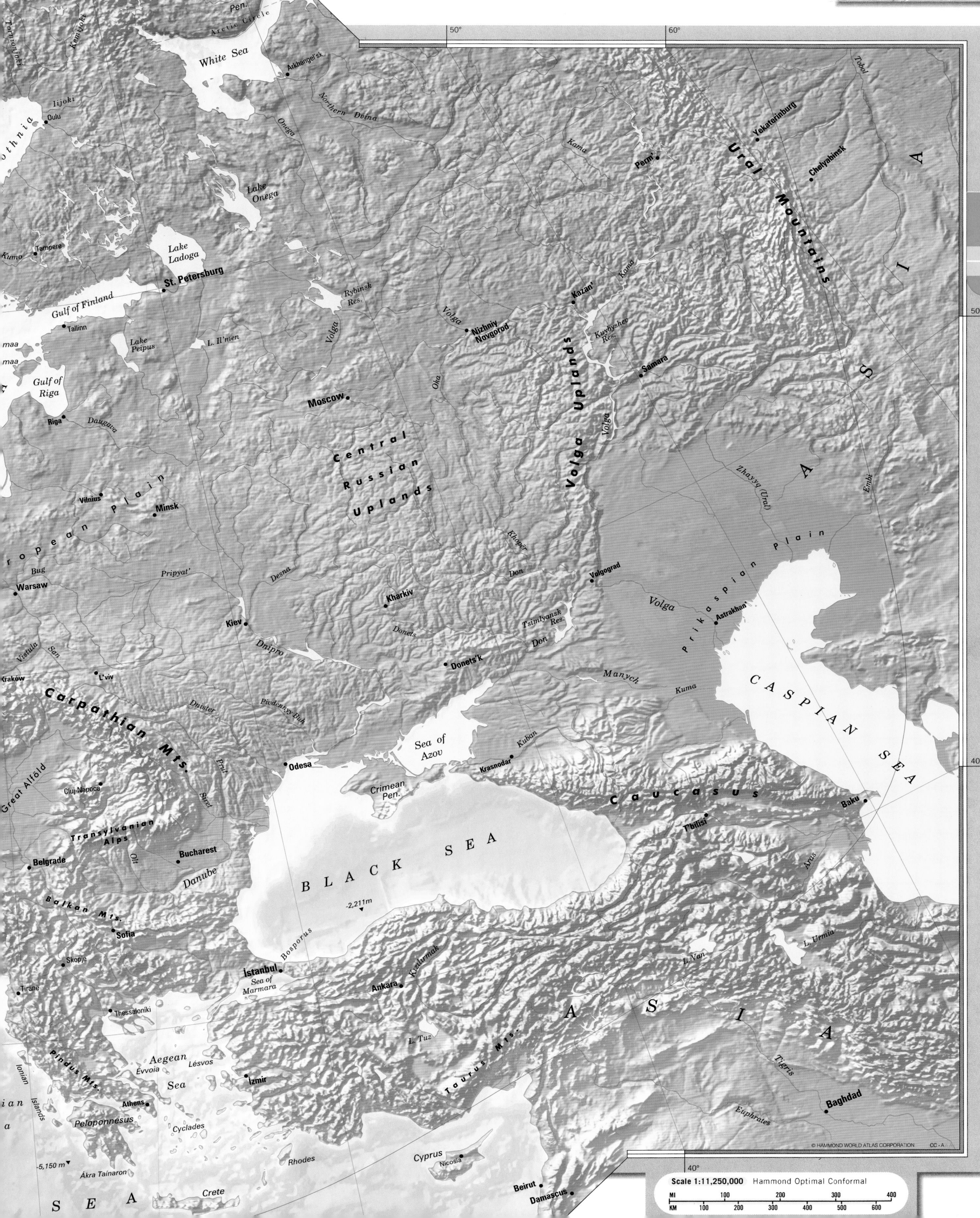

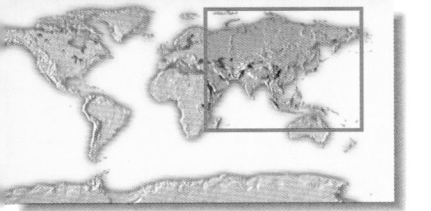

Asia

Although the Ural Mountains and the Caspian Sea form a boundary between Europe and Asia, geologists view both continents as part of the Eurasian Plate. The largest contiguous land mass on earth, this plate also comprises the Himalayas, the world's highest and most extensive mountain system. Deep ocean trenches sear the boundaries of the Pacific and Indo-Australian plates.

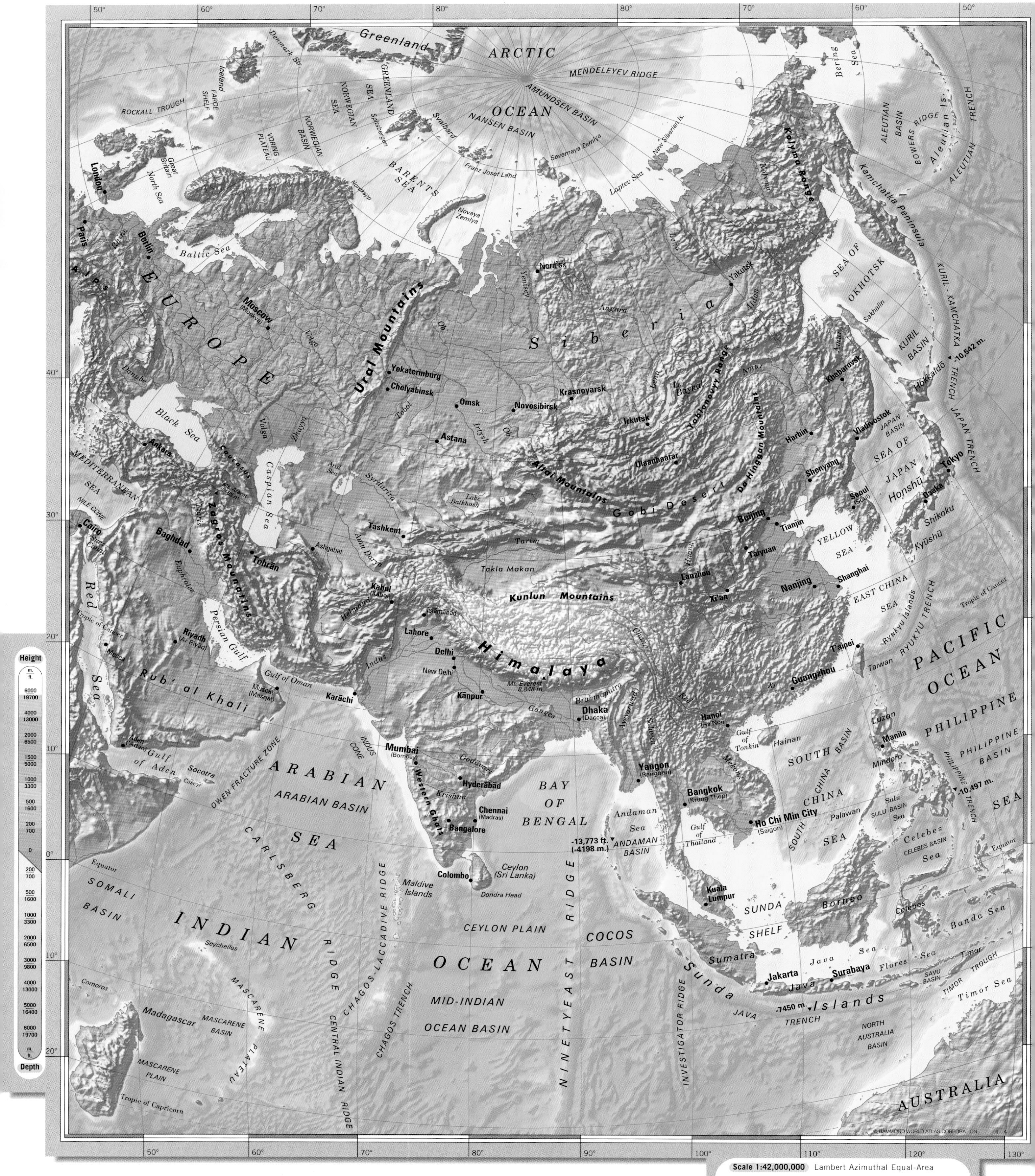

Height

m. ft.
6000 / 19700
4000 / 13000
2000 / 6500
1500 / 5000
1000 / 3300
500 / 1600
200 / 700
0
200 / 700
500 / 1600
1000 / 3300
2000 / 6500
3000 / 9800
4000 / 13000
5000 / 16400
6000 / 19700
m. ft.

Depth

ARCTIC OCEAN

MENDELEYEV RIDGE

AMUNDSEN BASIN

NANSEN BASIN

Greenland

Iceland

ROCKALL TROUGH

FAROE SHELF

GREENLAND SEA

NORWEGIAN SEA

NORWEGIAN BASIN

VORING PLATEAU

Denmark Str.

Svalbard

Spitsbergen

Nordkapp

Franz Josef Land

Novaya Zemlya

Severnaya Zemlya

New Siberian Is.

Laptev Sea

Kolyma

Bering Sea

ALEUTIAN BASIN

BOWERS RIDGE

Aleutian Is.

ALEUTIAN TRENCH

London

Paris

Berlin

Great Britain

North Sea

Baltic Sea

EUROPE

ALPS

Moscow (Moskva)

Volga

Ural Mountains

Ob

BARENTS SEA

Yenisey

Noril'sk

Lena

Siberia

Lena

Aldan

Kolyma Range

Kamchatka Peninsula

KURIL - KAMCHATKA TRENCH

SEA OF OKHOTSK

Sakhalin

KURIL BASIN

Hokkaidō ◄ -10,542 m.

JAPAN TRENCH

Black Sea

Caucasus

Ankara

MEDITERRANEAN SEA

NILE CONE

Cairo

Baghdad

Zagros Mountains

Tigris

Euphrates

Tehrān

Caspian Sea

Aral Sea

Syrdarya

Amu Darya

Tashkent

Ashgabat

Lake Balkhash

Altai Mountains

Yekaterinburg

Chelyabinsk

Omsk

Irtysh

Tobol

Ob

Astana

Novosibirsk

Krasnoyarsk

Irkutsk

Angara

Baikal

Yablonovyy Range

Ulaanbaatar

Gobi Desert

Da Hinggan Mountains

Amur

Khabarovsk

Harbin

Vladivostok

JAPAN BASIN

SEA OF JAPAN

Shenyang

Seoul (Sŏul)

Honshū

Tokyo

Osaka

Shikoku

Kyūshū

Kabul (Kābol)

Tarim

Takla Makan

Kunlun Mountains

Beijing

Tianjin

Taiyuan

Lanzhou

Xi'an

Nanjing

Shanghai

YELLOW SEA

EAST CHINA SEA

Tropic of Cancer

Ryukyu Islands

RYUKYU TRENCH

PACIFIC OCEAN

Red Sea

Mecca

Riyadh (Ar Riyāḍ)

Persian Gulf

Gulf of Oman

Muscat (Masqaṭ)

Karāchi

Indus

Islāmābād

Lahore

Delhi

New Delhi

Kānpur

Himalaya

Mt. Everest 8,848 m.

Ganges

Brahmaputra

Dhaka (Dacca)

Chang

Guangzhou

Taipei

Taiwan

PHILIPPINE BASIN

Rub' al Khali

Aden

Gulf of Aden

Socotra

Qeshm

OWEN FRACTURE ZONE

INDUS CONE

ARABIAN SEA

ARABIAN BASIN

Western Ghats

Mumbai (Bombay)

Godāvari

Krishna

Hyderābād

Chennai (Madras)

Bangalore

BAY OF BENGAL

Andaman Sea

ANDAMAN BASIN

-13,773 ft. (-4198 m.)

Yangon (Rangoon)

Salween

Mekong

Hanoi (Ha Noi)

Gulf of Tonkin

Hainan

Bangkok (Krung Thep)

SOUTH CHINA BASIN

Luzon

Manila

Mindoro

PHILIPPINE SEA

PHILIPPINE TRENCH -10,497 m.

SOMALI BASIN

CARLSBERG RIDGE

Equator

Seychelles

Comoros

Madagascar

MASCARENE PLATEAU

MASCARENE BASIN

MASCARENE PLAIN

Tropic of Capricorn

CHAGOS-LACCADIVE RIDGE

Maldive Islands

Colombo

Ceylon (Sri Lanka)

Dondra Head

CEYLON PLAIN

NINETYEAST RIDGE

CENTRAL INDIAN RIDGE

CHAGOS TRENCH

INDIAN OCEAN

MID-INDIAN OCEAN BASIN

COCOS BASIN

INVESTIGATOR RIDGE

Ho Chi Minh City (Saigon)

Palawan

Sulu Sea

SULU BASIN

Celebes

CELEBES BASIN

Celebes Sea

Equator

Kuala Lumpur

SOUTH CHINA SEA

SUNDA SHELF

Sumatra

Borneo

Banda Sea

Java

Jakarta

Surabaya

JAVA TRENCH

-7450 m.

Java

JAVA Islands

Flores Sea

Flores

Timor

SAVU BASIN

TIMOR TROUGH

Timor Sea

NORTH AUSTRALIA BASIN

Sunda

AUSTRALIA

© HAMMOND WORLD ATLAS CORPORATION

Scale 1:42,000,000 Lambert Azimuthal Equal-Area

MI		500	1000	1500
KM	500	1000	1500	2000

Vast highland basins and deserts stand in marked contrast to the fertile plains of the region. Deserts, such as the Gobi, dominate the northwestern part of this region, while the waters and floodplains of great Huang Ho (Yellow) and the Yangtze (Chang) Rivers in the east provide the basis for the cultivation of food crops that feed millions of people.

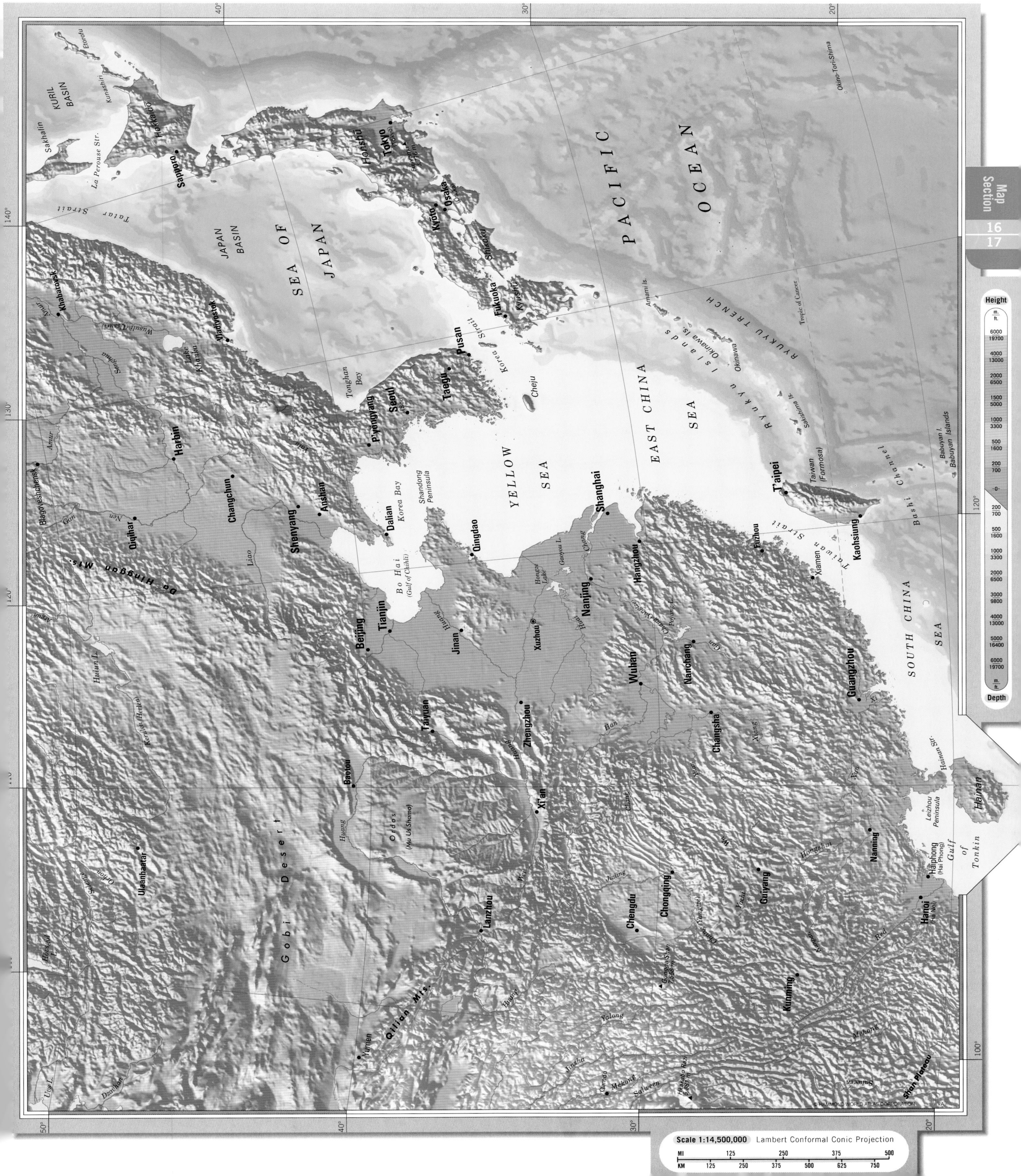

East Asia

Height

m. / ft.
6000 / 19700
4000 / 13000
2000 / 6500
1500 / 5000
1000 / 3300
500 / 1600
200 / 700
0
200 / 700
500 / 1600
1000 / 3300
2000 / 6500
3000 / 9800
5000 / 16400
6000 / 19700
m. / ft.

Depth

PACIFIC OCEAN

SEA OF JAPAN

JAPAN BASIN

KURIL BASIN

YELLOW SEA

EAST CHINA SEA

SOUTH CHINA SEA

Gobi Desert

RYUKYU TRENCH

Tropic of Cancer

Ryukyu Islands

Bashi Channel

Gulf of Tonkin

Bo Hai (Gulf of Chihli)

Korea Bay

Tatar Strait

La Perouse Str.

Korea Strait

Taiwan Strait

Shandong Peninsula

Leizhou Peninsula

Hainan Str.

Da Hinggan Mts.

Qilian Mts.

Shan Plateau

Ordos (Mu Us Shamo)

Sakhalin

Hokkaido

Honshu

Kyushu

Shikoku

Cheju

Taiwan (Formosa)

Hainan

Okino-Tori-Shima

Anami Is.

Okinawa I.

Babuyan Islands

Tokyo
Sapporo
Osaka
Kyoto
Fukuoka
Khabarovsk
Vladivostok
Harbin
Qiqihar
Changchun
Shenyang
Anshan
Dalian
Beijing
Tianjin
Jinan
Qingdao
Pyongyang
Seoul
Taegu
Pusan
Shanghai
Hangzhou
Nanjing
Xuzhou
Zhengzhou
Taiyuan
Baotou
Xi'an
Wuhan
Nanchang
Changsha
Fuzhou
Xiamen
Taipei
Kaohsiung
Guangzhou
Nanning
Guiyang
Kunming
Chongqing
Chengdu
Lanzhou
Hanoi (Ha Noi)
Haiphong (Hai Phong)
Ulaanbaatar
Blagoveshchensk

Scale 1:14,500,000   Lambert Conformal Conic Projection

MI   125   250   375   500
KM 125 250 375 500 625 750

Southeast Asia

Several tectonic plates converge in Southeast Asia to form an extended arc of islands adjacent to deep ocean trenches. Many of the islands are characterized by extreme volcanic activity.

Located on the continental shelf along the South China Sea is the vast delta (70,000 sq. km.) of the Mekong, the "Mother of Waters," whose course from the Tibetan Plateau to the sea measures 4,500 km.

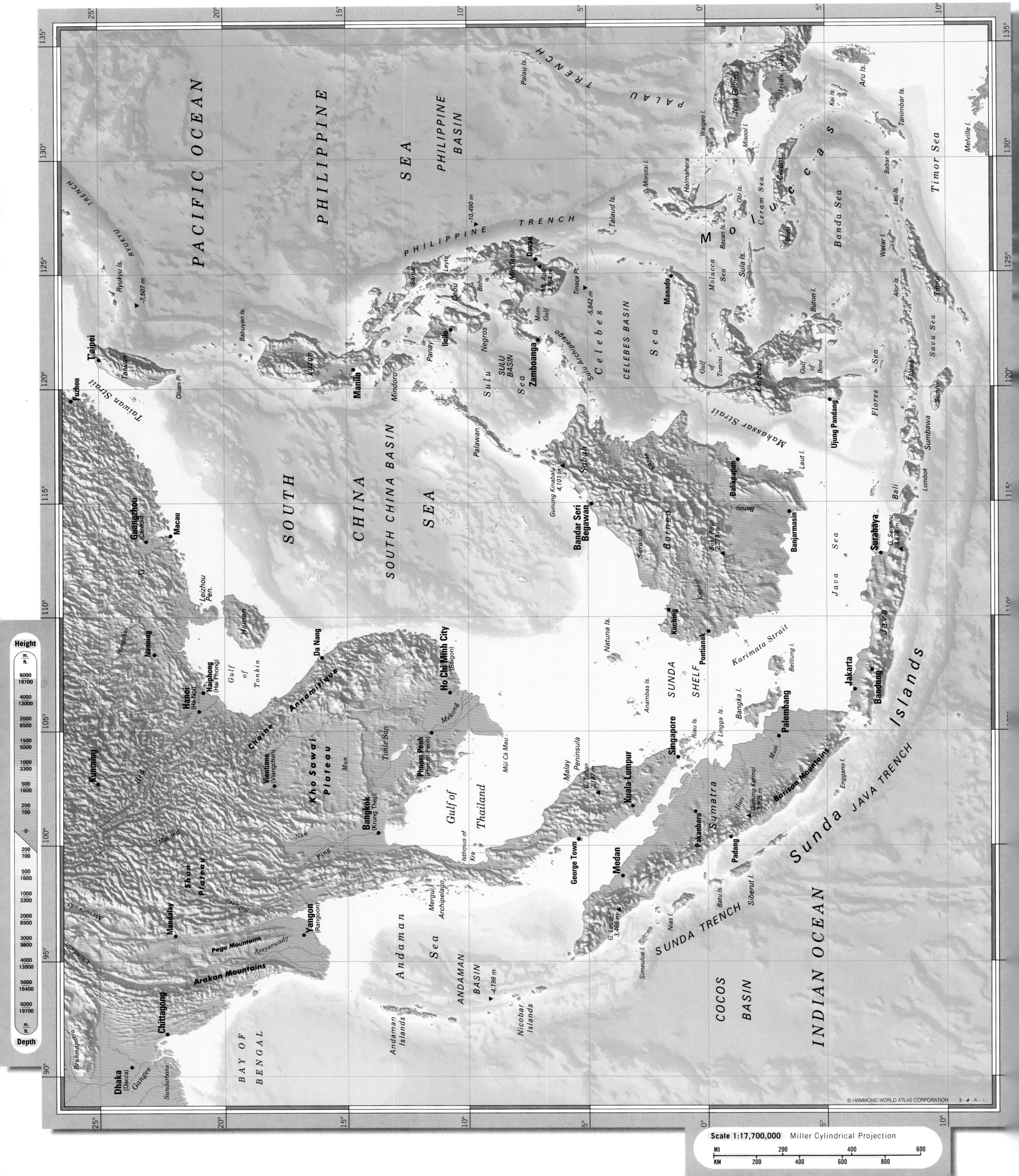

PACIFIC OCEAN

PHILIPPINE SEA

PHILIPPINE BASIN

RYUKYU TRENCH

▲ 7,607 m

PALAU TRENCH

Palau Is.

PHILIPPINE TRENCH

▲ -10,490 m

Moluccas

New Guinea

Irian Jaya

Waigeo I.

Misool I.

Obi Is.

Bacan Is.

Halmahera

Morotai I.

Kai Is.

Aru Is.

Tanimbar Is.

Melville I.

Timor Sea

Banda Sea

Ceram Sea

Ceram I.

Buru I.

Sula Is.

Molucca Sea

Taipei

Taiwan

Fuzhou

Taiwan Strait

Oluan Pt.

Babuyan Is.

Luzon

Manila

Mindoro

Samar

Leyte

Cebu

Bohol

Panay

Iloilo

Negros

Davao

Mindanao

Mt. Apo ▲ 2,954 m

Tinaca Pt.

Moro Gulf

Zamboanga

Sulu Archipelago

Sulu Sea

SULU BASIN

▲ -5,842 m

CELEBES SEA

CELEBES BASIN

Manado

Celebes

Gulf of Tomini

Buton I.

Molucca Sea

Saleyer I.

Wetar I.

Alor Is.

Leti Is.

Babar Is.

Flores Sea

Savu Sea

Timor

Gulf of Bone

Sumba

G. Semeru ▲ 3,676 m

SOUTH CHINA SEA

SOUTH CHINA BASIN

Palawan

Sabah

Gunung Kinabalu 4,101 m

Bandar Seri Begawan

Sarawak

Borneo

Barito

Bukit Raya 2,278 m

Banjarmasin

Makassar Strait

Laut I.

Balikpapan

Ujung Pandang

Java Sea

Bali

Lombok

Sumbawa

Surabaya

Java

Islands

Guangzhou (Canton)

Macau

Leizhou Pen.

Hainan

Gulf of Tonkin

Da Nang

Nanning

Hanoi (Ha Noi)

Haiphong (Hai Phong)

Natuna Is.

SUNDA SHELF

Kuching

Pontianak

Kapuas

Karimata Strait

Belitung I.

Billiton I.

Jakarta

Bandung

Ho Chi Minh City (Saigon)

Mekong

Phnom Penh (Phnum Penh)

Annamitique

Chaine

Tonle Sap

Mui Ca Mau

Anambas Is.

Riau Is.

Lingga Is.

Bangka I.

Palembang

Musi

Barisan Mountains

Enggano I.

Kuming

Xi

Vientiane (Viangchan)

Kho Sawai Plateau

Mun

Bangkok (Krung Thep)

Nan

Malay Peninsula

G. Tahan 2,187 m

Singapore

Kuala Lumpur

George Town

Medan

Pakanbaru

Sumatra

Gunung Kerinci 3,805 m

Padang

Hari

SUNDA JAVA TRENCH

Salween

Shan Plateau

Mekong

Ping

Isthmus of Kra

Gulf of Thailand

Mergui Archipelago

Nias I.

Batu Is.

Siberut I.

Simeulue I.

SUNDA TRENCH

INDIAN OCEAN

Mandalay

Irrawaddy

Pegu Mountains

Yangon (Rangoon)

Ayeyarwady

Arakan Mountains

Andaman Sea

Andaman Islands

ANDAMAN BASIN

▲ -4,198 m

Nicobar Islands

COCOS BASIN

Brahmaputra

Dhaka (Dacca)

Ganges

Sundarbans

BAY OF BENGAL

© HAMMOND WORLD ATLAS CORPORATION

Height	
m. ft.	
6000 19700	
4000 13000	
2000 6500	
1500 5000	
1000 3300	
500 1600	
200 700	
0	
200 700	
500 1600	
1000 3300	
2000 6500	
3000 9800	
4000 13000	
5000 16400	
6000 19700	
m. ft.	
Depth	

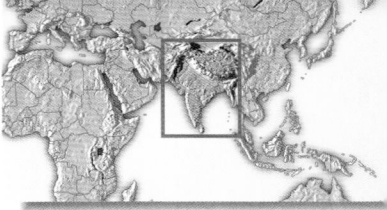

The collision of the Indian subcontinent with Eurasia about 50 million years ago gave birth to the Himalayas. Since that time, the Indian subcontinent has penetrated some 2,000 km into Eurasia, thrusting rock upward to form the world's loftiest mountain range, with peaks as high as 9,000 meters. Today, such mighty rivers as the Ganges (2,700 km long) flow from sources in the Himalayas.

Southern Asia

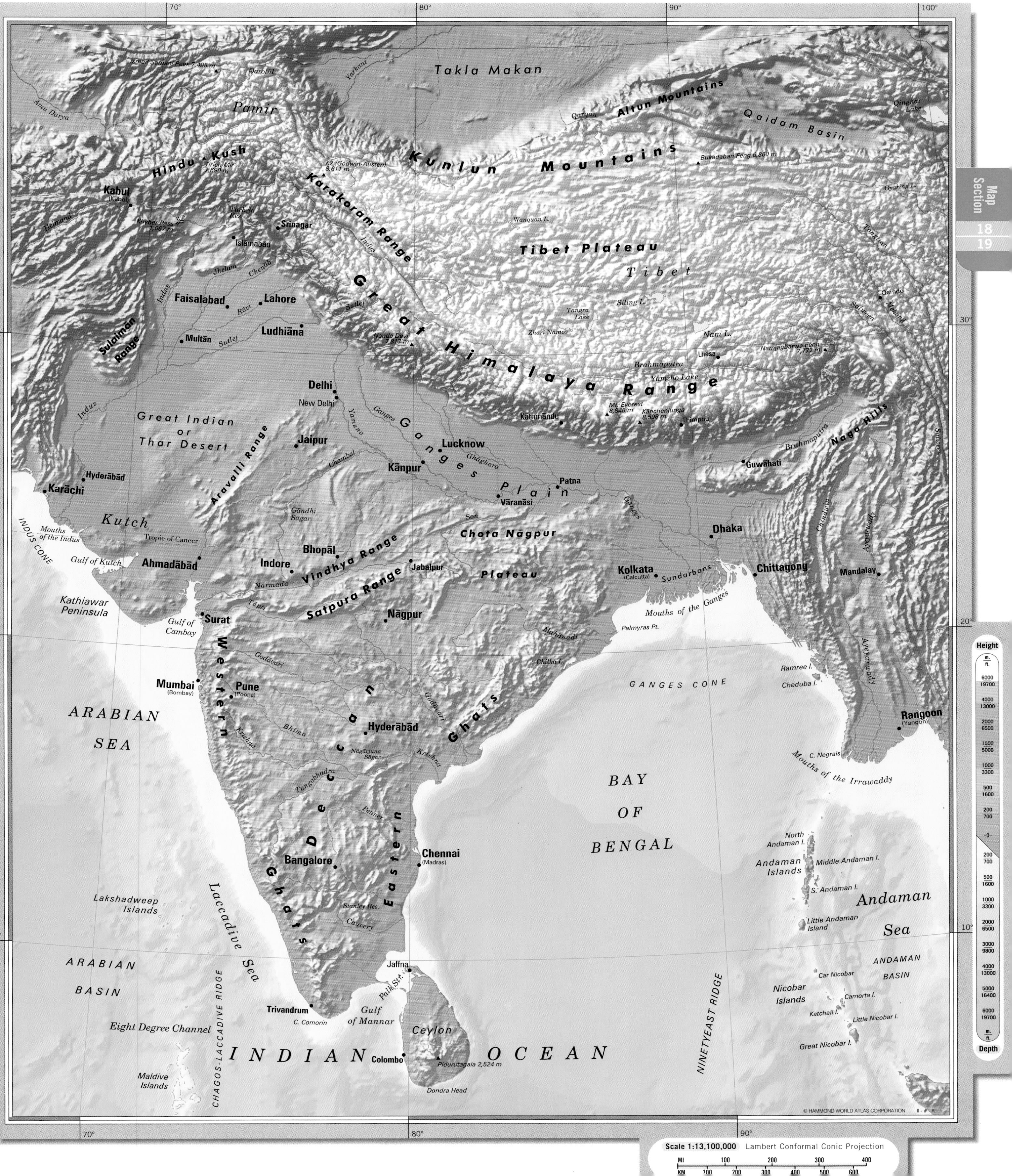

South Sakinai Peak 7,495 m
Pamir
Qamati
Yarkant
Takla Makan
Qaryan
Altun Mountains
Qaidam Basin
Qinghai Lake

Hindu Kush
Tirich Mir 7,690 m
Kunlun Mountains
Bukadaban Feng 6,860 m
Gyaring L.

Kabul
(Kabol)
K2 (Godwin-Austen) 8,611 m
Karakoram Range
Wanquan L.

Helmand
Khyber Pass 1,067 m
Srinagar
Indus
Tibet Plateau
Tibet

Islamabad
Jhelum
Chenab
Great Himalaya Range
Tangra Tso
Siling L.
Nam L.
Ostado
Meking

Faisalabad
Ravi
Lahore
Zhari Namco
Brahmaputra
Lhasa
Namjagbarwa Feng 7,782 m
Salween

Multan
Sutlej
Ludhiāna
Nanda Devi 7,817 m
Yamzho Lake

Indus
Sutlej
Delhi
Ganges
Kathmandu
Mt. Everest 8,848 m
Kanchenjunga 8,598 m
Thimphu
Naga Hills

Great Indian or Thar Desert
Aravalli Range
New Delhi
Yamuna
Ganges
Ghaghara
Lucknow
Brahmaputra
Guwāhati

Jaipur
Chambal
Kānpur
Ganges Plain
Patna

Hyderābād
Gāndhi Sāgar
Varānāsi
Son
Ganges
Dhaka

Karāchi
Kutch
Tropic of Cancer
Bhopāl
Vindhya Range
Chota Nāgpur
Kolkata (Calcutta)
Chittagong
Mandalay

INDUS CONE
Mouths of the Indus
Indore
Narmada
Satpura Range
Jabalpur
Plateau
Sundarbans

Gulf of Kutch
Ahmadābād
Tapti
Nāgpur
Mouths of the Ganges

Kathiawar Peninsula
Gulf of Cambay
Surat
Godāvari
Mahanadi
Chilka L.
Palmyras Pt.

Mumbai (Bombay)
Pune (Poona)
Western Ghats
Bhima
Hyderābād
Godavari
Gulf of Kutch
Chita
Krishna
GANGES CONE
Ramree I.
Cheduba I.
Ayeyarwaddy

ARABIAN SEA
Deccan
Nāgārjuna Sāgar
Krishna
Eastern Ghats
Rangoon (Yangon)

Bangalore
Tungabhadra
Pennar
C. Negrais
Mouths of the Irrawaddy

Lakshadweep Islands
Laccadive Sea
Ghats
Stanley Res.
Chennai (Madras)
BAY OF BENGAL
North Andaman I.
Andaman Islands
Middle Andaman I.
S. Andaman I.
Andaman Sea

ARABIAN BASIN
Trivandrum
C. Comorin
Gulf of Mannar
Jaffna
Palk Str.
Ceylon
Pidurutagala 2,524 m
Little Andaman Island
Car Nicobar
ANDAMAN BASIN
Nicobar Islands
Camorta I.
Katchall I.
Little Nicobar I.
Great Nicobar I.

Eight Degree Channel
CHAGOS-LACCADIVE RIDGE
Colombo
NINETYEAST RIDGE
INDIAN OCEAN

Maldive Islands
Dondra Head

© HAMMOND WORLD ATLAS CORPORATION

Height	
m.	ft.
6000	19700
4000	13000
2000	6500
1500	5000
1000	3300
500	1600
200	700
0	0
200	700
500	1600
1000	3300
2000	6500
3000	9800
4000	13000
5000	16400
6000	19700
m.	ft.
Depth	

Scale 1:13,100,000   Lambert Conformal Conic Projection

MI   100   200   300   400

KM   100   200   300   400   500   600

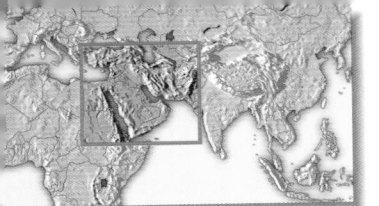

Near and Middle East

Some 25 million years ago, the Red Sea opened, separating the Arabian Peninsula from Africa. At some time in the distant future, a new arm of the sea may extend from the southern Red Sea through the Afar Depression into continental Africa. Today, the oil fields along the Persian Gulf and around the Caspian seaport of Baku hold about two-thirds of the world's known oil reserves.

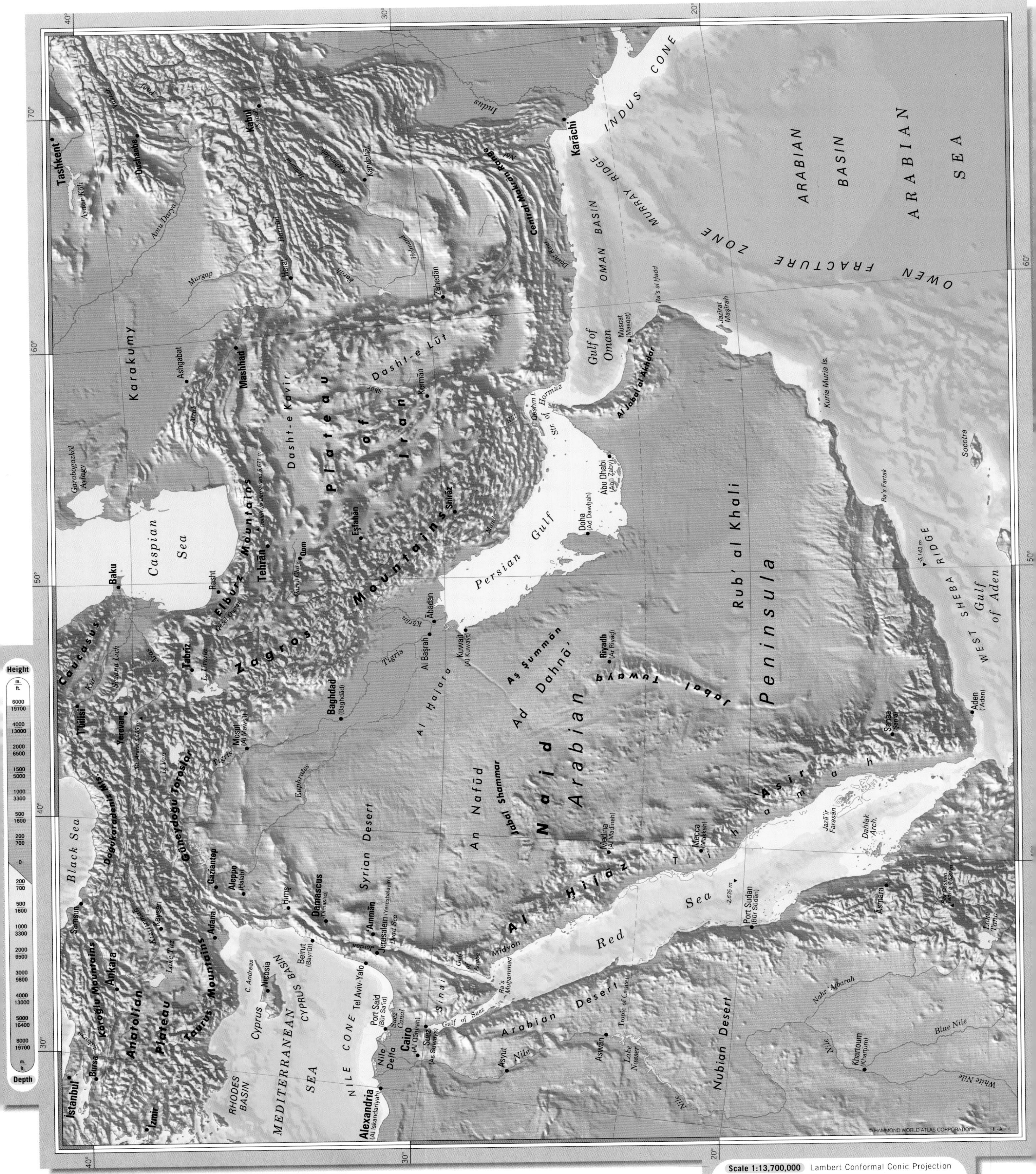

Height

m.
ft.
6000
19700
4000
13000
2000
6500
1500
5000
1000
3300
500
1600
200
700
-0-
200
700
500
1600
1000
3300
2000
6500
3000
9800
4000
13000
5000
16400
6000
19700
m.
ft.

Depth

Scale 1:13,700,000   Lambert Conformal Conic Projection

MI   100   200   300   400
KM   100 200 300 400 500 600

© HAMMOND WORLD ATLAS CORPORATION

III-A

frica comprises some 30 million square
kilometers - one-fifth of the world's
l land area. Except for the young Altas
untains, the continent consists of an an-
nt shelf divided into basins by low rises.

The African Sahara is the largest desert in
the world. The East African Rift System,
marked by the volcano Kilimanjaro (5,892 m)
and other major peaks, runs north to south
through the eastern half of the continent.

Africa

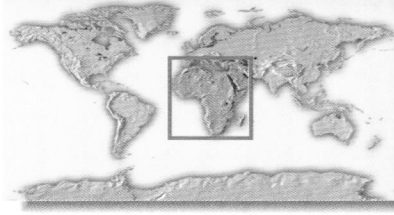

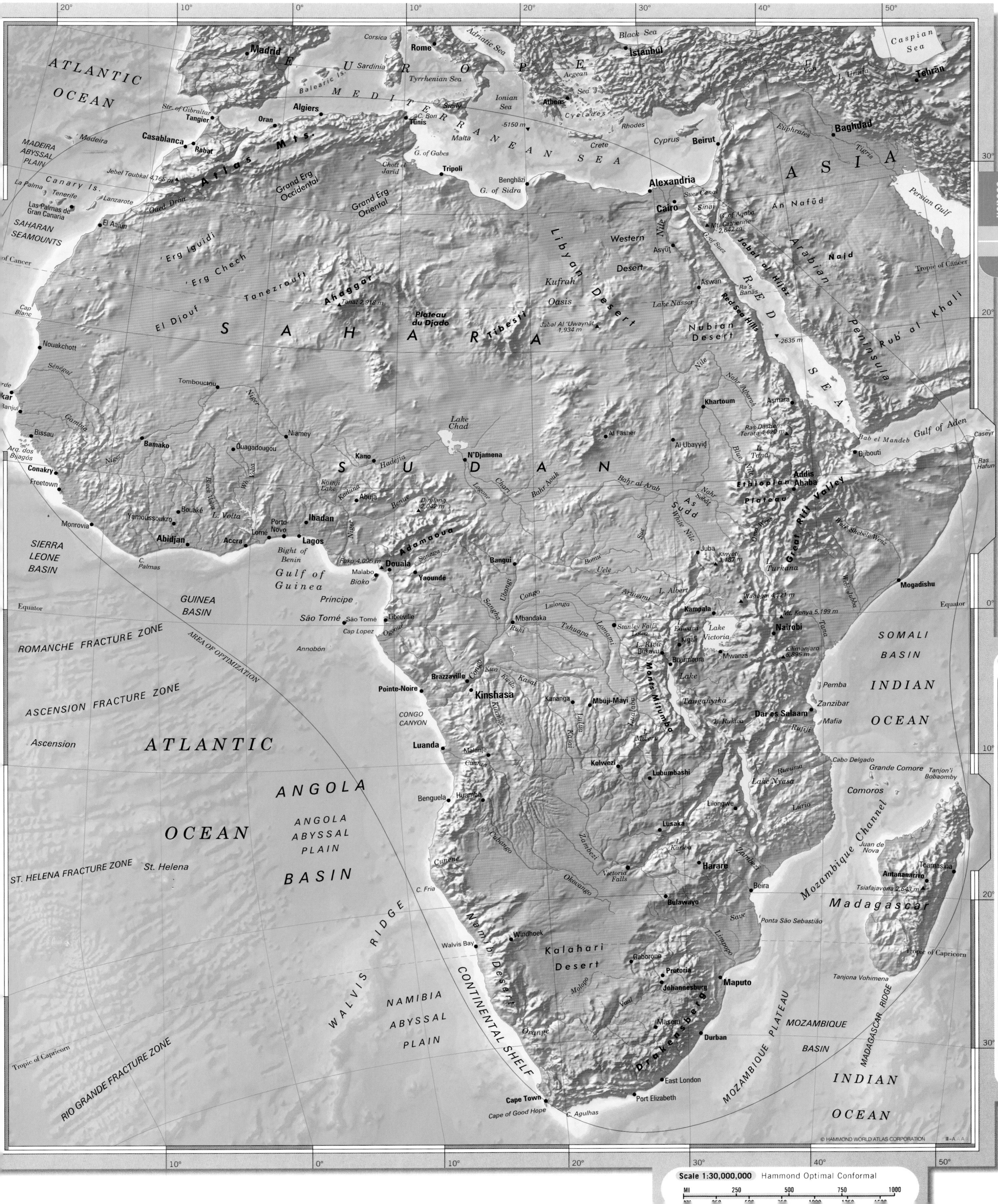

Scale 1:30,000,000 Hammond Optimal Conformal

© HAMMOND WORLD ATLAS CORPORATION

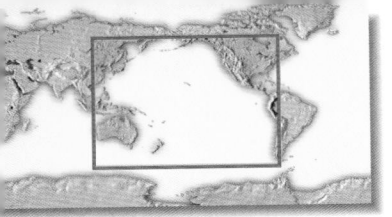

Australia and Pacific Ocean

Situated on the Indo-Australian Plate, the continent of Australia lies on a stable foundation. The earth is considerably more active off the coasts of New Zealand and Japan and around the Aleutians.

There the subduction of oceanic crust is accompanied by lively volcanic activity caused primarily by the breakup of the East Pacific Rise extending from the Baja Peninsula in California to the Antarctic.

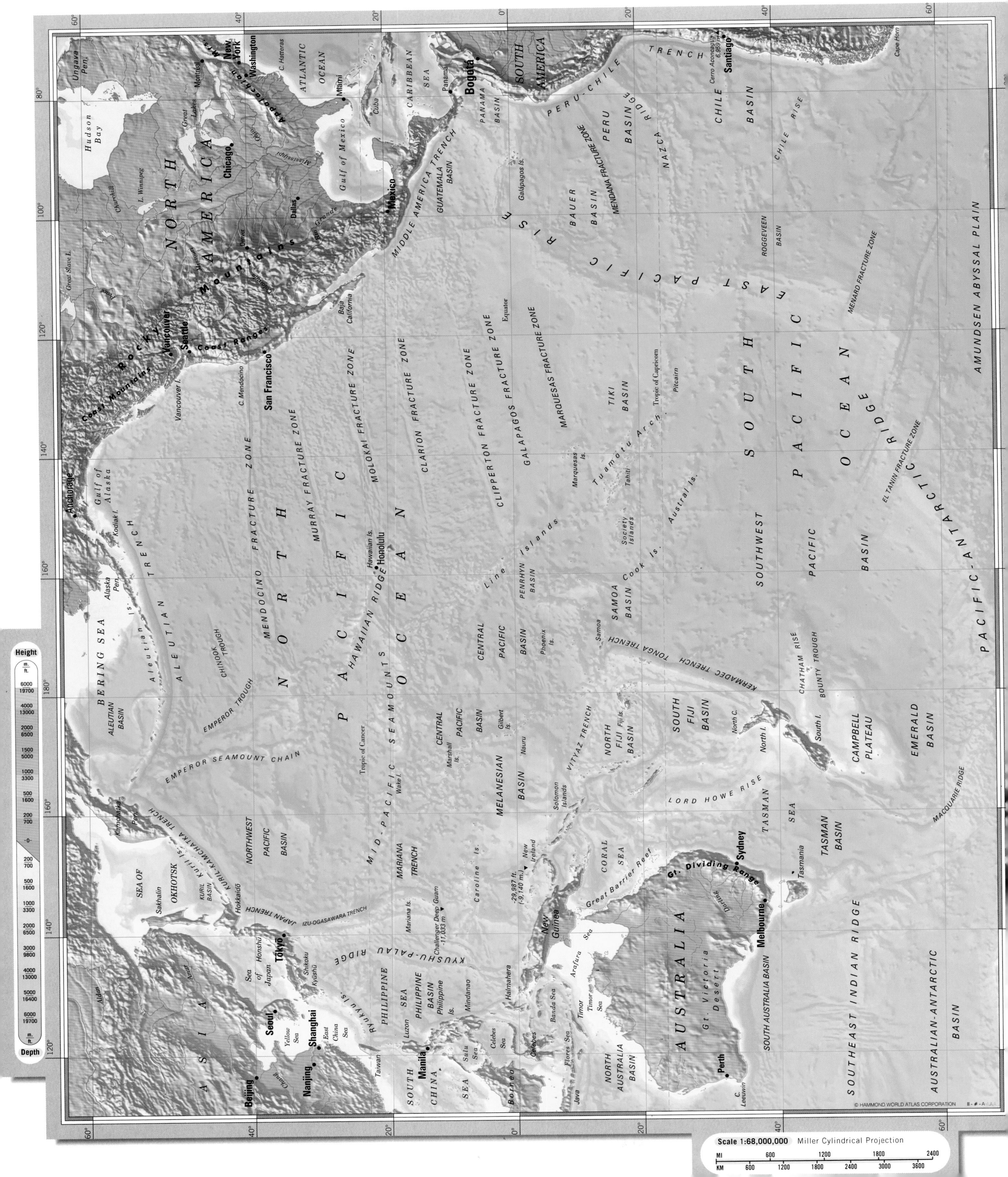

© HAMMOND WORLD ATLAS CORPORATION

Scale 1:68,000,000 Miller Cylindrical Projection

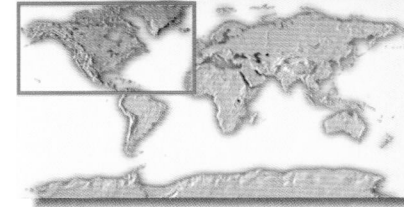
wo mountain ranges enclose the North American heartland: the old, heavily ...led Appalachian chain in the East and ...Rocky Mountains of the Cordillera sys-...in the West. The northernmost points of the continent are on Ellesmere Island and Greenland. Geographers place the southern continental boundary on the Isthmus of Tehuantepec in Mexico, although it is culturally a part of Central America.

Map Section 22 23

Height
m / ft
6000 / 19700
4000 / 13000
2000 / 6500
1500 / 5000
1000 / 3300
500 / 1600
200 / 700
-
200 / 700
1000 / 3300
2000 / 6500
3000 / 9800
4000 / 13000
5000 / 16400
6000 / 19700
m / ft
Depth

Scale 1:30,000,000   Hammond Optimal Conformal
MI   250   500   750   1000

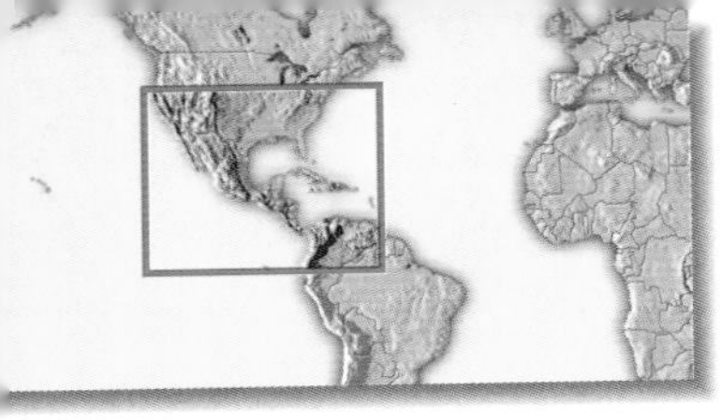

Middle America

North and South America are connected only by a narrow land bridge. Actually, the two land masses are separated by the relatively small Caribbean Plate, whose western boundary is defined by the East

Middle America Trench, which reaches a depth of 6662 m off the coast of Chiapas in Mexico. There, the Cocos Plate is thrust under the Caribbean Plate, causing considerable earthquake and volcanic activity.

© HAMMOND WORLD ATLAS CORPORATION

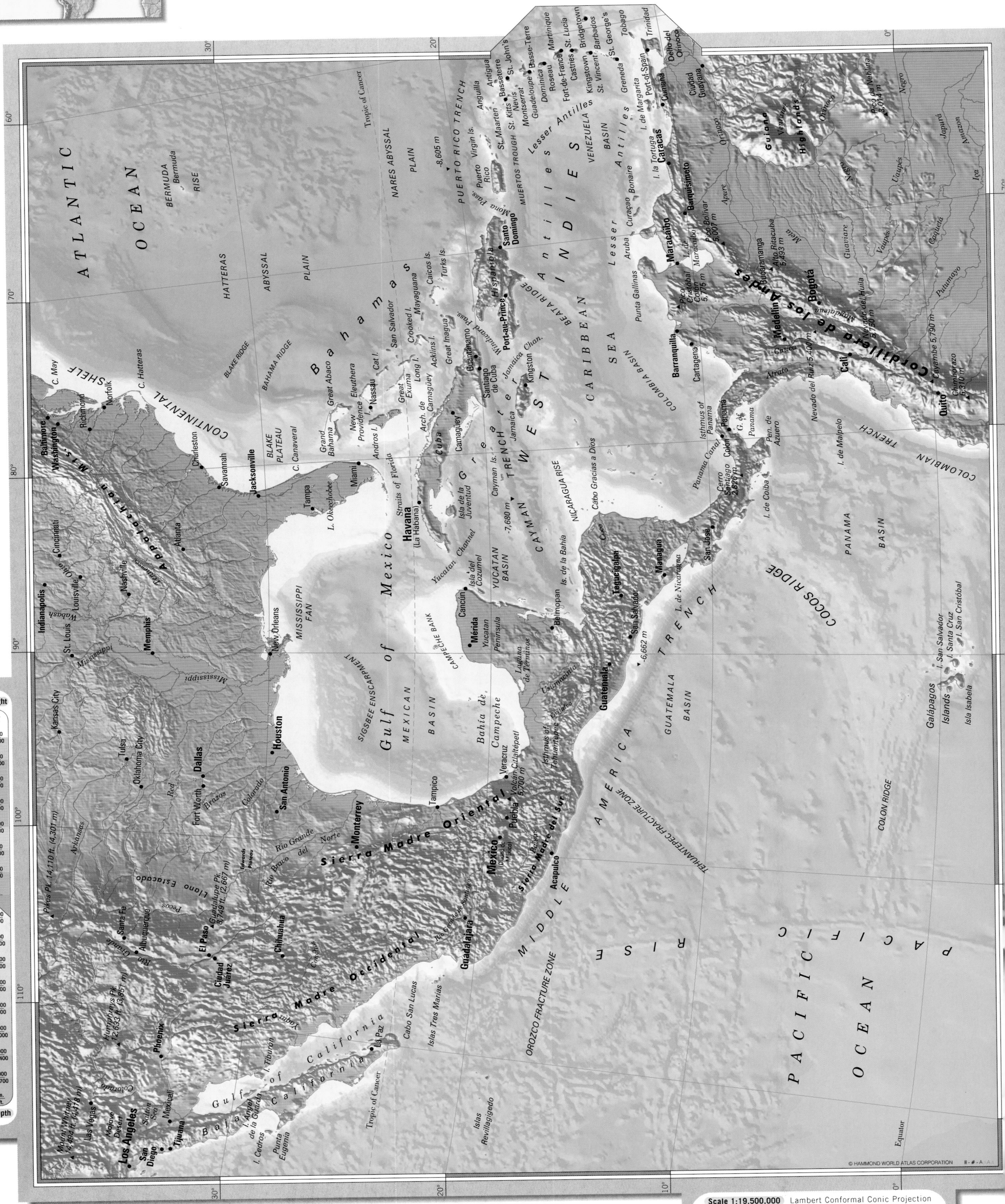

Scale 1:19,500,000 Lambert Conformal Conic Projection

The Andes, extending 7200 km from north to south, are a product of the subduction of the Nazca Plate beneath the South American Plate. Some 130 million years ago, a 7000-km-wide strip of Pacific seafloor disappeared into the earth's crust. The rock melted, and the magma rising to the surface formed the Andes range, with snow-capped volcanoes rising to more than 6,000 meters above sea level.

South America

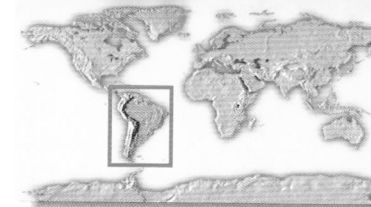

CARIBBEAN SEA

San José

Panama Canal

PANAMA

Isla de Malpelo

BASIN

Cabo Corrientes

Punta Galera

Equator

Gulf of Panama

Punta Aguja

PERU-CHILE TRENCH

PERU

BASIN

NAZCA RIDGE

PACIFIC

OCEAN

CHALLENGER FRACTURE ZONE

CHILE BASIN

Is. Juan Fernández

I. Alejandro Selkirk   I. Robinson Crusoe

CHILE RISE

Arch. de Los Chonos

Pen. Taitao
Cabo Tres Montes

Isla Wellington

Arch. Reina Adelaida

Strait of Magellan

Cape Horn

Punta Gallinas

Barranquilla

Maracaibo

L. de Maracaibo

Pico Bolívar 5,007 m

Bucaramanga

Medellín

Alto Ritacuba 5,493 m

Nevado del Tolima 5,215 m

Bogotá

Cali

Nevado del Huila 5,750 m

Quito

Chimborazo 6,267 m

Guayaquil

G. de Guayaquil

Cauca

Magdalena

Meta

Arauca

Orinoco

Guaviare

Salto Angostura

Vaupés

Caquetá

Negro

Putumayo

Napo

Iquitos

Marañón

Yavari

Juruá

Ucayali

Huallaga

La Montaña

Trujillo

Nevado Huascarán 6,768 m

Callao   Lima

Cusco

Madre de Díos

Beni

Mamoré

Guaporé

Iténez

Nevado Ancohuma 6,550 m

La Paz

Lake Titicaca

Arequipa

Altiplano

Arica

-8,064 m

Antofagasta

Tropic of Capricorn

Volcán Llullaillaco 6,723 m

San Miguel de Tucumán

Cerro Ojos del Salado 6,880 m

Valparaíso

Cerro Aconcagua 6,959 m

Mendoza

Santiago

Concepción

Puerto Montt

L. Nahuel Huapí

Isla Chiloé

G. Corcovado

Lago Buenos Aires

Pen. Taitao

Lago Argentino

Punta Arenas

Tierra del Fuego

C. San Diego

Willemstad

Caracas

G. de Venezuela

Port-of-Spain

Trinidad

Delta del Orinoco

Ciudad Guayana

Orinoco

Georgetown

Paramaribo

Cayenne

Salto del Ángel

Mt. Roraima 2,772 m

Pico de la Neblina 3,014 m

Rep. de Balbina

Manaus

Amazon

Amazon

Purus

Madeira

Xingu

Tapajós

Tocantins

Araguaia

Serra dos Parecis

Guaporé

Iténez

Planalto do

Mato Grosso

Campo Grande

Asunción

Paraguay

Pilcomayo

Bermejo

Salado del Norte

Paraná

Gran Chaco

Córdoba

Santa Fe

Rosario

Salado

Buenos Aires

La Plata

Río de la Plata

Montevideo

Cabo San Antonio

Bahía Blanca

Colorado

Negro

Golfo San Matías

Pen. Valdés

Chubut

Golfo San Jorge

Cabo Tres Puntas

Descado

Golfo San Jorge

Bahía Grande

West Falkland

East Falkland

Falkland Is.

Strait of Magellan

Guiana

Highlands

Orinoco

Branco

L I a n o s

Cordillera de los Andes

Cordillera de los Andes

Cordillera de los Andes

Pampas

Patagonia

S e l v a s

Selvas

Uaupés

B. de Marajó

Ilha de Marajó

Pará

Belém

São Luís

B. de São Marcos

Parnaíba

Teresina

Fortaleza

Natal

Cabo de São Roque

Recife

Maceió

Caatingas

Rep. de Sobradinho

São Francisco

Salvador

Brasília

Goiânia

Brazilian

Highlands

Belo Horizonte

Pico da Bandeira 2,890 m

Paraíba

Rio de Janeiro

São Paulo

Cabo de São Tomé

Cabo Frio

Santos

Curitiba

Serra do Mar

Iguaçu

Cataratas del Iguazú

Represa de Itaipú

Paraná

Uruguay

Pôrto Alegre

L. Mar Chiquita

DEMERARA ABYSSAL PLAIN

ATLANTIC

OCEAN

MID-ATLANTIC RIDGE

PARA ABYSSAL PLAIN

CEARA ABYSSAL PLAIN

Equator

I. Fernando de Noronha

BRAZIL

BASIN

SANTOS PLATEAU

Tropic of Capricorn

RIO GRANDE PLATEAU

ATLANTIC

ARGENTINE

BASIN

OCEAN

CONTINENTAL SHELF

-6,098 m

FALKLAND ESCARPMENT

© RAMMOND WORLD ATLAS CORPORATION

Scale 1:24,000,000   Lambert Azimuthal Equal-Area

MI   200   400   600   800
KM   200   400   600   800   1000   1200

Height

m.
ft.

6000 | 19700
4000 | 13000
2000 | 6500
1500 | 5000
1000 | 3300
500 | 1600
200 | 700
0
200 | 700
500 | 1600
1000 | 3300
2000 | 6500
3000 | 9800
4000 | 13000
5000 | 16400
6000 | 19700

m.
ft.

Depth

According to an estimate published by the United Nations, roughly 8 billion people will be living on earth in the year 2025 - the majority of them in Asia and Africa. Their environment will have changed dramatically in the interim. The growing global population requires a constantly increasing supply of food, energy, and clean drinking water. Progressive land development threatens the survival of numerous animal and plant species. Even today, wars and migration can often be traced to deteriorating environmental conditions.

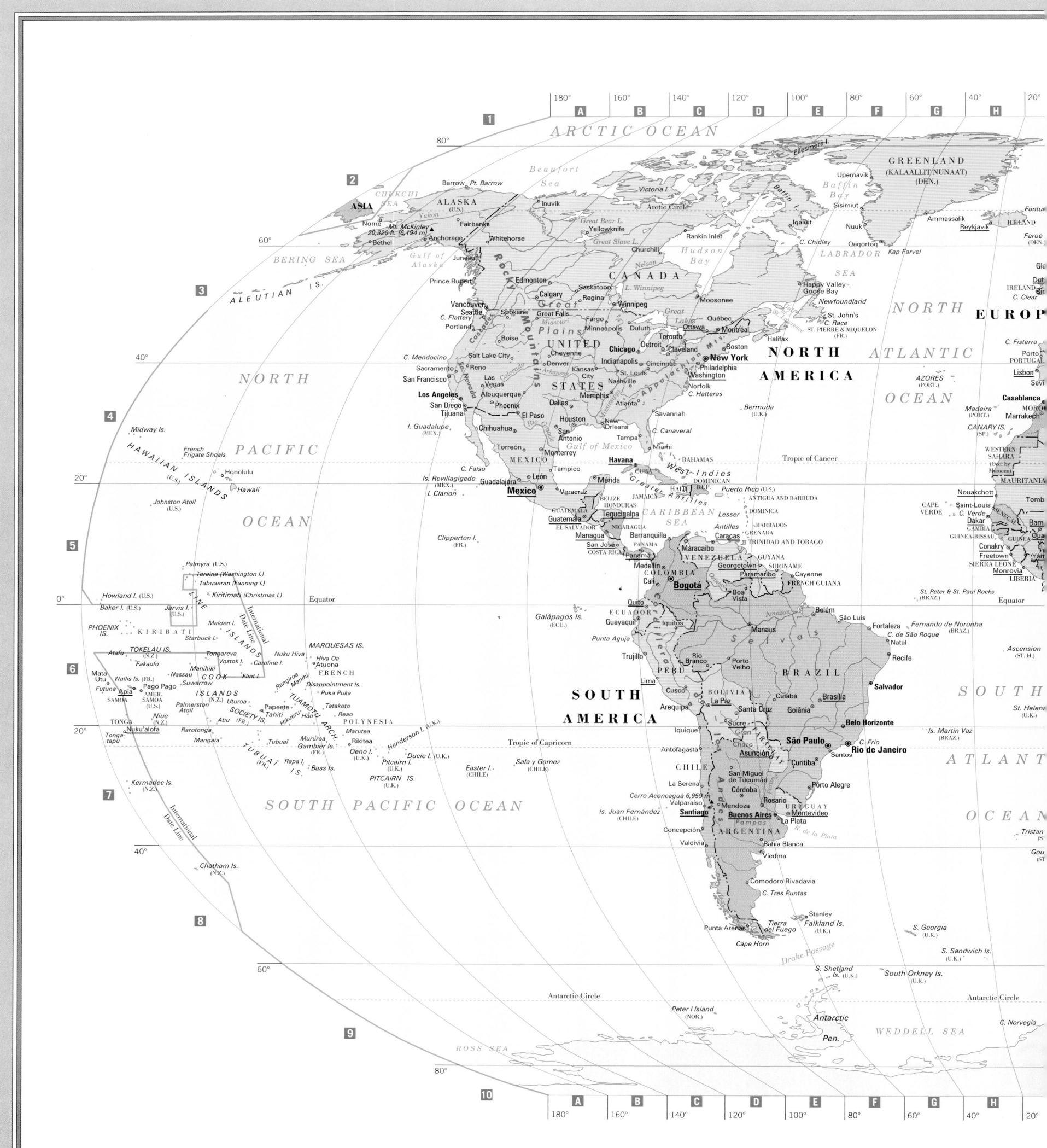

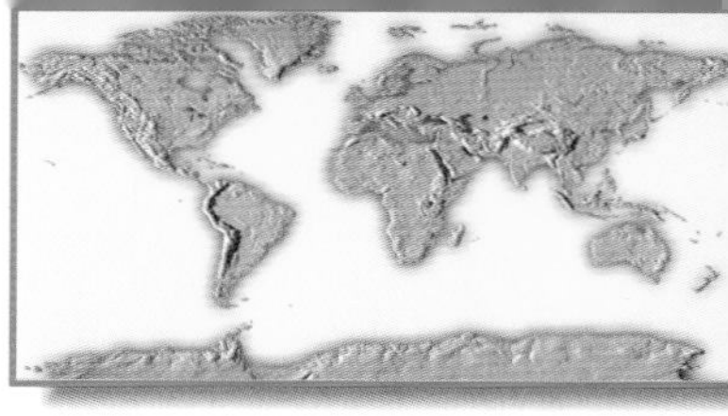

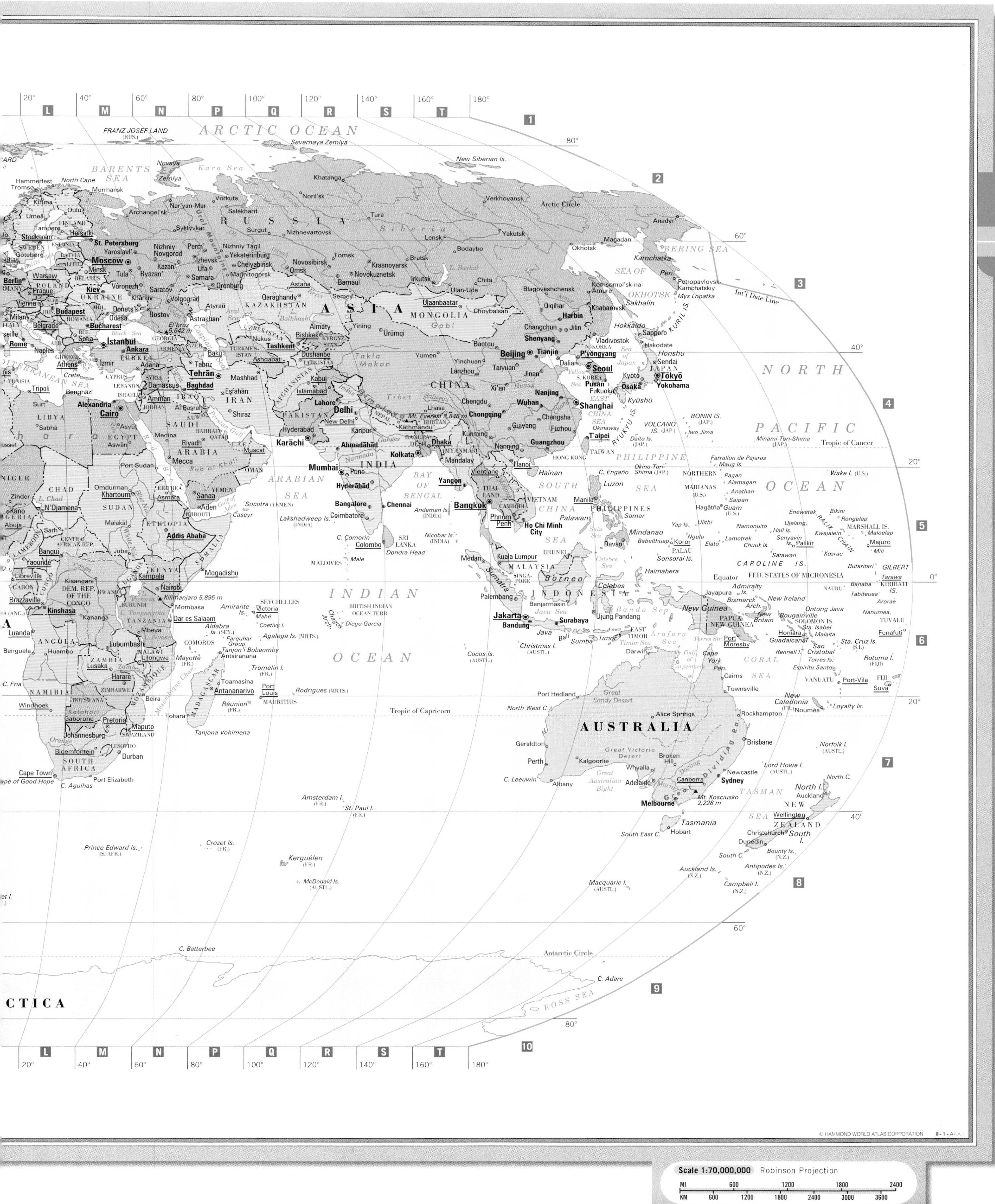

Scale 1:70,000,000   Robinson Projection

MI		600	1200	1800	2400
KM	600	1200	1800	2400	3000	3600

he four large peninsulas of the Peloponnesus extend like fingers into the Mediterranean south of the Gulf of Corinth. The peninsula as a whole is bounded by the Ionian Sea to the west and the Mirtöön Sea to the east. The ancient Greeks regarded Cape Taínaron, located at the tip of the central peninsula, as the end of the world. The Peloponnesus, the Gulf of Corinth, and the Pindus Mountains to the north are excellent examples of the effects of the upward and downward thrust of segments of the earth's crust caused by the collision of the African and Eurasian Plates.

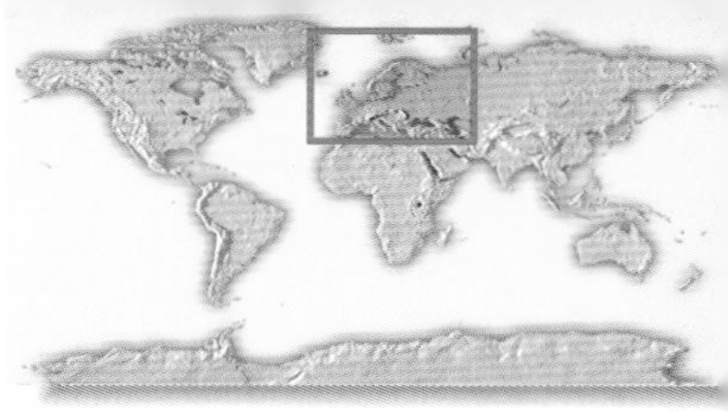

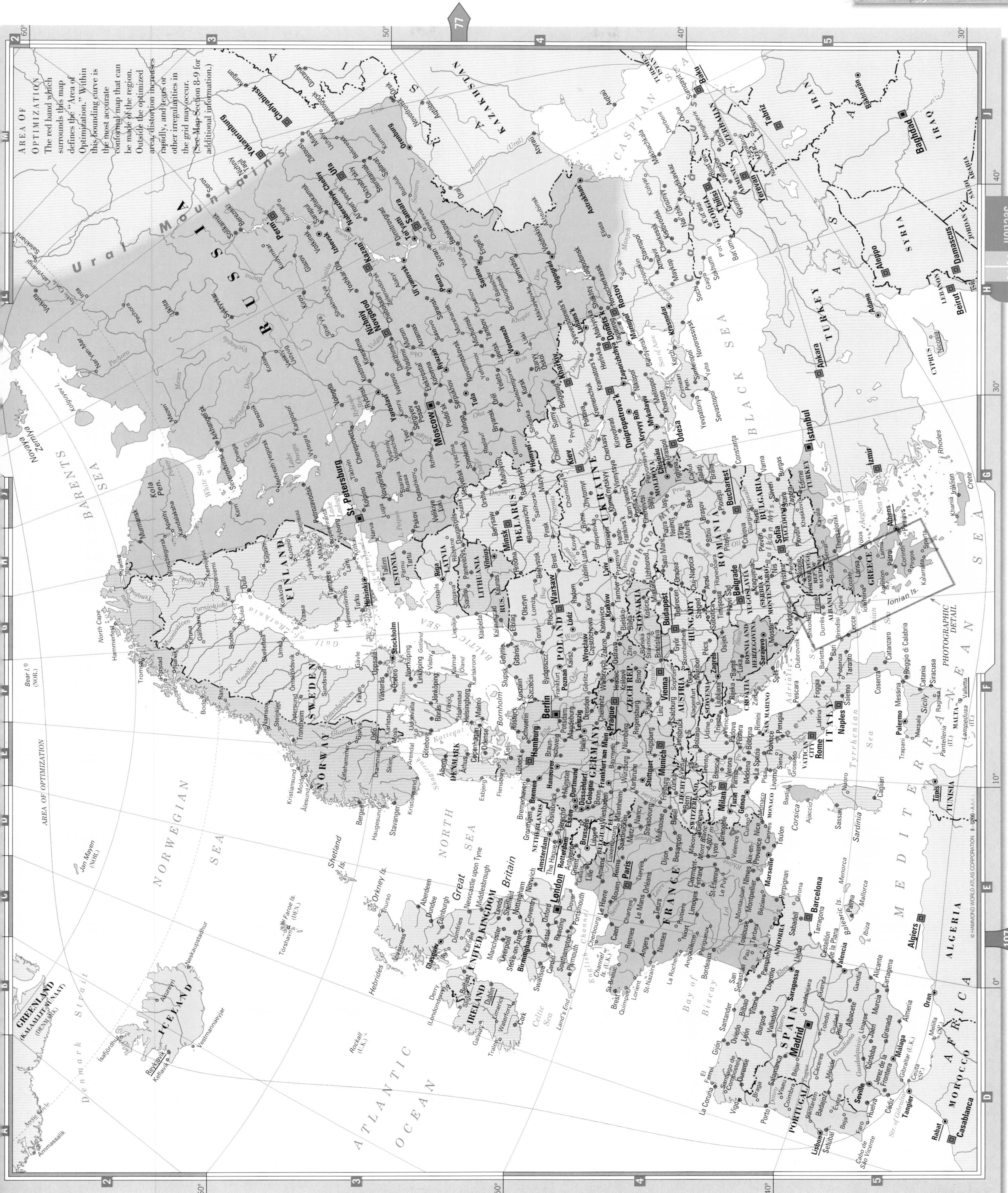

Population

■ Over 3,000,000   ● 500,000 - 999,999   ○ Under 100,000
□ 1,000,000 - 2,999,999   ● 100,000 - 499,999

Scale 1:18,000,000   Hammond Optimal Conformal

London, Paris

Both of these major commercial centers are situated on the banks of major rivers: the Thames and the Seine. With more than seven million inhabitants, Greater London is one of the largest cities on earth.

Though Paris itself has a population of only 2.5 million, its greater metropolitan area is home to some ten million people. The Channel Tunnel has reduced travel time from Paris to London to only a few hours.

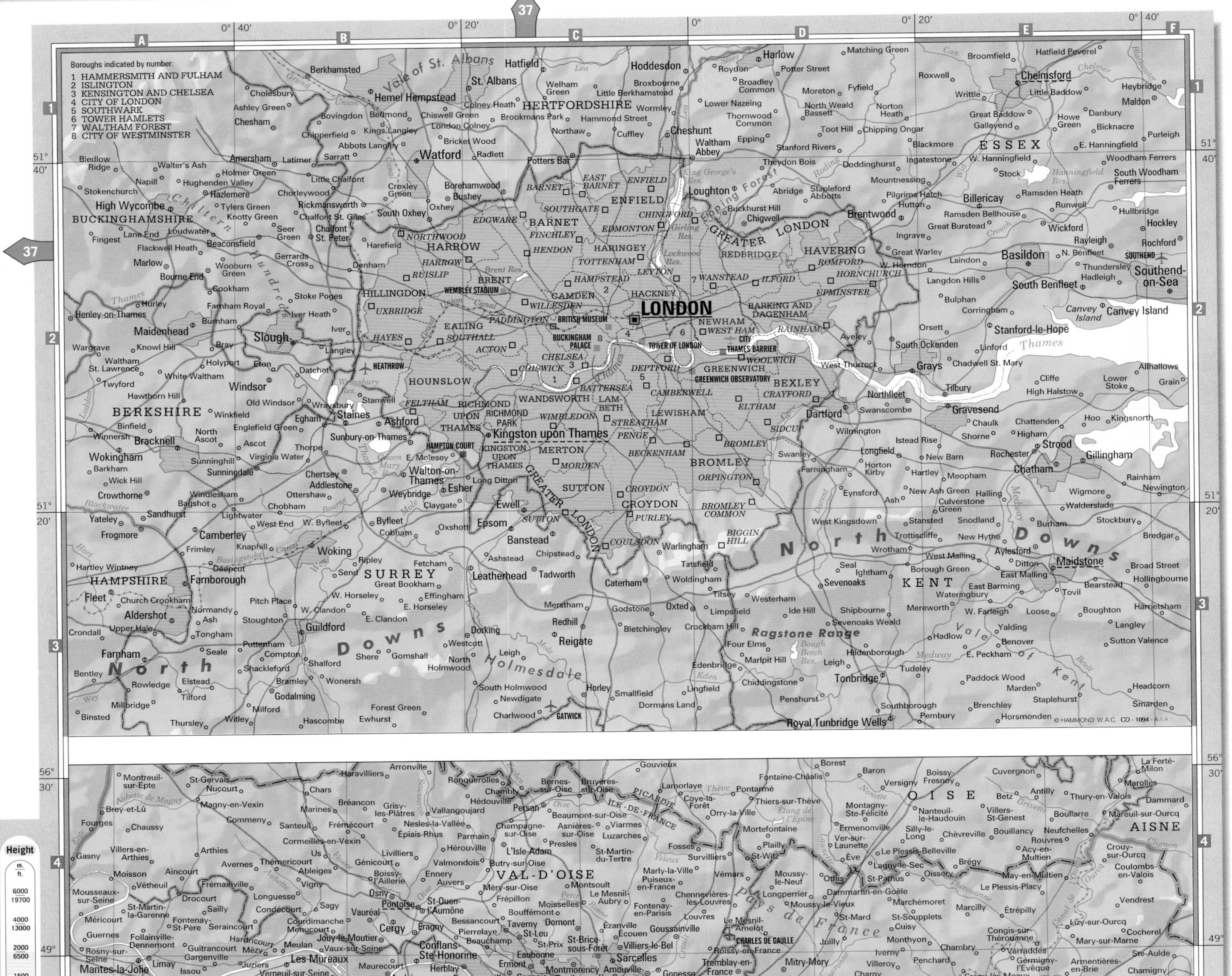

Boroughs indicated by number:
1 HAMMERSMITH AND FULHAM
2 ISLINGTON
3 KENSINGTON AND CHELSEA
4 CITY OF LONDON
5 SOUTHWARK
6 TOWER HAMLETS
7 WALTHAM FOREST
8 CITY OF WESTMINSTER

Height

m.	ft.
6000	19700
4000	13000
2000	6500
1500	5000
1000	3300
500	1600
200	700
0	0
200	700
500	1600
1000	3300
2000	6500
3000	9800
4000	13000
5000	16400
6000	19700

Depth

Population

- ■ Over 2,000,000
- ■ 1,000,000 - 1,999,999
- ● 500,000 - 999,999
- ● 250,000 - 499,999
- ● 100,000 - 249,999
- ● 30,000 - 99,999
- ⊙ 10,000 - 29,999
- ○ Under 10,000

Scale 1:500,000 Lambert Conformal Conic Projection

MI	5	10	15
KM	5	10	15	20

© HAMMOND W.A.C. CD - 1094 - AAA

© HAMMOND W.A.C. CD - 1095 - AAA

United Kingdom, Ireland

The British Isles are only 32 km from the European continent. Britain's isolated geographic position is due chiefly to its irregular coastline with its many steep, towering cliffs, which offers only very few points of access for ships. The most important commercial centers of the United Kingdom and Ireland developed where fjords and estuaries extend far into the island interior.

Scale 1:3,000,000 Lambert Conformal Conic Projection

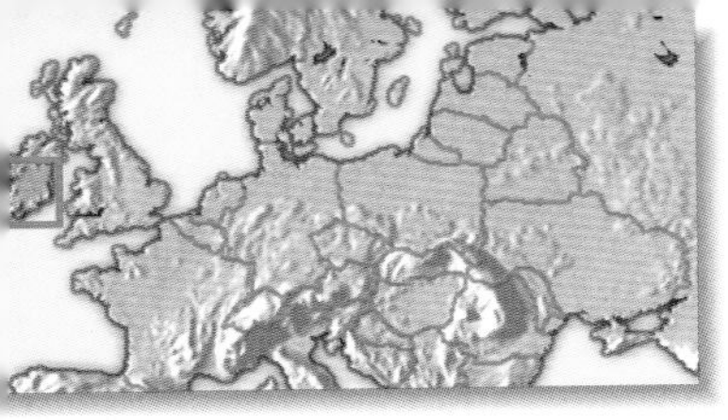

Central and Southern Ireland

The "Emerald Isle" of Ireland derives its name from the lush, evergreen vegetation that flourishes in Ireland's oceanic climate. Low-pressure centers passing over the island from the Atlantic bring substantial precipitation, which falls more frequently in the west than in the east. Moreover, the influence of the Gulf Stream keeps temperatures relatively mild even during the winter months.

Scale 1:1,000,000 Lambert Conformal Conic Projection

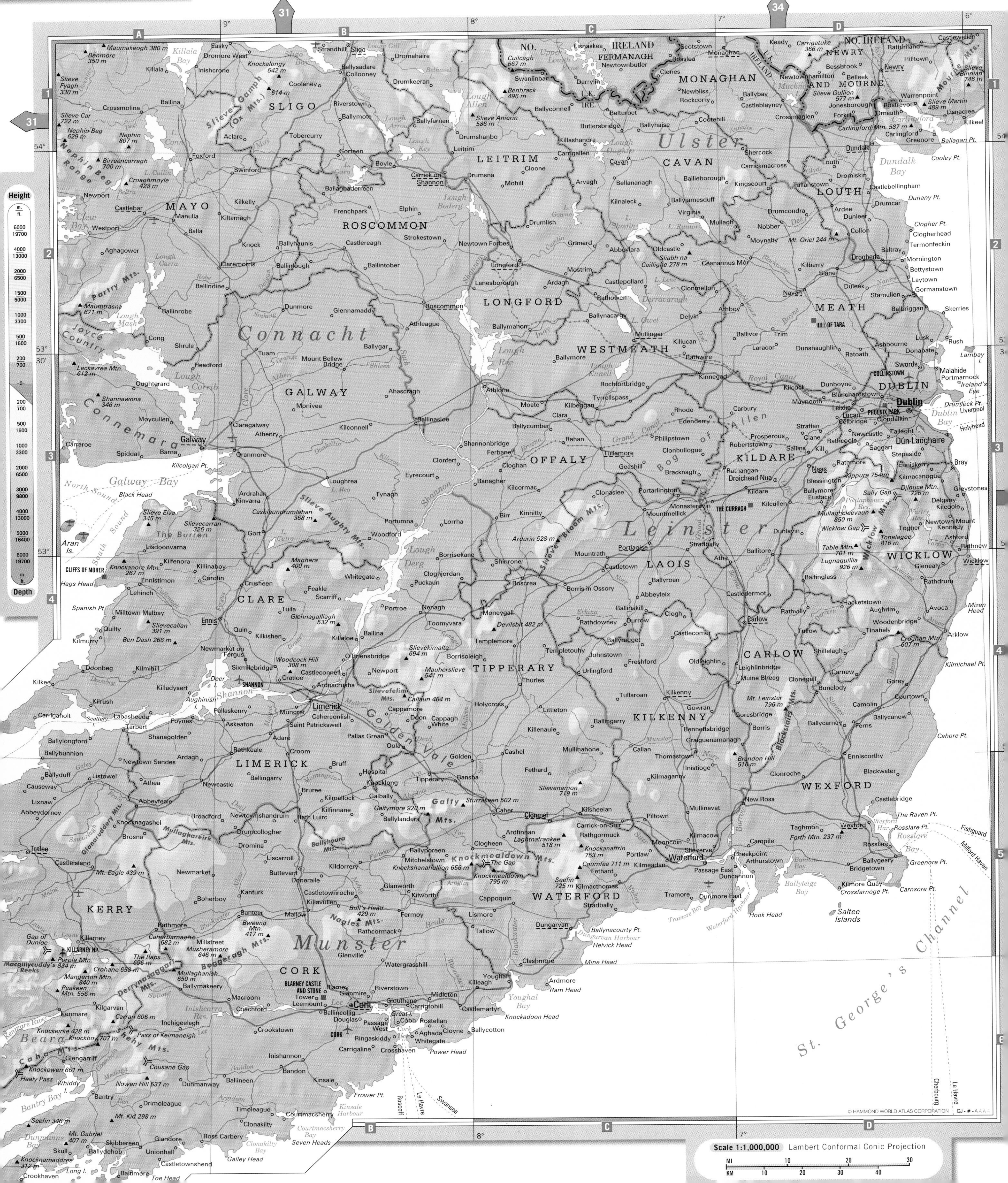

Glen Mòr, the largest linear fault in northern Scotland, divides central Scotland into the Northern Highlands and the Grampian Mountains to the south. Ben Nevis (1,343 m) is the highest peak in the Grampian range. The sparsely forested highlands covered by broad moors and heaths provide ideal grazing areas for sheep. Farmland is found primarily in the lowlands and along the coast.

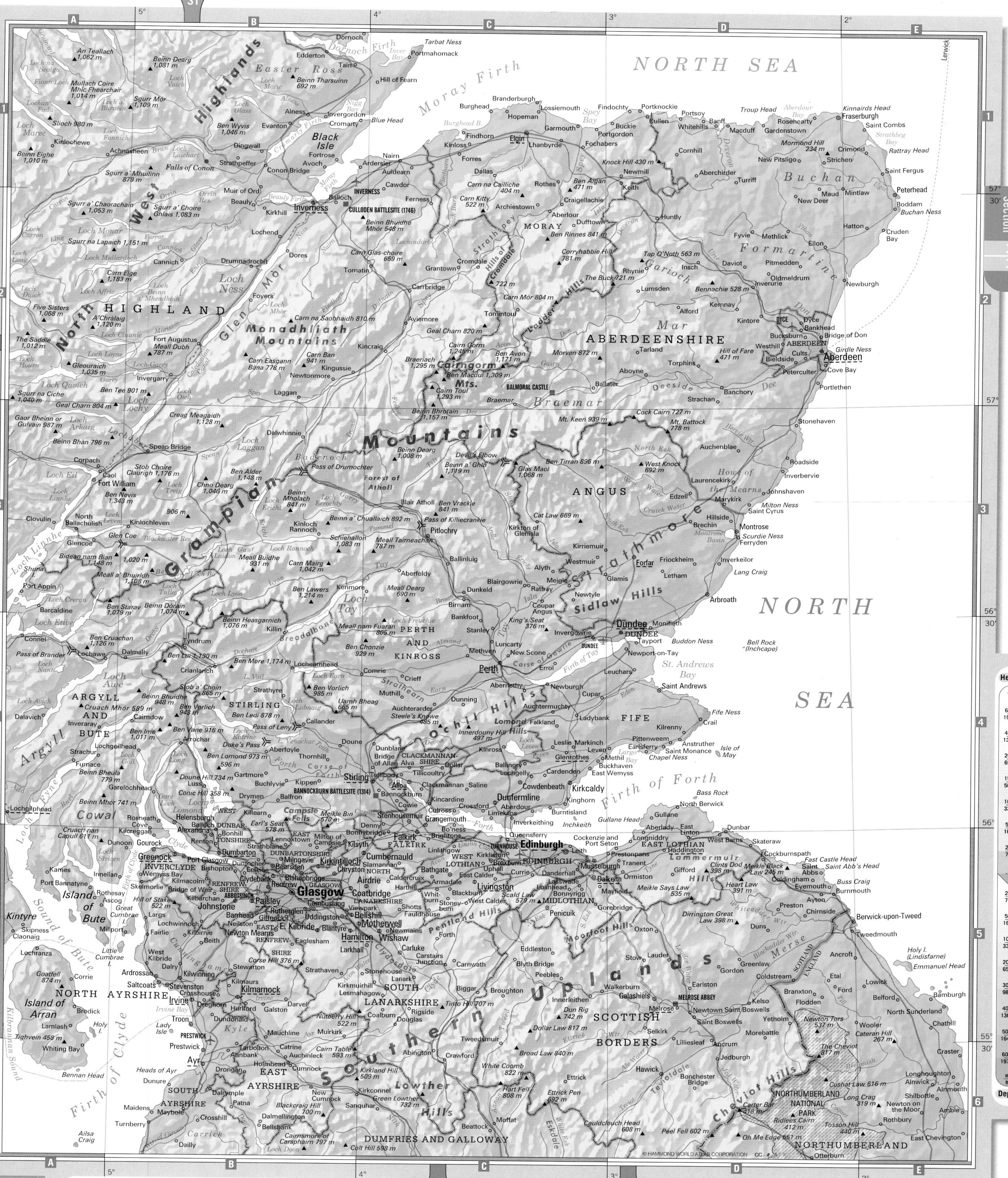

Population

▣ Over 2,000,000	◉ 500,000 - 999,999
▢ 1,000,000 - 1,999,999	◉ 250,000 - 499,999
◉ 100,000 - 249,999	○ 10,000 - 29,999
◉ 30,000 - 99,999	○ Under 10,000

Scale 1:1,000,000   Lambert Conformal Conic Projection

Height — Depth (m. / ft.)

6000 / 19700
4000 / 13000
2000 / 6500
1500 / 5000
1000 / 3300
500 / 1600
200 / 700
0
200 / 700
1000 / 3300
2000 / 6500
3000 / 9800
4000 / 13000
5000 / 16400
6000 / 19700

Lake District National Park offers a striking display of the diversity of the landscape of the British Isles. The park contains not only England's largest lake, Lake Windermere, but also its highest peak, Seafell Pike (978 m). Sheep graze on the lush, green meadows of this area. Although the landscape seems almost alpine, many of the lakes here lie below sea level.

During the Ice Age, a land bridge connected Great Britain and Ireland. When the waters rose again, the Irish Sea formed and separated the two large islands.

NORTH SEA

Scotland / Scottish Borders

SCOTTISH BORDERS — Cauldcleuch Head 608 m — Carter Bar 418 m — Ettrick Pen 692 m — Roan Fell 568 m — Sighty Crag 519 m — Peel Fell 602 m — Oh Me Edge 551 m — Tosson Hill 440 m

GALLOWAY — Newcastleton — Langholm — Canonbie — Eaglesfield — Eastriggs — Gretna — Bowness-on-Solway — Longtown — Brampton — Milton — Wigton — Caldbeck

Cumbria / Lake District

CUMBRIA — Carlisle — Wetheral — Penrith — Greystoke — Keswick — Skiddaw 931 m — Cold Fell 622 m — Alston — Collier Law 516 m

LAKE DISTRICT NAT'L PARK — Cumbrian Mts. — Scafell Pikes 978 m — High Street 829 m — Kirkstone Pass — Grasmere — Ambleside — Coniston — Windermere — Staveley — Kendal — Troutbeck

Ulverston — Barrow-in-Furness — Dalton-in-Furness — Askam in Furness — Grange — Arnside — Silverdale — Carnforth — Morecambe — Heysham — Lancaster — Morecambe Bay — Hilpsford Pt. — Rossall Pt. — Fleetwood — Knott End-on-Sea — Preesall — Thornton Cleveleys — BLACKPOOL — Lytham St. Anne's

Northumberland

NORTHUMBERLAND NATIONAL PARK — Kielder — Kielder Res. — Bellingham — Wark — Humshaugh — Otterburn — Newton on the Moor — Rothbury — Amble — Chevington — East Chevington — Druridge Bay — Ashington — Newbiggin-by-the-Sea — Pegswood — Morpeth — Bedlington — Blyth — Seaton Delaval — Whitley Bay — Tynemouth — North Shields — South Shields

HADRIAN'S WALL — HOUSESTEADS ROMAN FORT — Haltwhistle — Haydon Bridge — Hexham — Riding Mill — Prudhoe — Allendale

Tyne and Wear

NEWCASTLE UPON TYNE — NEWCASTLE INT'L — Gosforth — Longbenton — N. TYNESIDE — Wallsend — Walls End — Jarrow — GATESHEAD — Felling — Whickham — Ryton — Newburn — SUNDERLAND — Washington — Houghton-le-Spring — Silksworth — Hetton-le-Hole — Seaham

Durham

DURHAM — Chester-le-Street — Stanley — Consett — Lanchester — Sacriston — Brandon — Sherburn — Shotton — Easington — Peterlee — Horden — Blackhall Rocks — Wearhead — Stanhope — Wolsingham — Crook — Willington — Spennymoor — Bishop Auckland — Shildon — Ferryhill — Sedgefield — HARTLEPOOL — Seaton Carew — Fishburn — Trimdon — Cross Fell 893 m — Chapelfell Top 696 m — Cow Green Res.

Tees Valley / Cleveland

Stockton-on-Tees — DARLINGTON — Middlesbrough — Billingham — Greatham — Redcar — REDCAR AND CLEVELAND — Marske-by-the-Sea — Saltburn — Brotton — Loftus — Eston — Skelton — Guisborough — Nunthorpe — Hinderwell — Liverton — TEESIDE INT'L — Hurworth — Scotch Corner — Hutton Rudby — Whitby

Mickle Fell 790 m — Middleton-in-Teesdale — Mickleton — Eggleston — Barnard Castle — Bowes — Staindrop — Gainford — Newton Aycliffe — Thorpe Thewles

North Yorkshire

NORTH YORKSHIRE — Richmond — Reeth — Hipswell — Catterick — Northallerton — Leyburn — Bedale — Middleham — Thirsk — Rievaulx — Helmsley — Kirkbymoorside — Pickering — Thornton Dale — Scalby — Scarborough — Filey — Seamer — Easingwold — Hovingham — Malton

YORKSHIRE DALES NAT'L PARK — Great Shunner Fell 713 m — The Calf 677 m — Sedbergh — Millthrop — Hawes — Wensleydale — Crag Hill 686 m — Whernside 736 m — Buckden Pike 702 m — Pen-y-Ghent 693 m — Kettlewell — Kirkby Stephen — Brough — Appleby — Shap — Newby Bridge

CLEVELAND HILLS — NORTH YORK MOORS NAT'L PARK — Hambleton Hills — Goathland — Glaisdale — Cloughton — Robin Hood's Bay — Eastfield — Ayton — Vale of Pickering — Derwent

Ripon — FOUNTAINS ABBEY — Boroughbridge — Summer Bridge — Pateley Bridge — Grassington — Bolton Abbey — Skipton — Gargrave — Settle — Airton — Giggleswick — Bentham — Wennington — Melling — Dolphinholme — Slaidburn — Ward's Stone 560 m — Stocks Res.

Knaresborough — Harrogate — Wetherby — Tadcaster — Thornthwaite — Masham — Collingham — Bramhope — Otley — Ilkley — Guiseley — Baildon — Shipley — Bingley — Keighley — Silsden — Earby — Barnoldswick — Colne

York / East Riding

Vale of York — YORK MINSTER — York — Fulford — Huntington — Dunnington — Haxby — Stamford Bridge — Wilberfoss — Pocklington — Market Weighton — Bishop Wilton — Hutton Cranswick — Driffield — Kilham — Rudston — Nafferton — Bempton — Flamborough Head — Flamborough — Hunmanby — Bridlington — Skipsea — Leven — Aldbrough — Humbsrby

EAST RIDING OF YORKSHIRE — YORKSHIRE WOLDS — Holme upon Spalding Moor — Howden — Newport — Gilberdyke — Cottingham — Beverley — Brandesburton — Hornsea — Wolds

Bridlington Bay

Lancashire / Greater Manchester

LANCASHIRE — Preston — Fulwood — Bamber Bridge — Leyland — Chorley — Coppull — Standish-with-Langtree — Adlington — Croston — Southport — Ainsdale — Formby Pt. — Formby — Crosby — Bootle — Litherland — SEFTON — Skelmersdale — Ormskirk — Burscough — Maghull — Kirkby

Blackburn — Darwen — BLACKBURN WITH DARWEN — Accrington — Great Harwood — Clayton-le-Moors — Church — Oswaldtwistle — Haslingden — Rawtenstall — Bacup — Ramsbottom — Turton — Withnell — Wheelton — Brierfield — Nelson — Padiham — Burnley — Pendle Hill 557 m — Clitheroe — Whalley — Barrowford — Waddington — Longridge — Garstang

GREATER MANCHESTER — MANCHESTER — Salford — Stretford — TRAFFORD — Sale — Altrincham — STOCKPORT — Denton — Hyde — TAMESIDE — Ashton-under-Lyne — Stalybridge — Dukinfield — OLDHAM — Royton — Shaw — Middleton — Prestwich — Whitefield — BURY — Radcliffe — Heywood — ROCHDALE — Milnrow — Littleborough — Whitworth — BOLTON — Horwich — Westhoughton — Farnworth — Kearsley — Atherton — Leigh — Tyldesley — WIGAN — Hindley — Ince-in-Makerfield — Ashton-in-Makerfield — Billinge — Haydock — Newton-le-Willows — Golborne — Eccles — Irlam — Urmston — Worsley

Merseyside / Cheshire

MERSEYSIDE — LIVERPOOL — Wallasey — Birkenhead — WIRRAL — Heswall — Hoylake — West Kirby — Neston — ST. HELENS — Prescot — Huyton-with-Roby — Widnes — HALTON — Runcorn — Speke — Bebington

CHESHIRE — Ellesmere Port — Frodsham — Helsby — Northwich — Knutsford — Wilmslow — Alderley Edge — Poynton — Bollington — Macclesfield — Congleton — Sandbach — Middlewich — Winsford — Tarporley — Tarvin — Chester — Kelsall — Mouldsworth — Cheshire Plain — Hazel Grove — Marple — Chelford — Goostrey — Holmes Chapel — Alsager — Nantwich — Crewe — Haslington — Audlem — Malpas

Peak District / Derbyshire

PEAK DISTRICT NAT'L PARK — Kinder Scout 636 m — Glossop — Whaley Bridge — Chapel-en-le-Frith — New Mills — Buxton — Tideswell — Bakewell — Matlock — Wirksworth — Ashbourne — Hathersage — Eyam — Bamford

DERBYSHIRE — DERBY — Chesterfield — Dronfield — Eckington — Staveley — Clowne — Bolsover — Clay Cross — North Wingfield — Alfreton — Ripley — Belper — Duffield — Heanor — Ilkeston — Long Eaton — Swadlincote — Ashby-de-la-Zouch — Measham — Overseal

South/West Yorkshire

WEST YORKSHIRE — LEEDS — LEEDS AND BRADFORD — BRADFORD — Pudsey — Morley — Rothwell — Garforth — Castleford — Pontefract — Knottingley — Featherstone — WAKEFIELD — Horbury — Ossett — Dewsbury — Batley — Mirfield — Brighouse — Elland — Halifax — Sowerby Bridge — Todmorden — Hebden Bridge — Ripponden — CALDERDALE — Denholme — Queensbury — Holmfirth — Meltham — Marsden — HUDDERSFIELD — KIRKLEES — Skelmanthorpe — Denby Dale — Penistone — Stocksbridge — Chapeltown

SOUTH YORKSHIRE — SHEFFIELD — ROTHERHAM — Rawmarsh — Wath upon Dearne — Swinton — Mexborough — Conisbrough — DONCASTER — Bentley — Armthorpe — New Rossington — Thorne — Crowle — Stainforth — Hatfield — BARNSLEY — Wombwell — Hoyland Nether — Darton — Royston — Cudworth — Grimethorpe — South Kirkby — Hemsworth — South Elmsall — Adwick le Street — Askern

Lincolnshire / Humber

NORTH LINCOLNSHIRE — Scunthorpe — Brigg — Barton-upon-Humber — Goxhill — Immingham — Grimsby — Cleethorpes — Humberston — N.E. LINCOLNSHIRE — HUMBERSIDE INT'L — Spurn Head — Holderness — Patrington — Withernsea — Hedon — Hessle — KINGSTON UPON HULL — Hull — Barrow-upon-Humber

LINCOLNSHIRE — Lincoln — LINCOLNSHIRE WOLDS — Market Rasen — Louth — Mablethorpe — Sutton on Sea — Alford — Tetford — Horncastle — Woodhall Spa — Coningsby — Skegness — Spilsby — Wragby — Bardney — Nettleham — Saxilby — Gainsborough — North Wheatley — East Retford — Tuxford — Lincoln Heath — Lincolnshire Plain — Boston — Sleaford — Grantham — Barrowby — The Wash — The Fens — Holbeach — Spalding — Pinchbeck — Bourne — Long Sutton — Sutton Bridge

Nottinghamshire

NOTTINGHAMSHIRE — NOTTINGHAM — Arnold — Carlton — West Bridgford — Hucknall Torkard — Eastwood — Kirkby in Ashfield — Sutton in Ashfield — Mansfield — Mansfield Woodhouse — Warsop — Worksop — Newark-on-Trent — Southwell — Calverton — Bingham — Radcliffe on Trent — Keyworth — Ruddington

Wales / Shropshire / Staffordshire

WALES — Wrexham — Rhosllanerchrugog — Chirk — Gobowen — Oswestry — POWYS — Flint — Connah's Quay — Queensferry — Hawarden — Buckley — Mold — Brymbo — Gwersyllt — Bangor-is-y-Coed — Overton — Whitchurch — Ruabon — Cefn — Llay — Pen-y-cae

SHROPSHIRE — THE WREKIN — Market Drayton — Prees — Wem — Hodnet — Newport — Edgmond — Shawbury — Baschurch — Ruyton — Wheaton Aston — Woodseaves

STAFFORDSHIRE — STOKE-ON-TRENT — Newcastle-under-Lyme — Kidsgrove — Biddulph — Leek — Cheadle — Stone — Stafford — Rugeley — Uttoxeter — Blythe Bridge — Burton upon Trent — Barton-under-Needwood — Eccleshall — Gnosall — Penkridge — Abbots Bromley — Blithfield Res.

Leicestershire / Rutland

LEICESTERSHIRE — Loughborough — Shepshed — Coalville — Melton Mowbray — Ashfordby — Long Whatton — EAST MIDLANDS — Sileby — Mountsorrel — East Leake — Kegworth

RUTLAND — NORFOLK — St. Botolph — Terrington Saint Clement — Gedney — Holbeach

Scale 1:1,000,000   Lambert Conformal Conic Projection

MI 10 20 30
KM 10 20 30 40

© HAMMOND WORLD ATLAS CORPORATION   CC · A A A

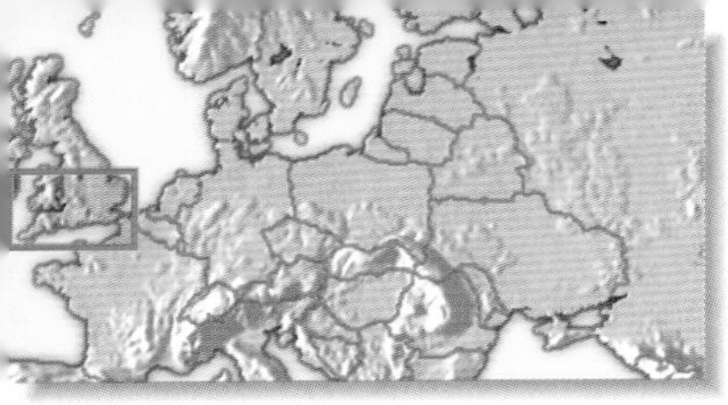

Southern Great Britain is traditionally
divided into two regions characterize
by yellow and green coloration. Yellow is
the eastern region, where wheat is grow
and, as in Spain, annual precipitation

Population

■ Over 2,000,000	● 500,000 - 999,999	◉ 100,000 - 249,999	○ 10,000 - 29,999
▣ 1,000,000 - 1,999,999	◎ 250,000 - 499,999	⊙ 30,000 - 99,999	○ Under 10,000

Height

m.
ft.

6000
19700

4000
13000

2000
6500

1500
5000

1000
3300

500
1600

200
700

-0-

200
700

500
1600

1000
3300

2000
6500

3000
9800

4000
13000

5000
16400

6000
19700

m.
ft.

Depth

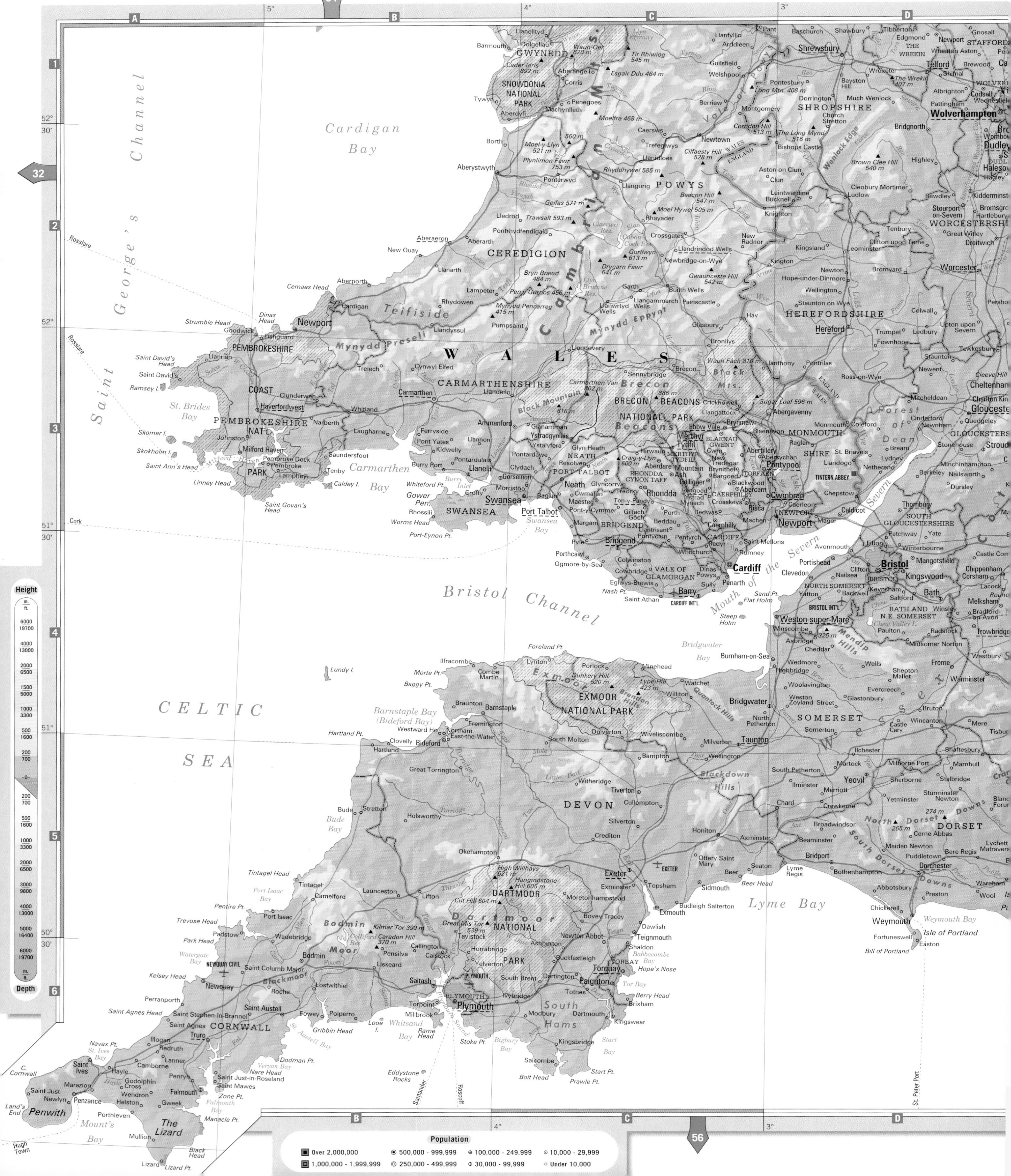

nts to no more than 500 mm in many s. Green is the western region, where s moving in from the sea bring rain e mountains. With elevations of over 0 m, the Welsh highlands extend as a broad peninsula far toward the west, forming a precipitation barrier that keeps the eastern lowlands dry. High humidity is the cause of frequent winter fog, which is thickened in places by air pollution.

Scale 1:1,000,000 Lambert Conformal Conic Projection

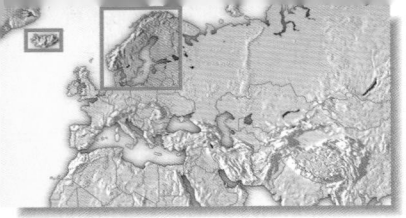

Scandinavia and Finland, Iceland

Marked by fjords, deep valleys, and lakes, the landscape of northern Europe was clearly shaped during the Ice Age. Although glaciers have long since receded in this region, the picture in Iceland is very different. The Vatnajöku Ice Cap covers an area of some 8,410 square kilometers, and melt caused by subglacial eruptions poses a significant danger to coastal settlements.

Scale 1:6,000,000   Lambert Conformal Conic Projection

© HAMMOND WORLD ATLAS CORPORATION

Helsinki, Copenhagen and Stockholm are situated at strategically favorable points on the Baltic Sea coast. With its many bays and rocky islands as well as Finland's largest harbor, Helsinki commands the entrance to the Gulf of Finland, Copenhagen the entrance to the Øresund. Stockholm, located where Lake Mälaren joins the Baltic Sea, is called the "Venice of the north" for its many waterways.

Map Section
38
39

UPPSALA

Uppsala
Österunda
Nysätra
Litslena
Grillby
Lillkyrka
Veckholm
Överselö
Selaön
Stallarholmen
Mariefred
Åkers styckebruk
Björnlunda
Gnesta
Torsåker
Vagnhärad
SÖDERMANLAND
Bogsta
Tystberga
Björnsund
Sjösa
-köping
Oxelösund

Knutby
Söderby-Karl
Björkö
Arholma
Norrtälje
Grädö
Spillersboda
Kapellskär
Furusund
Blidö
Svartlöga
Roslagen
Rådmansö

STOCKHOLM
Täby
Sollentuna
Roslags-Näsby
Sundbyberg
Solna Lidingö
Nacka
Skärholmen
Botkyrka
Huddinge
Salem
Södertälje
Tumba
Flemingsberg
Rönninge
Handen
Haninge
Västerhaninge
Tungelsta
Österhörna
Ditinäs

Dalarö
Ornö
Muskö
Nynäshamn
Utö
Utö
Ålö
Nåttarö
Torö
Askö

BALTIC SEA

LÄNSI-SUOMEN LÄÄNI
Hämeenlinna
Forssa
Tampella
LÄNSI-SUOMEN LÄÄNI
Hyvinkää
ETELÄ-SUOMEN LÄÄNI
Lahti
Hollola
Riihimäki
Mäntsälä
Järvenpää
Tuusula
Kerava
Nurmijärvi
Porvoo (Borgå)
Vihti
Lohja
Vantaa
Espoo (Esbo)
Helsinki (Helsingfors)
Suomenlinna

Gulf of Finland

Porkkala
Orslandet
Stockholm
Tallinn

40
38
41
61°
60°

DENMARK
Århus
Tirstrup
Ebeltoft
Samsø
Tranebjerg
Hindsholm
Martofte
FYN
Ullerslev
Nyborg
Korsør

Kattegat

Halmstad
HALLAND
Torekov
Båstad
Skälderviken
Ängelholm
Kullen
Mölle
Höganäs
Viken
KRISTIANSTAD
SWEDEN
Osby
Markaryd
Vittsjö
Bjärnum
Hästveda
Glimåkra
Broby
Hässleholm
Klippan
Åstorp
Helsingborg (Hälsingborg)
Bjuv
Skåne
Kristianstad
Åhus
Landskrona
Ven
MALMÖHUS
Lund
Eslöv
Höör
Malmö
KØBENHAVN
Copenhagen (København)
Frederiksberg
Dragør
Skanör
Falsterbo
Trelleborg
Ystad
Simrishamn

Sjælland
VEST-SJÆLLAND
ROSKILDE
Roskilde
Køge
Ringsted
Slagelse
STORSTRØM
Næstved

BALTIC SEA
Fakse Bugt
Køge Bugt
Hanöbukten

Height
m. ft.
6000 19700
4000 13000
2000 6500
1500 5000
1000 3300
500 1600
200 700
0
200 700
500 1600
1000 3300
2000 6500
3000 9800
4000 13000
5000 16400
6000 19700
m. ft.
Depth

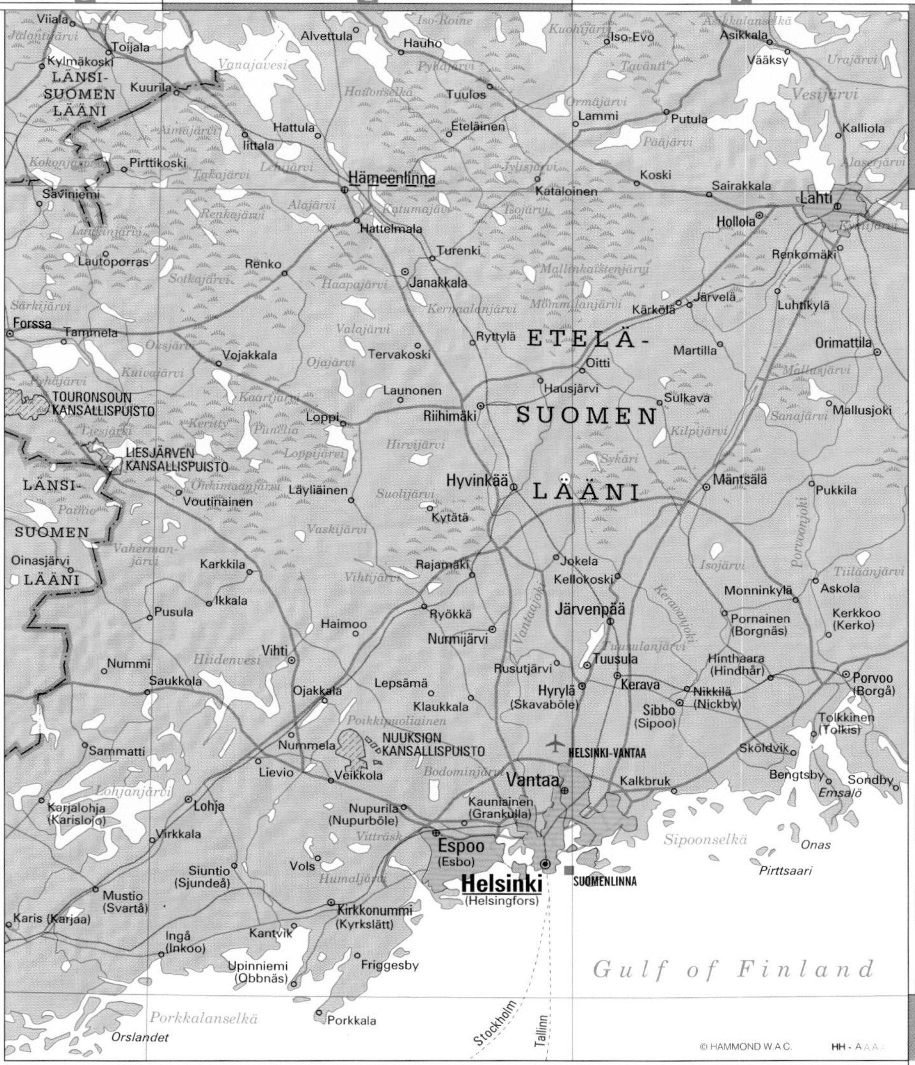

Population
- ■ Over 2,000,000
- ■ 1,000,000 - 1,999,999
- ● 500,000 - 999,999
- ● 250,000 - 499,999
- ◉ 100,000 - 249,999
- ◉ 30,000 - 99,999
- ⊙ 10,000 - 29,999
- ○ Under 10,000

Scale 1:1,000,000 Lambert Conformal Conic Projection

MI 10 20 30
KM 10 20 30 40

© HAMMOND W.A.C.

The Baltic Sea is connected to the North Sea by the Skagerrak and the Kattegat. Covering 390,000 square km (including the Kattegat), it has an average depth of 55 m and measures 459 m at its deepest point. Originally an inland lake, the Baltic is fed by the rivers of northern Europe and exchanges little water with the North Sea. Thus its salinity is low: 8 % at the surface. Tides play only a minor role in the region. At high tide, the water level rises no more than 40 cm in the Kattegat, between 20 and 30 cm in the Store Baelt, and only a few centimeters along the central coastlines.

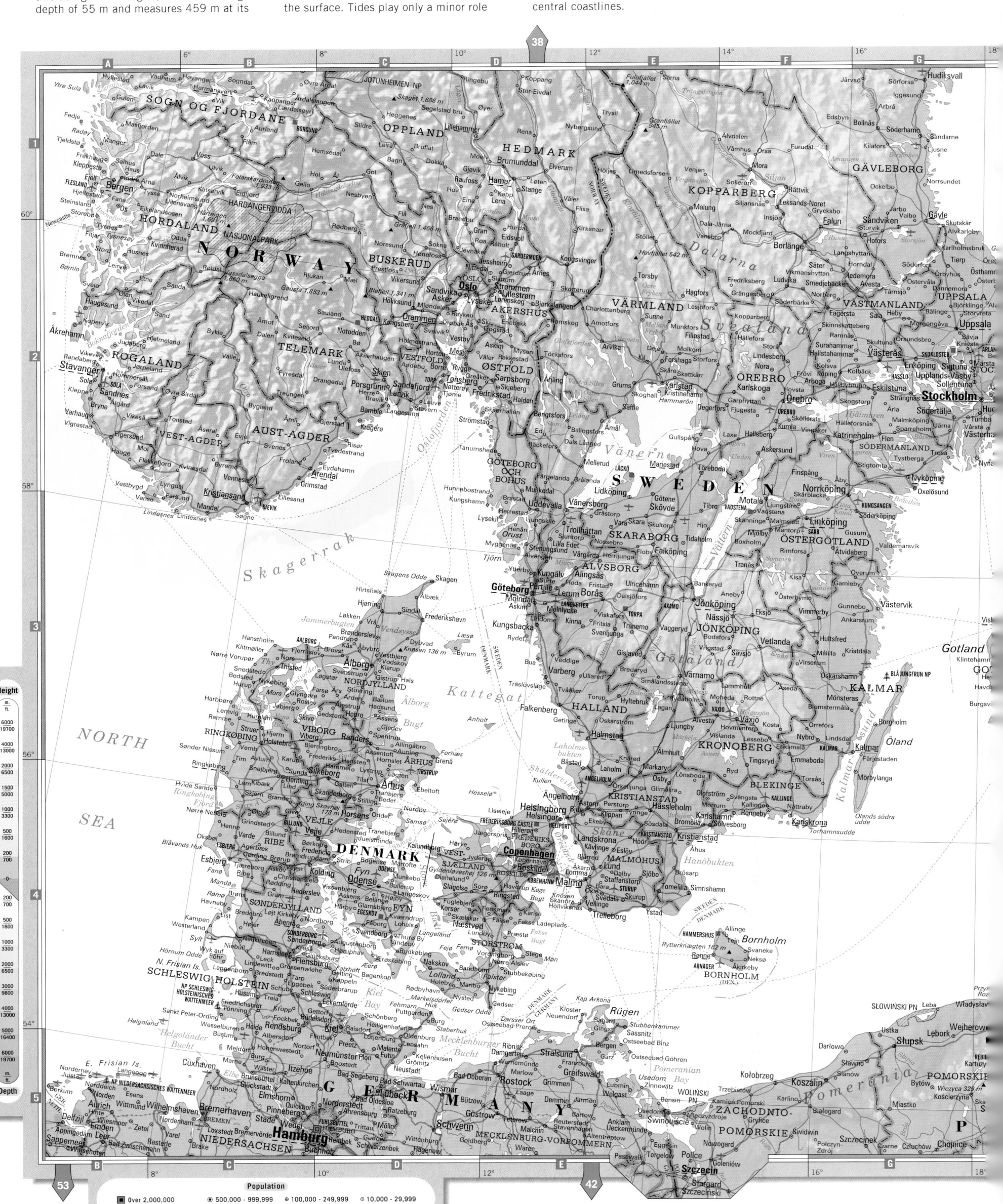

Height

m.	ft.
6000	19700
4000	13000
2000	6500
1500	5000
1000	3300
500	1600
200	700
-0-	
200	700
500	1600
1000	3300
2000	6500
3000	9800
5000	16400
6000	19700

Depth

Population

■ Over 2,000,000	◉ 500,000 - 999,999	◉ 100,000 - 249,999	○ 10,000 - 29,999
■ 1,000,000 - 1,999,999	◉ 250,000 - 499,999	◉ 30,000 - 99,999	○ Under 10,000

38

RESPUBLIKA KARELIYA

Gulf of Bothnia

J 20° K 22° L 24° M 26° N 28° P 30° Q 32°

Mäntyluoto Noormarkku Yiöjärvi Orivesi ISOJÄRVEN KP Kuhmoinen Sysmä Mäntyharju Ristiina Rautjärvi Elisenvaara Kurkijoki Vidlitsa Olonets Megrega

PORI Pirkkala Nokia Kangasala Tampere Kuohijärvi ITÄ-SUOMEN LÄÄNI Savitaipale Imatra Svetogorsk Kamennogorsk Priozersk **Lake Ladoga**

Pori Ulvila Vammala TAMPERE-PIRKKALA Lempäälä Valkeakoski Lammi Heinola Vuohijärvi Lappeenranta Joutseno L. Vuoksa Kuz'molovskiy Mys Volchiy Nos

Rauma Eurajoki Eura LÄNSI- Hämeenlinna Hollola Lahti Kuusankoski Valkeala Kouvola Salpausselkä Selznëvo Vyborg Zhitkovo LENINGRADSKAYA

SUOMEN Kauttua Säkylä Pyhäjärvi Forssa Janakkala Hauskärvi Orimattila Elimäki Anjalankoski Karhula Hamina Primorsk Vysotsk OBLAST'

Mynämäki LÄÄNI Jokioinen Tammela Loppi Riihimäki Mäntsälä Porvoo Kotka Vyborg Bay Zelenogorsk Pesochnyy Pargolovo Verkhniye Osel'ki

Uusikaupunki TURKU Raisio Lieto Somero Karkkila Vihti Tuusula Kerava Järvenpää (Borgå) Ushkovo Sestroretsk Repino **ST. PETERSBURG** Volkhov

Naantali Turku Kaarina Paimio Halikko Nummi HELSINKI-VANTAA Sibbo Kronshtadt Lisiy Nos Lomonosovo Mga Novaya Maluksa

Åland (Åbo) Pargas Salo Lohja Espoo (Sipoo) SUOMENLINNA Gogland Moshchnyy Seskar Petrodvorets PULKOVO Pushkin Kolpino Ul'yanovka Motokhovo

Eckerö Finström (Parainen) Perniö Pohja Kirkkonummi **Helsinki** (Helsingfors) Lomonosovo Strel'na Pavlovsk Tosno Ushaki Kirishi Budogoshch'

MARIEHAMN Houtskär Korpo (Pojo) Ekenäs (Kyrkslätt) Gostilitsy Kipen' Gatchina Susanino Vyritsa Grvady

hamn Marianhamina Korppoo Hanko (Tammisaari) FIN. RUS. **Gulf of Finland** Ust'-Luga Kotly Begunitsy Volosovo Yelizavetino Siverskiy

(Mariehamn) Lemland Föglö (Hangö) EST. EST. Juminda Nina Purikari Neem **Narva Bay** Luga Bay Kas'kovo Kommunar Chudovo

Ahvenanmaa Kökar Paldiski Keila Kolgakula LAHEMAA NP Kunda Kohtla-Järve Sillamäe Narva Ivangorod Kingisepp Toropets

Kõrgessaare Tahkuna Nina Rakvere Viru-Jaagupi Jõhvi Narva-Jõesuu Slantsy Os'mino Tēsovo-Netyl'skiy Malaya Vishera

Hiiumaa Kärdla Hullo Paivere Risti Maardu Raasiku Kehra Tapa Kadrina Tudu Iisaku **Narva Res.**

Tallinn ÜLEMISTE Kohila Rapla Järva-Jaani Mustvee Alajõe Gdov Lyady Strugi-Krasnyye Luga Dubrovka Batetskiy **Novgorod**

Pöösapää Neem Riguldi Vormsi Haapsalu Märjamaa Paide Koigi Jõgeva Kallaste Yamm Nikolayevo Utorgosh Shimsk **L. Il'men'**

Kullamaa Türi Põltsamaa Puurmani Koosa **Lake Peipus** Sol'tsy Staraya Russa Pola

Saaremaa Kärevere Tartu Mehikoorma EST. RUS. NOVGORODSKAYA OBLAST

Emmaste Muhu Kuivastu Lihula Kivi-Vigala Vändra Suure-Jaani Puhja Rõngu Elva Räpina **Lake Pskov** Pavy Dno Staraya Russa

Leisi Orissaare Virtsu Koonga Lavassaare Tootsi Viljandi Abja-Paluoja Otepää Veriora Värska Pskov Volot Poddor'ye

Kuressaare Pärnu Sindi Kilingi-Nõmme Mõisaküla Tõrva Kuutse Mägi 217 m Antsla Võru Pechory Novoizborsk Karamyshevo Porkhov Kholm

Salme Kihnu **ESTONIA** Vörtsjärv Ruhnu Ainaži Staicele Mazsalaca Valga Munamägi 318 m Apē Ostrov PSKOVSKAYA Dedovichi **RUSSIA**

Gotska Sandön GOTSKA SANDÖN NP Sõrve Säär Säare **Gulf of Riga** EST. LAT. Rūjiena Valka Gauja NP Alūksne Liepna Vilaka Chikhachëvo Pytalovo Novgorodka Novorzhev Podberez'ye **TVERSKAYA OBLAST'**

Kolkasrags Mazirbe Kolka Limbaži Valmiera Smiltene Lejasciems Vyshgorod Pushkinskiye Gory Opochka Kholm

BALTIC Ovīsi Dundaga Roja **GAUJA NP** Cēsis Rauna Gaujiena Gulbene Balvi Rugāji Loknya PSKOVSKAYA OBLAST'

Ventspils Valdemarpils Mērsrags SPILVE Sigulda Ligatne Jaunpiebalga Vecpiebalga Ceavine Vilaka Novosokol'niki Kun'ya **Velikiye Luki**

FÅRÖN Piltene Ugāle Talsi Engure **LATVIA** Ērgļi Madona Lubāna Kārsava Idritsa Sebezh

Fårösund Renda Kandava Tukums Jūrmala **Riga** Ogre Gaizina Kalns 311 m Barkava Viļāni Rēzekne Zilupe Nevel'

Pāvilosta SWEDEN LATVIA Sabile Kuldīga Saldus Dobele Jelgava Baldone Jaunjelgava Skrīveri Koknese Varakļāni Ludza Dagda **RUSSIA BELARUS'**

SEA Aizpute Durbe Skrunda Broceni Bene Olaine Iecava Bauska Skaistkalne Viesite Jēkabpils Līvāni Preiļi Malta Rundēni

Liepāja Grobiņa Vainode Auce Eleja Vecumnieki Zasa Aknīste Spoģi Dagda Dūdz Novosokol'niki

Nīca Priekule Ylakiai Mažeikiai Žagarē Joniškis Biržai Nereta Subate LATVIA BELARUS' Bigosovo

Rucava Skuodas Viekšniai Naujoji-Akmenė Pasvalys Pandėlys Juodupė Rokiškis Obeliai **Daugavpils** Krāslava Druya Verkhnedvinsk Polatsk Gorodok Surazh

Palanga Darbėnai Seda Papilė Gruzdžiai Kuršėnai Linkuva Pakruojis Vabalninkas Kupiškis Kamajai Dusetos Svedasai Skrudaliena Turmantas Druya Disna Navapolatsk

Kretinga Plungė Telšiai Varniai Radviliškis **Šiauliai** Joniškelis Kelme Šeduva Naujamiestis Troškūnai Anykščiai Zarasai Visaginas Dūkštas Miory Vetrino Polatsk **Vitsyebsk**

Klaipėda Gargždai Kražiai Tytuvenai Baisogala **Panevėžys** Ramygala Utena AUKŠTAITIJA NP Ignalina Sharkawshchyna VITSYEBSKAYA Ushachi Liozno

KURŠIU NERIJA NP Priekulė Švėkšna Šilalė Kelmė Seta Kavarskas Molėtai Švenčionys Adutiškis Pastavy Varapayeva Hlybokaye VOBLASTS' Beshankovichy

Neringa Šilutė Žemaičiu Naumiestis Raseiniai Skaudvilė Ariogala Kėdainiai Žeimiai Žely Giedraičiai Pabrade Švenčionėliai Lyntupy Krulevshchizna Chashniki Senno Orekhovsk

Kurshskaya Kosa Rusne Pagėgiai Tauragė Vandžiogala Jonava Širvintos Nemenčinė Naroch Dokshytsy Lyepyel' Bogushëvsk Ol'sha

Zelenogradsk Sovetsk Nemunas Neman Jurbarkas Vilkija **Kaunas** **Vilnius** Ostrovets Smorgon' Smarhon' Bobr Kokhanovo Orsha

Svetlogorsk Neman Zhilino Šakiai Kačerginė KAUNAS **LITHUANIA** TRAKAI NP Baltoji Voke Medininkai Krivichi Maladzyechna Barysaw **Dubrovno**

Yantarnyy Kurshskiy Zaliv Bol'shakovo Kudirkos-Naumiestis Kazlu Ruda Garliava Elektrenai Prienai Birštonas VILNIUS Jieznas Smorgon' Vileyka Zhodino Tolochin

Primorsk Svetlyy **RUSSIA** Chernyakhovsk Kybartai Vilkaviškis Šalčininkai Šumskas Pleshchenitsy Barán'

Kaliningrad Gvardeysk Gusev Marijampolė Balbieriškis Varėna Eišiškės Dieveniškes Gora Lysaya 342 m Zhodina **MAHILYOW**

Baltiysk KALININGRADSKAYA Mamonovo Bagrationovsk Novostroyevo Zheleznodorozhnyy Kalvarija Simnas Alytus Daugai Valkininkai Voronovo Volozhin Gorodok Smolevichi **Mahilyow**

Mierzeja OBLAST' RUSSIA POLAND Gołdap Lazdijai DZUKIJA NP Merkinė Vareña Voronovo Yuratishki Krasnoye Ostroshitskiy Gorodok Berezino MAHILYOWSKAYA

Wiślana Braniewo Bartoszyce Węgorzewo Szeszke-Wzgorza 309 m Suwałki Druskininkai Eišiškės Dzyatlava Zaslavl' Chervyen' VOBLASTS'

Elbląg Pieniężno Górowo Sejny Veisiejai Leipalingis HRODZYENSKAYA Ivyanets **Minsk** Rudensk Bykhaw

Tolkmicko Orneta Lidzbark Warmiński Korsze Kętrzyn Gizycko Olecko Augustów PODLASKIE Porech'ye Skidel' **Hrodna** Ozёry Shchuchin Lida VOBLASTS' MINSKAYA Dzerzhinsk Gresk Negoreloye

ELBLĄG Pasłęk Morąg Dobre Miasto Reszel Mrągowo Orzysz Ełk Grajewo Białostocka Voronovo MINSK Stolbtsy Novogrudok

Tczew Susz Ostróda **WARMIŃSKO-MAZURSKIE** Mikołajki Ruciane-Nida Dąbrowa Śniardwy Narew POLAND

POLAND Morąg Iława Biskupiec Barczewo Szczytno

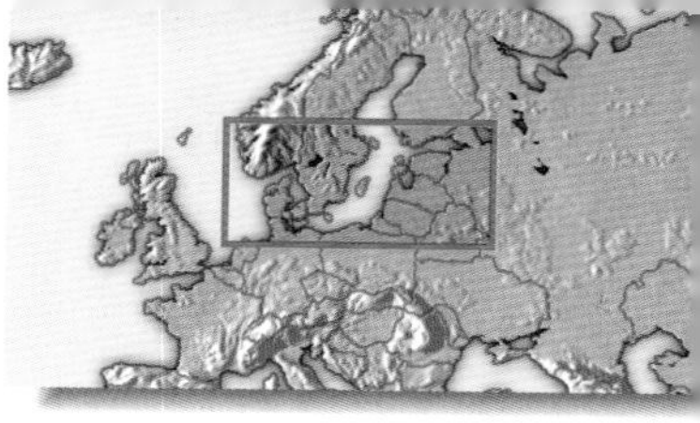

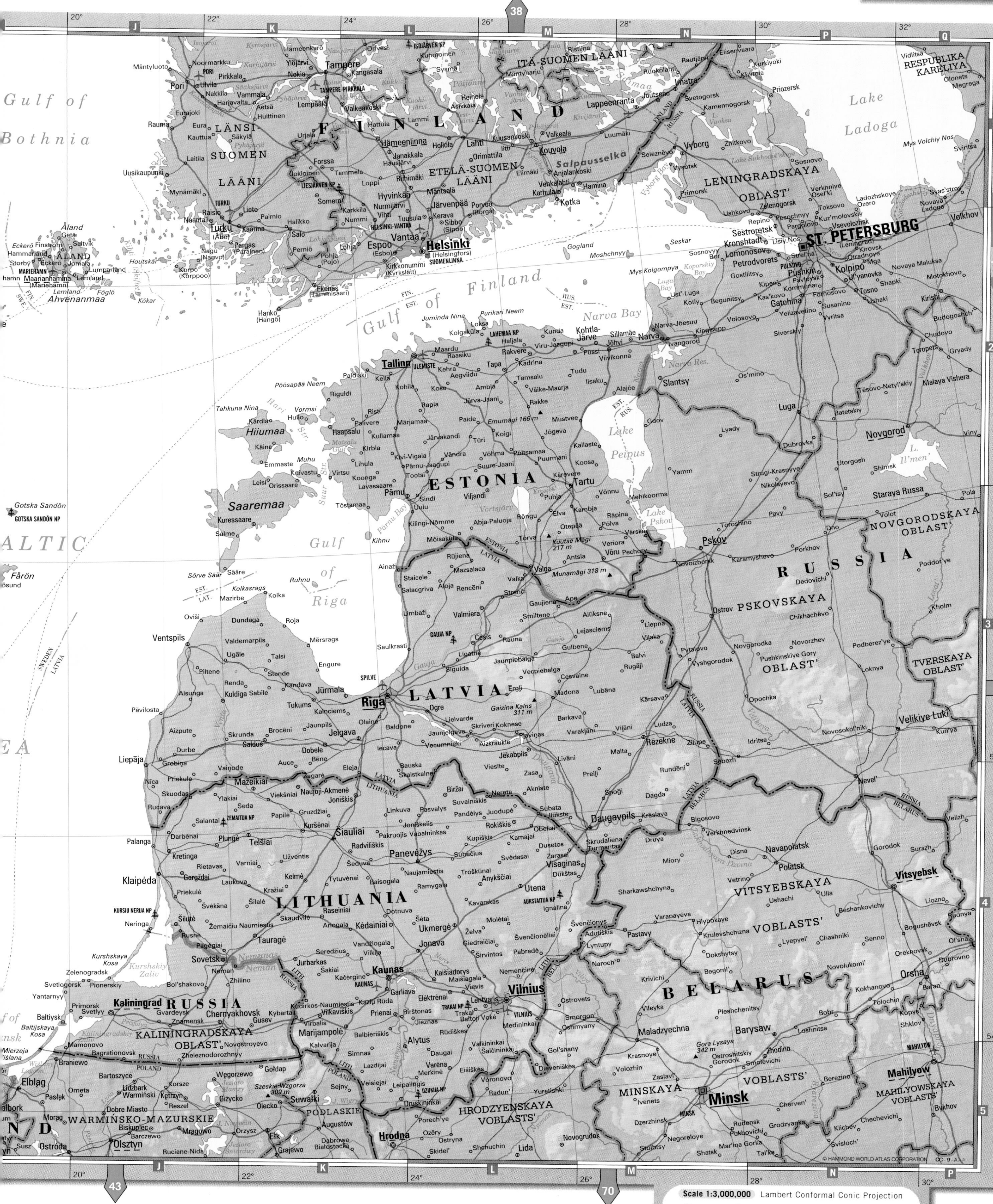

Scale 1:3,000,000 Lambert Conformal Conic Projection

MI 0 25 50 75 100

KM 0 25 50 75 100 125 150

© HAMMOND WORLD ATLAS CORPORATION

OC – 9 – A

Next to the Rhine, the Elbe (1,165 km) is the longest and busiest river in North Central Europe. Its drainage basin encompasses some 144,000 square km. The Elbe flows from its source at 1,500 m above sea in the Riesengebirge Range in the Czech Republic to its mouth in the North Sea at Cuxhaven in Germany where it reaches a width of 15 km. Hamburg marks the beginning of the long (100 km) Elbe estuary, in which tidal activity is significant as far up-river as Geesthacht. Although international treaties have brought some improvement in water quality, the Elbe is still one of the most heavily polluted rivers in Europe.

Scale 1:3,000,000 Lambert Conformal Conic Projection

About 1,200 km long and up to 250 km wide, the Alps are the largest mountain system in Europe. Their highest peak is Mont Blanc (4,807 m). The Alps occupy an area of 220,000 square km and form the watershed between the North Sea and the Mediterranean Sea along the north-south axis and between the Black Sea and the Mediterranean Sea to the east. Geologically speaking, the Alps are a young mountain system and continue to rise at a rate of several millimeters per year due to continental drift, growing higher as the African Plate presses against the European.

West Central Europe

Scale 1:3,000,000   Lambert Conformal Conic Projection

© Hammond World Atlas Corporation   CC-1015-AaA

The central core of the Iberian Peninsula is the Meseta plateau, which is almost completely surrounded by mountain ranges. This ring of mountains is encircled by narrow bands of coastal lowlands.

The topographic pattern is reflected in the vegetation. Sheep graze in the grassy areas and juniper groves of the sparse highlands where vast fields of wheat and sunflowers yield modest harvests. Olive groves and maquis-garrigue growth are the dominant features of lowland vegetation, which is interspersed with oaks. The valleys of rivers such as the Ebro and the Guadalquivir are intensely cultivated.

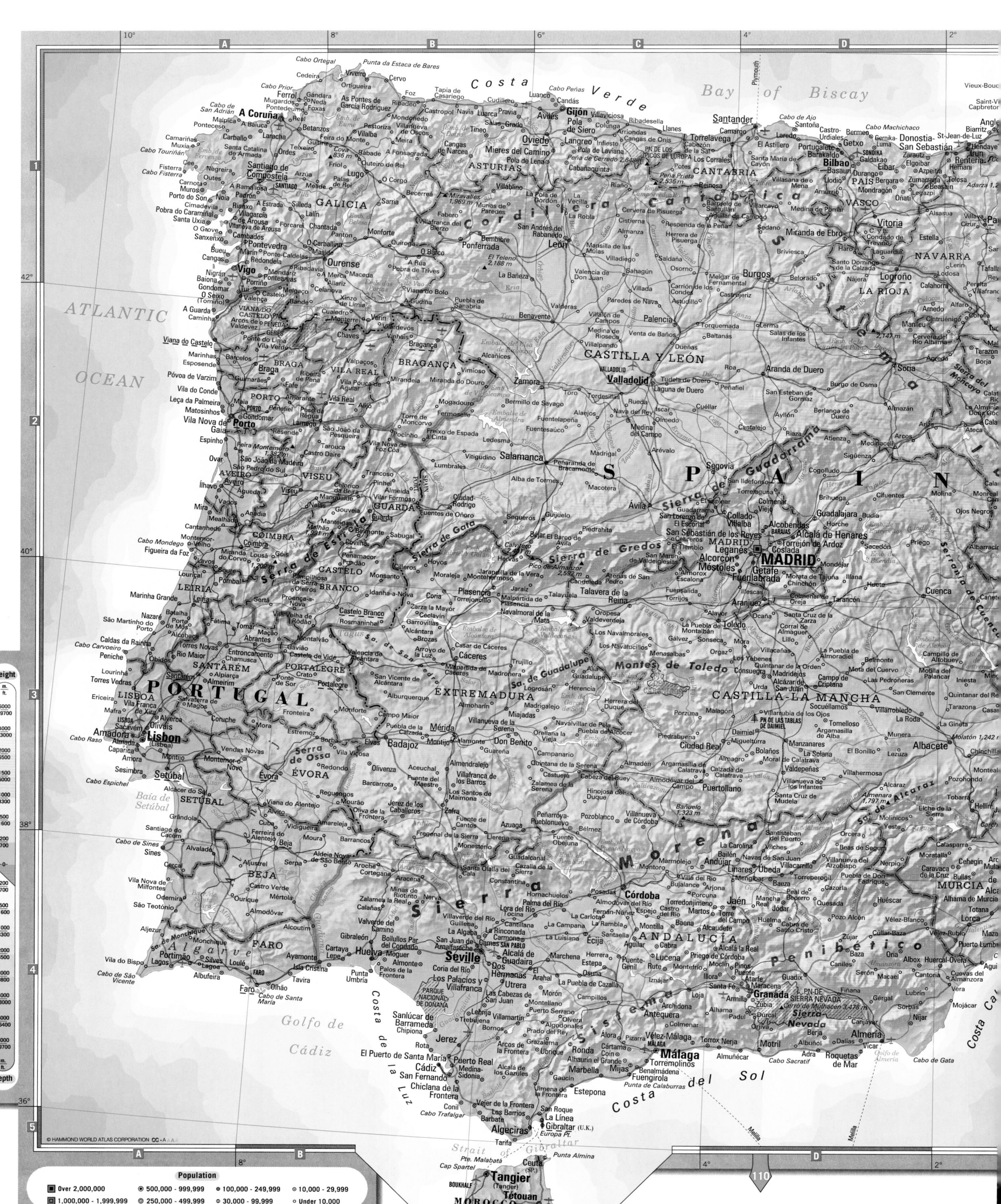

44   64

F   G   H   J

MIDI-PYRÉNÉES
BLAGNAC
Montauban
Toulouse
Castres
FRANCE
Albi
Ganges
Nîmes
Châteaurenard
Cavaillon
Pierrevert
Manosque
Apt
Grasse
CÔTE D'AZUR
Monaco
Nice
Antibes
Cannes
PROVENCE-ALPES-CÔTE D'AZUR
Aix-en-Provence
Arles
Salon-de-Provence
Marseille
Cap Croisette
Toulon
La Ciotat
Hyères
Côte d'Azur

Perpignan
LANGUEDOC-ROUSSILLON
Narbonne
Carcassonne
Foix
ANDORRA
Andorra la Vella
Figueres
Roses
Costa Brava
Girona (Gerona)

Gulf of Lion

Huesca
Saragossa
ARAGÓN
Lleida (Lérida)
CATALUÑA
Manresa
Terrassa
Sabadell
Mataró
Barcelona
L'Hospitalet de Llobregat
El Prat de Llobregat
Sitges
Tarragona
Reus
Costa Dorada

MEDITERRANEAN

Castellón de la Plana
VALENCIA
Valencia
Costa del Azahar
Gandía
Dénia
Alcoy
Benidorm
Alicante
Elche
Torrevieja
Costa Blanca
Cabo de Palos
Cartagena

Golfo de Valencia

Minorca (Menorca)
Ciutadella
Mahón
MENORCA
Pollença
Alcúdia
Sóller
Inca
Sa Pobla
Artà
Capdepera
Son Servera
Manacor
Mallorca
Palma de Mallorca
PALMA MALLORCA
Llucmajor
Campos
Felanitx
Santanyí
Cabo de ses Salinas
Cabrera
ISLAS BALEARES
Ibiza
Sant Antoni de Portmany
Santa Eulalia del Rio
San José
Ibiza (Eivissa)
Formentera

Balearic Islands (Islas Baleares)

SEA

ALGERIA
Bou Kadir

Barcelona inset (K / L):
Manresa
El Montcau
La Garriga
Sant Celoni
PARQUE NATURAL DEL MONTSENY
Montserrat 1,236 m
CATALUÑA
Terrassa
Sabadell
Granollers
Arenys de Mar
Mataró
Premià de Mar
Rubí
Montcada i Reixac
Badalona
Santa Coloma de Gramenet
Sant Adrià de Besòs
Barcelona
L'Hospitalet de Llobregat
CASTELL DE MONTJUIC
Viladecans
Gavà
El Prat de Llobregat
Castelldefels
Sitges
Vilanova i la Geltrú
MEDITERRANEAN SEA
Mahón
0   10 Mi / 0   10 Km
© HAMMOND W.A.C.   CD-1103 - A - A A

Madrid inset (M / N):
Siete Picos 2,138 m
Sierra de Guadarrama
Puerto de Navacerrada
CASTILLA-LA MANCHA
Guadarrama
Collado-Villalba
San Lorenzo de El Escorial
El Escorial
Galapagar
Torrelodones
Colmenar Viejo
San Sebastián de los Reyes
MADRID
Alcalá de Henares
Torrejón de Ardoz
Las Rozas de Madrid
Majadahonda
Pozuelo de Alarcón
Coslada
San Fernando de Henares
Boadilla del Monte
HORTALEZA
Villaviciosa de Odón
MADRID
VILLAVERDE
Alcorcón
Leganés
VALLECAS
Móstoles
Getafe
Fuenlabrada
Parla
Pinto
© HAMMOND W.A.C.   CD-1106 - A - A A

Azores inset (R / S):
Corvo
Santa Cruz das Flores
Flores
ATLANTIC
Santa Cruz da Graciosa
Graciosa
Terceira
LAJES
Praia da Vitória
Angra do Heroísmo
Faial
Horta
São Jorge
Velas
Calheta
São Roque do Pico
Ponta do Pico 2,351 m
Pico
Lajes
São Miguel
Ribeira Grande
Póvoação
NORDELA
Ponta Delgada
Vila Franca do Campo
AZORES (PORTUGAL)
OCEAN
Santa Maria
Vila do Porto
0   60 Mi / 0   60 Km
© HAMMOND W.A.C.   CD-1102 - A - A A

Lisbon inset (P / Q):
Ericeira
Vila Franca de Xira
Mafra
Malveira
Bucelas
Alhandra
Samora Correia
SANTARÉM
São João das Lampas
Montelavar
Loures
Sacavém
Colares
Sintra
Odivelas
LISBOA
Moscavide
Cabo da Roca
Serra de Sintra
Belas
Amadora
Alcochete
Cabo Raso
Paço de Queluz
ALFAMA
Montijo
Estoril
Carnaxide
BELÉM TOWER
Lisbon (Lisboa)
Rio Frio
Cascais
Parede
Oeiras
Almada
Baixa da Banheira
Pinhal Novo
Costa da Caparica
Barreiro
Moita
Caparica
Seixal
SETÚBAL
Amora
Palmela
São Lourenço
Setúbal
ATLANTIC OCEAN
Alfarim
Baía de Setúbal
Tróia
Cabo Espichel
Sesimbra
Outão
0   10 Mi / 0   10 Km
CD-1101 - A - A A

Scale 1:3,000,000   Lambert Conformal Conic Projection
MI 0   25   50   75   100
KM 0   25   50   75   100   125   150

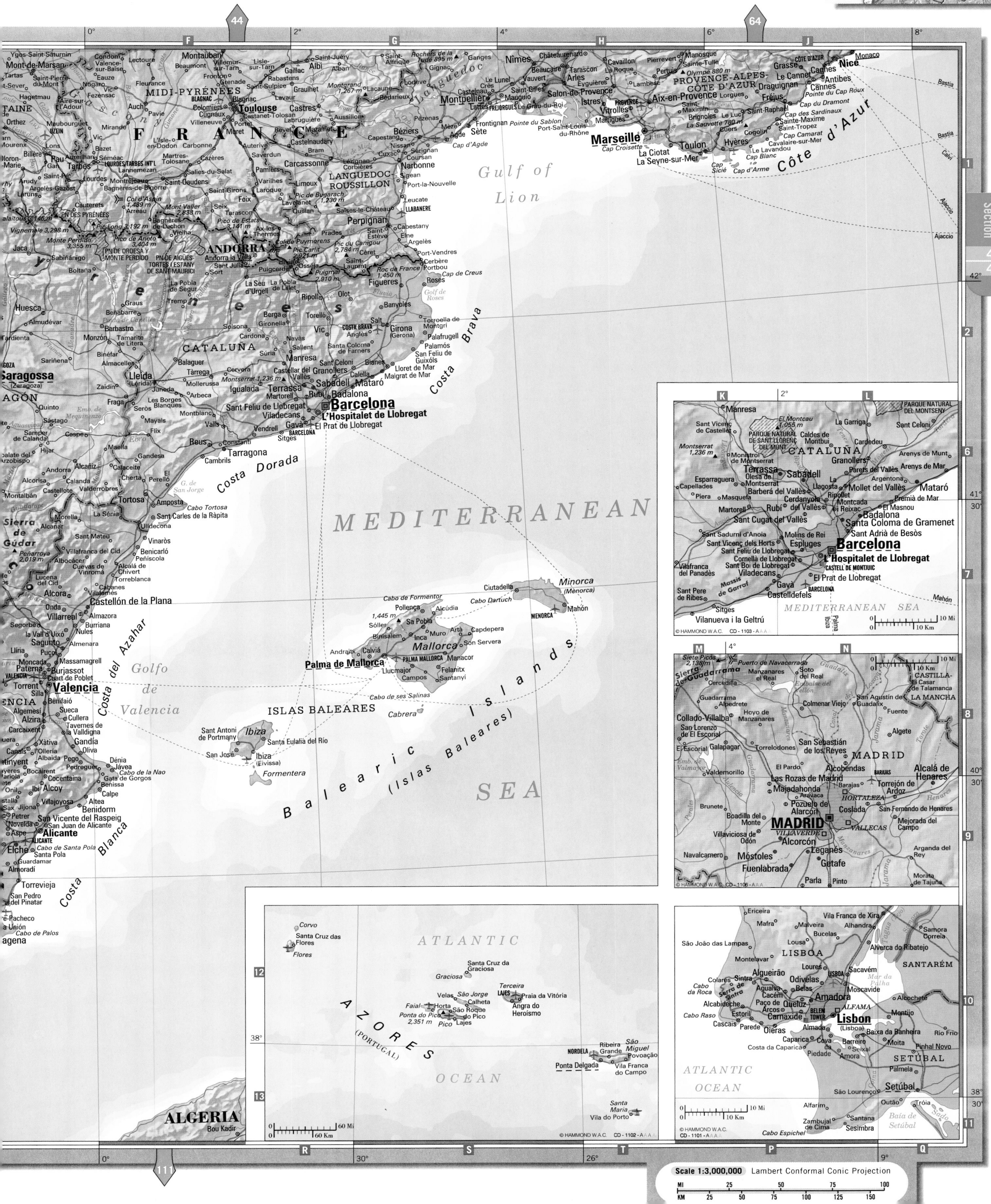

The once remarkably fertile and heavily forested Mediterranean region suffers today from soil erosion and a severe shortage of water. Deforestation began with the ancient Greeks and Romans, who needed huge quantities of wood for heating and ship-building. Forest fires are still a regular summer occurrence. The exposed soil is carried off by rain, thus depleting a valuable water storage medium.

Rivers often run dry during the summer months, particularly in the south, where rain does not fall for as much as six months at a time.

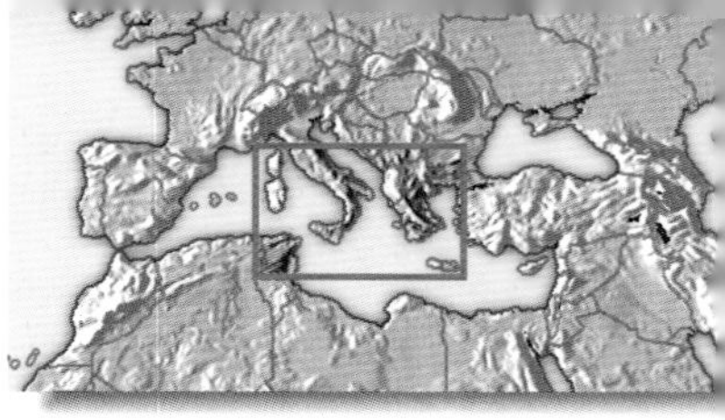

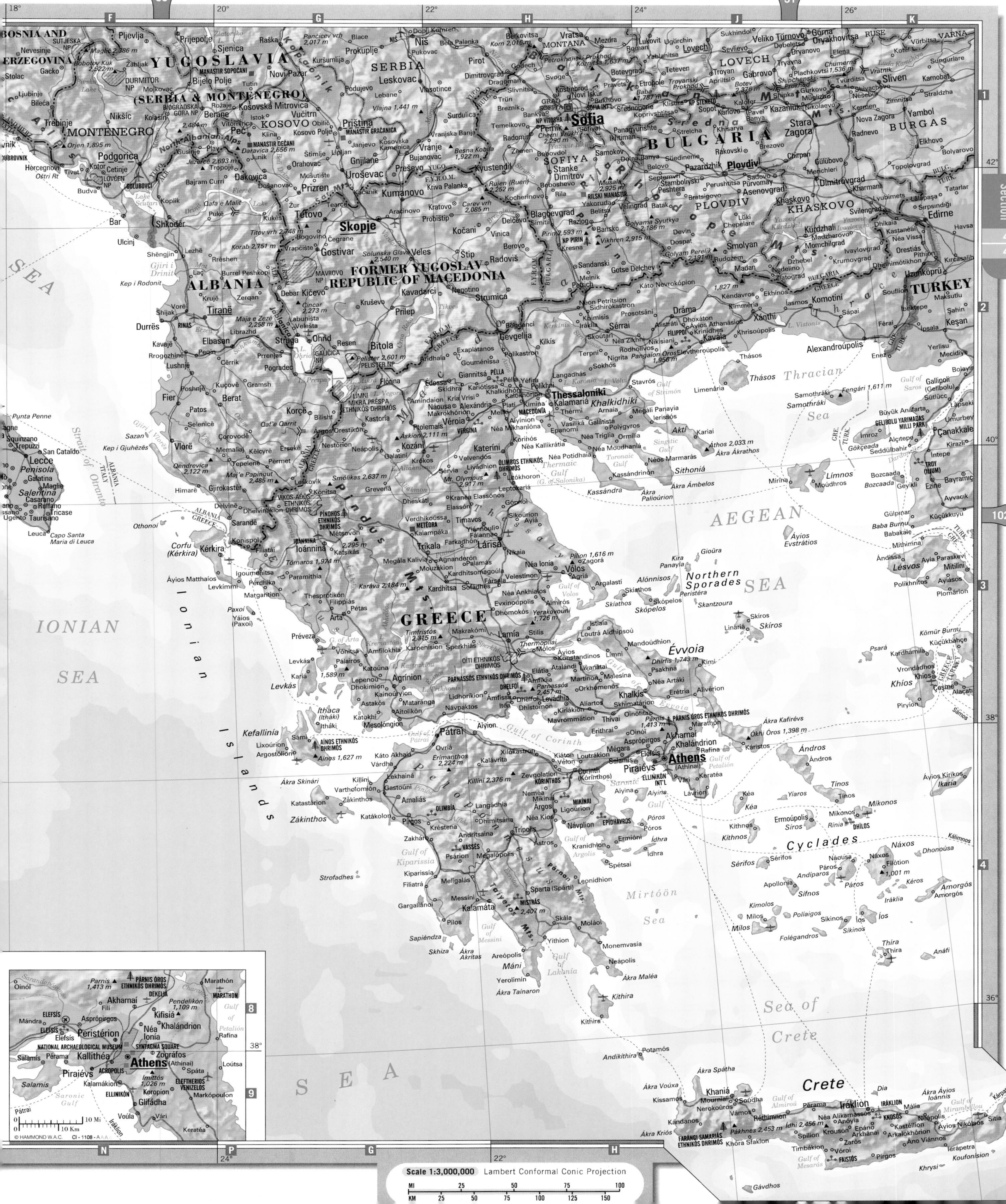

When the Alps and neighboring mountain ranges formed during the Tertiary some 65 million years ago, the folding process extended into the Mediterranean region, creating the Dinaric Alps on the western Balkan Peninsula. The ridges of these folds can be seen today along the Dalmatian coast, where they rise from the sea as elongated islands. The troughs of the folded range are covered by water.

The product of a similar upthrusting process, the Carpathians are cut by the Danube, which is 2,850 km long and second only to the Volga among the longest rivers of Europe.

Scale 1:3,000,000 Lambert Conformal Conic Projection

Netherlands, Northwestern Germany

In the 15th century, the Dutch began building a system of dykes to protect their land, much of which lies below sea level, from the sea. A massive seawall now separates the former North Sea bay of the Zuidersee from the North Sea, transforming it into a fresh-water lake-- the IJsselmeer. Parts of the lake have been drained, creating new areas of dry land known as polders.

Population
- ■ Over 2,000,000
- ● 500,000 - 999,999
- ● 100,000 - 249,999
- ◉ 10,000 - 29,999
- ● 250,000 - 499,999
- ● 30,000 - 99,999
- ○ Under 10,000

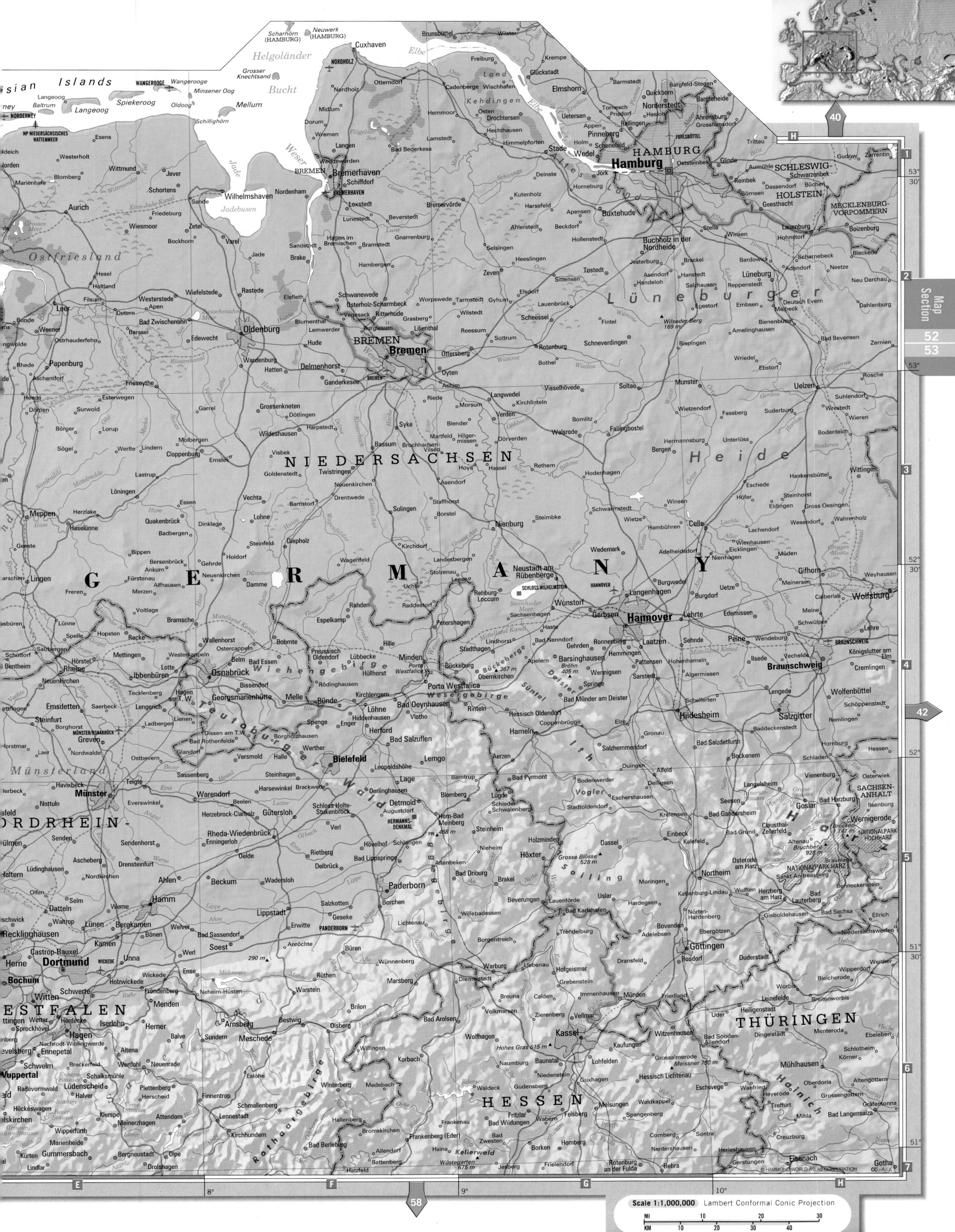

Frisian Islands
Helgoländer Bucht
Scharhörn (HAMBURG)
Neuwerk (HAMBURG)
Grosser Knechtsand
Wangerooge
Spiekeroog
Langeoog
Baltrum
Norderney
Minsener Oog
Mellum
Oldoog
Schillighörn
NP NIEDERSÄCHSISCHES WATTENMEER
Ostfriesland
Jadebusen
Cuxhaven
Brunsbüttel
Wilster
Elbe
Kehdingen
Glückstadt
Elmshorn
Norderstedt
Quickborn
Bargfeld-Stegen
Bargteheide
Ahrensburg
Uetersen
Pinneberg
Wedel
Stade
Buxtehude
HAMBURG
Hamburg
FUHLSBÜTTEL
SCHLESWIG-HOLSTEIN
MECKLENBURG-VORPOMMERN
Geesthacht
Lauenburg
Boizenburg
Reinbek
Buchholz in der Nordheide
Lüneburg
Lüneburger Heide
Wilseder Berg 169 m
Esens
Aurich
Wittmund
Jever
Schortens
Wilhelmshaven
Nordenham
Bremerhaven
BREMEN
BREMERHAVEN
Varel
Leer
Westerstede
Oldenburg
Delmenhorst
BREMEN
Bremen
Papenburg
Verden
Rotenburg
Soltau
Uelzen
Munster
Celle
NIEDERSACHSEN
Cloppenburg
Vechta
Meppen
Lingen
Nienburg
Neustadt am Rübenberge
Steinhuder Meer
Wunstorf
HANNOVER
Hannover
Langenhagen
Gifhorn
Wolfsburg
Braunschweig
BRAUNSCHWEIG
Wolfenbüttel
Salzgitter
Hildesheim
G E R M A N Y
Dümmer
Osnabrück
Rheine
Ibbenbüren
MÜNSTER/OSNABRÜCK
Greven
Münster
Münsterland
Teutoburger Wald
Wiehengebirge
Wesergebirge
Minden
Porta Westfalica
Bückeberge
Deister
Süntel
Bad Oeynhausen
Herford
Bielefeld
Gütersloh
Detmold
HERMANNS-DENKMAL
Hameln
Ith
Paderborn
PADERBORN
Eggegebirge
Höxter
Holzminden
Solling
Grosse Blösse 528 m
Northeim
Göttingen
Einbeck
Goslar
Harz
Brocken 1141 m
NATIONALPARK HOCHHARZ
NATIONALPARK HARZ
Wernigerode
SACHSEN-ANHALT
NORDRHEIN-WESTFALEN
Hamm
Recklinghausen
Dortmund
WICKEDE
Unna
Bochum
Witten
Hagen
Wuppertal
Lüdenscheid
Soest
Lippstadt
Warburg
Marsberg
Brilon
Meschede
Arnsberg
Möhnesee
Rothaargebirge
Winterberg
Bad Berleburg
Kassel
Hohes Gras 615 m
Meissner 750 m
Witzenhausen
HESSEN
Fritzlar
Bad Wildungen
Frankenberg (Eder)
Kellerwald
Wüstegarten 675 m
Rotenburg an der Fulda
Bebra
Eschwege
THÜRINGEN
Hainich
Mühlhausen
Bad Langensalza
Eisenach
Gotha
Heiligenstadt
Duderstadt
© HAMMOND WORLD ATLAS CORPORATION
53° 30'
53°
52° 30'
52°
51° 30'
51°
8°
9°
10°
E
F
G
H
1
2
3
4
5
6
7
40
42
58
Map Section
52
53
Scale 1:1,000,000
Lambert Conformal Conic Projection
MI 10 20 30
KM 10 20 30 40

An extension of the Middle Rhine Highlands, the Ardennes form a high plateau that stretches across much of northeastern Central Europe. Its highest point (694 m) is in the Hautes Fagnes (Belgium).

Exposed to the west, the heavily wooded, sparsely settled uplands dotted with numerous moors have a rugged climate. Average annual precipitation is 1,400 mm, and heavy snowfalls are common.

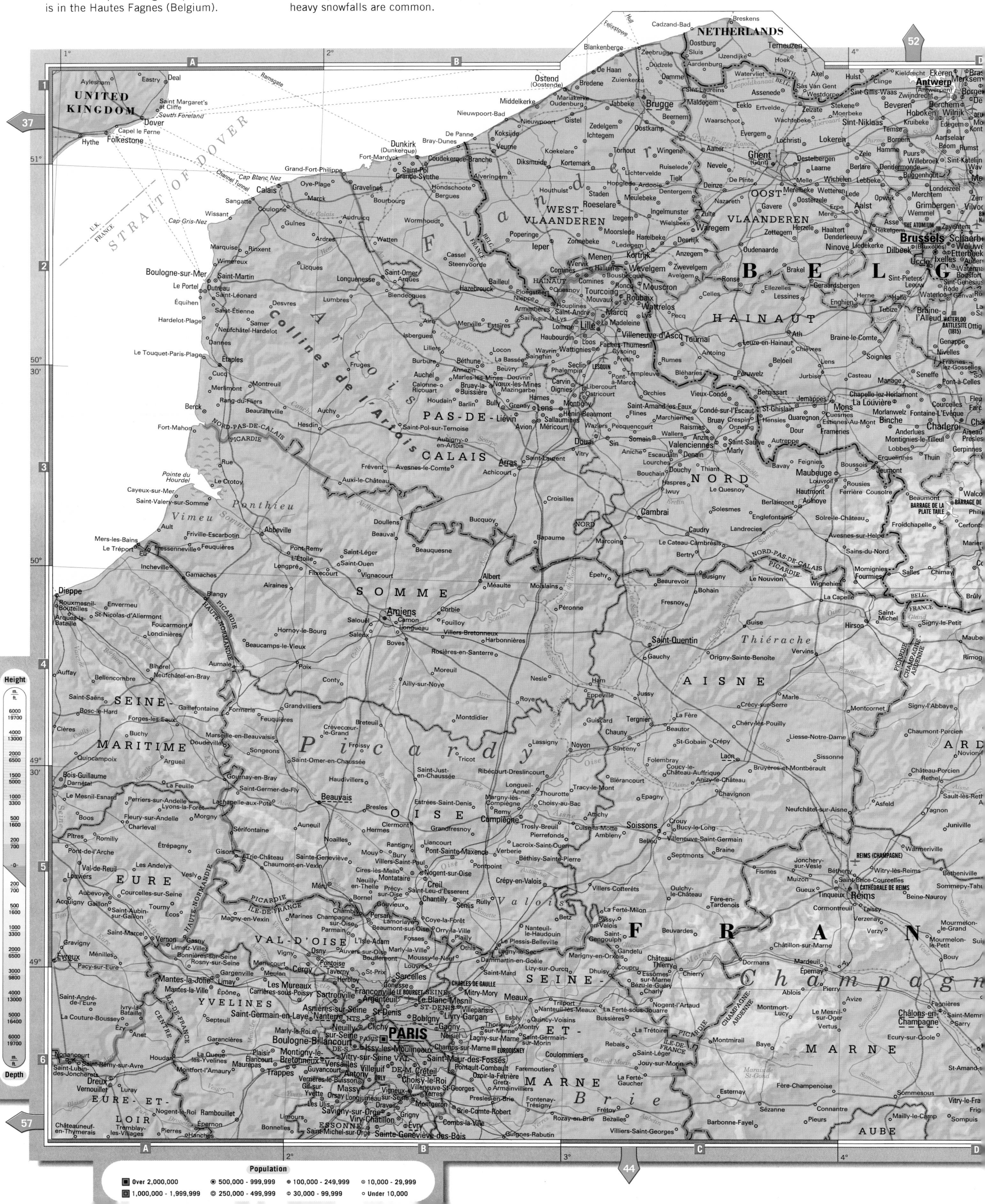

UNITED KINGDOM

NETHERLANDS

STRAIT OF DOVER

WEST-VLAANDEREN

OOST-VLAANDEREN

BELGIË

HAINAUT

NORD

PAS-DE-CALAIS

Collines de l'Artois

Ponthieu

Vimeu

SOMME

Picardy

AISNE

Thiérache

SEINE-MARITIME

EURE

OISE

VAL-D'OISE

YVELINES

ILE-DE-FRANCE

SEINE-ET-

MARNE

Brie

MARNE

AUBE

Champagne

Valois

HAUTE-NORMANDIE

PICARDIE

EURE-ET-LOIR

PARIS

Brussels
(Bruxelles)

Antwerp
(Antwerpen)

Ghent (Gent)

Lille

Amiens

Reims (CHAMPAGNE)

CATHÉDRALE DE REIMS

WATERLOO BATTLESITE (1815)

Height
m. / ft.
6000 / 19700
4000 / 13000
2000 / 6500
1500 / 5000
1000 / 3300
500 / 1600
200 / 700
-0-
200 / 700
500 / 1600
1000 / 3300
2000 / 6500
3000 / 9800
4000 / 13000
5000 / 16400
6000 / 19700
m. / ft.
Depth

Population
◼ Over 2,000,000   ◉ 500,000 - 999,999   ● 100,000 - 249,999   ◉ 10,000 - 29,999
◼ 1,000,000 - 1,999,999   ◉ 250,000 - 499,999   ● 30,000 - 99,999   ○ Under 10,000

NETHERLANDS

LIMBURG

Düsseldorf
Mönchengladbach

NORDRHEIN-WESTFALEN

Cologne (Köln)

Bonn

Aachen

MAASTRICHT
Maastricht

Liège

Verviers

Hautes Fagnes

L I È G E

Schneifel

E i f e l

G E R M A N Y

HESSEN

Wiesbaden

Mainz

RHEINLAND-PFALZ

Hunsrück

A r d e n n e s

LUXEMBOURG

DIEKIRCH

Oesling

GREVEN-MACHER

LUXEMBOURG

Trier

Koblenz

Bitburg

SAARLAND

Saarbrücken

Zweibrücken

Pfälzerwald

Landau in der Pfalz

Metz

MEUSE

MEURTHE-ET-MOSELLE

Nancy

MOSELLE

LORRAINE ALSACE

BAS-RHIN

Strasbourg

BADEN-WÜRTTEMBERG

Scale 1:1,000,000   Lambert Conformal Conic Projection

MI   10   20   30
KM   10   20   30   40

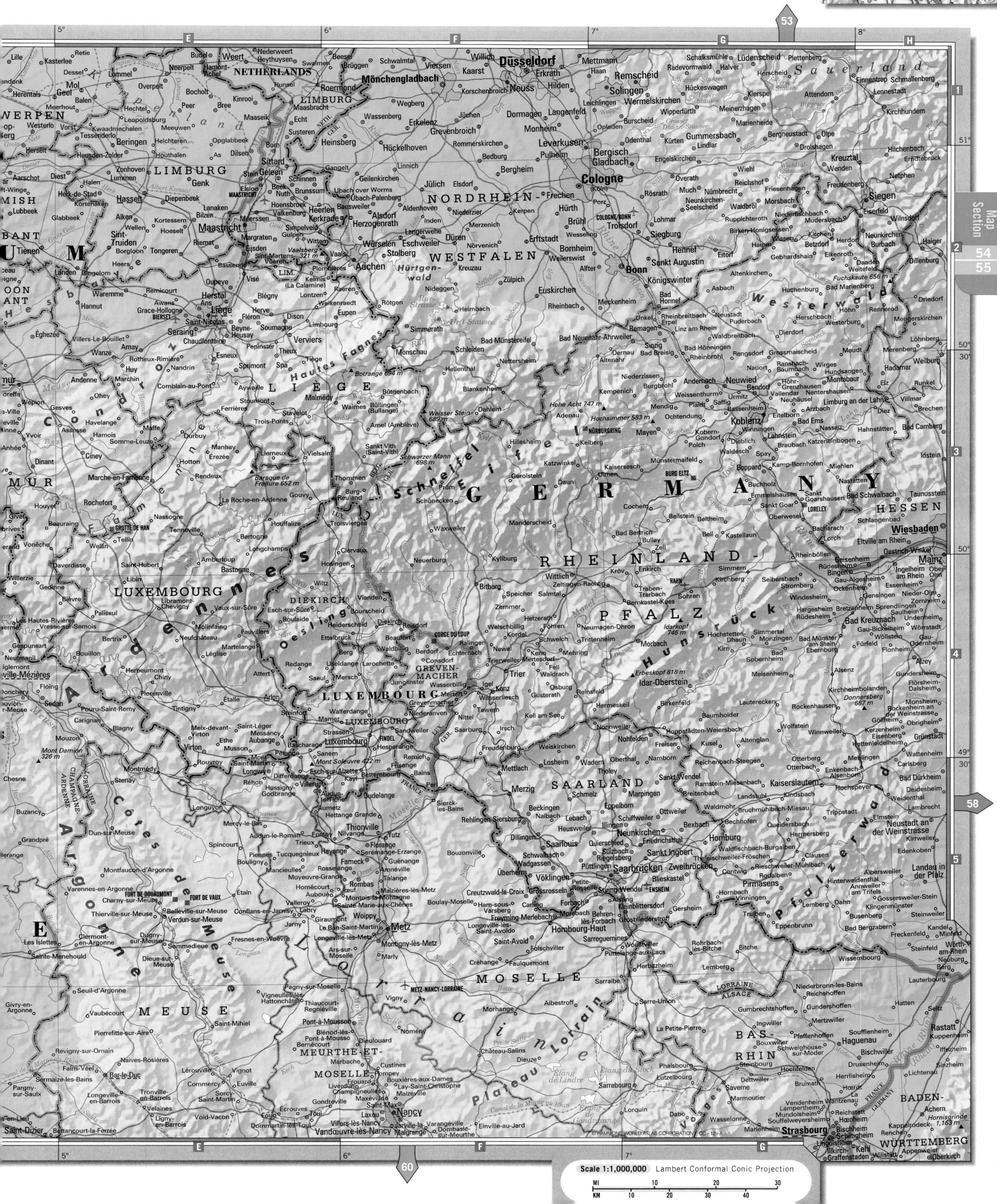

Tidal activity along the Channel coast of Normandy is unusually vigorous. In the Bay of Mont-Saint-Michel, the sea recedes several kilometers at low tide and rises roughly 15 m when the tide is in.

Normandy's gentle climate is favorable to agriculture, and vast fields of grain line the banks of the Seine and the Loire. The region is known for its orchards, which supply apples used in the production of cider and Calvados (apple brandy). Heaths, moors, and woodlands are prevalent in the highlands of Brittany, where the climate is much less agreeable.

Population

■ Over 2,000,000	◉ 500,000 - 999,999
▣ 1,000,000 - 1,999,999	◉ 250,000 - 499,999
● 100,000 - 249,999	○ 10,000 - 29,999
◦ 30,000 - 99,999	○ Under 10,000

Northwestern France

Scale 1:1,000,000 Lambert Conformal Conic Projection

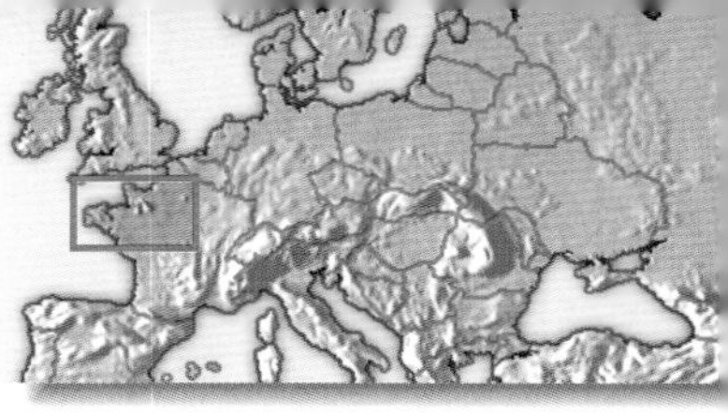

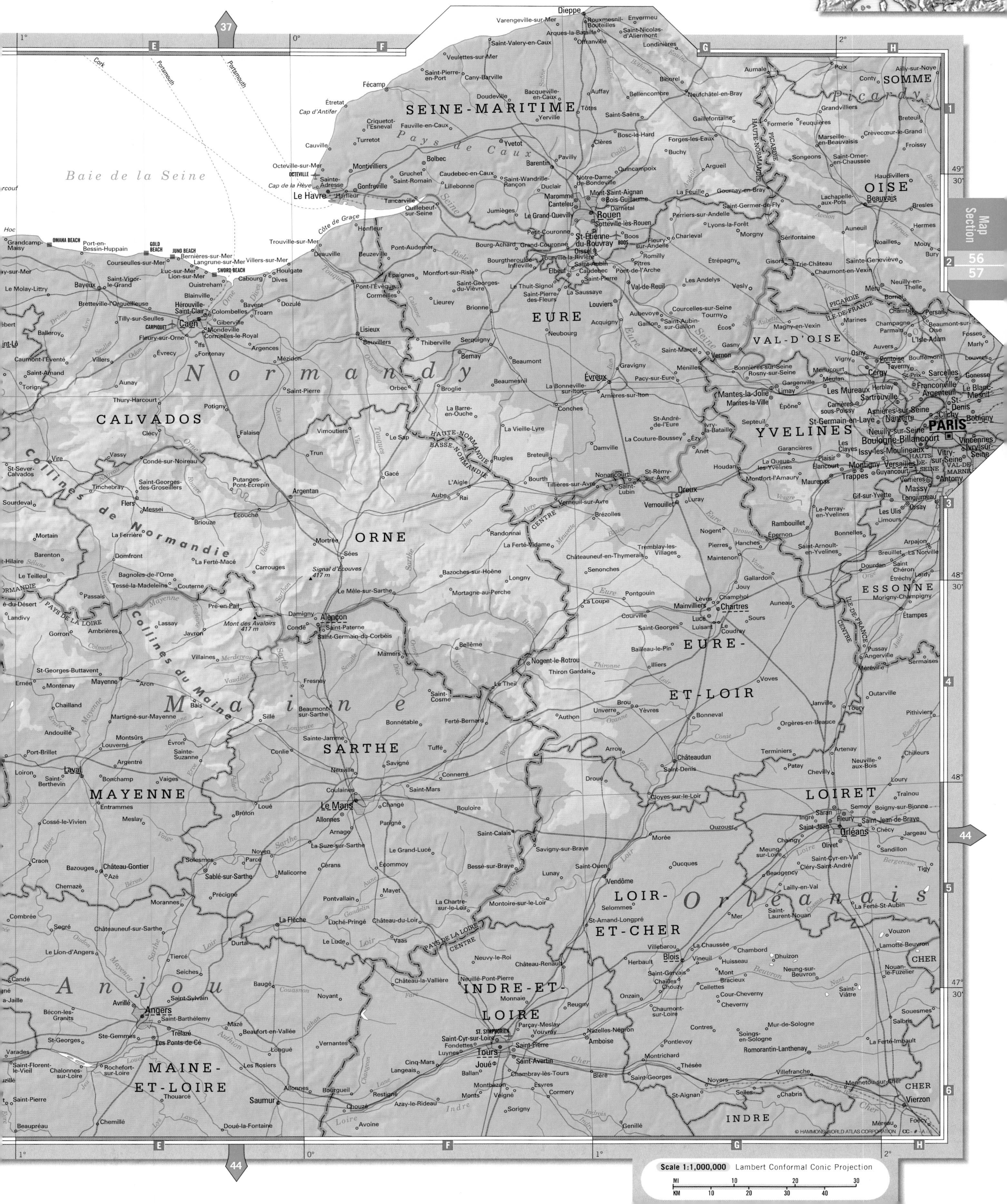

At first glance, the three neighboring central ranges of the Franconian-Thuringian uplands appear quite similar. The Fichtelgebirge, the Thüringer Wald and the Frankenwald are all covered by dense mountain forests. Yet each has its own unique features: the granite massifs of the Fichtelgebirge, the deep valleys that cut through the higher elevations of the Thüringer Wald, and the high plateaus of the Frankenwald. The central uplands extend eastward through the Erzgebirge, whose old mixed forests were largely destroyed by intensive mining and gave way to less robust coniferous growth.

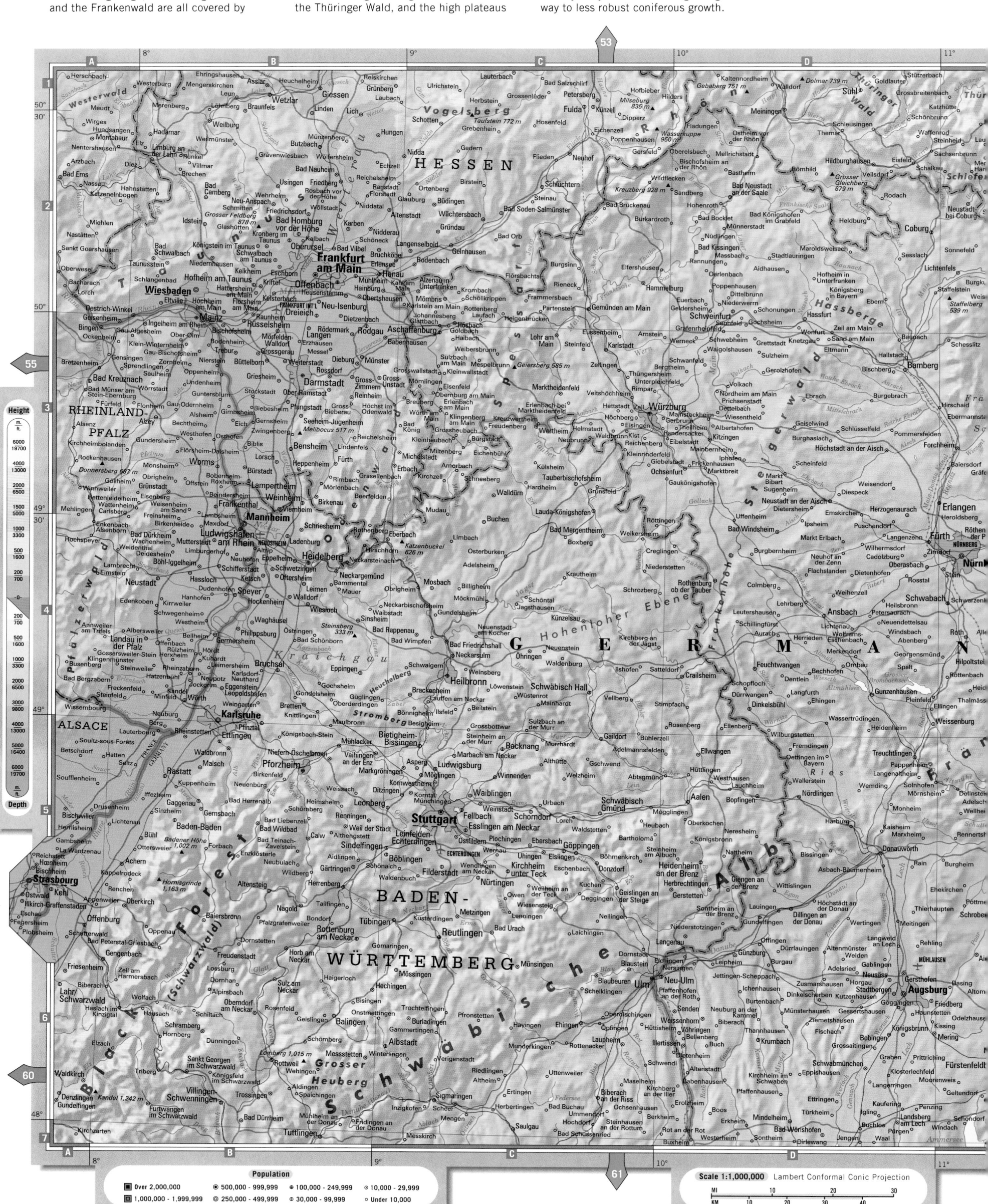

Population

■ Over 2,000,000	● 500,000 - 999,999	● 100,000 - 249,999	○ 10,000 - 29,999
■ 1,000,000 - 1,999,999	● 250,000 - 499,999	○ 30,000 - 99,999	○ Under 10,000

Scale 1:1,000,000 Lambert Conformal Conic Projection

MI   10   20   30

KM   10   20   30   40

Southern Germany, Czech Republic, Upper Austria

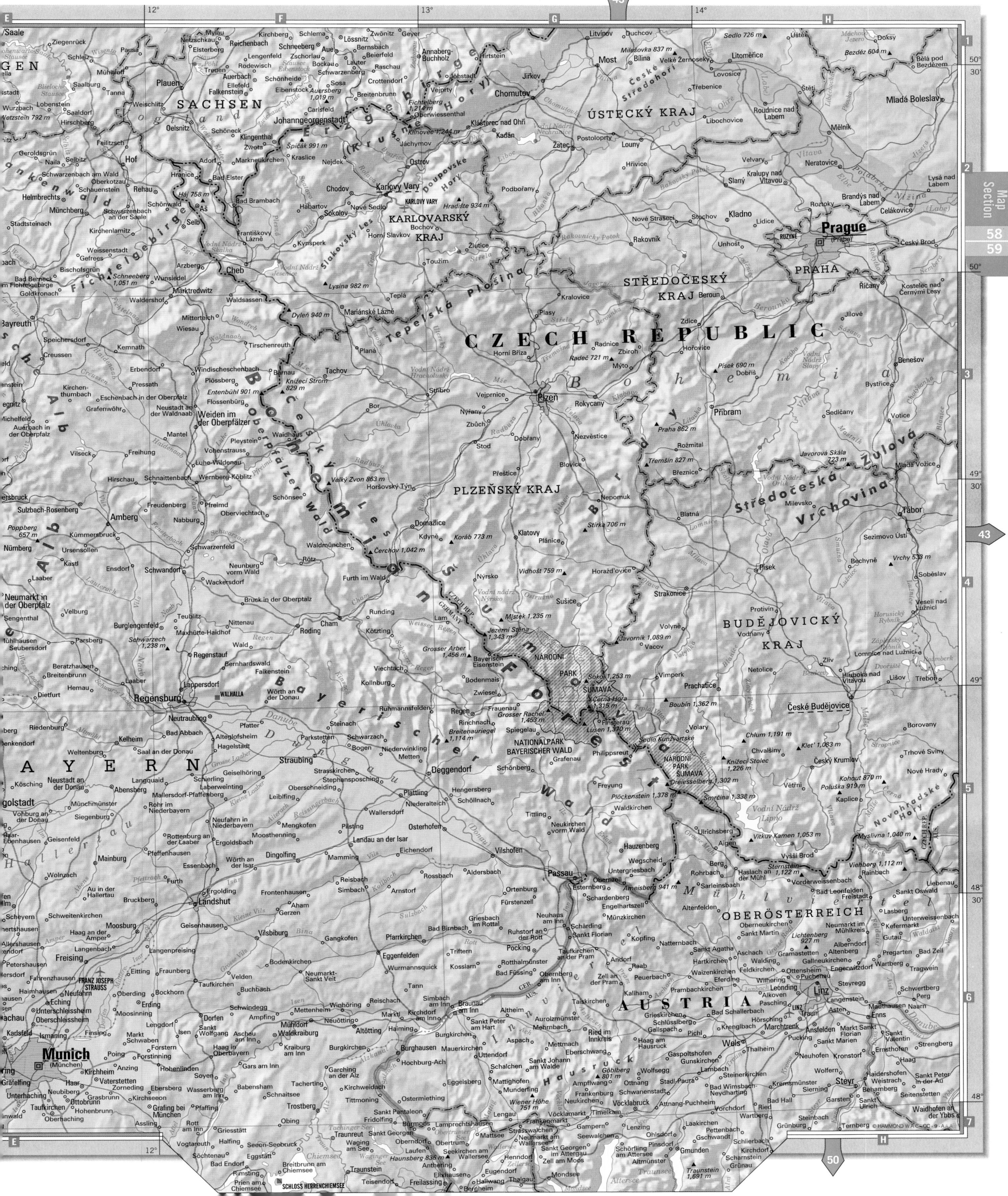

Map Section
58
59

Switzerland is the most important source and reservoir of drinking water in Central Europe. It borders on the two largest Alpine lakes - Lake Constance and Lake Geneva - and pre-Alpine central

Switzerland is dotted with many smaller lakes. Major rivers such as the Rhine and the Rhône flow from sources in Switzerland. Glaciers also provide huge storehouses of water. Covering some 125 square km,

the Aletsch Glacier, which descends from the Jungfraujoch, is the largest in the Alps. Its tongue has receded more than 1,000 m since the early 20th century.

Population

■ Over 2,000,000 ● 500,000 - 999,999 ● 100,000 - 249,999 ○ 10,000 - 29,999
▣ 1,000,000 - 1,999,999 ● 250,000 - 499,999 ● 30,000 - 99,999 ○ Under 10,000

Scale 1:1,000,000   Lambert Conformal Conic Projection

© HAMMOND WORLD ATLAS CORPORATION CC · 1018 · AAA

At the end of its course (652 km), the Po, the longest river on the Apennine Peninsula, empties into the Adriatic Sea south of Venice. Its drainage basin covers an area of about 75,000 square km. Fast-flowing tributaries descending from the Alps and the Apennines deposit heavy loads of sediment in the Po delta, which extends some 80 m farther into the sea every year. Numerous dams along the lower reaches of the river raise the riverbed above the level of the surrounding fertile plain. The Po often overflows its banks during periods of heavy rain in the spring and fall.

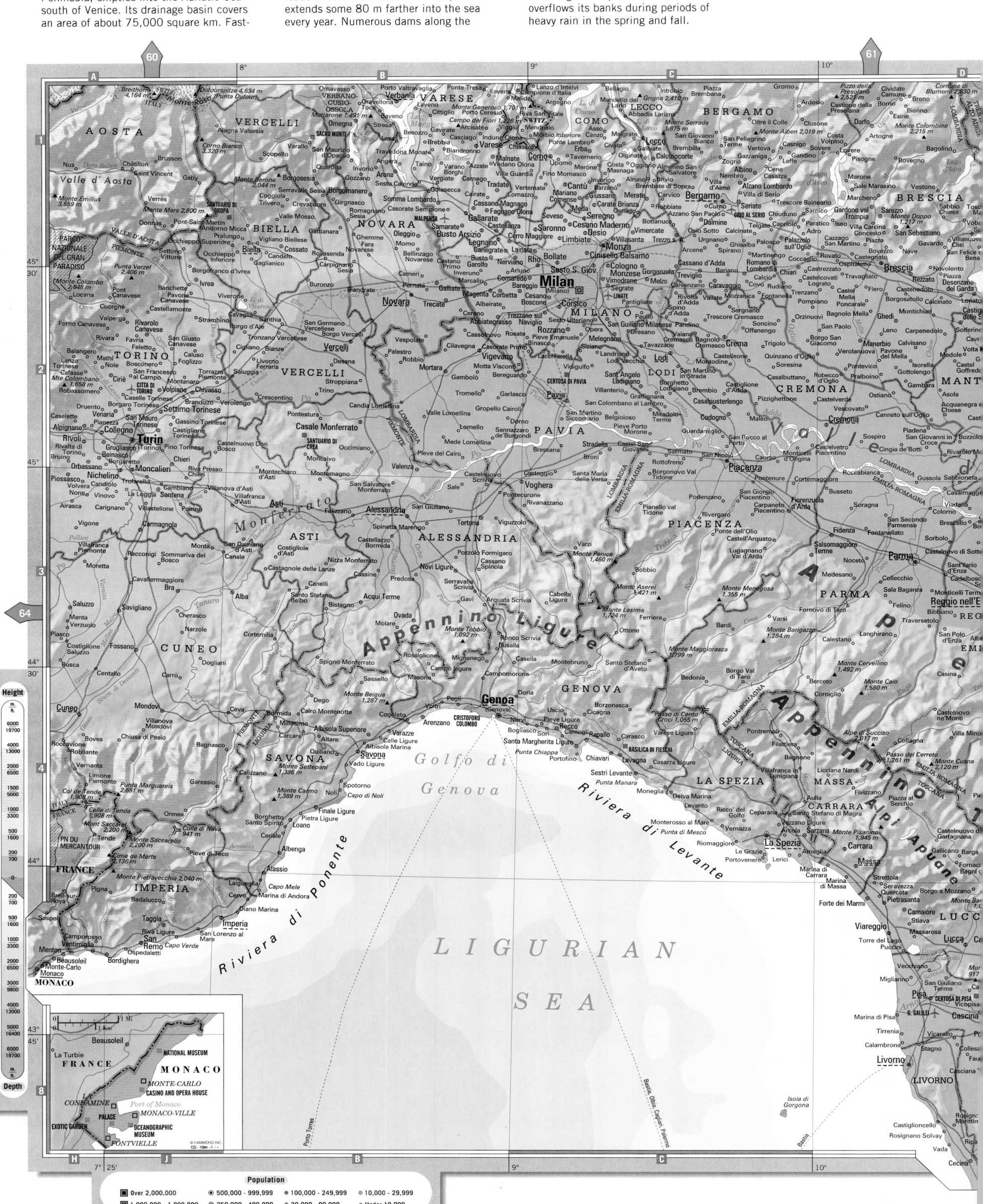

Northern Italy

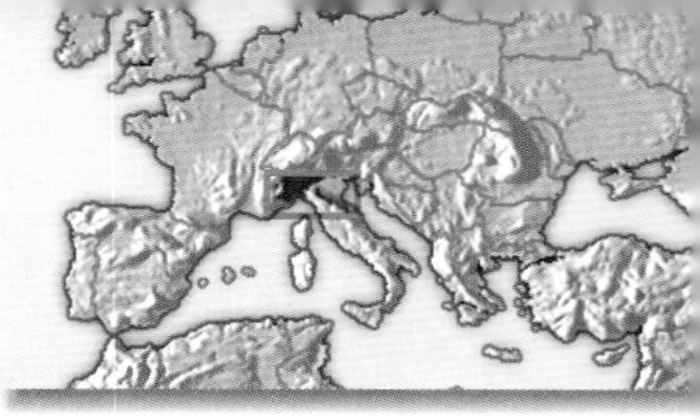

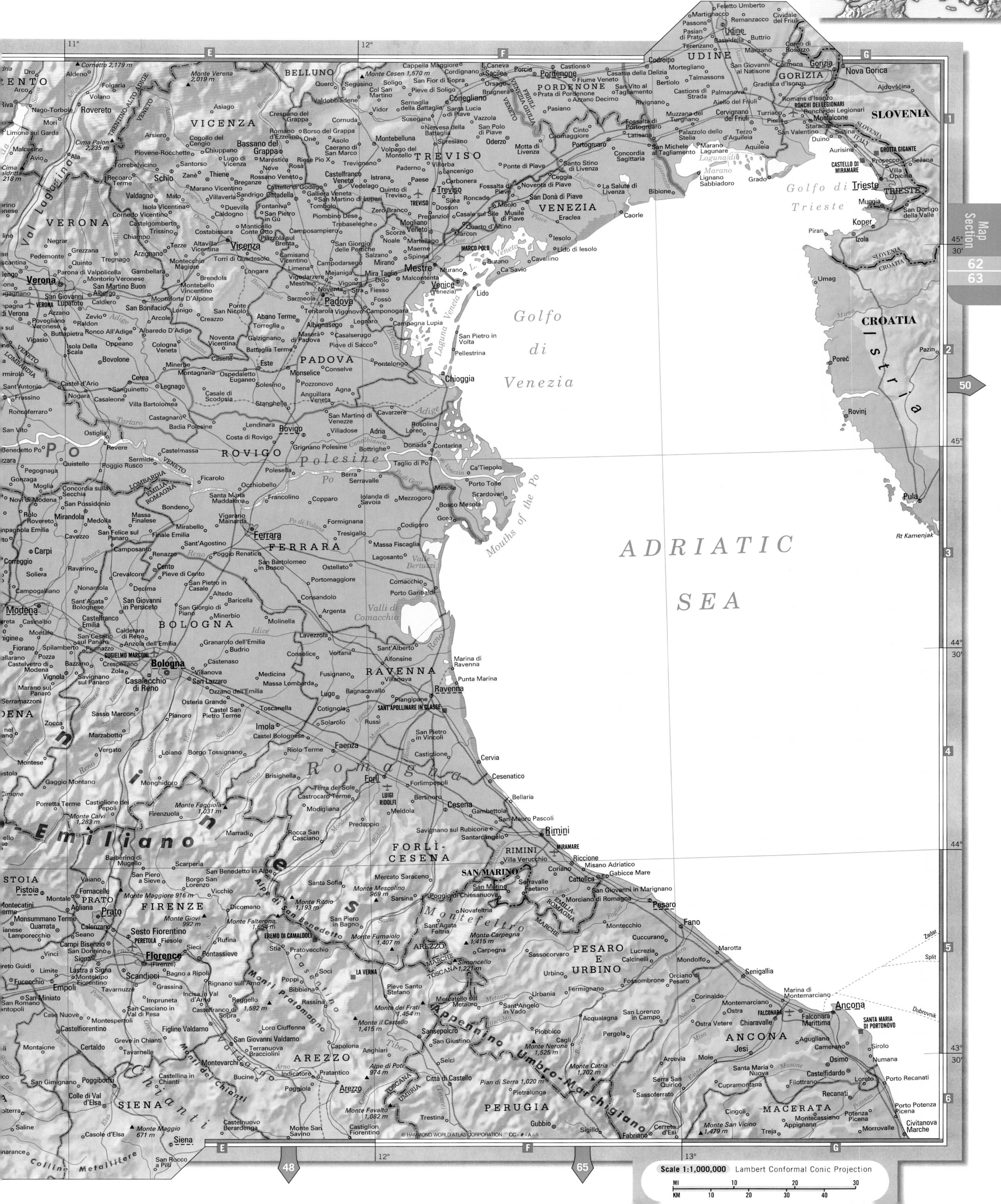

Southeastern France

The Alps dominate this region, with many peaks exceeding 3000 meters in height. Provence, to the south, features rugged terrain, fragrant lavender fields, and a spectacular coastline. The famed French Riviera (Côte d'Azur), which stretches from St-Tropez through Cannes and Nice to the Italian border, boasts some of the most fashionable resorts in the world.

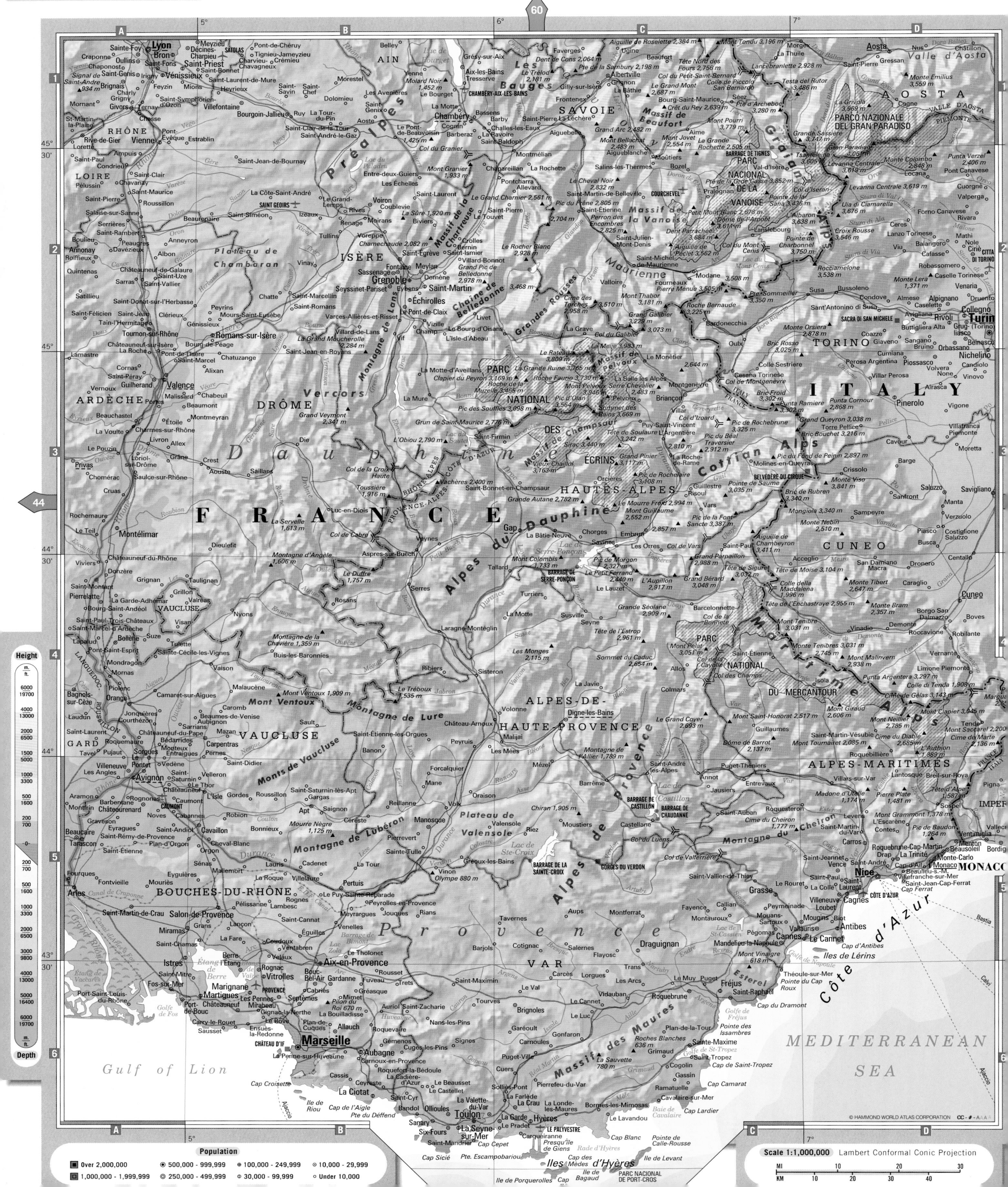

Height	
m. ft.	
6000 19700	
4000 13000	
2000 6500	
1500 5000	
1000 3300	
500 1600	
200 700	
0	
200 700	
500 1600	
1000 3300	
2000 6500	
3000 9800	
4000 13000	
5000 16400	
6000 19700	
m. ft.	
Depth	

Population
- Over 2,000,000
- 1,000,000 - 1,999,999
- 500,000 - 999,999
- 250,000 - 499,999
- 100,000 - 249,999
- 30,000 - 99,999
- 10,000 - 29,999
- Under 10,000

Scale 1:1,000,000 Lambert Conformal Conic Projection

MI 10 20 30
KM 10 20 30 40

© HAMMOND WORLD ATLAS CORPORATION

The Apennines, which cover an area roughly 1,500 km long and 150 km wide, have their own distinct climate. Average temperatures are lower while precipitation is heavier than elsewhere in the country.

In 1921, 292 square km in the southern reaches of this range of limestone formations were set aside as the Abbruzzi National Park, which remains a refuge for bears, wolves, and golden eagles.

Central Italy

© HAMMOND W.A.C. CG-1144

Population

| Over 2,000,000 | 500,000 - 999,999 | 100,000 - 249,999 | 10,000 - 29,999 |
| 1,000,000 - 1,999,999 | 250,000 - 499,999 | 30,000 - 99,999 | Under 10,000 |

Scale 1:1,000,000 Lambert Conformal Conic Projection

The Mediterranean Sea is connected to the Atlantic by the Straight of Gibraltar. It covers a total surface area of 3.02 million square km and reaches a maximum depth of 5,121 m west of the Peloponnesus.

Due to more rapid evaporation, salinity in the Mediterranean (39.1 % in the east) is higher than in the Atlantic. Consequently, a strong surface current carries low-saline water into the Mediterranean from the

Atlantic, while saltier water flows westward through the straight along the seafloor. The narrow passage between the two bodies of water also limits tidal activity in the Mediterranean.

Population			
▣ Over 2,000,000	◉ 500,000 - 999,999	◉ 100,000 - 249,999	◉ 10,000 - 29,999
▣ 1,000,000 - 1,999,999	◉ 250,000 - 499,999	◉ 30,000 - 99,999	○ Under 10,000

Height
m.
ft.
6000
19700
4000
13000
2000
6500
1500
5000
1000
3300
500
1600
200
700
-0-
200
700
500
1600
1000
3300
2000
6500
3000
9800
4000
13000
5000
16400
6000
19700
m.
ft.
Depth

Scale 1:6,000,000   Lambert Conformal Conic Projection

©HAMMOND WORLD ATLAS CORPORATION   CC-23-A A A

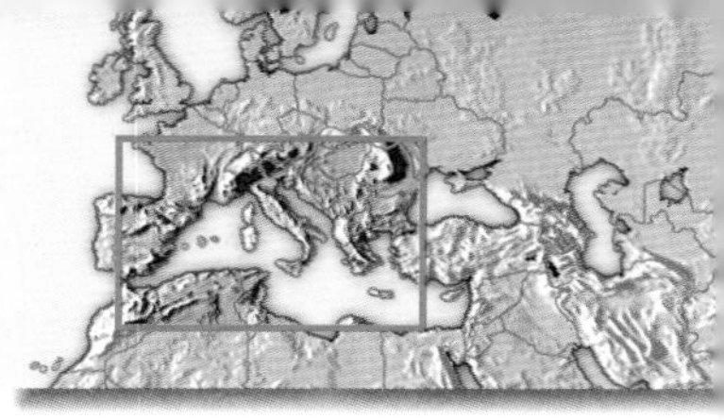

Receding ice left behind a landscape of lakes, morainic ridges, drumlins, and other glacial formations in northeastern Europe. The Finnish lake region alone comprises some 55,000 mostly shallow lakes.

Northeastern Europe is known for its vast woodlands. With 68 percent of its area covered by firs, pines, alders, and beeches, Finland is the most heavily forested country in Europe. The climate is continental for the most part, becoming subpolar in the north. Coastal waters begin to freeze over toward the end of the year. Tundra vegetation is predominant in the north.

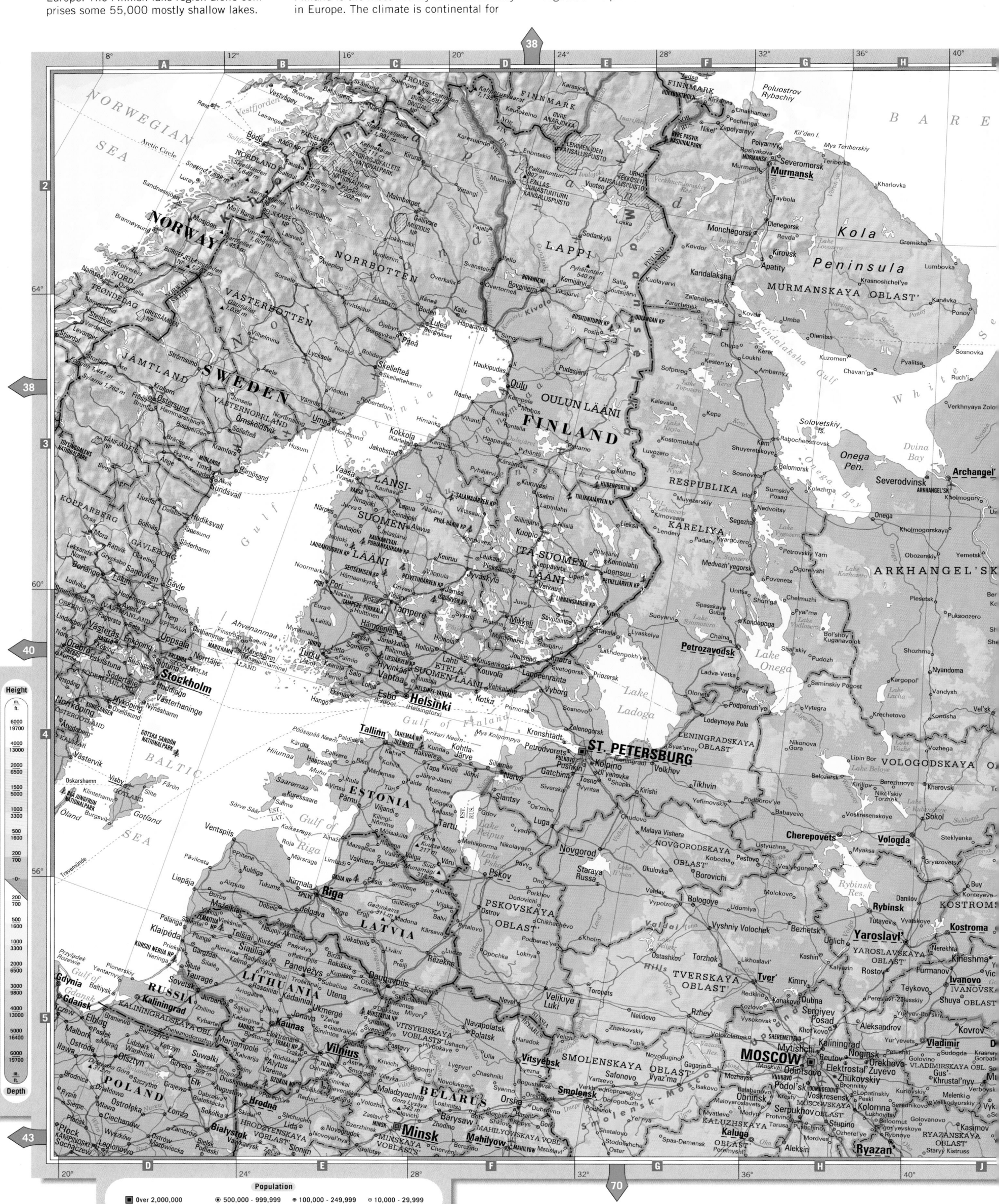

Map Section
68
69

Main Map

KARA SEA

Yugorskiy Peninsula
Pay-Khoy Mts.

Kolguyev Island

Pechora Bay
Kanin Pen.
Cheshskaya Bay

NENETSKIY AVT. OKRUG

Bol'shezemel'skaya Tundra

Malozemel'skaya Tundra

Timanskiy Tundra

Arctic Circle

Nar'yan-Mar
Vorkuta
VORKUTA

Gora Narodnaya 1,894 m.

RESPUBLIKA KOMI

R U S S I A

Ukhta
Sosnogorsk
Yarega

Syktyvkar

Northern Urals

KOMI-PERMYATSKIY AVTONOMNYY OKRUG

Kotlas
Koryazhma
Velikiy Ustyug

Solikamsk
Berezniki
PERMSKAYA OBLAST'

Kizel
Gubakha

Kirov
Kirovo-Chepetsk

Central Urals

Nizhniy Tagil

Krasnokamsk
Perm'

Glazov

Kudymkar

Chusovoy
Lys'va
Kungur

Yekaterinburg
Pervoural'sk
Kamensk-Ural'skiy

SVERDLOVSKAYA OBLAST'

KIROVSKAYA OBLAST'

Izhevsk
RESPUBLIKA UDMURTIYA
Votkinsk
Chaykovskiy

Sarapul
Mozhga

Yoshkar-Ola
Novocheboksarsk

RESPUBLIKA MARIY-EL

Neftekamsk

Naberezhnyye Chelny
Nizhnekamsk

RESPUBLIKA BASHKORTOSTAN

Chelyabinsk
Kopeysk
Zlatoust
Miass

CHELYABINSKAYA OBLAST'

TYUMENSKAYA OBLAST'
Tyumen'

KURGANSKAYA OBLAST'
Kurgan

Cheboksary
RESPUBLIKA CHUVASHIYA
Kazan'

RESPUBLIKA TATARSTAN

Ufa

Al'met'yevsk
Leninogorsk
Bugul'ma

Gora Yamantau 1,640 m.

Magnitogorsk

Ul'yanovsk

Nizhniy Novgorod (Gor'kiy)

NIZHEGORODSKAYA OBLAST'

KAZAKHSTAN
QOSTANAY

St. Petersburg Inset

Gulf of Finland
Helsinki

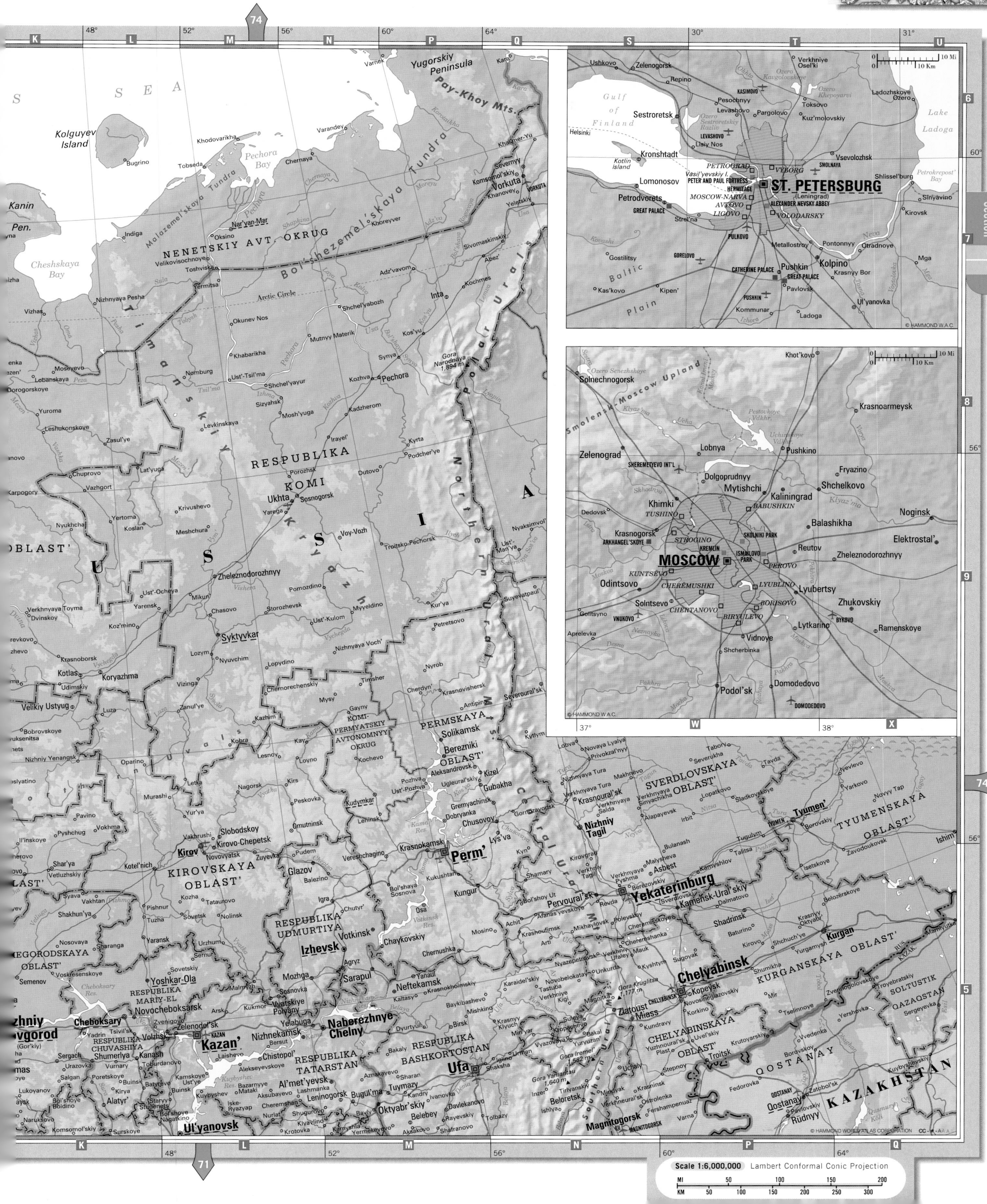

Sestroretsk
Kronshtadt
Kotlin Island
Lomonosov

ST. PETERSBURG (Leningrad)

PETROGRAD
HERMITAGE
PETER AND PAUL FORTRESS
MOSCOW-NARVA
AVTOVO
LIGOVO
VOLODARSKY
ALEXANDER NEVSKY ABBEY

Petrodvorets
GREAT PALACE
Strel'na
Pulkovo

CATHERINE PALACE
GREAT PALACE
Pushkin
Pavlovsk

Kolpino
Krasnyy Bor

Lake Ladoga

Baltic Plain

Moscow Inset

Solnechnogorsk
Zelenograd

Smolensk-Moscow Upland

Sheremetyevo Int'l
Dolgoprudnyy
Lobnya
Pushkino

Khimki
Mytishchi
Kaliningrad
Fryazino
Shchelkovo

Krasnogorsk
ARKHANGEL'SKOYE
STROGINO
KREMLIN
ISMAILOVO PARK
Balashikha
Noginsk
Elektrostal'

MOSCOW
Reutov
Zheleznodorozhnyy

Odintsovo
CHEREMUSHKI
PEROVO
Lyubertsy
Zhukovskiy

Solntsevo
LYUBLINO
BORISOVO
Lytkarino
BYKOVO

VNUKOVO
CHERTANOVO
BIRYULEVO
Ramenskoye

Aprelevka
Vidnoye
Shcherbinka

Podol'sk
Domodedovo
DOMODEDOVO

© HAMMOND W.A.C.

Scale 1:6,000,000 Lambert Conformal Conic Projection

© HAMMOND WORLD ATLAS CORPORATION

The Black Sea receives substantial flows of fresh water from such rivers as the Danube, the Don, and the Dnepr. Thus its salinity near the surface is only half that of the Atlantic. Salt-rich water also flows into this sea from the Mediterranean Sea along the floor of the Bosporus Strait. This stable, layered configuration produces an oxygen shortage at the bottom of the Black Sea that is hostile to living organisms.

By contrast, the Danube Delta teems with life. It is a paradise for birds - one of the last in Europe - and provides spawning grounds for over one hundred different species of fish.

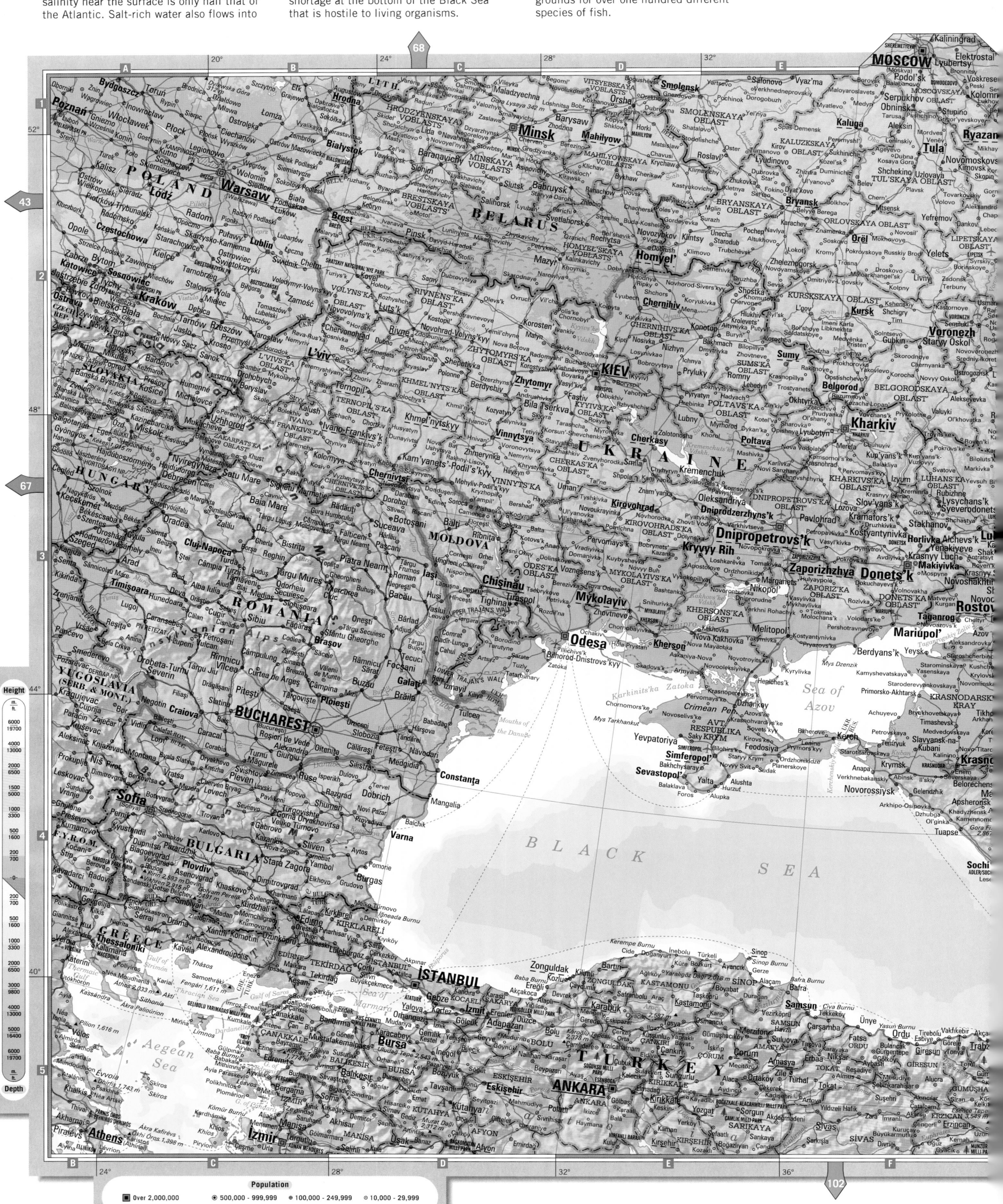

Scale 1:6,000,000 Lambert Conformal Conic Projection

MI 50 100 150 200
KM 50 100 150 200 250

Major countries / regions: RUSSIA, KAZAKHSTAN, UZBEKISTAN, TURKMENISTAN, GEORGIA, ARMENIA, AZERBAIJAN, IRAN

Seas: CASPIAN SEA, Aral Sea

Selected cities and places: Saransk, Penza, Ul'yanovsk, Tol'yatti, Samara, Novokuybyshevsk, Syzran', Saratov, Engel's, Volgograd (Stalingrad), Volzhskiy, Volgodonsk, Astrakhan', Elista, Stavropol', Cherkessk, Pyatigorsk, Nal'chik, Vladikavkaz, Grozny, Makhachkala, Kaspiysk, Derbent, Orenburg, Orsk, Novotroitsk, Magnitogorsk, Sterlitamak, Salavat, Oral, Aqtöbe, Atyraū, Aqtaū, Baku, Sumqayıt, Gäncä, Yerevan, T'bilisi, Rust'avi, Qostanay, Rūdnyy

© HAMMOND WORLD ATLAS CORPORATION

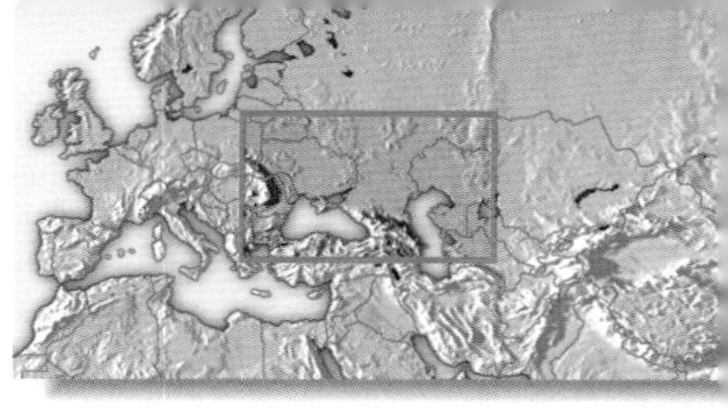

Northern Ukraine lies within a mixed-forest zone of oak, beech, and pine that gives way to a forest-steppe in the heartland, where the roots of trees reach groundwater at only a very few places.

The topography in the south is dominated by plains. The rich, black soil (chernozem) of the forest-steppes and plains yields bountiful harvests of wheat, barley, sugar beets, and sunflower seeds.

Ukraine holds the world's largest reserves of anthracite coal in the Donets River Basin, as well as rich deposits of iron and manganese ore.

34° H 36° J 38° K 40° L 42° M 44°

Ukraine

ANSKAYA OBLAST' Komarichi Suzemka Trosna Maloarkhangel'sk ORLOVSKAYA Terbuny LIPETSKAYA Khlevnoye OBLAST' Usman Dobrinka Mordovo TAMBOVSKAYA OBLAST' Uvarovo Turki Arkadak

Novoyamskoye Zheleznogorsk Dmitriyev-L'govskiy Fatezh Zolotukhino Novosil'skoye Ramon Krasnolesnyy Tokarevka Zherdevka Muchkapskiy Malinovka

Druzhba 242 m Sevsk Khomutovka Kalinovka Shchigry Kshenskiy VORONEZH Somovo 180 m Ertil SARATOVSKAYA

Novhorod-Sivers'kyy Chervone L'gov Imeni Karla Besedino Tim Gorshechnoye Novaya Usman Anna Rogachëvka Arkhangel'skoye Baychurovo 178 m Samoylovka

Hluhiv **Kursk** Lukhekhta Medvenka Solntsevo Siniye Lipyagi Novovoronezhskiy Bobrov Khrenovoye Talovaya Povorino Novonikolayevskiy

Khomutovka KURSKSKAYA OBLAST' Oboyan Prokhorovka Yakovlevo Korocha Ostrogozhsk Kamenka Novokhopërskiy Uryupinsk Novoanninskiy

Krolevets Shalyhyne Ryl'sk Bol'shoye Soldatskoye 276 m Skorodnoye Staryy Oskol Chernyanka Novyy Oskol Podgorenskiy 242 m Pavlovsk Kalach Nekhayevskiy Panfilovo Sennoy

Altynivka Putyvl' SUMS'KA Krasnopillya Lebedyn Trostyanets Chupakhivka Borisovka Razumnoye Shebekino Valuyki Rossosh Verkhniy Mamon Ryabovskiy Kumylzhenskaya VOLGOGRADSKAYA

Konotop Buryn Vorozhba Bilopillya **Sumy** Zhovtneve OBLAST' Okhtyrka Zolochiv **Belgorod** Ol'khovatka Boguchar Shumilinskaya Zimnyatskiy Frolovo

Romny Hadyach Komyshna Zin'kiv Bohodukhiv Vil'shany Kazacha Lopan' Vovchans'k Prykolotne Urazovo Mitrofanovka Taly Kazanskaya Serafimovich OBLAST'

POLTAVS'KA Zhovtneve Sharovka Peresechna Prudyanka Velykyy Burluk 220 m Troyits'ke Rovenki Radchenskoye Kantemirovka Veshenskaya Ilovlya

Myrhorod Romodan **Poltava** 202 m Opishnya Dykan'ka **Kharkiv** Chuhuyiv Kup'yans'k Pokrovs'ke Biloluts'k RUSSIA Chertkovo Don Kletskiy Sirotinskaya

Khorol Lyubotyn Merefa Birky Shevchenkove Kup'yans'k Vuzlovyy Markivka UKRAINE Millerovo Pervomayskoye Surovikino

Kobelyaky Nova Vodolaha Derhachi Balakliya Izyum Svatove Mistky Starobil'sk Bilovods'k Dëgtevo Kashary Ridge Nizhniy Chir

Kremenchuk Komsomol's'k Shyshaky KHARKIVS'KA Krasnohrad Lozova Barvinkove Kreminna LUHANS'KA Shchastya Stanychno-Luhans'ke Glubokiy Kamensk-Shakhtinskiy ROSTOVSKAYA Tatsinskiy Tsimlyansk Res.

OBLAST' Karlivka Sakhnovshchyna Krasnopavlivka Nova Astrakhan' Rubizhne Syeverodonets'k OBLAST' Hirs'ke Pervomaysk Gornyatskiy Morozovsk

Zhovti Vody Pereshchepyne Yur'yivka Yasynovata Soledar Popasna **Luhans'k** Molodohvardiys'k Krasnodon Belaya Kalitva

Verkhn'odniprovs'k Petrykivka Novomoskovs'k Ternivka Krasnyy Lyman Slov'yans'k Chasiv Yar Zolote Stakhanov Alchevs'k Donetsk Koksovyy Sinegorskiy

Dniprodzerzhyns'k Pidhorodne Pavlohrad Dobropillya Druzhkivka Kramators'k Artemivs'k Bryanka Artëmovsk Lutuhyne Likhovskoy Krasnyy Sulin

Verkhn'odniprovs'k P'yatykhatky **Dnipropetrovs'k** Petropavlivka Bilyts'ke Kostyantynivka Dzerzhyns'k Antratsyt Zverevo Novoshakhtinsk Shakhty

Verkhn'odniprovsk Tomakivka Krynychky Vasyl'kivka Novohrods'ke Horlivka Yenakiyeve Krasnyy Luch Sverdlovs'k Gukovo OBLAST' Volgodonsk

Kryvyy Rih Synel'nykove Pokrovs'ke Krasnoarmiys'k Selydove **Makiyivka** Kirovs'ke Shakhtars'k Rovenki Sokolovo-Kundryuchenskoye Konstantinovsk

Inhulets Marhanets **Zaporizhzhya** Novomykolayivka Kurakhove **Donets'k** Torez Snizhne Nahol'no-Tarasivka Novocherkassk Semikarakorsk Dubovskoye

Apostolove OBLAST' Tomakivka Orikhiv Velyka Novosilka Mar'inka Zuhres Ilovays'k Amvrosiyivka UKRAINE Mayskiy Kamenolomni Bagayevskiy Zimovniki

Nikopol' Zelenodol's'k DONETS'KA OBLAST' Volnovakha Dokuchayevs'k Komsomol's'ke Matveyev Kurgan **ROSTOV** Konstantinovskiy Orlovskiy

Kam'yanka- Dniprovs'ka Vasylivka Dniprorudne Hulyaypole Rozivka Andriyivka Pokrovskoye Anastasiyevka **Taganrog** Aksay Krasnoarmeyskiy

ZAPORIZ'KA Mykhaylivka Tokmak Komysh-Zorya Volodars'ke SARTANA Fëdorovka Novoazovs'k **Rostov** Bataysk Veselyy Res. Proletarsk Remontnoye

Velyka Bilozerka Mala Bilozerka Molochans'k Vesele MARIUPOL' Pershotravneve **Mariupol'** Azov 115 m Zernograd Yegorlykskaya Lake Manych-Gudilo

KHERSONS'KA Velyka Lepetykha Melitopol' Kostyantynivka Pryazovs'ke Yakymivka Aleksandrovka Leningradskaya Krylovskaya Pavlovskaya Belaya Glina RESPUBLIKA KALMYKIYA

Beryslav OBLAST' Nova Mayachka Chkalovo **Berdyans'k** Yeysk Staroshcherbinovskaya Staromninskaya Kanevskaya Novopokrovskaya Peschanokopskoye Gorodovikovsk Kievka

ZAPOVIDNYK ASKANIYA-NOVA Askaniya-Nova Novotroyits'ke Dolzhanskaya Staroderevyankovskaya Pavlovskaya Takhta Ipatovo

Kalanchak Henichens'k Kyrylivka Primorsko-Akhtarsk Kubano-Priazov Kanevskaya Kalnibolotskaya 46°

Perekops'kyy Armyans'k Achuyevo **Sea of Azov** Bryukhovetskaya Plain Tikhoretsk Novopokrovskaya Krasnogvardeyskoye STAVROPOL'SKIY

Krasnoperekops'k Dzhankoy Krasnohvardiys'ke Nyzhn'ohirs'kyy Sovets'kyy UKRAINE RUSSIA Timashevsk Vyselki Kropotkin Gul'kevichi KRAY Svetlograd

Rozdol'ne Pervomays'ke Nizhn'ohirs'kyy Mys Kazantip KRASNODARSKIY KRAY Kazanskaya Ladozhskaya Novokubansk Izobil'nyy

AVTONOMNA RESPUBLIKA Novoselivs'ke Azovs'ke Baherove Kerch Temryuk Slavyansk-na-Kubani Kalnino Vasyurinskaya Gora Strizhament 831 m

KRYM Crimean Peninsula Simferopol' Staryy Krym Feodosiya Kerchens'kyy Pivostriv Varenikovskaya Kuban' **Stavropol'** Armavir

Saky Sudak Anapa Anapskaya Krymsk **Krasnodar** Giaginskaya Kurganinsk Nevinnomyssk

Bakhchysaray Planers'ke Ordzhonikidze Verkhnebakanskiy KRASNODAR Yablonovskiy Belorechensk RESPUBLIKA Sovetskaya Kursavka

Sevastopol' Balaklava 1,254 m Kryms'ki Hory Novorossiysk Kabardinka ADYGEYA Maykop Gora Strizhament

Hora Roman Kosh 1,545 m **Yalta** Alushta Partenit Gelendzhik Gora Tkhab 905 m Apsheronsk Khanskaya Cherkessk

Foros Simeiz Alupka **SEA** Arkhipo-Osipovka Khadyzhensk RESPUBLIKA KARACHAYEVO-CHERKESIYA

Mys Sarych YALTYNS'KYY ZAPOVIDNYK Dzhubga Bar'umi Psebay Uchkeken 44°

34° H 36° J 38° K 40° L 42° M

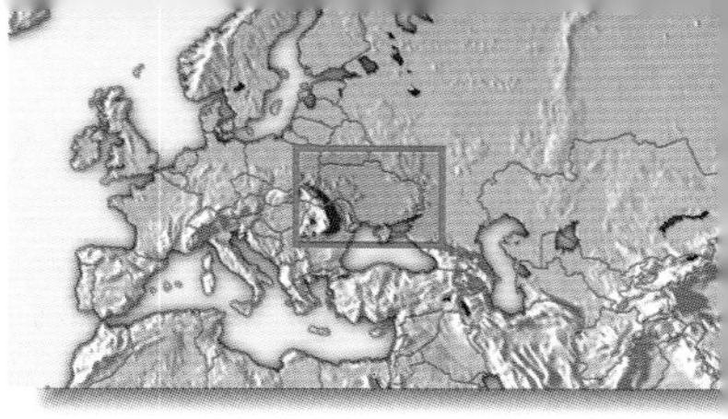

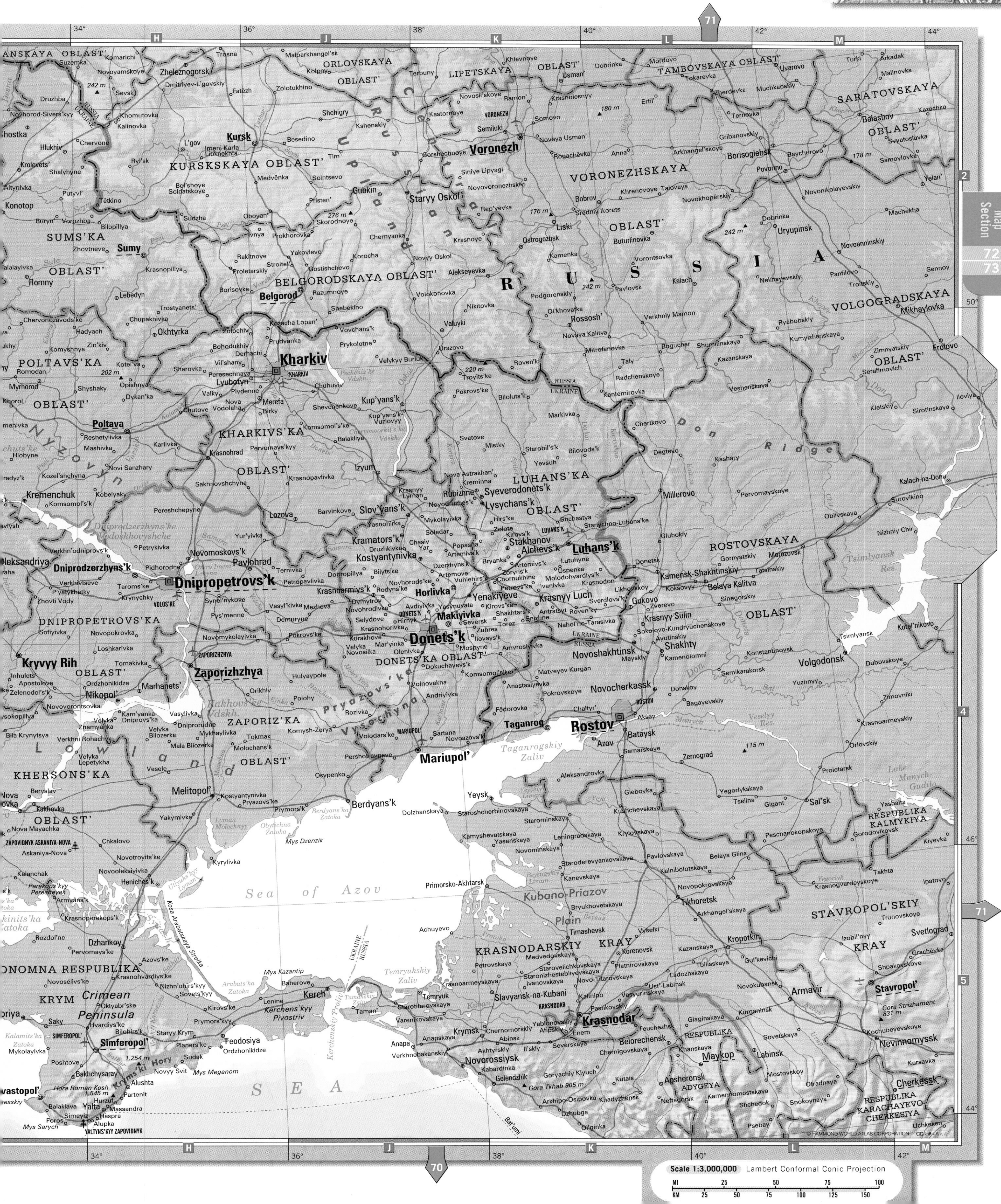

Russia measures more than 4,000 km from north to south and stretches across 9,600 km of territory from west to east - spanning nearly half the globe in the northern latitudes. The Russian landscape is dominated by vast plains west of the Yenisey River. The climate is predominantly continental and cool. The coldest temperatures in the northern hemisphere have been recorded near the villages of Oymyakon and Verkhoyansk in eastern Siberia. Long winters with little snow keep the ground frozen for much of the year in about two-thirds of the country, while the climate along the Black Sea coast is subtropical.

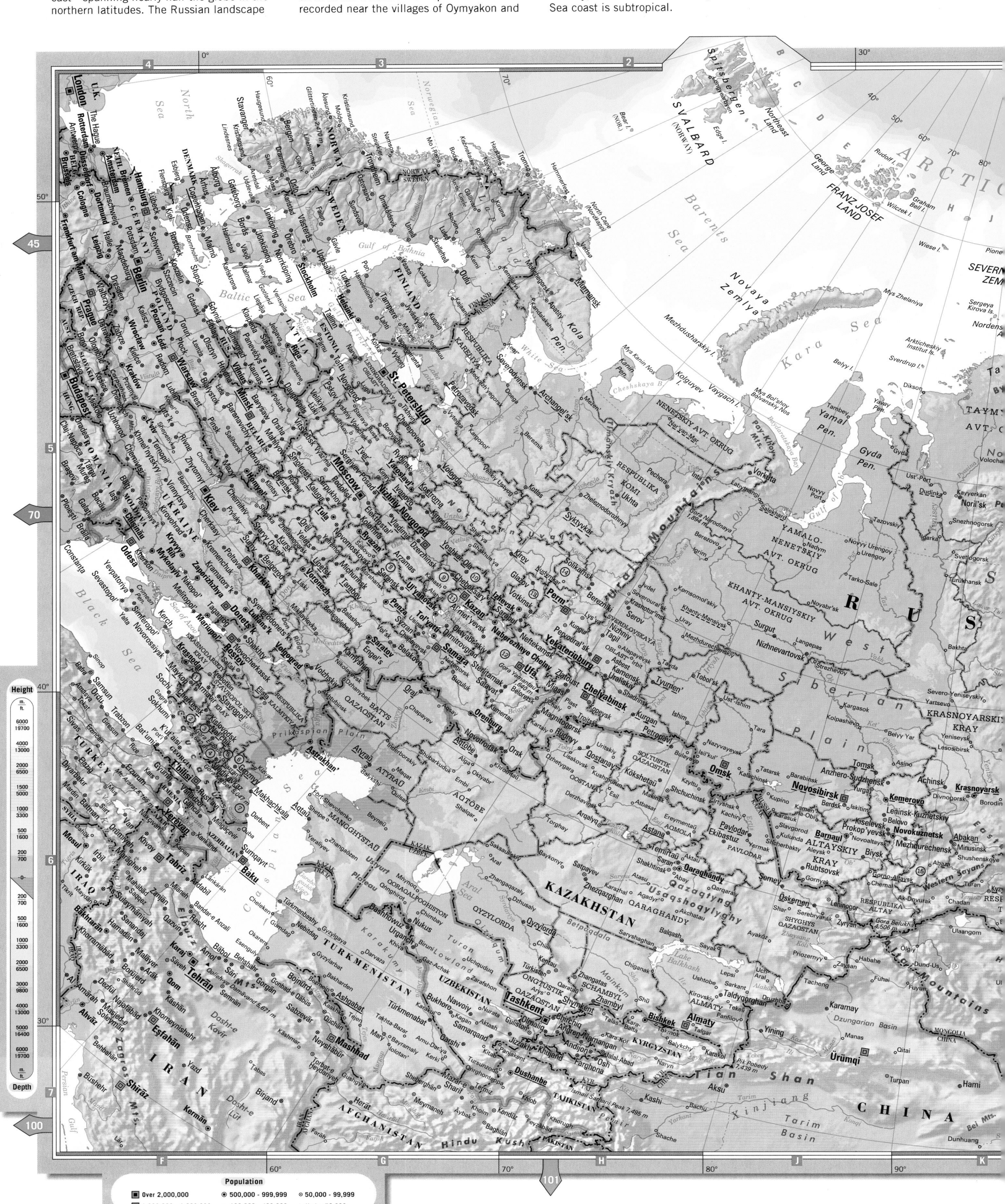

Population

- Over 2,000,000
- 1,000,000 - 1,999,999
- 500,000 - 999,999
- 100,000 - 499,999
- 50,000 - 99,999
- Under 50,000

Russia and Neighboring Countries

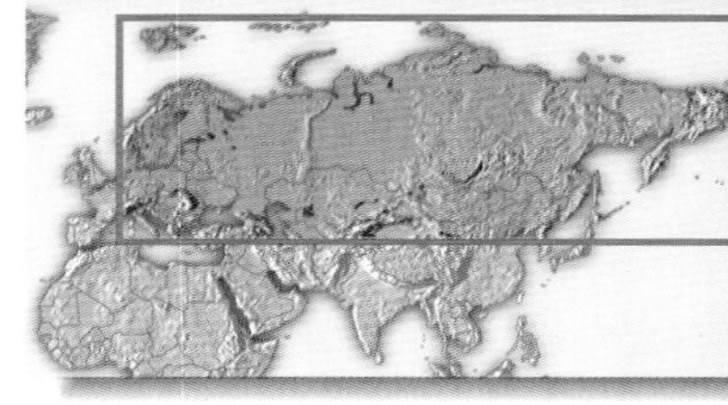

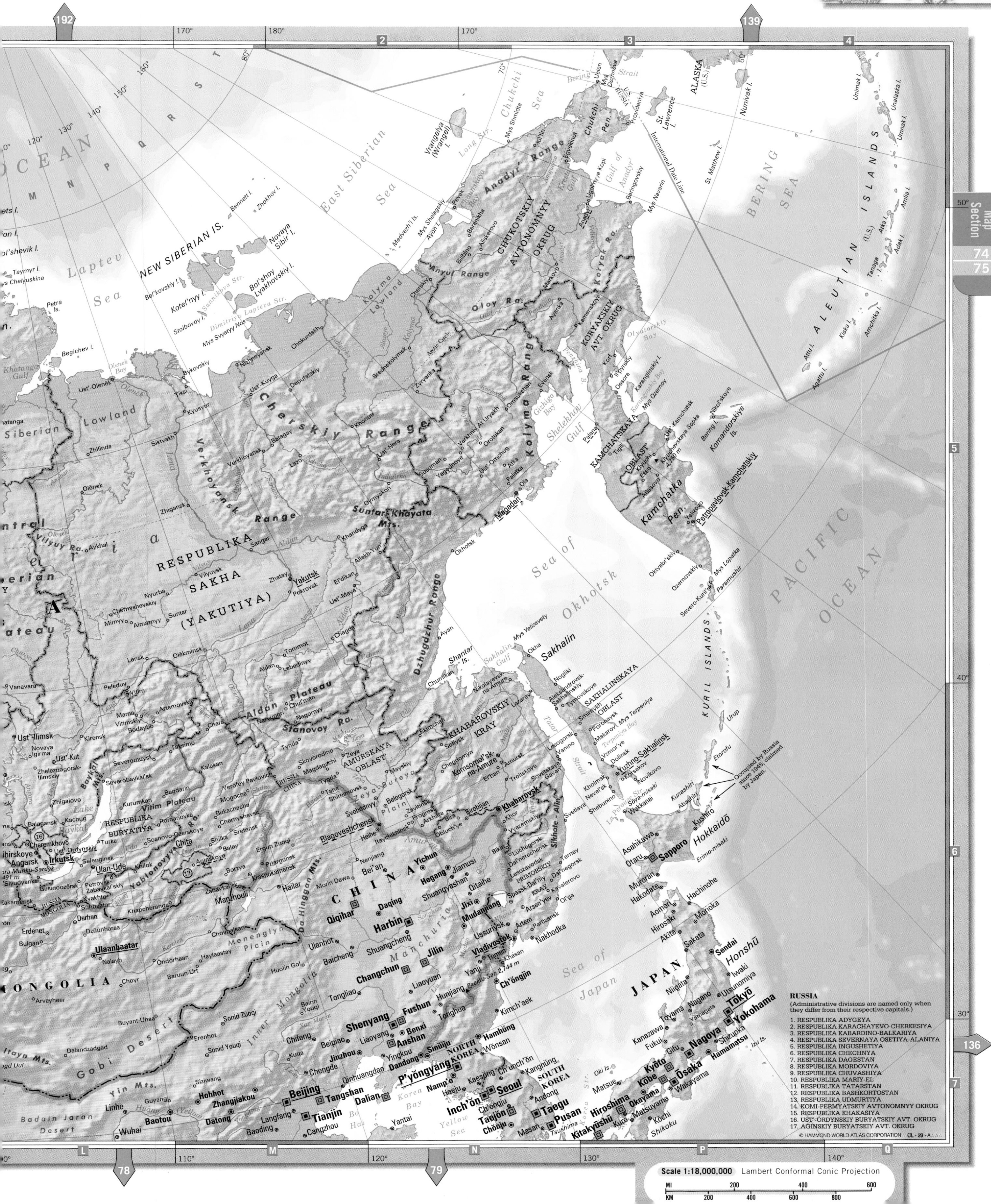

he Indus is the longest river in south-west Asia (3200 km), and its delta vers an area of 7,800 square km. The er flows from its source at an elevation 5,182 meters in the Trans-Himalayas and is fed by snowmelt and glacial melt-water from the mountains of the Tibet Plateau. After leaving the Himalayas, it flows onto the Punjab Plain and through a vast alluvial lowland before emptying into the Arabian Sea south of Hyderabad. Water levels on the Indus fluctuate with the rhythm of the monsoon rains. Dams and canals ensure a reliable supply of water to the world's largest irrigation zone.

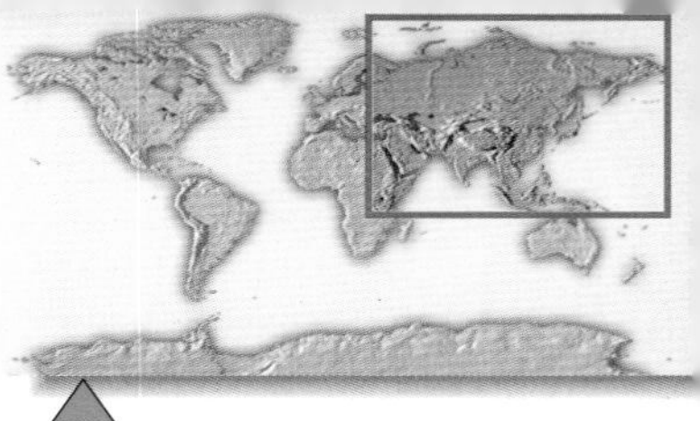

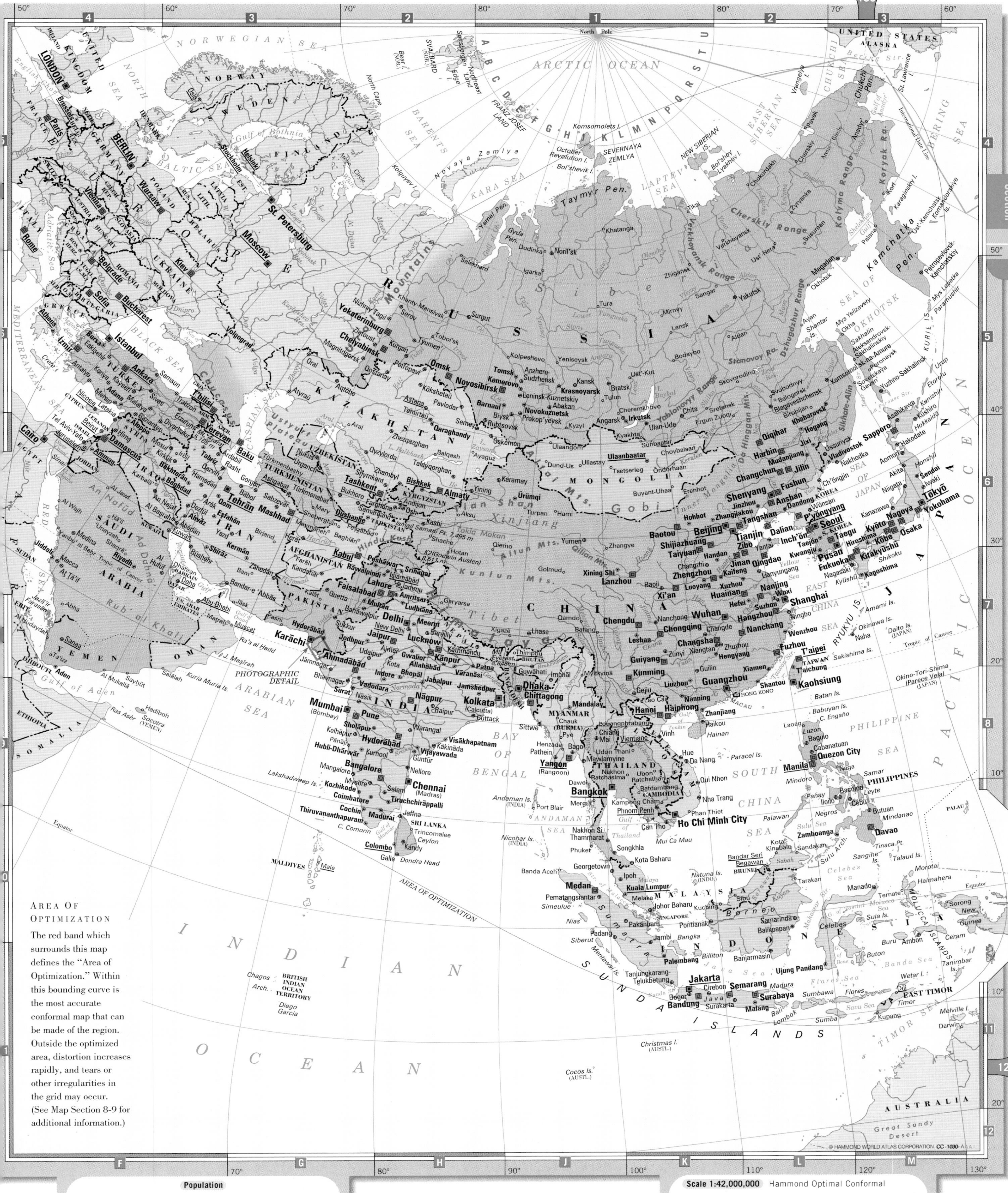

AREA OF OPTIMIZATION

The red band which surrounds this map defines the "Area of Optimization." Within this bounding curve is the most accurate conformal map that can be made of the region. Outside the optimized area, distortion increases rapidly, and tears or other irregularities in the grid may occur. (See Map Section 8-9 for additional information.)

Map Section 76 77

139

127

Population

- ■ Over 3,000,000
- ■ 1,000,000 - 2,999,999
- ⊙ 500,000 - 999,999
- ◉ 100,000 - 499,999
- ○ Under 100,000

Scale 1:42,000,000 Hammond Optimal Conformal

MI 500 1000 1500
KM 500 1000 1500 2000

© HAMMOND WORLD ATLAS CORPORATION CC-1030

Eastern Asia is the most populous region on Earth. Its most prominent topographic features are the plains and deserts of the central highlands, and its broad, fertile loess plains. The climate is controlled by monsoon winds. In the winter, the East Asian monsoon carries dry, cold air - often accompanied by dust storms - from a cold high-pressure center in the Asian heartland to the Pacific. Temperatures in China drop to below freezing north of the Qilian Shan in the winter, while warm, moist air flows inland from the sea during the summer.

Population

■ Over 2,000,000	● 500,000 - 999,999	● 100,000 - 249,999	○ 10,000 - 29,999
■ 1,000,000 - 1,999,999	● 250,000 - 499,999	● 30,000 - 99,999	○ Under 10,000

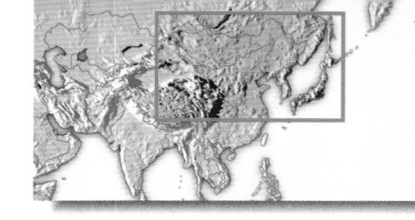

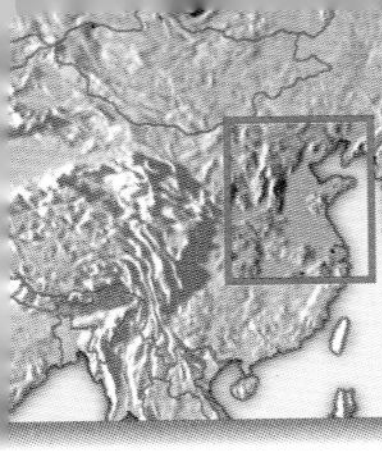

Northeastern China

The alluvial plain created by the Huang (Yellow) River is the cradle of Chinese civilization. Now lined by levees along its lower reaches, the river lies up to 10 m above the surrounding land.

The Huang has often overflowed its banks, causing devastating floods, and even changed its course, emptying into the sea at different points north and south of the Shandong Peninsula.

Population

▪	Over 2,000,000
▫	1,000,000 - 1,999,999
●	500,000 - 999,999
●	250,000 - 499,999
⊙	100,000 - 249,999
⊙	30,000 - 99,999
○	10,000 - 29,999
○	Under 10,000

Scale 1:6,000,000   Lambert Conformal Conic Projection

MI 50 100 150 200
KM 50 100 150 200 250 300

Height
m.   ft.
6000   19700
4000   13000
2000   6500
1500   5000
1000   3300
500   1600
200   700
0
200   700
500   1600
1000   3300
2000   6500
3000   9800
4000   13000
5000   16400
6000   19700
m.   ft.
Depth

© Hammond World Atlas Corporation   CD - 1039 - A - A.A.

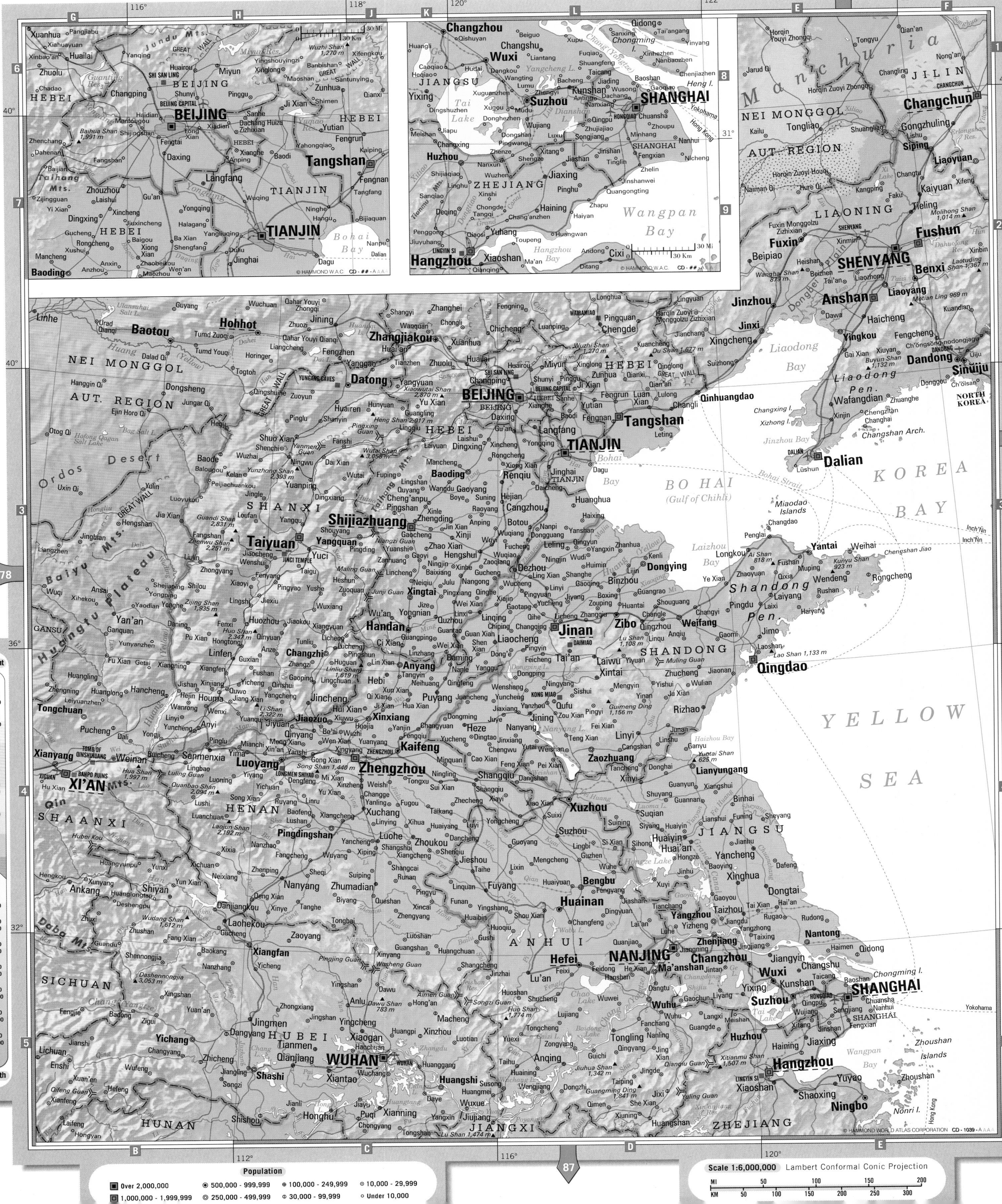

The Korean peninsula is the home of a distinct culture that was influenced early on by China and bears the indelible imprint of Buddhism. Korea was annexed [by] Japan in 1910 and divided into a communist north and a pro-western south in 1948. In the years since the end of the Korean War (1950-1953), South Korea has become a major industrial power.

Korea

CHINA · JILIN · MANCHURIA · LIAONING · Dongbei Plain

SHENYANG · Fushun · Anshan · Benxi · Liaoyang · Dandong · Yingkou

Liaodong Bay · Liaodong Peninsula · DALIAN · Dalian

KOREA BAY

NORTH KOREA · P'YŎNGYANG · Namp'o · Sariwŏn · Haeju · Kaesŏng · Hamhŭng · Wŏnsan · Sinŭiju · Kimch'aek · Ch'ŏngjin

HAMGYŎNG-BUKTO · YANGGANG-DO · CHAGANG-DO · HAMGYŎNG-NAMDO · P'YŎNGAN-BUKTO · P'YŎNGAN-NAMDO · HWANGHAE-BUKTO · HWANGHAE-NAMDO · KANGWŏN-DO

Armistice Line, 1953 · Demilitarized Zone · Panmunjom

SEA OF JAPAN · Tonghan Bay

SOUTH KOREA · SEOUL · INCH'ON · Suwŏn · Songnam · Anyang · Puch'on · Taejŏn · Chŏnju · TAEGU · Kwangju · PUSAN · Ulsan · Masan · Chinju · Ch'angwŏn · P'ohang

KYŎNGGI-DO · KANGWŎN-DO · CH'UNGCH'ŎNG-BUKTO · CH'UNGCH'ŎNG-NAMDO · CHŎLLA-BUKTO · CHŎLLA-NAMDO · KYŎNGSANG-BUKTO · KYŎNGSANG-NAMDO

Kyŏnggi Bay · YELLOW SEA · Cheju

SŎRAKSAN NAT'L PK. · ODAESAN NAT'L PK. · CHIRI-SAN NAT'L PARK · TADOHAE HAESANG NAT'L PARK · HALLYO HAESANG NAT'L PARK

CHINA · SHANDONG · Weihai · Qingdao · Yantai

Inset map

NORTH KOREA · SOUTH KOREA · KYŎNGGI-DO

SEOUL · INCH'ON · Puch'on · Anyang · Ansan · Suwŏn · Songnam · Kwangju · Kwangmyŏng · Uijŏngbu

PUK-AN-SAN NATIONAL PARK · NAMANSANSONG PROVINCIAL PARK · KOREAN FOLK VILLAGE

Kyŏnggi Bay

Height	
m. / ft.	
6000	19700
4000	13000
2000	6500
1500	5000
1000	3300
500	1600
200	700
0	0
200	700
500	1600
1000	3300
2000	6500
3000	9800
4000	13000
5000	16400
6000	19700
Depth	

Population
- ■ Over 2,000,000
- ■ 1,000,000 - 1,999,999
- ● 500,000 - 999,999
- ● 250,000 - 499,999
- ● 100,000 - 249,999
- ○ 30,000 - 99,999
- ○ 10,000 - 29,999
- ○ Under 10,000

Scale 1:3,000,000 · Lambert Conformal Conic Projection
MI 0 25 50 75 100
KM 0 25 50 75 100 125 150

Northern Japan

Hokkaidō, Japan's northernmost major island, is home to the Ainu, a people unrelated to the Japanese who also settled on Sakhalin and the Kuril Islands. Their origin is unknown. Long ago, the Ainu retreated to the fertile inland valleys to farm, hunt, and fish. Today, only 14,00 Ainu live on the island. Hokkaido hosted the Winter Olympics in 1972.

SEA OF JAPAN

SEA OF OKHOTSK

PACIFIC OCEAN

La Perouse Strait

RUSSIA / JAPAN

Kril'on Pen.
Aniva Bay
Tonino-Anivskiy Pen.
Mys Aniva
SAKHALINSKAYA OBLAST'
Mys Kril'on
Kril'on

Vulkan Chirip 1,589 m
Kuril'sk
Etoro

Sōya-misaki
Wakkanai
Noshappu-misaki
Rebun-tō
Rebun
RISHIRI-REBUN-SAROBETSU NP
Rishiri-tō
Rishiri
Teshio
Enbetsu
Esashi
Sarufutsu
Hamatombetsu
L. Kutcharo
Ōmu
Okoppe
Mombetsu
Yūbetsu

Kitami Mountains

Haboro
Tomamae
1,032 m
Nayoro
Shibetsu
Engaru
Tokoro
Abashiri
L. Notoro
L. Abashiri
Shari
SHIRETOKO NP
Shiretoko-misaki
Rausu
Occupied by Russia since 1945; claimed by Japan
Kunashiri-tō
Yuzhno-Kuril'sk
Gora Tyatya 1,819 m

Obira
Rumoi
Mashike
Fukagawa
Shokanbetsu-dake 1,492 m
Teshio-dake 1,558 m
Kamikawa
Asahikawa
Akabira
Takikawa
Sunagawa
Utashinai
Ashibetsu
Asahi-dake 2,290 m
DAISETSUZAN NAT'L PARK
Rubeshibe
Kitami
Bihoro
L. Kussharo
AKAN NP
Me-akan-dake 1,503 m
Teshikaga
Shibecha
KUSHIRO-SHITSUGEN NP
L. Mashū
Konsen Plateau
Nemuro Str.
Gora Golovnina 547 m
Golovnino
Habomai Islands
Shikotan-tō
Shpanberga Chan.
Taraku-jima
Suishō-tō
Shibotsu-jima
Yuri-tō
Nosappu-misaki
Nemuro
Nemuro Pen.
Ochiishi-misaki

HOKKAIDŌ

Kamui-misaki
Shakotan Pen.
Otaru
Ishikari
Ishikari Bay
Bibai
Mikasa
Iwamizawa
Kurisawa
Yubari
Furano
Ishikari Mts.
Shimukappu
Shimizu
Shintoku
Shimizu
Otofuke
Honbetsu
Ashoro
Obihiro
Ikeda
Urahoro
Shiranuka
Kushiro
Hamanaka
Akkeshi

Yoichi
Kutchan
JOZANKEI SPA
SHIKOTSU-TOYA NP
Sapporo
Eniwa
Chitose
CHITOSE
Naganuma
Ebetsu
Kitahiroshima
Hidaka
Hidaka Mountains
Horoshiri-dake 2,052 m
Taiki
Samani
Erimo
Erimo-misaki

Iwanai
Benkei-misaki
Suttsu
Yōtei-san 1,893 m
Shikotsu
L. Tōya
Tomakomai
Shiraoi
Mukawa
Mombetsu
Biratori
Shizunai
Urakawa
Hiro'o

Motsuta-misaki
Kariba-yama 1,520 m
Setana
Oshamambe
Abuta
Date
Noboribetsu
Muroran
Yakumo
Mori
Shikabe

Okushiri-tō
Okushiri
Kumaishi
Oshima Peninsula
Minamikayabe
Esan-misaki
Nanae
Kamiisco

Ō-shima
Dai-Segen-dake 1,072 m
Kikonai
Hakodate
Tsugaru Strait
Fukushima
Matsumae
HOKKAIDŌ
TŌHOKU
Shirakami-misaki
Ōma-zaki
Ōma
Ōhata
Shimokita Pen.
Shiriya-zaki

Honshū

Tappi-zaki
Kodomari
Tsugaru Pen.
Nakasato
Mimmaya
Hiranai
Rokkasho
Mutsu Bay
Ogawara

Goshogawara
Ajigasawa
Itayanagi
Kizukuri
Namioka
Aomori
AOMORI
Misawa
Momoishi
Hachinohe
Iwasaki
Iwaki-san 1,640 m
Hirosaki
Kuroishi
Hakkōda-san 1,585 m
Gonohe
Sannohe
Henashi-zaki
Owani
TOWADA-HACHIMANTAI NP
Ninohe
Kuji
Hachimori
Ōdate
Ichinohe
Kuzumaki
Noshiro
Takanosu
Kazuno
Nyūdo-zaki
Oga Pen.
Gojōnome
Ani
Iwate
Iwaizumi
Oga
TOWADA-HACHIMANTAI NP
Iwate-san 2,041 m
Tarō
AKITA
Tazawako
Miyako
Akita
Kakunodate
Shizukuishi
Morioka
Hayachine-san 1,914 m
Iwaizumi
Kawabe
Dewa Mts.
IWATE
Yamada
Honjō
Ōmagari
Yokote
Hanamaki
Kitakami Mts.
Otsuchi
Kisakata
Yashima
Jūmonji
Kitakami
Tōno
Kamaishi
Chōkai-san 2,237 m
Yuzawa
Mizusawa
Esashi
Ofunato
RIKUCHŪ-KAIGAN NP
Sakata
Yuza
Ōgachi
Ichinoseki
Rikuzentakata
Yuza
Kaneyama
Kesen'numa
Amarume
Shinjō
Mogami
Kurikoma-yama 1,628 m
Motoyoshi
Atsumi
Tsuruoka
Murayama
Shizugawa
YAMAGATA
Higashine
Furukawa
Onagawa
TŌHOKU
Sagae
Matsushima
Ishinomaki
CHŪBU
Tendō
Yamato
BANDAI
Gas-san 1,980 m
Izumi
MIYAGI
Wakuya
Ōshika Pen.
Murakami
Yamagata
Shiogama
Sendai Bay
NIIGATA
Kaminoyama
Sendai
Nakajō
Nagai
Zaō-san 1,841 m
Watari
Asahi-dake 1,870 m

Ishikari Bay
Uchiura Bay
Mutsu Bay

© HAMMOND WORLD ATLAS CORPORATION   CC-1036-A

Height

m. / ft.
6000 / 19700
4000 / 13000
2000 / 6500
1500 / 5000
1000 / 3300
500 / 1600
200 / 700
0
200 / 700
500 / 1600
1000 / 3300
2000 / 6500
3000 / 9800
4000 / 13000
5000 / 16400
6000 / 19700
m. / ft.

Depth

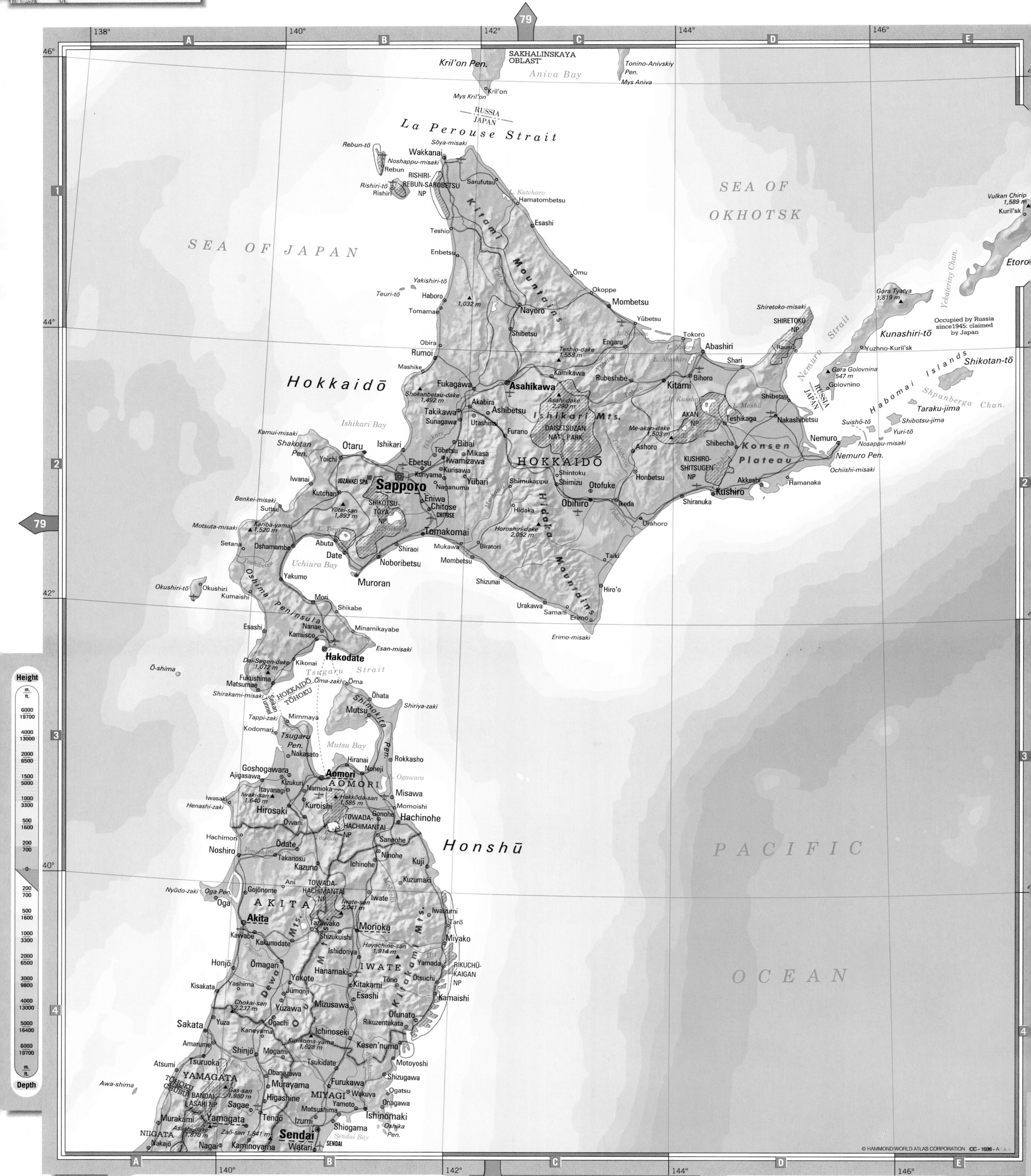

Population

■ Over 2,000,000	● 500,000 - 999,999	● 100,000 - 249,999	○ 10,000 - 29,999
▣ 1,000,000 - 1,999,999	● 250,000 - 499,999	● 30,000 - 99,999	○ Under 10,000

Scale 1:3,000,000   Lambert Conformal Conic Projection

MI   25   50   75   100
KM   25   50   75   100   125   150

okyo is one of the most densely populated cities on Earth. This modern tropolis is also a major Japanese commercial center, and its industrial region reads far beyond the city boundaries.

Osaka is the second-largest commercial and industrial center in Japan. The former capital, with its roughly 1,500 temples, is regarded as the heart of the Japanese culture.

Population	
■ Over 2,000,000	◉ 500,000 - 999,999
□ 1,000,000 - 1,999,999	◉ 250,000 - 499,999

◉ 100,000 - 249,999	○ 10,000 - 29,999
◎ 30,000 - 99,999	∘ Under 10,000

Scale 1:1,000,000   Lambert Conformal Conic Projection

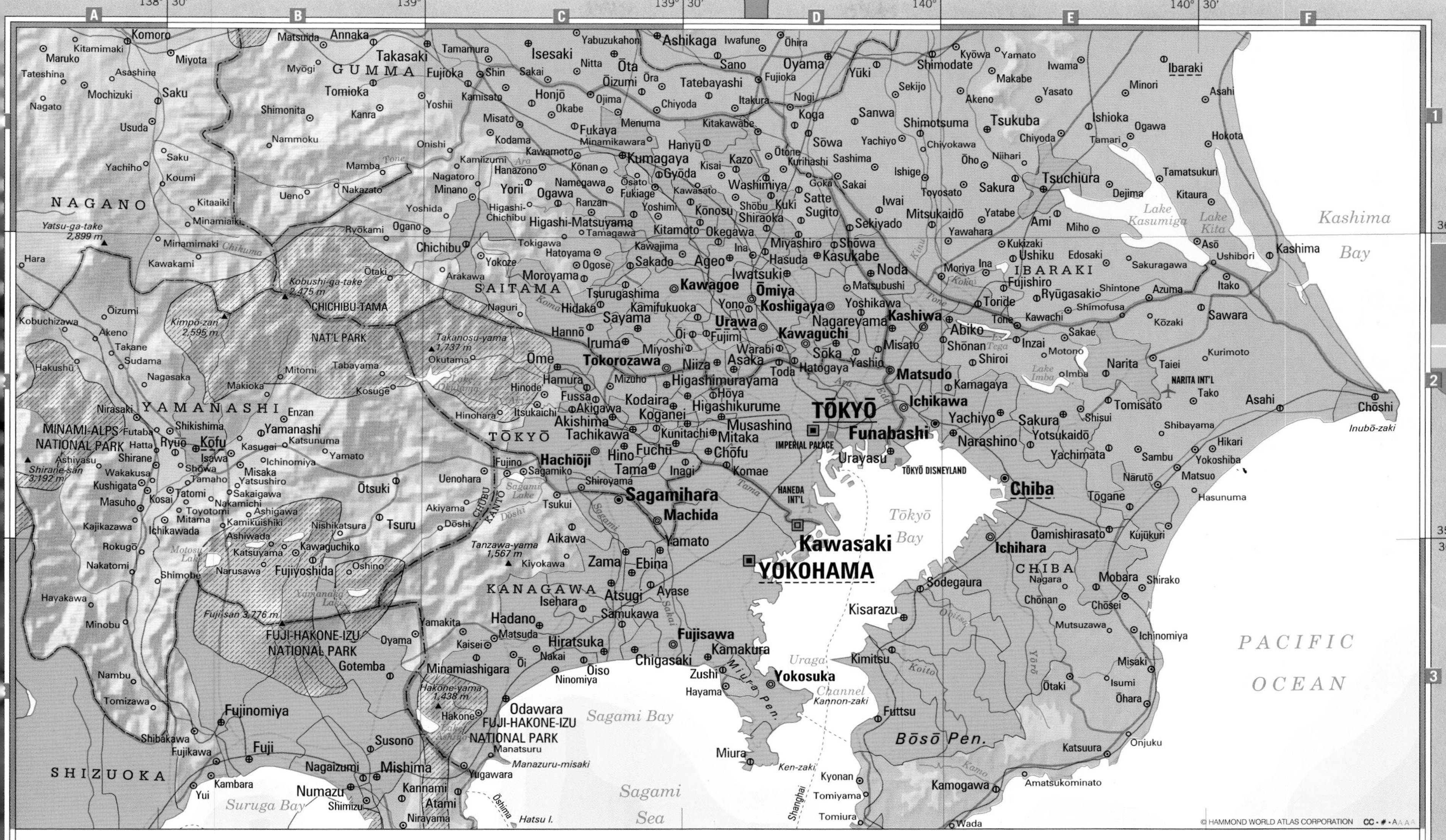

Height

m.	ft.
6000	19700
4000	13000
2000	6500
1500	5000
1000	3300
500	1600
200	700
0	0
200	700
500	1600
1000	3300
2000	6500
3000	9800
4000	13000
5000	16400
6000	19700

m. / ft.

Depth

© HAMMOND WORLD ATLAS CORPORATION

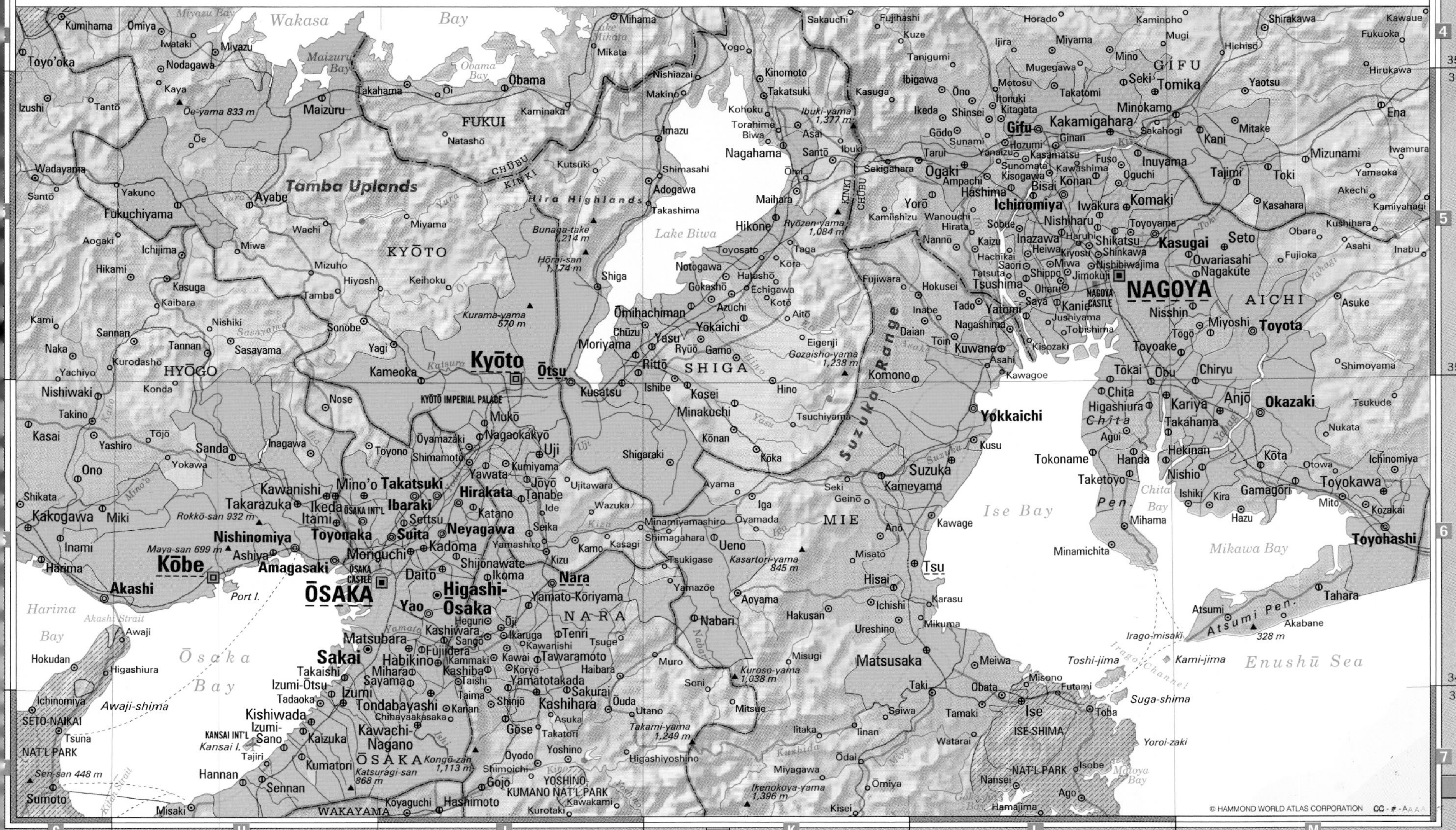

The heart of Japan's industrial might lies in four highly urbanized clusters, three of which are located on the southern coast of Honshu (Tokyo/Yokohama, Nagoya, Kobe/Osaka). The fourth cluster is located in northern Kyushu. Despite its lack of iron ore, coal, and petroleum and its limited arable land, Japan has become a major economic power since the end of World War II.

Using imported raw materials, skilled Japanese work force produces cars, electronics, optical equipment, textiles, and other quality products for the global market.

Continued on inset at right

Population

| ■ Over 2,000,000 | ⊙ 500,000 - 999,999 | ⊙ 100,000 - 249,999 | ∘ 10,000 - 29,999 |
| ☐ 1,000,000 - 1,999,999 | ⊙ 250,000 - 499,999 | ⊙ 30,000 - 99,999 | ∘ Under 10,000 |

Central and Southern Japan

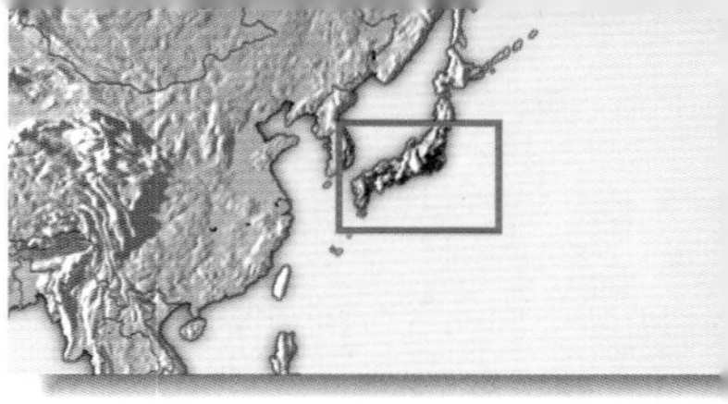

Map Section 84 85

E   138°   F   140°   G   142°   H   144°   J

MIYAGI
Ishinomaki
Yamoto Onagawa
Higashine Matsushima
Sagae Shiogama
YAMAGATA Tendo
Sendai
Yamagata Iwanuma
Kaminoyama Zaō-san 1,841 m SENDAI
Nakajo Takahata Shiroishi Watari
Shibata Yonezawa Sōma
Nagai Hobara

Awa-shima
Hajiki-zaki
Murakami
Asahi-dake 1,870 m
BANDAI-ASAHI
NP

Aikawa
Ryōtsu
Niigata
Niitsu Gosen Kitakata Nihonmatsu Namie
NIIGATA Shirone Aizu- Motomiya Miharu Ōtakine-yama 1,193 m
Tsubame Yamato Wakamatsu **Kōriyama** Towada
Nagaoka Kamo BANDAI-ASAHI Sukagawa Iwaki
Sanjo Mitsuke NP Tajima Yabuki Ishikawa **Iwaki**
Ojiya Nasu-dake 1,917 m Shirakawa

Sado
Sawasaki-bana Ogi
Suzu-misaki
Suzu Pen.
Toyama Bay
Nanao Namerikawa
Nyūzen **Toyama** Tate-yama 3,015 m
Himi Uozu
TOYAMA

Honshū

CHŪBU
TŌHOKU
KANTŌ

NIKKŌ NAT'L PARK
Nikkō Yaita Ōtawara Kita-Ibaraki
Imaichi Daigo Takahagi
Utsunomiya Hitachi-ōta Hitachi
Kanuma Mōka Kasama Katsuta
Tochigi Kasama Nakaminato
TOCHIGI Mito Ishioka Hokota
Oyama Koga **IBARAKI** Tsuchiura Kashima
Koshigaya Ryūgasaki Itako
Kawagoe **Urawa** Sawara Asahi
Sayama Kasukabe NARITA INT'L **Chōshi**
Tokorozawa **TŌKYŌ** Narita Inubō-zaki
Tachikawa **TŌKYŌ** **Chiba**
Chōfu **Kawaguchi** **CHIBA**
Hachiōji Kisarazu
Kawasaki Kimitsu
YOKOHAMA Futtsu
Sagamihara **Fujisawa** Ōtaki
KANAGAWA **Yokosuka** Bōsō
Hadano Chigasaki Pen. Katsuura
Isehara Kamakura Kyonan Kamogawa
Odawara Mishima Tomiyama
Atami Tateyama Nojima-zaki

NAGOYA AICHI
Toyota
Okazaki
Nishio Toyokawa
Hamakita
Toyohashi **Hamamatsu**
SHIZUOKA
Shizuoka FUJI-HAKONE-IZU NAT'L PARK
Fujieda Amagi-san 1,407 m
Yaizu Ō Island
Omae-zaki Shimoda Ōshima

Sagami Sea
Suruga Bay
Irō-zaki
CHŪBU KANTŌ

TŌKYŌ
Kōzu-shima
Miyake-jima
MIYAKEJIMA

J A P A N

Mikura-jima

FUJI-HAKONE-IZU NAT'L PARK
(JAPAN)
Hachijō-jima
Hachijō HACHIJŌJIMA
Izu Islands

Aoga-shima

Beyoneisu-retsugan

PACIFIC OCEAN
Sendai Bay

Inset: Kyūshū / Ryukyu Islands

Koshiki Is. Sendai Kokubu Miyakonojō
Kushikino Ijūin **KAGOSHIMA** Nichinan
Kagoshima Kaseda Kanoya Kōyama Kushima
Makurazaki Sata-misaki Tarumizu **Kyūshū**
Ōsumi Strait
Nishino'omote
Tanega-shima
Kaniyaku Yaku 1,935 m
Kuchino-shima Nakatane
Suwanose-jima Ōsumi Is.
Shanghai Tokara Islands
KAGOSHIMA

EAST CHINA SEA
Naze Amami-ōshima
Setouchi Kikai
Tokuno Amami
Tokunoshima
Okinoerabu
Yoron
Iheya Hedo-misaki
Ie Yonaha-dake 498 m
Motobu Nago Okinawa
Kumé Ginowan Gushikawa
Naha Urasoe
Itoman Kyan-zaki
Okinawa Is.

R y u k y u   I s l a n d s
(Nansei - Shotō)

Keelung Senkaku-Shotō
OKINAWA

Sakishima Islands Hirara
Yonaguni Tamara Miyako
Ishigaki Miyako Is.
Iriomote Ishigaki
Yaeyama Is.

Kitadaitō
Minamidaitō
Okidaitō
PACIFIC OCEAN

© HAMMOND W.A.C.

Scale 1:3,000,000   Lambert Conformal Conic Projection
MI   25   50   75   100
KM   25   50   75   100   125   150

0   60 Mi
0   60 Km

Southeastern China was once the most backward part of the country. Growth has accelerated in recent years, particularly in Guangzhou (Canton) - for many years the only city in China where foreign trade was possible - and Shenzhen, which benefits from its proximity to Hong Kong (a special administration of the People's Republic of China since 1997) and is now an autonomous economic district.

Taiwan, the island refuge of the Nationalist Chinese government since 1949, has developed into a major industrial power.

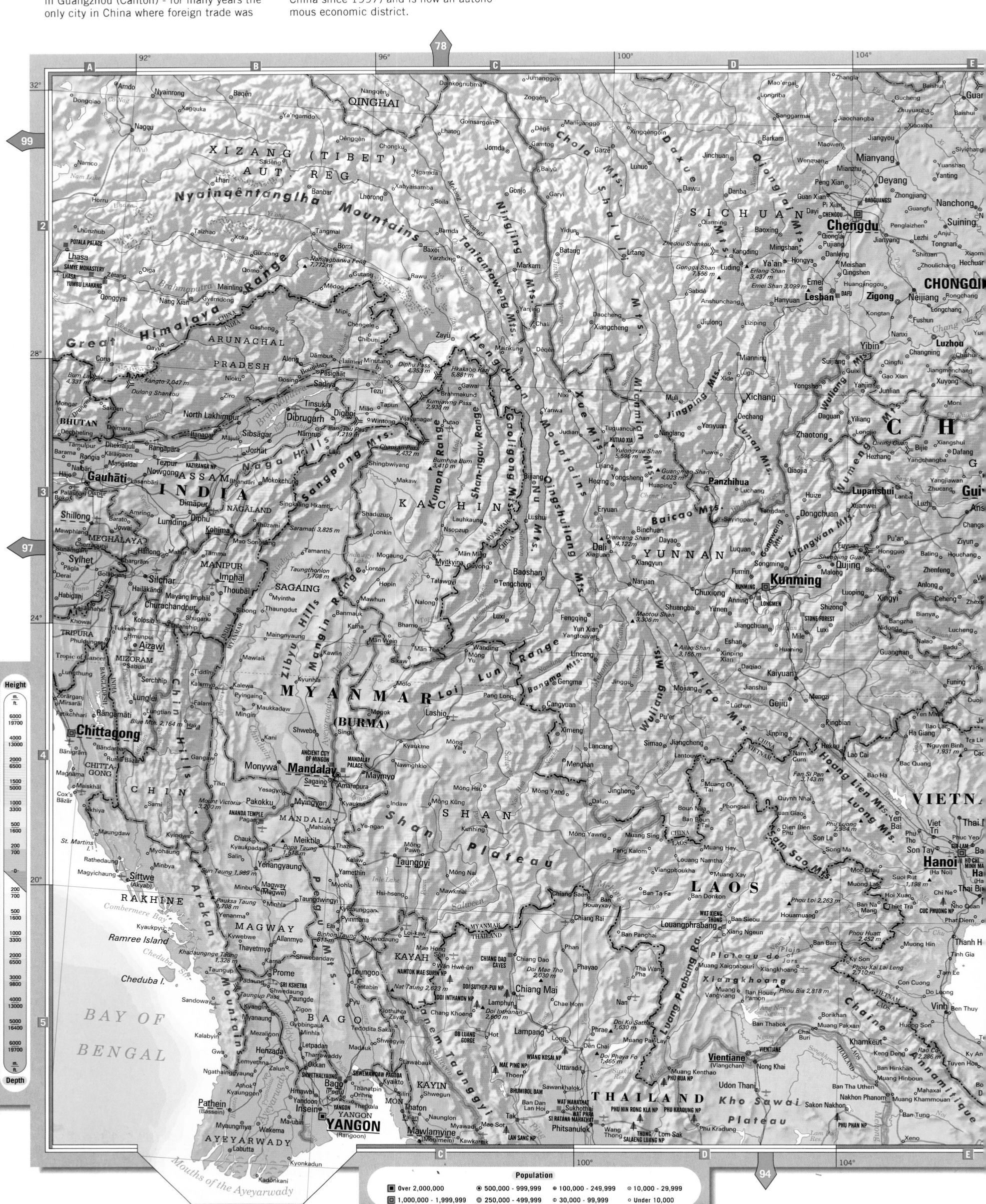

Population

■ Over 2,000,000	◉ 500,000 - 999,999	⊙ 100,000 - 249,999	○ 10,000 - 29,999
■ 1,000,000 - 1,999,999	◎ 250,000 - 499,999	◌ 30,000 - 99,999	○ Under 10,000

Height

m. ft.
6000 19700
4000 13000
2000 6500
1500 5000
1000 3300
500 1600
200 700
0
200 700
500 1600
1000 3300
2000 6500
3000 9800
4000 13000
5000 16400
6000 19700
m. ft.

Depth

108° 79 F 112° G 80 116° H 120°

SHAANXI
Wudang Shan 1,612 m
HENAN
ANHUI
NANJING
Hefei
JIANGSU
SHANGHAI

HUBEI
THREE GORGES DAM (U.C.)
Yichang
Shashi
WUHAN
Huangshi
Hangzhou

Changde
Yueyang
Nanchang
Jiujiang
ZHEJIANG
Ningbo

Changsha
HUNAN
Zhuzhou
Xiangtan
Pingxiang
JIANGXI
Fuzhou
FUJIAN

Hengyang
Leiyang
Chenzhou
Ganzhou
EAST CHINA SEA

Guilin
GUILIN
Liuzhou
Shaoguan
Xiamen
Quanzhou

T'AIPEI Keelung
TAIWAN
T'aichung

GUANGDONG
GUANGZHOU (Canton)
Foshan Dongguan
Shenzhen
Chaozhou
Shantou

Nanning
GUANGXI ZHUANGZU AUTONOMOUS REGION
Wuzhou
Jiangmen Zhongshan

Macau MACAU
Victoria HONG KONG
Kaohsiung

Zhanjiang

Leizhou Peninsula
SOUTH

Haikou HAIKOU

HAINAN
Hainan Dao
CHINA SEA

Gulf of Tonkin

Dongsha I. (Pratas I.) (CHINA) Pratas Reef

PHILIPPINES
Luzon

Tropic of Cancer

Paracel Islands (Sovereignty disputed)

Crescent Group
Amphitrite Group

Inset map — Hong Kong region:

GUANGDONG
Sheung Shui
Fanling
Shenzhen
GUANGDONG

Tin Shui Wai
Yuen Long
Tuen Mun
Tsuen Wan
Tai Po
Sha Tin
New Territories

HONG KONG
Kowloon
Victoria Hong Kong
CHEK LAP KOK
Lantau Island
Lantau Peak 934 m

SOUTH CHINA SEA

Macau

108° F 112° G 114° K L 114° 15' M 114° 30' H 120° J

Scale 1:6,000,000 Lambert Conformal Conic Projection
MI 50 100 150 200
KM 50 100 150 200 250 300

© HAMMOND W.A.C.

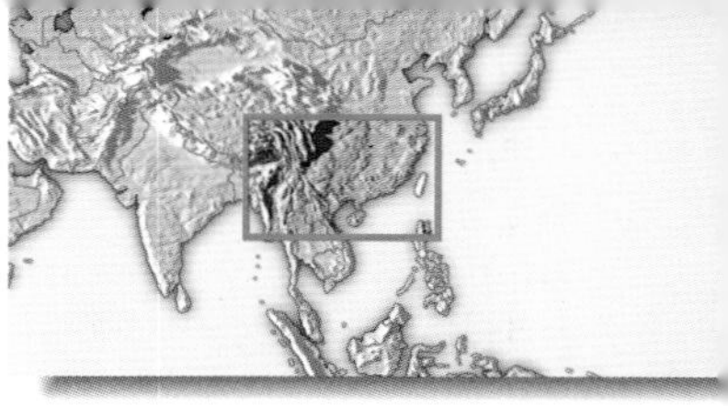

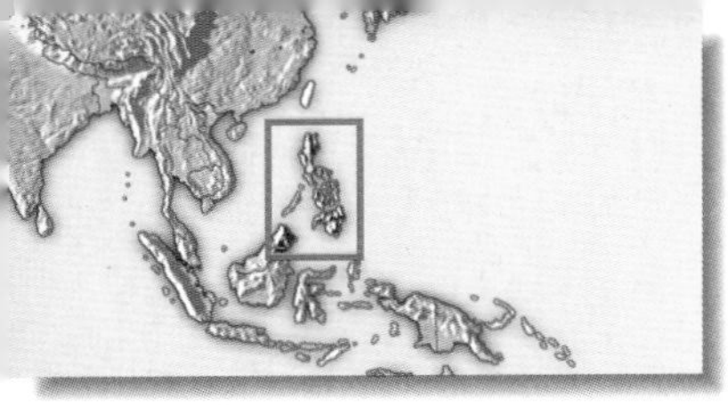

Philippines

Only ten percent of the 7,000 islands that comprise the Philippines are inhabited. The region was originally settled primarily by Malays. A Spanish dominion from 1565 until 1898, the islands became a bastion of Catholicism in Southeast A[...] The 48 years of U.S. rule that followed also left an indelible imprint on the isl[...] nation.

Height

m.	ft.
6000	19700
4000	13000
2000	6500
1500	5000
1000	3300
500	1600
200	700
0	0
200	700
500	1600
1000	3300
2000	6500
3000	9800
4000	13000
5000	16400
6000	19700

Depth

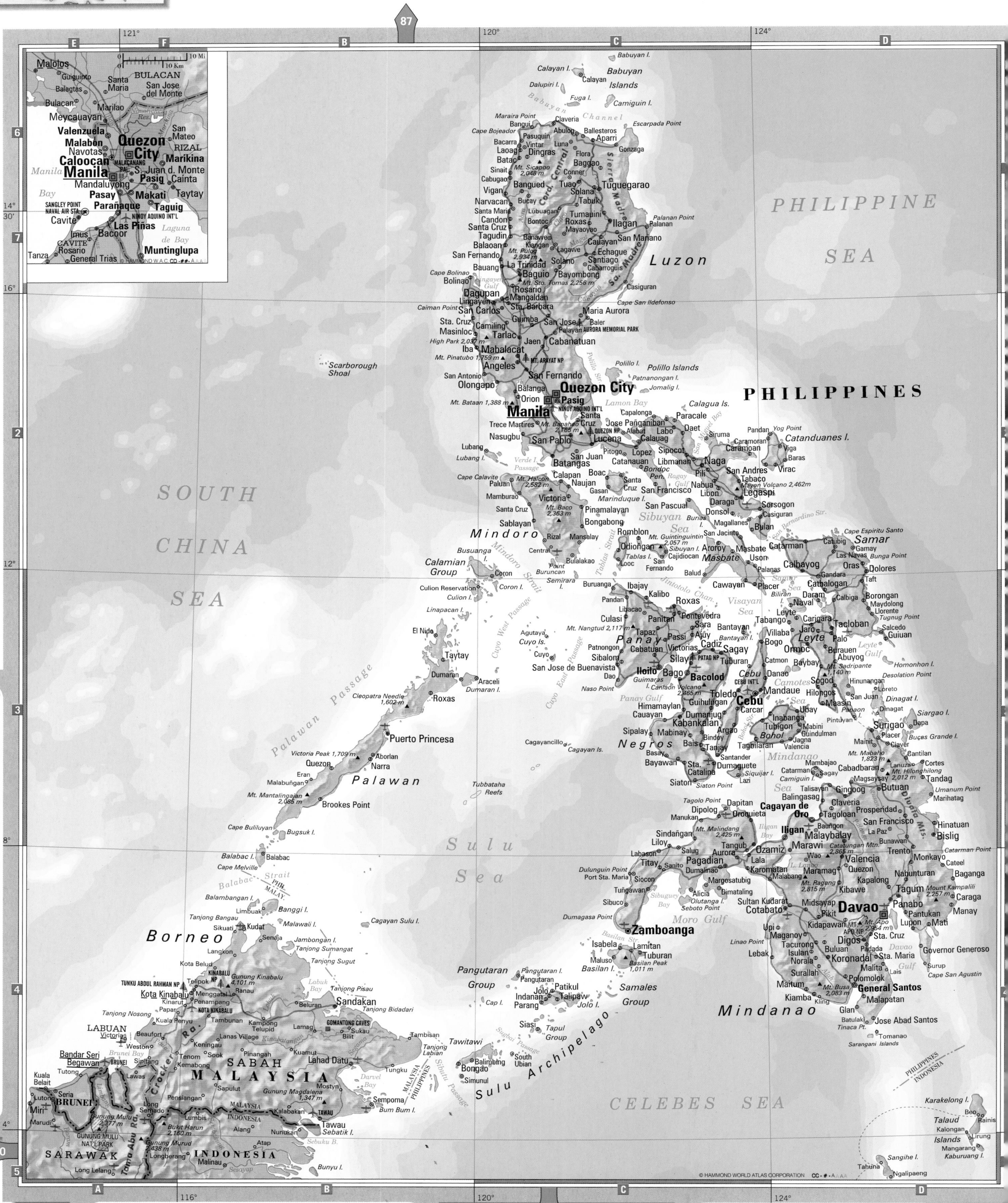

Population

■ Over 2,000,000	● 500,000 - 999,999
■ 1,000,000 - 1,999,999	● 250,000 - 499,999
● 100,000 - 249,999	○ 10,000 - 29,999
○ 30,000 - 99,999	○ Under 10,000

Scale 1:6,000,000 Lambert Conformal Conic Projection

© HAMMOND WORLD ATLAS CORPORATION

Malaysia and Indonesia are the easternmost outposts of Islam. Indonesia is now the most populous Islamic nation in the world. Only the Island of Bali has a predominantly Hindu population. A major producer of wood, tin, and rubber positioned along important international shipping routes, Malaysia has developed one of the most productive economies in the region.

Malaya, Sumatra, Java

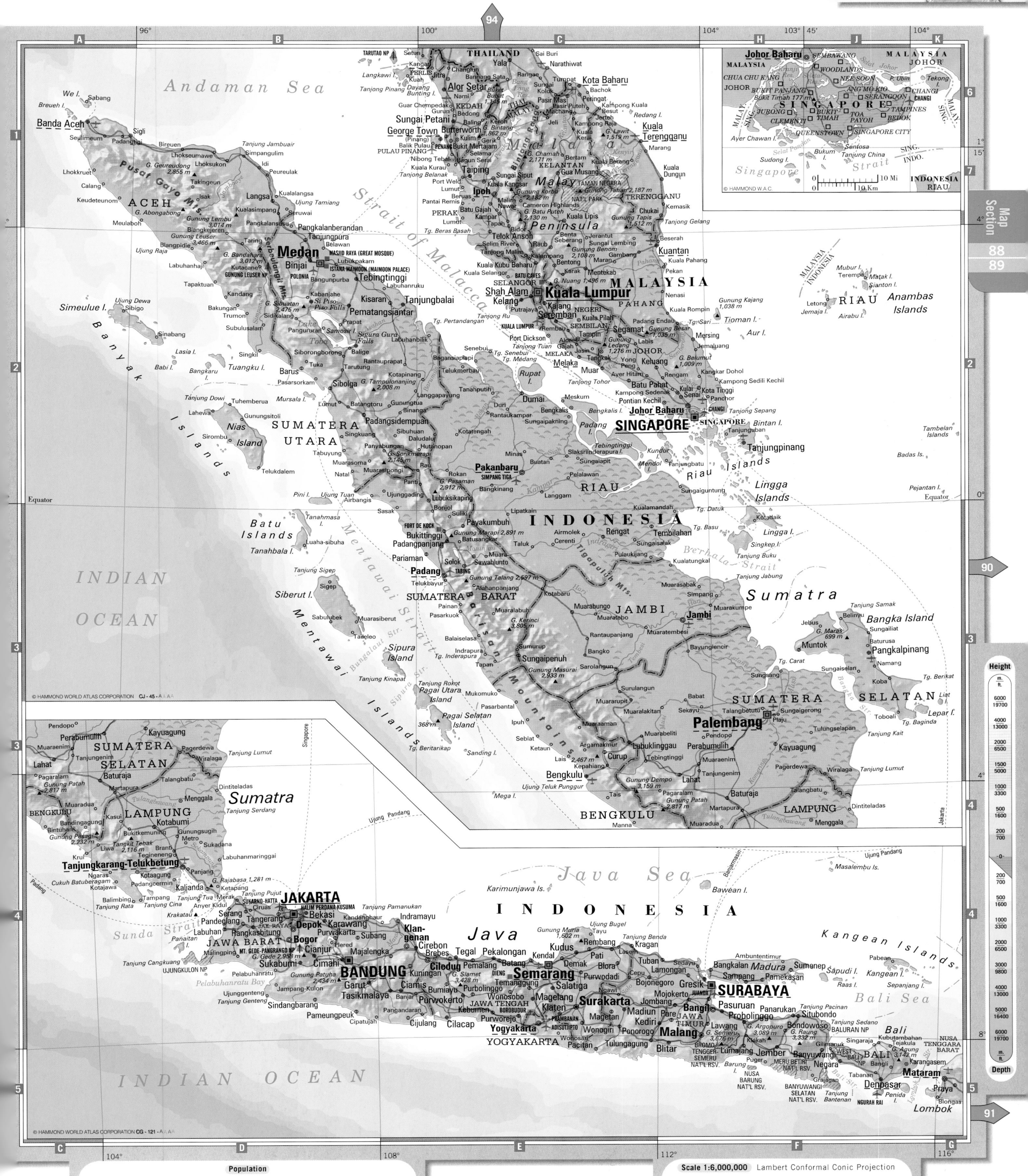

90

91

Population

■ Over 2,000,000   ● 500,000 - 999,999   ● 100,000 - 249,999   ◦ 10,000 - 29,999
■ 1,000,000 - 1,999,999   ◉ 250,000 - 499,999   ● 30,000 - 99,999   ◦ Under 10,000

Scale 1:6,000,000   Lambert Conformal Conic Projection

MI 50 100 150 200
KM 50 100 150 200 250 300

Height

m.   ft.
6000 19700
4000 13000
2000 6500
1500 5000
1000 3300
500   1600
200   700
0   0
200   700
1000 3300
2000 6500
3000 9800
4000 13000
5000 16400
6000 19700
m.   ft.
Depth

© HAMMOND WORLD ATLAS CORPORATION

Indonesia covers most of the Malaysian archipelago. The Greater Sunda Islands of Sumatra and Java are characterized by "spines" of steep folded mountain ranges that tower above broad floodplains.

The hot, tropical climate, with annual rainfall of about 6,000 mm, supports flourishing rain-forest growth that once covered over 60 percent of the land surface. Today, the rain forest has given way to secondary forest, alang-alang grass, and ferns - the result of extensive logging and burning. The best known of the roughly 200 active volcanoes in the region is Krakatoa, which last erupted in 1883, causing thousands of deaths.

Population

- ▣ Over 2,000,000
- ◉ 500,000 - 999,999
- ● 100,000 - 249,999
- ⊙ 10,000 - 29,999
- ▢ 1,000,000 - 1,999,999
- ◎ 250,000 - 499,999
- ○ 30,000 - 99,999
- ∘ Under 10,000

Scale 1:9,000,000   Lambert Conformal Conic Projection

© HAMMOND WORLD ATLAS CORPORATION   CD - 1047 - A-A-A

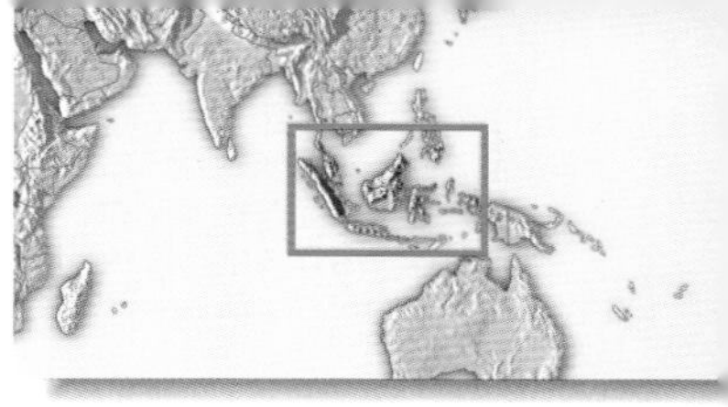

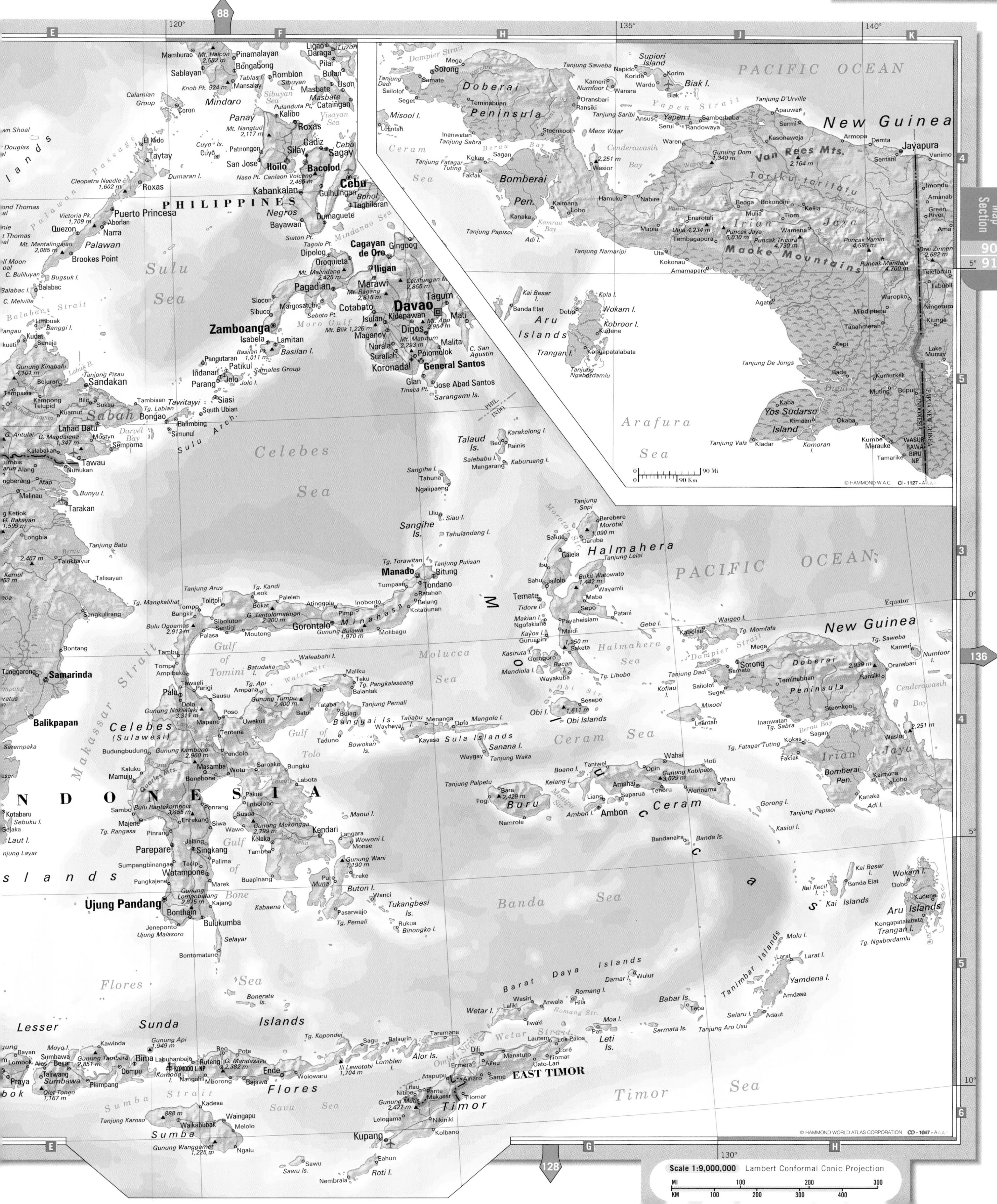

The map shows the Asian monsoon region, through which expansive air currents move in an alternating, semi-annual rhythm. ("Monsoon" comes from the Arabic "mausim," or "season [suitable for sea voyages].") The southwest monsoon that comes from the sea brings life-giving rains to this densely populated region during the summer. A rainless monsoon season causes severe famine, while extreme precipitation often results in flood disasters. Roughly half of the world's population lives in monsoon regions. Most working people in this part of the world are employed in subsistence agriculture, primarily in rice cultivation.

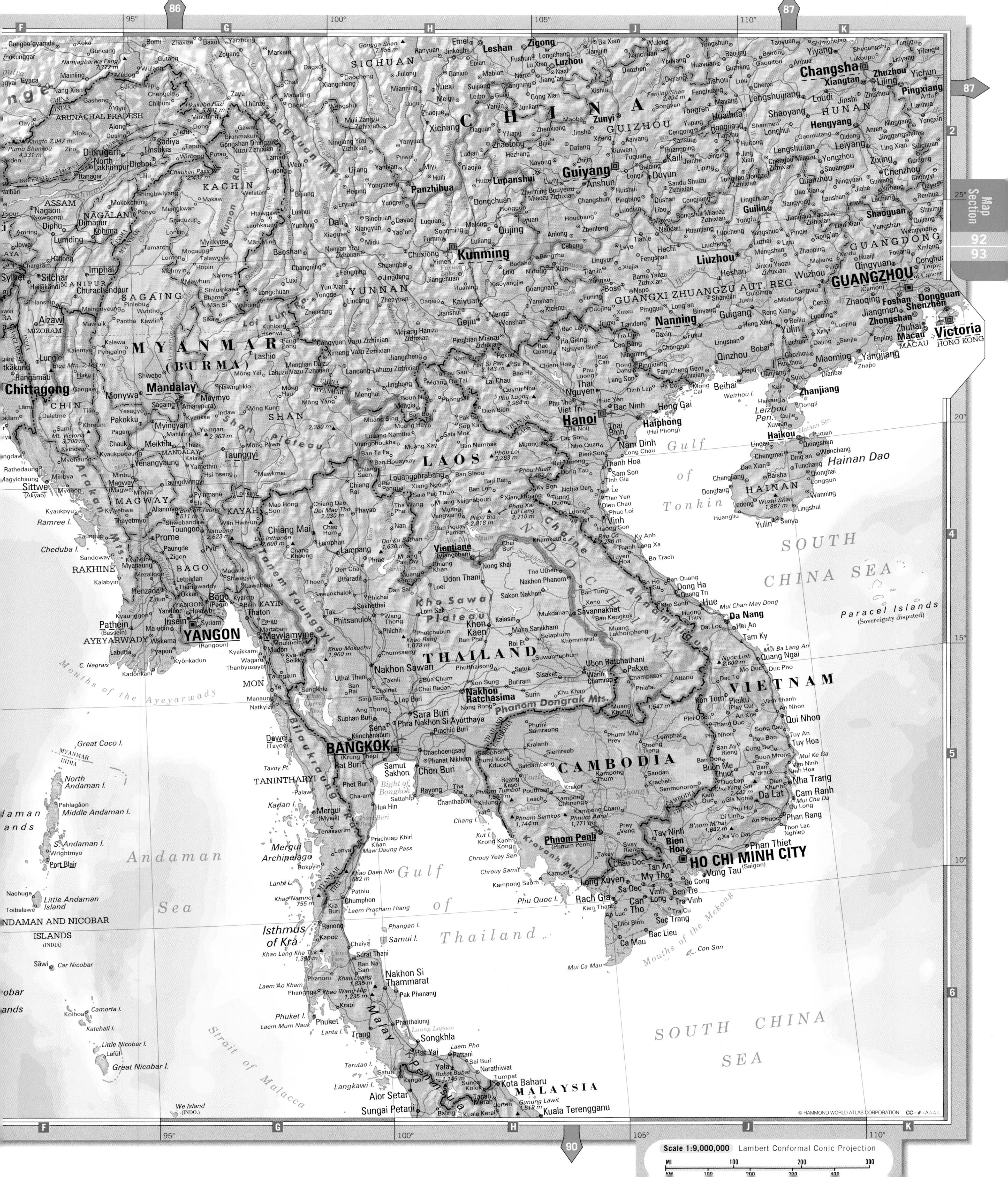

Scale 1:9,000,000 Lambert Conformal Conic Projection

© Hammond World Atlas Corporation

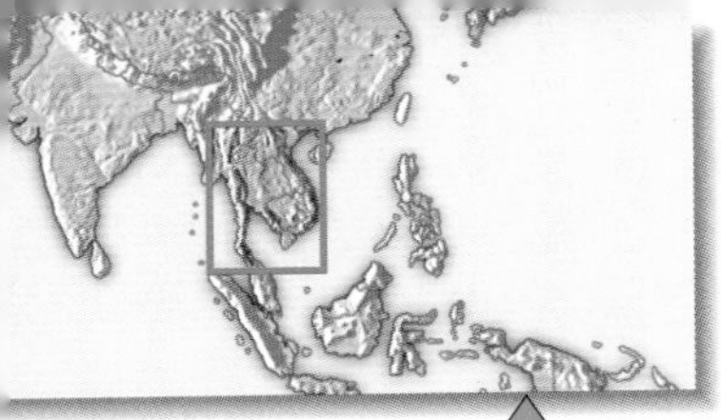

Indochina

The backbone of eastern India is formed by several mountain ranges to the southeast of the Himalayas that drain into the fertile plains of the Mekong, Salween, Irawadi, and Menam Chao Phraya rivers.

The region has a monsoon climate, with rainfall decreasing toward the interior. Vegetation ranges from dense tropical rain forest to moist and arid savannahs farther inland.

© HAMMOND WORLD ATLAS CORPORATION   CC - # - AAA-

Scale 1:6,000,000   Lambert Conformal Conic Projection

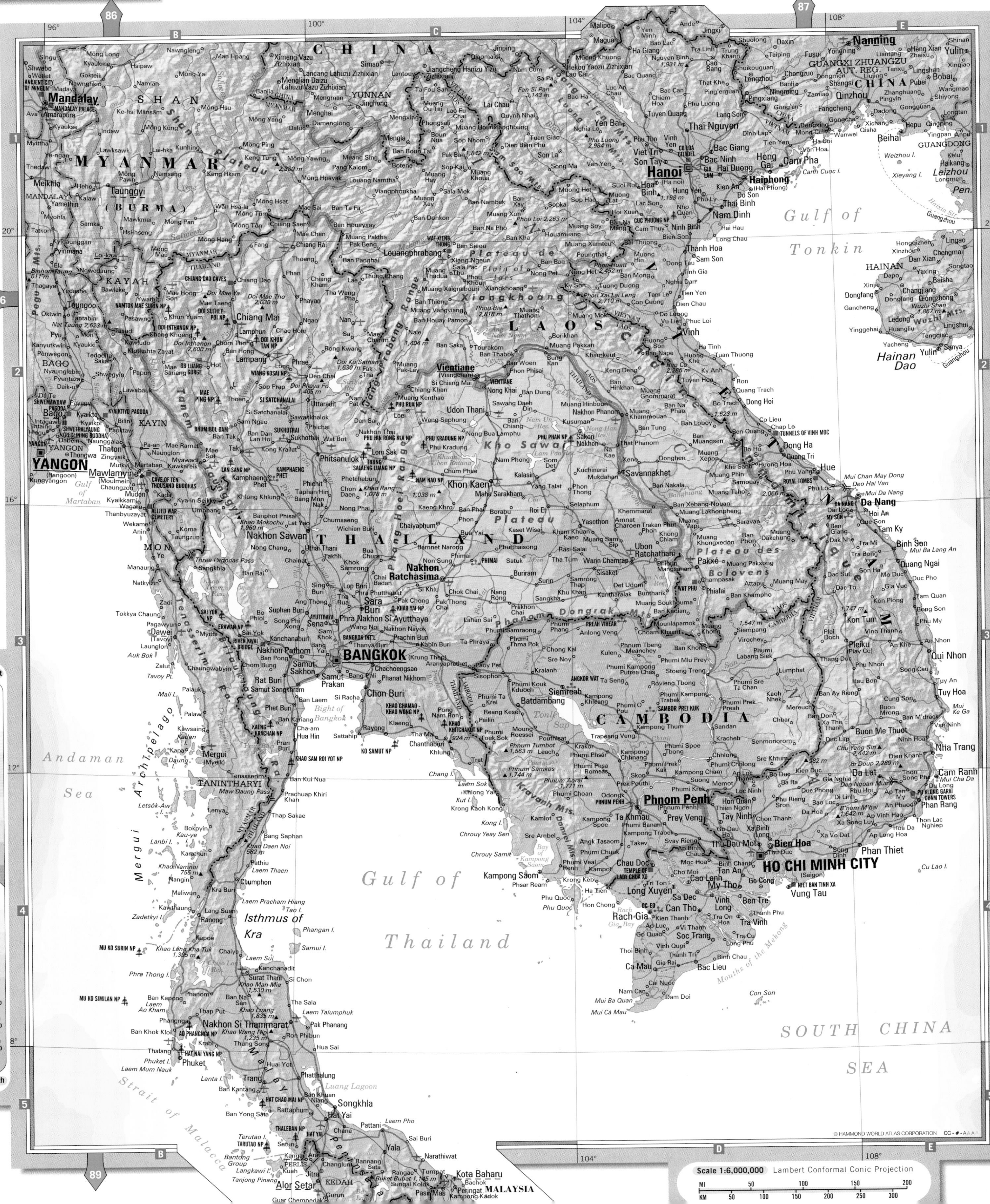

irtually no other country is as dependent upon monsoons as India. Monsoon ...ns are essential to the rice harvests that ...ed nearly a billion people. The southwest ...onsoon provides 90 percent of the region's precipitation (Cherrapunji holds the record, with 10,870 mm of rainfall per year). It also replenishes groundwater reserves that supply millions of people in India's metropolitan centers with drinking water.

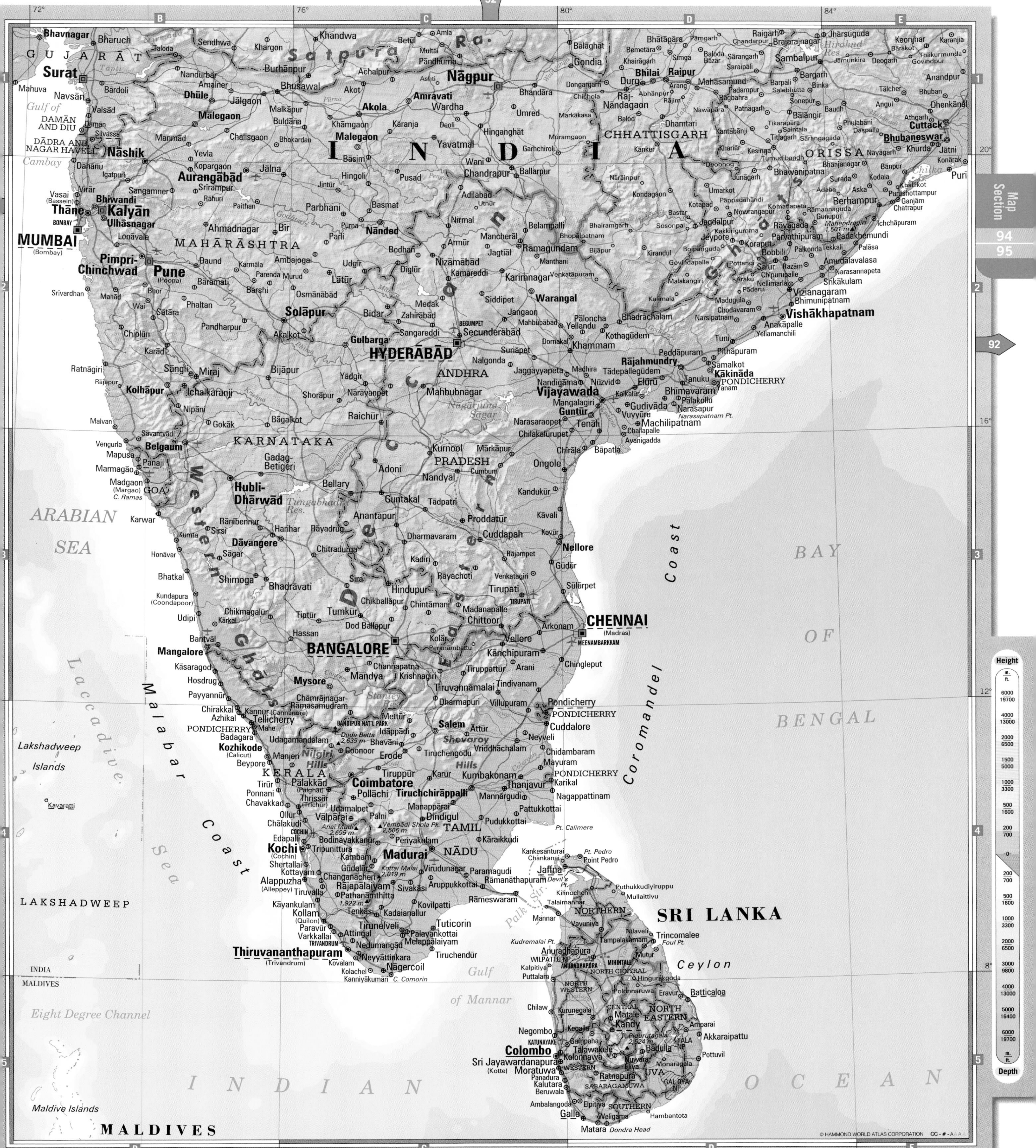

Southern India

Map Section 94 95

Scale 1:6,000,000 Lambert Conformal Conic Projection

Population	
■ Over 2,000,000	◉ 500,000 - 999,999	○ 100,000 - 249,999	○ 10,000 - 29,999
□ 1,000,000 - 1,999,999	◉ 250,000 - 499,999	○ 30,000 - 99,999	○ Under 10,000

© HAMMOND WORLD ATLAS CORPORATION

Over 2,700 km long, the Ganges flows from headwaters 4,000 meters above sea level in the Himalayas. It joins the Brahmaputra in Bengal, forming a fertile delta comprising some 56,000 square km.

Used intensively for irrigation, the river now carries much less water than in the past, especially during the dry months. The water shortage in the region is exacerbated by progressive deforestation in the

Himalayas, which has reduced the capacity to store monsoon rainwater. Water now runs off rapidly during the rainy season, causing frequent catastrophic flooding and taking thousands of lives.

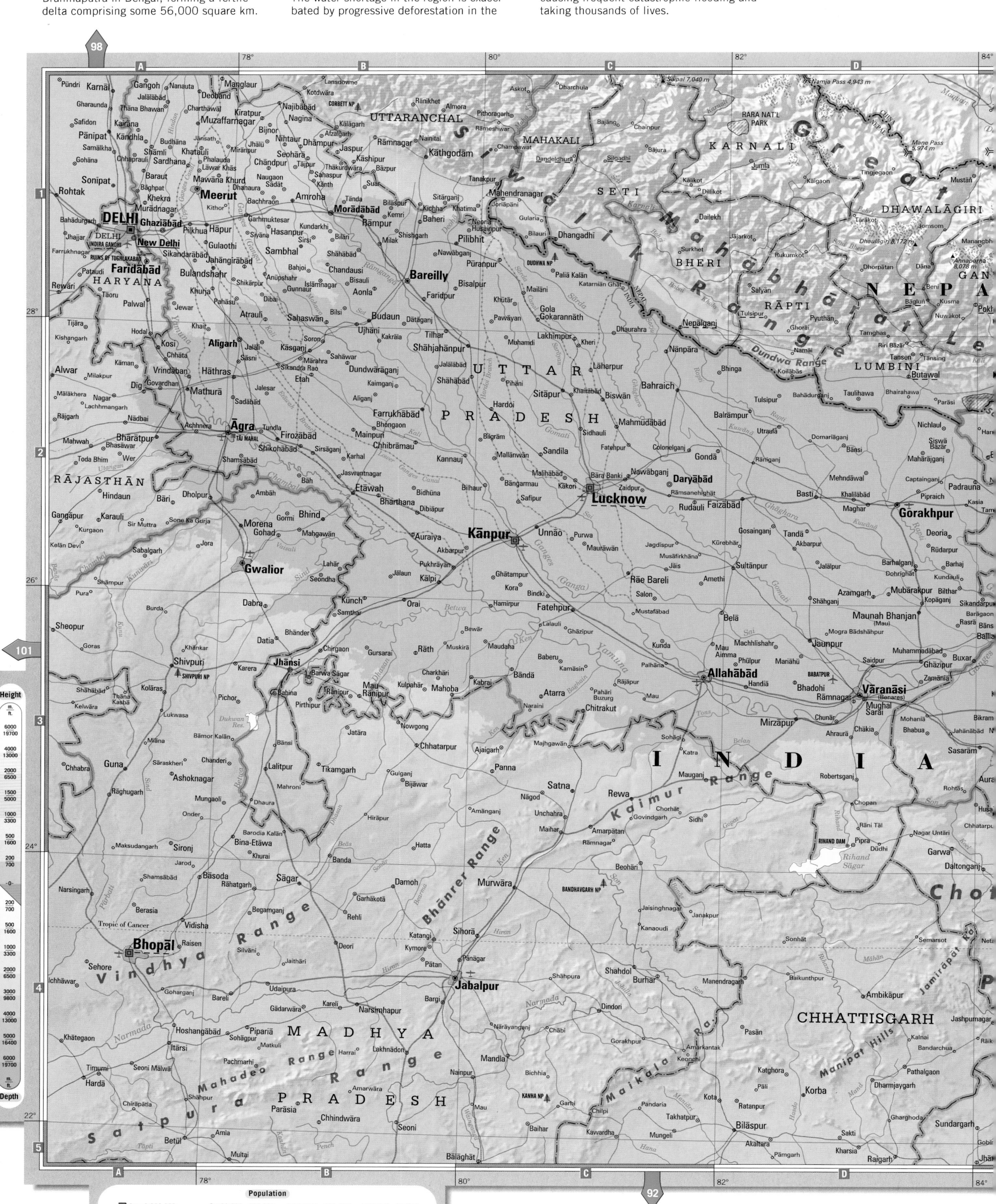

Population		
■ Over 2,000,000	◉ 500,000 - 999,999	◎ 100,000 - 249,999	○ 10,000 - 29,999
▣ 1,000,000 - 1,999,999	⊚ 250,000 - 499,999	◦ 30,000 - 99,999	○ Under 10,000

Scale 1:3,000,000   Lambert Conformal Conic Projection

© HAMMOND WORLD ATLAS CORPORATION

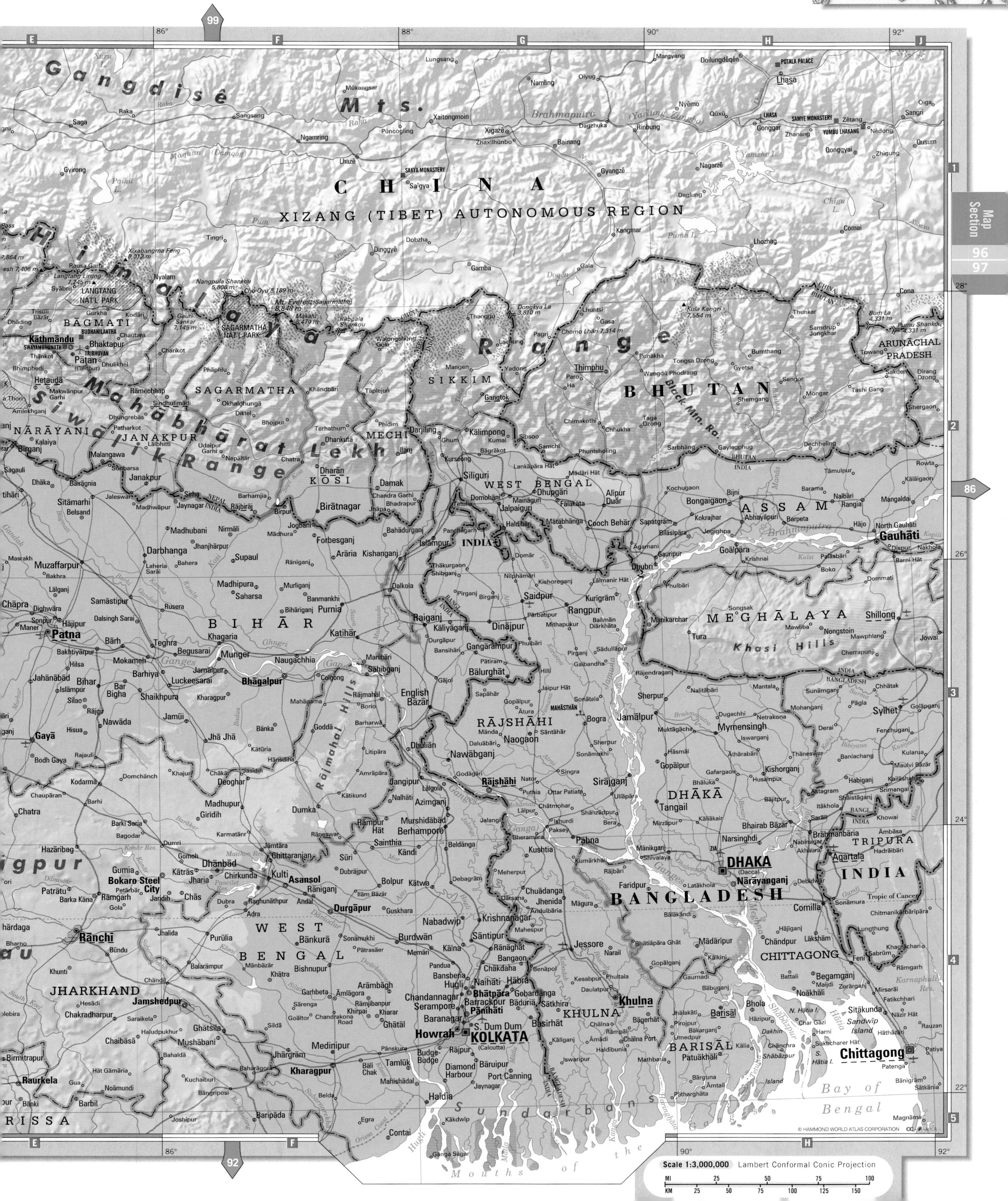

Punjab Plain

This plain, irrigated by a fan of eastern tributaries of the Indus, forms the granary of India and Pakistan. For thousands of years, a vast network of canals and dams has covered the plain. Thanks to this irrigation system, the Punjab is agricultural land and the most producti[ve] wheat and cotton-growing region in we[stern] India. Most of the area is in Pakistan, w[hich] gained independence from India in 194[7].

Height

m.	ft.
6000	19700
4000	13000
2000	6500
1500	5000
1000	3300
500	1600
200	700
- 0 -	
200	700
500	1600
1000	3300
2000	6500
3000	9800
4000	13000
5000	16400
6000	19700

Depth

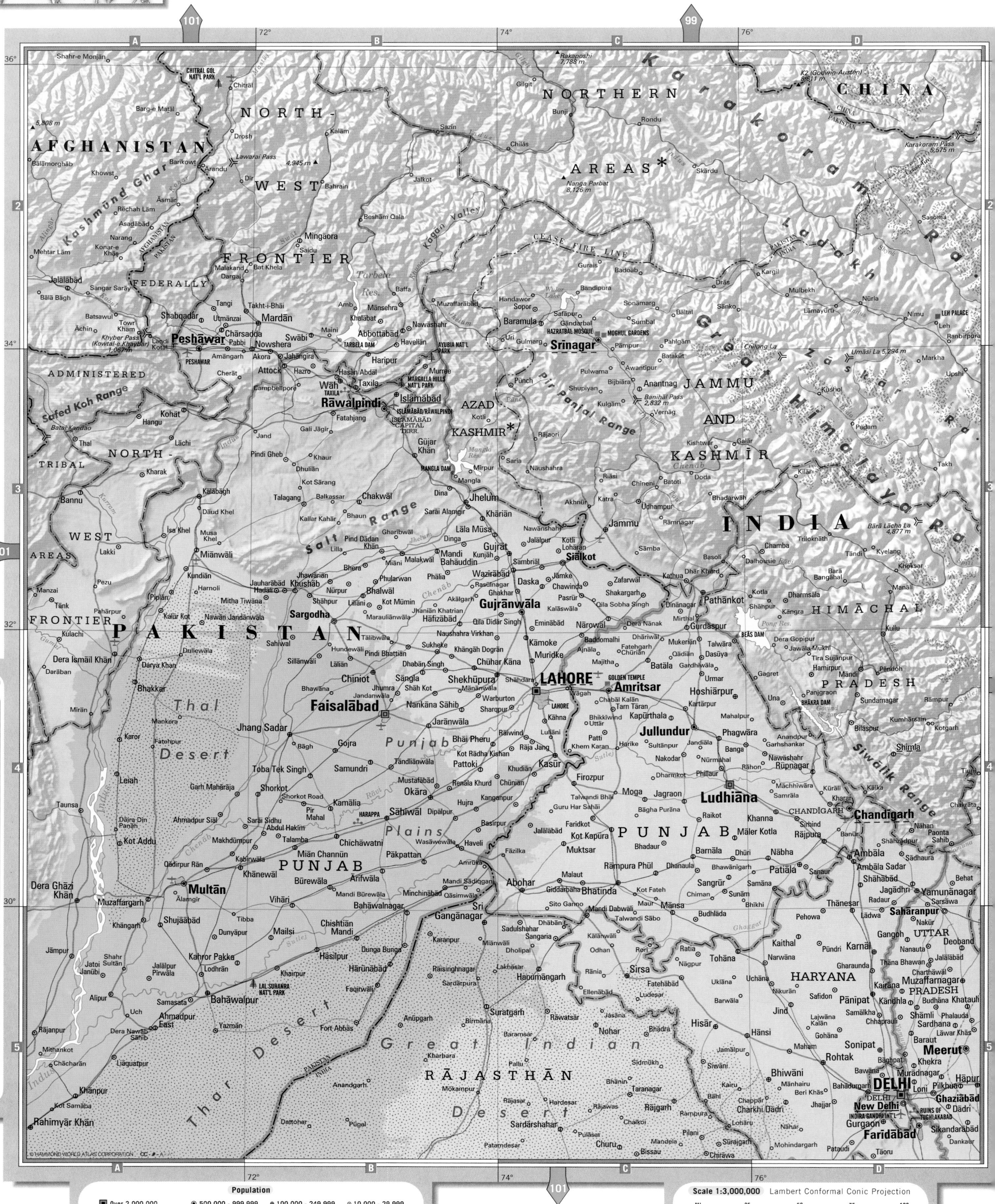

Population

- ■ Over 2,000,000
- ◉ 500,000 - 999,999
- ◉ 100,000 - 249,999
- ◦ 10,000 - 29,999
- ▣ 1,000,000 - 1,999,999
- ◉ 250,000 - 499,999
- ◎ 30,000 - 99,999
- • Under 10,000

*AZARD KASHMIR AND THE NORTHERN AREAS ARE ADMINISTERED BY PAKISTAN BUT DO NOT HAVE PROVINCIAL STATUS.

Scale 1:3,000,000 Lambert Conformal Conic Projection

MI 25 50 75 100

KM 25 50 75 100 125 150

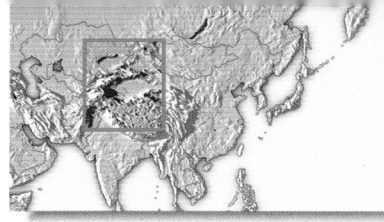

Central Asia

nown as the "Roof of the World,"
central Asia is dominated by the vast
ountain systems of the Hindu Kush, the
mir, the Tian Shan and the Himalayas,
tending over 2,400 km from Pakistan
to Bhutan. Here, the Indian plate thrusts
beneath the Asian continent, pushing
Tibet upward. The young mountain range
is still rising at a rate of about one
centimeter per year.

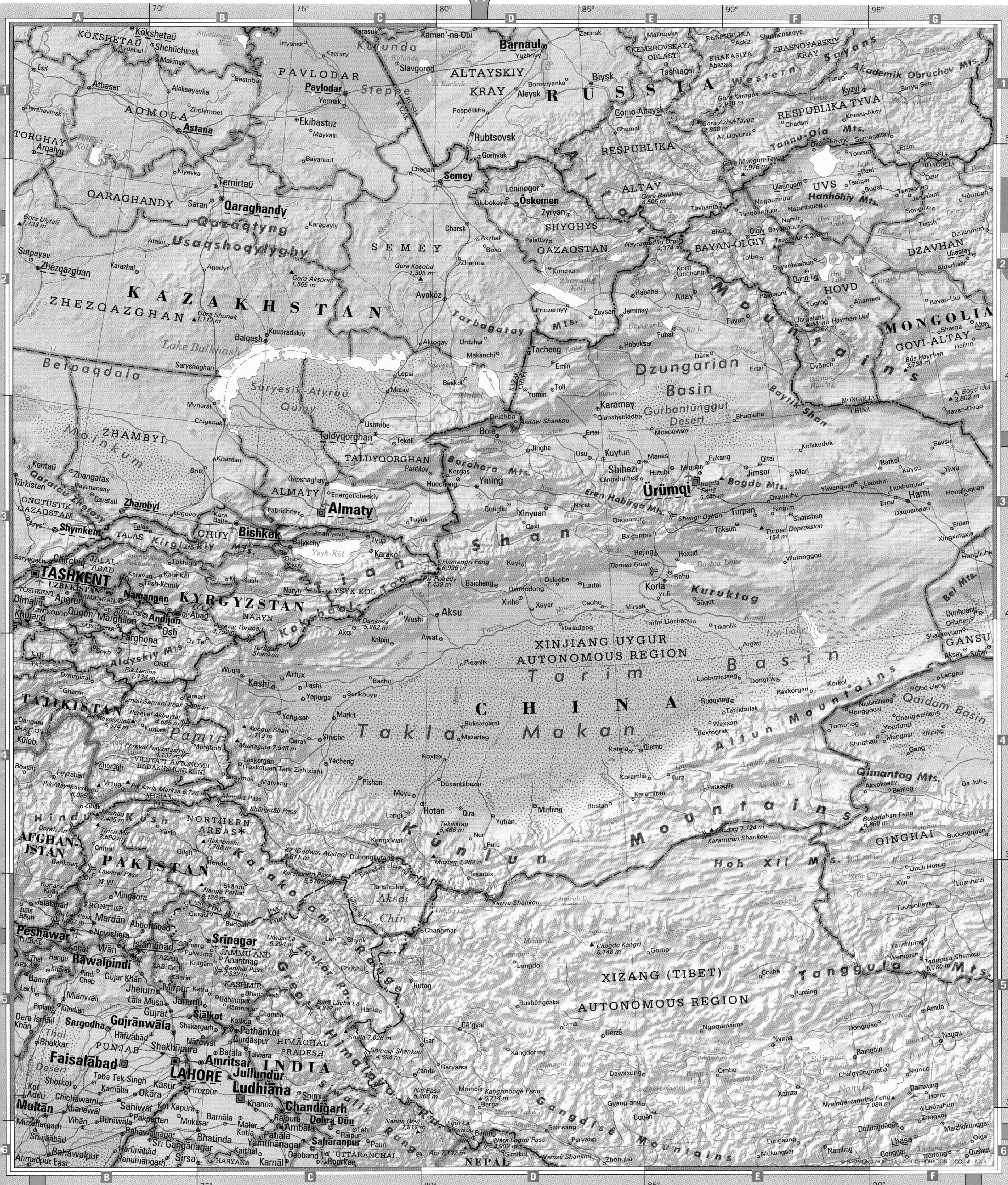

Scale 1:9,000,000   Lambert Conformal Conic Projection

Population

- ■ Over 2,000,000
- ● 500,000 - 999,999
- ● 100,000 - 249,999
- ○ 10,000 - 29,999
- □ 1,000,000 - 1,999,999
- ● 250,000 - 499,999
- ● 30,000 - 99,999
- ○ Under 10,000

*AZAD KASHMIR AND THE NORTHERN AREAS ARE ADMINISTERED
BY PAKISTAN BUT DO NOT HAVE PROVINCIAL STATUS.

Saudi Arabia occupies most of the Arabian Peninsula. Arid plains and deserts, such as the Rub' al Khali, cover ninety-nine percent of the country. Oases are found only at the foot of plateaus and near intermittently dry riverbeds known as wadis. A rift structure thrusts the southwestern edge of the peninsula abruptly upward from the Red Sea, forming an imposing escarpment, and then descends steeply toward the northeast. Water is extremely scarce. Sparse winter rains fall only in the north and in the Oman mountain region. The coastal areas, however, are very humid.

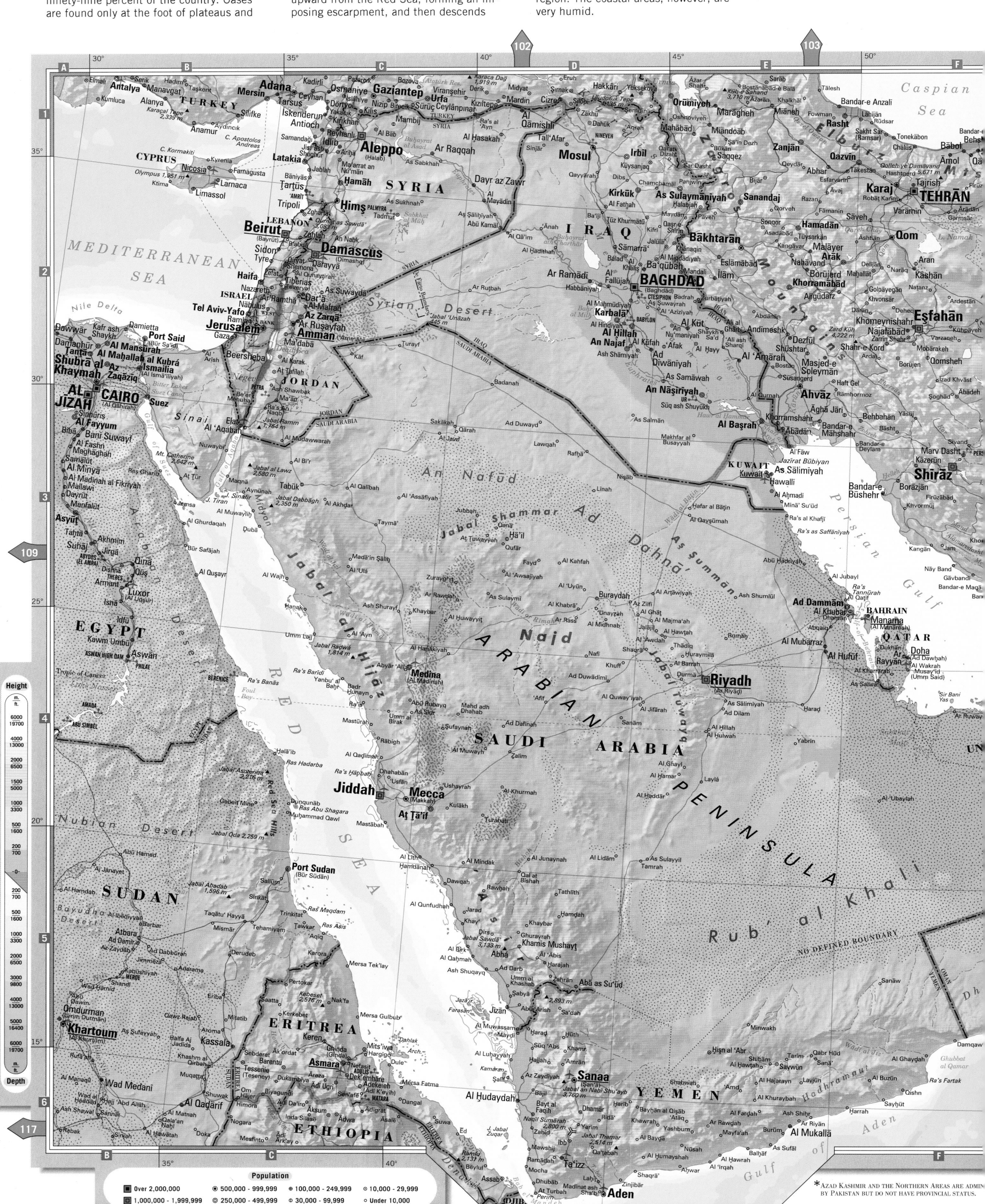

Population

■ Over 2,000,000   ◉ 500,000 - 999,999   ◉ 100,000 - 249,999   ○ 10,000 - 29,999
■ 1,000,000 - 1,999,999   ◉ 250,000 - 499,999   ● 30,000 - 99,999   ○ Under 10,000

*AZAD KASHMIR AND THE NORTHERN AREAS ARE ADMINISTERED BY PAKISTAN BUT DO NOT HAVE PROVINCIAL STATUS.

TURKMENISTAN

UZBEKISTAN

TAJIKISTAN

TAJIKISTAN

CHINA

Ashgabat

Mashhad

Neyshābūr

Sabzevār

AFGHANISTAN

Herāt

Kabul
(Kabol)

Hindu Kush

Peshawar

Rawalpindi

Islāmābād

Srinagar

JAMMU AND KASHMIR

Kandahār

Quetta

PAKISTAN

BALOCHISTĀN

Kermān

Zāhedān

LAHORE

Amritsar

Ludhiāna

Chandigarh

Faisalābād

Multān

Gujrānwāla

Sargodha

PUNJAB

DELHI

New Delhi

Meerut

Ghaziā-
bad

Faridābād

Bikaner

Jaipur

Jodhpur

RĀJASTHĀN

Great Indian

Desert
(Thar)

INDIA

Ajmer

Kota

Udaipur

Hyderabad

KARĀCHI

Mouths
of the Indus

AHMADĀBĀD

Vadodara
(Baroda)

GUJARĀT

Rājkot

Jāmnagar

Kathiāwar

Bhāvnagar

Indore

MADHYA PRADESH

Surat

Nāsik

Aurangābād

Kalyān

Thāna

MUMBAI
(Bombay)

Pune
(Poona)

Pimpri-Chinchwad

MAHĀRĀSHTRA

Sholāpur

Kolhāpur

Belgaum

KARNĀTAKA

Hubli-
Dhārwār

GOA

OMAN

Muscat
(Muscat)

Gulf of Oman

Gulf of
Maşirah

Kuria Muria Is.

ARABIAN SEA

Makran Coast

Tropic of Cancer

Scale 1:9,000,000   Lambert Conformal Conic Projection

MI   100   200   300

KM   100   200   300   400

© HAMMOND WORLD ATLAS CORPORATION

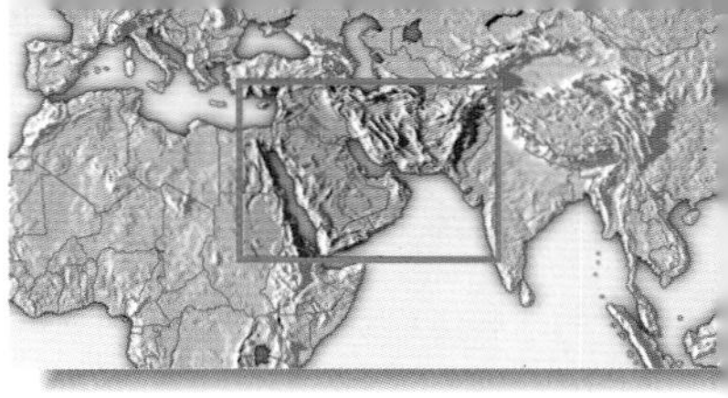

Both the Tigris and the Euphrates, the longest river in the Middle East (3,380 km), flow from sources in eastern Turkey and are of crucial geopolitical importance. Turkey uses the rivers for irrigation and hydroelectric power and can control the flow of water into neighboring countries with such large facilities as the Ataturk Dam. These two life-giving arteries of the Middle East converge to form the Shatt al Arab, which flows into the Persian Gulf. The world's largest oil reserves are located here in a total of 15 oil fields with known reserves of 1.5 billion tons each.

Scale 1:6,000,000 Lambert Conformal Conic Projection

MI 50 100 150 200

Eastern Mediterranean Region

The countries of the eastern Mediterranean region are faced with a constant shortage of water. Competition for water has always been a leading cause of conflicts in this part of the world. Citrus fruits are the most important products harvested in heavily irrigated strips of land along the coasts. Winter rains fall to the west of the uplands, while the higher plateaus and mountains offer only dry, sparse grazing.

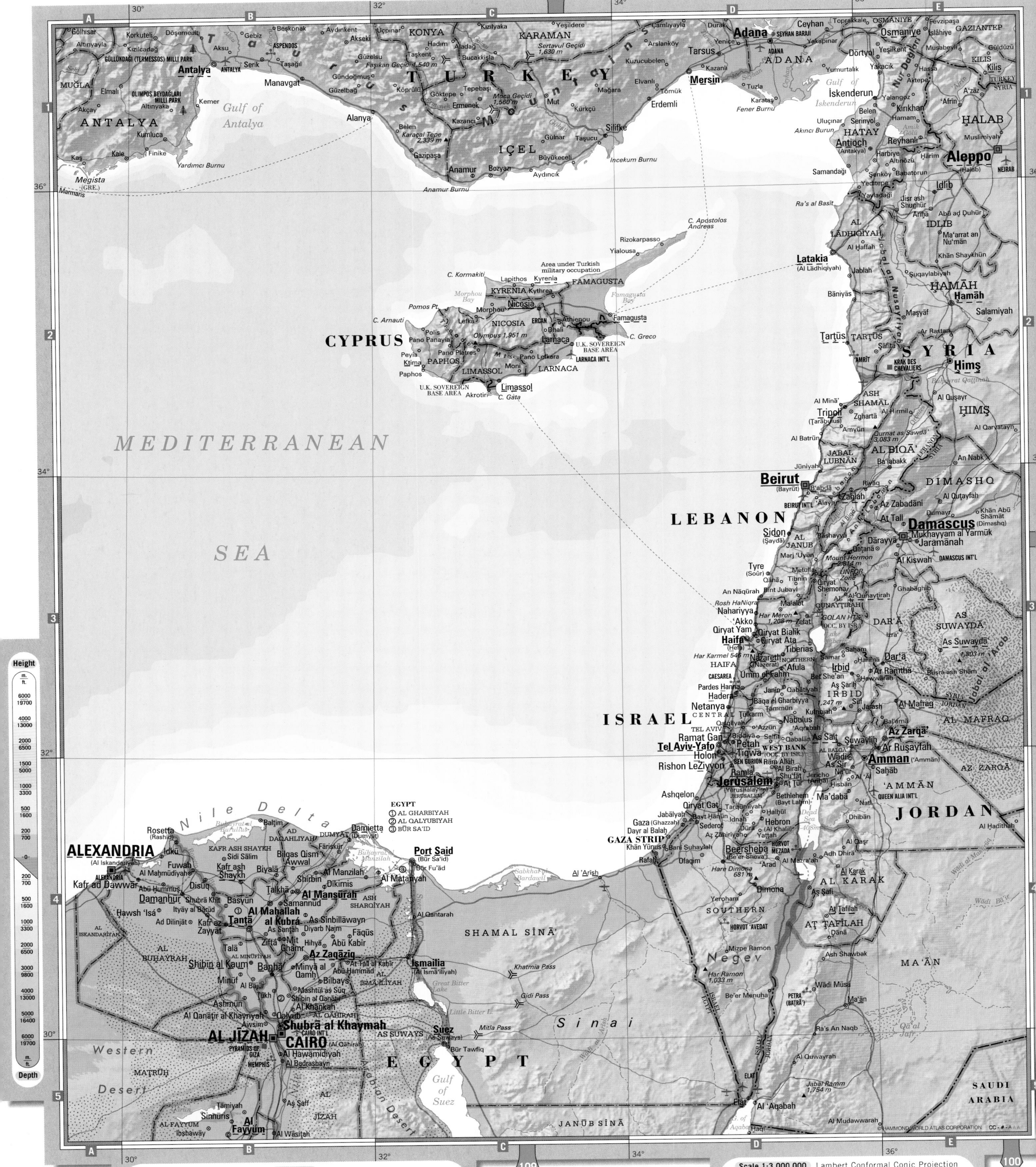

Scale 1:3,000,000 Lambert Conformal Conic Projection

Population
- Over 2,000,000
- 500,000 – 999,999
- 100,000 – 249,999
- 10,000 – 29,999
- 1,000,000 – 1,999,999
- 250,000 – 499,999
- 30,000 – 99,999
- Under 10,000

Height
m. / ft.
6000 / 19700
4000 / 13000
2000 / 6500
1500 / 5000
1000 / 3300
500 / 1600
200 / 700
0
200 / 700
500 / 1600
1000 / 3300
2000 / 6500
3000 / 9800
4000 / 13000
5000 / 16400
6000 / 19700
m. / ft.
Depth

wo tectonic plates glide past each other in the Jordan River Valley. The eastern te drifts northward along the western plate, ating a dislocation of about 105 km in the th. The fault line shifts westward in several places. There, the Earth's crust expands and sinks, a process that has given birth to the Lake of Genezareth, and the Dead Sea, whose surface lies at 408 m below sea level - the lowest point on the surface of the Earth.

104

Map Section

104
105

102

MEDITERRANEAN SEA

LEBANON

JABĀL LUBNĀN

AL JANŪB

AL BIQĀ'

Beirut (Bayrūt)

BEIRUT INT'L.

Sidon (Şaydā)

Tyre (Soûr)

Damascus (Dimashq)

DIMASHQ

SYRIA

DAR'Ā

AS SUWAYDĀ'

GOLAN HEIGHTS (OCCUPIED BY ISRAEL)

Lake Tiberias (Yam Kinneret)

Galilee

NORTHERN

Haifa (Hefa)

Nazareth (Nazeret)

CENTRAL

Netanya

Samaria

ISRAEL

WEST BANK*

Nābulus

Tel Aviv

Tel Aviv-Yafo

Ramat Gan

Bat Yam

Rishon LeZiyyon

Ashdod

Ramla

Rehovot

Ashqelon

Jerusalem (Yerushalayim)

JERUSALEM

Bethlehem (Bayt Laḥm)

Hebron (Al Khalīl)

GAZA STRIP*

Gaza (Ghazzah)

SOUTHERN

Khān Yūnus

Rafah

Sinai

Beersheba (Be'er Sheva)

IRBID

Irbid

AL MAFRAQ

Az Zarqā'

AZ ZARQĀ'

AL BALQĀ'

Amman ('Ammān)

'AMMĀN

JORDAN

AL KARAK

Dead Sea (-408m)

ISRAEL JORDAN

*WEST BANK AND GAZA STRIP ARE ISRAELI OCCUPIED WITH CURRENT STATUS SUBJECT TO THE ISRAELI-PALESTINIAN INTERIM AGREEMENT - PERMANENT STATUS TO BE DETERMINED

Scale 1:1,000,000   Lambert Conformal Conic Projection

MI   10   20   30

KM   10   20   30   40

Height	
m.	ft.
6000	19700
4000	13000
2000	6500
1500	5000
1000	3300
500	1600
200	700
0	-
200	700
500	1600
1000	3300
2000	6500
3000	9800
4000	13000
5000	16400
6000	19700
m.	ft.
Depth	

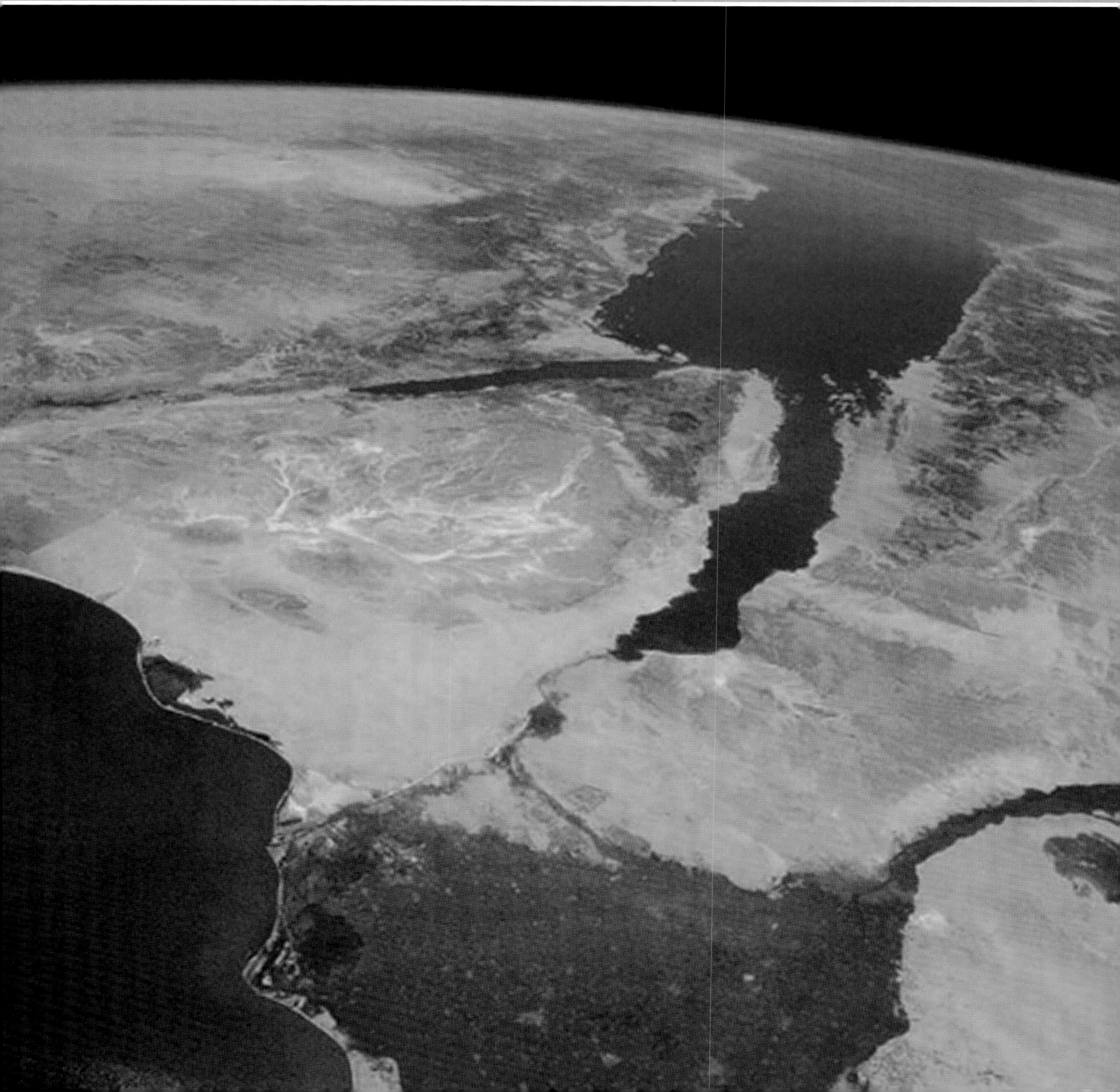

...aken from the southeast, this photograph shows the Nile Delta as a dark area in ...foreground. It extends from Cairo at the ...x of the delta to the Suez Canal (lower ...), which connects the Mediterranean Sea

and the Red Sea (upper middle). Desert-like areas are seen southwest of the delta and on the Sinai Peninsula. The Gulf of Aqaba protrudes like a spur from the Red Sea into the Arabian Peninsula.

This depression extends into the Jordan River Valley and the Dead Sea toward the north and widens beneath the Red Sea in the south.

PHOTOGRAPHIC DETAIL

Map Section

106
107

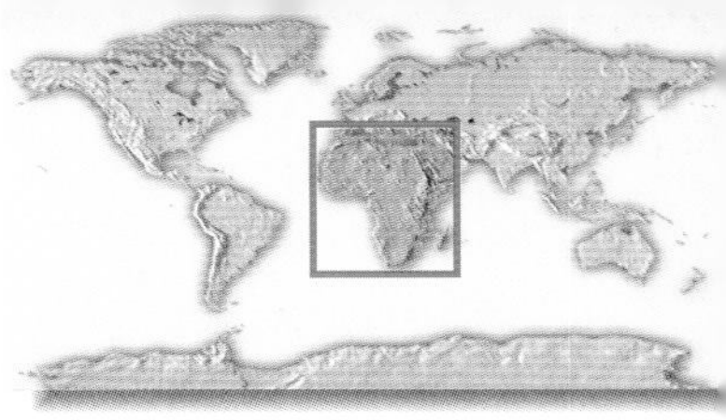

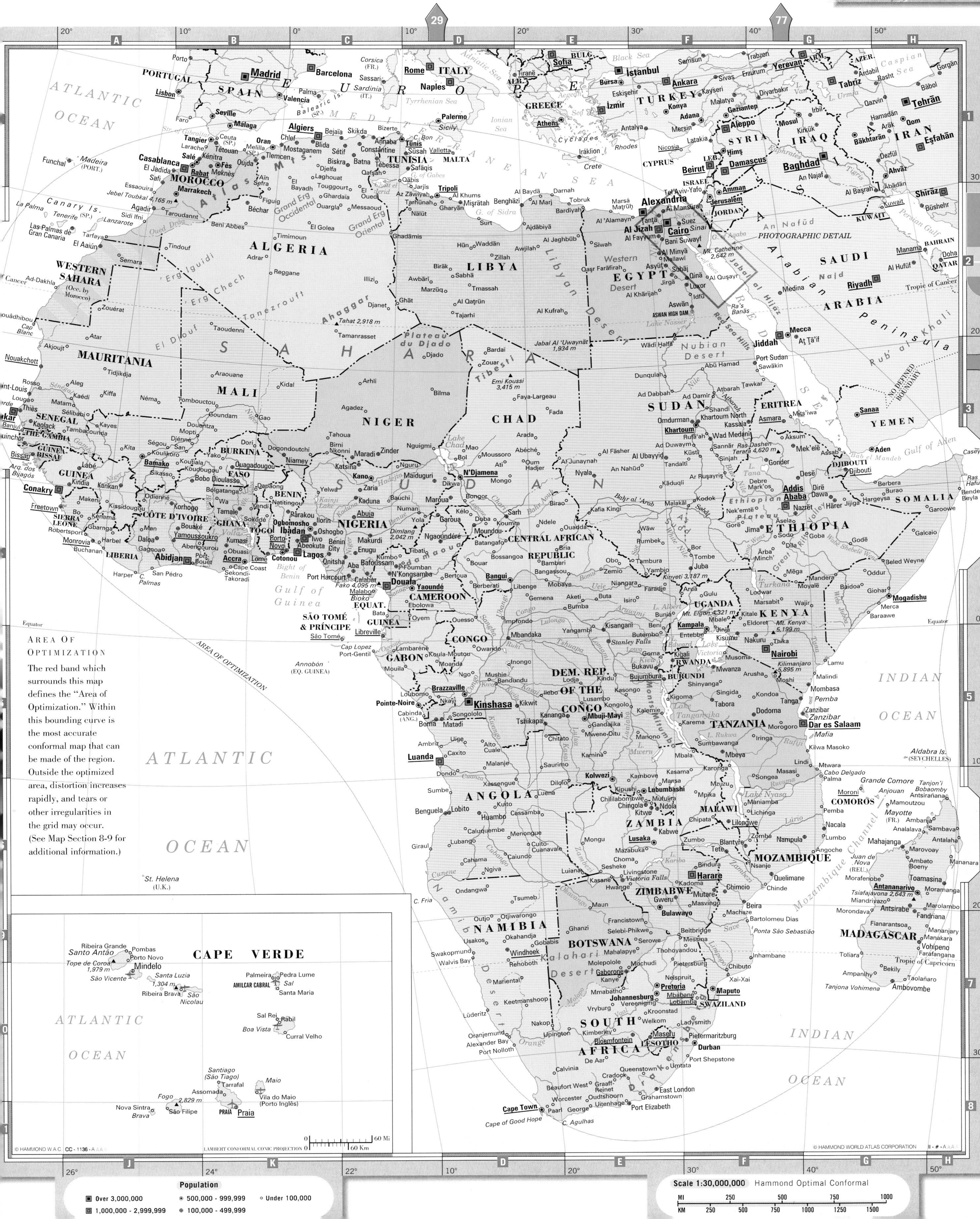

AREA OF OPTIMIZATION

The red band which surrounds this map defines the "Area of Optimization." Within this bounding curve is the most accurate conformal map that can be made of the region. Outside the optimized area, distortion increases rapidly, and tears or other irregularities in the grid may occur. (See Map Section 8-9 for additional information.)

CAPE VERDE

Population

■ Over 3,000,000	● 500,000 - 999,999
■ 1,000,000 - 2,999,999	● 100,000 - 499,999
	○ Under 100,000

Scale 1:30,000,000   Hammond Optimal Conformal

MI   250   500   750   1000
KM   250   500   750   1000   1250   1500

LAMBERT CONFORMAL CONIC PROJECTION

© HAMMOND W.A.C   CC - 1136 · A · A.A.

© HAMMOND WORLD ATLAS CORPORATION

The Tibesti range covers 100,000 square km of territory between northern Chad and the Libyan border. The range is a volcanic mountain system that rises steeply from the Sahara. This volcanic activity deep within the African continent is the result of a thermal anomaly in the earth's interior known as a hot spot. Hot springs and mud pools offer striking evidence of persisting geological activity in the region. Due to its height, the Tibesti range draws more rain than the surrounding areas and is known as the "emerald isle" of the Sahara.

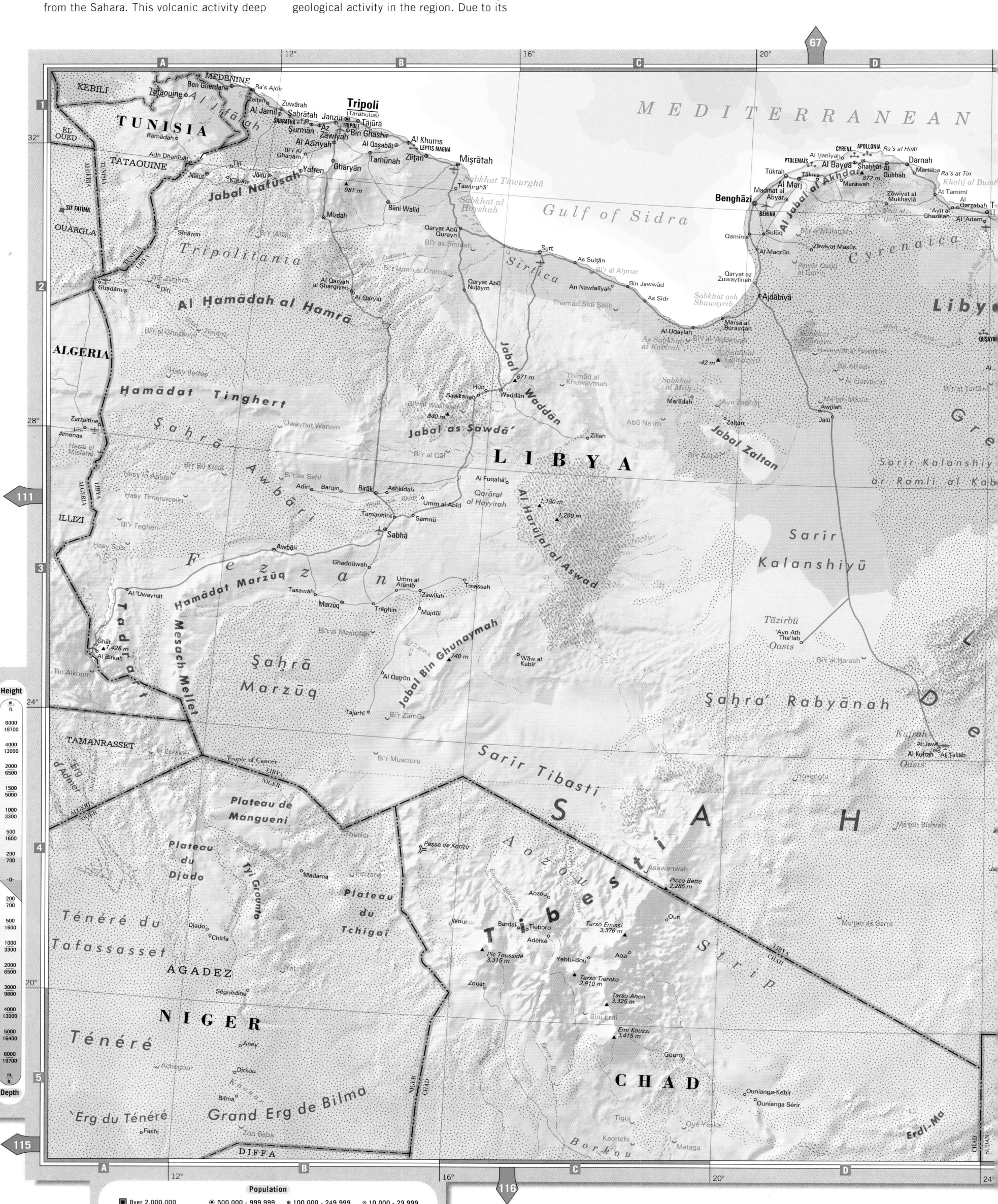

111

115

Height

m.
ft.
6000 19700
4000 13000
2000 6500
1500 5000
1000 3300
500 1600
200 700
-0-
200 700
500 1600
1000 3300
2000 6500
3000 9800
4000 13000
5000 16400
6000 19700
m.
ft.
Depth

Population

◾ Over 2,000,000 ⊙ 500,000 - 999,999 ⊙ 100,000 - 249,999 ○ 10,000 - 29,999
◼ 1,000,000 - 1,999,999 ⊙ 250,000 - 499,999 ⊙ 30,000 - 99,999 ○ Under 10,000

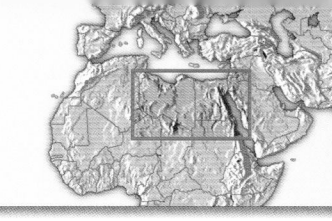

102

Map Section

108
109

102

100

EGYPT
① AL ISKANDARĪYAH
② KAFR ASH SHAYKH
③ AL GHARBĪYAH
④ AL MINŪFĪYAH
⑤ AD DAQAHLĪYAH
⑥ DUMYĀT
⑦ BŪR SAʿĪD
⑧ ASH SHARQĪYAH
⑨ AL ISMĀʿĪLĪYAH
⑩ AL QALYŪBĪYAH
⑪ AL QĀHIRAH
⑫ AL FAYYŪM
⑬ BANĪ SUWAYF

SEA

Gulf of Sollum
Sīdī Barrānī
Marsá Maṭrūḥ

Khalīj al ʿArab

ALEXANDRIA (Al Iskandarīyah)
Kafr ad Dawwār
Damanhūr
Shibīn al Kawm
AL BUHAYRAH
Minūf
CAIRO (Al Qāhirah)
AL JIZAH
PYRAMIDS OF GIZA
MEMPHIS
Ibshawāy
Sinnūris
Al Fayyūm
AL JIZAH
AS SUWAYS
Bibā
Banī Suwayf
Maghāghah
Al Fashn
Banī Mazār
Samālūṭ
AL MINYĀ
Al Minyā
Mallawī
Dayrūṭ
Abnūb
ASYŪṬ
Asyūṭ
Ṭaḥṭā
Akhmīm
Suhāj
SUHĀJ
Juhaynah
Al Marāghah
Jirjā
ABYDOS
At Balyanā
Dishnā
QINĀ
Qūṣ
THEBES
VALLEY OF THE KINGS
Luxor (Al Uqṣur)
At Karnak
LUXOR
Armant
Isnā
Idfū
Kawm Umbū
First Cataract
Aswān
ASWAN HIGH DAM
ASWĀN
Lake Nasser
ABU SIMBEL
El Ghāb

Qattara Depression
−74 m
MAṬRŪḤ
Siwa Oasis
Siwah
Al Wāḥāt al Baḥrīyah
Al Bawīṭī
Wāḥāt al Farāfirah
Qaṣr Farāfirah

Western
Desert
−427 m
Wāḥāt ad Dākhilah
Al Qaṣr
Mūṭ
Al Khārijah
Al Wāḥāt al Khārijah
Bārīs

EGYPT

AL WĀDĪ AL JADĪD

Hadabat al Jilf al Kabīr 1,098 m

Damietta (Dumyāṭ)
Al Manṣūrah
As Sinbillāwayn
Abū Kabīr
Zifta
Tanṭā
Al Manzilah
Port Said (Būr Saʿīd)
Al ʿArīsh
Ismailia (Al Ismāʿīlīyah)
Az Zaqāzīq
Banhā
Bilbays
CAIRO
Al Hawāmidīyah
Suez (As Suways)
Būr Tawfīq

SHAMĀL SĪNĀʾ
Suez Canal
Bitter Lakes
Khatmia Pass
Gidi Pass
Mitla Pass
Sinai

JANŪB SĪNĀʾ
Mt. Catherine 2,642 m
St. Catherine
Dhahab
Aṭ Ṭūr
Sharm ash Shaykh
Jemsa
Ras Gharib
Arabian
Desert
Jabal Shāʾib al Banāt 2,005 m
Būr Safājah
Al Ghurdaqah
Ra's Muḥammad
Jazīrat Tīrān

AL BAḤR AL AḤMAR
Marsá al ʿAlam
Ra's Abū Madd
Jabal Hamāṭah 1,977 m
Ra's Banās
BERENICE
Foul Bay
Ra's Hadarba

RED SEA

SYRIA
Damascus (Dimashq)
Ḍarayyā
LEBANON
Qiryat Shemona
Nahariyya
Haifa (Hefa)
Akko
Nazareth (Nazerat)
Zefat
ISRAEL
Netanya
Petaḥ Tiqwa
Tel Aviv-Yafo
Holon
Ramla
Jerusalem
Gaza (Ghazzah)
GAZA STRIP
Gaṭ
WEST BANK
Hebron (Al Khalīl)
Golan Heights
Har Meron 1,208 m
Irbid
Dar'ā
As Suwaydā'
Jabal ad Durūz 1,803 m
Amman
Az Zarqā'
Ar Ruṣayfah
Mādabā
Dhibān
Al Karak
Aṭ Ṭafīlah
Ash Shawbak
PETRA
Ma'ān
ELAT
Al ʿAqabah
Jabal Ramm 1,754 m
Al Mudawwarah
Ḥaql

JORDAN
Beersheba (Be'er Sheva)
Negev
Dimona
Be'er Menuḥa

IRAQ
Ar Rutbah
Ash Shabakaho
Turayf
Syrian Desert
Kāf
Sakākah
Al Jawf
Qārah

SAUDI ARABIA
An Nafūd
Al Bi'r
Tabūk
Al Akhḍar
Al Qalībah
Jabal al Lawz 2,580 m
Jabal Dabbāgh 2,350 m
Midyan
Al Muwaylíḥ
Ḍubā
Al Wajh
Ummal Lujj
Taymā'
Madā'in Ṣāliḥ
Al ʿUlā
Ash Shuray'
Khaybar
Hanak
Yanbu' al Baḥr
Jabal Raḍwā 1,814 m
Medina (Al Madīnah)
Abyār 'Alī
Al Musayjīd
Al Ḥamrā'
Badr Ḥunayn
Tropic of Cancer
As Sidr
Ar Rabad
Masṭūrah
Rābigh
Al Qaḍīmah
Jiddah
KING ABDUL AZIZ

Jabal al Ḥijāz

SUDAN
ASH SHAMĀLĪYAH
Wādī Ḥalfā
Second Cataract
Akasha East
Abri
Kosha
Dal Cataract
SEDEINGA TEMPLE
SULB TEMPLE
SESEBI
Dalqū
Jabal Kurur 1,240 m
Laqiya al Arba'in
'Uwaynāt
Kisū
Ṭaqab
Third Cataract
Kanīsah
ĀRFŪR
Jabal Abyaḍ

Nubian Desert

ASH SHARQĪYAH
Port Sudan (Būr Sūdān)
Muḥammad Qawl
Ras Abu Shagara
Gebeit Mine
Salālah
Suakin Arch.
Sawākin
Ra's Maqdam
Sinkāt
Trinkitat
Ra's Asis
Tokar
TOKAR GAME RESERVE
Aqīq
Ras Kasar
Jabal Oda 2,259 m
Jabal Asoteriba 2,216 m
Jabal ʾIs 1,851 m
Halā'ib

Nūbian Desert
Argo
Gharb Binna
Dunqulah
KAWA
Karbakā
Abū Hamad
Abū Dīs
Al Janayet
Mismār
Ṭaqatu Ḥayyā
Jabal Abadab 1,596 m
Bayudha Desert
Fourth Cataract
Kūraymah
Marawī
NURI
NAPATA
Kūrtī
Fifth Cataract
Al Ibēdiyya
Barbar
Mibērika
Karīmah
Dunqulah

Scale 1:6,000,000 Polyconic Projection

MI   0   50   100   150   200
KM   0   50   100   150   200   250

© HAMMOND WORLD ATLAS CORPORATION

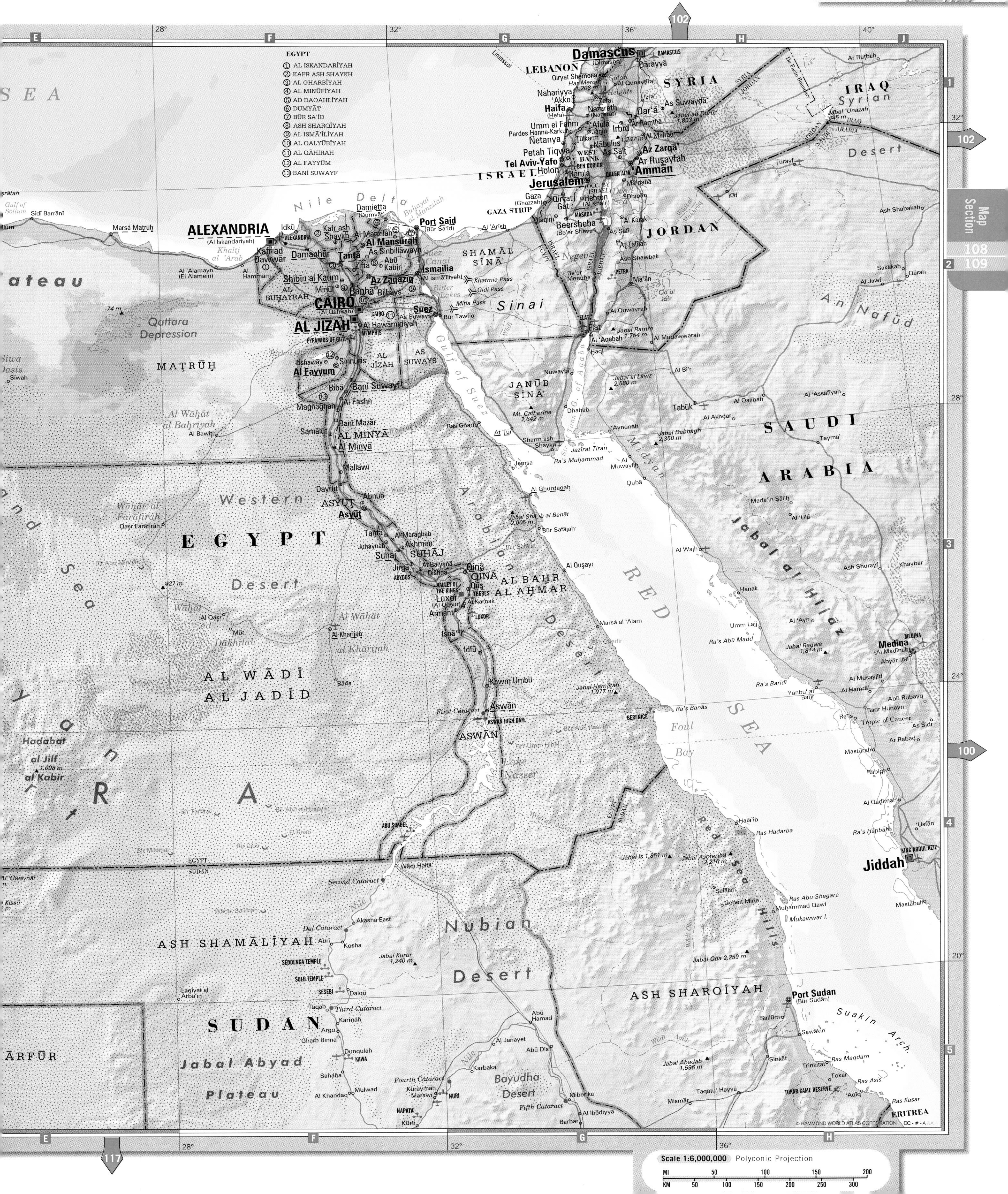

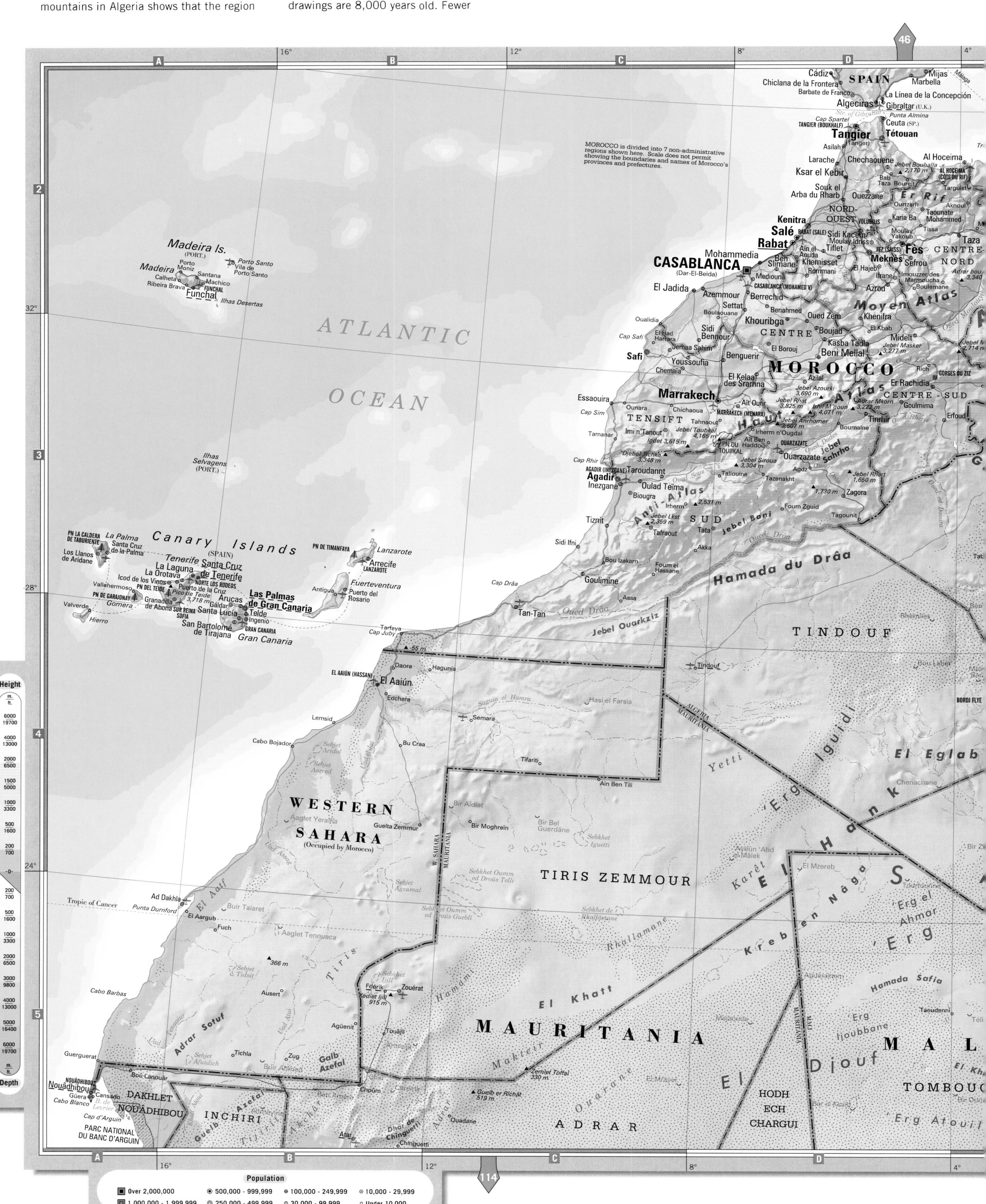

The Sahara, the world's largest desert, covers some 9.1 million square km. It is 4,670 km long and 1,760 km wide. Evidence found in the Tassili-n-Ajjer mountains in Algeria shows that the region was once covered by lush green vegetation. Prehistoric drawings feature images of elephants, buffalo, hippos, and crocodiles. The earliest of the more than 1,000 rock drawings are 8,000 years old. Fewer species are depicted as the drawings grow more recent. Thus the course of the Sahara's transformation into a desert can be traced from drawing to drawing.

MOROCCO is divided into 7 non-administrative regions shown here. Scale does not permit showing the boundaries and names of Morocco's provinces and prefectures.

Population

- ■ Over 2,000,000
- ■ 1,000,000 – 1,999,999
- ◉ 500,000 – 999,999
- ◉ 250,000 – 499,999
- ⊙ 100,000 – 249,999
- ⊙ 30,000 – 99,999
- ⊙ 10,000 – 29,999
- ○ Under 10,000

Height

m.
ft.

6000
19700

4000
13000

2000
6500

1500
5000

1000
3300

500
1600

200
700

-0-

200
700

500
1600

1000
3300

2000
6500

3000
9800

4000
13000

5000
16400

6000
19700

m.
ft.

Depth

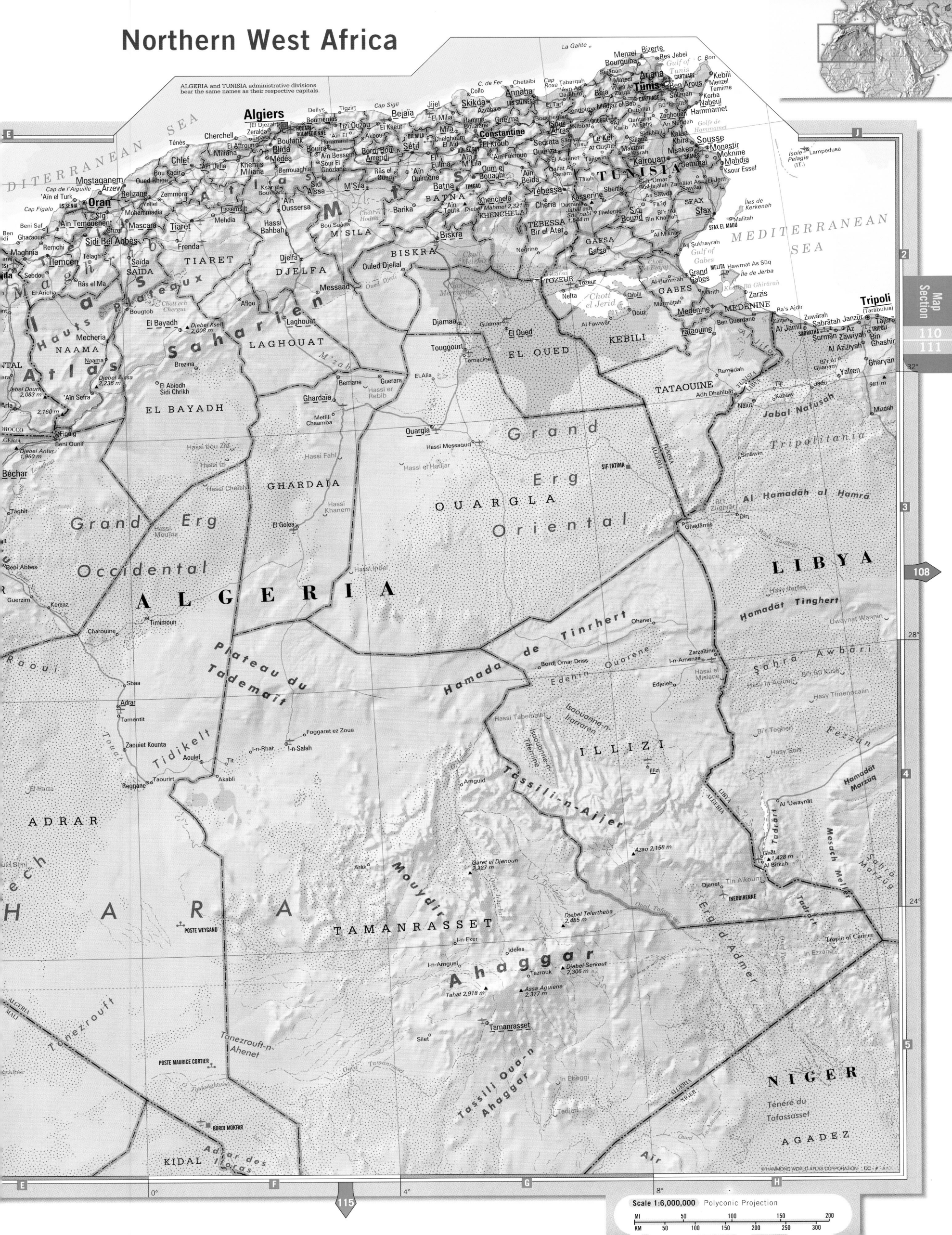

Northern West Africa

ALGERIA and TUNISIA administrative divisions bear the same names as their respective capitals.

MEDITERRANEAN SEA

Algiers (El Djezaïr)

Oran

TUNISIA

Tunis

Tripoli (Tarābulus)

MEDITERRANEAN SEA

Gulf of Gabes

Île de Jerba

ALGERIA

Hauts Plateaux

Atlas Saharien

NAAMA

SAIDA

TIARET

DJELFA

LAGHOUAT

EL BAYADH

GHARDAÏA

Grand Erg Occidental

Grand Erg Oriental

OUARGLA

EL OUED

BISKRA

TOZEUR

GABES

KEBILI

MEDÉNINE

TATAOUINE

LIBYA

Tripolitania

Al Hamādah al Hamrā

Jabal Nafusah

Hamādāt Tinghert

Fezzan

Plateau du Tademaït

Hamada de Tinrhert

Ḥamadāt Murzūq

ADRAR

Tidikelt

ILLIZI

Tassili-n-Ajjer

Erg d'Admer

Sahrā Murzūq

Saharā Awbāri

S A H A R A

TAMANRASSET

Mouydir

Ahaggar

Tassili Oua-n-Ahaggar

Tanezrouft

Tanezrouft-n-Ahenet

Tropic of Cancer

NIGER

Aïr

AGADEZ

Ténéré du Tafassasset

KIDAL

Adrar des Iforas

Scale 1:6,000,000   Polyconic Projection

© HAMMOND WORLD ATLAS CORPORATION

Northern Morocco, Algeria, Tunisia

The Atlas Mountains of northern Africa are a protective wall that shields northern Morocco, Algeria, and Tunisia against encroachment by the desert to the south. Moist air from the sea brings welcome rains. Many of the ports along the coast lie in the lee of capes formed by steeply sloping mountain ridges that jut sharply into the sea.

46

111

MOROCCO
① MOHAMMADIA-ZNATA
② BEN MSIK-SIDI OTHMANE
③ CASABLANCA-ANFA
④ AÏN CHOK-HAY MOHAMMADIA

Major labels

ATLANTIC OCEAN

MEDITERRANEAN SEA

SPAIN

MOROCCO

ALGERIA

TUNISIA

MALTA

Tangier — TANGER — Tétouan — TETOUAN — Al Hoceima — Nador — NADOR — Melilla (SP.) — Oujda — OUJDA — Oran — ORAN — Tlemcen — TLEMCEN — SIDI BEL ABBES — NAAMA

Kénitra — Salé — Rabat — CASABLANCA — Mohammedia — Meknès — MEKNES — Fès — FES — Taza — TAZA — FIGUIG

Algiers (ALGER) — BLIDA — MEDEA — AÏN DEFLA — Chlef — CHLEF — MOSTAGANEM — RELIZANE — Mascara — MASCARA — TIARET — SAÏDA — DJELFA — BOUIRA — TIZI OUZOU — Bejaïa — BEJAÏA — SETIF — Sétif — MILA — Constantine — BORDJ BOU ARRERIDJ — M'SILA — BATNA — Batna — BISKRA — OUM EL BOUAGHI

SKIKDA — Skikda — JIJEL — Jijel — Annaba — ANNABA — GUELMA — Guelma — SOUK AHRAS — Souk Ahras — CONSTANTINE — KHENCHELA — TEBESSA — AURES Mts.

Bizerte — BIZERTE — Tunis — TUNIS — CARTHAGE — NABEUL — Nabeul — BEJA — Béja — JENDOUBA — Jendouba — SILIANA — ZAGHOUAN — LE KEF — Le Kef — KAIROUAN — Kairouan — SOUSSE — Sousse — Monastir — MONASTIR — MAHDIA — Mahdia — KASSERINE — Kasserine — SIDI BOU ZID — SFAX

Sicily (IT.) — **MALTA** — Gozo — Strait of Sicily — Pantelleria (IT.) — Isole di Pelagie — Lampedusa

Height
m. / ft.
6000 / 19700
4000 / 13000
2000 / 6500
1500 / 5000
1000 / 3300
500 / 1600
200 / 700
-0-
200 / 700
500 / 1600
1000 / 3300
2000 / 6500
3000 / 9800
4000 / 13000
5000 / 16400
6000 / 19700
m. / ft.
Depth

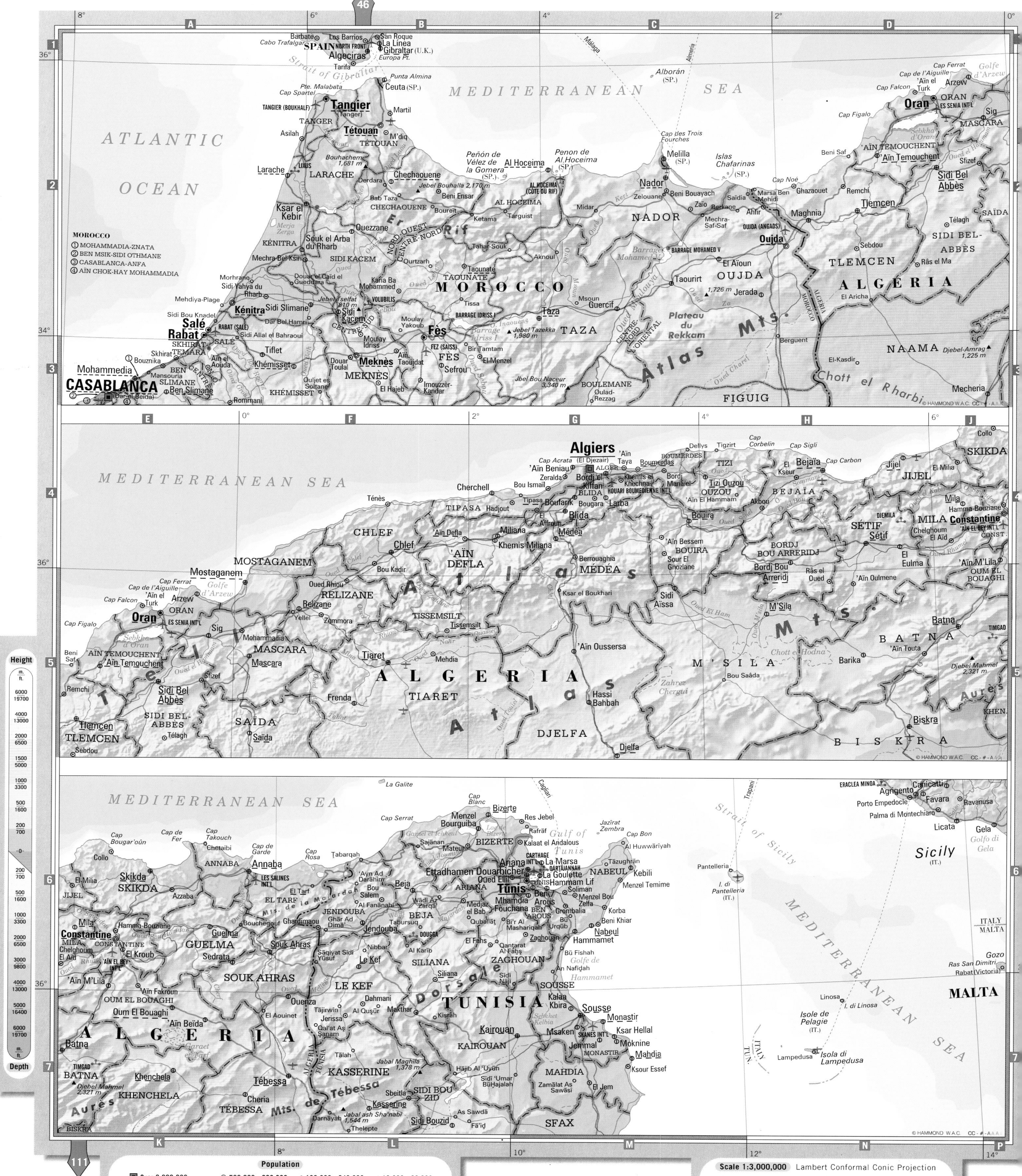

Population
■ Over 2,000,000
■ 1,000,000 - 1,999,999
● 500,000 - 999,999
● 250,000 - 499,999
⊚ 100,000 - 249,999
○ 30,000 - 99,999
◦ 10,000 - 29,999
· Under 10,000

Scale 1:3,000,000 Lambert Conformal Conic Projection

MI 25 50 75 100
KM 25 50 75 100 125 150

© HAMMOND W.A.C.

easuring 6,671 km from source to mouth, the Nile is the longest river Earth. Alternating periods of flooding d low water have shaped the lives of ple in the region for millennia.

A complex network of irrigation canals supplies the fertile Nile Delta with water. The Suez Canal in the northeast of the country serves as a vital link between the Mediterranean and Red seas.

Nile River Delta

MEDITERRANEAN SEA

Rosetta Mouth (Maşabb Rashīd)

Damietta Mouth (Maşabb Dumyāt)

Khalīj Abū Qīr

Buḥayrat al Burullus

ALEXANDRIA (Al Iskandarīyah)

CANOPUS
Abū Qīr
Al Ma'mūrah
Al Maks
Buḥayrat Maryūt

Rosetta (Rashīd)
Idkū

Port Saïd (Būr Sa'īd)
BŪR SA'ĪD

DUMYĀT
Damietta (Dumyāt)
Rās el-Barr

KAFR ASH SHAYKH

SHAMĀL SĪNĀ'

Damanhūr
Kafr ash Shaykh
Al Maḥallah al Kubrā
Al Manşūrah
Dikirnis

Tanţā
AL GHARBĪYAH
AD DAQAHLĪYAH

Kafr az Zayyāt
Zifta

Shibīn al Kawm
AL MINŪFĪYAH
Az Zaqāzīq
Ismailia (Al Ismā'īlīyah)

Banha
AL QALYŪBĪYAH
Bilbays

AL BUḤAYRAH

AL ISKANDARĪYAH

AL ISMĀ'ĪLĪYAH

Western Desert
AL JĪZAH

Great Bitter Lake

Shubrā al Khaymah
HELIOPOLIS
CAIRO INT'L

AL JĪZAH
CAIRO (Al Qāhirah)
Imbābah

AL QĀHIRAH

PYRAMIDS OF JĪZAH
MEMPHIS
Ḥulwān

Arabian Desert

AS SUWAYS

MAŢRŪḤ

Jabal Qaṭrānī

Birkat Qārūn

Al Fayyūm
BANĪ SUWAYF

AL JĪZAH

Jabal al Jalālah al Baḥrīyah

FAYYŪM

Banī Suwayf
AL BAḤR AL AḤMAR

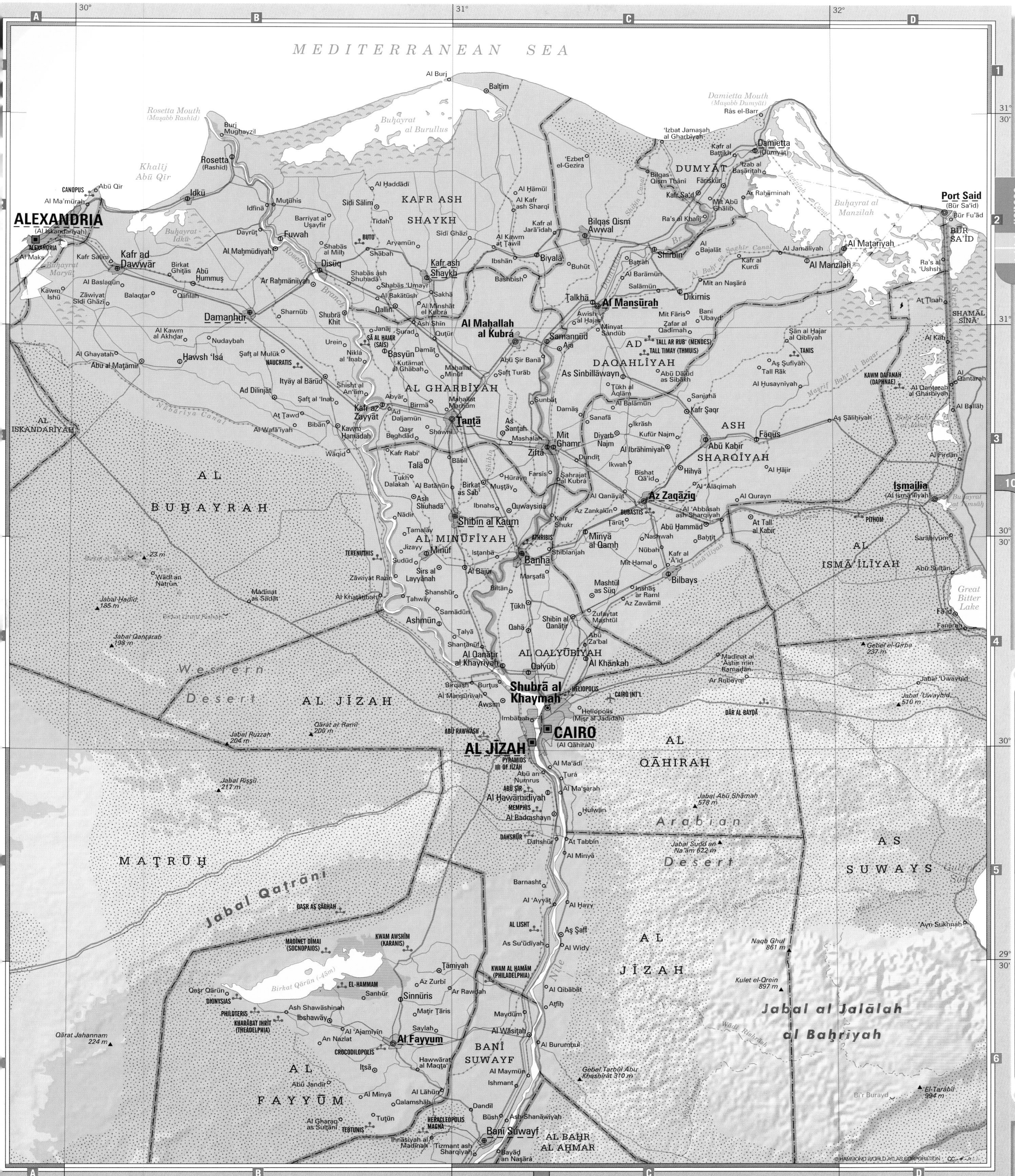

Population
- Over 2,000,000
- 1,000,000 - 1,999,999
- 500,000 - 999,999
- 250,000 - 499,999
- 100,000 - 249,999
- 30,000 - 99,999
- 10,000 - 29,999
- Under 10,000

Scale 1:1,000,000   Lambert Conformal Conic Projection

Height
m. / ft.
6000 / 19700
4000 / 13000
2000 / 6500
1500 / 5000
1000 / 3300
500 / 1600
200 / 700
0
Depth

109

Map Section
112
113

The course of the Niger could hardly be more unusual. The river descends from the Loma Mountains on the border between Sierra Leone and Guinea, but rather than flowing directly to the Atlantic, it pursues a circuitous route through Mali, Niger, and Nigeria before finally emptying into the Gulf of Guinea. With a length of 4,184 km, it is the third-longest river in Africa. The Niger deposits large quantities of sediment in its wide delta (20,000 square km), which lies above rich reserves of oil and natural gas. Nearly 90 percent of Nigeria's income comes from petroleum exports.

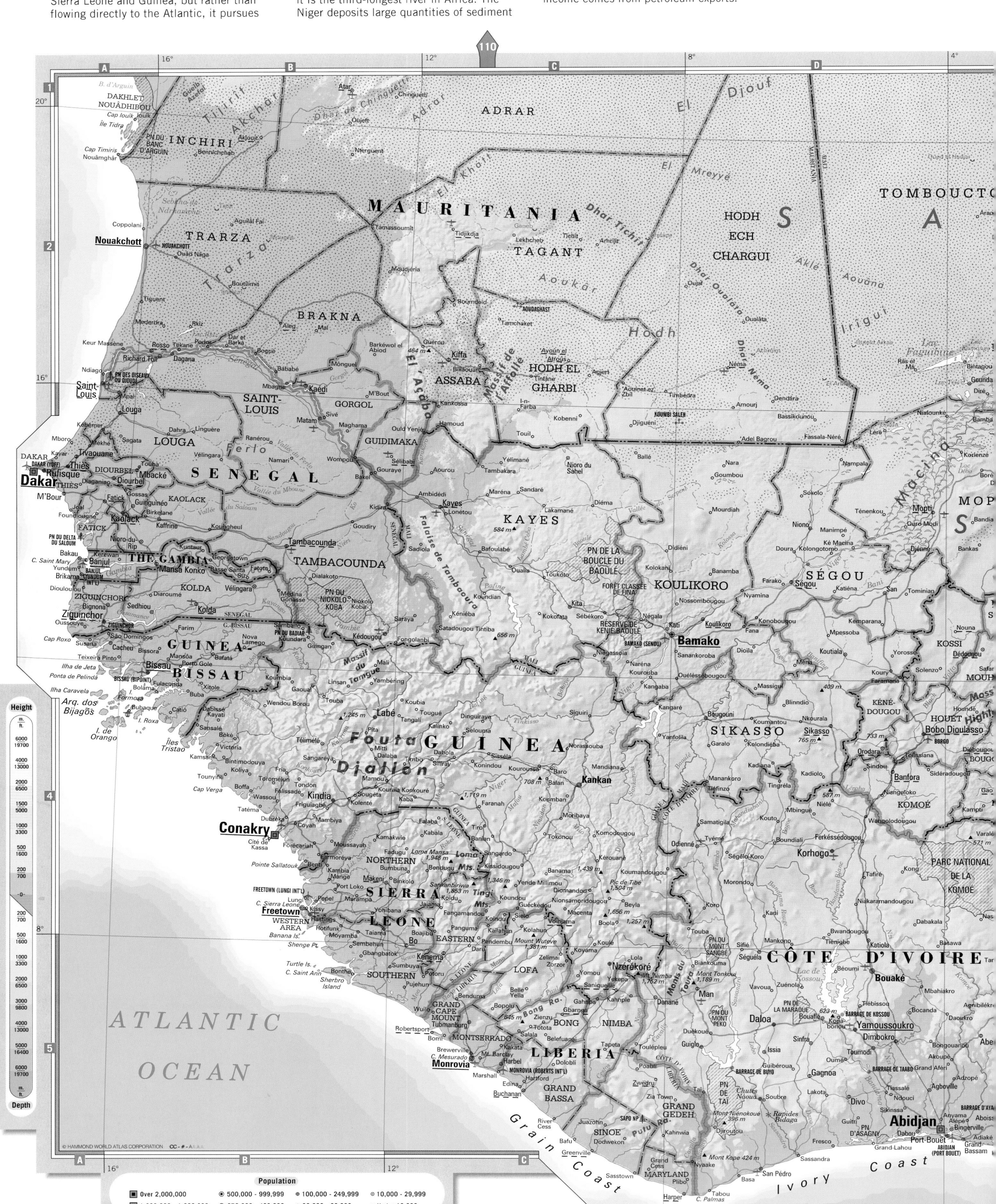

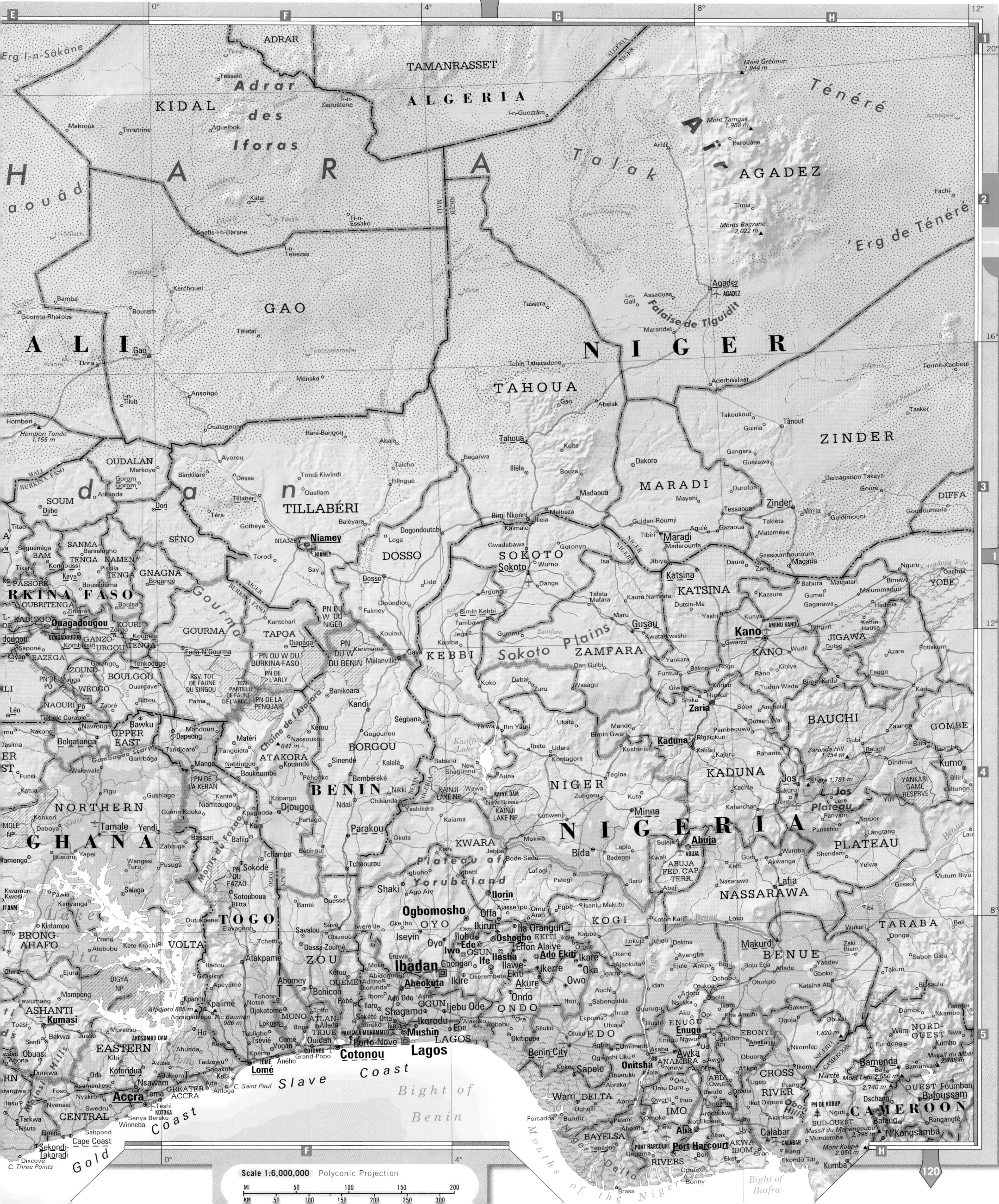

Like the bow of a ship, the Mandara Mountains of northern Cameroon extend into the arid plains of Nigeria and the swamplands of Chad. The wooded highland savannah is relatively fertile, as rainfall from May to November is sufficient to support agriculture. Some of this water flows into the riverless depression of the Chad Basin and Lake Chad, the large, shallow lake at its center. Lake Chad is one of the few fresh water reservoirs along the edge of the Sahel region, which encompasses substantial parts of Chad, Niger, and Sudan.

Population

■ Over 2,000,000 ⬤ 500,000 - 999,999 ⬤ 100,000 - 249,999 ⊙ 10,000 - 29,999
◻ 1,000,000 - 1,999,999 ⬤ 250,000 - 499,999 ⊙ 30,000 - 99,999 ○ Under 10,000

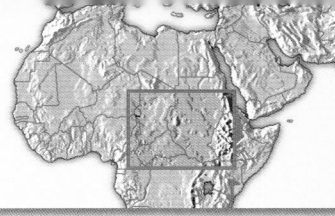

109

28°   32°   36°

RED SEA

E   F   G   H

Libyan
Desert

ASH SHAMĀLĪYAH

Ad Dabbāh   Nile   Kürti
Abū Dawm   Karora
                                        Mersa Tek'lay
                    Al Ibēdiyya   Mismār
          Qawz Abū Dulu   Barbar   Nak'fa
                              Atbara   Derudeb
              Ad Dāmir   Medruriet
Teiga   Az Zaydāb   Jimmēza   Pertokar
Plateau   Al Matammah   Adarama   Kebeset
                    MEROE   2,631 m
              Wad Hāmid   Eriba   Hoho
          Abū Dawm   Sixth Cataract   Qawz Rajab   Kerkebet
                                                    Saatta   ERITREA
                                        Mitatib   Ak'ordat   Engherne   Keren
ARFŪR   Ilay   AL KHARTŪM   SUDAN-ERITREA   16°   Sebderat   Mensura   1
Jabal Teljo   ASH SHARQĪYAH   Aroma   Kieru   Dukambiya   Himbirti
1,954 m   Hamrat ash   Omdurman   Khartoum North   Dighem   Guluy   Biyagundi   Barentu
          Shaykh   (Umm Durmān) (Al Khurtūm Bahri)   Halfa Aj   Om Hājer   Adi Kwal
Umm Qawzayn   Khartoum   Umm Dhibbān   Kassala   Jadīda   Adi Da'iro   Äksum
Mellit   Abū Shanab   KHARTOUM   Shurayk   Nogara   K'eftya
          Al Wazz   Aş Şafiyya   KHAZZĀN JABAL AL AWLIYĀ Aş Şufayyah   Inda Silase   2
Al Fasher   Sawdiri   Umm Inderaba   Al Masid   Muqatta   Mesfinto   SIMEN MTS.
                              Umm Dhibbān   Shuwak   NAT'L PARK
Umm Kaddādah   Jabal Katul   Al Qaţaynah   Al Husayhişah   Al Matnah   Debark'   Rās Dejen
          1,028 m   Umm   Na'ima   Al Musallamīyah   Qala'an Nahl Doka   Dabat   4,620 m
          Kagmar   Sayyālah   Wad Medani   Simen Mts.
'lyāl Bakhit   Nabalat al   Shabashah   Al Manaqil   Hajj 'Abd   Al Hawātah   Amba Giyorgis
          Hajanah   Ad Duwaym   Allah   Āykel   Azezo   Gonder
Dam Gamad   SUDAN   Umm Dam   Ash Shawal   As Sūki   Sinjah   Rumaylah   Degoma
Wad Bandah   Ba'shūm   Sennār   DINDER   El Gulut   Adis Zemen
          Al Ubayyid   SENNAR DAM   Dār 'Aqil   NAT'L   Delgi   Gorgora
Khuwayy   Umm Ruwābah   Kūsti   Rabak   AL WUSTA   PARK   Dinder Wenz   12°   Debre Tabor
An Nahūd   Sa'ata   Ar Rahad   Abū Rukbah   Abū Hugar   Wehni   Guna Terara
          Jabal ad Dayr   Al Jabalayn   Wad an   Ar Rusayris   4,231 m   Lake
Serambe   Abū Zabad   1,412 m   Keri Kera   Nail   Ad Damazin   Aytony   Tana
Ogr   KURDUFĀN   Geigar   Abū Kūk   ROSEIRES DAM   Delgi   Bahir Dar
Ad Du'ayn   Al Udayyah   Dilling   Rashād   Ar Rank   Khazzān   Bagusta   Blue Nile
          Dalāmi   Ar Rusayris   Dangila   Falls   Blue Nile
Al 'Umdah   Al Fūlah   Katla   Kurdufān   El Galhak   Abu Mendi   Adēt   Injibara
          Jabal Haybān   Al Lagowa   Bobuk   Belaya 3,131 m   Chagne   Mota
Ad Du'ayn   1,325 m   Al 'Abbāsiyah   Farnakah   Mertule
Buram   Abū Jābirah   Al Muglad   Haybān   Jibāl   El Galhak   Guba   Bikori   Maryam
          Barakah   Kāduqli   An Nūbah   Kurmuk   Abatimbo el   Chagne   Jiga   Debre Werk'   Tenta
Wādi Al Khadar   Kaloqi   Gumas   Burē   Talo   Bichena
Al Fifi   As Sumayh   Al Malamm   Talawdi   Qaysān   Debre Zeyit   4,413 m   Dejen
Gabras   Abyei   Kākā   Paloich   Asosa   Debre Mark'os
          Barakah   Belfodiyo   Goha Ts'iyon
                    Tungaru   Malut   ETHIOPIA   Gelila   Alibo
Mireigha   Bahr Al 'Arab   Kodok   Yelgu   Mendi   Gebre Guracha   DEBRE LIBANOS
          Riangnom   Bambesi   Fiche   MONASTERY
BAHR AL GHAZĀL   Buffalo   Tonga   Malakāl   Daga Post   Nejo   Goroch'an   Shambu   Kembolcha
          Bentiu   Cape   Fangak   Bēgi   3,276 m   Gēdo   ADDIS ABABA
Nyamlell   Wun Rog   Ghābat al   Abwong   SUDAN   Gimbi   Bako   (Ādīs Ābeba)
Wedweil   'Arab   Nyerol   Nāşir   Gidami   Ch'alchīs Terara   Sebeta   BOLE
          Gumbelē   Mogogh   Tulu Weleï   3,113 m   Nek'emtē
Uwayl   Gogrial   Meshra   Ayod   Jikawo   3,301 m   Guyi   Colba   Giyon
          'ar Raqq   Wa'th   Itang   Dembi Dolo   Bedelē   Tulu Bolo
Raga   Aluk   A 'ĀLĪ AN NĪL   GAMBELA   Bilo   Welk'it'ē   Guragē
Kangi   Kwajok   Adok   Duk Fadiat   Darbatta   NAT'L   Metu   Abelti   3,719 m
          Wun Shwai   Kongor   Tirgol   PARK   Gorē   Dembi   Butajira
Daym Zubayr   Agwok   Madeir   Akobo   Bichano   Suntu
          Wal Athiang   Tor   Gogo   Vuca
BAHR AL GHAZĀL   Jongley   Pibor Post   Jima   Āgaro   Jirēn
Wāw   Kawajena   Akelo   Shewa Gimira   Shebē   Hosa'ina
          Toni   Shambe   Lopaye   Sodo   ABIYATA-SHALA
J. DE FAUNE   SOUTHERN   Rumbek   Bor   Tēpi   Bonga   Waka   LAKES NAT'L PARK
ZEMONGO   NATIONAL   Bo River   Minkamman   BOMA NP   Ameya   Boditi
          PARK   Akot   Yirol   Malek   Cantiere   Maji'   Bulk'i   Sodo
HAUT-   Papiu   Towot   Mui   Ch'ench'a   Abaya
MBOMOU   Tambura   Mvolo   Tali Post   Tombe   Kenamuke   Kenamuke   Guge   Wendo
Ngouyo   Linqasi   Amadi   Medi   Terakeka   Swamp   Shasha   4,200 m   Dila
          Maridi   Al ISTIWĀ' ĪYAH   Kobowen   Arba Minch   NECHISAR
Mboki   Zamoi   Doruma   Lado   Swamp   Naita 2,139 m   OMO NAT'L   K'ey Āfer   NP
Bakia   Ukwatutu   Mongalla   Juba   Kapoeta   PARK   MAGO   Konso   Derba
Zapai   Yambio   Rejaf   Murle   Arbore   NP   Keranyu
          Aba   Luluba   Liwan   Mogige   Kelem   Carraiu
Digba   Usuma   Banda   Torit   Gingero   Yabēlo
          PN DE LA   Misa   Kapoeta   Lenia
ORIENTALE   GARAMBA   Yei   Nagishot   Lotuke   Todenyang   Gamud   4°
Ambili   Baranga   Duru   Lalyo   Loka   2,797 m   Faille   2,486 m
Api   Bambesa   Faradje   Kajo-Kaji   Kinyeti   Lokichokio   1,755 m   SIBILOI   Gamud
          NIMULE NP   Aba   3,187 m   Kakuma   1,585 m   NAT'L   Mega
Titule   Bazuru Mawiwi   Dramba   Opari   Lwala   Oropoi   Sogwass   PARK
          Nekalagba   Moyo   Nimule   Madi Opei   2,456 m   Sogwass   North I.
Zobia   Bangazeno   Watsa   Lamwa   Kaabong   2,086 m   L. Turkana   CENTRAL ISLAND NP
          Egbunda   Mungbere   1,927 m   Mugel 2,040 m   (L. Rudolf)   EASTERN
Doromo   Mawa   Gombari   Rom   Kidepo   MATHENIKO   Murua Nigithangar   North Horr   KENYA
          Arua   2,352 m   VALLEY NP   GAME RSV.   Chalbi
E CONGO   Gulu   Adranga   UGANDA   Kotido   RIFT   SOUTH ISLAND NP   Desert
          Maie   Aswa   Lolora   VALLEY   Mount Kulal   MARSABIT
          Tata   MORoto   1,437 m   Kalokol   2,293 m   NAT'L RSV.
                    Wiawer   Moroto   Lodwar
                    3,084 m   KENYA-ETHIOPIA

121   119

28°   32°   36°

E   F   G   H

© HAMMOND WORLD ATLAS CORPORATION

Scale 1:6,000,000   Polyconic Projection

MI   50   100   150   200
KM   50   100   150   200   250   300

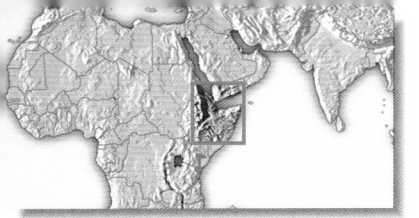

Ethiopia, Somalia

A hot spot beneath the Afar Depression in eastern Ethiopia gave birth to two young seas some 30 million years ago: the Gulf of Aden and the Red Sea. The volcanic islands in the Bab el Mandeb Strait bear witness to the geological forces that caused Africa and the Arabian Peninsula to drift apart. As they continue to diverge, the Red Sea is gradually becoming an ocean.

100
117
119

Height
m.	ft.
6000	19700
4000	13000
2000	6500
1500	5000
1000	3300
500	1600
200	700
0	0
200	700
500	1600
1000	3300
2000	6500
3000	9800
4000	13000
5000	16400
6000	19700

Depth

Population

■ Over 2,000,000	◉ 500,000 - 999,999	⦿ 100,000 - 249,999	◎ 10,000 - 29,999
■ 1,000,000 - 1,999,999	● 250,000 - 499,999	⊙ 30,000 - 99,999	○ Under 10,000

Scale 1:6,000,000 Polyconic Projection

MI 50 100 150 200
KM 50 100 150 200 250 300

© HAMMOND WORLD ATLAS CORPORATION

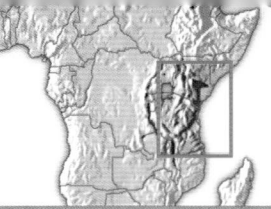

he East African Rift System runs from Ethiopia to Mozambique and splits [in]to two branches at Lake Victoria. The [ma]ny lakes in the region bear witness to [a] plate rift that began some 40 million years ago and is still in progress today. Its margin is lined by some of the highest mountains on the continent - most of them volcanoes like Kilimanjaro (5,895 m).

Height

m. / ft.
6000 / 19700
4000 / 13000
2000 / 6500
1500 / 5000
1000 / 3300
500 / 1600
200 / 700
0
200 / 700
500 / 1600
1000 / 3300
2000 / 6500
3000 / 9800
4000 / 13000
5000 / 16400
6000 / 19700
m. / ft.

Depth

123

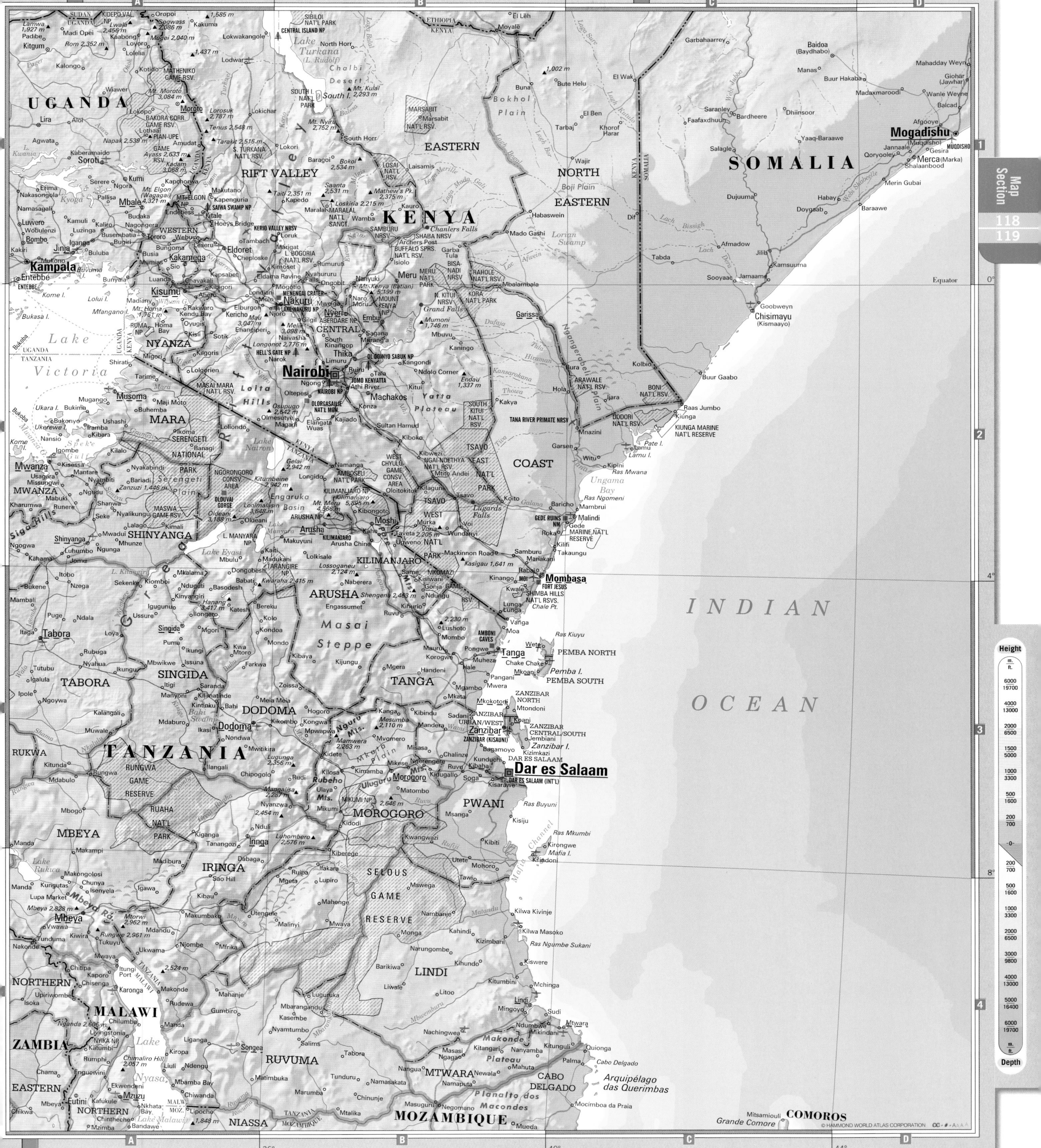

Population

■ Over 2,000,000	● 500,000 - 999,999
■ 1,000,000 - 1,999,999	● 250,000 - 499,999
	● 100,000 - 249,999
	◎ 30,000 - 99,999
	● 10,000 - 29,999
	○ Under 10,000

Scale 1:6,000,000   Polyconic Projection

| MI | 50 | 100 | 150 | 200 |
| KM | 50 | 100 | 150 | 200 | 250 | 300 |

© Hammond World Atlas Corporation

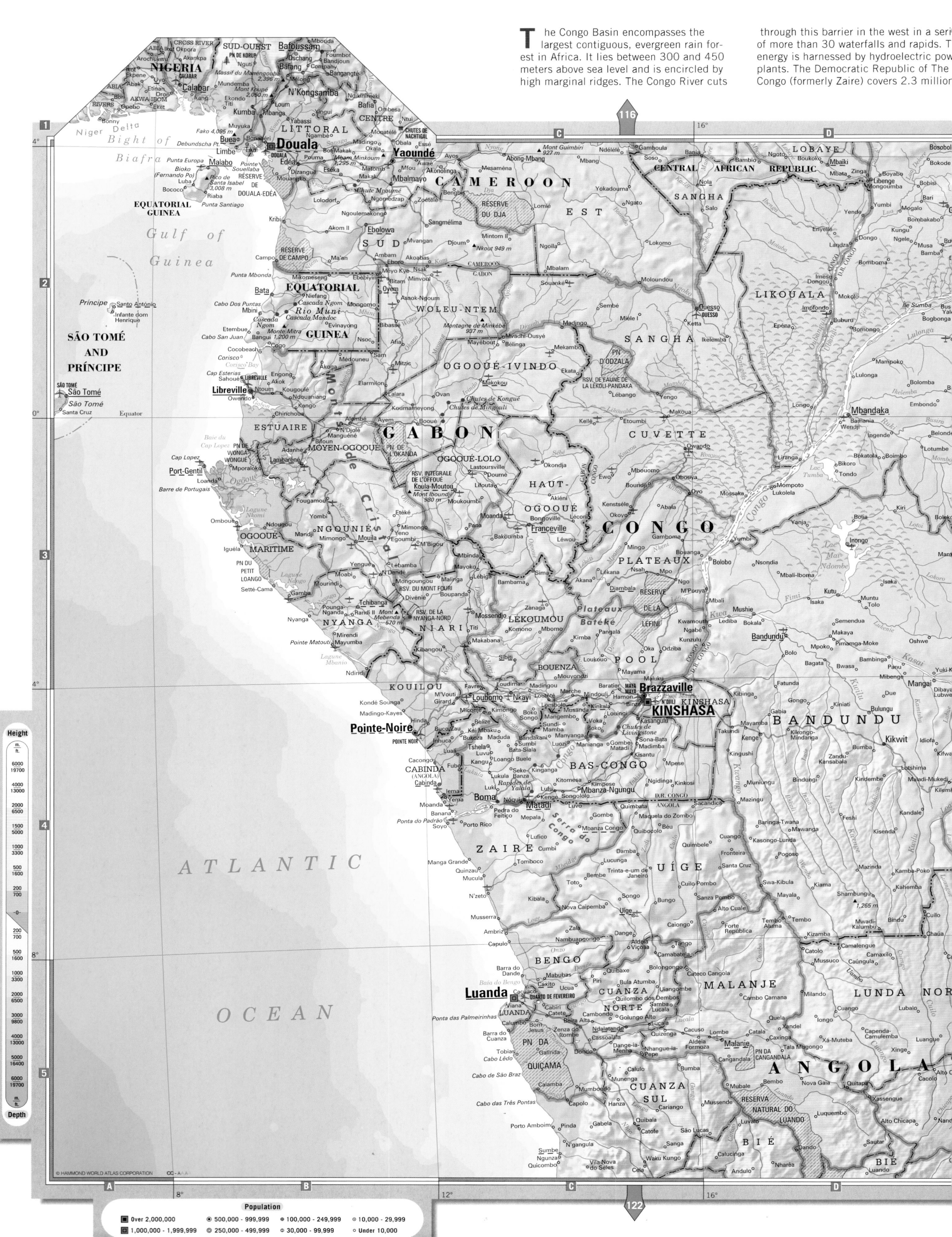

The Congo Basin encompasses the largest contiguous, evergreen rain forest in Africa. It lies between 300 and 450 meters above sea level and is encircled by high marginal ridges. The Congo River cuts through this barrier in the west in a seri of more than 30 waterfalls and rapids. T energy is harnessed by hydroelectric pow plants. The Democratic Republic of The Congo (formerly Zaire) covers 2.3 million

Height

m. ft.
6000 19700
4000 13000
2000 6500
1500 5000
1000 3300
500 1600
200 700
-0-
200 700
500 1600
1000 3300
2000 6500
3000 9800
4000 13000
5000 16400
6000 19700
m. ft.

Depth

Population
- ■ Over 2,000,000
- ● 500,000 - 999,999
- ● 100,000 - 249,999
- ○ 10,000 - 29,999
- ■ 1,000,000 - 1,999,999
- ● 250,000 - 499,999
- ● 30,000 - 99,999
- ○ Under 10,000

© HAMMOND WORLD ATLAS CORPORATION

square km of territory and occupies most
of the Congo Basin. An abundance of
arable land and mineral resources make
it potentially one of the richest countries
of Africa. It is, however, one of the poorest.

DEM. REP. OF THE CONGO

ORIENTALE

ÉQUATEUR

NORD-KIVU

SUD-KIVU

MANIEMA

KASAÏ-ORIENTAL

KASAÏ-OCCIDENTAL

KATANGA

SUDAN

UGANDA

RWANDA

BURUNDI

TANZANIA

ZAMBIA

MALAWI

Lake Albert

Lake Edward

Lake Victoria

Lake Kivu

Lake Tanganyika

Lake Mweru

Lake Rukwa

Lake Bangweulu

L. Nyasa

Great Rift Valley

Monts Mitumba

Monts Bleus

Monts Muhila

Monts Kundelungu

Marungu

Muchinga Mts.

Kampala

Kisangani

Kindu

Bukavu

Goma

Kigali

Bujumbura

Mwanza

Tabora

Mbeya

Kananga

Mbuji-Mayi

Kolwezi

Likasi

Lubumbashi

MARA · MWANZA · SHINYANGA · KIGOMA · TABORA · RUKWA · SINGIDA · MBEYA · NORTHERN · LUAPULA · EASTERN

Scale 1:6,000,000 Polyconic Projection

MI 50 100 150 200

KM 50 100 150 200 250 300

117
119
120
121
123
Map Section

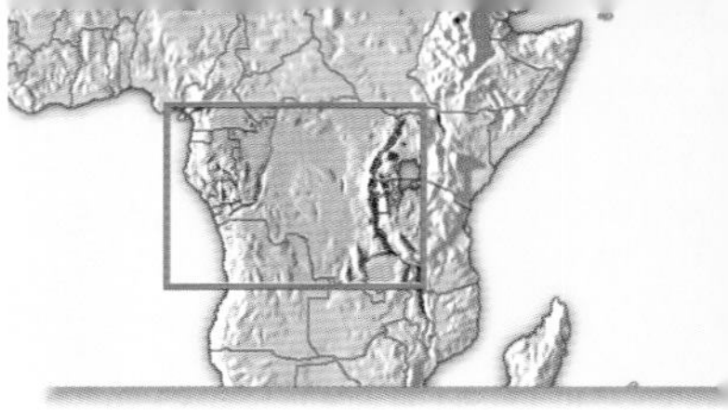

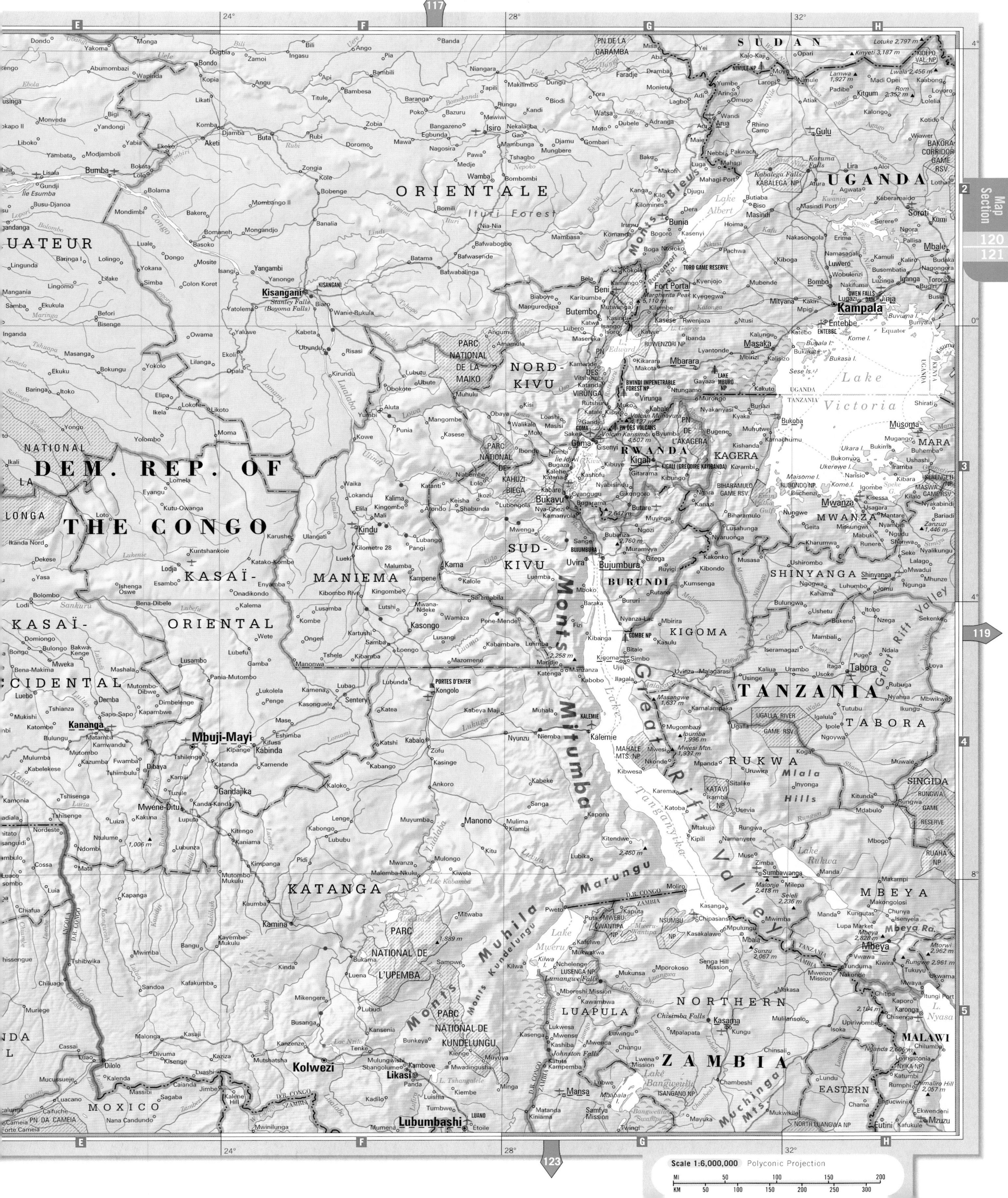

One of the most arid regions of the world is the Namib, a desert that stretches for more than 2,000 km along the western coast of Africa from Angola to South Africa. Annual precipitation here rarely exceeds 50 mm. The desert owes its existence to the cold Benguela Current and cool prevailing winds that carry very little moisture. The Namib is a diverse desert landscape. A prominent topographic feature is the Namib-Naukluft Park south from Walvis Bay, which encompasses some 34,000 square km of sand dunes with an abundant array of forms. Some star dunes here rise to heights of 550 meters.

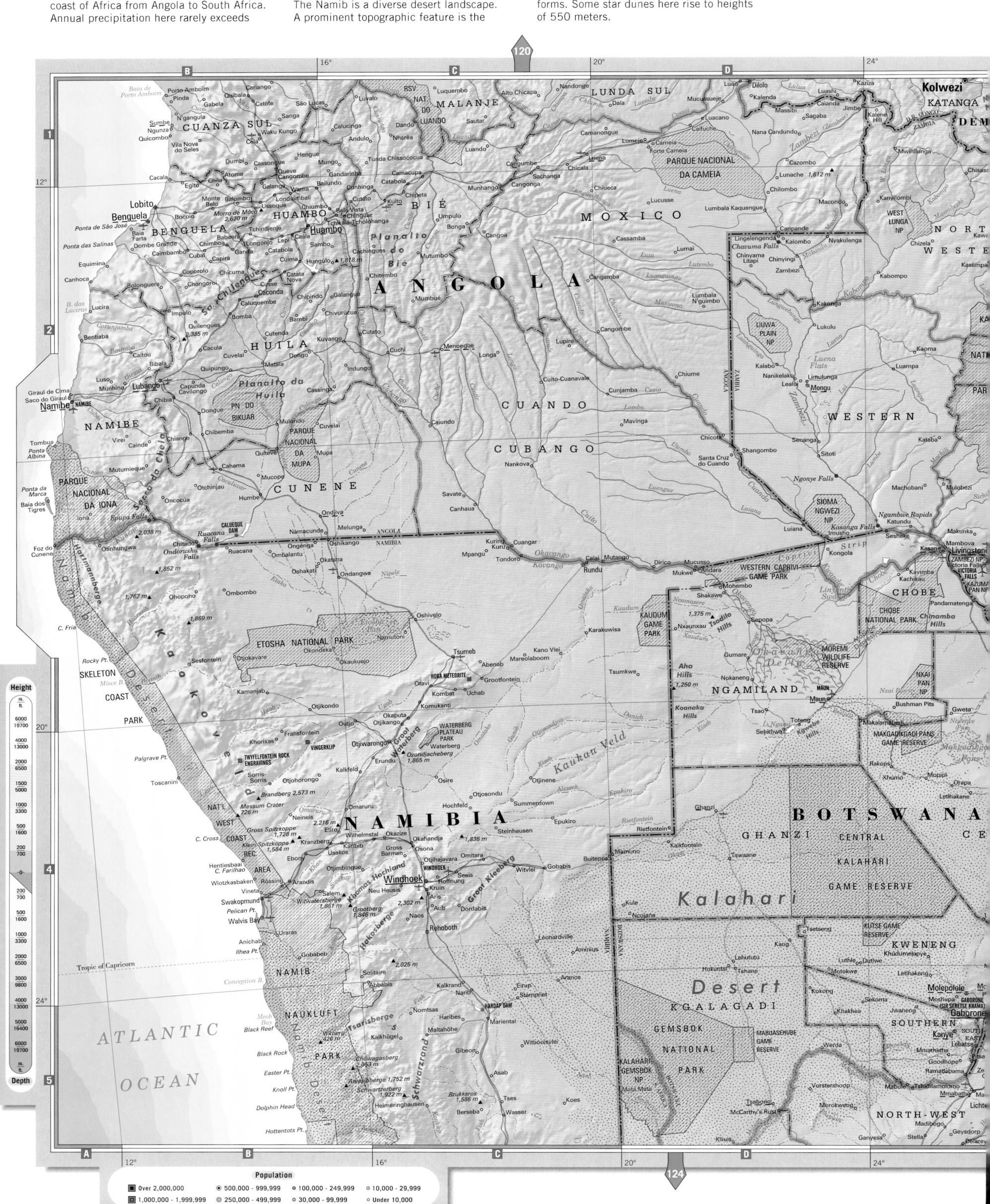

Height

m. / ft.
6000 / 19700
4000 / 13000
2000 / 6500
1500 / 5000
1000 / 3300
500 / 1600
200 / 700
0
200 / 700
500 / 1600
1000 / 3300
2000 / 6500
3000 / 9800
4000 / 13000
5000 / 16400
6000 / 19700
m. / ft.

Depth

Population

- ■ Over 2,000,000
- ◉ 500,000 - 999,999
- ● 100,000 - 249,999
- ⊚ 10,000 - 29,999
- ▣ 1,000,000 - 1,999,999
- ◉ 250,000 - 499,999
- ● 30,000 - 99,999
- ○ Under 10,000

South Central Africa

Scale 1:6,000,000 Polyconic Projection

© HAMMOND WORLD ATLAS CORPORATION

Extending from northern South Africa to the Cape Provinces, the Drakensberg mountains are among the most imposing and beautiful natural features of South Africa. Known as the Great Escarpment, the range comprises rock of different hardness that has been selectively eroded into impressive landscape formations. Billions of years old, the continental plate holds rich ore and diamond deposits that are intensively mined today. Madagascar - separated from the African continent - is the home of many plant and animal species that have developed in isolation and are found nowhere else in the world.

MOZAMBIQUE

GAZA

INHAMBANE

MAPUTO

KRUGER NP

Matola
Maputo

SWAZILAND

Mbabane
Manzini (MATSAPA)

MAPUTO INT'L

Cabo dos Correntes

Ponta Závora

Cabo de Santa Maria

Ponta do Ouro

Botelerpunt

IALANGA

ZULU-NATAL

Richard's Bay

Lake St. Lucia
Kaap Vidal
Leven Pt.
C. Saint Lucia
St. Lucia Estuary

SODWANA BAY NP

KwaMashu
Pinetown
Durban
DURBAN (LOUIS BOTHA)
Amanzimtoti
Umkomaas
Scottburgh

Port Shepstone
Uvongo Beach
Margate

INDIAN

OCEAN

COMOROS

Mitsamiouli
MARAYA Grande Comore
Hahaia
Moroni
Iconi
Foumbouni
Mohéli
Nioumachoua MOHÉLI

Mutsamudu OUANI
Sima Anjouan
Fomboni Domoni
Moya

Mamoudzou
Dembeni Dzaoudzi
Sada DZAOUDZI
Bandeli

MAYOTTE
(FRANCE)

Îles Glorieuses
(FRANCE)

Geyser Reef

Mozambique Channel

Juan de Nova
(FRANCE)

Nosy Chesterfield

Nosy Barren
(Barren Is.)

Tanjona Vilanandro

Tanjon'i Bobaomby
Andranovondrona

Antsiranana

PN MONTAGNE D'AMBRE
1,475 m
Sadjoavato

Tanjon' Andrantany
Tampon Ambohitra

Nosy Mitsio

Nosy Be
Dzamandzar
Ambanja

ANTSIRANANA

Tsaratanana Massif
Maromokotro
2,876 m

Bealanana
2,133 m

Mahajanga

MAHAJANGA

ANTANANARIVO

Antananarivo
IVATO

Antsirabe

TOAMASINA

Toamasina

MADAGASCAR

Miandrivazo

Fandriana

Ambositra

FIANARANTSOA

Fianarantsoa
Ifanadiana

PN DE L'ISALO
1,304 m

TOLIARA

Toliara
Betioky

Ambovombe
Amboasary

Tanjona Vohimena

INDIAN
OCEAN

Tropic of Capricorn

INDIAN

OCEAN

MAURITIUS

C. Malheureux
Triolet
Poudre d'Or

Port Louis
Beau Bassin
Quatre Bornes Curepipe
827 m
Rose Belle
Mahébourg
SIR SEEWOOSAGUR RAMGOOLAM
Souillac

MAURITIUS

RÉUNION
(FRANCE)

Saint-Denis
GILLOT
Saint-André
Saint-Benoît
Piton des Neiges
3,069 m
Le
Tampon
Piton de la Fournaise
2,631 m
Saint-Pierre
Saint-Joseph
Pointe des Cascades

Mascarene Islands

© H.W.A.C. CL 1140

© HAMMOND WORLD ATLAS CORPORATION CD-1143-A·A·A

Scale 1:6,000,000 Lambert Conformal Conic Projection

MI 50 100 150 200
KM 50 100 150 200 300

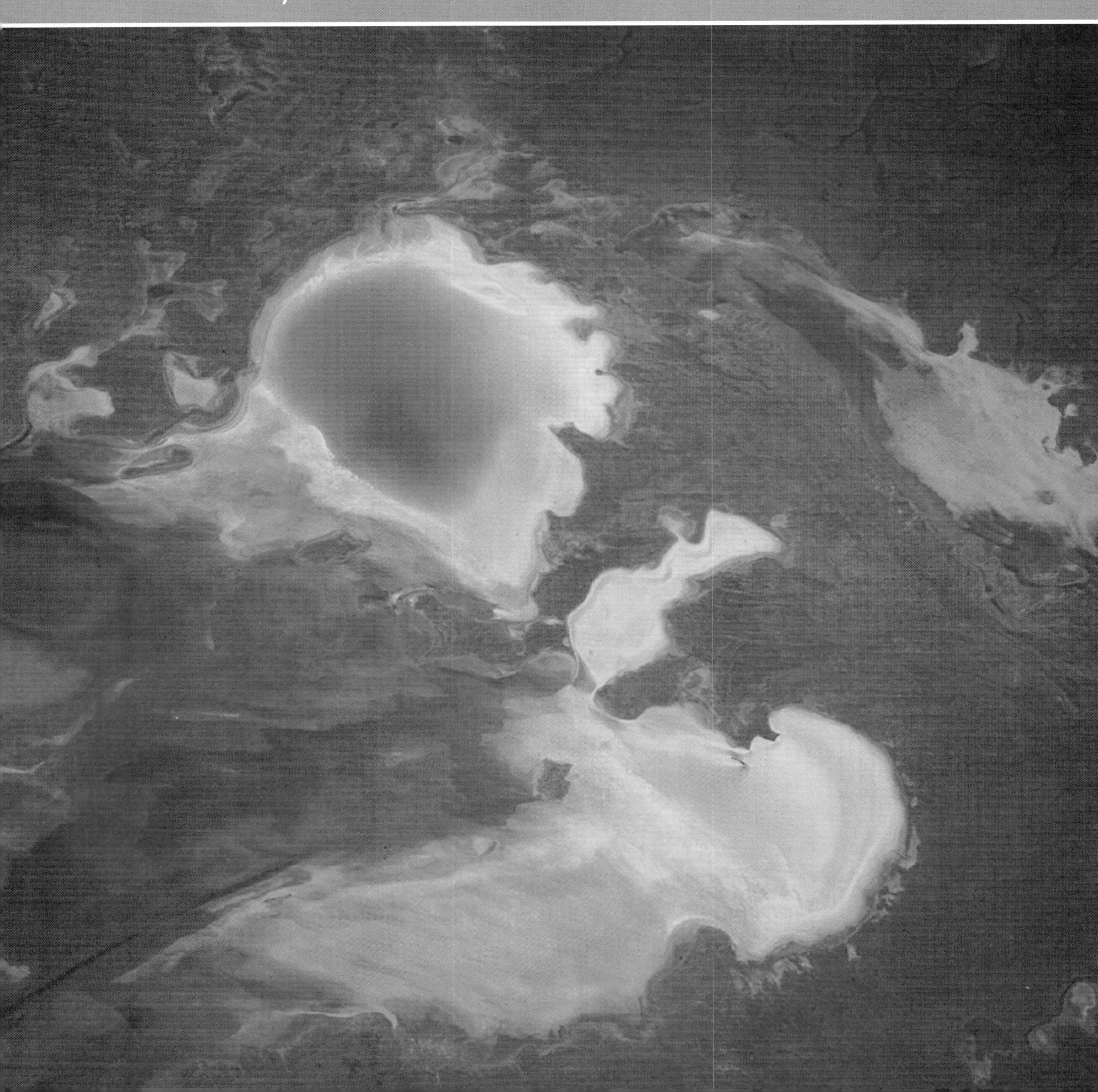

ake Eyre, located at the edge of the Victoria Desert, is the largest lake sin on the continent (8,900 square km), hough it fills with water only after heavy ns. For most of the year, the bed of this salt lake is dry. With depths of up to 16 m below sea level, it is the lowest point in Australia. The much larger northern basin shown on the left (the highly reflective areas) comprises two lakebeds. The western lobe is Belt Bay, and the eastern lobe is Madigan Bay. The coloration, especially of Madigan Bay, indicates that there was some water in this lobe at the time the image was taken.

Map Section 126 127

LAMBERT CONFORMAL CONIC PROJECTION

NEW ZEALAND

INDONESIA

EAST TIMOR

PAPUA NEW GUINEA

Port Moresby

SOLOMON ISLANDS

VANUATU

NEW CALEDONIA (FR.)

CORAL SEA ISLANDS TERRITORY (AUSTL.)

Great Barrier Reef

CORAL SEA

PACIFIC OCEAN

Arafura Sea

Gulf of Carpentaria

Timor Sea

Cape York Peninsula

Torres Strait

Arnhem Land

NORTHERN TERRITORY

Barkly Tableland

QUEENSLAND

Brisbane
Gold Coast
Ipswich

Sydney
Wollongong
Canberra
AUSTRALIAN CAPITAL TERR.

NEW SOUTH WALES

Great Dividing Range

Darling Downs

Grey Range

Simpson Desert

Channel Country

Tanami Desert

Alice Springs
Mount Zeil 1,511 m
MacDonnell Ranges
Uluru (Ayers Rock) 867 m
Musgrave Ras.
Mount Woodroffe 1,440 m

WESTERN AUSTRALIA

Gibson Desert

Great Victoria Desert

Great Sandy Desert

Kimberley Plateau

King Leopold Ras.

Hamersley Range

Nullarbor Plain

Great Australian Bight

SOUTH AUSTRALIA

Lake Eyre North
Lake Eyre South
Lake Torrens
Lake Gairdner
Lake Frome
Flinders Ranges

Adelaide

Murray

VICTORIA

Melbourne
Geelong
Ballarat

Bass Strait

King I.

TASMANIA

Hobart
Launceston
Mount Ossa 1,617 m

TASMAN SEA

Wilsons Promontory

Darling Range

Perth

INDIAN OCEAN

PHOTOGRAPHIC DETAIL

AREA OF OPTIMIZATION

AREA OF OPTIMIZATION
The red band which surrounds this map defines the "Area of Optimization." Within this bounding curve is the most accurate conformal map that can be made of the region. Outside the optimized area, distortion increases rapidly, and tears or other irregularities in the grid may occur.
(See Map Section 8-9 for additional information.)

Population
■ Over 2,000,000	◉ 500,000 - 999,999	○ 50,000 - 99,999
□ 1,000,000 - 1,999,999	⊕ 100,000 - 499,999	∘ Under 50,000

Scale 1:16,000,000   Hammond Optimal Conformal

| MI | 125 | 250 | 375 | 500 |
| KM | 125 250 | 500 | 625 | 750 |

© HAMMOND WORLD ATLAS CORPORATION

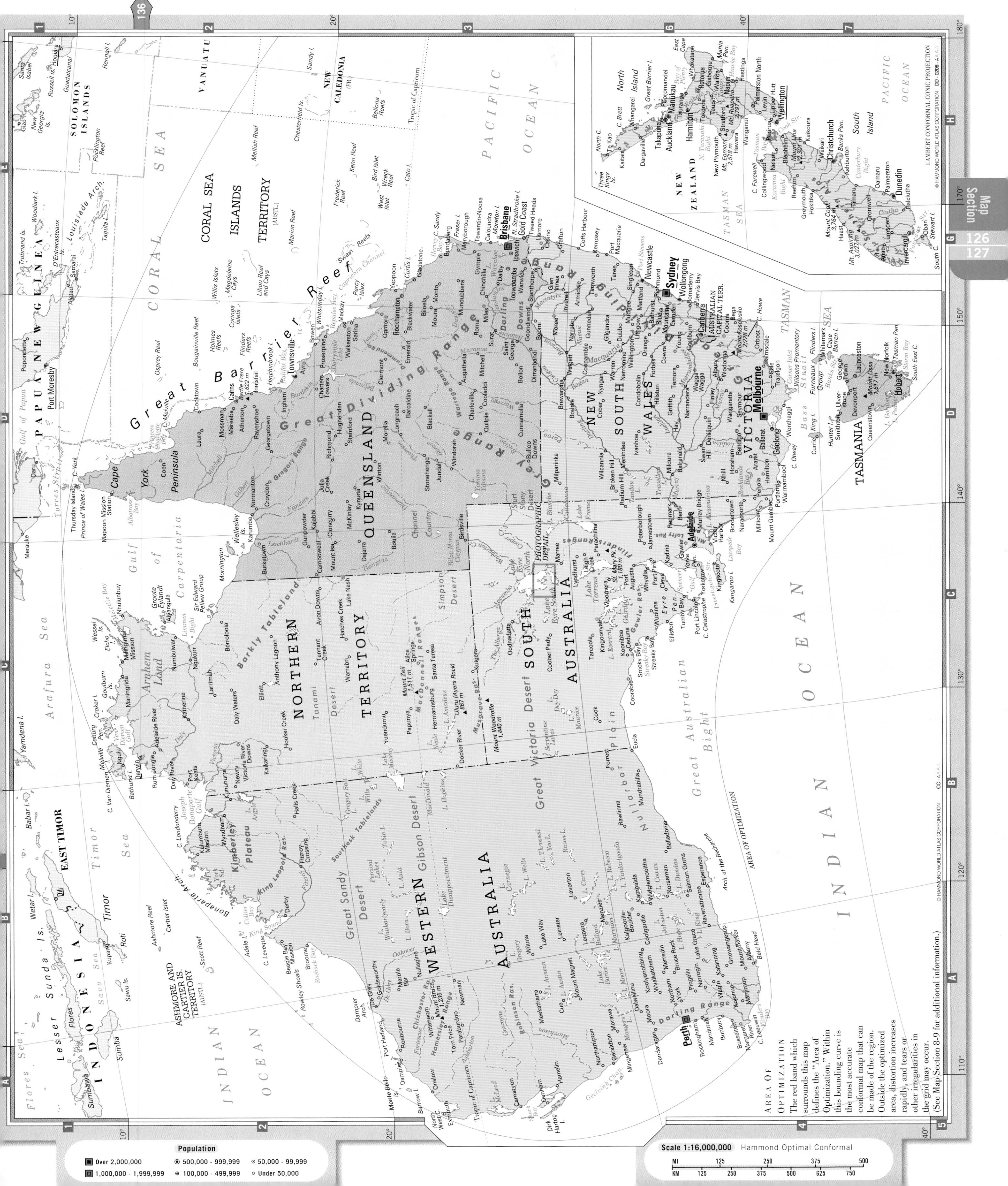

Papua New Guinea lies on the seam between the Indo-Australian and Pacific Plates. Consequently, it is a region of massive earthquakes, active volcanoes, and rugged mountain terrain that provides a unique natural refuge for plants and wildlife today. The tropical rain forest is home to rare birds of paradise and butterflies with wingspans of up to 25 cm. It is also the geographical boundary for many Australian species, including the duck-billed platypus of the order Monotremata. Most Papuans had no contact with modern civilization until 1933.

Papua New Guinea, Northern Australia

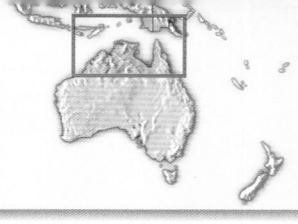

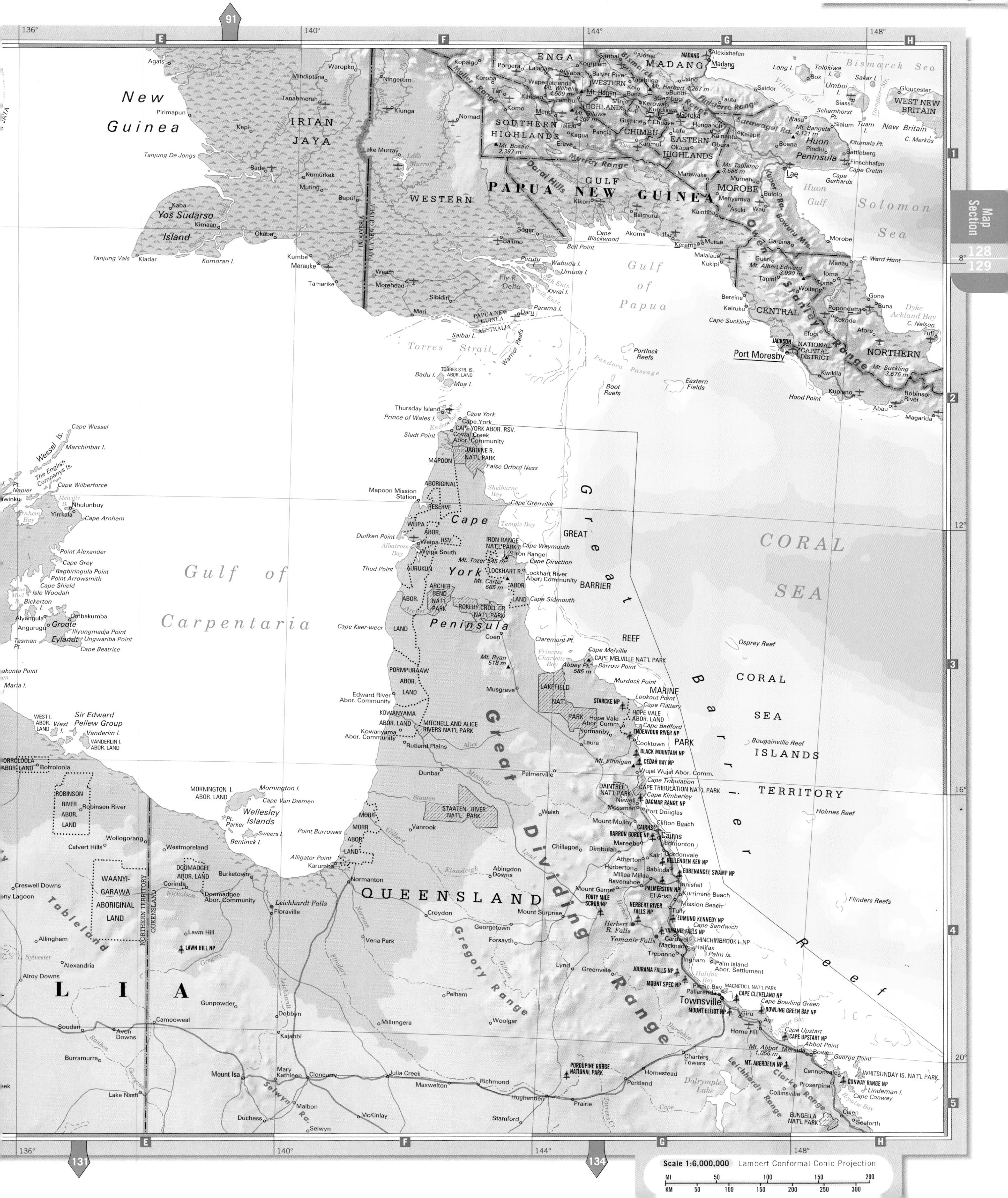

91
131
134
136°
140°
144°
148°
E
F
G
H
1
2
3
4
5
8°
12°
16°
20°
Map Section
128
129
New Guinea
IRIAN JAYA
Agats
Waropko
Mindiptana
Ningerum
Tanahmerah
Kiunga
Pirimapun
Kepi
Tanjung De Jongs
Lake Murray
Bade
Kumurkek
Muting
Bupul
WESTERN
Kaba
Yos Sudarso Island
Kimaan
Okaba
Tanjung Vals
Kladar
Komoran I.
Kumbe
Merauke
Tamarike
Weam
Morehead
Sibidiri
Mari
INDONESIA
PAPUA NEW GUINEA
ENGA
Kopiago
Porgera
Laiagam
Kompiam
Simbai
Aiome
MADANG
Madang
Alexishafen
Koroba
Wabag
Baiyer River
Tabibuga
Usino
Tari
Wapenamanda
Mt. Wilhelm 4,509 m
Mt. Hagen
Mt. Herbert 4,267 m
Bundi
Gembogl
WESTERN HIGHLANDS
Kandep
Nomad
Komo
Mendi
Mt. Giluwe 4,367 m
Kup
Kerowagi
Kundiawa
Goroka
SOUTHERN HIGHLANDS
Ialibu
Pangia
Gumine
CHIMBU
Chuave
Hengangi
Kagua
Mt. Bosavi 2,397 m
Erave
Karimui
Okapa
EASTERN HIGHLANDS
Obura
Lufa
Kainantu
Murray Range
Darai Hills
Kikori
GULF
PAPUA NEW GUINEA
Finisterre Range
Saidor
Sarawaget Ra.
Mt. Bangeta 4,121 m
Wasu
Kaiapit
Boana
Huon Peninsula
Pindiu
Sattleberg
Finschhafen
Cape Cretin
Marawaka
Mt. Tabletop 3,686 m
Mumeng
Lae
MOROBE
Menyamya
Aseki
Wau
Bulolo
Kaintiba
Huon Gulf
Cape Gerhards
Bismarck Sea
Long I.
Tolokiwa I.
Bok
Umboi I.
Sakar I.
Siassi
Gloucester
WEST NEW BRITAIN
Scharnhorst Pt.
Sialum
Tuam I.
New Britain
C. Merkus
Kitumala Pt.
Solomon Sea
Vitiaz Str.
Dampier Str.
Baimuru
Kikori
Sogeri
Balimo
Cape Blackwood
Akoma
Ihu
Kerema
Murua
Bell Point
Purutu
Wabuda I.
Umuda I.
Fly R. Delta
Kiwai I.
Parama I.
Daru
PAPUA NEW GUINEA
AUSTRALIA
Gulf of Papua
Malalaua
Kukipi
Garaina
Morobe
Guari
Mt. Albert Edward 3,990 m
Tapini
Woitape
Manau
C. Ward Hunt
Ioma
Koma
Owen Stanley Range
Kuper Ra.
Bowutu Mts.
Bereina
Kairuku
CENTRAL
Cape Suckling
Gona
Buna
Popondetta
Kokoda
Dyke Ackland Bay
C. Nelson
Afore
Tufi
Efogi
JACKSON
NATIONAL CAPITAL DISTRICT
Port Moresby
NORTHERN
Mt. Suckling 3,676 m
Kwikila
Kupiano
Hood Point
Robinson River
Abau
Magarida
Saibai I.
Torres Strait
Warrior Reefs
Portlock Reefs
Pandora Passage
Eastern Fields
Boot Reefs
Badu I.
TORRES STR. IS. ABOR. LAND
Moa I.
Thursday Island
Prince of Wales I.
Endeavour Str.
Cape York
CAPE YORK ABOR. RSV.
Cowal Creek Abor. Community
Sladt Point
JARDINE R. NAT'L PARK
MAPOON
False Orford Ness
ABORIGINAL
Mapoon Mission Station
Shelburne Bay
RESERVE
Cape Grenville
WEIPA
Cape
Temple Bay
Duifken Point
ABOR.
Albatross Bay
Weipa
RSV.
Weipa South
IRON RANGE NAT'L PARK
Cape Weymouth
Iron Range
Mt. Tozer 545 m
Cape Direction
Thud Point
AURUKUN
York
LOCKHART R.
Lockhart River Abor. Community
ARCHER BEND NAT'L PARK
Mt. Carter 665 m
ABOR.
LAND
Cape Sidmouth
ROKEBY-CROLL CR. NAT'L PARK
Cape Keer-weer
Peninsula
Coen
Claremont Pt.
Mt. Ryan 518 m
Princess Charlotte Bay
Cape Melville
CAPE MELVILLE NAT'L PARK
Abbey Pk. 585 m
Barrow Point
PORMPURAAW ABOR. LAND
Edward River Abor. Community
Musgrave
LAKEFIELD NAT'L PARK
Murdock Point
Lookout Point
Cape Flattery
STARCKE NP
HOPE VALE ABOR. LAND
Hope Vale Abor. Comm.
Cape Bedford
ENDEAVOUR RIVER NP
KOWANYAMA ABOR. LAND
MITCHELL AND ALICE RIVERS NAT'L PARK
Kowanyama Abor. Community
Rutland Plains
Alice
Normanby
Laura
Cooktown
BLACK MOUNTAIN NP
Mt. Finnigan
CEDAR BAY NP
Wujal Wujal Abor. Comm.
Cape Tribulation
DAINTREE NAT'L PARK
CAPE TRIBULATION NAT'L PARK
Cape Kimberley
Newell
DAGMAR RANGE NP
Mossman
Port Douglas
Mount Molloy
Clifton Beach
CAIRNS NP
BARRON GORGE NP
Cairns
Mareeba
Edmonton
Dimbulah
Gordonvale
Atherton
Kairi
BELLENDEN KER NP
Herberton
Babinda
Millaa Millaa
EUBENANGEE SWAMP NP
Ravenshoe
Innisfail
PALMERSTON NP
El Arish
Kurrimine Beach
Mount Garnet
FORTY MILE SCRUB NP
HERBERT RIVER FALLS NP
Tully
Mission Beach
EDMUND KENNEDY NP
Cape Sandwich
Herbert R. Falls
YAMANIE FALLS NP
Cardwell
HINCHINBROOK I. NP
Yamanie Falls
Mackna
Halifax
Trebonne
Palm Is.
Ingham
Palm Island Abor. Settlement
Halifax Bay
JOURAMA FALLS NP
MOUNT SPEC NP
Picnic Bay
MAGNETIC I. NAT'L PARK
Pallarenda
CAPE CLEVELAND NP
Townsville
MOUNT ELLIOT NP
Cape Bowling Green
BOWLING GREEN BAY NP
Giru
Ayr
Home Hill
Upstart Bay
Cape Upstart
CAPE UPSTART NP
Abbot Point
Mt. Abbot 1,056 m
Merinda
Bowen
George Point
MT. ABERDEEN NP
Cannonvale
WHITSUNDAY IS. NAT'L PARK
Proserpine
CONWAY RANGE NP
Lindeman I.
Cape Conway
Repulse Bay
Collinsville
Colen
Seaforth
EUNGELLA NAT'L PARK
Leichhardt Range
Clarke Range
Gulf of Carpentaria
Great Barrier Reef
GREAT BARRIER REEF MARINE PARK
CORAL SEA ISLANDS TERRITORY
CORAL SEA
Osprey Reef
Bougainville Reef
Holmes Reef
Flinders Reefs
Great Dividing Range
Gregory Range
QUEENSLAND
Palmerville
Dunbar
Mitchell
Staaten
STAATEN RIVER NAT'L PARK
Walsh
Vanrook
Chillagoe
MORR
MORR ABOR. LAND
Gilbert
Point Burrowes
Alligator Point
Karumba
Normanton
Einasleigh
Abingdon Downs
Lynd
Croydon
Mount Surprise
Georgetown
Forsayth
Vena Park
Norman
Flinders
Lynd
Greenvale
Pelham
Woolgar
Millungera
Dobbyn
Kajabbi
Burdekin
Charters Towers
Homestead
Pentland
Dalrymple Lake
PORCUPINE GORGE NATIONAL PARK
Julia Creek
Richmond
Maxwelton
Hughenden
Prairie
Torrens Cr.
Stamford
McKinlay
Cloncurry
Mary Kathleen
Mount Isa
Selwyn Ra.
Malbon
Selwyn
Duchess
Lake Nash
Burramurra
Soudan
Avon Downs
Ranken
Georgina
Camooweal
Gunpowder
Leichhardt
Lawn Hill
LAWN HILL NP
Leichhardt Falls
Floraville
Burketown
Doomadgee Abor. Community
DOOMADGEE ABOR. LAND
Corinda
Nicholson
Westmoreland
Mornington I.
MORNINGTON I. ABOR. LAND
Cape Van Diemen
Wellesley Islands
Pt. Parker
Sweers I.
Bentinck I.
Wollogorang
Calvert Hills
ROBINSON RIVER ABOR. LAND
Robinson River
WAANYI-GARAWA ABORIGINAL LAND
NORTHERN TERRITORY
QUEENSLAND
Creswell Downs
Tableland
Allingham
Alexandria
Alroy Downs
Gregory
Borroloola
BORROLOOLA ABOR. LAND
Sir Edward Pellew Group
West I.
WEST I. ABOR. LAND
Vanderlin I.
VANDERLIN I. ABOR. LAND
Maria I.
Cape Wessel
Wessel Is.
Marchinbar I.
The English Companys Is.
Cape Wilberforce
Pt. Napier
Melville B.
Nhulunbuy
Yirrkala
Arnhem Bay
Cape Arnhem
Point Alexander
Cape Grey
Bagbiringula Point
Point Arrowsmith
Cape Shield
Isle Woodah
Bickerton
Umbakumba
Alyangula
Angurugu
Groote Eylandt
Ilyungmadja Point
Ungwariba Point
Tasman Pt.
Cape Beatrice
L I A
Scale 1:6,000,000
Lambert Conformal Conic Projection
MI 50 100 150 200
KM 50 100 150 200 250 300

Australia is covered by more desert for its size than any other inhabited continent. Known collectively as the "outback," these desert regions are located primarily in the west and the interior. Many of the rivers that flow sporadically into the central basin seldom reach their terminal lakes, which are dry salt flats for most of the year. The basin has enormous groundwater reserves left over from the ice age, however. These are tapped from artesian wells to water grazing lands for sheep. Cultivation is possible only in a few coastal areas concentrated primarily around Perth and Adelaide. The isolated monolith of Ayers Rock rises from the plain in the Northern Territory. It is sacred to the Aborigine who call it Uluru.

Height

m. / ft.
6000 / 19700
4000 / 13000
2000 / 6500
1500 / 5000
1000 / 3300
500 / 1600
200 / 700
-0-
200 / 700
500 / 1600
1000 / 3300
2000 / 6500
3000 / 9800
4000 / 13000
5000 / 16400
6000 / 19700
m. / ft.

Depth

Population

■ Over 2,000,000	● 500,000 - 999,999	⊙ 100,000 - 249,999	○ 10,000 - 29,999
▣ 1,000,000 - 1,999,999	● 250,000 - 499,999	⊙ 30,000 - 99,999	○ Under 10,000

Western and Central Australia

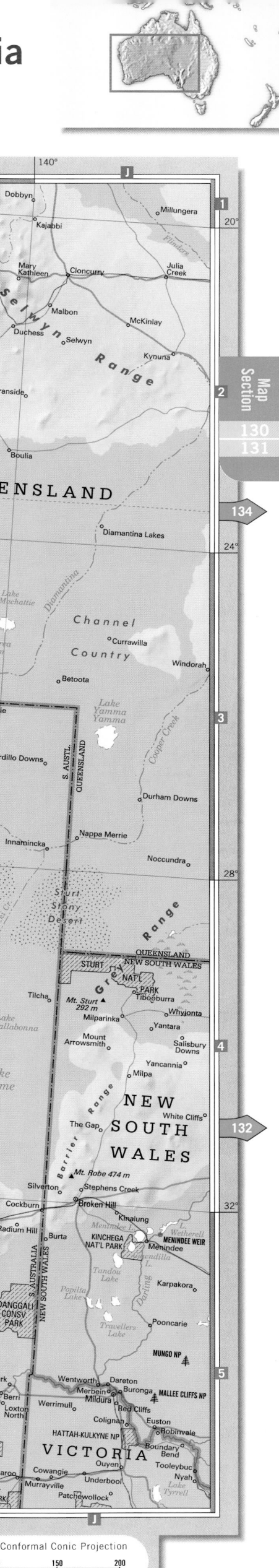

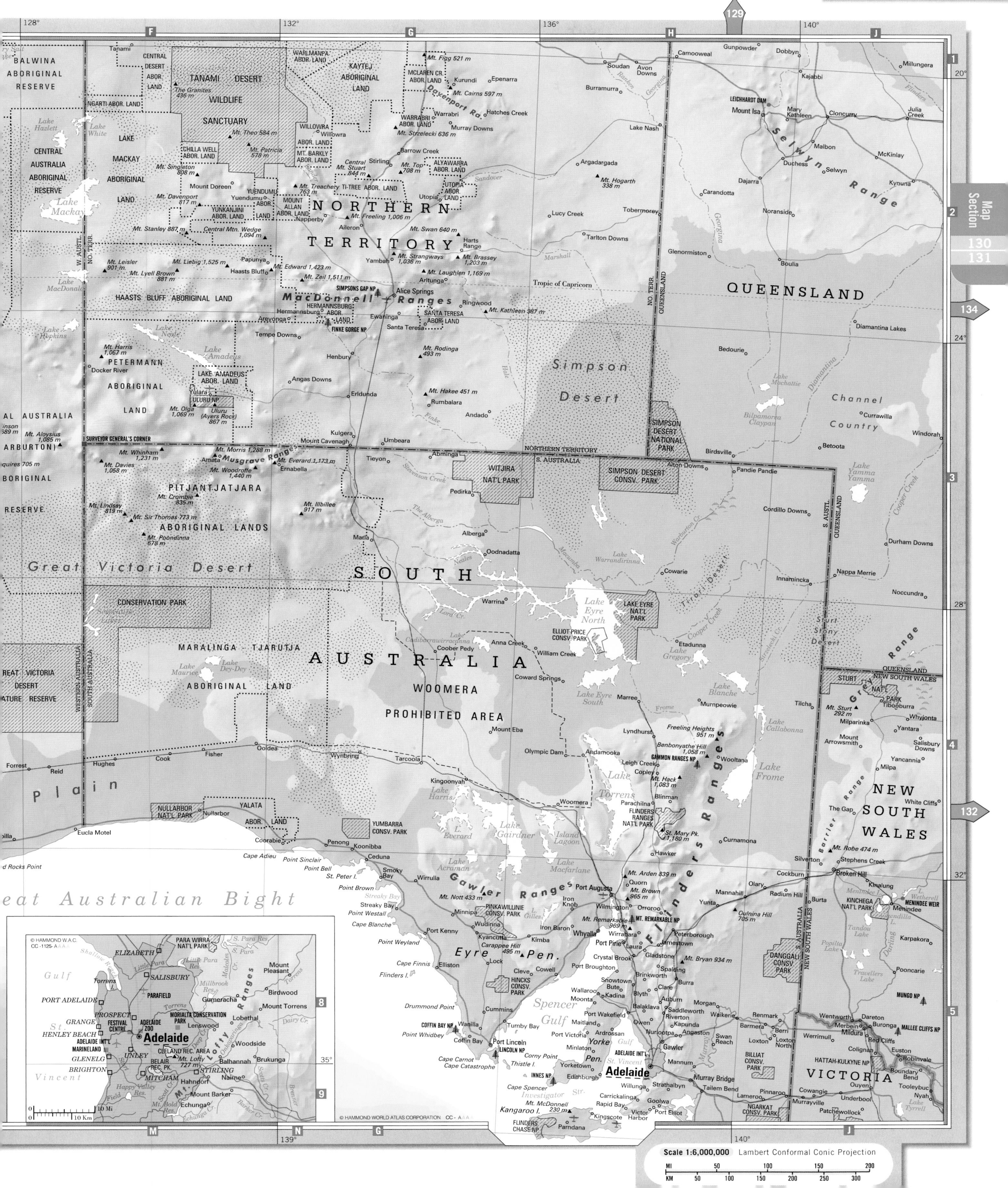

Scale 1:6,000,000 Lambert Conformal Conic Projection

Southeastern Australia

Tasmania lies within the cool-temperate West Wind Drift of the southern hemisphere. The resulting climate provides abundant precipitation and ideal conditions for fruit and berry cultivation. The northern area of southeastern Australia, where New South Wales merges with the monsoon region of Queensland, is much warmer. Areas of subtropical rain forest are also found along the northern coast.

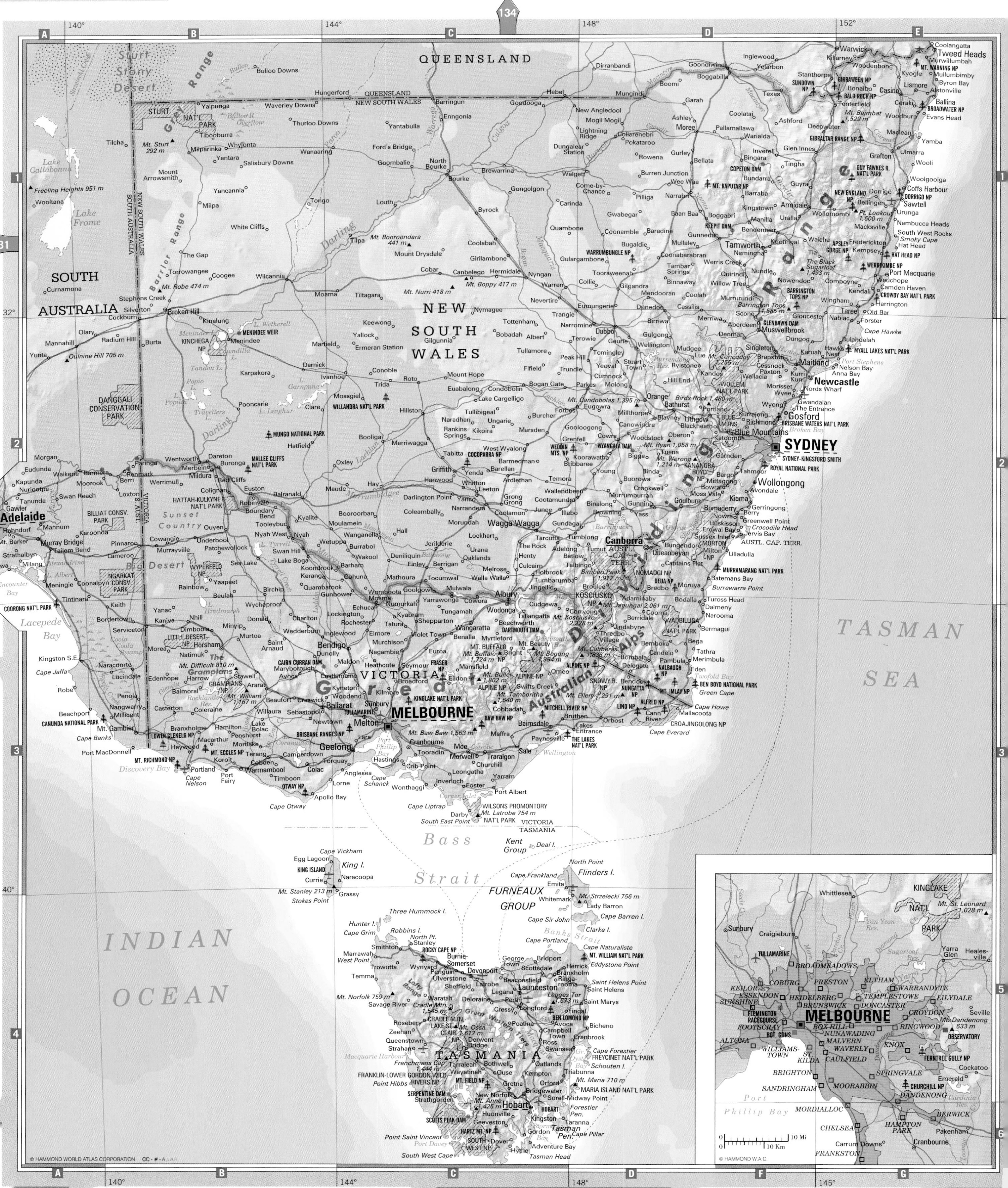

134

131

Height
m. ft.
6000 19700
4000 13000
2000 6500
1500 5000
1000 3300
500 1600
200 700
0
200 700
500 1600
1000 3300
2000 6500
3000 9800
4000 13000
5000 16400
6000 19700
m. ft.
Depth

Population

- Over 2,000,000
- 1,000,000 - 1,999,999
- 500,000 - 999,999
- 250,000 - 499,999
- 100,000 - 249,999
- 30,000 - 99,999
- 10,000 - 29,999
- Under 10,000

Scale 1:6,000,000 Lambert Conformal Conic Projection

MI 50 100 150 200
KM 50 100 150 200 250 300

© HAMMOND WORLD ATLAS CORPORATION

ue to its relatively pleasant climate and reliable rainfall, the region between ney and Melbourne is home to most tralians. Lush forests of eucalyptus found here, and the Blue Mountains west of Sydney are presumably named for the shimmering blue of indigenous eucalyptus trees. Mount Kosciusko, Australia's highest peak, rises to an elevation of 2,228 meters south of Canberra.

Map Section

132
133

Height

m.
ft.

6000
19700

4000
13000

2000
6500

1500
5000

1000
3300

500
1600

200
700

-0-

200
700

500
1600

1000
3300

2000
6500

3000
9800

4000
13000

5000
16400

6000
19700

m.
ft.

Depth

© HAMMOND WORLD ATLAS CORPORATION   CC - # - A - A

Scale 1:3,000,000   Lambert Conformal Conic Projection

MI   25   50   75   100

KM   25   50   75   100   125   150

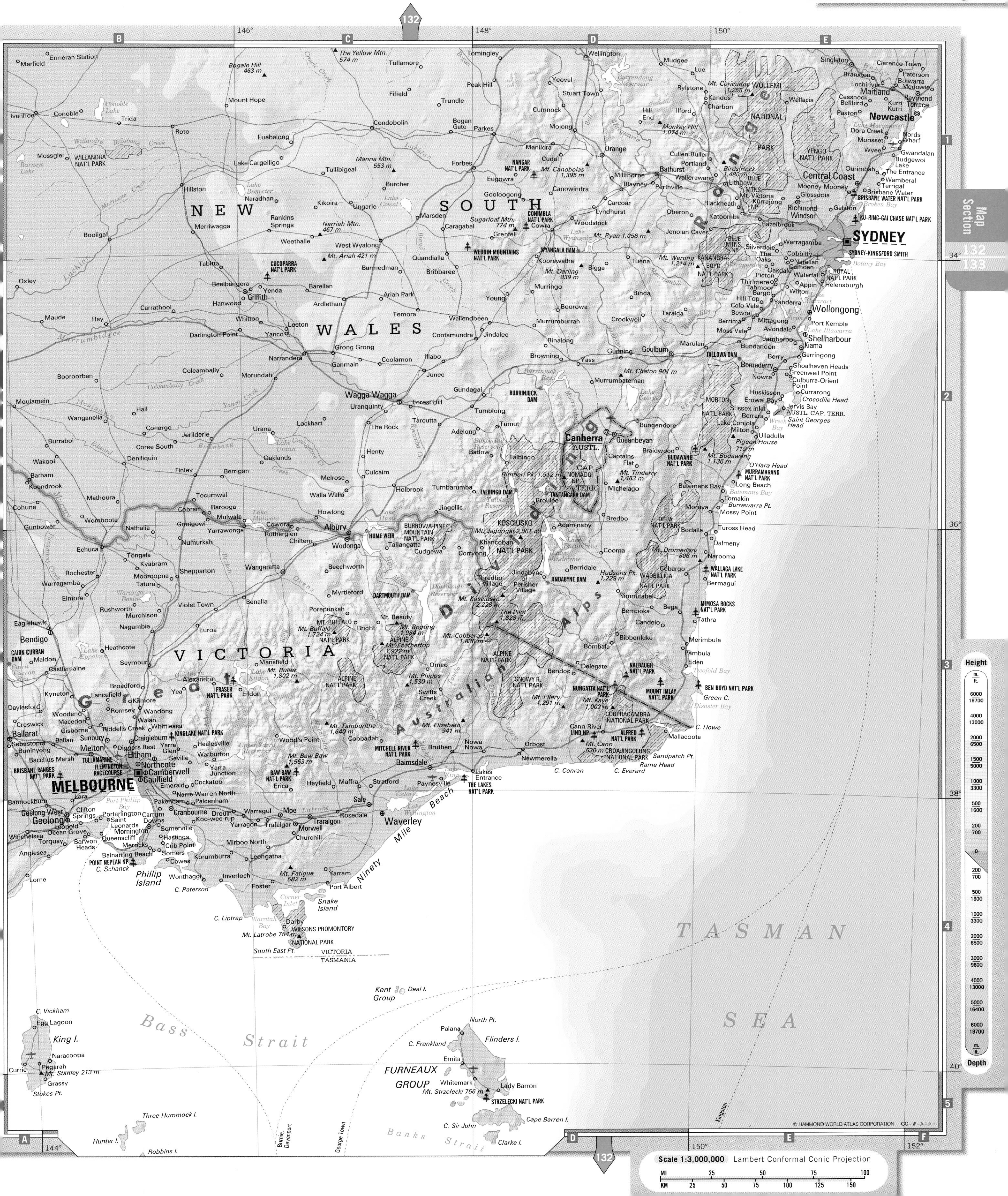

Northeastern Australia

The Great Barrier Reef is a complex of coral reefs, atolls, and shoals that runs along the northeastern coast of Australia for about 2,600 km. Its foundations lie on the shelf of the Coral Sea at depths of up to 180 m. Water levels and climatic conditions have a major impact on reef growth. A rapid rise in sea level endangers coral organisms, which cannot survive in depths below 55 m.

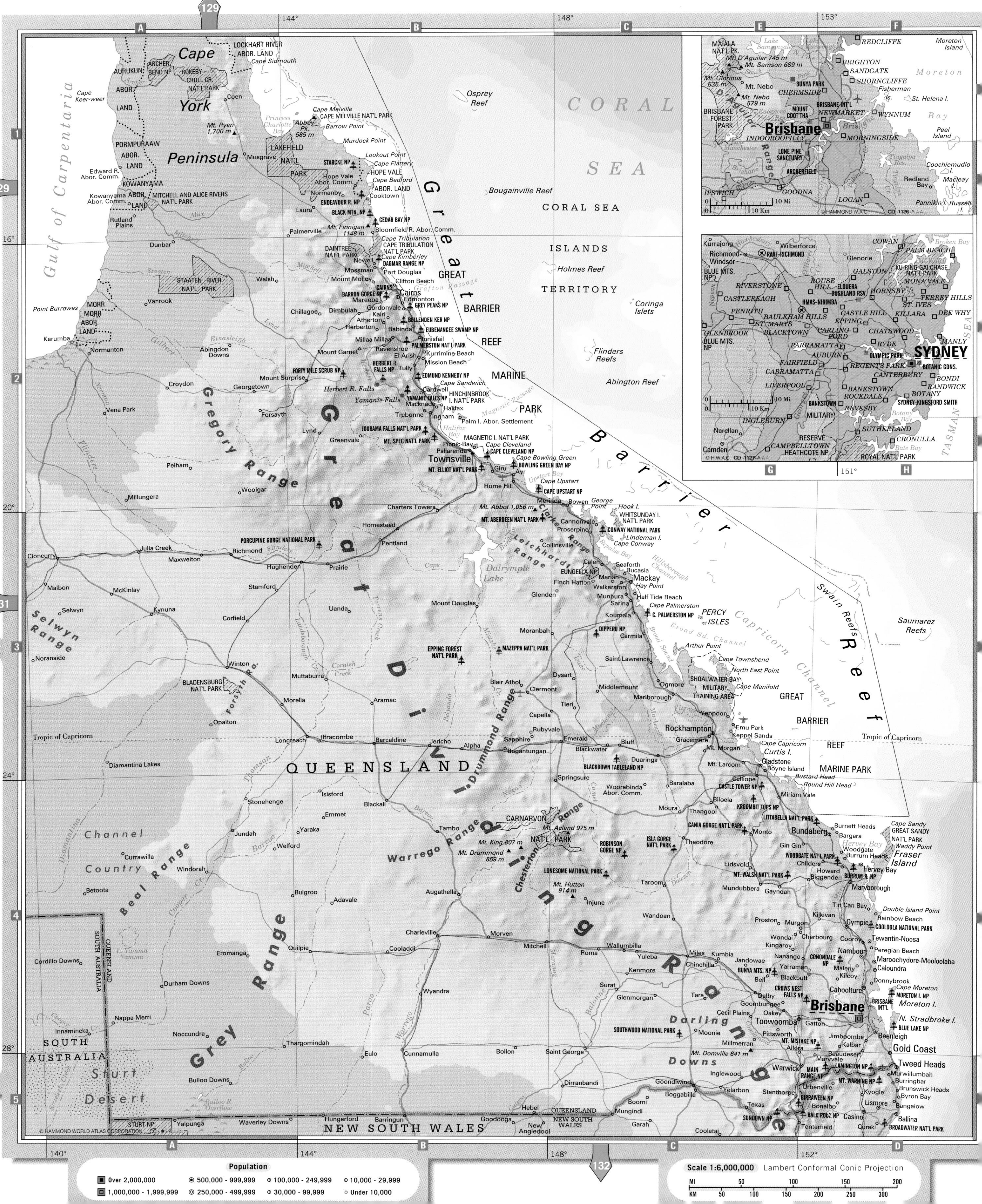

Height

m. / ft.
6000 / 19700
4000 / 13000
2000 / 6500
1500 / 5000
1000 / 3300
500 / 1600
200 / 700
-0-
200 / 700
500 / 1600
1000 / 3300
2000 / 6500
3000 / 9800
4000 / 13000
5000 / 16400
6000 / 19700
m. / ft.

Depth

Population

- ■ Over 2,000,000
- □ 1,000,000 - 1,999,999
- ⊛ 500,000 - 999,999
- ◉ 250,000 - 499,999
- ⊕ 100,000 - 249,999
- ⊙ 30,000 - 99,999
- ○ 10,000 - 29,999
- ∘ Under 10,000

Scale 1:6,000,000 Lambert Conformal Conic Projection

MI 50 100 150 200
KM 50 100 150 200 300

© HAMMOND WORLD ATLAS CORPORATION

ctive volcanoes, geysers, glaciers, fjords, sandy beaches, evergreen beach sts, ferns the size of trees, parrots - list of New Zealand's natural beauties s on and on. The North Island lies along the Pacific "Ring of Fire" and is therefore subject to volcanic eruptions. The South Island, where glaciers descend far into forested areas, is much calmer.

New Zealand

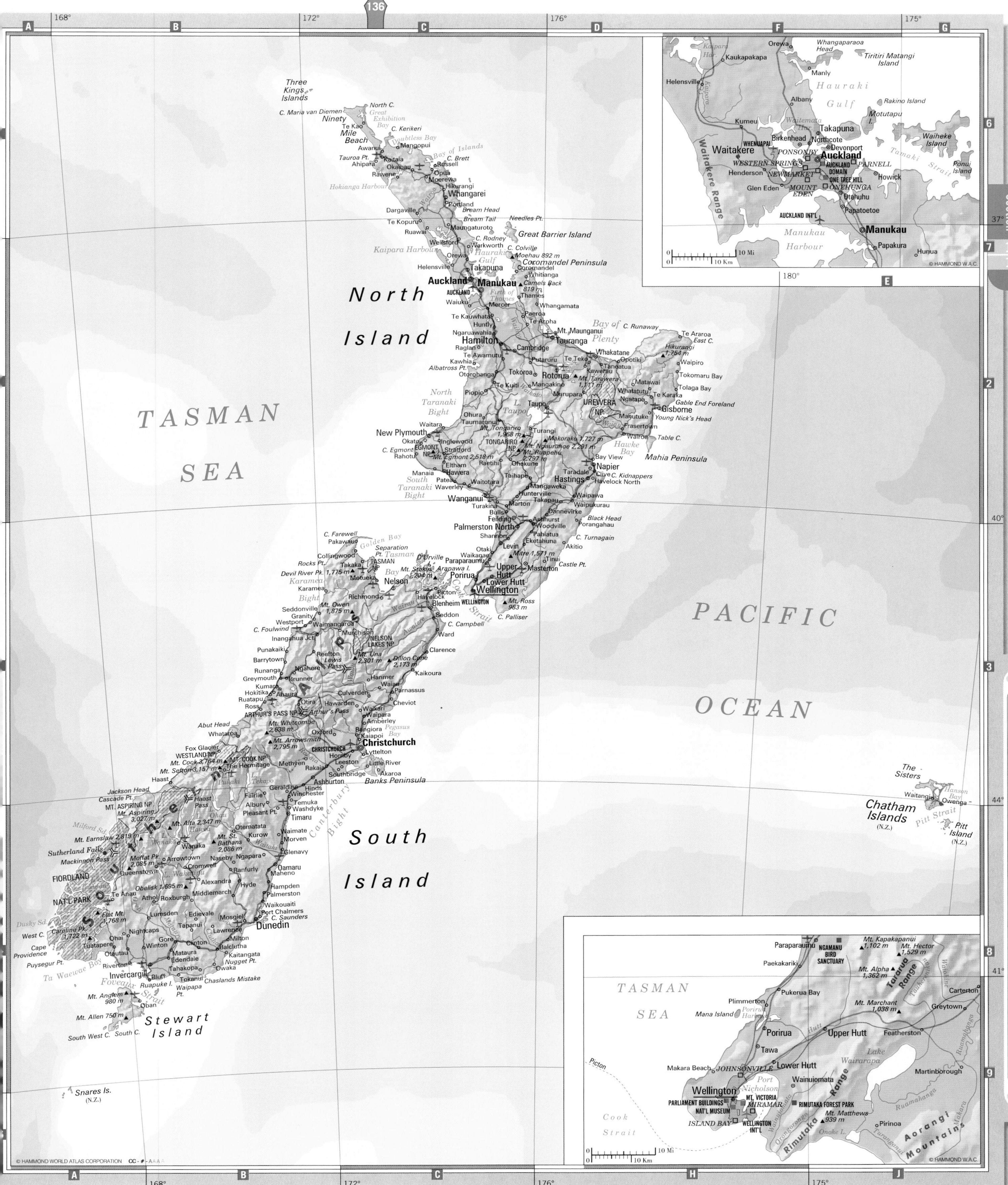

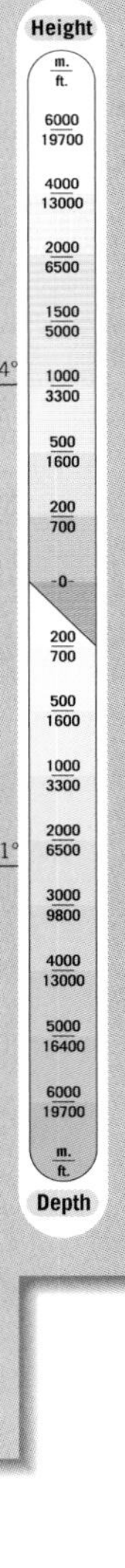

134
135

Map Section

North Island

South Island

TASMAN SEA

PACIFIC OCEAN

Three Kings Islands

Stewart Island

Chatham Islands (N.Z.)

Pitt Island (N.Z.)

The Sisters

Auckland inset:
Hauraki Gulf
Helensville
Kaukapakapa
Orewa
Whangaparaoa Head
Tiritiri Matangi Island
Manly
Albany
Rakino Island
Motutapu I.
Kumeu
Takapuna
Waiheke Island
Birkenhead
Northcote
Devonport
Ponui Island
WHENUAPAI
PONSONBY
Auckland
AUCKLAND
WESTERN SPRINGS
PARNELL
Waitakere
Henderson
NEWMARKET
DOMAIN
Howick
Glen Eden
MOUNT EDEN
ONEHUNGA
ONE TREE HILL
Pakuranga
AUCKLAND INT'L
Manukau
Papatoetoe
Manukau Harbour
Papakura
Hunua
© HAMMOND W.A.C.

Wellington inset:
TASMAN SEA
Paraparaumu
NGAMANU BIRD SANCTUARY
Mt. Kapakapanui 1,102 m
Mt. Hector 1,529 m
Paekakariki
Mt. Alpha 1,362 m
Tararua Range
Carterton
Pukerua Bay
Mt. Marchant 1,038 m
Greytown
Plimmerton
Porirua
Upper Hutt
Featherston
Mana Island
Tawa
Lower Hutt
Wainuiomata
Rimutaka Forest Park
Mt. Matthews 939 m
Martinborough
Picton
Makara Beach
JOHNSONVILLE
Port Nicholson
Wellington
PARLIAMENT BUILDINGS
NAT'L MUSEUM
MT. VICTORIA
MIRAMAR
WELLINGTON INT'L
ISLAND BAY
Cook Strait
Aorangi Mountains
Pirinoa
Rimutaka Range
Ruamahanga
© HAMMOND W.A.C.

Population

■ Over 2,000,000	● 500,000 - 999,999	● 100,000 - 249,999	○ 10,000 - 29,999
□ 1,000,000 - 1,999,999	● 250,000 - 499,999	● 30,000 - 99,999	• Under 10,000

Height
m. / ft.
6000 / 19700
4000 / 13000
2000 / 6500
1500 / 5000
1000 / 3300
500 / 1600
200 / 700
0
200 / 700
500 / 1600
1000 / 3300
2000 / 6500
3000 / 9800
4000 / 13000
5000 / 16400
6000 / 19700
m. / ft.
Depth

Scale 1:6,000,000   Lambert Conformal Conic Projection

MI   50   100   150   200
KM   50   100   150   200   300

© HAMMOND WORLD ATLAS CORPORATION

The Pacific Ocean is the largest body of water on Earth. It covers about 166 million square km, while the world's total land area amounts to only 150 million square km. It is more than twice the size of the Atlantic and Indian oceans and holds roughly 46% of the Earth's water. The ocean is by no means as peaceful as its name suggests. Tropical storms known as typhoons generate waves up to 34 m high. Evidently, Ferdinand Magellan, who gave the ocean its name in 1520, enjoyed calm seas on his voyage across the Pacific.

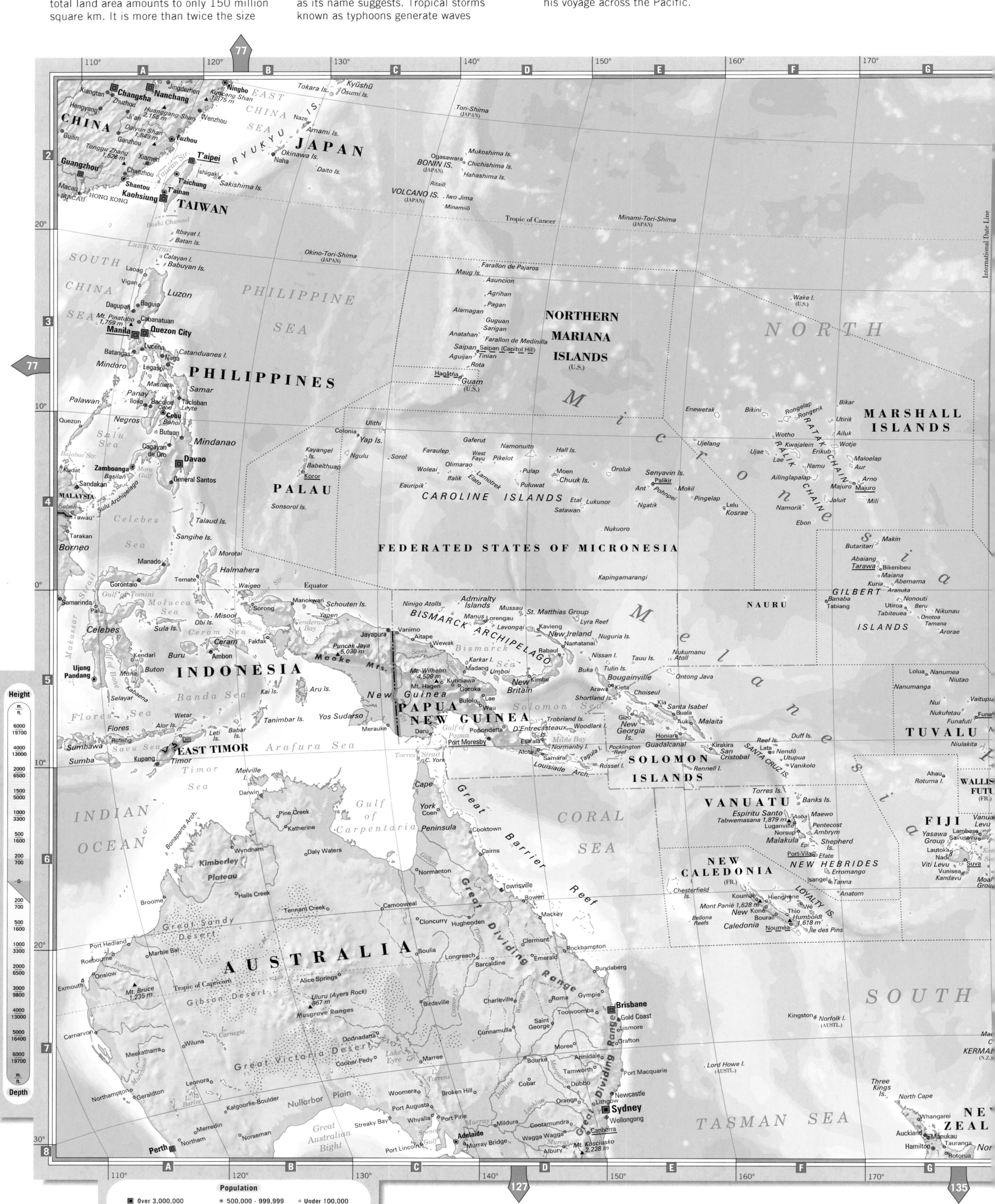

Central Pacific Ocean

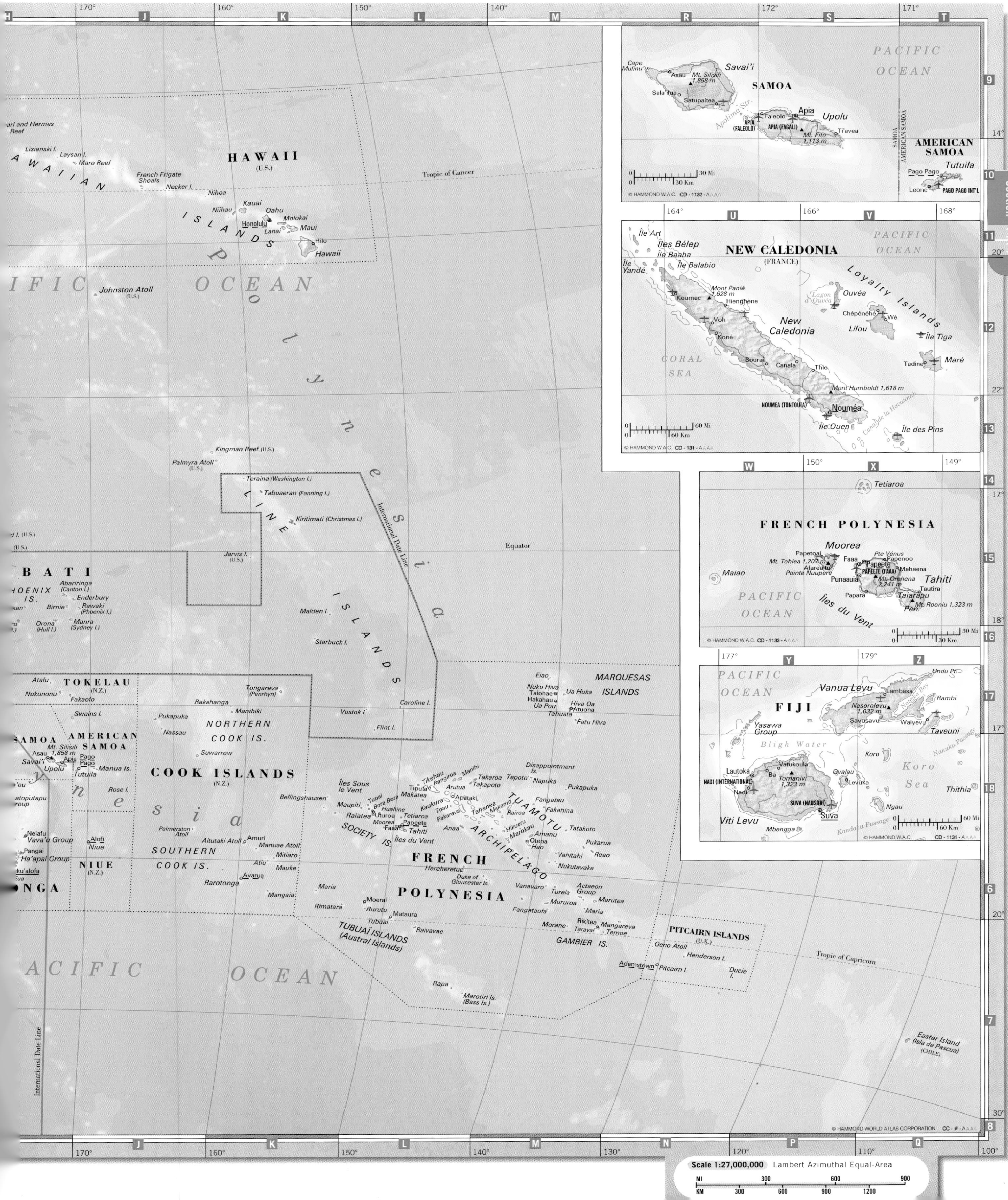

Main Map

H 170° J 160° K 150° L 140° M

HAWAII (U.S.)

Earl and Hermes Reef

Lisianski I.
Laysan I.
Maro Reef
French Frigate Shoals
Necker I.
Nihoa
Niihau Kauai Oahu
Honolulu Molokai
Lanai Maui
Hawaii Hilo

HAWAIIAN ISLANDS

Tropic of Cancer

Johnston Atoll (U.S.)

PACIFIC OCEAN

Polynesia

Kingman Reef (U.S.)
Palmyra Atoll (U.S.)

LINE ISLANDS

Teraina (Washington I.)
Tabuaeran (Fanning I.)
Kiritimati (Christmas I.)

Jarvis I. (U.S.)

International Date Line

Equator

I. (U.S.)

BATI
PHOENIX IS.
Abariringa (Canton I.)
Enderbury
Birnie Rawaki (Phoenix I.)
Orona (Hull I.) Manra (Sydney I.)

Malden I.

Starbuck I.

Vostok I.
Caroline I.
Flint I.

MARQUESAS ISLANDS
Eiao
Nuku Hiva Ua Huka
Taiohae Hiva Oa
Hakahau Atuona
Ua Pou Tahuata
Fatu Hiva

Atafu TOKELAU (N.Z.)
Nukunonu
Fakaofo
Swains I.

Tongareva (Penrhyn)
Rakahanga Manihiki
Pukapuka
Nassau
NORTHERN COOK IS.
Suwarrow

SAMOA AMERICAN SAMOA
Asau Mt. Silisili 1,858 m
Pago Pago
Savai'i Apia Pago
Upolu Tutuila Manua Is.
Rose I.

atoputapu Group

Ha'apai Group

ku'alofa
NGA

Neiafu
Vava'u Group
Alofi Niue
NIUE (N.Z.)

COOK ISLANDS (N.Z.)

Palmerston Atoll
Aitutaki Atoll Amuri Manuae Atoll
Mitiaro
SOUTHERN Atiu
COOK IS. Mauke
Rarotonga

Mangaia

Bellingshausen

Maupiti Tupai Bora Bora
Uturoa Huahine
Raiatea Tetiaroa
Moorea Papeete
Tahiti
Îles Sous le Vent
SOCIETY IS. Îles du Vent

Îles Sous le Vent

Tikehau Rangiroa Manihi
Tiputa Arutua Takaroa Tepoto Napuka
Makatea Takapoto
Kaukura Toau Fangatau
Fakarava Anaa Makemo Fakahina
Raroia
Tahanea
Anaa Marokau Tatakoto
Hikueru
Hao Otepa Pukarua
Hereheretue Vahitahi Reao
Duke of Gloucester Is. Nukutavake

TUAMOTU ARCHIPELAGO

Disappointment Is.

FRENCH POLYNESIA

Maria
Moerai
Rurutu
Rimatara
Mataura
Tubuai
Raivavae
TUBUAI ISLANDS (Austral Islands)

Vanavaro Tureia
Marutea
Mururoa Maria
Fangataufa Rikitea Mangareva
Morane Taravai Temoe
GAMBIER IS.

Actaeon Group

PITCAIRN ISLANDS (U.K.)

Oeno Atoll
Adamstown Henderson I.
Pitcairn I. Ducie I.

Tropic of Capricorn

Rapa
Marotiri Is. (Bass Is.)

ACIFIC OCEAN

Easter Island (Isla de Pascua) (CHILE)

International Date Line

170° J 160° K 150° L 140° M 130° N 120° P 110° Q 100°

Inset: Samoa

R 172° S 171° T

PACIFIC OCEAN

Cape Mulinu'u
Asau Mt. Silisili 1,858 m
Sala'ilua Savai'i SAMOA
Satupaitea
Apolima Str.
Faleolo Apia Upolu
APIA (FALEOLO)
APIA (FAGALI) Mt. Fito 1,113 m Ti'avea

AMERICAN SAMOA
Tutuila
Pago Pago
Leone PAGO PAGO INT'L

0 ——— 30 Mi
0 ——— 30 Km

© HAMMOND W.A.C.   CD - 1132 - A-A-A

Inset: New Caledonia

U 164° 166° V 168°

Île Art
Îles Bélep
Île Baaba
Île Yandé Île Balabio

NEW CALEDONIA (FRANCE)

PACIFIC OCEAN

Mont Panié 1,628 m
Koumac Hienghène
Voh
Koné New Caledonia

Loyalty Islands
Lagon d'Ouvéa Ouvéa
Chépénéhé Wé
Lifou Île Tiga
Tadine Maré

CORAL SEA

Bourail Canala Thio
Mont Humboldt 1,618 m

NOUMEA (TONTOUTA) Nouméa

Canal de la Havannah

Île Ouen Île des Pins

0 ——— 60 Mi
0 ——— 60 Km

© HAMMOND W.A.C.   CD - 131 - A-A-A

Inset: French Polynesia

W 150° X 149°

Tetiaroa

FRENCH POLYNESIA

Moorea
Papetoai Pte Vénus
Faaa Papenoo
Mt. Tohiea 1,207 m Papeete
Afareaitu PAPEETE (FAA'A) Mahaena
Pointe Nuupere Mt. Orohena 2,241 m Tahiti
Maiao Punaauia Tautira
Papara Taiarapu
Pen. Mt. Roouiu 1,323 m

PACIFIC OCEAN

Îles du Vent

0 ——— 30 Mi
0 ——— 30 Km

© HAMMOND W.A.C.   CD - 1133 - A-A-A

Inset: Fiji

Y 177° 179° Z

PACIFIC OCEAN

Undu Pt.
Vanua Levu Lambasa
Nasorolevu 1,032 m Rambi
Yasawa Group Savusavu Savusavu Bay
Waiyevu
Bligh Water Taveuni
Vatukoula
Lautoka Ba Tomanivi 1,323 m Ovalau Koro
NADI (INTERNATIONAL) Levuka
Nadi Koro Sea
Viti Levu
SUVA (NAUSORI) Ngau
Suva Thithia
Mbengga
Nanuku Passage
Kandavu Passage

0 ——— 60 Mi
0 ——— 60 Km

© HAMMOND W.A.C.   CD - 1131 - A-A-A

© HAMMOND WORLD ATLAS CORPORATION   CC - # - A-A-A

Scale 1:27,000,000 Lambert Azimuthal Equal-Area

MI   300   600   900
KM   300   600   900   1200

with a depth of 1.6 km, the Grand Canyon is one of the deepest river [gorg]es in the world. This image taken [tow]ard the west shows the Colorado River, [whi]ch has cut through rock billions of years

old to form the canyon. The Grand Canyon is 260 km long and averages about 16 km in width at the top but narrows to as few as 15 m in places along the valley floor. The river flows over 150 rapids on its course

through the canyon. The valley itself is only a few million years old. Visible in the image are the snow-covered Kaibab Plateau north of the canyon and the Coconino Plateau to the south.

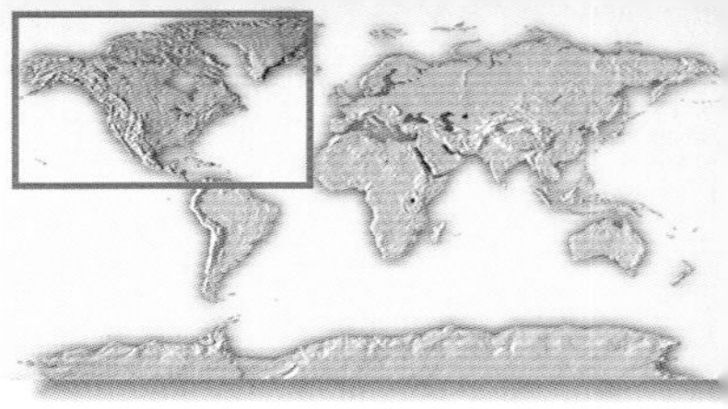

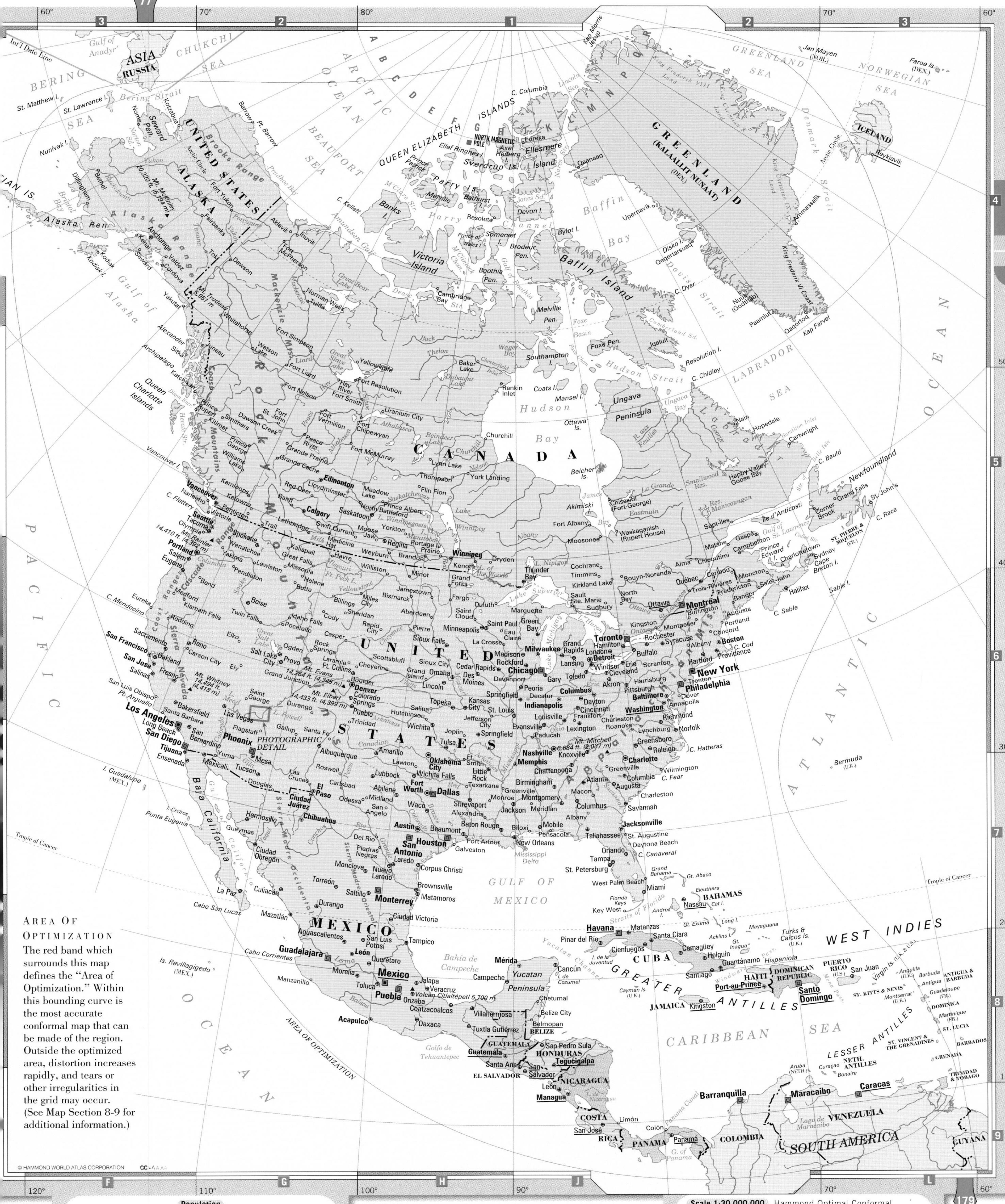

AREA OF
OPTIMIZATION
The red band which surrounds this map defines the "Area of Optimization." Within this bounding curve is the most accurate conformal map that can be made of the region. Outside the optimized area, distortion increases rapidly, and tears or other irregularities in the grid may occur. (See Map Section 8-9 for additional information.)

© HAMMOND WORLD ATLAS CORPORATION   CC · A · A · A

Population

■ Over 3,000,000	● 500,000 - 999,999	○ Under 100,000
■ 1,000,000 - 2,999,999	● 100,000 - 499,999	

Scale 1:30,000,000   Hammond Optimal Conformal

MI   250   500   750   1000
KM   250   500   750   1000   1250   1500

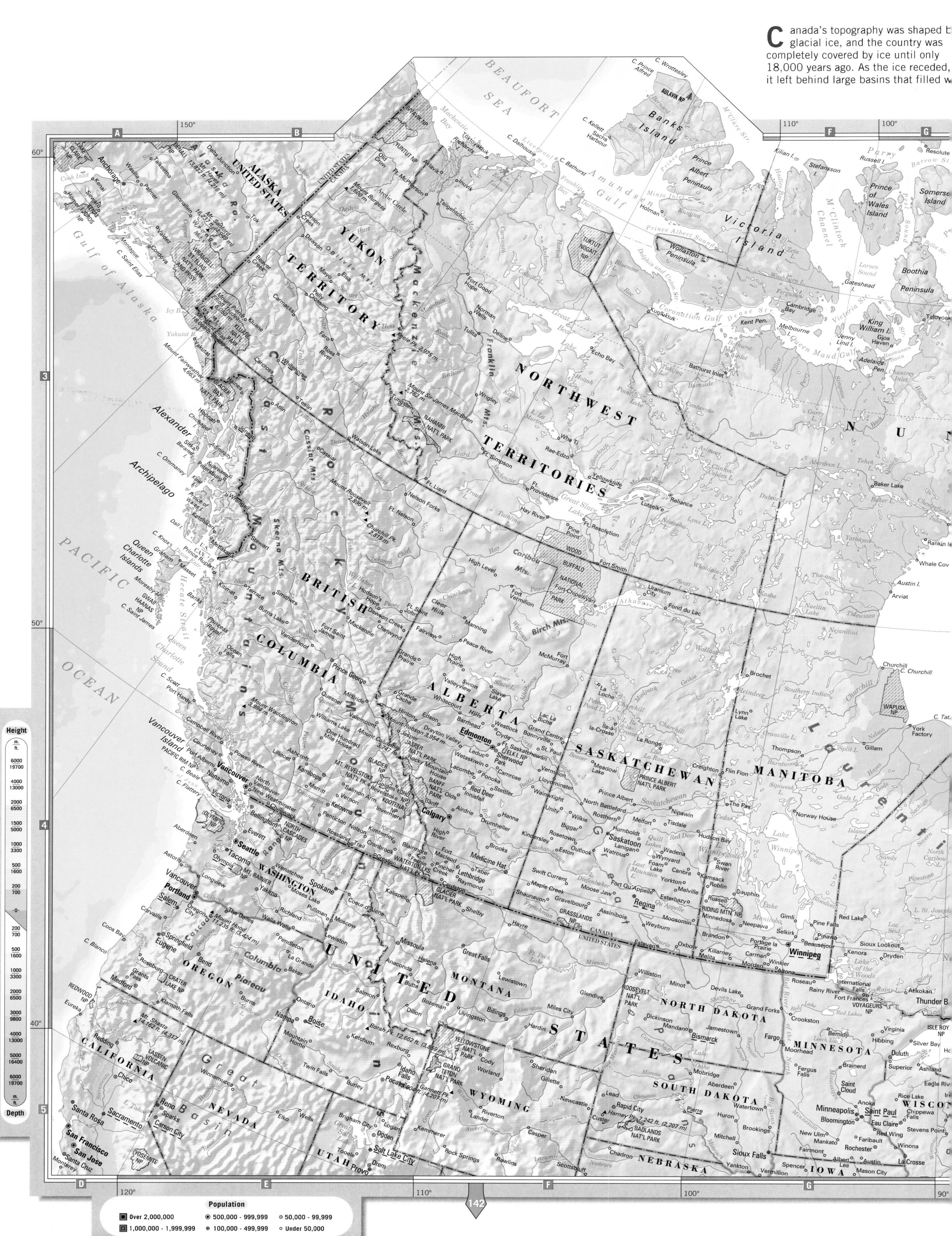

Population

Over 2,000,000   500,000 - 999,999   50,000 - 99,999
1,000,000 - 1,999,999   100,000 - 499,999   Under 50,000

Canada's topography was shaped b
glacial ice, and the country was
completely covered by ice until only
18,000 years ago. As the ice receded,
it left behind large basins that filled w
142

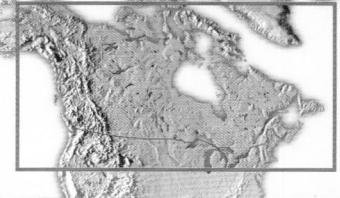

water. Today, Canada has more than [ ] million lakes. The country is larger [than] the United States but very thinly [popu]lated, as widespread settlement has [been] discouraged by the extremely short growing season north of the 55th parallel, the extremely poor, thin soils north of the St. Lawrence Valley, and low levels of precipitation in the northwestern coniferous forest and tundra region.

Scale 1:12,000,000 Lambert Conformal Conic Projection

The Rocky Mountains, the Mississippi River system, which flows along a course of more than 6,400 km from the north to the Gulf of Mexico, and the Great Lakes along the border to Canada are the most striking major landscape features of the United States. The geologically young Rocky Mountains extend nearly 4,800 km from Alaska through Canada and into New Mexico. The five Great Lakes form the largest contiguous area of fresh water in the world, covering some 245,000 square km. Lake Ontario and Lake Erie are joined by the spectacular Niagara Falls.

Population

■ Over 2,000,000 ● 500,000 - 999,999 ● 50,000 - 99,999
■ 1,000,000 - 1,999,999 ● 100,000 - 499,999 ○ Under 50,000

United States

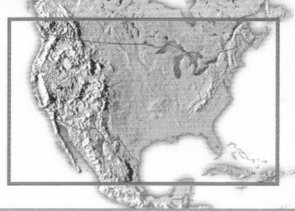

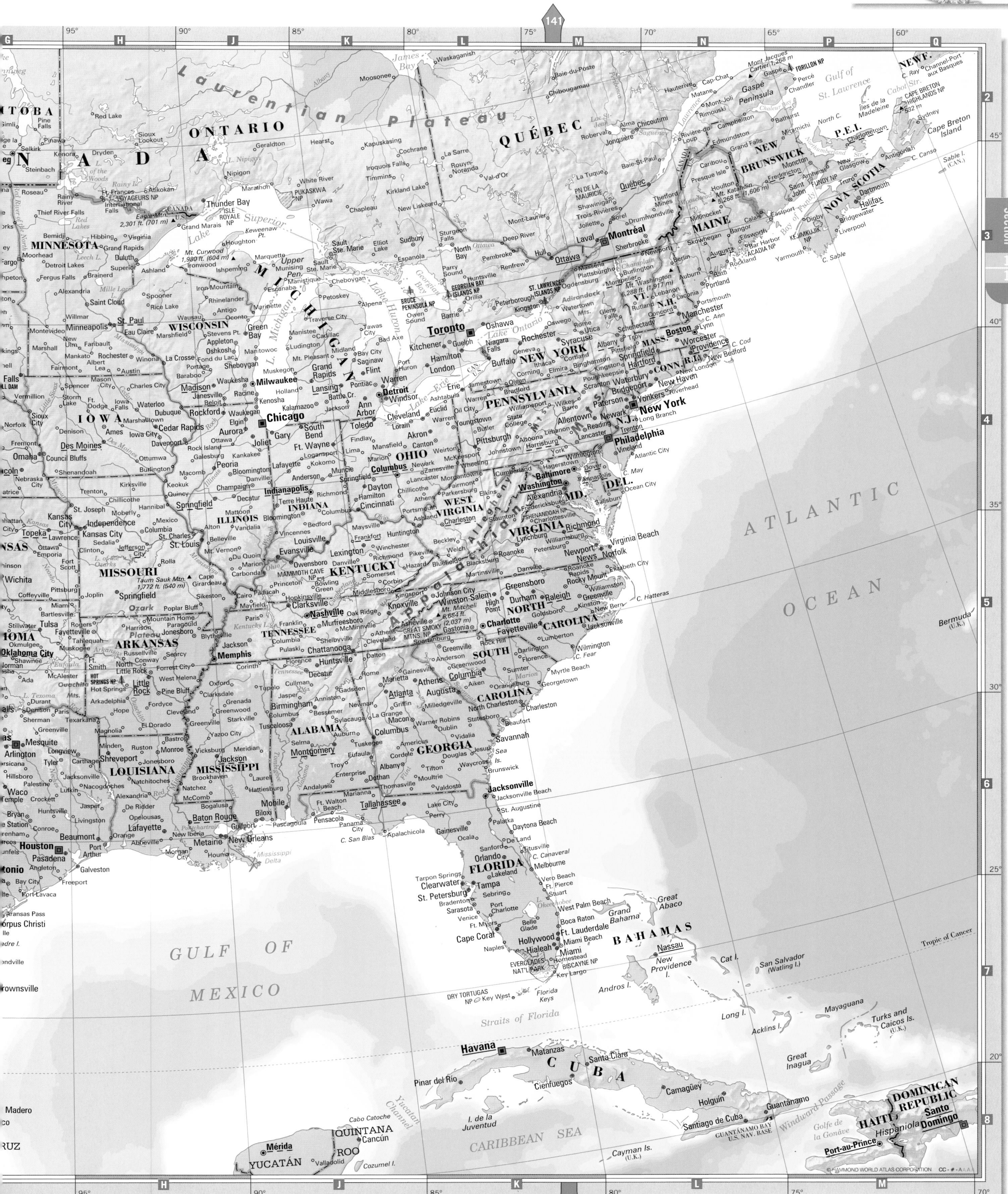

Scale 1:12,000,000 Lambert Conformal Conic Projection

MI 100 200 300 400

KM 100 200 300 400 500 600

Map Section 142 143

The glacier-covered Rocky Mountains, with peaks over 4,000 m high, and the volcanic Cascade Range are both products of a collision between the Pacific and North American plates. Over the course of the past several billion years, microplates have been pulverized, folded, hrust upward, or pressed deep into the earth along the line of convergence. Several thousand kilometers of the oceanic plate have disappeared beneath the North American continent. This rock melts and returns to the surface as lava through volcanoes like Mount Saint Helens and Mount Rainier.

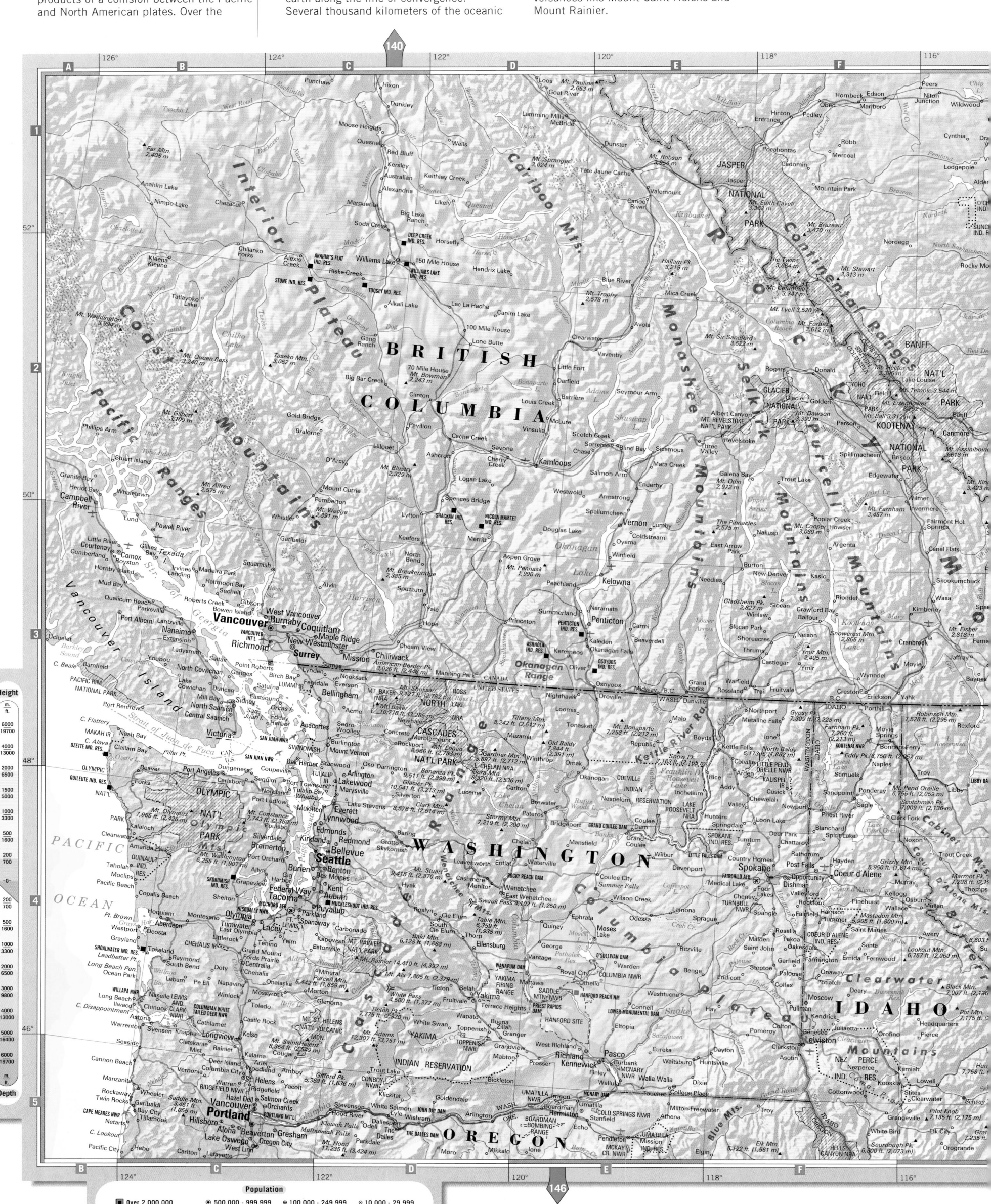

Population

◼ Over 2,000,000
◼ 1,000,000 - 1,999,999
● 500,000 - 999,999
● 250,000 - 499,999
● 100,000 - 249,999
● 30,000 - 99,999
● 10,000 - 29,999
○ Under 10,000

140

114° 112° 110° 108° 106° 104°

H J K L M N

Edmonton

ALBERTA

SASKATCHEWAN

Saskatoon

Prince Albert

Regina

Moose Jaw

Red Deer

Medicine Hat

Lethbridge

Cypress Hills

Great Sand Hills

Couteau Hills

Lake Diefenbaker

Missouri Coteau

GRASSLANDS NATIONAL PARK

CANADA
UNITED STATES

MONTANA

GLACIER NATIONAL PARK

WATERTON GLACIER INT'L PEACE PARK

BLACKFOOT INDIAN RES.

FT. BELKNAP INDIAN RESERVATION

FT. PECK INDIAN RESERVATION

ROCKY BOYS IND. RES.

Bearpaw Mts.

Great Falls

Helena

Butte

Missoula

Billings

G R E A T   P L A I N S

The Pine Hills

Ft. Peck Lake

CHARLES M. RUSSELL NAT'L WILD. REF.

UPPER MISSOURI RIVER BREAKS NM

Judith Mts.

Little Belt Mts.

Big Belt Mts.

CROW IND. RES.

NORTHERN CHEYENNE IND. RES.

LITTLE BIGHORN BATTLEFIELD NM

Mt. Haggin 10,664 ft. (3,250 m)

Warren Pk. 10,463 ft. (3,189 m)

Mt. Brown 6,958 ft. (2,121 m)

Baldy Mtn. 6,916 ft. (2,108 m)

Big Baldy Mtn. 9,175 ft. (2,797 m)

Highwood Baldy 7,625 ft. (2,324 m)

Granite Mtn. 7,608 ft. (2,319 m)

52°

50°

48°

46°

1

2

3

4

5

147

© HAMMOND WORLD ATLAS CORPORATION

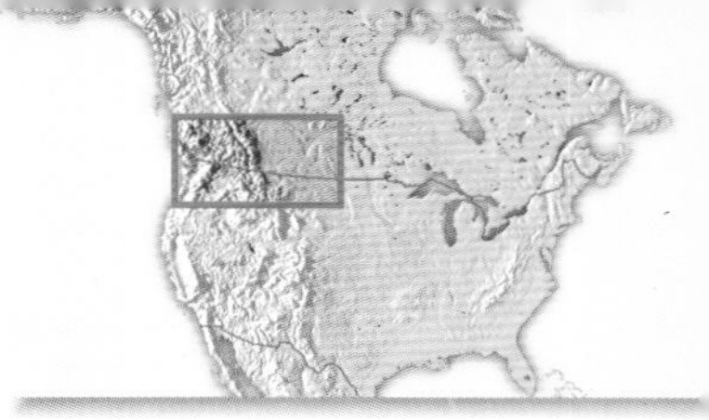

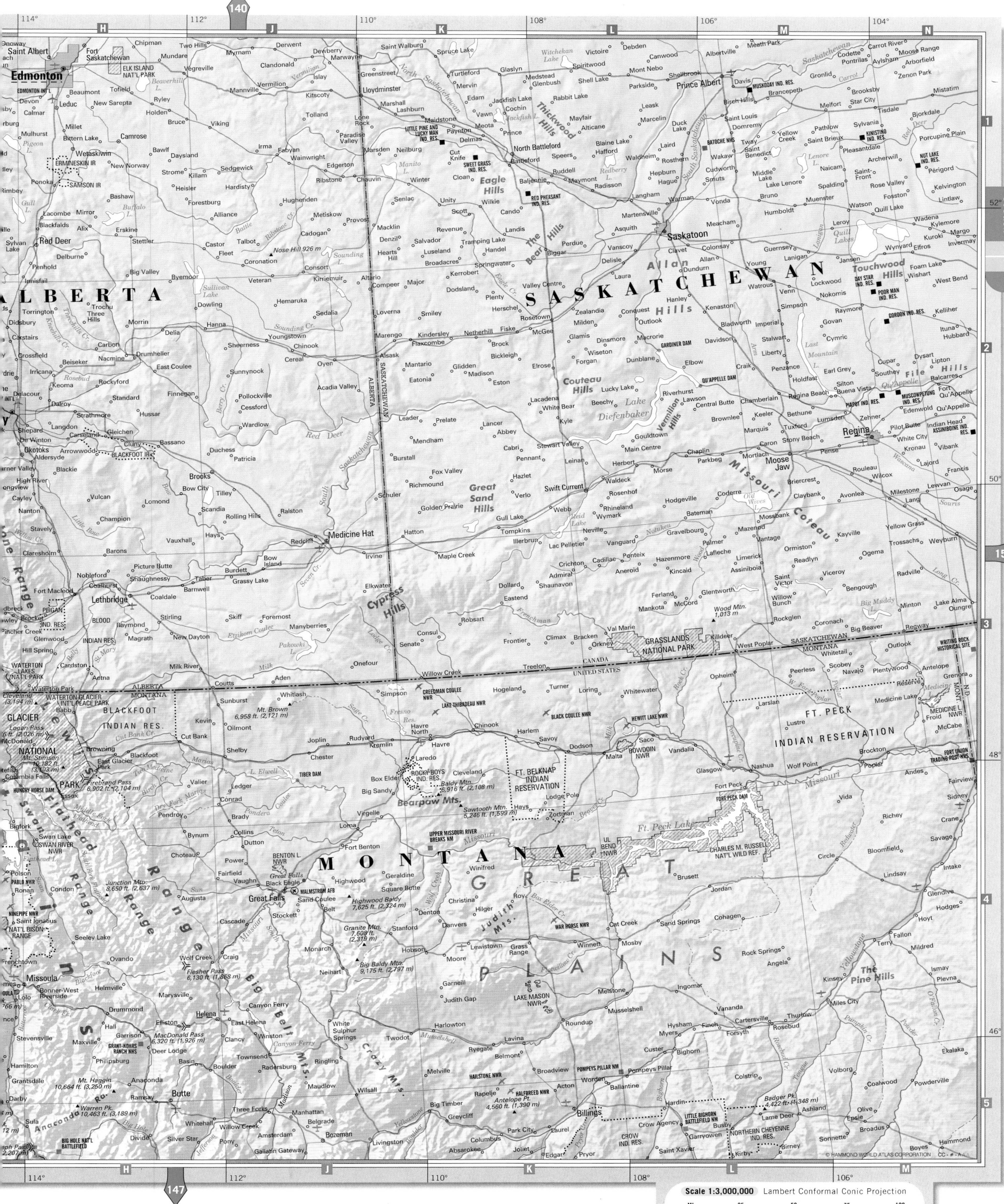

Scale 1:3,000,000   Lambert Conformal Conic Projection

MI   0   25   50   75   100

KM   0   25   50   75   100   125   150

Arid areas of North America, like the Great Basin and the nearby salt lakes, are most prevalent in the central western states, where high mountain chains hold back moisture-bearing winds.

Thus annual precipitation west of the Sierra Nevada can be as high as 1,300 m, while Reno on the rim of the Great Basin receives only about 150 m of precipitation a year. The Great Salt Lake is a remnant of

Lake Bonneville, an ice-age lake with depths of up to 330 m and a surface area of over 50,000 square km. Depending upon drainage, today the Great Salt Lake covers some 5,000 square km with a mean depth of three meters.

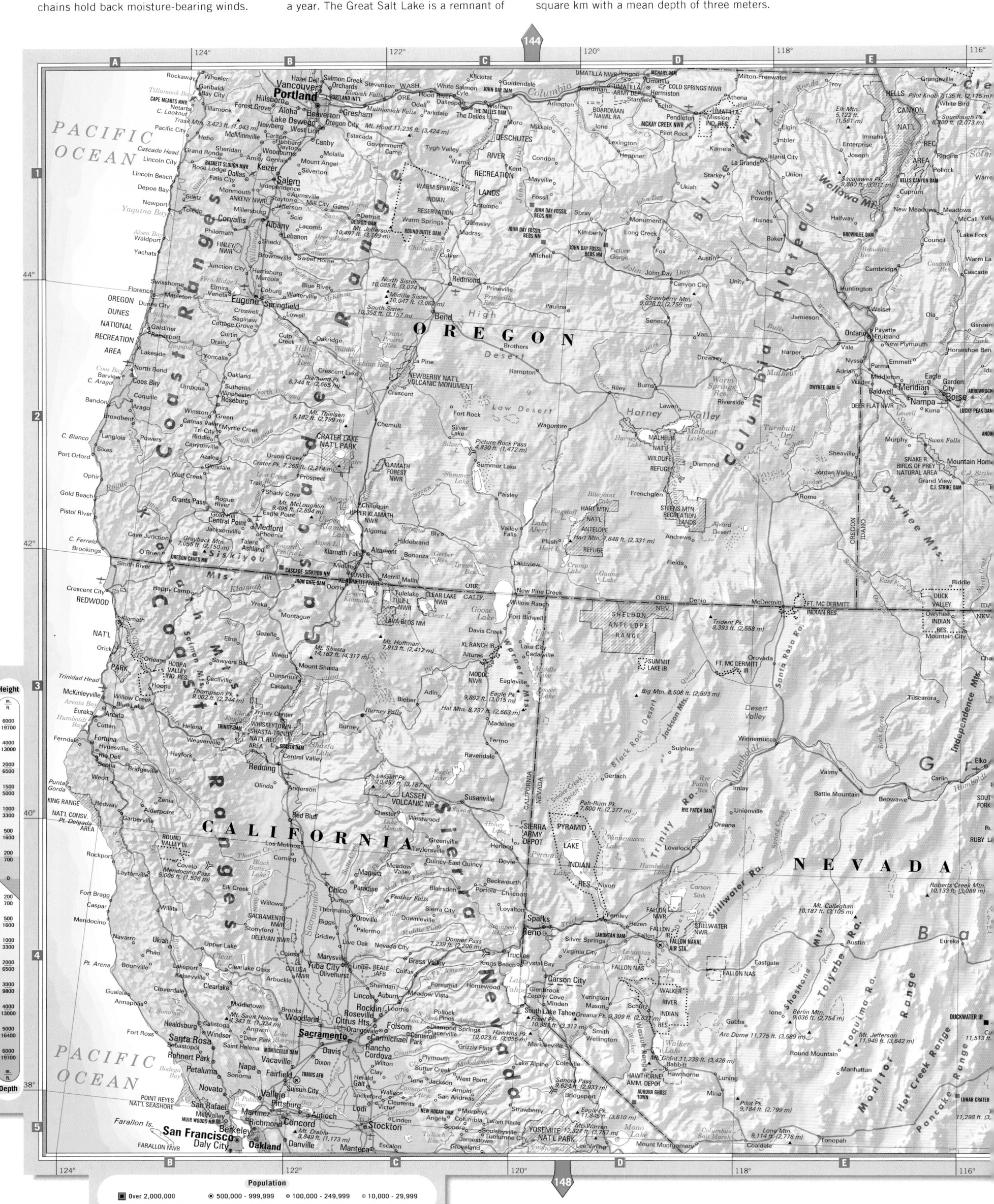

Population
■ Over 2,000,000   ● 500,000 - 999,999   ● 100,000 - 249,999   ○ 10,000 - 29,999
□ 1,000,000 - 1,999,999   ● 250,000 - 499,999   ○ 30,000 - 99,999   ∘ Under 10,000

Central Pacific and Western U.S.

Scale 1:3,000,000   Lambert Conformal Conic Projection

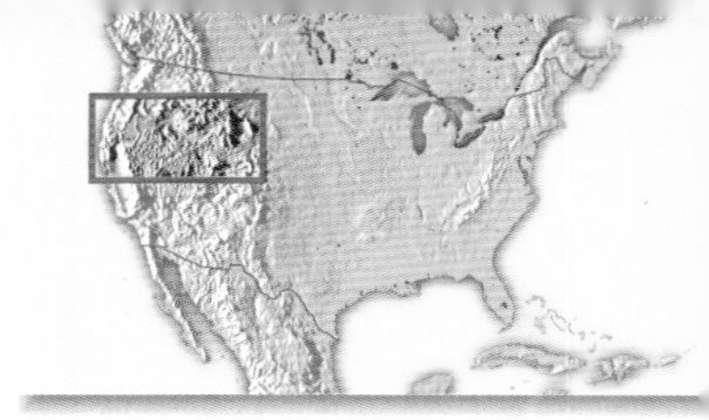

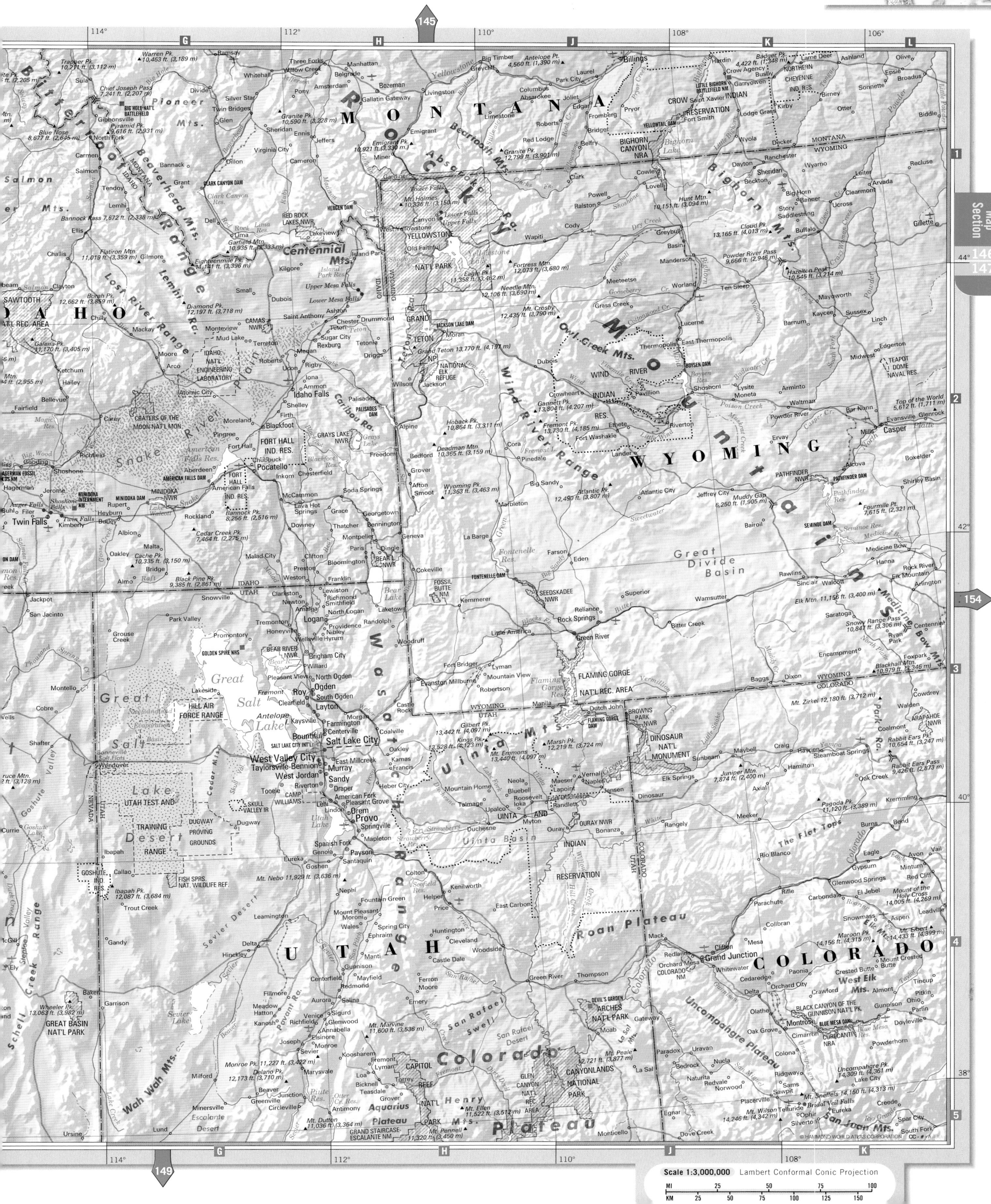

The world's most famous geologic fault runs straight through the state of California. The U.S. southwest is part of the Pacific Plate, which is drifting north-westward along the fault line at a rate of 5.6 cm per year. The San Andreas Fault is actually a bundle of parallel faults that extends north from the Gulf of Mexico to a point about 350 km north of San Francisco. The landscape bears the imprint of this plate movement: A number of valleys are sealed off; rainwater accumulates in the fracture zones and gives rise to characteristic bands of vegetation.

Height	
m. ft.	
6000 19700	
4000 13000	
2000 6500	
1500 5000	
1000 3300	
500 1600	
200 700	
-0-	
200 700	
500 1600	
1000 3300	
2000 6500	
3000 9800	
4000 13000	
5000 16400	
6000 19700	
m. ft.	
Depth	

Population
- ■ Over 2,000,000
- ■ 1,000,000 - 1,999,999
- ◉ 500,000 - 999,999
- ◉ 250,000 - 499,999
- ◉ 100,000 - 249,999
- ○ 30,000 - 99,999
- ◦ 10,000 - 29,999
- · Under 10,000

UTAH
COLORADO
ARIZONA
NEW MEXICO
SONORA
CHIHUAHUA

Phoenix
Tucson
Albuquerque
El Paso
Ciudad Juárez
Las Cruces
Flagstaff
Prescott
Santa Fe
Rio Rancho
Mesa
Tempe
Scottsdale
Glendale
Peoria
Sun City
Chandler
Gilbert

Grand Canyon National Park
Painted Desert
Kaibab Plateau
Kaibab Indian Reservation
Navajo Indian Reservation
Hopi Indian Reservation
San Carlos Indian Reservation
Fort Apache Indian Reservation
Papago Indian Reservation
Zion National Park
Bryce Canyon National Park
Canyonlands National Park
Capitol Reef National Park
Glen Canyon National Recreation Area
Monument Valley Navajo Tribal Park
Canyon de Chelly Nat'l Mon.
Petrified Forest National Park
Saguaro NP
Chaco Culture Nat'l Hist. Park
Mesa Verde NP
Aztec Ruins Nat'l Mon.
White Sands Missile Range
White Sands Nat'l Mon.
Barry M. Goldwater Air Force Range
Cabeza Prieta National Wildlife Refuge
Organ Pipe Cactus Nat'l Mon.
Gila Cliff Dwellings NM

Mogollon Plateau
Colorado Plateau
Aquarius Plateau
Kaibito Plateau
Coconino Plateau
Mazatzal Mts.
San Francisco Mts.
Sangre de Cristo Mts.
Rocky Mountains

Humphreys Pk. 12,633 ft. (3,851 m)
Mt. Taylor 11,301 ft. (3,445 m)
Mt. Graham 10,713 ft. (3,265 m)
Baldy Pk. 11,590 ft. (3,593 m)
Greens Pk. 10,210 ft. (3,112 m)
Uncompahgre Peak 14,309 ft. (4,361 m)
Mt. Wilson 14,246 ft. (4,342 m)

Four Corners Monument

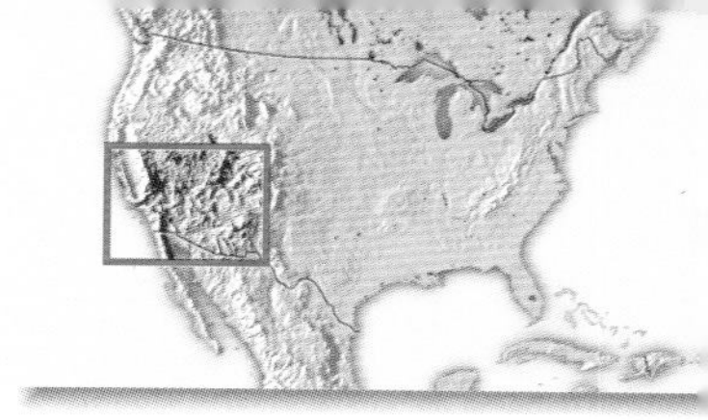

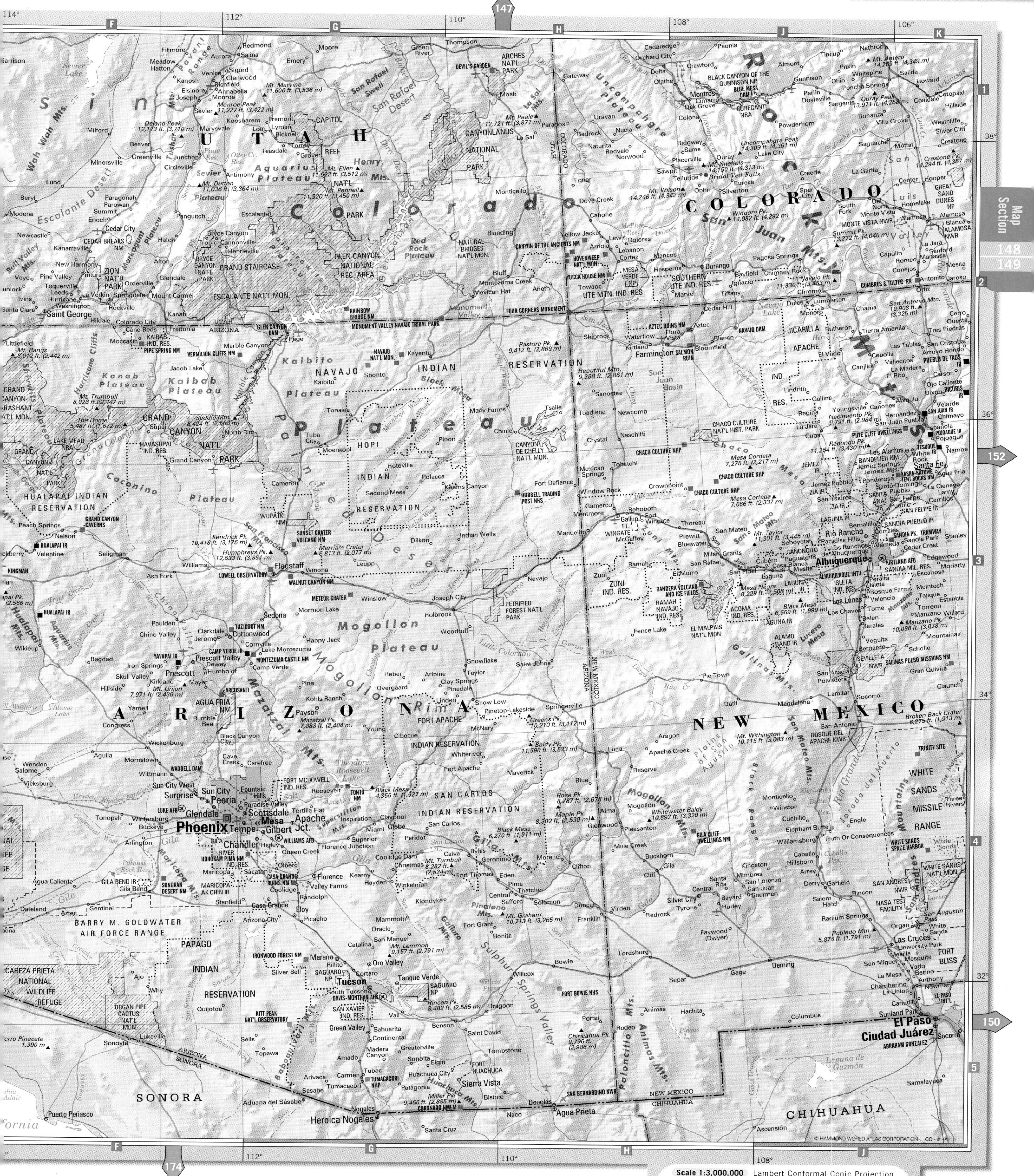

Scale 1:3,000,000 — Lambert Conformal Conic Projection

© Hammond World Atlas Corporation

The sensational discovery of the Spindle-top Oil Field in 1901 made Texas the principal source of energy in the United States. The Mississippi, the Rio Grande, and other rivers that drain the continental interior have dumped vast quantities of sediment into a deep trough in the coastal plain and the Gulf of Mexico (with depths of up to 15 km). The rich deposits of oil and natural gas located there are the product of great deposits of ancient organic material and the sealing effect of the layers of sediment, which inhibited the natural process of decomposition.

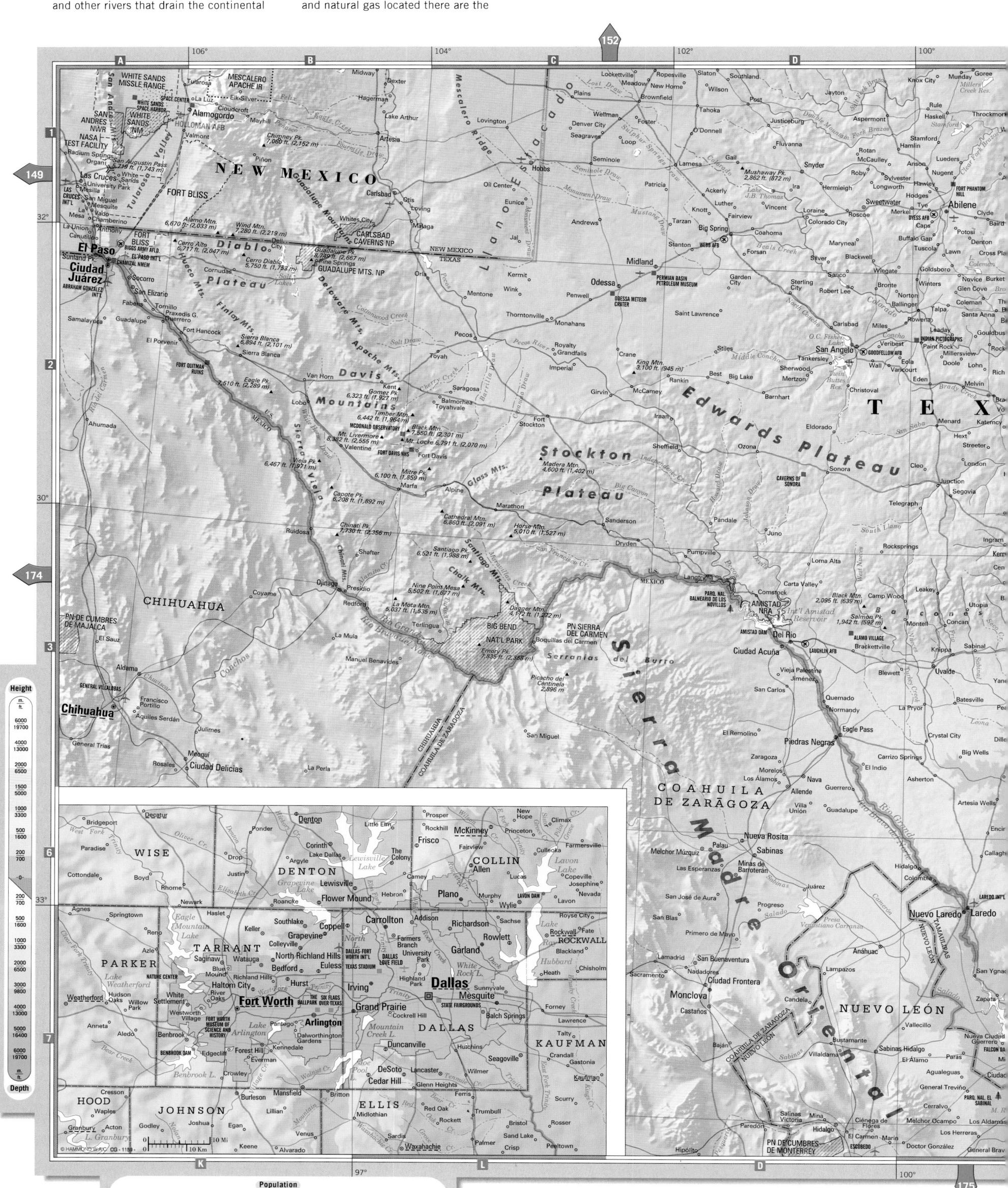

149

174

175

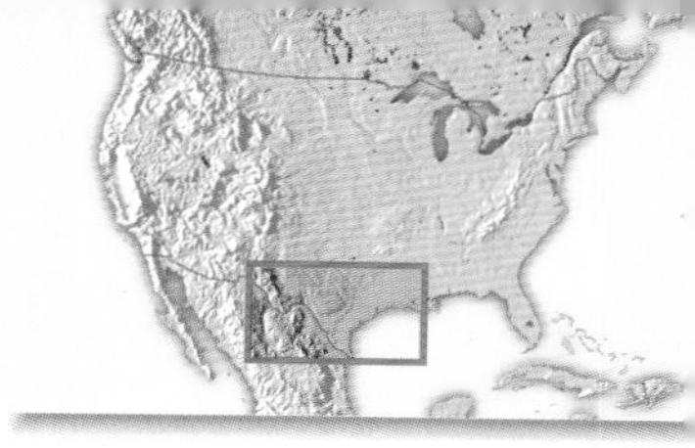

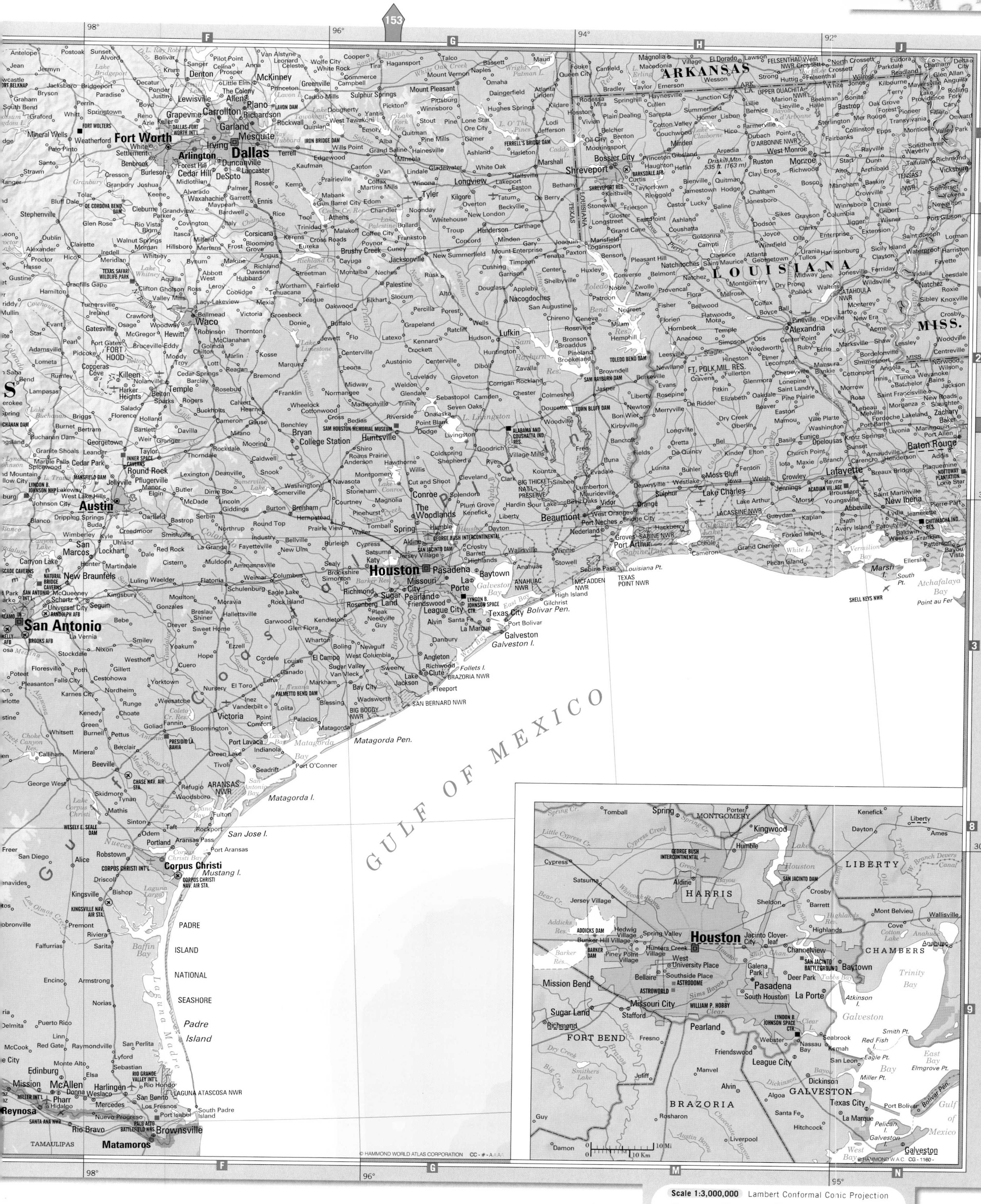

Scale 1:3,000,000   Lambert Conformal Conic Projection

Scarcity of water is the dominant charac- teristic of the Great Plains. So much water has been drawn from the Ogallala aquifer beneath the plateaus of Texas and New Mexico during the past few centuries that it would take several thousand years to restore the groundwater to its original level. Geologists estimate that available reserves will be exhausted within a few years. Without this essential water supply, some five million acres of irrigated land - on which 12 percent of all the cotton, corn, wheat and millet produced in the U.S. are grown - would no longer be arable.

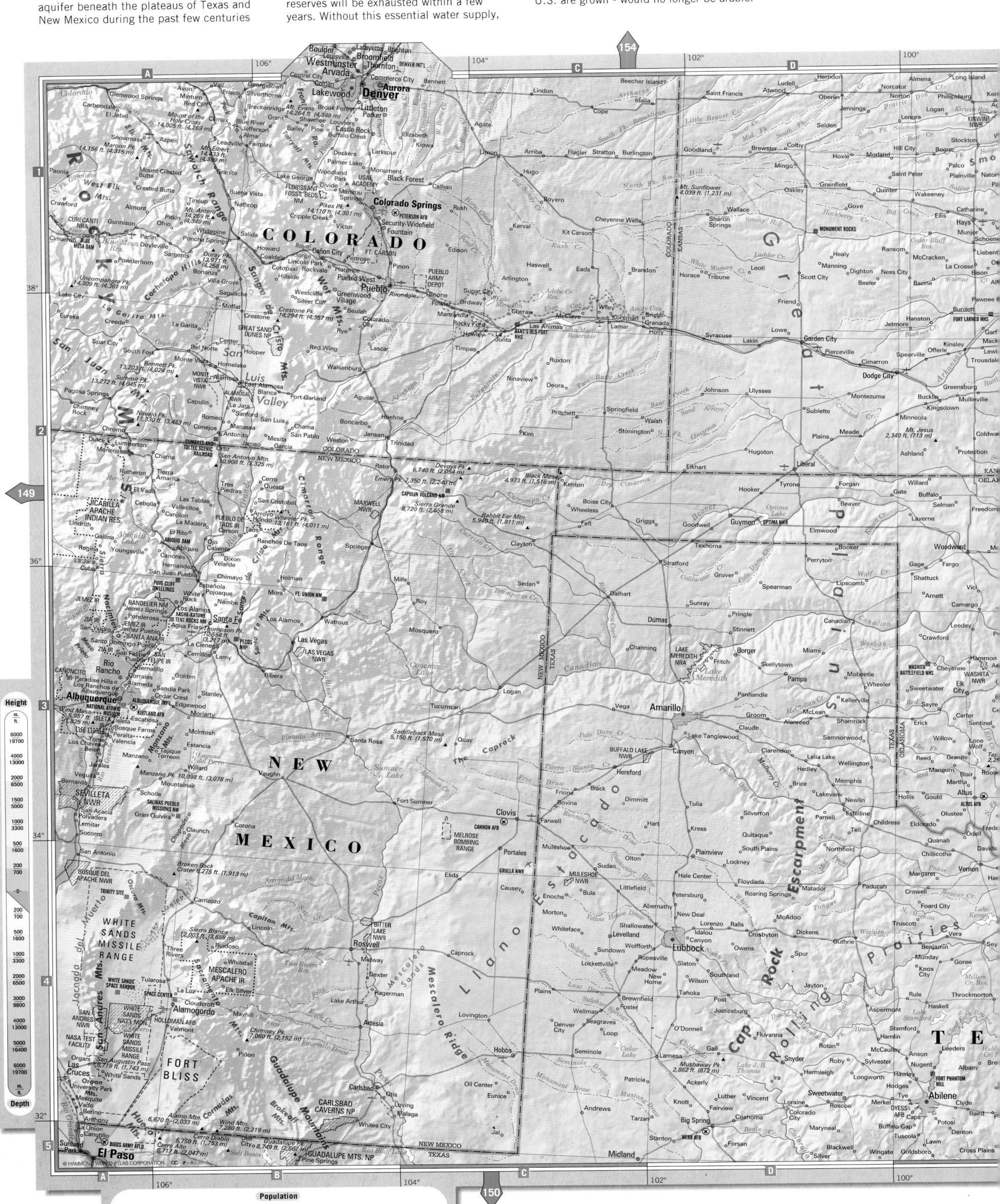

Population

■ Over 2,000,000	● 500,000 - 999,999

155

MISSOURI

ILLINOIS

OKLAHOMA

ARKANSAS

LOUISIANA

TEXAS

KANSAS

Saint Joseph · Kansas City · Independence · Overland Park · Olathe · Topeka · Lawrence · Manhattan · Junction City · Salina

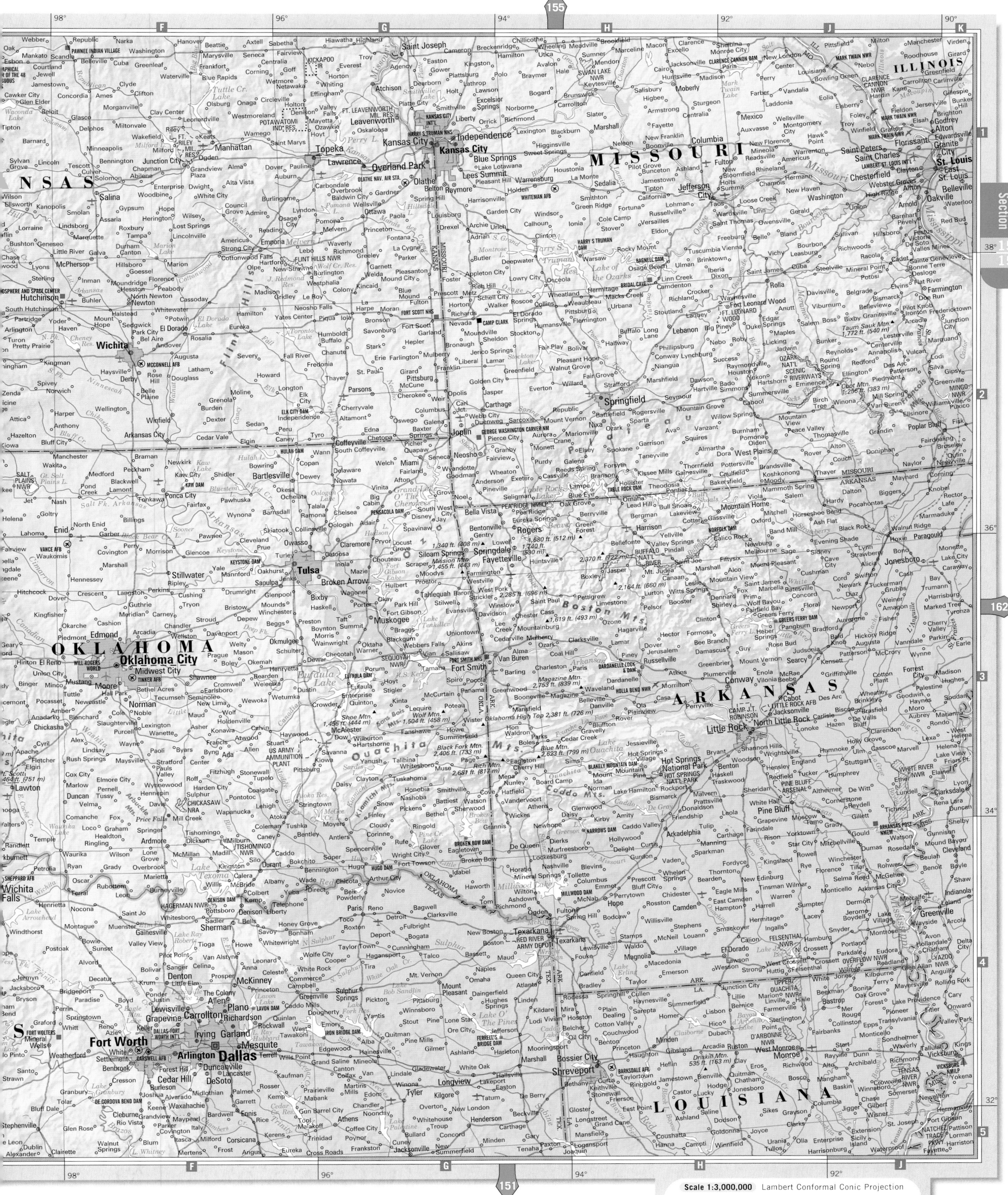

Wichita · Hutchinson · Enid · Stillwater · Tulsa · Broken Arrow · Muskogee · Oklahoma City · Midwest City · Norman · Shawnee · Ada · Lawton

Springfield · Joplin · Rogers · Springdale · Fayetteville · Fort Smith · Little Rock · North Little Rock · Hot Springs · Pine Bluff · Conway

Saint Louis · East St. Louis · Belleville · Jefferson City · Columbia · Sedalia

Fort Worth · Arlington · Dallas · Irving · Garland · Mesquite · Plano · Richardson · Carrollton · Lewisville · Denton · McKinney · Sherman · Denison · Paris · Texarkana · Shreveport · Bossier City · Longview · Tyler · Monroe

Wichita Falls

Scale 1:3,000,000   Lambert Conformal Conic Projection

MI 0 25 50 75 100

KM 0 25 50 75 100 125 150

Map Section 152 153

162

151

The Great Plains comprise one of the largest agricultural regions on Earth. Often plagued throughout their history by catastrophic droughts and erosion, the dry grassland states of the "Dust Bowl" were hardest hit in 1935, the year in which 908 hours of dust storms - the infamous "Black Blizzards" - ravaged the region, carrying away much of the exposed topsoil and depositing it as far away as the Atlantic Ocean. Overcultivation and poor land management were to blame for this disaster, which took a heavy toll in soil and arable land.

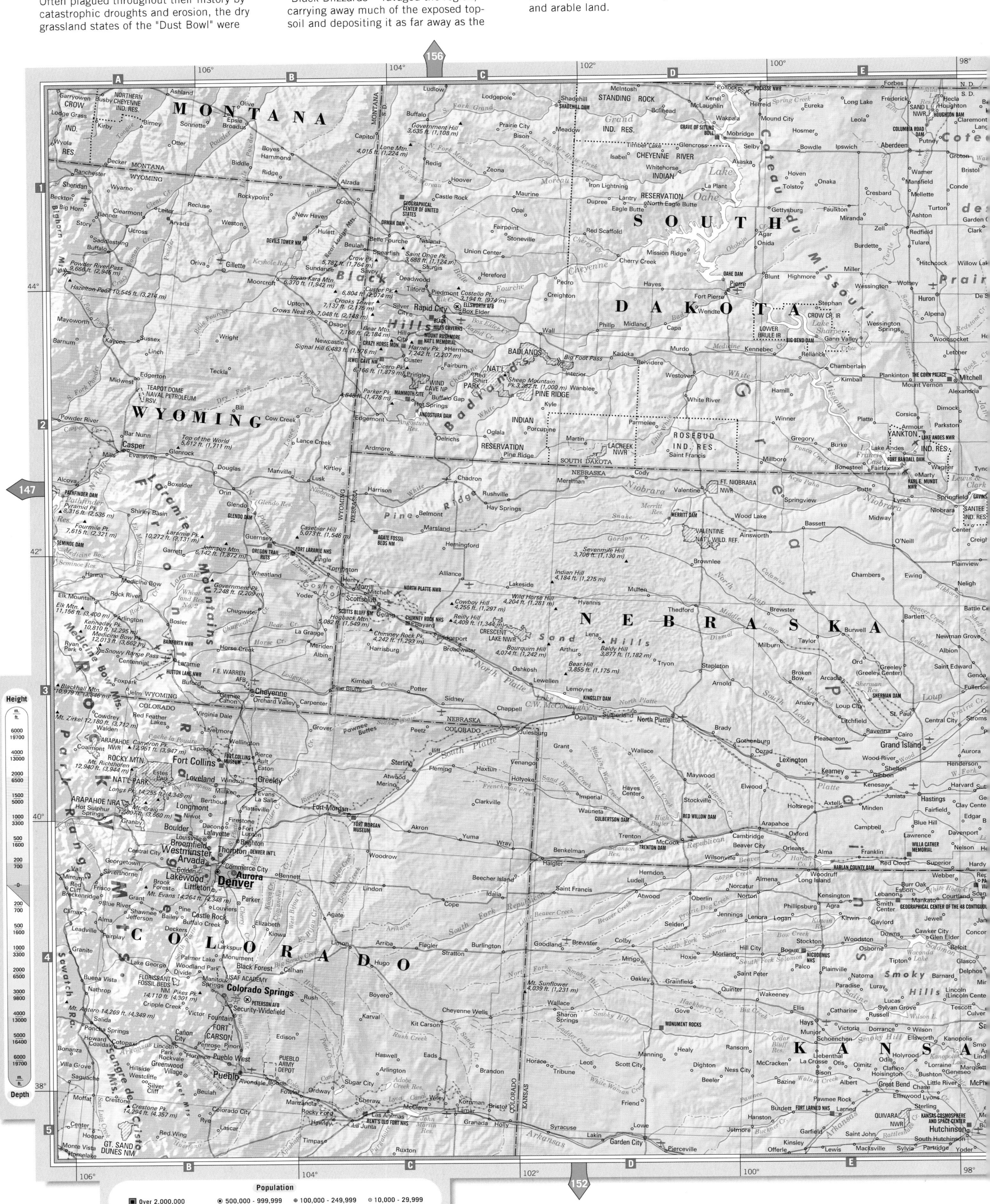

WISCONSIN

MINNESOTA

IOWA

ILLINOIS

MISSOURI

Minneapolis
Saint Paul
Milwaukee
Chicago
Madison
Rockford
Springfield
Des Moines
West Des Moines
Omaha
Council Bluffs
Lincoln
Sioux City
Cedar Rapids
Davenport
Rock Island
Moline
Peoria
Saint Louis
East St. Louis
Kansas City
Overland Park
Topeka
Lawrence
Independence
Saint Joseph
Leavenworth
La Crosse
Eau Claire
Green Bay
Appleton
Oshkosh
Rochester
Mankato
Waterloo

© HAMMOND WORLD ATLAS CORPORATION

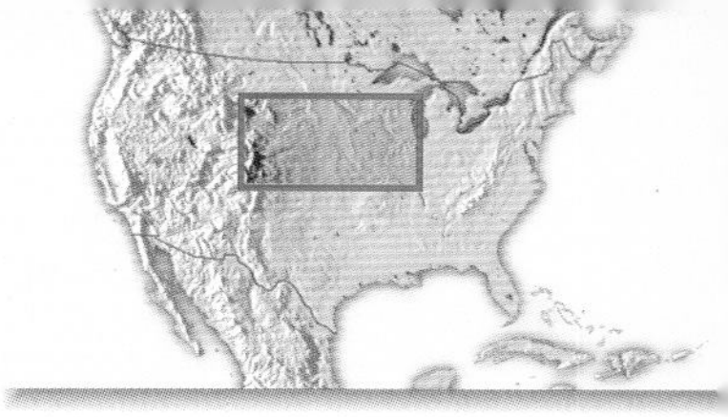

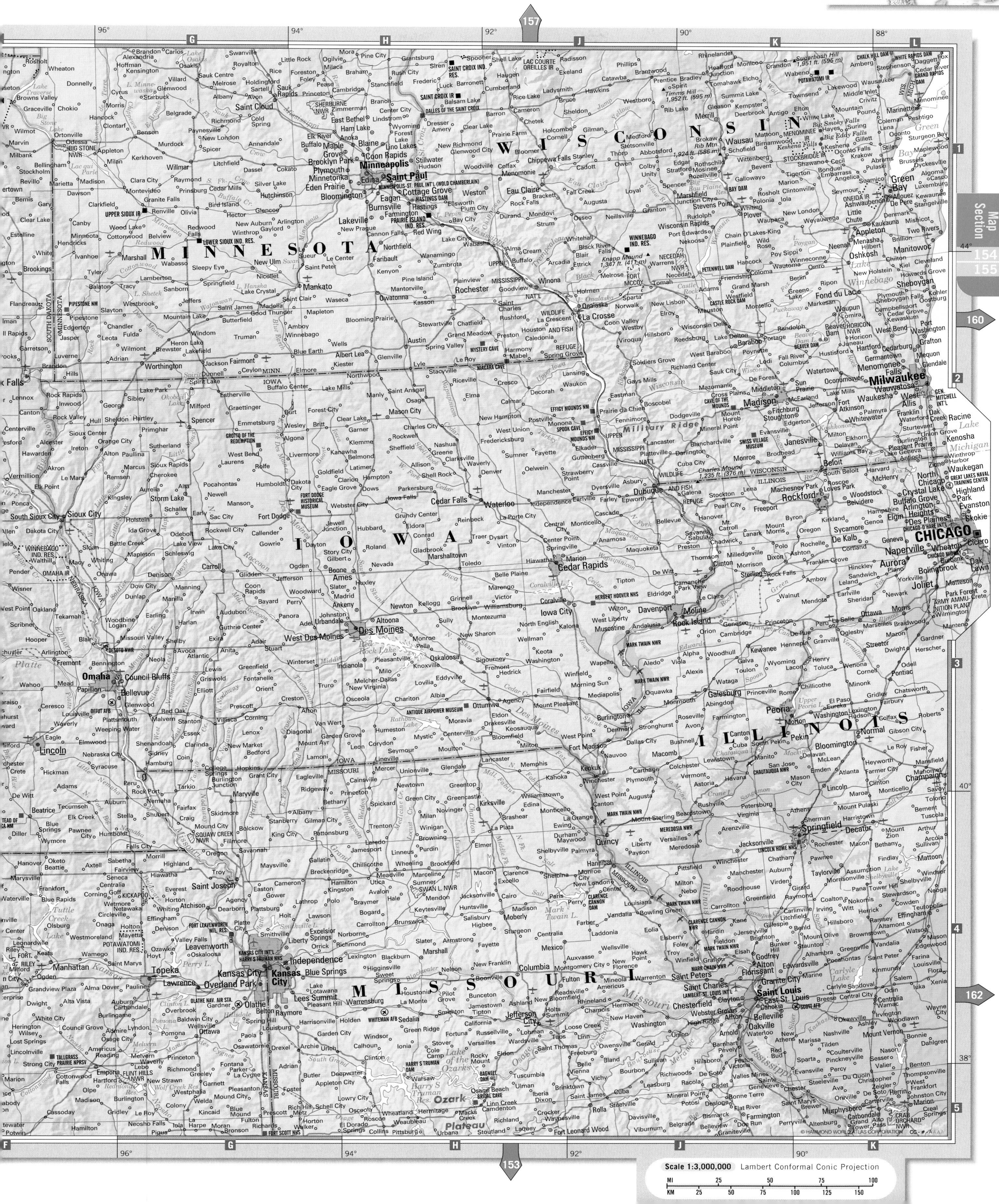

The drainage basins of the Hudson Bay, the Atlantic, and the Gulf of Mexico, to which the Mississippi flows, converge in Minnesota. The state's predominantly flat, rolling moraine topography and its continental climate are ideal for sheep and cattle grazing. The northern half of the state and much of the east are now densely forested again, the eastern region in particular having recovered from almost total deforestation in the early years of the 20th century. The fertile prairies of Manitoba and Saskatchewan to the north also offer prime land for wheat farming and cattle grazing.

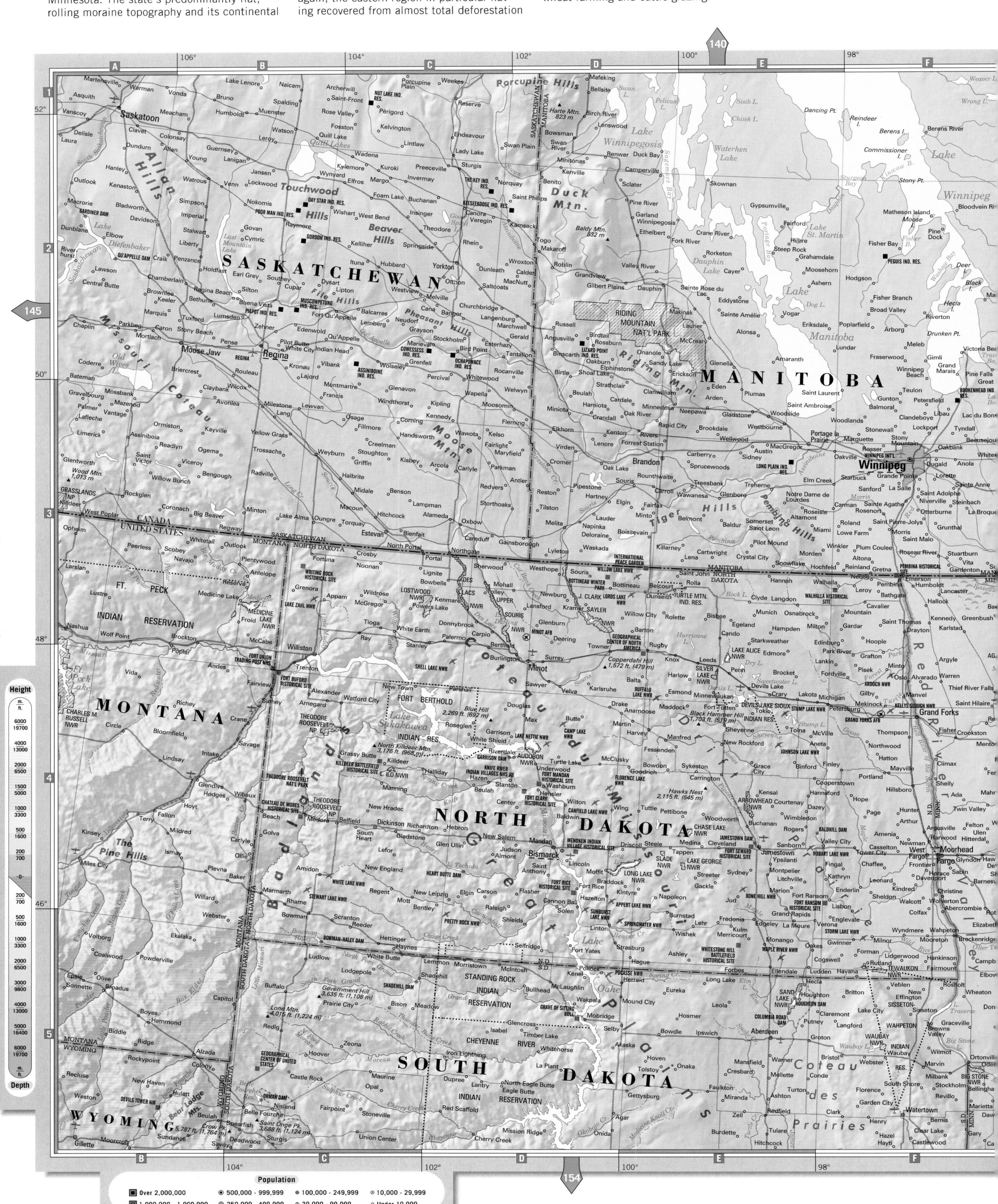

Height

m. ft.	
6000 19700	
4000 13000	
2000 6500	
1500 5000	
1000 3300	
500 1600	
200 700	
-0-	
200 700	
500 1600	
1000 3300	
2000 6500	
3000 9800	
4000 13000	
5000 16400	
6000 19700	
m. ft.	

Depth

Population
- ■ Over 2,000,000
- ■ 1,000,000 - 1,999,999
- ⊛ 500,000 - 999,999
- ⊛ 250,000 - 499,999
- ⊛ 100,000 - 249,999
- ◉ 30,000 - 99,999
- ◉ 10,000 - 29,999
- ○ Under 10,000

South Central Canada, North Central U.S.

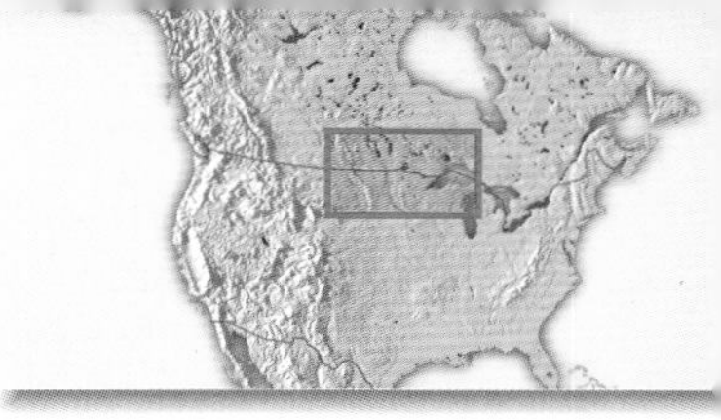

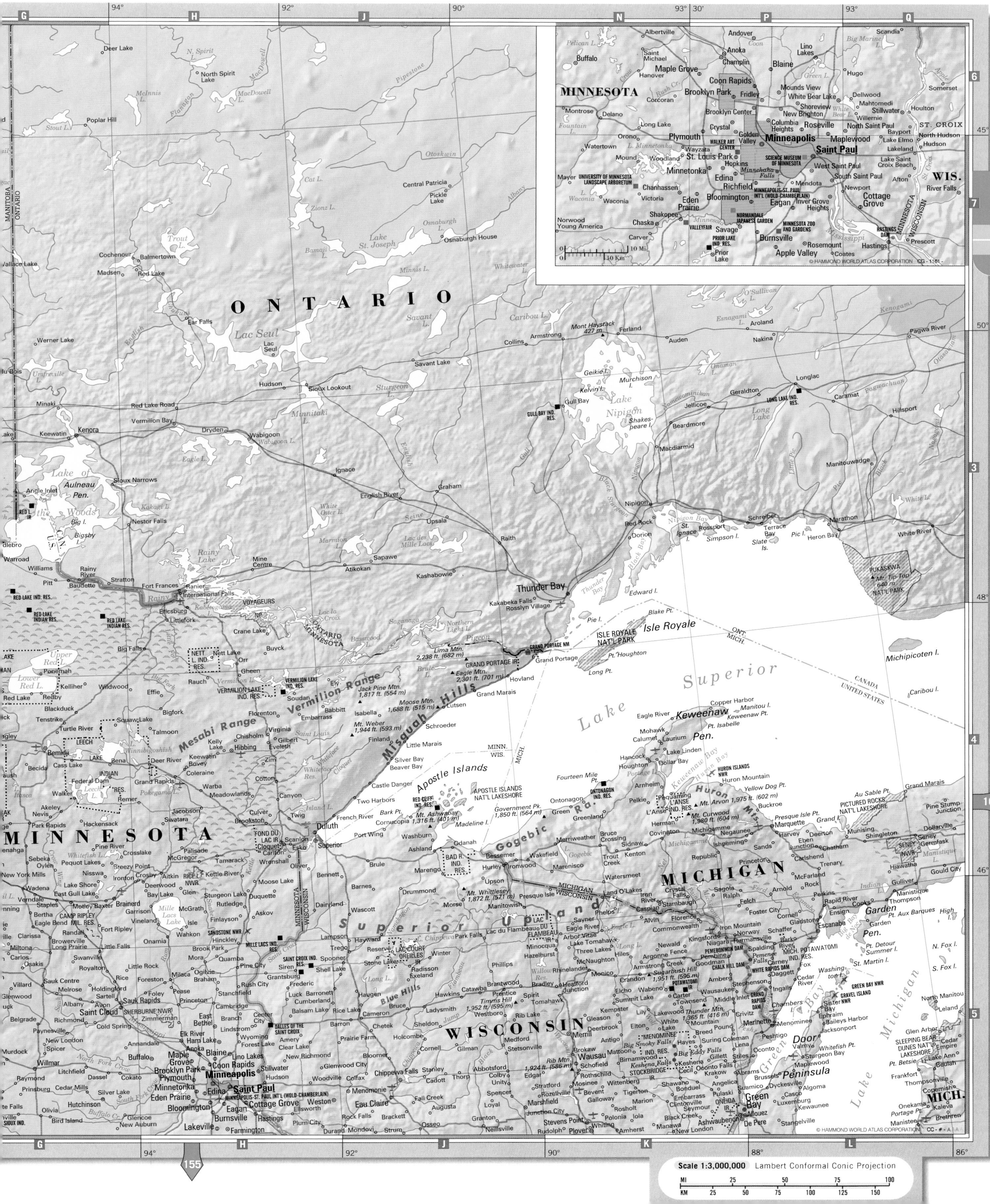

ONTARIO
MINNESOTA
MICHIGAN
WISCONSIN
MANITOBA
Lake Superior
Lake Michigan
Lake Nipigon
Lac Seul
Lake of the Woods
Rainy Lake
Isle Royale
Apostle Islands
Keweenaw Pen.
Garden Pen.
Door Peninsula
Green Bay
Mesabi Range
Vermilion Range
Misquah Hills
Gogebic Ra.
Huron Mts.
Superior Upland
Thunder Bay
Kenora
Dryden
Sioux Lookout
Fort Frances
International Falls
Duluth
Superior
Marquette
Nipigon
Marathon
Schreiber
Geraldton
Longlac
Minneapolis
Saint Paul
Saint Cloud
Eau Claire
Wausau
Green Bay
Escanaba
Ironwood
Houghton
Hibbing
Virginia
Bemidji
Grand Rapids
Brainerd
MINNESOTA
WIS.
Minneapolis
Saint Paul
Bloomington
Brooklyn Park
Coon Rapids
Plymouth
Maple Grove
Eagan
Burnsville
Minnetonka
Eden Prairie
Scale 1:3,000,000
Lambert Conformal Conic Projection
MI 25 50 75 100
KM 25 50 75 100 125 150
© HAMMOND WORLD ATLAS CORPORATION

Map Section 156 157
155
160

The low, undulating mountain chains of Newfoundland are part of the Appalachian system. Shaped by glacial action, the sparsely populated island highlands are covered by tundra and forest growth.

The waters around this island at the Gulf of St. Lawrence are rich in fish, as are those of Nova Scotia further south. The strongest tides in the world have been measured at the funnel-shaped mouth of

of the Bay of Fundy between Nova Scotia and Maine and New Brunswick to the east. The average difference between low and high tides here is 14.5 meters, with peaks of 16.3 meters.

141

Population

- ■ Over 2,000,000
- ◉ 500,000 - 999,999
- ● 100,000 - 249,999
- ⊙ 10,000 - 29,999
- ▣ 1,000,000 - 1,999,999
- ◎ 250,000 - 499,999
- ⊙ 30,000 - 99,999
- ○ Under 10,000

NEWFOUNDLAND

Gulf of St. Lawrence

Cabot Strait

ATLANTIC OCEAN

St. PIERRE & MIQUELON (FRANCE)

Avalon Peninsula

St. John's

SCOTIA

Cape Breton I.

Cape Breton Highlands

Lake Ontario

Lake Erie

ONTARIO

TORONTO

Mississauga

Brampton

Hamilton

NEW YORK

Buffalo

Niagara Falls

Saint Catharines

Montréal

Laval

Longueuil

Thanks to a relatively mild climate and an abundance of natural resources, the Great Lakes region is one of the most heavily populated areas of North America. Ontario is situated on the Canadian Shield -- a base of old ore-rich rock - and some of the world's largest deposits of nickel, copper, gold, silver, and platinum are located near Sudbury. The Appalachians farther south have large reserves of anthracite coal. Raw materials from these locations can be shipped easily through the Great Lakes or by river to the major industrial centers on the Atlantic Coast.

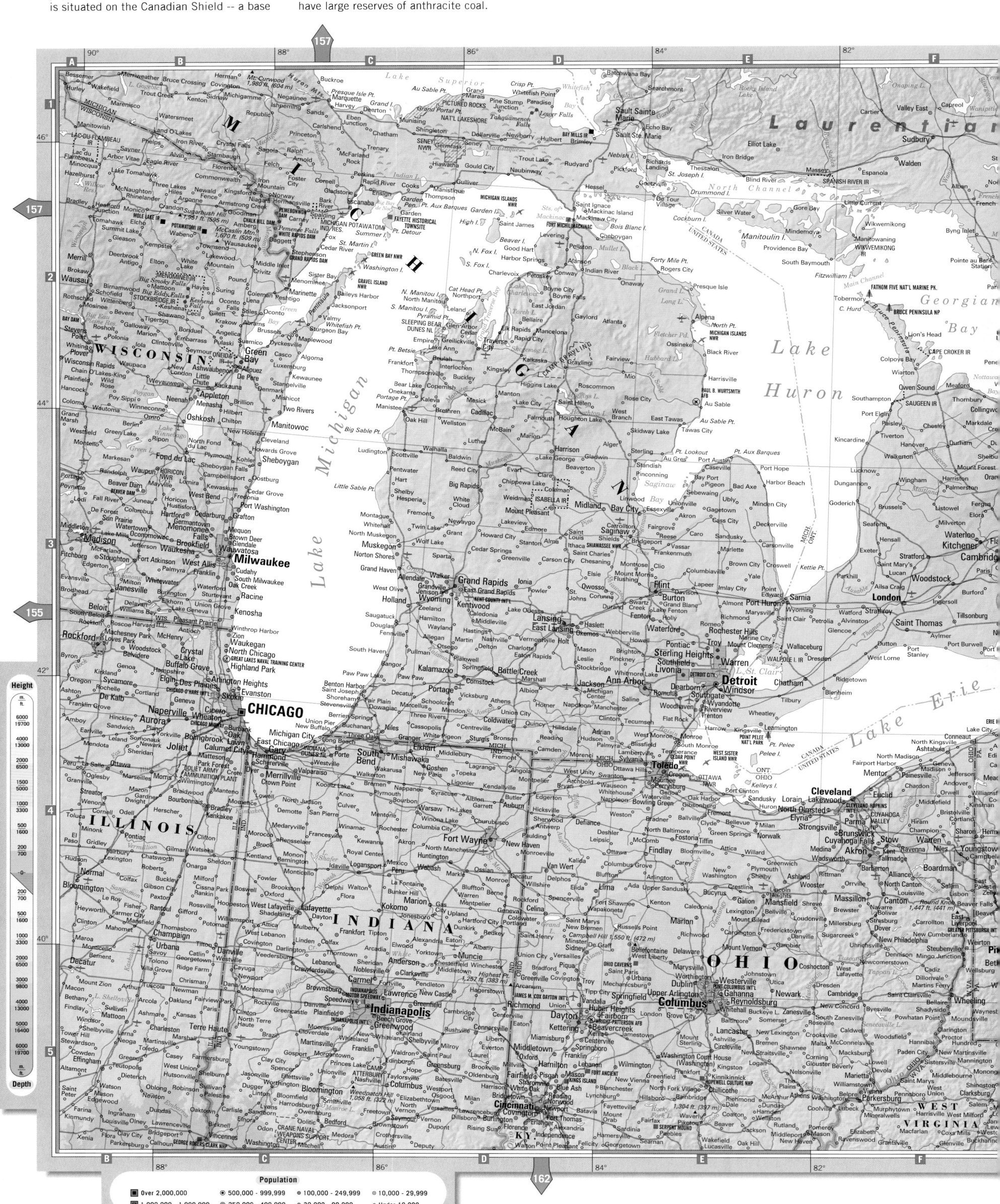

Great Lakes Region, Middle Atlantic U.S.

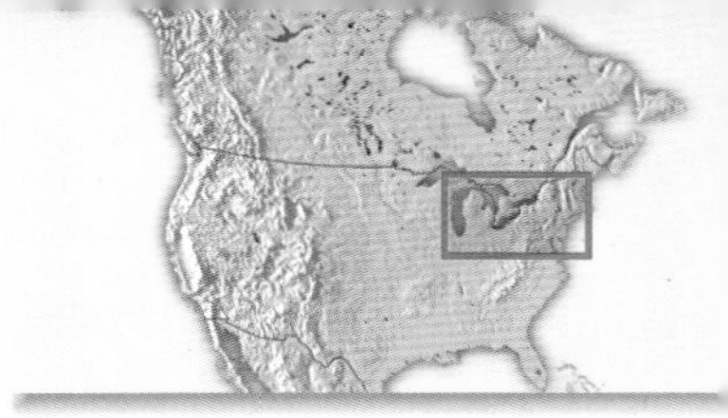

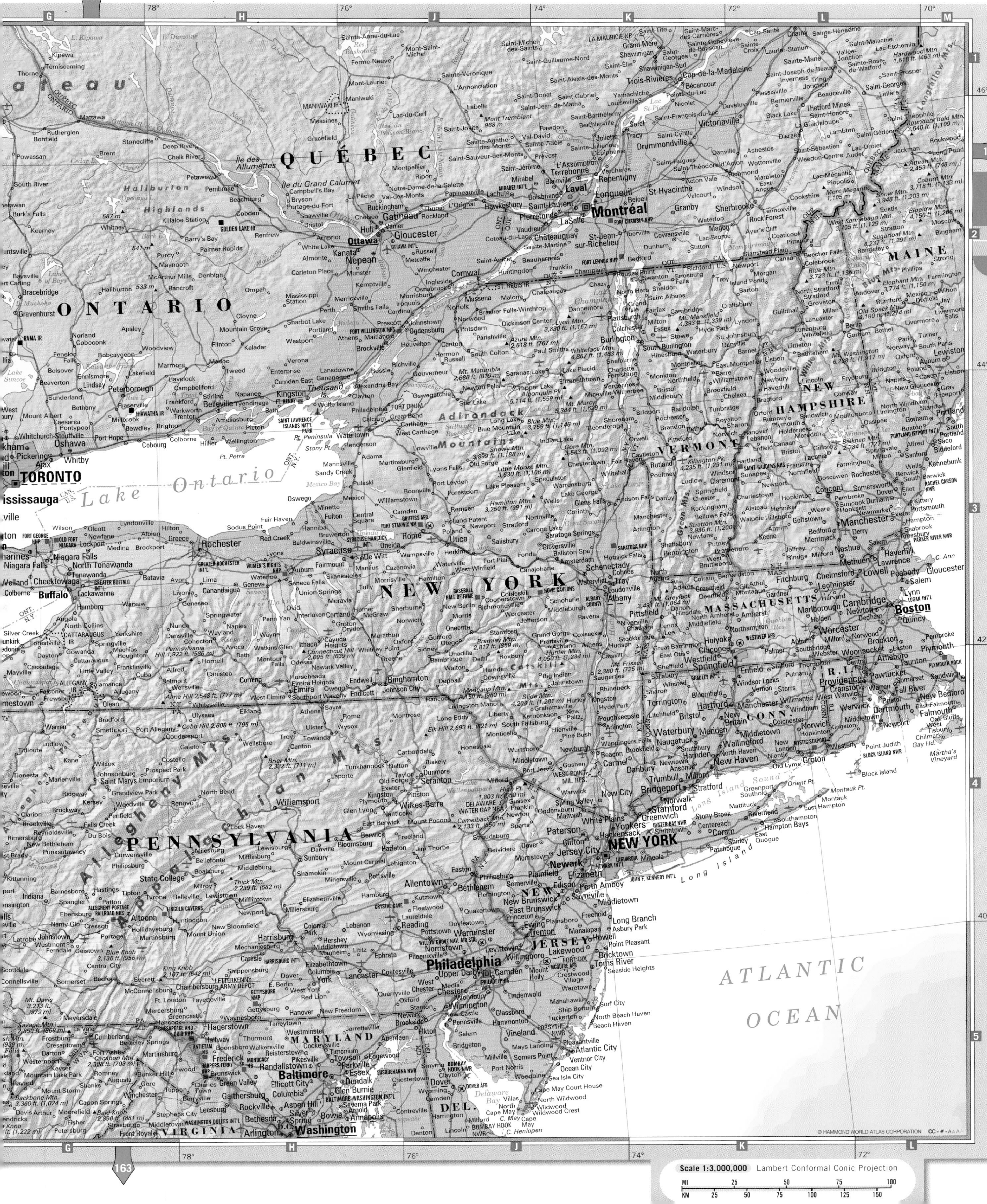

Scale 1:3,000,000   Lambert Conformal Conic Projection

© HAMMOND WORLD ATLAS CORPORATION

The mideastern region of the United States is dominated by the Appalachian Mountain system, a complex of low, rolling chains some 2,600 km long that separates the Atlantic coastal plain from the lowlands of the North American continent. They are broken by natural gaps in only a few places. Although the Appalachians bear a certain resemblance to the central mountain ranges of Europe, they are home to a much wider diversity of species - in part a consequence of the migration of animals toward the south along the northeast-southwest axis of the Appalachians during the last ice age.

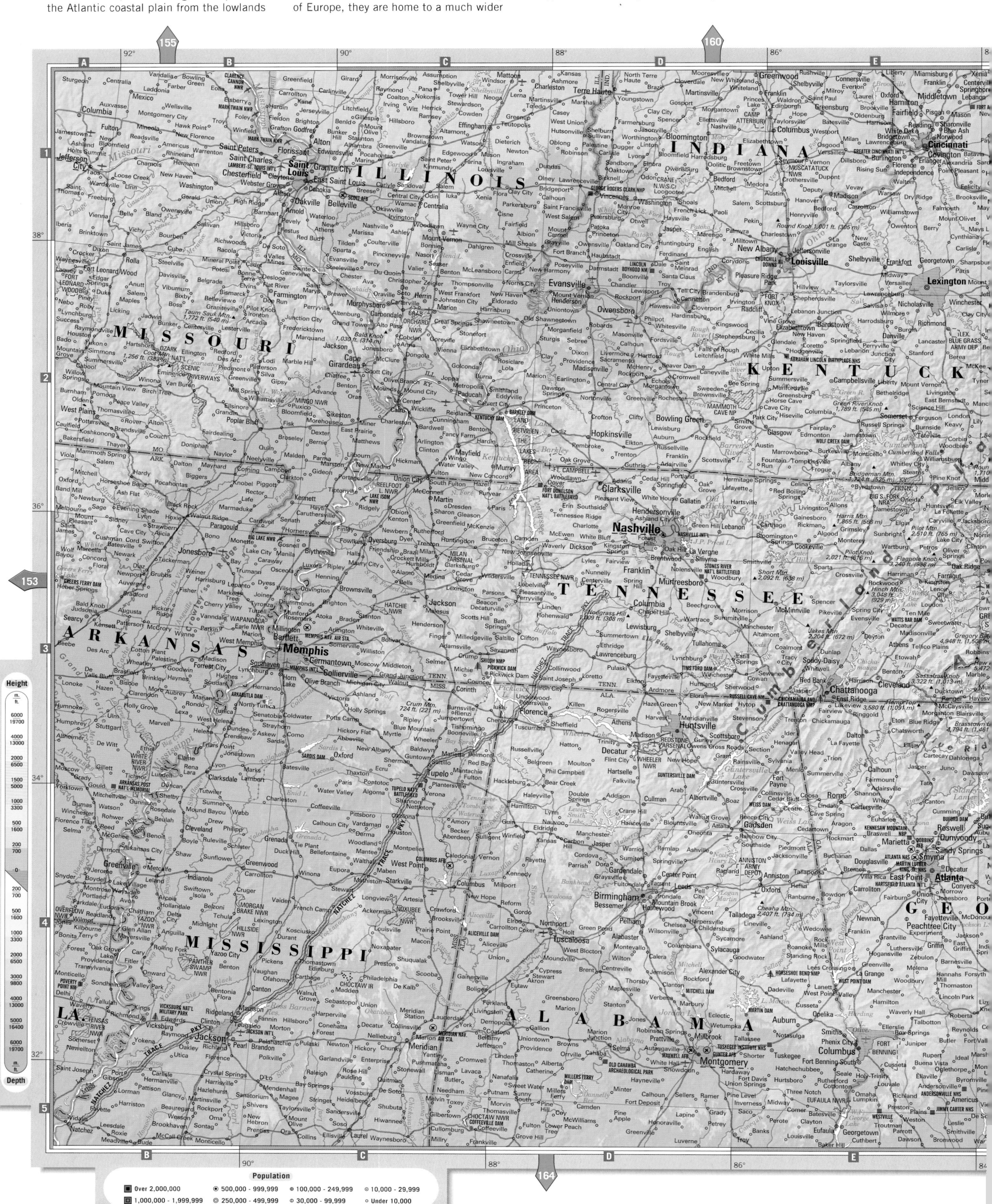

OHIO · **WEST VIRGINIA** · **VIRGINIA** · **MARYLAND** · **DELAWARE** · **N.J.**

NORTH CAROLINA · **SOUTH CAROLINA** · **GEORGIA**

Major cities: Baltimore · Washington · Annapolis · Richmond · Charlottesville · Lynchburg · Roanoke · Norfolk · Virginia Beach · Newport News · Portsmouth · Chesapeake · Charleston · Huntington · Winston-Salem · Greensboro · Durham · Raleigh · Charlotte · Fayetteville · Wilmington · Columbia · Augusta · Savannah

ATLANTIC OCEAN

CAPE HATTERAS NAT'L SEASHORE · CAPE LOOKOUT NAT'L SEASHORE · Cape Hatteras · Cape Lookout · Pamlico Sound · Albemarle Sound · Chesapeake Bay · Hilton Head Island · Myrtle Beach

Inset map — Atlanta area:
Atlanta · Marietta · Smyrna · Decatur · East Point · College Park · Roswell · Alpharetta · Duluth · Lawrenceville · Norcross
Counties: COBB · FULTON · GWINNETT · DEKALB · DOUGLAS · CLAYTON · HENRY · FAYETTE · COWETA · ROCKDALE · PAULDING
Six Flags Over Georgia · Hartsfield Atlanta Int'l · Stone Mountain Park

© HAMMOND WORLD ATLAS CORPORATION

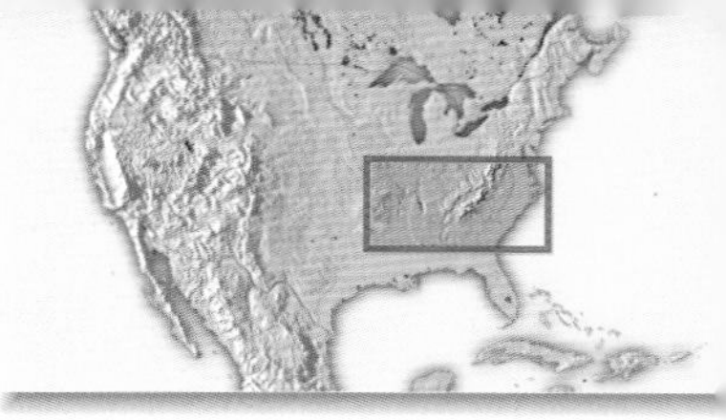

Scale 1:3,000,000   Lambert Conformal Conic Projection

161 · 162 · 163 · 165

The Mississippi is the mightiest river in North America and one of the longest in the world. Ordinarily, the river discharges more sediment into the Gulf of Mexico than waves, tides, and currents can carry away. Yet the "bird's-foot delta" and its vast wetlands are actually shrinking. Dredging and dams are partly responsible for this, but so is the river itself. The Mississippi has shifted its course back and forth several times during the last millennium and is now sending increasing amounts of sediment into an arm it abandoned some 3,800 years ago.

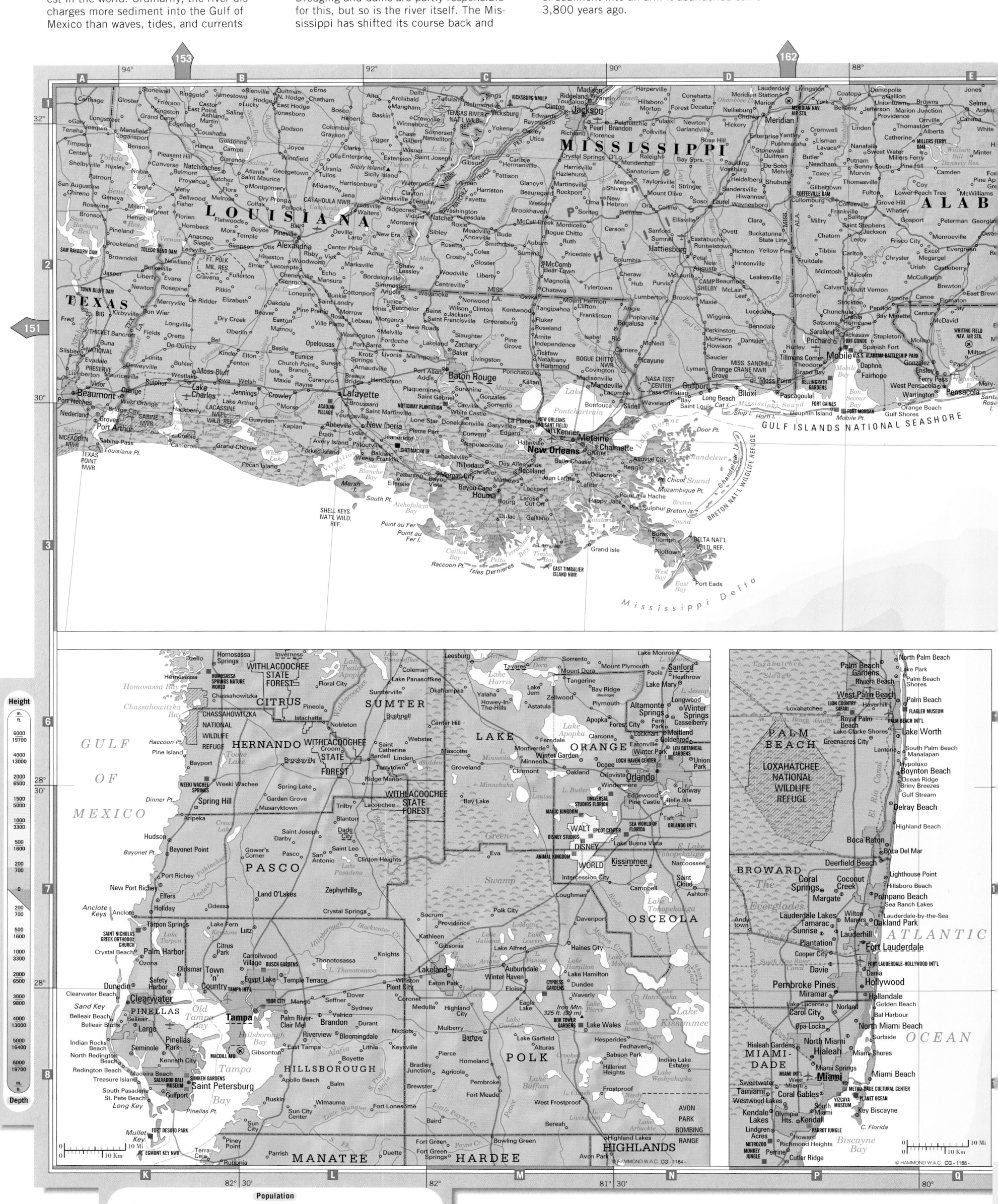

Population

■ Over 2,000,000	◉ 500,000 - 999,999	● 100,000 - 249,999	○ 10,000 - 29,999
▣ 1,000,000 - 1,999,999	◎ 250,000 - 499,999	⊙ 30,000 - 99,999	○ Under 10,000

163

86°		84°		82°		80°	

GEORGIA

FLORIDA

Columbus · Phenix City · FT. BENNING MIL. RES. · Fort Benning South · Tuskegee Institute NHS

Montgomery · Tuskegee · Hatchechubbee · Seale · Holy Trinity

EUFAULA NWR · Georgetown · Eufaula · Clayton

Dothan · Headland · Ozark · Enterprise

Albany · Dawson · Cuthbert · Fort Gaines · Blakely

Tallahassee · SAN LUIS ARCHAEOLOGICAL SITE · JIM WOODRUFF DAM

Thomasville · Cairo · Quitman · Valdosta · Lake Park

Panama City · TYNDALL AFB · Mexico Beach · Port Saint Joe · SAINT VINCENT NWR · Apalachicola · C. San Blas · St. George I.

ST. MARKS NWR · Apalachee Bay · Lighthouse Pt. · Dekle Beach

Perry · Steinhatchee · Horseshoe Beach · Suwannee · Cedar Key · LOWER SUWANNEE NWR

Live Oak · Lake City · White Springs · Jasper · OKEFENOKEE NAT'L WILDLIFE REFUGE · Fargo

Jacksonville · JACKSONVILLE INT'L · Baldwin · Jacksonville Beach · Atlantic Beach · MAYPORT NAV. AIR STA.

Savannah · Hinesville · Fort Stewart · FT. STEWART HUNTER ARMY AFLD · WASSAU NAT'L WILD. REF. · Skidaway Island · Ossabaw Island

Hilton Head · Hilton Head Island · PARRIS ISLAND MARINE BASE · SAVANNAH NWR · TYBEE NWR

Gainesville · High Springs · Newberry · Archer · Hawthorne · Palatka

Ocala · FLORIDA'S SILVER SPRINGS · Belleview · Silver Springs · OCALA NAT'L FOREST

Green Cove Springs · Middleburg · Orange Park · Penney Farms · Starke · CAMP BLANDING MIL. RES. · Keystone Hts.

Saint Augustine · CASTILLO DE SAN MARCOS NM · Anastasia I. · FORT MATANZAS NM · Hastings · Flagler Beach

Daytona Beach · Ormond Beach · Port Orange · New Smyrna Beach · Edgewater · Ponce Inlet

De Land · Deltona · Orange City · Lake Helen · Osteen · Sanford

CANAVERAL NAT'L SEASHORE · Titusville · MERRITT ISLAND NWR · KENNEDY SPACE CTR.

Orlando · WALT DISNEY WORLD · Kissimmee · Saint Cloud · ORLANDO INT'L · Winter Park · Altamonte Springs

Cocoa · Rockledge · Merritt Island · CAPE CANAVERAL AIR FORCE STATION · PATRICK AIR FORCE STATION · Satellite Beach · Indian Harbour Beach · Melbourne · West Melbourne · Palm Bay · Malabar

Leesburg · Lady Lake · Mount Dora · Tavares · Eustis · Bushnell

Spring Hill · Weeki Wachee Springs · Brooksville · New Port Richey · Hudson · Elfers

Tarpon Springs · Palm Harbor · Dunedin · Clearwater · Largo · Pinellas Park · Gulfport · Saint Petersburg · Saint Pete Beach

Tampa · TAMPA INT'L · BUSCH GARDENS · Plant City · Brandon · MACDILL AFB · FORT DESOTO PARK · SALVADOR DALI MUSEUM

Lakeland · Winter Haven · Auburndale · Bartow · Fort Meade · Bowling Green · Wauchula

Lake Wales · Frostproof · AVON PARK · Avon Park · Sebring · 2 BOMBING RANGE

Bradenton · Palmetto · Oneca · Anna Maria · Longboat Key · Sarasota · Siesta Key · RINGLING MUSEUM OF ART

Venice · Englewood · North Port · Port Charlotte · Punta Gorda · Arcadia · Zolfo Springs · Gardner

Cape Coral · North Fort Myers · Fort Myers · Lehigh Acres · Boca Grande · Gasparilla I. · PINE ISLAND NWR · Captiva I. · Sanibel I. · DARLING NWR

Bonita Springs · Naples Park · Golden Gate · Naples · East Naples · Immokalee · La Belle · Clewiston

Lake Okeechobee · Moore Haven · South Bay · Belle Glade · Pahokee · Canal Point · BRIGHTON SEMINOLE INDIAN RES.

BIG CYPRESS SEMINOLE INDIAN RES. · BIG CYPRESS NATIONAL PRESERVE · LOXAHATCHEE NAT'L WILD. REF.

Jupiter · Juno Beach · Palm Beach Gardens · Riviera Beach · West Palm Beach · Lake Worth · Greenacres City · Boynton Beach · Delray Beach · Boca Raton · Deerfield Beach · PALM BEACH INT'L · LION COUNTRY SAFARI

Fort Pierce · Port Saint Lucie · Jensen Beach · Stuart · Palm City · HOBE SOUND NWR · PELICAN ISLAND NWR · Vero Beach · Sebastian · Fellsmere · Gifford · North Hutchinson I. · Hutchinson I.

Coral Springs · Sunrise · Plantation · Pembroke Pines · Pompano Beach · Fort Lauderdale · FORT LAUDERDALE-HOLLYWOOD INT'L · Hollywood · Hallandale

MICCOSUKEE INDIAN RES. · Hialeah · Miami · Coral Gables · Kendall · Miami Beach · MIAMI INT'L · METROZOO · Perrine · Cutler Ridge

EVERGLADES NATIONAL PARK · Homestead · Florida City · Leisure City · BISCAYNE NAT'L PARK · Elliot Key · Key Largo

Cape Sable · Flamingo · Florida Bay · Plantation Key · Islamorada · Long Key · Layton · Grassy Key · Marathon

FLORIDA KEYS · GREAT WHITE HERON NAT'L WILDLIFE REFUGE · NAT'L KEY DEER REFUGE · Big Pine Key · Sugarloaf Key · Summerland Key · KEY WEST NAT'L WILDLIFE REFUGE · Key West · KEY WEST INT'L · KEY WEST NAV. AIR STA. · Marquesas Keys

DRY TORTUGAS NAT'L PK. · Dry Tortugas

ATLANTIC OCEAN

GULF OF MEXICO

Sea Islands

Map Section		
164		
165		

173

© Hammond World Atlas Corporation   CC - # - A A A

Scale 1:3,000,000 — Lambert Conformal Conic Projection

MI 25 50 75 100

KM 25 50 75 100 125 150

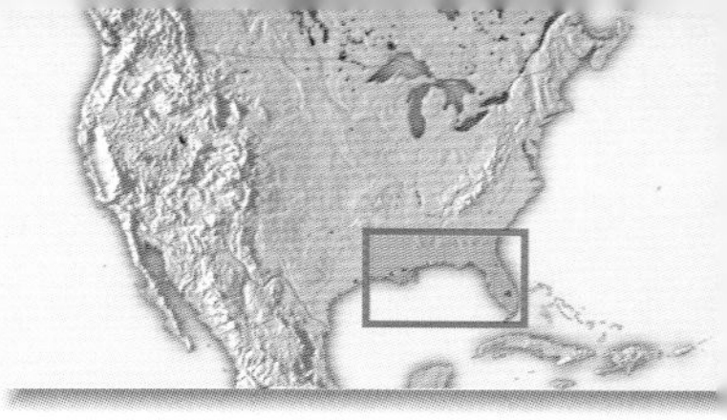

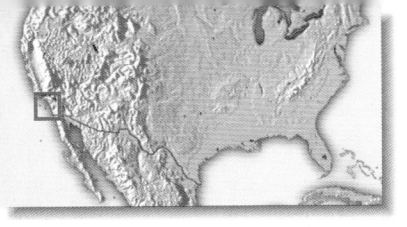

Los Angeles – San Diego

The sprawling metropolis of Los Angeles on California's West Coast extends over a distance of 184 km from Ventura to San Bernardino. The region its plagued by an increasingly severe shortage of water, since groundwater reserves are nearly exhaus Even the many reservoirs in the area ar barely able to meet the needs of local farmers and a rapidly growing populatic

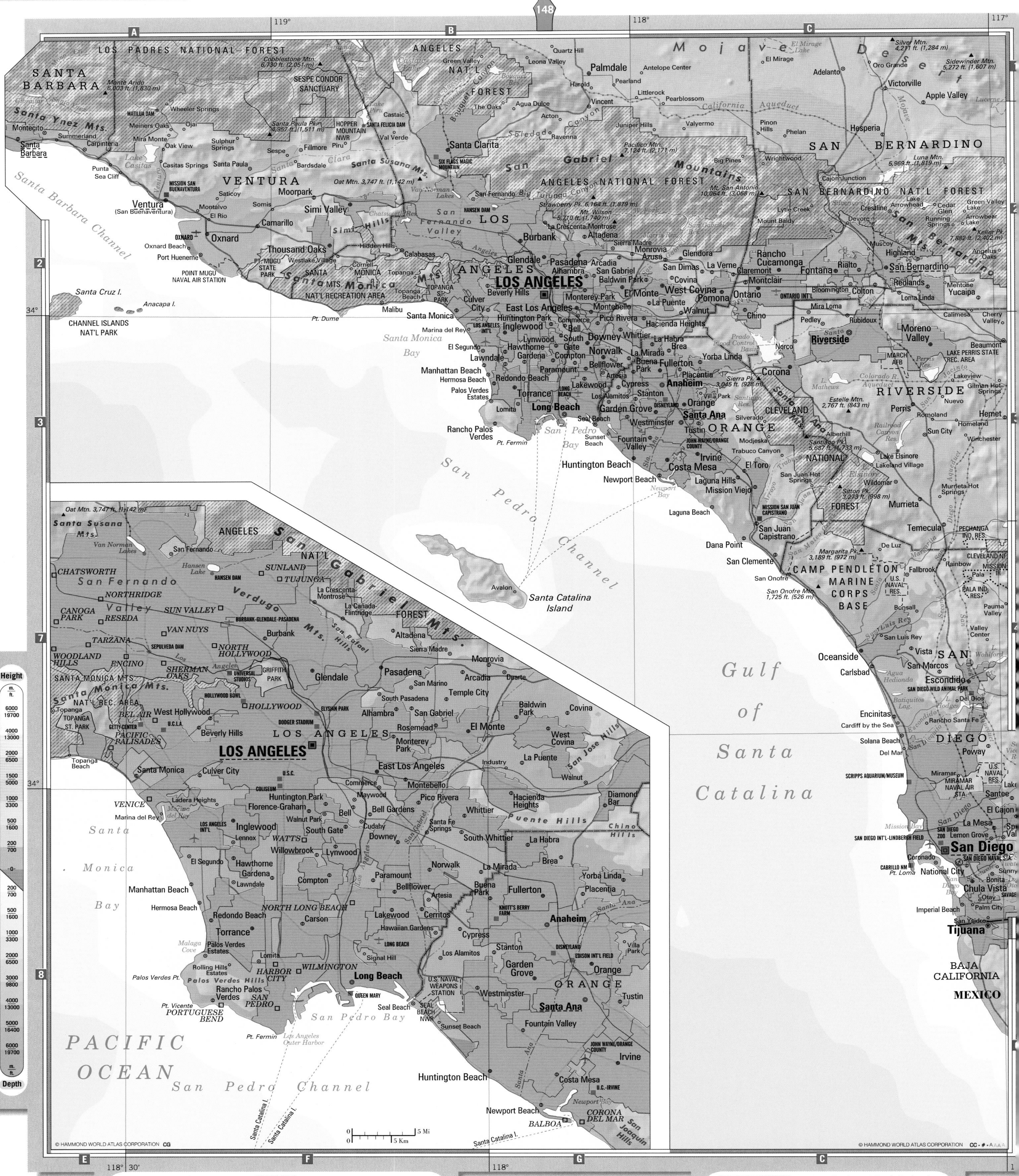

Population

- ■ Over 2,000,000
- ▣ 1,000,000 - 1,999,999
- ⊙ 500,000 - 999,999
- ◎ 250,000 - 499,999
- ⊕ 100,000 - 249,999
- ⊙ 30,000 - 99,999
- ⊙ 10,000 - 29,999
- ○ Under 10,000

Scale 1:1,000,000 Lambert Conformal Conic Projection

MI 10 20 30

KM 10 20 30 40

Four different roads to the future: Seattle has grown steadily in recent years through a steady influx of people into the less densely populated northwest. New technologies have created new jobs here and in Silicon Valley, the region between San Francisco and San Jose. Detroit relies on the automobile industry, and Chicago is already one of the world's leading commercial centers.

Seattle, San Francisco, Detroit, Chicago

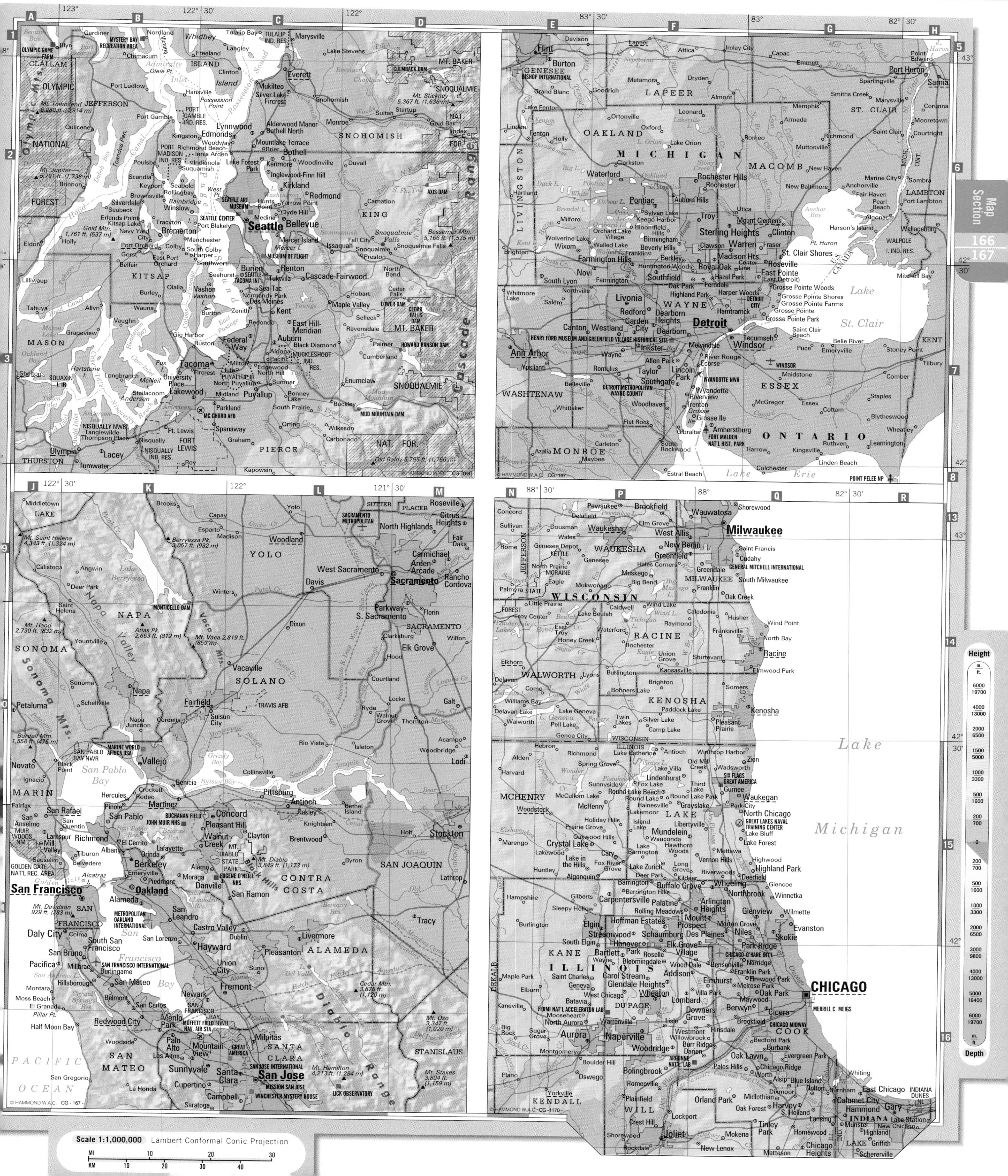

Map Section

166
167

Scale 1:1,000,000   Lambert Conformal Conic Projection

Height
m. / ft.
6000 / 19700
4000 / 13000
2000 / 6500
1500 / 5000
1000 / 3300
500 / 1600
200 / 700
0
Depth
200 / 700
500 / 1600
1000 / 3300
2000 / 6500
3000 / 9800
4000 / 13000
5000 / 16400
6000 / 19700

© HAMMOND W.A.C. CG-167

Roughly 18,000 years ago, the sea level along the East Coast of the United States was about 100 meters lower than it is today. The old valleys along the coast were "drowned" when the waters rose again and flooded the coastal plain. These sunken valleys are still recognizable today as long, funnel-shaped bays on the northern and middle Atlantic coasts. Raritan Bay at the mouth of the Hudson River and the Chesapeake and Delaware Bays are among the most prominent examples. They are actually estuaries with fluctuating salinity levels that provide a habitat for a unique range of fauna.

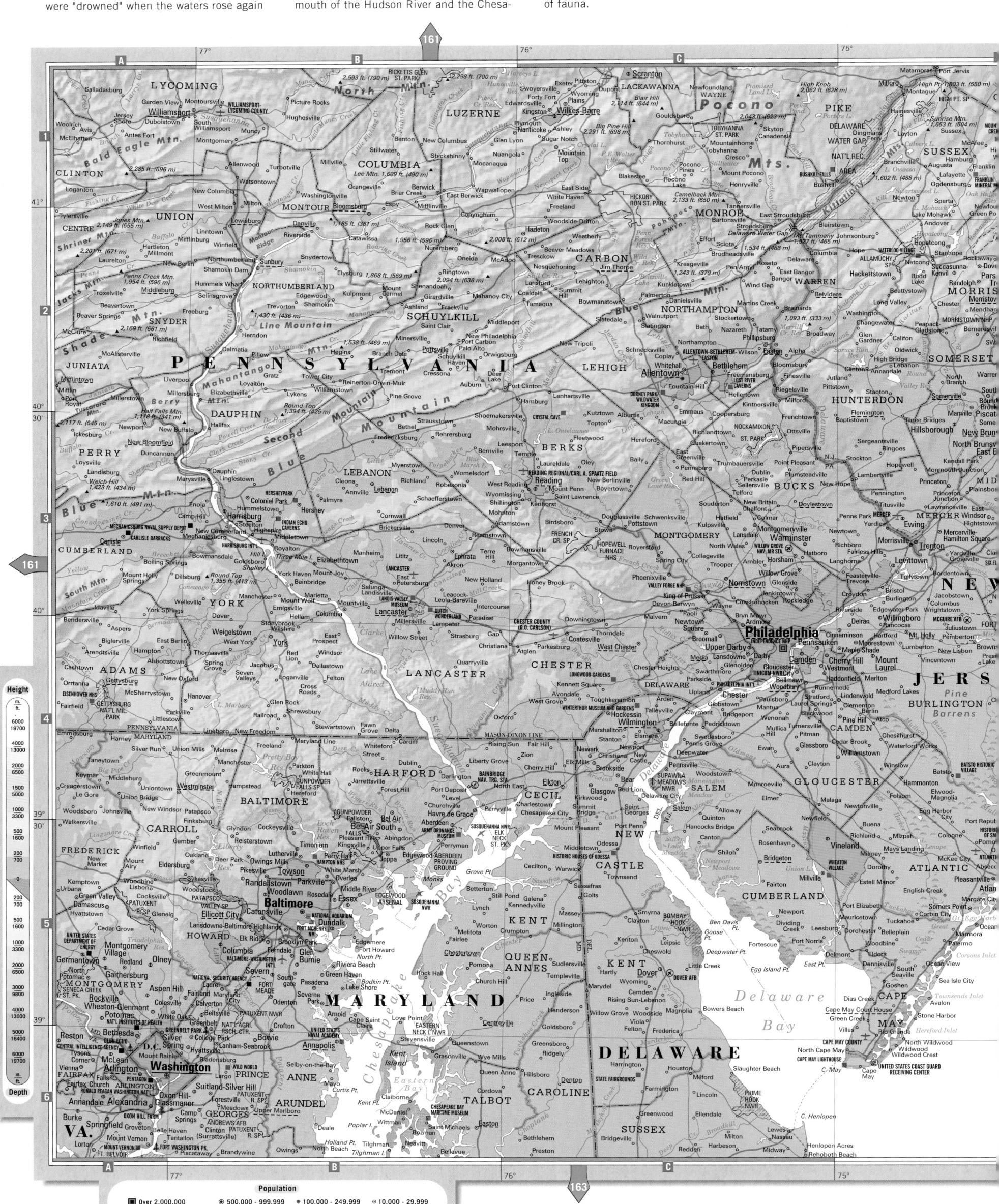

New York – Philadelphia – Washington

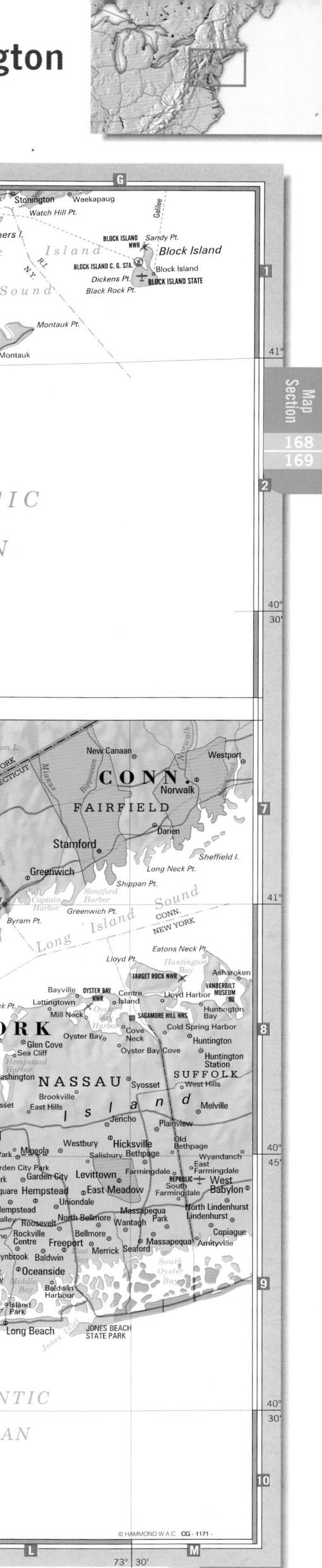

Map Section
168
169

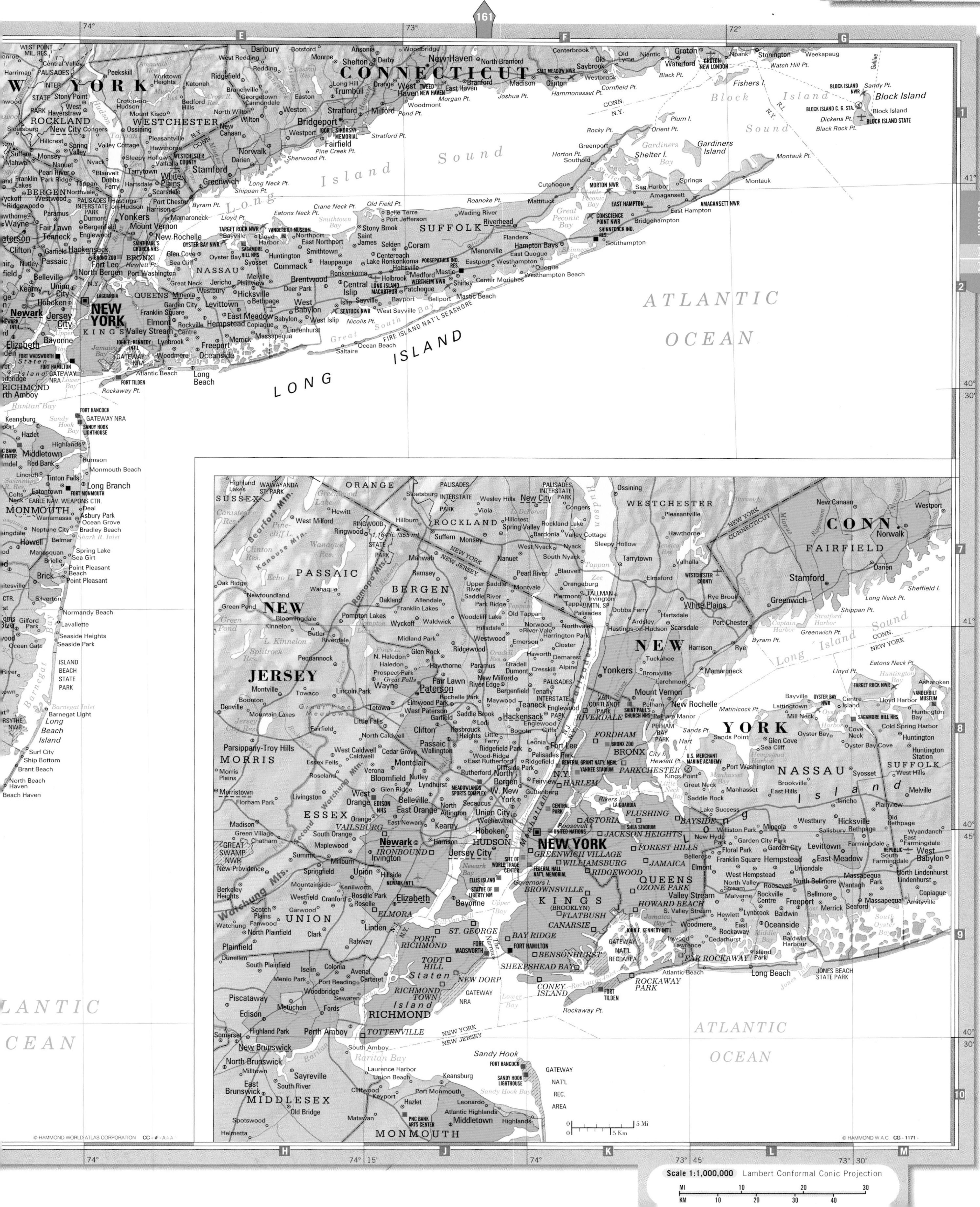

Scale 1:1,000,000 Lambert Conformal Conic Projection

MI 10 20 30
KM 10 20 30 40

Denver, Kansas City, New Orleans, Oklahoma City, Phoenix, San Antonio, Salt Lake City, St. Louis

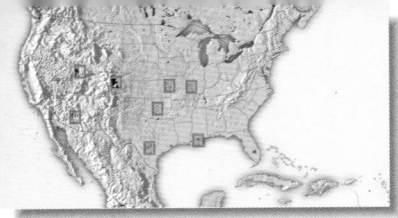

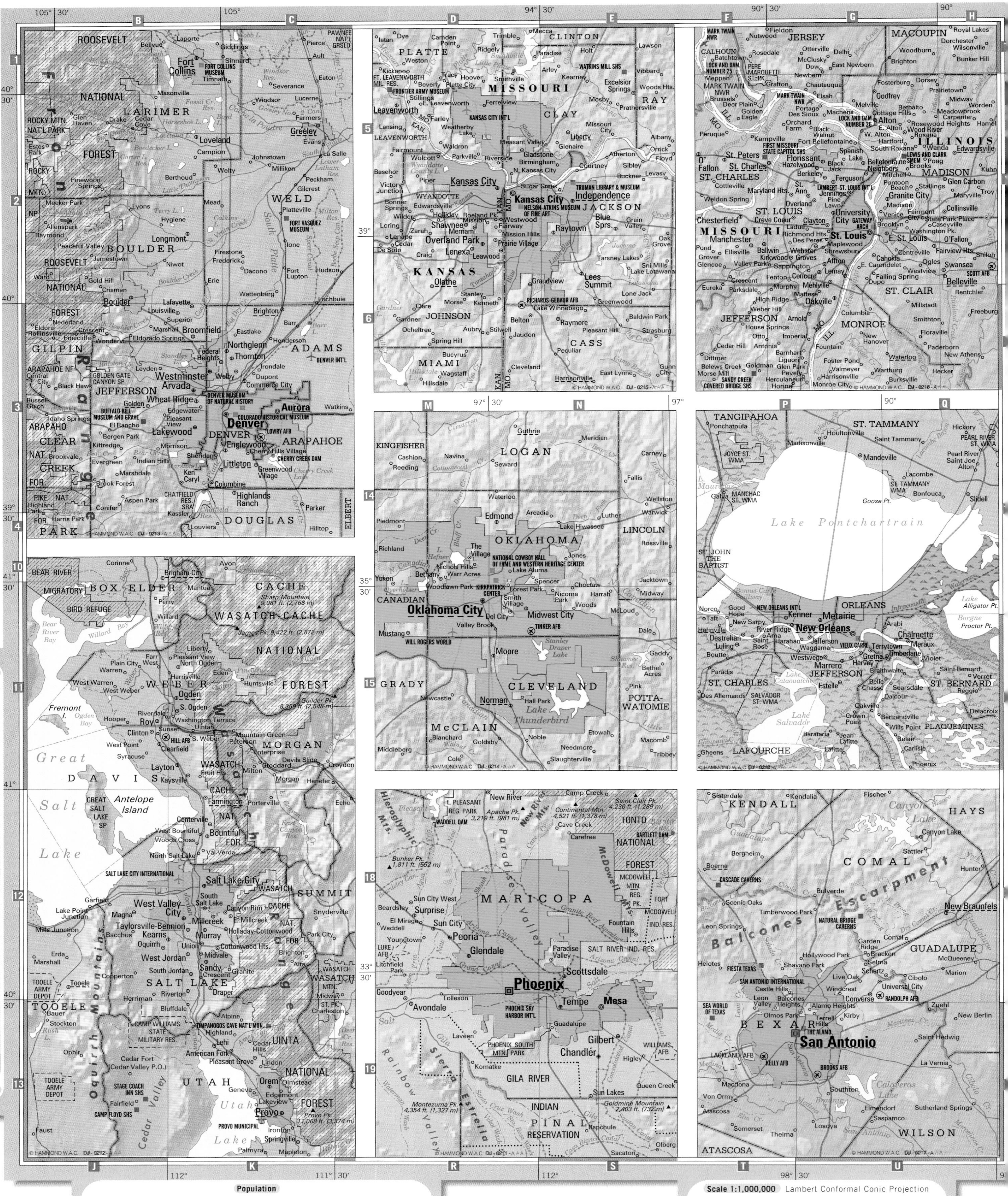

Population

- Over 2,000,000
- 1,000,000 - 1,999,999
- 500,000 - 999,999
- 250,000 - 499,999
- 100,000 - 249,999
- 30,000 - 99,999
- 10,000 - 29,999
- Under 10,000

Scale 1:1,000,000 Lambert Conformal Conic Projection

MI 0 10 20 30
KM 0 10 20 30 40

laska, the forty-ninth state of the U.S., comprises four major geographic zones. In the south, the heavily glaciated Alaska Range extends along the Pacific coast, with many fjords. Its highest peak is Mount McKinley, which at 6,194 meters is also the highest mountain in North America. The Brooks Range in the north extends eastward to the shores of the Beaufort Sea. The interior is dominated by the Yukon River system.

The island chain of the Aleutians is the most geologically active area in the region. Here, the Pacific Plate submerges beneath the continental plate along the Aleutian Trench.

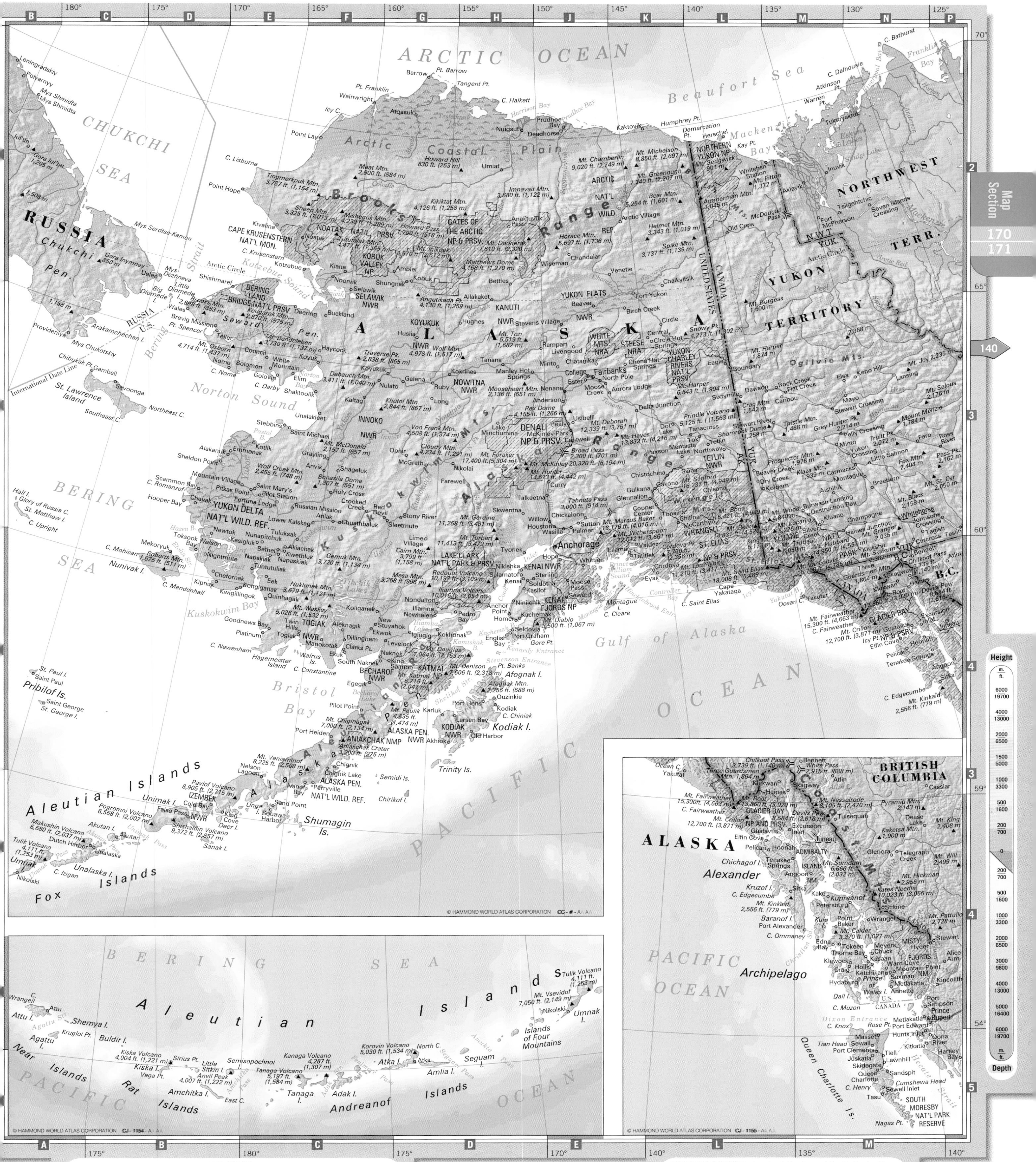

Alaska

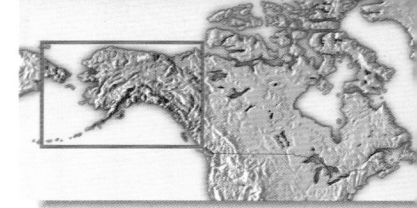

Height

m.
ft.
6000 19700
4000 13000
2000 6500
1500 5000
1000 3300
500 1600
200 700

0

200 700
500 1600
1000 3300
2000 6500
3000 9800
4000 13000
5000 16400
6000 19700

m.
ft.

Depth

Population

| ■ Over 2,000,000 | ◉ 500,000 - 999,999 | ⊕ 100,000 - 249,999 | ⊙ 10,000 - 29,999 |
| ▣ 1,000,000 - 1,999,999 | ◉ 250,000 - 499,999 | ⊙ 30,000 - 99,999 | ○ Under 10,000 |

Scale 1:9,000,000   Lambert Conformal Conic Projection

MI   100   200   300
KM   100   200   300   400

© HAMMOND WORLD ATLAS CORPORATION   CJ - 1154 - A - A

© HAMMOND WORLD ATLAS CORPORATION   CJ - 1155 - A & A.

Middle America

151 164 165 174

The isthmian tract between the United States and Colombia marks the transition from North America to South America. Geographically speaking, North America extends as far south as the Isthmus of Tehuantepec in Mexico. South America begins in the Rio Atrato Valley in Colom... In the interest of simplicity and for stati... cal reasons, Mexico is treated as part of North America, all of Colombia as part o...

Height

m.	ft.
6000	19700
4000	13000
2000	6500
1500	5000
1000	3300
500	1600
200	700
0	0
200	700
500	1600
1000	3300
2000	6500
3000	9800
4000	13000
5000	16400
6000	19700

Depth

MEXICO
① DISTRITO FEDERAL
② MÉXICO
③ MORELOS
④ TLAXCALA
⑤ QUERÉTARO DE ARTEAGA
⑥ AGUASCALIENTES

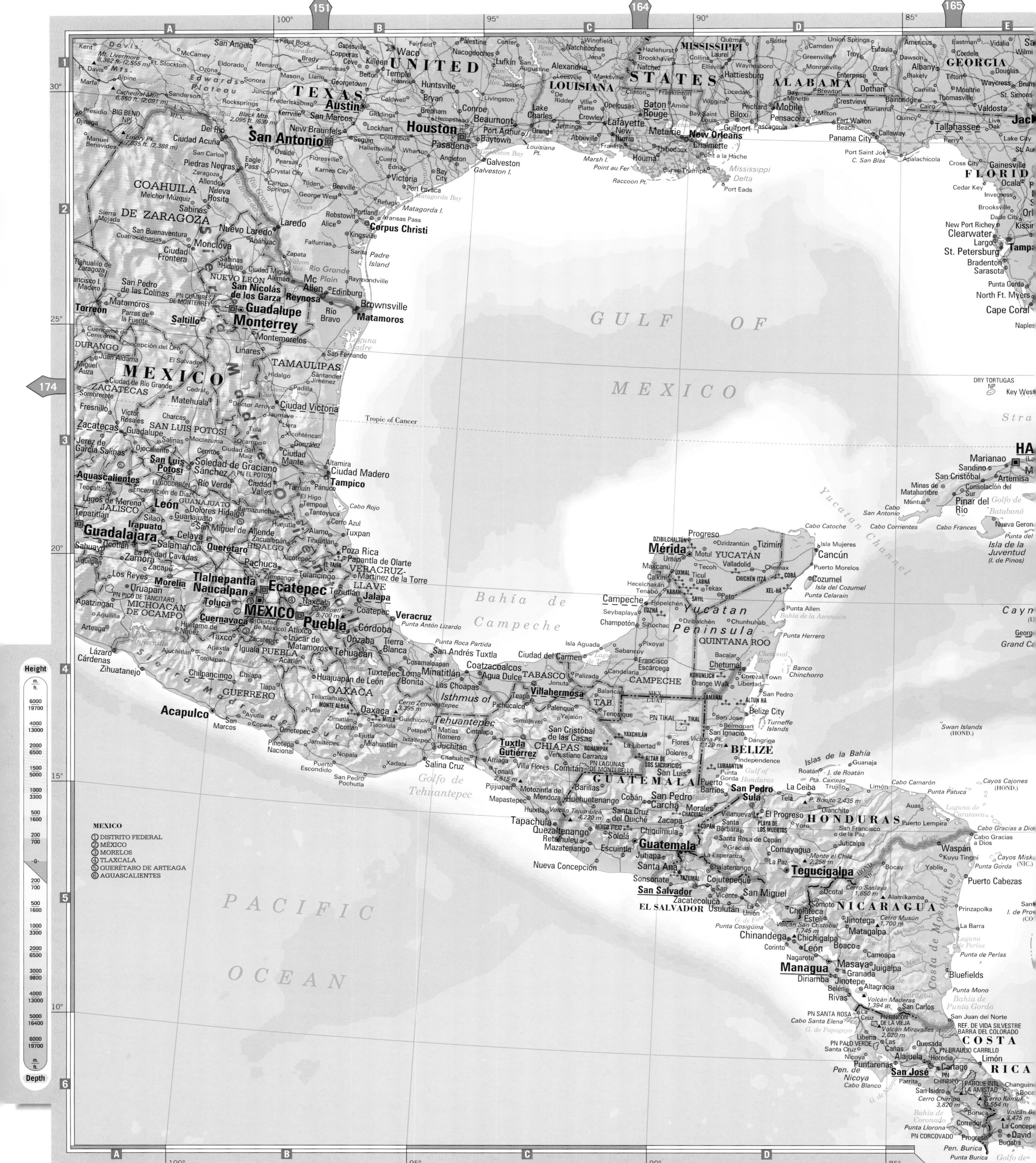

Population
- ■ Over 2,000,000
- ◉ 500,000 - 999,999
- ⊙ 100,000 - 249,999
- ○ 10,000 - 29,999
- ■ 1,000,000 - 1,999,999
- ◉ 250,000 - 499,999
- ⊙ 30,000 - 99,999
- ○ Under 10,000

UNITED STATES · TEXAS · LOUISIANA · MISSISSIPPI · ALABAMA · GEORGIA · FLORIDA

MEXICO · COAHUILA DE ZARAGOZA · NUEVO LEÓN · TAMAULIPAS · DURANGO · ZACATECAS · SAN LUIS POTOSÍ · JALISCO · GUANAJUATO · HIDALGO · VERACRUZ-LLAVE · MICHOACÁN DE OCAMPO · GUERRERO · OAXACA · CHIAPAS · TABASCO · CAMPECHE · YUCATÁN · QUINTANA ROO

GUATEMALA · BELIZE · HONDURAS · EL SALVADOR · NICARAGUA · COSTA RICA

GULF OF MEXICO · Bahía de Campeche · Yucatan Channel · Yucatan Peninsula · PACIFIC OCEAN · Golfo de Tehuantepec

San Antonio · Houston · Corpus Christi · Monterrey · Matamoros · Torreón · Saltillo · San Luis Potosí · Aguascalientes · León · Guadalajara · Querétaro · Morelia · Toluca · MEXICO · Puebla · Cuernavaca · Veracruz · Acapulco · Tampico · Ciudad Victoria · Mérida · Cancún · Cozumel · Campeche · Chetumal · Villahermosa · Tuxtla Gutiérrez · San Pedro Sula · Guatemala · San Salvador · Tegucigalpa · Managua · San José

Tropic of Cancer · New Orleans · Tallahassee · Clearwater · St. Petersburg · Tampa · Cape Coral

South America. The countries in between and the islands of the Caribbean
are referred to as Middle America.

DOMINICAN
REPUBLIC

PUERTO RICO

Virgin Islands

ATLANTIC

OCEAN

Leeward Islands

Isabela Charlotte Tortola I. Anegada (U.K.)
Aguadilla Arecibo San Juan Amalie (U.K.) Virgin Gorda
Mayagüez Utuado Bayamón Carolina St. Road Town The Valley Anguilla (U.K.)
Hormigueros Caguas Thomas V.I. Marigot St-Martin (GUAD.)
I. Mona Yabucoa El Yunque St. John (U.S.) Gustavia St-Barthélemy
C. Rojo 1,065 m V.I. NP (GUAD.)
Ponce Guayama US I. de Vieques Saba (N.A.) Oranjestad Codrington Barbuda
NAV. RES. (P.R.) Sint Eustatius (N.A.) Basseterre ANTIGUA
St. Croix Frederiksted Christiansted St. Kitts AND
(U.S.) BRIMSTONE HILL Charlestown Saint John's BARBUDA
ST. KITTS Nevis Pk. Nevis Boggy Pk. Falmouth
AND NEVIS 1,096 m 402 m Antigua

Montserrat Port-Louis Grande-Terre
(U.K.) Plymouth Basse-Terre Pointe-à-Pitre Guadeloupe
GUADELOUPE NP (FRANCE)
Soufrière Morne Constant
1,467 m 205 m Marie-Galante
Basse-Terre

Dominica Passage
Portsmouth Marigot
Morne Diablotin
DOMINICA 1,447 m
Roseau

Martinique Passage
Mt. Pelée
1,397 m Sainte-Marie
Saint-Pierre Martinique
FORT DESAIX (FRANCE)
Fort-de-France

St. Lucia Channel
Castries Gros Islet
Mt. Gimie ST. LUCIA
958 m Micoud
Vieux Fort

Soufrière St. Vincent Passage
1,234 m BARBADOS
St. Vincent Mt. Hillaby
Georgetown 336 m Bathsheba
Barrouallie Kingstown Bridgetown
ST. VINCENT Bequia
AND THE
GRENADINES

Carriacou

Canouan

Gouyave Mt. St. Catherine
Saint George's 840 m
GRENADA

Windward Islands

ATLANTIC

OCEAN

ATLANTIC

OCEAN

CARIBBEAN

SEA

West Palm
Beach
St. Lucie

Grand
Bahama
Freeport

Fort Lauderdale
Hollywood
Miami

Bimini
Is.

Berry Is.

BAHAMAS

Great Abaco

Eleuthera

Nassau
New Providence I.

Cat I.

Andros I.

Great
Exuma
Sound

Great Guana
Cay

San Salvador
(Watling I.)

Rum Cay

Tropic of Cancer

Aves I.
(VEN.)

Lesser

Antilles

CUBA

Caibarién
Cabaiguán
Morón
Sancti Ciego de Ávila
Spíritus Carlos Rojas Florida
Camagüey Nuevitas
Contramaestre Victoria de
las Tunas
G. de
Ana María Holguín
Bayamo Mayarí
Santa Cruz Julio A.
del Sur Mella San
Bartolomé Masó Palma Luis
Yara Soriano El Salvador
Cabo Cruz Pico Turquino Guantánamo
4,131 m GUANTÁNAMO BAY
Santiago de U.S. NAVAL BASE
Cuba

Long I.

Clarence Town

Crooked I.

Northeast Pt.

Acklins I.
Salina Pt.

Abraham's
Bay Mayaguana

BAHM.
TURKS.

Kew
Great Inagua Caicos Is.
Matthew
Town Little Inagua

Turks and
Caicos Is.
(U.K.)

Grand Turk

Turks Is.

Northeast Pt.

Southeast Pt.

La Asunción
NUEVA ESPARTA
Porlamar
VENEZUELA SUCRE
Cariaco El Pilar
Casanay Irapa

Is. Los Testigos

El Cerro
del Aripo
940 m
Port-of- Arima
Spain Güiria Chaguanas
Río Claro
Güiria San Fernando
Gulf of Point Fortín
Paria Pedernales Siparia
Fullarton

Tobago Charlotteville
Roxborough
Scarborough

TRINIDAD
AND
TOBAGO

Trinidad

© HAMMOND W.A.C. CC · # · A A A

Cayman Brac

JAMAICA
Montego Bay
Savanna-la-Mar Ocho Saint Ann's
Rios Bay
Spanish Port
Mandeville Town Antonio
May Pen Blue Mtn. Pk.
Kingston 2,256 m
Portland Pt.

Pedro Cays
(JAM.)

Serranilla
Bank (COL.)

Bajo Nuevo
(COL.)

Roncador Cay
(COL.)

Serrana Bank
(COL.)

Cabo Cruz

Windward Passage

Cap-Haïtien
Petite Rivière
de l'Artibonite
Jérémie Anse-d'Hainault
Dame Marie Pointe Ouest
Cap Tiburon
Chardonnières
Les Cayes Jacmel
Pointe à Gravois Pedernales
Cabo Falso

St-Louis Monte Puerto
du Nord Cristi Plata
Mao Cabo Francés Viejo
HAITI Santiago Sosúa
San Francisco DOMINICAN
Port-au-Prince La Vega de Macorís Cabo Samaná
Pico Duarte REPUBLIC
Las Matas 3,175 m El Seibo
de Farfán Bonao Hato Mayor Higüey
Azua La San Pedro de Macorís
Neiba SANTO Romana
Barahona DOMINGO
Cabo Rojo
Cabo Beata

Hispaniola

PUERTO RICO
(U.S.)

San Juan
Bayamón Carolina
Utuado Caguas
Mayagüez St. Croix
Guayama Christiansted
Ponce Saba (N.A.)

Virgin Is. Anegada (U.K.)
St. Thomas Road Town Tortola I. (U.K.)
(U.S.) Charlotte Amalie The Valley Anguilla (U.K.)
St. John St-Martin (FR.)
(U.S.) St. Maarten Philipsburg
(N.A.) Barbuda ANTIGUA
Codrington &
St. Kitts BARBUDA
ST. KITTS Basseterre Antigua
& NEVIS Charlestown Nevis Saint John's

Montserrat Guadeloupe
(U.K.) Plymouth Basse-Terre Grande-Terre
GUADELOUPE NP Pointe-à-Pitre (FRANCE)
Soufrière 1,467 m
Basse-Terre
Marie-Galante

DOMINICA Marigot
Roseau
(VEN.)

Aves I.
(VEN.)

Mont Pelée 1,397 m
Saint-Pierre Martinique
Fort-de-France (FRANCE)

Castries Gros Islet
ST. LUCIA Micoud
Vieux Fort Soufrière
1,234 m
ST. VINCENT & Kingstown Bridgetown
THE GRENADINES BARBADOS

GRENADA Carriacou
Saint George's Mt. St. Catherine
840 m

Windward Is.

Lesser Antilles

Leeward Is.

Lesser Antilles

CARIBBEAN

SEA

Greater

West

Indies

Lesser Antilles

Aruba NETH. Bonaire
(NETH.) Curaçao Kralendijk
Oranjestad NETH. El Roque
Willemstad ANTILLES (VEN.)
Islas I. La Orchila
Punta Gallinas Las Aves (VEN.)
Pen. de (VEN.) Islas
Cabo de la Vela Paraguaná Los Roques
Carrizal Jadacaquiva (VEN.)
Guajira Punta Cardón I. La Tortuga
Pen. Amuay (VEN.)
Cojoro Santa Ana I. La Blanquilla
Ríohacha Coro (VEN.) (VEN.)
Cabo de Maracaibo Puerto Cumarebo I. de Margarita
Santa Marta la Aguja Mitare Tucacas Juangriego La Asunción
Uribia Venezuela Chichiriviche Pen. de Porlamar
Barranquilla Cabimas Paria
Malambo Ciénaga Coro Cumaná Carúpano
Soledad PN SIERRA NEVADA Ciudad Ojeda Puerto Cabello Caracas San Antonio Güiria
Cartagena DE SANTA MARTA Maracaibo Valencia Maracay del Golfo Carúpano Port-of-
Turbaco Pico Cristóbal Siquisiqui Petare Guarenas Barcelona Quíbor Spain
Colón 5,775 m Lago Barquisimeto Valencia Los Teques Puerto La Arima &
San Jacinto de Mene Grande Tocuyito Turmero Cruz TOBAGO
El Carmen Maracaibo Acarigua San Carlos San José Anaco Sangre Grande
Sincelejo Machiques Trujillo de los Morros de Guaribe San José Trinidad
Corozal San Carlos VENEZUELA Zaraza de Guanipa Point
Chinú del Zulia Calabozo El Tigre Fortín
Montería San José Valle de la Pascua Maturín
Planeta Rica Agustín Guanare Santa María Tembladora
Cereté Codazzi PN SIERRA Pico Bolívar de Ipire Santa Cruz
Lorica Valledupar NEVADA 5,007 m Barinas de Guanipa
San Marcos Magangué Mérida Las Mercedes Ciudad Guayana
Sahagún El Banco Ejido El Samán de Apure Pariaguán Upata
COLOMBIA San Carlos Tovar Libertad Bruzual Barrancas El Palmar
El Porvenir Monte Carmelo Bocono PN Ciudad Delta del
Arjona Mompós Bocono AGUARO Bolívar Orinoco
Narganá Bruzual San Fernando GUARIQUITO Calcara de Orinoco Tumeremo
Ailigandi Plato Convención La Fría de Apure Mapire Guasipati
Isthmus of El Llano Aguachica Ayapel Arismendi Portuguesa Orinoco
Panama San Jacinto San PN SIERRA Achaguas
Panamá San Marcos Lagunillas © HAMMOND WORLD ATLAS CORPORATION CC · # · A A
Gulf of Cerro Chucantí NEVADA
Panama 1,439 m

PN DARIÉN
PN
PARAMILLO

Mexico has a unique blend of Native American and Spanish cultural heritages. Today, this Latin American culture is spreading north across the Rio Grande into the Anglo-American cultural region at an increasingly rapid pace. Bordered on the east and west by the parallel chains of the Sierra Madre Occidental and the Sierra Madre Oriental, Mexico's vast highlands are home to a large part of the Mexican population. The heavily urbanized area around Mexico City stretches from Guadalajara to Veracruz.

Population

- ■ Over 2,000,000
- ■ 1,000,000 - 1,999,999
- ● 500,000 - 999,999
- ● 250,000 - 499,999
- ● 100,000 - 249,999
- ● 30,000 - 99,999
- ○ 10,000 - 29,999
- ○ Under 10,000

Northern and Central Mexico

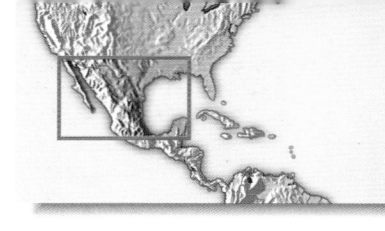

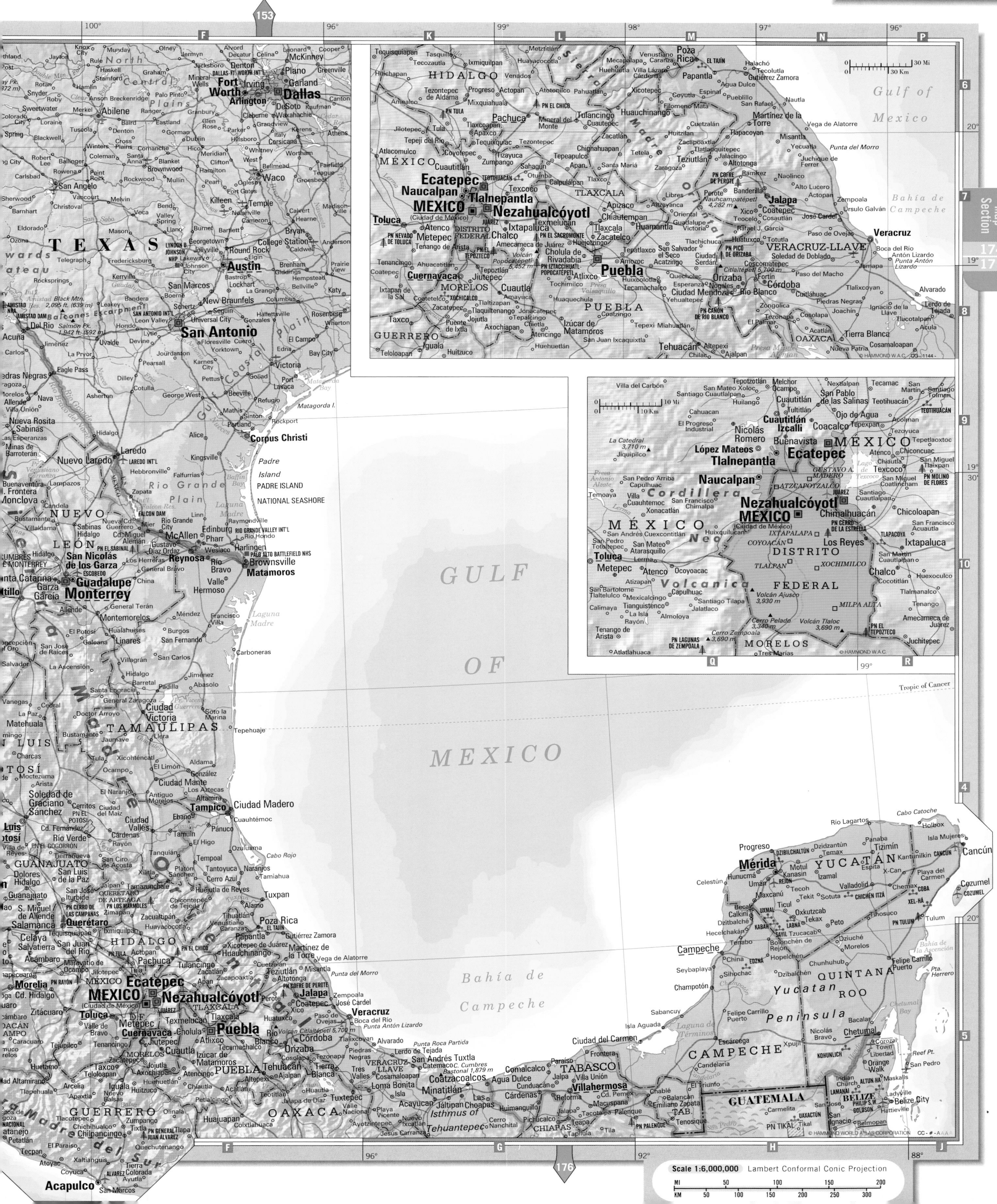

Map Section 174 175

Costa Rica, the "Rich Coast," differs from its neighbors in many ways. Stable political relationships have enabled the country to preserve a large part of its tropical rain forest, which receives abundant precipitation from the northeast trade wind on the Caribbean side. Though much more dry in comparison, the Pacific coastal region is known around the world for its splendid orchids. The long (50 km) Valle Central in the interior highlands has a particularly mild climate and fertile volcanic soil. This is Costa Rica's traditional coffee-growing region.

Population

■ Over 2,000,000	◉ 500,000 - 999,999
■ 1,000,000 - 1,999,999	◎ 250,000 - 499,999

● 100,000 - 249,999
◎ 30,000 - 99,999

◉ 10,000 - 29,999
○ Under 10,000

Height
m. ft.
6000 19700
4000 13000
2000 6500
1500 5000
1000 3300
500 1600
200 700
-0-
200 700
500 1600
1000 3300
2000 6500
3000 9800
4000 13000
5000 16400
6000 19700
m. ft.
Depth

Scale 1:6,000,000 — Lambert Conformal Conic Projection

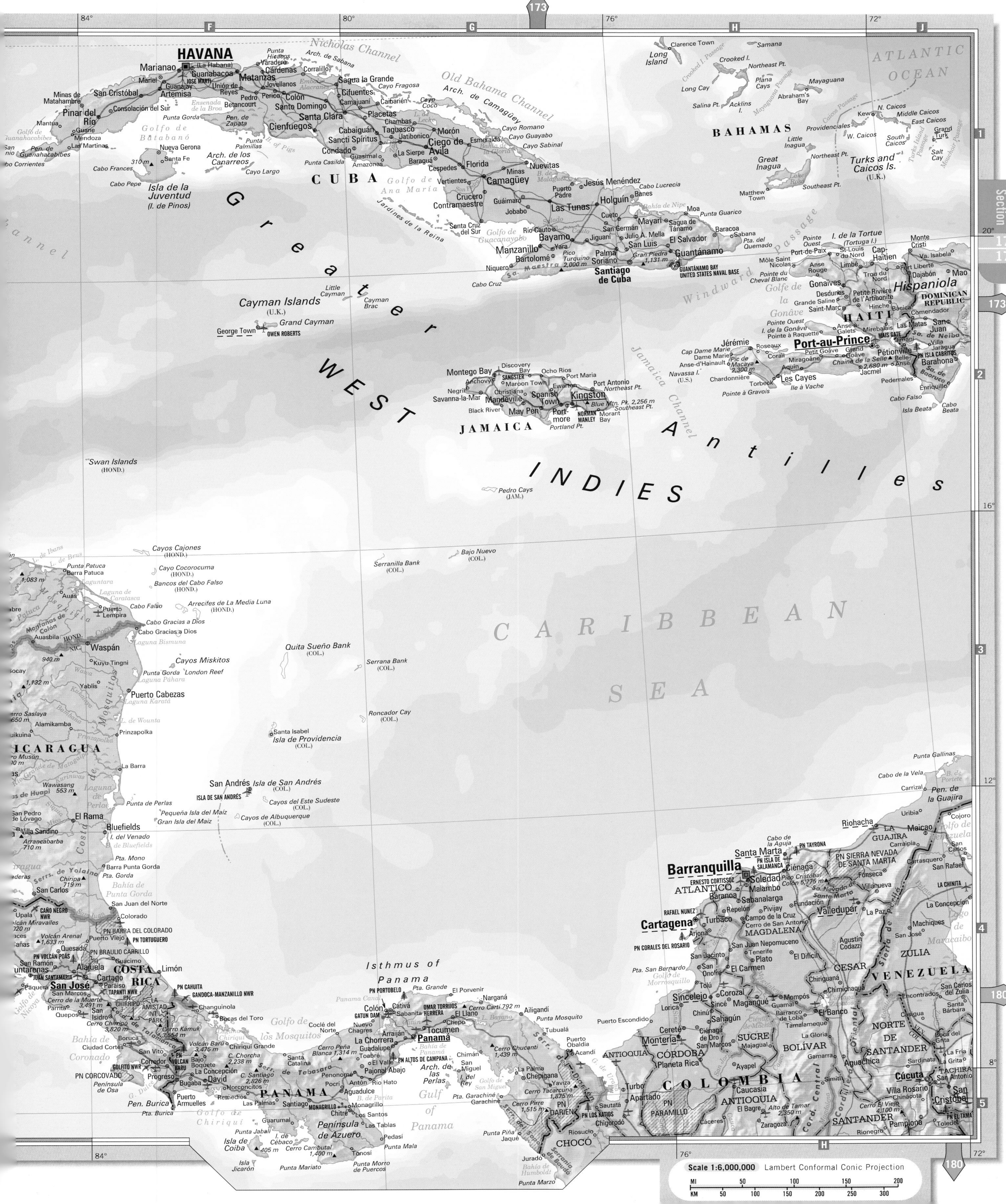

...he highest mountain peak in the Americas, with an elevation of 6,959 meters, glacier-covered Mount Aconcagua. This ...theastward-looking image shows the ...rth-south axis of the Andes along the border between Chile and Argentina. The narrow valley running east to west immediately south of Mount Aconcagua contains a section of the American Highway that connects Mendoza, Argentina, with Santiago, Chile. Although composed of volcanic material, Mount Aconcagua - unlike many of its neighbors in the Andes - is not a volcano itself.

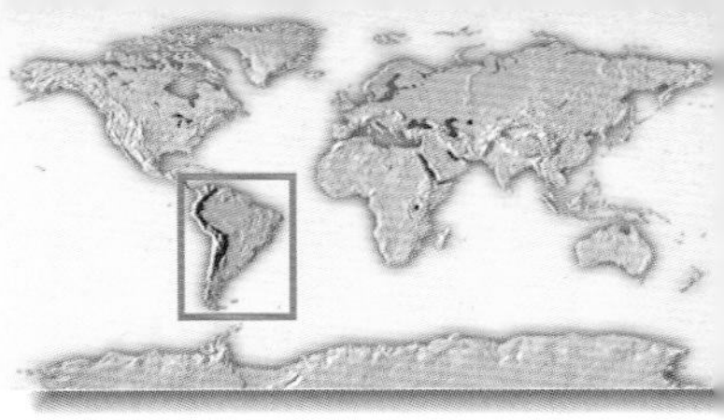

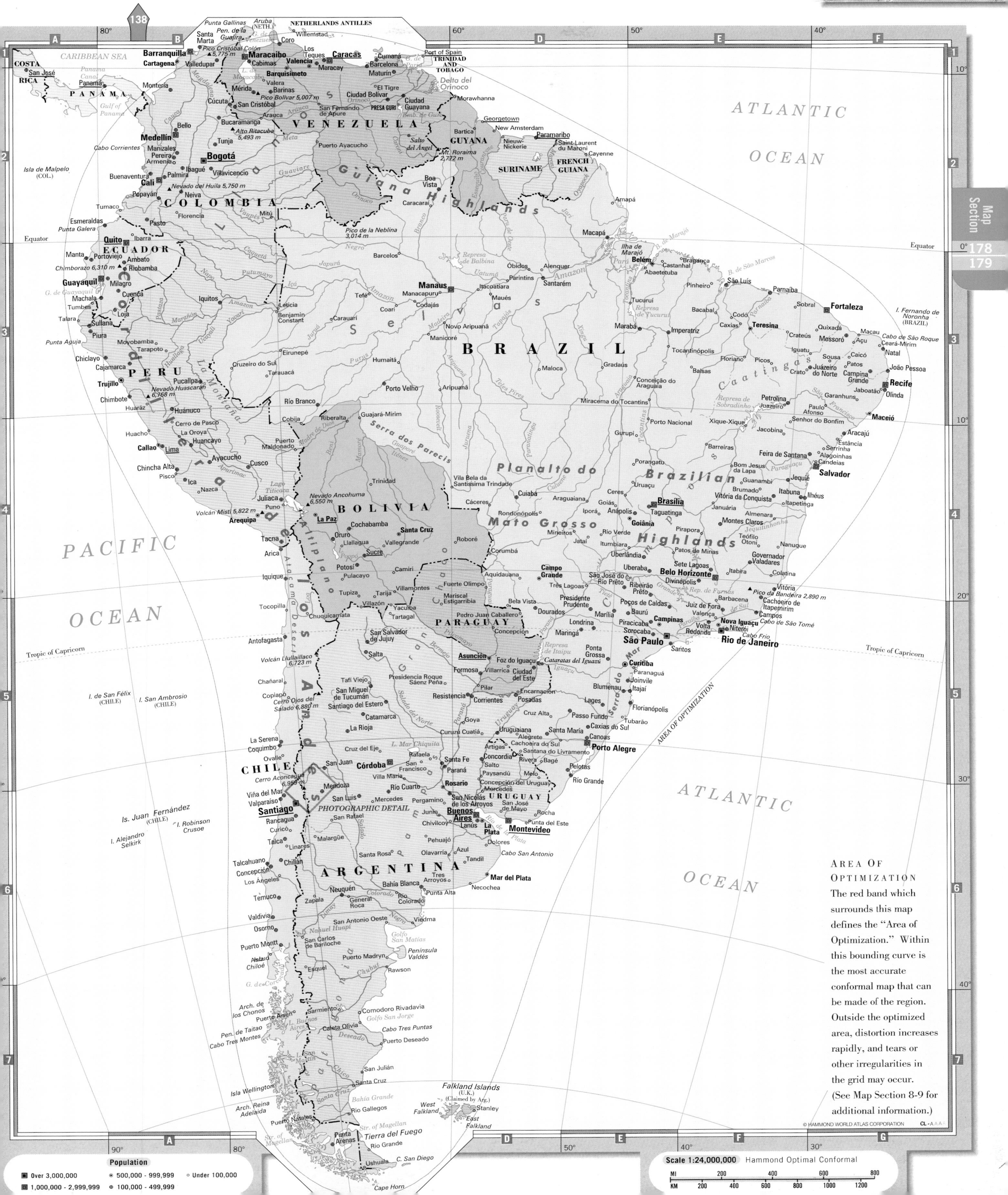

AREA OF OPTIMIZATION
The red band which surrounds this map defines the "Area of Optimization." Within this bounding curve is the most accurate conformal map that can be made of the region. Outside the optimized area, distortion increases rapidly, and tears or other irregularities in the grid may occur. (See Map Section 8-9 for additional information.)

CARIBBEAN SEA

ATLANTIC OCEAN

PACIFIC OCEAN

ATLANTIC OCEAN

Equator

Tropic of Capricorn

PANAMA
COSTA RICA
VENEZUELA
GUYANA
SURINAME
FRENCH GUIANA
COLOMBIA
ECUADOR
PERU
BRAZIL
BOLIVIA
PARAGUAY
CHILE
ARGENTINA
URUGUAY

NETHERLANDS ANTILLES
TRINIDAD AND TOBAGO

Pico Cristóbal Colón 5,775 m
Pico Bolívar 5,007 m
Alto Ritacuba 5,493 m
Nevado del Huila 5,750 m
Mt. Roraima 2,772 m
Pico de la Neblina 3,014 m
Chimborazo 6,310 m
Nevado Huascarán 6,768 m
Volcán Misti 5,822 m
Nevado Ancohuma 6,550 m
Pico da Bandeira 2,890 m
Volcán Llullaillaco 6,723 m
Cerro Ojos del Salado 6,880 m
Cerro Aconcagua 6,959 m

Bogotá · Caracas · Maracaibo · Barranquilla · Cartagena · Medellín · Cali · Quito · Guayaquil · Lima · Callao · Trujillo · Arequipa · La Paz · Sucre · Santa Cruz · Manaus · Belém · Fortaleza · Recife · Salvador · Brasília · Belo Horizonte · Rio de Janeiro · São Paulo · Curitiba · Porto Alegre · Asunción · Córdoba · Rosario · Buenos Aires · Montevideo · Santiago · Valparaíso · Mar del Plata

PHOTOGRAPHIC DETAIL

AREA OF OPTIMIZATION

Falkland Islands (U.K.) (Claimed by Arg.)
West Falkland · East Falkland · Stanley
Tierra del Fuego
Cape Horn
Str. of Magellan
Is. Juan Fernández (CHILE)
I. Robinson Crusoe
I. Alejandro Selkirk
Isla de Malpelo (COL.)
I. de San Félix (CHILE)
I. San Ambrosio (CHILE)
I. Fernando de Noronha (BRAZIL)

Population
■ Over 3,000,000
■ 1,000,000 - 2,999,999
⊙ 500,000 - 999,999
○ 100,000 - 499,999
∘ Under 100,000

Scale 1:24,000,000   Hammond Optimal Conformal
MI   200   400   600   800
KM 200 400 600 800 1000 1200

© HAMMOND WORLD ATLAS CORPORATION   CL-A

The Orinoco is fed by the third-largest drainage basin in South America, a region that covers 70 percent of Venezuela and 25 percent of Colombia. Extreme topographic contrasts and a warm, humid climate make this one of the world's most diverse landscapes. Water flows from the heights of snow-covered Pico Bolívar (5,007 m) through tropical jungle, over virtually treeless plains known as Llanos, and on to the flood plain of the Orinoco. Here lie the oil reserves of Venezuela, which are among the largest in the world. Farther south, in the Guiana Highlands, water plunges 979 meters from the top of a flat-topped plateau at Angel Falls, the highest waterfall in the world.

Map Section

180
181

2

3

4

182

5

CARIBBEAN SEA

Aves
DEPENDENCIAS FEDERALES (VEN.)
El Roque
I. La Orchila (VEN.)
s Roques (VEN.)
I. Blanquilla (VEN.)

GRENADA
Victoria — Carriacou
Sauteurs
Saint George's — Mt. St. Catherine 840 m
POINT SALINES

Is. Los Testigos (VEN.)

Tobago
576 m — Charlotteville
CROWN POINT — Roxborough
Scarborough

I. La Tortuga

NUEVA ESPARTA — **I. de Margarita**
Juangriego — La Asunción
PN LAGUNA DE LA RESTINGA — Porlamar
GRAL. S. MARINO — PN CERRO EL COPEY
I. Cubagua — I. Coche
PN PENÍNSULA DE PARIA

Caracas
Petare
Los Teques — MIRANDA
Victoria
Cúa
Ocumare del Tuy
ARAGUA
Juan de Morros
San José de Guaribe
Valle de Guanape
Lezama
El Sombrero
Chaguaramas
Las Mercedes
GUÁRICO
PN AGUARO-GUARIQUITO
San Mauricio
San Antonio
Santa Rita

Puerto La Cruz
Barcelona
Pozuelos
ANZOÁTEGUI
J. A. ANZOÁTEGUI
Puerto Píritu
Guanape
Onoto
Anaco
El Tigre
San Tomé
San José de Guanipa
Cantaura
Santa Clara
El Pao
La Canoa
Zuata

Cumaná
San Antonio del Golfo
SUCRE
PN MOCHIMA
San Antonio
Cariaco
Casanay
Carúpano
El Pilar — Irapa
Güiria
Pta. de Araya
Peh. de Araya
PN EL GUACHARO

PN PENÍNSULA DE PARIA
Blanchisseuse — Toco — Pta. Galera
Port-of-Spain — Arima
Chaguanas — PIARCO
Couva — **Trinidad**
San Fernando — Tabaquite
Point Fortin — Siparia
Fullarton — Río Claro
Pta. Galeota

TRINIDAD AND TOBAGO
Sangre Grande
Guiriquire

Gulf of Paria
Dragon's Mouth
Serpent's Mouth

ATLANTIC OCEAN

Pedernales
Macareo
Tucupita — **DELTA**
Barrancas — Santo Niño
Piacoa — La Esperanza
Delta del Orinoco
San Antonio de Tabasca
Uracoa

MONAGAS
Maturín
Aguisay
Punta de Mata
Témblador
Los Castillos
El Toro

Ciudad Guayana
El Pao
Ciudad Bolívar
Upata — El Palmar
El Miamo
La Horqueta — La Margarita
La Horqueta
Mount Everard
Baramanni
AMACURO
San José de Amacuro
Las Piedras
Mabaruma

PRESA GURI
Cerro Bolívar 802 m — Ciudad Piar
El Manteco
Guasipati
El Callao
Tumeremo

BARIMA-WAINI
Charity
POMEROON-SUPÉNAAM
Anna Regina
Queenstown
Suddie
Baramita

VENEZUELA
Guiana
Highlands

Cerro Guanay 2,300 m
Cerro Yavi 2,441 m
Salto Pará
El Casabe
Las Trincheras
La Paragua
El Dorado

BOLÍVAR
Salto Hacha
PARQUE — Salto del Ángel (Angel Falls)
Auyán-Tepui 1,890 — Cerro Venamo 2,950 m
Uruyén — Uonquén
NACIONAL — *La Gran Sabana*
Urimán — Roraim
Chimantá-Tepui 2,342 m — Monte Roraima 2,772 m
Apurúren — Perai-tepui
CANAIMA
Santa Maria de Erebató
Guaina
Santa Elena de Uairén
Icabarú

Carabobo
Tumereng
Cataratas de Surwakwima
Kamarang
Monte Ayanganna 2,042 m
Kangaruma
PN KAIETEUR
Tumatumari — Mahdia
Kwakwani

CUYUNI-MAZARUNI
Aurora
Cataratas de Kamaria
Bartica
Rockstone
Linden

ESSEQUIBO IS.-W. DEMERARA
Vreed-en-Hoop
Georgetown
TIMEHRI
Mahaica — Mahaicony Village
DEMERARA
MAHAICA
Fort Wellington
MAHAICA-BERBICE
New Amsterdam
Corriverton
Nieuw-Nickerie
Totness — CORONIE
NICKERIE
Calcutta — Groningen
Lelydorp

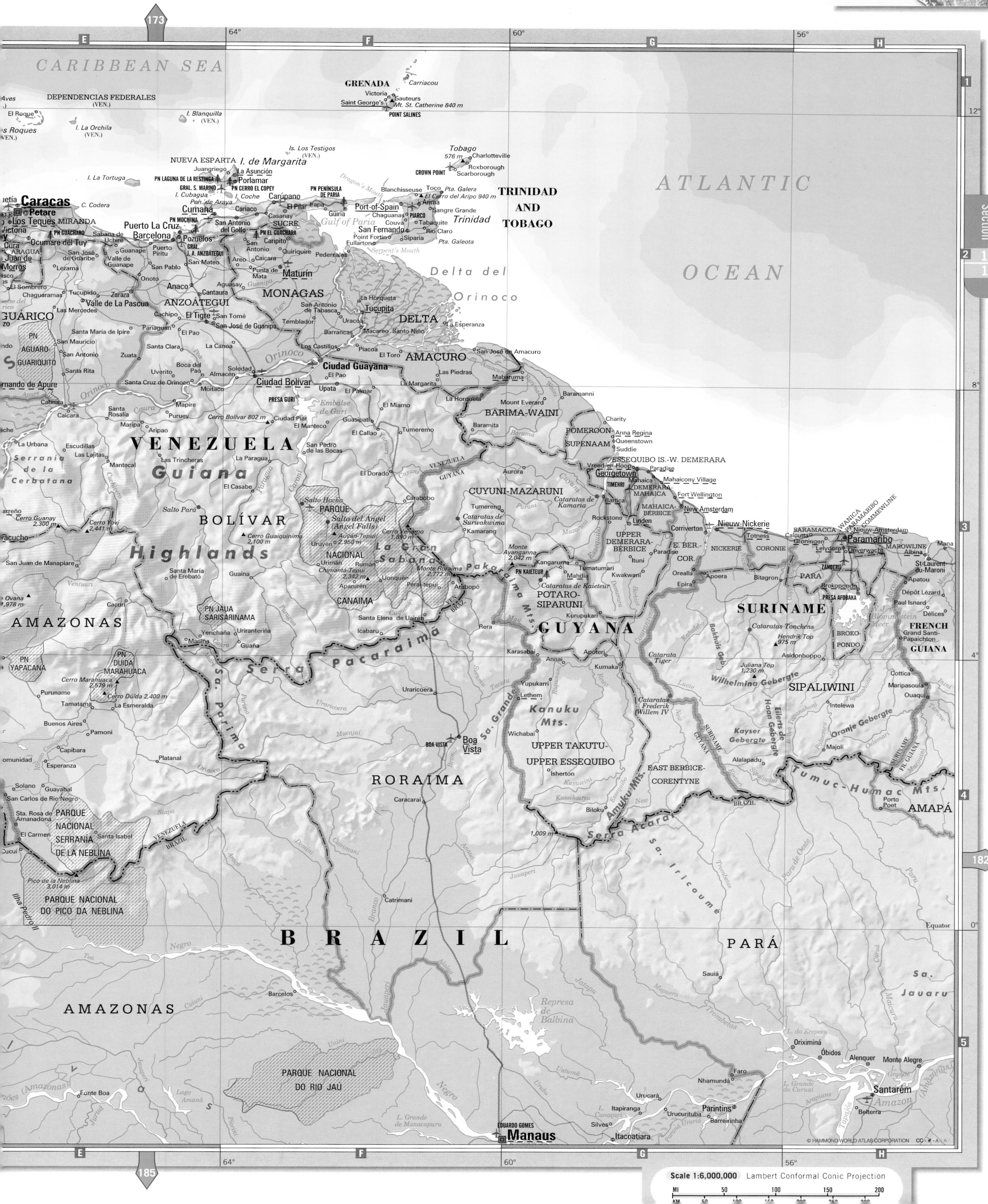

SURINAME
Paramaribo
WANICA — PARAMARIBO
Nieuw-Amsterdam
COMMEWLINE
Albina — Mana
St-Laurent-du-Maroni
MAROWIJNE
Apatou

GUYANA
POTARO-SIPARUNI
Kurupukari
Cataratas de Kaieteur
Kúrupung
Rera
Karasabai
Annai
Apoteri
Kumaka
Yupukarri
Lethem

UPPER DEMERARA-BERBICE
Ituni
Paradise
E. BER.-COR.
Apoera
Oealla
Epira

PARA
ZANDERIJ
Brokopondo — PRESA AFOBAKA
BROKO-PONDO
PARA

SIPALIWINI
Juliana Top 1,230 m
Wilhelmina Gebergte
Kayser Gebergte
Eilerts de Haan Gebergte
Oranje Gebergte
Cataratas Tonckens
Hendrik Top 975 m
Asidonhoppo
Alalapadu
Majoli

FRENCH GUIANA
Grand Santi-Papaïchton
Dépôt Lézard
Paul Isnard
Délices
Ouaqui
Maripasoula
Cottica

AMAZONAS
PN YAPACANA
PN DUIDA MARAHUACA
Cerro Marahuaca 2,579 m
Cerro Duida 2,400 m
Puruname
Tamatama
La Esmeralda
Buenos Aires
Pamoni
Capibara
Platanal
Solano
Guayabal
San Carlos de Río Negro
Sta. Rosa de Amanadona
Santa Isabel
El Carmen
Cucui
PARQUE NACIONAL SERRANÍA DE LA NEBLINA
Pico de la Neblina 3,014 m
PARQUE NACIONAL DO PICO DA NEBLINA

Serra Pacaraimá
Pakaraima Mts.
Sa. Parima

BOA VISTA
Boa Vista
Uraricoera
Uraricá
Caracaraí

RORAIMA
Catrimani

UPPER TAKUTU-UPPER ESSEQUIBO
Ishertón
Kanuku Mts.
Wichabai
Karasabai
Bilóku
Aishalton

EAST BERBICE-CORENTYNE
Cataratas Frederik Willem IV
Kwakwani
1,009 m

Serra Acaraí
Tumuc-Humac Mts.
Porto Poet

AMAPÁ

BRAZIL
AMAZONAS
Barcelos
Fonte Boa
PARQUE NACIONAL DO RIO JAÚ
Eduardo Gomes
Manaus

PARÁ
Sauiá
Oriximiná — Óbidos
Alenquer — Monte Alegre
Faro
Nhamundá
Parintins
Uricurá
Itapiranga
Uruará
Silves
Itacoatiara
Barreirinha
Santarém
Belterra

Rio Negro
Amazon
Represa de Balbina
L. Grande de Manacapuru
Represa de Curuá
Manaus

© HAMMOND WORLD ATLAS CORPORATION

Scale 1:6,000,000   Lambert Conformal Conic Projection
MI   50   100   150   200
KM

The Amazon Basin of northern Brazil comprises the world's largest rain forest, an area covering some 4.5 million square km. The Amazon, its more than 200 tributaries, and the vast rain forest are home to over one million different species of plants and animals. Millions of acres of this vital ecosystem are destroyed every year. Without its protective cover of foliage, the exposed, sensitive soil hardens into unfertile laterite and is subject to heavy erosion. The Amazon Basin has an average relative humidity of 90 percent and receives up to 4,000 mm of precipitation per year.

Guianas, Northern Brazil

Scale 1:6,000,000   Lambert Conformal Conic Projection

A unique feature of the climate of the west coast of South America is the El Niño phenomenon, which occurs about every three to seven years. At these times, temperatures rise in the equatorial coastal waters, drastically reducing the amount of nutrient-rich cold water that ascends from the depths to the surface and thus decimating the fish population. Unusually heavy rainfall in Peru and Ecuador resulting from El Niño has been known to cause severe landslides on the steep mountain slopes. The Andes reach their widest point in Bolivia, where the Cordillera Occidental and the Cordillera Oriental frame the expansive Bolivian highland, the Altiplano, which grows progressively more arid south of Lake Titicaca and culminates in a high desert.

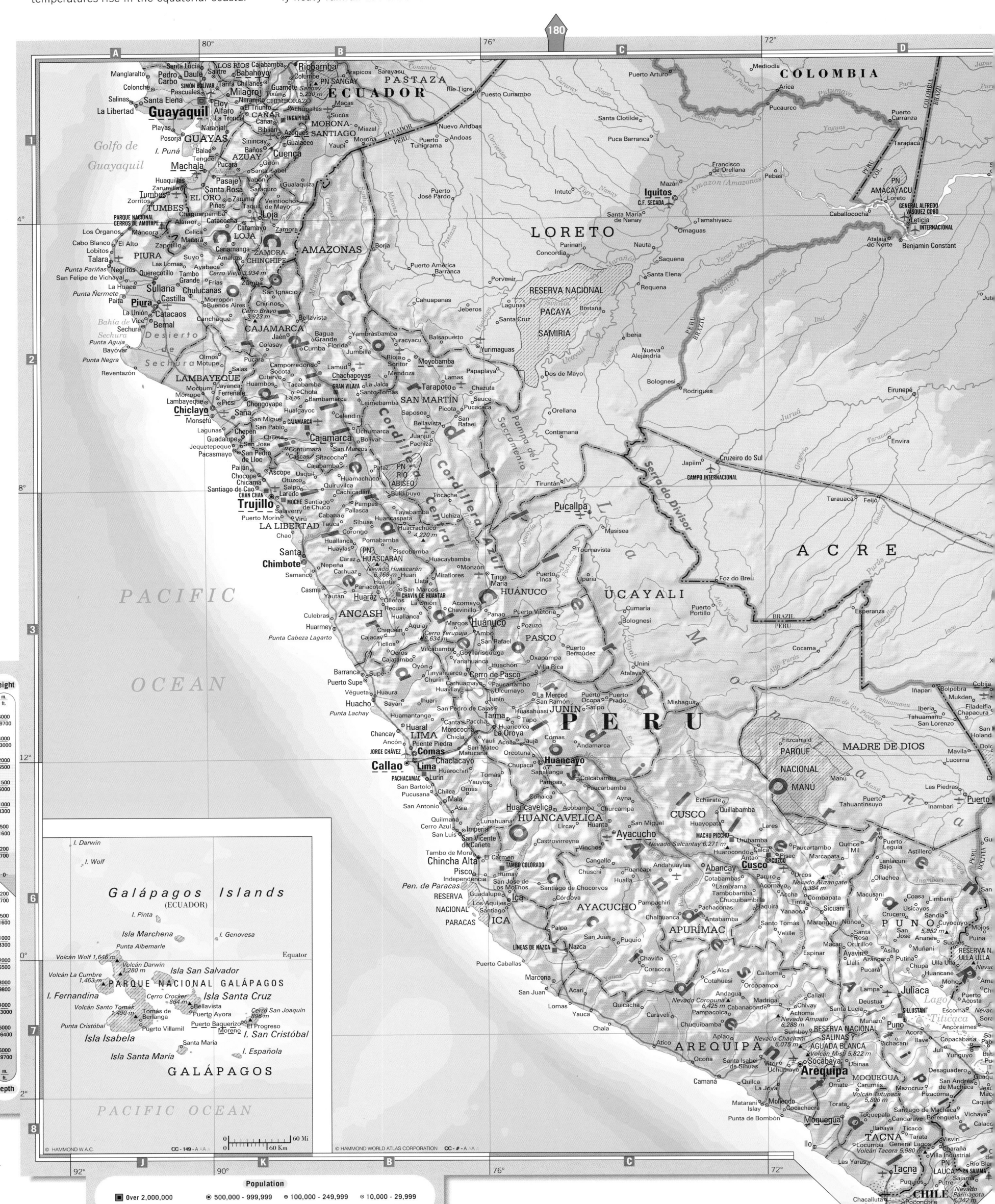

PARQUE NACIONAL DO RIO JAÚ

Sólimões (Amazonas)
Maraã
Igarapé Água Preta
Fonte Boa
L. Amanã
L. Piorini
L. Badajós
L. Grande de Manacapuru
Negro
EDUARDO GOMES
Manaus
Manacapuru
Careiro
Codajás
Anori
Itacoatiara
Nova Olinda do Norte
Silves
Itapiranga
Itacoatiara
Urucará
Urucurituba
Parintins
Barreirinha
Faro
Nhamundá
Urucuriá
Oriximiná
Óbidos
Alenquer
Santarém
Belterra
Juruti
Maués
Autazes
Borba
Antônio
Içá
Tefé
L. Tefé
Tefé
Coari
L. de Coari
Uruç
Uruá
Madeirinha

PARQUE NACIONAL DE AMAZÔNIA (TAPAJÓS)
Itaituba
Entre Rios

A M A Z O N A S

P A R Á

Carauari
Tapauá
Canutama
Tapauá
Pinhuã
Lábrea
Pauini
Pauini
Manicoré
Novo Aripuanã
Jacareacanga

B e l v a s

B R A Z I L

RESERVA FLORESTAL MUNDURUCÂNIA

Bôca do Acre
Humaitá
Sumaúma
Calama
Sa. de São João
Serra do Cachimbo

Porto Velho
Manoa
Abunã
Fortaleza
Puerto General Ovando
Triunfo
Villa Bella
Ariquemes
Alta Floresta

RONDÔNIA
Jaru
Ji-Paraná (Rondônia)
Presidente Médici
Cacoal
Espigão d'Oeste
Pimenta Bueno
Rolim de Moura
Aripuanã

RESERVA FLORESTAL DO JURUENA

Sinop

Rio Branco
Santos Mercado
Nuevo Mundo
Santo Domingo
San Pedro
Loma Alta
Guajará-Mirim
Guayaramerín
Riberalta
Las Piedras
Ivón
Pollar
PANDO
Nacebe
RESERVA NACIONAL MANURIPI HEATH
AMAZONICA
Maravillas
Sena
Concepción
Tres Mapajos
Santa Rosa
PARQUE NACIONAL DOS PÁCAAS NOVOS
Serra dos Pácaas Novos

Serra do Norte
Serra do Tombador
Serra dos Apiacás
RESERVA FLORESTAL
Serra dos Caiabis

MATO GROSSO

Asunción
Pedro
Bolívar
Todos Santos
Fortaleza
El Perú
Rosario
Alejandría
Mayo Mayo
Costa Marques
La Horquilla
Versalles
Remanso
Vilhena
Colorado do Oeste

Serra do Providência
Serra Grande
Serra dos Parecis

Benavides
Barrera
Cavinas
Yata
Carrito
Chalamama
Las Pampitas
San Joaquín
San Ramón
Exaltación
Mateguá
San Simón
Puerto Villazón
Piso Firme
Bella Vista
Arenápolis
Diamantino
Nortelândia
Nobres
Rosário Oeste

Laguna Rogaguado
José Agustín Palacios
Santa Ana
Soberanía
San Miguel
Nieve
Las Petas
El Pilar
Magdalena
Huacaraje
Bauris
Orobayaya
Puerto Alegre
Porvenir
Alto Paraguai
Tangará da Serra
Barra do Bugres

Laguna Huatunas
Yata
El Carmen

Laguna San Luis
La Esperanza
Huachi
San Cristóbal
San Martín
Puerto Frey
Monte Cristo
La Esperanza
El Pensamiento
Perseverancia
Vila Bela da Santíssima Trindade
Pontes e Lacerda
Nova Brasilândia
Acorizal

Planalto do Mato Grosso

B E N I
Llanos de Mojos
Reyes
San Borja
Chevejécure
San Ignacio
Puerto Leigue
San Pedro
Puerto Ballivián
San Javier
Trinidad
Puerto Almacén
Sachojere
San Andrés
San Antonio
Loreto
Yaguarú
Urubichá
La Unión
Puerto Arturo
Cuiabá
Várzea Grande
Santo Antônio do Levergo
Dom Aquino

Laguna Rogagua
La Embocada
Puerto Pando
Muchanes
Puerto Canoa
San Francisco
Puerto Calvimonte
San Lorenzo
Limoquije
Los Cusis
Santa María
San Pablo
Ascención
Cuyuchi
San Diego
BOLIVIA
San Ramón
La Esperanza
San Pedro de Cururu
Cáceres
Jaciara

PARQUE NACIONAL ISIBORO SÉCURE

Asunta
Irupana
Araopongo
Puerto Patiño
Puerto Torno
Puerto Velarde
San Javier
San Ignacio
Santa Rosa de la Roca
San Ignacio
Santa Ana
Las Petas
San Matías
Poconé
Poxoreo
Rondonópolis

COCHABAMBA
nevado Illimani 6,462 m
Inquisivi
Cajuata
Circuata
Quime
Independencia
Morochata
SAN JOSÉ DE LA BANDA
Corani
Sacaba
Quillacollo
Cochabamba
Punata
Arani
Pocona
Cerro Bravo 3,201 m

Paléduro
Yaco
Cavari
Lanza
Caxata
Colquiri
Tapacari
Tarata
Cliza
San Carlos
Pojo
Chimoré
Puerto Grether
Santa Rosa
San Ignacio del Sara
La Esperanza
Motacucito
Santa María
San Miguelito
Esperancita
Candelaria

Puerto Mamoré
Puerto Villarroel
Cuatro Ojos
Palmarito
Santa Rosa del Palmar
San Miguel
San Rafael
Caucas
Candelaria

SANTA CRUZ
San Javier
San Pedro
El Puente
Cañada Larga
Pozo del Tigre
El Cerro
Puesto de Pailas
San Luis

MATO GROSSO DO SUL
Itiquira

Buena Vista
Montero
Warnes
Portachuelo
Madrecitas
Tocomechi

Laguna Concepción
Laguna Mandioré

Barão de Melgaço

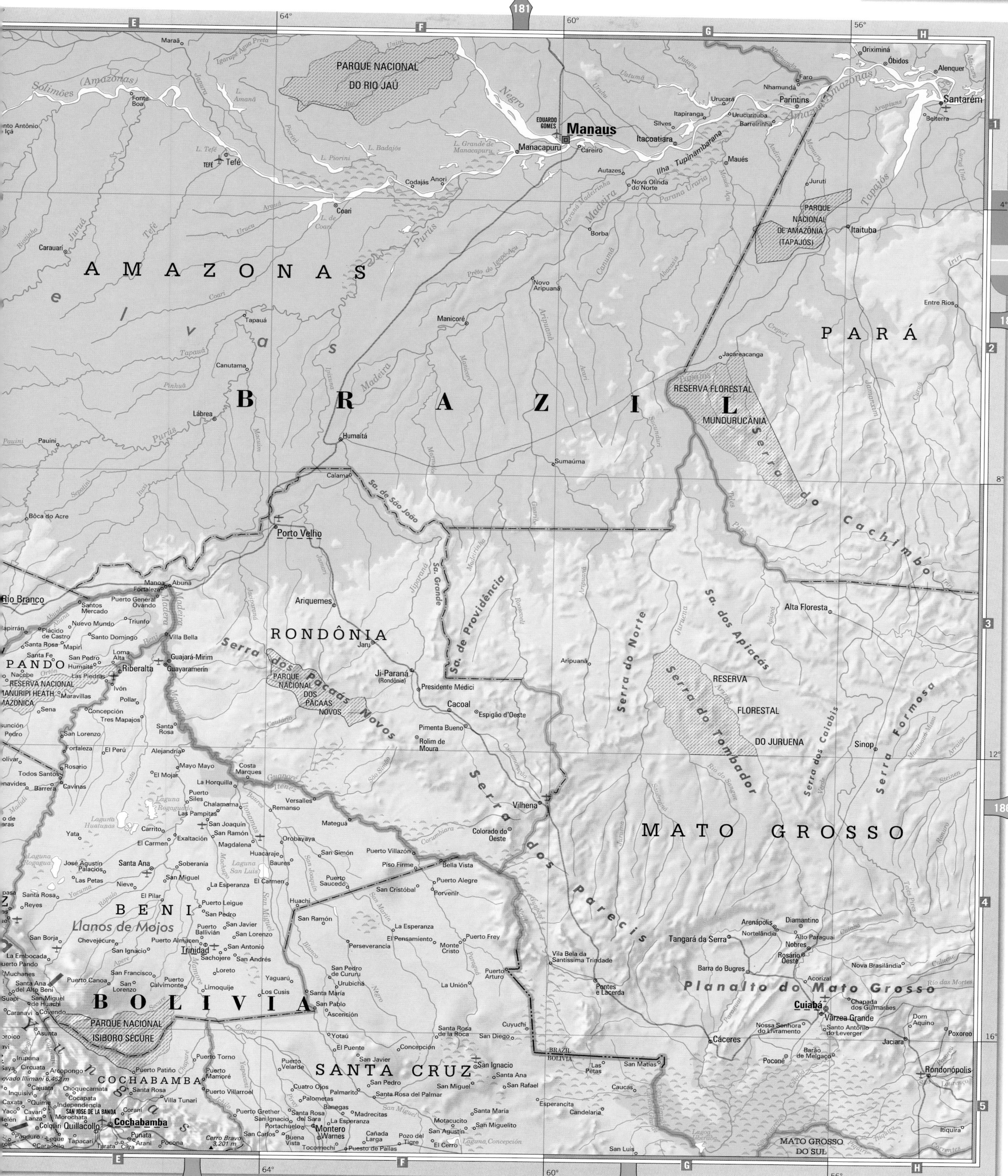

Scale 1:6,000,000 Lambert Conformal Conic Projection

MI   50   100   150   200
KM 50   100   150   200   250

Brazil is the fifth largest country on earth and covers nearly half of the South American continent. Its tropical-subtropical climate and extensive highlands provide ideal conditions for the cultivation of coffee.

The very old underlying rock is also rich in iron ore, gold, and diamonds. The most important energy source - water - is harnessed effectively in the Paraná River system (Itaipú hydroelectric plant). Substantial

oil reserves have been discovered off the coast near Rio de Janeiro. Eighty percent of the population lives in the cities, the largest of which are Sao Paulo and Rio de Janeiro.

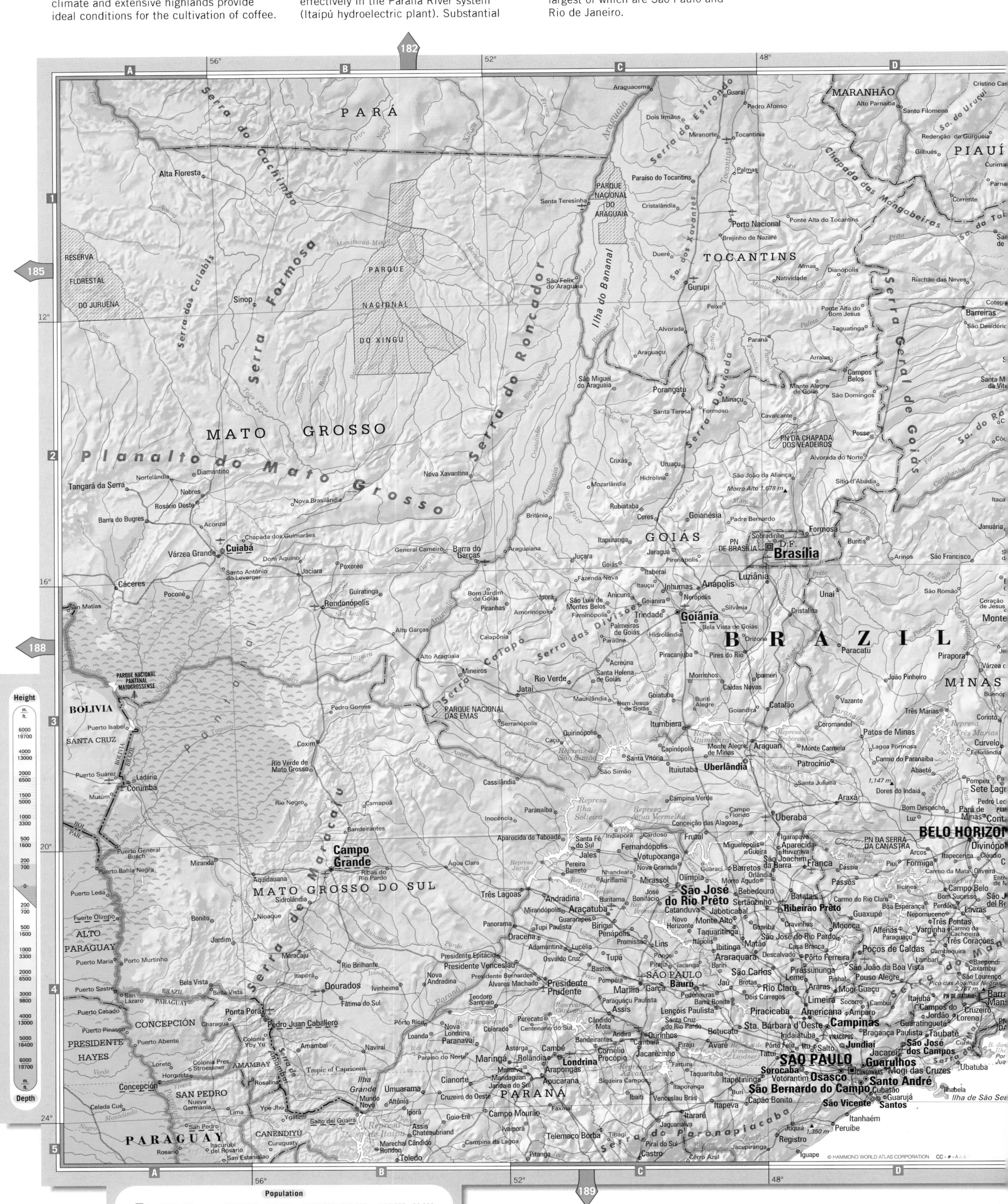

Population

■ Over 2,000,000   ● 500,000 - 999,999   ● 100,000 - 249,999   ○ 10,000 - 29,999

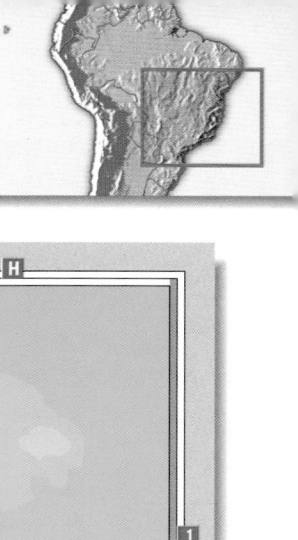

183

ATLANTIC OCEAN

Scale 1:6,000,000 Lambert Conformal Conic Projection

MI 50 100 150 200
KM 50 100 150 200 250 300

© HAMMOND WORLD ATLAS CORPORATION CC - 1150 - A

Map Section 186 187

Major places

PERNAMBUCO · Petrolina · Juazeiro · Paulo Afonso · Maceió · ALAGOAS · Arapiraca · Penedo · Aracajú · SERGIPE · São Cristóvão · Estância · Feira de Santana · Santo Amaro · Candeias · Camaçari · Simões Filho · SALVADOR · Valença · Jequié · Itabuna · Ilhéus · Canavieiras · Belmonte · Porto Seguro · Itamaraju · Nanuque · Caravelas

BAHIA · Irecê · Jacobina · Senhor do Bonfim · Morro do Chapéu · Seabra · PN CHAPADA DIAMANTINA · Brumado · Vitória da Conquista · Guanambi · Espinosa

Governador Valadares · ESPÍRITO SANTO · Colatina · Linhares · Serra · Vitória · Vila Velha · Guarapari · Cachoeiro de Itapemirim · Ipatinga · Coronel Fabriciano · Caratinga · Manhuaçu · PARQUE NACIONAL DO CAPARAÓ · Pico da Bandeira 2,899 m

RIO DE JANEIRO · Campos · Macaé · Cabo Frio · Nova Friburgo · Teresópolis · Duque de Caxias · Niterói · RIO DE JANEIRO

Tropic of Capricorn

Inset (São Paulo region)

Poços de Caldas · MINAS GERAIS · Juiz de Fora · Santos Dumont · São João Nepomuceno · Leopoldina · Cataguases · Três Corações · Varginha · Alfenas · Muzambinho · Guaxupé · Mococa · São José do Rio Pardo · Campinas · Jundiaí · Vinhedo · Valinhos · Americana · Amparo · Bragança Paulista · Atibaia · Guarulhos · Osasco · SÃO PAULO · Santo André · São Bernardo do Campo · Diadema · Mogi das Cruzes · São José dos Campos · Jacareí · Taubaté · Pindamonhangaba · Guaratinguetá · Lorena · Cruzeiro · Resende · Barra Mansa · Volta Redonda · Barra do Piraí · Vassouras · Petrópolis · Teresópolis · Nova Iguaçu · São João de Meriti · Nilópolis · Duque de Caxias · Itaguaí · Niterói · São Gonçalo · Magé · Itaboraí · RIO DE JANEIRO · PARQUE NACIONAL DA TIJUCA · Corcovado · Três Rios · Nova Friburgo · Juiz de Fora · Serra da Mantiqueira · Serra do Mar · PN DE ITATIAIA · Pico das Agulhas Negras 2,787 m · Angra dos Reis · Ilha Grande · Ubatuba · Caraguatatuba · Ilhabela · São Sebastião · Santos · São Vicente · Praia Grande · Guarujá · Itanhaém · Peruíbe · Ilha de Santo Amaro · Ilha de São Sebastião · Ilha de Alcatrazes

ATLANTIC OCEAN

Tropic of Capricorn

0 30 Mi
0 30 Km

The Gran Chaco, South America's vast heartland, through which the many tributaries of the Paraguay and the Paraná flow, has a hot, subtropical climate with heavy precipitation in the east and much drier conditions in the west. The winds blowing inland from the Pacific travel over cold ocean currents and thus carry little moisture. The prevailing climate has produced coastal deserts in Chile and Peru, where average precipitation often falls below 4 mm. One such desert is the Atacama, an arid region rich in ore deposits where the mean annual temperature is a moderate 66° F.

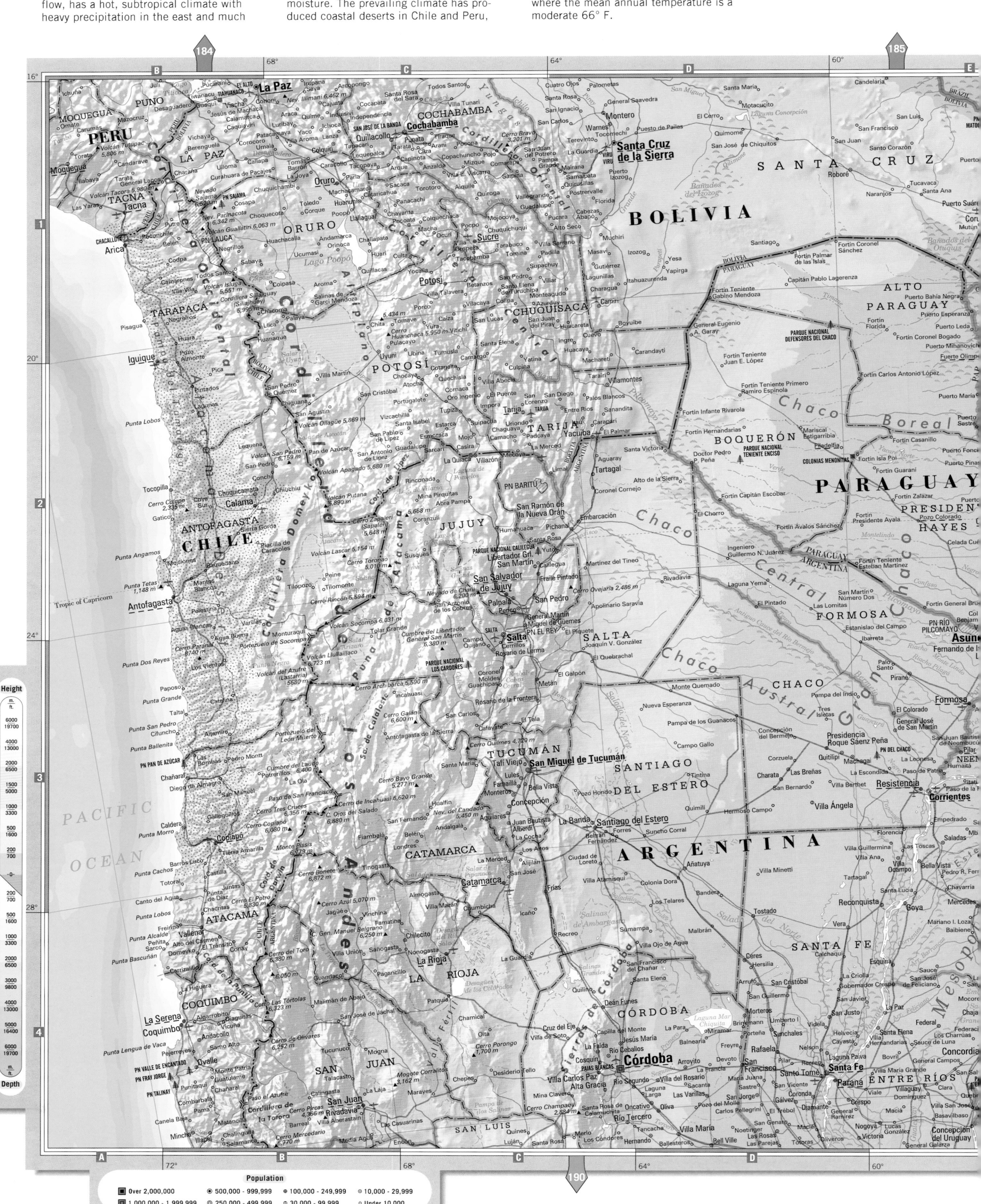

Population
■ Over 2,000,000   ◉ 500,000 - 999,999   ◎ 100,000 - 249,999   ⊙ 10,000 - 29,999
▣ 1,000,000 - 1,999,999   ⊚ 250,000 - 499,999   ⊙ 30,000 - 99,999   ○ Under 10,000

Scale 1:6,000,000   Lambert Conformal Conic Projection

© HAMMOND WORLD ATLAS CORPORATION

The expansive grasslands of Argentina, the Pampas, were probably covered with light forest growth before settlers began clearing the land for wheat farming and to provide grazing land for cattle. With good access to shipping routes, the area around the mouths of the Paraná and Uruguay rivers is one of South America's most important economic regions. Climatic conditions in the south are extreme, both in east Patagonia, with its salt swamps, and in Tierra del Fuego, where storms off Cape Horn have been the bane of seafarers for centuries.

URUGUAY

BRAZIL

RIO GRANDE DO SUL

SALTO

TACUAREMBÓ

CERRO LARGO

DURAZNO

FLORES

TREINTA Y TRES

LAVALLEJA

FLORIDA

ROCHA

MALDONADO

Montevideo

CARRASCO

PUNTA DEL ESTE (CAPITÁN CURBELO)

Punta del Este

PARQUE NACIONAL SANTA TERESA

Cabo Polonio

ENTRE RÍOS

URUGUAY

ARGENTINA

RÍO NEGRO

DURAZNO

PAYSANDÚ

TACUAREMBÓ

SORIANO

FLORES

FLORIDA

COLONIA

SAN JOSÉ

CANELONES

BUENOS AIRES

Tigre
Vicente López
San Fernando
General San Martín
Morón
Merlo
Avellaneda
Lanús
Lomas de Zamora
La Plata
Colonia del Sacramento
MONTEVIDEO
Montevideo

BUENOS AIRES

ATLANTIC OCEAN

0   30 Mi
0   30 Km

© HAMMOND W.A.C.   CD - 1175 - A A A

ATLANTIC OCEAN

Same scale as main map

ARGENTINA

SANTA CRUZ

Gran Altiplanicie Central

Patagonia

Cordillera de los Andes

AISÉN DEL GENERAL CARLOS IBÁÑEZ DEL CAMPO

PARQUE NACIONAL LAGUNA SAN RAFAEL

PN PERITO MORENO

PN LOS GLACIARES

PN BERNARDO O'HIGGINS

PN TORRES DEL PAINE

Río Gallegos

CHILE

MAGALLANES Y DE LA ANTÁRTICA CHILENA

PARQUE NACIONAL PALI AIKE

PARQUE NACIONAL LOS PINGÜINOS

Punta Arenas

Isla Grande de Tierra del Fuego

Río Grande

TIERRA DEL FUEGO, ANTÁRTIDA E ISLAS DEL ATLÁNTICO SUR

PN TIERRA DEL FUEGO

Ushuaia

PARQUE NACIONAL ALBERTO DE AGOSTINI

FALKLAND ISLANDS
(ISLAS MALVINAS)
(U.K. -- Claimed by Argentina)

West Falkland

East Falkland

Stanley

MOUNT PLEASANT

PACIFIC OCEAN

PN CABO DE HORNOS

Cape Horn

Drake Passage

© HAMMOND WORLD ATLAS CORPORATION   CD - 159 - A A

Scale 1:6,000,000   Lambert Conformal Conic Projection

MI   50   100   150   200
KM   50   100   150   200   250   300

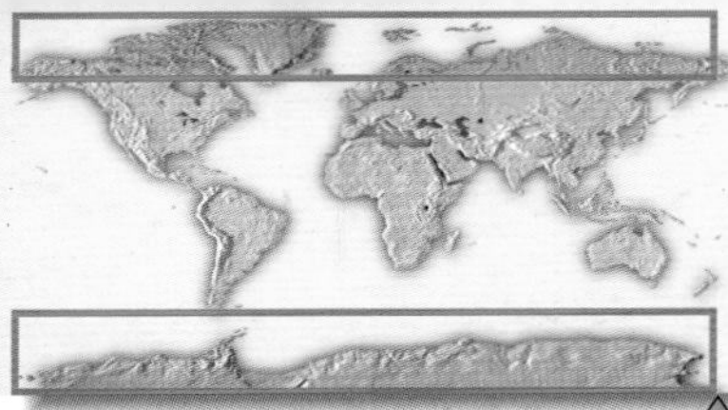

Arctic Regions, Antarctica

Polar climates extend from the poles in the direction of the equator up to a line along which average temperatures during the warmest month do not exceed 40° F. Except for Greenland, the Arctic is a landless region of sea and ice. Antarc… is the coldest, driest continent on earth… and has the highest average elevation. … record low temperature of -129.8° F wa… recorded at the Vostok Research Station…

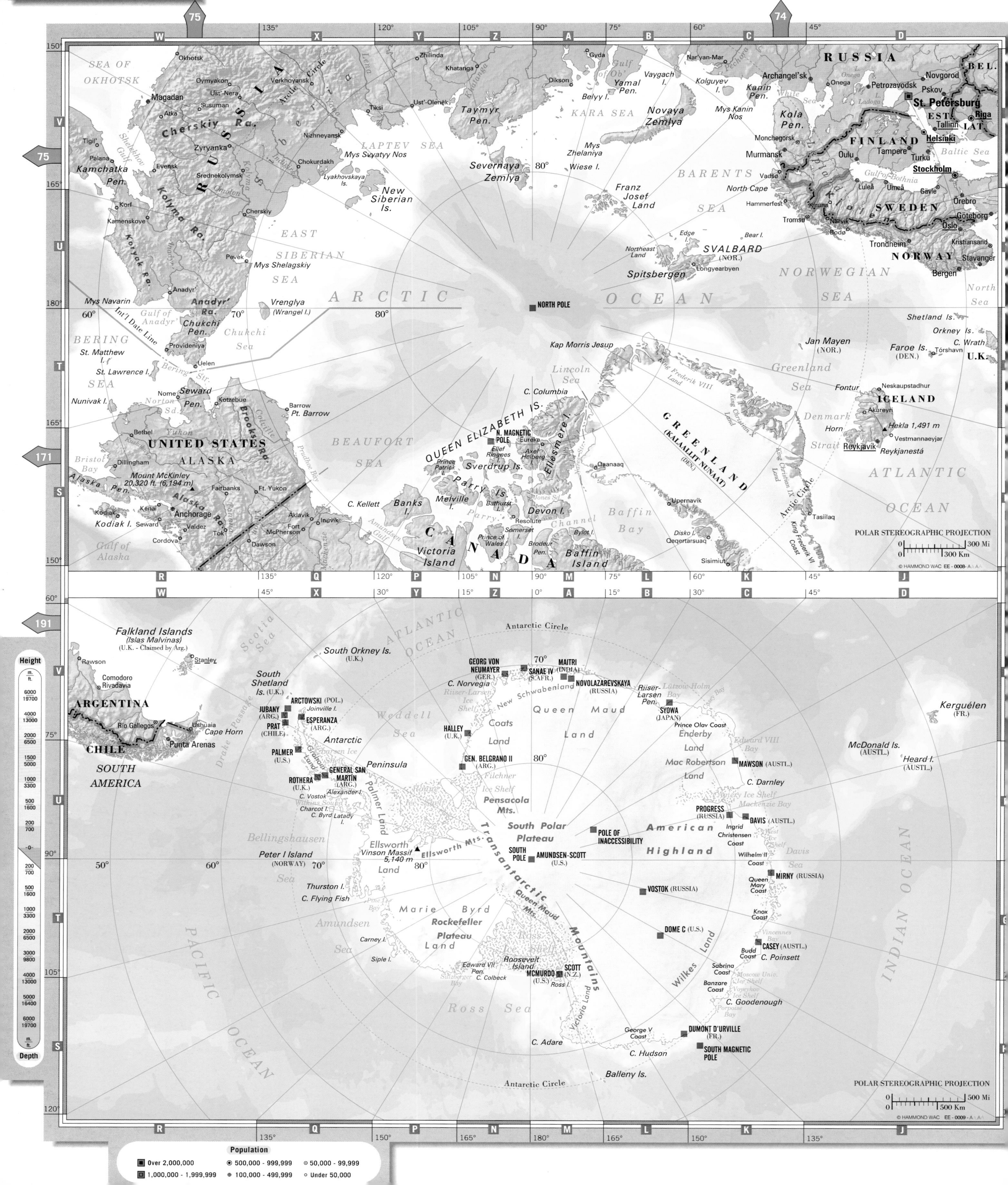

Statistical Tables and Index

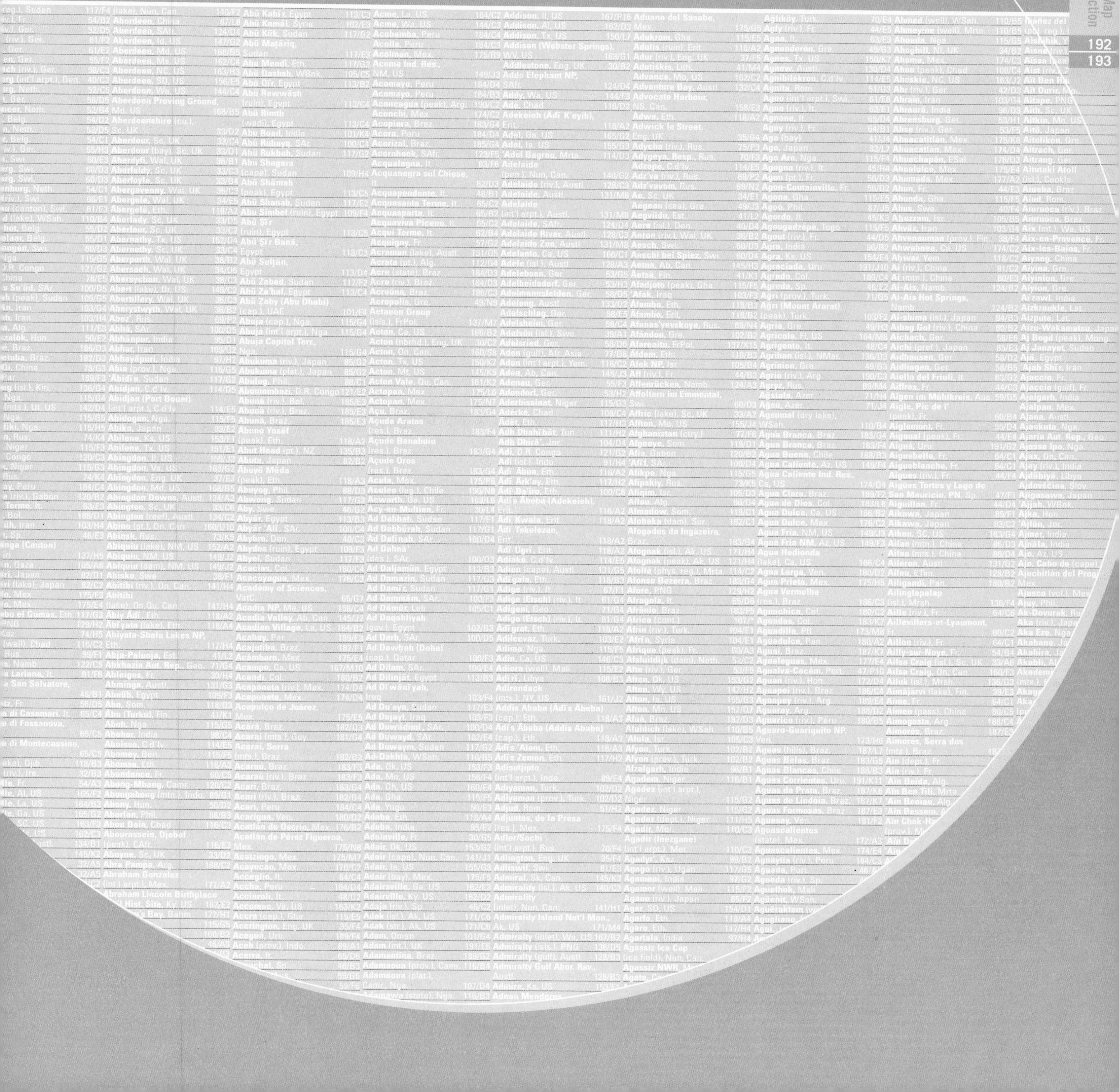

World Statistics

Elements of the Solar System

	Mean Distance from Sun: in Miles	in Kilometers	Period of Revolution around Sun	Period of Rotation on Axis	Equatorial Diameter in Miles	in Kilometers	Surface Gravity (Earth = 1)	Mass (Earth = 1)	Mean Density (Water = 1)	Number of Satellites
Mercury	35,990,000	57,900,000	87.97 days	58.7 days	3,032	4,880	0.38	0.055	5.4	0
Venus	67,240,000	108,200,000	224.70 days	243 days†	7,521	12,104	0.91	0.815	5.2	0
Earth	93,000,000	149,700,000	365.26 days	23h 56m	7,926	12,755	1.00	1.00	5.5	1
Mars	141,610,000	227,900,000	686.98 days	24h 37m	4,221	6,794	0.38	0.107	3.9	2
Jupiter	483,675,000	778,400,000	11.86 years	9h 55m	88,846	142,984	2.36	317.8	1.3	39
Saturn	890,800,000	1,433,500,000	29.46 years	10h 30m	74,898	120,536	0.92	95.2	0.7	30
Uranus	1,784,800,000	2,872,500,000	84.01 years	17h 14m†	31,763	51,118	0.89	14.5	1.3	21
Neptune	2,793,100,000	4,495,100,000	164.79 years	16h 6m	30,778	49,532	1.13	17.1	1.6	8
Pluto	3,647,000,000	5,870,000,000	247.70 years	6.4 days†	1,485	2,390	0.07	0.002	2.1	1

† Retrograde motion

Source: NASA, National Space Science Center

Dimensions of the Earth

	Area in: Sq. Miles	Sq. Kilometers
Superficial area	196,939,000	510,072,000
Land surface	57,506,000	148,940,000
Water surface	139,433,000	361,132,000

	Distance in: Miles	Kilometers
Equatorial circumference	24,902	40,075
Polar circumference	24,860	40,007
Equatorial diameter	7,926.4	12,756.4
Polar diameter	7,899.8	12,713.6
Equatorial radius	3,963.2	6,378.2
Polar radius	3,949.9	6,356.8

Volume of the Earth	2.6×10^{11} cubic miles	10.84×10^{11} cubic kilometers
Mass or weight	6.6×10^{21} short tons	6.0×10^{21} metric tons
Maximum distance from Sun	94,600,000 miles	152,000,000 kilometers
Minimum distance from Sun	91,300,000 miles	147,000,000 kilometers

Oceans and Major Seas

	Area in: Sq. Miles	Sq. Kms.	Greatest Depth in: Feet	Meters
Pacific Ocean	63,855,000	165,384,000	36,198	11,033
Atlantic Ocean	31,744,000	82,217,000	28,374	8,648
Indian Ocean	28,417,000	73,600,000	25,344	7,725
Arctic Ocean	5,427,000	14,056,000	17,880	5,450
Caribbean Sea	970,000	2,512,300	24,720	7,535
Mediterranean Sea	969,000	2,509,700	16,896	5,150
South China Sea	895,000	2,318,000	15,000	4,600
Bering Sea	875,000	2,266,250	15,800	4,800
Gulf of Mexico	600,000	1,554,000	12,300	3,750
Sea of Okhotsk	590,000	1,528,100	11,070	3,370
East China Sea	482,000	1,248,400	9,500	2,900
Yellow Sea	480,000	1,243,200	350	107
Sea of Japan	389,000	1,007,500	12,280	3,740
Hudson Bay	317,500	822,300	846	258
North Sea	222,000	575,000	2,200	670
Black Sea	185,000	479,150	7,365	2,245
Red Sea	169,000	437,700	7,200	2,195
Baltic Sea	163,000	422,170	1,506	459

The Continents

	Area in: Sq. Miles	Sq. Kms.	Percent of World's Land
Asia	17,159,867	44,444,100	29.8
Africa	11,701,147	30,306,000	20.3
North America	9,355,975	24,232,000	16.3
South America	6,879,916	17,819,000	12.0
Antarctica	5,500,000	14,245,000	9.6
Europe	4,066,019	10,531,000	7.1
Australia	2,967,893	7,686,850	5.1

Major Ship Canals

	Length in: Miles	Kms.	Minimum Depth in: Feet	Meters
Volga-Baltic, Russia	225	362	–	–
Baltic-White Sea, Russia	140	225	16	5
Suez, Egypt	100.76	162	42	13
Albert, Belgium	80	129	16.5	5
Moscow-Volga, Russia	80	129	18	6
Volga-Don, Russia	62	100	–	–
Göta, Sweden	54	87	10	3
Kiel (Nord-Ostsee), Germany	53.2	86	38	12
Panama Canal, Panama	50.72	82	41.6	13
Houston Ship, U.S.A.	50	81	36	11

Largest Islands

	Area in: Sq. Miles	Sq. Kms.
Greenland	840,000	2,175,600
New Guinea	305,000	789,950
Borneo	286,000	740,740
Madagascar	226,656	587,040
Baffin, Canada	195,928	507,454
Sumatra, Indonesia	164,000	424,760
Honshu, Japan	88,000	227,920
Great Britain	84,400	218,896
Victoria, Canada	83,896	217,290
Ellesmere, Canada	75,767	196,236
Celebes, Indonesia	72,986	189,034
South I., New Zealand	58,393	151,238
Java, Indonesia	48,842	126,501
North I., New Zealand	44,187	114,444
Cuba	42,803	110,860
Newfoundland, Canada	42,031	108,860
Luzon, Philippines	40,420	104,688
Iceland	39,768	103,000
Mindanao, Philippines	36,537	94,631
Ireland	32,589	84,406
Hokkaido, Japan	30,436	78,829
Sakhalin, Russia	29,500	76,405

	Area in: Sq. Miles	Sq. Kms.
Hispaniola, Haiti & Dom. Rep.	29,399	76,143
Banks, Canada	27,038	70,028
Ceylon, Sri Lanka	25,332	65,610
Tasmania, Australia	24,600	63,710
Svalbard, Norway	23,957	62,049
Devon, Canada	21,331	55,247
Novaya Zemlya (north isl.), Russia	18,600	48,200
Marajó, Brazil	17,991	46,597
Tierra del Fuego, Chile & Argentina	17,900	46,360
Alexander, Antarctica	16,700	43,250
Axel Heiberg, Canada	16,671	43,178
Melville, Canada	16,274	42,150
Southampton, Canada	15,913	41,215
New Britain, Papua New Guinea	14,100	36,519
Taiwan	13,836	35,835
Kyushu, Japan	13,770	35,664
Hainan, China	13,127	33,999
Prince of Wales, Canada	12,872	33,338
Spitsbergen, Norway	12,355	31,999
Vancouver, Canada	12,079	31,285
Timor, Indonesia	11,527	29,855
Sicily, Italy	9,926	25,708

	Area in: Sq. Miles	Sq. Kms.
Somerset, Canada	9,570	24,786
Sardinia, Italy	9,301	24,090
Shikoku, Japan	6,860	17,767
New Caledonia, France	6,530	16,913
Nordaustlandet, Norway	6,409	16,599
Samar, Philippines	5,050	13,080
Negros, Philippines	4,906	12,707
Palawan, Philippines	4,550	11,785
Panay, Philippines	4,446	11,515
Jamaica	4,232	10,961
Hawaii, United States	4,038	10,458
Viti Levu, Fiji	4,010	10,386
Cape Breton, Canada	3,981	10,311
Mindoro, Philippines	3,759	9,736
Kodiak, Alaska, U.S.A.	3,670	9,505
Cyprus	3,572	9,251
Puerto Rico, U.S.A.	3,435	8,897
Corsica, France	3,352	8,682
New Ireland, Papua New Guinea	3,340	8,651
Crete, Greece	3,218	8,335
Anticosti, Canada	3,066	7,941
Wrangel, Russia	2,819	7,301

Principal Mountains

Mountain	Height in: Feet	Meters
Everest, Nepal-China	29,028	8,848
K2 (Godwin Austen), Pakistan-China	28,250	8,611
Kanchenjunga, Nepal-India	28,208	8,598
Lhotse, Nepal-China	27,923	8,511
Makalu, Nepal-China	27,789	8,470
Dhaulagiri, Nepal	26,810	8,172
Nanga Parbat, Pakistan	26,660	8,126
Annapurna, Nepal	26,504	8,078
Nanda Devi, India	25,645	7,817
Rakaposhi, Pakistan	25,550	7,788
Kongur Shan, China	25,325	7,719
Tirich Mir, Pakistan	25,230	7,690
Gongga Shan, China	24,790	7,556
Ismail Samani Peak, Tajikistan	24,590	7,495
Pobedy Peak, Kyrgyzstan	24,406	7,439
Chomo Lhari, Bhutan-China	23,997	7,314
Muztag, China	23,891	7,282
Cerro Aconcagua, Argentina	22,831	6,959
Ojos del Salado, Chile-Argentina	22,572	6,880
Bonete, Chile-Argentina	22,546	6,872
Tupungato, Chile-Argentina	22,310	6,800

Mountain	Height in: Feet	Meters
Pissis, Argentina	22,241	6,779
Mercedario, Argentina	22,211	6,770
Huascarán, Peru	22,205	6,768
Llullaillaco, Chile-Argentina	22,057	6,723
Nevada Ancohuma, Bolivia	21,489	6,550
Chimborazo, Ecuador	20,561	6,267
McKinley, Alaska	20,320	6,194
Logan, Yukon, Canada	19,524	5,951
Cotopaxi, Ecuador	19,347	5,897
Kilimanjaro, Tanzania	19,340	5,895
El Misti, Peru	19,101	5,822
Pico Cristóbal Colón, Colombia	18,947	5,775
Huila, Colombia	18,865	5,750
Citlaltépetl (Orizaba), Mexico	18,700	5,700
Damavand, Iran	18,605	5,671
El'brus, Russia	18,510	5,642
St. Elias, Alaska, U.S.A.-Yukon, Canada	18,008	5,489
Dykh-tau, Russia	17,070	5,203
Batian (Kenya), Kenya	17,058	5,199
Ararat, Turkey	16,946	5,165
Vinson Massif, Antarctica	16,864	5,140

Mountain	Height in: Feet	Meters
Margherita (Ruwenzori), Africa	16,795	5,119
Kazbek, Georgia-Russia	16,558	5,047
Puncak Jaya, Indonesia	16,503	5,030
Blanc, France	15,771	4,807
Klyuchevskaya Sopka, Russia	15,584	4,750
Fairweather, Br. Col., Canada	15,300	4,663
Dufourspitze (Mte. Rosa), Italy-Switzerland	15,203	4,634
Ras Dashen, Ethiopia	15,157	4,620
Matterhorn, Switzerland	14,691	4,478
Whitney, California, U.S.A.	14,494	4,418
Elbert, Colorado, U.S.A.	14,433	4,399
Rainier, Washington, U.S.A.	14,410	4,392
Shasta, California, U.S.A.	14,162	4,317
Pikes Peak, Colorado, U.S.A.	14,110	4,301
Finsteraarhorn, Switzerland	14,022	4,274
Mauna Kea, Hawaii, U.S.A.	13,796	4,205
Mauna Loa, Hawaii, U.S.A.	13,677	4,169
Jungfrau, Switzerland	13,642	4,158
Grossglockner, Austria	12,457	3,797
Fujiyama, Japan	12,389	3,776
Cook, New Zealand	12,349	3,764

Longest Rivers

River	Length in: Miles	Kms.
Nile, Africa	4,145	6,671
Amazon, S. America	4,007	6,448
Mississippi-Missouri-Red Rock, U.S.A.	3,710	5,971
Chang Jiang (Yangtze), China	3,500	5,633
Ob'-Irtysh, Russia-Kazakhstan	3,362	5,411
Yenisey-Angara, Russia	3,100	4,989
Huang He (Yellow), China	2,950	4,747
Congo, Africa	2,780	4,474
Amur-Shilka-Onon, Asia	2,744	4,416
Lena, Russia	2,734	4,400
Mackenzie-Peace-Finlay, Canada	2,635	4,241
Paraná-La Plata, S. America	2,630	4,232
Mekong, Asia	2,610	4,200
Niger, Africa	2,580	4,152
Missouri-Red Rock, U.S.A.	2,564	4,125
Yenisey, Russia	2,500	4,028
Mississippi, U.S.A.	2,348	3,778
Murray-Darling, Australia	2,310	3,718
Volga, Russia	2,290	3,685
Madeira, S. America	2,013	3,240
Purus, S. America	1,995	3,211
Yukon, Alaska-Canada	1,979	3,185
Zambezi, Africa	1,950	3,138
São Francisco, Brazil	1,930	3,106
St. Lawrence, Canada-U.S.A.	1,900	3,058

River	Length in: Miles	Kms.
Rio Grande, Mexico-U.S.A.	1,885	3,034
Syrdar'ya-Naryn, Asia	1,859	2,992
Indus, Asia	1,800	2,897
Danube, Europe	1,775	2,857
Brahmaputra, Asia	1,700	2,736
Tocantins, Brazil	1,677	2,699
Salween, Asia	1,675	2,696
Euphrates, Asia	1,650	2,655
Xi (Si), China	1,650	2,655
Amu Darya, Asia	1,616	2,601
Nelson-Saskatchewan, Canada	1,600	2,575
Orinoco, S. America	1,600	2,575
Paraguay, S. America	1,584	2,549
Kolyma, Russia	1,562	2,514
Ganges, Asia	1,550	2,494
Zhayyq (Ural), Kazakhstan-Russia	1,509	2,428
Japurá, S. America	1,500	2,414
Arkansas, U.S.A.	1,450	2,334
Colorado, U.S.A.-Mexico	1,450	2,334
Negro, S. America	1,400	2,253
Dnepr (Dnyapro, Dnipro), Russia-Belarus-Ukraine	1,368	2,202
Orange, Africa	1,350	2,173
Ayeyarwady, Myanmar	1,325	2,132
Brazos, U.S.A.	1,309	2,107
Ohio-Allegheny, U.S.A.	1,306	2,102

River	Length in: Miles	Kms.
Kama, Russia	1,252	2,031
Don, Russia	1,222	1,967
Red, U.S.A.	1,222	1,966
Columbia, U.S.A.-Canada	1,214	1,953
Tigris, Asia	1,181	1,901
Darling, Australia	1,160	1,867
Angara, Russia	1,135	1,827
Sungari, Asia	1,130	1,819
Pechora, Russia	1,124	1,809
Snake, U.S.A.	1,038	1,670
Churchill, Canada	1,000	1,609
Pilcomayo, S. America	1,000	1,609
Uruguay, S. America	994	1,600
Platte-N. Platte, U.S.A.	990	1,593
Ohio, U.S.A.	981	1,578
Magdalena, Colombia	956	1,538
Pecos, U.S.A.	926	1,490
Oka, Russia	918	1,477
Canadian, U.S.A.	906	1,458
Colorado, Texas, U.S.A.	894	1,439
Dnister (Nistru), Ukraine-Moldova	876	1,410
Fraser, Canada	850	1,369
Rhine, Europe	820	1,319
Northern Dvina, Russia	809	1,302
Ottawa, Canada	790	1,271

Principal Natural Lakes

Lake	Area in: Sq. Miles	Sq. Kms.	Max. Depth in: Feet	Meters
Caspian Sea, Asia	143,243	370,999	3,264	995
Lake Superior, U.S.A.-Canada	31,820	82,414	1,329	405
Lake Victoria, Africa	26,628	69,215	270	82
Lake Huron, U.S.A.-Canada	23,010	59,596	748	228
Lake Michigan, U.S.A.	22,400	58,016	923	281
Aral Sea, Kazakhstan-Uzbekistan	15,830	41,000	213	65
Lake Tanganyika, Africa	12,650	32,764	4,700	1,433
Lake Baykal, Russia	12,162	31,500	5,316	1,620
Great Bear Lake, Canada	12,096	31,328	1,356	413
Lake Nyasa (Malawi), Africa	11,555	29,928	2,320	707
Great Slave Lake, Canada	11,031	28,570	2,015	614
Lake Erie, U.S.A.-Canada	9,940	25,745	210	64
Lake Winnipeg, Canada	9,417	24,390	60	18
Lake Ontario, U.S.A.-Canada	7,540	19,529	775	244
Lake Balkhash, Kazakhstan	7,081	18,340	87	27
Lake Chad, Africa*	7,000	18,130	25	8
Lake Ladoga, Russia	6,900	17,871	738	225
Lake Maracaibo, Venezuela	5,120	13,261	100	31
Lake Onega, Russia	3,761	9,741	377	115

Lake	Area in: Sq. Miles	Sq. Kms.	Max. Depth in: Feet	Meters
Lake Eyre, Australia*	3,500-0	9,065-0	–	–
Lake Titicaca, Peru-Bolivia	3,200	8,288	1,000	305
Lake Nicaragua, Nicaragua	3,100	8,029	230	70
Lake Athabasca, Canada	3,064	7,936	400	122
Reindeer Lake, Canada*	2,568	6,651	–	–
Lake Turkana (Rudolf), Africa	2,463	6,379	240	73
Ysyk-Köl, Kyrgyzstan	2,425	6,281	2,303	702
Lake Torrens, Australia*	2,230	5,776	–	–
Vänern, Sweden	2,156	5,584	328	100
Nettilling Lake, Canada*	2,140	5,543	–	–
Lake Winnipegosis, Canada	2,075	5,374	38	12
Lake Albert, Africa	2,075	5,374	160	49
Kariba Lake, Zambia-Zimbabwe	2,050	5,310	295	90
Lake Nipigon, Canada	1,872	4,848	540	165
Lake Mweru, Africa	1,800	4,662	60	18
Lake Manitoba, Canada	1,799	4,659	12	4
Lake Taymyr, Russia	1,737	4,499	85	26
Lake Khanka, China-Russia	1,700	4,403	33	10
Lake Kioga, Uganda	1,700	4,403	25	8
Lake of the Woods, U.S.A.-Canada	1,679	4,349	70	21

* Figures subject to great seasonal variations.

Population of Countries and Major Cities

The following pages include population figures for all countries, and cities with more than 100,000 inhabitants. All national capitals, regardless of size are also listed. Countries are listed alphabetically, and cities are grouped alphabetically within each country. Capitals are indicated with an asterisk (*). The population figures, given in thousands, represent the most current information available.

Country City	Population in thousands
A	
Afghanistan	**27,756**
Herāt	177
Kabul*	1,424
Mazār-e Sharīf	131
Qandahār	226
Albania	**3,545**
Tiranë*	244
Algeria	**3,545**
Algiers*	1,688
Annaba	228
Batna	185
Bechar	107
Bejaïa	118
Biskra	130
Blida	132
Chelif	130
Constantine	450
Mostaganem	115
Oran	599
Sétif	186
Sidi Bel-Abbes	155
Skikda	129
Tébessa	108
Tiaret	106
Tlemcen	108
Andorra	**68**
Andorra la Vella*	16
Angola	**10,593**
Luanda*	1,530
Antigua and Barbuda	**67**
Saint John's*	22
Argentina	**37,812**
Almirante Brown	449
Avellaneda	347
Bahía Blanca	240
Belén de Escobar	117
Berazateugi	245
Buenos Aires*	2,961
Catamaraca	110
Concordia	116
Córdoba	1,148
Corrientes	258
Florencio Varela	249
Formosa	154
General San Martín	408
General Sarmiento	647
Godoy Cruz	179
Guaymallén	201
Lanús	467
La Plata	520
La Rioja	104
Las Heras	146
Lomas de Zamora	573
Mar del Plata	512
Mariano Moreno	286
Mendoza	122
Merlo	386
Morón	642
Neuquén	167
Paraná	207
Pilar	113
Posadas	202
Quilmes	509
Resistencia	228
Río Cuarto	135
Rosario	895
Salta	367
San Fernando	141
San Isidro	249
San Juan	119
San Luis	110
San Miguel de Tucumán	471
San Nicolás de los Arroyes	115
San Salvador de Jujuy	181
Santa Fé	343
Santiago del Estero	189
Tigre	254
Vicente López	289
Villa Nueva	201
Armenia	**3,330**
Gyumri	120
Vanadzor	146
Yerevan*	1,199
Australia	**19,547**
Adelaide	957
Baulkham Hills	114
Brisbane	1146
Canberra*	276
Geelong	126
Gold Coast	226
Gosford	129
Hobart	127
Melbourne	2,762
Newcastle	262
Perth	1019
Salisbury	106
Stirling	173
Sydney	3,098
Townsville	101
Warringah	172
Waverley	118
Wollongong	211
Austria	**8,170**
Graz	238
Innsbruck	118
Linz	203
Salzburg	144
Vienna*	1,540
Azerbaijan	**7,798**
Baku*	1,149
Gäncä	281
Sumgayıt	235
B	
Bahamas, The	**301**
Nassau*	172
Bahrain	**656**
Manama*	140
Bangladesh	**133,377**
Barisāl	180
Chittagong	1,560
Comilla	184
Dhaka*	3,638
Dinājpur	137
Jamālpur	108
Jessore	176
Khulna	601
Mymensingh	189
Naogaon	105
Nārāyanganj	285
Nawābganj	130
Pābna	110
Rājshāhi	302
Rangpur	221
Saidpur	108
Sirājganj	100
Sylhet	110
Tangail	108
Barbados	**277**
Bridgetown*	7
Belarus	**10,335**
Babruysk	226
Baranavichy	170
Barysaw	152
Brest	287
Homyel'	503
Hrodna	295
Mahilyow	363
Mazyr	105
Minsk*	1,655
Orsha	125
Pinsk	128
Vitsyebsk	365
Belgium	**10,275**
Antwerp	468
Brugge	117
Brussels*	954
Charleroi	206
Ghent	230
Liège	195
Namur	103
Schaerbeek	103
Belize	**263**
Belmopan*	8
Benin	**6,788**
Cotonou	537
Djougou	134
Parakou	104
Porto-Novo*	179
Bhutan	**2,094**
Thimphu*	30
Bolivia	**8,445**
Cochabamba	404
El Alto	404
La Paz*	711
Oruro	183
Potosí	112
Santa Cruz de la Sierra	695
Sucre*	131
Bosnia & Herzegovina	**3,964**
Banja Luka	196
Doboj	103
Mostar	127
Prijedor	113
Sarajevo*	529
Tuzla	132
Zenica	146
Botswana	**1,591**
Gaborone*	175
Brazil	**176,030**
Alvorada	133
Americana	154
Anápolis	222
Aracaju	402
Araçatuba	146
Arapiraca	125
Araraquara	101
Barra Mansa	145
Baurú	254
Belém	765
Belo Horizonte	2,206
Betim	153
Blumenau	185
Boa Vista	119
Brasília*	1,493
Cachoeiro de Itapemirim	112
Campina Grande	298
Campinas	748
Campo Grande	516
Campos	276
Canoas	269
Carapicuíba	207
Caruaru	181
Cascavel	175
Caxias do Sul	263
Colombo	105
Contegem	196
Cuiabá	253
Curitiba	842
Diadema	305
Divinópolis	142
Dourados	117
Duque du Caxias	326
Embu	156
Feira de Santana	340
Florianópolis	192
Fortaleza	1,027
Foz do Iguaçu	186
Franca	228
Goiânia	912
Governador Valadares	210
Gravataí	167
Guarapuava	107
Guarulhos	545
Ilhéus	135
Imperatriz	210
Ipatinga	120
Itabuna	170
Itajaí	115
Itapevi	108
Itaquaquecetuba	165
Jacareí	143
Jequié	115
João Pessoa	497
Joinvile	326
Juazeiro do Norte	164
Juiz de Fora	378
Jundiaí	253
Lages	137
Limeira	177
Londrina	355
Luziânia	194
Macapá	147
Maceió	555
Manaus	1,006
Marabá	102
Maracanau	133
Marília	145
Maringá	226
Mauá	295
Mogi das Cruzes	126
Montes Claros	233
Mossoró	177
Muribeca dos Guararapes	201
Natal	460
Nilópolis	105
Niterói	401
Nova Friburgo	111
Nova Iguaçu	562
Novo Hamburgo	199
Olinda	341
Osasco	567
Passo Fundo	135
Parnaíba	105
Pelotas	261
Petrolina	124
Petrópolis	165
Piracicaba	223
Poços de Caldas	105
Ponta Grossa	220
Porto Alegre	1,237
Porto Velho	226
Presidente Prudente	158
Recife	1,297
Ribeirão Prêto	416
Rio Branco	167
Rio Claro	130
Rio de Janeiro	5,474
Rio Grande	158
Salvador	2,070
Santa Bárbara d'Oeste	140
Santa Maria	193
Santarém	168
Santo André	518
Santos	416
São Bernardo do Campo	550
São Caetano do Sul	149
São Carlos	101
São Gonçalo	296
São João de Meriti	221
São José do Rio Preto	263
São José dos Campos	386
São Luís	164
São Leopoldo	160
São Paulo	9,394
São Vicente	268
Sapucia do Sul	105
Sete Lagoas	138
Sorocaba	349
Suzano	110
Taboão da Serra	160
Taubaté	186
Teresina	556
Uberaba	199
Uberlândia	355
Uruguaiana	103
Vitória	184
Vila Velha Argolas	114
Vitória da Conquista	180
Volta Redonda	220
Brunei	**351**
Bandar Seri Begawan*	46
Bulgaria	**8,653**
Burgas	196
Dobrich	104
Pleven	131
Plovdiv	341
Ruse	170
Sliven	106
Sofia*	1,114
Stara Zagora	150
Varna	309
Burkina Faso	**12,603**
Bobo Dioulasso	229
Ouagadougou*	442
Burundi	**6,373**
Bujumbura*	235
C	
Cambodia	**12,775**
Phnom Penh*	620
Cameroon	**16,185**
Bafoussam	140
Bamenda	130
Douala	1,030
Garoua	170
Maroua	150
Ngaoundéré	100
N'Kongsamba	110
Yaoundé*	654
Canada	**31,902**
Abbotsford	105
Brampton	268
Burlington	137
Burnaby	179
Calgary	768
Cambridge	101
Coquitlam	102
Edmonton	616
Gatineau	101
Gloucester	104
Halifax	114
Hamilton	322
Kitchener	178
Laval	330
London	326
Longueuil	128
Markham	173
Mississauga	544
Montréal	1,016
Nepean	115
Oakville	128
Oshawa	134
Ottawa*	323
Québec	167
Regina	180
Richmond	149
Richmond Hill	102
Saint Catharines	131
Saint John's	102
Saskatoon	194
Surrey	304
Thunder Bay	114
Toronto	654
Vancouver	514
Vaughan	133
Windsor	198
Winnipeg	618
Cape Verde	**409**
Praia*	62
Central African Republic	**3,643**
Bangui*	597
Chad	**8,997**
Moundou	102
N'Djamena*	530
Sarh	113
Chile	**15,499**
Antofagasta	227
Arica	161
Barrancas	184
Calama	120
Chillán	146
Concepción	327
Coquimbo	115
Iquique	151
La Serena	109
Maipú	254
Osorno	114
Puente Alto	254
Puerto Montt	112
Punta Arenas	114
Quilpué	102
Rancagua	180
Renca	129
San Bernardo	191
Santiago*	4,298
Talca	161
Talcahuano	246
Temuco	211
Valdivia	114
Valparaíso	282
Viña del Mar	304
China	**1,284,304**
Acheng	193
Aksu	126
Anda	133
Ankang	129
Anqing	247
Anshan	1,215
Anshun	175
Anyang	395
Baicheng	214
Baiyin	199
Baoding	485
Baoji	325
Baotou	980
Bei'an	193
Beihai	116
Beijing*	5,715
Beipiao	190
Bengbu	441
Benxi	767
Binzhou	129
Cangzhou	222
Changchun	1,698
Changde	253
Changji	109
Changsha	1,077
Changshu	180
Changzhi	307
Changzhou	523
Chaoyang	218
Chaozhou	289
Chengde	243
Chengdu	1,719
Chenzhou	166
Chifeng	344
Chongqing	2,265
Chuzhou	120
Cixi	101
Da'an	124
Da Xian	185
Dali	134
Dalian	1,632
Dandong	525
Daqing	676
Datong	779
Deyang	171
Dezhou	183
Dongguan	271
Dongtai	131
Dongying	257
Dunhua	225
Duyun	130
Ezhou	137
Fengcheng	150
Foshan	291
Fuling	164
Fushun	1,210
Fuxin	623
Fuyang	161
Fuyu	174
Fuzhou	890
Ganzhou	219
Gejiu	212
Gongzhuling	218
Guangyuan	173
Guangzhou	2,892
Guigang	111
Guilin	371
Guiyang	1,009
Haicheng	196
Haikou	271
Hailar	176
Hailun	128
Hami	146
Handan	798
Hangzhou	1,119
Hanzhong	157
Harbin	2,468
Hebi	196
Hefei	733
Hegang	507
Hengyang	469
Heze	154
Hohhot	654
Honghu	130
Huadian	166
Huai'an	113
Huaibei	332
Huaihua	120
Huainan	674
Huaiyin	221
Huangshi	432
Huizhou	147
Hunjiang	475
Huzhou	398
Jiamusi	477
Ji'an	143
Jiangmen	219
Jiangyin	145
Jiaohe	172
Jiaozuo	386
Jiaxing	205
Jilin	1,038
Jinan	1,361
Jinchang	100
Jincheng	128
Jingdezhen	274
Jingmen	158
Jinhua	139
Jining (Nei Mong.)	248
Jining (Shandong)	190
Jinxi	349
Jinzhou	573
Jiujiang	284
Jiutai	173
Jixi	638
Kaifeng	503
Kaili	109
Kaiyuan	122
Karamay	194
Kashi	158
Korla	137
Kunming	1,108
Kunshan	100
Laiwu	186
Langfang	146
Lanzhou	1,205
Laohekou	108
Leiyang	129
Lengshuijiang	126
Leshan	333
Lianyuan	114
Lianyungang	352
Liaocheng	149
Liaoyang	485
Liaoyuan	341
Liling	107
Linchuan	161
Linfen	174
Linhe	131
Linyi	210
Liuzhou	602
Longyan	134
Loudi	121
Lu'an	137
Luohe	122
Luoyang	730
Lupanshui	342
Luzhou	262
Ma'anshan	297
Manzhouli	119
Maoming	162
Meihekou	205
Meizhou	120
Mianyang	250
Mudanjiang	562
Nanchang	1,026
Nanchong	179
Nanjing	2,114
Nanning	723
Nanping	188
Nantong	324
Nanyang	229
Neijiang	240
Ningbo	548
Panzhihua	407
Pingdingshan	442
Pingxiang	306
Puyang	120
Qingdao	1,317
Qingjiang	172
Qingyuan	134
Qinhuangdao	360
Qinzhou	105
Qiqihar	1,066
Qitaihe	218
Quanzhou	178
Qujing	163
Quzhou	105
Renqiu	128
Rizhao	109
Sanmenxia	114
Sanming	159
Shanghai	7,551
Shangqiu	159
Shangrao	127
Shangzhi	208
Shantou	558
Shaoguan	334
Shaoxing	180
Shaoyang	242
Shashi	277
Shenyang	3,588
Shenzhen	466
Sheung Shui-Fanling	201
Shihezi	160
Shijiazhuang	1,065
Shiyan	241
Shizuishan	245
Shuangyashan	392
Shuangcheng	131
Siping	310
Suihua	219
Suining	134
Suizhou	139
Suzhou (Anhui)	147
Suzhou (Jiangsu)	697
Tai'an	246
Taiyuan	1,514
Taizhou	151
Tangshan	1,042
Tianjin	4,521
Tianmen	138
Tianshui	238
Tieling	247
Tin Shui Wai	150
Tongchuan	259
Tonghua	321
Tongliao	247
Tongling	212
Tseung Kwan O	137
Ulanhot	152
Ürümqi	1071
Wafangdian	250
Wanxian	156
Weifang	359
Weinan	135
Wenzhou	204
Wuhai	261
Wuhan	3,177
Wuhu	419
Wuwei	125
Wuxi	806
Wuzhou	213
Xiamen	391
Xi'an	1,954
Xiangfan	390
Xiangtan	429
Xianning	110
Xiantao	124
Xianyang	328
Xiaogan	140
Xiaoshan	159
Xichang	133
Xingcheng	102
Xinghua	155
Xingtai	270
Xining	559
Xintai	209
Xinxiang	453
Xinyang	185
Xinyu	163
Xuchang	196
Xuzhou	795
Yan'an	106
Yancheng	239
Yangjiang	203
Yangquan	338
Yangzhou	306
Yanji	233

Country City	Population in thousands
Yantai	400
Yibin	241
Yichang	364
Yichun (Heilonjiang)	787
Yichun (Jiangxi)	134
Yinchuan	350
Yingkou	423
Yining	172
Yixing	186
Yiyang	180
Yong'an	109
Yuci	189
Yueyang	296
Yulin	130
Yumen	112
Yuyao	103
Zaozhuang	309
Zhangjiakou	525
Zhangzhou	178
Zhanjiang	384
Zhaodong	164
Zhaoqing	173
Zhengzhou	1,139
Zhenjiang	355
Zhongshan	256
Zhoukou	136
Zhuhai	162
Zhumadian	121
Zhuzhou	383
Zibo	864
Zigong	385
Zixing	107
Zunyi	269
Colombia	**41,008**
Armenia	211
Barrancabermeja	136
Barranquilla	1,000
Bello	260
Bogotá*	5,699
Bucaramanga	403
Buenaventura	187
Cali	1,625
Cartagena	576
Cúcuta	462
Dos Quebradas	115
Envigado	110
Floridablanca	177
Ibagué	336
Itagüí	168
Manizales	341
Medellín	1,485
Montería	182
Neiva	223
Palmira	189
Pasto	244
Pereira	329
Popayán	175
Santa Marta	211
Sincelejo	120
Soacha	181
Soledad	236
Tuluá	104
Tunjá	102
Valledupar	209
Villavicencio	190
Comoros	**614**
Moroni*	30
Congo, Dem. Rep. of the	**55,226**
Boma	264
Bukavu	210
Kananga	372
Kikwit	183
Kinshasa*	3,800
Kisangani	373
Kolwezi	545
Lubumbashi	739
Matadi	173
Mbandaka	166
Mbuji-Mayi	613
Panda-Likasi	146
Tshikapa	110
Congo, Rep. of the	**2,958**
Brazzaville*	938
Pointe-Noire	576
Costa Rica	**3,835**
San José*	279
Côte d'Ivoire	**16,805**
Abidjan	1,929
Bouaké	330
Daloa	122
Korhogo	109
Yamoussoukro*	107
Croatia	**4,391**
Osijek	130
Rijeka	168
Split	200
Zagreb*	868
Cuba	**11,224**
Bayamo	138
Camagüey	249
Ciego de Avila	101
Cienfuegos	130
Guantánamo	208
Havana*	2,176
Holguín	242
Las Tunas	127
Manzanillo	108
Marianao	128
Matanzas	123
Pinar del Río	129
Santa Clara	205
Santiago de Cuba	430
Victoria de las Tunas	115
Cyprus	**767**
Nicosia*	47
Czech Republic	**10,257**
Brno	379
Olomouc	103
Ostrava	319
Plzeň	166
Prague*	1,179
D	
Denmark	**5,369**
Ålborg	117
Århus	209
Copenhagen*	467
Odense	143
Djibouti	**473**
Djibouti*	200
Dominica	**70**
Roseau*	6
Dominican Republic	**8,722**
La Romana	140
San Francisco de Macorís	162
San Pedro de Macorís	125
Santiago de los Caballeros	365
Santo Domingo*	1,610
E	
East Timor	**840**
Dili*	13
Ecuador	**13,447**
Ambato	124
Cuenca	195
Esmeraldas	100
Guayaquil	1,513
Loja	111
Machala	146
Manta	130
Milagro	103
Portoviejo	153
Quito*	1,113
Riobamba	101
Santo Domingo de los Colorados	171
Egypt	**70,712**
Alexandria	3,380
Al Fayyum	250
Al Jīzah	2,144
Al Maḩallah al Kubrá	408
Al Manşūra	371
Al Minyā	208
Aswān	220
Asyūt	321
Az Zaqāzīq	287
Banhā	136
Banī Suwayf	179
Cairo*	6,663
Damanhūr	222
Ismailia	255
Kafr ad Dawwār	226
Luxor	146
Port Said	460
Qinā	141
Shibīn al Kaum	158
Shubrā al Khaymah	834
Suez	376
Suhāj	156
Tantā	380
El Salvador	**6,354**
Mejicanos	132
San Miguel	128
San Salvador*	415
Santa Ana	139
Soyapango	261
Equatorial Guinea	**498**
Malabo*	30
Eritrea	**4,466**
Asmara*	435
Estonia	**1,416**
Tallinn*	482
Tartu	114
Ethiopia	**67,673**
Addis Ababa*	2,316
Bahir Dar	116
Debrezit	117
Dessi	195
Dirē Dawa	195
Gonder	167
Hārer	123
Jimma	120
Mekele	120
Nazerit	147
F	
Fiji	**856**
Suva*	70
Finland	**5,184**
Esbo (Espoo)	191
Helsinki*	525
Oulu	109
Tampere	183
Turku	165
Vantaa	166
France	**59,766**
Aix-en-Provence	127
Amiens	136
Angers	146
Besançon	119
Bordeaux	213
Boulogne-Billancourt	102
Brest	153
Caen	116
Clermont-Ferrand	140
Dijon	152
Grenoble	154
Le Havre	197
Le Mans	148
Lille	178
Limoges	136
Lyon	422
Marseille	808
Metz	124
Montpellier	211
Mulhouse	110
Nancy	102
Nantes	252
Nice	346
Nîmes	134
Orléans	108
Paris*	2,175
Perpignan	108
Reims	185
Rennes	204
Rouen	105
Saint-Denis	122
Saint-Étienne	202
Strasbourg	256
Toulon	170
Toulouse	366
Tours	133
Villeurbanne	120
G	
Gabon	**1,233**
Libreville*	362
Gambia, The	**1,456**
Banjul*	42
Georgia	**4,961**
Bat'umi	136
K'ut'aisi	235
Rust'avi	159
Sokhumi	121
T'bilisi*	1,260
Germany	**82,163**
Aachen	242
Augsburg	257
Bergisch Gladbach	104
Berlin*	3,434
Bielefeld	319
Bochum	396
Bonn	292
Bottrop	119
Braunschweig	259
Bremen	551
Bremerhaven	130
Chemnitz	294
Cologne	954
Cottbus	126
Darmstadt	139
Dortmund	599
Dresden	491
Duisburg	535
Düsseldorf	576
Erfurt	209
Erlangen	102
Essen	627
Frankfurt am Main	645
Freiburg	191
Fürth	103
Gelsenkirchen	294
Gera	129
Göttingen	122
Hagen	214
Halle	310
Hamburg	1,652
Hamm	180
Hannover	513
Heidelberg	137
Heilbronn	116
Herne	178
Hildesheim	105
Ingolstadt	105
Jena	103
Karlsruhe	275
Kassel	194
Kiel	246
Koblenz	109
Köpenick	118
Krefeld	244
Leipzig	511
Leverkusen	161
Lübeck	215
Ludwigshafen	162
Magdeburg	279
Mainz	179
Mannheim	310
Moers	105
Mönchengladbach	259
Mülheim an der Ruhr	178
Munich	1,229
Münster	259
Neuss	147
Nürnberg	494
Oberhausen	224
Offenbach	115
Oldenburg	143
Osnabrück	163
Paderborn	121
Pforzheim	113
Potsdam	140
Recklinghausen	125
Regensburg	122
Remscheid	123
Reutlingen	104
Rostock	237
Saarbrücken	191
Salzgitter	118
Schwerin	122
Siegen	112
Solingen	166
Stuttgart	594
Ulm	115
Wiesbaden	271
Witten	106
Wolfsburg	128
Wuppertal	387
Würzburg	129
Zwickau	108
Ghana	**20,244**
Accra*	954
Kumasi	399
Tamale	136
Tema	100
Greece	**10,645**
Athens*	772
Iráklion	115
Kallithéa	114
Lárisa	113
Pátrai	153
Peristérion	137
Piraiévs	183
Thessaloníki	384
Grenada	**89**
Saint George's*	5
Guatemala	**13,314**
Guatemala*	823
Mixco	305
Quezaltenango	109
San Pedro Carchá	103
Villa Nueva	192
Guinea	**7,775**
Conakry*	950
Labé	110
Guinea-Bissau	**1,345**
Bissau*	109
Guyana	**698**
Georgetown*	72
Pickersgill	249
H	
Haiti	**7,064**
Port-au-Prince*	690
Honduras	**6,561**
San Pedro Sula	287
Tegucigalpa*	577
Hungary	**10,075**
Budapest*	2,017
Debrecen	212
Győr	129
Kecskemét	103
Miskolc	196
Nyíregyháza	114
Pécs	170
Szeged	175
Székesfehérvár	109
I	
Iceland	**279**
Reykjavík*	111
India	**1,045,845**
Abohar	107
Ādoni	136
Āgra	892
Agartala	157
Ahmadābād	2,877
Ahmadnagar	181
Aīzawl	155
Ajmer	403
Akola	328
Alīgarh	481
Allahābād	793
Alleppey	175
Alwar	205
Ambāla	119
Amravati	422
Amritsar	709
Amroha	137
Anand	110
Anantapur	175
Arrah	157
Asansol	262
Aurangābād	573
Bahraich	135
Bally	184
Bālurghāt	120
Bangalore	2,660
Bānkura	115
Baranagar	225
Bārāsat	170
Bareilly	587
Barrackpur	133
Basīrhāt	101
Beāwar	105
Belgaum	326
Bellary	245
Berhampore	115
Berhampur	210
Bhadrāvati	130
Bhāgalpur	253
Bhārātpur	105
Bharuch	133
Bhatinda	159
Bhātpāra	305
Bhavnagar	402
Bhilai	386
Bhīlwāra	184
Bhīmavaram	121
Bhind	110
Bhiwandi	379
Bhiwāni	122
Bhopāl	1,063
Bhubaneswar	412
Bhūj	102
Bhusawal	145
Bīdar	108
Bihar	201
Bijāpur	187
Bīkaner	416
Bilāspur	180
Bīr	112
Bokaro Steel City	334
Budaun	117
Bulandshahr	127
Burdwān	245
Burhānpur	173
Champdāni	101
Chandannagar	120
Chandigarh	504
Chandrapur	226
Chāpra	137
Chennai (Madras)	3,841
Chittoor	133
Cochin	565
Coimbatore	816
Cuddalore	145
Cuddapah	121
Cuttack	403
Darbhanga	218
Daryābād	270
Dāvangere	266
Dehra Dūn	270
Delhi	7,207
Dewās	164
Dhānbād	152
Dhūlia	278
Dibrugarh	120
Dindigul	182
Dombivli	103
Durg	151
Durgāpur	426
Elūrū	213
English Bāzār	139
Erode	160
Etāwah	124
Faizābād	124
Farīdābād	618
Farrukhābād	195
Fatehpur	118
Firozābād	215
Gadag-Betigeri	134
Gāndhīdhām	105
Gandhinagar	123
Gayā	292
Ghaziābād	454
Gondia	109
Gorakhpur	506
Gudivāda	102
Gulbarga	304
Guna	100
Guntakal	108
Guntūr	471
Gurgaon	121
Guwāhati	584
Gwalior	691
Hābra	100
Haldīa	100
Hālisahar	114
Hāpur	146
Hardwār	147
Hāthras	113
Hindupur	105
Hisār	173
Hooghly-Chinsura	152
Hoshiārpur	123
Howrah	950
Hubli-Dhārwār	648
Hyderābād	3,044
Ichalkaranji	215
Imphāl	199
Indore	1,092
Jabalpur	742
Jaipur	1,458
Jālgaon	242
Jālna	175
Jammu	206
Jāmnagar	342
Jamshedpur	461
Jaunpur	136
Jhānsi	301
Jodhpur	666
Jullundur	510
Junāgadh	130
Kākināda	280
Kalyān	1,015
Kāmārhāti	267
Kānchīpuram	145
Kanchrāpāra	100
Kānpur	1,874
Karīmnagar	149
Karnāl	174
Kāthgodām	104
Katihār	135
Khammam	128
Khandwa	145
Kharagpur	262
Kolhāpur	406
Kolkata (Calcutta)	4,400
Korba	125
Kota	537
Kozhikode (Calicut)	420
Krishnanagar	121
Kulti	109
Kumbakonam	139
Kurnool	237
Lātūr	197
Lucknow	1,619
Ludhiāna	1,043
Machilipatnam	159
Madurai	941
Mahbubnagar	117
Mālegaon	343
Mandya	120
Mangalore	273
Mathurā	227
Maunath Bhanjan	137
Medinipur	125
Meerut	754
Mira-Bhayandar	176
Miraj	122
Mirzāpur	169
Morādābād	429
Morena	147
Mumbai (Bombay)	9,926
Munger	150
Murwāra	163
Muzaffarnagar	241
Muzaffarpur	241
Mysore	481
Nabadwīp	125
Nadiād	167
Nāgercoil	190
Nāgpur	1,625
Naihāti	133
Nānded	275
Nandyāl	120
Nāsik	657
Navsāri	126
Nellore	317
New Bombay	350
New Delhi*	301
Nizāmābād	241
North Barrackpore	101
Ongole	101
Pālghāt	123
Pāli	137
Pānīpat	191
Pānihāti	276
Parbhani	190
Pathānkot	124
Patiāla	238
Patna	917
Pīlībhīt	107
Pimpri-Chinchwad	517
Pollāchi	115
Pondicherry	203
Porbandar	117
Proddatūr	134
Pune (Poona)	1,567
Purī	125
Purnia	115
Quilon	140
Rāe Bareli	130
Raichūr	158
Raiganj	151
Raipur	439
Rājahmundry	325
Rājapālaiyam	114
Rāj-Nāndagaon	125
Rāmagundam	215
Rāmpur	244
Rānchī	599
Ratlām	183
Raurkela	356
Rewa	129
Rishra	103
Rohtak	216
Sāgar	195
Sahāranpur	375
Salem	367
Sambalpur	131
Sambhal	151
Sāngli	193
Sāntipur	107
Satna	157
Secunderābād	171
Serampore	137
Shāhjahānpur	238
Shillong	132
Shimoga	179
Shivpurī	108
Sholāpur	604
Sīkar	148
Silchar	115
Silīguri	217
Sirsa	113
Sītāpur	122
Sonīpat	144
South Dum Dum	233
Sri Gangānagar	161
Srīnagar	606
Surat	1,499
Surendranagar	106
Tellicherry	104
Tenāli	144
Thāna	803
Thanjavur	202
Thiruvananthapuram	524
Tiruchchirāppalli	387
Tirunelveli	136
Tirupati	174
Tiruppūr	236
Tiruvannāmalai	109
Titāgarh	114
Tonk	100
Tumkūr	139
Tuticorin	200
Udaipur	309
Ujjain	362
Ulbāria	155
Ulhāsnagar	369
Unnāo	107
Uttarpara-Kotrung	101
Vadodara (Baroda)	1,031
Vālpārai	106
Vārānasi	929
Vellore	175
Vijayawada	702
Visākhapatnam	752

Country City	Population in thousands
Vizianagaram	160
Warangal	448
Wardha	103
Yamunānagar	144
Yavatmāl	109
Indonesia	**232,073**
Ambon	205
Balikpapan	309
Banda Aceh	143
Bandung	2,026
Bangil	386
Banjarmasin	443
Bekasi	146
Bengkulu	170
Binjai	127
Blitar	113
Bogor	271
Ciamis	105
Cianjur	109
Cibinong	264
Cilacap	142
Ciedug	293
Cimahi	197
Ciparay	135
Cirebon	225
Denpasar	210
Depok	382
Garut	146
Gorontalo	133
Gresik	102
Jakarta*	8,228
Jambi	301
Jayapura	101
Jember	115
Karawang	143
Kediri	235
Klangenan	291
Klaten	120
Kudus	183
Kupang	111
Madiun	166
Magelang	123
Majalaya	177
Malang	650
Manado	321
Mataram	276
Medan	1,685
Padang	477
Pakanbaru	341
Palangkaraya	113
Palembang	1,084
Pangkalpinang	108
Parepare	109
Pasuran	134
Pekalongan	227
Pematangsiantar	203
Pontianak	397
Probolinggo	131
Purwokerto	158
Salatiga	103
Samarinda	335
Semarang	1,004
Sukabumi	120
Surabaya	2,410
Surakarta	504
Tanjungbalai	108
Tanjungkarang-Telukbetung	458
Tanjungpinang	106
Tasikmalaya	194
Tebingtinggi	117
Tegal	226
Ujung Pandang	913
Yogyakarta	412
Iran	**66,623**
Āmol	155
Ahvāz	828
Arāk	379
Ardabīl	330
Bābol	153
Bākhtarān	666
Bandar-e `Abbās	384
Bandar-e Mushehr	141
Bīrjand	115
Bojnūrd	126
Borūjerd	212
Būshehr	141
Dezfūl	202
Eşfahān	1,221
Eslāmshahr	240
Gorgān	178
Hamadān	406
Īlām	137
Karaj	588
Kāshān	166
Kermān	350
Khomeynīshahr	127
Khorramābād	277
Khvoy	153
Malāyer	150
Marāgheh	129
Mashhad	1,964
Masjed-e Soleymān	109
Najafābād	182
Neyshābūr	155
Orūmīyeh	396
Qā'emshahr	133
Qazvīn	299
Qom	780
Rasht	374
Sabzevār	161
Sanandaj	271
Sārī	186
Shīrāz	1,043
Sīrjān	120
Tabrīz	1,166
Tajrīsh	157
Tehrān*	6,750
Yazd	306
Zāhedān	420
Zanjān	281
Iraq	**24,002**
Ad Dīwānīyah	196
Al `Amārah	209
Al Başrah	406
Al Ḩillah	269
Al Karrādah	236
Al Kūt	183
An Najaf	309
An Nāşirīyah	266
Ar Ramādī	193
As Sulaymānīyah	364
Baghdad*	3,841
Ba`qūbah	115
Dīwānīyah	196
Irbīl	486
Karbalā'	297
Kirkūk	419
Mosul	664
Ireland	**3,883**
Cork	127
Dublin*	478
Israel	**6,030**
Ashdod	128
Bat Yam	142
Beersheba	153
Bene Beraq	129
Ḥaifa	252
Ḥolon	164
Jerusalem*	591
Netanya	148
Petaḥ Tiqwa	153
Ramat Gan	122
Rishon LeẒiyyon	165
Tel Aviv-Yafo	356
Italy	**57,716**
Ancona	103
Bari	341
Bergamo	116
Bologna	412
Bolzano	100
Brescia	197
Cagliari	212
Catania	330
Catanzaro	104
Cosenza	104
Ferrara	111
Florence	402
Foggia	155
Genoa	676
La Spezia	102
Lecce	102
Livorno	171
Messina	272
Mestre	182
Milan	1,371
Modena	176
Monza	121
Naples	1,025
Novara	103
Padova	215
Palermo	697
Parma	174
Perugia	110
Pescara	129
Piacenza	102
Prato	167
Reggio di Calabria	178
Reggio nell'Emilia	109
Rimini	115
Rome*	2,693
Salerno	153
Sassari	120
Siracusa	125
Taranto	232
Torre del Greco	101
Trieste	231
Turin	962
Verona	253
Vicenza	109
J	
Jamaica	**2,680**
Kingston*	104
Japan	**126,975**
Abiko	121
Ageo	195
Aizu-Wakamatsu	119
Akashi	271
Akishima	105
Akita	302
Amagasaki	499
Anjō	142
Aomori	288
Asahikawa	364
Asaka	104
Ashikaga	168
Atsugi	197
Beppu	130
Chiba	829
Chigasaki	202
Chofū	181
Daitō	126
Ebina	106
Fuchū	209
Fuji	222
Fujieda	120
Fujinomiya	117
Fujisawa	350
Fukui	253
Fukuoka	1,237
Fukushima	278
Fukuyama	366
Funabashi	533
Gifu	410
Habikino	115
Hachiōji	466
Hachinohe	241
Hadano	156
Hakodate	311
Hamakita	811
Hamamatsu	535
Higashikurume	114
Higashimurayama	134
Higashi-Ōsaka	518
Himeji	454
Hino	166
Hirakata	391
Hiratsuka	245
Hirosaki	174
Hiroshima	1,086
Hitachi	202
Hōfu	118
Ibaraki	254
Ichihara	258
Ichikawa	437
Ichinomiya	262
Ikeda	104
Imabari	123
Iruma	138
Ise	104
Isesaki	116
Ishinomaki	122
Itami	186
Iwaki	356
Iwakuni	110
Iwatsuki	106
Izumi	148
Jōetsu	130
Kadoma	142
Kagoshima	537
Kakamigahara	130
Kakogawa	240
Kamakura	174
Kanazawa	443
Kariya	120
Kashihara	116
Kashiwa	305
Kasugai	267
Kasukabe	189
Katsuta	110
Kawachi-Nagano	109
Kawagoe	305
Kawaguchi	439
Kawanishi	141
Kawasaki	1,174
Kiryū	126
Kisarazu	123
Kishiwada	189
Kitakyūshū	1,026
Kitami	107
Kōbe	1,477
Kōchi	317
Kōfu	201
Kōriyama	315
Kodaira	164
Koganei	106
Kokubunji	101
Komaki	124
Komatsu	106
Koshigaya	285
Kumagaya	152
Kumamoto	579
Kurashiki	415
Kure	217
Kurume	228
Kushiro	210
Kyōto	1,461
Machida	349
Maebashi	286
Matsubara	136
Matsudo	456
Matsue	142
Matsumoto	201
Matsusaka	119
Matsuyama	443
Mino'o	122
Misato	128
Mishima	105
Mitaka	166
Mito	235
Miyakonojō	130
Miyazaki	287
Moriguchi	157
Morioka	235
Muroran	126
Musashino	139
Nagano	347
Nagaoka	186
Nagareyama	140
Nagasaki	445
Nagoya	2,155
Naha	305
Nara	349
Narashino	151
Neyagawa	257
Niigata	486
Niihama	129
Niiza	139
Nishinomiya	427
Nobeoka	130
Noda	114
Numazu	212
Obihiro	168
Odawara	193
Ōgaki	148
Ōita	409
Okayama	594
Okazaki	307
Okinawa	106
Ōme	126
Ōmiya	404
Ōmuta	150
Ōsaka	2,624
Ota	140
Otaru	167
Ōtsu	260
Oyama	142
Saga	170
Sagamihara	532
Sakai	814
Sakata	101
Sakura	145
Sapporo	1,672
Sasebo	247
Sayama	157
Sendai	918
Seto	126
Shimizu	242
Shimonoseki	263
Shizuoka	472
Sōka	206
Suita	345
Suzuka	174
Tachikawa	153
Takamatsu	330
Takaoka	175
Takarazuka	202
Takasaki	236
Takatsuki	360
Tama	144
Tokorozawa	303
Tokushima	263
Tokuyama	111
Tōkyō*	8,164
Tomakomai	152
Tomika	109
Tondabayashi	110
Tottori	142
Toyama	321
Toyohashi	338
Toyokawa	112
Toyonaka	410
Toyota	332
Tsu	157
Tsuchiura	127
Tsukuba	143
Ube	175
Ueda	119
Uji	177
Urawa	418
Urayasu	116
Utsunomiya	427
Wakayama	397
Yachiyo	149
Yaizu	112
Yamagata	249
Yamaguchi	129
Yamato	192
Yao	278
Yatsushiro	108
Yokkaichi	274
Yokohama	3,220
Yokosuka	433
Yonago	133
Zama	112
Jordan	**5,307**
Amman*	970
Ar Ruşayfah	137
Az Zarqā'	351
Irbid	208
K	
Kazakhstan	**16,742**
Aqtöbe	264
Almaty	1,176
Atyraū	149
Aqmola*	287
Aqtaū	174
Atyraū	151
Ekibastuz	141
Kökshetaū	144
Oral	220
Öskemen	334
Pavlodar	349
Petropavl	248
Qaraghandy	596
Qostanay	234
Qyzylorda	164
Rudnyy	130
Semey	342
Shymkent	404
Taldyqorghan	125
Temirtaū	213
Zhambyl	317
Zhezqazghan	108
Kenya	**31,139**
Kisumu	185
Mombasa	465
Nairobi*	1,346
Nakuru	163
Kiribati	**96**
Tarawa*	2
Korea, North	**22,224**
Ch'ŏngjin	754
Haeju	131
Hamhŭng	775
Kaesŏng	346
Kimch'aek	281
Nampŏ	691
P'yŏngyang*	2,639
Sariwŏn	130
Sinŭiju	500
Wŏnsan	350
Korea, South	**48,324**
Andong	117
Ansan	252
Anyang	481
Ch'angwŏn	323
Ch'echŏn	102
Cheju	233
Chinhae	120
Chinju	256
Ch'ŏnan	211
Ch'ŏngju	478
Chŏnju	517
Ch'unch'ŏn	174
Ch'ungju	128
Inch'ŏn	2,203
Iri	203
Kangnŭng	153
Kimhae	106
Kohŭng	217
Kumi	206
Kunp'o	100
Kunsan	218
Kuri	109
Kwangju (Kwangju-Jikhalsi)	1,236
Kwangju (Kyŏnggi-Do)	906
Kwangmyŏng	329
Kyŏngju	142
Masan	494
Mokp'o	243
Nonsan	226
P'ohang	318
Puch'on	668
Pusan	3,802
Seoul*	10,776
Sŏngnam	541
Sunch'ŏn	167
Suwŏn	665
Taegu	2,256
Taejŏn	1,183
Ŭijŏngbu	212
Ulsan	682
Wŏnju	173
Yŏsu	173
Kuwait	**2,112**
Al Jahrah	139
As Sālimīyah	116
Jalīb ash Shuyūkh	115
Kuwait*	31
Kyrgyzstan	**4,822**
Bishkek*	628
Osh	219
L	
Laos	**5,777**
Vientiane*	377
Latvia	**2,367**
Daugavpils	123
Liepāja	106
Riga*	865
Lebanon	**3,678**
Beirut*	1,000
Sidon	110
Tripoli	240
Lesotho	**2,208**
Maseru*	109
Liberia	**3,228**
Monrovia*	421
Libya	**5,369**
Benghāzī	446
Mişrātah	121
Tripoli*	590
Liechtenstein	**33**
Vaduz*	5
Lithuania	**3,601**
Kaunas	422
Klaipėda	204
Panevėžys	132
Šiauliai	148
Vilnius*	582
Luxembourg	**449**
Luxembourg*	75
M	
Macedonia, F.Y.R of	**2,055**
Gostivar	116
Skopje*	441
Madagascar	**16,473**
Amboasary	110
Ambovombe	144
Antananarivo*	676
Antsirabe	120
Betioky	140
Fandriana	135
Ifanadiana	102
Mahajanga	101
Toamasina	127
Vohipeno	106
Malawi	**10,702**
Blantyre	332
Lilongwe*	234
Malaysia	**22,662**
Alor Setar	125
George Town	219
Ipoh	383
Johor Baharu	329
Kelang	244
Kota Baharu	220
Kuala Lumpur*	1,145
Kuala Terengganu	229
Kuantan	198
Kuching	148
Petaling Jaya	255
Sandakan	126
Seremban	183
Shah Alam	102
Sibu	126
Sungai Petani	116
Taiping	183
Maldives	**320**
Male*	55
Mali	**11,340**
Bamako*	658
Malta	**379**
Valletta*	9
Marshall Islands	**74**
Majuro*	22
Mauritania	**2,829**
Nouakchott*	390
Mauritius	**1,200**
Port Louis*	144
Mexico	**103,400**
Acapulco de Juárez	515
Aguascalientes	440
Buenavista	115
Campeche	151
Cancún	168
Celaya	215
Chalco de Díaz Covarrubias	224
Chihuahua	516
Chimalhuacán	236
Ciudad Adolfo López Mateos	315
Ciudad Apodaca	113
Ciudad Juárez	790
Ciudad Madero	160
Ciudad Obregón	220
Ciudad Victoria	140
Coacalco de Berriozabal	151
Coatzacoalcos	199
Colima	107
Córdoba	137
Cuautitlán Izcalli	313
Cuautla Morelos	110
Cuernavaca	279
Culiacán Rosales	415
Durango de Victoria	348
Ecatepec de Morelos	1,218
Ensenada	169
Garza García	113
Gómez Palacio	164
Guadalajara	1,650
Guadalupe	535
Hermosillo	406
Heroica Matamoros	266
Heroica Nogales	106
Irapuato	265
Ixtapaluca	116
Jalapa Enríquez	279
La Paz	138
León	758
Los Mochis	163
Los Reyes Acaquilpan	135
Mazatlán	268
Mérida	529
Metepec	116
Mexicali	439
Mexico*	8,237
Minatitlán	145
Monclova	178
Monterrey	1,069
Morelia	428
Naucalpan de Juárez	846
Nezahualcóyotl	1,255
Nuevo Laredo	218
Oaxaca de Juárez	213
Orizaba	114
Pachuca de Soto	188
Poza Rica	164
Puebla de Zaragoza	1,007
Querétaro	387
Reynosa	266
Salamanca	123
Saltillo	421
San Luis Potosí	489
San Nicolás de los Garzas	437
Santa Catarina	163
Sánchez	124
Tampico	273
Tapachula	139
Tehuacán	139
Tepic	207
Tijuana	699
Tlalnepantla de Galeana	702
Tlaquepaque	151
Toluca de Lerdo	328
Tonalá	151
Torreón	439
Tuxtla Gutiérrez	290
Uruapan	188
Veracruz	439
Villahermosa	261
Villa Nicolás Romero	146
Zacatecas	100
Zamora de Hidalgo	110
Zapopan	668
Micronesia, Federated States of	**136**
Palikir*	6
Moldova	**4,435**
Bălţi	159
Chişinău*	665
Tighina (Bendery)	130
Tiraspol	182

Country / City	Population in thousands
Monaco	**32**
Monaco*	27
Mongolia	**2,694**
Ulaanbaatar*	575
Morocco	**31,168**
Agadir	261
Beni Mallal	140
Casablanca	2,541
El Aaiún	137
El Jadida	119
Fès	508
Kénitra	293
Khouribga	152
Ksar el Kebir	107
Marrakech	521
Meknès	378
Mohammedia	169
Nador	208
Oujda	362
Rabat*	917
Safi	262
Salé	579
Témara	126
Tangier	519
Taza	121
Tétouan	278
Mozambique	**19,608**
Beira	397
Chimoio	171
Maputo*	967
Matola	425
Nacala	158
Nampula	303
Quelimane	150
Myanmar (Burma)	**42,238**
Akyab	108
Bago (Pegu)	151
Insein	144
Mandalay	533
Mawlamyine (Moulmein)	220
Monywa	107
Pathein (Bassein)	144
Sittwe (Akyab)	108
Taunggyi	108
Yangon* (Rangoon)	2,513
N	
Namibia	**1,821**
Windhoek*	147
Nauru	**12**
Yaren (district)	0.4
Nepal	**25,874**
Biratnagar	129
Kāthmāndu*	421
Pātan (Lalitpur)	116
Netherlands	**16,068**
Amersfoort	104
Amsterdam*	713
Apeldoorn	149
Arnhem	133
Breda	127
Dordrecht	112
Eindhoven	194
Enschede	147
Groningen	169
Haarlem	150
Leiden	113
Maastricht	118
Nijmegen	146
Rotterdam	590
The Hague*	445
Tilburg	161
Utrecht	232
Zaandam	130
Zaanstad	131
Zoetermeer	101
New Zealand	**3,908**
Auckland	346
Christchurch	309
Dunedin	118
Hamilton	108
Manukau	254
North Shore	172
Waitakere	156
Wellington*	158
Nicaragua	**5,024**
Chinandega	118
León	160
Managua*	883
Masaya	121
Niger	**10,640**
Maradi	109
Niamey*	392
Zinder	120
Nigeria	**129,935**
Aba	271
Abeokuta	387
Abuja*	306
Ado Ekiti	325
Akure	147
Awka	101
Benin City	207
Bida	114
Calabar	158
Deba Habe	125
Ede	278
Effon Alaiye	139
Enugu	286
Gusau	143
Ibadan	1,295
Ife	269
Ijebu Ode	142
Ikare	128
Ikerre	221
Ikire	112
Ikirun	164
Ikorodu	167
Ila Orangun	239
Ilawe - Ekiti	167
Ilesha	342
Ilobu	180
Ilorin	431
Inisa	108
Iseyin	197
Iwo	335
Jos	185
Kaduna	310
Kano	700
Katsina	187
Kuma	134
Lafia	111
Lagos	1,347
Maiduguri	289
Makurdi	111
Minna	126
Mushin	302
Offa	178
Ogbomosho	660
Oka	130
Ondo	154
Onitsha	337
Oshogbo	441
Owo	166
Oyo	237
Port Harcourt	371
Sapele	126
Shagamu	106
Shaki	161
Shomolu	134
Sokoto	186
Warri	114
Zaria	345
Norway	**4,525**
Bergen	223
Oslo*	489
Stavanger	104
Trondheim	144
O	
Oman	**2,713**
Muscat*	67
P	
Pakistan	**147,663**
Bahāwalpur	180
Chiniot	106
Dera Ghāzi Khān	102
Faisalābād	1,104
Gujrānwāla	659
Gujrāt	155
Hyderābād	752
Islāmābād*	204
Jhang Sadar	196
Jhelum	106
Karāchi	5,076
Kasūr	156
Lahore	2,953
Lārkāna	124
Mardān	148
Mīrpur Khās	124
Multān	732
Nawābshāh	102
Okāra	127
Peshāwar	566
Quetta	286
Rahīmyār Khān	119
Rāwalpindi	795
Sāhīwāl	151
Sargodha	291
Shekhūpura	141
Siālkot	302
Sukkur	191
Wāh	127
Palau	**19**
Koror*	9
Panama	**2,882**
Panamá*	456
San Miguelito	282
Papua New Guinea	**5,172**
Port Moresby*	193
Paraguay	**5,884**
Asunción*	547
Ciudad del Este	134
San Lorenzo	133
Peru	**27,950**
Arequipa	625
Ayacucho	106
Cajamarca	112
Callao	512
Chiclayo	412
Chimbote	269
Chincha Alta	110
Comas	287
Cusco	256
Huancayo	258
Huánuco	119
Ica	161
Iquitos	275
Juliaca	143
Lima*	376
Piura	278
Pucallpa	172
Santa	146
Sullana	147
Tacna	174
Trujillo	509
Philippines	**76,104**
Angeles	234
Antipolo	346
Bacolod	402
Bacoor	251
Bago	132
Baguio	227
Baliuag	103
Batangas	212
Biñan	160
Binangonan	141
Bislig	104
Butuan	247
Cabanatuan	201
Cadiz	126
Cagayan de Oro	428
Cainta	202
Calamba	219
Calbayog	129
Caloocan	1,023
Cebu	662
Concepcion	101
Cotabato	147
Dagupan	126
Dasmariñas	262
Davao	1,007
Digos	107
General Santos	327
Ilagan	107
Iligan	273
Iloilo	335
Imus	177
Kabankalan	139
Koranadal	118
Lapu-Lapu	174
Las Pinas	413
Legaspi	142
Lipa	178
Lubao	110
Lucena	178
Mabalacat	130
Makati	484
Malabon	347
Malasiqui	101
Malaybalay	112
Malolos	47
Mandaluyong	287
Mandaue	195
Manila*	1,655
Marawi	114
Marikina	357
Meycauayan	137
Muntinglupa	400
Naga	127
Navotas	229
Olongapo	180
Ormoc	144
Ozamiz	102
Pagadian	125
Panabo	131
Parañaque	391
Pasay	409
Pasig	471
Puerto Princesa	130
Quezon City	1,989
Roxas	119
Sagay	128
San Carlos (Negros Occ.)	101
San Carlos (Pangasinan)	134
San Fernando	193
San Jose	101
San Jose del Monte	201
San Juan del Monte	124
San Miguel	108
San Pablo	184
San Pedro	189
Santa Maria	161
Santa Rosa	138
Sariaya	101
Silang	124
Silay	123
Surigao	105
Tacloban	167
Taguig	381
Tagum	157
Talisay	120
Tanauan	104
Tarlac	230
Taytay	145
Toledo	121
Tuguegarai	107
Urdaneta	100
Valencia	129
Valenzuela	437
Zamboanga	511
Poland	**38,625**
Białystok	268
Bielsko-Biała	181
Bydgoszcz	380
Bytom	230
Chorzów	132
Częstochowa	257
Dąbrowa Górnicza	135
Elblag	126
Gdańsk	462
Gdynia	251
Gliwice	212
Gorzów Wielkopolski	123
Grudziądz	102
Jastrzębie Zdroj	102
Kalisz	106
Katowice	366
Kielce	213
Koszalin	108
Kraków	746
Legnica	104
Łódź	849
Lublin	349
Olsztyn	161
Opole	127
Płock	121
Poznań	587
Radom	226
Ruda Śląska	169
Rybnik	142
Rzeszów	151
Słupsk	100
Sosnowiec	259
Szczecin	411
Tarnów	121
Toruń	201
Tychy	190
Wałbrzych	142
Warsaw*	1,651
Włocławek	121
Wodzisław Śląski	111
Wrocław	641
Zabrze	203
Zielona Góra	113
Portugal	**10,084**
Lisbon*	818
Porto	330
Q	
Qatar	**793**
Doha*	217
R	
Romania	**22,318**
Arad	190
Bacău	205
Baia Mare	149
Botoşani	126
Brăila	234
Braşov	324
Bucharest*	2,068
Buzău	148
Cluj-Napoca	329
Constanţa	351
Craiova	304
Drobeta-Turnu Severin	115
Focşani	101
Galaţi	326
Iaşi	344
Oradea	223
Piatra Neamţ	123
Piteşti	179
Ploieşti	253
Reşiţa	106
Rîmnicu Vîlcea	114
Satu Mare	132
Sibiu	165
Suceava	114
Timisoara	334
Tîrgu Mures	164
Russia	**144,979**
Abakan	158
Achinsk	122
Al'met'yevsk	137
Angarsk	268
Anzhero-Sudzhensk	105
Arkhangel'sk	410
Armavir	161
Arzamas	111
Astrakhan'	508
Balakovo	207
Balashikha	136
Barnaul	595
Belgorod	314
Belovo	112
Berezniki	197
Biysk	233
Blagoveshchensk	212
Bratsk	260
Bryansk	456
Cheboksary	446
Chelyabinsk	1,130
Cherepovets	318
Cherkessk	118
Chita	365
Dimitrovgrad	131
Dzerzhinsk	286
Elektrostal'	152
Engel's	185
Glazov	107
Groznyy	354
Irkutsk	630
Ivanovo	474
Izhevsk	652
Kaliningrad (Kalin.)	413
Kaliningrad (Moscow)	136
Kaluga	344
Kamensk-Ural'skiy	206
Kamyshin	128
Kansk	111
Kazan'	1,086
Kemerovo	513
Khabarovsk	608
Khimki	136
Kineshma	103
Kirov	491
Kiselevsk	125
Kislovodsk	110
Kolomna	162
Kolpino	145
Komsomol'sk-na-Amure	314
Kostroma	281
Kovrov	162
Krasnodar	636
Krasnoyarsk	917
Kurgan	360
Kursk	434
Kuznetsk	102
Leninsk-Kuznetskiy	131
Lipetsk	466
Lyubertsy	164
Magadan	138
Magnitogorsk	439
Makhachkala	325
Maykop	162
Mezhdurechensk	108
Miass	170
Michurinsk	106
Moscow*	8,527
Murmansk	454
Murom	125
Mytishchi	153
Naberezhnye Chelny	527
Nakhodka	164
Nal'chik	236
Neftekamsk	117
Nevinnomyssk	127
Nizhnekamsk	206
Nizhnevartovsk	245
Nizhniy Novgorod	1,425
Nizhniy Tagil	431
Noginsk	121
Noril'sk	170
Novgorod	233
Novocheboksarsk	123
Novocherkassk	187
Novokuybyshevsk	113
Novokuznetsk	597
Novomoskovsk	144
Novorossiysk	193
Novoshakhtinsk	106
Novosibirsk	1,424
Novotroitsk	108
Obninsk	106
Odintsovo	131
Oktyabr'skiy	108
Omsk	1,164
Orekhovo-Zuyevo	135
Orël	343
Orenburg	554
Orsk	275
Penza	548
Perm'	1,091
Pervoural'sk	143
Petropavlovsk-Kamchatskiy	265
Petrozavodsk	279
Podol'sk	204
Prokop'yevsk	265
Pskov	207
Pyatigorsk	128
Rostov	1,013
Rubtsovsk	171
Ryazan'	524
Rybinsk	251
Saint Petersburg	4,329
Salavat	156
Samara	1,232
Saransk	321
Sarapul	110
Saratov	899
Sergiyev Posad	115
Serov	102
Serpukhov	140
Severodvinsk	249
Shakhty	227
Shchelkovo	108
Smolensk	349
Sochi	328
Solikamsk	109
Staryy Oskol'	190
Stavropol'	333
Sterlitamak	255
Surgut	261
Syktyvkar	226
Syzran'	175
Taganrog	290
Tambov	311
Tol'yatti	682
Tomsk	498
Tula	534
Tver'	449
Tyumen'	491
Ufa	1,092
Ukhta	112
Ulan-Ude	364
Ul'yanovsk	664
Usol'ye-Sibirskoye	107
Ussuriysk	161
Ust'-Ilimsk	113
Velikiye Luki	116
Vladikavkaz	308
Vladimir	335
Vladivostok	637
Volgodonsk	183
Volgograd	997
Vologda	290
Volzhskiy	282
Vorkuta	111
Voronezh	899
Votkinsk	105
Yakutsk	196
Yaroslavl'	628
Yekaterinburg	1,351
Yelets	118
Yoshkar-Ola	248
Yuzhno-Sakhalinsk	160
Zelenograd	179
Zhukovskiy	101
Zlatoust	207
Rwanda	**7,398**
Kigali*	233
S	
Saint Kitts and Nevis	**39**
Basseterre*	13
Saint Lucia	**160**
Castries*	13
Saint Vincent and the Grenadines	**116**
Kingstown*	15
Samoa	**179**
Apia*	32
San Marino	**25**
San Marino*	3
Sao Tome and Principe	**170**
São Tomé*	43
Saudi Arabia	**23,513**
Ad Dammām	350
Al Hufūf	101
Aţ Ţā'if	410
Jiddah	1,500
Mecca	630
Medina	400
Riyadh*	1,800
Senegal	**10,590**
Dakar*	1,641
Kaolack	193
Saint Louis	132
Thiès	216
Zinguinchor	162
Seychelles	**80**
Victoria*	24
Sierra Leone	**5,615**
Freetown*	470
Singapore	**4,453**
Singapore*	3,462
Slovakia	**5,422**
Bratislava*	442
Košice	235
Slovenia	**1,933**
Ljubljana*	287
Maribor	105
Solomon Islands	**495**
Honiara*	30
Somalia	**7,753**
Mogadishu*	600
South Africa	**43,648**
Alexandra	125
Benoni	114
Bloemfontein	127
Boksburg	120
Botshabelo	178
Cape Town*	855
Carletonville	119
Daveyton	152
Diepmeadow	241
Durban	716
East London	102
Evaton	201
Germiston	134
Johannesburg	714
Katlehong	202
Kempton Park	107
Khayelitsa	190
KwaMashu	157
Lekoa	218
Mamelodi	155
Ntuzuma	102
Pietermaritzburg	156
Port Elizabeth	303
Pretoria*	526
Roodeport	163
Sandton	101
Soshanguve	146
Soweto	597
Tembisa	209
Umlazi	299
Virginia	118
Spain	**39,244**
Albacete	141
Alcalá de Henares	166
Alcorcón	142
Algeciras	104
Alicante	275
Almería	167
Badajoz	130
Badalona	219
Baracaldo	104
Barcelona	1,631
Bilbao	372
Burgos	166
Cádiz	155
Cartagena	180
Castellón de la Plana	139
Córdoba	316
Elche	191
Fuenlabrada	158
Getafe	144
Gijón	270
Granada	271
Huelva	145
Jaén	113
Jerez de la Frontera	190
La Coruña	255
La Laguna	125
Las Palmas de Gran Canaria	372
Leganés	178
León	147
L'Hospitalet de Llobregat	266
Lleida	114
Logroño	125
Madrid*	3,041
Málaga	531
Mataró	102
Móstoles	199

Country / City	Population in thousands
Murcia	342
Orense	109
Oviedo	202
Palma	322
Pamplona	182
Sabadell	189
Salamanca	167
San Sebastián	178
Santa Coloma de Gramenet	132
Santa Cruz de Tenerife	204
Santander	195
Saragossa	607
Seville	714
Tarragona	115
Terrassa	161
Valencia	764
Valladolid	337
Vigo	289
Vitoria	214
Sri Lanka	**19,577**
Colombo*	615
Dehiwala-Mount Lavinia	196
Galle	109
Jaffna	129
Kandy	104
Moratuwa	170
Sri Jayawardanapura (Kotte)	109
Sudan	**37,090**
Al Qaḑārif	189
Al Ubayyiḑ	228
Juba	115
Kassala	234
Khartoum*	925
Khartoum North	341
Nyala	112
Omdurman	229
Port Sudan	305
Wad Medanī	219
Suriname	**443**
Paramaribo*	180
Swaziland	**1,032**
Mbabane*	38
Sweden	**8,946**
Borås	102
Göteborg	433
Helsingborg	109
Jönköping	114
Linköping	122
Malmö	234
Norrköping	120
Örebro	121
Stockholm*	675
Uppsala	167
Västerås	120
Switzerland	**7,302**
Basel	174
Bern*	127
Geneva	174
Lausanne	116
Zürich	344
Syria	**17,156**
Aleppo	1,542
Al Mamishlī	113
Ar Raqqah	138
Damascus*	1,549
Dar'ā	180
Dayr az Zawr	133
Dūmā	131
Ḩamāh	273
Ḩimş	558
Idlib	113
Jaramānah	138
Latakia	303
Ţarţūs	137
T	
Taiwan	**22,548**
Changhua	165
Chiai	262
Chungli	270
Chutung	105
Fengshan	291
Fengyüan	121
Hsinchu	340
Hsinchuang	299
Hsintien	226
Hualien	108
Kaohsiung	1,424
Keelung (Chilung)	368
P'ingchen	147
P'ingtung	172
Sanchung	376
Shulin	112
T'aichung	850
T'ainan	706
T'aipei*	2,639
T'aoyüan	241
Yungho	250
Tajikistan	**6,720**
Dushanbe*	602
Khujand	163
Tanzania	**37,188**
Dar es Salaam*	1,361
Dodoma*	204
Mbeya	194
Mwanza	223
Tabora	214
Tanga	188
Zanzibar	158
Thailand	**62,354**
Bangkok*	5,876
Chiang Mai	167
Chon Buri	187
Khon Kaen	206
Nakhon Ratchasima	278
Nakhon Sawan	152
Nakhon Si Thammarat	112
Nonthaburi	233
Sara Buri	107
Songkhla	243
Togo	**5,286**
Lomé*	450
Tonga	**106**
Nuku'alofa*	21
Trinidad and Tobago	**1,164**
Port-of-Spain*	51
Tunisia	**9,816**
Al Qayrawān	103
Aryānah	153
Ettadhamen Douarhicher	149
Sūsah	125
Şafāqis	231
Tūnis*	674
Turkey	**67,309**
Adana	916
Adapazarı	171
Adıyaman	100
Ankara*	2,559
Antalya	378
Antioch	124
Aydın	107
Balıkesir	171
Batman	147
Bursa	835
Çorum	117
Denizli	204
Diyarbakır	381
Edirne	102
Elazığ	205
Erzurum	242
Eskişehir	413
Gaziantep	603
Gebze	159
İskenderun	155
Isparta	112
İstanbul	6,620
İzmir	1,757
İzmit	257
Kağıthane	269
Kahramanmaraş	228
Karabük	105
Kayseri	421
Kırıkkale	185
Konya	513
Kütahya	131
Malatya	282
Manisa	159
Mersin	422
Ordu	102
Osmaniye	122
Samsun	304
Sivas	222
Tarsus	188
Trabzon	144
Urfa	277
Uşak	105
Van	153
Zonguldak	117
Turkmenistan	**4,689**
Ashgabat*	407
Chärjew	164
Dashhowuz	114
Tuvalu	**11**
Funafuti*	2
U	
Uganda	**24,699**
Kampala*	774
Ukraine	**48,396**
Alchevs'k	127
Bila Tserkva	209
Berdyans'k	137
Cherkasy	308
Chernihiv	311
Chernivtsi	261
Dniprodzerzhyns'k	287
Dnipropetrovs'k	1,190
Donets'k	1,121
Horlivka	336
Ivano-Frankivs'k	230
Kam'yanets'-Podol's'kyy	106
Kerch	181
Kharkiv	1,622
Kherson	368
Khmel'nytskyy	250
Kirovohrad	280
Kiev*	2,643
Kostyantynivka	107
Kramators'k	203
Krasnyy Luch	114
Kremenchuk	245
Kryvyy Rih	729
Luhans'k	505
Luts'k	215
L'viv	807
Lysychans'k	127
Makiyivka	426
Mariupol'	523
Melitopol'	178
Mykolayiv	515
Nikopol'	160
Odesa	1,096
Oleksandriya	106
Pavlohrad	136
Poltava	324
Rivne	244
Sevastopol'	371
Simferopol'	357
Slov'yans'k	138
Stakhanov	113
Sumy	305
Syeverodonets'k	134
Ternopil'	225
Uzhhorod	125
Vinnytsya	384
Yenakiyeve	120
Yevpatoriya	108
Zaporizhzhya	898
Zhytomyr	299
United Arab Emirates	**2,446**
Abu Dhabi*	243
Al 'Ayn	102
Ash Shāriqah	125
Dubayy	266
United Kingdom	**61,454**
Aberdeen	219
Basildon	101
Belfast	295
Birmingham	966
Blackburn	106
Blackpool	146
Bolton	139
Bournemouth	155
Bradford	289
Brighton	125
Bristol	408
Cardiff	272
Coventry	299
Derby	224
Dudley	192
Dundee	151
Edinburgh	448
Glasgow	618
Gloucester	114
Hillingdon	231
Huddersfield	144
Ipswich	130
Kingston upon Hull	311
Kingston upon Thames	132
Leeds	424
Leicester	319
Liverpool	482
London*	6,680
Luton	172
Manchester	403
Middlesbrough	147
Newcastle upon Tyne	189
Newport	116
Northampton	180
Norwich	171
Nottingham	270
Oldham	104
Oxford	119
Peterborough	135
Plymouth	245
Poole	138
Portsmouth	175
Preston	178
Reading	213
Rotherham	121
Saint Helens	106
Sheffield	432
Slough	111
Southampton	210
Southend-on-Sea	159
Stockport	133
Stoke-on-Trent	267
Sunderland	183
Sutton Coldfield	106
Swansea	171
Swindon	145
Thanet	117
Walsall	175
Watford	113
West Bromwich	146
Wolverhampton	258
York	125
United States	**280,562**
Abilene	116
Akron	217
Albuquerque	449
Alexandria	128
Allentown	107
Amarillo	174
Amherst	117
Anaheim	328
Anchorage	260
Ann Arbor	114
Arlington (Tex.)	333
Arlington (Va.)	189
Arvada	102
Athens	101
Atlanta	417
Augusta	200
Aurora (Colo.)	276
Aurora (Ill.)	143
Austin	657
Bakersfield	247
Baltimore	651
Baton Rouge	228
Beaumont	114
Bellevue	110
Berkeley	103
Birmingham	243
Boise	186
Boston	589
Bridgeport	140
Brownsville	140
Buffalo	293
Burbank	100
Cambridge	101
Cape Coral	102
Carrollton	110
Cedar Rapids	121
Chandler	177
Charlotte	541
Chattanooga	156
Chesapeake	199
Chicago	2,896
Chula Vista	174
Cincinnati	331
Citrus Heights	107
Clarksville	103
Clearwater	109
Cleveland	478
Colorado Springs	361
Columbia	116
Columbus (Ga.)	186
Columbus (Ohio)	711
Concord	122
Coral Springs	118
Corona	125
Corpus Christi	277
Costa Mesa	109
Dallas	1,189
Daly City	104
Dayton	166
Denver	555
Des Moines	199
Detroit	951
Downey	107
Durham	187
East Los Angeles	124
Elizabeth	121
El Monte	116
El Paso	564
Erie	104
Escondido	134
Eugene	138
Evansville	122
Fayetteville	121
Flint	125
Fontana	129
Fort Collins	119
Fort Lauderdale	152
Fort Wayne	206
Fort Worth	535
Fremont	203
Fresno	428
Fullerton	126
Garden Grove	165
Garland	216
Gary	103
Gilbert	110
Glendale (Ariz.)	219
Glendale (Calif.)	195
Grand Prairie	128
Grand Rapids	198
Green Bay	102
Greensboro	224
Hampton	146
Hartford	122
Hayward	140
Henderson	175
Hialeah	226
Hollywood	139
Honolulu	372
Houston	1,954
Huntington Beach	190
Huntsville	158
Independence	113
Indianapolis	792
Inglewood	113
Irvine	143
Irving	192
Jackson	184
Jacksonville	736
Jersey City	240
Joliet	106
Kansas City (Kans.)	147
Kansas City (Mo.)	442
Knoxville	174
Lafayette	110
Lakewood	144
Lancaster	119
Lansing	119
Laredo	177
Las Vegas	478
Lexington	261
Lincoln	226
Little Rock	183
Livonia	101
Long Beach	462
Los Angeles	3,695
Louisville	256
Lowell	105
Lubbock	200
Madison	208
Manchester	107
McAllen	106
Memphis	650
Mesa	396
Mesquite	125
Metairie	146
Miami	362
Milwaukee	597
Minneapolis	383
Mobile	199
Modesto	189
Montgomery	202
Moreno Valley	142
Naperville	128
Nashville	570
Newark	274
New Haven	124
New Orleans	485
Newport News	180
New York	8,008
Norfolk	234
North Las Vegas	115
Norwalk	103
Oakland	399
Oceanside	161
Oklahoma City	506
Omaha	390
Ontario	158
Orange	129
Orlando	186
Overland Park	149
Oxnard	170
Palmdale	117
Paradise	186
Pasadena (Calif.)	134
Pasadena (Tex.)	142
Paterson	149
Pembroke Pines	137
Peoria (Ariz.)	108
Peoria (Ill.)	113
Philadelphia	1,518
Phoenix	1,321
Pittsburgh	335
Plano	222
Pomona	149
Portland	529
Portsmouth	101
Providence	174
Provo	105
Pueblo	102
Raleigh	276
Rancho Cucamonga (Cucamonga)	128
Reno	180
Richmond	198
Riverside	255
Rochester	220
Rockford	150
Sacramento	407
Saint Louis	348
Saint Paul	287
Saint Petersburg	248
Salem	137
Salinas	151
Salt Lake City	182
San Antonio	1,145
San Bernardino	185
San Diego	1,223
San Francisco	777
San Jose	895
Santa Ana	338
Santa Clara	102
Santa Clarita	151
Santa Rosa	148
Savannah	132
Scottsdale	203
Seattle	563
Shreveport	200
Simi Valley	111
Sioux Falls	124
South Bend	108
Spokane	196
Springfield (Ill.)	111
Springfield (Mass.)	152
Springfield (Mo.)	152
Stamford	117
Sterling Heights	124
Stockton	244
Sunnyvale	132
Sunrise Manor	156
Syracuse	147
Tacoma	194
Tallahassee	151
Tampa	303
Tempe	159
Thousand Oaks	117
Toledo	314
Topeka	122
Torrance	138
Tucson	487
Tulsa	393
Vallejo	117
Vancouver	144
Ventura	101
Virginia Beach	425
Waco	114
Warren	138
Washington, D.C.*	572
Waterbury	107
West Covina	105
West Valley City	109
Westminster	101
Wichita	344
Wichita Falls	104
Winston-Salem	186
Worcester	173
Yonkers	196
Uruguay	**3,387**
Montevideo*	1,360
Uzbekistan	**25,563**
Andijon	297
Angren	133
Bukhoro	228
Chirchiq	159
Farghona	198
Jizzakh	108
Marghilon	125
Namangan	312
Nawoiy	110
Nukus	175
Olmaliq	116
Qarshi	163
Qūqon	176
Samarqand	370
Tashkent*	2,094
Urganch	129
V	
Vanuatu	**196**
Port-Vila*	19
Vatican City	**1**
Vatican City*	1
Venezuela	**24,288**
Acarigua	117
Barcelona	222
Barinas	154
Barquisimeto	625
Baruta	183
Cabimas	166
Caracas*	1,822
Catia La Mar	100
Ciudad Bolívar	225
Ciudad Guayana	453
Coro	125
Cumaná	212
Guacara	101
Guarenas	134
Los Teques	141
Maracaibo	1,250
Maracay	354
Maturín	207
Mérida	171
Petare	338
Puerto Cabello	129
Puerto La Cruz	156
San Cristóbal	221
San Francisco	198
Turmero	174
Valencia	904
Vietnam	**81,098**
Bien Hoa	274
Cam Pha	105
Cam Ranh	118
Can Tho	208
Da Lat	103
Da Nang	370
Haiphong	450
Hanoi*	1,090
Ho Chi Minh City	2,900
Hong Gai	123
Hue	212
Long Xuyen	129
My Tho	105
Nam Dinh	166
Nha Trang	213
Phan Thiet	114
Qui Nhon	160
Rach Gia	138
Thai Nguyen	125
Vinh	111
Vung Tau	124
Y	
Yemen	**18,701**
Al Ḩudaydah	155
Al Mukallā	154
Aden	562
Sanaa*	972
Ta'izz	178
Yugoslavia (Serbia & Montenegro)	**11,210**
Belgrade*	1,555
Kragujevac	147
Niš	176
Novi Sad	179
Podgorica	118
Priština	125
Subotica	100
Uroševac	114
Z	
Zambia	**9,959**
Chingola	168
Kabwe	167
Kitwe	247
Lusaka*	982
Ndola	376
Zimbabwe	**11,377**
Bulawayo	622
Chitungwiza	275
Gweru	125
Harare*	1,189
Mutare	132
Uroševac	114
Areas of Special Sovereignty	
Hong Kong (China)	**7,303**
Kowloon	775
New Kowloon	1,527
Sha Tin	550
Tai Po	260
Tsuen Wan	700
Tuen Mun	432
Victoria*	1,251
Yuen Long	143
Macau (China)	**462**
Macau*	343
Puerto Rico (U.S.)	**3,958**
Bayamón	202
Carolina	162
Ponce	159
San Juan*	427

Foreign Geographic Terms

Foreign Term	Language	English Meaning
A		
Adrar	Berber	Mountains
Aiguille	French	Peak
Ákra	Greek	Cape
Altos	Spanish	Mountains
Älv, Älven	Swedish	River
Anse	French	Cove
Archipiélago	Spanish	Archipelago
Arcipelago	Italian	Archipelago
Arquipélago	Portuguese	Archipelago
Arrecife	Spanish	Reef
Arroyo	Spanish	Stream
'Ayn	Arabic	Spring
B		
Baai	Dutch	Bay
Bab	Arabic	Strait
Bach	German	Stream
Bælt	Danish	Strait
Bahía	Spanish	Bay
Baḥr	Arabic	River, Sea
Baia	Portuguese	Bay
Baie	French	Bay
Ballon	French	Dome
Bana	Japanese	Cape
Bañados	Spanish	Marsh
Bandar	Persian	Harbor
Barrage	French	Dam, Reservoir
Bassin	French	Basin
Bāţlāq	Persian	Marsh
Be'er	Hebrew	Well
Belt	German	Strait
Ben, Beinn	Gaelic	Mountain
Berg	Afrikaans, German	Mountain
Bi'r	Arabic	Well
Birkat	Arabic	Lake
Boca	Spanish	River Mouth
Bogd	Mongolian	Range
Bolsón	Spanish	Depression
Botn	Norwegian	Bay
Brazo	Spanish	River Branch
Bucht	German	Bay
Bugt	Danish	Bay
Buhayrat	Arabic	Lake, Lagoon
Bukit	Malay	Mountain
Bukt, Bukten	Swedish	Bay
Bulu	Indonesian	Mountain
Burj	Arabic	Hill
Burnu, Burun	Turkish	Cape
Busen	German	Bay
C		
Cabo	Portuguese, Spanish	Cape
Cañada	Spanish	Stream
Canal	Portuguese, Spanish	Channel
Canale	Italian	Canal
Cap	French	Cape
Capo	Italian	Cape
Cataratas	Spanish	Waterfalls
Catena	Spanish	Range
Causse	French	Upland
Cayos	Spanish	Cays
Cerro(s)	Spanish	Hill(s)
Chaîne	French	Range
Chapada	Portuguese	Hills
Chott	Arabic	Intermittent Lakes, Marshes
Chroüy	Cambodian	Cape
Chute(s)	French	Waterfall(s)
Ciénaga	Spanish	Marsh
Cima	Italian, Spanish	Peak
Cime	French	Peak
Città	Italian	City
Ciudad	Spanish	City
Co	Tibetan	Lake
Col	French	Pass
Colina(s)	Spanish	Hill(s)
Colle	Italian	Pass
Colline	Italian	Hills
Collines	French	Hills
Cordillera	Spanish	Range
Corno	Italian	Peak
Costa	Portuguese, Spanish	Coast
Côte	French	Coast, Ridge
Coteau	French	Hills
Csatorna	Magyar	Canal
Cuchilla	Spanish	Hills
Cumbre	Spanish	Peak
D		
Dağ, Daği	Turkish	Mountain
Dake	Japanese	Mountain
Dal, Dalen	Swedish	Valley
Damägheh	Persian	Cape
Daryächeh	Persian	Lake
Dasht	Persian	Desert
Desierto	Spanish	Desert
Détroit	French	Strait
Dhar	Arabic	Escarpment
Diep	Dutch	Channel
Dijk	Dutch	Dike
Ding	Chinese	Hill
Djebel	Arabic	Mountain(s)
Doi	Thai	Mountain
Dyb	Danish	Strait
E		
Eiland	Dutch	Island
Elv	Norwegian	River
Embalse	Spanish	Reservoir
Emi	Berber	Mountain
Enseada	Portuguese	Cove
Ensenada	Spanish	Cove
Erg	Arabic	Desert
Estrecho	Spanish	Strait
Étang	French	Lagoon
F		
Falaise	French	Cliff
Feld	German	Plain
Feng	Chinese	Mountain
Firth	Gaelic	Estuary
Fjärden	Swedish	Bay, Sound
Fjord, Fjorden	Norwegian	Inlet
Fjördhur	Icelandic	Bay
Fljót	Icelandic	River
Flói	Icelandic	Bay
Foci	Italian	River Mouths
G		
Gat	Danish, Dutch	Marine Channel
Gebirge	German	Range
Geçidi	Turkish	Pass
Gobi	Mongolian	Desert
Göl	Turkish	Lake
Golfe	French	Gulf
Golfo	Italian, Spanish	Gulf
Gora	Russian	Mountain
Got	Korean	Cape
Graben	German	Ditch
Guan	Chinese	Pass
Guelb	Arabic	Mountain
Gunung	Indonesian	Mountain
H		
Hai	Chinese	Sea
Hamada	Arabic	Desert
Ḩammādat	Arabic	Plateau
Ḩāmūn	Persian	Intermittent Salt Lake
Har	Hebrew	Mountain
Havet	Norwegian	Bay
Ḩawd	Arabic	Oasis
Hayk'	Amharic (Ethiopia)	Lake
Hegy	Magyar	Mountain
Heide	Arabic	Heath
Hoek	Dutch	Point
Höhe	German	Height
Holm	Danish, Swedish	Island
Horn	German	Point
Hornatina	Czech, Slovak	Plateau
Hory	Czech, Slovak	Range
Hügel	German	Hill
I		
Île(s)	French	Island(s)
Ilha(s)	Portuguese	Island(s)
Insel(n)	German	Island(s)
Irmak	Turkish	River
Isla(s)	Spanish	Island(s)
Isola, Isole	Italian	Island, Islands
J		
Jabal	Arabic	Mountains
Järvi	Finnish	Lake
Jazīrat, Jazā'ir	Arabic	Island, Islands
Jbel	Arabic	Mountain(s)
Jezero	Czech, Slovak	Lake
Jezioro	Polish	Lake
Jiao	Chinese	Cape
Jibāl	Arabic	Mountain(s)
Joki	Finnish	River
Jökull	Icelandic	Glacier
Jolgeh	Persian	Plain
K		
Kaap	Dutch	Cape
Kabīr	Persian	Mountains
Kanaal	Dutch	Canal
Kanal	German, Serbo-Croatian	Canal
Kangri	Tibetan	Peak
Kap	German	Cape
Kapp	Norwegian	Cape
Kavīr	Persian	Desert
Kawlat	Arabic	Mountain
Kawm	Arabic	Hill
Kep	Albanian	Cape
Khalīj	Arabic	Gulf
Khao	Thai	Mountain
Khatt	Arabic	Intermittent River
Khawr	Arabic	Intermittent River
Khazzān	Arabic	Dam
Khuan	Thai	Lake
Kloof	Dutch	Gap
Kogel	German	Mountain
Kop	Dutch	Peak
Kopf	German	Peak
Kreb	Arabic	Dune
Küh	Persian	Mountain
L		
La	Tibetan	Pass
Lac(s)	French	Lake(s)
Laem	Thai	Cape
Laga, Lagh	Swahili	Intermittent River
Lago(s)	Italian, Portuguese, Spanish	Lake(s)
Lagoa	Portuguese	Lake
Laguna	Spanish	Lagoon
Les	Czech	Mountains
Ling	Chinese	Mountain
Llano(s)	Spanish	Plain(s)
Loch, Lough	Gaelic	Inlet, Lake
M		
Mägi	Estonian	Mountain
Mare	Italian	Sea
Marsä	Arabic	Bay
Maşabb	Arabic	River Mouth
Maşrif	Arabic	Canal
Massif	French	Upland
Meer	Afrikaans, Dutch, German	Lake, Sea
Meseta	Spanish	Plateau
Mifraz	Hebrew	Bay
Misaki	Japanese	Cape
Mont(s)	French	Mountain(s)
Montagna	Italian	Mountain
Montagne(s)	French	Mountain(s)
Montaña(s)	Spanish	Mountain(s)
Monte	Italian, Portuguese, Spanish	Mountain
Montes	Portuguese, Spanish	Mountains
Monti	Italian	Mountains
Morne	French	Mountain
Morro	Portuguese, Spanish	Mountain
Mui	Vietnamese	Cape
Mys	Russian	Cape
N		
Nafūd	Arabic	Desert
Naḥal	Hebrew	River
Nahr	Arabic	River
Namakzär	Persian	Salt Flat
Neem	Estonian	Cape
Nek	Dutch	Pass
Nevado	Spanish	Snow-covered Peak
Nina	Estonian	Cape
Nos	Russian	Cape
Nosy	Malagasy	Island
O		
Ø, Øy	Norwegian	Island
Odde	Danish	Point
Óros	Greek	Mountain
Otok	Serbo-Croatian	Island
Ouadi, Oued	Arabic	Intermittent River
Ozero	Russian	Lake
P		
Pampa	Spanish	Plain
Pantanal	Portuguese, Spanish	Swamp
Pas	Dutch	Pass
Pas	French	Strait
Paso	Spanish	Pass
Passage	French	Marine Channel
Peña, Peñasco	Spanish	Peak
Pereval	Russian	Pass
Phnum	Cambodian	Mountain
Phou	Lao	Mountain
Pi	Chinese	Cape
Pic	French	Peak
Picacho	Spanish	Peak
Picco	Italian	Peak
Pico(s)	Portuguese, Spanish	Peak(s)
Pik	Russian	Peak
Pique	French	Peak
Piton	French	Mountain
Piz, Pizzo	Italian	Peak
Planalto	Portuguese	Plateau
Planina	Serbo-Croatian	Plain
Plato	Afrikaans	Plateau
Playa	Spanish	Beach
Plōsina	Czech	Plateau
Pointe	French	Point
Ponta	Portuguese	Point
Presa	Spanish	Dam, Reservoir
Presqu'île	French	Peninsula
Prokhod	Bulgarian	Pass
Promontorio	Italian	Promontory
Puncak	Indonesian	Mountain
Punt	Dutch	Point
Punta	Italian, Spanish	Point
Q		
Qanät	Arabic	Canal
Qiryat	Hebrew	City
Qolleh	Persian	Mountain
R		
Rada	Spanish	Anchorage
Rade	French	Anchorage
Rann	Hindi	Marsh
Rapides	French	Rapids
Ras, Ra's	Arabic	Cape
Recifes	Portuguese	Reefs
Represa	Portuguese	Dam, Reservoir
Retto	Japanese	Islands
Rio	Portuguese	River
Río	Spanish	River
Rivier	Dutch	River
Rivière	French	River
Rosh	Hebrew	Cape
Rt	Serbo-Croatian	Cape
S		
Sabana	Spanish	Savanna
Sabkhat	Arabic	Lagoon, Salt Marsh
Săgar	Hindi	Lake
Saguia	Arabic	Intermittent River
Şaḥrā'	Arabic	Desert
Saki	Japanese	Cape
Salar	Spanish	Salt Flat
Salina(s)	Spanish	Salt Flat(s)
Salto(s)	Portuguese, Spanish	Waterfall(s)
San	Japanese	Mountain
Sarīr	Arabic	Desert
Sebjet	Arabic	Dry Lake
Sebkha	Arabic	Salt Flat
See	German	Lake
Selkä	Finnish	Bay
Serra	Portuguese	Range
Serranía(s)	Spanish	Ridge(s)
Seto	Japanese	Strait
Sgurr	Gaelic	Mountain
Shan	Chinese	Mountain
Shankou	Chinese	Pass
Shaţţ	Arabic	Intermittent Lake
Shet'	Amharic (Ethiopia)	River
Shima	Japanese	Island
Shotō	Japanese	Islands
Sierra	Spanish	Range
Sistema	Spanish	Range
Sjö, Sjön	Swedish	Lake
Slieve	Gaelic	Mountain
Sø	Danish	Lake
Sommet	French	Peak
Sopka	Russian	Volcano
Spitze	German	Peak
Stausee	German	Reservoir
Stretto	Italian	Strait
Sund	Danish, Swedish	Sound
T		
Tal	German	Valley
Tall	Arabic	Mountain
Tanjona	Malagasy	Cape
Tanjung	Malay	Cape
Tanjung	Indonesian	Cape
Tassili	Berber	Plateau
Ténéré	Berber	Desert
Tepe	Turkish	Peak
Terara	Amharic (Ethiopia)	Mountain
Tō	Japanese	Island
Tó	Magyar	Lake
Tōge	Japanese	Pass
Tunturi	Finnish	Mountain
U		
Udde	Swedish	Point
Udolni	Czech	Reservoir
Uul	Mongolian	Mountain
Úval	Czech	Valley
V		
Val	French, Italian	Valley
Valle	Italian, Spanish	Valley
Vallée	French	Valley
Vallen	Dutch	Waterfall
Valli	Italian	Lagoon
Vatn	Norwegian	Lake
Veld	Dutch	Plain
Vig	Danish	Bay
Vik, Viken	Swedish	Bay
Vîrful	Romanian	Mountain
Vliet	Dutch	Channel
Vodoskhovyshche	Ukrainian	Reservoir
Volcán	Spanish	Volcano
Vrch	Serbo-Croatian	Mountain
Vrchy	Czech, Slovak	Range
Vysočina	Czech, Slovak	Plateau
W		
Wabē	Amharic (Ethiopia)	River
Wādī	Arabic	Intermittent River
Waḩāt	Arabic	Oasis
Wald	German	Forest, Mountains
Webi	Somali	River
Wenz	Amharic (Ethiopia)	River
Y		
Yam	Hebrew	Lake, Sea
Yama	Japanese	Mountain
Z		
Zaki	Japanese	Point
Zatoka	Ukranian	Gulf
Zee	Dutch	Lake, Sea
Zemlya	Russian	Land

Index of the World

This index is a comprehensive listing of the places and geographic features found in the atlas. Names are arranged in strict alphabetical order, without regard to hyphens or spaces. Every name is followed by the country or area to which it belongs. Except for cities, towns and cultural areas, all entries include a reference to feature type, such as province, river, island, peak, and so on. The page number and alpha-numeric code appear in blue to the right of each listing. The page number directs you to the largest scale map on which the name can be found. The code refers to the grid squares formed by the horizontal and vertical lines of latitude and longitude on each map. Following the letters from left to right and the numbers from top to bottom helps you to quickly locate the square containing the place or feature. Inset maps have their own alpha-numeric codes. Names on the map that are accompanied by a point symbol are indexed to the symbol's grid location. Other names are indexed in the grid in which the initial letter of the name falls. When a map name contains a subordinate or alternate name, both names are listed in the index. To conserve space and provide room for more entries, many abbreviations are used in this index. The primary abbreviations are listed below.

Index Abbreviations

A

Ab,Can	Alberta
Abor.	Aboriginal
Acad.	Academy
ACT	Australian Capital Territory
A.F.B.	Air Force Base
Afld.	Airfield
Afg.	Afghanistan
Afr.	Africa
Ak,US	Alaska
Al,US	Alabama
Alb.	Albania
Alg.	Algeria
Amm. Dep.	Ammunition Depot
And.	Andorra
Ang.	Angola
Angu.	Anguilla
Ant.	Antarctica
Anti.	Antigua and Barbuda
Ar,US	Arkansas
Arch.	Archipelago
Arg.	Argentina
Arm.	Armenia
Arpt.	Airport
Aru.	Aruba
ASam.	American Samoa
Ash.	Ashmore and Cartier Islands
Aus.	Austria
Austl.	Australia
Aut.	Autonomous
Az,US	Arizona
Azer.	Azerbaijan
Azor.	Azores

B

Bahm.	Bahamas, The
Bahr.	Bahrain
Bang.	Bangladesh
Bar.	Barbados
BC,Can	British Columbia
Bela.	Belarus
Belg.	Belgium
Belz.	Belize
Ben.	Benin
Berm.	Bermuda
Bfld.	Battlefield
Bhu.	Bhutan
Bol.	Bolivia
Bor.	Borough
Bosn.	Bosnia and Herzegovina
Bots.	Botswana
Braz.	Brazil
Brln.	British Indian Ocean Territory
Bru.	Brunei
Bul.	Bulgaria
Burk.	Burkina Faso
Buru.	Burundi
BVI	British Virgin Islands

C

Ca,US	California
CAfr.	Central African Republic
Camb.	Cambodia
Camr.	Cameroon
Can.	Canada
Can.	Canal
Canl.	Canary Islands
Cap.	Capital
Cap. Dist.	Capital District
Cap. Terr.	Capital Territory
Cay.	Cayman Islands
C.d'Iv.	Côte d'Ivoire
C.G.	Coast Guard
Chan.	Channel
Chl.	Channel Islands
Co.	County
Co,US	Colorado
Col.	Colombia
Com.	Comoros
Cont.	Continent
CpV.	Cape Verde Islands
CR	Costa Rica
Cr.	Creek
Cro.	Croatia
CSea.	Coral Sea Islands Territory
Ct,US	Connecticut
Ctr.	Center
Ctry.	Country
Cyp.	Cyprus
Czh.	Czech Republic

D

DC,US	District of Columbia
De,US	Delaware
Den.	Denmark
Depr.	Depression
Dept.	Department
Des.	Desert
DF	Distrito Federal
Dist.	District
Djib.	Djibouti
Dom.	Dominica
Dpcy.	Dependency
D.R.Congo	Democratic Republic of the Congo
DRep.	Dominican Republic

E

Ecu.	Ecuador
Emb.	Embankment
Eng.	Engineering
Eng,UK	England
EqG.	Equatorial Guinea
Erit..	Eritrea
ESal.	El Salvador
Est.	Estonia
Eth.	Ethiopia
ETim.	East Timor
Eur.	Europe

F

Falk.	Falkland Islands
Far.	Faroe Islands
Fed. Dist.	Federal District
Fin.	Finland
Fl,US	Florida
For.	Forest
Fr.	France
FrAnt.	French Southern and Antarctic Lands
FrG.	French Guiana
FrPol.	French Polynesia
FYROM	Former Yugoslav Rep. of Macedonia

G

Ga,US	Georgia
Galp.	Galapagos Islands
Gam.	Gambia, The
Gaza	Gaza Strip
GBis.	Guinea-Bissau
Geo.	Georgia
Ger.	Germany
Gha.	Ghana
Gib.	Gibraltar
Glac.	Glacier
Gov.	Governorate
Govt.	Government
Gre.	Greece
Grld.	Greenland
Gren.	Grenada
Grsld.	Grassland
Guad.	Guadeloupe
Guat.	Guatemala
Gui.	Guinea
Guy.	Guyana

H

Har.	Harbor
Hi,US	Hawaii
Hist.	Historic(al)
Hon.	Honduras
Hts.	Heights
Hun.	Hungary

I

Ia,US	Iowa
Ice.	Iceland
Id,US	Idaho
Il,US	Illinois
IM	Isle of Man
In,US	Indiana
Ind. Res.	Indian Reservation
Indo.	Indonesia
Int'l	International
Ire.	Ireland
Isl., Isls.	Island, Islands
Isr.	Israel
Isth.	Isthmus
It.	Italy

J

Jam.	Jamaica
Jor.	Jordan

K

Kaz.	Kazakhstan
Kiri.	Kiribati
Ks,US	Kansas
Kuw.	Kuwait
Ky,US	Kentucky
Kyr.	Kyrgyzstan

L

La,US	Louisiana
Lab.	Laboratory
Lag.	Lagoon
Lakesh.	Lakeshore
Lat.	Latvia
Lcht.	Liechtenstein
Ldg.	Landing
Leb.	Lebanon
Les.	Lesotho
Libr.	Liberia
Lith.	Lithuania
Lux.	Luxembourg

M

Ma,US	Massachusetts
Madg.	Madagascar
Madr.	Madeira
Malay.	Malaysia
Mald.	Maldives
Malw.	Malawi
Mart.	Martinique
May.	Mayotte
Mb,Can	Manitoba
Md,US	Maryland
Me,US	Maine
Mem.	Memorial
Mex.	Mexico
Mi,US	Michigan
Micr.	Micronesia, Federated States of
Mil.	Military
Mn,US	Minnesota
Mo,US	Missouri
Mol.	Moldova
Mon.	Monument
Mona.	Monaco
Mong.	Mongolia
Monts.	Montserrat
Mor.	Morocco
Moz.	Mozambique
Mrsh.	Marshall Islands
Mrta.	Mauritania
Mrts.	Mauritius
Ms,US	Mississippi
Mt.	Mount
Mt,US	Montana
Mtn., Mts.	Mountain, Mountains
Mun. Arpt.	Municipal Airport
Myan.	Myanmar

N

NAm.	North America
Namb.	Namibia
NAnt.	Netherlands Antilles
Nat'l	National
Nav.	Naval
NB,Can	New Brunswick
Nbrhd.	Neighborhood
NC,US	North Carolina
NCal.	New Caledonia
ND,US	North Dakota
Ne,US	Nebraska
Neth.	Netherlands
Nf,Can	Newfoundland
Nga.	Nigeria
NH,US	New Hampshire
NI,UK	Northern Ireland
Nic.	Nicaragua
NJ,US	New Jersey
NKor.	North Korea
NM,US	New Mexico
NMar.	Northern Mariana Islands
Nor.	Norway
NS,Can	Nova Scotia
Nv,US	Nevada
Nun.,Can	Nunavut
NW,Can	Northwest Territories
NY,US	New York
NZ	New Zealand

O

Obl.	Oblast
Oh,US	Ohio
Ok,US	Oklahoma
On,Can	Ontario
Or,US	Oregon

P

Pa,US	Pennsylvania
PacUS	Pacific Islands, U.S.
Pak.	Pakistan
Pan.	Panama
Par.	Paraguay
Par.	Parish
PE,Can	Prince Edward Island
Pen.	Peninsula
Phil.	Philippines
Phys. Reg.	Physical Region
Pitc.	Pitcairn Islands
Plat.	Plateau
PNG	Papua New Guinea
Pol.	Poland
Port.	Portugal
Poss.	Possession
Pkwy.	Parkway
PR	Puerto Rico
Pref.	Prefecture
Prov.	Province
Prsv.	Preserve
Pt.	Point

Q

Qu,Can	Quebec

R

Rec.	Recreation(al)
Ref.	Refuge
Reg.	Region
Rep.	Republic
Res.	Reservoir, Reservation
Reun.	Réunion
RI,US	Rhode Island
Riv.	River
Rom.	Romania
Rsv.	Reserve
Rus.	Russia
Rvwy.	Riverway
Rwa.	Rwanda

S

SAfr.	South Africa
Sam.	Samoa
SAm.	South America
SaoT.	São Tomé and Príncipe
SAr.	Saudi Arabia
Sc,UK	Scotland
SC,US	South Carolina
SD,US	South Dakota
Seash.	Seashore
Sen.	Senegal
Sey.	Seychelles
SGeo.	South Georgia and Sandwich Islands
Sing.	Singapore
Sk,Can	Saskatchewan
SKor.	South Korea
SLeo.	Sierra Leone
Slov.	Slovenia
Slvk.	Slovakia
SMar.	San Marino
Sol.	Solomon Islands
Som.	Somalia
Sp.	Spain
Spr., Sprs.	Spring, Springs
SrL.	Sri Lanka
Sta.	Station
StH.	Saint Helena
Str.	Strait
StK.	Saint Kitts and Nevis
StL.	Saint Lucia
StP.	Saint Pierre and Miquelon
StV.	Saint Vincent and the Grenadines
Sur.	Suriname
Sval.	Svalbard
Swaz.	Swaziland
Swe.	Sweden
Swi.	Switzerland

T

Tah.	Tahiti
Tai.	Taiwan
Taj.	Tajikistan
Tanz.	Tanzania
Ter.	Terrace
Terr.	Territory
Thai.	Thailand
Tn,US	Tennessee
Tok.	Tokelau
Trg.	Training
Trin.	Trinidad and Tobago
Trkm.	Turkmenistan
Trks.	Turks and Caicos Islands
Tun.	Tunisia
Tun.	Tunnel
Turk.	Turkey
Tuv.	Tuvalu
Twp.	Township
Tx,US	Texas

U

UAE	United Arab Emirates
Ugan.	Uganda
UK	United Kingdom
Ukr.	Ukraine
Uru.	Uruguay
US	United States
USVI	U.S. Virgin Islands
Ut,US	Utah
Uzb.	Uzbekistan

V

Va,US	Virginia
Val.	Valley
Van.	Vanuatu
VatC.	Vatican City
Ven.	Venezuela
Viet.	Vietnam
Vill.	Village
Vol.	Volcano
Vt,US	Vermont

W

Wa,US	Washington
Wal,UK	Wales
Wall.	Wallis and Futuna
WBnk.	West Bank
Wi,US	Wisconsin
Wild.	Wildlife, Wilderness
WSah.	Western Sahara
WV,US	West Virginia
Wy,US	Wyoming

Y

Yem.	Yemen
Yk,Can	Yukon Territory
Yugo.	Yugoslavia (Serbia & Montenegro)

Z

Zam.	Zambia
Zim.	Zimbabwe

A'alī an Nīl (pol. reg.), Sudan 117/F4
Aa (riv.), Fr. 54/B2
Aa (riv.), Ger. 52/D5
Aach (riv.), Ger. 61/F2
Aach, Ger. 61/E2
Aachen, Ger. 55/F2
Aalbach (riv.), Ger. 58/C3
Aalborg (int'l arpt.), Den. 40/C3
Aalburg, Neth. 52/C5
Aalen, Ger. 58/D5
Aalsmeer, Neth. 52/B4
Aalst, Belg. 54/D2
Aalten, Neth. 52/D5
Aalter, Belg. 54/C1
Aar (riv.), Ger. 55/H3
Aarau, Swi. 60/E3
Aarberg, Swi. 60/D3
Aarburg, Swi. 60/D3
Aardenburg, Neth. 54/C1
Aare (riv.), Swi. 66/E1
Aargau (canton), Swi. 61/E3
Aarred (lake), WSah. 110/B4
Aarschot, Belg. 55/D2
Aartselaar, Belg. 55/D1
Aarwangen, Swi. 60/D3
Aba, Nga. 115/G5
Aba, D.R. Congo 121/G2
Aba, China 78/E5
Abā as Su'ūd, SAr. 100/D5
Abadab (peak), Sudan 109/G5
Ābādān, Iran 103/G4
Ābādeh, Iran 103/H4
Abadla, Alg. 111/E3
Abádszalók, Hun. 50/E2
Abaeté, Braz. 186/D3
Abaetetuba, Braz. 182/D3
Abag Qi, China 78/G3
Abaí, Par. 189/F3
Abaiang (isl.), Kiri. 136/G4
Abaji, Nga. 115/G4
Abajo (mts.), Ut, US 142/D4
Abak, Nga. 115/G5
Abakaliki, Nga. 115/H5
Abakan, Rus. 74/K4
Abala, Niger 115/F3
Abala, Congo 120/C3
Abalak, Niger 115/G3
Aban, Rus. 74/K4
Abancay, Peru 184/C4
Abanga (riv.), Gabon 120/B2
Abano Terme, It. 63/E3
Abapó, Bol. 188/D1
Abar Kūh, Iran 103/H4
Abarán, Sp. 46/E3
Abariringa (Canton) (isl.), Kiri. 137/H5
'Abasān, Gaza 105/A6
Abashiri, Japan 82/D1
Abashiri (lake), Japan 82/C2
Abasolo, Mex. 175/F3
Abasolo, Mex. 175/E4
Abatimbo el Gumas, Eth. 117/G3
Abau, PNG 129/H2
Abay, Kaz. 74/H5
Abaya (well), Chad 116/C2
Abaza, Rus. 99/F1
Abbabis, Namb. 122/C5
Abbadia Lariana, It. 61/F6
Abbadia San Salvatore, It. 48/B1
Abbaretz, Fr. 56/D5
Abbazia di Casamari, It. 65/C4
Abbazia di Fossanova, It. 65/C5
Abbazia di Montecassino, It. 65/C5
Abbe (lake), Djib. 118/B3
Abbert (riv.), Ire. 32/B3
Abbeville, Fr. 54/A3
Abbeville, Al, US 165/F2
Abbeville, La, US 164/B3
Abbeville, Ga, US 165/G2
Abbeville, SC, US 163/F3
Abbeville, Ms, US 162/C3
Abbey (peak), Austl. 134/B1
Abbey, Sk, Can. 145/K2
Abbeydorney, Ire. 32/A5
Abbeyfeale, Ire. 32/A5
Abbeylara, Ire. 32/C2
Abbeyleix, Ire. 32/C4
Abbiategrasso, It. 62/B3
Abbot (mt.), Austl. 134/B3
Abbot (pt.), Austl. 129/H4
Abbots Bromley, Eng, UK 35/G6
Abbots Langley, Eng, UK 30/B1
Abbotsbury, Eng, UK 36/D5
Abbotsford, Wi, US 155/J1
Abbotsinch (int'l arpt.), Sc, UK 33/B5
Abbott, Tx, US 151/F2
Abbottābād, Pak. 98/B2
Abbottsburg, NC, US 163/H3
Abbottstown, Pa, US 168/B4
Abcoude, Neth. 52/B4
Ābdānān, Iran 100/E2
Abdul Hakīm, Pak. 98/B4
Abdulino, Rus. 71/K1
Abéché, Chad 116/D2
Abejorral, Col. 183/K7
Abel Erasmuspas (pass), SAfr. 123/F5
Ābeltī, Eth. 117/H3
Abemama (isl.), Kiri. 136/G4
Abenab, Namb. 122/C3
Abenberg, Ger. 58/D4
Abengourou, C.d'Iv. 114/E5
Åbenrå, Den. 40/C4
Abens (riv.), Ger. 42/F4
Abensberg, Ger. 59/E5
Abeokuta, Nga. 115/F5
Aber, Wal, UK 34/D5
Aber Wrac'h (riv.), Fr. 56/A3
Aberaeron, Wal, UK 36/B2
Aberangell, Wal, UK 36/C1
Aberarth, Wal, UK 36/B2
Abercarn, Wal, UK 36/C3
Aberchirder, Sc, UK 33/D1
Abercrombie, ND, US 156/F4
Abercrombie (riv.), Austl. 133/D2
Aberdare, Wal, UK 36/C3
Aberdare NP, Kenya 119/B2
Aberdaron, Wal, UK 34/D6
Aberdeen, Austl. 132/D2
Aberdeen, Sc, UK 33/D2
Aberdeen (co.), Sc, UK 33/D2
Aberdeen (lake), Nun, Can. 140/F2
Aberdeen, China 87/L8
Aberdeen, SAfr. 124/D4
Aberdeen, Id, US 147/G2
Aberdeen, Md, US 168/B5
Aberdeen, Ms, US 162/C4
Aberdeen, NC, US 163/H3
Aberdeen, SD, US 156/E5
Aberdeen, Wa, US 144/C4
Aberdeen Proving Ground, Md, US 168/B5
Aberdeenshire (co.), Sc, UK 33/D2
Aberdour, Sc, UK 33/C4
Aberdour (bay), Sc, UK 33/D1
Aberdyfi, Wal, UK 36/B1
Aberfeldy, Sc, UK 33/C3
Aberfoyle, Sc, UK 33/B4
Abergavenny, Wal, UK 36/C3
Abergele, Wal, UK 34/E5
Ābergelē, Eth. 118/A2
Aberlady, Sc, UK 33/D5
Aberlour, Sc, UK 33/C2
Abernathy, Tx, US 152/D4
Abernethy, Sc, UK 33/C4
Aberporth, Wal, UK 36/B2
Abersoch, Wal, UK 34/D6
Abersychan, Wal, UK 36/C3
Abert (lake), Or, US 146/C2
Abertillery, Wal, UK 36/C3
Aberystwyth, Wal, UK 36/B2
Abez', Rus. 69/P2
Abhá, SAr. 100/D5
Abhānpur, India 95/D1
Abhar, Iran 103/G2
Abhayāpuri, India 97/H2
Abia (prov.), Nga. 115/G5
'Ābidīn, Sudan 117/G2
Abidjan, C.d'Iv. 114/D5
Abidjan (Port Bouet) (int'l arpt.), C.d'Iv. 114/E5
Abidogun, Nga. 115/F5
Abiko, Japan 83/E2
Abilene, Ks, US 153/F1
Abilene, Tx, US 151/E1
Abingdon, Il, US 155/J3
Abingdon, Va, US 163/G2
Abingdon, Eng, UK 37/E3
Abingdon, Md, US 168/B5
Abingdon Downs, Austl. 134/A2
Abington, Sc, UK 33/C6
Abington (reef), Austl. 134/C2
Abino (pt.), On, Can. 160/U10
Abinsk, Rus. 73/K5
Abiquiu (lake), NM, US 152/A2
Abiquiu, NM, US 149/J2
Abiquiu (dam), NM, US 149/J2
Abisko, Swe. 38/F1
Abitibi (riv.), On, Can. 141/H4
Abitibi (lake), On,Qu, Can. 141/H4
Ābīy Ādī, Eth. 118/A2
Ābīyata (lake), Eth. 118/A4
Abiyata-Shala Lakes NP, Eth. 117/H4
Abja-Paluoja, Est. 41/L2
Abkhazia Aut. Rep., Geo. 71/G4
Ableiges, Fr. 30/H4
Abminga, Austl. 131/G3
Abnūb, Egypt 109/F3
Abo, Som. 118/D3
Åbo (Turku), Fin. 41/K1
Aboh, Nga. 115/G5
Abohar, India 98/C4
Aboisso, C.d'Iv. 114/E5
Abomey, Ben. 115/F5
Ābomsa, Eth. 118/A3
Abondance, Fr. 60/C5
Abong-Mbang, Camr. 120/C2
Abongabong (mtn.), Indo. 89/B1
Abony, Hun. 50/D2
Aborlan, Phil. 88/B3
Abou Deia, Chad 116/C3
Abourassein, Djebel (peak), CAfr. 116/E3
Aboyne, Sc, UK 33/D2
Abra Pampa, Arg. 188/C2
Abraham Gonzalez (int'l arpt.), Mex. 177/A2
Abraham Lincoln Birthplace Nat'l Hist. Site, Ky, US 162/E2
Abraham's Bay, Bahm. 177/H1
Abraka, Nga. 115/G5
Abrams, Wi, US 160/B2
Abrantes, Port. 46/A3
Abreojos (pt.), Mex. 174/B3
'Abrī, Sudan 109/F4
Abridge, Eng, UK 30/D2
Abrud, Rom. 51/F2
Abruzzi (pol. reg.), It. 65/C3
Abruzzi (prov.), It. 45/K5
Abruzzo, PN d', It. 48/C2
Absam, Aus. 61/H3
Absaroka (range), Mt,Wy, US 147/H1
Absarokee, Mt, US 147/J1
Absdorf, Aus. 51/N7
Absecon, NJ, US 168/D5
Abtsgmünd, Ger. 58/D5
Abū aḑ Ḑuhūr, Syria 104/E2
Abū al Maţāmīr, Egypt 113/B3
Abū 'Alī (isl.), SAr. 103/G5
Abū an Numrus, Egypt 113/C5
Abū 'Arīsh, SAr. 100/D5
Abū Dā'ūd as Sibākh, Egypt 113/C3
Abū Dawm, Sudan 117/F1
Abū Dawm, Sudan 117/G1
Abu Dhabi (int'l arpt.), UAE 101/F4
Abu Dhabi (Abū Ẓaby) (cap.), UAE 101/F4
Abū Dīs, Sudan 109/G5
Abū Ḩadrīyah, SAr. 103/G5
Abū Hamad, Sudan 109/G5
Abū Ḩammād, Egypt 113/C3
Abū Hugar, Sudan 117/G2
Abū Ḩummuş, Egypt 113/B2
Abū Jābirah, Sudan 117/E3
Abū Jandīr, Egypt 113/B6
Abū Jubayhah, Sudan 117/F3
Abū Kabīr, Egypt 113/C3
Abū Kamāl, Syria 102/E3
Abū Kūk, Sudan 117/G2
Abū Maţāriq, Sudan 117/E3
Abu Mendi, Eth. 117/G3
Abū Qashsh, WBnk. 105/C5
Abū Qīr, Egypt 113/B2
Abū Rawwāsh (ruin), Egypt 113/C4
Abū Rimth (wadi), Egypt 113/C4
Abu Road, India 101/K4
Abū Rubayq, SAr. 100/C4
Abū Rukbah, Sudan 117/G2
Abu Shagara (cape), Sudan 109/H4
Abū Shāmah (peak), Egypt 113/C5
Abū Shanab, Sudan 117/E2
Abu Simbel (ruin), Egypt 109/F4
Abū Şīr (ruin), Egypt 113/C5
Abū Şīr Banā, Egypt 113/C3
Abū Sulţān, Egypt 113/D4
Abū Zabad, Sudan 117/F2
Abū Za'bal, Egypt 113/C4
Abū Ẓaby (Abu Dhabi) (cap.), UAE 101/F4
Abuja (cap.), Nga. 115/G4
Abuja (int'l arpt.), Nga. 115/G4
Abuja Capital Terr., Nga. 115/G4
Abukuma (riv.), Japan 85/G2
Abukuma (plat.), Japan 85/G2
Abulog, Phil. 88/C1
Abumombazi, D.R. Congo 121/E2
Abuná (riv.), Bol. 185/E3
Abunã (riv.), Braz. 185/E3
Abunã, Braz. 185/E3
Ābune Yosēf (peak), Eth. 118/A2
Abut Head (pt.), NZ 135/B3
Abuta, Japan 82/B2
Ābuyē Mēda (peak), Eth. 118/A3
Abuyog, Phil. 88/D3
Abwong, Sudan 117/G3
Åby, Swe. 40/G2
Abyār, Egypt 113/B3
Abyār 'Alī, SAr. 100/C4
Åbybro, Den. 40/C3
Abydos (ruin), Egypt 109/F3
Abyei, Sudan 117/F3
Acacías, Col. 180/C4
Acacoyagua, Mex. 176/C3
Academy of Sciences, VatC. 65/G7
Acadia NP, Me, US 158/C4
Acadia Valley, Ab, Can. 145/J2
Acadian Village, La, US 164/B2
Acahay, Par. 189/E3
Acajutiba, Braz. 187/F1
Acámbaro, Mex. 175/E4
Acampo, Ca, US 167/M10
Acandí, Col. 180/B2
Acaponeta (riv.), Mex. 174/D4
Acaponeta, Mex. 174/D4
Acapulco de Juárez, Mex. 175/E5
Acará, Braz. 182/D3
Acarai (mts.), Guy. 181/G4
Acaraí, Serra (mts.), Braz. 182/B2
Acaraú, Braz. 183/F3
Acaraú (riv.), Braz. 183/F3
Acari, Braz. 183/G4
Acari (riv.), Braz. 182/B4
Acarí, Peru 184/C4
Acarigua, Ven. 180/D2
Acatlán de Osorio, Mex. 176/B2
Acatlán de Pérez Figueroa, Mex. 175/N8
Acatzingo, Mex. 175/M7
Acayucan, Mex. 176/C2
Acceglio, It. 64/C4
Accha, Peru 184/D4
Acciaroli, It. 48/D2
Accomac, Va, US 163/K2
Accra (cap.), Gha. 115/E5
Accrington, Eng, UK 35/F4
Aceguá, Uru. 189/F4
Aceh (prov.), Indo. 89/A1
Acerra, It. 65/D6
Aceuchal, Sp. 46/B3
Ach (riv.), Aus. 59/G6
Ach, Aus. 59/F6
Achaguas, Ven. 180/D3
Achalpur, India 95/C1
Achao, Chile 190/B4
Achar, Uru. 191/K10
Achegour (well), Niger 108/A5
Achen (pass), Ger. 61/H2
Acheng, China 79/K2
Achères, Fr. 30/J5
Acheron (riv.), Austl. 133/B3
Achhnera, India 96/A2
Achicourt, Fr. 54/B3
Achila, Bol. 184/D4
Achill (isl.), Ire. 30/N10
Achill Head (pt.), Ire. 30/N9
Achiltibuie, Sc, UK 31/R7
Achim, Ger. 53/G2
Achim, Ouadi (riv.), Chad 116/C1
Āchīn, Afg. 98/A2
Achinsk, Rus. 74/K4
Achit, Rus. 69/N4
Achmîm (well), Mrta. 114/D2
Achnasheen, Sc, UK 33/A1
Achoma, Peru 184/D4
A'chràlaig (peak), Sc, UK 33/A2
Achuapa, Nic. 176/E3
Achupallas, Ecu. 184/B1
Achuyevo, Rus. 73/J5
Achziv NP, Isr. 105/C2
Acigné, Fr. 56/D4
Acilia, It. 65/B4
Acireale, It. 48/D4
Ackerly, Tx, US 150/D1
Ackerman, Ms, US 162/C4
Acklins (isl.), Bahm. 139/K7
Ackworth Moor Top, Eng, UK 35/G4
Acland (mt.), Austl. 134/C4
Aclare, Ire. 32/B1
Acme, La, US 164/C2
Acme, Wa, US 144/C3
Acobamba, Peru 184/C4
Acolla, Peru 184/C3
Acolman, Mex. 175/R9
Acoma Ind. Res., NM, US 149/J3
Acomayo, Peru 184/D4
Acomayo, Peru 184/B3
Aconcagua (peak), Arg. 190/C2
Aconchi, Mex. 174/C2
Acopiara, Braz. 183/G4
Acora, Peru 184/D4
Acorizal, Braz. 185/G4
Acornhoek, SAfr. 123/F5
Acqualagna, It. 63/F6
Acquanegra sul Chiese, It. 62/D3
Acquapendente, It. 48/B1
Acquasanta Terme, It. 65/C2
Acquasparta, It. 65/B2
Acquaviva Piceno, It. 65/C2
Acqui Terme, It. 62/B4
Acquigny, Fr. 57/G2
Acraman (lake), Austl. 131/G5
Acrata (pt.), Alg. 112/G4
Acre (state), Braz. 184/D3
Acre (riv.), Braz. 184/D3
Acreúna, Braz. 186/C3
Acropolis, Gre. 49/N9
Actaeon Group (isls.), FrPol. 137/M7
Acton, Ca, US 166/B2
Acton (nbrhd.), Eng, UK 30/C2
Acton, On, Can. 160/S8
Acton, Tx, US 150/K7
Acton, Mt, US 145/K5
Acton Vale, Qu, Can. 161/K2
Actopan, Mex. 175/L6
Actopan, Mex. 175/N7
Açu, Braz. 183/G4
Açude Aratas (res.), Braz. 183/F4
Açude Banabuiu (res.), Braz. 183/G4
Açude Oros (res.), Braz. 183/G4
Acula, Mex. 175/P8
Aculeo (lag.), Chile 190/N8
Acworth, Ga, US 163/L6
Acy-en-Multien, Fr. 30/L4
Ad Dabbah, Sudan 117/F1
Ad Dabbūrah, Sudan 117/G1
Ad Dafīnah, SAr. 100/D4
Ad Dahnā' (des.), SAr. 100/D3
Ad Daljamūn, Egypt 113/B3
Ad Damazin, Sudan 117/G3
Ad Damīr, Sudan 117/G1
Ad Dammām, SAr. 100/F3
Ad Dāmūr, Leb. 105/C1
Ad Daqahlīyah (gov.), Egypt 102/B3
Ad Darb, SAr. 100/D5
Ad Dawḩah (Doha) (cap.), Qatar 100/F3
Ad Dilam, SAr. 100/E4
Ad Dilinjāt, Egypt 113/B3
Ad Dīwānīyah, Iraq 103/F4
Ad Du'ayn, Sudan 117/E3
Ad Dujayl, Iraq 103/F3
Ad Duwādimī, SAr. 100/D4
Ad Duwayd, SAr. 102/E4
Ad Duwaym, Sudan 117/G2
Ad-Dakhla, WSah. 110/B5
Ada, Ok, US 153/F3
Ada, Mn, US 156/F4
Ada, Oh, US 160/E4
Ada, Gha. 115/F5
Ada, Yugo. 50/E3
Ādaba, Eth. 118/A4
Adaba, India 95/E2
Adainville, Fr. 30/G5
Adair, Ok, US 153/G2
Adair (cape), Nun, Can. 141/J1
Adair, Ia, US 155/G3
Adair (bay), Mex. 175/F5
Adairsville, Ga, US 162/E3
Adairville, Ky, US 162/D2
Adaja (riv.), Sp. 46/C2
Adak (isl.), Ak, US 171/C6
Adak (str.), Ak, US 171/C6
Adam, Oman 101/G4
Adam (mt.), UK 191/E6
Adamantina, Braz. 189/G2
Adamaoua (prov.), Camr. 116/B4
Adamaoua (plat.), Camr., Nga. 107/D4
Adamawa (state), Nga. 116/B3
Adamello (peak), It. 61/G5
Adaminaby, Austl. 133/D3
Adamovka, Rus. 71/L2
Adams, NY, US 161/H3
Adams, Ma, US 161/K3
Adams, Ne, US 155/F3
Adams, Tn, US 162/D2
Adams, Wi, US 155/K2
Adams (mt.), Wa, US 144/D4
Adams (lake), BC, Can. 144/E2
Adams (riv.), BC, Can. 144/E2
Adams (co.), Pa, US 168/A4
Adams Run, SC, US 163/G4
Adamstown (cap.), Pitc. 137/M7
Adamstown, Pa, US 168/B3
Adamsville, Tn, US 162/C3
Adamsville, Tx, US 151/E2
Adamw (plat.), Nga. 115/H5
Aden ('Adan), Yem. 118/C2
'Adan (Aden), Yem. 118/C2
Adana (int'l arpt.), Turk. 102/C2
Adana, Turk. 102/C2
Adana (prov.), Turk. 102/C2
Adanhé, Gabon 120/B3
Adapazarı, Turk. 51/K5
Adarama, Sudan 117/G1
Adare, Ire. 32/B4
Adare (cape), Ant. 192/M
Adarza (peak), Fr. 46/E1
Adaut, Indo. 128/C2
Adavale, Austl. 134/B4
Add (riv.), Sc, UK 33/A4
Adda (riv.), Sudan 116/D3
Adda (riv.), It. 45/H4
Addicks (dam), Tx, US 151/M9
Addicks (res.), Tx, US 151/M9
Addis, La, US 164/C2
Addison, Il, US 167/P16
Addison, Al, US 162/D3
Addison, Tx, US 150/L7
Addison (Webster Springs), WV, US 163/G1
Addlestone, Eng, UK 30/B2
Addo Elephant NP, SAfr. 124/D4
Addy, Wa, US 144/F3
Adé, Chad 116/D2
Adekeieh (Ādī K'eyih), Erit. 118/A2
Adel, Ga, US 165/G2
Adel, Ia, US 155/G3
'Adel Bagrou, Mrta. 114/D3
Adelaide (pen.), Nun, Can. 140/G2
Adelaide (riv.), Austl. 128/C3
Adelaide, Austl. 131/M8
Adelaide (int'l arpt.), Austl. 131/M8
Adelaide, SAfr. 124/D4
Adelaide River, Austl. 128/C3
Adelaide Zoo, Austl. 131/M8
Adelanto, Ca, US 166/C1
Adèle (isl.), Austl. 128/A3
Adelebsen, Ger. 53/G5
Adelheidsdorf, Ger. 53/H3
Adelmannsfelden, Ger. 58/D5
Adelong, Austl. 133/D2
Adelschlag, Ger. 58/E5
Adelsheim, Ger. 58/C4
Adelsön (isl.), Swe. 39/A1
Adelsried, Ger. 58/D6
Aden (gulf), Afr.,Asia 77/D8
Aden (int'l arpt.), Yem. 118/C2
Aden, Ab, Can. 145/J3
Adenau, Ger. 55/F3
Adendorf, Ger. 53/H2
Aderbissinat, Niger 115/G3
Adèrké, Chad 108/C4
Ādēt, Eth. 117/H3
Adh Dhahībāt, Tun. 111/H2
Adh Dhirā', Jor. 104/D4
Adi, D.R. Congo 121/G2
Adi (isl.), Indo. 91/H4
Ādī Ābun, Eth. 118/A2
Ādī Ārk'ay, Eth. 117/H2
Ādī Da'iro, Eth. 100/C6
Ādīs Ābeba (Adekeieh), Erit. 118/A2
Ādī Kwala, Erit. 118/A2
Ādī Tekelezan, Erit. 118/A2
Ādī Ugrī, Erit. 118/A2
Adiaké, C.d'Iv. 114/E5
Adieu (cape), Austl. 131/G5
Ādīgala, Eth. 118/B3
Adige (riv.), It. 67/F1
Adige (Etsch) (riv.), It. 61/G4
Adigeni, Geo. 71/G4
Adigo (Etsch) (riv.), It. 61/G4
Ādīgrat, Eth. 118/A2
Adilcevaz, Turk. 103/E2
Adimo, Nga. 115/F5
Adin, Ca, US 146/C3
Adiora (well), Mali 115/E2
Adīrī, Libya 108/B3
Adirondack (mts.), NY, US 161/J2
Addis Ababa (Ādīs Ābeba) (cap.), Eth. 118/A3
Ādīs Ābeba (Addis Ababa) (cap.), Eth. 118/A3
Ādīs 'Alem, Eth. 118/A3
Ādīs Zemen, Eth. 117/H2
Adisutjipto (int'l arpt.), Indo. 89/E4
Adıyaman, Turk. 102/D2
Adıyaman (prov.), Turk. 102/D2
Adjud, Rom. 51/H2
Adjuntas, de la Presa (res.), Mex. 175/F4
Adler/Sochi (int'l arpt.), Rus. 70/F4
Adlington, Eng, UK 35/F4
Adliswil, Swi. 61/E3
Admiral, Sk, Can. 145/K3
Admirality (isl.), Ak, US 140/C3
Admirality (inlet), Nun, Can. 141/H1
Admirality Island Nat'l Mon., Ak, US 171/M4
Admiralty (inlet), Wa, US 167/B2
Admiralty (isls.), PNG 136/D5
Admiralty (gulf), Austl. 128/B3
Admiralty Gulf Abor. Rsv., Austl. 128/B3
Admire, Ks, US 153/F1
Adnan Menderes (int'l arpt.), Turk. 70/C5
Ado (riv.), Japan 83/J5
Ado Ekiti, Nga. 115/G5
Ado Odo, Nga. 115/F5
Adobe Creek (res.), Co, US 152/C1
Adogawa, Japan 83/K5
Adok, Sudan 117/F3
Adolfo López Mateos, Mex. 174/B3
Ādoni, India 95/C3
Adorf, Ger. 59/F2
Adoru, Nga. 115/G5
Adour (riv.), Fr. 66/D2
Adra, India 97/F4
Adra, Sp. 46/D4
Adranga, D.R. Congo 121/G2
Adrano, It. 48/D4
Adrar, Alg. 111/E4
Adrar (phys. reg.), Mrta. 114/B1
Adrar (pol. reg.), Mrta. 114/C1
Adrar (pol. reg.), Alg. 115/F1
Adrar (reg.), Mrta. 110/C5
Adrar (wilaya), Alg. 111/E4
Adrar bou Nasser (peak), Mor. 110/E2
Adrar Sotuf (mts.), WSah. 110/B5
Adré, Chad 116/D2
Adria, It. 63/F3
Adrian, Mo, US 153/G1
Adrian, Mi, US 160/D4
Adrian, Or, US 146/E2
Adrian, Mn, US 155/G2
Adrian, WV, US 163/G1
Adriatic (sea), Eur. 29/F4
Adro, It. 62/C2
Aduana del Sásabe, Mex. 175/G5
Adukrom, Gha. 115/E5
Adulis (ruin), Erit. 118/A2
Adur (riv.), Eng, UK 37/F5
Adutiškis, Lith. 41/M4
Advance, Mo, US 162/C2
Adventure Bay, Austl. 132/C4
Advocate Harbour, NS, Can. 158/E3
Ādwa, Eth. 118/A2
Adwick le Street, Eng, UK 35/G4
Adycha (riv.), Rus. 75/P3
Adygeya, Resp., Rus. 70/F3
Adzopé, C.d'Iv. 114/E5
Adz'va (riv.), Rus. 69/P2
Adz'vavom, Rus. 69/N2
Ae, Sc, UK 34/E1
Aegean (sea), Gre. 49/J3
Aegviidu, Est. 41/L2
Aerø (isl.), Den. 40/D4
Aeron (riv.), Wal, UK 36/B2
Aesch, Swi. 60/D3
Aeschi bei Spiez, Swi. 60/D4
Aetna, Ab, Can. 145/H3
Äetsä, Fin. 41/K1
Afadjoto (peak), Gha. 115/F5
'Afak, Iraq 103/F3
Āfambo, Eth. 118/B3
Āfambo, Erit. 118/B2
Afanas'yevskoye, Rus. 69/N4
Afándou, Gre. 102/B2
Afareaitu, FrPol. 137/X15
Āfdem, Eth. 118/B3
Afek NP, Isr. 105/B4
Aff (riv.), Fr. 44/B3
Affenrücken, Namb. 124/A3
Affoltern im Emmental, Swi. 60/D3
Affric (lake), Sc, UK 33/A2
Affton, Mo, US 155/J4
Afghanistan (ctry.) 77/F6
Afgooye, Som. 119/D1
Afia, Gabon 120/B2
'Afīf, SAr. 100/D4
Afikpo, Nga. 115/G5
Afipskiy, Rus. 73/K5
Afiqim, Isr. 105/D3
Aflou, Alg. 66/D4
Afmadow, Som. 119/C1
Afobaka (dam), Sur. 182/C1
Afogados da Ingàzeira, Braz. 183/G4
Afognak (isl.), Ak, US 171/H4
Afognak (peak), Ak, US 171/H4
Afollé (phys. reg.), Mrta. 114/C2
Afonso Bezerra, Braz. 183/G4
Afore, PNG 129/H2
Afragola, It. 65/D6
Afrânio, Braz. 183/F5
Africa (cont.) 107/*
Afrin (riv.), Turk. 104/E1
'Afrīn, Syria 104/E1
Afrique (peak), Fr. 60/A3
Afsluitdijk (dam), Neth. 52/C2
Afte (riv.), Ger. 53/F5
Afton, Ok, US 153/G2
Afton, Wy, US 147/H2
Afton, Ia, US 155/G3
Afton, Mn, US 157/Q7
Afuá, Braz. 182/D3
Afuidich (lake), WSah. 110/B5
'Afula, Isr. 105/C3
Afyon, Turk. 102/B2
Afyon (prov.), Turk. 102/B2
Afzalgarh, India 96/B1
Agadem, Niger 116/B1
Agades (int'l arpt.), Niger 115/G2
Agadez, Niger 115/G2
Agadez (dept.), Niger 111/H5
Agadir, Mor. 110/C3
Agadir (Inezgane) (int'l arpt.), Mor. 110/C3
Agadyr', Kaz. 99/B2
Agago (riv.), Ugan. 117/G5
Āgamani, India 97/G2
Agamor (well), Mali 115/F2
Agano (riv.), Japan 85/F2
Agar, SD, US 154/D1
Āgarfa, Eth. 118/A4
Āgaro, Eth. 117/H4
Agartala, India 97/H4
Agassiz Ice Cap (ice field), Nun, Can. 141/T6
Agassiz NWR, Mn, US 156/F3
Agate, Co, US 154/C4
Agate Fossil Beds Nat'l Mon., Ne, US 154/C2
Agats, Indo. 129/E1
Agattu (isl.), Ak, US 171/A5
Agattu (str.), Ak, US 171/A5
Agbabu, Nga. 115/G5
Agbor Bojiboji, Nga. 115/G5
Agboville, C.d'Iv. 114/D5
Ağcabädi, Azer. 103/F1
Ağdam, Azer. 103/F2
Ağdärä, Azer. 103/F1
Ağdaş, Azer. 71/H4
Agde, Fr. 44/E5
Agdz, Mor. 110/D3
Agen, Fr. 44/D4
Agency (lake), Or, US 146/B2
Agency, Mo, US 155/G4
Agency, Ia, US 155/H3
Ageo, Japan 83/D2
Ager (riv.), Aus. 59/G7
Agerӕk, Den. 40/C4
Āgere Maryam, Eth. 118/A4
Agerisee (lake), Swi. 61/E3
Agersø (isl.), Den. 39/H7
Ageyevo, Rus. 70/F1
Agger (riv.), Ger. 55/G1
Aggteleki NP, Slvk. 50/E1
Āghā Jārī, Iran 103/G4
Aghada, Ire. 32/B6
Aghagallon, NI, UK 34/B3
Aghagower, Ire. 32/A2
Agiabampo, Mex. 174/C3
Ağın, Turk. 102/D2
Aginskiy Buryatskiy (aut. okrug), Rus. 78/G1
Aginskoye, Rus. 78/G1
Agivey, NI, UK 34/B1
Agjert, Mrta. 114/C2
Agliana, It. 63/D6
Ağlıköy, Turk. 70/E4
Agly (riv.), Fr. 44/E5
Agna, It. 63/E3
Agnanderón, Gre. 49/G3
Agnes, Tx, US 150/K7
Agnew, Austl. 130/D4
Agnibilékrou, C.d'Iv. 114/E5
Agnita, Rom. 51/G3
Agno (int'l arpt.), Swi. 61/E6
Agno (riv.), It. 63/E1
Agnone, It. 65/D4
Agny (riv.), Fr. 64/B1
Ago (bay) 41/J4
Ago, Japan 83/L7
Ago Are, Nga. 115/F4
Agogna (riv.), It. 45/H4
Agon (pt.), Fr. 56/D3
Agon-Coutainville, Fr. 56/D2
Agona, Gha. 115/E5
Agoo, Phil. 87/J5
Agordo, It. 45/K3
Agougadzépe, Togo 115/F5
Agout (riv.), Fr. 44/D5
Āgra, India 96/B2
Agra, Ks, US 154/E4
Agraciada, Uru. 191/J10
Agrado, Col. 180/C4
Ágreda, Sp. 46/E2
Ağri (prov.), Turk. 71/G5
Ağrı (Mount Ararat) (peak), Turk. 103/F2
Agriá, Gre. 49/H3
Agricola, Fl, US 164/M8
Agrigento, It. 48/C4
Agrihan (isl.), NMar. 136/D3
Agrínion, Gre. 49/G3
Agrio (riv.), Arg. 190/C3
Agryz, Rus. 69/M4
Ağstafa, Azer. 71/H4
Ağsu, Azer. 71/J4
Agsumal (dry lake), WSah. 110/B4
Água Branca, Braz. 183/G4
Água Branca, Braz. 183/F4
Agua Buena, Chile 188/B3
Agua Caliente, Az, US 149/F4
Agua Caliente Ind. Res., Ca, US 174/D4
Água Clara, Braz. 189/F2
Agua de Dios, Col. 183/L8
Agua Dulce, Ca, US 166/B2
Agua Dulce, Mex. 176/C2
Agua Fria, NM, US 149/J3
Agua Fria NM, Az, US 149/F3
Agua Hedionda (lake), Ca, US 166/C4
Agua Larga, Ven. 180/D2
Agua Prieta, Mex. 175/H5
Agua Vermelha (res.), Braz. 186/C3
Aguachica, Col. 180/C2
Aguadas, Col. 183/K7
Aguadilla, PR 173/M8
Aguadulce, Pan. 180/A2
Aguaí, Braz. 187/K7
Agualeguas, Mex. 177/E4
Agualva-Cacém, Port. 47/P10
Aguan (riv.), Hon. 172/D4
Aguapeí (riv.), Braz. 186/C4
Aguapey (riv.), Arg. 189/E4
Aguaray, Arg. 188/D2
Aguarico (riv.), Peru 180/B5
Aguaro-Guariquito NP, Ven. 173/H6
Águas (hills), Braz. 187/L7
Águas Belas, Braz. 183/G5
Aguas Blancas, Chile 188/B3
Aguas Corrientes, Uru. 191/K11
Águas da Prata, Braz. 187/K6
Águas de Lindóia, Braz. 187/K7
Águas Formosas, Braz. 187/E3
Aguasay, Ven. 181/F2
Aguascalientes (state), Mex. 172/A3
Aguascalientes, Mex. 174/E4
Aguaytía (riv.), Peru 184/C3
Águeda, Port. 46/A2
Agueda (riv.), Sp. 46/B2
Aguelhok, Mali 115/F2
Agüenit, WSah. 110/B5
Aguêraktem (well), Mali 110/D5
Agugliano, It. 63/G6
Agui, Japan 83/L6
Aguié, Niger 115/G3
Aguijan (isl.), NMar. 136/D3
Aguila, Az, US 149/F4
Aguilâl Faï, Mrta. 114/B2
Aguilar, Co, US 152/B2
Aguilar, Sp. 46/C4
Aguilar de Campóo, Sp. 46/C1
Aguilares, Arg. 188/C3
Aguilas, Sp. 46/E4
Aguililla, Mex. 174/E5
Aguja (pt.), Peru 184/A2
Agulhas (cape), SAfr. 124/M11
Agulhas Negras, Pico das (peak), Braz. 187/M7
Agung (vol.), Indo. 89/F5
Agusan (riv.), Phil. 88/D3
Agustín Codazzi, Col. 180/C2
Agutaya, Phil. 88/C3
Agwata, Ugan. 119/A1
Agwok, Sudan 117/F4
Aha (hills), Bots. 122/D3
Ahaggar (mts.), Alg. 111/G5
Ahal (prov.), Trkm. 71/L5
Aham, Ger. 59/F5
Ahar, Iran 103/F2
Ahascragh, Ire. 32/B3
Ahau, Fiji 136/G6
Ahaura, NZ 135/B3
Ahaus, Ger. 52/E4
Aherlow (riv.), Ire. 32/B5
Ahero, Kenya 119/A2
Ahfir, Mor. 112/C2
Ahipara, NZ 135/C1
Ahırlı, Turk. 102/C2
Ahlat, Turk. 102/E2
Ahlen, Ger. 53/E5
Ahlerstedt, Ger. 53/G2
Ahmadābād, India 101/K4
Ahmadnagar, India 95/B2
Ahmadpur East, Pak. 98/A5
Ahmadpur Siāl, Pak. 98/A4
Ahmar (mts.), Eth. 118/B3
Ahmar, 'Erg el (des.), Mali 110/D4
Ahmed (well), WSah. 110/B5
Ahmeyine (well), Mrta. 110/B5
Ahoada, Nga. 115/G5
Ahoghill, NI, UK 34/B2
Ahome, Mex. 174/C3
Ahon (peak), Chad 108/C4
Ahoskie, NC, US 163/J2
Ahr (riv.), Ger. 42/D3
Ahram, Iran 103/G4
Ahraurā, India 96/D3
Ahrensburg, Ger. 53/H1
Ahse (riv.), Ger. 53/F5
Ahuacatitlán, Mex. 175/K8
Ahuacatlán, Mex. 174/D4
Ahuachapán, ESal. 176/D3
Ahualulco, Mex. 175/E4
Ahumada, Mex. 177/A2
Ahun, Fr. 44/E3
Ahunda, Gha. 115/F5
Åhus, Swe. 40/F4
Aḩuzzam, Isr. 105/B5
Ahvāz, Iran 103/G4
Ahvenanmaa (prov.), Fin. 38/F4
Ahwahnee, Ca, US 174/C2
Aḩwar, Yem. 118/C2
Ai (riv.), China 81/C2
Ai (mtn.), China 80/E3
Ai-Ais, Namb. 124/B2
Ai-Ais Hot Springs, Namb. 124/B2
Ai-shima (isl.), Japan 84/B3
Aibag Gol (riv.), China 80/B2
Aichach, Ger. 58/E6
Aichi (pref.), Japan 85/E3
Aidhausen, Ger. 58/D2
Aidlingen, Ger. 58/B5
Aiello del Friuli, It. 63/G2
Aiffres, Fr. 44/C3
Aigen im Mühlkreis, Aus. 59/G5
Aigle, Pic de l' (peak), Fr. 60/B4
Aiglemont, Fr. 55/D4
Aigoual (peak), Fr. 44/E4
Aiguá, Uru. 191/G2
Aiguebelle, Fr. 64/C1
Aigueblanche, Fr. 64/C1
Aigues (riv.), Fr. 44/F4
Aigües Tortes y Lago de San Mauricio, PN, Sp. 47/F1
Aiguillon, Fr. 44/D4
Aikawa, Japan 85/F1
Aikawa, Japan 83/C2
Aiken, SC, US 163/G4
Ailao (mtn.), China 86/D3
Ailao (mts.), China 86/D4
Aileron, Austl. 131/G2
Aileu, ETim. 128/B2
Ailigandí, Pan. 180/B2
Ailinglapalap (isl.), Mrsh. 136/F4
Aille (riv.), Fr. 64/C6
Aillevillers-et-Lyaumont, Fr. 60/C2
Aillon (riv.), Fr. 64/C1
Ailly-sur-Noye, Fr. 54/B4
Ailsa Craig (isl.), Sc, UK 33/A6
Ailsa Craig, On, Can. 160/F3
Ailuk (isl.), Mrsh. 136/G3
Aimäjärvi (lake), Fin. 39/E3
Aime, Fr. 64/C1
Aimen (pass), China 80/C5
Aimogasta, Arg. 188/C4
Aimorés, Braz. 187/E3
Aimorés, Serra dos (mts.), Braz. 187/E3
Ain (dept.), Fr. 64/B1
Ain (riv.), Fr. 44/F4
'Aïn Beïda, Alg. 112/K7
Aïn Ben Tili, Mrta. 110/C4
'Aïn Beniau, Alg. 112/G4
'Aïn Bessem, Alg. 112/G4
Aïn Chok-Hay Mohammadia (prov.), Mor. 112/A2
'Aïn Defla, Alg. 112/F4
'Aïn Defla (wilaya), Alg. 112/F4
Aïn el Aouda, Mor. 112/A3
'Aïn El Bey (int'l arpt.), Alg. 112/K6
'Aïn El Hammam, Alg. 112/H4
'Aïn el Turk, Alg. 112/D2
'Aïn Fakroun, Alg. 112/K6
'Aïn M'lila, Alg. 112/K6
'Aïn Oulmene, Alg. 112/H5
'Aïn Oussersa, Alg. 112/G5
'Aïn Sefra, Alg. 111/E2
Aïn Taoujdat, Mor. 112/B3
'Aïn Taya, Alg. 112/G4
'Aïn Temouchent, Alg. 112/D2
'Aïn Touta, Alg. 112/H5
Ainaro, ETim. 128/B2
Ainaži, Lat. 41/L3
Aincourt, Fr. 30/H4
Aínos (peak), Gre. 49/G3
Aínos Ethnikós Dhrimós, (nat'l. park), Gre. 49/G3
Ainsdale, Eng, UK 35/E4
Ainslie (lake), NS, Can. 159/G2
Ainsworth, Ne, US 154/E2
Aiome, PNG 129/G1
Aipe, Col. 180/C4
Aiquile, Bol. 188/C1
Aïr (plat.), Niger 111/G5
Air Force (isl.), Nun, Can. 141/J2
Airabu (isl.), Indo. 89/D2
Airaines, Fr. 54/A4
Airasca, It. 64/D3
Airbangis, Indo. 89/B2
Airdrie, Sc, UK 33/C5
Airdrie, Ab, Can. 145/G2
Aire (riv.), Eng, UK 35/G3
Aire, Canal d' (canal), Fr. 54/B2
Aire-sur-la-Lys, Fr. 54/B2
Aire-sur-l'Adour, Fr. 44/C5
Airgin Sum, China 78/G3
Airmolek, Indo. 89/C3
Airola, It. 65/D5
Airolo, Swi. 61/E4
Airton, Eng, UK 35/F3
Airuno, It. 62/C2
Airvault, Fr. 44/C3
Aisch (riv.), Ger. 45/J2
Aiseau-Presles, Belg. 55/D3
Aisén del General Carlos Ibáñez del Campo (pol. reg.), Chile 190/B5
Aishihik, Yk, Can. 171/L3
Aisne (riv.), Fr. 42/B4
Aïssa (peak), Alg. 111/E2
Aist (riv.), Aus. 59/H6
Aït Ben Haddou, Mor. 110/D3
Aït Ourir, Mor. 110/D3
Aitape, PNG 136/D5
Aith, Sc, UK 31/W13
Aitkin, Mn, US 157/H4
Aitō, Japan 83/K5
Aitolikón, Gre. 49/G3
Aitrach, Ger. 61/G2
Aitrang, Ger. 61/G2
Aitutaki Atoll (isl.), CookIs. 137/J6
Aiuaba, Braz. 183/F4
Aiud, Rom. 51/F2
Aiuruoca (riv.), Braz. 187/M7
Aiuruoca, Braz. 187/M6
Aix (mt.), Wa, US 144/D4
Aix-en-Provence, Fr. 64/B5
Aix-les-Bains, Fr. 64/B1
Aiyang, China 81/C2
Aíyina, Gre. 49/H4
Aiyínion, Gre. 49/H2
Aíyion, Gre. 49/H3
Aīzawl, India 86/B4
Aizkraukle, Lat. 41/L3
Aizpute, Lat. 41/J3
Aizu-Wakamatsu, Japan 85/F2
Aj Bogd (peak), Mong. 78/D3
Aj Janayet, Sudan 109/G5
Ajā, Egypt 113/C3
'Ajab Shīr, Iran 103/F2
Ajaccio, Fr. 48/A2
Ajaccio (gulf), Fr. 66/E2
Ajaigarh, India 96/C3
Ajalpan, Mex. 175/M8
Ajana, Austl. 130/B3
Ajaokuta, Nga. 115/G5
Ajaria Aut. Rep., Geo. 71/G4
Ajasse Ipo, Nga. 115/G4
Ajax, On, Can. 160/U8
Ajay (riv.), India 97/F3
Ajdābiyā, Libya 108/D2
Ajdovščina, Slov. 45/K4
Ajigasawa, Japan 82/B3
'Ajjah, WBnk. 105/C4
Ajka, Hun. 50/C2
'Ajlūn, Jor. 105/D4
Ajmer, India 92/B2
Ajnāla, India 98/C4
Ajo, Az, US 149/F4
Ajo, Cabo de (cape), Sp. 44/B5
Ajuchitlán del Progreso, Mex. 172/A4
Ajusco (vol.), Mex. 175/Q10
Ajuy, Phil. 88/C3
Ak-Dovurak, Rus. 99/F1
Aka (riv.), Japan 85/F1
Aka Eze, Nga. 115/G5
Akabane, Japan 83/M6
Akabira, Japan 82/C2
Akabli, Alg. 111/F4
Akademik Obruchev (mts.), Rus. 78/C1
Akagera, PN de l', Rwa. 121/G3
Akaishi-dake (peak), Japan 85/F3
Āk'ak'ī Besek'a, Eth. 118/A3
Akālgarh, Pak. 98/B3
Akalkot, India 95/C2
Akaltara, India 96/D4
Akan (lake), Japan 82/D2
Akan NP, Japan 82/D2
Akana, Congo 120/C3
Akankpa, Nga. 115/H5
Akaroa, NZ 135/C3
Åkarp, Swe. 40/E4
Akarsu, Turk. 102/D2
Akasha East, Sudan 109/F4
Akashi, Japan 83/G6
Akashi (str.), Japan 83/G6
Akaska, SD, US 156/D5
Akbarpur, India 96/D2
Akbarpur, India 96/B2
Akbaytal (pass), Taj. 99/B4
Akbou, Alg. 112/H4
Akçaabat, Turk. 70/F4
Akçakale, Turk. 102/D2
Akçakoca, Turk. 51/K5
Akçaova, Turk. 51/J5
Akçapınar, Turk. 102/D2
Akçay, Turk. 104/A1
Akchâr (phys. reg.), Mrta. 110/B5
Akchatau, Kaz. 74/H5
Akdağmadeni, Turk. 70/E5
Akdar, Al Jabal al (mts.), Libya 67/J4
Akechi, Japan 83/M5
Akeley, Mn, US 157/G4
Akelo, Sudan 117/G4
Akeno, Japan 83/A2
Akeno, Japan 83/E1
Åkers styckebruk, Swe. 39/A1
Åkersberga, Swe. 40/H2
Akershus (co.), Nor. 38/D3
Akershus Castle, Nor. 38/S8
Aketi, D.R. Congo 121/E2
Akhalk'alak'i, Geo. 71/G4
Akhalts'ikhe, Geo. 71/G4
Akharnaí, Gre. 49/N8
Akhaura, Bang. 97/H4
Akhelóos (riv.), Gre. 49/G3
Akhiok, Ak, US 171/H4
Akhisar, Turk. 70/C5
Akhmeta, Geo. 71/H4
Akhmīm, Egypt 109/F3
Akhnūr, India 98/C3
Akhtopol, Bul. 51/H4
Akhtuba (riv.), Rus. 71/H3
Akhtubinsk, Rus. 71/H2
Akhtyrskiy, Rus. 73/K5
Aki, Japan 84/C4
Aki (riv.), Japan 83/C2
Akiachak, Ak, US 171/F3
Akiéni, Gabon 120/C3
Akigawa, Japan 83/C2
Akimiski (isl.), On, Can. 141/H3
Akıncı (pt.), Turk. 104/D1
Akıncılar, Turk. 102/D1
Akins, Ok, US 153/G3
Åkirkeby, Den. 40/F4
Akishima, Japan 83/C2
Akita, Japan 82/B4
Akita (pref.), Japan 82/B4
Akitio, NZ 135/D3
Akiyama, Japan 83/C2
Akjoujt, Mrta. 114/B2
Akka, Mor. 110/C3
Akkerhaugen, Nor. 40/C2
Akkeshi, Japan 82/D2
Acre ('Akko), Isr. 105/C3
'Akko (Acre), Isr. 105/C3
Akkrum, Neth. 52/C2
Akkystau, Kaz. 71/K2
Aklavik, NW, Can. 171/L2
'Aklé 'Aouâna (dune), Mrta. 114/D2
Aknīste, Lat. 41/L3
Aknoul, Mor. 112/C2
Akō, Japan 84/D3
Akoabas, Camr. 120/C2
Akobo, Sudan 117/G4
Ākobo Wenz (riv.), Eth. 117/G4
Akoga, Gabon 120/B2

Alsip – Antani

Map Section

204
205

Alsip, Il, US 167/Q16
Alstahaug, Nor. 38/E2
Alstead, NH, US 161/K3
Alster (riv.), Ger. 53/H1
Alston, Eng, UK 35/F2
Alstonville, Austl. 132/E1
Alsunga, Lat. 41/J3
Alt (riv.), Eng, UK 35/F4
Alta, Nor. 38/G1
Ålta, Swe. 39/B1
Alta (mt.), NZ 135/B4
Alta, Ia, US 155/G2
Alta Gracia, Arg. 188/C4
Alta Vista, US 153/F1
Altach, Aus. 61/F3
Altadena, Ca, US 166/F7
Altagracia, Nic. 176/E4
Altagracia de Orituco, Ven. 183/P8
Altai (mts.), Asia 77/H5
Altai (mts.), China 74/J5
Altamache (riv.), Ga, US 172/E1
Altamira, Braz. 182/C3
Altamira, Chile 188/B3
Altamira, Mex. 176/B1
Altamira do Maranhão, Braz. 183/E4
Altamont, Il, US 162/C1
Altamont, Ks, US 153/G2
Altamont, Mb, Can. 156/E3
Altamont, Or, US 146/C2
Altamont, Tn, US 162/E3
Altamonte Springs, Fl, US 164/N6
Altamura, It. 48/E2
Altanteel, Mong. 78/C2
Altar (vol.), Ecu. 180/B5
Altar, Mex. 174/C2
Altar de los Sacrificios (ruin), Guat. 176/D2
Altar Wash (riv.), Az, US 149/G5
Altare, It. 62/B5
Altario, Ab, Can. 145/J2
Altavilla Irpina, It. 65/D6
Altavilla Vicentina, It. 63/E2
Altavista, US 163/H2
Altay, China 99/E2
Altay, Mong. 78/D2
Altay, Mong. 78/B2
Altay Resp., Rus. 74/J4
Altayskiy Kray, Rus. 99/C1
Altdorf, Swi. 61/E4
Altdorf bei Nürnberg, Ger. 59/E4
Altea, Sp. 47/E3
Altedo, It. 63/E4
Altena, Ger. 53/E6
Altenahr, Ger. 55/G2
Altenau (riv.), Ger. 53/F5
Altenau, Ger. 53/H5
Altenbeken, Ger. 53/F5
Altenberg bei Linz, Aus. 59/H6
Altenburg, Ger. 42/G3
Altenburg, Mo, US 162/C2
Altenfelden, Aus. 59/G6
Altenglan, Ger. 55/G4
Altengottern, Ger. 53/H6
Altenkirchen, Ger. 55/G2
Altenmarkt an der Triesting, Aus. 51/N7
Altenmünster, Ger. 58/D6
Altenstadt, Ger. 61/G2
Altenstadt, Ger. 61/G1
Altenstadt, Ger. 58/B2
Altensteig, Ger. 58/B5
Altentreptow, Ger. 51/G5
Alter do Chão, Braz. 182/C3
Alter Rhein (riv.), Ger. 52/D5
Altes Land (phys. reg.), Ger. 53/G1
Altha, Fl, US 165/F2
Altheim, Aus. 59/G6
Altheim, Ger. 61/F1
Altheimer, Ar, US 153/J3
Althengstett, Ger. 58/B5
Althofen, Aus. 45/L3
Althorpe, Eng, UK 35/H4
Althütte, Ger. 58/C5
Altındere NP, Turk. 70/F4
Altıntaş, Turk. 104/C1
Altıntaş, Turk. 102/B2
Altınyayla, Turk. 104/B1
Altıplanicie del Payón (rocks), Arg. 190/C3
Altiplano (plat.), Bol.,Peru 179/C4
Altiplano (plat.), Peru 185/D4
Altkirch, Fr. 60/D2
Altlandsberg, Ger. 42/G3
Altmark (phys. reg.), Ger. 42/F2
Altmühl (riv.), Ger. 45/J2
Altmünster, Aus. 59/G7
Altnaharra, Sc, UK 31/R7
Alto (peak), It. 61/G4
Alto, La, US 153/J4
Alto (peak), Braz. 186/D2
Alto, Tx, US 150/G2
Alto (mtn.), Tx, US 151/B2
Alto Araguaia, Braz. 186/B3
Alto Chicapa, Ang. 120/D5
Alto Cuaie, Ang. 120/D4
Alto Cuilo, Ang. 120/D5
Alto de la Sierra, Arg. 188/D2
Alto de Tamar (peak), Col. 180/C3
Alto del Carmen, Chile 188/B4
Alto Garças, Braz. 186/B3
Alto Longá, Braz. 183/F4
Alto Molócuè, Moz. 123/H2
Alto Paraguay (dept.), Par. 186/A4
Alto Paraná (dept.), Par. 189/F3
Alto Parnaíba, Braz. 183/E5
Alto Pencoso, Arg. 190/D2
Alto Purús (riv.), Peru 184/D3
Alto Santo, Braz. 183/G4
Alto Seco, Bol. 188/C1
Alto Yuruá (riv.), Peru 184/C3
Alton, Eng, UK 37/F4
Alton, Il, US 155/J4

Alton, Ia, US 155/F2
Alton, Mo, US 153/J2
Alton Downs, Austl. 131/H3
Alton, Ut, US 149/G2
Altona, Mb, Can. 156/D3
Altona, Ger. 53/H1
Altona (isl.), Japan 77/M7
Altona (isl.), Japan 85/K6
Altamira (lake), Braz. 181/E5
Altônia, Braz. 189/F2
Altoona, Pa, US 161/G4
Altoona, Wi, US 155/H3
Altopascio, It. 63/D6
Altos de Camapana NP, Pan. 188/C4
Altotonga, Mex. 175/M7
Altötting, Ger. 59/F6
Altrincham, Eng, UK 35/F5
Altrip, Ger. 58/B4
Altun (mts.), China 77/H6
Altun Ha (ruin), Belz. 176/D2
Alturas, Port. 46/A2
Alturas, It. 64/M8
Altus, Ok, US 152/E3
Altus (A.F.B.), Ok, US 152/E3
Altykarasu, Kaz. 71/K2
Altynivka, Ukr. 73/G2
Altynkul', Uzb. 71/L4
Altzayanca, Mex. 175/M7
Alucra, Turk. 102/D1
Aluk, Sudan 117/E3
Alum Fork (riv.), Ar, US 153/H3
Aluminé, Arg. 190/C3
Alunda, Swe. 40/F1
Alupka, Ukr. 70/E4
Alūs, Iraq 102/E3
Alushta, Turk. 73/H5
Aluta, D.R. Congo 121/F3
Alva, Ok, US 153/E2
Alva, Sc, UK 33/C4
Alva, Fl, US 165/H4
Alvalade, Port. 46/A4
Alvängen, Swe. 40/E3
Alvarado, Col. 183/C3
Alvarado, Mn, US 156/F3
Alvarado, Tx, US 150/K7
Alvares Machado, Braz. 189/E2
Alvarez, Arg. 190/E2
Alvaro Obregón, Presa (dam), Mex. 174/C2
Alvdal, Nor. 38/D3
Alvear, Arg. 189/E2
Alvechurch, Eng, UK 37/E2
Alverca, Port. 47/P10
Alveringem, Belg. 54/B1
Alvesta, Swe. 40/F3
Alviano (lake), It. 65/B2
Alvignano, It. 65/D5
Alvik, Nor. 40/B1
Alvin, BC, Can. 144/C3
Alvin, Tx, US 151/M9
Alvin, Wi, US 157/K5
Alvinston, On, Can. 160/T3
Alvito, Port. 46/B3
Älvsborg (co.), Swe. 38/E4
Älvsbyn, Swe. 38/D2
Alvord, L, Wal, UK 34/E5
Alvord (bay), Wa, US 144/C4
Alvord, Tx, US 153/F4
Alvord (des.), Or, US 146/C2
Amarillo, Tx, US 152/D3
American Bolder (peak), Wa, US 144/D3
American College, Id, US 65/G8
American Falls, Id, US 147/G2
American Falls (dam), Id, US 147/G2
American Falls (res.), Id, US 147/G2
American Fork, Ut, US 147/H3
American Highland (reg.), Ant. 192/F
American Samoa 137/T10
American South Fork (riv.), Ca, US 146/C4
American South Fork (riv.), Ca, US 149/J1
American North Fork (riv.), Ca, US 146/C4

Antanimora, Madg. 125/H9
Antar (peak), Alg. 111/E3
Antarctic (pen.), Ant. 192/W
Antarctic Circle 192/Z
Antarctica (cont.) 192/*
Antaritarika, Madg. 125/H9
Antas, Rio das (riv.), Braz. 189/G4
Antella, It. 63/E6
Antelope, Tx, US 153/E4
Antelope, Mt, US 156/B3
Antelope, Or, US 146/C1
Antelope (isl.), Ut, US 147/G3
Antelope (peak), Mt, US 145/K5
Antelope Center, Ca, US 166/C1
Antelope Mine, Zim. 123/F4
Antenor Navarro, Braz. 183/G4
Antequera, Sp. 46/C4
Antequera, Par. 189/E3
Antero (mt.), Co, US 149/J1
Antes Fort, Pa, US 168/A1
Anthering, Aus. 59/G7
Anthony, Ks, US 153/E2
Anthony, Fl, US 165/G3
Anthony, NM, US 150/A1
Anthony Lagoon, Austl. 129/D4
Anti-Atlas (mts.), Mor. 110/C3
Anti-Lebanon (mts.), Leb. 104/D3
Antibes, Fr. 64/D5
Anticosti, Ile d' (isl.), Qu, Can. 141/K4
Antiesen (riv.), Aus. 59/G6
Antietam Nat'l Bfld., Md, US 161/H5
Antifer (cape), Fr. 57/F1
Antigo, Wi, US 157/K5
Antigonish, NS, Can. 159/G3
Antigua, Sp. 110/B3
Antigua (isl.), Anti. 173/N8
Antigua and Barbuda (ctry.) 173/N8
Antigua Guatemala, Guat. 176/D3
Antiguo Cauce del Río Bermejo (riv.), Arg. 188/D3
Antiguo Morelos, Mex. 175/F4
Antilly, Fr. 30/L4
Anţilyās, Leb. 105/D1
Antimony, Ut, US 149/G1
Anting, China 80/L8
Antioch, Ca, US 146/C4
Antioch, Il, US 160/B3
Antioquia, Col. 180/C3
Antioquia (dept.), Col. 177/H5
Antipina, Rus. 69/N3
Antipodes (isls.), NZ 27/T8
Antique Airpower Museum, Ia, US 155/H3
Antisana (vol.), Ecu. 180/B5
Antler, Sk, Can. 156/D3
Antlers, Ok, US 153/G3
Antofagasta, Chile 188/B2
Antofagasta (pol. reg.), Chile 188/B2
Antofagasta de la Sierra, Arg. 188/C3
Antoing, Belg. 54/C2
Antokonosy Manambondro, Madg. 125/H8
Antón, Pan. 180/A2
Anton Lizardo (pt.), Mex. 175/P7
Antón Lizardo, Mex. 175/P7
Antongil (bay), Madg. 125/J6
Antonibe, Madg. 125/H6
Antoniesberg (peak), SAfr. 124/C4
Antonina do Norte, Braz. 183/G4
Antônio Carlos, Braz. 187/N6
Antonio de Biedma, Arg. 191/D5
Antônio João, Braz. 189/F2
Antonito, Co, US 149/J2
Antonovo, Bul. 51/H4
Antony, Fr. 30/J5
Antrain, Fr. 56/D4
Antratsyt, Ukr. 73/K3
Antrim (dist.), NI, UK 34/B2
Antrim (mts.), NI, UK 34/B1
Antrim, NI, UK 34/B2
Antrim, NH, US 161/L3
Antrodoco, It. 65/C3
Antronapiana, It. 60/E5
Antsakabary, Madg. 125/J6
Antsalova, Madg. 125/H7
Antsambalahy, Madg. 125/J6
Antsenavolo, Madg. 125/J8
Antsiafabositra, Madg. 125/H7
Antsirabato, Madg. 125/J6
Antsirabe, Madg. 125/H7
Antsirañana (prov.), Madg. 125/J6
Antsirañana, Madg. 125/J6
Antsla, Est. 41/M3
Antsohihy, Madg. 125/H6
Antubia, Gha. 114/E5
Antuco (vol.), Chile 190/C3
Antulai (mtn.), Malay. 91/E3
Antwerp, Oh, US 160/D4
Antwerp (Deurne) (int'l arpt.), Belg. 52/B6
Antwerpen, Belg. 52/B6
Anūpgarh, India 98/B5
Anūpshahr, India 96/B1
Anuradhapura, SrL. 95/D4
Anuradhapura (ruin), SrL. 95/D4
Anutt, Mo, US 153/J2
Anvik, Ak, US 171/F3
Anvil Peak (mt.), Ak, US 171/B6
Anxi, China 78/D3
Anxi, China 87/H3
Anxin, China 80/G7
Anyama, C.d'Iv. 114/D5
Anyang, SKor. 81/F7
Anyang (riv.), SKor. 81/F7
Anyang, China 80/C3
A'nyêmaqên (mts.), China 78/D4
Anyer Kidul, Indo. 89/D4
Anyi, China 80/B4
Anykščiai, Lith. 41/L4
Anyuan, China 87/H3
Anyuan, China 87/G3
Anyuy (riv.), Rus. 79/M2
Anza (riv.), It. 60/E6
Anzá, Col. 183/K6
'Anzah, WBnk. 105/C4
Anzaldo, Bol. 188/C1
Anze, China 80/C3
Anzegem, Belg. 54/C2
Anzhero-Sudzhensk, Rus. 74/J4
Anzhou, China 80/G7
Anzin, Fr. 54/C3
Anzing, Ger. 59/E6
Anzio, It. 65/B5
Anzoátegui (state), Ven. 181/E2
Anzoátegui, Ven. 180/D2
Anzoátegui (int'l arpt.), Ven. 181/E2
Anzoátegui, Col. 183/K8
Anzola dell'Emilia, It. 63/E4
Ao Kham (pt.), Thai. 94/B4
Ao Phangnga NP, Thai. 94/B4
Aoba (isl.), Van. 136/F6
Aoga (isl.), Japan 85/F4
Aogaki, Japan 83/H5
Aoiz, Sp. 44/C5
Aojiang, China 87/J3
Aomori, Japan 82/B3
Aomori (pref.), Japan 82/B3
Aonla, India 96/B1
Aoquanxu, China 87/G3
Aoral (peak), Camb. 94/D3
Aorangi (mts.), NZ 135/J9
Áos, Gre. 49/J4
Aosta, It. 64/D1
Aoste, Fr. 64/B1
Aouara, FrG. 182/C1
Aoudaghast (ruin), Mrta. 114/C2
'Aouînat ez Zbil, Mrta. 114/C2
Aouk-Aoukale, Rsv. de Faune de l', Chad 116/D3
Aoukar (phys. reg.), Mrta. 114/C2
Aoulef, Alg. 111/F4
Aourou, Mali 114/C3
Aouste-sur-Sye, Fr. 64/B3
Aoyama, Japan 83/K6
Aozi, Chad 108/C4
Aozou, Chad 108/C4
Aozou Strip (reg.), Chad 108/C4
Ap Binh Chau, Viet. 94/D4
Ap Loc Thanh, Viet. 94/D4
Ap Long Hoa, Viet. 94/E4
Ap Luc, Viet. 94/D4
Ap Tan My, Viet. 94/E4
Ap Vinh Hao, Viet. 94/E4
Apa (riv.), Braz.,Par. 186/A4
Apache, Ok, US 153/E3
Apache (mts.), Tx, US 151/B2
Apache (lake), Az, US 149/G4
Apache Creek, NM, US 149/H4
Apache Junction, Az, US 149/G4
Apagado (vol.), Bol.,Chile 188/C2
Apalachee (bay), Fl, US 165/F3
Apalachee (riv.), Ga, US 163/F4
Apalachicola, Fl, US 165/F3
Apalachicola (riv.), Fl, US 165/F2
Apan, Mex. 175/L7
Apanovka, Kaz. 71/M1
Apaporis (riv.), Col. 180/D5
Aparados da Serra, PN de, Braz. 189/G4
Aparecida, Braz. 189/H2
Aparecida do Taboado, Braz. 189/G2
Aparición, Ven. 180/D2
Aparri, Phil. 88/C1
Apartadó, Col. 180/B3
Aparurén, Ven. 181/F3
Apataki, FrPol. 137/L6
Apátfalva, Hun. 50/E2
Apatin, Yugo. 50/D3
Apatity, Rus. 68/G2
Apatou, FrG. 182/C1
Apatzingán de la Constitución, Mex. 174/E5
Apauwar, Indo. 91/J4
Apaxco, Mex. 175/K7
Apaxtla de Castrejon, Mex. 175/F5
Ape, Lat. 41/M3
Apeldoorn, Neth. 52/C4
Apelern, Ger. 53/G4
Apen, Ger. 53/E2
Apennines (mts.), It. 29/F4
Apensen, Ger. 53/G2
Apere (riv.), Bol. 185/E4
Apex, NC, US 163/H3
Apéyémé, Togo 115/F5
Aphrodisias (ruin), Turk. 102/B2
Api, D.R. Congo 121/F2
Api (riv.), D.R. Congo 121/F2
Api (cape), Indo. 91/F4
Api (cape), Indo. 90/C3
Api (peak), Indo. 91/E5
Api (peak), Nepal 99/D5
Apia (cap.), Sam. 137/S9
Apía, Col. 183/K7
Apia (Fagali) (int'l arpt.), Sam. 137/S9
Apia (Faleolo) (int'l arpt.), Sam. 137/S9
Apiacá (riv.), Braz. 185/G3
Apiacás, Serra dos (mts.), Braz. 185/G3
Apiaí, Braz. 189/G3
Apishapa (riv.), Co, US 154/B5
Apizaco, Mex. 175/L7
Aplao, Peru 184/C5
Apo (mt.), Phil. 88/D4
Apodi, Braz. 183/G4
Apoera, Sur. 181/G3
Apolima (str.), Sam. 137/R9
Apolinario Saravia, Arg. 188/C3
Apollo Bay, Austl. 132/B3
Apollo Beach, Fl, US 164/L8
Apollonía, Gre. 49/J4
Apollonia (ruin), Libya 67/J4
Apolo, Bol. 184/D4
Apopka (lake), Fl, US 165/H3
Apopka, Fl, US 164/M6
Aporé (riv.), Braz. 189/G1
Apore (riv.), Braz. 186/B3
Apostle (isls.), Wi, US 157/J4
Apostle Islands Nat'l Lakeshore, Wi, US 157/J4
Apóstoles, Arg. 189/F3
Apostolic Palace, VatC. 65/G7
Apostolos Andreas (cape), Cyp. 104/D2
Apostolove, Ukr. 73/G4
Apoteri, Guy. 181/G3
Appalachian (mts.), US 143/K4
Appam, ND, US 156/C3
Appelscha, Neth. 52/D3
Appen, Ger. 53/G1
Appennino Abruzzese (mts.), It. 65/C3
Appennino Ligure (mts.), It. 45/H4
Appennino Napoletano (mts.), It. 65/D4
Appennino Tosco-Emiliano (mts.), It. 45/J4
Appennino Umbro-Marchigiano (mts.), It. 45/K5
Appenweier, Ger. 60/D1
Appenzell, Swi. 61/F3
Appenzell (canton), Swi. 61/F3
Appert Lake Nat'l Wild. Ref., ND, US 156/D4
Appignano, It. 63/G7
Appin, Austl. 133/E2
Appingedam, Neth. 52/D2
Apple (riv.), Wi, US 157/Q6
Apple Valley, Ca, US 166/C1
Apple Valley, Mn, US 157/P7
Appleby, Eng, UK 35/F2
Appleby, Tx, US 151/G2
Appleby Magna, Eng, UK 37/E1
Appleton, Mn, US 155/F1
Appleton, NY, US 160/V9
Appleton, Wi, US 160/B2
Appleton City, Mo, US 153/G1
Appling, Ga, US 163/F4
Appomattox, Va, US 163/H2
Appomattox Court House Nat'l Hist. Park, Va, US 163/H2
Approuage (riv.), FrG. 182/C2
Aprelevka, Rus. 69/W9
Aprica, It. 61/G5
Aprica, Passo dell' (pass), It. 61/G5
Apricena, It. 48/D2
Aprilia, It. 65/B4
Apriltsi, Bul. 51/G4
Apsheronsk, Rus. 73/K5
Apsley, On, Can. 161/G2
Apsley (str.), Austl. 128/C2
Apsley Gorge NP, Austl. 132/E1
Apt, Fr. 64/B5
Apucarana, Braz. 189/G2
Apuiarés, Braz. 183/G3
Apulia (reg.), It. 67/H2
Apulo, Col. 183/L8
Apure (riv.), Ven. 173/H6
Apure (prov.), Ven. 180/D3
Apurímac (riv.), Peru 179/B4
Apurímac (dept.), Peru 184/C4
Āq Qal'eh, Iran 103/H2
Aqaba (gulf), Asia 77/B7
'Aqdā, Iran 103/H3
'Aqīq, Sudan 100/C5
Aqmola Oblast, Kaz. 99/A1
'Aqqābah, WBnk. 105/C4
Aqqikkol (lake), China 99/E4
'Aqrabah, WBnk. 105/C4
'Aqrah, Iraq 103/E2
Aqsay, Kaz. 71/K2
Aqtaū, Kaz. 71/J4
Aqtöbe, Kaz. 71/L2
Aqtöbe (int'l arpt.), Kaz. 71/L2
Aqtöbe Oblast, Kaz. 71/L3
Aqua Fria (riv.), Az, US 149/F4
Aquanaval (riv.), Mex. 174/E3
Aquapei (riv.), Braz. 189/G2
Aquarius (plat.), Ut, US 147/H4
Aquarius (mts.), Az, US 149/F3
Aquia, Peru 184/B3
Aquidabán (riv.), Par. 186/A4
Aquidauana, Braz. 189/F2
Aquidauana (riv.), Braz. 186/B3
Aquila, Swi. 61/E5
Aquileia, It. 63/G2
Aquiles Serdán, Mex. 177/B3
Aquilla, Tx, US 151/F2
Aquin, Haiti 177/H2
Aquino, It. 65/C5
Aquiraz, Braz. 183/G3
Aquitaine (pol. reg.), Fr. 44/C4
Ar (riv.), China 78/D4
Ar Horqin Qi, China 80/E2
Ar Rabaḑ, SAr. 109/H4
Ar Rafīd, Jor. 105/D3
Ar Rafīd, Syria 105/D3
Ar Rahad, Sudan 117/F2
Ar Raḩāminah, Egypt 113/C2
Ar Raḩmānīyah, Egypt 113/B2
Ar Ramādī, Iraq 103/E3
Ar Ramthā, Jor. 105/D3
Ar Rank, Sudan 117/G3
Ar Raqqah, Syria 102/D3
Ar Raqqah (prov.), Syria 102/D2
Ar Rashīdīyah, Leb. 105/C2
Ar Rass, SAr. 100/D3
Ar Rastan, Syria 104/E2
Ar Rawḑah, SAr. 100/D3
Ar Rawḑah, Yem. 118/C2
Ar Rawḑah, Egypt 113/B6
Ar Rāwuk, Yem. 118/D2
Ar Rayyān, Qatar 100/F3
Ar Rifā'ī, Iraq 103/F4
Ar Rīḩīyah, WBnk. 105/C6
Ar Riyāḑ (Riyadh) (cap.), SAr. 100/E4
Ar Riyān, Yem. 118/D2
Ar Rubayqī, Egypt 113/C4
Ar Rumaythah, Iraq 103/F4
Ar Rummān, Jor. 105/D4
Ar Ruşayfah, Jor. 105/E4
Ar Ruşayriş, Sudan 117/G3
Ar Ruţbah, Iraq 102/E3
Ar Ruways, Qatar 100/F3
Ar-Asgat, Mong. 78/F2
Ara (riv.), Ire. 32/B5
Ara (riv.), Japan 85/F2
Ara Terra, Eth. 118/B4
'Arab (gulf), Egypt 109/F2
Arab, Al, US 162/D3
'Arab (wadi), Jor. 105/D3
'Arabah (wadi), Egypt 109/G2
Araban, Turk. 102/D2
Arabatsk (bay), Ukr. 73/H5
Arabatsk Spit (pen.), Ukr. 73/H4
Arabi, Ga, US 165/G2
Arabian (sea), Asia 77/F8
Arabian (des.), Egypt 109/G3
Arabian (pen.), Asia 100/D3
Arabopó, Ven. 181/F3
Araç (riv.), Turk. 70/E4
Araç, Turk. 70/E4
Araça (riv.), Braz. 181/F4
Araca, Bol. 188/C1
Aracaju, Braz. 187/F1
Aracataca, Col. 180/C2
Aracati, Braz. 183/G4
Araçatuba, Braz. 189/G2
Araceli, Phil. 88/B3
Aracena, Sp. 46/B4
Aračinovo, FYROM 49/G1
Aracoiaba, Braz. 183/G4
Aracruz, Braz. 187/E3
Araçuaí, Braz. 187/E3
Araçuaí (riv.), Braz. 187/E3
Arad (prov.), Rom. 50/E2
Arad, Rom. 50/E2
Arada, Chad 116/D2
'Arādah, UAE 100/F4
Ārādān, Iran 103/H3
Arafali, Erit. 118/A2
Arafura (sea), Austl.,Indo. 128/D2
Aragats (peak), Arm. 71/H4
Araglin (riv.), Ire. 32/B5
Arago, Or, US 146/A2
Arago (cape), Or, US 146/A2
Aragón (reg.), Sp. 66/C2
Aragón (riv.), Sp. 66/C2
Aragon, NM, US 149/H4
Aragon, Ga, US 162/E3
Aragua (state), Ven. 181/E2
Araguacema, Braz. 182/D5
Araguaçu, Braz. 186/C2
Araguaia (riv.), Braz. 179/D3
Araguaia, PN do, Braz. 186/C1
Araguaiana, Braz. 186/C2
Araguaína, Braz. 182/D4
Araguari, Braz. 186/C3
Araguari (riv.), Braz. 182/D2
Araguari (riv.), Braz. 189/H1
Araguatins, Braz. 182/D4
Arai, Japan 85/F2
Araioses, Braz. 183/F3
Arāk, Iran 103/G3
Arak, Alg. 111/F4
Arakan (mts.), Myan. 93/F3
Arakawa, Japan 83/C2
Árakhthos (riv.), Gre. 49/G3
Araklı, Turk. 70/G4
Araku, India 95/D2
Aral, Kaz. 74/G5
Aral (sea), Kaz. 77/E5
Aralık, Turk. 103/F2
Aralsor (lake), Kaz. 71/H2
Aramac, Austl. 134/B3
Arāmbāgh, India 97/F4
Aramon, Fr. 64/A5
Ārān, Iran 103/G3
Aran (isls.), Ire. 31/P10
Aran Fawddwy (peak), Wal, UK 34/E6
Aranda de Duero, Sp. 46/D2
Arandelovac, Yugo. 50/E3
Arandis, Namb. 122/B4
Arandu, Pak. 98/A2
Arang, India 95/D1
Arani, Bol. 188/C1
Arani, India 95/C3
Aranjuez, Sp. 46/D2
Aranos, Namb. 122/C5
Aransas (riv.), Tx, US 151/F3
Aransas NWR, Tx, US 151/F3
Aransas Pass, Tx, US 151/F4
Arantina, Braz. 187/M6
Aranuka (isl.), Kiri. 136/G5
Aranyaprathet, Thai. 94/C3
Araouane, Mali 114/E2
Arapaho, Ok, US 152/E3
Arapahoe, Ne, US 154/E3
Arapahoe Nat'l Rec. Area, Co, US 154/A3
Arapahoe NWR, Co, US 147/K3
Arapawa (isl.), NZ 135/C3
Arapicos, Ecu. 184/B1
Arapiraca, Braz. 187/F1
Arapiuns (riv.), Braz. 181/H5
Arapongas, Braz. 189/G2
'Ar'ara, WBnk. 105/C4
Araracuara, Col. 180/C5
Araranguá, Braz. 189/G4
Araraquara, Braz. 189/G2
Araras, Braz. 189/H2
Ararat, Austl. 132/B3
Ararat, Mount (Ağrı) (peak), Turk. 103/F2
Arari, Braz. 183/E3
Arari (lake), Braz. 182/D3
Arāria, India 97/F2
Araripe, Chapada do (uplands), Braz. 183/F4
Araripina, Braz. 183/F4
Araruna, Braz. 183/H4
Aras (riv.), Iran 74/E6
Aras (riv.), Turk. 102/E2
Aratane (well), Mrta. 114/C2
Aratoca, Col. 180/C3
Aratuba, Braz. 183/G4
Arau, Malay. 94/C5
Arauá (riv.), Braz. 185/E2
Arauca (riv.), Col. 180/D3
Arauca (riv.), Col.,Ven. 181/E3
Arauca (dept.), Col. 180/D3
Arauca, Col. 180/D3
Arauco, Chile 190/B3
Arauquita, Col. 180/D3
Araure, Ven. 180/D2
Aravaca, Sp. 47/N9
Arawa, PNG 136/E5
Arawale Nat'l Reserve, Kenya 119/C2
Araxá, Braz. 186/D3
Araya (pen.), Ven. 181/E2
Arazatí, Uru. 191/K11
Ārba Minch', Eth. 117/H4
Ārbē Gona, Eth. 118/A4
Arbeca, Sp. 47/F2
Arbedo, Swi. 61/F5
Arbeláez, Col. 183/L8
Arbīl (gov.), Iraq 103/E3
Arboga, Swe. 40/F2
Arbois, Fr. 60/B4
Arbois, Mont d' (peak), Fr. 60/C6
Arboletes, Col. 180/B2
Arbon, Swi. 61/F2
Arbor Vitae, Wi, US 157/K5
Arbore, Eth. 117/H4
Arborfield, Sk, Can. 145/N1
Arborg, Mb, Can. 156/F2
Arbovale, WV, US 163/H1
Arbrå, Swe. 40/G1
Arbroath, Sc, UK 33/D3
Arbuckle (mts.), Ok, US 153/F3
Arbuckle (lake), Fl, US 165/H4
Arbuckle, Ca, US 146/B4
Arc (riv.), Fr. 44/F5
Arc (mtn.), Nv, US 146/E4
Arc-en-Barrois, Fr. 60/B2
Arc-et-Senans, Fr. 60/B3
Arc-lès-Gray, Fr. 60/B3
Arc-sur-Tille, Fr. 60/B3
Arcachon, Fr. 44/C4
Arcadia, Ca, US 166/F7
Arcadia, Fl, US 165/H4
Arcadia, In, US 160/C4
Arcadia, La, US 153/H4
Arcadia, Mo, US 162/B2
Arcadia, Ne, US 154/E3
Arcadia, NS, Can. 158/D4
Arcadia, Ok, US 153/F3
Arcadia, Wi, US 155/J1
Arcanum, Oh, US 160/D5
Arcata, Ca, US 146/A3
Arcata (bay), Ca, US 146/A3
Arce, It. 65/C4
Arceburgo, Braz. 187/K6
Arcelia, Mex. 175/E5
Arcen, Neth. 52/D6
Arcene, It. 62/C2
Arceto, It. 63/D4
Arcevia, It. 63/F7
Archangel (Arkhangel'sk), Rus. 68/J2
Archbold, Oh, US 160/D4
Archdale, NC, US 163/H3
Archena, Sp. 46/E3
Archer, Fl, US 165/G3
Archer (riv.), Austl. 129/F3
Archer Bend NP, Austl. 129/F3
Archer City, Tx, US 153/E4
Archerfield (arpt.), Austl. 134/E7
Archers Post, Kenya 119/B1
Arches, Fr. 60/C1
Arches NP, Ut, US 147/J4
Archibald, La, US 153/J4
Archibarca (peak), Arg. 188/C3
Archidona, Sp. 46/C4
Archie, Mo, US 153/G1
Archiestown, Sc, UK 33/C2
Archman, Trkm. 71/L5
Archman, Trkm. 71/L5
Arcipelago Toscano (isl.), It. 45/H5
Arcisate, It. 61/E6
Arco, It. 61/G6
Arco, Id, US 147/G2
Arco, Paso del (pass), Arg. 190/C3
Arcola, Sk, Can. 156/C3
Arcola, It. 62/C5
Arcola, Ms, US 162/B4
Arcole, It. 63/E3
Arcopongo, Bol. 188/C1
Arcos, Braz. 186/D4
Arcos de Jalón, Sp. 46/D2
Arcos de la Frontera, Sp. 46/C4
Arcos de Valdevez, Port. 46/A2
Arcosanti, Az, US 149/F3
Arcoverde, Braz. 183/G5
Arctic (ocean) 26/A1
Arctic Bay, Nun, Can. 141/H1
Arctic Circle 26/C2
Arctic Coastal (plain), Ak, US 171/F2
Arctic Red (riv.), NW, Can. 171/M2
Arctic Village, Ak, US 171/J2
Arctowski, Pol., Ant. 192/W
Arda (riv.), Bul. 70/C4
Arda (riv.), It. 63/C3
Ardabīl, Iran 103/G2
Ardabīl (gov.), Iran 103/G2
Ardagh, Ire. 32/A4
Ardagh, Ire. 32/C2
Ardahan, Turk. 71/G4
Ardakān, Iran 103/H3
Ardal, Iran 103/G4
Årdalstangen, Nor. 40/B1
Ardanuç, Turk. 71/G4
Ardatov, Rus. 68/J5
Arddleen, Wal, UK 36/C1
Ardea, It. 65/B4
Ardèche (dept.), Fr. 64/A3
Ardèche (riv.), Fr. 44/F4
Ardee, Ire. 34/B4
Arden, Mb, Can. 156/E2
Arden, Den. 40/C3
Arden (mt.), Austl. 131/H5
Arden, De, US 168/C4
Arden, Wa, US 144/F3
Arden-Arcade, Ca, US 167/M9
Ardennes (for.), Fr. 42/C4
Ardennes (dept.), Fr. 55/D4
Ardennes (for.), Belg. 44/F1
Ardennes, Canal des (canal), Fr. 55/D4
Ardenno, It. 61/F5
Arderin (peak), Ire. 32/C3
Ardersier, Sc, UK 33/B1
Ardeşen, Turk. 71/G4
Ardesio, It. 61/F6
Ardestān, Iran 103/H3
Ardez, Swi. 61/G4
Ardfinnan, Ire. 32/C5
Ardglass, NI, UK 34/C3
Ardila (riv.), Sp. 46/B3
Ardino, Bul. 51/G5
Ardivachar (pt.), Sc, UK 31/Q8
Ardle (riv.), Sc, UK 33/C3
Ardlethan, Austl. 133/C2
Ardmore, Ire. 32/C6
Ardmore, Ok, US 153/F3
Ardmore, Pa, US 168/C4
Ardmore, SD, US 154/C2
Ardmore, Tn, US 162/D3
Ardnacrusha, Ire. 32/B4
Ardnamurchan (pt.), Sc, UK 31/Q8
Ardoch Nat'l Wild. Ref., ND, US 156/F3
Ardon, Swi. 60/D5
Ardooie, Belg. 54/C2
Ardrahan, Ire. 32/B3
Ardres, Fr. 54/A2
Ardrossan, Sc, UK 33/B5
Ardrossan, Austl. 131/H5
Ards (pen.), Sc, UK 34/C3
Ards (dist.), NI, UK 34/C2
Ardsley, NY, US 169/K7
Åre, Swe. 38/E3
Areado, Braz. 187/K6
Arecibo, PR 173/M8
Areia Branca, Braz. 183/G4
Arena (pt.), Ca, US 146/B4
Arena de la Ventana Punta (pt.), Mex. 174/C3
Arenal (vol.), CR 177/E4
Arenápolis, Braz. 185/G4
Arenas de San Pedro, Sp. 46/C2
Arenas, Punta de (pt.), Arg. 191/C7
Arendal, Nor. 40/C2
Arendonk, Belg. 52/C6
Arendtsville, Pa, US 168/A4
Arenig Fawr (peak), Wal, UK 34/E6
Arenys de Mar, Sp. 47/L6
Arenzano, It. 62/B5
Arenzville, Il, US 155/J4
Areo, Ven. 181/F2
Areópolis, Gre. 49/H4
Arequipa, Peru 184/D5
Arequipa (dept.), Peru 184/C5
Arequito, Arg. 190/E2
Aresing, Ger. 58/E5
Arévalo, Sp. 46/C2
Areyonga, Austl. 131/G3
Āreza, Erit. 118/A2
Arezzo, It. 63/E7
Arezzo (prov.), It. 63/E5
Arfa' Deh, Iran 103/H3
Arga (riv.), Sp. 44/C5
Argadargada, Austl. 131/H2
Argalastí, Gre. 49/H3
Argamakmur, Indo. 89/C3
Argamasilla de Alba, Sp. 46/D3
Argamasilla de Calatrava, Sp. 46/C3
Argan, China 99/E3
Arganda, Sp. 47/N9
Argao, Phil. 88/C3
Argatone (peak), It. 65/C4
Argegno, It. 61/F6
Argelès-Gazost, Fr. 44/C5
Argelès-sur-Mer, Fr. 44/E5
Argelia, Col. 183/K7
Argen (riv.), Ger. 61/F2
Argenbühl, Ger. 61/F2
Argences, Fr. 57/E2
Argens (riv.), Fr. 45/G5
Argenta, It. 63/E4
Argenta, BC, Can. 144/F2
Argentan, Fr. 57/E3
Argentat, Fr. 44/D4
Argentera (peak), It. 64/D4
Argenteuil, Fr. 30/J5
Argentina (riv.), It. 62/A5
Argentina (ctry.) 179/C6
Argentino (lake), Arg. 191/B6
Argenton-sur-Creuse, Fr. 44/D3
Argentona, Sp. 47/L6
Argentré, Fr. 57/E4
Argeş (riv.), Rom. 70/C3
Argeş (prov.), Rom. 51/G3
Arghandab (riv.), Afg. 101/J2
Argideen (riv.), Ire. 32/B6
Argıthanı, Turk. 102/B2
Argo, Sudan 109/F5
Argolis (gulf), Gre. 67/J3
Argonne, Wi, US 157/K5
Argonne (for.), Fr. 42/C4
Argonne Nat'l Lab., Il, US 167/P16
Argopuro (peak), Indo. 89/F4
Árgos, Gre. 49/H4
Árgos Orestikón, Gre. 49/G2
Argostólion, Gre. 49/G3
Argueil, Fr. 57/G1
Arguello (pt.), Ca, US 142/B5
Arguenon (riv.), Fr. 56/C4
Argun (riv.), China,Rus 79/J1
Argungu, Nga. 115/G3
Argusville, ND, US 156/F4
Argut (riv.), Rus. 78/B2
Arguut, Mong. 78/E2
Argyle, Mn, US 156/F3
Argyle (lake), Austl. 128/C4
Argyle, Tx, US 150/K6
Argyll (reg.), Sc, UK 33/A4
Argyll and Bute (co.), Sc, UK 33/A4
Arhangay (prov.), Mong. 78/D2
Arhli, Niger 115/G2
Arholma (isl.), Swe. 39/C1
Arhreijît (well), Mrta. 110/B5
Arhrîjît, Mrta. 114/C2
Århus, Den. 40/D3
Århus (co.), Den. 40/D3
Ariah (mtn.), Austl. 133/C2
Ariah Park, Austl. 133/C2
Ariamsvlei, Namb. 124/B3
Ariari (riv.), Col. 180/C4
Arias, Arg. 190/E2
Aribinda, Burk. 115/E3
Arica, Col. 180/D5
Arica, Chile 188/B1
Arica (Chacalluta) (int'l arpt.), Chile 188/B1
Arıcak, Turk. 102/E2
Ariccia, It. 65/B4
Arichat, NS, Can. 159/G3
Arid (cape), Austl. 130/D5
Arida, Japan 84/D3
Aridhaía, Gre. 49/H2
Arido (peak), Ca, US 166/A1
Aridol (lake), WSah. 110/B4
Ariège (riv.), Fr. 44/D5
Ariel, Wa, US 144/C5
Arienzo, It. 65/D5
Arifiye, Turk. 51/K5
Ārifwāla, Pak. 98/B4
Arīḩā, Syria 104/E2
Arīḩā (Jericho), WBnk. 105/C5
Arikaree (riv.), Co, US 154/C4
Arilje, Yugo. 50/E4
Arima, Trin. 181/F2
Aringa, Ugan. 121/G2
Arinos (riv.), Braz. 185/G3
Arinos, Braz. 186/D2
Arinthod, Fr. 60/B5
Ario de Rosales, Mex. 175/E5
Ariogala, Lith. 41/K4
Aripao, Ven. 181/E3
Aripeka, Fl, US 164/K7
Aripine, Az, US 149/G3
Aripuanã, Braz. 185/G3
Aripuanã (riv.), Braz. 179/C3
Ariquemes, Braz. 185/F3
Aris, Namb. 122/C4
Arish, Austl. 134/B2
`Arīsh (wadi), Egypt 109/G2
Arismendi, Ven. 180/D2
Arissa, Eth. 118/B3
Ariton, Al, US 165/F2
Arivaca, Az, US 149/G5
Arivechi, Mex. 174/C2
Arivonimamo, Madg. 125/H7
Ariza, Sp. 46/D2
Arize (riv.), Fr. 47/F1
Arizona (state), US 142/D5
Arizona, Arg. 190/D2
Arizona City, Az, US 149/G4
Arizpe, Mex. 174/C2
Årjäng, Swe. 40/E2
Arjay, Ky, US 162/F2
Arjeplog, Swe. 38/F2
Arjona, Col. 180/C2
Arjona, Sp. 46/C4
Arkabutla (dam), Ms, US 162/B3
Arkadak, Rus. 71/G2
Arkadelphia, Ar, US 153/H3
Arkaig (lake), Sc, UK 33/A3
Arkalokhórion, Gre. 49/J5
Arkansas (riv.), US 143/K4
Arkansas (state), US 143/H4
Arkansas City, Ks, US 153/F2
Arkansas Post Nat'l Mem., Ar, US 153/J3
Arkansas, Salt Fork (riv.), Ok, US 153/F2
Arkanū (peak), Libya 108/E4
Arkhángelos, Gre. 102/B2
Arkhangel'sk (int'l arpt.), Rus. 68/J2
Arkhangel'skaya Oblast, Rus. 68/H3
Arkhangel'sk (Archangel), Rus. 68/J2
Arkhangel'skaya, Rus. 73/L5
Arkhangel'skoye, Rus. 69/W9
Arkhangel'skoye, Rus. 73/L2
Arkhara, Rus. 79/L2
Arkhipo-Osipovka, Rus. 70/F3
Arkhyz, Rus. 71/G4
Arklow, Ire. 34/B6
Arkona (cape), Ger. 40/E4
Arksey, Eng, UK 35/G4
Arkticheskiy Institut (isls.), Rus. 74/H2
Ärla, Swe. 40/G2
Arlanda (int'l arpt.), Swe. 40/G2
Arlanza (riv.), Sp. 46/C1
Arlazón (riv.), Sp. 46/D1
Arlbergpass (pass), Aus. 61/G3
Arles, Fr. 64/A5
Arlesheim, Swi. 60/D3
Arlington, Az, US 149/F4
Arlington, Co, US 152/C1
Arlington, Ga, US 165/F2
Arlington, Ks, US 153/E2
Arlington, Ky, US 162/C2
Arlington, Mn, US 155/G1
Arlington, Ne, US 155/F3
Arlington, NY, US 161/K4
Arlington, Oh, US 160/E4
Arlington, Or, US 144/D5
Arlington, SD, US 155/F1
Arlington, Tn, US 162/C3
Arlington, Tx, US 150/K7
Arlington (lake), Tx, US 150/K7
Arlington, Va, US 168/A6
Arlington, Vt, US 161/K3
Arlington, Wa, US 144/C3
Arlington Heights, Il, US 160/C3
Arló, Hun. 43/L4
Arlon, Belg. 55/E4
Arltunga, Austl. 131/G2
Arluno, It. 62/B2
Arly (riv.), Fr. 60/C6
Arm (riv.), Sk, Can. 145/M2
Armada, Mi, US 167/G6
Armadale (nbrhd.), Austl. 130/L7
Armadale, Sc, UK 33/C5
Armagh, NI, UK 34/B3
Armagh (dist.), NI, UK 34/B3
Armançon (riv.), Fr. 44/F3
Armando Laydner (res.), Braz. 186/C4
Armant, Egypt 109/G3
Armavir, Arm. 71/H4
Armavir, Rus. 73/L5
Armenia (ctry.) 77/D5
Armenia, Col. 183/K8
Armentières, Fr. 54/B2
Armentières-en-Brie, Fr. 30/M5
Armería, Mex. 174/E5
Armero, Col. 183/L8
Armidabán (riv.), Par. 189/E2
Armidale, Austl. 132/D1
Armilla, Sp. 46/D4
Arminto, Wy, US 147/K2
Armona, Ca, US 148/C2
Armopa, Indo. 91/J4
Armour, SD, US 154/E2
Armoy, NI, UK 34/B1
Armstrong, Arg. 190/E2
Armstrong, BC, Can. 144/E2
Armstrong, On, Can. 157/K2
Armstrong, Mo, US 155/H4
Armstrong, Tx, US 151/F4
Armstrong Creek, Wi, US 157/K5
Armthorpe, Eng, UK 35/G4
Ārmūr, India 95/C2
Armutlu, Turk. 51/J5
Army Ammunition Plant, Il, US 155/K3
Army Dep., Or, US 146/D1
Army Ordnance Museum, Md, US 168/B5
Armyans'k, Ukr. 73/G4
Arnage, Fr. 57/F5
Arnager (int'l arpt.), Den. 40/F4
Arnaía, Gre. 49/H2
Arnaud (riv.), Qu, Can. 141/J3
Arnaudville, La, US 164/C2
Arnauti (cape), Cyp. 104/C2
Arnavutköy, Turk. 103/M6
Arncott, Eng, UK 37/E3
Arnedo, Sp. 46/D1
Arnegard, ND, US 156/C4
Arneiroz, Braz. 183/F4
Arnett, Ok, US 152/E2
Arnheim, Mi, US 157/K4
Arnhem, Neth. 52/C5
Arnhem (cape), Austl. 129/E3
Arnhem (bay), Austl. 129/E3
Arnhem Land (reg.), Austl. 128/D3
Arnhem Land (reg.) 127/C2
Arnhem Land Abor. Land, Austl. 128/D3
Arnières-sur-Iton, Fr. 57/G3
Arno (riv.), It. 66/F2
Arnö, Swe. 39/A2
Arnö, Swe. 39/A1
Arno (isl.), Mrsh. 136/G4
Arnold, Eng, UK 35/G6
Arnold, Ca, US 146/C4
Arnold, Md, US 168/B5
Arnold, Mi, US 157/L4
Arnold, Mo, US 162/B1
Arnold, Ne, US 154/D3
Arnold (riv.), Austl. 128/D3
Arnoldstein, Aus. 45/K3
Arnon (riv.), Fr. 44/E3
Arnouville-lès-Gonesse, Fr. 30/K5
Arnprior, On, Can. 161/H2
Arnsberg, Ger. 53/F6
Arnside, Eng, UK 35/F3
Arnstein, Ger. 58/C3
Arnstorf, Ger. 59/F5
Aro Usu (cape), Indo. 128/C2
Aroab, Namb. 124/B2
Aroases, Braz. 183/F4
Aroche, Sp. 46/B4
Arochukwu, Nga. 115/G5
Aroland, On, Can. 157/L2
Arolsen, Ger. 53/G6
Aroma, Sudan 117/H2
Aroma, Bol. 188/C1
Aron, Fr. 57/E4
Aron (riv.), Fr. 44/E3
Arona, It. 62/B2
Aronde (riv.), Fr. 54/B5
Aroostook, NB, Can. 158/D2
Arorae (isl.), Kiri. 136/G5
Aroroy, Phil. 88/C2
Åros, Nor. 38/S8
Arosa, Swi. 61/F4
Aroser Rothern (peak), Swi. 61/F4
Ærøskøbing, Den. 40/D4
Arp, Ga, US 165/G2
Arpaçay, Turk. 71/G4
Arpajon, Fr. 30/J6
Arpajon-sur-Cère, Fr. 44/E4
Arqalyq, Kaz. 99/A1
Arquata Scrivia, It. 62/B4
Arque, Bol. 188/C1
Arques, Fr. 54/B2
Arques-la-Bataille, Fr. 57/G1
'Arrāba, Isr. 105/C3
'Arrābah, WBnk. 105/C4
Arrah, India 97/E3
Arraha, Eth. 118/B3
Arraias (riv.), Braz. 185/H3
Arraias, Braz. 186/D2
Arraiján, Pan. 180/B2
Arrais (riv.), Fr. 47/F1
Arram, Eng, UK 35/H4
Arran (isl.), Sc, UK 31/R8
Arrancabarba (peak), Nic. 177/E4
Arras, Fr. 54/B3
Arreau, Fr. 44/D5
Arrecifal, Col. 180/D4
Arrecife, Sp. 110/B3
Arrecifes, Arg. 190/E2
Arrée, Monts d' (mts.), Fr. 44/B2
Arresø (lake), Den. 39/J7
Arrey, NM, US 149/J4
Arriaga, Mex. 176/C2
Arriba, Co, US 154/C4
Arrington, Va, US 163/H2
Arriola, Co, US 149/H2
Arriondas, Sp. 46/C1
Arrochar, Sc, UK 33/B4
Arrone, It. 65/B2
Arrone (riv.), It. 65/B3
Arronville, Fr. 30/J4
Arroscia (riv.), It. 62/B4
Arrou, Fr. 57/G4
Arroux (riv.), Fr. 44/F3
Arrow (riv.), Eng, UK 36/C2
Arrowbear Lake, Ca, US 166/C2
Arrowhead (lake), Tx, US 153/E4
Arrowhead NWR, ND, US 156/E4
Arrowrock (res.), Id, US 146/F2
Arrowrock (dam), Id, US 146/F2
Arrowsmith (mt.), NZ 135/B3
Arrowsmith (pt.), Austl. 129/E3
Arrowtown, NZ 135/B4
Arrowwood, Ab, Can. 145/H2
Arroyito, Arg. 188/D4
Arroyo de la Luz, Sp. 46/B3
Arroyo del Macho (riv.), NM, US 152/B4
Arroyo Grande, Bol. 184/D3
Arroyo Grande, Ca, US 148/B3
Arroyo Hondo, NM, US 152/B2
Arroyo Hondo (riv.), Ca, US 167/L12
Arroyo Trabuco (riv.), Ca, US 166/C3
Arroyo Valle (brook), Ca, US 167/L11
Arrufó, Arg. 188/D4
Års, Den. 40/C3
Ars-sur-Moselle, Fr. 55/F5
Arsanjān, Iran 103/H4
Arsen'yev, Rus. 79/L3
Ārsī (prov.), Eth. 118/A4
Arsiero, It. 63/E2
Arsk, Rus. 69/L4
Arslanköy, Turk. 104/D1
Årsta havsbad, Swe. 39/B1
Árta, Gre. 49/G3
Arta (gulf), Gre. 49/G3
'Arta, Djib. 118/B3
Artá, Sp. 47/G3
Arteaga, Mex. 174/E5
Arteixo, Sp. 46/A1
Artem, Rus. 79/L3
Artemisa, Cuba 177/F1
Artemivs'k, Ukr. 73/K3
Artemove, Ukr. 73/J3
Artemovskiy, Rus. 75/M4
Artena, It. 65/B4
Artenay, Fr. 57/G4
Artesia, Ca, US 166/F8
Artesia, Ms, US 162/C4
Artesia, NM, US 152/B4
Artesia Wells, Tx, US 151/E3
Arth, Swi. 61/E3
Arthies, Fr. 30/H4
Arthur (riv.), Austl. 130/C5
Arthur (pt.), Austl. 134/C3
Arthur, ND, US 156/F4
Arthur, Ne, US 154/D3
Arthur, WV, US 163/H1
Arthur City, Tx, US 153/G4
Arthur Kill (riv.), US 169/J9
Arthur's Pass NP, NZ 135/B3
Arthurdale, WV, US 161/G5
Arthur's (pass), NZ 135/B3
Arthurstown, Ire. 32/D5
Arti, Rus. 69/N4
Artigas (dept.), Uru. 189/E4
Artigas, Uru. 189/E4
Art'ik, Arm. 103/E1
Artogne, It. 62/D2
Artois (reg.), Fr. 42/A3
Artova, Turk. 102/D1
Artsyz, Ukr. 51/J3
Artuby (riv.), Fr. 64/C5
Artur Nogueira, Braz. 187/J7
Arturo Merino Benitez (int'l arpt.), Chile 190/N8
Artux, China 99/C4
Artvin (prov.), Turk. 71/G4
Artvin, Turk. 71/G4
Artyom, Azer. 71/J4
Aru, D.R. Congo 121/G2
Aru (isls.), Indo. 128/D1
Arua, Ugan. 121/G2
Aruba (isl.), Aru., Neth. 179/B1
Arucas, Sp. 110/B3
Arudy, Fr. 44/C5
Arujá, Braz. 187/K8
Arun (riv.), China 97/F2
Arun (riv.), Eng, UK 37/F5
Arunāchal Pradesh (state), India 93/F2
Arundel, Eng, UK 37/F5
Aruppukkottai, India 95/C4
'Ārūrah, WBnk. 105/C4
Arus (cape), Indo. 91/F3
Arusha (prov.), Tanz. 119/B3
Arusha, Tanz. 119/B2
Arusha Chine, Tanz. 119/B2
Arusha NP, Tanz. 119/B2
Arutua (isl.), FrPol. 137/L6
Aruwimi (riv.), D.R. Congo 107/E4
Arvada, Co, US 154/B4
Arvada, Wy, US 154/A1
Arvagh, Ire. 32/C2
Arvan (riv.), Fr. 64/C2
Arvayheer, Mong. 78/E2
Arve (riv.), Fr. 60/C6
Arvidsjaur, Swe. 38/F2
Arviat, Nun, Can. 140/G2
Arvika, Swe. 40/E2
Arvin, Ca, US 148/C3
Arvon (mt.), Mi, US 157/K4
Arvonia, Va, US 163/H2
Arwala, Indo. 128/B1
Aryamūn, Egypt 113/B2
Aryānah, Tun. 48/B4
Aryānah (gov.), Tun. 48/A4
Arys', Kaz. 99/A3
Arz (riv.), Fr. 44/B3
Arzachena, It. 48/A2
Arzamas, Rus. 69/K5
Arzano, It. 65/D6
Arzbach, Ger. 55/G3
Arzberg, Ger. 59/F2
Ärzen, Ger. 53/G4
Arzew, Alg. 112/E5
Arzgir, Rus. 71/H3
Arzignano, It. 63/E2
Arzl im Pitztal, Aus. 61/G3
Arzúa, Sp. 46/A1
As, Belg. 55/E1
Aš, Czh. 59/F2
Ås, Nor. 40/D2
As Sabkhah, Syria 102/D3
As Sabkhat al Kabīrah (swamp), Libya 108/C2
Aş Şaff, Egypt 113/C5
Aş Şāfī, Jor. 104/D4
Aş Şāfiyah, Sudan 117/F2
Aş Şāliḩīyah, Syria 102/E3
Aş Şāliḩīyah, Egypt 113/C3
As Sālimīyah, Kuw. 103/G4
As Sallūm, Egypt 108/E2
As Salmān, Iraq 103/F4
As Salţ, Jor. 105/D4
As Salwá, SAr. 100/F4
As Samāwah, Iraq 103/F4
Aş Şanamayn, Syria 105/E2
As Sanţah, Egypt 113/C3
Aş Şarafand, Leb. 105/C2
Aş Şarīḩ, Jor. 105/D3
Aş Şawma'ah, Yem. 118/C2
As Sīb, Oman 101/G4
As Sidr, Libya 108/C2
As Sidr, SAr. 100/C4
As Sinbillāwayn, Egypt 113/C3
Aş Şubayḩī, Jor. 105/D4
As Sudd (reg.), Sudan 107/F4
As Sufāl, Yem. 118/D2
Aş Şufayyah, Sudan 117/G2
Aş Şufīyāh, Egypt 113/C3
As Sukhnah, Syria 102/D3
As Sukhnah, Jor. 105/E4
As Suki, Sudan 117/G2
As Sulaymānīyah, Iraq 103/F3
As Sulaymānīyah (gov.), Iraq 103/F3
As Sulaymī, SAr. 100/D3
As Sulayyil, SAr. 100/E4
As Sulţān, Libya 108/C2
As Sumayḩ, Sudan 117/E3

Aş Şummān (range), SAr. 103/F5
As Su'ūdīyah, Egypt 113/C5
As Suwāqah, Jor. 105/E6
Aş Şuwār, Syria 102/E3
As Suwaydā', Syria 105/F3
As Suwaydā' (gov.), Syria 105/E3
As Suwayq, Oman 101/G4
Aş Şuwayrah, Iraq 103/F3
As Suways (gov.), Egypt 109/G2
Asab, Namb. 122/C5
Asaba, Nga. 115/G5
Asad (lake), Syria 102/D2
Asadābād, Afg. 98/A2
Asadābād, Iran 103/G3
Asagny, PN d', C.d'Iv. 114/D5
Asahan (riv.), Indo. 90/A3
Asahi (riv.), Japan 84/C3
Asahi, Japan 85/G3
Asahi, Japan 83/M5
Asahi, Japan 83/L5
Asahi, Japan 83/F1
Asahi-dake (peak), Japan 82/C2
Asahikawa, Japan 82/C2
Asai, Japan 83/K5
Asaka, Japan 83/D2
Asake (riv.), Japan 83/K5
'Asal (depr.), Djib. 118/B3
Āsalē, Eth. 118/B2
'Asalūyeh, Iran 103/H5
Asama-yama (peak), Japan 85/F2
Asamankese, Gha. 115/E5
Asan (bay), SKor. 81/D4
Asankrangwa, Gha. 115/E5
Asansol, India 97/F4
Asashi-dake (peak), Japan 85/F1
Asashina, Japan 83/A1
Asau, Sam. 137/R9
Asawanwah (well), Libya 108/C4
Āsayita, Eth. 118/B3
Asbach, Ger. 55/G2
Asbach-Bäumenheim, Ger. 58/D5
Āsbe Teferī, Eth. 118/B3
Asbest, Rus. 69/P4
Asbestos, Qu, Can. 161/L2
Asbestos. (mts.), SAfr. 124/C3
Asbury, Ia, US 155/J2
Asbury Park, NJ, US 168/D3
Ascención (bay), Mex. 172/D4
Ascensión, Arg. 190/E2
Ascención, Bol. 185/F4
Ascensión, Mex. 175/J5
Ascension, NAnt. 180/D1
Ascensione, Monte dell (peak), It. 65/C2
Aschach (riv.), Aus. 59/G6
Aschach an der Donau, Aus. 59/H6
Aschaffenburg, Ger. 58/C3
Aschau am Inn, Ger. 59/F6
Ascheberg, Ger. 53/E5
Aschendorf, Ger. 53/E2
Aschersleben, Ger. 42/F3
Ascog, Sc, UK 33/A5
Ascoli Piceno (prov.), It. 65/C1
Ascoli Piceno, It. 65/C2
Ascoli Satriano, It. 48/D2
Ascona, Swi. 61/E5
Ascope, Peru 184/B2
Ascot, Eng, UK 30/B2
Āsebot, Eth. 118/B3
Åseda, Swe. 40/F3
Aseki, PNG 129/G1
Āsela, Eth. 118/A4
Åsele, Swe. 38/F2
Āsendabo, Eth. 117/H4
Asendorf, Ger. 53/G2
Asendorf, Ger. 53/F3
Asenovgrad, Bul. 51/G4
Åseral, Nor. 40/B2
Aserei (peak), It. 62/C4
Asfeld, Fr. 55/D5
Ash, Eng, UK 30/A3
Ash, Eng, UK 30/D3
Ash Flat, Ar, US 153/J2
Ash Fork, Az, US 149/F3
Ash Shabakah, Iraq 102/E4
Ash Shāghūr, Jor. 105/D5
Ash Shamal (gov.), Leb. 104/E2
Ash Shamālīyah (pol. reg.), Sudan 109/E4
Ash Shāmīyah, Iraq 103/F4
Ash Shanāwīyah, Egypt 113/C6
Ash Shāriqah, UAE 101/G3
Ash Sharqāt, Iraq 103/E3
Ash Sharqīyah (prov.), Sudan 109/G5
Ash Shaţrah, Iraq 103/F4
Ash Shawal, Sudan 117/G2
Ash Shawāshinah, Egypt 113/B6
Ash Shawbak, Jor. 104/D4
Ash Shaykh Sa'd, Syria 105/E3
Ash Shiḩr, Yem. 118/D2
Ash Shīn, Egypt 113/B2
Ash Shuhadā', Egypt 113/B3
Ash Shumlūl, SAr. 100/E3
Ash Shuqayq, SAr. 100/D5
Ash Shurayf, SAr. 100/C3
Asha, Nga. 115/F5
Ashampstead, Eng, UK 37/E4
Ashanti (pol. reg.), Gha. 115/E5
Ashanti (uplands), Gha. 114/E5
Asharoken, NY, US 169/M8
Ashbourne, Ire. 34/B4
Ashbourne, Eng, UK 35/G5
Ashburn, Ga, US 165/G2
Ashburton, NZ 135/B3
Ashburton, Eng, UK 36/C5
Ashburton (riv.), Austl. 127/A3
Ashburton Downs, Austl. 130/C2
Ashby, Mn, US 156/G4
Ashby (canal), Eng, UK 37/E1
Ashby-de-la-Zouch, Eng, UK 37/E1
Ashcroft, BC, Can. 144/D2
Ashdod, Isr. 105/B5
Ashdot Ya'aqov, Isr. 105/D3
Ashdown, Ar, US 153/G4
Asheboro, NC, US 163/H3
Asher, Ok, US 153/F3
Ashern, Mb, Can. 156/E2
Asherton, Tx, US 151/E3
Asheville, NC, US 163/F3
Ashfield, Austl. 133/E1
Ashford, Austl. 132/D1
Ashford, Ire. 34/B5
Ashford, Eng, UK 30/B2
Ashford, Eng, UK 37/G4
Ashford, Al, US 165/F2
Ashfordby, Eng, UK 37/F1
Ashgabat (cap.), Trkm. 101/G1
Ashgrove, On, Can. 160/T8
Ashhurst, NZ 135/C3
Ashibetsu, Japan 82/C2
Ashigawa, Japan 83/B2
Ashikaga, Japan 83/C1
Ashington, Eng, UK 35/G1
Ashino (lake), Japan 83/C3
Ashiwada, Japan 83/B3
Ashiya, Japan 83/H6
Ashiyasu, Japan 83/A2
Ashizuri-Misaki (cape), Japan 84/C4
Ashkal (lake), Tun. 112/L6
Ashkelon NP, Isr. 105/B5
Ashkhabad (int'l arpt.), Trkm. 101/G1
Ashkīdah, Libya 108/B3
Ashland, Al, US 162/E4
Ashland, Ks, US 152/E2
Ashland, Ky, US 163/F1
Ashland, La, US 153/H4
Ashland, Mo, US 153/H1
Ashland, Ms, US 162/C3
Ashland, Mt, US 145/L5
Ashland, NY, US 161/J3
Ashland, Oh, US 160/E4
Ashland, Or, US 146/B2
Ashland, Pa, US 168/B2
Ashland, Tx, US 151/G1
Ashland, Wi, US 157/J4
Ashland City, Tn, US 162/D2
Ashley, ND, US 156/E4
Ashley, Austl. 132/D1
Ashley, Il, US 162/C1
Ashley, Pa, US 168/C1
Ashley Green, Eng, UK 30/B1
Ashmore, Il, US 160/B5
Ashmore and Cartier Islands (terr.), Austl. 127/B2
Ashmore (reef), Austl. 128/A3
Ashmūn, Egypt 113/B4
Ashnola Ind. Res., BC, Can. 144/D3
Ashoknagar, India 96/A3
Ashoro, Japan 82/C2
Ashqelon, Isr. 105/B5
Ashstead, Eng, UK 30/C3
Ashta, India 92/C3
Ashtabula, Oh, US 160/F4
Ashtarak, Arm. 71/H4
Ashti, India 95/C1
Āshtīān, Iran 103/G3
Ashton, SAfr. 124/M10
Ashton, Fl, US 164/N7
Ashton, Id, US 147/H1
Ashton, Il, US 155/K3
Ashton, SD, US 154/E1
Ashton-In-Makerfield, Eng, UK 35/F5
Ashton-under-Lyne, Eng, UK 35/F5
Ashuapmushuan (riv.), Qu, Can. 158/A1
Ashville, Oh, US 160/E5
Ashville, Al, US 162/D4
Ashwabay (mt.), Wi, US 157/J4
Ashwaubenon, Wi, US 160/B2
Ashwell, Eng, UK 37/F2
Asia (cont.) 77/*
Asia, Peru 184/B4
Asiago, It. 61/H6
Asidonhoppo, Sur. 182/C2
Asikkala, Fin. 41/L1
Asikkalanselkä (lake), Fin. 39/F3
Asilah, Mor. 112/A2
Asillo, Peru 184/D4
Asina, It. 65/C4
Asinara (gulf), It. 48/A2
Asinara (isl.), It. 48/A2
Asino, Rus. 74/J4
Asipovichy, Bela. 70/D1
`Asīr (mts.), SAr. 100/D5
Asis (cape), Sudan 109/H5
Aska, India 95/E2
Aşkale, Turk. 102/E2
Askam in Furness, Eng, UK 35/E3
Askaniya-Nova, Ukr. 73/G4
Askeaton, Ire. 32/B4
Asker, Nor. 40/D2
Askern, Eng, UK 35/G4
Askersund, Swe. 40/F2
Askew, Ms, US 162/B3
Askham, SAfr. 124/C2
Askim, Nor. 40/D2
Askim, Swe. 40/D3
Áskion (peak), Gre. 49/G2
Askiz, Rus. 99/F1
Askja (crater), Ice. 38/P6
Askö (isl.), Swe. 39/A2
Askola, Fin. 39/F4
Askot, India 96/C1
Askov, Mn, US 157/H4
Askov, Den. 40/C4
Askvoll, Nor. 38/C3
Āsmār, Afg. 98/A2
Asmara (cap.), Erit. 118/A2
Asnæs, Den. 39/H7
Asnen (lake), Swe. 40/F3
Asnières-sur-Oise, Fr. 30/K4
Asnières-sur-Seine, Fr. 30/J5
Aso (riv.), It. 65/C1
Asō, Japan 83/E2
Aso NP, Japan 84/B4
Aso-san (peak), Japan 84/B4
Asola, It. 62/D3
Asolo, It. 63/E2
Āsosa, Eth. 117/G3
Asoteriba (peak), Sudan 109/H4
Asotin, Wa, US 144/F4
Aspach, Aus. 59/G6
Asparn, Aus. 51/N7
Aspatria, Eng, UK 35/E2
Aspe, Sp. 47/E3
Aspen (lake), Or, US 146/B2
Aspen Grove, BC, Can. 144/D3
Aspen Hill, Md, US 168/A5
Aspendos (ruin), Turk. 104/B1
Asperg, Ger. 58/C5
Aspermont, Tx, US 152/D4
Aspers, Pa, US 168/A4
Aspetuck (riv.), Ct, US 169/E1
Aspiring (mt.), NZ 135/B4
Aspres-sur-Buëch, Fr. 64/B3
Aspy (bay), NS, Can. 159/G2
Asquith, Sk, Can. 145/L1
Assa, Mor. 110/C3
Assa Aguiene (peak), Alg. 111/G5
Assab, Erit. 118/B2
Assam (state), India 93/F2
Assaouas, Niger 115/G2
Assaré, Braz. 183/G4
Assaria, Ks, US 153/F1
Assateague Island Nat'l Seashore, Md, US 163/K1
Asse, Belg. 55/D2
Assegairivier (riv.), SAfr. 123/F5
Assemini, It. 48/A3
Assen, Neth. 52/D3
Assenede, Belg. 54/C1
Assens, Den. 40/C4
Assens, Den. 40/D3
Assentoft, Den. 40/D3
Assesse, Belg. 55/E3
Assiniboia, Sk, Can. 145/M3
Assiniboine (riv.), Sk, Can. 156/D2
Assiniboine (riv.), Mb, Can. 140/F4
Assiniboine (mt.), Ab, Can. 144/G2
Assiniboine Ind. Res., Sk, Can. 156/C2
Assis, Braz. 189/G2
Assis Chateaubriand, Braz. 189/F3
Assisi, It. 65/B1
Assling, Ger. 59/F6
Asso, It. 62/C2
Assok-Ngoum, Gabon 120/B2
Assomada, CpV. 107/K10
Assou (riv.), Fr. 47/G1
Assumption, Il, US 155/K4
Astagram, Bang. 97/H3
Astakós, Gre. 49/G3
Astana (cap.), Kaz. 99/B1
Astara, Iran 103/G2
Astara, Azer. 71/J5
Astatula, Fl, US 164/M6
Asten, Aus. 59/H6
Asten, Neth. 52/C6
Asti (prov.), It. 62/B3
Astico (riv.), It. 63/E1
Astillero, Peru 184/D4
Astipálaia (isl.), Gre. 67/K3
Astipálaia, Gre. 67/K3
Astle, NB, Can. 158/D2
Aston, Eng, UK 37/E2
Aston on Clun, Eng, UK 36/D2
Astorga, Braz. 189/G2
Astoria (nbrhd.), NY, US 169/K8
Astoria, Il, US 155/J3
Astoria, Or, US 144/C4
Åstorp, Swe. 40/E3
Astra, Arg. 190/D5
Astrakhan', Rus. 71/J3
Astrakhanskaya Oblast, Rus. 71/H3
Astrodome, Tx, US 151/M9
Ástros, Gre. 49/H4
Astroworld, Tx, US 151/M9
Astudillo, Sp. 46/C1
Asturias (dist.), Sp. 46/B1
Astwood Bank, Eng, UK 37/E2
Asuka, Japan 83/J7
Asuke, Japan 83/M5
Asuncion (isl.), NMar. 136/D3
Asunción, Bol. 184/E3
Asunción (cap.), Par. 188/E3
Asunción (Silvio Pettirossi) (int'l arpt.), Par. 188/E3
Asunción Ixtaltepec, Mex. 172/B4
Asunden (lake), Swe. 40/F3
Asunta, Bol. 185/E5
Aswa (riv.), Ugan. 117/G5
Aswa, Ugan. 117/G5
Aswān (gov.), Egypt 109/G4
Aswān, Egypt 109/G3
Aswan High (dam), Egypt 109/G4
Asyūţ (gov.), Egypt 109/F3
Asyūţ, Egypt 109/F3
Asyūţī (wadi), Egypt 109/F3
Aszód, Hun. 51/R9
At Ta'mīn (gov.), Iraq 103/E3
At Tabbīn, Egypt 113/C5
Aţ Ţafīlah (gov.), Jor. 104/D4
Aţ Ţafīlah, Jor. 104/D4
Aţ Ţā'if, SAr. 100/D4
At Tall, Syria 105/E1
At Tall al Kabīr, Egypt 113/C3
Aţ Ţallāb, Libya 108/D3
At Tamīmī, Libya 67/J4
Aţ Ţawd, Egypt 113/B3
Aţ Ţayyibah, Leb. 105/D2
Aţ Ţayyibah, Jor. 105/D3
Aţ Ţīnah, Egypt 113/D2
Aţ Ţunayb, Jor. 105/D5
Aţ Ţūr, Egypt 109/G2
Aţ Ţūr, WBnk. 105/C5
At Turbah, Yem. 118/C2
Aţ Ţuwayshah, Sudan 117/E2
Aţ Ţuwayyah, SAr. 102/E5
Atabapo (riv.), Ven. 181/E4
Atacama (des.), Chile 179/B4
Atacama (pol. reg.), Chile 188/B4
Atacames, Ecu. 180/B4
Atafu (isl.), Tok. 137/H5
Atakpamé, Togo 115/F5
Atalaia do Norte, Braz. 184/D2
Atalándi, Gre. 49/H3
Atalaya, Peru 184/C3
Atamanovka, Kaz. 78/G1
Atambohobe, Madg. 125/H8
Atambua, Indo. 128/B2
Atami, Japan 85/F3
Atap, Indo. 91/E3
Atapupu, Indo. 128/B2
'Atāq, Yem. 118/C2
Atarfe, Sp. 46/D4
Atarra, India 96/C3
Atas Bogd (peak), Mong. 78/D3
Atascadero, Ca, US 148/B3
Atascosa (riv.), Tx, US 151/E3
Atascosa, Tx, US 150/E3
Atasu, Kaz. 99/B2
Atatürk (dam), Turk. 102/D2
Ataturk (int'l arpt.), Turk. 103/M7
Atatürk (res.), Turk 102/D2
Atauro (isl.), ETim. 128/B2
Ātaya, Eth. 118/A3
Atbara, Sudan 117/G1
Atbara (riv.), Eth. 117/H2
Atbara (riv.), Sudan 107/F3
'Atbarah, Nahr (riv.), Sudan 100/B5
Atbasar, Kaz. 99/A1
Atchafalaya (riv.), La, US 151/J2
Atchafalaya (bay), La, US 151/J3
Atchison, Ks, US 155/G4
Atco, NJ, US 168/D4
Atebubu, Gha. 115/E5
Ateca, Sp. 46/E2
Ateelva (riv.), Nor. 38/G1
Atén, Bol. 184/D4
Atencingo, Mex. 175/L8
Atenco, Mex. 175/Q10
Atenco, Mex. 175/R9
Atengo (riv.), Mex. 174/D4
Aterno (riv.), It. 65/C3
Atessa, It. 65/D3
Aţfīḩ, Egypt 113/C6
Atglen, Pa, US 168/C4
Ath, Belg. 54/C2
Athabasca (riv.), Ab, Can. 140/E3
Athabasca (lake), Ab,Sk, Can. 140/E3
Āthārabāri, Bang. 97/H3
Athboy, Ire. 32/D2
Athea, Ire. 32/A5
Athena, Or, US 144/E5
Athenry, Ire. 32/B3
Athens, On, Can. 161/J2
Athens (Athínai) (cap.), Gre. 49/N9
Athens, Al, US 162/D3
Athens, Ar, US 153/H3
Athens, NY, US 161/K3
Athens, Oh, US 160/E5
Athens, Pa, US 161/H4
Athens, Mi, US 160/D3
Athens, WV, US 163/G2
Athens, Tn, US 162/E3
Athens, Ga, US 163/F4
Athens, Il, US 155/K4
Athens, Tx, US 151/G1
Atherstone, Eng, UK 37/E1
Atherton, Eng, UK 35/F4
Atherton, Austl. 134/B2
Athgarh, India 95/E1
Athi (riv.), Kenya 119/B2
Athi River, Kenya 119/B2
Athienou, Cyp. 104/C2
Athínai (Athens) (cap.), Gre. 49/N9
Athis-Mons, Fr. 30/K5
Athleague, Ire. 32/B2
Athlone, Ire. 32/C3
Athok, Myan. 86/B5
Athol, Ma, US 161/K3
Athol, NZ 135/B4
Atholl (for.), Sc, UK 33/B3
Áthos (peak), Gre. 49/J2
Athribis (ruin), Egypt 113/C4
Athy, Ire. 32/D4
Ati, Chad 116/C2
Ati Ardébé, Chad 116/C2
Atiak, Ugan. 121/H2
Atibaia (riv.), Braz. 187/K7
Atibaia, Braz. 187/K8
Atico, Peru 184/C5
Atienza, Sp. 46/D2
Atikokan, On, Can. 157/J3
Atil, Mex. 174/C2
Atinggola, Indo. 91/F3
Atitlán (lake), Guat. 176/D3
Atiu (isl.), CookIs. 137/K7
Atizapan, Mex. 175/Q10
Atka, Rus. 75/R3
Atka (isl.), Ak, US 171/D5
Atka, Ak, US 171/D5
Atkarsk, Rus. 71/H2
Atkins, Ar, US 153/H3
Atkins, Va, US 163/G2
Atkinson (isl.), Tx, US 151/N9
Atlacomulco de Fabela, Mex. 175/K7
Atlanta, SAfr. 123/E5
Atlanta (cap.), Ga, US 163/M7
Atlanta, Il, US 155/K3
Atlanta, La, US 164/B2
Atlanta, Mi, US 160/D2
Atlanta, Tx, US 153/G4
Atlanta Botanical Garden, Ga, US 163/M7
Atlanta Nav. Air Sta., Ga, US 163/L7
Atlantic, NC, US 163/J3
Atlantic (ocean) 26/G3
Atlantic (peak), Wy, US 147/J2
Atlantic, Ia, US 155/G3
Atlantic (co.), NJ, US 168/D4
Atlantic Beach, Fl, US 165/H2
Atlantic Beach, NY, US 169/L9
Atlantic City, Wy, US 147/J2
Atlantic City, NJ, US 168/D5
Atlantic City International (arpt.), NJ, US 168/D5
Atlantic Highlands, NJ, US 169/J10
Atlantico (dept.), Col. 177/H4
Atlántida, Uru. 191/L11
Atlantique (prov.), Ben. 115/F5
Atlas (mts.), Afr. 66/C4
Atlas (peak), Ca, US 167/K10
Atlasovo, Rus. 75/R4
Atlatlahuaca, Mex. 175/Q10
Atlin, BC, Can. 171/M3
Atlin (lake), BC, Can. 171/M3
'Atlit, Isr. 105/B3
Atlixco, Mex. 175/L8
Atmore, Al, US 164/E2
Atnarko (riv.), BC, Can. 144/B1
Atocha, Bol. 188/C2
Atoka, Ok, US 153/F3
Atoka (res.), Ok, US 153/F3
Atoka, Tn, US 162/C3
Atome, Ang. 122/B1
Atomic City, Id, US 147/G2
Atondo, D.R. Congo 121/F3
Atotonilco, Mex. 175/L6
Atouila, 'Erg (des.), Mali 110/D5
Atoyac (riv.), Mex. 176/B2
Atoyac, Mex. 175/E5
Atqasuk, Ak, US 171/G1
Atrai (riv.), Bang. 97/G3
Atrak (riv.), Iran 74/F6
Ätran (riv.), Swe. 40/E3
Atrato (riv.), Col. 173/F6
Atrauli, India 96/B1
Atri, It. 65/C2
Atripalda, It. 65/D6
Atsugi, Japan 83/C3
Atsumi, Japan 83/M6
Atsumi (pen.), Japan 83/M6
Attalens, Swi. 60/C4
Attalla, Al, US 162/D3
Attapu, Laos 94/D3
Attapulgus, Ga, US 165/F2
Attawapiskat, On, Can. 141/H3
Attawapiskat (riv.), On, Can. 141/H3
Attean (mtn.), Me, US 161/L2
Attel (riv.), Ger. 59/F7
Attendorn, Ger. 53/E6
Atteridgeville, SAfr. 124/Q12
Attersee (lake), Aus. 45/K3
Attert, Belg. 55/E4
Attica, Ks, US 153/E2
Attica, Oh, US 160/E4
Attica, In, US 160/C4
Attica, Mi, US 167/F5
Attigliano, It. 65/B2
Attigny, Fr. 55/D5
'Attīl, WBnk. 105/C4
Attingal, India 95/C4
Attleboro, Ma, US 161/L4
Attleborough, Eng, UK 37/E1
Attnang-Puchheim, Aus. 59/G6
Attock, Pak. 98/B3
Attoyac (riv.), Tx, US 151/G2
Attu (isl.), Ak, US 171/A5
Āttūr, India 95/C4
Atuel (riv.), Arg. 190/D2
Atuntaqui, Ecu. 180/B4
Atuona, FrPol. 137/M5
Ātura, Bang. 97/G3
Atura, Ugan. 121/H2
Åtvidaberg, Swe. 40/G2
Atwater, Ca, US 148/B2
Atwood, Ok, US 153/F3
Atwood, Ks, US 154/D4
Atwood, Co, US 154/C3
Atyraū (int'l arpt.), Kaz. 71/J3
Atyraū, Kaz. 71/J3
Atyraū Oblast, Kaz. 71/J3
Atzcapotzalco (nbrhd.), Mex. 175/Q10
Au, Swi. 61/F3
Au, Aus. 61/F3
Au Gres, Mi, US 160/E2
Au in der Hallertau, Ger. 59/E5
Au Sable (riv.), Mi, US 160/E2
Au Sable (pt.), Mi, US 160/E2
Au Sable, Mi, US 160/E2
Auari (riv.), Braz. 181/E3
Auas, Hon. 177/E3
Auasbila, Hon. 177/E3
Aub, Namb. 122/C4
Aubá, ETim. 128/B2
Aubagne, Fr. 64/B6
Aubange, Belg. 55/E4
Aube, Fr. 57/F3
Aube (riv.), Fr. 42/C4
Aube (dept.), Fr. 55/D6
Aubepierre-Ozouer-le-Repos, Fr. 30/L6
Aubergenville, Fr. 30/H5
Auberry, Ca, US 148/C2
Aubert (peak), Swi. 60/C4
Aubervilliers, Fr. 30/K5
Aubetin (riv.), Fr. 54/C6
Aubette (riv.), Fr. 54/A5
Aubette de Magny (riv.), Fr. 30/H4
Aubevoye, Fr. 57/G2
Aubignon, Fr. 64/B4
Aubigny-en-Artois, Fr. 54/B3
Aubigny-sur-Nère, Fr. 44/E3
Aubin, Fr. 44/E4
Aubonne, Swi. 60/C5
Auboué, Fr. 55/E5
Aubrac (mts.), Fr. 44/E4
Aubrey, Ar, US 162/B3
Aubrives, Fr. 55/D3
Auburn, Austl. 131/H5
Auburn (nbrhd.), Austl. 134/H8
Auburn, Al, US 162/E4
Auburn, Ca, US 146/C4
Auburn, Ga, US 162/F3
Auburn, Il, US 155/K4
Auburn, In, US 160/D4
Auburn, Ks, US 153/G1
Auburn, Ky, US 162/D2
Auburn, Ma, US 161/L3
Auburn, Me, US 161/L2
Auburn, Ms, US 164/C2
Auburn, Ne, US 155/G3
Auburn, NY, US 161/H3
Auburn, Pa, US 168/B2
Auburn, Wa, US 144/C4
Auburn Hills, Mi, US 167/F6
Auburndale, Fl, US 164/M7
Aubusson, Fr. 44/E4
Aucá Mahuida (peak), Arg. 190/C3
Auce, Lat. 41/K3
Auch, Fr. 44/D5
Auchel, Fr. 54/B3
Auchenblae, Sc, UK 33/D3
Auchencairn, Sc, UK 34/E2
Auchi, Nga. 115/G5
Auchinleck, Sc, UK 33/B6
Auchterarder, Sc, UK 33/C4
Auchtermuchty, Sc, UK 33/C4
Auchy-lès-Hesdin, Fr. 54/B3
Aucilla (riv.), Fl, US 165/G2
Auckland (isls.), NZ 27/T8
Auckland (int'l arpt.), NZ 135/F6
Auckland, NZ 135/F6
Auckland Domain, NZ 135/F6
Aude (riv.), Fr. 66/D2
Auden, On, Can. 157/L2
Auderghem, Belg. 55/D2
Audet, Qu, Can. 158/B3
Audeux (riv.), Fr. 60/C3
Audience Hall, VatC. 65/G7
Audierne (bay), Fr. 44/A3
Audincourt, Fr. 60/C3
Audlem, Eng, UK 35/F6
Audley, Eng, UK 35/F5
Audo (range), Eth. 118/B4
Audruicq, Fr. 54/B2
Audubon, Ia, US 155/G3
Audubon NWR, ND, US 156/D4
Audun-le-Roman, Fr. 55/E5
Audun-le-Tiche, Fr. 55/E5
Aue (riv.), Ger. 53/E2
Aue, Ger. 59/F1
Auer (Ora), It. 61/H5
Auerbach, Ger. 59/F1
Auerbach in der Oberpfalz, Ger. 59/E3
Auersberg (peak), Ger. 59/F2
Aufess (riv.), Ger. 58/E3
Auffargis, Fr. 30/H5
Auffay, Fr. 57/G1
Augathella, Austl. 134/B4
Auger (falls), Id, US 147/F2
Augher, NI, UK 34/A3
Aughinish (isl.), Ire. 32/A4
Aughnacloy, NI, UK 34/B3
Aughrim, Ire. 34/B6
Auglaize (riv.), Oh, US 160/D4
Augrabies Falls NP, SAfr. 124/C3
Augrabiesvalle (falls), SAfr. 124/C3
Augsburg, Ger. 58/D6
Augsburg (Mühlhausen) (arpt.), Ger. 58/D6
Augub (peak), Namb. 124/A2
Augusta, Austl. 130/B5
Augusta, It. 48/D4
Augusta (gulf), It. 48/D4
Augusta, Ar, US 153/J3
Augusta, Ga, US 163/G4
Augusta, Il, US 155/J3
Augusta, Ks, US 153/F2
Augusta (cap.), Me, US 158/C3
Augusta, Mt, US 145/H4
Augusta, NJ, US 168/D1
Augusta, Wi, US 155/J1
Augusta, WV, US 161/G5
Augustdorf, Ger. 53/F5
Augustenborg, Den. 40/C4
Augustine Ind. Res., Ca, US 148/D4
Augusto César Sandino (int'l arpt.), Nic. 176/E3
Augustów, Pol. 41/K5
Augustus (mt.), Austl. 130/C3
Auk Bok (isl.), Myan. 94/B3
Aukam, Namb. 124/B2
Auki, Sol. 136/F5
Aukstatija NP, Lith. 41/M4
Aulander, NC, US 163/J2
Aulatsivik, North (isl.), Nf, Can. 141/K3
Aulatsivik, South (isl.), Nf, Can. 141/K3
Auld (lake), Austl. 127/B3
Auldearn, Sc, UK 33/C1
Aulencia (riv.), Sp. 47/M9
Aulendorf, Ger. 61/F2
Aulla, It. 62/C5
Aulnay-sous-Bois, Fr. 30/K5
Aulnay-sur-Mauldre, Fr. 30/H5
Aulne (riv.), Fr. 44/A2
Aulneau (pen.), On, Can. 157/G3
Aulnoy, Fr. 30/M5
Aulnoye-Aymeries, Fr. 54/C3
Aulnut (int'l arpt.), Fr. 44/E4
Ault (peak), Swi. 61/F4
Ault, Fr. 54/A3
Ault, Co, US 154/B3
Aumale, Fr. 54/A4
Aumetz, Fr. 55/E5
Aumsville, Or, US 146/B1
Aumühle, Ger. 53/H1
Auna, Nga. 115/G4
Aunay-sur-Odon, Fr. 57/E2
Aune (riv.), Fr. 57/F5
Auneau, Fr. 57/G4
Aunette (riv.), Fr. 54/B5
Auneuil, Fr. 54/B5
Auning, Den. 40/D3
Auob (riv.), Namb. 122/C5
Auobrivier (riv.), SAfr. 122/D5
Aups, Fr. 64/C5
Aur (isl.), Mrsh. 136/G4
Aur (isl.), Malay. 89/D2
Aura, NJ, US 168/C4
Aurach (riv.), Ger. 58/D3
Aurach, Ger. 58/D4
Auraiya, India 96/B2
Aurangābād, India 97/E3
Aurangābād, India 95/B2
Auray, Fr. 56/C5
Aureilhan, Fr. 44/D5
Aurelia, Ia, US 155/G2
Aurelian (wall), It. 65/G8
Aurès (mts.), Alg. 66/E4
Aurich, Ger. 53/E2
Auriflama, Braz. 189/G2
Aurillac, Fr. 44/E4
Auriol, Fr. 64/B6
Aurisina, It. 63/G2
Aurland, Nor. 40/B1
Aurolzmünster, Aus. 59/G6
Aurora, Braz. 183/G4
Aurora, On, Can. 161/G3
Aurora, Guy. 181/G3
Aurora, Phil. 88/C4
Aurora, Co, US 154/B4
Aurora, Il, US 160/B4
Aurora, Mo, US 153/H2
Aurora, NC, US 163/J3
Aurora, Ne, US 154/E3
Aurora, Ut, US 149/G1
Aurora Ghost Town, Nv, US 146/D4
Aurora Lodge, Ak, US 171/J3
Aurunci (mts.), It. 65/C5
Aus, Namb. 124/B2
Ausa (riv.), It. 63/G1
Ausable (riv.), On, Can. 160/F3
Auschwitz (Oświęcim), Pol. 43/K3
Ausert, WSah. 110/B5
Ausoni (mts.), It. 65/C5
Aussenkehr, Namb. 124/B3
Aussillon, Fr. 44/E5
Aust-Agder (co.), Nor. 38/C4
Austell, Ga, US 163/L7
Austin (lake), Austl. 127/A3
Austin, Mb, Can. 156/E3
Austin (isl.), Nun, Can. 140/G2
Austin, In, US 162/E1
Austin, Ky, US 162/D2
Austin, Mn, US 155/H2
Austin, Nv, US 146/E4
Austin, Or, US 146/D1
Austin (cap.), Tx, US 151/F2
Austin Bayou (riv.), Tx, US 151/M9
Austonio, Tx, US 151/G2
Austral (Tubuaï Islands) (isls.), FrPol. 137/K7
Australia (ctry.) 127/*
Australia (cont.) 127/*
Australian, BC, Can. 144/C1
Australian Capital Terr., Austl. 127/D4
Australind, Austl. 130/B5
Austria (ctry.) 29/F4
Austurhorn (pt.), Ice. 38/P7
Autaugaville, Al, US 162/D4
Autazes, Braz. 182/B3
Auterive, Fr. 44/D5
Authie (riv.), Fr. 42/B3
Authion (riv.), Fr. 57/E6
Authon-du-Perche, Fr. 57/F4
Autlán de Navarro, Mex. 174/D5
Automne (riv.), Fr. 54/B5
Autore (peak), It. 65/C4
Autreppe, Belg. 54/C3
Autun, Fr. 44/F3
Auvergne, Ar, US 153/J3
Auvergne (pol. reg.), Fr. 44/E4
Auvergne, Austl. 128/C3
Auvers-sur-Oise, Fr. 30/J4
Auvézère (riv.), Fr. 44/D4
Aux Barques (pt.), Mi, US 160/E2
Aux Barques (pt.), Mi, US 160/C2
Auxerre, Fr. 44/E3
Auxi-le-Château, Fr. 54/B3
Auxonne, Fr. 60/B3
Auxvasse, Mo, US 155/J4
Auyán-Tepuí (peak), Ven. 181/F3
Auyuittuq NP, Nun, Can. 141/K2
Auzangate (peak), Peru 184/D4
Ava, Mo, US 153/H2
Ava, Il, US 162/C2
Ava, Myan. 94/A1
Āvaj, Iran 103/G3
Avallon, Fr. 44/E3
Avaloirs (peak), Fr. 57/E4
Avalon, Ca, US 166/B4
Avalon (pen.), Nf, Can. 141/L4
Avalon, Mo, US 155/H4
Avalon, NJ, US 168/D5
Avanigadda, India 95/D2
Avanne-Aveney, Fr. 60/B3
Avaré, Braz. 189/G2
Avarua, NZ 137/K7
Avcilar, Turk. 103/M7
Avdiyivka, Ukr. 73/J3
Avebury, Eng, UK 37/E4
Avebury Stone Circle, Eng, UK 37/E4
Aveiro, Port. 46/A2
Aveiro (dist.), Port. 46/A2
Aveley, Eng, UK 30/D2
Avelgem, Belg. 54/C2
Avellaneda, Arg. 191/J11
Avellino, It. 65/D6
Avellino (prov.), It. 65/D6
Avelon (riv.), Fr. 54/A5
Aven (riv.), Fr. 56/B4
Avenal, Ca, US 148/B2
Avenches, Swi. 60/D4
Avenel, NJ, US 169/H9
Avernes, Fr. 30/H4
Aversa, It. 65/D6
Avery, Id, US 144/G4
Avery Island, La, US 164/C3
Aves (isl.), Ven. 173/J4
Avesnes-le-Comte, Fr. 54/B3
Avesnes-sur-Helpe, Fr. 54/C3
Avessac, Fr. 56/D5
Avesta, Swe. 40/G1
Aveyron (riv.), Fr. 44/D4
Avezzano, It. 65/C3
Avich (lake), Sc, UK 33/A4
Aviemore, Sc, UK 33/C2
Avigliana, It. 64/D2
Avignon, Fr. 64/A5
Aviḩayil, Isr. 105/B4
Ávila de los Caballeros, Sp. 46/C2
Avilés, Sp. 46/C1
Avio, It. 63/D2
Avion, Fr. 54/B3
Aviron (pt.), Nf, Can. 159/J2
Avis, Pa, US 168/A1
Avisio (riv.), It. 61/H5
Avize, Fr. 54/D6
Avlum, Den. 40/C3
Avoca (riv.), Ire. 34/B6
Avoca, Austl. 132/C4
Avoca, Austl. 132/B3
Avoca, Ia, US 155/G3
Avoca, NY, US 161/H3
Avoch, Sc, UK 33/B1
Avoine, Fr. 57/F6
Avola, It. 48/D4
Avola, BC, Can. 144/E2
Avon (lake), Austl. 133/E2
Avon (riv.), Fr. 30/L6
Avon (riv.), Eng, UK 36/C6
Avon (riv.), Sc, UK 33/C1
Avon, Al, US 165/F2
Avon, Il, US 155/J3
Avon, Mn, US 157/G5
Avon, Ms, US 162/B4
Avon, NC, US 163/K3
Avon, NY, US 161/H3
Avon Downs, Austl. 129/E5
Avon Park, Fl, US 164/M8
Avon Park Bombing Range, Fl, US 165/H4
Avon Valley NP, Austl. 130/C4
Avon Water (riv.), Sc, UK 33/B5
Avonbeg (riv.), Ire. 34/B6
Avondale, Co, US 152/B1
Avondale, Pa, US 168/C4
Avondale, Austl. 133/E2
Avonlea, Sk, Can. 156/B2
Avonmore (riv.), Ire. 34/B5
Avonmouth, Eng, UK 36/D3
Avraga, Mong. 78/F2
Avranches, Fr. 56/D3
Avre (riv.), Fr. 42/B4
Avrillé, Fr. 57/E5
Avrora, Azer. 103/G2
Avtovo (nbrhd.), Rus. 69/T7
Āvupalli, India 92/D4
Awa-shima (isl.), Japan 82/A4
Awaé, Camr. 120/B2
A'waj (riv.), Syria 104/E3
Awaji, Japan 83/H6
Awakaba, CAfr. 116/D3
Awans, Belg. 55/E2
Awantīpur, India 98/C3
Awanui, NZ 135/C1
Awara (plain), Kenya 118/B5
Āwarē, Eth. 118/C3
Āwasa, Eth. 118/A4
Āwash, Eth. 118/B3
Awash NP, Eth. 118/A3
Āwash Wenz (riv.), Eth. 117/H3
Awasibberge (peak), Namb. 122/B5
Awaso, Gha. 115/E5
Awat, China 99/D3
Awatere (riv.), NZ 135/C3
Awbārī (des.), Libya 111/H4
Awbārī, Libya 108/B3
Awbeg (riv.), Ire. 32/B5
Awdheegle, Som. 118/C5
Awe (lake), Sc, UK 33/A4
Awgu, Nga. 115/G5
Āwira Wenz (riv.), Eth. 118/A2
Awīsh al Ḩajar, Egypt 113/C2
Awjilah, Libya 108/D2
Awka, Nga. 115/G5
Awsīm, Egypt 113/C4
Ax-les-Thermes, Fr. 44/D5
Axamo (int'l arpt.), Swe. 40/F3
Axams, Aus. 61/H3
Axarfjördhur (inlet), Ice. 38/N6
Axbridge, Eng, UK 36/D4
Axel, Neth. 52/A6
Axel Heiberg (isl.), Nun, Can. 141/S7
Axial, Co, US 147/K3
Axim, Gha. 115/E5
Axios (riv.), Gre. 49/H2
Axis (dam), Wa, US 167/D2
Axixá do Tocantins, Braz. 182/E4
Axminster, Eng, UK 36/D5
Axochiapan, Mex. 175/L8
Axson, Ga, US 165/G2
Axtell, Ks, US 155/F4
Axtell, Ne, US 154/E3
Ay (riv.), Fr. 56/D2
Ay (riv.), Rus. 69/N5
Ay, Fr. 54/C5
Ayabaca, Peru 184/B2
Ayabe, Japan 83/H5
Ayacucho, Arg. 190/F3
Ayacucho, Peru 184/C4
Ayacucho (dept.), Peru 184/C4
Ayagöz, Kaz. 99/D2
Ayaguz (riv.), Kaz. 99/D2
Ayakkum (lake), China 99/E4
Ayama, Japan 83/K6
Ayamonte, Sp. 46/B4
Ayan, Rus. 75/P4
Ayancık, Turk. 70/E4
Ayanganna (mtn.), Guy. 181/G3
Ayangba, Nga. 115/G5
Ayanka, Rus. 75/S3
Ayapel, Col. 180/C2
Ayaş, Turk. 102/C1
Ayase, Japan 83/C3
Ayass (peak), Ugan. 119/A1
Ayaviri, Peru 184/D4
Āybak, Afg. 74/G6
Aybas, Kaz. 71/J3
Aybastı, Turk. 70/F4
Aydabul, Kaz. 99/A1
Ayden, NC, US 163/J3
Aydın, Turk. 102/A2
Aydin (prov.), Turk. 102/B2
Aydıncık, Turk. 102/C1
Aydıncık, Turk. 104/C1
Aydınkent, Turk. 104/B1
Aydinli, Turk. 103/N7
Āydora, Eth. 118/B3
Aydyrlinskiy, Rus. 71/L1
Āyelu (peak), Eth. 118/B3
Ayem, Gabon 120/B3
Ayer, Swi. 60/D5
Ayer Hitam, Malay. 89/C2
Ayer's Cliff, Qu, Can. 161/K2
Ayers Rock (Uluru) (peak), Austl. 131/F3
Ayeyarwady (state), Myan. 93/F4
Ayiá, Gre. 49/H3
Ayía Paraskeví, Gre. 49/K3
Ayiásos, Gre. 49/K3
Ayina (riv.), Congo 120/C2
Áyios Athanásios, Gre. 49/J2
Áyios Evstrátios (isl.), Gre. 67/K3
Áyios Ioánnis (cape), Gre. 49/J5
Áyios Kírikos, Gre. 49/K4
Áyios Konstandínos, Gre. 49/H3
Áyios Matthaíos, Gre. 49/F3
Áyios Nikólaos, Gre. 49/J5
Āykel, Eth. 117/H2
Aykhal, Rus. 75/M3
Aylesbury, Eng, UK 37/F3
Aylesford, NS, Can. 158/E3
Aylesford, Eng, UK 37/G4
Aylesham, Eng, UK 37/H4
Ayllón, Sp. 46/D2
Aylmer, On, Can. 160/F3
Aylmer (lake), NW, Can. 140/F2
Aylsham, Eng, UK 37/H1
Aylsham, Sk, Can. 145/N1
'Ayn Ad Darāhim, Tun. 112/L6
'Ayn al 'Arab, Syria 102/D2
'Ayn al Ghazālah, Libya 67/J4
'Ayn Ath Tha'lab, Libya 108/D3
'Ayn Sukhnah, Egypt 113/D5
Ayna, Peru 184/C4
Aynor, SC, US 163/H4
'Aynūnah, SAr. 109/G2
Ayod, Sudan 117/F3
Ayolas, Par. 189/E3
Ayon (isl.), Rus. 75/S3
Ayora, Sp. 47/E3
Ayorou, Niger 115/F3
Ayos, Camr. 120/C2
Ayotzintepec, Mex. 176/B2
'Ayoûn 'Abd el Mâlek (well), Mrta. 110/D4
'Ayoûn el 'Atroûs, Mrta. 114/C2
Ayr (riv.), Sc, UK 33/B5
Ayr, Sc, UK 33/B6
Ayr, Austl. 134/B2
Āysha, Eth. 118/B3
Ayton, Sc, UK 33/D5
Ayton, Eng, UK 35/H3
Āytony, Eth. 117/H3
Aytos, Bul. 51/H4
Aytré, Fr. 44/C3
Ayubia NP, Pak. 98/B3
Ayutinskiy, Rus. 73/L4
Ayutla, Mex. 174/D4
Ayutla de los Libres, Mex. 172/B4
Ayutthaya (ruin), Thai. 94/C3
Ayvacık, Turk. 49/K3
Aywaille, Belg. 55/E3
Az Zabābidah, WBnk. 105/C4
Az Zabadānī, Syria 105/E1
Aẓ Ẓāhirīyah, WBnk. 105/B6
Az Zankalūn, Egypt 113/C3
Az Zaqāzīq, Egypt 113/C3
Az Zarqā' (gov.), Jor. 104/E3
Az Zarqā', Jor. 105/E4
Az Zawāmil, Egypt 113/C4
Az Zāwiyah, Libya 67/G4
Az Zaydāb, Sudan 117/G1
Az Zaydīyah, Yem. 118/B2
Az Zilfī, SAr. 100/D3
Az Zrārīyah, Leb. 105/C2
Az Zubayr, Iraq 103/F4
Az Zurbī, Egypt 113/B6
Azad Kashmir (terr.), Pak. 98/B3
Āzādshahr, Iran 103/G3
Azahar (coast), Sp. 47/F3
Azalea, Or, US 146/B2
Azalia, Mi, US 167/E7
Azamgarh, India 96/D2
Azángaro (riv.), Peru 184/D4
Azángaro, Peru 184/D4
Azao (peak), Alg. 111/H4
Azaouâd (phys. reg.), Mali 115/E2
Azapa, Chile 184/D5
Āzar Shahr, Iran 103/F2
Āzarān, Iran 103/F2
Āzarbāyjān-e Gharbī (gov.), Iran 103/F2
Āzarbāyjān-e Sharqī (gov.), Iran 103/F2
Azare, Nga. 115/H4
Azay-le-Rideau, Fr. 57/F6
A'zāz, Syria 104/E1
Azemmour, Mor. 110/C2
Azerbaijan (ctry.) 77/D5
Āzezo, Eth. 117/H2
Azhikal, India 95/B4
Azhu-Tayga (peak), Rus. 99/E1
Azilal, Mor. 110/D3
Azīmganj, India 97/G3
Azizbekov, Arm. 103/F2
Azle, Tx, US 150/K7
Aznā, Iran 103/G3
Aznakayevo, Rus. 69/M5
Azogues, Ecu. 180/B5
Azores (dpcy.), Port. 47/R12
Azourki (peak), Mor. 110/D3
Azov (sea), Ukr.,Rus. 74/D5
Azov, Rus. 73/K4
Azovs'ke, Ukr. 73/H5
Azoyú, Mex. 176/B2
Azpeitia, Sp. 44/B5
Azrou, Mor. 110/D2
Aztec, NM, US 149/J2
Aztec, Az, US 149/F4
Aztec Ruins Nat'l Mon., NM, US 149/H2
Azua de Compostela, DRep. 173/G4
Azuaga, Sp. 46/C3
Azuara, Sp. 47/E2
Azuay (dept.), Ecu. 180/B5
Azuchi, Japan 83/K5
Azuero (pen.), Pan. 173/E6
Azufre (vol.), Chile 188/B3
Azufre, Paso el (pass), Chile 188/B4
Azuga, Rom. 51/G3
Azul (mtn.), CR 176/E4
Azul (riv.), Guat. 176/D2
Azul, Arg. 190/F3
Azul (peak), Arg. 188/B4
Azul (riv.), Mex. 175/H5
Azul, Cordillera (mts.), Peru 184/B2
'Aẓūm (wadi), Sudan 116/D2
Azuma, Japan 83/E2
Azuma-san (peak), Japan 85/G2
Azumaya-san (peak), Japan 85/F2
Azurduy, Bol. 188/C1
Azure (mtn.), NY, US 161/J2
Azusa, Ca, US 166/C2
Azzaba, Alg. 112/K6
Azzano, It. 63/D3
Azzano Decimo, It. 63/F2
Azzano San Paolo, It. 62/C2
Azzate, It. 62/B2
'Azzūn, WBnk. 105/C4

B

Bà (riv.), Sc, UK 33/B3
Ba, Fiji 137/Y18
Bà (riv.), China 78/F5
Ba Illi, Chad 116/C3
Ba Lang An (cape), Viet. 94/E3
Ba Quan (cape), Viet. 94/D4
Ba Ra, Viet. 94/D4
Ba Xian, China 80/H7
Baa, Indo. 128/A2
Baan Baa, Austl. 132/D1
Baar, Swi. 61/E3
Baargaal, Som. 118/D3
Baarle-Hertog, Belg. 52/B6
Baarle-Nassau, Neth. 52/B6
Baarn, Neth. 52/C4
Bab Taza, Mor. 112/B2
Baba (pt.), Turk. 51/K5
Baba (peak), Bul. 51/F4
Baba (mts.), Afg. 101/J2
Baba Burnu (pt.), Turk. 49/K3

Bababé – Banga

Bababé, Mrta. 114/B2
Babaçulândia, Braz. 182/E4
Babadag, Rom. 51/J3
Babadayhan, Trkm. 101/H1
Babaera, Ang. 122/B2
Babaeski, Turk. 51/H5
Babahoyo, Ecu. 180/B5
Babai Gaxun, China 78/E3
Babai Khola (riv.), Nepal 96/C1
Babakale, Turk. 49/K3
Babana, Nga. 115/F4
Babanango, SAfr. 125/E3
Babanūsah, Sudan 117/E3
Babar (isls.), Indo. 128/C1
Babar (isl.), Indo. 128/C1
Babat, Indo. 89/C3
Babati, Tanz. 119/A3
Babatorun, Turk. 104/E1
Babatpur (int'l arpt.), India 96/D3
Babayevo, Rus. 68/G4
Babb, Mt, US 145/H3
Babbacombe (bay), Eng, UK 36/C6
Babbitt, Mn, US 157/J4
Babbitt, Nv, US 146/D4
B'abdā, Leb. 105/D1
Babelthuap (isl.), Palau 136/C4
Babenhausen, Ger. 61/G1
Babenhausen, Ger. 58/B3
Babensham, Ger. 59/F6
Baberu, India 96/C3
Babi (isl.), Indo. 89/B2
Babia (peak), Pol. 70/A2
Babian (riv.), China 93/H3
Bābil (gov.), Iraq 103/F3
Bābil, Egypt 113/B3
Bābil (Babylon) (ruin), Iraq 103/F3
Babīna, India 96/B3
Babinda, Austl. 134/B2
Babine (riv.), BC, Can. 140/D3
Bābol, Iran 103/H2
Bābol Sar, Iran 103/H2
Baboquivari (mts.), Az, US 149/G5
Baboua, CAfr. 116/B4
Babson Park, Fl, US 164/M8
Bābuganj, Bang. 97/H4
Babura, Nga. 115/H3
Babushkin (nbrhd.), Rus. 69/W9
Babuyan (isl.), Phil. 77/M8
Babuyan (chan.), Phil. 88/C1
Babylon, NY, US 169/E2
Babylon (Bābil) (ruin), Iraq 103/F3
Bac Can, Viet. 94/D1
Bac Giang, Viet. 94/D1
Bac Lieu, Viet. 94/D4
Bac Ninh, Viet. 86/E4
Bac Quang, Viet. 86/E4
Bacaadweeyn, Som. 118/C4
Bacabal, Braz. 183/E4
Bacabal, Braz. 182/B4
Bacadéhuachi, Mex. 174/C2
Bacajá (riv.), Braz. 182/D4
Bacalar (lag.), Mex. 176/D2
Bacalar, Mex. 176/D2
Bacan (isl.), Indo. 91/G4
Bacarra, Phil. 88/C1
Bacău (prov.), Rom. 51/H2
Bacău, Rom. 72/D4
Baccarat, Fr. 60/C1
Bacchiglione (riv.), It. 63/E2
Bacchus Marsh, Austl. 133/B3
Bacerac, Mex. 174/C2
Bacharach, Ger. 55/G3
Bacheng, China 80/L8
Bachhraon, India 96/B1
Bachíniva, Mex. 174/D2
Bachok, Malay. 89/C1
Bachu, China 99/C4
Back (riv.), Nun, Can. 140/F2
Back (riv.), Md, US 168/B5
Back Bay, NB, Can. 158/D3
Back Bay Nat'l Wild. Ref., Va, US 163/K2
Bačka (reg.), Yugo. 67/H1
Bačka Palanka, Yugo. 50/D3
Bačka Topola, Yugo. 50/D3
Backbone (mtn.), Md, US 161/G5
Bäckefors, Swe. 40/E2
Backnang, Ger. 58/C5
Backwell, Eng, UK 36/D4
Baco (mt.), Phil. 88/C2
Bacobampa, Mex. 174/C3
Bacolod, Phil. 88/C3
Bacoor, Phil. 88/E7
Bacqueville-en-Caux, Fr. 57/F1
Bácsalmás, Hun. 50/D2
Bács-Kiskun (prov.), Hun. 50/D2
Bacup, Eng, UK 35/F4
Bacuri, Braz. 183/E3
Bād, Iran 103/H3
Bad (riv.), SD, US 154/D1
Bad Abbach, Ger. 59/F5
Bad Axe, Mi, US 160/E3
Bad Bellingen, Ger. 60/D2
Bad Bergzabern, Ger. 58/A4
Bad Berneck, Ger. 59/E2
Bad Bocklet, Ger. 58/D2
Bad Brambach, Ger. 59/F2
Bad Breisig, Ger. 55/G3
Bad Brückenau, Ger. 58/C2
Bad Buchau, Ger. 61/F1
Bad Camberg, Ger. 58/B2
Bad Doberan, Ger. 40/D4
Bad Driburg, Ger. 53/G5
Bad Dürkheim, Ger. 58/B4
Bad Dürrheim, Ger. 61/E1
Bad Ems, Ger. 55/G3
Bad Endorf, Ger. 59/F7
Bad Essen, Ger. 53/F4
Bad Freienwalde, Ger. 43/H2
Bad Gandersheim, Ger. 53/H5
Bad Grund, Ger. 53/H5
Bad Hall, Aus. 59/H6
Bad Harzburg, Ger. 53/H5
Bad Heilbrunn, Ger. 61/H2
Bad Herrenalb, Ger. 58/B5
Bad Hofgastein, Aus. 45/K3
Bad Homburg vor der Höhe, Ger. 58/B2
Bad Honnef, Ger. 55/G2
Bad Hönningen, Ger. 55/G2
Bad Karlshafen, Ger. 53/G5
Bad Kissingen, Ger. 58/D2
Bad Kohlgrub, Ger. 61/H2
Bad König, Ger. 58/C3
Bad Königshofen, Ger. 58/D2
Bad Kreuznach, Ger. 55/G4
Bad Krozingen, Ger. 60/D2
Bad Langensalza, Ger. 53/H6
Bad Lauterberg, Ger. 53/H5
Bad Leonfelden, Aus. 59/H5
Bad Liebenzell, Ger. 58/B5
Bad Lippspringe, Ger. 53/F3
Bad Marienberg, Ger. 55/G2
Bad Mergentheim, Ger. 58/C4
Bad Munder am Deister, Ger. 53/G4
Bad Münster am Stein, Ger. 55/G4
Bad Nauheim, Ger. 58/B2
Bad Nenndorf, Ger. 53/G4
Bad Neuenahr-Ahrweiler, Ger. 55/G2
Bad Neustadt an der Saale, Ger. 58/D2
Bad Oeynhausen, Ger. 53/F4
Bad Orb, Ger. 58/C2
Bad Peterstal-Griesbach, Ger. 60/E1
Bad Plaas, SAfr. 125/E2
Bad Pyrmont, Ger. 53/G5
Bad Ragaz, Swi. 61/F4
Bad Rappenau, Ger. 58/C4
Bad Reichenhall, Ger. 45/K3
Bad River Ind. Res., Wi, US 157/J4
Bad Rothenfelde, Ger. 53/F4
Bad Sachsa, Ger. 53/H5
Bad Salzdetfurth, Ger. 53/G4
Bad Salzschlirf, Ger. 58/C1
Bad Salzuflen, Ger. 53/F4
Bad Salzungen, Ger. 42/F3
Bad Sankt-Leonhard im Lavanttal, Aus. 45/L3
Bad Sassendorf, Ger. 53/F5
Bad Schallerbach, Aus. 59/G6
Bad Schwalbach, Ger. 55/H3
Bad Schwartau, Ger. 40/D5
Bad Segeberg, Ger. 40/D5
Bad Soden-Salmünster, Ger. 58/C2
Bad Sooden-Allendorf, Ger. 53/G6
Bad Tölz, Ger. 61/H2
Bad Vilbel, Ger. 58/B2
Bad Waldsee, Ger. 61/F2
Bad Wildungen, Ger. 53/G6
Bad Wimpfen, Ger. 58/C4
Bad Wimsbach-Neydharting, Aus. 59/G6
Bad Windsheim, Ger. 58/D3
Bad Wörishofen, Ger. 61/G1
Bad Wurzach, Ger. 61/F2
Bad Zell, Aus. 59/H6
Bad Zwischenahn, Ger. 53/F2
Badahe, China 93/H3
Badain Jaran (des.), China 75/L5
Badajós (lake), Braz. 185/F1
Badajoz, Sp. 46/B3
Badalona, Sp. 47/L7
Badalucco, It. 62/A5
Badanah, SAr. 100/D2
Badaohao, China 81/A2
Badas (isls.), Indo. 89/D2
Badbergen, Ger. 53/E3
Baddeck, NS, Can. 159/G2
Baddeckenstedt, Ger. 53/H4
Baddomalhi, Pak. 98/C4
Bade, Indo. 129/E1
Badeggi, Nga. 115/G4
Baden, Swi. 61/E3
Baden, Fr. 56/C5
Baden-Baden, Ger. 58/B5
Baden-Württemberg (state), Ger. 45/H2
Badener (peak), Ger. 58/B5
Badenoch (reg.), Sc, UK 33/B3
Badenweiler, Ger. 60/D2
Badgastein, Aus. 45/K3
Badger, Mn, US 156/F3
Badger (cr.), Co, US 154/C4
Badger (peak), Mt, US 145/L5
Badger's Quay, Nf, Can. 159/L1
Badgingarra NP, Austl. 130/B4
Badhoevedorp, Neth. 52/B4
Badia Polesine, It. 63/E3
Badiar, PN du, Gui. 114/B3
Badile (peak), It. 61/F5
Badīn, Pak. 101/J4
Badin (lake), NC, US 163/G3
Badin, NC, US 163/G3
Badiraguato, Mex. 174/D3
Badlands (hills), SD, US 154/C2
Badlands NP, SD, US 154/C2
Bado, Mo, US 153/H2
Badoāb, India 98/C2
Badong, China 87/F2
Badonviller, Fr. 60/C1
Badou, Togo 115/F5
Badovinci, Yugo. 50/D3
Badr Ḩunayn, SAr. 100/C4
Badrah, Iraq 103/F3
Bādrāh, Pak. 101/J3
Bādshāhpur, India 96/D3
Badu, China 87/G3
Badu, China 87/H3
Badu, China 87/H3
Badu, China 86/E3
Badua (riv.), India 97/F3
Badulla, SrL. 95/D5
Bāduriā, India 97/G4
Badwater (cr.), Wy, US 147/K2
Baekaezo (riv.), BC, Can. 144/C1
Baena, Sp. 46/C4
Baependi, Braz. 187/M6
Baerenkopf (peak), Fr. 60/C2
Baesweiler, Ger. 55/F2
Baeza, Sp. 46/D4
Bafatá, GBis. 114/B3
Baffa, Pak. 98/B2
Baffin (isl.), Can. 139/K2
Baffin (bay), Can. 139/K2
Bafia, Camr. 120/B1
Bafilo, Togo 115/F4
Bafing (riv.), Mali 114/C4
Bafoulabé, Mali 114/C3
Bāfq, Iran 103/H4
Bafra (cape), Turk. 70/E4
Bafra, Turk. 70/E4
Bāft, Iran 103/J4
Bafu, Libr. 114/C5
Bafwabalinga, D.R. Congo 121/F2
Bafwabogbo, D.R. Congo 121/F2
Bafwasende, D.R. Congo 121/F2
Bag Salt (lake), China 80/B3
Baga, Nga. 116/B2
Bagaces, CR 176/E4
Bagadó, Col. 180/B3
Bagaha, India 97/E2
Bāgalkot, India 95/B2
Bagamoyo, Tanz. 119/B3
Bagan, China 78/D5
Baganga, Phil. 88/D4
Bagansiapiapi, Indo. 89/C2
Bagarwa, Niger 115/G3
Bagata, D.R. Congo 120/D3
Bagayevskiy, Rus. 73/L4
Bagbag (cr.), Phil. 88/E6
Bāgbahra, India 95/D1
Bagbiringula (pt.), Austl. 129/E3
Bagda (mts.), China 99/E3
Bagdad, Az, US 149/F3
Bagdadi, Geo. 71/G4
Bagdarin, Rus. 78/G1
Bagé, Braz. 189/F4
Bagenkop, Den. 40/D4
Bāgerhāt, Bang. 97/G4
Baggao, Phil. 88/C1
Baggs, Wy, US 147/K3
Baggy (pt.), Eng, UK 36/B4
Bāgh, Pak. 98/B4
Bāgha Purāna, India 98/C4
Baghain (riv.), India 96/C3
Baghdad (cap.), Iraq 103/F3
Baghdādābād, Iran 103/H4
Bagheria, It. 48/C3
Bāghīn, Iran 103/J4
Baghlān, Afg. 101/J1
Bāghpat, India 98/D5
Bāghū, Iran 103/J5
Baginda (cape), Indo. 89/D3
Baginton (arpt.), Eng, UK 37/E2
Bağırpaşa (peak), Turk. 102/E2
Baglan, Wal, UK 36/C3
Bagley, Mn, US 157/G4
Bāglun, Nepal 96/D1
Bāgmati (riv.), India 97/E2
Bāgmati (zone), Nepal 97/E2
Bagn, Nor. 40/C1
Bagnacavallo, It. 63/F5
Bagnasco, It. 62/B5
Bagnell (dam), Mo, US 153/H1
Bagnères-de-Bigorre, Fr. 44/D5
Bagnères-de-Luchon, Fr. 44/D5
Bagneux, Fr. 30/J5
Bagni di Lucca, It. 62/D5
Bagni di Tivoli, It. 65/B4
Bagno a Ripoli, It. 63/E6
Bagnoles-de-L'Orne, Fr. 57/E3
Bagnolet, Fr. 30/K5
Bagnoli del Trigno, It. 65/D4
Bagnolo Cremasco, It. 62/C3
Bagnolo in Piano, It. 63/D4
Bagnolo Mella, It. 62/D3
Bagnolo San Vito, It. 63/D3
Bagnols-sur-Cèze, Fr. 64/A4
Bagnone, It. 62/C5
Bagnoregio, It. 65/B2
Bago, Phil. 88/C3
Bago (Pegu), Myan. 86/C5
Bagodar, India 97/E3
Bagoe (riv.), Mali 114/D3
Bagolino, It. 62/D2
Bagong, China 87/E3
Bāgrākot, India 97/G2
Bagrationovsk, Rus. 41/J4
Bagre, Braz. 182/D3
Bagshot, Eng, UK 30/A3
Bagua Grande, Peru 184/B2
Baguio, Phil. 88/C1
Baguirmi (reg.), Chad 116/C2
Bagun Serai, Malay. 89/C1
Bagusta, Eth. 117/H3
Bagwell, Tx, US 153/G4
Bagzane (peak), Niger 115/H2
Bāh, India 96/B2
Bahādurganj, Nepal 96/D2
Bahādurganj, India 97/F2
Bahādurgarh, India 98/D5
Bahaldā, India 97/F4
Bahamas (ctry.) 139/K7
Baharāgora, India 97/F4
Bahāwalnagar, Pak. 98/B5
Bahāwalpur, Pak. 98/A5
Bahçe, Turk. 102/D2
Bahçesaray, Turk. 103/E2
Bahera, India 97/F2
Baheri, India 96/B1
Baherove, Ukr. 73/J5
Bahi (swamp), Tanz. 119/A3
Bahi, Tanz. 119/A3
Bahía (state), Braz. 183/G5
Bahía Asunción, Mex. 174/B3
Bahía Blanca, Arg. 190/E3
Bahía Bustamante, Arg. 190/D5
Bahía de Caráquez, Ecu. 180/A5
Bahía de los Angeles, Mex. 174/B2
Bahía de Tortugas, Mex. 174/B3
Bahía Mansa, Chile 190/B4
Bahía San Blas, Arg. 190/E4
Bahía Solano, Col. 180/B3
Bahía Thetis, Arg. 191/D7
Bahía, Islas de la (isls.), Hon. 172/D4
Bahir Dar, Eth. 117/H3
Bahjoi, India 96/B1
Bāhl, India 98/C5
Bahlah, Oman 101/G4
Baḩr al 'Arab (riv.), Sudan 107/E3
Baḩr Al Ghazāl (pol. reg.), Sudan 117/E4
Baḩr Al Ghazāl (riv.), Sudan 117/F3
Baḩr al Milḩ (lake), Iraq 103/E3
Bahr Aouk (riv.), Chad 107/D4
Baḩr Az Zarāf (riv.), Sudan 117/F3
Bahr Azoum (riv.), Chad 116/D3
Bahr Bola (riv.), Chad 116/C3
Bahr el Ghazal (riv.), Chad 116/C2
Bahr Erguig (riv.), Chad 116/C3
Bahr Kéita (riv.), Chad 116/C3
Bahr Oulou (riv.), CAfr. 116/D3
Bahr Salamat (riv.), Chad 116/C3
Bahraich, India 96/C2
Bahrain (ctry.) 77/E7
Bahrain, Pak. 98/B2
Bahrain (int'l arpt.), Bahr. 100/F3
Bahrain (gulf), Asia 100/F3
Bahrām Chāh, Afg. 101/H3
Baḩṭīṭ, Egypt 113/C4
Bāhū Kalāt, Iran 101/H3
Bai (riv.), China 78/H3
Bai Thuong, Viet. 94/D2
Baia, It. 65/D6
Baia de Aramă, Rom. 51/F3
Baía dos Tigres, Ang. 122/A3
Baia Farta, Ang. 122/B2
Baia Mare, Rom. 51/F2
Baia Sprie, Rom. 51/F2
Baiano, It. 65/D6
Baião, Braz. 182/D3
Baibiene, Arg. 188/E4
Baïbokoum, Chad 116/B4
Baicao (mts.), China 86/D3
Baicheng, China 99/D3
Baicheng, China 79/J2
Băicoi, Rom. 51/G3
Baidishi, China 87/F3
Baidoa (Baydhabo), Som. 118/B5
Baidong (lake), China 80/D5
Baie Verte, Nf, Can. 141/L4
Baie-Saint-Paul, Qu, Can. 158/B2
Baie-Sainte-Anne, NB, Can. 158/E2
Baie-Trinité, Qu, Can. 158/D1
Baienfurt, Ger. 61/F2
Baiersbronn, Ger. 58/B5
Baiersdorf, Ger. 58/E3
Baifusi, China 87/F2
Baigorrita, Arg. 190/E2
Baigou, China 80/H7
Baigou (riv.), China 80/G7
Baihar, India 96/C4
Baihua (mtn.), China 80/G7
Ba'ījī, Iraq 103/E3
Baijian, China 80/G7
Baikunthpur, India 96/D4
Bailadores, Ven. 180/D2
Baildon, Eng, UK 35/G4
Băile Govora, Rom. 51/G3
Băile Herculane, Rom. 50/F3
Băile Olăneşti, Rom. 51/G3
Băile Tuşnad, Rom. 51/G2
Bailén, Sp. 46/D3
Băileşti, Rom. 51/F3
Bailey, Co, US 152/B1
Bailey, NC, US 163/H3
Baileys Harbor, Wi, US 160/C2
Bailicun, China 87/F3
Bailieborough, Ire. 32/D2
Bailleau-le-Pin, Fr. 57/G4
Bailleul, Fr. 54/B2
Bailmān Diārkhāta, Bang. 97/G3
Bailong, China 78/F5
Bailong (riv.), China 78/E5
Bailu (riv.), China 80/C4
Bailundo, Ang. 122/B2
Baima, China 78/E5
Baimangying, China 87/F3
Baimianxia, China 78/F5
Baimuru, PNG 129/G1
Bain (riv.), Eng, UK 35/H5
Bain-de-Bretagne, Fr. 56/D5
Bainang, China 97/G1
Bainbridge, Ga, US 165/F2
Bainbridge, NY, US 161/J3
Bainbridge, Oh, US 163/F1
Bainbridge, Pa, US 168/B3
Bainbridge (isl.), Wa, US 167/B2
Bainbridge Nav. Trg. Sta., Md, US 168/B4
Baines, West (riv.), Austl. 128/C4
Baingoin, China 99/E5
Bains, La, US 164/C2
Bains-les-Bains, Fr. 60/C2
Bains-sur-Oust, Fr. 56/C5
Baipadgué, Chad 116/B4
Baiquan, China 79/K2
Bā'ir (wadi), Jor. 104/E4
Bairab (lake), China 99/D4
Bairāgnia, India 97/E2
Baird, Fl, US 164/M8
Baird, Tx, US 150/E1
Baird Inlet (bay), Ak, US 171/F3
Bairnsdale, Austl. 133/C3
Bairoil, Wy, US 147/K2
Bais, Fr. 57/E4
Bais, Phil. 88/C3
Baïse (riv.), Fr. 44/D5
Baisha, China 87/H3
Baisha, China 87/G4
Baishaguan, China 87/H2
Baishaling, China 87/G2
Baishan, China 87/F3
Baishe, China 87/H3
Baishi (peak), China 87/H3
Baishui, China 86/E1
Baishui, China 78/F5
Baishui, China 87/G2
Baishuijiang, China 78/F5
Baisogala, Lith. 41/K4
Baisong (pass), China 87/H3
Baixa da Banheira, Port. 47/P10
Baixa Grande, Braz. 187/E2
Baixiang, China 80/C3
Baixo Guandu, Braz. 187/E3
Baiyanggou, China 81/B2
Baiyer River, PNG 129/G1
Baiyin, China 78/E4
Baiyu (mts.), China 80/B3
Baiyü, China 86/C2
Baiyun (int'l arpt.), China 87/G4
Baiyun, China 87/H3
Baja, Hun. 50/D2
Baja (pt.), Chile 191/B6
Baja (pt.), Mex. 174/B2
Baja California (pen.), Mex. 139/F6
Baja California (state), Mex. 174/B2
Baja California Sur (state), Mex. 174/B3
Bājah (gov.), Tun. 48/A4
Bājah, Tun. 112/L6
Baján, Mex. 177/D4
Bajāng, Nepal 96/C1
Bajánsenye, Hun. 50/C2
Bajawa, Indo. 91/F5
Bajestān, Iran 101/G2
Bājil, Yem. 118/B2
Bajilei, China 79/J3
Bajina Bašta, Yugo. 50/D4
Bājitpur, Bang. 97/H3
Bajmbat (mt.), Austl. 132/E1
Bajmok, Yugo. 50/D3
Bajo Boquete, Pan. 177/F4
Bajo de Gualicho (plain), Arg. 190/D4
Bajo de Sta. Rosa (plain), Arg. 190/D4
Bajo Nuevo (bank), Col. 173/F4
Bajo Palena, Chile 190/B4
Bajone (pt.), Moz. 123/J2
Bajos Caracoles, Arg. 191/C5
Bajram Curri, Alb. 50/E4
Bājura, Nepal 96/C1
Baka, Slvk. 50/C2
Bakaba, Chad 116/C4
Bakal, Rus. 69/N5
Bakala, CAfr. 116/D4
Bakali (riv.), D.R. Congo 120/D4
Bakaly, Rus. 69/M5
Bakanas (riv.), Kaz. 99/C2
Bakaoré, Chad 116/D2
Bakar, Cro. 45/L4
Bākarganj, Bang. 97/H4
Bakau, Gam. 114/A3
Bakayan (peak), Indo. 91/E3
Bakel, Sen. 114/B3
Bakel, Neth. 52/C5
Baker (peak), Ok, US 153/E3
Baker, Mt, US 156/B4
Baker, La, US 164/C2
Baker, Fl, US 164/E2
Baker (isl.), Pac., US 137/H4
Baker, Or, US 146/E1
Baker (lake), Nun, Can. 140/G2
Baker, Nv, US 147/F4
Baker, Ca, US 148/D3
Baker (riv.), Chile 191/B5
Baker (mt.), Wa, US 144/D3
Baker Hill, Al, US 165/F2
Baker Lake, Nun, Can. 140/G2
Bakere, D.R. Congo 121/E2
Bakersfield, Mo, US 153/H2
Bakersfield, Ca, US 148/C3
Bakersville, NC, US 163/F2
Bakewell, Eng, UK 35/G5
Bakhchysaray, Ukr. 73/G5
Bakhmach, Ukr. 73/G2
Bakhra, India 97/E2
Bakhshāyesh, Iran 103/F2
Bakhta, Rus. 74/J3
Bākhtarān, Iran 103/F3
Bakhtegān (lake), Iran 103/H4
Bakhtīārī (gov.), Iran 103/G4
Bakhtiyārpur, India 97/E3
Bakhuis (mts.), Sur. 181/G4
Bakia, CAfr. 117/E4
Bakkaflói (bay), Ice. 38/P6
Baklan, Turk. 102/B2
Bako, Eth. 117/H3
Bako, Eth. 117/H4
Bakokandi (riv.), D.R. Congo 117/F5
Bakony (mts.), Hun. 67/H1
Bakonyszombathely, Hun. 50/C2
Bakora Corridor Game Rsv., Ugan. 119/B2
Bakori, Nga. 115/G4
Bakouma, CAfr. 116/D4
Bakoumba, Gabon 120/C3
Bakovský Potok (riv.), Czh. 59/G2
Bakoye (riv.), Gui. 114/C4
Baku (cap.), Azer. 103/G1
Baku (int'l arpt.), Azer. 103/G1
Baku, D.R. Congo 121/G2
Bakungan, Indo. 89/B2
Bakwa-Kenge, D.R. Congo 121/E4
Bal Harbour, Fl, US 164/P11
Balâ, Turk. 102/C2
Bala, Wal, UK 34/E6
Bala, On, Can. 161/G2
Bālā Bāgh, Afg. 98/A2
Balabac, Phil. 88/B4
Balabac (isl.), Phil. 88/B4
Balabac (str.), Malay,Phil. 88/B4
Balabanovo, Rus. 68/H5
Balad, Iraq 103/F3
Balagansk, Rus. 78/E1
Bālāghāt, India 96/C5
Balagtas, Phil. 88/E6
Balaguer, Sp. 47/F2
Balaiselasa, Indo. 89/C3
Balaïtous (peak), Fr. 44/C5
Balaka, Malw. 123/G2
Bālākāndi, Bang. 97/H4
Balakhna, Rus. 69/J4
Balaklava, Ukr. 70/E3
Balaklava, Austl. 131/H5
Balakliya, Ukr. 73/J3
Balakovo, Rus. 71/H1
Bal'amā, Jor. 105/E4
Balambangan (isl.), Malay. 88/B4
Bālāmorghāb, Afg. 98/A2
Balan, Gui. 114/C4
Bălan, Rom. 72/C4
Balancán, Mex. 176/D2
Balanga, Phil. 88/C2
Balangala, D.R. Congo 120/D2
Balangero, It. 64/D2
Bālāngir, India 95/D1
Balantak, Indo. 91/F4
Balao, Ecu. 184/B1
Balaoan, Phil. 88/C1
Balaqṭar, Egypt 113/B2
Balarāmpur, India 97/F4
Balashikha, Rus. 69/W9
Balashov, Rus. 73/M2
Balasore (Baleshwar), India 92/E3
Balassagyarmat, Hun. 43/K4
Balatina, Mol. 72/D4
Balaton (lake), Hun. 67/H1
Balaton, Mn, US 155/G1
Balatonfenyves, Hun. 50/C2
Balatonföldvár, Hun. 50/C2
Balatonfüred, Hun. 50/C2
Balatonszabadi, Hun. 50/D2
Balatonszentgyörgy, Hun. 50/C2
Balaurin, Indo. 128/A2
Balaxani, Azer. 71/J4
Balbieriškis, Lith. 41/K4
Balbina (res.), Braz. 179/D3
Balboa (nbrhd.), Ca, US 166/G8
Balbriggan, Ire. 34/B4
Balcarce, Arg. 190/F3
Balcarres, Sk, Can. 156/C2
Balcary (pt.), Sc, UK 34/E2
Balch Springs, Tx, US 150/L7
Balchik, Bul. 51/J4
Balclutha, NZ 135/B4
Balcombe, Eng, UK 37/F4
Bald (hill), Il, US 162/C2
Bald (peak), Va, US 163/G2
Bald (pt.), Austl. 130/C5
Bald (mtn.), Wa, US 144/D4
Bald (peak), WV, US 163/H1
Bald Eagle Mtn. (mtn.), Pa, US 168/A1
Bald Knob, Ar, US 153/J3
Bald Rock NP, Austl. 132/E1
Baldhill (dam), ND, US 156/E4
Baldock, Eng, UK 37/F3
Baldone, Lat. 41/L3
Baldur, Mb, Can. 156/E3
Baldwin, Ga, US 163/F3
Baldwin, Fl, US 165/H2
Baldwin, La, US 164/C3
Baldwin, Mi, US 160/D3
Baldwin, ND, US 156/D4
Baldwin, NY, US 169/L9
Baldwin City, Ks, US 153/G1
Baldwin Harbour, NY, US 169/L9
Baldwin Park, Ca, US 166/G7
Baldwinsville, NY, US 161/H3
Baldwyn, Ms, US 162/C3
Baldy (mtn.), Can. 156/D2
Baldy (peak), Az, US 149/H4
Baldy (hill), Ne, US 154/D3
Baldy (mtn.), Mt, US 145/K3
Baldy Beacon (peak), Belz. 176/D2
Bale (prov.), Eth. 118/B4
Bale Mountains NP, Eth. 118/A4
Baleares (Balearic) (isls.), Sp. 47/G3
Balearic (isls.), Sp. 66/D3
Balearic (Baleares) (isls.), Sp. 47/G3
Baleia, Ponta da (pt.), Braz. 187/F3
Baleine, Rivièveà la (riv.), Qu, Can. 141/K3
Baleine,Grand Rivière de la (riv.), Qu, Can. 141/J3
Baleine,Petite Rivière de la (riv.), Qu, Can. 141/J3
Balen, Belg. 55/E1
Baler, Phil. 88/C2
Balerna, Swi. 61/F6
Balesa (riv.), Kenya 119/B1
Baleshwar (Balasore), India 92/E3
Baley, Rus. 78/H1
Baléyara, Niger 115/F3
Balezino, Rus. 69/M4
Balfour, SAfr. 124/E2
Balfour, BC, Can. 144/F3
Balfron, Sc, UK 33/B4
Balgatay, Mong. 78/D2
Balguntay, China 99/E3
Balḩāf, Yem. 118/D2
Balhannah, Austl. 131/M8
Balḩo, Djib. 118/B2
Bali (isl.), Indo. 77/L10
Bali, Camr. 115/H5
Bali, India 92/B2
Bali (str.), Indo. 89/F5
Bali (sea), Indo. 90/D5
Bāli Chak, India 97/F4
Balice (int'l arpt.), Pol. 43/K3
Balidianzi, China 81/C2
Baliem (riv.), Indo. 91/J4
Balige, Indo. 89/B2
Balik Pulau, Malay. 89/C1
Balıkesir, Turk. 70/C5
Balıkesir (prov.), Turk. 70/C5
Balikpapan, Indo. 91/E4
Balimbing, Indo. 89/D4
Balimbing, Phil. 88/B4
Balimo, PNG 129/F1
Baling, Malay. 89/C1
Baling, China 86/E3
Balingasag, Phil. 88/D3
Bälinge, Swe. 40/G2
Balingen, Ger. 61/E1
Balivanich, Sc, UK 31/Q8
Baljennie, Sk, Can. 145/L1
Balk, Neth. 52/C3
Balkan (prov.), Trkm. 71/K4
Balkan (mts.), Yugo.,Bul. 29/F3
Balkassar, Pak. 98/B3
Balkhash (lake), Kaz. 77/G5
Ball, La, US 164/B2
Ball (mt.), Ab, Can. 144/G2
Balla, Ire. 32/A2
Balladonia, Austl. 130/D5
Ballagan (pt.), Ire. 34/B4
Ballaghaderreen, Ire. 32/B2
Ballan, Austl. 133/B3
Ballan-Miré, Fr. 57/F6
Ballangen, Nor. 38/F1
Ballantine, Mt, US 145/K5
Ballantrae, Sc, UK 34/C1
Ballarat, Austl. 133/A3
Ballard (lake), Austl. 130/D4
Ballarpur, India 95/C2
Ballater, Sc, UK 33/C2
Ballaugh, IM, UK 34/D3
Ballé, Mali 114/C3
Ballenita (pt.), Chile 188/B3
Ballens, Swi. 60/C4
Balleny (isls.), Ant. 192/L
Balleroy, Fr. 57/E2
Ballerup, Den. 39/J7
Ballesteros, Phil. 88/C1
Ballesteros, Arg. 188/D5
Ballia, India 97/E3
Ballidu, Austl. 130/C4
Ballina, Austl. 132/E1
Ballina, Ire. 32/B4
Ballina, Ire. 32/A1
Ballinafad, On, Can. 160/S8
Ballinakill, Ire. 32/C4
Ballinamallard, NI, UK 31/Q9
Ballinasloe, Ire. 32/B3
Ballincollig, Ire. 32/B6
Ballinderry (riv.), NI, UK 34/B2
Ballindine, Ire. 32/B2
Ballineen, Ire. 32/B6
Ballingarry, Ire. 32/C4
Ballingarry, Ire. 32/B5
Ballinger, Tx, US 151/E2
Ballingry, Sc, UK 33/C4
Ballinlough, Ire. 32/B2
Ballinluig, Sc, UK 33/C3
Ballinrobe, Ire. 32/A2
Ballintober, Ire. 32/B2
Ballintoy, NI, UK 34/B1
Ballitore, Ire. 32/D4
Ballivián, Bol. 184/D5
Ballivor, Ire. 32/D2
Balloch, Sc, UK 33/B2
Balloch, Sc, UK 33/B5
Ballon d'Alsace (peak), Fr. 60/C2
Ballon de Sevance (peak), Fr. 60/C2
Ballston Spa, NY, US 161/K3
Ballville, Oh, US 160/E4
Bally, Pa, US 168/C3
Ballybay, Ire. 32/D1
Ballybunnion, Ire. 32/A4
Ballycanew, Ire. 32/D4
Ballycarney, Ire. 32/D4
Ballycarry, NI, UK 34/C2
Ballycastle, NI, UK 34/B1
Ballycastle, Ire. 31/P9
Ballyclare, NI, UK 34/B2
Ballyconnell, Ire. 32/C1
Ballycotton, Ire. 32/B6
Ballycumber, Ire. 32/C3
Ballydehob, Ire. 32/A6
Ballyduff, Ire. 32/A5
Ballyeaston, NI, UK 34/B2
Ballyfarnan, Ire. 32/B1
Ballygar, Ire. 32/B2
Ballygawley, NI, UK 34/A3
Ballygeary, Ire. 32/D5
Ballygowan, NI, UK 34/C3
Ballyhaise, Ire. 32/C1
Ballyhalbert, NI, UK 34/C3
Ballyhaunis, Ire. 32/B2
Ballyheigue, Ire. 30/P10
Ballyhoura (mts.), Ire. 32/B5
Ballyjamesduff, Ire. 32/C2
Ballykelly, NI, UK 34/A1
Ballylanders, Ire. 32/B5
Ballyliffin, Ire. 34/A1
Ballylongford, Ire. 32/A4
Ballymahon, Ire. 32/C2
Ballymakeery, Ire. 32/A6
Ballymena (dist.), NI, UK 34/B2
Ballymena, NI, UK 34/B2
Ballymoney, NI, UK 34/B1
Ballymoney (dist.), NI, UK 34/B1
Ballymore, Ire. 32/C3
Ballymore Eustace, Ire. 32/D3
Ballymote, Ire. 32/B1
Ballynacargy, Ire. 32/C2
Ballynacourty (pt.), Ire. 32/C5
Ballynahinch, NI, UK 34/C3
Ballynure, NI, UK 34/C2
Ballyporeen, Ire. 32/B5
Ballyquintin (pt.), NI, UK 34/C3
Ballyragget, Ire. 32/C4
Ballyroan, Ire. 32/C4
Ballysadare, Ire. 32/B1
Ballyshannon, Ire. 31/P9
Ballyteige (bay), Ire. 32/D5
Ballywalter, NI, UK 34/C2
Balm, Fl, US 164/L8
Balmaceda, Chile 190/C5
Balmaceda (peak), Chile 191/B6
Balmazújváros, Hun. 43/L5
Balmertown, On, Can. 157/H2
Balmhorn (peak), Swi. 60/D5
Balmoral, NB, Can. 158/D2
Balmoral, Mb, Can. 156/F2
Balmoral, Zam. 123/F2
Balmoral, Austl. 132/B3
Balmoral Castle, Sc, UK 33/C2
Balmorhea, Tx, US 151/C2
Balnarring Beach, Austl. 133/B4
Balnearia, Arg. 188/D4
Balneário Camboriú, Braz. 189/G3
Balneario Carrasco, Uru. 191/K11
Balneario Claromecó, Arg. 190/E3
Balneario de los Novillos, PN, Mex. 177/D3
Balochistān (reg.), Pak. 92/A2
Balod, India 95/D1
Baloda Bāzār, India 95/D1
Balombo, Ang. 122/B2
Balonne (riv.), Austl. 127/D3
Bālotra, India 101/K3
Balougou, China 80/B3
Balqash, Kaz. 99/C2
Balrāmpur, India 96/D2
Balranald, Austl. 132/B2
Balş, Rom. 51/G3
Balsall Common, Eng, UK 37/E2
Balsam Lake, Wi, US 157/H5
Bálsamo (pt.), Ecu. 180/A5
Balsapuerto, Peru 184/B2
Balsas (riv.), Mex. 139/G8
Balsas, Braz. 183/E4
Balsas (riv.), Braz. 183/E4
Balsorano Nuovo, It. 65/C4
Bålsta, Swe. 39/A1
Balsthal, Swi. 60/D3
Balta, ND, US 156/D3
Balta, Ukr. 72/E4
Bāltal, India 98/C2
Baltanás, Sp. 46/C2
Baltasar Brum, Uru. 189/E4
Baltay, Rus. 71/H1
Bălţi, Mol. 72/D4
Baltic (plain), Rus. 69/S7
Baltic (sea), Eur. 38/F5
Baltic Spit (bar), Rus.,Pol. 41/H4
Balṭīm, Egypt 113/C1
Baltimore, Ire. 32/A7
Baltimore, Md, US 168/B5
Baltimore (co.), Md, US 168/B4
Baltimore, Oh, US 160/E5
Baltimore-Washington (int'l arpt.), Md, US 168/B5
Baltinglass, Ire. 32/D4
Baltiysk, Rus. 41/H4
Baltoji Vokė, Lith. 41/L4
Baltray, Ire. 34/B4
Baltrum (isl.), Ger. 53/E1
Balud, Phil. 88/C2
Bælum, Den. 40/D3
Baluran NP, Indo. 89/F4
Bālurghāt, India 97/G3
Balvard, Iran 103/J4
Balve, Ger. 53/E6
Balvi, Lat. 41/M3
Balwina Aboriginal Reserve, Austl. 128/B5
Balya, Turk. 70/C5
Balykchy, Kyr. 74/H5
Balykshi, Kaz. 71/J3
Balzar, Ecu. 180/B5
Balzers, Lcht. 61/F3
Bam (prov.), Burk. 115/E3
Bam, Iran 101/G3
Bam (lake), China 99/F5
Bam, Rus. 79/J1
Bama, Nga. 116/B3
Bama Yaozu Zizhixian, China 87/E3
Bamaji (lake), On, Can. 157/J2
Bamako (cap.), Mali 114/D3
Bamako (Senou) (int'l arpt.), Mali 114/D3
Bamania, D.R. Congo 120/D3
Bamao, China 87/J2
Bamba, Mali 115/E2
Bamba, D.R. Congo 120/D2
Bambama, Congo 120/C3
Bambamarca, Peru 184/B2
Bambana (riv.), Nic. 177/E3
Bambara, Chad 116/C3
Bambara Maoundé, Mali 114/E3
Bambari, CAfr. 116/D4
Bamber Ridge, Eng, UK 35/F4
Bamberg, Ger. 58/D3
Bamberg, SC, US 163/G4
Bambesa, D.R. Congo 121/F2
Bambesi, Eth. 117/G3
Bambi, Ang. 122/B2
Bambili, D.R. Congo 121/F2
Bambinga, D.R. Congo 120/D3
Bambio, CAfr. 120/D2
Bamble, Nor. 40/C2
Bambouti, CAfr. 117/E4
Bambouto (mts.), Camr. 116/B4
Bambu, Eth. 117/G4
Bamburgh, Eng, UK 33/E5
Bamda, China 86/C2
Bamenda, Camr. 115/H5
Bamfield, BC, Can. 144/B3
Bamforth Nat'l Wild. Ref., Wy, US 154/B3
Bamingui, CAfr. 116/D4
Bamingui (riv.), CAfr. 116/C3
Bamingui-Bangoran (pref.), CAfr. 116/D3
Bamingui-Bangoran, PN de, CAfr. 116/C4
Bammental, Ger. 58/B4
Bamnet Narong, Thai. 94/C3
Bāmor Kalān, India 96/B3
Bampton, Eng, UK 36/C5
Bampūr (riv.), Iran 101/H3
Bamu (riv.), PNG 129/F1
Bamunka, Camr. 115/H5
Bamyili, Austl. 128/D3
Ban Ay Rieng, Viet. 94/E3
Ban Ban, Laos 86/D5
Ban Boun Tai, Laos 86/D4
Ban Chiang (ruin), Thai. 94/C2
Ban Dan Lan Hoi, Thai. 94/B2
Ban Don, Viet. 94/D3
Ban Donkon, Laos 86/D4
Ban Dung, Thai. 94/C2
Ban Hinkhan, Laos 94/D2
Ban Hong, Thai. 94/B2
Ban Houay Pamon, Laos 94/C2
Ban Houayxay, Laos 86/D4
Ban Kadian, Laos 94/D3
Ban Kantang, Thai. 94/B5
Ban Kapong, Thai. 94/B4
Ban Kariang, Thai. 94/B3
Ban Kengkok, Laos 93/J4
Ban Kha, Laos 94/C1
Ban Khampho, Laos 94/D3
Ban Khlong Yai, Thai. 94/C4
Ban Khok Kloi, Thai. 94/B4
Ban Khon, Laos 94/D3
Ban Khuan Niang, Thai. 94/B5
Ban Kui Nua, Thai. 94/B3
Ban Laem, Thai. 94/B3
Ban Len, Laos 93/H4
Ban Loboy, Laos 94/D2
Ban Mdrack, Viet. 94/E3
Ban Mong, Viet. 94/D2
Ban Muangsen, Laos 94/D2
Ban Na Mang, Laos 86/E4
Ban Na Phao, Laos 94/D2
Ban Na Pho, Laos 94/C1
Ban Na San, Thai. 94/B4
Ban Nakala, Laos 94/D2
Ban Nambak, Laos 94/C1
Ban Pak Phanang, Thai. 94/C4
Ban Panghai, Laos 86/D5
Ban Phai, Thai. 94/C2
Ban Phon, Laos 94/D3
Ban Pong, Thai. 94/B3
Ban Rai, Thai. 94/B3
Ban Saka, Laos 94/C2
Ban Sieou, Laos 86/D5
Ban Ta Fa, Laos 86/D4
Ban Tak, Thai. 94/B2
Ban Thabok, Laos 94/C2
Ban Thieng, Laos 94/C2
Ban Tung, Laos 94/D2
Ban Woen, Laos 94/C2
Ban Xay, Laos 94/C1
Ban Xebang-Nouan, Laos 94/D3
Ban Yong Sata, Thai. 94/B5
Bana (wadi), Yem. 118/C2
Banaba (isl.), Kiri. 136/F5
Bañado de Medina, Uru. 189/F5
Bañado de Rocha, Uru. 189/F4
Bañados de Izozog (swamp), Bol. 188/D1
Bañados de Otuquis (swamp), Bol. 188/E1
Banagher, Ire. 32/C3
Banagi, Tanz. 119/A2
Banahao (mt.), Phil. 88/C2
Banalia, D.R. Congo 121/F2
Banama, Gui. 114/C4
Banamba, Mali 114/D3
Banana, D.R. Congo 120/C4
Banana (isls.), SLeo. 114/B4
Bananal, Braz. 187/M7
Bananal (isl.), Braz. 186/C2
Bananeiras, Braz. 183/H4
Banar (riv.), Bang. 97/H3
Banarlı, Turk. 51/H5
Banās (riv.), India 92/C2
Banat (reg.), Rom.,Yugo. 67/J1
Banat (reg.), Yugo. 50/E3
Banatalor Game Ref., NB, Can. 158/D2
Banatsko Novo Selo, Yugo. 50/E3
Banawe, Phil. 88/C1
Banaz, Turk. 102/B2
Banbar, China 86/B2
Banbishan, China 80/H6
Banbridge, NI, UK 34/B3
Banbridge (dist.), NI, UK 34/B3
Banbury, Eng, UK 37/E2
Banc D'Arguin, Mrta. 110/A5
Banc D'Arguin, PN du, Mrta. 114/A2
Banchette, It. 62/A2
Banchory, Sc, UK 33/D2
Banco Chinchorro (isls.), Mex. 172/D4
Bancroft, La, US 150/H2
Bancroft, On, Can. 161/H2
Band Mill, Ar, US 153/J2
Banda (sea), Indo. 77/M10
Bāndā, India 96/C3
Banda, India 96/B3
Banda, D.R. Congo 117/E4
Banda (isls.), Indo. 91/H4
Banda Aceh, Indo. 89/A1
Banda Elat, Indo. 128/D1
Bandahara (peak), Indo. 89/B2
Bandai-san (peak), Japan 85/G2
Bandakani, D.R. Congo 120/C4
Bandama (riv.), C.d'Iv. 114/D5
Bandama Blanc (riv.), C.d'Iv. 114/D4
Bandama Rouge (riv.), C.d'Iv. 114/D4
Bandanaira, Indo. 91/G4
Bandar Abbas (int'l arpt.), Iran 103/J5
Bandar Beheshtī, Iran 101/H3
Bandar Seri Begawan (cap.), Bru. 88/A4
Bandar-e 'Abbās, Iran 103/J5
Bandar-e Anzalī, Iran 103/G2
Bandar-e Būshehr, Iran 103/G4
Bandar-e Chārak, Iran 103/H5
Bandar-e Deylam, Iran 103/G4
Bandar-e Gaz, Iran 103/H2
Bandar-e Kīāshahr, Iran 103/G2
Bandar-e Kong, Iran 103/H5
Bandar-e Lengeh, Iran 103/H5
Bandar-e Māhshahr, Iran 103/G4
Bandar-e Maqām, Iran 103/H5
Bandar-e Moghūyeh, Iran 101/F3
Bandar-e Rīg, Iran 103/G4
Bandar-e Torkeman, Iran 103/H2
Bāndarban, Bang. 86/B4
Bandarchua, India 96/D4
Bandawe, Malw. 123/G1
Bande, Sp. 46/B1
Bandeira do Sul, Braz. 187/K6
Bandeira, Pico da (peak), Braz. 187/E4
Bandeirantes, Braz. 189/F1
Bandeirantes, Braz. 189/G2
Bandeli, May. 125/H6
Bandelier Nat'l Mon., NM, US 149/J3
Bandera, Arg. 188/D4
Bandera, Tx, US 150/E3
Bandera Volcano and Ice Fields, NM, US 149/H3
Banderilla, Mex. 175/N7
Bandhavgarh NP, India 96/C4
Bandholm, Den. 40/D4
Bandiagara, Mali 114/E3
Bandingagung, Indo. 89/C3
Bandīpur, Nepal 97/E2
Bandipur NP, India 95/C4
Bandipura, India 98/C2
Bandirma (gulf), Turk. 51/H5
Bandırma, Turk. 51/H5
Bandjoun, Camr. 120/B1
Bandol, Fr. 64/B6
Bandon, Ire. 32/B6
Bandon (riv.), Ire. 32/B6
Bandon, Or, US 146/A2
Bandundu (pol. reg.), D.R. Congo 120/D4
Bandundu, D.R. Congo 120/D3
Bandung, Indo. 89/D4
Bandya, Austl. 130/D3
Banegas, Bol. 185/F5
Bāneh, Iran 103/F3
Bañeres, Sp. 47/E3
Banes, Cuba 177/H1
Banfangzi, China 78/F5
Banff, Ab, Can. 144/G2
Banff, Sc, UK 33/D1
Banff NP, Ab,BC, Can. 144/F2
Banfora, Burk. 114/D4
Bang, CAfr. 116/B4
Bang Lang (res.), Thai. 94/C5
Bang Mun Nak, Thai. 94/C2
Bang Phli, Thai. 94/C3
Bang Saphan, Thai. 94/B4
Bang Yai, Thai. 94/C3
Banga, India 98/C4

Bangalow, Austl. 134/D5
Bangaon, India 97/G4
Bangar, Phil. 87/J5
Bāngarmau, India 96/C2
Bangassou, CAfr. 116/D4
Bangau (cape), Malay. 88/B4
Bangazeno, D.R. Congo 121/F2
Bangeta (mt.), PNG 129/G1
Banggai (isls.), Indo. 91/F4
Banggong (lake), China 99/C5
Banghiang (riv.), Laos 94/D2
Bangil, Indo. 89/F4
Bangka (isl.), Indo. 77/K10
Bangka (str.), Indo. 90/B4
Bangkalan, Indo. 89/F4
Bangkaru (isl.), Indo. 89/B2
Bangkinang, Indo. 89/C2
Bangkir, Indo. 91/F3
Bangko, Indo. 89/C3
Bangkok (int'l arpt.), Thai. 94/C3
Bangkok (Krung Thep) (cap.), Thai. 94/C3
Bangkok, Bight of (bay), Thai. 93/H5
Bangladesh (ctry.) 77/H7
Bangli, Indo. 89/F5
Bangma (mts.), China 86/C4
Bangor, Sk, Can. 156/C2
Bangor, NI, UK 34/C2
Bangor, Wal, UK 34/D5
Bangor, Mi, US 160/C3
Bangor, Fr. 56/B6
Bangor, Me, US 141/K4
Bangor, Pa, US 168/C2
Bangor-is-y-Coed, Wal, UK 35/F6
Bangoran (riv.), CAfr. 116/C3
Bāngriposi, India 97/F4
Bangs (mt.), Az, US 149/F2
Bangs, Tx, US 150/E2
Bangu, D.R. Congo 121/E5
Bangued, Phil. 88/C1
Bangui (cap.), CAfr. 116/C4
Bangui (int'l arpt.), CAfr. 116/C4
Bangui, EqG. 120/B2
Bangui, Phil. 88/C1
Bangunpurba, Indo. 89/B2
Bangzha, China 86/E3
Banhā, Egypt 113/C4
Banhine, PN de, Moz. 123/G4
Baní, DRep. 173/G4
Bani, CAfr. 116/D4
Bani (riv.), Mali 114/D3
Banī Mazār, Egypt 109/F2
Banī Suhaylah, Gaza 105/A6
Banī Suwayf (gov.), Egypt 102/B3
Banī Suwayf, Egypt 113/C6
Banī 'Ubayd, Egypt 113/C2
Bāni Walīd, Libya 108/B2
Bani-Bangou, Niger 115/F3
Bania, CAfr. 120/D2
Baniachang, Bang. 97/H3
Banian, Gui. 114/C4
Bánica, DRep. 177/J2
Banifing (riv.), Mali 114/D3
Banihāl (pass), India 98/C3
Banikoara, Ben. 115/F4
Banisa, Kenya 118/B5
Banister (riv.), Va, US 163/H2
Bāniyās, Syria 104/D2
Banja Koviljača, Yugo. 50/D3
Banja Luka, Bosn. 50/C3
Banjar, Indo. 89/E4
Banjarmasin, Indo. 90/D4
Banjia, China 94/B1
Banjiang, China 87/F3
Banjul (cap.), Gam. 114/A3
Banjul (Yundum) (int'l arpt.), Gam. 114/A3
Bankä, Azer. 103/G2
Bānka, India 97/F3
Banka Banka, Austl. 128/D4
Bankas, Mali 114/E3
Bankengting, China 87/H3
Bankeryd, Swe. 40/F3
Bankfoot, Sc, UK 33/C3
Bankhead, Sc, UK 33/D2
Bankhead (lake), Al, US 162/D4
Bānki, India 97/E4
Bankilare, Niger 115/F3
Banks, Al, US 165/F2
Banks (pen.), NZ 127/H7
Banks (cape), Austl. 132/B3
Banks (isl.), Austl. 129/F2
Banks (str.), Austl. 127/D5
Banks (isl.), NW, Can. 139/E2
Banks (cape), Ak, US 171/H4
Banks (lake), Wa, US 144/E4
Banks (isls.), Van. 136/F6
Bankstown (arpt.), Austl. 134/G8
Bankstown (nbrhd.), Austl. 134/H8
Bānkurā, India 97/F4
Bankya, Bul. 49/H1
Banmankhi, India 97/F3
Banmauk, Myan. 86/B3
Banmian, China 87/H3
Bann (riv.), NI, UK 34/B3
Bann (riv.), Ire. 32/D4
Banna (riv.), It. 62/A3
Bannack, Mt, US 147/G1
Bannalec, Fr. 56/B5
Bannang Sata, Thai. 89/C1
Banner, Wy, US 147/K1
Banner, Ky, US 163/F2
Banning, Ca, US 148/D4
Bannock (pass), Id, US 147/G1
Bannockburn, Sc, UK 33/C4
Bannockburn, Austl. 133/B4
Bannockburn Battlesite, Sc, UK 33/C4
Bannow (bay), Ire. 32/D5
Bannu, Pak. 98/A3
Banon, Fr. 64/B4
Baños, Ecu. 184/B1
Banphot Phisai, Thai. 94/B3
Banpo Ruins, China 80/B4
Bānpur, India 95/E2
Bansberia, India 97/G4
Bānsdīh, India 97/E3
Bansha, Ire. 32/B5
Banshi, China 87/G3
Bānsi, India 96/B3
Bānsi, India 96/D2
Bansihāri, India 97/G3
Bansin, Ger. 40/F5
Bansko, Bul. 49/H2
Banskobystrický (pol. reg.), Slvk. 43/K4
Banstead, Eng, UK 30/C3
Bānswāra, India 92/B3
Bantayan (isl.), Phil. 88/C3
Bantayan, Phil. 88/C3
Banté, Ben. 115/F4
Banteer, Ire. 32/B5
Bantenan (cape), Indo. 89/F5
Bantong Group (isls.), Thai. 94/B5
Bantry, Ire. 32/A6
Bantry (bay), Ire. 32/A6
Bantvāl, India 95/B3
Bañuelo (peak), Sp. 46/C3
Banūr, India 98/D4
Banxi, China 87/F2
Banyak (isls.), Indo. 90/A3
Banyo, Camr. 116/A4
Banyoles, Sp. 47/G1
Banyuwangi, Indo. 89/F5
Banz, PNG 129/G1
Banzare (coast), Ant. 192/J
Banzart (lake), Tun. 48/A4
Banzart (Bizerte), Tun. 48/A4
Bao Ha, Viet. 86/E4
Bao Lac, Viet. 86/E4
Bao Loc, Viet. 94/D4
Baode, China 80/B3
Baodi, China 80/H7
Baoding, China 80/G7
Baofeng, China 80/C4
Baoguangsi, China 86/E2
Baoji, China 78/F5
Baojing, China 93/J2
Baokang, China 80/B5
Baoro, CAfr. 116/B4
Baoruco (mts.), DRep. 177/J2
Baoshan, China 86/C3
Baoshan, China 80/L8
Baotian, China 86/E3
Baotou, China 80/B2
Baoulé (riv.), Mali 114/C3
Baoxing, China 86/D2
Baoxinji, China 87/G1
Baoying, China 80/D4
Bāpatla, India 95/D3
Bapaume, Fr. 54/B3
Baptistown, NJ, US 168/C2
Bāqa el Gharbiyya, Isr. 105/C4
Baqên, China 78/C5
Ba'qūbah, Iraq 103/F3
Baquedano, Chile 188/B2
Bar, Yugo. 49/F1
Bar (riv.), Fr. 42/C4
Bar, Ukr. 72/D3
Bar Bigha, India 97/E3
Bar el Ksaïb (well), Mali 110/D5
Bar Harbor, Me, US 158/C3
Bar Hill, Eng, UK 37/G2
Bar-le-Duc, Fr. 55/E6
Bar-sur-Aube, Fr. 44/F2
Bar-sur-Seine, Fr. 44/F2
Bara, Swe. 40/E4
Bara, Indo. 91/G4
Barā Bangāhal, India 98/D3
Bāra Banki, India 96/C2
Bārā Lācha La (pass), India 98/D3
Baraawe, Som. 119/D1
Barabai, Indo. 90/E4
Barabinsk, Rus. 74/H4
Baraboo, Wi, US 155/K2
Baracaldo, Sp. 44/B5
Barachois, NB, Can. 158/E2
Barachois, Qu, Can. 158/E1
Barachois (pt.), NS, Can. 159/G3
Baracoa, Cuba 177/H1
Barada (riv.), Syria 104/E3
Baradero, Arg. 191/J10
Baradine, Austl. 132/D1
Barāgaon, India 97/E3
Baragoi, Kenya 119/B1
Baragua, Ven. 180/D2
Baraguá, Cuba 177/G1
Bārah, Sudan 117/F2
Barajas (int'l arpt.), Sp. 47/N9
Barajas, Sp. 47/N9
Barajevo, Yugo. 50/E3
Barāk (riv.), India 86/B3
Baraka, D.R. Congo 121/G4
Baraka (riv.), Sudan 117/H1
Barakah, Sudan 117/E3
Barākar (riv.), India 97/F3
Barakī Barak, Afg. 101/J2
Bārākot, India 95/E1
Baralaba, Austl. 134/C4
Baram (cape), Malay. 90/D3
Baram (riv.), Malay. 90/D3
Bar'am NP, Isr. 105/C2
Barama, India 97/H2
Barama (riv.), Guy. 181/G3
Baramanni, Guy. 181/G3
Baramita, Guy. 181/F3
Baramsar, India 98/C5
Baramula, India 98/C2
Baran', Bela. 41/P4
Bāran, India 92/C2
Baranagar, India 97/G4
Baranga, D.R. Congo 121/F2
Barani (well), Alg. 110/E4
Baranikha, Rus. 75/S3
Baranivka, Ukr. 72/D2
Barano d'Ischia, It. 65/C6
Baranoa, Col. 180/C2
Baranof (isl.), Ak, US 140/C3
Baranya (prov.), Hun. 50/C3
Barão de Cocais, Braz. 187/E3
Barão de Grajaú, Braz. 183/F4
Barão de Melgaço, Braz. 185/H5
Baraolt, Rom. 51/G2
Baraque de Fraiture (hill), Belg. 55/E3
Baras, Phil. 88/D2
Barat Daya (isls.), Indo. 91/G5
Barate, Indo. 128/A2
Baratier, Congo 120/C4
Barato, India 86/B3
Barauli, India 97/E2
Baraut, India 98/D5
Baraya, Col. 180/C4
Barbacena, Braz. 186/E4
Barbacoas, Col. 180/B4
Barbacoas, Ven. 183/P8
Barbados (ctry.) 139/M8
Barbalha, Braz. 183/G4
Barbaros, Turk. 51/H5
Barbas (cape), Mor. 110/A5
Barbastro, Sp. 47/F1
Barbate de Franco, Sp. 46/C4
Barbeau (peak), Nun, Can. 141/T6
Barbentane, Fr. 64/A5
Barberà del Vallès, Sp. 47/L6
Barberaz, Fr. 64/B1
Barberino di Mugello, It. 63/E6
Barberton, Oh, US 160/F4
Barberton, SAfr. 125/E2
Barbil, India 97/E4
Barbon, Eng, UK 35/F3
Barbona (peak), It. 62/D6
Barbosa, Col. 180/C3
Barbosa, Col. 183/K6
Barboursville, Va, US 163/H1
Barbourville, Ky, US 162/F2
Barbuda (isl.), Anti. 139/L8
Barby, Fr. 64/B1
Barcaldine, Sc, UK 33/A3
Barcaldine, Austl. 134/B3
Barcarena, Braz. 182/D3
Barcarrota, Sp. 46/B3
Barcău (riv.), Rom. 67/J1
Barcellona Pozzo di Gotto, It. 48/D3
Barcelona, Ven. 181/E2
Barcelona (int'l arpt.), Sp. 47/L7
Barcelona, Sp. 47/L7
Barcelonnette, Fr. 64/C4
Barcelos, Braz. 181/F5
Barcelos, Port. 46/A2
Barcin, Pol. 43/J2
Barclay, Tx, US 151/F2
Barcoo (riv.), Austl. 127/D3
Barcs, Hun. 50/C3
Barczewo, Pol. 41/J5
Bard, Ca, US 148/E4
Bärdä, Azer. 103/F1
Bardaï, Chad 108/C4
Bardas Blancas, Arg. 190/C2
Bardejov, Slvk. 43/L4
Bardeskan, Iran 101/G1
Bardheere, Som. 119/C1
Bardi, It. 62/C4
Bardīyah, Libya 108/E2
Bardney, Eng, UK 35/H5
Bārdoli, India 95/B1
Bardolino, It. 63/D2
Bardonecchia, It. 64/C2
Bardonia, NY, US 169/K7
Bardsdale, Ca, US 166/B2
Bardsey (isl.), Wal, UK 34/D6
Bardstown, Ky, US 162/E2
Bardwell, Ky, US 162/C2
Bardwell, Tx, US 151/F1
Bareeda, Som. 118/D3
Bareggio, It. 62/B3
Barei (wadi), Sudan 116/D2
Bareilly, India 96/B1
Bareli, India 96/B4
Barellan, Austl. 133/C2
Barendrecht, Neth. 52/B5
Barentin, Fr. 57/F1
Barenton, Fr. 57/E3
Barents (sea), Eur. 29/H1
Barentu, Erit. 117/H2
Bäretswil, Swi. 61/E3
Barfleur, Fr. 56/D1
Barfleur (pt.), Fr. 56/D1
Barg-e Matāl, Afg. 98/A2
Barga, It. 62/D5
Barga, China 99/D5
Bargara, Austl. 134/D4
Bargarh, India 95/D1
Barge, It. 64/D3
Bargfeld-Stegen, Ger. 53/H1
Bargi, India 96/B4
Bargo, Austl. 133/E2
Bargoed, Wal, UK 36/C3
Bargteheide, Ger. 53/H1
Bārguna, Bang. 97/H4
Barguzin (riv.), Rus. 78/G1
Bārh, India 97/E3
Barhaj, India 96/D2
Barhalganj, India 96/D2
Barham, Austl. 133/B2
Barhamjia, Nepal 97/F2
Barharwā, India 97/F3
Barhi, India 97/E3
Barhiya, India 97/F3
Bari, It. 48/E2
Bāri, India 96/A2
Bari, D.R. Congo 120/D2
Bari Sardo, It. 48/A3
Bariadi, Tanz. 119/A2
Bariano, It. 62/C2
Baricella, It. 63/E4
Barichara, Col. 180/C3
Baricho, Kenya 119/B2
Barigazzo (peak), It. 62/C4
Barika, Alg. 112/H5
Barikiwa, Tanz. 119/B4
Barīkowt, Afg. 98/A2
Barillas, Guat. 176/D3
Barima (riv.), Guy. 181/G2
Barima-Waini (pol. reg.), Guy. 181/F3
Barinas (state), Ven. 180/D2
Barinas, Ven. 180/D2
Baring, Wa, US 144/D4
Baringa, D.R. Congo 121/E3
Baringa I, D.R. Congo 121/E2
Baringa-Twana, D.R. Congo 120/D4
Barinitas, Ven. 180/D2
Baripāda, India 97/F5
Bariri, Braz. 189/G2
Bārīs, Egypt 109/F3
Barisakho, Geo. 71/H4
Barisāl, Bang. 97/H4
Barisāl (pol. reg.), Bang. 97/H4
Barisan (mts.), Indo. 90/B4
Barisciano, It. 65/C3
Barito (riv.), Indo. 90/D4
Baritu, PN, Arg. 188/C2
Barjols, Fr. 64/C5
Bark (pt.), Wi, US 157/J4
Bark (lake), On, Can. 161/G2
Bark (riv.), Wi, US 167/N13
Bark River, Mi, US 160/C2
Barka Kāna, India 97/E4
Barkam, China 86/D2
Barkava, Lat. 41/M3
Barker (cr.), Austl. 131/M9
Barker (dam), Tx, US 151/M9
Barker, NY, US 160/V9
Barkéwol el Abiod, Mrta. 114/B2
Barkham, Eng, UK 30/A2
Barki Saria, India 97/E3
Barking and Dagenham (bor.), Eng, UK 30/D2
Barkley (dam), Ky, US 162/C2
Barkley (sound), BC, Can. 144/B3
Barkley (lake), Ky, US 162/D2
Barkly East, SAfr. 124/D3
Barkly Tableland (plat.), Austl. 127/C2
Barkly West, SAfr. 124/D3
Barkol (Barkol Kazak Zizhixian), China 78/C3
Barkol Kazak Zizhixian (Barkol), China 78/C3
Barksdale (A.F.B.), La, US 153/H4
Barlaston, Eng, UK 35/F6
Barlby, Eng, UK 35/G4
Barlee (range), Austl. 130/B2
Barlee (lake), Austl. 127/A3
Barlee Range Nature Reserve, Austl. 130/B2
Barletta, It. 48/E2
Barlin, Fr. 54/B3
Barlinek, Pol. 43/H2
Barling, Ar, US 153/G3
Barmedman, Austl. 133/C2
Bārmer, India 101/K3
Barmera, Austl. 131/J5
Barmouth, Wal, UK 36/B1
Barmstedt, Ger. 53/G1
Barna, Ire. 32/A3
Barnāla, India 98/C4
Barnard, Ks, US 154/E4
Barnard Castle, Eng, UK 35/G2
Barnasht, Egypt 113/C5
Barnaul, Rus. 99/D1
Bärnbach, Aus. 45/L3
Barnegat (bay), NJ, US 168/D4
Barnegat, NJ, US 168/D4
Barnegat (inlet), NJ, US 168/D4
Barnegat Light, NJ, US 168/D4
Barnes, Wi, US 157/J4
Barnesboro, Pa, US 161/G4
Barnesville, Mn, US 156/F4
Barnesville, Ga, US 162/E4
Barnet, Vt, US 161/K2
Barnet (nbrhd.), Eng, UK 30/C2
Barneveld, Neth. 52/C4
Barneville-Carteret, Fr. 56/D2
Barney, Ga, US 165/G2
Barneys (lake), Austl. 133/B1
Barnhart, Mo, US 162/B1
Barnhart, Tx, US 151/D2
Barni Hāt, India 97/H2
Barnoldswick, Eng, UK 35/F4
Barnsdall, Ok, US 153/F2
Barnsley, Eng, UK 35/G4
Barnsley (co.), Eng, UK 35/G4
Barnstaple, Eng, UK 36/B4
Barnstaple (Bideford) (bay), Eng, UK 36/B4
Barnstorf, Ger. 53/F3
Barntrup, Ger. 53/G5
Barnum, Wy, US 147/K2
Barnwell, Ab, Can. 145/H3
Barnwell, SC, US 163/G4
Baro, Gui. 114/C4
Baro, Nga. 115/G4
Baro Wenz (riv.), Eth. 117/G3
Baroda (Vadodara), India 92/B3
Barodia Kalān, India 96/B3
Baron, Ok, US 153/G3
Baron, Fr. 30/L4
Barona Ranch Ind. Res., Ca, US 148/D4
Barone (peak), It. 62/B2
Barong, China 78/D5
Barons, Ab, Can. 145/H2
Barooga, Austl. 133/B2
Baroua, CAfr. 117/E4
Barow (riv.), Ire. 34/A5
Barowghīl (pass), Afg. 101/K1
Barpāli, India 95/D1
Barpeta, India 97/H2
Barqin, Libya 108/B3
Barquisimeto, Ven. 180/D2
Barquisimeto (int'l arpt.), Ven. 180/D2
Barr, Fr. 60/D1
Barr, Sc, UK 34/D1
Barra (isl.), Sc, UK 31/Q8
Barra, Braz. 187/E1
Barra Bonita, Braz. 189/G2
Barra del Colorado, PN, CR 172/E5
Barra do Bugres, Braz. 185/G4
Barra do Corda, Braz. 183/E4
Barra do Cuanza, Ang. 120/C5
Barra do Dande, Ang. 120/C5
Barra do Garças, Braz. 186/B2
Barra do Piraí, Braz. 187/N7
Barra do Ribeiro, Braz. 189/G4
Barra Head (pt.), Sc, UK 31/Q8
Barra Mansa, Braz. 187/M7
Barra Patuca, Hon. 177/E3
Barra Punta Gorda, Nic. 177/F4
Barra Velha, Braz. 189/G3
Barraba, Austl. 132/D1
Barrackpur, India 97/G4
Barrage d'Ayamé I (dam), C.d'Iv. 114/E5
Barrage d'Ayamé Li (dam), C.d'Iv. 114/E5
Barrage de Bimont (res.), Fr. 64/B5
Barrage de Buyo (dam), C.d'Iv. 114/D5
Barrage de Castillon (dam), Fr. 64/C5
Barrage de Chaudanne (dam), Fr. 64/C5
Barrage de Kossou (dam), C.d'Iv. 114/D5
Barrage de la Grande Dixence (dam), Swi. 60/D5
Barrage de la Plate Taile (dam), Belg. 55/D3
Barrage de la Sainte-Croix (dam), Fr. 64/C5
Barrage de Lagdo (dam), Camr. 116/B3
Barrage de l'Eau d'Heure (dam), Belg. 55/D3
Barrage de Mauvoisin (dam), Swi. 60/D6
Barrage de Mbakaou (dam), Camr. 116/B4
Barrage de Serre-Ponçon (dam), Fr. 64/C4
Barrage de Taabo (dam), C.d'Iv. 114/D5
Barrage de Tignes (dam), Fr. 64/C1
Barrage de Vouglans (dam), Fr. 60/B5
Barrage Idriss I (res.), Mor. 112/B2
Barrage Mohamed V (res.), Mor. 112/C2
Barragem da Chicamba Real (dam), Moz. 123/G3
Barragem de Cabora Bassa (dam), Moz. 123/G2
Barragem Paso Real (res.), Braz. 189/F4
Barranca, Peru 184/B2
Barranca, Peru 184/B3
Barranca de Upía, Col. 180/C3
Barranca del Cobre PN, Mex. 174/D3
Barrancabermeja, Col. 180/C3
Barrancas, Col. 180/C2
Barrancas, Ven. 181/F2
Barrancas, Arg. 190/C3
Barrancas, Chile 190/N8
Barrancas, Arroyo (cr.), Arg. 188/E4
Barranco de Loba, Col. 180/C2
Barrancos, Port. 46/B3
Barranquilla, Col. 180/C2
Barras, Col. 180/C4
Barras, Braz. 183/F4
Barre, Vt, US 161/K2
Barre de Portugais (pt.), Gabon 120/B3
Barreal, Arg. 188/B4
Barreiras, Braz. 186/D2
Barreirinha, Braz. 182/B3
Barreirinhas, Braz. 183/F3
Barreiro, Port. 47/P10
Barreiros, Braz. 183/H5
Barrême, Fr. 64/C5
Barren (isl.), Madg. 125/G7
Barren (riv.), Ky, US 162/D2
Barren (Nosy Barren) (isls.), Madg. 125/G7
Barren River (lake), Ky, US 162/D2
Barrera, Bol. 185/E4
Barretal, Mex. 175/F3
Barretos, Braz. 189/G2
Barrett, Tx, US 151/M9
Barrhead, Sc, UK 33/B5
Barrhead, Ab, Can. 140/E3
Barrhill, Sc, UK 34/D1
Barrie, On, Can. 161/G2
Barrier (range), Austl. 131/J4
Barrière, BC, Can. 144/D2
Barrilla Draw (riv.), Tx, US 151/C2
Barrington, Il, US 167/P15
Barrington Hills, Il, US 167/P15
Barrington Tops (peak), Austl. 132/D1
Barrington Tops NP, Austl. 132/D1
Barringun, Austl. 132/C1
Barrīyat al Uşayfir, Egypt 113/B2
Barro Duro, Braz. 183/F4
Barron, Wi, US 157/J5
Barron Gorge NP, Austl. 134/B2
Barronett, Wi, US 157/J5
Barros Luco, Chile 188/B3
Barroso, Braz. 186/E4
Barrouallie, StV. 173/N9
Barrow (isl.), Austl. 127/A3
Barrow (pt.), Austl. 134/B1
Barrow (str.), Nun, Can. 140/G1
Barrow (riv.), Ire. 32/D4
Barrow, Ak, US 171/G1
Barrow (pt.), Ak, US 171/G1
Barrow Creek, Austl. 131/G2
Barrow Island, Austl. 130/B2
Barrow-in-Furness, Eng, UK 35/E3
Barrowby, Eng, UK 35/H6
Barrowford, Eng, UK 35/F4
Barruelo de Santullán, Sp. 46/C1
Barry, Wal, UK 36/C4
Barry M. Goldwater Air Force Range, Az, US 149/F4
Barry's Bay, On, Can. 161/H2
Barrytown, NZ 135/B3
Barsakel'mes (lake), Uzb. 71/L4
Barsalogho, Burk. 115/E3
Bārshi, India 95/B2
Barsinghausen, Ger. 53/G4
Bårslöv, Swe. 39/J6
Barssel, Ger. 53/E2
Barstow, Ca, US 148/D3
Bartang (riv.), Taj. 99/B4
Bartenheim, Fr. 60/D2
Barth, Ger. 40/E4
Bartholomä, Ger. 58/C5
Bartholomäberg, Aus. 61/F3
Bartica, Guy. 181/G3
Bartın, Turk. 70/E4
Bartle Frere (peak), Austl. 127/D2
Bartlesville, Ok, US 153/G2
Bartlett, Il, US 167/P16
Bartlett, Tn, US 162/C3
Bartlett, Ne, US 154/E3
Bartlett, Tx, US 151/F2
Bartley, WV, US 163/G2
Bartolomé Masó, Cuba 177/G1
Bartolomeu Dias, Moz. 123/G4
Barton, ND, US 156/D3
Barton, Vt, US 161/K2
Barton, Md, US 161/G5
Barton under Needwood, Eng, UK 37/E1
Barton-in-the-Clay, Eng, UK 37/F3
Barton-upon-Humber, Eng, UK 35/H4
Bartonsville, Pa, US 168/C2
Bartoszyce, Pol. 41/J4
Bartow, Ger. 40/E5
Bartow, Fl, US 164/M8
Barú (vol.), Pan. 177/F4
Bāruipur, India 97/G4
Baruman (riv.), Indo. 89/C2
Barumun (riv.), Indo. 90/B3
Barus, Indo. 89/B2
Baruta, Ven. 183/P7
Baruth, Ger. 43/G2
Baruun Huuray (phys. reg.), Mong. 78/C2
Baruun-Urt, Mong. 78/G2
Baruunsuu, Mong. 78/F3
Barview, Or, US 146/A2
Barvinkove, Ukr. 73/J3
Barwa Sāgar, India 96/B3
Barwāha, India 92/C3
Barwāla, India 98/C5
Barwāni, India 92/B3
Barwick, Ga, US 165/G2
Barwon (riv.), Austl. 127/D3
Barwon Heads, Austl. 133/B4
Barycz (riv.), Pol. 43/J3
Barysaw, Bela. 41/N4
Barysh, Rus. 71/H1
Baryshivka, Ukr. 72/F2
Barzanò, It. 62/C2
Bas-Caraquet, NB, Can. 158/E2
Bas-Congo (pol. reg.), D.R. Congo 120/A4
Bas-Rhin (dept.), Fr. 60/D1
Basa, C.d'Iv. 114/D5
Basaldella, It. 63/G1
Basankusu, D.R. Congo 120/D2
Basarabeasca, Mol. 72/E4
Basauri, Sp. 44/B5
Basavilbaso, Arg. 191/J10
Basawa, C.d'Iv. 114/D4
Basay, Phil. 88/C3
Bascharage, Lux. 55/E4
Baschurch, Eng, UK 36/D1
Bascom, Fl, US 165/F2
Bascuñán (pt.), Chile 188/B4
Basdorf, Ger. 42/Q6
Baseball Hall of Fame, NY, US 161/J3
Basekpio, D.R. Congo 117/E4
Basel, Swi. 60/D2
Basel/Mulhouse (int'l arpt.), Fr. 60/D2
Baselga di Pinè, It. 61/H5
Baselice, It. 65/D5
Baselland (canton), Swi. 60/D3
Bashaw, Ab, Can. 145/H1
Bashbīsh, Egypt 113/C2
Bashee (riv.), SAfr. 124/E3
Bashi (chan.), Phil.,Tai. 87/J4
Bashkaus (riv.), Rus. 78/B1
Bashkortostan Resp., Rus. 74/F4
Bashmakovo, Rus. 71/G1
Bāsht, Iran 103/G4
Bashtanka, Ukr. 72/G4
Ba'shūm, Sudan 117/F2
Basilan (isl.), Phil. 88/C4
Basilan (str.), Phil. 88/C4
Basilan (peak), Phil. 88/C4
Basildon, Eng, UK 37/G3
Basile, La, US 164/B2
Basilica di Fieschi, It. 62/C5
Basilicata (reg.), It. 48/D2
Bāsim, India 95/C1
Basin, Wy, US 147/J1
Basin, Mt, US 145/H4
Basingstoke (canal), Eng, UK 30/A3
Basingstoke, Eng, UK 37/E4
Basīrhāt, India 97/G4
Basīrpur, Pak. 98/B4
Baška, Cro. 45/L4
Baskahegan (lake), Me, US 158/C3
Başkale, Turk. 103/F2
Baskatong (res.), Qu, Can. 161/J1
Baskerville (cape), Austl. 128/A4
Baskett Slough Nat'l Wild. Ref., Or, US 146/B1
Baskil, Turk. 102/D2
Baskin, La, US 153/J4
Başkomutan NP, Turk. 102/B2
Başköy, Turk. 102/D2
Basmat, India 95/C2
Bāsmenj, Iran 103/F2
Bāsoda, India 96/A4
Basodesh, Tanz. 119/A3
Basodino (peak), It. 61/E5
Basoko, D.R. Congo 121/E2
Basoli, India 98/C3
Basongo, D.R. Congo 121/E4
Basque Provinces (prov.), Sp. 44/B5
Bass (str.), Austl. 127/D4
Bass Is. (Marotiri) (isl.), FrPol. 137/L7
Bass River, NS, Can. 158/F3
Bass Rock (isl.), Sc, UK 33/D4
Bassae (Vassés) (ruin), Gre. 49/G4
Bassano, Ab, Can. 145/H2
Bassano del Grappa, It. 63/E2
Bassano Romano, It. 65/B3
Bassari, Togo 115/F4
Bassas da India (isl.), Reun., Fr. 123/H4
Basse Santa Su, Gam. 114/B3
Basse-Kotto (pref.), CAfr. 116/D4
Basse-Normandie (pol. reg.), Fr. 57/D3
Basse-Terre (isl.), Guad. 173/J4
Basse-Terre, Fr. 173/N8
Bassecourt, Swi. 60/D3
Bassein (riv.), Myan. 93/F4
Bassein (Pathein), Myan. 86/B5
Bassein (Vasai), India 101/K5
Bassenge, Belg. 55/E2
Bassenheim, Ger. 55/G3
Bassens, Fr. 64/B1
Bassenthwaite (lake), Eng, UK 35/E2
Basseterre (cap.), StK. 173/N8
Bassett, Tx, US 153/G4
Bassett, Ne, US 154/E2
Bassett, Va, US 163/H2
Bassikounou, Mrta. 114/D3
Bassum, Ger. 53/F3
Basswood (lake), Can.,US 157/J3
Båstad, Swe. 40/E3
Bastak, Iran 103/H5
Basţām, Iran 103/H2
Bastar, India 95/D2
Bastelicaccia, Fr. 48/A2
Bastheim, Ger. 58/D2
Bastī, India 96/D2
Bastia, Fr. 48/A1
Bastia, It. 65/B1
Bastogne, Belg. 55/E4
Bastos, Braz. 189/G2
Bastrop, La, US 153/J4
Bastrop, Tx, US 150/F2
Basu (cape), Indo. 89/C3
Basyūn, Egypt 113/B3
Bat Khela, Pak. 98/A2
Bat Shelomo, Isr. 105/B3
Bat Yam, Isr. 105/B4
Bata, EqG. 120/B2
Bata-Siala, D.R. Congo 120/C4
Bataan (mt.), Phil. 88/C2
Batabanó (gulf), Cuba 172/E3
Batac, Phil. 88/C1
Batagay, Rus. 75/P3
Batai (pass), Pak. 98/A3
Batak, Bul. 49/J2
Batakan, Indo. 90/D4
Batakūt, India 98/C3
Batāla, India 98/C4
Batalha, Port. 46/A3
Batalha, Braz. 183/F4
Batallas, Bol. 184/D5
Bataly, Kaz. 71/M1
Batama, D.R. Congo 121/F2
Batamshinskiy, Kaz. 71/L2
Batan (isls.), Phil. 77/M7
Batang, China 86/C2
Batang, Indo. 89/E4
Batangafo, CAfr. 116/C4
Batangas, Phil. 88/C2
Batangtoru, Indo. 89/B2
Bātāru, India 92/B2
Batatais, Braz. 189/H2
Batataria (bay), La, US 164/C3
Batavia, NY, US 161/G3
Batavia, Il, US 167/P16
Batavia, Oh, US 162/E1
Bataysk, Rus. 73/K4
Batchelor, La, US 164/C2
Batchelor, Austl. 128/C3
Batchwana Bay, On, Can. 160/D1
Bătdambang, Camb. 94/C3
Bate (bay), Austl. 134/H9
Bateman, Sk, Can. 145/L2
Batemans (bay), Austl. 133/E2
Batemans Bay, Austl. 133/E2
Batesburg-Leesville, SC, US 163/G4
Batesville, Al, US 165/F1
Batesville, Ar, US 153/J3
Batesville, In, US 160/D5
Batesville, Ms, US 162/C3
Batesville, Tx, US 151/E3
Batesville, Va, US 163/H2
Batetskiy, Rus. 41/P2
Bath (range), Austl. 129/D3
Bath, NS, Can. 158/D2
Bath, On, Can. 161/H2
Bath, Eng, UK 36/D4
Bath, Neth. 52/B6
Bath, NY, US 161/H3
Bath, Pa, US 168/C2
Bath (Berkeley Springs), WV, US 161/G5
Bath and Northeast Somerset, (co.), Eng, UK 36/D4
Bath Springs, Tn, US 162/C3
Batha (pref.), Chad 116/C2
Batha (riv.), Chad 116/C2
Batha de Laïri (riv.), Chad 116/C3
Bathgate, ND, US 156/F3
Bathgate, Sc, UK 33/C5
Bathmen, Neth. 52/D4
Bathsheba, Bar. 173/P9
Bathurst, NB, Can. 158/E2
Bathurst (inlet), Nun, Can. 140/F2
Bathurst (isl.), Nun, Can. 139/G2
Bathurst (cape), NW, Can. 171/N1
Bathurst, Austl. 133/D1
Bathurst (isl.), Austl. 128/C2
Bathurst Abor. Land, Austl. 128/C2
Bathurst Inlet, Nun, Can. 140/F2
Batī, Eth. 118/B3
Batian (peak), Kenya 119/B2
Bāţiāq-e Gāv Khūnī (lake), Iran 103/H3
Batié, Burk. 114/E4
Batik (mts.), China 78/C2
Bāţin (wadi), SAr. 100/E3
Batiquitos (lag.), Ca, US 166/C4
Batiscan (riv.), Qu, Can. 158/A2
Batley, Eng, UK 35/G4
Batlow, Austl. 133/D2
Batman, Turk. 102/E2
Batman (dam), Turk. 102/E2
Batna (wilaya), Alg. 111/G2
Batna, Alg. 112/J5
Batoche Nat'l Hist. Site, Sk, Can. 145/L1
Batoka, Zam. 123/E3
Baton Rouge (cap.), La, US 164/C2
Batopilas, Mex. 174/D3
Batoti, India 98/C3
Batouri, Camr. 116/B4
Batovi (riv.), Braz. 186/B2
Baţrā' (ruin), Jor. 104/D4
Baţrah, Egypt 113/C2
Batsawul, Afg. 98/A2
Båtsfjord, Nor. 38/J1
Batsto, NJ, US 168/D4
Batsto (riv.), NJ, US 168/D4
Batsto Historic Village, NJ, US 168/D4
Battaglia Terme, It. 63/E3
Battali, Bang. 97/H4
Battenberg, Ger. 53/F6
Bätterkinden, Swi. 60/D3
Battersby, Eng, UK 35/G3
Battersea (nbrhd.), Eng, UK 30/C2
Battiest, Ok, US 153/G3
Battipaglia, It. 65/D6
Battle (riv.), Ab,Sk, Can. 140/E3
Battle, Eng, UK 37/G5
Battle (riv.), Ab, Can. 145/J1
Battle Creek, Mi, US 160/D3
Battle Creek, Ne, US 154/F3
Battle Creek, Ia, US 155/G2
Battle Lake, Mn, US 157/G4
Battle Mountain, Nv, US 146/E3
Battleboro, NC, US 163/J2
Battlefield, Mo, US 153/H2
Battleford, Sk, Can. 145/K1
Battock (mt.), Sc, UK 33/D3
Batu (peak), Eth. 118/A4
Batu (isls.), Indo. 90/A4
Batu (peak), Malay. 90/D3
Batu (bay), Malay. 90/D3
Batu (cape), Indo. 91/E3
Batu Caves, Malay. 89/C2
Batu Gajah, Malay. 89/C1
Batu Pahat, Malay. 89/C2
Batu Puteh (peak), Malay. 89/C1
Batuco, Chile 190/N8
Batudaka (isl.), Indo. 91/F4
Batuensambang (peak), Indo. 90/D3
Batui, Indo. 91/F4
Batulaki, Phil. 88/D4
Batumi (int'l arpt.), Geo. 71/G4
Bat'umi, Geo. 71/G4
Baturaja, Indo. 89/D4
Baturino, Rus. 69/P5
Baturité, Braz. 183/G4
Baturusa, Indo. 89/D3
Baturyn, Ukr. 73/G2
Batusangkar, Indo. 89/C3
Batyrevo, Rus. 69/K5
Batys Qazaqstan, Kaz. 74/E5
Batys Qazaqstan Oblast, Kaz. 74/E5
Batz-sur-Mer, Fr. 56/C6
Bauang, Phil. 88/C1
Baubau, Indo. 128/A1
Bauchi (state), Nga. 115/H4
Bauchi, Nga. 115/H4
Baud, Fr. 56/B5
Baudette, Mn, US 157/G3
Baudh, India 95/E1
Baudó (riv.), Col. 180/B3
Baudó (mts.), Col. 177/G5
Baudon, Pic de (peak), Fr. 64/D5
Baugé, Fr. 57/E5
Baukau, ETim. 128/B2
Bauld (cape), Nf, Can. 141/L3
Baulkham Hills, Austl. 133/E1
Baulmes, Swi. 60/C4
Bauman (peak), Togo 115/F5
Baume-les-Dames, Fr. 60/C3
Baumholder, Ger. 55/G4
Baunach, Ger. 58/D3
Baunach (riv.), Ger. 58/D2
Baunatal, Ger. 53/G6
Baunei, It. 48/A2
Baungon, Phil. 88/D3
Baures, Bol. 185/F4
Baures (riv.), Bol. 185/E4
Baurú, Braz. 189/G2
Bauska, Lat. 41/L3
Bautino, Kaz. 71/J3
Bautzen, Ger. 43/H3
Bavans, Fr. 60/C3
Bavarian Alps (mts.), Aus., Ger. 67/F1
Bavay, Fr. 54/C3
Båven (lake), Swe. 40/G2
Baveno, It. 61/E6
Bavent, Fr. 57/E2
Baviácora, Mex. 174/C2
Bavilliers, Fr. 60/C2
Bavly, Rus. 69/M5
Baw Baw (mt.), Austl. 133/C3
Baw Baw NP, Austl. 133/C3
Bawan, Indo. 90/D4
Bawāna, India 98/D5
Bawang (cape), Indo. 90/C4
Bawean (isl.), Indo. 90/D5
Bawku, Gha. 115/E4
Bawlake, Myan. 94/B2
Bawlf, Ab, Can. 145/H1
Baxian, China 87/F1
Baxkorgan, China 99/F4
Baxley, Ga, US 165/G2
Baxoi, China 86/C2
Baxter, Mn, US 157/G4
Baxter Springs, Ks, US 153/G2
Bay (dam), Wi, US 155/K1
Bay, Ar, US 162/B3
Bay Bulls, Nf, Can. 159/L2
Bay City, Tx, US 151/G3
Bay City, Mi, US 160/E3
Bay City, Wi, US 155/H1
Bay City, Or, US 144/C5
Bay de Verde, Nf, Can. 159/L1
Bay Lake, Mn, US 157/H4
Bay Lake, Fl, US 164/M7
Bay L'Argent, Nf, Can. 159/K2
Bay Mills Ind. Res., Mi, US 160/D1
Bay Minette, Al, US 164/E2
Bay Port, Mi, US 160/E3
Bay Ridge (nbrhd.), NY, US 169/J9
Bay Ridge (Bayridge), Fl, US 164/M6
Bay Roberts, Nf, Can. 159/L2
Bay Saint Lawrence, NS, Can. 159/G2
Bay Saint Louis, Ms, US 164/D2
Bay Springs, Ms, US 164/D2
Bay Springs (lake), Ms, US 162/C3
Bay View, NZ 135/D2
Bayāḑ an Naşārá, Egypt 113/C6
Bayamo, Cuba 177/G1
Bayamón, PR 173/M8
Bayan, Indo. 91/E5
Bayan, Mong. 78/D2
Bayan, China 79/K2
Bayan Har (mts.), China 78/D5
Bayan Mod, China 78/E3
Bayan Obo, China 78/F3
Bayan Qagan, China 79/J2
Bayan-Ölgiy (prov.), Mong. 78/B2
Bayan-Ovoo, Mong. 78/C3
Bayan-Ulaan, Mong. 78/E2
Bayanaul, Kaz. 99/C1
Bayanbulag, Mong. 78/F2
Bayangol, Rus. 78/E1
Bayanhongor, Mong. 78/E2
Bayanhongor (prov.), Mong. 78/D3
Bayanhushuu, Mong. 78/C2
Bayanhushuu, Mong. 78/E2
Bayannuur, Mong. 99/F2
Bayano (lake), Pan. 177/G4
Bayansayr, Mong. 78/D2
Bayanterem, Mong. 78/G2
Bayantsagaan, Mong. 78/E2
Bayard, WV, US 161/G5
Bayard, NM, US 149/H4
Bayard, Ne, US 154/C3
Bayard, Ia, US 155/G3
Bayat, Turk. 70/E4
Bayawan, Phil. 88/C3
Baybach (riv.), Ger. 55/G3
Baybay, Phil. 88/D3
Bayboro, NC, US 163/J3
Bayburt (prov.), Turk. 70/F4
Bayburt, Turk. 102/E1
Baychunas, Kaz. 71/K3
Baychurovo, Rus. 73/M2
Baydaratskaya (bay), Rus. 74/G2
Baydhabo (Baidoa), Som. 118/B5
Baydrog (riv.), Mong. 78/D2
Bayel, Fr. 60/A1
Bayelsa (state), Nga. 115/G5
Bayerischer Wald (hills), Ger. 59/F4
Bayerischer Wald NP, Ger. 59/G5
Bayern (state), Ger. 42/F4
Bayeux, Fr. 57/E2
Bayeux, Braz. 183/H4
Bayfield, Co, US 149/J2
Baygorria (res.), Uru. 191/K10
Bayḩān al Qişāb, Yem. 118/C2
Baykal (mts.), Rus. 75/L4
Baykal (lake), Rus. 77/L4
Baykal, Rus. 78/E1
Baykal'sk, Rus. 78/E1
Baykan, Turk. 102/E2
Baykibashevo, Rus. 69/N5
Baykit, Rus. 74/K3
Baykonyr, Kaz. 74/G5
Baymak, Rus. 71/L1
Baynes Lake, BC, Can. 144/G3
Bayo Grande (peak), Arg. 188/C3
Bayombong, Phil. 88/C1
Bayon, Fr. 60/C1
Bayona, Sp. 46/A1
Bayonet (pt.), Fl, US 164/K7
Bayonet Point, Fl, US 164/K7
Bayonne, NJ, US 169/J9
Bayonne, Fr. 44/C5
Bayonne-Anglet (Biarritz) (arpt.), Fr. 44/C5
Bayou Bartholomew (riv.), Ar, US 162/B4
Bayou Cane, La, US 164/C3
Bayou D'arbonne (lake), La, US 151/H1
Bayou de View (riv.), Ar, US 162/B3
Bayou Lafourche (riv.), La, US 164/C3
Bayou Macon (riv.), La, US 162/B4
Bayou Meto (riv.), Ar, US 162/B3
Bayou Nezpique (bayou), La, US 151/H2
Bayou Phalia (riv.), Ms, US 162/B4
Bayou Pierre (riv.), La, US 151/H1
Bayou Pierre (riv.), Ms, US 162/A4
Bayou Queue de Tortue (riv.), La, US 164/B2
Bayou Teche (riv.), La, US 151/H2
Bayou Vista, La, US 164/C3
Bayóvar, Peru 184/A2
Bayport, Mn, US 157/Q6
Bayport, Fl, US 164/K6
Bayport, NY, US 169/E2
Bayramaly, Trkm. 101/H1
Bayramıç, Turk. 49/K3
Bayreuth, Ger. 59/E3
Bayridge (Bay Ridge), Fl, US 164/M6
Bayrūt (gov.), Leb. 105/C1
Bayrūt (Beirut) (cap.), Leb. 105/C1
Bays (lake), On, Can. 161/G2
Bayse (riv.), Fr. 47/E1
Bayşehir (lake), Turk. 102/B2
Bayside (nbrhd.), NY, US 169/K8
Bayston Hill, Eng, UK 36/D1
Baysville, On, Can. 161/G2
Bayswater (nbrhd.), Austl. 130/K6
Bayt al Faqīh, Yem. 118/B2
Bayt Fajjār, WBnk. 105/C5
Bayt Ḩanīnā, WBnk. 105/C5
Bayt Ḩānūn, Gaza 105/B5
Bayt Jālā, WBnk. 105/C5
Bayt Lāhiyah, Gaza 105/B5
Bayt Laḩm (Bethlehem), WBnk. 105/C5
Bayt Sāḩūr, WBnk. 105/C5
Baytown, Tx, US 151/N9
Bayudha (des.), Sudan 109/G5
Bayunglencir, Indo. 89/C3
Bayville, NY, US 169/L8
Baywood-Los Osos, Ca, US 148/B3
Bayy al Kabīr (wadi), Libya 108/B2
Bayzhansay, Kaz. 99/A3
Baza, Sp. 46/D4
Bazainville, Fr. 30/G5
Bazardüzü (peak), Azer. 71/H4

Bāzarg – Bern-Be

Bāzargān, Iran 103/F2
Bazarnyye Mataki, Rus. 69/L5
Bazarshulan, Kaz. 71/J2
Bazèga (prov.), Burk. 115/E4
Bazemont, Fr. 30/H5
Bazet, Fr. 44/D5
Bazhong, China 87/E2
Bazine, Ks, US 152/E1
Bazoches-sur-Hoëne, Fr. 57/F3
Bazouges, Fr. 57/E5
Bāzpur, India 96/B1
Bazuru, D.R. Congo 121/F2
Bazzano, It. 63/E4
Beach, ND, US 156/B4
Beach Haven, NJ, US 168/D4
Beach Meadows, NS, Can. 158/E3
Beachburg, On, Can. 161/H2
Beachport, Austl. 132/B3
Beachton, Ga, US 165/F2
Beachwood, NJ, US 168/D4
Beachy (pt.), Eng, UK 44/D1
Beachy (head), Eng, UK 37/G5
Beacon, NY, US 161/K4
Beacon, Tn, US 162/C3
Beacon (peak), Wal, UK 36/C2
Beacon Hill, Fl, US 165/F3
Beaconsfield, Austl. 132/C4
Beaconsfield, Qu, Can. 159/N7
Beaconsfield, Eng, UK 37/F3
Beagle (gulf), Austl. 128/C3
Beagle Bay Abor. Rsv., Austl. 128/A4
Beagle Bay Mission, Austl. 128/A4
Beal (range), Austl. 134/A4
Béal Traversier, Pic du (peak), Fr. 64/C3
Bealanana, Madg. 125/J6
Beale AFB, Ca, US 146/C4
Beals (cr.), Tx, US 151/D1
Beaminster, Eng, UK 36/D5
Beampingaratra (ridge), Madg. 125/H9
Beamsville, On, Can. 160/U9
Bear (hills), Sk, Can. 145/K1
Bear (isl.), Nor. 192/E
Bear (mt.), Ak, US 171/K3
Bear (mt.), Ak, US 171/K2
Bear (riv.), Ca, US 146/C4
Bear, De, US 168/C4
Bear (hill), Ne, US 154/D3
Bear (mtn.), SD, US 154/C2
Bear (lake), Ut, US 142/D3
Bear (cr.), Wy, US 154/B3
Bear Creek, Al, US 162/D3
Bear Lake, Mi, US 160/C2
Bear Lake NWR, Id, US 147/H2
Bear Lodge (mts.), Wy, US 154/B1
Bear River, NS, Can. 158/E3
Bear River (bay), Ut, US 147/G3
Bear River NWR, Ut, US 147/G3
Bear Town, Ms, US 164/C2
Beara (reg.), Ire. 32/A6
Bearden, Ar, US 153/H4
Bearden, Ok, US 153/F3
Beardmore, On, Can. 157/L3
Beardstown, Il, US 155/J3
Bearfort (mtn.), NJ, US 169/H7
Bearma (riv.), India 96/B4
Bearpaw (mts.), Mt, US 145/J3
Bearsden, Sc, UK 33/B5
Bearstead, Eng, UK 30/E3
Beartooth (mts.), Mt, US 147/H1
Beās (riv.), India 96/B3
Beas de Segura, Sp. 46/D3
Beasain, Sp. 44/B5
Beata (cape), DRep. 173/G4
Beata (pt.), DRep. 177/J2
Beata (isl.), Thai. 177/J2
Beatenberg, Swi. 60/D4
Beatrice, Zim. 123/F3
Beatrice, Ne, US 155/F3
Beatrice (cape), Austl. 129/E3
Beattie, Ks, US 155/F4
Beattock, Sc, UK 33/C6
Beatty, Nv, US 148/D2
Beattystown, NJ, US 168/D2
Beattyville, Ky, US 162/F2
Beau Bassin-Rose Hill, Mrts. 125/T15
Beaucaire, Fr. 64/A5
Beaucamps-le-Vieux, Fr. 54/A4
Beauceville, Qu, Can. 158/B2
Beauchamp, Fr. 30/J4
Beauchastel, Fr. 64/A3
Beaucourt, Fr. 60/C3
Beaudesert, Austl. 134/D4
Beaufort, Fr. 60/B4
Beaufort, Lux. 55/F4
Beaufort, Fr. 64/C1
Beaufort, Austl. 132/B3
Beaufort (sea), Can.,US 139/C2
Beaufort, Malay. 88/A4
Beaufort, SC, US 163/G4
Beaufort, NC, US 163/J3
Beaufort (inlet), NC, US 163/J3
Beaufort Castle (ruins), Leb. 105/D2
Beaufort Marine Corps Air Base, SC, US 163/G4
Beaufort West, SAfr. 124/C4
Beaufort-en-Vallée, Fr. 57/E6
Beaugency, Fr. 57/G5
Beauharnois, Qu, Can. 161/K2
Beauharnois (co.), Qu, Can. 159/M7
Beaujolais (mts.), Fr. 44/F4
Beaulieu, Eng, UK 37/E5
Beaulieu-sur-Mer, Fr. 64/D5
Beauly, Sc, UK 33/B2
Beauly (riv.), Sc, UK 33/B2
Beauly Firth (lake), Sc, UK 33/B2
Beaumaris, Wal, UK 34/D5
Beaumes-de-Venise, Fr. 64/B4
Beaumesnil, Fr. 57/F2
Beaumont, Fr. 56/D1
Beaumont, Belg. 55/D3
Beaumont, Ms, US 164/D2
Beaumont, Ca, US 166/D3
Beaumont, Fr. 44/E4
Beaumont, Ab, Can. 145/H1
Beaumont, Tx, US 151/G2
Beaumont-de-Lomagne, Fr. 44/D5
Beaumont-le-Roger, Fr. 57/F2
Beaumont-lès-Valence, Fr. 64/A3
Beaumont-sur-Oise, Fr. 30/J4
Beaumont-sur-Sarthe, Fr. 57/F4
Beaupréau, Fr. 57/E6
Beauquesne, Fr. 54/B3
Beauraing, Belg. 55/D3
Beaurainville, Fr. 54/A3
Beauregard, Ms, US 164/C2
Beaurepaire, Fr. 64/B2
Beaurevoir, Fr. 54/C4
Beausejour, Mb, Can. 156/F2
Beausoleil, Fr. 64/D5
Beautheil, Fr. 30/M5
Beautiful (mtn.), NM, US 149/H2
Beautor, Fr. 54/C4
Beauvais, Fr. 54/B5
Beauval, Fr. 54/B3
Beauvoir, Fr. 30/L6
Beaver (hills), Sk, Can. 156/C2
Beaver (riv.), Yk, Can. 140/D2
Beaver, Ak, US 171/J2
Beaver (lake), Ar, US 153/H2
Beaver (cr.), Co, US 154/C4
Beaver (cr.), Co,Ks, US 154/D4
Beaver, La, US 164/B2
Beaver (isl.), Mi, US 160/D2
Beaver (cr.), Ne, US 154/E3
Beaver, Oh, US 163/F1
Beaver, Ok, US 152/D2
Beaver, Pa, US 160/F4
Beaver, Ut, US 149/F1
Beaver (riv.), Ut, US 147/J4
Beaver, Wa, US 144/B3
Beaver (dam), Wi, US 155/K2
Beaver Bay, Mn, US 157/J4
Beaver City, Ne, US 154/E3
Beaver Creek, Yk, Can. 171/K3
Beaver Crossing, Ne, US 155/F3
Beaver Dam, Ky, US 162/D2
Beaver Dam, Wi, US 155/K2
Beaver Dam (lake), Wi, US 155/K2
Beaver Falls, Pa, US 160/F4
Beaver Meadows, Pa, US 168/C2
Beaver Springs, Pa, US 168/A2
Beaverbank, NS, Can. 158/F3
Beavercreek, Oh, US 160/D5
Beaverdam, Va, US 163/J2
Beaverdell, BC, Can. 144/E3
Beaverhead (mts.), Mt, US 147/G1
Beaverhead (riv.), Mt, US 147/G1
Beaverhill (lake), Ab, Can. 145/H1
Beaverton, On, Can. 161/G2
Beaverton, Mi, US 160/D3
Beaverton, Or, US 146/B1
Beavertown, Pa, US 168/A2
Beāwar, India 92/B2
Bebe, Tx, US 151/F3
Bébédjia, Chad 116/C3
Bebedouro, Braz. 189/G2
Beberibe, Braz. 183/G4
Bebington, Eng, UK 35/E5
Beboto, Chad 116/C3
Béboura Iii, CAfr. 116/C4
Bebra, Ger. 53/G7
Becal, Mex. 176/D1
Bécancour, Qu, Can. 161/K1
Beccles, Eng, UK 37/H2
Bečej, Yugo. 50/E3
Becerreá, Sp. 46/B1
Bechar, Alg. 111/E3
Bechar (wilaya), Alg. 110/E3
Becharof (lake), Ak, US 171/G4
Bechhofen, Ger. 55/G5
Bechhofen, Ger. 58/D4
Bechtheim, Ger. 58/B3
Bechyně, Czh. 59/H4
Becida, Mn, US 157/G4
Beckdorf, Ger. 53/G2
Beckenham (nbrhd.), Eng, UK 30/D2
Beckenried, Swi. 61/E4
Becker, Ms, US 162/C4
Beckingen, Ger. 55/F5
Beckingham, Eng, UK 35/H5
Beckley, WV, US 163/G2
Beckton, Wy, US 147/K1
Beckum, Ger. 53/F5
Beckville, Tx, US 151/G1
Beckwourth, Ca, US 146/C4
Beclean, Rom. 51/G2
Bécon-les-Granits, Fr. 57/E5
Becs de Bosson (peak), Swi. 60/D5
Bedale, Eng, UK 35/G3
Bédaoyo, Chad 116/C4
Bédarieux, Fr. 44/E5
Bédarrides, Fr. 64/A4
Bedaya, Chad 116/C3
Bedburg, Ger. 55/F2
Bedburg-Hau, Ger. 52/D5
Beddau, Wal, UK 36/C3
Beddgelert, Wal, UK 34/D5
Bedelē, Eth. 117/H3
Beder, Den. 40/D3
Bederkesa, Ger. 53/G1
Bederkesa, Ger. 53/F1
Bedēsa, Eth. 118/B3
Bedford (cape), Austl. 134/B1
Bedford, Qu, Can. 161/K2
Bedford, SAfr. 124/D4
Bedford, Eng, UK 37/F2
Bedford, Ia, US 155/G3
Bedford, In, US 162/D1
Bedford, Ky, US 162/E1
Bedford, NH, US 161/L3
Bedford, Pa, US 161/G4
Bedford, Tx, US 150/K7
Bedford, Va, US 163/H2
Bedford, Wy, US 147/H2
Bedford Hills, NY, US 169/E1
Bedford Level (phys. reg.), Eng, UK 37/F2
Bedford Park, Il, US 167/Q16
Bedfordshire (co.), Eng, UK 37/F2
Bedias, Tx, US 151/G2
Bédiondo, Chad 116/C3
Bedlington, Eng, UK 35/G1
Bedmond, Eng, UK 30/B1
Bedok (nbrhd.), Sing. 89/J6
Bedong, Malay. 89/C1
Bedonia, It. 62/C4
Bédouaram, Niger 116/B2
Bedourie, Austl. 131/H3
Bedretto, Swi. 61/E5
Bedrock, Co, US 149/H1
Bedsted, Den. 40/C3
Bedum, Neth. 52/D2
Bedwas, Wal, UK 36/C3
Bedworth, Eng, UK 37/E2
Bee (cr.), Eng, UK 107/F6
Bee Branch, Ar, US 153/H3
Bee Spring, Ky, US 162/D2
Beebe, Ar, US 153/J3
Beech Grove, In, US 160/C5
Beecher Falls, Vt, US 161/L2
Beecher Island, Co, US 154/C4
Beechgrove, Tn, US 162/D3
Beechworth, Austl. 133/C3
Beechy, Sk, Can. 145/L2
Beef Island (int'l arpt.), UK 173/M8
Beek, Neth. 55/E2
Beek, Neth. 52/C5
Beekman, La, US 153/J4
Beelbangera, Austl. 133/C2
Beelen, Ger. 53/F5
Beeler, Ks, US 152/D1
Beelitz, Ger. 42/P7
Beenleigh, Austl. 134/D4
Beer, Eng, UK 36/C5
Beer (pt.), Eng, UK 36/C5
Be'er Menuḥa, Isr. 104/D4
Be'er Sheva' (Beersheba), Isr. 105/B6
Beerato, Som. 118/C3
Beerfelden, Ger. 58/B3
Be'eri, Isr. 105/A6
Beernem, Belg. 54/C1
Beersheba (Be'er Sheva'), Isr. 105/B6
Beerzel, Belg. 55/D1
Beesel, Neth. 52/D6
Beeville, Tx, US 150/F3
Befale, D.R. Congo 121/E2
Befandriana, Madg. 125/G8
Befandriana, Madg. 125/J6
Befasy, Madg. 125/H8
Befori, D.R. Congo 121/E2
Beforona, Madg. 125/J7
Befotaka, Madg. 125/H8
Befotaka, Madg. 125/J6
Beg (lake), NI, UK 34/B2
Bega (riv.), Ger. 53/F5
Bega, Austl. 133/D3
Bega Veche (riv.), Cro. 50/E3
Begamganj, India 96/B4
Begamganj, Bang. 97/H4
Bégard, Fr. 56/B3
Begarslan (peak), Trkm. 71/K4
Begejci, Yugo. 50/E3
Beggs, Ok, US 153/F3
Bēgī, Eth. 117/G3
Begichev (isl.), Rus. 75/M2
Begna (riv.), Nor. 38/D3
Begoml', Bela. 41/N4
Begumpet (int'l arpt.), India 95/C2
Begunitsy, Rus. 41/N2
Begusarai, India 97/F3
Béhague (pt.), FrG. 182/D1
Behāla, India 92/E3
Behala (str.), Indo. 90/B4
Behamberg, Aus. 59/H6
Behara, Madg. 125/H9
Behat, India 98/D4
Behbahān, Iran 103/G4
Beheloka, Madg. 125/G8
Behenjy-Afovany, Madg. 125/H7
Behleg, China 78/C4
Béhoust, Fr. 30/H5
Behren-lès-Forbach, Fr. 55/F5
Behri (riv.), Nepal 96/C1
Behshahr, Iran 103/H2
Bei (mts.), China 74/K5
Bei'an, China 79/K2
Beiba, China 78/F5
Beibei, China 87/E2
Beida (riv.), China 78/D4
Beidianzi, China 81/A4
Beierfeld, Ger. 59/F1
Beigantang (isl.), Tai. 87/J3
Beigua (peak), It. 62/B5
Beiguo, China 80/L8
Beihai, China 87/F4
Beijing (prov.), China 78/H3
Beijing (cap.), China 80/H7
Beijing Capital (int'l arpt.), China 80/H6
Beilen, Neth. 52/D3
Beiling, China 87/G3
Beiliu, China 87/F4
Beilngries, Ger. 59/E4
Beilstein, Ger. 58/C4
Beilu (riv.), China 78/C5
Beilun (pass), China 87/E4
Bein Tharsuinn (peak), Sc, UK 33/B1
Beinamar, Chad 116/B3
Beinasco, It. 64/D2
Beindersheim, Ger. 58/B3
Beinn a' Chuallaich (peak), Sc, UK 33/B3
Beinn a' Ghlò (peak), Sc, UK 33/C3
Beinn a' Mheadhoin (lake), Sc, UK 33/B2
Beinn Bhàn (peak), Sc, UK 33/A3
Beinn Bheula (peak), Sc, UK 33/B4
Beinn Bhrotain (peak), Sc, UK 33/C2
Beinn Bhuidhe (peak), Sc, UK 33/B4
Beinn Bhuidhe Mhór (peak), Sc, UK 33/B2
Beinn Dearg (peak), Sc, UK 33/B1
Beinn Dearg (peak), Sc, UK 33/C3
Beinn Dòrain (peak), Sc, UK 33/B4
Beinn Eighe (peak), Sc, UK 33/A1
Beinn Heasgarnich (peak), Sc, UK 33/B3
Beinn Mholach (peak), Sc, UK 33/B3
Beinn Mhór (peak), Sc, UK 33/A4
Beinwil am See, Swi. 60/E3
Beipiao, China 80/E2
Beira (int'l arpt.), Moz. 123/G3
Beira, Moz. 123/G3
Beira Alta, Ang. 120/C5
Beirong, China 87/F2
Beiru (riv.), China 80/C4
Beirut (int'l arpt.), Leb. 105/C1
Beirut (Bayrūt) (cap.), Leb. 105/C1
Beiseker, Ab, Can. 145/H2
Beishan, China 78/D3
Beishan, China 87/F3
Beit Jann, Isr. 105/C3
Beitbridge, Zim. 123/F4
Beith, Sc, UK 33/B5
Beiuş, Rom. 50/F2
Beizhen, China 81/A2
Beja, Port. 46/B3
Beja (dist.), Port. 46/A4
Bejaïa, Alg. 112/H4
Bejaïa (wilaya), Alg. 112/H4
Béjar, Sp. 46/C2
Bejhi (riv.), Pak. 101/J3
Bekasi, Indo. 89/D4
Bekdash, Trkm. 71/K4
Békés (prov.), Hun. 50/E2
Békés, Hun. 50/E2
Békéscsaba, Hun. 50/E2
Bekilli, Turk. 102/B2
Bekily, Madg. 125/H9
Bekitro, Madg. 125/H9
Bekodoka, Madg. 125/H7
Bek'ojī, Eth. 118/A4
Bekopaka, Madg. 125/H7
Bekoropoka, Madg. 125/G8
Bekwai, Gha. 115/E5
Bel, La, US 164/B2
Bel Air, Md, US 168/B4
Bel Air South, Md, US 168/B5
Bel Aire, Ks, US 153/F2
Belá, Slvk. 43/K4
Bela, Pak. 101/J3
Bela, D.R. Congo 121/G2
Belā, India 92/D2
Bela Crkva, Yugo. 50/E3
Bela Cruz, Braz. 183/F3
Bela Palanka, Yugo. 50/F4
Bělá pod Bezdězem, Czh. 59/H1
Belā Pratāpgarh, India 96/C3
Bela Vista, Ang. 122/C2
Bela Vista, Braz. 189/E2
Bela Vista, Moz. 125/F2
Bela Vista de Goiás, Braz. 186/C3
Bela Vista do Paraíso, Braz. 189/G2
Belabérim (well), Niger 116/B2
Bélabo, Camr. 116/B4
Belair Rec. Pk., Austl. 131/M9
Belampalli, India 95/C2
Belan (riv.), India 96/D3
Belanak (cape), Malay. 89/C1
Belang, Indo. 91/F3
Belarus (ctry.) 29/G3
Belas, Port. 47/P10
Belawan, Indo. 89/B2
Belaya (riv.), Rus. 74/F4
Belaya (peak), Eth. 117/H3
Belaya Glina, Rus. 73/L4
Belaya Kalitva, Rus. 73/L3
Belbo (riv.), It. 62/B3
Bełchatów, Pol. 43/K3
Belchen (peak), Ger. 60/D2
Belcher, La, US 153/H4
Belcher (isls.), Can. 139/J4
Belcher (isls.), On, Can. 141/H3
Belcher (chan.), Nun, Can. 141/S7
Belchite, Sp. 47/E2
Belcourt, ND, US 156/E3
Belda, India 97/F4
Beldānga, India 97/G4
Belebey, Rus. 69/M5
Beled Weyne, Som. 118/C4
Belefuanai, Libr. 114/C5
Bélel, Camr. 116/B4
Belém, Braz. 183/H4
Belém, Braz. 182/D3
Belém de São Francisco, Braz. 183/G5
Belem Tower, Port. 47/P10
Belen, Turk. 104/E1
Belen, Turk. 104/C1
Belén, Nic. 172/D5
Belen, NM, US 149/J3
Belén, Uru. 188/E4
Belén, Chile 188/B1
Belén, Arg. 188/C3
Belén, Bol. 185/E5
Belén de Escobar, Arg. 191/J11
Belén de Umbría, Col. 183/K7
Belene, Bul. 51/G4
Bélep (isls.), NCal. 137/T11
Beles Wenz (riv.), Eth. 117/G3
Belesar (res.), Sp. 46/B1
Belev, Rus. 70/F1
Belfair, Wa, US 167/B3
Belfast (dist.), NI, UK 34/B2
Belfast (cap.), NI, UK 34/C2
Belfast, SAfr. 125/E2
Belfast Lough (bay), NI, UK 34/C2
Belfaux, Swi. 60/D4
Belfield, ND, US 156/C4
Bēlfodiyo, Eth. 117/G3
Belford, Eng, UK 33/E5
Belfort (dept.), Fr. 60/C2
Belfort, Fr. 60/C2
Belfountain, On, Can. 160/S8
Belfry, Mt, US 147/J1
Belgioioso, It. 62/C3
Belgium (ctry.) 29/E3
Belgorod, Rus. 73/J2
Belgorodskaya Oblast, Rus. 70/F2
Belgrade, Mn, US 157/G5
Belgrade, Mo, US 162/B2
Belgrade (Beograd) (cap.), Yugo. 50/E3
Belgreen, Al, US 162/D3
Belhavel (lake), Ire. 32/B1
Belhaven, NC, US 163/J3
Beli Drim (riv.), Yugo. 49/G1
Beli Drim (riv.), Alb. 50/E4
Beli Manastir, Cro. 50/D3
Beli Timok (riv.), Yugo. 50/F4
Belidzhi, Rus. 71/J4
Bélinga, Gabon 120/C2
Belington, WV, US 163/H1
Belinskiy, Rus. 71/G1
Belinyu, Indo. 89/D3
Belitsa, Bul. 49/H2
Belitung (isl.), Indo. 90/C4
Belize, Ang. 120/C4
Belize (riv.), Belz. 176/D2
Belize (ctry.) 139/J8
Belize City, Belz. 176/D2
Bélizon, FrG. 182/C1
Beljanica (peak), Yugo. 50/E3
Belk, Tx, US 153/G4
Belknap (mtn.), NH, US 161/L3
Bel'kovskiy (isl.), Rus. 75/N2
Bell, Ger. 55/G3
Bell (isl.), Nf, Can. 159/L2
Bell, Fl, US 165/G3
Bell, Ca, US 166/F8
Bell, Austl. 134/C4
Bell (pt.), Austl. 131/G5
Bell (riv.), Austl. 133/D1
Bell (riv.), Qu, Can. 141/J4
Bell (pen.), Nun, Can. 141/H2
Bell (pt.), PNG 129/F2
Bell Gardens, Ca, US 166/F8
Bell Rock (Inchcape) (isl.), Sc, UK 33/D4
Bell Ville, Arg. 188/D5
Bella Coola, BC, Can. 142/AA13
Bella Flor, Bol. 184/E3
Bella Vista, Arg. 188/E4
Bella Vista, Arg. 188/C3
Bella Vista, Bol. 185/F4
Bella Vista, Par. 189/E2
Bella Vista, Ar, US 153/G2
Bellac, Fr. 44/D3
Bellachat (peak), Fr. 64/C1
Bellaco, Uru. 191/K10
Bellaghy, NI, UK 34/B2
Bellagio, It. 61/F6
Bellaire, Oh, US 160/F4
Bellaire, Mi, US 160/D2
Bellaire, Tx, US 151/M9
Bellamy, Al, US 162/C4
Bellananagh, Ire. 32/C2
Bellano, It. 61/F5
Bellaria, It. 63/F5
Bellary, India 95/C3
Bellata, Austl. 132/D1
Bellavista (cape), It. 48/A3
Bellavista, Ecu. 184/J7
Bellavista, Peru 184/B2
Bellavista, Peru 184/B2
Bellbird, Austl. 133/E1
Belle, Mo, US 153/J1
Belle (riv.), On, Can. 167/G7
Belle, WV, US 163/G1
Belle Chasse, La, US 164/D3
Belle Fourche (res.), SD, US 156/C5
Belle Fourche, SD, US 154/C1
Belle Fourche (riv.), Wy,SD, US 154/"B2,
Belle Glade, Fl, US 165/H4
Belle Haven, Va, US 168/A6
Belle Isle, Fl, US 164/N7
Belle Isle (str.), NF, Can. 139/M4
Belle Plaine, Ks, US 153/F2
Belle Plaine, Ia, US 155/H3
Belle River, On, Can. 167/G7
Belle Terre, NY, US 169/E2
Belle Yella, Libr. 114/C5
Belle-Anse, Haiti 177/H2
Belle-Ile (isl.), Fr. 44/B3
Belle-Isle-en-Terre, Fr. 56/B3
Belleair, Fl, US 164/K8
Belleair Beach, Fl, US 164/K8
Belleair Bluffs, Fl, US 164/K8
Belleek, NI, UK 34/B3
Bellefontaine, Oh, US 160/E4
Bellefontaine, Ms, US 162/C4
Bellefonte, Ar, US 153/H2
Bellefonte, Pa, US 161/H4
Bellefonte, De, US 168/C4
Bellegarde-sur-Valserine, Fr. 60/B5
Bellême, Fr. 57/F4
Bellenberg, Ger. 61/G1
Bellencombre, Fr. 57/G1
Bellenden Ker NP, Austl. 134/B2
Belleoram, Nf, Can. 159/K2
Belleplain, NJ, US 168/D5
Bellerive-sur-Allier, Fr. 44/E3
Bellerose, NY, US 169/L9
Belleu, Fr. 54/C5
Belleview, Fl, US 165/G3
Belleview, Mo, US 162/B2
Belleville, On, Can. 161/H2
Belleville, Fr. 60/A5
Belleville, Ar, US 153/H3
Belleville, Il, US 162/C1
Belleville, Ks, US 154/F4
Belleville, Mi, US 167/E7
Belleville, NJ, US 169/J8
Belleville, Pa, US 161/H4
Belleville-sur-Meuse, Fr. 55/E5
Bellevue, Id, US 147/F2
Bellevue, Ia, US 155/J2
Bellevue, Md, US 168/B6
Bellevue, Ne, US 155/G3
Bellevue, Oh, US 160/E4
Bellevue, Wa, US 144/C4
Belley, Fr. 60/B6
Bellflower, Ca, US 166/F8
Bellheim, Ger. 58/B4
Bellignat, Fr. 60/B5
Bellinge, Den. 40/D4
Bellingen, Austl. 132/E1
Bellingham, Eng, UK 35/F1
Bellingham, Mn, US 155/F1
Bellingham, Wa, US 144/C3
Bellingrath Gardens and Home, Al, US 164/D2
Bellingshausen (sea), Ant. 192/U
Bellingshausen (isl.), FrPol. 137/K6
Bellingwolde, Neth. 53/E2
Bellinzago Novarese, It. 62/B2
Bellinzona, Swi. 61/F5
Belliveau Cove, NS, Can. 158/D3
Bellizzi, It. 65/D6
Bellmawr, NJ, US 168/C4
Bellmead, Tx, US 151/F2
Bellmore, NY, US 169/L9
Bello, Col. 183/K6
Bellona, It. 65/D5
Bellona Reefs (reef), NCal. 136/E7
Bellot (str.), Nun, Can. 140/G1
Bellows Falls, Vt, US 161/K3
Bellport, NY, US 169/F2
Bells, Tn, US 162/C3
Bells, Tx, US 153/F4
Bellsbank, Sc, UK 33/B6
Bellshill, Sc, UK 33/B5
Bellsite, Mb, Can. 156/D1
Belluno (prov.), It. 63/E1
Belluno, It. 45/K3
Bellville, SAfr. 124/L10
Bellville, Ga, US 163/G4
Bellville, Oh, US 160/E4
Bellville, Tx, US 150/F3
Bellwald, Swi. 60/E5
Bellwood, La, US 164/B2
Belly (riv.), Ab, Can. 145/H3
Belm, Ger. 53/F4
Belmar, NJ, US 168/D3
Bélmez, Sp. 46/C3
Belmond, Ia, US 155/H2
Belmont, Mb, Can. 156/E3
Belmont, NS, Can. 158/F3
Belmont, Ca, US 167/K11
Belmont, La, US 164/B2
Belmont, Ms, US 162/C3
Belmont, Mt, US 145/K4
Belmont, NC, US 163/G3
Belmont, Ne, US 154/C2
Belmont, NY, US 161/G3
Belmonte, Port. 46/B2
Belmonte, Sp. 46/D3
Belmonte, Braz. 187/F2
Belmopan (cap.), Belz. 176/D2
Belmullet, Ire. 31/P9
Belo, Madg. 125/G8
Belo Campo, Braz. 187/E2
Belo Horizonte, Braz. 186/E3
Belo Jardim, Braz. 183/G5
Belo-Tsiribihina, Madg. 125/H7
Beloeil, Belg. 54/C2
Beloeil, Qu, Can. 159/P6
Belogorsk, Rus. 79/K1
Beloha, Madg. 125/H9
Beloit, Ks, US 154/E4
Beloit, Wi, US 155/K2
Belokany, Azer. 71/H4
Béloko, CAfr. 116/B4
Belomorsk, Rus. 68/G2
Belondo-Kundu, D.R. Congo 120/D3
Beloomut, Rus. 68/H5
Beloozërsk, Bela. 70/C1
Belorado, Sp. 44/B5
Belorechensk, Rus. 73/K5
Belören, Turk. 102/C2
Beloretsk, Rus. 69/N5
Beloslav, Bul. 51/H4
Belovo, Bul. 49/J1
Belovo, Rus. 74/J4
Beloye (lake), Rus. 74/D3
Belozersk, Rus. 68/H3
Belozërskoye, Rus. 69/Q5
Belper, Eng, UK 35/G5
Belpre, Oh, US 160/F5
Belsand, India 97/E2
Belsay, Eng, UK 35/G1
Belt, Mt, US 145/J4
Belterra, Braz. 182/C3
Belterwijde (lake), Neth. 52/D3
Beltheim, Ger. 55/G3
Belton (lake), Tx, US 151/F2
Belton, Mo, US 153/G1
Belton, SC, US 163/F3
Belton, Eng, UK 37/H1
Belton, Tx, US 150/F2
Beltra (lake), Ire. 32/A2
Beltrán, Arg. 188/C3
Beltsville, Md, US 168/B5
Belturbet, Ire. 32/C1
Beltzville (lake), Pa, US 168/C2
Belukha (peak), Rus. 99/E2
Belumut (peak), Malay. 89/C2
Beluran, Malay. 88/B4
Belvedere, Ca, US 167/K11
Belvédère du Cirque, Fr. 64/D3
Belvedere Park, Ga, US 163/M7
Belvidere, SD, US 154/D2
Belvidere, Il, US 155/K2
Belvidere, NJ, US 168/C2
Belview, Mn, US 155/G1
Belvoir NP, Isr. 105/D3
Belwood, On, Can. 160/S8
Belyando (riv.), Austl. 127/D3
Belyayevka, Rus. 71/L2
Belynkovichi, Bela. 70/E1
Belyy (isl.), Rus. 192/A
Belyy Yar, Rus. 74/J4
Belyye Berega, Rus. 70/E1
Belz, Ukr. 72/C2
Belzig, Ger. 42/G2
Belzoni, Ms, US 162/B4
Bełżyce, Pol. 43/M3
Bémal, CAfr. 116/C4
Bemanevika, Madg. 125/J6
Bemanevika, Madg. 125/J6
Bemaraha (plat.), Madg. 125/H7
Bemarivo (riv.), Madg. 125/H7
Bembe, Ang. 120/C4
Bembéréké, Ben. 115/F4
Bembezi (riv.), Zim. 123/F3
Bembibre, Sp. 46/B1
Bembo, Ang. 120/D5
Bemboka, Austl. 133/D3
Bembridge, Eng, UK 37/E5
Bemebesi, Zim. 123/F4
Bemetāra, India 95/D1
Bemidji, Mn, US 157/G4
Bemis, SD, US 155/F1
Bemmel, Neth. 52/C5
Bempton, Eng, UK 35/H3
Ben Aigan (hill), Sc, UK 33/C1
Ben Alder (peak), Sc, UK 33/B3
Ben Améra (well), Mrta. 110/B5
Ben Avon (peak), Sc, UK 33/C2
Ben Boyd NP, Austl. 133/E3
Ben Chonzie (peak), Sc, UK 33/C4
Ben Cleuch (peak), Sc, UK 33/C4
Ben Cruachan (peak), Sc, UK 33/A4
Ben Dash (peak), Ire. 32/A4
Ben Davis (pt.), NJ, US 168/C5
Ben Giang, Viet. 94/D3
Ben Gurion (int'l arpt.), Isr. 105/B4
Ben Hope (peak), Sc, UK 31/R7
Ben Ime (peak), Sc, UK 33/B4
Ben Lawers (peak), Sc, UK 33/B3
Ben Ledi (peak), Sc, UK 33/B4
Ben Lomond (peak), Sc, UK 33/B4
Ben Lomond, Ca, US 148/A2
Ben Lomond NP, Austl. 132/C4
Ben Lui (peak), Sc, UK 33/B4
Ben Macdui (peak), Sc, UK 33/C2
Ben More (peak), Sc, UK 31/Q8
Ben More (peak), Sc, UK 33/B4
Ben More Assynt (peak), Sc, UK 31/R7
Ben Msik-Sidi Othmane (prov.), Mor. 112/A2
Ben Nevis (peak), Sc, UK 33/B3
Ben Quang, Viet. 94/D2
Ben Rinnes (peak), Sc, UK 33/C2
Ben Slimane, Mor. 110/D2
Ben Slimane (prov.), Mor. 112/A3
Ben Starav (peak), Sc, UK 33/A3
Ben Tee (peak), Sc, UK 33/B2
Ben Thuy, Viet. 86/E5
Ben Tirran (peak), Sc, UK 33/C3
Ben Tre, Viet. 94/D4
Ben Vane (peak), Sc, UK 33/B4
Ben Vorlich (peak), Sc, UK 33/B4
Ben Vrackie (peak), Sc, UK 33/C3
Ben Wyvis (peak), Sc, UK 33/B1
Ben Zohra (well), Alg. 110/E3
Bena, Mn, US 157/G4
Bena-Bendi, D.R. Congo 120/E4
Bena-Dibele, D.R. Congo 121/E4
Bena-Makima, D.R. Congo 121/E4
Benabarre, Sp. 47/F1
Benahmed, Mor. 110/D2
Benalla, Austl. 133/B3
Benalmádena, Sp. 46/C4
Benalto, Ab, Can. 144/G1
Benāpol, Bang. 97/G4
Benavente, Sp. 46/C1
Benavides, Bol. 185/E4
Benavides, Tx, US 151/E4
Benbane (pt.), NI, UK 34/B1
Benbecula (isl.), Sc, UK 31/Q8
Benbonyathe (peak), Austl. 131/H4
Benbrack (peak), Ire. 32/C1
Benbrook (lake), Tx, US 150/K7
Benbrook (dam), Tx, US 150/K7
Benbrook, Tx, US 150/K7
Benburb, NI, UK 34/B3
Benchley, Tx, US 151/F2
Bencubbin, Austl. 130/C4
Bend, Or, US 146/C1
Bend, Tx, US 151/E2
Benda (cape), Indo. 89/E4
Bende, Nga. 115/G5
Bendeleben (mt.), Ak, US 171/F2
Bendemeer, Austl. 132/D1
Bender Beyla, Som. 118/D3
Bender Cassim (Bosaaso), Som. 118/D3
Bendersville, Pa, US 168/A4
Bendery (Tighina), Mol. 72/E4
Bendigo, Austl. 133/B3
Bendoc, Austl. 133/D3
Bendorf, Ger. 40/C4
Bendugu, SLeo. 114/C4
Benduma, Libr. 114/C5
Bēne, Lat. 41/K3
Bene Beraq, Isr. 105/B4
Benedict (mt.), Nf, Can. 141/L3
Benediktbeuern, Ger. 61/H2
Benediktenwand (peak), Ger. 61/H2
Beneditinos, Braz. 183/F4
Benenitra, Madg. 125/H8
Benešov, Czh. 59/H3
Benevento (prov.), It. 65/D5
Benevento, It. 65/D5
Benfeld, Fr. 60/D1
Benga, Moz. 123/G3
Bengal (bay), Asia 77/H8
Bengal, Bay of (gulf), Asia 92/E4
Bengbis, Camr. 120/C2
Bengbu, China 80/D4
Benge, Wa, US 144/E4
Benghāzī, Libya 67/J4
Bengkalis, Indo. 89/C2
Bengkalis (isl.), Indo. 90/B3
Bengkayang, Indo. 90/C3
Bengkulu, Indo. 89/C3
Bengkulu (prov.), Indo. 89/C4
Bengo (riv.), Ang. 120/C5
Bengo (prov.), Ang. 120/C5
Bengo (bay), Ang. 120/C5
Bengough, Sk, Can. 156/B3
Bengtsby, Fin. 39/F4
Bengtsfors, Swe. 40/E2
Benguela, Ang. 122/B2
Benguela (prov.), Ang. 122/B2
Benguerir, Mor. 110/D2
Benguerua (isl.), Moz. 123/G4
Bengweulu (lake), Zam. 121/G5
Bengweulu (swamp), Zam. 121/G5
Beni, Nepal 96/D1
Beni, D.R. Congo 121/G2
Beni (riv.), Bol. 179/C4
Beni (dept.), Bol. 185/E4
Beni Abbes, Alg. 111/E3
Beni Bouayach, Mor. 112/C2
Beni Ensar, Mor. 112/B2
Beni Khiar, Tun. 112/M6
Beni Mellal, Mor. 110/D2
Beni Ounif, Alg. 111/E2
Beni Saf, Alg. 112/D2
Beni Tajit, Mor. 110/E2
Benicarló, Sp. 47/F2
Benicia, Ca, US 167/K10
Benidorm, Sp. 47/E3
Benifayó, Sp. 47/E3
Benin (ctry.) 107/C3
Benin City, Nga. 115/G5
Benina (int'l arpt.), Libya 67/J4
Benisa, Sp. 47/F3
Benisheikh, Nga. 116/B3
Benito, Mb, Can. 156/D2
Benito Juárez, Mex. 174/D2
Benjamin, Tx, US 152/E4
Benjamin Constant, Braz. 184/D2
Benjamín Hill, Mex. 174/C2
Benjamin, Isla (isl.), Chile 190/B5
Benkei-misaki (cape), Japan 82/B2
Benkelman, Ne, US 154/D3
Benld, Il, US 155/K4
Benllech, Wal, UK 34/D5
Benmore (peak), Ire. 32/A1
Bennachie (hill), Sc, UK 33/D2
Bennan (pt.), Sc, UK 33/A6
Benndale, Ms, US 164/D2
Benneckenstein, Ger. 53/H5
Bennett, BC, Can. 171/M3
Bennett (isl.), Rus. 75/Q2
Bennett, Co, US 154/B4
Bennett (peak), Co, US 152/A2
Bennett, Wi, US 157/J4
Bennettsbridge, Ire. 32/C4
Bennettsville, SC, US 163/H3
Bennichchab, Mrta. 114/B2
Bennington, Id, US 147/H2
Bennington, Ks, US 153/F1
Bennington, Ne, US 155/F3
Bennington, Ok, US 153/F3
Bennington, Vt, US 161/K3
Bénodet, Fr. 56/A5
Benoit, Ms, US 162/B4
Benom (peak), Malay. 89/C2
Bénoué (riv.), Camr. 116/B3
Bénoue, PN de la, Camr. 116/B3
Benover, Eng, UK 30/E3
Benoy, Chad 116/C3
Bensenville, Il, US 167/Q16
Bensheim, Ger. 58/B3
Benson, Mn, US 157/G5
Benson, La, US 150/H2
Benson, Sk, Can. 156/C3
Benson, Az, US 149/G5
Benson, NC, US 163/H3
Bensonhurst (nbrhd.), NY, US 169/K9
Benta (riv.), Hun. 51/Q10
Benta Seberang, Malay. 89/C1
Bentham, Eng, UK 35/F3
Bentheim, Ger. 53/E4
Benti, Gui. 114/B4
Bentiaba, Ang. 122/B2
Bentiaba (riv.), Ang. 122/B2
Bentinck (isl.), Austl. 129/E4
Bentiu, Sudan 117/F3
Bentley, ND, US 156/C4
Bentley, Ok, US 153/F3
Bentley, Eng, UK 35/G4
Bentley, Eng, UK 30/A3
Bento Gonçalves, Braz. 189/G4
Benton, Ar, US 153/H3
Benton, La, US 153/H4
Benton, Il, US 162/C2
Benton, Ms, US 162/B4
Benton, Ky, US 162/C2
Benton, Mo, US 162/C2
Benton, Tn, US 162/E3
Benton, Pa, US 168/B1
Benton Harbor, Mi, US 160/C3
Benton Lake NWR, Mt, US 145/J4
Bentong, Malay. 89/C2
Bentonia, Ms, US 162/B4
Bentonville, Ar, US 153/G2
Bentonville, Va, US 163/H1
Bent's Old Fort Nat'l Hist. Site, Co, US 152/C1
Benua Martinus, Indo. 90/D3
Benue (state), Nga. 115/H5
Benue (riv.), Nga. 107/C4
Benxi, China 81/B2
Benxi, China 81/C2
Beo, Indo. 91/G3
Beočin, Yugo. 50/D3
Beoga, Indo. 91/J4
Beograd (int'l arpt.), Yugo. 50/E3
Beograd (Belgrade) (cap.), Yugo. 50/E3
Beohāri, India 96/C3
Béoumi, C.d'Iv. 114/D5
Béoux (riv.), Fr. 64/B3
Beowawe, Nv, US 146/E3
Beppu (bay), Japan 84/B4
Beppu, Japan 84/B4
Bequia (isl.), StV. 173/N9
Bequimão, Braz. 183/E3
Bera, Bang. 97/G3
Beragh, NI, UK 34/A2
Beraketa, Madg. 125/H8
Beraketa, Madg. 125/H9
Beramanja, Madg. 125/J6
Beras Basah (cape), Malay. 89/C2
Berasia, India 96/A4
Berat, Alb. 49/F2
Beratus (peak), Indo. 91/E4
Beratzhausen, Ger. 59/E4
Berau (bay), Indo. 91/H4
Berau (riv.), Indo. 91/E3
Beravina, Madg. 125/H7
Berbenno di Valtellina, It. 61/F5
Berbera, Som. 118/C3
Berbérati, CAfr. 116/B4
Berbice (riv.), Guy. 181/G3
Berceto, It. 62/C4
Berchem, Belg. 52/B6
Bercher, Swi. 60/C4
Berching, Ger. 59/E4
Berchogur, Kaz. 71/L2
Berchtesgaden, Ger. 45/K3
Berchtesgaden, NP Ger. 45/K3
Berck, Fr. 54/A3
Berclair, Tx, US 151/F3
Berdale, Som. 118/C4
Berdorf, Lux. 55/F4
Berdsk, Rus. 74/J4
Berdyans'k, Ukr. 73/J4
Berdyansk (bay), Ukr. 73/J4
Berdychiv, Ukr. 72/E3
Béré, Chad 116/C3
Bere Regis, Eng, UK 36/D5
Berea, Ky, US 162/E2
Berea, Les. 124/D3
Bereah, Fl, US 164/M8
Berebere, Indo. 91/G3
Bereguardo, It. 62/C3
Berehomet, Ukr. 72/C3
Berehove, Ukr. 43/M4
Bereina, PNG 129/G2
Bereku, Tanz. 119/A3
Berekum, Gha. 115/E5
Berenguela, Bol. 188/B1
Berenice (ruin), Egypt 109/G4
Berens (isl.), Mb, Can. 156/F1
Berens River, Mb, Can. 156/F1
Berenty, Madg. 125/H8
Beresford, NB, Can. 158/E2
Beresford, SD, US 155/F2
Bereşti, Rom. 51/H2
Berettyóújfalu, Hun. 50/E2
Berevo, Madg. 125/H7
Berezan', Ukr. 72/F2
Berezhany, Ukr. 72/C3
Berezhnoye, Rus. 68/H4
Berezino, Bela. 41/N5
Berezivka, Ukr. 72/F4
Bereznik, Rus. 68/J3
Berezniki, Rus. 69/N4
Berezovo, Rus. 74/G3
Berëzovskiy, Rus. 69/P4
Berezovyy, Rus. 79/L1
Berg, Ger. 61/H2
Berg, Swi. 61/F2
Berg, Lux. 55/F4
Berg, Ger. 58/B5
Berg (riv.), SAfr. 124/B4
Berg bei Rohrbach, Aus. 59/G5
Berg en Dal, Sur. 182/C1
Berga, Sp. 47/F1
Bergama, Turk. 70/C5
Bergamo (prov.), It. 61/F6
Bergamo, It. 62/C2
Bergara, Sp. 46/D1
Bergatruete, Ger. 61/F2
Bergedorf, Ger. 53/H2
Bergen, Nor. 40/A1
Bergen, Ger. 40/E4
Bergen, Ger. 53/G3
Bergen, Neth. 52/B3
Bergen (co.), NJ, US 168/D2
Bergen aan Zee, Neth. 52/B3
Bergen op Zoom, Neth. 52/B5
Bergenfield, NJ, US 169/K8
Berger, Nor. 38/S9
Bergerac, Fr. 44/D4
Bergeresse (riv.), Fr. 57/H5
Bergeyk, Neth. 52/C6
Bergheim, Ger. 55/F2
Bergheim, Aus. 59/G7
Bergheim, Tx, US 151/E3
Bergisch Gladbach, Ger. 55/G2
Bergkamen, Ger. 53/E5
Bergman, Ar, US 153/H2
Bergnäset, Swe. 68/D2
Bergneustadt, Ger. 55/G1
Bergrheinfeld, Ger. 42/F4
Bergsbrunna, Swe. 39/A1
Bergse Maas (riv.), Neth. 52/B5
Bergshamra, Swe. 40/H2
Bergsvatnet (lake), Nor. 38/R9
Bergsviken, Swe. 38/G2
Bergtheim, Ger. 58/D3
Berguent, Mor. 112/C2
Bergues, Fr. 54/B2
Bergum, Neth. 52/D2
Bergumermeer (lake), Neth. 52/D2
Bergün-Bravuogn, Swi. 61/F4
Bergviken (lake), Swe. 40/G1
Berh, Mong. 78/G2
Berhala (str.), Indo. 89/C3
Berhampore, India 97/G3
Berhampur, India 95/E2
Beri Khās, India 98/D5
Berikat (cape), Indo. 89/D3
Bering (str.), Rus.,US 171/E3
Bering (isl.), Rus. 75/S4
Bering (sea), Asia,NAm. 171/D3
Beringen, Belg. 55/E1
Beringovskiy, Rus. 75/T3
Beritarikap (cape), Indo. 89/C3
Berja, Sp. 46/D4
Berkane, Mor. 112/C2
Berkel (riv.), Ger. 42/D2
Berkel, Neth. 52/B5
Berkeley, Eng, UK 36/D3
Berkeley Heights, NJ, US 169/H9
Berkeley Lake, Ga, US 163/M7
Berkeley Springs (Bath), WV, US 161/G5
Berkhamsted, Eng, UK 30/B1
Berkheim, Ger. 61/G1
Berkhout, Neth. 52/B3
Berkley, Mi, US 167/F6
Berkovitsa, Bul. 51/F4
Berks (co.), Pa, US 168/C3
Berkshire (co.), Eng, UK 37/E3
Berkshire Downs (hills), Eng, UK 37/E3
Berlaimont, Fr. 54/C3
Berlanga de Duero, Sp. 46/D2
Berlare, Belg. 54/D1
Berleburg, Ger. 53/F6
Berlicum, Neth. 52/C5
Berlin (cap.), Ger. 42/Q6
Berlin (state), Ger. 42/Q6
Berlin, Ga, US 165/G2
Berlin, NJ, US 168/D4
Berlin, Md, US 163/K1
Berlin (mtn.), Nv, US 146/E4
Berlin, Wi, US 155/K2
Bermagui, Austl. 133/E3
Bermejillo, Mex. 151/C5
Bermejo (riv.), Arg. 179/D5
Bermejo, Arg. 190/D1
Bermeo, Sp. 44/B5
Bermillo de Sayago, Sp. 46/B2
Bermuda (isl.), UK 139/L6
Bermudian (cr.), Pa, US 168/A4
Bern (canton), Swi. 60/D4
Bern (cap.), Swi. 60/D4
Bern-Belp (int'l arpt.), Swi. 60/D4

Black P – Borgo S

Black Pine (peak), Id, US 147/G2
Black Point, Ca, US 167/K10
Black Reef (pt.), Namb. 122/B5
Black River, Mi, US 160/E2
Black River, Jam. 177/G2
Black River Falls, Wi, US 155/J1
Black Rock (des.), Nv, US 146/D3
Black Rock, Ar, US 162/B2
Black Rock (pt.), RI, US 169/G1
Black Sea Lowland (lowland), Ukr. 72/E4
Black Sea Lowlands (reg.), Ukr. 51/J3
Black Sturgeon (riv.), On, Can. 157/K3
Black Sugarloaf (peak), Austl. 132/D1
Black Volta (riv.), Burk. 107/B4
Black Warrior (riv.), Al, US 162/D4
Black Warrior, Locust Fk. (riv.), Al, US 162/D4
Blackadder Water. (riv.), Sc, UK 33/D5
Blackall, Austl. 134/B4
Blackbeard Island NWR, Ga, US 165/H2
Blackberry (cr.), Il, US 167/P16
Blackburn, Eng, UK 35/F4
Blackburn, Sc, UK 33/C5
Blackburn, Mo, US 155/H4
Blackburne (int'l arpt.), UK 173/N8
Blackburn with Darwen (co.), Eng, UK 35/F4
Blackbutt, Austl. 134/D4
Blackcraig (peak), Sc, UK 33/B6
Blackdown (hills), Eng, UK 36/C5
Blackdown (hill), Eng, UK 37/F4
Blackdown Tableland NP, Austl. 134/C3
Blackduck, Mn, US 157/G4
Blackfalds, Ab, Can. 145/H1
Blackfoot (res.), Id, US 147/H2
Blackfoot, Id, US 147/G2
Blackfoot (riv.), Id, US 147/H2
Blackfoot, Mt, US 145/H3
Blackfoot Ind. Res., Mt, US 145/H3
Blackfoot Ind. Res., Ab, Can. 145/H2
Blackgum, Ok, US 153/G3
Blackhall Rocks, Eng, UK 35/G2
Blackheath, Austl. 133/E1
Blackie, Ab, Can. 145/H2
Blackland, Tx, US 150/L7
Blackmoor (upland), Eng, UK 36/B5
Blackmore, Eng, UK 30/D1
Blackpool, Eng, UK 35/E4
Blackpool (co.), Eng, UK 35/E4
Blackpool (arpt.), Eng, UK 35/E4
Blackrod, Eng, UK 35/F4
Blacks Fk. (riv.), Wy, US 147/J3
Blacks Harbour, NB, Can. 158/D3
Blacksburg, Va, US 163/G2
Blacksburg, SC, US 163/G3
Blackshear, Ga, US 165/G2
Blackshear (lake), Ga, US 162/F5
Blackstairs (mts.), Ire. 32/D5
Blackstone, Va, US 163/H2
Blacksville, Ga, US 163/M8
Blacktown (nbrhd.), Austl. 134/G8
Blackville, NB, Can. 158/E2
Blackville, SC, US 163/G4
Blackwater (riv.), Mo, Ire. 153/H1
Blackwater (riv.), Ire. 34/B4
Blackwater (res.), Sc, UK 33/B3
Blackwater, Ire. 32/D5
Blackwater (cr.), Fl, US 164/L7
Blackwater (riv.), Eng, UK 30/A2
Blackwater, Austl. 134/C3
Blackwater (riv.), Mo, US 155/H4
Blackwater (inlet), Eng, UK 37/G3
Blackwater Draw (riv.), Tx, US 152/C3
Blackwater NWR, Md, US 163/J1
Blackwell, Ok, US 153/F2
Blackwell, Tx, US 151/D1
Blackwells, Ga, US 163/L6
Blackwood (riv.), Austl. 130/B5
Blackwood (cape), PNG 129/G1
Blackwood, Wal, UK 36/C3
Blackwood, NJ, US 168/C4
Bladel, Neth. 52/C6
Bladenboro, NC, US 163/H3
Bladensburg, Md, US 168/B6
Bladensburg NP, Austl. 134/A3
Bladnoch (riv.), Sc, UK 34/D2
Bladworth, Sk, Can. 145/L2
Blaenau-Ffestiniog, Wal, UK 34/E6
Blaenau Gwent (co.), Wal, UK 36/C3
Blaenavon, Wal, UK 36/C3
Blagnac (int'l arpt.), Fr. 44/D5
Blagnac, Fr. 44/D5
Blagny, Fr. 55/E4
Blagodarniy, Rus. 71/G3
Blagoevgrad, Bul. 49/H1
Blagoveshchensk, Rus. 79/K1
Blain, Fr. 56/D6
Blaine, Tn, US 162/F2
Blaine, Mn, US 157/P6
Blaine Lake, Sk, Can. 145/L1
Blainville, Qu, Can. 159/N6
Blainville-sur-Orne, Fr. 57/E2
Blair, Ok, US 152/E3
Blair, Ne, US 155/F3
Blair, Wi, US 155/J1
Blair (hill), Pa, US 168/C1
Blair Athol, Austl. 134/B3
Blair Atholl, Sc, UK 33/C3
Blairgowrie, Sc, UK 33/C3
Blairmore, Ab, Can. 144/G3
Blairsden, Ca, US 146/C4
Blairstown, NJ, US 168/D2
Blairsville, Ga, US 162/F3
Blaise (riv.), Fr. 44/F2
Blaj, Rom. 51/F2
Blake (pt.), Mi, US 157/K3
Blakely, Pa, US 161/J4
Blakely, Ga, US 165/F2
Blakely Mountain (dam), Ar, US 153/H3
Blakeslee, Pa, US 168/C1
Blamont, Fr. 60/C3
Blanc (peak), Fr. 60/C6
Blanc (cape), Fr. 64/C6
Blanc Nez (cape), Fr. 54/A2
Blanca (peak), NM, US 152/B4
Blanca, Co, US 152/B2
Blanca (bay), Arg. 179/C6
Blanca (coast), Sp. 47/E4
Blanca (peak), Tx, US 151/B2
Blanca (pt.), Mex. 174/B2
Blanchard, Ok, US 153/F3
Blanchard, Id, US 144/F3
Blanchardstown, Ire. 34/B5
Blanchardville, Wi, US 155/K2
Blanche (peak), Swi. 60/D5
Blanche (riv.), Fr. 64/C4
Blanche (lake), Austl. 130/D2
Blanche (cape), Austl. 131/G5
Blanchester, Oh, US 160/E5
Blanchisseuse, Trin. 181/F2
Blanco (cr.), Tx, US 151/F3
Blanco (riv.), Tx, US 151/E2
Blanco (cape), Mor. 110/A5
Blanco (cape), CR 176/E4
Blanco, NM, US 149/J2
Blanco (cape), Or, US 142/A3
Blanco (lake), Chile 191/C7
Blanco (riv.), Arg. 188/B4
Blanco (riv.), Bol. 185/F4
Blanco, SAfr. 124/C4
Blanco, Tx, US 150/E2
Bland, Mo, US 153/J1
Bland, Va, US 163/G2
Bland (cr.), Austl. 133/C1
Blandford Forum, Eng, UK 36/D5
Blanding, Ut, US 149/H2
Blandy, Fr. 30/L6
Blanes, Sp. 47/G2
Blangkejeren, Indo. 89/B2
Blangpidie, Indo. 89/B2
Blangy-sur-Bresle, Fr. 54/A4
Blankenberge, Belg. 54/C1
Blankenese, Ger. 53/G1
Blankenfelde, Ger. 42/Q7
Blankenheim, Ger. 55/F3
Blanket, Tx, US 150/E2
Blanquilla (isl.), Ven. 173/J5
Blanquillo, Uru. 191/G2
Blansko, Czh. 43/J4
Blanton, Fl, US 164/L7
Blantyre, Sc, UK 33/B5
Blantyre, Malw. 123/G2
Blanzy, Fr. 44/F3
Blaricum, Neth. 52/C4
Blarney, Ire. 32/B6
Blarney Castle and Stone, Ire. 32/B6
Blas (peak), Swi. 61/E4
Blatná, Czh. 59/G4
Blato, Cro. 50/C4
Blatten, Swi. 60/D5
Blau (riv.), Ger. 58/C6
Blaubeuren, Ger. 58/C6
Blauen (peak), Ger. 60/D2
Blaustein, Ger. 58/C6
Blauvelt, NY, US 169/K7
Blåvands (pt.), Den. 40/C4
Blavet (riv.), Fr. 44/B3
Blaye, Fr. 44/C4
Blaye, The (Alderney) (arpt.), Chl, UK 56/C1
Blayney, Austl. 133/D1
Blaze (pt.), Austl. 128/C3
Bleckede, Ger. 53/H2
Bled, Slov. 45/L3
Bledlow Ridge, Eng, UK 30/A2
Blefjell (peak), Nor. 40/C2
Blégny, Belg. 55/E2
Bléharies, Belg. 54/C2
Bleiburg, Aus. 50/B2
Bleicherode, Ger. 53/H6
Bleik (peak), Ger. 61/G2
Bleiswijk, Neth. 52/B4
Blekinge (co.), Swe. 38/E4
Blendecques, Fr. 54/B2
Blender, Ger. 53/G3
Blenheim, On, Can. 160/F3
Blenheim, NZ 135/C3
Blénod-lès-Pont-à-Mousson, Fr. 55/F6
Bléone (riv.), Fr. 45/G4
Blera, It. 65/B3
Bléré, Fr. 57/G6
Blerick, Neth. 52/D6
Blesberg (peak), SAfr. 124/C4
Blessing, Tx, US 151/F3
Blessington, Ire. 34/B5
Bletchingley, Eng, UK 30/C3
Bletchley, Eng, UK 37/F3
Bletterans, Fr. 60/B4
Bleury, Fr. 30/H6
Bleus, Monts (mts.), D.R. Congo 121/G2
Blevins, Ar, US 153/H4
Blewbury, Eng, UK 37/E3
Blewett, Tx, US 151/D3
Blewett Falls (lake), NC, US 163/H3
Blida (wilaya), Alg. 112/G4
Blida, Alg. 112/G4
Blidö (isl.), Swe. 39/B1
Blidworth, Eng, UK 35/G5
Blies (riv.), Ger. 55/G5
Blieskastel, Ger. 55/G5
Bligh Water (bay), Fiji 137/Y18
Blik (mt.), Phil. 91/F2
Blind Bay, BC, Can. 144/E2
Blind River, On, Can. 160/E1
Blinman, Austl. 131/H4
Blinndio, Mali 114/D4
Blinnenhorn (peak), Swi. 61/E5
Bliss, Id, US 147/F2
Bliss (dam), Id, US 147/F2
Blissfield, NB, Can. 158/D2
Blissfield, Mi, US 160/E4
Blitar, Indo. 89/F5
Blithe (riv.), Eng, UK 35/F6
Blithfield (res.), Eng, UK 35/G6
Blitta, Togo 115/F4
Block (isl.), RI, US 169/F1
Block House, NS, Can. 158/E3
Block Island (sound), Ma, US 158/B5
Block Island (New Shoreham), RI, US 169/G1
Block Island C. G. Sta., RI, US 169/G1
Block Island Nat'l Wild. Ref., RI, US 169/G1
Block Island State (arpt.), RI, US 169/G1
Blodelsheim, Fr. 60/D2
Bloemendaal, Neth. 52/B4
Bloemfontein, SAfr. 124/D3
Bloemhof, SAfr. 124/D2
Bloemhofdam (res.), SAfr. 124/D2
Blois, Fr. 57/G5
Blokzijl, Neth. 52/C3
Blomberg, Ger. 53/G5
Blomberg, Ger. 53/E1
Blommestein (lake), Sur. 181/H3
Blomstermåla, Swe. 40/G3
Blonay, Swi. 60/C5
Blönduós, Ice. 38/N6
Blongas, Indo. 89/G5
Blood Indian Res., Ab, Can. 145/H2
Bloodvein (riv.), Mb,On, Can. 140/G3
Bloodvein River, Mb, Can. 156/F2
Bloody Foreland (pt.), Ire. 31/P9
Bloomer, Wi, US 155/J1
Bloomfield, Ct, US 161/K4
Bloomfield, Ia, US 155/H3
Bloomfield, In, US 162/D1
Bloomfield, Mo, US 162/C2
Bloomfield, Mt, US 156/B4
Bloomfield, Nf, Can. 159/L1
Bloomfield, NJ, US 169/J8
Bloomfield, NM, US 149/J2
Bloomfield Hills, Mi, US 167/F6
Blooming Grove, Tx, US 151/F1
Blooming Prairie, Mn, US 155/H2
Bloomingdale, Fl, US 164/L8
Bloomingdale, Ga, US 163/G4
Bloomingdale, Il, US 167/P16
Bloomingdale, NJ, US 169/H7
Bloomington, Ca, US 166/C2
Bloomington, Id, US 147/H2
Bloomington, Il, US 155/K3
Bloomington, In, US 160/C5
Bloomington, Mn, US 157/P7
Bloomington, Tx, US 151/F3
Bloomington Springs, Tn, US 162/E2
Bloomsburg, Pa, US 168/B2
Bloomsbury, NJ, US 168/C2
Bloomville, Oh, US 160/E4
Blora, Indo. 89/E4
Blotzheim, Fr. 60/D2
Blouberg (peak), SAfr. 123/F4
Blountstown, Fl, US 165/F2
Blountsville, Al, US 162/D3
Blountville, Tn, US 163/F2
Blovice, Czh. 59/G3
Blowering (res.), Austl. 133/D2
Blowing Rock, NC, US 163/G2
Bloxham, Eng, UK 37/E2
Bloxwich, Eng, UK 36/E1
Blšanka (riv.), Czh. 45/K1
Blūdān, Syria 105/E1
Bludenz, Aus. 61/F3
Blue (mtn.), Ar, US 153/G3
Blue (hills), Wi, US 157/J5
Blue (mtn.), NB, Can. 158/D2
Blue (hill), ND, US 156/D4
Blue (hill), Pa, US 161/G4
Blue (mtn.), NH, US 161/L2
Blue (mtn.), NY, US 161/J3
Blue, Az, US 149/H4
Blue (mts.), Or,Wa, US 142/C2
Blue (riv.), Co, US 154/A4
Blue (mtn.), India 86/B4
Blue and Gray Museum, Ga, US 165/G2
Blue Ash, Oh, US 162/E1
Blue Cypress (lake), Fl, US 165/H4
Blue Earth, Mn, US 155/G2
Blue Earth (riv.), Mn, US 155/G2
Blue Eye, Mo, US 153/H2
Blue Head (pt.), Sc, UK 33/C1
Blue Hill, Ne, US 154/E3
Blue Island, Il, US 167/Q16
Blue Lagoon NP, Zam. 123/E2
Blue Lake, Ca, US 146/B3
Blue Lake NP, Austl. 134/D4
Blue Marsh Lake (res.), Pa, US 168/B3
Blue Mesa (res.), Co, US 147/K4
Blue Mesa (dam), Co, US 149/J1
Blue Mound, Ks, US 153/G1
Blue Mound, Tx, US 150/K7
Blue Mountain (peak), Jam. 177/G2
Blue Mountain, Ms, US 162/C3
Blue Mountain (ridge), Pa, US 168/A3
Blue Mountain Lake, NY, US 161/J3
Blue Mountains, Austl. 133/E1
Blue Mud (bay), Austl. 129/D3
Blue Nile (riv.), Eth. 118/B3
Blue Nile (riv.), Eth.,Sudan 117/G2
Blue Nile (falls), Eth. 117/H3
Blue Nile (riv.), Sudan 107/F3
Blue Nose (peak), Mt, US 147/F1
Blue Rapids, Ks, US 155/F4
Blue Ridge, Ga, US 162/E3
Blue Ridge (mts.), Ga, US 162/G3
Blue Ridge Pky., US 163/G2
Blue River, Or, US 146/B1
Blue River, BC, Can. 144/E1
Blue Springs, Mo, US 155/G4
Blue Springs, Ne, US 155/F3
Bluebell, Ut, US 147/H3
Bluefield, WV, US 163/G2
Bluefield, Va, US 163/G2
Bluefields (bay), Nic. 177/F4
Bluefields, Nic. 177/F4
Bluejoint (lake), Or, US 146/D2
Bluenose (lake), Nun, Can. 140/E2
Bluestem (lake), Ok, US 153/F2
Bluestone (lake), WV, US 163/G2
Bluewater, NM, US 149/J3
Bluff (cr.), Ks,Ok, US 153/F2
Bluff, Austl. 134/C3
Bluff, NZ 135/B4
Bluff, Ut, US 149/H2
Bluff (peak), Austl. 130/C5
Bluff (pt.), Austl. 130/B3
Bluff (pt.), NC, US 163/J3
Bluff City, Ar, US 153/H4
Bluff City, Ks, US 153/F2
Bluff Dale, Tx, US 151/E1
Bluff Face (range), Austl. 128/B4
Bluffton, Ar, US 153/H3
Bluffton, In, US 160/D4
Bluffton, Oh, US 160/E4
Blum, Tx, US 151/F1
Blumberg, Ger. 61/E2
Blumberg, Ger. 42/Q6
Blumenau, Braz. 189/G3
Blumenthal, Ger. 53/G2
Blumenthal, Ger. 53/F2
Blümlisalp (peak), Swi. 60/D5
Blunt, SD, US 154/E1
Blustry (mt.), BC, Can. 144/D2
Bly, Or, US 146/C2
Blyn, Wa, US 167/B1
Blyth, Austl. 131/H5
Blyth, Eng, UK 35/G5
Blyth, Eng, UK 35/G1
Blyth Bridge, Sc, UK 33/C5
Blythe, Ca, US 148/E4
Blythe, Ga, US 163/F4
Blythe Bridge, Eng, UK 35/F6
Blytheswood, On, Can. 167/G7
Blytheville, Ar, US 162/C3
Bnom Mhai (peak), Viet. 94/D4
Bø, Nor. 40/C2
Bo, SLeo. 114/C5
Bo Duc, Viet. 94/D4
Bo Hai (Chihli) (gulf), China 75/M6
Bo Ho Su, Viet. 94/D2
Bo Phloi, Thai. 94/B3
Bo River, Sudan 117/E4
Bo Trach, Viet. 94/D2
Boa Esperança, Braz. 186/D4
Boa Esperança (res.), Braz. 183/E4
Boa Nova, Braz. 182/B5
Boa Viagem, Braz. 183/G4
Boa Vista (int'l arpt.), Braz. 181/F4
Boa Vista, Braz. 181/F4
Boa Vista (isl.), CpV. 107/K10
Boac, Phil. 88/C2
Boaco, Nic. 176/E3
Boadilla del Monte, Sp. 47/N9
Bo'ai, China 80/C4
Boajibu, SLeo. 114/C4
Boalsburg, Pa, US 161/H4
Boana, PNG 129/G1
Boano (isl.), Indo. 91/G4
Board Camp, Ar, US 153/G3
Boardman, Oh, US 160/F4
Boardman, Or, US 144/E5
Boardman Bombing Range, Or, US 144/E5
Boardman Naval Ra., Or, US 146/D1
Boas (riv.), Nun, Can. 141/H2
Boavita, Col. 180/C3
Boaz, Al, US 162/D3
Bob Sandlin (lake), Tx, US 153/G4
Boba, Hun. 50/C2
Bobadah, Austl. 132/C2
Bobai, China 87/F4
Bobaomby (cape), Madg. 125/J5
Bobbili, India 95/D2
Bobbio, It. 62/C4
Bobcaygeon, On, Can. 161/G2
Bobenge, D.R. Congo 121/F2
Bobenheim-Roxheim, Ger. 58/B3
Bobigny, Fr. 30/K5
Bobila, D.R. Congo 121/E2
Bobingen, Ger. 61/G1
Bobisi, D.R. Congo 120/D2
Böblingen, Ger. 58/C5
Bobo Dioulasso, Burk. 114/D4
Bobonong, Bots. 123/F4
Boboshevo, Bul. 49/H1
Bobotov Kuk (peak), Yugo. 50/D4
Bobovdol, Bul. 50/F4
Bobr, Bela. 41/N4
Bóbr (riv.), Pol. 43/H3
Bobrov, Rus. 73/L2
Bobrovskoye, Rus. 69/K3
Bobrovytsya, Ukr. 72/F2
Bobrynets', Ukr. 73/G3
Bobuk, Sudan 117/G3
Bobures, Ven. 180/D2
Boby (peak), Madg. 125/H8
Boca de Aroa, Ven. 180/D2
Boca de Pepé, Col. 180/B3
Boca del Grita, Ven. 180/C2
Boca del Guafo (chan.), Chile 190/B4
Boca del Mar, Fl, US 164/P10
Boca del Pao, Ven. 181/E2
Boca del Río, Mex. 175/N7
Bôca do Acre, Braz. 185/E3
Boca Grande, Fl, US 165/G4
Boca Raton, Fl, US 164/P10
Bocaina (mts.), Braz. 187/M7
Bocaina, Braz. 183/F4
Bocairente, Sp. 47/E3
Bocaiúva, Braz. 186/E3
Bocanda, C.d'Iv. 114/D5
Bocaranga, CAfr. 116/B4
Bocas del Toro, Pan. 177/F4
Bocay, Nic. 176/E3
Bocay (riv.), Nic. 176/E3
Bochil, Mex. 176/C2
Bochnia, Pol. 43/L4
Bocholt, Belg. 55/E1
Bocholt, Ger. 52/D5
Bochov, Czh. 59/G2
Bochum, SAfr. 123/F4
Bochum, Ger. 53/E6
Bockau, Ger. 59/F1
Bockenem, Ger. 53/H4
Bockenheim an der Weinstrasse, Ger. 55/H4
Bockhorn, Ger. 59/E6
Bockhorn, Ger. 53/F2
Bocking, Eng, UK 37/G3
Bococo, EqG. 120/B2
Bocoio, Ang. 122/B2
Boconó, Ven. 180/D2
Bocq (riv.), Belg. 55/D3
Boda, CAfr. 116/C4
Bodafors, Swe. 40/F3
Bodalla, Austl. 133/E3
Bodaybo, Rus. 75/M4
Bodcau (cr.), Ar, US 153/H4
Bodcaw, Ar, US 153/H4
Boddam, Sc, UK 33/E2
Boddington, Austl. 130/C5
Bode (riv.), Ger. 42/F3
Bode-Sadu, Nga. 115/G4
Bodega (bay), Ca, US 146/B4
Bodegraven, Neth. 52/B4
Bodélé (reg.), Chad 116/C1
Bodenheim, Ger. 58/B3
Bodenkirchen, Ger. 59/F6
Bodenmais, Ger. 59/G4
Bodensee (Constance) (lake), Swi.,Ger. 61/F2
Bodenteich, Ger. 53/H3
Bodfish, Ca, US 148/C3
Bodh Gaya, India 97/E3
Bodhan, India 95/C2
Bodie (isl.), NC, US 163/K3
Bodio, Swi. 61/E5
Bodkin (pt.), Md, US 168/B5
Bodmin, Eng, UK 36/B6
Bodmin Moor (upland), Eng, UK 36/B6
Bodø, Nor. 38/E2
Bodomijärvi (lake), Fin. 39/E4
Bodonchiyn (riv.), Mong. 78/C2
Bodoukpa, CAfr. 116/C4
Bodrog (riv.), Slvk.,Hun. 43/L4
Bodrum, Turk. 102/A2
Bódvaszilas, Hun. 43/L4
Boëge, Fr. 60/C5
Boegoeberg (peak), Namb. 124/A2
Boekel, Neth. 52/C5
Boende, D.R. Congo 121/E3
Boerne, Tx, US 151/E3
Boeuf (riv.), La, US 162/B4
Boffa, Gui. 114/B4
Bog of Allen (swamp), Ire. 34/A5
Boga, D.R. Congo 121/G2
Bogalo (mtn.), Austl. 133/C1
Bogalusa, La, US 164/D2
Bogamangon, CAfr. 116/C4
Bogan (riv.), Austl. 127/D4
Bogan Gate, Austl. 133/C1
Bogandé, Burk. 115/E3
Bogangolo, CAfr. 116/C4
Bogantungan, Austl. 134/B3
Bogard, Mo, US 155/H4
Bogata, Tx, US 153/G4
Bogatić, Yugo. 50/D3
Bogatoye, Rus. 71/J1
Bogatynia, Pol. 43/H3
Bogatyrëvo, Kaz. 71/J2
Boğazkale-Alacahöyük NP, Turk. 102/C1
Boğazlıyan, Turk. 102/C2
Bogbonga, D.R. Congo 120/D2
Bogcang (riv.), China 99/E5
Bogda (peak), China 99/E3
Bogda (mts.), China 78/B3
Bogdanci, FYROM 49/H2
Bogdanovka, Geo. 71/G4
Bogen, Nor. 38/F1
Bogen, Ger. 59/F5
Bogenfels, Namb. 124/A2
Bogenli, China 79/K2
Bogense, Den. 40/D4
Boggabilla, Austl. 134/C5
Boggabri, Austl. 132/D1
Boggeragh (mts.), Ire. 32/A5
Boggy (peak), Anti. 173/N8
Boglárlelle, Hun. 50/C2
Bogliasco, It. 62/C5
Bognor Regis, Eng, UK 37/F5
Bogny-sur-Meuse, Fr. 55/D4
Bogo, Camr. 116/B3
Bogo, Phil. 88/C3
Bogol Manyo, Eth. 118/B4
Bogong (mt.), Austl. 133/C3
Bogor, Indo. 89/D4
Bogoria Nat'l Rsv., Kenya 119/B1
Bogoro, D.R. Congo 121/G2
Bogoroud (well), Chad 116/B2
Bogotá (cap.), Col. 183/L8
Bogotá (riv.), Col. 183/L8
Bogota, NJ, US 169/J8
Bogovino, FYROM 49/G2
Bogra, Bang. 97/G3
Bogra (pol. reg.), Bang. 97/G3
Bogsta, Swe. 39/A2
Boguchar, Rus. 73/L3
Bogué, Mrta. 114/B2
Bogue, Ks, US 154/E4
Bogue Chitto (riv.), La, US 164/C2
Bogue Chitto, Ms, US 164/C2
Bogue Chitto NWR, La, US 164/C2
Bogue Homo (cr.), Ms, US 164/D2
Boguila Kota, CAfr. 116/C4
Bogushëvsk, Bela. 41/P4
Bohai (bay), China 80/D3
Bohain-en-Vermandois, Fr. 54/C4
Bohemia (reg.), Czh. 43/G4
Bohemian (for.), Czh.,Ger. 42/G4
Bohemian (for.), Ger.,Czh. 45/K2
Boherboy, Ire. 32/A5
Bohicon, Ben. 115/F5
Böhl-Iggelheim, Ger. 58/B4
Böhme (riv.), Ger. 53/G3
Böhmenkirch, Ger. 58/C5
Bohmte, Ger. 53/F4
Bohners Lake, Wi, US 167/P14
Bohodukhiv, Ukr. 73/H2
Bohol (isl.), Phil. 88/C3
Bohol (str.), Phil. 88/C3
Böhönye, Hun. 50/C2
Bohu, China 99/E3
Bohuslav, Ukr. 72/F3
Boiestown, NB, Can. 158/D2
Boigny-sur-Bionne, Fr. 57/H5
Boiling Springs, Pa, US 168/A3
Boiling Springs, SC, US 163/G3
Boimbo, D.R. Congo 120/D3
Boinu (riv.), Myan. 86/B4
Boipāriguda, India 95/D2
Boipeba (isl.), Braz. 187/F2
Boiro, Sp. 46/A1
Bois (isl.), Nf, Can. 159/K2
Bois Blanc (isl.), Mi, US 160/D2
Bois de Boulogne (dept.), Fr. 30/J5
Bois de Vincennes (dept.), Fr. 30/K5
Bois, Rio dos (riv.), Braz. 186/C3
Bois-d'Amont, Fr. 60/C4
Bois-d'Arcy, Fr. 30/J5
Bois-des-Filion, Qu, Can. 159/N6
Bois-Guillaume, Fr. 57/G2
Boisbriand, Qu, Can. 159/N6
Boise (riv.), Fr. 47/F1
Boise (mts.), Id, US 146/F2
Boise (riv.), Id, US 146/A3
Boise (cap.), Id, US 146/E2
Boise City, Ok, US 152/C2
Boissevain, Mb, Can. 156/D3
Boissevain, Va, US 163/G2
Boissy-Fresnoy, Fr. 30/L4
Boissy-L'Aillerie, Fr. 30/J4
Boissy-le-Châtel, Fr. 30/M5
Boissy-Saint-Léger, Fr. 30/K5
Boissy-Sans-Avoir, Fr. 30/H5
Boizenburg, Ger. 53/H2
Bojano, It. 65/D5
Bojeador (cape), Phil. 88/C1
Boji (plain), Kenya 119/B1
Bojkovice, Czh. 43/J4
Bojnūrd, Iran 103/J2
Bojonegoro, Indo. 89/E4
Boju, Nga. 115/G5
Boju Ega, Nga. 115/H5
Bok, PNG 129/G1
Bok Tower Gardens, Fl, US 164/M8
Bokala, D.R. Congo 120/D3
Bokapo Li, D.R. Congo 121/E2
Bokaro Steel City, India 97/F4
Bokat, Indo. 91/F3
Bokata, D.R. Congo 121/E2
Bokatola, D.R. Congo 120/D3
Bokchito, Ok, US 153/F3
Boké, Gui. 114/B4
Boké (pol. reg.), Gui. 114/B4
Bokele, D.R. Congo 121/E3
Bokengo, D.R. Congo 121/E2
Bokhan, Rus. 78/E1
Bokhol (plain), Kenya 119/B1
Boknafjorden (estu.), Nor. 38/C4
Boko, India 97/H3
Boko, Congo 120/C4
Boko, Kaz. 99/D2
Boko Songo, Congo 120/C4
Bokode, D.R. Congo 120/D2
Bokol (peak), Kenya 119/B1
Bokondini, Indo. 91/J4
Bokoro, Chad 116/C2
Bokote, D.R. Congo 120/E3
Bokpyin, Myan. 94/B4
Boksburg, SAfr. 124/Q13
Bokspits, Bots. 124/C2
Bokungu, D.R. Congo 121/E3
Bol, Chad 116/B2
Bol'shaya Khobda (riv.), Kaz. 71/K2
Bol'shaya Kinel' (riv.), Rus. 71/K1
Bol'shaya Ussurka (riv.), Rus. 79/L2
Bol'shoy Irgiz (riv.), Rus. 71/J1
Bol'shoy Uzen' (riv.), Rus. 71/J2
Bol'shoy Yenisey (riv.), Rus. 78/D1
Bolama, GBis. 114/B4
Bolama, D.R. Congo 121/E2
Bolān (pass), Pak. 101/J3
Bolaños de Calatrava, Sp. 46/D3
Bolayır, Turk. 51/H5
Bolbec, Fr. 57/F1
Bolckow, Mo, US 155/G3
Boldeşti-Scăeni, Rom. 51/H3
Boldon, Eng, UK 35/G2
Bole, Gha. 115/E4
Bole (int'l arpt.), Eth. 118/A3
Bole, China 99/D3
Bolekhiv, Ukr. 72/B3
Boleko, D.R. Congo 120/D3
Boleng (peak), Indo. 128/A2
Boles, Ar, US 153/G3
Bolesławiec, Pol. 43/H3
Boley, Ok, US 153/F3
Bolgatanga, Gha. 115/E4
Bolhrad, Ukr. 51/J3
Boli, China 79/L2
Bolia, D.R. Congo 120/D3
Boliden, Swe. 38/G2
Boligee, Al, US 162/C4
Bolinao (cape), Phil. 88/B1
Bolinao, Phil. 88/B1
Boling, Tx, US 151/G3
Bolingbrook, Il, US 160/B4
Bolivar (pen.), Tx, US 151/G3
Bolivar, Tx, US 153/F4
Bolivar, Mo, US 153/H2
Bolivar, Oh, US 160/F4
Bolívar (peak), Ven. 181/F3
Bolívar (state), Ven. 181/E3
Bolívar, Ecu. 180/A4
Bolívar, Col. 180/B3
Bolívar (dept.), Col. 180/C2
Bolívar (peak), Ven. 180/D2
Bolívar, Arg. 190/E3
Bolivar, Tn, US 162/C3
Bolívar, Bol. 185/E4
Bolívar, Peru 184/B2
Bolivia (ctry.) 179/C4
Bolivia, NC, US 163/H3
Böljane (riv.), Swe. 39/K6
Bolkhov, Rus. 70/F1
Bollate, It. 62/C2
Bollène, Fr. 64/A4
Bolligen, Swi. 60/D4
Bollin (riv.), Eng, UK 35/F5
Bollington, Eng, UK 35/F5
Bollmora, Swe. 39/B1
Bollnäs, Swe. 40/G1
Bollon, Austl. 134/B5
Bollullos Par del Condado, Sp. 46/B4
Bolmen (lake), Swe. 40/E3
Bolney, Eng, UK 37/F5
Bolnisi, Geo. 71/H4
Bolo, D.R. Congo 120/D3
Bolobo, D.R. Congo 120/D3
Bologna, It. 63/E5
Bologna (prov.), It. 63/E3
Bologne, Fr. 60/B1
Bolognesi, Peru 184/C3
Bolognesi, Peru 184/C2
Bologoye, Rus. 68/G4
Bolomba, D.R. Congo 120/D2
Bolombo (riv.), D.R. Congo 121/E2
Bolombo, D.R. Congo 121/E3
Bolon', Rus. 79/M2
Bolon' (lake), Rus. 79/M2
Bolonchén de Rejón, Mex. 176/D2
Bolongongo, Ang. 120/C5
Bolonguera, Ang. 122/B2
Bolpebra, Bol. 184/D3
Bolpur, India 97/F4
Bolsena (lake), It. 48/B1
Bolsena, It. 65/A2
Bol'shakovo, Rus. 41/J4
Bol'shaya Belozërka, Ukr. 73/H4
Bol'shaya Breëstovitsa, Bela. 43/N2
Bol'shaya Chernigovka, Rus. 71/J1
Bol'shaya Damba, Kaz. 71/J3
Bol'shaya Rogovaya (riv.), Rus. 69/P2
Bol'shaya Sosnova, Rus. 69/M4
Bol'shaya Synya (riv.), Rus. 69/N2
Bol'shaya Znamenka, Ukr. 73/H4
Bol'shevik (isl.), Rus. 77/H2
Bol'shevik, Bela. 70/D1
Bol'shezemel'skaya, (tundra), Rus. 69/M2
Bol'shoy Bolvanskiy Nos (pt.), Rus. 74/F2
Bol'shoy Kuganavolok, Rus. 68/H3
Bol'shoy Lyakhov (isl.), Rus. 77/P2
Bol'shoy Lyakhovskiy (isl.), Rus. 75/Q2
Bol'shoy Ut, Rus. 69/N4
Bol'shoy Yenisey (riv.), Rus. 99/G1
Bol'shoye Boldino, Rus. 69/K5
Bol'shoye Nagatkino, Rus. 69/K5
Bol'shoye Soldatskoye, Rus. 73/H2
Bolsover, Eng, UK 35/G5
Bolsover, On, Can. 161/G2
Bolsward, Neth. 52/C2
Bolt (pt.), Eng, UK 36/C6
Boltaña, Sp. 47/F1
Boltigen, Swi. 60/D4
Bolton, Eng, UK 35/F4
Bolton (co.), Eng, UK 35/F4
Bolton, On, Can. 160/T8
Bolton Abbey, Eng, UK 35/G4
Bolu, Turk. 70/D4
Bolu (prov.), Turk. 70/D4
Bolungavík, Ice. 38/M6
Bolus Head (pt.), Ire. 30/N11
Bolvadin, Turk. 104/E1
Bolwarra, Austl. 133/E1
Bóly, Hun. 50/D3
Bolyarovo, Bul. 51/H4
Bolzano, It. 61/H5
Bolzano-Bozen (prov.), It. 61/H4
Bom Conselho, Braz. 183/G5
Bom Despacho, Braz. 186/D3
Bom Jardim de Goiás, Braz. 186/B3
Bom Jardin de Minas, Braz. 187/M6
Bom Jesus, Ang. 120/C5
Bom Jesus, Braz. 189/G4
Bom Jesus, Braz. 183/E5
Bom Jesus, Braz. 183/H4
Bom Jesus da Gurguéia, Serra (mts.), Braz. 187/E1
Bom Jesus da Lapa, Braz. 187/E2
Bom Jesus de Goiás, Braz. 186/C3
Bom Jesus do Gurgueia, Serra do (mts.), Braz. 183/F5
Bom Jesus do Itabapoana, Braz. 187/E4
Bom Jesus dos Perdões, Braz. 187/K8
Bom Sucesso, Braz. 186/D4
Boma, D.R. Congo 120/C4
Boma NP, Sudan 117/G4
Bomaderry, Austl. 133/E2
Bomaneh, D.R. Congo 121/E2
Bomba, Ang. 122/B2
Bombakabo, D.R. Congo 120/D2
Bombala, Austl. 133/D3
Bombala (riv.), Austl. 133/D3
Bombay (Mumbai), India 101/K5
Bombay Hook NWR, De, US 168/C5
Bomberai (pen.), Indo. 91/H4
Bombo, Ugan. 121/H2
Bomboma, D.R. Congo 120/D2
Bombombi, D.R. Congo 121/F2
Bomboyo, Chad 116/B2
Bomerano, It. 65/D6
Bomi, Libr. 114/C5
Bomi, China 86/B2
Bomili, D.R. Congo 121/F2
Bomlitz, Ger. 53/G3
Bømlo (isl.), Nor. 40/A2
Bomokandi (riv.), D.R. Congo 121/F2
Bomongo, D.R. Congo 120/D2
Bomu (riv.), D.R. Congo 107/E4
Bon Air, Va, US 163/J2
Bon Secour (bay), Al, US 164/E2
Bon Wier, Tx, US 151/H2
Bon, Cap (Ra's aţ Ţīb) (cape), Tun. 48/B4
Bon-Encontre, Fr. 44/D4
Bona (mt.), Ak, US 171/K3
Bonāb, Iran 103/J4
Bonabéri, Camr. 120/B1
Bonaduz, Swi. 61/F4
Bonaire (isl.), NAnt. 139/L8
Bonalbo, Austl. 132/E1
Bonampak (ruin), Mex. 176/D2
Bonanza, Ut, US 147/J3
Bonanza, Or, US 146/C2
Bonanza, Co, US 149/J1
Bonanza (peak), Wa, US 144/D3
Bonao, DRep. 173/G4
Bonaparte (arch.), Austl. 128/B3
Bonaparte (riv.), BC, Can. 144/D2
Bonaparte (lake), BC, Can. 144/D2
Bonaparte (mt.), Wa, US 144/E3
Bonaparte (isls.), Austl. 127/B2
Bonasila Dome (mt.), Ak, US 171/F3
Bonaventure, Qu, Can. 158/E1
Bonaventure (riv.), Qu, Can. 158/E1
Bonavista, Nf, Can. 159/L1
Bonavista (cape), Nf, Can. 159/L1
Bonavista (bay), Nf, Can. 159/L1
Boncarbo, Co, US 152/B2
Bonchamp-lès-Laval, Fr. 57/E4
Bonchester Bridge, Sc, UK 33/D6
Boncourt, Swi. 60/D3
Bond, Co, US 147/K4
Bondari, Rus. 71/G1
Bondeno, It. 63/E4
Bondi (nbrhd.), Austl. 134/H8
Bondo, D.R. Congo 121/E2
Bondoc (pen.), Phil. 88/C2
Bondoukou, C.d'Iv. 114/E4
Bondowoso, Indo. 89/F4
Bonduel, Wi, US 155/K1
Bone (gulf), Indo. 77/M10
Bone (cape), Tun. 112/M6
Bone Hill Nat'l Wild. Ref., ND, US 156/E4
Bonebone, Indo. 91/F4
Bonefro, It. 65/D4
Bönen, Ger. 53/E5
Bonerate (isls.), Indo. 91/F5
Bo'ness, Sc, UK 33/C4
Bonesteel, SD, US 154/E2
Bonete (peak), Arg. 188/B3
Bonfield, On, Can. 161/G1
Bonfol, Swi. 60/D3
Bonfouca, La, US 164/D2
Bong (co.), Libr. 114/C5
Bong (range), Libr. 114/C5
Bong (lake), China 99/F5
Bong Son, Viet. 94/E3
Bonga, Ang. 122/C2
Bonga, Eth. 117/H4
Bongabong, Phil. 88/C2
Bongaigaon, India 97/H2
Bongandanga, D.R. Congo 121/E2
Bongao, Phil. 88/B4
Bonggi (isl.), Malay. 91/E2
Bongka (riv.), Indo. 91/F4
Bongo, D.R. Congo 121/E4
Bongo, D.R. Congo 120/E2
Bongolava (uplands), Madg. 125/H7
Bongor, Chad 116/B3
Bongou (riv.), CAfr. 116/D4
Bongouanou, C.d'Iv. 114/D5
Bongoville, Gabon 120/C3
Bonham, Tx, US 153/F4
Bonheiden, Belg. 55/D1
Bonhill, Sc, UK 33/B5
Boni, Mali 115/E3
Boni Nat'l Rsv., Kenya 119/C2
Bonifacio, Fr. 48/A2
Bonifacio (str.), Fr.,It. 66/F2
Bonifay, Fl, US 165/F2
Bönigen, Swi. 60/D4
Bonin (isls.), Japan 136/C2
Bonita, Az, US 149/H4
Bonita, Ca, US 166/C5
Bonita, La, US 153/J4
Bonita Springs, Fl, US 165/H4
Bonito (peak), Hon. 176/E3
Bonito, Braz. 183/H5
Bonito, Braz. 189/E2
Bonito de Santa Fé, Braz. 183/G4
Bonjol, Indo. 89/C3
Bonn, Ger. 55/G2
Bonndorf im Schwarzwald, Ger. 61/E2
Bonne, Fr. 60/C5
Bonne (riv.), Fr. 64/B3
Bonne Terre, Mo, US 162/B2
Bonneau, SC, US 163/H4
Bonnefjorden (fd.), Nor. 38/S8
Bonnelles, Fr. 30/J6
Bonner-West Riverside, Mt, US 145/H4
Bonners Ferry, Id, US 144/F3
Bonnet (lake), Mb, Can. 156/F2
Bonnétable, Fr. 57/F4
Bonneuil-sur-Marne, Fr. 30/K5
Bonneval, Fr. 57/G4
Bonneville, Fr. 60/C5
Bonney Lake, Wa, US 167/C3
Bonnie, Il, US 162/C1
Bonnie Doone, NC, US 163/H3
Bonnières-sur-Seine, Fr. 57/G2
Bonnieux, Fr. 64/B5
Bönnigheim, Ger. 58/C4
Bonnybridge, Sc, UK 33/C5
Bonnyman, Ky, US 163/F2
Bonnyrigg, Sc, UK 33/C5
Bonnyville, Ab, Can. 140/E3
Bono, Ar, US 162/B3
Bonorva, It. 48/A2
Bons-en-Chablais, Fr. 60/C5
Bonsall, Ca, US 166/C4
Bontang, Indo. 91/E3
Bontberg (peak), SAfr. 124/C4
Bontebok NP, SAfr. 124/C4
Bonthain, Indo. 91/E5
Bonthe, SLeo. 114/B5
Bontoc, Phil. 88/C1
Bontomatane, Indo. 91/F5
Bonyeri, Gha. 114/E5
Bonyhád, Hun. 50/D2
Bonzart (lake), Tun. 112/L6
Booker, Tx, US 152/D2
Booker T. Washington Nat'l Mon., Va, US 163/H2
Boola, Gui. 114/C4
Boolaloo, Austl. 130/B2
Booligal, Austl. 133/B1
Boom, Belg. 55/D1
Boomi, Austl. 134/C5
Boone, Co, US 152/B1
Boone (riv.), Ia, US 155/H2
Boone, Ia, US 155/H2
Boone, NC, US 163/G2
Boone (dam), Tn, US 163/F2
Booneville, Ar, US 153/H3
Booneville, Ky, US 162/F2
Booneville, Ms, US 162/C3
Boonsboro, Md, US 161/H5
Boonton, NJ, US 169/H8
Bööntsagaan (lake), Mong. 78/D2
Boonville, Ca, US 146/B4
Boonville, In, US 162/D1
Boonville, Mo, US 155/H4
Boonville, NY, US 161/J3
Boopi (riv.), Bol. 185/E5
Boorabbin NP, Austl. 130/D4
Boorama, Som. 118/B3
Booroondara (mt.), Austl. 132/C1
Booroorban, Austl. 133/B2
Boorowa, Austl. 133/D2
Boos, Fr. 57/G2
Boos (int'l arpt.), Fr. 57/G2
Boos, Ger. 61/G1
Boostedt, Ger. 40/D4
Booster, Ar, US 153/H3
Boot Reefs (reef), PNG 129/G2
Boothia (pen.), Nun, Can. 140/G1
Boothia (gulf), Can. 139/H2
Bootjack, Ca, US 148/C2
Bootle, Eng, UK 35/E5
Booué, Gabon 120/B3
Bopa, Ben. 115/F5
Bopfingen, Ger. 58/D5
Bopili, D.R. Congo 121/E2
Bopolu, Libr. 114/C5
Boppard, Ger. 55/G3
Boppy (mt.), Austl. 132/C1
Boqueirão, Serra do (mts.), Braz. 187/E1
Boqueron (dept.), Par. 188/D2
Boquete (peak), Arg. 190/C4
Boquilla (res.), Mex. 174/D3
Boquillas del Carmen, Mex. 151/C3
Bor, Czh. 59/F3
Bor, Rus. 69/K4
Bor, Sudan 117/F4
Bor, Turk. 102/C2
Bor, Yugo. 50/F3
Bor Ul (mts.), China 74/K5
Bora Bora (isl.), FrPol. 137/K6
Borabu, Thai. 94/C2
Borah (peak), Id, US 147/G1
Borås, Swe. 40/E3
Borāzjān, Iran 103/G4
Borba, Braz. 182/B4
Borba, Port. 46/B3
Borbera (riv.), It. 62/B3
Borbona, It. 65/C2
Borbonnais (reg.), Fr. 44/D3
Borbore (riv.), It. 62/B3
Borča, Yugo. 50/E3
Borcea Branch (riv.), Rom. 51/H3
Borchen, Ger. 53/F5
Borçka, Turk. 71/G4
Borculo, Neth. 52/D4
Borda da Mata, Braz. 187/K7
Bordeaux, Fr. 44/C4
Bordelonville, La, US 164/C2
Borden, PE, Can. 158/F2
Borden (pen.), Nun, Can. 141/H1
Borden, Austl. 130/C5
Borden (isl.), NW, Can. 141/R7
Bordentown, NJ, US 168/D3
Bordertown, Austl. 132/B3
Bordighera, It. 64/D5
Bordj Bou Arreridj, Alg. 112/H4
Bordj Bou Arreridj (wilaya), Alg. 112/H4
Bordj el Kiffan, Alg. 112/G4
Bordj Manaïel, Alg. 112/G4
Bordj Moktar, Alg. 111/F5
Bordj Omar Driss, Alg. 111/G3
Bordj Sainte-Marie, Alg. 110/E4
Bordon, Eng, UK 37/F4
Boré, Mali 114/E3
Borē, Eth. 118/A4
Borehamwood, Eng, UK 30/C2
Borest, Fr. 30/L4
Boretto, It. 62/D4
Borgå (Porvoo), Fin. 41/L1
Borgaretto, It. 62/A2
Borgarnes, Ice. 38/N7
Borgaro Torinese, It. 62/A2
Børgefjell NP, Nor. 38/E2
Borgentreich, Ger. 53/G5
Borger, Tx, US 152/D3
Börger, Ger. 53/E3
Borger, Neth. 52/D3
Borgerhout, Belg. 52/B6
Borges Blanques, Sp. 47/F2
Borghetto Lodigiano, It. 62/C3
Borghetto Santo Spirito, It. 62/B5
Borgholm, Swe. 40/G3
Borgholzhausen, Ger. 53/F4
Borghorst, Ger. 53/E4
Borgloon, Belg. 55/E2
Borgnäs (Pornainen), Fin. 39/F4
Borgne (riv.), Swi. 60/D5
Borgne (lake), La, US 164/D3
Borgo, It. 61/H5
Borgo, Fr. 48/A1
Borgo (int'l arpt.), Burk. 114/D4
Borgo a Mozzano, It. 62/D6
Borgo Maggiore, SMar. 63/F6
Borgo Sabotino, It. 65/B5
Borgo San Dalmazzo, It. 64/D4
Borgo San Giacomo, It. 62/C3

Borgo San Lorenzo, It. 63/E6
Borgo Tossignano, It. 63/E5
Borgo Val di Taro, It. 62/C5
Borgo Vercelli, It. 62/B3
Borgofranco d'Ivrea, It. 62/A1
Borgomanero, It. 62/B2
Borgonovo Val Tidone, It. 62/C3
Borgosatollo, It. 62/D3
Borgosesia, It. 62/B2
Borgou (prov.), Ben. 115/F4
Borgund, Nor. 40/B1
Bori, Nga. 115/G5
Borikhan, Laos 94/C2
Borinskoye, Rus. 70/F1
Borio, India 97/F3
Borisoglebsk, Rus. 73/M2
Borisovka, Rus. 73/J2
Borisovo (nbrhd.), Rus. 69/W9
Borispol (int'l arpt.), Ukr. 72/F2
Borja, Sp. 46/E2
Borja, Peru 184/B2
Borken, Ger. 53/G6
Borken, Ger. 52/D5
Børkop, Den. 40/C4
Borkou (reg.), Chad 108/C5
Borkou-Ennedi-Tibesti (pref.), Chad 116/C1
Borkum (isl.), Ger. 52/D1
Borkum, Ger. 52/D1
Borkum (arpt.), Ger. 52/D1
Borlänge, Swe. 40/F1
Bormes-les-Mimosas, Fr. 64/C6
Bormida, It. 62/B5
Bormida (riv.), It. 45/H4
Bormida di Millesimo (riv.), It. 62/B4
Bormio, It. 61/G5
Born, Neth. 55/E1
Borna, Ger. 42/G3
Borndiep (chan.), Neth. 52/C2
Borne (riv.), Fr. 60/C6
Borne, Neth. 52/D4
Bornel, Fr. 54/B5
Bornem, Belg. 55/D1
Borneo (isl.), Indo.,Malay. 77/L9
Borneo (isl.), Indo. 91/E3
Bornheim, Ger. 55/G2
Bornholm (co.), Den. 40/F4
Bornholm (isl.), Swe.,Den. 29/F3
Bornholmsgat (chan.), Den.,Swi. 43/H1
Borno, It. 61/G6
Borno (state), Nga. 116/B2
Bornos, Sp. 46/C4
Börnsen, Ger. 53/H2
Bornus (plain), Nga. 116/B2
Boro (riv.), Sudan 117/E3
Borobudur (ruin), Indo. 89/E4
Borodino, Rus. 74/K4
Borodino, Ukr. 51/J2
Borodyanka, Ukr. 72/E2
Borohoro (mts.), China 99/D3
Boromo, Burk. 114/E4
Boron, Ca, US 148/D3
Borongan, Phil. 88/D3
Borough Green, Eng, UK 30/D3
Boroughbridge, Eng, UK 35/G3
Borovany, Czh. 59/H5
Borovichi, Rus. 68/G4
Borovlyanka, Rus. 99/D1
Borovo, Cro. 50/D3
Borovo, Bul. 51/G4
Borovsk, Rus. 70/F1
Borovskiy, Rus. 69/Q4
Borovskoy, Kaz. 69/Q5
Borraan, Som. 118/D3
Borre, Nor. 40/D2
Borrego Springs, Ca, US 148/D4
Borris, Ire. 32/D4
Borris in Ossory, Ire. 32/C4
Borrisokane, Ire. 32/B4
Borrisoleigh, Ire. 32/C4
Borrnida (riv.), It. 62/B3
Borroloola, Austl. 129/E4
Borroloola Abor. Land, Austl. 129/D4
Borşa, Rom. 51/F2
Borsec, Rom. 72/C4
Borshchiv, Ukr. 72/D3
Borshchovochnyy (mts.), Rus. 79/H1
Borso del Grappa, It. 63/E2
Borsod-Abaúj-Zemplén (co.), Hun. 43/L4
Borssele, Neth. 52/A6
Borstel, Ger. 53/F3
Bort-les-Orgues, Fr. 44/E4
Bortala (riv.), China 99/D3
Borth, Wal, UK 36/B2
Boruca, CR 177/F4
Borūjen, Iran 103/G4
Borūjerd, Iran 103/G3
Børup, Den. 39/H7
Boryslav, Ukr. 43/M4
Boryspil', Ukr. 72/F2
Borzna, Ukr. 72/G2
Borzonasca, It. 62/C5
Borzya, Rus. 78/H1
Bosa, It. 48/A2
Bosaaso (Bender Cassim), Som. 118/D3
Bosanska Dubica, Bosn. 50/C3
Bosanska Gradiška, Bosn. 50/C3
Bosanska Kostajnica, Bosn. 50/C3
Bosanska Krupa, Bosn. 50/C3
Bosanski Brod, Bosn. 50/D3
Bosanski Petrovac, Bosn. 50/C3
Bosanski Šamac, Bosn. 50/D3
Bošany, Slvk. 43/K4
Bosavi (mt.), PNG 129/F1
Bosc-le-Hard, Fr. 57/G1
Boscawen, NH, US 161/L3
Bosco, La, US 153/H4
Bosco, It. 65/B1
Bosco Mesola, It. 63/F4
Boscobel, Wi, US 155/J2
Bosconero, It. 62/A2
Boscoreale, It. 65/D6
Bose, China 87/E4
Bosham, Eng, UK 37/F5
Boshnyakovo, Rus. 79/N2
Boshof, SAfr. 124/D3
Boshrūyeh, Iran 103/J3
Boskoop, Neth. 52/B4
Boskovice, Czh. 43/J4
Bosler, Wy, US 154/B3
Bosna (riv.), Bosn. 50/D3
Bosnia and Herzegovina (ctry.) 29/F4
Bošnjaci, Cro. 50/D3
Bōsō (pen.), Japan 85/G3
Bosobolo, D.R. Congo 116/C4
Bososama, D.R. Congo 116/D4
Bosporus (str.), Turk. 70/D4
Bosporus (riv.), Turk. 103/N6
Bosque del Apache Nat'l Wild Ref., NM, US 149/J4
Bosque Farms, NM, US 149/J3
Bosques Petrificados, Mon. Natural, Arg. 191/C5
Boss, Mo, US 162/B2
Bossangoa, CAfr. 116/C4
Bossembele, CAfr. 116/C4
Bossentélé, CAfr. 116/C4
Bossier City, La, US 153/H4
Bosso, Niger 116/B2
Bossut (cape), Austl. 128/A4
Bostān, Iran 103/G4
Bostan, China 99/D4
Bostānābād-e Bālā, Iran 103/F2
Bosten (lake), China 99/E3
Boston (mts.), Ar, US 153/H3
Boston, Tx, US 153/G4
Boston, Eng, UK 35/H6
Boston, Ga, US 165/G2
Boston (cap.), Ma, US 158/B4
Bostwick, Fl, US 165/H3
Bosut (riv.), Cro. 50/D3
Boswell, In, US 160/C4
Boswil, Swi. 61/E3
Bot Makak, Camr. 120/B2
Botād, India 101/K4
Botany, Austl. 133/E1
Botelerpunt (pt.), SAfr. 125/F2
Botelhos, Braz. 187/K6
Botene, Laos 94/C1
Botev (peak), Bul. 51/G4
Botevgrad, Bul. 51/F4
Bothaspas (pass), SAfr. 125/E2
Bothaville, SAfr. 124/D2
Bothel, Eng, UK 35/E2
Bothel, Ger. 53/G2
Bothell, Wa, US 167/C2
Bothenhampton, Eng, UK 36/D5
Bothnia (gulf), Swe.,Fin. 192/E
Bothwell, Austl. 132/C4
Botkyrka, Swe. 39/A1
Botletle (riv.), Bots. 122/D4
Botlikh, Rus. 71/H4
Botoşani, Rom. 72/D4
Botoşani (prov.), Rom. 51/H2
Botou, China 80/D3
Botrange (peak), Belg. 55/F3
Botrivier, SAfr. 124/L11
Botsford, Ct, US 169/E1
Botswana (ctry.) 107/E7
Bottanuco, It. 62/C2
Botte Donato (peak), It. 48/E3
Bottesford, Eng, UK 35/H6
Bottesford, Eng, UK 35/H4
Botticino, It. 62/D2
Bottineau, ND, US 156/D3
Bottineau Winter Park, ND, US 156/D3
Bottrighe, It. 63/F3
Bottrop, Ger. 52/D5
Botucatu, Braz. 189/G2
Botwood, Nf, Can. 159/K1
Bötzow, Ger. 42/Q6
Bou (riv.), C.d'Iv. 114/D4
Bou Arfa, Mor. 111/E2
Boû Djébéha (well), Mali 114/E2
Bou Hamdane, Oued (riv.), Alg. 112/K6
Bou Ismaïl, Alg. 112/G4
Bou Izakarn, Mor. 110/C3
Bou Kadir, Alg. 112/F4
Bou Laber (well), Alg. 110/D4
Boû Lanouâr, Mrta. 110/A5
Bou Naceur (peak), Mor. 112/C3
Bou Regreg (riv.), Mor. 112/A3
Bou Saâda, Alg. 112/H5
Bou Salem, Tun. 112/L6
Bou Sellam, Oued (riv.), Alg. 112/H4
Bouaflé, C.d'Iv. 114/D5
Bouafle, Fr. 30/H5
Bouaké, C.d'Iv. 114/D5
Bouali, CAfr. 116/C4
Bouanga, Congo 120/D3
Bouar, CAfr. 116/B4
Bouba Ndjida, PN de, Camr. 116/B3
Boubín (peak), Czh. 59/G5
Bouc-Bel-Air, Fr. 64/B6
Bouca, CAfr. 116/C4
Bouchain, Fr. 54/C3
Bouchegouf, Alg. 112/K6
Boucherville, Qu, Can. 159/P6
Bouches-du-Rhône (dept.), Fr. 64/A5
Bouchet (mtn.), Fr. 64/D3
Boucle Du Baoulé, PN de la, Mali 114/C3
Boudenib, Mor. 110/E3
Boudi, Eth. 118/B4
Boudreaux (lake), La, US 164/C3
Boudry, Swi. 60/C4
Bouenza (riv.), Congo 120/C3
Bouenza (pol. reg.), Congo 120/C3
Boufarik, Alg. 112/G4
Bouffémont, Fr. 30/J4
Bougainville (cape), Austl. 128/B3
Bougainville (reef), Austl. 127/D2
Bougainville (isl.), PNG 136/E5
Bougainville (reef), PNG 129/G3
Bougainville (cape), UK 191/F6
Bougara, Alg. 112/G4
Bougar'oûn (cape), Alg. 112/K6
Bough Beech (res.), Eng, UK 30/D3
Boughton, Eng, UK 30/E3
Bougouni, Mali 114/D4
Bougouriba (prov.), Burk. 114/E4
Bougtob, Alg. 66/D4
Bouguenais, Fr. 44/C3
Bouhachem (peak), Mor. 112/B2
Bouhalla (peak), Mor. 112/B2
Bouillancy, Fr. 30/L4
Bouillon, Belg. 55/E4
Bouira, Alg. 112/G4
Bouira (wilaya), Alg. 112/G4
Boujad, Mor. 110/D2
Boukhalf (Tangier) (int'l arpt.), Mor. 112/B2
Boukoko, CAfr. 120/D2
Boukoumbé, Ben. 115/F4
Boulaide, Lux. 55/E4
Boulaouane, Mor. 110/C2
Boulay-Moselle, Fr. 55/F5
Boulazac, Fr. 44/D4
Boulder (riv.), Mt, US 147/H1
Boulder, Co, US 154/B3
Boulder, Mt, US 145/H4
Boulder City, Nv, US 148/E3
Boulder Creek, Ca, US 148/A2
Boulder Hill, Il, US 167/P16
Boulemane, Mor. 110/D2
Boulemane (prov.), Mor. 112/C3
Bouleurs, Fr. 30/L5
Boulgo (prov.), Burk. 115/E4
Boulia, Austl. 131/H2
Boulieu-lès-Annonay, Fr. 64/A2
Bouligny, Fr. 55/E5
Boulkiemde (prov.), Burk. 115/E3
Boullarre, Fr. 30/M4
Boulogne (riv.), Fr. 44/C3
Boulogne-Billancourt, Fr. 30/J5
Boulogne-sur-Mer, Fr. 54/A2
Bouloire, Fr. 57/F5
Boulsa, Burk. 115/E3
Boulsworth (hill), Eng, UK 35/F4
Boumalne, Mor. 110/D3
Boumba (riv.), Camr. 120/C2
Boûmdeïd, Mrta. 114/C2
Boumerdas (wilaya), Alg. 112/G4
Boumerdas, Alg. 112/G4
Boun Nua, Laos 86/D4
Bouna, C.d'Iv. 114/E4
Bound Brook, NJ, US 168/D2
Boundary, Yk, Can. 171/K3
Boundary (peak), Nv, US 142/C4
Boundary Bald (mtn.), Me, US 161/L2
Boundary Bend, Austl. 132/B2
Boundiali, C.d'Iv. 114/D4
Boundji, Congo 120/C3
Bountiful, Ut, US 147/H3
Boupanda, Congo 120/C3
Bouquet (res.), Ca, US 166/B1
Bouquet (canyon), Ca, US 166/B2
Bourail, NCal. 137/U12
Bourbeuse (riv.), Mo, US 155/J4
Bourbon, Mo, US 153/J1
Bourbon, In, US 160/C4
Bourbon l'Archambault, Fr. 44/E3
Bourbonnais, Il, US 160/C4
Bourbonnais (reg.), Fr. 66/D1
Bourbonne-les-Bains, Fr. 60/B2
Bourbourg, Fr. 54/B2
Bourbre (riv.), Fr. 64/B1
Bourbriac, Fr. 56/B4
Bourdonné, Fr. 30/G5
Boureït, Mor. 112/B2
Bourem, Mali 115/E2
Bouressa (riv.), Mali 115/F2
Bourg, La, US 164/C3
Bourg-Achard, Fr. 57/F2
Bourg-de-Péage, Fr. 64/B2
Bourg-en-Bresse, Fr. 60/B5
Bourg-lès-Valence, Fr. 64/A3
Bourg-Saint-Andéol, Fr. 64/A4
Bourg-Saint-Maurice, Fr. 64/C1
Bourg-Saint-Pierre, Swi. 60/D6
Bourganeuf, Fr. 44/D4
Bourges, Fr. 44/E3
Bourget (lake), Fr. 60/B6
Bourgneuf (bay), Fr. 44/B3
Bourgogne (canal), Fr. 60/B3
Bourgogne (pol. reg.), Fr. 44/F3
Bourgoin-Jallieu, Fr. 64/B1
Bourgtheroulde-Infreville, Fr. 57/F2
Bourgueil, Fr. 57/F6
Bourke, Austl. 132/C1
Bourmont, Fr. 60/B1
Bourne (riv.), Fr. 64/B2
Bourne, Eng, UK 37/F1
Bourne (riv.), Eng, UK 37/E4
Bourne End, Eng, UK 37/F3
Bournemouth, Eng, UK 37/E5
Bournemouth (co.), Eng, UK 37/E5
Bournemouth (arpt.), Eng, UK 37/E5
Bournville, Eng, UK 37/E2
Bourquim (hill), Ne, US 154/D3
Bourscheid, Lux. 55/F4
Bourtanger Moor (reg.), Ger. 53/E3
Bourth, Fr. 57/F3
Bourton on the Water, Eng, UK 37/E3
Bousbecque, Fr. 54/C2
Bouse, Az, US 149/E4
Bousso, Chad 116/C3
Boussois, Fr. 54/D3
Boussouma, Burk. 115/E3
Boutilimit, Mrta. 114/B2
Bouvard (cape), Austl. 130/B5
Bouvet (isl.), Nor. 27/K8
Bouvron, Fr. 56/D6
Bouxières-aux-Dames, Fr. 55/F6
Bouxwiller, Fr. 55/G6
Bouza, Niger 115/G3
Bouzillé, Fr. 57/D6
Bouznika, Mor. 112/A3
Bouzonville, Fr. 55/F5
Bovalino, It. 48/E3
Bovegno, It. 62/D2
Boven Tapanahoni (riv.), Sur. 181/H4
Boven Tappanahoni (riv.), Sur. 182/C2
Boven-Hardinxveld, Neth. 52/B5
Bovenden, Ger. 53/G5
Bovenkarspel, Neth. 52/C3
Bovenwijde (lake), Neth. 52/D3
Boves, Fr. 54/B4
Boves, It. 64/D4
Bovey, Mn, US 157/H4
Bovey Tracey, Eng, UK 36/C5
Bovezzo, It. 62/D2
Bovina, Tx, US 152/C3
Bovingdon, Eng, UK 30/B1
Bovino, It. 50/B5
Bovolone, It. 63/E3
Bovril, Arg. 188/E4
Bow (riv.), Ab, Can. 140/E3
Bow (cr.), Ks, US 154/E4
Bow (riv.), Ab, Can. 145/H2
Bow City, Ab, Can. 145/H2
Bow Island, Ab, Can. 145/J3
Bow River Abor. Land, Austl. 128/B4
Bowbells, ND, US 156/C3
Bowdle, SD, US 156/E5
Bowdoin NWR, Mt, US 145/L3
Bowdon, ND, US 156/E4
Bowdon, Eng, UK 35/F5
Bowdon, Ga, US 162/E4
Bowen, Austl. 134/C3
Bowen, Arg. 190/D2
Bowen Island, BC, Can. 144/C3
Bowers Beach, De, US 168/C5
Bowes, Eng, UK 35/G3
Bowie, Tx, US 153/F4
Bowie, Az, US 149/H4
Bowie, Md, US 168/B6
Bowling Green, Oh, US 160/E4
Bowling Green, Fl, US 164/M8
Bowling Green (cape), Austl. 134/B2
Bowling Green, Ky, US 162/D2
Bowling Green, Mo, US 155/J4
Bowling Green, Va, US 163/J1
Bowling Green Bay NP, Austl. 134/B2
Bowman, ND, US 156/C4
Bowman (bay), Nun, Can. 141/J2
Bowman, Ga, US 163/F3
Bowman (mt.), BC, Can. 144/D2
Bowman-Haley (dam), ND, US 156/C5
Bowman-Haley (lake), ND, US 156/C4
Bowmansdale, Pa, US 168/B3
Bowmanstown, Pa, US 168/C2
Bowmansville, Pa, US 168/B3
Bowmanville, On, Can. 160/V8
Bowmore, Sc, UK 31/Q9
Bowness-on-Solway, Eng, UK 35/E2
Bowokan (isls.), Indo. 91/F4
Bowral, Austl. 133/E2
Bowring, Ok, US 153/F2
Bowron (riv.), BC, Can. 144/D1
Bowsman, Mb, Can. 156/D1
Bowutu (mts.), PNG 129/G1
Bowwood, Zam. 122/E3
Box Elder (riv.), Mt, US 156/B5
Box Elder (cr.), SD, US 154/C3
Box Elder (cr.), Co, US 154/B3
Box Elder, SD, US 154/C1
Box Elder, Mt, US 145/J3
Box Hill (nbrhd.), Austl. 132/G5
Box Springs, Ga, US 162/E4
Boxberg, Ger. 58/C4
Boxelder, Wy, US 154/B2
Boxholm, Swe. 40/F2
Boxing, China 80/D3
Boxley, Ar, US 153/H3
Boxmeer, Neth. 52/C5
Boxodoi, China 78/H3
Boxtel, Neth. 52/C5
Boxum, Neth. 52/C2
Boyabat, Turk. 70/E4
Boyabo, D.R. Congo 120/D2
Boyabo, D.R. Congo 116/C5
Boyaca (dept.), Col. 180/C3
Boyalık, Turk. 103/M6
Boyanup, Austl. 130/B5
Boyarka, Ukr. 72/F2
Boyce, La, US 164/B2
Boychinovtsi, Bul. 51/F4
Boyd, Tx, US 150/K6
Boydell, Ar, US 153/J4
Boyds, Wa, US 144/E3
Boydton, Va, US 163/H2
Boye, China 80/C3
Boyer (riv.), Ia, US 155/G2
Boyero, Co, US 154/C4
Boyertown, Pa, US 168/C3
Boyes, Mt, US 154/B1
Boyette, Fl, US 164/L8
Boykins, Va, US 163/J2
Boyle, Ire. 32/B2
Boyle, Ms, US 162/B4
Boyne (riv.), Ire. 34/B4
Boyne City, Mi, US 160/D2
Boyne Falls, Mi, US 160/D2
Boyne Island, Austl. 134/C3
Boynton, Ok, US 153/G3
Boynton Beach, Fl, US 164/P9
Boysen (res.), Wy, US 147/J2
Boysen (dam), Wy, US 147/J2
Boyuibe, Bol. 188/D2
Boyup Brook, Austl. 130/C5
Boz (pt.), Turk. 51/J5
Bozcaada, Turk. 49/K3
Bozcaada (isl.), Gre. 49/J3
Bozel, Fr. 64/C2
Bozeman, Mt, US 147/H1
Bozhai, China 87/F3
Bozkir, Turk. 102/C2
Bozkurt, Turk. 70/E4
Bozman, Md, US 168/B6
Bozoum, CAfr. 116/C4
Bozova, Turk. 102/D2
Bozüyük, Turk. 104/E1
Bozyazı, Turk. 104/C1
Bozzolo, It. 62/D3
Bra, It. 62/A3
Braan (riv.), Sc, UK 33/C3
Bråån (riv.), Swe. 39/K7
Brabourne Lees, Eng, UK 37/G4
Brač (isl.), Cro. 48/E1
Bracciano (lake), It. 48/B1
Bracciano, It. 65/B3
Bracebridge, On, Can. 161/G2
Bracieux, Fr. 57/G5
Bracigliano, It. 65/D6
Brackel, Ger. 53/H2
Bracken, Sk, Can. 145/K3
Brackenheim, Ger. 58/C4
Brackett, Wi, US 155/J1
Brackettville, Tx, US 151/D3
Brackley, Eng, UK 37/E2
Bracknagh, Ire. 32/C3
Bracknell, Eng, UK 37/F4
Bracknell Forest (co.), Eng, UK 37/F4
Brackwede, Ger. 53/F5
Braço do Norte, Braz. 189/G4
Braço Menor do Araguaia (riv.), Braz. 186/C2
Brad, Rom. 51/F2
Bradano (riv.), It. 50/B5
Bradda (pt.), IM, UK 34/D3
Braddock, ND, US 156/D4
Braden, Tn, US 162/C3
Bradenton, Fl, US 165/G4
Bradford, Eng, UK 35/G4
Bradford (co.), Eng, UK 35/G4
Bradford, Ar, US 153/J3
Bradford, Oh, US 160/D4
Bradford, Pa, US 161/G4
Bradford, Vt, US 161/K3
Bradford West Gwillimbury, On, Can. 161/G2
Bradford-on-Avon, Eng, UK 36/D4
Brading, Eng, UK 37/E5
Bradley, Wi, US 157/K5
Bradley, Ar, US 153/H4
Bradley (int'l arpt.), Ct, US 161/K4
Bradley, Il, US 160/C4
Bradley, Ca, US 148/B3
Bradley Beach, NJ, US 168/D3
Bradley Junction, Fl, US 164/M8
Bradner, Oh, US 160/E4
Brady (cr.), Tx, US 151/E2
Brady, Ne, US 154/D3
Brady, Mt, US 145/J3
Brady, Tx, US 151/E2
Braeburn, Yk, Can. 171/L3
Braemar (reg.), Sc, UK 33/C2
Braemar, Sc, UK 33/C2
Braeriach (peak), Sc, UK 33/C2
Braga, Port. 46/A2
Braga (dist.), Port. 46/A2
Bragado, Arg. 190/E2
Bragança, Port. 46/B2
Bragança (dist.), Port. 46/B2
Bragança, Braz. 183/E3
Bragança Paulista, Braz. 187/K7
Bragg Creek, Ab, Can. 144/G2
Braggs, Ok, US 153/G3
Bragin, Bela. 72/F2
Braham, Mn, US 157/H5
Brahmakund, India 86/C3
Brāhmanbāria, Bang. 97/H4
Brahmaputra (riv.), Asia 77/J7
Braich-y-Pwll (pt.), Wal, UK 34/D6
Braid (riv.), NI, UK 34/B2
Braidwood, Il, US 160/B4
Braidwood, Austl. 133/D2
Brăila, Rom. 51/H3
Brăila (prov.), Rom. 51/H3
Brainard, Ne, US 155/F3
Brainards, NJ, US 168/C2
Braine, Fr. 54/C5
Braine-l'Alleud, Belg. 55/D2
Braine-le-Comte, Belg. 55/D2
Brainerd, Mn, US 157/G4
Braintree, Eng, UK 37/G3
Braithwaithe (pt.), Austl. 128/D2
Brajarajnagar, India 95/D1
Brak (riv.), SAfr. 124/C3
Brak (riv.), SAfr. 124/D3
Brake, Ger. 53/F2
Brakel, Belg. 54/C2
Brakel, Ger. 53/G5
Brakel, Neth. 52/C5
Brakna (pol. reg.), Mrta. 114/B2
Brålanda, Swe. 40/E2
Bralorne, BC, Can. 144/C2
Bram (peak), It. 64/D4
Bram, Fr. 44/E5
Bramalea, On, Can. 160/T8
Braman, Ok, US 153/F2
Bramdrupdam, Den. 40/C4
Bramhope, Eng, UK 35/G4
Bramley (mtn.), NY, US 161/J3
Bramley, Eng, UK 30/B3
Brampton, Eng, UK 35/F2
Brampton, On, Can. 160/T8
Bramsche, Ger. 53/F4
Bramstedt, Ger. 53/F2
Bran (riv.), Sc, UK 33/A1
Branam, Gha. 115/E5
Brancaleone-Marina, It. 48/E4
Brancepeth, Sk, Can. 145/M1
Branch, Mn, US 157/H5
Branch, Nf, Can. 159/L2
Branch, La, US 164/B2
Branch Dale, Pa, US 168/B2
Branch, North (riv.), Md, US 168/B5
Branch, South (riv.), WV, US 163/H1
Branchville, NJ, US 168/D1
Branchville, Ct, US 169/E1
Branco (riv.), Braz. 179/C2
Brand, Aus. 61/F3
Brandberg (peak), Namb. 122/B4
Brandbu, Nor. 40/D1
Brande, Den. 40/C4
Brandenburg, Ger. 42/G2
Brandenburg (state), Ger. 42/P6
Brandenburg, Ky, US 162/D2
Brander, Pass of (pass), Sc, UK 33/A4
Branderburgh, Sc, UK 33/C1
Brandesburton, Eng, UK 35/H4
Brandfort, SAfr. 124/D3
Brandizzo, It. 62/A2
Brandon, Mb, Can. 156/E3
Brandon (peak), Ire. 32/D5
Brandon, Eng, UK 35/G2
Brandon, Eng, UK 37/G2
Brandon, Co, US 152/C1
Brandon, Fl, US 164/L8
Brandon, Mn, US 157/G5
Brandon, Ms, US 162/C4
Brandon, SD, US 155/F2
Brandon, Vt, US 161/K3
Brandsen, Arg. 191/J11
Brandsville, Mo, US 153/J2
Brandvlei, SAfr. 124/C3
Brandýs nad Labem, Czh. 59/H2
Brandywine, Md, US 168/B6
Brandywine (riv.), Pa, US 168/C4
Brandywine, WV, US 163/H1
Branford, Fl, US 165/G3
Branford, Ct, US 169/F1
Branges, Fr. 60/B4
Braniewo, Pol. 41/H4
Brannenburg, Ger. 45/K3
Bransgore, Eng, UK 37/E5
Branson, Mo, US 153/H2
Brant (co.), On, Can. 160/S9
Brant Beach, NJ, US 168/D4
Brantford, On, Can. 160/S9
Branti, Indo. 89/D4
Brantley, Al, US 165/E2
Brantwood, Wi, US 157/J5
Branxholm, Austl. 132/C4
Branxholme, Austl. 132/B3
Branxton, Austl. 133/E1
Branxton, Eng, UK 33/D5
Branzoll (Bronzolo), It. 61/H4
Brasfield, Ar, US 153/J3
Brashear, Mo, US 155/H3
Brasher Falls-Winthrop, NY, US 161/J2
Brasiléia, Braz. 184/D3
Brasília (cap.), Braz. 186/D2
Brasília de Minas, Braz. 186/D3
Brasilia, PN de, Braz. 186/C2
Braşov, Rom. 51/G3
Braşov (prov.), Rom. 51/G3
Brass, Nga. 115/G5
Brasschaat, Belg. 52/B6
Brassey (mt.), Austl. 131/G2
Brasstown Bald (peak), Ga, US 162/F3
Brastad, Swe. 40/D2
Braswell, Ga, US 162/E4
Brat (isl.), Cro. 67/H2
Bratislava (cap.), Slvk. 50/C1
Bratislava (Ivanka) (int'l arpt.), Slvk. 50/C1
Bratislavský (pol. reg.), Slvk. 43/J4
Bratsigovo, Bul. 49/J1
Bratsk, Rus. 75/L4
Brats'ke, Ukr. 72/F4
Bratslav, Ukr. 72/E3
Brattleboro, Vt, US 161/K3
Bratunac, Bosn. 50/D3
Braubach, Ger. 55/G3
Braulio Carrillo, PN, CR 172/E5
Braunau am Inn, Aus. 59/G6
Braunfels, Ger. 58/B1
Braunlage, Ger. 53/H5
Bräunlingen, Ger. 61/E2
Braunschweig, Ger. 53/H4
Braunschweig (arpt.), Ger. 53/H4
Braunton, Eng, UK 36/B4
Brava (coast), Sp. 47/G2
Brava (pt.), Chile 191/C7
Brava (isl.), CpV. 107/J11
Brava (pt.), Uru. 191/K11
Brave, Pa, US 160/F5
Bråviken (inlet), Swe. 40/G2
Bravo (peak), Bol. 188/C1
Bravo (peak), Peru 184/B2
Bravo del Norte (riv.), Mex. 172/A2
Brawley, Ca, US 148/E4
Bray (pt.), Ire. 34/B5
Bray, Ire. 34/B5
Bray, Eng, UK 30/A2
Bray (isl.), Nun, Can. 141/J2
Bray-Dunes, Fr. 54/B1
Braye (riv.), Fr. 44/D3
Braymer, Mo, US 155/H4
Brazeau (riv.), Ab, Can. 144/F1
Brazeau (mt.), Ab, Can. 144/F1
Brazey-en-Plaine, Fr. 60/B3
Brazil, In, US 160/C5
Brazil (ctry.) 179/D3
Brazil, Tn, US 162/C3
Brazilian Highlands (uplands), Braz. 179/E4
Brazo Casiquiare (riv.), Ven. 181/E4
Brazo Sur (riv.), Arg. 191/C6
Brazópolis, Braz. 187/L7
Brazoria (co.), Tx, US 151/M9
Brazoria NWR, Tx, US 151/G3
Brazos (riv.), US 139/H6
Brazos, Double Mountain Fork (riv.), Tx, US 152/D4
Brazos, Salt Fork (riv.), Tx, US 152/D4
Brazzaville (cap.), Congo 120/C4
Brčko, Bosn. 50/D3
Brda (riv.), Pol. 40/G5
Brdy (mts.), Czh. 43/G4
Brea, Ca, US 166/G8
Breadalbane (dist.), Sc, UK 33/B4
Breakenridge (mt.), BC, Can. 144/D3
Bream (pt.), NZ 135/C1
Bream, Eng, UK 36/D3
Bream Tail (pt.), NZ 135/C2
Breamish (riv.), Eng, UK 33/D6
Bréancon, Fr. 30/J4
Bréau, Fr. 30/L6
Breaux Bridge, La, US 164/C2
Breaza, Rom. 51/G3
Brebbia, It. 62/B2
Brebes, Indo. 89/E4
Brécey, Fr. 57/D3
Brech, Fr. 56/C5
Brêche (riv.), Fr. 54/B5
Brechen, Ger. 58/B2
Brechin, Sc, UK 33/D3
Brecht, Belg. 52/B6
Breckenridge, Mn, US 156/F4
Breckenridge, Mo, US 155/H4
Breckenridge, Tx, US 151/E1
Breckerfeld, Ger. 53/E6
Breckland (phys. reg.), Eng, UK 37/G2
Brecknock (pen.), Chile 191/C7
Brecon, Wal, UK 36/C3
Brecon Beacons (mts.), Wal, UK 36/C3
Bréda (riv.), Fr. 64/C2
Breda, Neth. 52/B5
Bredaryd, Swe. 40/E3
Bredasdorp, SAfr. 124/M11
Bredbo, Austl. 133/D2
Bredebro, Den. 40/C4
Bredene, Belg. 54/B1
Bredgar, Eng, UK 30/F3
Bredstedt, Ger. 40/C4
Bree, Belg. 55/E1
Breë (riv.), SAfr. 124/B4
Breeches (cr.), Pa, US 168/A3
Breed, Wi, US 157/K5
Breese, Il, US 162/C1
Breezand, Neth. 52/B3
Breezy Point, Mn, US 157/G4
Breg (riv.), Ger. 42/E5
Bregagno (peak), It. 61/F5
Bregalinca (riv.), FYROM 49/H2
Breganze, It. 63/E2
Bregenz, Aus. 61/F3
Bregenzer Ache (riv.), Aus. 61/F3
Bregovo, Bul. 50/F3
Brégy, Fr. 30/L4
Bréhal, Fr. 56/D3
Breidhafjördhur (bay), Ice. 38/M6
Breil-Brigels, Swi. 61/F4
Breil-sur-Roya, Fr. 64/D5
Breisach, Ger. 60/D1
Breitbrunn am Chiemsee, Ger. 59/F7
Breitenauriegel (peak), Ger. 59/G5
Breitenbach, Swi. 60/D3
Breitenbach, Ger. 55/G5
Breitenbrunn, Ger. 59/E4
Breitenbrunn, Ger. 59/F2
Breitenfurt bei Wien, Aus. 51/N7
Breitenworbis, Ger. 53/H6
Breithorn (peak), Swi. 60/D5
Breithorn (peak), Swi. 60/D6
Brejinho de Nazaré, Braz. 186/C1
Brejo, Braz. 183/F3
Brejo do Cruz, Braz. 183/G4
Brejo Santo, Braz. 183/G4
Brembate di Sopra, It. 62/C2
Brembilla, It. 62/C2
Brembio, It. 62/C3
Brembo (riv.), It. 61/F6
Bremen, Ger. 53/F2
Bremen (int'l arpt.), Ger. 53/F2
Bremen (state), Ger. 40/C5
Bremen, Ga, US 162/E4
Bremen, In, US 160/C4
Bremen, Oh, US 160/E5
Bremer (riv.), Austl. 134/E7
Bremerhaven, Ger. 53/F1
Bremerhaven (arpt.), Ger. 53/F1
Bremerton, Wa, US 144/C4
Bremervörde, Ger. 53/G2
Bremgarten, Swi. 61/E3
Bremgarten bei Bern, Swi. 60/D4
Bremnes, Nor. 40/A2
Bremond, Tx, US 151/F2
Bremsa (riv.), Nor. 38/R8
Brenchley, Eng, UK 30/E3
Brend (riv.), Ger. 58/D2
Brendel (lake), Mi, US 167/E7
Brendola, It. 63/E3
Brendon (hills), Eng, UK 36/C4
Brenham, Tx, US 151/F2
Brenne (riv.), Fr. 42/C5
Brenner (pass), Aus. 61/H4
Brenner (riv.), Austl. 131/N9
Brenno (riv.), Swi. 61/E5
Breno, It. 61/G6
Brent, On, Can. 161/G1
Brent (riv.), Eng, UK 30/B2
Brent (bor.), Eng, UK 30/C2
Brent (res.), Eng, UK 30/C2
Brent, Al, US 162/D4
Brenta (peak), It. 61/G5
Brenta (riv.), It. 45/J4
Brenton, WV, US 163/G2
Brentwood, Eng, UK 30/D2
Brentwood, Ca, US 167/L11
Brentwood, Tn, US 162/D2
Brentwood, NY, US 169/E2
Brenz (riv.), Ger. 58/D5
Brescello, It. 62/D4
Brescia (prov.), It. 61/G6
Brescia, It. 62/D2
Breskens, Neth. 54/C1
Breslau, Tx, US 151/F3
Bresle (riv.), Fr. 44/D1
Bresles, Fr. 54/B5
Bresque (riv.), Fr. 64/C5
Bressana, It. 62/C3
Bressanone, It. 45/J3
Bressay (isl.), Sc, UK 31/W13
Bressuire, Fr. 44/C3
Brest, Bela. 43/M2
Brest (int'l arpt.), Bela. 43/M2
Brest, Fr. 56/A4
Brestskaya Voblasts, Bela. 70/C1
Bretagne (pt.), Fr. 125/T15
Bretagne (pol. reg.), Fr. 44/B2
Bretagne, Monts de (mts.), Fr. 44/B2
Bretaña, Peru 184/C2
Breteuil, Fr. 57/F3
Breteuil, Fr. 54/B4
Brethren, Mi, US 160/C2
Brétigny-sur-Orge, Fr. 30/J6
Breton, Ab, Can. 144/G1
Breton (cape), NS, Can. 159/H3
Breton (isls.), La, US 164/D3
Breton (sound), La, US 164/D3
Breton Cove, NS, Can. 159/G2
Breton Nat'l Wild. Ref., La, US 164/D3
Brett (cape), NZ 135/C1
Brett (riv.), Eng, UK 37/G2
Brettach (riv.), Ger. 58/C4
Bretten, Ger. 58/B4
Bretteville-L'Orgueilleuse, Fr. 57/E2
Bretzenheim, Ger. 55/G4
Breuberg, Ger. 58/C3
Breueh (isl.), Indo. 89/A1
Breugel, Neth. 52/C5
Breuillet, Fr. 30/J6
Breukelen, Neth. 52/B4
Breuna, Ger. 53/G6
Breuvannes-en-Bassigny, Fr. 60/B1
Brevard, NC, US 163/F3
Breves, Braz. 182/D3
Brevig Mission, Ak, US 171/E2
Brevik, Nor. 40/C2
Brevik, Swe. 39/B1
Brevoort (isl.), Nun, Can. 141/K2
Brewarrina, Austl. 132/C1
Brewer, Mo, US 162/C2
Brewerton, NY, US 161/H3
Brewerville, Libr. 114/C5
Brewood, Eng, UK 36/D1
Brewster (cape), Austl. 128/B3
Brewster (lake), Austl. 133/C1
Brewster, Fl, US 164/M8
Brewster, Ks, US 154/D4
Brewster, Mn, US 155/G2
Brewster, Ne, US 154/E3
Brewster, Oh, US 160/F4
Brewster, Wa, US 144/E3
Brewton, Al, US 164/E2
Brey-et-Lû, Fr. 30/G4
Breyten, SAfr. 125/E2
Brežice, Slov. 50/B3
Brezina, Alg. 111/F2
Březnice, Czh. 59/G3
Breznik, Bul. 50/F4
Brezoi, Rom. 51/G3
Brézolles, Fr. 57/G3
Brezovo, Bul. 51/G4
Bria, CAfr. 116/D4
Briançon, Fr. 64/C3
Briar Creek, Pa, US 168/B1
Briare, Fr. 44/E3
Bribbaree, Austl. 133/C2
Bric de Rubren (peak), Fr. 64/C3
Bric Rosso (peak), It. 64/D3
Brice, Tx, US 152/D3
Briceni, Mol. 72/D3
Brickerville, Pa, US 168/B3
Bricket Wood, Eng, UK 30/B1
Brickley (brook), Austl. 130/L7
Bricktown, NJ, US 168/D3
Bricquebec, Fr. 56/D2
Bridal Cave, Mo, US 153/H1
Bridal Veil (falls), Co, US 149/J2
Bride, IM, UK 34/D3
Bride (riv.), Ire. 32/B5
Bridge, Id, US 147/G2
Bridge (riv.), BC, Can. 144/C2
Bridge City, Tx, US 151/H2
Bridge of Allan, Sc, UK 33/C4
Bridge of Don, Sc, UK 33/D2
Bridge of Weir, Sc, UK 33/B5
Bridgehampton, NY, US 169/F2
Bridgeman (mtn.), Ky, US 162/E2
Bridgend, Wal, UK 36/C3
Bridgend (co.), Wal, UK 36/C3
Bridgeport, Ca, US 146/D4
Bridgeport, Ct, US 169/E1
Bridgeport, Il, US 162/D1
Bridgeport, Mi, US 160/E3
Bridgeport, Ne, US 154/C3
Bridgeport, NJ, US 168/C4
Bridgeport, Tx, US 150/K6
Bridgeport (lake), Tx, US 151/F1
Bridgeport, Wa, US 144/E3
Bridgeport, WV, US 160/F5
Bridger, Mt, US 147/J1
Bridgeton, NJ, US 168/C5
Bridgetown, Ire. 32/D5
Bridgetown, NS, Can. 158/E3
Bridgetown, Oh, US 162/E1
Bridgetown, Austl. 130/C5
Bridgetown (cap.), Bar. 173/P9
Bridgeville, Qu, Can. 158/E1
Bridgeville, Ca, US 146/B3
Bridgeville, De, US 168/C6
Bridgewater, Austl. 132/C4
Bridgewater, NS, Can. 158/E3
Bridgewater, Va, US 163/H1
Bridgnorth, Eng, UK 36/D1
Bridgton, Me, US 161/L2
Bridgwater, Eng, UK 36/D4
Bridgwater (bay), Eng, UK 36/C4
Bridlington (bay), Eng, UK 35/H3
Bridlington, Eng, UK 35/H3
Bridport, Austl. 132/C4
Bridport, Eng, UK 36/D5
Bridport, Vt, US 161/K3
Brie (reg.), Fr. 42/B4
Brie-Comte-Robert, Fr. 30/K5
Briec, Fr. 56/A4
Brieg Brzeg, Pol. 43/J3
Brielle, Neth. 52/B5
Brielle, NJ, US 168/D3
Brienz, Swi. 60/E4
Brier (isl.), Ns., Can. 158/D3
Brier (cr.), Ga, US 163/G4
Brier (mtn.), Pa, US 161/H4
Brier, Wa, US 167/C2
Briercrest, Sk, Can. 145/M2
Brierfield, Eng, UK 35/F4
Brieselang, Ger. 42/Q6
Brig, Swi. 60/D5
Brigach (riv.), Ger. 58/B7
Brigantine, NJ, US 168/D5
Brigg, Eng, UK 35/H4
Briggs, Tx, US 150/F2
Briggs Corner, NB, Can. 158/E2
Brigham City, Ut, US 147/G3
Brighouse, Eng, UK 35/G4
Brighstone, Eng, UK 37/E5
Bright, Austl. 133/C3
Brightlingsea, Eng, UK 37/H3
Brighton (nbrhd.), Austl. 131/M9
Brighton (nbrhd.), Austl. 132/G5
Brighton (nbrhd.), Austl. 134/F6
Brighton, On, Can. 161/H2
Brighton, Eng, UK 37/F5
Brighton, Co, US 154/B4
Brighton, Il, US 155/J4
Brighton, Mi, US 160/E3
Brighton, Tn, US 162/C3
Brighton, Wi, US 167/P14
Brighton and Hove (co.), Eng, UK 37/F5
Brightons, Sc, UK 33/C5
Brignais, Fr. 64/A1
Brignoles, Fr. 64/C6
Brihante (riv.), Braz. 189/F2
Brihuega, Sp. 46/D2
Briis-sous-Forges, Fr. 30/J6
Brikama, Gam. 114/A3
Brilhante (riv.), Braz. 186/B4
Brill, Eng, UK 37/E3
Brillion, Wi, US 160/B2
Brilon, Ger. 53/F6
Brimington, Eng, UK 35/G5
Brimley, Mi, US 160/D1
Brimstone Hill NP, StK. 173/N8
Brindisi, It. 49/E2
Brinkley, Ar, US 153/J3
Brinkmann, Arg. 188/D4
Brinktown, Mo, US 153/H1
Brinkworth, Austl. 131/H5
Brinkworth, Eng, UK 36/E3
Brinnon, Wa, US 167/B2
Brinson, Ga, US 165/F2
Briny Breezes, Fl, US 164/P9
Brion (isl.), Qu, Can. 159/G2
Brión, Sp. 46/A1
Brione, Swi. 61/E5
Briones (res.), Ca, US 167/K11
Brionne, Fr. 57/F2
Briouze, Fr. 57/E3
Brisbane, Austl. 134/F6
Brisbane (int'l arpt.), Austl. 134/F6
Brisbane (riv.), Austl. 134/E7
Brisbane Forest Park, Austl. 134/E6
Brisbane Ranges NP, Austl. 133/B3
Brisbane Water, Austl. 133/E1
Brisbane Water NP, Austl. 133/E1
Brisco, BC, Can. 144/F2
Brisighella, It. 63/E5
Brissago, Swi. 61/E5
Bristol, NB, Can. 158/D2
Bristol, Qu, Can. 161/H2
Bristol, Eng, UK 36/D4
Bristol (co.), Eng, UK 36/D4
Bristol (chan.), Eng, Wal, UK 36/B4
Bristol (bay), Ak, US 171/F4
Bristol (lake), Ca, US 148/E3
Bristol, Co, US 152/C1
Bristol, Ct, US 161/K4
Bristol, Fl, US 165/F2
Bristol, Ga, US 165/G2
Bristol, NH, US 161/L3
Bristol, Pa, US 168/D3
Bristol, RI, US 161/L4
Bristol, SD, US 156/F5
Bristol, Tn, US 163/F2
Bristol, Tx, US 150/L7
Bristol, Vt, US 161/K2
Bristolville, Oh, US 160/F4
Bristow, Ok, US 153/F3
Britânia, Braz. 186/C2
British (mts.), Ak, US 142/Y12
British Columbia (prov.), Can. 140/D3
British Empire (range), Nun, Can. 141/S6
British Indian Ocean Terr. (terr.), UK 77/G10
British Mountains (range), Can.,Ak, US 171/K2
British Museum, Eng, UK 30/C2
Brits, SAfr. 123/E5
Britstown, SAfr. 124/C3
Britt, Ia, US 155/H2
Brittany (reg.), Fr. 44/B3
Britton, SD, US 156/F5
Britton, Tx, US 150/K7
Brive-la-Gaillarde, Fr. 44/D4
Brives-Charensac, Fr. 44/E4
Briviesca, Sp. 44/B5
Brivio, It. 62/C2
Brixham, Eng, UK 36/C6
Brixworth, Eng, UK 37/F2
Brlik, Kaz. 99/B3
Brněnský (pol. reg.), Czh. 43/J4
Beneěov, Czh. 59/H3
Brnik (int'l arpt.), Slov. 45/L3
Brno, Czh. 43/J4
Broa (bay), Cuba 177/F1
Broad (riv.), Ga, US 163/F4
Broad Arrow, Austl. 130/D4
Broad Law (peak), Sc, UK 33/C6
Broad Sound (isls.), Austl. 134/C2
Broad Street, Eng, UK 30/E3
Broad Valley, Mb, Can. 156/F2
Broadacres, Sk, Can. 145/K1
Broadbent, Or, US 146/A2
Broaddus, Tx, US 151/G2
Broadford, Ire. 32/B5
Broadford, Austl. 133/B3
Broadkill (riv.), De, US 168/C6
Broadley Common, Eng, UK 30/D1
Broadmeadows (nbrhd.), Austl. 132/F5
Broadstairs, Eng, UK 37/H4
Broadstone, Eng, UK 36/E5
Broadus, Mt, US 154/B1
Broadview, Mt, US 145/K4
Broadwater, Ne, US 154/C3
Broadwater NP, Austl. 132/E1
Broadway (hill), Eng, UK 37/E3
Broadway, NJ, US 168/C2
Broadwindsor, Eng, UK 36/D5
Broby, Swe. 39/L6
Broc, Swi. 60/D4
Brocēni, Lat. 41/K3
Brochet, Mb, Can. 140/F3
Brock (isl.), NW, Can. 141/R7
Brock, Sk, Can. 145/K2
Brocken (peak), Ger. 53/H5
Brockenhurst, Eng, UK 37/E5
Brocket, ND, US 156/E3
Brocket, Ab, Can. 145/H3
Brockman (mt.), Austl. 130/C2
Brockport, NY, US 161/H3
Brockton, Mt, US 156/B3
Brockton, Ma, US 161/L3
Brockville, On, Can. 161/J2
Brockway, Pa, US 161/G4
Brocton, NY, US 161/G3
Brodeur (pen.), Nun, Can. 140/G1
Brodhead, Wi, US 155/K2
Brodhead (cr.), Pa, US 168/C1
Brodheadsville, Pa, US 168/C2
Brodick, Sc, UK 33/A5

Map Section
212
213

Brodni – Bwindi

Brodnica, Pol. 43/K2
Brody, Ukr. 72/C2
Broek in Waterland, Neth. 52/B4
Broek Op Langedijk, Neth. 52/B3
Brogden, NC, US 163/H3
Broglie, Fr. 57/F2
Bröhn (peak), Ger. 53/G4
Brokaw, Wi, US 155/K1
Broken (bay), Austl. 132/D2
Broken (riv.), Austl. 133/B3
Broken Arrow, Ok, US 153/G2
Broken Back (crater), NM, US 149/J4
Broken Bow (dam), Ok, US 153/G3
Broken Bow, Ok, US 153/G3
Broken Bow (lake), Ok, US 153/G3
Broken Bow, Ne, US 154/E3
Broken Hill, Austl. 132/B1
Brokenhead Ind. Res., Mb, Can. 156/F2
Brokeoff (mts.), NM, US 152/B4
Brokopondo, Sur. 182/C1
Brokopondo (dist.), Sur. 181/H3
Brome, Ger. 42/F2
Bromley (nbrhd.), Eng, UK 30/D2
Bromley, Zim. 123/F3
Bromley Common (nbrhd.), Eng, UK 30/D3
Bromölla, Swe. 40/F3
Bromsgrove, Eng, UK 36/D2
Bromskirchen, Ger. 53/F6
Bromyard, Eng, UK 36/D2
Bron, Fr. 60/A6
Bronaugh, Mo, US 153/G2
Brøndby, Den. 39/J7
Brønderslev, Den. 40/C3
Brong-Ahafo (pol. reg.), Gha. 115/E5
Broni, It. 62/C3
Bronkhorstspruit, SAfr. 124/E2
Bronllys, Wal, UK 36/C2
Brønnøy, Nor. 38/E2
Brøns, Den. 40/C4
Bronschhofen, Swi. 61/F3
Bronson, Ks, US 153/G2
Bronson, Fl, US 165/G3
Bronson, Mi, US 160/D4
Bronson, Tx, US 151/G2
Bronte, It. 48/D4
Bronte, On, Can. 160/T9
Bronte, Tx, US 150/D2
Bronwood, Ga, US 165/F2
Bronx (bor.), NY, US 169/E2
Bronx Zoo, NY, US 169/K8
Bronxville, NY, US 169/K8
Bronzolo (Branzoll), It. 61/H5
Brook, In, US 160/C4
Brook Forest, Co, US 154/B4
Brook Park, Mn, US 157/H5
Brookdale, Mb, Can. 156/E2
Brookdale, SC, US 163/G4
Brookeland, Tx, US 151/H2
Brooker, Fl, US 165/G3
Brooke's Point, Phil. 88/B3
Brookfield, Ct, US 161/K4
Brookfield, Il, US 167/Q16
Brookfield, Mo, US 155/H4
Brookfield, Vt, US 161/K2
Brookfield, Wi, US 160/B3
Brookhaven, Ms, US 164/C2
Brookings, Or, US 146/A2
Brookings, SD, US 155/F1
Brooklet, Ga, US 163/G4
Brooklyn, Ms, US 164/D2
Brooklyn, Ia, US 155/H3
Brooklyn (bor.), NY, US 168/D2
Brooklyn Center, Mn, US 157/P6
Brooklyn Park, Mn, US 157/P6
Brooklyn Park, Md, US 168/B5
Brookmans Park, Eng, UK 30/C1
Brookneal, Va, US 163/H2
Brooks (mt.), Ak, US 171/E2
Brooks (range), Ak, US 171/F2
Brooks, Ca, US 146/B4
Brooks, Ab, Can. 145/J2
Brooks (A.F.B.), Tx, US 151/E3
Brooksby, Sk, Can. 145/M1
Brookshire, Tx, US 151/G3
Brookside, De, US 168/C4
Brookston, Mn, US 157/H4
Brookston, In, US 160/C4
Brooksville, Fl, US 164/L6
Brooksville, Ky, US 162/E1
Brooksville, Ms, US 162/C4
Brookton, Austl. 130/C5
Brookville, In, US 160/D5
Brookville, Pa, US 161/G4
Brookville, NY, US 169/L8
Brookville (lake), In, US 162/E1
Broomall, Pa, US 168/C4
Broome, Austl. 128/A4
Broomfield, Eng, UK 30/E1
Broomfield, Co, US 154/B4
Broons, Fr. 56/C4
Brørup, Den. 40/C4
Brösarp, Swe. 40/F4
Broseley, Mo, US 162/B2
Brosna, Ire. 32/A5
Brosna (riv.), Ire. 32/C3
Brossard, Qu, Can. 159/P7
Brotas, Braz. 189/G2
Brothers, Or, US 146/C2
Brotton, Eng, UK 35/H2
Brou, Fr. 57/G4
Brough, Eng, UK 35/F2
Brough (pt.), Sc, UK 31/V14
Brougham, On, Can. 160/U8
Broughshane, NI, UK 34/B2
Broughton, Sc, UK 33/C5
Broughton, Eng, UK 37/F2
Broughton in Furness, Eng, UK 35/E3
Broughton Street, Eng, UK 37/G4
Broulee, Austl. 133/D2
Broulkou (well), Chad 116/C1
Broussard, La, US 164/C2
Brousseval, Fr. 60/A1
Brouwersdam (dam), Neth. 52/A5
Brouwershaven, Neth. 52/A5
Brovary, Ukr. 72/F2
Brovst, Den. 40/C3
Broward (co.), Fl, US 164/P10
Browerville, Mn, US 157/G4
Brown (pt.), Austl. 131/G5
Brown (mt.), Austl. 131/H5
Brown (pt.), Wa, US 144/B4
Brown (mt.), Mt, US 145/J3
Brown City, Mi, US 160/E3
Brown Clee (hill), Eng, UK 36/D2
Brown Deer, Wi, US 160/C3
Browndell, Tx, US 151/H2
Brownfield, Tx, US 152/C4
Brownhills, Eng, UK 37/E1
Browning, Mo, US 155/H3
Browning, Mt, US 145/H3
Browning, Austl. 133/D2
Brownlee (dam), Id, US 146/E1
Brownlee (res.), Id, US 146/E1
Brownlee, Ne, US 154/D2
Brownlee, Sk, Can. 145/L2
Browns, Al, US 162/D4
Browns Mills, NJ, US 168/D4
Browns Park NWR, Co, US 147/J3
Browns Valley, Mn, US 156/F5
Brownsburg, In, US 160/C5
Brownsea (isl.), Eng, UK 37/E5
Brownstown, Il, US 162/C1
Brownstown, In, US 162/D1
Brownsville, Ky, US 162/D2
Brownsville (nbrhd.), NY, US 169/K9
Brownsville, Or, US 146/B1
Brownsville, Tn, US 162/C3
Brownsville, Tx, US 150/F5
Brownsville, Wa, US 167/B2
Brownwood (lake), Tx, US 151/E2
Brownwood, Tx, US 150/E2
Broxbourne, Eng, UK 30/C1
Broxburn, Sc, UK 33/C5
Broxton, Ga, US 165/G2
Broye (riv.), Swi. 60/C4
Broyle (cape), Nf, Can. 159/L2
Brozas, Sp. 46/B3
Bruay-la-Buissière, Fr. 54/B3
Bruay-sur-L'Escaut, Fr. 54/C3
Bruce, Wi, US 157/J5
Bruce (pen.), On, Can. 160/F2
Bruce (mt.), Austl. 130/C2
Bruce, Ab, Can. 145/H1
Bruce Crossing, Mi, US 157/K4
Bruce Peninsula NP, On, Can. 161/F2
Bruce Rock, Austl. 130/C4
Bruceton, Tn, US 162/C2
Bruceville-Eddy, Tx, US 151/F2
Bruchberg (peak), Ger. 53/H5
Bruche (riv.), Fr. 45/G2
Bruchhausen-Vilsen, Ger. 53/G3
Bruchköbel, Ger. 58/B2
Bruchmühlbach-Miesau, Ger. 55/G5
Bruchsal, Ger. 58/B4
Brucht (riv.), Ger. 53/G5
Bruck, Aus. 51/P7
Bruck an der Grossglocknerstrasse, Aus. 45/K3
Bruck an der Mur, Aus. 45/L3
Bruckberg, Ger. 59/F5
Brue (riv.), Eng, UK 36/D4
Bruff, Ire. 32/B5
Bruflat, Nor. 40/C1
Brügg, Swi. 60/D3
Brugg, Swi. 60/E3
Brugge, Belg. 54/C1
Brüggen, Ger. 52/D6
Brugnera, It. 63/F2
Brühl, Ger. 55/F2
Bruin, Ky, US 163/F1
Bruinisse, Neth. 52/B5
Bruino, It. 64/D2
Brukkaros (peak), Namb. 124/B2
Brukunga, Austl. 131/M8
Brule (lake), Mn, US 157/J4
Brule, Wi, US 157/J4
Brûlon, Fr. 57/E5
Brûly, Belg. 55/D4
Brumado, Braz. 187/E2
Brumath, Fr. 55/G6
Brummānā, Leb. 105/D1
Brummen, Neth. 52/D4
Brumunddal, Nor. 40/D1
Brundall, Eng, UK 37/H1
Brundidge, Al, US 165/F2
Brune (riv.), Fr. 54/C4
Bruneau (riv.), Id, US 146/F2
Brunei (ctry.) 77/L9
Brunei (bay), Bru. 88/A4
Brunei (int'l arpt.), Bru. 88/A4
Brunete, Sp. 47/M9
Brunette (isl.), Nf., Can. 159/J2
Brunflo, Swe. 38/E3
Bruni, Tx, US 151/E4
Brunico, It. 45/J3
Brünigpass (pass), Swi. 60/E4
Bruning, Ne, US 154/F3
Brunn am Gebirge, Aus. 51/N7
Brunna, Swe. 39/A1
Brunner, NZ 135/B3
Bruno, Sk, Can. 145/M1
Brunoy, Fr. 30/K5
Brunsbüttel, Ger. 53/G1
Brunson, SC, US 163/G4
Brunssum, Neth. 55/E2
Brunstatt, Fr. 60/D2
Brunswick (nbrhd.), Austl. 132/F5
Brunswick (pen.), Chile 191/C7
Brunswick, Ga, US 165/H2
Brunswick, Md, US 161/H5
Brunswick, Mo, US 155/H4
Brunswick, Oh, US 160/F4
Brunswick Heads, Austl. 134/D5
Brunswick Junction, Austl. 130/B5
Bruree, Ire. 32/B5
Brus (lake), Nic. 177/E3
Brusartsi, Bul. 50/F4
Brusenets, Rus. 69/K3
Brusett, Mt, US 145/L4
Brushy (cr.), Tx, US 151/F2
Brushy Creek, Tx, US 150/G2
Brusio, Swi. 61/G5
Brusque, Braz. 189/G3
Brussels (int'l arpt.), Belg. 55/D2
Brussels, Wi, US 160/C2
Brussels, On, Can. 160/F3
Brussels (Bruxelles) (cap.), Belg. 55/D2
Brusson, It. 62/A1
Bruthen, Austl. 133/C3
Bruton, Eng, UK 36/D4
Bruxelles (Brussels) (cap.), Belg. 55/D2
Bruyères, Fr. 60/C1
Bruyères-le-Châtel, Fr. 30/J6
Bruyères-sur-Oise, Fr. 30/J4
Bruz, Fr. 56/D4
Bruzual, Ven. 180/D2
Bryan, Oh, US 160/D4
Bryan (mt.), Austl. 131/H5
Bryan, Tx, US 150/F2
Bryanka, Ukr. 73/K3
Bryansk, Rus. 70/E1
Bryanskskaya Oblast, Rus. 70/E1
Bryant, Ar, US 153/H3
Bryce Canyon, Ut, US 149/F2
Bryce Canyon NP, Ut, US 149/F2
Brymbo, Wal, UK 35/E5
Bryn Brawd (peak), Wal, UK 36/C2
Bryn Mawr, Pa, US 168/C3
Bryne, Nor. 40/A2
Brynithel, Wal, UK 36/C3
Brynmawr, Wal, UK 36/C3
Bryson, Tx, US 153/E4
Bryson, Qu, Can. 161/H2
Bryson City, NC, US 163/F3
Bryukhovetskaya, Rus. 73/K5
Brzeg Dolny, Pol. 43/J3
Brzesko, Pol. 43/L4
Brzozów, Pol. 43/M4
Bū Athlah (well), Libya 108/D2
Bu Craa, WSah. 110/B4
Bū Fīshah, Tun. 48/B4
Bū Kūsā (well), Libya 108/A3
Bū 'Urqūb, Tun. 48/B4
Bua, Swe. 40/E3
Bua (riv.), Malw. 123/G2
Bua Chum, Thai. 94/C3
Bua Yai, Thai. 94/C3
Buala, Sol. 136/E5
Buang, Indo. 90/D4
Buapinang, Indo. 91/F4
Buatan, Indo. 89/C2
Buaya (riv.), Indo. 129/E2
Buba, GBis. 114/B4
Bubanza, Buru. 121/G3
Bubaque, GBis. 114/B4
Bubastis (ruin), Egypt 113/C3
Bubendorf, Swi. 60/D3
Bubikon, Swi. 61/E3
Bubry, Fr. 56/B5
Bubu (riv.), Tanz. 119/A3
Buburu, D.R. Congo 120/D2
Bubye (riv.), Zim. 123/F4
Buc, Fr. 30/J5
Bucak, Turk. 102/B2
Bucakkişla, Turk. 104/C1
Bucaramanga, Col. 180/C3
Bucas Grande (isl.), Phil. 88/D3
Bucasia, Austl. 134/C3
Bucay, Phil. 88/C1
Buccaneer (arch.), Austl. 128/A4
Bucelas, Port. 47/P10
Buch, Ger. 61/G1
Bucha, Ukr. 72/F2
Buchach, Ukr. 72/C3
Buchan (reg.), Sc, UK 33/D1
Buchan (gulf), Nun, Can. 141/J1
Buchan (riv.), Austl. 133/D3
Buchan Ness (pt.), Sc, UK 33/E2
Buchanan, Sk, Can. 156/C2
Buchanan, ND, US 156/E4
Buchanan (lake), Tx, US 151/E2
Buchanan, Mi, US 160/C4
Buchanan, Libr. 114/C5
Buchanan, Ga, US 162/E4
Buchanan (dam), Tx, US 151/E2
Buchanan, Va, US 163/H2
Buchanan Dam, Tx, US 151/E2
Buchanan Field (arpt.), Ca, US 167/K11
Buchans, Nf, Can. 159/J1
Bucharest (Burcureşti) (cap.), Rom. 72/D5
Buchbach, Ger. 59/F6
Büchen, Ger. 53/H2
Buchen, Ger. 58/C3
Buchenberg, Ger. 61/G2
Buchenzi, Tanz. 121/H3
Buchholz, Ger. 55/G3
Buchholz, Ger. 42/Q6
Buchholz in der Nordheide, Ger. 53/G2
Buchloe, Ger. 61/G1
Buchlyvie, Sc, UK 33/B4
Buchon (pt.), Ca, US 148/B3
Buchs, Swi. 61/F3
Buchy, Fr. 57/G1
Bucine, It. 63/E7
Buckatunna, Ms, US 164/D2
Buckatunna (cr.), Ms, US 162/C4
Buckden Pike (peak), Eng, UK 35/F3
Bückeburg, Ger. 53/G4
Buckeye, Az, US 149/F4
Buckeye Lake, Oh, US 160/E5
Buckfastleigh, Eng, UK 36/C6
Buckhannon, WV, US 163/G1
Buckhaven, Sc, UK 33/C4
Buckholts, Tx, US 151/F2
Buckhorn, NM, US 149/H4
Buckhurst Hill, Eng, UK 30/D2
Buckie, Sc, UK 33/D1
Buckingham, Qu, Can. 161/J2
Buckingham, Eng, UK 37/F3
Buckingham, Va, US 163/H2
Buckingham Palace, Eng, UK 30/C2
Buckland, Qu, Can. 158/B2
Buckland, Ak, US 171/F2
Buckle (pt.), Austl. 128/B3
Buckley, Wal, UK 35/E5
Buckley, Il, US 160/B4
Buckley, Mi, US 160/D2
Buckley, Wa, US 167/C3
Bucklin, Ks, US 152/E2
Bucknell, Eng, UK 36/D2
Buckner (cr.), Ks, US 154/E4
Buckroe, Mi, US 157/L4
Bucks (co.), Pa, US 168/C3
Bucksburn, Sc, UK 33/D2
Buco-Zau, Ang. 120/C4
Bucquoy, Fr. 54/B3
Buctouche, NB, Can. 158/E2
Bucureşti (co.), Rom. 51/G3
Bucureşti (Bucharest) (cap.), Rom. 51/H3
Bucy-le-Long, Fr. 54/C5
Bucyrus, Oh, US 160/E4
Buda, Tx, US 151/F2
Buda-Koshelëvo, Bela. 70/D1
Budai hegy (hill), Hun. 51/Q9
Budaka, Ugan. 119/A1
Budakeszi, Hun. 51/Q9
Budaörs, Hun. 51/R10
Budapest (co.), Hun. 51/R9
Budapest (cap.), Hun. 51/R9
Budarino, Kaz. 71/J2
Budaun, India 96/B1
Budawang (mt.), Austl. 133/E2
Budawang NP, Austl. 133/D2
Budd (coast), Ant. 192/H
Budd (inlet), Wa, US 167/B3
Budd Lake, NJ, US 168/D2
Buddi, Eth. 118/B4
Buddon Ness (pt.), Sc, UK 33/D4
Buddusò, It. 48/A2
Bude, Ms, US 164/C2
Bude, Eth. 118/B4
Bude, Eng, UK 36/B5
Bude (bay), Eng, UK 36/B5
Budějovický (pol. reg.), Czh. 43/H4
Budel, Neth. 52/C6
Büdelsdorf, Ger. 40/C4
Budge-Budge, India 97/G4
Budgewoi Lake, Austl. 133/E1
Budhāna, India 98/D5
Budhanilantha, Nepal 97/E2
Budhlāda, India 98/C5
Budia, Sp. 46/D2
Büdingen, Ger. 58/C2
Budjala, D.R. Congo 120/D2
Budleigh Salterton, Eng, UK 36/C5
Budogoshch', Rus. 41/Q2
Budongquan, China 99/F4
Budrio, It. 63/E4
Budungbudung, Indo. 91/E4
Budva, Yugo. 49/F1
Budzhak (reg.), Mol.,Ukr. 67/L1
Buea, Camr. 120/B1
Buellton, Ca, US 148/B3
Buelna (int'l arpt.), Mex. 174/D4
Buena, Wa, US 144/D4
Buena, NJ, US 168/D4
Buena Esperanza, Arg. 190/D2
Buena Fe, Ecu. 180/B5
Buena Park, Ca, US 166/G8
Buena Vista, Sk, Can. 156/B2
Buena Vista, Ven. 180/D3
Buena Vista, Ga, US 162/E4
Buena Vista, Bol. 185/F5
Buena Vista, Uru. 189/F5
Buena Vista, Va, US 163/H2
Buena Vista Lake Bed, Ca, US 148/C3
Buenaventura, Col. 180/B4
Buenaventura, Mex. 174/D2
Buenavista, Mex. 175/Q9
Bueno (riv.), Chile 190/B4
Bueno Brandão, Braz. 187/K7
Buenópolis, Braz. 186/D3
Buenos Aires, Col. 180/B4
Buenos Aires (lake), Arg.,Chile 179/B7
Buenos Aires, Col. 180/D4
Buenos Aires, Col. 180/C4
Buenos Aires, Ven. 181/E4
Buenos Aires (prov.), Arg. 190/E3
Buenos Aires (cap.), Arg. 191/J11
Buenos Aires, Peru 184/B2
Buenos Aires (Jorge Newbery) (int'l arpt.), Arg. 191/J11
Buenos Aires (Ministro Pistarini) (int'l arpt.), Arg. 191/J11
Buerarema, Braz. 187/F2
Buesaco, Col. 180/B4
Buet (peak), Fr. 60/C5
Bueu, Sp. 46/A1
Buffalo (mt.), Austl. 133/C3
Buffalo (lake), Ab, Can. 145/H1
Buffalo (riv.), SAfr. 125/E2
Buffalo, Ks, US 153/G2
Buffalo, Mo, US 153/H2
Buffalo (cr.), Mn, US 155/G1
Buffalo, Mn, US 157/N6
Buffalo, NY, US 160/V10
Buffalo, Ok, US 152/E2
Buffalo, SC, US 163/G3
Buffalo, SD, US 156/C5
Buffalo, Tx, US 151/F2
Buffalo (mtn.), Va, US 163/G2
Buffalo, Wi, US 155/J1
Buffalo, WV, US 163/G1
Buffalo, Wy, US 147/K1
Buffalo Cape, Sudan 117/F3
Buffalo Center, Ia, US 155/H2
Buffalo Creek, Co, US 152/B1
Buffalo Gap, SD, US 154/C2
Buffalo Gap, Tx, US 151/E1
Buffalo Grove, Il, US 160/C3
Buffalo Lake Nat'l Wildlife Res., Tx, US 152/C3
Buffalo Lake Nat'l Wild. Ref., ND, US 156/E3
Buffalo Nat'l River, Ar, US 153/H2
Buffalo River Overflow (swamp), Austl. 132/B1
Buffalo Sprs. Nat'l Rsv., Kenya 119/B1
Buffelsrivier (riv.), SAfr. 124/B3
Buffum (lake), Fl, US 164/M8
Buford, Ga, US 162/E3
Buford, Wy, US 154/B3
Buford (dam), Ga, US 162/E3
Buftea, Rom. 51/G3
Bug (riv.), Pol. 74/C4
Bug (riv.), Eur. 43/L2
Buga, Col. 180/B4
Bugaba, Pan. 177/F4
Bugac, Hun. 50/D2
Bugala (isl.), Ugan. 121/H3
Bugalagrande, Col. 180/B3
Bugaldie, Austl. 132/D1
Bugarach, Pic de (peak), Fr. 47/G1
Bugarama, Rwa. 121/G3
Bugat, Mong. 78/C2
Bugat, Mong. 78/C2
Bugaza, D.R. Congo 121/G3
Bugbrooke, Eng, UK 37/E2
Buğdaylı, Turk. 51/H5
Bugdayly, Trkm. 103/H2
Bugel (pt.), Indo. 89/E4
Bugene, Tanz. 121/G3
Buggenhout, Belg. 55/D1
Bugiri, Ugan. 119/A1
Bugojno, Bosn. 50/C3
Bugrino, Rus. 69/L1
Bugsuk (isl.), Phil. 91/E2
Bugul'ma, Rus. 69/M5
Buguruslan, Rus. 71/K1
Buh (riv.), China 78/D4
Buh (riv.), Ukr. 43/M3
Buḩayrat ath Tharthār (res.), Iraq 103/E3
Buhemba, Tanz. 119/A2
Buhera, Zim. 123/F3
Buhl, Fr. 60/D2
Bühl, Ger. 61/E2
Buhl, Id, US 147/F2
Buhler, Ks, US 153/F1
Buhler, La, US 164/B2
Bühler (riv.), Ger. 58/C4
Bühlerzell, Ger. 58/C5
Buhuşi, Rom. 72/D4
Buhūt, Egypt 113/C2
Bui (dam), Gha. 115/E4
Bui Gorge (res.), Gha. 115/E4
Bui NP, Gha. 115/E4
Buies Creek, NC, US 163/H3
Buiksloot, Neth. 52/B4
Builth Wells, Wal, UK 36/C2
Buin (peak), Swi. 61/G4
Buin, Chile 190/N8
Buinsk, Rus. 69/K5
Buinsk, Rus. 69/L5
Buíque, Braz. 183/G5
Buis-les-Baronnies, Fr. 64/B4
Buitepos, Namb. 122/C4
Bujalance, Sp. 46/C4
Bujanovac, Yugo. 50/E4
Bujumbura (cap.), Buru. 121/G3
Bujumbura (int'l arpt.), Buru. 121/G3
Buk, Pol. 43/J2
Buka (isl.), PNG 136/E5
Bukachacha, Rus. 78/H1
Bukadaban (peak), China 99/F4
Bukakata, Ugan. 121/H3
Bukama, D.R. Congo 121/F5
Būkān, Iran 103/F2
Bukasa (isl.), Ugan. 119/A2
Bukavu, D.R. Congo 121/G3
Bukene, Tanz. 121/H4
Buket Bubat (peak), Malay. 89/C1
Bukhoro, Uzb. 74/G6
Bukhovo, Bul. 49/H1
Bukhtarma (riv.), Kaz. 78/B2
Bukima, Tanz. 119/A2
Bukit Mertajam, Malay. 89/C1
Bukit Panjang, Sing. 89/J6
Bukit Timah (peak), Sing. 89/J6
Bukit Timah (nbrhd.), Sing. 89/J6
Bukitkemuning, Indo. 89/D4
Bukittinggi, Indo. 89/C3
Bükki NP, Hun. 70/B2
Bukoba, Tanz. 121/G3
Bukonyo, Tanz. 121/H3
Bukoza, Ang. 120/C4
Buksamaral, China 99/D4
Buku (cape), Indo. 89/D3
Bukuru, Nga. 115/H4
Bula, Tx, US 152/C4
Bula Atumba, Ang. 120/C5
Bulacan (prov.), Phil. 88/F6
Bulacan, Phil. 88/E6
Bülach, Swi. 61/E2
Bulagi, Indo. 91/F4
Bulahdelah, Austl. 132/E2
Bulalakao, Phil. 88/C2
Bulan, Ky, US 163/F2
Bulan, Phil. 88/C2
Bulanash, Rus. 69/P4
Bulancak, Turk. 70/F4
Bulandshahr, India 96/A1
Bulanık, Turk. 102/E2
Bulawa (peak), Indo. 91/F3
Bulawayo, Zim. 123/F4
Bulawayo (int'l arpt.), Zim. 123/F4
Bulayevo, Kaz. 74/H4
Buldan, Turk. 102/B2
Buldāna, India 95/C1
Buldibuyo, Peru 184/B3
Buldir (isl.), Ak, US 171/B5
Bule, Eth. 118/A4
Bulembu, Swaz. 125/E2
Bulgan, Mong. 78/E1
Bulgan, Mong. 78/E2
Bulgan, Mong. 78/E3
Bulgan (prov.), Mong. 78/E2
Bulgan (riv.), Mong. 78/C2
Bulgaria (ctry.) 29/G4
Bŭlgarovo, Bul. 51/H4
Bulgheria (peak), It. 48/D2
Bulgroo, Austl. 134/A4
Buliluyan (cape), Phil. 88/B3
Bulimba (cr.), Austl. 134/F7
Bulk'ī, Eth. 117/H4
Bulkington, Eng, UK 37/E2
Bull (pt.), NI, UK 34/B1
Bull (isl.), SC, US 165/H1
Bull (riv.), BC, Can. 144/G3
Bull Shoals, Ar, US 153/H2
Bull Shoals (lake), Ar, US 153/H2
Bull Valley (mts.), Ut, US 149/F2
Bullange, Belg. 55/F3
Bullard, Tx, US 151/G1
Bullas, Sp. 46/E3
Bullaxaar, Som. 118/C3
Bulle, Swi. 60/D4
Buller (mt.), Austl. 133/C3
Bullerön (isl.), Swe. 39/B1
Bullerup, Den. 40/D4
Bullfinch, Austl. 130/C4
Bullhead, SD, US 156/D5
Bullhead City, Az, US 148/E3
Bullion, Fr. 30/H6
Bullock, NC, US 163/H2
Bulloo (riv.), Austl. 127/D3
Bulloo Downs, Austl. 134/A5
Bulloo River Overflow (swamp), Austl. 134/A5
Bulls, NZ 135/C3
Bullsbrook East, Austl. 130/L6
Bully (riv.), Or, US 146/E1
Bully-les-Mines, Fr. 54/B3
Bulnayn (mts.), Mong. 78/D2
Bulnes, Chile 190/B3
Bulolo, PNG 129/G1
Bulongo, D.R. Congo 121/E4
Bulphan, Eng, UK 30/E2
Bultfontein, SAfr. 124/D3
Buluan, Phil. 88/D4
Buluba, Ugan. 119/A1
Bulukumba, Indo. 91/F5
Bulungu, D.R. Congo 121/E4
Bulungu, D.R. Congo 120/D4
Bulungwa, Tanz. 121/H4
Bum Bum (isl.), Malay. 88/B4
Bumba, D.R. Congo 121/E2
Bumba, Ang. 120/C5
Bumba, D.R. Congo 120/D4
Bumbah (gulf), Libya 67/J4
Bumble Bee, Az, US 149/F3
Bumbuna, SLeo. 114/C4
Bumhpa (peak), Myan. 86/C3
Bumiayu, Indo. 89/E4
Bumtang (riv.), Bhu. 97/H2
Bumthang, Bhu. 97/H2
Buna, Kenya 119/B1
Buna, PNG 129/H2
Buna, Tx, US 151/H2
Bunaga-take (peak), Japan 83/J5
Bunawan, Phil. 88/D3
Bunazi, Tanz. 121/G3
Bunbury, Austl. 130/B5
Bunceton, Mo, US 153/H1
Bunclody, Ire. 32/D4
Bundaberg, Austl. 134/D4
Bundanoon, Austl. 133/E2
Bundarra, Austl. 132/D1
Bunde, Ger. 53/E2
Bünde, Ger. 53/F4
Bunde, Ger. 53/F4
Būndi, India 92/C2
Bundi, PNG 129/G1
Bundoran, Ire. 31/P9
Būndu, India 97/E4
Bung Kan, Thai. 94/C2
Bunga (pt.), Phil. 88/D2
Bungalaut (str.), Indo. 89/B3
Bungay, Eng, UK 37/H2
Bungendore, Austl. 133/D2
Bungku, Indo. 91/F4
Bungo, Ang. 120/C4
Bungoma, Kenya 119/A1
Bunguran (isl.), Indo. 90/C3
Bunia, D.R. Congo 121/G2
Buninyong, Austl. 133/A3
Bunji, Pak. 98/C2
Bunkeflo Strand, Swe. 39/J7
Bunker, Mo, US 153/J2
Bunker Hill, In, US 160/C4
Bunker Hill, WV, US 161/G5
Bunker Hill, Il, US 155/K4
Bunker Hill Village, Tx, US 151/M9
Bunkeya, D.R. Congo 121/F5
Bunkie, La, US 164/B2
Bunnell, Fl, US 165/H3
Bunnik, Neth. 52/C4
Buñol, Sp. 47/E3
Bunschoten, Neth. 52/C4
Buntharik, Thai. 94/D3
Buntingford, Eng, UK 37/F3
Bunya, Austl. 134/E6
Bunya, Swaz. 125/E2
Bunya Mountains NP, Austl. 134/C4
Bunyala, Kenya 119/A1
Bünyan, Turk. 102/C2
Bunyu (isl.), Indo. 91/E3
Buochs, Swi. 61/E4
Buon Me Thuot, Viet. 94/E3
Buon Mrong, Viet. 94/E3
Buonconvento, It. 45/J5
Bupul, Indo. 129/F1
Buqayq, SAr. 100/E3
Buqde Caqable, Som. 118/C4
Buquim, Braz. 187/F1
Būr Fu'ād, Egypt 113/D2
Bur Sa'id (gov.), Egypt 104/C4
Būr Safājah, Egypt 109/G3
Būr Sa'īd (gov.), Egypt 109/F1
Būr Sa'īd (Port Said), Egypt 113/D2
Būr Sūdān (Port Sudan), Sudan 109/H5
Būr Tawfīq, Egypt 104/C5
Bura, Kenya 119/B2
Buram, Sudan 117/E3
Burang, China 99/D5
Burannoye, Rus. 71/K2
Burano, It. 63/F3
Burano (riv.), It. 63/F5
Burao (Burco), Som. 118/C3
Burāq, Syria 105/E2
Buras-Triumph, La, US 164/D3
Burauen, Phil. 88/D3
Buraydah, SAr. 100/D3
Burbach, Ger. 55/H2
Burbank, Il, US 160/C4
Burbank, Ca, US 166/F7
Burbank, Wa, US 144/E4
Burbank-Glendale-Pasadena (arpt.), Ca, US 166/F7
Burbure, Fr. 54/B2
Burcher, Austl. 133/C1
Burco (Burao), Som. 118/C3
Burda, India 96/A3
Burdekin (riv.), Austl. 127/D2
Burdell (mtn.), Ca, US 167/J10
Burden, Ks, US 153/F2
Burdett, Ks, US 152/E1
Burdett, Ab, Can. 145/J3
Burdette, SD, US 154/E1
Burdur, Turk. 102/B2
Burdur (lake), Turk. 102/B2
Burdur (prov.), Turk. 102/B2
Burdwān, India 97/F4
Burē, Eth. 117/H3
Burē, Eth. 117/G3
Bure (riv.), Eng, UK 37/H1
Büren, Ger. 53/F5
Buren, Neth. 52/C5
Buren, Neth. 52/C2
Büren an der Aare, Swi. 60/D3
Bürengiyn (mts.), Mong. 78/E2
Bures-sur-Yvette, Fr. 30/J5
Būrewāla, Pak. 98/B4
Bureya (riv.), Rus. 75/P4
Bureya (mts.), Rus. 79/L2
Burford, On, Can. 160/F3
Burford, Eng, UK 37/E3
Burg, Ger. 40/D4
Burg, Ger. 40/C4
Burg, Ger. 42/F2
Burgas (prov.), Bul. 49/K1
Burgas (bay), Bul. 67/K2
Burgas, Bul. 51/H4
Burgas (int'l arpt.), Bul. 51/H4
Burgau, Ger. 58/D6
Burgaw, NC, US 163/J3
Burgazada (riv.), Turk. 103/M7
Burgberg im Allgäu, Ger. 61/G2
Burgbernheim, Ger. 58/D4
Burgbrohl, Ger. 55/G3
Burgdorf, Swi. 60/D3
Burgdorf, Ger. 53/H4
Burgebrach, Ger. 58/D3
Burgenland (prov.), Aus. 43/J5
Burgeo, Nf, Can. 159/J2
Burgersdorp, SAfr. 124/D3
Burges (mt.), Austl. 130/D4
Burgess (mt.), Yk, Can. 171/L2
Burgess Hill, Eng, UK 37/F5
Burgfjället (peak), Swe. 38/E2
Burgh le Marsh, Eng, UK 35/J5
Burghaslach, Ger. 58/D3
Burghausen, Ger. 59/F6
Burghead (bay), Sc, UK 33/C1
Burghead, Sc, UK 33/C1
Burgheim, Ger. 58/E5
Burgin, Ky, US 162/E2
Burgkirchen, Aus. 59/G6
Burgkirchen an der Alz, Ger. 59/F6
Burgkunstadt, Ger. 58/E2
Bürglen, Swi. 61/F2
Burglengenfeld, Ger. 59/F4
Burglesum, Ger. 53/F2
Burgos, Sp. 46/D1
Burgos, Mex. 175/F3
Burgsinn, Ger. 58/C2
Burgstall (Postal), It. 61/H4
Burgsteinfurt, Ger. 53/E4
Burgsvik, Swe. 40/H3
Burgundy (reg.), Fr. 66/E1
Burgwedel, Ger. 53/G3
Burhābalang (riv.), India 97/F4
Burham, Eng, UK 30/E3
Burhan Budai (mts.), China 78/D4
Burhaniye, Turk. 70/C5
Burhānpur, India 95/C1
Burhar-Dhanpuri, India 96/C4
Burhi Dihing (riv.), India 86/B3
Burhi Gandok (riv.), India 97/E2
Buri (pen.), Erit. 118/A2
Buri, Braz. 189/G2
Burias (isl.), Phil. 88/C2
Buribay, Rus. 71/L2
Burica (pen.), Pan. 172/E6
Burica (pt.), Pan. 177/F4
Burien, Wa, US 144/C4
Burin, Nf, Can. 159/K2
Burin (pen.), Nf, Can. 141/L4
Buriram, Thai. 94/C3
Buritama, Braz. 189/G2
Buriti, Braz. 183/F3
Buriti Alegre, Braz. 186/C3
Buriti Bravo, Braz. 183/F4
Buriti dos Lopes, Braz. 183/F3
Buritis, Braz. 186/D2
Buritizeiro, Braz. 189/H1
Burj Mughayzil, Egypt 113/B2
Burjasot, Sp. 47/E3
Burkardroth, Ger. 58/C2
Burkburnett, Tx, US 153/E3
Burke, SD, US 154/E2
Burke, Va, US 163/J1
Bürkelkopf (peak), Aus. 61/G4
Burkes Garden, Va, US 163/G2
Burkesville, Ky, US 162/E2
Burketown, Austl. 129/E4
Burkett, Tx, US 150/E2
Burkeville, Tx, US 151/H2
Burkeville, Va, US 163/H2
Burkina Faso (ctry.) 107/B3
Burk's Falls, On, Can. 161/G2
Burladingen, Ger. 61/F1
Burleigh, Tx, US 150/F3
Burleson, Tx, US 150/K7
Burley, Id, US 147/G2
Burley, Wa, US 167/B3
Burli, Kaz. 71/K2
Burlin (pen.), Nf, Can. 159/K2
Burlingame, Ks, US 153/G1
Burlingame, Ca, US 167/K11
Burlington, On, Can. 160/T9
Burlington, Co, US 154/C4
Burlington, Ia, US 155/J3
Burlington, Il, US 167/N15
Burlington, Ks, US 153/G1
Burlington, Ky, US 162/E1
Burlington, NC, US 163/H2
Burlington, ND, US 156/D3
Burlington (co.), NJ, US 168/D4
Burlington, NJ, US 168/D3
Burlington, Ok, US 153/E2
Burlington, Vt, US 161/K2
Burlington, Wi, US 160/B3
Burlington, Wa, US 144/C3
Burlington Junction, Mo, US 155/G3
Burlöv, Swe. 39/K7
Burma (Myanmar) (ctry.) 77/J7
Bürmoos, Aus. 59/F7
Burna, Ky, US 162/C2
Burnaby, BC, Can. 144/C3
Burnas (lake), Ukr. 51/K3
Burnell, Tx, US 151/F3
Burnet, Tx, US 150/E2
Burnett Heads, Austl. 134/D4
Burney, Ca, US 146/C3
Burney (falls), Ca, US 146/C3
Burney (peak), Chile 191/B7
Burneyville, Ok, US 153/F4
Burnham, Mo, US 153/J2
Burnham, Il, US 167/Q16
Burnham, Eng, UK 30/B2
Burnham-on-Crouch, Eng, UK 37/G3
Burnham-on-Sea, Eng, UK 36/D4
Burnie-Somerset, Austl. 132/C4
Burnley, Eng, UK 35/F4
Burnmouth, Sc, UK 33/D5
Burns, Or, US 146/D2
Burns, Co, US 147/K4
Burns Flat, Ok, US 152/E3
Burnside (riv.), Nun, Can. 140/E2
Burnside, Ky, US 162/E2
Burnside, Sur. 182/B1
Burnstad, ND, US 156/E4
Burnsville, NC, US 163/F3
Burnsville, WV, US 163/G1
Burnsville, Ms, US 162/C3
Burnsville, Mn, US 157/P7
Burnt Islands, Nf, Can. 159/H2
Burntisland, Sc, UK 33/C4
Burntwood (riv.), Mb, Can. 140/G3
Burntwood, Eng, UK 37/E1
Buronga, Austl. 132/B2
Buronzo, It. 62/B3
Burpee Game Ref., NB, Can. 158/D3
Burqā, WBnk. 105/C4
Burqin (riv.), China 78/B2
Burqin, China 78/B2
Burqīn, WBnk. 105/C4
Burqush, Syria 105/D2
Burr Oak, Ks, US 154/E4
Burr Ridge, Il, US 167/Q16
Burra, Austl. 131/H5
Burraboi, Austl. 133/B2
Burragorang (lake), Austl. 133/E2
Burramurra, Austl. 131/H2
Burrel, Alb. 49/G2
Burren Junction, Austl. 132/D1
Burrewarra (pt.), Austl. 133/E2
Burriana, Sp. 47/E3
Burringbar, Austl. 134/D5
Burrinjuck (dam), Austl. 133/D2
Burro (cr.), Az, US 149/F3
Burroburro (riv.), Guy. 182/B1
Burrow (pt.), Sc, UK 34/D2
Burrowa-Pine Mountain NP, Austl. 133/C3
Burrowes (pt.), Austl. 134/A2
Burrum Heads, Austl. 134/D4
Burrum River NP, Austl. 134/D4
Burry (inlet), Wal, UK 36/B3
Burry Port, Wal, UK 36/B3
Bursa (prov.), Turk. 70/D5
Burscheid, Ger. 55/G1
Burscough, Eng, UK 35/F4
Burshtyn, Ukr. 72/C3
Bürstadt, Ger. 58/B3
Burstall, Sk, Can. 145/K2
Burt, Ia, US 155/G2
Burt, NY, US 160/V9
Burta, Austl. 131/J5
Burtenbach, Ger. 58/D6
Burton, BC, Can. 144/F3
Burton, NS, Can. 158/D3
Burton, Eng, UK 37/E5
Burton (lake), Ga, US 163/F3
Burton, Mi, US 160/E3
Burton, SC, US 163/G4
Burton, Tx, US 151/F2
Burton, Wa, US 167/C3
Burton Latimer, Eng, UK 37/F2
Burton upon Trent, Eng, UK 37/E1
Burtts Corner, NB, Can. 158/D2
Burṭus, Egypt 113/C4
Buru (isl.), Indo. 77/M10
Buruanga, Phil. 88/C3
Burullus (lake), Egypt 104/B4
Burūm, Yem. 118/D2
Burun Shibertuy (peak), Rus. 78/F2
Buruncan (pt.), Phil. 88/C2
Burundi (ctry.) 107/E5
Bururi, Buru. 121/G3
Burutu, Nga. 115/G5
Burwell, Ne, US 154/E3
Burwell, Eng, UK 37/G2
Bury, Fr. 54/B5
Bury, Eng, UK 35/F4
Bury (co.), Eng, UK 35/F4
Bury, Eng, UK 37/F5
Bury Saint Edmunds, Eng, UK 37/G2
Buryatia, Resp., Rus. 78/F1
Buryn', Ukr. 73/G2
Burynshyk (pt.), Kaz. 71/J3
Büs Hayrhan (peak), Mong. 78/C2
Busa (mt.), Phil. 88/D4
Busalla, It. 62/B4
Busanga, D.R. Congo 121/F5
Busca, It. 64/D3
Busch Gardens, Fl, US 164/L7
Busch Gardens, Va, US 163/J2
Busembatia, Ugan. 119/A1
Busenberg, Ger. 55/G5
Buseno, Swi. 61/F5
Būsh, Egypt 113/C6
Bush (riv.), Md, US 168/B5
Bush Kill (riv.), Pa, US 168/C1
Būshehr (gov.), Iran 103/G4
Bushêngcaka, China 99/D5
Bushey, Eng, UK 30/B2
Bushimaie (riv.), D.R. Congo 121/E4
Bushkill, Pa, US 168/C1
Bushkill Falls, Pa, US 168/C1
Bushman Pits, Bots. 122/E4
Bushmanland (reg.), SAfr. 124/B3
Bushmills, NI, UK 34/B1
Bushnell, Fl, US 164/L6
Bushnell, Il, US 155/J3
Bushton, Ks, US 153/E1
Busia, Kenya 119/A1
Busigny, Fr. 54/C3
Businga, D.R. Congo 121/E2
Busira (riv.), D.R. Congo 120/D3
Bus'k, Ukr. 72/C3
Buskerud (co.), Nor. 38/D3
Busko-Zdrój, Pol. 43/L3
Buşrá ash Shām, Syria 105/E3
Buss Craig (pt.), Sc, UK 33/D5
Busselton, Austl. 130/B5
Busseri (riv.), Sudan 117/E4
Busseto, It. 62/D4
Bussi sul Tirino, It. 65/C3
Bussolengo, It. 63/D3
Bussoleno, It. 64/D2
Bussum, Neth. 52/C4
Bustamante, Mex. 151/D4
Bustamante (pt.), Arg. 191/C6
Bustamante, Mex. 175/F4
Bustard (pt.), Austl. 134/C4
Buşteni, Rom. 51/G3
Busto Arsizio, It. 62/B2
Busto Garolfo, It. 62/B2
Busu Kwanga, D.R. Congo 120/E2
Busu Melo, D.R. Congo 120/E2
Busu Yale, D.R. Congo 120/D2
Busu-Djanoa, D.R. Congo 121/E2
Busuanga (isl.), Phil. 88/B2
Büsum, Ger. 40/C4
Busunu, Gha. 115/E4
Buta, D.R. Congo 121/F2
Buta Ranquil, Arg. 190/C3
Butajīra, Eth. 118/A3
Butare, Rwa. 121/G3
Butaritari (isl.), Kiri. 136/G4
Butawal, Nepal 96/D2
Bute (isl.), Sc, UK 33/A5
Bute, Austl. 131/H5
Bute (inlet), BC, Can. 144/B2
Bute Helu, Kenya 119/B1
Büteeliyn (mts.), Mong. 78/E2
Butembo, D.R. Congo 121/G2
Bütgenbach, Belg. 55/F3
Butha-Buthe, Les. 124/E3
Buti, It. 62/D6
Butiaba, Ugan. 121/G2
Butler, Al, US 164/D1
Butler (lake), Fl, US 164/M7
Butler, Ga, US 162/E4
Butler, In, US 160/D4
Butler, Mo, US 153/G1
Butler, NJ, US 169/H8
Butler, Pa, US 161/G4
Butler, Tx, US 150/F2
Butlersbridge, Ire. 32/C1
Butmir (int'l arpt.), Bosn. 50/D4
Butner, NC, US 163/H2
Buto (ruin), Egypt 113/B2
Butry-sur-Oise, Fr. 30/J4
Bütschelegg (peak), Swi. 60/D4
Bütschwil, Swi. 61/F3
Butt of Lewis (pt.), Sc, UK 31/Q7
Buttahatchee (riv.), Al,Ms, US 162/C4
Buttapietra, It. 63/D3
Butte, ND, US 156/D4
Butte (cr.), Ca, US 146/C4
Butte, Ne, US 154/E2
Butte-Silver Bow County, Mt, US 145/H4
Büttelborn, Ger. 58/B3
Butter (cr.), Or, US 146/D1
Butterfield, Mn, US 155/G2
Butters, NC, US 163/H3
Butterworth, Malay. 89/C1
Butterworth, SAfr. 124/E4
Buttes, Swi. 60/C4
Buttevant, Ire. 32/B5
Buttigliera Alta, It. 64/D2
Buttonwillow, Ca, US 148/C3
Buttrio, It. 63/G1
Butuan, Phil. 88/D3
Butung (isl.), Indo. 77/M10
Buturlinovka, Rus. 73/L2
Butzbach, Ger. 58/B2
Bützow, Ger. 40/D5
Buëch (riv.), Fr. 44/F4
Buuhoodle, Som. 118/C3
Buulo Berde, Som. 118/C5
Buur Gaabo, Som. 119/C2
Buur Hakaba, Som. 119/D1
Buvuma (isl.), Ugan. 119/A1
Buxar, India 96/D3
Buxheim, Ger. 61/G2
Buxtehude, Ger. 53/G2
Buxton, Eng, UK 35/G5
Buxton, Me, US 161/L3
Buy, Rus. 68/J4
Buyant, Mong. 78/D2
Buyant-Uhaa, Mong. 78/G3
Buyck, Mn, US 157/H3
Buynaksk, Rus. 71/H4
Buyr (lake), Mong. 79/H2
Buyuan (riv.), China 86/D4
Büyük Anafarta, Turk. 49/K2
Büyükada, Turk. 51/J5
Büyükada (isl.), Turk. 103/N7
Büyükarmutlu, Turk. 102/D2
Büyükçekmece (lake), Turk. 103/M6
Büyükçekmece, Turk. 103/M6
Büyükeceli, Turk. 104/C1
Büyükkarıştıran, Turk. 51/H5
Buyukly, Rus. 79/N2
Büyükyurt, Turk. 102/D2
Buyun Shan (peak), China 81/B2
Buyuni (pt.), Tanz. 119/B3
Buz'kyy Lyman (estu.), Ukr. 72/F4
Buzachi (pen.), Kaz. 71/J3
Buzançais, Fr. 44/D3
Buzancy, Fr. 55/D5
Buzău (riv.), Rom. 70/C3
Buzău, Rom. 51/H3
Buzău (prov.), Rom. 51/H3
Búzi (riv.), Moz. 123/G3
Buziaş, Rom. 50/E3
Búzios (isl.), Braz. 187/L8
Buz'kyy Lyman (estu.), Ukr. 51/K2
Büzmeyin, Trkm. 101/G1
Buzsák, Hun. 50/C2
Buzuluk, Rus. 71/K1
Buzzard Roost (dam), SC, US 163/G3
Bwandougou, C.d'Iv. 114/D4
Bwasa, D.R. Congo 120/D3
Bweeng (mtn.), Ire. 32/B5
Bwindi Impenetrable Forest NP, Tanz. 121/G3

Byala – Cany-Ba

Byala, Bul. 51/G4
Byala, Bul. 51/H4
Byala Slatina, Bul. 51/F4
Byam Martin (isl.), Nun, Can. 141/R7
Byam Martin (chan.), Nun, Can. 141/R7
Byarezina (riv.), Bela. 68/E5
Byaroza, Bela. 70/C1
Byars, Ok, US 153/F3
Bydgoszcz, Pol. 43/J2
Byemoor, Ab, Can. 145/H2
Byers, Ks, US 152/E2
Byesville, Oh, US 160/F5
Byfield, Eng, UK 37/E2
Byfleet, Eng, UK 30/B3
Byford, Austl. 130/L7
Bygland, Nor. 40/B2
Bykhov, Bela. 41/P5
Bykle, Nor. 40/B2
Bykovo, Rus. 71/H2
Bykovo (int'l arpt.), Rus. 69/X9
Bykovskiy, Rus. 75/N2
Bylas, Az, US 149/G4
Bylchau, Wal, UK 34/E5
Bylot (isl.), Can. 139/K2
Bylot (isl.), Nun, Can. 141/J1
Byng, Ok, US 153/F3
Byng Inlet, On, Can. 160/F2
Bynum, Tx, US 151/F2
Bynum, Mt, US 145/H4
Bynum Run (riv.), Md, US 168/B4
Byram (lake), NY, US 169/L7
Byram (pt.), Ct, US 169/L8
Byram (riv.), Ct, US 169/E1
Byrd (cape), Ant. 192/U
Byrd, US, Ant. 192/S
Byrdstown, Tn, US 162/E2
Byremo, Nor. 40/B2
Byrock, Austl. 132/C1
Byromville, Ga, US 162/F4
Byron, Ca, US 167/L11
Byron, Il, US 155/K2
Byron, Ga, US 162/F4
Byron (isl.), Chile 191/B5
Byron Bay, Austl. 134/D5
Byrranga (mts.), Rus. 74/K2
Byrum, Den. 40/D3
Bystice (riv.), Czh. 59/F2
Bystrá (peak), Slvk. 43/K4
Bystřice, Czh. 59/H3
Bytantay (riv.), Rus. 75/N3
Bytom, Pol. 43/K3
Bytów, Pol. 40/G4
Byumba, Rwa. 121/G3

C

C (canal), Co, US 149/H1
C.F. Secada (int'l arpt.), Peru 184/C1
C.J. Strike (res.), Id, US 146/E2
C.J. Strike (dam), Id, US 146/E2
C.W. McConaughy (lake), Ne, US 154/C3
Ca (riv.), Viet. 93/J4
Ca Mau (cape), Viet. 94/D4
Ca Mau, Viet. 94/D4
Caacupé, Par. 189/E3
Caaguazú (dept.), Par. 189/E3
Caaguazú, Par. 189/E3
Caála, Ang. 122/B2
Caatingas (phys. reg.), Braz. 179/E3
Caazapá, Par. 189/E3
Caazapá (dept.), Par. 189/E3
Cabadbaran, Phil. 88/D3
Cabaiguán, Cuba 177/G1
Caballo, NM, US 149/J4
Caballo (res.), NM, US 149/J4
Caballococha, Peru 184/D1
Caban-Coch (res.), Wal, UK 36/C2
Cabana, Peru 184/B3
Cabanaconde, Peru 184/D4
Cabañaquinta, Sp. 46/C1
Cabanatuan, Phil. 88/C2
Cabanes, Sp. 47/F2
Cabannes, Fr. 64/A5
Cabano, Qu, Can. 158/C2
Cabarroguis, Phil. 88/C1
Cabatuan, Phil. 88/C3
Cabedelo, Braz. 183/H4
Cabella Ligure, It. 62/C4
Cabestany, Fr. 44/E5
Cabeza del Buey, Sp. 46/C3
Cabeza Lagarto (pt.), Peru 184/B3
Cabeza Prieta Nat'l. Wild. Ref., Az, US 149/F4
Cabezas, Bol. 188/D1
Cabezón de la Sal, Sp. 46/C1
Cabildo, Arg. 190/E3
Cabimas, Ven. 180/D2
Cabinda, Ang. 120/C4
Cabinda (prov.), Ang. 120/B4
Cabinet (mts.), Mt, US 144/G3
Cabiri, Ang. 120/C5
Cabo, Braz. 183/H5
Cabo Blanco, Arg. 191/D5
Cabo Blanco, Peru 184/A2
Cabo Bojador, WSah. 110/B4
Cabo Corrientes, Cabo (cape), Mex. 174/D4
Cabo de Hornos, PN, Chile 191/D7
Cabo Delgado (prov.), Moz. 119/B4
Cabo Delgado (prov), Moz. 123/H2
Cabo do Norte (cape), Braz. 182/D2
Cabo Falso (bank), Hon. 177/F3
Cabo Frio, Braz. 187/E4
Cabo Gracias a Dios, Nic. 177/F3
Cabo Orange, PN do, Braz. 182/D2
Cabo San Lucas, Mex. 174/C4
Cabo Verde, Braz. 187/K6
Cabonga (res.), Qu, Can. 141/J4
Cabool, Mo, US 153/H2
Caboolture, Austl. 134/D4
Cabora Bassa (lake), Moz. 123/F2
Cabot, Ar, US 153/H3
Cabot (str.), NS,NF, Can. 141/K4
Cabourg, Fr. 57/E2
Cabra, Sp. 46/C4
Cabra Corral (res.), Arg. 188/C3
Cabra de Santo Cristo, Sp. 46/D4
Cabramatta (nbrhd.), Austl. 134/G8
Cabras, It. 48/A3
Cabrera, Isla de (isl.), Sp. 66/D3
Cabri, Sk, Can. 145/K2
Cabriel (riv.), Sp. 46/E3
Cabriès, Fr. 64/B6
Cabrillo Nat'l Mon., Ca, US 166/C5
Cabrobó, Braz. 183/G5
Cabruta, Ven. 181/E3
Cabudare, Ven. 180/D2
Cabugao, Phil. 88/C1
Cabure, Ven. 180/D2
Caçador, Braz. 189/G3
Čačak, Yugo. 50/E4
Cacala, Ang. 122/B1
Cacalotán, Mex. 174/D4
Caçapava, Braz. 187/L8
Caçapava do Sul, Braz. 189/F4
Cacapon (mtn.), WV, US 161/G5
Cacapon (riv.), WV, US 163/H1
Caccia (cape), It. 48/A2
Cacequi, Braz. 189/F4
Cáceres, Col. 180/C3
Cáceres, Sp. 46/B3
Cáceres, Braz. 185/G5
Cachapoal (riv.), Chile 190/N9
Cacharí, Arg. 191/J12
Cache, Ok, US 153/E3
Cache (cr.), Ca, US 146/B4
Cache (peak), Id, US 147/G2
Cache Creek, BC, Can. 144/D2
Cache la Poudre (riv.), Co, US 154/B3
Cache Slough (riv.), Ca, US 167/L10
Cacheu, GBis. 114/A3
Cachicadán, Peru 184/B3
Cachimbo, Serra do (mts.), Braz. 182/B4
Cachingues, Ang. 122/C2
Cachipo, Ven. 181/E2
Cachoeira Alta, Braz. 189/G1
Cachoeira de Minas, Braz. 187/L7
Cachoeira do Arari, Braz. 182/D3
Cachoeira do Sul, Braz. 189/F4
Cachoeira Paulista, Braz. 187/L7
Cachoeiras de Macacu, Braz. 187/P7
Cachoeirinha, Braz. 189/G4
Cachoeiro de Itapemirim, Braz. 187/E4
Cachorras, Col. 180/C4
Cachos (pt.), Chile 188/B3
Cacoal, Braz. 185/F3
Cacolo, Ang. 120/D5
Caconda, Ang. 122/B2
Caconde, Braz. 187/K6
Cacongo, Ang. 120/C4
Caçu, Braz. 186/C3
Cacuaco, Ang. 120/C5
Cacula, Ang. 122/B2
Caculuvar (riv.), Ang. 122/B3
Cacuri, Ven. 181/E3
Cacuso, Ang. 120/C5
Cadaadle, Som. 118/C3
Čadca, Slvk. 43/K4
Caddo (mts.), Ar, US 153/H3
Caddo (riv.), Ar, US 153/H3
Caddo, Ok, US 153/F3
Caddo, Tx, US 151/E1
Caddo Mills, Tx, US 153/F4
Caddo Valley, Ar, US 153/H3
Cadelbosco di Sopra, It. 62/D4
Cadelle (peak), It. 61/F5
Cadenberge, Ger. 53/G1
Cadenet, Fr. 64/B5
Cader Idris (peak), Wal, UK 36/C1
Cadet, Mo, US 162/B2
Cadibarrawirracanna (lake), Austl. 131/G4
Cadillac, Mi, US 160/D2
Cadillac, Sk, Can. 145/L3
Cadiz, Oh, US 160/F4
Cádiz, Sp. 46/B4
Cádiz (gulf), Port.,Sp. 46/B4
Cadiz, Ca, US 148/E3
Cadiz, Ky, US 162/D2
Cadiz (lake), Ca, US 148/E3
Cadiz, Phil. 88/C3
Cadnam, Eng, UK 37/E5
Cadogan, Ab, Can. 145/J1
Cadolzburg, Ger. 58/D4
Cadomin, Ab, Can. 144/F1
Cadott, Wi, US 155/J1
Cadria (peak), It. 61/G6
Cadwell, Ga, US 163/F4
Cadzand-Bad, Neth. 54/C1
Caen, Fr. 57/E2
Caen (bay), Fr. 44/C2
Caerano di San Marco, It. 63/F2
Caerleon, Wal, UK 36/D3
Caernarfon, Wal, UK 34/D5
Caernarfon (bay), Wal, UK 34/D5
Caernarfon Castle, Wal, UK 34/D5
Caerphilly, Wal, UK 36/C3
Caerphilly (co.), Wal, UK 36/C3
Caersws, Wal, UK 36/C1
Caesarea, On, Can. 161/G2
Caesarea NP, Isr. 105/B3
Caeté, Braz. 187/E3
Cafarnaum, Braz. 187/E1
Cafasse, It. 64/D2
Cafayate, Arg. 188/C3
Cagayan (isls.), Phil. 88/C3
Cagayan de Oro, Phil. 88/D3
Cagayan Sulu (isl.), Phil. 88/B4
Cagayancillo, Phil. 88/C3
Cagli, It. 63/F6
Cagliari, It. 48/A3
Cagliari (gulf), It. 66/F3
Cagne (riv.), Fr. 64/D5
Cagnes-sur-Mer, Fr. 64/D5
Cagoyan (riv.), Phil. 88/C1
Cagua, Ven. 183/N7
Caguán (riv.), Col. 180/C4
Caguas, PR 173/M8
Caha (mts.), Ire. 32/A6
Cahaba, Al, US 162/D4
Cahaba (riv.), Al, US 162/D4
Cahama, Ang. 122/B3
Caher, Ire. 32/C5
Caherbarnagh (peak), Ire. 32/A5
Caherconlish, Ire. 32/B4
Cahirsiveen, Ire. 30/N11
Cahokia, Il, US 155/J4
Cahone, Co, US 149/H2
Cahore (pt.), Ire. 32/D4
Cahors, Fr. 44/D4
Cahuacan, Mex. 175/Q9
Cahuapanas, Peru 184/B2
Cahuilla Ind. Res., Ca, US 148/D4
Cahuinari (riv.), Col. 180/D5
Cahuita, PN, CR 177/F4
Cahul, Mol. 51/J3
Cai (riv.), Braz. 189/G4
Cai Nuoc, Viet. 94/D4
Caia, Moz. 123/G3
Caiabis, Serra dos (mts.), Braz. 185/G4
Caianda, Ang. 121/E5
Caiapó (riv.), Braz. 186/C3
Caiapó, Serra (mts.), Braz. 186/B3
Caiapônia, Braz. 186/C3
Caiazzo, It. 65/D5
Caibarién, Cuba 177/G1
Caicara, Ven. 181/F2
Caicara, Ven. 181/E3
Caiçara, Braz. 183/H4
Caicedo, Col. 183/K6
Caicedonia, Col. 183/K8
Caicó, Braz. 183/G4
Caicos (isls.), Uk 173/G3
Caicos Passage (chan.), Bahm. 177/H1
Caieiras, Braz. 187/K8
Caifuche, Ang. 122/D1
Cailloma, Peru 184/D4
Caillou (bay), La, US 164/C3
Caillou (lake), La, US 164/C3
Cailly (riv.), Fr. 54/A4
Caiman (pt.), Phil. 88/B2
Caimbambo, Ang. 122/B2
Cainde, Ang. 122/B2
Caine (riv.), Bol. 188/C1
Cainnyigoin, China 78/E5
Cainsville, Mo, US 155/H3
Cainta, Phil. 88/F6
Caio (peak), It. 62/D5
Caiongo, Ang. 120/C4
Cairate, It. 62/B2
Cairn (mt.), Ak, US 171/G3
Cairn Curran (res.), Austl. 133/A3
Cairn Curran (dam), Austl. 133/A3
Cairn Gorm (peak), Sc, UK 33/C2
Cairn Table (peak), Sc, UK 33/B6
Cairn Toul (peak), Sc, UK 33/C2
Cairndow, Sc, UK 33/B4
Cairngorm (mts.), Sc, UK 33/B2
Cairnryan, Sc, UK 34/C2
Cairns (int'l arpt.), Austl. 134/B2
Cairns, Austl. 134/B2
Cairns (mt.), Austl. 131/G2
Cairnsmore of Carsphairn (peak), Sc, UK 33/B6
Cairo, Ga, US 165/F2
Cairo (peak), It. 65/C4
Cairo, Mo, US 155/H4
Cairo, Ne, US 154/E3
Cairo, Il, US 162/C2
Cairo (int'l arpt.), Egypt 113/C4
Cairo (Al Qāhirah) (cap.), Egypt 113/C4
Cairo Montenotte, It. 62/B5
Caister-on-Sea, Eng, UK 37/H1
Caistor, Eng, UK 35/H5
Caistor Centre, On, Can. 160/T9
Caistorville, On, Can. 160/T9
Caitou, Ang. 122/B2
Caiuana (bay), Braz. 182/D3
Caiundo, Ang. 122/C2
Caixi, China 87/H3
Caiza, Bol. 188/C2
Caizi (lake), China 80/D5
Cajabamba, Ecu. 180/B5
Cajabamba, Peru 184/B2
Cajacay, Peru 184/B3
Cajamarca (ruin), Peru 184/B2
Cajamarca (dept.), Peru 184/B2
Cajamarca, Peru 184/B2
Cajapió, Braz. 183/E3
Cajari, Braz. 183/E3
Cajatambo, Peru 184/B3
Cajazeiras, Braz. 183/G4
Cajibío, Col. 180/B4
Cajidiocan, Phil. 88/C2
Cajón (pt.), Cuba 177/E1
Cajon Junction, Ca, US 166/C2
Cajones (isl.), Nic. 177/F2
Caju (isl.), Braz. 183/F3
Cajuapara (riv.), Braz. 183/E4
Cajuata, Bol. 188/C1
Çal, Turk. 102/B2
Cala d'Oliva, It. 48/A2
Cala, Piombo, Punta di (pt.), It. 66/F3
Calabar (int'l arpt.), Nga. 115/H5
Calabar, Nga. 115/H5
Calabasas, Ca, US 166/B2
Calabash, NC, US 163/H4
Calabozo, Ven. 181/E2
Calabria (pol. reg.), It. 67/H3
Calabria, Parco Nazionale della, It. 48/D3
Calaburras (pt.), Sp. 46/C4
Calaceite, Sp. 47/F2
Calacoto, Bol. 184/D5
Calafat, Rom. 50/F4
Calagua (isls.), Phil. 88/C2
Calahorra, Sp. 46/E1
Calaí, Ang. 122/C3
Calais, Fr. 54/A2
Calais, Me, US 141/K4
Calais, Canal de (canal), Fr. 54/A2
Calama, Braz. 185/F3
Calama, Chile 188/B2
Calamar, Col. 180/C4
Calamar, Col. 180/C2
Calamarca, Bol. 188/B1
Calamba, Ang. 120/C5
Calambrone, It. 62/D6
Calamian Gr. (isls.), Phil. 91/E1
Calamian Group (isls.), Phil. 88/B2
Calamocha, Sp. 46/E2
Calamonte, Sp. 46/B3
Calamus (riv.), Ne, US 154/E2
Călan, Rom. 50/F3
Calañas, Sp. 46/B4
Calanda, Sp. 47/E2
Calang, Indo. 89/A1
Calangianus, It. 48/A2
Calapan, Phil. 88/C2
Calapooia (riv.), Or, US 146/B1
Călăraşi (prov.), Rom. 51/H3
Călăraşi, Rom. 51/H3
Călăraşi, Mol. 72/E4
Calarcá, Col. 183/K8
Calasparra, Sp. 46/E3
Calatayud, Sp. 46/E2
Calatorao, Sp. 46/E2
Calauag, Phil. 88/C2
Calaveras (res.), Ca, US 167/L12
Calaveras (riv.), Ca, US 146/C4
Calavite (cape), Phil. 88/C2
Calavon (riv.), Fr. 64/B5
Calayan (isl.), Phil. 88/C1
Calbayog, Phil. 88/D2
Calberlah, Ger. 53/H4
Calbiga, Phil. 88/D3
Calbuco, Chile 190/B4
Calca, Peru 184/D4
Calcasieu (lake), La, US 151/H3
Calcasieu (riv.), La, US 151/H2
Calceta, Ecu. 180/A5
Calchaquí, Arg. 188/D4
Calchaquí (riv.), Arg. 188/C3
Calci, It. 62/D6
Calcinate, It. 62/C2
Calcinato, It. 62/D3
Calcinelli, It. 63/F6
Calcio, It. 62/C3
Calcium, NY, US 161/J2
Calçoene, Braz. 182/D2
Calcutta, India 97/G4
Calcutta (int'l arpt.), India 97/G4
Calcutta, Sur. 181/H3
Caldaro (Kaltern), It. 45/J3
Caldas (dept.), Col. 180/C3
Caldas, Col. 183/K6
Caldas, Braz. 187/K6
Caldas da Rainha, Port. 46/A3
Caldas Novas, Braz. 186/C3
Caldbeck, Eng, UK 35/E2
Calden, Ger. 53/G6
Calder, Sk, Can. 156/D2
Calder (riv.), Eng, UK 35/F4
Calder (mt.), Ak, US 171/M4
Caldera, Chile 188/B3
Calderara di Reno, It. 63/E4
Calderas, Ven. 180/D2
Caldercruix, Sc, UK 33/C5
Calderdale (co.), Eng, UK 35/F4
Caldes de Montbui, Sp. 47/L6
Caldew (riv.), Eng, UK 35/F2
Caldicot, Wal, UK 36/D3
Caldiero, It. 63/E3
Çaldıran, Turk. 103/E2
Caldogno, It. 63/E2
Caldonazzo, It. 61/H6
Caldono, Col. 180/B4
Caldwell, Id, US 146/E2
Caldwell, NJ, US 169/H8
Caldwell, Oh, US 160/F5
Caldwell, Tx, US 150/F2
Caldwell, Wi, US 167/P14
Caldy (isl.), Eng, UK 36/B3
Caledon, NI, UK 34/B3
Caledon, SAfr. 124/L11
Caledon, On, Can. 160/T8
Caledon (riv.), SAfr. 124/D3
Caledon East, On, Can. 160/T8
Caledonia (hills), NB, Can. 158/E3
Caledonia, Mi, US 160/D3
Caledonia, Mn, US 155/J2
Caledonia, Ms, US 162/C4
Caledonia, NS, Can. 158/E3
Caledonia, Oh, US 160/E4
Caledonia, Wi, US 167/P14
Caledonian (canal), Sc, UK 33/B2
Calella, Sp. 47/G2
Calen, Austl. 134/C3
Calenzana, Fr. 48/A1
Calenzano, It. 63/E6
Calera, Ok, US 153/F4
Calera, Al, US 162/D4
Calera de Tango, Chile 190/N8
Calestano, It. 62/D4
Caleta Clarencia, Chile 191/C7
Caleta de Campos, Mex. 174/E5
Caleta Olivia, Arg. 190/D5
Caletones, Chile 190/N9
Calf of Man (isl.), IM, UK 34/C3
Calgary (int'l arpt.), Ab, Can. 145/G2
Calgary, Ab, Can. 145/G2
Calhan, Co, US 154/B4
Calheta, Port. 110/A2
Calheta, Azor., Port. 47/S12
Calhoun, Al, US 164/E1
Calhoun, Ga, US 162/E3
Calhoun, Il, US 162/C1
Calhoun, Ky, US 162/D2
Calhoun, Mo, US 153/H1
Calhoun City, Ms, US 162/C4
Calhoun Falls, SC, US 163/F3
Cali, Col. 180/B4
Calico Ghost Town, Ca, US 148/D3
Calico Rock, Ar, US 153/H2
Calicut (Kozhikode), India 95/B4
Calida (coast), Sp. 46/E4
Caliente, Nv, US 148/E2
Califon, NJ, US 168/D2
California, Mo, US 153/H1
California (aqueduct), Ca, US 167/L11
California (gulf), Mex. 139/F6
California (state), US 142/C4
California (aqueduct), Ca, US 148/B2
California, Md, US 163/J1
California City, Ca, US 148/D3
Calilegua, Arg. 188/C2
Calilegua, PN, Arg. 188/C2
Călimăneşti, Rom. 51/G3
Calimaya, Mex. 175/Q10
Calimere (pt.), India 95/C4
Calimesa, Ca, US 166/C2
Calingasta, Arg. 188/B4
Calion, Ar, US 153/H4
Calipatria, Ca, US 148/E4
Calistoga, Ca, US 146/B4
Calitri, It. 48/D2
Calixa-Lavallée, Qu, Can. 159/P6
Calizzano, It. 62/B5
Calkiní, Mex. 176/D1
Çalköy, Turk. 102/B2
Callac, Fr. 56/B4
Callaghan (mt.), Nv, US 146/E4
Callaghan, Tx, US 151/E4
Callahan, Fl, US 165/H2
Callahonna (lake), Austl. 127/D3
Callalli, Peru 184/D4
Callan, Ire. 32/C4
Callander, Sc, UK 33/B4
Callantsoog, Neth. 52/B3
Callao, Peru 184/B4
Callao, Ut, US 147/G4
Callao, Va, US 163/J2
Callapa, Bol. 188/B1
Callaun (peak), Ire. 32/B4
Callaway, Mn, US 156/G4
Callaway, Fl, US 165/F2
Calle Larga, Chile 190/N8
Callender, Ia, US 155/G2
Callian, Fr. 64/C5
Calliham, Tx, US 151/E3
Callington, Eng, UK 36/B5
Calliope, Austl. 134/C4
Callosa de Segura, Sp. 47/E3
Calmar, Ia, US 155/J2
Calmar, Ab, Can. 145/H1
Calne, Eng, UK 36/E4
Calolziocorte, It. 62/C2
Calonga (riv.), Ang. 122/B2
Calonne (riv.), Fr. 57/F2
Calonne-Ricouart, Fr. 54/B3
Caloocan, Phil. 88/E6
Caloosahatchee (riv.), Fl, US 165/H4
Caloosahatchee Nat'l Wild. Ref., Fl, US 165/H4
Calore (riv.), It. 67/G2
Caloundra, Austl. 134/D4
Calpe, Sp. 47/F3
Calpulálpan, Mex. 175/L7
Calstock, Eng, UK 36/B6
Caltagirone, It. 48/D4
Caltanissetta, It. 48/D4
Caltavuturo, It. 48/C4
Caluango, Ang. 120/D5
Calucinga, Ang. 122/C1
Calueque (dam), Ang. 122/B3
Calulo, Ang. 120/C5
Calumbo, Ang. 120/C5
Calumet, Mi, US 157/K4
Calumet (riv.), Il, US 167/Q16
Calumet City, Il, US 160/C4
Calumet Sag (chan.), Il, US 167/Q16
Caluquembe, Ang. 122/B2
Caluso, It. 62/A2
Caluula (pt.), Som. 118/D3
Caluula, Som. 118/D3
Calva, Az, US 149/G4
Calvados (dept.), Fr. 57/E3
Calvary, Ga, US 165/F2
Calvello, It. 48/D2
Calvenzano, It. 62/C3
Calvert, Nf, Can. 159/L2
Calvert, Al, US 164/D2
Calvert, Tx, US 151/F2
Calvert City, Ky, US 162/C2
Calvert Hills, Austl. 129/E4
Calverton, Eng, UK 35/G5
Calverton, Md, US 168/B5
Calvi, Fr. 48/A1
Calvi (peak), It. 63/E5
Calvi Risorta, It. 65/D5
Calviá, Sp. 47/G3
Calvilli (peak), It. 65/C5
Calvillo, Mex. 174/E4
Calvin, Ok, US 153/F3
Calvinia, SAfr. 124/B3
Calvisano, It. 62/D3
Calvitero (peak), Sp. 46/C2
Calw, Ger. 58/B5
Calzada de Calatrava, Sp. 46/D3
Cam or Rhee (riv.), Eng, UK 37/F2
Cam Pha, Viet. 87/E4
Cam Ranh, Viet. 94/E4
Cam Thuy, Viet. 94/D1
Camabatela, Ang. 120/C5
Camaçari, Braz. 187/F2
Camacho, Bol. 188/C2
Camacho, Bol. 185/E3
Camacho, Mex. 174/E3
Camacupa, Ang. 122/C2
Camaguán, Ven. 181/E2
Camagüey (arch.), Cuba 173/F3
Camagüey, Cuba 177/G1
Camaiore, It. 62/D6
Camajuaní, Cuba 177/G1
Camalengue, Ang. 120/D5
Camalu, Mex. 174/A2
Camamu, Braz. 187/F2
Camaná, Peru 184/C5
Camanche (res.), Ca, US 146/C4
Camanche, Ia, US 155/J3
Camanducaia, Braz. 187/K7
Camanongue, Ang. 122/D1
Camapuã, Braz. 189/F1
Camaquã, Braz. 189/G4
Camaquã (riv.), Braz. 189/F4
Camarat (cape), Fr. 64/C6
Camaret-sur-Aigues, Fr. 64/A4
Camaret-sur-Mer, Fr. 56/A4
Camargo, Ok, US 152/E2
Camargo, Sp. 46/D1
Camargo, Bol. 188/C2
Camarillo, Ca, US 166/A2
Camariñas, Sp. 46/A1
Camarón (cape), Hon. 177/E3
Camarones (bay), Arg. 190/D5
Camarones, Arg. 190/D5
Camarones, Chile 188/B1
Camas, Sp. 46/B4
Camas NWR, Id, US 147/G2
Camas Prairie (grsld.), Id, US 144/F4
Camas Valley, Or, US 146/B2
Camatagua, Ven. 183/P8
Camaxilo, Ang. 120/D5
Cambados, Sp. 46/A1
Cambará, Braz. 189/G2
Cambay (gulf), India 92/B3
Cambé, Braz. 189/G2
Camberley, Eng, UK 30/A3
Camberwell (nbrhd.), Eng, UK 30/C2
Camberwell, Austl. 133/B3
Cambiano, It. 62/A3
Cambo (riv.), Ang. 120/D5
Cambo Camana, Ang. 120/D5
Cambodia (ctry.) 77/K8
Cambondo, Ang. 120/C5
Camborne, Eng, UK 36/A6
Cambrai, Fr. 54/C3
Cambria, Ca, US 148/B3
Cambrian (mts.), Wal, UK 34/E5
Cambridge (gulf), Austl. 128/C3
Cambridge, On, Can. 160/F3
Cambridge (int'l arpt.), Eng, UK 37/G2
Cambridge, Eng, UK 37/G2
Cambridge, NZ 135/C2
Cambridge, Id, US 146/E1
Cambridge, Il, US 155/J3
Cambridge, Ma, US 161/L3
Cambridge, Md, US 163/J1
Cambridge, Mn, US 157/H5
Cambridge, Ne, US 154/D3
Cambridge, Oh, US 160/F4
Cambridge, Vt, US 161/K2
Cambridge Bay, Nun, Can. 140/F2
Cambridge City, In, US 160/D5
Cambridge Springs, Pa, US 160/F4
Cambridge-Narrows, NB, Can. 158/E3
Cambridgeshire (co.), Eng, UK 37/F2
Cambrils, Sp. 47/F2
Cambuí, Braz. 187/K7
Cambulo, Ang. 121/E4
Cambuquira, Braz. 187/L6
Cambuslang, Sc, UK 33/B5
Cambutal (mtn.), Pan. 180/A3
Camden, Austl. 134/G9
Camden (sound), Austl. 128/A3
Camden (co.), Eng, UK 30/C2
Camden, Al, US 164/E2
Camden, Ar, US 153/H4
Camden, De, US 168/C5
Camden, Mi, US 160/D4
Camden, NC, US 163/J2
Camden, NJ, US 168/C4
Camden (co.), NJ, US 168/C4
Camden, NY, US 161/J3
Camden, SC, US 163/G3
Camden, Tn, US 162/C2
Camden, Tx, US 151/G2
Camden East, On, Can. 161/H2
Camden Haven, Austl. 132/E1
Camdenton, Mo, US 153/H1
Cameia, Ang. 122/D1
Cameia, PN da, Ang. 121/E5
Cameia, PN da, Ang. 122/D1
Camel (riv.), Eng, UK 36/B6
Camelback (mtn.), Pa, US 168/C1
Camelford, Eng, UK 36/B5
Camels Back (peak), NZ 135/C2
Camenca, Mol. 72/E3
Camerano, It. 63/G6
Cameri, It. 62/B3
Camerino, It. 65/C1
Camerón (riv.), Mex. 151/D4
Cameron (isl.), Nun, Can. 141/R7
Cameron, Az, US 149/G3
Cameron (peak), Co, US 154/B3
Cameron, La, US 164/B3
Cameron, Mo, US 155/G4
Cameron, Mt, US 147/H1
Cameron, Tx, US 151/F2
Cameron, Wi, US 157/J5
Cameron Highlands, Malay. 89/C1
Cameron Park, Ca, US 146/C4
Cameroon (ctry.) 107/D4
Cameroon Highlands (uplands), Nga. 116/A4
Cametá, Braz. 182/D3
Camey, Tx, US 150/L6
Camfield, Austl. 128/C4
Camicia (peak), It. 65/C3
Camiguin (isl.), Phil. 88/C1
Camiling, Phil. 88/C2
Camilla, Ga, US 165/F2
Camilo Aldao, Arg. 190/E2
Caminha, Port. 46/A2
Camiranga, Braz. 183/E3
Camiri, Bol. 188/D2
Camisano Vicentino, It. 63/E2
Camissombo, Ang. 121/E5
Çamlıdere, Turk. 70/E4
Çamlık NP, Turk. 102/C2
Camlin (riv.), Ire. 32/C2
Çamlıyayla, Turk. 104/D1
Camo-Camo, Moz. 123/G4
Camoapa, Nic. 176/E3
Camocim, Braz. 183/F3
Camogli, It. 62/C5
Camolin, Ire. 32/D4
Camon, Fr. 54/B4
Camooweal, Austl. 129/E4
Camopi, FrG. 182/C2
Camopi (riv.), FrG. 182/C2
Camorta (isl.), India 93/F6
Camoruco, Col. 180/D3
Camotes (sea), Phil. 88/D3
Camp Angelus (Angelus Oaks), Ca, US 166/D2
Camp Atterbury, In, US 162/D1
Camp Blanding Mil. Res., Fl, US 165/G3
Camp Grayling, Mi, US 160/D2
Camp Hill, Pa, US 168/B3
Camp J.T. Robinson, Ar, US 153/H3
Camp Lake, Wi, US 167/P14
Camp Lake Nat'l Wild. Ref., ND, US 156/D4
Camp Lejeune, NC, US 163/J3
Camp Lejeune Marine Base, NC, US 163/J3
Camp Pendleton, Ca, US 148/D4
Camp Ripley Mil. Res., Mn, US 157/G4
Camp Roberts, Ca, US 148/B3
Camp Shelby, Ms, US 164/D2
Camp Springs, Md, US 168/B6
Camp Verde, Az, US 149/G3
Camp Verde Ind. Res., Az, US 149/G3
Camp Williams, Ut, US 147/G3
Camp Wood, Tx, US 151/D3
Campagna di Roma (reg.), It. 65/B4
Campagna Lupia, It. 63/F3
Campagnano di Roma, It. 65/B3
Campagnola Emilia, It. 63/D4
Campamento, Uru. 189/E4
Campana (isl.), Chile 191/B6
Campana, Arg. 191/J11
Campanario, Sp. 46/C3
Campanario (peak), Arg. 190/C2
Campanella (cape), It. 65/D6
Campanha, Braz. 187/L6
Campania (prov.), It. 48/D2
Campbell (cape), NZ 135/C3
Campbell (isl.), NZ 27/T8
Campbell, Ca, US 167/L12
Campbell, Fl, US 164/N7
Campbell, Mn, US 156/F4
Campbell, Mo, US 162/B2
Campbell (hill), Oh, US 160/E4
Campbell, Oh, US 160/F4
Campbell, Ne, US 154/E3
Campbell, Tx, US 153/G4
Campbell Town, Austl. 132/C4
Campbellford, On, Can. 161/H2
Campbellpore, Pak. 98/B3
Campbell's Bay, Qu, Can. 161/H2
Campbellsport, Wi, US 160/B3
Campbellsville, Ky, US 162/E2
Campbellton, NB, Can. 158/D1
Campbellton, Fl, US 165/F2
Campbelltown (nbrhd.), Austl. 134/G9
Campbellville, On, Can. 160/T9
Campbeltown, Sc, UK 31/R9
Campbon, Fr. 56/D6
Campden, On, Can. 160/U9
Campeche (state), Mex. 172/C4
Campeche, Mex. 176/D2
Campeche (bay), Mex. 139/H7
Campello sul Clitunno, It. 65/B2
Camperdown, Austl. 132/B3
Camperville, Mb, Can. 156/D2
Campestre, Braz. 187/K6
Campi Bisenzio, It. 63/E6
Campidano (range), It. 48/A3
Campile, Ire. 32/D5
Campillo de Altobuey, Sp. 46/E3
Campillos, Sp. 46/C4
Campina da Lagoa, Braz. 189/F3
Campina Grande, Braz. 183/H4
Campina Verde, Braz. 186/C3
Campinas, Braz. 187/J7
Campione d'Italia, It. 61/E6
Campli, It. 65/C2
Camplong, Indo. 128/A2
Campo, Camr. 120/B2
Campo, Ca, US 148/D4
Campo (int'l arpt.), Braz. 184/C2
Campo Belo, Braz. 186/D4
Campo de Criptana, Sp. 46/D3
Campo de la Cruz, Col. 180/C2
Campo dei Fiori (peak), It. 62/B2
Campo Erê, Braz. 189/F3
Campo Florido, Braz. 189/G1
Campo Formoso, Braz. 187/E1
Campo Gallo, Arg. 188/D3
Campo Grande, Braz. 189/F2
Campo Ind. Res., Ca, US 148/D4
Campo Largo, Braz. 189/G3
Campo Ligure, It. 62/B4
Campo Limpo Paulista, Braz. 187/K8
Campo Maior, Port. 46/B3
Campo Maior, Braz. 183/F4
Campo Mourão, Braz. 189/F3
Campo Quijano, Arg. 188/C3
Campo Redondo, Braz. 183/G4
Campo Tencia (peak), Swi. 61/E5
Campo Tizzoro, It. 63/D5
Campoalegre, Col. 180/C4
Campobasso (prov.), It. 65/D4
Campobasso, It. 65/D4
Campobello (isl.), Ns., Can. 158/D3
Campodarsego, It. 63/E3
Campodolcino, It. 61/F5
Campogalliano, It. 63/D4
Campomorone, It. 62/B4
Camponogara, It. 63/F3
Camporosso, It. 62/A5
Camporredondo (res.), Sp. 46/C1
Camporredondo, Peru 184/B2
Campos (phys. reg.), Braz. 179/D5
Campos Belos, Braz. 186/D2
Campos de Hielo Norte (glacier), Chile 191/B5
Campos de Hielo Sur (glacier), Chile 191/B6
Campos del Puerto, Sp. 47/G3
Campos do Jordão, Braz. 187/L7
Campos dos Goytacazes, Braz. 187/E4
Campos Novos, Braz. 189/G3
Campos Sales, Braz. 183/F4
Camposampiero, It. 63/E2
Camposanto, It. 63/E4
Camposauro (peak), It. 65/D5
Campotosto (lake), It. 65/C3
Campsie Fells (hills), Sc, UK 33/B4
Campti, La, US 164/B2
Campton, Ky, US 163/F2
Camrose, Ab, Can. 145/H1
Çan, Turk. 70/C4
Can (riv.), Eng, UK 30/E1
Can Tho, Viet. 94/D4
Cana, Sk, Can. 156/C2
Canaan, Ar, US 153/H3
Canaan, Vt, US 161/L2
Canaan (riv.), NB, Can. 158/E2
Canaan, NH, US 161/K3
Canaan Game Ref., NB, Can. 158/E2
Canaçari (lake), Braz. 181/G5
Canacari (lake), Braz. 182/B3
Canada (ctry.) 139/G4
Cañada de Gómez, Arg. 190/E2
Cañada Larga, Bol. 185/F5
Cañada Nieto, Uru. 191/J10
Cañada Rosquín, Arg. 190/E2
Canadensis, Pa, US 168/C1
Canadian, Tx, US 152/D3
Canadian (riv.), US 139/G6
Canadian, North (riv.), Ok, US 142/F4
Cañadón de las Vacas, Arg. 191/C6
Cañadon Grande (mts.), Arg. 190/C5
Cañadón Seco, Arg. 190/D5
Canaima, PN, Ven. 181/F3
Canajoharie, NY, US 161/J3
Çanakkale, Turk. 49/K2
Çanakkale (prov.), Turk. 70/C5
Canal Flats, BC, Can. 144/G2
Canal Point, Fl, US 165/H4
Canala, NCal. 137/U12
Canalbianco (riv.), It. 63/E2
Canale, It. 62/A3
Canale Cavour (canal), It. 62/B2
Canals, Sp. 47/E3
Canals, Arg. 190/E2
Canandaigua, NY, US 161/H3
Cananea, Mex. 174/C2
Canaos (riv.), Braz. 189/G3
Cañar (dept.), Ecu. 180/B5
Cañar, Ecu. 184/B1
Canard (riv.), On, Can. 167/G7
Canarsie (nbrhd.), NY, US 169/K9
Canary (isls.), Sp. 110/A3
Canary (isls.) 107/A2
Cañas, CR 176/E4
Cañasgordas, Col. 180/B3
Canatlán de las Manzanas, Mex. 174/D3
Canaveral (pen.), Fl, US 165/H3
Canaveral (cape), Fl, US 165/H3
Canaveral Nat'l Seashore, Fl., US 165/H3
Canavieiras, Braz. 187/F2
Canbelego, Austl. 132/C1
Canberra (cap.), Austl. 133/D2
Canby, Or, US 146/B1
Canby, Mn, US 155/F1
Cancale, Fr. 56/D3
Cance (riv.), Fr. 64/A2
Cancello-Arnone, It. 65/D5
Canchaque, Peru 184/B2
Canche (riv.), Fr. 44/E1
Cancun (int'l arpt.), Mex. 176/E1
Cancún, Mex. 176/E1
Candarave, Peru 188/B1
Çandarli (gulf), Gre. 102/A2
Candás, Sp. 46/C1
Candás, Sp. 46/B1
Candé, Fr. 57/D5
Candeias, Braz. 187/F2
Candela, Mex. 151/D4
Candelaria (riv.), Mex. 176/D2
Candelaria, Mex. 176/D2
Candelaria, Arg. 190/D2
Candelária, Braz. 189/F4
Candelaria, Bol. 188/E1
Candeleda, Sp. 46/C2
Candelo, It. 62/B2
Candelo, Austl. 133/D3
Candia Lomellina, It. 62/B3
Candiac, Qu, Can. 159/N7
Cândido Mendes, Braz. 183/E3
Cândido Mota, Braz. 189/G2
Canding (cape), Indo. 90/D5
Candiolo, It. 64/D3
Çandır, Turk. 102/C2
Candler-McAfee, Ga, US 163/M7
Candlewood, NJ, US 168/D3
Cando, ND, US 156/E3
Cando, Sk, Can. 145/K1
Candon, Phil. 88/C1
Cane (cr.), Ga, US 165/G2
Cane Beds, Az, US 149/F2
Cane Field (int'l arpt.), Dom. 173/N9
Canegrate, It. 62/B2
Canela, Braz. 189/G4
Canela Baja, Chile 188/B4
Canelli, It. 62/B4
Canelones (dept.), Uru. 191/F2
Canelones, Uru. 191/K11
Canepina, It. 65/B3
Cañete, Sp. 46/E2
Canete, Río de (riv.), Peru 184/B4
Caneva, It. 63/F2
Caney (cr.), Tx, US 151/G3
Caney, Ok, US 153/F3
Caney, Ks, US 153/G2
Caney (riv.), Ks,Ok, US 175/F2
Caneyville, Ky, US 162/D2
Canfield, Ar, US 153/H4
Canfield Lake Nat'l Wild. Ref., ND, US 156/D4
Cangallo, Peru 184/C4
Cangamba, Ang. 122/C2
Cangandala, Ang. 120/D5
Cangas, Sp. 46/A1
Cangas de Narcea, Sp. 46/B1
Cangas de Onís, Sp. 46/C1
Cangkuang (cape), Indo. 89/D4
Cango Caves, SAfr. 124/C4
Cangoa, Ang. 122/C2
Cangombe, Ang. 122/D2
Cangonga, Ang. 122/C2
Cangqian, China 87/H3
Cangrejo (peak), Arg. 191/B6
Cangshan, China 80/D4
Cangshan, China 79/J1
Canguaretama, Braz. 183/H4
Canguçu, Braz. 189/F4
Cangumbe, Ang. 122/C1
Cangwu, China 93/K3
Cangyuan (Cangyuan Vazu Zizhixian), China 86/C4
Cangzhou, China 80/D3
Canh Cuoc (isl.), Viet. 94/D1
Canhaua, Ang. 122/C3
Canhoca, Ang. 122/B2
Canhotinho, Braz. 183/G5
Cania Gorge NP, Austl. 134/C4
Caniapiscau (lake), Qu, Can. 141/K3
Caniapiskau (riv.), Qu, Can. 141/J3
Canicatti, It. 48/C4
Canigou, Pic du (peak), Fr. 44/E5
Canik (mts.), Turk. 102/C1
Caniles, Sp. 46/D4
Canim Lake, BC, Can. 144/D2
Canindé, Braz. 183/G4
Canindé (riv.), Braz. 183/F4
Canindeyú (dept.), Par. 186/B5
Canino, It. 48/B1
Canistear (res.), NJ, US 169/H7
Canisteo, NY, US 161/H3
Cañitas de Felipe Pescador, Mex. 174/E4
Canjáyar, Sp. 46/D4
Canje (riv.), Guy. 182/B1
Canjilon, NM, US 149/J2
Cankhor, Som. 118/C3
Çankırı, Turk. 70/E4
Çankırı (prov.), Turk. 70/E4
Canlaon (vol.), Phil. 88/C3
Canmore, Ab, Can. 144/G2
Cann (mtn.), Austl. 133/D3
Cann (riv.), Austl. 133/D3
Cann River, Austl. 133/D3
Canna (isl.), Sc, UK 31/Q8
Cannara, It. 65/B2
Canne (ruin), It. 48/E2
Cannel City, Ky, US 163/F2
Cannelton, In, US 162/D2
Canner (riv.), Fr. 55/F5
Cannero Riviera, It. 61/E5
Cannes, Fr. 64/D5
Canneto sull'Oglio, It. 62/D3
Cannich, Sc, UK 33/B2
Canning (peak), Austl. 130/C4
Canning (riv.), Austl. 130/K7
Canning (dam), Austl. 130/L7
Cannobio, It. 61/E5
Cannock, Eng, UK 36/D1
Cannon (A.F.B.), NM, US 152/C3
Cannon Ball, ND, US 156/D4
Cannon Beach, Or, US 144/C5
Cannon Falls, Mn, US 155/H1
Cannonball (riv.), ND, US 156/D4
Cannondale, Ct, US 169/E1
Cannonvale, Austl. 134/C3
Cannonville, Ut, US 149/F2
Caño Guaritico (riv.), Ven. 180/D3
Caño Negro Nat'l Wild. Ref., CR 177/E4
Canoas, Braz. 189/G4
Canobolas (mt.), Austl. 133/D1
Canoe, Al, US 164/E2
Canoe River, BC, Can. 144/E1
Canoga Park (nbrhd.), Ca, US 166/E7
Canoinhas, Braz. 189/G3
Canon City, Co, US 152/B1
Cañón de Río Blanco, PN, Mex. 175/M8
Cañón del Sumidero, PN, Mex. 176/C2
Cañon Largo (riv.), NM, US 149/J2
Canonbie, Sc, UK 35/F1
Cañoncito Ind. Res., NM, US 149/J3
Canones, NM, US 149/J2
Canoochee (riv.), Ga, US 165/G1
Canopus (ruin), Egypt 113/B2
Canora, Sk, Can. 156/C2
Canosa di Puglia, It. 48/E2
Canouan (isl.), StV. 173/N9
Canowindra, Austl. 133/D1
Cansado, Mrta. 110/A5
Canso, NS, Can. 159/G3
Canso (cape), NS, Can. 159/G3
Canta, Peru 184/B3
Cantabria (prov.), Sp. 44/B5
Cantabria (dist.), Sp. 46/C1
Cantal (mass.), Fr. 44/E4
Cantalejo, Sp. 46/D2
Cantanhede, Port. 46/A2
Cantanhede, Braz. 183/E3
Cantaura, Ven. 181/E2
Canteleu, Fr. 57/G2
Canterbury (nbrhd.), Austl. 134/H8
Canterbury, Eng, UK 37/H4
Canterbury Bight (bay), NZ 127/H7
Canterbury Cathedral, Eng, UK 37/H4
Cantiere, Eth. 117/G4
Cantil, Ca, US 148/D3
Cantilan, Phil. 88/D3
Cantillana, Sp. 46/C4
Canto del Agua, Chile 188/B4
Canto do Buriti, Braz. 183/F5
Canton, Ga, US 162/E3
Canton, Il, US 155/J3
Canton, Ks, US 153/F1
Canton, Mi, US 167/E7
Canton, Mo, US 155/J3
Canton, Ms, US 162/B4
Canton, NC, US 163/F3
Canton, NJ, US 168/C5
Canton, NY, US 161/J2
Canton, Oh, US 160/F4
Canton, Ok, US 153/E2
Canton (lake), Ok, US 153/E2
Canton, Pa, US 161/H4
Canton, SD, US 155/F2
Canton, Tx, US 151/G1
Canton (Abariringa) (isl.), Kiri. 137/H5
Cantoria, Sp. 46/D4
Cantù, It. 62/C2
Cantwell, Ak, US 171/J3
Cañuelas, Arg. 191/J11
Canumã (riv.), Braz. 182/B4
Canunda NP, Austl. 132/B3
Canutama, Braz. 185/E2
Canutillo, Tx, US 151/A2
Canvey (isl.), Eng, UK 30/E2
Canvey Island, Eng, UK 37/G3
Canwood, Sk, Can. 145/L1
Cany-Barville, Fr. 57/F1

Map Section
214
215

Catema – Chartre
216
217
Map Section

Catemaco (lake), Mex. 176/C2
Catemaco, Mex. 176/C2
Catende, Braz. 183/H5
Cateran (hill), Eng, UK 33/E5
Caterham, Eng, UK 30/C3
Caterham and Warlingham, Eng, UK 37/F4
Catete, Ang. 120/C5
Catfish (cr.), Fl, US 164/N8
Catharine, Ks, US 152/E1
Cathcart, SAfr. 124/D4
Cathedral (mtn.), Tx, US 151/C2
Cathedral City, Ca, US 148/D4
Cathédrale de Reims, Fr. 54/D5
Catherine (peak), Egypt 109/G2
Catherine, Al, US 162/D4
Catherine Palace, Rus. 69/T7
Cathlamet, Wa, US 144/C4
Ca'Tiepolo, It. 63/F4
Catierick, Eng, UK 35/G3
Catingueira, Braz. 183/G4
Catió, GBis. 114/B4
Cativá, Pan. 177/G4
Catlettsburg, Ky, US 163/F1
Catlin, Il, US 160/C4
Catmon, Phil. 88/D3
Cato (isl.), Aus. 127/E3
Catoche, Cabo (cape), Mex. 176/E1
Catofe, Ang. 120/C5
Catolé do Rocha, Braz. 183/G4
Catolo, Ang. 120/D5
Catonsville, Md, US 168/B5
Catoosa, Ok, US 153/G2
Catria (peak), It. 63/F7
Catriló, Arg. 190/E3
Catrimani, Braz. 181/F4
Catrimani (riv.), Braz. 181/F4
Catrine, Sc, UK 33/B6
Catshill, Eng, UK 36/D2
Catskill, NY, US 161/K3
Catskill (mts.), NY, US 161/J3
Cattaraugus, NY, US 161/G3
Cattaraugus Ind. Res., NY, US 161/G3
Cattawissa (cr.), Pa, US 168/B2
Cattolica, It. 63/F6
Catu, Braz. 187/F2
Catubig, Phil. 88/D2
Catuípe, Braz. 189/F4
Cauale (riv.), Ang. 120/D4
Cauayan, Phil. 88/C3
Cauayan, Phil. 88/C1
Cauca (riv.), Col. 180/C3
Cauca (riv.), Col. 179/B2
Cauca (dept.), Col. 180/B4
Caucagua, Ven. 180/D3
Caucagua, Ven. 183/P7
Caucaia, Braz. 183/G3
Caucas, Bol. 185/G5
Caucasia, Col. 180/C3
Caucasus (mts.), Geo.,Rus. 71/G4
Caucasus (mts.), Geo. 74/F6
Caucasus (mts.), Asia 102/E1
Caudan, Fr. 56/B5
Caudebec-en-Caux, Fr. 57/F1
Caudebec-lès-Elbeuf, Fr. 57/G2
Caudete, Sp. 47/E3
Caudry, Fr. 54/C3
Cauese, Montes (mts.), Moz. 123/F2
Cauldcleuch Head (peak), Sc, UK 33/D6
Caulfield, Mo, US 153/H2
Caulfield, Austl. 133/B3
Caulnes, Fr. 56/C4
Caumont (arpt.), Fr. 64/A5
Caumont-L'Éventé, Fr. 57/E2
Caumont-sur-Durance, Fr. 64/A5
Caúngula, Ang. 120/D5
Cauquenes, Chile 190/B2
Caura (riv.), Ven. 181/E3
Cauresi (riv.), Moz. 123/G3
Cauron (riv.), Fr. 64/B6
Causapscal, Qu, Can. 158/D1
Căuşeni, Mol. 72/E4
Causeway, Ire. 32/A5
Causey, NM, US 152/C4
Caussade, Fr. 44/D4
Cautário (riv.), Braz. 185/F3
Cauterets, Fr. 44/C5
Cauto (riv.), Cuba 177/G1
Cauvery (riv.), India 92/C5
Cauville, Fr. 57/F1
Cava de'Tirreni, It. 65/D6
Cava d'Ispica (ruin), It. 48/D4
Cávado (riv.), Port. 46/A2
Cavaglià, It. 62/B3
Cavaillon, Fr. 64/B5
Cavalaire-sur-Mer, Fr. 64/C6
Cavalcante, Braz. 186/D2
Cavalese, It. 61/H5
Cavalier, ND, US 156/F3
Cavalla (Cavally) (riv.), Libr. 114/D5
Cavallermaggiore, It. 62/A3
Cavallino, It. 63/F3
Cavallo, Capo al (cape), Fr. 48/A1
Cavally (riv.), C.d'Iv. 114/C5
Cavally (Cavalla) (riv.), Libr. 114/D5
Cavan, Ire. 32/C2
Cavari, Bol. 185/E5
Cavarzere, It. 63/F3
Cave, It. 65/B4
Cave City, Ar, US 153/J3
Cave City, Ky, US 162/E2
Cave Creek, Az, US 149/G4
Cave Junction, Or, US 146/B2
Cave of Ten Thousand Buddhas, Myan. 94/B2
Cave Of The Mounds, Wi, US 155/K2
Cave Run (lake), Ky, US 163/F1
Cave Spring, Va, US 163/G2
Cave Spring, Ga, US 162/E3
Caverns of Sonora, Tx, US 151/D2
Cavezzo, It. 63/E4
Caviana (isl.), Braz. 182/D2
Cavinas, Bol. 185/E4
Cavite (co.), Phil. 88/E7
Cavite, Phil. 88/E7
Cavnic, Rom. 51/F2
Cavour, It. 64/D3
Cavriana, It. 62/D3
Cawayan, Phil. 88/C3
Cawdor, Sc, UK 33/C1
Cawker City, Ks, US 154/E4
Cawood, Eng, UK 35/G4
Cawston, Eng, UK 37/H1
Caxambu, Braz. 187/M6
Caxata, Bol. 185/E5
Caxias, Braz. 183/F4
Caxias do Sul, Braz. 189/G4
Caxinas (pt.), Hon. 176/E2
Caxinga, Ang. 120/D5
Caxito, Ang. 120/C5
Çay, Turk. 102/B2
Çayağzı, Turk. 103/N6
Çayağzi (riv.), Turk. 103/N6
Cayambe, Ecu. 180/B4
Cayambe (vol.), Ecu. 180/B4
Cayastá, Arg. 188/D4
Cayce, SC, US 163/G4
Çaycuma, Turk. 70/E4
Çayeli, Turk. 71/G4
Cayenne (cap.), FrG. 182/C1
Cayenne (dist.), FrG. 182/C1
Cayer, Mb, Can. 156/E2
Cayeux-sur-Mer, Fr. 54/A3
Çayırhan, Turk. 51/K5
Çaylar, Turk. 102/E2
Cayley, Ab, Can. 145/H2
Cayman (isls.), UK 139/J8
Cayman Brac (isl.), UK 173/F4
Caynabo, Som. 118/C3
Cayo Coco (isl.), Cuba 177/G1
Cayo Cocorocuma (isl.), Hon. 177/F3
Cayo Fragosa (isl.), Cuba 177/G1
Cayo Guayabo (isl.), Cuba 177/G1
Cayo Largo (isl.), Cuba 177/F1
Cayo Romano (isl.), Cuba 177/G1
Cayo Sabinal (isl.), Cuba 177/G1
Cayos Arcas (isl.), Mex. 176/D1
Cayos Cajones (isl.), Hon. 172/E4
Cayos de Albuquerque (isl.), Col. 177/F3
Cayos del Este Sudeste (isl.), Col. 177/F3
Cayos Miskitos (isl.), Nic. 172/E5
Cayucos, Ca, US 148/B3
Cayuga, In, US 160/C5
Cayuga (lake), NY, US 161/H3
Cayuga (cr.), NY, US 160/V10
Cayuga, Tx, US 150/G2
Cayuga Heights, NY, US 161/H3
Cazalla de la Sierra, Sp. 46/C4
Cazenovia, NY, US 161/J3
Cazères, Fr. 44/D5
Cazin, Bosn. 50/B3
Cazis, Swi. 61/F4
Cazombo, Ang. 122/D1
Cazones (riv.), Mex. 176/B1
Cazorla, Sp. 46/D4
Cazula, Moz. 123/G2
Cazzago San Martino, It. 62/D2
Cea (riv.), Sp. 46/C1
Ceanannus Mór (Kells), Ire. 32/D2
Ceará (state), Braz. 183/F4
Ceará-Mirim, Braz. 183/H4
Cébaco (isl.), Pan. 177/F5
Ceballos, Mex. 174/D3
Cebolla, NM, US 149/J2
Cebollatí, Uru. 191/G2
Cebollati (riv.), Uru. 191/G2
Cebreros, Sp. 46/C2
Cebu, Phil. 88/C3
Cebu (isl.), Phil. 88/C3
Cebu (int'l arpt.), Phil. 88/C3
Ceccano, It. 65/C4
Cecil, Wi, US 155/K1
Cecil (co.), Md, US 168/C4
Cecil Macks (pass), Swaz. 125/E2
Cecil Plains, Austl. 134/C4
Cecil Rhodes (mt.), Austl. 130/D3
Cecilia, Ky, US 162/E2
Cecilton, Md, US 168/C5
Cecilville, Ca, US 146/B3
Cecina (riv.), It. 63/D6
Cecina, It. 45/J5
Cecita (lake), It. 48/E3
Ceclavín, Sp. 46/B3
Cedar (lake), Tx, US 152/C4
Cedar, Mi, US 160/D2
Cedar (lake), On, Can. 161/G1
Cedar (mtn.), Ca, US 167/L11
Cedar (lake), Sk,Mb, Can. 140/F3
Cedar (mts.), Ut, US 147/G3
Cedar (riv.), Ne, US 154/E3
Cedar (cr.), Ia, US 155/H3
Cedar (riv.), Mn, US 155/G1
Cedar (riv.), Ia, US 155/H2
Cedar (isl.), Md, US 163/K2
Cedar Bay NP, Austl. 134/B1
Cedar Bayou (riv.), Tx, US 151/M8
Cedar Bluff, Al, US 162/E3
Cedar Bluff (res.), Ks, US 154/E4
Cedar Breaks Nat'l Mon., Ut, US 149/F2
Cedar Brook, NJ, US 168/D4
Cedar City, Ut, US 149/F2
Cedar Creek, Ar, US 153/H3
Cedar Creek (peak), Id, US 147/G2
Cedar Creek (res.), Tx, US 175/F1
Cedar Crest, NM, US 149/J3
Cedar Falls (dam), Wa, US 167/D3
Cedar Falls, Wa, US 167/D3
Cedar Falls, Ia, US 155/H2
Cedar Glen, Ca, US 166/C2
Cedar Grove, Wi, US 160/C3
Cedar Grove, NJ, US 169/J8
Cedar Grove, Tn, US 162/C3
Cedar Grove, Md, US 168/A5
Cedar Hill, NM, US 149/J2
Cedar Hill, Tn, US 162/D2
Cedar Hill, Tx, US 150/L7
Cedar Island, NC, US 163/J3
Cedar Island NWR, NC, US 163/J3
Cedar Key, Fl, US 165/G3
Cedar Mills, Mn, US 155/G1
Cedar Park, Tx, US 151/F2
Cedar Point Nat'l Wild. Ref., Oh, US 160/E4
Cedar Rapids, Ia, US 155/J3
Cedar River, Mi, US 160/C2
Cedar Springs, Mi, US 160/D3
Cedar Springs, Tx, US 151/F2
Cedar Vale, Ks, US 153/F2
Cedarburg, Wi, US 160/C3
Cedaredge, Co, US 149/J1
Cedarhurst, NY, US 169/L9
Cedartown, Ga, US 162/E3
Cedarville, Ar, US 153/G3
Cedarville, Ca, US 146/C3
Cedegolo, It. 61/G5
Cedeira, Sp. 46/A1
Cedral, Mex. 175/E4
Cedro, Braz. 183/G4
Cedros (isl.), Mex. 139/F7
Ceduna, Austl. 131/G5
Cee, Sp. 46/A1
Ceel Afweyne, Som. 118/C3
Ceel Buur, Som. 118/C4
Ceel Dheere, Som. 118/C5
Ceel Xamurre, Som. 118/D4
Ceeldheere, Som. 118/C4
Ceerigaabo (Erigabo), Som. 118/C3
Cefalù, It. 48/D3
Cefn-Mawr, Wal, UK 35/E6
Cefni (riv.), Wal, UK 34/D5
Cega (riv.), Sp. 46/C2
Ceggia, It. 63/F2
Cegléd, Hun. 50/D2
Čegrane, FYROM 49/G2
Cehegín, Sp. 46/E3
Ceheng Bouyeizu Zizhixian, China 86/E3
Cehu Silvaniei, Rom. 51/F2
Ceiriog (riv.), Wal, UK 35/E6
Çekerek (riv.), Turk. 70/F4
Çekerek, Turk. 102/C1
Cela, Ang. 122/B1
Celada Cué, Par. 188/E2
Celákovice, Czh. 59/H2
Celano, It. 65/C3
Celanova, Sp. 46/B1
Celaya, Mex. 175/E4
Celbridge, Ire. 32/D3
Celebes (isl.), Indo. 77/L10
Celebes (sea), Asia 77/M9
Celebes (Sulawesi) (isl.), Indo. 91/E4
Celendín, Peru 184/B2
Celenza Valfortore, It. 65/D4
Celeste, Tx, US 153/F4
Celestún, Mex. 176/D1
Celica, Ecu. 184/B2
Céligny, Swi. 60/C5
Celina, Tx, US 153/F4
Celina, Oh, US 160/D4
Celina, Tn, US 162/E2
Celje, Slov. 50/B2
Cella, Sp. 46/E2
Celldömölk, Hun. 50/C2
Celle (riv.), Fr. 42/B4
Celle, Ger. 53/H3
Celle Ligure, It. 62/B5
Celles, Belg. 54/C2
Cellettes, Fr. 57/G5
Cellole, It. 65/C5
Čelopek, FYROM 50/E5
Celorico da Beira, Port. 46/B2
Celtic (sea), Eur. 31/P11
Cemaes (pt.), Wal, UK 36/B2
Cemaru (peak), Indo. 90/D3
Cembra, It. 61/H5
Cenajo (res.), Sp. 46/E3
Cenderawasih (bay), Indo. 91/H4
Cene, It. 62/C2
Cenepa (riv.), Peru 184/B1
Çengerli, Turk. 102/D2
Cengong, China 93/J2
Cenia, Sp. 47/F2
Ceno (riv.), It. 62/C3
Centallo, It. 64/D3
Centenario do Sul, Braz. 189/G2
Centennial (mts.), Id, US 147/G1
Centennial Wash (riv.), Az, US 149/F4
Center, Co, US 149/J2
Center, Mo, US 155/J4
Center, ND, US 156/D4
Center, Ne, US 154/F2
Center, Ok, US 153/F3
Center, Tx, US 151/G2
Center City, Mn, US 157/H5
Center Hill, Fl, US 164/M6
Center Hill (lake), Tn, US 162/E2
Center Moriches, NY, US 169/F2
Center Point, Al, US 162/D4
Center Point, Ia, US 155/J2
Center Point, La, US 164/B2
Center Point, Tx, US 151/E3
Centerbrook, Ct, US 169/F1
Centereach, NY, US 169/E2
Centerfield, Ut, US 147/H4
Centerville, Ga, US 162/F4
Centerville, Ga, US 163/M7
Centerville, In, US 160/D5
Centerville, Ia, US 155/H3
Centerville, Mo, US 162/B2
Centerville, Oh, US 160/D5
Centerville, Ok, US 152/E3
Centerville, SD, US 155/F2
Centerville, Tn, US 162/D3
Centerville, Tx, US 151/G2
Centerville, Tx, US 151/G2
Centerville, Ut, US 147/H3
Cento, It. 63/E4
Cento Croci, Passo di (pass), It. 62/C5
Central (peak), Arg. 190/C4
Central (dist), Bots. 122/E4
Central, Braz. 187/E1
Central (mass.), Fr. 44/E4
Central (pol. reg.), Gha. 115/E5
Central (dist.), Isr. 105/B4
Central (prov.), Kenya 119/B2
Central (dept.), Par. 188/E3
Central, Phil. 88/C2
Central (prov.), PNG 129/G2
Central (prov.), SrL. 95/D5
Central (int'l arpt.), Ukr. 72/F4
Central, Ak, US 171/K2
Central, Az, US 149/H4
Central, NM, US 149/H4
Central African Republic (ctry.) 107/D4
Central Australia (Warburton) Abor. Rsv., Austl. 131/E3
Central Australia Abor. Land, Austl. 131/F2
Central Butte, Sk, Can. 145/L2
Central City, Co, US 154/B4
Central City, Il, US 162/C1
Central City, Ky, US 162/D2
Central City, Ia, US 155/J2
Central City, Ne, US 154/F3
Central City, Pa, US 161/G4
Central Desert Abor. Rsv., Austl. 131/F2
Central Desert Aboriginal Land, Austl. 128/C4
Central Falls, RI, US 161/L4
Central Intelligence Agency Fed. Govt. Res., Va, US 168/A6
Central Island NP, Kenya 117/H5
Central Islip, NY, US 169/E2
Central Kalahari Game Reserve, Bots. 122/D4
Central Makrān (range), Pak. 101/H3
Central Mount Stuart (peak), Austl. 131/G2
Central Mount Wedge (peak), Austl. 131/F2
Central Park, NY, US 169/K8
Central Patricia, On, Can. 157/J2
Central Point, Or, US 146/B2
Central Russian Uplands (uplands), Rus. 73/J1
Central Saanich, BC, Can. 144/C3
Central Siberian (plat.), Rus. 75/L3
Central Square, NY, US 161/H3
Central Ural (mts.), Rus. 69/N4
Central Valley, Ca, US 146/B3
Central Valley, NY, US 168/D1
Centralia, Il, US 162/C1
Centralia, Ks, US 155/F4
Centralia, Mo, US 155/H4
Centralia, Wa, US 144/C4
Centre (prov.), Camr. 116/A4
Centre (pol. reg.), Fr. 44/D3
Centre (pol. reg.), Mor. 110/D2
Centre, Al, US 162/E3
Centre (co.), Pa, US 168/A2
Centre Island, NY, US 169/L8
Centre Nord (pol. reg.), Mor. 110/D2
Centre Sud (pol. reg.), Mor. 110/D3
Centre-Nord (pol. reg.), Mor. 112/B2
Centre-Sud (pol. reg.), Mor. 112/B2
Centreville, Al, US 162/D4
Centreville, Md, US 168/B5
Centreville, Mi, US 160/D4
Centreville, Ms, US 164/C2
Centreville, NS, Can. 158/E3
Century, Fl, US 164/E2
Cenxi, China 93/K3
Cepagatti, It. 65/D3
Ceparana, It. 62/C5
Cepet (cape), Fr. 64/B6
Čepin, Cro. 50/D3
Ceprano, It. 65/C4
Cepu, Indo. 89/E3
Ceram (isl.), Indo. 91/G4
Ceram (sea), Indo. 91/G4
Cerano, It. 62/B3
Cérans-Foulletourte, Fr. 57/F5
Ceraso (cape), It. 48/A2
Cerbat (mts.), Az, US 149/E3
Cerbère, Fr. 44/E5
Cercal, Port. 46/A4
Cercedilla, Sp. 47/M8
Cerchio, It. 65/C3
Čerchov (peak), Czh. 59/F4
Cerdanyola del Vallès, Sp. 47/L7
Cère (riv.), Fr. 44/E4
Cerea, It. 63/E3
Cereal, Ab, Can. 145/J2
Ceredigion (co.), Wal, UK 36/B3
Cerenti, Indo. 89/C3
Ceres, Arg. 188/D4
Ceres, Braz. 186/C2
Ceres, It. 64/D2
Ceres, SAfr. 124/L10
Ceres, Ca, US 148/B2
Ceresco, Ne, US 155/F3
Cerese, It. 63/D3
Céreste, Fr. 64/B5
Céret, Fr. 44/E5
Cereté, Col. 180/C2
Cerfone (riv.), It. 63/E6
Cerfontaine, Belg. 55/D3
Cergy, Fr. 30/J4
Ceriale, It. 62/B5
Cerignola, It. 48/D2
Cerisy-la-Salle, Fr. 56/D2
Çerkeş, Turk. 70/E4
Çerkezköy, Turk. 51/J5
Çermik, Turk. 102/D2
Černá (riv.), Czh. 59/H5
Černá (peak), Czh. 59/G5
Cernavodă, Rom. 51/J3
Cernay, Fr. 60/D2
Cernay-la-Ville, Fr. 30/H5
Cerne Abbas, Eng, UK 36/D5
Cernier, Swi. 60/C3
Cérou (riv.), Fr. 44/D4
Cerralvo, Mex. 151/E4
Cerralvo (isl.), Mex. 174/C3
Cerreto di Spoleto, It. 65/B2
Cerreto Guidi, It. 63/D6
Cerreto Sannita, It. 65/D5
Cerreto, Passo del (pass), It. 62/D5
Cerrig-y-Druidion, Wal, UK 34/E5
Cërrik, Alb. 49/F2
Cerrillos, NM, US 149/J3
Cerrillos, Arg. 188/C3
Cerrito, Par. 188/E3
Cerritos, Ca, US 166/F8
Cerritos, Mex. 175/E4
Cerro, NM, US 152/B2
Cerro Azul, Mex. 176/B1
Cêrro Azul, Braz. 189/G3
Cerro Azul, Peru 184/B4
Cerro Castillo, Chile 191/B6
Cerro Chato, Uru. 191/G2
Cerro Colorados (res.), Arg. 190/C3
Cêrro Corá, Braz. 183/G4
Cerro de la Estrella, PN, Mex. 175/Q10
Cerro de las Armas, Uru. 191/K11
Cerro de las Campanas, PN, Mex. 175/E4
Cerro de Pasco, Peru 184/B3
Cerro de San Antonio, Col. 180/C2
Cerro Dorotea, Chile 191/B6
Cerro El Copey, PN, Ven. 181/F2
Cerro Largo (dept.), Uru. 189/F5
Cerro Maggiore, It. 62/B2
Cerro Nanchital, Mex. 176/C2
Cerro Sombrero, Chile 191/C7
Cerros de Amotape, PN, Peru 184/A2
Certaldo, It. 63/E6
Certosa di Pavia, It. 62/C3
Certosa di Pisa, It. 62/D6
Cervantes, Austl. 130/B4
Cervaro, It. 65/C5
Cervaro (riv.), It. 50/B5
Cervati (peak), It. 48/D2
Cervellino (peak), It. 62/D4
Cervera, Sp. 47/F2
Cervera de Pisuerga, Sp. 46/C1
Cervera del Río Alhama, Sp. 46/E1
Cerveteri, It. 65/B4
Cerveyrette (riv.), Fr. 64/C3
Cervia, It. 63/F5
Cervignano del Friuli, It. 63/G2
Cervina (peak), It. 61/H4
Cervinara, It. 65/D5
Cervione, Fr. 48/A1
Cervo (riv.), It. 62/B1
Cervo, It. 62/B6
Cervo, Sp. 66/B2
Cervo (hills), Braz. 187/K7
Cesana Torinese, It. 64/C3
Cesano, It. 65/B3
Cesano (riv.), It. 63/F6
Cesano Boscone, It. 62/C3
Cesano Maderno, It. 62/C2
César (riv.), Col. 173/G5
César (dept.), Col. 180/C2
Cesar (prov.), Col. 177/H4
Cesen (peak), It. 63/F2
Cesena, It. 63/F5
Cesenatico, It. 63/F5
Cēsis, Lat. 41/L3
České Budějovice, Czh. 59/H5
Ceské Středohoří (mts.), Czh. 59/G2
Českomoravská Vysočina (mts.), Czh. 43/H4
Český Brod, Czh. 59/H2
Český Krumlov, Czh. 59/H5
Český Les Sumava (mts.), Czh. 59/F3
Česma (riv.), Cro. 50/C3
Çeşme, Turk. 49/K3
Cessford, Ab, Can. 145/J2
Cessnock, Austl. 133/E1
Cesson, Fr. 30/K6
Cesson-Sévigné, Fr. 56/D4
Cestohowa, Tx, US 151/F3
Cestos (riv.), Libr. 114/C5
Cesvaine, Lat. 41/M3
Cetara, It. 65/D6
Cetina (riv.), Cro. 50/C4
Cetinje, Yugo. 50/D4
Çetinkaya, Turk. 102/D2
Çetmi, Turk. 102/B2
Céu Azul, Braz. 189/F3
Ceurda del Pozo (res.), Sp. 46/D2
Ceuta, Sp. 112/B2
Ceva, It. 62/B5
Cevedale (peak), It. 61/G5
Cévennes (mts.), Fr. 44/E4
Cevio, Swi. 61/E5
Ceyhan, Turk. 104/C2
Ceylânpınar, Turk. 102/E2
Ceylon (isl.), SrL. 77/H9
Ceylon, Mn, US 155/G2
Ceyreste, Fr. 64/B6
Ceyzériat, Fr. 60/B5
Cèze (riv.), Fr. 44/F4
Ch'o (isl.), NKor. 81/C3
Ch'ok'ē (mts.), Eth. 118/A3
Ch'ungman (riv.), NKor. 81/C2
Cha Da (cape), Viet. 94/E4
Cha-am, Thai. 94/B3
Cha'anpu, China 87/F2
Chabāl Kalān, India 98/C4
Chabás, Arg. 190/E2
Chabeuil, Fr. 64/B3
Chābi, India 96/C4
Chabjuwardoo (bay), Austl. 130/B2
Chablé, Mex. 176/D2
Chabris, Fr. 57/G6
Chacabuco, Arg. 190/E2
Chacalluta, Chile 184/D5
Chacalluta (Arica) (int'l arpt.), Chile 188/B1
Chacao, Chile 190/B4
Chachani (peak), Peru 184/D5
Chachapoyas, Peru 184/B2
Chācharān, Pak. 98/A5
Chachoengsao, Thai. 94/C3
Chaclacayo, Peru 184/B3
Chaco (dept.), Arg. 188/D3
Chaco (riv.), NM, US 149/H2
Chaco (mesa), NM, US 149/J3
Chaco Austral (plain), Arg. 188/D3
Chaco Boreal (plain), Par. 188/D2
Chaco Central (plain), Arg. 188/D2
Chaco Culture Nat'l Hist. Park, NM, US 149/J2
Chaco Culture Nat'l Hist. Park, NM, US 149/H3
Chaco Culture Nat'l Hist. Park, NM, US 149/J3
Chaco, PN del, Arg. 188/E3
Chacoma, Bol. 188/B1
Chacritas, Chile 188/B4
Chacujal (ruin), Guat. 176/D3
Chad (lake), Afr. 116/B2
Chad (lake), Niger 107/D3
Chad (ctry.) 107/D3
Chadan, Rus. 99/F1
Chadao, China 80/G6
Chadbourn, NC, US 163/H3
Chadiza, Zam. 123/G2
Chadlington, Eng, UK 37/E3
Chadong, China 87/F2
Chadron, Ne, US 154/C2
Chadwell Saint Mary, Eng, UK 30/E2
Chadwick, Il, US 155/K2
Chae Hom, Thai. 94/B2
Chaedong-nodongjagu, NKor. 81/D3
Chaeryŏng, NKor. 81/C3
Chafarinas (isl.), Sp. 112/C2
Chaffee, ND, US 156/F4
Chaffee, Mo, US 162/C2
Chafurray, Col. 180/C4
Chāgai, Pak. 101/H3
Chagan, Kaz. 99/C1
Chagang-do (prov.), NKor. 81/D2
Chagda, Rus. 75/P4
Chagdo Kangri (mtn.), China 99/D5
Chagne, Eth. 117/H3
Chagny, Fr. 44/F3
Chagos (arch.), BIOT, UK 77/G10
Chaguanas, Trin. 181/F2
Chaguaramas, Ven. 183/P8
Chaguarpamba, Ecu. 184/B1
Chaguaya, Bol. 188/C2
Chagyl, Trkm. 71/K4
Cha'gyüngoinba, China 99/F5
Chahuites, Mex. 176/C2
Chai Badan, Thai. 94/C3
Chaibāsā, India 97/E4
Chailland, Fr. 57/E4
Chailles, Fr. 57/G5
Chailly-en-Brie, Fr. 30/M5
Chain, SKor. 81/E5
Chain O'Lakes-King, Wi, US 155/K1
Chainat, Thai. 94/C3
Chaîne Annamitique (mts.), Laos 93/H4
Chaîne Annamitique (mts.), Laos,Viet. 94/D2
Chaîne de Belledonne (range), Fr. 64/B2
Chaîne de l'atacora (mts.), Ben. 115/F4
Chaine de la Selle (peak), Haiti 177/J2
Chaingy, Fr. 57/G5
Chainpur, Nepal 96/C1
Chaiya, Thai. 94/B4
Chaiyaphum, Thai. 94/C3
Chajarí, Arg. 188/E4
Chākāi, India 97/F3
Chakari, Zim. 123/F3
Chākdaha, India 97/G4
Chake Chake, Tanz. 119/B3
Chākia, India 96/D3
Chakradharpur, India 97/E4
Chakrāta, India 98/D4
Chakwāl, Pak. 98/B3
Chala, Peru 184/C4
Chalain (lake), Fr. 60/B4
Chalais, Swi. 60/D5
Chālakudi, India 95/C4
Chalamama, Bol. 185/E4
Chalaronne (riv.), Fr. 60/A5
Chalatenango, ESal. 176/D3
Chalbi (des.), Kenya 119/B1
Chalchihuites, Mex. 174/E4
Ch'alchīs (peak), Eth. 117/H3
Chalchyn (riv.), Mong. 79/H2
Chalco, Mex. 175/R10
Chale (pt.), Kenya 119/B3
Chaleur (bay), NB,,Qu, Can. 158/D2
Chalfont, Pa, US 168/C3
Chalfont Saint Giles, Eng, UK 30/B2
Chalfont Saint Peter, Eng, UK 30/B2
Chalhuanca, Peru 184/C4
Chali, China 86/C2
Chalifert (canal), Fr. 30/L5
Chalindrey, Fr. 60/B2
Chaling, China 87/G3
Chalinguita, Chile 188/B4
Chalinze, Tanz. 119/B3
Chālisgaon, India 95/B1
Chalk (mts.), Tx, US 151/C3
Chalk Hill (dam), Mi, US 157/L5
Chalk River, On, Can. 161/H1
Chalkar, Kaz. 71/J2
Chalkoi, India 98/C5
Chalkyitsik, Ak, US 171/K2
Challana, Bol. 184/D4
Challans, Fr. 44/C3
Challapalle, India 95/D2
Challapata, Bol. 188/C1
Challenger (mts.), Nun, Can. 141/T6
Challes-les-Eaux, Fr. 64/B1
Challis, Id, US 147/F1
Challock, Eng, UK 37/G4
Chalmette, La, US 164/D3
Chalna, Rus. 68/G3
Chālna, Bang. 97/G4
Chālna Port, Bang. 97/G4
Chalon-sur-Saône, Fr. 60/A4
Chalonnes-sur-Loire, Fr. 57/E6
Châlons-sur-Marne, Fr. 55/D6
Châlonvillars, Fr. 60/C2
Chaltyr', Rus. 73/K4
Chālūs, Iran 103/G2
Cham, Swi. 61/E3
Cham, Ger. 59/F4
Cham (riv.), Ger. 59/F4
Chama, Co, US 152/B2
Chama, Zam. 119/A4
Chama, NM, US 149/J2
Chama (riv.), NM, US 149/J2
Chamah (peak), Malay. 89/C1
Chaman, Pak. 101/J2
Chaman Bīd, Iran 103/J2
Chamba, India 98/D3
Chambal (riv.), India 92/C2
Chambaran (plat.), Fr. 44/F4
Chambas, Cuba 177/G1
Chamberino, NM, US 150/A1
Chamberlain (lake), Me, US 158/C2
Chamberlain, SD, US 154/E2
Chamberlain, Uru. 191/K10
Chamberlain, Sk, Can. 145/M2
Chamberlin (mt.), Ak, US 171/K2
Chambers (bay), Austl. 128/C3
Chambers (isl.), Mi, US 157/L5
Chambers, Ne, US 154/E2
Chambers (cr.), Tx, US 151/F1
Chambers (co.), Tx, US 151/N9
Chambersburg, Pa, US 161/H5
Chambéry, Fr. 64/B1
Chambéry-Aix-les-Bains (arpt.), Fr. 64/B1
Chambeshi, Zam. 121/G5
Chambeshi (riv.), Zam. 121/G5
Chambeyron, Aiguille de (peak), Fr. 64/C3
Chambishi, Zam. 123/F2
Chamblee, Ga, US 163/M7
Chambly, Fr. 30/J4
Chambly, Qu, Can. 159/P7
Chambord, Fr. 57/G5
Chambourcy, Fr. 30/J5
Chambray-lès-Tours, Fr. 57/F6
Chambry, Fr. 30/L5
Chamchamāl, Iraq 103/F3
Chamechaude (peak), Fr. 64/B2
Chameis, Namb. 124/A2
Chamical, Arg. 188/C4
Chamigny, Fr. 30/M5
Chamizal Nat'l Mem., Tx, US 151/A2
Chamizo, Uru. 191/L11
Cha'mo Hāyk' (lake), Eth. 117/H4
Chamois, Mo, US 153/J1
Chamonix-Mont-Blanc, Fr. 60/C6
Champ-sur-Drac, Fr. 64/B2
Champagne, Yk, Can. 171/L3
Champagne (reg.), Fr. 42/C4
Champagne (Reims) (arpt.), Fr. 54/D5
Champagne-Ardenne (pol.reg), Fr. 44/F2
Champagne-sur-Oise, Fr. 30/J4
Champagney, Fr. 60/C2
Champagnole, Fr. 60/B4
Champaign, Il, US 160/B4
Champaqui (peak), Arg. 188/C4
Champasak, Laos 94/D3
Champawat, India 96/C1
Champdeuil, Fr. 30/L6
Champeaux, Fr. 30/L6
Champéry, Swi. 60/C5
Champex, Swi. 60/D5
Champhol, Fr. 57/G4
Champigneulles, Fr. 55/F6
Champigny-sur-Marne, Fr. 30/K5
Champion, Oh, US 160/F4
Champion, Ab, Can. 145/H2
Champlain, NY, US 161/K2
Champlain (lake), NY,Vt, US 143/M3
Champlin, Mn, US 157/P6
Champlitte, Fr. 60/B2
Champotón, Mex. 176/D2
Champotón (riv.), Mex. 176/D2
Champs-sur-Marne, Fr. 30/K5
Champsevraine, Fr. 60/B2
Champtoceaux, Fr. 56/D6
Champvans, Fr. 60/B3
Chāmrājnagar-Rāmasamu-dram, India 95/C4
Chamusca, Port. 46/A3
Chan Chan (ruin), Peru 184/B3
Chan May Dong (cape), Viet. 94/E2
Chana, Thai. 94/C5
Chañaral, Chile 188/B4
Chañaral, Chile 188/B3
Chança (riv.), Port. 46/B4
Chancay, Peru 184/B3
Chance Cove (pt.), Nf, Can. 159/L2
Chance Harbour, NB, Can. 158/D3
Chānchra, Bang. 97/H4
Chanco, Chile 190/B2
Chancy, Swi. 60/B5
Chandalar, Ak, US 171/J2
Chandalar (riv.), Ak, US 171/J2
Chandannagar, India 97/G4
Chandarpur, India 95/D1
Chandausi, India 96/B1
Chandeleur (isls.), La, US 164/D3
Chandeleur (sound), La, US 164/D3
Chanderi, India 96/B3
Chandīgarh (state), India 98/D4
Chandīgarh, India 98/D4
Chāndil, India 97/F4
Chandlees (riv.), Braz. 184/D3
Chandler, Qu, Can. 158/E1
Chandler (lake), Ak, US 171/H2
Chandler, Az, US 149/G4
Chandler, In, US 162/D1
Chandler, Mn, US 155/G2
Chandler, Ok, US 153/F3
Chandler, Tx, US 151/G1
Chandolin, Swi. 60/D5
Chāndpur, India 96/B1
Chāndpur, Bang. 97/H4
Chandra Garhi, Nepal 97/G2
Chandrakona Road, India 97/F4
Chanduy, Ecu. 180/A5
Chang (riv.), China 77/L6
Chang (isl.), Camb. 93/H5
Chang (lake), China 80/C5
Chang (Yangtze) (riv.), China 80/D5
Chang Khoeng, Thai. 86/C5
Changan, SKor. 81/E5
Changanācheri, India 95/C4
Changane (riv.), Moz. 123/G4
Chang'anzhen, China 80/L9
Changara, Moz. 123/G3
Changbai (peak), China 81/E2
Changbai (mts.), NKor. 79/K3
Changbai Chaoxianzu Zizhixian, China 81/E2
Changchun, China 79/K3
Changdang (lake), China 80/D5
Changdao, China 80/E3
Changde, China 87/F2
Ch'angdo, NKor. 81/D3
Changé, Fr. 57/F5
Changeon (riv.), Fr. 57/F6
Changewater, NJ, US 168/D2
Changfeng, China 80/D4
Changgang, NKor. 81/D2
Changge, China 80/C4
Changgi-ap (cape), SKor. 84/A2
Changhai, China 81/B3
Changhang, SKor. 81/D4
Changhowŏn, SKor. 81/D4
Changhua, Tai. 87/J3
Changhŭng, SKor. 81/D5
Changhŭng, NKor. 81/E2
Changi (nbrhd.), Sing. 89/J6
Changi (int'l arpt.), Sing. 89/J6
Changis-sur-Marne, Fr. 30/M5
Changjiang, China 87/F5
Changjiang Zhongxiayou (plain), China 87/G2
Changjin (lake), NKor. 81/D2
Changjin (res.), NKor. 81/D2
Changjin, NKor. 81/D2
Changle, China 87/J2
Changle, China 80/D3
Changle, China 87/E2
Changli, China 80/D3
Changling, China 80/E1
Changlingji, China 87/G1
Changlingzi, China 81/B3
Changlingzi, China 79/J4
Changlingzi, China 79/J4
Changliushui, China 78/F4
Changlun, Malay. 94/C5
Changmar, China 99/C5
Changning, China 93/G3
Changning, China 86/E2
Ch'angnyŏng, SKor. 81/E5
Changping, China 80/H6
Changp'ung-ŭp, NKor. 81/D3
Changqing, China 80/D3
Changsan-got (cape), NKor. 81/C3
Changsha, China 87/G2
Changshan, China 87/H4
Changshan (arch.), China 79/J4
Changsheng, China 87/G3
Changshoudian, China 87/G2
Changshu, China 80/L8
Changshun, China 87/E3
Changsŏng, SKor. 81/D5
Changsu, SKor. 81/D5
Changsŭngp'o, SKor. 81/E5
Changtu, China 80/F2
Changuinola, Pan. 177/F4
Changweiliang, China 78/C4
Ch'angwŏn, SKor. 81/E5
Changwu, China 78/F4
Changxing, China 80/K8
Changyang, China 87/F2
Changyi, China 80/D3
Changyŏn, NKor. 81/C3
Changyuan, China 80/C4
Changzhi, China 80/C3
Changzhou, China 80/K8
Chanhassen, Mn, US 157/N7
Chankanai, SrL. 95/C4
Chanlers (falls), Kenya 119/B1
Channapatna, India 95/C3
Channel (isls.), UK 29/D4
Channel Country (phys. reg.), Austl. 127/C3
Channel Islands NP, Ca, US 166/A3
Channel Islands NP, Ca, US 148/C3
Channel Tunnel (tun.), Eng, UK,Fr. 37/H5
Channel-Port aux Basques, Nf, Can. 159/H2
Channelview, Tx, US 151/M9
Channing, Tx, US 152/C3
Chantada, Sp. 46/B1
Chanteloup-les-Vignes, Fr. 30/J5
Chantepie, Fr. 56/D4
Chanthaburi, Thai. 94/C3
Chantilly, Fr. 54/B5
Chantraine, Fr. 60/C1
Chantrey (inlet), Nun, Can. 140/G2
Chanute, Ks, US 153/G2
Chao (riv.), China 78/H3
Chao (lake), China 80/D5
Chao, Peru 184/B3
Chao Phraya (riv.), Thai. 94/C3
Chaobai (riv.), China 79/H4
Chaor (riv.), China 79/J2
Chaoyang, China 87/H4
Chaoyang, China 80/E2
Chaozhou, China 87/H4
Chap Le, Viet. 94/D2
Chapacura, Bol. 184/D3
Chapada Diamantina, PN, Braz. 187/E2
Chapada dos Guimarães, Braz. 186/B2
Chapada dos Veadeiros, PN da, Braz. 186/D2
Chapadinha, Braz. 183/F3
Chapala (lake), Mex. 174/E4
Chapala, Mex. 174/E4
Chapará (riv.), Bol. 188/C1
Chaparé (riv.), Bol. 185/E5
Chapareillan, Fr. 64/B2
Chaparral, Col. 180/C4
Chaparrosa, Mex. 174/E4
Chapayev, Kaz. 71/J2
Chapayevsk, Rus. 71/J1
Chapecó, Braz. 189/F3
Chapecó (riv.), Braz. 189/F3
Chapel en le Frith, Eng, UK 35/G5
Chapel Hill, Tn, US 162/D3
Chapel Hill, Ga, US 163/L7
Chapel Hill, NC, US 163/H3
Chapel Ness (pt.), Sc, UK 33/D4
Chapel Saint Leonards, Eng, UK 35/J5
Chapelfell Top (peak), Eng, UK 35/F2
Chapelle-lez-Herlaimont, Belg. 55/D3
Chapeltown, Eng, UK 35/G5
Chaplain (lake), Wa, US 167/D2
Chapleau, On, Can. 141/H4
Chaplin, Sk, Can. 145/L2
Chaplin (riv.), Ky, US 162/E2
Chaplygin, Rus. 70/F1
Chapman, Ks, US 153/F1
Chapman, Al, US 164/E2
Chapmanville, WV, US 163/F2
Chaponost, Fr. 64/A1
Chappār, India 98/D5
Chappell, Ne, US 154/C3
Chāpra, India 97/E3
Char (well), Mrta. 110/B5
Char Gāzi, Bang. 97/H4
Chara, Rus. 75/M4
Chara (riv.), Rus. 75/M4
Charagua, Bol. 188/D1
Charagua, Par. 189/E2
Charambirá (pt.), Col. 180/B3
Charaña, Bol. 188/B1
Charandra (riv.), Gre. 49/N8
Ch'arants'avan, Arm. 103/F1
Charata, Arg. 188/D3
Charbon, Austl. 133/D1
Charcas, Mex. 175/E4
Charcot (isl.), Ant. 192/U
Chard, Eng, UK 36/D5
Chardon, Oh, US 160/F4
Chardonniēre, Haiti 177/H2
Charente (riv.), Fr. 66/C1
Chargrām, Bang. 93/F3
Chari (riv.), Chad 107/D3
Chari-Baguirmi (pref.), Chad 116/B3
Chārīkār, Afg. 101/J1
Charikot, Nepal 97/F2
Chariton (riv.), Mo,Ia, US 155/H3
Chariton, Ia, US 155/H3
Charity, Guy. 181/G3
Charkhāri, India 96/B3
Charkhi Dādri, India 98/D5
Charlbury, Eng, UK 37/E3
Charlemagne, Qu, Can. 159/P6
Charlemont, NI, UK 34/B3
Charleroi, Belg. 55/D3
Charleroi, Pa, US 161/G4
Charleroi à Bruxelles, Canal de (canal), Belg. 55/D2
Charles (isl.), Qu, Can. 141/J2
Charles (hill), Il, US 155/J2
Charles (pt.), Austl. 128/C3
Charles (peak), Austl. 130/D5
Charles (mt.), Austl. 130/C3
Charles (cape), Va, US 163/K2
Charles City, Ia, US 155/H2
Charles City, Va, US 163/J2
Charles de Gaulle (int'l arpt.), Fr. 30/K4
Charles Fuhr, Arg. 191/C6
Charles H. Russell NWR, Mt, US 156/A4
Charles M. Russell Nat'l Wild Ref., Mt, US 145/L4
Charles Town, WV, US 161/H5
Charleston, Ar, US 153/G3
Charleston, Il, US 160/B5
Charleston, Mo, US 162/C2
Charleston, Ms, US 162/B3
Charleston, Nv, US 146/F3
Charleston (peak), Nv, US 148/E2
Charleston, SC, US 163/H4
Charleston (A.F.B.), SC, US 163/G4
Charleston (cap.), WV, US 163/G1
Charlestown, StK. 173/N8
Charlestown, NH, US 161/K3
Charlestown, In, US 162/E1
Charlestown, Md, US 168/C4
Charleval, Fr. 57/G2
Charleville, Austl. 134/B4
Charleville-Mézières, Fr. 55/D4
Charlevoix, Mi, US 160/D2
Charlevoix (lake), Mi, US 160/D2
Charlotte (lake), BC, Can. 144/B1
Charlotte (har.), Fl, US 165/G4
Charlotte, Mi, US 160/D3
Charlotte, Tn, US 162/D2
Charlotte, Vt, US 161/K2
Charlotte, NC, US 163/G3
Charlotte, Tx, US 150/E3
Charlotte Amalie, USVI 173/M8
Charlotte Court House, Va, US 163/H2
Charlotte Hall, Md, US 163/J1
Charlotte/Douglas (int'l arpt.), NC, US 163/G3
Charlottenberg, Swe. 40/E2
Charlottenburg, Ger. 42/Q6
Charlottesville, Va, US 163/H1
Charlottetown (cap.), PE, Can. 158/F2
Charlotteville, Trin. 181/F2
Charlton, Austl. 132/B3
Charlton (isl.), On, Can. 141/H3
Charlton Kings, Eng, UK 36/D3
Charlwood, Eng, UK 30/C3
Charly, Fr. 54/C6
Charly, Fr. 64/A1
Charmco, WV, US 163/G1
Charmes (res.), Fr. 60/B2
Charmes, Fr. 60/C1
Charmes-sur-Rhône, Fr. 64/A3
Charmey, Swi. 60/D4
Charnay-lès-Mâcon, Fr. 44/F3
Charny, Qu, Can. 158/B2
Charny, Fr. 30/L5
Charny-sur-Meuse, Fr. 55/E5
Charolais, Monts du (mts.), Fr. 44/F3
Charouine, Alg. 111/E3
Charquemont, Fr. 60/C3
Chars, Fr. 30/H4
Chārsadda, Pak. 98/A2
Charsk, Kaz. 99/D2
Charters Towers, Austl. 134/B3
Charthāwāl, India 98/D5
Chartres, Fr. 57/G4
Chartres, UK 191/E6
Chartres-de-Bretagne, Fr. 56/D4

Chrysler, Al, US 164/E2
Chryston, Sc, UK 33/B5
Chrzanów, Pol. 43/K3
Chu (riv.), Viet. 94/D2
Chu Yang Sin (peak), Viet. 94/E3
Chua Chu Kang (nbrhd.), Sing. 89/H6
Chuādanga, Bang. 97/G4
Chualar, Ca, US 148/B2
Chuanchang, China 87/H3
Chuansha, China 80/L8
Chuanshi, China 87/H3
Chuathbaluk, Ak, US 171/G3
Chuave, PNG 129/G1
Chubbuck, Id, US 147/G2
Chubut (riv.), Arg. 179/C7
Chubut (prov.), Arg. 190/C4
Chucanti (peak), Pan. 180/B2
Chuchkovo, Rus. 71/G1
Chudovo, Rus. 41/P2
Chūgoku (mts.), Japan 84/C3
Chūgoku (prov.), Japan 84/B4
Chugwater, Wy, US 154/B3
Chugwater (cr.), Wy, US 154/B3
Chūhar Kāna, Pak. 98/B4
Chuhuyiv, Ukr. 73/J3
Chukai, Malay. 89/C1
Chukch (sea), Asia, NAm. 75/U3
Chukchagirskoye (lake), Rus. 79/M1
Chukchi (sea), Rus. 77/T3
Chukchi (pen.), Rus. 77/T3
Chukotskiy Aut. Okrug, Rus. 75/S3
Chukou, China 87/G3
Chukuni (riv.), On, Can. 157/H2
Chula, Ga, US 165/G2
Chula Vista, Ca, US 166/C5
Chul'man, Rus. 75/N4
Ch'ulp'o, SKor. 81/D5
Chulucanas, Peru 184/A2
Chulym (riv.), Rus. 74/J4
Chulyshman (riv.), Rus. 78/B1
Chum Phae, Thai. 94/C2
Chuma, Bol. 184/D4
Chūmar, India 101/L2
Chumbicha, Arg. 188/C4
Chumerna (peak), Bul. 51/G4
Chumikan, Rus. 75/P4
Chumphon, Thai. 94/B4
Chumsaeng, Thai. 94/C3
Chumunjin, SKor. 81/E4
Chuna (riv.), Rus. 74/K4
Chunan, Tai. 87/J3
Chunār, India 96/D3
Chunchi, China 87/H3
Ch'unch'ŏn, SKor. 81/D4
Chunchula, Al, US 164/D2
Ch'ungch'ŏng-bukto (prov.), SKor. 81/D4
Ch'ungch'ŏng-namdo (prov.), SKor. 81/D4
Chunggang, NKor. 81/D2
Chunghsinghsintsun, Tai. 87/J4
Chunghwa, NKor. 81/C3
Ch'ungju, SKor. 81/D4
Ch'ungju (lake), SKor. 84/A2
Ch'ungmu, SKor. 81/E5
Chungnang (nbrhd.), SKor. 81/G6
Chŭngsan, NKor. 81/C3
Chungu, Zam. 121/G5
Chunheji, China 87/G1
Chunhuhub, Mex. 176/D2
Chūniān, Pak. 98/B4
Chunky, Ms, US 162/C4
Chunshui, China 87/G4
Chunya (riv.), Rus. 75/L3
Chunya, Tanz. 119/A4
Ch'unyang, SKor. 81/E4
Chupa, Rus. 68/G2
Chupa, Peru 184/D4
Chupaca, Peru 184/C4
Chupadera Mesa (mesa), NM, US 152/A3
Chupakhivka, Ukr. 73/H2
Chuprovo, Rus. 69/K2
Chuquibamba, Peru 184/C4
Chuquibambilla, Peru 184/C4
Chuquicamata, Chile 188/B2
Chuquichambi, Bol. 188/C1
Chuquichuqui, Bol. 188/C1
Chuquisaca (dept.), Bol. 188/C2
Chur, Swi. 61/F4
Churachandpur, India 86/B3
Churcampa, Peru 184/C4
Church, Eng, UK 35/F4
Church Crookham, Eng, UK 30/A3
Church Hill, Md, US 168/C5
Church Point, La, US 164/B2
Church Stretton, Eng, UK 36/D1
Churchbridge, Sk, Can. 156/D2
Churchill, Austl. 133/C4
Churchill (riv.), Can. 139/H4
Churchill (cape), Mb, Can. 140/G3
Churchill (riv.), Sk, Can. 140/F3
Churchill (lake), Sk, Can. 140/F3
Churchill, Mb, Can. 140/G3
Churchill (peak), BC, Can. 140/D3
Churchill Downs, Ky, US 162/E1
Churchill Falls, Nf, Can. 141/K3
Churchill NP, Austl. 132/G5
Churchville, Va, US 163/H1
Churchville, Md, US 168/B4
Churia Ghats (mts.), Nepal 97/E2
Churín, Peru 184/B3
Churnet (riv.), Eng, UK 35/G5
Churu, India 98/C5
Churubusco, In, US 160/D4
Churuguara, Ven. 180/D2
Churumuco de Morelos, Mex. 175/E5
Churwalden, Swi. 61/F4
Chuschi, Peru 184/C4
Chushul, India 99/C5
Chusovaya (riv.), Rus. 69/N4
Chusovoy, Rus. 69/N4
Chute-aux-Outardes, Qu, Can. 158/C1
Chutove, Ukr. 73/H3
Chutyr', Rus. 69/M4
Chuvashiya, Resp., Rus. 74/E4
Chuviscar (riv.), Mex. 151/B3
Chuwang-san NP, SKor. 84/A2
Chuxiong, China 86/D3
Chuya (riv.), Rus. 78/B1
Chuzhou, China 87/H1
Chūzu, Japan 83/K5
Chvalšiny, Czh. 59/H5
Chyhyryn, Ukr. 72/G3
Ci Xian, China 80/C3
Ciadîr-Lunga, Mol. 51/J2
Ciamis, Indo. 89/E3
Ciampino, It. 65/B4
Ciampino (int'l arpt.), It. 65/B4
Cianjur, Indo. 89/D4
Cianorte, Braz. 189/F2
Cibecue, Az, US 149/G3
Cibola Nat'l Wild Ref., Az,Ca, US 148/E4
Cicagna, It. 62/C5
Cicciano, It. 65/D6
Cicero, Il, US 160/C4
Cicero (peak), SD, US 154/C2
Cícero Dantas, Braz. 187/F1
Ćićevac, Yugo. 50/E4
Cide, Turk. 70/E4
Ciechanów, Pol. 43/L2
Ciechocinek, Pol. 43/K2
Ciego de Ávila, Cuba 177/G1
Ciénaga, Col. 180/C2
Ciénaga de Oro, Col. 180/C2
Ciénega de Flores, Mex. 151/D5
Cienfuegos, Cuba 177/F1
Cieplice Śląskie Zdrój, Pol. 43/H3
Cieszyn, Pol. 43/K4
Cieza, Sp. 46/E3
Çifteler, Turk. 102/B2
Cifuentes, Cuba 177/F1
Cifuentes, Sp. 46/D2
Cifuncho, Chile 188/B3
Cigánd, Hun. 43/L4
Cigliano, It. 62/B3
Cigno (riv.), It. 65/D4
Cigüela (riv.), Sp. 46/D3
Cihanbeyli, Turk. 102/C2
Cihuatlán, Mex. 174/D5
Cijara (res.), Sp. 46/C3
Cijulang, Indo. 89/E3
Cilacap, Indo. 89/E3
Cilavegna, It. 62/B3
Çıldır (lake), Turk. 71/G4
Ciledug, Indo. 89/E3
Cilfaesty (peak), Wal, UK 36/C2
Cilleros, Sp. 46/B2
Cima, Ca, US 148/E3
Cima della Laurasca (peak), It. 61/E5
Cima de'Piazzi (peak), It. 61/G5
Cima la Casina (peak), It. 61/G4
Cimahi, Indo. 89/D4
Cimarron (range), NM, US 152/B2
Cimarron, Ks, US 152/D2
Cimarron (cr.), NM, US 152/B2
Cimarron (riv.), Ks,Ok, US 142/G4
Cimarron, Co, US 149/J1
Cimarron, North Fork (riv.), Co,Ks, US 152/C2
Cime de Gélas (peak), Fr. 64/D4
Cime de Marte (peak), Fr. 64/D4
Cime des Torches (peak), Fr. 64/C2
Cime du Cheiron (peak), Fr. 64/C5
Cime du Diable (peak), Fr. 64/D4
Cimino (peak), It. 65/B3
Cimişlia, Mol. 72/E4
Cimone (peak), It. 63/D5
Cîmpeni, Rom. 51/F2
Cîmpia Turzii, Rom. 51/F2
Cîmpina, Rom. 51/G3
Cîmpulung, Rom. 51/G3
Cîmpulung Moldovenesc, Rom. 72/C4
Cina (cape), Indo. 89/D4
Çınar, Turk. 102/E2
Çınarcık, Turk. 51/J5
Cinaruco (riv.), Ven. 180/D3
Cinca (riv.), Sp. 66/D2
Cincar (peak), Bosn. 50/C4
Cincinnati, Oh, US 162/E1
Cinco Chañares, Arg. 190/D4
Cinco Saltos, Arg. 190/C3
Cinderford, Eng, UK 36/D3
Cîndrelu (peak), Rom. 51/F3
Çine, Turk. 102/B2
Ciney, Belg. 55/E3
Cingia de'Botti, It. 62/D3
Cingoli, It. 63/G7
Cinisello Balsamo, It. 62/C2
Cinnaminson, NJ, US 168/D4
Cinq-Mars-la-Pile, Fr. 57/F6
Cintalapa de Figueroa, Mex. 176/C2
Cinto (peak), Fr. 48/A1
Cinto Caomaggiore, It. 63/F2
Cintruénigo, Sp. 46/E1
Čiovo (isl.), Cro. 50/C4
Cipatujah, Indo. 89/D4
Cipolletti, Arg. 190/D3
Circeo (peak), It. 65/C5
Circeo Parco Nazionale del, It. 48/C2
Circle, Ak, US 171/K2
Circle, Mt, US 145/M4
Circle Hot Springs, Ak, US 171/K2
Circleville, Oh, US 160/E5
Circleville, Ut, US 149/F1
Circleville, Ks, US 155/G4
Circuata, Bol. 185/E5
Cirebon, Indo. 89/E3
Cirencester, Eng, UK 36/E3
Cires-lès-Mello, Fr. 54/B5
Ciriè, It. 64/D2
Cirò Marina, It. 49/E3
Ciron (riv.), Fr. 44/C4
Ciruas, Indo. 89/D4
Cisco, Tx, US 151/E1
Ciserano, It. 62/C2
Cisnădie, Rom. 51/G3
Cisne, Il, US 162/C1
Cisneros, Col. 180/C3
Cisnes (riv.), Chile 190/B5
Cisse (riv.), Fr. 44/D3
Cissna Park, Il, US 160/C4
Cistern, Tx, US 151/F3
Cisterna di Latina, It. 65/B4
Cistierna, Sp. 46/C1
Cité de Kassa, Gui. 114/B4
Citlaltépetl (vol.), Mex. 175/M7
Citra, Fl, US 165/G3
Citronelle, Al, US 164/D2
Citrus (co.), Fl, US 164/L6
Citrus Heights, Ca, US 146/C4
Citrus Park, Fl, US 164/K7
Citrusdal, SAfr. 124/L10
Città del Vaticano (cap.), VatC. 65/B4
Città della Pieve, It. 65/B2
Città di Castello, It. 63/F7
Citta di Torino (int'l arpt.), It. 64/D2
Cittadella, It. 63/E2
Cittaducale, It. 65/B3
Cittanova, It. 48/E3
Citta'Sant'Angelo, It. 65/D2
Cittiglio, It. 61/E6
City (int'l arpt.), NI, UK 34/C2
City (isl.), NY, US 169/K8
City Beach (nbrhd.), Austl. 130/K6
Ciudad Acuña, Mex. 151/D3
Ciudad Altamirano, Mex. 175/E5
Ciudad Bolívar, Ven. 181/F2
Ciudad Bolivia, Ven. 180/D2
Ciudad Camargo, Mex. 151/E4
Ciudad Camargo, Mex. 174/D3
Ciudad Constitución, Mex. 174/C3
Ciudad Cortés, CR 177/F4
Ciudad Cuauhtémoc, Mex. 176/B1
Ciudad de Dolores Hidalgo, Mex. 175/E4
Ciudad de Loreto, Arg. 188/C4
Ciudad de México (Mexico) (cap.), Mex. 175/Q10
Ciudad de Nutrias, Ven. 180/D2
Ciudad de Río Grande, Mex. 174/E4
Ciudad del Carmen, Mex. 176/D2
Ciudad del Este, Par. 189/F3
Ciudad del Maíz, Mex. 175/F4
Ciudad Delicias, Mex. 151/B3
Ciudad Fernández, Mex. 175/E4
Ciudad Frontera, Mex. 151/D4
Ciudad Guayana, Ven. 181/F2
Ciudad Guzmán, Mex. 174/E5
Ciudad Hidalgo, Mex. 176/C3
Ciudad Hidalgo, Mex. 175/E5
Ciudad Insurgentes, Mex. 174/C3
Ciudad Ixtepec, Mex. 176/C2
Ciudad Juárez, Mex. 151/A2
Ciudad Lerdo, Mex. 174/E3
Ciudad Madero, Mex. 176/B1
Ciudad Mante, Mex. 175/F4
Ciudad Mendoza, Mex. 175/M8
Ciudad Miguel Alemán, Mex. 151/E4
Ciudad Obregón, Mex. 174/C3
Ciudad Ojeda, Ven. 180/D2
Ciudad Pemex, Mex. 176/C2
Ciudad Piar, Ven. 181/F3
Ciudad Real, Sp. 46/D3
Ciudad Rodrigo, Sp. 46/B2
Ciudad Serdán, Mex. 175/M8
Ciudad Valles, Mex. 176/B1
Ciudad Victoria, Mex. 175/F4
Ciutadella de Menorca, Sp. 47/G3
Civa Burnu (pt.), Turk. 70/F4
Civate, It. 62/C2
Civezzano, It. 61/H5
Cividale del Friuli, It. 45/K3
Cividate Camuno, It. 61/G6
Civita Castellana, It. 65/B3
Civitavecchia, It. 48/B1
Civitella del Tronto, It. 65/C2
Civitella Roveto, It. 65/C4
Civray, Fr. 44/D3
Çivril, Turk. 102/B2
Cixi, China 80/L9
Cize, Fr. 60/B4
Cizre, Turk. 102/E2
Cizre (dam), Turk. 102/E2
Cizur, Sp. 46/E1
Clackamas (riv.), Or, US 146/B1
Clackmannan, Sc, UK 33/C4
Clackmannanshire (co.), Sc, UK 33/C4
Clacton-on-Sea, Eng, UK 37/H3
Claerwen (res.), Wal, UK 36/C2
Claflin, Ks, US 153/E1
Claiborne (lake), La, US 151/H1
Claiborne, Md, US 168/B6
Claie (riv.), Fr. 56/C5
Clain (riv.), Fr. 44/D3
Clair Engle (lake), Ca, US 146/B3
Claire (lake), Ab, Can. 140/E3
Clairefontaine-en-Yvelines, Fr. 30/H6
Clairette, Tx, US 151/E1
Clairton, Pa, US 161/G4
Clairvaux-les-Lacs, Fr. 60/B4
Claise (riv.), Fr. 44/D3
Clallam (co.), Wa, US 167/A2
Clallam Bay, Wa, US 144/B3
Clamart, Fr. 30/J5
Clamecy, Fr. 44/E3
Clancy, Mt, US 145/J4
Clandeboye, Mb, Can. 156/F2
Clandonald, Ab, Can. 145/J1
Clane, Ire. 32/D3
Clanfield, Eng, UK 37/F5
Clanton, Al, US 162/D4
Clanwilliam, Mb, Can. 156/E2
Clanwilliam, SAfr. 124/B4
Claonig, Sc, UK 33/A5
Clapier (peak), Fr. 64/D4
Clapier du Peyron (peak), Fr. 64/C3
Clara (pt.), Arg. 190/D4
Clara, Arg. 188/E4
Clara, Ire. 32/C3
Clara, Ms, US 164/D2
Clara City, Mn, US 155/G1
Claravale, Austl. 128/C3
Clarcona, Fl, US 164/N6
Clare (riv.), Ire. 32/B3
Clare (isl.), Ire. 30/N10
Clare (co.), Ire. 32/B4
Clare, Mi, US 160/D3
Clare, Austl. 132/B2
Clare, Austl. 131/H5
Clarée (riv.), Fr. 64/C2
Claregalway, Ire. 32/B3
Claremont (pt.), Austl. 129/F3
Claremont, Ca, US 166/C2
Claremont, SD, US 156/E5
Claremont, NH, US 161/K3
Claremore, Ok, US 153/G2
Claremorris, Ire. 32/A2
Clarence (riv.), Austl. 132/D4
Clarence, La, US 164/B2
Clarence, NZ 135/C3
Clarence, Mo, US 155/H4
Clarence (str.), Austl. 128/C3
Clarence, NY, US 160/V9
Clarence (pt.), Nun, Can. 141/T7
Clarence Cannon (dam), Mo, US 155/J4
Clarence Cannon Nat'l Wildlife Res., Mo, US 153/J1
Clarence Cannon Nat'l Wild. Ref., Mo, US 155/J4
Clarence Town, Bahm. 173/G3
Clarence Town, Austl. 133/E1
Clarendon, Tx, US 152/D3
Clarendon, Ar, US 153/J3
Clarenville, Nf, Can. 159/L1
Claresholm, Ab, Can. 145/H2
Clarinda, Ia, US 155/G3
Clarington, Oh, US 160/F5
Clarion, Pa, US 161/G4
Clarion, Ia, US 155/H2
Clarion (isl.), Mex. 174/B5
Clarissa, Mn, US 157/G4
Clark, NJ, US 169/H9
Clark, Wy, US 147/J1
Clark, SD, US 154/F1
Clark (mtn.), Wa, US 144/D3
Clark, Tx, US 151/G2
Clark (cr.), Pa, US 168/B3
Clark Canyon (dam), Mt, US 147/G1
Clark Canyon (res.), Mt, US 147/G1
Clark Fk. (riv.), Mt, US 145/H4
Clark Fork (riv.), Id, US 140/E4
Clark Fork, Id, US 144/F3
Clark Fork (riv.), Mt, US 144/G3
Clark Mil. Res., Mo, US 153/G2
Clarkdale, Az, US 149/F3
Clarkdale, Ga, US 163/L7
Clarke (range), Austl. 129/G5
Clarke (lake), Pa, US 168/B4
Clarkesville, Ga, US 163/F3
Clarkfield, Mn, US 155/G1
Clarks, La, US 164/B1
Clarks Fk. Yellowstone (riv.), Wy,Mt, US 147/J1
Clark's Harbour, NS, Can. 158/E4
Clarks Hill, SC, US 163/F4
Clarksburg, WV, US 160/F5
Clarksburg, Ca, US 167/L10
Clarksburg, Tn, US 162/C3
Clarksburg, NJ, US 168/D3
Clarksdale, Ms, US 162/B3
Clarkson, On, Can. 160/T8
Clarks Point, Ak, US 171/G4
Clarkston, Mi, US 167/F6
Clarkston, Ut, US 147/G3
Clarkston, Ga, US 163/M7
Clarkston, Wa, US 144/F4
Clarksville, Ar, US 153/H3
Clarksville, Ia, US 155/H2
Clarksville, In, US 160/D4
Clarksville, Tn, US 162/D2
Clarksville, Tx, US 153/G4
Clarksville, Va, US 163/H2
Clarkton, Mo, US 162/C2
Clarkton, NC, US 163/H3
Clarkville, Co, US 154/C3
Claro, Swi. 61/F5
Claro (riv.), Braz. 186/C3
Clashmore, Ire. 32/C6
Clatskanie, Or, US 144/C4
Clatteringshaws Loch (lake), Sc, UK 34/D1
Claude, Tx, US 152/D3
Cláudio, Braz. 186/D4
Claudy, NI, UK 34/A2
Claunch, NM, US 149/K3
Clausen, Ger. 55/G5
Clausthal-Zellerfeld, Ger. 53/H5
Claver, Phil. 88/D3
Claveria, Phil. 88/D3
Claveria, Phil. 88/C1
Clavet, Sk, Can. 145/L1
Clawson, Mi, US 167/F6
Claxton, Ga, US 163/G4
Clay, La, US 153/H4
Clay (pt.), IM, UK 34/D3
Clay, Ca, US 146/C4
Clay, Ky, US 162/D2
Clay, WV, US 163/G1
Clay Center, Ne, US 154/E3
Clay Center, Ks, US 155/F4
Clay City, In, US 160/C5
Clay City, Il, US 162/C1
Clay City, Ky, US 162/F2
Clay Cross-North Wingfield, Eng, UK 35/G5
Clay Springs, Az, US 149/G3
Claybank, Sk, Can. 145/M2
Claydon, Eng, UK 37/H2
Claye-Souilly, Fr. 30/L5
Claygate, Eng, UK 30/C2
Clayhatchee, Al, US 165/F2
Claymont, De, US 168/C4
Claypool, Az, US 149/G4
Clayton, Al, US 165/F2
Clayton, Ca, US 167/L11
Clayton, De, US 168/C5
Clayton (co.), Ga, US 163/M7
Clayton, Ga, US 163/F3
Clayton, Id, US 147/F1
Clayton, La, US 164/C2
Clayton, Mo, US 155/J4
Clayton, NJ, US 168/C4
Clayton, NC, US 163/H3
Clayton, NM, US 152/C2
Clayton, NY, US 161/H2
Clayton, Ok, US 153/G3
Clayton-le-Moors, Eng, UK 35/F4
Clé (stream), Arg. 191/J10
Cle Elum, Wa, US 144/D4
Clear (hills), Ab, Can. 140/E3
Clear (cape), Ire. 31/P11
Clear (lake), Ca, US 146/B3
Clear (riv.), Tx, US 151/M9
Clear (cr.), Wy, US 147/K1
Cleare (cape), Ak, US 171/J4
Clear Fork (riv.), Tx, US 175/E1
Clear Fork Trinity (riv.), Tx, US 150/K7
Clear Lake, Ia, US 155/H2
Clear Lake, SD, US 155/F1
Clear Lake, Wi, US 157/H5
Clear Lake NWR, Ca, US 146/C3
Clearfield, Ut, US 147/G3
Clearfield, Ky, US 163/F1
Clearlake, Ca, US 146/B4
Clearlake Oaks, Ca, US 146/B4
Clearmont, Wy, US 147/K1
Clearwater (riv.), Id, US 146/F1
Clearwater (mts.), Id, US 142/C2
Clearwater, Fl, US 164/K8
Clearwater (riv.), BC, Can. 144/D2
Clearwater, Wa, US 144/B4
Clearwater, BC, Can. 144/D2
Clearwater, Id, US 144/G4
Clearwater (lake), Mo, US 162/B2
Clearwater Beach, Fl, US 164/K8
Cleator Moor, Eng, UK 34/E2
Cleburne, Tx, US 151/F1
Clécy, Fr. 57/E3
Cléden-Cap-Sizun, Fr. 56/A4
Cléder, Fr. 56/A3
Cleethorpes, Eng, UK 35/H4
Cleeve (hill), Eng, UK 36/D3
Cleland Rec. Area, Austl. 131/M8
Clément, FrG. 182/C2
Clementi (nbrhd.), Sing. 89/J6
Clementon, NJ, US 168/D4
Clements, Ca, US 146/C4
Clementsport, NS, Can. 158/E3
Clemmons, NC, US 163/G2
Clemson, SC, US 163/F3
Clendenin, WV, US 163/G1
Cleo, Tx, US 151/E2
Cleo (Cleo Springs), Ok, US 153/E2
Cleo Springs (Cleo), Ok, US 153/E2
Cleobury Mortimer, Eng, UK 36/D2
Cleona, Pa, US 168/B3
Cleopatra Needle (peak), Phil. 88/B3
Clères, Fr. 57/G1
Clérieux, Fr. 64/A2
Clermont, Qu, Can. 158/B2
Clermont, Fr. 54/B5
Clermont, Fl, US 164/M6
Clermont, Austl. 134/B3
Clermont-en-Argonne, Fr. 55/E5
Clermont-Ferrand, Fr. 44/E4
Clerval, Fr. 60/C3
Clervaux, Lux. 55/F3
Cléry-Saint-André, Fr. 57/G5
Cles, It. 61/H5
Cleve, Austl. 131/H5
Clevedon, Eng, UK 36/D4
Cleveland (cape), Austl. 134/B2
Cleveland (hills), Eng, UK 35/G3
Cleveland, Fl, US 165/H4
Cleveland, Ga, US 162/F3
Cleveland, Ms, US 162/B4
Cleveland, Mt, US 145/K3
Cleveland (mt.), Mt, US 145/H3
Cleveland, ND, US 156/E4
Cleveland, Ok, US 153/F2
Cleveland, Oh, US 160/F4
Cleveland, SC, US 163/F3
Cleveland, Tn, US 162/E3
Cleveland, Tx, US 151/G2
Cleveland, Ut, US 147/H4
Cleveland, Wi, US 160/C3
Cleveland National Forest, Ca, US 166/C3
Cleveland-Hopkins (int'l arpt.), Oh, US 160/F4
Clevelândia, Braz. 189/F3
Clevelândia do Norte, Braz. 182/D2
Clew (bay), Ire. 32/A2
Clewiston, Fl, US 165/H4
Clichy, Fr. 30/J5
Clichy-sous-Bois, Fr. 30/K5
Clifden, Ire. 30/F10
Cliff, NM, US 149/H4
Cliffe, Eng, UK 30/E2
Cliffs of Moher, Ire. 32/A4
Cliffside Park, NJ, US 169/K8
Cliffwood, NJ, US 169/J10
Clifton, La, US 164/C2
Clifton, Il, US 160/C4
Clifton, NJ, US 169/J8
Clifton, Co, US 147/J4
Clifton, Az, US 149/H4
Clifton, Id, US 147/G2
Clifton, Ks, US 155/F4
Clifton, Tn, US 162/D3
Clifton, Eng, UK 36/D4
Clifton, Tx, US 150/F2
Clifton Beach, Austl. 134/B2
Clifton Forge, Va, US 163/H2
Clifton Springs, Austl. 133/B4
Clifton-on-Teme, Eng, UK 36/D2
Clifty, Ky, US 162/D2
Clignon (riv.), Fr. 54/C5
Climax, Sk, Can. 145/K3
Climax, Ga, US 165/F2
Climax, Mn, US 156/F4
Climax, Tx, US 150/L6
Clinch (lake), Fl, US 164/M8
Clinch (riv.), Va, US 163/F2
Clinge, Neth. 52/B6
Clingmans (mtn.), Tn, US 163/F3
Clinton, NZ 135/B4
Clinton, BC, Can. 144/D2
Clinton, Ar, US 153/H3
Clinton, Ct, US 169/F1
Clinton, Ia, US 155/J3
Clinton, Il, US 155/K3
Clinton, In, US 160/C5
Clinton (lake), Ks, US 155/G4
Clinton, Ky, US 162/C2
Clinton, La, US 164/C2
Clinton, NC, US 163/H3
Clinton, Mo, US 153/H1
Clinton, Mi, US 160/E3
Clinton (riv.), Mi, US 167/F6
Clinton, Mi, US 167/G6
Clinton, Ms, US 162/B4
Clinton (res.), NJ, US 168/D1
Clinton, NJ, US 168/D2
Clinton, Ok, US 152/E3
Clinton (co.), Pa, US 168/A1
Clinton, SC, US 163/G3
Clinton, Tn, US 162/E2
Clinton, Wa, US 167/C2
Clinton (Surrattsville), Md, US 163/J1
Clinton Creek, Yk, Can. 140/B2
Clinton Heights, Fl, US 164/L7
Clinton, Mid. Branch (riv.), Mi, US 167/G6
Clinton, North Branch (riv.), Mi, US 167/G6
Clinton-Colden (lake), NW, Can. 140/F2
Clintonville, Wi, US 155/K1
Clints Dod (hill), Sc, UK 33/D5
Clintwood, Va, US 163/F2
Clio, Al, US 165/F2
Clio, Mi, US 160/E3
Clio, SC, US 163/H3
Clipston, Eng, UK 37/F2
Clisbako (riv.), BC, Can. 144/C1
Clitheroe, Eng, UK 35/F4
Clitunno (riv.), It. 65/B2
Clive, NZ 135/D2
Cliza, Bol. 188/C1
Cloan, Sk, Can. 145/K1
Cloates (pt.), Austl. 130/B2
Clocolan, SAfr. 124/D3
Clogh, Ire. 32/C4
Cloghan, Ire. 32/C3
Clogheen, Ire. 32/B5
Clogher (pt.), Ire. 32/D2
Clogherhead, Ire. 34/B4
Cloghjordan, Ire. 32/B4
Cloghy, NI, UK 34/C3
Clohars-Carnoët, Fr. 56/B5
Clonakilty, Ire. 32/B6
Clonakilty (bay), Ire. 32/B6
Clonaslee, Ire. 32/C3
Clonbullogue, Ire. 32/C3
Cloncurry, Austl. 134/A3
Clondalkin, Ire. 34/B5
Clonegall, Ire. 32/D4
Clones, Ire. 32/C1
Clonfert, Ire. 32/B3
Clonmany, Ire. 34/A1
Clonmel, Ire. 32/C5
Clonmellon, Ire. 32/C2
Clonroche, Ire. 32/D5
Clontarf, Mn, US 155/G1
Cloone, Ire. 32/C2
Cloppenburg, Ger. 53/F3
Clopton, Al, US 165/F2
Cloquet (riv.), Mn, US 157/J4
Cloquet, Mn, US 157/H4
Cloridorme, Qu, Can. 158/E1
Clos-Fontaine, Fr. 30/M6
Closeburn, Sc, UK 34/E1
Closter, NJ, US 169/K8
Cloud (peak), Wy, US 147/K1
Cloudcroft, NM, US 152/B4
Cloudy (mt.), Ak, US 171/G3
Cloudy, Ok, US 153/G3
Cloughmills, NI, UK 34/B2
Cloughton, Eng, UK 35/H3
Clover, SC, US 163/G3
Clover Lick, WV, US 163/H1
Cloverdale, In, US 160/C5
Cloverdale, Ca, US 146/B4
Cloverleaf, Tx, US 151/M9
Cloverport, Ky, US 162/D2
Clovis, NM, US 152/C3
Clovis, Ca, US 148/C2
Clovulin, Sc, UK 33/A3
Clowne, Eng, UK 35/G5
Cloyes-sur-le-Loir, Fr. 57/G4
Cloyne, Ire. 32/B6
Cloyne, On, Can. 161/H2
Cluanie (lake), Sc, UK 33/A2
Cluj (co.), Rom. 51/F2
Cluj-Napoca, Rom. 51/F2
Clun, Eng, UK 36/C2
Clunderwen, Wal, UK 36/B3
Cluny, Ab, Can. 145/H2
Cluses, Fr. 60/C5
Clusko (riv.), BC, Can. 144/B1
Clusone, It. 61/F6
Clute, Tx, US 150/G3
Clutha (riv.), NZ 127/G7
Clwyd (riv.), Wal, UK 35/E5
Clwydian (range), Wal, UK 35/E5
Clydach, Wal, UK 36/C3
Clyde, Ab, Can. 140/E3
Clyde (riv.), NS, Can. 158/E4
Clyde (riv.), Sc, UK 33/B5
Clyde, Ks, US 153/F1
Clyde, ND, US 156/E3
Clyde, Oh, US 160/E4
Clyde, Tx, US 150/E1
Clyde Hill, Wa, US 167/C2
Clyde, Firth of (inlet), Sc, UK 31/R8
Clydebank, Sc, UK 33/B5
Clydesdale (valley), Sc, UK 33/C5
Clywedog (riv.), Wal, UK 36/C2
CN Tower, On, Can. 160/U8
Co Lieu, Viet. 94/D2
Co Loa Citadel, Viet. 94/D1
Co Nag (lake), China 99/F5
Côa (riv.), Port. 46/B2
Coacalco, Mex. 175/Q9
Coachella, Ca, US 148/D4
Coachella (canal), Ca, US 148/E4
Coachford, Ire. 32/B6
Coagh, NI, UK 34/B2
Coahoma, Tx, US 151/D1
Coahuayana de Hidalgo, Mex. 174/E5
Coahuila, Mex. 174/B1
Coahuila de Zaragoza (state), Mex. 151/D3
Coal (valley), Nv, US 148/E2
Coal (mtn.), WV, US 163/G2
Coal (riv.), WV, US 163/G1
Coal City, WV, US 163/G2
Coal Hill, Ar, US 153/H3
Coalburn, Sc, UK 33/C5
Coalcomán de Matamoros, Mex. 174/E5
Coaldale, Ab, Can. 145/H3
Coaldale, Co, US 152/B1
Coaldale, Pa, US 168/C2
Coalgate, Ok, US 153/F3
Coalhurst, Ab, Can. 145/H3
Coalinga, Ca, US 148/B2
Coalisland, NI, UK 34/B2
Coalmont, Tn, US 162/E3
Coalton, Oh, US 163/F1
Coalton, Il, US 155/K4
Coalville, Ut, US 147/H3
Coalville, Eng, UK 37/E1
Coalwood, Mt, US 145/M5
Coaraci, Braz. 187/F2
Coari (riv.), Braz. 185/E2
Coari, Braz. 185/F2
Coari (lake), Braz. 185/F2
Coarsegold, Ca, US 148/C2
Coasa, Peru 184/D4
Coast (prov.), Kenya 119/B2
Coast (mts.), Can.,US 139/D4
Coast (range), US 139/E6
Coast (mts.), BC,Yk, Can. 140/C2
Coastal (plain), US 163/G4
Coatbridge, Sc, UK 33/B5
Coatepec, Mex. 175/N7
Coatepec Harinas, Mex. 175/K8
Coates, Mn, US 157/P7
Coatesville, Pa, US 168/C4
Coatetelco, Mex. 175/K8
Coaticook, Qu, Can. 161/L2
Coatopa, Al, US 162/C4
Coats, Ks, US 152/E2
Coats (isl.), Nun, Can. 141/H2
Coats (isl.), Can. 139/J3
Coats Land (pol. reg.), Ant. 192/Y
Coatzacoalcos, Mex. 176/C2
Coatzingo, Mex. 175/L8
Coazze, It. 64/D2
Coba (ruin), Mex. 176/E1
Cobán, Guat. 176/D3
Cobar, Austl. 132/C1
Cobargo, Austl. 133/D3
Cobb (hill), Pa, US 161/H4
Cobb (co.), Ga, US 163/L6
Cobbadah, Austl. 133/C3
Cobberas (mt.), Austl. 133/D3
Cobberas-Tingaringy NP, Austl. 133/D3
Cobbitty, Austl. 133/E2
Cobblestone (mtn.), Ca, US 166/B1
Cobbtown, Ga, US 163/F4
Cobden, On, Can. 161/H2
Cobden, Austl. 132/B3
Cobden, Il, US 162/C2
Cobequid (mts.), NS, Can. 158/F3
Cóbh, Ire. 32/B6
Cobham, Eng, UK 30/B3
Cobija, Bol. 184/D3
Cobleskill, NY, US 161/J3
Coboconk, On, Can. 161/G2
Cobourg, On, Can. 161/G3
Cobourg (pen.), Austl. 128/D2
Cobquecura, Chile 190/B3
Cobram, Austl. 133/B2
Cobre, Nv, US 147/F3
Cóbuè, Moz. 123/G2
Coburg (nbrhd.), Austl. 132/F5
Coburg (pen.) Austl. 127/C2
Coburg (isl.), Nun, Can. 141/T7
Coburg, Ger. 58/D2
Coburg, Or, US 146/B1
Coburn (mtn.), Me, US 161/L2
Coca, Ecu. 180/B5
Coca (riv.), Ecu. 180/B5
Cocachacra, Peru 184/D5
Cocal, Braz. 183/F3
Cocalico (cr.), Pa, US 168/B3
Cocama, Peru 184/D3
Cocapata, Bol. 188/C1
Coccaglio, It. 62/C2
Cocentaina, Sp. 47/E3
Cochabamba, Bol. 188/C1
Cochabamba (dept.), Bol. 185/E5
Coche (isl.), Ven. 181/F2
Cochem, Ger. 55/G3
Cochenour, On, Can. 157/H2
Cocherel, Fr. 30/M4
Cochetopa (hills), Co, US 152/A1
Cochin, Sk, Can. 145/K1
Cochran, Ga, US 163/F4
Cochrane, On, Can. 141/H4
Cochrane, Ab, Can. 144/G2
Cochranton, Pa, US 160/F4
Cock Cairn (peak), Sc, UK 33/D3
Cockatoo, Austl. 132/G5
Cockburn, Austl. 131/J5
Cockburn (cape), Austl. 128/D2
Cockburn (sound), Austl. 130/K7
Cockburn (chan.), Chile 191/B7
Cockburn (isl.), On, Can. 160/E2
Cockburnspath, Sc, UK 33/D5
Cockenzie, Sc, UK 33/D5
Cockermouth, Eng, UK 35/E2
Cockeysville, Md, US 168/B5
Cockrell Hill, Tx, US 150/L7
Cockscomb (peak), SAfr. 124/D4
Coclé del Norte, Pan. 177/F4
Coco (riv.), Hon. 172/E5
Coco (riv.), Nic. 176/E3
Cocoa, Fl, US 165/H3
Cocobeach, Gabon 120/B2
Cocodrie (lake), La, US 164/B2
Coconino (plat.), Az, US 149/F3
Coconut Creek, Fl, US 164/P10
Cocopah Ind. Res., Az, US 148/E4
Cocoparra NP, Austl. 133/C2
Cocorná, Col. 183/K6
Cocos (isls.), Austl. 77/J11
Côcos, Braz. 186/D2
Cocotitlán, Mex. 175/R10
Cocula, Mex. 174/E4
Cod (isl.), Nf, Can. 141/K3
Codajás, Braz. 185/F1
Codegua, Chile 190/N9
Codera (cape), Ven. 183/P7
Coderre, Sk, Can. 145/L2
Codette, Sk, Can. 145/M1
Codigoro, It. 63/F4
Codlea, Rom. 51/G3
Codó, Braz. 183/F4
Codogno, It. 62/C3
Codorus (cr.), Pa, US 168/B4
Codpa, Chile 188/B1
Codrington, Anti. 173/N8
Codroy, Nf, Can. 159/H2
Codsall, Eng, UK 36/D1
Cody, Ne, US 154/D2
Cody, Wy, US 147/J1
Coeburn, Va, US 163/F2
Coelemu, Chile 190/B3
Coelho Neto, Braz. 183/F4
Coello, Col. 183/L8
Coen, Austl. 134/A1
Coeroeni (riv.), Sur. 182/B2
Coesfeld, Ger. 53/E5
Coeur d'Alene, Id, US 144/F4
Coeur D'Alene (mts.), Mt, US 144/G4
Coeur d'Alene (lake), Id, US 144/F4
Coeur d'Alene Ind. Res., Id, US 144/F4
Coevorden, Neth. 52/D3
Coffee City, Tx, US 151/G1
Coffeepot (lake), Wa, US 144/E4
Coffeeville (dam), Al, US 164/D2
Coffeeville, Al, US 164/D2
Coffeeville, Ms, US 162/C4
Coffeyville, Ks, US 153/G2
Coffin Bay, Austl. 131/G5
Coffin Bay NP, Austl. 131/G5
Coffs Harbour, Austl. 132/E1
Cofield, NC, US 163/J2
Cofre de Perote, PN, Mex. 175/M7
Cogealac, Rom. 51/J3
Coggeshall, Eng, UK 37/G3
Coggiola, It. 62/B2
Coghinas (lake), It. 48/A2
Cognac, Fr. 44/C4
Cogne, It. 64/D1
Cognin, Fr. 64/B1
Cogo, Gabon 120/B2
Cogoleto, It. 62/B5
Cogolin, Fr. 64/C6
Cogollo del Cengio, It. 63/E2
Cogolludo, Sp. 46/D2
Cogswell, ND, US 156/F4
Cohagen, Mt, US 145/L4
Cohansey (riv.), NJ, US 168/C5
Cohocton, NY, US 161/H3
Cohoes, NY, US 161/K3
Cohoni, Bol. 188/C1
Cohuna, Austl. 133/B2
Cohunu NP, Austl. 130/L7
Coiba, Isla de (isl.), Pan. 172/E6
Coig (riv.), Arg. 191/C6
Coignières, Fr. 30/H5
Coihaique, Chile 190/B5
Coihueco, Chile 190/C3
Coimbra, Port. 46/A2
Coimbra (dist.), Port. 46/A2
Coín, Sp. 46/C4
Coin, Ia, US 155/G3
Coina (riv.), Port. 47/P10
Coinjock, NC, US 163/K2
Coipasa, Bol. 188/B1
Coise (riv.), Fr. 44/F4
Cojedes (state), Ven. 180/D2
Cojimíes, Ecu. 180/A4
Cojoro, Ven. 180/D2
Cojudo Blanco (peak), Arg. 191/C5
Cojutepeque, ESal. 176/D3
Čoka, Yugo. 50/E3
Cokato, Mn, US 155/G1
Coker, Al, US 162/D4
Cokeville, Wy, US 147/H2
Col d'Aspin (pass), Fr. 47/F1
Col de Cabre (pass), Fr. 64/B3
Col de la Bonnete (pass), Fr. 64/C4
Col de la Cayolle (pass), Fr. 64/C4
Col de la Croix Haute (pass), Fr. 64/B3
Col de la Faucille (pass), Fr. 60/C5
Col de la Forclaz (pass), Swi. 60/D5
Col de la Givrine (pass), Swi. 60/C5
Col de Montgenèvre (pass), Fr. 64/C3
Col de Puymorens (pass), Fr. 44/D5
Col de Saales (pass), Fr. 60/D1
Col de Tende (pass), Fr. 62/A4
Col de Valferriére (pass), Fr. 64/C5
Col de Vars (pass), Fr. 64/C3
Col des Aravis (pass), Fr. 60/C6
Col des Champs (pass), Fr. 64/C4
Col des Mosses (pass), Swi. 60/D5
Col d'Iseran (pass), Fr. 64/D2
Col d'Ispéguy (pass), Fr. 44/C5
Col d'Izoard (pass), Fr. 64/C3
Col du Ballon (pass), Fr. 60/C2
Col du Bonhomme (pass), Fr. 60/D1
Col du Galibier (pass), Fr. 64/C2
Col du Grand Saint-Bernard (pass), Swi. 60/D6
Col du Granier (pass), Fr. 64/B2
Col du Luens (pass), Fr. 64/C5
Col du Mollendruz (pass), Swi. 60/C4
Col du Mont Cenis (pass), Fr. 64/C2
Col du Petit-Saint-Bernard (pass), Fr. 64/C1
Col du Pillon (pass), Swi. 60/D5
Col San Martino, It. 63/F2
Colac, Austl. 132/B3
Colares, Port. 47/P10
Colares, Braz. 182/D3
Colasay, Peru 184/B2
Colatina, Braz. 187/E3
Colba, Eth. 117/G3
Colbeck (cape), Ant. 192/P
Colbert, Ok, US 153/F4
Colborne, On, Can. 161/H3
Colbún, Chile 190/C2
Colby, Ks, US 154/D4
Colby, Wa, US 167/B2
Colby, Wi, US 155/J1
Colca (riv.), Peru 184/D4
Colcabamba, Peru 184/C4
Colchester, On, Can. 167/G8
Colchester, Ct, US 161/K4
Colchester, Vt, US 161/K2
Colchester, Il, US 155/J3
Colchester, Eng, UK 37/G3
Cold Bay, Ak, US 171/F4
Cold Fell (peak), Eng, UK 35/F2
Cold Spring, Mn, US 157/G5
Cold Spring Harbor, NY, US 169/M8
Cold Springs NWR, Or, US 146/D1
Coldingham, Sc, UK 33/D5
Coldspring, Tx, US 151/G2
Coldstream, BC, Can. 144/E2
Coldstream, Sc, UK 33/D5
Coldwater, On, Can. 161/G2
Coldwater, Ks, US 152/E2
Coldwater, Mi, US 160/D4
Coldwater, Ms, US 162/C3
Coldwater (riv.), Ms, US 162/C3
Coldwater, Oh, US 160/D4
Coldwater (cr.), Tx, US 152/D2
Cole (riv.), Eng, UK 37/E3
Cole, Ok, US 153/F3
Cole Camp, Mo, US 153/H1
Coleambally, Austl. 133/B2
Coleambally (cr.), Austl. 133/B2
Colebrook, NH, US 161/L2
Coleford, Eng, UK 36/D3
Coleman, Ab, Can. 144/G3
Coleman, Fl, US 164/L6
Coleman, Ga, US 165/F2
Coleman, Mi, US 160/D3
Coleman, Tx, US 150/E2
Coleman (lake), Tx, US 151/E1
Coleman, Ok, US 153/F3
Coleman, Wi, US 160/B2
Çölemerik, Turk. 103/E2
Colenso, SAfr. 125/E3
Coleraine, Mn, US 157/H4
Coleraine (dist.), NI, UK 34/B1
Coleraine, NI, UK 34/B1
Coleraine, Austl. 132/B3
Coleridge, Ne, US 155/F2
Coleroon (riv.), India 95/C4
Coles, Ms, US 164/C2
Colesberg, SAfr. 124/D3
Coleshill, Eng, UK 37/E1
Colesville, Md, US 168/A5
Coleto Cr. (res.), Tx, US 151/F3
Coleville, Ca, US 146/D4
Colfax, Ca, US 146/C4
Colfax, Il, US 155/K3
Colfax, In, US 160/C4
Colfax, La, US 164/B2
Colfax, ND, US 156/F4
Colfax, Tx, US 151/G1
Colfax, Wi, US 155/J1
Colfax, Wa, US 144/F4
Colfiorito, It. 65/B1
Colgate (cape), Nun, Can. 141/S6
Colgong, India 97/F3
Colhué Huapí (lake), Arg. 190/C5
Colico, It. 61/F5
Colignan, Austl. 132/B2
Coligny, Fr. 60/B5
Coligny, SAfr. 124/D2
Colijnsplaat, Neth. 52/A5
Colima, Mex. 174/E5
Colima (state), Mex. 174/D5
Colina, Chile 190/N8
Colinas, Braz. 183/E4
Colinas de Goiás, Braz. 182/D5
Colinas do Tocantins, Braz. 182/D5
Coliseum, Ca, US 166/F8
Coll (isl.), Sc, UK 31/Q8
Collado-Villalba, Sp. 47/N8
Collagna, It. 62/D5
Collana, Bol. 184/D5
Collarenebri, Austl. 132/D1
Collbran, Co, US 147/K4
Colle de Piccolo San Bernardo (pass), It. 64/C1
Colle della Maddalena (pass), It. 64/C4
Colle di Nava (pass), It. 62/A4
Colle di Tenda (pass), It. 64/D4
Colle di Val d'Elsa, It. 63/E7
Colle Isarco (Gossensass), It. 61/H4
Colle Sannita, It. 65/D5
Colle Sestriere, It. 64/C3
Collecchio, It. 62/D4
Colleen Bawn, Zim. 123/F4
Colleferro, It. 65/C4
College, Ak, US 171/J3
College Park, Ga, US 163/M7
College Park, Md, US 168/B6
College Place, Wa, US 144/E4
College Springs, Ia, US 155/G3
College Station, Tx, US 150/F2
Collegeville, Pa, US 168/C3
Collegno, It. 64/D2
Collelongo, It. 65/C4
Collesalvetti, It. 62/D6
Colletorto, It. 65/D4
Colleyville, Tx, US 150/K7
Colli a Volturno, It. 65/D4
Collie, Austl. 132/D1
Collie, Austl. 130/C5
Collier (range), Austl. 130/C3
Collier (bay), Austl. 127/B2
Collier Range NP, Austl. 130/C3
Collierville, Tn, US 162/C3
Colliford (res.), Eng, UK 36/B5
Collin (co.), Tx, US 150/L6
Collingham, Eng, UK 35/G4
Collingham, Eng, UK 35/H5
Collingwood, On, Can. 160/F2
Collingwood, NZ 135/C3
Collins, On, Can. 157/K2
Collins, Ga, US 163/F4
Collins, Mo, US 153/H2
Collins, Ms, US 164/D2
Collins, Mt, US 145/J4
Collins (riv.), Tn, US 162/E3
Collinston, La, US 153/J4
Collinstown (int'l arpt.), Ire. 34/B5
Collinsville, Austl. 134/B3
Collinsville, Al, US 162/E3
Collinsville, Ca, US 167/L10
Collinsville, Ms, US 162/C4

Collinsville, Ok, US 153/G2
Collinsville, Va, US 163/H2
Collinwood, Tn, US 162/D3
Collo, Alg. 112/K6
Collombey, Swi. 60/C5
Collon, Ire. 34/B4
Collonges, Fr. 60/B5
Collooney, Ire. 32/B1
Collpa, Bol. 188/C1
Colma, Ca, US 167/K11
Colman, SD, US 155/F2
Colmar, Fr. 60/D1
Colmar, Pa, US 168/C3
Colmars, Fr. 64/C4
Colmberg, Ger. 58/D4
Colmenar, Sp. 46/C4
Colmenar de Oreja, Sp. 46/D2
Colmenar Viejo, Sp. 47/N8
Colmesneil, Tx, US 151/G2
Colmillo (cape), Chile 191/B6
Colmonell, Sc, UK 34/D1
Colmont (riv.), Fr. 57/E4
Colne (riv.), Eng, UK 35/G4
Colne, Eng, UK 35/F4
Colne (riv.), Eng, UK 37/G3
Colney Heath, Eng, UK 30/C1
Colo (riv.), Austl. 133/E1
Colo Vale, Austl. 133/E2
Cologna Spiaggia, It. 65/C2
Cologna Veneta, It. 63/E3
Cologne, It. 62/C2
Cologne, NJ, US 168/D5
Cologne (Kölm), Ger. 45/G1
Cologne/Bonn (int'l arpt.), Ger. 55/G2
Cologno Monzese, It. 62/C2
Coloma, Wi, US 155/K1
Colombelles, Fr. 57/E2
Colombes, Fr. 30/J5
Colombey-les-Belles, Fr. 60/B1
Colombia (ctry.) 179/A2
Colombia, Col. 180/C4
Colombia, Mex. 151/E4
Colombier, Swi. 60/C4
Colombine (peak), It. 62/D2
Colombis (peak), Fr. 64/C3
Colombo (peak), It. 64/D2
Colombo, Braz. 189/G3
Colombo (cap.), SrL. 95/C5
Colomiers, Fr. 44/D5
Colomoncagua, Hon. 176/D3
Colón, Arg. 190/E2
Colón, Arg. 188/E5
Colón, Cuba 177/F1
Colón (mts.), Hon. 177/E3
Colón, Pan. 177/G4
Colón, Uru. 191/G2
Colon Koret, D.R. Congo 121/E2
Colona, Co, US 149/J1
Colonche, Ecu. 184/A1
Colonelganj, India 96/C2
Colonia, Micr. 136/C4
Colonia, NJ, US 169/H9
Colonia (dept.), Uru. 190/F2
Colonia Barón, Arg. 190/E3
Colonia Benjamín Aceval, Par. 188/E3
Colonia del Sacramento, Uru. 191/K11
Colonia Dora, Arg. 188/D4
Colonia Gobernador Ayala, Arg. 190/C3
Colonia Josefa, Arg. 190/D3
Colonia Juárez, Mex. 174/C2
Colonia Las Heras, Arg. 190/C5
Colonia Lavalleja, Uru. 189/E4
Colônia Leopoldina, Braz. 183/H5
Colonia Presidente Stroessner, Par. 189/E2
Colonia Yby Yu, Par. 189/F2
Colonial Beach, Va, US 163/J1
Colonial Heights, Va, US 163/J2
Colonial NHP, Va, US 163/J2
Colonial Park, Pa, US 168/B3
Colonna, It. 65/B4
Colonsay (isl.), Sc, UK 31/Q8
Colonsay, Sk, Can. 145/M2
Colony, Ks, US 153/G1
Colony, Wy, US 154/B1
Colorado, CR 177/F4
Colorado (peak), Arg. 191/C6
Colorado, Braz. 189/G2
Colorado (riv.), Mex. 175/B1
Colorado (riv.), US 139/H6
Colorado (riv.), Mex.,US 149/F2
Colorado (plat.), Ut, US 147/H4
Colorado (state), US 142/E4
Colorado (canal), Co, US 154/B4
Colorado City, Co, US 152/B2
Colorado City, Az, US 149/F2
Colorado City, Tx, US 151/D1
Colorado do Oeste, Braz. 185/F4
Colorado Nat'l Mon., Co, US 147/J4
Colorado River (aqueduct), Ca, US 148/E3
Colorado River Ind. Res., Az,Ca, US 148/E3
Colorado Springs, Co, US 152/B1
Colorno, It. 62/D4
Colostre (riv.), Fr. 64/B5
Colotlán, Mex. 174/E4
Colpoys Bay, On, Can. 160/F2
Colquechaca, Bol. 188/C1
Colquiri, Bol. 188/C1
Colquitt, Ga, US 165/F2
Colrain, Ma, US 161/K3
Colson (pt.), Belz. 176/D2
Colstrip, Mt, US 145/L5
Colt (hill), Sc, UK 33/B6
Coltauco, Chile 190/N9
Coltishall, Eng, UK 37/H1
Colton, Ca, US 166/C2
Colton, Ut, US 147/H4
Colton, Wa, US 144/F4
Colts Neck, NJ, US 168/D3
Coluene (riv.), Braz. 179/D4
Columbe, Ecu. 184/B1
Columbia (mt.), Ab, Can. 144/F1
Columbia (riv.), US 139/E5
Columbia, Al, US 165/F2
Columbia, Ky, US 162/E2
Columbia, La, US 153/H4
Columbia, Md, US 168/B5
Columbia, Mo, US 155/H4
Columbia, Ms, US 164/D2
Columbia, NC, US 163/J3
Columbia, NJ, US 168/C2
Columbia (co.), Pa, US 168/B1
Columbia, Pa, US 168/B3
Columbia (plat.), Or, US 140/E4
Columbia (plat.), Or, US 146/D2
Columbia (cap.), SC, US 163/G3
Columbia, Tn, US 162/D3
Columbia (riv.), Wa, US 142/B2
Columbia City, In, US 160/D4
Columbia City, Or, US 144/C5
Columbia Falls, Mt, US 145/G3
Columbia Heights, Mn, US 157/P6
Columbia NWR, Wa, US 144/E4
Columbia Reach (lake), BC, Can. 144/F2
Columbia Road (dam), SD, US 156/E5
Columbian White Tailed Deer Nat'l Wild. Ref., Or, US 144/C4
Columbiana, Al, US 162/D4
Columbiaville, Mi, US 160/E3
Columbine (cape), SAfr. 124/K10
Columbretes (isls.), Sp. 66/D3
Columbus, Ar, US 153/H4
Columbus, Ga, US 162/E4
Columbus, In, US 160/D5
Columbus, Ks, US 153/G2
Columbus, Ms, US 162/C4
Columbus (lake), Ms, US 162/C4
Columbus (A.F.B.), Ms, US 162/C4
Columbus, NC, US 163/F3
Columbus, Ne, US 155/F3
Columbus, NJ, US 168/D3
Columbus, NM, US 149/J5
Columbus (cap.), Oh, US 160/E5
Columbus, Wi, US 155/K2
Columbus, Tx, US 150/F3
Columbus Grove, Oh, US 160/D4
Columbus Salt Marsh (salt marsh), Nv, US 146/D4
Colunga, Sp. 46/C1
Colupo (peak), Chile 188/B2
Colusa, Ca, US 146/B4
Colusa NWR, Ca, US 146/B4
Colville (lake), NW, Can. 140/D2
Colville (cape), NZ 135/C2
Colville (riv.), Ak, US 171/H2
Colville, Wa, US 144/F3
Colville Ind. Res., Wa, US 144/E3
Colvos (passg.), Wa, US 167/B3
Colwall, Eng, UK 36/D2
Colwinston, Wal, UK 36/C4
Colwyn Bay, Wal, UK 34/E5
Comacchio, It. 63/F4
Comacchio (lag.), It. 45/K4
Comai, China 97/H1
Comala, Mex. 174/E5
Comalcalco, Mex. 176/C2
Comanche, Ok, US 153/F3
Comanche (cr.), Co, US 154/B4
Comanche (res.), Ca, US 148/B1
Comanche, Tx, US 150/E2
Comandante Luis Piedra Buena, Arg. 191/C6
Comandante Nicanor Otamendi, Arg. 190/F3
Comănești, Rom. 72/D4
Comar Gambon, Som. 118/C5
Comarapa, Bol. 188/C1
Comarnic, Rom. 51/G3
Comas, Peru 184/B3
Comas, Peru 184/C3
Comayagua, Hon. 176/E3
Comayagua (mts.), Hon. 176/D3
Combahee (riv.), SC, US 163/G4
Combapata, Peru 184/D4
Combarbalá, Chile 188/B4
Combe Martin, Eng, UK 36/B4
Combeaufontaine, Fr. 60/B2
Comber, On, Can. 167/G7
Comber, NI, UK 34/C2
Combermere (bay), Myan. 86/B5
Comblain-au-Pont, Belg. 55/E3
Combloux, Fr. 60/C6
Combourg, Fr. 56/D4
Comboyne, Austl. 132/E1
Combrée, Fr. 57/D5
Combrit, Fr. 56/A5
Combs (riv.), Fr. 56/C5
Combs, Ky, US 163/F2
Combs-la-Ville, Fr. 30/K6
Comé, Ben. 115/F5
Come-By-Chance, Austl. 132/D1
Comemoração (riv.), Braz. 185/F3
Comendador, DRep. 177/J2
Comer, Al, US 165/F1
Comfort, Tx, US 151/E3
Comilla, Bang. 97/H4
Comilla (pol. reg.), Bang. 97/H4
Comines, Fr. 54/C2
Comines, Belg. 54/B2
Comino (isl.), Malta 48/L6
Comitán de Domínguez, Mex. 176/C2
Commack, NY, US 169/E2
Commentry, Fr. 44/E3
Commeny, Fr. 30/H4
Commerce, Tx, US 153/G4
Commerce, Ca, US 166/F7
Commerce, Ga, US 163/F3
Commerce City, Co, US 154/B4
Commercy, Fr. 55/E6
Commewijne (dist.), Sur. 181/H3
Commissioner (isl.), Mb, Can. 156/F1
Committee (bay), Nun, Can. 141/H2
Commonwealth, Wi, US 157/K5
Como, It. 61/F6
Como (lake), It. 66/F1
Como (lake), Wi, US 167/P14
Como, Wi, US 167/P14
Como, Ms, US 162/C3
Comodoro Rivadavia, Arg. 190/D5
Comoé (prov.), Burk. 114/D4
Comoé, PN de la, C.d'Iv. 114/D4
Comorin (cape), India 95/C4
Comoros (ctry.) 107/G6
Comox, BC, Can. 144/B3
Company, Camr. 120/B1
Compeer, Ab, Can. 145/J2
Compiègne, Fr. 54/B5
Compomarino, It. 66/E4
Compostela, Mex. 174/D4
Comprida (isl.), Braz. 189/H3
Compton, Ca, US 166/F8
Compton, Eng, UK 30/B3
Comrat, Mol. 51/J2
Comrie, Sc, UK 33/C4
Comstock, Mi, US 160/D3
Comstock, Tx, US 151/D3
Comunanza, It. 65/C2
Comunidad, Ven. 181/E4
Con Cuong, Viet. 94/D2
Con Son (isl.), Viet. 93/J6
Cona, China 93/F2
Conaica, Peru 184/C4
Conakry (cap.), Gui. 114/B4
Conakry (pol. reg.), Gui. 114/B4
Conakry (int'l arpt.), Gui. 114/B4
Conambo (riv.), Ecu. 180/B5
Conargo, Austl. 133/B2
Conay, Chile 188/B4
Conboy NWR, Wa, US 144/D5
Conca (riv.), It. 63/F5
Concan, Tx, US 151/E3
Concarneau, Fr. 56/B5
Conceição das Alagoas, Braz. 189/G1
Conceição de Macabu, Braz. 187/E4
Conceição do Araguaia, Braz. 182/D5
Conceição do Coité, Braz. 187/F1
Conceição do Mato Dentro, Braz. 187/E3
Conceição do Rio Verde, Braz. 187/L6
Conceição dos Ouros, Braz. 187/L7
Concepción, Arg. 188/E4
Concepción, Arg. 188/C3
Concepción, Bol. 185/E3
Concepción, Bol. 185/F5
Concepción (lake), Bol. 185/F5
Concepción (lag.), Bol. 188/D1
Concepción, Chile 190/B3
Concepción (pt.), Mex. 174/C3
Concepción (bay), Mex. 174/B3
Concepción, Par. 188/E2
Concepción (dept.), Par. 186/A4
Concepción de La Vega, DRep. 173/G4
Concepción del Bermejo, Arg. 188/D3
Concepción del Oro, Mex. 175/E3
Concepción del Uruguay, Arg. 191/J10
Conception (bay), Nf, Can. 159/L2
Conception (pt.), Ca, US 148/B3
Conception (bay), Namb. 122/B4
Concesio, It. 62/D2
Concession, Zim. 123/F3
Conchal, Braz. 187/J7
Conchas (lake), NM, US 152/B3
Conches, Fr. 30/L5
Conches-en-Ouche, Fr. 57/F3
Conchi, Chile 188/B2
Conchillas, Uru. 191/J11
Concho (riv.), Tx, US 151/D2
Conchos (riv.), Mex. 139/G7
Concón, Chile 190/N8
Concord, Ar, US 153/J3
Concord, Fl, US 165/F2
Concord, NC, US 163/G3
Concord (cap.), NH, US 161/L3
Concord, Tx, US 150/G1
Concord, Va, US 163/H2
Concord, Wi, US 167/N13
Concordia, Ks, US 154/F4
Concordia, Arg. 188/E4
Concórdia, Braz. 189/F3
Concordia, Col. 183/K6
Concordia, Mex. 174/D4
Concordia, Peru 184/C2
Concordia Sagittaria, It. 63/F2
Concordia sulla Secchia, It. 63/D4
Concrete, Wa, US 144/D3
Condado, Cuba 177/G1
Condamine, Austl. 134/C3
Condamine (riv.), Austl. 127/E3
Condar, Col. 180/C5
Conde, SD, US 154/E1
Conde, Braz. 187/F1
Condé-sur-L'Escaut, Fr. 54/C3
Condé-sur-Noireau, Fr. 57/E3
Condé-sur-Sarthe, Fr. 57/F4
Condé-sur-Vesgre, Fr. 30/G5
Condé-sur-Vire, Fr. 57/D2
Condécourt, Fr. 30/H4
Condeúba, Braz. 187/E2
Condino, It. 61/G6
Condobolin, Austl. 133/C1
Condom, Fr. 44/D5
Condon, Or, US 146/C1
Condon, Mt, US 145/H4
Condor, Ab, Can. 144/G1
Condove, It. 64/D2
Condrieu, Fr. 64/A2
Condroz (plat.), Belg. 42/C3
Conecuh (riv.), Al, US 164/E2
Conegliano, It. 63/F2
Conehatta, Ms, US 162/C4
Conejos, Co, US 149/J2
Conejos (riv.), Co, US 149/J2
Conequh (riv.), Al, US 162/E5
Conesa, Arg. 190/E2
Conestoga (riv.), Pa, US 168/B3
Conewago (lake), Pa, US 168/A3
Conewago (cr.), Pa, US 168/B4
Coney Island (nbrhd.), NY, US 169/K9
Confins (int'l arpt.), Braz. 186/E3
Conflans-en-Jarnisy, Fr. 55/E5
Conflans-Sainte-Honorine, Fr. 30/J5
Confuso (riv.), Par. 188/E3
Cong, Ire. 32/A2
Congaree Swamp Nat'l Mon., SC, US 163/G4
Congers, NY, US 169/K7
Conghua, China 87/G4
Congis-sur-Thérouanne, Fr. 30/L4
Congjiang, China 87/F3
Congleton, Eng, UK 35/F5
Congo (riv.), Afr. 120/C4
Congo, Braz. 183/G4
Congo (ctry.) 107/D5
Congo (riv.), D.R. Congo 107/D5
Congo (Zaire) (riv.) 107/D4
Congonhal, Braz. 187/K7
Congonhas (int'l arpt.), Braz. 187/K8
Congonhas, Braz. 189/J2
Congress, Az, US 149/F3
Conguel (pt.), Fr. 56/B6
Conguillío, PN, Chile 190/C3
Conic (hill), Sc, UK 33/B4
Cónico (peak), Arg. 190/C4
Conie (riv.), Fr. 57/G4
Conil de la Frontera, Sp. 46/B4
Conimbla NP, Austl. 133/D1
Coningsby, Eng, UK 35/H5
Conisbrough, Eng, UK 35/G5
Coniston, Eng, UK 35/E3
Conley, Ga, US 163/M7
Conlie, Fr. 57/E4
Conlig, NI, UK 34/C2
Conn (lake), Nun, Can. 141/J1
Conn (lake), Ire. 32/A1
Connacht (reg.), Ire. 32/B2
Connah's Quay, Wal, UK 35/E5
Connantre, Fr. 54/C6
Conneaut, Oh, US 160/F4
Connecticut (riv.), US 158/A4
Connecticut (state), US 143/M3
Connecticut (hill), NY, US 161/H3
Connel, Sc, UK 33/A4
Connell, Wa, US 144/E4
Connellsville, Pa, US 161/G4
Connemara (dist.), Ire. 32/A3
Connemara NP, Ire. 31/P10
Conner, Phil. 88/C1
Connerré, Fr. 57/F4
Connersville, In, US 160/D5
Cono Grande (peak), Arg. 191/C6
Conoble, Austl. 133/B1
Conoble (lake), Austl. 133/B1
Conocoto, Ecu. 180/B5
Conodoguinet (cr.), Pa, US 168/A3
Conon, Falls of (falls), Sc, UK 33/B1
Cononbridge, Sc, UK 33/B1
Conondale NP, Austl. 134/D4
Čonoplja, Yugo. 50/D3
Conover, NC, US 163/G3
Conquest, Sk, Can. 145/L2
Conrad, Ia, US 155/H2
Conrad, Mt, US 145/J3
Conran (cape), Austl. 133/D3
Conroe (lake), Tx, US 151/G2
Conroe, Tx, US 151/G2
Consandolo, It. 63/E4
Conscience Point Nat'l Wild. Ref., NY, US 169/F2
Consdorf, Lux. 55/F4
Conselheiro Lafaiete, Braz. 186/E4
Conselheiro Pena, Braz. 187/E3
Conselice, It. 63/E4
Conselve, It. 63/E3
Conservation Park, Austl. 131/F4
Consett, Eng, UK 35/G2
Conshohocken, Pa, US 168/C3
Consolación del Sur, Cuba 177/F1
Consort, Ab, Can. 145/J1
Constance (lake), Swi.,Ger. 61/F2
Constance (mt.), Wa, US 144/C4
Constance (Bodensee) (lake), Swi.,Ger. 61/F2
Constant (mtn.), Fr. 173/N9
Constanta (prov.), Rom. 51/H3
Constanța, Rom. 51/J3
Constantí, Sp. 47/F2
Constantina, Sp. 46/C4
Constantine, Alg. 112/K6
Constantine (cape), Ak, US 171/G4
Constitución (res.), Uru. 191/K10
Constitución, Chile 190/B2
Constitución de 1857, PN, Mex. 174/B2
Constitution, Ga, US 163/M7
Constitution de 1857, PN, Mex. 148/E5
Consuegra, Sp. 46/D3
Consul, Sk, Can. 145/K3
Contai, India 97/F5
Contamana, Peru 184/C2
Contarina, It. 63/F3
Contas, Rio de (riv.), Braz. 187/E2
Contegem, Braz. 186/D3
Contes, Fr. 64/D5
Conthey, Swi. 60/D5
Contigliano, It. 65/B3
Continental, Az, US 149/G5
Continentals (range), Ab, Can. 144/F1
Contoy (isl.), Mex. 176/E1
Contra Costa (canal), Ca, US 167/L10
Contra Costa (co.), Ca, US 167/L11
Contramaestre, Cuba 177/G1
Contratación, Col. 180/C3
Contrecoeur, Qu, Can. 159/P6
Contreras (res.), Sp. 46/E3
Contres, Fr. 57/G6
Contrexéville, Fr. 60/B1
Controller (bay), Ak, US 171/J3
Contulmo, Chile 190/B3
Contumazá, Peru 184/B2
Contwig, Ger. 55/G5
Contwoyko (lake), Nun, Can. 140/F2
Conty, Fr. 54/B4
Convención, Col. 180/C2
Convent, La, US 164/C2
Convento San Francesco, It. 65/B3
Conversano, It. 49/E2
Converse, La, US 150/H2
Conway (cape), Austl. 134/C3
Conwy, Wal, UK 34/E5
Conwy (co.), Wal, UK 34/E5
Conwy (riv.), Wal, UK 34/E5
Conwy (bay), Wal, UK 34/D5
Conway, Ar, US 153/H3
Conway, Fl, US 164/N6
Conway, Mi, US 160/D2
Conway, Mo, US 153/H2
Conway, NH, US 161/L3
Conway, SC, US 163/H4
Conway NP, Austl. 134/C3
Conyers, Ga, US 163/M7
Conyngham, Pa, US 168/B2
Coober Pedy, Austl. 131/G4
Cooch Behār, India 97/G2
Coochiemudlo (isl.), Austl. 134/F7
Coogee, Austl. 132/B1
Cook, Austl. 131/F4
Cook (bay), Chile 191/C7
Cook (str.), NZ 127/H7
Cook (mt.), NZ 135/B3
Cook (inlet), Ak, US 140/A3
Cook (co.), Il, US 167/Q16
Cook Is. (terr.), CookIs. 137/J6
Cooke (mt.), Austl. 130/C5
Cookeville, Tn, US 162/E2
Cookham, Eng, UK 30/A2
Cookhouse, SAfr. 124/D4
Cooks, Mi, US 160/C2
Cookshire, Qu, Can. 161/L2
Cookstown, NI, UK 34/B2
Cookstown (dist.), NI, UK 34/B2
Cooksville, Md, US 168/A5
Cooktown, Austl. 134/B1
Coola Coola (swamp), Austl. 132/B3
Coolabah, Austl. 132/C1
Cooladdi, Austl. 134/B4
Coolah, Austl. 132/D1
Coolamon, Austl. 133/C2
Coolaney, Ire. 32/B1
Coolangatta, Austl. 132/E1
Coolatai, Austl. 132/D1
Cooley (pt.), Ire. 34/B4
Coolgardie, Austl. 130/D4
Coolibah, Austl. 128/C3
Coolidge, Ga, US 165/G2
Coolidge (dam), Az, US 149/G4
Coolidge, Tx, US 151/F2
Coolidge Dam, Az, US 149/G4
Cooloola NP, Austl. 134/D4
Cooloongup (lake), Austl. 130/K7
Coolville, Oh, US 163/G1
Cooma, Austl. 133/D3
Coon (cr.), Il, US 167/N15
Coon (riv.), Mn, US 157/P6
Coon Rapids, Ia, US 155/G3
Coon Rapids, Mn, US 157/P6
Coon Valley, Wi, US 155/J2
Coon, East Branch (cr.), Mi, US 167/G6
Coonabarabran, Austl. 132/D1
Coonalpyn, Austl. 132/A2
Coonamble, Austl. 132/D1
Coonana Abor. Land, Austl. 130/D4
Coondapoor (Kundapura), India 101/K6
Coongan Abor. Land, Austl. 130/C2
Cooper, Tx, US 153/G4
Cooper (cr.), Austl. 131/J3
Cooper (mt.), BC, Can. 144/F2
Cooper City, Fl, US 164/P10
Cooper (brook), Austl. 127/C3
Coopersburg, Pa, US 168/C2
Cooperstown, ND, US 156/E4
Cooperstown, NY, US 161/J3
Coopracambra NP, Austl. 133/D3
Coorabie, Austl. 131/G4
Coordewandy (peak), Austl. 130/C3
Coorong NP, Austl. 132/A3
Coorow, Austl. 130/C4
Cooroy, Austl. 134/D4
Coos (bay), Or, US 146/A2
Coos Bay, Or, US 146/A2
Coosa, Ga, US 162/E3
Coosa (riv.), Al, US 162/D4
Coosawattee (riv.), Ga, US 162/E3
Coot (mtn.), Mo, US 153/J2
Cootamundra, Austl. 133/D2
Cootehill, Ire. 32/C1
Coot'tha (mt.), Austl. 134/E6
Copacabana, Col. 183/K6
Copacabana, Bol. 184/D5
Copachuncho, Bol. 188/C1
Copahué (vol.), Chile 190/C3
Copainalá, Mex. 176/C2
Copala, Mex. 172/B4
Copalis Beach, Wa, US 144/B4
Copan, Ok, US 153/G2
Copán (ruin), Hon. 176/D3
Copano (bay), Tx, US 151/F3
Cope (cape), Sp. 46/E4
Cope, Co, US 154/C4
Copeland (isl.), NI, UK 34/C2
Copemish, Mi, US 160/D2
Copenhagen (København) (cap.), Den. 39/J7
Coper, Col. 183/L7
Copertino, It. 49/F2
Copeton (dam), Austl. 132/D1
Copeville, Tx, US 150/L6
Copiague, NY, US 169/M9
Copiapó (peak), Chile 188/B3
Copiapó (riv.), Chile 188/B3
Copiapó, Chile 188/B3
Coplay, Pa, US 168/C2
Copley, Austl. 131/H4
Coporolo, Ang. 122/B2
Coporolo (riv.), Ang. 122/B2
Copparo, It. 63/E4
Coppell, Tx, US 150/K7
Coppename (riv.), Sur. 181/H3
Coppenbrügge, Ger. 53/G4
Copper (riv.), Ak, US 140/B2
Copper Center, Ak, US 171/J3
Copper Harbor, Mi, US 157/L4
Copperas Cove, Tx, US 150/F2
Copperbelt (prov.), Zam. 123/E2
Copperdahl (hill), ND, US 156/D3
Coppermine (riv.), NW,Nun, Can. 140/E2
Coppet, Swi. 60/C5
Coppolani, Mrta. 114/A2
Coppull, Eng, UK 35/F4
Copşa Mică, Rom. 51/G2
Coqên, China 99/E5
Coquet (riv.), Eng, UK 33/D6
Coquet Dale (valley), Eng, UK 35/G1
Coquille, Or, US 146/A2
Coquille (riv.), Or, US 146/A2
Coquimbo (pol. reg.), Chile 188/B4
Coquimbo, Chile 188/B4
Coquitlam, BC, Can. 144/C3
Cora, Wy, US 147/J2
Corabia, Rom. 51/G4
Coração de Jesus, Braz. 186/D3
Coracora, Peru 184/C4
Corail, Haiti 177/H2
Coraki, Austl. 132/E1
Coral (sea) 127/D2
Coral Gables, Fl, US 164/P11
Coral Harbour, Nun, Can. 141/H2
Coral Sea Islands Territory (terr.), Austl. 127/E2
Coral Springs, Fl, US 164/P10
Corales del Rosario, PN, Col. 180/C2
Coralville, Ia, US 155/J3
Coram, NY, US 169/E2
Corambá (riv.), Braz. 189/G1
Corani, Bol. 185/E5
Corantijne (riv.), Sur. 182/B1
Coranzulí, Arg. 188/C2
Corato, It. 48/E2
Coray, Fr. 56/B4
Corbara (lake), It. 65/B2
Corbeil-Essonnes, Fr. 30/K6
Corbélia, Braz. 189/F3
Corbelin (cape), Alg. 112/H4
Corbenay, Fr. 60/C2
Corbet (peak), Swi. 61/F5
Corbett NP, India 96/B1
Corbetta, It. 62/B3
Corbie, Fr. 54/B4
Corbière (pt.), Chl, UK 56/C2
Corbieres (mts.), Fr. 44/E5
Corbin, Ky, US 162/E2
Corbin City, NJ, US 168/D5
Corbridge, Eng, UK 35/F2
Corby, Eng, UK 37/F2
Corchiano, It. 65/B3
Corcoran, Ca, US 148/C2
Corcoran, Mn, US 157/N6
Corcovado, CR 177/E4
Corcovado (gulf), Chile 179/B7
Corcovado (vol.), Chile 190/B4
Corcovado, Braz. 187/N7
Corcovado, PN, CR 172/E6
Cord, Ar, US 153/J3
Cord. de la Punilla (mts.), Chile 188/B4
Cord. de Lipez (mts.), Bol. 188/C2
Cordata (mesa), NM, US 149/J3
Cordeiro, Braz. 187/E4
Cordele, Ga, US 165/G2
Cordele, Tx, US 151/F3
Cordelia, Ca, US 167/K10
Cordell (New Cordell), Ok, US 152/E3
Cordenons, It. 45/K4
Cordignano, It. 63/F2
Cordilheiras, Serra das (mts.), Braz. 182/D4
Cordillera (mts.), Sp. 66/B2
Cordillera (dept.), Par. 189/E3
Cordillera Central (mts.), Phil. 88/C1
Cordillera Darwin (mts.), Chile 188/B4
Cordillera de la Costa (mts.), Ven. 183/N8
Cordillera de los Andes (mts.), SAm. 188/B1
Cordillera de los Picachos, PN, Col. 180/C4
Cordillera Domeyko (mts.), Chile 188/B3
Cordillera Neo Volcanica (mts.), Mex. 175/Q10
Cordillera Occidental (mts.), Ecu. 180/B5
Cordillera Oriental (mts.), Col. 177/G7
Cordillera Oriental (mts.), SAm. 188/C1
Cordillera Real (mts.), Peru 184/C3
Cordillo Downs, Austl. 134/A4
Córdoba (dept.), Col. 177/H4
Córdoba, Sp. 46/C4
Córdoba (plain), SAm. 190/E2
Córdoba (prov.), Arg. 188/D4
Córdoba, Arg. 188/C4
Córdoba, Mex. 175/N8
Córdoba (Pajas Blancas) (int'l arpt.), Arg. 188/C4
Cordón. de la Totora (mts.), Arg. 188/B4
Córdova, Peru 184/C4
Cordova, Ak, US 171/J3
Cordova, Al, US 162/D4
Cordova, Md, US 168/C6
Cordova Peak (mt.), Ak, US 171/J3
Core Banks (isl.), NC, US 163/J3
Coreaú, Braz. 183/F3
Coree South, Austl. 133/B2
Corella, Sp. 46/E1
Coremas, Braz. 183/G4
Corentyne (riv.), Guy. 182/B2
Corfield, Austl. 134/A3
Corfu (Kérkira) (isl.), Gre. 67/H3
Corgémont, Swi. 60/D3
Corgo, Sp. 46/B1
Cori, It. 65/B4
Coria, Sp. 46/B3
Coria del Río, Sp. 46/B4
Coriano, It. 63/F6
Coribe, Braz. 186/D2
Coricudgy (mt.), Austl. 133/E1
Corigliano Calabro, It. 48/E3
Corinaldo, It. 63/G6
Corinda, Austl. 129/E4
Coringa Islets (isls.), Austl. 134/C2
Coringa Islets (isl.), Austl. 127/D2
Corinne, Ok, US 153/G3
Corinth, NY, US 161/K3
Corinth (gulf), Gre. 67/J3
Corinth, Ms, US 162/C3
Corinth, Tx, US 150/K6
Corinth (Kórinthos) (ruin), Gre. 49/H4
Corinto, Nic. 176/E3
Corinto, Braz. 186/D3
Corisco (bay), EqG. 120/B2
Corisco (isl.), EqG. 120/B2
Corixa Grande (riv.), Braz. 185/G5
Cork (int'l arpt.), Ire. 32/B6
Cork (har.), Ire. 32/B6
Cork, Ire. 32/B6
Corkscrew (swamp), Fl, US 165/H4
Corleone, It. 48/C4
Corleto Perticara, It. 48/E2
Çorlu, Turk. 51/H5
Cormeilles, Fr. 57/F2
Cormeilles-en-Vexin, Fr. 30/J4
Cormelles-le-Royal, Fr. 57/E2
Cormery, Fr. 57/F6
Cormons, It. 63/G2
Cormontreuil, Fr. 54/D5
Corn Palace, The, SD, US 154/E2
Cornaca, Bol. 188/C2
Cornacchia (peak), It. 65/C4
Cornaredo, It. 62/C3
Cornas, Fr. 64/A3
Cornberg, Ger. 53/G6
Corndon (peak), Wal, UK 36/C1
Cornedo Vicentino, It. 63/E2
Cornelia, Ga, US 163/F3
Cornélio Procópio, Braz. 189/G2
Cornelius Grinnel (bay), Nun, Can. 141/K2
Cornell, Ca, US 166/B2
Cornell, Mi, US 160/C2
Cornell, Wi, US 155/J1
Cornell, Il, US 155/K3
Cornella, Sp. 47/L7
Corner (inlet), Austl. 127/D4
Corner Brook, Nf, Can. 159/J1
Cornerstone, Ar, US 153/J3
Cornesti, Mol. 72/E4
Cornetto (peak), It. 61/H6
Cornfield (pt.), Ct, US 169/F1
Cornhill, Sc, UK 33/D1
Corniglio, It. 62/D5
Cornimont, Fr. 60/C2
Corning, Sk, Can. 156/C3
Corning, Ar, US 162/B2
Corning, Ca, US 146/B4
Corning, Ks, US 155/F4
Corning, Ia, US 155/G3
Corning, NY, US 161/H3
Corning, Oh, US 160/E5
Cornish (cr.), Austl. 134/B3
Corno (peak), It. 65/B2
Corno (riv.), It. 65/B2
Corno alle Scale (peak), It. 45/J4
Corno di Rosazzo, It. 63/G2
Cornone di Blumone (peak), It. 61/G6
Cornour (peak), It. 64/D3
Cornú (peak), Arg. 191/D7
Cornucopia, Wi, US 157/J4
Cornuda, It. 63/F2
Cornudas (mts.), NM, US 152/B4
Cornudas, Tx, US 151/B2
Cornville, Az, US 149/G3
Cornwall, On, Can. 161/J2
Cornwall (isl.), Nun, Can. 141/S7
Cornwall (co.), Eng, UK 36/A6
Cornwall (cape), Eng, UK 36/A6
Cornwall, Pa, US 168/B3
Cornwallis (isl.), Nun, Can. 141/S7
Cornwell, Fl, US 165/H4
Cornwerd, Neth. 52/C2
Corny (pt.), Austl. 131/H5
Coro, Ven. 180/D2
Coroatá, Braz. 183/E4
Corocoro, Bol. 188/B1
Corofin, Ire. 32/A4
Coroico, Bol. 184/E5
Coromandel, NZ 135/C2
Coromandel (pen.), NZ 135/C2
Coromandel (coast), India 92/D5
Coromandel, Braz. 186/D3
Coron (isl.), Phil. 88/C3
Coron, Phil. 88/C2
Corona, NM, US 152/B3
Corona, Ca, US 166/C3
Corona del Mar (nbrhd.), Ca, US 166/G8
Coronach, Sk, Can. 145/M3
Coronado, Ca, US 166/C5
Coronado (bay), CR 172/E6
Coronado Nat'l Mem., Az, US 149/G5
Coronation (gulf), Nun, Can. 140/E2
Coronation, Ab, Can. 145/J1
Coronation, SAfr. 125/E2
Coronda, Arg. 188/D4
Coronel, Chile 190/B3
Coronel Bogado, Par. 189/E3
Coronel Cornejo, Arg. 188/D2
Coronel Dorrego, Arg. 190/E3
Coronel Fabriciano, Braz. 187/E3
Coronel Moldes, Arg. 190/D2
Coronel Moldes, Arg. 188/C3
Coronel Oviedo, Par. 189/E3
Coronel Pringles, Arg. 190/E3
Coronel Suárez, Arg. 190/E3
Coronel Vidal, Arg. 190/F3
Coronel Vivida, Braz. 189/F3
Coronet, Fl, US 164/L8
Corongo, Peru 184/B3
Coronie (dist.), Sur. 181/G3
Coropuna (peak), Peru 184/C4
Çorovodë, Alb. 49/G2
Corozal, Belz. 176/D2
Corozal, Col. 180/C2
Corozo Pando, Ven. 181/E2
Corpach, Sc, UK 33/A3
Corps-Nuds, Fr. 56/D5
Corpus, Arg. 189/F3
Corpus Christi (lake), Tx, US 151/E3
Corpus Christi (bay), Tx, US 151/F4
Corpus Christi (int'l arpt.), Tx, US 175/F3
Corpus Christi, Tx, US 151/F4
Corpus Christi Nav. Air Sta., Tx, US 151/F4
Corque, Bol. 188/C1
Corral, Chile 190/B3
Corral de Almaguer, Sp. 46/D3
Corral de Bustos, Arg. 190/E2
Corrales, Col. 180/C3
Corrales, NM, US 149/J3
Corralillo, Cuba 177/F1
Corralitos (peak), Arg. 188/C4
Corre, Fr. 60/C2
Correa, Arg. 190/E2
Corredor, CR 177/F4
Correggio, It. 63/D4
Corrella (lake), Austl. 129/D4
Corrente (riv.), Braz. 186/C3
Corrente, Braz. 186/D1
Correntes (riv.), Braz. 185/H5
Correntes, Cabo das (cape), Moz. 123/G5
Corrib (lake), Ire. 32/A3
Corrie, Sc, UK 33/A5
Corrientes, Arg. 188/E3
Corrientes (prov.), Arg. 189/E4
Corrientes (pt.), Col. 180/B3
Corrientes (cape), Cuba 177/E1
Corrientes (riv.), Ecu. 180/B5
Corrientes (riv.), Peru 184/C1
Corrigan, Tx, US 151/G2
Corrigin, Austl. 130/C5
Corringham, Eng, UK 30/E2
Corris, Wal, UK 36/C1
Corriverton, Guy. 181/G3
Corry, Pa, US 161/G4
Corryhabbie (peak), Sc, UK 33/C2
Corryong, Austl. 133/C3
Corse (cape), Fr. 48/A1
Corse (hill), Sc, UK 33/B5
Corse (dept.), Fr. 45/H5
Corserine (peak), Sc, UK 34/D1
Corseul, Fr. 56/C4
Corsewall (pt.), NI, UK 34/C1
Corsham, Eng, UK 36/D4
Corsica, SD, US 154/E2
Corsica (isl.), Fr. 29/E4
Corsicana, Tx, US 151/F1
Corsico, It. 62/C3
Corsons (inlet), NJ, US 168/D5
Cortada (mesa), NM, US 149/J3
Cortaillod, Swi. 60/C4
Cortaro, Az, US 149/G4
Cortegana, Sp. 46/B4
Cortemaggiore, It. 62/C4
Cortemilia, It. 62/B4
Cortes, Phil. 88/D3
Cortez, Co, US 149/H2
Cortina d'Ampezzo, It. 45/K3
Cortines, Arg. 191/J11
Cortland, NY, US 161/H3
Cortland, Oh, US 160/F4
Cortland, Il, US 155/K3
Corubal (riv.), GBis. 114/B3
Coruche, Port. 46/A3
Çoruh (riv.), Turk. 71/G4
Çorum, Turk. 70/E4
Çorum (prov.), Turk. 70/E4
Corumbá, Braz. 188/E1
Corumbá (riv.), Braz. 186/C3
Corumbaú (pt.), Braz. 187/F3
Corumbiara (riv.), Braz. 185/F4
Corunna, Mi, US 160/D3
Corunna, On, Can. 167/H6
Coruripe, Braz. 187/F1
Corvallis, Or, US 146/B1
Corvaro, It. 65/C3
Corve (riv.), Eng, UK 36/D2
Corvo (peak), It. 65/C3
Corvo (isl.), Azor., Port. 47/R12
Corwen, Wal, UK 35/E6
Corydon, In, US 162/D1
Corydon, Ia, US 155/H3
Corzoneso, Swi. 61/E5
Corzuela, Arg. 188/D3
Cosalá, Mex. 174/D3
Cosamaloapan, Mex. 175/P8
Cosapa, Bol. 188/B1
Cosautlán, Mex. 175/N7
Coscapa, Bol. 184/D5
Coscerno (peak), It. 65/B2
Coscomatepec, Mex. 175/M7
Cosenza, It. 48/E3
Coshocton, Oh, US 160/F4
Cosigüina (pt.), Nic. 176/E3
Coslada, Sp. 47/N9
Cosmit Ind. Res., Ca, US 148/D4
Cosmo Newberry Aboriginal Rsv., Austl. 130/D3
Cosmópolis, Braz. 187/J7
Cosne d'Allier, Fr. 44/E3
Cosne-Cours-sur-Loire, Fr. 44/E3
Cosolapa, Mex. 175/N8
Cospeito, Sp. 46/B1
Cosquín, Arg. 188/C4
Cossa, Ang. 121/E4
Cossato, It. 62/B2
Cossé-le-Vivien, Fr. 57/E5
Cosson (riv.), Fr. 44/D3
Cossonay, Swi. 60/C4
Costa Azul, Uru. 191/G2
Costa Brava (int'l arpt.), Sp. 47/G2
Costa da Caparica, Port. 47/P10
Costa de Mosquitos (phys. reg.), Nic. 177/E4
Costa del Sol (coast), Sp. 66/B3
Costa di Rovigo, It. 63/E3
Costa Marques, Braz. 185/E4
Costa Masnaga, It. 62/C2
Costa Mesa, Ca, US 166/G8
Costa Rica (ctry.) 139/J8
Costa Rica, Bol. 184/D3
Costa Smeralda (int'l arpt.), It. 48/A2
Costa Volpino, It. 62/D2
Costabissara, It. 63/E2
Costello, Pa, US 161/G4
Costello (peak), SD, US 154/C1
Costessey, Eng, UK 37/H1
Costești, Rom. 51/G3
Costigliole d'Asti, It. 62/B4
Costiglione Saluzzo, It. 64/D3
Cosumnes (riv.), Ca, US 146/C4
Cotabambas, Peru 184/C4
Cotabato, Phil. 88/D4
Cotacachi (peak), Ecu. 180/B4
Cotacajes (riv.), Bol. 185/E5
Cotagaita, Bol. 188/C2
Cotahuasi, Peru 184/C4
Cotatumbo (riv.), Col. 177/H4
Cote Blanche (bay), La, US 164/C3
Côte d'Azur (coast), Fr. 47/J1
Côte d'Or (uplands), Fr. 44/F3
Côte d'Azur (int'l arpt.), Fr. 64/D5
Côte de Grace (coast), Fr. 57/F2
Côte de Hautmont (hill), Fr. 60/B1
Côte D'Ivoire (ctry.) 107/B4
Côte du Rif (Al Hoceima) (int'l arpt.), Mor. 112/C2
Côte-Saint-Luc, Qu, Can. 159/N7
Coteau des Prairies (plat.), SD, US 154/E1
Coteau du Missouri (plat.), SD, US 154/D1
Coteau-du-Lac, Qu, Can. 159/M7
Coteau-Landing, Qu, Can. 159/M7
Cotegipe, Braz. 186/D2
Cotentin (pen.), Fr. 44/C2
Cotento (peak), It. 65/C4
Côtes de Meuse (uplands), Fr. 42/C4
Côtes-D'Armor (dept.), Fr. 56/B4
Cothi (riv.), Wal, UK 36/B3
Cotia, Braz. 187/K8
Cotignac, Fr. 64/C5
Cotignola, It. 63/E5
Cotonou (int'l arpt.), Ben. 115/F5
Cotonou, Ben. 115/F5
Cotopaxi, Co, US 152/B1
Cotopaxi (vol.), Ecu. 180/B5
Cotopaxi (dept.), Ecu. 180/B5
Cotopaxi, PN, Ecu. 180/B5
Cotswolds (hills), Eng, UK 36/D3
Cottage Grove, Or, US 146/B2
Cottage Grove, Mn, US 157/Q7
Cottageville, SC, US 163/G4
Cottam, On, Can. 167/G7
Cottbus, Ger. 43/H3
Cottel (isl.), Nf, Can. 159/L1
Cottenham, Eng, UK 37/G2
Cotter, Ar, US 153/H2
Cottica, Sur. 182/C2
Cotton, Mn, US 157/H4
Cotton (lake), Tx, US 151/N9
Cotton Bowl (State Fair Park), Tx, US 150/L7
Cotton Plant, Ar, US 153/J3
Cotton Valley, La, US 153/H4
Cottondale, Fl, US 165/F2
Cottondale, Tx, US 150/K6
Cottonport, La, US 164/B2
Cottonton, Al, US 162/E4
Cottonwood, Al, US 165/F2
Cottonwood, Az, US 149/F3
Cottonwood, Id, US 144/F4
Cottonwood (riv.), Ks, US 155/F4
Cottonwood, Mn, US 155/G1
Cottonwood (riv.), Mn, US 155/G1
Cottonwood, Tx, US 151/F2
Cottonwood (cr.), Wy, US 147/J2
Cottonwood Falls, Ks, US 153/F1
Cottonwood Wash (riv.), Az, US 149/G3
Cottsloe (nbrhd.), Austl. 130/K6
Cotulla, Tx, US 151/E3
Couasnon (riv.), Fr. 57/E5
Coubert, Fr. 30/L6
Coublevie, Fr. 64/B2
Couch, Mo, US 153/J2
Couchey, Fr. 60/A3
Couchwood, La, US 153/H4
Coudekerque-Branche, Fr. 54/B1
Coudersport, Pa, US 161/G4
Coudoux, Fr. 64/B5
Couëron, Fr. 56/D6
Couesnon (riv.), Fr. 56/D4
Cougar, Wa, US 144/C4
Coulaines, Fr. 57/F4
Coulee City, Wa, US 144/E4
Coulee Dam, Wa, US 144/E4
Coulee Dam NRA, Wa, US 144/E3
Coulogne, Fr. 54/A2
Coulomb (pt.), Austl. 128/A4
Coulomb Pt. Nature Rsv., Austl. 128/A4
Coulombs-en-Valois, Fr. 30/M4
Coulommes, Fr. 30/L5
Coulommiers, Fr. 54/C6
Coulon (riv.), Fr. 64/B5
Coulonge (riv.), Qu, Can. 161/H1
Coulounieix-Chamiers, Fr. 44/D4
Coulsdon (nbrhd.), Eng, UK 30/C3
Coulterville, Ca, US 148/B2
Coulterville, Il, US 162/C1
Coumfea (peak), Ire. 32/C5
Counamama, FrG. 182/C1
Counce, Tn, US 162/C3
Council, Ak, US 171/F3
Council, Id, US 146/E1
Council Bluffs, Ia, US 155/G3
Council Grove, Ks, US 153/F1
Country Homes, Wa, US 144/F4
Coupar Angus, Sc, UK 33/C3
Coupeville, Wa, US 144/C3
Coupvray, Fr. 30/L5
Cour-Cheverny, Fr. 57/G5
Courantyne (riv.), Sur. 181/G3
Courantyne (riv.), Guy.,Sur. 179/D2
Courantyne (riv.), Guy. 182/B1
Courbevoie, Fr. 30/J5
Courcelles, Belg. 55/D3

Courcelles-sur-Seine, Fr. 57/G2
Courchevel (arpt.), Fr. 64/C2
Courcouronnes, Fr. 30/K6
Courdimanche, Fr. 30/H4
Courgenay, Swi. 60/D3
Courgent, Fr. 30/G5
Courmayeur, It. 60/C6
Cournon-d'Auvergne, Fr. 44/E4
Courpalay, Fr. 30/L6
Courrendlin, Swi. 60/D3
Courroux, Swi. 60/D3
Coursan, Fr. 44/E5
Courseulles-sur-Mer, Fr. 57/E2
Courtelary, Swi. 60/D3
Courtenay, ND, US 156/E4
Courtepin, Swi. 60/D4
Courthézon, Fr. 64/A4
Courtice, On, Can. 160/V8
Courtisols, Fr. 55/D6
Courtland, Ca, US 167/L10
Courtland, Ks, US 154/F4
Courtland, Va, US 163/J2
Courtmacsherry, Ire. 32/B6
Courtmacsherry (bay), Ire. 32/B6
Courtney, Tx, US 151/F2
Courtomer, Fr. 30/L6
Courtown, Ire. 32/D4
Courtright, On, Can. 167/H6
Courville-sur-Eure, Fr. 57/G4
Cousance, Fr. 60/B4
Cousane (pass), Ire. 32/A6
Coushatta, La, US 164/B1
Cousolre, Fr. 55/D3
Coutances, Fr. 56/D2
Couteau (hills), Sk, Can. 145/L2
Couterne, Fr. 57/E3
Coutevroult, Fr. 30/L5
Couto de Magalhães, Braz. 182/D5
Coutras, Fr. 44/C4
Coutts, Ab, Can. 145/J3
Couva, Trin. 181/F2
Couvet, Swi. 60/C4
Couvin, Belg. 55/D3
Couzeix, Fr. 44/D4
Covadonga, PN, Sp. 46/C1
Covasna (prov.), Rom. 51/G3
Covasna, Rom. 51/H3
Cove, Ar, US 153/G3
Cove, Sc, UK 33/B5
Cove, Tx, US 151/N9
Cove Bay, Sc, UK 33/D2
Cove Gap, WV, US 163/F1
Cove Neck, NY, US 169/L8
Covelo, Ca, US 146/B4
Covendo, Bol. 185/E4
Coventry, Eng, UK 37/E2
Coventry (co.), Eng, UK 37/E2
Coventry (canal), Eng, UK 37/E1
Covered, Turk. 103/M6
Covesville, Va, US 163/H2
Covilhã, Port. 46/B2
Covina, Ca, US 166/G7
Covington, Ga, US 162/F4
Covington, In, US 160/C4
Covington, Ky, US 162/E1
Covington, La, US 164/C2
Covington, Mi, US 157/K4
Covington, Ok, US 153/F2
Covington, Oh, US 160/D4
Covington, Tn, US 162/C3
Covington, Tx, US 151/F1
Covington, Va, US 163/H2
Covo, It. 62/C3
Cow (cr.), Or, US 146/B2
Cow Creek, Wy, US 154/B2
Cow Green (res.), Eng, UK 35/F2
Cowal (reg.), Sc, UK 33/A4
Cowal (lake), Austl. 133/C1
Cowal Creek Aboriginal Community, Austl. 129/F2
Cowan, Tn, US 162/D3
Cowan (nbrhd.), Austl. 134/H8
Cowan (lake), Austl. 127/B4
Cowangie, Austl. 132/B2
Cowansville, Qu, Can. 161/K2
Cowaramup, Austl. 130/B5
Coward Springs, Austl. 131/H4
Cowarie, Austl. 131/H3
Cowboy (hill), Ne, US 154/C3
Cowbridge, Wal, UK 36/C4
Cowden, Il, US 155/K4
Cowdenbeath, Sc, UK 33/C4
Cowee (mts.), NC, US 163/F3
Cowell, Austl. 131/H5
Cowes, Eng, UK 37/E5
Cowes, Austl. 133/B4
Cowessess Ind. Res., Sk, Can. 156/C2
Coweta (co.), Ga, US 163/L8
Cowhouse (cr.), Tx, US 151/E2
Cowichan (lake), BC, Can. 144/B3
Cowie, Sc, UK 33/C4
Cowlesville, NY, US 160/W10
Cowley, Wy, US 147/J1
Cowley, Ab, Can. 145/G3
Cowlitz (riv.), Wa, US 144/D4
Cowora, Austl. 133/C3
Cowpens Nat'l Bfld., SC, US 163/G3
Cowra, Austl. 133/D1
Cox City, Ok, US 153/F3
Coxhoe, Eng, UK 35/G2
Coxilha de Santana (hills), Braz. 189/F4
Coxim, Braz. 189/F1
Coxim (riv.), Braz. 186/B3
Cox's Bāzār, Bang. 93/F3
Cox's Cove, Nf, Can. 159/H1
Coxs Mills, WV, US 163/G1
Coxsackie, NY, US 161/K3
Coy, Al, US 164/E2
Coy Aike, Arg. 191/C6
Coya, Chile 190/N9
Coya Sur, Chile 188/B2
Coyah, Gui. 114/B4
Coyame, Mex. 151/B3
Coyanosa Draw (riv.), Tx, US 151/C2
Coye-la-Forêt, Fr. 30/K4
Coyoacán (nbrhd.), Mex. 175/R10
Coyote (cr.), Ca, US 167/L12
Coyotepec, Mex. 175/K7
Coyuca de Benítez, Mex. 175/E5
Coyutla, Mex. 175/M6
Cozad, Ne, US 154/E3
Cozhê, China 99/E5
Cozumel, Mex. 176/E1
Cozumel (int'l arpt.), Mex. 176/E1
Cozumel (isl.), Mex. 139/J7
Crab (cr.), Wa, US 144/E4
Crab Orchard Nat'l Wild. Ref., Il, US 155/K5
Crab Orchard NWR, Il, US 162/C2
Crabapple, Ga, US 163/M6
Cradle (mtn.), Austl. 132/C4
Cradock, SAfr. 124/D4
Craftsbury, Vt, US 161/K2
Crag (mt.), Yk, Can. 171/K3
Crag (peak), Eng, UK 35/F3
Craig, Ak, US 171/M4
Craig, Co, US 147/K3
Craig (mt.), Co, US 154/B3
Craig, Mo, US 155/G3
Craig, Mt, US 145/J4
Craig (cr.), Va, US 163/G2
Craigavad, NI, UK 34/C2
Craigavon (dist.), NI, UK 34/B3
Craigavon, NI, UK 34/B3
Craigellachie, Sc, UK 33/C2
Craigieburn, Austl. 132/F5
Craigsville, WV, US 163/G1
Craigsville, Va, US 163/H1
Craik, Sk, Can. 145/M2
Crail, Sc, UK 33/D4
Crailsheim, Ger. 58/D4
Craiova, Rom. 51/F3
Cramalina (peak), Swi. 61/E5
Cramlington, Eng, UK 35/G1
Cran-Gevrier, Fr. 60/C6
Crana (riv.), Ire. 34/A1
Cranborne Chase (for.), Eng, UK 36/D5
Cranbourne, Austl. 132/G6
Cranbrook, Austl. 132/D4
Cranbrook, Austl. 130/C5
Cranbrook, BC, Can. 144/G3
Cranbury, NJ, US 168/D3
Crandall, Mb, Can. 156/D2
Crandall, Tx, US 150/L7
Crandon, Wi, US 157/K5
Crane, Mt, US 156/B4
Crane, Mo, US 153/H2
Crane (lake), Il, US 155/J3
Crane, Tx, US 150/C2
Crane Hill, Al, US 162/D3
Crane Lake, Mn, US 157/H3
Crane Naval Weapons Support Center, In, US 160/C5
Crane Neck (pt.), NY, US 169/E2
Crane NWSC, In, US 162/D1
Crane Prairie (res.), Or, US 146/C2
Crane River, Mb, Can. 156/E2
Cranfills Gap, Tx, US 150/F2
Cranford, NJ, US 169/H9
Cranleigh, Eng, UK 37/F4
Cranston, RI, US 161/L4
Craon, Fr. 57/E5
Craponne (canal), Fr. 64/A5
Craponne, Fr. 64/A1
Crary, ND, US 156/E3
Crasna (riv.), Rom. 50/F2
Crasnoe, Mol. 72/E4
Craster, Eng, UK 33/E6
Crater (peak), Or, US 146/B2
Crater (lake), Or, US 146/B2
Crater Lake NP, Or, US 146/B2
Craters Of The Moon Nat'l Mon., Id, US 147/G2
Crateús, Braz. 183/F4
Crati (riv.), It. 48/E3
Cratloe, Ire. 32/B4
Crato, Port. 46/B3
Crato, Braz. 183/G4
Cravens, La, US 164/B2
Cravinhos, Braz. 189/H2
Crawford, Co, US 149/J1
Crawford, Ga, US 163/F4
Crawford, Ms, US 162/C4
Crawford, Ok, US 152/E3
Crawford, Sc, UK 33/C6
Crawford, Tx, US 151/F2
Crawford Bay, BC, Can. 144/F3
Crawfordsville, In, US 160/C4
Crawfordville, Fl, US 165/F2
Crawfordville, Ga, US 163/F4
Crawley, Eng, UK 37/F4
Cray (riv.), Eng, UK 30/D2
Crayford (nbrhd.), Eng, UK 30/D2
Crazy (mts.), Mt, US 145/J4
Crazy Horse Monument, SD, US 154/C2
Crazy Woman (cr.), Wy, US 147/K1
Creag Meagaidh (peak), Sc, UK 33/B3
Creagerstown, Md, US 168/A4
Creal Springs, Il, US 162/C2
Cream, Wi, US 155/J1
Creasy (Mifflinville), Pa, US 168/B1
Creazzo, It. 63/E3
Crêches-sur-Saône, Fr. 60/A5
Crécy-sur-Serre, Fr. 54/C4
Credit (riv.), On, Can. 160/T8
Crediton, Eng, UK 36/C5
Cree (riv.), Sc, UK 34/D2
Cree (lake), Sk, Can. 140/F3
Cree (riv.), Sk, Can. 140/F3
Creede, Co, US 149/J2
Creedman Coulee Nat'l Wild. Ref., Mt, US 145/K3
Creedmoor, Tx, US 151/F2
Creek (Pryor), Ok, US 153/G2
Creel, Mex. 174/D3
Creelman, Sk, Can. 156/C3
Creemore, On, Can. 160/F2
Creetown, Sc, UK 34/D2
Creglingen, Ger. 58/D4
Crégy-lès-Meaux, Fr. 30/L5
Créhange, Fr. 55/F5
Créhen, Fr. 56/C3
Creighton, Sk, Can. 140/F3
Creighton, Ne, US 154/F2
Creighton, SD, US 154/C1
Creignish, NS, Can. 159/G3
Creil, Fr. 54/B5
Crema, It. 62/C3
Crémieu, Fr. 60/B6
Cremlingen, Ger. 53/H4
Cremona, It. 62/D3
Cremona (prov.), It. 62/C2
Cremona, Ab, Can. 144/G2
Crenshaw, Ms, US 162/B3
Creola, Al, US 164/D2
Creole, La, US 164/B3
Crepaja, Yugo. 50/E3
Crepori (riv.), Braz. 182/B4
Crépy, Fr. 54/C4
Creran (lake), Sc, UK 33/A3
Cres (isl.), Cro. 67/G1
Cres, Cro. 45/L4
Cresaptown, Md, US 161/G5
Cresbard, SD, US 154/E1
Crescent, Ok, US 153/F3
Crescent (lake), Fl, US 165/H3
Crescent, Or, US 146/C2
Crescent City, Fl, US 165/H3
Crescent City, Ca, US 146/A3
Crescent Group (isls.), Asia 87/F5
Crescent Lake, Or, US 146/C2
Crescent Lake Nat'l. Wild. Ref., Ne, US 154/C3
Crescentino, It. 62/B3
Cresco, Ia, US 155/H2
Cresco, Pa, US 168/C1
Crespano del Grappa, It. 63/E2
Crespellano, It. 63/E4
Crespières, Fr. 30/H5
Crespin, Fr. 54/C3
Crespo, Arg. 188/D5
Cresskill, NJ, US 169/K8
Cresson, Pa, US 161/G4
Cresson, Tx, US 150/K7
Cressona, Pa, US 168/B2
Cressy, Austl. 132/C4
Crest, Fr. 64/B3
Crest Hill, Il, US 167/P16
Crestline, Ca, US 166/C2
Crestline, Oh, US 160/E4
Creston, Nf, Can. 159/K2
Creston, Ca, US 148/B3
Creston, Ia, US 155/G3
Creston, BC, Can. 144/F3
Crestone, Co, US 152/B2
Crestone (peak), Co, US 152/B2
Crestview, Fl, US 164/E2
Crestwood Village, NJ, US 168/D4
Creswell, Eng, UK 35/G5
Creswell, Or, US 146/B2
Creswell Downs, Austl. 129/D4
Creswick, Austl. 133/A3
Crêt de la Neige (peak), Fr. 60/B5
Crêt du Nu (peak), Fr. 60/B5
Crêt du Rey (peak), Fr. 64/C1
Crete, Il, US 160/C4
Crete (sea), Gre. 67/K3
Crete, Ne, US 155/F3
Crete (isl.), Gre. 29/G5
Créteil, Fr. 30/K5
Cretin (cape), PNG 129/G1
Creuch (hill), Sc, UK 33/B5
Creus (cape), Sp. 47/G1
Creuse (riv.), Fr. 66/D1
Creussen (riv.), Ger. 59/E3
Creussen, Ger. 59/E3
Creutzwald-la-Croix, Fr. 55/F5
Creuzburg, Ger. 53/H6
Crevacuore, It. 62/B2
Crevalcore, It. 63/E4
Crèvecœur-le-Grand, Fr. 54/B4
Crevillente, Sp. 47/E3
Crevoladossola, It. 61/E5
Crewe, Eng, UK 35/F5
Crewe, Va, US 163/H2
Crewkerne, Eng, UK 36/D5
Crews (lake), Fl, US 164/K7
Crianlarich, Sc, UK 33/B4
Crib Point, Austl. 133/B4
Criccieth, Wal, UK 34/D6
Crichton, Sk, Can. 145/L3
Criciúma, Braz. 189/G4
Cricket, NC, US 163/G2
Crickhowell, Wal, UK 36/C3
Cricklade, Eng, UK 37/E3
Crieff, Sc, UK 33/C4
Criffell (hill), Sc, UK 34/E2
Crikvenica, Cro. 45/L4
Crillon (mt.), Ak, US 171/L4
Crimean (pen.), Rom. 51/L3
Crimean (mts.), Ukr. 73/H5
Crimond, Sc, UK 33/E1
Cripple Creek, Co, US 152/B1
Criquetot-L'Esneval, Fr. 57/F1
Crisenoy, Fr. 30/L6
Crisfield, Md, US 163/K2
Crisp (pt.), Mi, US 160/D1
Crisp, Tx, US 150/L7
Crissier, Swi. 60/C4
Crissiumal, Braz. 189/F3
Crissolo, It. 64/D3
Cristal, Monts de (mts.), Gabon 120/B2
Cristalândia, Braz. 186/C1
Cristalina, Braz. 186/D3
Cristalinho (riv.), Braz. 186/C2
Cristina, Braz. 187/L7
Cristino Castro, Braz. 183/E5
Cristóbal (pt.), Ecu. 184/J7
Cristóbal Colón (peak), Col. 180/C2
Cristoforo Colombo (int'l arpt.), It. 62/B5
Cristuru Secuiesc, Rom. 51/G2
Crişul Negru (riv.), Rom. 50/E2
Crişul Repede (riv.), Rom. 72/B4
Crivitz, Wi, US 160/B2
Crixás, Braz. 186/C2
Crixás-Açu (riv.), Braz. 186/C2
Crna Reka (riv.), FYROM 49/G2
Črnomelj, Slov. 50/B3
Croaghmoyle (peak), Ire. 32/A2
Croatia (ctry.) 29/F4
Croce (peak), It. 61/H5
Croce, Pico di (peak), It. 61/H4
Croche (peak), Fr. 60/C6
Croche (riv.), Qu, Can. 158/A1
Crocker, Mo, US 153/H2
Crocker (range), Malay. 91/E3
Crocker (peak), Ecu. 184/J7
Crocketford, Sc, UK 34/E1
Crockett, Ca, US 167/K10
Crockett, Tx, US 151/G2
Crockett Mills, Tn, US 162/C3
Crockham Hill, Eng, UK 30/D3
Crocodile (pt.), Austl. 133/E2
Crocodilopolis (ruin), Egypt 113/B6
Crodo, It. 61/E5
Crofton, Ky, US 162/D2
Crofton, Md, US 168/B6
Crofty, Wal, UK 36/B3
Croghan (mtn.), Ire. 34/B6
Crohane (peak), Ire. 32/A6
Croisette (cape), Fr. 64/B6
Croisic (bay), Fr. 56/C6
Croisic (pt.), Fr. 56/C6
Croisilles, Fr. 54/B3
Croissy-Beaubourg, Fr. 30/K5
Croix (lake), On, Can. 157/J3
Croix Rousse (peak), Fr. 64/D2
Croker (cape), Austl. 128/D2
Croker (isl.), Austl. 127/C2
Crolles, Fr. 64/B2
Cromarty, Sc, UK 33/B1
Cromarty Firth (bay), Sc, UK 33/B1
Crombie (mt.), Austl. 131/F3
Cromdale, Sc, UK 33/C2
Cromdale (hills), Sc, UK 33/C2
Cromer, Mb, Can. 156/D3
Cromer, Eng, UK 37/H1
Cromwell, NZ 135/B4
Cromwell, Al, US 162/C4
Cromwell, Ky, US 162/D2
Cromwell, Ok, US 153/F3
Crondall, Eng, UK 30/A3
Crong A Na (riv.), Viet. 94/D3
Cronulla (nbrhd.), Austl. 134/H9
Crook, Eng, UK 35/G2
Crooked (isl.), Bahm. 173/G3
Crooked (isl.), Fl, US 165/F3
Crooked (lake), Fl, US 165/H4
Crooked (cr.), Ks, US 152/D2
Crooked (riv.), Or, US 146/C1
Crooked Creek, Ak, US 171/G3
Crooked Island Passage (chan.), Bahm. 177/H1
Crookhaven, Ire. 32/A7
Crooks, SD, US 155/F2
Crooks Tower (peak), SD, US 154/C1
Crookston, Mn, US 156/F4
Crookstown, Ire. 32/B6
Crooksville, Oh, US 160/E5
Crookwell, Austl. 133/D2
Croom, Ire. 32/B4
Croom, Fl, US 164/L6
Crosby, Mn, US 157/H4
Crosby, ND, US 156/C3
Crosby, Eng, UK 35/E5
Crosby, Ms, US 164/C2
Crosby (mt.), Wy, US 147/J2
Crosby, Tx, US 151/M9
Crosbyton, Tx, US 152/D4
Cross (cape), Namb. 122/B4
Cross, Tx, US 151/F2
Cross Anchor, SC, US 163/G3
Cross City, Fl, US 165/G3
Cross Fell (peak), Eng, UK 35/F2
Cross Hill, SC, US 163/G3
Cross Plains, Wi, US 155/K2
Cross Plains, Tx, US 151/E1
Cross River (state), Nga. 115/H5
Cross River (res.), NY, US 169/E1
Cross Roads, Tx, US 151/G1
Cross Roads, Pa, US 168/B4
Crossett, Ar, US 153/J4
Crossfarnoge (pt.), Ire. 32/D5
Crossfield, Ab, Can. 145/G2
Crossford, Sc, UK 33/C4
Crossgar, NI, UK 34/C3
Crossgates, Wal, UK 36/C2
Crosshaven, Ire. 32/B6
Crosshill, Sc, UK 33/B6
Crosshouse, Sc, UK 33/B5
Crosskeys, Wal, UK 36/C3
Crosslake, Mn, US 157/G4
Crossmaglen, NI, UK 32/D1
Crossmichael, Sc, UK 34/E2
Crossmolina, Ire. 32/A1
Crossroads, Ire. 31/P9
Crossville, Il, US 162/C1
Crossville, Al, US 162/E3
Crossville, Tn, US 162/E3
Crosswicks (cr.), NJ, US 168/D3
Crostolo (riv.), It. 62/D3
Croston, Eng, UK 35/F4
Croswell, Mi, US 160/E3
Crothersville, In, US 162/E1
Croton-Harmon (Croton-On-Hudson), NY, US 169/E1
Croton-On-Hudson (Croton-Harmon), NY, US 169/E1
Crotone, It. 49/E3
Crottendorf, Ger. 59/F1
Croult (riv.), Fr. 30/K5
Crouy, Fr. 54/C5
Crouy-sur-Ourcq, Fr. 30/M4
Crow (cr.), Co, US 154/B3
Crow (riv.), Mn, US 157/N6
Crow (peak), SD, US 154/C1
Crow Creek Ind. Res., SD, US 154/E1
Crow Ind. Res., Mt, US 147/J1
Crow Ind. Res., Mt, US 145/K5
Crow Wing (riv.), Mn, US 157/G4
Crow, North Fork (riv.), Mn, US 157/G5
Crow, North Fork (riv.), Mn, US 155/G1
Crow, South Fork (riv.), Mn, US 157/G5
Crow, South Fork (riv.), Mn, US 155/G1
Crowborough, Eng, UK 37/G4
Crowder, Ok, US 153/G3
Crowdy Bay NP, Austl. 132/E1
Crowe (riv.), On, Can. 161/H2
Crowell, Tx, US 152/E4
Crowheart, Wy, US 147/J2
Crowie (cr.), Austl. 133/C1
Crowland, Eng, UK 37/F1
Crowle, Eng, UK 35/H4
Crowley (lake), Ca, US 148/C2
Crowley, La, US 164/B2
Crowley, Tx, US 150/K7
Crowley's (ridge), Ar, US 162/B3
Crown Point, In, US 160/C4
Crown Point (int'l arpt.), Trin. 181/F2
Crown Prince Frederik (isl.), Nun, Can. 141/H1
Crownpoint, NM, US 149/H3
Crows Nest (peak), SD, US 154/C1
Crows Nest Falls NP, Austl. 134/D4
Crowther (cr.), Austl. 133/D2
Crowthorne, Eng, UK 37/F4
Crowville, La, US 153/J4
Croxley Green, Eng, UK 30/B2
Croydon (bor.), Eng, UK 30/C2
Croydon (nbrhd.), Eng, UK 30/C2
Croydon, Austl. 134/A2
Croydon (nbrhd.), Austl. 132/G5
Croydon, Pa, US 168/D3
Crozet (isls.), Fr. 27/M8
Crozon, Fr. 56/A4
Cruach Mhór (peak), Sc, UK 33/A4
Cruach nan Capull (peak), Sc, UK 33/A5
Cruas, Fr. 64/A3
Crucero, Peru 184/D4
Cruden Bay, Sc, UK 33/E2
Cruger, Ms, US 162/B4
Cruick Water (riv.), Sc, UK 33/D3
Crum (mtn.), Ms, US 162/C3
Crumlin, NI, UK 34/B2
Crummock Water (lake), Eng, UK 35/E2
Crump (lake), Or, US 146/D2
Crump, Tn, US 162/C3
Crumpton, Md, US 168/C5
Cruseilles, Fr. 60/C5
Crusheen, Ire. 32/B4
Crusnes (riv.), Fr. 55/E5
Cruz (cape), Cuba 177/G2
Cruz Alta, Arg. 190/E2
Cruz Alta (peak), Port. 47/P10
Cruz Alta, Braz. 189/F4
Cruz del Eje, Arg. 188/C4
Cruz Grande, Mex. 176/B2
Cruzeiro, Braz. 187/M7
Cruzeiro do Oeste, Braz. 189/F2
Cruzeiro do Sul, Braz. 184/C2
Cruzeta, Braz. 183/G4
Cruzília, Braz. 187/M6
Crvenka, Yugo. 50/D3
Cryn-y-Brain (peak), Wal, UK 35/E5
Crystal, NM, US 149/H2
Crystal, Mn, US 157/P6
Crystal (lake), Pa, US 168/C1
Crystal Bay, Nv, US 146/D4
Crystal Beach, Fl, US 164/K7
Crystal Brook, Austl. 131/H5
Crystal Cave, Pa, US 168/C2
Crystal City, Mb, Can. 156/E3
Crystal City, Tx, US 151/E3
Crystal Falls, Mi, US 157/K4
Crystal Hill, Va, US 163/H2
Crystal Lake, Fl, US 165/F2
Crystal Lake, Il, US 160/B3
Crystal River, Fl, US 165/G3
Crystal Springs, Ms, US 164/C2
Crystal Springs, Fl, US 164/L7
Crystal Springs (res.), Ca, US 167/K11
Csenger, Hun. 43/M5
Csepreg, Hun. 50/C2
Csongrád, Hun. 50/E2
Csorna, Hun. 50/C2
Csorvás, Hun. 50/E2
Csóványos (peak), Hun. 50/D2
Csurgó, Hun. 50/C2
Ctesiphon (ruin), Iraq 103/F3
Cu Lao (isl.), Viet. 94/E4
Cuajinicuilapa, Mex. 176/B2
Cualedro, Sp. 46/B2
Cuamba, Moz. 123/H2
Cuanavale (riv.), Ang. 122/C2
Cuando (riv.), Ang. 122/D3
Cuangar, Ang. 122/C3
Cuango, Ang. 120/D5
Cuango, Ang. 120/D4
Cuango (riv.), Ang. 120/D5
Cuanza (riv.), Ang. 107/D6
Cuanza Norte (prov.), Ang. 120/C5
Cuanza Sul (prov.), Ang. 120/C5
Cuareim (riv.), Braz. 189/E4
Cuaró, Uru. 189/F4
Cuart de Poblet, Sp. 47/E3
Cuarto (riv.), Arg. 190/D2
Cuatir (riv.), Ang. 122/C2
Cuatro Ojos, Bol. 188/D1
Cuauhtémoc, Mex. 174/E5
Cuauhtémoc, Mex. 174/D2
Cuautepec, Mex. 175/L6
Cuautitlán, Mex. 175/Q9
Cuautitlán Izcalli, Mex. 175/Q9
Cuautla, Mex. 175/L8
Cuba (ctry.) 139/J7
Cuba, Il, US 155/J3
Cuba, Ks, US 154/F4
Cuba, Mo, US 153/J1
Cuba, NM, US 149/J2
Cuba, NY, US 161/G3
Cuba, Port. 46/B3
Cuba City, Wi, US 155/J2
Cubagua (isl.), Ven. 181/E2
Cubal, Ang. 122/B2
Cubal (riv.), Ang. 122/B2
Cuballing, Austl. 130/C5
Cubango (riv.), Ang. 107/D6
Cubatão, Braz. 187/K8
Cubati, Braz. 183/G4
Cubero, NM, US 149/J3
Çubuk, Turk. 102/C1
Cuc Phuong NP, Viet. 86/E4
Cucamonga (Rancho Cucamonga), Ca, US 166/C2
Cuccurano, It. 63/F6
Cucharas (riv.), Co, US 152/B2
Cuchi, Ang. 122/C2
Cuchi (riv.), Ang. 122/C2
Cuchilla Caraguatá, Uru. 189/F5
Cuchillo, NM, US 149/J4
Cuchillo-Có, Arg. 190/D3
Cuchivero (riv.), Ven. 181/E3
Cuchumatanes (mts.), Guat. 176/D3
Cuckfield, Eng, UK 37/F4
Cuckmere (riv.), Eng, UK 37/G5
Cucuí, Braz. 181/E4
Cúcuta, Col. 180/C3
Cucuyagua, Hon. 176/D3
Cudahy, Wi, US 160/C3
Cudahy, Ca, US 166/F8
Cudal, Austl. 133/D1
Cuddalore, India 95/C4
Cuddington, Eng, UK 35/F5
Cudgewa, Austl. 133/C3
Cudillero, Sp. 46/B1
Cudrefin, Swi. 60/D4
Cudworth, Eng, UK 35/G4
Cudworth, Sk, Can. 145/M1
Cue, Austl. 130/C3
Cuebe (riv.), Ang. 122/C2
Cueio (riv.), Ang. 122/D2
Cueli (riv.), Ang. 122/C2
Cuéllar, Sp. 46/C2
Cuéllar-Baza, Sp. 46/D4
Cuenca, Ecu. 180/B5
Cuenca, Sp. 46/D2
Cuencamé de Ceniceros, Mex. 174/E3
Cuengo (riv.), Ang. 120/D5
Cuernavaca, Mex. 175/K8
Cuero, Tx, US 151/F3
Cuers, Fr. 64/C6
Cuesmes, Belg. 54/C3
Cueto, Cuba 177/H1
Cuetzalán, Mex. 175/M6
Cueva de la Quebrada del Toro, PN, Ven. 180/D2
Cuevas de Vinromá, Sp. 47/F2
Cuevas del Almanzora, Sp. 46/E4
Cuevo, Bol. 188/D2
Cuffley, Eng, UK 30/C1
Cufré, Uru. 191/K11
Cuges-les-Pins, Fr. 64/B6
Cugir, Rom. 51/F3
Cuglieri, It. 48/A2
Cugnaux, Fr. 44/D5
Cugo (riv.), Ang. 120/D4
Cuiabá, Braz. 186/A2
Cuiabá (riv.), Braz. 185/G5
Cuicas, Ven. 180/D2
Cuijk, Neth. 52/C5
Cuilapa, Guat. 176/D3
Cuilcagh (peak), NI, UK 32/C1
Cuilco (riv.), Guat. 176/C3
Cuillin (sound), Sc, UK 31/Q8
Cuilo, Ang. 120/D4
Cuilo (riv.), Ang. 120/C4
Cuilo Pombo, Ang. 120/C4
Cuima, Ang. 122/B2
Cuisance (riv.), Fr. 60/B4
Cuise-la-Motte, Fr. 54/C5
Cuiseaux, Fr. 60/B5
Cuisery, Fr. 60/A4
Cuisy, Fr. 30/L4
Cuité, Braz. 183/G4
Cuitláhuac, Mex. 175/N8
Cuito (riv.), Ang. 122/C2
Cuito-Cuanavale, Ang. 122/C2
Cuiuni (riv.), Braz. 181/E5
Cujmir, Rom. 50/F3
Cukuh Batuberagam (cape), Indo. 89/C4
Culasi, Phil. 88/C3
Culbertson (dam), Ne, US 154/D3
Culburra-Orient Point, Austl. 133/E2
Culcairn, Austl. 133/C2
Culdaff (riv.), Ire. 34/A1
Culdaff, Ire. 34/A1
Culebras, Peru 184/B3
Culemborg, Neth. 52/C5
Culfa, Azer. 103/F2
Culgoa (riv.), Austl. 127/D3
Culiacán Rosales, Mex. 174/D3
Culion (isl.), Phil. 88/B3
Culion Reservation, Phil. 88/C3
Culiseu (riv.), Braz. 186/B2
Cullen, Arg. 191/C7
Cullen, La, US 153/H4
Cullen, Sc, UK 33/D1
Cullen, Va, US 163/H2
Cullen Bullen, Austl. 133/E1
Cullenagh (riv.), Ire. 32/A4
Culleoka, Tx, US 150/L6
Cullera, Sp. 47/E3
Culleredo, Sp. 46/A1
Cullin (lake), Ire. 32/A2
Cullinan, SAfr. 123/F5
Cullman, Al, US 162/D3
Culloden Battlesite, Sc, UK 33/B2
Cullomburg, Al, US 164/D2
Cullompton, Eng, UK 36/C5
Cullowhee, NC, US 163/F3
Cully, Swi. 60/C5
Cullybackey, NI, UK 34/B2
Culmback (dam), Wa, US 167/D2
Culmore, NI, UK 34/A1
Culoz, Fr. 60/B6
Culp Creek, Or, US 146/B2
Culpeper, Va, US 163/J1
Culpina, Bol. 188/C2
Culross, Sc, UK 33/C4
Culta, Bol. 188/C1
Cultra (lake), Ire. 32/B3
Cults, Sc, UK 33/D2
Culuene (riv.), Braz. 185/H4
Culver (pt.), Austl. 130/E5
Culver, Ks, US 153/F1
Culver, In, US 160/C4
Culver, Mn, US 157/H4
Culver, Or, US 146/C1
Culver City, Ca, US 166/F7
Culverden, NZ 135/C3
Culvers (lake), NJ, US 168/D1
Culverstone Green, Eng, UK 30/E3
Cumã (bay), Braz. 183/E3
Cumaná, Ven. 181/E2
Cumane (riv.), Fr. 64/B2
Cumaría, Peru 184/C3
Cumba, Peru 184/B2
Cumbal, Col. 180/B4
Cumberland (isl.), Ga, US 165/H2
Cumberland, Md, US 161/G5
Cumberland, Wa, US 167/D3
Cumberland, Wi, US 157/H5
Cumberland (riv.), Ky,Tn, US 143/J4
Cumberland (pen.), Nun, Can. 141/K2
Cumberland (sound), Nun, Can. 141/K2
Cumberland (falls), Ky, US 162/E2
Cumberland, Ky, US 163/F2
Cumberland, BC, Can. 144/B3
Cumberland (co.), NJ, US 168/A3
Cumberland (plat.), US 162/D3
Cumberland (lake), Ky, US 162/E2
Cumberland, Va, US 163/H2
Cumberland Gap NHP, NC,Va, US 163/F2
Cumberland Island Nat'l Seashore, Ga, US 165/H2
Cumbernauld, Sc, UK 33/C5
Cumbi, Ang. 120/C4
Cumbre del Laudo (peak), Arg. 188/B3
Cumbre del Libertador General San Martín (peak), Arg. 188/C3
Cumbres and Toltec Railroad, Co, US 149/J2
Cumbres Bastonal, Cerro (peak), Mex. 176/C2
Cumbres de Majalca, PN, Mex. 174/D2
Cumbres de Monterrey, PN, Mex. 172/A2
Cumbres de Monterrey, PN, Mex. 174/E3
Cumbria (co.), Eng, UK 35/E2
Cumbrian (mts.), Eng, UK 35/E2
Cumbum, India 95/C3
Cumiana, It. 64/D3
Cumming, Ga, US 162/E3
Cummins, Austl. 131/G5
Cumnock, Sc, UK 33/B6
Cumnock, Austl. 133/D1
Cumpas, Mex. 174/C2
Çumra, Turk. 102/C2
Cuñapirú, Uru. 191/G1
Cuñaré, Col. 180/C4
Cunaviche, Ven. 181/E3
Cunco, Chile 190/B3
Cunde (riv.), Ang. 122/C2
Cundeelee Abor. Rsv., Austl. 130/D4
Cunderdin, Austl. 130/C4
Cundinamarca (dept.), Col. 180/C3
Cunduacán, Mex. 176/C2
Cunene (prov.), Ang. 122/B3
Cunene (riv.), Ang. 107/D6
Cuneo (prov.), It. 62/A3
Cuneo, It. 64/D4
Cuneo (prov.), Fr. 64/D3
Cuney, Tx, US 150/G1
Cung Son, Viet. 94/E3
Cunha, Braz. 187/M8
Cunhinga, Ang. 122/C2
Cunhinga (riv.), Ang. 122/C1
Cunjamba, Ang. 122/D2
Cunnamulla, Austl. 134/B5
Cunningham, Ks, US 153/E2
Cunningham, Ky, US 162/C2
Cunningham, Tx, US 153/G4
Cunninghame (reg.), Sc, UK 33/B5
Čuokkaraš'ša (peak), Nor. 38/H1
Cuorgnè, It. 64/D2
Cuozhen, China 87/H2
Cupar, Sk, Can. 156/B2
Cupar, Sc, UK 33/C4
Cupello, It. 65/D3
Cupertino, Ca, US 167/K12
Cupra Marittima, It. 65/C1
Cupramontana, It. 63/G7
Ćuprija, Yugo. 50/E4
Cuprija, Yugo. 50/E4
Cuprum, Id, US 146/E1
Cuquenán (riv.), Ven. 181/F3
Curaçá, Braz. 183/G5
Curaçao (isl.), Neth. 173/H5
Curacautín, Chile 190/C3
Curacaví, Chile 190/N8
Curahuara de Carangas, Bol. 184/D5
Curahuara de Pacajes, Bol. 188/B1
Curanilahue, Chile 190/B3
Curaray (riv.), Peru 180/C5
Curaray (riv.), Peru 180/B5
Curaray (riv.), Ecu.,Peru 184/C1
Curarén, Hon. 176/E3
Curaumilla (pt.), Chile 190/N8
Curcubăta (peak), Rom. 51/F2
Cure (riv.), Fr. 42/B5
Curecanti National Recreation Area, Co, US 147/K4
Curecanti Natl'l Rec. Area, Co, US 152/A1
Curepipe, Mrts. 125/T15
Curepto, Chile 190/B2
Curiche Grande (riv.), Bol. 185/G5
Curicó, Chile 190/C2
Curimatá, Braz. 186/D1
Curitiba, Braz. 189/G3
Curitibanos, Braz. 189/G3
Curnamona, Austl. 131/H4
Curno, It. 62/C2
Curoca (riv.), Ang. 122/B3
Curone (riv.), It. 62/C3
Currais Novos, Braz. 183/G4
Curral Velho, CpV. 107/K10
Curralinho, Braz. 182/D3
Currant (mtn.), Nv, US 146/F4
Currant, Nv, US 146/F4
Currarong, Austl. 133/E2
Currawilla, Austl. 134/A4
Current (riv.), Mo, US 162/B2
Currie, Austl. 133/A4
Currie, Sc, UK 33/C5
Currie, Nv, US 147/F3
Currituck, NC, US 163/J2
Currituck (sound), NC, US 163/K2
Curry, Ak, US 171/H3
Curtea de Argeş, Rom. 51/G3
Curtici, Rom. 50/E2
Curtin, Or, US 146/B2
Curtina, Uru. 189/E5
Curtis (riv.), Austl. 134/D4
Curtis (isl.), NZ 136/G8
Curtis, Sp. 46/A1
Curtis, Ar, US 153/H4
Curtis, La, US 153/H4
Curtis (pt.), Md, US 168/B6
Curú Nat'l Wild. Ref., CR 177/E4
Curuá (riv.), Braz. 182/C4
Curuá (isl.), Braz. 182/D2
Curuá (riv.), Braz. 181/H5
Curuá Una (riv.), Braz. 181/H5
Curuçá, Braz. 182/E3
Curuçú (riv.), Braz. 184/D2
Curup, Indo. 89/C3
Cururupu, Braz. 183/E3
Curuzú Cuatiá, Arg. 188/E4
Curvelo, Braz. 186/D3
Curwensville, Pa, US 161/G4
Curwood (mt.), Mi, US 157/K4
Cusco, Peru 184/D4
Cusco (dept.), Peru 184/C4
Cushendall, NI, UK 34/B1
Cusher (riv.), NI, UK 34/B3
Cushet Law (peak), Eng, UK 33/D6
Cushing, Ok, US 153/F3
Cushing, Tx, US 151/G2
Cushman, Ar, US 153/J3
Cusick, Wa, US 144/F3
Cusna (peak), It. 62/D5
Cussava (riv.), Ang. 122/B2
Cusse, Ang. 122/B2
Cusset, Fr. 44/E3
Cusseta, Ga, US 162/E4
Cusseta, Al, US 162/E4
Custer (peak), SD, US 154/C1
Custer, SD, US 154/C2
Custer, Mt, US 145/L4
Custer City, Ok, US 152/E3
Custines, Fr. 55/F6
Custódia, Braz. 183/G5
Cut (hill), Eng, UK 36/C5
Cut and Shoot, Tx, US 151/G2
Cut Bank, Mt, US 145/H3
Cut Bank (cr.), Mt, US 145/H3
Cut Knife, Sk, Can. 145/K1
Cut Off, La, US 164/C3
Cutato, Ang. 122/C2
Cutato, Ang. 122/C2
Cutato (riv.), Ang. 120/D5
Cutchogue, NY, US 169/F2
Cutenda, Ang. 122/B2
Cutervo, Peru 184/B2
Cuthbert, Ga, US 165/F2
Cutler Ridge, Fl, US 165/H5
Cutral-Có, Arg. 190/C3
Cutro, It. 49/E3
Cuttack, India 95/E1
Cutten, Ca, US 146/A3
Cuvelai, Ang. 122/B2
Cuvergnon, Fr. 30/L4
Cuvette (pol. reg.), Congo 120/C3
Cuvier (cape), Austl. 130/B3
Cuvo (riv.), Ang. 122/B1
Cuxac, Fr. 47/G1
Cuxhaven, Ger. 53/F1
Cuyabeno, Ecu. 180/C5
Cuyahoga (riv.), Oh, US 160/F4
Cuyahoga Falls, Oh, US 160/F4
Cuyahoga Valley Nat'l Park, Oh, US 160/F4
Cuyama (riv.), Ca, US 148/B3
Cuyapaipe Ind. Res., Ca, US 148/D4
Cuyo (isls.), Phil. 91/F1
Cuyo, Phil. 88/C3
Cuyo East Passage (chan.), Phil. 88/C3
Cuyo West Passage (chan.), Phil. 88/C3
Cuyocuyo, Peru 184/D4
Cuyuchi, Bol. 185/F4
Cuyuni (riv.), Guy. 181/G3
Cuyuni (riv.), Ven. 181/F3
Cuyuni-Mazaruni (pol. reg.), Guy. 181/F3
Cuzco (ruin), Peru 184/D4
Cwm, Wal, UK 36/C3
Cwmafan, Wal, UK 36/C3
Cwmbran, Wal, UK 36/C3
Cyangugu, Rwa. 121/G3
Cyclades (isls.), Gre. 67/K3
Cymric, Sk, Can. 156/B2
Cynthia, Ab, Can. 144/G1
Cynthiana, Ky, US 162/E1
Cynwyl Elfed, Wal, UK 36/B3
Cypress (hills), Ab, Can. 145/J3
Cypress, Al, US 162/D4
Cypress, Ca, US 166/F8
Cypress (lake), Fl, US 164/N7
Cypress, Tx, US 151/M9
Cypress (cr.), Tx, US 151/M8
Cypress Gardens, Fl, US 164/M8
Cyprus (ctry.) 77/C6
Cyrenaica (reg.), Libya 67/J5
Cyrene (ruin), Libya 67/J4
Cyril, Ok, US 153/E3
Cyril E. King (int'l arpt.), USVI 173/M8
Cyrus, Mn, US 157/G5
Cysoing, Fr. 54/C2
Cywyn (riv.), Wal, UK 36/B3
Czaplinek, Pol. 43/J2
Czarna Białostocka, Pol. 43/M2
Czarnków, Pol. 43/J2
Czech Republic (ctry.) 29/F4
Częstochowa, Pol. 43/K3
Człuchów, Pol. 40/G5

D

D'Aguilar (range), Austl. 134/E6
D'Arcachon,Bassin di (lag.), Fr. 44/C4
D'Arcy, BC, Can. 144/C2
D' Ouvéa (lag.), NCal. 137/V12
D'Urville (isl.), NZ 135/C3
D. F. Malan (Cape Town) (int'l arpt.), SAfr. 124/L10
D.C. (fed. dist.), US 163/J1
Da (riv.), China 78/D5
Da (Black) (riv.), Viet. 86/E4
Da Hinggan (mts.), China 77/M5
Da Hoa, Viet. 94/D4
Da Juh, China 78/C4
Da Lat, Viet. 94/E4
Da Nang, Viet. 94/E2
Da Nang (cape), Viet. 94/E2
Da Qaidam, China 78/D4
Da Te, Myan. 94/B2
Da Xian, China 87/E2
Daaden, Ger. 55/G2
Da'an, China 79/J2
Daba (mts.), China 78/F5
Dabaga, Tanz. 119/A4
Dabai, Nga. 115/G4
Dabajuro, Ven. 180/D2
Dabakala, C.d'Iv. 114/D4
Dabas, Hun. 50/D2
Dabat, Eth. 117/H2
Dabeiba, Col. 180/B3
Dabeibu, China 87/H2
Dabein, Myan. 94/B2
Dabendorf, Ger. 42/Q7
Dabhoi, India 92/B3
Dabie (mts.), China 87/G2
Dabissé Kayati, Gui. 114/B4
Dabo, Fr. 55/G6
Dabob (bay), Wa, US 167/B2
Daboji, China 79/K3
Dabola, Gui. 114/C4
Daborow, Som. 118/D4
Dabou, C.d'Iv. 114/D5
Daboya, Gha. 115/E4
Dabra, India 96/B3
Dąbrowa Białostocka, Pol. 41/K5
Dąbrowa Górnicza, Pol. 43/K3
Dabu, China 87/G3
Dăbuleni, Rom. 51/G4
Dac Sut, Viet. 94/D3
Dac To, Viet. 94/D3
Dacca (Dhaka) (cap.), Bang. 97/H4
Dachang, China 80/L8
Dachang Huizu Zizhixian, China 80/H7
Dachau, Ger. 59/E6
Dacheng, China 87/G2
Dacono, Co, US 154/B3
Dadanawa, Guy. 182/B2
Dade (co.), Fl, US 164/P11
Dade City, Fl, US 164/L7
Dades, Oued (riv.), Mor. 110/D3
Dadeville, Al, US 162/E4
Dadi (cape), Indo. 91/H4
Ḑadnah, UAE 101/G3
Dadong, China 94/E1
Dādra and Nagar Haveli (state), India 92/B4
Dādri, India 98/D5
Dādu, Pak. 101/J3
Dadu (riv.), China 78/E5
Daduru (riv.), SrL. 92/C6
Daen Noi (peak), Thai. 94/B4
Dăeni, Rom. 51/J3
Daet, Phil. 88/C2
Dafang, China 86/E3
Dafanhe, China 81/B1
Dafeng, China 80/E4
Dafna, Isr. 105/D2
Dafu, China 86/D2
Dafu, China 87/H2
Dag, India 92/C3
Daga Medo, Eth. 118/B4
Daga Post, Sudan 117/G3
Dagaio, Eth. 118/B4
Dagana, Sen. 114/B2
Dağardı, Turk. 102/B2
Dağbaşı, Turk. 102/D2
Dagda, Lat. 41/M3
Dage, D.R. Congo 121/E2
Dagestan, Resp., Rus. 71/H4
Dagestanskiye Ogni, Rus. 71/J4
Daggaboersnek (pass), SAfr. 124/D4
Dagger (mtn.), Tx, US 151/C3
Daggett, Mi, US 160/C2
Daglung, China 97/H1
Dagmar Range NP, Austl. 134/B2
Dagneux, Fr. 60/B6
Dagny, Fr. 30/M5
Dagongcha, China 78/D4
Dagu, China 80/H7
Daguan, China 87/E3
Daguan, China 86/D3
D'Aguilar (mt.), Austl. 134/E6
Dagujia, China 81/C1
Daguokui (peak), China 79/K2
Dagupan, Phil. 88/C1
Daguragu Abor. Land, Austl. 128/C4
Dagxoi, China 93/G2
Dagzê (lake), China 99/E5
Dagzhuka, China 97/G1
Dahana (des.), SAr. 77/D7
Dāhānu, India 95/B2
Daharki, Pak. 92/A2
Dahei (riv.), China 80/B2
Daheiding (peak), China 79/K2
Dahekou, China 78/F5
Dahenan, China 80/G7
Dahlak (arch.), Erit. 118/B1
Dahlem, Ger. 55/F3
Dahlem, Ger. 42/Q7
Dahlenburg, Ger. 53/H2
Dahlgren, Il, US 162/C1
Dahlonega, Ga, US 162/F3
Dahmani, Tun. 112/L7
Dahme (riv.), Ger. 43/G3
Dahn, Ger. 55/G5
Dahongliutan, China 99/C4
Dahongqi, China 81/B2
Dahra, Sen. 114/B3
Dahshūr, Egypt 113/C5
Dahshūr (ruin), Egypt 113/C5
Dahūk, Iraq 103/E2
Dahūk (gov.), Iraq 103/E2
Dahuofang (res.), China 80/D2
Dahushan, China 81/B2
Dai (isl.), Indo. 128/C1
Dai (isl.), China 87/J2
Dai (lake), China 80/C2
Dai Loc, Viet. 94/E3
Dai Xian, China 80/C3
Dai-Segen-dake (peak), Japan 82/B3
Dai-sen (peak), Japan 84/C3
Daian, Japan 83/L5
Daicheng, China 80/D3
Daigo, Japan 85/G2
Daik-u, Myan. 94/B2
Dā'il, Syria 105/E3

Dailek – Dera Is

Dailekh, Nepal 96/C1
Dailly, Sc, UK 33/B6
Daimiao, China 80/D3
Daimiel, Sp. 46/D3
Daingerfield, Tx, US 153/G4
Dainkognubma, China 78/D5
Daintree NP, Austl. 129/G4
Daiō-zaki (pt.), Japan 85/E3
Dāira Dīn Panāh, Pak. 98/A4
Daireaux, Arg. 190/E3
Dairy (cr.), Austl. 131/N8
Dairyland, Wi, US 157/H4
Daisen-Oki NP, Japan 84/C3
Daisetsuzan NP, Japan 82/C2
Daisy, Ok, US 153/G3
Daisy, Ar, US 153/H3
Daisy, Ky, US 163/F2
Daito (isl.), Japan 77/N7
Daitō, Japan 83/J6
Daiyun (peak), China 87/H3
Dajabón, DRep. 177/J2
Dajarra, Austl. 131/H2
Dajing, China 93/K3
Dak Nhe, Viet. 94/D3
Dakar (cap.), Sen. 114/A3
Dakar (pol. reg.), Sen. 114/A3
Dakar (Yoff) (int'l arpt.), Sen. 114/A3
Dakeng, China 87/G3
Daketa Shet' (riv.), Eth. 118/B4
Dakhin Shābāzpur (isl.), Bang. 97/H4
Dakhlet Nouadhibou (pol. reg.), Mrta. 110/A5
Dakoro, Niger 115/G3
Dakota (co.), Mn, US 157/P7
Dakota City, Ia, US 155/G2
Dakota City, Ne, US 155/F2
Dakovica, Yugo. 50/E4
Dakovo, Cro. 50/D3
Dal (riv.), Swe. 74/B3
Dal Cataract (falls), Sudan 109/F4
Dala, Ang. 120/E5
Dala-Järna, Swe. 40/F1
Dalaas, Aus. 61/F3
Dalaba, Gui. 114/B4
Dalad Qi, China 80/B2
Dalai (lake), China 78/H3
Dalaman, Turk. 102/B2
Dalaman (int'l arpt.), Turk. 102/B2
Dalāmī, Sudan 117/F3
Dalandzadgad, Mong. 78/E3
Dalangwan, China 87/G4
Dalaoba, China 99/D3
Dalarna (reg.), Swe. 38/E3
Dalarö, Swe. 39/B1
Dalatangi (pt.), Ice. 38/Q6
Dalavich, Sc, UK 33/A4
Dalbeattie, Sc, UK 34/E2
Dalby, Austl. 134/C4
Dalby, Swe. 40/E4
Dalby, Swe. 39/K7
Dalby-Söderskog NP, Swe. 39/K7
Dalcross (int'l arpt.), Sc, UK 33/B1
Dale, Nor. 40/A1
Dale, In, US 162/D1
Dale, Tx, US 150/F3
Dale, SC, US 163/G4
Dale City, Va, US 163/J1
Dale Hollow (lake), Tn, US 162/E2
Dalen, Nor. 40/C2
Dalen, Neth. 52/D3
Daleside, SAfr. 124/Q13
Daletme, Myan. 93/F3
Daleville, Al, US 165/F2
Dalfsen, Neth. 52/D3
Dalgan (riv.), Ire. 32/B2
Dalgaranger (mt.), Austl. 130/C3
Dalhart, Tx, US 152/C2
Dalhousie, NB, Can. 158/D1
Dalhousie, India 98/C3
Dalhousie (cape), NW, Can. 140/D1
Dali, China 80/B4
Dali (riv.), China 78/F4
Dali, China 86/D3
Dalian (bay), China 81/A3
Dalian, China 81/A3
Dalian (int'l arpt.), China 80/E3
Daliang, China 78/E4
Dalías, Sp. 46/D4
Daliburgh, Sc, UK 31/Q8
Dalidag (peak), Azer. 103/F2
Daling (riv.), China 79/H3
Dāliyat el Karmil, Isr. 105/C3
Dalizi, China 81/D2
Dalj, Cro. 50/D3
Dalkeith, Sc, UK 33/C5
Dalkola, India 97/F3
Dall (isl.), Ak, US 140/C3
Dall (lake), Ak, US 171/F3
Dallas, Sc, UK 33/C1
Dallas, Ga, US 162/E4
Dallas, Or, US 146/B1
Dallas (co.), Tx, US 150/L7
Dallas, Tx, US 150/L7
Dallas City, Il, US 155/J3
Dallas Love Field (arpt.), Tx, US 150/L7
Dallas-Fort Worth (int'l arpt.), Tx, US 150/K7
Dallastown, Pa, US 168/B4
Dalles of the Saint Croix, Mn, US 157/H5
Dallesport, Wa, US 146/C1
Dallgow, Ger. 42/Q6
Dallol Bosso (riv.), Niger,Mali 115/F3
Dalmally, Sc, UK 33/B4
Dalmatia (reg.), Cro. 67/G1
Dalmatia, Pa, US 168/B2
Dalmatovo, Rus. 69/P4
Dalmellington, Sc, UK 33/B6
Dalmeny, Austl. 133/E3
Dalmine, It. 62/C2
Dal'negorsk, Rus. 79/M3
Dal'nerechensk, Rus. 79/L2
Daloa, C.d'Iv. 114/D5
Dalol, Eth. 118/B2
Dalqū, Sudan 109/F4
Dalroy, Ab, Can. 145/H2
Dalry, Sc, UK 33/B5
Dalrymple, Sc, UK 33/B6
Dalrymple (lake), Austl. 127/D3
Dals Långed, Swe. 40/E2
Dalsingh Sarai, India 97/E3
Dalsjöfors, Swe. 40/E3
Dalton, Ar, US 162/B2
Dalton, Ga, US 162/E3
Dalton, Mn, US 156/G4
Dalton, Ma, US 161/K3
Dalton, Pa, US 161/J4
Dalton-in-Furness, Eng, UK 35/E3
Daltonganj, India 97/E3
Dalu, China 78/E4
Daluābāri, Bang. 97/G3
Daludalu, Indo. 89/C2
Daluo (peak), China 87/G4
Dalupiri (isl.), Phil. 88/C1
Dalvík, Ice. 38/N6
Dalwallinu, Austl. 130/C4
Dalwhinnie, Sc, UK 33/B3
Dalworthington Gardens, Tx, US 150/K7
Daly (bay), Nun, Can. 140/G2
Daly (riv.), Austl. 128/C3
Daly (riv.) 127/C2
Daly R. Wild. Sanct., Austl. 128/C3
Daly River, Austl. 128/C3
Daly River Aboriginal Land, Austl. 128/C3
Daly Waters, Austl. 128/D4
Dalyup, Austl. 130/D5
Dam (riv.), China 99/F5
Dam Doi, Viet. 94/D4
Dam Gamad, Sudan 117/E2
Damagaram Takaya, Niger 115/H3
Damāgheh-ye Kūh (pt.), Iran 103/J5
Damak, Nepal 97/F2
Damān and Diu (state), India 92/B3
Damanhūr, Egypt 113/B2
Damara, CAfr. 116/C4
Damāş, Egypt 113/C3
Damasak, Nga. 116/B2
Damascus, Ar, US 153/H3
Damascus, Ga, US 165/F2
Damascus, Va, US 163/G2
Damascus (int'l arpt.), Syria 105/F2
Damascus, Md, US 168/A5
Damascus (Dimashq) (cap.), Syria 105/E1
Damāţ, Egypt 113/B3
Damaturu, Nga. 116/A3
Damavānd (mtn.), Iran 103/H3
Damāvand, Iran 103/H3
Damaying, China 87/G3
Damba, Ang. 120/C4
Dambach-la-Ville, Fr. 60/D1
Dambaslar, Turk. 51/H5
Dāmbuk, India 86/B2
Dame Marie (cape), Haiti 177/H2
Dame Marie, Haiti 177/H2
Damenglong, China 94/C1
Damerham, Eng, UK 37/E5
Dameron, Md, US 163/J1
Dāmghān, Iran 103/H2
Damietta (Dumyāţ) (mouth), Egypt 113/C1
Damietta Branch (riv.), Egypt 104/B4
Damigny, Fr. 57/F4
Daming (mtn.), China 87/F4
Daming, China 87/G3
Daming, China 80/C3
Damintun, China 81/B2
Damion (peak), Fr. 55/D4
Dāmiyā, Jor. 105/D4
Dammard, Fr. 30/M4
Dammartin-en-Goële, Fr. 30/L4
Dammastock (peak), Swi. 61/E4
Damme, Belg. 54/C1
Damme, Ger. 53/F3
Dāmodar (riv.), India 92/E3
Damoh, India 96/B4
Damon, Tx, US 151/M9
Damongo, Gha. 115/E4
Damparis, Fr. 60/B3
Dampier, Austl. 130/C2
Dampier (str.), Indo. 91/H4
Dampier (arch.), Austl. 127/A2
Dampier Downs, Austl. 128/A4
Dampierre, Fr. 60/B3
Dampierre, Fr. 30/H5
Dampierre-sur-Salon, Fr. 60/B2
Damprichard, Fr. 60/C3
Damqawt, Yem. 100/F5
Damqog (Maquan) (riv.), China 96/E1
Damrei (mts.), Camb. 94/C4
Damsterdiep (riv.), Neth. 52/D2
Damvant, Swi. 60/C3
Damville, Fr. 57/G3
Damwoude, Neth. 52/D2
Damxung, China 99/F5
Dan (riv.), China 78/G5
Dan, Isr. 105/D2
Dan (riv.), NC, US 162/H2
Dan Gulbi, Nga. 115/G4
Dan Sai, Thai. 94/C2
Dan Xian, China 87/F5
Ḑānā, Jor. 104/D4
Dana, In, US 160/C5
Dāna, Nepal 96/D1
Dana Point, Ca, US 166/C4
Danakil (reg.), Djib. 118/B3
Danané, C.d'Iv. 114/C5
Danao, Phil. 88/D3
Danba, China 86/D2
Danbury, Eng, UK 37/G3
Danbury, Ct, US 161/K4
Danbury, NC, US 163/G2
Danbury, Tx, US 150/G3
Danby, Vt, US 161/K3
Danby (lake), Ca, US 148/E3
Dancheng, China 80/C4
Dancing (pt.), Mb, Can. 156/E1
Dandaragan, Austl. 130/B4
Dande (riv.), Ang. 120/C5
Dandeldhurā, Nepal 96/C1
Dandenaong (cr.), Austl. 132/G5
Dandenong (nbrhd.), Austl. 132/G5
Dandenong (mt.), Austl. 132/G5
Danderhall, Sc, UK 33/C5
Dandīl, Egypt 113/C6
Dando, Ang. 122/C1
Dandong, China 81/C2
Dandridge, Tn, US 163/F2
Dane (riv.), Eng, UK 35/F5
Dang (riv.), China 78/D4
Dangal, Erit. 118/B2
Dangara, Taj. 99/A4
Dangayos (pt.), Phil. 87/J5
Dange, Nga. 115/G3
Dange, Ang. 120/C4
Dange-ia-Menha, Ang. 120/C5
Danger (pt.), SAfr. 124/L11
Danggali Conservation Park, Austl. 132/B2
Dangila, Eth. 117/H3
Dangkou, China 80/L8
Dangme (riv.), Bhu. 86/A3
Dangriga, Belz. 176/D2
Dangshan, China 80/D4
Dangtu, China 80/D5
Dangur, Eth. 117/H3
Dangyang, China 87/F2
Dania, Fl, US 164/P10
Danieb (riv.), Namb. 122/D4
Danielskuil, SAfr. 124/C3
Danielsville, Ga, US 163/F3
Danielsville, Pa, US 168/C2
Danilov, Rus. 68/J4
Daning, China 80/B3
Danjiangkou, China 80/B4
Danjiangkou (res.), China 78/G5
Danjoutin, Fr. 60/C2
Ḑank, Oman 101/G4
Dankaur, India 98/D5
Dankhar Gompa, India 101/L2
Dankov, Rus. 70/F1
Dankova (peak), Kyr. 99/C3
Danleng, China 86/D2
Danlí, Hon. 176/E3
Dannelly (res.), Al, US 162/D4
Dannemora, Swe. 40/G1
Dannemora, NY, US 161/K2
Dannenberg, Ger. 42/F2
Dannes, Fr. 54/A2
Dannevirke, NZ 135/D3
Dannhauser, SAfr. 125/E3
Dano, Burk. 114/E4
Dansville, NY, US 161/H3
Dantzler, Ms, US 164/D2
Danube (riv.), Yugo. 70/B3
Danube (riv.), Hun.,Rom. 72/D5
Danube (riv.), Eur. 67/K1
Danube (riv.), Aus. 29/F4
Danube (Donau) (riv.), Ger.,Aus. 45/H2
Danube, Delta of the (delta), Rom.,Ukr. 67/L1
Danube, Mouths of the (mouth), Rom.,Ukr. 70/D3
Danville, Qu, Can. 161/K2
Danville, Ar, US 153/H3
Danville, Il, US 160/C4
Danville, In, US 160/C5
Danville, Ky, US 162/E2
Danvers, Mt, US 145/K4
Danville, Oh, US 160/E4
Danville, Pa, US 168/B2
Danville, Va, US 163/H2
Danville, Vt, US 161/K2
Danville, Wa, US 144/E3
Dao, Phil. 88/C3
Dao Xian, China 87/F3
Daocheng, China 86/D2
Daodou'ao, China 87/J2
Daora, WSah. 110/B4
Daoshui, China 87/F4
D'Aosta (valley), It. 62/A1
Daotiandi, China 79/L2
Daoukro, C.d'Iv. 114/E5
Daoulas, Fr. 56/A4
Daoura, Oued ed (riv.), Alg. 110/D3
Daozhen, China 87/E2
Dapa, Phil. 88/D3
Dapaong, Togo 115/F4
Daphne, Al, US 164/E2
Dapingying, China 87/F2
Dapitan, Phil. 88/C3
Dapo, China 94/E2
Dapuzi, China 87/F3
Daqiao, China 86/D4
Daqiao, China 87/H3
Daqing, China 79/K2
Daqing (riv.), China 80/H7
Daqiu, China 87/H3
Daqu (isl.), China 87/J2
Daquanwan, China 78/C3
Dār al Bayḑā (ruin), Egypt 113/C4
Dār 'Aqīl, Sudan 117/G2
Dar Bel Hamri, Mor. 112/B2
Dar el Barka, Mrta. 114/B2
Dar es Salaam (prov.), Tanz. 119/B3
Dar es Salaam (int'l arpt.), Tanz. 119/B3
Dar es Salaam (cap.), Tanz. 119/B3
Dar Rounga (reg.), CAfr. 116/D3
Dar-e Rūd, Iran 103/J4
Dar-el-Beida (Casablanca), Mor. 110/D2
Dar'ā, Syria 105/E3
Dar'ā (prov.), Syria 105/E3
Dārāb, Iran 103/H4
Darāban, Pak. 98/A4
Darabani, Rom. 72/D3
Daraga, Phil. 88/C2
Daragodleh, Som. 118/C3
Darai (hills), PNG 129/F1
Daram, Phil. 88/D3
Dārān, Iran 103/G3
Darasun, Rus. 78/G1
Đaravica (peak), Yugo. 50/E4
Dārayyā, Syria 105/E2
Darbatta, Eth. 117/G4
Darbėnai, Lith. 41/J3
Darbhanga, India 97/E2
Darby, Austl. 133/C4
Darby (cape), Ak, US 171/F3
Darby, Fl, US 164/L7
Darby, Mt, US 145/G4
Darby, Pa, US 168/C4
Darda, Cro. 50/D3
Dardanelle, Ar, US 153/H3
Dardanelle (dam), Ar, US 153/H3
Dardanelles (str.), Turk. 70/C4
Darebin (cr.), Austl. 132/G5
Darent (riv.), Eng, UK 30/D3
Dareton, Austl. 132/B2
Darfield, BC, Can. 144/D2
Darfo, It. 61/G6
Dārfūr (pol. reg.), Sudan 109/E5
Dargai, Pak. 98/A2
Dargaville, NZ 135/C1
Argentière, Aiguille d' (peak), Swi. 60/D6
Dargle (riv.), Ire. 34/B5
Dargo (riv.), Austl. 133/C3
D'Arguin (bay), Mrta. 114/A1
Darhan (peak), Mong. 78/F2
Darhan, Mong. 78/F2
Darhan Muminggan Lianheqi, China 78/G3
Darie (hills), Som. 118/C3
Darien, Ga, US 165/H2
Darien, Il, US 167/P16
Darien, Ct, US 169/M7
Darién (mts.), Pan. 177/G4
Darién, PN, Pan. 173/F6
Darjazīn, Iran 103/G3
Darjiling, India 97/G2
Darkan, Austl. 130/C5
Darlag, China 78/D5
Darling (lake), ND, US 156/D3
Darling, SAfr. 124/L10
Darling (mtn.), Austl. 133/D2
Darling (range), Austl. 127/A4
Darling (riv.), Austl. 127/D4
Darling Downs (range), Austl. 134/C3
Darling Downs (reg.), Austl. 127/D3
Darling Nat'l Wild. Ref., Fl, US 165/G4
Darlington, Eng, UK 35/G2
Darlington (co.), Eng, UK 35/G2
Darlington, In, US 160/C4
Darlington, Wi, US 155/J2
Darlington, SC, US 163/H3
Darlington, Md, US 168/B4
Darlington Point, Austl. 133/C2
D'Armainvilliers (pond), Fr. 30/L5
Darmstadt, Ger. 58/B3
Darmstadt, In, US 162/D1
Darnah, Libya 67/J4
Darnāyah, Tun. 112/L7
Darnétal, Fr. 57/G2
Darney, Fr. 60/C1
Darnick, Austl. 132/B2
Darnley (cape), Ant. 192/E
Darnley (bay), NW, Can. 140/D2
Daroca, Sp. 46/E2
Darongjiang, China 87/F3
Darongtang, China 87/F2
Darras Hall, Eng, UK 35/G1
Darregueira, Arg. 190/E3
Darreh Gaz, Iran 101/G1
Darreh-ye Shahr, Iran 103/F3
Darrington, Wa, US 144/D3
Dārsana, Bang. 97/G4
Darsser (cape), Ger. 40/E4
Dart (riv.), Eng, UK 36/C6
Dart, West (riv.), Eng, UK 36/C6
Dartford, Eng, UK 30/D2
Dartington, Eng, UK 36/C6
Dartmoor (upland), Eng, UK 36/B5
Dartmoor NP, Eng, UK 44/A1
Dartmouth (dam), Austl. 133/C3
Dartmouth, NS, Can. 158/F3
Dartmouth, Eng, UK 36/C6
Dartmouth, Ma, US 161/L4
Darton, Eng, UK 35/G4
Dartowo, Pol. 40/G4
Dartuch (cape), Sp. 47/G3
Daru, SLeo. 114/C5
Daru, PNG 129/F2
Daruba, Indo. 91/G3
Daruvar, Cro. 50/C3
Darvel, Sc, UK 33/B5
Darvel (bay), Malay. 91/E3
Darwen, Eng, UK 35/F4
Darwendale, Zim. 123/F3
Darwin, Austl. 128/C3
Darwin (int'l arpt.), Austl. 128/C3
Darwin, Ca, US 148/D2
Darwin (bay), Chile 190/B5
Darwin (isl.), Ecu. 184/J6
Darwin (vol.), Ecu. 184/J7
Darya Khan, Pak. 98/A4
Daryābād, India 96/C2
Dārzīn, Iran 101/G3
Dashahe, China 79/K3
Dashanzui, China 79/K3
Dashengtang (peak), China 79/H3
Dashennongjia (peak), China 80/B5
Dasher, Ga, US 165/G2
Dashhowuz, Trkm. 74/F5
Dashi, China 87/H2
Dashowuz (prov.), Trkm. 71/L4
Dasht Kaur (riv.), Pak. 101/H3
Dasht-e Kavīr (des.), Iran 74/F6
Dasht-e Lūt (des.), Iran 74/F6
Dasht-e Mārgow (des.), Afg. 101/H2
Dasima, Gha. 115/E4
Dasing, Ger. 58/E6
Daska, Pak. 98/C3
Daspalla, India 95/E1
Dassa-Zoumé, Ben. 115/F5
Dassel, Ger. 53/G5
Dassel, Mn, US 155/G1
Dassendorf, Ger. 53/H1
Dasseneiland (isl.), SAfr. 124/B4
Dasūya, India 98/C4
Dat Do, Viet. 94/D4
Datadian, Indo. 90/E3
Dātāganj, India 96/B1
Datchet, Eng, UK 30/B2
Date, Japan 82/B2
Dateland, Az, US 149/F4
Datia, India 96/B3
Datian (peak), China 87/F4
Datil, NM, US 149/J3
Datong (riv.), China 78/D4
Datong, China 80/C2
Datong, China 78/E4
Datong (mts.), China 78/D4
Datong, China 78/G3
Datteln, Ger. 53/E5
Dattohar, India 98/B5
Datu (cape) 90/C3
Datuk (cape), Indo. 89/C2
Dāud Khel, Pak. 98/A3
Daugai, Lith. 41/L4
Daugava (riv.), Lat. 74/C4
Daugavpils, Lat. 41/M4
Daugherty Field (Long Beach) (arpt.), Ca, US 166/F8
Daulatpur, Bang. 97/G4
Daule (riv.), Ecu. 180/B5
Daule, Ecu. 180/B5
Daun, Ger. 55/F3
Daung (isl.), Myan. 94/B3
Dauphin, Mb, Can. 156/D2
Dauphin (riv.), Mb, Can. 156/E2
Dauphin (lake), Mb, Can. 156/E2
Dauphin (cape), NS, Can. 159/G2
Dauphin (co.), Pa, US 168/B3
Dauphin, Pa, US 168/B3
Dauphin Island, Al, US 164/D2
Dauphine (reg.), Fr. 66/E1
Dauphiné (range), Fr. 44/F4
Daura, Nga. 115/H3
Däväçi, Azer. 71/J4
Davao, Phil. 88/D4
Davao (gulf), Phil. 88/D4
Dāvarzan, Iran 103/J2
Davegoriale, Som. 118/C3
Davel, SAfr. 125/E2
Daveluyville, Qu, Can. 161/K1
Davenda, Rus. 79/H1
Davenport, ND, US 156/F4
Davenport, Ok, US 153/F3
Davenport, Fl, US 164/M7
Davenport, Ia, US 155/J3
Davenport, Ne, US 154/F3
Davenport (range), Austl. 128/D5
Davenport (mt.), Austl. 131/F2
Davenport, Wa, US 144/E4
Daventry, Eng, UK 37/E2
Daverdisse, Belg. 55/E3
Daveyton, SAfr. 124/E2
Davézieux, Fr. 64/A2
Davgaard-Jensen Land (phys. reg.), Grld. 141/T6
David, Pan. 177/F4
David City, Ne, US 155/F3
David-Gorodok, Bela. 72/D1
Davidson, Ar, US 153/G3
Davidson, Ok, US 152/E3
Davidson (mt.), Ca, US 167/J11
Davidson, Sk, Can. 145/M2
Davidson, NC, US 163/G3
Davie, Fl, US 164/P10
Davies (mt.), Austl. 131/F3
Davilla, Tx, US 151/F2
Daviot, Sc, UK 33/D2
Davis (sea), Ant. 192/F
Davis, Austl., Ant. 192/F
Davis (str.), Can.,Grld. 141/L2
Davis, Sk, Can. 145/M1
Davis (dam), Az, US 148/E3
Davis, Ca, US 146/C4
Davis (cr.), Mi, US 167/E7
Davis, Ok, US 153/F3
Davis (mt.), Pa, US 161/G5
Davis (mts.), Tx, US 142/F5
Davis, WV, US 163/H1
Davis Cove, Nf, Can. 159/K2
Davis Creek, Ca, US 146/C3
Davis Dam, Az, US 148/E3
Davis-Monthan (A.F.B.), Az, US 149/G4
Davisboro, Ga, US 163/F4
Davison, Mi, US 160/E3
Davisville, Mo, US 162/B2
Davlekanovo, Rus. 69/M5
Davo (riv.), C.d'Iv. 114/D5
Davos, Swi. 61/F4
Dawa, China 81/B2
Dawa Wenz (riv.), Eth. 118/B4
Dawan, China 87/F4
Dawangja (isl.), China 81/B3
Dawaxung, China 99/E5
Dawei (Tavoy), Myan. 94/B3
Dawen (riv.), China 78/H4
Dawlish, Eng, UK 36/C5
Dawqah, SAr. 100/D5
Dawson (riv.), Austl. 127/D3
Dawson (mt.), BC, Can. 144/F2
Dawson, Yk, Can. 171/L3
Dawson (isl.), Chile 191/C7
Dawson, Ga, US 165/F2
Dawson, Mo, US 153/H2
Dawson, Mn, US 155/F1
Dawson, Tx, US 151/F2
Dawson Creek, BC, Can. 140/D3
Dawson Springs, Ky, US 162/D2
Dawsonville, Ga, US 162/E3
Dawu, China 86/D2
Dawu, China 80/C5
Dawu (mtn.), China 80/C5
Dawujiang, China 87/E3
Dax, Fr. 44/C5
Daxin, China 94/D1
Daxing, China 87/F3
Daxing, China 80/H7
Daxue (mts.), China 78/E5
Day Star Ind. Res., Sk, Can. 156/B2
Dayang (riv.), China 81/B2
Dayang, China 87/F4
Dayang Bunting (isl.), Thai. 89/B1
Dayao, China 86/D3
Daye, China 87/G2
Dayi, China 86/D2
Daying, China 81/D1
Daying (riv.), China 93/G3
Daylesford, Austl. 133/B3
Daylight (pass), Ca, US 148/D2
Daym Zubayr, Sudan 117/E4
Daymán (riv.), Uru. 189/E4
Dayong, China 87/F3
Dayong, China 87/F2
Dayr Abū Sa'īd, Jor. 105/D3
Dayr al Balaḩ, Gaza 105/A6
Dayr al Ghuşūn, WBnk. 105/C4
Dayr al Qamar, Leb. 105/D1
Dayr 'Allā, Jor. 105/D4
Dayr az Zawr, Syria 102/E3
Dayr Az Zawr (prov.), Syria 102/D3
Dayr Ballūţ, WBnk. 105/C4
Dayr Dibwān, WBnk. 105/C5
Dayr Sharaf, WBnk. 105/C4
Dayrūt, Egypt 109/F3
Dayrūţ, Egypt 113/B2
Daysland, Ab, Can. 145/H1
Dayton, Ia, US 155/G2
Dayton, In, US 160/C4
Dayton, NJ, US 168/D3
Dayton, NY, US 161/G3
Dayton, Oh, US 160/D5
Dayton, Or, US 146/B1
Dayton, Tn, US 162/E3
Dayton, Tx, US 151/N8
Dayton, Va, US 163/H1
Dayton, Wa, US 144/F4
Dayton, Wy, US 147/K1
Daytona Beach, Fl, US 165/H3
Dayu (isl.), China 87/J3
Dayu, China 87/G3
Dayuan, China 87/J2
Dayushupu, China 81/A2
Dazey, ND, US 156/E4
Dazhengjiatun, China 81/B3
Dazhizhu Dau (isl.), China 87/K8
Dazhu, China 87/E2
De Aar, SAfr. 124/D3
De Bary, Fl, US 165/H3
De Berry, Tx, US 151/G1
De Bilt, Neth. 52/C4
De Cocksdorp, Neth. 52/B2
De Cordova Bend (dam), Tx, US 151/F1
De Doorns, SAfr. 124/L10
De Forest, Wi, US 155/K2
De Funiak Springs, Fl, US 165/E2
De Gaulle, CAfr. 116/B4
De Graff, Oh, US 160/E4
De Gray (lake), Ar, US 153/H3
De Grey (riv.), Austl. 128/A5
De Grey, Austl. 130/C2
De Haan, Belg. 54/C1
De Hart (res.), Pa, US 168/B3
De Hoge Veluwe, NP, Neth. 52/C4
De Jongs (cape), Indo. 129/E1
De Kalb (co.), Il, US 167/N16
De Kalb, Il, US 155/K3
De Kalb, Ms, US 162/C4
De Koog, Neth. 52/B2
De La Vassako-Bolo, Rsv. Nat. Int., CAfr. 116/C3
De Lacs (riv.), ND, US 156/D3
De Land, Fl, US 165/H3
De Las Ánimas (pt.), Mex. 174/B2
De Leijen (lake), Neth. 52/D2
De Leon (lake), Fr. 44/C4
De Leon, Tx, US 150/E1
De Lier, Neth. 52/B5
Déljne, NW, Can. 140/D2
De Luz, Ca, US 166/C4
De Meern, Neth. 52/C4
De Motte (Demotte), In, US 160/C4
De Panne, Belg. 54/B1
De Peel (phys. reg.), Neth. 52/C6
De Pere, Wi, US 160/B2
De Pinte, Belg. 54/C2
De Pue, Il, US 155/K3
De Queen, Ar, US 153/G3
De Quincy, La, US 164/B2
De Ridder, La, US 164/B2
De Smet, SD, US 154/F1
De Soto, Ga, US 165/F2
De Soto, Il, US 162/C2
De Soto, Mo, US 162/B1
De Soto, Ms, US 164/D2
De Tour Village, Mi, US 160/E2
De Valls Bluff, Ar, US 153/J3
De Wijk, Neth. 52/D3
De Winton, Ab, Can. 145/G2
De Witt, Ar, US 153/J3
De Witt, NY, US 161/H3
De Witt, Ne, US 155/F3
De Witt, Ia, US 155/J3
Dead (riv.), Ire. 32/B4
Dead (lake), Fl, US 165/F2
Dead (sea), (Asia) 105/C5
Deadhorse, Ak, US 171/J1
Deadman (mtn.), Wy, US 147/H2
Deadman (peak), Austl. 130/C2
Deadwood, SD, US 154/C1
Deal (isl.), Austl. 132/C3
Deal, NJ, US 168/D3
Deal Island, Md, US 163/K1
Deale, Md, US 168/B6
Dean (for.), Eng, UK 36/D3
Dean (riv.), BC, Can. 144/B1
Deán Funes, Arg. 188/C4
Deanmill, Austl. 130/C5
Deanville, Tx, US 150/F2
Dearborn, Mi, US 160/E3
Dearborn, Mo, US 155/G4
Dearborn Heights, Mi, US 167/F7
Dearing, Ga, US 163/F4
Dearne, Eng, UK 35/G4
Deary, Id, US 144/F4
Dease (riv.), BC, Can. 140/D3
Dease (str.), Nun, Can. 139/F3
Dease Lake, BC, Can. 142/Z13
Death (valley), Ca, US 148/D2
Death Valley, Ca, US 148/D2
Death Valley NP, Ca,Nv, US 148/D2
Deauville, Fr. 57/F2
Deavgay (peak), Rus. 103/F1
Deba Habe, Nga. 116/A3
Debagrām, India 97/G4
Debar, FYROM 49/G2
Debark', Eth. 117/H2
Debauch (mt.), Ak, US 171/G3
Debaysīma, Erit. 118/B2
Debden, Sk, Can. 145/L1
Debelets, Bul. 51/G4
Deben (riv.), Eng, UK 37/H2
Debenham, Eng, UK 37/H2
Debert, NS, Can. 158/F3
Dębica, Pol. 43/L3
Debīdwār, Bang. 97/H4
Dęblin, Pol. 43/L3
Dębno, Pol. 43/H2
Deborah (mt.), Ak, US 171/J3
Debre Birhan, Eth. 118/A3
Debre Lībanos Monastery, Eth. 118/A3
Debre Mark'os, Eth. 117/H3
Debre Sīna, Eth. 118/A3
Debre Tabor, Eth. 117/H3
Debre Zebīt, Eth. 118/A3
Debre Zeyit, Eth. 118/A3
Debre Zeyit, Eth. 117/G3
Debrecen, Hun. 43/L5
Debub, Eth. 118/A2
Debundscha (pt.), Camr. 120/B1
DeBurgh (lake), Austl. 129/D4
Decatur, Al, US 162/D3
Decatur, Ga, US 163/M7
Decatur, Il, US 155/K4
Decatur, In, US 160/D4
Decatur, Mi, US 160/D3
Decatur, Ms, US 162/C4
Decatur, Tn, US 162/E3
Decatur, Tx, US 150/K6
Decaturville, Tn, US 162/C3
Decazeville, Fr. 44/E4
Deccan (plat.), India 92/C5
Dechang, China 86/D3
Dechheling, Bhu. 97/H2
Decima, It. 63/E4
Děčín, Czh. 43/H3
Décines-Charpieu, Fr. 60/A6
Decize, Fr. 44/E3
Decker, Mt, US 147/K1
Deckers, Co, US 152/B1
Deckerville, Mi, US 160/E3
Decorah, Ia, US 155/J2
Deddington, Eng, UK 37/E3
Dedemsvaart, Neth. 52/D3
Deder, Eth. 118/B3
Dedham, Ma, US 161/L3
Dedo (peak), Arg. 190/C5
Dédougou, Burk. 114/E3
Dedovichi, Rus. 41/N3
Dedovsk, Rus. 69/W9
Dedu, China 79/K2
Dedza, Malw. 123/G2
Dee (riv.), Sc, UK 33/C3
Dee Why (nbrhd.), Austl. 134/H8
Deel (riv.), Ire. 34/A4
Deep (cr.), Austl. 131/M8
Deep (cr.), De, US 168/C6
Deep (riv.), NC, US 163/H3
Deep Brook, NS, Can. 158/E3
Deep Creek Ind. Res., BC, Can. 144/C1
Deep Fork (riv.), Ok, US 153/F3
Deep Red (cr.), Ok, US 153/E3
Deep River, On, Can. 161/H1
Deep Springs, Ca, US 148/D2
Deepcut, Eng, UK 30/F3
Deeping Saint James, Eng, UK 37/F1
Deepwater, Mo, US 153/H1
Deepwater, Austl. 132/D1
Deepwater (pt.), De, US 168/C5
Deepwater, NJ, US 168/C4
Deer (isl.), Mb, Can. 156/F2
Deer (isl.), Ire. 32/A4
Deer (isl.), Ak, US 171/F5
Deer (cr.), Ms, US 153/J4
Deer Flat NWR, Id, US 146/E2
Deer Island, Or, US 144/C5
Deer Lake, On, Can. 157/G1
Deer Lake, Nf, Can. 159/J1
Deer Lake, Pa, US 168/B2
Deer Lodge, Mt, US 145/H4
Deer Park, Ca, US 146/B4
Deer Park, Il, US 167/P15
Deer Park, Md, US 168/B5
Deer Park, NY, US 169/E2
Deer Park, Tx, US 151/M9
Deer Park, Wa, US 144/F4
Deer River, Mn, US 157/H4
Deerbrook, Wi, US 157/K5
Deerfield, Ma, US 161/K3
Deerfield, Il, US 167/P15
Deerfield Beach, Fl, US 164/P10
Deering, Ak, US 171/F2
Deering, ND, US 156/D3
Deerlijk, Belg. 54/C2
Deerton, Mi, US 157/L4
Deerwood, Mn, US 157/H4
Deesa, India 101/K4
Deeside (valley), Sc, UK 33/D2
Deex Nugaaleed (riv.), Som. 118/C3
Defensores del Chaco, PN, Par. 188/D2
Defiance, Oh, US 160/D4
Deganwy, Wal, UK 34/E5
Dêgê, China 86/C2
Degeberga, Swe. 39/L7
Degeh Bur, Eth. 118/B3
Dégelis, Qu, Can. 158/C2
Degema, Nga. 115/G5
Degerfors, Swe. 40/F2
Degersheim, Swi. 61/F3
Deggendorf, Ger. 59/F5
Deggingen, Ger. 58/C5
Dego, It. 62/B5
Degoma, Eth. 117/H2
DeGrey (riv.), Austl. 130/C2
Dëgtevo, Rus. 73/L3
Deh Bīd, Iran 103/H4
Deh Dasht, Iran 103/G4
Deh-e Shīr, Iran 103/H4
Dehaj, Iran 103/H4
Dehalak (isl.), Erit. 118/A2
Dehalak Marine NP, Erit. 118/B2
Dehāqān, Iran 103/G4
Dehdez, Iran 103/G4
Deheq, Iran 103/G3
Dehlorān, Iran 103/F3
Dehri, India 97/E3
Dehua, China 87/H3
Dehui, China 79/K3
Deidesheim, Ger. 58/B4
Deil, Neth. 52/C5
Deinste, Ger. 53/G1
Deinze, Belg. 54/C2
Deister (mts.), Ger. 53/G4
Deiva Marina, It. 62/C5
Dej, Rom. 51/F2
Deje, Swe. 40/E2
Dejiang, China 87/F2
Dejima, Japan 83/E1
Dekalb (co.), Ga, US 163/M7
Dekelia (arpt.), Gre. 49/N8
Dekemhare (Dek'emhāre), Erit. 118/A2
Dek'emhāre (Dekemhare), Erit. 118/A2
Dekese, D.R. Congo 121/E3
Dekina, Nga. 115/G5
Dekle Beach, Fl, US 165/G3
Dékoa, CAfr. 116/C4
Del Campillo, Arg. 190/D2
Del Carril, Arg. 191/J11
Del Dios, Ca, US 166/C4
Del Gran Paradiso, It. 62/A2
Del Mar, Ca, US 166/C5
Del Norte, Co, US 149/J2
Del Puerte (cr.), Ca, US 167/M12
Del Rio, Tx, US 151/D3
Del Valle, Arg. 190/E2
Del Valle (lake), Ca, US 167/L11
Del Vallo Mazara (valley), It. 48/C4
Delacour, Ab, Can. 145/H2
Delacroix, La, US 164/D3
Delafield, Wi, US 167/P13
Delamar (lake), Nv, US 148/E2
Delano, Ca, US 148/C3
Delano, Mn, US 157/N6
Delano (peak), Ut, US 149/F1
Delareyville, SAfr. 124/D2
Delavan (lake), Wi, US 167/P14
Delavan, Il, US 155/K3
Delavan, Wi, US 155/K2
Delavan Lake, Wi, US 167/N14
Delaware (state), US 143/L4
Delaware (bay), US 163/K1
Delaware (riv.), US 161/J4
Delaware (riv.), Ks, US 155/G4
Delaware, NJ, US 168/C2
Delaware, Oh, US 160/E4
Delaware, Ok, US 153/G2
Delaware (co.), Pa, US 168/C4
Delaware (pass), Pa, US 168/C2
Delaware (mts.), Tx, US 151/B2
Delaware City, De, US 168/C4
Delaware Water Gap Nat'l Rec. Area, NJ,Pa, US 161/J4
Delbrück, Ger. 53/F5
Delburne, Ab, Can. 145/H1
Delčevo, FYROM 49/H2
Delcommune (lake), D.R. Congo 121/F5
Delden, Neth. 52/D4
Delebio, It. 61/F5
Delegate, Austl. 133/D3
Delémont, Swi. 60/D3
Delevan NWR, Ca, US 146/B4
Delft, Neth. 52/B4
Delfzijl, Neth. 52/D2
Delgada (pt.), Ca, US 146/A3
Delgada (pt.), Arg. 190/E4
Delgado (cape), Moz. 119/C4
Delgany, Ire. 34/B5
Delger (riv.), Mong. 78/D2
Delgī, Eth. 117/H2
Delhi, Ca, US 148/B2
Delhi, India 98/D5
Delhi, NY, US 161/J3
Delhi (state), India 92/C2
Déli, Chad 116/B3
Delia, Ab, Can. 145/H2
Delice, Turk. 102/C2
Delice (riv.), Turk. 70/E5
Délices, FrG. 182/C1
Delight, Ar, US 153/H3
Delījān, Iran 103/G3
Delingha, China 78/D4
Delisle, Qu, Can. 158/B1
Delisle, Sk, Can. 145/L2
Dell, Mt, US 147/G1
Dell City, Tx, US 151/B2
Dell Rapids, SD, US 155/F2
Delligsen, Ger. 53/G5
Dellwood, Mn, US 157/Q6
Dellys, Alg. 112/G4
Delmar, De, US 163/K1
Delmas, SAfr. 124/Q13
Delmas, Sk, Can. 145/K1
Delme (riv.), Ger. 53/F3
Delmenhorst, Ger. 53/F2
Delmiro Gouveia, Braz. 183/G5
Delmita, Tx, US 151/E4
Delmont, NJ, US 168/D5
Delnice, Cro. 45/L4
Deloraine, Mb, Can. 156/D3
Deloraine, Austl. 132/C4
Delphi, In, US 160/C4
Delphi (Dhelfoí) (ruin), Gre. 49/H3
Delphos, Oh, US 160/D4
Delphos, Ks, US 154/F4
Delportshoop, SAfr. 124/D3
Delran, NJ, US 168/D4
Delray Beach, Fl, US 164/P10
Delson, Qu, Can. 159/N7
Delta (state), Nga. 115/G5
Delta, Co, US 149/H1
Delta, Pa, US 168/B4
Delta, Ut, US 147/G4
Delta City, Ms, US 162/B4
Delta del Tigre, Uru. 191/K11
Delta du Saloum, PN du, Sen. 114/A3
Delta Junction, Ak, US 171/J3
Delta Nat'l Wild. Ref., La, US 164/D3
Delta-Mendota (canal), Ca, US 167/M11
Delton, Mi, US 160/D3
Deltona, Fl, US 165/H3
Delvin, Ire. 32/C2
Delvinë, Alb. 49/G3
Delyatyn, Ukr. 72/C3
Dëma (riv.), Rus. 69/M5
Demak, Indo. 89/E4
Demanda (range), Sp. 46/D1
Demarcation (pt.), Ak, US 171/K2
Demarest, NJ, US 169/K8
Demba, D.R. Congo 121/E4
Dembech'a, Eth. 117/H3
Dembeni, May. 125/H6
Dembī, Eth. 117/H3
Dembī Dolo, Eth. 117/G3
Dembia, CAfr. 116/E4
Demer (riv.), Belg. 42/C3
Demerara (riv.), Guy. 181/G3
Demerara-Mahaica (pol. reg.), Guy. 181/G3
Demerval Lobão, Braz. 183/F4
Deming, NM, US 149/J4
Demini (riv.), Braz. 181/F4
Demirci, Turk. 102/B2
Demirkent, Turk. 102/C2
Demirköy, Turk. 51/H5
Demirtaş, Turk. 51/J5
Demmin, Ger. 40/E5
Democratic Republic of the Congo (ctry.) 107/E5
Demone (valley), It. 48/D4
Demonte, It. 64/D4
Demopolis, Al, US 162/D4
Demotte (De Motte), In, US 160/C4
Dempo (peak), Indo. 89/C4
Dempster (pt.), Austl. 130/D5
Demta, Indo. 91/K4
Demuryne, Ukr. 73/J3
Den Burg, Neth. 52/B2
Den Chai, Thai. 94/C2
Den Ham, Neth. 52/D4
Den Helder, Neth. 52/B3
Den Oever, Neth. 52/C3
Denain, Fr. 54/C3
Denair, Ca, US 148/B2
Denakil (reg.), Eth. 100/D6
Denali National Park and Preserve, Ak, US 171/H3
Denan, Eth. 118/B4
Denbigh, On, Can. 161/H2
Denbigh, Wal, UK 35/E5
Denbighshire (co.), Wal, UK 35/E5
Denby Dale, Eng, UK 35/G4
Dendâra, Mrta. 114/D2
Dender (riv.), Belg. 42/B3
Denderleeuw, Belg. 55/D2
Dendermonde, Belg. 55/D1
Dendron, SAfr. 123/F4
Denekamp, Neth. 52/E4
Deng Xian, China 80/C4
Dengfeng, China 80/C4
Dengjiatang, China 87/G3
Dengkou, China 78/F3
Dêngqên, China 86/B2
Dengta, China 87/G3
Denguéno, CAfr. 116/C4
Denham, Eng, UK 30/B2
Denham (sound), Austl. 130/B3
Denham, Austl. 130/B3
Denholme, Eng, UK 35/G4
Denia, Sp. 47/F3
Deniliquin, Austl. 133/B2
Denio, Nv, US 146/D3
Denison (mt.), Ak, US 171/H4
Denison (dam), Ok, US 153/F4
Denison, Ks, US 155/G4
Denison, Ia, US 155/G2
Denison, Tx, US 153/F4
Denizli, Turk. 102/B2
Denizli (prov.), Turk. 102/B2
Denkendorf, Ger. 59/E5
Denklingen, Ger. 61/G2
Denman, Austl. 132/D2
Denmark (str.), Grld.,Ice. 139/R3
Denmark, Ia, US 155/J3
Denmark, Austl. 130/C5
Denmark (ctry.) 29/E3
Denmark, SC, US 163/G4
Denmark, Wi, US 160/C2
Dennard, Ar, US 153/H3
Dennilton, SAfr. 123/F5
Dennison, Oh, US 160/F4
Dennisville, NJ, US 168/D5
Denny, Sc, UK 33/C4
Denpasar, Indo. 89/F5
Dent de Cons (peak), Fr. 64/C1
Dent de Lys (peak), Swi. 60/C4
Dent d'Hérens (peak), It. 60/D6
Dentergem, Belg. 54/C2
Dentlein am Forst, Ger. 58/D4
Denton, Eng, UK 35/F5
Denton, Eng, UK 37/G5
Denton, Ga, US 165/G2
Denton, Md, US 168/C6
Denton, Mt, US 145/K4
Denton, Tx, US 150/K6
Denton (co.), Tx, US 150/K6
Denton (cr.), Tx, US 151/F1
D'Entrecasteaux (isls.), PNG 136/D5
D'Entrecasteaux (pt.), Austl. 130/B5
Dents du Midi (peak), Swi. 60/C5
Dentsville, SC, US 163/G3
Denver (cap.), Co, US 154/B4
Denver, Ia, US 155/H2
Denver, Pa, US 168/B3
Denver City, Tx, US 152/C4
Denver International (int'l arpt.), Co, US 152/B1
Denville, NJ, US 168/D2
Denzil, Sk, Can. 145/K1
Denzlingen, Ger. 60/D1
Deoband, India 98/D5
Deobhog, India 95/D2
Deoghar, India 97/F3
Deohā (riv.), India 96/B1
Deolāli, India 92/B4
Deoli, India 92/C2
Deoli, India 95/C1
Deolia, India 92/B2
Déols, Fr. 44/D3
Deora, Co, US 152/C2
Deorī, India 96/B4
Deoria, India 96/D2
Dependencias Federales (state), Ven. 181/E1
Depew, Ok, US 153/F3
Depew, NY, US 160/V10
Depoe Bay, Or, US 146/A1
Depok, Indo. 90/C5
Deport, Tx, US 153/G4
Deposit, NY, US 161/J3
Dépôt Lézard, FrG. 182/C1
Dépression de Mourdi (depr.), Chad 116/D1
Deptford (nbrhd.), Eng, UK 30/C2
Deputatskiy, Rus. 75/P3
Deputy, In, US 162/E1
Dêqên, China 86/C2
Deqing, China 80/L9
Dera, D.R. Congo 121/G2
Dera Ghāzi Khān, Pak. 98/A4
Dera Gopipur, India 98/D4
Dera Ismāīl Khān, Pak. 98/A4

Derā Nānak, India 98/C3
Dera Nawāb Sāhib, Pak. 98/A5
Derai, Bang. 97/H3
Deram Shet' (riv), Eth. 118/A3
Derazhnya, Ukr. 72/D3
Derbent, Rus. 71/J4
Derby, Austl. 128/A4
Derby, Eng, UK 35/G6
Derby (co.), Eng, UK 35/G6
Derby, Ct, US 169/E1
Derby, Ks, US 153/F2
Derbyshire (co.), Eng, UK 35/G6
Derdap NP, Yugo. 50/F3
Derdara, Mor. 112/B2
Derdepoort, SAfr. 123/E5
Derecske, Hun. 50/E2
Dereköy, Turk. 51/H5
Dereköy (riv.), Turk. 103/M6
Derendingen, Swi. 60/D3
Deresgē, Eth. 118/A2
Dergachi, Rus. 71/J2
Derhachi, Ukr. 73/J2
Derik, Turk. 102/E2
Derinkuyu, Turk. 102/C2
Derkul, Kaz. 71/J2
Derma, Ms, US 162/C4
Dermott, Ar, US 153/J4
Dernau, Ger. 55/G2
Déroute, Passage de la (Chan), Fr., UK 44/B2
Derravaragh (lake), Ire. 32/C2
Derreen (riv.), Ire. 32/D4
Derrevaragh (lake), Ire. 34/A4
Derry, NH, US 161/L3
Derry, NM, US 149/J4
Derryboy, NI, UK 34/C3
Derrylin, NI, UK 32/C1
Derrynasaggart (mts.), Ire. 32/A6
Dersingham, Eng, UK 37/G1
Derudeb, Sudan 117/H1
Deruta, It. 65/B2
Dervaig, Sc, UK 31/Q8
Derval, Fr. 56/D5
Derventa, Bosn. 50/C3
Dervio, It. 61/F5
Dervock, NI, UK 34/B1
Derwent (riv.), Austl. 132/C4
Derwent, Ab, Can. 145/J1
Derwent (res.), Eng, UK 35/F2
Derwent (riv.), Eng, UK 35/E2
Derwent Bridge, Austl. 132/C4
Derwent Water (lake), Eng, UK 35/E2
Derzhavīnsk, Kaz. 99/A1
Des Allemands, La, US 164/C3
Des Arc, Ar, US 153/J3
Des Arc, Mo, US 162/B2
Des Lacs NWR, ND, US 156/C3
Des Moines (riv.), Ia, Mn, US 143/H3
Des Moines (int'l arpt.), Ia, US 155/H3
Des Moines (cap.), Ia, US 155/H3
Des Moines, Wa, US 144/C4
Des Moines, East Fork (riv.), Ia, US 155/G2
Des Plaines, Il, US 160/C3
Desaguadero, Peru 188/B1
Desaguadero (riv.), Bol. 185/E9
Desagües de los Colorados, Arg. 188/C4
Desagües del Río Salvage, Arg. 188/C4
Desana, It. 62/B3
Desborough, Eng, UK 37/F2
Descabezado Grande (vol.), Chile 190/C2
Descalvado, Braz. 189/H2
Descartes, Fr. 44/D3
Deschutes (riv.), Or, US 146/C1
Deschutes River Recreation Lands, Or, US 146/C1
Desdunes, Haiti 177/H2
Dese (riv.), It. 63/F2
Desē, Eth. 118/A3
Deseado (riv.), Arg. 179/C7
Deseado (cape), Chile 191/B7
Desengaño (pt.), Arg. 191/D6
Desenzano del Garda, It. 62/D3
Deseret Depot, Ut, US 147/G3
Désert (riv.), Qu, Can. 161/H1
Desert (valley), Nv, US 146/D3
Desert (lake), Nv, US 148/E2
Desert Center, Ca, US 148/E4
Desert Hot Springs, Ca, US 148/D4
Désertines, Fr. 44/E3
Deshengpu, China 80/B4
Deshler, Oh, US 160/E4
Desiderio Tello, Arg. 188/C4
Desio, It. 62/C2
Desloge, Mo, US 162/B2
Desna (riv.), Rus. 69/W9
Desolación (isl.), Chile 191/B7
Desolation (pt.), Phil. 88/D3
Desoto, Tx, US 150/L7
Desoto Nat'l Wild.Ref., Ne, US 155/F3
Despatch, SAfr. 124/D4
Déssa, Niger 115/F3
Dessau, Ger. 42/G3
Dessel, Belg. 52/C6
Dessoubre (riv.), Fr. 60/C3
Destelbergen, Belg. 54/C1
Destêrro, Braz. 183/G4
Destin, Fl, US 164/E2
Destruction Bay, Can. 171/L3
Desulo, It. 48/A2
Desvres, Fr. 54/A2
Det Udom, Thai. 94/D3
Deta, Rom. 50/E3
Dete, Zim. 123/E3
Detern, Ger. 53/E2
Detmold, Ger. 53/F5
Detour (pt.), Mi, US 160/C2
Detrital Wash (riv.), Az, US 148/E3
Detroit (riv.), Can.,US 167/F7
Detroit, Mi, US 160/E3
Detroit, Or, US 146/B1
Detroit (dam), Or, US 146/B1
Detroit (lake), Or, US 146/B1
Detroit, Tx, US 153/G4
Detroit City (arpt.), Mi, US 167/G7
Detroit Lakes, Mn, US 156/G4
Detroit Metropolitan Wayne County (int'l arpt.), Mi, US 160/E3
Dettelbach, Ger. 58/D3
Dettifoss (falls), Ice. 38/P6
Dettwiller, Fr. 55/G6
Deua NP, Austl. 133/D2
Deuil-la-Barre, Fr. 30/J5
Deûle (riv.), Fr. 54/B2
Deurne, Belg. 52/B6
Deurne, Neth. 52/C6
Deurne (Antwerp) (int'l arpt.), Belg. 52/B6
Deustua, Peru 184/D4
Deutsch Evern, Ger. 53/H2
Deutsch Wagram, Aus. 51/P7
Deutschkreutz, Aus. 50/C2
Deutschlandsberg, Aus. 50/B2
Deux-Montagnes, Qu, Can. 159/N6
Deux-Montagnes (lake), Qu, Can. 159/M7
Deux-Montagnes (co.), Qu, Can. 159/M6
Deva, Rom. 50/F3
Dévaványa, Hun. 50/E2
Develi, Turk. 102/C2
Deventer, Neth. 52/D4
Deveron (riv.), Sc, UK 33/D2
Devil River (peak), NZ 135/C3
Devil's Playground (des.), Ca, US 148/E3
Deville, Fr. 55/D4
Deville, La, US 164/B2
Devil's (isl.), FrG. 182/C1
Devils (riv.), Mex. 175/E2
Devil's (pt.), SrL. 95/D4
Devils (lake), ND, US 156/E3
Devils (riv.), Tx, US 151/D3
Devil's Elbow (pass), Sc, UK 33/C3
Devil's Garden, Ut, US 149/H1
Devils Lake, ND, US 156/E3
Devils Paw (mt.), Ak, US 171/M4
Devils Postpile Nat'l Mon., Ca, US 148/C2
Devils Tower Nat'l Mon., Wy, US 154/B1
Devilsbit (peak), Ire. 32/C4
Devin, Bul. 49/J2
Devine, Tx, US 151/E3
Devizes, Eng, UK 36/E4
Devnya, Bul. 51/H4
Devola, Oh, US 160/F5
Devoll (riv.), Alb. 67/J2
Devoll (riv.), Alb.,Gre. 50/E5
Devon, Ab, Can. 145/H1
Devon (isl.), Nun, Can. 141/H1
Devon (isl.), Can. 139/J2
Devon (riv.), Sc, UK 33/C4
Devon (co.), Eng, UK 36/C5
Devon-Berwyn, Pa, US 168/C3
Devonport, Austl. 132/C4
Devonport, NZ 135/F6
Devore, Ca, US 166/C2
Devoto, Arg. 188/D4
Devoys (peak), NM, US 152/C2
Devrek (riv.), Turk. 70/D4
Devrek, Turk. 70/D4
Devrez (riv.), Turk. 70/E4
Devure (riv.), Zim. 123/F3
Dewa (pt.), Indo. 89/A2
Dewa (mts.), Japan 82/B4
Dewar, Ok, US 153/G3
Dewās, India 92/C3
Dewberry, Ab, Can. 145/J1
Dewetsdorp, SAfr. 124/D3
Dewey, Ok, US 153/G2
Dewey, Az, US 149/F3
Deweyville, Tx, US 151/H2
Dewsbury, Eng, UK 35/G4
Dexter, Ks, US 153/F2
Dexter, NM, US 152/B4
Dexter, Mo, US 162/C2
Dexter, Ga, US 163/F4
Dey-Dey (lake), Austl. 127/C3
Deyang, China 86/E2
Deyhūk, Iran 103/J3
Deyyer, Iran 103/G5
Dez (riv.), Iran 74/E6
Dezfūl, Iran 103/G3
Dezhneva (cape), Rus. 142/W12
Dezhou, China 80/D3
Dhābān, India 98/C5
Dhabān Singh, Pak. 98/B4
Dhāding, Nepal 97/E2
Dhahab, Egypt 109/G2
Dhahabān, SAr. 100/C4
Dhahran (int'l arpt.), SAr. 100/F3
Dhahran, SAr. 100/D5
Dhākā (pol. div.), Bang. 97/G4
Dhāka, India 97/E2
Dhākā (pol. reg.), Bang. 97/H4
Dhākā (Dacca) (cap.), Bang. 97/H4
Dhaleswari (riv.), Bang. 97/H4
Dhali, Cyp. 104/C2
Dhamār, Yem. 118/C2
Dhāmpur, India 96/B1
Dhamtari, India 95/D1
Dhanaula, India 98/C4
Dhanaura, India 96/B1
Dhānbād, India 97/F4
Dhangadhī, Nepal 96/C1
Dhankutā, Nepal 97/F2
Dhār, India 92/C3
Dhar de Chinguetti (cliff), Mrta. 110/B5
Dhār Khurd, India 98/C3
Dhar Néma (cliff), Mrta. 114/D2
Dhar Oualâta (cliff), Mrta. 114/D2
Dhar Tîchît (cliff), Mrta. 114/C2
Dharampur, India 92/B3
Dharān, Nepal 97/F2
Dharchula, Nepal 96/C1
Dhāri, India 101/K4
Dhārīwāl, India 98/C4
Dharmapuri, India 95/C3
Dharmavaram, India 95/C3
Dharmjaygarh, India 96/D4
Dharmkot, India 98/C4
Dharmsāla, India 98/D3
Dhasan (riv.), India 96/B3
Dhaulāgiri (zone), Nepal 96/D1
Dhaulāgiri (peak), Nepal 96/D1
Dhaura, India 96/B3
Dhaurahra, India 96/C1
Dhekiajuli, India 86/B3
Dhelfoí, Gre. 49/H3
Dhelfoí (Delphi) (ruin), Gre. 49/H3
Dhelvinákion, Gre. 49/G3
Dheskáti, Gre. 49/G3
Dheune (riv.), Fr. 60/A4
Dhī Qār (gov.), Iraq 103/F4
Dhībān, Jor. 105/D5
Dhidhimótikhon, Gre. 51/H5
Dhiinsoor, Som. 119/C1
Dhíkaia, Gre. 51/H5
Dhílos (ruin), Gre. 49/J4
Dhimitsána, Gre. 49/H4
Dhírfis (peak), Gre. 49/H3
Dhístomon, Gre. 49/H3
Dhlo Dhlo (ruin), Zim. 123/F3
Dhofar (reg.), Oman 100/F5
Dhokímion, Gre. 49/G3
Dholipal, India 98/C5
Dholka, India 101/K4
Dholpur, India 96/A2
Dhomokós, Gre. 49/H3
Dhonoúsa (isl.), Gre. 49/J4
Dhorāji, India 101/K4
Dhorpātan, Nepal 96/D1
Dhoxáton, Gre. 49/J2
Dhronbach (riv.), Ger. 55/F4
Dhubāb, Yem. 118/B2
Dhubri, India 97/G2
Dhuizon, Fr. 57/G5
Dhūlia, India 95/B1
Dhuliān, Pak. 98/B3
Dhuliān, India 97/F3
Dhulikhel, Nepal 97/E2
Dhungrebās, Nepal 97/E2
Dhupgāri, India 97/G2
Dhūri, India 98/C4
Dhuudo, Som. 118/D3
Dhuudo (riv.), Som. 118/D3
Dhuusamarreeb (Dusa Marreb), Som. 118/C4
Di Linh, Viet. 94/E4
Dia (isl.), Gre. 49/J5
Diablo (mt.), Ak, US 171/H4
Diablo (range), Ca, US 148/B2
Diablo (mtn.), Tx, US 151/B2
Diablo, Punta del (pt.), Uru. 191/G2
Diablotin (peak), Dom. 173/N9
Diadema, Braz. 187/K8
Diadema Argentina, Arg. 190/D5
Diaganiao, Sen. 114/A3
Diagonal, Ia, US 155/G3
Diaguitas, Chile 188/B4
Dialakoto, Sen. 114/B3
Diamante (riv.), Arg. 190/D2
Diamante, Arg. 188/D5
Diamantina, Braz. 187/E3
Diamantina (riv.), Austl. 127/D3
Diamantina Lakes, Austl. 134/A3
Diamantina, Chapada (hills), Braz. 187/E1
Diamantino, Braz. 185/G4
Diamond (cr.), Austl. 132/G5
Diamond (peak), Id, US 147/G1
Diamond, Or, US 146/D2
Diamond (peak), Or, US 146/B2
Diamond Bar, Ca, US 166/G8
Diamond Harbour, India 97/G4
Diamond Springs, Ca, US 146/C4
Dian (lake), China 86/D3
Dianalund, Den. 40/D4
Dianbai, China 87/F4
Diancang (mtn.), China 86/D3
Dianjiang, China 87/E2
Diano Marina, It. 62/B6
Dianópolis, Braz. 186/D1
Dianshan (lake), China 80/L8
Diapaga, Burk. 115/F3
Diaroumé, Sen. 114/B3
Dias Creek, NJ, US 168/D5
Diavolezza (peak), Swi. 61/F5
Diaz, Ar, US 153/J3
Dibai, India 96/B1
Dibaya, D.R. Congo 121/E4
Dibaya-Lubwe, D.R. Congo 120/D4
Dibbin NP, Jor. 105/D4
Dibella (well), Niger 116/B1
Dibeng, SAfr. 124/C2
Dibiāpur, India 96/B2
Dībīlē, Eth. 118/B3
Diboll, Tx, US 150/G2
Dibrugarh, India 86/B3
Dibs, Iraq 103/F3
Dickens, Tx, US 152/D4
Dickens (pt.), RI, US 169/G1
Dickinson, ND, US 156/C4
Dickinson, Tx, US 151/M9
Dickinson Bayou (riv.), Tx, US 151/M9
Dickinson Center, NY, US 161/J2
Dickson, Ab, Can. 144/G1
Dickson, Ok, US 153/F3
Dickson, Tn, US 162/D2
Dicle (dam), Turk. 102/E2
Dicomano, It. 63/E6
Didam, Neth. 52/D5
Didcot, Eng, UK 37/E3
Didhav, Eth. 118/B2
Didiéni, Mali 114/C3
Didig Sala, Eth. 118/A2
Didinga (hills), Sudan 117/G4
Didsbury, Ab, Can. 145/G2
Dīdwāna, India 101/K3
Didyma (ruin), Turk. 102/A2
Die, Fr. 64/B3
Die Berg (peak), SAfr. 123/F5
Dieblich, Ger. 55/G3
Diébougou, Burk. 114/E4
Dieburg, Ger. 58/B3
Diedersdorf, Ger. 42/Q7
Diefenbaker (lake), Sk, Can. 140/F3
Diefenbaker (lake), Sk, Can. 145/L2
Diego de Almagro (isl.), Chile 191/B6
Diego de Almagro, Chile 188/B3
Diego Garcia (isl.), UK 77/G10
Diekirch, Lux. 55/F4
Diekirch (dist.), Lux. 55/E4
Diéma, Mali 114/C3
Diemen, Neth. 52/B4
Diemtigen, Swi. 60/D4
Dien Bien, Viet. 86/D4
Dien Chau, Viet. 94/D2
Dien Khanh, Viet. 94/E3
Dieng (ruin), Indo. 89/E4
Diepenbeek, Belg. 55/E2
Diepenveen, Neth. 52/D4
Diepholz, Ger. 53/F3
Diepoldsau, Swi. 61/F3
Dieppe, Fr. 57/G1
Dieppe, NB, Can. 158/E2
Dierdorf, Ger. 55/G2
Dieren, Neth. 52/D4
Dierks, Ar, US 153/G3
Diespeck, Ger. 58/D3
Diessen am Ammersee, Ger. 61/H2
Diest, Belg. 55/E2
Dietenheim, Ger. 61/G1
Dietenhofen, Ger. 58/D4
Dieterich, Il, US 162/C1
Dietersheim, Ger. 58/D3
Dietfurt an der Altmühl, Ger. 59/E4
Dietikon, Swi. 61/E3
Dietmannsried, Ger. 61/G2
Dietzenbach, Ger. 58/B2
Dieue-sur-Meuse, Fr. 55/E5
Dieulefit, Fr. 64/B3
Dieulouard, Fr. 55/F6
Dieuze, Fr. 55/F6
Dieveniškės, Lith. 41/L4
Diever, Neth. 52/D3
Diez, Ger. 58/B2
Dif, Kenya 119/C1
Diffa, Niger 116/B2
Diffa (dept.), Niger 116/B2
Differdange, Lux. 55/E4
Difficult (mt.), Austl. 132/B3
Dīg, India 96/A2
Digba, D.R. Congo 117/E4
Digboi, India 86/B3
Digby, NS, Can. 158/E3
Digby Neck (pen), Ns, Can. 158/D3
Diggers Rest, Austl. 133/B3
Dighem, Sudan 117/G2
Dighton, Ks, US 152/D1
Dighwāra, India 97/E3
Dīglūr, India 95/C2
Digne-les-Bains, Fr. 64/C4
Digoin, Fr. 44/E3
Digor, Turk. 103/E1
Digos, Phil. 88/D4
Digul (riv.), Indo. 91/K4
Digya NP, Gha. 115/E5
Dihang (riv.), India 86/B2
Dihun, Eth. 118/B4
Dijon, Fr. 60/A3
Dik, Chad 116/C3
Dikhil, Djib. 118/B3
Dikirnis, Egypt 113/C2
Diklosmta (peak), Geo. 71/H4
Diksmuide, Belg. 54/B1
Dikson, Rus. 74/J2
Diktel, Nepal 97/F2
Dikwa, Nga. 116/B2
Dīla, Eth. 118/A4
Dilbeek, Belg. 55/D2
Dilek Yarımadası NP, Turk. 102/A2
Dili (cap.), ETim. 128/B2
Dilijan, Arm. 71/H4
Dilkon, Az, US 149/G3
Dillenburg, Ger. 55/H2
Diller, Ne, US 155/F3
Dilley, Tx, US 151/E3
Dillia (riv.), Niger 116/A2
Dillikot, Nepal 96/C1
Dilling, Sudan 117/F2
Dillingen, Ger. 55/F5
Dillingen an der Donau, Ger. 58/D5
Dillingham, Ak, US 171/G4
Dillnås, Swe. 39/A1
Dillon, Mt, US 147/G1
Dillon, SC, US 163/H3
Dillon Cone (peak), NZ 135/C3
Dillonvale, Oh, US 160/F4
Dillsboro, In, US 162/E1
Dillsburg, Pa, US 168/A3
Dilolo, D.R. Congo 121/E5
Dilsen, Belg. 55/E1
Dimako, Camr. 116/B4
Dimāpur, India 86/B3
Dimaro, It. 61/G5
Dimas, Mex. 174/D4
Dimashq (prov.), Syria 105/E1
Dimashq (Damascus) (cap.), Syria 105/E1
Dimataling, Phil. 88/C4
Dimbaza, SAfr. 124/D4
Dimbelenge, D.R. Congo 121/E4
Dimbokro, C.d'Iv. 114/D5
Dimboola, Austl. 132/B3
Dîmboviţa (prov.), Rom. 51/G3
Dîmboviţa (riv.), Rom. 72/C5
Dimbulah, Austl. 134/B2
Dime Box, Tx, US 151/F2
Dimitriya Lapteva (str.), Rus. 75/P2
Dimitrovgrad, Rus. 71/J1
Dimitrovgrad, Yugo. 51/F4
Dimitrovgrad, Bul. 51/G4
Dimlang (peak), Nga. 116/A3
Dimmitt, Tx, US 152/C3
Dimock, SD, US 154/F2
Dimovo, Bul. 51/F4
Dina, Pak. 98/B3
Dinach, Som. 118/D3
Dinagat, Phil. 88/D3
Dinagat (isl.), Phil. 91/G1
Dinājpur (pol. reg.), Bang. 97/G3
Dinājpur, Bang. 97/G3
Dinan, Fr. 56/C4
Dīnānagar, India 98/C3
Dinant, Belg. 55/D3
Dinar, Turk. 102/B2
Dinard, Fr. 56/C3
Dinaric Alps (mts.), Cro. 50/C3
Dinas (pt.), Wal, UK 36/B2
Dinas Powys, Wal, UK 36/C4
Dinder NP, Sudan 117/G2
Dinder Wenz (riv.), Eth. 117/G2
Dindima, Nga. 115/H4
Dindori, India 96/C4
Dinga, Pak. 98/B3
Ding'an, China 87/F5
Dingbian, China 78/F4
Dingelstädt, Ger. 53/H6
Dinggyê, China 97/F1
Dingjiang, China 87/G3
Dingjiasuo, China 79/J5
Dingle, Ire. 30/F10
Dingle (bay), Ire. 30/N10
Dingle, Id, US 147/H2
Dingmans Ferry, Pa, US 168/D1
Dingolfing, Ger. 59/F5
Dingras, Phil. 88/C1
Dingshuzhen, China 80/K8
Dingtao, China 80/C4
Dinguiraye, Gui. 114/C4
Dingwall, Sc, UK 33/B1
Dingwall, NS, Can. 159/G2
Dingxi, China 78/E4
Dingxiang, China 80/C3
Dingxing, China 80/G7
Dingyuan, China 80/D4
Dinh Lap, Viet. 94/D1
Dinkel (riv.), Ger. 53/E4
Dinkelsbühl, Ger. 58/D4
Dinkelscherben, Ger. 58/D6
Dinklage, Ger. 53/F3
Dinnebito Wash (riv.), Az, US 149/G2
Dinner (pt.), Fl, US 164/K7
Dinnington, Eng, UK 35/G1
Dinokana, SAfr. 122/E5
Dinosaur, Co, US 147/J3
Dinosaur Nat'l Monument, Co, US 147/J3
Dinslaken, Ger. 52/D5
Dinsmore, Sk, Can. 145/L2
Dintel Mark (riv.), Neth. 52/B5
Dintenloord, Neth. 52/B5
Dintiteladas, Indo. 89/D4
Dinuba, Ca, US 148/C2
Dinwiddie, Va, US 163/J2
Dinxperlo, Neth. 52/D5
Dioïla, Mali 114/D3
Diomandou, Gui. 114/C4
Dion (riv.), Gui. 114/C4
Dionysias (ruin), Egypt 113/B6
Diósd, Hun. 51/Q10
Diouloulou, Sen. 114/A3
Dioundiou, Niger 115/F3
Diourbel (pol. reg.), Sen. 114/A3
Diourbel, Sen. 114/A3
Dīpālpur, Pak. 98/B4
Diphu, India 86/B3
Diphu (pass), India 86/C2
Diplo, Pak. 101/J4
Dipni (dam), Turk. 102/E2
Dipolog, Phil. 88/C3
Dipperu NP, Austl. 134/C3
Dipperz, Ger. 58/C1
Dique (canal), Col. 177/H4
Dīr, Pak. 98/A2
Dira (well), Chad 116/B2
Dirang Dzong, India 97/J2
Diré, Mali 114/E2
Dirē Dawa, Eth. 118/B3
Direct, Tx, US 153/G4
Direction (cape), Austl. 129/F3
Diriamba, Nic. 176/E4
Dirico, Ang. 122/D3
Dirj, Libya 111/H3
Dirk Hartog (isl.), Austl. 127/A3
Dirkou, Niger 108/B5
Dirksland, Neth. 52/B5
Dirlewang, Ger. 61/G2
Dirranbandi, Austl. 134/C5
Dirrington Great Law (hill), Sc, UK 33/D5
Ḍirs, SAr. 100/D5
Dirty Devil (riv.), Ut, US 147/H4
Disappointment (lake), Austl. 127/B3
Disappointment (isls.), FrPol. 137/L6
Disappointment (cape), Wa, US 144/B4
Disaster (bay), Austl. 133/D3
Discovery (bay), Austl. 132/B3
Discovery Bay, Jam. 177/G2
Disentis-Mustér, Swi. 61/E4
Disgrazi (peak), It. 61/F5
Dishman, Wa, US 144/F4
Dishnā, Egypt 109/G3
Disko (isl.), Grld. 139/M3
Disko (Qeqertarsuaq) (isl.), Grld. 141/L2
Disley, Eng, UK 35/F5
Dismal (riv.), Ne, US 154/D3
Disna, Bela. 41/N4
Disney, Ok, US 153/G2
Disney Studios, Fl, US 164/M7
Disneyland, Ca, US 166/G8
Dison, Belg. 55/E2
Dispur, India 93/F2
Disraëli, Qu, Can. 158/B3
Diss, Eng, UK 37/H2
Dissen am Teutoburger Wald, Ger. 53/F4
Distington, Eng, UK 34/E2
Distrito Especial (cap. dist.), Col. 183/L8
Distrito Federal (fed. dist.), Braz. 186/D2
Distrito Federal (fed. dist.), Col. 180/C3
Distrito Federal (fed. dist.), Mex. 172/A5
Distrito Federal (fed. dist.), Ven. 181/E2
Disūq, Egypt 113/B2
Ditang, China 80/L9
Ditchling Beacon (hill), Eng, UK 37/F5
Dittaino (riv.), It. 48/D4
Dittelbrunn, Ger. 58/D2
Ditton, Eng, UK 30/E3
Ditzingen, Ger. 58/C5
Diu, India 92/B3
Diuata (mts.), Phil. 88/D3
Diva (riv.), Yugo. 50/D4
Dīvān Darreh, Iran 103/F3
Divatte (riv.), Fr. 56/D6
Dive (riv.), Fr. 44/D3
Divénié, Congo 120/C3
Dives (riv.), Fr. 57/E2
Dives-sur-Mer, Fr. 57/E2
Divette (riv.), Fr. 56/D1
Divide, Co, US 152/B1
Divide, Mt, US 147/G1
Dividing Creek, NJ, US 168/C5
Divinolândia, Braz. 187/K6
Divinópolis, Braz. 186/D4
Divisa Nova, Braz. 187/K6
Divisões, Serra das (mts.), Braz. 186/C3
Divisor, Serra do (mts.), Braz.,Peru 184/C2
Divnogorsk, Rus. 74/K4
Divnoye, Rus. 71/G3
Divo, C.d'Iv. 114/D5
Divonne-les-Bains, Fr. 60/C5
Divriği, Turk. 102/D2
Divuma, D.R. Congo 121/E5
Dix (lake), Swi. 60/D5
Dixcove, Gha. 115/E5
Dixfield, Me, US 161/L2
Dixie, Ga, US 165/G2
Dixie, Al, US 164/E2
Dixie, Id, US 146/F1
Dixie, Wa, US 144/E4
Dixmoor, Il, US 167/Q16
Dixon, Ca, US 146/C4
Dixon, Ky, US 162/D2
Dixon, Il, US 155/K3
Dixon, Mt, US 144/G4
Dixon, NM, US 152/B2
Dixon, Mo, US 153/H2
Dixcn, Wy, US 147/K3
Dixon Entrance (chan.), Can.,US 139/D4
Diyadin, Turk. 103/E2
Diyāla (gov.), Iraq 103/F3
Diyarb Najm, Egypt 113/C3
Diyarbakır, Turk. 102/E2
Diyarbakir (prov.), Turk. 102/E2
Dizangué, Camr. 120/B2
Dja (riv.), Camr. 116/B5
Djado, Niger 108/B4
Djado (plat.), Niger 107/D2
Djakotomé, Ben. 115/F5
Djamaa, Alg. 111/G2
Djamba, D.R. Congo 121/F2
Djambala, Congo 120/C3
Djamu, D.R. Congo 121/G2
Djanet, Alg. 111/H4
Djebel Tichka (peak), Mor. 110/C3
Djebel-Amrag (mtn.), Alg. 112/D3
Djébrène, Chad 116/C3
Djédaa, Chad 116/C2
Djedi, Oued (riv.), Alg. 111/G2
Djelfa, Alg. 66/D4
Djema, CAfr. 117/E4
Djemila (ruin), Alg. 112/H4
Djénné, Mali 114/D3
Djerem (riv.), Camr. 116/B4
Djermaya, Chad 116/B2
Djibo, Burk. 115/E3
Djibouti (cap.), Djib. 118/B3
Djibouti (ctry.) 107/G3
Djiguéni, Mrta. 114/C3
Djiouce (mtn.), Ire. 32/D3
Djiroutou, C.d'Iv. 114/D5
Djohong, Camr. 116/B4
Djouab (riv.), Congo 120/C2
Djoué (riv.), Congo 120/C3
Djougou, Ben. 115/F4
Djoum, Camr. 120/C2
Djugu, D.R. Congo 121/G2
Djúpivogur, Ice. 38/P7
Djurö, Swe. 39/B1
D'Lo, Ms, US 164/D2
Dmanisi, Geo. 71/H4
Dmitriyev-L'govskiy, Rus. 73/H1
Dmitriyevskiy, Kaz. 71/L2
Dmytrivka, Ukr. 73/G2
Dnepr (riv.), Rus. 74/D4
Dnestrovsc, Mol. 72/E4
Dnieper (lowland), Ukr. 72/F2
Dnieper (upland), Ukr. 72/E3
Dnipro (riv.), Ukr. 29/H3
Dniprodzerzhyns'ke Vodoskhovyshche (res.), Ukr. 73/H3
Dniprodzerzhyns'k, Ukr. 73/H3
Dnipropetrovs'k, Ukr. 73/H3
Dnipropetrovs'ka Oblast (Ukr. 70/E2
Dniprorudne, Ukr. 73/H4
Dniprovs'kyy Lyman (estu.), Ukr. 51/K2
Dnister (riv.), Eur. 74/C5
Dnister (riv.), Ukr. 42/M4
Dnistrovs'kyy Lyman (estu.), Ukr. 51/K2
Dno, Rus. 41/N3
Dnyapro (riv.), Bela. 41/P4
Do (lake), Mali 115/E3
Do (riv.), China 78/D5
Do Gonbadān, Iran 103/G4
Do Luong, Viet. 94/D2
Do Rāh (pass), Afg. 101/K1
Do Son, Viet. 94/D1
Doa, Moz. 123/G3
Doaktown, NB, Can. 158/D2
Doany, Madg. 125/J6
Doba, Chad 116/C3
Dobbins (A.F.B.), Ga, US 163/L7
Dobbs Ferry, NY, US 169/K7
Dobbyn, Austl. 129/F4
Dobele, Lat. 41/K3
Döbeln, Ger. 42/G3
Doberai (pen.), Indo. 91/H4
Dobiegniew, Pol. 43/H2
Dobo, Indo. 128/D1
Dobogo-kó (peak), Hun. 51/Q9
Doboj, Bosn. 50/D3
Dobřany, Czh. 59/G3
Dobre Miasto, Pol. 41/J5
Dobrich, Bul. 51/H4
Dobrinka, Rus. 71/G1
Dobrinka, Rus. 73/L1
Dobříš, Czh. 59/H3
Dobromyl', Ukr. 43/M4
Dobropillya, Ukr. 73/J3
Dobrovnik, Slov. 50/C2
Dobruja (reg.), Bul.,Rom. 67/K2
Dobrush, Bela. 70/D1
Dobryanka, Rus. 69/N4
Dobryanka, Ukr. 72/F1
Dobson, NC, US 163/G2
Dobzha, China 97/G1
Doce (riv.), Braz. 187/E3
Dochart (riv.), Sc, UK 33/B4
Dock Junction, Ga, US 165/H2
Docker River, Austl. 131/F3
Docking, Eng, UK 37/G1
Doctor Arroyo, Mex. 175/E4
Doctor Cecilio Báez, Par. 189/E3
Doctor Coss, Mex. 151/E5
Doctor González, Mex. 151/E5
Doctor Pedro P. Peña, Par. 188/D2
Doctor Petru Groza, Rom. 50/F2
Dod Ballāpur, India 95/C3
Doda (riv.), India 98/D3
Doda, India 98/C3
Doda Betta (peak), India 95/C4
Dodder (riv.), Ire. 34/B5
Doddinghurst, Eng, UK 30/D2
Dodge, Tx, US 151/G2
Dodge City, Ks, US 152/D2
Dodger Stadium, Ca, US 166/F7
Dodgeville, Wi, US 155/J2
Dodman (pt.), Eng, UK 36/B6
Dodola, Eth. 118/A4
Dodoma (prov.), Tanz. 119/A3
Dodoma, Tanz. 119/A3
Dodori Nat'l Rsv., Kenya 119/C2
Dodsland, Sk, Can. 145/K2
Dodson, La, US 164/B1
Dodson, Mt, US 145/K3
Dodwekon, Libr. 114/C5
Dodworth, Eng, UK 35/G4
Doe Run, Mo, US 162/B2
Doel, Belg. 52/B6
Doerun, Ga, US 165/G2
Doesburg, Neth. 52/D4
Doetinchem, Neth. 52/D5
Dofa, Indo. 91/G4
Dog (lake), Mb, Can. 156/E2
Dog (isl.), Fl, US 165/F3
Dog (riv.), BC, Can. 144/C2
Dogai Coring (lake), China 99/E5
Dogana, SMar. 63/F6
Doğanhisar, Turk. 102/B2
Doğankent (riv.), Turk. 70/F4
Doğanşar, Turk. 102/D1
Doğanşehir, Turk. 102/D2
Doğanyurt, Turk. 70/E4
Döğer, Turk. 102/B2
Dogliani, It. 62/A3
Dōgo (isl.), Japan 79/L4
Dogondoutchi, Niger 115/G3
Doğubayazıt, Turk. 103/F2
Doğukaradeniz (mts.), Turk. 102/D1
Doha (int'l arpt.), Qatar 100/F3
Doha (Ad Dawḩah) (cap.), Qatar 100/F3
Dohad, India 92/B3
Dohrīghāt, India 96/D2
Doi Inthanon NP, Thai. 86/C5
Doi Khun Tan NP, Thai. 94/B2
Doi Suthep-Pui NP, Thai. 86/C5
Doimara, India 86/B3
Doiras (res.), Sp. 46/B1
Dois Córregos, Braz. 189/G2
Dois de Julho (int'l arpt.), Braz. 187/F2
Dois Irmãos do Tocantins, Braz. 182/D5
Dois Irmãos, Serra (mts.), Braz. 183/F5
Dois Vizinhos, Braz. 189/F3
Doische, Belg. 55/D3
Doka, Sudan 117/G2
Dokka, Nor. 40/D1
Dokkum, Neth. 52/D2
Dokkumer Ee (riv.), Neth. 52/C2
Dokshitsy, Bela. 41/M4
Doksy, Czh. 59/H1
Dokuchayevs'k, Ukr. 73/J4
Dol-de-Bretagne, Fr. 56/D3
Dolan Springs, Az, US 148/E3
Dolbeau, Qu, Can. 158/A1
Dolcedorme (peak), It. 48/E3
Dole, Fr. 60/B3
Dolent (peak), Swi. 60/D6
Dolgellau, Wal, UK 36/C1
Dolgoprudnyy, Rus. 69/W9
Doli, India 92/B2
Dolianova, It. 48/A3
Dolinsk, Rus. 79/N2
Dolinskoye, Ukr. 72/E4
Dolj (prov.), Rom. 51/F3
Dollar, Sc, UK 33/C4
Dollar Bay, Mi, US 157/K4
Dollar Law (peak), Sc, UK 33/C5
Dollard, Sk, Can. 145/K3
Dollard (Dollart) (bay), Neth.,Ger. 53/E2
Dollard-des-Ormeaux, Qu, Can. 159/N7
Dollart (Dollard) (bay), Neth.,Ger. 53/E2
Dollarville, Mi, US 160/D1
Doller (riv.), Fr. 42/D5
Dollnstein, Ger. 58/E5
Dolmance Palace, Turk. 103/M6
Dolmar (peak), Ger. 58/D1
Dolmen (ruin), It. 48/E2
Dolna Banya, Bul. 51/F4
Dolni Dŭbnik, Bul. 51/G4
Dolní Kounice, Czh. 45/M2
Dolnośląskie (prov.), Pol. 43/J3
Dolo (riv.), It. 62/D4
Dolo, It. 63/F3
Dolo, Eth. 118/B4
Dolo, Indo. 91/E4
Dolo Odo, Eth. 118/B4
Dolobli, Libr. 114/C5
Dolomieu, Fr. 64/B1
Dolomite Alps (mts.), It. 67/F1
Dolon (riv.), Fr. 64/A2
Doloon, Mong. 78/F3
Dolores, Arg. 190/F3
Dolores, Bol. 184/D3
Dolores, Guat. 176/D2
Dolores, Phil. 88/D2
Dolores, Uru. 191/J10
Dolores, Co, US 149/H2
Dolores (riv.), Co, US 147/J4
Dolores, Ven. 180/D2
Dolphin (pt.), Namb. 122/B5
Dolphin (cape), UK 191/F6
Dolphin and Union (str.), Nun, Can. 140/E2
Dolphinholme, Eng, UK 35/F4
Dölsach, Aus. 45/K3
Dolton, Il, US 167/Q16
Dolyna, Ukr. 72/C3
Dolyns'ka, Ukr. 73/G3
Dolzhanskaya, Rus. 73/J4
Dom (peak), Indo. 91/J4
Dom (peak), Swi. 60/D5
Dom Aquino, Braz. 186/B2
Dom Carlos (pt.), Moz. 123/G4
Dom Noi (res.), Thai. 94/D3
Dom Pedrito, Braz. 189/F4
Doma, Zim. 123/F3
Domanivka, Ukr. 72/F4
Domār, Bang. 97/G2
Domariāganj, India 96/D2
Domasi, Malw. 123/G2
Domat-Ems, Swi. 61/F4
Domažlice, Czh. 59/F4
Dombarovskiy, Rus. 71/L2
Dombasle-sur-Meurthe, Fr. 55/F6
Dombay-Ul'gen (peak), Geo. 71/G4
Dombe Grande, Ang. 122/B2
Dombes (lake), Fr. 60/B5
Dombey (cape), Austl. 128/C3
Domboshawa, Zim. 123/F3
Dombóvár, Hun. 50/D2
Dombrád, Hun. 50/E1
Domburg, Sur. 182/C1
Domburg, Neth. 52/A5
Domchānch, India 97/E3
Dome, Az, US 148/E4
Dome (peak), Az, US 149/F2
Dome C, US, Ant. 192/J
Dôme de Barrot (peak), Fr. 64/C4
Dôme de l'Arpont (peak), Fr. 64/C2
Domène, Fr. 64/B2
Domérat, Fr. 44/E3
Domeyko, Chile 188/B4
Domfront, Fr. 57/E3
Domínguez, Arg. 188/E4
Dominica (ctry.) 139/L8
Dominica Passage (chan.), Dom.,Guad. 173/N9
Dominican Republic (ctry.) 139/K8
Dominion, NS, Can. 159/G2
Domiongo, D.R. Congo 121/E4
Dommartin-lès-Remiremont, Fr. 60/C2
Dommartin-lès-Toul, Fr. 55/E6
Dommati, India 97/H3
Dommel (riv.), Belg. 55/E1
Domo, Eth. 118/C4
Domodedovo, Rus. 69/W9
Domodedovo (int'l arpt.), Rus. 69/W9
Domodossola, It. 61/E5
Domohāni, India 97/G2
Domoni, Com. 125/H6
Domont, Fr. 30/J4
Dompu, Indo. 91/E5
Domremy, Sk, Can. 145/M1
Domrémy-la-Pucelle, Fr. 60/B1
Dömsöd, Hun. 50/D2
Domusnovas, It. 48/A3
Domuyo (vol.), Arg. 190/C3
Domvilk (mt.), Austl. 134/C5
Domžale, Slov. 45/L3
Don (cape), Austl. 128/C2
Don (riv.), Eng, UK 35/G5
Don (riv.), Sc, UK 33/D2
Don (ridge), Rus. 74/E5
Don (riv.), Rus. 29/J4
Don Benito, Sp. 46/C3
Don Pedro (res.), Ca, US 148/B2
Dona Ana, Moz. 123/G3
Donabate, Ire. 34/B5
Donada, It. 63/F3
Donaghadee, NI, UK 34/C2
Donaghmore, NI, UK 34/B2
Donald, Austl. 132/B3
Donald, BC, Can. 144/F2
Donaldson, Ar, US 153/H3
Donaldsonville, La, US 164/C2
Donalsonville, Ga, US 165/F2
Doñana, PN, Sp. 46/B4
Donath, Swi. 61/F4
Donau (Danube) (riv.), Aus.,Ger. 45/H2
Donaueschingen, Ger. 61/E2
Donauwörth, Ger. 58/D5
Doncaster (nbrhd.), Austl. 132/G5
Doncaster, Eng, UK 35/G4
Doncaster (co.), Eng, UK 35/G4
Donchery, Fr. 55/D4
Dondo, D.R. Congo 116/D4
Dondo, Moz. 123/G3
Dondo, Ang. 120/C5
Dondra Head (pt.), SrL. 95/D5
Donduseni, Mol. 72/D3
Donegal (bay), Ire. 31/P9
Donegal, Ire. 31/P9
Donegal (dist.), Ire. 34/A1
Doneraile, Ire. 32/B5
Donets (riv.), Rus. 71/G2
Donets' (riv.), Ukr. 73/J3
Donetsk (int'l arpt.), Ukr. 73/J3
Donets'ka Oblast, Ukr. 70/F3
Donetsk, Rus. 73/L3
Donets'k, Ukr. 73/J3
Dong (riv.), China 78/E3
Dong, India 93/G2
Dong (riv.), Viet. 93/J5
Dong Dang, Viet. 93/J3
Dong Ha, Viet. 94/D2
Dong Hoi, Viet. 94/D2
Dong Noi (riv.), Viet. 94/D4
Dong Tau, Viet. 94/D2
Dong Ujimqin Qi, China 78/H2
Donga (riv.), Nga. 115/H4
Donga, Nga. 115/H5
Dongai (riv.), Camr. 116/A4
Dongar Parāsia, India 96/B4
Dongara, Austl. 130/B4
Dongargarh, India 95/D1
Dongbei (plain), China 80/E2
Dongchuan, China 86/D3
Dong'e, China 80/D3
Dongen, Neth. 52/B5
Donges, Fr. 56/C6
Dongfang, China 94/E2
Dongfang, China 87/F5
Donggou, China 81/C3
Dongguan, China 87/G4
Dongguang, China 80/D3
Donghai, China 80/D4
Donghen, Laos 94/D2
Donghezhen, China 80/L8
Dongio, Swi. 61/E5
Dongjia, China 87/G2
Dongjing (riv.), China 87/G2
Dongjingling, China 81/B2
Dongkeng, China 87/H3
Dongkya (pass), China 97/G2
Dongli, China 93/K3
Dongliao (riv.), China 80/F2
Donglük, China 99/E4
Dongmen, China 94/D1
Dongming, China 80/C4
Dongnan (plat.), China 87/F4
Dongo, It. 61/F5
Dongo, D.R. Congo 120/D2
Dongo, D.R. Congo 121/E2
Dongo, Ang. 122/B2
Dongo-Kuma, D.R. Congo 120/E2
Dongobesh, Tanz. 119/A3
Dongola, Il, US 162/C2
Dongou, Congo 120/D2
Dongping, China 80/D4
Dongqiao, China 99/F5
Dongsha (isl.), China 87/H4
Dongsha (Pratas) (isl.), China 87/H4
Dongshajiao, China 87/J2
Dongshan (isl.), China 87/H4
Dongshan, China 80/L8
Dongshao, China 87/G3
Dongsheng, China 80/B3
Dongtai, China 80/E4
Dongtiao (riv.), China 80/L9
Dongting (lake), China 87/G2
Dongtingxi, China 87/F2
Dongue, Ang. 122/B2
Dongxing, China 94/D1
Dongxing, China 87/F3
Dongying, China 80/D3
Dongzhen, China 78/E4
Dongzhi, China 87/H2
Donie, Tx, US 151/F2
Donihue, Chile 190/N9
Donington, Eng, UK 35/H6
Doniphan, Mo, US 162/B2
Donjek (riv.), Yk, Can. 140/C2
Donji Komren, Yugo. 50/E4
Donji Vakuf, Bosn. 50/C3
Donk, Neth. 52/C5
Donna, Tx, US 151/E4
Donnas, It. 62/A1
Donnelly, Mn, US 156/F5
Donner (pass), Ca, US 146/C4
Donner und Blitzen (riv.), Or, US 146/D2
Donnersberg (peak), Ger. 55/G4
Donnybrook, ND, US 156/D3
Donnybrook, Austl. 134/D4
Donnybrook, Austl. 130/B5
Donon (peak), Fr. 60/D1
Donora, Pa, US 161/G4
Donoratico, It. 45/J5
Donskoy, Rus. 73/L4
Donsol, Phil. 88/C2
Donville-les-Bains, Fr. 56/D3
Donyan (riv.), Myan. 86/B5
Donzdorf, Ger. 58/C5
Donzère, Fr. 64/A4
Donzy, Fr. 44/E3
Doole, Tx, US 151/E2
Dooleena (peak), Austl. 130/C2
Doomadgee Abor. Land, Austl. 129/E4
Doomadgee Aboriginal Community, Austl. 129/E4
Doon, Ire. 32/B4
Doon (lake), Sc, UK 33/B6
Doon (riv.), Sc, UK 33/B6
Doon Doon Abor. Land, Austl. 128/C4
Doonbeg (riv.), Ire. 32/A4
Doonbeg, Ire. 32/A4
Doonerak (mt.), Ak, US 171/H2
Door (pen.), Wi, US 157/L5
Door (pt.), La, US 164/D2
Doorn, Neth. 52/C4
Doorn (riv.), SAfr. 124/B3
Doppo (peak), It. 62/D2
Doqên (lake), China 97/G1
Dora, Mo, US 153/H2
Dora (lake), Fl, US 164/M6
Dora, Al, US 162/D4
Dora (lake), Austl. 127/B3
Dora Baltea (riv.), It. 64/D1
Dora Creek, Austl. 133/E1
Dora di Rhêmes (riv.), It. 64/D1
Dora Riparia (riv.), It. 45/G4
Dorada (coast), Sp. 47/F2
Dorāh Ān (pass), Pak. 99/B4
Doraville, Ga, US 163/M7
Dorchester, NB, Can. 158/E3
Dorchester (cape), Nun, Can. 141/J2
Dorchester, Eng, UK 36/D5
Dorchester, Ne, US 155/F3
Dorchester, NJ, US 168/D5
Dorchester, SC, US 163/G4
Dordabis, Namb. 122/C4
Dordogne (riv.), Fr. 66/D1
Dordrecht, Neth. 52/B5
Dordrecht, SAfr. 124/D3
Dore (mts.), Fr. 44/E4
Dore (riv.), Fr. 44/E4
Dores, Sc, UK 33/B2
Dores do Indaiá, Braz. 186/D3
Dorfen (riv.), Ger. 59/E6
Dorfen, Ger. 59/F6
Dorgali, It. 48/A2
Dörgön (lake), Mong. 78/C2
Dori, Burk. 115/E3
Doria, It. 62/B5
Dorion, On, Can. 157/K3
Dorion, Qu, Can. 159/M7
Dorking, Eng, UK 30/C3
Dorlisheim, Fr. 60/D1
Dormagen, Ger. 55/F1
Dormans, Fr. 54/C5
Dormans Land, Eng, UK 30/D3
Dornach, Swi. 60/D3
Dornakal, India 95/D2
Dornbirn, Aus. 61/F3
Dorney Park/ Wildwater Kingdom, Pa, US 168/C2
Dornhan, Ger. 61/E1

Dorno – Eastma

Dorno, It. 62/B3
Dornoch, Sc, UK 33/B1
Dornoch Firth (inlet), Sc, UK 33/B1
Dornod (prov.), Mong. 78/G2
Dornogovĭ (prov.), Mong. 78/F3
Dornstadt, Ger. 58/C6
Dornstetten, Ger. 58/B6
Doro, Mali 115/E2
Dorog, Hun. 51/Q9
Dorogobuzh, Rus. 68/G5
Dorogorskoye, Rus. 69/K2
Dorohoi, Rom. 72/D4
Doromo, D.R. Congo 121/F2
Doron de Chavière (riv.), Fr. 64/C2
Dorothy, NJ, US 168/D5
Dorowa Mining Lease, Zim. 123/F3
Dörpen, Ger. 53/E3
Dorra, Djib. 118/B2
Dorrance, Ks, US 153/E1
Dorre (isl.), Austl. 130/B3
Dorridge, Eng, UK 37/E2
Dorrigo, Austl. 132/E1
Dorrigo NP, Austl. 132/E1
Dorrington, Eng, UK 36/D1
Dorris, Ca, US 146/C3
Dorsale (mts.), Tun. 66/F4
Dorsbach (riv.), Ger. 58/B2
Dorset (co.), Eng, UK 36/D5
Dorsten, Ger. 52/D5
Dortan, Fr. 60/B5
Dortches, NC, US 163/J2
Dortmund, Ger. 53/E5
Dortmund (Wickede) (int'l arpt.), Ger. 53/E5
Dortmund-Ems (canal), Ger. 53/E4
Dörtyol, Turk. 104/E1
Dorum, Ger. 53/F1
Doruma, D.R. Congo 117/E4
Dorval, Qu, Can. 159/N7
Dörverden, Ger. 53/G3
Dos Bahias (cape), Arg. 190/D5
Dos de Mayo, Peru 184/C2
Dos Hermanas, Sp. 46/C4
Dos Palos, Ca, US 148/B2
Dos Pozos, Arg. 190/D4
Dos Puntas (cape), EqG. 120/B2
Dos Quebradas, Col. 183/K8
Dos Reyes (pt.), Chile 188/B3
Döşemealtı, Turk. 104/B1
Dosewallips (riv.), Wa, US 167/A2
Dōshi (riv.), Japan 83/C2
Dōshi, Japan 83/C2
Dosing, India 86/B3
Dospat, Bul. 49/J2
Dosse (riv.), Ger. 42/G2
Dosso (dept.), Niger 115/F3
Dosso, Niger 115/F3
Dosson, It. 63/F2
Dossor, Kaz. 71/K3
Dothan, Al, US 165/F2
Dot Lake, Ak, US 171/K3
Dötlingen, Ger. 53/F3
Dotnuva, Lith. 41/K4
Döttingen, Swi. 61/E2
Doty, Wa, US 144/C4
Douai, Fr. 54/C3
Douala, Camr. 120/B1
Douala (int'l arpt.), Camr. 120/B1
Douar el Cäid el Gueddara, Mor. 112/A2
Douar Toulal, Mor. 112/B3
Douarnenez (bay), Fr. 44/A2
Douarnenez, Fr. 56/A4
Double Island (pt.), Austl. 134/D4
Double Mtn. Fork (riv.), Tx, US 175/E1
Double Springs, Al, US 162/D3
Doubs, Fr. 60/C4
Doubs (dept.), Fr. 60/C3
Doubs (riv.), Fr. 66/E1
Doubtful (bay), Austl. 128/B3
Doubtful Island (bay), Austl. 130/C5
Doubtless (bay), NZ 135/C1
Doucette, Tx, US 151/G2
Douchy-les-Mines, Fr. 54/C3
Doudeville, Fr. 57/F1
Doue, Fr. 30/M5
Doué-la-Fontaine, Fr. 57/E6
Douentza, Mali 114/E3
Dougga (ruin), Tun. 112/L6
Dougherty, Tx, US 153/G4
Douglas, Austl. 128/C3
Douglas (lake), BC, Can. 144/D2
Douglas, Ire. 32/B6
Douglas, SAfr. 124/C3
Douglas (cap.), IM, UK 34/D3
Douglas, Sc, UK 33/C5
Douglas (mt.), Ak, US 171/H4
Douglas, Az, US 149/H5
Douglas (co.), Ga, US 163/L7
Douglas, Ga, US 165/G2
Douglas, Mi, US 160/C3
Douglas, ND, US 156/D4
Douglas (lake), Tn, US 163/F3
Douglas, Wy, US 154/B2
Douglass, Ks, US 153/F2
Douglass, Tx, US 151/G2
Douglassville, Pa, US 168/C3
Douglastown, NB, Can. 158/E2
Douglasville, Ga, US 163/L7
Dougou, China 87/G1
Doujiang, China 87/F3
Doulaincourt-Saucourt, Fr. 60/B1
Doullens, Fr. 54/B3
Doumé, Camr. 116/B4
Doumé, Gabon 120/C3
Doumé (riv.), Camr. 116/B4
Dounby, Sc, UK 31/V14
Doune (peak), Sc, UK 33/B4
Doune, Sc, UK 33/B4
Doupovské Hory (mts.), Czh. 45/K1
Dour, Belg. 54/C3
Doura, Mali 114/D3
Dourada, Serra (mts.), Braz. 186/C2
Dourados, Braz. 189/F2
Dourados (riv.), Braz. 186/B4
Dourbali, Chad 116/B3
Dourdan, Fr. 30/J6
Dourdou (riv.), Fr. 44/E4
Dourdoura, Chad 116/D3
Dourh (peak), Mor. 111/E2
Douro (riv.), Port. 66/B2
Douron (riv.), Fr. 56/B3
Dousman, Wi, US 167/P13
Doussard, Fr. 60/C6
Douvaine, Fr. 60/C5
Douve (riv.), Fr. 56/D2
Douvrin, Fr. 54/B2
Doux (riv.), Fr. 44/F4
Douze (riv.), Fr. 44/C4
Dove Creek, Co, US 149/H2
Dover, Austl. 132/C4
Dover (pt.), Austl. 130/E5
Dover, Eng, UK 37/H4
Dover (str.), UK,Fr. 44/D1
Dover, Ar, US 153/H3
Dover (A.F.B.), De, US 168/C5
Dover (cap.), De, US 168/C5
Dover, Fl, US 164/L8
Dover, Ks, US 153/G1
Dover, NH, US 161/L3
Dover, NJ, US 168/D2
Dover, Oh, US 160/F4
Dover, Ok, US 153/F3
Dover, Pa, US 168/B4
Dover, Tn, US 162/D2
Dover Bluff, Ga, US 165/H2
Doveridge, Eng, UK 35/G6
Dovrefjell NP, Nor. 38/D3
Dovsk, Bela. 70/D1
Dow, Ok, US 153/G3
Dow City, Ia, US 155/G3
Dowagiac, Mi, US 160/C4
Dowerin, Austl. 130/C4
Dowghā'ī, Iran 101/G1
Dowi (cape), Indo. 89/B2
Dowlatābād, Iran 103/J4
Dowling, Ab, Can. 145/H2
Down (dist.), NI, UK 34/C3
Downers Grove, Il, US 167/P16
Downey, Ca, US 166/F8
Downey, Id, US 147/G2
Downham Market, Eng, UK 37/G1
Downieville, Ca, US 146/C4
Downingtown, Pa, US 168/C4
Downpatrick, NI, UK 34/C3
Downs, Ks, US 154/E4
Downsville, NY, US 161/J3
Downton, Eng, UK 37/E4
Dows, Ia, US 155/H2
Dowshī, Afg. 101/J1
Doygaab, Som. 119/C1
Doyle, Ca, US 146/C3
Doylestown, Pa, US 168/C3
Doyleville, Co, US 149/J1
Dōzen (isl.), Japan 84/C3
Dozier, Al, US 165/E2
Dozulé, Fr. 57/E2
Drâa (cape), Mor. 110/C3
Drâa, Oued (riv.), Mor. 107/B2
Drac (riv.), Fr. 44/F4
Dracena, Braz. 189/G2
Drachten, Neth. 52/D2
Drăgăneşti-Olt, Rom. 51/G3
Drăgăşani, Rom. 51/G3
Dragoman, Bul. 51/F4
Dragon's Mouth (str.), Trin.,Ven. 181/F2
Dragoon, Az, US 149/G4
Dragør, Den. 39/J7
Draguignan, Fr. 64/C5
Drain, Or, US 146/B2
Drake, ND, US 156/D4
Drake (passg) 192/V
Drake (passg.), SAm. 191/D8
Drakensberg (mts.), SAfr. 107/E8
Drakesville, Ia, US 155/H3
Dráma, Gre. 49/J2
Dramba, D.R. Congo 121/G2
Drammen, Nor. 40/D2
Drammensfjorden (fd.), Nor. 38/R8
Dramselva (riv.), Nor. 38/R8
Drance (riv.), Swi. 60/D5
Drancy, Fr. 30/K5
Drangedal, Nor. 40/C2
Dranse (riv.), Fr. 60/C5
Dransfeld, Ger. 53/G5
Drap, Fr. 64/D5
Draper, Ut, US 147/H3
Draperstown, NI, UK 34/B2
Drās, India 98/C2
Drau (riv.), Aus. 45/K3
Drava (riv.), Cro. 50/C2
Dráva (riv.), Hun. 50/C3
Drava (riv.), Slov. 45/L3
Draveil, Fr. 30/K5
Drawa (riv.), Pol. 43/H2
Drawienski NP, Pol. 43/H2
Drawsko Pomorskie, Pol. 43/H2
Drayton, ND, US 156/F3
Drayton Valley, Ab, Can. 144/G1
Dreghorn, Sc, UK 33/B5
Drei Zinnen (peak), PNG 91/K4
Dreiesselberg (peak), Ger. 59/G5
Dreisam (riv.), Ger. 60/D2
Drensteinfurt, Ger. 53/E5
Drenthe (prov.), Neth. 52/D3
Drentse Hoofdvaart (riv.), Neth. 52/D3
Drentwede, Ger. 53/F3
Dresano, It. 62/C3
Dresden, Ger. 74/B4
Dresden, Oh, US 160/E4
Dresden, On, Can. 160/E3
Dresden, Tn, US 162/C2
Dresser, Wi, US 155/H1
Dreux, Fr. 57/G3
Drew, Ms, US 162/B4
Drews (res.), Or, US 146/C2
Drewsey, Or, US 146/D2
Drexel, Mo, US 153/G1
Dreyer, Tx, US 151/F3
Drezdenko, Pol. 43/H2
Driebergen, Neth. 52/C4
Driedorf, Ger. 55/H2
Driffield, Eng, UK 35/H4
Drift Prairie (grsld.), ND, US 156/E4
Driggs, Id, US 147/H2
Drigh Road, Pak. 101/J4
Drimoleague, Ire. 32/A6
Drin (gulf), Alb. 49/F2
Drin (riv.), Alb. 67/H2
Drina (riv.), Bosn.,Yugo 67/H2
Dripping Springs, Tx, US 151/E2
Driscoll, ND, US 156/D4
Driscoll, Tx, US 151/F4
Driskill (mtn.), La, US 153/H4
Drniš, Cro. 50/C4
Dro, It. 61/G6
Drøbak, Nor. 40/D2
Drobeta-Turnu Severin, Rom. 50/F3
Drochia, Mol. 72/D3
Drochtersen, Ger. 53/G1
Drocourt, Fr. 30/H4
Drogheda, Ire. 34/B4
Drogichin, Bela. 72/C1
Drohobych, Ukr. 72/B3
Droichead Nuadh, Ire. 32/D3
Droitwich, Eng, UK 36/D2
Drolshagen, Ger. 55/G1
Dromahaire, Ire. 32/B1
Drôme (riv.), Fr. 57/E2
Drôme (dept.), Fr. 64/B3
Dromedary (mt.), Austl. 133/E3
Dromina, Ire. 32/B5
Dromiskin, Ire. 34/B4
Dromore (riv.), Ire. 34/A3
Dromore, NI, UK 34/B3
Dromore West, Ire. 32/B1
Dronero, It. 64/D4
Dronfield, Eng, UK 35/G5
Drongan, Sc, UK 33/B6
Dronne (riv.), Fr. 44/D4
Dronten, Neth. 52/C3
Drop, Tx, US 150/K6
Dropt (riv.), Fr. 44/D4
Drosh, Pak. 98/A2
Droskovo, Rus. 70/F1
Drottningholm Palace, Swe. 39/A1
Droué, Fr. 57/G4
Drouette (riv.), Fr. 54/A6
Drouin, Austl. 133/B4
Druento, It. 64/D2
Druid Hills, Ga, US 163/M7
Drum (inlet), NC, US 163/J3
Drumaness, NI, UK 34/C3
Drumbeg, NI, UK 34/C2
Drumcar, Ire. 34/B4
Drumcollogher, Ire. 32/B5
Drumcondra, Ire. 32/D2
Drumheller, Ab, Can. 145/H2
Drumkeeran, Ire. 32/B1
Drumleck (pt.), Ire. 34/B5
Drumlish, Ire. 32/C2
Drummond (mt.), Austl. 134/B4
Drummond (pt.), Austl. 131/G5
Drummond (range), Austl. 127/D3
Drummond, NB, Can. 158/D2
Drummond, Id, US 147/H2
Drummond (isl.), MI, US 160/E1
Drummond, Mt, US 145/H4
Drummond, Wi, US 157/J4
Drummonds, Tn, US 162/C3
Drummondville, Qu, Can. 161/K2
Drummore, Sc, UK 34/D2
Drumnadrochit, Sc, UK 33/B2
Drumnakilly, NI, UK 34/A2
Drumochter, Pass of (pass), Sc, UK 33/B3
Drumright, Ok, US 153/F3
Drumshanbo, Ire. 32/B1
Drumsna, Ire. 32/B2
Drunen, Neth. 52/C5
Drunken (pt.), Mb, Can. 156/F2
Druridge (bay), Eng, UK 35/G1
Drusenheim, Fr. 55/G6
Druskininkai, Lith. 41/K4
Druten, Neth. 52/C5
Druya, Bela. 41/M4
Druzhba, Kaz. 99/D2
Druzhba, Ukr. 73/G1
Druzhkivka, Ukr. 73/J3
Drvar, Bosn. 50/C3
Drwęca (riv.), Pol. 43/K2
Dry (lake), ND, US 156/E3
Dry (cr.), Ca, US 146/C4
Dry Cimarron (riv.), Ok, US 152/C2
Dry Creek, Yk, Can. 171/K3
Dry Creek, La, US 164/B2
Dry Fork (riv.), Wy, US 154/B1
Dry Fork Marias (riv.), Mt, US 145/H3
Dry Prong, La, US 164/B2
Dry Ridge, Ky, US 162/E1
Dry Run, Oh, US 163/F1
Dry Tortugas (isl.), Fl, US 165/G5
Dry Tortugas Nat'l Pk., Fl, US 172/E3
Dryanovo, Bul. 51/G4
Dryden, On, Can. 157/H3
Dryden, Mi, US 167/F6
Dryden, NY, US 161/H3
Dryden, Tx, US 151/C2
Dryden, Va, US 163/F2
Drygarn Fawr (peak), Wal, UK 36/C2
Drymen, Sc, UK 33/B4
Drysdale (riv.), Austl. 128/B3
Drysdale River NP, Austl. 128/B3
Du (riv.), China 78/G5
Du Bois, Pa, US 161/G4
Du Dja, Réserve, Camr. 116/B5
Du Long, Viet. 94/E4
Du Page (co.), Il, US 167/P16
Du Page (riv.), Il, US 167/P16
Du Page, East Branch (riv.), Il, US 167/P16
Du Quoin, Il, US 162/C1
Duaringa, Austl. 134/C3
Duarte (peak), DRep. 173/G4
Duarte, Ca, US 166/G7
Ḑubā, SAr. 109/G3
Dubach, La, US 153/H4
Dubai (int'l arpt.), UAE 101/G3
Dubăsari, Mol. 72/E4
Dubawnt (riv.), NW, Can. 140/F2
Dubawnt (lake), Nun, Can. 140/F2
Dubawnt (lake), Can. 139/G3
Dubayy, UAE 101/G3
Dubele, D.R. Congo 121/G2
Dübendorf, Swi. 61/E3
Dübener Heide (phys. reg.), Ger. 42/G3
Dubino, It. 61/F5
Dublin (cap.), Ire. 34/B5
Dublin (co.), Ire. 34/B5
Dublin, Ca, US 167/L11
Dublin, Ga, US 163/F4
Dublin, Md, US 168/B4
Dublin, Oh, US 160/E4
Dublin, Pa, US 168/C3
Dublin, Tx, US 151/E1
Dublin, Va, US 163/G2
Dubna, Rus. 70/F1
Dubna, Rus. 68/H4
Dubnica nad Váhom, Slvk. 43/K4
Dubno, Ukr. 72/C2
Dubois, Wy, US 147/J2
Dubois, Id, US 147/G1
Duboistown, Pa, US 168/A1
Dubossary (res.), Mol. 51/J2
Dubovskiy, Rus. 71/G2
Dubovskoye, Rus. 73/M4
Dubovyy Umët, Rus. 71/J1
Dubra, India 97/F4
Dubrājpur, India 97/F4
Dubréka, Gui. 114/B4
Dubrovka, Rus. 70/E1
Dubrovka, Rus. 41/P2
Dubrovnik (int'l arpt.), Yugo. 50/D4
Dubrovnik, Cro. 50/D4
Dubrovno, Bela. 41/P4
Dubrovytsya, Ukr. 72/D2
Dubulu, D.R. Congo 116/D4
Dubuque, Ia, US 155/J2
Duc Lap, Viet. 94/D3
Duc Pho, Viet. 94/E3
Duc Phong, Viet. 94/D4
Duchcov, Czh. 59/G1
Duchesne, Ut, US 147/H3
Duchesne (riv.), Ut, US 147/H3
Duchess, Austl. 131/H2
Duchess, Ab, Can. 145/J2
Ducie (isl.), Pitc. 137/N7
Duck (lake), Mi, US 167/E7
Duck (cr.), Nv, US 147/F4
Duck (riv.), Tn, US 162/D3
Duck Bay, Mb, Can. 156/D1
Duck Hill, Ms, US 162/C4
Duck Lake, Sk, Can. 145/L1
Duck Mtn. (mtn.), Mb, Can. 156/D2
Duck Valley Ind. Res., Id, US 146/E2
Duckabush (riv.), Wa, US 167/A2
Ducktown, Tn, US 162/E3
Duckwater, Nv, US 146/F4
Duckwater Ind. Res., Nv, US 148/E1
Duclair, Fr. 57/F2
Duda (riv.), Col. 180/C4
Duddon (riv.), Eng, UK 35/E3
Dudelange, Lux. 55/F5
Dudenhofen, Ger. 58/B4
Duderstadt, Ger. 53/H5
Dudh Kosi (riv.), Nepal 97/F2
Dūdhi, India 96/D3
Dudhwa NP, India 96/C1
Dudignac, Arg. 190/E2
Düdingen, Swi. 60/D4
Dudinka, Rus. 74/J3
Dudley, Eng, UK 36/D1
Dudley (co.), Eng, UK 36/D1
Dudub, Eth. 118/C4
Dudzele, Belg. 54/C1
Due, D.R. Congo 120/D4
Due West, SC, US 163/F3
Duékoué, C.d'Iv. 114/D5
Dueñas, Sp. 46/C2
Duenweg, Mo, US 153/G2
Dueré, Braz. 186/C1
Duette, Fl, US 164/L8
Dueville, It. 63/E2
Dufaja (riv.), Kenya 119/B2
Duff (isls.), Sol. 136/F5
Duffel, Belg. 55/D1
Dufferin (co.), On, Can. 160/S8
Duffield, Eng, UK 35/G6
Duff's Corners, On, Can. 160/S9
Dufftown, Sc, UK 33/C2
Dufour (Dufourspitze) (peak), Swi. 62/A1
Dufourspitze (Dufour) (peak), Swi. 62/A1
Dugachhi, Bang. 97/H3
Dugald, Mb, Can. 156/F3
Dugbia, D.R. Congo 121/F2
Dugdemona (riv.), La, US 151/H1
Dugger, In, US 162/D1
Dugi (isl.), Cro. 45/L4
Dugi Otok (isl.), Cro. 67/G2
Dugny-sur-Meuse, Fr. 55/E5
Dugo Selo, Cro. 50/C3
Dugu, Eth. 118/B3
Dugway, Ut, US 147/G3
Dugway Proving Grounds, Ut, US 147/G3
Duich (lake), Sc, UK 33/A2
Duida (peak), Ven. 181/E4
Duida Marahuaca, PN, Ven. 181/E4
Duifken (pt.), Austl. 129/F3
Duingen, Ger. 53/G4
Duino, It. 63/G2
Duisburg, Ger. 52/D6
Duitama, Col. 180/C3
Duiven, Neth. 52/D5
Duivendrecht, Neth. 52/B4
Dujuuma, Som. 119/C1
Duk Fadiat, Sudan 117/F4
Dukafulu, Eth. 118/A4
Dukambīya, Erit. 117/H2
Duke, Mo, US 153/H2
Duke of Gloucester (isls.), FrPol. 137/L7
Duke's (pass), Sc, UK 33/B4
Dukhān, Qatar 100/F3
Dukielska (Dukla Pass) (pass), Pol. 43/L4
Dukla Pass (Dukielska) (pass), Pol. 43/L4
Dūkštas, Lith. 41/M4
Dula, D.R. Congo 116/D4
Dulac, La, US 164/C3
Dulan, China 78/D4
Dulce (riv.), Arg. 188/D4
Dulce, NM, US 149/J2
Dulce (gulf), Pan. 177/F4
Dulce Nombre de Culmí, Hon. 176/E3
Dule, Erit. 118/A2
Duleek, Ire. 34/B4
Dŭlgopol, Bul. 51/H4
Duliu (riv.), China 93/J2
Duliu, China 80/H7
Dullewāla, Pak. 98/A4
Dullstroom, SAfr. 123/F5
Dülmen, Ger. 53/E5
Dulnain (riv.), Sc, UK 33/C2
Dulong (pass), China 86/B3
Dulovo, Bul. 51/H4
Dulunguin (pt.), Phil. 88/C4
Duluth, Mn, US 157/H4
Duluth, Ga, US 163/M6
Dulverton, Eng, UK 36/C4
Dūmā, Syria 105/E1
Dūmā, WBnk. 105/C4
Dumagasa (pt.), Phil. 88/C4
Dumaguete, Phil. 88/C3
Dumai, Indo. 89/C2
Dumalinao, Phil. 88/C4
Dumanjug, Phil. 88/C3
Dumaran, Phil. 88/B3
Dumaran (isl.), Phil. 91/E1
Dumas, Tx, US 152/D3
Dumas, Ar, US 153/J4
Ḑumayr, Syria 104/E3
Ḑumayr, Syria 105/F1
Dumbarton, Sc, UK 33/B5
Dumbi, D.R. Congo 120/D4
Dumbi, Ang. 122/B1
Ďumbier (peak), Slvk. 43/K4
Dumbleyung, Austl. 130/C5
Dumbrăveni, Rom. 51/G2
Dume (pt.), Ca, US 166/B2
Dumei, China 87/H3
Dumfries, Sc, UK 34/E1
Dumfries and Galloway (co.), Sc, UK 33/C6
Duminichi, Rus. 70/E1
Dumka, India 97/F3
Dumlu, Turk. 71/G4
Dummar, Syria 105/E1
Dümmer (lake), Ger. 53/F3
Dumoine (riv.), Qu, Can. 161/H1
Dumoine (lake), Qu, Can. 141/J4
Dumont, NJ, US 169/K8
Dumont d'Urville, Fr., Ant. 192/K
Dumraon, India 97/E3
Dumri, India 97/F4
Dumyat (gov.), Egypt 102/B3
Dumyāţ (Damietta), Egypt 113/C2
Dumyāţ, Massabb (Damietta) (mouth), Egypt 113/C1
Dún Laoghaire, Ire. 34/B5
Dun Rig (peak), Sc, UK 33/C5
Dunaföldvár, Hun. 50/D2
Dunaharaszti, Hun. 51/R10
Dunajec (riv.), Pol. 43/L4
Dunakeszi, Hun. 51/R9
Dunany (pt.), Ire. 34/B4
Dunaszekcso, Hun. 50/D2
Dunaújváros, Hun. 50/D2
Dunavecse, Hun. 50/D2
Dunavtsi, Bul. 50/F4
Dunayivtsi, Ukr. 72/D3
Dunbar, Sc, UK 33/D5
Dunbar, Austl. 134/A2
Dunblane, Sk, Can. 145/L2
Dunblane, Sc, UK 33/C4
Dunboyne, Ire. 34/B5
Duncan, Ok, US 153/F3
Duncan, Az, US 149/H4
Duncan, Ms, US 162/B3
Duncan, BC, Can. 144/C3
Duncannon, Ire. 32/D5
Duncannon, Pa, US 168/A3
Duncansby Head (pt.), Sc, UK 31/V14
Duncanville, Tx, US 150/L7
Dund-Us, Mong. 78/C2
Dundaga, Lat. 41/K3
Dundalk (bay), Ire. 34/B4
Dundalk, Ire. 34/B4
Dundalk, On, Can. 160/F2
Dundalk, Md, US 168/B5
Dundas (lake), Austl. 130/D5
Dundas (str.), Austl. 128/C2
Dundas (pen.), NW, Can. 141/R7
Dundas, On, Can. 160/T9
Dundas, Oh, US 163/F1
Dundas, Il, US 162/C1
Dundee, SAfr. 125/E3
Dundee, Sc, UK 33/D4
Dundee (co.), Sc, UK 33/D4
Dundee (arpt.), Sc, UK 33/C4
Dundee, Fl, US 164/M7
Dundee, Ms, US 162/B3
Dundee, Tx, US 152/E4
Dundgovi (prov.), Mong. 78/F2
Dundīţ, Egypt 113/C3
Dundonald, Sc, UK 33/B5
Dundrum (bay), NI, UK 34/C3
Dundrum, NI, UK 34/C3
Dundurn, Sk, Can. 145/L2
Dundwa (range), Nepal 96/D2
Dundwārāganj, India 96/B2
Dunedin, NZ 135/B4
Dunedin, Fl, US 164/K7
Dunedoo, Austl. 132/D2
Dunellen, NJ, US 169/H9
Dunes City, Or, US 146/A2
Dunfanaghy, Ire. 31/Q9
Dunfermline, Sc, UK 33/C4
Dunga Bunga, Pak. 98/B5
Dungalear Station, Austl. 132/D1
Dungannon, NI, UK 34/B3
Dungannon (co.), NI, UK 34/B3
Dungannon, On, Can. 160/F3
Dungarpur, India 92/B3
Dungarvan, Ire. 32/C5
Dungarvan (har.), Ire. 32/C5
Dungau (reg.), Ger. 59/F5
Dungeness (pt.), Arg. 191/C7
Dungeness (pt.), Eng, UK 37/G5
Dungeness, Wa, US 144/C3
Dungiven, NI, UK 34/B2
Dunglow, Ire. 31/P9
Dungog, Austl. 132/D2
Dungu, D.R. Congo 121/G2
Dungu (riv.), D.R. Congo 117/F5
Dunham, Qu, Can. 161/K2
Dunhua, China 79/K3
Dunhuang, China 78/C3
Dunkeld, Sc, UK 33/C3
Dunkellin (riv.), Ire. 32/B3
Dunkerque (Dunkirk), Fr. 44/E1
Dunkery (hill), Eng, UK 36/C4
Dunkirk, NY, US 161/G3
Dunkirk, In, US 160/D4
Dunkirk (Dunkerque), Fr. 44/E1
Dunkley, BC, Can. 144/C1
Dunkwa, Gha. 115/E5
Dunlap, Tn, US 162/E3
Dunlap, Ia, US 155/G3
Dunlavin, Ire. 32/D3
Dunleath, Sk, Can. 156/C2
Dunleer, Ire. 34/B4
Dunloe, Gap of (pass), Ire. 32/A5
Dunloy, NI, UK 34/B2
Dunmanus (bay), Ire. 32/A6
Dunmanway, Ire. 32/A6
Dunmore, Ire. 32/B2
Dunmore, Pa, US 161/J4
Dunmore, WV, US 163/H1
Dunmore East, Ire. 32/C5
Dunmurry, NI, UK 34/B2
Dunn, La, US 153/J4
Dunn, NC, US 163/H3
Dunnamanagh, NI, UK 34/A2
Dunnamore, NI, UK 34/B2
Dunnell, Mn, US 155/G2
Dunnellon, Fl, US 165/G3
Dünnern (riv.), Swi. 60/D3
Dunnet Head (pt.), Sc, UK 31/V14
Dunning, Sc, UK 33/C4
Dunningen, Ger. 61/E1
Dunnington, Eng, UK 35/H4
Dunnsville, Va, US 163/J2
Dunnville, On, Can. 160/T10
Dunolly, Austl. 132/B3
Dunoon, Sc, UK 33/B5
Dunqulah, Sudan 109/F5
Dunqunāb, Sudan 100/C4
Dunragit, Sc, UK 34/D2
Duns, Sc, UK 33/D5
Dunsborough, Austl. 130/B5
Dunscore, Sc, UK 34/E1
Dunseith, ND, US 156/D3
Dunseverick, NI, UK 34/B1
Dunshaughlin, Ire. 34/B4
Dunsmuir, Ca, US 146/B3
Dunstable, Eng, UK 37/F3
Dunster, BC, Can. 144/E1
Duntocher, Sc, UK 33/B5
Dunure, Sc, UK 33/B6
Dunville, Nf, Can. 159/L2
Dunwoody, Ga, US 163/M7
Dunyāpur, Pak. 98/A5
Duobukur (riv.), China 79/J1
Duojing, China 87/E4
Duolun, China 78/H3
Dupont, In, US 162/E1
Dupont, Pa, US 168/C1
Dupree, SD, US 154/D1
Dupuy (cape), Austl. 130/B2
Duque Bacelar, Braz. 183/F4
Duque de Caxias, Braz. 187/N7
Duque de York (isl.), Chile 191/A6
Duquette, Mn, US 157/H4
Dūrā, WBnk. 105/C5
Durack (range), Austl. 128/B4
Durack (riv.), Austl. 128/B4
Durağan, Turk. 70/E4
Durak, Turk. 104/D1
Durand, Mi, US 160/E3
Durand, Wi, US 155/J1
Durango (state), Mex. 172/A3
Durango, Sp. 44/B5
Durango, Co, US 149/J2
Durango de Victoria, Mex. 174/D3
Duranillin, Austl. 130/C5
Durant, Ok, US 153/F4
Durant, Fl, US 164/L8
Durant, Ms, US 162/C4
Durazno (dept.), Uru. 191/F2
Durazno, Uru. 191/K10
Durban, SAfr. 125/E3
Durban (Louis Botha) (int'l arpt.), SAfr. 125/E3
Durbanville, SAfr. 124/L10
Durbe, Lat. 41/J3
Durbion (riv.), Fr. 60/C1
Durbuy, Belg. 55/E3
Dúrcal, Sp. 46/D4
Durdevac, Cro. 50/C2
Durdevo, Yugo. 50/E3
Durdur (riv.), Som. 118/B3
Düre, China 99/E2
Dureji, Pak. 101/J3
Düren, Ger. 55/F2
Durg, India 95/D1
Durgāpur, India 97/G3
Durgāpur, India 97/F4
Durgerdam, Neth. 52/B4
Durham, On, Can. 160/F2
Durham (co.), On, Can. 160/V8
Durham (co.), Eng, UK 35/F2
Durham, Eng, UK 35/G2
Durham, Ca, US 146/C4
Durham, Ks, US 153/F1
Durham, Mo, US 155/J4
Durham, NC, US 163/H3
Durham, NH, US 161/L3
Durham Bridge, NB, Can. 158/D2
Durham Downs, Austl. 134/A4
Duri, Indo. 89/C2
Durlston (pt.), Eng, UK 36/E5
Ḑurmā, SAr. 100/E4
Durmitor NP, Yugo. 49/F1
Durnford (pt.), WSah. 110/B5
Duror, Sc, UK 33/A5
Dürrenroth, Swi. 60/D3
Durrës, Alb. 49/F2
Durrington, Eng, UK 37/E4
Dürrlauingen, Ger. 58/D6
Durrow, Ire. 32/C4
Dürrwangen, Ger. 58/D4
Dursley, Eng, UK 36/D3
Dursunbey, Turk. 70/D5
Durtal, Fr. 57/E5
Duru, D.R. Congo 117/F4
Durugu, D.R. Congo 116/C4
Durukhsi, Eth. 118/C3
Durusu (lake), Turk. 103/M6
Durusu, Turk. 103/M6
Durūz (peak), Syria 109/H1
D'Urville (cape), Indo. 91/J4
Dusa Marreb (Dhuusamarreeb), Som. 118/C4
Dusanovo, Yugo. 49/G1
Dusetos, Lith. 41/L4
Dushak, Trkm. 101/H1
Dushan, China 87/E3
Dushanbe (cap.), Taj. 74/G6
Dusheti, Geo. 71/H4
Dushui (riv.), China 87/E3
Dusky (sound), NZ 135/A4
Düsseldorf (int'l arpt.), Ger. 52/D6
Düsseldorf, Ger. 52/D6
Dusti, Taj. 101/J1
Dustin, Ok, US 153/F3
Duszniki-Zdrój, Pol. 43/J3
Dutch (riv.), Eng, UK 35/H4
Dutch (cr.), BC, Can. 144/F2
Dutch Harbor, Ak, US 171/E5
Dutch John, Ut, US 147/J3
Dutch Wonderland, Pa, US 168/B3
Dutlwe, Bots. 122/D4
Dutoitspiek (peak), SAfr. 124/L10
Dutovo, Rus. 69/N3
Dutse, Nga. 115/H4
Dutsen Wai, Nga. 115/H4
Dutsin-Ma, Nga. 115/G3
Dutton, On, Can. 160/F3
Dutton (mt.), Ut, US 149/F1
Dutton, Mt, US 145/J4
Dutukpene, Gha. 115/F4
Duvall, Wa, US 167/D2
Duvno, Bosn. 50/C4
Düxanbibazar, China 99/D4
Duxun, China 87/H4
Duyang, China 87/E3
Duyun, China 87/E3
Dūz, Tun. 66/F4
Düzce, Turk. 51/K5
Düzici, Turk. 102/D2
Dve Mogili, Bul. 51/G4
Dvina (bay), Rus. 68/H2
Dvinskoy, Rus. 69/K3
Dvořiště (lake), Czh. 59/H4
Dvorníky, Slvk. 50/C1
Dwārka, India 101/J4
Dwārkeswar (riv.), India 97/F4
Dwight, Ks, US 153/F1
Dwight, Il, US 160/B4
Dworshak (res.), Id, US 144/F4
Dwyer (Faywood), NM, US 149/H4
Dwyfor (riv.), Wal, UK 34/D6
Dwyka (riv.), SAfr. 124/C4
Dyat'kovo, Rus. 70/E1
Dybvad, Den. 40/D3
Dyce, Sc, UK 33/D2
Dyce (int'l arpt.), Sc, UK 33/D2
Dyckesville, Wi, US 160/C2
Dyer, In, US 160/C4
Dyer (cape), Nun, Can. 141/K2
Dyer, Nv, US 148/C2
Dyer, Tn, US 162/C2
Dyer (cape), Chile 191/B6
Dyersburg, Tn, US 162/C2
Dyersville, Ia, US 155/J2
Dyess, Ar, US 162/B3
Dyess (A.F.B.), Tx, US 151/E1
Dyfed (co.), Wal, UK 36/B2
Dyffryn, Wal, UK 34/D6
Dyfi (riv.), Wal, UK 36/C1
Dyje (riv.), Czh. 43/J4
Dykan'ka, Ukr. 73/H3
Dyke Ackland (bay) 129/H2
Dykh-tau (peak), Rus. 71/G4
Dyle (riv.), Belg. 42/C3
Dyleň (peak), Czh. 59/F3
Dylewska (peak), Pol. 43/K2
Dymchurch, Eng, UK 37/G4
Dymer, Ukr. 72/F2
Dymytrov, Ukr. 73/J3
Dysart, Sk, Can. 156/B2
Dysart, Austl. 134/C3
Dysart, Ia, US 155/H2
Dysselsdorp, SAfr. 124/C4
Dyul'tydag (peak), Rus. 71/H4
Dyurtyuli, Rus. 69/M5
Dzalanyama (range), Moz. 123/G2
Dzamandzar, Madg. 125/J6
Dzaoudzi (cap.), May. 125/H6
Dzaoudzi (int'l arpt.), May. 125/H6
Dzavhan (riv.), Mong. 78/C2
Dzavhan (prov.), Mong. 78/D2
Dzel, Mong. 99/F2
Dzenzik (pt.), Ukr. 73/J4
Dzerzhinsk, Rus. 68/J4
Dzerzhinsk, Bela. 41/M5
Dzerzhyns'k, Ukr. 73/J3
Dzerzhyns'k, Ukr. 72/D2
Dzhalinda, Rus. 79/J1
Dzhambeyty, Kaz. 71/K2
Dzhanga, Trkm. 103/H1
Dzhankoy, Ukr. 73/H5
Dzhanybek, Kaz. 71/H2
Dzharylgach (gulf), Ukr. 51/L2
Dzhebel, Bul. 49/J2
Dzhebrail, Azer. 103/F2
Dzhirgatal', Taj. 99/B4
Dzhubga, Rus. 70/F3
Dzhugdzhur (range), Rus. 77/N4
Dzhusaly, Kaz. 74/G5
Działdowo, Pol. 43/L2
Dzibalchén, Mex. 176/D2
Dzibilchaltún (ruin), Mex. 176/D1
Dzidzantún, Mex. 176/D1
Dzierżoniów, Pol. 43/J3
Dzitbalché, Mex. 176/D1
Dziuché, Mex. 176/D2
Dzöölön, Mong. 78/D1
Dzukija NP, Lith. 41/L4
Dzungarian (basin), China 74/J5
Dzur, Mong. 78/D2
Dzüünbayan, Mong. 78/G3
Dzüünbulag, Mong. 78/G2
Dzüünharaa, Mong. 78/F2
Dzüünhövöö, Mong. 99/F1
Dzuunmod, Mong. 78/F2

E

E.D.F. (canal), Fr. 64/B5
E.T. Joshua (int'l arpt.), StV. 173/N9
Eads, Co, US 152/C1
Eagan, Mn, US 157/P7
Eagle (riv.), Nf, Can. 141/L3
Eagle (cr.), Sk, Can. 145/K2
Eagle (hills), Sk, Can. 145/K1
Eagle (mt.), Ire. 32/A5
Eagle, Ak, US 171/K3
Eagle (lake), Ca, US 146/C3
Eagle (mts.), Ca, US 148/E4
Eagle (peak), Ca, US 146/C3
Eagle (peak), Ca, US 146/D4
Eagle, Co, US 147/K4
Eagle (riv.), Co, US 147/K4
Eagle, Id, US 146/E2
Eagle (cr.), Ky, US 162/E1
Eagle (mtn.), Mn, US 157/J4
Eagle, Ne, US 155/F3
Eagle (peak), Tx, US 151/B2
Eagle (pt.), Tx, US 151/N9
Eagle, Wi, US 167/P14
Eagle (peak), Wy, US 147/H1
Eagle Bend, Mn, US 157/G4
Eagle Butte, SD, US 154/D1
Eagle Crags (peak), Ca, US 148/D3
Eagle Grove, Ia, US 155/H2
Eagle Lake, Fl, US 164/M8
Eagle Lake, Tx, US 150/F3
Eagle Mills, Ar, US 153/H4
Eagle Mountain (lake), Tx, US 153/F4
Eagle Pass, Tx, US 151/D3
Eagle Point, Or, US 146/B2
Eagle River, Mi, US 157/K4
Eagle River, Wi, US 157/K5
Eagle Rock, Va, US 163/H2
Eaglehawk, Austl. 133/B3
Eaglesfield, Sc, UK 35/E1
Eaglesham, Sc, UK 33/B5
Eagleton, Ar, US 153/G3
Eagletown, Ok, US 153/G3
Eagleville, Ca, US 146/C3
Eagleville, Mo, US 155/H3
Eahun, Indo. 128/A2
Eakly, Ok, US 153/E3
Ealing (bor.), Eng, UK 30/B2
Ear Falls, On, Can. 157/H2
Earby, Eng, UK 35/F4
Earith, Eng, UK 37/G2
Earl Grey, Sk, Can. 156/B2
Earl Stonham, Eng, UK 37/H2
Earle, Ar, US 162/B3
Earle Nav. Weapons Ctr., NJ, US 168/D3
Earlimart, Ca, US 148/C3
Earling, Ia, US 155/G3
Earlington, Ky, US 162/D2
Earls Barton, Eng, UK 37/F2
Earls Colne, Eng, UK 37/G3
Earl's Seat (peak), Sc, UK 33/B4
Earlsboro, Ok, US 153/F3
Earlsferry, Sc, UK 33/D4
Earlston, Sc, UK 33/D5
Earltown, NS, Can. 158/F3
Earlville, Ia, US 155/J2
Earlville, Il, US 155/K3
Early, Ia, US 155/G2
Early, Tx, US 150/E2
Earn (riv.), Sc, UK 33/C4
Earn (lake), Sc, UK 33/B4
Earnslaw (mt.), NZ 135/B4
Earp, Ca, US 148/E3
Easington, Eng, UK 35/G2
Easingwold, Eng, UK 35/G3
Easky, Ire. 32/B1
Easley, SC, US 163/F3
East (mt.), Austl. 130/D4
East (cape), NZ 135/D2
East (cape), Ak, US 171/B6
East (mesa), Ca, US 148/E4
East (cape), Fl, US 165/H5
East (pt.), NJ, US 168/C5
East (riv.), NY, US 169/K8
East (bay), Tx, US 151/G3
East (passg.), Wa, US 167/C3
East Alamosa, Co, US 152/B2
East Alligator (riv.), Austl. 128/D3
East Anglia (reg.), Eng, UK 37/H2
East Angus, Qu, Can. 161/L2
East Arrow Park, BC, Can. 144/F2
East Ayrshire (co.), Sc, UK 33/B6
East Baines (riv.), Austl. 128/C3
East Bangor, Pa, US 168/C2
East Barming, Eng, UK 30/E3
East Barnet (nbrhd.), Eng, UK 30/C2
East Berbice-Corentyne (pol. reg.), Guy. 181/G3
East Bergholt, Eng, UK 37/H3
East Berlin, Pa, US 168/B4
East Bernstadt, Ky, US 162/E2
East Berwick, Pa, US 168/B1
East Bethel, Mn, US 157/H5
East Bijou (cr.), Co, US 154/B4
East Brady, Pa, US 161/G4
East Brewton, Al, US 164/E2
East Brunswick, NJ, US 169/H10
East Cache (cr.), Ok, US 153/E3
East Caicos (isl.), UK 177/J1
East Calder, Sc, UK 33/C5
East Camden, Ar, US 153/H4
East Carbon, Ut, US 147/H4
East Chevington, Eng, UK 33/E6
East Chicago, In, US 160/C4
East China (sea), Asia 77/M6
East Clandon, Eng, UK 30/B3
East Coulee, Ab, Can. 145/H2
East Dart (riv.), Eng, UK 36/C5
East Dereham, Eng, UK 37/G1
East Detroit (East Pointe), Mi, US 167/G7
East Dismal (swamp), NC, US 163/J3
East Dublin, Ga, US 163/F4
East Dumbartonshire (co.), Sc, UK 33/B5
East Falkland (isl.), UK 179/D8
East Falmouth, Ma, US 161/L4
East Farmingdale, NY, US 169/M9
East Flat Rock, NC, US 163/F3
East Fork (riv.), Tx, US 153/F4
East Fork Chandalar (riv.), Ak, US 171/J2
East Fork Trinity (riv.), Tx, US 150/L6
East Frisian (isls.), Neth. 42/D2
East Frisian (isls.), Ger. 40/B5
East Ghor (canal), Jor. 105/D4
East Glacier Park, Mt, US 145/H3
East Glen (riv.), Eng, UK 35/H6
East Grand Rapids, Mi, US 160/D3
East Greenville, Pa, US 168/C3
East Griffin, Ga, US 162/E4
East Grinstead, Eng, UK 37/F4
East Gull Lake, Mn, US 157/G4
East Hampton, NY, US 169/F2
East Hampton (arpt.), NY, US 169/F2
East Hanningfield, Eng, UK 30/E2
East Haven, Ct, US 169/F1
East Helena, Mt, US 145/J4
East Hill-Meridian, Wa, US 167/C3
East Hills, NY, US 169/L8
East Hodge, La, US 164/B1
East Horseley, Eng, UK 30/B3
East Jordan, Mi, US 160/D2
East Kilbride, Sc, UK 33/B5
East Korea (bay), NKor. 79/K4
East Lamma (chan.), China 87/L8
East Lansing, Mi, US 160/D3
East Las Vegas, Nv, US 148/E2
East Leake, Eng, UK 35/G6
East Linton, Sc, UK 33/D5
East Liverpool, Oh, US 160/F4
East London, SAfr. 124/D4
East Los Angeles, Ca, US 166/F7
East Lothian (co.), Sc, UK 33/D5
East Malling, Eng, UK 30/E3
East Meadow, NY, US 169/L9
East Midlands (int'l arpt.), Eng, UK 35/G6
East Millcreek, Ut, US 147/H3
East Mojave Nat'l Scenic Area, Ca, US 148/E3
East Molesey, Eng, UK 30/B2
East Montpelier, Vt, US 161/K2
East Naples, Fl, US 165/H4
East Newark, NJ, US 169/J9
East Nishnabotna (riv.), Ia, US 155/G3
East Nodaway (riv.), Ia, US 155/G3
East Northport, NY, US 169/E2
East Olympia, Wa, US 144/C4
East Orange, NJ, US 169/J8
East Otis, Ma, US 161/K3
East Palatka, Fl, US 165/H3
East Palestine, Oh, US 160/F4
East Peckham, Eng, UK 30/E3
East Petersburg, Pa, US 168/B3
East Point, La, US 150/H1
East Point, Ga, US 163/M7
East Pointe (East Detroit), Mi, US 167/G7
East Port Orchard, Wa, US 167/B2
East Prairie, Mo, US 162/C2
East Prospect, Pa, US 168/B4
East Quogue, NY, US 169/F2
East Riding of Yorkshire (co.), Eng, UK 35/H4
East Renfrewshire (co.), Sc, UK 33/B5
East Retford, Eng, UK 35/H5
East Ridge, Tn, US 162/E3
East Rockaway, NY, US 169/L9
East Rockingham, NC, US 163/H3
East Rutherford, NJ, US 169/J8
East Saint Louis, Il, US 155/J4
East Siberian (sea), Rus. 75/S2
East Side, Pa, US 168/C1
East Stroudsburg, Pa, US 168/C2
East Sussex (co.), Eng, UK 37/G5
East Tampa, Fl, US 164/L8
East Tawas, Mi, US 160/E2
East Thermopolis, Wy, US 147/J2
East Timbalier Island Nat'l Wild. Ref.,La, US 164/C3
East Timor (ctry.) 128/B2
East Troy, Wi, US 167/P14
East Walker (riv.), Ca, Nv, US 146/D4
East Walker (riv.), Ca,Nv, US 148/C1
East Wemyss, Sc, UK 33/C4
East Wenatchee, Wa, US 144/D4
East Windsor, NJ, US 168/D3
East Wittering, Eng, UK 37/F5
East York (city), On, Can. 160/U8
East-the-Water, Eng, UK 36/B4
Eastabuchie, Ms, US 164/D2
Eastbourne, Eng, UK 37/G5
Eastend, Sk, Can. 145/K3
Easter (pt.), Namb. 122/B5
Easter (Isla de Pascua) (isl.), Chile 137/Q7
Eastern (pt.), Nf, Can. 159/H2
Eastern (pol. reg.), Gha. 115/E5
Eastern (chan.), Japan 84/A4
Eastern (prov.), Kenya 119/B1
Eastern (prov.), SLeo. 114/C4
Eastern (prov.), SrL. 95/D5
Eastern (plain), Eng, UK 35/H4
Eastern (bay), Md, US 168/B6
Eastern Fields (reef), PNG 129/G2
Eastern Ghats (mts.), India 92/C5
Eastern Highlands (prov.), PNG 129/G1
Eastern Neck Island NWR, Md, US 168/B5
Eastern Sayans (mts.), Rus. 74/K4
Eastfield, Eng, UK 35/H3
Eastgate, Nv, US 146/E4
Eastland, Tx, US 151/E1
Eastleigh, Eng, UK 37/E5
Eastleigh (int'l arpt.), Eng, UK 37/E5
Eastmain (riv.), Can. 139/K4

Eastmain (riv.), Qu, Can. 141/J3
Eastman, Ga, US 163/F4
Eastman, Wi, US 155/J2
Easton, Eng, UK 36/D5
Easton, Ca, US 148/C2
Easton, Ct, US 169/E1
Easton (res.), Ct, US 169/E1
Easton, Ma, US 161/L3
Easton, La, US 164/B2
Easton, Md, US 163/J1
Easton, Mo, US 155/G4
Easton, Pa, US 168/C2
Easton, Tx, US 151/G1
Eastport, NY, US 169/F2
Eastriggs, Sc, UK 35/E2
Eastry, Eng, UK 37/H4
Eastsound, Wa, US 144/C3
Eastville, Va, US 163/K2
Eastwood, Eng, UK 35/G6
Eatington, Eng, UK 37/E2
Eaton, Co, US 154/B3
Eaton, In, US 160/D4
Eaton, Oh, US 160/D5
Eaton Park, Fl, US 164/M7
Eaton Rapids, Mi, US 160/D3
Eaton Socon, Eng, UK 37/F2
Eatonia, Sk, Can. 145/K2
Eatons Neck (pt.), NY, US 169/M8
Eatonton, Ga, US 163/F4
Eatontown, NJ, US 168/D3
Eatonville, Fl, US 164/N6
Eatonville, Wa, US 144/C4
Eau (riv.), Eng, UK 35/H5
Eau Claire (lake), Qu, Can. 141/J3
Eau Claire (riv.), Wi, US 155/J1
Eau Claire, Wi, US 155/J1
Eau d'Heure (riv.), Belg. 55/D3
Eaubonne, Fr. 30/J5
Eaulne (riv.), Fr. 54/A4
Eauripik (isl.), Micr. 136/D4
Eauze, Fr. 44/D5
Ebalo (riv.), D.R. Congo 116/D5
Ebano, Mex. 176/B1
Ebble (riv.), Eng, UK 37/E4
Ebbw Vale, Wal, UK 36/C3
Ebebiyín, EqG. 120/B2
Ebeggi (well), Alg. 111/G5
Ebéjico, Col. 183/K6
Ebeleben, Ger. 53/H6
Ebeltoft, Den. 40/D3
Ebeltoft Vig (bay), Swe. 39/G6
Eben Junction, Mi, US 157/L4
Ebensburg, Pa, US 161/G4
Ebensee, Aus. 50/A2
Eberbach, Ger. 58/B4
Ebergassing, Aus. 51/P7
Ebergötzen, Ger. 53/H5
Ebermannstadt, Ger. 58/E3
Ebern, Ger. 58/D2
Ebernburg, Ger. 55/G4
Ebersbach an der Fils, Ger. 58/C5
Ebersberg, Ger. 59/E6
Eberschwang, Aus. 59/G6
Ebersheim, Fr. 60/D1
Eberswalde-Finow, Ger. 43/G2
Ebetsu, Japan 82/B2
Ebian, China 93/H2
Ebina, Japan 83/C3
Ebingen, Ger. 61/F1
Ebinur (lake), China 99/D3
Ebnat-Kappel, Swi. 61/F3
Ebo (lake), Mali 114/E3
Ebola (riv.), D.R. Congo 121/E2
Ebolowa, Camr. 120/B2
Ebon (isl.), Mrsh. 136/F4
Ebony, Namb. 122/B4
Ebony, Va, US 163/J2
Ebonyi (state), Nga. 141/H5
Eboro, Gabon 120/B2
Ebrach, Ger. 58/D3
Ebreichsdorf, Aus. 51/N8
Ebro, Mn, US 157/G4
Ebro (riv.), Sp. 29/D4
Ebron (riv.), Fr. 64/B3
Ebstorf, Ger. 53/H2
Ecatepec, Mex. 175/Q9
Ecclefechan, Sc, UK 35/E1
Eccles, Eng, UK 35/F5
Eccles, WV, US 163/G2
Eccleshall, Eng, UK 35/F6
Echague, Phil. 88/C1
Echallens, Swi. 60/C4
Echarate, Peru 184/C4
Echaz (riv.), Ger. 58/C6
Éché Fadadinga (riv.), Niger 115/H3
Éché Téfidinga (riv.), Niger 116/B2
Echigawa, Japan 83/K5
Eching, Ger. 59/E6
Échirolles, Fr. 64/B2
Echo, La, US 164/B2
Echo (lake), NJ, US 168/D1
Echo Bay, On, Can. 160/D1
Echo Bay, NW, Can. 140/E2
Echols, Ky, US 162/D2
Echt, Neth. 55/E1
Echterdingen (int'l arpt.), Ger. 58/C5
Echternach, Lux. 55/F4
Echuca, Austl. 133/B3
Echunga, Austl. 131/M9
Echunga (cr.), Austl. 131/M9
Echzell, Ger. 58/B2
Écija, Sp. 46/C4
Ečka, Yugo. 50/E3
Eckernförde, Ger. 40/C4
Eckerö, Fin. 41/H1
Eckerö (isl.), Fin. 41/H1
Eckington, Eng, UK 35/G5
Eckington, Eng, UK 36/D2
Eckville, Ab, Can. 144/G1
Eclectic, Al, US 162/D4
Eclipse Sound (bay), Nun, Can. 141/H1
Écommoy, Fr. 57/F5
Ecorse, Mi, US 167/F7
Ecorse (riv.), Mi, US 167/F7
Écos, Fr. 57/G2
Écouché, Fr. 57/E3
Écouen, Fr. 30/K4
Ecquevilly, Fr. 30/H5
Ecrins, PN, Fr. 45/G4
Ecrosnes, Fr. 30/H6
Écrouves, Fr. 55/E6
Ecru, Ms, US 162/C3
Ecuador (ctry.) 179/A2
Ecublens, Swi. 60/C4
Ed, Swe. 40/D2
Ēd, Erit. 118/B2
Edam, Neth. 52/C3
Edam, Sk, Can. 145/K1
Edapalli, India 95/C4
Eday (isl.), Sc, UK 31/V14
Edchera, Mor. 110/B4
Edderton, Sc, UK 33/B1
Eddleston, Sc, UK 33/C5
Eddy (peak), Id, US 144/F3
Eddystone, Mb, Can. 156/E2
Eddystone (pt.), Austl. 132/D4
Eddystone Rocks (isls.), Eng, UK 36/B6
Eddyville, Ia, US 155/H3
Eddyville, Ky, US 162/C2
Ede, Nga. 115/G5
Ede, Neth. 52/C4
Edéa, Camr. 120/B2
Edegem, Belg. 55/D1
Edehin Ouarene (des.), Alg. 111/G4
Edéia, Braz. 189/G1
Edelény, Hun. 43/L4
Edemissen, Ger. 53/H4
Eden, Austl. 133/D3
Eden, Mb, Can. 156/E2
Eden (riv.), Sc, UK 33/D4
Eden, Az, US 149/H4
Eden, Md, US 163/K1
Eden, NC, US 163/H2
Eden, Tx, US 150/E2
Eden, Wy, US 147/J2
Eden Mills, On, Can. 160/S8
Eden Prairie, Mn, US 157/P7
Edenbridge, Eng, UK 30/D3
Edenburg, SAfr. 124/D3
Edendale, NZ 135/B4
Edendale, SAfr. 125/E3
Edenderry, Ire. 32/C3
Edenhope, Austl. 132/B3
Edenkoben, Ger. 58/B4
Edenside (valley), Eng, UK 35/F2
Edenton, NC, US 163/J2
Edenwold, Sk, Can. 156/B2
Eder (riv.), Ger. 42/E3
Eder-Stausee (lake), Ger. 53/F6
Edewecht, Ger. 53/E2
Edgar, Mt, US 147/J1
Edgar, Ne, US 154/F3
Edgar, Wi, US 155/K1
Edgar (mt.), Austl. 130/D2
Edgar Springs, Mo, US 153/J2
Edgard, La, US 164/C2
Edgartown, Ma, US 158/B5
Edgbaston, Eng, UK 37/E2
Edge (isl.), Sval. 192/E
Edgecliff, Tx, US 150/K7
Edgecumbe (cape), Ak, US 171/L4
Edgefield, La, US 164/B1
Edgefield, SC, US 163/G4
Edgeley, ND, US 156/E4
Edgell (isl.), Nun, Can. 141/K2
Edgemere, Md, US 168/B5
Edgemont, SD, US 154/C2
Edgerton, Ab, Can. 145/J1
Edgerton, Mn, US 155/F2
Edgerton, Oh, US 160/D4
Edgerton, Wi, US 155/K2
Edgerton, Wy, US 154/A2
Edgewater, BC, Can. 144/F2
Edgewater, Fl, US 165/H3
Edgewater Park, NJ, US 168/D3
Edgewood, Fl, US 164/N7
Edgewood, Il, US 162/C1
Edgewood, Md, US 168/B5
Edgewood, NM, US 149/J3
Edgewood, Pa, US 168/B2
Edgewood, Tx, US 151/G1
Edgewood Arsenal, Md, US 168/B5
Edgewood-North Hill, Wa, US 167/C3
Edgmond, Eng, UK 36/D1
Edgware (nbrhd.), Eng, UK 30/C2
Édhessa, Gre. 49/H2
Edievale, NZ 135/B4
Edina, Libr. 114/C5
Edina, Mo, US 155/H3
Edina, Mn, US 157/P7
Edinboro, Pa, US 160/F4
Edinburgh (cap.), Sc, UK 33/C5
Edinburgh (co.), Sc, UK 33/C5
Edinburg, ND, US 156/F3
Edinburg, Ms, US 162/C4
Edinburg, Tx, US 151/E4
Edinburg, Va, US 163/H1
Edinburgh, In, US 160/D5
Edinet, Mol. 72/D3
Edingeni, Malw. 123/G2
Edirne (prov.), Turk. 70/C4
Edirne, Turk. 51/H5
Edison, Co, US 152/B1
Edison, Ga, US 165/F2
Edison, NJ, US 169/H9
Edison, Ca, US 148/C3
Edison Nat'l Hist. Site, NJ, US 169/J8
Edisto, SC, US 163/G4
Edisto (isl.), SC, US 163/G4
Edisto (riv.), SC, US 163/G4
Edisto Island, SC, US 163/G4
Edisto, South Fork (riv.), SC, US 163/G4
Edith Cavell (mt.), BC, Can. 144/E1
Edithburgh, Austl. 131/H5
Edjeleh, Alg. 111/H4
Édjérir (riv.), Mali 115/F2
Edmond, Ok, US 153/F3
Edmonds, Wa, US 144/C4
Edmondt, FrG. 182/C1
Edmonton (nbrhd.), Eng, UK 30/C2
Edmonton, Austl. 134/B2
Edmonton (cap.), Ab, Can. 145/H1
Edmonton, Ky, US 162/E2
Edmonton (int'l arpt.), Ab, Can. 145/H1
Edmore, ND, US 156/E3
Edmore, Mi, US 160/D3
Edmund Kennedy NP, Austl. 134/B2
Edmundston, NB, Can. 158/C2
Edna, Ks, US 153/G2
Edna, Tx, US 151/F3
Edna Bay, Ak, US 171/M4
Edo (state), Nga. 115/G5
Edo (riv.), Japan 83/D2
Edolo, It. 61/G5
Edom, Tx, US 151/G1
Edosaki, Japan 83/E2
Edremit (gulf), Gre.,Turk. 70/C5
Edsbro, Swe. 39/B1
Edsbyn, Swe. 40/F1
Eduardo Castex, Arg. 190/D2
Eduardo Gomes (int'l arpt.), Braz. 182/A3
Edward (isl.), On, Can. 157/K3
Edward (mt.), Austl. 131/F2
Edward (riv.), Austl. 133/B2
Edward (lake), D.R. Congo, Ugan. 107/E5
Edward River Abor. Community, Austl. 134/A1
Edward VII (pen.), Ant. 192/P
Edward VIII (bay), Ant. 192/D
Edwards (plat.), Tx, US 142/F5
Edwards, Ms, US 162/B4
Edwards (riv.), Il, US 155/J3
Edwards (A.F.B.), Ca, US 148/C3
Edwardsville, Il, US 155/K4
Edwardsville, Pa, US 168/C1
Edwin, Al, US 165/F2
Edzell, Sc, UK 33/D3
Edzná (ruin), Mex. 176/D2
Eefde, Neth. 52/D4
Eek, Ak, US 171/F3
Eeklo, Belg. 54/C1
Eel (riv.), Ca, US 146/B4
Eel, South Fork (riv.), Ca, US 146/B3
Eelde-Paterswolde, Neth. 52/D2
Eem (riv.), Neth. 52/C4
Eemenes, Neth. 52/C4
Eems (Ems) (riv.), Ger., Neth. 52/D2
Eemshaven (har.), Neth. 52/D2
Eemskanaal (riv.), Neth. 52/D2
Eersel, Neth. 52/C6
Efate (isl.), Van. 136/F6
Eferding, Aus. 59/H6
Effie, Mn, US 157/H4
Effigy Mounds Nat'l Mon., Ia, US 155/J2
Effingham, Eng, UK 30/B3
Effingham, Il, US 162/C1
Effingham, Ks, US 155/G4
Effingham, On, Can. 160/U9
Effon Alaiye, Nga. 115/G5
Effort, Pa, US 168/C2
Efogi, PNG 129/G2
Eforie, Rom. 51/J3
Efringen-Kirchen, Ger. 60/D2
Egadi (isls.), It. 67/G3
Egan (riv.), Ger. 58/D5
Egan, Tx, US 150/K7
Egaña, Uru. 191/K10
Egbe, Nga. 115/G4
Egbunda, D.R. Congo 121/F2
Egegik, Ak, US 171/G4
Egeland, ND, US 156/E3
Eger (riv.), Ger. 42/G3
Eger, Hun. 43/L5
Egeskov, Den. 40/D4
Egestorf, Ger. 53/H2
Egg, Aus. 61/F3
Egg, Swi. 61/E3
Egg Harbor City, NJ, US 168/D4
Egg Island (pt.), NJ, US 168/C5
Egg Lagoon, Austl. 133/A4
Eggebek, Ger. 40/C4
Eggegebirge (ridge), Ger. 53/F5
Eggelsberg, Aus. 59/F6
Eggenburg, Aus. 45/L2
Eggenfelden, Ger. 59/F6
Eggenstein-Leopoldshafen, Ger. 58/B4
Eggesin, Ger. 40/F5
Eggiwil, Swi. 60/D4
Egglescliffe, Eng, UK 35/G3
Eggleston, Eng, UK 35/G2
Eggstätt, Ger. 59/F7
Egham, Eng, UK 30/B2
Éghezée, Belg. 55/D2
Egilsstadhir, Ice. 38/P6
Egito, Ang. 122/B2
Egiyn (riv.), Mong. 78/E1
Égletons, Fr. 44/E4
Eglinton, NI, UK 34/A1
Eglinton (isl.), NW, Can. 141/Q7
Eglinton (Londonderry) (arpt.), UK 34/A1
Eglisau, Swi. 61/E2
Eglwys-Brewis, Wal, UK 36/C4
Égly, Fr. 30/J6
Egmond aan Zee, Neth. 52/B3
Egmont (bay), PE, Can. 158/E2
Egmont (mt.), NZ 135/C2
Egmont (cape), NZ 135/C2
Egmont Key Nat'l Wild. Ref., Fl, US 164/K8
Egmont NP, NZ 135/C2
Egna (Neumarkt), It. 61/H5
Egnach, Swi. 61/F2
Egnar, Co, US 149/H2
Egoumbi, Gabon 120/B3
Egra, India 97/F5
Egremont, Eng, UK 34/E3
Eğridir, Turk. 102/B2
Eğridir (lake), Turk. 102/B2
Éguas, Rio das (riv.), Braz. 186/D2
Éguilles, Fr. 64/B5
Egvekinot, Rus. 75/U3
Egypt (ctry.) 107/E2
Egypt Lake, Fl, US 164/L7
Eha Amufu, Nga. 115/G5
Ehebach (riv.), Ger. 58/D3
Ehekirchen, Ger. 58/D5
Ehime (pref.), Japan 84/C4
Ehingen, Ger. 61/F1
Ehingen, Ger. 58/D4
Ehrenberg, Az, US 148/E4
Ehrhardt, SC, US 163/G4
Ehringshausen, Ger. 58/B1
Ehrwald, Aus. 61/G3
Eiao (isl.), FrPol. 137/L5
Eibar, Sp. 44/B5
Eibelstadt, Ger. 58/C3
Eibenstock, Ger. 59/F1
Eibergen, Neth. 52/D4
Eich, Ger. 58/B3
Eichel (riv.), Fr. 55/G6
Eichenau, Ger. 58/E6
Eichenbühl, Ger. 58/C3
Eichendorf, Ger. 59/F5
Eichenzell, Ger. 58/C2
Eichstätt, Ger. 58/E5
Eichwalde, Ger. 42/Q7
Eicklingen, Ger. 53/H3
Eid, Nor. 38/C3
Eidelstedt, Ger. 53/G1
Eidfjord, Nor. 40/B1
Eidsfoss, Nor. 38/R9
Eidsvold, Austl. 134/C4
Eidsvoll, Nor. 40/D1
Eifel (plat.), Ger. 42/D3
Eiffel Flats, Zim. 123/F3
Eiffel Tower, Fr. 30/J5
Eigenji, Japan 83/K5
Eiger (peak), Swi. 60/D4
Eigersund, Nor. 40/A2
Eigg (isl.), Sc, UK 31/Q8
Eight Degree (chan.), India,Mald. 95/B5
Eighteenmile (peak), Id, US 147/G1
Eighty Mile Beach (beach), Austl. 128/A4
Eijerlandse Gat (chan.), Neth. 52/B2
Eijsden, Neth. 55/E2
Eikelandsosen, Nor. 40/A1
Eikeren (lake), Nor. 38/R9
Eil, Loch (inlet), Sc, UK 33/A3
Eildon, Austl. 133/B3
Eilerts de Haan (mts.), Sur. 181/G4
'Ein Māhil, Isr. 105/C3
Eina, Nor. 40/D1
Einbeck, Ger. 53/G5
Eindhoven (int'l arpt.), Neth. 52/C6
Eindhoven, Neth. 52/C6
Einsiedeln, Swi. 61/E3
Einville-au-Jard, Fr. 55/F6
Eirunepé, Braz. 184/D2
Eirup, Namb. 122/C5
Eisack (Isarco) (riv.), It. 61/H4
Eisch (riv.), Lux. 55/E4
Eiseb (riv.), Namb. 122/C4
Eisenach, Ger. 53/H7
Eisenberg, Ger. 58/B3
Eisenerz, Aus. 45/L3
Eisenhower (mt.), Ab, Can. 144/G2
Eisenhower Nat'l Hist. Site, Pa, US 168/A4
Eisenhüttenstadt, Ger. 43/H2
Eisenstadt, Aus. 50/C2
Eiserfeld, Ger. 55/G2
Eisfeld, Ger. 58/D2
Eisingen, Ger. 58/C3
Eišiškės, Lith. 41/L4
Eislingen, Ger. 58/C5
Eitelborn, Ger. 55/G3
Eiter (riv.), Ger. 53/F3
Eitorf, Ger. 55/G2
Eitting, Ger. 59/E6
Ejea de los Caballeros, Sp. 47/E1
Ejeda, Madg. 125/H9
Ejido, Ven. 180/D2
Ejin Horo Qi, China 80/B3
Ejin Qi, China 78/E3
Ejule, Nga. 115/G5
Ejura, Gha. 115/E5
Ejutla de Crespo, Mex. 176/B2
Ekalaka, Mt, US 156/B5
Ekang, Nga. 115/H5
Ekata, Gabon 120/C2
Ekeby, Swe. 40/E3
Ekeby, Swe. 39/A1
Ekenäs (Tammisaari), Fin. 41/K2
Ekeren, Belg. 52/B6
Ekerö, Swe. 39/A1
Eket, Nga. 120/A1
Eketahuna, NZ 135/C3
Ekhínos, Gre. 49/J2
Ekibastuz, Kaz. 99/C1
Ekimchan, Rus. 79/L1
Ekma, India 97/E3
Ekoko, D.R. Congo 121/E2
Ekoli, D.R. Congo 121/F3
Ekoln (lake), Swe. 39/A1
Ekondo Titi, Camr. 120/B1
Ekpoma, Nga. 115/G5
Eksjö, Swe. 40/F3
Ekuk, Ak, US 171/G4
Ekuku, D.R. Congo 121/E3
Ekukula, D.R. Congo 121/E2
Ekwan (riv.), On, Can. 141/H3
Ekwendeni, Malw. 123/G1
Ekwok, Ak, US 171/G4
El Aaiún, WSah. 110/B4
El Aaiún (Hassan) (int'l arpt.), WSah. 110/B4
El Aargub, WSah. 110/B5
El Aatf (reg.), WSah. 110/B5
El Abanico, Chile 190/C3
El Abiodh Sidi Chrikh, Alg. 111/F2
Ēl Ābrēd, Eth. 118/C4
El Affroun, Alg. 112/G4
El Aïoun, Mor. 112/C2
El Alamein (Al 'Alamayan), Egypt 109/F2
El Álamo, Mex. 151/E4
El Alia, Alg. 111/G2
El Alto, Peru 184/A2
El Alto (int'l arpt.), Bol. 188/B1
El Amparo de Apure, Ven. 180/D3
El Anegado, Ecu. 180/A5
El Aouinet, Alg. 112/K7
El Arahal, Sp. 46/C4
El Arhlaf (well), Mrta. 114/D2
El Aricha, Alg. 112/D2
El Arrayán, Chile 190/N8
El Astillero, Sp. 46/D1
El Avila, PN, Ven. 183/P7
El Bagre, Col. 180/C3
El Banco, Col. 180/C2
El Barco, Sp. 46/B1
El Barco de Ávila, Sp. 46/C2
El Baúl, Ven. 180/D2
El Bayadh (wilaya), Alg. 111/F2
El Bayadh, Alg. 111/F2
El Ben, Kenya 119/C1
El Bolsón, Arg. 190/C4
El Bonillo, Sp. 46/D3
El Borouj, Mor. 110/D2
El Burgo de Osma, Sp. 46/D2
El Caín, Arg. 190/C4
El Cajon, Ca, US 166/D5
El Cajón (res.), Hon. 176/E3
El Calafate, Arg. 191/B6
El Callao, Ven. 181/F3
El Campo, Tx, US 151/F3
El Capitan (peak), Mt, US 144/G4
El Carmen, Bol. 185/F4
El Carmen, Bol. 185/E4
El Carmen, Chile 190/B3
El Carmen, Col. 180/B3
El Carmen, Mex. 151/D5
El Carmen, Peru 184/B4
El Carmen, Ven. 181/E4
El Carmen de Bolívar, Col. 180/C2
El Casabe, Ven. 181/F3
El Casar de Talamanca, Sp. 47/N8
El Centro Nav. Air Facility, Ca, US 148/D4
El Cerrito, Ca, US 167/K11
El Cerrito, Col. 180/B4
El Cerrito, Arg. 191/C6
El Cerro, Bol. 188/D1
El Cerro del Aripo (peak), Trin. 181/F2
El Cerrón (peak), Ven. 180/D2
El Chico, PN, Mex. 175/L6
El Chorro, Arg. 188/D2
El Cocuy, Col. 180/C3
El Cocuy (dept.), Col. 180/C3
El Colegio, Col. 183/L8
El Colorado, Arg. 188/E3
El Cóndor, Arg. 191/C7
El Cuy, Arg. 190/C3
El Der (riv.), Som. 118/C3
El Dere, Eth. 118/B4
El Descanso, Mex. 148/D4
El Difícil, Col. 180/C2
El Djezair (Algiers) (cap.), Alg. 112/G4
El Djouf (des.), Alg. 110/D5
El Dorado, Ks, US 153/F2
El Dorado, Ar, US 153/H4
El Dorado (lake), Ks, US 153/F2
El Dorado, Ven. 181/F3
El Dorado, Mex. 174/D3
El Dorado Springs, Mo, US 153/G2
El Edén, Ecu. 180/B5
El Eglab (plat.), Alg. 110/D4
El Empedrado, Ven. 180/D2
El Escorial, Sp. 47/M8
El Espinar, Sp. 46/C2
El Eulma, Alg. 112/H4
El Fahs, Tun. 112/L6
El Ferrol, Sp. 46/A1
El Fuerte, Mex. 174/C3
El Fureidīs, Isr. 105/B3
El Galhak, Sudan 117/G3
El Galpón, Arg. 188/C3
El Gogorrón, PN, Mex. 172/A3
El Golea, Alg. 111/F3
El Golfete (lake), Guat. 176/D3
El Granada, Ca, US 167/K11
El Grullo, Mex. 174/D5
El Guachara, PN, Ven. 181/F2
El Guapo, Ven. 183/P7
El Gulut, Eth. 117/G2
El Had Harrara, Mor. 110/C2
El Hajeb, Mor. 112/B3
El Hank (cliff), Mali, 110/D4
El Harino, Pan. 180/A2
El Harta (well), Alg. 111/E4
El Higo, Mex. 176/B1
El Indio, Tx, US 151/D3
El Jadida, Mor. 110/C2
El Kbab, Mor. 110/D2
El Kelaâ des Srarhna, Mor. 110/D2
Ēl Kerē, Eth. 118/B4
El Khatt (depr.), Mrta. 114/C2
El Khnâchîch (cliff), Mali 110/E5
Ēl K'oran, Eth. 118/C4
El Kroub, Alg. 112/K6
El Kseur, Alg. 112/H4
Ēl Lēh, Eth. 118/A5
El Libertador General Bernardo O'Higgins (pol. reg.), Chile 190/N8
El Limón, Mex. 175/F4
El Mahia (phys. reg.), Mali 111/E5
El Maitén, Arg. 190/C4
El Mallaile, Eth. 118/B4
El Malpais Nat'l Mon., NM, US 149/H3
El Manteco, Ven. 181/F3
El Manzanito, Chile 190/N8
El Manzano, Chile 190/N9
El Medera, Eth. 118/B4
El Messir (well), Chad 116/C2
El Miamo, Ven. 181/F3
El Milia, Alg. 112/J4
El Mirage, Ca, US 166/C1
El Mirage (lake), Ca, US 148/D3
El Mojar, Bol. 185/E4
El Montcau (peak), Sp. 47/K6
El Monte, Ca, US 166/F7
El Morrito (pt.), Chile 190/C1
El Morro, NM, US 149/H3
El Mrâyer (well), Mrta. 110/C5
El Mreyyé (phys. reg.), Mrta. 114/C2
El Mzereb (well), Mali 110/D4
El Naranjo de Carlos Sarabia, Mex. 175/F4
El Nayar, Mex. 174/D4
El Nevado (peak), Arg. 190/C2
El Nido, Ca, US 148/B2
El Nido, Phil. 88/B3
El Olivar Alto, Chile 190/N9
El Oro (dept.), Ecu. 184/A1
El Oso, Ven. 182/A1
El Oued (wilaya), Alg. 111/G2
El Oued, Alg. 111/G2
El Palmar, Ven. 181/F3
El Palmar, Bol. 188/D2
El Palmar, Mex. 175/N8
El Palmar, PN, Arg. 188/E4
El Pao, Ven. 181/F2
El Pao, Ven. 181/E2
El Pao, Ven. 183/M8
El Paraíso, Hon. 176/E3
El Paraíso, Col. 180/C4
El Paraíso, Mex. 175/E5
El Pardo, Sp. 47/N8
El Paso, Il, US 155/K3
El Paso, Tx, US 151/A2
El Paso de Robles (Paso Robles), Ca, US 148/B3
El Paso International (int'l arpt.), Tx, US 151/A2
El Pato, Col. 180/C4
El Pensamiento, Bol. 185/F4
El Perú, Bol. 185/E4
El Pilar, Ven. 181/F2
El Pilar, Bol. 185/E4
El Pintado, Arg. 188/D3
El Piquete, Arg. 188/C3
El Plumerillo (Mendoza) (int'l arpt.), Arg. 190/C2
El Portal, Ca, US 148/C2
El Porvenir, Mex. 151/B2
El Porvenir, Pan. 180/B2
El Porvenir, Ven. 180/D3
El Porvenir, Mex. 148/D4
El Potosí, Mex. 175/E3
El Potosí, PN, Mex. 172/B3
El Prat de Llobregat, Sp. 47/L7
El Progreso, Guat. 176/D3
El Progreso, Hon. 176/E3
El Progreso, Ecu. 184/K7
El Progreso Industrial, Mex. 175/Q9
El Puente, Bol. 185/F5
El Puente, Bol. 188/C2
El Puerto de Santa María, Sp. 46/B4
El Pun, Ecu. 180/B4
El Quebrachal, Arg. 188/C3
El Quelite, Mex. 174/D4
El Quisco, Chile 190/N8
El Rama, Nic. 177/E3
El Rastro, Ven. 183/N8
El Remolino, Mex. 151/D3
El Reno, Ok, US 153/F3
El Rey, PN, Arg. 188/C3
El Rio, Ca, US 166/A2
El Rio (canal), Fl, US 164/P10
El Rito, NM, US 149/J2
El Roble, Pan. 180/A2
El Roque, Ven. 181/E2
El Rosario de Arriba, Mex. 174/B2
El Sabinal, PN, Mex. 151/E4
El Sacromonte, PN, Mex. 175/L7
El Salado, Col. 183/K8
El Salado, Arg. 191/D6
El Salto, Mex. 174/D4
El Salvador, Cuba 177/H1
El Salvador (int'l arpt.), ESal. 176/D3
El Salvador (ctry.) 139/H8
El Salvador, Mex. 175/E3
El Samán de Apure, Ven. 180/D3
El Sauz, Mex. 151/A3
El Sauzal, Mex. 174/A2
El Segundo, Ca, US 166/F8
El Shab (well), Egypt 109/F4
El Socorro, Col. 180/D3
El Sombrero, Arg. 190/C5
El Sombrero, Ven. 183/N8
El Sosneado, Arg. 190/C2
El Tabo, Chile 190/N8
El Tajín (ruin), Mex. 175/M6
El Tala, Arg. 188/C3
El Tama, PN, Ven. 180/C3
El Tambo, Ecu. 180/B5
El Tarf (wilaya), Alg. 112/K6
El Tarf, Alg. 112/L6
El Teleno (peak), Sp. 46/B1
El Tepozteco, PN, Mex. 175/R10
El Tiemblo, Sp. 46/C2
El Tigre, Ven. 181/E2
El Tocuyo, Ven. 180/D2
El Toro, Ca, US 166/C3
El Toro, Ven. 181/F2
El Toro, Tx, US 151/F3
El Tránsito, Chile 188/B4
El Trébol, Arg. 188/D5
El Triunfo, Mex. 176/D2
El Triunfo, Ecu. 180/B5
El Tucuche (peak), Trin. 181/F2
El Tuito, Mex. 174/D4
El Tuparro, PN, Col. 180/D3
El Vado, NM, US 149/J2
El Valle, Pan. 180/A2
El Venado (isl.), Nic. 177/F4
El Viejo, Nic. 176/E3
El Viejo (peak), Col. 180/C3
El Vigía, Ven. 180/D2
El Vínculo, Ven. 180/D1
El Volcán, Chile 190/N8
El Wak, Kenya 119/C1
El Yagual, Ven. 180/D3
El Yunque (peak), PR 173/M8
El Zacatón, Mex. 174/E4
El Zurdo, Arg. 191/C6
El'ton (lake), Rus. 71/H2
El-Gezira, 'Erg, Egypt 113/C2
El-Girba (peak), Egypt 113/D4
El-Hammam (ruin), Egypt 113/B6
El-Kasdir, Alg. 112/D3
El-Menzel, Mor. 112/B3
El-Tarâbîl (peak), Egypt 113/D6
Ela, Myan. 86/C5
El'Acâba (pol. reg.), Mrta. 114/C2
Elaho (riv.), BC, Can. 144/C2
Elaine, Ar, US 162/B3
Elan (riv.), Wal, UK 36/C2
Élancourt, Fr. 30/H5
Elands (riv.), SAfr. 123/E5
Elandsrivier (riv.), SAfr. 124/Q12
Elangata Wuas, Kenya 119/B2
Elarmilon, Gabon 120/B2
Elassón, Gre. 49/H3
Elat (int'l arpt.), Isr. 104/D5
Elat, Isr. 109/G2
Elátia, Gre. 49/H3
Elato (isl.), Micr. 136/D4
Elavagnon, Togo 115/F5
Elazığ, Turk. 102/D2
Elazığ (prov.), Turk. 102/D2
Elba, Al, US 165/E2
Elba (isl.), It. 48/B1
El'ban, Rus. 79/M1
Elbasan, Alb. 49/G2
Elbbach (riv.), Ger. 55/G2
Elbe (riv.), Ger. 29/F3
Elbe (Labe) (riv.), Czh.,Ger. 43/H2
Elbe-Seitenkanaal (canal), Ger. 53/H2
Elbert, Tx, US 152/E4
Elberton, Ga, US 163/F3
Elbeuf, Fr. 57/G2
Elbigenalp, Aus. 61/G3
Elbląg, Pol. 41/H4
Elbow (riv.), Ab, Can. 144/G2
Elbow, Sk, Can. 145/L2
Elbow Lake, Mn, US 156/G5
El'brus (peak), Rus. 71/G4
Elburg, Neth. 52/C4
Elburgon, Kenya 119/A2
Elburn, Il, US 167/N16
Elburz (mts.), Iran 74/E6
Elche, Sp. 47/E3
Elche de la Sierra, Sp. 46/D3
Elchingen, Ger. 58/D6
Elcho, Wi, US 157/K5
Elcho (isl.), Austl. 129/D2
Elcho (isl.) 127/C2
Eld (inlet), Wa, US 167/A3
Elda, Sp. 47/E3
Eldama Ravine, Kenya 119/A1
Elde (riv.), Ger. 42/G2
Eldersburg, Md, US 168/B5
El'dikan, Rus. 75/P3
Eldivan, Turk. 70/E4
Eldon, Mo, US 153/H1
Eldon, Wa, US 167/A2
Eldon, Ia, US 155/H3
Eldora, Ia, US 155/H2
Eldora, NJ, US 168/D5
Eldorado, Arg. 189/F3
Eldorado, Braz. 189/G3
Eldorado, Braz. 189/F2
Eldorado (int'l arpt.), Col. 183/L8
Eldorado, Il, US 162/C2
Eldorado, Ok, US 152/E3
Eldorado, Tx, US 151/D2
Eldoret, Kenya 119/A1
Eldridge, Al, US 162/D4
Eldridge, Ia, US 155/J3
Eleanor, WV, US 163/G1
Electra, Tx, US 152/E3
Elefsís, Gre. 49/N8
Elefsís (arpt.), Gre. 49/N8
Elefsís (ruin), Gre. 49/N8
Eleja, Lat. 41/K3
Elek, Hun. 50/E2
Elėktrėnai, Lith. 41/L4
Elektrostal', Rus. 69/X9
Elele, Nga. 115/G5
Elena, Arg. 190/D2
Elena, Bul. 51/G4
Elephant (mtn.), Me, US 161/L2
Elephant Butte, NM, US 149/J4
Elephant Butte (res.), NM, US 149/J4
Elesbão Veloso, Braz. 183/F4
Eleşkirt, Turk. 103/E2
Eleuthera (isl.), Bahm. 139/K7
Eleven Point (riv.), Mo,Ar, US 153/J2
Elevtheroúpolis, Gre. 49/J2
Elfers, Fl, US 164/K7
Elfershausen, Ger. 58/C2
Elfin Cove, Ak, US 171/L4
Elfrida, On, Can. 160/T9
Elfros, Sk, Can. 156/C2
Elgg, Swi. 61/E3
Elgin, Mb, Can. 156/D3
Elgin, Sc, UK 33/C1
Elgin, Az, US 149/G5
Elgin, Il, US 160/B3
Elgin, Ks, US 153/F2
Elgin, ND, US 156/D4
Elgin, Nv, US 148/E2
Elgin, Ok, US 153/E3
Elgin, Or, US 146/E1
Elgin, SC, US 163/G3
Elgin, Tn, US 162/E2
Elgin, Tx, US 150/F2
Elgin Mills, On, Can. 160/U8
Elgóibar, Sp. 44/B5
Elgon (Wagagai) (peak), Ugan. 119/A1
Elias Garcia, Ang. 120/E5
Elida, NM, US 152/C4
Elida, Oh, US 160/D4
Elie, Sc, UK 33/D4
Elila (riv.), D.R. Congo 121/F3
Elila, D.R. Congo 121/F3
Elim, Ak, US 171/F3
Elim, SAfr. 124/L11
Elimäki, Fin. 41/M1
Eling, Eng, UK 37/E5
Eliot, Me, US 161/L3
Elipa, D.R. Congo 121/E3
Elisenvaara, Rus. 41/N1
Eliseu Martins, Braz. 183/F5
Elista, Rus. 71/H3
Elixhausen, Aus. 59/G7
Elizabeth (mtn.), Austl. 133/C3
Elizabeth (nbrhd.), Austl. 131/M8
Elizabeth (bay), Namb. 124/A2
Elizabeth, Co, US 154/B4
Elizabeth, Ga, US 163/L7
Elizabeth, La, US 164/B2
Elizabeth (isls.), Ma, US 158/B5
Elizabeth, Mn, US 156/F4
Elizabeth, NJ, US 169/J9
Elizabeth (cr.), Tx, US 150/K6
Elizabeth, WV, US 163/G1
Elizabeth City, NC, US 163/J2
Elizabethan Village Hist. Site, Austl. 130/L7
Elizabethton, Tn, US 163/F2
Elizabethtown, Il, US 162/C2
Elizabethtown, In, US 162/E1
Elizabethtown, Ky, US 162/E2
Elizabethtown, NC, US 163/H3
Elizabethtown, Pa, US 168/B3
Elizabethtown, NY, US 161/K2
Elizabethville, Pa, US 168/B2
Elizondo, Sp. 44/C5
Ełk, Pol. 41/K5
Elk (riv.), BC, Can. 144/G2
Elk (riv.), Al,Tn, US 162/D3
Elk (mts.), Co, US 147/K4
Elk (mtn.), Or, US 146/E1
Elk (hill), Pa, US 161/J4
Elk (riv.), WV, US 163/G1
Elk City, Ks, US 153/G2
Elk City (dam), Ks, US 153/G2
Elk City, Ok, US 152/E3
Elk Creek, Ca, US 146/B4
Elk Creek, Ne, US 155/F3
Elk Grove, Ca, US 167/M10
Elk Grove Village, Il, US 167/P16
Elk Mills, Md, US 168/C4
Elk NP, Ab, Can. 145/H1
Elk Point, SD, US 155/F2
Elk Rapids, Mi, US 160/D2
Elk Ridge, Md, US 168/B5
Elk Ridge (ridge), Tn, US 162/D3
Elk River, Mn, US 157/H5
Elk Silver, NM, US 152/B4
Elk Slough (riv.), Ca, US 167/L10
Elk Springs, Co, US 147/J3
Elk Valley, Tn, US 162/E2
Elkader, Ia, US 155/J2
Elkenroth, Ger. 55/G2
Elkford, BC, Can. 144/G2
Elkhart, Ks, US 152/D2
Elkhart, In, US 160/D4
Elkhart, Tx, US 150/G2
Elkhorn, Mb, Can. 156/D3
Elkhorn (riv.), Ne, US 143/G3
Elkhorn, Wi, US 155/K2
Elkhovo, Bul. 51/H4
Elkin, NC, US 163/G2
Elkins, WV, US 163/H1
Elkland, Pa, US 161/H4
Elko, Nv, US 146/F3
Elko, BC, Can. 144/G3
Elkton, Ky, US 162/D2
Elkton, Md, US 168/C4
Elkton, Tn, US 162/D3
Elkton, Va, US 163/H1
Elkview, WV, US 163/G1
Elkwater, Ab, Can. 145/J3
Ellamar, Ak, US 171/J3
Elland, Eng, UK 35/G4
Ellaville, Ga, US 162/E4
Ellé (riv.), Fr. 56/B5
Elle (riv.), Ger. 55/F2
Ellef Ringnes (isl.) 139/G2
Ellefeld, Ger. 59/F2
Ellen (riv.), Eng, UK 35/E2
Ellen (mt.), Ut, US 149/G1
Ellenābād, India 98/C5
Ellenberg, Ger. 58/D4
Ellendale, Austl. 128/B4
Ellendale, De, US 168/C6
Ellendale, ND, US 156/E4
Ellensburg, Wa, US 144/D4
Ellenton, Ga, US 165/G2
Ellenville, NY, US 161/J4
Ellenwood, Ga, US 163/M7
Eller (riv.), Ger. 53/H5
Ellerbach (riv.), Ger. 55/G4
Ellerbe, NC, US 163/H3
Ellero (riv.), It. 62/A4
Ellerslie, Ga, US 162/E4
Ellerslie, La, US 164/C3
Ellerslie, PE, Can. 158/F2
Ellery (mt.), Austl. 133/D3
Ellesmere (isl.), Can. 139/J2
Ellesmere Port, Eng, UK 35/F5
Ellettsville, In, US 160/C5
Ellezelles, Belg. 54/C2
Elliant, Fr. 56/B4
Ellice (riv.), Nun, Can. 140/F2
Ellicott City, Md, US 168/B5
Ellijay, Ga, US 162/E3
Ellington, Mo, US 162/B2
Ellinikón (int'l arpt.), Gre. 49/N9
Ellinwood, Ks, US 153/E1
Elliot, SAfr. 124/D3
Elliot Key (isl.), Fl, US 165/H5
Elliot Lake, On, Can. 160/E1
Elliot Price Consv. Park, Austl. 131/H4
Elliott, Ia, US 155/G3
Elliott, Austl. 128/D4
Elliott, SC, US 163/G3
Elliott (peak), Va, US 163/H1
Ellis, Id, US 147/F1
Ellis, Ks, US 152/E1
Ellis (co.), Tx, US 150/L7
Ellis Island, NJ,NY, US 169/J9
Ellisras, SAfr. 123/E4
Elliston, Austl. 131/G5
Elliston, Mt, US 145/H4
Ellisville, Ms, US 164/D2
Ellon, Sc, UK 33/D2
Elloree, SC, US 163/G4
Elloughton, Eng, UK 35/H4
Ellrich, Ger. 53/H5
Ellsinore, Mo, US 162/B2
Ellsworth, Ks, US 153/E1
Ellsworth (mts.), Ant. 192/U
Ellsworth (A.F.B.), SD, US 154/C1
Ellsworth, Wi, US 155/H1
Ellsworth Land (phys. reg.), Ant. 192/U
Ellwangen, Ger. 58/D5
Elm, Swi. 61/F4
Elm (lake), SD, US 156/E5
Elm (riv.), SD, US 154/E1
Elm City, NC, US 163/J3
Elm Creek, Mb, Can. 156/F3
Elm Fork (riv.), Ok, US 152/E3
Elm Fork (riv.), Tx, US 150/L6
Elm Grove, Wi, US 167/P13
Elma, Ia, US 155/H2
Elma, NY, US 160/V10
Elmadağ, Turk. 70/E5
Elmalı, Turk. 104/A1
Elmas (int'l arpt.), It. 48/A3
Elmer, La, US 164/B2
Elmer, Mo, US 155/H4
Elmer, NJ, US 168/C4
Elmgrove (pt.), Tx, US 151/N9
Elmhurst, Il, US 167/Q16
Elmina, Gha. 115/E5
Elmira, NY, US 161/H3
Elmira, Or, US 146/B1
Elmira Heights, NY, US 161/H3
Elmo, Mt, US 144/G4
Elmont, NY, US 169/L9
Elmora (nbrhd.), NJ, US 169/J9
Elmore, Mn, US 155/G2
Elmore, Austl. 133/B3
Elmore City, Ok, US 153/F3
Elmsdale, PE, Can. 158/E2
Elmsdale, NS, Can. 158/F3
Elmsford, NY, US 169/K7
Elmshorn, Ger. 53/G1
Elmstein, Ger. 55/G5
Elmswell, Eng, UK 37/G2
Elmvale, On, Can. 161/G2
Elmwood, Ok, US 152/D2
Elmwood, Ne, US 155/F3
Elmwood Park, Il, US 167/Q16
Elmwood Park, NJ, US 169/J8
Elmwood Park, Wi, US 167/Q14
Elne, Fr. 44/E5
Elnora, In, US 162/D1
Elói Mendes, Braz. 187/L6
Eloise, Fl, US 164/M8
Elon College, NC, US 163/H2
Elora, On, Can. 160/F3
Elora, Tn, US 162/D3
Élorn (riv.), Fr. 44/A2
Elortondo, Arg. 190/E2
Elorza, Ven. 180/D3
Elouera Nat'l Rsv., Austl. 134/H8
Elowah (falls), Or, US 144/D5
Eloy, Az, US 149/G4
Eloy Alfaro, Ecu. 180/B5
Éloyes, Fr. 60/C1
Elphin, Ire. 32/B2
Elphinstone, Mb, Can. 156/D2
Elqui (riv.), Chile 188/B4
Elrod, Al, US 162/D4
Elrose, Sk, Can. 145/K2
Elroy, Wi, US 155/J2
Elroy, NC, US 163/J3
Elsa (riv.), Sp. 67/B2
Elsa (res.), Sp. 46/B2
Elsa, Yk, Can. 171/L3
Elsa, Tx, US 151/F4
Elsah, Il, US 155/J4
Elsberry, Mo, US 155/J4
Elsdorf, Ger. 55/F2
Elsdorf, Ger. 53/G2
Else (riv.), Ger. 53/F4
Elsen (lake), China 99/F4
Elsenfeld, Ger. 58/C3
Elsenz (riv.), Ger. 58/B4
Elsey, Mo, US 153/H2
Elsfleth, Ger. 53/F2
Elsie, Mi, US 160/D3
Elsinore (lake), Ca, US 166/C3
Elsinore, Ut, US 149/F1
Elsloo, Neth. 55/E2
Elsmere, De, US 168/C4
Elst, Neth. 52/C5
Elstal, Ger. 42/Q6
Elstead, Eng, UK 37/F4
Elsterberg, Ger. 59/F1
Eltari (int'l arpt.), Indo. 128/A2
Eltham (nbrhd.), Eng, UK 30/D2
Eltham, NZ 135/C2
Eltham, Austl. 133/B3
Eltmann, Ger. 58/D3
Elton, Wi, US 157/K5
Elton, La, US 164/B2
Eltopia, Wa, US 144/E4
Eltville am Rhein, Ger. 58/B2
Elva, Est. 41/M2
Elvanlı, Turk. 104/D1
Elvas, Port. 46/B3
Elven, Fr. 56/C5
Elverum, Nor. 40/D1
Elvins, Mo, US 162/B2
Elvire (mt.), Austl. 130/C2
Elvo (riv.), It. 62/B2
Elwell (lake), Mt, US 145/J3
Elwood, In, US 160/D4
Elwood, Ne, US 154/E3
Elwood-Magnolia, NJ, US 168/D4
Elwy (riv.), Wal, UK 34/E5
Ely, Eng, UK 37/G2
Ely, Mn, US 157/J4
Ely, Nv, US 147/F4
Elyaqim, Isr. 105/C3
Elyashiv, Isr. 105/B4
Elyria, Oh, US 160/E4
Elysburg, Pa, US 168/B2
Elysian Park, Ca, US 166/F7
Elz, Ger. 58/B2
Elz (riv.), Ger. 58/B6
Elzach, Ger. 60/E1
Elzbach (riv.), Ger. 55/G3
Elze, Ger. 53/G4
Emajõgi (riv.), Est. 41/M2
Emām Taqī, Iran 101/G1
Emāmshahr, Iran 103/H2
Emån (riv.), Swe. 40/F3
Emancé, Fr. 30/H6
Emas, PN das, Braz. 186/B3
Emba (riv.), Kaz. 70/K3
Embarcación, Arg. 188/C2
Embarras (riv.), Il, US 162/C1
Embarrass, Mn, US 157/H4
Embarrass, Wi, US 155/K1
Embi, Kaz. 71/L2
Embi (riv.), Kaz. 74/F5
Embira (riv.), Braz. 184/D3
Embondo, D.R. Congo 120/D2
Emborcação (res.), Braz. 186/D3
Embrach, Swi. 61/E3
Embrun, Fr. 64/C3
Embsen, Ger. 53/H2
Embu, Kenya 119/B2
Emden, Il, US 155/K3
Emden, Ger. 53/E2
Emei (peak), China 86/D2
Emeishan, China 86/D2
Emerald, Austl. 134/C3
Emerald, Austl. 132/G5
Emeriau (pt.), Austl. 128/A4
Emerson, Mb, Can. 156/F3
Emerson, Ar, US 153/H4
Emerson, NJ, US 169/J8
Emery (peak), NM, US 152/C2
Emery, SD, US 154/F2
Emery, Ut, US 149/G1
Emeryville, On, Can. 167/G7
Emeryville, Ca, US 167/K11
Emet, Turk. 102/B2
Emida, Id, US 144/F4
Emigrant (peak), Mt, US 147/H1
Emigrant, Mt, US 147/H1
Emigsville, Pa, US 168/B3
Emilia-Romagna (pol. reg.), It. 45/J4
Emiliano Zapata, Mex. 176/D2
Emilius (peak), It. 64/D1
Emin, China 99/D2
Emin (riv.), China 99/D2
Eminābād, Pak. 98/C3

Eminence, Mo, US 153/J2
Emir Pasha (gulf), Tanz. 121/G3
Emirdağ, Turk. 102/B2
Emirgazi, Turk. 102/C2
Emissi, Tarso (peak), Chad 108/C4
Emita, Austl. 133/C4
Emlembe (peak), Swaz. 125/E2
Emlenton, Pa, US 161/G4
Emlichheim, Ger. 52/D3
Emma (riv.), Sur. 181/H4
Emmaboda, Swe. 40/F3
Emmanuel Head (pt.), Eng, UK 33/E5
Emmaste, Est. 41/K2
Emmaus, Pa, US 168/C2
Emme (riv.), Swi. 60/D4
Emmeloord, Neth. 52/C3
Emmen, Neth. 52/D3
Emmendingen, Ger. 60/D1
Emmental (valley), Swi. 60/D3
Emmer (riv.), Ger. 53/G4
Emmer-Compascuum, Neth. 52/E3
Emmerbach (riv.), Ger. 53/E5
Emmerich, Ger. 52/D5
Emmet, Ar, US 153/H4
Emmet, Austl. 134/B4
Emmetsburg, Ia, US 155/G2
Emmett, Mi, US 167/G6
Emmett, Id, US 146/E2
Emmingen-Liptingen, Ger. 61/E2
Emmitsburg, Md, US 168/A4
Emmonak, Ak, US 171/F3
Emmons (mt.), Ut, US 147/H3
Emneth, Eng, UK 37/G1
Emód, Hun. 50/E2
Emory, Tx, US 153/G4
Emory (peak), Tx, US 151/C3
Emosson (lake), Swi. 60/C5
Empalme, Mex. 174/C3
Empangeni, SAfr. 125/E3
Empedrado, Chile 190/B2
Empedrado, Arg. 188/E3
Empire, Mi, US 160/C2
Empire, Ga, US 163/F4
Empoli, It. 63/D6
Emporia, Ks, US 153/F1
Emporia, Va, US 163/J2
Emporium, Pa, US 161/G4
'Emrānī, Iran 101/G2
Ems (riv.), Ger. 42/D2
Ems (Eems) (riv.), Ger.,Neth. 52/D2
Ems-Jade (canal), Ger. 53/E2
Emsbüren, Ger. 53/E4
Emsdetten, Ger. 53/E4
Emskirchen, Ger. 58/D3
Emsland (reg.), Ger. 42/D2
Emstek, Ger. 53/F3
Emu, China 79/K3
Emu Park, Austl. 134/C3
Emumägi (hill), Est. 41/M2
Emur (riv.), China 79/J1
Emyvale, Ire. 34/B3
'En Gedi, Isr. 105/C6
'En Harod, Isr. 105/C3
Ena, Japan 85/E3
Enangiperi, Kenya 119/A2
Enarotali, Indo. 91/J4
Enbetsu, Japan 82/B1
Encampment, Wy, US 147/K3
Encantada, Cerro (peak), Mex. 174/B3
Encantada, Cerro de la (peak), Mex. 174/B2
Encarnación, Par. 189/F3
Encarnación de Díaz, Mex. 174/E4
Enchi, Gha. 114/E5
Encinal, Tx, US 151/E3
Encinitas, Ca, US 166/C4
Encino (nbrhd.), Ca, US 166/E7
Encino, Tx, US 150/E4
Enciso, Col. 180/C3
Enciso, Col. 180/D4
Encón, Arg. 188/C5
Encontrados, Ven. 180/C2
Encounter (bay), Austl. 132/A2
Encruzilhada do Sul, Braz. 189/F4
Encs, Hun. 43/L4
Endau (peak), Kenya 119/B2
Ende (isl.), Indo. 128/A2
Ende, Indo. 128/A2
Endeavour, Sk, Can. 156/C1
Endeavour (str.), Austl. 129/F2
Endeavour River NP, Austl. 134/B1
Endebess, Kenya 119/A1
Enderbury (isl.), Kiri. 137/H5
Enderby, BC, Can. 144/E2
Enderby Land (phys. reg.), Ant. 192/D
Enderlin, ND, US 156/F4
Endicott, NY, US 161/H3
Endicott, Wa, US 144/F4
Endingen, Ger. 60/D1
Endwell (Hooper), NY, US 161/H3
Endyalgourt (isl.), Austl. 128/C2
Ene (riv.), Peru 184/C3
Eneabba, Austl. 130/B4
Enebakk, Nor. 40/D2
Enem, Rus. 73/K5
Energeticheskiy, Kaz. 99/C3
Energetik, Rus. 71/L2
Enewetak (isl.), Mrsh. 136/F3
Enez, Turk. 49/K2
Enfield, NS, Can. 158/F3
Enfield (nbrhd.), Eng, UK 30/C2
Enfield (bor.), Eng, UK 30/C2
Enfield, Ct, US 161/K4
Enfield, Il, US 162/C1
Enfield, NC, US 163/J2
Enfield, NH, US 161/K3
Enga (prov.), PNG 129/F1
Engaño (cape), Phil. 77/M8
Engaru, Japan 82/C1
Engaruka (basin), Tanz. 119/A2
Engassumet, Tanz. 119/B3
Engcobo, SAfr. 124/E3
Engelberg, Swi. 61/E4
Engelhartszell, Aus. 59/G5
Engel's, Rus. 71/H2
Engelskirchen, Ger. 55/G2
Engelsmanplaat (isl.), Neth. 52/D2
Engen, Ger. 61/E2
Engenheiro Paulo de Frontin, Braz. 187/N7
Enger, Ger. 53/F4
Engerwitzdorf, Aus. 59/H6
Enggano (isl.), Indo. 90/B5
Enghershatu (peak), Erit. 100/C5
Enghien, Belg. 54/D2
Engi, Swi. 61/F4
England, Ar, US 153/J3
England, Eng, UK 35/F4
England, UK 36/D2
Engle, NM, US 149/J4
Englefield Green, Eng, UK 30/B2
Englefontaine, Fr. 54/C3
Englevale, ND, US 156/F4
Englewood, Fl, US 165/G4
Englewood, NJ, US 169/K8
Englewood Cliffs, NJ, US 169/K8
English (riv.), On, Can. 157/H2
English, In, US 162/D1
English (chan.), UK,Fr. 29/D4
English Bay, Ak, US 171/H4
English Bāzār, India 97/G3
English Creek, NJ, US 168/D5
English Harbour West, Nf, Can. 159/K2
English River, On, Can. 157/J3
Englishtown, NJ, US 168/D3
Engong, Gabon 120/B2
Engucwini, Malw. 119/A4
Énguera, Sp. 47/E3
Engure, Lat. 41/K3
Enguri (riv.), Geo. 71/G4
Enhtal, Mong. 78/F2
Enid, Ok, US 153/F2
Enid (lake), Ms, US 162/C3
Enigma, Ga, US 165/G2
Eniwa, Japan 82/B2
Enka, NC, US 163/F3
Enkenbach-Alsenborn, Ger. 55/G5
Enkhuizen, Neth. 52/C3
Enkirch, Ger. 55/G4
Enköping, Swe. 40/G2
Enna, It. 48/D4
Enné, Ouadi (riv.), Chad 116/C2
Ennedi (plat.), Chad 116/D1
Ennell, Lough (lake), Ire. 32/C3
Ennepe (riv.), Ger. 53/E6
Ennepetal, Ger. 53/E6
Enneri Bardagué (riv.), Chad 108/C4
Enneri Blaka (riv.), Niger 108/B4
Enneri Ké (riv.), Chad 108/C5
Enneri Maro (riv.), Chad 108/C5
Enneri Yébiqué (riv.), Chad 108/C4
Enneri Zergamouchi (riv.), Niger 108/B4
Ennery, Fr. 30/J4
Enngonia, Austl. 132/C1
Enningerloh, Ger. 53/F5
Ennis, Ire. 32/B4
Ennis, Mt, US 147/H1
Ennis, Tx, US 151/F1
Enniscorthy, Ire. 32/D5
Enniskerry, Ire. 34/B5
Enniskillen, NI, UK 31/Q9
Ennismore, On, Can. 161/G2
Ennistimon, Ire. 32/A4
Enns (riv.), Aus. 43/H5
Enns, Aus. 59/H6
Ennuye (riv.), Fr. 64/B4
Enoch, Ut, US 149/F2
Enochs, Tx, US 152/C4
Enogger (res.), Austl. 134/E6
Enola, Ar, US 153/H3
Enola, Pa, US 168/B3
Enontekiö, Fin. 38/G1
Enoree, SC, US 163/G3
Enoree (riv.), SC, US 163/G3
Enosburg Falls, Vt, US 161/K2
Enping, China 87/G4
Enrekang, Indo. 91/E4
Enrick (riv.), Sc, UK 33/B2
Enrique Carbó, Arg. 191/J10
Enriquillo, DRep. 177/J2
Enschede, Neth. 52/D4
Ensdorf, Ger. 59/E4
Ense, Ger. 53/E5
Enseleni, SAfr. 125/F3
Ensenada, Arg. 191/K11
Ensenada, Mex. 174/A2
Ensheim (arpt.), Ger. 55/G5
Ensheim (Saarbrücken) (arpt.), Ger. 55/G5
Enshi, China 87/F2
Ensign, Mi, US 160/C2
Ensisheim, Fr. 60/D2
Enskär (isl.), Swe. 39/A2
Ensley, Fl, US 164/E2
Ensuès-la-Redonne, Fr. 64/B6
Entebbe, Ugan. 121/H2
Entebbe (int'l arpt.), Ugan. 121/H2
Entenbühl (peak), Ger. 59/F3
Enterprise, On, Can. 161/H2
Enterprise, Al, US 165/F2
Enterprise, Ks, US 153/F1
Enterprise, La, US 164/C2
Enterprise, Ms, US 162/C4
Enterprise, Ok, US 153/G3
Enterprise, Or, US 146/E1
Entiat, Wa, US 144/D4
Entlebuch, Swi. 60/E4
Entraigues-sur-Sorgue, Fr. 64/A5
Entrance, Ab, Can. 144/F1
Entre Lagos, Chile 190/B4
Entre Ríos (prov.), Arg. 188/E4
Entre Ríos, Bol. 188/C2
Entre Rios, Braz. 182/C4
Entre Rios, Braz. 187/F1
Entre Ríos (mts.), Hon. 176/E3
Entre Rios de Minas, Braz. 186/D4
Entre Vientos, Chile 191/C7
Entre-Deux-Guiers, Fr. 64/B2
Entre-Rios, Moz. 123/H2
Entrevaux, Fr. 64/C5
Entroncamento, Port. 46/A3
Entry (isl.), Qu, Can. 159/G2
Entwistle, Ab, Can. 144/G1
Entzheim, Fr. 60/D1
Entzheim (Strasbourg) (int'l arpt.), Fr. 60/D1
Enu (isl.), Indo. 128/D1
Enugu, Nga. 115/G5
Enugu Ngwo, Nga. 115/G5
Enumclaw, Wa, US 167/D3
Enushū (sea), Japan 83/M6
Envermeu, Fr. 57/G1
Envigado, Col. 183/K6
Envira, Braz. 184/D2
Enyamba, D.R. Congo 121/F3
Enyang, China 87/E2
Enyellé, Congo 120/D2
Enz (riv.), Ger. 42/E4
Enza (riv.), It. 62/D4
Enzan, Japan 85/F3
Enzbach (riv.), Ger. 55/F4
Enzersdorf an der Fischa, Aus. 51/P7
Enzklösterle, Ger. 58/B5
Eola, Tx, US 150/D2
Eolia, Mo, US 155/J4
Épaignes, Fr. 57/F2
Epalinges, Swi. 60/C4
Epáno Arkhánai, Gre. 49/J5
Epanomí, Gre. 49/H2
Epcot Center, Fl, US 164/M7
Epe, Nga. 115/F5
Epe, Neth. 52/C4
Épehy, Fr. 54/C3
Epéna, Congo 120/D2
Epenarra, Austl. 129/D5
Épernay, Fr. 54/C5
Épernon, Fr. 57/G3
Epfig, Fr. 60/D1
Ephesus (ruin), Turk. 67/K3
Ephraim, Wi, US 157/L5
Ephraim, Ut, US 147/H4
Ephrata, Pa, US 168/B3
Ephrata, Wa, US 144/E4
Epi (isl.), Van. 136/F6
Épiais-Rhus, Fr. 30/J4
Epídhavros (Epidaurus) (ruin), Gre. 49/H4
Épinal, Fr. 60/C1
Épinal (Mirecourt) (arpt.), Fr. 60/C1
Épinay-sur-Orge, Fr. 30/J6
Épinay-sur-Seine, Fr. 30/J5
Epira, Guy. 181/G3
Epirus (reg.), Gre. 67/J3
Epomeo (vol.), It. 65/C6
Épône, Fr. 54/A6
Eppalock (lake), Austl. 133/B3
Eppelborn, Ger. 55/F5
Eppelheim, Ger. 58/B4
Eppenbrunn, Ger. 55/G5
Eppeville, Fr. 54/C4
Epping, Eng, UK 30/D1
Epping (for.), Eng, UK 30/D2
Epping (nbrhd.), Austl. 134/H8
Epping Forest NP, Austl. 134/B3
Eppingen, Ger. 58/B4
Eppishausen, Ger. 61/G1
Epps, La, US 153/J4
Epsie, Mt, US 145/M5
Epsom, Eng, UK 30/C3
Epsom and Ewell, Eng, UK 37/F4
Epte (riv.), Fr. 54/A4
Epukiro, Namb. 122/C4
Epukiro (riv.), Namb. 122/D4
Epulu (riv.), D.R. Congo 121/G2
Epupa (falls), Ang. 122/B3
Epworth, Eng, UK 35/H4
Epworth, Ia, US 155/J2
Eqlīd, Iran 103/H4
Equateur (pol. reg.), D.R. Congo 116/D5
Equator (fall), Ecu. 180/A4
Equatorial Guinea (ctry.) 107/C4
Équeurdreville-Hainneville, Fr. 56/D1
Équihen-Plage, Fr. 54/A2
Equimina, Ang. 122/B2
Er (lake), China 93/H2
Er (isl.), Fr. 56/B3
Er Rachidia, Mor. 110/D3
Er Reina, Isr. 105/C3
Er Rif (mts.), Mor. 66/B4
Era (riv.), It. 63/A5
Era (riv.), PNG 129/G1
Eraclea (ruin), It. 48/E2
Eraclea, It. 63/F2
Eraclea Minoa (ruin), It. 48/C4
Éragny, Fr. 30/J4
Eran, Phil. 88/B3
Erandique, Hon. 176/D3
Erath, La, US 164/B3
Erave (riv.), PNG 129/G1
Erave, PNG 129/F1
Erawan NP, Thai. 94/B3
Erba, It. 62/C2
Erbaa, Turk. 70/F4
Erbach, Ger. 58/B3
Erbendorf, Ger. 59/F3
Erbeskopf (peak), Ger. 55/G4
Ercan (int'l arpt.), Cyp. 104/C2
Ercé-en-Lamée, Fr. 56/D5
Erçek, Turk. 103/E2
Erçek (lake), Turk. 103/E2
Ercilla, Chile 190/B3
Erciş, Turk. 103/E2
Erciyes (peak), Turk. 102/C2
Erclin (riv.), Fr. 54/C3
Ercolano, It. 65/D6
Érd, Hun. 51/Q10
Erdao (riv.), China 79/K3
Erdek (gulf), Turk. 51/H5
Erdek, Turk. 51/H5
Erdemli, Turk. 104/D1
Erdenet, Mong. 78/E2
Erdenetsogt, Mong. 78/F3
Erdi (well), Chad 108/C4
Erdi-Ma (upland), Chad 108/D5
Erding, Ger. 59/E6
Erdre (riv.), Fr. 44/C3
Erdweg, Ger. 58/E6
Erechim, Braz. 189/F3
Ereen Davaanï (mts.), Mong. 78/G2
Ereğli, Turk. 102/C2
Ereğli, Turk. 51/K5
Ereke, Indo. 91/F4
Eremo delle Carceri, It. 65/B1
Eremo di Camaldoli, It. 63/E6
Erenhaberga (mts.), China 99/D3
Erenler, Turk. 51/K5
Erentepe, Turk. 102/E2
Erepecu (lake), Braz. 181/H5
Ērer Shet' (riv.), Eth. 118/B3
Eresma (riv.), Sp. 46/C2
Erétria, Gre. 49/H3
Erevan (int'l arpt.), Arm. 103/F1
Ereymentaū, Kaz. 74/H4
Érezée, Belg. 55/E3
Erfa (riv.), Ger. 58/C3
Erfoud, Mor. 110/D3
Erft (riv.), Ger. 42/D3
Erftstadt, Ger. 55/F2
Erfurt, Ger. 42/F3
`Erg Chech (des.), Mali,Alg. 107/B2
Erg du Djourab (des.), Chad 116/C2
`Erg Iguidi (des.), Alg.,Mrta. 110/D4
Ergene Nehri (riv.), Turk. 51/H5
Ērgli, Lat. 41/L3
Ergué-Gabéric, Fr. 56/A4
Ergun (riv.), China,Rus 79/J1
Ergun Youqi, China 79/J1
Ergun Zuoqi, China 79/J1
Erhard, Mn, US 156/F4
Erhlin, Tai. 87/J4
Erhulai, China 81/C2
Eriba, Sudan 117/H1
Erica, Neth. 52/D3
Erica, Austl. 133/C3
Ericeira, Port. 47/P10
Ericht (lake), Sc, UK 33/B3
Ericht (riv.), Sc, UK 33/B3
Erick, Ok, US 152/E3
Erickson, Mb, Can. 156/E2
Erickson, BC, Can. 144/F3
Ericsburg, Mn, US 157/H3
Erie, Ks, US 153/G2
Erie (int'l arpt.), Pa, US 160/F3
Erie, Pa, US 160/F3
Erie (lake), Can.,US 139/J5
Erie (canal), NY, US 160/V9
Erie (co.), NY, US 160/V10
Erie NWR, Pa, US 161/G4
Erigabo (Ceerigaabo), Som. 118/C3
Eriksdale, Mb, Can. 156/E2
Eriksmalå, Swe. 40/F3
Erikub (isl.), Mrsh. 136/F4
Erima, Ugan. 121/H2
Erímanthos (peak), Gre. 49/G4
Erimo, Japan 82/C2
Erimo-misaki (cape), Japan 82/C3
Erin, Tn, US 162/D2
Erin, On, Can. 160/S8
Erithraí, Gre. 49/H3
Eritrea (ctry.) 107/F3
Erkelenz, Ger. 55/F1
Erken (isl.), Swe. 41/H1
Erken (lake), Swe. 39/B1
Erkheim, Ger. 61/G1
Erkina (riv.), Ire. 32/C4
Erkner, Ger. 42/Q7
Erkrath, Ger. 52/D6
Erlach, Swi. 60/D3
Erlands Point-Kitsap Lake, Wa, US 167/B2
Erlang (peak), China 86/D2
Erlangen, Ger. 58/E3
Erlanger, Ky, US 162/E1
Erlau (riv.), Ger. 59/G5
Erldunda, Austl. 131/G3
Erlenbach (riv.), Ger. 58/B4
Erlenbach am Main, Ger. 58/C3
Erlenbach bei Marktheidenfeld, Ger. 58/C3
Erlenbach im Simmental, Swi. 60/D4
Erlinsbach, Swi. 60/E3
Erlongshan, China 79/K2
Erlongshan (res.), China 80/F2
Erme (riv.), Eng, UK 36/C6
Ermelo, Neth. 52/C4
Ermelo, SAfr. 125/E2
Ermenek (riv.), Turk. 104/C1
Ermenek, Turk. 104/C1
Ermenonville, Fr. 30/L4
Ermera, ETim. 128/B2
Ermeran Station, Austl. 133/B1
Ermineskin Ind. Res., Ab, Can. 145/H1
Ermióni, Gre. 49/H4
Ermont, Fr. 30/J5
Ermoúpolis, Gre. 49/J4
Erms (riv.), Ger. 58/C6
Ernabella, Austl. 131/G3
Erndtebrück, Ger. 55/H2
Ernée, Fr. 57/E4
Ernée (riv.), Fr. 44/C2
Ernesto Cortissoz (int'l arpt.), Col. 180/C2
Ernsthofen, Aus. 59/H6
Erode, India 95/C4
Erolzheim, Ger. 61/G1
Eromanga, Austl. 134/A4
Eros, La, US 153/H4
Erowal Bay, Austl. 133/E2
Erpe, Belg. 54/C2
Erpel, Ger. 55/G2
Erpengdianzi, China 81/C2
Erpu, China 78/C3
Erquelinnes, Belg. 55/D3
Erquy, Fr. 56/C3
Errego, Moz. 123/H3
Errigal (mtn.), Ire. 31/P9
Erris Head (pt.), Ire. 31/P9
Erro (riv.), It. 62/B4
Errochty (lake), Sc, UK 33/B3
Errol, Sc, UK 33/C4
Errol, NH, US 161/L2
Erromango (isl.), Van. 136/F6
Erse (riv.), Ger. 53/H4
Ersekë, Alb. 49/G2
Ershibadu, China 87/H2
Erskine, Mn, US 156/F4
Erskine, Ab, Can. 145/H1
Erstein, Fr. 60/D1
Erstfeld, Swi. 61/E4
Ertai, China 99/D3
Ertai, China 78/B2
Ertil', Rus. 73/L2
Ertingen, Ger. 61/F1
Ertis (riv.), Kaz. 74/H4
Ertix (riv.), China 78/B2
Ertvelde, Belg. 54/C1
Eruh, Turk. 102/E2
Erundu, Namb. 122/C4
Eruwa, Nga. 115/F5
Erval, Braz. 189/F5
Erval d'Oeste, Braz. 189/G3
Ervália, Braz. 187/E4
Ervay, Wy, US 147/K2
Erve (riv.), Fr. 57/E4
Ervia (riv.), It. 64/D5
Erwin, Tn, US 163/F2
Erwin, NC, US 163/H3
Erwitte, Ger. 53/F5
Eryuan, China 86/C3
Erzen (riv.), Alb. 49/F2
Erzgebirge (Krušné Hory) (mts.), Czh.,Ger. 45/K1
Erzhausen, Ger. 58/B3
Erzin, Rus. 78/D1
Erzincan, Turk. 102/D2
Erzincan (prov.), Turk. 102/D2
Erzurum, Turk. 102/E2
Erzurum (prov.), Turk. 102/E1
Es Senia (int'l arpt.), Alg. 112/E5
Esa'ala, PNG 136/E5
Esambo, D.R. Congo 121/E3
Esan-misaki (cape), Japan 82/B3
Esashi, Japan 82/B3
Esashi, Japan 82/C1
Esashi, Japan 82/B4
Esbiye, Turk. 70/F4
Esbjerg (int'l arpt.), Den. 40/C4
Esbjerg, Den. 40/C4
Esbly, Fr. 30/L5
Esbo (Espoo), Fin. 41/L1
Esbon, Ks, US 154/E4
Escabosa, NM, US 149/J3
Escada, Braz. 183/H5
Escalante, Ut, US 149/G2
Escalante (des.), Ut, US 147/G4
Escalante (riv.), Ut, US 149/G2
Escalón, Mex. 174/D3
Escalona, Sp. 46/C2
Escambia (riv.), Fl, US 164/E2
Escampobariou (pt.), Fr. 64/C6
Escanaba (riv.), Mi, US 157/L4
Escanaba, Mi, US 160/C2
Escarpada (pt.), Phil. 88/C1
Escatawpa (riv.), Ms, US 164/D2
Escaudain, Fr. 54/C3
Escaut (riv.), Fr. 42/B3
Esch (riv.), Fr. 55/E6
Esch-sur-Alzette, Lux. 55/E4
Esch-sur-Sure, Lux. 55/E4
Eschach (riv.), Ger. 61/E1
Eschau, Fr. 60/D1
Eschborn, Ger. 58/B2
Eschede, Ger. 53/H3
Eschen, Lcht. 61/F3
Eschenbach, Ger. 58/C5
Eschenbach in der Oberpfalz, Ger. 59/E3
Eschershausen, Ger. 53/G5
Esches (riv.), Fr. 54/B5
Escholzmatt, Swi. 60/D4
Eschwege, Ger. 53/H6
Eschweiler, Ger. 55/F2
Escobedo (int'l arpt.), Mex. 151/D5
Escoma, Bol. 184/D4
Escondido, Ca, US 166/C4
Escondido (cr.), Ca, US 166/C4
Escoutay (riv.), Fr. 64/A3
Escudillas, Ven. 181/E3
Escuinapa de Hidalgo, Mex. 174/D4
Escuintla, Guat. 176/D3
Esdraelon (plain), Isr. 105/C3
Eséka, Camr. 120/B2
Esenboga (int'l arpt.), Turk. 102/C1
Esence (peak), Turk. 102/D2
Esenguly, Trkm. 103/H2
Esens, Ger. 53/E1
Esera (riv.), Sp. 47/F1
Eşfahān, Iran 103/G3
Eşfahān (gov.), Iran 103/H3
Esfandak, Iran 101/H3
Esfarāyen, Iran 103/J2
Esfarvarīn, Iran 103/G3
Esgair Ddu (peak), Wal, UK 36/C1
Esh, Eng, UK 35/G2
Esh Winning, Eng, UK 35/G2
Esha Ness (cape), Sc, UK 31/W13
Eshan Yizu Zizhixian, China 86/D3
Esher, Eng, UK 30/B2
Eshimba, D.R. Congo 121/F4
Eshkol NP, Isr. 105/A6
Eshowe, SAfr. 125/E3
Eshtehārd, Iran 103/G3
Esil (riv.), Kaz. 77/F4
Esil, Kaz. 99/A1
Esine, It. 61/G6
Esino (riv.), It. 63/G6
Esira, Madg. 125/H9
Esk (riv.), Eng, UK 35/E2
Esk, North (riv.), Sc, UK 33/C5
Esk, South (riv.), Sc, UK 33/C5
Esk, South (riv.), Austl. 132/C4
Eskdale (valley), Sc, UK 33/C6
Eskifjördhur, Ice. 38/Q6
Eskil, Turk. 102/C2
Eskilstuna, Swe. 40/G2
Eskimalatya, Turk. 102/D2
Eskimo (lakes), NW, Can. 140/C2
Eskipazar, Turk. 70/E4
Eskişehir, Turk. 102/B2
Eskişehir (prov.), Turk. 102/B2
Esko, Mn, US 157/H4
Esla (riv.), Sp. 46/C1
Eslāmābād, Iran 103/F3
Eslāmābād, Iran 103/G2
Eslohe, Ger. 53/F6
Eslöv, Swe. 40/E4
Eslöv, Swe. 39/K7
Eşme, Turk. 102/B2
Esmeralda, Cuba 177/G1
Esmeraldas (dept.), Ecu. 180/B4
Esmeraldas, Ecu. 180/B4
Esmond, ND, US 156/E3
Esmont, Va, US 163/H2
Esmoraca, Bol. 188/C2
Esnagami (lake), On, US 157/L2
Esneux, Belg. 55/E2
Espada (pt.), Col. 180/D1
Espakeh, Iran 101/H3
Espalion, Fr. 44/E4
Espanola, On, Can. 160/F1
Española (isl.), Ecu. 184/K7
Española, NM, US 149/J3
Esparraguera, Sp. 47/K6
Esparta, Hon. 176/E3
Esparto, Ca, US 167/K9
Espejo, Sp. 46/C4
Espelkamp, Ger. 53/F4
Esperança, Braz. 183/H4
Esperance (bay), Den. 40/E4
Esperance (bay), Austl. 130/D5
Esperance, Austl. 130/D5
Esperance (int'l arpt.), Neth. 173/N8
Esperancita, Bol. 185/F5
Esperantina, Braz. 183/F3
Esperantinópolis, Braz. 183/E4
Esperanza, Arg. 191/C6
Esperanza, Arg., Ant. 192/W
Esperanza (mts.), Hon. 176/E3
Esperanza, Mex. 175/M8
Esperanza, Mex. 174/C3
Esperanza, Peru 184/D3
Esperanza, Uru. 191/K10
Esperanza, Ven. 181/E4
Esperia, It. 65/C5
Espichel (cape), Port. 47/P11
Espigão d'Oeste, Braz. 185/F3
Espinal, Col. 180/C3
Espinal, Mex. 175/M6
Espinar, Peru 184/D4
Espinhaço, Serra do (mts.), Braz. 187/E4
Espinho, Port. 46/A2
Espinillo (pt.), Uru. 191/F2
Espinosa, Braz. 187/E2
Espírito Santo (state), Braz. 187/E3
Espíritu Santo (bay), Cuba 176/E2
Espiritu Santo (isl.), Mex. 174/C3
Espiritu Santo (cape), Phil. 88/D2
Espiritu Santo (isl.), Van. 136/F6
Espita, Mex. 176/D1
Esplanada, Braz. 187/F1
Espluga de Francolí, Sp. 47/E2
Espluges, Sp. 47/L7
Espoo (Esbo), Fin. 41/L1
Esposende, Port. 46/A2
Esprit-Saint, Qu, Can. 158/C1
Espungabera, Moz. 123/G4
Espy, Pa, US 168/B1
Esqueda, Mex. 174/C2
Esquel, Arg. 190/C4
Esquina, Arg. 188/E4
Esrum Sø (lake), Den. 39/J6
Essaouira, Mor. 110/C3
Esse (riv.), Ger. 53/G5
Essé, Camr. 120/B1
Essen, Belg. 52/B6
Essen, Ger. 53/E3
Essen, Ger. 52/E6
Essenbach, Ger. 59/F5
Essendon (mt.), Austl. 130/D3
Essendon (nbrhd.), Austl. 132/F5
Essenheim, Ger. 55/H4
Essequibo (riv.), Guy. 179/D2
Essequibo Island-West Demerara (pol. reg.), Guy. 181/G3
Essex (co.), On, Can. 167/G7
Essex, On, Can. 167/G7
Essex (co.), Eng, UK 30/E1
Essex, Ca, US 148/E3
Essex, Ia, US 155/G3
Essex, Md, US 168/B5
Essex, Mt, US 145/H3
Essex (co.), NJ, US 168/D2
Essex, Vt, US 161/K2
Essex Fells, NJ, US 169/H8
Essexville, Mi, US 160/E3
Essie, Ky, US 163/F2
Esslingen, Ger. 58/C5
Esso, Rus. 75/R4
Essômes-sur-Marne, Fr. 54/C5
Essonne (riv.), Fr. 44/E2
Est (prov.), Camr. 116/B5
Est, Canal de l' (canal), Fr. 55/E5
Estaca de Bares, Punta de la (cape), Sp. 66/B2
Estacada, Or, US 146/B1
Estación Santa Engracia, Mex. 175/F3
Eşţahbān, Iran 103/H4
Estaires, Fr. 54/B2
Estancia, NM, US 149/J3
Estância, Braz. 187/F1
Estancia Carmen, Arg. 191/D7
Estanislao del Campo, Arg. 188/D3
Estarca, Bol. 188/C2
Estats, Pico de (peak), Sp. 44/D5
Estavayer-le-Lac, Swi. 60/C4
Estcourt, SAfr. 125/E3
Este, It. 63/E3
Este, Punta del (pt.), Cuba 172/E3
Esteio, Braz. 189/G4
Estelí, Nic. 176/E3
Estell Manor (Risley), NJ, US 168/D5
Estella, Sp. 44/B5
Estelle (mtn.), Ca, US 166/C3
Estelline, Tx, US 152/D3
Estelline, SD, US 155/F1
Estepa, Sp. 46/C4
Estepona, Sp. 46/C4
Ester, Ak, US 171/J3
Esterel (upland), Fr. 64/C6
Esterhazy, Sk, Can. 156/C2
Esterias (cape), Gabon 120/B2
Esternay, Fr. 54/C6
Estero (pt.), Ca, US 148/B3
Estero de Agiabampo (lag.), Mex. 174/C3
Estéron (riv.), Fr. 45/G5
Esteros de Iberá (swamp), Arg. 188/E4
Esterwegen, Ger. 53/E3
Estes Park, Co, US 154/B3
Estevan, Sk, Can. 156/C3
Estherville, Ia, US 155/G2
Estill, SC, US 163/G4
Estill Springs, Tn, US 162/D3
Estinnes-au-Mont, Belg. 55/D3
Esto, Fl, US 165/F2
Eston, Sk, Can. 145/K2
Eston and South Bank, Eng, UK 35/G2
Estonia (ctry.) 29/G3
Estoril, Port. 47/P10
Estrablin, Fr. 64/A1
Estral Beach, Mi, US 167/F8
Estrées-Saint-Denis, Fr. 54/B5
Estrêla, Braz. 189/G4
Estrella (pt.), Mex. 174/B2
Estremadura (reg.), Sp. 66/B3
Estremoz, Port. 46/B3
Estrondo, Serra do (mts.), Braz. 182/D5
Estuna, Swe. 39/B1
Esturaire (prov.), Gabon 120/B3
Esvres, Fr. 57/F6
Esztergom, Hun. 50/D2
Eţ Ţaiyiba, Isr. 105/C4
Eţ Ţīra, Isr. 105/B4
Étables-sur-Mer, Fr. 56/C3
Etadunna, Austl. 131/H4
Etah, India 96/B2
Étain, Fr. 55/E5
Etaka (riv.), Namb. 122/B3
Etal, Eng, UK 33/D5
Etal (isl.), Micr. 136/E4
Étalle, Belg. 55/E4
Étampes, Fr. 57/H4
Étaples, Fr. 54/A2
Etāwah, India 96/B2
Etāwah Branch (riv.), India 96/B2
Etchojoa, Mex. 174/C3
Etéké, Gabon 120/B3
Etel (riv.), Fr. 56/B5
Étel, Fr. 56/B5
Etelïnen, Fin. 39/E4
Etembue, EqG. 120/B2
Ethe, Belg. 55/E4
Ethel, Ar, US 162/B3
Ethel Creek, Austl. 130/D2
Ethelbert, Mb, Can. 156/D2
Ethete, Wy, US 147/J2
Ethiopia (ctry.) 107/F4
Ethiopian (plat.), Eth. 107/F4
Ethiopian Seminary, VatC. 65/F7
Ethridge, Tn, US 162/D3
Eti (riv.), Japan 83/K5
Etili, Turk. 51/H6
Etinan, Nga. 120/A1
Etiro, Namb. 122/B4
Étival-Clairefontaine, Fr. 60/C1
Etive, Loch (inlet), Sc, UK 33/A4
Etna (peak), It. 48/D4
Etna, Ca, US 146/B3
Etne, Nor. 40/A2
Etobicoke (co), On, Can. 160/T8
Étoile, D.R. Congo 123/E1
Étoile-sur-Rhône, Fr. 64/A3
Etolin (str.), Ak, US 171/E3
Eton, Eng, UK 30/B2
Eton, Ga, US 162/E3
Etorofu (isl.), Rus. 77/P5
Etosha NP, Namb. 122/B3
Etosha Pan (salt pan), Namb. 122/C3
Etoumbi, Congo 120/C3
Etowah, Tn, US 162/E3
Etowah (riv.), Ga, US 162/E3
Étréchy, Fr. 57/H3
Etrek (riv.), Trkm. 103/H2
Étrelles, Fr. 57/D4
Étrépagny, Fr. 57/G2
Étrépilly, Fr. 30/L4
Étretat, Fr. 57/F1
Etropole, Bul. 51/G4
Etroubles, It. 60/D6
Etsch (Adigo) (riv.), It. 61/G4
Ettadhamen Douarhicher, Tun. 112/M6
Ettelbruck, Lux. 55/F4
Etten-Leur, Neth. 52/B5
Ettenheim, Ger. 60/D1
Etterbeek, Belg. 55/D2
Etters (Goldsboro), Pa, US 168/B3
Ettlingen, Ger. 58/B5
Ettrick, Sc, UK 33/C6
Ettrick, Wi, US 155/J1
Ettrick Pen (peak), Sc, UK 33/C6
Ettrick Water (riv.), Sc, UK 33/C5
Ettringen, Ger. 61/G1
Etzikom Coulee (riv.), Ab, Can. 145/J3
Eu, Fr. 54/A3
'Eua (isl.), Tonga 137/H7
Euabalong, Austl. 133/C1
Eubenangee Swamp NP, Austl. 134/B2
Euchiniko (riv.), BC, Can. 144/C1
Eucla, Austl. 131/F4
Euclid, Oh, US 160/F4
Euclides da Cuhna, Braz. 187/F1
Eucumbene (lake), Austl. 133/D3
Eudunda, Austl. 132/A2
Euerbach, Ger. 58/D2
Eufaula, Al, US 165/F2
Eufaula (dam), Ok, US 153/G3
Eufaula, Ok, US 153/G3
Eufaula (lake), Ok, US 143/G4
Eugendorf, Aus. 59/G7
Eugene, Or, US 146/B1
Eugene O'Neill NHS, Ca, US 167/L11
Eugenia (pt.), Mex. 174/B3
Eugowra, Austl. 133/D1
Euharlee, Ga, US 162/E3
Euless, Tx, US 150/K7
Eulo, Austl. 134/B5
Eulonia, Ga, US 165/H2
Eume (res.), Sp. 46/B1
Eumungerie, Austl. 132/D1
Eungella NP, Austl. 134/C3
Eunice, La, US 164/B2
Eunice, NM, US 150/C1
Eupen, Belg. 55/F2
Euphrates (riv.), Iraq,Syria 77/D6
Euphrates (riv.), Syria,Iraq 100/C1
Eupora, Ms, US 162/C4
Eura, Fin. 41/K1
Eurajoki, Fin. 41/J1
Eure (dept.), Fr. 54/A5
Eure (riv.), Fr. 44/D2
Eure-et-Loir (dept.), Fr. 54/A6
Eureka (sound), Nun, Can. 141/S7
Eureka, Co, US 149/J2
Eureka, Il, US 155/K3
Eureka, Ks, US 153/F2
Eureka, Mt, US 144/G3
Eureka, Nv, US 146/F4
Eureka, SD, US 156/E5
Eureka, Tx, US 151/F1
Eureka, Ut, US 147/G4
Eureka, Wa, US 144/E4
Eureka Springs, Ar, US 153/H2
Euroa, Austl. 133/B3
Eurodisney, Fr. 30/L5
Euron (riv.), Fr. 60/C1
Europa (pt.), EqG. 120/B2
Europa (isl.), Fr. 123/J4
Europa (pt.), Gib. 46/C4
Europabrücke, Aus. 61/H3
Europe (cont.) 29/*
Europoort, Neth. 52/B5
Euskirchen, Ger. 55/F2
Eussenheim, Ger. 58/C3
Eustis, Fl, US 165/H3
Eustis, Me, US 161/L2
Euston, Austl. 132/B2
Eutaw, Al, US 162/D4
Eutin, Ger. 40/D4
Eutini, Malw. 123/G1
Euville, Fr. 55/E6
Euxton, Eng, UK 35/F4
Eva, Fl, US 164/M7
Eva Downs, Austl. 129/D4
Evadale, Tx, US 151/G2
Evander, SAfr. 124/E2
Evans (mt.), Co, US 152/B1
Evans, La, US 164/B2
Evans (str.), Nun, Can. 141/H2
Evans, Co, US 154/B3
Evans, WV, US 163/G1
Evans, Ga, US 163/F4
Evans Head, Austl. 132/E1
Evansburg, Ab, Can. 144/G1
Evanston, Il, US 160/C3
Evanston, Wy, US 147/H3
Evansville, Ar, US 153/G3
Evansville, Il, US 162/C1
Evansville, In, US 162/D2
Evansville, Mn, US 157/G4
Evansville, Wi, US 155/K2
Evant, Tx, US 150/E2
Evanton, Sc, UK 33/B1
Evart, Mi, US 160/D3
Evaton, SAfr. 124/D2
Evaz, Iran 103/H5
Ève, Fr. 30/L4
Evel (riv.), Fr. 56/C5
Eveleth, Mn, US 157/H4
Even Yehuda, Isr. 105/B4
Evening Shade, Ar, US 153/J2
Evenlode (riv.), Eng, UK 37/E3
Evensk, Rus. 75/R3
Evenkiyskiy Aut. Okrug, Rus. 75/R3
Evensville, Tn, US 162/E3
Everard (lake), Austl. 131/G4
Everard (mt.), Austl. 131/G3
Everard (cape), Austl. 133/D3
Evercreech, Eng, UK 36/D4
Everest, Ks, US 155/G4
Everest (Sagarmatha) (mtn.), China,Nepal 97/F2
Everett, Ga, US 165/H2
Everett, Pa, US 161/G4
Everett, Wa, US 144/C4
Evergem, Belg. 54/C1
Everglades City, Fl, US 165/H5
Everglades NP, Fl, US 165/H5
Evergreen, Al, US 164/E2
Evergreen Park, Il, US 167/Q16
Everman, Tx, US 150/K7
Eversholt, Eng, UK 37/F3
Everson, Wa, US 144/C3
Everswinkel, Ger. 53/E5
Everton, Mo, US 153/H2
Everton, In, US 160/D5
Evesham, Eng, UK 37/E2
Évian-les-Bains, Fr. 60/C5
Evinayong, EqG. 120/B2
Évinos (riv.), Gre. 49/G3
Evje, Nor. 40/B2
Evolène, Swi. 60/D5
Évora (dist.), Port. 46/A3
Évora, Port. 46/B3
Évran, Fr. 56/D4
Evre (riv.), Fr. 57/D6
Évrecy, Fr. 57/E2
Évreux, Fr. 57/G2
Évron, Fr. 57/E4
Evrótas (riv.), Gre. 49/H4
Évry, Fr. 30/K6
Evvoia (gulf), Gre. 70/B5
Evvoia (isl.), Gre. 70/B5
Évvoia (gulf), Gre. 49/H3
Evxinoúpolis, Gre. 49/H3
Ewan, NJ, US 168/C4
Ewaninga, Austl. 131/G2
Ewarton, Jam. 177/G2
Ewaso Ng'iro (riv.), Kenya 119/B1
Ewaso Ngiro (riv.), Kenya 119/A2
Ewell, Eng, UK 30/C3
Ewell, Md, US 163/J2
Ewenkizu Zizhiqi, China 79/H2
Ewhurst, Eng, UK 30/B3
Ewing, Mo, US 155/J3
Ewing, Ky, US 162/F1
Ewing, Ne, US 154/E2
Ewing, NJ, US 168/D3
Ewo, Congo 120/C3
Exaltación, Bol. 185/E4
Exaplátanos, Gre. 49/H2
Excel, Al, US 164/E2
Excello, Mo, US 155/H4
Excelsior Springs, Mo, US 155/G4
Excursion Inlet, Ak, US 171/L4
Exe (riv.), Eng, UK 36/C4
Exeland, Wi, US 157/J5
Exeter, On, Can. 160/F3
Exeter, Eng, UK 36/C5
Exeter (arpt.), Eng, UK 36/C5
Exeter, Ca, US 148/C2
Exeter, Mo, US 153/H2
Exeter, Ne, US 154/F3
Exeter, NH, US 161/L3
Exeter, Pa, US 161/J4
Exira, Ia, US 155/G3
Exminster, Eng, UK 36/C5
Exmoor (upland), Eng, UK 36/C4
Exmoor NP, Eng, UK 36/C4
Exmore, Va, US 163/K2
Exmouth (gulf), Austl. 130/B2
Exmouth, Austl. 130/B2
Exmouth (pen.), Chile 191/B6
Exmouth, Eng, UK 36/C5
Experiment, Ga, US 162/E4
Exploits (riv.), Nf, Can. 159/J1
Extension, La, US 164/C2
Extension, BC, Can. 144/C3
Extrema, Braz. 187/K7
Extrême Nord (prov.), Camr. 116/B3
Exu, Braz. 183/G4
Exuma (sound), Bahm. 173/F3
Eyach (riv.), Ger. 58/B6
Eyak, Ak, US 171/J3
Eyam, Eng, UK 35/G5
Eyangu, D.R. Congo 121/E3
Eyasi (lake), Tanz. 119/A2
Eyb (riv.), Ger. 58/C5
Eybens, Fr. 64/B2
Eydehamn, Nor. 40/C2
Eye, Eng, UK 37/H2
Eye (brook), Eng, UK 37/F1
Eyemouth, Sc, UK 33/D5
Eyguières, Fr. 64/B5
Eyl, Som. 118/D4
Eyn Hemed (ruin), Isr. 105/C5
Eyn Hemeo NP, Isr. 105/C5
Eynsford, Eng, UK 30/D2
Eyragues, Fr. 64/A5
Eyre, Austl. 130/E5
Eyre (pen.), Austl. 131/G5
Eyre, North (lake), Austl. 131/H4
Eyre, South (lake), Austl. 131/H4
Eyrecourt, Ire. 32/B3
Eyrieux (riv.), Fr. 64/A3
Eyüp (nbrhd.), Turk. 103/M6
Eyüp, Turk. 103/M6
Ézanville, Fr. 30/K4
Ezequiel Ramos Mexía (res.), Arg. 190/C3
Ezhou, China 87/G2
Ezine, Turk. 49/K3
Ézy-sur-Eure, Fr. 57/G3
Ezzane (well), Alg. 108/A4
Ezzell, Tx, US 151/F3

F

F.D. Roosevelt (int'l arpt.), NAnt. 173/N8
F.E. Walter (res.), Pa, US 168/C1
F.E. Warren (A.F.B.), Wy, US 154/B3
Faaa, FrPol. 137/X15
Faaa (Papeete) (int'l arpt.), FrPol. 137/X15
Faafaxdhuun, Som. 119/C1
Fabbrico, It. 63/D4
Fabens, Tx, US 151/A2
Fabero, Sp. 46/B1
Fåborg, Den. 40/D4
Fabrica di Roma, It. 65/B3
Fabrichnyy, Kaz. 99/C3
Fabyan, Ab, Can. 145/J1
Facatativá, Col. 183/L8
Faches-Thumesnil, Fr. 54/C2
Facundo, Arg. 190/C5
Fada (lake), Sc, UK 33/A1
Fada, Chad 116/D1
Fada-N'Gourma, Burk. 115/F3
Fadghamī, Syria 102/E3
Fadugu, SLeo. 114/C4
Faenza, It. 63/E5
Faetano, SMar. 63/F6
Fafa (riv.), CAfr. 116/C4
Fafe, Port. 46/A2
Fafen Shet' (riv.), Eth. 118/C4
Fagali (Apia) (int'l arpt.), Sam. 137/S9
Făgăraş, Rom. 51/G3
Fagersta, Swe. 40/F2
Fagerstrand, Nor. 38/S8
Faggiola (peak), It. 63/E5
Faggo, Nga. 115/H4
Fagnano (lake), Arg. 191/D7
Fagnano Olona-Bergoro, It. 62/B2
Fagnières, Fr. 55/D6
Faguibine (lake), Mali 114/D2
Fagundes, Braz. 182/C4
Fahl (well), Alg. 111/F3
Fahrenzhausen, Ger. 59/E6
Faial (isl.), Azor., Port. 47/S12
Faiano, It. 65/D6
Fā'id, Egypt 113/D4
Faido, Swi. 61/E5
Faille, Eth. 118/A4
Failsworth, Eng, UK 35/F4
Fains-Véel, Fr. 55/E6
Fair Bluff, NC, US 163/H3
Fair Grove, Mo, US 153/H2
Fair Haven, Mi, US 167/G6
Fair Haven, NY, US 161/H3
Fair Haven, Vt, US 161/K3
Fair Hill, Md, US 168/C4
Fair Isle (isl.), Sc, UK 31/W14
Fair Lawn, NJ, US 169/J8
Fair Oaks, Ca, US 167/M9
Fair Oaks, Ga, US 163/L7
Fair Plain, Mi, US 160/C3
Fair Play, Mo, US 153/H2
Fairbanks, Ak, US 171/J3
Fairbanks, La, US 153/H4
Fairborn, Oh, US 160/D5
Fairburn, Ga, US 163/L7
Fairburn, SD, US 154/C2
Fairbury, Il, US 155/K3
Fairbury, Ne, US 155/F3
Fairchild (A.F.B.), Wa, US 144/F4
Fairdealing, Mo, US 162/B2
Fairfax, Ok, US 153/F2
Fairfax, Mb, Can. 156/D3
Fairfax, Vt, US 161/K2
Fairfax, Ca, US 167/J11
Fairfax, Mo, US 155/G3
Fairfax, Oh, US 162/F1
Fairfax, SD, US 154/E2
Fairfax, SC, US 163/G4
Fairfax, Va, US 168/A6
Fairfax (co.), Va, US 168/A6
Fairfield (nbrhd.), Austl. 134/G8
Fairfield, Ca, US 146/B4
Fairfield, Ct, US 169/E1

Fairfield (co.), Ct, US 169/L7
Fairfield, Ia, US 155/J3
Fairfield, Id, US 147/F2
Fairfield, Il, US 162/C1
Fairfield, Mt, US 145/J4
Fairfield, NC, US 163/J3
Fairfield, Ne, US 154/E3
Fairfield, NJ, US 169/H8
Fairfield, Oh, US 160/D5
Fairfield, Pa, US 168/A4
Fairfield, Tx, US 151/F3
Fairfield, Va, US 163/H2
Fairfield, Wa, US 144/F4
Fairfield Bay, Ar, US 153/H3
Fairford, Mb, Can. 156/E2
Fairford, Eng, UK 37/E3
Fairgrove, Mi, US 160/E3
Fairhope, Al, US 164/E2
Fairland, In, US 160/D5
Fairland, Md, US 168/B5
Fairland, Ok, US 153/G2
Fairlawn, Va, US 163/G2
Fairlee, Md, US 168/B5
Fairless Hills, Pa, US 168/D3
Fairlie, Sc, UK 33/B5
Fairlie, NZ 135/B4
Fairlight, Sk, Can. 156/D3
Fairlight, Eng, UK 37/G5
Fairmead, Ca, US 148/B2
Fairmont, WV, US 160/F5
Fairmont, Mn, US 155/G2
Fairmont, NC, US 163/H3
Fairmont Hot Springs, BC, Can. 144/G2
Fairmount, ND, US 156/F4
Fairmount, NY, US 161/H3
Fairmount, Ga, US 162/E3
Fairplains, NC, US 163/G2
Fairplay, Ky, US 162/E2
Fairpoint, SD, US 154/C1
Fairport Harbor, Oh, US 160/F4
Fairton, NJ, US 168/C5
Fairvale, NB, Can. 158/E3
Fairview, Ab, Can. 140/E3
Fairview, Ga, US 162/E3
Fairview, Ks, US 155/G4
Fairview, Mt, US 156/B4
Fairview, Mo, US 153/G2
Fairview, Mi, US 160/D2
Fairview, NJ, US 169/K8
Fairview, Ok, US 153/E2
Fairview, Tn, US 162/D3
Fairview, Tx, US 150/L6
Fairview, Tx, US 151/D1
Fairview (peak), Zim. 123/G3
Fairview Park, In, US 160/C5
Fairweather (mt.), Can.,US 171/L4
Fairweather (cape), Ak, US 171/L4
Faisalābād, Pak. 98/B4
Faison, NC, US 163/H3
Faistós (ruin), Gre. 49/J5
Faizābād, India 96/D2
Fajardo, PR 173/M8
Fak Tha, Thai. 94/C2
Fakahina (isl.), FrPol. 137/M6
Fakaofo (isl.), Tok. 137/H5
Fakarava (isl.), FrPol. 137/L6
Fakfak, Indo. 91/H4
Fako (peak), Camr. 120/B1
Fakse, Den. 40/E4
Fakse Ladeplads, Den. 40/E4
Faku, China 80/E2
Fal (riv.), Eng, UK 36/B6
Falaba, SLeo. 114/C4
Falaise, Fr. 57/E3
Fālākāta, India 97/G2
Falam, Myan. 86/B4
Falāmah, WBnk. 105/C4
Falán, Col. 183/L7
Fálanna, Gre. 49/H3
Falciano del Massico, It. 65/C5
Fălciu, Rom. 51/J2
Falcon (cape), Alg. 112/D2
Falcon (res.), Mex., US 172/B2
Falcon (dam), Tx, US 151/E4
Falcón (state), Ven. 180/D2
Falcon Lake, Mb, Can. 157/G3
Falconara (arpt.), It. 63/G6
Falconara Marittima, It. 63/G6
Falconer, NY, US 161/G3
Falémé (riv.), Mali 114/C3
Faleolo, Sam. 137/S9
Faleolo (Apia) (int'l arpt.), Sam. 137/S9
Faleşti, Mol. 72/D4
Falfurrias, Tx, US 150/E4
Falissadé, Gui. 114/B4
Falkenberg, Swe. 40/E3
Falkensee, Ger. 42/G6
Falkenstein, Ger. 59/F2
Falkenstein, Ger. 59/F4
Falkirk, Sc, UK 33/C5
Falkirk (co.), Sc, UK 33/C5
Falkland, Sc, UK 33/C4
Falkland (isls.), UK 179/C8
Falkland Sound (str.), UK 191/E7
Falköping, Swe. 40/E2
Falkville, Al, US 162/D3
Fall (riv.), Ks, US 153/F2
Fall City, Wa, US 167/D2
Fall Creek, Wi, US 155/J1
Fall River, Ks, US 153/F2
Fall River, Ma, US 161/L4
Fall River, Wi, US 155/K2
Fallbrook, Ca, US 166/C4
Fallere (peak), It. 60/D6
Fallingbostel, Ger. 53/G3
Fallon, Mt, US 156/B4
Fallon, Nv, US 146/D4
Fallon Ind. Res., Nv, US 146/D4
Fallon Naval Air Station, Nv, US 146/D4
Falls Church, Va, US 168/A6
Falls City, Ne, US 155/G3
Falls City, Or, US 146/B1
Falls City, Tx, US 151/E3
Falls Creek, Pa, US 161/G4
Falls Lake (res.), NC, US 163/H2
Falls of Rough, Ky, US 162/D2
Fallston, Md, US 168/B4
Falmey, Niger 115/F3
Falmouth, Anti. 173/N8
Falmouth, Eng, UK 36/A6
Falmouth (bay), Eng, UK 36/A6
Falmouth, Ky, US 162/E1
Falmouth, Ma, US 161/L4
Falmouth, Mi, US 160/D2
Falmouth, NS, Can. 158/E3
Falmouth, Va, US 163/J1
False Cape Bossut (cape), Austl. 128/A4
False Orford Ness (cape), Austl. 129/F2
False Pass, Ak, US 171/F5
Falshöft (pt.), Ger. 40/C4
Falso (cape), Hon. 177/F3
Falso Cabo de Hornos (cape), Chile 191/C7
Falso, Cabo (cape), Mex. 174/C4
Falster (isl.), Den. 38/E5
Falsterbo, Den. 39/J7
Falterona (peak), It. 63/E6
Fălticeni, Rom. 72/D4
Falun, Swe. 40/F1
Famagusta (dist.), Cyp. 104/C2
Famagusta, Cyp. 104/C2
Famagusta (bay), Cyp. 104/C2
Famaillá, Arg. 188/C3
Famakah, Sudan 117/G3
Fāmanīn, Iran 100/E1
Famatina, Arg. 188/C4
Fameck, Fr. 55/F5
Famenne (reg.), Belg. 55/E3
Family (lake), Mb, Can. 157/G2
Famoso, Ca, US 148/C3
Fan Si Pan (peak), Viet. 86/D4
Fana, Nor. 40/A1
Fana, Mali 114/D3
Fanārah, Egypt 113/D4
Fanchang, China 80/D5
Fancy Farm, Ky, US 162/C2
Fandriana, Madg. 125/H8
Fane (riv.), Ire. 32/D2
Fang, Thai. 94/B2
Fang Xian, China 80/B4
Fangak, Sudan 117/F3
Fangamadou, Gui. 114/C4
Fangatau (isl.), FrPol. 137/L6
Fangataufa (isl.), FrPol. 137/L7
Fangcheng, China 80/C4
Fangcheng Gezu Zizhixian, China 87/F4
Fangcun, China 87/H3
Fangdao, China 87/H3
Fangdou (mts.), China 87/E2
Fangjiatun, China 79/J3
Fangliao, Tai. 87/J4
Fangshan, China 80/B3
Fangshan, China 80/G7
Fangxi, China 87/G2
Faniria, Madg. 125/H8
Fanjing (peak), China 87/F3
Fannich (lake), Sc, UK 33/A1
Fannie (lake), Fl, US 164/M7
Fannin, Ms, US 162/C4
Fannin, Tx, US 151/F3
Fanning (Tabuaeran) (isl.), Kiri. 137/K4
Fanø (isl.), Den. 40/C4
Fano, It. 63/G6
Fanshan, China 87/J3
Fanshawe, Ok, US 153/G3
Fanshi, China 80/C3
Fanwood, NJ, US 169/H9
Faqīrwāli, Pak. 98/B5
Faqqū'ah, WBnk. 105/C3
Fāqūs, Egypt 113/K7
Far (mtn.), BC, Can. 144/B1
Far Rockaway (nbrhd.), NY, US 169/K9
Fara in Sabina, It. 65/B2
Fara Novarese, It. 62/B2
Faradje, D.R. Congo 121/G2
Farafangana, Madg. 125/H8
Farāh, Afg. 74/G6
Farāh (riv.), Afg. 74/G6
Fa'rah (wadi), WBnk. 105/C4
Farako, Mali 114/D4
Farallon (isls.), Ca, US 146/B5
Farallón Centinela (isl.), Ven. 183/F7
Farallon de Medinilla (isl.), NMar. 136/D3
Farallon de Pajaros (isl.), NMar. 136/D2
Farallon NWR, Ca, US 146/B5
Farallones de Cali, PN, Col. 180/B4
Faramana, Burk. 114/D3
Faranah, Gui. 114/C4
Faranah (pol. reg.), Gui. 114/C4
Farángi Samariás NP, Gre. 49/H5
Faraony (riv.), Madg. 125/H8
Farasan (isls.), Sudan 117/B4
Faraulep (isl.), Micr. 136/D4
Farber, Mo, US 155/J4
Farciennes, Belg. 55/D3
Fare (riv.), Fr. 57/F5
Fareham, Eng, UK 37/E5
Farellones, Chile 190/N8
Faremoutiers, Fr. 54/C6
Farentuna, Swe. 39/A1
Farewell (cape), NZ 135/C3
Farewell, Ak, US 171/H3
Farfa (riv.), It. 65/B3
Färgelanda, Swe. 40/E2
Farghona, Uzb. 99/B4
Fargo, Ga, US 165/G2
Fargo, ND, US 156/F4
Fargo, Ok, US 152/E2
Faribault, Mn, US 155/H1
Farīdābād, India 98/D5
Farīdkot, India 98/C4
Farīdpur, India 96/B1
Farīdpur (pol. reg.), Bang. 97/G4
Farīdpur, Bang. 97/G4
Farihao (cape), Namb. 122/B4
Farim, GBis. 114/B3
Farina, Il, US 162/C1
Farindale, Ar, US 153/H3
Färingsö (isl.), Swe. 39/A1
Fāriskūr, Egypt 113/C2
Farit (peak), Eth. 118/A3
Färjestaden, Swe. 40/G3
Farkadhón, Gre. 49/H3
Farkasgyepű, Hun. 50/C2
Farkwa, Tanz. 119/A4
Farley, Ia, US 155/J2
Farlington, Ks, US 153/G2
Farmer City, Il, US 155/K3
Farmers Branch, Tx, US 150/L7
Farmersburg, In, US 160/C5
Farmersville, Tx, US 150/L6
Farmerville, La, US 153/H4
Farmingdale, NJ, US 168/D3
Farmingdale, NY, US 169/M9
Farmington, Ar, US 153/G2
Farmington, De, US 168/C6
Farmington, Il, US 155/J3
Farmington, Me, US 161/L2
Farmington, Mi, US 167/F7
Farmington, Mn, US 155/H1
Farmington, Mo, US 162/B2
Farmington, NH, US 161/L3
Farmington, NM, US 149/H2
Farmington, Ut, US 147/H3
Farmington, Wa, US 144/F4
Farmington Hills, Mi, US 167/E6
Farmoréya, Gui. 114/B4
Farmville, NC, US 163/J3
Farmville, Va, US 163/H2
Farnborough, Eng, UK 37/F4
Farnham (mt.), BC, Can. 144/G2
Farnham, Eng, UK 37/F4
Farnham (peak), Id, US 144/F3
Farnham Royal, Eng, UK 30/B2
Farningham, Eng, UK 30/D2
Farnworth, Eng, UK 35/F4
Faro, Braz. 182/B3
Faro (riv.), Camr. 116/B4
Faro, Yk, Can. 171/M3
Faro (int'l arpt.), Port. 46/B4
Faro, Port. 46/B4
Faro (dist.), Port. 46/A4
Faro, PN de, Camr. 116/B3
Faroe (isls.), Den. 192/G
Fårön (isl.), Swe. 41/H3
Farösund, Swe. 41/H3
Farquhar (cape), Austl. 130/B2
Farragut, Tn, US 162/E3
Farranfore (arpt.), Ire. 32/A5
Farrāshband, Iran 103/H4
Farrokh Shahr, Iran 103/G3
Farroupilha, Braz. 189/G4
Farrukhābād, India 96/B2
Farrukhnagar, India 96/A1
Fārs (gov.), Iran 103/H4
Fársala, Gre. 49/H3
Fārsān, Iran 103/G3
Farsīs, Egypt 113/C3
Farsø, Den. 40/C3
Farson, Wy, US 147/J2
Farsund, Nor. 40/B2
Fartura, Braz. 189/G2
Farum, Swe. 39/J7
Farwell, Tx, US 152/C3
Fasā, Iran 103/H4
Fasano, It. 49/E2
Faşıkan (pass), Turk. 104/C1
Fassala-Néré, Mrta. 114/D3
Fassberg, Ger. 53/H3
Fast Castle (pt.), Sc, UK 33/D5
Fastiv, Ukr. 72/E2
Fatagar Tuting (cape), Indo. 91/H4
Fatehjang, Pak. 98/B3
Fate, Tx, US 150/L7
Fate, Monte delle (peak), It. 65/C5
Fatehābād, India 98/C5
Fatehgarh Chūriān, India 98/C4
Fatehpur, Pak. 98/A4
Fatehpur, India 96/C3
Fatehpur, India 96/C2
Fatëzh, Rus. 73/H1
Fathom Five NP, On, Can. 161/F2
Fatick (pol. reg.), Sen. 114/A3
Fatick, Sen. 114/A3
Fatigue (mt.), Austl. 133/C4
Fátima, Port. 46/A3
Fátima do Sul, Braz. 189/F2
Fātir (wadi), Leb. 105/D1
Fatoto, Gam. 114/B3
Fatsa, Turk. 70/F4
Fatu Hiva (isl.), FrPol. 137/M6
Fatunda, D.R. Congo 120/D4
Faucilles (mts.), Fr. 42/C4
Faughan (riv.) 34/A2
Faugh, It. 62/D6
Fauldhouse, Sc, UK 33/C5
Faulkton, SD, US 154/E1
Faulquemont, Fr. 55/F5
Faure (isl.), Austl. 130/B3
Făurei, Rom. 51/H3
Fauske, Nor. 38/E2
Fauville-en-Caux, Fr. 57/F1
Fauvillers, Belg. 55/E4
Favalto (peak), It. 63/F7
Favara, It. 48/C4
Fave (riv.), Fr. 60/C1
Faverges, Fr. 60/C6
Faverney, Fr. 60/C2
Faversham, Eng, UK 37/G4
Favières, Fr. 30/C5
Favignana, It. 48/C4
Favira, It. 62/A2
Favrieux, Fr. 30/G5
Fawley, Eng, UK 37/E5
Fawn (riv.), On, Can. 140/H3
Fawn Grove, Pa, US 168/B4
Fawumang, Gha. 115/E5
Faxaflói (bay), Ice. 38/M7
Faxinal, Braz. 189/F3
Faya-Largeau, Chad 116/C1
Fayd, SAr. 102/E5
Fayence, Fr. 64/C5
Fayette, Al, US 162/D3
Fayette (co.), Ga, US 163/M8
Fayette, Ia, US 155/J2
Fayette, Mo, US 155/H4
Fayette, Ms, US 164/C2
Fayette Historical Townsite, Mi, US 160/C2
Fayetteville, Ar, US 153/G2
Fayetteville, Ga, US 163/M8
Fayetteville, NC, US 163/H3
Fayetteville, Oh, US 162/F1
Fayetteville, Pa, US 161/H5
Fayetteville, Tn, US 162/D3
Fayetteville, Tx, US 151/F3
Fayetteville, WV, US 163/G1
Fayl-la-Forêt, Fr. 60/B2
Fayrā, Yem. 118/B2
Faywood (Dwyer), NM, US 149/H4
Fazao, Monts du (mts.), Togo 115/F4
Fazao, PN du, Togo 115/F4
Fazenda Nova, Braz. 186/C3
Fāzilka, India 98/C4
Fdérik, Mrta. 110/B5
Feakle, Ire. 32/B4
Feale (riv.), Ire. 32/A5
Fear (cape), NC, US 163/J4
Feasterville-Trevose, Pa, US 168/D3
Feather (riv.), Ca, US 146/C4
Feather (falls), Ca, US 146/C4
Feather, Mid. Fk. (riv.), Ca, US 146/C4
Featherston, NZ 135/J9
Featherstone, Eng, UK 35/G4
Featherstone, Zim. 123/F3
Feathertop (mt.), Austl. 133/C3
Fécamp, Fr. 57/F1
Fecht (riv.), Fr. 60/D1
Federación, Arg. 188/E4
Federal, Arg. 188/E4
Federal Dam, Mn, US 157/G4
Federal Hall Nat'l Mem., NY, US 169/K9
Federal Way, Wa, US 144/C4
Federally Admin. Tribal Areas, Pak. 98/A2
Federalsburg, Md, US 163/K1
Federsee (lake), Ger. 58/C6
Fedhaven, Fl, US 164/N8
Fedīs, Eth. 118/B3
Fedje, Nor. 40/A1
Fëdorovka, Kaz. 69/P5
Fëdorovka, Kaz. 71/J2
Fëdorovka, Rus. 46/A4
Fëdorovka, Rus. 71/J1
Fëdorovka, Rus. 73/K4
Fedscreek, Ky, US 163/F2
Feeny, NI, UK 34/A2
Feerfeer, Som. 118/C4
Fegersheim, Fr. 58/A6
Fégréac, Fr. 56/C5
Fehérgyarmat, Hun. 50/F2
Fehmarn (isl.), Den. 40/D4
Fehmarn Belt (str.), Den. 42/F1
Fei Huang (riv.), China 80/D4
Fei Xian, China 80/D4
Feia (lake), Braz. 187/E4
Feicheng, China 80/D3
Feidong, China 80/D5
Feignies, Fr. 54/C3
Feijó, Braz. 184/D3
Feilding, NZ 135/C3
Feillans, Fr. 60/A5
Feira, Port. 46/A2
Feira de Santana, Braz. 187/F2
Feistritz (riv.), Aus. 45/L3
Feixi, China 80/D5
Fejér (co.), Hun. 50/D2
Fejø (isl.), Den. 40/D4
Feke, Turk. 102/C2
Feketić, Yugo. 50/D3
Felanitx, Sp. 47/G3
Felch, Mi, US 157/L5
Feldafing, Ger. 61/H2
Feldaist (riv.), Aus. 59/H6
Feldberg (peak), Ger. 60/E2
Feldkirch, Aus. 61/F3
Feldkirchen an der Donau, Aus. 59/H6
Feldkirchen bei Graz, Aus. 50/B2
Feldkirchen in Kärnten, Aus. 45/L3
Feletto, It. 62/A2
Feletto Umberto, It. 63/G1
Feliciano, Arroyo (brook), Arg. 188/E4
Felicity, Oh, US 162/E1
Felino, It. 62/D4
Felipe Carrillo Puerto, Mex. 176/D2
Felix (riv.), NM, US 151/B1
Felixburg, Zim. 123/F3
Felixdorf, Aus. 50/C2
Felixlândia, Braz. 186/D3
Felixstowe, Eng, UK 37/H3
Felizzano, It. 62/B4
Fell, Ger. 58/C3
Fellbach, Ger. 58/C5
Felling, Eng, UK 35/G2
Fellows, Ca, US 148/C3
Fellsmere, Fl, US 165/H4
Felsberg, Ger. 53/G6
Felsberg, Swi. 61/F4
Felsenthal, Ar, US 153/H4
Felt, Ok, US 152/C2
Feltham (nbrhd.), Eng, UK 30/B2
Felton, Ca, US 148/A2
Felton, Ca, US 145/A2
Felton, De, US 168/C5
Felton, Mn, US 156/F4
Feltre, It. 63/E1
Feltwell, Eng, UK 37/G2
Fema (peak), It. 65/C2
Femø (isl.), Den. 40/D4
Femundsmarka NP, Nor. 38/D3
Fen (riv.), China 78/G5
Fénay, Fr. 60/B3
Fence, Wi, US 157/K5
Fence Lake, NM, US 149/H3
Fenchuganj, Bang. 97/H3
Fene, Sp. 46/A1
Fenelon Falls, On, Can. 161/G2
Fener (pt.), Turk. 104/D1
Feng Xian, China 78/F5
Feng Xian, China 80/D4
Fengári (peak), Gre. 49/J2
Fengcheng, China 81/C2
Fengchuihudie (peak), China 87/G3
Fenggeling, China 78/F5
Fenghuang, China 93/J2
Fenghuang, China 87/E3
Fengjie, China 87/F2
Fengkou, China 87/G2
Fengle (riv.), China 80/D5
Fengle, China 87/E2
Fenglin, China 87/H3
Fenglin, Tai. 87/J3
Fenglingdu, China 78/G5
Fengnan, China 80/J7
Fengning, China 80/D2
Fengqing, China 86/C3
Fengqiu, China 80/C4
Fengrun, China 80/J7
Fengshan, China 93/J3
Fengshan, China 79/H3
Fengshan, China 87/F3
Fengshuba (res.), China 87/G3
Fengshui (peak), China 79/J1
Fengtai, China 80/H7
Fengtian, China 87/G3
Fengtian, China 87/G3
Fengxian, China 80/L9
Fengxiang, China 78/F5
Fengyang, China 80/D4
Fengyüan, Tai. 87/J3
Fengzhen, China 80/C2
Fengzhou, China 78/F5
Feni, Bang. 97/H4
Fenimore Pass (str.), Ak, US 171/C5
Fenner, Ca, US 148/E3
Fennimore, Wi, US 155/J2
Fennville, Mi, US 160/C3
Fenoarivo Atsinanana, Madg. 125/J7
Fenshui (pass), China 87/H3
Fenshui Guan (pass), China 87/H4
Fenshuizhen, China 87/F2
Fensmark, Den. 40/D4
Fensterbach (riv.), Ger. 59/F4
Fenton, La, US 164/B2
Fenton, Mi, US 160/E3
Fenton (lake), Mi, US 167/E7
Fenwick, WV, US 163/G1
Fenxi, China 80/B3
Fenyang, China 80/B3
Feodosiya, Ukr. 73/H5
Férai, Gre. 51/H5
Ferbane, Ire. 32/C3
Ferdinand, In, US 162/D1
Ferdinandshof, Ger. 43/G2
Ferdows, Iran 101/G2
Fère-Champenoise, Fr. 54/C6
Fère-en-Tardenois, Fr. 54/C5
Ferentillo, It. 65/B2
Ferentino, It. 65/C4
Ferento (ruin), It. 65/B3
Fereydūn Shahr, Iran 103/G3
Fergus (riv.), Ire. 32/B4
Fergus, On, Can. 160/F3
Fergus Falls, Mn, US 156/F4
Ferguson (lake), Nun, Can. 140/F2
Ferguson, Ky, US 162/E2
Ferihegy (int'l arpt.), Hun. 50/D2
Ferkessédougou, C.d'Iv. 114/D4
Ferlach, Aus. 45/L3
Ferland, On, Can. 157/K2
Ferland, Sk, Can. 145/L3
Ferland-et-Boilleau, Qu, Can. 158/B1
Ferlo (valley), Sen. 114/B3
Fermanagh (dist.), NI, UK 34/A3
Fermanville, Fr. 56/D1
Ferme-Neuve, Qu, Can. 161/J1
Fermeuse, Nf, Can. 159/L2
Fermi Nat'l Accelerator Lab., Il, US 167/P16
Fermignano, It. 63/F6
Fermin (pt.), Ca, US 166/F8
Fermo, It. 65/C1
Fermoselle, Sp. 46/B2
Fermoy, Ire. 32/B5
Fern Park, Fl, US 164/N6
Fern Ridge (lake), Or, US 146/B1
Fernán-Núñez, Sp. 46/C4
Fernández, Arg. 188/D3
Fernandina (isl.), Ecu. 184/J7
Fernandina Beach, Fl, US 165/H2
Fernando de la Mora, Par. 188/E3
Fernando de Noronha (isl.), Braz. 179/F3
Fernando Po (Bioko) (isl.), EqG. 120/B2
Fernandópolis, Braz. 189/G2
Ferndale, Ca, US 146/A3
Ferndale, Fl, US 164/M6
Ferndale, Md, US 168/B5
Ferndale, Mi, US 167/F7
Ferndale, Pa, US 161/G4
Ferndale, Wa, US 144/C3
Ferndown, Eng, UK 37/E5
Ferness, Sc, UK 33/C2
Ferney-Voltaire, Fr. 60/C5
Fernie, BC, Can. 144/G3
Fernley, Nv, US 146/D4
Fernpass (pass), Aus. 61/G3
Ferns, Ire. 32/D4
Ferntree Gully NP, Austl. 132/G5
Fernwood, Id, US 144/F4
Ferrandina, It. 48/E2
Ferrara, It. 63/E4
Ferrara (prov.), It. 63/E4
Ferrat (cape), Fr. 64/D5
Ferrat (cape), Alg. 112/E5
Ferreira do Alentejo, Port. 46/A3
Ferreira Gomes, Braz. 182/D2
Ferrell's Bridge (dam), Tx, US 153/G4
Ferrelo (cape), Or, US 146/A2
Ferreñafe, Peru 184/B2
Ferret (cape), Fr. 62/A4
Ferrette, Fr. 60/D3
Ferriday, La, US 164/C2
Ferriere, It. 62/C4
Ferrière-la-Grande, Fr. 55/E3
Ferrières, Belg. 55/E3
Ferris, Tx, US 150/L7
Ferrisburg, Vt, US 161/K2
Ferron, Ut, US 147/H4
Ferrum, Va, US 163/G2
Ferry Pass, Fl, US 164/E2
Ferryden, Sc, UK 33/D3
Ferryfield (int'l arpt.), Eng, UK 37/G5
Ferryhill, Eng, UK 35/G2
Ferryland, Nf, Can. 159/L2
Ferryside, Wal, UK 36/B3
Fershampenuaz, Rus. 69/N5
Ferté-Bernard, Fr. 57/F4
Fertile, Mn, US 156/F4
Fertő (Neusiedler) (lake), Aus. 45/M3
Ferwerd, Neth. 52/C2
Fès (prov.), Mor. 112/B3
Fès, Mor. 112/B3
Fesches-le-Châtel, Fr. 60/C2
Feshi, D.R. Congo 120/D4
Feshie (riv.), Sc, UK 33/C2
Fessenden, ND, US 156/D4
Fessenheim, Fr. 60/D2
Festival Centre, Austl. 131/M8
Festus, Mo, US 162/B1
Fet, Nor. 38/T8
Fetcham, Eng, UK 30/B3
Feteşti, Rom. 51/H3
Fethaland (pt.), Sc, UK 31/W13
Fethard, Ire. 32/C5
Fethard, Ire. 32/C5
Fethiye, Turk. 102/B2
Fetsund, Nor. 38/T8
Feucherolles, Fr. 30/H5
Feucht, Ger. 58/E4
Feuchtwangen, Ger. 58/D4
Feuilles (lake), Qu, Can. 141/J3
Feuilles, Rivière aux (riv.), Qu., Can. 139/K4
Feuquières, Fr. 54/A4
Feuquières-en-Vimeu, Fr. 54/A3
Feurs, Fr. 44/F4
Fevzipaşa, Turk. 104/E1
Feyzābād, Afg. 99/B4
Feyzin, Fr. 64/A1
Fez (Saiss) (int'l arpt.), Mor. 112/B3
Fezzane (well), Niger 108/B4
Ffestiniog, Wal, UK 34/E6
Fiambalá, Arg. 188/C3
Fianarantsoa, Madg. 125/H8
Fianarantsoa (prov.), Madg. 125/H8
Fianga, Chad 116/B3
Fiano Romano, It. 65/B3
Fiastrone (riv.), It. 65/C1
Ficarolo, It. 63/E4
Fichē, Eth. 118/A3
Fichtelberg (peak), Ger. 59/F2
Fichtelgebirge (mts.), Ger. 42/F3
Fichtelnaab (riv.), Ger. 59/E3
Ficksburg, SAfr. 124/D3
Ficulle, It. 65/B2
Fidenza, It. 62/D4
Fié (riv.), Gui. 114/C4
Field (isl.), Austl. 128/D3
Field (riv.), Austl. 131/M9
Field, Ab, Can. 144/F2
Field, On, Can. 160/F1
Fieldon, Il, US 155/J4
Fields, La, US 164/B2
Fields, Or, US 146/D2
Fieni, Rom. 51/G3
Fier, Alb. 49/F2
Fier (riv.), Fr. 60/B6
Fierzë (lake), Alb. 49/G1
Fiesch, Swi. 60/E5
Fiesole, It. 63/E6
Fiesso, It. 63/F3
Fiesso Umbertiano, It. 63/E4
Fife (co.), Sc, UK 33/D4
Fife, Wa, US 167/C3
Fife, Ga, US 163/L7
Fife Ness (pt.), Sc, UK 33/D4
Fifield, Austl. 133/C1
Fifth Cataract (falls), Sudan 109/G5
Fiftysix, Ar, US 153/H3
Figalo (cape), Alg. 112/D2
Figari, Fr. 48/A2
Figeac, Fr. 44/E4
Figg (mt.), Austl. 128/D5
Figline Valdarno, It. 63/E6
Figtree, Zim. 123/F4
Figueira da Foz, Port. 46/A2
Figueres, Sp. 47/G1
Figuig, Mor. 111/E2
Figuig (prov.), Mor. 112/C3
Figuil, Camr. 116/B3
Fiherenana (riv.), Madg. 125/G8
Fijāj (lake), Tun. 66/F4
Fiji (ctry.) 137/Y17
Fīk', Eth. 118/B3
Filabusi, Zim. 123/F4
Filadelfia, Col. 183/K7
Filadélfia, Braz. 183/E4
Filadelfia, Par. 188/D2
Filadelfia, Bol. 184/D3
Filandia, Col. 183/K8
Filattiera, It. 62/C5
Filchner Ice Shelf, Ant. 192/Y
File (hills), Sk, Can. 145/M2
Filer, Id, US 147/F2
Filey (bay), Eng, UK 35/H3
Filey, Eng, UK 35/H3
Filí, Gre. 49/N8
Filiaşi, Rom. 51/F3
Filiatá, Gre. 49/G3
Filiatrá, Gre. 49/G4
Filicudi (isl.), It. 48/D3
Filingué, Niger 115/F3
Filippiás, Gre. 49/G3
Filippoi (ruin), Gre. 49/J2
Filipstad, Swe. 40/F2
Filisur, Swi. 61/F4
Fillière (riv.), Fr. 60/C6
Fillmore, Sk, Can. 156/C3
Fillmore, Ca, US 166/B2
Fillmore, Ut, US 149/F1
Fillmore, Mo, US 155/G3
Filo (mt.), Sam. 137/S9
Filomeno Mata, Mex. 175/M6
Filótion, Gre. 49/J4
Filottrano, It. 63/G7
Fils (riv.), Ger. 58/C5
Filsum, Ger. 53/E2
Filton, Eng, UK 36/D3
Fīltu, Eth. 118/B4
Fimi (riv.), D.R. Congo 120/D3
Fina, Rsv. de, Mali 114/C3
Finale Emilia, It. 63/E4
Finale Ligure, It. 62/B5
Fiñana, Sp. 46/D4
Fincastle, Va, US 163/H2
Finch, Mt, US 145/J4
Finch Hatton, Austl. 134/C3
Finchley (nbrhd.), Eng, UK 30/C2
Findel (int'l arpt.), Lux. 55/F4
Findhorn, Sc, UK 33/C1
Findhorn (riv.), Sc, UK 33/C2
Findlay, Oh, US 160/E4
Findlay, Il, US 155/K4
Findochty, Sc, UK 33/D1
Finesville, NJ, US 168/C2
Fingal, ND, US 156/E4
Fingal, Austl. 132/C4
Finger, Tn, US 162/C3
Finger Lakes, NY, US 161/H3
Fingest, Eng, UK 30/A2
Fingoè, Moz. 123/F2
Finhaut, Swi. 60/C5
Finike, Turk. 104/B1
Finistère (dept.), Fr. 56/A4
Finisterre, Sp. 46/A1
Finisterre (cape), Sp. 46/A1
Finisterre (range), PNG 129/G1
Finjasjön (lake), Swe. 39/K6
Finke (riv.), Austl. 131/G3
Finke Gorge NP, Austl. 131/G3
Finkenwerder, Ger. 53/G1
Finksburg, Md, US 168/B5
Finland (ctry.) 38/H3
Finland (gulf), Eur. 74/C4
Finland, Mn, US 157/J4
Finlay (mts.), Tx, US 151/B2
Finlay (riv.), BC, Can. 140/D3
Finlayson, Mn, US 157/H4
Finley, Austl. 133/B2
Finley, ND, US 156/F4
Finley, Ok, US 153/G3
Finley, Tn, US 162/C2
Finley, Wa, US 144/E4
Finley NWR, Or, US 146/B1
Finn (riv.), Ire. 31/Q9
Finnegan, Ab, Can. 145/H2
Finnentrop, Ger. 53/E6
Finnigan (mt.), Austl. 134/B1
Finnis (cape), Austl. 131/G5
Finnmark (co.), Nor. 38/G1
Fino (riv.), It. 65/C2
Fino Mornasco, It. 62/C2
Fins, Oman 101/G4
Finschhafen, PNG 129/G1
Finsing, Ger. 59/E6
Finspång, Swe. 40/F2
Finsteraarhorn (peak), Swi. 60/E4
Finstown, Sc, UK 31/V14
Finström, Fin. 41/H1
Fintel, Ger. 53/G2
Fintona, NI, UK 34/A3
Fioio (riv.), It. 65/C4
Fionn Loch (lake), Sc, UK 33/A1
Fionnay, Swi. 60/D5
Fiora (riv.), It. 45/J5
Fiorano, It. 63/D4
Fiordland NP, NZ 135/A4
Fiorenzuola d'Arda, It. 62/C4
Fiori, Monte de (peak), It. 65/C2
Fiq, Syria 105/D3
Fircrest, Wa, US 167/C3
Fire Island Nat'l Seashore, NY, US 169/E2
Firebaugh, Ca, US 148/B2
Firebrand (pass), Mt, US 145/H3
Firenze (prov.), It. 63/E5
Firenze (Florence), It. 63/E6
Firenzuola, It. 63/E5
Firesteel (cr.), SD, US 154/E1
Firestone, Co, US 154/B3
Firmat, Arg. 190/E2
Firmi, Fr. 44/E4
Firminópolis, Braz. 186/C3
Firminy, Fr. 44/F4
Firozābād, India 98/C5
Firozpur, India 98/C4
First Cataract (falls), Egypt 109/G3
Firth, Id, US 147/G2
Firth of Forth (inlet), Sc, UK 33/C4
Firth of Lorn (inlet), Sc, UK 31/Q8
Firth of Tay (inlet), Sc, UK 33/C4
Firth of Thames (inlet), NZ 135/C2
Fīrūz Kūh, Iran 103/H3
Fīrūzābād, Iran 103/H4
Firyuza, Trkm. 101/G1
Fischa (riv.), Aus. 51/P7
Fischach, Ger. 61/G1
Fischamend Markt, Aus. 51/P7
Fischbacher Alpen (mts.), Aus. 45/L3
Fischbek, Ger. 53/G2
Fischen im Allgäu, Ger. 61/G3
Fisenge, Zam. 123/F2
Fish (riv.), Namb. 122/C5
Fish Camp, Ca, US 148/C2
Fishburn, Eng, UK 35/G2
Fisher, Austl. 131/F4
Fisher (bay), Mb, Austl. 156/F2
Fisher (mt.), BC, Can. 144/G3
Fisher (str.), Nun, Can. 141/H2
Fisher, Ar, US 162/B3
Fisher, Il, US 160/B4
Fisher, La, US 164/B2
Fisher, Mn, US 156/F4
Fisher, WV, US 163/H1
Fisher Bay, Mb, Can. 156/F2
Fisher Branch, Mb, Can. 156/F2
Fisherman (isl.), Austl. 134/F6
Fishermans Island Nat'l Wild. Ref., Va, US 163/K2
Fishers (isl.), NY, US 169/G1
Fishersville, Va, US 163/H1
Fishguard, Wal, UK 36/B3
Fishing (lake), Mb, Can. 157/G1
Fishing (cr.), NC, US 163/J2
Fisht (peak), Rus. 70/F4
Fishtoft, Eng, UK 35/J6
Fisk, Mo, US 162/B2
Fiske, Sk, Can. 145/K2
Fisksätra, Swe. 39/B1
Fismes, Fr. 54/C5
Fitchburg, Ma, US 161/L3
Fitchburg, Wi, US 155/K2
Fitful Head (pt.), Sc, UK 31/W14
Fitjar, Nor. 40/A2
Fitjja, Swe. 39/A1
Fitton (mt.), Yk, Can. 171/L2
Fitz Roy, Arg. 190/D5
Fitzcarrald, Peru 184/D3
Fitzgerald, Ga, US 165/G2
Fitzgerald River NP, Austl. 130/C5
Fitzhugh, Ok, US 153/F3
Fitzroy (peak), Arg. 191/B6
Fitzroy, UK 191/F6
Fitzroy (riv.), Austl. 128/B2
Fitzroy Crossing, Austl. 128/B4
Fitzwilliam (isl.), On, Can. 160/E2
Fitzwilliam (str.), NW, Can. 141/R7
Fiuggi, It. 65/C4
Fiume Veneto, It. 63/F2
Fiumicino, It. 65/B4
Five Forks, Ga, US 163/M7
Five Islands, NS, Can. 158/E3
Five Sisters (peak), Sc, UK 33/A2
Fivemile (cr.), Wy, US 147/J2
Fivemiletown, NI, UK 34/A3
Fivizzano, It. 62/D5
Fizi, D.R. Congo 121/G4
Fizuli, Azer. 71/H5
Fjell, Nor. 40/A1
Fjellstrand, Nor. 38/S8
Fjerritslev, Den. 40/C3
Fjugesta, Swe. 40/F2
Flå, Nor. 40/C1
Flachslanden, Ger. 58/D4
Flackwell Heath, Eng, UK 30/A2
Fladden, Ger. 58/D1
Fladungen, Ger. 58/D1
Flagler, Co, US 154/C4
Flagler Beach, Fl, US 165/H3
Flagler Museum, Fl, US 164/P9
Flagpole (peak), Tn, US 162/E2
Flagstaff, Az, US 149/G3
Flagstaff (lake), Or, US 146/D2
Flåm, Nor. 40/B1
Flambeau (riv.), Wi, US 157/J5
Flamborough Head (pt.), Eng, UK 35/H3
Flamborough, Eng, UK 35/H3
Flamborough, On, Can. 160/T9
Fläming (hills), Ger. 42/G2
Flaming Gorge (dam), Ut, US 147/J3
Flaming Gorge (res.), Ut.,Wy, US 147/J3
Flaming Gorge NRA, Wy, US 147/J3
Flamingo, Fl, US 165/H5
Flamingo Field (int'l arpt.), NAnt. 180/D1
Flanagan (riv.), On, Can. 157/H1
Flanders (reg.), Belg.,Fr. 54/B2
Flanders, NY, US 169/F2
Flandes, Col. 183/L8
Flandreau, SD, US 155/F1
Flärdläng (isl.), Swe. 39/B1
Flasher, ND, US 156/D4
Flat (mt.), NZ 135/A4
Flat Bay, Nf, Can. 159/H1
Flat Creek, Yk, Can. 171/L3
Flat Holm (isl.), Eng, UK 36/C4
Flat River, Mo, US 162/B2
Flat Rock, Mi, US 167/E8
Flat Rock, NC, US 163/G3
Flatbush (nbrhd.), NY, US 169/K9
Flateby, Nor. 38/T8
Flathead (lake), Mt, US 145/H4
Flathead (range), Mt, US 145/H3
Flathead (riv.), Mt, US 144/G4
Flathead Indian Res., Mt, US 144/G4
Flathead, South Fork (riv.), Mt, US 145/H4
Flatiron (mtn.), Id, US 147/G1
Flatonia, Tx, US 151/F3
Flattery (cape), Austl. 134/B1
Flattery (cape), Wa, US 142/A2
Flatwillow (cr.), Mt, US 145/K4
Flatwoods, La, US 164/B2
Flatwoods, Ky, US 163/F1
Flavio Alfaro, Ecu. 180/B5
Flawil, Swi. 61/F3
Flaxcombe, Sk, Can. 145/K2
Flaxlanden, Fr. 60/D2
Flayosc, Fr. 64/C5
Fleet, Eng, UK 37/F4
Fleet, Ab, Can. 145/J1
Fleetwood, Eng, UK 35/E4
Fleetwood, Pa, US 168/C3
Flekkefjord, Nor. 40/B2
Fleming, Sk, Can. 156/D2
Fleming, Co, US 154/C3
Fleming-Neon, Ky, US 163/F2
Flemingsberg, Swe. 39/A1
Flemingsburg, Ky, US 162/F1
Flemington, Mo, US 153/H2
Flemington, NJ, US 168/D2
Flemington Racecourse, Austl. 132/F5
Flemish Brabant (prov.), Belg. 55/D2
Flen, Swe. 40/G2
Flensburg, Ger. 40/C4
Flero, It. 62/D3
Fleron, Belg. 55/E2
Flers, Fr. 56/E3
Flesher (pass), Mt, US 145/H4
Flesk (riv.), Ire. 32/A5
Flesland (int'l arpt.), Nor. 40/A1
Fletcher, Ok, US 153/E3
Fletcher (pond), Mi, US 160/E2
Fletcher, NC, US 163/F3
Fletschhorn (peak), Swi. 60/D5
Fleurance, Fr. 44/D5
Fleurier, Swi. 60/C4
Fleurus, Belg. 55/D3
Fleury-les-Aubrais, Fr. 57/G5
Fleury-sur-Andelle, Fr. 57/G2
Fleury-sur-Orne, Fr. 57/E2
Flevoland (isl.), Neth. 42/C2
Flevoland (prov.), Neth. 52/C4
Flexenpass (pass), Aus. 61/G3
Flieden, Ger. 58/C2
Flieden (riv.), Ger. 58/C2
Fliess, Aus. 61/G3
Flimby, Eng, UK 34/E2
Flims, Swi. 61/F4
Flin Flon, Mb, Can. 140/F3
Flinders (range), Austl. 131/H5
Flinders (bay), Austl. 130/B5
Flinders (isl.), Austl. 127/D4
Flinders (riv.), Austl. 127/D2
Flinders Chase NP, Austl. 131/H5
Flinders Ranges (mts.), Austl. 127/C4
Flinders Ranges NP, Austl. 131/H4
Flinders Reefs (isls.), Austl. 134/C2
Flinders Reefs (isls.), Austl. 129/H4
Flines-lez-Raches, Fr. 54/C3
Flint, Wal, UK 35/E5
Flint (isl.), Kiri. 137/K6
Flint (lake), Nun, Can. 141/J2
Flint (riv.), Ga, US 163/M8
Flint (hills), Ks, US 153/F2
Flint, Mi, US 160/E3
Flint City, Al, US 162/D3
Flint Hills Nat'l Wild. Ref., Ks, US 155/G4
Flint, South Branch (riv.), Mi, US 167/E6
Flintbek, Ger. 40/D4
Flinton, On, Can. 161/H2
Flintshire (co.), Wal, UK 35/E5
Flippen, Ga, US 163/M8
Flisa, Nor. 40/E1
Flitwick, Eng, UK 37/F2
Flix, Sp. 47/F2
Flixecourt, Fr. 54/B3
Flize, Fr. 55/D4
Flo, Tx, US 151/G2
Floby, Swe. 40/E2
Floda, Swe. 40/E3
Flodden, Eng, UK 33/D5
Flögelner See (riv.), Ger. 53/F1
Flöha (riv.), Ger. 43/G3
Floing, Fr. 55/D4
Flomaton, Al, US 164/E2
Flonheim, Ger. 58/B3
Flora (mt.), Austl. 130/C2
Flora, Nor. 38/C3
Flora, Il, US 162/C1
Flora, In, US 160/C4
Flora, La, US 164/B2
Flora, Ms, US 162/B4
Flora, Phil. 88/C1
Flora (mtn.), Wa, US 144/D3
Flora Vista, NM, US 149/H2
Floral, Ar, US 153/J3
Floral City, Fl, US 164/G6
Floral Park, NY, US 169/L9
Florala, Al, US 165/E2
Florange, Fr. 55/F5
Florânia, Braz. 183/G4
Floraville, Austl. 129/E4
Floreffe, Belg. 55/D3
Florence (Firenze), It. 63/E6
Florence, Al, US 162/D3
Florence, Ar, US 153/J4
Florence, Az, US 149/G4
Florence, Co, US 152/B1
Florence, Ks, US 153/F1
Florence, Ky, US 162/E1
Florence, Ms, US 162/B4
Florence, Mt, US 145/G4
Florence, Or, US 146/A2
Florence, SC, US 163/H3
Florence, SD, US 155/F1
Florence, Tx, US 151/F2
Florence, Wi, US 157/K5
Florence Junction, Az, US 149/G4
Florence Lake Nat'l Wild. Ref., ND, US 156/D4
Florence-Graham, Ca, US 166/F8
Florenceville, NB, Can. 158/D2
Florencia, Col. 180/C4
Florencia, Arg. 188/E4
Florennes, Belg. 55/D3
Florentino Ameghino, Arg. 190/D4
Florenton, Mn, US 157/H4
Florenville, Belg. 55/E4
Flores (isl.), Azor., Port. 47/R12
Flores, Braz. 183/G4
Flores, Guat. 176/D2
Flores (isl.), Indo. 77/M10
Flores (sea), Indo. 77/L10
Flores (dept.), Uru. 191/F2
Flores, Braz. 183/F4
Flores, Arroyo de los (cr.), Arg. 190/E3
Floresta, Braz. 183/G5
Floreşti, Mol. 72/E4
Floresville, Tx, US 151/E3
Florham Park, NJ, US 169/H8
Floriano, Braz. 183/F4
Florianópolis, Braz. 189/G3
Florida, Bol. 184/D4
Florida, Bol. 188/D1
Florida, Col. 180/B4
Florida, Cuba 177/G1
Florida (str.), Cuba,US 143/K7
Florida, Hon. 176/D3
Florida, Peru 184/B2
Florida, Uru. 191/K11
Florida (dept.), Uru. 191/F2
Florida (state), US 143/K6
Florida (cape), Fl, US 164/P11
Florida, NY, US 168/D1
Florida City, Fl, US 165/H5
Florida Keys (isls.), Fl, US 165/H5
Florida Keys (isls.), Fl, US 139/J7
Florida Negra, Arg. 191/D6
Florida's Silver Springs, Fl, US 165/G3
Floridablanca, Col. 180/C3
Floridia, It. 48/D4
Florin, Ca, US 167/M10
Florina, Gre. 49/G2
Florissant, Mo, US 155/J4
Florissant Fossil Beds Nat'l Monument, Co, US 152/B1
Florissant Fossil Beds Nat'l Mon., Co, US 154/B4
Flörsbachtal, Ger. 58/C2
Flörsheim am Main, Ger. 58/B2
Flörsheim-Dalsheim, Ger. 58/B3
Florstadt, Ger. 58/B2
Flossenbürg, Ger. 59/F3
Flottsund, Swe. 39/A1
Flower Mound, Tx, US 150/K6
Floyd (riv.), Ia, US 155/F2
Floyd, Va, US 163/G2
Floyd, Ga, US 163/L7
Floydada, Tx, US 152/D4
Fluchthorn (peak), Aus. 61/G4
Flüelapass (pass), Swi. 61/F4
Flüelen, Swi. 61/E4
Fluessen (lake), Neth. 52/C3
Fluker, La, US 164/C2
Flume (riv.), Fr. 56/D4
Flums, Swi. 61/F3
Flushing, Mi, US 160/E3
Flushing (nbrhd.), NY, US 169/K8
Fluvanna, Tx, US 152/D4
Fly (riv.), PNG 129/F2
Fly River (delta), PNG 129/F2
Flying Fish (cape), Ant. 192/T
Fnjóská (riv.), Ice. 38/P6
Foam Lake, Sk, Can. 156/C2
Foard City, Tx, US 152/E4
Foča, Bosn. 50/D4
Fochabers, Sc, UK 33/C1
Fochville, SAfr. 124/P13
Fockbek, Ger. 40/C4
Focşani, Rom. 51/H3

Foëcy – Fuente

Foëcy, Fr. 57/H6
Fog (bay), Austl. 128/C3
Fogang, China 93/K3
Foggaret ez Zoua, Alg. 111/F4
Foggia, It. 48/D2
Fogi, Indo. 91/G4
Foglia (riv.), It. 63/F5
Fogliano (lake), It. 65/B5
Foglizzo, It. 62/A2
Föglö (isl.), Fin. 41/J3
Fogo (isl.), CpV. 107/J10
Fohnsdorf, Aus. 45/L3
Föhren, Ger. 55/F4
Foix, Fr. 44/D5
Fokino, Rus. 70/E1
Folarskardnuten (peak), Nor. 40/B1
Folda (inlet), Nor. 38/E2
Földeák, Hun. 50/E2
Folégandros (isl.), Gre. 67/K3
Folembray, Fr. 54/C4
Foley, Mn, US 157/H5
Foley, Fl, US 165/G2
Foley (isl.), Nun, Can. 141/J2
Foley, Mo, US 155/J4
Folgaria, It. 61/H6
Foligno, It. 65/B2
Foligno, It. 65/B2
Folkestone, Eng, UK 37/H4
Folkston, Ga, US 165/G2
Follainville-Dennemont, Fr. 30/H4
Follets (isl.), Tx, US 151/G3
Follonica (gulf), It. 45/J5
Folly Beach, SC, US 163/H4
Folschviller, Fr. 55/F5
Folsom (dam), Ca, US 148/B1
Folsom (lake), Ca, US 146/C4
Folsom, Ca, US 146/C4
Folsom, NJ, US 168/D4
Folteşti, Rom. 51/J3
Fomboni, Com. 125/G6
Fómeque, Col. 183/M8
Fomin, Rus. 71/G3
Fond de Peinin, Pic du (peak), Fr. 64/C3
Fond du Lac, Sk, Can. 140/F3
Fond du Lac (riv.), Sk, Can. 140/F3
Fond du Lac, Wi, US 155/K2
Fond du Lac Ind. Res., Mn, US 157/H4
Fonda, NY, US 161/J3
Fondettes, Fr. 57/F6
Fondi (lake), It. 65/C5
Fondi, It. 65/C5
Fondo, It. 61/H5
Fongen (peak), Nor. 38/D3
Fongolanbi, Sen. 114/B3
Fonni, It. 48/A2
Fonsagrada, Sp. 46/B1
Fonseca (gulf), Nic. 172/D5
Fonseca, Col. 180/C2
Font Sancte, Pic de la (peak), Fr. 64/C3
Fontaine, Fr. 64/B2
Fontaine-Châalis, Fr. 30/L4
Fontaine-lès-Dijon, Fr. 60/A3
Fontaine-lès-Luxeuil, Fr. 60/C2
Fontaine-l'Evêque, Belg. 55/D3
Fontana, Ca, US 166/C2
Fontana, Ks, US 153/G1
Fontana (lake), NC, US 162/F3
Fontanarossa, It. 65/E5
Fontanarossa (int'l arpt.), It. 48/D4
Fontanella, It. 62/C3
Fontanellato, It. 62/D4
Fontanelle, Ia, US 155/G3
Fontaniva, It. 63/E2
Fonte Boa, Braz. 181/E5
Fontenailles, Fr. 30/L6
Fontenais, Swi. 60/D3
Fontenay-en-Parisis, Fr. 30/K4
Fontenay-le-Comte, Fr. 44/C3
Fontenay-le-Fleury, Fr. 30/J5
Fontenay-le-Marmion, Fr. 57/E2
Fontenay-les-Briis, Fr. 30/J6
Fontenay-Saint-Père, Fr. 30/H4
Fontenay-sous-Bois, Fr. 30/K5
Fontenay-Trésigny, Fr. 30/L5
Fontenelle (res.), Wy, US 147/H2
Fontenelle (dam), Wy, US 147/H2
Fontibón, Col. 183/L8
Fontoy, Fr. 55/F5
Fontur (pt.), Ice. 38/P6
Fontvieille, Fr. 64/A5
Fontvieille, Mona. 62/J8
Footscray (nbrhd.), Austl. 132/F5
Foping, China 78/F5
Foraker (mt.), Ak, US 171/H3
Forbach, Fr. 55/F5
Forbach, Ger. 58/B5
Forbes, ND, US 156/E5
Forbes (mt.), BC, Can. 144/F2
Forbes, Austl. 133/D1
Forbesganj, India 97/F2
Forcados, Nga. 115/G5
Forcalquier, Fr. 64/B5
Forcarey, Sp. 46/A1
Forchheim, Ger. 58/E3
Ford (riv.), Mi, US 157/L4
Ford, Eng, UK 33/D5
Ford (cape), Austl. 128/C3
Ford City, Ca, US 148/C3
Fordate (isl.), Indo. 128/D1
Førde, Nor. 38/C3
Fordham (nbrhd.), NY, US 169/K8
Fordingbridge, Eng, UK 37/E5
Fordoche, La, US 164/C2
Fords, NJ, US 169/H9
Ford's Bridge, Austl. 132/C1
Fords Prairie, Wa, US 144/C4
Fordsville, Ky, US 162/D2
Fordville, ND, US 156/F3
Fordyce, Ar, US 153/H4
Forécariah, Gui. 114/B4
Foreland (pt.), Eng, UK 36/C4
Foreland, The (pt.), Eng, UK 37/E5
Foremost, Ab, Can. 145/J3
Foreness (pt.), Eng, UK 37/H4
Forest, La, US 153/J4
Forest (riv.), ND, US 156/F3
Forest, Ms, US 162/C4
Forest, Tx, US 151/G2
Forest City, Fl, US 164/N6
Forest City, Ia, US 155/H2
Forest City, NC, US 163/G3
Forest Green, Eng, UK 30/B3
Forest Grove, Me, US 146/B1
Forest Hill, Austl. 133/C2
Forest Hill, Md, US 168/B4
Forest Hill, Tx, US 150/K7
Forest Hill, WV, US 163/G2
Forest Hills (nbrhd.), NY, US 169/K9
Forest Hills, Tn, US 162/D2
Forest Lake, Mn, US 157/H5
Forest Park, Ga, US 163/M7
Forestbrook, SC, US 163/H4
Forestburg, Ab, Can. 145/H1
Foresthill, Ca, US 146/C4
Forestier (cape), Austl. 132/D4
Forestier (pen.), Austl. 132/D4
Foreston, Mn, US 157/H5
Forestport, NY, US 161/J3
Forestville, Qu, Can. 158/C1
Forestville, NY, US 161/G3
Forestville, Md, US 168/B6
Forét (bay), Fr. 56/B5
Forêt du Day NP, Djib. 118/B3
Forez (mts.), Fr. 44/E4
Forfar, Sc, UK 33/D3
Forgan, Ok, US 152/D2
Forgan, Sk, Can. 145/L2
Forges-les-Bains, Fr. 30/J6
Forges-les-Eaux, Fr. 57/G1
Forggensee (lake), Ger. 61/G2
Forillon NP, Qu, Can. 158/E1
Forino, It. 65/D6
Forio, It. 65/C6
Fork Res. (lake), Tx, US 151/G1
Fork River, Mb, Can. 156/D2
Forked Deer, South Fork (riv.), Tn, US 162/C3
Forked Island, La, US 164/B3
Forked River, NJ, US 168/D4
Forkill, NI, UK 34/B3
Forkland, Al, US 162/D4
Forks, Wa, US 144/B4
Forlì, It. 63/F5
Forlì (prov.), It. 63/F4
Forlimpopoli, It. 63/F5
Forman, ND, US 156/F4
Formartine (reg.), Sc, UK 33/D2
Formazza, It. 61/E5
Formby, Eng, UK 35/E4
Formby (pt.), Eng, UK 35/E4
Formello, It. 65/B3
Formentera, Isla de (isl.), Sp. 66/D3
Formentor (cape), Sp. 47/G3
Former Yugoslav Republic of Macedonia (Macedonia) (ctry.) 29/G4
Formerie, Fr. 54/A4
Formia, It. 65/C5
Formiga, Braz. 186/D4
Formigine, It. 63/D4
Formignana, It. 63/E4
Formosa (prov.), Arg. 188/D3
Formosa, Arg. 188/E3
Formosa, Braz. 186/D2
Formosa (isl.), GBis. 114/B4
Formosa (peak), SAfr. 124/C4
Formosa, Ar, US 153/H3
Formosa, Serra (mts.), Braz. 185/H4
Formoso (riv.), Braz. 186/C1
Formoso, Braz. 186/C2
Fornacelle, It. 63/E6
Fornaci di Barga, It. 62/D5
Fornæs (cape), Den. 40/D3
Fornebu (int'l arpt.), Nor. 40/D2
Forney, Tx, US 150/L7
Forno Canavese, It. 64/D2
Fornosovo, Rus. 41/P2
Fornovo di Taro, It. 62/D4
Foro (riv.), It. 65/D3
Foro Burunga, Sudan 116/D2
Foros, Ukr. 70/E3
Forres, Sc, UK 33/C1
Forres, Arg. 188/D3
Forrest, Austl. 131/F4
Forrest City, Ar, US 162/B3
Forrest River Abor. Rsv., Austl. 128/B3
Forrest River Mission, Austl. 128/B3
Forrest Station, Mb, Can. 156/E3
Forsan, Tx, US 151/D1
Forsand, Nor. 40/B2
Forsayth, Austl. 134/A2
Forshaga, Swe. 40/E2
Forssa, Fin. 41/K1
Forster, Austl. 132/E2
Forstern, Ger. 59/E6
Forstinning, Ger. 59/E6
Forsyth, Mo, US 153/H2
Forsyth (range), Austl. 134/A3
Forsyth, Ga, US 162/F4
Forsyth, Mt, US 145/L4
Forsythe NWR, NJ, US 161/J5
Forsythe NWR, NJ, US 168/D5
Fort Polk Mil. Res., La, US 151/H2
Fort A.P. Hill, Va, US 163/J1
Fort Abbās, Pak. 98/B5
Fort Albany, On, Can. 141/H3
Fort Ancient, Oh, US 160/D5
Fort Apache, Az, US 149/H4
Fort Apache Ind. Res., Az, US 149/G3
Fort Ashby, WV, US 161/G5
Fort Atkinson, Wi, US 155/K2
Fort Augustus, Sc, UK 33/B2
Fort Beaufort, SAfr. 124/D4
Fort Beauséjour Nat'l Hist. Park, NB, Can. 158/E3
Fort Belknap, Tx, US 153/E4
Fort Belknap Ind. Res., Mt, US 145/K3
Fort Belvoir, Va, US 168/A6
Fort Bend (co.), Tx, US 151/M9
Fort Benning, Ga, US 162/E4
Fort Benning Mil. Res., Ga, US 165/F1
Fort Benning South, Ga, US 162/E4
Fort Benton, Mt, US 145/J4
Fort Berthold Ind. Res., ND, US 156/C4
Fort Bidwell, Ca, US 146/C3
Fort Bliss (mil. res.), NM, US 149/J4
Fort Bowie Nat'l Hist. Site, Az, US 149/H4
Fort Bragg, Ca, US 146/B4
Fort Bragg, NC, US 163/H3
Fort Branch, In, US 162/D1
Fort Bridger, Wy, US 147/H3
Fort Buford Historical Site, ND, US 156/C4
Fort Campbell, Tn,Ky, US 162/D2
Fort Carson, Co, US 152/B1
Fort Carson, Co, US 154/B4
Fort Chambly Nat'l Hist. Park, Qu, Can. 159/P7
Fort Chipewyan, Ab, Can. 140/E3
Fort Clark Historical Site, ND, US 156/D4
Fort Collins, Co, US 154/B3
Fort Collins Museum, Co, US 154/B3
Fort Conde, Al, US 164/D2
Fort Davis, Al, US 162/E4
Fort Davis, Tx, US 151/C2
Fort Davis Nat'l Hist. Site, Tx, US 151/C2
Fort de Douaumont, Fr. 55/E5
Fort de Kock, Indo. 89/C3
Fort de Vaux, Fr. 55/E5
Fort Defiance, Az, US 149/H3
Fort Deposit, Al, US 164/E2
Fort Desaix Mil. Res., Fr. 173/N9
Fort Desoto Park, Fl, US 164/K8
Fort Dix, NJ, US 161/J4
Fort Dodge, Ia, US 155/G2
Fort Dodge Historical Museum, Ia, US 155/G2
Fort Donelson Nat'l Bfld., Tn, US 162/D2
Fort Drum, NY, US 161/J2
Fort Duchesne, Ut, US 147/J3
Fort Erie, On, Can. 160/V10
Fort Frances, On, Can. 157/H3
Fort Frederica Nat'l Mon., Ga, US 165/H2
Fort Gaines, Al, US 164/D2
Fort Gaines, Ga, US 165/F2
Fort Garland, Co, US 152/B2
Fort Gates, Tx, US 150/F2
Fort Gay, WV, US 163/F1
Fort George Nat'l Hist. Park, On, Can. 160/U9
Fort Gibson, Ok, US 153/G3
Fort Gibson (lake), Ok, US 153/G2
Fort Good Hope, NW, Can. 140/D2
Fort Gordon, Ga, US 163/F4
Fort Grant, Az, US 149/H4
Fort Green, Fl, US 164/M8
Fort Green Springs, Fl, US 164/M8
Fort Hall, Id, US 147/G2
Fort Hall Ind. Res., Id, US 147/G2
Fort Hancock, NJ, US 169/J10
Fort Hancock, Tx, US 151/B2
Fort Hood, Tx, US 151/F2
Fort Howard, Md, US 168/B5
Fort Huachuca, Az, US 149/G5
Fort Hunter Liggett, Ca, US 148/B3
Fort Independence Ind. Res., Ca, US 148/C2
Fort Irwin (mil. res.), Ca, US 148/D3
Fort Jackson, SC, US 163/G3
Fort Jesus, Kenya 119/B3
Fort Knox, Ky, US 162/E2
Fort Laramie (canal), Wy, US 154/B2
Fort Laramie Nat'l Hist.Site, Wy, US 154/B2
Fort Larned Nat'l Hist. Site, Ks, US 152/E1
Fort Lauderdale, Fl, US 164/P10
Fort Lauderdale-Hollywood (int'l arpt.), Fl, US 164/P10
Fort Lawn, SC, US 163/G3
Fort Leavenworth Mil. Res., Ks, US 153/G1
Fort Lee, NJ, US 169/K8
Fort Lennox Nat'l Hist. Park, Qu, Can. 161/K2
Fort Leonard Wood, Mo, US 153/H2
Fort Lewis, Wa, US 167/B3
Fort Liard, NW, Can. 140/D2
Fort Liberté, Haiti 177/J2
Fort Lonesome, Fl, US 164/L8
Fort Loudon, Pa, US 161/H5
Fort Lupton, Co, US 154/B3
Fort Lyon (canal), Co, US 154/C4
Fort Macleod, Ab, Can. 145/H3
Fort Madison, Ia, US 155/J3
Fort Malden Nat'l Hist. Park, On, Can. 167/F7
Fort Mandan Historical Site, ND, US 156/D4
Fort Matanzas Nat'l Mon., Fl, US 165/H3
Fort Mc Dermitt Ind. Res., Nv, US 146/D3
Fort McCoy, Fl, US 165/H3
Fort McCoy (fort), Wi, US 155/J1
Fort McDowell Ind. Res., Az, US 149/G4
Fort McHenry Nat'l Mon., Md, US 168/B5
Fort McMurray, Ab, Can. 140/E3
Fort McPherson, NW, Can. 171/M2
Fort Meade, Fl, US 164/M8
Fort Meade, Md, US 168/B5
Fort Michilimackinac, Mi, US 160/D2
Fort Mill, SC, US 163/G3
Fort Missoula, Mt, US 145/G4
Fort Mojave Ind. Res., Az,Ca, US 148/E3
Fort Morgan, Al, US 164/D2
Fort Morgan, Co, US 154/C3
Fort Morgan Museum, Co, US 154/C3
Fort Motte, SC, US 163/G4
Fort Moultrie, SC, US 163/H4
Fort Myers, Fl, US 165/H4
Fort Nelson (riv.), BC, Can. 140/D3
Fort Nelson, BC, Can. 142/AA13
Fort Niobrara NWR, Ne, US 154/D2
Fort Nottingham, SAfr. 125/E3
Fort Payne, Al, US 162/E3
Fort Peck (lake), Mt, US 139/G5
Fort Peck, Mt, US 145/L3
Fort Peck (dam), Mt, US 145/L4
Fort Peck Ind. Res., Mt, US 145/L3
Fort Phantom Hill, Tx, US 151/E1
Fort Pierce, Fl, US 165/H4
Fort Pierre, SD, US 154/D1
Fort Plain, NY, US 161/J3
Fort Portal, Ugan. 121/G2
Fort Providence, NW, Can. 140/E2
Fort Pulaski Nat'l Mon., Ga, US 163/G4
Fort Qu'Appelle, Sk, Can. 156/C2
Fort Quitman Ruins, Tx, US 151/B2
Fort Raleigh Nat'l Hist. Site, NC, US 163/K3
Fort Randall (dam), SD, US 154/E2
Fort Ransom, ND, US 156/F4
Fort Ransom Historical Site, ND, US 156/F4
Fort Resolution, NW, Can. 140/E2
Fort Rice, ND, US 156/D4
Fort Rice Historical Site, ND, US 156/D4
Fort Riley (fort), Ks, US 155/F4
Fort Riley Mil. Res., Ks, US 153/F1
Fort Ripley, Mn, US 157/G4
Fort Rixon, Zim. 123/F4
Fort Rock, Or, US 146/C2
Fort Ross, Ca, US 146/B4
Fort Rucker Military Res., Al, US 165/f2
Fort Saint James, BC, Can. 140/D3
Fort Saint John, BC, Can. 140/D3
Fort Scott, Ks, US 153/G2
Fort Scott Nat'l Hist. Site, Ks, US 153/G2
Fort Seward Historical Site, ND, US 156/E4
Fort Seybert, WV, US 163/H1
Fort Shawnee, Oh, US 160/D4
Fort Sill Mil. Res., Ok, US 153/E3
Fort Simpson, NW, Can. 140/D2
Fort Smith, Ar, US 153/G3
Fort Smith, NW, Can. 140/E2
Fort Smith, Mt, US 147/K1
Fort Smith Nat'l Hist. Site, Ar, US 153/G3
Fort Stanwix Nat'l Mon., NY, US 161/J3
Fort Stewart, Ga, US 165/H2
Fort Stockton, Tx, US 151/C2
Fort Sumner, NM, US 152/B3
Fort Sumter Nat'l Mon., SC, US 163/H4
Fort Thomas, Az, US 149/H4
Fort Thomas, Ky, US 160/D5
Fort Tilden, NY, US 169/K9
Fort Totten, ND, US 156/E4
Fort Totten Indian Res., ND, US 156/E4
Fort Towson, Ok, US 153/G3
Fort Union Nat'l Mon., NM, US 152/B3
Fort Union Trading Post Nat'l Hist. Site, Mt, US 156/B3
Fort Valley, Ga, US 162/F4
Fort Vermilion, Ab, Can. 140/E3
Fort Wadsworth, NY, US 169/J9
Fort Walton Beach, Fl, US 164/E2
Fort Washakie, Wy, US 147/J2
Fort Washington (park), Md, US 168/A6
Fort Wayne, In, US 160/D4
Fort Wellington Nat'l Hist. Park, On, Can. 161/J2
Fort White, Fl, US 165/G3
Fort William, Sc, UK 33/A3
Fort Wingate, NM, US 149/H3
Fort Wingate (mil. res.), NM, US 149/H3
Fort Worth, Tx, US 150/K7
Fort Worth Museum of Science and History, Tx, US 150/K7
Fort Yates, ND, US 156/D4
Fort Yukon, Ak, US 171/J2
Fort Yuma Ind. Res., Ca, US 148/E4
Fort-de-France, Guad. 173/N9
Fort-Foureau, Camr. 116/B2
Fort-George (Chisasibi), Qu, Can. 141/J3
Fort-Mahon-Plage, Fr. 54/A3
Fort-Mardyck, Fr. 54/B1
Fort-Shevchenko, Kaz. 71/J3
Fortaleza, Bol. 185/E3
Fortaleza, Bol. 185/E4
Fortaleza, Braz. 183/G3
Fortaleza dos Nogueiras, Braz. 183/E4
Fortaleza Santa Teresa, Uru. 191/G2
Forte Cameia, Ang. 122/D1
Forte dei Marmi, It. 62/D6
Forte República, Ang. 120/D4
Fortescue (riv.), Austl. 130/C2
Fortescue, NJ, US 168/C5
Forth (mtn.), Ire. 32/D5
Forth (riv.), Sc, UK 33/B4
Forth, Sc, UK 33/C5
Fortín, Mex. 175/N8
Fortín Ávalos Sánchez, Par. 188/D2
Fortín Capitán Escobar, Par. 188/D2
Fortín Carlos Antonio López, Par. 188/E2
Fortín Casanillo, Par. 188/E2
Fortín Coronel Bogado, Par. 188/E2
Fortín Coronel Sánchez, Par. 188/E1
Fortín Florida, Par. 188/E2
Fortín General Bruguez, Par. 188/E3
Fortín Guaraní, Par. 188/E2
Fortín Hernandarias, Par. 188/D2
Fortín Infante Rivarola, Par. 188/D2
Fortín Isla Poi, Par. 188/E2
Fortín Palmar de las Islas, Par. 188/D1
Fortín Presidente Ayala, Par. 188/E2
Fortín Teniente Esteban Martínez, Par. 188/E3
Fortín Teniente Gabino Mendoza, Par. 188/D2
Fortín Teniente Juan E. López, Par. 188/D2
Fortín Teniente Primero Ramiro Espínola, Par. 188/D2
Fortín Uno, Arg. 190/D3
Fortín Zalazar, Par. 188/E2
Forton, Eng, UK 35/F4
Fortore (riv.), It. 48/D2
Fortress (mtn.), Wy, US 147/J1
Fortress of Louisbourg Nat'l Hist. Park, NS, Can. 159/G3
Fortrose, Sc, UK 33/B1
Fortuna, Arg. 190/D2
Fortuna, Braz. 183/E4
Fortuna, Ca, US 146/A3
Fortuna, Mo, US 153/H1
Fortuna, ND, US 156/C3
Fortuna Ledge, Ak, US 171/F3
Fortune (bay), Nf, Can. 159/K2
Fortune, Nf, Can. 159/K2
Fortuneswell, Eng, UK 36/D5
Fortville, In, US 160/D5
Forty Fort, Pa, US 168/C1
Forty Mile (pt.), Mi, US 160/E2
Forty Mile Scrub NP, Austl. 134/B2
Fortymile Wash (riv.), Nv, US 148/D2
Forūr (isl.), Iran 103/H5
Fos (gulf), Fr. 64/A6
Fos-sur-Mer, Fr. 64/A6
Fosca, Col. 183/M8
Foshan, China 87/G4
Fosheim (pen.), Nun, Can. 141/S7
Foso, Gha. 115/E5
Foss (riv.), Eng, UK 35/G3
Fossacesia, It. 65/D3
Fossalta di Piave, It. 63/F2
Fossalta di Portogruaro, It. 63/F2
Fossano, It. 62/A3
Fosses, Fr. 30/K4
Fosses-la-Ville, Belg. 55/D3
Fossil, Or, US 146/C1
Fossil Butte Nat'l Mon., Wy, US 147/H3
Fossò, It. 63/F3
Fossombrone, It. 63/F6
Fosston, Sk, Can. 156/C1
Fosston, Mn, US 156/G4
Foster, Austl. 133/C4
Foster, Mo, US 153/G1
Foster, Tx, US 152/C4
Foster City, Mi, US 157/L5
Fostoria, Oh, US 160/E4
Fót, Hun. 51/R9
Fotan, China 87/H3
Fotokol, Camr. 116/B2
Foucarmont, Fr. 54/A4
Foucherans, Fr. 60/B3
Fouesnant, Fr. 56/A5
Foug, Fr. 55/E6
Fougamou, Gabon 120/B3
Fougères, Fr. 56/D4
Fougerolles, Fr. 60/C2
Fouilloy, Fr. 54/B4
Fouke, Ar, US 153/H4
Foul (pt.), SrL. 95/D4
Foula (isl.), Sc, UK 31/V13
Foulness (riv.), Eng, UK 35/H4
Foulness (pt.), Eng, UK 37/G3
Foulness (isl.), Eng, UK 37/G3
Foulsham, Eng, UK 37/H1
Foulwind (cape), NZ 135/B3
Foum el Hassane, Mor. 110/C3
Foum Zguid, Mor. 110/D3
Foumbouni, Com. 125/G5
Foundiougne, Sen. 114/A3
Fountain, Co, US 152/B1
Fountain, Fl, US 165/F2
Fountain (cr.), Co, US 154/B4
Fountain (lake), Mn, US 157/N6
Fountain Green, Ut, US 147/H4
Fountain Hill, Pa, US 168/C2
Fountain Hills, Az, US 149/G4
Fountain Inn, SC, US 163/F3
Fountain Run, Ky, US 162/E2
Fountain Valley, Ca, US 166/G8
Fountains Abbey, Eng, UK 35/G3
Four Corners Monument, US 149/H2
Four Elms, Eng, UK 30/D3
Four Lakes, Wa, US 144/F4
Four Mountains (isls.), Ak, US 171/D5
Fourchambault, Fr. 44/E3
Fourche La Fave (riv.), Ar, US 153/H3
Fourcroy (cape), Austl. 128/C2
Fourges, Fr. 30/G4
Fourmies, Fr. 54/D4
Fourmile (peak), Wy, US 147/K2
Fourmile Draw (riv.), NM, US 151/B1
Fourneaux, Fr. 64/C2
Fourques, Fr. 64/A5
Fourteen Mile (pt.), Mi, US 157/K4
Fourth Cataract (falls), Sudan 109/G5
Fouta Djallon (phys. reg.), Gui. 114/B4
Foveaux (str.), NZ 127/G7
Fowey (riv.), Eng, UK 36/B6
Fowey, Eng, UK 36/B6
Fowler, Ca, US 148/C2
Fowler, Co, US 152/B1
Fowler, In, US 160/C4
Fowler, Mi, US 160/D3
Fowlkes, Tn, US 162/C3
Fowman, Iran 103/G2
Fownhope, Wal, UK 36/D2
Fox (mtn.), Yk., Can. 171/M3
Fox (isls.), Ak, US 171/E5
Fox, Ar, US 153/H3
Fox (lake), Il, US 155/K2
Fox, Mi, US 160/C2
Fox, Ok, US 153/F3
Fox, Or, US 146/D1
Fox (isl.), Wa, US 167/B3
Fox (riv.), Wi, US 157/K5
Fox (riv.), Wi,Il, US 155/"K2,
Fox Glacier, NZ 135/B3
Fox Harbour, Nf, Can. 159/L2
Fox Lake, Il, US 167/P15
Fox River Grove, Il, US 167/P15
Fox Valley, Sk, Can. 145/K2
Foxe (pen.), Can. 139/K3
Foxe (chan.), Can. 139/K3
Foxe Basin (chan.), Can. 139/K3
Foxen (lake), Swe. 40/D2
Foxford, Ire. 32/A2
Foxton, Eng, UK 37/G2
Foyers, Sc, UK 33/B2
Foyle (riv.) 34/A2
Foynes, Ire. 32/A4
Foz, Sp. 46/B1
Foz do Breu, Braz. 184/C3
Foz do Cunene, Ang. 122/A3
Foz do Iguaçu, Braz. 189/F3
Frackville, Pa, US 168/B2
Fraga, Sp. 47/F2
Fraiburgo, Braz. 189/G3
Fraile Muerto, Uru. 189/F5
Fraile Pintado, Arg. 188/C2
Fraisans, Fr. 60/B3
Fraize, Fr. 60/D1
Frameries, Belg. 54/C3
Framlingham, Eng, UK 37/H2
Frammersbach, Ger. 58/C2
Franca, Braz. 189/H2
Francavilla al Mare, It. 65/D3
Francavilla Fontana, It. 49/E2
Francavilla in Sinni, It. 48/E2
France (ctry.) 29/E4
Frances (cape), Cuba 177/F1
Frances (lake), Yk, Can. 140/C2
Francés Viejo (cape), DRep. 173/H4
Francesville, In, US 160/C4
Franceville, Gabon 120/C3
Franche-Comté (pol. reg.), Fr. 60/B5
Francia, Uru. 191/K10
Francis, Sk, Can. 156/C2
Francis, Ok, US 153/F3
Francis, Ut, US 147/H3
Francis Case (lake), SD, US 154/E2
Francisco de Orellana, Peru 184/C1
Francisco Escárcega, Mex. 176/D2
Francisco I. Madero, Mex. 151/C5
Francisco Javier Mina, Mex. 174/C3
Francisco Portillo, Mex. 151/B3
Francisco Sá, Braz. 187/E3
Francisco Zarco, Mex. 174/A1
Francistown (int'l arpt.), Bots. 123/E4
Francistown, Bots. 123/E4
Franco da Rocha, Braz. 187/K8
Francolino, It. 63/E4
Franconville, Fr. 30/J5
Franeker, Neth. 52/C2
Frangy, Fr. 60/B5
Frank Hahn NP, Austl. 130/C5
Franken Wald (for.), Ger. 59/E2
Frankenau, Ger. 53/F6
Frankenberg-Eder, Ger. 53/F6
Frankenburg am Hausruck, Aus. 59/G6
Frankenhöhe (mts.), Ger. 42/F4
Frankenmarkt, Aus. 59/G7
Frankenmuth, Mi, US 160/E3
Frankenthal, Ger. 58/B3
Frankford, On, Can. 161/H2
Frankford, De, US 163/K1
Frankfort, SAfr. 124/E2
Frankfort, In, US 160/C4
Frankfort, Ks, US 155/F4
Frankfort (cap.), Ky, US 162/E1
Frankfort, Mi, US 160/C2
Frankfort, Oh, US 160/E5
Frankfurt (int'l arpt.), Ger. 58/B2
Frankfurt, Ger. 43/H2
Frankfurt am Main, Ger. 58/B2
Fränkische Alb (mts.), Ger. 42/F4
Fränkische Rezat (riv.), Ger. 58/D4
Fränkische Saale (riv.), Ger. 42/E3
Fränkische Schweiz (reg.), Ger. 42/F4
Fränkische Schweiz (reg.), Ger. 45/J2
Frankland (cape), Austl. 133/C4
Franklin (bay), NW, Can. 140/D2
Franklin (mts.), NW, Can. 140/D2
Franklin, Qu, Can. 161/K2
Franklin (cape), Ak, US 171/G1
Franklin, Az, US 149/H4
Franklin, Ga, US 162/E4
Franklin, Id, US 147/H2
Franklin, In, US 160/C5
Franklin, Ks, US 153/G2
Franklin, Ky, US 162/D2
Franklin, La, US 164/C3
Franklin, Mi, US 167/F6
Franklin, NC, US 163/F3
Franklin, Ne, US 154/E3
Franklin, NH, US 161/L3
Franklin, NJ, US 168/D1
Franklin, Oh, US 160/D5
Franklin, Pa, US 161/G4
Franklin, Tn, US 162/D3
Franklin, Tx, US 151/F2
Franklin, Va, US 163/J2
Franklin, Wi, US 160/B3
Franklin, WV, US 163/H1
Franklin D. Roosevelt (lake), Wa, US 144/E3
Franklin Grove, Il, US 155/K3
Franklin Lakes, NJ, US 169/J7
Franklin Mineral Museum, NJ, US 168/D1
Franklin Park, Il, US 167/Q16
Franklin Square, NY, US 169/L9
Franklin-Lower Gordon Wild Rivers NP, Austl. 132/C4
Franklinton, La, US 164/C2
Franklinton, NC, US 163/H2
Franklinville, NY, US 161/G3
Frankston (nbrhd.), Austl. 132/G6
Frankston, Tx, US 150/G1
Franksville, Wi, US 167/Q14
Frankville, Al, US 164/D2
Franois, Fr. 60/B3
Franquelin, Qu, Can. 158/D1
Franschhoek, SAfr. 124/L10
Fransfontein, Namb. 122/B4
Fransisco Beltrão, Braz. 189/F3
Fransisco Morato, Braz. 187/K8
Františkovy Lázně, Czh. 59/F2
Franz Josef Land (isls.), Rus. 192/C
Franz Joseph Strauss (int'l arpt.), Ger. 59/E6
Franzburg, Ger. 40/E4
Frascati, It. 65/B4
Fraser (mt.), Austl. 130/C3
Fraser (isl.), Austl. 127/E3
Fraser (riv.), BC, Can. 144/D2
Fraser, Mi, US 167/G6
Fraser NP, Austl. 133/B3
Fraserburg, SAfr. 124/C3
Fraserburgh, Sc, UK 33/D1
Frasertown, NZ 135/D2
Fraserville, On, Can. 161/G2
Fraserwood, Mb, Can. 156/F2
Frasne, Fr. 60/C4
Frasnes-lez-Gosselies, Belg. 55/D2
Frassine (riv.), It. 63/E2
Frassino, It. 63/D3
Frasso Telesino, It. 65/D5
Frastanz, Aus. 61/F3
Frati, Monte dei (peak), It. 63/F6
Frauenfeld, Swi. 61/E2
Fraunberg, Ger. 59/F6
Fray Bentos, Uru. 191/J10
Fray Jorge, PN, Chile 188/B4
Fray Marcos, Uru. 191/L11
Frazier Downs Abor. Land, Austl. 128/A4
Frazier Park, Ca, US 148/C3
Frechen, Ger. 55/F2
Freckenfeld, Ger. 58/B4
Fred (mt.), Les. 124/E3
Fred, Tx, US 151/G2
Fredensborg, Den. 39/J7
Frederic, Wi, US 157/H5
Frederica, De, US 168/C6
Fredericia, Den. 40/C4
Frederick (reef), Austl. 127/E3
Frederick, Md, US 161/H5
Frederick (co.), Md, US 168/A5
Frederick, Ok, US 152/E3
Frederick, SD, US 154/E1
Fredericksburg, Ia, US 155/H2
Fredericksburg, Pa, US 168/B3
Fredericksburg, Tx, US 151/E2
Fredericksburg, Va, US 163/J1
Fredericksburg and Spotsylvania Nat'l Mil. Park, Va, US 163/J1
Frederickton, Austl. 132/E1
Fredericktown, Oh, US 160/E4
Fredericktown, Mo, US 162/B2
Frederico Westphalen, Braz. 189/F3
Fredericton (cap.), NB, Can. 158/D3
Fredericton Junction, NB, Can. 158/D3
Frederik Willem IV (falls), Sur. 181/G4
Frederiks, Den. 40/C3
Frederiksberg, Den. 39/H7
Frederiksberg, Den. 39/J7
Frederiksborg (co.), Den. 40/E4
Frederiksborg Castle (Frederiksborg Slot), Den. 40/E4
Frederiksborg Slot (Frederiksborg Castle), Den. 40/E4
Frederikshavn, Den. 40/D3
Frederikssund, Den. 39/J7
Frederiksted, USVI 173/M8
Frederiksværk, Den. 39/J7
Fredersdorf bei Berlin, Ger. 42/Q7
Fredonia, ND, US 156/E4
Fredonia, Ks, US 153/G2
Fredonia, Wi, US 160/C3
Fredonia, NY, US 161/G3
Fredonia, Az, US 149/F2
Fredonia, Col. 183/K7
Fredonia (Biscoe), Ar, US 153/J3
Fredriksberg, Swe. 40/F1
Fredrikstad, Nor. 40/D2
Free State (prov.), SAfr. 124/P13
Freeburg, Mo, US 153/J1
Freeburg, Pa, US 168/B2
Freedom, Ok, US 152/E2
Freedom, Wy, US 147/H2
Freehold, NJ, US 168/D3
Freel (peak), Ca, US 146/D4
Freeland, Md, US 168/B4
Freeland, Pa, US 168/C1
Freeland, Wa, US 167/B1
Freeling (mt.), Austl. 131/G2
Freeling Heights (peak), Austl. 131/H4
Freelton, On, Can. 160/S9
Freeman, SD, US 154/F2
Freemansburg, Pa, US 168/C2
Freeport, Bahm. 173/F2
Freeport, Fl, US 165/E2
Freeport, Il, US 155/K2
Freeport, Me, US 161/L3
Freeport, NY, US 169/L9
Freeport, Pa, US 161/G4
Freeport, Tx, US 150/G3
Freer, Tx, US 151/E4
Freetown (cap.), SLeo. 114/B4
Freetown, In, US 162/D1
Freetown (Lungi) (int'l arpt.), SLeo. 114/B4
Fregenal de la Sierra, Sp. 46/B3
Fregene, It. 65/B4
Fréhel (cape), Fr. 56/C3
Frei Inocêncio, Braz. 187/E3
Freib Mulde (riv.), Ger. 42/G3
Freiberg, Ger. 43/G3
Freiburg, Ger. 60/D2
Freiburg, Ger. 53/G1
Freienbach, Swi. 61/E3
Freigné, Fr. 57/D5
Freihung, Ger. 59/E3
Freilassing, Ger. 59/F7
Freinsheim, Ger. 58/B3
Freire, Chile 190/B3
Freirina, Chile 188/B4
Freisen, Ger. 55/G4
Freising, Ger. 59/E6
Freistadt, Aus. 59/H5
Freital, Ger. 43/G3
Freixo de Espada à Cinta, Port. 46/B2
Frejorgues (int'l arpt.), Fr. 44/E5
Fréjus, Fr. 64/C6
Frekhaug, Nor. 40/A1
Frémainfille, Fr. 30/H4
Fremantle (nbrhd.), Austl. 130/K7
Fremdingen, Ger. 58/D5
Frémécourt, Fr. 30/J4
Fremington, Eng, UK 36/B4
Fremont, Ia, US 155/H3
Fremont, In, US 160/D4
Fremont, Mi, US 160/D3
Fremont, NC, US 163/J3
Fremont, Ne, US 155/F3
Fremont, Oh, US 160/E4
Fremont (riv.), Ut, US 147/H4
Fremont (isl.), Ut, US 147/G3
Fremont, Ut, US 149/G1
Fremont (lake), Wy, US 147/J2
Fremont (peak), Wy, US 147/J2
French (riv.), On, Can. 160/F1
French (cr.), Pa, US 168/C3
French Broad (riv.), Tn, US 163/F3
French Camp, Ms, US 162/C4
French Cr. SP, Pa, US 168/C3
French Frigate Shoals (bar), Hi, US 137/J2
French Guiana (dpcy.), FrG. 181/H3
French Lick, In, US 162/D1
French Polynesia (terr.), Fr. 137/L6
French River, On, Can. 160/F1
French River, Mn, US 157/J4
Frenchburg, Ky, US 162/F2
Frenchglen, Or, US 146/D2
Frenchman (riv.), Can.,US 140/F4
Frenchman (cr.), Co, US 154/C3
Frenchman (riv.), Sk, Can. 145/K3
Frenchman's (bay), On, Can. 160/U8
Frenchmans Cap (peak), Austl. 132/C4
Frenchpark, Ire. 32/B2
Frenchtown, Mt, US 144/G4
Frenchtown, NJ, US 168/C2
Frenda, Alg. 112/F5
Frêne, Pic du (peak), Fr. 64/C2
Frépillon, Fr. 30/J4
Freren, Ger. 53/E4
Fresco, C.d'Iv. 114/D5
Fresco (riv.), Braz. 182/D4
Freshford, Ire. 32/C4
Freshwater, Nf, Can. 159/L2
Freshwater, Eng, UK 37/E5
Fresia, Chile 190/B4
Fresnay-sur-Sarthe, Fr. 57/F4
Fresnes, Fr. 30/J5
Fresnes-en-Woëvre, Fr. 55/E5
Fresnillo, Mex. 174/E4
Fresno, Col. 183/K7
Fresno, Ca, US 148/C2
Fresno (riv.), Ca, US 148/B2
Fresno, Tx, US 151/M9
Fresno (res.), Mt, US 145/J3
Fresnoy-le-Grand, Fr. 54/C4
Fresse-sur-Moselle, Fr. 60/C2
Fressenneville, Fr. 54/A3
Fresta, Swe. 39/A1
Fretani (mts.), It. 65/D3
Fretin, Fr. 54/C2
Freuchie (lake), Sc, UK 33/C3
Freudenberg, Ger. 55/G2
Freudenberg, Ger. 59/E4
Freudenberg, Ger. 58/C3
Freudenburg, Ger. 55/F4
Freudenstadt, Ger. 61/E1
Frévent, Fr. 54/B3
Frewena, Austl. 129/D4
Frewsburg, NY, US 161/G3
Freycinet (har.), Austl. 130/B3
Freycinet NP, Austl. 132/D4
Freyming-Merlebach, Fr. 55/F5
Freyre, Arg. 188/D4
Freystadt, Ger. 59/E4
Freyung, Ger. 59/G5
Fria, Gui. 114/B4
Fria (cape), Namb. 122/B3
Friant, Ca, US 148/C2
Friant (dam), Ca, US 148/C2
Friant-Kern (canal), Ca, US 148/C3
Friars Point, Ms, US 162/B3
Frías, Peru 184/B2
Frías, Arg. 188/C4
Fribourg, Swi. 60/D4
Fribourg (canton), Swi. 60/D4
Frick, Swi. 60/E3
Frickenhausen am Main, Ger. 58/D3
Friday Harbor, Wa, US 144/C3
Fridingen an der Donau, Ger. 61/E1
Fridley, Mn, US 157/P6
Fridolfing, Ger. 59/F6
Friedberg, Ger. 58/B2
Friedberg, Ger. 58/D6
Friedeburg, Ger. 53/E2
Friedland, Ger. 53/G6
Friedrichsdorf, Ger. 58/B2
Friedrichshafen (arpt.), Ger. 61/F2
Friedrichshafen, Ger. 61/F2
Friedrichstadt, Ger. 40/C4
Friedrichsthal, Ger. 55/G5
Frielendorf, Ger. 53/G7
Friend, Ks, US 152/D1
Friend, Ne, US 155/F3
Friendship, Ar, US 153/H3
Friendship, Tn, US 162/C3
Friendship, Wi, US 155/K2
Friendswood, Tx, US 151/M9
Frierson, La, US 150/H1
Friesenhagen, Ger. 55/G2
Friesenheim, Ger. 60/D1
Friesland (prov.), Neth. 52/C2
Friesoythe, Ger. 53/E2
Friggesby, Fin. 39/E4
Frignano, It. 65/D6
Frignicourt, Fr. 55/D6
Friguiagbé, Gui. 114/B4
Frimley, Eng, UK 30/A3
Frinton, Eng, UK 37/H3
Frio (riv.), Tx, US 175/F2
Frio Draw (riv.), NM,Tx, US 152/C3
Friockheim, Sc, UK 33/D3
Friol, Sp. 46/B1
Friona, Tx, US 152/C3
Frisange, Lux. 55/F4
Frisco, Tx, US 150/L6
Frisco City, Al, US 164/E2
Frissell (mt.), Ct, US 161/K3
Fristad, Swe. 40/E3
Fritch, Tx, US 152/D3
Fritsla, Swe. 40/E3
Fritzlar, Ger. 53/G6
Friuli (reg.), It. 67/G1
Friuli-Venezia Giula (prov.), It. 45/K3
Friville-Escarbotin, Fr. 54/A3
Frizington, Eng, UK 34/E2
Frobisher (bay), Nun, Can. 141/K2
Frodsham, Eng, UK 35/F5
Frogmore, Eng, UK 30/A3
Frogue, Ky, US 162/E2
Frohavel (inlet), Nor. 38/D3
Frohnleiten, Aus. 45/L3
Froid, Mt, US 156/B3
Froid (mtn.), Fr. 64/C3
Froid-Chapelle, Belg. 55/D3
Froideconche, Fr. 60/C2
Froissy, Fr. 54/B4
Froland, Nor. 40/C2
Frolovo, Rus. 71/G2
Fromberg, Mt, US 147/J1
Frome (lake), Austl. 127/D4
Frome (riv.), Austl. 131/H4
Frome (riv.), Eng, UK 36/D2
Frome, Eng, UK 36/D4
Frome (riv.), Eng, UK 36/D5
Froncles, Fr. 60/B1
Front (range), Co, US 154/B3
Front Royal, Va, US 163/H1
Fronteira, Ang. 120/D4
Fronteira, Port. 46/B3
Frontenex, Fr. 64/C1
Frontenhausen, Ger. 59/F5
Frontera, Mex. 176/C2
Frontera Comalapa, Mex. 176/C3
Frontier, ND, US 156/F4
Frontier, Sk, Can. 145/K3
Frontignan, Fr. 44/E5
Fronton, Fr. 44/D5
Frosinone (prov.), It. 65/C4
Frosinone, It. 65/C4
Frösö, Swe. 38/E3
Frosolone, It. 65/D4
Frost, Tx, US 151/F1
Frostburg, Md, US 161/G5
Frostproof, Fl, US 164/M8
Frösunda, Swe. 39/B1
Frotey-lès-Vesoul, Fr. 60/C2
Frouard, Fr. 55/F6
Frövi, Swe. 40/F2
Frower (pt.), Ire. 32/B6
Frøya (isl.), Nor. 38/D3
Frozen (str.), Nun, Can. 141/H2
Fruges, Fr. 54/B2
Fruitdale, Al, US 164/D2
Fruitland, On, Can. 160/T9
Fruitland, Id, US 146/E1
Fruitland, Md, US 163/K1
Fruitvale, BC, Can. 144/F3
Fruitvale, Wa, US 144/D4
Frunze (int'l arpt.), Kyr. 99/B3
Frunzens'ke, Ukr. 73/H5
Frunzivka, Ukr. 72/E4
Fruška Gora (mts.), Cro.,Yugo. 67/H1
Fruška Gora NP, Cro. 50/D3
Frutal, Braz. 189/G1
Frutigen, Swi. 60/D4
Frutillar, Chile 190/B4
Fruvik, Swe. 39/B1
Fryazino, Rus. 69/X9
Frýdek-Místek, Czh. 43/K4
Fryeburg, Me, US 161/L2
Fu Xian, China 80/B4
Fu'an, China 87/H3
Fubo, Ang. 120/C4
Fucecchio, It. 63/D6
Fuch, WSah. 110/B5
Fucheng, China 80/D3
Fuchū, Japan 84/C3
Fuchū, Japan 83/C2
Fuchun, China 87/H2
Fuchun (riv.), China 80/D5
Fude, China 87/H3
Fuding, China 87/J3
Fuengirola, Sp. 46/C4
Fuenlabrada, Sp. 47/N9
Fuensalida, Sp. 46/C2
Fuente, Sp. 47/N8
Fuente de Cantos, Sp. 46/B3
Fuente del Maestre, Sp. 46/B3
Fuente Obejuna, Sp. 46/C3
Fuentelapeña, Sp. 46/C2

Fuente – George

Fuentes de Oñoro, Sp. 46/B2
Fuentesaúco, Sp. 46/C2
Fuerte (riv.), Mex. 174/C3
Fuerte Olimpo, Par. 188/E2
Fuerteventura (isl.), Canl., Sp. 110/B3
Fufang, China 87/H3
Fuga (isl.), Phil. 88/C1
Fuglebjerg, Den. 40/D4
Fugong, China 93/G2
Fugou, China 80/C4
Fuhai, China 99/E2
Fuhlsbüttel (Hamburg) (int'l arpt.), Ger. 53/G1
Fuhne (riv.), Ger. 42/F3
Fuhse (riv.), Ger. 53/H4
Fuji, Japan 85/F3
Fuji (riv.), Japan 85/F3
Fuji-Hakone-Izu NP, Japan 85/F3
Fuji-san (peak), Japan 85/F3
Fujian (prov.), China 87/H3
Fujieda, Japan 85/F3
Fujihashi, Japan 83/K4
Fujiidera, Japan 83/J6
Fujikawa, Japan 83/B3
Fujimi, Japan 83/D2
Fujino, Japan 83/C2
Fujinomiya, Japan 83/B3
Fujioka, Japan 85/F2
Fujioka, Japan 83/M5
Fujioka, Japan 83/D1
Fujisawa, Japan 85/F3
Fujishiro, Japan 83/E2
Fujiwara, Japan 83/K5
Fujiyoshida, Japan 85/F3
Fukagawa, Japan 82/C2
Fukang, China 99/E3
Fukaya, Japan 83/C1
Fukiage, Japan 83/C1
Fukuchiyama, Japan 83/H5
Fukue, Japan 84/A4
Fukue (isl.), Japan 79/K5
Fukui, Japan 84/E2
Fukui (pref.), Japan 84/E3
Fukuoka (pref.), Japan 84/B4
Fukuoka, Japan 84/B4
Fukuoka (int'l arpt.), Japan 84/B4
Fukuoka, Japan 83/M4
Fukuroi, Japan 85/E3
Fukushima, Japan 85/G2
Fukushima (pref.), Japan 85/F2
Fukushima, Japan 82/B3
Fukuyama, Japan 84/C3
Fulacunda, GBis. 114/B4
Fūlādī (mtn.), Afg. 101/J2
Fulbourn, Eng, UK 37/G2
Fulbright, Tx, US 153/G4
Fulda (riv.), Ger. 42/E3
Fulda, Ger. 58/C1
Fulda, Mn, US 155/G2
Fulford, Eng, UK 35/G4
Fuling, China 87/E2
Fullarton, Trin. 181/F2
Fullerton, La, US 164/B2
Fullerton, Ca, US 166/G8
Fullerton, Ne, US 154/F3
Fullerton (Whitehall), Pa, US 168/C2
Fully, Swi. 60/D5
Fulpmes, Aus. 61/H3
Fulton, Al, US 164/E2
Fulton, Ar, US 153/H4
Fulton (co.), Ga, US 163/M7
Fulton, Ky, US 162/C2
Fulton, Ks, US 153/G1
Fulton, Mo, US 153/J1
Fulton, Ms, US 162/C3
Fulton, NY, US 161/H3
Fulton, On, Can. 160/T9
Fulton, Tx, US 150/F3
Fultondale, Al, US 162/D4
Fulufjället (peak) 40/E1
Fuluo, China 87/F3
Fulwood, Eng, UK 35/F4
Fumaiolo (peak), It. 63/F6
Fumay, Fr. 55/D4
Fumel, Fr. 44/D4
Fumin, China 86/D3
Funabashi, Japan 83/D2
Funafuti (cap.), Tuv. 136/G5
Funafuti (isl.), Tuv. 136/G5
Funan, China 80/C4
Funchal (int'l arpt.), Port. 110/A2
Funchal, Port. 110/A2
Fundación, Col. 180/C2
Fundão, Port. 46/B2
Fundong, Camr. 115/H5
Fundy (bay), NB,NS, Can. 141/K4
Fundy NP, NB, Can. 158/E3
Funhalouro, Moz. 123/G4
Funing, China 80/D4
Funing, China 86/E4
Funshion (riv.), Ire. 32/B5
Funsi, Gha. 115/E4
Funston, Ga, US 165/G2
Funtua, Nga. 115/G4
Funza, Col. 183/L8
Fuorn, Pass dal (Ofenpass) (pass), Swi. 61/G4
Fuping, China 80/C3
Fuqiao, China 80/L8
Fuqū', Jor. 105/D6
Fuquan, China 93/J2
Fur (riv.), China 81/C2
Furan (riv.), Fr. 60/B6
Furancungo, Moz. 123/G2
Furano, Japan 82/C2
Fure (riv.), Fr. 64/B2
Fürfeld, Ger. 55/G4
Furmanov, Rus. 68/J4
Furmanovo, Kaz. 71/J2
Furnace, Sc, UK 33/A4
Furnas (res.), Braz. 179/E5
Furneaux Group (isls.), Austl. 127/D4
Fürstenau, Ger. 53/E3
Fürstenfeld, Aus. 50/C2
Fürstenfeldbruck, Ger. 58/E6
Fürstenwalde, Ger. 43/H2
Fürth, Ger. 58/B3
Furth, Ger. 59/F5
Fürth, Ger. 58/D4
Furth im Wald, Ger. 59/F4
Furtwangen im Schwarzwald, Ger. 60/E1
Furudal, Swe. 40/F1
Furukawa, Japan 82/B4
Furulund, Swe. 39/K7
Furusund, Swe. 39/B1
Fury and Hecla (str.), Nun, Can. 141/H2
Fusagasugá, Col. 183/L8
Fushan, China 80/B4
Fushan, China 80/E3
Fushi, China 87/H3
Fushi, China 87/F3
Fushu, China 87/H3
Fushun, China 81/B2
Fushun, China 86/E2
Fushuncheng, China 81/B2
Fusignano, It. 63/E5
Fusio, Swi. 61/E5
Fuso, Japan 83/L5
Fusong, China 79/K3
Fussa, Japan 83/C2
Füssen, Ger. 61/G2
Fusui, China 94/D1
Futaba, Japan 83/A2
Futaleufú, Chile 190/C4
Futami, Japan 83/L7
Futog, Yugo. 50/D3
Futrono, Chile 190/B4
Futtsu, Japan 85/F3
Futuna (isl.), Wall. 136/H6
Fuveau, Fr. 64/B6
Fuwah, Egypt 113/B2
Fuxian (lake), China 93/H3
Fuxin, China 80/E2
Fuxin Monggolzu Zizhixian, China 80/E2
Fuxing, China 87/E2
Fuyang, China 80/C4
Fuyang, China 87/H4
Fuyi (riv.), China 87/F3
Fuyu, China 79/J2
Fuyu, China 79/J2
Fuyuan, China 86/E3
Fuyun, China 78/B2
Fuzhou, China 87/H3
Fuzhoucheng, China 81/A3
Fwamba, D.R. Congo 121/E4
Fyfield, Eng, UK 30/D1
Fyn (isl.), Den. 38/D5
Fyn (co.), Den. 40/D4
Fyne, Loch (inlet), Sc, UK 33/A5
Fyresdal, Nor. 40/C2
Fysingen (lake), Swe. 39/A1
Fyvie, Sc, UK 33/D2

G

Ga, Gha. 115/E4
Ga Vache (isl.), Haiti 177/H2
Gaalkacyo (Galcaio), Som. 118/C4
Gaast, Neth. 52/C2
Gabarus, NS, Can. 159/G3
Gabas (riv.), Fr. 44/C5
Gabbs, Nv, US 146/E4
Gabčíkovo, Slvk. 50/C2
Gabela, Ang. 120/C5
Gabes (gulf), Tun. 107/D1
Gabia, D.R. Congo 120/D4
Gabicce Mare, It. 63/F6
Gable End (pt.), NZ 135/D2
Gablingen, Ger. 58/D6
Gablitz, Aus. 51/N7
Gabon (riv.), Gabon 120/B2
Gabon (ctry.) 107/C5
Gaborone (cap.), Bots. 122/E5
Gaborone (Sir Seretse Khama) (int'l arpt.), Bots. 122/E5
Gabras, Sudan 117/E3
Gabriel (mt.), Ire. 32/A6
Gabriel Leyva Solano, Mex. 174/C3
Gabrovo, Bul. 51/G4
Gaby, It. 62/A1
Gacé, Fr. 57/F3
Gachsārān, Iran 103/G4
Gackle, ND, US 156/E4
Gacko, Bosn. 50/D4
Gădăbăy, Azer. 103/F1
Gādarwāra, India 96/B4
Gadmen, Swi. 61/E4
Gadrut, Azer. 71/H5
Gadsden, Az, US 148/E4
Gadsden, Al, US 162/D3
Gadstrup, Den. 39/J7
Gadzema, Zim. 123/F3
Gadzi, CAfr. 116/C4
Găeşti, Rom. 51/G3
Gaeta, It. 65/C5
Gaeta (gulf), It. 48/C2
Gafargaon, Bang. 97/H3
Gaferut (isl.), Micr. 136/D4
Gaffney, SC, US 163/G3
Gagal, Chad 116/B3
Gagarawa, Nga. 115/H3
Gagarin, Rus. 68/G5
Gage, Ok, US 152/E2
Gage, NM, US 149/H4
Gagetown, NB, Can. 158/D3
Gagetown, Mi, US 160/E3
Gaggenau, Ger. 58/B5
Gaggio Montano, It. 63/D5
Gaglianico, It. 62/B2
Gagnoa, C.d'Iv. 114/D5
Gagny, Fr. 30/K5
Gagra, Geo. 70/G4
Gagret, India 98/D4
Gahanna, Oh, US 160/E4
Gahnpa, Libr. 114/C5
Gai Xian, China 81/B2
Gaibandha, Bang. 97/G3
Gaichtpass (pass), Aus. 61/G3
Gaidain'goinba, China 78/D4
Gail (riv.), Aus. 45/K3
Gail (riv.), It. 50/A2
Gail, Tx, US 150/D1
Gaildorf, Ger. 58/C5
Gaillac, Fr. 44/D5
Gaillefontaine, Fr. 57/G1
Gaillon, Fr. 57/G2
Gailtaler (mts.), Aus. 45/K3
Gaiman, Arg. 190/D4
Gaimersheim, Ger. 59/E5
Gainesboro, Tn, US 162/E2
Gainesville, Al, US 162/C4
Gainesville, Fl, US 165/G3
Gainesville, Ga, US 162/F3
Gainesville, Mo, US 153/H2
Gainesville, Tx, US 153/F4
Gainford, Eng, UK 35/G2
Gainsborough, Sk, Can. 156/D3
Gainsborough, Eng, UK 35/H5
Gairdner (lake), Austl. 127/C4
Gairezi (riv.), Zim. 123/G3
Gairn (riv.), Sc, UK 33/C2
Gais, Swi. 61/F3
Gaiserwald, Swi. 61/F3
Gaithersburg, Md, US 163/J1
Gaizina (peak), Lat. 41/L3
Gājol, India 97/G3
Gakarosa (peak), SAfr. 124/C2
Gakem, Nga. 115/H5
Gakona, Ak, US 171/J3
Gal Oya NP, SrL. 95/D5
Gala, China 97/G1
Galan (peak), Arg. 188/C3
Galana (riv.), Kenya 119/B2
Galand, Iran 103/H2
Galanga, Ang. 122/B2
Galangue, Ang. 122/C2
Galapagar, Sp. 47/M8
Galápagos (isls.), Ecu. 184/J6
Galápagos (dept.), Ecu. 184/J7
Galápagos, PN, Ecu. 184/J7
Galār, India 98/C3
Galashiels, Sc, UK 33/D5
Galaţi (prov.), Rom. 51/H3
Galaţi, Rom. 51/J3
Galatina, It. 49/F2
Galatiní, Gre. 49/G2
Galátista, Gre. 49/H2
Galatone, It. 49/F2
Galaure (riv.), Fr. 64/A2
Galax, Va, US 163/G2
Galb Azefal (hill), WSah. 110/B5
Galbally, Ire. 32/B5
Galbiate, It. 62/C2
Galcaio (Gaalkacyo), Som. 118/C4
Galdácano, Sp. 46/D1
Gáldar, Sp. 110/B3
Galeana, Mex. 175/E3
Galela, Indo. 91/G3
Galena, Ak, US 171/G3
Galena (peak), Id, US 147/F2
Galena, Il, US 155/J2
Galena, Ks, US 153/G2
Galena, Md, US 168/C5
Galena, Mo, US 153/H2
Galena Bay, BC, Can. 144/F2
Galena Park, Tx, US 151/M9
Galeota (pt.), Trin. 181/F2
Galera (pt.), Trin. 181/F2
Galera (pt.), Ecu. 180/A4
Galera (pt.), Chile 190/B3
Galesburg, Il, US 155/J3
Galeton, Pa, US 161/H4
Galey (riv.), Ire. 32/A5
Galga (riv.), Hun. 51/R9
Galgamácsa, Hun. 51/R9
Galgorm, NI, UK 34/B2
Gali, Geo. 71/G4
Gali Jāgīr, Pak. 98/B3
Galich, Rus. 68/J4
Galicia (reg.), Sp. 66/A2
Galičica NP, FYROM 49/G2
Galičica NP, Alb. 50/E5
Gālīkash, Iran 103/H2
Galilee (reg.), Isr. 105/C3
Galileo Galilei (int'l arpt.), It. 62/D6
Galim, Camr. 116/B4
Galinakopf (peak), Aus. 61/F3
Galinda, Ang. 120/C5
Galion, Oh, US 160/E4
Galiuro (mts.), Az, US 149/G4
Galiwinku, Austl. 129/D3
Gallan Head (pt.), Sc, UK 31/Q7
Gallarate, It. 62/B2
Gallardon, Fr. 57/G3
Gallatin (riv.), Mt, US 147/H1
Gallatin, Mo, US 155/H4
Gallatin, Tn, US 162/D2
Gallatin Gateway, Mt, US 147/H1
Gallegos (riv.), Arg. 191/C6
Galleguillos, Chile 188/B3
Galley Head (pt.), Ire. 32/B6
Galleyend, Eng, UK 30/E1
Galliano, La, US 164/C3
Galliate, It. 62/B3
Gallicano, It. 62/D5
Galliera Veneta, It. 63/E2
Gallina, NM, US 149/J2
Gallinas (riv.), NM, US 152/B3
Gallinas (pt.), Col. 180/D1
Gallinas (mts.), NM, US 149/J3
Gallion, Al, US 162/D4
Gallipoli, It. 49/E2
Gallipoli (pen.), Turk. 67/K2
Gallipolis, Oh, US 163/F1
Gällivare, Swe. 38/G2
Gallneukirchen, Aus. 59/H6
Gallo (lake), It. 61/G4
Gallo (cape), It. 48/C3
Galloway, Wi, US 155/K1
Gallspach, Aus. 59/G6
Galluis, Fr. 30/H5
Gallup, NM, US 149/H3
Gallur, Sp. 46/E2
Gally (riv.), Fr. 30/H5
Gålö (isl.), Swe. 39/B1
Gal'on, Isr. 105/B5
Galston, Sc, UK 33/B5
Galston (nbrhd.), Austl. 134/H8
Galston, Austl. 133/E1
Galt, Ca, US 146/C4
Galten, Den. 40/C3
Galty (mts.), Ire. 32/B5
Galtymore (peak), Ire. 32/B5
Galva, Ks, US 153/F1
Galva, Il, US 155/J3
Galvarino, Chile 190/B3
Galveston (isl.), Tx, US 172/C2
Galveston (bay), Tx, US 172/C2
Galveston, Tx, US 151/N9
Galveston (co.), Tx, US 151/M9
Gálvez, Sp. 46/C3
Gálvez, Arg. 188/D5
Galway, Ire. 32/A3
Galway (bay), Ire. 31/P10
Galway (co.), Ire. 32/B3
Galway (Carnmore) (arpt.), Ire. 32/B3
Galzignano, It. 63/E3
Gam (riv.), Viet. 93/J3
Gamaches, Fr. 54/A4
Gamagara (riv.), SAfr. 124/C2
Gamagōri, Japan 83/M6
Gamarra, Col. 180/C2
Gamay, Phil. 88/D2
Gamba, China 97/G1
Gamba, D.R. Congo 121/F4
Gamba, Gabon 120/B3
Gambaga, Gha. 115/E4
Gambaga Scarp (cliff), Gha. 115/E4
Gambais, Fr. 30/H5
Gambang, Malay. 89/C2
Gambara, It. 62/D3
Gambat, Pak. 92/A2
Gambatesa, It. 65/D5
Gambēla, Eth. 117/G3
Gambell, Ak, US 171/D3
Gambella NP, Eth. 117/G3
Gambellara, It. 63/E3
Gamber, Md, US 168/B5
Gambettola, It. 63/F5
Gambia (riv.), Sen. 114/A3
Gambia (riv.), Gam. 107/A3
Gambia (ctry.) 107/A3
Gambier (cape), Austl. 128/C2
Gambier (isls.), FrPol. 137/M7
Gambier, Oh, US 160/E4
Gámbita, Col. 180/C3
Gambo, Nf, Can. 159/K1
Gambolò, It. 62/B3
Gamboma, Congo 120/C3
Gamboula, CAfr. 116/B4
Gambsheim, Fr. 58/A5
Gameleira, Braz. 183/H5
Gamerco, NM, US 149/H3
Gamewell, NC, US 163/G3
Gaming, Aus. 45/L3
Gamka (riv.), SAfr. 124/C4
Gamkab (riv.), Namb. 124/B3
Gamleby, Swe. 40/G3
Gamlingay, Eng, UK 37/F2
Gammel Ølstykke, Den. 39/J7
Gammelstad, Swe. 68/D2
Gammertingen, Ger. 61/F1
Gammon Ranges NP, Austl. 131/H4
Gamo, Japan 83/K5
Gamo Gofa (pol. reg.), Eth. 117/H4
Gampaha, SrL. 95/C5
Gampern, Aus. 59/G7
Gamtog, China 86/C2
Gamud (peak), Eth. 118/A4
Gan, Fr. 44/C5
Gan (riv.), China 79/J1
Gan Gan, Arg. 190/C4
Gan Hashlosha NP, Isr. 105/C4
Ganado, Tx, US 151/F3
Gananoque, On, Can. 161/H2
Ganāveh, Iran 103/G4
Ganbashao, China 87/E3
Gäncä, Azer. 71/H4
Gancheng, China 94/E2
Ganda, Ang. 122/B2
Gandajika, D.R. Congo 121/E4
Gandak (riv.), India 97/E2
Gandaki (zone), Nepal 96/D1
Gandara, Phil. 88/D2
Gāndarbal, India 98/C2
Gandarinha, Ang. 122/C1
Gandelin (riv.), Fr. 57/F5
Gander (lake), Nf, Can. 159/K1
Gander, Nf, Can. 159/K1
Ganderkesee, Ger. 53/F2
Gandesa, Sp. 47/F2
Gāndhi Sāgar (res.), India 92/B3
Gāndhīhām, India 101/K4
Gandhinagar, India 101/K4
Gandía, Sp. 47/E3
Gandino, It. 62/C2
Gandisê (mts.), China 97/E1
Gandjo, D.R. Congo 121/G3
Gandoca-Manzanillo Nat'l Wild. Ref., CR 177/F4
Gandy, Ut, US 147/G4
Ganeb (well), Mrta. 114/C2
Ganesh (mtn.), China 97/E1
Ganeshganj, India 92/C2
Gang, China 99/F4
Gang Ranch, BC, Can. 144/C2
Ganga (Ganges) (riv.), India 96/B1
Gānga Sāgar, India 97/G5
Gangala-Na-Bodio, D.R. Congo 116/D5
Gangāpur, India 92/C2
Gangara, Niger 115/H3
Gangārāmpur, India 97/G3
Gangaw, Myan. 86/B4
Gangca, China 78/E4
Gangdisê (mts.), China 99/D5
Gangelt, Ger. 55/F2
Ganges (riv.), Asia 77/A5
Ganges, BC, Can. 144/C3
Ganges, Fr. 44/E5
Ganges (Ganga) (riv.), India 96/B1
Ganges, Mouths of the (delta), India,Bang. 92/E3
Gangi, It. 48/D4
Gangkofen, Ger. 59/F6
Gango (riv.), Ang. 120/C5
Gangoh, India 98/D5
Gangtok, India 97/G2
Gangtou, China 87/H3
Ganjām, India 95/E2
Ganjingzi, China 81/A3
Ganløse, Den. 39/J7
Ganluo, China 93/H2
Ganmain, Austl. 133/C2
Gann Valley, SD, US 154/E1
Gannan, China 79/J2
Gannat, Fr. 44/E3
Gannett (peak), Wy, US 147/J2
Ganquan, China 80/B3
Gansbaai, SAfr. 124/L11
Gänserndorf, Aus. 51/P7
Gansu (prov.), China 78/D4
Gantheaume (pt.), Austl. 128/A4
Gantrisch (peak), Swi. 60/D4
Gantsevichi, Bela. 70/C1
Gantt, Al, US 165/E2
Gantt, SC, US 163/F3
Ganxitang, China 87/F3
Ganye, Nga. 116/A3
Ganyesa, SAfr. 124/D2
Ganyu, China 80/D4
Ganyushkino, Kaz. 71/J3
Ganzhou, China 87/G3
Ganzlin, Ger. 42/G2
Ganzourgou (prov.), Burk. 115/E3
Gao, Niger 115/G3
Gao, Mali 115/E2
Gao (pol. reg.), Mali 115/F2
Gao, D.R. Congo 121/G2
Gao Xian, China 86/E2
Gao'an, China 87/G2
Gaobei, China 87/G3
Gaocheng, China 80/C3
Gaochun, China 80/D5
Gaojian, China 87/J2
Gaolan (isl.), China 87/G4
Gaolan, China 78/E4
Gaoligong (mts.), Myan. 86/C3
Gaoling, China 81/A4
Gaomi, China 80/D3
Gaomutang, China 87/F3
Gaoping, China 80/C4
Gaoqiao, China 80/L8
Gaoqing, China 80/D3
Gaoqitou, China 87/F2
Gaor Bheinn (Gulvain) (peak), Sc, UK 33/A3
Gaotai, China 78/D4
Gaotang, China 80/D3
Gaotian, China 87/H3
Gaoua, Burk. 114/E4
Gaoual, Gui. 114/B4
Gaoxingxu, China 87/G3
Gaoyang, China 80/C3
Gaoyi, China 80/C3
Gaoyou (lake), China 79/H5
Gaoyou, China 80/D4
Gaozhou, China 87/F4
Gap, Fr. 64/C3
Gap, Pa, US 168/B4
Gap Mills, WV, US 163/G2
Gapeau (riv.), Fr. 64/B6
Gar, China 99/C5
Gar (riv.), China 78/C5
Gara (lake), Ire. 32/B2
Garabogazköl, Trkm. 71/K4
Garabogazköl (gulf), Trkm. 74/F5
Garacad, Som. 118/D4
Garachiné, Pan. 180/B2
Garachiné (pt.), Pan. 177/G4
Garah, Austl. 132/D1
Garai (riv.), Bang. 92/E3
Garaina, PNG 129/G1
Garajonay, PN de, Sp. 110/A3
Garalo, Mali 114/D4
Garamba, PN de la, D.R. Congo 117/F4
Garancières, Fr. 54/A6
Garango, Burk. 115/E4
Garanhuns, Braz. 183/G5
Garba, CAfr. 116/D3
Garba Tula, Kenya 119/B1
Garbahaarrey, Som. 118/B5
Garber, Ok, US 153/F2
Garberville, Ca, US 146/B3
Garbsen, Ger. 53/G4
Garça, Braz. 189/G2
Garças, Rio das (riv.), Braz. 186/B3
Garching an der Alz, Ger. 59/F6
Garcia, Co, US 152/B2
Garcia de Sota (res.), Sp. 46/C3
Gard (dept.), Fr. 64/A4
Gard (riv.), Fr. 66/E1
Garda, It. 63/D2
Garda (lake), It. 65/F1
Gardabani, Geo. 71/H4
Gardanne, Fr. 64/B6
Gardar, ND, US 156/F3
Gardelegen, Ger. 42/F2
Garden (isl.), Austl. 130/K7
Garden (pen.), Mi, US 157/L5
Garden (isl.), Mi, US 160/D2
Garden, Mi, US 160/C2
Garden (riv.), On, Can. 160/E1
Garden City, Ga, US 163/G4
Garden City, Id, US 146/E2
Garden City, Ks, US 152/D2
Garden City, Mi, US 167/F7
Garden City, Mo, US 153/G1
Garden City, NY, US 169/L9
Garden City, SD, US 154/F1
Garden City, Tx, US 151/D2
Garden City Beach, SC, US 163/H4
Garden City Park, NY, US 169/L9
Garden Grove, Ca, US 166/G8
Garden Grove, Fl, US 164/L7
Garden Grove, Ia, US 155/H3
Garden Valley, Id, US 146/F1
Garden View, Pa, US 168/A1
Gardena, Ca, US 166/F8
Gardendale, Al, US 162/D4
Gardenstown, Sc, UK 33/D1
Gardenton, Mb, Can. 156/F3
Gardēz, Afg. 101/J2
Gardhīwāla, India 98/C4
Gardi, Ga, US 165/H2
Gardiner (dam), Sk, Can. 145/L2
Gardiner, Mt, US 147/H1
Gardiner, Or, US 146/A2
Gardiner, Wa, US 167/B1
Gardiners (isl.), NY, US 169/F1
Gardiners (bay), NY, US 169/F1
Gardner, Ks, US 153/G1
Gardner, Il, US 160/B4
Gardner (lake), Me, US 158/D3
Gardner, Ma, US 161/L3
Gardner, Fl, US 165/H4
Gardner (mtn.), Wa, US 144/D3
Gardner (Nikumaroro) (isl.), Kiri. 137/H5
Gardone val Trompia, It. 62/D2
Gare Favre, Congo 120/C4
Gare Girard, Congo 120/C4
Gare Loch (inlet), Sc, UK 33/B4
Gareat el Tarf (salt pan), Alg. 112/K7
Garelochhead, Sc, UK 33/B4
Garéoult, Fr. 64/C6
Garessio, It. 62/B5
Garet el Djenoun (peak), Alg. 111/G4
Garfield, Ks, US 152/E1
Garfield, NJ, US 169/J8
Garfield (lake), Fl, US 164/M8
Garfield (mtn.), Mt, US 147/G1
Garfield, NM, US 149/J4
Garfield, Ga, US 163/F4
Garfield, Tx, US 151/F2
Garfield, Wa, US 144/F4
Gärflotta (isl.), Swe. 39/A2
Garforth, Eng, UK 35/G4
Gargaliánoi, Gre. 49/G4
Gargan (peak), Fr. 44/D4
Gargas, Fr. 64/B5
Gargenville, Fr. 54/A6
Garges-lès-Gonesse, Fr. 30/K5
Gargnano, It. 63/D2
Gargrave, Eng, UK 35/F4
Gargždai, Lith. 41/J4
Garh Mahārāja, Pak. 98/A4
Garhākotā, India 96/B4
Garhbeta, India 97/F4
Garhchiroli, India 95/C1
Garhi, India 96/C4
Garhmuktesar, India 96/B1
Garhshankar, India 98/D4
Garibaldi, Braz. 189/G4
Garibaldi, Or, US 144/C5
Garibaldi, BC, Can. 144/C3
Garies, SAfr. 124/B3
Garigliano (riv.), It. 65/C5
Garioch (reg.), Sc, UK 33/D2
Garissa, Kenya 119/B2
Garland, Mb, Can. 156/D2
Garland, Ks, US 153/G2
Garland, Tx, US 150/L7
Garland, NC, US 163/H3
Garlandville, Ms, US 162/C4
Garlasco, It. 62/B3
Garliava, Lith. 41/K4
Garlieston, Sc, UK 34/D2
Garmeh, Iran 103/J2
Garmisch-Partenkirchen, Ger. 61/H3
Garmouth, Sc, UK 33/C1
Garmsār, Iran 103/H3
Garmuda, Eth. 118/C4
Garneill, Mt, US 145/K4
Garner, Ia, US 155/H2
Garner, NC, US 163/H3
Garneton, Zam. 123/F2
Garnett, Ks, US 153/G1
Garnett, SC, US 163/G4
Garnish, Nf, Can. 159/K2
Garnpung (lake), Austl. 132/B2
Garonne (riv.), Fr. 66/D1
Garoowe, Som. 118/D3
Garopaba, Braz. 189/G4
Garou (lake), Mali 115/E2
Garoua, Camr. 116/B3
Garoua (int'l arpt.), Camr. 116/B3
Garoua Boulaï, Camr. 116/B4
Garphyttan, Swe. 40/F2
Garraf (mts.), Sp. 47/K7
Garreg, Wal, UK 34/D6
Garrel, Ger. 53/F3
Garretson, SD, US 155/F2
Garrett, In, US 160/D4
Garrett, Tx, US 151/F1
Garrett, Wy, US 154/B2
Garrison, Mo, US 153/H2
Garrison, Mn, US 157/H4
Garrison, ND, US 156/D4
Garrison (dam), ND, US 156/D4
Garrison, Ky, US 163/F1
Garrison, Mt, US 145/H4
Garrison, Tx, US 151/G2
Garrison, Ut, US 147/F4
Garron (pt.), NI, UK 34/C1
Garrovillas, Sp. 46/B3
Garry (lake), Sc, UK 33/B2
Garry (riv.), Sc, UK 33/A2
Garry (bay), Nun, Can. 141/H2
Garry (lake), Nun, Can. 140/F2
Gars am Inn, Ger. 59/F6
Gars am Kamp, Aus. 43/H4
Garsen, Kenya 119/C2
Garstang, Eng, UK 35/F4
Garsten, Aus. 59/H6
Garte (riv.), Ger. 53/H6
Gartempe (riv.), Fr. 44/D3
Garth, Wal, UK 36/C2
Gartmore, Sc, UK 33/B4
Gärtringen, Ger. 58/B5
Garut, Indo. 89/D4
Garvagh, NI, UK 34/B2
Garwa, India 96/D3
Garwolin, Pol. 43/L3
Garwood, NJ, US 169/H9
Garwood, Tx, US 150/F3
Gary, In, US 160/C4
Gary, SD, US 155/F1
Gary, Tx, US 151/G1
Gary, WV, US 163/G2
Garyarsa, China 99/D5
Garyi, China 86/C2
Garyville, La, US 164/C2
Garz, Ger. 40/E4
Garza García, Mex. 175/E3
Garzê, China 86/D2
Garzón, Col. 180/C4
Gas, Fr. 30/G6
Gas (lake), China 99/F4
Gas City, In, US 160/D4
Gas-san (peak), Japan 82/B4
Gasa, Bhu. 97/G2
Gæsafjöll (peak), Ice. 38/P6
Gasan, Phil. 88/C2
Gaschurn, Aus. 61/G4
Gasconade (riv.), Mo, US 155/J4
Gasconde (riv.), Mo, US 153/H2
Gascony (reg.), Fr. 66/D2
Gascoyne (mt.), Austl. 130/C3
Gascoyne (riv.), Austl. 127/A3
Gascoyne Junction, Austl. 130/B3
Gash (riv.), Erit. 117/H2
Gashaka, Nga. 116/A4
Gasheng, India 86/B2
Gasny, Fr. 57/G2
Gaspar (str.), Indo. 90/C4
Gaspard (riv.), BC, Can. 144/C2
Gasparilla (isl.), Fl, US 165/G4
Gaspé, Qu, Can. 158/E1
Gaspé (bay), Qu, Can. 158/E1
Gaspé (pen.), Qu, Can. 141/K4
Gaspoltshofen, Aus. 59/G6
Gasport, NY, US 160/V9
Gassin, Fr. 64/C6
Gassino Torinese, It. 62/A2
Gassville, Ar, US 153/H2
Gastins, Fr. 30/M6
Gaston, NC, US 163/J2
Gaston (lake), NC, US 163/H2
Gastonia, Tx, US 150/L7
Gastonia, NC, US 163/G3
Gastoúni, Gre. 49/G4
Gat, Isr. 105/B5
Gata (cape), Cyp. 104/C2
Gata (cape), Sp. 46/D4
Gata (mts.), Sp. 46/B2
Gata de Gorgos, Sp. 47/F3
Gatchina, Rus. 41/P2
Gate, Ok, US 152/D2
Gate City, Va, US 163/F2
Gatehouse-Of-Fleet, Sc, UK 34/D2
Gates, Or, US 146/B1
Gates of The Arctic NP and Prsv., Ak, US 171/G2
Gateshead (isl.), Nun, Can. 140/F1
Gateshead, Eng, UK 35/G2
Gateshead (co.), Eng, UK 35/G2
Gatesville, Tx, US 150/F2
Gatesville, NC, US 163/J2
Gateway, Co, US 149/H1
Gateway, Or, US 146/C1
Gateway NRA, NJ, US 169/K9
Gateway NRA, NJ, US 168/D2
Gathright (dam), Va, US 163/H2
Gaths Mine, Zim. 123/F4
Gatico, Chile 188/B2
Gatineau, Qu, Can. 161/J2
Gatineau (riv.), Qu, Can. 161/J1
Gatineau (riv.), Qu, Can. 141/J4
Gatlinburg, Tn, US 163/F3
Gatow, Ger. 42/Q7
Gattendorf, Aus. 45/M2
Gatteville-le-Phare, Fr. 56/D1
Gattianara, It. 62/B2
Gatton, Austl. 134/D4
Gatún (lake), Pan. 177/G4
Gatún (dam), Pan. 177/G4
Gatvand, Iran 103/G3
Gatwick (int'l arpt.), Eng, UK 30/C3
Gau Algesheim, Ger. 58/B3
Gau Bischofsheim, Ger. 58/B3
Gau Odernheim, Ger. 58/B3
Gaubickelheim, Ger. 55/H4
Gauchy, Fr. 54/C4
Gaucín, Sp. 46/C4
Gauja (riv.), Est.,Lat. 41/L3
Gauja NP, Lat. 41/L3
Gaujiena, Lat. 41/M3
Gaukönigshofen, Ger. 58/C3
Gauley (riv.), WV, US 163/G1
Gaunless (riv.), Eng, UK 35/G2
Gaupne, Nor. 38/C3
Gaur (riv.), Sc, UK 33/B3
Gauri Sankar (peak), Nepal 97/F2
Gauripur, India 97/G2
Gaurnadi, Bang. 97/H4
Gause, Tx, US 151/F2
Gausta (peak), Nor. 40/C2
Gauteng (prov.), SAfr. 123/F5
Gauting, Ger. 59/E6
Gavà, Sp. 47/L7
Gavardo, It. 62/D2
Gavāter, Iran 101/H3
Gāvbandī, Iran 103/H5
Gávdhos (isl.), Gre. 67/K4
Gave de Pau (riv.), Fr. 47/E1
Gavel-Långsjön (lake), Swe. 39/B1
Gavere, Belg. 54/C2
Gāvgān, Iran 103/F2
Gavi, It. 62/B4
Gavião, Port. 46/B3
Gavins Point (dam), SD, US 154/F2
Gaviota, Ca, US 148/B3
Gavirate, It. 62/B2
Gävle, Swe. 40/G1
Gävleborg (co.), Swe. 38/E3
Gavray, Fr. 56/D3
Gawai, Myan. 86/C3
Gawler, Austl. 131/H5
Gawler Ranges (mts.), Austl. 127/C4
Gawso, Gha. 115/E5
Gaxun (lake), China 78/D3
Gay, Rus. 71/L2
Gay (peak), WV, US 163/G1
Gaya, Niger 115/F4
Gayā, India 97/E3
Gaya (riv.), China 79/K3
Gayam, Chad 116/C3
Gayaza, Ugan. 121/G3
Gaylegphug, Bhu. 97/H2
Gaylord, Ks, US 154/E4
Gaylord, Mi, US 160/D2
Gaylord, Mn, US 155/G1
Gayndah, Austl. 134/C4
Gayny, Rus. 69/M3
Gays Mills, Wi, US 155/J2
Gayville, SD, US 155/F2
Gaz, Iran 103/G3
Gaz-Achak, Trkm. 74/G5
Gaza (prov.), Moz. 123/G4
Gaza (Ghazzah) 105/A5
Gaza Strip 105/A6
Gazanjyk, Trkm. 71/K5
Gazanjyk, Trkm. 103/H2
Gazaoua, Niger 115/G3
Gazelle, Ca, US 146/B3
Gazeran, Fr. 30/H6
Gaziantep, Turk. 102/D2
Gaziantep (prov.), Turk. 102/D2
Gaziköy, Turk. 51/H5
Gazimur (riv.), Rus. 79/H1
Gazipaşa, Turk. 104/C1
Gazon de Faing (peak), Fr. 60/D1
Gazzaniga, It. 62/C2
Gbadolite, D.R. Congo 116/D4
Gbangbatok, SLeo. 114/B5
Gbarnga, Libr. 114/C5
Gboko, Nga. 115/H5
Gbongan, Nga. 115/G5
Gd Res de Vioreau (res.), Fr. 56/D5
Gdansk (gulf), Pol. 68/C5
Gdańsk, Pol. 40/H4
Gdov, Rus. 41/M2
Gdynia, Pol. 40/H4
Ge (lake), China 80/D5
Geal Charn (peak), Sc, UK 33/C2
Geal Charn (peak), Sc, UK 33/A3
Geary, NB, Can. 158/D3
Geary, Ok, US 153/E3
Geashill, Ire. 32/C3
Geba Wenz (riv.), Eth. 117/G3
Gebaberg (peak), Ger. 58/D1
Gebe (isl.), Indo. 91/G3
Gebeit Mine, Sudan 109/H4
Gebhardshain, Ger. 55/G2
Gebilu, Eth. 118/B3
Gebiz, Turk. 104/B1
Gebra-Hainleite, Ger. 53/H6
Gebre Guracha, Eth. 118/A3
Gedara (Umm Qays) (ruin), Jor. 105/D3
Gede (peak), Indo. 89/D4
Gede, Kenya 119/C2
Gedera, Isr. 105/B5
Gedern, Ger. 58/C2
Gedi (riv.), Turk. 67/K3
Gedi Ruins Nat'l Mon., Kenya 119/B2
Gedikbulak, Turk. 103/E2
Gedinne, Belg. 55/D4
Gediz, Turk. 102/B2
Gediz (riv.), Turk. 102/A2
Gedlegubē, Eth. 118/C4
Gēdo, Eth. 117/H3
Gedser, Den. 40/D4
Gedser (cape), Den. 40/D4
Gedsted, Den. 40/C3
Geel, Belg. 55/E1
Geelong, Austl. 133/B4
Geelong West, Austl. 133/B4
Geelvink (chan.), Austl. 127/A3
Geertruidenberg, Neth. 52/B5
Geeste (riv.), Ger. 53/F1
Geeste, Ger. 53/E3
Geestemünde, Ger. 53/F1
Geesthacht, Ger. 53/H2
Geeveston, Austl. 132/C4
Gefrees, Ger. 59/E2
Gegeya Shet' (riv.), Eth. 118/A2
Gê'gyai, China 99/D5
Gehrde, Ger. 53/F3
Gehrden, Ger. 53/G4
Geidam, Nga. 116/A2
Geifas (peak), Wal, UK 36/C2
Geigar, Sudan 117/G3
Geikie (isl.), On, Can. 157/K2
Geikie (riv.), Sk, Can. 140/F3
Geikie Gorge NP, Austl. 128/B4
Geilenkirchen, Ger. 55/F2
Geilo, Nor. 40/C1
Geinō, Japan 83/K6
Geiselhöring, Ger. 59/F5
Geiselwind, Ger. 58/D3
Geisenfeld, Ger. 59/E5
Geisenhausen, Ger. 59/F6
Geisenheim, Ger. 55/G4
Geislingen, Ger. 61/E1
Geislingen an der Steige, Ger. 58/C5
Geistown, Pa, US 161/G4
Geita, Tanz. 121/H3
Gejiu, China 86/D4
Gekeng, China 87/H3
Gel (riv.), Sudan 117/F4
Gela, It. 48/D4
Gela (gulf), It. 48/D4
Geladī, Eth. 118/C4
Gelai (peak), Tanz. 119/B2
Gelang (cape), Malay. 89/C1
Gelderland (prov.), Neth. 52/C4
Geldermalsen, Neth. 52/C5
Geldern, Ger. 52/D5
Geldersheim, Ger. 58/D2
Geldrop, Neth. 52/C6
Geleen, Neth. 55/E2
Gelemso, Eth. 118/B3
Gelendost, Turk. 102/B2
Gelendzhik, Rus. 73/K5
Gelibolu, Turk. 51/H5
Gelibolu Yarımadas NP, Turk. 49/K2
Gelīla, Eth. 117/H3
Gelincik (peak), Turk. 103/E2
Gelinggang, Indo. 90/D4
Gelligaer, Wal, UK 36/C3
Gelnhausen, Ger. 58/C2
Gelsenkirchen, Ger. 52/E5
Geltendorf, Ger. 61/H1
Gelterkinden, Swi. 60/D3
Gelting, Ger. 40/C4
Gemas, Malay. 90/B3
Gembloux, Belg. 55/D2
Gembogl, PNG 129/G1
Gemena, D.R. Congo 120/D2
Gémenos, Fr. 64/B6
Gemert, Neth. 52/C5
Gemlik (gulf), Turk. 51/J5
Gemlik, Turk. 51/J5
Gemona del Friuli, It. 45/K3
Gemsbok NP, Bots. 122/D5
Gemuk (mt.), Ak, US 171/G3
Gemünden am Main, Ger. 58/C2
Gen (riv.), China 78/J1
Genalē Wenz (riv.), Eth. 118/B4
Genappe, Belg. 55/D2
Genargentu (mts.), It. 48/A2
Genarp, Swe. 39/K7
Genay, Fr. 60/A6
Genazzano, It. 65/B4
Genç, Turk. 102/E2
Gendringen, Neth. 52/D5
Gendt, Neth. 52/C5
Genemuiden, Neth. 52/D3
General Acha, Arg. 190/D3
General Alfredo Vasquez Cobo (int'l arpt.), Col. 184/D2
General Alvear, Arg. 190/D2
General Alvear, Arg. 190/E3
General Arenales, Arg. 190/E2
General Artigas, Par. 189/E3
General Belgrano, Arg. 190/F2
General Belgrano II, Arg., Ant. 192/X
General Bravo, Mex. 151/E5
General Cabrera, Arg. 190/E2
General Campos, Arg. 188/E4
General Carneiro, Braz. 186/B2
General Carrera (lake), Chile 190/B5
General Cepeda, Mex. 175/E3
General Conesa, Arg. 190/D4
General Deheza, Arg. 190/E2
General Edward Lawrence Logan (Logan Int'l) (int'l arpt.), Ma, US 161/L3
General Enrique Godoy, Arg. 190/D3
General Eugenio A. Garay, Par. 188/D2
General Francisco Villa, Mex. 175/F3
General Galarza, Arg. 191/J10
General Grant Grove, Ca, US 148/C2
General Grant Nat'l Mem., NY, US 169/K8
General José de San Martín, Arg. 188/E3
General Juan Álvarez, PN, Mex. 175/F5
General Juan José Rios, Mex. 174/C3
General Juan Madariaga, Arg. 191/F3
General La Madrid, Arg. 190/E3
General Lagos, Chile 188/B1
General Las Heras, Arg. 191/J11
General Lavalle, Arg. 191/K12
General Manuel Belgrano (peak), Arg. 188/C4
General Martín Miguel de Güemes, Arg. 188/C3
General Mitchell (int'l arpt.), Wi, US 160/C3
General Pico, Arg. 190/E2
General Pinto, Arg. 190/E2
General Ramírez, Arg. 188/D5
General Roca, Arg. 190/D3
General Saavedra, Bol. 188/D1
General Sampaio, Braz. 183/G4
General San Martín, Arg., Ant. 192/V
General San Martín, Arg. 190/E3
General San Martín, Arg. 191/J11
General Santiago Marino (int'l arpt.), Ven. 181/F2
General Santos, Phil. 88/D4
General Sherman Tree, Ca, US 148/C2
General Terán, Mex. 175/F3
General Treviño, Mex. 151/E4
General Trías, Mex. 151/A3
General Trias, Phil. 88/E7
General Viamonte, Arg. 190/E2
General Villalobas (int'l arpt.), Mex. 151/B3
General Villegas, Arg. 190/E2
General Zaragoza, Mex. 175/F4
General-Toshevo, Bul. 51/J4
Generoso (peak), Swi. 61/F6
Genesee, Id, US 144/F4
Genesee (co.), Mi, US 167/E6
Genesee (riv.), NY, US 161/G3
Genesee, Wi, US 167/P14
Genesee Depot, Wi, US 167/P14
Geneseo, Ks, US 153/E1
Geneseo, NY, US 161/H3
Geneseo, Il, US 155/J3
Genet, Eth. 118/A3
Geneva (Léman) (lake), Fr. 45/G3
Geneva (lake), Fr.,Swi. 66/E1
Geneva (Genève), Swi. 45/G3
Geneva (int'l arpt.), Swi. 60/C5
Geneva, Al, US 165/F2
Geneva, Id, US 147/H2
Geneva, Il, US 160/B4
Geneva, In, US 160/D4
Geneva, Ne, US 154/F3
Geneva, NY, US 161/H3
Geneva, Oh, US 160/F4
Geneva, Tx, US 151/H2
Genève, Swi. 60/C5
Genève (canton), Swi. 60/C5
Gengding (mtn.), China 87/E3
Gengenbach, Ger. 60/E1
Genglou, China 87/G4
Gengma Daizu Vazu Zizhixian, China 86/C4
Gengzhuang, China 81/B2
Génicourt, Fr. 30/J4
Genil (riv.), Sp. 66/B3
Genillé, Fr. 57/G6
Génissieux, Fr. 64/B2
Genk, Belg. 55/E2
Genlis, Fr. 60/B3
Gennach (riv.), Ger. 61/G2
Gennep, Neth. 52/C5
Gennevilliers, Fr. 30/J5
Genoa (riv.), Austl. 133/D3
Genoa (Genova), It. 62/B5
Genoa, Ne, US 154/F3
Genoa, Il, US 155/K2
Genoa, Oh, US 160/E4
Genoa City, Wi, US 167/P14
Genola, Ut, US 147/H4
Génova, Col. 183/K8
Genova (Genoa), It. 62/B5
Genova (prov.), It. 62/C4
Genova (gulf), It. 66/F1
Genovesa (isl.), Ecu. 184/K6
Gensingen, Ger. 55/G4
Gent (Ghent), Belg. 54/C1
Gent-Brugge Kanaal (canal), Belg. 54/C1
Genteng, Indo. 90/D5
Genteng (cape), Indo. 89/D4
Gentofte, Den. 39/J7
Gentry, Ar, US 153/G2
Genval, Belg. 55/D2
Genzano di Roma, It. 65/B4
Geographe (bay), Austl. 130/B5
Geographe (chan.), Austl. 130/B3
Geographical Center of North America, ND, US 156/D3
Geographical Center of the 48 Contiguous States, Ks, US 154/E4
Geographical Center of United States, SD, US 154/C1
Geok-Tepe, Trkm. 103/J2
Georg von Neumayer, Ger., Ant. 192/Z
George (pt.), Austl. 134/C3
George (lake), Austl. 131/D2
George (riv.), Can. 139/L4
George (riv.), Qu, Can. 141/K3
George, SAfr. 124/C4
George (lake), Ugan. 121/G3
George, Ia, US 155/F2
George, Wa, US 144/E4
George Land (isl.), Rus. 74/E2
George Rogers Clark Nat'l Hist. Park, In, US 162/D1
George Town, Austl. 132/C4
George Town (cap.), Cay. 177/F2
George Town, Malay. 89/C1
George V (coast), Ant. 192/L
George Washington Birthplace Nat'l Mon., Va, US 163/J1
George Washington Carver Nat'l Mon., Mo, US 153/G2

Map Section 228 229

George – Goshen
George West, Tx, US 151/E3
Georgensmünd, Ger. 58/E4
Georges (riv.), Austl. 134/G9
Georgetown, Austl. 134/A2
Georgetown, On, Can. 160/T8
Georgetown, PE, Can. 159/F2
Georgetown, Gam. 114/B3
Georgetown (cap.), Guy. 181/G3
Georgetown, StV. 173/N9
Georgetown, Co, US 154/B4
Georgetown, Ct, US 169/E1
Georgetown, De, US 163/K1
Georgetown, Fl, US 165/H3
Georgetown, Ga, US 165/F2
Georgetown, Ga, US 165/H2
Georgetown, Id, US 147/H2
Georgetown, Il, US 160/C5
Georgetown, Ky, US 162/E1
Georgetown, La, US 164/B2
Georgetown, Oh, US 162/F1
Georgetown, SC, US 163/H4
Georgetown, Tx, US 151/F2
Georgi Traykov, Bul. 51/H4
Georgia (ctry.) 77/D5
Georgia (str.), BC, Can. 144/B3
Georgia (state), US 143/K5
Georgia Agrirama, Ga, US 165/G2
Georgian (bay), On, Can. 141/H4
Georgian Bay Islands NP, On, Can. 160/F2
Georgiana, Al, US 164/E2
Georgina (riv.), Austl. 127/C3
Georgsmarienhütte, Ger. 53/F4
Gepatsch (lake), Aus. 61/G4
Gera, Ger. 42/G3
Geraardsbergen, Belg. 54/C2
Geral de Goiás, Serra (mts.), Braz. 186/D1
Geral, Serra (mts.), Braz. 189/G3
Gerald, Sk, Can. 156/D2
Gerald, Mo, US 153/J1
Geraldine, NZ 135/B4
Geraldine, Mt, US 145/J4
Geraldton, Austl. 130/B4
Geraldton, On, Can. 157/L3
Gérardmer, Fr. 60/C1
Gerasdorf bei Wien, Aus. 51/N7
Gerāsh, Iran 103/H5
Gerber (res.), Or, US 146/C2
Gerbéviller, Fr. 60/C1
Gerbier de Jonc (peak), Fr. 44/F4
Gerbrunn, Ger. 58/C3
Gerdau (riv.), Ger. 53/H3
Gerdine (mt.), Ak, US 171/H3
Gère (riv.), Fr. 64/B2
Gerede, Turk. 70/E4
Geres, Iles D' (isls.), Fr. 66/E2
Geretsried, Ger. 61/H2
Gérgal, Sp. 46/D4
Gerger, Turk. 102/D2
Gerhards (cape), PNG 129/G1
Gerik, Malay. 89/C1
Gering, Ne, US 154/C3
Gerlach, Nv, US 146/D3
Gerlachovský Štít (peak), Slvk. 43/L4
Gerlafingen, Swi. 60/D3
Germantown, Md, US 168/A5
Germantown, Tn, US 162/C3
Germantown, Wi, US 160/B3
Germany (ctry.) 29/E3
Germering, Ger. 59/E6
Germersheim, Ger. 58/B4
Germfask, Mi, US 160/D1
Germigny-L'Evêque, Fr. 30/L5
Germinaga, It. 61/E6
Germiston, SAfr. 124/E2
Gernsbach, Ger. 58/B5
Geroldsgrün, Ger. 59/E2
Gerolsbach, Ger. 59/E5
Gerolstein, Ger. 55/F3
Gerolzhofen, Ger. 58/D3
Geronimo, Az, US 149/G4
Gerpinnes, Belg. 55/D3
Gerra (Verzasca), Swi. 61/E5
Gerrards Cross, Eng, UK 30/B2
Gerringong, Austl. 133/E2
Gers (riv.), Fr. 44/D5
Gersau, Swi. 61/E4
Gersfeld, Ger. 58/C2
Gersheim, Ger. 55/G5
Gerspenz (riv.), Ger. 58/B3
Gerstetten, Ger. 58/E5
Gerstheim, Fr. 60/D1
Gersthofen, Ger. 58/D6
Gerstungen, Ger. 53/H7
Gervais, Or, US 146/B1
Gervanne (riv.), Fr. 64/B3
Gervasio, Uru. 191/G2
Gerze, Turk. 70/E4
Gêrzê, China 99/D5
Gescher, Ger. 52/E5
Geseke, Ger. 53/F5
Gesher, Isr. 105/D3
Gesher Ha Ziw, Isr. 105/C2
Gesira, Som. 119/D1
Gespunsart, Fr. 55/D4
Gessertshausen, Ger. 58/D6
Gesso (riv.), It. 62/A4
Gesso (riv.), Fr. 64/D4
Gesves, Belg. 55/E3
Geta, Fin. 41/H1
Getafe, Sp. 47/N9
Getai, China 80/B4
Gete (riv.), Belg. 55/E2
Getinge, Swe. 40/E3
Gettorf, Ger. 40/C4
Gettysburg, Pa, US 161/H5
Gettysburg, SD, US 154/E1
Gettysburg Nat'l Mil. Park, Pa, US 168/A4
Getúlio Vargas, Braz. 189/F3
Geul (riv.), Neth. 55/E2
Geureudong (peak), Indo. 89/B1
Geurie, Austl. 132/D2
Gevar'am, Isr. 105/B5
Gevaş, Turk. 103/E2
Gevelsberg, Ger. 53/E6
Gevgelija, FYROM 49/H2
Gewanē, Eth. 118/B3
Gex, Fr. 60/C5
Geyer, Ger. 59/F1
Geyersberg (peak), Ger. 58/C3
Geyikli, Turk. 49/K3
Geysdorp, SAfr. 124/D2
Geyser (reef), Madg. 125/H6
Geyve, Turk. 51/K5
Gez (riv.), China 99/B4
Ghabāghib, Syria 105/E2
Ghābat al 'Arab, Sudan 117/F3
Ghadāmis, Libya 111/H3
Ghaddūwah, Libya 108/B3
Ghaggar (riv.), India 98/C5
Ghaghara (riv.), India 96/C2
Ghāghra, India 97/E4
Ghakhar, Pak. 98/C3
Ghana (ctry.) 107/B4
Ghantiāli, India 101/K3
Ghanzi, Bots. 122/D4
Ghanzi (dist.), Bots. 122/D4
Ghār Ad Dimā', Tun. 112/L6
Gharaunda, India 98/D5
Gharb Binna, Sudan 109/F5
Gharbah (wadi), Egypt 113/C5
Gharbī, Jazīrat al (isl.), Tun. 66/F4
Ghardaïa, Alg. 111/F2
Ghardaïa (wilaya), Alg. 111/F3
Ghardimaou, Tun. 112/L6
Gharghoda, India 96/D4
Gharībwāl, Pak. 98/B3
Gharm, Taj. 99/B4
Gharqābād, Iran 103/G3
Gharyān, Libya 67/G4
Ghāt, Libya 111/H4
Ghātāl, India 97/F4
Ghātampur, India 96/C2
Ghātsīla, India 97/F4
Ghayl Bā Wazīr, Yem. 118/D2
Ghazaouet, Alg. 112/D2
Ghaziābād, India 98/D5
Ghāzīpur, India 96/D3
Ghāzīpur, India 96/C3
Ghaznī, Afg. 101/J2
Ghazzah (Gaza), Gaza 105/A5
Ghedi, It. 62/D3
Gheen, Mn, US 157/H4
Ghemme, It. 62/B2
Ghent (Gent), Belg. 54/C1
Gheorghe Gheorghiu-Dej, Rom. 51/H2
Gheorgheni, Rom. 72/C4
Gherla, Rom. 51/F2
Gheura, India 101/K3
Ghilarza, It. 48/A2
Ghinda (Gīnda), Erit. 118/A2
Ghio (lake), Arg. 190/C5
Ghirārah (gulf), Gabon 111/H2
Ghisalba, It. 62/C2
Ghisonaccia, Fr. 48/A1
Gholson, Tx, US 151/F2
Ghora Bāri, Pak. 101/J4
Ghorāi, Nepal 96/D1
Ghost Town, Nv, US 148/D2
Ghotki, Pak. 92/A2
Ghugri (riv.), India 97/F3
Ghum, India 97/G2
Ghurayrah, SAr. 100/D5
Ghūrīān, Afg. 101/H2
Ghuwaybah (wadi), Egypt 113/D5
Gia Lam (int'l arpt.), Viet. 86/E4
Gia Nghia, Viet. 94/D4
Gia Rai, Viet. 94/D4
Gia Vuc, Viet. 94/E3
Giaginskaya, Rus. 73/L5
Gianicolo (hill), It. 65/G8
Giannutri (isl.), It. 48/B1
Giant Sequoia Nat'l Mon., Ca, US 148/C2
Giant's Castle (peak), SAfr. 124/E3
Giant's Causeway, NI, UK 34/B1
Giarre, It. 48/D4
Giaveno, It. 64/D2
Giba'i Shet' (riv.), Eth. 118/A2
Gibb River, Austl. 128/B4
Gibbon, Ne, US 154/E3
Gibbonsville, Id, US 147/G1
Gibbstown, NJ, US 168/C4
Gībē Shet' (riv.), Eth. 117/H4
Gībē Wenz (riv.), Eth. 117/H3
Gibeon, Namb. 122/C5
Giberville, Fr. 57/E2
Gibloux (peak), Swi. 60/D4
Gibraleón, Sp. 46/B4
Gibraltar (pt.), Eng, UK 35/J5
Gibraltar, Ven. 173/G6
Gibraltar (res.), Ca, US 166/A1
Gibraltar, Mi, US 167/F7
Gibraltar (cap.), Gib. 46/C4
Gibraltar (str.), Mor.,Sp. 29/D5
Gibraltar Range NP, Austl. 132/E1
Gibsland, La, US 153/H4
Gibson, Ga, US 163/F4
Gibson, Austl. 130/D5
Gibson, NC, US 163/H3
Gibson (des.), Austl. 127/B3
Gibson City, Il, US 160/B4
Gibson Desert Nature Reserve, Austl. 130/E3
Gibsonburg, Oh, US 160/E4
Gibsonia, Fl, US 164/M7
Gibsons, BC, Can. 144/C3
Gibsonton, Fl, US 164/L8
Gīdamī, Eth. 117/G3
Giddarbāha, India 98/C4
Gidden (lake), Fl, US 164/L6
Giddings, Tx, US 151/F2
Gideon, Mo, US 162/C2
Gidollē, Eth. 117/H4
Giebelstadt, Ger. 58/C3
Gieboldehausen, Ger. 53/H5
Giedraičiai, Lith. 41/L4
Gien, Fr. 44/E3
Giengen an der Brenz, Ger. 58/D5
Gier (riv.), Fr. 44/F4
Giessbachfälle (falls), Swi. 60/E4
Giessen (riv.), Fr.,Ger. 60/D1
Giessen, Ger. 58/B1
Giessendam, Neth. 52/B5
Gieten, Neth. 52/D2
Giethoorn, Neth. 52/D3
Gif-sur-Yvette, Fr. 30/J5
Gīfān, Iran 103/J2
Gifford, Sc, UK 33/D5
Gifford, Fl, US 165/H4
Gifford, Il, US 160/B4
Gifford (riv.), Nun, Can. 141/H1
Gifford (peak), Wa, US 144/D5
Gifford, SC, US 163/G4
Giffre (riv.), Fr. 60/C5
Gifhorn, Ger. 53/H4
Gifu, Japan 83/L5
Gig Harbor, Wa, US 144/C4
Gigant, Rus. 73/L4
Gigante, Col. 180/C4
Giggleswick, Eng, UK 35/F3
Giglio (isl.), It. 67/F2
Gignac, Fr. 47/G1
Gignac-la-Nerthe, Fr. 64/B6
Gijón, Sp. 46/C1
Gikongoro, Rwa. 121/G3
Gil de Vilches, PN, Chile 190/C2
Gila (riv.), Az, NM, US 149/G4
Gila, NM, US 149/H4
Gila (mts.), Az, US 149/G4
Gila Bend, Az, US 149/F4
Gila Bend Ind. Res., Az, US 149/F4
Gila Cliff Dwellings Nat'l Mon., NM, US 149/H4
Gīlān (gov.), Iran 103/G2
Gīlān-e Gharb, Iran 103/F3
Gilat, Isr. 105/B6
Gilberdyke Newport, Eng, UK 35/H4
Gilbert (riv.), Austl. 127/D2
Gilbert (mt.), BC, Can. 144/B2
Gilbert (isls.), Kiri. 136/G5
Gilbert, Az, US 149/G4
Gilbert, Ia, US 155/H2
Gilbert, La, US 164/C1
Gilbert, Mn, US 157/H4
Gilbert (peak), Ut, US 147/H3
Gilbert Plains, Mb, Can. 156/D2
Gilbertown, Al, US 164/D2
Gilberts, Il, US 167/P15
Gilbjerg (pt.), Den. 39/J6
Gilbués, Braz. 183/E5
Gilby, ND, US 156/F3
Gilching, Ger. 58/E6
Gilchrist, Tx, US 151/G3
Gilé, Moz. 123/H3
Gilfach Gôch, Wal, UK 36/C3
Gilford, NI, UK 34/B3
Gilford, NH, US 161/L3
Gilford Park, NJ, US 168/D4
Gilgandra, Austl. 132/D1
Gilgil, Kenya 119/B2
Gilgit (riv.), Pak. 98/C1
Gilgit, Pak. 98/C2
Gilgit (riv.), India 99/B4
Gilgunnia, Austl. 132/C2
Gilimanuk, Indo. 89/F5
Gill, Ma, US 161/K3
Gill, Lough (lake), Ire. 32/B1
Gillam, Mb, Can. 140/G3
Gilleleje, Den. 39/J6
Gilles (lake), Austl. 131/H5
Gillespie, Il, US 155/K4
Gillett, Ar, US 153/J3
Gillett, Wi, US 160/B2
Gillett, Tx, US 151/F3
Gillette, Wy, US 154/B1
Gillies Bay, BC, Can. 144/B3
Gillingham, Eng, UK 37/G4
Gillot (int'l arpt.), Fr. 125/S15
Gilly, Swi. 60/C5
Gilly-sur-Isère, Fr. 64/C1
Gilman, Wi, US 157/J5
Gilman, Il, US 160/C4
Gilman City, Mo, US 155/H3
Gilman Hot Springs, Ca, US 166/D3
Gilmer, Tx, US 151/G1
Gilmore, Id, US 147/G1
Gīlo Wenz (riv.), Eth. 117/G4
Gilqit (riv.), Pak. 101/K1
Gilroy, Ca, US 148/B2
Giluwe (mt.), PNG 129/F1
Gilyuy (riv.), Rus. 79/K1
Gilze, Neth. 52/B5
Gīmbī, Eth. 117/G3
Gimbsheim, Ger. 58/B3
Gimel, Swi. 60/C4
Gimie (mt.), StL. 173/N9
Gimli, Mb, Can. 156/F2
Gimo, Swe. 40/H1
Gimone (riv.), Fr. 47/F1
Gin Gin, Austl. 134/C4
Ginan, Japan 83/L5
Gīnch'ī, Eth. 118/A3
Gīnda (Ghinda), Erit. 118/A2
Gingelom, Belg. 55/E2
Gingero, Eth. 117/H4
Gingin, Austl. 130/B4
Gingindlovu, SAfr. 125/E3
Gingoog, Phil. 88/D3
Gingst, Ger. 40/E4
Gīnīr, Eth. 118/B4
Ginneken, Neth. 52/B5
Ginnosar, Isr. 105/D3
Ginosa, It. 48/E2
Ginowan, Japan 85/J7
Gioia (gulf), It. 48/D3
Gioia dei Marsi, It. 65/C4
Gioia del Colle, It. 48/E2
Gioia Tauro, It. 48/D3
Giornico, Swi. 61/E5
Gioūra (isl.), Gre. 49/J3
Gioveretto (peak), It. 61/G5
Giovi (peak), It. 63/E6
Gipping (riv.), Eng, UK 37/G2
Gipsy, Mo, US 162/B2
Girard, Ks, US 153/G2
Girard, Pa, US 160/F3
Girard, Il, US 155/K4
Girardot, Col. 183/L8
Girardota, Col. 183/K6
Girardville, Qu, Can. 158/A1
Girardville, Pa, US 168/B2
Giraud (peak), Fr. 64/D4
Giraul, Ang. 122/B2
Giraul (riv.), Ang. 122/B2
Giraumont, Fr. 55/E5
Girawa, Eth. 118/B3
Girdle Ness (pt.), Sc, UK 33/D2
Giresun (prov.), Turk. 70/F4
Giresun, Turk. 70/F4
Girgnasco, It. 62/B2
Giri (riv.), D.R. Congo 120/D2
Gīrīdīh, India 97/F3
Girifalco, It. 48/E3
Girilambone, Austl. 132/C1
Girling (res.), Eng, UK 30/C2
Giromagny, Fr. 60/C2
Girón, Ecu. 180/B5
Girón, Col. 180/C3
Girona, Sp. 47/G2
Gironcourt-sur-Vraine, Fr. 60/B1
Gironde (riv.), Fr. 66/C1
Gironella, Sp. 47/F1
Girraween NP, Austl. 132/D1
Giru, Austl. 134/B2
Giruá, Braz. 189/F4
Girvan, Sc, UK 34/D1
Girvin, Tx, US 151/C2
Gisborne, NZ 135/D2
Gisborne, Austl. 133/B3
Gisenyi, Rwa. 121/G3
Gislaved, Swe. 40/E3
Gisors, Fr. 54/A5
Gissi, It. 65/D3
Gistel, Belg. 54/B1
Gistrup, Den. 40/D3
Gitarama, Rwa. 121/G3
Gitega, Buru. 121/G3
Gittsfjället (peak), Swe. 38/E2
Giubiasco, Swi. 61/F5
Giugliano in Campania, It. 65/D6
Giulianello, It. 65/B4
Giulianova, It. 65/C2
Giurgeni, Rom. 51/H3
Giurgiu, Rom. 51/G4
Giurgiu (prov.), Rom. 51/G3
Giussano, It. 62/C2
Giv'at Brenner, Isr. 105/B5
Giv'at Hayyim, Isr. 105/B4
Giv'atayim, Isr. 105/B4
Give, Den. 40/C4
Givet, Fr. 55/D3
Givors, Fr. 64/A1
Giwa, Nga. 115/G4
Giyani, SAfr. 123/F4
Gizhiga (bay), Rus. 75/R3
Gizo, Sol. 136/E5
Giżycko, Pol. 41/J4
Gjerdrum, Nor. 40/D1
Gjerlev, Den. 40/D3
Gjerstad, Nor. 40/C2
Gjirokastër, Alb. 49/G2
Gjoa Haven, Nun, Can. 140/G2
Gjøvik, Nor. 40/D1
Glabbeek, Belg. 55/E2
Glace Bay, NS, Can. 159/H2
Glacier (peak), Wa, US 144/D3
Glacier, BC, Can. 144/F2
Glacier Bay NP, Ak, US 142/Z13
Glacier NP, Mt, US 145/H3
Glacier NP, BC, Can. 144/F2
Gladbeck, Ger. 52/D5
Gladbrook, Ia, US 155/H2
Glade Spring, Va, US 163/G2
Gladewater, Tx, US 151/G1
Gladsakse, Den. 39/J7
Gladsheim (peak), BC, Can. 144/F3
Gladstone, Mb, Can. 156/E2
Gladstone, ND, US 156/C4
Gladstone, Mi, US 160/C2
Gladstone, Austl. 134/C3
Gladstone, Austl. 131/H5
Gladwin, Mi, US 160/D3
Gladys, Va, US 163/H2
Glafsfjorden (lake), Swe. 40/D2
Glaisdale, Eng, UK 35/H3
Glamis, Sc, UK 33/D3
Glamis, Ca, US 148/E4
Glamis, Sk, Can. 145/L2
Glamsbjerg, Den. 40/D4
Glan (riv.), Ger. 42/D4
Glan, Phil. 88/D4
Glanamman, Wal, UK 36/C3
Glanaruddery (mts.), Ire. 32/A5
Glancy, Ms, US 164/C2
Gland, Swi. 60/C5
Gland (riv.), Fr. 55/D4
Glandon (riv.), Fr. 64/C2
Glandore, Ire. 32/A6
Glandorf, Ger. 53/F4
Glanmire, Ire. 32/B6
Glænø (isl.), Den. 39/H7
Glanworth, Ire. 32/B5
Glärnisch (range), Swi. 61/E3
Glarus, Swi. 61/F3
Glarus (canton), Swi. 61/E4
Glarus Alps (range), Swi. 45/H3
Glas Maol (peak), Sc, UK 33/C3
Glasbury, Wal, UK 36/C2
Glasco, Ks, US 154/F4
Glasgow, Sc, UK 33/B5
Glasgow (co.), Sc, UK 33/B5
Glasgow, De, US 168/C4
Glasgow, Ky, US 162/E2
Glasgow, Mt, US 145/L3
Glasgow, Va, US 163/H2
Glashütten, Ger. 58/B2
Glaslyn (riv.), Wal, UK 34/D6
Glaslyn, Sk, Can. 145/K1
Glass (lake), Sc, UK 33/B1
Glass (riv.), Sc, UK 33/B2
Glass (mts.), Tx, US 151/C2
Glassboro, NJ, US 168/C4
Glastonbury, Eng, UK 36/D4
Glatt (riv.), Swi. 61/E1
Glatt (riv.), Ger. 58/B6
Glattbach, Ger. 58/C3
Glattfelden, Swi. 61/E2
Glavinitsa, Bul. 51/H4
Glazoué, Ben. 115/F5
Glazov, Rus. 69/M4
Gleason, Wi, US 157/K5
Gleason, Tn, US 162/C2
Glebovka, Rus. 73/K4
Gleichen, Ab, Can. 145/H2
Gleisdorf, Aus. 50/B2
Glems (riv.), Ger. 58/C5
Glemsford, Eng, UK 37/G2
Glen, Mn, US 157/H4
Glen (riv.), Eng, UK 35/H6
Glen, Mt, US 147/G1
Glen (canyon), Ut, US 149/G2
Glen Allan, Ms, US 162/B4
Glen Allen, Va, US 163/J2
Glen Arbor, Mi, US 160/D2
Glen Burnie, Md, US 168/B5
Glen Canyon (dam), Az, US 149/G2
Glen Canyon Nat'l Rec. Area, Az,Ut, US 147/H4
Glen Coe (pass), Sc, UK 33/B3
Glen Cove, NY, US 169/L8
Glen Cove, Tx, US 150/E2
Glen Echo (park), Md, US 168/A6
Glen Eden, NZ 135/F6
Glen Elder, Ks, US 154/E4
Glen Flora, Tx, US 151/F3
Glen Gardner, NJ, US 168/D2
Glen Haven, Ga, US 163/M7
Glen Innes, Austl. 132/D1
Glen Lyon, Pa, US 168/B1
Glen Mòr (valley), Sc, UK 33/B2
Glen Ridge, NJ, US 169/J8
Glen Rock, NJ, US 169/J8
Glen Rock, Pa, US 168/B4
Glen Rose, Tx, US 151/F1
Glen Ullin, ND, US 156/D4
Glen Williams, On, Can. 160/T8
Glenan (isl.), Fr. 44/A3
Glenarm (riv.), NI, UK 34/C2
Glenarm, NI, UK 34/C2
Glenavon, Sk, Can. 156/C2
Glenavy, NI, UK 34/B2
Glenavy, NZ 135/B4
Glenbawn (dam), Austl. 132/D2
Glenboro, Mb, Can. 156/E3
Glenbrook, Nv, US 146/D4
Glenbrook (nbrhd.), Austl. 134/G8
Glenburn, ND, US 156/D3
Glenbush, Sk, Can. 145/L1
Glencaple, Sc, UK 34/E2
Glenclova, Zim. 123/F3
Glencoe, Ok, US 153/F2
Glencoe, Sc, UK 33/A3
Glencoe, On, Can. 160/F3
Glencoe, Il, US 167/Q15
Glencoe, Mn, US 155/G1
Glencoe, SAfr. 125/E3
Glencross, SD, US 156/D5
Glendale, Wi, US 160/C3
Glendale, Ca, US 166/F7
Glendale, Zim. 123/F3
Glendale, Az, US 149/F4
Glendale, Or, US 146/B2
Glendale, Ut, US 149/F2
Glendale, Ky, US 162/E2
Glendale, Mo, US 155/H3
Glendale, Tx, US 151/G2
Glendale Heights, Il, US 167/P16
Glenden, Austl. 134/C3
Glendive, Mt, US 156/B4
Glendo (dam), Wy, US 154/B2
Glendo (res.), Wy, US 154/B2
Glendo, Wy, US 154/B2
Glendon, NC, US 163/H3
Glendora, Ca, US 166/C2
Glendun (riv.), NI, UK 34/B1
Glenealy, Ire. 34/B6
Glenelg, Sc, UK 31/R8
Glenelg (riv.), Austl. 132/B3
Glenelg (nbrhd.), Austl. 131/M8
Glenelg, Md, US 168/B5
Glenella, Mb, Can. 156/E2
Glenelly (riv.) 34/A2
Glenfield, NY, US 161/J3
Glengarriff, Ire. 32/A6
Glengarry (range), Austl. 130/C3
Glenluce, Sc, UK 34/D2
Glenmere (lake), NY, US 168/D1
Glenmora, La, US 164/B2
Glenmorgan, Austl. 134/C4
Glenn Heights, Tx, US 150/L7
Glennallen, Ak, US 171/J3
Glennamaddy, Ire. 32/B2
Glenns Ferry, Id, US 147/F2
Glennville, Ga, US 165/H2
Glennville, Ca, US 148/C3
Glenolden, Pa, US 168/C4
Glenoma, Wa, US 144/C4
Glenora, BC, Can. 171/M4
Glenorie, Austl. 134/H8
Glenormiston, Austl. 131/H2
Glenpool, Ok, US 153/F3
Glenrock, Wy, US 154/B2
Glenrothes, Sc, UK 33/C4
Glens Falls, NY, US 161/K3
Glenshane (pass), NI, UK 34/B2
Glenside, Pa, US 168/C3
Glenties, Ire. 31/P9
Glentrool, Sc, UK 34/D1
Glentworth, Sk, Can. 145/L3
Glenveagh NP, Ire. 31/Q9
Glenview, Il, US 167/Q15
Glenville, Ire. 32/B5
Glenville, WV, US 163/G1
Glenville, Mn, US 155/H2
Glenwood, Ab, Can. 145/H3
Glenwood, Al, US 165/E2
Glenwood, Ar, US 153/H3
Glenwood, Ga, US 163/F4
Glenwood, Ia, US 155/G3
Glenwood, Mn, US 157/G5
Glenwood, NM, US 149/H4
Glenwood, NJ, US 168/D1
Glenwood, Ut, US 149/G1
Glenwood City, Wi, US 155/H1
Gleouraich (peak), Sc, UK 33/A2
Glidden, Ia, US 155/G2
Glidden, Sk, Can. 145/K2
Glifádha, Gre. 49/N9
Glimåkra, Swe. 40/F3
Glina, Cro. 50/C3
Glinde, Ger. 53/H1
Glindow, Ger. 42/P7
Glitra (riv.), Nor. 38/R8
Glitrevatn (lake), Nor. 38/R8
Gliwice, Pol. 43/K3
Globe, Az, US 149/G4
Glockturm (peak), Aus. 61/G4
Glodeni, Mol. 72/D4
Gloggnitz, Aus. 43/H5
Głogów, Pol. 43/J3
Głogówek, Pol. 43/J3
Glomma (riv.), Nor. 38/D3
Glonn (riv.), Ger. 58/E6
Gloria (bay), Cuba 177/G1
Glorious (mt.), Austl. 134/E6
Glory of Russia (cape), Ak, US 142/V12
Glossodia, Austl. 133/E1
Glossop, Eng, UK 35/G5
Gloster, La, US 150/H1
Gloster, Ms, US 164/C2
Gloster, Ga, US 163/M7
Glostrup, Den. 39/J7
Glotovka, Rus. 71/H1
Gloucester, Ma, US 161/L3
Gloucester, On, Can. 161/J2
Gloucester, Austl. 132/D1
Gloucester, PNG 129/H1
Gloucester, Eng, UK 36/D3
Gloucester (co.), NJ, US 168/C4
Gloucester (Gloucester Court House), Va, US 163/J2
Gloucester City, NJ, US 168/C4
Gloucester Court House (Gloucester), Va, US 163/J2
Gloucester Point, Va, US 163/J2
Gloucestershire (co.), Eng, UK 36/D3
Glouster, Oh, US 160/E5
Glouthane, Ire. 32/B6
Glover, Ok, US 153/G3
Glover (isl.), Nf, Can. 159/J1
Glovers Reef (reef), Belz. 176/E2
Gloversville, NY, US 161/J3
Glovertown, Nf, Can. 159/K1
Głowno, Pol. 43/K3
Głubczyce, Pol. 43/J3
Glubokiy, Rus. 73/L3
Glubokoye, Kaz. 99/D1
Głuchołazy, Pol. 43/J3
Glücksburg, Ger. 40/C4
Glückstadt, Ger. 53/G1
Glumslöv, Swe. 39/J7
Glumsø, Den. 39/H7
Glyde (riv.), Ire. 32/D2
Glyn Heath, Wal, UK 36/C3
Glyncorrwg, Wal, UK 36/C3
Glyndon, Mn, US 156/F4
Glyndon, Md, US 168/B5
Glyngøre, Den. 40/C3
Glynn, NI, UK 34/C2
Gmünd, Aus. 43/H4
Gmunden, Aus. 59/G7
Gnagna (prov.), Burk. 115/E3
Gnarrenburg, Ger. 53/G2
Gnesta, Swe. 39/A1
Gnezdovo, Rus. 70/D1
Gniew, Pol. 41/H5
Gniezno, Pol. 43/J2
Gnjilane, Yugo. 50/E4
Gnosall, Eng, UK 36/D1
Gnowangerup, Austl. 130/C5
Gō (riv.), Japan 84/C3
Go Cong, Viet. 94/D4
Go Dau Ha, Viet. 94/D4
Go Quao, Viet. 94/D4
Goa (state), India 92/B4
Goageb, Namb. 124/B2
Goālpāra, India 97/H2
Goāltor, India 97/F4
Goat Fell (peak), Sc, UK 33/A5
Goat River, BC, Can. 144/D1
Goathland, Eng, UK 35/H3
Goba, Eth. 118/A4
Goba, Moz. 125/F2
Gobabeb, Namb. 122/B4
Gobabis, Namb. 122/C4
Gobardānga, India 97/G4
Gobernador Castro, Arg. 190/F2
Gobernador Costa, Arg. 190/C5
Gobernador Crespo, Arg. 188/D4
Gobernador Duval, Arg. 190/D3
Gobernador Gregores, Arg. 191/C6
Gobernador Ingeniero Valetín Virasoro, Arg. 189/E4
Gobernador Mansilla, Arg. 191/J10
Gobi (des.), China,Mon 77/K5
Gobindpur, India 97/E5
Göblberg (peak), Aus. 59/G6
Gobō, Japan 84/D4
Gobowen, Eng, UK 35/E6
Goch, Ger. 52/D5
Gochas, Namb. 124/B2
Gochsheim, Ger. 58/D2
Goda, Eth. 118/B4
Godāgāri, Bang. 97/G3
Godalming, Eng, UK 37/F4
Godāvari (riv.), India 77/G8
Godbout, Qu, Can. 158/D1
Goddā, India 97/F3
Godē, Eth. 118/B4
Godeanu (peak), Rom. 50/F3
Godech, Bul. 50/F4
Goderich, On, Can. 160/F3
Godfrey, Il, US 155/J4
Godhra, India 92/B3
Godinlabe, Som. 118/C4
Godinne, Belg. 55/D3
Godley, Tx, US 150/K7
Godmanchester, Eng, UK 37/F2
Gōdo, Japan 83/L5
Gödölló, Hun. 43/K5
Godolphin Cross, Eng, UK 36/A6
Godoy Cruz, Arg. 190/C2
Gods (lake), Mb, Can. 140/G3
Gods (riv.), Mb, Can. 140/G3
Gods Mercy (bay), Nun, Can. 141/H2
Godstone, Eng, UK 30/C3
Godthåb (Nuuk), Grld. 139/M3
Godwin Austen (K2) (peak), Pak. 98/D2
Goeree (isl.), Neth. 52/A5
Goes, Neth. 52/A5
Goessel, Ks, US 153/F1
Goetzville, Mi, US 160/D1
Goff, Ks, US 155/G4
Goffstown, NH, US 161/L3
Gofitskoye, Rus. 71/G3
Gogebic (range), Mi, US 157/J4
Gogebic (lake), Mi, US 157/K4
Göggingen, Ger. 58/D6
Gogland (isl.), Rus. 41/M1
Gogo, Eth. 117/G4
Gogo, Austl. 128/B4
Gogogogo, Madg. 125/H9
Gogōme, Japan 82/B4
Gogounou, Ben. 115/F4
Gogra (riv.), India 92/D2
Gogrial, Sudan 117/F3
Goha Ts'iyon, Eth. 118/A3
Gohad, India 96/B2
Gohāna, India 98/D5
Goharganj, India 96/A4
Gohbach (riv.), Ger. 53/G3
Goiana, Braz. 183/H4
Goiandira, Braz. 186/C3
Goianésia, Braz. 186/C2
Goiânia, Braz. 186/C3
Goianinha, Braz. 183/H4
Goianira, Braz. 186/C3
Goiás, Braz. 186/C2
Goiás (state), Braz. 186/C2
Goiatuba, Braz. 186/C3
Goil (lake), Sc, UK 33/B4
Goinsargoin, China 86/C2
Goio-Erê, Braz. 189/F3
Goirle, Neth. 52/C5
Góis, Port. 46/A2
Goito, It. 63/D3
Gojam (prov.), Eth. 117/H3
Gojeb Wenz (riv.), Eth. 117/H4
Gojō, Japan 84/D3
Gojra, Pak. 98/B4
Gok (riv.), Turk. 70/E4
Goka, Japan 83/D1
Gokāk, India 95/B2
Gokase (riv.), Japan 84/B4
Gokashō, Japan 83/K5
Gokasho (bay), Japan 83/L7
Gökçeada (isl.), Turk. 102/A1
Gökçebey, Turk. 51/L5
Gökçekaya (dam), Turk. 102/B1
Göksu (riv.), Turk 102/D2
Göksun, Turk. 102/D2
Gokteik, Myan. 94/B1
Göktepe, Turk. 104/C1
Gokwe, Zim. 123/F3
Gol, Nor. 40/C1
Gola, India 97/E4
Gola Gokarannāth, India 96/C1
Golan Hts. (reg.), Syria 104/D3
Golasecca, It. 62/B2
Gölbaşı, Turk. 102/D2
Gölbaşı, Turk. 102/C2
Golbey, Fr. 60/C1
Golborne, Eng, UK 35/F5
Golconda, Il, US 162/C2
Gölcük, Turk. 51/J5
Gold (coast), Gha. 115/E5
Gold (mtn.), Wa, US 167/B2
Gold (cr.), BC, Can. 144/G3
Gold Bar, Wa, US 167/D2
Gold Beach, Fr. 57/E2
Gold Beach, Or, US 146/A2
Gold Bridge, BC, Can. 144/C2
Gold Coast, Austl. 134/D5
Gold Hill, Or, US 146/B2
Gold Point, Nv, US 148/D2
Goldach, Swi. 61/F3
Gołdap, Pol. 41/K4
Goldbach, Ger. 58/C3
Goldberg, Ger. 40/E5
Golden, NM, US 152/A3
Golden, Ire. 32/B4
Golden (bay), NZ 135/C3
Golden, Co, US 154/B4
Golden, BC, Can. 144/F2
Golden Beach, Fl, US 164/P11
Golden City, Mo, US 153/G2
Golden Gate, Fl, US 165/H4
Golden Gate (chan.), Ca, US 167/J11
Golden Gate Highlands NP, SAfr. 124/D3
Golden Gate Nat'l Recreation Area, Ca., US 148/A2
Golden Lake Ind. Res., On, Can. 161/H2
Golden Prairie, Sk, Can. 145/K2
Golden Rock (int'l arpt.), StK. 173/N8
Golden Spike Nat'l Hist. Site, Ut, US 147/G3
Golden Temple, India 98/C4
Golden Vale (plain), Ire. 32/B4
Golden Valley, Zim. 123/F3
Golden Valley, Mn, US 157/P6
Goldendale, Wa, US 144/D5
Goldene Aue (reg.), Ger. 42/F3
Goldenrod, Fl, US 164/N6
Goldenstedt, Ger. 53/F3
Goldfield, Nv, US 148/D2
Goldfield, Ia, US 155/H2
Goldkronach, Ger. 59/E2
Goldlauter, Ger. 58/D1
Goldonna, La, US 164/B1
Goldsboro, Tx, US 150/E1
Goldsboro, Md, US 168/C5
Goldsboro, NC, US 163/J3
Goldsboro (Etters), Pa, US 168/B3
Goldsworthy, Austl. 130/C2
Goldthwaite, Tx, US 151/E2
Göle, Turk. 71/G4
Goleniów, Pol. 40/F5
Golfito Nat'l Wild. Ref., CR 177/F4
Golfo Aranci, It. 48/A2
Golfo de Santa Clara, Mex. 174/B2
Gölhısar, Turk. 102/B2
Goliad, Tx, US 151/F3
Golinda, Tx, US 151/F2
Golitsyno, Rus. 69/W9
Gölköy, Turk. 70/F4
Gollach (riv.), Ger. 58/D3
Göllheim, Ger. 58/B3
Gölmarmara, Turk. 102/A2
Golmud, China 78/C4
Gololcha, Eth. 118/B3
Golomoti Station, Malw. 123/G2
Golovanovo, Rus. 68/J5
Golovin, Ak, US 171/F3
Golovino, Rus. 68/J5
Golovnina (peak), Rus. 82/D2
Golovnino, Rus. 82/D2
Golpāyegān, Iran 103/G3
Gölpazarı, Turk. 51/K5
Gols, Aus. 45/M3
Gol'shany, Bela. 41/M4
Goltry, Ok, US 153/E2
Golts, Md, US 168/C5
Golub-Dobrzyń, Pol. 43/K2
Golubovci (int'l arpt.), Yugo. 50/D4
Golungo Alto, Ang. 120/C5
Golva, ND, US 156/C4
Golyam Perelik (peak), Bul. 49/J2
Golyama Kamchiya (riv.), Bul. 51/H4
Golyama Syutkya (peak), Bul. 49/J2
Goma (int'l arpt.), D.R. Congo 121/G3
Goma, D.R. Congo 121/G3
Gomantong Caves, Malay. 88/B4
Gomaringen, Ger. 58/C6
Gomati (riv.), India 96/C2
Gombari, D.R. Congo 121/G2
Gombe (riv.), Tanz. 121/G4
Gombe, Ang. 120/C4
Gombe NP, Tanz. 121/G4
Gombe-Matadi, D.R. Congo 120/C4
Gomera (isl.), Sp. 110/A4
Gomez (peak), Tx, US 151/B2
Gómez Farías, Mex. 174/D2
Gómez Palacio, Mex. 174/E3
Gomīshān, Iran 100/F1
Gommern, Ger. 42/F2
Gomo, China 99/E5
Gomoh, India 97/F4
Goms (valley), Swi. 60/E5
Gomshall, Eng, UK 30/B3
Gomshall, Eng, UK 37/F4
Gona, PNG 129/H2
Gonābād, Iran 101/G2
Gonaïves, Haiti 177/H2
Gonarezhou NP, Zim. 123/F4
Gonâve (gulf), Haiti 173/G4
Gonâve (isl.), Haiti 177/H2
Gonbad-e Qābūs, Iran 103/H2
Gönc, Hun. 43/L4
Gonçalves Dias, Braz. 183/E4
Gondā, India 96/C2
Gondal, India 101/K4
Gondelsheim, Ger. 58/B4
Gonder, Eth. 117/H2
Gonder (pol. reg.), Eth. 117/H2
Gondola Point, NB, Can. 158/E3
Gondomar, Port. 46/A2
Gondomar, Sp. 46/A1
Gondrecourt-le-Château, Fr. 60/B1
Gondreville, Fr. 55/E6
Gondrexange (lake), Fr. 55/F6
Gönen, Turk. 70/C4
Gonesse, Fr. 30/K5
Gonfaron, Fr. 64/C6
Gonfreville-L'Orcher, Fr. 57/F1
Gong Xian, China 93/H2
Gong Xian, China 80/C4
Gong'an, China 87/F3
Gongbo'gyamda, China 93/F2
Gongchangling, China 81/B2
Gongche, China 87/F4
Gongga (peak), China 86/D2
Gonggar, China 97/H1
Gongguan, China 87/F4
Gonghe, China 78/E4
Gongliu, China 99/D3
Gongo, D.R. Congo 120/D4
Gongola (riv.), Nga. 115/H4
Gongolgon, Austl. 132/C1
Gongping, China 87/G4
Gongshan Drungzu Nuzu Zizhixian, China 93/G2
Gongtian, China 87/G2
Gongwan (mts.), China 86/D3
Gongxi, China 87/G3
Gongzhuling, China 80/F2
Goñi, Uru. 191/K10
Gonja, Tanz. 119/B3
Gonjo, China 86/C2
Gónnoi, Gre. 49/H3
Gonohe, Japan 82/B3
Gonubie, SAfr. 124/D4
Gonvick, Mn, US 157/G4
Gonyú, Hun. 50/C2
Gonzaga, It. 63/D4
Gonzaga, Phil. 88/C1
Gonzales, La, US 164/C2
Gonzales, Ca, US 148/B2
Gonzales, Tx, US 151/F3
Gonzalez, Fl, US 164/E2
González, Mex. 175/F4
Goobweyn, Som. 119/C2
Goochland, Va, US 163/J2
Good Hart, Mi, US 160/D2
Good Hope, Cape of (cape), SAfr. 124/L11
Good Spirit (lake), Sk, Can. 156/C2
Goodenough (cape), Ant. 192/J
Goodes, Ga, US 163/L7
Goodfellow (A.F.B.), Tx, US 151/D2
Goodhope, Bots. 122/E5
Gooding, Id, US 147/F2
Goodland, Fl, US 165/H5
Goodland, Ks, US 154/D4
Goodman, Mo, US 153/G2
Goodman, Wi, US 157/K5
Goodna (nbrhd.), Austl. 134/E7
Goodnews Bay, Ak, US 171/F4
Goodooga, Austl. 132/C1
Goodrich, Mi, US 167/F6
Goodrich, ND, US 156/D4
Goodrich, Tx, US 151/G2
Goodridge, Mn, US 156/G3
Goodview, Mn, US 155/J1
Goodwater, Al, US 162/D4
Goodwell, Ok, US 152/D2
Goodwick, Wal, UK 36/B2
Goodwin, Ar, US 162/B3
Goodwood, SAfr. 124/L10
Gooimeer (lake), Neth. 52/C4
Goole, Eng, UK 35/H4
Goolgowi, Austl. 133/B2
Gooloogong, Austl. 133/D1
Goolwa, Austl. 131/H5
Goomalling, Austl. 130/C4
Goombalie, Austl. 132/C1
Goombungee, Austl. 134/C4
Goondiwindi, Austl. 134/C5
Goongarrie NP, Austl. 130/D4
Goor, Neth. 52/D4
Goose (riv.), ND, US 156/F4
Goose (lake), Ca, US 142/B3
Goose (cr.), Id, US 147/G2
Goose (pt.), De, US 168/C5
Goose Creek, SC, US 163/G4
Goose Green, UK 191/F6
Gooseberry (cr.), Wy, US 147/J1
Goostrey, Eng, UK 35/F5
Gopālganj, India 97/E2
Gopālganj, Bang. 97/G4
Gopālpur, Bang. 97/G3
Gopat (riv.), India 96/D3
Göppingen, Ger. 58/C5
Góra, Pol. 43/J3
Góra Kalwaria, Pol. 43/L3
Gorakhpur, India 96/D2
Gorakhpur, India 96/C4
Goras, India 96/A3
Goražde, Bosn. 50/D4
Gorchs, Arg. 191/J11
Gorczański NP, Pol. 43/L4
Gorda (pt.), Cuba 177/F1
Gorda (pt.), Nic. 177/F3
Gorda (pt.), Nic. 177/F4
Gorda (pt.), Ca, US 146/A3
Gordes, Fr. 64/B5
Gordevio, Swi. 61/E5
Gordeyevka, Rus. 70/D1
Gordil, CAfr. 116/D3
Gørding, Den. 40/C4
Gordo, Al, US 162/D4
Gordola, Swi. 61/E5
Gordon, Sc, UK 33/D5
Gordon, Al, US 165/F2
Gordon, Austl. 132/C4
Gordon, Ga, US 163/F4
Gordon (cr.), Ne, US 154/D2
Gordon (lake), Austl. 127/D5
Gordon Downs, Austl. 128/C4
Gordon Ind. Res., Sk, Can. 156/B2
Gordonsbaai, SAfr. 124/L11
Gordonsville, Va, US 163/H1
Gordonvale, Austl. 134/B2
Gore, Va, US 161/G5
Gore (mtn.), NY, US 161/J3
Goré, Chad 116/C4
Gorē, Eth. 117/G3
Gore, NZ 135/B4
Gore Bay, On, Can. 160/E2
Gore Point (cape), Ak, US 171/H4
Gorebridge, Sc, UK 33/C5
Goree, Tx, US 152/E4
Görele, Turk. 70/F4
Gorelovo (arpt.), Rus. 69/T7
Goresbridge, Ire. 32/D4
Goreville, Il, US 162/C2
Gorey, Ire. 32/D4
Gorey, Chl, UK 56/C2
Gorgān, Iran 103/H2
Gorgān (riv.), Iran 103/H2
Gorge du Loup, Lux. 55/F4
Gorges du Verdon, Fr. 64/C5
Gorges du Ziz, Mor. 110/D2
Gorgol (riv.), Mrta. 114/B2
Gorgol (pol. reg.), Mrta. 114/B3
Gorgona, Isola di (isl.), It. 62/C6
Gorgonzola, It. 62/C2
Gorgora, Eth. 117/H2
Gorham, Me, US 161/L3
Gorham, NH, US 161/L2
Gori, Geo. 71/H4
Gorinchem, Neth. 52/B5
Goring, Eng, UK 37/E3
Goring-by-Sea, Eng, UK 37/F5
Goris, Arm. 103/F2
Gorizia, It. 63/G2
Gorizia (prov.), It. 63/G1
Gorj (prov.), Rom. 51/F3
Gor'kiy (res.), Rus. 68/J4
Gørlev, Den. 39/H7
Gorlice, Pol. 43/L4
Görlitz, Ger. 43/H3
Gorllwyn (peak), Wal, UK 36/C2
Gorman, Ca, US 148/C3
Gorman, Tx, US 151/E1
Gormanstown, Ire. 34/B4
Gormī, India 96/B2
Gormley, On, Can. 160/U8
Gorna Oryakhovitsa, Bul. 51/G4
Gorner (glacier), Swi. 60/D6
Gornji Milanovac, Yugo. 50/E3
Gornji Vakuf, Bosn. 50/C4
Gorno-Altaysk, Rus. 99/E1
Gornozavodsk, Rus. 69/N4
Gornyak, Rus. 70/F1
Gornyak, Rus. 99/D1
Gornyatskiy, Rus. 73/L3
Gornyy, Rus. 79/L3
Gornyy Balykley, Rus. 71/H2
Gornyy Zerentuy, Rus. 79/H1
Goro, It. 63/F4
Goro, Eth. 118/B4
Goroch'an (peak), Eth. 117/H3
Gorodets, Rus. 69/J4
Gorodok, Bela. 41/N4
Gorodovikovsk, Rus. 73/L4
Gorogoro, Indo. 91/G4
Goroka, PNG 129/G1
Gorom Gorom, Burk. 115/E3
Goromonzi, Zim. 123/F3
Gorong (isl.), Indo. 91/H4
Gorongoza, Moz. 123/G3
Gorongoza, PN da, Moz. 123/G3
Gorontalo, Indo. 91/F3
Goronyo, Nga. 115/G3
Gorredijk, Neth. 52/D3
Gorreh, Iran 103/G4
Gorron, Fr. 57/E4
Gorseinon, Wal, UK 36/B3
Gorshechnoye, Rus. 73/K2
Gorskoye, Ukr. 73/K3
Gorssel, Neth. 52/D4
Gorst, Wa, US 167/B2
Gort, Ire. 32/B3
Gorteen, Ire. 32/B2
Gortin, NI, UK 34/A2
Görwihl, Ger. 60/E2
Goryachiy Klyuch, Rus. 73/K5
Goryn' (riv.), Ukr. 70/C2
Gorzano (peak), It. 65/C2
Gorzów Wielkopolski, Pol. 43/H2
Gos, Eth. 118/C3
Gosainganj, India 96/D2
Göschenen, Swi. 61/E4
Gōse, Japan 83/J7
Gosen, Japan 85/F2
Gosford, Austl. 133/E1
Gosforth, Eng, UK 35/G2
Goshen, In, US 160/D4
Goshen, NY, US 161/J4
Goshen, NS, Can. 159/G3

Goshen – Gros-Mo

Goshen, Ut, US 147/H4
Goshen, NJ, US 168/D5
Goshen Hole (lowland), Ne, Wy, US 154/B4
Goshogawara, Japan 82/B3
Goshute (lake), Nv, US 147/F3
Goshute (valley), Nv, US 147/F3
Goshute Ind. Res., Nv,Ut, US 147/F4
Goslar, Ger. 53/H5
Gosnell, Ar, US 162/C3
Gospić, Cro. 50/B3
Gosport, In, US 160/C5
Gosport, Al, US 164/E2
Gosport, Eng, UK 37/E5
Gossas, Sen. 114/A3
Gossau, Swi. 61/F3
Gossensass (Colle Isarco), It. 61/H4
Gossersweiler-Stein, Ger. 55/G5
Gostepriimnyy, Rus. 71/M2
Gostilitsy, Rus. 69/S7
Gostishchevo, Rus. 73/J2
Gostivar, FYROM 49/G2
Gostyń, Pol. 43/J3
Gostynin, Pol. 43/K2
Göta (riv.), Swe. 40/G2
Gota, Eth. 118/B3
Götaland (reg.), Swe. 40/E3
Gotebo, Ok, US 152/E3
Göteborg, Swe. 40/D3
Göteborg Och Bohus (co.), Swe. 38/D4
Gotel (mts.), Nga.,Cam. 116/A4
Gotemba, Japan 85/F3
Götene, Swe. 40/E2
Gotha, Ger. 53/H7
Gothenburg, Ne, US 154/D3
Gothèye, Niger 115/F3
Gotland (isl.), Swe. 74/B4
Gotland (co.), Swe. 38/F4
Gotō (isls.), Japan 79/K5
Gotse Delchev, Bul. 49/H2
Gotska Sandön (isl.), Swe. 41/H2
Gotska Sandön NP, Swe. 41/H2
Gōtsu, Japan 84/C3
Gottenheim, Ger. 60/D1
Göttingen, Ger. 53/G5
Gottmadingen, Ger. 61/E2
Gottolengo, It. 62/D3
Gottröta, Swe. 39/B1
Götzis, Aus. 61/F3
Gouarec, Fr. 56/B4
Goubangzi, China 81/A2
Gouda, SAfr. 124/L10
Gouda, Neth. 52/B4
Goudiry, Sen. 114/B3
Gouesnou, Fr. 56/A4
Gouessant (riv.), Fr. 56/C4
Gouet (riv.), Fr. 56/C4
Gough (isl.), StH 26/J7
Gough, Ga, US 163/F4
Gouin (res.), Qu, Can. 141/J4
Goulais (riv.), On, Can. 160/D1
Goulburn (isls.) 127/C2
Goulburn, Austl. 133/D2
Goulburn, North (isl.), Austl. 128/D2
Goulburn, South (isl.), Austl. 128/D2
Gould, Ok, US 152/E3
Gould, Ar, US 153/J4
Gould (mt.), Austl. 130/C3
Gould City, Mi, US 160/D1
Gouldbusk, Tx, US 150/E2
Goulds, Nf, Can. 159/L2
Gouldsboro, Pa, US 168/C1
Gouldtown, Sk, Can. 145/L2
Goulfey, Camr. 116/B2
Goulimine, Mor. 110/C3
Goulmima, Mor. 110/D3
Goulou (peak), China 87/E3
Goulou (mts.), China 87/F4
Goumbou, Mali 114/D3
Gouménissa, Gre. 49/H2
Goundam, Mali 114/E2
Goundi, Chad 116/C3
Gounou Gaya, Chad 116/B3
Goupillières, Fr. 30/H5
Gouraye, Mrta. 114/B3
Gourcy, Burk. 115/E3
Gourdon, Fr. 44/D4
Gouré, Niger 115/H3
Gourin, Fr. 56/B4
Gourits (riv.), SAfr. 124/C4
Gourma (prov.), Burk. 115/F3
Gourma (phys. reg.), Burk. 115/F3
Gourma Rharous, Mali 115/E2
Gournay-en-Bray, Fr. 54/A5
Gouro, Chad 108/C5
Gourock, Sc, UK 33/B5
Goussainville, Fr. 30/K4
Gouvêa, Braz. 187/E3
Gouveia, Port. 46/B2
Gouverneur, NY, US 161/J2
Gouvieux, Fr. 30/K4
Gouville-sur-Mer, Fr. 56/D2
Gouvy, Belg. 55/E3
Gouyave, Gren. 173/N9
Govan, Sk, Can. 156/B2
Govardhan, India 96/A2
Gove (Gove City), Ks, US 152/D1
Gove City (Gove), Ks, US 152/D1
Goverla (peak), Ukr. 72/C3
Governador Archer, Braz. 183/E4
Governador Celso Ramos, Braz. 189/G3
Governador Dix-Sept Rosado, Braz. 183/G4
Governador Eugênio Barros, Braz. 183/E4
Governador Valadares, Braz. 187/E3
Government (hill), SD, US 156/C5
Government (peak), Mi, US 157/K4
Government (peak), Wy, US 154/B3
Government Camp, Or, US 146/C1
Government Palace, VatC. 65/G7
Governor Generoso, Phil. 88/D4
Governors (isl.), NY, US 169/J9
Govĭ Altayn (mts.), Mong. 75/K5
Govi-Altay (prov.), Mong. 78/D2
Govind Sāgar (res.), India 98/D4
Govindapalle, India 95/D2
Govindgarh, India 96/C3
Govindpur, India 95/E1
Gowanda, NY, US 161/G3
Gower, Mo, US 155/G4
Gower (pen.), Wal, UK 36/B3
Gower's Corner, Fl, US 164/L7
Gowk, Iran 101/G3
Gowna (lake), Ire. 32/C2
Gowran, Ire. 32/C4
Gowrie, Ia, US 155/G2
Goxhill, Eng, UK 35/H4
Goya, Arg. 188/E4
Göyçay, Azer. 71/H4
Goyen (riv.), Fr. 56/A4
Goyllarisquizga, Peru 184/B3
Göynük, Turk. 51/K5
Goyt (riv.), Eng, UK 35/F5
Göytäpä, Azer. 103/G2
Goz Beïda, Chad 116/D2
Goz Sassulko (dune), CAfr. 116/D3
Gozaisho-yama (peak), Japan 83/K5
Gözeli, Turk. 102/D2
Gozha (lake), China 99/D5
Gozo (isl.), Malta 67/G3
Gozzano, It. 62/B2
Graaff-Reinet, SAfr. 124/D4
Graafschap (phys. reg.), Neth. 52/D4
Graæted, Den. 39/J6
Graauw, Neth. 52/B6
Graben, Ger. 61/G1
Graberberg (peak), Namb. 124/B2
Grabouw, SAfr. 124/L11
Grabow, Ger. 42/F2
Graça Aranha, Braz. 183/E4
Gračac, Cro. 50/B3
Gračanica, Bosn. 50/D3
Grace, Id, US 147/H2
Grace City, ND, US 156/E4
Gracefield, Qu, Can. 161/H1
Gracemere, Austl. 134/C3
Gracemont, Ok, US 153/E3
Graceville, Mn, US 156/F5
Graceville, Fl, US 165/F2
Grächen, Swi. 60/D5
Grachev Kust, Rus. 71/J2
Grachëvka, Rus. 73/M5
Gracias, Hon. 176/D3
Gracias a Dios (cape), Hon. 177/F3
Graciosa (isl.), Azor., Port. 47/S12
Gradačac, Bosn. 50/D3
Gradaús, Braz. 182/D4
Gradaús, Serra dos (mts.), Braz. 182/D5
Gradisca d'Isonzo, It. 63/G2
Grado, It. 63/G2
Grädö, Swe. 39/C1
Grado, Sp. 46/B1
Grady, Ar, US 153/J3
Grady, Ok, US 153/F3
Grady, Al, US 165/E2
Graettinger, Ia, US 155/G2
Gräfelfing, Ger. 59/E6
Grafenau, Ger. 59/G5
Gräfenberg, Ger. 58/E3
Grafenrheinfeld, Ger. 58/D3
Gräfentonna, Ger. 53/H6
Grafenwöhr, Ger. 59/E3
Graffignana, It. 62/C3
Grafing bei München, Ger. 59/E6
Gråfjell (peak), Nor. 40/C1
Graford, Tx, US 153/E4
Grafrath, Ger. 61/H1
Grafton, Austl. 132/E1
Grafton, NB, Can. 158/D2
Grafton, Il, US 155/J4
Grafton, ND, US 156/F3
Grafton, Wi, US 160/C3
Grafton, WV, US 160/F5
Grafton Passage, Austl. 134/B2
Gragnano, It. 65/D6
Graham, On, Can. 157/J3
Graham, Ok, US 153/F3
Graham, Tx, US 153/E4
Graham (lake), Me, US 158/C3
Graham, Fl, US 165/G3
Graham (mt.), Az, US 149/H4
Graham (isl.), BC, Can. 140/C3
Graham (isl.), Nun, Can. 141/S7
Graham, NC, US 163/H2
Graham Bell (isl.), Rus. 74/G1
Graham Land (phys. reg.), Ant. 192/V
Grahamdale, Mb, Can. 156/E2
Grahamstown, SAfr. 124/D4
Grahamsville, NY, US 161/J4
Graian Alps (range), Fr. 66/E1
Graiguenamanagh, Ire. 32/D4
Grain (coast), Libr. 114/C5
Grain, Eng, UK 37/G4
Grainau, Ger. 61/H3
Grainfield, Ks, US 154/D4
Grajagan, Indo. 89/F5
Grajaú, Braz. 183/E4
Grajaú (riv.), Braz. 183/E4
Grajewo, Pol. 41/K5
Gram, Den. 40/C4
Gramada, Bul. 50/F4
Gramastetten, Aus. 59/H6
Gramat (plat.), Fr. 44/D4
Gramat, Fr. 44/D4
Gramatneusiedl, Aus. 51/N7
Grammont (peak), Fr. 64/D5
Grampian (mts.), Sc, UK 33/B3
Grampians NP, Austl. 132/B3
Gramsbergen, Neth. 52/D3
Gramsh, Alb. 49/G2
Gran, Nor. 40/D1
Gran (des.), Mex. 148/E4
Gran Altiplanicie Central (plat.), Arg. 191/C6
Gran Bajo de San Julián (plain), Arg. 191/C6
Gran Bajo Oriental (plain), Arg. 190/C5
Gran Canaria (int'l arpt.), Sp. 110/B4
Gran Canaria (isl.), Sp. 110/B4
Gran Chaco (plain), SAm. 179/C5
Gran Isla del Maíz (isl.), Nic. 177/F3
Gran Laguna Salada (lag.), Arg. 190/D5
Gran Paradiso (peak), It. 64/D1
Gran Paradiso, PN (Nat'l Parc), It. 45/G4
Gran Piedra (hill), Cuba 177/H2
Gran Pilastro (peak), It. 45/J3
Gran Quivira, NM, US 149/J3
Gran Sasso d'Italia (mts.), It. 65/C3
Gran Vilaya (ruin), Peru 184/B2
Grana (riv.), It. 64/D4
Granada, Co, US 152/C1
Granada, Col. 180/C4
Granada, Nic. 176/E4
Granada, Sp. 46/D4
Granadilla de Abona, Sp. 110/A3
Granados, Mex. 174/C2
Granard, Ire. 32/C2
Granarolo dell'Emilia, It. 63/E4
Granbury (lake), Tx, US 151/E1
Granbury, Tx, US 151/F1
Granby, Mo, US 153/G2
Granby, Qu, Can. 161/K2
Granby, Co, US 154/B3
Granby (riv.), BC, Can. 144/E3
Grand (isl.), Mi, US 157/L4
Grand (lake), Nb, Can. 158/E2
Grand (falls), Kenya 119/B2
Grand (lake), Nf, Can. 141/L4
Grand (riv.), Ia,Mo, US 155/G3
Grand (canal), China 80/D4
Grand Aféri, C.d'Iv. 114/E5
Grand Arc (peak), Fr. 64/C1
Grand Bahama (isl.), Bahm. 139/K7
Grand Bank, Nf, Can. 159/K2
Grand Bassa (co.), Libr. 114/C5
Grand-Bassam, C.d'Iv. 114/E5
Grand Bay, NB, Can. 158/D3
Grand Bay, Al, US 164/D2
Grand Bérard (peak), Fr. 64/C4
Grand Blanc, Mi, US 160/E3
Grand Brière (swamp), Fr. 56/C6
Grand Calumet (isl.), Qu, Can. 161/H2
Grand Canal d'Alsace (canal), Fr. 60/D2
Grand Cane, La, US 150/H1
Grand Canyon, Az, US 149/F2
Grand Canyon (canyon), Az, US 149/F2
Grand Canyon Caverns, Az, US 149/F3
Grand Canyon Nat'l Park, Az, US 149/F2
Grand Canyon-Parashant Nat'l Mon., Ut, US 149/F2
Grand Cape Mount (co.), Libr. 114/C5
Grand Cayman (isl.), Cay. 172/E4
Grand Centre, Ab, Can. 140/E3
Grand Cess, Libr. 114/C5
Grand-Charmont, Fr. 60/C2
Grand Chenier, La, US 164/B3
Grand Colombier (peak), Fr. 60/B6
Grand Combine (peak), Swi. 60/D6
Grand Coulee (dam), Wa, US 144/E4
Grand Coulee, Wa, US 144/E4
Grand-Couronne, Fr. 57/G2
Grand Drumont (peak), Fr. 60/C2
Grand Erg de Bilma (des.), Niger 108/B5
Grand Erg Occidental (des.), Alg. 107/C1
Grand Erg Oriental (des.), Alg. 107/C1
Grand Eyvia (riv.), It. 64/D1
Grand Falls, NB, Can. 158/D2
Grand Falls, Nf, Can. 159/K1
Grand Forks (A.F.B.), ND, US 156/F4
Grand Forks, ND, US 156/F4
Grand Forks, BC, Can. 144/E3
Grand-Fort-Philippe, Fr. 54/B2
Grand-Fougeray, Fr. 56/D5
Grand Galibier (peak), Fr. 64/C2
Grand Goâve, Haiti 177/H2
Grand Gorge, NY, US 161/J3
Grand Harbour, NB, Can. 158/D3
Grand Haven, Mi, US 160/C3
Grand Island, Ne, US 154/E3
Grand Isle, Vt, US 161/K2
Grand Isle, La, US 164/D3
Grand Jide (co.), Libr. 114/D5
Grand Junction, Co, US 147/J4
Grand Junction, Tn, US 162/C3
Grand-Lahou, C.d'Iv. 114/D5
Grand Manan (isl.), NB, Can. 158/D3
Grand Marais, Mn, US 157/J4
Grand Marais, Mb, Can. 156/F2
Grand Marsh, Wi, US 155/K2
Grand Meadow, Mn, US 155/H2
Grand Mont (pt.), Fr. 56/C5
Grand Mont Ruan (peak), Fr. 60/C5
Grand Mound, Wa, US 144/C4
Grand Muveran (peak), Swi. 60/D5
Grand North Fork (riv.), SD, US 156/C5
Grand Parpaillon (peak), Fr. 64/C4
Grand Pic de Belledonne (peak), Fr. 64/B2
Grand Pinier (peak), Fr. 64/C3
Grand-Popo, Ben. 115/F5
Grand Portage, Mn, US 157/K4
Grand Portage Ind. Res., Mn, US 157/J4
Grand Portage Nat'l Mon., Mn, US 157/K4
Grand Portal (pt.), Mi, US 160/C1
Grand Prairie, Tx, US 150/L7
Grand Prairie (plain), Ar, US 162/B3
Grand Pré Nat'l Hist. Park, NS, Can. 158/E3
Grand Queyron (peak), Fr. 64/D3
Grand Rapids, Mn, US 157/H4
Grand Rapids, ND, US 156/E4
Grand Rapids (dam), Mi, US 160/C2
Grand Rapids, Mi, US 160/D3
Grand Rhône (riv.), Fr. 44/F5
Grand Ronde, Or, US 146/B1
Grand Ronde (riv.), Wa, US 144/F4
Grand Russel (chan.), UK 56/C2
Grand Saline, Tx, US 151/G1
Grand Santi, FrG. 182/C1
Grand South Fork (riv.), SD, US 156/C5
Grand Staircase-Escalante Nat'l Mon., Ut, US 149/F2
Grand Taureau (peak), Fr. 60/C4
Grand Teton (peak), Wy, US 147/H2
Grand Teton NP, Wy, US 147/H2
Grand Tower, Il, US 162/C2
Grand Traverse (bay), Mi, US 160/D2
Grand Valley, On, Can. 160/S8
Grand Veymont (peak), Fr. 64/B3
Grand View, Id, US 146/E2
Grand, East Fork (riv.), Ia, Mo, US 155/G3
Grand, South Fork (riv.), SD, US 154/C1
Grandcamp-Maisy, Fr. 57/D2
Grandcour, Swi. 60/C4
Grande (peak), It. 48/C4
Grande (peak), NM, US 152/C2
Grande (peak), It. 65/C3
Grande (bay), Arg. 179/C8
Grande (pt.), Pan. 177/G4
Grande (riv.), Uru. 191/K10
Grande (isl.), Braz. 186/B4
Grande (pt.), Chile 188/B3
Grande (lake), Braz. 181/H5
Grande Autane (peak), Fr. 64/C3
Grande Cache, Ab, Can. 140/E3
Grande Comore (isl.) 107/G6
Grande de Curuaí (lake), Braz. 182/C3
Grande de Gurupá (isl.), Braz. 182/D3
Grande de Manacapuru (lake), Braz. 182/A3
Grande de Tierra del Fuego (isl.), Chile,Arg. 191/D7
Grande do Curuaí (lake), Braz. 181/H5
Grande Pointe, Mb, Can. 156/F3
Grande Prairie, Ab, Can. 140/E3
Grande Ronde (riv.), Or, US 146/E1
Grande Saline, Haiti 177/H2
Grande Sassière (peak), Fr. 64/D1
Grande Séolane (peak), Fr. 64/C4
Grande, Serra (mts.), Braz. 181/F4
Grande-Anse, Qu, Can. 158/A2
Grande-Cascapédia, Qu, Can. 158/E1
Grande-Entrée, Qu, Can. 159/G2
Grande-Rivière, Qu, Can. 158/E1
Grande-Synthe, Fr. 54/B1
Grande-Terre (isl.), Guad. 173/J4
Grande-Vallée, Qu, Can. 158/E1
Grandes Jorasses (peak), It. 60/D6
Grandes Rousses (range), Fr. 64/C2
Grandfalls, Tx, US 151/C2
Grandfield, Ok, US 153/E3
Grandfresnoy, Fr. 54/B5
Grandin, Mo, US 162/B2
Grândola, Port. 46/A3
Grandpuits-Bailly-Carrois, Fr. 30/L6
Grandson, Swi. 60/C4
Grandview, Mb, Can. 156/D2
Grandview, Tx, US 151/F1
Grandview, Wa, US 144/E4
Grandview Park, Pa, US 161/G4
Grandview Plaza, Ks, US 153/F1
Grandvillars, Fr. 60/C2
Grandville, Mi, US 160/D3
Grandvilliers, Fr. 54/A4
Grâne, Fr. 64/A3
Graneros, Chile 190/N9
Graney (riv.), Ire. 32/B4
Granfjället (peak), Swe. 40/E1
Grange (riv.), Ire. 32/B3
Grange, Eng, UK 35/F3
Grange (nbrhd.), Austl. 131/M8
Grange, Mont de (peak), Fr. 60/C5
Grangemouth, Sc, UK 33/C4
Granger (mt.), Yk, Can. 171/L3
Granger, In, US 160/C4
Granger, Tx, US 151/F2
Granger, Wa, US 144/D4
Granges-sur-Vologne, Fr. 60/C1
Grängesberg, Swe. 40/F1
Grangeville, Id, US 144/F5
Granier (peak), Fr. 64/B2
Granite, Ok, US 152/E3
Granite (peak), Mt, US 147/J1
Granite (peak), Mt, US 147/G1
Granite (mtn.), Mt, US 145/J4
Granite Bay, BC, Can. 144/B2
Granite Canon, Wy, US 154/B3
Granite City, Il, US 155/J4
Granite Falls, Mn, US 155/G1
Granite Shoals, Tx, US 151/E2
Graniteville, Mo, US 162/B2
Granity, NZ 135/B3
Granja, Braz. 183/F3
Grankulla (Kauniainen), Fin. 39/E4
Grannis, Ar, US 153/G3
Granollers, Sp. 47/L6
Grans, Fr. 64/B5
Grant, Al, US 162/D3
Grant, Co, US 152/B1
Grant, Mi, US 160/D3
Grant, Mt, US 147/G1
Grant, Ne, US 154/D3
Grant (range), Nv, US 146/F4
Grant (mt.), Nv, US 146/D4
Grant City, Mo, US 155/G3
Grant-Kohrs Ranch Nat'l Hist. Site, Mt, US 145/H4
Grantham, Eng, UK 35/H6
Grantley Adams (int'l arpt.), Bar. 173/P9
Granton, Wi, US 155/J1
Grantown-on-Spey, Sc, UK 33/C2
Grants, NM, US 149/J3
Grants Pass, Or, US 146/B2
Grantsboro, NC, US 163/J3
Grantsburg, Wi, US 157/H5
Grantsdale, Mt, US 145/G4
Grantsville, WV, US 163/G1
Grantville, Ga, US 162/E4
Granville, Fr. 56/D3
Granville (lake), Mb, Can. 140/F3
Granville, Il, US 155/K3
Granville Ferry, NS, Can. 158/E3
Grapeland, Tx, US 151/G2
Grapeview, Wa, US 167/B3
Grapeview, Wa, US 144/C4
Grapevine, Ar, US 153/H3
Grapevine (lake), Tx, US 150/K6
Grapevine, Tx, US 150/K7
Gras-Ellenbach, Ger. 58/B3
Grasberg, Ger. 53/F2
Grasbrunn, Ger. 59/E6
Graskö (isl.), Swe. 39/C1
Graskop, SAfr. 123/F5
Grasmere, Eng, UK 35/E3
Grasmere, SAfr. 124/P13
Grasmere, BC, Can. 144/G3
Grasø (isl.), Swe. 40/H1
Grasonville, Md, US 168/B6
Grass (lake), Il, US 167/P15
Grass Creek, Wy, US 147/J2
Grass Range, Mt, US 145/K4
Grass Valley, Ca, US 146/C4
Grasse, Fr. 64/C5
Grassie, On, Can. 160/T9
Grassina, It. 63/E6
Grassington, Eng, UK 35/G3
Grasslands NP, Sk, Can. 145/L3
Grassy (peak), WV, US 163/G1
Grassy, Austl. 133/B5
Grassy Butte, ND, US 156/C4
Grassy Key (isl.), Fl, US 165/H5
Grassy Lake, Ab, Can. 145/J3
Grassy Park, SAfr. 124/L11
Grästorp, Swe. 40/E2
Grates Cove, Nf, Can. 159/L1
Gratkorn, Aus. 50/B2
Gratz, Pa, US 168/B2
Graubünden (canton), Swi. 61/F4
Graulhet, Fr. 44/E5
Graus, Sp. 47/F1
Gravatá, Braz. 183/H5
Grave, Neth. 52/C5
Grave of Sitting Bull, SD, US 156/D5
Gravedona, It. 61/F5
Gravel Island Nat'l Wild. Ref., Wi, US 160/C2
Gravelbourg, Sk, Can. 145/L3
Gravelines, Fr. 54/B2
Gravellona Toce, It. 61/E6
Gravelly, Ar, US 153/H3
Gravelotte, SAfr. 123/F4
Gravenhurst, On, Can. 161/G2
Grävenwiesbach, Ger. 58/B2
Gravesend, Eng, UK 30/E2
Graveson, Fr. 64/A5
Gravigny, Fr. 57/G2
Gravina di Puglia, It. 48/E2
Gray, Fr. 60/B3
Gray, Me, US 161/L3
Gray, Ga, US 163/F4
Grayback (mtn.), Or, US 146/B2
Grayland, Wa, US 144/B4
Grayling, Ak, US 171/F3
Grayling, Mi, US 160/D2
Grays, Eng, UK 30/E2
Grays (lake), Id, US 147/H2
Grays (har.), Wa, US 144/B4
Grays Lake NWR, Id, US 147/H2
Grayslake, Il, US 167/P15
Grayson, Sk, Can. 156/C2
Grayson, La, US 164/B1
Grayson, Ky, US 163/F1
Graysville, Al, US 162/D4
Grayville, Il, US 162/D1
Graz, Aus. 50/B2
Grazalema, Sp. 46/C4
Grazzanise, It. 65/D5
Greåker, Nor. 40/D2
Gréasque, Fr. 64/B6
Great (plain), US 152/D1
Great (isl.), Ire. 32/B6
Great (bay), NH, US 158/B4
Great (falls), NJ, US 169/J8
Great (lake), Austl. 132/C4
Great (basin), Nv, US 142/C4
Great (basin), Nv, US 140/E4
Great (falls), Mt, US 145/J4
Great Abaco (isl.), Bahm. 139/K7
Great Alföld (plain), Hun. 67/J1
Great Alföld (plain), Hun., Yugo. 50/D2
Great America, Ca, US 167/L12
Great Australian Bight (bay), Austl. 127/B4
Great Baddow, Eng, UK 30/E1
Great Bahama (bank), Bahm. 173/F2
Great Barford, Eng, UK 37/F2
Great Barrier (isl.), NZ 127/H6
Great Barrier (reef), Austl. 127/D2
Great Barrier Reef Marine Park, Austl. 129/G3
Great Barrington, Ma, US 161/K3
Great Barton, Eng, UK 37/G2
Great Basin NP, Nv, US 147/F4
Great Bear (lake), NW, Can. 140/D2
Great Bend, Ks, US 153/E1
Great Bend, NY, US 161/J2
Great Bitter (lake), Egypt 104/C4
Great Bookham, Eng, UK 30/B3
Great Brak (riv.), SAfr. 124/C3
Great Britain (isl.), UK 29/D3
Great Burstead, Eng, UK 30/E2
Great Cedar (swamp), NJ, US 168/D5
Great Coco (isl.), Myan. 93/F5
Great Cornard, Eng, UK 37/G2
Great Cumbrae (isl.), Sc, UK 33/B5
Great Dismal Swamp NWR, Va, US 163/J2
Great Divide (basin), Wy, US 147/J2
Great Dividing (range), Austl. 127/D2
Great Dunmow, Eng, UK 37/G3
Great Egg (har.), NJ, US 168/D5
Great Egg Harbor (riv.), NJ, US 168/D4
Great Exhibition (bay), NZ 135/C1
Great Exuma (isl.), Bahm. 139/K7
Great Falls, Mb, Can. 156/F2
Great Falls, Mt, US 145/J4
Great Falls, SC, US 163/G3
Great Fish (riv.), SAfr. 124/D4
Great Fish (pt.), SAfr. 124/D4
Great Gransden, Eng, UK 37/F2
Great Guana Cay (isl.), Bahm. 173/F3
Great Harwood, Eng, UK 35/F4
Great Himalaya (range), Asia 92/D2
Great Inagua (isl.), Bahm. 139/K7
Great Indian (des.), India,Pak. 92/B2
Great Karoo (plat.), SAfr. 124/C4
Great Kei (riv.), SAfr. 124/D4
Great Lakes Nav. Trg. Sta., Il, US 160/C3
Great Miami (riv.), Oh, US 160/D4
Great Milton, Eng, UK 37/E3
Great Mis Tor (hill), Eng, UK 36/B5
Great Missenden, Eng, UK 37/F3
Great Moose (lake), Me, US 158/C3
Great Mosque (Masjid Raya), Indo. 89/B2
Great Neck, NY, US 169/L8
Great Nicobar (isl.), India 93/F6
Great Ouse (riv.), Eng, UK 37/E2
Great Palace, Rus. 69/S7
Great Palace, Rus. 69/T7
Great Peconic (bay), NY, US 169/F2
Great Pee Dee (riv.), SC, US 163/H3
Great Piece Meadows (swamp), NJ, US 169/H8
Great Rift (valley), Afr. 121/G4
Great Ruaha (riv.), Tanz. 119/A3
Great Sacandara (lake), NY, US 161/J3
Great Salt (lake), Ut, US 139/F5
Great Salt Lake (des.), Ut, US 142/D3
Great Salt Plains (lake), Ok, US 153/E2
Great Sand (hills), Sk, Can. 145/K2
Great Sand Dunes Nat'l Park, Co, US 149/K2
Great Sand Sea (des.), Egypt,Libya 108/D2
Great Sandy (des.), Austl. 127/B2
Great Scarcies (riv.), SLeo. 114/B4
Great Shelford, Eng, UK 37/G2
Great Shunner Fell (peak), Eng, UK 35/F3
Great Slave (lake), NW, Can. 139/F3
Great Smoky Mountains NP, Tn, US 162/F3
Great South (bay), US 169/E2
Great Stour (riv.), Eng, UK 37/G4
Great Torrington, Eng, UK 36/B5
Great Victoria (des.), Austl. 127/B3
Great Victoria Desert Nature Reserve, Austl. 131/E4
Great Village, NS, Can. 158/F3
Great Wall (wall), China 78/F4
Great Warley, Eng, UK 30/D2
Great Wass (isl.), Me, US 158/D3
Great Western Tiers (mts.), Austl. 132/C4
Great White Heron Nat'l Wildlife Refuge, Fl, US 165/H5
Great Winterhoek (peak), SAfr. 124/L10
Great Witley, Eng, UK 36/D2
Great Yarmouth, Eng, UK 37/H1
Great Zab (riv.), Iraq 103/E2
Great Zimbabwe (ruin), Zim. 123/F4
Greater Accra (pol. reg.), Gha. 115/F5
Greater Antilles (isls.), NAm. 139/J7
Greater Barsuki (des.), Kaz. 71/L3
Greater Buffalo (int'l arpt.), NY, US 160/V10
Greater Cincinnati (int'l arpt.), Oh, US 162/E1
Greater London (co.), Eng, UK 30/D2
Greater Manchester (co.), Eng, UK 35/F4
Greater Pittsburgh (int'l arpt.), Pa, US 160/F4
Greater Rochester (int'l arpt.), NY, US 161/H3
Greater Sunda (isls.), Indo. 90/C4
Greaterville, Az, US 149/G5
Greatham, Eng, UK 35/G2
Grebenhain, Ger. 58/C2
Grebenstein, Ger. 53/G6
Grébon (peak), Niger 115/H2
Grecco, Uru. 191/K10
Greco (cape), Cyp. 104/D2
Greco (peak), It. 65/C4
Greding, Ger. 59/E4
Gredos (mts.), Sp. 46/C2
Grée (riv.), Fr. 192/G
Greece, NY, US 161/H3
Greece (ctry.) 29/G5
Greeley, Ks, US 153/G1
Greeley, Co, US 154/B3
Greeley (Greeley Center), Ne, US 154/E3
Greeley Center (Greeley), Ne, US 154/E3
Greeleyville, SC, US 163/H4
Greely Ford (ford), Nun, Can. 141/S6
Green, Mi, US 157/K4
Green (lake), Wi, US 160/B3
Green (mts.), Vt, US 161/K3
Green (pond), NJ, US 169/H7
Green (riv.), Ut,Wy, US 142/E4
Green, Or, US 146/B2
Green (bay), Wi, US 155/L1
Green, Tx, US 151/F3
Green (swamp), NC, US 163/H3
Green (cape), Austl. 133/E3
Green Bay, Wi, US 160/B2
Green Bay Nat'l Wild. Ref., Wi, US 160/C2
Green City, Mo, US 155/H3
Green Cove Springs, Fl, US 165/H3
Green Creek, NJ, US 168/D5
Green Forest, Ar, US 153/H2
Green Haven, Md, US 168/B5
Green Hill, Tn, US 162/D2
Green Lake, Wi, US 155/K2
Green Lake, Tx, US 150/F3
Green Lane (res.), Pa, US 168/C3
Green Lowther (peak), Sc, UK 33/C6
Green Peter (lake), Or, US 146/B1
Green Pond, Al, US 162/D4
Green Pond, NJ, US 168/D1
Green Ridge, Mo, US 153/H1
Green River, Wy, US 147/J3
Green River, Ut, US 149/G1
Green River (hill), Ky, US 162/E2
Green River, PNG 91/K4
Green River, On, Can. 160/U8
Green River (lake), Ky, US 162/E2
Green Springs, Oh, US 160/E4
Green Valley, Md, US 161/H5
Green Valley, Ca, US 166/B1
Green Valley, Az, US 149/G5
Green Valley Lake, Ca, US 166/C2
Green Village, NJ, US 169/H9
Greenacres, Ca, US 148/C3
Greenacres City, Fl, US 164/P9
Greenbelt (park), Md, US 168/B6
Greenbelt, Md, US 168/B6
Greenbrier, Ar, US 153/H3
Greenbrier (riv.), WV, US 163/G2
Greenbush, Mn, US 156/F3
Greenbushes, Austl. 130/C5
Greencastle, Ire. 34/B1
Greencastle, In, US 160/C5
Greencastle, Pa, US 161/H5
Greencastle, Mo, US 155/H3
Greendale, Wi, US 167/Q14
Greene, NY, US 161/J3
Greene, Ia, US 155/H2
Greeneville, Tn, US 163/F2
Greenfield, Ca, US 148/B2
Greenfield, Ia, US 155/G3
Greenfield, Il, US 155/J4
Greenfield, In, US 160/D5
Greenfield, Mo, US 153/H2
Greenfield, Ma, US 161/K3
Greenfield, Nf, Can. 158/E3
Greenfield, Oh, US 160/E5
Greenfield, Tn, US 162/C2
Greenfield, Wi, US 167/P14
Greenfield Park, Qu, Can. 159/P7
Greenisland, NI, UK 34/C2
Greenland, Mi, US 157/K4
Greenland (sea) 139/R2
Greenland (Kalaallit Nunaat) (dpcy.), Den. 139/N2
Greenlaw, Sc, UK 33/D5
Greenleaf, Ks, US 155/F4
Greenmount, Md, US 168/B4
Greenock, Sc, UK 33/B5
Greenore (pt.), Ire. 32/D5
Greenore, Ire. 34/B3
Greenough (riv.), Austl. 130/B4
Greenough (mt.), Ak, US 171/K2
Greenport, NY, US 169/F1
Greens (peak), Az, US 149/H3
Greens Bayou (riv.), Tx, US 151/M9
Greensboro, Al, US 162/D4
Greensboro, Fl, US 165/F2
Greensboro, Ga, US 163/F4
Greensboro, Md, US 168/C6
Greensboro, NC, US 163/H2
Greensburg, Ks, US 152/E2
Greensburg, Pa, US 161/G4
Greensburg, La, US 164/C2
Greensburg, In, US 160/D5
Greensburg, Ky, US 162/E2
Greenspond, Nf, Can. 159/L1
Greenstreet, Sk, Can. 145/K1
Greensville, On, Can. 160/T9
Greentop, Mo, US 155/H3
Greenup, Ky, US 163/F1
Greenup, Il, US 162/C1
Greenvale, Austl. 134/B2
Greenville, Libr. 114/C5
Greenville, Al, US 164/E2
Greenville, Ca, US 146/C3
Greenville, Fl, US 165/G2
Greenville, Ga, US 162/E4
Greenville, Ky, US 162/D2
Greenville, Il, US 155/K4
Greenville, Mi, US 160/D3
Greenville, Mo, US 162/B2
Greenville, Ms, US 162/B4
Greenville, NC, US 163/J3
Greenville, Oh, US 160/D4
Greenville, SC, US 163/F3
Greenville, Tx, US 153/F4
Greenville, Ut, US 149/F1
Greenwater (riv.), Wa, US 167/D3
Greenwell Point, Austl. 133/E2
Greenwich, Oh, US 160/E4
Greenwich (pt.), Ct, US 169/L8
Greenwich (bor.), Eng, UK 30/D2
Greenwich, Ct, US 169/L7
Greenwich Observatory, Eng, UK 30/D2
Greenwich Village (nbrhd.), NY, US 169/K9
Greenwood, On, Can. 160/U8
Greenwood, Ar, US 153/G3
Greenwood, De, US 168/C6
Greenwood, Fl, US 165/F2
Greenwood, In, US 160/C5
Greenwood, Ms, US 162/B4
Greenwood, SC, US 163/F3
Greenwood (lake), SC, US 163/F3
Greenwood Lake, NY, US 168/D1
Greenwood Village, Co, US 152/B1
Greer, SC, US 163/F3
Greers Ferry (dam), Ar, US 153/J3
Greers Ferry, Ar, US 153/H3
Greers Ferry (lake), Ar, US 162/A3
Greeson (lake), Ar, US 153/H3
Grefrath, Ger. 52/D6
Gregoire Kayibanda (Kigali) (int'l arpt.), Rwa. 121/G3
Gregório (riv.), Braz. 184/D2
Gregory (peak), NC, US 162/F3
Gregory, SD, US 154/E2
Gregory (riv.), Austl. 129/E4
Gregory (range), Austl. 127/D2
Gregory (lake), Austl. 127/B3
Gregory Lake Abor. Land, Austl. 128/B5
Greifswald, Ger. 40/E4
Greifwalder Bodden (bay), Ger. 43/G1
Greilickville, Mi, US 160/D2
Greimberg (peak), Aus. 45/L3
Gremikha, Rus. 68/H1
Gremyachinsk, Rus. 69/N4
Grenå, Den. 40/D3
Grenada (ctry.) 139/L8
Grenada, Ms, US 162/C4
Grenada (lake), Ms, US 162/C4
Grenade, Fr. 44/D5
Grenay, Fr. 54/B3
Grenchen, Swi. 60/D3
Grenfell, Sk, Can. 156/C2
Grenfell, Austl. 133/D1
Grennach (riv.), Ger. 58/D6
Grenoble, Fr. 64/B2
Grenola, Ks, US 153/F2
Grenora, ND, US 156/C3
Grenville (cape), Austl. 129/F2
Grenzach-Wyhlen, Ger. 60/D2
Gréoux-les-Bains, Fr. 64/B5
Gresham, Or, US 146/B1
Gresham Park, Ga, US 163/M7
Gresik, Indo. 89/F4
Gressåmoen NP (nat'l park), Nor. 68/B2
Gressåmoen NP, Nor. 38/E2
Gressan, It. 64/D1
Gresse (riv.), Fr. 64/B3
Gresston, Ga, US 165/G1
Grésy-sur-Aix, Fr. 64/B1
Greta (riv.), Eng, UK 35/E2
Gretna, Austl. 132/C4
Gretna, Mb, Can. 156/F3
Gretna, Sc, UK 35/E2
Gretna, Fl, US 165/F2
Gretna, La, US 164/C3
Gretna, Va, US 163/H2
Gretton, Eng, UK 37/F1
Grettstadt, Ger. 58/D3
Gretz-Armainvilliers, Fr. 30/L5
Greve (riv.), It. 63/E5
Greve, Den. 39/J7
Greve in Chianti, It. 63/E6
Grevelingendam (dam), Neth. 52/B5
Greven, Ger. 53/E4
Grevená, Gre. 49/G2
Grevenbroich, Ger. 55/F1
Grevenmacher (dist.), Lux. 55/F4
Grevenmacher, Lux. 55/F4
Grevesmühlen, Ger. 42/F2
Grevlingen (chan.), Neth. 52/A5
Grey (pt.), NI, UK 34/C2
Grey (riv.), Nf, Can. 159/J2
Grey (cape), Austl. 129/E3
Grey (range), Austl. 127/D3
Grey Abbey, NI, UK 34/C2
Grey Peaks NP, Austl. 134/B2
Grey River, Nf, Can. 159/J2
Greybull (riv.), Wy, US 147/J1
Greybull, Wy, US 147/J1
Greycliff, Mt, US 145/K5
Greylingstad, SAfr. 124/E2
Greylock (mt.), Ma, US 161/K3
Greymouth, NZ 135/B3
Greystoke, Eng, UK 35/F2
Greystones, Ire. 34/B5
Greytown, NZ 135/J9
Greytown, SAfr. 125/E3
Grez-Doiceau, Belg. 55/D2
Grezzana, It. 63/E2
Gribanovskiy, Rus. 73/L2
Gribbin (pt.), Eng, UK 36/B6
Gribingui (riv.), CAfr. 116/C4
Gribingui (pref.), CAfr. 116/C4
Gribingui-Bamingui, Rsv. de Faune du, CAfr. 116/C4
Gridley, Ks, US 153/G1
Gridley, Ca, US 146/C4
Gridley, Il, US 155/K3
Griefensee (lake), Swi. 61/E3
Griekwastad, SAfr. 124/C3
Griend (isl.), Neth. 52/C2
Gries am Brenner, Aus. 61/H3
Griesheim, Ger. 58/B3
Grieskirchen, Aus. 59/G6
Griesskogel (peak), Aus. 61/H3
Griesstätt, Ger. 59/F7
Griffin, Sk, Can. 156/C3
Griffin (lake), Fl, US 164/M6
Griffin, Ga, US 162/E4
Griffiss (A.F.B.), NY, US 161/J3
Griffith, In, US 167/R16
Griffith, Austl. 133/C2
Griffith Park, Ca, US 166/F7
Griffithville, Ar, US 153/J3
Grifton, NC, US 163/J3
Griggs, Ok, US 152/C2
Grigna (peak), It. 61/F6
Grignan, Fr. 64/A4
Grignano Polesine, It. 63/E3
Grignon, Fr. 64/C1
Grigny, Fr. 64/A1
Grigny, Fr. 30/K6
Grigoriopol, Mol. 72/E4
Grigor'yevskoye, Rus. 68/H5
Grijalva (riv.), Mex. 176/C2
Grijpskerk, Neth. 52/D2
Grillby, Swe. 39/A1
Grillon, Fr. 64/A4
Grim (cape), Austl. 132/C4
Grimari, CAfr. 116/D4
Grimaud (riv.), Fr. 64/C6
Grimaud, Fr. 64/C6
Grimbergen, Belg. 55/D2
Grimesland, NC, US 163/J3
Grimethorpe, Eng, UK 35/G4
Grimisuat, Swi. 60/D5
Grimmen, Ger. 40/E4
Grimsby, Eng, UK 35/H4
Grimsby, On, Can. 160/T9
Grimselpass (pass), Swi. 61/E4
Grimsey (isl.), Ice. 38/N6
Grimsley, Tn, US 162/E2
Grimstad, Nor. 40/C2
Grindavík, Ice. 38/M7
Grindelwald, Swi. 60/E4
Grindsted, Den. 40/C4
Grinnel (pen.), Nun, Can. 141/S7
Grinnell, Ia, US 155/H3
Grintavec (peak), Slov. 45/L3
Griqualand East (reg.), SAfr. 124/E3
Griqualand West (reg.), SAfr. 124/C2
Gris-Nez (cape), Fr. 54/A2
Grise Fiord, Nun, Can. 141/S7
Grisslehamn, Swe. 41/H1
Griswold, Ia, US 155/G3
Grisy-les-Plâtres, Fr. 30/J4
Grisy-Suisnes, Fr. 30/L5
Grivaï Pamia, CAfr. 116/C4
Grivette (riv.), Fr. 30/L4
Grizzly (bay), Ca, US 167/K10
Grizzly (mtn.), Id, US 144/F4
Grizzly Flats, Ca, US 146/C4
Grmeč (mts.), Bosn. 50/C3
Groaíras, Braz. 183/F3
Grobbendonk, Belg. 52/B6
Gröben, Ger. 42/Q7
Gröbenzell, Ger. 59/E6
Grobiņa, Lat. 41/J3
Groblersdal, SAfr. 123/F5
Groblershoop, SAfr. 124/C3
Grödby, Swe. 39/A1
Grodków, Pol. 43/J3
Grodzisk Wielkopolski, Pol. 43/J2
Grodzyanka, Bela. 41/N5
Groenlo, Neth. 52/D4
Groesbeck, Tx, US 151/F2
Groesbeek, Neth. 52/C5
Groix, Fr. 56/B5
Groix (isl.), Fr. 44/B3
Grójec, Pol. 43/L3
Grömitz, Ger. 40/D4
Gromo, It. 61/F6
Gronau, Ger. 53/G4
Gronau, Ger. 52/E4
Grong Grong, Austl. 133/C2
Groningen (prov.), Neth. 52/D2
Groningen, Sur. 182/C1
Groningen, Neth. 52/D2
Gronlait (peak), It. 61/H5
Gronlid, Sk, Can. 145/M1
Grono, Swi. 61/F5
Groom, Tx, US 152/D3
Groot Kleeberg (mts.), Namb. 122/C4
Groot Marico (riv.), SAfr. 123/E5
Groot Waterberg (mts.), Namb. 122/C4
Groot-Letabarivier (riv.), SAfr. 123/F4
Groot-Marico, SAfr. 122/E5
Groot-Marico (riv.), SAfr. 124/D2
Grootberg (peak), Namb. 122/B4
Grootdraaidam (res.), SAfr. 124/Q13
Groote Eylandt (isl.), Austl. 127/C2
Grootegast, Neth. 52/D2
Grootfontein, Namb. 122/C3
Grootgeluk, SAfr. 123/E4
Grootvloer (salt pan), SAfr. 124/C3
Gropello Cairoli, It. 62/B3
Gros Islet, StL. 173/N9
Gros Morne (peak), Nf, Can. 141/L4
Gros Morne NP, Nf, Can. 159/J1
Gros Ventre (riv.), Wy, US 147/H2
Gros-Morne, Qu, Can. 158/E1

Map Section
230
231

Halibu – Hedmar

Haliburton, On, Can. 161/G2
Haliburton Highlands (uplands), On, Can. 161/G2
Halifax, Eng, UK 35/G4
Halifax (cap.), NS, Can. 158/F3
Halifax (int'l arpt.), NS, Can. 158/F3
Halifax, Austl. 134/B2
Halifax, NC, US 163/J2
Halifax, Pa, US 168/B3
Halifax, Va, US 163/H2
Halifax (bay), Austl. 127/D2
Halikko, Fin. 41/K1
Halīl (riv.), Iran 101/G3
Halim Perdana Kusuma (int'l arpt.), Indo. 89/D4
Haliun, Mong. 78/D2
Haljala, Est. 41/M2
Häljarp, Swe. 39/J7
Halkett (cape), Ak, US 171/H1
Hall, Austl. 133/B2
Hall (pt.), Austl. 128/B3
Hall (isls.), Micr. 136/E4
Hall (pen.), Nun, Can. 141/K2
Hall (isl.), Ak, US 171/D3
Hall, Mt, US 145/H4
Hall Beach, Nun, Can. 141/H2
Hall Park, Ok, US 153/F3
Halla-san (peak), SKor. 79/K5
Halladale (riv.), Sc, UK 31/S7
Hallam (peak), BC, Can. 144/E1
Hallam (Hellam), Pa, US 168/B4
Halland (co.), Swe. 38/E4
Hallandale, Fl, US 164/P11
Hällbybrunn, Swe. 40/G2
Halle, Ger. 74/B4
Halle, Belg. 55/D2
Halle, Ger. 53/F4
Halle-Neustadt, Ger. 42/F3
Halleck, Nv, US 146/F3
Hällefors, Swe. 40/F2
Hälleforsnäs, Swe. 40/G2
Hallein, Aus. 45/K3
Hallenberg, Ger. 53/F6
Hallertau (reg.), Ger. 59/E5
Hallettsville, Tx, US 151/F3
Halley, UK, Ant. 192/Y
Halliday, ND, US 156/C4
Halling, Eng, UK 30/E3
Hallingdalselvi (riv.), Nor. 40/C1
Hallock, Mn, US 156/F3
Halls, Tn, US 162/C3
Halls Creek, Austl. 128/B4
Hallsberg, Swe. 40/F2
Hallstahammar, Swe. 40/G2
Hallstavik, Swe. 40/H1
Hallsville, Tx, US 151/G1
Hallu (riv.), Fr. 42/B4
Halluin, Fr. 54/C2
Hallum, Neth. 52/C2
Hallwang, Aus. 59/G7
Hallwilersee (lake), Swi. 60/E3
Hallyŏ Haesang NP, SKor. 84/A3
Halmahera (isl.), Indo. 77/M9
Halmahera (sea), Indo. 91/G4
Halmstad, Swe. 40/E3
Ḩalq al Wādī, Tun. 48/B4
Ḩalq al Wādī, Tun. 67/F4
Hals, Den. 40/D3
Hälsingborg (Helsingborg), Swe. 40/E3
Halstead, Ks, US 153/F1
Halstead, Eng, UK 37/G3
Halsteren, Neth. 52/B5
Haltang (riv.), China 78/C4
Haltemprice, Eng, UK 35/H4
Haltern, Ger. 53/E5
Haltom City, Tx, US 150/K7
Halton (co.), On, Can. 160/T8
Halton (co.), Eng, UK 35/F5
Halton Hills, On, Can. 160/T8
Haltwhistle, Eng, UK 35/F2
Haludpukhur, India 97/F4
Halver, Ger. 53/E6
Halverder Aa (riv.), Ger. 53/E4
Ham, Fr. 54/C4
Ham, Chad 116/B3
Ham Lake, Mn, US 157/H5
Ham River, Namb. 124/B3
Ham, Oued El (riv.), Alg. 112/G5
Ham-sous-Varsberg, Fr. 55/F5
Hamada, Japan 84/C3
Hamada de Tinrhert (plat.), Alg. 111/G4
Hamada du Drâa (plat.), Alg. 110/D3
Hamada Safia (plat.), Mali 110/D5
Hamadān, Iran 103/G3
Hamadān (gov.), Iran 103/G3
Hamādat Marzūq (plat.), Libya 111/H4
Ḩamādat Tinghert (uplands), Libya 111/H3
Ḩamāh, Syria 104/E2
Ḩamāh (prov.), Syria 104/E2
Hamajima, Japan 83/L7
Hamakita, Japan 85/E3
Hamam, Turk. 104/E1
Hamamatsu, Japan 85/E3
Hamami (reg.), Mrta. 110/C5
Hamanaka, Japan 82/D2
Hamar, Nor. 40/D1
Ḩamāţah (peak), Egypt 109/G3
Hamath Tiberias NP, Isr. 105/D3
Hamatombetsu, Japan 82/C1
Hambergen, Ger. 53/F2
Hamble, Eng, UK 37/E5
Hambleton (hills), Eng, UK 35/G3
Hambühren, Ger. 53/G3
Hamburg, Ar, US 153/J4
Hamburg (state), Ger. 40/D5
Hamburg, NY, US 161/G3
Hamburg, Ger. 53/G1
Hamburg, Ia, US 155/G3
Hamburg, Pa, US 168/C2
Hamburg, NJ, US 168/D1
Hamburg (Fuhlsbüttel) (int'l arpt.), Ger. 53/G1
Ḩamḑ (wadi), SAr. 100/C3
Ḩamḑah, SAr. 100/D5
Ḩamdānah, SAr. 100/D5
Hamden, Ct, US 161/K4
Hamden, NY, US 161/J3
Hamden, Oh, US 163/F1
Häme (prov.), Fin. 38/G3
Hämeenkyrö, Fin. 41/K1
Hämeenlinna, Fin. 41/L1
Hamelin, Austl. 130/B3
Hamelin Pool (bay), Austl. 130/B3
Hameln, Ger. 53/G4
Hamero Hadad, Eth. 118/B4
Hamersley (range), Austl. 127/A3
Hamersley Range NP, Austl. 130/C2
Hamersville, Oh, US 162/F1
Hamford Water (inlet), Eng, UK 37/H3
Hamgyŏng (mts.), NKor. 79/K3
Hamgyŏng-bukto (prov.), NKor. 81/E2
Hamgyŏng-namdo (prov.), NKor. 81/D2
Hamhŭ-si (prov.), NKor. 81/D3
Hamhŭng, NKor. 81/D3
Hami, China 78/C3
Ḩamīdīyeh, Iran 103/G4
Hamill, SD, US 154/E2
Hamilton, Austl. 132/B3
Hamilton, On, Can. 160/T9
Hamilton (har.), On, Can. 160/T9
Hamilton (inlet), Nf, Can. 139/M4
Hamilton, NZ 135/C2
Hamilton, Sc, UK 33/B5
Hamilton, Al, US 162/D3
Hamilton (mt.), Ca, US 167/L12
Hamilton, Co, US 147/K3
Hamilton (lake), Fl, US 164/M7
Hamilton, Ga, US 162/E4
Hamilton, Ks, US 153/F2
Hamilton, Mi, US 160/C3
Hamilton, Mo, US 155/H4
Hamilton, Mt, US 145/G4
Hamilton, NY, US 161/J3
Hamilton (mtn.), NY, US 161/J3
Hamilton, Oh, US 160/D5
Hamilton, Tx, US 151/E2
Hamilton Mil. Res., NY, US 169/J9
Hamilton-Wentworth (co.), On, Can. 160/S9
Ḩamīm (wadi), Libya 108/D2
Hamina, Fin. 41/M1
Hamiota, Mb, Can. 156/D2
Hamīrpur, India 98/D4
Hamīrpur, India 96/C3
Hamju, NKor. 81/D3
Hamlet, NC, US 163/H3
Hamlin, Tx, US 152/D4
Hamlin, WV, US 163/F1
Hamm, Ger. 55/G2
Hamm, Ger. 58/B3
Hamm, Ger. 53/E5
Hamma-Bouziane, Alg. 112/K6
Ḩammām Al Anf, Tun. 48/B4
Ḩammāmāt (gulf), Gabon 111/H1
Ḩammāmāt (gulf), Tun. 66/F3
Hammanskraal, SAfr. 123/F5
Hammarland, Fin. 41/H1
Hammarön (isl.), Swe. 40/E2
Hammarsjön (lake), Swe. 39/L7
Hammarstrand, Swe. 38/F3
Hamme, Belg. 55/D1
Hamme (riv.), Ger. 53/F2
Hammel, Den. 40/C3
Hammelburg, Ger. 58/C2
Hammer (cr.), Pa, US 168/B3
Hammerfest, Nor. 38/G1
Hammershus, Den. 40/F4
Hammersmith and Fulham (bor.), Eng, UK 30/A1
Hammett, Id, US 146/F2
Hamminkeln, Ger. 52/D5
Hammon, Ok, US 152/E3
Hammonasset (pt.), Ct, US 169/F1
Hammond, In, US 160/C4
Hammond, La, US 164/C2
Hammond, Mt, US 154/B1
Hammond Street, Eng, UK 30/C1
Hammonton, NJ, US 168/D4
Hamnvik, Nor. 38/F1
Hamois, Belg. 55/E3
Hamon, Congo 120/C4
Hamont-Achel, Belg. 52/C6
Hamoud, Mrta. 114/C3
Hampden, ND, US 156/E3
Hampden, NZ 135/B4
Hampden Sydney, Va, US 163/H2
Hampshire, Il, US 155/K2
Hampshire Downs (hills), Eng, UK 37/E4
Hampstead (nbrhd.), Eng, UK 30/C2
Hampstead, Md, US 168/B4
Hampton, Ar, US 153/H4
Hampton, Fl, US 165/G3
Hampton, Ia, US 155/H2
Hampton, NB, Can. 158/E3
Hampton, NH, US 161/L3
Hampton, Or, US 146/C2
Hampton, Pa, US 168/A4
Hampton, SC, US 163/G4
Hampton, Tn, US 163/F2
Hampton, Va, US 163/J2
Hampton Bays, NY, US 169/F2
Hampton Court, Eng, UK 30/C2
Hampton Nat'l Hist. Site, Md, US 168/B5
Hampton Park (nbrhd.), Austl. 132/G6
Hampton Roads (est.), Va, US 163/J2
Hamp'yŏng, SKor. 81/D5
Ḩamrat ash Shaykh, Sudan 117/E2
Hamtramck, Mi, US 167/F7
Hamuku, Indo. 91/J4
Hamura, Japan 83/C2
Hamyang, SKor. 81/D5
Hamyŏl, SKor. 81/D4
Han (riv.), China 77/M6
Hana (riv.), India 96/C5
Hanahan, SC, US 163/G4
Hanainef, Erit. 118/B2
Hanak, Turk. 71/G4
Ḩanak, SAr. 109/H3
Hanamaki, Japan 82/B4
Hanan, Eth. 118/C4
Hanang (peak), Tanz. 119/A3
Hanau, Ger. 58/B2
Hanazono, Japan 83/C1
Hanceville, Al, US 162/D3
Hancheng, China 80/B4
Hanches, Fr. 57/G3
Hancock (lake), Fl, US 164/M8
Hancock, Md, US 161/G5
Hancock, Mi, US 157/K4
Hancock, Mn, US 156/G5
Hancock, NY, US 161/J4
Hancock, Wi, US 155/K1
Hancocks Bridge, NJ, US 168/C5
Handa, Japan 83/L6
Handae-ri, NKor. 81/D2
Handan, China 80/C3
Handawor, India 98/C2
Handel, Sk, Can. 145/K1
Handeloh, Ger. 53/G2
Handen, Swe. 39/B1
Handeni, Tanz. 119/B3
Handiā, India 96/D3
Handsworth, Sk, Can. 156/C3
Handsworth, Eng, UK 37/E1
Hanford, Ca, US 148/C2
Hanford Reach Nat'l Mon., Wa, US 144/E4
Hanford Site, Wa, US 144/E4
Hangayn (mts.), Mong. 74/K5
Hanggin Qi, China 80/B3
Hanging Rock (mtn.), NC, US 163/G2
Hangingstone (hill), Eng, UK 36/C5
Hangklip (cape), SAfr. 124/L11
Hangman (cr.), Wa, US 144/F4
Hangö (Hanko), Fin. 41/K2
Hangu, Pak. 98/A3
Hangu, China 80/H7
Hangzhou, China 80/L9
Hangzhou (bay), China 80/L9
Hanhofen, Ger. 58/B4
Hanhöhiy (mts.), Mong. 78/C2
Hani, Turk. 102/E2
Haninge, Swe. 40/H2
Hanja (riv.), Ang. 122/B2
Hanjalipan, Indo. 90/D4
Hanjiang, China 87/H3
Hankensbüttel, Ger. 53/H3
Hankey, SAfr. 124/D4
Hankinson, ND, US 156/F4
Hanko (Hangö), Fin. 41/K2
Hanle, India 99/C5
Hanley, Sk, Can. 145/L2
Hanmer, NZ 135/C3
Hann (mt.), Austl. 128/B3
Hanna, La, US 164/B2
Hanna, Ab, Can. 145/J2
Hannaford, ND, US 156/E4
Hannah, ND, US 156/E3
Hannahs Mill, Ga, US 162/E4
Hannan, Japan 83/H7
Hannibal, Oh, US 160/F5
Hannibal, NY, US 161/H3
Hannibal, Mo, US 155/J4
Hanningfield (res.), Eng, UK 30/E2
Hannō, Japan 83/C2
Hannover, Ger. 53/G4
Hannover (int'l arpt.), Ger. 53/G4
Hannut, Belg. 55/E2
Hanöbukten (bay), Swe. 38/E5
Hanoi (Ha Noi) (cap.), Viet. 86/E4
Hanover, On, Can. 160/F2
Hanover (isl.), Chile 191/B6
Hanover, SAfr. 124/D3
Hanover, Il, US 155/J2
Hanover, In, US 162/E1
Hanover, Ks, US 155/F4
Hanover, Mn, US 157/N6
Hanover, NH, US 161/K3
Hanover, Pa, US 168/B4
Hanover, Va, US 163/J2
Hanover Park, Il, US 167/P16
Hānsdiha, India 97/F3
Hansen (dam), Ca, US 166/F7
Hanshan, China 80/D5
Hānsi, India 98/C5
Hanska (lake), Mn, US 155/G1
Hanson (bay), NZ 135/E3
Hanstedt, Ger. 53/H2
Hanstholm, Den. 40/C3
Hanston, Ks, US 152/E1
Hansville, Wa, US 167/B2
Hantengri Feng (peak), China 99/D3
Hantsport, NS, Can. 158/E3
Hantzsch (riv.), Nun, Can. 141/J2
Hanumāngarh, India 98/C5
Hanuy (riv.), Mong. 78/E2
Hanwood, Austl. 133/C2
Hanyū, Japan 83/D1
Hanyuan, China 86/D2
Hanza, Ang. 120/C5
Hanzhong, China 78/F5
Hao (isl.), FrPol. 137/L6
Haoshan, China 87/G3
Haouach, Ouadi (riv.), Chad 116/D1
Håøya (isl.), Nor. 38/S8
Haparanda, Swe. 68/E2
Hapch'ŏn, SKor. 81/E5
Hapeville, Ga, US 163/M7
Happy Camp, Ca, US 146/B3
Happy Jack, La, US 164/D3
Happy Jack, Az, US 149/G3
Happy Valley (res.), Austl. 131/M9
Happy Valley-Goose Bay, Nf, Can. 141/K3
Haptŏk, SKor. 81/D4
Hāpur, India 96/A1
Ḩaql, SAr. 109/G2
Haquira, Peru 184/C4
Har (lake), Mong. 78/C2
Har Karmel (peak), Isr. 105/C3
Har Meron (peak), Isr. 105/C3
Har Nur, China 79/J2
Har Ramon (peak), Isr. 104/D4
Har Tavor (peak), Isr. 105/C3
Har Us (lake), Mong. 78/C2
Har-Ayrag, Mong. 78/F2
Har-Us (riv.), Mong. 78/D2
Hara, Japan 83/A2
Haraa (riv.), Mong. 78/F2
Ḩaraḑ, SAr. 100/E4
Ḩaraḑ, Yem. 118/B1
Ḩarajah, SAr. 100/D5
Haramachi, Japan 85/G2
Harappa (ruin), Pak. 98/B4
Harare (cap.), Zim. 123/F3
Harare (int'l arpt.), Zim. 123/F3
Haravilliers, Fr. 30/J4
Haraz, Chad 116/C2
Haraze-Mangueigne, Chad 116/D3
Harbel, Libr. 114/C5
Harbeson, De, US 168/C6
Harbin, China 79/K2
Harbiye, Turk. 104/E1
Harbonnières, Fr. 54/B4
Harboøre, Den. 40/C3
Harbor Beach, Mi, US 160/E3
Harbor City (nbrhd.), Ca, US 166/F8
Harbor Springs, Mi, US 160/D2
Harbour Breton, Nf, Can. 159/K2
Harbour Grace, Nf, Can. 159/L2
Harbour Main, Nf, Can. 159/L2
Harburg, Ger. 53/G2
Harburg, Ger. 58/D5
Harbury, Eng, UK 37/E2
Hårby, Den. 40/D4
Hard, Aus. 61/F3
Hardā, India 92/C3
Hardangervidda NP, Nor. 40/B1
Hardap (dam), Namb. 122/C5
Hardau (riv.), Ger. 53/H3
Hardaway, Al, US 162/E4
Hardee (co.), Fl, US 164/M8
Hardeeville, SC, US 163/G4
Hardegsen, Ger. 53/G5
Hardelot-Plage, Fr. 54/A2
Harden City, Ok, US 153/F3
Hardenberg, Neth. 52/D3
Harderwijk, Neth. 52/C4
Hardesar, India 98/C5
Hardheim, Ger. 58/C3
Hardin, Ky, US 162/C2
Hardin, Il, US 155/J4
Hardin, Mt, US 145/L5
Hardin, Tx, US 151/G2
Harding, SAfr. 125/E3
Harding (res.), Ga, US 162/E4
Hardinsburg, Ky, US 162/D2
Hardisty, Ab, Can. 145/J1
Hardoi, India 96/C2
Hardoi Branch (riv.), India 96/C2
Hardricourt, Fr. 30/H4
Hardscrabble Wash (riv.), Az, US 149/H3
Hardtner, Ks, US 153/E2
Hardwār, India 101/L3
Hardwick, Ga, US 163/F4
Hardwood (mtn.), Me, US 161/L1
Hardy, Ar, US 153/J2
Hardy, Ne, US 154/F3
Hardy (pen.), Chile 191/C7
Hare Bay, Nf, Can. 159/K1
Hare Dimona (peak), Isr. 104/D4
Harefield, Eng, UK 30/B2
Harelbeke, Belg. 54/C2
Haren, Neth. 52/D2
Haren, Ger. 53/E3
Hārer, Eth. 118/B3
Harerge (prov.), Eth. 118/B3
Harewa, Eth. 118/B3
Harfleur, Fr. 57/F1
Harford (co.), Md, US 168/B4
Hargele, Eth. 118/B4
Hargesheim, Ger. 55/G4
Hargeville, Fr. 30/H5
Hargeysa, Som. 118/C3
Hargeysa (int'l arpt.), Som. 118/C3
Harghita (prov.), Rom. 51/G2
Harghita (peak), Rom. 51/G2
Hargīgo, Erit. 118/A2
Harhorin, Mong. 78/E2
Hari (str.), Est. 41/K2
Hari (river), Indo. 89/C3
Hari (riv.), Indo. 90/B4
Ḩarīb, Yem. 118/C2
Haribes, Namb. 122/C5
Harihar, India 95/B3
Hariharganj, India 97/E3
Harīke, India 98/C4
Ḩārim, Syria 104/E1
Harima (sea), Japan 84/D3
Harima (bay), Japan 83/G6
Harima, Japan 83/G6
Ḩarīmā, Jor. 105/D3
Haringey (bor.), Eng, UK 30/C2
Haringhāta (riv.), Bang. 97/G4
Haringvliet (chan.), Neth. 52/B5
Haringvlietdam (dam), Neth. 52/B5
Harīpur, Pak. 98/B3
Harīrūd (riv.), Afg. 77/F6
Ḩāris, WBnk. 105/C4
Harisal, India 92/C3
Harjavalta, Fin. 41/K1
Harker Heights, Tx, US 151/F2
Harlan, Ky, US 163/F2
Harlan, Ia, US 155/G3
Harlan Co. (lake), Ne, US 154/E3
Harlan County (dam), Ne, US 154/E3
Harlech, Wal, UK 34/D6
Harlem (nbrhd.), NY, US 169/K8
Harlem, Ga, US 163/F4
Harlem, Mt, US 145/K3
Harleston, Eng, UK 37/H2
Harleton, Tx, US 151/G1
Hårlev, Den. 39/J7
Harleyville, SC, US 163/G4
Harlingen, Neth. 52/C2
Harlingen, Tx, US 150/F4
Harlington, Eng, UK 37/F3
Harlow, ND, US 156/E3
Harlow, Eng, UK 30/D1
Harlowton, Mt, US 145/K4
Harmannsdorf, Aus. 51/N7
Harmelen, Neth. 52/B4
Harmony, Mn, US 155/H2
Harnātānr, India 97/E2
Harnes, Fr. 54/B3
Harney (valley), Or, US 146/D2
Harney (lake), Or, US 146/D2
Harney (peak), SD, US 154/C2
Harney, Md, US 168/A4
Harni, Bang. 97/H4
Harnoli, Pak. 98/A3
Harö (isl.), Swe. 39/B1
Haro, Sp. 44/B5
Haro (cape), Mex. 174/C3
Harold, Ca, US 166/B1
Harpenden, Eng, UK 37/F3
Harper, Libr. 114/D5
Harper (mt.), Yk, Can. 171/L3
Harper (mt.), Ak, US 171/K3
Harper (lake), Ca, US 148/D3
Harper, Ks, US 153/E2
Harper, Or, US 146/E2
Harper, Tx, US 151/E2
Harper, Wa, US 167/B2
Harper Woods, Mi, US 167/F7
Harpers Ferry Nat'l Hist. Park, WV, US 161/H5
Harpersville, Al, US 162/D4
Harperville, Ms, US 162/C4
Harpeth (riv.), Tn, US 162/D2
Harpstedt, Ger. 53/F3
Harqin Qi, China 79/H3
Harqin Zuoyi Monggolzu Zizhixian, China 80/D2
Ḩarrah, Yem. 118/D2
Harrai, India 96/B4
Harran, Turk. 102/D2
Ḩarrān al 'Awāmīd, Syria 105/F2
Harrell, Ar, US 153/H4
Harricana (riv.), Qu, Can. 141/J4
Harrietsham, Eng, UK 30/F3
Harrietts Bluff, Ga, US 165/H2
Harriman, Tn, US 162/E3
Harriman, NY, US 168/D1
Harrington, Austl. 132/E1
Harrington, De, US 168/C6
Harrington Park, NJ, US 169/K8
Harris (isl.), Sc, UK 31/Q8
Harris (lake), Austl. 131/G4
Harris (mtn.), Tn, US 162/E2
Harris (mt.), Austl. 131/F3
Harris (co.), Tx, US 151/M9
Harrisburg, Or, US 146/B1
Harrisburg, Ne, US 154/C3
Harrisburg, Il, US 162/C2
Harrisburg, Ar, US 162/B3
Harrisburg (cap.), Pa, US 168/B3
Harrisburg (arpt.), Pa, US 168/B3
Harrislee, Ger. 40/C4
Harrismith, SAfr. 124/E3
Harrison (cape), Nf, Can. 141/L3
Harrison (lake), BC, Can. 144/C3
Harrison (bay), Ak, US 171/H1
Harrison, Ar, US 153/H2
Harrison, Ga, US 163/F4
Harrison, Id, US 144/F4
Harrison, Mi, US 160/D2
Harrison, Ne, US 154/C2
Harrison, NJ, US 169/J9
Harrison, NY, US 169/L8
Harrison, Oh, US 160/D5
Harrison, Tn, US 162/E3
Harrisonburg, La, US 164/C2
Harrisonburg, Va, US 163/H1
Harrisonville, Mo, US 153/G1
Harriston, On, Can. 160/F3
Harriston, Ms, US 164/C2
Harristown, Il, US 155/K4
Harrisville, Ms, US 164/C2
Harrisville, Mi, US 160/E2
Harrisville, WV, US 163/G1
Harrodsburg, In, US 162/D1
Harrodsburg, Ky, US 162/E2
Harrogate, Eng, UK 35/G4
Harrogate-Shawnee, Tn, US 162/F2
Harrold, Tx, US 152/E3
Harrow, On, Can. 160/E3
Harrow (bor.), Eng, UK 30/B2
Harrow (nbrhd.), Eng, UK 30/C2
Harrow, Austl. 132/B3
Harry S Truman (dam), Mo, US 153/H1
Harry S Truman (res.), Mo, US 155/H4
Harry S Truman Nat'l Hist. Site, Mo, US 155/G4
Harsefeld, Ger. 53/G2
Harsewinkel, Ger. 53/F5
Harskamp, Neth. 52/C4
Harson's Island, Mi, US 167/G6
Hart, Tx, US 152/C3
Hart, Mi, US 160/C3
Hart (riv.), Eng, UK 30/A3
Hart (isl.), NY, US 169/K8
Hart (lake), Or, US 146/C2
Hart (riv.), Yk, Can. 140/C2
Hart (mtn.), Or, US 146/D2
Hart (mt.), Austl. 128/B4
Hart Fell (peak), Sc, UK 33/C6
Hart Mtn. Nat'l Antelope Refuge, Or, US 146/D2
Ḩartā, Jor. 105/D3
Hartbeesrivier (riv.), SAfr. 124/C3
Harte (mtn.), Can. 156/D1
Hårteigen (peak), Nor. 40/B1
Hartelkanaal (riv.), Neth. 52/B5
Hartford, Libr. 114/C5
Hartford, Al, US 165/F2
Hartford (cap.), Ct, US 161/K4
Hartford, Ks, US 153/G1
Hartford, Ky, US 162/D2
Hartford, NJ, US 168/D4
Hartford, Wi, US 160/B3
Hartford City, In, US 160/D4
Hartheim, Ger. 60/D2
Harthill, Sc, UK 33/C5
Hartington, Ne, US 155/F2
Hartkirchen, Aus. 59/H6
Hartland, NB, Can. 158/D2
Hartland, Vt, US 161/K3
Hartland, Mi, US 167/E6
Hartland (pt.), Eng, UK 36/B4
Hartland, Eng, UK 36/B4
Hartlebury, Eng, UK 36/D2
Hartlepool, Eng, UK 35/G2
Hartlepool (co.), Eng, UK 35/G2
Hartleton, Pa, US 168/A2
Hartley, Eng, UK 30/D2
Hartley, Ia, US 155/G2
Hartley Bay, BC, Can. 171/N5
Hartley Wintney, Eng, UK 30/A3
Hartly, De, US 168/C5
Hartmannberge (mts.), Namb. 122/B3
Hartney, Mb, Can. 156/D3
Harts, WV, US 163/F1
Harts (riv.), SAfr. 122/E5
Harts Range, Austl. 131/G2
Hartsdale, NY, US 169/K7
Hartselle, Al, US 162/D3
Hartsfield Atlanta Int'l (int'l arpt.), Ga, US 163/M7
Hartshill, Eng, UK 37/E1
Hartshorn, Mo, US 153/J2
Hartshorne, Ok, US 153/G3
Hartsön (isl.), Swe. 39/A2
Hartstene (isl.), Wa, US 167/B3
Hartsville, Tn, US 162/D2
Hartsville, SC, US 163/G3
Hartville, Mo, US 153/H2
Hartwell (dam), Ga, US 163/F3
Hartwell, Ga, US 163/F3
Hartwell (res.), SC, US 163/F3
Hartz Mountain NP, Austl. 132/C4
Haruhi, Japan 83/L5
Harun (peak), Indo. 88/A4
Hārūnābād, Pak. 98/B5
Hārūt (riv.), Afg. 101/H2
Harvard, Ma, US 161/L3
Harvard, Il, US 155/K2
Harvard, Ne, US 154/E3
Harvest, Al, US 162/D3
Harvey, ND, US 156/E4
Harvey, Mi, US 157/L4
Harvey, NB, Can. 158/E3
Harvey, Il, US 167/Q16
Harvey, Austl. 130/B5
Harveys (lake), Pa, US 168/B1
Harwich, Eng, UK 37/H3
Harwood, ND, US 156/F4
Harworth, Eng, UK 35/G5
Haryana (state), India 99/C6
Harz (mts.), Ger. 42/F3
Hasan (peak), Turk. 102/C2
Hasan Abdāl, Pak. 98/B3
Hasanpur, India 96/B1
Ḩāşbayyā, Leb. 105/D2
Hasbrouck Heights, NJ, US 169/J8
Hascombe, Eng, UK 30/B3
Hasdo (riv.), India 96/D4
Hase (riv.), Ger. 42/D2
Hasel (riv.), Ger. 58/D1
Haselünne, Ger. 53/E3
Hasenmatt (peak), Swi. 60/D3
Hashaat, Mong. 78/E2
Hashima, Japan 83/L5
Hashimoto, Japan 84/D3
Hashtgerd, Iran 103/G3
Hasi el Farsía (well), WSah. 110/C4
Hāsilpur, Pak. 98/B5
Haskell, Ok, US 153/G3
Haskell, Tx, US 152/E4
Haskell, Ar, US 153/H3
Haslach an der Mühl, Aus. 59/H5
Haslach im Kinzigtal, Ger. 60/E1
Hasle bei Burgdorf, Swi. 60/D3
Haslemere, Eng, UK 37/F4
Hasler (cr.), Mi, US 167/F6
Haslet, Tx, US 150/K7
Haslett, Mi, US 160/D3
Haslev, Den. 39/H7
Haslingden, Eng, UK 35/F4
Haslington, Eng, UK 35/F5
Hasloh, Ger. 53/G1
Hāsmāi, Bang. 97/G3
Haspra, Ukr. 73/H5
Haspres, Fr. 54/C3
Hassa, Turk. 104/E1
Hassan (El Aaiún) (int'l arpt.), WSah. 110/B4
Hassayampa (riv.), Az, US 149/F3
Hassberge (hills), Ger. 58/D2
Hasse, Tx, US 150/E2
Hassel, Ger. 53/G3
Hassel Sound (str.), Nun, Can. 141/S7
Hasselt, Belg. 55/E2
Hasselt, Neth. 52/D3
Hassfurt, Ger. 58/D2
Hassi Bahbah, Alg. 112/G5
Hassi bou Zid (well), Alg. 111/F3
Hassi el Hadjar (well), Alg. 111/G3
Hassi el Mislane (well), Alg. 111/H4
Hassi er Rebib (well), Alg. 111/G2
Hassi Messaoud, Alg. 111/G3
Hässleholm, Swe. 40/E3
Hasslo (int'l arpt.), Swe. 40/G2
Hassloch, Ger. 58/B4
Haste, Ger. 53/G4
Hastings, Fl, US 165/H3
Hastings, Mi, US 160/D3
Hastings, Pa, US 161/G4
Hastings, SLeo. 114/B4
Hastings, NZ 135/D2
Hastings, Ne, US 154/E3
Hastings, Mn, US 157/Q7
Hastings (dam), Mn, US 157/Q7
Hastings, Eng, UK 37/G5
Hastings, Austl. 133/B4
Hastings Battlesite, Eng, UK 37/G5
Hastings-On-Hudson, NY, US 169/K7
Hästveda, Swe. 39/K6
Hasuda, Japan 83/D2
Hasunuma, Japan 83/E2
Hasvik, Nor. 38/G1
Haswell, Co, US 152/C1
Hat (mtn.), Ca, US 146/C3
Hat Chao Mai NP, Thai. 94/B5
Hāt Gāmāria, India 97/E4
Hat Head, Austl. 132/E1
Hat Head NP, Austl. 132/E1
Hat Nai Yang NP, Thai. 94/B5
Hat Yai, Thai. 94/C5
Hat Yai (int'l arpt.), Thai. 94/C5
Hatansuudal, Mong. 78/E3
Hatashō, Japan 83/K5
Hatavch, Mong. 78/G2
Hatay (prov.), Turk. 104/D1
Hatboro, Pa, US 168/C3
Hatch, Ut, US 149/F2
Hatch, NM, US 149/J4
Hatchechubbee, Al, US 162/E4
Hatcher (peak), Arg. 191/B6
Hatches Creek, Austl. 131/G2
Hatchie (riv.), Tn, US 162/C3
Hatchie NWR, Tn, US 162/C3
Hatchineha (lake), Fl, US 165/H3
Haţeg, Rom. 50/F3
Hatfield, Ar, US 153/G3
Hatfield, Eng, UK 30/C1
Hatfield, Austl. 132/B2
Hatfield, Pa, US 168/C3
Hatfield Peverel, Eng, UK 30/E1
Hatgal, Mong. 78/E1
Hāthāzāri, Bang. 97/H4
Hathersage, Eng, UK 35/G5
Hāthras, India 96/B2
Hātia (riv.), Bang. 97/H4
Hātia, North (isl.), Bang. 97/H4
Hātia, South (isl.), Bang. 97/H4
Hato (int'l arpt.), NAnt. 180/D1
Hato Corozal, Col. 180/D3
Hato Mayor, DRep. 173/H4
Hatogaya, Japan 83/D2
Hatoyama, Japan 83/C2
Hatsu (isl.), Japan 83/C3
Hatta, India 96/B3
Hatta, Japan 83/A2
Hattah-Kulkyne NP, Austl. 131/J5
Hattelmala, Fin. 39/E4
Hattem, Neth. 52/D4
Hatten, Fr. 55/G6
Hatten, Ger. 53/F2
Hatteras, NC, US 163/K3
Hatteras (isl.), NC, US 163/K3
Hattersheim am Mein, Ger. 58/B2
Hattiesburg, Ms, US 164/D2
Hattieville, Belz. 176/D2
Hattingen, Ger. 53/E6
Hatton, ND, US 156/F4
Hatton, Sc, UK 33/E2
Hatton, Eng, UK 35/G6
Hatton, Ut, US 149/F1
Hatton, Al, US 162/D3
Hatton, Sk, Can. 145/K2
Hattula, Fin. 41/L1
Håtuna, Swe. 39/A1
Hatvan, Hun. 50/D2
Hatzenbühl, Ger. 58/B4
Hatzfeld, Ger. 53/F6
Hau Bon, Viet. 94/E3
Hau Giang (riv.), Viet. 94/D4
Haubourdin, Fr. 54/B2
Haubstadt, In, US 162/D1
Haud (reg.), Eth. 118/C4
Hauge, Nor. 40/B2
Haugen, Wi, US 157/J5
Haugesund, Nor. 40/A2
Haughton, La, US 153/H4
Hauho, Fin. 39/E3
Haukeligrend, Nor. 40/B2
Haukipudas, Fin. 68/E2
Haune (riv.), Ger. 42/E3
Haunsberg (peak), Aus. 59/F7
Haunstetten, Ger. 58/D6
Hauonselkä (lake), Fin. 39/E3
Hauppauge, NY, US 169/E2
Hauraki (gulf), NZ 135/C2
Haus, Nor. 40/A1
Hausach, Ger. 60/E1
Hausjärvi, Fin. 41/L1
Hausleiten, Aus. 51/N7
Hausstock (peak), Swi. 61/F4
Haut Atlas (mts.), Mor. 110/D3
Haut-Ogooue (prov.), Gabon 120/C3
Haut-Rhin (dept.), Fr. 60/D2
Haut-Zaïre, D.R. Congo 121/F2
Haute-Kotto (pref.), CAfr. 116/D4
Haute-Normandie (pol. reg.), Fr. 44/D2
Haute-Sangha (pref.), CAfr. 116/B4
Haute-Saône (dept.), Fr. 60/B2
Haute-Savoie (dept.), Fr. 60/C5
Hautefeuille, Fr. 30/L5
Hautes Fagnes (uplands), Belg. 55/E3
Hautes-Alpes (dept.), Fr. 64/C3
Hauteurs de Gâtine (uplands), Fr. 44/C3
Hauteville-Lompnes, Fr. 60/B6
Hautmont, Fr. 54/C3
Hautsx (plat.), Alg. 111/E2
Hautsx (plat.), Alg.,Mor. 66/C4
Havana, ND, US 156/F5
Havana, Fl, US 165/F2
Havana, Il, US 155/J3
Havannah, Canal de la (chan.), NCal. 137/V13
Havant, Eng, UK 37/F5
Havasu (lake), Az, Ca, US 148/E3
Havasu Nat'l Wild Ref., Az, US 148/E3
Havasupai Ind. Res., Az, US 149/F2
Havdhem, Swe. 40/H3
Havdrup, Den. 40/E4
Havel (riv.), Ger. 43/G2
Havel (canal), Ger. 42/P6
Havelange, Belg. 55/E3
Haveli, Pak. 98/B4
Haveliān, Pak. 98/B2
Havelländischer Grosser Hauptkanal (canal), Ger. 42/P6
Havelock, NB, Can. 158/E2
Havelock, On, Can. 161/H2
Havelock, NZ 135/C3
Havelock, NC, US 163/J3
Havelock North, NZ 135/D2
Havelte, Neth. 52/D3
Haven, Ks, US 153/F2
Havencore (isl.), Eng, UK 37/G3
Haverfordwest, Wal, UK 36/B3
Haverhill, NH, US 161/K2
Haverhill, Ma, US 161/L3
Haverhill, Fl, US 164/P9
Haverhill, Eng, UK 37/G2
Havering (bor.), Eng, UK 30/D2
Haviland, Ks, US 152/E2
Ḩavīq, Iran 103/G2
Havířov, Czh. 43/K4
Havixbeck, Ger. 53/E5
Havlíčkuv Brod, Czh. 43/H4
Havneby, Den. 40/C4
Havnehage (isl.), Den. 39/G7
Hâvre (riv.), Fr. 56/D6
Havre, Mt, US 145/K3
Havre de Grace, Md, US 168/B4
Havre North, Mt, US 145/K3
Havre-Aubert, Qu, Can. 159/G2
Havre-Saint-Pierre, Qu, Can. 141/K3
Havsa, Turk. 51/H5
Havza, Turk. 70/E4
Haw (peak), NC, US 162/E3
Haw (riv.), NC, US 163/H2
Hawaii (state), US 142/S10
Hawaii (isl.), Hi, US 142/U11
Hawaii Volcanoes Nat'l Pk., Hi, US 142/U11
Hawaiian (isls.), US 137/H2
Hawaiian Gardens, Ca, US 166/F8
Ḩawallī, Kuw. 103/G4
Hawarden, Wal, UK 35/E5
Hawarden, NZ 135/C3
Hawarden, Ia, US 155/F2
Hawea (lake), NZ 135/B4
Hawera, NZ 135/C2
Hawes, Eng, UK 35/F3
Hawesville, Ky, US 162/D2
Haweswater (res.), Eng, UK 35/F2
Hawick, Sc, UK 33/D6
Hawk Point, Mo, US 155/J4
Hawke (bay), NZ 127/H6
Hawke (cape), Austl. 132/E2
Hawker, Austl. 131/H4
Hawkesbury, On, Can. 161/J2
Hawkesbury (pt.), Austl. 128/D2
Hawkesbury (riv.), Austl. 134/G8
Hawkins, Wi, US 157/J5
Hawkins (peak), Ca, US 146/D4
Hawkinsville, Ga, US 163/F4
Hawks Nest (peak), ND, US 156/E4
Hawks Nest, Austl. 132/E2
Hawksbill (mtn.), Va, US 163/H1
Hawley, Mn, US 156/F4
Hawley, Co, US 152/C2
Hawley, Tx, US 151/E1
Haworth, Ok, US 153/G4
Haworth, NJ, US 169/K8
Hawr al Ḩammār (lake), Iraq 103/F4
Ḩawsh 'Īsá, Egypt 113/B3
Hawston, SAfr. 124/L11
Hawthorn Hill, Eng, UK 30/A2
Hawthorn Woods, Il, US 167/P15
Hawthorne, Ca, US 166/F8
Hawthorne, Fl, US 165/G3
Hawthorne, NJ, US 169/J8
Hawthorne, NY, US 169/K8
Hawthorne, Nv, US 146/D4
Hawthorne, Tx, US 151/G2
Hawthorne Ammunition Depot, Nv, US 146/D4
Ḩawwārah, Jor. 105/D3
Hawwārat al Maqţa', Egypt 113/B6
Hawzēn, Eth. 118/A2
Haxby, Eng, UK 35/G3
Haxtun, Co, US 154/C3
Hay, Austl. 133/B2
Hay (cape), Austl. 128/C3
Hay (pt.), Austl. 134/C3
Hay (riv.), Austl. 131/A1
Hay (riv.), Can. 139/F4
Hay (riv.), Ab, BC, Can. 140/E3
Hay, Wal, UK 36/C2
Hay, Wa, US 144/F4
Hay River, NW, Can. 140/E2
Hay Springs, Ne, US 154/C2
Hayachine-san (peak), Japan 82/B4
Hayakawa, Japan 83/A3
Hayama, Japan 83/D3
Hayange, Fr. 55/F5
Haybān (peak), Sudan 117/F3
Haybān, Sudan 117/F3
Haybes, Fr. 55/D4
Haycock, Ak, US 171/F2
Haydān (wadi), Jor. 105/D5
Hayden, Az, US 149/G4
Hayden, Co, US 147/K3
Hayden, Id, US 144/F4
Hayden-Rhodes (aqueduct), Az, US 149/F4
Haydock, Eng, UK 35/F5
Haydon Bridge, Eng, UK 35/F2
Hayes (riv.), Mb, Can. 140/G3
Hayes (nbrhd.), Eng, UK 30/B2
Hayes (pen.), Grld. 141/T7
Hayes (mt.), Ak, US 171/J3
Hayes, SD, US 154/D1
Hayes, Wi, US 160/B2
Hayes Center, Ne, US 154/D3
Hayesville, NC, US 162/F3
Hayfork, Ca, US 146/B3
Hayingen, Ger. 61/F1
Hāyk' (lake), Eth. 117/H4
Haylaastay, Mong. 75/M5
Hayle (riv.), Eng, UK 36/A6
Hayle, Eng, UK 36/A6
Hayling (isl.), Eng, UK 37/F5
Haylow, Ga, US 165/G2
Haymana, Turk. 102/C2
Haynes, ND, US 156/C5
Haynes, Ar, US 162/B3
Haynesville, La, US 153/H4
Hayneville, Al, US 162/D4
Haynin, Yem. 118/D2
Hayrabolu, Turk. 51/H5
Hays, Ks, US 152/E1
Hays, Ab, Can. 145/J2
Hays, Mt, US 145/K4
Haystack (peak), On, Can. 157/K2
Haysville, Ks, US 153/F2
Haysville, In, US 162/D1
Haysyn, Ukr. 72/E3
Hayti, Mo, US 162/C2
Hayti, SD, US 155/F1
Hayvoron, Ukr. 72/E3
Hayward, Wi, US 157/J4
Haywards Heath, Eng, UK 37/F5
Haywood, Ok, US 153/G3
Hazār (mtn.), Iran 103/J4
Hazard, Ky, US 163/F2
Hazāribag, India 97/E4
Hazebrouck, Fr. 54/B2
Hazel, SD, US 154/F1
Hazel, Ky, US 162/C2
Hazel Dell, Wa, US 144/C5
Hazel Green, Al, US 162/D3
Hazel Grove, Eng, UK 35/F5
Hazel Hill, NS, Can. 159/G3
Hazel Park, Mi, US 167/F7
Hazelbrook, Austl. 133/E1
Hazeldean, NB, Can. 158/D2
Hazelhurst, Wi, US 157/K5
Hazelton, ND, US 156/D4
Hazelton, Ks, US 153/E2
Hazelton (peak), Wy, US 147/K1
Hazen (str.), NW,Nun, Can. 141/R7
Hazen (bay), Ak, US 171/E3
Hazen, Ar, US 153/J3
Hazen, ND, US 156/D4
Hazen, Nv, US 146/D4
Hazenmore, Sk, Can. 145/L3
Hāzipur, Bang. 97/H4
Hazlehurst, Ga, US 165/G2
Hazlehurst, Ms, US 164/C2
Hazlemere, Eng, UK 30/A2
Hazlet, NJ, US 169/J10
Hazlet, Sk, Can. 145/K2
Hazleton, Pa, US 168/C2
Hazlett (lake), Austl. 131/F2
Hazor, Isr. 105/D3
Hazratbal Mosque, India 98/C2
Hazro, Pak. 98/B3
Hazu, Japan 83/M6
He (riv.), China 93/K2
He Xian, China 87/F3
He Xian, China 80/D5
Heacham, Eng, UK 37/G1
Head of Bay d'Espoir, Nf, Can. 159/K2
Head of Saint Margarets Bay, NS, Can. 158/F3
Headcorn, Eng, UK 37/G4
Headford, Ire. 32/A3
Headingley, Eng, UK 35/G4
Headland, Al, US 165/F2
Headlands, Zim. 123/G3
Headquarters, Id, US 144/G4
Heads of Ayr (pt.), Sc, UK 33/B6
Heafford Junction, Wi, US 157/K5
Healdsburg, Ca, US 146/B4
Healdton, Ok, US 153/F3
Healesville, Austl. 132/G5
Healy (pass), Ire. 32/A6
Healy, Ak, US 171/J3
Healy, Ks, US 152/D1
Heanor, Eng, UK 35/G6
Heany Junction, Zim. 123/F4
Heard (isl.), Austl. 192/E
Hearne, Tx, US 151/F2
Hearst, On, Can. 141/H4
Heart (riv.), ND, US 156/C4
Heart Butte (dam), ND, US 156/D4
Heart Law (hill), Sc, UK 33/D5
Hearts Hill, Sk, Can. 145/K1
Heath (pt.), QU, Can. 159/G1
Heath, Tx, US 150/L7
Heathcote, Austl. 133/B3
Heathcote NP, Austl. 134/G9
Heatherton, Nf, Can. 159/H1
Heathfield, Eng, UK 37/G5
Heathrow, Fl, US 164/N6
Heathrow (int'l arpt.), Eng, UK 30/B2
Heathsville, Va, US 163/J2
Hebbronville, Tx, US 151/E4
Hebbs Cross, NS, Can. 158/E3
Hebden Bridge, Eng, UK 35/F4
Hebei (prov.), China 78/G4
Hebel, Austl. 132/C1
Heber, Az, US 149/G3
Heber, Ca, US 148/E4
Heber City, Ut, US 147/H3
Heber Springs, Ar, US 153/H3
Hebert, La, US 164/C1
Hebertshausen, Ger. 59/E6
Hebgen (lake), Mt, US 147/H1
Hebgen (dam), Mt, US 147/H1
Hebi, China 80/C4
Hebo, Or, US 146/B1
Hebrides (sea), Sc, UK 31/Q8
Hebrides (isls.), UK 29/D3
Hebron, NS, Can. 158/D4
Hebron, ND, US 156/C4
Hebron, Il, US 167/P15
Hebron, Ne, US 154/F3
Hebron, Tx, US 150/L6
Hebron (Al Khalīl), WBnk. 105/C5
Heby, Swe. 40/G2
Hecate (str.), BC, Can. 139/D4
Hecelchakán, Mex. 176/D1
Hechi, China 87/F3
Hechingen, Ger. 58/B6
Hechtel, Belg. 55/E1
Hechthausen, Ger. 53/G1
Hechuan, China 87/E2
Heckington, Eng, UK 35/H6
Hecla, SD, US 156/E5
Hecla (isl.), Mb, Can. 156/F2
Hecla and Griper (bay), NW, Can. 141/R7
Hector, Ar, US 153/H3
Hector, Mn, US 155/G1
Hector (mt.), NZ 135/J8
Hector (mt.), Ab, Can. 144/F2
Hecun, China 87/H2
Heddal, Nor. 40/C2
Hédé, Fr. 56/D4
Hedehusene, Den. 39/J7
Hedel, Neth. 52/C5
Hedemora, Swe. 40/F1
Hedensted, Den. 40/C4
Hedi (res.), China 87/F4
Hedley, Tx, US 152/D3
Hedmark (co.), Nor. 38/D3

Map Section
232
233

Hollis – Hutchi
Map Section 234 235

Hollis, Ak, US 171/M4
Hollis, Ok, US 152/E3
Hollister, Mo, US 153/H2
Hollister, Ca, US 148/B2
Hollister (mt.), Austl. 130/B2
Hollister, NC, US 163/J2
Hollogne-aux-Pierres, Belg. 55/E2
Hollola, Fin. 41/L1
Holloman (A.F.B.), NM, US 152/A4
Hollum, Neth. 52/C2
Höllviksnäs, Swe. 40/E4
Holly, Co, US 152/C1
Holly, Mi, US 160/E3
Holly, Wa, US 167/B2
Holly Grove, Ar, US 153/J3
Holly Hill, Fl, US 165/H3
Holly Hill, SC, US 163/G4
Holly Ridge, NC, US 163/J3
Holly Springs, Ms, US 162/C3
Hollysloot, Neth. 52/C4
Hollywood, Ar, US 153/H3
Hollywood (nbrhd.), Ca, US 166/F7
Hollywood, Fl, US 164/P10
Hollywood, SC, US 163/G4
Hollywood Bowl, Ca, US 166/F7
Hollywood Park, Tx, US 150/E3
Holm, Ger. 53/G1
Holman, NM, US 152/B2
Holman, NW, Can. 140/E1
Hólmavík, Ice. 38/N6
Holmdel, NJ, US 168/D3
Holme upon Spalding Moor, Eng, UK 35/H4
Holmen, Wi, US 155/J2
Holmenkollen, Nor. 38/S8
Holmer Green, Eng, UK 30/A2
Holmes (mt.), Wy, US 147/H1
Holmes (riv.), BC, Can. 144/E1
Holmes Chapel, Eng, UK 35/F5
Holmes Reef (reef), Austl. 129/H4
Holmes Reefs (isl.), Austl. 127/D2
Holmesdale (valley), Eng, UK 30/C3
Holmestrand, Nor. 40/D2
Holmfirth, Eng, UK 35/G4
Holmhead, Sc, UK 33/B6
Holmsbu, Nor. 38/S9
Holmsjön (lake), Swe. 38/F3
Holmsund, Swe. 38/G3
Holmsvatnet (lake), Nor. 38/R9
Hölö, Swe. 39/A1
Holoby, Ukr. 72/C2
Holon, Isr. 105/B4
Holoog, Namb. 124/B2
Holroyd, Austl. 133/E1
Holsfjorden (lake), Nor. 38/R8
Holstebro, Den. 40/C3
Holstein, Ia, US 155/G2
Holston (riv.), Tn, US 162/F3
Holston Ordnance Works Fed. Govt. Res., Tn, US 163/F2
Holston, North Fork (riv.), Va, US 163/F2
Holsworthy, Eng, UK 36/B5
Holt, Fl, US 164/E2
Holt, Mi, US 160/D3
Holt, Ca, US 167/M11
Holt, Al, US 162/D4
Holt, Mo, US 155/G4
Holt, Eng, UK 37/H1
Holtålen, Nor. 38/D3
Holte, Den. 39/J7
Holten, Neth. 52/D4
Holtland, Ger. 53/E2
Holton, Ks, US 155/G4
Holts Summit, Mo, US 153/H1
Holtsville, NY, US 169/E2
Holtville, NB, Can. 158/D2
Holtville, Ca, US 148/E4
Holwerd, Neth. 52/C2
Holy (isl.), Sc, UK 33/A5
Holy Cross, Ak, US 171/G3
Holy Trinity, Al, US 162/E4
Holycross, Ire. 32/C4
Holyhead, Wal, UK 34/D5
Holyoke, Ma, US 161/K3
Holyoke, Co, US 154/C3
Holyport, Eng, UK 30/A2
Holyrood, Ks, US 153/E1
Holyrood, Nf, Can. 159/L2
Holywell, Wal, UK 35/E5
Holywood, NI, UK 34/C2
Holzminden, Ger. 53/G5
Holzwickede, Ger. 53/E5
Hom (riv.), Namb. 124/B3
Homa (mt.), Kenya 119/A2
Homa Bay, Kenya 119/A2
Homathko (riv.), BC, Can. 144/B2
Homberg, Ger. 53/G6
Homberg, Ger. 52/D6
Hombori, Mali 115/E3
Hombori Tondo (peak), Mali 115/E3
Hombourg-Haut, Fr. 55/F5
Homburg, Ger. 55/G5
Home (bay), Nun, Can. 141/K2
Home Hill, Austl. 134/B2
Homécourt, Fr. 55/E5
Homelake, Co, US 149/J2
Homeland, Ga, US 165/G2
Homeland, Ca, US 166/C3
Homeland, Fl, US 164/M8
Homer, La, US 153/H4
Homer, Mi, US 160/D3
Homer, NY, US 161/H3
Homer, Ga, US 163/F3
Homer, Ak, US 171/H4
Homerville, Ga, US 165/G2
Homestead, Fl, US 165/H5
Homestead, Austl. 134/B3
Homestead of America Nat'l Mon., Ne, US 155/F3
Homewood, Il, US 167/Q16
Homewood, Ca, US 146/C4
Homewood, Al, US 162/D4
Homib (riv.), Erit. 100/C5
Hommersåk, Nor. 40/A2
Homochitto (riv.), Ms, US 162/B5
Homoíne, Moz. 123/G4
Homonhon (isl.), Phil. 88/D3
Homosassa (bay), Fl, US 164/K6
Homosassa, Fl, US 164/K6
Homosassa Springs, Fl, US 164/K6
Homosassa Springs Nature World, Fl, US 164/K6
Homyel', Bela. 70/D1
Homyel'skaya Voblasts, Bela. 70/D1
Hon, Ar, US 153/G3
Hon Chong, Viet. 94/D4
Hon Quan, Viet. 94/D4
Honbetsu, Japan 82/C2
Honda, Col. 183/L7
Honddu (riv.), Wal, UK 36/C2
Hondeklipbaai, SAfr. 124/B3
Hondo, Japan 84/B4
Hondo (riv.), Belz. 176/D2
Hondo, Tx, US 151/E3
Hondo Creek (res.), Tx, US 151/E3
Hondschoote, Fr. 54/B2
Hondsrug (hills), Neth. 42/D2
Hondsrug (reg.), Neth. 52/D3
Honduras (gulf), NAm. 172/D4
Honduras (ctry.) 139/J8
Honea Path, SC, US 163/F3
Hønefoss, Nor. 40/D1
Honesdale, Pa, US 161/J4
Honey (cr.), Wi, US 167/N14
Honey (lake), Ca, US 146/C3
Honey Brook, Pa, US 168/C3
Honey Creek, Wi, US 167/P14
Honey Grove, Tx, US 153/G4
Honeybourne, Eng, UK 37/E2
Honeyville, Ut, US 147/G3
Honfleur, Fr. 57/F2
Hong (isl.), SKor. 81/C5
Høng, Den. 39/H7
Hong (lake), China 80/C5
Hong (riv.), China 80/C4
Hong (Red) (riv.), Viet. 86/E4
Hong Gai, Viet. 87/E4
Hong Kong (dpcy.), China 77/L7
Hong Kong (int'l arpt.), China 87/G4
Hong Kong (isl.), China 87/L7
Hongam-nodongjagu, NKor. 81/E1
Hong'an, China 80/C5
Hongchang, China 81/B2
Hongch'ŏn, SKor. 81/D4
Hongdu (riv.), China 93/J2
Hongdu, China 87/F4
Honggouzi, China 78/C4
Hongguo, China 86/E3
Honghu, China 87/G2
Hongjiang, China 87/F3
Honglai, China 87/H3
Hongliu (riv.), China 78/F4
Hongliuhe, China 78/C3
Hongliuquan, China 78/D3
Honglu, China 87/H3
Hongqi, China 81/B2
Hongqiao, China 87/J2
Hongqiao (int'l arpt.), China 80/L8
Hongqizhen, China 94/E2
Hongshui (riv.), China 93/J3
Hongsŏng, SKor. 81/D4
Hongtian, China 87/H3
Hongtong, China 80/B3
Honguedo Passage, (chan.), Qu, Can. 141/K4
Honguedo Passage, Qu, Can. 158/E1
Hongwŏn, NKor. 81/D2
Hongya, China 86/D2
Hongyan, China 87/F2
Hongyang, China 87/H4
Hongyuan, China 78/E5
Hongze (lake), China 79/H5
Hongze, China 80/D4
Hœnheim, Fr. 55/G6
Honiara (cap.), Sol. 136/E5
Honiton, Eng, UK 36/C5
Honjō, Japan 82/B4
Honjō, Japan 83/C1
Honobia, Ok, US 153/G3
Honolulu (cap.), Hi, US 142/W11
Honoraville, Al, US 165/E2
Hönow, Ger. 42/Q6
Honshu (isl.), Japan 75/Q6
Honshū (isl.), Japan 77/P6
Hontianske Nemce, Slvk. 50/D1
Hoo, Eng, UK 30/E2
Hood (mt.), Ca, US 167/J10
Hood (canal), Wa, US 167/B2
Hood, Ca, US 167/L10
Hood (mt.), Or, US 146/C1
Hood (pt.), Austl. 130/C5
Hood (pt.), PNG 129/G2
Hood (co.), Tx, US 150/K7
Hood River, Or, US 144/D5
Hoofddorp, Neth. 52/B4
Hoogeloon, Neth. 52/C6
Hoogeveen, Neth. 52/D3
Hoogeveense Vaart (canal), Neth. 52/D3
Hoogezand, Neth. 52/D2
Hooghly (riv.), India 97/F5
Hooghly-Chinsura, India 97/G4
Hoogkarspel, Neth. 52/C3
Hooglede, Belg. 54/C2
Hoogstraten, Belg. 52/B6
Hook (sound), Austl. 134/C3
Hook, Eng, UK 37/F4
Hook Head (pt.), Ire. 32/D5
Hooker, Ok, US 152/D2
Hooker Creek, Austl. 128/C4
Hooker Creek Abor. Land, Austl. 128/C4
Hooksett, NH, US 161/L3
Hoonah, Ak, US 171/L4
Hoopa, Ca, US 146/B3
Hoopa Valley Ind. Res., Ca, US 146/B3
Hooper, Co, US 152/B2
Hooper, Ne, US 155/F3
Hooper (Endwell), NY, US 161/H3
Hooper Bay, Ak, US 171/E3
Hoopeston, Il, US 160/C4
Hoople, ND, US 156/F3
Hoopstad, SAfr. 124/D2
Höör, Swe. 40/E4
Hoorn, Neth. 52/C3
Hoornse Hop (bay), Neth. 52/C3
Hoosick Falls, NY, US 161/K3
Hoover (dam), Az, US 142/D4
Hoover (peak), WV, US 163/F2
Hoover, SD, US 154/C1
Höövör, Mong. 78/G2
Hopa, Turk. 71/G4
Hopatcong, NJ, US 168/D2
Hopatcong (lake), NJ, US 168/D2
Hope (lake), Austl. 127/A4
Hope, BC, Can. 144/D3
Hope, Wal, UK 35/E5
Hope, Ak, US 171/J3
Hope, Ar, US 153/H4
Hope, In, US 160/D5
Hope, Ks, US 153/F1
Hope, ND, US 156/F4
Hope, NJ, US 168/D2
Hope, Tx, US 151/F3
Hope Mills, NC, US 163/H3
Hope Vale Abor. Land, Austl. 129/G3
Hope Vale Aboriginal Community, Austl. 134/B1
Hope-under-Dinmore, Eng, UK 36/D2
Hopedale, Nf, Can. 141/K3
Hopelchén, Mex. 176/D2
Hopeman, Sc, UK 33/C1
Hopes Advance (cape), Qu, Can. 141/K2
Hope's Nose (pt.), Eng, UK 36/C6
Hopetoun, Austl. 130/D5
Hopetown, SAfr. 124/D3
Hopewell, NS, Can. 159/F3
Hopewell, NJ, US 168/D3
Hopewell, Va, US 163/J2
Hopewell Cape, NB, Can. 158/E3
Hopewell Culture Nat'l Mon., Oh, US 160/E5
Hopewell Furnace NHS, Pa, US 168/C3
Hopi Ind. Res., Az, US 149/G2
Hopin, Myan. 86/C3
Hôpital-Camfrout, Fr. 56/A4
Hopkins (lake), Austl. 131/F3
Hopkins (riv.), Austl. 132/B3
Hopkins, Mo, US 155/G3
Hopkins, Mn, US 157/P7
Hopkinsville, Ky, US 162/D2
Hopkinton, RI, US 161/L4
Hopkinton, NH, US 161/L3
Hoppecke (riv.), Ger. 53/F6
Hoppegarten, Ger. 42/Q6
Hopper Mtn. NWR, Ca, US 166/B2
Hoppstädten-Weiersbach, Ger. 55/G4
Hopsten, Ger. 53/E4
Hoquiam, Wa, US 144/C4
Hor, China 78/E4
Horace (mt.), Ak, US 171/J2
Horace, ND, US 156/F4
Horadiz, Azer. 103/F2
Horado, Japan 83/L4
Hōrai-san (peak), Japan 83/J5
Horasan, Turk. 102/E1
Horatio, Ar, US 153/G4
Horažd'ovice, Czh. 59/G4
Horb am Neckar, Ger. 58/B6
Horbat Qesari (ruin), Isr. 104/D3
Horbourg-Wihr, Fr. 60/D1
Hörbranz, Aus. 61/F2
Horbury, Eng, UK 35/G4
Hörby, Swe. 39/K7
Horche, Sp. 46/D2
Horconcitos, Pan. 177/F4
Horcones (riv.), Arg. 188/C3
Hordaland (co.), Nor. 38/C3
Horden, Eng, UK 35/G2
Hœrdt, Fr. 55/G6
Hördt, Ger. 58/B4
Horezu, Rom. 51/G3
Horgau, Ger. 58/D6
Horgen, Swi. 61/E3
Hörh (peak), Mong. 78/F3
Horicon, Wi, US 155/K2
Horicon NWR, Wi, US 155/K2
Horinger, China 80/B2
Horiult, Mong. 78/E2
Horizontina, Braz. 189/F3
Horley, Eng, UK 30/C3
Horlivka, Ukr. 73/K3
Hormigüeros, PR 173/M8
Hormozgān (gov.), Iran 103/J5
Hormūd-e Mīr Khūnd, Iran 103/H5
Hormuz (str.), Oman 101/G3
Horn (isl.), Ms, US 164/D2
Horn (pt.), Ice. 192/H
Horn Lake, Ms, US 162/B3
Horn-Bad Meinberg, Ger. 53/F5
Hornachuelos, Sp. 46/C4
Hornád (riv.), Slvk. 43/L4
Hornavan (lake), Swe. 38/F2
Hornbach, Ger. 55/G5
Hornbæk, Den. 39/J6
Hornbeck, La, US 164/B2
Hornbeck, Ab, Can. 144/F1
Hornberg, Ger. 61/E1
Hornburg, Ger. 53/H4
Hornby, NZ 135/C3
Hornby, On, Can. 160/T8
Hornby Island, BC, Can. 144/B3
Horncastle, Eng, UK 35/H5
Hornchurch (nbrhd.), Eng, UK 30/D2
Horndal, Swe. 40/G1
Horné Saliby, Slvk. 50/C1
Horneburg, Ger. 53/G1
Hornell, NY, US 161/H3
Hornersville, Mo, US 162/B2
Horní Bříza, Czh. 59/G3
Horní Slavkov, Czh. 59/F2
Hornisgrinde (peak), Ger. 58/B5
Hornitos, Ca, US 148/B2
Hornos, (cape), Chile 191/D7
Hornoy-le-Bourg, Fr. 54/A4
Hornsby (nbrhd.), Austl. 134/H8
Hornsea, Eng, UK 35/H4
Hornslet, Den. 40/D3
Hörnum (cape), Ger. 40/C4
Horodenka, Ukr. 72/C3
Horodnya, Ukr. 72/F2
Horodok, Ukr. 72/D3
Horodok, Ukr. 72/B3
Horodyshche, Ukr. 72/F3
Horokhiv, Ukr. 72/C2
Horoshiri-dake (peak), Japan 82/C2
Hořovice, Czh. 59/G3
Horqin Youyi Zhongqi, China 79/J2
Horqin Zuoyi Houqi, China 80/E2
Horqin Zuoyi Zhongqi, China 80/E1
Horqueta, Par. 189/E2
Horrabridge, Eng, UK 36/B5
Hörsching, Aus. 59/H6
Horse (cr.), Co, US 154/B4
Horse (mtn.), Tx, US 151/C2
Horse Cave, Ky, US 162/E2
Horse Creek, Wy, US 154/B3
Horse Shoe Run, WV, US 161/G5
Horsefly, BC, Can. 144/D1
Horsefly (riv.), BC, Can. 144/D1
Horsefly (lake), BC, Can. 144/D1
Horseheads, NY, US 161/H3
Horsens, Den. 40/C4
Horseshoe Beach, Fl, US 165/G3
Horseshoe Bend, Ar, US 153/J2
Horseshoe Bend, Id, US 146/E2
Horseshoe Bend Nat'l Mil. Park, Al, US 162/E4
Horsethief (cr.), BC, Can. 144/F2
Horsey (isl.), Eng, UK 37/H3
Horsforth, Eng, UK 35/G4
Horsham, Austl. 132/B3
Horsham, Eng, UK 37/F4
Horsham, Pa, US 168/C3
Hørsholm, Den. 39/J7
Horsmonden, Eng, UK 30/E3
Horšovský Týn, Czh. 59/F3
Horst, Ger. 53/H2
Horst, Neth. 52/D6
Hörstel, Ger. 53/E4
Horstmar, Ger. 53/E4
Horta, Azor., Port. 47/S12
Hortaleza (nbrhd.), Sp. 47/N9
Horten, Nor. 40/D2
Hortense, Ga, US 165/H2
Hortes, Fr. 60/B2
Hortobágyi NP, Hun. 70/B3
Horton, Mo, US 153/G2
Horton (riv.), NW, Can. 140/D2
Horton, Ks, US 155/G4
Horton (pt.), NY, US 169/F1
Horton Kirby, Eng, UK 30/D2
Høruphav, Den. 40/C4
Horusický Rybnik (lake), Czh. 59/H4
Hørve, Den. 40/D4
Hørve, Den. 39/H7
Horvot 'Avedat (ruin), Isr. 104/D4
Horvot Dor, Isr. 105/B3
Horw, Swi. 61/E3
Horwich, Eng, UK 35/F4
Hosa'ina, Eth. 117/H4
Hösbach, Ger. 58/C2
Hosdrug, India 95/B3
Hosenfeld, Ger. 58/C1
Hosenofu (well), Libya 108/D4
Hoséré Vokré (peak), Camr. 116/B3
Hosford, Fl, US 165/F2
Hoshāb, Pak. 101/H3
Hoshangābād, India 96/A4
Hoshcha, Ukr. 72/D2
Hoshiārpur, India 98/C4
Hosingen, Lux. 55/F3
Hosmer, SD, US 156/E5
Hosmer, BC, Can. 144/G3
Hospental, Swi. 61/E4
Hospital, Ire. 32/B5
Hospital, Chile 190/N8
Hosston, La, US 153/H4
Hosszúpereszteg, Hun. 50/C2
Hoste (isl.), Chile 191/C7
Hostomel', Ukr. 72/F2
Hoswick, Sc, UK 31/W13
Hot, Thai. 94/B2
Hot Creek (range), Nv, US 146/E4
Hot Springs, SD, US 154/C2
Hot Springs NP, Ar, US 153/H3
Hot Springs Village, Ar, US 153/H3
Hot Sulphur Springs, Co, US 154/A3
Hotaka, Japan 85/E2
Hotaka-dake (peak), Japan 85/E2
Hotan (riv.), China 99/D4
Hotan, China 99/C4
Hotazel, SAfr. 124/C2
Hotevilla, Az, US 149/G3
Hotham (cape), Austl. 128/C3
Hoti, Indo. 91/H4
Hot'kovo, Rus. 69/W8
Hotont, Mong. 78/E2
Hottah (lake), NW, Can. 140/E2
Hottentot (bay), Namb. 124/A2
Hottentots (pt.), Namb. 122/B5
Hotton, Belg. 55/E3
Hou (riv.), China 78/F5
Houamuang, Laos 86/D4
Houari Boumedienne (int'l arpt.), Alg. 112/G4
Houat (isl.), Fr. 56/C6
Houchang, China 87/E3
Houdain, Fr. 54/B3
Houdan, Fr. 57/G3
Houdan, Fr. 30/G5
Houet (prov.), Burk. 114/D4
Houffalize, Belg. 55/E3
Houghton, SD, US 156/E5
Houghton (pt.), Mi, US 157/K4
Houghton (dam), SD, US 156/E5
Houghton, Mi, US 157/K4
Houghton, NY, US 161/G3
Houghton (lake), Mi, US 160/D2
Houghton Lake, Mi, US 160/D2
Houghton-le-Spring, Eng, UK 35/G2
Houilles, Fr. 30/J5
Houlgate, Fr. 57/E2
Houlton, Me, US 141/K4
Houlton, Wi, US 157/Q6
Houma, La, US 164/C3
Houma, China 80/B4
Houndé, Burk. 114/E4
Houplines, Fr. 54/B2
Hourn, Loch (inlet), Sc, UK 33/A2
Hourtin, Fr. 44/C4
Housatonic (riv.), Ct, US 169/E1
House (range), Ut, US 142/D4
Housesteads Roman Fort, Eng, UK 35/F1
Houssen, Fr. 60/D1
Houston, De, US 168/C6
Houston, Fl, US 165/G2
Houston, Mn, US 155/J2
Houston, Mo, US 153/J2
Houston, Ms, US 162/C4
Houston, Tx, US 151/M9
Houston (lake), Tx, US 151/G2
Houston Intercontinental (int'l arpt.), Tx, US 151/M9
Houston Ship (chan.), Tx, US 151/M9
Houstonia, Mo, US 153/H1
Houtbaai, SAfr. 124/L11
Houten, Neth. 52/C4
Houthalen, Belg. 55/E1
Houthulst, Belg. 54/B2
Houtman Abrolhos (isl.), Austl. 130/B4
Houtribdijk (dam), Neth. 52/C3
Houtskär (isl.), Fin. 41/J1
Houyet, Belg. 55/E3
Houyingzi, China 81/B2
Houzhenzi, China 78/F5
Hov, Nor. 40/D1
Hova, Swe. 40/F2
Hovd (prov.), Mong. 78/C2
Hove, Eng, UK 37/F5
Hövelhof, Ger. 53/F5
Hoven, SD, US 154/E1
Hovenweep Nat'l Mon., Co, US 149/H2
Hoveton, Eng, UK 37/H1
Hovfjället (peak), Swe. 40/E1
Hovingham, Eng, UK 35/H3
Hovland, Mn, US 157/K4
Hovmantorp, Swe. 40/F3
Hövsgöl (prov.), Mong. 99/G2
Hövsgöl (lake), Mong. 78/E1
Hovsta, Swe. 40/F2
Howa, Oued (riv.), Chad 116/D2
Howar (wadi), Sudan 117/E1
Howard, Austl. 134/D4
Howard (isl.), Austl. 129/D2
Howard, NB, Can. 158/E2
Howard, Co, US 152/B1
Howard, Fl, US 164/P11
Howard, Ks, US 153/F2
Howard (co.), Md, US 168/B5
Howard, SD, US 154/F1
Howard Beach (nbrhd.), NY, US 169/K9
Howard City, Mi, US 160/D3
Howard Draw (riv.), Tx, US 151/D2
Howard Hanson (res.), Wa, US 167/D3
Howard Hanson (dam), Wa, US 167/D3
Howard Prairie (lake), Or, US 146/B2
Howards Grove, Wi, US 160/C3
Howden, Eng, UK 35/H4
Howe, Ok, US 153/G3
Howe, Tx, US 153/F4
Howe (sound), BC, Can. 144/C3
Howe (cape), Austl. 133/D3
Howe Caverns, NY, US 161/J3
Howe Green, Eng, UK 30/E1
Howe of the Mearns (reg.), Sc, UK 33/D3
Howell, Mi, US 160/E3
Howell, NJ, US 168/D3
Howey-in-the-Hills, Fl, US 164/M6
Howick, NZ 135/F6
Howick, SAfr. 125/E3
Howison, Ms, US 164/D2
Howland (isl.), Pac., US 137/H4
Howley, Nf, Can. 159/J1
Howlong, Austl. 133/C2
Howrah, India 97/G4
Howser, BC, Can. 144/F2
Hoxie, Ks, US 154/D4
Hoxie, Ar, US 162/B2
Höxter, Ger. 53/G5
Hoxud, China 99/E3
Hoy (isl.), Sc, UK 31/V14
Hoya, Ger. 53/G3
Hōya, Japan 83/D2
Høyanger, Nor. 40/B1
Hoyerswerda, Ger. 43/H3
Hoylake, Eng, UK 35/E5
Hoyland Nether, Eng, UK 35/G4
Hoyo de Manzanares, Sp. 47/N8
Hoyos, Sp. 46/B2
Hoyoux (riv.), Belg. 55/E3
Hoyt, NB, Can. 158/D3
Hoyt, Mt, US 156/B4
Hoyt, Ok, US 153/G3
Hoyt, Ks, US 155/G4
Hoyt Tamir (riv.), Mong. 78/E2
Hozumi, Japan 83/L5
Hracholusky (res.), Czh. 59/F3
Hradec Králové, Czh. 43/H3
Hradište (peak), Czh. 59/G2
Hradyz'k, Ukr. 73/G3
Hranice, Czh. 59/F2
Hrasnica, Bosn. 50/D4
Hrastnik, Slov. 50/B2
Hrazdan, Arm. 103/F1
Hrebinka, Ukr. 73/G1
Hrebinky, Ukr. 72/F3
Hřivice, Czh. 59/G2
Hrodna, Bela. 41/K5
Hrodzyenskaya Voblasts, Bela. 68/E5
Hrolleifsborg (peak), Ice. 38/M6
Hron (riv.), Slvk. 70/A2
Hronov, Czh. 43/J3
Hrubieszów, Pol. 72/B2
Hrubý Jeseník (mts.), Czh.,Pol. 43/J3
Hrútafjöll (peak), Ice. 38/P6
Hrymayliv, Ukr. 72/D3
Hsenwi, Myan. 93/G3
Hsi-hseng, Myan. 86/C4
Hsinchu, Tai. 87/J3
Hsipaw, Myan. 94/B1
Hsüeh (peak), Tai. 87/J3
Htawgaw, Myan. 93/G2
Hts-de-Seine (dept.), Fr. 57/H3
Hu Xian, China 78/F5
Hua (peak), China 80/B4
Hua Hin, Thai. 94/B3
Hua Sai, Thai. 94/C4
Hua Xian, China 80/C4
Huab (riv.), Namb. 122/B3
Huacaraje, Bol. 185/F4
Huacareta, Bol. 188/D2
Huacaya, Bol. 188/D2
Huacaybamba, Peru 184/B3
Huachacalla, Bol. 188/B1
Huacheng, China 87/G3
Huachi, China 78/F4
Huachi, Bol. 185/F4
Huacho, Peru 184/B3
Huachón, Peru 184/C3
Huachuan, China 79/L2
Huachuca (mts.), Az, US 149/G5
Huachuca City, Az, US 149/G5
Huacrachuco, Peru 184/B3
Huade, China 78/G3
Huadian, China 79/K3
Huadianzi, China 81/C2
Huahine (isl.), FrPol. 137/K6
Huai (riv.), China 80/C4
Huai Yot, Thai. 94/B5
Huai'an, China 80/C2
Huai'an, China 80/D4
Huaibei, China 78/H5
Huaibin, China 80/C4
Huaihua, China 87/F3
Huaiji, China 87/G4
Huailai, China 80/G6
Huainan, China 80/D4
Huaining, China 87/H2
Huairen, China 80/C3
Huairou, China 80/H6
Huaiyang, China 80/C4
Huaiyin, China 80/D4
Huaiyin, China 80/D4
Huaiyuan, China 80/D4
Huajicori, Mex. 174/D4
Huajuapan de León, Mex. 176/B2
Hualahuises, Mex. 175/F3
Hualañé, Chile 190/C2
Hualapai (peak), Az, US 149/F3
Hualapai (mts.), Az, US 149/F3
Hualapai Ind. Res., Az, US 149/F3
Hualfín, Arg. 188/C3
Hualgayoc, Peru 184/B2
Hualien, Tai. 87/J4
Hualla, Peru 184/C4
Huallaga (riv.), Peru 179/B3
Huallanca, Peru 184/B3
Huamachuco, Peru 184/B2
Huamantanga, Peru 184/B3
Huamantla, Mex. 175/M7
Huambo, Ang. 122/B2
Huambo (dist.), Ang. 122/B2
Huambos, Peru 184/B2
Huan (riv.), China 80/C5
Huan Xian, China 78/F4
Huanan, China 79/L2
Huanaque, Bol. 188/B2
Huancané, Peru 184/D4
Huancapi, Peru 184/C4
Huancaspata, Peru 184/B3
Huancavelica, Peru 184/C4
Huancavelica (dept.), Peru 184/C4
Huancayo, Peru 184/C4
Huanchaca (peak), Bol. 188/C2
Huang (riv.), China 77/L6
Huang (Yellow) (riv.), China 78/G4
Huangbayi, China 78/F5
Huangbei, China 87/H3
Huangchuan, China 80/C4
Huangcun, China 87/F3
Huanggang (peak), China 87/H3
Huanggang, China 87/G2
Huanghua, China 80/D3
Huangjinbu, China 87/H2
Huangjinggou, China 86/E2
Huangli, China 80/K8
Huangling, China 80/B4
Huangliu, China 87/F5
Huanglong, China 80/B4
Huanglong, China 87/G3
Huanglongtan, China 80/B4
Huangmao (peak), China 87/H3
Huangmei, China 87/G2
Huangniupu, China 78/F5
Huangpi, China 87/G2
Huangping, China 93/J2
Huangqi (lake), China 80/C2
Huangshan, China 87/H2
Huangshi, China 87/G2
Huangshidu, China 87/H3
Huangtang (lake), China 80/C5
Huangtianpu, China 87/F3
Huangtu (plat.), China 80/B4
Huangtudian, China 87/F2
Huanguelén, Arg. 190/E3
Huangwan, China 80/L9
Huangyunpu, China 80/B4
Huangzhai, China 87/H2
Huangzhan, China 87/G2
Huangzhong, China 78/E4
Huaning, China 86/D3
Huanjiang, China 93/J3
Huanren, China 81/C2
Huanta, Peru 184/C4
Huantai, China 80/D3
Huántar, Peru 184/B3
Huantunas (lake), Bol. 185/E4
Huánuco, Peru 184/B3
Huánuco (dept.), Peru 184/C3
Huanuni, Bol. 188/C1
Huanxi, China 87/G3
Huapi (mts.), Nic. 176/E3
Huaping, China 86/D3
Huaqiaozhen, China 78/F5
Huaquechula, Mex. 175/L8
Huaquillas, Ecu. 184/A1
Huara, Chile 188/B1
Huaral, Peru 184/B3
Huaraz, Peru 184/B3
Huari, Bol. 188/C1
Huari, Peru 184/B3
Huaricolca, Peru 184/C3
Huarina, Bol. 184/D5
Huarmey, Peru 184/B3
Huarochirí, Peru 184/B4
Huarocondo, Peru 184/C4
Huásabas, Mex. 174/C2
Huasahuasi, Peru 184/C3
Huascarán (peak), Peru 184/B3
Huascaran, PN, Peru 184/B3
Huasco (riv.), Chile 188/B4
Huashi (mts.), China 87/G3
Huashi, China 87/G3
Huatabampo, Mex. 174/C3
Huatong, China 81/A2
Huatuxco, Mex. 175/N7
Huauchinango, Mex. 175/L6
Huaura, Peru 184/B3
Huautla de Jiménez, Mex. 176/B2
Huayacocotla, Mex. 175/L6
Huayang, China 87/J2
Huayangzhen, China 78/F5
Huaying, China 87/E2
Huaylas, Peru 184/B3
Huayllay, Peru 184/B3
Huayopata, Peru 184/C4
Huayuan, China 81/D1
Huayuan, China 93/J2
Huayuan, China 87/G2
Huazhaizi, China 78/E4
Huazhou, China 93/K3
Huazi, China 81/B2
Hub, Ms, US 164/D2
Hubbard, Sk, Can. 156/C2
Hubbard (mt.), Ak, US 171/L3
Hubbard, Ia, US 155/H2
Hubbard (lake), Mi, US 160/E2
Hubbard, Or, US 146/B1
Hubbard, Tx, US 151/F2
Hubbard Creek (res.), Tx, US 151/E1
Hubbards, NS, Can. 158/E3
Hubbell Trading Post Nat'l Hist. Site, Az, US 149/H3
Hubei (pass), China 80/B4
Huber Heights, Oh, US 160/D5
Hubli-Dhārwār, India 95/B3
Huch'ang, NKor. 81/D2
Hückelhoven, Ger. 55/F1
Hückeswagen, Ger. 55/G1
Hucknall, Eng, UK 35/G5
Hudai, China 80/L8
Huddersfield, Eng, UK 35/G4
Huddinge, Swe. 40/G2
Hude, Ger. 53/F2
Hudiksvall, Swe. 40/G1
Hudson (cape), Ant. 192/L
Hudson (bay), Can. 139/J3
Hudson, On, Can. 157/H2
Hudson, Qu, Can. 159/M7
Hudson (str.), Nun,Qu, Can. 141/J2
Hudson, Fl, US 164/K7
Hudson, Il, US 155/K3
Hudson, Mi, US 160/D4
Hudson, NC, US 163/G3
Hudson (co.), NJ, US 169/J9
Hudson, NY, US 161/K3
Hudson (riv.), NJ, NY, US 161/K3
Hudson (lake), Ok, US 153/G2
Hudson, Tx, US 151/G2
Hudson, Wi, US 157/Q7
Hudson Bay, Sk, Can. 140/F3
Hudson Falls, NY, US 161/K3
Hudson Oaks, Tx, US 150/K7
Hudsons (peak), Austl. 133/D3
Hudson's Hope, BC, Can. 140/D3
Hue, Viet. 94/D2
Hueco (mts.), Tx, US 151/B2
Huedin, Rom. 51/F2
Huehuetenango, Guat. 176/D3
Huehuetla, Mex. 175/L6
Huehuetlán, Mex. 175/L8
Huejotzingo, Mex. 175/L7
Huejuquilla el Alto, Mex. 174/E4
Huejutla de Reyes, Mex. 176/B1
Huelgoat, Fr. 56/B4
Huelma, Sp. 46/D4
Huelva (riv.), Sp. 46/B4
Huelva, Sp. 46/B4
Huequi (vol.), Chile 190/B4
Huercal-Overa, Sp. 46/E4
Huerfano (riv.), Co, US 154/B5
Huesca, Sp. 47/E1
Huéscar, Sp. 46/D4
Huesos (stream), Arg. 190/F3
Huetamo de Nuñez, Mex. 175/E5
Huete, Sp. 46/D2
Huexoculco, Mex. 175/R10
Hüfingen, Ger. 61/E2
Huger, SC, US 163/H4
Hugh Town, Eng, UK 31/Q12
Hughenden, Austl. 134/B3
Hughenden, Ab, Can. 145/J1
Hughenden Valley, Eng, UK 30/A2
Hughes, Arg. 190/E2
Hughes, Ak, US 171/H2
Hughes, Ar, US 162/B3
Hughes, Austl. 131/F4
Hughes Springs, Tx, US 153/G4
Hughesville, Pa, US 168/B1
Hughson, Ca, US 148/B2
Huglfing, Ger. 61/H2
Hugli (riv.), India 92/E3
Hugo, Ok, US 153/G3
Hugo (lake), Ok, US 153/G3
Hugo (dam), Ok, US 153/G3
Hugo, Co, US 154/C4
Hugo, Mn, US 157/Q6
Hugoton, Ks, US 152/D2
Huguan, China 80/C3
Hui (riv.), China 79/H2
Hui Xian, China 80/C4
Huib-Hock (plat.), Namb. 124/B2
Huichapan, Mex. 175/K6
Hŭich'ŏn, NKor. 81/D2
Huila (dept.), Col. 180/C4
Huila (dept.), Ang. 122/B2
Huilango, Mex. 175/Q9
Huili, China 93/H2
Huimanguillo, Mex. 176/C2
Huimin, China 80/D3
Huinan, China 79/K3
Huinca Renancó, Arg. 190/D2
Huining, China 78/F4
Hŭisaek-pong (peak), NKor. 81/D2
Huishui, China 93/J2
Huisne (riv.), Fr. 44/D2
Huisseau-sur-Cosson, Fr. 57/G5
Huissen, Neth. 52/C5
Huitong, China 93/J2
Huittinen, Fin. 41/K1
Huitzilan, Mex. 175/M7
Huitzuco, Mex. 175/K8
Huixcolotla, Mex. 175/M8
Huixquilucan, Mex. 175/Q10
Huixtla, Mex. 176/C3
Huize, China 86/D3
Huizen, Neth. 52/C4
Huizhou, China 87/G4
Hujirt, Mong. 78/E2
Hujra, Pak. 98/B4
Hŭksan (arch.), SKor. 79/J5
Hukuntsi, Bots. 122/D4
Hulah (dam), Ok, US 153/F2
Hulah (lake), Ok, US 153/F2
Hulan, China 79/K2
Hulan (riv.), China 79/K2
Hulbert, Ok, US 153/G3
Hulbert, Mi, US 160/D1
Hulett, Wy, US 154/B1
Hull (riv.), Eng, UK 35/H4
Hull, Qu, Can. 161/J2
Hull, Ia, US 155/F2
Hull (Orona) (isl.), Kiri. 137/H5
Hullbridge, Eng, UK 30/E2
Hüllhorst, Ger. 53/F4
Hullo, Est. 41/K2
Hulst, Neth. 52/B6
Hultsfred, Swe. 40/F3
Hulu (riv.), China 78/F4
Hulun (lake), China 78/H2
Hulwān, Egypt 113/C5
Hulyaypole, Ukr. 73/J4
Huma (riv.), China 75/N4
Huma, China 79/K1
Humahuaca, Arg. 188/C2
Humaitá, Par. 188/E3
Humaitá, Braz. 185/F2
Humaitá, Bol. 185/E3
Humaljärvi (lake), Fin. 39/E4
Humansdorp, SAfr. 124/D4
Humansville, Mo, US 153/H2
Humay, Peru 184/C4
Humbe, Ang. 122/B3
Humber (riv.), Eng, UK 35/H4
Humber (riv.), Nf, Can. 158/J1
Humber (bay), On, Can. 160/U8
Humber, West (riv.), On, Can. 160/T8
Humberside (arpt.), Eng, UK 35/H4
Humberston, Eng, UK 35/H4
Humberto de Campos, Braz. 183/F3
Humble, Tx, US 151/M9
Humboldt, Sk, Can. 145/M1
Humboldt (bay), Col. 177/G5
Humboldt (peak), NCal. 137/V12
Humboldt, Az, US 149/F3
Humboldt (bay), Ca, US 146/A3
Humboldt, Ks, US 153/G2
Humboldt, Ia, US 155/G2
Humboldt, Mn, US 156/F3
Humboldt, Ne, US 155/G3
Humboldt (lake), Nv, US 146/D3
Humboldt (riv.), Nv, US 142/C3
Humboldt, Tn, US 162/C3
Humboldt, North Fork (riv.), Nv, US 146/F3
Hume (dam), Austl. 133/C3
Hūmedān, Iran 101/G3
Humenné, Slvk. 43/L4
Humeston, Ia, US 155/H3
Humlebæk, Den. 39/J7
Humlum, Den. 40/C3
Hummels Wharf, Pa, US 168/B2
Hummelstown, Pa, US 168/B3
Humnoke, Ar, US 153/J3
Humphrey, Ar, US 153/J3
Humphrey, On, Can. 161/G2
Humphrey, Ne, US 154/F3
Humphrey Point (cape), Ak, US 171/K2
Humphreys (peak), Az, US 149/G3
Humphreys (mt.), Ca, US 148/C2
Humpty Doo, Austl. 128/C3
Humshaugh, Eng, UK 35/F1
Hūn, Libya 108/B2
Hun (riv.), China 79/J3
Húnaflói (bay), Ice. 38/N6
Hunan (prov.), China 93/K2
Hunchun, China 79/L3
Hundested, Den. 39/H7
Hundewāli, Pak. 98/B4
Hundred, WV, US 160/F5
Hundred Fifty Mile House, BC, Can. 144/D1
Hundred Mile House, BC, Can. 144/D2
Hundsangen, Ger. 55/G3
Hunedoara (prov.), Rom. 50/F3
Hunedoara, Rom. 50/F3
Hünenberg, Swi. 61/E3
Hung Yen, Viet. 94/D1
Hungaroring, Hun. 51/R9
Hungary (ctry.) 29/F4
Hungen, Ger. 58/B2
Hungerford, Austl. 132/C1
Hungerford, Eng, UK 37/E4
Hŭnghae, SKor. 81/E4
Hŭngnam, NKor. 81/D3
Hŭngnyŏng-nodongjagu, NKor. 81/D3
Hungry (peak), Id, US 144/G4
Hungry Horse (dam), Mt, US 145/G3
Hungulo, Ang. 122/C2
Hüngüy (riv.), Mong. 78/C2
Hunjiang, China 81/D2
Hunkui, Nga. 115/G4
Hunmanby, Eng, UK 35/H3
Hunnebostrand, Swe. 40/D2
Hunsel, Neth. 52/C6
Hunsrück (mts.), Ger. 42/D4
Hunstanton, Eng, UK 37/G1
Hunt (mtn.), Wy, US 147/K1
Hunte (riv.), Ger. 42/E2
Hunter (mt.), Ak, US 171/H3
Hunter, ND, US 156/F4
Hunter (mtn.), NY, US 161/J3
Hunter (riv.), Austl. 132/D2
Hunter, Tx, US 150/E3
Hunter (isl.), Austl. 127/D5
Hunter Army Afld., Ga, US 165/H1
Hunterdon (co.), NJ, US 168/C2
Hunters, Wa, US 144/E3
Hunters Creek Village, Tx, US 151/M9
Huntersville, NC, US 163/G3
Hunterville, NZ 135/C2
Huntingburg, In, US 162/D1
Huntingdon, Qu, Can. 161/J2
Huntingdon, Eng, UK 37/F2
Huntingdon, Tn, US 162/C2
Huntingdon, Pa, US 161/G4
Huntington, Eng, UK 35/G4
Huntington, In, US 160/D4
Huntington, NY, US 169/M8
Huntington (bay), NY, US 169/M8
Huntington, Or, US 146/E1
Huntington (cr.), Pa, US 168/B1
Huntington, Tx, US 150/G2
Huntington, Ut, US 147/H4
Huntington, WV, US 163/F1
Huntington Bay, NY, US 169/M8
Huntington Beach, Ca, US 166/G8
Huntington Park, Ca, US 166/F8
Huntington Station, NY, US 169/M8
Huntington Woods, Mi, US 167/F7
Huntland, Tn, US 162/D3
Huntley, Il, US 167/P15
Huntly, Sc, UK 33/D2
Huntly, NZ 135/C2
Hunts Inlet, BC, Can. 171/M4
Hunts Point, Wa, US 167/C2
Huntsville, On, Can. 161/G2
Huntsville, Al, US 162/D3
Huntsville, Ar, US 153/H2
Huntsville, Mo, US 155/H4
Huntsville (res.), Pa, US 168/B1
Huntsville, Tn, US 162/E2
Huntsville, Tx, US 151/G2
Huntsville, Wa, US 144/E4
Hunua, NZ 135/G7
Hunucmá, Mex. 176/D1
Hünxe, Ger. 52/D5
Hunyuan, China 80/C3
Huo (mtn.), China 80/B3
Huo (mtn.), China 80/D5
Huocheng, China 99/D3
Huojia, China 80/C4
Huolin Gol, China 79/H2
Huolongmen, China 79/K2
Huolupu, China 87/E2
Huon (gulf), PNG 129/G1
Huon (pen.), PNG 129/G1
Huong Hoa, Viet. 94/D2
Huong Khe, Viet. 94/D2
Huong Son, Viet. 94/D2
Huong Thuy, Viet. 93/J4
Huonville, Austl. 132/C4
Huoqiu, China 80/D4
Huoshan, China 80/D5
Huotong, China 87/H3
Huozhou, China 80/B3
Ḩuraymilā, SAr. 100/E3
Hūrayn, Egypt 113/B3
Hurd (cape), On, Can. 160/F2
Hurdal, Nor. 40/D1
Hurdiyo, Som. 118/D3
Hurdle Mills, NC, US 163/H2
Hure Qi, China 80/E2
Hurepoix (reg.), Fr. 30/H6
Hurley, Wi, US 157/J4
Hurley (riv.), Ire. 34/B4
Hurley, Ms, US 164/D2
Hurley, NY, US 161/J4
Hurley, Eng, UK 30/A2
Hurley, NM, US 149/H4
Hurlford, Sc, UK 33/B5
Hurlock, Md, US 163/K1
Huron (bay), Mi, US 157/K4
Huron (mts.), Mi, US 157/K4
Huron, Oh, US 160/E4
Huron (pt.), Mi, US 167/G6
Huron (riv.), Mi, US 167/E7
Huron, Ca, US 148/B2
Huron (lake), Can.,US 139/J5
Huron, SD, US 154/E1
Huron Islands Nat'l Wild. Ref., Mi, US 157/K4
Huron Mountain, Mi, US 157/L4
Hurricane (lake), ND, US 156/E3
Hurricane, Al, US 164/E2
Hurricane, Ut, US 149/F2
Hurricane, WV, US 163/F1
Hurricane (cliffs), Az, US 149/F2
Hurshat Tal NP, Isr. 105/D2
Hurst, Tx, US 150/K7
Hurstville, Austl. 133/E1
Hurtaut (riv.), Fr. 54/D4
Hürtgenwald (reg.), Ger. 55/F2
Hürth, Ger. 55/F2
Hurtsboro, Al, US 162/E4
Hurum, Nor. 38/S9
Hurup, Den. 40/C3
Huruta, Eth. 118/A3
Hurworth, Eng, UK 35/G3
Hurzuf, Ukr. 70/E3
Husainābād, India 97/E3
Husainpur, Bang. 97/H3
Huslia, Ak, US 171/G2
Húsavík, Ice. 38/P6
Ḩusayyāt al Fawākhir (well), Libya 108/D2
Husbands Bosworth, Eng, UK 37/E2
Husby-Långhundra, Swe. 39/B1
Hushan, China 87/H2
Husher, Wi, US 167/Q14
Hushi, China 87/H3
Huşi, Rom. 72/E4
Huskisson, Austl. 133/E2
Husnes, Nor. 40/A2
Hussar, Ab, Can. 145/H2
Hussigny-Godbrange, Fr. 55/E5
Hustisford, Wi, US 155/K2
Husum, Ger. 40/C4
Husum, Swe. 38/F3
Husyatyn, Ukr. 72/D3
Hutag, Mong. 78/E2
Hutanopan, Indo. 89/C2
Hutchins, Tx, US 150/L7
Hutchinson, Ks, US 153/F1

Hutchi – Irene

Hutchinson (isl.), Fl, US 165/H4
Hutchinson, Mn, US 155/G1
Ḩūth, Yem. 118/B1
Hutiaoxia, China 86/D3
Hutsonville, Il, US 160/C5
Hutt (riv.), NZ 135/J9
Huttig, Ar, US 153/H4
Hüttisheim, Ger. 61/F1
Hüttlingen, Ger. 58/D5
Huttoft, Eng, UK 35/J5
Hutton, Eng, UK 30/E2
Hutton (mt.), Austl. 134/C4
Hutton Cranswick, Eng, UK 35/H4
Hutton Lake Nat'l Wild. Ref., Wy, US 154/B3
Hutton Rudby, Eng, UK 35/G3
Huttonville, On, Can. 160/T8
Huttwil, Swi. 60/D3
Hutubi, China 99/E3
Hutuo (riv.), China 80/C3
Huveane (riv.), Fr. 47/H1
Huveaune (riv.), Fr. 64/B6
Huwan, China 87/G2
Ḩuwwārah, WBnk. 105/G4
Huxi, China 87/G3
Huxley, Tx, US 151/H2
Huxley, Ia, US 155/H3
Huy, Belg. 55/E2
Huyton-with-Roby, Eng, UK 35/F5
Hūzgān, Iran 103/G4
Huzhou, China 80/L9
Hvammstangi, Ice. 38/N6
Hvannadalshnúkur (peak), Ice. 38/P7
Hvar, Cro. 50/C4
Hvar (isl.), Cro. 67/H2
Hvardiys'ke, Ukr. 73/H5
Hvide Sande, Den. 40/C4
Hvidovre, Den. 39/J7
Hvítá (riv.), Ice. 38/N7
Hvitsten, Nor. 38/S9
Hvittingfoss, Nor. 38/R9
Hvolsvöllur, Ice. 38/N7
Hwach'ŏn, SKor. 81/D3
Hwadae, NKor. 81/E2
Hwange, Zim. 123/E3
Hwange (Wankie) NP, Zim. 123/E3
Hwanghae-bukto (prov.), NKor. 81/D3
Hwanghae-namdo (prov.), NKor. 81/C3
Hwangju (riv.), NKor. 81/C3
Hwangju, NKor. 81/C3
Hwap'yŏng, NKor. 81/D2
Hwasun, SKor. 81/D5
Hyades (peak), Chile 190/B5
Hyak, Wa, US 144/D4
Hyangsan, NKor. 81/D2
Hyannis, Ne, US 154/D2
Hyargas (lake), Mong. 78/C2
Hyattstown, Md, US 168/A5
Hyattsville, Md, US 168/B6
Hyco (res.), NC, US 163/H2
Hydaburg, Ak, US 171/M4
Hyde, Eng, UK 35/F5
Hyde, NZ 135/B4
Hyde Park, Vt, US 161/K2
Hyde Park, NY, US 161/K4
Hyden, Ky, US 163/F2
Hyden, Austl. 130/C5
Hyder, Ak, US 171/M4
Hyderābād, India 95/C2
Hyderābād, Pak. 101/J3
Hydesville, Ca, US 146/A3
Hyères (riv.), Fr. 56/B4
Hyères (bay), Fr. 64/C6
Hyères, Fr. 64/C6
Hyères, Iles d' (isls.), Fr. 66/E2
Hyesan, NKor. 81/E2
Hyland (riv.), Yk, Can. 140/D2
Hyllestad, Nor. 40/A1
Hyltebruk, Swe. 40/E3
Hylton (hill), Ky, US 163/F2
Hyō-no-sen (peak), Japan 84/D3
Hyōgo (pref.), Japan 84/D3
Hyŏndŭng-san (peak), SKor. 81/G6
Hypoluxo, Fl, US 164/P9
Hyrra Banda, CAfr. 116/D4
Hyrum, Ut, US 147/H3
Hyrylä (Skavaböle), Fin. 39/F4
Hysham, Mt, US 145/L4
Hythe, Austl. 132/C4
Hythe, Eng, UK 37/E5
Hythe, Eng, UK 37/H4
Hytop, Al, US 162/D3
Hyūga, Japan 84/B4
Hyvinkää, Fin. 41/L1

I

I-n-Amenas, Alg. 111/H3
I-n-Amguel, Alg. 111/G5
I-n-Azaoua, Oued (riv.), Niger 111/H5
I-n-Chaouâg (wadi), Mali 115/F2
I-n-Dagouber (well), Mali 111/E5
I-n-Échaï (well), Mali 115/E1
I-n-Eker, Alg. 111/G4
I-n-Farba, Mrta. 114/C3
I-n-Gall, Niger 115/G2
I-n-Guezzâm, Alg. 115/G2
I-n-Milach (well), Mali 115/E2
I-n-Rhar, Alg. 111/F4
I-n-Sâkâne, 'Erg (des.), Mali 115/E1
I-n-Salah, Alg. 111/F4
I-n-Tassik (well), Mali 115/F2
I-n-Tebezas, Mali 115/F2
I-n-Tileft, Mali 115/E3
Iabalo, Eth. 118/B4
Iacanga, Braz. 189/G2
Iaco (riv.), Braz. 184/D3
Iaçu, Braz. 187/E2
Iâf di Montasio (peak), It. 45/K3
Iakora, Madg. 125/H8
Ialibu, PNG 129/F1
Ialomiţa (riv.), Rom. 70/C3
Ialomita (prov.), Rom. 51/H3
Ianakafy, Madg. 125/H8
Ianapera, Madg. 125/H8
Iargara, Mol. 72/E4
Iaşi (prov.), Rom. 51/H2
Iaşi, Rom. 72/D4
Íasmos, Gre. 49/J2
Iatt (lake), La, US 164/B2
Iba, Phil. 88/B2
Ibadan, Nga. 115/F5
Ibagué, Col. 183/K8
Ibaiti, Braz. 189/G2
Ibajay, Phil. 88/C3
Ibanda, Ugan. 121/G3
Ibans (lake), Nic. 177/E3
Ibapah (peak), Ut, US 147/G4
Ibapah, Ut, US 147/G3
Ibar (riv.), Yugo. 50/E4
Ibara, Japan 84/C3
Ibaraki (pref.), Japan 85/F2
Ibaraki, Japan 83/E1
Ibaraki, Japan 83/J6
Ibarra, Ecu. 180/B4
Ibarreta, Arg. 188/E3
Ibb, Yem. 118/C2
Ibba (riv.), Sudan 117/F4
Ibbenbüren, Ger. 53/E4
'Ibbīn, Jor. 105/D4
Ibdekkene (riv.), Mali 115/F2
Ibenga (riv.), Congo 120/D2
Iberia, Mo, US 153/H1
Iberia, Peru 184/D3
Iberia, Peru 184/C2
Ibérico, Sistema (mts.), Sp. 66/C2
Iberville, Qu, Can. 159/P7
Ibeto, Nga. 115/G4
Ibi, Nga. 115/H4
Ibi, Sp. 47/E3
Ibi (riv.), Japan 79/M4
Ibiapada, Serra da (mts.), Braz. 183/F3
Ibiapina, Braz. 183/F3
Ibicaraí, Braz. 187/F2
Ibicuí (riv.), Braz. 189/E4
Ibicuy, Arg. 191/J10
Ibigawa, Japan 83/L5
I'billīn, Isr. 105/C3
Ibimirim, Braz. 183/G5
Ibirapuitã (riv.), Braz. 189/F4
Ibirubá, Braz. 189/F4
Ibitinga, Braz. 189/G2
Ibiúna, Braz. 187/J8
Ibiza (isl.), Sp. 47/F3
Ibiza, Sp. 47/F3
Ibiza (isl.), Sp. 29/E5
Ibnahs, Egypt 113/C3
Ibo (riv.), Japan 84/D3
Ibo, Moz. 123/J2
Ibondo, D.R. Congo 121/G3
Iboro, Nga. 115/F5
Ibotirama, Braz. 187/E2
Iboundji (peak), Gabon 120/B3
Ibrā', Oman 101/G4
Ibrah (wadi), Sudan 117/E3
Ibrány, Hun. 43/L4
'Ibrī, Oman 101/G4
İbriktepe, Turk. 51/H5
Ibshān, Egypt 113/C2
Ibshawāy, Egypt 113/B6
Ibstock, Eng, UK 37/E1
Ibu, Indo. 91/G3
Ibuki, Japan 83/K5
Ibuki-yama (peak), Japan 83/K5
Iça (riv.), SAm. 179/D3
Ica, Peru 184/C4
Ica (dept.), Peru 184/C4
Icabarú, Ven. 181/F3
Içana (riv.), Braz. 180/E4
Icaño, Arg. 188/C4
Icaraíma, Braz. 189/F2
Icatu, Braz. 183/E3
Icel (prov.), Turk. 104/C1
Iceland (ctry.) 29/B2
Ichalkaranji, India 95/B2
Ichāmati (riv.), Bang. 97/G3
Ichenhausen, Ger. 58/D6
Icheu, Nga. 115/G5
Ichhāwar, India 96/A4
Ichihara, Japan 83/E3
Ichijima, Japan 83/H5
Ichikawa, Japan 83/D2
Ichikawada, Japan 83/B2
Ichilo (riv.), Bol. 185/E5
Ichinohe, Japan 82/B3
Ichinomiya, Japan 83/G7
Ichinomiya, Japan 83/L5
Ichinomiya, Japan 83/E3
Ichinomiya, Japan 83/B2
Ichinomiya, Japan 83/M6
Ichinoseki, Japan 82/B4
Ichishi, Japan 83/K6
Ichnya, Ukr. 73/G1
Ichoca, Bol. 188/C1
Ich'ŏn, SKor. 81/D4
Ich'ŏn, NKor. 81/D3
Ichtegem, Belg. 54/C1
Ichuña, Peru 188/B1
Ickesburg, Pa, US 168/A3
Icó, Braz. 183/G4
Icod de los Vinos, Sp. 110/A3
Iconi, Com. 125/G5
Icononzo, Col. 183/L8
Icy (bay), Ak, US 140/B3
Icy (cape), Ak, US 171/F1
Icy (pt.), Ak, US 171/L4
Icy (str.), Ak, US 171/L4
Ida Grove, Ia, US 155/G2
Idabel, Ok, US 153/G4
Idabo, Eth. 118/B4
Idah, Nga. 115/G5
Idaho (state), US 142/C3
Idaho City, Id, US 146/F2
Idaho Falls, Id, US 147/G2
Idaho Nat'l Engineering Laboratory, Id, US 147/G2
Idalia, Co, US 154/C4
Idalou, Tx, US 152/D4
Idanha-a-Nova, Port. 46/B3
Idāppādi, India 95/C4
Idar, India 92/B3
Idar-Oberstein, Ger. 55/G4
Idarkopf (peak), Ger. 55/G4
Idaville, In, US 160/C4
Idaville, Pa, US 168/A3
Ide, Japan 83/J6
Ide Hill, Eng, UK 30/D3
Ideal, Ga, US 162/E4
Idel', Rus. 68/G2
Ideles, Alg. 111/G5
Ider, Al, US 162/E3
Ider, Mong. 78/D2
Ider (riv.), Mong. 78/D2
Idfīnā, Egypt 113/B2
Idfū, Egypt 109/G3
Ídhi (peak), Gre. 49/J5
Ídhra, Gre. 49/H4
Idi, Indo. 89/B1
Idice (riv.), It. 63/E4
Idiofa, D.R. Congo 120/D4
Idiroko, Nga. 115/F5
Idkū (lake), Egypt 113/B2
Idkū, Egypt 113/B2
Idle (riv.), Eng, UK 35/H5
Idlib, Syria 104/E2
Idlib (prov.), Syria 104/E2
Idnah, WBnk. 105/B5
Idrija, Slov. 45/L4
Idriss I (dam), Mor. 112/B2
Idritsa, Rus. 41/N3
Idro (lake), It. 62/D1
Idstein, Ger. 58/B2
Idyllwild-Pine Cove, Ca, US 148/D4
Ie (isl.), Japan 85/J7
Iecava, Lat. 41/L3
Iema, Ang. 120/C4
Ieper, Belg. 54/B2
Ierápetra, Gre. 49/J5
Ierissós, Gre. 49/H2
Ierna, Slvk. 72/B3
Iesolo, It. 63/F2
Ifakara, Tanz. 119/B4
Ifaki, Nga. 115/G5
Ifalik (isl.), Micr. 136/D4
Ifanadiana, Madg. 125/H8
Ife, Nga. 115/G5
Iferfes (well), Libya 111/H3
Iferouâne, Niger 115/H2
Iffeldorf, Ger. 61/H2
Iffezheim, Ger. 58/B5
Ifon, Nga. 115/G5
Iforas, Adrar des (mts.), Alg.,Mali 111/F5
Ifrane, Mor. 110/D2
Ifs, Fr. 57/E2
Iga, Japan 83/K6
Iga (riv.), Japan 83/K6
Igal, Hun. 50/C2
Igalula, Tanz. 121/H4
Iganga, Ugan. 119/A1
Igara Paraná (riv.), Col. 180/C5
Igarapava, Braz. 189/H2
Igarapé Açu, Braz. 183/E3
Igarapé Água Preta (riv.), Braz. 185/E1
Igarapé Grande, Braz. 183/E4
Igarapé-Miri, Braz. 182/D3
Igarassu, Braz. 183/H4
Igaratá, Braz. 187/K8
Igarka, Rus. 74/J3
Igarra, Nga. 115/G5
Igawa, Tanz. 119/A4
Igbetti, Nga. 115/G4
Igboho, Nga. 115/F4
Igdet (peak), Mor. 110/C3
Iğdır, Turk. 103/F2
Igel, Ger. 55/F4
Iggesund, Swe. 40/G1
Ightham, Eng, UK 30/D3
Igikpak (mt.), Ak, US 171/H2
Igis, Swi. 61/F4
Igiugig, Ak, US 171/G4
Iglesias, It. 48/A3
Igli, Alg. 111/E3
Igling, Ger. 61/G1
Iglino, Rus. 69/N5
Igloolik, Nun, Can. 141/H2
Ignace, On, Can. 157/J3
Ignacio, Ca, US 167/J10
Ignacio, Co, US 149/J2
Ignacio de la Llave, Mex. 175/P8
Ignacio Zaragoza, Mex. 174/D2
Ignalina, Lith. 41/M4
İğneada, Turk. 51/H5
İğneada Burnu (cape), Turk. 51/J5
Igney, Fr. 60/C1
Ignon (riv.), Fr. 60/A2
Igny, Fr. 30/J5
Igombe (riv.), Tanz. 119/A3
Igombe, Tanz. 121/H3
Igor I. Sikorsky Memorial (arpt.), Ct, US 169/E1
Igora Paraná (riv.), Col. 184/C1
Igoumenítsa, Gre. 49/G3
Igra, Rus. 69/M4
Igreja Nova, Braz. 187/F1
Igrim, Rus. 74/G3
Iguaçu (riv.), Braz. 179/D5
Iguaçu, PN do, Braz. 189/F3
Iguaí, Braz. 187/E2
Iguala, Mex. 175/K8
Igualada, Sp. 47/F2
Iguape, Braz. 189/H3
Iguape, Ribeira do (riv.), Braz. 186/C5
Iguatemi (riv.), Braz. 186/B4
Iguatu, Braz. 183/G4
Iguazú (int'l arpt.), Arg. 189/F3
Iguéla, Gabon 120/B3
Iguetti (lake), Mrta. 110/C4
Igugunu, Tanz. 119/A3
Iharana, Madg. 125/J6
Iheya (isl.), Japan 85/J7
Ihhayrhan, Mong. 78/F2
Ihiala, Nga. 115/G5
Ihnāsiyah al Madīnah, Egypt 113/B6
Ihosy, Madg. 125/H8
Ihotry (lake), Madg. 125/G8
Ihu, PNG 129/G1
Ihuari, Peru 184/B3
Ihuo, Nga. 115/G5
Ii, Fin. 68/E2
Ii (riv.), Fin. 74/C3
Iida, Japan 85/E3
Iidaan, Som. 118/D4
Iide-san (peak), Japan 85/F2
Iijoki (riv.), Fin. 68/F2
Iinan, Japan 83/K7
Iisaku, Est. 41/M2
Iisalmi, Fin. 68/E3
Iitaka, Japan 83/K7
Iittala, Fin. 39/E3
Iitti, Fin. 41/M1
Iiyama, Japan 85/F2
Iizuka, Japan 84/B4
Ijara, Kenya 119/C2
Ijebu Ode, Nga. 115/F5
Ijill (lake), Mrta. 110/B5
Ijill (peak), Mrta. 110/B5
Ijira, Japan 83/L4
IJlst, Neth. 52/C2
IJmeer (bay), Neth. 52/C4
Ijmuiden, Neth. 52/B4
Ijnaoun (well), Mrta. 114/B2
Ijoki (riv.), Fin. 38/H2
Ijoubbane, 'Erg (des.), Mali 110/D5
IJssel (riv.), Neth. 52/C3
Ijsselmeer (lake), Neth. 42/C2
Ijsselmuiden, Neth. 52/C3
Ijsselstein, Neth. 52/C4
Ijuí (riv.), Braz. 189/F4
Ijuí, Braz. 189/F4
Ijūin, Japan 84/B5
Ijzendijke, Neth. 54/C1
Ijzer (riv.), Belg. 42/B3
Ik (riv.), Rus. 69/M5
Ikahavo (plat.), Madg. 125/H7
Ikalamavony, Madg. 125/H8
Ikali, D.R. Congo 121/E3
Ikamba, Tanz. 121/G4
Ikanda Nord, D.R. Congo 121/E3
Ikang, Nga. 120/B1
Ikare, Nga. 115/G5
Ikaría (isl.), Gre. 67/K3
Ikaría (isl), Gre. 102/A2
Ikaruga, Japan 83/J6
Ikasi, Tanz. 119/A3
Ikeda, Japan 84/C3
Ikeda, Japan 82/C2
Ikeda, Japan 83/H6
Ikeda, Japan 83/L5
Ikeja, Nga. 115/F5
Ikela, D.R. Congo 121/E3
Ikelemba (riv.), D.R. Congo 120/D2
Ikelemba, Congo 120/D2
Ikem, Nga. 115/G5
Ikenokoya-yama (peak), Japan 83/K7
Ikerre, Nga. 115/G5
Ikhtiman, Bul. 51/F4
Iki (isl.), Japan 84/A4
Iki (chan.), Japan 84/A4
Iki-Burul, Rus. 71/H3
Ikire, Nga. 115/G5
Ikirun, Nga. 115/G5
İkizce, Turk. 102/C2
İkizdere, Turk. 71/G4
Ikkala, Fin. 39/E4
Ikole, Nga. 115/G5
Ikom, Nga. 115/H5
Ikoma, Tanz. 119/A2
Ikoma, Japan 83/J6
Ikongo, Madg. 125/H8
Ikopa (riv.), Madg. 125/H7
Ikorodu, Nga. 115/F5
Ikot Ekpene, Nga. 115/G5
Ikot Okpora, Nga. 115/H5
Ikozi, D.R. Congo 121/F3
Ikrāsh, Egypt 113/C3
Iksāl, Isr. 105/C3
Ikungi, Tanz. 119/A3
Ikungu, Tanz. 119/A3
Ikuno, Japan 84/D3
Ikwah, Egypt 113/C3
Ila Orangun, Nga. 115/G4
Ilabaya, Peru 188/B1
Ilagala, Tanz. 121/G4
Ilagan, Phil. 88/C1
Ilaka, Madg. 125/H8
Ilaka, Madg. 125/J7
Īlām, Iran 103/F3
Ilam, Nepal 97/F2
Īlām (gov.), Iran 103/F3
Ilām Bāzār, India 97/F4
Ilan, Tai. 87/J3
Ilangali, Tanz. 119/A3
Ilanz, Swi. 61/F4
Ilaro, Nga. 115/F5
Ilave, Peru 184/D5
Iława, Pol. 43/K2
Ilawe-Ekiti, Nga. 115/G5
'Ilay, Sudan 117/F1
Ilchester, Eng, UK 36/D4
Ile (riv.), Kaz. 77/G5
Ile Art (isl.), NCal. 137/T11
Ile aux Coudres (isl.), Qu, Can. 158/B2
Ile aux Grues (isl.), Qu, Can. 158/B2
Ile aux Lièvres (isl.), QU, Can. 158/C2
Ile Baaba (isl.), NCal. 137/T11
Ile Balabio (isl.), NCal. 137/U12
Ile Callot (isl.), Fr. 56/B3
Ile d' Orléans (isl.), Qu, Can. 158/B2
Ile d'Anticosti (isl.), Can. 139/L5
Ile de Bagaud (isl.), Fr. 64/C7
Ile de Batz (isl.), Fr. 56/A3
Ile de Bréhat (isl.), Fr. 56/C3
Ile de Levant (isl.), Fr. 64/C6
Ile de Porquerolles (isl.), Fr. 64/C7
Ile de Riou (isl.), Sp. 64/B6
Ile des Pins (isl.), NCal. 136/F7
Ile Esumba (isl.), D.R. Congo 121/E2
Ile Idjwe (isl.), D.R. Congo 121/G3
Ile Tidra (isl.), Mrta. 114/A2
Ile Tiga (isl.), NCal. 137/V12
Ile Yandé (isl.), NCal. 137/T12
Île-à-la-Crosse, Sk, Can. 140/F3
Île-de-France (pol. reg.), Fr. 54/A6
Ile-de-Montréal (co.), Qu, Can. 159/N6
Ile-Jésus (co.), Qu, Can. 159/N6
Île-Perrot (isl.), Qu, Can. 159/N7
Ilebo, D.R. Congo 121/E4
Ilek, Rus. 71/K2
Ilek (riv.), Rus. 71/K2
Ilen (riv.), Ire. 32/A6
Iles Chausey (isl.), Fr. 56/D3
Iles de la Madeleine (isl.), Qu, Can. 159/F2
Iles de Lérins (isls.), Fr. 64/D5
Iles du Vent (isls.), FrPol. 137/L6
Îles Ehotilés, PN des, C.d'Iv. 114/E5
Iles Glorieuses (isls.), Reun. 125/H5
Iles sous le Vent (isls.), FrPol. 137/K6
Iles Tristao (isls.), Gui. 114/B4
Ilesha, Nga. 115/G5
Ilfacombe, Austl. 134/B3
Ilfis (riv.), Swi. 60/D4
Ilford (nbrhd.), Eng, UK 30/D2
Ilford, Austl. 133/D1
Ilfracombe, Eng, UK 36/B4
Ilgaz, Turk. 70/E4
Ilgın, Turk. 102/B2
Ilha Caravela (isl.), GBis. 114/A4
Ilha de Jeta (isl.), GBis. 114/A4
Ilha de Marajó (isl.), Braz. 179/D3
Ilha do Bazaruto (isl.), Moz. 123/G4
Ilha Grande (bay), Braz. 186/D4
Ilha Solteira (res.), Braz. 186/C3
Ilhabela, Braz. 187/L8
Ilhas Desertas (isl.), Port. 110/A2
Ilhas Selvagens (isl.), Sp. 110/A3
Ílhavo, Port. 46/A2
Ilhea (pt.), Namb. 122/B4
Ilhéus, Braz. 187/F2
Iliamna, Ak, US 171/H4
Iliamna (lake), Ak, US 171/G4
Iliamna (mt.), Ak, US 171/H3
İliç, Turk. 102/D2
Ilıca, Turk. 71/G5
Ilicínea, Braz. 186/D4
Iliff, Co, US 154/C3
Iligan, Phil. 88/D3
Iligan (bay), Phil. 88/C3
Ilijaš, Bosn. 50/D4
Iliniza (peak), Ecu. 180/B5
Il'inskiy, Rus. 79/N2
Il'inskoye, Rus. 69/K4
Iliomar, ETim. 128/B2
Ilirska Bistrica, Slov. 45/L4
Ilısu (dam), Turk. 102/E2
Ilisu (res.), Turk. 102/E2
Ilium (Troy) (ruin), Turk. 49/K3
Ilkeston, Eng, UK 35/G6
Īlkhchī, Iran 103/F2
Ilkley, Eng, UK 35/G4
Ill (riv.), Fr. 45/G3
Ill (riv.), Aus. 45/H3
Illabo, Austl. 133/C2
Illana, Sp. 46/D2
Illapel, Chile 188/B4
Illasi (riv.), It. 63/E1
Illawarra (lake), Austl. 133/E2
Illbillee (mt.), Austl. 131/G3
Ille (riv.), Fr. 56/D4
Ille-et-Vilaine (dept.), Fr. 56/D4
Illéla, Niger 115/G3
Illela, Nga. 115/G3
Iller (riv.), Ger. 45/J2
Illerbrun, Sk, Can. 145/K3
Illertissen, Ger. 61/G1
Illescas, Sp. 46/D2
Illet (riv.), Fr. 56/D4
Illichivs'k, Ukr. 72/F4
Illiers-Combray, Fr. 57/G4
Illigh (pt.), Som. 118/D4
Illimani (peak), Bol. 188/C1
Illingen, Ger. 55/G5
Illinois (riv.), Il, US 143/J3
Illinois (state), US 143/J4
Illinois (riv.), Il, US 155/K3
Illizi, Alg. 111/H4
Illizi (wilaya), Alg. 111/G4
Illkirch-Graffenstaden, Fr. 60/D1
Illmensee, Ger. 61/F2
Illnau, Swi. 61/E3
Illogan, Eng, UK 36/A6
Illora, Sp. 46/D4
Illovo, SAfr. 125/E3
Illushi, Nga. 115/G5
Illyungmadja (pt.), Austl. 129/E3
Illzach, Fr. 60/D2
Ilm (riv.), Ger. 42/F4
Ilmajoki, Fin. 38/G3
Ilme (riv.), Ger. 53/G5
Il'men (lake), Rus. 74/D4
Ilmenau (riv.), Ger. 53/H2
Ilminster, Eng, UK 36/D5
Ilo, Peru 184/D5
Ilobu, Nga. 115/G5
Iloca, Chile 190/B2
Iloilo, Phil. 88/C3
Ilongero, Tanz. 119/A3
Ilorin, Nga. 115/G4
Ilovays'k, Ukr. 73/K4
Ilovlya, Rus. 71/G2
Ilovlya (riv.), Rus. 71/H2
Ilpendam, Neth. 52/B4
Il'pyrskiy, Rus. 75/S4
Ilsan, SKor. 81/F6
Ilse (riv.), Ger. 53/H5
Ilsede, Ger. 53/H4
Ilsenburg, Ger. 53/H5
Ilsfeld, Ger. 58/C4
Ilshofen, Ger. 58/C4
Il'skiy, Rus. 73/K5
Īlubabor (pol. reg.), Eth. 117/G4
Ilūkste, Lat. 41/M4
Ilwaco, Wa, US 144/B4
Ilwaki, Indo. 128/B1
Ilyas Burnu (pt.), Turk. 51/H5
Ilych (riv.), Rus. 69/N3
Ilz (riv.), Ger. 43/G4
Imabari, Japan 84/C3
Imaichi, Japan 85/F2
Imaloto (riv.), Madg. 125/H8
İmamoğlu, Turk. 102/C2
Imandra (lake), Rus. 38/J2
Imanombo, Madg. 125/H9
Imari, Japan 84/A4
Imatong (mts.), Sudan 117/G4
Imatra, Fin. 41/N1
Imazu, Japan 83/K5
Imba (lake), Japan 83/E2
Imba, Japan 83/E2
Imbābah, Egypt 113/C4
Imbabura (prov.), Ecu. 180/B4
Imbaimadai, Guy. 182/A1
Imbituba, Braz. 189/G4
Imbler, Or, US 146/E1
Imeni 26 Bakinskikh Komissarov, Trkm. 71/K5
Imeni Chapayeva, Trkm. 101/H1
Imeni Karla Libknekhta, Rus. 73/H2
Imeni Moskvy (canal), Rus. 69/W8
Imerimandroso, Madg. 125/J7
Imese, D.R. Congo 120/D2
Īmī, Eth. 118/B4
Imi n'tanout, Mor. 110/C3
İmişli, Azer. 103/G2
Imittós (peak), Gre. 49/N9
Imja (isl.), SKor. 81/C5
Imjin (riv.), NKor. 79/K4
Imlay, Nv, US 146/D3
Imlay City, Mi, US 160/E3
Immeln (lake), Swe. 39/L6
Immendingen, Ger. 61/E2
Immenhausen, Ger. 53/G6
Immenstaad am Bodensee, Ger. 61/F2
Immenstadt im Allgäu, Ger. 61/G2
Immingham, Eng, UK 35/H4
Immokalee, Fl, US 165/H4
Imnaha (riv.), Or, US 146/E1
Imnaha, Or, US 146/E1
Imnavait (mt.), Ak, US 171/J2
Imo (state), Nga. 115/G5
Imola, It. 63/E5
Imonda, PNG 91/K4
Imouzzer des Marmoucha, Mor. 110/D2
Imouzzèr-Kandar, Mor. 112/B3
Imperatriz, Braz. 183/E4
Imperia, It. 62/B6
Imperia (prov.), It. 64/D5
Imperial (dam), Az, US 148/E4
Imperial (res.), Az,Ca, US 148/E4
Imperial, Ne, US 154/D3
Imperial (valley), Ca, US 148/E4
Imperial, Peru 184/B4
Imperial, Tx, US 151/C2
Imperial, Sk, Can. 145/M2
Imperial Beach, Ca, US 166/C5
Imperial Nat'l Wild Ref., Az,Ca, US 148/E4
Imperial Palace, Japan 83/D2
Impero (riv.), It. 62/B5
Impfondo, Congo 120/D2
Imphāl, India 86/B3
Imphy, Fr. 44/E3
Impora, Bol. 188/C2
Impruneta, It. 63/E6
Impulo, Ang. 122/B2
İmrali (isl.), Turk. 51/J5
İmranlı, Turk. 102/D2
İmroz, Gre. 49/J2
Imshil, SKor. 81/D5
Imst, Aus. 61/G3
Imuris, Mex. 174/C2
Imus, Phil. 88/E7
Imus (riv.), Phil. 88/E7
Imusho, Zam. 122/D3
In Agiuel (well), Libya 108/A3
Ina (riv.), Pol. 40/F5
Ina, Japan 85/E3
Ina (riv.), Japan 83/H6
Ina, Japan 83/E2
Ina, Japan 83/D2
Inabanga, Phil. 88/D3
Inabe, Japan 83/L5
Inabu, Japan 83/M5
Inagawa, Japan 83/H6
Inagi, Japan 83/D2
Inaha, Ga, US 165/G2
Inajá, Braz. 183/G5
Inaja Ind. Res., Ca, US 148/D4
Inambari (riv.), Peru 184/D4
Inambari, Peru 184/D4
Inami, Japan 83/G6
Inangahua Junction, NZ 135/B3
Inanwatan, Indo. 91/H4
Inaouene (riv.), Mor. 112/B2
Iñapari, Peru 184/D3
Inarjärvi (lake), Fin. 38/H1
Inău (peak), Rom. 51/G2
Inawashiro (lake), Japan 85/F2
Inazawa, Japan 83/L5
Inca, Sp. 47/G3
Incahuasi, Arg. 188/C3
Incahuasi, Cerro de (peak), Chile 188/B3
Incekum (pt.), Turk. 104/C1
Inch'on-jikhalsi (prov.), SKor. 81/D4
Inchcape (Bell Rock) (isl.), Sc, UK 33/D4
Inchelium, Wa, US 144/E3
Incheville, Fr. 54/A3
Inchigeelagh, Ire. 32/A6
Inchinnan, Sc, UK 33/B5
Inchkeith (isl.), Sc, UK 33/C4
Inchnadamph, Sc, UK 31/R7
Inch'ŏn, SKor. 81/F7
Inchope, Moz. 123/G3
İncirliova, Turk. 102/A2
Incisa in Val d'Arno, It. 63/E6
Incomati (riv.), Moz. 123/G5
Inconfidentes, Braz. 187/K7
Incudine, Mont l' (peak), Fr. 48/A2
Ind. Dunes NL, In, US 160/C4
Inda Silasē, Eth. 100/C6
Indaiatuba, Braz. 189/H2
Indalsälven (riv.), Swe. 38/E3
Indanan, Phil. 88/C4
Indaw, Myan. 86/C4
Indawgyi (lake), Myan. 86/C3
Inde (riv.), Ger. 55/F2
Inden, Ger. 55/F2
Independence, Belz. 176/D2
Independence, Ca, US 148/C2
Independence, Ia, US 155/J2
Independence, Ks, US 153/G2
Independence, Ky, US 162/E1
Independence, La, US 164/C2
Independence, Mo, US 155/G4
Independence (mts.), Nv, US 146/E3
Independence, Or, US 146/B1
Independence (cr.), Tx, US 151/C2
Independence, Va, US 163/G2
Independence Nat'l Hist. Park, Pa, US 168/C4
Independencia, Peru 184/B4
Independencia, Bol. 188/C1
Independência, Braz. 183/F4
Inder (lake), Kaz. 71/K2
Inderapura (cape), Indo. 89/C3
Inderborskiy, Kaz. 71/J2
Index, Wa, US 167/D2
India (ctry.) 77/G7
Indian (lake), Mi, US 157/L4
Indian (ocean) 27/N6
Indian (hill), Ne, US 154/D2
Indian (cr.), Ga, US 163/M7
Indian Brook, NS, Can. 159/G2
Indian Church, Belz. 176/D2
Indian Echo Caverns, Pa, US 168/B3
Indian Harbour Beach, Fl, US 165/H3
Indian Head, Sk, Can. 156/C2
Indian Lake, NY, US 161/J3
Indian Lake Estates, Fl, US 164/N8
Indian Pictographs, Tx, US 151/E2
Indian River, Mi, US 160/D2
Indian Rocks Beach, Fl, US 164/K8
Indian Springs, Ga, US 162/F4
Indian Valley, Va, US 163/G2
Indian Wells, Az, US 149/G3
Indiana, Pa, US 161/G4
Indiana (state), US 143/J4
Indianapolis (cap.), In, US 160/C5
Indianapolis (int'l arpt.), In, US 160/C5
Indianapolis Motor Speedway, In, US 160/C5
Indianola, Ga, US 165/G2
Indianola, Wa, US 167/B2
Indianola, Ia, US 155/H3
Indianola, Ms, US 162/B4
Indianola, Tx, US 150/F3
Indiantown, Fl, US 165/H4
Indiaporã, Braz. 189/G1
Indicatore, It. 63/E7
Indiga, Rus. 69/L2
Indigirka (riv.), Rus. 77/P3
Inđija, Yugo. 50/E3
Indio, Ca, US 148/D4
Indira Gandhi (int'l arpt.), India 98/D5
Indochina (reg.), Asia 94/C1
Indonesia (ctry.) 77/K10
Indooroopilly (nbrhd.), Austl. 134/E7
Indore, India 92/C3
Indragiri (riv.), Indo. 90/B4
Indragiri (river), Indo. 89/C3
Indramayu, Indo. 89/E4
Indramayu (cape), Indo. 90/C5
Indrapura, Indo. 89/C3
Indrāvati (riv.), India 92/D4
Indre (dept.), Fr. 57/G6
Indre (riv.), Fr. 44/D3
Indre Arna, Nor. 40/A1
Indre-et-Loire (dept.), Fr. 57/F5
Indrois (riv.), Fr. 44/D3
Indungo, Ang. 122/C2
Induno Olona, It. 61/E6
Indus (riv.), Asia 77/G6
Industry, Ca, US 166/G7
Industry, Tx, US 150/F3
İnebolu, Turk. 70/E4
İnece, Turk. 51/H5
İnecik, Turk. 51/H5
Inedbirenne (int'l arpt.), Alg. 111/H4
Iner (riv.), Ger. 58/C3
Ineu, Rom. 50/E2
Inez, Ky, US 163/F2
Inez, Tx, US 151/F3
Inezgane, Mor. 110/C3
Inezgane (Agadir) (int'l arpt.), Mor. 110/C3
Infanta (cape), SAfr. 124/C4
Infante dom Henrique, SaoT. 120/A2
Infiernillo (res.), Mex. 172/A4
Infiernillo, Presa del (dam), Mex. 174/E5
Infiesto, Sp. 46/C1
Ingá, Braz. 183/H4
Ingå (Inkoo), Fin. 39/E4
Ingalls, Mi, US 157/L5
Ingalls, Ar, US 153/H4
Inganda, D.R. Congo 121/E3
Ingapirca (ruin), Ecu. 180/B5
Ingarö (isl.), Swe. 39/B1
Ingarö, Swe. 39/B1
Ingasu, D.R. Congo 121/F2
Ingatestone, Eng, UK 30/E2
Ingelmunster, Belg. 54/C2
Ingende, D.R. Congo 120/D3
Ingeniero Guillermo N. Juárez, Arg. 188/D2
Ingeniero Jacobacci, Arg. 190/C4
Ingeniero Luiggi, Arg. 190/D2
Ingenio, Sp. 110/B4
Ingersheim, Fr. 60/D1
Ingersoll, On, Can. 160/F3
Ingettolgoy, Mong. 78/E2
Inggen, China 78/E3
Ingham, Austl. 134/B2
Ingleburn (nbrhd.), Austl. 134/G9
Ingleside, On, Can. 161/J2
Ingleside, Md, US 168/C5
Ingleton, Eng, UK 35/G2
Inglewood, Ca, US 166/F8
Inglewood, Austl. 132/B3
Inglewood, Austl. 134/C5
Inglewood, NZ 135/C2
Inglewood, On, Can. 160/T8
Inglewood-Finn Hill, Wa, US 167/C2
Inglis, Fl, US 165/G3
Ingmarsö (isl.), Swe. 39/B1
Ingoda (riv.), Rus. 75/M4
Ingoldmells, Eng, UK 35/J5
Ingolstadt, Ger. 59/E5
Ingomar, Mt, US 145/L4
Ingonish, NS, Can. 159/G2
Ingonish Beach, NS, Can. 159/G2
Ingraham, Il, US 162/C1
Ingram, Tx, US 151/E2
Ingrave, Eng, UK 30/E2
Ingré, Fr. 57/G5
Ingre, Bol. 188/D2
Ingrid Christianson (coast), Ant. 192/F
Ingulets (riv.), Ukr. 73/G3
Ingushetia, Resp., Rus. 75/Q6
Ingwavuma, SAfr. 125/E2
Ingwiller, Fr. 55/G6
Inhacalunga, Ang. 121/E5
Inhambane, Moz. 123/G4
Inhambane (prov.), Moz. 123/G4
Inhaminga, Moz. 123/G3
Inhapim, Braz. 187/E3
Inharrime, Moz. 123/G5
Inhassoro, Moz. 123/G4
Inhuca, Ang. 120/C4
Inhulets', Ukr. 73/G4
Inhuma, Braz. 183/F4
Inhumas, Braz. 186/C3
Iniesta, Sp. 46/E3
Inifel (well), Alg. 111/F3
Inini (riv.), FrG. 181/H4
Inini, FrG. 182/C2
Inírida (riv.), Col. 180/D4
Inishannon, Ire. 32/B6
Inishbofin (isl.), Ire. 30/N10
Inishcarra (res.), Ire. 32/A6
Inishcrone, Ire. 32/A1
Inishmaan (arpt.), Ire. 32/A3
Inishmeer (arpt.), Ire. 32/A3
Inishowen (pt.), Ire. 34/B1
Inishowen (pen.), Ire. 34/A1
Inistioge, Ire. 32/C5
Inje, SKor. 81/E3
Injibara, Eth. 117/H3
Injune, Austl. 134/C4
Inkerman, NB, Can. 158/E2
Inkhil, Syria 105/E2
Inkisi (riv.), D.R. Congo 120/C4
Inkom, Id, US 147/G2
Inkoo (Ingå), Fin. 39/E4
Inkster, Mi, US 167/F7
Inland (sea), Japan 84/C4
Inle (lake), Myan. 93/G3
Inman, Ks, US 153/F1
Inman, SC, US 163/F3
Inn (riv.), Aus. 45/J3
Inn (riv.), Aus.,Ger. 42/G5
Inn (riv.), Eur. 67/F1
Inn (riv.), Ger. 45/K2
Inn (riv.), Swi. 45/J3
Innamincka, Austl. 134/A4
Innbach (riv.), Aus. 59/H6
Innellan, Sc, UK 33/B5
Inner (sound), Sc, UK 31/R8
Inner (chan.), Belz. 176/D2
Inner Hebrides (isls.), Sc, UK 31/Q8
Inner Mongolia (reg.), China 77/L5
Inner Space Caverns, Tx, US 151/F2
Innerdouny (hill), Sc, UK 33/C4
Innerleithen, Sc, UK 33/C5
Innerste (riv.), Ger. 53/G4
Innertkirchen, Swi. 61/E4
Innes NP, Austl. 131/H5
Innichen (San Candito), It. 45/K3
Innis, La, US 164/C2
Innisfail, Austl. 134/B2
Innisfail, Ab, Can. 145/H1
Innoko (riv.), Ak, US 171/G3
Innsbruck, Aus. 61/H3
Innviertel (reg.), Aus. 59/G6
Inny (riv.), Ire. 32/C2
Inny (riv.), Eng, UK 36/B5
Ino, Japan 84/C4
Inobonto, Indo. 91/F3
Inocência, Braz. 189/G1
Inola, Ok, US 153/G2
Inongo, D.R. Congo 120/D3
İnönü, Turk. 102/B2
Inowrocław, Pol. 43/K2
Inquisivi, Bol. 188/C1
Insch, Sc, UK 33/D2
Inscription (cape), Austl. 130/B3
Insein, Myan. 86/C5
Inshāş ar Raml, Egypt 113/C4
Insinger, Sk, Can. 156/C2
Insiza, Zim. 123/F3
Insjön, Swe. 40/F1
Inspiration, Az, US 149/G4
Insu, Gha. 115/E5
Int'l Amistad (res.), Mex.,US 151/D3
Inta, Rus. 69/N2
Intagaw, Myan. 94/B2
Intaing, Myan. 94/B2
Intake, Mt, US 156/B4
Intelewa, Sur. 182/C2
Intendente Alvear, Arg. 190/E2
İntepe, Turk. 49/K2
Intercession City, Fl, US 164/M7
Intercourse, Pa, US 168/B3
Interior, SD, US 154/D2
Interior (plat.), BC, Can. 144/B1
Interlaken, Swi. 60/D4
Interlaken, NY, US 161/H3
Interlochen, Mi, US 160/D2
Internacional (int'l arpt.), Braz. 184/D2
Internacional (int'l arpt.), Mex. 175/E5
International Falls, Mn, US 157/H3
International Peace Garden, ND, US 156/D3
Inthanon (peak), Thai. 86/C5
Intich'o, Eth. 118/A2
Întorsura Buzăului, Rom. 51/H3
Intragna, Swi. 61/E5
Introbio, It. 61/F6
Intuto, Peru 184/C1
Inubō-zaki (pt.), Japan 85/G3
Inukjuak, Qu, Can. 141/J3
Inutil (bay), Chile 191/C7
Inuvik, Yk, Can. 171/M2
Inuyama, Japan 83/L5
Inver (bay), Sc, UK 33/C1
Inver Grove Heights, Mn, US 157/P7
Inveraray, Sc, UK 33/A4
Inverbervie, Sc, UK 33/D3
Invercargill, NZ 135/B4
Inverclyde (co.), Sc, UK 33/B5
Inverell, Austl. 132/D1
Invergarry, Sc, UK 33/B2
Invergordon, Sc, UK 33/B1
Invergowrie, Sc, UK 33/C4
Inverie, Sc, UK 31/R8
Inverigo, It. 62/C2
Inverkeilor, Sc, UK 33/D3
Inverkeithing, Sc, UK 33/C4
Inverloch, Austl. 133/B4
Invermay, Sk, Can. 156/C2
Invermere, BC, Can. 144/F2
Invermoriston, IM, UK 34/D3
Inverness, Qu, Can. 158/B2
Inverness, Sc, UK 33/B2
Inverness, Fl, US 165/G3
Inverness, NS, Can. 159/G2
Inverness, Al, US 165/F1
Inveruno, It. 62/B2
Inverurie, Sc, UK 33/D2
Inverway, Austl. 128/C4
Investigator (str.), Austl. 127/C4
Invorio, It. 62/B2
Inwood, WV, US 161/G5
Inwood, NY, US 169/L9
Inwood, Ia, US 155/F2
Inyan Kara (mtn.), Wy, US 154/B1
Inyanga, Zim. 123/G3
Inyangani (peak), Zim. 123/G3
Inyati, Zim. 123/F3
Inyo (mts.), Ca, US 148/D2
Inyokern, Ca, US 148/D3
Inyonga, Tanz. 121/H4
Inza, Rus. 71/H1
Inzai, Japan 83/E2
Inzer, Rus. 69/N5
Inzhavino, Rus. 71/G1
Inzia (riv.), D.R. Congo 120/D4
Inzigkofen, Ger. 61/F1
Inzing, Aus. 61/H3
Inzinzac-Lochrist, Fr. 56/B5
Iō-shima (isl.), Japan 84/B5
Ioánnina, Gre. 49/G3
Ioánnina (int'l arpt.), Gre. 49/G3
Ioka, Ut, US 147/H3
Iola, Ks, US 153/G2
Iola, Wi, US 155/K1
Iolotan', Trkm. 101/H1
Ioma, PNG 129/G2
Iona (isl.), Sc, UK 31/Q8
Iona, Ang. 122/B3
Iona, Id, US 147/H2
Iona, PN da, Ang. 122/A3
Ione, Nv, US 146/E4
Ione, Or, US 146/D1
Ione, Ca, US 146/C4
Ione, Wa, US 144/F3
Ione Wash (riv.), Nv, US 148/D1
Iongo, Ang. 120/D5
Ionia, Mo, US 153/H1
Ionia, Mi, US 160/D3
Ionian (sea), Gre. 67/H3
Ionian (isls.), Gre. 29/F5
Íos (isl.), Gre. 67/K3
Iota, La, US 164/B2
Iouîk, Mrta. 114/A2
Iouîk (cape), Mrta. 114/A2
Iowa, La, US 164/B2
Iowa (state), US 143/H3
Iowa (riv.), Ia, US 155/H2
Iowa City, Ia, US 155/J3
Iowa Falls, Ia, US 155/H2
Iowa Park, Tx, US 153/E4
Ipameri, Braz. 186/C3
Ipanema, Braz. 187/E3
Ipanguaçu, Braz. 183/G4
Iparia, Peru 184/C3
Ipatinga, Braz. 187/E3
Ipatovo, Rus. 71/G3
Ipaumirim, Braz. 183/G4
Ipel' (riv.), Slvk. 43/K4
Ipel' (riv.), Hun. 50/D1
Iphofen, Ger. 58/D3
Ipiales, Col. 180/B4
Ipiaú, Braz. 187/F2
Ipirá, Braz. 187/F2
Ipixuna (riv.), Braz. 185/G2
Ipoh, Malay. 89/C1
Ipole, Tanz. 121/H4
Ipoly (riv.), Hun. 43/K4
Ipolyszög, Hun. 50/D1
Iporá, Braz. 186/C3
Iporã, Braz. 189/F2
Ippy, CAfr. 116/D4
Ipsala, Turk. 51/H5
Ipsheim, Ger. 58/D3
Ipswich, SD, US 156/E5
Ipswich (nbrhd.), Austl. 134/E7
Ipswich, Eng, UK 37/H2
Ipu, Braz. 183/F4
Ipueiras, Braz. 183/F4
Ipuh, Indo. 89/C3
Ipuiúna, Braz. 187/K7
Ipumba (hill), Tanz. 121/G4
Ipun, Isla (isl.), Chile 190/B5
Ipupiara, Braz. 187/E1
Iqaluit, (cap.), Nun, Can. 141/K2
Iquique, Chile 188/B2
Iquitos, Peru 184/C1
Ira, Tx, US 151/D1
Iraan, Tx, US 151/D2
Iracoubo, FrG. 182/C1
Irago (chan.), Japan 83/L6
Irago-misaki (cape), Japan 83/M6
Iraí, Braz. 189/F3
Iráklia, Gre. 49/H2
Iráklia (isl.), Gre. 49/J4
Iráklion (int'l arpt.), Gre. 49/J5
Iráklion, Gre. 49/J5
Iramba, Tanz. 119/A2
Iran (ctry.) 77/E6
Iran (mts.), Indo.,Malay. 90/D3
Īrān Shāh, Iran 103/F2
Irapa, Ven. 181/F2
Irapuato, Mex. 175/E4
Iraq (ctry.) 77/B6
Irati, Braz. 189/G3
Irauçuba, Braz. 183/G3
Irayel', Rus. 69/M2
Irbid (gov.), Jor. 104/D3
Irbid, Jor. 105/D3
Irbīl, Iraq 103/F2
Irbit, Rus. 69/P4
Irdyn', Ukr. 72/F3
Irecê, Braz. 187/E1
Iredell, Tx, US 150/F2
Ireland, Tx, US 150/F2
Ireland (ctry.) 29/D3
Ireland's Eye (isl.), Ire. 34/B5
Iremel' (peak), Rus. 69/N5
Irene, SAfr. 123/F5

Ireton – Jaunpa

Ireton, Ia, US 155/F2
Irfon (riv.), Wal, UK 36/C2
Irgiz, Kaz. 71/M2
Irharhar, Oued (riv.), Alg. 111/G4
Irhazer Oua-n-Agadez (riv.), Niger 115/G2
Irherm, Mor. 110/C3
Irherm n'Ougdal, Mor. 110/D3
Iri, SKor. 81/D5
Irian Jaya (reg.), Indo. 91/H4
Irian Jaya (prov.), Indo. 129/E1
Iriba, Chad 116/D2
Iricoume (mts.), Braz. 181/G4
Irig, Yugo. 50/D3
Irigny, Fr. 64/A1
Irîgui (phys. reg.), Mali 114/D2
Iriklinskiy, Rus. 71/L2
Iriklinskiy (res.), Rus. 71/L2
Iringa (prov.), Tanz. 119/A4
Iringa, Tanz. 119/A3
Iriomote (isl.), Japan 85/G8
Iriri (riv.), Braz. 182/C4
Iriri Novo (riv.), Braz. 186/B1
Iriri-Novo (riv.), Braz. 182/C5
Irish (sea), Ire.,UK 34/C4
Irish Vale, NS, Can. 159/G3
Irituía, Braz. 183/E3
Irkliyiv, Ukr. 73/G3
Irkut (riv.), Rus. 78/E1
Irkutsk, Rus. 78/E1
Irkutsk (int'l arpt.), Rus. 78/E1
Irkutskaya Oblast, Rus. 78/E1
Irlam, Eng, UK 35/F5
Irma, Ab, Can. 145/J1
Irmo, SC, US 163/G3
Irō-zaki (pt.), Japan 85/F3
Iroise (bay), Fr. 44/A2
Iron (mtn.), Fl, US 164/M8
Iron (mtn.), Id, US 147/F2
Iron Baron, Austl. 131/H5
Iron Bridge (dam), Tx, US 153/G4
Iron Bridge, On, Can. 160/E1
Iron City, Ga, US 165/F2
Iron City, Tn, US 162/D3
Iron Gate (dam), Ca, US 146/B3
Iron Knob, Austl. 131/H5
Iron Lightning, SD, US 154/D1
Iron Mountain, Mi, US 157/K5
Iron Range, Austl. 129/F3
Iron Range NP, Austl. 129/F3
Iron River, Mi, US 157/K4
Iron Springs, Az, US 149/F3
Ironbound (nbrhd.), NJ, US 169/J9
Irondale, Al, US 162/D4
Ironton, Mn, US 157/H4
Ironton, Oh, US 163/F1
Ironton, Mo, US 162/B2
Ironwood, Mi, US 157/J4
Ironwood Forest Nat'l Mon., Az, US 149/G4
Iroquois, On, Can. 161/J2
Iroquois Falls, On, Can. 141/H4
Irpin', Ukr. 72/F2
Irput' (riv.), Rus. 70/E1
Irrawaddy (riv.), Myan. 77/J7
Irricana, Ab, Can. 145/H2
Irrigon, Or, US 144/E5
Irrua, Nga. 115/G5
Irsch, Ger. 55/F4
Irsen (riv.), Ger. 55/F3
Irsina, It. 48/E2
Irt (riv.), Eng, UK 35/E3
Irthing (riv.), Eng, UK 35/F1
Irthlingborough, Eng, UK 37/F2
Irtysh (riv.), Rus. 77/G4
Irtyshsk, Kaz. 99/C1
Iruma, Japan 83/C2
Irumu, D.R. Congo 121/G2
Irún, Sp. 44/C5
Irupana, Bol. 188/C1
Irvine, Sc, UK 33/B5
Irvine (bay), Sc, UK 33/B5
Irvine (riv.), Sc, UK 33/B5
Irvine, Ca, US 166/G8
Irvine, Ky, US 162/F2
Irvine, Ab, Can. 145/J3
Irvines Landing, BC, Can. 144/B3
Irving, Il, US 155/K4
Irving, Tx, US 150/L7
Irvington, NJ, US 169/J9
Irvington, NY, US 169/K7
Irvington, Ky, US 162/D2
Irvington, Il, US 162/C1
Irwin, Ia, US 155/G3
Irwin, Austl. 130/B4
Irwin, SC, US 163/G3
Irwinton, Ga, US 163/F4
Is (peak), Sudan 109/G4
Is-sur-Tille, Fr. 60/B2
Isa, Nga. 115/G3
Īsa Khel, Pak. 98/A3
Isabel, SD, US 156/D5
Isabel, Ks, US 153/E2
Isabel, La, US 164/D2
Isabela, Phil. 88/C4
Isabela (isl.), Ecu. 184/J7
Isabela, PR 173/M8
Isabelia (mts.), Nic. 176/E3
Isabella, Ok, US 153/E2
Isabella, Mn, US 157/J4
Isabella (bay), Nun, Can. 141/K2
Isabella (lake), Ca, US 148/C3
Isabella Ind. Res., Mi, US 160/D3
Isabelle (pt.), Mi, US 157/L4
Isaccea, Rom. 51/J3
Isachsen (cape), Nun, Can. 141/R7
Isachsen, Nun, Can. 141/R7
Ísafjardhardjúp (inlet), Ice. 38/M6
Ísafjördhur, Ice. 38/M6
Isahaya, Japan 84/B4
Isak, Indo. 89/B1
Isaka, D.R. Congo 120/D3
Isaka, D.R. Congo 120/D3
Isakovo, Rus. 68/G5
Isalo Ruiniform (mass.), Madg. 125/H8
Isalo, PN de l', Madg. 125/H8
Isana (riv.), Col. 180/D4
Isandhlwana Battlesite, SAfr. 125/E3
Isangano NP, Zam. 121/G5
Isangel, Van. 136/F6
Isangi, D.R. Congo 121/F2
Isango-Isoro, D.R. Congo 121/G3
Isanlu Makutu, Nga. 115/G4
Isaouanne-n-Irarraren (des.), Alg. 111/G4
Isaouanne-n-Tifernine (des.), Alg. 111/G4
Isar (riv.), Aus. 61/H3
Isarco (riv.), It. 45/J3
Isarco (Eisack) (riv.), It. 61/H4
Isaszeg, Hun. 51/R9
Isawa, Japan 83/B2
Isbergues, Fr. 54/B2
Iscar, Sp. 46/C2
Ischgl, Aus. 61/G3
Ischia, It. 65/C6
Ischia (isl.), It. 65/C6
Isclero (riv.), It. 65/D5
Ise (riv.), Ger. 53/H3
Ise (bay), Japan 85/E3
Ise, Japan 83/L7
Ise (riv.), Eng, UK 37/F2
Ise-Shima NP, Japan 85/E3
Isehara, Japan 85/F3
Isel (riv.), Aus. 67/G1
Iselin, NJ, US 169/H9
Isen (riv.), Ger. 42/G4
Isen, Ger. 59/F6
Isenthal, Swi. 61/E4
Isenyela, Tanz. 119/A4
'Iseo (lake), It. 62/C1
Iseo, It. 62/D2
Iseo (lake), It. 45/J4
Iseramagazi, Tanz. 121/H4
Isère (dept.), Fr. 60/B6
Isère (riv.), Fr. 44/F4
Iserlohn, Ger. 53/E6
Isernia, It. 65/D4
Isernia (prov.), It. 65/D4
Isesaki, Japan 85/F2
Iset' (riv.), Rus. 69/Q4
Isetskoye, Rus. 69/Q4
Iseyin, Nga. 115/F5
Isfahan (int'l arpt.), Iran 103/G3
'Isfiyā, Isr. 105/C3
Ishenga Oswe, D.R. Congo 121/E3
Isherton, Guy. 181/G4
Ishi (riv.), Japan 83/J7
Ishibashi, Japan 85/F2
Ishibe, Japan 83/K5
Ishidoriya, Japan 82/B4
Ishigaki (isl.), Japan 85/G8
Ishige, Japan 85/F2
Ishikari, Japan 82/B2
Ishikari (riv.), Japan 82/B2
Ishikari (bay), Japan 82/B2
Ishikari (mts.), Japan 82/C2
Ishikawa, Japan 85/G2
Ishikawa (pref.), Japan 85/E2
Ishiki, Japan 83/M6
Ishim, Rus. 69/R4
Ishim (riv.), Rus. 74/H4
Ishimbay, Rus. 71/L1
Ishinomaki, Japan 82/B4
Ishioka, Japan 85/G2
Ishizuchi-san (peak), Japan 84/C4
Ishlya, Rus. 69/N5
Ishmant, Egypt 113/C6
Ishøj, Den. 39/J7
Ishpeming, Mi, US 157/L4
Ishurdi, Bang. 97/G3
Isiboro Secure, PN (riv.), Bol. 185/E4
Isidoro Noblía, Uru. 189/F4
Isigny-le-Buat, Fr. 57/D3
Isigny-sur-Mer, Fr. 57/D2
Isil'kul', Rus. 74/H4
Isiolo, Kenya 119/B1
Isiro, D.R. Congo 121/F2
Isisford, Austl. 134/B4
Iskandarūnah, Leb. 105/C2
Iske-Ryazyap, Rus. 69/L5
İskenderun (gulf), Turk. 104/D1
İskenderun, Turk. 104/E1
İskilip, Turk. 70/E4
Iskininskiy, Kaz. 71/K3
Iskitim, Rus. 74/J4
Iskŭr (res.), Bul. 49/H1
Iskŭr (riv.), Bul. 49/H1
Iskŭr (riv.), Aus. 51/G4
Iskŭr (riv.), Bul. 67/K2
Iskur (lake), Hun. 51/F4
Iskushuban, Som. 118/D3
Isla (riv.), Sc, UK 33/C3
Isla, Mex. 176/C2
Isla Aguada, Mex. 176/D2
Isla Cabritos, PN, DRep. 177/J2
Isla Cedros, Mex. 174/B2
Isla Cristina, Sp. 46/B4
Isla de Maipo, Chile 190/N8
Isla de Salamanca, PN, Col. 180/C2
Isla de San Andrés (int'l arpt.), Col. 177/F3
Isla Gorge NP, Austl. 134/C4
Isla Guamblin, PN, Chile 190/B5
Isla Isabela, PN, Mex. 174/D4
Isla Magdalena, PN, Chile 190/B5
Isla Mujeres, Mex. 176/E1
Islām Kot, Pak. 101/K4
Islāmābād (cap.), Pak. 98/B3
Islāmābād (cap. terr.), Pak. 98/B3
Islāmābād/Rāwalpindi (int'l arpt.), Pak. 98/B3
Islāmnagar, India 96/B1
Islamorada, Fl, US 165/H5
Islāmpur, India 97/G2
Islāmpur, India 97/E3
Island (lake), Mn, US 157/H4
Island (co.), Wa, US 167/B2
Island (lake), Mb, Can. 140/G3
Island Bay (nbrhd.), NZ 135/H9
Island Bay Nat'l Wild. Ref., Fl, US 165/G4
Island Beach State Park, NJ, US 168/D4
Island City, Or, US 146/D1
Island Lagoon (lake), Austl. 131/H4
Island Lake, Il, US 167/P15
Island Park, NY, US 169/L9
Island Park, Id, US 147/H1
Island Park (res.), Id, US 147/H1
Island Pond, Vt, US 161/L2
Islands (bay), NF, Can. 158/H1
Islands (bay), NZ 135/C1
Islay (isl.), Sc, UK 31/Q9
Islay, Peru 184/C5
Islay, Ab, Can. 145/J1
Isle, Mn, US 157/H4
Isle au Haut (isl.), Me, US 158/C3
Isle aux Morts, Nf, Can. 159/H2
Isle Madame (isl.), Ns., Can. 159/G3
Isle of Anglesey (co.), Wal, UK 34/D5
Isle of Ely (phys. reg.), Eng, UK 37/G2
Isle of Man (Ronaldsway) (arpt.), IM, UK 34/D3
Isle of Portland (pen.), Eng, UK 36/D5
Isle of Thanet (phys. reg.), Eng, UK 37/H4
Isle of Whithorn, Sc, UK 34/D2
Isle of Wight (co.), Eng, UK 37/E5
Isle of Wight, Va, US 163/J2
Isle Royale (isl.), Mi, US 157/K3
Isle Royale NP, Mi, US 157/K3
Isle Wooden (isl.), Austl. 129/E3
Isleham, Eng, UK 37/G2
Isles Dernieres (isls.), La, US 164/C3
Isleta, NM, US 149/J3
Isleta Ind. Res., NM, US 149/J3
Isleten, Swi. 61/E4
Isleton, Ca, US 167/L10
Islington (bor.), Eng, UK 30/A1
Islip, NY, US 169/E2
Isluga (vol.), Chile 188/B1
Ismā'īlīyah (canal), Egypt 113/C4
Ismailovo Park, Rus. 69/W9
Ismail Samani (peak), Taj. 99/B4
Ismaning, Ger. 59/E6
İsmayıllı, Azer. 71/J4
Isnā, Egypt 109/G3
Isny, Ger. 61/G2
Iso-Evo, Fin. 39/F3
Iso-Roine (lake), Fin. 39/E3
Isoanala, Madg. 125/H8
Isobe, Japan 83/L7
Isojärven NP, Fin. 41/L1
Isojärvi (lake), Fin. 41/J1
Isoka, Zam. 121/H5
Isola, Fr. 64/D4
Isola, Ms, US 162/B4
Isola del Gran Sasso d'Italia, It. 65/C3
Isola del Liri, It. 65/C4
Isola della Scala, It. 63/D3
Isola di Capo Rizzuto, It. 49/E3
Isola Vicentina, It. 63/E2
Isole (riv.), Fr. 56/B5
Isonzo (riv.), It. 63/G1
Isorella, It. 62/D3
Isparta, Turk. 102/B2
Isparta (prov.), Turk. 102/B2
Isperikh, Bul. 51/H4
Ispir, Turk. 71/G4
Israel (ctry.) 77/C6
Issac (lake), BC, Can. 144/D1
Issac (riv.), Austl. 127/D3
Issano, Guy. 182/B1
Issaquah, Wa, US 167/C2
Issaquah (cr.), Wa, US 167/C2
Issé, Fr. 56/D5
Issel (riv.), Ger. 52/D5
Isselburg, Ger. 52/D5
Issenheim, Fr. 60/D2
Issia, C.d'Iv. 114/D5
Issoire, Fr. 44/E4
Issou, Fr. 30/H5
Issum, Ger. 52/D5
Issuna, Tanz. 119/A3
Issutugan (riv.), Som. 118/C3
Issy-les-Moulineaux, Fr. 30/J5
Istachatta, Fl, US 164/L6
Istállós-Kó (peak), Hun. 50/E1
Istana Maimoon (Maimoon Palace), Indo. 89/B2
İstanbul (prov.), Turk. 70/D4
İstanbul, Turk. 103/M6
Isṭanhā, Egypt 113/C4
Istead Rise, Eng, UK 30/E2
Istiaía, Gre. 49/H3
Istmina, Col. 180/B3
Istok, Yugo. 50/E4
Istokpaga (lake), Fl, US 165/H4
Istra (riv.), Rus. 69/W9
Istrana, It. 63/F2
Istranca (mts.), Turk. 67/K2
Istres, Fr. 64/A5
Istria (reg.), Cro. 67/G1
Istria (pen.), Cro. 45/K4
Isulan, Phil. 88/D4
Isumi, Japan 83/E3
Iswarganj, Bang. 97/H3
Iswarīpur, Bang. 97/G4
Isyangulovo, Rus. 71/L1
Itá Ibaté, Arg. 189/E3
Itabaiana, Braz. 187/F1
Itabaiana, Braz. 183/H4
Itabaianinha, Braz. 187/F1
Itaberaba, Braz. 187/E2
Itaberaí, Braz. 186/C3
Itabira, Braz. 187/E3
Itabirito, Braz. 186/E4
Itaboraí, Braz. 187/P7
Itabuna, Braz. 187/F2
Itacaiunas (riv.), Braz. 182/D4
Itacajá, Braz. 182/E5
Itacarambi, Braz. 186/D2
Itacoatiara, Braz. 182/B3
Itacuaí (riv.), Braz. 184/D2
Itacuruba, Braz. 183/G5
Itacurubí del Rosario, Par. 189/E3
Itaga, Tanz. 121/H4
Itagibá, Braz. 187/F2
Itaguaí, Braz. 187/N7
Itaguatins, Braz. 183/E4
Itagüí, Col. 183/K6
Itahuazurenda, Bol. 188/D1
Itaí, Braz. 189/G2
Itaíba, Braz. 183/G5
Itaiçaba, Braz. 183/G4
Itainópolis, Braz. 183/F4
Itaiópolis, Braz. 189/G3
Itaipu (res.), Braz.,Par. 179/D5
Itaipú (dam), Par. 189/F3
Itaituba, Braz. 182/C4
Itajaí, Braz. 189/G3
Itajaí (riv.), Braz. 189/G3
Itajubá, Braz. 187/L7
Itākhola, Bang. 97/H3
Itako, Japan 85/G3
Itakura, Japan 83/D1
Itala, Som. 118/C5
Italy, Tx, US 151/F1
Italy (ctry.) 29/F4
Itamaraju, Braz. 187/F3
Itambacuri, Braz. 187/E3
Itambé, Braz. 183/H4
Itambé, Braz. 187/E2
Itambé, Pico de (peak), Braz. 187/E3
Itami, Japan 83/H6
Itamonte, Braz. 187/M7
Itampolo, Madg. 125/G9
Itanagar, India 86/B3
Itang, Eth. 117/G3
Itanhaém, Braz. 187/K9
Itanhomi, Braz. 187/E3
Itapagé, Braz. 183/G3
Itaparica (isl.), Braz. 187/F2
Itapé, Braz. 187/F2
Itapé, Par. 189/E3
Itapecerica, Braz. 186/D4
Itapecuru-Mirim, Braz. 183/E3
Itapemirim, Braz. 187/E4
Itaperuna, Braz. 187/E4
Itapetim, Braz. 183/G4
Itapetinga, Braz. 187/E2
Itapetininga, Braz. 189/G2
Itapeva, Braz. 189/G2
Itapevi, Braz. 187/K8
Itapicuru (riv.), Braz. 183/F4
Itapipoca, Braz. 183/G3
Itapira, Braz. 187/K7
Itapiranga, Braz. 182/B3
Itapiranga, Braz. 189/F3
Itapitanga, Braz. 187/F2
Itapiúna, Braz. 183/G4
Itápolis, Braz. 189/G2
Itaporã, Braz. 189/F2
Itaporã do Tocantins, Braz. 182/D5
Itaporanga, Braz. 189/G2
Itapúa (dept.), Par. 189/F3
Itapuranga, Braz. 186/C2
Itaquaquecetuba, Braz. 187/K8
Itaqui, Braz. 189/E4
Itarantim, Braz. 187/E2
Itararé, Braz. 189/G3
Itariri, Braz. 187/J9
Itārsi, India 96/A4
Itasca (lake), Mn, US 157/G4
Itasca, Tx, US 151/F1
Itatí, Arg. 188/E3
Itatiaia, PN de, Braz. 187/M7
Itatiba, Braz. 187/K7
Itaú, Bol. 188/D2
Itauçu, Braz. 186/C3
Itaueira, Braz. 183/F4
Itaueira (riv.), Braz. 183/F5
Itayanagi, Japan 82/B3
Itbayat, Phil. 87/J4
Itbayat (isl.), Phil. 87/J4
Itchen (riv.), Eng, UK 37/E4
Itéa, Gre. 49/H3
Itembiri (riv.), D.R. Congo 121/E2
Iténez (riv.), Bol. 179/C4
Ith (hills), Ger. 53/G4
Ithaca, Mi, US 160/D3
Ithaca, NY, US 161/H3
Ithaca (Itháki) (isl.), Gre. 49/G3
Itháki, Gre. 49/G3
Ithon (riv.), Wal, UK 36/C2
Itigi, Tanz. 119/A3
Itiquira (riv.), Braz. 185/H5
Itiruçu, Braz. 187/E2
Itō, Japan 85/F3
Itobo, Tanz. 119/A3
Itoigawa, Japan 85/E2
Itoko, D.R. Congo 121/E3
Itoman, Japan 85/J7
Iton (riv.), Fr. 44/D2
Itonamas (riv.), Bol. 185/E4
Itondy, Madg. 125/H7
Itonuki, Japan 83/L5
Itororó, Braz. 187/E2
Itremo, Madg. 125/H8
Itri, It. 65/C5
Iṭsā, Egypt 113/B6
Itsukaichi, Japan 83/C2
Itter (riv.), Ger. 53/F6
Itterbeck, Ger. 52/D3
Ittiri, It. 48/A2
Itu, Nga. 115/G5
Itu, Braz. 189/H2
Ituango, Col. 180/C3
Ituberá, Braz. 187/F2
Ituí (riv.), Braz. 184/D2
Ituiutaba, Braz. 186/C3
Itumbiara (res.), Braz. 186/C3
Itumbiara, Braz. 186/C3
Itumirim, Braz. 187/M6
Ituna, Sk, Can. 156/C2
Itungi Port, Tanz. 119/A4
Ituni, Guy. 181/G3
Itupiranga, Braz. 182/D4
Ituporanga, Braz. 189/G3
Iturama, Braz. 189/G1
Iturbe, Par. 189/E3
Ituri (riv.), D.R. Congo 121/F2
Ituri Forest (for.), D.R. Congo 121/F2
Itutinga (res.), Braz. 187/M6
Ituverava, Braz. 189/H2
Ituxi (riv.), Braz. 185/E3
Ituzaingó, Uru. 191/K11
Ityāy al Bārūd, Egypt 113/B3
Itz (riv.), Ger. 42/F3
Iuka, Ks, US 153/E2
Iuka, Il, US 162/C1
Iuka, Ms, US 162/C3
Iul'tin, Rus. 142/V12
Iva, SC, US 163/F3
Ivaí (riv.), Braz. 186/B4
Ivaiporã, Braz. 189/G3
Ivalojoki (riv.), Fin. 38/H1
Ivančice, Czh. 45/M2
Ivanec, Cro. 50/C2
Ivangorod, Rus. 41/N2
Ivangrad, Yugo. 50/D4
Ivanhoe, Mn, US 155/F1
Ivanhoe, Va, US 163/G2
Ivanhoe, Austl. 128/C3
Ivanhoe, Austl. 133/B1
Ivanivka, Ukr. 73/K3
Ivanjica, Yugo. 50/E4
Ivanjska, Bosn. 50/C3
Ivanka (Bratislava) (int'l arpt.), Slvk. 50/C1
Ivankiv, Ukr. 72/E2
Ivankovo, Cro. 50/D3
Ivano-Frankivs'k, Ukr. 72/C3
Ivano-Frankivs'k (int'l arpt.), Ukr. 72/C3
Ivano-Frankivs'ka Oblast, Ukr. 70/C2
Ivanov, Ukr. 72/E3
Ivanof Bay, Ak, US 171/G4
Ivanovka, Rus. 69/M5
Ivanovo, Bela. 70/C1
Ivanovo, Rus. 68/J4
Ivanovskaya, Rus. 73/K5
Ivanovskaya Oblast, Rus. 68/J4
Ivanpah (lake), Nv, US 148/E3
Ivato (int'l arpt.), Madg. 125/H7
Ivato, Madg. 125/H8
Ivatsevichi, Bela. 70/C1
Ivaylovgrad (res.), Bul. 49/J2
Ivaylovgrad, Bul. 51/H5
Ivdel, Rus. 74/G3
Ivel, Ky, US 163/F2
Ivenets, Bela. 41/M5
Iver, Eng, UK 30/B2
Iver Heath, Eng, UK 30/B2
Iveragh (pen.), Ire. 30/P11
Iverny, Fr. 30/L5
Ivey, Ga, US 163/F4
Ivindo (riv.), Gabon 120/C2
Ivinheima (riv.), Braz. 186/B4
Ivinheima, Braz. 189/F2
Ivins, Ut, US 149/F2
Ivnya, Rus. 73/J2
Ivö (isl.), Swe. 39/L6
Ivohibe, Madg. 125/H8
Ivón, Bol. 185/E3
Ivondro (riv.), Madg. 125/J7
Ivösjön (lake), Swe. 40/F3
Ivrea, It. 62/A2
İvrindi, Turk. 70/C5
Ivry-la-Bataille, Fr. 57/G3
Ivry-sur-Seine, Fr. 30/K5
Ivujivik, Qu, Can. 141/J2
Ivvavik NP, Yk, Can. 171/K2
Ivybridge, Eng, UK 36/C6
Iwafune, Japan 83/D1
Iwai, Japan 85/F2
Iwaizumi, Japan 82/B4
Iwaki, Japan 85/G2
Iwaki-san (peak), Japan 82/B3
Iwakuni, Japan 84/C3
Iwakura, Japan 83/L5
Iwama, Japan 83/E1
Iwami, Japan 84/D3
Iwamizawa, Japan 82/B2
Iwamura, Japan 83/M5
Iwanai, Japan 82/B2
Iwanuma, Japan 85/G1
Iwasaki, Japan 82/A3
Iwata, Japan 85/E3
Iwataki, Japan 83/H4
Iwate, Japan 82/B4
Iwate (pref.), Japan 82/B4
Iwate-san (peak), Japan 82/B4
Iwatsuki, Japan 83/D2
Iwere Ile, Nga. 115/F5
Iwo, Nga. 115/G5
Iwo Jima (isl.), Japan 136/D2
Iwŏn, NKor. 81/E2
Iwuy, Fr. 54/C3
Ixcán (riv.), Guat. 176/D3
Ixelles, Belg. 55/D2
Ixiamas, Bol. 184/D4
Ixmiquilpan, Mex. 175/K6
Ixopo, SAfr. 125/E3
Ixtapalapa (nbrhd.), Mex. 175/Q10
Ixtapaluca, Mex. 175/L7
Ixtapan de la Sal, Mex. 175/K8
Ixtlán del Río, Mex. 174/D4
Ixworth, Eng, UK 37/G2
Iya (riv.), Rus. 78/D1
'Iyādh, Yem. 118/C2
'Iyāl Bakhīt, Sudan 117/F2
Iyevlevo, Rus. 69/Q4
Iyo, Japan 84/C4
Iyo (sea), Japan 84/B4
'Izab al Başāriţah, Egypt 113/C2
Izabal (lake), Guat. 172/D4
Īzad Khvāst, Iran 103/H4
Izamal, Mex. 176/D1
'Izbat Jamaşah al Gharbīyah, Egypt 113/C2
Izberbash, Rus. 71/H4
Izeaux, Fr. 64/B2
Izegem, Belg. 54/C2
Izhevsk, Rus. 69/M4
Izhma (riv.), Rus. 69/M2
Izhora (riv.), Rus. 69/T7
Izi (well), Alg. 111/F3
Izigan (cape), Ak, US 171/E5
Izkī, Oman 101/G4
Izmayil, Ukr. 51/J3
İzmir (prov.), Turk. 70/C5
İzmit, Turk. 51/J5
İzmit (gulf), Turk. 51/J5
Iznájar, Sp. 46/C4
İznik, Turk. 51/J5
İznik (lake), Turk. 51/J5
Izobil'noye, Rus. 71/K2
Izobil'nyy, Rus. 73/L5
Izola, Slov. 63/G2
Izozog, Bol. 188/D1
Izra', Syria 105/E3
Izsák, Hun. 50/D2
Iztaccíhuatl-Popocatépetl, PN, Mex. 175/L7
Izu (isls.), Japan 75/P6
Izu (pen.), Japan 85/F3
Izúcar de Matamoros, Mex. 175/L8
Izuhara, Japan 84/A3
Izumi, Japan 84/B4
Izumi, Japan 82/B4
Izumi, Japan 83/H7
Izumi-Ōtsu, Japan 83/H7
Izumi-Sano, Japan 83/H7
Izumo, Japan 84/C3
Izunagaoka, Japan 83/B3
Izushi, Japan 83/G5
Izvestkovyy, Rus. 79/L2
Izyaslav, Ukr. 72/D2
Izyum, Ukr. 73/J3

J

J. B. Thomas (lake), Tx, US 152/D4
J. Clark Sayler NWR, ND, US 156/D3
J. Ḩanīsh al Kabīr (isl.), Yem. 118/B2
J. Jabal Zuqar (isl.), Yem. 118/B2
J. Lee (lake), Ar, US 153/H4
J. P. Priest (lake), Tn, US 162/D2
J. Paul Getty Museum, Ca, US 166/E7
Jääsjärvi (lake), Fin. 41/M1
Jaba', WBnk. 105/C4
Jabal Abu Rujmayn (mts.), Syria 102/D3
Jabal Abyad (plat.), Sudan 109/F5
Jabal ad-Dayr (peak), Sudan 117/F2
Jabal Ajlūn (mts.), Jor. 105/D4
Jabal al 'Arab (mts.), Syria 104/E3
Jabal al Bārūk (peak), Leb. 105/D1
Jabal al Jaw'alīyāt (peak), Jor. 105/E6
Jabal al Lawz (peak), SAr. 109/G2
Jabal al Mudaysīsāt (peak), Jor. 105/E5
Jabal an Nabī Shu'ayb (peak), Yem. 118/B2
Jabal an Nusayriyab (mts.), Syria 104/E2
Jabal ar Ruwaq (mts.), Syria 102/D3
Jabal as Sawdā' (mts.), Libya 108/B2
Jabal ash Shām (peak), Oman 101/G4
Jabal ash Sha'nabī (peak), Tun. 112/L7
Jabal ash Shaykh (peak), Leb. 105/D2
Jabal 'Aybāl (peak), WBnk. 105/C4
Jabal Bin Ghunaymah (mts.), Libya 108/B3
Jabal Dabbāgh (peak), SAr. 109/G3
Jabāl Lubnan (gov.), Leb. 105/D1
Jabal Marrah (mts.), Sudan 116/E2
Jabal Nafūsah (mts.), Libya 111/H3
Jabal Qaţrānī (mts.), Egypt 113/B5
Jabal Raḑwá (peak), SAr. 109/H3
Jabal Ramm (peak), Jor. 104/D5
Jabal Thamar (peak), Yem. 118/C2
Jabal 'Unāzah (peak), SAr. 102/D3
Jabal 'Uwaybid, Egypt 113/D4
Jabal Waddān (mts.), Libya 108/C2
Jabal Zaltan (mts.), Libya 108/C2
Jabal'āmil (peak), Leb. 105/C2
Jabalí (pt.), Pan. 177/F5
Jabalón (riv.), Sp. 66/C3
Jabalpur, India 96/B4
Jabalyāh, Gaza 105/B5
Jabālyah, Gaza 105/A5
Jabbeke, Belg. 54/C1
Jabbūl (lake), Syria 102/D3
Jabiru, Austl. 128/D3
Jabjabah (wadi), Sudan 100/B4
Jablah, Syria 104/D2
Jablanica (mts.), Alb. 49/G2
Jablanica, Bosn. 50/C4
Jablonec nad Nisou, Czh. 43/H3
Jaboatão dos Guararapes, Braz. 183/H5
Jaboticabal, Braz. 189/G2
Jabron (riv.), Fr. 64/B4
Jabsar Gaxun, China 78/D4
Jabuka, Yugo. 50/E3
Jabung (cape), Indo. 89/D3
Jaca, Sp. 47/E1
Jacaré (riv.), Braz. 187/E1
Jacareacanga, Braz. 182/B4
Jacareí, Braz. 187/L8
Jacarèzinho, Braz. 189/G2
Jaceel (riv.), Som. 118/D3
Jáchal (riv.), Arg. 188/B4
Jáchymov, Czh. 59/F2
Jaciara, Braz. 186/B2
Jacinto Arauz, Arg. 190/E3
Jacinto City, Tx, US 151/M9
Jaciparaná (riv.), Braz. 185/E3
Jack, Al, US 165/E2
Jack Lee (lake), Ar, US 151/H1
Jack Pine (mtn.), Mn, US 157/J4
Jackfish (lake), Sk, Can. 145/K1
Jackfish Lake, Sk, Can. 145/K1
Jackman, Me, US 161/L2
Jackpot, Nv, US 147/F3
Jacks Fk. (riv.), Mo, US 162/B2
Jacks Mtn. (range), Pa, US 168/A2
Jacksboro, Tx, US 153/E4
Jacksboro, Tn, US 162/E2
Jackson (int'l arpt.), PNG 129/G2
Jackson, Al, US 164/E2
Jackson, Ca, US 146/C4
Jackson, Ga, US 162/F4
Jackson (lake), Ga, US 162/E4
Jackson, Ky, US 163/F2
Jackson, La, US 164/C2
Jackson, Mi, US 160/D3
Jackson, Mn, US 155/G2
Jackson, Mo, US 162/C2
Jackson (cap.), Ms, US 162/B4
Jackson, NC, US 163/J2
Jackson (mts.), Nv, US 146/D3
Jackson, Oh, US 163/F1
Jackson, Tn, US 162/C3
Jackson, Wy, US 147/H2
Jackson Head (pt.), NZ 135/B3
Jackson Heights (nbrhd.), NY, US 169/K9
Jackson Lake (dam), Wy, US 147/H2
Jacksonport, Wi, US 160/C2
Jacksonville, Al, US 162/E4
Jacksonville, Ar, US 153/H3
Jacksonville, Fl, US 165/H2
Jacksonville (int'l arpt.), Fl, US 165/H2
Jacksonville, Ga, US 165/G2
Jacksonville, Il, US 155/J4
Jacksonville, Or, US 146/B2
Jacksonville, Mo, US 155/H4
Jacksonville, NC, US 163/J3
Jacksonville, Tx, US 150/G2
Jacksonville Beach, Fl, US 165/H2
Jacksonville Nav. Air Sta., Fl, US 165/H2
Jacmel, Haiti 177/H2
Jacob Lake, Az, US 149/F2
Jacobābād, Pak. 101/J3
Jacobina, Braz. 187/E1
Jacobsdal, SAfr. 124/D3
Jacobson, Mn, US 157/H4
Jacobstown, NJ, US 168/D3
Jacobus, Pa, US 168/B4
Jácome, Ven. 183/P8
Jacona de Plancarte, Mex. 174/E5
Jacques Cartier (peak), Qu, Can. 158/E1
Jacques-Cartier (riv.), Qu, Can. 158/B2
Jacquet River, NB, Can. 158/D2
Jacuí (riv.), Braz. 189/F4
Jacuípe (riv.), Braz. 187/F1
Jacupiranga, Braz. 189/H3
Jacura, Ven. 180/D2
Jadacaquiva, Ven. 180/D2
Jaddi (pt.), Pak. 101/H3
Jade (bay), Ger. 42/E2
Jade (riv.), Ger. 53/F1
Jade, Ger. 53/F2
Jadebusen (bay), Ger. 53/F2
Jadito Wash (riv.), Az, US 149/G3
Jādū, Libya 108/B2
Jadwin, Mo, US 153/J2
Jaén, Sp. 46/D4
Jaen, Phil. 88/C2
Jaén, Peru 184/B2
Jaffa (cape), Austl. 132/A3
Jaffna, SrL. 95/C4
Jaffray, BC, Can. 144/G3
Jaffrey, NH, US 161/K3
Jagādhri, India 98/D4
Jagdīspur, India 96/C2
Jagdīspur, India 97/E3
Jagersfontein, SAfr. 124/D3
Jægerspris, Den. 40/D4
Jægerspris, Den. 39/H7
Jaggayyapeta, India 95/D2
Jagna, Phil. 88/D3
Jagraon, India 98/C4
Jagst (riv.), Ger. 45/J2
Jaguaquara, Braz. 187/F2
Jaguarão (riv.), Braz. 191/G2
Jaguarão, Braz. 189/F5
Jaguaretama, Braz. 183/G4
Jaguari, Braz. 189/F4
Jaguari (riv.), Braz. 189/F4
Jaguariaíva, Braz. 189/G3
Jaguaribara, Braz. 183/G4
Jaguaribe, Braz. 183/G4
Jaguaribe (riv.), Braz. 183/G4
Jaguariúna, Braz. 187/K7
Jaguaruana, Braz. 183/G4
Jagüé, Arg. 188/B4
Jagungal (mt.), Austl. 133/D3
Jahānābād, India 96/D3
Jahānābād, India 97/E3
Jahāngīra, Pak. 98/B3
Jahāngīrābād, India 96/B1
Jahleel (pt.), Austl. 128/C2
Jahrom, Iran 103/H4
Jai (brook), Sur. 181/H4
Jaiama, SLeo. 114/C4
Jaicós, Braz. 183/F4
Jailolo, Indo. 91/G3
Jailu (riv.), China 80/C4
Jaimalsar, India 92/B2
Jainca, China 78/E4
Jaipur, India 92/C2
Jaipur Hāt, Bang. 97/G3
Jāis, India 96/C2
Jaisalmer, India 101/K3
Jaisinghnagar, India 96/C4
Jaithāri, India 96/B4
Jājapur, India 92/E3
Jājarkot, Nepal 96/D1
Jājarm, Iran 103/J2
Jajce, Bosn. 50/C3
Jakarta (cap.), Indo. 89/D4
Jakes (mtn.), Tn, US 162/E3
Jakin, Ga, US 165/F2
Jakobsberg, Swe. 39/A1
Jakobstad (Pietarsaari), Fin. 68/D3
Jal, NM, US 150/C1
Jala, Mex. 174/D4
Jalacingo, Mex. 175/M7
Jalaid Qi, China 79/J2
Jalājil, SAr. 100/E3
Jalal-Abad, Kyr. 99/B3
Jalālābād, India 98/C4
Jalālābād, Afg. 98/A2
Jalālābād, India 98/D5
Jalālābād, India 96/B2
Jalāli, India 96/B2
Jalālpur, Pak. 98/C3
Jalālpur, India 96/D2
Jalālpur Pīrwāla, Pak. 98/A5
Jalamah, Isr. 105/C3
Jalang, Indo. 91/F4
Jalangi (riv.), India 97/G3
Jalangi, India 97/G3
Jålanti (lake), Fin. 39/D3
Jalapa, Mex. 176/C2
Jalapa, Guat. 176/D3
Jalapa, Mex. 175/N7
Jalatlaco, Mex. 175/Q10
Jālaun, India 96/B2
Jalbūn, WBnk. 105/C4
Jaldhāka (riv.), India 97/G2
Jales, Braz. 189/G2
Jalesar, India 96/B2
Jaleswar, Nepal 97/E2
Jalīb ash Shuyūkh, Kuw. 103/F4
Jalingo, Nga. 116/A3
Jalisco, Mex. 174/D4
Jāliţah, Jazīrat (isl.), Tun. 66/F3
Jalkot, Pak. 98/B2
Jallouvre, Pic de (peak), Fr. 60/C6
Jalon (riv.), Sp. 46/E2
Jālor, India 101/K3
Jalostotitlán, Mex. 174/E4
Jalpa, Mex. 174/E4
Jalpa de Méndez, Mex. 176/C2
Jalpaiguri, India 97/G2
Jalpan de Serra, Mex. 175/F4
Jaltenango de la Paz, Mex. 176/C3
Jaltepec (riv.), Mex. 176/C2
Jáltipan de Morelos, Mex. 176/C2
Jālū, Libya 108/D2
Jālūd, WBnk. 105/C4
Jaluit (isl.), Mrsh. 136/F4
Jalūlā', Iraq 103/F3
Jam, Iran 103/H5
Jamaame, Som. 119/C1
Jamaare (riv.), Nga. 115/H3
Jamaica (chan.), Jam. 173/F4
Jamaica (nbrhd.), NY, US 169/K9
Jamaica (ctry.) 139/K8
Jamaica (bay), NY, US 168/K9
Jamālpur, India 98/C5
Jamālpur, Bang. 97/G3
Jamālpur, India 97/F3
Jamanxim (riv.), Braz. 182/C4
Jamapa, Mex. 175/N7
Jamari (riv.), Braz. 185/F3
Jamberoo, Austl. 133/E2
Jambi (prov.), Indo. 89/C3
Jambi, Indo. 89/C3
Jāmbo, India 92/B2
Jamboaye (riv.), Indo. 89/B1
Jambongan (isl.), Malay. 88/B4
Jambuair (cape), Indo. 89/B1
James (bay), Qu, Can. 139/J4
James (pt.), Chile 190/B5
James (riv.), SD, US 154/E1
James (lake), NC, US 163/F3
James City, NC, US 163/J3
James M. Cox Dayton (int'l arpt.), Oh, US 160/D5
James Ross (str.), Nun, Can. 140/G1
Jamesburg, NJ, US 168/D3
Jamesport, Mo, US 155/H4
Jamestown, Austl. 131/H5
Jamestown, Ks, US 154/F4
Jamestown, Ky, US 162/E2
Jamestown, La, US 153/H4
Jamestown, Mo, US 153/H1
Jamestown (dam), ND, US 156/E4
Jamestown, ND, US 156/E4
Jamestown, NY, US 161/G3
Jamestown, Oh, US 160/E5
Jamestown, Tn, US 162/E2
Jamestown Nat'l Hist. Site, Va, US 163/J2
Jamesville, Va, US 163/K2
Jamieson, Or, US 146/E1
Jamīrāpāt (range), India 96/D4
Jāmke, Pak. 98/C3
Jammāl, Tun. 48/B5
Jammerbugt (bay), Den. 40/C3
Jammerland (bay), Den. 39/G7
Jammu, India 98/C3
Jammu and Kashmīr (state), India 99/C5
Jāmnagar, India 101/K4
Jampang-Kulon, Indo. 89/D4
Jāmpur, Pak. 98/A5
Jamshedpur, India 97/F4
Jāmtāra, India 97/F4
Jämtland (co.), Swe. 38/E3
Jamuda, Eth. 118/A4
Jamūi, India 97/F3
Jamuna (riv.), Bang. 97/G3
Jāmunkira, India 95/E1
Jan Kempdorp, SAfr. 124/D2
Jan Mayen (isl.), Nor. 192/G
Jan Smuts (Johannesburg) (int'l arpt.), SAfr. 124/E2
Janāj, Egypt 113/B3
Janakkala, Fin. 41/L1
Janakpur, India 96/C4
Janakpur (zone), Nepal 97/E2
Janakpur, Nepal 97/E2
Janaúba, Braz. 187/E2
Janaucu (isl.), Braz. 182/D2
Jand, Pak. 98/B3
Jandaia, Braz. 189/G1
Jandaia do Sul, Braz. 189/G2
Jandanwāla, Pak. 98/B4
Jandaq, Iran 103/H3
Jandiāla, India 98/C4
Jandikot (arpt.), Austl. 130/K7
Jandowae, Austl. 134/C4
Jándula (riv.), Sp. 46/C4
Jane (brook), Austl. 130/L6
Jane Lew, WV, US 163/G1
Janesville, Wi, US 155/K2
Jangamo, Moz. 123/G5
Jangaon, India 95/C2
Jangipur, India 97/G3
Janikowo, Pol. 43/K2
Janīn, WBnk. 105/C4
Janja, Bosn. 50/D3
Janjevo, Yugo. 50/E4
Jannaale, Som. 119/D1
Janos, Mex. 174/C2
Jánoshalma, Hun. 50/D2
Jánosháza, Hun. 50/C2
Janów Lubelski, Pol. 43/M3
Jānsath, India 96/A1
Jansen, Sk, Can. 156/B2
Jansen, Co, US 152/B2
Jansenville, SAfr. 124/D4
Januária, Braz. 186/D2
Janville, Fr. 57/G4
Janvry, Fr. 30/J6
Janzé, Fr. 56/D5
Janzūr, Libya 67/G4
Jaora, India 92/C3
Japan (sea), Asia 77/N5
Japan (ctry.) 77/N6
Japanese Alps NP, Japan 85/E2
Japiim, Braz. 184/C2
Japurá (riv.), Braz. 179/C3
Jaqué, Pan. 180/B3
Jarābulus, Syria 102/D2
Jarad, SAr. 100/D5
Jaraguá, Braz. 186/C2
Jaraíz de la Vera, Sp. 46/C2
Jarales, NM, US 149/J3
Jarama (riv.), Sp. 46/D2
Jaramānah, Syria 105/E2
Jaramillo, Arg. 191/D5
Jarandilla de la Vera, Sp. 46/C2
Jarānwāla, Pak. 98/B4
Jarash, Jor. 105/D4
Jarbah, Jazīrat (isl.), Tun. 67/F4
Jarbidge, Nv, US 146/F3
Järbo, Swe. 40/G1
Jarby (pt.), IM, UK 34/D3
Jardas al 'Abīd, Libya 67/J4
Jardim, Braz. 189/E2
Jardim, Braz. 183/G4
Jardim do Seridó, Braz. 183/G4
Jardín, Col. 183/K7
Jardín América, Arg. 189/F3
Jardine (riv.), Austl. 129/F2
Jardine R. Nat'l Park, Austl. 129/F2
Jardines de la Reina (arch.), Cuba 177/G1
Jargalant, Mong. 78/E2
Jargalant, Mong. 99/F2
Jargalant, Mong. 78/D2
Jargeau, Fr. 57/H5
Jari (riv.), Braz. 179/D2
Jaridih, India 97/F4
Jarjīs, Tun. 67/F4
Järlåsa, Swe. 39/A1
Jarmen, Ger. 40/E5
Järna, Swe. 40/G2
Jarny, Fr. 55/E5
Jaro, Phil. 88/D3
Jarocin, Pol. 43/J3
Jarod, India 96/A4
Jaroměř, Czh. 43/H3
Jarosław, Pol. 43/M3
Jaroso, Co, US 152/B2
Jarratt, Va, US 163/J2
Jarrettsville, Md, US 168/B4
Jarrow, Eng, UK 35/G2
Jars (plain), Laos 94/C2
Jartai, China 78/F4
Jaru, Braz. 185/F3
Jarud Qi, China 80/E1
Järva-Jaani, Est. 41/L2
Järvakandi, Est. 41/L2
Järvelä, Fin. 39/F4
Järvenpää, Fin. 41/L1
Jarville-la-Malgrange, Fr. 55/F6
Jarvis (isl.), Pac., US 137/J5
Jarvisburg, NC, US 163/K2
Järvsö, Swe. 40/G1
Jás-Nagykun-Szonok (co.), Hun. 43/L5
Jasāna, India 98/C5
Jasenagykun-Seolnok (prov.), Hun. 50/E2
Jashpurnagar, India 97/E4
Jasidih, India 97/F3
Jasin, Malay. 89/C2
Jāsk, Iran 101/G3
Jasło, Pol. 43/L4
Jason (isl.), Mald. 191/E6
Jasonville, In, US 160/C5
Jasper, Ab, Can. 144/E1
Jasper, Al, US 162/D4
Jasper, Ar, US 153/H2
Jasper, Fl, US 165/G2
Jasper, Ga, US 162/E3
Jasper, In, US 162/D1
Jasper, Mn, US 155/F2
Jasper, Mo, US 153/G2
Jasper, Tn, US 162/E3
Jasper, Tx, US 151/H2
Jasper NP, Ab, Can. 144/E1
Jaspur, India 96/B1
Jastrebarsko, Cro. 50/B3
Jastrowie, Pol. 43/J2
Jastrzębie Zdroj, Pol. 43/K4
Jaswantnagar, India 96/B2
Jászapáti, Hun. 43/L5
Jászárokszállás, Hun. 50/D2
Jászberény, Hun. 43/K5
Jataí, Braz. 186/C3
Jatapu (riv.), Braz. 181/G5
Jatāra, India 96/B3
Jataté (riv.), Mex. 176/D2
Jāti, Pak. 101/J4
Jati, Braz. 183/G4
Jatibonico, Cuba 177/G1
Játiva, Sp. 47/E3
Jātni, India 95/E1
Jatoi Janūbi, Pak. 98/A5
Jaú (riv.), Braz. 181/F5
Jaú, Braz. 189/G2
Jaua Sarisarinama, PN, Ven. 181/E3
Jauaperi (riv.), Braz. 181/F5
Jauaperi (riv.), Braz. 181/E5
Jauaru (mts.), Braz. 181/H5
Jaubert (cape), Austl. 128/A4
Jaudy (riv.), Fr. 56/B3
Jauharābād, Pak. 98/B3
Jauja, Peru 184/C3
Jaumave, Mex. 175/F4
Jaun, Swi. 60/D4
Jaunay-Clan, Fr. 44/D3
Jaunjelgava, Lat. 41/L3
Jaunpass (pass), Swi. 60/D4

Map Section
236
237

Jaunpi – Kailu

Jaunpiebalga, Lat. 41/M3
Jaunpils, Lat. 41/K3
Jaunpur, India 96/D3
Jauru (riv.), Braz. 186/A3
Jausiers, Fr. 64/C5
Java (isl.), Indo. 77/K10
Java (sea), Indo. 77/K10
Javari (riv.), Braz. 184/C2
Jávea, Sp. 47/F3
Javier (isl.), Chile 191/B5
Javier de Viana, Uru. 189/E4
Javorie (peak), Slvk. 50/D1
Javornice (riv.), Czh. 59/G2
Javorník (peak), Czh. 59/G4
Javorová Skála (peak), Czh. 59/H3
Javron-les-Chapelles, Fr. 57/E4
Jawāla Mukhi, India 98/D4
Jawhar, Som. 118/C5
Jawi, Indo. 90/C4
Jawor, Pol. 43/J3
Jay, Ok, US 153/G2
Jay, Me, US 161/L2
Jay, Fl, US 164/E2
Jayanca, Peru 184/B2
Jayapura, Indo. 91/K4
Jaynagar, India 97/G4
Jaynagar, India 97/F2
Jayton, Tx, US 152/D4
Jaywick, Eng, UK 37/H3
Jazīrat Būbiyan (isl.), Kuw. 103/G4
Jazīrat Maşīrah (isl.), Oman 77/F5
Jazzīn, Leb. 105/D1
JB Thomas (lake), Tx, US 151/D1
Jbel Bani (mts.), Mor. 110/D3
Jean, Tx, US 153/E4
Jean Lafitte, La, US 164/C3
Jeanerette, La, US 164/C3
Jebba, Nga. 115/G4
Jeberos, Peru 184/B2
Jebjerg, Den. 40/C3
Jebus, Indo. 89/D3
Jed Water (riv.), Sc, UK 33/D6
Jedburgh, Sc, UK 33/D6
Jedlicze, Pol. 43/L4
Jędrzejów, Pol. 43/L3
Jeetze (riv.), Ger. 42/F2
Jeffers, Mn, US 155/G1
Jeffers, Mt, US 147/H1
Jefferson, Al, US 162/D4
Jefferson, Ga, US 163/F3
Jefferson, Oh, US 160/F4
Jefferson, Ia, US 155/G2
Jefferson (riv.), Mt, US 147/H1
Jefferson, NC, US 163/G2
Jefferson (mt.), Nv, US 146/E4
Jefferson, NY, US 161/J3
Jefferson, Or, US 146/B1
Jefferson (mt.), Or, US 146/C1
Jefferson, Tx, US 153/G4
Jefferson (co.), Wi, US 167/N14
Jefferson, Wi, US 155/K2
Jefferson, Va, US 163/J2
Jefferson City (cap.), Mo, US 153/H1
Jefferson City, Tn, US 163/F2
Jeffersonville, In, US 162/E1
Jeffersonville, Ky, US 162/F2
Jeffersonville, Ga, US 163/F4
Jeffrey, WV, US 163/G2
Jeffrey City, Wy, US 147/K2
Jeffrey's, Nf, Can. 159/H1
Jeffreys Bay, SAfr. 124/D4
Jega, Nga. 115/G3
Jegenstorf, Swi. 60/D3
Jeinemeni (peak), Chile 190/B5
Jejui Guazú (riv.), Par. 186/A5
Jēkabpils, Lat. 41/L3
Jekyll (isl.), Ga, US 165/H2
Jelcz-Laskowice, Pol. 43/J3
Jelence, Slvk. 50/D1
Jelenia Gora (prov.), Czh.,Ger. 43/E2
Jelenia Góra, Pol. 43/H3
Jelep (pass), China 92/E2
Jelgava, Lat. 41/K3
Jeli, Malay. 89/C1
Jelka, Slvk. 50/C1
Jellico, Tn, US 162/E2
Jellicoe, On, Can. 157/L3
Jelm, Wy, US 154/A3
Jelow Gīr, Iran 103/F3
Jeløya (isl.), Nor. 38/S9
Jelsi, It. 65/D4
Jema Shet' (riv.), Eth. 117/H3
Jemaa Sahim, Mor. 110/C2
Jemaja (isl.), Indo. 89/D2
Jemaluang, Malay. 89/C2
Jemappes, Belg. 54/C3
Jember, Indo. 89/F5
Jembiani, Tanz. 119/B3
Jemez (mts.), NM, US 149/J3
Jemez (riv.), NM, US 149/J3
Jemez Ind. Res., NM, US 149/J3
Jemez Pueblo, NM, US 149/J3
Jemez Springs, NM, US 149/J3
Jeminay, China 99/E2
Jemison, Al, US 162/D4
Jempang (lake), Indo. 91/E4
Jemsa, Egypt 109/G3
Jena, Ger. 42/F3
Jena, La, US 164/B2
Jenaz, Swi. 61/F4
Jenbach, Aus. 45/J3
Jendouba, Tun. 112/L6
Jendouba (gov.), Tun. 112/L6
Jeneponto, Indo. 91/E5
Jengen, Ger. 61/G2
Jenison, Mi, US 160/D3
Jenkins, Ky, US 163/F2
Jenkintown, Pa, US 168/C3
Jenks, Ok, US 153/G2
Jennersdorf, Aus. 50/C2
Jennings, La, US 164/B2
Jennings, Fl, US 165/G2
Jennings, Ks, US 154/D4
Jenny, Sur. 182/C1
Jenny Lind (isl.), Nun, Can. 140/F2
Jenolan Caves, Austl. 133/E1
Jens Muck (isl.), Nun, Can. 141/H2
Jensen, Ut, US 147/J3
Jensen Beach, Fl, US 165/H4
Jeppener, Arg. 191/J11
Jequetepeque, Peru 184/B2
Jequié, Braz. 187/E2
Jequitaí, Braz. 186/D3
Jequitinhonha (riv.), Braz. 179/E4
Jequitinhonha, Braz. 187/E3
Jerada, Mor. 112/C2
Jerantut, Malay. 89/C2
Jerdera, Indo. 128/D1
Jérémie, Haiti 177/H2
Jeremoabo, Braz. 187/F1
Jerer Shet' (riv.), Eth. 118/B3
Jerez de García Salinas, Mex. 174/E4
Jerez de la Frontera, Sp. 46/B4
Jerez de los Caballeros, Sp. 46/B3
Jericho, NY, US 169/L8
Jericho, Austl. 134/B3
Jericho (Arīḩā), WBnk. 105/C5
Jericó, Col. 183/K7
Jericó, Braz. 183/G4
Jerico Springs, Mo, US 153/G2
Jerilderie, Austl. 133/B2
Jerissa, Tun. 112/L7
Jermyn, Tx, US 153/E4
Jerome, Ar, US 153/J4
Jerome, Id, US 147/F2
Jerome, Az, US 149/F3
Jerramungup, Austl. 130/C5
Jersey (isl.), Chl, UK 44/B2
Jersey City, NJ, US 169/J9
Jersey City (res.), NJ, US 169/H8
Jersey Shore, Pa, US 168/A1
Jersey Village, Tx, US 151/M9
Jerseyville, Il, US 155/J4
Jerteh, Malay. 89/C1
Jerumenha, Braz. 183/F4
Jerusalem (dist.), Isr. 104/D4
Jerusalem, Ar, US 153/H3
Jerusalem (arpt.), WBnk. 105/C5
Jerusalem (Yerushalayim) (cap.), Isr. 105/C5
Jervis (inlet), BC, Can. 144/C2
Jervis Bay, Austl. 133/E2
Jerzu, It. 48/A3
Jesberg, Ger. 53/G6
Jesenice (res.), Czh. 59/F2
Jesenice, Slov. 45/L3
Jesi, It. 63/G6
Jessheim, Nor. 40/D1
Jessieville, Ar, US 153/H3
Jessore, Bang. 97/G4
Jessore (pol. reg.), Bang. 97/G4
Jessup (lake), Fl, US 165/H3
Jesuânia, Braz. 187/L6
Jesup, Ga, US 165/H2
Jesus (mt.), Ks, US 152/E2
Jésus (isl.), Qu, Can. 159/N6
Jesús, Par. 189/F3
Jesús Carranza, Mex. 176/C2
Jesús de Machaca, Bol. 188/B1
Jesús María, Col. 183/M7
Jesús María, Arg. 188/C4
Jesús Menéndez, Cuba 177/G1
Jet, Ok, US 153/E2
Jetmore, Ks, US 152/E1
Jetpur, India 101/K4
Jettingen-Scheppach, Ger. 58/D6
Jetzendorf, Ger. 59/E6
Jeu (riv.), Fr. 57/E6
Jeumont, Fr. 55/D3
Jevenstedt, Ger. 42/E1
Jever, Ger. 53/E1
Jevnaker, Nor. 40/D1
Jewar, India 96/A1
Jewel Cave Nat'l Mon., SD, US 154/C2
Jewell, Ks, US 154/E4
Jewell Junction, Ia, US 155/H2
Jewett, Tx, US 151/F2
Jezerce (peak), Alb. 50/D4
Jezerní Stěna (peak), Czh. 59/G4
Jeziorak (lake), Pol. 43/K2
Jhā Jhā, India 97/F3
Jhajjar, India 98/D5
Jhal Jhao, Pak. 101/J3
Jhālakāti, Bang. 97/H4
Jhālawār, India 92/C3
Jhalida, India 97/E4
Jhālū, India 96/B1
Jhang Sadar, Pak. 98/B4
Jhaniān Khatrian, Pak. 98/B3
Jhanjhārpur, India 97/F2
Jhānsi, India 96/B3
Jhāpa, Nepal 97/F2
Jhārgrām, India 97/F4
Jharia, India 97/F4
Jharkhand (state), India 92/D3
Jhārsuguda, India 97/E5
Jhawāriān, Pak. 98/B3
Jhelum, Pak. 98/B3
Jhelum (riv.), Pak. 98/B3
Jhelum (riv.), India 99/B5
Jhenida, Bang. 97/G4
Jhumra, Pak. 98/B4
Ji (riv.), China 78/D5
Ji Xian, China 80/C4
Ji Xian, China 80/H6
Ji-Paraná, Braz. 185/F3
Jia Xian, China 80/B3
Jiading, China 80/L8
Jiahe, China 93/K2
Jialing (riv.), China 77/K6
Jialu (riv.), China 78/G5
Jiamusi, China 79/L2
Ji'an, China 81/D2
Jian (riv.), China 87/H3
Ji'an, China 87/G3
Jianchang, China 81/C2
Jianchang, China 80/D2
Jiancheng, China 87/F4
Jiang (riv.), China 94/E1
Jiang Xian, China 80/B4
Jiang'an, China 93/J2
Jiangcheng Hanizu Yizu Zizhixian, China 86/D4
Jiangchuan, China 86/D3
Jiangdu, China 80/D4
Jianghua Yaozu Zizhixian, China 87/F3
Jiangjiadian, China 79/H3
Jiangjin, China 87/E2
Jiangjunhe, China 78/G5
Jiangjunshi, China 81/A3
Jiangjuntai, China 78/D3
Jiangkou, China 87/J2
Jiangkou, China 87/F2
Jiangkou, China 87/G3
Jiangkouzhen, China 87/F2
Jiangling, China 87/G2
Jiangmen, China 87/G4
Jiangmenchang, China 86/E2
Jiangning, China 80/D5
Jiangsu (prov.), China 79/H5
Jiangwan, China 87/G3
Jiangxi (prov.), China 80/C5
Jiangxiang, China 87/H1
Jiangya, China 87/F2
Jiangyin, China 80/E5
Jiangyong, China 87/F3
Jiangyou, China 86/E2
Jianhe, China 93/J2
Jianhu, China 80/D4
Jianli, China 87/G2
Jian'ou, China 87/H3
Jianping, China 79/H3
Jianshi, China 87/F2
Jianshui, China 86/D4
Jianyang, China 86/E2
Jianyang, China 87/H3
Jiaochangba, China 86/D1
Jiaocheng, China 80/C3
Jiaohe, China 79/K3
Jiaojiang, China 87/J2
Jiaokou, China 80/C3
Jiaolai (riv.), China 79/J3
Jiaonan, China 80/D4
Jiaotou, China 87/J2
Jiaozuo, China 80/C4
Jiapu, China 80/K8
Jiashan, China 80/D4
Jiashan, China 80/L9
Jiashi, China 99/C4
Jiaxiang, China 80/D4
Jiaxing, China 80/L9
Jiaya, China 87/F3
Jiayin, China 79/L2
Jiayou, China 87/E3
Jiayu, China 87/G2
Jiayuguan, China 78/D4
Jiazi, China 87/H4
Jibāl An Nūbah (mts.), Sudan 117/F3
Jibāl Múāb (mts.), Jor. 105/D5
Jibiya, Nga. 115/G3
Jibóia, Braz. 180/D4
Jibou, Rom. 51/F2
Jicarilla Apache Ind. Res., NM, US 149/J2
Jicarón (isl.), Pan. 177/F5
Jičín, Czh. 43/H3
Jidali (riv.), Som. 118/C3
Jiddah, SAr. 100/C4
Jidong, China 79/L2
Jiehualong, China 87/G3
Jieshi, China 87/G4
Jieshipu, China 78/F4
Jieshou, China 80/C4
Jiexiu, China 80/B3
Jieyang, China 87/H4
Jieznas, Lith. 41/L4
Jifnā, WBnk. 105/C5
Jiga, Eth. 117/H3
Jigalong Abor. Land, Austl. 130/D2
Jigawa (prov.), Nga. 115/H4
Jigger, La, US 164/C1
Jiggs, Nv, US 146/F3
Jiguaní, Cuba 177/G1
Jiguanshan, China 81/C1
Jigzhi, China 78/E5
Jihlava, Czh. 43/H4
Jihlava (riv.), Czh. 45/L2
Jihlavský (pol. reg.), Czh. 43/H4
Jiiqley, Som. 118/C4
Jijel (wilaya), Alg. 112/H4
Jijel, Alg. 112/H4
Jijia (riv.), Rom. 70/C3
Jijiga, Eth. 118/B3
Jijona, Sp. 47/E3
Jikawo, Eth. 117/G3
Jilhava (riv.), Czh. 43/H4
Jili (lake), China 78/B2
Jilib, Som. 119/C1
Jilin (prov.), China 79/K3
Jilin, China 79/K3
Jiliu (riv.), China 79/J1
Jiloca (riv.), Sp. 46/E2
Jilotepec, Mex. 175/K7
Jílové u Prahy, Czh. 59/H3
Jim Thorpe, Pa, US 168/C2
Jim Woodruff (dam), Fl, US 165/F2
Jīma, Eth. 117/H4
Jimaní, DRep. 177/J2
Jimbe, Ang. 121/E5
Jimbolia, Rom. 50/E3
Jimboomba, Austl. 134/D4
Jimei, China 87/H3
Jimena de la Frontera, Sp. 46/C4
Jiménez, Mex. 151/D3
Jiménez, Mex. 174/D3
Jimingsi, China 87/F2
Jimmēza, Sudan 117/G1
Jimmy Carter Nat'l Hist. Site, Ga, US 165/F1
Jimo, China 80/E3
Jimokuji, Japan 83/L5
Jimsar, China 99/E3
Jin (riv.), China 93/K2
Jin Xian, China 81/A3
Jin Xian, China 80/C3
Jinan, China 80/D3
Jin'an, China 87/H2
Jinchang, China 78/E4
Jincheng, China 81/A2
Jincheng, China 80/C4
Jinchuan, China 86/D2
Jinchuan, China 79/K3
Jinci Temple, China 80/C3
Jīnd, India 98/D5
Jindabyne (lake), Austl. 133/D3
Jindabyne (dam), Austl. 133/D3
Jindabyne, Austl. 133/D3
Jindalee, Austl. 133/D2
Jindřichuv Hradec, Czh. 43/H4
Jinfosi, China 78/D4
Jing (riv.), China 78/F5
Jing Xian, China 87/H2
Jing Xian, China 87/F3
Jingbian, China 80/B3
Jingde, China 87/H2
Jingdezhen, China 87/H2
Jingdong, China 93/H3
Jingellic, Austl. 133/C2
Jinggangshan, China 87/G3
Jinggu, China 86/D4
Jinghai, China 87/H4
Jinghai, China 80/H7
Jinghaiwei, China 81/B4
Jinghe, China 99/D3
Jinghong, China 86/D4
Jingjiang, China 80/E4
Jingle, China 80/B3
Jingmen, China 80/C5
Jingning, China 78/F4
Jingping (mts.), China 86/D3
Jingshan, China 80/C5
Jingtai, China 78/E4
Jingxi, China 87/E4
Jingyou, China 78/G4
Jingyu, China 79/K3
Jingyuan, China 78/E4
Jinhu, China 80/D4
Jinhua, China 87/H2
Jining, China 80/D4
Jining, China 80/C2
Jinja, Ugan. 119/A1
Jinjie, China 87/E4
Jinka, Eth. 117/H4
Jinkouhe, China 93/H2
Jinlansi, China 87/G3
Jinmen (isl.), Tai. 87/H3
Jinotega, Nic. 176/E3
Jinotepe, Nic. 176/E4
Jinping, China 86/D4
Jinping, China 87/F3
Jinqian (riv.), China 78/F5
Jinsha (riv.), China 77/J7
Jinsha, China 93/J2
Jinsha, China 87/H2
Jinshan, China 80/L9
Jinshanwei, China 80/L9
Jinshi, China 87/F2
Jinshui, China 78/F5
Jintan, China 80/D5
Jintang, China 87/G2
Jintotolo (chan.), Phil. 88/C3
Jintūr, India 95/C2
Jinxi, China 87/H3
Jinxi, China 80/E2
Jinxiang, China 80/D4
Jinxiu Yaozu Zizhixian, China 93/K3
Jinyun, China 87/J2
Jinzhai, China 80/C5
Jinzhou (bay), China 81/A3
Jinzhou, China 80/E2
Jiparana (riv.), Braz. 185/F3
Jipijapa, Ecu. 180/A5
Jiquilpan de Juárez, Mex. 174/E5
Jiquipilco, Mex. 175/Q9
Jīrēn, Eth. 117/H4
Jirgā, Egypt 109/F3
Jirin Gol, China 79/H3
Jiřkov, Czh. 59/G1
Jīroft, Iran 101/G3
Jīsh, Isr. 105/C2
Jishan, China 80/B4
Jishou, China 87/F2
Jisr ash Shughūr, Syria 104/E2
Jitan, China 87/G3
Jitra, Malay. 89/C1
Jiu (riv.), Rom. 70/B3
Jiucheng, China 87/E2
Jiudongshan, China 87/H4
Jiufeng, China 87/H3
Jiugong (mtn.), China 87/G2
Jiuhua (mtn.), China 87/H2
Jiujiang, China 87/G2
Jiulianshan, China 87/G3
Jiuling (mts.), China 87/G2
Jiulong, China 86/D2
Jiun (riv.), China 87/F4
Jiurongcheng, China 81/B4
Jiutai, China 79/K3
Jiutang, China 87/F4
Jiutepec, Mex. 175/K8
Jiuwan (mts.), China 87/E3
Jiuxincheng, China 80/G7
Jiuyongshou, China 78/F5
Jiuyuhang, China 80/K9
Jiuzhan, China 79/K1
Jīwani, Pak. 101/H3
Jixi, China 79/L2
Jixi, China 87/H2
Jixian, China 79/L2
Jiyang, China 80/D3
Jiyuan, China 80/C4
Jiz' (wadi), Yem. 100/F5
Jīzān, SAr. 100/D5
Jizayy, Egypt 113/B4
Jize, China 80/C3
Jizera (riv.), Czh. 43/H3
Jizl (wadi), SAr. 100/C3
Jizō-zaki (pt.), Japan 84/C3
Jizzakh, Uzb. 74/G5
Jmijin (riv.), SKor. 81/F6
Joaçaba, Braz. 189/G3
Joachín, Mex. 175/N8
Joaíma, Braz. 187/E3
Joal, Sen. 114/A3
Joana Peres, Braz. 182/D3
Joanna, SC, US 163/G3
João Câmara, Braz. 183/H4
João Lisboa, Braz. 183/E4
João Monlevade, Braz. 187/E3
João Pessoa, Braz. 183/H4
João Pinheiro, Braz. 186/D3
Joaquim Távora, Braz. 189/G2
Joaquin, Tx, US 151/G2
Joaquín V. González, Arg. 188/C3
Jobabo, Cuba 177/G1
Jocassee (dam), SC, US 163/F3
Jockgrim, Ger. 58/B4
Jocón, Hon. 176/E3
Jódar, Sp. 46/D4
Jodhpur, India 92/B2
Jodoigne, Belg. 55/D2
Joe, Mt, US 156/B4
Joe Pool (lake), Tx, US 150/L7
Joensuu, Fin. 68/F3
Jōetsu, Japan 85/F2
Jogbani, India 97/F2
Jõgeva, Est. 41/M2
Joggins, NS, Can. 158/E3
Joghdān, Iran 101/G3
Jogighpa, India 97/H2
Johannesberg, Ger. 58/C2
Johannesburg, Ca, US 148/D3
Johannesburg, SAfr. 124/E2
Johannesburg (Jan Smuts) (int'l arpt.), SAfr. 124/E2
Johanngeorgenstadt, Ger. 59/F2
Johilla (riv.), India 96/C4
John Day (riv.), Or, US 142/B2
John Day, Or, US 146/D1
John Day (dam), Or, US 144/D5
John Day Fossil Beds Nat'l Mon., Or, US 146/C1
John Day Fossil Beds Nat'l Mon., Or, US 146/D1
John Day, North Fork (riv.), Or, US 146/D1
John F. Kennedy (int'l arpt.), NY, US 169/K9
John Forrest NP, Austl. 130/L6
John H. Kerr (dam), Va, US 163/H2
John Martin (res.), Co, US 154/C4
John O'Groats, Sc, UK 31/S7
John Wayne/Orange County (int'l arpt.), Ca, US 166/G8
Johnshaven, Sc, UK 33/D3
Johnson (mtn.), Wy, US 154/B2
Johnson (co.), Tx, US 150/K7
Johnson (cr.), NY, US 160/V9
Johnson (Johnson City), Ks, US 152/D2
Johnson City, NY, US 161/J3
Johnson City, Tn, US 163/F2
Johnson City, Tx, US 150/E2
Johnson Draw (riv.), Tx, US 151/D2
Johnson Lake Nat'l Wild. Ref., ND, US 156/E4
Johnsonburg, Pa, US 161/G4
Johnsonburg, NJ, US 168/D2
Johnsons Crossing, Yk, Can. 171/M3
Johnsonville (nbrhd.), NZ 135/H9
Johnsonville, SC, US 163/H4
Johnston (falls), Zam. 121/G5
Johnston, Ia, US 155/H3
Johnston, Wal, UK 36/B3
Johnston (lake), Austl. 127/B4
Johnston, SC, US 163/G4
Johnston Atoll (isl.), Pac., US 137/J3
Johnston City, Il, US 162/C2
Johnstone, Sc, UK 33/B5
Johnstown, Ire. 32/C4
Johnstown, Oh, US 160/E4
Johnstown, NY, US 161/J3
Johnstown, On, Can. 161/J2
Johnstown, Pa, US 161/G4
Johnsville, Md, US 168/A4
Johor (state), Malay. 89/C2
Johor (river), Malay. 89/C2
Johor (str.), Malay.,Sing. 89/J6
Johor Baharu, Malay. 89/J6
Jöhstadt, Ger. 59/G1
Joigny, Fr. 44/E3
Joiner, Ar, US 162/B3
Joinvile, Braz. 189/G3
Joinville, Fr. 60/B1
Joinville (isl.), Can. 192/Ant.
Jojutla, Mex. 175/K8
Jokau, Sudan 117/G3
Jokela, Fin. 39/E4
Jokioinen, Fin. 41/K1
Jokkmokk, Swe. 38/F2
Jökulsargljufur NP, Ice. 38/P6
Jolanda di Savoia, It. 63/E4
Jolfā, Iran 103/F2
Jolgeh-ye Khūzestan (plain), Iran 103/G4
Joliet, Il, US 160/B4
Joliet, Mt, US 147/J1
Joliet Army Ammo. Plant, Il, US 160/B4
Joliette, Qu, Can. 161/K1
Jollyville, Tx, US 151/F2
Jolo (isl.), Phil. 91/F2
Jolo, Phil. 88/C4
Jomala, Fin. 41/H1
Jomalig (isl.), Phil. 88/C2
Jombang, Indo. 89/F4
Jombo (riv.), Ang. 120/D5
Jomda, China 86/C2
Jomo Kenyatta (int'l arpt.), Kenya 119/B2
Jomsom, Nepal 96/D1
Jomu, Tanz. 119/A2
Jona, Swi. 61/E3
Jonacatepec, Mex. 175/L8
Jonava, Lith. 41/L4
Jonchery-sur-Vesle, Fr. 54/C5
Jones, La, US 153/J4
Jones (inlet), NY, US 169/L9
Jones (sound), Can. 139/J2
Jones, Al, US 162/D4
Jones (mtn.), Pa, US 168/A2
Jones Beach State Park, NY, US 169/L9
Jonesboro, La, US 153/H4
Jonesboro, In, US 160/D4
Jonesboro, Il, US 162/C2
Jonesboro, Ar, US 162/B3
Jonesboro, Ga, US 163/M7
Jonesborough, NI, UK 34/B3
Jonesborough, Tn, US 163/F2
Jonestown, Ms, US 162/B3
Jonesville, La, US 164/C2
Jonesville, Va, US 163/F2
Jonesville, NC, US 163/G2
Jonglei, Sudan 117/F4
Joniškelis, Lith. 41/L3
Joniškis, Lith. 41/K3
Jönköping (co.), Swe. 38/E4
Jönköping, Swe. 40/F3
Jonquière, Qu, Can. 158/B1
Jonquières, Fr. 64/A4
Jonuta, Mex. 172/C4
Joondalup (lake), Austl. 130/K6
Joplin, Mo, US 153/G2
Joplin, Mt, US 145/J3
Joppa, Il, US 162/C2
Joppa (Joppatowne), Md, US 168/B5
Joppatowne (Joppa), Md, US 168/B5
Jora, India 96/A2
Jordan (riv.), Isr.,Jor. 104/D4
Jordan (ctry.) 77/C6
Jordan (riv.), Or, US 147/E2
Jordan (riv.), Jor. 105/D4
Jordan, On, Can. 160/U9
Jordan, Mt, US 145/L4
Jordan (cr.), Pa, US 168/C2
Jordan (lake), Al, US 162/D4
Jordan Station, On, Can. 160/U9
Jordan Valley, Or, US 146/E2
Jordbro, Swe. 39/B1
Jorge (cape), Chile 191/B6
Jorge Chavez (int'l arpt.), Peru 184/B4
Jorge Newbury (Buenos Aires) (int'l arpt.), Arg. 191/J11
Jorhāt, India 86/B3
Joriāpāni, Nepal 96/C1
Jork, Ger. 53/G1
Jornada del Muerto (val.), NM, US 152/A4
Jørpeland, Nor. 40/B2
Jos, Nga. 115/H4
Jos (plat.), Nga. 115/H4
Jose Abad Santos, Phil. 88/D4
José Agustín Palacios, Bol. 185/E4
José Batlle y Ordóñez, Uru. 191/G2
José Bonifácio, Braz. 189/G2
José Cardel, Mex. 175/N7
José de Freitas, Braz. 183/F4
José Enrique Rodó, Uru. 191/K10
José María Córdova (int'l arpt.), Col. 183/K6
José María Morelos, Mex. 176/D2
Jose Marti (int'l arpt.), Cuba 177/F1
Jose Panganiban, Phil. 88/C2
José Pedro Varela, Uru. 191/G2
José, South (dept.), Uru. 191/F2
Josefa Camejo (int'l arpt.), Ven. 180/D2
Joseph, Or, US 146/E1
Joseph, Ut, US 149/F1
Joseph Bonaparte (gulf), Austl. 127/B2
Joseph City, Az, US 149/G3
Josephine, Tx, US 150/L6
Joshin-Etsu Kogen NP, Japan 85/F2
Joshipur, India 97/F5
Joshua, Tx, US 150/K7
Joshua (pt.), Ct, US 169/F1
Joshua Tree, Ca, US 148/D3
Joshua Tree NP, Ca, US 148/D4
Jossa (riv.), Ger. 58/C2
Josselin, Fr. 56/C5
Jotunheimen NP, Nor. 40/C1
Jouanne (riv.), Fr. 44/C2
Jouarre, Fr. 30/M5
Joué-lès-Tours, Fr. 57/F6
Joué-sur-Erdre, Fr. 56/D6
Jœuf, Fr. 55/F5
Jouques, Fr. 64/B5
Jourama Falls NP, Austl. 134/B2
Jourdanton, Tx, US 150/E3
Joure, Neth. 52/C3
Joutseno, Fin. 41/N1
Joutsijärvi, Fin. 68/E2
Joux (lake), Swi. 60/C4
Jouy, Fr. 57/G3
Jouy-en-Josas, Fr. 30/J5
Jouy-le-Châtel, Fr. 30/M6
Jouy-le-Moutier, Fr. 30/J4
Jouy-sur-Morin, Fr. 54/C6
Jovellanos, Cuba 177/F1
Jovet (peak), Fr. 64/C2
Joveyn (riv.), Iran 101/G1
Jow Khvāh, Iran 103/J3
Jowai, India 93/F2
Jowsheqān-e Qālī, Iran 103/G3
Joy (mt.), Yk, Can. 171/M3
Joyce, La, US 164/B2
Joyce's Country (dist.), Ire. 32/A2
Jōyō, Japan 83/J6
Jozankei Spa, Japan 82/B2
Ju (riv.), China 78/G5
Ju Xian, China 80/D4
Juan Aldama, Mex. 174/E3
Juan Bautista Alberdi, Arg. 188/C3
Juan de Fuca (str.), BC, Can.,US 140/D4
Juan de Nova (isl.), Fr. 107/G6
Juan Fernández (isls.), Chile 179/A6
Juan Fernández, Arg. 190/F3
Juan Jackson, Uru. 191/K10
Juan José Paso, Arg. 190/E2
Juan L. Lacaze, Uru. 191/K11
Juan Santamaria (int'l arpt.), CR 177/E4
Juancheng, China 80/C4
Juancho Yrausquin (int'l arpt.), Neth. 173/N8
Juanda (int'l arpt.), Indo. 89/F4
Juangriego, Ven. 181/F2
Juanjuí, Peru 184/B2
Juárez, Mex. 151/D4
Juárez, Arg. 190/F3
Juarez (arpt.), Mex. 175/Q10
Juaso, Gha. 115/E5
Juazeirinho, Braz. 183/G4
Juazeiro, Braz. 183/F5
Juazeiro do Norte, Braz. 183/G4
Juazohn, Libr. 114/C5
Juba, Sudan 117/F4
Jubany, Arg., Ant. 192/W
Jubbah, SAr. 102/E4
Jübek, Ger. 42/E1
Jubones (riv.), Ecu. 184/B1
Juby (cape), Mor. 110/B4
Júcar (riv.), Sp. 66/C3
Juçara, Braz. 186/C2
Jucás, Braz. 183/G4
Jüchen, Ger. 55/F1
Juchipila, Mex. 174/E4
Juchique de Ferrer, Mex. 175/N7
Juchitán de Zaragoza, Mex. 176/C2
Juchitepec, Mex. 175/R10
Jucurutu, Braz. 183/G4
Jud, ND, US 156/E4
Judaberg, Nor. 40/A2
Judenburg, Aus. 45/L3
Judian, China 86/C3
Judith (mts.), Mt, US 145/K4
Judith Gap, Mt, US 145/K4
Judson, ND, US 156/D4
Judsonia, Ar, US 153/J3
Juelsminde, Den. 40/D4
Jufrah (wadi), Egypt 113/C4
Jugon-les-Lacs, Fr. 56/C4
Juḩā, SAr. 118/B1
Juhaynah, Egypt 109/F3
Juicai (mtn.), China 87/F3
Juigalpa, Nic. 176/E3
Juilly, Fr. 30/L4
Juine (riv.), Fr. 44/E2
Juishui, Tai. 87/J4
Juist (isl.), Ger. 52/D1
Juist, Ger. 52/E1
Juist (arpt.), Ger. 52/E1
Juiz de Fora, Braz. 187/N6
Juizhen, China 87/H3
Jujurieux, Fr. 60/B5
Jujuy (prov.), Arg. 188/C2
Julbach, Ger. 59/F6
Julesburg, Co, US 154/C3
Juli, Peru 184/D5
Julia Creek, Austl. 134/A3
Juliaca, Peru 184/D4
Juliaetta, Id, US 144/F4
Julian, Ca, US 148/D4
Julian Alps (mts.), It. 45/K3
Juliana (lake), Fl, US 164/M7
Juliana Top (peak), Sur. 182/B2
Jülich, Ger. 55/F2
Juliff, Tx, US 151/M9
Julimes, Mex. 151/B3
Julio A. Mella, Cuba 177/H1
Júlio de Castilhos, Braz. 189/F4
Juliustown, NJ, US 168/D3
Jullouville, Fr. 56/D3
Jullundur, India 98/C4
Julu, China 80/C3
Juma (riv.), China 78/H4
Jumanggoin, China 86/C1
Jumbilla, Peru 184/B2
Jumbo, Zim. 123/F3
Jumeauville, Fr. 30/H5
Jumièges, Fr. 57/F2
Jumilla, Sp. 46/E3
Jūmīn (wadi), Tun. 112/L6
Juminda (pt.), Est. 41/L2
Jumla, Nepal 96/D1
Jümme (riv.), Ger. 53/E2
Jūmonji, Japan 82/B4
Jump (riv.), Wi, US 155/J1
Jumpertown, Ms, US 162/C3
Jūn, Leb. 105/C1
Junāgadh, India 101/K4
Jūnāgarh, India 95/D2
Junan, China 80/D4
Juncal (peak), Chile 190/N8
Junction, Ut, US 149/F1
Junction (mtn.), Mt, US 145/H4
Junction, Tx, US 151/E2
Junction City, Ar, US 153/H4
Junction City, Ks, US 153/F1
Junction City, Ky, US 162/E2
Junction City, La, US 150/H1
Junction City, Mo, US 162/B2
Junction City, Or, US 146/B1
Junction City, Wi, US 155/K1
Jundah, Austl. 134/A4
Jundiaí, Braz. 187/K8
Jundu (mts.), China 80/H6
June Lake, Ca, US 148/C2
Juneau, Wi, US 155/K2
Juneau (cap.), Ak, US 171/M4
Juneda, Sp. 47/F2
Junee, Austl. 133/C2
Jungar Qi, China 80/B3
Jungfrau (peak), Swi. 60/D4
Jungfraujoch, Swi. 60/D4
Jungkat, Indo. 90/C3
Junglinster, Lux. 55/F4
Juniata (riv.), Pa, US 161/H4
Juniata, Ne, US 154/E3
Juniata (co.), Pa, US 168/A2
Junik, Yugo. 50/E4
Junín, Ecu. 180/A5
Junín, Col. 180/B4
Junín, Arg. 190/E2
Junín, Arg. 190/C2
Junín, Peru 184/B3
Junín (dept.), Peru 184/C3
Junín de los Andes, Arg. 190/C3
Junior, WV, US 163/H1
Juniper, NB, Can. 158/D2
Juniper (mtn.), Co, US 147/J3
Juniper, Ga, US 162/E4
Juniper Hills, Ca, US 166/C2
Junipero Serra (peak), Ca, US 148/B2
Jūniyah, Leb. 104/D3
Junji (pass), China 80/C3
Junkou, China 87/H3
Junlian, China 86/E2
Juno, Ga, US 162/E3
Juno, Tx, US 151/D2
Juno Beach, Fr. 57/E2
Juno Beach, Fl, US 165/H4
Junpu, China 87/H2
Junsele, Swe. 38/F3
Juntas, Chile 188/B4
Ju'nyunggoin, China 78/D5
Juodupė, Lith. 41/L3
Juparanã (lake), Braz. 187/E3
Jupiá (res.), Braz. 186/C4
Jupiter, Fl, US 165/H4
Jupiter (riv.), Qu, Can. 158/F1
Jupiter (mt.), Wa, US 167/A2
Juquiá, Braz. 189/H3
Juquitiba, Braz. 187/J8
Jur (riv.), Sudan 117/F3
Jur pri Bratislave, Slvk. 50/C1
Jura (dept.), Fr. 60/B4
Jura (canton), Swi. 60/D3
Jura (isl.), Sc, UK 31/Q9
Jura (pen.), Sc, UK 31/R8
Jura (mts.), Fr. 66/E1
Juradó, Col. 180/B3
Jurançon, Fr. 44/C5
Jurbarkas, Lith. 41/K4
Jurbise, Belg. 54/C2
Jurien, Austl. 130/B4
Jūrmala, Lat. 41/K3
Jurong (nbrhd.), Sing. 89/H6
Juruá (riv.), Braz. 179/C3
Juruena (riv.), Braz. 179/D4
Juruena, Res. Florestal do, Braz. 185/G3
Juruti, Braz. 182/B3
Jushi, China 87/F4
Jushiyama, Japan 83/L5
Jushui, China 87/H3
Juskatla, BC, Can. 171/M5
Jussey, Fr. 60/B2
Jussy, Swi. 60/C5
Jussy, Fr. 54/C4
Justice, WV, US 163/G2
Justiceburg, Tx, US 152/D4
Justin, Tx, US 150/K6
Justo Daract, Arg. 190/D2
Jutaí (riv.), Braz. 181/E5
Jutaí, Braz. 184/D2
Jutiapa, Guat. 176/D3
Juticalpa, Hon. 176/E3
Jutland (pen.), Den. 38/D4
Jutland, NJ, US 168/D2
Juventud, Isla de la (Isla de Pinos) (isl.), Cuba 172/E3
Juye, China 80/D4
Jūyom, Iran 103/H4
Juzhang (riv.), China 80/C5
Juziers, Fr. 30/H4
Južna Morava (riv.), Yugo. 50/E4
Juzur Qarqannah (isl.), Congo 111/H2
Jwaneng, Bots. 122/E5
Jwayyā, Leb. 105/C2
Jyderup, Den. 40/D4
Jylisjärvi (lake), Fin. 39/E3
Jyllinge, Den. 39/J7

K

K'ok'a (lake), Eth. 118/A3
K2 (Godwin Austen) (peak), Pak. 98/D2
Ka (isl.), NKor. 81/C3
Ka Lae (cape), Hi, US 142/U11
Kaabong, Ugan. 117/G5
Kaakhka, Trkm. 101/G1
Kaap Plato (plat.), SAfr. 124/C3
Kaapmuiden, SAfr. 123/F5
Kaarina, Fin. 41/K1
Kaarst, Ger. 52/D6
Kaartjärvi (lake), Fin. 39/E4
Kaba, Gui. 114/C4
Kaba, Hun. 50/E2
Kaba, Indo. 129/E1
Kaba (riv.), China 99/E2
Kabadak (riv.), Bang. 97/G4
Kabaena (isl.), Indo. 91/F5
Kabah (ruin), Mex. 176/D1
Kabala, SLeo. 114/C4
Kabale, Ugan. 121/G3
Kabalega (falls), Ugan. 121/G2
Kabalega NP, Ugan. 121/G2
Kabalo, D.R. Congo 121/F4
Kabamba (lake), D.R. Congo 121/F5
Kabambare, D.R. Congo 121/F4
Kabango, D.R. Congo 121/F4
Kabanjahe, Indo. 89/B2
Kabankalan, Phil. 88/C3
Kabardinka, Rus. 73/J5
Kabardino-Balkariya, Resp., Rus. 75/Q6
Kabare, D.R. Congo 121/G3
Kābāw, Libya 108/A2
Kabba, Nga. 115/G5
Kabeke, D.R. Congo 121/G4
Kabelekese, D.R. Congo 121/E4
Kaberamaido, Ugan. 119/A1
Kabeta, D.R. Congo 121/F3
Kabetawa, Niger 116/B2
Kabetogama (lake), Mn, US 157/H3
Kabeya Maji, D.R. Congo 121/F4
Kabī, Eth. 118/A3
Kabin Buri, Thai. 94/C3
Kabinda, D.R. Congo 121/F4
Kabīr Kūh (mts.), Iran 103/F3
Kabīr, Oued el (riv.), Alg. 112/H4
Kabīrwāla, Pak. 98/A4
Kabkābīyah, Sudan 116/E2
Kableshkovo, Bul. 51/H4
Kabo, CAfr. 116/C4
Kabobo, D.R. Congo 121/G4
Kābol (Kābul) (cap.), Afg. 101/J2
Kabolaa, Indo. 91/H4
Kabompo, Zam. 122/E2
Kabompo (riv.), Zam. 122/D2
Kabong, Malay. 90/D3
Kabongo, D.R. Congo 121/F4
Kabrai, India 96/C3
Kābul (riv.), Afg. 101/J2
Kābul (Kābol) (cap.), Afg. 101/J2
Kabunda, D.R. Congo 123/F2
Kaburuang (isl.), Indo. 91/G3
Kabūshīyah, Sudan 117/G1
Kabwe, Zam. 123/F2
Kačanik, Yugo. 49/G1
Kačergine, Lith. 41/K4
Kachalola, Zam. 123/F2
Kachemak, Ak, US 171/H4
Kachemak (bay), Ak, US 171/H4
Kachia, Nga. 115/G4
Kachikau, Bots. 122/E3
Kachin (state), Myan. 93/G2
Kachiry, Kaz. 99/C1
Kachug, Rus. 78/F1
Kaçkar Daği (peak), Turk. 71/G4
Kada, Myan. 94/B2
Kadam (peak), Ugan. 119/A1
Kadam (isl.), Myan. 93/G5
Kadăn, Czh. 59/G2
Kadan (isl.), Myan. 94/B3
Kadavu (isl.), Fiji 136/G6
Kadaya, Rus. 79/H1
Kadéï (riv.), CAfr. 116/B4
Kadesa, Indo. 91/F5
Kadiana, Mali 114/D4
Kadiköy (nbrhd.), Turk. 103/N7
Kadina, Austl. 131/H5
Kadınhanı, Turk. 102/C2
Kadiogo (prov.), Burk. 115/E3
Kadiolo, Mali 114/D4
Kadirli, Turk. 102/D2
Kadışehri, Turk. 102/C1
Kadoka, SD, US 154/D2
Kadoma, Zim. 123/F3
Kadoma, Japan 83/J6
Kadônkani, Myan. 93/G4
Kadoshkino, Rus. 71/H1
Kadrina, Est. 41/M2
Kaduna (state), Nga. 115/G4
Kaduna, Nga. 115/G4
Kaduna (riv.), Nga. 107/C4
Kāduqli, Sudan 117/F3
Kadzharan, Arm. 71/H5
Kadzherom, Rus. 69/M2
Kaech'ŏn, NKor. 81/C3
Kaédi, Mrta. 114/B2
Kaehwa-ri, NKor. 81/D2
Kaélé, Camr. 116/B3
Kaeng Khro, Thai. 94/C2
Kaeng Krachan NP, Thai. 94/B3
Kaep'ung, NKor. 81/D4
Kaesŏng, NKor. 81/D3
Kaesŏng-si (prov.), NKor. 81/D4
Kafakumba, D.R. Congo 121/E5
Kafanchan, Nga. 115/H4
Kafar Jar Ghar (mts.), Afg. 101/J2
Kaffraria (reg.), SAfr. 124/D4
Kaffrine, Sen. 114/B3
Kafia Kingi, Sudan 116/E3
Kafirévs (cape), Gre. 49/J3
Kafr ad Dawwār, Egypt 113/B2
Kafr al 'ā'id, Egypt 113/C4
Kafr al Baţţīkh, Egypt 113/C2
Kafr al Jarā'idah, Egypt 113/C2
Kafr al Kurdī, Egypt 113/C2
Kafr Ash Shaykh (gov.), Egypt 109/F1
Kafr ash Shaykh, Egypt 113/B2
Kafr az Zayyāt, Egypt 113/B3
Kafr Kannā, Isr. 105/C3
Kafr Mandā, Isr. 105/C3
Kafr Qari', Isr. 105/C3
Kafr Qāsim, Isr. 105/B4
Kafr Rabī', Egypt 113/B3
Kafr Sa'd, Egypt 113/C2
Kafr Salīm, Egypt 113/B2
Kafr Şaqr, Egypt 113/C3
Kafr Shukr, Egypt 113/C3
Kafr Yāsīf, Isr. 105/C3
Kafu (riv.), Ugan. 121/G2
Kafubu (riv.), D.R. Congo 123/E1
Kafue (dam), Zam. 123/F2
Kafue, Zam. 123/F2
Kafue (riv.), Zam. 122/E2
Kafue Flats (swamp), Zam. 123/E2
Kafue Gorge (res.), Zam. 123/E2
Kafue NP, Zam. 122/E2
Kafukule, Malw. 123/G1
Kafulwe, Zam. 121/G5
Kaga, Japan 84/E2
Kaga Bandoro, CAfr. 116/C4
Kagan, Uzb. 74/G6
Kāgān (valley), Pak. 98/B2
Kagang, China 78/E4
Kagawa (pref.), Japan 84/D3
Kagera (riv.), Tanz. 121/G3
Kågeröd, Swe. 39/K7
Kağıthane, Turk. 103/M6
Kâğithane (riv.), Turk. 103/M6
Kağızman, Turk. 103/E1
Kagmar, Sudan 117/F2
Kagoshima (int'l arpt.), Japan 84/B5
Kagoshima (bay), Japan 84/B5
Kagoshima, Japan 84/B5
Kagoshima (dept.), Japan 85/L5
Kagua, PNG 129/F1
K'aha, Eth. 118/B3
Kahama, Tanz. 121/H3
Kaharlyk, Ukr. 72/F3
Kahayan (riv.), Indo. 90/D4
Kahe, Tanz. 119/B2
Kahemba, D.R. Congo 120/D4
Kahindi, Tanz. 119/B4
Kahl am Main, Ger. 58/C2
Kahmsara (riv.), Rus. 78/D1
Kāhna, Pak. 98/C4
Kahnple, Libr. 114/C5
Kahnūj, Iran 101/G3
Kahnwia, Libr. 114/C5
Kahoka, Mo, US 155/J3
Kahoolawe (isl.), Hi, US 142/T10
Kahperusvaara (peak), Fin. 38/G1
Kahramanmaraş, Turk. 102/D2
Kahramanmaraş (prov.), Turk. 102/D2
Kahror Pakka, Pak. 98/A5
Kâhta, Turk. 102/D2
Kahuku (pt.), Hi, US 142/T10
Kahului, Hi, US 142/T10
Kahuzi-Biega, PN de, D.R. Congo 121/F3
Kai (isls.), Indo. 91/H5
Kai Besar (isl.), Indo. 91/H5
Kai Kecil (isl.), Indo. 91/H5
Kai Mbaku, D.R. Congo 120/C4
Kaiama, Nga. 115/F4
Kaiapit, PNG 129/G1
Kaiapoi, NZ 135/C3
Kaibab (plat.), Az, US 149/F2
Kaibab Ind. Res., Az, US 149/F2
Kaibara, Japan 83/H5
Kaibito, Az, US 149/G2
Kaibito (plat.), Az, US 149/G2
Kaidu (riv.), China 99/D3
Kaieteur (falls), Guy. 181/G3
Kaieteur NP, Guy. 181/G3
Kaifeng, China 80/C4
Kāigaon, Nepal 96/D1
Kaijiang, China 87/E2
Kaikalūr, India 95/D2
Kaikoura, NZ 135/C3
Kailahun, SLeo. 114/C4
Kaili, China 87/E3
Kailu, China 80/E2

Kailua – Kavīr-e
Map Section 238 239

Kailua, Hi, US 142/T11
Kaimar, China 78/D5
Kaimganj, India 96/B2
Kaimur (range), India 96/C3
Käina, Est. 41/K2
Kainab (riv.), Namb. 124/B2
Kainach (riv.), Aus. 50/B2
Kainan, Japan 84/D3
Kainantu, PNG 129/G1
Kaindu, Zam. 123/E2
Kainji (dam), Nga. 115/G4
Kainji (lake), Nga. 107/C3
Kainji Lake NP, Nga. 115/F4
Kainoúryion, Gre. 49/G3
Kaintiba, PNG 129/G1
Kaipara (riv.), NZ 135/F6
Kaiparowits (plat.), Ut, US 149/G2
Kaiping, China 80/J7
Kairāna, India 98/D5
Kairi, Austl. 134/B2
Kairu, India 98/C5
Kairuku, PNG 129/G2
Kaisei, Japan 83/C3
Kaiseregg (peak), Swi. 60/D4
Kaisersesch, Ger. 55/G3
Kaiserslautern, Ger. 55/G5
Kaisheim, Ger. 58/D5
Kaišiadorys, Lith. 41/L4
Kait (cape), Indo. 89/D3
Kaitaia, NZ 135/C1
Kaitangata, NZ 135/B4
Kaithal, India 98/D5
Kaiti, Tanz. 119/A2
Kaiwi (chan.), Hi, US 142/T10
Kaiyang, China 93/J2
Kaiyuan, China 80/F2
Kaiyuan, China 86/D4
Kaizu, Japan 83/L5
Kaizuka, Japan 83/H7
Kajaani, Fin. 74/C3
Kajabbi, Austl. 129/F5
Kajang (peak), Malay. 89/D2
Kajang, Malay. 89/C2
Kajang, Indo. 91/F5
Kaji-san (peak), SKor. 84/A3
Kajiado, Kenya 119/B2
Kajikazawa, Japan 83/A2
Kajo-Kaji, Sudan 121/G2
Kajuru, Nga. 115/G4
Kākā, Sudan 117/G3
Kakabeka Falls, On, Can. 157/K3
Kakada (well), Chad 116/B1
Kakadu NP, Austl. 128/D3
Kakagi (lake), On, Can. 157/H3
Kakamas, SAfr. 124/C3
Kakamega, Kenya 119/A1
Kakamigahara, Japan 83/L5
Kakanj, Bosn. 50/D3
Kakata, Libr. 114/C5
Kākdwīp, India 97/G5
Kake, Ak, US 171/M4
Kaketsa (mt.), BC, Can. 171/M4
Kākhk, Iran 101/G2
Kakhovka, Ukr. 72/G4
Kakhovs'ke Vodoskhovyshche (res.), Ukr. 70/E3
Kakielo, D.R. Congo 123/F2
Kākināda, India 95/D2
Kakiri, Ugan. 121/H2
Kakkirigumma, India 95/D2
Kako (riv.), Japan 83/G6
Kakogawa, Japan 83/G6
Kakonga, Zam. 122/D2
Kakonko, Tanz. 121/G3
Kākori, India 96/C2
Kakrāla, India 96/B2
Kakrima (riv.), Gui. 114/B4
Kaktovik, Ak, US 171/K1
Kaku, India 92/B2
Kakuda, Japan 85/G2
Kakuma, Kenya 117/G5
Kakumbi, Zam. 123/F2
Kakuna, D.R. Congo 121/E4
Kakunodate, Japan 82/B4
Kakuri, Nga. 115/G4
Kakuto, Ugan. 121/G3
Kakya, Kenya 119/B2
Kāl-e Shūr (riv.), Iran 103/J2
Kalā Chāy, Iran 103/G2
Kala-i-Mor, Trkm. 101/H1
Kalaa Kebira, Tun. 48/B5
Kalaallit Nunaat (Greenland) (dpcy.), Den. 139/N2
Kālābāgh, Pak. 98/A3
Kalabahi, Indo. 128/B2
Kalabakan, Malay. 88/B4
Kalabo, Zam. 122/D2
Kalabyin, Myan. 86/B5
Kalach, Rus. 73/L2
Kalach-na-Donu, Rus. 71/G2
Kalachinsk, Rus. 74/H4
Kaladan (riv.), Myan. 93/F3
Kaladar, On, Can. 161/H2
Kālāgarh, India 96/B1
Kalahari (des.), Namb. 107/D7
Kalahari-Gemsbok NP, SAfr. 124/C2
Kalaiya, Nepal 97/E2
Kalakan, Rus. 75/M4
Kalalé, Ben. 115/F4
Kalāleh, Iran 103/H2
Kalaloch, Wa, US 144/B4
Kalām, Pak. 98/B2
Kalama, Wa, US 144/C4
Kalamákion, Gre. 49/N8
Kalamaloué, PN de, Camr. 116/B2
Kalamare, Bots. 123/E4
Kalamariá, Gre. 49/H2
Kalamáta, Gre. 49/H4
Kalamazoo (riv.), Mi, US 160/D3
Kalamazoo, Mi, US 160/D3
Kalamitsk (bay), Ukr. 73/G5
Kalampáka, Gre. 49/G3
Kalanchak, Ukr. 73/G4
Kalandy, Madg. 125/J6
Kalangali, Tanz. 119/A3
Kalanguy, Rus. 78/H1
Kālānwāli, India 98/C5
Kalaotoa (isl.), Indo. 128/A1
Kalasin, Thai. 94/C2
Kalāswāla, Pak. 98/C3
Kalāt, Pak. 101/J3
Kalaupapa, Hi, US 142/T10
Kalávrita, Gre. 49/H3
Kalaw, Myan. 86/C4
Kalbā, UAE 101/G3
Kälbäcär, Azer. 103/F1
Kalbach, Ger. 58/B2
Kalbar, Austl. 134/D4
Kalbarri, Austl. 130/B3
Kalbarri NP, Austl. 130/B3
Kaldakvísl (riv.), Ice. 38/N7
Kale, Turk. 104/A1
Kale, Turk. 102/D1
Kalecik, Turk. 102/C1
Kaleden, BC, Can. 144/E3
Kaledupa (isl.), Indo. 128/A1
Kalefeld, Ger. 53/H5
Kalehe, D.R. Congo 121/G3
Kalema, D.R. Congo 121/F4
Kalemie (int'l arpt.), D.R. Congo 121/G4
Kalemie, D.R. Congo 121/G4
Kalemyo, Myan. 86/B4
Kalenda, D.R. Congo 121/E5
Kalety, Pol. 43/K3
Kaleva, Mi, US 160/C2
Kalevala, Rus. 68/F2
Kalewa, Myan. 86/B4
Kaleya, Zam. 123/E2
Kalgoorlie-Boulder, Austl. 130/D4
Kāli (riv.), India 96/B1
Kali (riv.), India 96/B2
Kāli (riv.), Nepal 96/D2
Kālia, Bang. 97/H4
Kāliākair, Bang. 97/H3
Kalianda, Indo. 89/D4
Kalibo, Phil. 88/C3
Kalida, Oh, US 160/D4
Kālīganj, Bang. 97/G4
Kālikot, Nepal 96/C1
Kalima, D.R. Congo 121/F3
Kalimala, India 95/D2
Kalimantan (reg.), Indo. 90/D4
Kálimnos, Gre. 67/K3
Kālimpong, India 97/G2
Kaliningrad, Rus. 69/W9
Kaliningrad, Rus. 41/J4
Kaliningradskaya Oblast, Rus. 68/D5
Kalinino, Rus. 73/K5
Kalininsk, Rus. 71/H2
Kalinkavichy, Bela. 72/E1
Kalinko, Gui. 114/C4
Kalinovka, Rus. 73/H2
Kaliro, Ugan. 119/A1
Kalis, Som. 118/D3
Kalisizo, Ugan. 121/G3
Kalispel Ind. Res., Wa, US 144/F3
Kalispell, Mt, US 144/G3
Kalisz, Pol. 43/K3
Kaliua, Tanz. 121/G4
Kalix, Swe. 68/D2
Kalixälven (riv.), Swe. 38/G2
Kāliyāganj, India 97/G3
Kālka, India 98/D4
Kalkaringi, Austl. 128/C4
Kalkaska, Mi, US 160/D2
Kalkbruk, Fin. 39/F4
Kalkfeld, Namb. 122/C4
Kalkfontein, Bots. 122/D4
Kalkhügel, Namb. 122/C5
Kālkini, Bang. 97/H4
Kalkrand, Namb. 122/C5
Kallar Kahār, Pak. 98/B3
Kallaste, Est. 41/M2
Kallham, Aus. 59/G6
Kallinge, Swe. 40/F3
Kallinge (int'l arpt.), Swe. 40/F3
Kalliola, Fin. 39/F4
Kallithéa, Gre. 49/N9
Kallsjön (lake), Swe. 38/E3
Kalmalo, Nga. 115/G3
Kalmar (co.), Swe. 38/F4
Kalmar (int'l arpt.), Swe. 40/G3
Kalmar, Swe. 40/G3
Kalmar, Swe. 39/A1
Kalmarsund (sound), Swe. 40/G3
Kalmthout, Belg. 52/B6
Kalmykia, Resp., Rus. 74/E5
Kalmykovo, Kaz. 71/J2
Kālna, India 97/G4
Kalnai, India 96/D4
Kalnciems, Lat. 41/K3
Kalni (riv.), Bang. 97/H3
Kalnibolotskaya, Rus. 73/L4
Kalocsa, Hun. 50/D2
Kalofer, Bul. 49/J1
Kalokhórion, Gre. 49/H2
Kaloko, D.R. Congo 121/F4
Kālol, India 101/K4
Kalole, D.R. Congo 121/F3
Kalombo, Zam. 122/D2
Kalomo, Zam. 123/E3
Kalona, Ia, US 155/J3
Kalongan, Indo. 88/D4
Kalongo, Ugan. 119/A1
Kalogi, Sudan 117/F3
Kālpi, India 96/B2
Kalpin, China 99/C3
Kalpitiya, SrL. 95/C4
Kalsdorf bei Graz, Aus. 50/B2
Kaltag, Ak, US 171/G3
Kaltasy, Rus. 69/M5
Kaltbrunn, Swi. 61/F3
Kaltenleutgeben, Aus. 51/N7
Kaltennordheim, Ger. 58/D1
Kaltern (Caldaro), It. 45/J3
Kalu (riv.), SrL. 92/D6
Kaluga, Rus. 68/H5
Kaluku, Indo. 91/E4
Kalulushi, Zam. 123/F2
Kalumburu Abor. Rsv., Austl. 128/B3
Kalumburu Mission, Austl. 128/B3
Kalumpang, Malay. 89/C2
Kalundborg, Den. 40/D4
Kalundborg (inlet), Den. 39/G7
Kalungu, Ugan. 121/G3
Kalungwishi (riv.), Zam. 121/G5
Kalūr Kot, Pak. 98/A3
Kalush, Ukr. 72/C3
Kaluzhkaya Oblast, Rus. 68/G5
Kalvarija, Lith. 41/K4
Kalwelwe, Zam. 123/F2
Kalyān, India 92/B4
Kalyazin, Rus. 68/H4
Kalynivka, Ukr. 72/E3
Kama (res.), Rus. 69/M4
Kama, D.R. Congo 121/F3
Kama, Myan. 86/B5
Kama (riv.), Rus. 29/K3
Kamachumu, Tanz. 121/G3
Kamagaya, Japan 83/E2
Kamaishi, Japan 82/B4
Kamajai, Lith. 41/L4
Kamakura, Japan 83/D3
Kamakusa, Guy. 182/A1
Kamakwie, SLeo. 114/B4
Kamalampaka, Tanz. 121/G4
Kamālia, Pak. 98/B4
Kaman, Turk. 102/C2
Kāman, India 96/A2
Kamande, D.R. Congo 121/G3
Kamango (lake), Mali 114/E2
Kamango, D.R. Congo 121/G2
Kamanjab, Namb. 122/B3
Kamanyola, D.R. Congo 121/G3
Kamaran (isl.), Yem. 118/B2
Kamarang, Guy. 181/F3
Kāmāreddi, India 95/C2
Kāmārhāti, India 92/E3
Kamaria (falls), Guy. 181/G3
Kamas, Ut, US 147/H3
Kamāsin, India 96/C3
Kamativi, Zim. 123/E3
Kamba, Nga. 115/G3
Kamba-Poko, D.R. Congo 120/D4
Kambalda, Austl. 130/D4
Kambam, India 95/C4
Kambar, Pak. 92/A2
Kambara, Japan 83/B3
Kambaswana, D.R. Congo 121/E4
Kambia, SLeo. 114/B4
Kambja, Est. 41/M2
Kambove, D.R. Congo 121/F5
Kambuno (peak), Indo. 91/F4
Kamchatka (pen.), Rus. 77/Q4
Kamchatskaya Oblast, Rus. 75/R4
Kamchiya (riv.), Bul. 70/C4
Kamela, Or, US 146/D1
Kamen, Ger. 53/E5
Kamen'-na-Obi, Rus. 99/D1
Kamena, D.R. Congo 121/F4
Kamende, D.R. Congo 121/F4
Kamenets, Bela. 43/M2
Kameničná, Slvk. 50/D2
Kamenjak, Rt (cape), Cro. 45/K4
Kamenka, Kaz. 71/J2
Kamenka, Rus. 71/H1
Kamenka, Rus. 69/K2
Kamenka, Rus. 73/K2
Kamenka, Rus. 79/M3
Kamennogorsk, Rus. 41/N1
Kamennomostskaya, Rus. 73/L5
Kameno, Bul. 51/H4
Kamenolomni, Rus. 73/L4
Kamensk-Shakhtinskiy, Rus. 73/L3
Kamensk-Ural'skiy, Rus. 69/P4
Kamenskoye, Rus. 75/S3
Kameoka, Japan 83/J5
Kameri, Indo. 91/H4
Kames, Sc, UK 33/A5
Kameyama, Japan 83/K6
Kami, Japan 83/G5
Kami (isl.), Japan 83/M6
Kami-koshiki (isl.), Japan 84/A5
Kamiah, Id, US 144/F4
Kamień Pomorski, Pol. 40/F5
Kamieskroon, SAfr. 124/B3
Kamifukuoka, Japan 83/D2
Kamiisco, Japan 82/B3
Kamiishizu, Japan 83/K5
Kamiizumi, Japan 83/C1
Kamiji, D.R. Congo 121/E4
Kamikawa, Japan 82/C2
Kamikuishiki, Japan 83/B2
Kamin'-Kashyrs'kyy, Ukr. 72/C2
Kamina, D.R. Congo 121/F5
Kaminaka, Japan 83/J5
Kaminoho, Japan 83/M4
Kaminoyama, Japan 85/G1
Kamisato, Japan 83/C1
Kamishak (bay), Ak, US 171/H4
Kamiyahagi, Japan 83/M5
Kamiyaku, Japan 85/L5
Kamla (riv.), India 97/F3
Kamloops, BC, Can. 144/D2
Kamlot, Camb. 94/C4
Kammaki, Japan 83/J6
Kamnik, Slov. 45/L3
Kamo, Arm. 103/F1
Kamo, Japan 85/F2
Kamo (riv.), Japan 83/E3
Kamo, Japan 83/J6
Kamogawa, Japan 85/G3
Kamojima, Japan 84/D3
Kāmoke, Pak. 98/C4
Kamonia, D.R. Congo 121/E4
Kamp (riv.), Aus. 43/H4
Kamp-Bornhofen, Ger. 55/G3
Kamp-Lintfort, Ger. 52/D5
Kampala (cap.), Ugan. 121/H2
Kampalili (mt.), Phil. 88/D4
Kampar, Malay. 89/C1
Kampar (riv.), Indo. 90/B3
Kampar (river), Indo. 89/C2
Kampen, Ger. 40/C4
Kampen, Neth. 52/C3
Kampene, D.R. Congo 121/F3
Kamphaeng Phet, Thai. 94/C5
Kamphaeng Phet (ruin), Thai. 94/B2
Kamp'o, SKor. 81/E5
Kampong Cham, Camb. 94/D4
Kampong Chhnang, Camb. 94/D3
Kampong Kadok, Malay. 94/C5
Kampong Khleang, Camb. 94/D3
Kampong Kuala Besut, Malay. 89/C1
Kampong Raja, Malay. 89/C1
Kampong Saom (bay), Camb. 90/B1
Kampóng Saom, Camb. 94/C4
Kampong Sedenak, Malay. 89/C2
Kampong Sedili Kechil, Malay. 89/D2
Kampong Spoe, Camb. 94/D4
Kampong Tampasis, Malay. 91/E2
Kampong Telupid, Malay. 88/B4
Kampong Thum, Camb. 94/D3
Kampong Trabek, Camb. 94/D4
Kampot, Camb. 94/D4
Kampti, Burk. 114/E4
Kamrau (bay), Indo. 91/H4
Kamsack, Sk, Can. 156/D2
Kamsar, Gui. 114/B4
Kamsdorf, Ger. 59/E1
Kamskoye Ust'ye, Rus. 69/L5
Kamsuuma, Som. 119/C1
Kamtsha (riv.), D.R. Congo 120/D4
Kamui-misaki (cape), Japan 82/B2
Kámuk (mtn.), CR 177/F4
Kamuli, Ugan. 119/A1
Kamuzu (Lilongwe) (int'l arpt.), Malw. 123/G2
Kamwandu, D.R. Congo 121/E4
Kam'yanets'-Podil's'kyy, Ukr. 72/D3
Kam'yanka, Ukr. 73/G3
Kam'yanka-Buz'ka, Ukr. 72/C2
Kam'yanka-Dniprovs'ka, Ukr. 73/H4
Kāmyārān, Iran 103/F3
Kamyshevatskaya, Rus. 73/J4
Kamyshin, Rus. 71/H2
Kamyshla, Rus. 69/M5
Kamyshlov, Rus. 69/P4
Kamyzyak, Rus. 71/J3
Kanaaupscow (riv.), Qu, Can. 141/J3
Kanab, Ut, US 149/F2
Kanab (plat.), Az, US 149/F2
Kanab (cr.), Az, US 149/F2
Kanaga (mt.), Ak, US 171/C6
Kanairiktok (riv.), Nf, Can. 141/K3
Kanākir, Syria 105/E2
Kanan, Japan 83/J7
Kananga, D.R. Congo 121/E4
Kanaoudi, India 96/C4
Kanarraville, Ut, US 149/F2
Kanash, Rus. 69/K5
Kanasin, Mex. 176/D1
Kanata, On, Can. 161/J2
Kanawake Ind. Res., Qu, Can. 159/N7
Kanawha, Ia, US 155/H2
Kanawha (riv.), WV, US 163/F1
Kanazawa, Japan 85/E2
Kanazi, Tanz. 121/G3
Kanchanaburi, Thai. 94/B3
Kanchanadit, Thai. 94/B4
Kānchenjunga (peak), Nepal 92/E2
Kānchīpuram, India 95/C3
Kandahār, Afg. 101/J2
Kanda-Kanda, D.R. Congo 121/E4
Kandalaksha, Rus. 68/G2
Kandalaksha (gulf), Rus. 38/K2
Kandale, D.R. Congo 120/D4
Kandang, Indo. 89/B2
Kandanghaur, Indo. 89/D4
Kándanos, Gre. 49/H5
Kandava, Lat. 41/K3
Kandavu Passage, Fiji 137/Y18
Kandé, Togo 115/F4
Kandel (peak), Ger. 60/E1
Kandel, Ger. 58/B4
Kandep, PNG 129/F1
Kander (riv.), Swi. 60/D4
Kandern, Ger. 60/D2
Kandersteg, Swi. 60/D5
Kandhkot, Pak. 101/J3
Kāndhla, India 98/D5
Kandi, Ben. 115/F4
Kāndi, India 97/G4
Kandi, D.R. Congo 121/G2
Kandi (cape), Indo. 91/F3
Kandıra, Turk. 51/K5
Kandos, Austl. 133/D1
Kandrāch, Pak. 101/J3
Kandreho, Madg. 125/H7
Kandry, Rus. 69/M5
Kandukūr, India 95/C3
Kandy, SrL. 95/D5
Kane, Pa, US 161/G4
Kane (co.), Il, US 167/P16
Kane, Il, US 155/J4
Kane (basin), Grld. 141/T7
Kanem (reg.), Chad 116/B2
Kanem (pref.), Chad 116/B2
Kaneohe, Hi, US 142/W11
Kaneville, Il, US 167/N16
Kanëvka, Rus. 68/H2
Kanevskaya, Rus. 73/K4
Kaneyama, Japan 82/B4
Kang, Bots. 122/D4
Kanga (riv.), Bang. 97/G5
Kanga, D.R. Congo 121/G2
Kanga, Tanz. 119/B3
Kangaba, Mali 114/C4
Kangal, Turk. 102/D2
Kangān, Iran 103/H5
Kangān, Iran 101/G3
Kangan Abor. Land, Austl. 130/C2
Kanganpur, Pak. 98/C4
Kangar, Malay. 94/C5
Kangaré, Mali 114/C4
Kangaroo (isl.), Austl. 127/C4
Kangaruma, Guy. 181/G3
Kangasala, Fin. 41/L1
Kangāvar, Iran 103/F3
Kangbao, China 78/G3
Kangding, China 86/D2
Kangdong (nbrhd.), SKor. 81/G6
Kangean (isl.), Indo. 89/F4
Kangean (isls.), Indo. 89/F4
Kangen (riv.), Sudan 117/G4
Kangendala, PN da, Ang. 120/D5
Kanggye, NKor. 81/D2
Kanggyŏng, SKor. 81/D4
Kanghwa, SKor. 81/F6
Kangi, Sudan 117/E3
Kangiqcliniq (Rankin Inlet), Nun, Can. 140/G2
Kangiqsualujjuaq, Qu, Can. 141/K3
Kangiqsujuaq, Qu, Can. 141/J2
Kangirsuk, Qu, Can. 141/J2
Kangjin, SKor. 81/D5
Kangkar Dohol, Malay. 89/C2
Kangmar, China 97/G1
Kangnam (mts.), NKor. 81/C2
Kangnam, NKor. 81/C3
Kangnam (nbrhd.), SKor. 81/G6
Kangnŭng, SKor. 84/A2
Kangnyŏng, NKor. 81/C4
Kango, Gabon 120/B2
Kangondi, Kenya 119/B2
Kangping, China 80/E2
Kāngra, India 98/D3
Kangrinboqê (peak), China 99/D5
Kangsŏ, NKor. 81/C3
Kangsŏ (nbrhd.), SKor. 81/F6
Kangto (peak), China 86/B3
Kangu, D.R. Congo 120/C4
Kangwŏn-do (prov.), NKor. 81/D3
Kangwŏn-do (prov.), SKor. 84/A2
Kangxiwar, China 99/C4
Kanha NP, India 96/C4
Kanhān (riv.), India 92/C3
Kanholmsfjärden (sound), Swe. 39/B1
Kani, C.d'Iv. 114/D4
Kani, Myan. 86/B4
Kani, Japan 83/M5
Kaniama, D.R. Congo 121/F4
Kanie, Japan 83/L5
Kanin (pen.), Rus. 192/C
Kanin Nos, Rus. 68/J1
Kanin Nos (pt.), Rus. 74/E3
Kaningo, Kenya 119/B2
Kaniv, Ukr. 72/F3
Kaniva, Austl. 132/B3
Kanivs'ke Vodoskhovyshche (res.), Ukr. 72/F2
Kanjiža, Yugo. 50/E2
Kankakee, Il, US 160/C4
Kankakee (riv.), Il, US 160/C4
Kankan (pol. reg.), Gui. 114/C4
Kankan, Gui. 114/C4
Kānker, India 95/D1
Kankesanturai, SrL. 95/D4
Kankossa, Mrta. 114/C3
Kanmen, China 87/J2
Kanmuri-yama (peak), Japan 84/C3
Kannami, Japan 83/B3
Kannapolis, NC, US 163/G3
Kannauj, India 96/B2
Kannon-zaki (pt.), Japan 83/D3
Kannus, Fin. 68/D3
Kano (state), Nga. 115/H4
Kano, Nga. 115/H4
Kano Vlei, Namb. 122/C3
Kanona, Zam. 123/F2
Kanoneiland, SAfr. 124/C3
Kan'onji, Japan 84/C3
Kanopolis, Ks, US 153/E1
Kanopolis (lake), Ks, US 154/E4
Kanosh, Ut, US 149/F1
Kanouse (mtn.), NJ, US 169/H7
Kanowit, Malay. 90/D3
Kanoya, Japan 84/B5
Kānpur, India 96/C2
Kanra, Japan 83/B1
Kansai (int'l arpt.), Japan 83/H7
Kansai (isl.), Japan 83/H7
Kansarokana (riv.), Kenya 119/B2
Kansas, Il, US 160/C5
Kansas (state), US 143/G4
Kansas (riv.), US 143/G4
Kansas, Al, US 162/D4
Kansas City, Ks, US 155/G4
Kansas City (int'l arpt.), Mo, US 155/G4
Kansas City, Mo, US 155/G4
Kansas Cosmosphere and Space Center, Ks, US 153/F1
Kansasville, Wi, US 167/P14
Kansenia, D.R. Congo 121/F5
Kansk, Rus. 74/K4
Kansŏng, SKor. 81/E3
Kantābānji, India 95/D1
Kantchari, Burk. 115/F3
Kantemirovka, Rus. 73/K3
Kānth, India 96/B1
Kantharalak, Thai. 94/D3
Kantō (prov.), Japan 85/F2
Kantunilkin, Mex. 176/E1
Kanturk, Ire. 32/B5
Kantvik, Fin. 39/E4
Kanuku (mts.), Guy. 181/G4
Kanuma, Japan 85/F2
Kanyanga, Gha. 115/E4
Kanye, Bots. 122/E5
Kanyilombi, Zam. 122/E2
Kanyutkwin, Myan. 94/B2
Kanzenze, D.R. Congo 121/F5
Kanzi, China 81/B3
Kaoh Nhek, Camb. 94/D3
Kaohsiung (int'l arpt.), Tai. 87/J4
Kaohsiung, Tai. 87/J4
Kaolack (pol. reg.), Sen. 114/B3
Kaolack, Sen. 114/A3
Kaolinovo, Bul. 51/H4
Kaoma, Zam. 122/E2
Kaongweshi (riv.), D.R. Congo 121/E5
Kaortchi (well), Chad 108/C5
Kaouadja, CAfr. 116/D4
Kaouar (reg.), Niger 108/B5
Kapa, Myan. 94/B3
Kapakapanui (mt.), NZ 135/J8
Kapalala, Zam. 123/F2
Kapalong, Phil. 88/D4
Kapambwe, D.R. Congo 121/E4
Kapan, Arm. 103/F2
Kapanga, D.R. Congo 121/E5
Kapaonik (mts.), Yugo. 49/G1
Kapchorwa, Ugan. 119/A1
Kapedo, Kenya 119/B1
Kapellen, Belg. 52/B6
Kapellshamn (isl.), Swe. 39/J6
Kapellskär, Swe. 39/C1
Kapenguria, Kenya 119/A1
Kapengwe, Zam. 123/F2
Kapfenberg, Aus. 45/L3
Kapidaği (pen.), Turk. 51/H5
Kapingamarangi (isl.), Micr. 136/E4
Kapiri Mposhi, Zam. 123/F2
Kapiskau (riv.), On, Can. 141/H3
Kaplan, La, US 164/B3
Kaplice, Czh. 59/H5
Kapoe, Thai. 94/B4
Kapoeta, Sudan 117/G4
Kapona, D.R. Congo 121/G4
Kaporo, Malw. 119/A4
Kapos (riv.), Hun. 50/C2
Kaposvár, Hun. 50/C2
Kapowsin, Wa, US 144/C4
Kapp, Nor. 40/D1
Kappeln, Ger. 40/C4
Kappl, Aus. 61/G3
Kapsabet, Kenya 119/A1
Kapsan, NKor. 81/E2
Kapuas (riv.), Indo. 90/C4
Kapuas Hulu (mts.), Indo.,Malay. 90/D3
Kapunda, Austl. 131/H5
Kapūrthala, India 98/C4
Kapuskasing, On, Can. 141/H4
Kaputa, Zam. 121/G5
Kapuvár, Hun. 50/C2
Kapydzhik (peak), Azer. 103/F2
Kap'yŏng, SKor. 81/D4
Kara (riv.), Rus. 69/Q1
Kara, Rus. 69/Q1
Kara, Togo 115/F4
Kara (sea), Rus. 192/A
Kara K'orē, Eth. 118/A3
Kara-Balta, Kyr. 99/B3
Kara-Kala, Trkm. 103/J2
Kara-Köl, Kyr. 99/B3
Kara-Saki (pt.), Japan 84/A3
Karaali, Turk. 102/C2
Karaart, Taj. 99/B4
Karabau, Kaz. 71/K2
Karabiğa, Turk. 51/H5
Karabra (riv.), Indo. 91/H4
Karabudakhkent, Rus. 71/H4
Karabük, Turk. 70/E4
Karabula, Rus. 74/K4
Karabulak, Rus. 71/H4
Karaburun, Turk. 51/J5
Karaca (peak), Turk. 102/D2
Karacadağ, Turk. 51/H5
Karacaköy, Turk. 51/J5
Karaçal (peak), Turk. 104/C1
Karacaoğlan, Turk. 51/H5
Karachala, Azer. 71/J5
Karachayevo-Cherkesiya, Resp., Rus. 75/Q6
Karachev, Rus. 70/E1
Karachi (int'l arpt.), Pak. 101/J4
Karāchi, Pak. 101/J4
Karād, India 95/B2
Karadere, Turk. 51/K5
Karagayly, Kaz. 99/C2
Karaginskiy (isl.), Rus. 77/R4
Karagoš (peak), Rus. 99/E1
Karaidel'skiy, Rus. 69/N5
Kāraikkudi, India 95/C4
Karaj, Iran 103/G3
Karak, Malay. 89/C2
Karakax (riv.), China 99/C4
Karakelong (isl.), Indo. 91/G3
Karakhoto (ruin), China 78/E3
Karakol, Kyr. 99/C3
Karakoram (pass), India 98/D2
Karakoram (range), India 99/C4
Karakoro (riv.), Mali 114/C3
Karakorum (pass), China 101/L1
Karakorum (ruin), Mong. 78/E2
Karaköse, Turk. 103/E2
Karaköy, Turk. 102/E2
Karakul', Uzb. 74/G6
Karakul' (lake), Taj. 99/B4
Karakumy (des.), Trkm. 74/F5
Karakuwisa, Namb. 122/C3
Karakyon (peak), Trkm. 103/H1
Karakyr (peak), Trkm. 101/H1
Karam (riv.), Indo. 91/E4
Karamagay, China 78/B2
Karaman, Turk. 102/C2
Karaman (prov.), Turk. 102/C2
Karamay, China 99/D2
Karambi, Tanz. 121/G3
Karamea, NZ 135/C3
Karamea Bight (bay), NZ 127/H7
Karamet-Niyaz, Trkm. 101/H1
Karamiran, China 99/E4
Karamiran (pass), China 99/E4
Karamiran (riv.), China 99/D4
Karamürsel, Turk. 51/J5
Karamyshevo, Rus. 41/N3
Karangasem, Indo. 89/F5
Karanginskiy (isl.), Rus. 75/S4
Karanginskiy (bay), Rus. 75/S4
Karanjia, India 95/E1
Karanpur, India 98/B5
Karapelit, Bul. 51/H4
Karapınar, Turk. 102/C2
Karasabai, Guy. 181/G3
Karaşar, Turk. 70/E4
Karasburg, Namb. 124/B3
Karasjohka-Karasjok, Nor. 38/H1
Karasu, Turk. 51/K5
Karasu, Japan 83/L6
Karasuk, Rus. 99/C1
Karatá (lag.), Nic. 177/F3
Karatal (riv.), Kaz. 99/C2
Karataş, Turk. 104/D1
Karatau (mts.), Kaz. 99/A3
Karathuri, Myan. 94/B4
Karatobe, Kaz. 71/K2
Karaton, Kaz. 71/K3
Karatoya (riv.), Bang. 97/G3
Karatsu, Japan 84/A4
Karauli, India 96/A2
Karaurgan, Turk. 102/E1
Karáva (peak), Gre. 49/G3
Karavan, Kyr. 99/B3
Karawang, Indo. 89/D4
Karayaka, Turk. 70/F4
Karayazı, Turk. 102/E2
Karazhal, Kaz. 99/B2
Karbaka, Sudan 109/G5
Karbalā', Iraq 103/F3
Karbalā (gov.), Iraq 103/E3
Karben, Ger. 58/B2
Karcag, Hun. 50/E2
Kardhámila, Gre. 49/K3
Kardhítsa, Gre. 49/G3
Kardhitsomagoúla, Gre. 49/G3
Kärdla, Est. 41/K2
Kareha (riv.), India 97/E3
Karelī, India 96/B4
Karelia (reg.), Rus. 38/J2
Kareliya, Resp., Rus. 74/D3
Karema, Tanz. 121/G4
Karenga (riv.), Rus. 78/H1
Karera, India 96/B3
Karesuando, Swe. 38/G1
Karêt (reg.), Mrta. 110/D4
Kärevere, Est. 41/M2
Kargala, Rus. 71/K2
Kargasok, Rus. 74/J4
Kargı, Turk. 70/E4
Kargil, India 98/D2
Kargopol', Rus. 68/H3
Karhal, India 96/B2
Karhijärvi (lake), Fin. 41/K1
Karhula, Fin. 41/M1
Kariá, Gre. 49/G3
Karia Ba Mohammed, Mor. 112/B2
Kariaí, Gre. 49/J2
Karianga, Madg. 125/H8
Kariba, Zam.,Zim. 123/F3
Kariba (dam), Zim. 123/F3
Kariba (lake), Zim. 107/E6
Kariba-yama (peak), Japan 82/A2
Karibib, Namb. 122/B4
Karibumba, D.R. Congo 121/G2
Karikal, India 95/C4
Karimama, Ben. 115/F3
Karimata (str.), Indo. 90/C4
Karimata (isl.), Indo. 90/D4
Karīmnagar, India 95/C2
Karimui, PNG 129/G1
Karimunjawa Islands (isls.), Indo. 90/D5
Karin, Som. 118/C3
Karin, Som. 118/D3
Kariótissa, Gre. 49/H2
Karis (Karjaa), Fin. 39/D4
Karise, Den. 40/E4
Karisimbi (vol.), D.R. Congo 121/G3
Karislojo (Karjalohja), Fin. 39/D4
Káristos, Gre. 49/J3
Kariya, Japan 83/L6
Karjaa (Karis), Fin. 39/D4
Karjalohja (Karislojo), Fin. 39/D4
Karkaar (mts.), Som. 118/D3
Karkar (isl.), PNG 136/D5
Karkinits'ka Zatoka (gulf), Ukr. 70/D3
Karkkila, Fin. 41/L1
Kärkölä, Fin. 39/F4
Karkonski NP, Pol. 43/H3
Karkur, Isr. 105/B4
Karl E. Mundt NWR, SD, US 154/E2
Karla Marksa (peak), Taj. 99/B4
Karleby (Kokkola), Fin. 68/D3
Karlholmsbruk, Swe. 40/G1
Karlino, Pol. 40/F4
Karlivka, Ukr. 73/H3
Karlo-Libknekhtovsk, Ukr. 73/K3
Karlovac, Cro. 50/B3
Karlovo, Bul. 51/G4
Karlovy Vary, Czh. 59/F2
Karlovy Vary (arpt.), Czh. 59/F2
Karlovarský (pol. reg.), Czh. 42/G3
Karlsdorf-Neuthard, Ger. 58/B4
Karlsfeld, Ger. 59/E6
Karlshamn, Swe. 40/F3
Karlshuld, Ger. 58/E5
Karlskoga, Swe. 40/F2
Karlskron, Ger. 59/E5
Karlskrona, Swe. 40/F3
Karlslunde Strand, Den. 39/J7
Karlsruhe, ND, US 156/D3
Karlsruhe, Ger. 58/B4
Karlstad, Mn, US 156/F3
Karlstad, Swe. 40/E2
Karlstadt, Ger. 58/C3
Karlstein am Main, Ger. 58/C2
Karluk, Ak, US 171/H4
Karmah, Sudan 109/F5
Karmāla, India 95/B2
Karmatānr, India 97/F3
Karmi'el, Isr. 105/C3
Karnāl, India 98/D5
Karnali (zone), Nepal 96/C1
Karnali (riv.), Nepal 96/C1
Karnaphuli (res.), Bang. 97/H4
Karnataka (state), India 92/C4
Karnes City, Tx, US 151/F3
Karnobat, Bul. 51/H4
Kärnten (prov.), Aus. 45/K3
Karo, Chad 116/C3
Karoi, Zim. 123/F3
Karomatan, Phil. 88/C4
Karonga, Malw. 119/A4
Karoo NP, SAfr. 124/D4
Karoo NP, SAfr. 124/C4
Karoonda, Austl. 132/A2
Karor, Pak. 98/A4
Karora, Sudan 100/C5
Karoso (cape), Indo. 91/E5
Karpakora, Austl. 132/B2
Kárpathos, Gre. 67/K4
Kárpathos (isl.), Gre. 102/A3
Karpatskiy NP, Ukr. 72/C3
Karpenísion, Gre. 49/G3
Karpogory, Rus. 69/K3
Karratha, Austl. 130/C2
Kars (riv.), Turk. 71/G4
Kars, Turk. 103/E1
Kars (prov.), Turk. 71/G4
Kars (riv.), SAfr. 124/M11
Kars (prov.), Geo. 103/E1
Kärsämäki, Fin. 68/E3
Karsantı, Turk. 102/C2
Kārsava, Lat. 41/M3
Kårsta, Swe. 39/B1
Kartaly, Rus. 71/M1
Kartārpur, India 98/C4
Kartushi, D.R. Congo 121/F4
Kartuzy, Pol. 40/H4
Karuah, Austl. 132/D2
Karuma (falls), Ugan. 121/H2
Karumba, Austl. 134/A2
Karūn (riv.), Iran 74/E6
Karunjie, Austl. 128/B4
Karup, Den. 40/C3
Karūr, India 95/C4
Karushe, D.R. Congo 121/F3
Karval, Co, US 152/C1
Karviná, Czh. 43/K4
Karwar, India 95/B3
Karymskoye, Rus. 78/G1
Kaş, Turk. 104/A1
Kås, Den. 40/C3
Kas, Sudan 116/E2
Kasaan, Ak, US 171/M4
Kasagi, Japan 83/J6
Kasahara, Japan 83/M5
Kāsai (riv.), India 97/F4
Kasai, Japan 84/D3
Kasai (riv.), D.R. Congo 107/D5
Kasai Occidental (pol. reg.), D.R. Congo 121/E4
Kasai Oriental (pol. reg.), D.R. Congo 121/E3
Kasaji, D.R. Congo 121/E5
Kasakalawe, Zam. 121/G5
Kasalu, Zam. 123/E2
Kasama, Japan 85/G2
Kasama, Zam. 121/G5
Kasamatsu, Japan 83/L5
Kasane, Bots. 122/E3
Kasanga (falls), Zam. 122/E3
Kasanga, Tanz. 121/G5
Kasangulu, D.R. Congo 120/C4
Kasanka NP, Zam. 123/F2
Kasaoka, Japan 84/C3
Kasar (cape), Sudan 109/H5
Kasartori-yama (peak), Japan 83/K6
Kasba (lake), NW,Nun, Can. 140/F2
Kasba Tadla, Mor. 110/D2
Kaseda, Japan 84/B5
Kaseke, D.R. Congo 123/E1
Kasembe, Tanz. 119/B4
Kasempa, Zam. 122/E2
Kasenga, D.R. Congo 121/G5
Kasenyi, D.R. Congo 121/G2
Kasese, Ugan. 121/G2
Kasese, D.R. Congo 121/F3
Kaset Wisai, Thai. 94/C3
Kāsganj, India 96/B2
Kashabowie, On, Can. 157/J3
Kashaf (riv.), Iran 101/H1
Kasha-Katuwe Tent Rocks Nat'l Mon., NM, US 149/J3
Kāshān, Iran 103/G3
Kashary, Rus. 73/L3
Kashi, China 99/C4
Kashiba, Zam. 121/G5
Kashiba, Japan 83/J6
Kashihara, Japan 83/J6
Kashima, Japan 85/G3
Kashima, Japan 84/B4
Kashima (bay), Japan 83/F1
Kashin, Rus. 68/H4
Kāshīpur, India 96/B1
Kashiwa, Japan 83/D2
Kashiwara, Japan 83/J6
Kashiwazaki, Japan 85/F2
Kāshmar, Iran 101/G1
Kashmūnd Ghar (range), Afg. 98/A2
Kashof (riv.), Iran 103/J2
Kashofu, D.R. Congo 121/G3
Kasia, India 96/D2
Kasidiji (riv.), D.R. Congo 121/E5
Kasigau (peak), Kenya 119/B2
Kasigluk, Ak, US 171/F3
Kasilof, Ak, US 171/H3
Kasimov, Rus. 68/J5
Kasimovo (arpt.), Rus. 69/T6
Kasindi, D.R. Congo 121/G2
Kasinge, D.R. Congo 121/F4
Kasiruta (isl.), Indo. 91/G4
Kasiui (isl.), Indo. 91/H4
Kasiya, Malw. 123/G2
Kaskaskia (riv.), Il, US 155/K4
Kas'kovo, Rus. 41/N2
Kaslo, BC, Can. 144/F3
Kasonaweja, Indo. 91/J4
Kasongan, Indo. 90/D4
Kasongo, D.R. Congo 121/F4
Kasongo-Lunda, D.R. Congo 120/D4
Kasonguele, D.R. Congo 121/F4
Kásos (isl.), Gre. 102/A3
Kaspi, Geo. 71/H4
Kaspichan, Bul. 51/H4
Kaspiysk, Rus. 71/H4
Kaspiyskiy, Rus. 71/H3
Kassala, Sudan 117/H2
Kassándra (pen.), Gre. 70/B5
Kassándria, Gre. 49/H2
Kassel, Ger. 53/G6
Kassikaityu (riv.), Guy. 181/G4
Kasson, Mn, US 155/H1
Kastamonu (prov.), Turk. 70/E4
Kastamonu, Turk. 70/E4
Kastanéai, Gre. 51/H5
Kaštel Stari, Cro. 50/C4
Kaštel Sućurac, Cro. 50/C4
Kastellaun, Ger. 55/G3
Kastéllion, Gre. 49/J5
Kasterlee, Belg. 52/B6
Kastl, Ger. 59/E4
Kastön (isl.), Swe. 39/B1
Kastoría, Gre. 49/G2
Kastornoye, Rus. 73/K2
Kastrakíou (lake), Gre. 49/G3
Kastrup, Den. 39/J7
Kasuga, Japan 83/K5
Kasuga, Japan 83/H5
Kasugai, Japan 83/B2
Kasugai, Japan 83/L5
Kasui, Indo. 89/D4
Kasukabe, Japan 85/F3
Kasuku (riv.), D.R. Congo 121/F3
Kasulu, Tanz. 121/G4
Kasumiga (lake), Japan 85/G2
Kasungu, Malw. 123/G2
Kasungu NP, Malw. 123/G2
Kasupe, Malw. 123/G2
Kasūr, Pak. 98/C4
Kat O Chau (isl.), China 87/M6
Kataba, Zam. 122/E3
Katagum (riv.), Nga. 116/A2
Katako-Kombe, D.R. Congo 121/F3
Katákolon, Gre. 49/G4
Katale, D.R. Congo 121/G3
Kataloinen, Fin. 39/E4
Katana, D.R. Congo 121/G3
Katanda, D.R. Congo 121/E4
Katanda, D.R. Congo 121/G3
Katanga, (pol. reg.), D.R. Congo 121/F5
Katangi, India 96/B4
Katanning, Austl. 130/C5
Katano, Japan 83/J6
Katanti, D.R. Congo 121/F3
Katarniān Ghāt, India 96/C1
Katastárion, Gre. 49/G4
Katavi NP, Tanz. 121/G4
Katchall (isl.), India 93/F6
Katea, D.R. Congo 121/F4
Katea, D.R. Congo 121/E4
Katebo, Ugan. 121/H3
Katemcy, Tx, US 151/E2
Katenga, D.R. Congo 121/G4
Kateríni, Gre. 49/H2
Kates Needle (mt.), Ak, US 171/M4
Katesh, Tanz. 119/A3
Katete, Malw. 123/G2
Katete, Zam. 123/G2
Katghora, India 96/D4
Katha, Myan. 86/C3
Katherine, Az, US 148/E3
Katherine, Austl. 128/D3
Katherine (riv.), Austl. 128/D3
Katherine Gorge NP, Austl. 128/D3
Kāthgodām, India 96/B1
Kathiawar (pen.), India 101/K4
Kathleen, Ga, US 165/G1
Kathleen, Fl, US 164/L7
Kathleen (mt.), Austl. 131/G2
Kāthmāndu (cap.), Nepal 97/E2
Kathryn, ND, US 156/F4
Kathua, India 98/C3
Kati, Mali 114/C3
Katiéna, Mali 114/D3
Katihār, India 97/F3
Kātikund, India 97/F3
Katiola, C.d'Iv. 114/D4
Katla, Sudan 117/F3
Katlehong, SAfr. 124/E2
Katlenburg-Lindau, Ger. 53/H5
Katma, China 99/E4
Katmai (mt.), Ak, US 171/H4
Katmai NP, Ak, US 171/G4
Káto Akhaía, Gre. 49/G3
Káto Nevrokópion, Gre. 49/H2
Katoba, Tanz. 121/G4
Katokhí, Gre. 49/G3
Katombe, D.R. Congo 121/E4
Katonah, NY, US 169/E1
Katonga (riv.), Ugan. 121/G2
Katoomba, Austl. 133/E1
Katoúna, Gre. 49/G3
Katowice, Pol. 43/K3
Katra, India 98/C3
Katra, India 96/C3
Kātrās, India 97/F4
Katrichev, Rus. 71/H2
Katrine (lake), Sc, UK 33/B4
Katrineholm, Swe. 40/G2
Katsepe, Madg. 125/H6
Katshi, D.R. Congo 121/F4
Katsikás, Gre. 49/G3
Katsina (state), Nga. 115/G3
Katsina, Nga. 115/G3
Katsina Ala (riv.), Nga. 115/H5
Katsina Ala, Nga. 115/H5
Katsunuma, Japan 83/B2
Katsura (riv.), Japan 83/J5
Katsuragi, Japan 84/D3
Katsuragi-san (peak), Japan 83/H7
Katsuta, Japan 85/G2
Katsuura, Japan 85/G3
Katsuyama, Japan 84/E2
Katsuyama, Japan 83/B3
Kattegat (str.), Den. 29/F3
Katua, Gha. 115/E4
Katul (mtn.), Sudan 117/F2
Katumajävi (lake), Fin. 39/E4
Katumbi, Malw. 119/A4
Katun' (riv.), Rus. 78/B1
Katunayake (int'l arpt.), SrL. 95/C5
Katun'chuya (riv.), Rus. 99/E1
Katundu, Zam. 122/E3
Kātūria, India 97/F3
Katuta Kampemba, Zam. 121/G5
Kātwa, India 97/G4
Katwa, D.R. Congo 121/G2
Katwe-Kabatooro, Ugan. 121/G3
Katwijk aan Zee, Neth. 52/B4
Katy, Tx, US 151/G3
Katzenbach (riv.), Ger. 58/B4
Katzenbuckel (peak), Ger. 58/C4
Katzenelnbogen, Ger. 55/G3
Katzhütte, Ger. 58/D1
Katzwinkel, Ger. 55/F3
Kau-ye (isl.), Myan. 94/B4
Kauai (isl.), Hi, US 142/S9
Kauai (chan.), Hi, US 142/S10
Kaudum (riv.), Namb. 122/D3
Kaudum Game Park, Namb. 122/D3
Kaufbeuren, Ger. 61/G2
Kaufering, Ger. 61/G1
Kaufman (co.), Tx, US 150/L7
Kaufman, Tx, US 151/F1
Kaufungen, Ger. 53/G6
Kauhava, Fin. 68/D3
Kauiki (pt.), Hi, US 142/U10
Kaukapakapa, NZ 135/F6
Kaukauna, Wi, US 160/B2
Kaukaveld (uplands), Namb. 122/B3
Kaukura (isl.), FrPol. 137/L6
Kaulashishi (hill), Zam. 123/F2
Kaulsdorf, Ger. 59/E1
Kaumba, D.R. Congo 121/F5
Kaunas (res.), Lith. 41/L4
Kaunas, Lith. 41/K4
Kaunas (int'l arpt.), Lith. 41/K4
Kauniainen (Grankulla), Fin. 39/E4
Kaupanger, Nor. 40/B1
Kaura Namoda, Nga. 115/G3
Kauro, Kenya 119/B1
Kauttua, Fin. 41/K1
Kavadarci, FYROM 49/H2
Kavajë, Alb. 49/F2
Kavála, Gre. 49/J2
Kavalerovo, Rus. 79/M3
Kāvali, India 95/C3
Kavango (riv.), Namb. 122/C3
Kavār, Iran 103/H4
Kavarna, Bul. 51/J4
Kavarskas, Lith. 41/L4
Kavgolovskoye (lake), Rus. 69/T6
Kavieng, PNG 136/E5
Kavimba, Bots. 122/E3
Kavīr-e Bāfq (Salt pan), Iran 103/H4

Kavīr-e – Kimch'ŏ

Kavīr-e Namak (Salt pan), Iran 103/J3
Kävlinge, Swe. 40/E4
Kävlingeån (riv.), Swe. 39/K7
Kaw (lake), Ok, US 153/F2
Kaw (dam), Ok, US 153/F2
Kaw, FrG. 182/C1
Kaw City, Ok, US 153/F2
Kawa (ruin), Sudan 109/F5
Kawa, Myan. 86/C5
Kawabe, Japan 82/B4
Kawachi, Japan 83/E2
Kawachi-Nagano, Japan 83/J7
Kawage, Japan 83/L6
Kawagoe, Japan 85/F3
Kawagoe, Japan 83/L5
Kawaguchi, Japan 85/F3
Kawaguchiko, Japan 83/B3
Kawai, Japan 83/J6
Kawajena, Sudan 117/F4
Kawajima, Japan 83/C2
Kawakami, Japan 83/B2
Kawakami, Japan 83/J7
Kawamata, Japan 85/G2
Kawambwa, Zam. 121/G5
Kawamoto, Japan 83/C1
Kawana, Zam. 122/E2
Kawanishi, Japan 83/J6
Kawanishi, Japan 83/H6
Kawardha, India 96/C4
Kawartha Lakes, On, Can. 161/G2
Kawasaki, Japan 85/F3
Kawasato, Japan 83/D1
Kawashima, Japan 83/L5
Kawaue, Japan 83/M4
Kawerau, NZ 135/D2
Kawhia, NZ 135/C2
Kawich (peak), Nv, US 148/D2
Kawinda, Indo. 91/E5
Kawkabān, Yem. 118/B2
Kawkareik, Myan. 94/B2
Kawlin, Myan. 86/B4
Kawludo, Myan. 94/B2
Kawm Dafanah (ruin), Egypt 113/D3
Kawm Ḩamādah, Egypt 113/B3
Kawm Ishū, Egypt 113/A2
Kawm Umbū, Egypt 109/G3
Kawsaing, Myan. 94/B3
Kawthaung, Myan. 94/B4
Kax (riv.), China 74/J5
Kay, Rus. 69/M4
Kaya, SKor. 81/E5
Kaya, Burk. 115/E3
Kaya, Japan 83/H5
Kaya-san (peak), SKor. 81/D4
Kayadibi, Turk. 102/C2
Kayagangiri (peak), CAfr. 116/B4
Kayah (state), Myan. 93/G4
Kayamba (hills), Zam. 123/E2
Kayan (riv.), Indo. 77/L9
Kayanga (riv.), Sen. 114/B3
Kayangel (isls.), Palau 136/C4
Kāyankulam, India 95/C4
Kayar, Sen. 114/A3
Kayasa, Indo. 91/F4
Kaycee, Wy, US 147/K2
Kaye (mtn.), Austl. 133/D3
Kayembe-Mukulu, D.R. Congo 121/E5
Kayenta, Az, US 149/G2
Kayes, Mali 114/C3
Kayes (pol. reg.), Mali 114/C3
Kayin (state), Myan. 93/G4
Kayl, Lux. 55/F5
Kaymaz, Turk. 51/K5
Kaynarca, Turk. 51/J5
Kaynaşlı, Turk. 51/K5
Kayoa (isl.), Indo. 91/G3
Kaysatskoye, Rus. 71/H2
Kayser (mts.), Sur. 181/G4
Kayseri, Turk. 102/C2
Kayseri (prov.), Turk. 102/C2
Kaysersberḡ, Fr. 60/D1
Kaysville, Ut, US 147/H3
Kaytej Aboriginal Land, Austl. 128/D5
Kayuagung, Indo. 89/D3
Kayville, Sk, Can. 156/B3
Kayyerkan, Rus. 74/J3
Kazachka, Rus. 73/M2
Kazakhstan (ctry.) 77/E4
Kazan', Rus. 69/L5
Kazan (int'l arpt.), Rus. 69/L5
Kazan (riv.), Nun, Can. 140/F2
Kazancı, Turk. 104/C1
Kazanka, Ukr. 73/G4
Kazanlı, Turk. 104/D1
Kazanlŭk, Bul. 51/G4
Kazanskaya, Rus. 73/L3
Kazanskaya, Rus. 73/L5
Kazantip (cape), Ukr. 73/H5
Kazaure, Nga. 115/H3
Kazbegi, Geo. 71/H4
Kazbek (peak), Geo. 71/H4
Kāzerūn, Iran 103/G4
Kazgar (riv.), China 99/C3
Kazhim, Rus. 69/L3
Kazimierza Wielka, Pol. 43/L3
Kâzımkarabekir, Turk. 102/C2
Kazincbarcika, Hun. 43/L4
Kaziranga NP, India 86/B3
Kaziza, D.R. Congo 121/E5
Kazlų Rūda, Lith. 41/K4
Kazo, Japan 83/D1
Kaztalovka, Kaz. 71/J2
Kazuma Pan NP, Zim. 122/E3
Kazumba, D.R. Congo 121/E4
Kazuno, Japan 82/B3
Kazy, Trkm. 71/L5
Kdyně, Czh. 59/G4
Ke Ga (cape), Viet. 94/E3
Ké Macina, Mali 114/D3
Ke-hsi Mānsām, Myan. 94/B1
Kéa, Gre. 49/J4
Keady, NI, UK 34/B3
Keams Canyon, Az, US 149/G3
Keansburg, NJ, US 169/J10
Kearney, On, Can. 161/G2
Kearney, Ne, US 154/E3
Kearny (pt.), NI, UK 34/C3
Kearny, NJ, US 169/J8
Kearny, Az, US 149/G4
Kearsley (cr.), Mi, US 167/E5
Keats, Ks, US 155/F4
Keavy, Ky, US 162/E2
Kebbi (state), Nga. 115/G4
Kébémer, Sen. 114/A3
Kebnekaise (peak), Swe. 38/F2
K'ebri Dehar, Eth. 118/C4
Kebumen, Indo. 89/E4
Kecel, Hun. 50/D2
Keçiborlu, Turk. 102/B2
Kecskemét, Hun. 50/D2
Kedah (state), Malay. 94/C5
Kėdainiai, Lith. 41/K4
Kedgwick, NB, Can. 158/D2
Kedgwick Game Refuge, NB, Can. 158/D2
Kediri, Indo. 89/E4
Kedong, China 79/K2
Kédougou, Sen. 114/B3
Kędzierzyn-Koźle, Pol. 43/K3
Keefers, BC, Can. 144/D2
Keego Harbor, Mi, US 167/F6
Keele (peak), Yk, Can. 140/C2
Keele (riv.), NW, Can. 140/D2
Keeler, Ca, US 148/D2
Keeler, Sk, Can. 145/M2
Keelung, Japan 85/G8
Keelung (Chilung), Tai. 87/J3
Keen (mt.), Sc, UK 33/D3
Keene, NH, US 161/K3
Keene, Ca, US 148/C3
Keene, Tx, US 150/K7
Keep River NP, Austl. 128/C3
Keepit (dam), Austl. 132/D1
Keer-Weer (cape), Austl. 134/A1
Keeseekoose Ind. Res., Sk, Can. 156/D2
Keetmanshoop, Namb. 124/B2
Keewatin, On, Can. 157/G3
Keewatin, Mn, US 157/H4
Keewong, Austl. 132/C2
Kefa (pol. reg.), Eth. 117/H4
Kefallinía (isl.), Gre. 67/J3
Kefamenanu, Indo. 128/B2
Kefar Blum, Isr. 105/D2
Kefar Gil'adi, Isr. 105/D2
Kefar Ruppin, Isr. 105/D4
Kefar Sava, Isr. 105/B4
Kefar Vitkin, Isr. 105/B4
Keffi, Nga. 115/G4
Keffin Hausa, Nga. 115/H3
Keflavik (int'l arpt.), Ice. 38/M7
Keflavík, Ice. 38/M7
K'eftya, Eth. 117/H2
Kegalla, SrL. 95/D5
Kegworth, Eng, UK 35/G6
Kehl, Ger. 60/D1
Kehra, Est. 41/L2
Kehrsatz, Swi. 60/D4
Keighley, Eng, UK 35/G4
Keihoku, Japan 83/J5
Keila, Est. 41/L2
Keilor (nbrhd.), Austl. 132/F5
Keimaneigh (pass), Ire. 32/A6
Keimoes, SAfr. 124/C3
Keisha, D.R. Congo 121/F3
Keïta, Niger 115/G3
Keith, Sc, UK 33/D1
Keith, Austl. 132/B3
Keith (cape), Austl. 128/C2
Keithley Creek, BC, Can. 144/D1
Keithville, La, US 150/H1
Keizer, Me, US 146/B1
Kejimkujik NP, NS, Can. 158/E3
Kékes (peak), Hun. 43/K5
K'elafo, Eth. 118/C4
Kelan, China 80/B3
Kelān Devī, India 92/C2
Kelang (isl.), Indo. 91/G4
Kelang, Malay. 89/C2
Kelantan (state), Malay. 89/C1
Kelantan (riv.), Malay. 89/C1
Kelberg, Ger. 55/F3
Këlcyrë, Alb. 49/G2
Kelem, Eth. 117/G4
Keles, Turk. 70/D5
Kelheim, Ger. 59/E5
Kelila, Indo. 91/J4
Kelkheim, Ger. 58/B2
Kelkit, Turk. 70/F4
Kelkıt (riv.), Turk. 102/D1
Kell, Ger. 55/F4
Kellé, Congo 120/C3
Kellen, Ger. 52/D5
Kellenhusen, Ger. 40/D4
Keller (peak), Ca, US 166/C2
Keller (lake), NW, Can. 140/D2
Keller, Tx, US 150/K7
Kellerberrin, Austl. 130/C4
Kellerville, Tx, US 152/D3
Kelleys (isl.), On, US 160/E4
Kelleytown, Ga, US 163/M7
Kelliher, Mn, US 157/G4
Kelliher, Sk, Can. 156/C2
Kellogg, Ia, US 155/H3
Kellogg, Id, US 144/F4
Kellokoski, Fin. 39/F4
Kells, NI, UK 34/B2
Kells (Ceannannus Mór), Ire. 32/D2
Kelly (A.F.B.), Tx, US 151/E3
Kelly Lake, Mn, US 157/H4
Kellys Slough Nat'l Wild. Ref., ND, US 156/F4
Kelmė, Lith. 41/K4
Kel'mentsi, Ukr. 72/D3
Kélo, Chad 116/B3
Kelowna, BC, Can. 144/E3
Kelsall, Eng, UK 35/F5
Kelsey (pt.), Eng, UK 36/A6
Kelseyville, Ca, US 146/B4
Kelso, Sk, Can. 156/D3
Kelso, Sc, UK 33/D5
Kelso, Ca, US 148/E3
Kelso, Wa, US 144/C4
Kelsterbach, Ger. 58/B2
Kelu, China 87/F4
Keluang, Malay. 89/C2
Kelvedon, Eng, UK 37/G3
Kelvin (isl.), On, Can. 157/K3
Kelvington, Sk, Can. 156/C1
Kelwāra, India 96/A3
Kelyexeed, Som. 118/D3
Kem' (riv.), Rus. 74/D3
Kem', Rus. 68/G2
Kemabong, Malay. 88/A4
Kemah, Turk. 70/F5
Kemah, Tx, US 151/M9
Kemaliye, Turk. 102/D2
Kemalpaşa, Turk. 71/G4
Kemasik, Malay. 89/C1
Kémata I, Chad 116/C3
Kematen an der Ybbs, Aus. 59/H6
Kematen in Tirol, Aus. 61/H3
Kembé, CAfr. 116/D4
Kemble, Eng, UK 36/D3
Kembolcha, Eth. 118/A3
Kembolcha, Eth. 117/H3
Kembs, Fr. 60/D2
Kemecse, Hun. 43/L4
Kemena (riv.), Malay. 90/D3
Kemence, Hun. 43/K4
Kemer, Turk. 104/B1
Kemerburgaz, Turk. 103/M6
Kemerhisar, Turk. 102/C2
Kemerovo, Rus. 74/J4
Kemerovskaya Oblast, Rus. 74/J4
Kemi, Fin. 74/C3
Kemijärvi, Fin. 68/E2
Kemijoki (riv.), Fin. 38/H2
Kemmerer, Wy, US 147/H3
Kemnath, Ger. 59/E3
Kemnay, Sc, UK 33/D2
Kemo-Gribingui (pref.), CAfr. 116/C4
Kemp, Ok, US 153/F4
Kemp (lake), Tx, US 152/E4
Kemp, Tx, US 151/F1
Kemparana, Mali 114/D3
Kempele, Fin. 68/E2
Kempen, Ger. 52/D6
Kempenich, Ger. 55/G3
Kempenland (phys. reg.), Belg. 52/C6
Kempisch Kanaal (canal), Belg. 55/E1
Kempsey, Austl. 132/E1
Kempster, Wi, US 157/K5
Kempston, Eng, UK 37/F2
Kempten, Ger. 61/G2
Kempton, Austl. 132/C4
Kempton Park, SAfr. 124/Q13
Kemptown, Md, US 168/A5
Kemptville, On, Can. 161/J2
Kemri, India 96/B1
Kemul (peak), Indo. 91/E3
Ken (lake), Sc, UK 34/D1
Ken (riv.), India 96/C3
Ken-zaki (pt.), Japan 83/D3
Kenadsa, Alg. 111/E3
Kenai, Ak, US 171/H3
Kenai Fjords NP, Ak, US 171/H4
Kenamuke (swamp), Sudan 117/G4
Kenansville, NC, US 163/J3
Kenaston, Sk, Can. 145/L2
Kenbridge, Va, US 163/H2
Kendal, Eng, UK 35/F3
Kendal, Indo. 89/E4
Kendale Lakes, Fl, US 164/P11
Kendall (co.), Il, US 167/P16
Kendall, Austl. 132/E1
Kendall, Fl, US 164/P11
Kendall Park, NJ, US 168/D3
Kendallville, In, US 160/D4
Kéndavros, Gre. 49/J2
Kendégué, Chad 116/C3
Kendel (riv.), Ger. 52/D5
Kendleton, Tx, US 151/G3
Kendrāpāra, India 92/E3
Kendrick, Fl, US 165/G3
Kendrick (peak), Az, US 149/G3
Kendrick, Id, US 144/F4
Kendu Bay, Kenya 119/A2
Kénédougou (prov.), Burk. 114/D4
Kenedy, Tx, US 151/F3
Kenefick, Tx, US 151/N8
Kenel, SD, US 156/D5
Kenema, SLeo. 114/C5
Kenesaw, Ne, US 154/E3
Keng Deng, Laos 94/D2
Keng Hkam, Myan. 94/B1
Keng Tung, Myan. 94/B1
Kenge, D.R. Congo 120/C4
Kenge, D.R. Congo 120/D4
Kenhardt, SAfr. 124/C3
Kenhorst, Pa, US 168/C3
Kéniéba, Mali 114/C3
Kenilworth, NJ, US 169/H9
Kenilworth, Ut, US 147/H4
Kenilworth, Eng, UK 37/E2
Keningau, Malay. 88/B4
Kénitra (prov.), Mor. 112/A2
Kénitra, Mor. 112/A2
Kenli, China 80/D3
Kenly, NC, US 163/H3
Kenmare, ND, US 156/C3
Kenmare, Ire. 32/A6
Kenmare (riv.), Ire. 32/A6
Kenmore, Sc, UK 33/C3
Kenmore, Wa, US 167/C2
Kenmore, Austl. 134/C4
Kenmore, NY, US 160/V10
Kenn, Ger. 55/F4
Kenn (reef) 127/E3
Kennaday (peak), Wy, US 154/A3
Kennard, Tx, US 151/G2
Kennebec (riv.), Me, US 158/C3
Kennebec, SD, US 154/E2
Kennebunk, Me, US 161/L3
Kennedale, Tx, US 150/K7
Kennedy (range), Austl. 130/B3
Kennedy (chan.), Nun, Can. 141/T6
Kennedy, Sk, Can. 156/C2
Kennedy, Al, US 162/D4
Kennedy, Mn, US 156/F3
Kennedy Entrance (str.), Ak, US 171/H4
Kennedy Space Ctr., Fl, US 165/H3
Kennedyville, Md, US 168/C5
Kennelbach, Aus. 61/F3
Kennemerduinen, NP de, Neth. 52/B4
Kenner, La, US 164/C3
Kennesaw, Ga, US 163/L6
Kennesaw Mountain Nat'l Bfld. Park, Ga, US 163/L7
Kennet (riv.), Eng, UK 37/E4
Kennet and Avon (canal), Eng, UK 36/D4
Kenneth City, Fl, US 164/K8
Kennett, Mo, US 162/B2
Kennett Square, Pa, US 168/C4
Kennewick, Wa, US 144/E4
Keno Hill, Yk, Can. 171/L3
Kenogami (riv.), On, US 157/M2
Kenogami (riv.), On, Can. 157/M2
Kenogami (riv.), On, Can. 141/H3
Kenora, On, Can. 157/G3
Kenosha, Wi, US 160/C3
Kenosha (co.), Wi, US 167/P14
Kensal, ND, US 156/E4
Kensett, Ar, US 153/J3
Kensico (res.), NY, US 169/K7
Kensington, Mn, US 157/G5
Kensington, PE, Can. 158/F2
Kensington, Ks, US 154/E4
Kensington and Chelsea (bor.), Eng, UK 30/A1
Kenstséle, Congo 120/C3
Kent (pen.), Nun, Can. 140/F2
Kent (co.), On, Can. 167/G6
Kent (co.), Eng, UK 37/G4
Kent (riv.), Eng, UK 35/F3
Kent (isl.), Md, US 168/B6
Kent (pt.), Md, US 168/B6
Kent (lake), Mi, US 167/E7
Kent, Oh, US 160/F4
Kent, Or, US 146/C1
Kent, Tx, US 150/B2
Kent, Wa, US 144/C4
Kent County (int'l arpt.), Mi, US 160/D3
Kentaū, Kaz. 99/A3
Kenting NP, Tai. 87/J4
Kentland, In, US 160/C4
Kenton, Mb, Can. 156/D3
Kenton, De, US 168/C5
Kenton, Mi, US 157/K4
Kenton, Oh, US 160/E4
Kenton, Ok, US 152/C2
Kenton, Tn, US 162/C2
Kentucky (lake), Ky, US 143/J4
Kentucky (state), US 143/J4
Kentucky (dam), Ky, US 162/C2
Kentucky (riv.), Ky, US 162/E1
Kentucky, Middle Fork (riv.), Ky, US 163/F2
Kentucky, North Fork (riv.), Wy, US 147/K2
Kentville, NS, Can. 158/E3
Kentwood, Mi, US 160/D3
Kentwood, La, US 164/C2
Kenville, Mb, Can. 156/D1
Kenwood, Ga, US 163/M7
Kenya (ctry.) 107/F4
Kenyon, Mn, US 155/H1
Kenzingen, Ger. 60/D1
Keokuk, Ia, US 155/J3
Keoma, Ab, Can. 145/H2
Keonchi, India 96/C4
Keonjhar, India 95/E1
Keosauqua, Ia, US 155/J3
Keota, Ia, US 155/J3
Keowee (dam), SC, US 163/F3
Keowee (lake), SC, US 163/F3
Kep i Gjuhëzës (cape), Alb. 49/F2
Kep i Rodonit (cape), Alb. 49/F2
Kepa, Rus. 68/G2
Kepahiang, Indo. 89/C3
Kepi, Indo. 129/E1
Kępno, Pol. 43/J3
Keppel Sands, Austl. 134/C3
Kerala (state), India 92/C5
Kéran, PN de la, Togo 115/F4
Kerang, Austl. 132/B2
Keranyu, Eth. 118/A4
Keratéa, Gre. 49/N9
Kerava, Fin. 41/L1
Keravanjoki (riv.), Fin. 39/F4
Kerch, Ukr. 73/J5
Kerch' (str.), Ukr.,Rus. 70/F3
Kerch' (pen.), Ukr. 73/H5
Kerchouel, Mali 115/F2
Kerdonis (pt.), Fr. 56/B6
Kerema, PNG 129/G1
Keremeos, BC, Can. 144/E3
Kerempe (pt.), Turk. 70/E4
Kerempe Burnu (cape), Turk. 102/C1
Keren, Erit. 100/C5
Kerens, Tx, US 151/F1
Kerepestarcsa, Hun. 51/R9
Keret, Rus. 68/G2
Keret' (lake), Rus. 38/K2
Kerewan, Gam. 114/A3
Kerguélen (isl.), Fr. 27/N8
Kerhonkson, NY, US 161/J4
Keri Kera, Sudan 117/G2
Kericho, Kenya 119/A2
Kerikeri (cape), NZ 135/C1
Kerinci (peak), Indo. 89/C3
Kerio (riv.), Kenya 119/B1
Kerio Valley Nat'l Rsv., Kenya 119/A1
Keritty (lake), Fin. 39/E4
Keriya (pass), China 99/D4
Keriya (riv.), China 99/D4
Kerkdriel, Neth. 52/C5
Kerkebet, Erit. 117/H1
Kerken, Ger. 52/D6
Kerkhoven, Mn, US 155/G1
Kerki, Trkm. 74/G6
Kerkínis (lake), Gre. 49/H2
Kérkira, Gre. 49/F3
Kérkira (Corfu) (isl.), Gre. 67/H3
Kerkkoo (Kerko), Fin. 39/F4
Kerko (Kerkkoo), Fin. 39/F4
Kerkrade, Neth. 55/F2
Kerkwijk, Neth. 52/C5
Kerlouan, Fr. 56/A3
Kermadec (isls.), NZ 136/G8
Kermān, Iran 103/J4
Kerman, Ca, US 148/B2
Kermān (gov.), Iran 103/J4
Kermānshāhan (gov.), Iran 103/F3
Kermen, Bul. 51/H4
Kermit, Tx, US 151/C2
Kern (riv.), Ca, US 148/C2
Kern Nat'l Wild Ref., Ca, US 148/C2
Kernaalanjärvi (lake), Fin. 39/E4
Kernersville, NC, US 163/G2
Kerns, Swi. 61/E4
Kernville, Ca, US 148/C3
Keroh, Malay. 89/C1
Kéros (isl.), Gre. 49/J4
Kérou, Ben. 115/F4
Kérouané, Gui. 114/C4
Kerowagi, PNG 129/G1
Kerpen, Ger. 55/F2
Kerr (dam), Mt, US 144/G4
Kerr (res.), NC, US 162/H2
Kerrobert, Sk, Can. 145/K2
Kerrville, Tx, US 151/E2
Kerry (co.), Ire. 32/A5
K'ersa, Eth. 118/B3
Kersey, Pa, US 161/G4
Kersley, BC, Can. 144/C1
Kert (riv.), Mor. 112/C2
Kerteminde, Den. 39/G7
Kerulen (riv.), Mong. 77/L5
Kerulen (Herlen) (riv.), Mong. 78/G2
Kerzaz, Alg. 111/E3
Kerzenheim, Ger. 55/H4
Kerzers, Swi. 60/D4
Kesabpur, Bang. 97/G4
Keşan, Turk. 51/H5
Kesch (peak), Swi. 61/F4
Kesen'numa, Japan 82/B4
Kesgrave, Eng, UK 37/H2
Keshan, China 79/K2
Keshena, Wi, US 155/K1
Keshena (falls), Wi, US 155/K1
Keshod, India 92/B3
Kesinga, India 95/D1
Keski-Suomi (prov.), Fin. 38/H3
Keskin, Turk. 102/C2
Kesselbach (riv.), Ger. 58/D5
Kessingland, Eng, UK 37/H2
Kesten'ga, Rus. 68/F2
Kesteren, Neth. 52/C5
Keswick, Eng, UK 35/E2
Keszthely, Hun. 50/C2
Ket' (riv.), Rus. 74/J4
Keta (riv.), Rus. 74/K3
Keta, Gha. 115/F5
Ketama, Mor. 112/B2
Ketapang, Indo. 89/D4
Ketaun, Indo. 89/C3
Ketchikan, Ak, US 171/M4
Ketchum, Id, US 147/F2
Kété, Camr. 116/B4
Kete Krachi, Gha. 115/E5
Ketelmeer (lake), Neth. 52/C3
Kétou, Ben. 115/F5
Kętrzyn, Pol. 41/J4
Ketsch, Ger. 58/B4
Ketta, Congo 120/C2
Kettering, Oh, US 160/D5
Kettering, Eng, UK 37/F2
Kettle (pt.), On, Can. 160/E3
Kettle (riv.), Wa, US 144/E3
Kettle Falls, Wa, US 144/E3
Kettle Moraine State Forest, Wi, US 167/P14
Kettle River, Mn, US 157/H4
Kettle River (range), Wa, US 144/E3
Kettleman City, Ca, US 148/C2
Kettlewell, Eng, UK 35/F3
Ketzin, Ger. 42/P7
Keudeteunom, Indo. 89/A1
Keuka (lake), NY, US 161/H3
Keukenhof, Neth. 52/B4
Keur Massène, Mrta. 114/A2
Kévé, Togo 115/F5
Kevelaer, Ger. 52/D5
Kevin, Mt, US 145/J3
Kew, UK 177/H1
Kewanee, Il, US 155/K3
Kewanna, In, US 160/C4
Kewaskum, Wi, US 160/B3
Kewaunee, Wi, US 160/C2
Keweenaw (pen.), Mi, US 157/K4
Keweenaw (pt.), Mi, US 157/L4
Keweenaw (bay), Mi, US 157/K4
K'ey Āfer, Eth. 117/H4
Key Biscayne, Fl, US 164/P11
Key Largo (isl.), Fl, US 165/H5
Key Largo, Fl, US 165/H5
Key West (int'l arpt.), Fl, US 165/H5
Key West, Fl, US 172/E3
Key West Nat'l Wildlife Refuge, Fl, US 165/G5
Key West Nav. Air Sta., Fl, US 165/H5
Keya Paha (riv.), Ne, SD, US 154/E2
Keyhole (res.), Wy, US 154/B1
Keyi, China 99/D3
Keyling (inlet), Austl. 128/C3
Keymar, Md, US 168/A4
Keynsham, Eng, UK 36/D4
Keyport, NJ, US 169/J10
Keyport, Wa, US 167/B2
Keyser, WV, US 161/G5
Keystone (dam), Ok, US 153/F2
Keystone (lake), Ok, US 153/F2
Keystone Heights, Fl, US 165/G3
Keysville, Fl, US 164/L8
Keysville, Va, US 163/H2
Keytesville, Mo, US 155/H4
Keytū, Iran 103/G3
Keyworth, Eng, UK 35/G6
Kezi, Zim. 123/F4
Kežmarok, Slvk. 43/L4
Kgalagadi (dist.), Bots. 122/D5
Kgatleng (prov.), Bots. 122/E4
Kgwebe (hills), Bots. 122/D4
Khaanziir (cape), Som. 118/C3
Khabab, Syria 105/E2
Khabarikha, Rus. 69/M2
Khabarovsk, Rus. 79/M2
Khabarovskiy Kray, Rus. 75/P4
Khadari (wadi), Sudan 117/E3
Khadaungnge (peak), Myan. 86/B5
Khadyzhensk, Rus. 73/K5
Khagaria, India 97/F3
Khagrāchari, Bang. 97/H4
Khair, India 96/A2
Khairābād, India 96/C2
Khairāgarh, India 95/D1
Khairpur, Pak. 98/B5
Khairpur, Pak. 101/J3
Khaishi, Geo. 71/G4
Khajuri, India 97/F3
Khākā (Xingkāi) (lake), Rus. 79/L3
Khakasiya, Resp., Rus. 75/Q6
Khakhea, Bots. 122/D5
Khalābat, Pak. 98/B2
Khalándrion, Gre. 49/N8
Khalīlābād, India 96/D2
Khalkhāl, Iran 103/G2
Khalkhidhikhi (pen.), Gre. 49/H2
Khalkidhón, Gre. 49/H2
Khalkís, Gre. 49/H3
Khallikot, India 95/E2
Khal'mer-yu, Rus. 69/P1
Khalūf, Oman 101/G4
Kham Khuan Kaeo, Thai. 94/D3
Khamar-Daban (mts.), Rus. 78/E1
Khambhāliya, India 101/J4
Khambhat, India 101/K4
Khāmgaon, India 95/C1
Khamīs Mushayţ, SAr. 100/D5
Khamkeut, Laos 94/D2
Khamr, Yem. 118/B2
Khan (riv.), Namb. 122/B4
Khān Abū Shāmāt, Syria 104/E3
Khān al 'Arūs, Syria 105/F1
Khan Arnabah, Syria 105/D2
Khān Dannūn, Syria 105/E2
Khān Shaykhūn, Syria 104/E2
Khān Yūnus, Gaza 105/A6
Khānābād, Afg. 101/J1
Khānaqīn, Iraq 103/F3
Khancoban, Austl. 133/D3
Khāndbāri, Nepal 97/F2
Khandwa, India 95/C1
Khandyga, Rus. 75/P3
Khanem (well), Alg. 111/F3
Khānewāl, Pak. 98/A4
Khāngāh Dogrān, Pak. 98/B4
Khāngarh, Pak. 98/A5
Khaniá, Gre. 49/J5
Khanka (lake), Rus. 75/P5
Khanka (lake), China,Rus 77/N5
Khānkar, India 96/A3
Khanna, India 98/D4
Khanovey, Rus. 69/P2
Khānpur, Pak. 98/A5
Khanskaya, Rus. 73/K5
Khantau, Kaz. 99/B3
Khanty-Mansiysk, Rus. 74/G3
Khanty-Mansiyskiy Aut. Okrug, Rus. 74/G3
Khao Chamao-Khao Wong NP, Thai. 94/C3
Khao Khitchakut NP, Thai. 94/C3
Khao Laem (res.), Thai. 93/G4
Khao Sam Roi Yot NP, Thai. 94/B3
Khao Yai NP, Thai. 94/C3
Khapcheranga, Rus. 78/G2
Kharabali, Rus. 71/H3
Kharābat Ihrīt (ruin), Egypt 113/B6
Kharagpur, India 97/F4
Kharagpur, India 97/F3
Kharak, Pak. 98/A3
Khārān, Pak. 101/J3
Kharānoq, Iran 103/H3
Kharar, India 98/D4
Kharar, India 97/F4
Khārās, WBnk. 105/C5
Kharbara, India 98/B5
Kharbatā, WBnk. 105/C5
Khargon, India 95/B1
Khāriān, Pak. 98/B3
Khariār, India 95/D1
Kharīţ (wadi), Egypt 109/G3
Khārk (isl.), Iran 103/G4
Kharkiv, Ukr. 73/J3
Kharkiv (int'l arpt.), Ukr. 73/J3
Kharkivs'ka Oblast, Ukr. 70/F2
Kharlovka, Rus. 68/H1
Kharmanli, Bul. 51/G5
Kharovsk, Rus. 68/J4
Kharrour (riv.), Mor. 112/B2
Kharsia, India 96/D5
Khartoum (int'l arpt.), Sudan 117/G2
Khartoum (Al Khurtum) (cap.), Sudan 117/G2
Khartoum North (Al Kharţūm Baḩrī), Sudan 117/G2
Kharumwa, Tanz. 121/H3
Kharv-e 'Olyā, Iran 103/J2
Khasan, Rus. 79/L3
Khasavyurt, Rus. 71/H4
Khāsh (riv.), Afg. 101/H2
Khashm al Qirbah, Sudan 117/G2
Khashuri, Geo. 71/G4
Khasi (hills), India 97/H3
Khaskovo (pol. reg.), Bul. 49/J2
Khaskovo (prov.), Bul. 51/G5
Khaskovo, Bul. 51/G5
Khatanga (gulf), Rus. 75/L2
Khatanga, Rus. 75/L2
Khatanga (riv.), Rus. 192/Z
Khatauli, India 98/D5
Khātegaon, India 96/A4
Khatīma, India 96/B1
Khatmia (pass), Egypt 104/C4
Khātra, India 97/F4
Khatt Atoui (riv.), Mrta. 110/B5
Khaur, Pak. 98/B3
Khāvda, India 101/J4
Khawr Abū Ḩabl (riv.), Sudan 117/F2
Khawr Fakkān, UAE 101/G3
Khawr Langeb (riv.), Sudan 117/H1
Khawr Nanaam (riv.), Sudan 117/G4
Khawr Veveno (riv.), Sudan 117/G4
Khawrah, Yem. 100/E6
Khay', SAr. 100/D5
Khaybar (pass), Afg. 98/A2
Khaybar, SAr. 100/D5
Khaybar, SAr. 100/C3
Khazzān Ar Ruşayriş (res.), Sudan 117/G3
Khazzān Darbandīkhān (res.), Iraq 103/F3
Khazzān Dūkān (res.), Iraq 103/F3
Khazzān Jabal Al Awliyā (dam), Sudan 117/G2
Khe Sanh, Viet. 94/D2
Khekra, India 98/D5
Khem Karan, India 98/C4
Khemis el Khechna, Alg. 112/G4
Khemis Miliana, Alg. 112/G4
Khémisset (prov.), Mor. 112/A3
Khémisset, Mor. 112/A3
Khemmarat, Thai. 94/D2
Khenchela (wilaya), Alg. 111/G2
Khenchela, Alg. 112/K7
Khénifra, Mor. 110/D2
Khepoyarvi (lake), Rus. 69/T6
Kherāmeh, Iran 103/H4
Kheri, India 96/C2
Khersān (riv.), Iran 100/F2
Kherson, Ukr. 73/G4
Kherson (int'l arpt.), Ukr. 72/G4
Khersonesskiy (cape), Ukr. 73/G5
Khersons'ka Oblast, Ukr. 70/E3
Khezrī, Iran 101/G2
Khiitola, Rus. 41/N1
Khilok, Rus. 78/G1
Khilok (riv.), Rus. 78/F1
Khimki, Rus. 69/W9
Khíos, Gre. 49/K3
Khíos (isl.), Gre. 70/C5
Khirbat Jābīr, Jor. 105/E3
Khirbat Qumrān (ruin), WBnk. 105/C5
Khirbat Umm al Jimāl (ruin), Jor. 105/E4
Khirpai, India 97/F4
Khisarya, Bul. 51/G4
Khisfīn, Syria 105/D3
Khiv, Rus. 71/H4
Khiva, Uzb. 74/G5
Khlebarovo, Bul. 51/H4
Khlevnoye, Rus. 73/K1
Khlong Khlung, Thai. 94/B2
Khlung, Thai. 94/C3
Khmel'nyts'ka Oblast, Ukr. 70/C2
Khmel'nytskyy, Ukr. 72/D3
Khmil'nyk, Ukr. 72/D3
Kho Sawai (plat.), Thai. 93/H4
Khobi, Geo. 71/G4
Khodoriv, Ukr. 72/C3
Khodovarikha, Rus. 69/M1
Khojak (pass), Pak. 101/J2
Khok Samrong, Thai. 94/C3
Khoksar, India 98/D3
Kholm, Rus. 41/P3
Kholm, Afg. 101/J1
Kholmogorskaya, Rus. 68/J3
Kholmogory, Rus. 68/J2
Kholmsk, Rus. 79/N2
Kholombidzo (falls), Malw. 123/G2
Kholtoson, Rus. 78/E1
Khomām, Iran 103/G2
Khomas Hochland (mts.), Namb. 122/B4
Khomeyn, Iran 103/G3
Khomeynīshahr, Iran 103/G3
Khomutovka, Rus. 73/H1
Khon Kaen, Thai. 94/C2
Khong Chiam, Thai. 94/D3
Khoni, Geo. 71/G4
Khonj, Iran 103/H5
Khonuu, Rus. 75/Q3
Khopër (riv.), Rus. 74/E4
Khor (riv.), Rus. 75/P5
Khor, Rus. 79/L2
Khor Angar, Djib. 118/B2
Khóra Sfakíon, Gre. 49/J5
Khorāsān (gov.), Iran 103/J3
Khoreyver, Rus. 69/N2
Khorinsk, Rus. 78/F1
Khorixas, Namb. 122/B4
Khorof Harar, Kenya 119/C1
Khorol, Ukr. 73/G3
Khorol', Rus. 79/L3
Khorramābād, Iran 103/G3
Khorramshahr, Iran 103/G4
Khorugh, Taj. 99/B4
Khosheutovo, Rus. 71/H3
Khosrowābād, Iran 103/G4
Khosrowshahr, Iran 103/F2
Khot'kovo, Rus. 68/H4
Khotol (mt.), Ak, US 171/G3
Khotyn, Ukr. 72/D3
Khouribga, Mor. 110/D2
Khovu-Aksy, Rus. 78/C1
Khowai, India 93/F3
Khowst, Afg. 98/A2
Khoyniki, Bela. 72/E2
Khrenovoye, Rus. 73/L2
Khreum, Myan. 93/F3
Khrisoúpolis, Gre. 49/J2
Khromtaū, Kaz. 71/L2
Khrysi (isl.), Gre. 49/J5
Khrystynivka, Ukr. 72/E3
Khu Khan, Thai. 94/D3
Khuan Ubon Ratana (lake), Thai. 94/C2
Khuchni, Rus. 71/H4
Khudiān, Pak. 98/C4
Khudumelapye, Bots. 122/E4
Khuff, SAr. 100/D4
Khuis, Bots. 124/C2
Khujand, Taj. 99/A3
Khulna (pol. div.), Bang. 97/G4
Khulna, Bang. 97/G4
Khulo, Geo. 71/G4
Khun Yuam, Thai. 94/B2
Khunti, India 97/E4
Khurai, India 96/B3
Khurda, India 95/E1
Khurja, India 96/A1
Khūsf, Iran 101/G2
Khushāb, Pak. 98/B3
Khust, Ukr. 43/M4
Khūtār, India 96/C1
Khuwayy, Sudan 117/F2
Khūzami, India 86/B3
Khuzdār, Pak. 101/J3
Khūzestān (gov.), Iran 103/G4
Khvalynka, Rus. 79/L3
Khvonsār, Iran 103/G3
Khvor, Iran 103/H3
Khvormūj, Iran 103/G4
Khvorostyanka, Rus. 71/J1
Khvoy, Iran 103/F2
Khwaja Rawash (int'l arpt.), Afg. 101/J2
Khyber (pass), Pak. 98/A2
Khyrdalan, Azer. 71/J4
Kia, Sol. 136/E5
Kiama, D.R. Congo 120/D4
Kiama, Austl. 133/E2
Kiamba, Phil. 88/D4
Kiambi, D.R. Congo 121/G4
Kiamichi (riv.), Ok, US 153/G3
Kiamichi (mts.), Ok, US 153/G3
Kiana, Ak, US 171/F2
Kiangan, Phil. 88/C1
Kiangara, Madg. 125/H7
Kianjavato, Madg. 125/H8
Kiáton, Gre. 49/H3
Kibaha, Tanz. 119/B3
Kibæk, Den. 40/C3
Kibala, Ang. 120/C4
Kibali (riv.), D.R. Congo 117/F5
Kibamba, D.R. Congo 121/F4
Kibanga, D.R. Congo 121/G4
Kibangou, Congo 120/C3
Kibar, India 101/L2
Kibara, Tanz. 119/A2
Kibau, Tanz. 119/A4
Kibawe, Phil. 88/D4
Kibaya, Tanz. 119/B3
Kibbee, Ga, US 163/F4
Kibblesworth, Eng, UK 35/G2
Kiberege, Tanz. 119/B3
Kibergneset (pt.), Nor. 38/J1
Kibi, Gha. 115/E5
Kibigori, Kenya 119/A2
Kibindu, Tanz. 119/B3
Kibinga, D.R. Congo 120/D4
Kibiti, Tanz. 119/B3
Kibiya, Nga. 115/H4
Kibo (peak), Tanz. 119/B2
Kiboga, Ugan. 121/G2
Kiboko, Kenya 119/B2
Kibombo Rive, D.R. Congo 121/F3
Kibondo, Tanz. 121/G3
Kibongoto, Tanz. 119/B2
Kibre Mengist, Eth. 118/A4
Kıbrısçık, Turk. 51/K5
Kibungo, Rwa. 121/G3
Kibuye, Rwa. 121/G3
Kibwesa, Tanz. 121/G4
Kibwezi, Kenya 119/B2
Kičevo, FYROM 49/G2
Kichha, India 96/B1
Kickapoo (riv.), Wi, US 155/J2
Kickapoo Ind. Res., Ks, US 155/G4
Kid (mt.), Ire. 32/A6
Kidal, Mali 115/F2
Kidal (pol. reg.), Mali 115/F2
Kidapawan, Phil. 88/D4
Kidderminster, Eng, UK 36/D2
Kidepo Valley NP, Ugan. 117/G5
Kidete, Tanz. 119/B3
Kidira, Sen. 114/B3
Kidnappers (cape), NZ 135/D2
Kidodi, Tanz. 119/B3
Kidsgrove, Eng, UK 35/F5
Kidugallo, Tanz. 119/B3
Kidwelly, Wal, UK 36/B3
Kiel (bay), Den. 38/D5
Kiel, Ger. 40/D4
Kiel, Wi, US 160/B3
Kielce, Pol. 43/L3
Kielder, Eng, UK 35/F1
Kielder (res.), Eng, UK 35/F1
Kieldrecht, Belg. 52/B6
Kiémbara, Burk. 114/E3
Kiembe, D.R. Congo 121/F5
Kien An, Viet. 94/D1
Kien Duc, Viet. 94/D4
Kien Thanh, Viet. 94/D4
Kienge, D.R. Congo 121/F5
Kierspe, Ger. 55/G1
Kiester, Mn, US 155/H2
Kiev (Kyyiv) (cap.), Ukr. 72/F3
Kiffa, Mrta. 114/C2
Kifisiá, Gre. 49/N8
Kifrī, Iraq 103/F3
Kifusa, D.R. Congo 121/F4
Kifwanzondo, D.R. Congo 120/D4
Kigali (cap.), Rwa. 121/G3
Kigali (Gregoire Kayibanda) (int'l arpt.), Rwa. 121/G3
Kiganga, Tanz. 119/A3
Kiği, Turk. 102/E2
Kigoma, Tanz. 121/G4
Kigoma (pol. reg.), Tanz. 121/G4
Kigye, SKor. 81/E4
Kihnu (isl.), Est. 41/L2
Kihti (str.), Fin. 41/J1
Kihundo, Tanz. 119/B4
Kihurio, Tanz. 119/B3
Kii (chan.), Japan 84/D4
Kii (mts.), Japan 84/D4
Kiines (riv.), China 99/D3
Kijang, SKor. 81/E5
Kijungu, Tanz. 119/B3
Kikai (isl.), Japan 85/L6
Kikarara, Ugan. 121/G3
Kikiktat (mt.), Ak, US 171/H2
Kikinda, Yugo. 50/E3
Kikki, Pak. 101/H3
Kikoira, Austl. 133/C1
Kikombo, Tanz. 119/A3
Kikonai, Japan 82/B3
Kikongo-Mndanga, D.R. Congo 120/D4
Kikori (riv.), PNG 129/F1
Kikori, PNG 129/G1
Kikwit, D.R. Congo 120/D4
Kil, Swe. 40/E2
Kil'den (isl.), Rus. 38/K1
Kilafors, Swe. 40/G1
Kilaguni, Kenya 119/B2
Kilalo, Tanz. 119/A2
Kilār, India 98/D3
Kilbarchan, Sc, UK 33/B5
Kilbeggan, Ire. 32/C3
Kilberry, Ire. 32/D2
Kilbirnie, Sc, UK 33/B5
Kilbrannan (sound), Sc, UK 33/A5
Kilbride, Nf, Can. 159/L2
Kilbride, On, Can. 160/T9
Kilchoan, Sc, UK 31/Q8
Kilchu, NKor. 81/E2
Kilcock, Ire. 32/D3
Kilcolgan (pt.), Ire. 32/A3
Kilconnell, Ire. 32/B3
Kilcoole, Ire. 34/B5
Kilcormac, Ire. 32/C3
Kilcoy, Austl. 134/D4
Kilcreggan, Sc, UK 33/B5
Kilcrow (riv.), Ire. 32/B3
Kilcullen, Ire. 32/D3
Kildare, Tx, US 153/G4
Kildare, Ire. 32/D3
Kildeer, Il, US 167/P15
Kil'den (isl.), Rus. 68/G1
Kildonan, Zim. 123/F3
Kildorrery, Ire. 32/B5
Kilembe, D.R. Congo 120/D4
Kilembe Estates, Ugan. 121/G2
Kilfenora, Ire. 32/A4
Kilfinnane, Ire. 32/B5
Kilgarvan, Ire. 32/A6
Kilgore, Id, US 147/H1
Kilgore, Tx, US 151/G1
Kilgoris, Kenya 119/A2
Kilham, Eng, UK 35/H3
Kilian (isl.), Nun, Can. 140/F1
Kilifi, Kenya 119/B2
Kilimanjaro (int'l arpt.), Tanz. 119/B2
Kilimanjaro (prov.), Tanz. 119/B2
Kilimanjaro NP, Tanz. 119/B2
Kilimatinde, Tanz. 119/A3
Kilimli, Turk. 70/D4
Kilindoni, Tanz. 119/B3
Kilingi-Nõmme, Est. 41/L2
Kilinochchi, SrL. 95/D4
Kilis, Turk. 104/E1
Kiliugaån (riv.), Swe. 39/L6
Kiliya, Ukr. 51/J3
Kilkee, Ire. 32/A4
Kilkeel, NI, UK 34/B3
Kilkelly, Ire. 32/B2
Kilkenny, Ire. 32/C4
Kilkenny (co.), Ire. 34/A6
Kilkís, Gre. 49/H2
Kilkishen, Ire. 32/B4
Kilkivan, Austl. 134/D4
Kill, Ire. 32/D3
Kill Devil Hills, NC, US 163/K2
Kill Van Kull (riv.), NJ,NY, US 169/J9
Killadysert, Ire. 32/A4
Killala (bay), Ire. 32/A1
Killala, Ire. 32/A1
Killaloe, Ire. 32/B4
Killaloe Station, On, Can. 161/H2
Killam, Ab, Can. 145/J1
Killamarsh, Eng, UK 35/G5
Killara (nbrhd.), Austl. 134/H8
Killarney, Mb, Can. 156/E3
Killarney, Ire. 32/A5
Killarney, Austl. 132/E1
Killarney, Austl. 128/C4
Killarney NP, Ire. 32/A5
Killashandra, Ire. 32/C1
Killavullen, Ire. 32/B5
Killdeer, ND, US 156/C4
Killdeer, Sk, Can. 145/L3
Killdeer Battlefield Historical Site, ND, US 156/C4
Killeagh, Ire. 32/C6
Killearn, Sc, UK 33/B4
Killeen, Tx, US 150/F2
Killen, Al, US 162/D3
Killenaule, Ire. 32/C4
Killian, La, US 164/C2
Killiecrankie, Pass of (pass), Sc, UK 33/C3
Killin, Sc, UK 33/B4
Killinaboy, Ire. 32/A4
Killinchy, NI, UK 34/C3
Killinek (isl.), Nun, Can. 141/K2
Killington (peak), Vt, US 161/K3
Killíni (peak), Gre. 49/H4
Killíni, Gre. 49/G4
Killough, NI, UK 34/C3
Killucan, Ire. 32/C2
Killybegs, Ire. 31/P9
Killyclogher, NI, UK 34/A2
Killyleagh, NI, UK 34/C3
Kilmacanogue, Ire. 34/B5
Kilmacolm, Sc, UK 33/B5
Kilmacow, Ire. 32/C5
Kilmacthomas, Ire. 32/C5
Kilmaganny, Ire. 32/C5
Kilmallock, Ire. 32/B5
Kilmar Tor (hill), Eng, UK 36/B5
Kilmarnock, Sc, UK 33/B5
Kilmarnock, Va, US 163/J2
Kilmaurs, Sc, UK 33/B5
Kilmeadan, Ire. 32/C5
Kilmichael (pt.), Ire. 34/B6
Kilmihill, Ire. 32/A4
Kilmore, Austl. 133/B3
Kilmore Quay, Ire. 32/D5
Kilmurry, Ire. 32/A4
Kilnaleck, Ire. 32/C2
Kilninver, Sc, UK 31/R8
Kilo, D.R. Congo 121/G2
Kilombero (riv.), Tanz. 119/B4
Kilometre 28, D.R. Congo 121/F3
Kilomines, D.R. Congo 121/G2
Kilosa, Tanz. 119/B3
Kilpijärvi (lake), Fin. 39/F4
Kilpisjärvi, Fin. 38/G1
Kilraghts, NI, UK 34/B1
Kilrea, NI, UK 34/B2
Kilrenny, Sc, UK 33/D4
Kilronan, Ire. 31/P10
Kilrush, Ire. 32/A4
Kilsheelan, Ire. 32/C5
Kilsyth, Sc, UK 33/B5
Kiltamagh, Ire. 32/A2
Kilwa, D.R. Congo 121/G5
Kilwa (isl.), Zam. 121/G5
Kilwa Kivinje, Tanz. 119/B4
Kilwa Masoko, Tanz. 119/B4
Kilwaughter, NI, UK 34/C2
Kilwinning, Sc, UK 33/B5
Kilworth, Ire. 32/B5
Kim, Co, US 152/C2
Kimaan, Indo. 129/E1
Kimali, Tanz. 119/A2
Kimamba, Tanz. 119/B3
Kimba, Austl. 131/H5
Kimba, Congo 120/C3
Kimball, Ne, US 154/C3
Kimball, SD, US 154/E2
Kimbe, PNG 136/E5
Kimberley (cape), Austl. 134/B2
Kimberley, BC, Can. 144/G3
Kimberley, SAfr. 124/D3
Kimberley (plat.), Austl. 127/B2
Kimberly, Id, US 147/F2
Kimberly, Or, US 146/D1
Kimch'aek, NKor. 81/E2
Kimch'ŏn, SKor. 81/E4

Kimhae, SKor. 84/A3
Kimhae (int'l arpt.), SKor. 84/A3
Kími, Gre. 49/J3
Kimi, Camr. 116/A4
Kímina, Gre. 49/H2
Kimitsu, Japan 85/F3
Kimje, SKor. 81/D5
Kimméria, Gre. 49/J2
Kimmirut, Nun, Can. 141/K2
Kimnyangjang-ni, SKor. 81/G7
Kímolos (isl.), Gre. 49/J4
Kimongo, Congo 120/C4
Kimoset, Kenya 119/A1
Kimovaara, Rus. 68/F3
Kimovsk, Rus. 70/F1
Kimpanga, D.R. Congo 121/F4
Kimpese, D.R. Congo 120/C4
Kimp'o, SKor. 81/F6
Kimp'o (int'l arpt.), SKor. 81/F6
Kimpō-zan (peak), Japan 83/B2
Kimry, Rus. 68/H4
Kinabalu (peak), Malay. 88/B4
Kinabalu NP, Malay. 88/B4
Kinabatangan (riv.), Malay. 91/E2
Kinaliada (isl.), Turk. 103/M7
Kinalung, Austl. 132/B2
Kinango, Kenya 119/B3
Kinapat (cape), Indo. 89/B3
Kinard, Fl, US 165/F2
Kinards, SC, US 163/G3
Kinarut, Malay. 88/B4
Kinbasket (lake), BC, Can. 144/E1
Kinbrace, Sc, UK 31/S7
Kincaid, Sk, Can. 145/L3
Kincaid, Ks, US 153/G1
Kincardine, Sc, UK 33/C4
Kincardine, On, Can. 160/F2
Kinchafoonee (cr.), Ga, US 165/F1
Kincolith, BC, Can. 171/N4
Kincraig, Sc, UK 33/C2
Kinda, D.R. Congo 121/F5
Kindambi, D.R. Congo 120/E4
Kindberg, Aus. 45/L3
Kindembe, D.R. Congo 120/D4
Kinder, La, US 164/B2
Kinder Scout (peak), Eng, UK 35/G5
Kindersley, Sk, Can. 145/K2
Kindia (pol. reg.), Gui. 114/B4
Kindia, Gui. 114/B4
Kinding, Ger. 59/E5
Kindred, ND, US 156/F4
Kindsbach, Ger. 55/G5
Kindu, D.R. Congo 121/F3
Kinel', Rus. 71/J1
Kineshma, Rus. 68/J4
Kineton, Eng, UK 37/E2
King (isl.), Austl. 127/D4
King (lake), Austl. 130/C5
King (mt.), Austl. 134/B4
King (riv.), Austl. 133/C3
King (sound), Austl. 127/B2
King (mt.), BC, Can. 171/N4
King (isl.), NZ 127/H6
King, NC, US 163/G2
King (hill), Pa, US 161/G4
King (mtn.), Tx, US 151/C2
King (co.), Wa, US 167/D2
King Abdul Aziz (int'l arpt.), SAr. 109/H4
King And Queen Court House, Va, US 163/J2
King Christian (isl.), Nun, Can. 141/R7
King Christian IX Land (reg.), Grld. 139/P3
King Christian X Land (reg.), Grld. 139/Q2
King City, Ca, US 148/B2
King City, Mo, US 155/G3
King City, On, Can. 160/T8
King Cove, Ak, US 171/F4
King Frederik VI Coast (reg.), Grld. 139/N3
King Frederik VIII Land (reg.), Grld. 139/Q2
King George (isls.), FrPol. 137/L6
King George (mt.), BC, Can. 144/G2
King George, Va, US 163/J1
King George Is. (isls.), Qu, Can. 141/J3
King George's (res.), Eng, UK 30/C2
King Hussein (arpt.), Jor. 105/E4
King Khaled (int'l arpt.), SAr. 100/E4
King Leopold (range), Austl. 128/B4
King of Prussia, Pa, US 168/C3
King Peak (mt.), Yk, Can. 171/K3
King Salmon, Ak, US 171/G4
King William (isl.), Nun, Can. 140/G2
King William, Va, US 163/J2
King William's Town, SAfr. 124/D4
Kinganga, D.R. Congo 120/C4
Kingaroy, Austl. 134/C4
Kingfisher, Ok, US 153/F3
Kinghorn, Sc, UK 33/C4
Kingisepp, Rus. 41/N2
Kinglake NP, Austl. 132/G5
Kingman, Ks, US 153/E2
Kingman, Az, US 149/E3
Kingman (reef), Pac., US 137/J4
Kingombe, D.R. Congo 121/F3
Kingoonyah, Austl. 131/G4
Kings (peak), Ut, US 147/H3
Kings, Ms, US 162/B4
Kings (riv.), Ca, US 148/C2
Kings (cr.), Tx, US 150/L7
Kings Beach, Ca, US 146/C4
Kings Canyon NP, Ca, US 148/C2
Kings Island, Oh, US 160/D5
Kings Langley, Eng, UK 30/B1
King's Lynn, Eng, UK 37/G1
Kings Mountain, NC, US 163/G3
Kings Mountain Nat'l Mil. Park, SC, US 163/G3
Kings Park, Austl. 130/K6
Kings Point, NY, US 169/L8
King's Seat (hill), Sc, UK 33/C4
Kings Sutton, Eng, UK 37/E2
Kingsbridge, Eng, UK 36/C6
Kingsburg, Ca, US 148/C2
Kingsbury, Tx, US 151/F3
Kingsclere, Eng, UK 37/E4
Kingscote, Austl. 131/H5
Kingscourt, Ire. 32/D2
Kingsdown, Ks, US 152/E2
Kingsford, Mi, US 157/K5
Kingsland, Eng, UK 36/D2
Kingsland, Ar, US 153/H4
Kingsland, Ga, US 165/H2
Kingsland, Tx, US 151/E2
Kingsley, Mi, US 160/D2
Kingsley (dam), Ne, US 154/D3
Kingsley, Ia, US 155/G2
Kingsnorth, Eng, UK 30/E2
Kingsport, Tn, US 163/F2
Kingston, Austl. 132/C4
Kingston, Austl. 136/F7
Kingston, On, Can. 161/H2
Kingston (cap.), Jam. 177/G2
Kingston, La, US 164/B1
Kingston, Mo, US 155/G4
Kingston, NM, US 149/J4
Kingston, NY, US 161/K4
Kingston, Oh, US 160/E5
Kingston, Ok, US 153/F4
Kingston, Pa, US 168/C1
Kingston, RI, US 161/L4
Kingston, Tn, US 162/E3
Kingston, Wa, US 167/B2
Kingston S.E., Austl. 132/A3
Kingston Springs, Tn, US 162/D2
Kingston upon Hull, Eng, UK 35/H4
Kingston upon Hull (co.), Eng, UK 35/H4
Kingston upon Thames, Eng, UK 30/C2
Kingston Upon Thames (bor.), Eng, UK 30/C2
Kingstown, Austl. 132/D1
Kingstown (cap.), StV. 173/N9
Kingstree, SC, US 163/H4
Kingsville, On, Can. 160/E3
Kingsville, Tx, US 151/F4
Kingsville, Md, US 168/B5
Kingsville Nav. Air Sta., Tx, US 151/F4
Kingswear, Eng, UK 36/C6
Kingswood, Ky, US 162/D2
Kingswood, Eng, UK 36/D4
Kington, Eng, UK 36/D2
Kingushi, D.R. Congo 120/D4
Kingussie, Sc, UK 33/B2
Kingwood, WV, US 161/G5
Kingwood, Tx, US 151/M8
Kiniama, D.R. Congo 123/F1
Kiniati, D.R. Congo 120/D4
Kınık, Turk. 70/C5
Kinistino Ind. Res., Sk, Can. 145/M1
Kinkaid (mt.), Ak, US 171/L4
Kinkaid (lake), Il, US 162/C2
Kinkala, Congo 120/C4
Kinki (prov.), Japan 84/D3
Kinkosi, D.R. Congo 120/C4
Kinloch Rannoch, Sc, UK 33/B3
Kinlochewe, Sc, UK 33/A1
Kinlochleven, Sc, UK 33/B3
Kinloss, Sc, UK 33/C1
Kinmel, Wal, UK 34/E5
Kinmundy, Il, US 162/C1
Kinna, Swe. 40/E3
Kinnairds (pt.), Sc, UK 33/D1
Kinnegad, Ire. 32/C3
Kinnelon, NJ, US 169/H8
Kinnelon (lake), NJ, US 169/H8
Kinneret, Isr. 105/D3
Kinnikinnick, Oh, US 160/E5
Kinnitty, Ire. 32/C3
Kino (riv.), Japan 84/D3
Kinomoto, Japan 83/K5
Kinrooi, Belg. 55/E1
Kinross, Sc, UK 33/C4
Kinsach (riv.), Ger. 59/F4
Kinsale (har.), Ire. 32/B6
Kinsale, Ire. 32/B6
Kinsale, On, Can. 160/U8
Kinsarvik, Nor. 40/B1
Kinsey, Mt, US 145/M4
Kinshasa (pol. reg), D.R. Congo 120/C4
Kinshasa (cap.), D.R. Congo 120/C4
Kinsley, Ks, US 152/E2
Kinsman, Oh, US 160/F4
Kinston, Al, US 165/E2
Kinston, NC, US 163/J3
Kinta, Ok, US 153/G3
Kintampo, Gha. 115/E4
Kintinku, Tanz. 119/A3
Kintnersville, Pa, US 168/C2
Kintore, Sc, UK 33/D2
Kintyre, ND, US 156/E4
Kintyre (isl.), Sc, UK 31/R8
Kintzheim, Fr. 60/D1
Kinu (riv.), Japan 85/F2
Kinvarra, Ire. 32/B3
Kinwow (bay), Mb, Can. 156/F2
Kinyangiri, Tanz. 119/A3
Kinyeti (peak), Sudan 117/G5
Kinzig (riv.), Ger. 42/E4
Kiomboi, Tanz. 119/A3
Kiowa, Ok, US 153/G3
Kiowa, Ks, US 153/E2
Kiowa (cr.), Co, US 154/B4
Kiowa, Co, US 154/B4
Kipange, D.R. Congo 121/F4
Kiparissía, Gre. 49/G4
Kiparissía (gulf), Gre. 67/J3
Kipawa (lake), Qu, Can. 161/G1
Kipawa, Qu, Can. 161/G1
Kipen', Rus. 69/S7
Kipili, Tanz. 121/G4
Kipilingu, D.R. Congo 123/F2
Kipini, Kenya 119/C2
Kipkarren (riv.), Kenya 119/A1
Kipling, Sk, Can. 156/C2
Kipnuk, Ak, US 171/F4
Kippel, Swi. 60/D5
Kippen, Sc, UK 33/B4
Kippens, Nf, Can. 159/H1
Kippure (peak), Ire. 34/B5
Kipti, Ukr. 72/F2
Kipushi, D.R. Congo 123/E1
Kira, Japan 83/M6
Kira Panayía (isl.), Gre. 49/H3
Kirakira, Sol. 136/F6
Kirandul, India 95/D2
Kiranomena, Madg. 125/H7
Kīratpur, India 96/B1
Kirawa, Nga. 116/B3
Kirazlı, Turk. 49/K2
Kirbla, Est. 41/K2
Kirby, Ar, US 153/H3
Kirby, Mt, US 147/K1
Kirbyville, Tx, US 151/H2
Kırcasalih, Turk. 51/H5
Kirchberg, Swi. 60/D3
Kirchberg, Swi. 61/F3
Kirchberg, Ger. 55/G4
Kirchberg, Ger. 59/F1
Kirchberg an der Iller, Ger. 61/G1
Kirchberg an der Jagst, Ger. 58/C4
Kirchdorf, Ger. 53/F3
Kirchdorf an der Krems, Aus. 59/H7
Kirchen, Ger. 55/G2
Kirchenlamitz, Ger. 59/E2
Kirchenthumbach, Ger. 59/E3
Kirchheim, Ger. 61/G1
Kirchheim bei München, Ger. 59/E6
Kirchheim unter Teck, Ger. 58/C5
Kirchheimbolanden, Ger. 58/B3
Kirchhundem, Ger. 53/F6
Kirchlengern, Ger. 53/F4
Kirchlinteln, Ger. 53/G3
Kirchsee (lake), Ger. 61/H2
Kirchseeon, Ger. 59/E6
Kirchweidach, Ger. 59/F6
Kirchzarten, Ger. 60/D2
Kirchzell, Ger. 58/C3
Kircubbin, NI, UK 34/C3
Kircudbright (bay), Sc, UK 34/D2
Kirensk, Rus. 75/L4
Kirgiz Steppe (upland), Kaz. 74/F5
Kirgizskiy (mts.), Kyr. 99/B3
Kiri, D.R. Congo 120/D3
Kiriákion, Gre. 49/H3
Kiribati (ctry.) 136/H5
Kırık, Turk. 102/E1
Kırıkhan, Turk. 104/E1
Kırıkkale, Turk. 102/C2
Kırıkkale (prov.), Turk. 102/C2
Kirikkuduk, China 78/C3
Kirillov, Rus. 68/H4
Kirishi, Rus. 41/Q2
Kirishima-Yaku NP, Japan 84/B5
Kirishima-yama (peak), Japan 84/B5
Kiritimati (Christmas) (isl.), Kiri. 137/K4
Kırkağaç, Turk. 70/C5
Kirkburton, Eng, UK 35/G4
Kirkby, Eng, UK 35/F5
Kirkby in Ashfield, Eng, UK 35/G5
Kirkby Lonsdale, Eng, UK 35/F3
Kirkby Stephen, Eng, UK 35/F3
Kirkbymoorside, Eng, UK 35/H3
Kirkcaldy, Sc, UK 33/C4
Kirkcolm, Sc, UK 34/C2
Kirkconnel, Sc, UK 33/C6
Kirkcowan, Sc, UK 34/D2
Kirkcudbright, Sc, UK 34/D2
Kirke Hvalsø, Den. 39/H7
Kirkee, India 92/B4
Kirkenær, Nor. 40/E1
Kirkham, Eng, UK 35/F4
Kirkhill, Sc, UK 33/B2
Kirkinner, Sc, UK 34/D2
Kirkintilloch, Sc, UK 33/B5
Kirkkonummi (Kyrkslätt), Fin. 41/L1
Kirkland, Qu, Can. 159/N7
Kirkland (hill), Sc, UK 33/C6
Kirkland, Az, US 149/F3
Kirkland, Il, US 155/K2
Kirkland, Wa, US 144/C4
Kirkland Lake, On, Can. 141/H4
Kırklar (peak), Turk. 70/C5
Kırklareli, Turk. 51/H5
Kırklareli (prov.), Turk. 51/H5
Kirklees (co.), Eng, UK 35/G4
Kirkliston, Sc, UK 33/C5
Kirkmichael, IM, UK 34/D3
Kirkmuirhill, Sc, UK 33/C5
Kirkstone (pass), Eng, UK 35/F3
Kirksville, Mo, US 155/H3
Kirkton of Glenisla, Sc, UK 33/C3
Kirkūk, Iraq 103/F3
Kirkwall, Sc, UK 31/V14
Kirkwood, SAfr. 124/D4
Kirkwood, De, US 168/C4
Kirn, Ger. 55/G4
Kirongwe, Tanz. 119/B3
Kiropa, Tanz. 119/A4
Kirov, Rus. 69/L4
Kirov, Rus. 70/E1
Kirovo-Chepetsk, Rus. 69/L4
Kirovohrad, Ukr. 73/G3
Kirovohrads'ka Oblast, Ukr. 70/D2
Kirovsk, Bela. 70/D1
Kirovsk, Rus. 68/G2
Kirovsk, Rus. 69/U7
Kirovs'k, Ukr. 73/K3
Kirovskaya Oblast, Rus. 69/P5
Kirovs'ke, Ukr. 73/H5
Kirovs'ke, Ukr. 73/K3
Kirovskiy, Rus. 71/J3
Kirovskiy, Kaz. 74/H5
Kirovskiy, Rus. 79/L2
Kirriemuir, Sc, UK 33/D3
Kirriemuir, Ab, Can. 145/J2
Kirrweiler, Ger. 58/B4
Kirs, Rus. 69/M4
Kirsanov, Rus. 71/G1
Kırşehir, Turk. 102/C2
Kırşehir (prov.), Turk. 102/C2
Kirtland, NM, US 149/H2
Kirtland (A.F.B.), NM, US 149/J3
Kirtley, Wy, US 154/B2
Kirton, Eng, UK 35/H6
Kirton in Lindsey, Eng, UK 35/H5
Kiruna, Swe. 38/G2
Kirundu, D.R. Congo 121/F3
Kirwin (res.), Ks, US 154/E4
Kirwin, Ks, US 154/E4
Kirwin Nat'l Wildlife Res., Ks, US 152/E1
Kirya, Rus. 69/K5
Kiryū, Japan 85/F2
Kisa, Swe. 40/F3
Kisai, Japan 83/D1
Kisakata, Japan 82/A4
Kisangani, D.R. Congo 121/F2
Kisangani (int'l arpt.), D.R. Congo 121/F2
Kisantu, D.R. Congo 120/C4
Kisar (isl.), Indo. 128/B1
Kisaran, Indo. 89/B2
Kisarawe, Tanz. 119/B3
Kisarazu, Japan 85/F3
Kisauni (Zanzibar) (int'l arpt.), Tanz. 119/B3
Kisber, Hun. 43/K5
Kisbey, Sk, Can. 156/C3
Kisei, Japan 83/K7
Kiselevsk, Rus. 74/J4
Kisenda, D.R. Congo 120/D4
Kisenge, D.R. Congo 121/E5
Kisessa, Tanz. 119/A2
Kīsh, Iran 103/H5
Kīsh (isl.), Iran 103/H5
Kishanda, Tanz. 121/G3
Kishanganj, India 97/F2
Kishangarh, India 96/A2
Kishangarh, India 92/B2
Kishi, Nga. 115/F4
Kishiwada, Japan 83/H7
Kishoreganj, Bang. 97/G3
Kishorganj, Bang. 97/H3
Kishtwar, India 98/C3
Kishwaukee (riv.), Il, US 167/N15
Kisi, D.R. Congo 121/G3
Kisigo (riv.), Tanz. 119/A3
Kisii, Kenya 119/A2
Kisiju, Tanz. 119/B3
Kisiwani, Tanz. 119/B3
Kiska (isl.), Ak, US 75/T4
Kiska (mt.), Ak, US 171/B5
Kiskissink, Qu, Can. 158/A2
Kiskőrös, Hun. 50/D2
Kiskunfélegyháza, Hun. 50/D2
Kiskunhalas, Hun. 50/D2
Kiskunmajsa, Hun. 50/D2
Kiskunsági Nemzeti NP, Hun. 50/D2
Kislovodsk, Rus. 71/G4
Kismaayo, Som. 119/C2
Kismaayo (Chisimayu), Som. 119/C2
Kiso (riv.), Japan 85/E3
Kisogawa, Japan 83/L5
Kisoro, Ugan. 121/G3
Kisozaki, Japan 83/L5
Kisrah, Tun. 112/L7
Kíssamos, Gre. 49/H5
Kissee Mills, Mo, US 153/H2
Kissidougou, Gui. 114/C4
Kissimmee, Fl, US 164/N7
Kissimmee (lake), Fl, US 165/H4
Kissimmee (riv.), Fl, US 165/H4
Kissing, Ger. 58/D6
Kisslegg, Ger. 61/F2
Kissū (peak), Sudan 108/E4
Kissy, SLeo. 114/B4
Kist, Ger. 58/C3
Kisújszállás, Hun. 50/E2
Kisumu, Kenya 119/A2
Kisvárda, Hun. 43/M4
Kiswere, Tanz. 119/B4
Kit Carson, Co, US 152/C1
Kita, Mali 114/C3
Kita (lake), Japan 85/G2
Kita-Ibaraki, Japan 85/G2
Kitaaiki, Japan 83/B1
Kitab, Uzb. 74/G6
Kitadaitō (isl.), Japan 85/L8
Kitagata, Japan 83/L5
Kitakami, Japan 82/B4
Kitakami (mts.), Japan 82/B4
Kitakami (riv.), Japan 82/B4
Kitakata, Japan 85/F2
Kitakawabe, Japan 83/D1
Kitakyūshū, Japan 84/B4
Kitale, Kenya 119/A1
Kitami, Japan 82/C2
Kitami (mts.), Japan 79/N2
Kitamimaki, Japan 83/A1
Kitamoto, Japan 83/D1
Kitan (str.), Japan 83/G7
Kitangari, Tanz. 119/B4
Kitangiri (lake), Tanz. 119/A3
Kitaura, Japan 83/F1
Kitchener, On, Can. 160/F3
Kite, Ga, US 163/F4
Kitendwe, D.R. Congo 121/G4
Kitengo, D.R. Congo 121/F4
Kitgum, Ugan. 121/H2
Kíthira, Gre. 49/H4
Kíthira (isl.), Gre. 67/J3
Kíthnos, Gre. 49/J4
Kíthnos (isl.), Gre. 67/K3
Kithor, India 96/A1
Kitim, Jor. 105/D4
Kitimat, BC, Can. 142/AA13
Kitkatla, BC, Can. 171/M5
Kitomesa, D.R. Congo 120/C4
Kitsap (co.), Wa, US 167/B3
Kitscoty, Ab, Can. 145/J1
Kitsman', Ukr. 72/C3
Kitt Peak National Observatory, Az, US 149/G5
Kittanning, Pa, US 161/G4
Kittatinny (mts.), NJ, US 168/C1
Kittery, Me, US 161/L3
Kitty Hawk, NC, US 163/K2
Kitu, D.R. Congo 121/F4
Kitui, Kenya 119/B2
Kitui Nat'l Rsv., Kenya 119/B2
Kitumala (pt.), PNG 129/G1
Kitumbeine (peak), Tanz. 119/B2
Kitumbini, Tanz. 119/B4
Kitunda, Tanz. 119/A3
Kitunguli, Tanz. 119/C4
Kitwe, Zam. 123/F2
Kitzbühel, Aus. 45/K3
Kitzingen, Ger. 58/D3
Kiunga, Kenya 119/C2
Kiunga, PNG 129/F1
Kiunga Marine Nat'l Res., Kenya 119/C2
Kiuruvesi, Fin. 68/E3
Kiuyu (pt.), Tanz. 119/B3
Kivalina, Ak, US 171/F2
Kivalo (mts.), Fin. 38/H2
Kivertsi, Ukr. 72/C2
Kivi-Vigala, Est. 41/L2
Kivijärvi (lake), Fin. 41/M1
Kivik, Swe. 39/L7
Kiviõli, Est. 41/M2
Kivu (lake), D.R. Congo 107/E5
Kiwai (isl.), PNG 129/F2
Kiwela, D.R. Congo 121/F4
Kiwira, Tanz. 119/A4
Kiyevka, Rus. 71/G3
Kiyevka, Kaz. 99/B1
Kıyıköy, Turk. 51/J5
Kiyokawa, Japan 83/C3
Kiyosu, Japan 83/L5
Kizamba, D.R. Congo 120/D5
Kizel, Rus. 69/N4
Kizëma, Rus. 69/K3
Kizhaba, Azer. 103/G2
Kizil (riv.), China 74/H6
Kızılcadağ, Turk. 104/A1
Kızılcahamam, Turk. 70/E4
Kızıldag NP, Turk. 102/B2
Kızılhisar, Turk. 102/B2
Kızılırmak (riv.), Turk. 70/E4
Kizil'skoye, Rus. 71/L1
Kızıltepe, Turk. 102/E2
Kızılyaka, Turk. 102/C2
Kizimbani, Tanz. 119/B4
Kizimkazi, Tanz. 119/B3
Kizlyar, Rus. 71/H4
Kizu (riv.), Japan 84/E3
Kizu, Japan 83/J6
Kizukuri, Japan 82/B3
Kizyl-Aatrek, Trkm. 103/H2
Kizyl-Su, Trkm. 103/H2
Kjeller, Nor. 38/T8
Kjerkestinden (peak), Nor. 38/F1
Kjevik (int'l arpt.), Nor. 40/C2
Kjølen (mts.), Nor. 38/E2
Klabava (riv.), Czh. 59/G3
Kladanj, Bosn. 50/D3
Kladar, Indo. 129/E2
Kladno, Czh. 59/H2
Kladovo, Yugo. 50/F3
Klaeng, Thai. 94/C3
Klagenfurt, Aus. 45/L3
Klaipėda, Lith. 41/J4
Klakah, Indo. 89/F5
Klamath (riv.), Ca, US 142/B3
Klamath, Ca, US 146/A3
Klamath (mts.), Ca,Or, US 146/B2
Klamath Falls, Or, US 146/C2
Klamath Forest NWR, Or, US 146/C2
Klåmmingen (lake), Swe. 39/A1
Klangenan, Indo. 89/E4
Klapmuts, SAfr. 124/L10
Klar (riv.), Swe. 74/B4
Klarälven (riv.), Swe. 38/E3
Klarup, Den. 40/D3
Klaserie, SAfr. 123/F5
Klášterec nad Ohří, Czh. 59/G2
Klaten, Indo. 89/E4
Klatovy, Czh. 59/G4
Klaukkala, Fin. 39/E4
Klaus, Aus. 61/F3
Klausen (Chiusa), It. 61/H4
Klausenpass (pass), Swi. 61/E4
Klawock, Ak, US 171/M4
Klaza (mt.), Yk, Can. 171/L3
Klazienaveen, Neth. 52/E3
Kleena Kleene, BC, Can. 144/B2
Klein Karas, Namb. 124/B2
Klein Spitzkoppe (peak), Namb. 122/B4
Klein Vaaldoorn, Namb. 124/B3
Klein-Letabarivier (riv.), SAfr. 123/F4
Kleinblittersdorf, Ger. 55/G5
Kleinburg, On, Can. 160/T8
Kleine Elster (riv.), Ger. 43/G3
Kleine Emme (riv.), Swi. 60/E4
Kleine Gete (riv.), Belg. 55/D2
Kleine Laber (riv.), Ger. 59/F5
Kleine Nete (riv.), Belg. 55/D1
Kleinheubach, Ger. 58/C3
Kleinlützel, Swi. 60/D3
Kleinmachnow, Ger. 42/Q7
Kleinmond, SAfr. 124/L11
Kleinolifants (riv.), SAfr. 124/Q12
Kleinrinderfeld, Ger. 58/C3
Kleinsee, SAfr. 124/B3
Kleinwallstadt, Ger. 58/C3
Kleinwinternheim, Ger. 58/B3
Klemme, Ia, US 155/H2
Kleppe, Nor. 40/A2
Kleppestø, Nor. 40/A1
Klerksdorp, SAfr. 124/D2
Klesiv, Ukr. 72/D2
Klet' (peak), Czh. 59/H5
Kletnya, Rus. 70/E1
Kletskiy, Rus. 73/M3
Kleve, Ger. 52/D5
Klichev, Bela. 41/N5
Klichka, Rus. 79/H1
Klickitat (riv.), Wa, US 144/D4
Klickitat, Wa, US 144/D5
Klimovichi, Bela. 70/D1
Klimovo, Rus. 70/E1
Klina, Yugo. 50/E4
Klinaklini (riv.), BC, Can. 144/B2
Kling, Phil. 88/D4
Klingenberg am Main, Ger. 58/C3
Klingenmünster, Ger. 58/B4
Klingenthal, Ger. 59/F2
Klínovec (peak), Czh. 59/F2
Klintehamn, Swe. 40/H3
Klintsy, Rus. 70/E1
Klip (riv.), SAfr. 124/E2
Klippan, Swe. 40/E3
Klipplaat, SAfr. 124/D4
Klisura, Bul. 51/G4
Klitmøller, Den. 40/C3
Kljajićevo, Yugo. 50/D3
Ključ, Bosn. 50/C3
Kłodawa, Pol. 43/K2
Kłodzko, Pol. 43/J3
Klondike, Ga, US 163/M7
Klondyke, Az, US 149/G4
Klöntaler-See (lake), Swi. 61/E3
Kloosterzande, Neth. 52/B6
Kloster, Ger. 40/E4
Klosterbach (riv.), Ger. 53/F3
Klosterlechfeld, Ger. 61/G1
Klosterneuburg, Aus. 51/N7
Klosters, Swi. 61/F4
Klosterwappen (peak), Aus. 43/H5
Kloten, Swi. 61/E3
Klothuhta Zayat, Myan. 86/C5
Klötze, Ger. 42/F2
Kluane, Yk, Can. 171/L3
Kluane NP, Yk, Can. 171/K3
Kluczbork, Pol. 43/K3
Klundert, Neth. 52/B5
Klukshu, Yk, Can. 171/L3
Klukwan, Ak, US 171/L3
Klyavlino, Rus. 69/M5
Klyaz'ma (riv.), Rus. 68/J4
Klyuchevskaya (peak), Rus. 75/S4
Klyuchi, Rus. 75/R4
Knaphill, Eng, UK 30/B3
Knapp (hill), Wi, US 155/J1
Knappa, Or, US 144/C4
Knapstad, Nor. 38/T9
Knäred, Swe. 40/E3
Knaresborough, Eng, UK 35/G3
Knebworth, Eng, UK 37/F3
Kneehills (cr.), Ab, Can. 145/H2
Knetzgau, Ger. 58/D3
Knezha, Bul. 51/G4
Knife (riv.), ND, US 156/C4
Knife River Indian Villages Nat'l Hist. Site, ND, US 156/D4
Knight (inlet), BC, Can. 144/B2
Knighton, Wal, UK 36/C2
Knights, Fl, US 164/L7
Knightsen, Ca, US 167/L11
Knin, Cro. 50/C3
Knippa, Tx, US 151/E3
Knislinge, Swe. 39/L6
Knittelfeld, Aus. 45/L3
Knittlingen, Ger. 58/B4
Knivsta, Swe. 40/G2
Knížecí Stolec (peak), Czh. 59/H5
Knížecí Strom (peak), Czh. 59/F3
Knjaževac, Yugo. 50/F4
Knob (peak), Phil. 91/F1
Knob (cape), Austl. 130/C5
Knobby (pt.), Austl. 130/B4
Knobel, Ar, US 162/B2
Knoch (hill), Sc, UK 33/D1
Knock, Ire. 32/B2
Knockadoon Head (pt.), Ire. 32/C6
Knockalongy (peak), Ire. 32/B1
Knockanaffrin (peak), Ire. 32/C5
Knockanore (mtn.), Ire. 32/A4
Knockboy (peak), Ire. 32/A6
Knockcloghrim, NI, UK 34/B2
Knockeirke (peak), Ire. 32/A6
Knocklong, Ire. 32/B5
Knockmealdown (peak), Ire. 32/C5
Knockmealdown (mts.), Ire. 32/B5
Knocknagashel, Ire. 32/A5
Knocknamaddree (peak), Ire. 32/A7
Knockowen (peak), Ire. 32/A6
Knockshanahullion (peak), Ire. 32/B5
Knoll (pt.), Namb. 122/B5
Knøsen (peak), Den. 40/D3
Knösen (pt.), Swe. 40/E4
Knosós (Knossos) (ruin), Gre. 49/J5
Knossos (Knosós) (ruin), Gre. 49/J5
Knott, Tx, US 151/D1
Knott End, Eng, UK 35/F4
Knottingley, Eng, UK 35/G4
Knott's Berry Farm, Ca, US 166/G8
Knotts Island, NC, US 163/K2
Knotty Green, Eng, UK 30/B2
Knowl Hill, Eng, UK 30/A2
Knowsley (co.), Eng, UK 35/F5
Knox, ND, US 156/E3
Knox, Pa, US 161/G4
Knox, In, US 160/C4
Knox (coast), Ant. 192/G
Knox (cape), BC, Can. 140/C3
Knox (nbrhd.), Austl. 132/G5
Knox City, Tx, US 152/E4
Knoxville, Ms, US 164/C2
Knoxville, Ia, US 155/H3
Knoxville, Tn, US 162/F3
Knoxville, Ga, US 162/F4
Knutby, Swe. 39/B1
Knutsford, Eng, UK 35/F5
Knysna, SAfr. 124/C4
Ko (riv.), Sen. 114/B3
Ko (peak), Rus. 79/M2
Ko Samut NP, Thai. 94/C3
Ko-saki (pt.), Japan 84/A3
Koanaka (hills), Bots. 122/D4
Koani, Tanz. 119/B3
Koāth, India 97/E3
Koba, Indo. 89/D3
Kobar Sink (depr.), Eth. 118/B2
Kobayashi, Japan 84/B5
Kōbe, Japan 83/H6
Kobelyaky, Ukr. 73/H3
København (int'l arpt.), Den. 40/E4
København (co.), Den. 39/J7
København (Copenhagen) (cap.), Den. 39/J7
Kobenni, Mrta. 114/C3
Kobern-Gondorf, Ger. 55/G3
Kobipato (peak), Indo. 91/G4
Koblach, Aus. 61/F3
Koblenz, Swi. 61/E2
Koblenz, Ger. 55/G3
K'obo, Eth. 118/A2
Kobowan (swamp), Sudan 117/G4
Kobozha, Rus. 68/G4
Kobra, Rus. 69/L3
Kobroor (isl.), Indo. 91/H5
Kobryn, Bela. 70/C1
Kobu, SKor. 81/D5
Kobuchizawa, Japan 83/A2
Kobuk, Ak, US 171/G2
Kobuk (riv.), Ak, US 171/G2
Kobuk Valley NP, Ak, US 171/G2
K'obulet'i, Geo. 71/G4
Kobushi-ga-take (peak), Japan 85/F3
Kocába (riv.), Czh. 59/H3
Kocaeli (prov.), Turk. 70/D4
Koçalı, Turk. 102/D2
Kočani, FYROM 49/H2
Kocapınar, Turk. 103/E2
Kočevje, Slov. 45/L4
Koch (isl.), Nun, Can. 141/J2
Koch'ang, SKor. 81/D5
Koch'ang, SKor. 81/D5
Kochel am See, Ger. 61/H2
Kochelsee (lake), Ger. 61/H2
Kochen'ga, Rus. 69/J3
Kocher (riv.), Ger. 45/H2
Kocherinovo, Bul. 49/H1
Kochetovka, Rus. 71/G1
Kochevo, Rus. 69/M4
Kōchi (pref.), Japan 84/C4
Kōchi, Japan 84/C4
Kochmes, Rus. 69/P2
Kochubey, Rus. 71/H3
Kochubeyevskoye, Rus. 73/L5
Kochugaon, India 97/H2
Kodaira, Japan 83/C2
Kodala, India 95/E2
Kodama, Japan 83/C1
Kodāri, Nepal 97/E2
Kodarmā, India 97/E3
Kodiak, Ak, US 171/H4
Kodiak (isl.), Ak, US 171/H4
Kodinār, India 101/K4
Kodomari, Japan 82/B3
Kodry (hills), Mol. 51/H2
Kodyma, Ukr. 72/E3
Koekelare, Belg. 54/B1
Koel (riv.), India 92/D3
Koes, Namb. 124/B2
Koesan, SKor. 81/D4
Koetari (riv.), Sur. 181/G4
Kofa (mts.), Az, US 149/E4
Kofa NWR, Az, US 149/E4
Kofçaz, Turk. 51/H5
Kofelē, Eth. 118/A4
Koffiefontein, SAfr. 124/D3
Kofiau (isl.), Indo. 91/G4
Koforidua, Gha. 115/E5
Kōfu, Japan 85/F3
Koga, Japan 85/F2
Koga, Tanz. 121/H4
Koganei, Japan 83/D2
Kogarah, Austl. 133/E1
Køge (bay), Den. 40/E4
Kogi, Nga. 115/G4
Kogon (riv.), Gui. 114/B4
Kŏgum (isl.), SKor. 81/D5
Kohāt, Pak. 98/A3
Kohila, Est. 41/L2
Kohīma, India 86/B3
Kohkīlūyeh and Bovīr Aḩmadi (gov.), Iran 103/G4
Kohler, Wi, US 160/C3
Kohls Ranch, Az, US 149/G3
Kohoku, Japan 83/K5
Kohout (peak), Czh. 59/H5
Kohtla-Järve, Est. 41/M2
Kohŭng, SKor. 81/D5
Kohunlich (ruin), Mex. 176/D2
Koichab (riv.), Namb. 122/B5
Koidern, Yk, Can. 171/K3
Koidu, SLeo. 114/C4
Koigi, Est. 41/L2
Koihoa, India 93/F6
Koilābās, Nepal 96/D2
Koímisis, Gre. 49/H2
Koindu, SLeo. 114/C4
Koito, Kenya 119/B2
Koito (riv.), Japan 83/D3
Koiva (riv.), Lat. 41/M3
Kŏje (isl.), SKor. 84/A3
Kojonup, Austl. 130/C5
Kojšovská (peak), Slvk. 43/L4
Kok (riv.), Myan. 94/B1
Kōka, Japan 83/K6
K'ok'a Gidib (dam), Eth. 118/A3
Kokai (riv.), Japan 83/E2
Kökar (isl.), Fin. 41/J3
Kokas, Indo. 91/H4
Kokemäenjoki (riv.), Fin. 41/J1
Kokhonak, Ak, US 171/H4
Kokhanovo, Bela. 41/N4
Kokkola (Karleby), Fin. 68/D3
Koknese, Lat. 41/L3
Koko, Nga. 115/G5
Koko, Nga. 115/G4
Kokoda, PNG 129/G2
Kokofata, Mali 114/C3
Kokola, D.R. Congo 121/G2
Kokomo, In, US 160/C4
Kokonau, Indo. 91/J4
Kokong, Bots. 122/D5
Kokonjärvi (lake), Fin. 39/D3
Kokrajhar, India 97/H2
Koksan, NKor. 81/D3
Kokshaal-Tau (mts.), Kyr. 99/C3
Kökshetaū, Kaz. 99/A1
Koksijde, Belg. 54/B1
Koksoak (riv.), Qu, Can. 141/K3
Koksovyy, Rus. 73/L3
Kokstad, SAfr. 124/E3
Kokubu, Japan 84/B5
Kokuy, Rus. 79/H1
Kol, PNG 129/G1
Kola (isl.), Indo. 91/H5
Kola (riv.), Rus. 68/G1
Kola (pen.), Rus. 192/D
Kolachel, India 95/C4
Kolahun, Libr. 114/C4
Kolaka, Indo. 91/F4
Kolāras, India 96/A3
Kolašin, Yugo. 50/D4
Kolbäck, Swe. 40/G2
Kolbano, Indo. 128/B2
Kolbio, Kenya 119/C2
Kolbotn, Nor. 38/S8
Kolbus, Sudan 116/D2
Kolbuszowa, Pol. 43/L3
Kolda, Sen. 114/B3
Kolda (pol. reg.), Sen. 114/B3
Kolding, Den. 40/C4
Kole, D.R. Congo 121/F2
Kolebira, India 97/E4
Kölen (mts.), Swe. 38/E2
Kolenté, Gui. 114/B4
Kolepom (Yos Sudarso) (isl.), Indo. 136/C5
Kolezhma, Rus. 68/G2
Kolgaküla, Est. 41/L2
Kolgompya (cape), Rus. 41/N2
Kolguyev (isl.), Rus. 192/C
Koliba (riv.), Gui. 114/B3
Koliganek, Ak, US 171/G4
Kolín, Czh. 43/H3
Kolind, Den. 39/G6
Koliya, Gui. 114/B4
Kolka, Lat. 41/K3
Kolkasrags (pt.), Lat. 41/K3
Kolkhozabad, Taj. 101/J1
Kollbach (riv.), Ger. 59/F5
Kollnburg, Ger. 59/F4
Kollum, Neth. 52/D2
Kolmanskop, Namb. 124/A2
Köln (Cologne), Ger. 55/F2
Kolno, Pol. 43/L2
Koło, Pol. 70/A1
Kolo, Tanz. 119/A3
Kołobrzeg, Pol. 40/F4
Kolofata, Camr. 116/B3
Kologriv, Rus. 69/K4
Kolokani, Mali 114/C3
Kololo, Eth. 118/B4
Kolomna, Rus. 68/H5
Kolomyya, Ukr. 72/C3
Kolondiéba, Mali 114/D4
Kolongotomo, Mali 114/D3
Kolonnawa, SrL. 95/C5
Kolosib, India 86/B3
Kolossa (riv.), Mali 114/D3
Kolpashevo, Rus. 74/J4
Kolpino, Rus. 69/T7
Kolpny, Rus. 70/F1
Kolpyta, Ukr. 72/F2
Kolsva, Swe. 40/F2
Kolubara (riv.), Yugo. 50/D3
Koluszki, Pol. 43/K3
Koluton (riv.), Kaz. 99/A1
Kolva (riv.), Rus. 69/N2
Kolwezi, D.R. Congo 121/F5
Kolyma (riv.), Rus. 77/Q3
Kolyma (range), Rus. 77/Q3
Kolyma Lowland (plain), Rus. 75/R2
Kolyshley, Rus. 71/H1
Kom (peak), Bul. 51/F4
Kom (riv.), Gabon 120/C2
Koma, Myan. 94/B3
Koma (riv.), Japan 83/C2
Komádi, Hun. 50/E2
Komadugu Gana (riv.), Nga. 115/H4
Komadugu Yobe (riv.), Nga. 115/H3
Komae, Japan 83/D2
Komagane, Japan 85/E3
Komaki, Japan 83/L5
Komaki (arpt.), Japan 83/L5
Komanda, D.R. Congo 121/G2
Komandorskiye (isls.), Rus. 77/R4
Komarichi, Rus. 73/H1
Komarin, Bela. 72/F2
Komárno, Slvk. 50/D2
Komárom, Hun. 50/D2
Komárom-Esztergom (prov.), Hun. 50/D2
Komatipoort, SAfr. 123/F5
Komatirivier (riv.), SAfr. 124/Q13
Komatlapeta, India 95/D2
Komatsu, Japan 84/E2
Komatsu (int'l arpt.), Japan 84/E2
Komatsushima, Japan 84/D3
Komba, D.R. Congo 121/E2
Kombat, Namb. 122/C3
Kombe, D.R. Congo 121/F4
Kombissiri, Burk. 115/E3
Kome (isl.), Ugan. 119/A2
Komering (riv.), Indo. 89/D4
Komi-Permyatskiy Aut. Okrug, Rus. 69/M2
Komjatice, Slvk. 43/K4
Komló, Hun. 50/D2
Kommetjie, SAfr. 124/L11
Kommunar, Rus. 41/P2
Komo, PNG 129/F1
Komodo (isl.), Indo. 91/E5
Komodo Island NP, Indo. 91/E5
Komodougou, Gui. 114/C4
Komoé (riv.), C.d'Iv. 114/E5
Komono, Congo 120/C3
Komono, Japan 83/L5
Komoran (isl.), Indo. 91/J5
Komoro, Japan 83/A1
Komotiní, Gre. 49/J2
Kompasberg (peak), SAfr. 124/D3
Kompiam, PNG 129/F1
Komsomolets (isl.), Rus. 77/J1
Komsomol's'k, Ukr. 73/G3
Komsomol'sk-na-Amure, Rus. 79/M1
Komsomol's'ke, Ukr. 73/J3
Komsomol's'ke, Ukr. 73/K4
Komsomol'skiy, Rus. 69/P2
Komsomol'skiy, Rus. 69/K5
Komsomol'skiy, Kaz. 71/K3
Komsomol'skiy, Rus. 74/G3
Komsomol'skiy, Rus. 71/H3
Komsomol'skoye, Rus. 71/H2
Komukanti, Namb. 122/C3
Kömür (pt.), Turk. 49/K3
Komysh-Zorya, Ukr. 73/J4
Komyshnya, Ukr. 73/G2
Kon (riv.), Kaz. 99/A2
Kon Plong, Viet. 94/E3
Kon Tum, Viet. 94/D3
Konabonou, C.d'Iv. 114/D5
Konakovo, Rus. 68/H4
Kōnan, Japan 83/K6
Kōnan, Japan 83/L5
Kōnan, Japan 83/C1
Konar (riv.), Afg. 98/A2
Konār (riv.), India 97/E4
Konār (res.), India 97/E4
Konar-e Khāş, Afg. 98/A2
Konārak, Iran 101/H3
Konārak, India 95/E2
Konawa, Ok, US 153/F3
Konaweha (riv.), Indo. 91/F4
Konda (riv.), Rus. 78/G1
Konda, Japan 83/H6
Kondagaon, India 95/D2
Kondé Sounga, Congo 120/B4
Kondinin, Austl. 130/C5
Kondoa, Tanz. 119/A3
Kondopoga, Rus. 68/G3
Kondūz, Afg. 74/G6
Koné, NCal. 137/U12
Konetsgor'ye, Rus. 68/J3
Kong, C.d'Iv. 114/D4
Kong (isl.), Camb. 94/C4
Kong (riv.), Laos 94/D3
Kong Kong (riv.), Sudan 117/G4
Kong Krailat, Thai. 94/B2
Kong Miao, China 80/D4
Kongapatalabata, Indo. 128/D1
Kongbo, CAfr. 116/D4
Kongiganak, Ak, US 171/F4
Kongju, SKor. 81/D4
Kongnŭg (riv.), SKor. 81/F6
Kongō-zan (peak), Japan 83/J7
Kongola, Namb. 122/D3
Kongolo, D.R. Congo 121/F4
Kongor, Sudan 117/F4
Kongoussi, Burk. 115/E3
Kongsberg, Nor. 40/C2
Kongsvinger, Nor. 40/E1
Kongtan, China 86/E2
Kongué, Chutes de (falls), Gabon 120/C2
Kongur (peak), China 99/C4
Kongwa, Tanz. 119/B3
Koniecpol, Pol. 43/K3
Königs Wusterhausen, Ger. 42/Q7
Königsberg in Bayern, Ger. 58/D2
Königsberg-Stein, Ger. 58/B5
Königsbronn, Ger. 58/D5
Königsbrunn, Ger. 61/G1
Königsdorf, Ger. 61/H2
Königsfeld im Schwarzwald, Ger. 61/E1
Königslutter am Elm, Ger. 53/H4
Königstein im Taunus, Ger. 58/B2
Königswinter, Ger. 55/G2
Konin, Pol. 43/K2
Konindou, Gui. 114/C4
Konispol, Alb. 49/G3
Kónitsa, Gre. 49/G2
Köniz, Swi. 60/D4
Konjic, Bosn. 50/C4
Könkämäeno (riv.), Fin. 68/D1
Konkiep (riv.), Namb. 122/C5
Konkiep, Namb. 124/B2
Konkola, Zam. 123/E2
Konkori, Gha. 115/E4
Konkouré (riv.), Gui. 114/B4
Konkourou-Bamingui, Rsv. de Faune du, CAfr. 116/D4
Konnevesi, Fin. 68/E3
Konobougou, Mali 114/D3
Konolfingen, Swi. 60/D4
Konosha, Rus. 68/J3
Kōnosu, Japan 83/D1
Konotop, Ukr. 73/G2
Konqi (riv.), China 74/J5
Konsen (plat.), Japan 82/D2
Końskie, Pol. 43/L3
Konso, Eth. 117/H4
Konstancin-Jeziorna, Pol. 43/L2
Konstantinovka, Ukr. 73/H3
Konstantinovsk, Rus. 73/L4
Konstantynówłódzki, Pol. 43/K3
Konstanz, Ger. 61/F2
Kontagora, Nga. 115/G4
Kontcha, Camr. 116/B4
Konteyevo, Rus. 68/J4
Kontich, Belg. 55/D1
Kontiolahti, Fin. 68/F3
Konuralp, Turk. 51/K5
Kóny, Hun. 50/C2
Konya, Turk. 102/C2
Konya (prov.), Turk. 102/C2
Konz, Ger. 55/F4
Konza, Kenya 119/B2
Koo-wee-rup, Austl. 133/B4
Koocenusa (lake), Mt, US 144/G3
Koog aan de Zaan, Neth. 52/B4
Koolpinyah, Austl. 128/C3
Koolyanobbing, Austl. 130/C4
Koondrook, Austl. 133/B2
Koonga, Est. 41/L2
Koonibba, Austl. 131/G4
Koontz Lake, In, US 160/C4
Kooparmora, Swe. 39/B1
Koorawatha, Austl. 133/D2
Koorda, Austl. 130/C4
Koosa, Est. 41/M2
Koosharem, Ut, US 149/G1
Kooskia, Id, US 144/G4
Kootenai Nat'l Wild. Ref., Id, US 144/F3
Kootenay (lake), BC, Can. 140/E3
Kootenay (riv.), BC, Can. 144/G2
Kootenay NP, BC, Can. 144/F2
Kootingal, Austl. 132/D1
Kop (pass), Turk. 102/E1
Kopāganj, India 96/D2
Kopaigo, PNG 129/F1
Kopargaon, India 95/B2
Kopargo, Ben. 115/F4
Kópavogur, Ice. 38/N7
Kope (peak), C.d'Iv. 114/D5
Köpenick, Ger. 42/Q7
Koper, Slov. 45/K4
Kopervik, Nor. 40/A2
Kopeysk, Rus. 69/P5
Kopfing im Innkreis, Aus. 59/G6
Kopia, D.R. Congo 121/E2
Kopili (riv.), India 86/B3
Köping, Swe. 40/G2
Koplik, Alb. 49/F1
Kopondei (cape), Indo. 128/A2
Koporskiy (bay), Rus. 41/N2
Koppang, Nor. 40/D1
Kopparberg (co.), Swe. 38/E3
Kopparberg, Swe. 40/F2
Koppi (riv.), Rus. 79/M2
Koppies, SAfr. 124/D2

Koprivnica, Cro. 50/C2
Koprivshtitsa, Bul. 51/G4
Kopru (riv.), Turk. 104/B1
Köprülü, Turk. 104/C1
Köprülü Kanyon NP, Turk. 102/B2
Kop'ung, NKor. 81/C2
Kopyl', Bela. 70/C1
Kopys', Bela. 41/P4
Kor (riv.), Iran 100/F2
Kora, India 96/C2
Kōra, Japan 83/K5
Kora NP, Kenya 119/B2
Korab (peak), Alb. 49/G2
Koráb (peak), Czh. 59/G4
Korablino, Rus. 70/G1
K'orahē, Eth. 118/C4
Korakuen Garden, Japan 84/C3
Koraluk (riv.), Nf, Can. 141/K3
Koramlik, China 99/E4
Korana (riv.), Cro. 45/L4
Korazim NP, Isr. 105/D3
Korba, India 96/D4
Korbach, Ger. 53/F6
K'orbeta, Eth. 118/A2
Korbu (peak), Malay. 89/C1
Korçë, Alb. 49/G2
Korčula (isl.), Cro. 67/H2
Korčula, Cro. 50/C4
Korčulanski Kanal (chan.), It. 48/E1
Korčulanski Kanal (chan.), Cro. 50/C4
Kord Kūy, Iran 103/H2
Kordel, Ger. 55/F4
Kordestān (gov.), Iran 103/F3
Korea (bay), China,NKor. 75/N6
Korea (str.), Japan,Skor. 75/P6
Korean Folk Village, SKor. 81/G7
Korem, Eth. 118/A2
Korenovsk, Rus. 73/K5
Korets', Ukr. 72/D2
Korf, Rus. 75/S3
Korgas, China 99/D3
Korhogo, C.d'Iv. 114/D4
Korido, Indo. 91/J4
Korienzé, Mali 114/E3
Korim, Indo. 91/J4
Korinós, Gre. 49/H2
Kórinthos (Corinth), Gre. 49/H4
Kórinthos (Corinth) (ruin), Gre. 49/H4
Kóris-Hegy (peak), Hun. 50/C2
Köritz, Ger. 42/G2
Kōriyama, Japan 85/G2
Korizo, Passe de (pass), Chad 108/B4
Korkino, Rus. 69/P5
Korkodon (riv.), Rus. 75/R3
Korkuteli, Turk. 104/B1
Korla, China 99/E3
Kormakiti (cape), Cyp. 104/C2
Körmend, Hun. 50/C2
Kornat (isl.), Cro. 45/L5
Körner, Ger. 53/H6
Korneuburg, Aus. 51/N7
Kornman, Co, US 152/C1
Korntal-Münchingen, Ger. 58/C5
Kornwestheim, Ger. 58/C5
Koro, C.d'Iv. 114/D4
Koro, Mali 114/E3
Koro (sea), Fiji 137/Z18
Koro Toro, Chad 116/C1
Koroba, PNG 129/F1
Korocha, Rus. 73/J2
Köroğlu (peak), Turk. 70/D4
Korogwe, Tanz. 119/B3
Koroit, Austl. 132/B3
Koronadal, Phil. 88/D4
Korónia (lake), Gre. 49/H2
Koronowo, Pol. 43/J2
Koropíon, Gre. 49/N9
Koror (cap.), Palau 136/C4
Körös (riv.), Hun. 50/E2
Korosten', Ukr. 72/E2
Korostyshiv, Ukr. 72/E2
Korotaikha (riv.), Rus. 69/P1
Korovin (mt.), Ak, US 171/D5
Korovino, Rus. 71/K1
Korpo (Korppoo), Fin. 41/J1
Korppoo (Korpo), Fin. 41/J1
Korsakov, Rus. 79/N2
Korschenbroich, Ger. 52/D6
Korsö (isl.), Swe. 39/B1
Korsør, Den. 40/D4
Korsun'-Shevchenkivs'kyy, Ukr. 72/F3
Korsze, Pol. 41/J4
Kortemark, Belg. 54/C1
Kortenaken, Belg. 55/E2
Kortenberg, Belg. 55/D2
Kortessem, Belg. 55/E2
Korti Linchang, China 99/E2
Kortrijk, Belg. 54/C2
Kortsevo, Rus. 68/J4
Korumburra, Austl. 133/B4
Korup, PN de, Camr. 115/H5
Koryak (range), Rus. 77/R3
Koryakskiy Aut. Okrug, Rus. 75/S3
Koryazhma, Rus. 69/K3
Kōryō, Japan 83/J6
Koryŏng, SKor. 81/E5
Koryukivka, Ukr. 72/G2
Kós, Gre. 102/A2
Kós (isl.), Gre. 102/A2
Kosai, Japan 85/E3
Kosai, Japan 83/A2
Kosan, NKor. 81/D3
Kosaya Gora, Rus. 70/F1
Koschagyl, Kaz. 71/K3
Kösching, Ger. 59/E5
Kościan, Pol. 43/J2
Kościerzyna, Pol. 40/G4
Kosciusko, Ms, US 162/C4
Kosciusko (mt.), Austl. 133/D3
Köse, Turk. 102/D1
Kose, Est. 41/L2
Kosei, Japan 83/K6
Kosha, Sudan 109/F4
Koshigaya, Japan 85/F3
Koshiki (isls.), Japan 85/K5
Koshkar, Kaz. 71/K3
Koshkonong, Mo, US 153/J2
Koshkonong (lake), Wi, US 155/K2
Kosi (zone), Nepal 97/F2
Kosi, India 96/A2
Kosi (riv.), India 92/E2
Košice, Slvk. 43/L4
Košický (pol. reg.), Slvk. 43/L4
Kosiv, Ukr. 72/C3
Koski, Fin. 39/F3
Koskinoú, Gre. 102/B2
Koslan, Rus. 69/L3
Kosoba (peak), Kaz. 99/C2
Kosŏng, SKor. 81/E5
Kosŏng, NKor. 81/E3
Kosovo (reg.), Yugo. 49/G1
Kosovo (prov.), Yugo. 50/E4
Kosovo Polje, Yugo. 50/E4
Kosovska Kamenica, Yugo. 50/E4
Kosovska Mitrovica, Yugo. 50/E4
Kosový (riv.), Czh. 59/F3
Kosrae (isl.), Micr. 136/F4
Kosse, Tx, US 151/F2
Kossi (prov.), Burk. 114/D3
Kossou (lake), C.d'Iv. 114/D5
Kosta, Swe. 40/F3
Kostelec nad Černými Lesy, Czh. 59/H3
Koster, SAfr. 124/D2
Kostinbrod, Bul. 51/F4
Kostomuksha, Rus. 68/F2
Kostopil', Ukr. 72/D2
Kostromskaya Oblast, Rus. 68/J4
Kostroma (riv.), Rus. 68/J4
Kostroma, Rus. 68/J4
Kostrzyn, Pol. 43/H2
Kostrzyn, Pol. 43/J2
Kostyantynivka, Ukr. 73/J3
Kostyantynivka, Ukr. 73/H4
Kostyukovichi, Bela. 70/E1
Kosuge, Japan 83/B2
Kos'va (riv.), Rus. 69/N4
Kos'yu (riv.), Rus. 69/N2
Kos'yu, Rus. 69/N2
Koszalin, Pol. 40/G4
Kószeg, Hun. 50/C2
Kot Addu, Pak. 98/A4
Kot Fateh, India 98/C4
Kot Kapūra, India 98/C4
Kot Mūmin, Pak. 98/B3
Kot Rādha Kishan, Pak. 98/C4
Kot Samāba, Pak. 98/A5
Kot Sārang, Pak. 98/B3
Kota, India 96/D4
Kota, India 92/C2
Kōta, Japan 83/M6
Kota Baharu, Malay. 89/C1
Kota Belud, Malay. 88/B4
Kota Kinabalu (int'l arpt.), Malay. 88/B4
Kota Kinabalu, Malay. 88/B4
Kota Tinggi, Malay. 89/C2
Kotaagung, Indo. 89/D4
Kotabaru, Indo. 91/E4
Kotabaru, Indo. 89/C3
Kotabesi, Indo. 90/D4
Kotabumi, Indo. 89/D4
Kotabunan, Indo. 91/F3
Kotadaik, Indo. 89/D3
Kotajawa, Indo. 89/D4
Kotapād, India 95/D2
Kotapinang, Indo. 89/C2
Kotatengah, Indo. 89/C2
Kotdwāra, India 96/B1
Kotel, Bul. 51/H4
Kotel'nich, Rus. 69/L4
Kotel'nikovo, Rus. 71/G3
Kotel'nyy (isl.), Rus. 75/P2
Kotel'va, Ukr. 73/H2
Kotgarh, India 98/D4
Kothagūdem, India 95/D2
Köthen, Ger. 42/F3
Kotido, Ugan. 119/A1
Kotka, Fin. 41/M1
Kotla, India 98/D3
Kotlas, Rus. 69/K3
Kotli, Pak. 98/B3
Kotli Lohārān, Pak. 98/C3
Kotlik, Ak, US 171/F3
Kotlin (isl.), Rus. 69/S7
Kotly, Rus. 41/N2
Kotō, Japan 83/K5
Kotoka (int'l arpt.), Gha. 115/E5
Koton Karifi, Nga. 115/G4
Kotor, Yugo. 50/D4
Kotor Varoš, Bosn. 50/C3
Kotovo, Rus. 71/H2
Kotovsk, Rus. 71/G1
Kotovs'k, Ukr. 72/E4
Kotri, Pak. 101/J3
Kottai Malai (peak), India 95/C4
Kottayam, India 95/C4
Kotte (Sri Jayawardanapura), SrL. 95/C5
Kotto (riv.), CAfr. 116/D4
Kotuy (riv.), Rus. 77/K3
Kotzebue, Ak, US 171/F2
Kotzebue (sound), Ak, US 171/E2
Kötzting, Ger. 59/F4
Kouandé, Ben. 115/F4
Kouango, CAfr. 116/C4
Kouba Olanga, Chad 116/C2
Koubia, Gui. 114/C4
Kouchibouguac (bay), Nb, Can. 158/E2
Kouchibouguac NP, NB, Can. 158/E2
Koudougou, Burk. 115/E3
Koufonísion (isl.), Gre. 49/J5
Kougarok (mt.), Ak, US 171/E2
Kougoulé, Gabon 120/B2
Kouhu, Tai. 87/J4
Kouilou, Congo 120/B4
Kouilou (riv.), Congo 120/C3
Koukdjuak (riv.), Nun, Can. 141/J2
Kouki, CAfr. 116/C4
Koukourou, CAfr. 116/D4
Koula-Moutou, Gabon 120/C3
Koulé, Gui. 114/C4
Koulikoro (pol. reg.), Mali 114/C3
Koulikoro, Mali 114/D3
Koulou, Niger 115/F3
Koulountou (riv.), Sen. 114/B3
Koum, Camr. 116/B3
Koumac, NCal. 137/U12
Koumala, Austl. 134/C3
Koumameyong, Gabon 120/B2
Koumandougou, Gui. 114/D4
Koumantou, Mali 114/D4
Koumban, Gui. 114/C4
Koumbi Saleh (ruin), Mrta. 114/D3
Koumbia, Gui. 114/B4
Koumi, Japan 83/A1
Koumra, Chad 116/C3
Koundara, Gui. 114/B3
Koundé, CAfr. 116/B4
Koundian, Mali 114/C3
Koundou, Gui. 114/C4
Koungheul, Sen. 114/B3
Kouno, Chad 116/C3
Kounradskiy, Kaz. 99/C2
Kountze, Tx, US 151/G2
Koupé (peak), Camr. 120/B1
Koupela, Burk. 115/E3
Kouraïa Konkouré, Gui. 114/B4
Kouritenga (prov.), Burk. 115/E3
Kourou, FrG. 182/C1
Kourouba, Mali 114/C3
Kouroussa, Gui. 114/C4
Koury, Mali 114/D3
Koussi (peak), Chad 108/C5
Koutiala, Mali 114/D3
Kouto, C.d'Iv. 114/D4
Kouvola, Fin. 41/M1
Kouyou (riv.), Congo 120/C3
Kovačica, Yugo. 50/E3
Kovada Gölü NP, Turk. 102/B2
Kovalam, India 95/C4
Kovashi (riv.), Rus. 69/S7
Kovda, Rus. 68/G2
Kovdor, Rus. 68/F2
Kovdozero (lake), Rus. 38/J2
Kovel', Ukr. 72/C2
Kovilj, Yugo. 50/E3
Kovilpatti, India 95/C4
Kovrov, Rus. 68/J4
Kovūr, India 95/C3
Kovylkino, Rus. 71/G1
Kowanyama Abor. Land, Austl. 129/F3
Kowanyama Aboriginal Community, Austl. 134/A1
Kowe, D.R. Congo 121/F3
Kowkcheh (riv.), Afg. 99/A4
Kowloon, China 87/G4
Kowŏn, NKor. 79/K4
Kowt-e 'Ashrow, Afg. 101/J2
Koxlax, China 99/D4
Kōyaguchi, Japan 83/J7
Koyama, Gui. 114/C5
Kōyama, Japan 84/B5
Koyang, SKor. 81/F6
Koynare, Bul. 51/G4
Koyuk, Ak, US 171/F3
Koyukuk (riv.), Ak, US 171/H2
Kozacha Lopan', Ukr. 73/J2
Kozakai, Japan 83/M6
Kōzaki, Japan 83/E2
Kozaklı, Turk. 102/C2
Kozan, Turk. 102/C2
Kozáni, Gre. 49/G2
Kozara NP, Aus. 50/C3
Kozel'shchyna, Ukr. 73/G3
Kozel'sk, Rus. 70/E1
Kozha, Rus. 69/L4
Kozhikode (Calicut), India 95/B4
Kozhozero (lake), Rus. 68/H3
Kozhva, Rus. 69/N2
Kozhva (riv.), Rus. 69/M2
Kozienice, Pol. 43/L3
Kozloduy, Bul. 51/F4
Kozlovo, Rus. 68/H4
Kozlu, Turk. 70/D4
Kozluk, Turk. 102/E2
Koźmin, Pol. 43/J3
Koz'mino, Rus. 69/L3
Koznitsa (peak), Bul. 51/F4
Kozova, Ukr. 72/C3
Kōzu (isl.), Japan 85/F3
Kożuchów, Pol. 43/H3
Kozyatyn, Ukr. 72/E3
Kpagouda, Togo 115/F4
Kpalimé, Togo 115/F5
Kpandu, Gha. 115/F5
Kpémé, Togo 115/F5
Kra (isth.), Myan. 93/G6
Kra Buri, Thai. 94/B4
Kraai (riv.), SAfr. 124/D3
Kraaifontein, SAfr. 124/L10
Krabbendijke, Neth. 52/B6
Krabbfjärden (sound), Swe. 39/A2
Krabi, Thai. 94/B4
Kracheh, Camb. 94/D3
Kragan, Indo. 89/E4
Kragerø, Nor. 40/C2
Kragujevac, Yugo. 50/E3
Kraiburg am Inn, Ger. 59/F6
Kraichbach (riv.), Ger. 58/B4
Kraichgau (reg.), Ger. 45/H2
Krailling, Ger. 59/E6
Krakatau (vol.), Indo. 89/D4
Krakor, Camb. 94/D3
Kraków, Pol. 43/K3
Krakow, Wi, US 160/B2
Kråkstad, Nor. 38/S8
Kralanh, Camb. 94/C3
Kralendijk, NAnt. 180/D1
Kraljevo, Yugo. 50/E4
Kralkızı (dam), Turk. 102/E2
Královéhradecký (pol. reg.), Czh. 43/H3
Kralovice, Czh. 59/G3
Kralupy nad Vltavou, Czh. 59/H2
Kramators'k, Ukr. 73/J3
Kramer, ND, US 156/D3
Kramfors, Swe. 38/F3
Krammer (chan.), Neth. 52/B5
Kranéa Elassónos, Gre. 49/G3
Kranebitten (int'l arpt.), Aus. 61/H3
Kranenburg, Ger. 52/D5
Kranídhion, Gre. 49/H4
Kranj, Slov. 45/L3
Kranji (res.), Sing. 89/H6
Kranskop, SAfr. 125/E3
Kranzberg, Namb. 122/B4
Krapkowice, Pol. 43/J3
Krāslava, Lat. 41/M4
Kraslice, Czh. 59/F2
Krasnaya Gorbatka, Rus. 68/J5
Krasnaya Sloboda, Bela. 70/C1
Krasne, Ukr. 72/C3
Krasni Okny, Ukr. 72/E4
Kraśnik, Pol. 43/M3
Kraśnik Fabryczny, Pol. 43/M3
Krasninsk, Rus. 69/N5
Krasnoarmeysk, Rus. 71/H2
Krasnoarmeysk, Rus. 69/W9
Krasnoarmeyskaya, Rus. 73/K5
Krasnoarmeyskiy, Rus. 73/M4
Krasnoarmiys'k, Ukr. 73/J3
Krasnoborsk, Rus. 69/K3
Krasnodar (int'l arpt.), Rus. 73/K5
Krasnodar, Rus. 73/K5
Krasnodarskiy Kray, Rus. 74/D5
Krasnodon, Ukr. 73/K3
Krasnogorsk, Rus. 69/W9
Krasnogvardeyskoye, Rus. 73/L5
Krasnohorivka, Ukr. 73/J3
Krasnohrad, Ukr. 73/H3
Krasnohvardiys'ke, Ukr. 73/H5
Krasnokamensk, Rus. 79/H1
Krasnokamsk, Rus. 69/M4
Krasnokholmskiy, Rus. 69/M5
Krasnolesnyy, Rus. 73/K2
Krasnooskol'skoye (res.), Ukr. 73/J3
Krasnopavlivka, Ukr. 73/J3
Krasnoperekops'k, Ukr. 73/G5
Krasnopillya, Ukr. 73/H2
Krasnoshchel'ye, Rus. 68/H2
Krasnoslobodsk, Rus. 71/G1
Krasnoslobodsk, Rus. 71/H2
Krasnotur'insk, Rus. 74/G4
Krasnoufimsk, Rus. 69/N4
Krasnoural'sk, Rus. 69/P4
Krasnovishersk, Rus. 69/N3
Krasnowodsk (int'l arpt.), Trkm. 103/H1
Krasnowodsk (Türkmenbashi), Trkm. 103/H2
Krasnoyarsk, Rus. 74/K4
Krasnoyarskiy, Rus. 71/L2
Krasnoyarskiy Kray, Rus. 74/K4
Krasnoye, Bela. 41/M4
Krasnoye, Rus. 73/K2
Krasnyy Bor, Rus. 69/T7
Krasnyy Chikoy, Rus. 78/F1
Krasnyy Gulyay, Rus. 71/J1
Krasnyy Kholm, Rus. 71/K2
Krasnyy Klyuch, Rus. 69/N5
Krasnyy Kut, Rus. 71/H2
Krasnyy Luch, Ukr. 73/K3
Krasnyy Lyman, Ukr. 70/F2
Krasnyy Oktyabr', Rus. 69/Q5
Krasnyy Sulin, Rus. 73/L4
Krasnyy Yar, Rus. 71/J3
Krasnyy Yar, Rus. 71/J1
Krasnyy Yar, Rus. 71/H2
Krasyliv, Ukr. 72/D3
Kratovo, FYROM 49/H1
Krautheim, Ger. 58/C4
Kravanh (mts.), Camb. 93/H5
Kraynovka, Rus. 71/H4
Kražiai, Lith. 41/K4
Kreb en Nâga (cliff), Mali 110/D5
Krechetovo, Rus. 68/H3
Kreck (riv.), Ger. 58/D2
Krefeld, Ger. 52/D6
Kreiensen, Ger. 53/G5
Kremastón (lake), Gre. 49/G3
Křemelna (riv.), Czh. 59/G4
Kremenchuk, Ukr. 73/G3
Kremenchuts'ke Vdskl. (res.), Ukr. 70/E2
Kremenets', Ukr. 72/C2
Kreminna, Ukr. 73/K3
Kremlin, Rus. 69/W9
Kremlin, Mt, US 145/J3
Kremmen, Ger. 42/Q6
Kremmling, Co, US 147/K3
Krempe, Ger. 53/G1
Krems an der Donau, Aus. 43/H4
Kremsmünster, Aus. 59/H6
Krenglbach, Aus. 59/G6
Kresgeville, Pa, US 168/C2
Kresna, Bul. 49/H2
Kress, Tx, US 152/D3
Kressbronn am Bodensee, Ger. 61/F2
Kresta (gulf), Rus. 75/T3
Kréstena, Gre. 49/G4
Kresty, Rus. 68/H5
Kretinga, Lith. 41/J4
Kreuzau, Ger. 55/F2
Kreuzberg (peak), Ger. 58/C2
Kreuzlingen, Swi. 61/F2
Kreuztal, Ger. 55/G2
Kreuzwertheim, Ger. 58/C3
Kría Vrísi, Gre. 49/H2
Kribi, Camr. 120/B2
Krieglach, Aus. 45/L3
Kriens, Swi. 61/E3
Kriftel, Ger. 58/B2
Kril'on (pen.), Rus. 82/B1
Kril'on (cape), Rus. 82/C1
Kril'on, Rus. 82/C1
Krim-Krim, Chad 116/B3
Krimpen aan de Ijssel, Neth. 52/B5
Krinídhes, Gre. 49/J2
Kriós (cape), Gre. 49/H5
Krishna (riv.), India 77/G8
Krishnagiri, India 95/C3
Krishnai, India 97/H2
Krishnanagar, India 97/G4
Kristdala, Swe. 40/G3
Kristiansand, Nor. 40/B2
Kristianstad (co.), Swe. 38/E4
Kristianstad (int'l arpt.), Swe. 40/F4
Kristianstad, Swe. 40/F3
Kristiansund, Nor. 38/C3
Kristinehamn, Swe. 40/F2
Kriva Palanka, FYROM 49/H1
Krivichi, Bela. 41/M4
Krivushevo, Rus. 69/L3
Krk (isl.), Cro. 67/G1
Krk, Cro. 45/L4
Krnov, Czh. 43/J3
Krokodil (riv.), SAfr. 123/F5
Krokodilrivier (riv.), SAfr. 123/E5
Krokom, Swe. 38/E3
Krókos, Gre. 49/G2
Krokstadelva, Nor. 38/R8
Krolevets', Ukr. 73/G2
Krombach, Ger. 58/C2
Kroměříž, Czh. 43/J4
Kromy, Rus. 70/E1
Kronach, Ger. 59/E2
Kronau, Sk, Can. 156/B2
Kronberg im Taunus, Ger. 58/B2
Krong Kaoh Kong, Camb. 94/C4
Krong Keb, Camb. 94/D4
Kronoberg (co.), Swe. 38/E4
Kronshtadt, Rus. 69/S6
Kronstorf, Aus. 59/H6
Kroombit Tops NP, Austl. 134/C4
Kroonstad, SAfr. 124/D2
Kropachevo, Rus. 69/N5
Kropotkin, Rus. 73/L5
Kropp, Ger. 40/C4
Krosno, Pol. 43/L4
Krosno Odrzańskie, Pol. 43/H2
Krotoszyn, Pol. 43/J3
Krotovka, Rus. 69/L5
Krottenkopf (peak), Aus. 61/G3
Krotz Springs, La, US 164/C2
Krousón, Gre. 49/J5
Kröv, Ger. 55/G4
Krško, Slov. 50/B3
Kruckau (riv.), Ger. 53/G1
Kruger NP, SAfr. 123/F4
Krugersdorp, SAfr. 124/P13
Kruglitsa (peak), Rus. 69/N5
Krugloi (cape), Ak, US 171/A5
Krui, Indo. 89/C3
Kruibeke, Belg. 52/B6
Kruin, Namb. 122/C4
Kruiningen, Neth. 52/B6
Kruisfontein, SAfr. 124/D4
Krujë, Alb. 49/F2
Krulevshchina, Bela. 41/M4
Krum, Tx, US 153/F4
Krumbach, Ger. 61/G1
Krummenau, Swi. 61/F3
Krumovgrad, Bul. 51/G5
Krün, Ger. 61/H3
Krung Thep (Bangkok) (cap.), Thai. 94/C3
Kruså, Den. 40/C4
Krusenstern (cape), Ak, US 171/F2
Kruševac, Yugo. 50/E4
Kruševo, FYROM 49/G2
Krušné Hory (Erzgebirge) (mts.), Czh.,Ger. 45/K1
Kruszwica, Pol. 43/K2
Krutoyarskiy, Rus. 69/P5
Kruzof (isl.), Ak, US 171/L4
Krychaw, Bela. 70/D1
Krylovskaya, Rus. 73/K4
Krym, Aut. Rep., Ukr. 73/G5
Krymsk, Rus. 73/K5
Krynica, Pol. 43/L4
Krynychky, Ukr. 73/H3
Kryve Ozero, Ukr. 72/F4
Kryvyy Rih, Ukr. 73/G4
Kryzhopil', Ukr. 72/E3
Krzna (riv.), Pol. 43/M3
Krzyż, Pol. 43/J2
Ksar el Boukhari, Alg. 112/G5
Ksar el Kebir, Mor. 112/B2
Ksel (peak), Alg. 111/F2
Ksen'yevka, Rus. 79/H1
Kshenskiy, Rus. 73/J2
Ktima, Cyp. 104/C2
Ku Sathan (peak), Thai. 94/C2
Ku-Ring-Gai Chase NP, Austl. 133/E1
Ku-Ring-Gai NP, Austl. 134/H8
Kuah, Malay. 94/B5
Kuai (riv.), China 78/H5
Kuala Belait, Bru. 90/D3
Kuala Berang, Malay. 89/C1
Kuala Dungun, Malay. 89/C1
Kuala Kangsar, Malay. 89/C1
Kuala Kelawang, Malay. 89/C2
Kuala Kerai, Malay. 89/C1
Kuala Kubu Baharu, Malay. 89/C2
Kuala Kurau, Malay. 89/C1
Kuala Lipis, Malay. 89/C1
Kuala Lumpur (int'l arpt.), Malay. 89/C2
Kuala Lumpur (cap.), Malay. 89/C2
Kuala Pahang, Malay. 89/C2
Kuala Penyu, Malay. 88/A4
Kuala Pilah, Malay. 89/C2
Kuala Rompin, Malay. 89/C2
Kuala Selangor, Malay. 89/C2
Kuala Terengganu, Malay. 89/C1
Kualalangsa, Indo. 89/B1
Kualamandah, Indo. 89/C3
Kualasimpang, Indo. 89/B1
Kualatungkal, Indo. 89/C3
Kuam, SKor. 81/G6
Kuamut, Malay. 88/B4
Kuancheng, China 80/D2
Kuandian, China 81/C2
Kuantan, Malay. 89/C2
Kuban' (riv.), Rus. 74/D5
Kubano-Priazov (plain), Rus. 73/K5
Kubaysah, Iraq 102/E3
Kubbum, Sudan 116/D3
Kubenskoye (lake), Rus. 68/H4
Kubokawa, Japan 84/C4
Kubrat, Bul. 51/H4
Kubumesaai, Indo. 90/E3
Kubutambahan, Indo. 89/F5
Kučevo, Yugo. 50/E3
Kuchaiburi, India 97/F4
Kuchen (peak), Aus. 61/G3
Kuchen, Ger. 58/C5
Kuchinarai, Thai. 94/D2
Kuching, Malay. 90/D3
Kuchino (isl.), Japan 85/K6
Kuchinoerabu (isl.), Japan 84/A5
Kuchl, Aus. 45/K3
Kūchnay Darvīshān, Afg. 101/H2
Kuçovë, Alb. 49/F2
Küçükbahçe, Turk. 49/K3
Küçükcekmece (lake), Turk. 103/M6
Küçükkuyu, Turk. 49/K3
Kuda, Indo. 90/D3
Kudamatsu, Japan 84/B3
Kudan, Nga. 115/G4
Kudara, Taj. 99/B4
Kudat, Malay. 88/B4
Kudene, Indo. 128/D1
Kudirkos-Naumiestis, Lith. 41/K4
Kudremalai (pt.), SrL. 95/C4
Kudus, Indo. 89/E4
Kudymkar, Rus. 69/M4
Kufrah (oasis), Libya 108/D3
Kufrinjah, Jor. 105/D4
Kufstein, Aus. 45/K3
Kufūr Najm, Egypt 113/C3
Kugaaruk, Nun, Can. 141/H2
Kugarchi, Rus. 71/L1
Kugluktuk, Nun, Can. 140/E2
Kuhardt, Ger. 58/B4
Kühbach, Ger. 58/E6
Kūhdasht, Iran 103/F3
Kūhestak, Iran 103/J5
Kuhmo, Fin. 68/F2
Kuhmoinen, Fin. 41/L1
Kūhpāyeh, Iran 103/H3
Kuikuina, Nic. 177/E3
Kuinder of Tjonger (riv.), Neth. 52/C3
Kuiseb (riv.), NAmb. 122/B4
Kuishan (mtn.), China 87/F4
Kuitan, China 87/G4
Kuito, Ang. 122/C2
Kuiu (isl.), Ak, US 140/C3
Kuivajärvi (lake), Fin. 39/D4
Kuivastu, Est. 41/K2
Kujang, NKor. 81/D3
Kujawsko Pomorskie (prov.), Pol. 43/K2
Kujawy (reg.), Pol. 43/K2
Kuji, Japan 82/B3
Kujū-san (peak), Japan 84/B4
Kujūkuri, Japan 83/E2
Kukalaya (riv.), Nic. 177/E3
Kukawa, Nga. 116/B2
Kuke (riv.), China 86/C3
Kukës, Alb. 49/G1
Kuki, Japan 85/F2
Kukipi, PNG 129/G2
Kukizaki, Japan 83/E2
Kukkia (lake), Fin. 41/L1
Kukmor, Rus. 69/L4
Kukushtan, Rus. 69/N4
Kūl (riv.), Iran 100/C3
Kula, Bul. 50/F4
Kula, Turk. 102/B2
Kula, Yugo. 50/D3
Kula Kangri (peak), Bhu. 97/H1
Kulachi, Pak. 98/A4
Kulagino, Kaz. 71/J2
Kulai, Malay. 89/C2
Kulākh, SAr. 100/D4
Kulal (mt.), Kenya 119/B1
Kulaly (isl.), Kaz. 71/J3
Kulandag (mts.), Trkm. 71/K4
Kularua, Bang. 97/J3
Kulashi, Geo. 71/G4
Kuldīga, Lat. 41/J3
Kule, Bots. 122/D4
Kulebaki, Rus. 68/J5
Kulen, Camb. 94/D3
Kulen Shet' (riv.), Eth. 118/B3
Kulet el-Qrein (peak), Egypt 113/C6
Kulgām, India 98/C3
Kulgera, Austl. 131/G3
Kulgunino, Rus. 71/L1
Kulim, Malay. 89/C1
Kulin, Austl. 130/C5
Kullamaa, Est. 41/L2
Kullen (cape), Swe. 40/E3
Kullu, India 98/D4
Kulm, ND, US 156/E4
Kulma (wadi), Sudan 116/D2
Kulmbach, Ger. 59/E2
Kŭlob, Taj. 99/A4
Kuloy (riv.), Rus. 69/J2
Kuloy, Rus. 68/J3
Kuloy, Rus. 69/J2
Kulpahār, India 96/B3
Kulpmont, Pa, US 168/B2
Kulpsville, Pa, US 168/C3
Kul'sary, Kaz. 71/K3
Külsheim, Ger. 58/C3
Kulsi (riv.), India 97/H2
Kulti, India 97/F4
Kulu, Turk. 102/C2
Kulunda, Rus. 74/H4
Kulunda (lake), Rus. 99/C1
Kulunda (riv.), Rus. 99/D1
Kulunda Steppe (plain), Kaz. 99/C1
Kulykivka, Ukr. 72/F2
Kŭm (riv.), SKor. 81/D4
Kuma (riv.), Rus. 74/E5
Kumagaya, Japan 85/F2
Kumai, India 97/G2
Kumaishi, Japan 82/A2
Kumak, Rus. 71/M2
Kumaka, Guy. 181/G4
Kumamoto (int'l arpt.), Japan 84/B4
Kumamoto (pref.), Japan 84/B4
Kumamoto, Japan 84/B4
Kumano (riv.), Japan 84/D4
Kumano, Japan 84/E4
Kumanovo, FYROM 49/G1
Kumār (riv.), Bang. 97/G4
Kumara, NZ 135/B3
Kumārkhāli, Bang. 97/G4
Kumasi, Gha. 115/E5
Kumatori, Japan 83/H7
Kumba, Camr. 120/B1
Kumbakonam, India 95/C4
Kumbe, Indo. 129/F2
Kumbia, Austl. 134/C4
Kŭmch'on, SKor. 81/F6
Kumé (isl.), Japan 85/J7
Kumertau, Rus. 71/K1
Kumeu, NZ 135/F6
Kŭmgang, NKor. 81/D3
Kumgang-san (peak), NKor. 81/E3
Kumhārsain, India 98/D4
Kŭmho (riv.), SKor. 81/E5
Kŭmhwa, SKor. 81/D3
Kumi, SKor. 81/E4
Kumi, Ugan. 119/A1
Kumihama, Japan 83/G4
Kumiyama, Japan 83/J6
Kumjawng (pass), India 86/C3
Kumköy, Turk. 103/N6
Kumla, Swe. 40/F2
Kumla, Swe. 39/B1
Kumluca, Turk. 104/B1
Kümmersbruck, Ger. 59/E4
Kumon (range), Myan. 93/G2
Kŭmsan, SKor. 81/D4
Kŭmsanp'o, NKor. 81/C3
Kumsenga, Tanz. 121/G3
Kumta, India 95/B3
Kumurkek, Indo. 129/F1
Kumylzhenskaya, Rus. 73/M3
Kuna, Id, US 146/E2
Kunashiri (isl.), Rus. 75/Q5
Kūnch, India 96/B3
Kunchha, Nepal 97/E1
Kunda, Est. 41/M2
Kunda, India 96/C3
Kundapura (Coondapoor), India 101/K6
Kundarkhi, India 96/B1
Kundauli, India 96/D2
Kundelungu, Monts (mts.), D.R. Congo 121/F5
Kundelungu, PN de, D.R. Congo 121/F5
Kundiān, Pak. 98/A3
Kundiawa, PNG 129/G1
Kundla, India 101/K4
Kundravy, Rus. 69/P5
Kunduchi, Tanz. 119/B3
Kundur (isl.), Indo. 89/C2
Kunene (riv.), Namb. 122/B3
Kungälv, Swe. 40/D3
Kungsangen (int'l arpt.), Swe. 40/G2
Kungsängen, Swe. 39/A1
Kungsbacka, Swe. 40/E3
Kungshamn, Swe. 40/D2
Kungu, D.R. Congo 120/D2
Kungu, Zam. 121/G5
Kungur, Rus. 69/N4
Kungutas, Tanz. 119/A4
Kungyangon, Myan. 94/B2
Kunhegyes, Hun. 50/E2
Kunhing, Myan. 86/C4
Kunimi-dake (peak), Japan 84/B4
Kuningan, Indo. 89/E4
Kunishiri (isl.), Rus. 77/P5
Kunitachi, Japan 83/C2
Kunjāh, Pak. 98/B3
Kunjirap (pass), China 101/L1
Kunkletown, Pa, US 168/C2
Kunlong, Myan. 93/G3
Kunlun (mts.), China 77/H6
Kunlun (pass), China 99/C4
Kunmadaras, Hun. 43/L5
Kunming (int'l arpt.), China 86/D3
Kunming, China 86/D3
Kunmunya Abor. Rsv., Austl. 128/B3
Kunp'o, SKor. 81/F7
Kunsan, SKor. 81/D5
Kunshan, China 80/L8
Kunszentmárton, Hun. 50/E2
Kuntaur, Gam. 114/B3
Kuntsëvo (nbrhd.), Rus. 69/W9
Kuntshankoie, D.R. Congo 121/E3
Kunu (riv.), India 101/L3
Kununurra, Austl. 128/C3
Kunwāri (riv.), India 96/A2
Kunwi, SKor. 81/E4
Kun'ya, Rus. 41/P3
Kunya, Nga. 115/H3
Kunyu (mtn.), China 80/E3
Künzell, Ger. 58/C1
K'unzila, Eth. 117/H3
Kunzulu, D.R. Congo 120/D3
Kunžvartské (pass), Czh. 59/G5
Kuocang (peak), China 87/J2
Kuohijärvi (lake), Fin. 41/L1
Kuolayarvi, Rus. 68/F2
Kuolimo (lake), Fin. 41/M1
Kuopio, Fin. 68/E3
Kuopio (prov.), Fin. 38/H3
Kup, PNG 129/G1
Kupa (riv.), Cro. 45/L4
Kupang, Indo. 128/A2
Kuper (range), PNG 129/G1
Kupiano, PNG 129/H2
Kupino, Rus. 74/H4
Kupiškis, Lith. 41/L4
Kuppenheim, Ger. 58/B5
Kupreanof (isl.), Ak, US 140/C3
Kup'yans'k, Ukr. 73/J3
Kup'yans'k-Vuzlovyy, Ukr. 73/J3
Kuqa, China 75/M5
Kür (riv.), Azer. 74/E6
Kur (riv.), Rus. 79/M1
Kurakh, Rus. 71/H4
Kurakhove, Ukr. 73/J4
Kurakino, Rus. 71/H1
Kūrālī, India 98/D4
Kurama-yama (peak), Japan 83/J5
Kurashiki, Japan 84/C3
Kuraymah, Sudan 109/F5
Kurayoshi, Japan 84/C3
Kurayyimah, Jor. 105/D4
Kurchum, Kaz. 99/D2
Kürdämir, Azer. 103/G1
Kurdistan (reg.), Asia 74/E6
Kurdufān (pol. reg.), Sudan 117/F2
Kŭrdzhali (res.), Bul. 49/J2
Kŭrdzhali, Bul. 51/G5
Küre, Turk. 70/E4
Kure, Japan 84/C3
Kure (isl.), Hi, US 136/H2
Küre (mts.), Turk 102/C1
Kūrebhār, India 96/D2
Kuressaare, Est. 41/K2
Kureyka (riv.), Rus. 74/K3
Kurgan, Rus. 69/Q5
Kurganskaya Oblast, Rus. 69/P5
Kurganinsk, Rus. 73/L5
Kurgaon, India 96/A2
Kuri, SKor. 81/G6
Kuria (isl.), Kiri. 136/G4
Kuria Muria (isls.), Oman 77/F5
Kurīgrām, Bang. 97/G3
Kurihashi, Japan 83/D1
Kurikoma-yama (peak), Japan 82/B4
Kuril (isls.), Rus. 77/Q5
Kurilovka, Rus. 71/J2
Kuril'sk, Rus. 82/E1
Kurimoto, Japan 83/F2
Kuring Kuru, Namb. 122/C3
Kurinwas (riv.), Nic. 177/E3
Kurisawa, Japan 82/B2
Kuriyama, Japan 82/B2
Kürkçü, Turk. 104/C1
Kurkiyoki, Rus. 41/N1
Kurlovskiy, Rus. 68/J5
Kurmuk, Eth. 117/G3
Kurnool, India 95/C3
Kuro (nbrhd.), SKor. 81/F7
Kuro-shima (isl.), Japan 84/A5
Kurodashō, Japan 83/G5
Kuroishi, Japan 82/B3
Kuroiso, Japan 85/G2
Kuroki, Sk, Can. 156/C2
Kurort-Darasun, Rus. 78/G1
Kuroso-yama (peak), Japan 83/K6
Kurotaki, Japan 83/J7
Kurow, NZ 135/B4
Kurrajong, Austl. 134/G8
Kurram (riv.), Pak. 101/K2
Kurri Kurri, Austl. 133/E1
Kurrimine Beach, Austl. 134/B2
Kursavka, Rus. 73/M5
Kuršėnai, Lith. 41/K3
Kurseong, India 97/G2
Kursiu Nerija NP, Lith. 41/J4
Kursk, Rus. 73/J2
Kurskaya Spit (bar), Lith.,Rus. 41/J4
Kurskiy (lag.), Lith.,Rus. 43/L1
Kurskiy (lag.), Lith. 41/J4
Kurskskaya Oblast, Rus. 70/E2
Kuršumlija, Yugo. 50/E4
Kurşunlu, Turk. 70/E4
Kurtalan, Turk. 102/E2
Kürten, Ger. 55/G1
Kurtköy, Turk. 103/N7
Kuru (riv.), Bhu. 97/H2
Kuru (riv.), Sudan 117/E3
Kuruca (pass), Turk. 102/E2
Kuruçay, Turk. 102/D2
Kuruçay (riv.), Turk. 71/G4
Kuruktag (mts.), China 78/B3
Kuruman, SAfr. 124/C2
Kurumansrivier (riv.), SAfr. 124/C2
Kurume, Japan 84/B4
Kurumkan, Rus. 78/G1
Kurundi, Austl. 131/G2
Kurupukari, Guy. 181/G3
Kurur (peak), Sudan 109/F4
Kurwongbah (lake), Austl. 134/E6
Kur'ya, Rus. 69/N3
Kurye, SKor. 81/D5
Kuryong (riv.), NKor. 81/C3
Kuryongp'o-ri, SKor. 81/E5
Kuşadası, Turk. 102/A2
Kusakan, Kaz. 71/M1
Kusatsu, Japan 83/J5
Kusel, Ger. 55/G4
Kushālgarh, India 101/K4
Kushchevskaya, Rus. 73/K4
Kusheriki, Nga. 115/G4
Kushida (riv.), Japan 83/K7
Kushigata, Japan 83/A2
Kushihara, Japan 83/M5
Kushikino, Japan 84/B5
Kushima, Japan 84/B5
Kushimoto, Japan 84/D4
Kushiro (riv.), Japan 82/D2
Kushiro, Japan 82/D2
Kushiro-Shitsugen NP, Japan 82/D2
Kushmurun (lake), Kaz. 69/Q5
Kushol, India 98/D3
Kushtia, Bang. 97/G4
Kushtia (pol. reg.), Bang. 97/G4
Kushui (riv.), China 78/F4
Kushum (riv.), Kaz. 71/J2
Kusiyana (riv.), Bang. 97/H3
Kuskokwim (bay), Ak, US 171/F4
Kuskokwim (mts.), Ak, US 171/G3
Kuskokwim (riv.), Ak, US 171/F3
Kusma, Nepal 96/D1
Küsnacht, Swi. 61/E3
Kusŏng, NKor. 81/C3
Kussharo (lake), Japan 82/C2
Küssnacht am Rigi, Swi. 61/E3
Kustarevka, Rus. 71/G1
Küstenkanal (canal), Ger. 53/E3
Kusterdingen, Ger. 58/C5
Kūstī, Sudan 117/G2
Kusu, Japan 83/L6
Kusuman, Thai. 94/D2
Kut (isl.), Camb. 93/H5
Kuta, Nga. 115/G4
Kutacane, Indo. 89/B2
Kütahya, Turk. 102/B2
Kütahya (prov.), Turk. 102/B2
Kutais, Rus. 73/K5
K'ut'aisi (int'l arpt.), Geo. 71/G4
K'ut'aisi, Geo. 71/G4
Kutāmat al Ghābah, Egypt 113/B3
Kutch (gulf), India 92/A3
Kutch (reg.), India 92/A3
Kutchan, Japan 82/B1
Kutcharo (lake), Japan 82/C1
Kutenholz, Ger. 53/G2
Kutiwenji, Nga. 115/G4
Kutná Hora, Czh. 43/H4
Kutno, Pol. 43/K2
Kutse Game Reserve, Bots. 122/D4
Kutsuki, Japan 83/J5
Küttigen, Swi. 60/E3
Kutu, D.R. Congo 120/D3
Kutu-Owanga, D.R. Congo 121/E3
Kutulik, Rus. 78/E1
Kutum, Sudan 117/E2
Kutzenhausen, Ger. 58/D6
Kutztown, Pa, US 168/C2
Kuujjua (riv.), NW, Can. 140/E1
Kuujjuaq, Qu, Can. 141/K3
Kuujjuarapik, Qu, Can. 141/J3
Kuuli-Mayak, Trkm. 103/H1
Kuurila, Fin. 39/E3
Kuusamo, Fin. 38/J2
Kuusankoski, Fin. 41/M1
Kuutse (hill), Est. 41/M2
Kuvandyk, Rus. 71/L2
Kuvango, Ang. 122/C2
Kuwait (cap.), Kuw. 103/F4
Kuwait (ctry.) 77/D7
Kuwait (int'l arpt.), Kuw. 103/F4
Kuwānā (riv.), India 92/D2
Kuwana, Japan 83/L5
Kuybyshev, Rus. 69/L5
Kuybyshev (res.), Rus. 74/E4
Kuybyshevka, Ukr. 72/F4
Kuybyshevskiy, Kaz. 69/Q5
Kuye (riv.), China 78/G4
Kūysanjaq, Iraq 103/F2
Küysu, China 78/C3
Kuyto (lake), Rus. 38/J2
Kuytun, China 99/E3
Kuytun (riv.), China 99/D3
Kuyu Tingni, Nic. 177/F3
Kuyuwini (riv.), Guy. 181/G4
Kuze, Japan 83/K4
Kuzitrin (riv.), Ak, US 171/E2
Kuz'molovskiy, Rus. 69/T6
Kuznetsk, Rus. 71/H1
Kuzomen', Rus. 68/H2
Kuzovatovo, Rus. 71/H1
Kuzucubelen, Turk. 104/D1
Kuzumaki, Japan 82/B3
Kvaløy (isl.), Nor. 38/F1
Kværndrup, Den. 40/D4
Kvarner (gulf), Cro. 67/G1
Kvarneric (chan.), Cro. 50/B3
Kvigtinden (peak), Nor. 38/E2
Kvinesdal, Nor. 40/B2
Kvinnherad, Nor. 40/B2
Kviteseid, Nor. 40/C2
Kwa (riv.), D.R. Congo 107/D5
Kwa Mtoro, Tanz. 119/A3
Kwaadmechelen, Belg. 55/E1
Kwach'ŏn, SKor. 81/F7
Kwail, NKor. 81/C3
Kwajalein (isl.), Mrsh. 136/F4
Kwajok, Sudan 117/F3
Kwakoegron, Sur. 182/C1
Kwaksan, NKor. 81/C3
Kwakwani, Guy. 181/G3
Kwale, Kenya 119/B3
Kwali, Nga. 115/G4
Kwam al Ḩamām (ruin), Egypt 113/C6
Kwam Awshīm (ruin), Egypt 113/B5
Kwamashu, SAfr. 125/E3
Kwamen Kwesi, Gha. 115/E4
Kwamouth, D.R. Congo 120/D3
Kwanak-san (peak), SKor. 81/F7
Kwando (riv.), Namb. 122/D3
Kwangch'ŏn, SKor. 81/D4
Kwangju, SKor. 81/D5
Kwangju, SKor. 81/G7
Kwangju-jikhalsi (prov.), SKor. 81/D5
Kwangmyŏng, SKor. 81/F7
Kwango (riv.), D.R. Congo 107/D5
Kwangwazi, Tanz. 119/B3
Kwangyang, SKor. 81/D5
Kwania (lake), Ugan. 119/A1
Kwansan, SKor. 81/D5
Kwara (state), Nga. 115/G4
Kwaraha (peak), Tanz. 119/A3
Kwatarkwashi, Nga. 115/G3
Kwazulu Natal (prov.), SAfr. 125/E3
Kwekwe, Zim. 123/F3
Kweneng (dist.), Bots. 122/E4
Kwenge (riv.), D.R. Congo 120/D4
Kwethluk, Ak, US 171/F3
Kwidzyn, Pol. 41/H5
Kwigillingok, Ak, US 171/F4
Kwīha, Eth. 118/A2
Kwikila, PNG 129/G2
Kwilu (riv.), D.R. Congo 107/D5
Kwinana, Austl. 130/K7
Kwitara (riv.), Guy. 182/B2
Ky Anh, Viet. 94/D2
Ky Son, Viet. 94/D2
Kya-in Seikkyi, Myan. 94/B2
Kyabé, Chad 116/C3
Kyabram, Austl. 133/B3
Kyaikkami, Myan. 94/B2
Kyaikpi, Myan. 94/B2
Kyaiktiyo Pagoda, Myan. 94/B2
Kyaikto, Myan. 86/C5
Kyaka, Tanz. 121/G3
Kyakhta, Rus. 78/F1
Kyalite, Austl. 132/B2
Kyan-zaki (cape), Japan 85/J7
Kyancutta, Austl. 131/G5
Kyangin, Myan. 86/B5
Kyargozero, Rus. 68/G3
Kyaukki, Myan. 94/B2
Kyaukme, Myan. 86/C4
Kyaukpadaung, Myan. 86/B4
Kyaukpyu, Myan. 86/B5
Kyaukse, Myan. 86/C4
Kyaunggon, Myan. 86/B5
Kybartai, Lith. 41/K4
Kyeamba (cr.), Austl. 133/C2
Kyegegwa, Ugan. 121/G2
Kyelang, India 98/D3
Kyenjojo, Ugan. 121/G2
Kyeryong-san NP, SKor. 81/D4
Kyidaunggan, Myan. 86/C5
Kyikug, China 78/E4
Kyindwe, Myan. 86/B4
Kyjov, Czh. 43/J4
Kyle (reg.), Sc, UK 33/B5
Kyle, SD, US 154/C2
Kyle, Sk, Can. 145/K2
Kyle, Tx, US 151/F3
Kylemore, Sk, Can. 156/C2
Kyll (riv.), Ger. 42/D3
Kylmäkoski, Fin. 39/D3
Kym (riv.), Eng, UK 37/F2
Kymi (prov.), Fin. 38/H3
Kymijärvi (lake), Fin. 39/F4
Kymijoki (riv.), Fin. 41/M1
Kymore, India 96/B4
Kyn, Rus. 69/N4
Kyneton, Austl. 133/B3
Kynšperk nad Ohří, Czh. 59/F2
Kynuna, Austl. 134/A3
Kyoga (lake), Ugan. 119/A1
Kyōga-misaki (cape), Japan 84/D3
Kyogle, Austl. 134/D5
Kyonan, Japan 85/F3

Kyŏngan (riv.), SKor. 81/G7
Kyŏngbok Palace, SKor. 81/F6
Kyŏnggi (bay), SKor. 81/C4
Kyŏnggi-Do (prov.), SKor. 81/D4
Kyŏngju, SKor. 84/A3
Kyŏngju NP, SKor. 81/E5
Kyŏngju NP, SKor. 84/A3
Kyŏngsan, SKor. 84/A3
Kyŏngsang-bukto (prov.), SKor. 81/E4
Kyŏngsang-namdo (prov.), SKor. 81/E5
Kyŏngsŏng, NKor. 81/E2
Kyônkadun, Myan. 86/B5
Kyōto (pref.), Japan 84/D3
Kyōto, Japan 83/J5
Kyōtō Imperial Palace, Japan 83/J6
Kyōwa, Japan 83/E1
Kyrenia, Cyp. 104/C2
Kyrenia (dist.), Cyp. 104/C2
Kyrgyzstan (ctry.) 77/G5
Kyritz, Ger. 42/G2
Kyrkslätt (Kirkkonummi), Fin. 41/L1
Kyrösjärvi (lake), Fin. 41/K1
Kyrta, Rus. 69/N2
Kyrykuduk, Kaz. 71/J2
Kyrylivka, Ukr. 73/H4
Kyshtym, Rus. 69/P5
Kythrea, Cyp. 104/C2
Kytlym, Rus. 69/N4
Kytätä, Fin. 39/E4
Kyunhla, Myan. 86/B4
Kyūshū (isl.), Japan 77/M6
Kyūshū Highlands (uplands), Japan 84/B4
Kyustendil, Bul. 49/H1
Kyusyur, Rus. 75/N2
Kywebwe, Myan. 86/B5
Kyyiv (Kiev) (cap.), Ukr. 72/F2
Kyyivs'ka Oblast, Ukr. 70/D2
Kyyivs'ke Vodoskhovyshche (res.), Ukr. 70/D2
Kyzyl, Rus. 78/C1
Kzyltu, Kaz. 74/H4

L

L' Achigan (riv.), Qu, Can. 159/N6
L'Anguille (riv.), Ar, US 162/B3
L'Anse, Mi, US 157/K4
L'Aquila (prov.), It. 65/C3
L'Aquila, It. 65/C3
L' Ariana (lake), Fl, US 164/M7
L'Artois, Collines de (hills), Fr. 42/A3
L'Assomption (riv.), Qu, Can. 159/P6
L'Assomption (co.), Qu, Can. 159/N6
L'Hongrin (lake), Swi. 60/D5
L'Oriental (pol. reg.), Mor. 111/E2
La Algaba, Sp. 46/B4
La Almunia de Doña Godina, Sp. 46/E2
La Amistad Int'l Park, CR 172/E6
La Araucanía (pol. reg.), Chile 190/B3
La Ascensión, Mex. 175/F3
La Asturiana, Arg. 190/D3
La Asunción, Ven. 181/F2
La Aurora (int'l arpt.), Guat. 176/D3
La Baie, Qu, Can. 158/B1
La Banda, Arg. 188/C3
La Bañeza, Sp. 46/C1
La Barge, Wy, US 147/H2
La Barra, Nic. 177/F3
La Barra, Uru. 191/G2
La Barre-en-Ouche, Fr. 57/F3
La Bassée, Fr. 54/B2
La Bâthie, Fr. 64/C1
La Bâtie-Neuve, Fr. 64/C3
La Baule-Escoublac, Fr. 56/C6
La Belle, Fl, US 165/H4
La Birse (riv.), Swi. 60/D3
La Blanquilla (isl.), Ven. 181/E2
La Bocana, Mex. 174/B3
La Bonneville-sur-Iton, Fr. 57/G3
La Bouilladisse, Fr. 64/B6
La Bresse, Fr. 60/C2
La Broque, Fr. 60/D1
La Broquerie, Mb, Can. 156/F3
La Cadière-d'Azur, Fr. 64/B6
La Caldera de Taburiente, PN, Sp. 110/A3
La Calera, Col. 183/M8
La Calera, Chile 190/N8
La Campana, Sp. 46/C4
La Campana, PN, Chile 190/N8
La Cañada (peak), Cuba 177/F1
La Canada-Flintridge, Ca, US 166/F7
La Canoa, Ven. 181/F2
La Capelle, Fr. 54/C4
La Carlota, Sp. 46/C4
La Carlota, Arg. 190/E2
La Carolina, Sp. 46/D3
La Catedral (peak), Mex. 175/Q9
La Ceiba, Ven. 180/D3
La Ceiba (int'l arpt.), Hon. 176/E3
La Ceiba, Hon. 176/E3
La Ceja, Col. 183/K6
La Celle-les-Bordes, Fr. 30/H6
La Celle-Saint-Cloud, Fr. 30/J5
La Celle-sur-Morin, Fr. 30/L5
La Center, Ky, US 162/C2
La Chapelle-de-Guinchay, Fr. 60/A5
La Chapelle-des-Marais, Fr. 56/C6
La Chapelle-Saint-Luc, Fr. 44/F2
La Chapelle-sur-Erdre, Fr. 56/D6
La Chartre-sur-le-Loir, Fr. 57/F5
La Chaussée-Saint-Victor, Fr. 57/G5
La Chaux-de-Bonds, Swi. 60/C3
La Chinita (int'l arpt.), Ven. 180/D2
La Chorrera, Col. 180/C5
La Cienega, NM, US 149/J3
La Ciotat, Fr. 64/B6
La Ciudad, PN, Mex. 174/D4
La Clusaz, Fr. 60/C6
La Cocha, Arg. 188/C3
La Colle-sur-Loup, Fr. 64/D5
La Concepción, Pan. 177/F4
La Concepción, Nic. 176/E4
La Concepcíon, Ven. 180/D2
La Condamine (nbrhd.), Mona. 62/J8
La Coronilla, Uru. 191/G2
La Coruña, Sp. 46/A1
La Côte-Saint-André, Fr. 64/B2
La Couronne, Fr. 44/D4
La Couture-Boussey, Fr. 57/G3
La Crau, Fr. 64/C6
La Crèche, Fr. 44/C3
La Crescent, Mn, US 155/J2
La Crescenta-Montrose, Ca, US 166/F7
La Criolla, Arg. 188/D4
La Croche, Qu, Can. 158/A2
La Croix-en-Brie, Fr. 30/M6
La Crosse, Ks, US 152/E1
La Crosse, Wi, US 155/J2
La Crosse, Va, US 163/H2
La Cruz, Col. 180/B4
La Cruz, CR 176/E4
La Cruz, Uru. 191/K10
La Cruz, Chile 190/N8
La Cruz, Mex. 174/D4
La Cuchilla, Uru. 189/F5
La Cumbre (vol.), Ecu. 184/J7
La Cygne, Ks, US 153/G1
La Dôle (peak), Swi. 60/C5
La Dorada, Col. 183/L7
La Doré, Qu, Can. 158/A1
La Dormida, Arg. 190/D2
La Durande (peak), Fr. 66/D1
La Embocada, Bol. 185/E4
La Escondida, Arg. 190/C3
La Escondida, Arg. 188/E3
La Esmeralda, Ven. 181/E4
La Esperanza, Arg. 190/C4
La Esperanza, Bol. 185/F4
La Esperanza, Bol. 185/F5
La Esperanza, Bol. 185/E4
La Esperanza, Hon. 176/D3
La Esperanza, Ven. 181/F2
La Estanzuela, Uru. 191/K11
La Estrada, Sp. 46/A1
La Estrella, Chile 190/N9
La Falda, Arg. 188/C4
La Fare-les-Oliviers, Fr. 64/B5
La Farlède, Fr. 64/C6
La Fayette, Ga, US 162/E3
La Fère, Fr. 54/C4
La Ferrière-aux-Étangs, Fr. 57/E3
La Ferté-Gaucher, Fr. 54/C6
La Ferté-Imbault, Fr. 57/G6
La Ferté-Macé, Fr. 57/E3
La Ferté-Milon, Fr. 30/M7
La Ferté-Sous-Jouarre, Fr. 54/C6
La Ferté-St-Aubin, Fr. 57/G5
La Ferté-Vidame, Fr. 57/F3
La Flèche, Fr. 57/E5
La Follette, Tn, US 162/E2
La Fontaine, In, US 160/D4
La Francia, Arg. 188/D4
La Fría, Ven. 180/C2
La Gacilly, Fr. 56/C5
La Garde, Fr. 64/C6
La Garde-Adhémar, Fr. 64/A4
La Garita (mts.), Co, US 152/A2
La Garita, Co, US 149/J2
La Garriga, Sp. 47/L6
La Gineta, Sp. 46/E3
La Glacerie, Fr. 56/D1
La Gloria, Col. 180/C2
La Gloria, Tx, US 151/E4
La Gran Sabana (plain), Ven. 181/F3
La Grand Moucherolle (peak), Fr. 64/B2
La Grande (riv.), Qu, Can. 141/J3
La Grande (riv.), Can. 139/K4
La Grande, Or, US 146/D1
La Grande Rochette (peak), Fr. 64/C2
La Grande Ruine (peak), Fr. 64/C3
La Grange, Austl. 128/A4
La Grange, Ga, US 162/E4
La Grange, Ky, US 162/E1
La Grange, Mo, US 155/J3
La Grange, NC, US 163/J3
La Grange, Tx, US 151/F3
La Grange, Wy, US 154/B3
La Grave, Fr. 64/C2
La Grita, Ven. 177/J4
La Grivola (peak), It. 64/D1
La Grue Bayou (riv.), Ar, US 162/B3
La Gruyère (lake), Swi. 60/D4
La Guadeloupe, Qu, Can. 158/B3
La Guaira, Ven. 183/P7
La Guajira (pen.), Col. 177/H4
La Guajira (dept.), Col. 177/H4
La Guardia, Sp. 46/A2
La Guardia, Arg. 188/C4
La Guardia, Bol. 188/D1
La Guardia (int'l arpt.), NY, US 169/K8
La Guerche-de-Bretagne, Fr. 56/D5
La Habana (Havana) (cap.), Cuba 172/E3
La Habra, Ca, US 166/G8
La Harpe, Ks, US 153/G2
La Have (riv.), NS, Can. 158/E3
La Haye-du-Puits, Fr. 56/D2
La Haye-Pesnel, Fr. 56/D3
La Higuera, Chile 188/B4
La Honda, Ca, US 167/K12
La Horqueta, Ven. 181/F3
La Horqueta, Ven. 181/F2
La Horquilla, Bol. 185/E4
La Houssaye-en-Brie, Fr. 30/L5
La Huaca, Peru 184/A2
La Huacana, Mex. 175/E5
La Huerta, Mex. 174/D5
La Isla, Mex. 175/Q10
La Jalca, Peru 184/B2
La Jara, NM, US 149/J2
La Jara, Co, US 149/K2
La Javie, Fr. 64/C4
La Jolla Ind. Res., Ca, US 148/D4
La Joya, Bol. 188/C1
La Joya, Peru 184/D5
La Joya de los Sachas, Ecu. 180/B5
La Junta, Co, US 152/C2
La Junta, Mex. 174/D2
La Juventud (isl.), Cuba 139/J7
La Laguna, Sp. 110/A3
La Laja, Arg. 188/B4
La Léchère, Fr. 64/C1
La Leonesa, Arg. 188/E3
La Libertad, Guat. 176/D2
La Libertad, Hon. 176/E3
La Libertad, Ecu. 180/A5
La Libertad (dept.), Peru 184/B3
La Ligua, Chile 190/C2
La Línea de la Concepción, Sp. 46/C4
La Llagosta, Sp. 47/L6
La Lobería, Arg. 190/E4
La Loche, Sk, Can. 140/F3
La Loggia, It. 62/A3
La Londe-les-Maures, Fr. 64/C6
La Loupe, Fr. 57/G4
La Louvière, Belg. 55/D3
La Luisiana, Sp. 46/C4
La Machine, Fr. 44/E3
La Maddalena, It. 48/A2
La Madeleine, Fr. 54/C2
La Madera, NM, US 149/J2
La Magdalena, Col. 183/L6
La Malbaie, Qu, Can. 158/B2
La Mancha (reg.), Sp. 66/C3
La Margarita, Ven. 181/F2
La Marque, Tx, US 151/N9
La Martre (lake), NW, Can. 140/E2
La Masica, Hon. 176/E3
La Mauricie NP, Qu, Can. 158/A2
La Media Luna (isls.), Hon. 177/F3
La Meije (peak), Fr. 64/C2
La Mensura (peak), Col. 180/C4
La Merca, Sp. 46/B1
La Merced, Bol. 188/C2
La Merced, Peru 184/C3
La Merced, Arg. 188/C4
La Mesa, Ca, US 166/C5
La Mesa (int'l arpt.), Hon. 176/E3
La Mesa, Ven. 180/D2
La Mesa, Col. 188/L8
La Mesa, NM, US 150/A1
La Mira, Mex. 174/E5
La Mirada, Ca, US 166/F8
La Moine (riv.), Il, US 155/J3
La Monna (peak), It. 65/C4
La Montaña (phys. reg.), Peru 179/B3
La Monte, Mo, US 153/H1
La Mota (mtn.), Tx, US 151/C3
La Motte, Fr. 56/C4
La Motte-d'Aveillans, Fr. 64/B3
La Motte-du-Caire, Fr. 64/C4
La Motte-Servolex, Fr. 64/B1
La Moure, ND, US 156/E4
La Mula, Mex. 151/B3
La Mure, Fr. 64/B3
La Negra, Arg. 190/C3
La Neuveville, Swi. 60/D3
La Norville, Fr. 30/J6
La Ola, Chile 188/B3
La Orchila (isl.), Ven. 173/H5
La Orotava, Sp. 110/A3
La Oroya, Peru 184/C3
La Palma, Pan. 177/G4
La Palma, Col. 183/L7
La Palma (isl.), Sp. 107/A2
La Paloma, Uru. 191/G2
La Pampa (prov.), Arg. 190/D3
La Para, Arg. 188/D4
La Paragua, Ven. 181/F3
La Paz, Arg. 190/D2
La Paz, Arg. 188/E4
La Paz (cap.), Bol. 188/B1
La Paz (dept.), Bol. 184/D4
La Paz, Col. 180/C3
La Paz, Col. 180/C2
La Paz, Hon. 176/E3
La Paz, Mex. 174/C3
La Paz (bay), Mex. 174/C3
La Paz, Phil. 88/D3
La Paz, Uru. 191/K11
La Paz, Uru. 191/K11
La Pêche, Qu, Can. 161/H2
La Pedrera, Col. 180/D5
La Peña, Pan. 172/E6
La Peña, Col. 183/L7
La Penne-sur-Huveaune, Fr. 64/B6
La Perla, Mex. 151/B3
La Perouse (str.), Japan,Rus. 77/P5
La Petite-Raon, Fr. 60/C1
La Piedad Cavadas, Mex. 174/E4
La Pine, Or, US 146/C2
La Place, La, US 164/C2
La Plant, SD, US 154/D1
La Plata, Arg. 191/K11
La Plata, Col. 180/C4
La Plata (riv.), Co, US 149/H2
La Plata, Md, US 163/J1
La Plata, Mo, US 155/H3
La Pobla de Lillet, Sp. 47/F1
La Pocatière, Qu, Can. 158/B2
La Poile, Nf, Can. 159/H2
La Pola de Gordón, Sp. 46/C1
La Porte, In, US 160/C4
La Porte, Tx, US 151/M9
La Porte City, Ia, US 155/H2
La Posta Ind. Res., Ca, US 148/D4
La Prairie (co.), Qu, Can. 159/N7
La Prairie, Qu, Can. 159/P7
La Pryor, Tx, US 151/E3
La Puebla, Sp. 47/G3
La Puebla de Almoradiel, Sp. 46/D3
La Puebla de Cazalla, Sp. 46/C4
La Puebla de Montalbán, Sp. 46/C3
La Puente, Ca, US 166/G7
La Puntilla (pt.), Ecu. 180/A5
La Quebrada, Ven. 180/D2
La Queue-les-Yvelines, Fr. 54/A6
La Quiaca, Arg. 188/C2
La Rambla, Sp. 46/C4
La Ravoire, Fr. 64/B1
La Reforma, Arg. 190/D3
La Reforma, Mex. 174/C3
La Rinconada, Sp. 46/C4
La Rioja (dist.), Sp. 46/C3
La Rioja (prov.), Arg. 188/C4
La Rioja, Arg. 188/C4
La Robla, Sp. 46/C1
La Roche, Swi. 60/D4
La Roche-Bernard, Fr. 56/C5
La Roche-de-Glun, Fr. 64/A3
La Roche-de-Rame, Fr. 64/C3
La Roche-en-Ardenne, Belg. 55/E3
La Roche-Maurice, Fr. 56/A4
La Roche-sur-Foron, Fr. 60/C5
La Roche-sur-Yon, Fr. 44/C3
La Rochelle, Fr. 44/C3
La Rochette, Fr. 64/C2
La Roda, Sp. 46/D3
La Romana, DRep. 173/H4
La Ronge, Sk, Can. 140/F3
La Roque-d'Anthéron, Fr. 64/B5
La Rotta, It. 63/D6
La Rúa, Sp. 46/B1
La Rumorosa, Mex. 148/D4
La Sabana, Ven. 183/P7
La Sal, Ut, US 149/H1
La Sal (mts.), Ut, US 147/J4
La Salle, Mb, Can. 156/F3
La Salle, Co, US 154/B3
La Salle, Il, US 155/K3
La Salle les Alpes, Fr. 64/C3
La Salute di Livenza, It. 63/F2
La Sara, Arg. 191/C7
La Sarraz, Swi. 60/C4
La Sarre, Qu, Can. 141/J4
La Saussaye, Fr. 57/F2
La Sauvette (peak), Fr. 64/C6
La Serena, Chile 188/B4
La Servelle (peak), Fr. 64/B3
La Seu d'Urgell, Sp. 47/F1
La Seyne-sur-Mer, Fr. 64/B6
La Sierpe, Cuba 177/G1
La Sila (mts.), It. 48/E3
La Silueta (peak), Chile 191/B7
La Solana, Sp. 46/D3
La Souterraine, Fr. 44/D3
La Spezia, It. 62/C5
La Spezia (prov.), It. 62/C4
La Sûre (peak), Fr. 64/B2
La Suze-sur-Sarthe, Fr. 57/F5
La Tabatière, Qu, Can. 141/L3
La Tebaida, Col. 183/K8
La Teste, Fr. 44/C4
La Tête à l'Ane (peak), Fr. 60/C6
La Thuile, It. 64/C1
La Tigra, PN, Hon. 176/E3
La Toma, Arg. 190/D2
La Tortue (isl.), Haiti 177/H1
La Tortuga (isl.), Ven. 181/E2
La Tour-d'Aigues, Fr. 64/B5
La Tour-de-Peilz, Swi. 60/C5
La Tour-de-Trême, Swi. 60/D4
La Tour-du-Pin, Fr. 64/B1
La Tranca, Arg. 190/D2
La Tremblade, Fr. 44/C4
La Trinidad, Phil. 88/C1
La Trinitaria, Mex. 176/C2
La Trinité, Fr. 64/D5
La Trinité-des-Monts, Qu, Can. 158/C1
La Trinité-Porhoët, Fr. 56/C4
La Troncal, Ecu. 180/B5
La Troya (riv.), Arg. 188/B4
La Turballe, Fr. 56/C6
La Turbie, Fr. 62/H8
La Uníon, Ven. 180/E2
La Unión, ESal. 176/E3
La Unión, Col. 180/B4
La Unión, Sp. 47/E4
La Unión, Chile 190/B4
La Unión, Col. 183/K7
La Unión, Bol. 185/F4
La Unión, Peru 184/A2
La Unión, Peru 184/B3
La Union, NM, US 150/A2
La Unión, Mex. 175/E5
La Urbana, Ven. 181/E3
La Vale, Md, US 161/G5
La Valette-du-Var, Fr. 64/B6
La Vecilla, Sp. 46/C1
La Vega, Col. 183/L8
La Vergne, Tn, US 162/D2
La Verkin, Ut, US 149/F2
La Verna, It. 63/E6
La Verne, Ca, US 166/C2
La Vernia, Tx, US 151/E3
La Verrière, Fr. 30/H5
La Victoria, Col. 180/B4
La Victoria, Ven. 180/D3
La Victoria, Col. 183/J8
La Victoria, Ven. 183/N7
La Vieille-Lyre, Fr. 57/F3
La Vieja (riv.), Col. 183/K8
La Virginia, Col. 183/K8
La Voulte-sur-Rhône, Fr. 64/A3
La Vraie-Croix, Fr. 56/C5
La Wantzenau, Fr. 55/G6
Laa an der Thaya, Aus. 45/M2
Laaber, Ger. 59/E4
Laage, Ger. 40/E5
Laakirchen, Aus. 59/G7
Laarne, Belg. 54/C1
Laas (Lasa), It. 61/G4
Laas Caanood, Som. 118/C3
Laas Dhaareed, Som. 118/C3
Laas Qoray, Som. 118/D3
Laatzen, Ger. 53/G4
Laax, Swi. 61/F4
Labadieville, La, US 164/C3
Labang, Malay. 90/D3
Labasheeda, Ire. 32/A4
Labason, Phil. 88/C3
L'Abbaye, Swi. 60/C4
Labdah (Leptis Magna) (ruin), Libya 45/G3
Labé (pol. reg.), Gui. 114/B4
Labé, Gui. 114/B4
Labe (Elbe) (riv.), Czh.,Ger. 43/H2
Labelle, Qu, Can. 161/J1
Laberweinting, Ger. 59/F5
Labian (cape), Malay. 88/B4
Labin, Cro. 45/L4
Labinsk, Rus. 73/L5
Labis, Malay. 89/C2
Labná (ruin), Mex. 176/D1
Labo, Phil. 88/C2
Laborde, Arg. 190/E2
Laborec (riv.), Slvk. 43/L4
Labota, Indo. 91/F4
Labouglé, Arg. 188/E4
Laboulaye, Arg. 190/E2
Labrador (reg.), Can. 139/L4
Labrador (sea), Can., NAm 139/M4
Labrador City, Nf, Can. 141/K3
Lábrea, Braz. 185/E2
Labrieville, Qu, Can. 158/C1
Labruguière, Fr. 44/E5
Labry, Fr. 55/E5
Labuan (terr.), Bru. 88/A4
Labuhan, Indo. 89/D4
Labuhanbajo, Indo. 91/E5
Labuhanbilik, Indo. 89/C2
Labuhanhaji, Indo. 89/B2
Labuhanmaringgai, Indo. 89/D4
Labuhanruku, Indo. 89/B2
Labuk (riv.), Malay. 91/E2
Labuk (bay), Malay. 91/E2
Labuništa, FYROM 49/G2
Labutta, Myan. 86/B5
Läby, Swe. 39/A1
Labytnangi, Rus. 74/G3
Laç, Alb. 49/F2
Lac (pref.), Chad 116/B2
Lac Afwein (riv.), Kenya 119/B1
Lac Court Oreilles Ind. Res., Wi, US 157/J5
Lac du Bonnet, Mb, Can. 156/F2
Lac du Flambeau, Wi, US 157/K5
Lac du Flambeau Ind. Res., Wi, US 157/K4
Lac La Biche, Ab, Can. 140/E3
Lac La Hache, BC, Can. 144/D2
Lac la Martre, NW, Can. 140/E2
Lac Pelletier, Sk, Can. 145/L3
Lac Seul, On, Can. 157/H2
Lac Son, Viet. 94/D1
Lac Thien, Viet. 90/C1
Lac-Alouette, Qu, Can. 159/N6
Lac-au-Saumon, Qu, Can. 158/D1
Lac-aux-Sables, Qu, Can. 158/A2
Lac-Beauport, Qu, Can. 158/B2
Lac-Bouchette, Qu, Can. 158/A1
Lac-Brome, Qu, Can. 161/K2
Lac-des-Aigles, Qu, Can. 158/C2
Lac-Drolet, Qu, Can. 158/B3
Lac-du-Cerf, Qu, Can. 161/J1
Lac-Édouard, Qu, Can. 158/A2
Lac-Etchemin, Qu, Can. 158/B2
Lac-Mégantic, Qu, Can. 158/B3
Lacadena, Sk, Can. 145/K2
L'Acadie, Qu, Can. 159/P7
Lacantum (riv.), Mex. 176/D2
Lacassine Nat'l Wild. Ref., La, US 151/H2
Lacaune, Fr. 44/E5
Laccadive (sea), Asia 92/B5
Lacchiarella, It. 62/C3
Lacco Ameno, It. 65/C6
Lacepede (bay), Austl. 127/C4
Lacerdónia, Moz. 123/G3
Laces (Latsch), It. 61/G4
Lacey, Ar, US 153/J4
Lacey, Wa, US 144/C4
Lach Bissigh (riv.), Som. 119/C1
Lach Dera (riv.), Som. 119/C1
Lacha (lake), Rus. 68/H3
Lachapelle-aux-Pots, Fr. 54/A5
Lachay (pt.), Peru 184/B3
Lachen, Swi. 61/E3
Lachenaie, Qu, Can. 159/N6
Lachendorf, Ger. 53/H3
Lachhmangarh, India 96/A2
Lāchi, Pak. 98/A3
Lachine, Qu, Can. 159/N7
Lachlan (riv.), Austl. 127/D4
Lachte (riv.), Ger. 53/H3
Lachung, India 97/G2
Lachute, Qu, Can. 161/J2
Laçin, Azer. 103/F2
Lackawanna, NY, US 160/V10
Lackawanna (co.), Pa, US 168/C1
Lackland (A.F.B.), Tx, US 151/E3
Läckö, Swe. 40/E2
Laclubar, ETim. 128/B2
Lacob ti-Duyong (mt.), Phil. 87/J5
Lacock, Eng, UK 36/D4
Lacomb, Or, US 146/B1
Lacombe, La, US 164/D2
Lacombe, Ab, Can. 145/H1
Lacon, Il, US 155/K3
Laconia, NH, US 161/L3
Lacoochee, Fl, US 164/L7
Lacreek Nat'l Wild. Ref., SD, US 154/D2
Lacroix-Saint-Ouen, Fr. 54/B5
Lacross (isl.), Austl. 128/C3
Lacy-Lakeview, Tx, US 151/F2
Ladakh (mts.), India 101/L2
Ladário, Braz. 188/E1
Ladbergen, Ger. 53/E4
Ladder (hills), Sc, UK 33/C2
Ladder (cr.), Ks, Co, US 154/D4
Laddonia, Mo, US 155/J4
Lądek-Zdrój, Pol. 43/J3
Ladenburg, Ger. 58/B4
Ladera Heights, Ca, US 166/F8
Ladismith, SAfr. 124/C4
Ladispoli, It. 65/B4
Lado, Sudan 117/F4
Ladoga, Rus. 69/T7
Ladoga (lake), Rus. 192/D
Ladoix-Serrigny, Fr. 60/A3
Ladozhskaya, Rus. 73/K5
Ladozhskoye Ozero, Rus. 69/U6
Ladrillero (mtn.), Chile 191/B7
Ladson, SC, US 163/G4
Ladva-Vetka, Rus. 68/G3
Lādwa, India 98/D5
Lady Barron, Austl. 133/D5
Lady Isle (isl.), Sc, UK 33/B5
Lady Lake, Sk, Can. 156/C1
Lady Lake, Fl, US 165/H3
Ladybank, Sc, UK 33/C4
Ladybower (res.), Eng, UK 35/G5
Ladybrand, SAfr. 124/D3
Ladysmith, Wi, US 157/J5
Ladysmith, BC, Can. 144/C3
Ladysmith, SAfr. 125/E3
Ladyville, Belz. 175/H5
Ladyzhyn, Ukr. 72/E3
Lae (isl.), Mrsh. 136/F4
Lae, Thai. 94/C2
Laer, Ger. 53/E4
Lafayette, Al, US 162/E4
Lafayette, Ca, US 167/K11
Lafayette, Co, US 154/B4
Lafayette, In, US 160/C4
Lafayette, La, US 164/B2
Lafayette, NJ, US 168/D1
Lafayette, Or, US 144/C5
Lafayette, Tn, US 162/D2
Lafe, Ar, US 162/B2
Lafia, Nga. 115/H4
Lafiagi, Nga. 115/G4
Lafitte, La, US 164/C3
Lafleche, Sk, Can. 145/L3
Lafnitz (riv.), Aus. 45/L3
Lafontaine, Qu, Can. 159/M6
Lāfūl, India 93/F6
Laga (mts.), It. 65/C2
Laga Balal (riv.), Kenya 117/H5
Laga Mado Gali (riv.), Kenya 119/B1
Laga Merille (riv.), Kenya 119/B1
Lagacéville, NB, Can. 158/E2
Lagamar, Braz. 189/H1
Lagan, Swe. 40/E3
Lagan (riv.), NI, UK 34/B3
Lagan (riv.), Swe. 40/E3
Lagarto, Braz. 187/F1
Lagawe, Phil. 88/C1
Lagbo, D.R. Congo 121/G2
Lagdo (lake), Camr. 116/B3
Lage, Ger. 53/F5
Lage Vaart (canal), Neth. 52/C4
Lågen (riv.), Nor. 40/C1
Lages, Braz. 189/G3
Laggan, Sc, UK 33/B2
Laggan (lake), Sc, UK 33/B3
Lagh Bogal (riv.), Kenya 118/A5
Lagh Bor (riv.), Kenya 118/A5
Lagh Kutulo (riv.), Kenya 119/C1
Laghouat (wilaya), Alg. 111/F2
Laghouat, Alg. 111/F2
Laghtnafrankee (peak), Ire. 32/C5
Lagnieu, Fr. 60/B6
Lagnö (isl.), Swe. 39/B1
Lagny-le-Sec, Fr. 30/L4
Lagny-sur-Marne, Fr. 30/L5
Lago Cardiel, Arg. 191/C6
Lago da Pedra, Braz. 183/E4
Lago de Atitlán, PN, Guat. 176/D3
Lago Piratuba, Reserva Biológica do, Bol. 182/B4
Lago Posadas, Arg. 191/C5
Lago Puelo, PN, Arg. 190/C4
Lago Verde, Chile 190/C5
Lago Viedma, Arg. 191/B6
Lagoa, Port. 46/A4
Lagoa da Prata, Braz. 189/H2
Lagoa Formosa, Braz. 186/D3
Lagoa Vermelha, Braz. 189/G4
Lagoda (lake), Rus. 38/J3
Lagodekhi, Geo. 71/H4
Lagonegro, It. 48/D2
Lagord, Fr. 44/C3
Lagos, Nga. 115/F5
Lagos (state), Nga. 115/F5
Lagos, Port. 46/A4
Lagos de Moreno, Mex. 174/E4
Lagosanto, It. 63/F4
Lagrange, In, US 160/D4
Laguardia, Sp. 44/B5
Laguna (cr.), Ca, US 167/M10
Laguna, NM, US 149/J3
Laguna (dam), Az, US 148/E4
Laguna (mts.), Ca, US 148/D4
Laguna (bay), Phil. 88/F7
Laguna, Braz. 189/G4
Laguna Atascosa NWR, Tx, US 151/F4
Laguna Beach, Fl, US 165/F2
Laguna Beach, Ca, US 166/C3
Laguna Blanca, PN, Arg. 190/C3
Laguna de Duero, Sp. 46/C2
Laguna de la Restinga, PN, Ven. 181/E2
Laguna del Laja, PN, Chile 190/C3
Laguna del Rey, Mex. 174/E3
Laguna Grande, Arg. 190/D4
Laguna Grande, Arg. 191/C6
Laguna Hills, Ca, US 166/C3
Laguna Ind. Res., NM, US 149/J3
Laguna Larga, Arg. 188/D4
Laguna Paiva, Arg. 188/D4
Laguna San Rafael, PN, Chile 190/B5
Laguna Verde, Chile 190/N8
Laguna Yema, Arg. 188/D3
Lagunas, Chile 188/B2
Lagunas, Peru 184/B2
Lagunas, Peru 184/C2
Lagunas de Chacahua, PN, Mex. 176/B2
Lagunas de Montebello, Mex. 172/C4
Lagunas de Zempoala, PN, Mex. 175/Q10
Lagundo (Algund), It. 61/H4
Lagunetas, Ven. 180/D2
Lagunillas, Ven. 180/D2
Lagunillas, Chile 190/N8
Lagunillas, Bol. 188/D1
Laguntara (lag.), Hon. 177/E3
Lagushao, China 81/C2
Lahad Datu, Malay. 88/B4
Lahan Sai, Thai. 94/C3
Lahār, India 96/B2
Lāharpur, India 96/C2
Lahat, Indo. 89/C3
Laheria Sarāi, India 97/E2
Lahewa, Indo. 89/B2
Laḩij, Yem. 118/C2
Lāhījān, Iran 103/G2
Lahn (riv.), Ger. 42/E3
Lahnstein, Ger. 55/G3
Laholm, Swe. 40/E3
Laholms (bay), Den. 40/F3
Lahoma, Ok, US 153/E2
Lahontan (res.), Nv, US 146/D4
Lahontan (dam), Nv, US 146/D4
Lahore, Pak. 98/C4
Lahore (int'l arpt.), Pak. 98/C4
Lahr, Ger. 60/D1
Lāhrūd, Iran 103/F2
Lahti, Fin. 41/L1
Laï, Chad 116/C3
Lai Chau, Viet. 94/C1
Lai-hka, Myan. 94/B1
Laiagam, PNG 129/F1
Lai'an, China 80/D4
Laichingen, Ger. 58/C5
Laidon (lake), Sc, UK 33/B3
Laifeng Tujiazu Zizhixian, China 87/F2
L'Aigle, Fr. 57/F3
Laigueglia, It. 62/B6
Laihia, Fin. 38/G3
Lailly-en-Val, Fr. 57/G5
Lainate, It. 62/C2
Laindon, Eng, UK 30/E2
Laingsburg, SAfr. 124/C4
Lainioälven (riv.), Swe. 38/G1
Laird, Sk, Can. 145/L1
Lais, Indo. 89/C3
Lais, Phil. 88/D4
Laisamis, Kenya 119/B1
Laishevo, Rus. 69/L5
Laishui, China 80/G7
Laisvall, Swe. 38/F2
Laitila, Fin. 41/J1
Laives (Leifers), It. 61/H5
Laiwu, China 80/D3
Laixi, China 80/E3
Laiyang, China 80/E3
Laiyuan, China 80/C3
Laizhou (bay), China 80/D3
Laja (lake), Chile 190/C3
Lajas, Peru 184/B2
Lajatico, It. 63/D7
Laje, Braz. 187/E1
Lajeado, Braz. 189/G4
Lajedo, Braz. 183/G5
Lajes, Azor., Port. 47/S12
Lajes (int'l arpt.), Azor., Port. 47/S12
Lajes, Braz. 183/G4
Lajing (pass), Nepal 97/E1
Lajord, Sk, Can. 156/B2
Lajosmizse, Hun. 50/D2
Lāju, India 86/B3
Lajwāna Kalān, India 98/D5
Lakamané, Mali 114/C3
Lakato, Madg. 125/J7
Lake (co.), Fl, US 164/M6
Lake (co.), Il, US 167/P15
Lake Mason NWR, Mt, US 145/K4
Lake Minchumina, Ak, US 171/H3
Lake Woodruff Nat'l Wild. Ref., Fl, US 165/H3
Lake Alfred, Fl, US 164/M7
Lake Alice NWR, ND, US 156/E3
Lake Alma, Sk, Can. 156/B3
Lake Alpine, Ca, US 146/C4
Lake Amadeus Abor. Land, Austl. 131/F3
Lake Andes, SD, US 154/E2
Lake Andes Nat'l Wild. Ref., SD, US 154/E2
Lake Ann, Mi, US 160/D2
Lake Arrowhead, Ca, US 166/C2
Lake Arthur, NM, US 152/B4
Lake Arthur, La, US 164/B2
Lake Barrington, Il, US 167/P15
Lake Beulah, Wi, US 167/P14
Lake Bluff, Il, US 167/Q15
Lake Boga, Austl. 132/B2
Lake Bolac, Austl. 132/B3
Lake Buena Vista, Fl, US 164/M7
Lake Butler, Fl, US 165/G2
Lake Cargelligo, Austl. 133/C1
Lake Catherine, Il, US 167/P15
Lake Charles, La, US 164/B2
Lake City, Ar, US 162/B3
Lake City, Ca, US 146/C3
Lake City, Co, US 149/J1
Lake City, Fl, US 165/G2
Lake City, Ga, US 163/M7
Lake City, Ia, US 155/G2
Lake City, Mi, US 160/D2
Lake City, Mn, US 155/H1
Lake City, Pa, US 160/F3
Lake City, SC, US 163/H4
Lake City, SD, US 156/F5
Lake City, Tn, US 162/E2
Lake Clark NP, Ak, US 142/X12
Lake Clarke Shores, Fl, US 164/P9
Lake Conjola, Austl. 133/E2
Lake Cowichan, BC, Can. 144/B3
Lake Creek (riv.), Ut, US 147/G4
Lake Crystal, Mn, US 155/G1
Lake Dallas, Tx, US 150/K6
Lake Delton, Wi, US 155/K2
Lake District NP, Eng, UK 35/E2
Lake Elmo, Mn, US 157/Q7
Lake Elsinore, Ca, US 166/C3
Lake Fenton, Mi, US 160/E3
Lake Fern, Fl, US 164/K7
Lake Forest, Il, US 167/Q15
Lake Forest Park, Wa, US 167/C2
Lake Fork (riv.), Ut, US 147/H3
Lake Fork, Id, US 146/E1
Lake Garfield, Fl, US 164/M8
Lake Geneva, Wi, US 160/B3
Lake George, Co, US 152/B1
Lake George, NY, US 161/K3
Lake George, Mi, US 160/D3
Lake George NWR, ND, US 156/E4
Lake Grace, Austl. 130/C5
Lake Hamilton, Ar, US 153/H3
Lake Hamilton, Fl, US 164/M7
Lake Havasu City, Az, US 148/E3
Lake Helen, Fl, US 165/H3
Lake Hughes, Ca, US 148/C3
Lake Ilo NWR, ND, US 156/C4
Lake in the Hills, Il, US 167/P15
Lake Isom Nat'l Wild. Ref., Tn, US 162/C2
Lake Jackson, Tx, US 150/G3
Lake Jem, Fl, US 164/M6
Lake King, Austl. 130/C5
Lake Lenore, Sk, Can. 145/M1
Lake Linden, Mi, US 157/K4
Lake Lotawana, Mo, US 153/G1
Lake Louise, Ab, Can. 144/F2
Lake Lucerne, Fl, US 164/P11
Lake Macleod, Austl. 130/B3
Lake Malawi NP, Malw. 123/G2
Lake Mary, Fl, US 164/N6
Lake Mburo NP, Ugan. 121/G3
Lake McDonald, Mt, US 145/H3
Lake Mead Nat'l Rec. Area, Az, Nv, US 148/E2
Lake Meredith Nat'l Rec. Area, Tx, US 152/D3
Lake Mills, Ia, US 155/H2
Lake Mills, Wi, US 155/K2
Lake Mohawk, NJ, US 168/D1
Lake Monroe, Fl, US 164/N6
Lake Montezuma, Az, US 149/G3
Lake Murray, PNG 129/F1
Lake Nakuru NP, Kenya 119/B2
Lake Nash, Austl. 131/H2
Lake Nettie Nat'l Wild. Ref., ND, US 156/D4
Lake Odessa, Mi, US 160/D3
Lake Orion, Mi, US 167/F6
Lake Oswego, Or, US 146/B1
Lake Panasoffkee, Fl, US 164/L6
Lake Park, Mn, US 156/F4
Lake Park, Ga, US 165/G2
Lake Park, Ia, US 155/G2
Lake Park, Fl, US 164/P9
Lake Placid, NY, US 161/K2
Lake Placid, Fl, US 165/H4
Lake Pleasant, NY, US 161/J3
Lake Preston, SD, US 155/F1
Lake Ronkonkoma, NY, US 169/E2
Lake Saint Croix Beach, Mn, US 157/Q7
Lake Shore, Mn, US 157/G4
Lake Shore, Md, US 168/B5
Lake Station, In, US 167/R16
Lake Stevens, Wa, US 144/C3
Lake Success, NY, US 169/L8
Lake Tanglewood, Tx, US 152/D3
Lake Thibadeau Nat'l Wild. Ref., Mt, US 145/K3
Lake Tomahawk, Wi, US 157/K5
Lake Toxaway, NC, US 163/F3
Lake View, Ar, US 153/J3
Lake View, Ia, US 155/G2
Lake Villa, Il, US 167/P15
Lake Waccamaw, NC, US 163/H3
Lake Wales, Fl, US 164/M8
Lake Way, Austl. 130/D3
Lake Worth, Fl, US 164/P9
Lake Zahl Nat'l Wild. Ref., ND, US 156/C3
Lake Zurich, Il, US 167/P15
Lakefield, On, Can. 161/G2
Lakefield, Mn, US 155/G2
Lakefield NP, Austl. 129/F3
Lakehills, Tx, US 150/E3
Lakehurst, NJ, US 168/D3
Lakehurst Nav. Air Eng. Ctr., NJ, US 168/D3
Lakeland, Ga, US 165/G2
Lakeland, La, US 164/C2
Lakeland, Fl, US 164/M7
Lakeland, Mn, US 157/Q7
Lakeland Village, Ca, US 166/C3
Lakemoor, Il, US 167/P15
Lakenheath, Eng, UK 37/G2
Lakeport, Ca, US 146/B4
Lakeport, Tx, US 151/G1
Lakes Entrance, Austl. 133/D3
Lakesfjorden (inlet), Nor. 38/H1
Lakeside, Ca, US 166/D5
Lakeside, Mt, US 144/G3
Lakeside, Ne, US 154/C2
Lakeside, Or, US 146/A2
Lakeside, Ut, US 147/G3
Lakeside, Va, US 163/J2
Laketown, Ut, US 147/H3
Lakeview, Ar, US 153/H2
Lakeview, Ca, US 166/C3
Lakeview, Ga, US 162/E3
Lakeview, Mi, US 160/D3
Lakeview, Mt, US 147/H1
Lakeview, Or, US 146/C2
Lakeview, Tx, US 152/D3
Lakeview Estates, Ga, US 163/M7
Lakeville (lake), Mi, US 167/F6
Lakeville, Mn, US 155/H1
Lakeway, Tx, US 151/F2
Lakewood, Ca, US 166/F8
Lakewood, Co, US 154/B4
Lakewood, Il, US 167/P15
Lakewood, NJ, US 168/D3
Lakewood, NY, US 161/G3
Lakewood, Oh, US 160/F4
Lakewood, Wa, US 144/C3
Lakewood, Wi, US 157/K5
Lakhāsar, India 98/B5
Lakhemaa NP, Est. 41/L2
Lakhīmpur, India 96/C2
Lakhnādon, India 96/B4
Lakhpat, India 101/J4
Lakhva, Bela. 72/D1
Laki (vol.), Ice. 38/N7
Lakin, Ks, US 152/D2
Lakki, Pak. 98/A3
Lakkíon, Gre. 67/K3
Lakonía (gulf), Gre. 67/J3
Lakor (isl.), Indo. 128/C2
Lakota, ND, US 156/E3
Lakota, C.d'Iv. 114/D5
Lakshadweep (isls.), India 77/F8
Lakshadweep (terr.), India 92/B6
Lākshām, Bang. 97/H4
Lal Suhanra NP, Pak. 98/B5
Lala, Phil. 88/C4
Lāla Mūsa, Pak. 98/B3
Lalago, Tanz. 119/A2
Lālajīn, Iran 103/G3
Lalana (riv.), Madg. 125/H8
Lalang (riv.), Indo. 90/B4
Lâlapaşa, Turk. 51/H5
Lalara, Gabon 120/B2
Lalauli, India 96/C3
L'Albaron (peak), Fr. 64/D2
Lālbhitti, Nepal 97/E2
Lālganj, India 97/E3
Lālgola, India 97/G3
Lālī, Iran 103/G3
Lāliān, Pak. 98/B4
Lalībela, Eth. 118/A2
Laliki, Indo. 128/B1
Lalín, Sp. 46/A1
Lalin (riv.), China 79/K3
Lalinde, Fr. 44/D4
Lalitpur, India 96/B3
Lalitpur (Pāţan), Nepal 97/E2
Lalla Rookh Abor. Land, Austl. 130/C2
Lālmanir Hāt, Bang. 97/G3
Lālpur, Bang. 97/G3
Lalyo, Sudan 117/F4
Lam Pao (res.), Thai. 86/D5
Lāma, Bang. 93/F3
Lamachan (peak), Sc, UK 34/D1
Lamadi, China 93/G2
Lamadrid, Mex. 151/D4
Lamag, Malay. 88/B4
Lamakera, Indo. 128/A2
Lamaline, Nf, Can. 159/K2
Lamanai (ruin), Belz. 176/D2
Lamandau (riv.), Indo. 90/D4
Lamar, Ar, US 153/H3
Lamar, Mo, US 153/G2
Lamar, Co, US 152/C1
Lamar, SC, US 163/G3
Lamarche, Fr. 60/B1
Lamarche-sur-Saône, Fr. 60/B3
Lamarque, Arg. 190/D3
Lamas, Peru 184/B2
Lamastre, Fr. 64/A3
Lāmayūrū, India 98/D2
Lambach, Aus. 59/G6
Lamballe, Fr. 56/C4
Lambaré, Par. 188/E3
Lambaréné, Gabon 120/B3
Lambari, Braz. 187/L6
Lambasa, Fiji 137/Z17
Lambay (isl.), Ire. 34/B5
Lambayeque (dept.), Peru 184/A2
Lambayeque, Peru 184/B2
Lambé Coba (riv.), Mali 114/C3
Lambeg, NI, UK 34/B3
Lambert, Ms, US 162/B3
Lambert-St. Louis (int'l arpt.), Mo, US 155/J4
Lamberton, Mn, US 155/G1
Lambert's Bay, SAfr. 124/B4
Lambertville, Mi, US 160/E4
Lambertville, NJ, US 168/D3
Lambesc, Fr. 64/B5
Lambeth (bor.), Eng, UK 30/C2
Lambourn, Eng, UK 37/E3
Lambrama, Peru 184/C4
Lambrecht, Ger. 58/B4
Lambro (riv.), It. 62/C2
Lambsburg, Va, US 163/G2
Lambsheim, Ger. 58/B3
Lambton, Qu, Can. 158/B3
Lambton (co.), On, Can. 167/H6
Lame Deer, Mt, US 145/L5
Lamego, Port. 46/B2
Lamentin (int'l arpt.), Fr. 173/N9
Lamèque, NB, Can. 158/E2
Lameroo, Austl. 131/J5
Lamesa, Tx, US 150/D1
Lamía, Gre. 49/H3
Lamine (riv.), Mo, US 153/H1
Lamington (riv.), NJ, US 168/D2
Lamington NP, Austl. 134/D5
Lamitan, Phil. 88/C4
Lamlash, Sc, UK 33/A5
Lamma (isl.), China 87/L8
Lammefjord (inlet), Den. 39/H7
Lammermuir (hills), Sc, UK 33/D5
Lammhult, Swe. 40/F3
Lammi, Fin. 41/L1
Lamming Mills, BC, Can. 144/D1
Lamoille, Nv, US 146/F3
Lamon (bay), Phil. 88/C2
Lamona, Wa, US 144/E4
Lamone (riv.), It. 45/J4
Lamongan, Indo. 89/F4
Lamoni, Ia, US 155/H3
Lamont, Ok, US 153/F2
Lamont, Fl, US 165/G2
Lamont, Ca, US 148/C3
Lamorlaye, Fr. 30/K4
Lamotrek (isl.), Micr. 136/D4
Lamotte-Beuvron, Fr. 57/H5
Lampa, Chile 190/N8
Lampa, Peru 184/D4
Lampang, Thai. 94/B2
Lampasas, Tx, US 151/E2
Lampasas (riv.), Tx, US 175/F2
Lampaul-Plouarzel, Fr. 56/A4
Lampazos de Naranjo, Mex. 151/D4
Lampe, Mo, US 153/H2
Lampedusa, It. 48/C5
Lampedusa (isl.), It. 29/F5
Lampertheim, Ger. 58/B3
Lampeter, Wal, UK 36/B2
Lampeter, Pa, US 168/B4
Lamphey, Wal, UK 36/B3
Lamphun, Thai. 94/B2
Lampman, Sk, Can. 156/C3
Lamporecchio, It. 63/D6
Lampson, Wi, US 157/J5
Lampung (prov.), Indo. 89/D4
Lamstedt, Ger. 53/G1
Lamu, Kenya 119/C2
Lamu (isl.), Kenya 119/C2
Lamud, Peru 184/B2
Lamwa (peak), Ugan. 117/G5
Lamy, NM, US 152/B3
Lan (isl.), Tai. 87/J4
Lan Sang NP, Thai. 94/B2
Lana, It. 61/H4
Lana, Río de la (riv.), Mex. 176/C2
Lanai (isl.), Hi, US 142/T10
Lanaken, Belg. 55/E2
Lanao (lake), Phil. 88/D4
Lanark, Sc, UK 33/C5
Lanark, Il, US 155/K2
Lanas Village, Malay. 88/B4
Lanba, China 86/E3
Lanbi (isl.), Myan. 93/G5
Lancang (riv.), China 86/C2
Lancang (Mekong) (riv.), China 78/D5
Lancashire (plain), Eng, UK 35/E4
Lancashire (co.), Eng, UK 35/F4
Lancaster (sound), Nun, Can. 141/H1
Lancaster, Eng, UK 35/F3
Lancaster, Ca, US 148/C3
Lancaster, Ky, US 162/E2
Lancaster, Mn, US 156/F3
Lancaster, Mo, US 155/H3
Lancaster, NH, US 161/L2
Lancaster, NY, US 160/V10
Lancaster, Oh, US 160/E5
Lancaster (arpt.), Pa, US 168/B3

Map Section

Lancas – Lenora

Lancaster (co.), Pa, US 168/B4
Lancaster, Pa, US 168/B3
Lancaster, SC, US 163/G3
Lancaster, Tx, US 150/L7
Lancaster, Va, US 163/J2
Lancaster, Wi, US 155/J2
Lance (cr.), Wy, US 154/B2
Lance Creek, Wy, US 154/B2
Lancebranlette (peak), Fr. 64/C1
Lancefield, Austl. 133/B3
Lancelin, Austl. 130/B4
Lancenigo, It. 63/F2
Lancer, Sk, Can. 145/K2
Lanchester, Eng, UK 35/G2
Lanch'khut'i, Geo. 71/G4
Lanciano, It. 65/D3
L'Ancienne-Lorette, Qu, Can. 158/B2
Lanco, Chile 190/B3
Lançon-Provence, Fr. 64/B5
Łańcut, Pol. 43/M3
Lancy, Swi. 60/C5
Land Between The Lakes Recreation Area, Ky, US 162/C2
Land Kehdingen (reg.), Ger. 53/G1
Land O'Lakes, Fl, US 164/L7
Land O'Lakes, Wi, US 157/K4
Landau an der Isar, Ger. 59/F5
Landau in der Pfalz, Ger. 58/B4
Landeck, Aus. 61/G3
Landen, Belg. 55/E2
Lander, Wy, US 147/J2
Landerneau, Fr. 56/A4
Landes (reg.), Fr. 44/C4
Landes de Lanvaux (mts.), Fr. 44/B3
Landesbergen, Ger. 53/G3
Landi Kotal, Pak. 98/A2
Landis, Sk, Can. 145/K1
Landis Valley Museum, Pa, US 168/B3
Landisburg, Pa, US 168/A3
Landivisiau, Fr. 56/A3
Landivy, Fr. 57/D4
Landrecies, Fr. 54/C3
Landri Sales, Braz. 183/F4
Landriano, It. 62/C3
Landrum, SC, US 163/F3
Land's End (pt.), Eng, UK 36/A6
Landsberg, Ger. 61/G1
Landsborough (cr.), Austl. 134/B3
Landser, Fr. 60/D2
Landshut, Ger. 59/F5
Landskrona, Swe. 40/E4
Landsmeer, Neth. 52/B4
Landstuhl, Ger. 55/G5
Landvetter (int'l arpt.), Swe. 40/E3
Landza, Congo 120/D2
Lane (riv.), Fr. 57/F6
Lane End, Eng, UK 30/A2
Lanercost, Eng, UK 35/F2
Lanesborough, Ire. 32/C2
Lanester, Fr. 56/B5
Lanett, Al, US 162/E4
Lang, Sk, Can. 156/B3
Lang Craig (pt.), Sc, UK 33/D3
Lang Kha Tuk (peak), Thai. 94/B4
Lang Son, Viet. 87/E4
Lang Suan, Thai. 94/B4
Langadhás, Gre. 49/H2
Langádia, Gre. 49/H4
Langano (lake), Eth. 118/A4
Langara, Indo. 91/F4
Langdon, ND, US 156/E3
Langdon, Ab, Can. 145/H2
Langdon Hills, Eng, UK 30/E2
Langeac, Fr. 44/E4
Langeais, Fr. 57/F6
Langebaanweg, SAfr. 124/L10
Langeberg (mts.), SAfr. 124/L10
Langeland (isl.), Ger. 40/D4
Langelsheim, Ger. 53/H5
Langen (lake), Nor. 38/S8
Langen, Ger. 58/B3
Langen, Ger. 53/F1
Langenaltheim, Ger. 58/D5
Langenargen, Ger. 61/F2
Langenau, Ger. 58/D5
Langenbach, Ger. 59/E6
Langenberg, Ger. 53/E6
Langenburg, Sk, Can. 156/D2
Längenfeld, Aus. 61/G3
Langenfeld, Ger. 55/F1
Langenhagen, Ger. 53/G4
Langenhorn, Ger. 40/C4
Langenlois, Aus. 43/H4
Langenpreising, Ger. 59/E6
Langenselbold, Ger. 58/C2
Langenstein, Aus. 59/H6
Langenthal, Swi. 60/D3
Langenwang, Aus. 45/L3
Langenzenn, Ger. 58/D3
Langenzersdorf, Aus. 51/N7
Langeoog (isl.), Ger. 53/E1
Langeoog, Ger. 53/E1
Langepas, Rus. 74/H3
Langerringen, Ger. 61/G1
Langeskov, Den. 40/D4
Langesund, Nor. 40/C2
Langeten (riv.), Swi. 60/D3
Langfang, China 80/H7
Langford, SD, US 156/F5
Langfurth, Ger. 58/D4
Langgam, Indo. 89/B2
Langgapayung, Indo. 89/B2
Langgar, China 78/C6
Langham, Eng, UK 37/F1
Langham, Sk, Can. 145/L1
Langhirano, It. 62/D4
Langholm, Sc, UK 35/F1
Langhorne, Pa, US 168/D3
Langjökull (glacier), Ice. 38/N7
Langkawi (isl.), Thai. 93/G6
Langkon, Malay. 88/B4
Langley, Eng, UK 30/E3
Langley, Eng, UK 30/B2
Langley, Wa, US 167/C1
Langley (A.F.B.), Va, US 163/J2
Langlois, Or, US 146/A2
Langnau im Emmental, Swi. 60/D4
Langney (pt.), Eng, UK 37/G5
Langogne, Fr. 44/E4
Langon, Fr. 56/D5
Långön (isl.), Swe. 39/A2
Langon, Fr. 44/C4
Langøya (isl.), Nor. 38/E1
Langqên (riv.), China 99/C5
Langquaid, Ger. 59/F5
Langres, Fr. 60/B2
Langres, de (plat.), Fr. 66/E1
Langru, China 99/C4
Langrune-sur-Mer, Fr. 57/E2
Langsa, Indo. 89/B1
Langshyttan, Swe. 40/G1
Langstaff, On, Can. 160/U8
Langston, Ok, US 153/F3
Langtang, Nga. 115/H4
Langtang, China 87/F2
Langtang Lirung (peak), Nepal 97/E1
Langtang NP, Nepal 97/E1
Langtou, China 81/C2
Langtry, Tx, US 151/D3
Languedoc (reg.), Fr. 66/D2
Languedoc-Roussillon (pol. reg.), Fr. 44/E5
Langueux, Fr. 56/C3
Languidic, Fr. 56/B5
Langwedel, Ger. 53/G3
Langweid an Lech, Ger. 58/E6
Langwies, Swi. 61/F4
Langxi, China 80/D5
Lanham-Seabrook, Md, US 168/B6
Lanigan (riv.), Sk, Can. 145/M2
Lanigan, Sk, Can. 145/M2
Lanin (vol.), Arg. 190/C3
Lanin, PN, Arg. 190/C3
Lankāpāra Hāt, India 97/G2
Länkäran, Azer. 103/G2
Lankin, ND, US 156/F3
Lankou, China 87/G4
Lanlacuni Bajo, Peru 184/D4
Lanmeur, Fr. 56/B3
Länna, Swe. 39/A1
Lannemezan (plat.), Fr. 44/D5
Lannemezan, Fr. 47/F1
Lanner, Eng, UK 36/A6
Lannilis, Fr. 56/A3
Lannion, Fr. 56/B3
Lannion (bay), Fr. 44/B2
Lannion (Servel) (arpt.), Fr. 56/B3
L'Annonciation, Qu, Can. 161/J1
Lanouée, Fr. 56/C4
Lans, Montagne de (mts.), Fr. 64/B3
Lansdale, Pa, US 168/C3
Lansdowne, On, Can. 161/H2
Lansdowne, India 96/B1
Lansdowne, Pa, US 168/C4
Lansdowne-Baltimore Highlands, Md, US 168/B5
L'Anse Ind. Res., Mi, US 157/K4
Lansford, ND, US 156/D3
Lansford, Pa, US 168/C2
Lanshan, China 87/G3
Lansing, Yk, Can. 171/M3
Lansing, Il, US 167/Q16
Lansing, Ia, US 155/J2
Lansing (cap.), Mi, US 160/D3
Lanslebourg-Mont-Cenis, Fr. 64/C2
Lanta (isl.), Thai. 93/G6
Lantana, Fl, US 164/P9
Lantang, China 87/G4
Lantau (isl.), China 87/K7
Lantau (peak), China 87/K8
Lantau (chan.), China 87/K8
Lanterne (riv.), Fr. 60/C2
Lantosque, Fr. 64/D5
Lantouy, Laos 86/D4
Lantry, SD, US 154/D1
Lantz, NS, Can. 158/F3
Lantzville, BC, Can. 144/B3
Lanús, Arg. 191/J11
Lanusei, It. 48/A3
Lanuvio, It. 65/B4
Lanuza, Phil. 88/D3
Lanvallay, Fr. 56/C4
Lanvéoc, Fr. 56/A4
Lanxi, China 79/K2
Lanxi, China 87/H2
Lanza, Bol. 188/C1
Lanzara, It. 65/D6
Lanzarote (int'l arpt.), Sp. 110/B3
Lanzarote (isl.), Canl., Sp. 107/A2
Lanžhot, Czh. 43/J4
Lanzhou, China 78/E4
Lanzo d'Intelvi, It. 61/F6
Lanzo Torinese, It. 64/D2
Lao (mts.), China 81/D2
Lao (riv.), China 87/G2
Lao (peak), China 80/E3
Lao Cai, Viet. 86/D4
Lao Fu Chai, Laos 94/C1
Laoag, Phil. 88/C1
Laobian, China 81/B2
Laocheng, China 78/F5
Laodao (riv.), China 87/G2
Laodaodian, China 79/K1
Laoguanzui, China 87/G2
Laoha (riv.), China 79/H3
Laohekou, China 80/B4
Laohutun, China 81/A3
Laojun (mtn.), China 80/B4
Laoling, China 81/D2
Laon, Fr. 54/C4
Laos (ctry.) 77/K8
Laoshan, China 80/E3
Laotuding (peak), China 81/C2
Laou (riv.), Mor. 112/B2
Lapa, Braz. 189/G3
Lapalud, Fr. 64/A4
Lapataia, Arg. 191/C7
Lapeer, Mi, US 160/E3
Lapeer (co.), Mi, US 167/F6
Lapia, Nga. 115/G4
Lapine, Al, US 165/E2
Lapinlahti, Fin. 68/E3
Lapithos, Cyp. 104/C2
Lapland (reg.), Nor. 68/C1
Lapland (reg.), Eur. 74/B3
Lapland (reg.), Swe. 192/D
Lapoint, Ut, US 147/J3
Laporte, Pa, US 161/H4
Laporte, Co, US 154/B3
Lapotina (mtn.), Rus. 79/N1
Lappeenranta, Fin. 41/N1
Lappersdorf, Ger. 59/F4
Lappi (prov.), Fin. 38/H2
Lâpseki, Turk. 49/K2
Laptev (sea), Rus. 77/M2
Lapua, Fin. 68/D3
Lapundra, India 101/K3
Lăpuşna, Mol. 72/E4
Lapy, Pol. 43/M2
Laqīyat al Arba'īn, Sudan 135/F4
Laquey, Mo, US 153/H2
Lār, Iran 103/H5
Lara (state), Ven. 180/D2
Lara, Austl. 133/B4
Laracha, Sp. 46/A1
Larache (prov.), Mor. 112/B2
Larache, Mor. 112/A2
Laracor, Ire. 32/D2
Laragne-Montéglin, Fr. 64/B4
Lārak (isl.), Iran 103/J5
Laramie (mts.), Wy, US 154/B2
Laramie, Wy, US 154/B3
Laramie (riv.), Wy, US 154/B3
Laramie (peak), Wy, US 154/B2
Laranjeiras do Sul, Braz. 189/F3
Larantuka, Indo. 128/A2
Larat (isl.), Indo. 91/H5
Larat, Indo. 128/C1
Larba, Alg. 112/G4
Larchmont, NY, US 169/K8
l'Arcouest (pt.), Fr. 56/B3
Lærdalsøyri, Nor. 40/B1
Lardier (cape), Fr. 64/C6
Laredo, Sp. 44/B5
Laredo, Mo, US 155/H3
Laredo, Peru 184/B3
Laredo, Mt, US 145/K3
Laredo, Tx, US 151/E4
Laredo (int'l arpt.), Tx, US 151/E4
Laren, Neth. 52/C4
Lares, Peru 184/C4
Larga (lag.), Tx, US 151/F4
L'Argentière-la-Bessée, Fr. 64/C3
Largo (bay), Sc, UK 33/D4
Largo, Fl, US 164/K8
Largo (cr.), NM, US 149/H3
Largo, Md, US 168/B6
Largs, Sc, UK 33/B5
Largue (riv.), Fr. 60/D2
Lariang (riv.), Indo. 91/E4
Lariano, It. 65/B4
Larino, It. 65/D4
Lárisa, Gre. 49/H3
Lark (riv.), Eng, UK 37/G2
Lark Harbour, Nf, Can. 159/H1
Lārkāna, Pak. 101/J3
Larkhall, Sc, UK 33/C5
Larkspur, Ca, US 167/J11
Larkspur, Co, US 154/B4
L'Arly, PN de, Burk. 115/F4
Larmor-Plage, Fr. 56/B5
Larnaca, Cyp. 104/C2
Larnaca (int'l arpt.), Cyp. 104/C2
Larnaca (dist.), Cyp. 104/C2
Larne, NI, UK 34/C2
Larne (dist.), NI, UK 34/C2
Larne Lough (inlet), NI, UK 34/C2
Larned, Ks, US 152/E1
Larochette, Lux. 55/F4
Laropi, Ugan. 121/G2
Laroque-d'Olmes, Fr. 44/D5
Larose, La, US 164/C3
Larreynaga, Nic. 176/E3
Larrimah, Austl. 128/D3
Larroque, Arg. 191/J10
Larrys (cr.), Pa, US 168/A1
Larry's River, NS, Can. 159/G3
Larsen Bay, Ak, US 171/H4
Larsen Ice Shelf, Ant. 192/V
Larsen Sound (bay), Nun, Can. 140/G1
Larslan, Mt, US 145/L3
Larto, La, US 164/C2
Laruns, Fr. 44/C5
Larvik, Nor. 40/D2
Las Animas, Co, US 152/C1
Las Aves (isls.), Ven. 173/H5
Las Bayas, Arg. 190/C4
Las Bombas, Chile 188/B3
Las Breñas, Arg. 188/D3
Las Cabezas de San Juan, Sp. 46/C4
Las Cabras, Chile 190/N9
Las Casuarinas, Arg. 188/B4
Las Cruces, NM, US 149/J4
Las Cruces (int'l arpt.), NM, US 174/D1
Las Delicias, Ven. 180/C3
Las Esperanzas, Mex. 151/D4
Las Flores, Arg. 190/F3
Las Guacamayas, Mex. 174/E5
Las Hermosas, PN, Col. 180/C4
Las Higueras, Arg. 190/D2
Las Juntas, Col. 180/C4
Las Lajas (peak), Arg. 190/C3
Las Lajas, Arg. 190/C3
Las Lajitas, Ven. 181/E3
Las Lomas, Peru 184/A2
Las Lomitas, Arg. 188/D3
Las Margaritas, Mex. 176/D2
Las Martinas, Cuba 177/E1
Las Mercedes, Ven. 181/E2
Las Minas (peak), Hon. 176/D3
Las Montañitas, Ven. 180/D3
Las Navas, Phil. 88/D2
Las Nieves, Mex. 174/D3
Las Orquídeas, PN, Col. 180/B3
Las Palmas, Pan. 177/F4
Las Palmas (riv.), Mex. 148/D4
Las Palmas de Cocalán, PN, Chile 190/N9
Las Palmas de Gran Canaria, Sp. 110/B3
Las Pampitas, Bol. 185/E4
Las Parejas, Arg. 188/D5
Las Pedroñeras, Sp. 46/D3
Las Perdices, Arg. 190/E2
Las Perlas (arch.), Pan. 177/G4
Las Petas, Bol. 185/E4
Las Petas, Bol. 185/G5
Las Piedras, Ven. 180/C2
Las Piedras, Ven. 181/F2
Las Piedras, Uru. 191/K11
Las Piedras, Peru 184/D4
Las Piedras, Bol. 185/E3
Las Pinas, Phil. 88/E7
Las Pipinas, Arg. 191/F2
Las Plumas, Arg. 190/D4
Las Rosas, Mex. 176/C2
Las Rosas, Arg. 188/D5
Las Rozas de Madrid, Sp. 47/N9
Las Tablas, Pan. 180/A3
Las Tablas, NM, US 149/J2
Las Tórtolas (peak), Chile 188/B4
Las Toscas, Uru. 189/F5
Las Toscas, Arg. 188/E4
Las Trincheras, Ven. 181/E3
Las Varas, Mex. 174/D4
Las Varillas, Arg. 188/D4
Las Vegas, NM, US 152/B3
Las Vegas, Nv, US 148/E2
Las Vegas Nat'l Wildlife Reserve, NM, US 152/B3
Las Yaras, Peru 188/B1
Lasa (Laas), It. 61/G4
Lasahau, Indo. 128/A1
Lasalle, Qu, Can. 159/N7
Lasan, Indo. 90/E3
Lasanbāri, India 86/B3
Lasberg, Aus. 59/H6
Lascano, Uru. 191/G2
Lascar (vol.), Chile 188/C2
Lascar, Co, US 152/B2
Lasem, Indo. 89/E4
Lashburn, Sk, Can. 145/K1
Lashio, Myan. 86/C4
Lashkar Gāh, Afg. 101/H2
Lashmanka, Rus. 69/L5
Lasia (isl.), Indo. 89/B2
Lasne-Chapelle-Saint-Lambert, Belg. 55/D2
Læsø (isl.), Den. 40/D3
Lasolo (riv.), Indo. 91/F4
Lassay-les-Châteaux, Fr. 57/E4
Lassen (peak), Ca, US 146/C3
Lassen Volcanic NP, Ca, US 146/C3
L'Assomption, Qu, Can. 159/P6
Lasswade, Sc, UK 33/C5
Last Mtn. (lake), Sk, Can. 145/M2
Lastoursville, Gabon 120/C3
Lastovo (isl.), Cro. 48/E1
Lastovo, Cro. 50/C4
Lastovski Kanal (canal), Cro. 48/E1
Lastra a Signa, It. 63/E6
Lästringe, Swe. 39/A2
Lastrup, Ger. 53/E3
Lat Yao, Thai. 94/B3
Lata, Sol. 136/F6
Latacunga, Ecu. 180/B5
Latady (isl.), Ant. 192/U
Latākhola, Bang. 97/H4
Latakia (Al Lādhiqīyah), Syria 104/D24
L'Atakora (prov.), Ben. 115/F4
Lātehār, India 97/E4
Latemar (peak), It. 61/H5
Laterrière, Qu, Can. 158/B1
Laterza, It. 48/E2
Latexo, Tx, US 151/G2
Latham, Ks, US 153/F2
Lathan (riv.), Fr. 44/C3
Lathrop, Ca, US 167/M11
Lathrop, Mo, US 155/G4
Latimer, Eng, UK 30/B2
Latimer, Ia, US 155/H2
Latina, It. 65/B5
Latina (prov.), It. 65/C5
Latina Scalo, It. 65/B4
Latisana, It. 63/G2
Latium (reg.), It. 67/G2
Laton, Ca, US 148/C2
Latorica (riv.), Slvk.,Ukr. 43/M4
Latouche Treville (cape), Austl. 128/A4
Latrobe, Pa, US 161/G4
Latrobe, Austl. 132/C4
Latrobe (mt.), Austl. 133/C4
Latsch (Laces), It. 61/G4
Lattes, Fr. 44/E5
Lattingtown, NY, US 169/L8
Lātūr, India 95/C2
Latvia (ctry.) 29/G3
Lat'yuga, Rus. 69/L2
Lau Group (isl.), Fiji 136/H6
Laubach, Ger. 58/B1
Lauca, PN, Chile 184/D5
Lauca, PN, Chile 188/B1
Lauch (riv.), Fr. 45/G3
Lauchert (riv.), Ger. 58/C6
Lauchheim, Ger. 58/D5
Lauda-Königshofen, Ger. 58/C3
Lauder, Mb, Can. 156/D3
Lauder, Sc, UK 33/D5
Lauderdale (lakes), Wi, US 167/N14
Lauderdale, Ms, US 162/C4
Lauderdale Lakes, Fl, US 164/P10
Lauderdale-by-the-Sea, Fl, US 164/P10
Lauderhill, Fl, US 164/P10
Laudun, Fr. 64/A4
Lauenbrück, Ger. 53/G2
Lauenburg, Ger. 53/H2
Lauenen, Swi. 60/D5
Lauenförde, Ger. 53/H5
Lauer (riv.), Ger. 58/D2
Lauf, Ger. 58/E3
Laufach, Ger. 58/C2
Laufen, Swi. 60/D3
Laufen, Ger. 59/F7
Laufenburg, Swi. 60/E2
Lauffen am Neckar, Ger. 58/C4
Laugharne, Wal, UK 36/B3
Laughlen (mt.), Austl. 131/G2
Laughlin (A.F.B.), Tx, US 151/D3
Lauhanvuoren NP, Fin. 68/D3
Lauhkaung, Myan. 86/C3
Lauingen, Ger. 58/D5
Laukuva, Lith. 41/K4
Launceston, Austl. 132/C4
Launceston, Eng, UK 36/B5
Laune (riv.), Ire. 32/A5
Launette (riv.), Fr. 30/L4
Launglon, Myan. 94/B3
Launonen, Fin. 39/E4
Laupen, Swi. 60/D4
Lauperswil, Swi. 60/D4
Laupheim, Ger. 61/F1
L'Aupillon (peak), Fr. 64/C4
Laura, Austl. 134/B1
Laura, Austl. 131/H5
Laura, Sk, Can. 145/L2
Laureana di Borrello, It. 48/E3
Laurel, De, US 163/K1
Laurel, Fl, US 165/G4
Laurel, In, US 160/D5
Laurel, Md, US 168/B5
Laurel, Ms, US 164/D2
Laurel, Ne, US 155/F2
Laurel, Va, US 163/J2
Laurel Bay, SC, US 163/G4
Laurel Hill, Fl, US 165/E2
Laurel Springs, NJ, US 168/C4
Laureldale, Pa, US 168/C3
Laurelton, Pa, US 168/A2
Laurelvale, NI, UK 34/B3
Laurence Harbor, NJ, US 169/J10
Laurencekirk, Sc, UK 33/D3
Laurens, Ia, US 155/G2
Laurens, SC, US 163/F3
Laurentian (plat.), On, Can. 140/G3
Laurentides, Qu, Can. 159/N6
Laurier, Mb, Can. 156/E2
Laurier-Station, Qu, Can. 158/B2
Laurieston, Sc, UK 34/D2
Laurinburg, NC, US 163/H3
Lauris, Fr. 64/B5
Laurium, Mi, US 157/K4
Lauriya Nandangarh, India 97/E2
Lauro, It. 65/D6
Lausanne, Swi. 60/C4
Lauscha, Ger. 58/E2
Laut (isl.), Indo. 91/E4
Lautaro, Chile 190/B3
Lautem, ETim. 128/B2
Lauter (riv.), Ger. 42/E3
Lauter (riv.), Fr.,Ger. 58/B4
Lauter, Ger. 59/F1
Lauterach (riv.), Ger. 59/E4
Lauterbach (riv.), Ger. 58/E2
Lauterbach, Ger. 58/C1
Lauterbourg, Fr. 58/B5
Lauterbrunnen, Swi. 60/D4
Lauterecken, Ger. 55/G4
L'Authion (peak), Fr. 64/D4
Lautoka, Fiji 137/Y18
Lautoporras, Fin. 39/E4
Lauve, Nor. 40/D2
Lauwers (chan.), Neth. 52/D1
Lauwersmeer (lake), Neth. 52/D2
Lava Beds Nat'l Mon., Ca, US 146/C3
Lava Hot Springs, Id, US 147/G2
Lavaca (riv.), Tx, US 151/F3
Lavaca (bay), Tx, US 151/F3
Lavaca, Al, US 162/C4
Lavagna, It. 62/C5
Lavagna (riv.), It. 62/C4
Laval, Fr. 57/E4
Laval, Qu, Can. 159/N6
Lavalleja (dept.), Uru. 191/G2
Lavallette, NJ, US 168/D4
Lāvān (isl.), Iran 103/H5
Lavans-lès-Saint-Claude, Fr. 60/B5
Lavant (riv.), Aus. 45/L3
Lavapié (pt.), Chile 190/B3
Lavaraty, Madg. 125/H8
Lavassaare, Est. 41/L2
Lavaur, Fr. 44/D5
Lavelanet, Fr. 44/D5
Lavello, It. 48/D2
Lavena, It. 61/E6
Laveno, It. 61/E6
Laverne, Ok, US 152/E2
Laverton, Austl. 130/D4
Lavey, Swi. 60/D5
Lavezzola, It. 63/E4
Lavik, Nor. 40/A1
Lavillette, NB, Can. 158/E2
Lavina, Mt, US 145/K4
Lavino (riv.), It. 63/E4
Lavis, It. 61/H5
Lavon (dam), Tx, US 150/L6
Lavon, Tx, US 150/L6
Lavonia, Ga, US 163/F3
Lavos, Port. 46/A2
Lavras, Braz. 186/D4
Lavras da Mangabeira, Braz. 183/G4
Lávrion, Gre. 49/J4
Lavushi Manda NP, Zam. 123/F2
Lawa (riv.), FrG.,Sur. 182/C2
Lawa (riv.), FrG. 181/H4
Lawabauk, Myan. 86/C5
Lawang, Indo. 89/F4
Lāwar Khās, India 96/A1
Lawarai (pass), Pak. 98/A2
Lawas, Malay. 88/A4
Lawdar, Yem. 118/C2
Lawen, Or, US 146/D2
Lawit (peak), Malay. 89/C1
Lawit (mtn.), Indo. 90/D3
Lawksawk, Myan. 94/B1
Lawn, Nf, Can. 159/K2
Lawn, Tx, US 151/E1
Lawn Hill, Austl. 129/E4
Lawn Hill NP, Austl. 129/E4
Lawndale, Ca, US 166/F8
Lawnhill, BC, Can. 171/M5
Lawqah, SAr. 103/E4
Lawra, Gha. 114/E4
Lawrence, Ks, US 153/G1
Lawrence, In, US 160/C5
Lawrence, Ma, US 161/L3
Lawrence, NY, US 169/L9
Lawrence, NZ 135/B4
Lawrence, Ne, US 154/E3
Lawrence, Tx, US 150/L7
Lawrence Park, Pa, US 160/F3
Lawrence Station, NB, Can. 158/D3
Lawrenceburg, Ky, US 162/E1
Lawrenceburg, Tn, US 162/D3
Lawrenceburg, In, US 162/E1
Lawrencetown, NI, UK 34/B3
Lawrenceville, Il, US 162/D1
Lawrenceville, Ga, US 163/N7
Lawrenceville, NJ, US 168/D3
Lawrenceville, Va, US 163/J2
Lawson, Ar, US 153/H4
Lawson, Mo, US 155/G4
Lawson, Sk, Can. 145/L2
Lawtey, Fl, US 165/G2
Lawton, Ok, US 153/E3
Lawu (peak), Indo. 90/D5
Lax, Ga, US 165/G2
Laxå, Swe. 40/F2
Laxey, IM, UK 34/D3
Laxou, Fr. 55/F6
Lay (riv.), Fr. 44/C3
Lay-Saint-Christophe, Fr. 55/F6
Laya (riv.), Rus. 69/N2
Layar (cape), Indo. 91/E4
Laye (riv.), Fr. 64/B4
Layjūn, Yem. 118/D2
Laylān, Iraq 103/F3
Läyliäinen, Fin. 39/E4
Layon (riv.), Fr. 44/C3
Laysan (isl.), Hi, US 137/H2
Layton, Fl, US 165/H5
Layton, Ut, US 147/H3
Layton, NJ, US 168/D1
Laytonville, Ca, US 146/B4
Laytown, Ire. 34/B4
Lazarev, Rus. 75/Q4
Lazarevac, Yugo. 50/E3
Lázaro Cárdenas, Mex. 148/E5
Lázaro Cárdenas, Mex. 174/B2
Lázaro Cárdenas, Mex. 174/E5
Lazdijai, Lith. 41/K4
Lazi, Phil. 88/C3
Lazio (prov.), It. 45/J5
Lazise, It. 63/D3
Lazo, Rus. 75/P3
Lazonby, Eng, UK 35/F2
Le Ban-Saint-Martin, Fr. 55/F5
Le Beausset, Fr. 64/B6
Le Bic, Qu, Can. 158/C1
Le Blanc, Fr. 44/D3
Le Blanc-Mesnil, Fr. 30/K5
Le Bono, Fr. 56/C5
Le Bourg-d'Oisans, Fr. 64/C2
Le Bourget (Paris), (Arpt.) 30/*
Le Bourget-du-Lac, Fr. 64/B1
Le Breuil, Fr. 44/F3
Le Cannet, Fr. 64/D5
Le Cannet-des-Maures, Fr. 64/C6
Le Castellet, Fr. 64/B6
Le Cateau-Cambrésis, Fr. 54/C3
Le Center, Mn, US 155/H1
Le Chasseral (peak), Swi. 60/D3
Le Chasseron (peak), Swi. 60/C4
Le Chesnay, Fr. 30/J5
Le Chesne, Fr. 55/D4
Le Cheval Blanc (peak), Fr. 60/C5
Le Cheval Noir (peak), Fr. 64/C2
Le Cheylard, Fr. 44/F4
Le Claire, Ia, US 155/J3
Le Conquet, Fr. 56/A4
Le Cornate (peak), It. 45/J5
Le Coudray, Fr. 57/G4
Le Crès, Fr. 47/G1
Le Creusot, Fr. 44/F3
Le Croisic, Fr. 56/C6
Le Crotoy, Fr. 54/A3
Le Duffre (peak), Fr. 64/B4
Le Faouët, Fr. 56/B4
Le Fœil, Fr. 56/C4
Le Folgoët, Fr. 56/A3
Le Gore, Md, US 168/A4
Le Goulet, NB, Can. 158/E2
Le Grammont (peak), Swi. 60/C5
Le Grand (peak), Fr. 64/C1
Le Grand, Ca, US 148/B2
Le Grand (cape), Austl. 130/D5
Le Grand Ballon (peak), Fr. 60/D2
Le Grand Charnier (peak), Fr. 64/C2
Le Grand Coyer (peak), Fr. 64/C4
Le Grand-Lemps, Fr. 64/B2
Le Grand-Lucé, Fr. 57/F5
Le Grand-Quevilly, Fr. 57/G2
Le Grau-du-Roi, Fr. 44/F5
Le Grazie, It. 62/C5
Le Harve-Octeville (arpt.), Fr. 57/F1
Le Havre, Fr. 57/F1
Le Landeron, Swi. 60/D3
Le Lauzet-Ubaye, Fr. 64/C4
Le Lavandou, Fr. 64/C6
Le Lion-D'Angers, Fr. 57/E5
Le Locle, Swi. 60/C3
Le Loroux-Bottereau, Fr. 56/D6
Le Luc, Fr. 64/C6
Le Lude, Fr. 57/F5
Le Mans, Fr. 57/F4
Le Mars, Ia, US 155/F2
Le Mée-sur-Seine, Fr. 30/K6
Le Mêle-sur-Sarthe, Fr. 57/F3
Le Mesnil-Amelot, Fr. 30/K4
Le Mesnil-Aubry, Fr. 30/K4
Le Mesnil-Esnard, Fr. 54/A5
Le Mesnil-le-Roi, Fr. 30/J5
Le Mesnil-Saint-Denis, Fr. 30/H5
Le Mesnil-sur-Oger, Fr. 54/D6
Le Molay-Littry, Fr. 57/E2
Le Môle (peak), Fr. 60/C5
Le Monêtier-les-Bains, Fr. 64/C3
Le Mont-Saint-Michel, Fr. 56/D3
Le Morond (peak), Fr. 60/C4
Le Moure de la Gardille (peak), Fr. 44/E4
Le Mourre Froid (peak), Fr. 64/C3
Le Murge (mts.), It. 48/E2
Le Muy, Fr. 64/C6
Le Noirmont (peak), Fr. 60/C4
Le Noirmont, Swi. 60/C3
Le Noirmont (peak), Swi. 60/C5
Le Nouvion-en-Thiérache, Fr. 54/C3
Le Palais, Fr. 56/B6
Le Palais-sur-Vienne, Fr. 44/D4
Le Palyvestre (arpt.), Fr. 64/C6
Le Passage, Fr. 44/D4
Le Pellerin, Fr. 56/D6
Le Perray-en-Yvelines, Fr. 30/H5
Le Petit Ballon (peak), Fr. 60/D2
Le Petit Ferrand (peak), Fr. 64/C4
Le Plessis-Belleville, Fr. 30/L4
Le Plessis-Feu-Aussoux, Fr. 30/M5
Le Plessis-Placy, Fr. 30/L4
Le Pont-de-Beauvoisin, Fr. 64/B1
Le Pont-de-Claix, Fr. 64/B2
Le Pontet, Fr. 64/A5
Le Port, Fr. 125/S15
Le Portel, Fr. 54/A2
Le Pouliguen, Fr. 56/C6
Le Pouzin, Fr. 64/A3
Le Pradet, Fr. 64/C6
Le Puy-en-Velay, Fr. 44/E4
Le Puy-Sainte-Réparade, Fr. 64/B5
Le Quesnoy, Fr. 54/C3
Le Raizet (int'l arpt.), Fr. 173/N8
Le Rateau (peak), Fr. 64/C2
Le Relecq-Kerhuon, Fr. 56/A4
Le Rocher Blanc (peak), Fr. 64/C2
Le Rouret, Fr. 64/D5
Le Rove, Fr. 64/B6
Le Roy, Ks, US 153/G1
Le Roy, Mn, US 155/H2
Le Roy, Il, US 155/K3
Le Russey, Fr. 60/C3
Le Sap, Fr. 57/F3
Le Suchet (peak), Swi. 60/C4
Le Sueur, Mn, US 155/H1
Le Tampon, Fr. 125/S15
Le Teil, Fr. 64/A3
Le Teilleul, Fr. 57/E3
Le Theil, Fr. 57/F4
Le Tholonet, Fr. 64/B5
Le Tholy, Fr. 60/C1
Le Thor, Fr. 64/A5
Le Thuit-Signol, Fr. 57/F2
Le Touquet-Paris-Plage, Fr. 54/A2
Le Touvet, Fr. 64/B2
Le Tréboux (peak), Fr. 64/B4
Le Trélod (peak), Fr. 64/C1
Le Tréport, Fr. 54/A3
Le Val, Fr. 64/C6
Le Val-d'Ajol, Fr. 60/C2
Le Vésinet, Fr. 30/J5
Le Vigan, Fr. 44/E5
Le'an (riv.), China 87/H2
Lea (riv.), Eng, UK 37/F3
Lea (Lee) (riv.), Eng, UK 30/C1
Leach, Camb. 94/C3
Leach (riv.), Eng, UK 37/E3
Leacock-Leola-Bareville, Pa, US 168/B3
Lead, SD, US 140/F4
Lead Hill, Ar, US 153/H2
Leaday, Tx, US 150/E2
Leadbetter (pt.), Wa, US 144/B4
Leadenham, Eng, UK 35/H5
Leader, Sk, Can. 145/K2
Leader Water (riv.), Sc, UK 33/D5
Leadon (riv.), Eng, UK 36/D3
Leaf, Ms, US 164/D2
Leaf (riv.), Ms, US 162/C5
Leaghur (lake), Austl. 132/B2
League City, Tx, US 151/M9
Leah, Ga, US 163/F4
Leakesville, Ms, US 164/D2
Leakey, Tx, US 151/E3
Lealui, Zam. 122/D2
Leam (riv.), Eng, UK 37/E2
Leamington, On, Can. 160/E3
Leamington, Ut, US 147/G4
Leander (pt.), Austl. 130/B4
Leander, Tx, US 151/F2
Leandro N. Alem, Arg. 189/F3
Leane (lake), Ire. 32/A5
Leaota (peak), Rom. 51/G3
Learmonth, Austl. 130/B2
Leary, Ga, US 165/F2
Leasburg, Mo, US 153/J1
Leask, Sk, Can. 145/L1
Leatherhead, Eng, UK 30/C3
Leavenworth, Ks, US 155/G4
Leavenworth, Wa, US 144/D4
Leba, Pol. 40/G4
Lebach, Ger. 55/F5
Lebak, Phil. 88/D4
Lebam, Wa, US 144/C4
Lébamba, Gabon 120/B3
Lebane, Yugo. 50/E4
Lébango, Congo 120/C2
Lebanon (ctry.) 77/C6
Lebanon (mts.), Leb. 104/D3
Lebanon (co.), US 169/B2
Lebanon, Co, US 149/H2
Lebanon, In, US 160/C4
Lebanon, Ks, US 154/E4
Lebanon, Ky, US 162/E2
Lebanon, Mo, US 153/H2
Lebanon, NH, US 161/K3
Lebanon, NJ, US 168/D2
Lebanon, Oh, US 160/D5
Lebanon, Or, US 146/B1
Lebanon, Pa, US 168/B3
Lebanon, Tn, US 162/D2
Lebanon, Va, US 163/F2
Lebanon Junction, Ky, US 162/E2
Lebbeke, Belg. 55/D2
Lebeau, La, US 164/C2
Lebec, Ca, US 148/C3
Lebedinyy, Rus. 75/N4
Lebedyan', Rus. 70/F1
Lebedyn, Ukr. 73/H2
Lebene (riv.), Mor. 112/B2
Lébény, Hun. 50/C2
Lébiga, Congo 120/C3
Lebo, Ks, US 153/G1
Lebombo (mts.), SAfr. 123/F5
Lębork, Pol. 40/G4
Lebowakgomo, SAfr. 123/F5
Lebrija, Sp. 46/B4
Lebu, Chile 190/B3
Leça da Palmeira, Port. 46/A2
Lecce, It. 49/F2
Lecce nei Marsi, It. 65/C4
Lecco (lake), It. 62/C1
Lech, Aus. 61/G3
Lech (riv.), Ger. 67/F1
Lechang, China 93/K2
Lechbruck, Ger. 61/G2
Leche (lake), Cuba 177/G1
Lechlade, Eng, UK 37/E3
Lechtaler Alps (mts.), Aus. 61/G3
Leck, Ger. 40/C4
Leckavrea (mtn.), Ire. 32/A3
Lecompte, La, US 164/B2
Léconi, Gabon 120/C3
Lectoure, Fr. 44/D5
Łęczna, Pol. 43/M3
Leda (riv.), Ger. 53/E2
Ledang (peak), Malay. 89/C2
Ledbury, Eng, UK 36/D2
Lede, Belg. 54/C2
Ledegem, Belg. 54/C2
Ledesma, Sp. 46/B2
Ledge Point, Austl. 130/B4
Ledger, Mt, US 145/J3
Lediba, D.R. Congo 120/D3
Lêdo (cape), Ang. 120/C5
Ledong, China 87/F5
Ledro (lake), It. 61/G6
Ledu (peak), It. 61/F5
Leduc, Ab, Can. 145/H1
Lee (riv.), Ire. 32/A6
Lee (Lea) (riv.), Eng, UK 30/C1
Lee, Fl, US 165/G2
Lee, Ma, US 161/K3
Lee (mtn.), Pa, US 168/B1
Lee Creek, Ar, US 153/G3
Leech (lake), Mn, US 143/H2
Leedale, Ab, Can. 144/G1
Leedey, Ok, US 152/E3
Leeds, Eng, UK 35/G4
Leeds (co.), Eng, UK 35/G4
Leeds, Al, US 162/D4
Leeds, ND, US 156/E3
Leeds, Ut, US 149/F2
Leeds and Bradford (int'l arpt.), Eng, UK 35/G4
Leeds and Liverpool (canal), Eng, UK 35/G4
Leeds Point, NJ, US 168/D5
Leegebruch, Ger. 42/Q6
Leek, Eng, UK 35/F5
Leek, Neth. 52/D2
Leeman, Austl. 130/B4
Leemount, Ire. 32/B6
Leer, Ger. 53/E2
Leerdam, Neth. 52/C5
Leersum, Neth. 52/C4
Lees Crossing, Ga, US 162/E4
Lees Summit, Mo, US 153/G1
Leesburg, Ga, US 165/F2
Leesburg, Fl, US 164/M6
Leesburg, Va, US 163/J1
Leesburg, NJ, US 168/D5
Leesdale, Ms, US 164/C2
Leese, Ger. 53/G3
Leesport, Pa, US 168/C3
Leeston, NZ 135/C3
Leesville, La, US 164/B2
Leesville (lake), Va, US 163/H2
Leesville (dam), Va, US 163/H2
Leeton, Austl. 133/C2
Leeu (riv.), SAfr. 124/L10
Leeudoringstad, SAfr. 124/D2
Leeuwarden, Neth. 52/C2
Leeuwin (cape), Austl. 130/B5
Leeuwin-Naturaliste NP, Austl. 130/B5
Leeville, La, US 164/C3
Leeward (isls.), NAm. 173/J4
Leff (riv.), Fr. 44/B2
Leffe, It. 62/C2
Léfini (riv.), Congo 120/C3
Lefka, Cyp. 104/C2
Lefo (peak), Camr. 115/H5
Lefor, ND, US 156/C4
Lefroy (lake), Austl. 130/D4
Left Hand, WV, US 163/G1
Legana, Austl. 132/C4
Leganés, Sp. 47/N9
Legaspi, Phil. 88/C2
Legau, Ger. 61/G2
Legazpia, Sp. 44/B5
Legges Tor (peak), Austl. 132/C4
Legionowo, Pol. 43/L2
Léglise, Belg. 55/E4
Legnago, It. 63/E3
Legnaro, It. 63/E3
Legnica, Pol. 43/J3
Legnone (peak), It. 61/F5
Léguer (riv.), Fr. 56/B3
Leh, India 98/D2
Leh Palace, India 98/D2
Lehi, Ut, US 147/H3
Lehigh, Ok, US 153/F3
Lehigh (riv.), Pa, US 161/J4
Lehigh (co.), Pa, US 168/C2
Lehigh Acres, Fl, US 165/H4
Lehighton, Pa, US 168/C2
Lehijärvi (lake), Fin. 39/E3
Lehinch, Ire. 32/A4
Léhon, Fr. 56/C4
Lehr, ND, US 156/E4
Lehrberg, Ger. 58/D4
Lehrte, Ger. 53/G4
Lehututu, Bots. 122/D4
Lei (riv.), China 93/K2
Leia (riv.), It. 65/A3
Leiah, Pak. 98/A4
Leiblfing, Ger. 59/F5
Leibnitz, Aus. 50/B2
Leibo, China 93/H2
Leicester, Eng, UK 37/E1
Leicester (co.), Eng, UK 37/E1
Leicestershire (co.), Eng, UK 35/H6
Leichhardt (dam), Austl. 131/H2
Leichhardt (falls), Austl. 129/E4
Leichhardt (riv.), Austl. 129/F4
Leichlingen, Ger. 55/G1
Leiden, Neth. 52/B4
Leiderdorp, Neth. 52/B4
Leidschendam, Neth. 52/B4
Leigh, Eng, UK 35/F5
Leigh, Eng, UK 30/D3
Leigh, Eng, UK 30/C3
Leigh Creek, Austl. 131/H4
Leighlinbridge, Ire. 32/D4
Leighton Buzzard, Eng, UK 37/F3
Leigong (mtn.), China 87/F3
Leimebamba, Peru 184/B2
Leimen, Ger. 58/B4
Leimersheim, Ger. 58/B4
Leinan, Sk, Can. 145/L2
Leine (riv.), Ger. 42/D3
Leinefelde, Ger. 53/H6
Leinfelden-Echterdingen, Ger. 58/C5
Leinster (reg.), Ire. 34/A5
Leinster (mt.), Ire. 32/D4
Leinster, Austl. 130/D3
Leintwardine, Eng, UK 36/D2
Leipheim, Ger. 58/D6
Leipsic, Oh, US 160/E4
Leipsic (riv.), De, US 168/C5
Leipsic, De, US 168/C5
Leipzig, Ger. 74/B4
Leira, Nor. 40/C1
Leiranger, Nor. 38/E2
Leiria, Port. 46/A3
Leiria (dist.), Port. 46/A3
Leirsund, Nor. 38/T8
Leirvik, Nor. 40/A2
Leisi, Est. 41/K2
Leisler (mt.), Austl. 131/F2
Leiston-cum-Sizewell, Eng, UK 37/H2
Leisure City, Fl, US 165/H5
Leitchfield, Ky, US 162/D2
Leiter, Wy, US 154/A1
Leith, Sc, UK 33/C5
Leith (hill), Eng, UK 30/B3
Leitha (riv.), Aus. 43/J5
Leitrim (co.), Ire. 32/C2
Leitrim, Ire. 32/B2
Leixlip, Ire. 34/B5
Leiyang, China 87/G3
Leiyuanzhen, China 80/B4
Leizhou (pen.), China 93/J3
Lejasciems, Lat. 41/M3
Lejpalingis, Lith. 41/K4
Lek (riv.), Neth. 42/C3
Lékana, Congo 120/C3
Lekhainá, Gre. 49/G4
Lekhcheb, Mrta. 114/C2
Lekkerkerk, Neth. 52/B5
Lekki (lag.), Nga. 115/G5
Lékoli-Pandaka, Rsv. de Faune de la, Congo 120/C2
Lekoni, Gabon 120/C3
Lekóti (riv.), Congo 120/C3
Lekoumou (pol. reg.), Congo 120/C3
Leksands-Noret, Swe. 40/F1
Leksozero (lake), Rus. 38/J3
Leku, Eth. 118/A4
Lelai (cape), Indo. 91/G3
Leland, Mi, US 160/D2
Leland, Ms, US 162/B4
Leland, Il, US 155/K3
Leland, NC, US 163/H3
Lelång (lake), Swe. 40/E2
Lel'chitsy, Bela. 72/E2
Leleque, Arg. 190/C4
Lelia Lake, Tx, US 152/D3
Leling, China 80/D3
Lelintah, Indo. 91/H4
Lelogama, Indo. 128/A2
Lelu, Micr. 136/F4
Lelydorp, Sur. 182/C1
Lelystad, Neth. 52/C3
Lem, Den. 40/C3
Lema (peak), It. 61/E5
Lema Shilindi, Eth. 118/B4
Léman (Geneva) (lake), Fr. 60/C5
Lemberg (peak), Ger. 61/E1
Lemberg, Sk, Can. 156/C2
Lemberg, Ger. 55/G5
Lembu (peak), Indo. 89/B1
Leme, Braz. 189/H2
Lemenjoen NP, Fin. 38/H1
Lemeshkino, Rus. 71/H2
Lemgo, Ger. 53/F4
Lemhi, Id, US 147/G1
Lemhi (range), Id, US 147/G1
Lemitar, NM, US 149/J3
Lemland (isl.), Fin. 41/H2
Lemland, Fin. 41/J1
Lemmer, Neth. 52/C3
Lemmon, SD, US 156/C5
Lemmon (mt.), Az, US 149/G4
Lemon Grove, Ca, US 166/C5
Lemon Springs, NC, US 163/H3
Lemoore, Ca, US 148/C2
Lemoore Nav. Air Sta., Ca, US 148/B2
Lemoyne, Ne, US 154/D3
Lempa (riv.), ESal. 176/D3
Lempäälä, Fin. 41/K1
Lempdes, Fr. 44/E4
Lemro (riv.), Myan. 86/B4
Lemsid, WSah. 110/B4
Lemva (riv.), Rus. 69/P2
Lemvig, Den. 40/C3
Lemwerder, Ger. 53/F2
Lemyethna, Myan. 86/B5
Lena (riv.), Rus. 77/M3
Lena, Mb, Can. 156/E3
Lena, Nor. 40/D1
Lena, Wi, US 160/B2
Lena, Il, US 155/K2
Lena, Ne, US 154/D3
Lena, SC, US 163/G4
Lenape (lake), NJ, US 168/D5
Lençóis Maranhenses, PN dos, Braz. 183/F3
Lençóis Paulista, Braz. 189/G2
Lendery, Rus. 68/F3
Lendinara, It. 63/E3
Lene (lake), Ire. 32/C2
Lengau, Aus. 59/G6
Lengdorf, Ger. 59/F6
Lenge, D.R. Congo 121/F4
Lengede, Ger. 53/H4
Lengenfeld, Ger. 59/F1
Lengerich, Ger. 53/E4
Lenggries, Ger. 61/H2
Lenghu, China 78/C4
Lengnau, Swi. 60/D3
Lengshuijiang, China 87/F3
Lengshuitan, China 87/F3
Lengua de Vaca (pt.), Chile 188/B4
Lengué Namobessie (riv.), Camr. 120/C2
Lengwe NP, Malw. 123/G3
Lengzipu, China 81/B2
Lenhartsville, Pa, US 168/C2
Lenia, Eth. 117/H4
Lenina (lake), Ukr. 73/H3
Lenina (peak), Taj. 99/B4
Leninabad (int'l arpt.), Taj. 99/A3
Lenine, Ukr. 73/H5
Leningradskaya, Rus. 73/K4
Leningradskaya Oblast, Rus. 68/G3
Leningradskiy, Rus. 142/U12
Leninogor, Kaz. 99/D1
Leninogorsk, Rus. 69/M5
Leninsk, Rus. 69/M4
Leninsk-Kuznetskiy, Rus. 74/J4
Leninskiy, Rus. 70/F1
Leninskoye, Kaz. 71/L2
Leninskoye, Rus. 79/L2
Leninváros, Hun. 43/L5
Lenk, Swi. 60/D5
Lenne (riv.), Ger. 55/G1
Lennestadt, Ger. 53/F6
Lenningen, Ger. 58/C5
Lennox (hills), Sc, UK 33/B5
Lennox, Ca, US 166/F8
Lennox, SD, US 155/F2
Lennox (isl.), Chile 191/D7
Lennoxtown, Sc, UK 33/B5
Lennoxville, Qu, Can. 161/L2
Leno, It. 62/D3
Lenoir, NC, US 163/G3
Lenoir City, Tn, US 162/E3
Lenola, It. 65/C5
Lenora, Ks, US 154/D4

Lenore – Little
Map Section
244
245

Lenore, Mb, Can. 156/D3
Lenore (lake), Sk, Can. 145/M1
Lenox, Ma, US 161/K3
Lenox, Ga, US 165/G2
Lenox, Ia, US 155/G3
Lens, Swi. 60/D5
Lens, Fr. 54/B3
Lens, Belg. 54/C2
Lensahn, Ger. 40/D4
Lensk, Rus. 75/M3
Lenswood, Mb, Can. 156/D1
Lenswood, Austl. 131/M8
Lent, Neth. 52/C5
Lentekhi, Geo. 71/G4
Lenting, Ger. 59/E5
Lentini, It. 48/D4
Lentvaris, Lith. 41/L4
Lenvik, Nor. 38/F1
Lenwood, Ca, US 148/D3
Leny, Pass of (pass), Sc, UK 33/B4
Lenya, Myan. 94/B4
Lenzburg, Swi. 60/E3
Lenzing, Aus. 59/G7
Lenzkirch, Ger. 61/E2
Léo, Burk. 115/E4
Leoben, Aus. 45/L3
Leográ (riv.), It. 63/E1
Leok, Indo. 91/F3
Leola, SD, US 156/E5
Leola, Ar, US 153/H3
Leominster, Ma, US 161/L3
Leominster, Eng, UK 36/D2
Leon, Ok, US 153/F4
Leon (riv.), Tx, US 172/B1
León, Nic. 176/E3
León, Sp. 46/C1
Leon, Ia, US 155/H3
Leon (int'l arpt.), Mex. 174/C3
León, Mex. 175/E4
León Muerto (pass), Chile 188/B3
Leon Valley, Tx, US 151/E3
Leon-Guanajuato (int'l arpt.), Mex. 175/E4
Leona (riv.), Tx, US 151/E3
Leona, Tx, US 151/G2
Leona Valley, Ca, US 165/B1
Leonard, ND, US 156/F4
Leonard, Tx, US 153/F4
Leonard, Mi, US 167/F6
Leonardo, NJ, US 169/J10
Leonardo da Vinci (int'l arpt.), It. 65/B4
Leonardtown, Md, US 163/J1
Leonardville, Namb. 122/C4
Leonardville, Ks, US 155/F4
Leonberg, Ger. 58/C5
Leonding, Aus. 59/H6
Leone (peak), It. 60/E5
Leone, ASam. 137/T10
Leones, Arg. 190/E2
Leonessa, It. 65/B2
Leonforte, It. 48/D4
Leongatha, Austl. 133/B4
Leonia, NJ, US 169/K8
Leonídhion, Gre. 49/H4
Leonora, Austl. 130/D4
Leopold, Austl. 133/B4
Leopoldina, Braz. 187/P6
Leopoldkanaal (riv.), Belg. 54/C1
Leopoldsburg, Belg. 55/E1
Leopoldsdorf, Aus. 51/N7
Leopoldsdorf im Marchfelde, Aus. 51/P7
Leopoldshöhe, Ger. 53/F4
Leota, Mn, US 155/F2
Leoti, Ks, US 152/D1
Leova, Mol. 72/E4
Lepaera, Hon. 176/D3
Lépanges-sur-Vologne, Fr. 60/C1
Lepanto, Ar, US 162/B3
Lepar (isl.), Indo. 89/D3
Lepe, Sp. 46/B4
Lepenoú, Gre. 49/G3
Lephepe, Bots. 122/E4
Lepi, Ang. 122/B2
L'Epine (pond), Fr. 30/K4
Leping, China 87/H2
L'Épiphanie, Qu, Can. 159/P6
Lepontine Alps (mts.), Swi. 66/F1
Lepreau Game Ref., NB, Can. 158/D3
Lepsämä, Fin. 39/E4
Lepsi, Kaz. 99/C2
Lepsy (riv.), Kaz. 99/C2
Leptis Magna (Labdah) (ruin), Libya 45/G3
Leptokariá, Gre. 49/H2
Leque, Bol. 185/E5
Lequena, Chile 188/B2
Lequepalca, Bol. 188/C1
Lequire, Ok, US 153/G3
Lera (peak), It. 64/D2
Léraba (riv.), Burk. 114/D4
Lercara Friddi, It. 48/C4
Lerdo de Tejada, Mex. 176/C2
Léré, Chad 116/B3
Lere, Nga. 115/H4
Léré, Mali 114/D3
Leribe, Les. 124/E3
Lerici, It. 62/C5
Lérida, Col. 180/D4
Lérida, Col. 183/L8
Lerik, Azer. 103/G2
Lerín, Sp. 46/E1
Lerma, Sp. 46/D1
Lerma (riv.), Mex. 139/G7
Lerma, Mex. 175/Q10
Lermoos, Aus. 61/G3
Lérouville, Fr. 55/E6
Leroux Wash (riv.), Az, US 149/G3
Leroy, ND, US 156/F3
Leroy, Al, US 164/E2
Leroy, Sk, Can. 145/M1
Leroy, Tx, US 151/F2
Lerum, Swe. 40/E3
Lerwick, Sc, UK 31/W13
Léry, Qu, Can. 159/N7
Les Alignements de Carnac, Fr. 56/B5
Les Alluets-le-Roi, Fr. 30/H5
Les Andelys, Fr. 57/G2
Les Angles, Fr. 64/A5
Les Arcs, Fr. 64/C6
Les Avenières, Fr. 64/B1
Les Bauges (upland), Fr. 64/C1
Les Bois, Swi. 60/C3
Les Breuleux, Swi. 60/D3
Les Bréviaires, Fr. 30/H5
Les Cayes, Haiti 177/H2
Les Cèdres, Qu, Can. 159/M7
Les Clayes-sous-Bois, Fr. 30/H5
Les Contamines-Montjoie, Fr. 60/C6
Les Diablerets (range), Swi. 60/D5
Les Échelles, Fr. 64/B2
Les Escoumins, Qu, Can. 158/C1
Les Essarts-le-Roi, Fr. 30/H5
Les Gets, Fr. 60/C5
Les Haudères, Swi. 60/D5
Les Hautes-Rivières, Fr. 55/D4
Les Herbiers, Fr. 44/C3
Les Islettes, Fr. 55/E5
Les Mées, Fr. 64/B4
Les Mesnuls, Fr. 30/H5
Les Minquier (isl.), UK 56/C3
Les Molières, Fr. 30/J6
Les Monges (peak), Fr. 64/C4
Les Mosses, Swi. 60/D5
Les Mureaux, Fr. 54/A6
Les Orres, Fr. 64/C3
Les Pennes-Mirabeau, Fr. 64/B6
Les Pieux, Fr. 56/D2
Les Ponts-de-Cé, Fr. 57/E6
Les Ponts-de-Martel, Swi. 60/C4
Les Rosiers, Fr. 57/E6
Les Rousses, Fr. 60/C5
Les Sables-d'Olonne, Fr. 44/C3
Les Salines (int'l arpt.), Alg. 112/K6
Les Sept Iles (isl.), Fr. 56/B3
Les Touches, Fr. 56/D6
Les Ulis, Fr. 30/J5
Les Verrières, Swi. 60/C4
Lesa, It. 62/B2
L'Escarène, Fr. 64/D5
Leselidze, Geo. 70/G4
Leseru, Kenya 119/A1
Leshan, China 86/D2
Leshukonskoye, Rus. 69/K2
Lésigny, Fr. 30/K5
Lesima (peak), It. 62/C4
Lesja, Nor. 38/D3
Lesjöfors, Swe. 40/F2
Lesko, Pol. 43/M4
Leskovac, Yugo. 50/E4
Leskovik, Alb. 49/G2
Leslie, Ar, US 153/H3
Leslie, Sc, UK 33/C4
Leslie, Ga, US 165/F2
Leslie, Mi, US 160/D3
Lesmahagow, Sc, UK 33/C5
Lesneven, Fr. 56/A3
Lešnica, Yugo. 50/D3
Lesnoy, Rus. 69/M4
Lesogorsk, Rus. 79/N2
Lesopil'noye, Rus. 79/L2
Lesosibirsk, Rus. 74/K4
Lesotho (ctry.) 107/E7
Lesozavodsk, Rus. 79/L2
Lesparre-Médoc, Fr. 44/C4
Lesquin (int'l arpt.), Fr. 54/C2
Lessay, Fr. 56/D2
Lesse (riv.), Belg. 42/C3
Lessebo, Swe. 40/F3
Lesser Antilles (isls.), NAm. 139/L8
Lesser Caucasus (mts.), Asia 71/G4
Lesser Slave (lake), Ab, Can. 140/E3
Lesser Sunda (isls.), Indo. 91/E5
Lessines, Belg. 54/C2
Lessley, Ms, US 164/C2
Lesterville, Mo, US 162/B2
Lesung (peak), Indo. 90/D3
Lésvos (isl.), Gre. 70/C5
Leswalt, Sc, UK 34/C2
Leszno, Pol. 43/J3
Letaba, SAfr. 123/F4
L'Étang-du-Nord, Qu, Can. 159/G2
Létavértes, Hun. 50/E2
Letcher, SD, US 154/E2
Letchworth, Eng, UK 37/F3
Lete (riv.), It. 65/D5
Letegge (peak), It. 65/C1
Letham, Sc, UK 33/D3
Lethbridge, Ab, Can. 145/H3
Lethe (riv.), Ger. 53/F2
Lethem, Guy. 181/G4
Leti (isls.), Indo. 128/B2
Leti (isl.), Indo. 128/B2
Leticia, Col. 184/D2
Leting, China 80/D3
L'Etivaz, Swi. 60/D5
Letka, Rus. 69/L4
Letlhakane, Bots. 122/E4
Letlhakeng, Bots. 122/E5
Letnitsa, Bul. 51/G4
L'Étoile, Fr. 54/B3
Letong, Indo. 89/D2
Letpadan, Myan. 86/B5
Letschin, Ger. 43/H2
Letsôk-Aw (isl.), Myan. 90/A1
Letterkenny, Ire. 31/Q9
Letterkenny Army Depot, Pa, US 161/H4
Lettomanoppello, It. 65/D5
Letychiv, Ukr. 72/D3
Leu Botanical Gardens, Fl, US 164/N6
Leuca, It. 49/F3
Leucate, Fr. 44/E5
Leuchars, Sc, UK 33/D4
Leuk, Swi. 60/D5
Leukerbad, Swi. 60/D5
Leun, Ger. 58/B1
Leupp, Az, US 149/G3
Leurbost, Sc, UK 31/Q7
Leusden-Zuid, Neth. 52/C4
Leuser (peak), Indo. 89/A2
Leutershausen, Ger. 58/D4
Leutkirch im Allgäu, Ger. 61/G2
Leuven (Louvain), Belg. 55/D2
Leuze-en-Hainaut, Belg. 54/C2
Levádhia, Gre. 49/H3
Levallois-Perret, Fr. 30/J5
Levanger, Nor. 38/D3
Levanna Centrale (peak), Fr. 64/D2
Levante, Riviera di (coast), Fr. 62/C4
Levanto, It. 62/C5
Levashovo, Rus. 69/T6
Levashovo (arpt.), Rus. 69/T6
Levee No. 33 (canal), Fl, US 164/P10
Level (isl.), Chile 190/B5
Level, Md, US 168/B4
Levelland, Tx, US 152/C4
Levelock, Ak, US 171/G4
Leven, Sc, UK 33/D4
Leven, Eng, UK 35/H4
Leven (lake), Sc, UK 33/A3
Leven (riv.), Sc, UK 33/C4
Leven (lake), Sc, UK 33/C4
Leven (pt.), SAfr. 125/F2
Levens, Fr. 64/D5
Leventina (Prato), Swi. 61/E5
Leveque (cape), Austl. 128/A4
Lever (riv.), Braz. 186/C1
Leverburgh, Sc, UK 31/Q8
Levering, Mi, US 160/D2
Leverkusen, Ger. 55/F1
Lèves, Fr. 57/G4
Levice, Slvk. 50/D1
Levico Terme, It. 61/H5
Levier, Fr. 60/C4
Levin, NZ 135/C3
Lévis, Qu, Can. 158/B2
Lévis-Saint-Nom, Fr. 30/H5
Levittown, NY, US 169/L9
Levittown, Pa, US 168/D3
Levkás, Gre. 49/G3
Levkás (isl.), Gre. 67/J3
Levkímmi, Gre. 49/G3
Levkinskaya, Rus. 69/L2
Levoča, Slvk. 43/L4
Levrier (bay), Mrta. 110/A5
Levski, Bul. 51/G4
Levuka, Fiji 137/Y18
Levy (lake), Fl, US 165/G3
Lewellen, Ne, US 154/C3
Lewes, Eng, UK 37/G5
Lewin Brzeski, Pol. 43/J3
Lewis (hill), Nf, Can. 159/H1
Lewis (hills), Nf, Can. 159/H1
Lewis (isl.), Sc, UK 31/Q7
Lewis, Ks, US 152/E2
Lewis (pass), NZ 135/C3
Lewis, Co, US 149/H2
Lewis, Ia, US 155/G3
Lewis (riv.), Wa, US 144/D4
Lewis and Clark (lake), SD,Ne, US 154/E2
Lewis and Clark NWR, Wa, US 144/C4
Lewis Smith (lake), Al, US 162/D3
Lewisburg, Ky, US 162/D2
Lewisburg, WV, US 163/G2
Lewisburg, Tn, US 162/D3
Lewisburg, [illegible]
Lewisham (bor.), Eng, UK 30/C2
Lewisport, Ky, US 162/D2
Lewisporte, Nf, Can. 159/K1
Lewiston, Me, US 158/B3
Lewiston, Ut, US 147/H3
Lewiston, NY, US 160/U9
Lewiston, Id, US 144/F4
Lewiston Woodville, NC, US 163/J2
Lewistown, Pa, US 161/H4
Lewistown, Il, US 155/J3
Lewistown, Mt, US 145/K4
Lewisville (lake), Tx, US 151/F1
Lewisville, Tx, US 150/L6
Lewotobi (peak), Indo. 128/A2
Léwou, Gabon 120/C3
Lewvan, Sk, Can. 156/B2
Lex (riv.), Fr. 47/F1
Lexa, Ar, US 162/B3
Lexington, Ga, US 163/F4
Lexington, Il, US 155/K3
Lexington, Ky, US 162/E1
Lexington, Oh, US 160/E4
Lexington, Ok, US 153/F3
Lexington, Or, US 146/D1
Lexington, Mo, US 155/H4
Lexington, Ms, US 162/B4
Lexington, Ne, US 154/E3
Lexington, NC, US 163/G3
Lexington, SC, US 163/G4
Lexington, Tn, US 162/C3
Lexington, Tx, US 151/F2
Lexington, Va, US 163/H2
Lexington Blue Grass Army Depot, Ky, US 162/E2
Lexington Park, Md, US 163/J1
Leyburn, Eng, UK 35/G3
Leye, China 87/E3
Leyland, Eng, UK 35/F4
Leysdown, Eng, UK 37/G4
Leysin, Swi. 60/D5
Leyte (isl.), Phil. 77/M8
Leyte (gulf), Phil. 88/D3
Leyte, Phil. 88/D3
Leyton (nbrhd.), Eng, UK 30/C2
Leytron, Swi. 60/D5
Lez (riv.), Fr. 44/F4
Leżajsk, Pol. 43/M3
Lezama, Ven. 183/P8
Lèze (riv.), Fr. 64/B5
Lezhë, Alb. 49/F2
Lezhi, China 86/E2
Lézignan-Corbières, Fr. 44/E5
Lezuza, Sp. 46/D3
L'gov, Rus. 73/H2
Lhanbyrd, Sc, UK 33/C1
Lhari, China 86/B2
Lhasa (riv.), China 99/F6
Lhasa (int'l arpt.), China 99/F5
Lhatog, China 86/C2
Lhazê, China 97/F1
L'Hermitage, Fr. 56/D4
Lhokkruet, Indo. 89/A1
Lhokseumawe, Indo. 89/B1
Lhoksukon, Indo. 89/B1
L'Hospitalet de Llobregat, Sp. 47/L7
Lhozhag, China 97/H1
Lhuntsi, Bhu. 97/G2
Lhünzê, China 93/G2
Li, Thai. 94/B2
Li (riv.), China 93/K2
Li (mtn.), China 80/B4
Li ani (riv.), Leb. 105/C2
Li Xian, China 87/F2
Lian (riv.), China 87/E3
Lian Xian, China 87/G3
Liancheng, China 87/H3
Liancourt, Fr. 54/B5
Liancourt Rocks (isl.), Asia 84/B2
Liang, Indo. 91/G4
Liangcheng, China 80/C2
Liangcun, China 87/G3
Liangdong, China 87/F4
Lianghekou, China 87/F2
Liangjia, China 81/B2
Liangjiadian, China 81/A3
Liangpran (peak), Indo. 90/D3
Liangshui, China 81/C2
Liangting, China 78/F5
Liangwan (mts.), China 86/D3
Liangzhen, China 78/F4
Liangzi (lake), China 80/C5
Lianhua (mts.), China 87/G4
Lianhua, China 93/K2
Lianjiang, China 93/K3
Lianjiang, China 87/H3
Lianjiangkou, China 87/G3
Liannan Yaozu Zizhixian, China 87/G3
Lianping, China 87/G3
Lianpu, China 87/H3
Lianshanguan, China 81/B2
Lianshui, China 80/D4
Liantang, China 94/E1
Liantang, China 87/F3
Liantang, China 80/L8
Lianyun (peak), China 87/G2
Lianyungang, China 80/D4
Liao (riv.), China 77/M5
Liaocheng, China 80/C3
Liaodong (pen.), China 81/A3
Liaodong (isls.), China 80/E3
Liaodong (gulf), China 79/J3
Liaodun, China 78/C3
Liaoning (prov.), China 79/J3
Liaoyang, China 81/B2
Liaoyuan, China 79/K3
Liaozhong, China 81/B2
Liāquatpur, Pak. 98/A5
Liard (riv.), Can. 139/E3
Liat (isl.), Indo. 89/D3
Libacao, Phil. 88/C3
Líbano, Col. 183/K8
Libau, Mb, Can. 156/F2
Libby (dam), Mt, US 144/G3
Libby, Mt, US 144/G3
Liběchovka (riv.), Czh. 59/H2
Libenge, D.R. Congo 120/D2
Liberal, Ks, US 152/D2
Liberal, Mo, US 153/G2
Libercourt, Fr. 54/C3
Liberdade, Braz. 187/M7
Liberdade (riv.), Braz. 186/B1
Liberec, Czh. 43/H3
Liberecký (pol. reg.), Czh. 43/H3
Liberi (arpt.), It. 65/D3
Liberia, CR 176/E4
Liberia (ctry.) 107/B4
Libertad, Belz. 176/D2
Libertad, Ven. 180/D2
Libertad, Uru. 191/K11
Libertad de Orituco, Ven. 183/P8
Libertador General San Martín, Arg. 188/C2
Liberty, Il, US 155/J4
Liberty, In, US 160/D5
Liberty, Ky, US 162/E2
Liberty (res.), Md, US 168/B5
Liberty, Mo, US 155/G4
Liberty, Ms, US 164/C2
Liberty, NC, US 163/H3
Liberty, NY, US 161/J4
Liberty, Ok, US 153/F4
Liberty, Sk, Can. 145/M2
Liberty, Tx, US 151/H2
Liberty, Tx, US 151/N8
Liberty (co.), Tx, US 151/N9
Liberty Grove, Md, US 168/B4
Libertyville, Al, US 165/E2
Libertyville, Il, US 167/P15
Libin, Belg. 55/E4
Libmanan, Phil. 88/C2
Libo, China 87/E3
Libobo (cape), Indo. 91/G4
Liboc (riv.), Czh. 43/G3
Libochovice, Czh. 59/H2
Liboko, D.R. Congo 121/E2
Libon, Phil. 88/C2
Librazhd, Alb. 49/G2
Libres, Mex. 175/M7
Libreville (cap.), Gabon 120/B2
Libreville (int'l arpt.), Gabon 120/B2
Libu, China 87/F4
Libya (ctry.) 107/D2
Libyan (plat.), Egypt,Libya 108/D2
Libyan (des.), Egypt,Libya 107/E2
Licantén, Chile 190/B2
Licata, It. 48/C4
Licciana Nardi, It. 62/D5
Lice, Turk. 102/E2
Lich, Ger. 58/B1
Licheng, China 80/D3
Licheng, China 80/C3
Lichfield, Eng, UK 37/E1
Lichinga, Moz. 123/G2
Lichtenau, Ger. 53/F5
Lichtenau, Ger. 58/B5
Lichtenau, Ger. 58/D4
Lichtenberg, Ger. 42/Q6
Lichtenburg, SAfr. 124/D2
Lichtenfels, Ger. 58/D2
Lichtenrade, Ger. 42/Q7
Lichtensteig, Swi. 61/F3
Lichtenvoorde, Neth. 52/D5
Lichterfelde, Ger. 42/Q7
Lichtervelde, Belg. 54/C1
Lichuan, China 87/F2
Lichuan, China 87/H3
Lick Observatory, Ca, US 167/L12
Licking, Mo, US 153/J2
Licking (riv.), Ky, US 162/E1
Licques, Fr. 54/A2
Licun, China 87/F4
Licungo (riv.), Moz. 123/H2
Lida, Bela. 41/L5
Lidao, China 81/B4
Liddell Water (riv.), Sc, UK 35/F1
Liddes, Swi. 60/D6
Liddon (gulf), NW, Can. 141/R7
Lidgerwood, ND, US 156/F4
Lidhoríkion, Gre. 49/H3
Lidice, Czh. 59/H2
Lidingö, Swe. 40/H2
Lidköping, Swe. 40/E2
Lidlington, Eng, UK 37/F2
Lido, Niger 115/F3
Lido, It. 63/F3
Lido di Iesolo, It. 63/F2
Lido di Ostia, It. 65/B4
Lidzbark, Pol. 43/K2
Lidzbark Warmiński, Pol. 41/J4
Lié (riv.), Fr. 56/C4
Liebenau, Ger. 53/G6
Liebenau, Aus. 59/H5
Liebenbergsvlei (riv.), SAfr. 124/E2
Liebenthal, Ks, US 152/E1
Liebig (mt.), Austl. 131/F2
Liechtenstein (ctry.) 29/E4
Liedekerke, Belg. 55/D2
Liège, Belg. 55/E2
Liège (prov.), Belg. 55/E3
Lieksa, Fin. 68/F3
Lielvarde, Lat. 41/L3
Lienden, Neth. 52/C5
Lienen, Ger. 53/E4
Lienz, Aus. 45/K3
Liepāja, Lat. 41/J3
Liepna, Lat. 41/M3
Lier, Belg. 55/D1
Lierbyen, Nor. 38/R8
Lierneux, Belg. 55/E3
Lies (riv.), Belg. 44/E1
Lieser (riv.), Ger. 55/F3
Liesjärven NP, Fin. 41/K1
Liesjärven NP, Fin. 39/D4
Liesse-Notre-Dame, Fr. 54/C4
Liestal, Swi. 60/D3
Lieto, Fin. 41/K1
Lieurey, Fr. 57/F2
Liévin, Fr. 54/B3
Lievio, Fin. 39/E4
Lièvre (riv.), Qu, Can. 161/J1
Liez (lake), Fr. 60/B2
Liezen, Aus. 45/L3
Lifake, D.R. Congo 121/E2
Lifau, ETim. 128/B2
Liffey (riv.), Ire. 34/B5
Liffol-le-Grand, Fr. 60/B1
Lifford, Ire. 31/Q9
Liffré, Fr. 56/D4
Lifou (isl.), NCal. 137/V12
Lifouta, Gabon 120/C3
Lifton, Eng, UK 36/B5
Liganga, Tanz. 119/A4
Ligao, Phil. 91/F1
Līgatne, Lat. 41/L3
Lighthouse (pt.), Fl, US 165/F3
Lighthouse Point, Fl, US 164/P10
Lightning Ridge, Austl. 132/C1
Lightwater, Eng, UK 30/B3
Lignano Sabbiadoro, It. 63/G2
Lignite, ND, US 156/C3
Ligny-en-Barrois, Fr. 55/E6
Ligoncio (peak), It. 61/F5
Ligonha (riv.), Moz. 123/H2
Ligonier, In, US 160/D4
Ligoúrion, Gre. 49/H4
Ligovo (nbrhd.), Rus. 69/T7
Liguria (pol. reg.), It. 62/B4
Ligurian (sea), Eur. 66/F2
Lihou Reef and Kays (isl.), Austl. 127/E2
Lihue, Hi, US 142/S10
Lihula, Est. 41/K2
Lijiang Naxizu Zizhixian, China 86/D3
Lijin, China 80/D3
Likasi, D.R. Congo 121/F5
Likati, D.R. Congo 121/E2
Likely, BC, Can. 144/D1
Likhoslavl', Rus. 68/G4
Likhovskoy, Rus. 73/L3
Likimi, D.R. Congo 121/E2
Likoma (isl.), Malw. 123/G2
Likoto, D.R. Congo 121/E3
Likouala (pol. reg.), Congo 120/D2
Likouala (riv.), Congo 120/C2
Likouala aux Herbes (riv.), Congo 120/D2
Likouala Mossaka (riv.), Congo 120/D3
Likova (riv.), Rus. 69/W9
Likstammen (lake), Swe. 39/A2
Liku, Indo. 90/C3
Lilanga, D.R. Congo 121/E3
Lilbourn, Mo, US 162/C2
Lilburn, Ga, US 163/M7
L'Île-Perrot, Qu, Can. 159/N7
L'Île-Rousse, Fr. 48/A1
Liliāni, Pak. 98/B3
Lilienthal, Ger. 53/F2
Liling, China 93/K2
Lilla, Pak. 98/B3
Lilla Edet, Swe. 40/E2
Lille, Fr. 54/C2
Lille, Belg. 52/B6
Lille Bælt (chan.), Ger. 40/C4
Lille Værløse, Den. 39/J7
Lillebonne, Fr. 57/F1
Lillehammer, Nor. 40/D1
Lillerød, Den. 39/J7
Lillers, Fr. 54/B2
Lillesand, Nor. 40/C2
Lillestrøm, Nor. 40/D2
Lillian, Tx, US 150/K7
Lillie, La, US 153/H4
Lilliesleaf, Sc, UK 33/D5
Lillington, NC, US 163/H3
Lilliwaup, Wa, US 167/A3
Lillkyrka, Swe. 39/A1
Lillo, Sp. 46/D3
Lillooet (riv.), BC, Can. 144/C2
Lillooet, BC, Can. 144/D2
Lilongwe (cap.), Malw. 123/G2
Lilongwe (Kamuzu) (int'l arpt.), Malw. 123/G2
Liloy, Phil. 88/C3
Lily, Wi, US 157/K5
Lily, Ky, US 162/E2
Lilydale (nbrhd.), Austl. 132/G5
Lim (riv.), Yugo. 49/F1
Lima, Arg. 191/J11
Lima (riv.), It. 63/D4
Lima, Par. 189/E2
Lima (cap.), Peru 184/B4
Lima (dept.), Peru 184/B3
Lima (riv.), Port. 47/A2
Lima (mtn.), Mn, US 157/J3
Lima, Mt, US 147/G1
Lima (res.), Mt, US 147/G1
Lima, NY, US 161/H3
Lima, Oh, US 160/D4
Lima Duarte, Braz. 187/N6
Limache, Chile 190/N8
Limal, Bol. 188/C2
Liman, Rus. 71/H3
Limanowa, Pol. 43/L4
Limassol (dist.), Cyp. 104/C2
Limassol, Cyp. 104/C2
Limavady (dist.) 34/A2
Limavady, NI, UK 34/B1
Limay, Fr. 57/G3
Limay (riv.), Arg. 179/C7
Limay Mahuida, Arg. 190/D3
Limbach, Ger. 58/C4
Limbang (riv.), Malay. 88/A4
Limbani, Peru 184/D4
Limbara (peak), It. 48/A2
Limbaži, Lat. 41/L3
Limbdi, India 101/K4
Limbe, Camr. 120/B1
Limbe, Malw. 123/G2
Limbé, Haiti 177/H2
Limbiate, It. 62/C2
Limbourg, Belg. 55/E2
Limbuak, Malay. 88/B4
Limbunya, Austl. 128/C4
Limburg (prov.), Belg. 55/E1
Limburg an der Lahn, Ger. 58/B2
Limburgerhof, Ger. 58/B4
Lime Village, Ak, US 171/G3
Limedsforsen, Swe. 40/E1
Limehouse, On, Can. 160/T8
Limeira, Braz. 189/H2
Limekilns, Sc, UK 33/C4
Limena, It. 63/E3
Limenária, Gre. 49/J2
Limerick (co.), Ire. 32/B5
Limerick, Ire. 32/B4
Limerick, Sk, Can. 145/L3
Limestone, Ar, US 153/H3
Limestone (lake), Tx, US 151/F2
Limestone, Mt, US 147/J1
Limfjorden (chan.), Den. 40/C3
Limidario (peak), It. 61/E5
Limington, Me, US 161/L3
Limite, It. 63/D6
Limmat (riv.), Swi. 61/E3
Limmen Bight (riv.), Austl. 129/D3
Limmen Bight (bay), Austl. 127/C2
Límni, Gre. 49/H3
Límnos (isl.), Gre. 70/C5
Limoeiro, Braz. 183/H4
Limoeiro do Norte, Braz. 183/G4
Limoges, Fr. 44/D4
Limogne (plat.), Fr. 44/D4
Limón, Hon. 176/E3
Limón, CR 177/F4
Limon, Co, US 154/C4
Limone Piemonte, It. 64/D4
Limone sul Garda, It. 63/D2
Limoquije, Bol. 185/E4
Limours, Fr. 30/J6
Limousin (mts.), Fr. 44/D4
Limousin (pol. reg.), Fr. 44/D4
Limoux, Fr. 44/E5
Limpopo (riv.), Afr. 123/G5
Limpopo (riv.), Moz. 107/F7
Limpsfield, Eng, UK 30/D3
Limu (mtn.), China 87/F5
Limu, China 87/F3
Limulunga, Zam. 122/D2
Limuru, Kenya 119/B2
Lin Xian, China 80/C3
Līnah, SAr. 103/E4
Linakhamari, Rus. 68/F1
Linanäs, Swe. 39/B1
Linao (pt.), Phil. 88/C4
Linapacan (isl.), Phil. 88/B3
Linard (peak), Swi. 61/G4
Linares, Sp. 46/D3
Linares, Chile 190/C2
Linares, Mex. 175/F3
Linariá, Gre. 49/J3
Linate (int'l arpt.), It. 62/C3
Lincang, China 86/D4
Linch, Wy, US 154/A2
Lincheng, China 80/C3
Linchuan, China 87/H3
Lincoln, Arg. 190/E2
Lincoln (sea), Can. 139/L1
Lincoln, On, Can. 160/U9
Lincoln, Eng, UK 35/H5
Lincoln, Ca, US 146/C4
Lincoln, De, US 168/C6
Lincoln, Il, US 155/K3
Lincoln, ND, US 156/D4
Lincoln (cap.), Ne, US 155/F3
Lincoln, NH, US 161/L2
Lincoln, NM, US 152/B4
Lincoln, Tx, US 151/F2
Lincoln, Pa, US 168/B3
Lincoln (Lincoln Center), Ks, US 153/E1
Lincoln Beach, Or, US 146/A1
Lincoln Boyhood Nat'l Mem., In, US 162/D1
Lincoln Caverns, Pa, US 161/G4
Lincoln Center (Lincoln), Ks, US 153/E1
Lincoln City, Or, US 146/A1
Lincoln Heath (woodld.), Eng, UK 35/H5
Lincoln Heights, Oh, US 160/E4
Lincoln Home Nat'l Hist. Site, Il, US 155/K4
Lincoln NP, Austl. 131/G5
Lincoln Park, Co, US 152/B1
Lincoln Park, NJ, US 169/H8
Lincoln Park, Mi, US 167/F7
Lincoln Park, Ga, US 162/E4
Lincolnshire (co.), Eng, UK 35/H5
Lincolnshire Wolds (grsld.), Eng, UK 35/H4
Lincolnton, Ga, US 163/F4
Lincolnton, NC, US 163/G3
Lincolnville, Ks, US 153/F1
Lincroft, NJ, US 168/D3
Lind, Den. 40/C3
Lind NP, Austl. 133/D3
Linda, Ca, US 146/C4
Lindale, Ga, US 162/E3
Lindale, Tx, US 151/G1
Lindau, Swi. 61/E3
Lindau, Ger. 61/F2
Linde (riv.), Neth. 52/D3
Lindeman (chan.), Austl. 134/C3
Lindeman (isl.), Austl. 129/H5
Linden, Ger. 58/B1
Linden, Guy. 181/G3
Linden, Al, US 162/D4
Linden, Az, US 149/G3
Linden, Fl, US 164/L6
Linden, In, US 160/C4
Linden, Mi, US 167/E6
Linden, NJ, US 169/J9
Linden, Tn, US 162/D3
Linden, Tx, US 153/G4
Linden Beach, On, Can. 167/G7
Lindenberg im Allgäu, Ger. 61/F2
Lindenfels, Ger. 58/B3
Lindenhurst, Il, US 167/P15
Lindenhurst, NY, US 169/E2
Lindenwold, NJ, US 168/D4
Lindern, Ger. 53/E3
Lindesberg, Swe. 40/F2
Lindesnes (cape), Nor. 40/B3
Lindesnes, Nor. 40/B2
Lindewitt, Ger. 40/C4
Lindgren Acres, Fl, US 164/P11
Lindholm (isl.), Den. 39/G7
Lindhorst, Ger. 53/E5
Líndhos (ruin), Gre. 102/B2
Lindi (riv.), D.R. Congo 121/F2
Lindi (prov.), Tanz. 119/B4
Lindi, Tanz. 119/B4
Lindian, China 79/J2
Lindlar, Ger. 55/G1
Lindley, SAfr. 124/D2
Lindome, Swe. 40/E3
Lindon, Ut, US 147/H3
Lindon, Co, US 154/C4
Lindre (lake), Fr. 55/F6
Lindrith, NM, US 149/J2
Lindsay (mt.), Austl. 130/C5
Lindsay (mt.), Austl. 131/F3
Lindsay, On, Can. 161/G2
Lindsay, Ca, US 148/C2
Lindsay, Mt, US 156/B4
Lindsay, Ok, US 153/F3
Lindsborg, Ks, US 153/F1
Lindsdal, Swe. 40/G3
Lindstrom, Mn, US 157/H5
Line (isls.), Kiri. 137/J4
Line Mountain (mtn.), Pa, US 168/B2
Líneas de Nazca, Peru 184/C4
Lineboro, Md, US 168/B4
Lineville, Al, US 162/E4
Lineville, Ia, US 155/H3
Linfen, China 80/B3
Linford, Eng, UK 30/E2
Ling (riv.), Sc, UK 33/A2
Ling Xian, China 93/K2
Ling Xian, China 80/D3
Linganore (cr.), Md, US 168/A5
Lingao, China 87/F5
Lingayen, Phil. 88/C1
Lingayen (gulf), Phil. 88/B1
Lingbao, China 80/B4
Lingbi, China 80/D4
Lingchuan, China 93/K2
Lingchuan, China 80/C4
Linge (riv.), Neth. 52/C5
Lingelengenda, Zam. 122/D2
Lingen, Ger. 53/E3
Lingfield, Eng, UK 30/C3
Lingga (isls.), Indo. 90/B3
Lingga (isl.), Indo. 89/D3
Linghu, China 80/L9
Lingle, Wy, US 154/B2
Linglestown, Pa, US 168/B3
Lingma, China 87/E4
Lingolsheim, Fr. 60/D1
Lingomo, D.R. Congo 121/E2
Lingqiu, China 80/C3
Lingshan, China 80/C3
Lingshan, China 87/F4
Lingshi, China 80/B3
Lingshui, China 87/F5
Lingtou, China 87/H3
Linguère, Sen. 114/B3
Lingunda, D.R. Congo 121/E2
Lingwu, China 78/F4
Lingxi, China 87/J3
Lingyin Si, China 80/L9
Lingyuan, China 80/D2
Lingyun, China 93/J3
Linhai, China 79/J1
Linhai, China 87/J2
Linhares, Braz. 187/E3
Linhe, China 78/F3
Linière, Qu, Can. 158/B2
Linjiang, China 81/D2
Linköping, Swe. 40/F2
Linkuva, Lith. 41/K3
Linlithgow, Sc, UK 33/C5
Linliu (mtn.), China 80/C3
Linn, Mo, US 153/J1
Linn, Tx, US 151/E4
Linn Creek, Mo, US 153/H1
Linneus, Mo, US 155/H4
Linney (pt.), Wal, UK 36/A3
Linnhe (lake), Sc, UK 33/A3
Linnich, Ger. 55/F2
Linntown, Pa, US 168/B2
Lino Lakes, Mn, US 157/P6
Linosa, It. 48/C5
Linosa (isl.), It. 48/C5
Linosa (isl.), It. 112/N7
Linqasi, Sudan 117/E4
Linqing, China 80/C3
Linqu, China 80/D3
Linquan, China 80/C4
Linru, China 80/C4
Lins, Braz. 189/G2
Linsan, Gui. 114/B4
Linschoten, Neth. 52/B4
Linshu, China 80/D4
Linshui, China 78/D4
Linta (riv.), Madg. 125/H9
Linth (riv.), Swi. 61/F3
Linthal, Swi. 61/F4
Lintlaw, Sk, Can. 156/C1
Linton, ND, US 156/D4
Linton, In, US 162/D1
Linton, Eng, UK 37/G2
Linville, La, US 153/H4
Linwood, Eng, UK 35/H5
Linwood, Mi, US 160/E3
Linwu, China 93/K2
Linxi, China 80/C3
Linxia, China 78/E4
Linyanti (swamp), Bots. 122/D3
Linyi, China 80/D4
Linyi, China 80/D3
Linyi, China 80/B4
Linying, China 80/C4
Linz (int'l arpt.), Aus. 59/H6
Linz, Aus. 59/H6
Linz am Rhein, Ger. 55/G2
Linze, China 78/E4
Linzhang, China 80/C3
Lioma, Moz. 123/H2
Lion (gulf), Fr.,Sp. 66/E2
Lion Country Safari, Fl, US 164/P9
Lion-sur-Mer, Fr. 57/E2
Lions Den, Zim. 123/F3
Lion's Head, On, Can. 160/F2
Lioppa, Indo. 128/B1
Lioto, CAfr. 116/D4
Liozno, Bela. 41/P4
Lipari, It. 48/D3
Lipari (isl.), It. 67/G3
Lipari (isls.), It. 67/G3
Lipatkain, Indo. 89/C3
Lipcani, Mol. 72/D3
Liperi, Fin. 68/F3
Lipetsk (int'l arpt.), Rus. 70/F1
Lipetsk, Rus. 70/F1
Lipetskaya Oblast, Rus. 70/F1
Lipez (riv.), Bol. 188/C2
Liphook, Eng, UK 37/F4
Lipin Bor, Rus. 68/H3
Liping, China 87/F3
Lipljan, Yugo. 50/E4
Lipno, Pol. 43/K2
Lipno (res.), Czh. 59/H5
Lipno, UN (lake), Czh. 45/L2
Lipobane (pt.), Moz. 123/H3
Lipoche, Moz. 123/G1
Lipomo, It. 62/C2
Lipova, Rom. 50/E2
Lippe (riv.), Ger. 42/D3
Lippstadt, Ger. 53/F5
Lipscomb, Tx, US 152/D2
Lipsko, Pol. 72/A2
Lipton, Sk, Can. 156/C2
Liptovská Lúžna, Slvk. 43/K4
Liptovský Svätý Mikuláš, Slvk. 43/K4
Liptrap (cape), Austl. 133/B4
Lipu, China 87/F3
Lipu La (pass), India 99/D5
Lira, Ugan. 121/H2
Liranga, Congo 120/D3
Lirangwe, Malw. 123/G2
Lircay, Peru 184/C4
Liré, Fr. 57/D6
Liri (riv.), It. 48/C2
Liria, Sp. 47/E3
Liro (riv.), It. 61/F5
Lirung, Indo. 88/D5
Lisala, D.R. Congo 121/E2
Lisboa (dist.), Port. 46/A3
Lisboa (int'l arpt.), Port. 47/P10
Lisboa (Lisbon) (cap.), Port. 47/P10
Lisbon, La, US 153/H4
Lisbon, Md, US 168/A5
Lisbon, Me, US 161/L2
Lisbon, ND, US 156/F4
Lisbon, NH, US 161/L2
Lisbon, Oh, US 160/F4
Lisbon (Lisboa) (cap.), Port. 47/P10
Lisburn (dist.), NI, UK 34/B3
Lisburn, NI, UK 34/B2
Lisburne (cape), Ak, US 171/E2
Liscarroll, Ire. 32/B5
Liscomb Game Sanctuary, NS, Can. 159/F3
Lisdoonvarna, Ire. 32/A3
Liseleje, Den. 40/D3
Lisha (riv.), China 93/H2
Lishe (riv.), China 86/D3
Lishu, China 80/F2
Lishui, China 87/H2
Lisianski (isl.), Hi, US 137/H2
Lisieux, Fr. 57/F2
Lisiy Nos, Rus. 69/T6
Liskeard, Eng, UK 36/B6
Liski, Rus. 73/K2
Lisle, Il, US 167/P16
L'Isle-Adam, Fr. 30/J4
L'Isle-d'Abeau, Fr. 64/B2
L'Isle-en-Dodon, Fr. 44/D5
L'Isle-sur-la-Sorgue, Fr. 64/B5
L'Isle-sur-le-Doubs, Fr. 60/C3
Lisle-sur-Tarn, Fr. 44/D5
L'Isle-Verte, Qu, Can. 158/C1
L'Islet, Qu, Can. 158/B2
Lisman, Al, US 162/C4
Lismore, Ire. 32/C5
Lismore, Austl. 132/E1
Lisnacree, NI, UK 34/B3
Lisnaskea, NI, UK 32/C1
Lišov, Czh. 59/H4
Lispeszentadorján, Hun. 50/C2
Liss, Eng, UK 37/F4
Lisse, Neth. 52/B4
Lisses, Fr. 30/K6
List, Ger. 40/C4
Lister (riv.), Ger. 53/E6
Listowel, Ire. 32/A5
Listowel, On, Can. 160/F3
Listvyanka, Rus. 78/E1
Lit. Scarcies (riv.), SLeo. 114/B4
Litang (riv.), China 93/H2
Litang, China 86/D2
Līţānī (riv.), Leb. 104/D3
Litani (riv.), Sur.,FrG. 182/C2
Litavka (riv.), Czh. 59/G3
Litchfield, Austl. 128/C3
Litchfield, Ct, US 161/K4
Litchfield, Il, US 155/K4
Litchfield, Mn, US 155/G1
Litchfield, Ne, US 154/E3
Litchville, ND, US 156/E4
Liteta, Zam. 123/F2
Lith, Neth. 52/C5
Litherland, Eng, UK 35/F5
Lithgow, Austl. 133/E1
Lithia, Fl, US 164/L8
Lithia Springs, Ga, US 163/L7
Lithonia, Ga, US 163/M7
Lithuania (ctry.) 29/G3
Litija, Slov. 45/L3
Litipāra, India 97/F3
Lititz, Pa, US 168/B3
Litókhoron, Gre. 49/H2
Litoměřice, Czh. 59/H1
Litoo, Tanz. 119/B4
Litovko, Rus. 79/M2
Litslena, Swe. 39/A1
Littabella NP, Austl. 134/D4
Littau, Swi. 61/E3
Little (lake), La, US 164/C3
Little (mtn.), SC, US 163/F3
Little (riv.), Ga, US 162/B5
Little America, Wy, US 147/J3
Little Andaman (isl.), India 93/F5
Little Arkansas (riv.), Ks, US 153/F1
Little Arkansas (riv.), Ks, US 154/E4
Little Baddow, Eng, UK 30/E1
Little Beaver (cr.), Co, US 154/D4
Little Berkhamstead, Eng, UK 30/C1
Little Bighorn (riv.), Mt, Wy, US 147/K1
Little Birch, WV, US 163/G1
Little Bitter (lake), Egypt 104/C4
Little Blue (riv.), Ne, US 154/F3
Little Bow (riv.), Ab, Can. 145/H2
Little Calumet (riv.), Il, US 167/Q16
Little Catalina, Nf, Can. 159/L1
Little Cayman (isl.), Cay. 173/E4
Little Chalfont, Eng, UK 30/B2
Little Chute, Wi, US 160/B2
Little Colorado (riv.), Az, US 149/H3
Little Creek, De, US 168/C5
Little Cumbrae (isl.), Sc, UK 33/A5
Little Current, On, Can. 160/F2
Little Cypress (cr.), Tx, US 151/M8
Little Deschutes (riv.), Or, US 146/C2
Little Desert NP, Austl. 132/B3
Little Diomede (isl.), Ak, US 171/E2
Little Egg (har.), NJ, US 168/D4
Little Elm, Tx, US 150/L6
Little Falls, Mn, US 157/G5
Little Falls, NJ, US 169/J8
Little Falls (dam), Wa, US 144/F4
Little Ferry, NJ, US 169/J8
Little Fishing (cr.), Pa, US 168/B1
Little Fork (riv.), Mn, US 157/H3
Little Fort, BC, Can. 144/D2
Little Gombi, Nga. 116/B3
Little Grand Rapids, Mb, Can. 157/G1
Little Heart's Ease, Nf, Can. 159/L1
Little Inagua (isl.), Bahm. 173/G3
Little Kanawha (riv.), WV, US 163/G1
Little Karoo (valley), SAfr. 124/C4
Little Lake, Ca, US 148/D3
Little Lehigh (riv.), Pa, US 168/C3
Little Manatee (riv.), Fl, US 164/L8
Little Manatee, South Fork (riv.), Fl, US 164/L8
Little Marais, Mn, US 157/J4
Little Minch (str.), Sc, UK 31/Q8
Little Missouri (riv.), Ar, US 153/H3
Little Missouri (riv.), Mt,Wy, US 154/B1
Little Moose (mtn.), NY, US 161/J3
Little Muddy (riv.), ND, US 156/C3
Little Muncy (cr.), Pa, US 168/B1
Little Neck (bay), NY, US 169/K8
Little Nemaha (riv.), Ne, US 155/F3
Little Nicobar (isl.), India 93/F6
Little Ocmulgee (riv.), Ga, US 163/F4
Little Para (res.), Austl. 131/M8
Little Para (riv.), Austl. 131/M8
Little Patuxent (riv.), Md, US 168/B5
Little Payne (cr.), Fl, US 164/M8
Little Peconic (bay), NY, US 169/F2
Little Pee Dee (riv.), SC, US 163/H3
Little Pend Orielle NWR, Wa, US 144/F3
Little Pic (riv.), On, Can. 157/L3
Little Pine and Lucky Man Ind. Res., Sk, Can. 145/K1
Little Pisgah (mtn.), NC, US 163/F3
Little Powder (riv.), Mt, US 147/L1
Little Prairie, Wi, US 167/N14
Little Red (riv.), Ar, US 153/J3
Little River, BC, Can. 144/B3
Little River, NZ 135/C3
Little River, Ks, US 153/E1
Little River, SC, US 163/H4
Little Rock, Mn, US 157/G5
Little Rock (cap.), Ar, US 153/H3
Little Rock (A.F.B.), Ar, US 153/H3
Little Rock (cr.), Il, US 167/N16
Little Sable (pt.), Mi, US 160/C3
Little Salmon, Yk, Can. 171/L3
Little Sark (isl.), UK 56/C2
Little Schuylkill (riv.), Pa, US 168/B2
Little Sioux (riv.), Ia, US 143/G3
Little Sioux, West Fork (riv.), Ia, US 155/F2
Little Sitkin (isl.), Ak, US 171/B5
Little Snake (riv.), Co, US 147/J3
Little St. George (isl.), Fl, US 165/F3
Little Stour (riv.), Eng, UK 37/H4
Little Stukeley, Eng, UK 37/F2
Little Swatara (cr.), Pa, US 168/B3
Little Tallapoosa (riv.), Al, US 162/E4
Little Valley, NY, US 161/G3

Little – Loznic

Little Wabash (riv.), Il, US 162/C1
Little White (riv.), SD, US 154/D2
Little Wichita (riv.), Tx,Ok, US 153/E4
Little Wind (riv.), Wy, US 147/J2
Little Wood (riv.), Id, US 147/F2
Little Zab (riv.), Iraq 103/E3
Littleborough, Eng, UK 35/F4
Littlefield, Tx, US 152/C4
Littlefield, Az, US 149/F2
Littlefork, Mn, US 157/H3
Littlehampton, Eng, UK 37/F5
Littleport, Eng, UK 37/G2
Littlerock, Ca, US 166/C1
Littlerock, Wa, US 144/C4
Littlestown, Pa, US 168/A4
Littleton, Ire. 32/C4
Littleton, NH, US 161/L2
Littleton, Co, US 154/B4
Littoral (prov.), Camr. 116/A4
Litvínov, Czh. 59/G1
Lityn, Ukr. 72/E3
Liu (riv.), China 75/N6
Liuba, China 78/F5
Liuche, China 87/G3
Liuchen, China 87/F4
Liucheng, China 93/J3
Liudongqiao, China 87/H2
Liudu, China 79/J5
Liuhe, China 79/K3
Liuheng (isl.), China 87/J2
Liujing, China 94/E1
Liukou, China 87/H2
Liukuei, Tai. 87/J4
Liuli, Tanz. 119/A4
Liulin, China 80/B3
Liushi, China 87/G3
Liushuquan, China 99/F3
Liuwa Plain NP, Zam. 122/D2
Liuxi (riv.), China 87/G4
Liuyang, China 93/K2
Liuyang (riv.), China 87/G2
Liuzhou, China 87/F3
Liuzigang, China 87/G2
Livádhion, Gre. 49/H2
Livanátai, Gre. 49/H3
Līvāni, Lat. 41/M3
Live Oak, Fl, US 165/G2
Live Oak, Ca, US 146/C4
Livengood, Ak, US 171/J2
Livenza (riv.), It. 63/F2
Liverdun, Fr. 55/F6
Liverdy-en-Brie, Fr. 30/L5
Livermore, Co, US 154/B3
Livermore, Me, US 161/L2
Livermore, Ky, US 162/D2
Livermore, Ia, US 155/G2
Livermore (mt.), Tx, US 151/B2
Livermore Falls, Me, US 161/L2
Liverpool (nbrhd.), Austl. 134/G8
Liverpool, NS, Can. 158/E3
Liverpool (bay), NW, Can. 140/C1
Liverpool (cape), Nun, Can. 141/J1
Liverpool, Eng, UK 35/F5
Liverpool (co.), Eng, UK 35/F5
Liverpool (bay), Wal, UK 35/E5
Liverpool, Pa, US 168/B2
Liverpool, Tx, US 151/M9
Liverton, Eng, UK 35/H2
Livet-et-Gavet, Fr. 64/B2
Livigno, It. 61/G4
Livilliers, Fr. 30/J4
Livingston, Guat. 176/D3
Livingston, Sc, UK 33/C5
Livingston, Al, US 162/C4
Livingston, Ca, US 148/B2
Livingston (lake), Fl, US 164/M8
Livingston, Ky, US 162/E2
Livingston, La, US 164/C2
Livingston (co.), Mi, US 167/E6
Livingston, Mt, US 147/H1
Livingston, NJ, US 169/H8
Livingston, Tn, US 162/E2
Livingston, Tx, US 151/G2
Livingston (lake), Tx, US 151/G2
Livingston Manor, NY, US 161/J4
Livingstone, Zam. 122/E3
Livingstone (range), Ab, Can. 144/G2
Livingstone Memorial, Zam. 123/F2
Livingstone, Chutes de (falls), Congo 120/C4
Livingstonia, Malw. 119/A4
Livno, Bosn. 50/C4
Livny, Rus. 70/F1
Livojoki (riv.), Fin. 38/H2
Livonia, Mi, US 160/E3
Livonia, La, US 164/C2
Livonia, NY, US 161/H3
Livorno, It. 62/D6
Livorno (prov.), It. 62/D6
Livorno Ferraris, It. 62/B3
Livramento do Brumado, Braz. 187/E2
Livron-sur-Drôme, Fr. 64/A3
Livry-Gargan, Fr. 30/K5
Ľivs'ka (prov.), Ukr. 43/M4
Liwa, Chad 116/B2
Liwa, Indo. 89/D4
Liwale, Tanz. 119/B4
Liwan, Sudan 117/G4
Liwonde, Malw. 123/G2
Liwonde NP, Malw. 123/G2
Lixin, China 87/H3
Lixin, China 80/D4
Lixnaw, Ire. 32/A5
Lixoúrion, Gre. 49/G3
Lixus (ruin), Mor. 112/A2
Liyang, China 80/D5
Liyong, China 87/G3
Lizard, Eng, UK 36/A7
Lizard (pt.), Eng, UK 36/A7
Lizard Point Ind. Res., Sk, Can. 156/D2
Lizella, Ga, US 162/F4
Lizifang, China 81/B3
Liziping, China 86/D2
Lizy-sur-Ourcq, Fr. 54/C5
Ljubic, Yugo. 50/E4
Ljubija, Bosn. 50/C3
Ljubinje, Bosn. 50/D4
Ljubljana (cap.), Slov. 45/L3
Ljubuški, Bosn. 50/C4
Ljungan (riv.), Swe. 38/F3
Ljungby, Swe. 40/E3
Ljungbyhed, Swe. 39/K6
Ljungsbro, Swe. 40/F2
Ljungskile, Swe. 40/D2
Ljusnan (riv.), Swe. 38/E3
Ljusne, Swe. 40/G1
Ljustero (isl.), Swe. 41/H2
Ljusterö, Swe. 39/B1
Lkst (peak), Mor. 110/C3
Llabanere (int'l arpt.), Fr. 44/E5
Llaillay, Chile 190/N8
Llaima (vol.), Chile 190/C3
Llallagua, Bol. 188/C1
Llalli, Peru 184/D4
Llanberis, Wal, UK 34/D5
Llanberis, Pass of (pass), Wal, UK 34/D5
Llancañelo (lake), Arg. 190/C2
Llandeilo, Wal, UK 36/C3
Llandogo, Wal, UK 36/D3
Llandovery, Wal, UK 36/C3
Llandrillo, Wal, UK 34/E6
Llandrindod Wells, Wal, UK 36/C2
Llandudno, Wal, UK 34/E5
Llandyssul, Wal, UK 36/B2
Llanelltyd, Wal, UK 36/C1
Llanenddwyn, Wal, UK 34/D6
Llanerchymedd, Wal, UK 34/D5
Llanes, Sp. 46/C1
Llanfair-Pwllgwyngyll, Wal, UK 34/D5
Llanfairfechan, Wal, UK 34/E5
Llanfyllin, Wal, UK 36/C1
Llangammarch Wells, Wal, UK 36/C2
Llangattock, Wal, UK 36/C3
Llangollen, Wal, UK 35/E6
Llangurig, Wal, UK 36/C2
Llanidloes, Wal, UK 36/C2
Llanllyfni, Wal, UK 34/D5
Llano (riv.), Tx, US 151/E2
Llano, Tx, US 151/E2
Llano Estacado (plain), US 142/F5
Llanos (plain), Col.,Ven. 179/B2
Llanquihue (lake), Chile 190/B4
Llanrhaeadr, Wal, UK 35/E5
Llanrian, Wal, UK 36/A3
Llanrwst, Wal, UK 34/E5
Llanthony, Wal, UK 36/C3
Llanuwchllyn, Wal, UK 34/E6
Llata, Peru 184/B3
Llay, Wal, UK 35/F5
Lledrod, Wal, UK 36/C2
Lleida, Sp. 47/F2
Llera de Canales, Mex. 175/F4
Llerena, Sp. 46/B3
Lleyn (pen.), Wal, UK 34/D6
Llica, Bol. 188/B1
Llico, Chile 190/B3
Llivia, Sp. 44/D5
Llobregat (riv.), Sp. 47/F1
Llodio, Sp. 44/B5
Llorente, Phil. 88/D3
Lloret de Mar, Sp. 47/G2
Llorona (pt.), CR 172/E6
Lloyd (pt.), NY, US 169/M8
Lloyd Harbor, NY, US 169/M8
Lloydminster, Sk, Can. 145/K1
Lloyds (riv.), Nf, Can. 159/J1
Lluchmayor, Sp. 47/G3
Llullaillaco (vol.), Arg.,Chile 188/B3
Llwchwr (riv.), Wal, UK 36/B3
Llyn Alaw (lake), Wal, UK 34/D5
Llyn Brenig (lake), Wal, UK 34/E5
Llyn Brianne (res.), Wal, UK 36/C2
Llyn Efyrnwy (lake), Wal, UK 34/E6
Llyn Tegid (lake), Wal, UK 34/E6
Llyn Trawsfynydd (lake), Wal, UK 34/D6
Llynfi (riv.), Wal, UK 36/C3
Lo Wu, China 87/L6
Loa (riv.), Chile 179/C5
Loa, Ut, US 149/G1
Loanda, Gabon 120/B3
Loanda, Braz. 189/F2
Loange (riv.), D.R. Congo 120/D4
Loango Buele, D.R. Congo 120/C4
Loanhead, Sc, UK 33/C5
Loano, It. 62/B5
Loaoya (canal), Sp. 47/N8
Loashi, D.R. Congo 121/G3
Lobanskaya, Rus. 69/K2
Lobatse, Bots. 122/E5
Lobbes, Belg. 55/D3
Lobelville, Tn, US 162/D3
Lobenstein, Ger. 59/E2
Loberia, Arg. 190/F3
Lobethal, Austl. 131/M8
Lobez, Pol. 43/H2
L'Obiou (peak), Fr. 64/B3
Lobito, Ang. 122/B2
Lobitos, Peru 184/A2
Lobnya, Rus. 69/W8
Lobo (riv.), C.d'Iv. 114/D5
Lobo, Tx, US 150/B2
Lobos, Arg. 191/J11
Lobos (pt.), Chile 188/B2
Lobos (pt.), Chile 188/B4
Lobos, Punta de (pt.), Chile 190/M9
Lobva, Rus. 69/P4
Loc (riv.), Fr. 56/C5
Loc Ninh, Viet. 94/D4
Locana, It. 64/D2
Locarno, Swi. 61/E5
Loch Haven Center, Fl, US 164/N6
Loch na Sealga (sea), Sc, UK 33/A1
Loch Raven (res.), Md, US 168/B5
Lochaber (reg.), Sc, UK 33/A3
Lochans, Sc, UK 34/D2
Locharbriggs, Sc, UK 34/E1
Lochau, Aus. 61/F2
Lochawe, Sc, UK 33/A4
Lochboisdale, Sc, UK 31/Q8
Lochearnhead, Sc, UK 33/B4
Lochem, Neth. 52/D4
Lochend, Sc, UK 33/B2
Loches, Fr. 44/D3
Lochgelly, Sc, UK 33/C4
Lochgilphead, Sc, UK 33/A4
Lochgoilhead, Sc, UK 33/B4
Lochiel, SAfr. 125/E2
Lochindorb (lake), Sc, UK 33/C2
Lochinvar, Austl. 133/E1
Lochinvar NP, Zam. 123/E2
Lochmaben, Sc, UK 34/E1
Lochmaddy, Sc, UK 31/Q8
Lochów, Pol. 43/L2
Lochranza, Sc, UK 33/A5
Lochristi, Belg. 54/C1
Lochsa (riv.), Id, US 144/G4
Lochwinnoch, Sc, UK 33/B5
Lochy (lake), Sc, UK 33/B3
Lochy (riv.), Sc, UK 33/B3
Lock, Austl. 131/G5
Lock Haven, Pa, US 161/H4
Locke, Ca, US 167/L10
Locke (mt.), Tx, US 151/B2
Lockeford, Ca, US 146/C4
Lockeport, NS, Can. 158/E4
Lockerbie, Sc, UK 35/E1
Lockesburg, Ar, US 153/G4
Lockettville, Tx, US 152/C4
Lockhart, Fl, US 164/N6
Lockhart, Tx, US 150/F3
Lockhart, Austl. 133/C2
Lockhart Abor. Land, Austl. 129/F3
Lockhart Abor. Rsv., Austl. 134/A1
Lockhart River Aboriginal Community, Austl. 129/F3
Lockington, Austl. 132/C3
Lockney, Tx, US 152/D3
Locknitz (riv.), Ger. 42/F2
Lockport, Mb, Can. 156/F2
Lockport, La, US 164/C3
Lockport, Il, US 167/P16
Lockport, NY, US 160/V9
Lockwood, Sk, Can. 156/B2
Lockwood (res.), Eng, UK 30/C2
Locmariaquer, Fr. 56/C5
Locminé, Fr. 56/C5
Loco, Ok, US 153/F3
Locoal-Mendon, Fr. 56/B5
Locon, Fr. 54/B2
Locquirec, Fr. 56/B3
Locri, It. 48/E3
Locronan, Fr. 56/A4
Loctudy, Fr. 56/A5
Locumba, Peru 184/D5
Locust (cr.), Mo, Ia, US 155/H3
Locust Grove, Ok, US 153/G2
Lod, Isr. 105/B5
Lodan (cr.), Ne, US 155/F2
Lodde (riv.), Swe. 39/K7
Löddeköpinge, Swe. 39/K7
Loddon (riv.), Austl. 132/B3
Loddon (riv.), Eng, UK 37/E4
Loddon, Eng, UK 37/H1
Lodenice (riv.), Czh. 59/H2
Lodève, Fr. 44/E5
Lodeynoye Pole, Rus. 68/G3
Lodge (cr.), Ab, Can. 145/J3
Lodge Grass, Mt, US 147/K1
Lodge Pole, Mt, US 145/K3
Lodgepole, SD, US 156/C5
Lodgepole (cr.), Wy, Ne, US 154/B3
Lodgepole, Ab, Can. 144/G1
Lodhrān, Pak. 98/A5
Lodi, It. 62/C3
Lodi, D.R. Congo 121/E4
Lodi, Ca, US 146/C4
Lodi, NJ, US 169/J8
Lodi, Mo, US 162/B2
Lodi, Tx, US 153/G4
Lodi, Wi, US 155/K2
Lodi Vecchio, It. 62/C3
Lodja, D.R. Congo 121/E3
Lodosa, Sp. 46/D1
Lodrino, Swi. 61/E5
Lodwar, Kenya 119/A1
Łódź, Pol. 43/K3
Łódzkie, (prov.), Pol. 43/K3
Loei, Thai. 94/C2
Loenen, Neth. 52/C4
Loengo, D.R. Congo 121/F4
Loeriesfontein, SAfr. 124/B3
Lofa (riv.), Libr. 114/C5
Lofa (co.), Libr. 114/C5
Löffingen, Ger. 61/E2
Lofonda, D.R. Congo 121/E2
Lofoten (isle.), Nor. 38/D2
Loftus, Eng, UK 35/H2
Lofty (range), Austl. 130/C3
Lofty (mt.), Austl. 131/M8
Loga, Niger 115/F3
Logan (nbrhd.), Austl. 134/F7
Logan (Trudeau) (mt.), Yk, Can. 171/K3
Logan, Ia, US 155/G3
Logan, Ks, US 155/E4
Logan (pass), Mt, US 145/H3
Logan, NM, US 152/C3
Logan, Oh, US 160/E5
Logan, Ut, US 147/H3
Logan (mt.), Wa, US 144/D3
Logan, WV, US 163/G2
Logan Int'l (General Edward Lawrence Logan) (int'l arpt.), Ma, US 161/L3
Logan Lake, BC, Can. 144/D2
Logan Martin (lake), Al, US 162/D4
Logansport, La, US 150/H2
Logansport, In, US 160/C4
Loganton, Pa, US 168/A1
Loganville, Ga, US 162/F4
Loganville, Pa, US 168/B4
Logatec, Slov. 45/L4
Loge (riv.), Ang. 120/C4
Loggieville, NB, Can. 158/E2
Logone (riv.), Chad 107/D3
Logone Birni, Camr. 116/B3
Logone Occ. (riv.), Chad 116/B4
Logone Oriental (riv.), Chad 116/C3
Logone-Occidental (pref.), Chad 116/B3
Logone-Oriental (pref.), Chad 116/B3
Lograto, It. 62/D3
Logroño, Sp. 44/B5
Logrosán, Sp. 46/C3
Løgstør, Den. 40/C3
Løgten, Den. 40/D3
Lohals, Den. 40/D4
Lohārdaga, India 97/E4
Lohāru, India 98/C5
Lohatlha, SAfr. 124/C3
Lohāwat, India 92/B2
Lohfelden, Ger. 53/G6
Lohja, Fin. 41/L1
Lohjanjärvi (lake), Fin. 41/K1
Lohman, Mo, US 153/H1
Lohmar, Ger. 55/G2
Lohn, Tx, US 151/E2
Löhnberg, Ger. 58/B1
Lohne, Ger. 53/F4
Lohne, Ger. 53/F3
Loholoho, Indo. 91/F4
Lohr, Ger. 58/C3
Loi-kaw, Myan. 86/C5
Loiano, It. 63/E5
Loica, Chile 190/N9
Loile (riv.), D.R. Congo 121/E3
Loing (riv.), Fr. 42/B5
Loir (riv.), Fr. 44/D3
Loir-et-Cher (dept.), Fr. 57/G5
Loire (dept.), Fr. 64/A2
Loire (riv.), Fr. 29/E4
Loire-Atlantique (dept.), Fr. 56/D6
Loiret (dept.), Fr. 57/G5
Loiron, Fr. 57/E4
Loisin (riv.), Fr. 55/E5
Loita (hills), Kenya 119/A2
Loja, Sp. 46/C4
Loja, Ecu. 184/B2
Loja (prov.), Ecu. 184/B2
Løjt Kirkeby, Den. 40/C4
Loka, Sudan 117/F4
Lokandu, D.R. Congo 121/F3
Lökåö (isl.), Swe. 39/B1
Lökbatan, Azer. 103/G1
Lokeren, Belg. 54/D1
Lokhvytsya, Ukr. 73/G2
Lokichar, Kenya 119/A1
Lokichokio, Kenya 117/G4
Lokitaung, Kenya 117/G4
Lokka, Fin. 68/E2
Løkken, Den. 40/C3
Loknya, Rus. 41/P3
Loko, Nga. 115/G5
Lokofe, D.R. Congo 121/E3
Lokoja, Nga. 115/G5
Lokolama, D.R. Congo 120/D3
Lokolia, D.R. Congo 121/E3
Lokolo (riv.), D.R. Congo 120/D3
Lokomby, Madg. 125/H8
Lokomo, Camr. 120/C2
Lokopo, Ugan. 119/A1
Lokori, Kenya 119/B1
Lokoro (riv.), D.R. Congo 120/D3
Lökösháza, Hun. 50/E2
Lokossa, Ben. 115/F5
Lokot', Rus. 70/E1
Loks (isl.), Nun, Can. 141/K2
Loksa, Est. 41/L2
Lokwakangole, Kenya 117/G5
Lola, Gui. 114/C5
Lola, Ky, US 162/C2
Lolelia, Ugan. 117/G5
Lolgorien, Kenya 119/A2
Lolingo, D.R. Congo 121/E2
Loliondo, Tanz. 119/A2
Lolita, Tx, US 151/F3
Lolkisale, Tanz. 119/B2
Lolland (isl.), Den. 38/D5
Lollar, Ger. 58/B3
Lolo, D.R. Congo 121/E2
Lolo (riv.), Gabon 120/C3
Lolo, D.R. Congo 121/F3
Lolo, Mt, US 145/G4
Lolo (peak), Mt, US 144/G4
Lolodorf, Camr. 120/B2
Lolua, Tuv. 136/G5
Lolui (isl.), Ugan. 119/A2
Lom, Nor. 38/D3
Lom, Bul. 51/F4
Lom (riv.), Camr. 116/B4
Lom Sak, Thai. 94/C2
Loma (pt.), Ca, US 166/C5
Loma (mts.), SLeo. 114/C4
Loma, Mt, US 145/J4
Loma Alta, Bol. 185/E3
Loma Alta, Tx, US 151/D3
Loma Bonita, Mex. 176/C2
Loma Linda, Ca, US 166/C2
Loma Mansa (peak), SLeo. 114/C4
Loma Negra, Arg. 190/E3
Lomami (riv.), D.R. Congo 107/E5
Lomas, Peru 184/C4
Lomas de Zamora, Arg. 191/J11
Lomazzo, It. 62/C2
Lomba (riv.), Ang. 122/D2
Lombard, Il, US 167/P16
Lombarda, Serra (mts.), Braz. 182/D2
Lombardia (pol.reg.), It. 61/E6
Lombardia (pol. reg.), It. 45/H4
Lombardia, Mex. 174/E5
Lombe, Ang. 120/D5
Lombe, Indo. 128/A1
Lomblen (isl.), Indo. 91/F5
Lombok, Indo. 91/E5
Lombok (isl.), Indo. 91/E5
Lombok (str.), Indo. 89/F5
Lombolo, Congo 120/C4
Lomé (cap.), Togo 115/F5
Lomé (int'l arpt.), Togo 115/F5
Lomela (riv.), D.R. Congo 121/E3
Lomela, D.R. Congo 121/E3
Lomello, It. 62/B3
Lometa, Tx, US 151/E2
Lomié, Camr. 120/C2
Lomira, Wi, US 160/B3
Lomita, Ca, US 166/F8
Lomma (riv.), Nor. 38/S8
Lomma, Swe. 40/E4
Lomme, Fr. 54/B2
Lommel, Belg. 52/C6
Lomnice (riv.), Czh. 59/G4
Lomnice nad Lužnicí, Czh. 59/H4
Lomond (lake), Sc, UK 33/B4
Lomond (hills), Sc, UK 33/C4
Lomond, Ab, Can. 145/H2
Lomone (riv.), It. 63/E4
Lomonosov, Rus. 69/S7
Lompobatang (peak), Indo. 91/E5
Lompoc, Ca, US 148/B3
Łomża, Pol. 43/M2
Lonato, It. 62/D3
Lonāvale, India 95/B2
Loncoche, Chile 190/B3
Loncopué, Arg. 190/C3
Londerzeel, Belg. 55/D2
Londiani, Kenya 119/A2
Londinières, Fr. 57/G1
London, On, Can. 160/F3
London (cap.), UK 30/C2
London, Ky, US 162/E2
London, Oh, US 160/E5
London, Tx, US 151/E2
London Bridge, Az, US 148/E3
London Colney, Eng, UK 30/C1
London (reef), Nic. 177/F3
London, City of (bor.), Eng, UK 30/A1
Londonderry (dist.) 34/A2
Londonderry, NI, UK 34/A2
Londonderry (cape), Austl. 128/B3
Londonderry (isl.), Chile 191/C7
Londonderry (Eglinton) (arpt.), UK 34/A1
Londres, Arg. 188/C3
Londrina, Braz. 189/G2
Londuimbali, Ang. 122/B2
Lone (mtn.), SD, US 156/C5
Lone (riv.), Ger. 58/C5
Lone Butte, BC, Can. 144/D2
Lone Grove, Ok, US 153/F3
Lone Pine, Ca, US 148/C2
Lone Pine Ind. Res., Ca, US 148/C2
Lone Pine Sanct., Austl. 134/E7
Lone Rock, Sk, Can. 145/K1
Lone Star, Tx, US 153/G4
Lone Star, La, US 164/C2
Lone Wolf, Ok, US 152/E3
Lonepine, La, US 164/B2
Lonesome NP, Austl. 134/C4
Lonétou, Mali 114/C3
Long (isl.), Bahm. 139/K7
Long (isl.), Nf., Can. 158/K2
Long (pt.), On, Can. 160/F3
Long (cr.), Sk, Can. 145/M3
Long (riv.), China 87/F3
Long (peak), Fr. 47/F1
Long (isl.), Ire. 32/A7
Long (isl.), PNG 129/G1
Long (str.), Rus. 75/T2
Long, Thai. 94/B2
Long (lake), Sc, UK 33/A2
Long (mtn.), Wal, UK 36/C1
Long, Ak, US 171/G3
Long (pt.), Mi, US 157/K4
Long (lake), ND, US 156/D4
Long (isl.), NY, US 169/K9
Long Beach, In, US 160/C4
Long Beach, Ms, US 164/D2
Long Beach, Ca, US 166/F8
Long Beach, NY, US 169/L9
Long Beach, On, Can. 160/U10
Long Beach (pen.), Wa, US 144/B4
Long Beach, Wa, US 144/B4
Long Beach (isl.), NJ, US 168/D4
Long Beach, Austl. 133/E2
Long Beach, NC, US 163/H4
Long Beach (Daugherty Field) (arpt.), Ca, US 166/F8
Long Branch, NJ, US 168/E3
Long Buckby, Eng, UK 37/E2
Long Cay (isl.), India 177/H1
Long Chau, Viet. 87/E4
Long Crag (hill), Eng, UK 33/E6
Long Creek, Or, US 146/D1
Long Crendon, Eng, UK 37/F3
Long Ditton, Eng, UK 30/C2
Long Eaton, Eng, UK 35/G6
Long Eddy, NY, US 161/J4
Long Grove, Il, US 167/P15
Long Hill, Ct, US 169/E1
Long Island, Ks, US 154/E4
Long Island MacArthur (arpt.), NY, US 169/E2
Long Ketiok, Indo. 91/E3
Long Key (isl.), Fl, US 165/H5
Long Lake, SD, US 156/E5
Long Lake, NY, US 161/J3
Long Lake Ind. Res., On, Can. 157/L3
Long Lake NWR, ND, US 156/D4
Long Lane, Mo, US 153/H2
Long Lelang, Malay. 88/A5
Long Mynd, The (hill), Eng, UK 36/D1
Long Neck (pt.), Ct, US 169/M7
Long Phu, Viet. 94/D4
Long Plain Ind. Res., Mb, Can. 156/E3
Long Pond, Me, US 161/L2
Long Prairie, Mn, US 157/G5
Long Range (mts.), Nf, Can. 159/H2
Long Semado, Malay. 88/A4
Long Sutton, Eng, UK 35/J6
Long Valley, NJ, US 168/D2
Long Xian, China 78/F5
Long Xuyen, Viet. 94/D4
Long, Loch (inlet), Sc, UK 33/B4
Longa, Ang. 122/C2
Longa (riv.), Ang. 120/C5
Longá (riv.), Braz. 183/F3
Long'an, China 93/J3
Longare, It. 63/E3
Longaví, Chile 190/C2
Longberang, Indo. 91/E3
Longbia, Indo. 91/E3
Longboat Key, Fl, US 165/G4
Longboh, Indo. 90/E3
Longbranch, Wa, US 167/B3
Longchamps, Belg. 55/E3
Longchang, China 86/E2
Longchuan, China 93/G3
Longchuan (riv.), China 86/C3
Longchuan, China 87/G3
Longdale, Ok, US 153/E2
Longde, China 78/F4
Longdongping, China 87/F2
Longeau (riv.), Fr. 55/E5
Longeuve (riv.), Fr. 57/E4
Longeville-en-Barrois, Fr. 55/E6
Longeville-lès-Metz, Fr. 55/F5
Longeville-lès-Saint-Avold, Fr. 55/F5
Longfellow (mts.), Me, US 158/B3
Longfield, Eng, UK 30/D2
Longford (co.), Ire. 32/C2
Longford, Ire. 32/C2
Longford, Austl. 132/C4
Longgang, China 87/H3
Longguang, China 87/E4
Longgun, China 87/F5
Longhoughton, Eng, UK 33/E6
Longhua (pass), China 87/F3
Longhua, China 80/D2
Longhui, China 87/F3
Longido, Tanz. 119/B2
Longjiang, China 79/J2
Longjie, China 86/E3
Longjumeau, Fr. 30/J5
Longkou, China 80/E3
Longlac, On, Can. 157/L3
Longli, China 93/J2
Longmen, China 94/E1
Longmen, China 86/D3
Longmen Shiyao, China 80/C4
Longmont, Co, US 154/B3
Longnan, China 87/G3
Longniddry, Sc, UK 33/D5
Longnor, Eng, UK 35/G5
Longny-au-Perche, Fr. 57/F3
Longo, Congo 120/D2
Longonjo, Ang. 122/B2
Longonot (peak), Kenya 119/B2
Longperrier, Fr. 30/K4
Longpont-sur-Orge, Fr. 30/J6
Longport, NJ, US 168/D5
Longpré-les-Corps-Saints, Fr. 54/A3
Longquan, China 87/H2
Longreach, Austl. 134/B3
Longriba, China 78/E5
Longridge, Eng, UK 35/F4
Longs (peak), Co, US 154/B3
Longshan, China 87/F2
Longshou (mts.), China 78/E4
Longstreet, La, US 150/H1
Longtan, China 87/F4
Longton, Ks, US 153/F2
Longtown, Eng, UK 35/F2
Longué-Jumelles, Fr. 57/E6
Longueau, Fr. 54/B4
Longueil-Annel, Fr. 54/B5
Longuenesse, Fr. 54/B2
Longuesse, Fr. 30/H4
Longueuil, Qu, Can. 159/P6
Longuyon, Fr. 55/E5
Longvic, Fr. 60/B3
Longview, Ms, US 162/C4
Longview, Tx, US 151/G1
Longview, Wa, US 144/C4
Longview, Ab, Can. 145/G2
Longville, La, US 164/B2
Longwo, China 87/G4
Longwood, Fl, US 164/N6
Longwood, NC, US 163/H3
Longwood Gardens, Pa, US 168/C4
Longworth, Tx, US 151/D1
Longwy, Fr. 55/E4
Longxi, China 78/E4
Longxingshi, China 87/G3
Longyan, China 87/H3
Longyearbyen, Nor. 74/B2
Longyou, China 87/H2
Longzhou, China 94/D1
Loni, India 98/D5
Lonigo, It. 63/E3
Löningen, Ger. 53/E3
Lonkin, Myan. 86/C3
Lonneker, Neth. 52/D4
Lonoke, Ar, US 153/J3
Lonquimay, Arg. 190/E3
Lons, Fr. 44/C5
Lons-le-Saunier, Fr. 60/B4
Lönsboda, Swe. 40/F3
Lonton, Myan. 86/C3
Lontzen, Belg. 55/F2
Lonza (riv.), Swi. 60/D5
Looc, Phil. 88/C2
Looe (isl.), Eng, UK 36/B6
Loogootee, In, US 162/D1
Lookout (pt.), Mi, US 160/E2
Lookout (pt.), Austl. 134/B1
Lookout (cape), Or, US 146/B1
Lookout (mtn.), Id, US 144/G4
Lookout (pt.), Md, US 163/J1
Lookout (cape), NC, US 163/J3
Loolmalasin (peak), Tanz. 119/A2
Looma, Austl. 128/B4
Loomis, Ca, US 146/C4
Loomis, Wa, US 144/E3
Loon Lake, Wa, US 144/F3
Loon op Zand, Neth. 52/C5
Loop, Tx, US 152/C4
Loop Head (pt.), Ire. 30/P10
Loos, Fr. 54/C2
Loos, BC, Can. 144/D1
Loose, Eng, UK 30/E3
Loose Creek, Mo, US 153/J1
Lop (lake), China 78/C3
Lop Buri, Thai. 94/C3
Lopary, Madg. 125/H8
Lopatin, Rus. 71/H4
Lopatinskiy, Rus. 68/H5
Lopatkovo, Rus. 69/P4
Lopaye, Sudan 117/G4
Lopeno, Tx, US 151/E4
Loperhet, Fr. 56/A4
Lopez (cape), Gabon 120/B3
Lopez (pt.), Ca, US 148/B2
Lopez, Phil. 88/C2
López Mateos, Mex. 175/Q9
Lopik, Neth. 52/B5
Lopori (riv.), D.R. Congo 121/E2
Lopphavet (bay), Nor. 38/G1
Loppi, Fin. 41/L1
Loppijärvi (lake), Fin. 39/E4
Lopukhovka, Rus. 71/H2
Lopydino, Rus. 69/M3
Lora (cr.), Austl. 131/G4
Lora del Río, Sp. 46/C4
Lorain, Oh, US 160/E4
Loraine, Tx, US 151/D1
Loralai, Pak. 101/J2
Lorca, Sp. 46/E4
Lorch, Ger. 55/G3
Lorch, Ger. 58/C5
Lord Howe (isl.), Austl. 136/E8
Lordegān, Iran 103/G4
Lords Lake Nat'l Wild. Ref., ND, US 156/D3
Lordsburg, NM, US 149/H4
Loré, ETim. 128/B2
Lorelei, Ger. 55/G3
Lorena, Braz. 187/L7
Lorengau, PNG 136/D5
Lørenskog, Nor. 40/D2
Lorentz (riv.), Indo. 91/J5
Lorentzsluizen (dam), Neth. 52/C2
Lorenzo, Tx, US 152/D4
Lorenzo Geyres, Uru. 190/F2
Loreo, It. 63/F3
Lorestān (gov.), Iran 103/G3
Loreto, It. 63/G7
Loreto, Ecu. 180/B5
Loreto (state), Peru 180/C5
Loreto, Phil. 88/D3
Loreto, Braz. 183/E4
Loreto, Col. 184/D1
Loreto, Bol. 185/E4
Loreto, Par. 189/E2
Loreto, Mex. 174/C3
Loreto (int'l arpt.), Mex. 174/C3
Loreto, Mex. 174/E4
Loreto Aprutino, It. 65/C3
Lorette, Mb, Can. 156/F3
Lorette, Fr. 64/A1
Loretteville, Qu, Can. 158/B2
Loretto, Tn, US 162/D3
Loretto, Ky, US 162/E2
Lorgues, Fr. 64/C6
Lorian (swamp), Kenya 119/B1
Lorica, Col. 180/C2
Lorient, Fr. 56/B5
Lorient (Lann-Bihoue) (arpt.), Fr. 56/B5
L'Oriental (pol. reg.), Mor. 112/C3
L'Orignal, On, Can. 161/J2
Lorillard (riv.), Nun, Can. 140/G2
Lorinci, Hun. 43/K5
Loring, Mt, US 145/L3
Loriol-sur-Drôme, Fr. 64/A3
Loris, SC, US 163/H3
Lorman, Ms, US 164/C2
Lorne, Austl. 133/A4
Lorne Park, On, Can. 160/T8
Loro Ciuffenna, It. 63/E6
Lorosuk (peak), Kenya 119/A1
Lorquin, Fr. 55/G6
Lörrach, Ger. 60/D2
Lorrain (plat.), Fr. 42/D4
Lorraine (pol. reg.), Fr. 60/C1
Lorraine, Ks, US 153/E1
Lorraine (reg.), Fr. 55/E5
Lorraine (pol.reg.), Fr. 44/G2
Lorraine, Qu, Can. 159/N6
Lorrha, Ire. 32/B3
Lorsch, Ger. 58/B3
Lorton, Eng, UK 35/E2
Lorton, Va, US 163/J1
Loruk, Kenya 119/B1
Lorup, Ger. 53/E3
Los Alamitos, Ca, US 166/F8
Los Alamos, NM, US 152/B3
Los Álamos, Mex. 151/D3
Los Alamos, NM, US 149/J3
Los Alamos, Ca, US 148/B3
Los Aldamas, Mex. 151/E4
Los Alerces, PN, Arg. 190/C4
Los Altos, Ca, US 167/K12
Los Altos, Arg. 188/C4
Los Amates, Guat. 176/D3
Los Andes, Col. 180/B4
Los Andes, Chile 190/N8
Los Angeles (co.), Ca, US 166/B2
Los Angeles (riv.), Ca, US 166/B2
Los Angeles (int'l arpt.), Ca, US 166/F8
Los Angeles, Ca, US 166/F7
Los Ángeles, Chile 190/B3
Los Angeles (aqueduct), Ca, US 148/C3
Los Angeles Outer (har.), Ca, US 166/F8
Los Aquijes, Peru 184/C4
Los Aztecas, Mex. 175/F4
Los Banos, Ca, US 148/B2
Los Barrios, Sp. 46/C4
Los Canarreos (arch.), Cuba 177/F1
Los Cardales, Arg. 191/J11
Los Cardoñes, PN, Arg. 188/C3
Los Castillos, Ven. 181/F2
Los Cerrillos, Uru. 191/K11
Los Charrúas, Arg. 188/E4
Los Chaves, NM, US 149/J3
Los Chonos (arch.), Chile 179/B7
Los Cóndores, Arg. 188/C5
Los Corrales de Buelna, Sp. 46/C1
Los Coyotes Ind. Res., Ca, US 148/D4
Los Cusis, Bol. 185/E4
Los Estados (isl.), Arg. 191/D7
Los Fresnos, Tx, US 150/F4
Los Glaciares, PN, Arg. 191/B6
Los Herreras, Mex. 151/E5
Los Katios, PN, Col. 180/B3
Los Lagos, Chile 190/B3
Los Lagos (pol. reg.), Chile 190/B4
Los Llanos de Aridane, Sp. 110/A3
Los Lunas, NM, US 149/J3
Los Mármoles, PN, Mex. 176/B1
Los Menucos, Arg. 190/C4
Los Mochis, Mex. 174/C3
Los Molinos, Ca, US 146/B3
Los Monos, Arg. 190/C5
Los Mosquitos (gulf), Pan. 177/F4
Los Muermos, Chile 190/B4
Los Navalmorales, Sp. 46/C3
Los Navalucillos, Sp. 46/C3
Los Nevados, PN, Col. 183/K8
Los Olmos (cr.), Tx, US 151/E4
Los Órganos, Peru 184/A2
Los Padres National Forest, Ca, US 166/A1
Los Palacios y Villafranca, Sp. 46/C4
Los Palos, ETim. 128/B2
Los Pingüinos, PN, Chile 191/C7
Los Pinos (riv.), Co, US 152/A2
Los Planes, Mex. 174/C3
Los Ranchos de Albuquerque, NM, US 149/J3
Los Reyes, Mex. 175/R10
Los Reyes de Salgado, Mex. 174/E5
Los Riecillos, Chile 190/N8
Los Ríos (prov.), Ecu. 184/B1
Los Roques (isls.), Ven. 173/H5
Los Santos, Pan. 180/A3
Los Santos de Maimona, Sp. 46/B3
Los Sauces, Chile 190/B3
Los Tamariscos, Arg. 190/C5
Los Taques, Ven. 180/D2
Los Telares, Arg. 188/D4
Los Teques, Ven. 183/N7
Los Testigos (isls.), Ven. 181/F2
Los Vientos, Chile 188/B3
Los Vilos, Chile 190/C1
Los Yébenes, Sp. 46/D3
Losai Nat'l Rsv., Kenya 119/B1
Losheim, Ger. 55/F4
Loshkarëvka, Ukr. 73/H4
Loshnitsa, Bela. 41/N4
Łosice, Pol. 43/M2
Losinj (isl.), Cro. 67/G1
Lošinj (isl.), Cro. 45/L4
Loskiria (peak), Kenya 119/B1
Losne, Fr. 60/B3
Losone, Swi. 61/E5
Lossburg, Ger. 61/E1
Losser, Neth. 52/E4
Lossie (riv.), Sc, UK 33/C1
Lossiemouth, Sc, UK 33/C1
Lössnitz, Ger. 59/F1
Lossoganeu (hill), Tanz. 119/B3
Lost (lake), La, US 164/C3
Lost (riv.), Or, US 146/C2
Lost Creek (res.), Or, US 146/B2
Lost Creek, WV, US 163/G1
Lost Creek, Ky, US 163/F2
Lost Draw (riv.), Tx, US 151/C1
Lost Hills, Ca, US 148/C3
Lost Mountain, Ga, US 163/L7
Lost River (range), Id, US 147/G1
Lost River Caverns, Pa, US 168/C2
Lost Springs, Ks, US 153/F1
Lostallo, Swi. 61/F5
Lostwithiel, Eng, UK 36/B6
Lostwood NWR, ND, US 156/C3
Losynivka, Ukr. 72/F2
Lot (riv.), Fr. 66/D1
Lota, Chile 190/B3
Løten, Nor. 40/D1
Lotfābād, Iran 101/G1
Lothaa, Ugan. 119/A1
Lotikipi (plain), Kenya 117/G4
Loto, D.R. Congo 121/E3
Lotogipi (swamp), Kenya 117/G4
Lotoi (riv.), D.R. Congo 120/D3
Lotsane (riv.), Bots. 123/E4
Lott, Tx, US 151/F2
Lotte, Ger. 53/E4
Lotuke (peak), Sudan 117/G4
Lotumbe, D.R. Congo 120/D3
Lou (riv.), China 80/B5
Louang Namtha, Laos 86/D4
Louangphrabang, Laos 86/D5
Louann, Ar, US 153/H4
Loubomo, Congo 120/C4
Loudéac, Fr. 56/C4
Loudi, China 87/F3
Loudima, Congo 120/C4
Loudon, Tn, US 162/E3
Loudonville, NY, US 161/K3
Loudonville, Oh, US 160/E4
Loudun, Fr. 44/D3
Loudwater, Eng, UK 30/A2
Loué, Fr. 57/E4
Loue (riv.), Fr. 44/F3
Louessé (riv.), Congo 120/C3
Louet (riv.), Fr. 57/E6
Loufan, China 80/B3
Louga, Sen. 114/A3
Louga (pol.reg.), Sen. 114/B3
Lough Foyle (lake), UK 34/A1
Loughborough, Eng, UK 37/E1
Loughbrickland, NI, UK 34/B3
Lougheed (isl.), Nun, Can. 141/R7
Loughgall, NI, UK 34/B3
Loughman, Fl, US 164/M7
Loughrea, Ire. 32/B3
Loughton, Eng, UK 30/D2
Louhans, Fr. 60/B4
Louingi, Congo 120/C4
Louis Botha (Durban) (int'l arpt.), SAfr. 125/E3
Louis Creek, BC, Can. 144/D2
Louis Trichardt, SAfr. 123/F4
Louisa (lake), Fl, US 164/M7
Louisa, Ky, US 163/F1
Louisa, Va, US 163/H1
Louisbourg, NS, Can. 159/H3
Louisburg, Ks, US 153/G1
Louisburg, NC, US 163/H2
Louisdale, NS, Can. 159/G3
Louise, Tx, US 151/F3
Louiseville, Qu, Can. 161/K1
Louisiade (arch.), PNG 136/E6
Louisiana (pt.), La, US 151/H3
Louisiana (state), US 143/H5
Louisiana, Mo, US 155/J4
Louisville, Al, US 165/F2
Louisville, Co, US 154/B4
Louisville, Ga, US 163/F4
Louisville, Il, US 162/C1
Louisville, Ky, US 162/E1
Louisville, Ms, US 162/C4
Louisville, Ne, US 155/F3
Louisville, Oh, US 160/F4
Loukhi, Rus. 68/G2
Loukkos (riv.), Mor. 112/A2
Loukouo, Congo 120/C3
Loulé, Port. 46/A4
Loum, Camr. 120/B1
Louny, Czh. 59/G2
Loup (riv.), Fr. 64/C5
Loup (riv.), Ne, US 154/E3
Loup City, Ne, US 154/E3
Lourches, Fr. 54/C3
Lourdes, Nf, Can. 159/H1
Lourdes, Fr. 44/C5
Lourdes/Tarbes (int'l arpt.), Fr. 44/D5
Loures, Port. 47/P10
Louriçal, Port. 46/A2
Lourinhã, Port. 46/A3
Loury, Fr. 57/H4
Lousã, Port. 46/A2
Lousa, Port. 47/Q10
Loushan (pass), China 87/E2
Loutété, Congo 120/C4
Louth, Ire. 34/B4
Louth, Eng, UK 35/H5
Louth (co.), Ire. 34/B4
Louth, Austl. 132/C1
Loutrá Aidhipsoú, Gre. 49/H3
Loutrákion, Gre. 49/H4
Louts (riv.), Fr. 47/E1
Loútsa, Gre. 49/P9
Louvain (Leuven), Belg. 55/D2
Louvale, Ga, US 162/E4
Louveira, Braz. 187/K8
Louverné, Fr. 57/E4
Louviers, Fr. 57/G2
Louviers, Co, US 154/B4
Louvigné-de-Bais, Fr. 56/D4
Louvigné-du-Désert, Fr. 57/D4
Louvres, Fr. 30/K4
Louvroil, Fr. 54/C3
Lovaart (riv.), Belg. 54/B1
Lovat' (riv.), Rus. 68/F4
Lovat' (riv.), Bela.,Rus. 41/P3
Lovćen NP, Yugo. 49/F1
Lovćenac, Yugo. 50/D3
Love Point, Md, US 168/B5
Lovech (prov.), Bul. 49/J1
Lovech, Bul. 51/G4
Lovejoy, Ga, US 163/M8
Lovelady, Tx, US 151/G2
Loveland, Co, US 154/B3
Lovell, Wy, US 147/J1
Lovelock, Nv, US 146/D3
Lovere, It. 62/D2
Loverna, Sk, Can. 145/K2
Loves Park, Il, US 155/K2
Lovilia, Ia, US 155/H3
Loving, NM, US 150/B1
Lovingston, Va, US 163/H2
Lovington, NM, US 152/C4
Lovios, Sp. 46/A2
Lövő, Hun. 50/C2
Lovosice, Czh. 59/H1
Lovozero (lake), Rus. 68/G2
Lóvua, Ang. 120/E4
Low (des.), Or, US 146/C2
Low (cape), Nun, Can. 141/H2
Lowa (riv.), D.R. Congo 107/E5
Lowdham, Eng, UK 35/H6
Lowe, Ks, US 152/D1
Lowe Farm, Mb, Can. 156/F3
Lowell, Ar, US 153/G2
Lowell, In, US 160/C4
Lowell, Oh, US 160/F5
Lowell (lake), Id, US 146/E2
Lowell, Or, US 146/B2
Lowell, Id, US 144/G4
Lowell Observatory, Az, US 149/G3
Löwen (riv.), Namb. 124/B2
Löwenstein, Ger. 58/C4
Lower (falls), Mi, US 160/D1
Lower (dam), Wa, US 167/D3
Lower (lake), Ca, US 146/C3
Lower (falls), Wy, US 147/H1
Lower (bay), NJ, US 168/D2
Lower Arrow (lake), BC, Can. 144/E3
Lower Brailes, Eng, UK 37/E2
Lower Brule Ind. Res., SD, US 154/D1
Lower Engadine (valley), Swi. 61/G4
Lower Ganges (canal), India 96/B2
Lower Glenelg NP, Austl. 132/B3
Lower Granite (gorge), Az, US 149/E2
Lower Heyford, Eng, UK 37/E3
Lower Hutt, NZ 135/H9
Lower Kalskag, Ak, US 171/F3
Lower Klamath (lake), Ca, US 146/C3
Lower Klamath NWR, Or, US 146/C2
Lower Mesa (falls), Id, US 147/H1
Lower Monumental (dam), Wa, US 144/E4
Lower Nazeing, Eng, UK 30/D1
Lower Otay (lake), Ca, US 166/D5
Lower Peach Tree, Al, US 164/E2
Lower Red (lake), Mn, US 157/G4
Lower Rhine (riv.), Neth. 52/C5
Lower Rouge (riv.), Mi, US 167/E7
Lower Sioux Ind. Res., Mn, US 155/G1
Lower Stoke, Eng, UK 30/E2
Lower Suwannee Nat'l Wild. Ref., Fl, US 165/G3
Lower Trajan's Wall (wall), Mol.,Ukr. 51/J3
Lower Tunguska (riv.), Rus. 77/J3
Lower Wedgeport, NS, Can. 158/E4
Lower West Pubnico, NS, Can. 158/E4
Lower Zambezi NP, Zam. 123/F2
Lowery (lake), Fl, US 164/M7
Lowestoft, Eng, UK 37/H2
Lowick, Eng, UK 33/E5
Łowicz, Pol. 43/K2
Lowman, Id, US 146/F1
Lowry City, Mo, US 153/H1
Lowther (hills), Sc, UK 33/C6
Lowville, NY, US 161/J3
Lowville, On, Can. 160/T9
Loxahatchee, Fl, US 164/P9
Loxahatchee National Wildlife Refuge, Fl, US 165/H4
Loxahatchee Slough (swamp), Fl, US 164/P9
Loxstedt, Ger. 53/F2
Loxton, Austl. 131/J5
Loxton, SAfr. 124/C3
Loxton North, Austl. 131/J5
Loya, Tanz. 119/A3
Loyal, Wi, US 155/J1
Loyall, Ky, US 163/F2
Loyalton, Ca, US 146/C4
Loyalton, Pa, US 168/B2
Loyalty (isls.), NCal. 136/F7
Loyettes, Fr. 60/B6
Loyev, Bela. 72/F2
Loyne (lake), Sc, UK 33/A2
Loyno, Rus. 69/M4
Loyoro, Ugan. 117/G5
Loysville, Pa, US 168/A3
Loznica, Yugo. 50/D3

Loznitsa, Bul. 51/H4
Lozova, Ukr. 73/J3
Lozovik, Yugo. 50/E3
Lozym, Rus. 69/L3
Lü (isl.), Tai. 87/J4
Lu (riv.), China 80/C5
Lu (mtn.), China 80/D3
Lu (peak), China 87/G2
Lu Xian, China 93/J2
Lua (riv.), Congo 116/C5
Lua (riv.), D.R. Congo 120/D2
Lua Dekere (riv.), D.R. Congo 120/D2
Luabo, Moz. 123/H3
Luacano, Ang. 122/D1
Luachimo, Ang. 121/E4
Luachimo (riv.), Ang. 121/E5
Luaco, Ang. 121/E4
Luaha-Sibuha, Indo. 89/B3
Luala (riv.), Moz. 123/H3
Lualaba (riv.), D.R. Congo 107/E5
Luale, D.R. Congo 121/E2
Luali, D.R. Congo 120/C4
Luama (riv.), D.R. Congo 121/F4
Luambe NP, Zam. 123/G2
Luampa, Zam. 122/E2
Luampa (riv.), Zam. 122/E2
Luan (riv.), China 75/M5
Lu'an, China 80/D5
Luan Xian, China 80/D3
Luancheng, China 87/F4
Luanchuan, China 80/B4
Luanco, Sp. 46/C1
Luanda (prov.), Ang. 120/C5
Luanda, Kenya 119/A1
Luanda (cap.), Ang. 120/C5
Luando (riv.), Ang. 120/D5
Luando, Ang. 122/C1
Luando, Rsv. Nat. do, Ang. 120/D5
Luang (peak), Thai. 94/B4
Luang (lag.), Malay. 93/H6
Luangue (riv.), Ang. 120/D4
Luangue, Ang. 120/D5
Luanguinga (riv.), Ang. 122/D2
Luangwa (riv.), Zam. 121/G5
Luanhaizi, China 78/C5
Luano (int'l arpt.), D.R. Congo 123/E1
Luanping, China 80/D2
Luanshya, Zam. 123/F2
Luao (riv.), D.R. Congo 121/E5
Luao, Ang. 121/E5
Luapula (riv.), Zam. 121/G5
Luapula (prov.), Zam. 121/G5
Luarca, Sp. 46/B1
Luashi, D.R. Congo 121/E5
Luatize (riv.), Moz. 123/F2
Luau (riv.), Ang. 121/E5
Luba, EqG. 120/B2
Lubaantun (ruin), Belz. 176/D2
Lubaczów, Pol. 43/M3
Lubalo, Ang. 120/D5
Lubań, Pol. 43/H3
Lubāna, Lat. 41/M3
Lubang (isl.), Phil. 88/B2
Lubang, Phil. 88/C2
Lubango, D.R. Congo 121/F3
Lubango, Ang. 122/B2
Lubansenshi (riv.), Zam. 121/G5
Lubao, D.R. Congo 121/F4
Lubartów, Pol. 43/M3
Lubawa, Pol. 43/K2
Lübbecke, Ger. 53/F4
Lubbeek, Belg. 55/D2
Lubbock, Tx, US 152/D4
Lubeck, WV, US 163/G1
Lubefu (riv.), D.R. Congo 121/E4
Lubefu, D.R. Congo 121/F4
Lubelska (uplands), Pol. 43/M3
Lubelskie (prov.), Pol. 43/M3
Lubenka, Kaz. 71/K2
Lubero, D.R. Congo 121/G3
Lubero (riv.), D.R. Congo 121/G3
Lubéron, Montagne de (mts.), Fr. 64/B5
Lubi (riv.), D.R. Congo 121/E4
Lubień Kujawski, Pol. 43/K2
Lubika, D.R. Congo 121/G4
Lubilash (riv.), D.R. Congo 121/E5
Lubin, Pol. 43/J3
Lublin, Pol. 43/M3
Lubliniec, Pol. 43/K3
Lubmin, Ger. 40/E4
Lubnaig (lake), Sc, UK 33/B4
Lubny, Ukr. 73/G2
Luboń, Pol. 43/J2
Lubongola, D.R. Congo 121/F3
Lubrín, Sp. 46/D4
Lubsko, Pol. 43/H3
Lubuagan, Phil. 88/C1
Lububu, D.R. Congo 121/F4
Lubudi (riv.), D.R. Congo 121/E4
Lubudi, D.R. Congo 121/F5
Lubue (riv.), D.R. Congo 120/D4
Lubuklinggau, Indo. 89/C3
Lubukpakam, Indo. 89/B2
Lubuksikaping, Indo. 89/C2
Lubumbashi, D.R. Congo 123/E1
Lubunda, D.R. Congo 121/F4
Lubunza, D.R. Congo 121/E4
Lubuskie (prov.), Pol. 43/H2
Lubutu, D.R. Congo 121/F3
Lubwe, Zam. 121/G5
Luc An Chau, Viet. 94/D1
Luc-en-Diois, Fr. 64/B3
Luc-sur-Mer, Fr. 57/E2
Lucala, Ang. 120/C5
Lucala (riv.), Ang. 120/C5
Lucan, Ire. 34/B5
Lucan, On, Can. 160/F3
Lucania (mt.), Yk, Can. 171/K3
Lücaoshan, China 78/D4
Lucapa, Ang. 121/E5
Lucas, Ks, US 153/E1
Lucas, Tx, US 150/L6
Lucas González, Arg. 191/J10
Lucasville, Oh, US 163/F1
Lucca (prov.), It. 62/D5
Lucca, It. 62/D6
Lucciana, Fr. 48/A1
Lucé, Fr. 57/G4
Luce (bay), Sc, UK 34/D2
Luce Bayou (riv.), Tx, US 151/M8
Lucedale, Ms, US 164/D2
Lucélia, Braz. 189/G2
Lucena, Sp. 46/C4
Lucena, Phil. 88/C2
Lucena del Cid, Sp. 47/E2
Lučenec, Slvk. 43/K4
Lucens, Swi. 60/C4
Lucerna, Peru 184/D4
Lucerne (lake), Ca, US 166/C1
Lucerne, Wy, US 147/J2
Lucerne, Wa, US 144/D3
Lucerne (Luzern), Swi. 45/H3
Lucerne (Vierwaldstättersee) (lake), Swi. 61/E3
Lucero (lake), NM, US 152/A4
Lucero (mesa), NM, US 149/J3
Luchang, China 86/D3
Luché-Pringé, Fr. 57/F3
Luchegorsk, Rus. 79/L2
Lucheng, China 80/C3
Lucheng, China 87/E3
Lucheringo (riv.), Moz. 123/G2
Lüchow, Ger. 42/F2
Luchuan, China 93/K3
Lüchun, China 86/D4
Lucia, Ca, US 148/B2
Lucie (riv.), Sur. 182/B2
Lucile, Ga, US 165/F2
Lucindale, Austl. 132/B3
Lucira, Ang. 122/B2
Luciras (bay), Ang. 122/B2
Lucito, It. 65/D4
Luck, Wi, US 157/H5
Luckeesarai, India 97/F3
Luckenwalde, Ger. 43/G2
Lucknow, On, Can. 160/F3
Lucknow, India 96/C2
Lucky, La, US 153/H4
Lucky Lake, Sk, Can. 145/L2
Lucky Peak (dam), Id, US 146/E2
Luco dei Marsi, It. 65/C4
Lucomagno, Passo del (pass), Swi. 61/E4
Lücongpo, China 78/G5
Lucrecia (cape), Cuba 177/H1
Lucrezia, It. 63/F6
Lucunga, Ang. 120/C4
Lucusse, Ang. 122/D2
Lucy Creek, Austl. 131/H2
Ludden, ND, US 156/E4
Ludell, Ks, US 154/D4
Lüdenscheid, Ger. 53/E6
Lüderitz, Namb. 124/A2
Ludesar, India 98/C5
Ludesch, Aus. 61/F3
Ludgershall, Eng, UK 37/E4
Ludhiāna, India 98/C4
Ludian, China 93/H2
Luding, China 86/D2
Ludinghausen, Ger. 53/E5
Ludington, Mi, US 160/C3
Ludlow, SD, US 156/C5
Ludlow, Pa, US 161/G4
Ludlow, Vt, US 161/K3
Ludlow, Ca, US 148/D3
Ludlow, Eng, UK 36/D2
Ludogorie (reg.), Bul. 51/H4
Ludowici, Ga, US 165/H2
Luduş, Rom. 51/G2
Ludvika, Swe. 40/F1
Ludwigs (canal), Ger. 59/E4
Ludwigsburg, Ger. 58/C5
Ludwigsfelde, Ger. 42/Q7
Ludwigshafen, Ger. 61/F2
Ludwigshafen, Ger. 58/B4
Ludwigslust, Ger. 42/F2
Ludwigsstadt, Ger. 59/E2
Ludza, Lat. 41/M3
Lue, Austl. 133/D1
Luebo, D.R. Congo 121/E4
Lueders, Tx, US 151/E1
Lueki, D.R. Congo 121/F3
Luemba (riv.), Ang. 121/E5
Luemba, D.R. Congo 121/G3
Luembe (riv.), Ang. 122/D1
Luembi (riv.), D.R. Congo 121/F4
Luena, D.R. Congo 121/F5
Luena, Ang. 122/C1
Luena (riv.), Zam. 122/D2
Luena (flats), Zam. 122/D2
Luengue (riv.), Ang. 122/D3
Luenha (riv.), Moz. 123/G3
Lueta (riv.), D.R. Congo 121/E4
Lüeyang, China 78/F5
Lufa, PNG 129/G1
Lufeng, China 87/G4
Lufico, Ang. 120/C4
Lufira (riv.), D.R. Congo 121/F5
Lufkin, Tx, US 150/G2
Lufu, D.R. Congo 120/C4
Lufupa (riv.), Zam. 122/E2
Luga (bay), Rus. 41/N2
Luga (riv.), Rus. 41/N2
Luga, Rus. 41/N2
Luga, D.R. Congo 121/G2
Lugagnano, It. 63/D3
Lugagnano Val d'Arda, It. 62/C4
Lugano, Swi. 61/E6
Lugano (lake), It. 61/E6
Luganville, Van. 136/F6
Lugards (falls), Kenya 119/B2
Lugavčina, Yugo. 50/E3
Lugazi, Ugan. 121/H2
Lügde, Ger. 53/G5
Lugela, Moz. 123/H3
Lugenda (riv.), Moz. 123/H2
Lugg (riv.), Wal, UK 36/C2
Lugg (riv.), Eng, UK 36/D2
Lugnaquillia (peak), Ire. 34/B6
Lugo, It. 63/E5
Lugo, Sp. 46/B1
Lugo di Vicenza, It. 63/E2
Lugoff, SC, US 163/G3
Lugogo (riv.), Ugan. 121/H2
Lugoj, Rom. 50/E3
Lugovoy, Kaz. 99/B3
Lugovskoye, Rus. 71/H2
Lugrin, Fr. 60/C5
Lugu, China 86/D2
Lugulu (riv.), D.R. Congo 121/F3
Lugunga (peak), Tanz. 119/B3
Luguruka, Tanz. 119/B4
Luhans'k (int'l arpt.), Ukr. 73/K3
Luhans'k, Ukr. 73/K3
Luhans'ka Oblast, Ukr. 70/F2
Lühe (riv.), Ger. 53/H2
Luhe (riv.), Ger. 59/F3
Luhe, China 80/D4
Luhe-Wildenau, Ger. 59/F3
Luhit (riv.), India 86/C3
Luhombero (peak), Tanz. 119/B3
Luhongshi, China 87/F3
Luhtikylä, Fin. 39/F4
Luhumbo, Tanz. 119/A2
Luhuo, China 86/D2
Luhyny, Ukr. 72/E2
Lui (riv.), Zam. 122/D2
Luia, Ang. 121/E5
Luia (riv.), Moz. 123/G2
Luia (riv.), Moz. 122/D2
Luiana, Ang. 122/D3
Luiana (riv.), Ang. 122/D3
Luichart (lake), Sc, UK 33/B1
Luidaogou, China 81/D2
Luie (riv.), D.R. Congo 120/D4
Luigi Ridolfi (arpt.), It. 63/F5
Luilaka (riv.), D.R. Congo 121/E3
Luilu (riv.), D.R. Congo 121/E4
Luino, It. 61/E6
Luis B. Sánchez, Mex. 174/B1
Luís Correia, Braz. 183/F3
Luís Domingues, Braz. 183/E3
Luis Munoz (int'l arpt.), PR 173/M8
Luisant, Fr. 57/G4
Luiza, D.R. Congo 121/E4
Luján, Arg. 191/J11
Luján, Arg. 188/C5
Lujiang, China 80/D5
Lukácsháza, Hun. 50/C2
Lukala (riv.), D.R. Congo 120/D4
Lukanga (swamp), Zam. 123/E2
Lukavac, Bosn. 50/D3
Luke (A.F.B.), Az, US 149/F4
Luke (mt.), Austl. 130/C3
Lukenie (riv.), D.R. Congo 120/D3
Lukeville, Az, US 149/F5
Lukhovitsy, Rus. 68/H5
Lŭki, Bul. 49/J2
Luki, D.R. Congo 120/C4
Lukolela, D.R. Congo 120/D3
Lukolela, D.R. Congo 121/F4
Lukoupu, China 87/G2
Lukovit, Bul. 51/G4
Łuków, Pol. 43/M3
Lukoyanov, Rus. 69/K5
Lukuga (riv.), D.R. Congo 121/F4
Lukula, D.R. Congo 120/C4
Lukula (riv.), D.R. Congo 120/C4
Lukulu, Zam. 122/D2
Lukulu (riv.), Zam. 121/G5
Lukunor (isl.), Micr. 136/E4
Lukusashi (riv.), Zam. 123/F2
Lukusuzi NP, Zam. 123/G2
Lukwasa, India 96/A3
Lukwesa, Zam. 121/G5
Luleå, Swe. 68/D2
Luleälven (riv.), Swe. 38/G2
Lüleburgaz, Turk. 51/H5
Lules, Arg. 188/C3
Luliang, China 93/H2
Luliāni, Pak. 98/C4
Lulimba, D.R. Congo 121/G4
Luling (pass), China 80/B4
Luling, Tx, US 150/F3
Lulong, China 80/D3
Lulonga, D.R. Congo 120/D2
Lulonga (riv.), D.R. Congo 107/E4
Lulsgate (int'l arpt.), Eng, UK 36/D4
Lulua (riv.), D.R. Congo 107/E5
Luluba, Sudan 117/F4
Lumai, Ang. 122/D2
Lumajang, Indo. 89/F5
Lumajangdong (lake), China 99/D5
Lumangwe (falls), Zam. 121/G5
Lumbala Kaquengue, Ang. 122/D2
Lumbala N'guimbo, Ang. 122/D2
Lumbe (riv.), Zam. 122/E3
Lumber (riv.), SC, US 163/H3
Lumber City, Ga, US 165/G2
Lumberton, Ms, US 164/D2
Lumberton, NC, US 163/H3
Lumberton, NJ, US 168/D4
Lumberton, NM, US 149/J2
Lumberton, Tx, US 151/G2
Lumbini (zone), Nepal 96/D2
Lumbis, Indo. 88/B4
Lumbo, Moz. 123/J2
Lumbovka, Rus. 68/J2
Lumbrales, Sp. 46/B2
Lumbrein, Swi. 61/F4
Lumbres, Fr. 54/B2
Lumby, BC, Can. 144/E2
Lumding, India 86/B3
Lumeje, Ang. 122/D1
Lumigny-Nesles-Ormeaux, Fr. 30/L5
Luminárias, Braz. 187/M6
Lummen, Belg. 55/E2
Lummi Ind. Res., Wa, US 144/C3
Lumparland, Fin. 41/J1
Lumphat, Camb. 94/D3
Lumpkin, Ga, US 165/F1
Lumsden, Sk, Can. 156/B2
Lumsden, Sc, UK 33/D2
Lumsden, NZ 135/B4
Lumu, China 80/L8
Lumut, Malay. 89/C1
Lumut, Indo. 89/B2
Lumut (cape), Indo. 89/D3
Lumut, Malay. 89/C1
Luna (mtn.), Ca, US 166/C2
Luna, NM, US 149/H4
Luna, Phil. 88/C1
Lunache, Ang. 122/D2
Lunahuaná, Peru 184/B4
Lunan (mts.), China 86/D3
Lunar Crater, Nv, US 146/F4
Lunay, Fr. 57/F5
Luncarty, Sc, UK 33/C4
Lund, Swe. 40/E4
Lund, Nv, US 147/F4
Lund, Ut, US 149/F1
Lund, BC, Can. 144/B3
Lunda, Swe. 39/B1
Lunda Norte (prov.), Ang. 120/D5
Lunda Sul (prov.), Ang. 121/E5
Lundar, Mb, Can. 156/E2
Lundazi, Zam. 123/G2
Lundbreck, Ab, Can. 145/G3
Lundby, Den. 40/D4
Lunde, Nor. 40/C2
Lundell, Ar, US 162/B3
Lundi (riv.), Zim. 123/F3
Lundu, Zam. 121/H5
Lundy (isl.), Eng, UK 36/B4
Lune (riv.), Eng, UK 35/F2
Lune (riv.), Eng, UK 35/F2
Lune (riv.), Ger. 53/F2
Lüneburg, Ger. 53/H2
Lüneburger Heide (reg.), Ger. 42/F2
Lunel, Fr. 44/F5
Lünen, Ger. 53/E5
Lunenburg, NS, Can. 158/E3
Lunenburg, Vt, US 161/L2
Lunenburg, Va, US 163/H2
Lunestedt, Ger. 53/F2
Lunéville, Fr. 45/G2
Lung (riv.), Ire. 32/B2
Lung Kwu Chau (isl.), China 87/K7
Lunga (riv.), Zam. 123/E2
Lunga, West (riv.), Zam. 121/F5
Lunga-Lunga, Kenya 119/B3
Lungdo, China 99/D5
Lungern, Swi. 60/E4
Lungi, SLeo. 114/B4
Lungi (Freetown) (int'l arpt.), SLeo. 114/B4
Lunglei, India 93/F3
Lungsang, China 99/E6
Lungtian, India 86/B4
Lungue-Bungo (riv.), Ang. 122/C2
Lungwebungu (riv.), Zam. 122/D2
Luni (riv.), India 92/B3
Luning, Nv, US 146/D4
Lunino, Rus. 71/H1
Luninyets, Bela. 70/C1
Lunita, La, US 150/H2
Lunkinjärvi (lake), Fin. 39/D4
Lünne, Ger. 53/E4
Luntai, China 99/D3
Lunzu, Malw. 123/G2
Luo (riv.), China 78/F4
Luobei, China 79/L2
Luobuzhuang, China 99/E4
Luocheng, China 87/F3
Luodian, China 87/E3
Luoding, China 87/F4
Luofu (peak), China 87/G4
Luohe, China 80/C4
Luojing, China 93/K3
Luoma (lake), China 80/D4
Luonan, China 87/F5
Luongo (riv.), Zam. 121/G5
Luoning, China 80/B4
Luoping, China 86/E3
Luoqiao, China 87/H3
Luoqing (riv.), China 87/F3
Luoshan, China 80/C4
Luoshuikan, China 87/F2
Luotian, China 87/G2
Luoxu, China 87/F4
Luoyang, China 87/F3
Luoyang, China 80/C4
Luoyukou, China 80/B3
Luozi, D.R. Congo 120/C4
Lupa Market, Tanz. 119/A4
Lupane, Zim. 123/E3
Lupanshui, China 86/E3
Lupeni, Rom. 51/F3
Lupire, Ang. 122/C2
Lupiro, Tanz. 119/B4
Lupon, Phil. 88/D4
Luputa, D.R. Congo 121/E4
Luqa (int'l arpt.), Malta 48/L7
Luqu, China 78/E5
Luquan, China 86/D3
Luquembo, Ang. 120/D5
Lūrah (riv.), Afg. 101/J2
Luraville, Fl, US 165/G2
Luray, Fr. 57/G3
Luray, Ks, US 154/E4
Luray, Va, US 163/H1
Lure, Fr. 60/C2
Lure, Montagne de (mts.), Fr. 64/B4
Lurgan, NI, UK 34/B3
Luri, Fr. 48/A1
Luribay, Bol. 188/C1
Lurín, Peru 184/B4
Lúrio, Moz. 123/J2
Lúrio (riv.), Moz. 107/F6
Lurnfeld, Aus. 45/K3
Lurøy, Nor. 38/E2
Lurton, Ar, US 153/H3
Lusahunga, Tanz. 121/G3
Lusaka (cap.), Zam. 123/F2
Lusaka (int'l arpt.), Zam. 123/F2
Lusaka (prov.), Zam. 123/F2
Lusamba, D.R. Congo 121/F4
Lusambo, D.R. Congo 121/E4
Lusangi, D.R. Congo 121/F4
Luseland, Sk, Can. 145/K1
Lusemfwa (riv.), Zam. 123/F2
Lusen (peak), Ger. 59/G5
Lusenga NP, Zam. 121/G5
Lush (mt.), Austl. 128/B4
Lushan, China 80/C4
Lushi, China 80/B4
Lushiko (riv.), D.R. Congo 120/D4
Lushnjë, Alb. 49/F2
Lushoto, Tanz. 119/B3
Lushui, China 86/C3
Lüshun, China 80/E3
Lusignan, Fr. 44/D3
Lusk, Ire. 34/B4
Lusk, Wy, US 154/B2
Luso, Ang. 122/B2
Luss, Sc, UK 33/B4
Lustenau, Aus. 61/F3
Lustre, Mt, US 145/M3
Lutang, China 87/G3
Lutembo (riv.), Ang. 122/D2
Luther, Mi, US 160/D2
Luther (pass), Ca, US 148/B1
Luther, Tx, US 151/D1
Luthern, Swi. 60/D3
Luthersville, Ga, US 162/E4
Lutherville, Md, US 168/B5
Luthle, Bots. 122/D4
Lütjehorn (isl.), Ger. 52/D1
Lütjenburg, Ger. 40/D4
Luton, Eng, UK 37/F3
Luton (co.), Eng, UK 37/F3
Luton (int'l arpt.), Eng, UK 37/F3
Lutong, Malay. 90/D3
Lutry, Swi. 60/C5
Łutselk'e, NW, Can. 140/E2
Lutsen, Mn, US 157/J4
Lutshi, D.R. Congo 121/F4
Lutshima, D.R. Congo 120/D4
Lutshima (riv.), D.R. Congo 120/D4
Luts'k, Ukr. 72/C2
Lutter (riv.), Ger. 53/F5
Lutterbach, Fr. 60/D2
Lutterworth, Eng, UK 35/G6
Lutuhyne, Ukr. 73/K3
Lutz (riv.), Aus. 61/F3
Lutz, Fl, US 164/L7
Lützow-Holm (bay), Ant. 192/C
Luumäki, Fin. 41/M1
Luuq, Som. 118/B5
Luvalo, Ang. 120/D5
Luverne, Al, US 165/E2
Luverne, Mn, US 155/F2
Luvo, Ang. 120/C4
Luvozero, Rus. 68/F2
Luvu, D.R. Congo 120/C4
Luvua (riv.), D.R. Congo 121/G4
Luwegu (riv.), Tanz. 119/B4
Luwembe, Zam. 123/F2
Luwero, Ugan. 121/H2
Luwingu, Zam. 121/G5
Lux, Fr. 60/A4
Luxapallila (cr.), Al, US 162/C4
Luxembourg (cap.), Lux. 55/F4
Luxembourg (prov.), Belg 55/E4
Luxembourg (ctry.) 29/E4
Luxemburg, Wi, US 160/C2
Luxeuil-les-Bains, Fr. 60/C2
Luxi, China 87/F2
Luxi, China 86/C3
Luxi, China 86/D3
Luxico (riv.), Ang. 120/D4
Luxikou, China 87/G2
Luxomni, Ga, US 163/M7
Luxor (int'l arpt.), Egypt 135/G3
Luxora, Ar, US 162/C3
Luxu, China 87/F4
Luxu, China 80/L8
Luy (riv.), Fr. 47/E1
Lüyang, China 81/A2
Luye (riv.), Fr. 64/C3
Luyi, China 80/C4
Luynes, Fr. 57/F6
Luz (coast), Port.,Sp. 46/B4
Luz, Braz. 186/D3
Luza (riv.), Rus. 69/L3
Luza, Rus. 69/K3
Luzarches, Fr. 30/K4
Luzein, Swi. 61/F4
Luzern, Swi. 61/E3
Luzern (canton), Swi. 60/E3
Luzern (Lucerne), Swi. 45/H3
Luzerne (co.), Pa, US 168/B1
Luzhai, China 93/J3
Luzhi, China 86/E3
Lüzhi (riv.), China 86/D3
Luzhou, China 86/E2
Luziânia, Braz. 186/D3
Luzilândia, Braz. 183/F3
Luzinga, Ugan. 119/A1
Lužnice (riv.), Czh. 43/H4
Luzon (isl.), Phil. 114/C1
Luzon (str.), Phil. 136/A3
Lužuice (riv.), Czh. 45/L2
Luzzara, It. 63/D4
Luzzi, It. 48/E3
L'viv, Ukr. 72/C3
L'vivs'ka Oblast, Ukr. 72/B2
Lwala (peak), Ugan. 117/G5
Lwena Mission, Zam. 121/G5
Lwi (riv.), Myan. 94/C1
Lyady, Rus. 41/N2
Lyakhovichi, Bela. 70/C1
Lyantonde, Ugan. 121/G3
Lyapin (riv.), Rus. 69/P2
Lychett Matravers, Eng, UK 36/D5
Lycksele, Swe. 38/F2
Lycoming (co.), Pa, US 168/A1
Lydd, Eng, UK 37/G5
Lydenburg, SAfr. 123/F5
Lydia, La, US 164/C3
Lydney, Eng, UK 36/D3
Lyell (mt.), BC, Can. 144/F2
Lyell Brown (mt.), Austl. 131/F2
Lyepel', Bela. 41/N4
Lyford, Tx, US 151/F4
Lykens, Pa, US 168/B2
Lyle, Mn, US 155/H2
Lyle, Wa, US 144/D5
Lyles, Tn, US 162/D3
Lyleton, Mb, Can. 156/D3
Lyman, Ms, US 164/D2
Lyman, Wy, US 147/H3
Lyman, Ut, US 149/G1
Lyman, SC, US 163/F3
Lyme (bay), Eng, UK 44/B1
Lyme Regis, Eng, UK 36/D5
Lymington, Eng, UK 37/E5
Lymm, Eng, UK 35/F5
Łyna (riv.), Pol. 43/L1
Lynas (pt.), Wal, UK 34/D5
Lynbrook, NY, US 169/L9
Lynch, Ne, US 154/E2
Lynch, Md, US 168/B5
Lynch Station, Va, US 163/H2
Lynchburg, Mo, US 153/H2
Lynchburg, Ms, US 162/B3
Lynchburg, Oh, US 162/F1
Lynchburg, Tn, US 162/D3
Lynchburg, Va, US 163/H2
Lynches (riv.), SC, US 163/G3
Lynd, Austl. 134/B2
Lynden, Wa, US 144/C3
Lyndhurst, NJ, US 169/J8
Lyndhurst, Austl. 131/H4
Lyndhurst, Eng, UK 37/E5
Lyndhurst, Austl. 133/D1
Lyndon, Ks, US 153/G1
Lyndon, Vt, US 161/K2
Lyndon, Austl. 130/B2
Lyndon B. Johnson (lake), Tx, US 151/E2
Lyndon B. Johnson Nat'l Hist. Park, Tx, US 151/E2
Lyndon B. Johnson Space Center, Tx, US 151/M9
Lyndonville, NY, US 161/G3
Lyne (riv.), Eng, UK 35/F1
Lyness, Sc, UK 31/V14
Lyngby, Den. 39/J7
Lyngdal, Nor. 40/B2
Lynge, Den. 39/J7
Lyngen (inlet), Nor. 38/G1
Lynn, Ar, US 153/J2
Lynn, Ma, US 161/L3
Lynn, Al, US 162/D3
Lynn Haven, Fl, US 165/F2
Lynn Lake, Mb, Can. 140/F3
Lynnwood, Wa, US 144/C4
Lynton, Eng, UK 36/C4
Lyntupy, Bela. 41/M4
Lynwood, Ca, US 166/F8
Lynx (lake), NW, Can. 140/F2
Lyon (riv.), Sc, UK 33/B3
Lyon (lake), Sc, UK 33/B3
Lyon (mtn.), NY, US 161/K2
Lyon, Fr. 64/A1
Lyon, Ms, US 162/B3
Lyon (Satolas) (int'l arpt.), Fr. 60/B6
Lyon (canal), Co, US 152/C1
Lyonne (riv.), Fr. 64/B2
Lyons, Ks, US 153/E1
Lyons, NY, US 161/H3
Lyons, Wi, US 167/P14
Lyons (riv.), Austl. 130/C3
Lyons, In, US 162/D1
Lyons, Ga, US 163/F4
Lyons Falls, NY, US 161/J3
Lyons-la-Forêt, Fr. 57/G2
Lype (hill), Eng, UK 36/C4
Lypovets', Ukr. 72/E3
Lyra (reef), PNG 136/E5
Lys (riv.), It. 62/A1
Lys (riv.), Fr. 44/E1
Lys-lez-Lannoy, Fr. 54/C2
Lysá (peak), Czh. 43/K4
Lysá nad Labem, Czh. 59/H2
Lysaker, Nor. 40/D2
Lysaya (hill), Bela. 41/M4
Lysekil, Swe. 40/D2
Lyseren (lake), Nor. 38/T8
Łysica (peak), Pol. 43/L3
Lysina (peak), Czh. 59/F2
Lysite, Wy, US 147/K2
Lyss, Swi. 60/D3
Lystrup, Den. 40/D3
Lys'va, Rus. 69/N4
Lysychans'k, Ukr. 73/K3
Lysyye Gory, Rus. 71/H2
Lytham Saint Anne's, Eng, UK 35/E4
Lytkarino, Rus. 69/W9
Lytle (cr.), Ca, US 166/C2
Lytle, Tx, US 150/E3
Lytle Creek, Ca, US 166/C2
Lyttelton, NZ 135/C3
Lytton, BC, Can. 144/D2
Lyuban', Bela. 70/D1
Lyubar, Ukr. 72/D3
Lyubech, Ukr. 72/F2
Lyubertsy, Rus. 69/W9
Lyubeshiv, Ukr. 72/C2
Lyubimets, Bul. 51/H5
Lyublino (nbrhd.), Rus. 69/W9
Lyuboml', Ukr. 72/C2
Lyubotyn, Ukr. 73/H3
Lyudinovo, Rus. 70/E1
Lywd (riv.), Wal, UK 36/C3

M

M'Clintock (chan.), Can. 139/G2
M'Sila (wilaya), Alg. 111/F2
M. Aleman (res.), Mex. 172/B4
M. R. Gómez, Presa (dam), Mex. 151/E4
Ma (riv.), Viet. 86/E4
Ma-ubin, Myan. 86/B5
Ma'ād, Jor. 105/D3
Ma'alot-Tarshiha, Isr. 105/C2
Ma'ān (gov.), Jor. 104/E4
Ma'ān, Jor. 104/D4
Maan, Camr. 120/B2
Ma'an, China 80/L9
Maanĭt, Mong. 78/E2
Maanĭt, Mong. 78/F2
Maanselkä (mts.), Fin. 38/H1
Ma'anshan, China 80/D5
Maardu, Est. 41/L2
Maarheeze, Neth. 52/C6
Maarianhamina (Mariehamn), Fin. 41/H1
Ma'arrat an Nu'mān, Syria 104/E2
Maarssen, Neth. 52/C4
Maartensdijk, Neth. 52/C4
Maas (riv.), Belg. 42/C4
Maas (riv.), Neth. 52/C5
Maasbracht, Neth. 55/E1
Maasbree, Neth. 52/D6
Maaseik, Belg. 55/E1
Maasin, Phil. 88/D3
Maassluis, Neth. 52/B5
Maasstroom, SAfr. 123/F4
Maastricht, Neth. 55/E2
Maastricht (int'l arpt.), Neth. 55/E2
Maave, Moz. 123/G4
Ma'ayan Harod NP, Isr. 105/C3
Maba, Indo. 91/G3
Mababe (depr.), Bots. 122/D3
Mabaho (mt.), Phil. 88/D3
Mabalacat, Phil. 88/C2
Mabalane, Moz. 123/G4
Mabank, Tx, US 151/F1
Mabaruma, Guy. 181/G2
Mabating, China 93/G2
Mabechi (riv.), Japan 82/B3
Mabel, Mn, US 155/J2
Maben, Ms, US 162/C4
Mabian, China 93/H2
Mabie, WV, US 163/H1
Mabili (riv.), Congo 120/C2
Mabinay, Phil. 88/C3
Mabini, Phil. 88/D3
Mablethorpe, Eng, UK 35/J5
Mableton, Ga, US 163/L7
Mabopane, SAfr. 124/Q12
Mabote, Moz. 123/G4
Mabou, NS, Can. 159/G2
Mabroûk, Mali 115/E2
Mabton, Wa, US 144/E4
Mabu (peak), Moz. 123/H3
Mabuasehube Game Reserve, Bots. 122/D5
Mabubas, Ang. 120/C5
Mabuki, Tanz. 119/A2
Mabule, Bots. 124/D2
Mac. Robertson Land (phys. reg.), Ant. 192/D
Macá (peak), Chile 190/B5
Macachín, Arg. 190/E3
Macaé, Braz. 187/E4
Macael, Sp. 46/D4
Macaíba, Braz. 183/H4
Macalister (riv.), Austl. 133/C3
Macaloge, Moz. 123/G2
Mação, Port. 46/A3
Macapá, Braz. 182/D2
Macapá (int'l arpt.), Braz. 182/D3
Macará, Ecu. 184/B2
Macaravita, Col. 180/C3
Macareo Santo Niño, Ven. 181/F2
Macari, Peru 184/D4
Macarthur, Austl. 132/B3
Macas, Ecu. 180/B5
Macau (dpcy.), Port. 77/L7
Macau (cap.), Macau 87/G4
Macau, Braz. 183/G4
Macauley (isl.), NZ 136/G7
Macaya (riv.), Col. 180/C4
Macaya, Pic de (peak), Haiti 177/H2
MacBride (lake), Ia, US 155/J3
Maccagno, It. 61/E5
Maccan, NS, Can. 158/E3
Maccarese, It. 65/B4
Macclenny, Fl, US 165/G2
Macclesfield (canal), Eng, UK 35/F5
Macclesfield, Eng, UK 35/F5
Macdhui (peak), SAfr. 124/D3
Macdiarmid, On, Can. 157/K3
MacDill (A.F.B.), Fl, US 164/K8
MacDonald (lake), Austl. 131/F2
Macdonald (peak), Mt, US 145/H4
Macdonald (lake), Austl. 127/B3
MacDonald (riv.), Austl. 133/E1
MacDonnell Ranges (mts.), Austl. 127/C3
MacDowell (lake), On, Can. 157/H1
MacDowell (riv.), On, Can. 157/H1
Macduff, Sc, UK 33/D1
Maceda, Sp. 46/B1
Macedon, Austl. 133/B3
Macedonía (int'l arpt.), Gre. 49/H2
Macedonia, Ar, US 153/H4
Macedonia (reg.), Gre.,FYROM 67/J2
Maceió, Braz. 187/G1
Maceió (pt.), Braz. 183/G4
Macenta, Gui. 114/C4
Macerata (prov.), It. 65/C1
Maces Bay, NB, Can. 158/D3
Macfarlan, WV, US 163/G1
Macfarlane (lake), Austl. 131/H5
Macgillycuddy's Reeks (mts.), Ire. 32/A6
MacGregor, Mb, Can. 156/E3
Macha, Bol. 188/C1
Machacamarca, Bol. 188/C1
Machache (peak), Les. 124/D3
Machachi, Ecu. 180/B5
Machado (swamp), Col. 177/H4
Machado, Braz. 187/L6
Machadodorp, SAfr. 125/E2
Machaerus (Mukāwir) (ruin), Jor. 105/D5
Machagai, Arg. 188/D3
Machaíla, Moz. 123/G4
Machakos, Kenya 119/B2
Machala, Ecu. 184/B1
Machalí, Chile 190/N9
Machalilla, PN, Ecu. 180/A5
Machang, Malay. 89/C1
Machanga, Moz. 123/G4
Machaquilá (riv.), Guat. 176/D2
Macharetí, Bol. 188/D2
Machattie (lake), Austl. 131/H3
Machaze, Moz. 123/G4
Machecoul, Fr. 44/C3
Macheke, Zim. 123/F3
Machekha, Rus. 73/M2
Machemma (ruin), SAfr. 123/F4
Machen, Wal, UK 36/C3
Macheng, China 80/C5
Machesney Park, Il, US 155/K2
Māchhīwāra, India 98/D4
Machhlīshahr, India 96/D3
Machi, China 78/F5
Machias, NY, US 161/G3
Machichaco (cape), Sp. 44/B5
Machico, Port. 110/A2
Machida, Japan 83/C2
Machili (riv.), Zam. 122/E3
Machilipatnam, India 95/D2
Machiques, Ven. 180/C2
Machobani, Zam. 122/E3
Machovo Jezero (lake), Czh. 59/H1
Machu Picchu (ruin), Peru 184/C4
Machupo (riv.), Bol. 185/E4
Machynlleth, Wal, UK 36/C1
Maciá, Arg. 188/E5
Macia, Moz. 123/G5
Maciel, Arg. 188/D5
Măcin, Rom. 51/J3
Macina (phys. reg.), Mali 114/D3
Macintyre (riv.), Austl. 127/E3
Mack, Co, US 147/J4
Mackay, Austl. 134/C3
Mackay, Id, US 147/G2
Mackay (lake), Austl. 127/B3
MacKenzie (bay), Ant. 192/E
Mackenzie, Austl. 134/C3
Mackenzie (riv.), Can. 139/E3
Mackenzie, BC, Can. 140/D3
Mackenzie (bay), NW,Yk, Can. 171/L2
Mackenzie (riv.), NW, Can. 140/D2
Mackenzie (mts.), Can. 139/D3
Mackenzie King (isl.), NW, Can. 141/R7
Mackin (riv.), BC, Can. 144/C1
Mackinac (str.), Mi, US 160/D2
Mackinac Island, Mi, US 160/D2
Mackinaw (riv.), Il, US 155/K3
Mackinaw City, Mi, US 160/D2
Mackinnon (pass), NZ 135/A4
Mackinnon Road, Kenya 119/B2
Macklin, Sk, Can. 145/K1
Macmillan (riv.), Yk, Can. 171/L3
Macknade, Austl. 134/B2
Macks Creek, Mo, US 153/H2
Macksburg, Oh, US 160/F5
Macksville, Ks, US 152/E2
Macksville, Austl. 132/E1
Macland, Ga, US 163/L7
Maclean, Austl. 132/E1
Maclear, SAfr. 124/E3
Macleay (isl.), Austl. 134/F7
Macleod (lake), Austl. 130/B3
MacNutt, Sk, Can. 156/D2
Macomb (co.), Mi, US 167/G6
Macomb, Il, US 155/J3
Macomer, It. 48/A2
Macomia, Moz. 123/J2
Macon (cr.), Mi, US 167/E7
Mâcon, Fr. 44/F3
Macon, Mo, US 155/H4
Macon, Il, US 155/K4
Macon, Ga, US 162/F4
Macon, Ms, US 162/C4
Macon, North Branch (cr.), Mi, US 167/E7
Maconcourt, Fr. 60/B1
Macondo, Ang. 122/D2
Macondo (riv.), Ang. 122/D2
Macosquin, NI, UK 34/B1
Macotera, Sp. 46/C2
Macoun, Sk, Can. 156/C3
Macoupin (cr.), Il, US 155/J4
Macouria, FrG. 182/C1
Macovane (pt.), Moz. 123/G4
Macquarie (isl.), Austl. 27/S8
Macquarie (lake), Austl. 133/E1
Macquarie (riv.), Austl. 127/D5
Macroom, Ire. 32/B6
Macrorie, Sk, Can. 145/L2
MacTier, On, Can. 161/G2
Macuelizo, Hon. 176/D3
Macuim (riv.), Braz. 185/E2
Macuira, PN, Col. 180/D1
Macuma (riv.), Ecu. 184/B1
Macumba (riv.), Austl. 127/C3
Macungie, Pa, US 168/C2
Macusani, Peru 184/D4
Macuspana, Mex. 176/C2
Macuzari, Presa (dam), Mex. 174/C3
Macy, Ne, US 155/F2
Mad (riv.), Ca, US 146/B3
Mādabā, Jor. 105/D5
Madagali, Nga. 116/B3
Madagascar (ctry.) 107/G7
Madā'in Şāliḩ, SAr. 135/H3
Madama, Niger 108/B4
Madan, Bul. 49/J2
Madanapalle, India 95/C3
Madang (int'l arpt.), PNG 129/G1
Madang (prov.), PNG 129/G1
Madanīyīn (gov.), Tun. 111/H2
Madanīyīn, Tun. 66/F4
Madao, China 78/F5
Madaoua, Niger 115/G3
Madaras, Hun. 50/D2
Mādāri Hāt, India 97/G2
Mādārīpur, Bang. 97/H4
Madarounfa, Niger 115/G3
Madauk, Myan. 86/C5
Madawaska (riv.), On, Can. 161/H2
Madaxmaroodi, Som. 119/D1
Madaya, Myan. 94/B1
Madayevo, Rus. 69/K5
Maddaket, Ma, US 158/B5
Maddaloni, It. 65/D5
Madden (dam), Pan. 180/B2
Madden, Ms, US 162/C4
Maddock, ND, US 156/E4
Made, Neth. 52/B5
Madeir, Sudan 117/F4
Madeira (isl.), Port. 110/A2
Madeira (riv.), Braz. 179/C3
Madeira (isl.), Madr., Port. 107/A1
Madeira Beach, Fl, US 164/K8
Madeira Park, BC, Can. 144/B3
Madeirinha (riv.), Braz. 185/F3
Mädelegabel (peak), Ger. 61/G3
Madeleine (riv.), Qu, Can. 158/E1
Madeleine, Iles de la (isl.), Qu, Can. 141/K4
Madelia, Mn, US 155/G1
Madeline (isl.), Wi, US 157/J4
Madeline, Ca, US 146/C3
Maden, Turk. 102/D2
Mäder, Aus. 61/F3
Madera, Ca, US 148/B2
Madera (riv.), Bol. 185/E3
Madera (mtn.), Tx, US 151/C2
Madera, Mex. 174/C2
Madera Canyon, Az, US 149/G5
Maderas (vol.), Nic. 176/E4
Madgaon (Margao), India 95/B3
Madhipura, India 97/F3
Madhira, India 95/D2
Madhubani, India 97/F2
Madhumati (riv.), Bang. 97/G4
Madhupur, India 97/F3
Mādhura, India 97/F2
Madhwāpur, India 97/E2
Madhya Pradesh (state), India 92/C3
Madi Opei, Ugan. 117/G5
Madiany, Kenya 119/A2
Madibogo, SAfr. 124/D2
Madibura, Tanz. 119/A4
Madidi (riv.), Bol. 185/E4
Madihui, China 78/G4
Madikwe, SAfr. 123/E5
Madill, Ok, US 153/F3
Madimba, D.R. Congo 120/C4
Madīnat al Abyār, Libya 67/J4
Madīnat al 'Āshir min Ramaḑān, Egypt 113/C4
Madīnat as Sādāt, Egypt 113/B4
Madīnat ash Sha'b, Yem. 118/C2
Madīnat ath Thawrah, Syria 102/D3
Madīnet Dīmai (ruin), Egypt 113/B5
Madingo, Congo 120/B1
Madingo-Kayes, Congo 120/C4
Madingou, Congo 120/C4
Madirovalo, Madg. 125/H7
Madison, Ks, US 153/F1
Madison, Oh, US 160/F4
Madison, Fl, US 165/G2
Madison, Ca, US 167/K9
Madison, NJ, US 169/H9
Madison (riv.), Mt, US 142/D2
Madison, Ga, US 163/F4
Madison, Mn, US 155/F1
Madison, SD, US 155/F1
Madison, Ne, US 154/F3
Madison, Ms, US 162/B4
Madison, Al, US 162/D3
Madison, WV, US 163/G1
Madison, Mo, US 155/H4
Madison (cap.), Wi, US 155/K2
Madison, Ar, US 162/B3
Madison, In, US 162/E1
Madison, Sk, Can. 145/K2
Madison, Va, US 163/H1
Madison, Ct, US 169/F1
Madison Heights, Mi, US 167/F6
Madison Heights, Va, US 163/H2
Madisonville, La, US 164/C2
Madisonville, Tn, US 162/E3
Madisonville, Ky, US 162/D2
Madisonville, Tx, US 151/G2
Madiun, Indo. 89/E4
Madjingo, Gabon 120/C2
Mado Gashi, Kenya 119/B1
Madoc, On, Can. 161/H2
Madoi, China 78/D5
Madon (riv.), Fr. 42/D4
Madona, Lat. 41/M3
Madone d'Utelle (peak), Fr. 64/D5
Madong, China 93/K3
Madongchuan, China 78/F4
Madras, Or, US 146/C1
Madras (Chennai), India 95/D3
Madre (lag.), Tx, US 172/B2
Madre (lag.), Mex. 175/F3
Madre de Deus de Minas, Braz. 187/M6
Madre de Dios (riv.), Bol.,Peru 179/C4
Madre de Dios (isl.), Chile 191/A6
Madre de Dios (dept.), Peru 184/D3
Madrecitas, Bol. 185/F5
Madrid (dist.), Sp. 46/C2
Madrid, Ia, US 155/H3
Madrid (cap.), Sp. 47/N9
Madrid, Col. 183/L8
Madridejos, Sp. 46/D3
Madrigal, Peru 184/D4
Madrigal de las Altas Torres, Sp. 46/C2
Madrigalejo, Sp. 46/C3
Madrisahorn (peak), Swi. 61/F4
Madroñera, Sp. 46/C3
Madsen, On, Can. 157/H2
Maduda, D.R. Congo 120/C4
Madugula, India 95/D2
Madukani, Tanz. 119/A2
Madura (isl.), Indo. 77/L10
Madura, Austl. 130/E4
Madurai, India 95/C4
Madzharovo, Bul. 51/G5
Mae Chan, Thai. 94/B1
Mae Charim, Thai. 94/C2
Mae Hong Son, Thai. 86/C5
Mae Ping NP, Thai. 94/B2
Mae Ramat, Thai. 94/B2
Mae Sai, Thai. 94/B1
Mae Sariang, Thai. 94/B2
Mae Sot, Thai. 94/B2
Mae Taeng, Thai. 94/B2
Mae Tho (peak), Thai. 94/B2
Mae Ya (mtn.), Thai. 94/B2
Maebashi, Japan 85/F2
Maella, Sp. 47/F2
Maengsan, NKor. 81/D3
Maenza, It. 65/C4
Maep'o, SKor. 81/E4
Maerne, It. 63/F2
Maeser, Ut, US 147/J3
Maevatanana-Ambanivohitra, Madg. 125/H7
Maewo (isl.), Van. 136/F6
Mafeking, Mb, Can. 156/D1
Mafeteng, Les. 124/D3
Maffe, Belg. 55/E3
Maffra, Austl. 133/C3
Mafia (isl.), Tanz. 119/C3
Mafia (chan.), Tanz. 119/B4
Mafikeng, SAfr. 124/D2
Máfil, Chile 190/B3
Mafou (riv.), Gui. 114/C4
Mafra, Port. 47/P10
Mafra, Braz. 189/G3
Mafungabusi (plat.), Zim. 123/F3
Magadan, Rus. 75/R4
Magadanskaya Oblast, Rus. 75/R4
Magadi, Kenya 119/B2
Magadino, Swi. 61/E5
Magalhães de Almeida, Braz. 183/F3
Magalia, Ca, US 146/C4
Magalies Berg (mts.), SAfr. 124/P12
Magaliesburg, SAfr. 124/P12
Magallanes, Phil. 88/C2
Magallanes y Antártica Chilena (prov.), Chile 191/C7
Magamba, CAfr. 116/D4
Magangué, Col. 180/C2
Maganoy, Phil. 88/D4
Mağara, Turk. 104/C1
Magaria, Niger 115/H3
Magarida, PNG 129/H2
Magat (riv.), Phil. 88/C1
Magazine, Ar, US 153/H3
Magazine (mtn.), Ar, US 153/H3
Magdagachi, Rus. 79/K1
Magdalena (dept.), Col. 177/H4
Magdalena (riv.), Col. 179/B2
Magdalena, NM, US 149/J3
Magdalena (peak), Malay. 88/B4
Magdalena, Arg. 191/K11
Magdalena, Bol. 185/E4
Magdalena de Kino, Mex. 174/C2
Magdeburg, Ger. 74/B4
Magdeburger Börde (ledge), Ger. 42/F2
Magdelaine Cays (isl.), Austl. 127/E2
Magé, Braz. 187/N7
Mage-shima (isl.), Japan 84/B5
Magee (isl.), NI, UK 34/C2
Magee, Ms, US 164/D2

Magela, Madg. 125/H7
Magelang, Indo. 89/E4
Magellan (str.), Arg.,Chile 179/B8
Magen, Isr. 105/A6
Magenta (lake), Austl. 130/C5
Magereya (isl.), Nor. 38/H1
Magetan, Indo. 89/E4
Maggia (riv.), Swi. 61/E5
Maggia, Swi. 61/E5
Maggio (peak), It. 63/E7
Maggiorasca (peak), It. 62/C4
Maggiore (peak), It. 65/D5
Maggiore (peak), It. 65/D3
Maggiore (peak), It. 63/E6
Maggiore (lake), It. 66/F1
Maghâghah, Egypt 114/B3
Maghama, Mrta. 114/B3
Maghar, India 96/D2
Maghâr, Isr. 105/C3
Maghdûshah, Leb. 105/C1
Maghera (peak), Ire. 32/B4
Maghera, NI, UK 34/B2
Magherafelt, NI, UK 34/B2
Magherafelt (co.), NI, UK 34/B2
Maghila, Tun. 112/L7
Maghnia, Alg. 112/D2
Magic (res.), Id, US 147/F2
Magic Kingdom, Fl, US 164/M7
Magilligan, NI, UK 34/B1
Magilligan (pt.), NI, UK 34/B1
Magione, It. 65/B1
Maglaj, Bosn. 50/D3
Magliano de'Marsi, It. 65/C3
Magliano Sabina, It. 65/B3
Maglič (peak), Yugo. 50/D4
Maglie, It. 49/F2
Maglod, Hun. 51/R10
Magnac-Laval, Fr. 44/D3
Magnet, Ga, US 163/M7
Magnetawan, On, Can. 161/G2
Magnetawan (riv.), On, Can. 160/F2
Magnetic Passage, Austl. 134/B2
Magnitka, Rus. 69/N5
Magnitogorsk, Rus. 69/N5
Magnitogorsk (int'l arpt.), Rus. 69/N5
Magnolia, Ar, US 153/H4
Magnolia, De, US 168/C5
Magnolia, Ms, US 151/G2
Magny-en-Vexin, Fr. 54/A5
Magny-les-Hameaux, Fr. 30/J5
Mago NP, Eth. 117/H4
Mágoé, Moz. 123/F2
Magog, Qu, Can. 161/K2
Magor, Wal, UK 36/D3
Magoye, Zam. 123/E3
Magra (riv.), It. 62/C4
Magrath, Ab, Can. 145/H3
Magreta, It. 63/D4
Magsaysay, Phil. 88/D3
Maguan, China 94/D1
Maguarinho (cape), Braz. 182/D3
Magude, Moz. 123/G5
Magugnano, It. 63/D2
Mágura, Bang. 97/G4
Magway (state), Myan. 93/F4
Magway (Magwe), Myan. 86/B4
Magwe (Magway), Myan. 86/B4
Magyichaung, Myan. 86/B4
Magyichaung, Chad 116/C3
Maha Sarakham, Thai. 94/C2
Mahâbâd, Iran 103/F2
Mahabe, Madg. 125/H7
Mahabe, Madg. 125/H8
Mahâbhârat (range), Nepal 96/C1
Mahaboboka, Madg. 125/H7
Mahâd, India 95/B2
Mahadday Weyn, Som. 118/B3
Mahadeo (range), India 96/A4
Mahaena, FrPol. 137/X15
Mahâgama, India 96/E3
Mahagi, D.R. Congo 121/G2
Mahagi-Port, D.R. Congo 121/G2
Mahaica-Berbice (pol. reg.), Guy. 181/G3
Mahaicony Village, Guy. 181/G3
Mahajamba (bay), Madg. 125/H7
Mahajamba (riv.), Madg. 125/H7
Mahajanga, Madg. 125/H6
Mahajanga (prov.), Madg. 125/H6
Mahajilo (riv.), Madg. 125/H7
Mahakali (zone), Nepal 96/C1
Mahakam (riv.), Indo. 91/E3
Mahalapye, Bots. 123/E4
Mahale Mts. NP, Tanz. 121/G3
Maḥallah, Iran 103/G3
Maḥallat Marḥūm, Egypt 113/B3
Maḥallat Minûf, Egypt 113/B3
Mahalpur, India 98/D4
Maham, India 98/D5
Mahān, Iran 103/J4
Mahān (riv.), India 96/D3
Mahanadi (riv.), India 92/D3
Mahananda (riv.), India 97/F3
Mahandiabani (riv.), C.d'Iv. 114/D4
Mahanje, Tanz. 119/A4
Mahanoro, Madg. 125/J7
Mahanoy (cr.), Pa, US 168/B2
Mahanoy City, Pa, US 168/B2
Mahantago (cr.), Pa, US 168/B2
Mahantango (mtn.), Pa, US 168/B2
Mahao, China 79/K3
Mahārājganj, India 97/E3
Mahārājpur, India 92/C3
Mahārāshtra (state), India 92/B4
Mahāsāmund, India 95/D1
Mahāsthān (ruin), Bang. 97/G3
Mahasoabe, Madg. 125/H8
Maḥaṭṭat Dab'ah, Jor. 125/H7
Mahavavy (riv.), Madg. 125/H7
Mahawa, India 96/B1
Mahaxai, Laos 86/E5
Mahazoarivo, Madg. 125/H8

Mahazoma, Madg. 125/H7
Mahbūbābād, India 95/D2
Mahbūb adh Dhahab, SAr. 100/D3
Mahdia, Guy. 181/G3
Mahe, India 101/L2
Mahébourg, Mrts. 125/T15
Mahendragiri, India 95/E2
Mahendranagar, Nepal 96/C1
Mahenge, Tanz. 119/B4
Maheno, NZ 135/B4
Mahesāna, India 101/K4
Mahespur, Bang. 97/G4
Mahezhen, China 78/E4
Mahgawān, India 96/B2
Mahia (pen.), NZ 127/H6
Mahia e Zezê (peak), Alb. 49/G2
Mahihip, Bela. 41/P5
Mahitsy, Madg. 125/H7
Mahlberg, Ger. 60/D1
Mahlow, Ger. 42/U7
Mahmel (peak), Alg. 66/E4
Mahmūd-e 'Erāqī, Afg. 101/J1
Maḥmūdiye, Turk. 102/B2
Mahmun, Mn, US 156/D4
Mahnomen, Mn, US 156/D4
Mahoba, India 96/B3
Mahomet, Il, US 160/B3
Mahon (riv.), Ire. 32/C5
Mahón, Sp. 47/N9
Mahone Bay, NS, Can. 158/E3
Mahoning (riv.), Oh, US 160/D3
Mahroni, India 96/B3
Maḥtomedi, Mn, US 157/O6
Mahuangou, China 78/D4
Mahur, India 86/B3
Mahusekwa, Zim. 123/F3
Mahuta, Tanz. 119/B4
Mahwah, India 96/A2
Mahwah, NJ, US 169/J7
Maḥwît, Egypt 114/B3
Mai-Ndombe (lake), D.R. Congo 120/D3
Maia, Port. 46/A2
Maia, It. 63/D1
Maiala Nat'l Pk., Austl. 134/E3
Maials, Sp. 47/F2
Maiana (isl.), Kiri. 136/G4
Maicao, Col. 180/C2
Maîche, Fr. 60/C3
Maicuru (riv.), Braz. 181/H5
Maiden (cr.), Pa, US 168/B2
Maidenhead, Eng, UK 36/D5
Maidens, Sc, UK 33/B6
Maidi, Ire. 91/G3
Maidstone, On, Can. 167/G7
Maidstone, Eng, UK 37/G4
Maidstone, Sk, Can. 145/K1
Maiduguri, Nga. 116/B3
Maie, D.R. Congo 121/G2
Maienfeld, Swi. 61/F4
Maigatari, Nga. 115/H4
Maigue (riv.), Ire. 32/B4
Maihar, India 96/C3
Maihara, Japan 83/K5
Maijdi, Bang. 97/H4
Maikala (range), India 96/C4
Maiko (riv.), D.R. Congo 121/F3
Maiko, PN de la, D.R. Congo 121/F3
Maikoor (riv.), Indo. 128/D1
Maikurgi, Chad 116/C3
Maimānah, Afg. 101/H2
Maimbung, Phil. 88/D3
Mailāni, India 96/C1
Mailly-le-Camp, Fr. 55/D6
Maimoon Palace (Istana Maimoon), Indo. 89/B2
Mailsi, Pak. 98/B5
Maimoon, Indo. 89/B2
Main (riv.), NI, UK 34/B2
Main (riv.), Ger. 42/E4
Main Centre, Sk, Can. 145/L2
Main Range NP, Austl. 134/D4
Main-à-Dieu, NS, Can. 159/H2
Main-Donau (canal), Ger. 58/D2
Maïnaguri, India 97/F2
Mainbernheim, Ger. 58/D2
Maincy, Fr. 30/L6
Maine (riv.), Ire. 32/A5
Maine (reg.), Fr. 44/C2
Maine (gulf), Fr. 159/D4
Maine (state), US 143/N2
Maine, Collines du (hill), Fr. 44/C2
Maïné-Soroa, Niger 116/B2
Maingkwan, Myan. 93/G2
Maïngnyaung, Myan. 86/B4
Mainhausen, Ger. 58/D2
Maini, Fr. 88/D3
Mainit, Phil. 88/D3
Mainkung, China 94/B3
Mainland (isl.), Sc, UK 31/V14
Mainling, China 94/B2
Minoru, Austl. 128/C2
Mainpurī, India 96/B2
Mainstockheim, Ger. 58/D2
Maintenon, Fr. 30/L6
Maintirano, Madg. 125/H7
Mainvilliers, Fr. 57/G4
Maio (isl.), CpV. 107/K10
Maisí, Cuba 177/H2
Mais Gate (int'l arpt.), Haiti 177/H2
Maisach, Ger. 59/T15
Maisome (isl.), Tanz. 121/G3
Maison-Rouge, Fr. 30/M6
Maisoncelles-en-Brie, Fr. 30/M5

[... index continues across multiple columns ...]

Manzan – Maubou
Map Section
248
249

Manzanita Ind. Res., Ca, US 148/D4
Manzano, It. 63/G2
Manzano (peak), NM, US 149/J3
Manzano, NM, US 149/J3
Manzano (mts.), NM, US 149/J3
Manzanola, Co, US 152/C1
Manzanza, D.R. Congo 121/G4
Manzhouli, China 79/H2
Manziana, It. 65/B3
Manzil Bū Zalafah, Tun. 48/B4
Manzil Tamīn, Tun. 48/B4
Manzilah (lake), Egypt 104/B4
Manzilah (canal), Egypt 113/C2
Manzini, Swaz. 125/E2
Manzini (Matsapa) (int'l arpt.), Swaz. 125/E2
Mao, Chad 116/B2
Mao Songsang, India 86/B3
Maoba, China 93/J2
Maobaguan, China 78/F5
Maodianzi, China 81/C2
Mao'ergai, China 78/E5
Maojing, China 78/F4
Maoke (mts.), Indo. 91/J4
Maoming, China 87/F4
Maoniushan, China 78/D4
Maoshan, China 80/H6
Maotian, China 78/F5
Maotou (peak), China 86/D3
Maowen Qiangzu Zizhixian, China 86/D2
Maoyang, China 87/H3
Maozhou, China 80/H7
Mapai, Moz. 123/F4
Mapam (lake), China 99/D5
Mapane, Indo. 91/F4
Mapastepec, Mex. 176/C3
Mapi (riv.), Indo. 91/J5
Mapia, Indo. 91/J4
Mapimí, Bolsón de (depr.), Mex. 174/D3
Mapire, Ven. 181/E3
Mapiri, Bol. 185/E3
Mapiri, Bol. 184/D4
Maple (peak), Az, US 149/H4
Maple (riv.), Ia, US 155/G2
Maple, On, Can. 160/T8
Maple Creek, Sk, Can. 145/K3
Maple Grove, Qu, Can. 159/N7
Maple Grove, Mn, US 157/P6
Maple Park, Il, US 167/N16
Maple Ridge, BC, Can. 144/C3
Maple River Nat'l Wild. Ref., ND, US 156/E4
Maple Shade, NJ, US 168/D4
Maple Valley, Wa, US 167/C3
Maples, Mo, US 153/J2
Maplesville, Al, US 162/D4
Mapleton, Ut, US 147/H3
Mapleton, Or, US 146/B1
Mapleton, Ia, US 155/G2
Mapleton, Mn, US 155/H2
Maplewood, Wi, US 160/C2
Maplewood, NJ, US 169/H9
Maplewood, Mn, US 157/P6
Map'o (nbrhd.), SKor. 81/F6
Mapoon Aboriginal Reserve, Austl. 129/F2
Mapoon Mission Station, Austl. 129/F2
Maporal, Ven. 180/D3
Mappsville, Va, US 163/K2
Mapuera (riv.), Braz. 181/G5
Mapumolo, SAfr. 125/E3
Maputa, SAfr. 125/F2
Maputo (int'l arpt.), Moz. 125/F2
Maputo (riv.), Moz. 123/G5
Maputo (prov.), Moz. 123/G5
Maputo (cap.), Moz. 125/F2
Maqat, Kaz. 71/K3
Maqdam (cape), Sudan 135/H5
Maqên, China 78/D5
Maquan (riv.), China 99/D6
Maquan (Damqog) (riv.), China 96/E1
Maquela do Zombo, Ang. 120/C4
Maquinchao, Arg. 190/C4
Maquoketa, Ia, US 155/J2
Maquoketa (riv.), Ia, US 155/J2
Maquoketa, North Fork (riv.), Ia, US 155/J2
Mar (reg.), Sc, UK 33/D2
Mar (mts.), Braz. 179/E5
Mar Chiquita (lag.), Arg. 188/D4
Mar de Ajó, Arg. 191/F3
Mar del Plata, Arg. 190/F3
Mar del Tuyú, Arg. 191/F3
Mar-Mac, NC, US 163/H3
Mara (riv.), Tanz. 119/A2
Mara (prov.), Tanz. 119/A2
Mara, Guy. 182/B1
Mara Creek, BC, Can. 144/E2
Maraã, Braz. 185/E1
Marabá, Braz. 182/D4
Maracá (isl.), Braz. 182/D2
Maracaibo (lake), Ven. 179/B2
Maracaibo, Ven. 180/D2
Maracaju, Braz. 189/F2
Maracaju, Serra de (mts.), Braz. 186/B4
Maracanã, Braz. 183/E3
Maracanaquará (plat.), Braz. 182/C3
Maracás, Braz. 187/E2
Maracay, Ven. 183/N7
Maracena, Sp. 46/D4
Marādah, Libya 108/C2
Maradi (dept.), Afr. 115/G2
Maradi, Niger 115/G3
Marāgheh, Iran 103/F2
Mārahra, India 96/B2
Marahuaca (peak), Ven. 181/E4
Maraira (pt.), Phil. 88/C1
Marais de St-Gond (swamp), Fr. 54/C6
Marais des Cygnes (riv.), Ks, Mo, US 153/G1
Marajó (bay), Braz. 179/E3
Marajó (isl.), Braz. 179/E3
Maralal, Kenya 119/B1
Maralal Nat'l Sanct., Kenya 119/B1
Marali, CAfr. 116/C4
Maralik, Arm. 103/E1
Maralinga-Tjarutja Aboriginal Land, Austl. 131/F4
Maramag, Phil. 88/D4
Marambaia (isl.), Braz. 187/N8
Marampa, SLeo. 114/B4
Maramureş (co.), Rom. 43/M5
Maran, Malay. 89/C2
Marana (lag.), Cro. 63/G1
Marana, Az, US 149/G4
Marand, Iran 103/F2
Marandet, Niger 115/G2
Marang, Malay. 89/C1
Marangani, Peru 184/D4
Maranguape, Braz. 183/G3
Maranhão (riv.), Braz. 186/C2
Maranhão (state), Braz. 183/E5
Marano di Napoli, It. 65/D6
Marano Lagunare, It. 63/G2
Marano sul Panaro, It. 63/D5
Marano Vicentino, It. 63/E2
Maranoa (riv.), Austl. 127/D3
Marañón (riv.), Peru 179/B3
Marans, Fr. 44/C3
Maraoue, PN de la, C.d'Iv. 114/D5
Marapanim, Braz. 182/E3
Marapi (peak), Indo. 89/C3
Maras (peak), Indo. 89/D3
Mărăşeşti, Rom. 51/H3
Marathón, Gre. 49/N8
Marathón (arpt.), Gre. 49/N8
Marathon, Fl, US 165/H5
Marathon, On, Can. 157/L3
Marathon, NY, US 161/H3
Marathon, Tx, US 150/C2
Marau, Braz. 189/F4
Marauliānwāla, Pak. 98/B3
Maravatío de Ocampo, Mex. 175/E5
Maravilha, Braz. 189/F3
Maravillas (cr.), Tx, US 151/C3
Maravillas, Bol. 185/E3
Marāwah, Libya 67/J4
Marawaka, PNG 129/G1
Marawī, Sudan 135/F5
Marawi, Phil. 88/D3
Marayes, Arg. 188/C4
Marazion, Eng, UK 36/A6
Marbach, Swi. 60/D4
Marbach am Neckar, Ger. 58/C5
Marbache, Fr. 55/F6
Marbella, Sp. 46/C4
Marble (canyon), Az, US 149/G2
Marble, NC, US 162/F3
Marble Bar, Austl. 130/C2
Marble Canyon, Az, US 149/G2
Marble Falls, Tx, US 150/E2
Marble Hall, SAfr. 123/F5
Marble Hill, Mo, US 162/C2
Marblemount, Wa, US 144/D3
Marbleton, Qu, Can. 161/L2
Marbleton, Wy, US 147/H2
Marburg (lake), Pa, US 168/B4
Marbury, Al, US 162/D4
Marcali, Hun. 50/C2
Marcallo, It. 62/B3
Marcapata, Peru 184/D4
Marcelin, Sk, Can. 145/L1
Marceline, Mo, US 155/H4
Marcelino Ramos, Braz. 189/G3
Marcella, Ar, US 153/J3
Marcellina, It. 65/B3
Marcellus, Mi, US 160/D3
March (A.F.B.), Ca, US 166/C3
March, Eng, UK 37/G1
Marchant (mt.), NZ 135/J9
Marche (pol. reg.), It. 65/C2
Marche, Congo 120/C4
Marche (mts.), Fr. 44/d3
Marche-en-Famenne, Belg. 55/E3
Marchémoret, Fr. 30/L4
Marchena, Sp. 46/C4
Marchena (isl.), Ecu. 184/J6
Marcheno, It. 62/D2
Marches (reg.), It. 67/G2
Marchiennes, Fr. 54/C3
Marchin, Belg. 55/E3
Marchinbar (isl.), Austl. 129/E2
Marchtrenk, Aus. 59/H6
Marchwell, Sk, Can. 156/D2
Marciana Marina, It. 48/B1
Marcianise, It. 65/D5
Marcilly, Fr. 30/L4
Marcilly-sur-Tille, Fr. 60/B2
Marck, Fr. 54/A2
Marckolsheim, Fr. 60/D1
Marco, Fl, US 165/H5
Marco (isl.), Fl, US 165/H5
Marco, Braz. 183/F3
Marco Polo (int'l arpt.), It. 63/F3
Marcoing, Fr. 54/C3
Marcola, Or, US 146/B1
Marcon, It. 63/F2
Marcona, Peru 184/C4
Marconi (mt.), BC, Can. 144/G2
Marcos Juárez, Arg. 190/E2
Marcosli (riv.), BC, Can. 144/C1
Marcoussis, Fr. 30/J6
Marcovia, Hon. 176/E3
Marcq-en-Barœul, Fr. 54/C2
Marcus, Ia, US 155/G2
Marcus Baker (mt.), Ak, US 171/J3
Marcy (mt.), NY, US 161/K2
Mardān, Pak. 98/B2
Marden, Eng, UK 30/E3
Mardeuil, Fr. 54/C5
Mardin, Turk. 102/E2
Mardin (prov.), Turk. 102/E2
Maré (isl.), NCal. 137/W12
Marecchia (riv.), It. 63/F5
Marechal Cândido Rondon, Braz. 189/F3
Marechal Deodoro, Braz. 187/G1
Maree (lake), Sc, UK 31/R8
Mareeba, Austl. 134/B2
Mareham le Fen, Eng, UK 35/H5
Mareil-sur-Mauldre, Fr. 30/H5
Marek, Indo. 91/F4
Maréna, Mali 114/C3
Marengo, Wi, US 157/J4
Marengo, Il, US 167/N15
Marengo, Ia, US 155/H3
Marengo, In, US 162/D1
Marengo, Sk, Can. 145/K2
Marenisco, Mi, US 157/K4
Marennes, Fr. 44/C4
Mareolaboom, Namb. 122/C3
Marerano, Madg. 125/H8
Maresfield, Eng, UK 37/G5
Mareuil-sur-Ourcq, Fr. 30/M4
Marfa, Tx, US 151/B2
Marfield, Austl. 133/B1
Marfino, Rus. 71/J3
Margalla Hills NP, Pak. 98/B3
Margam, Wal, UK 36/C3
Marganets', Ukr. 73/H4
Margao (Madgaon), India 95/B3
Margaree, NS, Can. 159/G2
Margaree Valley, NS, Can. 159/G2
Margaret, Tx, US 152/E3
Margaret (riv.), Austl. 128/B4
Margaret (mt.), Austl. 130/C2
Margaret River, Austl. 130/B5
Margarita (peak), Ca, US 166/C4
Margarita (isl.), Ven. 181/F2
Margarita, Isla de (isl.), Trin. 173/J5
Margarítion, Gre. 49/G3
Margate, Eng, UK 37/H4
Margate, Fl, US 164/P10
Margate, SAfr. 125/E3
Margate City, NJ, US 168/D5
Margeride (mts.), Fr. 44/E4
Margeta (cape), Indo. 128/B2
Margherita (peak), Ugan. 121/G2
Marghilon, Uzb. 99/B3
Marghita, Rom. 50/F2
Margny-lès-Compiègne, Fr. 54/B5
Margo, Sk, Can. 156/C2
Margog Caka (lake), China 99/E5
Margos, Peru 184/B3
Margosatubig, Phil. 88/C4
Margraten, Neth. 55/E2
Marguareis (peak), It. 64/D4
Marguerite, BC, Can. 144/C1
Margyang, China 97/H1
Mari, PNG 129/F2
Mari, Braz. 183/H4
Maria, Qu, Can. 158/E1
Maria (mt.), Austl. 132/D4
Maria (isl.), Austl. 129/D3
Maria Aurora, Phil. 88/C2
María Cleófas (isl.), Mex. 174/D4
Maria da Fé, Braz. 187/L7
Maria Island NP, Austl. 132/D4
Maria Juana, Arg. 188/D4
María Madre (isl.), Mex. 174/D4
María Magdalena (isl.), Mex. 174/D4
Maria van Diemen (cape), NZ 135/C1
Mariāhū, India 96/D3
Mariakani, Kenya 119/B2
Mariakerke, Belg. 54/B1
Marialva, Braz. 186/C4
Marian, Austl. 134/C3
Marianao, Cuba 177/F1
Marianna, Fl, US 165/F2
Marianna, Ar, US 162/B3
Mariano Comense, It. 62/C2
Mariano I. Loza, Arg. 188/E4
Mariánské Lázně, Czh. 59/F3
Mariarano, Madg. 125/H6
Marias (riv.), Mt, US 145/H3
Mariato (pt.), Pan. 180/A3
Ma'rib, Yem. 118/C2
Maribo, Den. 40/D4
Maribor, Slov. 50/B2
Maricá, Braz. 187/P7
Maricopa, Ca, US 148/C3
Maricopa, Az, US 149/F4
Maricopa (mts.), Az, US 149/F4
Maricopa Ak Chin Ind. Res., Az, US 149/F4
Maridalsvatn (lake), Nor. 38/S8
Marīdī, Sudan 117/F4
Marié (riv.), Braz. 181/E5
Marie Byrd Land (phys. reg.), Ant. 192/S
Marie-Galante (isl.), Dom. 173/J4
Mariefred, Swe. 39/A1
Mariehamn (int'l arpt.), Fin. 41/H1
Mariehamn (Maarianhamina), Fin. 41/H1
Marieholm, Swe. 39/K7
Mariel, Cuba 177/F1
Marienbourg, Belg. 55/D3
Mariënburg, Sur. 182/C1
Mariendorf, Ger. 42/Q7
Marienfelde, Ger. 42/Q7
Marienhafe, Ger. 53/E1
Marienheide, Ger. 55/G1
Mariental, Namb. 122/C5
Marienville, Pa, US 161/G4
Mariestad, Swe. 40/E2
Marietta, Ga, US 163/L7
Marietta, Mn, US 155/F1
Marietta, Ms, US 162/C3
Marietta, Oh, US 160/F5
Marietta, Ok, US 153/F4
Marietta, Pa, US 168/B3
Marieval, Sk, Can. 156/C2
Marigat, Kenya 119/A1
Marigliano, It. 65/D6
Marignane, Fr. 64/B6
Marigot, Fr. 173/N8
Marigot, Dom. 173/N9
Marihatag, Phil. 88/D3
Marijampolė, Lith. 41/K4
Marikina, Phil. 88/F6
Marikina (riv.), Phil. 88/F6
Marilao, Phil. 88/E6
Marília, Braz. 189/G2
Mariluz, Braz. 189/F3
Marín, Mex. 151/D5
Marin (co.), Ca, US 167/J10
Marín, Sp. 46/A1
Marin-Epagnier, Swi. 60/D3
Marina, It. 48/D3
Marina, Ca, US 148/B2
Marina del Rey (harbor), Ca, US 166/F8
Marina del Rey, Ca, US 166/F8
Marina di Andora, It. 62/B6
Marina di Carrara, It. 62/D5
Marina di Massa, It. 62/D5
Marina di Montemarciano, It. 63/G6
Marina di Pisa, It. 62/D6
Marina di Ravenna, It. 63/F5
Marina di Vasto, It. 65/D3
Mar'ina Gorka, Bela. 41/N5
Marinduque (isl.), Phil. 88/C2
Marine, Il, US 155/K4
Marine City, Mi, US 160/E3
Marine Nat'l Res., Kenya 119/C2
Marine World Africa USA, Ca, US 167/K10
Marineland, Austl. 131/M8
Marineland of Florida, Fl, US 165/H3
Marines, Fr. 30/H4
Marinette, Wi, US 160/C2
Maringa (riv.), D.R. Congo 121/E2
Maringá, Braz. 189/G2
Maringouin, La, US 164/C2
Maringuè, Moz. 123/G3
Marinha Grande, Port. 46/A3
Marinhas, Port. 46/A2
Marino, It. 65/B4
Marion (reef), Austl. 127/E2
Marion, Al, US 162/D4
Marion, Ar, US 162/B3
Marion (cr.), Fl, US 164/M7
Marion (lake), Fl, US 164/M7
Marion, Ia, US 155/J2
Marion, Il, US 162/C2
Marion, In, US 160/D4
Marion, Ks, US 153/F1
Marion, Ky, US 162/C2
Marion, La, US 153/H4
Marion, Mi, US 160/D2
Marion, Ms, US 162/C4
Marion, NC, US 163/F3
Marion, ND, US 156/E4
Marion, Oh, US 160/E4
Marion, SC, US 163/H3
Marion (lake), SC, US 143/K5
Marion, SD, US 155/F2
Marion, Va, US 163/G2
Marion, Wi, US 155/K1
Marion Bridge, NS, Can. 159/G3
Marion Junction, Al, US 162/D4
Marionville, Mo, US 153/H2
Maripa, Ven. 181/E3
Maripa, FrG. 182/D2
Maripasoula, FrG. 182/C2
Mariposa, Ca, US 148/C2
Mariposa Grove, Ca, US 148/C2
Mariquita, Col. 183/L7
Mariscal Estigarribia, Par. 188/D2
Mariscal Sucre (int'l arpt.), Ecu. 180/B5
Marissa, Il, US 162/C1
Mārith, Tun. 66/F4
Maritime Alps (mts.), Fr. 66/E1
Maritsa (riv.), Bul. 70/C4
Maritsa (riv.), Turk. 51/H5
Mariupol', Ukr. 73/J4
Mariupol (int'l arpt.), Ukr. 73/J4
Mariy-El, Resp., Rus. 74/E4
Marj 'Uyūn, Leb. 105/D2
Märjamaa, Est. 41/L2
Mark (riv.), Belg. 52/B6
Mark Twain (lake), Mo, US 155/H4
Mark Twain Nat'l Wild. Ref., Il, Ia, US 155/J3
Mark Twain Nat'l Wild. Ref., Il, Mo, US 155/J4
Marka (riv.), Ger. 53/E3
Marka, Som. 119/D1
Mārkā, Jor. 105/D5
Markagunt (plat.), Ut, US 149/F2
Markākasa, India 95/D1
Markakol (lake), Kaz. 78/D4
Markam, China 86/C2
Mārkāpur, India 95/C3
Markaryd, Swe. 40/E3
Markazī (gov.), Iran 103/G3
Markdale, On, Can. 160/F2
Markdorf, Ger. 61/F2
Marked Tree, Ar, US 162/B3
Markelsdorfer (pt.), Ger. 40/D4
Marken (isl.), Neth. 52/C4
Markerwaard (polder), Neth. 52/C3
Markesan, Wi, US 155/K2
Market Bosworth, Eng, UK 37/E1
Market Deeping, Eng, UK 37/F1
Market Drayton, Eng, UK 35/F6
Market Harborough, Eng, UK 37/F2
Market Rasen, Eng, UK 35/H5
Market Weighton, Eng, UK 35/H4
Markethill, NI, UK 34/B3
Markgroningen, Ger. 58/C5
Markha, India 98/D3
Markham, On, Can. 159/S8
Markham (bay), Nun, Can. 141/J2
Markham (riv.), PNG 129/G1
Markham, Tx, US 151/F3
Marki, Pol. 43/L2
Markinch, Sc, UK 33/C4
Markit, China 99/C4
Markivka, Ukr. 73/K3
Markle, In, US 160/D4
Markleeville, Ca, US 146/D4
Marknesse, Neth. 52/C3
Markneukirchen, Ger. 59/F2
Markópoulon, Gre. 49/N9
Markounda, CAfr. 116/C4
Markova, Rus. 78/E1
Markovac, Yugo. 50/E3
Markovo, Rus. 75/S3
Markoye, Burk. 115/F3
Marks, Rus. 71/H2
Marks, Ms, US 162/B3
Marksville, La, US 164/B2
Markt Bibart, Ger. 58/D3
Markt Erlbach, Ger. 58/D4
Markt Indersdorf, Ger. 59/E6
Markt Rettenbach, Ger. 61/G2
Markt Sankt Florian, Aus. 59/H6
Markt Schwaben, Ger. 59/E6
Marktbreit, Ger. 58/D3
Marktheidenfeld, Ger. 58/C3
Marktl, Ger. 59/F6
Marktoberdorf, Ger. 61/G2
Marktredwitz, Ger. 59/F3
Marl, Ger. 53/E5
Marla, Austl. 131/G3
Marlboro, Ab, Can. 144/F1
Marlboro, NJ, US 168/D3
Marlboro (Upper Marlboro), Md, US 168/B6
Marlborough, Ma, US 161/L3
Marlborough, Austl. 134/C3
Marlborough, Eng, UK 37/E4
Marle, Fr. 54/C4
Marlengo (Marling), It. 61/H4
Marlenheim, Fr. 55/G6
Marles-en-Brie, Fr. 30/L5
Marles-les-Mines, Fr. 54/B3
Marlette, Mi, US 160/E3
Marlin, Tx, US 151/F2
Marling (Marlengo), It. 61/H4
Marlinton, WV, US 163/G1
Marlow, Ok, US 153/F3
Marlow, Ger. 40/E4
Marlow, Eng, UK 37/F3
Marlow, Ga, US 163/G4
Marlpit Hill, Eng, UK 30/D3
Marlton, NJ, US 168/D4
Marly, Fr. 54/C3
Marly, Fr. 55/F5
Marly-la-Ville, Fr. 30/K4
Marly-le-Roi, Fr. 30/J5
Marmaduke, Ar, US 162/B2
Marmagão, India 95/B3
Marmande, Fr. 44/D4
Marmara (sea), Turk. 70/D4
Marmara (isl.), Turk. 67/K2
Marmara, Turk. 51/H5
Marmaraereğlisi, Turk. 51/H5
Marmaris, Turk. 102/B2
Marmarth, ND, US 156/C4
Marmelos, Rio dos (riv.), Braz. 182/A4
Marmet, WV, US 163/G1
Marmion (lake), On, Can. 157/J3
Marmion (lake), Austl. 130/D4
Marmirolo, It. 63/D3
Marmolada (peak), It. 45/J3
Marmolejo, Sp. 46/C3
Marmontana (peak), It. 61/F5
Marmora, On, Can. 161/H2
Marmora, NJ, US 168/D5
Marmot (peak), Mt, US 144/G4
Marmoutier, Fr. 55/G6
Marnay, Fr. 60/B3
Marnaz, Fr. 60/C5
Marne, Ger. 40/C5
Marne (dept.), Fr. 54/C6
Marne (riv.), Fr. 42/C4
Marne au Rhin, Canal de la (canal), Fr. 55/D6
Marneuli, Geo. 71/H4
Marnhull, Eng, UK 36/D5
Maro, Chad 116/C3
Maro (reef), Hi, US 137/H2
Maroa, Ven. 181/E4
Maroa, Il, US 155/K3
Maroantsetra, Madg. 125/J6
Marofandilia, Madg. 125/H8
Marokau (isl.), FrPol. 137/L6
Marolambo, Madg. 125/J8
Maroldsweisach, Ger. 58/D2
Marolles, Fr. 30/M4
Marolles-en-Brie, Fr. 30/M5
Marolles-en-Hurepoix, Fr. 30/J6
Maromme, Fr. 57/G2
Maromokotro (peak), Madg. 125/J6
Marondera, Zim. 123/F3
Marone, It. 62/D2
Maroni (riv.), FrG., Sur. 179/D2
Maroni (riv.), Sur., FrG. 182/C1
Maroni (riv.), Sur. 181/H3
Maroochydore-Mooloolaba, Austl. 134/D4
Maroon Town, Jam. 177/G2
Maropaika, Madg. 125/H8
Marostica, It. 63/E2
Marotandrano, Madg. 125/J7
Marotiri (Bass Is.) (isl.), FrPol. 137/L7
Marotta, It. 63/G6
Maroua, Camr. 116/B3
Marouini (riv.), FrG. 181/H4
Marovato, Madg. 125/J6
Marovato, Madg. 125/J6
Marovoay, Madg. 125/H7
Marowijne (dist.), Sur. 181/H3
Marpingen, Ger. 55/G5
Marple, Eng, UK 35/F5
Marqên Gangri (peak), China 78/D5
Marquan (riv.), China 92/E2
Marquand, Mo, US 162/B2
Marquard, SAfr. 124/D3
Marquarie (riv.), Austl. 132/C1
Marquesas (isls.), FrPol. 137/M5
Marquesas Keys (isls.), Fl, US 165/G5
Marquetalia, Col. 183/K7
Marquette, Mi, US 157/L4
Marquette, Ks, US 153/F1
Marquette, Mb, Can. 156/F2
Marquez, Tx, US 151/F2
Marquis, Sk, Can. 145/M2
Marquise, Fr. 54/A2
Marracuene, Moz. 125/F2
Marradi, It. 63/E5
Marrah (peak), Sudan 116/E2
Marrakech, Mor. 110/D3
Marrakech (Menara) (int'l arpt.), Mor. 110/C3
Marrawah, Austl. 132/C4
Marree, Austl. 131/H4
Marromeu, Moz. 123/G3
Marrowbone, Ky, US 162/E2
Marrowie (cr.), Austl. 133/B1
Marrupa, Moz. 123/H2
Mars, Pa, US 160/F4
Mars (peak), It. 62/A1
Mars Hill, NC, US 163/F3
Marsá al 'Alam, Egypt 135/G3
Marsá al Burayqah, Libya 108/C2
Marsa Ben Mehidi, Alg. 112/C2
Marsá Matrūh, Egypt 135/E2
Marsabit, Kenya 119/B1
Marsabit Nat'l Rsv., Kenya 117/H5
Marsabit National Reserve, Kenya 118/A5
Marşafā, Egypt 113/C4
Marsala, It. 48/C4
Marsange (riv.), Fr. 30/L5
Marsannay, Fr. 60/A3
Marsberg, Ger. 53/F6
Marsciano, It. 65/B2
Marsden, Eng, UK 35/G4
Marsden, Sk, Can. 145/K1
Marsden, Austl. 133/C1
Marsdiep Texelstroom (chan.), Neth. 52/B3
Marseille, Fr. 64/B6
Marseille au Rhône (canal), Fr. 64/A5
Marseille-en-Beauvaisis, Fr. 54/A4
Marseilles, Il, US 155/K3
Marsella, Col. 183/K8
Marsh (mtn.), Md, US 161/G5
Marsh (isl.), La, US 172/C2
Marsh (peak), Ut, US 147/J3
Marsh (cr.), Pa, US 168/F1
Marsh Gibbon, Eng, UK 37/E3
Marshall, Ok, US 153/F2
Marshall, Ar, US 153/H3
Marshall, Il, US 160/C5
Marshall, Mi, US 160/D3
Marshall, Libr. 114/C5
Marshall (riv.), Austl. 131/H2
Marshall, Mo, US 155/H4
Marshall, NC, US 163/F3
Marshall, Mn, US 155/G1
Marshall, Sk, Can. 145/K1
Marshall, Tx, US 151/G1
Marshall Islands (ctry.) 136/G3
Marshallton, De, US 168/C4
Marshalltown, Ia, US 155/H2
Marshallville, Ga, US 162/F4
Marshfield, Mo, US 153/H2
Marshfield, Wi, US 155/J1
Marshyhope (cr.), Md, US 168/C6
Marske-by-the-Sea, Eng, UK 35/G2
Marsland, Ne, US 154/C2
Märsta, Swe. 40/G2
Marston, Mo, US 162/C2
Marsyandi (riv.), Nepal 97/E1
Marta, It. 48/B1
Marta (mts.), Col. 177/H4
Martaban, Myan. 94/B2
Martaban (gulf), Myan. 94/B2
Martano (peak), It. 65/B2
Martap, Camr. 116/B4
Martapura, Indo. 89/D4
Martapura, Indo. 90/D4
Marte R. Gomez, Mex. 174/C3
Martelange, Belg. 55/E4
Martellago, It. 63/F2
Martensville, Sk, Can. 145/L1
Martfeld, Ger. 53/G3
Martha, Ok, US 152/E3
Martha, Ky, US 163/F1
Martha's Vineyard (isl.), Ma, US 158/B5
Martignacco, It. 63/G1
Martigné-Ferchaud, Fr. 56/D5
Martigné-sur-Mayenne, Fr. 57/E4
Martigny, Swi. 60/D5
Martigny-les-Bains, Fr. 60/B1
Martigues, Fr. 64/B6
Martil, Mor. 112/B2
Martilla, Fin. 39/F4
Martin, ND, US 156/D4
Martin, La, US 164/B1
Martin, Mi, US 160/D3
Martin, SD, US 154/D2
Martin (dam), Al, US 162/E4
Martin, Tn, US 162/C2
Martin (lake), Al, US 162/E4
Martín Chico, Uru. 191/J11
Martin Luther King, Jr. Nat'l Hist. Site, Ga, US 163/M7
Martina Franca, It. 49/E2
Martinborough, NZ 135/J9
Martindale, Tx, US 150/F3
Martinengo, It. 62/C2
Martinez, Ca, US 146/B4
Martinez, Ga, US 163/F4
Martínez de la Torre, Mex. 175/M6
Martínez del Tineo, Arg. 188/C2
Martinique (isl.), Fr. 139/L8
Martinique Passage (chan.), Dom.,Mart. 173/N9
Martínon, Gre. 49/H3
Martinópole, Braz. 183/F3
Martins, Braz. 183/G4
Martins Creek, Pa, US 168/C2
Martins Ferry, Oh, US 160/F4
Martins Mills, Tx, US 151/G1
Martinsburg, WV, US 161/H5
Martinsburg, Pa, US 161/G4
Martinsburg, NY, US 161/J3
Martinsicuro, It. 65/C2
Martinsville, Il, US 160/C5
Martinsville, Ms, US 164/C2
Martinsville, In, US 160/C5
Martinsville, Va, US 163/H2
Martock, Eng, UK 36/D5
Martofte, Den. 40/D4
Marton, NZ 135/C3
Martorell, Sp. 47/K7
Martos, Sp. 46/D4
Martovce, Slvk. 50/D2
Martres-Tolosane, Fr. 44/D5
Martūba, Libya 67/J4
Martuk, Kaz. 71/L2
Martuni, Arm. 71/H4
Marty, SD, US 154/E2
Martynovo, Kaz. 71/J2
Maru, Nga. 115/G3
Marudi, Malay. 88/A4
Marugame, Japan 84/C3
Maruim, Braz. 187/F1
Maruko, Japan 85/F2
Marulan, Austl. 133/E2
Marulanda, Col. 183/K7
Marum, Neth. 52/D2
Marumba, Tanz. 123/H1
Marungu (mts.), D.R. Congo 121/G5
Maruoka, Japan 84/E2
Marutea (isl.), FrPol. 137/M7
Marv Dasht, Iran 103/H4
Marvel, Co, US 149/H2
Marvell, Ar, US 162/B3
Marvin, SD, US 155/F1
Marvine (mt.), Ut, US 149/G1
Marwayne, Ab, Can. 145/J1
Marxheim, Ger. 58/D5
Mary (lake), Ms, US 164/C2
Mary, Trkm. 101/H1
Mary Anne Passage, Austl. 130/B2
Mary Esther, Fl, US 164/E2
Mary Kathleen, Austl. 131/H2
Mary-sur-Marne, Fr. 30/M4
Maryānaj, Iran 103/G3
Maryang, China 99/C4
Maryborough, Austl. 134/D4
Maryborough, Austl. 132/B3
Marydale, SAfr. 124/C3
Marydel, Md, US 168/C5
Maryfield, Sk, Can. 156/D3
Mar'yinka, Ukr. 73/J4
Marykirk, Sc, UK 33/D3
Maryland (co.), Libr. 114/C5
Maryland (state), US 143/L4
Maryland City, Md, US 168/B5
Maryland Junction, Zim. 123/F3
Maryland Line, Md, US 168/B4
Maryneal, Tx, US 151/D1
Maryport, Eng, UK 34/E2
Marystown, Nf, Can. 159/K2
Marysvale, Ut, US 149/F1
Marysville, Mi, US 160/E3
Marysville, Oh, US 160/E4
Marysville, Ca, US 146/C4
Marysville, Ks, US 155/F4
Marysville, Wa, US 144/C3
Marysville, Mt, US 145/H4
Marysville, Pa, US 168/B3
Maryūt (lake), Egypt 113/A2
Maryvale, Austl. 134/D5
Maryville, Tn, US 162/F3
Maryville, Mo, US 155/G3
Marzabotto, It. 63/E5
Marzano (peak), It. 48/D2
Marzo (pt.), Col. 180/B3
Marzūq, Libya 108/B3
Marzūq (des.), Libya 108/B3
Masabit Nat'l Rsv., Kenya 119/B1
Masada (ruin), Isr. 135/G2
Masada NP, Isr. 105/C6
Masagan (riv.), Som. 118/C3
Masai Mara Nat'l Rsv., Kenya 119/A2
Masai Steppe (grsld.), Tanz. 119/B3
Masaka, Ugan. 121/G3
Masākin, Tun. 48/B5
Masalembu Besar (isl.), Indo. 89/F4
Masallı, Azer. 103/G2
Masamagrell, Sp. 47/E3
Masamba, Indo. 91/F4
Masan, SKor. 81/E5
Masan-ni, SKor. 81/F7
Masanga, D.R. Congo 121/E3
Masangwe (hill), Tanz. 121/G4
Masaryktown, Fl, US 164/L7
Masasi, Tanz. 119/B4
Masavi, Bol. 188/D1
Masaya, Nic. 176/E4
Masbate, Phil. 88/C2
Masbate (isl.), Phil. 88/C2
Mascara, Alg. 112/F5
Mascarene (isls.), Mrts 125/T15
Mascot, Tn, US 162/F2
Mascota, Mex. 174/D4
Mascotte, Fl, US 164/M6
Mascouche, Qu, Can. 159/N6
Mase, D.R. Congo 121/F4
Masela (isl.), Indo. 128/C2
Maselheim, Ger. 61/F1
Maserà di Padova, It. 63/E3
Masereka, D.R. Congo 121/G3
Maseru (cap.), Les. 124/D3
Maseru (Moshoeshoe) (int'l arpt.), Les. 124/D3
Masevaux, Fr. 60/D2
Masfjorden, Nor. 40/A1
Masha, China 87/H3
Mashaba, Zim. 123/F4
Mashad (int'l arpt.), Iran 101/G1
Mashala, D.R. Congo 121/E4
Mashalah, Egypt 113/C3
Masham, Eng, UK 35/G3
Mashhad, Iran 101/G1
Mashike, Japan 82/B2
Mashivka, Ukr. 73/H3
Mashīz, Iran 103/J4
Māshkīd (riv.), Iran 101/H3
Mashonaland Central (prov.), Zim. 123/F3
Mashonaland East (prov.), Zim. 123/F3
Mashonaland West (prov.), Zim. 123/F3
Mashqharah, Leb. 105/D1
Mashtūl as Sūq, Egypt 113/C4
Mashū (lake), Japan 82/D2
Masiaca, Mex. 174/C3
Maside, Sp. 46/A1
Masīlah (wadi), Yem. 118/D2
Masim (peak), Rus. 71/L1
Masindi, Ugan. 121/G2
Masindi Port, Ugan. 121/H2
Masinloc, Phil. 88/B2
Masis, Arm. 103/F1
Masisea, Peru 184/C3
Masisi, D.R. Congo 121/G3
Masjed-e Soleymān, Iran 103/G4
Masjid Raya (Great Mosque), Indo. 89/B2
Mask (lake), Ire. 32/A2
Maskall, Belz. 176/D2
Maskan (cape), Som. 118/B3
Masker (peak), Mor. 110/D2
Maskin, Oman 101/G4
Maskūtān, Iran 101/G3
Masnou, Sp. 47/L7
Masoala (pen.), Madg. 125/J6
Masoala (cape), Madg. 125/J6
Masoarivo, Madg. 125/H7
Mason, Il, US 162/C1
Mason, Mi, US 160/D3
Mason, Nv, US 146/D4
Mason, Oh, US 160/D5
Mason, Ok, US 153/F3
Mason, Tx, US 151/E2
Mason (co.), Wa, US 167/A3
Mason (lake), Wa, US 167/B3
Mason, WV, US 163/F1
Mason and Dixon Line, Pa, US 168/B4
Mason City, Il, US 155/K3
Mason City, Ia, US 155/H2
Masonboro, NC, US 163/J3
Masone, It. 62/B5
Masontown, Pa, US 161/G5
Masonville, Ky, US 162/D2
Masquefa, Sp. 47/K6
Masrakh, India 97/E2
Maşrif Baḩr al Baqar (canal), Egypt 113/C3
Massa, It. 62/D5
Massa Finalese, It. 63/E4
Massa Fiscaglia, It. 63/F4
Massa Lombarda, It. 63/E5
Massa Lubrense, It. 65/D6
Massa Marittima, It. 48/B1
Massa Martana, It. 65/B2
Massa-Carrara (prov.), It. 62/C4
Massachusetts (bay), Ma, US 158/B4
Massachusetts (state), US 143/M3
Massaciuccoli (lake), It. 62/D5
Massafra, It. 49/E2
Massaguet, Chad 116/B2
Massakory, Chad 116/B2
Massandra, Ukr. 73/H5
Massangena, Moz. 123/G4
Massapê, Braz. 183/F3
Massapequa, NY, US 169/M9
Massapequa Park, NY, US 169/M9
Massarosa, It. 62/D6
Massbach, Ger. 58/D2
Massena, NY, US 161/J2
Massenya, Chad 116/C3
Masset, BC, Can. 171/M4
Massey, On, Can. 160/E1
Massey (sound), Nun, Can. 141/S7
Massey, Md, US 168/C5
Massibi, Ang. 121/E5
Massif Central (upland), Fr. 66/D1
Massif de Beaufort (mass.), Fr. 64/C1
Massif de Champsaur (mass.), Fr. 64/C3
Massif de Guéra (peak), Chad 116/C3
Massif de la Chartreuse (mass.), Fr. 64/B2
Massif de la Vanoise (mass.), Fr. 64/C2
Massif de l''Assâba (mass.), Mrta. 114/C2
Massif de Pelvoux (mass.), Fr. 64/C3
Massif de Termit (mass.), Niger 116/A1
Massif des Bongos (uplands), CAfr. 116/D3
Massif des Maures (mass.), Fr. 64/C6
Massif du Manéngouba (peak), Camr. 115/H5
Massif du Tamgue (mass.), Gui. 114/B3
Massigui, Mali 114/D4
Massillon, Oh, US 160/F4
Massinga, Moz. 123/G4
Massingir, Moz. 123/G4
Massy, Fr. 30/J5
Mastābah, SAr. 100/C4
Mastadon (mtn.), Id, US 144/G4
Maştağa, Azer. 71/J4
Masterton, NZ 135/C3
Mastgat (chan.), Neth. 52/B5
Mastic, NY, US 169/F2
Mastic Beach, NY, US 169/F2
Mastník (riv.), Czh. 59/H3
Mastūj (riv.), Pak. 98/A2
Mastung, Pak. 101/J3
Mastūrah, SAr. 100/C4
Masuda, Japan 84/B3
Masuguru, Tanz. 123/H1
Masuho, Japan 83/A2
Masurai (peak), Indo. 89/C3
Masvingo, Zim. 123/F4
Masvingo (prov.), Zim. 123/F4
Maswa Game Rsv., Tanz. 119/A2
Maşyāf, Syria 104/E2
Mat (riv.), Alb. 49/F2
Mata, D.R. Congo 121/E4
Mata Bia (peak), ETim. 128/B2
Mata de Guanábano, Ven. 180/D3
Mata Grande, Braz. 183/G5
Mata Mata, SAfr. 124/C2
Mata Utu, Wall. 137/H6
Matabeleland North (prov.), Zim. 123/E3
Matabeleland South (prov.), Zim. 123/F4
Mātābhānga, India 97/G2
Matadi, D.R. Congo 120/C4
Matador, Tx, US 152/D3
Matagalpa, Nic. 176/E3
Matagorda, Tx, US 151/G3
Matagorda (pen.), Tx, US 151/G3
Matagorda (bay), Tx, US 172/B2
Matagorda (isl.), Tx, US 172/B2
Matak (isl.), Indo. 89/D2
Matala, Ang. 122/B2
Matam, Sen. 114/B3
Matamba, D.R. Congo 121/E4
Mataméye, Niger 115/H3
Matamoras, Pa, US 168/D1
Matamoros, Mex. 174/E3
Ma'ţan as Sarra (well), Libya 108/D4
Matancilla, Chile 188/B4
Matanda, Zam. 123/F1
Matandu (riv.), Tanz. 119/B4
Matane, Qu, Can. 158/D1
Matane (riv.), Qu, Can. 158/D1
Matanga, Madg. 125/H8
Matanzas, Cuba 172/E3
Matão, Braz. 189/G2
Matape (riv.), Mex. 174/C2
Matapédia, Qu, Can. 158/D2
Mataquito (riv.), Chile 190/C2
Matara (ruin), Erit. 100/C6
Matara, Erit. 118/A2
Mataram, Indo. 91/E5
Mataránga, Gre. 49/G3
Matarani, Peru 184/C5
Mataranka, Austl. 128/D3
Mataró, Sp. 47/L6
Matatiele, SAfr. 124/E3
Mataura, FrPol. 137/L7
Mataura, NZ 135/B4
Mataura (riv.), NZ 135/B4
Matawai, NZ 135/D2
Matawan, NJ, US 169/J10
Matawin (riv.), Qu, Can. 158/A2
Matay, Kaz. 71/L3
Matay, Kaz. 99/C2
Matching Green, Eng, UK 30/D1
Matecaña (int'l arpt.), Col. 183/K8
Mateguá, Bol. 185/F4
Matehuala, Mex. 175/E4
Mateke (hills), Zim. 123/F4
Matera, It. 48/E2
Matéri, Ben. 115/F4
Maternillos (pt.), Cuba 173/F3
Matese (lake), It. 65/D5
Matese (mts.), It. 65/D5
Mátészalka, Hun. 43/M5
Matetsi, Zim. 122/E3
Mathay, Fr. 60/C3
Mathbaria, Bang. 97/G4
Matheniko Game Rsv., Ugan. 117/G5
Matheson Island, Mb, Can. 156/F2
Mathews, La, US 164/C3
Mathews (lake), Ca, US 166/C3
Mathew's (peak), Kenya 119/B1
Mathews, Va, US 163/J2
Mathi, It. 64/D2
Mathis, Tx, US 151/F3
Mathiston, Ms, US 162/C4
Mathoura, Austl. 133/B2
Mathurā, India 96/A2
Mati, Phil. 88/D4
Matias Barbosa, Braz. 187/N6
Matias Olímpio, Braz. 183/F3
Matías Romero, Mex. 176/C2
Matignon, Fr. 56/C3
Matíguas, Nic. 176/E3
Matilija (dam), Ca, US 166/A2
Matimbuka, Tanz. 119/A4
Matinha, Braz. 183/E4
Matinicock (pt.), NY, US 169/L8
Mātir, Tun. 48/A4
Maţir Ţāris, Egypt 113/B6
Matiyuri (riv.), Ven. 180/D3
Matkuli, India 96/B4
Mātla (riv.), India 97/G5
Matlock, Eng, UK 35/G5
Maţmāţah, Tun. 66/F4
Matn (riv.), Leb. 105/D1
Mato Grosso (plat.), Braz. 179/D4
Mato Grosso (state), Braz. 182/A5
Mato Grosso do Sul (state), Braz. 185/G5
Mato Grosso, Meseta do (plat.), Braz. 185/G4
Mato Verde, Braz. 187/E2
Matobo (Matopos) NP, Zim. 123/F4
Matões, Braz. 183/F4
Matolo-Rio, Moz. 125/F2
Matomb, Camr. 120/B2
Matombo, Tanz. 119/B3
Matopos, Zim. 123/F4
Matopos (Matobo) NP, Zim. 123/F4
Matosinhos, Port. 46/A2
Matoury, FrG. 182/C1
Matouti (pt.), Gabon 120/B3
Matoya (bay), Japan 83/L7
Maţraḩ, Oman 101/G4
Matrei am Brenner, Aus. 61/H3
Matrei in Osttirol, Aus. 45/K3
Matriz de Camaragibe, Braz. 183/H5
Matroosberg (peak), SAfr. 124/L10
Matsalu (gulf), Est. 41/K2
Matsapa (Manzini) (int'l arpt.), Swaz. 125/E2
Matsiatra (riv.), Madg. 125/H8
Matsoandakana, Madg. 125/J6
Matsubara, Japan 83/J6
Matsubushi, Japan 83/D2
Matsuda, Japan 83/C3
Matsudo, Japan 83/D2
Matsue, Japan 84/C3
Matsuida, Japan 83/B1
Matsumae, Japan 82/B3
Matsumoto, Japan 85/E2
Matsuo, Japan 83/E2
Matsusaka, Japan 83/L6
Matsushima, Japan 82/B4
Matsutō, Japan 84/E2
Matsuyama, Japan 84/C4
Matt, Swi. 61/F4
Mattamuskeet (lake), NC, US 163/J3
Mattamuskeet Nat'l Wild. Ref., NC, US 163/J3
Mattaponi (riv.), Va, US 163/J2
Mattarello, It. 61/H6
Mattawa, On, Can. 161/G1
Mattawa, Wa, US 144/E4
Matterhorn (peak), It.,Swi. 60/D6
Mattertal (valley), Swi. 60/D5
Matteson, Il, US 160/C4
Matthew Town, Bahm. 177/H1
Matthews, Mo, US 162/C2
Matthews (mt.), NZ 135/J9
Matthews, NC, US 163/G3
Matthews Dome (mt.), Ak, US 171/H2
Mattie (lake), Fl, US 164/M7
Mattig (riv.), Aus. 59/G6
Mattighofen, Aus. 59/G6
Mattituck, NY, US 169/F2
Mattmarksee (lake), Swi. 60/D5
Mattō, Japan 84/E2
Mattock (riv.), Ire. 34/B4
Mattoon, Wi, US 155/K1
Mattsee, Aus. 59/G7
Matucana, Peru 184/B3
Matumbla (mt.), NY, US 161/J2
Matundwe (range), Malw.,Moz. 123/G3
Maturín, Ven. 181/F2
Matusadona NP, Zim. 123/F3
Matutum (mt.), Phil. 91/G2
Matveyev Kurgan, Rus. 73/K4
Matzen, Aus. 51/P7
Mau, India 96/C3
Mau, India 96/C4
Mau (peak), Kenya 119/A2
Maú (riv.), Guy. 181/G3
Maú (riv.), Guy.,Ven. 182/B1
Mau Aimma, India 96/C3
Mau Rānīpur, India 96/B3
Mau-é-Ele, Moz. 123/G5
Maúa, Moz. 123/H2
Maubert-Fontaine, Fr. 55/D4
Maubeuge, Fr. 54/C3
Maubourguet, Fr. 44/D5

Merrim – Mīt an N

Merriman, Ne, US 154/D2
Merriott, Eng, UK 36/D5
Merritt (isl.), Fl, US 165/H3
Merritt (dam), Ne, US 154/D2
Merritt (res.), Ne, US 154/D2
Merritt, BC, Can. 144/D2
Merritt Island, Fl, US 165/H3
Merritt Island Nat'l Wild. Ref., Fl, US 165/H3
Merriwa, Austl. 132/D2
Merriwagga, Austl. 133/B1
Merriweather, Mi, US 157/K4
Merryville, La, US 164/B2
Mers-les-Bains, Fr. 54/A3
Mersa Fatma, Erit. 118/B2
Mersa Gulbub, Erit. 118/A1
Mersa Tek'lay, Erit. 100/C5
Mersch, Lux. 55/F4
Merse (reg.), Sc, UK 33/D5
Mersey (riv.), Eng, UK 35/F5
Merseyside (co.), Eng, UK 35/F5
Mershon, Ga, US 165/G2
Mersin, Turk. 104/D1
Mersin Galgalo, Eth. 118/C4
Mersing, Malay. 89/C2
Mērsrags, Lat. 41/K3
Merstham, Eng, UK 30/C3
Mertens, Tx, US 151/F1
Mertert, Lux. 55/F4
Mertesdorf, Ger. 55/F4
Merthyr Tydfil, Wal, UK 36/C3
Merthyr Tydfil (co.), Wal, UK 36/C3
Mértola, Port. 46/B4
Merton (bor.), Eng, UK 30/C2
Mertzon, Tx, US 151/D2
Mertzwiller, Fr. 55/G6
Méru, Fr. 54/B5
Meru, Kenya 119/B1
Meru (mt.), Tanz. 119/B2
Meru NP, Kenya 119/B1
Meruoca, Braz. 183/F3
Merville, Fr. 54/B2
Mervin, Sk, Can. 145/K1
Merwedekanaal (riv.), Neth. 52/C5
Méry-sur-Oise, Fr. 30/J4
Merzen, Ger. 53/E4
Merzenich, Ger. 55/F2
Merzifon, Turk. 70/E4
Merzig, Ger. 55/F5
Mesa (peak), Arg. 191/C6
Mesa (mt.), Ak, US 171/G3
Mesa, Az, US 149/G4
Mesa, Co, US 147/J4
Mesa Prieta (mesa), NM, US 152/A3
Mesa Verde NP, Co, US 149/H2
Mesabi (range), Mn, US 157/H4
Mesach Mellet (hills), Libya 111/H4
Mesagne, It. 49/E2
Mesaména, Camr. 120/C2
Mesarás (gulf), Gre. 49/J5
Mescalero (ridge), NM, US 152/C4
Mescalero Sands (des.), NM, US 152/B4
Meschede, Ger. 53/F6
Mesco, Punta di (pt.), It. 62/C5
Mescolino (peak), It. 63/F6
Meseta de Montemayor (plat.), Arg. 190/D5
Mesfinto, Eth. 117/H2
Meshchura, Rus. 69/L3
Meshgīn Shahr, Iran 103/F2
Meshra'ar Raqq, Sudan 117/F3
Mesick, Mi, US 160/D2
Mesilla, NM, US 149/J4
Mesita, Co, US 152/B2
Mesita, NM, US 149/J3
Meskum, Indo. 89/C2
Meslay-du-Maine, Fr. 57/E5
Mesola, It. 63/F4
Mesolóngion, Gre. 49/G3
Mesomeloka, Madg. 125/J8
Mesopotamia (reg.), Iraq 100/D2
Mesopotamia (reg.), Arg 188/E4
Mesoraca, It. 48/E3
Mespelbrunn, Ger. 58/C3
Mesquer, Fr. 56/C6
Mesquite, NM, US 149/J4
Mesquite, Tx, US 150/L7
Mesrouh (peak), Mor. 110/E2
Messaad, Alg. 66/D4
Messac, Fr. 56/D5
Messalo (riv.), Moz. 123/H2
Messancy, Belg. 55/E4
Messei, Fr. 57/E3
Messel, Ger. 58/B3
Messina, It. 48/D3
Messina (str.), It. 67/G3
Messina, SAfr. 123/F4
Messines, Qu, Can. 161/H1
Messinge (riv.), Moz. 123/G2
Messini, Gre. 49/H4
Messini (gulf), Gre. 67/J3
Messkirch, Ger. 61/F2
Messstetten, Ger. 61/E1
Messum Crater (peak), Namb. 122/B4
Messy, Fr. 30/L5
Mesta (riv.), Bul. 51/F5
Mestia, Geo. 71/G4
Město, Czh. 59/F3
Mestre, It. 63/F3
Mestrino, It. 63/E3
Mesudiye, Turk. 70/F4
Mesumba (peak), Tanz. 119/B3
Mesurado (cape), Libr. 114/C5
Meta, It. 65/D6
Meta (dept.), Col. 180/C4
Meta (riv.), Col.,Ven. 179/C2
Meta Incognita (pen.), Nun, Can. 141/K2
Metabetchouan, Qu, Can. 158/B1
Métabetchouane (riv.), Qu, Can. 158/B2
Metacáua (pt.), Moz. 123/J2
Metahāra, Eth. 118/A3
Metairie, La, US 164/C3
Metaline Falls, Wa, US 144/F3
Metallifere, Colline (mts.), It. 63/D6
Metallostroy, Rus. 69/T7
Metamora, Mi, US 167/F6
Metán, Arg. 188/C3
Metangula, Moz. 123/G2
Metapontum (ruin), It. 48/E2
Metauro (riv.), It. 45/K5
Metcalfe, On, Can. 161/J2
Metcalfe, Ms, US 162/B4
Meteghan, NS, Can. 158/D3
Meteghan River, NS, Can. 158/D3
Metelen, Ger. 53/E4
Metema, Eth. 117/H2
Meteor Crater, Az, US 149/G3
Metéora, Gre. 49/G3
Metepec, Mex. 175/Q10
Metheringham, Eng, UK 35/H5
Methil, Sc, UK 33/C4
Methlick, Sc, UK 33/D2
Methow (riv.), Wa, US 144/D3
Methuen, Ma, US 161/L3
Methuen (mt.), Austl. 128/B3
Methven, Sc, UK 33/C4
Methven, NZ 135/B3
Metica (riv.), Col. 180/C4
Metiskow, Ab, Can. 145/J1
Metković, Cro. 50/C4
Metlakatla, BC, Can. 171/M4
Metlakatla, Ak, US 171/M4
Metlatonoc, Mex. 176/B2
Metlili Chaamba, Alg. 111/F2
Metoro, Moz. 123/H2
Metro, Indo. 89/D4
Metro Toronto Zoo, On, Can. 160/U8
Metro-Dade Cultural Center, Fl, US 164/P11
Metropolis, Il, US 162/C2
Metropolitana de Santiago (pol. reg.), Chile 190/N8
Metrozoo, Fl, US 164/P11
Métsovon, Gre. 49/G3
Mettawa, Il, US 167/Q15
Mettenheim, Ger. 59/F6
Metter, Ga, US 163/F4
Mettet, Belg. 55/D3
Mettingen, Ger. 53/E4
Mettlach, Ger. 55/F4
Mettler, Ca, US 148/C3
Mettmach, Aus. 59/G6
Mettmann, Ger. 52/D6
Mettūr, India 95/C4
Metu, Eth. 117/G3
Metuchen, NJ, US 169/H9
Metulla, Isr. 105/D2
Metz, Mo, US 153/G2
Metz, Fr. 55/F5
Metz-Nancy-Lorraine (int'l arpt.), Fr. 55/F6
Metzingen, Ger. 58/C5
Metztitlán, Mex. 175/L6
Meu (riv.), Fr. 56/C4
Meudon, Fr. 30/J5
Meudt, Ger. 55/G3
Meulaboh, Indo. 89/B1
Meulan, Fr. 30/H4
Meulebeke, Belg. 54/C2
Meung-sur-Loire, Fr. 57/G5
Meurthe (riv.), Fr. 60/C1
Meurthe-et-Moselle (dept.), Fr. 55/E6
Meuse (riv.), Fr. 42/C4
Meuse (dept.), Fr. 55/E6
Meuvette (riv.), Fr. 57/F3
Meuzin (riv.), Fr. 60/A3
Mevasseret Ẕiyyon, Isr. 105/C5
Mexborough, Eng, UK 35/G5
Mexia, Tx, US 151/F2
Mexiana (isl.), Braz. 182/D2
Mexicalcingo, Mex. 175/Q10
Mexican Hat, Ut, US 149/H2
Mexican Springs, NM, US 149/H3
Mexico (bay), NY, US 161/H3
Mexico, Me, US 161/L2
Mexico, NY, US 161/H3
Mexico, In, US 160/C4
México (state), Mex. 172/A5
Mexico, Mo, US 155/J4
Mexico (ctry.) 139/G7
Mexico (gulf), NAm. 139/H7
Mexico (Ciudad de México) (cap.), Mex. 175/Q10
Mexico Beach, Fl, US 165/F3
Meximieux, Fr. 60/B6
Meybod, Iran 103/H3
Meycauayan, Phil. 88/E6
Meydān-e Gel (lake), Iran 103/H4
Meyers Chuck, Ak, US 171/M4
Meyersdale, Pa, US 161/G5
Meyerton, SAfr. 124/Q13
Meylan, Fr. 64/B2
Meymaneh, Afg. 101/H1
Méyo Kyé, Gabon 120/B2
Meyrargues, Fr. 64/B5
Meyrin, Swi. 60/C5
Meythet, Fr. 60/C6
Meythet (Annecy) (arpt.), Fr. 60/C6
Meyzieu, Fr. 60/A6
Mezaligon, Myan. 86/B5
Mezdra, Bul. 51/F4
Mèze, Fr. 44/E5
Mézel, Fr. 64/C5
Mezen', Rus. 69/K2
Mezen' (bay), Rus. 69/J2
Mezen' (riv.), Rus. 74/E3
Mezha (riv.), Bela. 41/P4
Mezhdurechensk, Rus. 74/J4
Mezhdurechenskiy, Rus. 74/G4
Mezhdusharskiy (isl.), Rus. 74/E2
Mezhova, Ukr. 73/J3
Mézidon-Canon, Fr. 57/E2
Mézières-sur-Seine, Fr. 30/H5
Mezoberény, Hun. 50/E2
Mezokovácsháza, Hun. 50/E2
Mezőkövesd, Hun. 43/L5
Mezőtúr, Hun. 50/E2
Mezquital (riv.), Mex. 174/D4
Mézy, Fr. 30/H5
Mezzana (peak), It. 61/G5
Mezzocorona, It. 61/H5
Mezzolombardo, It. 61/H5
Mfangano (isl.), Kenya 119/A2
Mfou, Camr. 120/B2
Mfrika, Tanz. 119/A4
Mga, Rus. 69/U7
Mga (riv.), Rus. 69/U7
Mgachi, Rus. 79/N1
Mgambo, Tanz. 119/B3
Mgera, Tanz. 119/B3
Mgeta, Tanz. 119/B4
Mglin, Rus. 70/E1
Mgori, Tanz. 119/A3
M'goun (peak), Mor. 110/D3
Mhamdia Fūshānah, Tun. 48/B4
Mhòr (lake), Sc, UK 33/B2
Mhow, India 92/C3
Mhunze, Tanz. 119/A2
Mi (riv.), China 80/D3
Mi Xian, China 80/C4
Mi-shima (isl.), Japan 84/B3
Miahuatlán de Porfirio Díaz, Mex. 176/B2
Miajadas, Sp. 46/C3
Miaméré, CAfr. 116/C3
Miami, Tx, US 152/D3
Miami, Mb, Can. 156/E3
Miami, Ok, US 153/G2
Miami (canal), Fl, US 165/H4
Miami, Az, US 149/G4
Miami, Fl, US 164/P11
Miami (int'l arpt.), Fl, US 164/P11
Miami (riv.), Oh, US 162/E1
Miami Beach, Fl, US 164/P11
Miami Shores, Fl, US 164/P11
Miami Springs, Fl, US 164/P11
Miamisburg, Oh, US 160/D5
Miān Channūn, Pak. 98/B4
Miāna, India 96/A3
Miancaowan, China 78/D4
Mianchi, China 80/B4
Mīāndasht, Iran 103/J2
Mīāndoāb, Iran 103/F2
Miandrivazo, Madg. 125/H7
Mīāneh, Iran 103/F2
Mianhu, China 87/H4
Miāni, Pak. 98/B3
Mianmian (mts.), China 86/D2
Mianning, China 86/D2
Mianus (riv.), Ct, US 169/E1
Miānwāli, India 98/B5
Miānwāli, Pak. 98/A3
Mianyang, China 86/E2
Mianzhu, China 86/E2
Miāo, India 86/C3
Miao'er (peak), China 87/F3
Miaoshi, China 87/F2
Miarinarivo, Madg. 125/H7
Miarinarivo, Madg. 125/J7
Miary, Madg. 125/G8
Miass, Rus. 69/P5
Miass (riv.), Rus. 69/P5
Miastko, Pol. 40/G4
Miazal, Ecu. 184/B1
Mibenge, D.R. Congo 120/D3
Miberika, Sudan 135/G5
Mica Creek, BC, Can. 144/E1
Micanopy, Fl, US 165/G3
Micay, Col. 180/B4
Micco, Fl, US 165/H4
Miccosukee, Fl, US 165/F2
Miccosukee Ind. Res., Fl, US 165/H4
Michalovce, Slvk. 43/L4
Michaud (pt.), NS, Can. 159/G3
Michel (bay), Fr. 44/C2
Michelago, Austl. 133/D2
Michelfeld, Ger. 59/E3
Michelson (mt.), Ak, US 171/K2
Michelstadt, Ger. 58/C3
Michendorf, Ger. 42/Q7
Michie, Tn, US 162/C3
Michigamme (lake), Mi, US 157/K4
Michigamme, Mi, US 157/K4
Michigan, ND, US 156/E3
Michigan (lake), US 139/J5
Michigan (state), US 143/J2
Michigan Center, Mi, US 160/D3
Michigan City, In, US 160/C4
Michigan City, Ms, US 162/C3
Michigan Islands Nat'l Wild. Ref., Mi, US 160/D2
Michipicoten (isl.), On, Can. 157/M4
Michoacán de Ocampo (state), Mex. 172/A4
Michurin, Bul. 51/H4
Michurinsk, Rus. 71/G1
Mickle Fell (peak), Eng, UK 35/F2
Mickleton, Eng, UK 35/F2
Mico (riv.), Nic. 172/E5
Miconje, Ang. 120/C4
Micoud, StL. 173/N9
Micronesia (ctry.) 136/D4
Micronesia (reg.) 136/E3
Mid Yell, Sc, UK 31/W13
Midal (well), Niger 115/G2
Midale, Sk, Can. 156/C3
Midar, Mor. 112/C2
Middelburg, Neth. 52/A5
Middelburg, SAfr. 124/D3
Middelburg, SAfr. 125/E2
Middelharnis, Neth. 52/B5
Middelkerke, Belg. 54/B1
Middenmeer, Neth. 52/B3
Middle (ridge), Nf, Can. 159/K1
Middle (bay), NY, US 169/L9
Middle (lake), Ca, US 146/C3
Middle (mtn.), WV, US 163/G1
Middle Andaman (isl.), India 93/F5
Middle Caicos (isl.), UK 177/J1
Middle Concho (riv.), Tx, US 151/D2
Middle Fabius (riv.), Mo, US 155/H3
Middle Inlet, Wi, US 160/C2
Middle Lake, Sk, Can. 145/M1
Middle Loup (riv.), Ne, US 154/D3
Middle Pease (riv.), Tx, US 152/D3
Middle Raccoon (riv.), Ia, US 155/G3
Middle River, Mn, US 156/F3
Middle River, Md, US 168/B5
Middle Sister (peak), Or, US 146/C1
Middle Stewiacke, NS, Can. 158/F3
Middle Yuba (riv.), Ca, US 146/C4
Middlebourne, WV, US 160/F5
Middlebro, Mb, Can. 157/G3
Middleburg, Fl, US 165/H2
Middleburg, Pa, US 168/A2
Middleburg, Md, US 168/A4
Middleburgh, NY, US 161/J3
Middlebury, Vt, US 161/K2
Middlebury, In, US 160/D4
Middlefield, Oh, US 160/F4
Middlefield, Ma, US 161/K3
Middleham, Eng, UK 35/G3
Middlemarch, NZ 135/B4
Middlemount, Austl. 134/C3
Middleport, Oh, US 163/F1
Middleport, NY, US 160/W9
Middleport, Pa, US 168/B2
Middlesboro, Ky, US 162/F2
Middlesbrough, Eng, UK 35/G2
Middlesex (reg.), Eng, UK 37/F4
Middlesex, NJ, US 168/D2
Middlesex, NC, US 163/H3
Middleton, Eng, UK 35/F4
Middleton, NS, Can. 158/E3
Middleton, Id, US 146/E2
Middleton, Wi, US 155/K2
Middleton, Tn, US 162/C3
Middleton Cheney, Eng, UK 37/E2
Middleton-in-Teesdale, Eng, UK 35/F2
Middletown, NI, UK 34/B3
Middletown, NY, US 161/J4
Middletown, In, US 160/D4
Middletown, Ct, US 161/K4
Middletown, Oh, US 160/D5
Middletown, RI, US 161/L4
Middletown, NJ, US 169/J10
Middletown, Ca, US 146/B4
Middletown, Pa, US 168/B3
Middletown, Va, US 163/H1
Middletown, De, US 168/C5
Middleville, Mi, US 160/D3
Middlewich, Eng, UK 35/F5
Middlewood, NS, Can. 158/E3
Midelt, Mor. 110/D2
Midhurst, Eng, UK 37/F5
Midi (canal), Fr. 44/D5
Midi-Pyrénées (pol.reg.), Fr. 44/D4
Midkiff, WV, US 163/F1
Midland, Mi, US 160/D3
Midland, On, Can. 161/G2
Midland, Wa, US 167/C3
Midland, Or, US 146/C2
Midland, SD, US 154/D1
Midland (nbrhd.), Austl. 130/L6
Midland (int'l arpt.), Tx, US 174/E2
Midland, Tx, US 151/C2
Midland City, Al, US 165/F2
Midland Park, NJ, US 169/J8
Midlands (prov.), Zim. 123/F3
Midleton, Ire. 32/B6
Midlothian (co.), Sc, UK 33/C5
Midlothian, Il, US 167/Q16
Midlothian, Tx, US 150/L7
Midlum, Ger. 53/F1
Midnight, Ms, US 162/B4
Midongy Atsimo, Madg. 125/H8
Midou (riv.), Fr. 44/C5
Midsayap, Phil. 88/D4
Midsomer Norton, Eng, UK 36/D4
Midu, China 93/H2
Midville, Ga, US 163/F4
Midway (isls.), Pac., US 136/H2
Midway, BC, Can. 144/E3
Midway, Al, US 165/F1
Midway, De, US 168/C6
Midway, Fl, US 165/F2
Midway, Ga, US 165/H2
Midway, Ky, US 162/E1
Midway, La, US 164/B2
Midway, Ne, US 154/E2
Midway, NM, US 152/B4
Midway, Tx, US 151/G2
Midwest, Wy, US 154/A2
Midwest City, Ok, US 153/F3
Midyan (reg.), SAr. 100/C3
Midyat, Turk. 102/E2
Midžor (peak), Yugo. 51/F4
Mie (pref.), Japan 84/E3
Mie, Japan 84/B4
Miechów, Pol. 70/B2
Międzychód, Pol. 43/H2
Międzylesie, Pol. 43/J3
Międzyrzec Podlaski, Pol. 43/M3
Międzyrzecz, Pol. 43/H2
Międzyzdroje, Pol. 40/F5
Miehlen, Ger. 55/G3
Miéle I, Congo 120/C2
Mielec, Pol. 43/L3
Mier, Mex. 151/E4
Miercurea Ciuc, Rom. 51/G2
Mieres, Sp. 46/C1
Miesbach, Ger. 45/J3
Mī'ēso, Eth. 118/B3
Mifflin, Pa, US 168/A2
Mifflinburg, Pa, US 168/A2
Mifflintown, Pa, US 161/H4
Mifflinville (Creasy), Pa, US 168/B1
Mifraẕ Hefa (bay), Isr. 105/B3
Migdal, Isr. 105/D3
Migdal Ha'emeq, Isr. 105/C3
Migdol, SAfr. 124/D2
Migennes, Fr. 44/E3
Migliarino, It. 62/D6
Mignanego, It. 62/B4
Mignano Monte Lungo, It. 65/C5
Mignovillard, Fr. 60/C4
Migori (riv.), Kenya 119/A2
Migori, Kenya 119/A2
Miguel Alemán, Mex. 174/C2
Miguel Aleman, Presa (dam), Mex. 175/M8
Miguel Alves, Braz. 183/F4
Miguel Auza, Mex. 174/E3
Miguel Calmon, Braz. 187/E1
Miguel Hidalgo (int'l arpt.), Mex. 174/E4
Miguel Hidalgo (res.), Mex. 174/C3
Miguel Pereira, Braz. 187/N7
Miguel Riglos, Arg. 190/E3
Miguelete, Uru. 191/K11
Miguelópolis, Braz. 189/G2
Miguelturra, Sp. 46/D3
Migŭm, SKor. 81/G6
Mihama, Japan 84/D3
Mihama, Japan 83/L6
Mihara, Japan 84/C3
Mihara, Japan 83/J6
Miharu, Japan 85/G2
Mihintale (ruin), SrL. 95/D4
Mihla, Ger. 53/H6
Miho, Japan 83/E2
Mihrābpur, Pak. 101/J3
Mijares (riv.), Sp. 47/E2
Mijas, Sp. 46/C4
Mijdāḩah, Yem. 118/D2
Mijdrecht, Neth. 52/B4
Mikasa, Japan 82/B2
Mikashevichi, Bela. 70/C1
Mikata, Japan 83/J4
Mikata (lake), Japan 83/J4
Mikawa (bay), Japan 83/M6
Mikengere, D.R. Congo 121/F5
Mikese, Tanz. 119/B3
Mikhaylov, Rus. 70/F1
Mikhaylovka, Rus. 73/M2
Mikhaylovsk, Rus. 69/N4
Mikhmoret, Isr. 105/B4
Miki, Japan 83/G6
Mikínai, Gre. 49/H4
Mikínai (Mycenae) (ruin), Gre. 49/H4
Mikindani, Tanz. 119/C4
Mikkalo, Or, US 146/C1
Mikkeli (prov.), Fin. 38/H3
Mikomeseng, EqG. 120/B2
Míkonos, Gre. 49/J4
Míkonos (isl.), Gre. 49/J4
Mikope, D.R. Congo 121/E4
Mikri Prespa NP, Gre. 49/G2
Mikuma, Japan 83/L6
Mikumi, Tanz. 119/B3
Mikumi NP, Tanz. 119/B3
Mikun', Rus. 69/L3
Mikuni, Japan 84/E2
Mikuni-tōge (pass), Japan 85/F2
Mikura (isl.), Japan 85/F4
Mila, Alg. 66/E3
Mila (wilaya), Alg. 112/H4
Milaca, Mn, US 157/H5
Milagres, Braz. 183/G4
Milagro, Ecu. 180/B5
Milak, India 96/B1
Milakpur, India 96/A2
Milam, Tx, US 151/H2
Milan, NH, US 161/L2
Milan, Oh, US 160/E4
Milan, Ga, US 165/G1
Milan, NM, US 149/J3
Milan, Tn, US 162/C3
Milan, Mn, US 155/G1
Milan, Mo, US 155/H3
Milan, In, US 162/E1
Milan (Milano), It. 45/H4
Milando, Ang. 120/D5
Milang, Austl. 132/A2
Milange, Moz. 123/G3
Milano (prov.), It. 62/C2
Milano, Tx, US 151/F2
Milano (Milan), It. 45/H4
Milas, Turk. 102/A2
Milazzo, It. 48/D3
Milbank, SD, US 155/F1
Milborne Port, Eng, UK 36/D5
Milburn, Ok, US 153/F3
Milburn, Ne, US 154/E3
Milden, Sk, Can. 145/L2
Mildenhall, Eng, UK 37/G2
Mildred, Mt, US 156/B4
Mildura, Austl. 132/B2
Mīlē, Eth. 118/B3
Mile, China 86/D3
Mīlē Wenz (riv.), Eth. 118/B3
Milepa, Tanz. 121/G5
Miles, Austl. 134/C4
Miles, Tx, US 151/D2
Miles City, Mt, US 145/M4
Milesburg, Pa, US 161/H4
Milešovka (peak), Czh. 59/G1
Milestone, Sk, Can. 156/B3
Miletto (peak), It. 65/D5
Milevsko, Czh. 59/H4
Milford, Ire. 32/B4
Milford, NI, UK 34/B3
Milford, NH, US 161/L3
Milford, Ma, US 161/L3
Milford, Ga, US 165/F2
Milford, Il, US 160/C4
Milford, Pa, US 161/J4
Milford, Mi, US 167/E6
Milford (sound), NZ 135/A4
Milford, Ut, US 149/F1
Milford, Ks, US 155/F4
Milford (lake), Ks, US 155/F4
Milford, Ia, US 155/G2
Milford, Ne, US 155/F3
Milford, Tx, US 151/F1
Milford, Ct, US 169/E1
Milford, De, US 168/C6
Milford, NJ, US 168/C2
Milford Haven (inlet), Wal., UK 36/A3
Milford Haven, Wal, UK 36/A3
Milford Station, NS, Can. 158/F3
Milford-on-Sea, Eng, UK 37/E5
Mili (isl.), Mrsh. 136/G4
Miliana, Alg. 112/G4
Milicz, Pol. 43/J3
Milikapiti, Austl. 128/C2
Milingimbi Mission, Austl. 129/D3
Military (ridge), Wi, US 155/J2
Milk (riv.), Mt, Can., US 140/F4
Milk (hill), Eng, UK 37/E4
Milk River, Ab, Can. 145/H3
Mill (isl.), Nun, Can. 141/J2
Mill, Neth. 52/C5
Mill (riv.), Ct, US 169/E1
Mill (cr.), Ct, US 169/F1
Mill Bay, BC, Can. 144/C3
Mill City, Or, US 146/B1
Mill Creek, Ok, US 153/F3
Mill Creek, WV, US 163/H1
Mill Neck, NY, US 169/L8
Mill Shoals, Il, US 162/C1
Mill Spring, Mo, US 162/B2
Mill Village, NS, Can. 158/E3
Millaa Millaa, Austl. 134/B2
Millau, Fr. 44/E4
Millboro, SD, US 154/E2
Millboro, Va, US 163/G1
Millbrae, Ca, US 167/K11
Millbridge, Eng, UK 30/A3
Millbrook, On, Can. 161/G2
Millbrook, Al, US 162/D4
Millbrook (res.), Austl. 131/M8
Millbrook, Eng, UK 36/B6
Millburn, NJ, US 169/H9
Millburne, Wy, US 147/H3
Mille Îles (riv.), Qu, Can. 159/N6
Mille Lacs (lake), Mn, US 143/H2
Mille Lacs Ind. Res., Mn, US 157/H4
Milledgeville, Ga, US 163/F4
Milledgeville, Il, US 155/K3
Milledgeville, Tn, US 162/C3
Millen, Ga, US 163/G4
Miller (peak), Az, US 149/G5
Miller, SD, US 154/E1
Miller (pt.), Tx, US 151/N9
Miller (int'l arpt.), Tx, US 175/F3
Millerovo, Rus. 73/L3
Millers Creek (res.), Tx, US 151/E1
Millers Ferry, Al, US 164/E1
Millers Ferry (dam), Al, US 164/E1
Millersburg, Oh, US 160/F4
Millersburg, Or, US 146/B1
Millersburg, Pa, US 168/B2
Millerstown, Pa, US 168/A2
Millersview, Tx, US 150/E2
Millersville, Pa, US 168/B4
Millerton (lake), Ca, US 148/C2
Millertown, Nf, Can. 159/J1
Millerville, Mn, US 157/G4
Millesimo, It. 62/B5
Millet, Ab, Can. 145/H1
Millett, Tx, US 151/E3
Milleur (pt.), Sc, UK 34/C1
Millevaches (plat.), Fr. 44/D4
Millgrove, On, Can. 160/T9
Millicent, Austl. 132/B3
Milligan, Fl, US 164/E2
Milliken, Co, US 154/B3
Millingen aan de Rijn, Neth. 52/D5
Millington, Tn, US 162/C3
Millington, Md, US 168/C5
Millinocket, Me, US 141/K4
Millisle, NI, UK 34/C2
Millmerran, Austl. 134/C4
Millmont, Pa, US 168/A2
Millom, Eng, UK 35/E3
Millport, Sc, UK 33/B5
Millport, Al, US 162/C4
Millry, Al, US 164/D2
Mills, NM, US 152/B2
Millsboro, De, US 163/K1
Millstone, WV, US 163/G1
Millstone (riv.), NJ, US 168/D3
Millstream-Chichester NP, Austl. 130/C2
Millstreet, Ire. 32/A5
Millthorpe, Austl. 133/D1
Millthrop, Eng, UK 35/F3
Milltown, NJ, US 169/H10
Milltown, In, US 162/D1
Milltown Malbay, Ire. 32/A4
Milltown-Head of Bay d'Espoir, Nf, Can. 159/K2
Millungera, Austl. 134/A2
Millville, Oh, US 160/D5
Millville, NJ, US 168/C5
Millville, Pa, US 168/B1
Millwood (dam), Ar, US 153/H4
Millwood (lake), Ar, US 153/G4
Millwood, Ga, US 165/G2
Millwood, WV, US 163/G1
Milmay, NJ, US 168/D5
Milnathort, Wal, UK 35/E5
Milne (bay), PNG 136/E5
Milngavie, Sc, UK 33/B5
Milnor, ND, US 156/F4
Milnrow, Eng, UK 35/F4
Milo (riv.), Gui. 114/C4
Milo, Ia, US 155/H3
Mílos, Gre. 49/J4
Mílos (isl.), Gre. 67/K3
Milpa, Austl. 132/B1
Milpa Alta (nbrhd.), Mex. 175/Q10
Milparinka, Austl. 131/J4
Milroy, In, US 160/D5
Milroy, Pa, US 161/H4
Milseburg (peak), Ger. 58/C1
Milstead, Ga, US 163/N7
Miltenberg, Ger. 58/C3
Milton, ND, US 156/E3
Milton, Eng, UK 35/F2
Milton, NH, US 161/L3
Milton, Vt, US 161/K2
Milton, Fl, US 164/E2
Milton, Wa, US 167/C3
Milton, NZ 135/B4
Milton, Ia, US 155/H3
Milton, Il, US 155/J4
Milton, Wi, US 155/K2
Milton, On, Can. 160/T8
Milton, Eng, UK 37/G4
Milton, Austl. 133/E2
Milton, Pa, US 168/B1
Milton Heights, On, Can. 160/T8
Milton Keynes, Eng, UK 37/F2
Milton Keynes (co.), Eng, UK 37/F2
Milton Ness (pt.), Sc, UK 33/D3
Milton of Campsie, Sc, UK 33/B5
Milton-Freewater, Or, US 144/E5
Miltona, Mn, US 157/G4
Miltonvale, Ks, US 154/F4
Miluo (riv.), China 87/G2
Milverton, On, Can. 160/F3
Milverton, Eng, UK 36/C4
Milwaukee, Wi, US 160/C3
Milwaukee (co.), Wi, US 167/P14
Milz (riv.), Ger. 58/D2
Mimbres, NM, US 149/J4
Mimbres (riv.), NM, US 149/J4
Mimet, Fr. 64/B6
Mimi (riv.), Japan 84/B4
Mimizan, Fr. 44/C4
Mimmaya, Japan 82/A3
Mimongo, Gabon 120/B3
Mimongo, Gabon 120/B3
Mimosa Rocks NP, Austl. 133/D3
Min (riv.), China 78/E5
Min Xian, China 78/E5
Min-Kush, Kyr. 99/B3
Mina, Mex. 151/D4
Mina, Nv, US 146/D4
Mîna (riv.), Alg. 112/F5
Mina Clavero, Arg. 188/C4
Mina Pirquitas, Arg. 188/C2
Mīnā' Su'ūd, Kuw. 103/G4
Mīnāb, Iran 103/J5
Minaçu, Braz. 186/C2
Minahasa (isl.), Indo. 91/F3
Minaki, On, Can. 157/G3
Minakuchi, Japan 83/K6
Minamata, Japan 84/B4
Minami Alps NP, Japan 85/F3
Minami-tori-shima (isl.), Japan 136/E2
Minamiaiki, Japan 83/B1
Minamiashigara, Japan 83/C3
Minamichita, Japan 83/L6
Minamidaitō (isl.), Japan 85/L8
Minamiiō (isl.), Japan 136/D2
Minamikawara, Japan 83/C1
Minamimaki, Japan 83/A2
Minamiyamashiro, Japan 83/J6
Minano, Japan 83/C1
Minas, Cuba 177/G1
Minas (peak), Ecu. 180/B5
Minas, Uru. 191/G2
Minas, Indo. 89/C2
Minas de Barroterán, Mex. 151/D4
Minas de Corrales, Uru. 189/F4
Minas de Matahambre, Cuba 177/F1
Minas de Ríotinto, Sp. 46/B4
Minas Gerais (state), Braz. 186/D3
Minatitlán, Mex. 176/C2
Minbu, Myan. 86/B4
Minbya, Myan. 86/B4
Minch, The (North Minch) (str.), Sc, UK 31/Q8
Mincha, Chile 188/B4
Minchinābād, Pak. 98/B4
Minchinhampton, Eng, UK 36/D3
Minchinmávida (vol.), Chile 190/B4
Mincio (riv.), It. 63/D2
Minco, Ok, US 153/F3
Mindanao (isl.), Phil. 77/M9
Mindanao (sea), Phil. 91/F2
Mindel (riv.), Ger. 42/F4
Mindelheim, Ger. 61/G1
Mindelo, CpV. 107/J10
Mindemoya, On, Can. 160/E2
Minden, La, US 153/H4
Minden, Ger. 53/F4
Minden, Nv, US 146/D4
Minden, Ne, US 154/E3
Minden, Tx, US 151/G1
Minden City, Mi, US 160/E3
Mindif, Camr. 116/B3
Mindiptana, Indo. 129/F1
Mindoro (isl.), Phil. 77/L8
Mindoro (str.), Phil. 88/C2
Mindouli, Congo 120/C4
Mindyak, Rus. 69/N5
Mine Centre, On, Can. 157/H3
Mine Head (pt.), Ire. 32/C6
Minehead, Eng, UK 36/C4
Mineiros, Braz. 186/B3
Mineola, NY, US 169/L8
Mineola, Mo, US 155/J4
Mineola, Tx, US 151/G1
Miner, Mt, US 147/H1
Miner, Mo, US 162/C2
Mineral, Tx, US 150/F3
Mineral, Wa, US 144/C4
Mineral del Monte, Mex. 175/L6
Mineral Point, Mo, US 162/B2
Mineral Point, Wi, US 155/J2
Mineral Springs, Ar, US 153/H4
Mineral Wells, Tx, US 151/E1
Mineral'nye Vody, Rus. 71/G3
Mineralnyye Vody (int'l arpt.), Rus. 71/G3
Mineralwells, WV, US 163/G1
Minerbe, It. 63/E3
Minerbio, It. 63/E4
Minerbio (pt.), Fr. 45/H5
Minersville, Ut, US 149/F1
Minersville, Pa, US 168/B2
Minetto, NY, US 161/H3
Mineville-Witherbee, NY, US 161/K2
Minfeld, Ger. 58/B4
Minfeng, China 99/D4
Ming (riv.), China 93/J3
Mingäçevir, Azer. 71/H4
Mingäçevir Su Anbari (res.), Azer. 71/H4
Mingala, CAfr. 116/D4
Mingāora, Pak. 98/B2
Mingenew, Austl. 130/B4
Mingin, Myan. 86/B4
Minglanilla, Sp. 46/E3
Mingo, Congo 120/C3
Mingo, Ks, US 154/D4
Mingo Junction, Oh, US 160/F4
Mingo NWR, Mo, US 162/B2
Mingouli, Chutes de (falls), Gabon 120/C2
Mingoyo, Tanz. 119/B4
Mingshan, China 86/D2
Mingshui, China 78/D3
Mingshui, China 79/K2
Mingun, Ancient City of, Myan. 86/B4
Minhang, China 80/L8
Minhe, China 78/E4
Minhla, Myan. 86/B5
Minhla, Myan. 86/B5
Minho (riv.), Port. 46/A1
Miniāri, India 92/B2
Minidoka (dam), Id, US 147/G2
Minidoka Internment Nat'l Mon., Id, US 147/F2
Minigwal (lake), Austl. 130/D4
Minilya, Austl. 130/B2
Minīn, Syria 105/E1
Miniota, Mb, Can. 156/D2
Ministro Pistarini (Buenos Aires) (int'l arpt.), Arg. 191/J11
Minitonas, Mb, Can. 156/D1
Minj, PNG 129/G1
Minkamman, Sudan 117/F4
Minkébé, Montagne de (peak), Gabon 120/C2
Minlaton, Austl. 131/H5
Minle, China 78/E4
Minna, Nga. 115/G4
Minneapolis, Ks, US 154/F4
Minneapolis, Mn, US 157/P7
Minneapolis-St.Paul (Wold-Chamberlain) (int'l arpt.), Mn, US 157/P7
Minnedosa, Mb, Can. 156/E2
Minnehaha (lake), Fl, US 164/M6
Minnehaha (falls), Mn, US 157/P7
Minneola, Ks, US 152/D2
Minneola, Fl, US 164/M6
Minneola (lake), Fl, US 164/M6
Minneota, Mn, US 155/G1
Minnequa (canal), Co, US 154/B4
Minnesota (state), US 143/G2
Minnesota (riv.), Mn, US 155/G1
Minnesota Zoo and Gardens, Mn, US 157/P7
Minnetonka, Mn, US 157/P7
Minnetonka (lake), Mn, US 157/N7
Minnewaska (lake), Mn, US 155/G1
Minnewaukan, ND, US 156/E3
Minnigaff, Sc, UK 34/D2
Minnipa, Austl. 131/G5
Minnis (lake), On, Can. 157/J2
Minnitaki (lake), On, Can. 157/H3
Miño (riv.), Sp. 46/A1
Mino, Japan 83/L4
Mino'o (riv.), Japan 83/H6
Minobu, Japan 85/F3
Minocqua, Wi, US 157/K5
Minokamo, Japan 83/M5
Minonk, Il, US 155/K3
Mino'o, Japan 83/H6
Minorca (Menorca) (isl.), Sp. 47/H2
Minori, It. 65/D6
Minori, Japan 83/E1
Minot, ND, US 156/D3
Minot (A.F.B.), ND, US 156/D3
Minqin, China 78/E4
Minqing, China 87/H3
Minquan, China 80/C4
Minsener Oog (isl.), Ger. 53/F1
Minsk (cap.), Bela. 41/M5
Minsk (int'l arpt.), Bela. 41/M5
Minskaya Voblasts, Bela. 41/M5
Mińsk Mazowiecki, Pol. 43/L2
Minster, Oh, US 160/D4
Minster, Eng, UK 37/H4
Mint Hill, NC, US 163/G3
Minta, Camr. 116/B4
Minter, Al, US 164/E1
Mintlaw, Sc, UK 33/E1
Minto, Mb, Can. 156/D3
Minto, NB, Can. 158/D2
Minto (inlet), NW, Can. 140/D1
Minto, Yk, Can. 171/L3
Minto, Ak, US 171/J2
Minto, ND, US 156/F3
Mintom Li, Camr. 120/C2
Minton, Sk, Can. 156/B3
Minturnae (ruin), It. 65/C5
Minturno, It. 65/C5
Mīnūdasht, Iran 103/H2
Minūf, Egypt 113/B4
Minusinsk, Rus. 74/K4
Minusio, Swi. 61/E5
Minutang, India 86/C2
Minvoul, Gabon 120/C2
Minwakh, Yem. 100/E5
Minxiao, China 87/F3
Minyā al Qamḩ, Egypt 113/C3
Min'yar, Rus. 69/N5
Minyat Sandūb, Egypt 113/C3
Minyip, Austl. 132/B3
Mio, Mi, US 160/D2
Mions, Fr. 64/A1
Miory, Bela. 41/M4
Mipi, India 86/B2
Miquan, China 99/E3
Miquelon, Nf, Fr. 159/J2
Mir, Rus. 69/P5
Mira, La, US 153/H4
Mira (riv.), NS, Can. 158/G3
Mira (riv.), Col. 180/B4
Mira (riv.), Port. 46/A4
Mira, Port. 46/A2
Mira Loma, Ca, US 166/C2
Mira Monte, Ca, US 166/A2
Mira Taglio, It. 63/F3
Mirabel (int'l arpt.), Can. 159/M6
Mirabel, Qu, Can. 159/M6
Mirabella Eclano, It. 65/D5
Mirabello, It. 63/E4
Miracema, Braz. 187/E4
Miradolo Terme, It. 62/C3
Mirador (pass), Chile 190/C4
Mirador, Braz. 183/E4
Miraflores, Col. 180/C4
Miraflores, Col. 180/C3
Miraflores, Peru 184/B3
Miraflores, Mex. 174/C4
Miragoâne, Haiti 177/H2
Miraj, India 95/B2
Miramar, Ca, US 166/C5
Miramar, Arg. 190/F3
Miramar (nbrhd.), NZ 135/H9
Miramar, Arg. 188/D4
Miramar, Fl, US 164/P11
Miramar Naval Air Station, Ca, US 166/C5
Miramare (arpt.), It. 63/F5
Miramas, Fr. 64/A5
Mirambéllou (gulf), Gre. 49/J5
Miramichi (bay), NB, Can. 158/E2
Miramichi, South West (riv.), NB, Can. 158/D2
Miramont-de-Guyenne, Fr. 44/D4
Mīrān, Pak. 98/A4
Miranda, It. 65/D4
Miranda, SD, US 154/E1
Miranda, Braz. 189/E2
Miranda (riv.), Braz. 186/A3
Miranda de Ebro, Sp. 44/B5
Miranda do Corvo, Port. 46/A2
Miranda do Douro, Port. 46/B2
Mirande, Fr. 44/D5
Mirandela, Port. 46/B2
Mirandiba, Braz. 183/G5
Mirando City, Tx, US 151/E4
Mirandópolis, Braz. 189/G2
Mirano, It. 63/F3
Miranorte, Braz. 182/D5
Mīrānpur, India 96/A1
Mirassol, Braz. 189/G2
Miravalles (vol.), CR 176/E4
Miravalles (peak), Sp. 46/B1
Mirbāţ, Oman 101/F5
Mirboo North, Austl. 133/C4
Mirebalais, Haiti 177/H2
Mirebeau, Fr. 60/B3
Mirecourt, Fr. 60/C1
Mirecourt (Épinal) (arpt.), Fr. 60/C1
Mireigha, Sudan 117/E3
Mirendi, Gabon 120/B3
Mirfield, Eng, UK 35/G4
Miri, Malay. 90/D3
Miriam Vale, Austl. 134/C4
Mirim (lake), Braz. 189/F5
Mirimire, Ven. 180/D2
Mírina, Gre. 49/J3
Miriñay (riv.), Arg. 188/E4
Mirinzal, Braz. 183/E3
Miritiparaná (riv.), Col. 180/D5
Mirna (riv.), Cro. 63/G5
Mirnyy, Rus. 75/M3
Mirnyy, Rus., Ant. 192/G
Mirow, Ger. 42/G2
Mīrpur, Pak. 98/B3
Mirria, Niger 115/H3
Mirror, Ab, Can. 145/H1
Mirror (lake), NJ, US 168/D4
Mirsali, China 99/E3
Mirthal, India 98/C3
Mirtóön (sea), Gre. 49/H4
Miryang, SKor. 84/A3
Mirzaani, Geo. 71/H4
Mirzāpur, Bang. 97/H3
Mirzāpur, India 96/D3
Misa (riv.), It. 63/G5
Misa, D.R. Congo 121/G1
Misaka, Japan 83/B2
Misaki, Japan 84/D3
Misaki, Japan 83/E3
Misano Adriatico, It. 63/F6
Misantla, Mex. 175/N7
Misasa, Tanz. 119/B3
Misato, Japan 83/D2
Misato, Japan 83/C1
Misato, Japan 83/K6
Misawa, Japan 82/B3
Miscano (riv.), It. 65/D5
Miscou (pt.), Qu, Can. 158/E1
Miscou (isl.), NB, Can. 158/E2
Miscou Centre, NB, Can. 158/E2
Misere (lake), La, US 164/B3
Misgār, Pak. 101/K1
Mishagua, Peru 184/C3
Mishan, China 79/L2
Mishawaka, In, US 160/C4
Misheguk (mt.), Ak, US 171/F2
Mishicot, Wi, US 160/C2
Mishima, Japan 85/F3
Mishkino, Rus. 69/M5
Mishmar Hanegev, Isr. 105/B6
Mishmar Hayarden, Isr. 105/D3
Misilmeri, It. 48/C3
Misiones (dept.), Arg. 189/E3
Miskolc, Hun. 43/L4
Mismār, Sudan 100/C5
Misono, Japan 83/L6
Misool (isl.), Indo. 91/H4
Misquah (hills), Mn, US 157/J4
Miṣr al Jadīdah, Egypt 113/C4
Miṣrātah, Libya 67/G4
Miṣrātah (pt.), Libya 67/K5
Missão Velha, Braz. 183/G4
Missillac, Fr. 56/C6
Missinaibi (riv.), On, Can. 141/H3
Mission (mtn.), Ok, US 153/G2
Mission (bay), Ca, US 166/C5
Mission, Or, US 146/D1
Mission, BC, Can. 144/C3
Mission, Tx, US 151/E4
Mission Beach, Austl. 134/B2
Mission Bend, Tx, US 151/M9
Mission Ind. Res., Ca, US 166/C4
Mission Ridge, SD, US 154/D1
Mission San Buenaventura, Ca, US 166/A2
Mission San Jose, Ca, US 167/L12
Mission San Juan Capistrano, Ca, US 166/C3
Mission San Luis Obispo de Tolosa, Ca, US 148/B3
Mission San Miguel Arcangel, Ca, US 148/B3
Mission Viejo, Ca, US 166/C3
Mississagi (riv.), On, Can. 160/E1
Mississauga, On, Can. 160/T8
Mississippi (sound), Al,Ms, US 164/D2
Mississippi (riv.), US 139/H6
Mississippi (delta), US 139/J7
Mississippi (state), US 143/H5
Mississippi (pt.), Austl. 130/D5
Mississippi Sandhill Crane NWR, Ms, US 164/D2
Mississippi Station, On, Can. 161/H2
Missoula, Mt, US 145/H4
Missouri (riv.), US 139/F5
Missouri (state), US 143/H4
Missouri City, Tx, US 151/M9
Missouri Valley, Ia, US 155/G3
Missungwi, Tanz. 119/A2
Mist, Or, US 144/C5
Mistake (cr.), Austl. 134/B3
Mistake Creek, Austl. 128/C4
Mistaken (pt.), Nf, Can. 159/L2
Mistassini, Qu, Can. 158/A1
Mistassini (lake), Qu, Can. 141/J3
Mistatim, Sk, Can. 145/N1
Misti (vol.), Peru 184/D5
Mistissini, Qu, Can. 141/J3
Mistley, Eng, UK 37/H3
Mistrás (ruin), Gre. 49/H4
Mistretta, It. 48/D4
Misty Fjords Nat'l Mon., Ak, US 171/M4
Misugi, Japan 83/K6
Miswa, Zam. 123/F2
Mīt Abū Ghālib, Egypt 113/C2
Mīt an Naṣārá, Egypt 113/C2

Map Section
250
251

Mīt Fāris, Egypt 113/C2
Mīt Ghamr, Egypt 113/C3
Mīt Ḩamal, Egypt 113/C4
Mita, Punta de (pt.), Mex. 174/D4
Mitaka, Japan 83/D2
Mitake, Japan 83/M5
Mitama, Japan 83/B2
Mitare, Ven. 180/D2
Mitatib, Sudan 117/H1
Mitcham (nbrhd.), Austl. 131/M9
Mitcheldean, Eng, UK 36/D3
Mitchell, Ar, US 153/H2
Mitchell, Austl. 134/B4
Mitchell, Or, US 146/C1
Mitchell, Ne, US 154/C3
Mitchell (dam), Al, US 162/D4
Mitchell, SD, US 154/E2
Mitchell (mt.), NC, US 163/F3
Mitchell, In, US 162/D1
Mitchell (range), Austl. 129/D3
Mitchell (riv.), Austl. 127/D2
Mitchell (lake), Al, US 162/D4
Mitchell and Alice Rivers NP, Austl. 129/F3
Mitchell Bay, On, Can. 167/H7
Mitchell River NP, Austl. 133/C3
Mitchellville, Ar, US 153/J4
Mitchelstown, Ire. 32/B5
Mitha Tiwāna, Pak. 98/B3
Mithankot, Pak. 98/A5
Mithapukur, Bang. 97/G3
Mithi, Pak. 101/J4
Mithimna, Gre. 49/K3
Mitiaro (isl.), Cookls. 137/K6
Mitilíni, Gre. 49/K3
Mitla (ruin), Mex. 176/B2
Mito, Japan 85/G2
Mito, Japan 83/M6
Mitomi, Japan 83/B2
Mitra (peak), EqG. 120/B2
Mitre (peak), NZ 135/C3
Mitre (pen.), Arg. 191/D7
Mitre (peak), Tx, US 151/C2
Mitrofanovka, Rus. 73/K3
Mitry-Mory, Fr. 30/K5
Mitsamiouli, Com. 125/G5
Mitshibu, D.R. Congo 121/E4
Mitsinjo, Madg. 125/H7
Mits'iwa, Erit. 118/A2
Mitsue, Japan 83/K7
Mitsukaidō, Japan 85/F2
Mitsuke, Japan 85/F2
Mitta Mitta (riv.), Austl. 133/C3
Mittagong, Austl. 133/E2
Mittagspitze (peak), Aus. 61/F3
Mittainville, Fr. 30/G5
Mittelberg, Aus. 61/G3
Mittelland (canal), Ger. 53/F4
Mittelradde (riv.), Ger. 53/E3
Mittenwald, Ger. 61/H3
Mittersill, Aus. 45/K3
Mitterteich, Ger. 59/F3
Mitti, Gui. 114/B4
Mittlere-Isar (canal), Ger. 59/E6
Mittweida, Ger. 42/G3
Mitú, Col. 180/D4
Mituas, Col. 180/D4
Mitumba, Monts (mtns.), D.R. Congo 121/G3
Mituosi, China 87/G2
Mitwaba, D.R. Congo 121/F5
Mitwitz, Ger. 58/E2
Mityana, Ugan. 121/H2
Mitzic, Gabon 120/B2
Miura, Japan 83/D3
Miura (pen.), Japan 83/D3
Mivtaḥim, Isr. 105/A6
Miwa, Japan 83/L5
Miwa, Japan 83/H5
Mixco Viejo (ruin), Guat. 176/D3
Mixquiahuala, Mex. 175/K6
Mixteco (riv.), Mex. 176/B2
Miya (riv.), Japan 83/K7
Miyagawa, Japan 83/K7
Miyagi (pref.), Japan 82/B4
Miyake (isl.), Japan 85/F3
Miyako, Japan 82/B4
Miyako (isls.), Japan 85/H8
Miyako (isl.), Japan 85/H8
Miyakonojō, Japan 84/B5
Miyaly, Kaz. 71/K2
Miyama, Japan 83/L4
Miyama, Japan 83/J5
Miyanojō, Japan 84/B5
Miyashiro, Japan 83/D2
Miyazaki, Japan 84/B5
Miyazaki (pref.), Japan 84/B4
Miyazu (bay), Japan 83/H4
Miyazu, Japan 83/H4
Miyi, China 93/H2
Miyoshi, Japan 84/C3
Miyoshi, Japan 83/D3
Miyoshi, Japan 83/D2
Miyoshi, Japan 83/M5
Miyota, Japan 83/B1
Miyun (res.), China 80/H6
Miyun, China 80/H6
Mizdah, Libya 108/B2
Mizen (pt.), Ire. 34/B6
Mizhhir'ya, Ukr. 72/B3
Mizil, Rom. 51/H3
Miziya, Bul. 51/F4
Mizoch, Ukr. 72/D2
Mizoram (state), India 93/F3
Mizpah (cr.), Mt, US 156/B5
Mizpah, NJ, US 168/D5
Mizpe Ramon, Isr. 104/D4
Mizque, Bol. 188/C1
Mizuho, Japan 83/C2
Mizuho, Japan 83/H5
Mizunami, Japan 83/M5
Mizusawa, Japan 82/B4
Mjöån (riv.), Swe. 39/K7
Mjölby, Swe. 40/F2
Mjøndalen, Nor. 40/D2
Mjörn (lake), Swe. 40/E3
Mjøsa (lake), Nor. 38/D3
Mkalama, Tanz. 119/A3
Mkata, Tanz. 119/B3
Mkata (plain), Tanz. 119/B3
Mkoani, Tanz. 119/B3
Mkokotoni, Tanz. 119/B3
Mkomazi Game Rsv., Tanz. 119/B3
Mkombo (riv.), Tanz. 121/G4
Mkondoa (riv.), Tanz. 119/B3
Mkorn (peak), Mor. 110/D3
Mkumbi (pt.), Tanz. 119/B3
Mkushi, Zam. 123/F2
Mkushi (riv.), Zam. 123/F2
Mkuze (riv.), SAfr. 125/F2
Mkuze, SAfr. 125/F2
Mladá Boleslav, Czh. 59/H2
Mladá Vožice, Czh. 59/H3
Mladenovac, Yugo. 50/E3
Mlala (hills), Tanz. 121/G4
Mława, Pol. 43/L2
Mljet (isl.), Cro. 67/H2
Mljet NP, Cro. 50/C4
Mlolo, Zam. 123/G2
Mmabatho, SAfr. 124/D2
Mmadinare, Bots. 123/E4
Mmamabula, Bots. 123/E4
Mmathethe, Bots. 122/E5
Mnazini, Kenya 119/C2
Mnyera (riv.), Tanz. 119/A4
Mo Duc, Viet. 94/E3
Moa (riv.), SLeo. 114/C5
Moa, Tanz. 119/B3
Moa, Cuba 177/H1
Moa (isl.), Indo. 128/B2
Moab, Ut, US 149/H1
Moabi, Gabon 120/B3
Moala Group (isl.), Fiji 136/G6
Moama, Austl. 132/C1
Moamba, Moz. 125/F2
Moaña, Sp. 46/A1
Moanda, Gabon 120/C3
Moanda, D.R. Congo 120/B4
Moapa River Ind. Res., Nv, US 148/E2
Moate, Ire. 32/C3
Mobara, Japan 83/E3
Mobārakeh, Iran 103/G3
Mobaye, CAfr. 116/D4
Mobeetie, Tx, US 152/D3
Moberly, Mo, US 155/H4
Mobile, Al, US 164/D2
Mobile (bay), Al, US 164/D2
Mobile (pt.), Al, US 164/D2
Mobridge, SD, US 156/D5
Moc Chau, Viet. 86/E4
Moc Hoa, Viet. 94/D4
Moca (pass), Turk. 104/C1
Mocache, Ecu. 180/B5
Mocajuba, Braz. 182/D3
Moçambique, Moz. 123/J2
Mocanaqua, Pa, US 168/B1
Moccasin, Az, US 149/F2
Mocha (riv.), Rus. 69/W9
Mocha, Yem. 118/B2
Moche (ruin), Peru 184/B3
Mochima, PN, Ven. 181/E2
Mochizuki, Japan 83/A1
Mochudi, Bots. 122/E5
Mochumí, Peru 184/B2
Mociu, Rom. 51/G2
Möckeln (lake), Swe. 40/E3
Mockfjärd, Swe. 40/F1
Möckmühl, Ger. 58/C4
Mocksville, NC, US 163/G3
Moclín, Sp. 46/D4
Moclips, Wa, US 144/B4
Mocoa, Col. 180/B4
Mococa, Braz. 187/J6
Mocoretá, Arg. 188/E4
Mocorito, Mex. 174/D3
Moctezuma, Mex. 175/E4
Moctezuma, Mex. 174/C2
Mocuba, Moz. 123/H3
Modane, Fr. 64/C2
Modāsa, India 92/B3
Modbury, Eng, UK 36/C6
Modderrivier (riv.), SAfr. 124/D3
Model Village, Ire. 32/B6
Modena, It. 63/D4
Modena (prov.), It. 63/D4
Modena, Ut, US 149/F2
Moder (riv.), Fr. 45/G2
Modesto, Ca, US 148/B2
Modica, It. 48/D4
Modigliana, It. 63/E5
Modjamboli, D.R. Congo 121/E2
Modjeska, Ca, US 166/C3
Modjigo (reg.), Niger 116/B1
Mödling, Aus. 51/N7
Modoc, SC, US 163/F4
Modoc NWR, Ca, US 146/C3
Modot, Mong. 78/F2
Modriča, Bosn. 50/D3
Modugno, It. 48/E2
Moe, Austl. 133/C4
Moeb (bay), Namb. 124/A2
Moehau (hill), NZ 135/C2
Moel Fammau (peak), Wal, UK 35/E5
Moel Fferna (peak), Wal, UK 35/E6
Moel Hywel (peak), Wal, UK 36/C2
Moel Sych (peak), Wal, UK 35/E6
Moel-y-Llyn (peak), Wal, UK 36/C2
Moëlan-sur-Mer, Fr. 56/B5
Moelfre (peak), Wal, UK 36/C1
Moelv, Nor. 40/D1
Moen, Nor. 38/F1
Moen, Micr. 182/C1
Moengo, Sur. 182/C1
Moenkopi, Az, US 149/G2
Moenkopi Wash (riv.), Az, US 149/G2
Moerai (isl.), FrPol. 137/K7
Moerbeke, Belg. 54/C1
Moerdijk, Neth. 52/B5
Moerewa, NZ 135/C1
Moers, Ger. 52/D6
Moervaart (riv.), Belg. 54/C1
Moesa (riv.), Swi. 61/F5
Moffat, Sc, UK 33/C6
Moffat (peak), NZ 135/B4
Moffat, Co, US 149/K2
Moffett Field Nav. Air Sta., Ca, US 167/K12
Moffit, ND, US 156/D4
Moga, India 98/C4
Mogadishu (cap.), Som. 118/C5
Mogadouro, Port. 46/B2
Mogalo, D.R. Congo 120/D2
Mogami, Japan 82/B4
Mogami (riv.), Japan 82/B4
Mogapinyana, Bots. 123/E4
Mogaung, Myan. 86/C3
Mogent (riv.), Sp. 47/L6
Mogglingen, Ger. 58/C5
Moghul Gardens, India 98/C3
Mogi das Cruzes, Braz. 187/K8
Mogi-Guaçu (riv.), Braz. 187/K7
Mogi-Guaçu, Braz. 187/K7
Mogi-Mirim, Braz. 187/K7
Mogige, Eth. 117/H4
Mogil Mogil, Austl. 132/D1
Mogilno, Pol. 43/J2
Mogincual, Moz. 123/J2
Moglia, It. 63/D4
Mogliano, It. 65/C1
Mogliano Veneto, It. 63/F2
Möglingen, Ger. 58/C5
Mogna, Arg. 188/B4
Mogocha, Rus. 79/H1
Mogogh, Sudan 117/F3
Mogok, Myan. 86/C4
Mogollon, NM, US 149/H4
Mogollon (mts.), NM, US 149/H4
Mogollon (rim), Az, US 149/G3
Mogollon (plat.), Az, US 149/G3
Mogolrivier (riv.), SAfr. 123/E4
Mogoro, It. 48/A3
Mogotes (pt.), Arg. 190/F3
Mogotio, Kenya 119/A2
Mogotón (peak), Nic. 176/E3
Mogoytuy, Rus. 78/G1
Moguer, Sp. 46/B4
Mogzon, Rus. 78/G1
Mohács, Hun. 50/D3
Mohaeli (isl.), Com. 125/G6
Mohales Hoek, Les. 124/D3
Mohall, ND, US 156/D3
Mohamed V (dam), Mor. 112/C2
Mohamed V (Casablanca) (int'l arpt.), Mor. 110/D2
Moḩammadābād, Iran 103/J3
Mohammadia, Alg. 112/F5
Mohammadia-Znata (prov.), Mor. 112/A2
Mohammedia, Mor. 112/A3
Mohanganj, Bang. 97/H3
Mohaniā, India 96/D3
Mohave (lake), Nv, US 148/E3
Mohawk, Mi, US 157/K4
Mohawk (riv.), NY, US 161/J3
Mohawk (lake), NJ, US 168/D1
Moheda, Swe. 40/F3
Mohembo, Bots. 122/D3
Mohican (cape), Ak, US 171/E3
Mohill, Ire. 32/C2
Mohindargarh, India 98/D5
Möhlin, Swi. 60/D2
Möhne (riv.), Ger. 53/F6
Möhnestausee (lake), Ger. 53/F5
Mohnton, Pa, US 168/C3
Mohnyin, Myan. 93/G3
Moho, Peru 184/D4
Mohoro, Tanz. 119/B4
Mohrsville, Pa, US 168/C3
Mohyliv-Podil's'kyy, Ukr. 72/D3
Moi, Nor. 40/B2
Moi (int'l arpt.), Kenya 119/B3
Moiano, It. 65/D5
Moie, It. 63/G6
Moincêr, China 99/D5
Moineşti, Rom. 72/D4
Moinkum (des.), Kaz. 74/H5
Moinsi (hills), Gha. 115/E5
Moira (riv.), On, Can. 161/H2
Moirans, Fr. 64/B2
Moirans-en-Montagne, Fr. 60/B5
Mõisaküla, Est. 41/L2
Moisant Field (New Orleans) (int'l arpt.), La, US 164/C3
Moisdon-la-Rivière, Fr. 56/D5
Moisie (riv.), Qu, Can. 141/K3
Moislains, Fr. 54/B4
Moissac, Fr. 44/D4
Moïssala, Chad 116/C3
Moisselles, Fr. 30/K4
Moisson, Fr. 30/G4
Mota, Port. 47/Q10
Moitaco, Ven. 181/E3
Mojā (isl.), Swe. 39/B1
Möja, Swe. 39/B1
Mojácar, Sp. 46/E4
Mojave (des.), Ca, US 142/C5
Mojave, Ca, US 148/C3
Mojave (riv.), Ca, US 148/D3
Mojiang Hanizu Zizhixian, China 86/D4
Mojkovac, Yugo. 50/D4
Mojo, Eth. 118/A3
Mojo, Bol. 188/C2
Mojocoya, Bol. 188/C1
Mojokerto, Indo. 89/F4
Mojos, Bol. 184/D4
Mojos, Llanos de (plain), Bol. 185/E4
Moju (riv.), Braz. 182/D3
Moju, Braz. 182/D3
Mōka, Japan 85/F2
Mokameh, India 97/E3
Mokampur, India 98/B5
Mokelumne (aqueduct), Ca, US 167/M11
Mokelumne (riv.), Ca, US 146/C4
Mokena, Il, US 167/Q16
Mokhotlong, Les. 124/E3
Mokhovoye, Rus. 70/F1
Mokil (isl.), Micr. 136/E4
Mokochu (peak), Thai. 94/B3
Mokokchūng, India 86/B3
Mokolo, Camr. 116/B3
Mokolo, D.R. Congo 120/D2
Mokp'o, SKor. 81/D5
Mokrin, Yugo. 50/E3
Moksha (riv.), Rus. 71/G1
Mokumbusu, D.R. Congo 121/E2
Mokwa, Nga. 115/G4
Mol, Yugo. 50/E3
Mol, Belg. 52/C6
Mola di Bari, It. 49/E2
Molalla, Or, US 146/B1
Moláoi, Gre. 49/H4
Molard Noir (peak), Fr. 64/B1
Molare, It. 62/B4
Molas, Punta (pt.), Mex. 176/E1
Molat (isl.), Cro. 50/B3
Molatón (peak), Sp. 46/E3
Molbergen, Ger. 53/E3
Mold, Wal, UK 35/E5
Moldava (reg.), Rom. 51/H2
Moldavian Carpathian (range), Rom. 51/G2
Molde, Nor. 38/C3
Moldova (riv.), Rom. 51/G2
Moldova (ctry.) 29/G4
Moldova Nouă, Rom. 50/E3
Moldoveanu (peak), Rom. 51/G3
Mole (riv.), Fr. 64/C6
Mole (riv.), Eng, UK 30/B3
Mole, D.R. Congo 121/G3
Mole (riv.), Eng, UK 36/C5
Mole Lake Ind. Res., Wi, US 160/B2
Mole NP, Gha. 115/E4
Môle Saint-Nicolas, Haiti 177/H2
Molegbe, D.R. Congo 116/D4
Molena, Ga, US 162/E4
Molepolole, Bots. 122/E5
Molėtai, Lith. 41/L4
Molfetta, It. 48/E2
Molibagu, Indo. 91/F3
Molina, Sp. 46/E2
Molina, Chile 190/C2
Molina de Segura, Sp. 46/E3
Moline, Ks, US 153/F2
Moline, Il, US 155/J3
Molinella, It. 63/E4
Molines-en-Queyras, Fr. 64/C3
Molinfaing, Belg. 55/E4
Molinicos, Sp. 46/D3
Molino, Fl, US 164/E2
Molino de Flores, PN, Mex. 175/R9
Molins de Rei, Sp. 47/L7
Moliro, D.R. Congo 121/G5
Molise (reg.), It. 67/G2
Molkom, Swe. 40/E2
Möll (riv.), Aus. 45/K3
Mollakänd, Azer. 103/G1
Mölle, Swe. 39/J6
Møllebjerg (peak), Den. 38/D5
Mollendo, Peru 184/C5
Mollerussa, Sp. 47/F2
Molles (pt.), Chile 190/C2
Molles, Uru. 191/K10
Mollet del Vallès, Sp. 47/L6
Mollis, Swi. 61/F3
Mölnbo, Swe. 39/A1
Mölndal, Swe. 40/E3
Mölnlycke, Swe. 40/E3
Molo, Kenya 119/A2
Molo, Myan. 86/C4
Molochans'k, Ukr. 73/H4
Molochnoye (lake), Ukr. 73/H4
Molócue (riv.), Moz. 123/H3
Molodezhnaya, Rus., Ant. 192/D
Molodohvardiys'k, Ukr. 73/K3
Mologa (riv.), Rus. 68/G4
Molokai (isl.), Hi, US 142/T10
Molokovo, Rus. 68/H4
Moloma (riv.), Rus. 69/L4
Molong, Austl. 133/D1
Molopo (riv.), Bots. 107/E7
Moloporivier (riv.), SAfr. 122/D5
Mólos, Gre. 49/H3
Moloundou, Camr. 120/C2
Molsheim, Fr. 60/D1
Molteno, SAfr. 124/D3
Molu (isl.), Indo. 91/H5
Molucca (sea), Asia 77/M10
Molucca (isls.), Indo. 77/M10
Moluccas (arch.), Indo. 91/G3
Molveno, It. 61/G5
Molveno (lake), It. 61/G5
Moma, D.R. Congo 121/E3
Moma, Moz. 123/H3
Mombaça, Braz. 183/G4
Mombongo Li, D.R. Congo 121/F2
Mombasa, Kenya 119/B3
Mombetsu, Japan 82/C1
Mombetsu, Japan 82/C2
Mombo, Tanz. 119/B3
Momboyo (riv.), D.R. Congo 120/D3
Mömbris, Ger. 58/C2
Momchilgrad, Bul. 51/G5
Momence, Il, US 160/C4
Momfafa (cape), Indo. 91/H4
Momignies, Belg. 55/D3
Mömlingen, Ger. 58/C3
Mommilanjärvi (lake), Fin. 39/E4
Momo, It. 62/B2
Momoishi, Japan 82/C3
Mompós, Col. 180/C2
Mompoto, D.R. Congo 120/D3
Møn (isl.), Den. 38/E5
Mon, Myan. 94/B2
Mon (state), Myan. 93/G4
Mon (riv.), Myan. 93/F3
Mon (state), Viet. 86/C5
Mona (passg.), NAm. 139/L8
Mona (isl.), PR 173/M8
Mona Quimbundo, Ang. 120/D5
Mona Vale (nbrhd.), Austl. 134/H8
Monaco (cap.), Mona. 62/J8
Monaco (ctry.) 29/E4
Monaco, Port of (har.), Mona. 62/J8
Monadhliath (mts.), Sc, UK 33/B2
Monaepa (pt.), Moz. 123/H3
Monagas (state), Ven. 181/F2
Monaghan (co.), Ire. 34/A3
Monaghan, Ire. 32/D1
Monagrillo, Pan. 180/A3
Monagrillo (ruin), Pan. 180/A2
Monahans, Tx, US 151/C2
Monango, ND, US 156/E4
Monapo, Moz. 123/J2
Monar (lake), Sc, UK 33/A2
Monaragala, SrL. 95/D5
Monarch, Mt, US 145/J4
Monashee (mts.), BC, Can. 144/E2
Monasterevin, Ire. 32/C3
Monatélé, Camr. 120/B1
Moncada, Sp. 47/E3
Moncalvo, It. 62/B3
Monção, Braz. 183/E3
Moncayo (range), Sp. 46/E2
Mönch (peak), Swi. 60/D4
Mönchegorsk, Rus. 68/G2
Mönchengladbach, Ger. 52/D6
Monchique (mts.), Port. 46/A4
Monchique, Port. 46/A4
Moncks Corner, SC, US 163/G4
Monclova, Mex. 174/E3
Moncontour, Fr. 56/C4
Moncton, NB, Can. 158/E2
Mondego (riv.), Port. 46/A2
Mondego (cape), Port. 46/A2
Mondéjar, Sp. 46/D2
Mondeville, Fr. 57/E2
Mondimbi, D.R. Congo 121/E2
Mondo, Chad 116/B2
Mondo, Tanz. 119/A3
Mondolfo, It. 63/G6
Mondoñedo, Sp. 46/B1
Mondorf-les-Bains, Lux. 55/F4
Mondovi, It. 62/A4
Mondovi, Wi, US 155/J1
Mondragon, Fr. 64/A4
Mondragón, Sp. 44/B5
Mondragone, It. 65/C5
Mondsee (lake), Aus. 59/G7
Mondsee, Aus. 59/G7
Mondy, Rus. 78/E1
Moneglia, It. 62/C5
Monemvasia, Gre. 49/H4
Monero, NM, US 149/J2
Mones Cazón, Arg. 190/E3
Monesterio, Sp. 46/B3
Moneta, Wy, US 147/K2
Monett, Mo, US 153/H2
Monette, Ar, US 153/J3
Money (pt.), Sc, UK 34/C2
Moneygall, Ire. 32/C4
Moneymore, NI, UK 34/B2
Moneyreagh, NI, UK 34/C2
Monferrato (reg.), It. 45/H4
Monforte, Port. 46/B3
Monforte, Sp. 46/B1
Mong Cai, Viet. 87/E4
Möng Hang, Myan. 94/B1
Möng Hpāyak, Myan. 94/B1
Möng Hsat, Myan. 94/B1
Möng Hsu, Myan. 86/C4
Möng Küng, Myan. 86/C4
Möng Long, Myan. 94/B1
Möng Maü, Myan. 94/B2
Möng Nai, Myan. 86/C4
Möng Pan, Myan. 94/B1
Möng Pawn, Myan. 86/C4
Möng Ping, Myan. 94/B1
Möng Tōn, Myan. 94/B1
Möng Tūm, Myan. 94/B1
Möng Yai, Myan. 86/C4
Möng Yang, Myan. 86/C4
Möng Yawng, Myan. 86/D4
Möng Yu, Myan. 86/C4
Monga, Tanz. 119/B4
Monga, D.R. Congo 116/D4
Mongaguá, Braz. 187/K9
Mongala (riv.), D.R. Congo 121/E2
Mongalla, Sudan 117/F4
Mongandjo, D.R. Congo 121/F2
Mongar, Bhu. 97/H2
Mongaup (mtn.), NY, US 161/J3
Mongers (lake), Austl. 130/C4
Monggümp'o, NKor. 81/C3
Monghidoro, It. 63/E5
Mongioia (peak), It. 64/C3
Mongo, Chad 116/C2
Mongo (riv.), Gui. 114/C4
Mongolia (ctry.) 77/J5
Mongomo, EqG. 120/B2
Mongororo, Chad 116/D2
Mongoumba, CAfr. 120/D2
Mongoungou, Gabon 120/B3
Mongu, Zam. 122/D2
Möngüel, Mrta. 114/B2
Mönh Hayrhan (peak), Mong. 78/C2
Mönh Sarĭdag (peak), Mong. 78/E1
Monhegan (isl.), Me, US 158/C4
Monheim, Ger. 55/F1
Monheim, Ger. 58/D5
Moni, Cyp. 104/C2
Moni, China 86/E3
Moniaive, Sc, UK 34/E1
Monico, Wi, US 157/K5
Monieltu, D.R. Congo 121/E2
Monifieth, Sc, UK 33/D4
Moniquirá, Col. 180/C3
Monistrol de Montserrat, Sp. 47/K6
Monistrol-sur-Loire, Fr. 44/F4
Monitor (range), Nv, US 146/E4
Monitor, Wa, US 144/D4
Monivea, Ire. 32/B3
Monkayo, Phil. 88/D4
Monkey (pt.), Nic. 177/F4
Monkey (mtn.), Austl. 133/D1
Monkey Bay, Malw. 123/G2
Monkey Jungle, Fl, US 164/P11
Monkey Mia, Austl. 130/B3
Monkey River Town, Belz. 176/D2
Mońki, Pol. 43/M2
Monkoto, D.R. Congo 121/E3
Monks (isl.), Md, US 168/B5
Monkton, Vt, US 161/K2
Monmouth, Il, US 155/J3
Monmouth, Or, US 146/B1
Monmouth Beach, NJ, US 168/E3
Monmouth Junction, NJ, US 168/D3
Monmouth Mil. Res., NJ, US 168/D3
Monmouthshire (co.), Wal, UK 36/D3
Monmow (riv.), Eng, UK 36/C2
Monnaie, Fr. 57/F5
Monnickendam, Neth. 52/C4
Monninkylä, Fin. 39/F4
Mono (cr.), Ca, US 166/A1
Mono (riv.), Togo 115/F5
Mono (prov.), Ben. 115/F5
Mono (lake), Ca, US 146/D4
Mono Road, On, Can. 160/T8
Monocacy (riv.), Md, US 168/A4
Monocacy Nat'l Bfld., Md, US 161/H5
Monon, In, US 160/C4
Monona, Ia, US 155/J2
Monongah, WV, US 160/F5
Monongahela (riv.), WV, US 160/G5
Monopoli, It. 49/E2
Monor, Hun. 50/D2
Monóvar, Sp. 47/E3
Monreal del Campo, Sp. 46/E2
Monreale, It. 48/C3
Monroe, La, US 153/H4
Monroe, In, US 160/D4
Monroe, Mi, US 160/E4
Monroe, Wa, US 167/C2
Monroe (peak), Ut, US 149/F1
Monroe, Ut, US 149/F1
Monroe, Ia, US 155/H3
Monroe, Ga, US 162/F4
Monroe, Wi, US 155/K2
Monroe, Ct, US 169/E1
Monroe, NY, US 168/D1
Monroe, NC, US 163/G3
Monroe (lake), In, US 162/D1
Monroe City, Mo, US 155/J4
Monroe City, In, US 162/D1
Monroe Mil. Res., Va, US 163/J2
Monroeville, In, US 160/D4
Monroeville, Al, US 164/E2
Monroeville, Pa, US 161/G4
Monroeville, NJ, US 168/C4
Monrovia (cap.), Libr. 114/C5
Monrovia, Ca, US 166/G7
Monrovia (Roberts) (int'l arpt.), Libr. 114/C5
Mons, Belg. 54/C3
Monsanto, Port. 46/B2
Monschau, Ger. 55/F2
Monse, Indo. 91/F4
Monsefú, Peru 184/B2
Monsenhor Hipólito, Braz. 183/F4
Monsenhor Tabosa, Braz. 183/F4
Monsey, NY, US 169/J7
Monsheim, Ger. 58/B3
Monster, Neth. 52/B4
Mönsteras, Swe. 40/G3
Monsummano Terme, It. 63/D6
Mont Belvieu, Tx, US 151/N9
Mont Fouri, Rsv. Du, Gabon,Congo 120/B3
Mont Nebo, Sk, Can. 145/L1
Mont Peko, PN du, C.d'Iv. 114/D5
Mont Sangbé, PN du, C.d'Iv. 114/D4
Mont Ventoux (range), Fr. 64/B4
Mont-Carmel, Qu, Can. 158/C2
Mont-de-Marsan, Fr. 44/C5
Mont-Joli, Qu, Can. 158/C1
Mont-Laurier, Qu, Can. 161/J1
Mont-Près-Chambord, Fr. 57/G5
Mont-Royal, Qu, Can. 159/N6
Mont-Saint-Aignan, Fr. 57/G2
Mont-Saint-Martin, Fr. 55/E4
Mont-Saint-Michel, Qu, Can. 161/J1
Mont-Sous-Vaudrey, Fr. 60/B4
Montà, It. 62/A3
Monta Fon (mts.), Aus. 61/F3
Montabaur, Ger. 55/G3
Montagnana, It. 63/E3
Montagne d'Ambre NP, Madg. 125/J6
Montagny-Sainte-Félicité, Fr. 30/L4
Montague (sound), Austl. 128/B3
Montague, PE, Can. 159/F2
Montague (isl.), Mex. 148/E5
Montagu, SAfr. 124/M10
Montague, Yk,Can. 171/L3
Montague (isl.), Ak, US 171/J4
Montague (str.), Ak, US 171/J4
Montague, Ca, US 146/B3
Montague, Ma, US 161/K3
Montague, Mi, US 160/C3
Montague, NJ, US 168/D1
Montague, Tx, US 153/F4
Montaigu, Fr. 44/C3
Montaione, It. 63/D6
Montalba, Tx, US 150/G2
Montalbán, Sp. 47/E2
Montalbano Jonico, It. 48/E2
Montale, It. 63/E6
Montale, It. 63/D4
Montalieu-Vercieu, Fr. 60/B6
Montalvão, Port. 46/B3
Montalvo, Ca, US 166/A2
Montana, Swi. 60/D5
Montana (prov.), Bul. 49/H1
Montana (prov.), Slov. 51/F4
Montana, Bul. 51/F4
Montana (state), US 142/D2
Montanaro, It. 62/A2
Montanha, Braz. 187/M5
Montara, Ca, US 167/J11
Montargis, Fr. 44/E2
Montataire, Fr. 54/B5
Montauban, Fr. 56/C4
Montauban, Fr. 44/D4
Montauk, NY, US 169/G1
Montauk (pt.), NY, US 169/G1
Montauroux, Fr. 64/C5
Montbard, Fr. 44/F3
Montbazon, Fr. 57/F6
Montbéliard, Fr. 60/C2
Montblanc, Sp. 47/F2
Montcada i Reixac, Sp. 47/L7
Montcalm, WV, US 163/G2
Montceau-les-Mines, Fr. 44/F3
Montclair, Ca, US 166/C2
Montclair, NJ, US 169/J8
Montcornet, Fr. 54/D4
Montdidier, Fr. 54/B4
Monte Albán (ruin), Mex. 176/B2
Monte Alegre, Braz. 183/H4
Monte Alegre, Braz. 182/C3
Monte Alegre de Goiás, Braz. 186/D2
Monte Alegre de Minas, Braz. 186/C3
Monte Alegre do Piauí, Braz. 183/E5
Monte Alto, Braz. 189/G2
Monte Alto, Tx, US 151/F4
Monte Azul, Braz. 187/E2
Monte Belo, Ang. 122/B2
Monte Carmelo, Ven. 180/D2
Monte Carmelo, Braz. 186/D3
Monte Caseros, Arg. 188/E4
Monte Comán, Arg. 190/D2
Monte Cristo, Bol. 185/F4
Monte di Procida, It. 65/D6
Monte Dourado, Braz. 182/C3
Monte Escobedo, Mex. 174/E4
Monte Etna (Mount Etna) (vol.), It. 48/D4
Monte León, Arg. 191/C6
Monte Maíz, Arg. 190/E2
Monte Pascoal, PN de, Braz. 187/F3
Monte Patria, Chile 188/B4
Monte Porzio Catone, It. 65/B4
Monte Quemado, Arg. 188/D3
Monte Rosa (mts.), It. 60/D6
Monte San Biagio, It. 65/C5
Monte San Giusto, It. 65/C1
Monte San Savino, It. 63/E7
Monte Sant'angelo, It. 48/D2
Monte Urano, It. 65/C1
Monte Verde, Bol. 184/D3
Monte Vista, Co, US 149/J2
Monte Vista Nat'l Wild. Ref., Co, US 149/J2
Monte-Carlo, Mona. 62/J8
Monteagudo, Bol. 188/D1
Montealegre, Sp. 46/E3
Montebello, Ca, US 166/F7
Montebello, Col. 183/K7
Montebello (isls.), Austl. 127/A3
Montebello Vincentino, It. 63/E3
Montebelluna, It. 63/F2
Montebourg, Fr. 56/D2
Montebruno, It. 62/C4
Montecarlo, Arg. 189/F3
Montecassiano, It. 63/G7
Montecatini Terme, It. 63/D6
Montecavolo, It. 62/D4
Montecchio, It. 63/F6
Montecchio Magiore, It. 63/E2
Montecelio, It. 65/B3
Montechiaro d'Asti, It. 62/B3
Montecilfone, It. 65/D4
Montecito, Ca, US 166/A2
Montecompatri, It. 65/B4
Montecorvino Rovella, It. 65/D6
Montecristo (isl.), It. 48/B1
Montecristo, PN, ESal. 176/D3
Montefalcione, It. 65/D6
Montefalco, It. 65/B2
Montefalcone di Val Fortore, It. 65/E5
Montefalcone nel Sannio, It. 65/D4
Montefeltro (reg.), It. 63/F5
Montefiascone, It. 65/B2
Monteforte D'Alpone, It. 63/E3
Monteforte Irpino, It. 65/D6
Montefrío, Sp. 46/C4
Montegiorgio, It. 65/C1
Montego Bay, Jam. 177/G2
Montegranaro, It. 65/C1
Montegrotto Terme, It. 63/E3
Montehermoso, Sp. 46/B2
Monteiro, Braz. 183/G4
Montejinni, Austl. 128/C4
Montelavar, Port. 47/P10
Montelibretti, It. 65/B3
Montélimar, Fr. 64/A3
Montelindo (riv.), Par. 186/A4
Montell, Tx, US 151/D3
Montellano, Sp. 46/C4
Montello, Nv, US 147/F3
Montello, Wi, US 155/K2
Montelupo Fiorentino, It. 63/E6
Montemagno, It. 62/B4
Montemarciano, It. 63/G6
Montemiletto, It. 65/D5
Montemor-o-Novo, Port. 46/A3
Montemor-o-Velho, Port. 46/A2
Montemorelos, Mex. 175/F3
Montemuro (peak), Port. 46/A2
Montenay, Fr. 57/E4
Montendre, Fr. 44/C4
Montenegro (reg.), Yugo. 67/H2
Montenegro, Chile 190/N8
Montenegro, Col. 183/K8
Montenegro, Braz. 189/G4
Montenero di Bisaccia, It. 65/D4
Montepuez (riv.), Moz. 123/H2
Montepuez, Moz. 123/H2
Montepulciano, It. 48/B1
Montereau-sur-le-Jard, Fr. 30/L6
Monterey, La, US 164/C2
Monterey (bay), Ca, US 142/B4
Monterey, Tn, US 162/E2
Monterey, Va, US 163/H1
Monterey Park, Ca, US 166/F7
Monteria, Col. 180/C2
Montero, Bol. 188/D1
Monteroduni, It. 65/D4
Monteros, Arg. 188/C3
Monterosso (peak), It. 61/G4
Monterosso al Mare, It. 62/C5
Monterotondo, It. 65/B3
Monterrey, Sp. 46/B2
Monterrey, Mex. 175/E3
Montes (pt.), Arg. 191/C6
Montes Altos, Braz. 183/E4
Montes Claros, Braz. 186/E3
Montesano, Wa, US 144/C4
Montesarchio, It. 65/D5
Montescaglioso, It. 48/E2
Montese, It. 63/D5
Montesilvano Marina, It. 65/D2
Montespertoli, It. 63/E6
Montesson, Fr. 30/J5
Monteux, Fr. 64/A4
Montevallo, Al, US 162/D4
Montevarchi, It. 63/E6
Montevideo, Mn, US 155/G1
Montevideo (dept.), Uru. 191/K11
Montevideo (cap.), Uru. 191/K11
Montevideo, Id, US 147/G2
Montévrain, Fr. 30/L5
Montezuma, Ks, US 152/D2
Montezuma, In, US 160/C5
Montezuma (slough), Ca, US 167/K10
Montezuma, Ia, US 155/H3
Montezuma (cr.), Ut, US 149/H2
Montezuma, Ga, US 162/E4
Montezuma Castle Nat'l Mon., Az, US 149/G3
Montezuma Creek, Ut, US 149/H2
Montfermeil, Fr. 30/K5
Montferrand-le-Château, Fr. 60/B3
Montferrat, Fr. 64/C5
Montfoort, Neth. 52/B4
Montfort, Fr. 56/D4
Montfort (ruin), Isr. 105/C2
Montfort-L'Amaury, Fr. 54/A6
Montfort-sur-Risle, Fr. 57/F2
Montfrin, Fr. 64/A5
Montgenèvre, Fr. 64/C3
Montgeron, Fr. 30/K5
Montgomery, Ga, US 165/H2
Montgomery, La, US 164/B2
Montgomery, Il, US 167/P16
Montgomery, WV, US 163/G1
Montgomery (cap.), Al, US 162/D4
Montgomery, Wal, UK 36/C1
Montgomery, Tx, US 151/G2
Montgomery, Pa, US 168/B1
Montgomery (co.), Md, US 168/A5
Montgomery City, Mo, US 155/J4
Montgomery Village, Md, US 168/A5
Montgomeryville, Pa, US 168/C3
Montgrand (peak), Fr. 44/E5
Monthermé, Fr. 55/D4
Monthey, Swi. 60/C5
Monthureux-sur-Saône, Fr. 60/B1
Monthyon, Fr. 30/L4
Monticelli d'Ongina, It. 62/D3
Monticelli Terme, It. 62/D4
Monticello, Ar, US 153/J4
Monticello, La, US 153/J4
Monticello, In, US 160/C4
Monticello, Ms, US 164/C2
Monticello, Fl, US 165/G2
Monticello, NY, US 161/J4
Monticello (dam), Ca, US 146/B4
Monticello, Ut, US 149/H2
Monticello, Ia, US 155/J2
Monticello, Ky, US 162/E2
Monticello, Ga, US 162/F4
Monticello, Mo, US 155/J3
Monticello, NM, US 149/J4
Monticello, Va, US 163/H2
Monticello Conte Otto, It. 63/E2
Montichiari, It. 62/D3
Montier-en-Der, Fr. 60/A1
Montignies-le-Tilleul, Belg. 55/D3
Montigny-en-Gohelle, Fr. 54/B3
Montigny-le-Bretonneux, Fr. 30/J5
Montigny-le-Roi, Fr. 60/B2
Montigny-les-Metz, Fr. 55/F5
Montijo, Sp. 46/B3
Montijo, Port. 47/Q10
Montilla, Sp. 46/C4
Montivilliers, Fr. 57/F1
Montlebon, Fr. 60/C3
Montlhéry, Fr. 30/J6
Montluçon, Fr. 44/E3
Montluel, Fr. 60/B6
Montmagny, Qu, Can. 158/B2
Montmartre, Sk, Can. 156/C2
Montmédy, Fr. 55/E4
Montmélian, Fr. 64/C1
Montmerle-sur-Saône, Fr. 60/A5
Montmeyran, Fr. 64/A3
Montmirail, Fr. 54/C6
Montmorency, Fr. 30/J5
Montmorillon, Fr. 44/D3
Montmorot, Fr. 60/B4
Monto, Austl. 134/C4
Montodine, It. 62/C3
Montoir-de-Bretagne, Fr. 56/C6
Montoire-sur-le-Loir, Fr. 57/F5
Montois-la-Montagne, Fr. 55/F5
Montone (riv.), It. 63/E4
Montopoli, It. 63/D6
Montorio al Vomano, It. 65/C2
Montorio Veronese, It. 63/E3
Montoro, Sp. 46/C3
Montour (ridge), Pa, US 168/B2
Montour, Pa, US 168/B1
Montour Falls, NY, US 161/H3
Montoursville, Pa, US 168/B1
Montpelier, ND, US 156/E4
Montpelier, Oh, US 160/D4
Montpelier, In, US 160/D4
Montpelier (cap.), Vt, US 161/K2
Montpelier, Id, US 147/H2
Montpelier, Ms, US 162/C4
Montpellier, Qu, Can. 161/J2
Montpellier, Fr. 44/E5
Montréal, Qu, Can. 159/N6
Montréal-Est, Qu, Can. 159/N6
Montréal-la-Cluse, Fr. 60/B5
Montréal-Nord, Qu, Can. 159/N6
Montréjeau, Fr. 44/D5
Montrésor, Fr. 57/G6
Montreuil, Fr. 54/A3
Montreuil, Fr. 30/K5
Montreuil-Bellay, Fr. 44/C3
Montreuil-sur-Epte, Fr. 30/G4
Montreux, Swi. 60/C5
Montreux-Château, Fr. 60/C2
Montrevault, Fr. 57/D6
Montrevel-en-Bresse, Fr. 60/B5
Montrichard, Fr. 57/G6
Montricher, Swi. 60/C5
Montrose (lake), Mo, US 153/G1
Montrose, Ar, US 153/J4
Montrose (basin), Sc, UK 33/D3
Montrose, Sc, UK 33/D3
Montrose, Mi, US 160/E3
Montrose, Pa, US 161/J4
Montrose, Co, US 149/J1
Montrose, Mn, US 157/N6
Montrose, Va, US 163/J1
Montrouge, Fr. 30/J5
Montry, Fr. 30/L5
Monts, Fr. 57/F6
Montseny, PN, Sp. 47/L6
Montserrado (co.), Libr. 114/C5
Montserrat (peak), Sp. 66/D2
Montserrat (dpcy.), UK 139/M8
Montserrat (isl.), Monts., UK 173/M8
Montsinéry, FrG. 182/C1
Montsoult, Fr. 30/J4
Montsûrs, Fr. 57/E4
Montuiri, Sp. 47/G3
Monturaqui, Chile 188/B3
Montvale, NJ, US 169/J7
Montverde, Fl, US 164/M6
Montville, NJ, US 169/H8
Monument, Co, US 152/B1
Monument, Or, US 146/D1
Monument (valley), Ut, US 149/G2
Monument Draw (riv.), Tx, US 151/C1
Monument Rocks, Ks, US 152/D1
Monument Valley Navajo Tribal Park, Ut, US 149/G2
Monveda, D.R. Congo 121/E2
Monywa, Myan. 86/B4
Monza, It. 62/C2
Monze, Zam. 123/E3
Monzingen, Ger. 55/G4
Monzón, Sp. 47/F2
Monzón, Peru 184/B3
Moody, Mo, US 153/J2
Moody, Tx, US 151/F2
Moodys, Ok, US 153/G2
Mooirivier, SAfr. 125/E3
Mook, Neth. 52/C5
Mookane, Bots. 123/E4
Mool (riv.), SAfr. 124/P13
Mooloo Downs, Austl. 130/C3
Moomaw (lake), WV, US 163/G2
Mooncoin, Ire. 32/C5
Mooney Mooney, Austl. 133/E1
Moonie, Austl. 134/C4
Moonta, Austl. 131/H5
Moora, Austl. 130/C4
Moorabbin (nbrhd.), Austl. 132/G5
Moorcroft, Wy, US 154/B1
Moordrecht, Neth. 52/B5
Moore, Ok, US 153/F3
Moore, Id, US 147/G2
Moore, Ut, US 149/G1
Moore, Mt, US 145/K4
Moore (lake), Austl. 127/A2
Moore Haven, Fl, US 165/H4
Moore River NP, Austl. 130/B4
Moorea (isl.), FrPol. 137/K6
Moorefield, WV, US 163/H1
Mooreland, Ok, US 152/E2
Moorenweis, Ger. 61/H1
Moores Creek Nat'l Bfld., NC, US 163/H3
Moorestown, NJ, US 168/D3
Mooresville, In, US 160/C5
Mooresville, NC, US 163/G3
Mooreton, ND, US 156/F4
Mooretown, On, Can. 167/H6
Moorfoot (hills), Sc, UK 33/C5
Moorhead, Mn, US 156/F4
Mooring, Tx, US 150/F2
Mooringsport, La, US 150/H1
Moorook, Austl. 132/B2
Mooroopna, Austl. 133/B3
Moorpark, Ca, US 166/B2
Moorreesburg, SAfr. 124/L10
Moorslede, Belg. 54/C2
Moosburg, Ger. 59/E6
Moose (mtn.), Mn, US 157/J4
Moose (isl.), Mb, Can. 156/F2
Moose (riv.), Me, US 158/B3
Moose Creek, Ak, US 171/J3
Moose Heights, BC, Can. 144/C1
Moose Jaw, Sk, Can. 145/M2
Moose (mtn.), Sk, Can. 156/C3
Moose Pass, Ak, US 171/J3
Moose Range, Sk, Can. 145/N1
Moosehead (lake), Me, US 143/N2
Mooseheart (mt.), Ak, US 171/H3
Mooseheart, Il, US 167/P16
Moosehorn, Mb, Can. 156/E2
Moosehorn NWR, Me, US 158/D3
Moosinning, Ger. 59/E6
Moosomin, Sk, Can. 156/D2
Moosonee, On, Can. 141/H3
Moosseedorf, Swi. 60/D3
Moosthenning, Ger. 59/F5
Mopeia, Moz. 123/G3
Mopipi, Bots. 122/E4
Mopti, Mali 114/D3
Mopti (pol. reg.), Mali 114/E3
Moqor, Afg. 101/J2
Moquegua, Peru 184/D5
Moquegua (dept.), Peru 184/D5
Moquehuá, Arg. 191/J11
Mor (riv.), India 97/F4
Mór, Hun. 50/D2
Mora, NM, US 152/B3
Mora, Mn, US 157/H5
Mora (riv.), NM, US 152/B3
Mora, Swe. 40/F1
Mora, Camr. 116/B3
Mora, La, US 164/B2
Mora, Sp. 46/D3
Mora, Port. 46/A3
Mora de Rubielos, Sp. 47/E2
Morača (riv.), Yugo. 49/F1
Morada Nova, Braz. 183/G4
Morādābād, India 96/B1
Morada Nova, Braz. 183/G4
Moraes, PN, Chile 190/P8
Morafenobe, Madg. 125/H7
Morág, Pol. 41/H5
Moraga, Ca, US 167/K11
Mórahalom, Hun. 50/D2
Morainvilliers, Fr. 30/H5
Moral de Calatrava, Sp. 46/D3
Moraleda, Canal de (chan.), Chile 190/B5
Moraleja, Sp. 46/B2
Morales, Guat. 176/D3
Moramanga, Madg. 125/J7
Moran, Ks, US 153/G2
Moran, Wy, US 147/H2
Moran, Tx, US 151/E1
Moranbah, Austl. 134/C3
Morangis, Fr. 30/K5
Morannes, Fr. 57/E5
Morano Calabro, It. 48/E3
Morant Bay, Jam. 177/G2
Morar (lake), Sc, UK 31/R8
Morarano Chrome, Madg. 125/J7
Morat (lake), Swi. 60/D4
Morata de Tajuña, Sp. 47/N9
Moratalla, Sp. 46/E3
Moratuwa, SrL. 95/C5
Morava (riv.), Yugo. 49/G1
Morava (riv.), Czh. 43/J4
Morāveh Tappeh, Iran 103/H2
Moravia (reg.), Czh. 43/J4
Moravia, Ia, US 161/H3
Moravia, Ia, US 155/H3
Moravica (riv.), Yugo. 51/F3
Moravian Falls, NC, US 163/G2
Moravská Třebová, Czh. 43/J4
Moravské Budějovice, Czh. 43/H4
Morawa, Austl. 130/C4
Moray (range), Austl. 128/C3

Moray (co.), Sc, UK	33/C2	Morley, Tn, US	162/E2	Mortcerf, Fr.	30/L5	Motherwell, Sc, UK
Moray Firth		Morlupo, It.	65/B3	Morte (pt.), Eng, UK	60/B3	Motian (mtn.), China
(inlet), Sc, UK	33/B1	Mormant, Fr.	30/L6	Morte (pt.), Eng, UK	36/B4	Motīhāri, India
Morbach, Ger.	55/G4	Mormon (peak), Nv, US	148/E2	Morteau, Fr.	60/C3	Motilla del Palancar, Sp.
Morbegno, It.	61/F5	Mormon (mts.), Nv, US	148/E2	Mortefontaine, Fr.	30/K4	Motley, Mn, US
Morbier, Fr.	60/C4	Mormon Lake, Az, US	149/G3	Mortegliano, It.	63/G2	Motloutse, Bots.
Morbihan (gulf), Fr.	56/B5	Mormond (hill), Sc, UK	33/D1	Morteros, Arg.	188/D4	Motloutse (riv.), Bots.
Morbihan (dept.), Fr.	56/B5	Mornac, Fr.	64/A1	Mortes, Rio das	185/H4	Moto, D.R. Congo
Morbio Inferiore, Swi.	61/F6	Mornas, Fr.	64/A4			Motobu, Japan
Morbras (riv.), Fr.	30/K5	Morning Sun, Ia, US	155/H3	Mortimer, Eng, UK	37/E4	Motohovo, Rus.
Mörbylånga, Swe.	40/G3	Morningstar (riv.), Ire.	32/B5	Mortlach, Sc, UK	145/L2	Mount Hope, Ks, US
Morcenx, Fr.	44/C4	Mornington (isl.), Chile	191/A6	Mortlake, Austl.	132/B3	Mount Hope, WV, US
Morciano di Romagna, It.	63/F6	Mornington, Austl.	133/C3	Morton, Tx, US	152/C4	Mount Hope, Austl.
Morclan, Pic de		Mornington, Austl.	133/C3	Morton, Ms, US	162/C4	Mount Horeb, Wi, US
(peak), Fr.	60/C5	Mornington (isl.), Austl.	127/C2	Morton, Il, US	155/K3	Mount Ida, Ar, US

[The remaining dense index entries continue in multi-column format across the page.]

Mun'gyŏng, SKor. 81/E4
Munhango, Ang. 122/C2
Munhino, Ang. 122/B2
Munich, ND, US 156/E3
Munich (München), Ger. 59/E6
Munising, Mi, US 157/L4
Muniungu, D.R. Congo 120/D4
Munjor, Ks, US 152/E1
Munka-Ljungby, Swe. 39/J6
Munkebo, Den. 40/D4
Munkedal, Swe. 40/D2
Munkfors, Swe. 40/E2
Munku-Sardyk (peak), Rus. 75/L4
Munku-Sasan (peak), Rus. 78/D1
Münnerstadt, Ger. 58/D2
Muñoz Gamero (pen.), Chile 191/B7
Munsan, SKor. 81/F6
Münsingen, Swi. 60/D4
Münsingen, Ger. 58/C6
Munsön (isl.), Swe. 39/A1
Munster, Fr. 60/D1
Münster, Swi. 61/E5
Munster (riv.), Ire. 32/C4
Munster (reg.), Ire. 32/B5
Münster, Ger. 58/B3
Munster, On, Can. 161/J2
Munster, Ger. 53/H3
Munster, In, US 167/R16
Münster, Ger. 53/E5
Münster/Osnabrück (int'l arpt.), Ger. 53/E4
Münstereifel, Ger. 55/F2
Münsterhausen, Ger. 58/D6
Münsterland (reg.), Ger. 42/D2
Münstermaifeld, Ger. 55/G3
Muntele Mare (peak), Rom. 51/F2
Muntendam, Neth. 52/D2
Muntinglupa, Phil. 88/F7
Muntok, Indo. 89/D3
Müntschemier, Swi. 60/D4
Muntu, D.R. Congo 120/D3
Münzenberg, Ger. 58/B2
Münzkirchen, Aus. 59/G6
Munzur Vadisi NP, Turk. 102/D2
Muong Het, Laos 94/D1
Muong Hin, Viet. 86/E5
Muong Khuong, Viet. 94/D1
Muong Lat, Viet. 86/E4
Muonio, Fin. 38/G2
Muonioälven (riv.), Swe. 38/G1
Muotathal, Swi. 61/E4
Mupa, Ang. 122/B3
Mupa, PN da, Ang. 122/B2
Muping, China 80/E3
Muqaddan (wadi), Sudan 117/F1
Muqaṭṭa', Sudan 117/G2
Muqeibila, Isr. 105/C3
Müqtädir, Azer. 71/J4
Mur (riv.), Aus. 67/G1
Mûr-de-Bretagne, Fr. 56/C4
Mur-de-Sologne, Fr. 57/G6
Mura (riv.), Slov.,Hun. 50/C2
Muradiye, Turk. 103/E2
Murādnagar, India 98/D5
Murakami, Japan 85/F1
Murallón (peak), Chile 191/B6
Muramgaon, India 95/D1
Muramvya, Buru. 121/G3
Murang'a, Kenya 119/B2
Murano, It. 63/F3
Murashi, Rus. 69/L4
Murat (peak), Turk. 102/B2
Muratlı, Turk. 102/E2
Muratlı, Turk. 51/H5
Murayama, Japan 82/B4
Mürcheh Khvort, Iran 103/G3
Murchison (isl.), On, Can. 157/K3
Murchison, NZ 135/C3
Murchison, Austl. 133/B3
Murchison (mt.), Austl. 130/C3
Murchison (riv.), Austl. 127/A3
Murchison Downs, Austl. 130/C3
Murcia (pol. reg.), Sp. 46/E4
Murcia, Sp. 47/E4
Murderkill (riv.), De, US 168/C6
Murdo, SD, US 154/D2
Murdochville, Qu, Can. 158/E1
Murdock (pt.), Austl. 134/B1
Murdock, Mn, US 155/G1
Mürefte, Turk. 51/H5
Mureş (riv.), Rom. 70/B3
Mureş (prov.), Rom. 51/G2
Muret, Fr. 44/D5
Murewa, Zim. 123/F3
Murfreesboro, Ar, US 153/H3
Murfreesboro, Tn, US 162/D3
Murfreesboro, NC, US 163/J2
Murg (riv.), Ger. 55/H6
Murgap (riv.), Trkm. 74/G6
Murgenella Wildlife Sanctuary, Austl. 128/D2
Murghob, Taj. 99/B4
Murgon, Austl. 134/C4
Murgoo, Austl. 130/C3
Muri, Swi. 61/E3
Muri, China 78/D4
Muri bei Bern, Swi. 60/D4
Muria (peak), Indo. 89/E4
Muriaé, Braz. 187/E4
Murias de Paredes, Sp. 46/B1
Murici, Braz. 183/H5
Murīdke, Pak. 98/C4
Muriege, Ang. 121/E5
Müritz (lake), Ger. 42/G2
Murka, Kenya 119/B2
Murle, Eth. 117/H4
Murlīganj, India 97/F3
Murmansk (int'l arpt.), Rus. 68/G1
Murmansk, Rus. 68/G1
Murmanskaya Oblast Rus. 38/J1
Murmashi, Rus. 68/G1
Murnau, Ger. 61/H2
Murnpeowie, Austl. 131/H4
Muro, Sp. 47/G3
Muro, Japan 83/K6
Muro Lucano, It. 48/D2
Murom, Rus. 68/J5
Murongo, Tanz. 121/G3
Muroran, Japan 82/B2
Muros, Sp. 46/A1
Muroto, Japan 84/D4
Muroto-zaki (pt.), Japan 84/D4
Murowana Goślina, Pol. 43/J2
Murphy, Id, US 146/E2
Murphy, NC, US 162/E3
Murphy, Tx, US 150/L6
Murphys, Ca, US 146/C4
Murphysboro, Il, US 162/C2
Murphytown, WV, US 163/G1
Murr (riv.), Ger. 58/C5
Murra, Nic. 176/E3
Murramarang NP, Austl. 133/E2
Murray, Ut, US 147/H3
Murray, Ky, US 162/C2
Murray (lake), PNG 129/F1
Murray (range), PNG 129/F1
Murray, Id, US 144/G4
Murray (riv.), Austl. 127/D4
Murray Bridge, Austl. 131/H5
Murray Downs, Austl. 131/G2
Murray River, PE, Can. 159/F2
Murraysburg, SAfr. 124/C3
Murrayville, Austl. 132/B2
Murrayville, Ga, US 162/F3
Murree, Pak. 98/B3
Mürren, Swi. 60/D4
Murrhardt, Ger. 58/C5
Murrieta, Ca, US 166/C3
Murrieta Hot Springs, Ca, US 166/C3
Murringo, Austl. 133/D2
Murrumbateman, Austl. 133/D2
Murrumbidgee (riv.), Austl. 127/D4
Murrumburrah, Austl. 133/D2
Murrupula, Moz. 123/H2
Murrurundi, Austl. 132/D1
Mursala (isl.), Indo. 89/B2
Murshidābād, India 97/G3
Murska Sobota, Slov. 50/C2
Murtala Muhammed (int'l arpt.), Nga. 115/F5
Murtaröl (peak), Swi. 61/G4
Murten, Swi. 60/D4
Murtle (riv.), BC, Can. 144/D1
Murtoa, Austl. 132/B3
Murton, Eng, UK 35/G2
Murua, PNG 129/G1
Murua Ngithigerr (mts.), Kenya 117/G5
Murud (peak), Malay. 88/A5
Murud, India 95/C2
Murupara, NZ 135/D2
Mururoa (isl.), FrPol. 137/M7
Murwāra, India 96/C4
Murwillumbah, Austl. 134/D5
Mürz (riv.), Aus. 43/H5
Mürzzuschlag, Aus. 43/H5
Muş, Turk. 102/E2
Muş (prov.), Turk. 102/E2
Musa, D.R. Congo 120/D2
Musa Khel, Pak. 98/A3
Musabeyli, Turk. 104/E1
Musāfirkhāna, India 96/C2
Musā'id, Libya 108/E2
Musala (peak), Bul. 49/H1
Musan, NKor. 81/E1
Musanda, D.R. Congo 120/C4
Musandam (pen.), Oman 103/H5
Musasa, Tanz. 121/G3
Musashino, Japan 83/D2
Musay'īd, Qatar 100/F4
Musaymir, Yem. 118/C2
Muscat (cap.), Oman 101/G4
Muscatatuck NWR, In, US 162/E1
Muscatine, Ia, US 155/J3
Musciuru (well), Libya 108/B4
Musconetcong (riv.), NJ, US 168/C2
Muscoot (res.), NY, US 169/E1
Muscowpetung Ind. Res., Sk, Can. 156/B2
Muscoy, Ca, US 166/C2
Muse, Ok, US 153/G3
Muse, Tanz. 121/G4
Museum of Flight, Wa, US 167/C2
Musgrave (range), Austl. 127/C3
Musgrave, Austl. 134/A1
Musgravetown, Nf, Can. 159/L1
Mushābani, India 97/F4
Mushāsh (wadi), Isr. 105/C5
Mushaway (peak), Tx, US 151/D1
Musheramore (peak), Ire. 32/B5
Mushie, D.R. Congo 120/D3
Mushin, Nga. 115/F5
Musholm (bay), Den. 39/H7
Musi (river), Indo. 89/C3
Musi (riv.), Indo. 90/B4
Musile di Piave, It. 63/F2
Musinga (peak), Col. 180/B3
Muskego, Wi, US 167/P14
Muskegon, Mi, US 160/C3
Muskegon (riv.), Mi, US 160/D3
Muskingum (riv.), Oh, US 160/E4
Muskirā, India 96/B3
Muskö (isl.), Swe. 39/B1
Muskoday Ind. Res., Sk, Can. 145/M1
Muskogee, Ok, US 153/G3
Muskrat (cr.), Wy, US 147/K2
Muslimīyah, Syria 104/E1
Musofu, Zam. 123/F2
Musoka (lake), On, Can. 161/G2
Musoma, Tanz. 119/A2
Musone (riv.), It. 63/G6
Musquodoboit Harbour, NS, Can. 158/F3
Mussau (isl.), PNG 136/D5
Mussel Fk. (riv.), Mo, US 155/H3
Musselburgh, Sc, UK 33/C5
Musselshell (riv.), Mt, US 142/E2
Musselshell, Mt, US 145/K4
Mussende, Ang. 120/D5
Musserra, Ang. 120/C4
Mussomeli, It. 48/C4
Musson, Belg. 55/E4
Mussuco, Ang. 120/D5
Mussuma (riv.), Ang. 122/D2
Mustafābād, Pak. 98/B4
Mustafābad, India 96/C3
Mustafakemalpaşa, Turk. 70/D4
Mustahīl, Eth. 118/C4
Müstair, Swi. 61/G4
Mustān, Nepal 96/D1
Mustang, Ok, US 153/F3
Mustang (isl.), Tx, US 151/F4
Muşţāy, Egypt 113/C3
Mustayevo, Rus. 71/K2
Musters (lake), Arg. 190/C5
Mustio (Svartå), Fin. 39/D4
Mustvee, Est. 41/M2
Musu-dan (pt.), NKor. 81/E2
Musún (mtn.), Nic. 176/E3
Müsüslü, Azer. 103/F1
Mušutište, Yugo. 49/G1
Muswellbrook, Austl. 132/D2
Mut, Turk. 104/C1
Mūt, Egypt 135/F3
Mutá, Ponta do (pt.), Braz. 187/F2
Mutambara, Zim. 123/G3
Mutango, Ang. 122/D3
Mutare, Zim. 123/G3
Mutenge, Zam. 123/F2
Mutepatepa, Zim. 123/F3
Muthill, Sc, UK 33/C4
Muting, Indo. 129/F1
Mutis (peak), Indo. 128/B2
Mutkyi, Myan. 94/B2
Mutnyy Materik, Rus. 69/M2
Mutoko, Zim. 123/G3
Mutombo, D.R. Congo 121/E4
Mutombo-Dibwe, D.R. Congo 121/E4
Mutombo-Mukulu, D.R. Congo 121/F4
Mutria (peak), It. 65/D5
Mutsamudu, Com. 125/H6
Mutshatsha, D.R. Congo 121/F5
Mutsu, Japan 82/B3
Mutsu (bay), Japan 82/B3
Mutsuzawa, Japan 83/E3
Muttaburra, Austl. 134/B3
Muttekopf (peak), Aus. 61/G3
Muttenz, Swi. 60/D2
Mutters, Aus. 61/H3
Mutterstadt, Ger. 58/B4
Muttler (peak), Swi. 61/G4
Muttonville, Mi, US 167/G6
Mutu (mtn.), Indo. 128/A2
Muţūhis, Egypt 113/B2
Mutum, Braz. 187/E3
Mutumbo, Ang. 122/C2
Mutumieque, Ang. 122/B3
Mutún, Bol. 188/E1
Mutur, SrL. 95/D4
Mutwanga, D.R. Congo 121/G2
Mutzig, Fr. 60/D1
Muwale, Tanz. 119/A3
Muyezerskiy, Rus. 68/F3
Muyinga, Buru. 121/G3
Mŭynoq, Uzb. 74/F5
Muyuka, Camr. 120/B1
Muyumba, D.R. Congo 121/F4
Muyuya, D.R. Congo 121/F5
Muzaffarābād, Pak. 98/B2
Muzaffargarh, Pak. 98/A4
Muzaffarnagar, India 98/D5
Muzaffarpur, India 97/E2
Muzambinho, Braz. 187/K6
Muzat (riv.), China 99/D3
Muzillac, Fr. 56/C5
Muzo, Col. 183/L7
Muzoka, Zam. 123/E3
Muzon (cape), Ak, US 171/M4
Muztag (peak), China 99/D4
Muztagata (peak), China 99/C4
Muzzana del Turgnano, It. 63/G2
Mvadhi-Ousyé, Gabon 120/C2
Mvangane, Camr. 120/B2
Mvolo, Sudan 117/F4
Mvomero, Tanz. 119/B3
Mvoung (riv.), Gabon 120/C2
M'vouti, Congo 120/C4
Mvuma, Zim. 123/F3
Mwadi-Kalumbu, D.R. Congo 120/D4
Mwadingusha, D.R. Congo 121/F5
Mwadui, Tanz. 119/A2
Mwami, Zim. 123/F3
Mwana (cape), Kenya 119/C2
Mwana-Ndeke, D.R. Congo 121/F4
Mwanza (gulf), Tanz. 119/A2
Mwanza, Malw. 123/G2
Mwanza (prov.), Tanz. 121/H3
Mwanza, Tanz. 121/H3
Mwanza, D.R. Congo 121/F4
Mwase Lundaz, Zam. 123/G2
Mwaya, Tanz. 119/B4
Mwaya, Tanz. 119/A4
Mweelrea (peak), Ire. 31/P10
Mweiga, Kenya 119/B2
Mweka, D.R. Congo 121/E4
Mwenda, Zam. 121/G5
Mwene-Ditu, D.R. Congo 121/E4
Mwenezi, Zim. 123/F4
Mwenezi (riv.), Zim. 123/F4
Mwenga, D.R. Congo 121/G3
Mwense, Zam. 121/G5
Mwenzo Mission, Zam. 121/H5
Mwera, Tanz. 119/B3
Mweru (lake), D.R. Congo 107/E5
Mweru-Wantipa (lake), D.R. Congo 121/G5
Mweru-Wantipa NP, Zam. 121/G5
Mwesi (mtn.), Tanz. 121/G4
Mwesi, Tanz. 121/G4
Mwimba, Tanz. 121/G5
Mwimba, D.R. Congo 121/E5
Mwinilunga, Zam. 122/E1
Mwitikira, Tanz. 119/A3
Mwombezhi (riv.), Zam. 122/E2
My Son Temples (ruin), Viet. 94/E3
My Tho, Viet. 94/D4
Myaksa, Rus. 68/H4
Myall Lakes NP, Austl. 132/E2
Myanaung, Myan. 86/B5
Myanmar (Burma) (ctry.) 77/J7
Myatlevo, Rus. 68/G5
Myaungmya, Myan. 86/B5
Myawadi, Myan. 94/B2
Mycenae (Mikínai) (ruin), Gre. 49/H4
Myebon, Myan. 93/F3
Myeik (Mergui), Myan. 94/B3
Myers, Mt, US 145/L4
Myerstown, Pa, US 168/B3
Myggenäs, Swe. 40/D2
Myingyan, Myan. 86/B4
Myintha, Myan. 86/B3
Myitinge (riv.), Myan. 86/C4
Myitkyinā, Myan. 86/C3
Myitta, Myan. 94/B3
Myittha, Myan. 94/B1
Myittha (riv.), Myan. 86/B4
Myjava, Slvk. 43/J4
Mykhaylivka, Ukr. 73/H4
Mykolayiv, Ukr. 72/B3
Mykolayiv, Ukr. 73/G4
Mykolayiv (int'l arpt.), Ukr. 72/G4
Mykolayivka, Ukr. 73/G5
Mykolayivs'ka Oblast, Ukr. 70/D3
Mykulyntsi, Ukr. 72/C3
Mylau, Ger. 59/F1
Mymensingh, Bang. 97/H3
Mymensingh (pol. reg.), Bang. 97/H3
Mynämäki, Fin. 41/J1
Mynaral, Kaz. 99/B2
Mynydd Eppynt (mts.), Wal, UK 36/C2
Mynydd Pencarreg (peak), Wal, UK 36/B2
Mynydd Preseli (mtn.), Wal, UK 36/B3
Myōgi, Japan 83/B1
Myohaung, Myan. 86/B4
Myohla, Myan. 86/C4
Myōkō-san (peak), Japan 85/F2
Myŏngch'ŏn, NKor. 81/E2
Myŏnggan, NKor. 81/E2
Myrhorod, Ukr. 73/G3
Myrnam, Ab, Can. 145/J1
Myronivka, Ukr. 72/F3
Myrtle, Ms, US 162/C3
Myrtle (isl.), Md, US 163/K2
Myrtle Beach, SC, US 163/H4
Myrtle Creek, Or, US 146/B2
Myrtleford, Austl. 133/C3
Mysen, Nor. 40/D2
Mysingen (bay), Swe. 39/B2
Myślenice, Pol. 43/K4
Myślibórz, Pol. 43/H2
Myslivna (peak), Czh. 59/H5
Mysore, India 95/C3
Mystery Bay Rec. Area, Wa, US 167/B1
Mystery Cave, Mn, US 155/H2
Mystic, Ga, US 165/G2
Mystic, Ia, US 155/H3
Mystic Island, NJ, US 168/D4
Mystic Seaport, Ct, US 161/L4
Mysy, Rus. 69/M3
Myszków, Pol. 43/K3
Mytishchi, Rus. 69/W9
Mýto, Czh. 59/G3
Myton, Ut, US 147/H3
Myyeldino, Rus. 69/M3
M'zab (reg.), Alg. 66/D4
Mže (riv.), Czh. 42/G4
Mzimba, Malw. 123/G1
Mzuzu, Malw. 123/G1

N

N'Djamena (cap.), Chad 116/B2
Na (riv.), Viet. 94/C1
Na Kae, Thai. 94/D2
Naaldwijk, Neth. 52/B4
Naama, Alg. 111/E2
Naantali, Fin. 41/K1
Naarden, Neth. 52/C4
Naarn im Machlande, Aus. 59/H6
Naas, Ire. 32/D3
Nabā (peak), Jor. 105/D5
Nababeep, SAfr. 124/B3
Nabadwīp, India 97/G4
Nabalat al Ḩajanah, Sudan 117/F2
Nabari, Japan 83/K6
Nabari (riv.), Japan 83/K6
Nabberu (lake), Austl. 130/D3
Nabburg, Ger. 59/F4
Naberera, Tanz. 119/B3
Naberezhnye Chelny, Rus. 69/M5
Nābha, India 98/D4
Nabiac, Austl. 132/E2
Nabīnagar, Bang. 97/H4
Nabire, Indo. 91/J4
Nabón, Ecu. 184/B1
Naboomspruit, SAfr. 123/F5
Nabua, Phil. 88/C2
Nābul, Tun. 48/B4
Nābul (gov.), Tun. 48/B4
Nābulus, WBnk. 105/C4
Nabunturan, Phil. 88/D4
Nacala, Moz. 123/J2
Nacaome, Hon. 176/E3
Nacebe, Bol. 185/E3
Nachi-Katsuura, Japan 84/D4
Nachingwea, Tanz. 119/B4
Náchod, Czh. 43/J3
Nachrodt-Wiblingwerde, Ger. 53/E6
Nachtigal, Chutes de (falls), Camr. 120/B1
Nachuge, India 93/F5
Nacimiento, Chile 190/B3
Nacimiento (peak), NM, US 149/J2
Nacimiento (res.), Ca, US 148/B3
Nacka, Swe. 39/B1
Nackawic, NB, Can. 158/D2
Nacmine, Ab, Can. 145/H2
Naco, Mex. 149/H5
Nacogdoches, Tx, US 151/G2
Nácori Chico, Mex. 174/C2
Nacozari de García, Mex. 174/C2
Nadadores, Mex. 151/D4
Nādbai, India 96/A2
Nadder (riv.), Eng, UK 36/D4
Nadi (int'l arpt.), Fiji 137/Y18
Nadi, Fiji 137/Y18
Nadiād, India 92/B3
Nādir, Egypt 113/B3
Nădlac, Rom. 50/E2
Nador, Mor. 112/C2
Nador (prov.), Mor. 112/C2
Nadur, Malta 48/L6
Nadvirna, Ukr. 72/C3
Nadvoitsy, Rus. 68/G3
Nadym, Rus. 74/H3
Naejang-san NP, SKor. 81/D5
Näfels, Swi. 61/F3
Nafferton, Eng, UK 35/H4
Nafī, SAr. 100/D3
Naftalan, Azer. 103/F1
Naga, Phil. 88/C2
Naga (hills), India 86/B3
Nagagami (riv.), On, Can. 157/M3
Nagahama, Japan 84/C4
Nagahama, Japan 83/K5
Nagai, Japan 85/G1
Nagaizumi, Japan 83/B3
Nagakute, Japan 83/M5
Nāgāland (state), India 93/F2
Nagambie, Austl. 133/B3
Nagano, Japan 85/F2
Nagano (pref.), Japan 85/E3
Naganuma, Japan 82/B2
Nagaoka, Japan 85/F2
Nagaokakyō, Japan 83/J6
Nagaon (Nowgong), India 86/B3
Nagappattinam, India 95/C4
Nagar, India 96/A2
Nagar Pārkar, Pak. 101/K4
Nagar Untāri, India 96/D3
Nagara (riv.), Japan 85/E3
Nagara, Japan 83/E3
Nagareyama, Japan 83/D2
Nāgārjuna Sāgar (res.), India 92/C4
Nagarote, Nic. 172/D5
Nagarzê, China 97/H1
Nagasaka, Japan 83/A2
Nagasaki, Japan 84/A4
Nagasaki (int'l arpt.), Japan 84/A4
Nagasaki (pref.), Japan 84/A4
Nagasaki Peace, Japan 84/A4
Nagashima, Japan 83/L5
Nagato, Japan 84/B3
Nagato, Japan 83/A1
Nagatoro, Japan 83/C1
Nāgaur, India 92/B2
Nāgda, India 92/C3
Nagele, Neth. 52/C3
Nāgercoil, India 95/C4
Nagīna, India 96/B1
Nagir, Pak. 101/K1
Nagishot, Sudan 117/G4
Nagles (mts.), Ire. 32/B5
Nago, Japan 85/J7
Nago-Torbole, It. 61/G6
Nāgod, India 96/C3
Nagold, Ger. 58/B5
Nagold (riv.), Ger. 58/B5
Nagongera, Ugan. 119/A1
Nagorno-Karabakh (prov.), Arm. 71/H5
Nagornyy, Rus. 75/N4
Nagorsk, Rus. 69/L4
Nagosira, D.R. Congo 121/F2
Nagoya, Japan 83/L5
Nagoya Castle, Japan 83/L5
Nagpula (pass), China 97/F1
Nāgpur, India 98/C5
Nāgpur, India 95/C1
Nagqu (riv.), China 78/C5
Nagqu, China 86/B2
Nags Head, NC, US 163/K3
Nagu (Nauvo), Fin. 41/J1
Naguri, Japan 83/C2
Nagy-Milic (peak), Hun. 43/L4
Nagyatád, Hun. 50/C2
Nagybatony, Hun. 50/D2
Nagyecsed, Hun. 43/M5
Nagyhalász, Hun. 50/E1
Nagykanizsa, Hun. 50/C2
Nagykáta, Hun. 50/D2
Nagykőrös, Hun. 50/D2
Naha, Japan 85/J7
Nahabuan, Indo. 90/D3
Naḩal Shillo (wadi), Isr. 105/C4
Nāhan, India 98/D4
Nahanni NP, NW, Can. 140/D2
Nāhar, India 98/D5
Nahariyya, Isr. 105/C3
Nahatlatch (riv.), BC, Can. 144/C3
Nahāvand, Iran 103/G3
Naḩel Soreq (riv.), Isr. 105/B5
Naḩḩālīn, WBnk. 105/C5
Nahol'no-Tarasivka, Ukr. 73/K3
Nahouri (prov.), Burk. 115/E4
Nahr Ad Dindar (riv.), Sudan 117/G2
Nahr Ar Rahad (riv.), Sudan 117/G2
Nahr aş Şafā (riv.), Leb. 105/C1
Nahr Ouassel (riv.), Alg. 112/F5
Nahuel Huapi (lake), Arg. 179/B7
Nahuel Huapí, PN, Arg. 190/C4
Nahuelbuta, PN, Chile 190/B3
Nahuentúe, Chile 190/B3
Nahunta, Ga, US 165/H2
Naica, Mex. 174/D3
Naicam, Sk, Can. 145/M1
Naiguatá, Ven. 183/P7
Naihāti, India 97/G4
Naij Gol (riv.), China 78/C4
Naij Tal, China 78/C4
Naikliu, Indo. 128/A2
Naila, Ger. 59/E2
Nailsea, Eng, UK 36/D4
Nailsworth, Eng, UK 36/D3
Nā'im (well), Libya 108/C2
Na'ima, Sudan 117/G2
Naiman Qi, China 80/E2
Nā'īn, Iran 103/H3
Nain, Nf, Can. 141/K3
Nainital, India 96/B1
Nainpur, India 96/C4
Naintré, Fr. 44/D3
Nairn (riv.), Sc, UK 33/B2
Nairn, Sc, UK 33/C1
Nairne, Austl. 131/M9
Nairobi (cap.), Kenya 119/B2
Nairobi NP, Kenya 119/B2
Naita (peak), Eth. 117/G4
Naivasha, Kenya 119/B2
Naives-Rosières, Fr. 55/E6
Najafābād, Iran 103/G3
Najd (des.), SAr. 102/E5
Nájera, Sp. 46/D1
Naju, SKor. 81/D5
Naka (riv.), Japan 84/D4
Naka, Japan 83/G5
Nakadōri (isl.), Japan 84/A4
Nakai, Japan 83/C3
Nakajō, Japan 85/F1
Nakamichi, Japan 83/B2
Nakaminato, Japan 85/G2
Nakamura, Japan 84/C4
Nakano, Japan 85/F2
Nakano (lag.), Japan 84/C3
Nakasato, Japan 82/B3
Nakashibetsu, Japan 82/D2
Nakasongola, Ugan. 121/H2
Nakatane, Japan 85/L5
Nakatomi, Japan 83/A3
Nakatsu, Japan 84/B4
Nakatsugawa, Japan 85/E3
Nakazato, Japan 83/B1
Nak'fa, Erit. 100/C5
Nakhodka, Rus. 79/L3
Nakhola, India 97/J2
Nakhon Nayok, Thai. 94/C3
Nakhon Pathom, Thai. 94/C3
Nakhon Phanom, Thai. 94/D2
Nakhon Ratchasima, Thai. 94/C3
Nakhon Sawan, Thai. 94/C3
Nakhon Si Thammarat, Thai. 94/B4
Nakhon Thai, Thai. 94/C2
Nakhtarāna, India 101/J4
Nakifuma, Ugan. 121/H2
Nakina, On, Can. 157/L2
Nakkila, Fin. 41/J1
Nakło nad Notecią, Pol. 43/J2
Naknek, Ak, US 171/G4
Nakodar, India 98/C4
Nakonde, Zam. 121/H5
Nakong, Gha. 115/E4
Nakop, Namb. 124/B3
Naksan-sa, SKor. 81/E3
Nakskov, Den. 40/D4
Naktong, SKor. 81/E4
Naktong (riv.), SKor. 84/A3
Nakūr, India 98/D5
Nakuru, Kenya 119/B2
Nakusp, BC, Can. 144/F2
Nāl (riv.), Pak. 101/J3
Nalao, China 86/E3
Nalayh, Mong. 78/F2
Nalázi, Moz. 123/G5
Nalbach, Ger. 55/F5
Nalbāri, India 97/H2
Nalbaugh NP, Austl. 133/D3
Nal'chik, Rus. 71/G4
Nalchik (int'l arpt.), Rus. 71/G4
Nale, Laos 94/C2
Nalgonda, India 95/C2
Nalhāti, India 97/F3
Nalitābāri, Bang. 97/H3
Naliya, India 101/J4
Nallıhan, Turk. 51/K5
Nalón (riv.), Sp. 46/B1
Nalong, Myan. 86/C3
Nālūt, Libya 111/H3
Nam (riv.), SKor. 81/D5
Nam (riv.), NKor. 81/D3
Nam (lake), China 99/E5
Nam Can, Viet. 94/D4
Nam Cum, Viet. 86/D4
Nam Dinh, Viet. 87/E4
Nam Nao NP, Thai. 94/C2
Nam Pat, Thai. 94/C2
Nam Phong, Thai. 94/C2
Nam Un (res.), Thai. 94/C2
Namacunde, Ang. 122/B3
Namacurra, Moz. 123/H3
Namadzi, Malw. 123/G2
Namāi, Nepal 96/D2
Namak (lake), Iran 103/G3
Namakzār-e Shahdād (salt pan), Iran 103/J4
Namang, Indo. 89/D3
Namanga, Kenya 119/B2
Namangan, Uzb. 99/B3
Namansansong Provicial Park, SKor. 81/G7
Namanyere, Tanz. 121/G4
Namapa, Moz. 123/H2
Namaputa, Tanz. 119/B4
Namaqualand (reg.), SAfr. 124/B3
Namari, Sen. 114/B3
Namaripi (cape), Indo. 91/J4
Namarrói, Moz. 123/H2
Namasagali, Ugan. 119/A1
Namasakata, Tanz. 123/H1
Namatanai, PNG 136/E5
Nambanje, Tanz. 119/B4
Nambe, NM, US 149/K3
Namborn, Ger. 55/G4
Nambour, Austl. 134/D4
Nambu, Japan 83/A3
Nambuangongo, Ang. 120/C5
Nambucca Heads, Austl. 132/E1
Nambung NP, Austl. 130/B4
Namco, China 99/F5
Namdae (riv.), NKor. 81/E2
Namdalseid, Nor. 38/D2
Nämdö (isl.), Swe. 39/B1
Nämdöfjärden (sound), Swe. 39/B1
Namegawa, Japan 83/C1
Namekagon (riv.), Wi, US 157/J4
Namentenga (prov.), Burk. 115/E3
Namerikawa, Japan 85/E2
Nametil, Moz. 123/H2
Namewaminikan (riv.), On, Can. 157/L3
Namhae (isl.), SKor. 81/D5
Namhae, SKor. 81/D5
Nami, Malay. 89/C1
Namib (des.), Namb. 107/D6
Namib-Naukluft Park, Namb. 122/B4
Namibe (int'l arpt.), Ang. 122/B2
Namibe, Ang. 122/B2
Namibe (dist.), Ang. 122/B2
Namibia (ctry.) 107/D7
Namie, Japan 85/G2
Namioka, Japan 82/B3
Namir, Mong. 78/C2
Namitete, Malw. 123/G2
Namja (pass), Nepal 99/D6
Namjagbarwa (peak), China 86/B2
Namlan, Myan. 94/B1
Namling, China 99/E6
Namloser Wetterspitze (peak), Aus. 61/G3
Nammoku, Japan 83/B1
Namnoi (peak), Myan. 94/B4
Namoi (riv.), Austl. 127/D4
Namonuito (isl.), Micr. 136/D4
Namorik (isl.), Mrsh. 136/F4
Namorona, Madg. 125/J8
Nampa, Id, US 146/E2
Nampala, Mali 114/D3
Namp'o, NKor. 81/C3
Nampula, Moz. 123/H2
Nampula (prov.), Moz. 123/H2
Namp'yŏng, SKor. 81/D5
Namrole, Indo. 91/G4
Nāmrup, India 86/B3
Namsa-ri, NKor. 81/D2
Namsang, Myan. 94/B1
Namsê (pass), China 99/D6
Namsos, Nor. 38/D2
Namtok Mae Surin NP, Thai. 86/C5
Namu (isl.), Mrsh. 136/F4
Namúli (mts.), Moz. 123/H2
Namuno, Moz. 123/H2
Namur (prov.), Belg. 55/D3
Namur, Belg. 55/D3
Namutoni, Namb. 122/C3
Namwala, Zam. 123/E2
Namwŏn, SKor. 81/D5
Namysłów, Pol. 43/J3
Nan, Thai. 94/C2
Nan (mts.), China 87/G3
Nan (riv.), China 78/F5
Nan (riv.), Thai. 87/F4
Nan'ao (isl.), China 87/H4
Nana Barya (riv.), Chad 116/C4
Nana Barya, Rsv. de Faune, CAfr. 116/C4
Nana Candundo, Ang. 122/D1
Nana-Mambéré (pref.), CAfr. 116/B4
Nanae, Japan 82/B3
Nanafalia, Al, US 162/D4
Nanaimo, BC, Can. 144/C3
Nanam, NKor. 81/E2
Nanango, Austl. 134/D4
Nanao, Japan 85/E2
Nanauta, India 98/D5
Nanay (riv.), Peru 184/C1
Nanbaozhen, China 80/L8
Nancagua, Chile 190/C2
Nancha, China 79/K2
Nanchang, China 87/G2
Nancheng, China 87/H3
Nanchong, China 86/E2
Nanchong, China 87/E2
Nanchuan, China 87/E2
Nancy, Fr. 55/F6
Nanda Devi (peak), India 99/C5
Nandan, China 93/J3
Nandashan, China 87/G2
Nānded, India 95/C2
Nandi Mill, Zim. 123/F4
Nandigāma, India 95/D2
Nanding (riv.), China 93/G3
Nandonge, Ang. 120/D5
Nandrin, Belg. 55/E3
Nandu, China 87/F4
Nandu (riv.), China 87/F5
Nandy, Fr. 30/K6
Nandyāl, India 95/C3
Nanfen, China 81/B2
Nanfeng, China 87/H3
Nang (isl.), Phil. 87/J4
Nang Rong, Thai. 94/C3
Nang Xian, China 86/B2
Nanga Parbat (peak), Pak. 98/C2
Nanga-Eboko, Camr. 116/B4
Nangalili, Indo. 91/F5
Nangamahap, Indo. 90/D4
Nangamentebah, Indo. 90/D3
Nangapinoh, Indo. 90/D4
Nangar NP, Austl. 133/D1
Nangata (pt.), Moz. 123/J2
Nangin, Myan. 94/B4
Nangis, Fr. 30/M6
Nangnim (mts.), NKor. 81/D2
Nangnim, NKor. 81/D2
Nangong, China 80/C3
Nangqên, China 78/D5
Nangtud (mt.), Phil. 88/C3
Nangua, Tanz. 119/B4
Nanguanling, China 81/A3
Nangwarry, Austl. 132/B3
Nanhsi, Tai. 87/J4
Nanhuang, China 81/A4
Nanhui, China 80/L8
Nanikelako, Zam. 122/D2
Nanjian Yizu Zizhixian, China 86/D3
Nanjiangkou, China 87/F4
Nanjing, China 80/D4
Nanka (riv.), Myan. 86/C4
Nankāna Sāhib, Pak. 98/B4
Nankoku, Japan 84/C4
Nankou, China 87/H3
Nankova, Ang. 122/C3
Nanlan (riv.), China 86/D4
Nanle, China 80/C3
Nanling, China 87/H2
Nanlinqiao, China 87/G2
Nanliu (riv.), China 93/J3
Nanlou (peak), China 79/K3
Nannestad, Nor. 40/D1
Nannine, Austl. 130/C3
Nanning, China 87/F4
Nannō, Japan 83/L5
Nannup, Austl. 130/B5
Nanny (riv.), Ire. 34/B4
Nanpan (riv.), China 86/E3
Nānpāra, India 96/C2
Nanpi, China 80/D3
Nanping, China 87/H3
Nanpu, China 80/J7
Nans-les-Pins, Fr. 64/B6
Nansei, Japan 83/L7
Nansemond Nat'l Wild. Ref., Va, US 163/J2
Nansen (sound), Nun, Can. 141/S6
Nansheng, China 87/H3
Nansio, Tanz. 119/A2
Nant (riv.), Fr. 57/G5
Nant (lake), Sc, UK 33/A4
Nantai, China 81/B2
Nantai-san (peak), Japan 85/F2
Nanterre, Fr. 30/J5
Nantes, Fr. 56/D6
Nantes à Brest (canal), Fr. 56/B4
Nanteuil-le-Haudouin, Fr. 30/L4
Nanteuil-lès-Meaux, Fr. 54/B6
Nantian, China 87/H3
Nantian, China 87/J2
Nanticoke, On, Can. 160/F3
Nanticoke, Pa, US 168/B1
Nanton, Ab, Can. 145/H2
Nantong, China 80/E4
Nantong, China 87/J1
Nantou, China 87/K6
Nantua, Fr. 60/B5
Nantucket, Ma, US 158/B5
Nantucket (isl.), Ma, US 158/C5
Nantucket (sound), Ma, US 158/B5
Nantucket Nat'l Wild. Ref., Ma, US 158/B5
Nantúpi, Moz. 123/H2
Nantwich, Eng, UK 35/F5
Nanty-Glo, Pa, US 161/G4
Nanuet, NY, US 169/J7
Nanuku Passage (chan.), Fiji 137/Y18
Nanumanga (isl.), Tuv. 136/G5
Nanumea (isl.), Tuv. 136/G5
Nanuque, Braz. 187/E3
Nanwon (res.), China 80/C4
Nanxi, China 86/E2
Nanxiang, China 80/L8
Nanxing, China 78/F5
Nanxun, China 80/L9
Nanyamba, Tanz. 119/B4
Nanyang, China 80/D4
Nanyang (lake), China 78/H4
Nanyang, China 80/C4
Nanyue, China 87/G3
Nanyuki, Kenya 119/B1
Nanzamu, China 81/C2
Nanzhang, China 80/B5
Nanzhao, China 80/C4
Nao, Cabo de la (cape), Sp. 47/F3
Não-Me-Toque, Braz. 189/F4
Naococane (lake), Qu, Can. 141/J3
Naogaon, Bang. 97/G3
Naokot, Pak. 92/A3
Naoli (riv.), China 79/L2
Naolinco, Mex. 175/N7
Naos, Namb. 122/C4
Naoua (falls), C.d'Iv. 114/D5
Náousa, Gre. 49/J4
Náousa, Gre. 49/H2
Naozhou (isl.), China 87/F4
Napa (riv.), Ca, US 167/K10
Napa (valley), Ca, US 167/K9
Napa (co.), Ca, US 167/K10
Napa, Ca, US 146/B4
Napa Junction, Ca, US 167/K10
Napak (peak), Ugan. 119/A1
Napakiak, Ak, US 171/F3
Napanee, On, Can. 161/H2
Napata (ruin), Sudan 135/F5
Napavine, Wa, US 144/C4
Nape, Laos 94/D2
Naperville, Il, US 160/B4
Napf (peak), Swi. 60/D4
Napido, Indo. 91/J4
Napier, SAfr. 124/L11
Napier, NZ 135/D2
Napier (pt.), Austl. 129/D2
Napier (mt.), Austl. 128/C4
Napier Broome (bay), Austl. 128/B3
Napierville (co.), Qu, Can. 159/N7
Napill, Eng, UK 30/A2
Napinka, Mb, Can. 156/D3
Naples (Napoli), It. 65/D6
Naples, Fl, US 165/H4
Naples, Id, US 144/F3
Naples, Me, US 161/L3
Naples, NY, US 161/H3
Naples, Tx, US 153/G4
Naples, Ut, US 147/J3
Naples Park, Fl, US 165/H4
Napo (prov.), Ecu. 180/B5
Napo (riv.), Ecu. 180/B5
Napo (riv.), Ecu.,Peru 179/B3
Napo (riv.), Peru 180/C5
Napo, China 93/J3
Napoleon, ND, US 156/E4
Napoleon, Oh, US 160/D4
Napoleon, Mi, US 160/D3
Napoleonville, La, US 164/C3
Napoli (gulf), It. 48/C2
Napoli (prov.), It. 65/D6
Napoli (Naples), It. 65/D6
Napoule (gulf), Fr. 64/C5
Nappa Merrie, Austl. 134/A4
Nappanee, In, US 160/C4
Napperby, Austl. 131/G2
Napton-on-the-Hill, Eng, UK 37/E2
Napuka (isl.), FrPol. 137/L6
Naqb Ghul (peak), Egypt 113/C5
Naqīl Sumārah (pass), Yem. 118/C2
Nara, Mali 114/D3
Nāra (riv.), Pak. 101/J4
Nara, Japan 83/J6
Nara Logna (pass), Nepal 99/D5
Naracoopa, Austl. 133/B4
Naracoorte, Austl. 132/B3
Naradhan, Austl. 133/C1
Narail, Bang. 97/G4
Naraini, India 96/C3
Nārāinpur, India 95/D2
Naramata, BC, Can. 144/E3
Naranbulag, Mong. 99/F2
Narang, Afg. 98/A2
Naranjal, Ecu. 180/B5
Naranjito, Ecu. 184/B1
Naranjos, Mex. 176/B1
Naranjos, Bol. 188/E1
Narāq, Iran 103/G3
Narasannapeta, India 95/E2
Narasapatnam (pt.), India 95/D2
Narasapur, India 95/D2
Narasaraopet, India 95/D2
Narashino, Japan 83/E2
Narat, China 99/D3
Narathiwat, Thai. 94/C5
Nārāyanganj, India 96/C4
Nārāyanganj, Bang. 97/H4
Nārāyani (zone), Nepal 97/E2
Narayani (riv.), Nepal 97/E2
Narbonne, Fr. 44/E5
Narceo (riv.), Sp. 46/B1
Narcoossee, Fl, US 164/N7
Nardò, It. 49/F2
Nare (pt.), Eng, UK 36/B6
Narellan, Austl. 134/G9
Narembeen, Austl. 130/C5
Naréna, Mali 114/C3
Nares (str.), Can.,Grld. 139/K2
Narew (riv.), Pol. 68/D5
Narganá, Pan. 180/B2
Narib, Namb. 122/C5
Narinda, Madg. 125/H6
Narinda (bay), Madg. 125/H6
Nariño (dept.), Col. 180/B4
Nariño, Col. 183/K7
Narita (int'l arpt.), Japan 85/G3
Narita, Japan 83/E2
Nariz (peak), Chile 191/C7
Narka, Ks, US 154/F4
Narkatiāganj, India 97/E2
Narmada (riv.), India 77/G7
Narman, Turk. 71/G4
Nærnes, Nor. 38/S8
Narni, It. 65/B2
Naro Moru, Kenya 119/B2
Naroch', Bela. 41/M4
Narodnaya (peak), Rus. 69/P2
Narok, Kenya 119/A2
Narón, Sp. 46/A1
Narooma, Austl. 133/E3
Narovlya, Bela. 72/E2
Nārowāl, Pak. 98/C3
Nærøy, Nor. 38/D2
Närpes (Närpiö), Fin. 68/D3
Närpiö (Närpes), Fin. 68/D3
Narra, Phil. 88/B3
Narrabri, Austl. 132/D1
Narrandera, Austl. 133/C2
Narre Warren North, Austl. 133/B3
Narriah (mtn.), Austl. 133/C1
Narrogin, Austl. 130/C5
Narromine, Austl. 132/D2
Narrows (dam), Ar, US 153/H3
Narrows (riv.), NY, US 169/J9
Narrows, Va, US 163/G2
Narsimhapur, India 96/B4
Narsingarh, India 92/C3
Narsinghdi, Bang. 97/H4
Narsī Patnam, India 95/D2
Nartuby (riv.), Fr. 64/C5
Narubis, Namb. 124/B2
Naruksovo, Rus. 69/K5
Narungombe, Tanz. 119/B4
Narusawa, Japan 83/B3
Naruto, Japan 84/D3
Narutō, Japan 83/E2
Narva (riv.), Est.,Rus. 68/E4
Narva (res.), Rus. 68/F4
Narva (bay), Rus.,Est. 41/M2
Narva, Est. 41/N2
Narva (riv.), Rus. 41/M2
Narva-Jõesuu, Est. 41/N2
Narvacan, Phil. 88/C1
Narvik, Nor. 38/F1
Narwāna, India 98/D5
Nar'yan-Mar, Rus. 69/M2
Naryn (riv.), Kyr. 74/H5
Naryn, Kyr. 99/C3
Naryn Khuduk, Rus. 71/H3
Narzole, It. 62/A3
NASA Test Center, Ms, US 164/D2
NASA Test Facility, NM, US 152/A4
NASA Wallops Space Ctr., Va, US 163/K2
Nasarawa, Nga. 115/G4
Năsăud, Rom. 51/G2
Naschel, Arg. 190/D2
Naschitti, NM, US 149/H2
Naseby, NZ 135/B4
Naselle, Wa, US 144/C4
Nash, Ok, US 153/E2
Nash, Eng, UK 37/F3
Nash (pt.), Wal, UK 36/C4
Nashoba, Ok, US 153/G3
Nashua, NH, US 161/L3
Nashua, Ia, US 155/H2
Nashua, Mt, US 145/L3
Nashville, Ar, US 153/H4
Nashville, Ga, US 165/G2
Nashville, In, US 160/C5
Nashville, Mi, US 160/D3
Nashville (int'l arpt.), Tn, US 162/D2
Nashville (cap.), Tn, US 162/D2
Nashville, Il, US 162/C1
Nashville, NC, US 163/J3
Nashwah, Egypt 113/C3
Našice, Cro. 50/D3
Nasielsk, Pol. 43/L2
Nasijärvi (lake), Fin. 41/K1
Nasikonis (cape), Indo. 128/A2
Nāşir, Sudan 117/G3
Nasīrābād, India 92/B2
Naso (pt.), Phil. 88/C3
Nason, Il, US 162/C1
Nasori (Suva) (int'l arpt.), Fiji 137/Y18
Nasorolevu (peak), Fiji 137/Z17
Nasosnyy, Azer. 71/J4
Nāsriganj, India 97/E3
Nass (riv.), BC, Can. 171/N4
Nassach (riv.), Ger. 58/D2
Nassau, Ger. 55/G3
Nassau (sound), Fl, US 165/H2
Nassau (cap.), Bahm. 173/F2
Nassau (isl.), CookIs. 137/J6
Nassau (bay), Chile 191/D7
Nassau, De, US 168/C6
Nassau (co.), NY, US 169/E2
Nassau Bay, Tx, US 151/M9
Nassawadox, Va, US 163/K2
Nasser (lake), Egypt 107/E2
Nassereith, Aus. 61/G3
Nassian, C.d'Iv. 114/E4
Nässjö, Swe. 40/F3
Nassogne, Belg. 55/E3
Nassoukou, Ben. 115/F4
Nastapoka (isls.), Qu, Can. 141/J3
Nastätten, Ger. 55/G3
Næstved, Den. 40/D4
Nasu-dake (peak), Japan 85/F2
Nasugbu, Phil. 88/C2
Nat (peak), Myan. 86/C5

Nat'l West Coast Rec. Area, Namb. 122/B4
Nata, Bots. 122/E4
Natá, Pan. 180/A2
Natagaima, Col. 180/C4
Natal, Indo. 89/B2
Natal, Braz. 183/H4
Natalbany, La, US 164/C2
Natalia, Tx, US 151/E3
Naṭanz, Iran 103/G3
Natashō, Japan 83/J5
Natashquan (riv.), Qu, Can. 141/K3
Natchez, La, US 164/B2
Natchez, Ms, US 164/C2
Natchez Trace (pkwy), Ms, US 153/J5
Natchez Trace, US 162/C4
Natchitoches, La, US 164/B2
Naters, Swi. 60/D5
Natewa (bay), Fiji 137/Z17
Nathalia, Austl. 133/B3
Nathalie, Va, US 163/H2
Nāthdwāra, India 92/B3
Nathenje, Malw. 123/G2
Nathrop, Co, US 149/J1
Natimuk, Austl. 132/B3
National Agriculture Rsch. Ctr., Md, US 168/B6
National Aquarium, Md, US 168/B5
National Archaeological Museum, Gre. 49/N8
National Atomic Musuem, NM, US 152/A3
National Capital District (cap. dist.), PNG 129/G2
National City, Ca, US 166/C5
National Elk (refuge), Wy, US 147/H2
National Exhibition Centre, Eng, UK 37/E2
National Institutes of Health, Md, US 168/A6
National Mine, Mi, US 157/L4
National Museum, Mona. 62/J8
National Security Agency, Md, US 168/B5
Natitingou, Ben. 115/F4
Natividade, Braz. 186/D1
Natkyizin, Myan. 94/B3
Natl, Jor. 105/D5
Nat'l Bison Range, Mt, US 145/G4
Nat'l Key Deer Refuge Nat'l Wild. Ref., Fl, US 165/H5
Nat'l Museum, NZ 135/H9
Natoma, Ks, US 154/E4
Nator, Bang. 97/G3
Natron (lake), Tanz. 119/A2
Nåttarö (isl.), Swe. 39/B2
Natternbach, Aus. 59/G6
Nattheim, Ger. 58/D5
Nättraby, Swe. 40/F3
Natuna (isls.), Indo. 77/K9
Natural Bridge Caverns, Tx, US 151/E3
Natural Bridges Nat'l Mon., Ut, US 149/H2
Naturaliste (chan.), Austl. 130/B3
Naturaliste (cape), Austl. 132/D4
Naturaliste (cape), Austl. 130/B5
Nature Center, Tx, US 150/K7
Nature Reserve, Austl. 130/C2
Nature Reserve, Austl. 130/C4
Nature Reserve, Austl. 130/C5
Nature Reserve, Austl. 130/E5
Naturita, Co, US 149/H1
Naturno (Naturns), It. 61/G4
Naturns (Naturno), It. 61/G4
Naubinway, Mi, US 160/D1
Naucalpan, Mex. 175/Q10
Naucelle, Fr. 44/E4
Naucratis (ruin), Egypt 113/B3
Nauders, Aus. 61/G4
Naudesnek (pass), SAfr. 124/E3
Nauen, Ger. 42/P6
Naugachhia, India 97/F3
Naugaon Sādāt, India 96/B1
Naugatuck, Ct, US 161/K4
Nauhcampatépetl (vol.), Mex. 175/M7
Nauheim, Ger. 58/B3
Naujamiestis, Lith. 41/L4
Naujan, Phil. 88/C2
Naujoji-Akmenė, Lith. 41/K3
Naumburg, Ger. 42/F3
Naumburg, Ger. 53/G6
Naunggala, Myan. 94/B2
Naunglon, Myan. 94/B2
Nauort, Ger. 55/G3
Nā'ūr, Jor. 105/D5
Nauru (ctry.) 136/F5
Nāushahra, India 98/C3
Naushahra Virkhan, Pak. 98/B4
Naushki, Rus. 78/F1
Nauta, Peru 184/C2
Nautla, Mex. 175/N6
Nauvo (Nagu), Fin. 41/J1
Nauvoo, Il, US 155/J3
Nauvoo, Al, US 162/D4
Nava, Mex. 151/D3
Nava del Rey, Sp. 46/C2
Navajo, Mt, US 156/B3
Navajo (riv.), NM,Co, US 152/A2
Navajo (dam), NM, US 149/J2
Navajo, Az, US 149/H3
Navajo (peak), Co, US 149/J2
Navajo (lake), NM, US 149/J2
Navajo Ind. Res., Az,NM, US 149/G2
Navajo Nat'l Mon., Az, US 149/G2
Naval, Phil. 88/D3
Naval Res., Ca, US 166/C4
Navalcarnero, Sp. 47/M9
Navalmoral de la Mata, Sp. 46/C3
Navalvillar de Pela, Sp. 46/C3
Navapolatsk, Bela. 41/N4
Navarin (cape), Rus. 75/T3
Navarino (isl.), Chile 191/C7
Navarra (reg.), Sp. 46/D1
Navarre, Oh, US 160/F4
Navarro, Ca, US 146/B4
Navarro, Arg. 191/J11
Navàs, Sp. 47/F2
Navas de San Juan, Sp. 46/D3
Navasota, Tx, US 151/F2
Navasota (riv.), Tx, US 175/F2
Navassa (isl.), Myan. 177/H2
Navax (pt.), Eng, UK 36/A6
Nave, It. 62/D2
Navenne, Fr. 60/C2
Navia (riv.), Sp. 46/B1
Navia, Sp. 46/B1
Navidad (riv.), Tx, US 151/F3
Navidad, Chile 190/N8
Naviraí, Braz. 189/F2
Navlya, Rus. 70/E1
Năvodari, Rom. 51/J3
Navojoa, Mex. 174/C3
Navolato, Mex. 174/D3
Navotas, Phil. 88/E6
Návpaktos, Gre. 49/G3
Návplion, Gre. 49/H4
Navrongo, Gha. 115/E4
Navy Board (inlet), Nun, Can. 141/H1
Navy Yard City, Wa, US 167/B2
Nawā, Syria 105/E3
Nawābganj, India 96/B1
Nawābganj, India 96/C2
Nawābganj, Bang. 97/G3
Nawābshāh, Pak. 101/J3
Nawāda, India 97/E3
Nawān Jandānwāla, Pak. 98/A3
Nawānshahr, India 98/C3
Nawāpāra, India 95/D1
Nawāshahr, India 98/D4
Nawāshahr, Pak. 98/B2
Nawnghkio, Myan. 86/C4
Nawngleng, Myan. 94/B1
Nawoiy, Uzb. 74/G5
Naxçıvan, Azer. 103/F2
Naxçivan Aut. Rep., Azer. 103/F2
Naxi, China 93/J2
Náxos, Gre. 49/J4
Náxos (isl.), Gre. 67/K3
Nāy Band, Iran 103/H5
Nāy Band, Iran 103/J3
Naya, Col. 180/B4
Nayāgarh, India 95/E1
Nayarit (state), Mex. 174/D4
Nayland, Eng, UK 37/G3
Naylor, Mo, US 162/B2
Nayong, China 93/J2
Nayoro, Japan 82/C1
Nayramadlïn (peak), Mong. 99/E2
Naytahwaush, Mn, US 157/G4
Nayuci, Malw. 123/G2
Nayzatash (pass), Taj. 99/B4
Nazaré, Port. 46/A3
Nazaré, Braz. 182/E4
Nazaré da Mata, Braz. 183/H4
Nazaré do Piauí, Braz. 183/F4
Nazaré Paulista, Braz. 187/K8
Nazareth, Belg. 54/C2
Nazareth, Pa, US 168/C2
Nazas, Mex. 174/D3
Nazas (riv.), Mex. 174/D3
Nazca, Peru 184/C4
Naze, Japan 85/K6
Nazelles-Négron, Fr. 57/F6
Naẕerat, Isr. 105/C3
Naẕerat 'Illit, Isr. 105/C3
Nazilli, Turk. 102/B2
Nāzir Hāt, Bang. 97/H4
Nazko (riv.), BC, Can. 144/C1
Nazran', Rus. 71/H4
Nazrēt, Eth. 118/A3
Nazyvayevsk, Rus. 74/H4
Ncamasere (riv.), Bots. 122/D3
Nchanga, Zam. 123/E2
Nchelenge, Zam. 121/G5
Ncheu, Malw. 123/G2
Nchisi, Malw. 123/G2
Ncojane, Bots. 122/D4
Ndabala, Zam. 123/F2
Ndala, Tanz. 119/A3
Ndalatando, Ang. 120/C5
Ndali, Ben. 115/F4
Ndele, CAfr. 116/D3
Ndélélé, Camr. 120/C1
N'Dendé, Gabon 120/B3
Ndende (isl.), Sol. 136/F6
Ndengu, Tanz. 119/A4
Ndiago, Mrta. 114/A2
Ndikiniméki, Camr. 120/B1
Ndim, CAfr. 116/B4
Ndindi, Gabon 120/B3
N'Djamena (int'l arpt.), Chad 116/B2
N'Djili (int'l arpt.), D.R. Congo 120/C4
N'Djolé, Gabon 120/B3
Ndogo (lag.), Gabon 120/B3
Ndola, Zam. 123/F2
Ndolo Corner, Kenya 119/B2
Ndombi, D.R. Congo 121/E4
Ndouaniang, Gabon 120/B2
Ndouci, C.d'Iv. 114/D5
Ndougou, Gabon 120/B3
Ndrhamcha (lake), Mrta. 114/B2
Ndu, D.R. Congo 116/D4
Nduguti, Tanz. 119/A3
Nduli, Tanz. 119/A3
Ndumbwe, Tanz. 119/B4
Ndungu, Tanz. 119/B3
Né (riv.), Fr. 44/C4
Néa Alikarnassós, Gre. 49/J5
Néa Ankhíalos, Gre. 49/H3
Néa Artáki, Gre. 49/H3
Néa Ionía, Gre. 49/H3
Néa Ionía, Gre. 49/N8
Néa Kallikrátia, Gre. 49/H2
Néa Kíos, Gre. 49/H4
Néa Mikhanióna, Gre. 49/H2
Néa Moudhaniá, Gre. 49/H2
Néa Potídhaia, Gre. 49/H2
Néa Tríglia, Gre. 49/H2
Néa Víssa, Gre. 51/H5
Néa Zíkhni, Gre. 49/H2
Neagh (lake), NI, UK 34/B2
Neah Bay, Wa, US 144/B3
Neale (lake), Austl. 131/F3
Neale (lake) 127/C3
Neales (riv.), Austl. 131/G3
Neamţ (prov.), Rom. 51/H2
Neaophli-le-Château, Fr. 30/H5
Neápolis, Gre. 49/J5
Neápolis, Gre. 49/H4
Neápolis, Gre. 49/G2
Near (isls.), Ak, US 171/A5
Neath, Wal, UK 36/C3
Neath (riv.), Wal, UK 36/C3
Neath Port Talbot (co.), Wal, UK 36/C3
Neavitt, Md, US 168/B6
Nebbi, Ugan. 121/G2
Nebel-Horn (peak), Ger. 61/G3
Nebikon, Swi. 60/D3
Nebin (peak), It. 64/D3
Nebish (isl.), Mi, US 160/D1
Nebitdag, Trkm. 103/H2
Neblina (peak), Braz. 181/E4
Nebo, Mo, US 153/H2
Nebo, SAfr. 123/F5
Nebo (mt.), Ut, US 147/H4
Nebo, Il, US 155/J4
Nebo (mt.), Austl. 134/E6
Nebraska (state), US 142/F3
Nebraska City, Ne, US 155/G3
Nebrodi (mts.), It. 48/C4
Necedah, Wi, US 155/J1
Necedah Nat'l Wild. Ref., Wi, US 155/J1
Nechako (riv.), BC, Can. 140/D3
Nechayane, Ukr. 72/F4
Neche, ND, US 156/F3
Neches (riv.), Tx, US 143/G5
Neches, Tx, US 150/G2
Nechisar NP, Eth. 117/H4
Nechranice (res.), Czh. 59/G2
Neckar (riv.), Ger. 42/D4
Neckarbischofsheim, Ger. 58/B4
Neckargemünd, Ger. 58/B4
Neckarsteinach, Ger. 58/B4
Neckarsulm, Ger. 58/C4
Necker (isl.), Hi, US 137/J2
Necochea, Arg. 190/F3
Necoclí, Col. 180/B2
Necropoli (ruin), It. 65/B3
Neda, Sp. 46/A1
Nedelino, Bul. 49/J2
Nedelišće, Cro. 50/C2
Nederland, Tx, US 151/H3
Nederweert, Neth. 52/C6
Nedlands (nbrhd.), Austl. 130/K6
Nedumangād, India 95/C4
Nee Soon (nbrhd.), Sing. 89/J6
Neede, Neth. 52/D4
Needham, Al, US 164/D2
Needham Market, Eng, UK 37/H2
Needingworth, Eng, UK 37/F2
Needle (mtn.), Wy, US 147/J1
Needles (pt.), NZ 135/C2
Needles, Ca, US 148/E3
Needles, BC, Can. 144/E3
Needles, The, Eng, UK 37/E5
Needville, Tx, US 151/G3
Neely Henry (lake), Al, US 162/D4
Neelyville, Mo, US 162/B2
Neembucú (dept.), Par. 188/E3
Neenah, Wi, US 155/K1
Neepawa, Mb, Can. 156/E2
Neerabup NP, Austl. 130/K6
Neerpelt, Belg. 52/C6
Neetze, Ger. 53/H2
Neetze (riv.), Ger. 53/H2
Nefas Mewch'a, Eth. 118/A3
Nefasīt, Erit. 118/A2
Neffelbach (riv.), Ger. 55/F2
Neftah, Tun. 66/E4
Neftçala, Azer. 103/G2
Neftegorsk, Rus. 71/J1
Neftegorsk, Rus. 73/K5
Neftekamsk, Rus. 69/M4
Neftekumsk, Rus. 71/H3
Nefud (des.), SAr. 77/B7
Nefyn, Wal, UK 34/D6
Nega Nega, Zam. 123/F2
Négala, Mali 114/C3
Negara, Indo. 89/F5
Negara, Indo. 90/E4
Negaunee, Mi, US 157/L4
Negba, Isr. 105/B5
Negēlē, Eth. 118/A4
Negēlē, Eth. 118/A4
Negeri Sembilan (state), Malay. 89/C2
Negev (reg.), Isr. 104/D4
Negoiu (peak), Rom. 51/G3
Negomano, Moz. 123/H1
Negoreloye, Bela. 41/M5
Negotin, Yugo. 50/F3
Negotino, FYROM 49/H2
Negra (pt.), Belz. 176/D2
Negra (mesa), NM, US 149/J3
Negra (pt.), Peru 184/A2
Negrais (cape), Myan. 93/F4
Negrar, It. 63/D2
Negreet, La, US 164/B2
Negreira, Sp. 46/A1
Negreiros, Chile 188/B1
Negreşti, Rom. 72/D4
Negril, Jam. 177/G2
Negrillos, Bol. 188/B1
Negrine, Alg. 66/E4
Negritos, Peru 184/A2
Negro (peak), Arg. 190/C3
Negro (riv.), Uru. 191/J11
Negro (brook), Uru. 191/K10
Negro (riv.), Bol. 185/F4
Negro (riv.), Braz. 182/A3
Negro (riv.), Par. 188/E3
Negros (isl.), Phil. 77/M9
Neguac, NB, Can. 158/E2
Nehalem (riv.), Or, US 144/C5
Nehbandān, Iran 101/H2
Neheim-Hüsten, Ger. 53/E6
Nei Monggol (plat.), China 78/G3
Nei Monggol (aut. reg.), China 78/E3
Neiafu, Tonga 137/H6
Neiba, DRep. 173/G4
Neiba (mts.), DRep. 177/J2
Neiderösterreich (prov.), Aus. 45/L2
Neihart, Mt, US 145/J4
Neihuang, China 80/C4
Neijiang, China 86/E2
Neilburg, Sk, Can. 145/K1
Neillier (peak), Fr. 64/D4
Neillsville, Wi, US 155/J1
Neil's Harbour, NS, Can. 159/G2
Neilston, Sc, UK 33/B5
Neineis, Namb. 122/B4
Neiqiu, China 80/C3
Neira, Col. 183/K7
Neisse (riv.), Ger. 43/H3
Neiva, Col. 180/C4
Neixiang, China 80/B4
Nejanilini (lake), Mb, Can. 140/G3
Nejdek, Czh. 59/F2
Nejo, Eth. 117/G3
Nejrab (int'l arpt.), Syria 104/E1
Nekā, Iran 103/H2
Nekalagba, D.R. Congo 121/G2
Nek'emtē, Eth. 117/H3
Nekhayevskiy, Rus. 73/L2
Nekoosa, Wi, US 155/K1
Nekrasovo, Rus. 71/H2
Nekselø (isl.), Den. 39/H7
Neksø, Den. 40/F4
Nelas, Port. 46/B2
Nelidovo, Rus. 68/G4
Neligh, Ne, US 154/E2
Nellieburg, Ms, US 162/C4
Nellimarla, India 95/D2
Nellingen, Ger. 58/C5
Nellis Air Force Range, Nv, US 148/D2
Nellore, India 95/C3
Nelson, Arg. 188/D4
Nelson (cape), Austl. 132/B3
Nelson, BC, Can. 144/F3
Nelson (riv.), Mb, Can. 140/G3
Nelson (str.), Chile 191/B6
Nelson, NZ 135/C3
Nelson (cape), PNG 129/H2
Nelson, Eng, UK 35/F4
Nelson, Wal, UK 36/C3
Nelson (isl.), Ak, US 171/E3
Nelson, Az, US 149/F3
Nelson, Mo, US 155/H4
Nelson, Ne, US 154/E3
Nelson Bay, Austl. 132/E2
Nelson Forks, BC, Can. 140/D3
Nelson Lagoon, Ak, US 171/F4
Nelson Lakes NP, NZ 135/C3
Nelson-Miramichi, NB, Can. 158/E2
Nelsonville, Oh, US 160/E5
Nelspruit, SAfr. 123/F5
Néma, Mrta. 114/D2
Nemaha, Ne, US 155/G3
Neman, Rus. 41/K4
Neman (riv.), Rus. 43/M1
Neman (Nemunas) (riv.), Eur. 41/K4
Nembrala, Indo. 128/A2
Nembro, It. 62/C2
Neméa, Gre. 49/H4
Nemenčinė, Lith. 41/L4
Nemi, It. 65/B4
Nemingha, Austl. 132/D1
Nemira (peak), Rom. 51/H2
Nemocón, Col. 183/M7
Nemor (riv.), China 79/K2
Nemours, Fr. 44/E2
Nemunas (riv.), Lith. 68/D5
Nemunas (Neman) (riv.), Eur. 41/K4
Nemuro (str.), Japan,Rus. 79/P3
Nemuro (pen.), Japan 82/D2
Nemuro, Japan 82/D2
Nemyriv, Ukr. 72/B2
Nemyriv, Ukr. 72/E3
Nen (riv.), China 77/M5
Nenagh (riv.), Ire. 32/B4
Nenagh, Ire. 32/B4
Nenana, Ak, US 171/J3
Nenasi, Malay. 89/C2
Nendaz, Swi. 60/D5
Nene (riv.), Eng, UK 35/J6
Nenetskiy Aut. Okrug, Rus. 69/M2
Nenjiang, China 79/K2
Nentershausen, Ger. 55/G3
Nentershausen, Ger. 53/G6
Nenzing, Aus. 61/F3
Neola, Ut, US 147/H3
Neola, Ia, US 155/G3
Néon Petrítsion, Gre. 49/H2
Neoria Husainpur, India 96/B1
Néos Marmarás, Gre. 49/H2
Neosho, Mo, US 153/G2
Neosho (riv.), US 143/G4
Neosho Falls, Ks, US 153/G1
Nepal (ctry.) 77/H7
Nepālganj, Nepal 96/C1
Nepāltār, Nepal 97/F2
Nepanagar, India 92/C3
Nepean, On, Can. 161/J2
Nepean (riv.), Austl. 134/G8
Nepeña, Peru 184/B3
Nepessina (lake), Mi, US 167/F6
Nephi, Ut, US 147/H4
Nephin (peak), Ire. 32/A1
Nephin Beg (range), Ire. 32/A1
Nephin Beg (peak), Ire. 32/A1
Nepi, It. 65/B3
Nepisiguit (bay), NB, Can. 158/E2
Nepisiguit (riv.), NB, Can. 158/D2
Nepoko (riv.), D.R. Congo 121/G2
Nepomuceno, Braz. 186/D4
Nepomuk, Czh. 59/G4
Neptune City, NJ, US 168/D3
Nera (riv.), It. 45/K5
Nérac, Fr. 44/D4
Neratovice, Czh. 59/H2
Nercha (riv.), Rus. 78/H1
Nerchinsk, Rus. 78/H1
Nerekhta, Rus. 68/J4
Neresheim, Ger. 58/D5
Nereta, Lat. 41/L3
Nereto, It. 65/C2
Neretva (riv.), Bosn.,Cro. 67/H2
Neretva (riv.), Bosn. 50/D4
Neringa, Lith. 41/J4
Neris (riv.), Lith. 68/E5
Nerja, Sp. 46/D4
Ñermete (pt.), Peru 184/A2
Nerokoúros, Gre. 49/J5
Nerone (peak), It. 63/F6
Nerópolis, Braz. 186/C3
Nerpio, Sp. 46/D3
Nersingen, Ger. 58/D6
Nerva, Sp. 46/B4
Nervesa della Battaglia, It. 63/F2
Nervi, It. 62/C5
Nerviano, It. 62/B2
Neryungri, Rus. 75/N4
Nes, Nor. 40/C1
Nes, Nor. 40/D1
Nes, Neth. 52/C2
Nes Ẕiyyona, Isr. 105/B5
Nesbyen, Nor. 40/C1
Nescopeck (cr.), Pa, US 168/C1
Nesebŭr, Bul. 51/H4
Neshaminy (cr.), Pa, US 168/C3
Nesher, Isr. 105/C3
Neskaupstadhur, Ice. 38/Q6
Nesle, Fr. 54/B4
Nesles-la-Vallée, Fr. 30/J4
Nesodden, Nor. 38/S8
Nespelem, Wa, US 144/E3
Nesque (riv.), Fr. 64/B4
Nesquehoning, Pa, US 168/C2
Ness (riv.), Sc, UK 33/B2
Ness (lake), Sc, UK 33/B2
Ness City, Ks, US 152/E1
Nesselrode (mt.), Ak, US 171/M4
Nesselwang, Ger. 61/G2
Nesslau, Swi. 61/F3
Nesterovka, Rus. 71/K1
Neston, Eng, UK 35/E5
Nestor Falls, On, Can. 157/H3
Nestore (riv.), It. 65/B1
Nestórion, Gre. 49/G2
Néstos (riv.), Gre. 67/K2
Nesvizh, Bela. 70/C1
Net (riv.), Mi, US 157/K4
Netanya, Isr. 105/B4
Netarhāt, India 97/E4
Netarts, Or, US 144/C5
Netawaka, Ks, US 155/G4
Netcong, NJ, US 168/D2
Nethe (riv.), Ger. 53/G5
Netherend, Eng, UK 36/D3
Netherhill, Sk, Can. 145/K2
Netherlands (ctry.) 29/E2
Netherlands Antilles (isls.), StL. 139/L8
Netishyn, Ukr. 72/D2
Netivot, Isr. 105/B6
Netley, Eng, UK 37/E5
Netolice, Czh. 59/H4
Netphen, Ger. 55/H2
Netrakona, Bang. 97/H3
Netstal, Swi. 61/F3
Nett Lake, Mn, US 157/H3
Nett Lake Ind. Res. (lake), Mn, US 157/H3
Nette (riv.), Ger. 52/D6
Nettebach (riv.), Ger. 55/G3
Nettersheim, Ger. 55/F3
Nettetal, Ger. 52/D6
Nettilling (lake), Nun, Can. 141/J2
Nettleham, Eng, UK 35/H5
Nettleton, Ms, US 162/C3
Nettuno, It. 65/B5
Netzschkau, Ger. 59/F1
Neu Darchau, Ger. 53/H2
Neu Heusis, Namb. 122/C4
Neu Zittau, Ger. 42/Q7
Neu-Isenburg, Ger. 58/B2
Neu-Ostheim (Mannheim) (arpt.), Ger. 58/B4
Neu-Ulm, Ger. 58/D6
Neubiberg, Ger. 59/E6
Neubourg, Fr. 57/F2
Neubrandenburg, Ger. 43/G2
Neubrunn, Ger. 58/C3
Neubulach, Ger. 58/B5
Neuburg, Ger. 58/B5
Neuburg an der Donau, Ger. 58/E5
Neuburg an der Kammel, Ger. 61/G1
Neuchâtel (canton), Swi. 60/C4
Neuchâtel, Swi. 60/C4
Neuchâtel, de (lake), Fr. 66/E1
Neudorf, Sk, Can. 156/C2
Neuenbürg, Ger. 58/B5
Neuenburg am Rhein, Ger. 60/D2
Neuendettelsau, Ger. 58/D4
Neuendorf, Ger. 40/E4
Neuenhagen, Ger. 42/Q6
Neuenhaus, Ger. 52/D3
Neuenkirchen, Ger. 53/F3
Neuenkirchen, Ger. 53/F3
Neuenkirchen, Ger. 53/E4
Neuenrade, Ger. 53/E6
Neuenstadt am Kocher, Ger. 58/C4
Neuenstein, Ger. 58/C4
Neuerburg, Ger. 55/F3
Neuf-Brisach, Fr. 60/D1
Neufahrn bei Freising, Ger. 59/E6
Neufchâteau, Fr. 60/B1
Neufchâteau, Belg. 55/E4
Neufchâtel-en-Bray, Fr. 57/G1
Neufchâtel-Hardelot, Fr. 54/A2
Neufchelles, Fr. 30/M4
Neufmanil, Fr. 55/D4
Neufmoutiers-en-Brie, Fr. 30/L5
Neugablonz, Ger. 61/G2
Neuhaus am Inn, Ger. 59/G6
Neuhaus am Rennweg, Ger. 58/E1
Neuhaus-Schierschnitz, Ger. 58/E2
Neuhäusel, Ger. 55/G3
Neuhausen am Rheinfall, Swi. 61/E2
Neuhof, Ger. 58/C2
Neuhof an der Zenn, Ger. 58/D4
Neuhofen, Ger. 58/B4
Neuhofen an der Krems, Aus. 59/H6
Neuillé-Pont-Pierre, Fr. 57/F5
Neuilly-en-Thelle, Fr. 54/B5
Neuilly-L'Évêque, Fr. 60/B2
Neuilly-sur-Marne, Fr. 30/K5
Neuilly-sur-Seine, Fr. 30/J5
Neukirchen, Ger. 40/C4
Neukirchen an der Vöckla, Aus. 59/G6
Neukirchen vorm Wald, Ger. 59/G5
Neukölln, Ger. 42/Q7
Neumarkt (Enga), It. 61/H5
Neumarkt am Wallersee, Aus. 59/G7
Neumarkt im Mühlkreis, Aus. 59/H6
Neumarkt in der Oberpfalz, Ger. 59/E4
Neumarkt-Sankt Veit, Ger. 59/F6
Neumünster, Ger. 40/C4
Neung-sur-Beuvron, Fr. 57/G5
Neunkirch, Swi. 61/E2
Neunkirchen, Ger. 55/H2
Neunkirchen, Ger. 55/G5
Neunkirchen, Aus. 45/M3
Neunkirchen-Seelscheid, Ger. 55/G2
Neupotz, Ger. 58/B4
Neuquén, Arg. 190/C3
Neuquén (riv.), Arg. 190/C3
Neuquén (prov.), Arg. 190/C3
Neuruppin, Ger. 42/G2
Neusäss, Ger. 58/D6
Neuse (riv.), NC, US 163/J3
Neusiedl am See, Aus. 45/M3
Neusiedler (lake), Aus. 43/J5
Neusiedler (Fertő) (lake), Aus. 45/M3
Neuss, Ger. 52/D6
Neustadt, Ger. 42/G2
Neustadt, Ger. 55/G2
Neustadt am Rübenberge, Ger. 53/G3
Neustadt an der Aisch, Ger. 58/D3
Neustadt an der Donau, Ger. 59/E5
Neustadt an der Waldnaab, Ger. 59/F3
Neustadt an der Weinstrasse, Ger. 58/B4
Neustadt bei Coburg, Ger. 58/E2
Neustadt in Holstein, Ger. 40/D4
Neustift im Stubaital, Aus. 61/H3
Neustrelitz, Ger. 42/G2
Neutraubling, Ger. 59/F5
Neuvic, Fr. 44/E4
Neuville-aux-Bois, Fr. 57/H4
Neuville-sur-Saône, Fr. 60/A6
Neuville-sur-Sarthe, Fr. 57/F4
Neuvy-le-Roii, Fr. 57/F5
Neuwied, Ger. 55/G3
Neuzelle, Ger. 43/H2
Neva (riv.), Rus. 41/P2
Nevada, Mo, US 153/G2
Nevada (mts.), Col. 177/H4
Nevada (state), US 142/C4
Nevada, Ia, US 155/H2
Nevada, Tx, US 150/L6
Nevada City, Ca, US 146/C4
Nevada del Huila, PN, Col. 180/C4
Nevada Test Site, Nv, US 148/D2
Nevada, PN, Ven. 180/D2
Nevado de Chañi (peak), Arg. 188/C3
Nevado de Colima (peak), Mex. 174/E5
Nevado de Colima PN, Mex. 174/D5
Nevado de Cumbal (peak), Col. 180/B4
Nevado de Toluca, PN, Mex. 175/K7
Nevado del Candado (peak), Arg. 188/C3
Nevado del Huila (peak), Col. 180/C4
Nevado del Ruiz (peak), Col. 183/K8
Nevado del Tolima (peak), Col. 183/K8
Nevatim, Isr. 105/B6
Nevel', Rus. 41/N3
Nevele, Belg. 54/C1
Nevel'sk, Rus. 79/N2
Never, Rus. 79/J1
Nevers, Fr. 44/E3
Nevertire, Austl. 132/C1
Nevesinje, Bosn. 50/D4
Neville, Sk, Can. 145/L3
Nevinnomyssk, Rus. 73/L5
Nevis, Mn, US 157/G4
Nevis (isl.), UK 173/J4
Nevis (int'l arpt.), StK. 173/N8
Nevis (peak), StK. 173/N8
Nevola (riv.), It. 63/G5
Nevşehir, Turk. 102/C2
Nevşehir (prov.), Turk. 102/C2
New (riv.), Guy. 181/G4
New (riv.), NC, US 163/J3
New Abbey, Sc, UK 34/E2
New Albany, Ms, US 162/C3
New Albany, In, US 162/E1
New Alfresford, Eng, UK 37/E4
New Amsterdam, Guy. 181/G3
New Ancholme (riv.), Eng, UK 35/H4
New Angledool, Austl. 132/C1
New Ash Green, Eng, UK 30/D2
New Athens, Il, US 162/C1
New Auburn, Mn, US 155/G1
New Augusta, Ms, US 164/D2
New Baltimore, Mi, US 167/G6
New Barn, Eng, UK 30/E2
New Bedford, Ma, US 161/L4
New Berlin, NY, US 161/J3
New Berlin, Wi, US 167/P14
New Berlin, Pa, US 168/B2
New Berlinville, Pa, US 168/C3
New Bern, NC, US 163/J3
New Bethlehem, Pa, US 161/G4
New Bloomfield, Mo, US 153/H1
New Bloomfield, Pa, US 161/H4
New Boston, Tx, US 153/G4
New Boston, Oh, US 163/F1
New Braunfels, Tx, US 150/E3
New Bremen, Oh, US 160/D4
New Brighton, Mn, US 157/P6
New Britain (isl.), PNG 136/D5
New Britain, Ct, US 161/K4
New Britain, Pa, US 168/C3
New Brunswick, NJ, US 169/H10
New Brunswick (prov.), Can. 141/K4
New Buffalo, Mi, US 160/C4
New Buffalo, Pa, US 168/B3
New Buildings, NI, UK 34/A2
New Bussa, Nga. 115/G4
New Caledonia (terr.), Fr. 136/F6
New Caledonia (isl.), NCal. 136/F7
New Canaan, Ct, US 169/M7
New Carlisle, Qu, Can. 158/E1
New Castile (reg.), Sp. 66/C3
New Castle, In, US 160/D5
New Castle, Pa, US 160/F4
New Castle, Ky, US 162/E1
New Castle, Va, US 163/G2
New Castle, De, US 168/C4
New Castle (co.), De, US 168/C5
New Chicago, In, US 167/R16
New City, NY, US 169/K7
New Columbia, Pa, US 168/B1
New Columbus, Pa, US 168/B1
New Concord, Oh, US 160/F5
New Concord, Ky, US 162/C2
New Cordell (Cordell), Ok, US 152/E3
New Cumberland, WV, US 160/F4
New Cumberland, Pa, US 168/B3
New Cumnock, Sc, UK 33/B6
New Dayton, Ab, Can. 145/H3
New Deal, Tx, US 152/D4
New Deer, Sc, UK 33/D1
New Delhi (cap.), India 98/D5
New Denver, BC, Can. 144/F3
New Dorp (nbrhd.), NY, US 169/J9
New Edinburg, Ar, US 153/H4
New Effington, SD, US 156/F5
New Egypt, NJ, US 168/D3
New Ellenton, SC, US 163/G4
New England, ND, US 156/C4
New England NP, Austl. 132/E1
New Era, La, US 164/C2
New Exchequer (dam), Ca, US 148/B2
New Florence, Mo, US 155/J4
New Franklin, Mo, US 155/H4
New Freedom, Pa, US 168/B4
New Galloway, Sc, UK 34/D1
New Georgia (isls.), Sol. 136/E5
New Georgia (sound), Sol. 136/E5
New Germany, NS, Can. 158/E3
New Glasgow, NS, Can. 159/F3
New Glasgow, Qu, Can. 159/N6
New Gloucester, Me, US 161/L3
New Gretna, NJ, US 168/D4
New Guinea (isl.), Indo.,PNG 77/N10
New Hampshire (state), US 143/M3
New Hampton, Ia, US 155/H2
New Hanover (isl.), PNG 136/D5
New Hanover, SAfr. 125/E3
New Harbour, NS, Can. 159/G3
New Harmony, Ut, US 149/F2
New Harmony, In, US 162/D1
New Haven, Ct, US 161/K4
New Haven, In, US 160/D4
New Haven, Mi, US 167/G6
New Haven, WV, US 163/G1
New Haven, Il, US 162/C2
New Haven, Mo, US 155/J4
New Haven, Ky, US 162/E2
New Haven, Wy, US 154/B1
New Hebrides (isls.), Van. 136/F6
New Hebron, Ms, US 164/D2
New Hogan (dam), Ca, US 146/C4
New Holland, Pa, US 168/B3
New Holstein, Wi, US 160/B3
New Home, Tx, US 152/D4
New Hope, Ms, US 162/C4
New Hope, Al, US 162/D3
New Hope, Ga, US 163/L7
New Hope, Tx, US 150/L6
New Hope, NC, US 163/H3
New Hope, NC, US 163/J3
New Hope, Pa, US 168/D3
New Hradec, ND, US 156/C4
New Hyde Park, NY, US 169/L9
New Hythe, Eng, UK 30/E3
New Iberia, La, US 164/C2
New Ireland (isl.), PNG 136/E5
New Jersey (state), US 143/M3
New Johnsonville, Tn, US 162/D2
New Kensington, Pa, US 161/G4
New Kent, Va, US 163/J2
New Kowloon, China 87/L7
New Leipzig, ND, US 156/D4
New Lenox, Il, US 167/Q16
New Lexington, Oh, US 160/E5
New Lima, Ok, US 153/F3
New Lisbon, Wi, US 155/J2
New Lisbon, NJ, US 168/D4
New Liskeard, On, Can. 141/J4
New London, Ct, US 161/K4
New London, Wi, US 155/K1
New London, Mn, US 155/G1
New London, Mo, US 155/J4
New London, Tx, US 151/G1
New Lowell, On, Can. 160/G2
New Madrid, Mo, US 162/C2
New Market, Ia, US 155/G3
New Market, Al, US 162/D3
New Market, Va, US 163/H1
New Market, Md, US 168/A5
New Martinsville, WV, US 160/F5
New Meadows, Id, US 146/E1
New Mexico (state), US 142/E5
New Milford, NJ, US 169/J8
New Mills, Eng, UK 35/F5
New Norcia, Austl. 130/C4
New Norfolk, Austl. 132/C4
New Norway, Ab, Can. 145/H1
New Orleans, La, US 164/C3
New Orleans (Moisant Field) (int'l arpt.), La, US 164/C3
New Oxford, Pa, US 168/A4
New Paltz, NY, US 161/J4
New Paris, In, US 160/D4
New Pekin (Pekin), In, US 162/D1
New Philadelphia, Oh, US 160/F4
New Philadelphia, Pa, US 168/B2
New Pine Creek, Or, US 146/C3
New Pitsligo, Sc, UK 33/D1
New Plymouth, NZ 135/C2
New Plymouth, Id, US 146/E2
New Port Richey, Fl, US 164/K7
New Prague, Mn, US 155/H1
New Providence (isl.), Bahm. 173/F3
New Providence, NJ, US 169/H9
New Quay, Wal, UK 36/B2
New Radnor, Wal, UK 36/C2
New Richmond, Qu, Can. 158/E1
New Richmond, Wi, US 155/H1
New River Gorge Nat'l Riv., WV, US 163/G2
New Roads, La, US 164/C2
New Rochelle, NY, US 169/K8
New Rockford, ND, US 156/E4
New Romney, Eng, UK 37/G5
New Ross, Ire. 32/D5
New Ross, NS, Can. 158/E3
New Rossington, Eng, UK 35/G5
New Salem, ND, US 156/D4
New Sarepta, Ab, Can. 145/H1
New Schwabenland (phys. reg.), Ant. 192/Z
New Scone, Sc, UK 33/C4
New Shagunnu, Nga. 115/G4
New Sharon, Ia, US 155/H3
New Shoreham (Block Island), RI, US 169/G1
New Shrewsbury (Tinton Falls), NJ, US 168/D3
New Siberian (isls.), Rus. 77/N2
New Smyrna Beach, Fl, US 165/H3
New South Wales (state), Austl. 127/D4
New Straitsville, Oh, US 160/E5
New Strawn (Strawn), Ks, US 153/G1
New Stuyahok, Ak, US 171/G4
New Summerfield, Tx, US 150/G2
New Tazewell, Tn, US 162/F2
New Town, ND, US 156/C4
New Tredegar, Wal, UK 36/C3
New Tripoli, Pa, US 168/C2
New Ulm, Mn, US 155/G1
New Ulm, Tx, US 150/F3
New Vienna, Oh, US 160/E5
New Virginia, Ia, US 155/H3
New Washington, Oh, US 160/E4
New Waterford, NS, Can. 159/G2
New Westminster, BC, Can. 144/C3
New Whiteland, In, US 160/C5
New Windsor, Md, US 168/A4
New York, NY, US 169/K9
New York (state), US 143/L3
New York Mills, Mn, US 157/G4
New Zealand (ctry.) 127/H6
Newala, Tanz. 119/B4
Newald, Wi, US 157/K5
Newark, Ar, US 153/J3
Newark, Oh, US 160/E4
Newark, NJ, US 169/J9
Newark (int'l arpt.), NJ, US 169/J9
Newark, Ca, US 167/K11
Newark (bay), NJ, US 169/J9
Newark, Il, US 155/K3
Newark, Tx, US 150/K6
Newark, De, US 168/C4
Newark Valley, NY, US 161/H3
Newark-on-Trent, Eng, UK 35/H5
Newaygo, Mi, US 160/D3
Newberg, Or, US 146/B1
Newbern, Tn, US 162/C2
Newberry, Fl, US 165/G3
Newberry, Mi, US 160/D1
Newberry, SC, US 163/G3
Newberry Nat'l Volcanic Mon., Or, US 146/C2
Newbiggin-by-the-Sea, Eng, UK 35/G1
Newbliss, Ire. 32/C1
Newbridge-on-Wye, Wal, UK 36/C2
Newburg, ND, US 156/D3
Newburg, Ar, US 153/J2
Newburgh, Sc, UK 33/E2
Newburgh, Sc, UK 33/C4
Newburgh, NY, US 161/J4
Newburn, Eng, UK 35/G2
Newbury, Vt, US 161/K2
Newbury, Eng, UK 37/E4
Newby Bridge, Eng, UK 35/F3
Newcastle, Austl. 133/E1
Newcastle, NB, Can. 158/E2
Newcastle, SAfr. 125/E2
Newcastle (int'l arpt.), Eng, UK 35/G1
Newcastle, NI, UK 34/C3
Newcastle, Ire. 34/B5
Newcastle, Ire. 32/A5
Newcastle, Ok, US 153/F3
Newcastle, Tx, US 153/E4
Newcastle, Ut, US 149/F2
Newcastle, Wy, US 154/B2
Newcastle upon Tyne, Eng, UK 35/G2
Newcastle upon Tyne (co.), Eng, UK 35/G1
Newcastle Waters, Austl. 128/D4
Newcastle-under-Lyme, Eng, UK 35/F6
Newcastleton, Sc, UK 35/F1
Newcomb, NM, US 149/H2
Newcomerstown, Oh, US 160/F4
Newdegate, Austl. 130/C5
Newdigate, Eng, UK 30/C3
Newe Yam, Isr. 105/B3
Newel, Ger. 55/F4
Newell, Austl. 134/B2
Newell, Ia, US 155/G2
Newellton, La, US 164/C1
Newenham (cape), Ak, US 171/F4
Newent, Eng, UK 36/D3
Newfane, Vt, US 161/K3
Newfane, NY, US 160/V9
Newfield, NJ, US 168/C4
Newfoundland, NJ, US 169/H7
Newfoundland (isl.), Can. 139/M5
Newfoundland (prov.), Can. 141/K3
Newfoundland, Pa, US 168/C1
Newfoundland Evaporation (basin), Ut, US 147/G3
Newgulf, Tx, US 151/G3
Newhalem, Wa, US 144/D3
Newhalen, Ak, US 171/H4
Newham (bor.), Eng, UK 30/D2
Newhaven, Eng, UK 37/F5
Newhope, Ar, US 153/H3
Newick, Eng, UK 37/G5
Newington, Eng, UK 30/F3
Newington, Ga, US 163/G4
Newkirk, Ok, US 153/F2
Newland, NC, US 163/G2
Newlin, Tx, US 152/D3
Newllano, La, US 164/B2
Newlyn, Eng, UK 36/A6
Newmains, Sc, UK 33/C5
Newman, ND, US 156/F4
Newman, Il, US 160/C5
Newman, NM, US 149/J4
Newman (mt.), Austl. 130/C2
Newman, Austl. 130/C2
Newman Grove, Ne, US 154/F3
Newmarket, Ire. 32/A5
Newmarket, NH, US 161/L3
Newmarket, On, Can. 161/G2
Newmarket (nbrhd.), Austl. 134/F6
Newmarket (nbrhd.), NZ 135/F6
Newmarket, Eng, UK 37/G2
Newmarket on Fergus, Ire. 32/B4
Newmerella, Austl. 133/D3
Newmill, Sc, UK 33/D1
Newnan, Ga, US 162/E4
Newnans (lake), Fl, US 165/G3
Newnham, Eng, UK 36/D3
Newport, Qu, Can. 158/E1
Newport, Ire. 32/B4
Newport, Ire. 32/A2
Newport, Eng, UK 36/D1
Newport, Eng, UK 37/E5
Newport, Wal, UK 36/D3
Newport (co.), Wal, UK 36/D3
Newport, Wal, UK 36/B2
Newport, Ar, US 153/J3
Newport (bay), Ca, US 166/C3
Newport, De, US 168/C4
Newport, In, US 160/C5
Newport, Ky, US 160/D5
Newport, Mn, US 157/P7
Newport, NC, US 163/J3
Newport, NH, US 161/K3
Newport, NJ, US 168/C5
Newport, NY, US 161/J3
Newport, Or, US 146/A1
Newport, Pa, US 168/A3
Newport, RI, US 161/L4
Newport, Tn, US 163/F3
Newport, Vt, US 161/K2
Newport, Wa, US 144/F3
Newport Beach, Ca, US 166/G8
Newport Meadows (lake), NJ, US 168/C5
Newport News, Va, US 163/J2
Newport Pagnell, Eng, UK 37/F2
Newport-On-Tay, Sc, UK 33/D4
Newquay, Eng, UK 36/A6
Newquay Civil (arpt.), Eng, UK 36/A6
Newry (dist.), NI, UK 34/B3
Newry, NI, UK 34/B3
Newry (canal), NI, UK 34/B3
Newry, Austl. 128/C4
Newtok, Ak, US 171/F3
Newton, Eng, UK 36/D2
Newton, Ks, US 153/F1
Newton, Sc, UK 35/E1
Newton, Ga, US 165/F2
Newton, Ma, US 161/L3
Newton, Tx, US 151/H2
Newton, Ut, US 147/H3
Newton, Il, US 162/C1
Newton, Ms, US 162/C4
Newton, Ia, US 155/H3
Newton, NC, US 163/G3
Newton, NJ, US 168/D1
Newton (co.), Ga, US 163/M7
Newton Abbot, Eng, UK 36/C5
Newton Aycliffe, Eng, UK 35/G2
Newton Falls, NY, US 161/J2
Newton Mearns, Sc, UK 33/B5
Newton on the Moor, Eng, UK 33/E6
Newton Stewart, Sc, UK 34/D2
Newton Tors (hill), Eng, UK 33/D5
Newton-le-Willows, Eng, UK 35/F5
Newtonmore, Sc, UK 33/B2
Newtonville, NJ, US 168/D4
Newtown, Ire. 32/B5
Newtown, Ct, US 161/K4
Newtown, Austl. 132/B3
Newtown, Mo, US 155/H3
Newtown, Wal, UK 36/C1
Newtown, Pa, US 168/D3
Newtown Forbes, Ire. 32/C2
Newtown Mount Kennedy, Ire. 34/B5
Newtown Saint Boswells, Sc, UK 33/D5
Newtown Sandes, Ire. 32/A4
Newtown Square, Pa, US 168/C4
Newtownabbey, NI, UK 34/C2
Newtownards, NI, UK 34/C2
Newtownbutler, NI, UK 32/C1
Newtownhamilton, NI, UK 34/B3
Newtownstewart, NI, UK 34/A2
Newtyle, Sc, UK 33/C3
Newville, Al, US 165/F2
Nextlalpan, Mex. 175/Q9
Neyagawa, Japan 83/J6
Neyrīz, Iran 103/H4
Neyshābūr, Iran 101/G1
Neyva (riv.), Rus. 69/P4
Neyveli, India 95/C4
Neyyāttinkara, India 95/C4
Nez de Jobourg (pt.), Fr. 56/D1
Nez Perce Ind. Res., Id, US 144/F4
Nezahualcóyotl, Mex. 175/Q10
Nezlobnaya, Rus. 71/G3

Neznay – Northe

Neznayka (riv.), Rus. 69/W9
Nezperce, Id, US 144/F4
Nezvěstice, Czh. 59/G3
Ngabang, Indo. 90/C3
Ngabé, Congo 120/D3
Ngabordamlu (cape), Indo. 128/D1
Ngabu, Malw. 123/G3
Ngabwe, Zam. 123/E2
Ngaga, Tanz. 119/B4
Ngahere, NZ 135/B3
Ngai-Ndethya Nat'l Rsv., Kenya 119/B2
Ngalipaeng, Indo. 91/G3
Ngaloua, Niger 116/B2
Ngalu, Indo. 91/F6
Ngama, Chad 116/C3
Ngamanu Bird Sanct., NZ 135/J8
Ngambé, Camr. 120/B1
Ngambwe (falls), Zam. 122/E3
Ngamda, China 86/C2
Ngami (lake), Bots. 122/D4
Ngamiland (dist.), Bots. 122/D3
Ngamring, China 97/F1
Nganda (peak), Malw. 119/A4
Ngangerabeli (plain), Kenya 119/B2
Ngangla Ringco (lake), China 99/D5
Ngangzê (lake), China 99/E5
Nganha, Montagne de (peak), Camr. 116/B4
Ngao, Thai. 94/B2
Ngaoundal, Camr. 116/B4
Ngaoundéré, Camr. 116/B4
Ngapara, NZ 135/B4
Ngara, Tanz. 121/G3
Ngaras, Indo. 89/D4
Ngarkat Consv. Park, Austl. 131/J5
Ngaruawahia, NZ 135/C2
Ngatapa, NZ 135/D2
Ngathainggyaung, Myan. 86/B5
Ngatik (isl.), Micr. 136/E4
Ngato, Camr. 120/C2
Ngau (isl.), Fiji 137/Y18
Ngauruhoe (vol.), NZ 135/C2
Ngawi, Indo. 89/E4
Ngele, D.R. Congo 120/D2
Ngerengere, Tanz. 119/B3
Nghia Dan, Viet. 94/D2
Nghia Lo, Viet. 94/D1
Ngidinga, D.R. Congo 120/C4
Ngiva, Ang. 122/B3
Ngo, Congo 120/C3
Ngoan Muc (pass), Viet. 94/E4
Ngoc Linh (peak), Viet. 93/J4
Ngofakiaha, Indo. 91/G3
Ngogwa, Tanz. 121/H3
Ngoïla, Camr. 120/C2
Ngoko (riv.), Camr. 120/C2
Ngolo, Chutes de (falls), CAfr. 116/D4
Ngom (falls), EqG. 120/B2
Ngom (falls), EqG. 120/B2
Ngomahuru, Zim. 123/F4
Ngomedzap, Camr. 120/B2
Ngomeni (cape), Kenya 119/C2
Ngong, Kenya 119/B2
Ngonye (falls), Zam. 122/D3
Ngoqumaima, China 99/E5
Ngora, Ugan. 119/A1
Ngoring (lake), China 78/D5
Ngorongoro Consv. Area, Tanz. 119/A2
Ngoto, CAfr. 120/D2
Ngotwane (riv.), Bots. 123/E5
Ngoulemakong, Camr. 120/B2
Ngounié (riv.), Gabon 120/B3
Ngounié (prov.), Gabon 120/B3
Ngoura, Chad 116/C2
Ngouri, Chad 116/B2
Ngourti, Niger 116/B2
N'Goutcheï (well), Chad 116/C1
Ngouyo, CAfr. 117/E4
Ngoywa, Tanz. 121/H4
Ngozi, Buru. 121/G3
Ngudu, Tanz. 119/A2
Nguélémendouka, Camr. 116/B4
Nguigmi, Niger 116/B2
Nguiu, Austl. 128/C2
Ngukurr, Austl. 129/D3
Ngulu (isl.), Micr. 136/C4
Ngumbe Sukani (pt.), Tanz. 119/B4
Ngundu Halt, Zim. 123/F4
Ngunga, Tanz. 119/A2
Ngunza, Ang. 122/B1
Ngurah Rai (int'l arpt.), Indo. 89/F5
Nguru (mts.), Tanz. 119/B3
Nguti, Camr. 115/H5
Nguyen Binh, Viet. 86/E4
Ngwedaung, Myan. 86/C5
Ngwenya (peak), Swaz. 125/E2
Ngwerere, Zam. 123/F2
Nha Trang, Viet. 94/E3
Nhamunda (riv.), Braz. 179/D3
Nhamundá, Braz. 182/B3
Nhandeara, Braz. 189/G2
Nhandugue (riv.), Moz. 123/G3
Nhangue-ia-Pepe, Ang. 120/C5
Nharêa, Ang. 122/C1
Nhia (riv.), Ang. 120/C5
Nhill, Austl. 132/B3
Nhlangano, Swaz. 125/E2
Nho Quan, Viet. 86/E4
Nhulunbuy, Austl. 129/E3
Nia-Nia, D.R. Congo 121/F2
Niabembe, D.R. Congo 121/F3
Niafounké, Mali 114/E3
Niagara, Wi, US 157/L5
Niagara (falls), Can.,US 160/U9
Niagara (co.), On, Can. 160/U9
Niagara (riv.), On, Can. 160/U9
Niagara Cave, Mn, US 155/H2
Niagara Falls, On, Can. 160/U9
Niagara Falls, NY, US 160/U9
Niagara-on-the-Lake, On, Can. 160/U9
Niagassola, Gui. 114/C3
Niakaramandougou, C.d'Iv. 114/D4
Niamey (int'l arpt.), Niger 115/F3
Niamey (cap.), Niger 115/F3
Niamey (dept.), Niger 115/F3
Niamtougou, Togo 115/F4
Niandan (riv.), Afr. 115/G5
Niangara, D.R. Congo 121/F2
Niangay (lake), Mali 114/E3
Niangoloko, Burk. 114/D4
Niangua (riv.), Mo, US 153/H2
Niangua, Mo, US 153/H2
Niangzi (pass), China 80/C3
Niantic, Ct, US 161/K4
Niari (pol. reg.), Congo 120/B3
Niari (riv.), Congo 120/C3
Nias (isl.), Indo. 77/J9
Niassa (prov.), Moz. 119/A4
Nibbar, Tun. 112/L6
Nibley, Ut, US 147/H3
Nibong Tebal, Malay. 89/C1
Nīca, Lat. 41/J3
Nicaragua (lake), Nic. 139/J8
Nicaragua (ctry.) 139/J8
Nicastro-Sambiase, It. 48/E3
Nicatous (lake), Me, US 158/C3
Nice, Fr. 64/D5
Niceville, Fl, US 165/E2
Nichelino, It. 64/D3
Nicheng, China 80/L9
Nichinan, Japan 84/B5
Nichlaul, India 96/D2
Nicholas (chan.), Bang. 177/F1
Nicholasville, Ky, US 162/E2
Nicholls, Ga, US 165/G2
Nichols, Fl, US 164/L8
Nichols, SC, US 163/H3
Nicholson (range), Austl. 130/C3
Nicholson, Austl. 128/C4
Nicholson (riv.), Austl. 129/E4
Nickby (Nikkilä), Fin. 39/F4
Nickelsville, Va, US 163/F2
Nickerie (dist.), Sur. 181/G3
Nickerie (riv.), Sur. 181/G3
Nickol (bay), Austl. 130/C2
Nicobar (isls.), India 77/J9
Nicodemus Nat'l Hist. Site, Ks, US 154/E4
Nicola Mameet Ind. Res., BC, Can. 144/D2
Nicolás Bravo, Mex. 176/D2
Nicolás Romero, Mex. 175/Q9
Nicolet, Qu, Can. 161/K1
Nicollet, Mn, US 155/G1
Nicolls (pt.), NY, US 169/E2
Nicosia, It. 48/D4
Nicosia (dist.), Cyp. 104/C2
Nicosia (cap.), Cyp. 104/C2
Nicotera, It. 48/D3
Nicoya (pen.), CR 172/D6
Nicoya (gulf), CR 172/D6
Nicoya, CR 176/E4
Nictau, NB, Can. 158/D2
Nictaux, NS, Can. 158/E3
Nidau, Swi. 60/D3
Nidd (riv.), Eng, UK 35/G3
Nidd (riv.), Eng, UK 35/G4
Nidda, Ger. 58/B2
Nidda (riv.), Ger. 42/E3
Niddatal, Ger. 58/B2
Nidder (riv.), Ger. 58/C2
Nideggen, Ger. 55/F2
Nidong, China 86/E3
Nidwalden (canton), Swi. 61/E4
Nidzica, Pol. 43/L2
Niebüll, Ger. 40/C4
Nied (riv.), Fr. 45/G2
Niedenstein, Ger. 53/G6
Nieder-Olm, Ger. 55/H4
Niederanven, Lux. 55/F4
Niederbipp, Swi. 60/D3
Niederbronn-les-Bains, Fr. 55/G6
Niedere Tauern (mts.), Aus. 67/G1
Niederfischbach, Ger. 55/G2
Niederlausitz (reg.), Ger. 43/G3
Niedernhausen, Ger. 58/B2
Niederösterreich (prov.), Aus. 50/B2
Niedersachsen (state), Ger. 40/C5
Niedersächsisches Wattenmeer NP, Ger. 53/E1
Niedersachswerfen, Ger. 53/H5
Niederstetten, Ger. 58/C4
Niederstotzingen, Ger. 58/D5
Niederurnen, Swi. 61/F3
Niederwerrn, Ger. 58/D2
Niederwinkling, Ger. 59/F5
Niederzier, Ger. 55/F2
Niederzissen, Ger. 55/G3
Niefang, EqG. 120/B2
Niefern-Öschelbronn, Ger. 58/B5
Niegocin (lake), Pol. 41/J5
Nieheim, Ger. 53/G5
Niélé, C.d'Iv. 114/D4
Niem, CAfr. 116/B4
Niemba, D.R. Congo 121/G4
Niemodlin, Pol. 43/J3
Nienburg, Ger. 53/G3
Nienhagen, Ger. 53/H3
Niénokoué (peak), C.d'Iv. 114/D5
Nieppe, Fr. 54/B2
Niéri (riv.), Sen. 114/B3
Niers (riv.), Ger. 55/F1
Nierstein, Ger. 58/B3
Niet Ban Tinh Xa, Viet. 94/D4
Nieuw Krai Ker, Indo. 128/D1
Nieuw-Amsterdam, Sur. 182/C1
Nieuw-Bergen, Neth. 52/D5
Nieuw-Buinen, Neth. 52/D3
Nieuw-Loosdrecht, Neth. 52/C4
Nieuw-Nickerie, Sur. 181/G3
Nieuw-Schoonebeek, Neth. 52/D3
Nieuw-Vossemeer, Neth. 52/B5
Nieuwe Pekela, Neth. 52/D2
Nieuwegein, Neth. 52/C4
Nieuwendam, Neth. 52/B4
Nieuwerkerk aan de Ijssel, Neth. 52/B5
Nieuweschans, Neth. 53/E2
Nieuwkoop, Neth. 52/B4
Nieuwleusen, Neth. 52/D3
Nieuwoudtville, SAfr. 124/B3
Nieuwpoort, Belg. 54/B1
Nieuwpoort-Bad, Belg. 54/B1
Nieve, Bol. 185/E4
Nieves, Mex. 174/E3
Nīfī Ya'qūb, WBnk. 105/C5
Niğde, Turk. 102/C2
Niğde (prov.), Turk. 102/C2
Nigel, SAfr. 124/E2
Niger (delta), Nga. 115/G5
Niger (riv.), Nga. 114/C4
Niger (ctry.) 107/C3
Niger (riv.), Afr. 107/C4
Niger, Mouths of the, Nga. 115/G5
Nigeria (ctry.) 107/C4
Nigg (bay), Sc, UK 33/B1
Nightcaps, NZ 135/B4
Nighthawk, Wa, US 144/E3
Nightmute, Ak, US 171/F3
Nigrán, Sp. 46/A1
Nigríta, Gre. 49/H2
Nīḩā (peak), Leb. 105/D1
Nihoa (isl.), Hi, US 137/J2
Nihonmatsu, Japan 85/G2
Nihtaur, India 96/B1
Nii (isl.), Japan 85/F3
Niigata, Japan 85/F2
Niigata (int'l arpt.), Japan 85/F2
Niigata (pref.), Japan 82/A4
Niihama, Japan 84/C4
Niihari, Japan 83/E1
Niihau (isl.), Hi, US 142/R10
Niimi, Japan 84/C3
Niitsu, Japan 85/F2
Niiza, Japan 83/D2
Níjar, Sp. 46/D4
Nijkerk, Neth. 52/C4
Nijlen, Belg. 55/D1
Nijmegen, Neth. 52/C5
Nijverdal, Neth. 52/D4
Níkaia, Gre. 49/H3
Nikel', Rus. 38/J1
Nikel'tau, Kaz. 71/L2
Nikiniki, Indo. 128/B2
Nikishka, Ak, US 171/H3
Nikísiani, Gre. 49/J2
Nikitovka, Rus. 73/K2
Nikki, Ben. 115/F4
Nikkilä (Nickby), Fin. 39/F4
Nikkō, Japan 85/F2
Nikkō NP, Japan 85/F2
Niklá al 'Inab, Egypt 113/B3
Niklasdorf, Aus. 45/L3
Nikolaevo, Bul. 51/G4
Nikolai, Ak, US 171/H3
Nikolayevka, Rus. 71/H1
Nikolayevka, Ukr. 72/F4
Nikolayevka, Ukr. 73/J3
Nikolayevo, Rus. 41/N2
Nikolayevsk, Rus. 71/H2
Nikolayevsk-na-Amure, Rus. 75/Q4
Nikol'sk, Rus. 71/H1
Nikolski, Ak, US 171/E5
Nikol'skiy Torzhok, Rus. 68/H4
Nikol'skoye, Rus. 71/H3
Nikol'skoye, Rus. 75/S4
Nikonga (riv.), Tanz. 121/G3
Nikonova Gora, Rus. 68/H3
Nikopol', Ukr. 73/H4
Nikopol, Bul. 51/G4
Niksar, Turk. 70/F4
Nīkshahr, Iran 101/H3
Nikšić, Yugo. 50/D4
Nikumaroro (Gardner) (isl.), Kiri. 137/H5
Nikunau (isl.), Kiri. 136/G5
Nikurān, India 98/D5
Nila (isl.), Indo. 128/C1
Niland, Ca, US 148/E4
Nilaveli, SrL. 95/D4
Nile (riv.), Afr. 107/F2
Nile (delta), Egypt 100/B2
Niles, Il, US 167/Q15
Niles, Mi, US 160/C4
Niles, Oh, US 160/F4
Ni'līn, WBnk. 105/C5
Nilo, Col. 183/L8
Nilópolis, Braz. 187/N7
Nilphāmāri, Bang. 97/G3
Nilsiä, Fin. 68/F3
Nilvange, Fr. 55/F5
Nīmach, India 92/B3
Nīmāj, India 92/B2
Niman (riv.), Rus. 79/L1
Nimba (co.), Libr. 114/C5
Nimba (peak), C.d'Iv. 114/C5
Nîmes, Fr. 44/F5
Nimmitabel, Austl. 133/D3
Nimpo Lake, BC, Can. 144/B1
Nimrod's Fortress (ruin), Syria 105/D2
Nimsbach (riv.), Ger. 55/F4
Nimu, India 98/D2
Nimule, Sudan 121/H2
Nimule NP, Sudan 121/G2
Nin, Cro. 50/B3
Ninaview, Co, US 152/C2
Nīnawā (gov.), Iraq 102/E3
Nīnawá (Nineveh) (ruin), Iraq 103/E2
Nine Point (mesa), Tx, US 151/C3
Ninepin Group (isls.), China 87/M8
Ninepipe Nat'l Wild. Ref., Mt, US 145/G4
Ninety Mile Beach (isl.), NZ 135/C1
Ninety Mile Beach (coast), Austl. 133/C4
Ninety Six, SC, US 163/F3
Ninety Six Nat'l Hist. Site, SC, US 163/F3
Nineveh (Mīnawá) (ruin), Iraq 103/E2
Ninfa (ruin), It. 65/B4
Ninfas (pt.), Arg. 190/D4
Ning'an, China 79/K3
Ningbo, China 80/E5
Ningerum, PNG 129/F1
Ninggang, China 87/G3
Ningguo, China 87/H2
Ninghe, China 80/H7
Ningjin, China 80/C3
Ningjin, China 80/D3
Ningjing (mts.), China 86/C2
Ninglang Yizu Zizhixian, China 86/D3
Ningling, China 80/C4
Ningming, China 87/E4
Ningwu, China 80/C3
Ningxia Zizhiqu (aut. reg.), China 78/F4
Ningyang, China 80/D4
Ningyuan, China 93/K2
Ninh Binh, Viet. 94/D1
Ninh Hoa, Viet. 94/E3
Ninian (riv.), Fr. 56/C4
Ninilchik, Ak, US 171/H3
Niningo (isls.), PNG 136/D5
Ninnescah (riv.), Ks, US 153/F2
Ninohe, Japan 82/B3
Ninomiya, Japan 83/C3
Ninove, Belg. 54/D2
Ninoy Aquino (int'l arpt.), Phil. 88/F6
Nioaque, Braz. 189/F2
Nioaque (riv.), Braz. 186/A4
Niobrara, Ne, US 154/E2
Niobrara (riv.), Ne,Wy, US 154/B2
Niokolo Koba, Sen. 114/B3
Niokolo-Koba, PN du, Sen. 114/B3
Nioku, India 86/B3
Niong (peak), Camr. 116/B4
Niono, Mali 114/D3
Nionsamoridougou, Gui. 114/C4
Nioro du Sahel, Mali 114/C3
Nioro-du-Rip, Sen. 114/B3
Niort, Fr. 44/C3
Nioumachoua, Com. 125/G6
Nipāni, India 95/B2
Nipawin, Sk, Can. 140/F3
Nipe (bay), Cuba 177/H1
Nipele (riv.), Namb. 122/C3
Nipigon (bay), On, Can. 157/K3
Nipigon (riv.), On, Can. 157/K3
Nipigon, On, Can. 157/K3
Nipigon (lake), On, Can. 140/G3
Nipissing (lake), On, Can. 141/J4
Nipomo, Ca, US 148/B3
Nippersink (cr.), Il, US 167/P15
Nipton, Ca, US 148/E3
Niqually (riv.), Wa, US 144/C4
Ñiquén, Chile 190/C3
Niquero, Cuba 177/G1
Nīr, Iran 103/F2
Nir Yizhaq, Isr. 105/A6
Nirasaki, Japan 85/F3
Nirayama, Japan 83/B3
Ñireguao, Chile 190/C5
Nirimba Army Afld., Austl. 134/G8
Nirmal, India 95/C2
Nirmāli, India 97/F2
Niš, Yugo. 50/E4
Niš (int'l arpt.), Yugo. 50/E4
Nişāb, SAr. 103/F4
Nişāb, Yem. 118/C2
Nišava (riv.), Yugo. 49/H1
Niscemi, It. 48/D4
Nishiazai, Japan 83/K5
Nishibiwajima, Japan 83/L5
Nishiharu, Japan 83/L5
Nishikatsura, Japan 83/B2
Nishiki (riv.), Japan 84/B3
Nishiki, Japan 83/H5
Nishinomiya, Japan 83/H6
Nishino'omote, Japan 84/B5
Nishio, Japan 83/M6
Nishiwaki, Japan 83/G6
Nisko, Pol. 43/M3
Nisland, SD, US 154/C1
Nisporeni, Mol. 72/E4
Nisqually (riv.), Wa, US 167/B3
Nisqually, Wa, US 167/B3
Nisqually Ind. Res., Wa, US 167/B3
Nisqually Nat'l Wild. Ref., Wa, US 144/C4
Nisqually Reach (str.), Wa, US 167/B3
Nissan (isl.), PNG 136/E5
Nissan, Fr. 47/G1
Nisser (lake), Nor. 40/C2
Nisshin, Japan 83/M5
Nissum (bay), Den. 40/C3
Nisswa, Mn, US 157/G4
Nistru (riv.), Mol.,Ukr. 72/D3
Nistru (riv.), Mol. 51/H1
Nitelva (riv.), Nor. 38/S8
Niterói, Braz. 187/N7
Nith (riv.), Sc, UK 33/C6
Nith (riv.), Sc, UK 34/E1
Nithsdale (valley), Sc, UK 34/E1
Niti (pass), India 99/C5
Nítibe, ETim. 128/B2
Niton Junction, Ab, Can. 144/G1
Nitra (riv.), Slvk. 43/K4
Nitriansky (pol. reg.), Slvk. 43/K4
Nitsa (riv.), Rus. 69/P4
Nitta, Japan 83/C1
Nittedal, Nor. 40/D1
Nittel, Ger. 55/F4
Nittenau, Ger. 59/F4
Niuafo'ou (isl.), Tonga 137/H6
Niuatoputapu Group (isls.), Tonga 137/H6
Niubiziliang, China 99/F4
Niuchang, China 87/E3
Niue (terr.), NZ 137/H7
Niue (isl.), Niue 137/J6
Niulakita (isl.), Tuv. 136/G6
Niulan (riv.), China 93/H2
Niumaowu, China 81/C2
Niut (peak), Indo. 90/C3
Niutao (isl.), Tuv. 136/G5
Niutou (isl.), China 87/J2
Niutoudian, China 87/F1
Niuwudu (cape), Indo. 128/A2
Niuxintai, China 81/B2
Niuzhuang, China 81/B2
Nivå, Den. 39/J7
Nivelles, Belg. 55/D2
Nivernais (hill), Fr. 44/E3
Niverville, Mb, Can. 156/F3
Niverville, NY, US 161/K3
Niwot, Co, US 154/B3
Nixa, Mo, US 153/H2
Nixi, China 86/C3
Nixon, Nv, US 146/D4
Nixon, Tx, US 151/F3
Niya (riv.), China 99/D4
Niyodo (riv.), Japan 84/C4
Nizāmābād, India 95/C2
Nizhegorodskaya Oblast, Rus. 71/G1
Nizhnekama (res.), Rus. 69/M4
Nizhnekamsk, Rus. 69/L5
Nizhneudinsk, Rus. 75/K4
Nizhnevartovsk, Rus. 74/H3
Nizhneyansk, Rus. 75/P2
Nizhniy Baskunchak, Rus. 71/H2
Nizhniy Chir, Rus. 71/G2
Nizhniy Lomov, Rus. 71/G1
Nizhniy Novgorod, Rus. 69/K4
Nizhniy Tagil, Rus. 69/N4
Nizhniy Yenangsk, Rus. 69/K4
Nizhnyaya Pesha, Rus. 69/K2
Nizhnyaya Tura, Rus. 69/N4
Nizhnyaya Voch', Rus. 69/M3
Nizhyn, Ukr. 72/F2
Nizip, Turk. 102/D2
Nízke Tatry NP, Slvk. 70/A2
Nizwá, Oman 101/G4
Nizza Monferrato, It. 62/B4
Nizzanim, Isr. 105/B5
Njardhvík, Ice. 38/M7
Njombe, Tanz. 119/A4
Njombe (riv.), Tanz. 119/A3
Njoro, Kenya 119/A2
Nkandla, SAfr. 125/E3
Nkayi, Congo 120/C4
Nkeni (riv.), Congo 120/C3
Nkhata Bay, Malw. 123/G1
Nkhotakota, Malw. 123/G2
Nkomfap, Nga. 115/H5
Nkomi (lag.), Gabon 120/B3
Nkonde, Tanz. 121/G4
N'Kongsamba, Camr. 120/B1
Nkourala, Mali 114/D4
Nkout (peak), Camr. 120/C2
Nkululu (riv.), Tanz. 119/A3
Nkusi (riv.), Ugan. 121/G2
Nmai (riv.), Myan. 93/G2
Nnewi, Nga. 115/G5
Noailles, Fr. 54/B5
Noākhāli (pol. reg.), Bang. 97/H4
Noākhāli, Bang. 97/H4
Noale, It. 63/F2
Noāmundi, India 97/E4
Noank, Ct, US 169/F1
Noatak, Ak, US 171/F2
Noatak (riv.), Ak, US 171/F2
Nobber, Ire. 32/D2
Nobeoka, Japan 84/B4
Noble, Ok, US 153/F3
Noble, La, US 150/H2
Nobleford, Ab, Can. 145/H3
Noblesville, In, US 160/C4
Nobleton, Fl, US 164/L6
Nobleton, On, Can. 160/T8
Noboa, Ecu. 180/A5
Noboribetsu, Japan 82/B2
Nobres, Braz. 185/G4
Nocatee, Fl, US 165/H4
Noccundra, Austl. 134/A4
Noce (riv.), It. 61/G5
Nocelleto, It. 65/D5
Nocera Inferiore, It. 65/D6
Nocera Superiore, It. 65/D6
Nocera Umbra, It. 65/B1
Noceto, It. 62/D4
Noci, It. 49/E2
Nockamixon St. Park, Pa, US 168/C3
Nocona, Tx, US 153/F4
Noda, Japan 83/D2
Nodagawa, Japan 83/H4
Nodaway (riv.), Mo, US 155/G3
Nødebo, Den. 39/J7
Nodgrass (hill), Tn, US 162/D3
Noé (cape), Alg. 112/D2
Noel, Mo, US 153/G2
Noëlville, On, Can. 160/F1
Noetinger, Arg. 188/D5
Nogales, Az, US 149/G5
Nogales, Mex. 175/M8
Nogara, It. 63/E3
Nogara, Eth. 117/H2
Nogaro, Fr. 44/C5
Nogat (riv.), Pol. 41/H4
Nogata, Japan 84/B4
Nogent, Fr. 60/B1
Nogent-l'Artaud, Fr. 54/C6
Nogent-le-Roi, Fr. 57/G3
Nogent-le-Rotrou, Fr. 57/F4
Nogent-sur-Oise, Fr. 54/B5
Nogi, Japan 83/D1
Noginsk, Rus. 69/X9
Nogliki, Rus. 75/Q4
Nogoa (riv.), Austl. 134/B4
Nogodan-san (peak), SKor. 81/D5
Nogoonnuur, Mong. 99/F2
Nogoyá, Arg. 188/E5
Nógrád (co.), Hun. 43/K5
Nogwak-san (peak), SKor. 84/A2
Nohar, India 98/C5
Noheji, Japan 82/B3
Nohfelden, Ger. 55/G4
Nohkú, (pt.), Mex. 176/E2
Nohwa, SKor. 79/K5
Noi (riv.), Viet. 93/J5
Noi (riv.), Laos 94/D2
Noidans-lès-Vesoul, Fr. 60/C2
Noire (riv.), Qu, Can. 161/H1
Noireau (riv.), Fr. 57/E3
Noires, (mts.), Fr. 44/B2
Noirmoutier (isl.), Fr. 44/B3
Noisiel, Fr. 54/B6
Noisy-le-Grand, Fr. 30/K5
Noisy-le-Mec, Fr. 30/K5
Noisy-le-Roi, Fr. 30/J5
Nojima-zaki (pt.), Japan 85/F3
Nokaneng, Bots. 122/D3
Nokia, Fin. 41/K1
Nokilalaki (peak), Indo. 91/F4
Nokomis, Sk, Can. 156/B2
Nokomis, Il, US 155/K4
Nokou, Chad 116/B2
Nola, It. 65/D6
Nola, CAfr. 120/D2
Nolan (riv.), Tx, US 150/K7
Nolanville, Tx, US 150/F2
Nole, It. 64/D2
Nolensville, Tn, US 162/D3
Noli, It. 62/B5
Noli, Capo di (cape), It. 62/B5
Nolichucky (riv.), Tn, US 163/F2
Nolin River (lake), Ky, US 162/D2
Nolinsk, Rus. 69/L4
Noma, Fl, US 165/F2
Nomad, PNG 129/F1
Nomadgi NP, Austl. 132/D2
Nombre de Dios (mts.), Hon. 176/E3
Nombre de Dios, Mex. 174/D4
Nomburg, Rus. 69/L2
Nome, Ak, US 171/E3
Nome (cape), Ak, US 171/F3
Nomény, Fr. 55/F6
Nomexy, Fr. 60/C1
Nomgon, Mong. 78/F3
Nomo-misaki (cape), Japan 84/B5
Nomo-zaki (pt.), Japan 84/A4
Nomtsas, Namb. 122/C5
Non Sung, Thai. 94/C3
Nonacho (lake), NW, Can. 140/F2
Nonancourt, Fr. 57/G3
Nonantola, It. 63/E4
Nondalton, Ak, US 171/H4
Nondwa, Tanz. 119/A3
None, It. 64/D3
Nonette (riv.), Fr. 54/B5
Nong Bua Lamphu, Thai. 94/C2
Nong Chang, Thai. 94/B3
Nong Han (res.), Thai. 94/D2
Nong Het, Laos 94/C2
Nong Khai, Thai. 94/C2
Nong Pet, Laos 94/C2
Nong Phai, Thai. 94/C3
Nong'an, China 79/K3
Nongempulu, D.R. Congo 121/E3
Nongenturi, D.R. Congo 120/D3
Nongoma, SAfr. 125/E2
Nongstoin, India 97/H3
Nonnweiler, Ger. 55/F4
Nonoava, Mex. 174/D3
Nonogasta, Arg. 188/C4
Nonouti (isl.), Kiri. 136/G5
Nonri (isl.), China 80/E5
Nonsan, SKor. 81/D4
Nontron, Fr. 44/D4
Nooksack, Wa, US 144/C3
Noonan, ND, US 156/C3
Noonday, Tx, US 151/G1
Noonkanbah Abor. Land, Austl. 128/B4
Noord Holland (prov.), Neth. 52/B3
Noord-Brabant (prov.), Neth. 52/C5
Noordbeveland (isl.), Neth. 52/A5
Noorderhaaks (isl.), Neth. 52/B3
Noordhollandsch Kan. (riv.), Neth. 52/B3
Noordoewer, Namb. 124/B3
Noordostpolder (polder), Neth. 52/C3
Noordwijk aan Zee, Neth. 52/B4
Noordwijk-Binnen, Neth. 52/B4
Noordwijkerhout, Neth. 52/B4
Noordzeekan. (canal), Neth. 52/B4
Noormarkku, Fin. 41/J1
Noorvik, Ak, US 171/F2
Nóqui, Ang. 120/C4
Nor Achin, Arm. 103/F1
Nora, Swe. 40/F2
Nora, Va, US 163/F2
Nora (riv.), Rus. 79/L1
Norala, Phil. 88/D4
Noranside, Austl. 131/J2
Norassouba, Gui. 114/C4
Norberg, Swe. 40/F1
Norberto de la Riestra, Arg. 191/J11
Norborne, Mo, US 155/H4
Norcatur, Ks, US 154/D4
Norchia (ruin), It. 65/A3
Norcia, It. 65/C2
Norco, Ca, US 166/C3
Norcross, Ga, US 163/M7
Nord (prov.), Fr. 54/C3
Nord (prov.), Camr. 116/B3
Nord (riv.), Qu, Can. 159/M6
Nord, (canal), Fr. 54/B4
Nord-Ostsee (Kiel) (canal), Ger. 53/G1
Nord-Ouest (prov.), Camr. 115/H5
Nord-Ouest (pol. reg.), Mor. 112/B2
Nord-Pas-de-Calais (pol. reg.), Fr. 37/H6
Nord-Radde (riv.), Ger. 53/E3
Nord-Sud Kanal (canal), Ger. 53/E3
Nord-Trøndelag (co.), Nor. 38/E2
Nordborg, Den. 40/C4
Nordby, Den. 40/D4
Norddeich, Ger. 53/E1
Nordegg, Ab, Can. 144/F1
Nordegg (riv.), Ab, Can. 144/G1
Nordela (int'l arpt.), Azor., Port. 47/T13
Norden, Ger. 53/E1
Nordenham, Ger. 53/F1
Nordenskjöld (arch.), Rus. 74/J2
Norderney (isl.), Neth. 53/E1
Norderney (arpt.), Ger. 53/E1
Norderney, Ger. 53/E1
Norderstedt, Ger. 53/G1
Nordeste, Ang. 121/E4
Nordhausen, Ger. 42/F3
Nordheim, Tx, US 151/F3
Nordholz, Ger. 53/F1
Nordhorn, Ger. 53/E4
Nordhouse, Fr. 60/D1
Nordjylland (co.), Den. 40/C3
Nordkapp, Nor. 38/H1
Nordkapp (cape), Nor. 38/H1
Nordkinn (pt.), Nor. 38/H1
Nordkirchen, Ger. 53/E5
Nordland (co.), Nor. 38/E2
Nordland, Wa, US 144/C3
Nördlingen, Ger. 58/D5
Nordmaling, Swe. 38/F3
Nordreisa, Nor. 38/G1
Nordrhein-Westfalen (state), Ger. 40/E3
Nords Wharf, Austl. 133/E1
Nordwalde, Ger. 53/E4
Nore (riv.), Ire. 32/C4
Nore, Pic de (peak), Fr. 44/E5
Noresund, Nor. 40/C1
Norfolk (dam), Ar, US 153/H2
Norfolk, NY, US 161/J2
Norfolk (isl.), Austl. 136/F7
Norfolk (mt.), Austl. 132/C4
Norfolk, Ne, US 154/F2
Norfolk, Va, US 163/J2
Norfolk Broads (swamp), Eng, UK 37/H1
Norfolk Nav. Base, Va, US 163/J2
Norg, Neth. 52/D2
Norheimsund, Nor. 40/B1
Norias, Tx, US 151/F4
Norikura-dake (peak), Japan 85/E2
Noril'sk, Rus. 74/J3
Norland, On, Can. 161/G2
Norlina, NC, US 163/H2
Norma, It. 65/B4
Normal, Il, US 155/K3
Norman (riv.), Austl. 129/F4
Norman, Ar, US 153/H3
Norman (lake), NC, US 163/G3
Norman, Ok, US 153/F3
Norman Manley (int'l arpt.), Jam. 177/G2
Norman Park, Ga, US 165/G2
Norman Wells, NW, Can. 140/D2
Normanby, Austl. 134/B1
Normanby (isl.), PNG 136/E6
Normandale Japanese Garden, Mn, US 157/P7
Normandie, Collines de (hill), Fr. 57/E3
Normandin, Qu, Can. 158/A1
Normandy, Eng, UK 30/B3
Normandy (reg.), Fr. 44/C2
Normandy, Tx, US 151/D3
Normandy Beach, NJ, US 168/D4
Normandy Park, Wa, US 167/C3
Normangee, Tx, US 151/F2
Norman's Cove, Nf, Can. 159/L2
Normanton, Austl. 134/A2
Normanton South, Eng, UK 35/G4
Norotshama (peak), Namb. 124/B3
Norquay, Sk, Can. 156/C2
Ñorquinco, Arg. 190/C4
Norrbotten (co.), Swe. 38/F2
Nørre Alslev, Den. 40/D4
Nørre Nebel, Den. 40/C4
Nørre Vorupør, Den. 40/C3
Norridge, Il, US 167/Q16
Norris, Tn, US 162/E2
Norris (lake), Tn, US 162/F2
Norris City, Il, US 162/C2
Norristown, Pa, US 168/C3
Norrköping, Swe. 40/G2
Norrland (reg.), Swe. 38/F2
Norröra (isl.), Swe. 39/C1
Norrsunda, Swe. 39/A1
Norrsundet, Swe. 40/G1
Norrtälje, Swe. 41/H2
Nors, Den. 40/C3
Norseman, Austl. 130/D5
Norsjö, Swe. 38/F2
Norsup, Van. 136/F6
Nort-sur-Erdre, Fr. 56/D6
Norte (pt.), Arg. 191/F3
Norte (pt.), Arg. 190/E4
Norte de Santander (dept.), Col. 177/H4
Norte de Santander (dept.), Col. 177/H4
Norte Los Rodeos (int'l arpt.), Sp. 110/A3
Norte, Canal do (chan.), Braz. 182/D2
Norte, Serra do (mts.), Braz. 185/G3
Nortelândia, Braz. 185/G4
Nörten-Hardenberg, Ger. 53/G5
North (pt.), Austl. 130/B4
North (pt.), Austl. 132/C4
North (pt.), Austl. 133/C4
North (cape), NS, Can. 158/F2
North (cape), NS, Can. 159/G2
North (chan.), On, Can. 160/E1
North (isl.), Kenya 117/G4
North (cape), NZ 135/C1
North (isl.), NZ 135/C2
North (sound), Sc, UK 31/V14
North (sea), Sc, UK 33/D4
North (chan.), UK 34/C1
North (cape), Ak, US 171/D5
North (pt.), Mi, US 160/E2
North (bay), Me, US 158/C
North (lake), Tx, US 150/L7
North, SC, US 163/G4
North (pt.), Md, US 168/B5
North Adams, Ma, US 161/K3
North Albanian Alps (mts.), Alb.,Yugo. 67/H2
North America (cont.) 139/*
North Amherst, Ma, US 161/K3
North Andaman (isl.), India 93/F5
North Anna (riv.), Va, US 163/J1
North Arlington, NJ, US 169/J8
North Ascot, Eng, UK 30/A2
North Atlanta, Ga, US 163/M7
North Augusta, SC, US 163/G4
North Aurora, Il, US 167/P16
North Ayrshire (co.), Sc, UK 33/A5
North Baldy (peak), Wa, US 144/F3
North Ballachulish, Sc, UK 33/A3
North Baltimore, Oh, US 160/E4
North Battleford, Sk, Can. 145/K1
North Bay, On, Can. 161/G1
North Bay, Wi, US 167/Q14
North Beach, Md, US 168/B6
North Beach Haven, NJ, US 168/D4
North Bellmore, NY, US 169/L9
North Bend, BC, Can. 144/D3
North Bend, Or, US 146/A2
North Bend, Pa, US 161/H4
North Bend, Wa, US 167/D3
North Benfleet, Eng, UK 30/E2
North Bergen, NJ, US 169/J8
North Berwick, Sc, UK 33/D4
North Bosque (riv.), Tx, US 151/F2
North Bourke, Austl. 132/C1
North Branch, NJ, US 168/D2
North Branford, Ct, US 169/F1
North Brunswick, NJ, US 168/D3
North Caicos (isl.), UK 177/J1
North Caldwell, NJ, US 169/J8
North Canadian (riv.), Ok, US 153/E2
North Canton, Oh, US 160/F4
North Cape May, NJ, US 168/D6
North Caribou (lake), On, Can. 140/H3
North Carolina (state), US 143/L4
North Cascades NP, Wa, US 144/D3
North Central (plain), Tx, US 175/F1
North Central (prov.), SrL. 95/D4
North Charleston, SC, US 163/H4
North Chicago, Il, US 160/C3
North Collins, NY, US 161/G3
North Concho (riv.), Tx, US 151/D2
North Cowichan, BC, Can. 144/C3
North Crossett, Ar, US 153/J4
North Dakota (state), US 142/F2
North Dandalup, Austl. 130/B5
North Decatur, Ga, US 163/M7
North Dorset Downs (uplands), Eng, UK 36/D5
North Down (dist.), NI, UK 34/C2
North Druid Hills, Ga, US 163/M7
North Eagle Butte, SD, US 154/D1
North East (pt.), Austl. 134/C3
North East, Md, US 168/C4
North East, Pa, US 161/G3
North Eastern (prov.), Kenya 118/B5
North Edwards, Ca, US 148/D3
North Elmham, Eng, UK 37/G1
North English, Ia, US 155/H3
North Enid, Ok, US 153/F2
North Entrance (inlet), PNG 129/F2
North Esk (riv.), Sc, UK 33/D3
North Fabius (riv.), Mo,Ia, US 155/H3
North Fond du Lac, Wi, US 160/B3
North Foreland (pt.), Eng, UK 37/H4
North Fork (riv.), Ok, US 152/E3
North Fork (cr.), Tx, US 153/G4
North Fork (riv.), Tx, US 152/D4
North Fork, Ca, US 148/C2
North Fork, Id, US 147/G1
North Fork Kuskokwim (riv.), Ak, US 171/H3
North Fork Village, Oh, US 160/E5
North Fort Myers, Fl, US 165/H4
North Fox (isl.), Mi, US 157/M5
North Frisian (isls.), Ger. 42/D1
North Front (int'l arpt.), UK 110/D1
North Gauhāti, India 97/H2
North Haledon, NJ, US 169/J8
North Harlowe, NC, US 163/J3
North Haven, Ct, US 161/K4
North Head, NB, Can. 158/D3
North Hero, Vt, US 161/K2
North Highlands, Ca, US 167/L9
North Hodge, La, US 164/B1
North Hollywood (nbrhd.), Ca, US 166/F7
North Holmwood, Eng, UK 30/C3
North Horr, Kenya 117/H5
North Hudson, Wi, US 157/Q7
North Hutchinson (isl.), Fl, US 165/H4
North Hykeham, Eng, UK 35/H5
North Judson, In, US 160/C4
North Killdeer (mtn.), ND, US 156/C4
North Kingsville, Oh, US 160/F4
North Korea (ctry.) 79/J3
North Lakhimpur, India 86/B3
North Lanarkshire (co.), Sc, UK 33/C5
North Las Vegas, Nv, US 148/E2
North Lincolnshire (co.), Eng, UK 35/H4
North Lindenhurst, NY, US 169/M9
North Little Rock, Ar, US 153/H3
North Logan, Ut, US 147/H3
North Long Beach (nbrhd.), Ca, US 166/F8
North Loup (riv.), Ne, US 154/D2
North Luangwa NP, Zam. 121/H5
North Madison, Oh, US 160/F4
North Manchester, In, US 160/D4
North Manitou (isl.), Mi, US 160/C2
North Manitou, Mi, US 160/D2
North Miami, Fl, US 164/P11
North Miami Beach, Fl, US 164/P11
North Minch (The Minch) (str.), Sc, UK 31/Q8
North Mtn. (mtn.), Pa, US 168/B1
North Muskegon, Mi, US 160/C3
North Myrtle Beach, SC, US 163/H4
North New River (canal), Fl, US 164/P10
North Newton, Ks, US 153/F1
North Ogden, Ut, US 147/H3
North Olmsted, Oh, US 160/F4
North Pacific (ocean) 26/A4
North Palm Beach, Fl, US 164/P9
North Pease (riv.), Tx, US 152/D3
North Pelham, On, Can. 160/U9
North Petherton, Eng, UK 36/C4
North Pine (riv.), Austl. 134/E6
North Plainfield, NJ, US 169/H9
North Platte (riv.), Wy, US 147/K3
North Platte, Ne, US 154/D3
North Platte Nat'l Wild.Ref., Ne, US 154/C3
North Pole 192/G
North Pole, Magnetic 192/N
North Pole, Ak, US 171/J3
North Port, Fl, US 165/G4
North Portal, Sk, Can. 156/C3
North Potomac, Md, US 168/A5
North Powder, Or, US 146/E1
North Prairie, Wi, US 167/P14
North Puyallup, Wa, US 167/C3
North Raccoon (riv.), Ia, US 155/G2
North Redington Beach, Fl, US 164/K8
North Richland Hills, Tx, US 150/K7
North Rim, Az, US 149/F2
North Ronaldsay (isl.), Sc, UK 31/V14
North Rustico, PE, Can. 158/F2
North Saanich, BC, Can. 144/C3
North Saint Paul, Mn, US 157/Q6
North Saskatchewan (riv.), Ab,Sk, Can. 140/E3
North Saskatchewan (riv.), Sk, Can. 145/K1
North Shields, Eng, UK 35/G2
North Siberian Lowland (plain), Rus. 74/K2
North Sister (peak), Or, US 146/C1
North Skunk (riv.), Ia, US 155/H3
North Somercotes, Eng, UK 35/J5
North Somerset (co.), Eng, UK 36/D4
North Spirit Lake, On, Can. 157/H1
North Stratford, NH, US 161/L2
North Sulphur (riv.), Tx, US 153/F4
North Sunderland, Eng, UK 33/E5
North Sydney, NS, Can. 159/G2
North Taranaki Bight (bay), NZ 127/H6
North Terre Haute, In, US 160/C5
North Thompson (riv.), BC, Can. 144/E2
North Thoresby, Eng, UK 35/H5
North Tidworth, Eng, UK 37/E4
North Tolsta, Sc, UK 31/Q7
North Tonawanda, NY, US 160/V9
North Tunica, Ms, US 162/B3
North Tyne (riv.), Eng, UK 35/F1
North Uist (isl.), Sc, UK 31/Q8
North Umpqua (riv.), Or, US 146/B2
North Valley Stream, NY, US 169/L9
North Vancouver, BC, Can. 140/D4
North Vernon, In, US 160/D5
North Wales, Pa, US 168/C3
North Walsham, Eng, UK 37/H1
North Weald Bassett, Eng, UK 30/D1
North West (cape), Austl. 130/B2
North West Frontier (prov.), Pak. 99/B4
North West Highlands (uplands), Sc, UK 31/R8
North Western (prov.), SrL. 95/C5
North Wheatley, Eng, UK 35/H5
North Wichita (riv.), Tx, US 152/E4
North Wildwood, NJ, US 168/D6
North Wilkesboro, NC, US 163/G2
North Wilton, Ct, US 169/E1
North Windham, Me, US 161/L3
North Wingfield, Eng, UK 35/G5
North York (city), On, Can. 160/T8
North York Moors NP, Eng, UK 35/G3
North Yorkshire (co.), Eng, UK 35/G3
North-East (dist.), Bots. 123/E4
North-West (prov.), SAfr. 122/E5
North-West Frontier (co.), India 98/A3
Northallerton, Eng, UK 35/G3
Northam, Austl. 130/C4
Northam, Eng, UK 36/B4
Northampton, Austl. 130/B4
Northampton, Eng, UK 37/F2
Northampton, Ma, US 161/K3
Northampton (co.), Pa, US 168/C2
Northampton, Pa, US 168/C2
Northampton Uplands (uplands), Eng, UK 37/E2
Northamptonshire (co.), Eng, UK 37/E2
Northaw, Eng, UK 30/C1
Northbrook, Il, US 167/Q15
Northcliffe, Austl. 130/C5
Northcote, NZ 135/F6
Northcote, Austl. 133/B3
Northeast (pt.), Bahm. 173/G3
Northeast (pt.), Bahm. 177/H1
Northeast (pt.), Jam. 177/G2
Northeast (cape), Ak, US 171/E3
Northeast Land (isl.), Nor. 74/C2
Northeast Land (isl.), Sval. 192/E
Northeast Lincolnshire (co.), Eng, UK 35/H5
Northeim, Ger. 53/G5

Northern (dist.), Isr. 105/C3
Northern (pol. reg.), Gha. 115/E4
Northern (reg.), Malw. 119/A4
Northern (prov.), PNG 129/H2
Northern (prov.), SLeo. 114/B4
Northern (prov.), SrL. 95/D4
Northern Areas (terr.), Pak. 99/B4
Northern Cape (prov.), SAfr. 124/C3
Northern Cheyenne Ind. Res., Mt, US 147/K1
Northern Cook (isls.), CookIs. 137/J6
Northern Dvina (riv.), Rus. 29/J2
Northern Ireland, NI, UK 32/D1
Northern Light (lake), On, Can. 157/J3
Northern Marianas (dpcy.), US 136/D3
Northern Peninsula. Abor. Rsv., Austl. 129/F2
Northern Province (prov.), SAfr. 124/E2
Northern Sporades (isls.), Gre. 67/K3
Northern Territory (terr.), Austl. 127/C2
Northern Ural (hills), Rus. 69/K4
Northern Ural (mts.), Rus. 69/N3
Northern Urals (hills), Rus. 74/E4
Northfield, Tx, US 152/D3
Northfield, Vt, US 161/K2
Northfield, NH, US 161/L3
Northfield, Mn, US 155/H1
Northfleet, Eng, UK 30/D2
Northgate, Sk, Can. 156/C3
Northport, Al, US 162/D4
Northport, Mi, US 160/D2
Northport, Wa, US 144/F3
Northport (Old Northport), NY, US 169/E2
Northridge (nbrhd.), Ca, US 166/E7
Northrup, Tx, US 151/F2
Northumberland (co.), Eng, UK 33/D6
Northumberland (str.), NB,PE, Can. 158/E2
Northumberland, Pa, US 168/B2
Northumberland (co.), Pa, US 168/B2
Northumberland NP, Eng, UK 33/D6
Northvale, NJ, US 169/K7
Northville, NY, US 161/J3
Northville, Mi, US 167/E7
Northway, Ak, US 171/K3
Northwest (cape), Fl, US 165/H5
Northwest Gander (riv.), Nf, Can. 159/K1
Northwest Territories (terr.), Can. 142/E2
Northwestern (prov.), Zam. 122/E2
Northwich, Eng, UK 35/F5
Northwood, ND, US 156/F4
Northwood (nbrhd.), Eng, UK 30/B2
Northwood, Ia, US 155/H2
Norton, NB, Can. 158/E3
Norton, Zim. 123/F3
Norton (bay), Ak, US 171/F3
Norton (sound), Ak, US 171/E3
Norton, Ks, US 154/E4
Norton, Va, US 163/F2
Norton, Tx, US 151/D2
Norton, WV, US 163/H1
Norton Bridge, Eng, UK 35/F6
Norton Heath, Eng, UK 30/D1
Norton Shores, Mi, US 160/C3
Nortonville, Ky, US 162/D2
Nortorf, Ger. 40/C4
Norval, On, Can. 160/T8
Norvegia (cape), Ant. 192/Y
Nörvenich, Ger. 55/F2
Norwalk (riv.), Ct, US 169/M7
Norwalk, Ca, US 166/F8
Norwalk, Ct, US 169/M7
Norwalk, Oh, US 160/E4
Norwalk, Wi, US 155/J2
Norway, Mi, US 157/L5
Norway, Me, US 161/L2
Norway (ctry.) 29/E2
Norway House, Mb, Can. 140/G3
Norwegian (bay), Nun, Can. 141/S7
Norwegian (sea), Eur. 29/D2
Norwich (int'l arpt.), Eng, UK 37/H1
Norwich, Eng, UK 37/H1
Norwich, Ct, US 161/K4
Norwich, Ks, US 153/F2
Norwich, NY, US 161/J3
Norwich, Vt, US 161/K3
Norwood, Co, US 149/H1
Norwood, La, US 164/C2
Norwood, Ma, US 161/L3
Norwood, Mn, US 157/N7
Norwood, NC, US 163/G3
Norwood, NY, US 161/J2
Norwood, NJ, US 169/K8
Norwood, Oh, US 162/E1
Nos Emine (cape), Bul. 51/H4
Nos Kaliakra (pt.), Bul. 51/J4
Nos Maslen Nos (pt.), Bul. 51/H4
Nosappu-misaki (cape), Japan 82/D2
Nose, Japan 83/H6
Nose (hill), Ab, Can. 145/J1
Noshappu-misaki (cape), Japan 82/B1
Noshiro, Japan 82/B3
Nosivka, Ukr. 72/F2
Nosŏng, SKor. 81/D5
Nosong (cape), Malay. 88/A4
Nosop (riv.), Bots. 122/D5
Nosovaya, Rus. 69/K4
Noşratābād, Iran 101/G3
Noss Head (pt.), Sc, UK 31/S7
Nossa Senhora da Glória, Braz. 187/F1
Nossa Senhora do Livramento, Braz. 185/G4
Nossebro, Swe. 40/E2
Nossob (riv.), Namb. 122/C4
Nossobrivier (riv.), SAfr. 122/D5
Nossombougou, Mali 114/D3
Nosy Barren (Barren Islands) (isls.), Madg. 125/G7
Nosy Be (isl.), Madg. 125/H6
Nosy Chesterfield (isl.), Madg. 125/G7
Nosy Mitsio (isl.), Madg. 125/J6
Nosy Saint. Marie (isl.), Madg. 125/J7
Nosy-Varika, Madg. 125/J8
Notaresco, It. 65/C2
Notasulga, Al, US 162/E4
Notch (cape), Chile 191/B6
Notec (riv.), Pol. 43/J2
Noto, It. 48/D4
Noto (valley), It. 48/D4
Noto (gulf), It. 48/D4
Noto (pen.), Japan 85/E2
Noto Antica (ruin), It. 48/D4
Notodden, Nor. 40/C2
Notogawa, Japan 83/K5
Notoro (lake), Japan 82/C1
Notre Dame (mts.), Qu, Can. 158/B3
Notre Dame, Fr. 30/K5
Notre Dame (mts.), On, Can. 141/J4
Notre Dame (bay), Nf, Can. 141/L4
Notre Dame de Lourdes, Mb, Can. 156/E3
Notre-Dame-de-Bondeville, Fr. 57/G1
Notre-Dame-de-Île-Perrot, Qu, Can. 159/N7
Notre-Dame-de-la-Salette, Qu, Can. 161/J2
Notre-Dame-des-Monts, Qu, Can. 158/B2
Notre-Dame-du-Lac, Qu, Can. 158/C2
Notsé, Togo 115/F5
Nott (mt.), Austl. 131/G5
Nottawasaga (bay), On, Can. 160/F2
Nottaway (riv.), Qu, Can. 141/J3
Nøtterøy, Nor. 40/D2
Nottingham, Eng, UK 35/G6
Nottingham (isl.), Nun, Can. 141/H2
Nottingham (co.), Eng, UK 35/G6
Nottinghamshire (co.), Eng, UK 35/G5
Nottoway, Va, US 163/H2
Nottoway (riv.), Va, US 163/J2
Nottoway Plantation, La, US 164/C2
Nottuln, Ger. 53/E5
Notukeu (riv.), Sk, Can. 145/L3
Nouabalé (riv.), Congo 120/D2
Nouâdhibou, Mrta. 110/A5
Nouadhibou (int'l arpt.), Mrta. 110/A5
Nouakchott (cap.), Mrta. 114/B2
Nouakchott (int'l arpt.), Mrta. 114/B2
Nouâmghâr, Mrta. 114/A2
Nouan-le-Fuzelier, Fr. 57/H5
Noue (riv.), Fr. 47/F1
Nouméa (cap.), NCal. 137/V13
Noumea (Tontouta) (int'l arpt.), NCal. 137/V13
Nouna, Burk. 114/E3
Noupoort, SAfr. 124/D3
Nouvelle, Qu, Can. 158/D1
Nouvion-sur-Meuse, Fr. 55/D4
Nœux-les-Mines, Fr. 54/B3
Nouzonville, Fr. 55/D4
Nova Andradina, Braz. 189/F2
Nova Astrakhan', Ukr. 73/K3
Nova Basan', Ukr. 72/F2
Nova Borova, Ukr. 72/E2
Nova Brasilândia, Braz. 186/B2
Nova Caipemba, Ang. 120/C4
Nova Cruz, Braz. 183/H4
Nová Dubnica, Slvk. 43/K4
Nova Friburgo, Braz. 187/E4
Nova Gaia, Ang. 120/D5
Nova Gorica, Slov. 63/G2
Nova Gradiška, Cro. 50/C3
Nova Granada, Braz. 189/G2
Nova Iguaçu, Braz. 187/N7
Nova Kakhovka, Ukr. 72/G4
Nova Lamego, GBis. 114/B3
Nova Levante (Welshnofen), It. 61/H5
Nova Lima, Braz. 186/E3
Nova Londrina, Braz. 186/B4
Nova Lusitânia, Moz. 123/G3
Nova Mambone, Moz. 123/G4
Nova Mayachka, Ukr. 73/G4
Nova Odesa, Ukr. 72/F4
Nova Olinda, Braz. 183/G4
Nova Olinda do Norte, Braz. 182/B3
Nova Pazova, Yugo. 50/E3
Nova Praha, Ukr. 73/G3
Nova Prata, Braz. 189/G4
Nova Russas, Braz. 183/F4
Nova Scotia (prov.), Can. 141/K4
Nova Sintra, CpV. 107/J11
Nova Sofala, Moz. 123/G4
Nova Timboteua, Braz. 183/E3
Nova Ushytsya, Ukr. 72/D3
Nova Varoš, Yugo. 50/D4
Nova Vodolaha, Ukr. 73/H3
Nova Xavantina, Braz. 186/B2
Nova Zagora, Bul. 51/H4
Novaci, Rom. 51/F3
Novafeltria, It. 63/F6
Novaliches (res.), Phil. 88/F6
Novara, It. 62/B3
Novate Mezzola, It. 61/F5
Novato, Ca, US 146/B4
Novaya Igirma, Rus. 75/L4
Novaya Ivanovka, Ukr. 51/J3
Novaya Kalitva, Rus. 73/L2
Novaya Kazanka, Kaz. 71/J2
Novaya Ladoga, Rus. 41/Q1
Novaya Lyalya, Rus. 69/P4
Novaya Maluksa, Rus. 41/P2
Novaya Sibir' (isl.), Rus. 75/R2
Novaya Usman', Rus. 73/K2
Novaya Zemlya (isl.), Rus. 192/C
Nove, It. 63/E2
Nové Hrady, Czh. 59/H5
Nové Město nad Váhom, Slvk. 43/J4
Nové Sedlo, Czh. 59/F2
Nové Strašecí, Czh. 59/G2
Nové Zámky, Slvk. 50/D2
Novelda, Sp. 47/E3
Novellara, It. 63/D4
Noventa, It. 63/E3
Noventa di Piave, It. 63/F2
Noventa Vicentina, It. 63/E3
Noves, Fr. 64/A5
Novgorod, Rus. 68/F4
Novgorodka, Rus. 41/N3
Novgorodskaya Oblast, Rus. 68/G4
Novgorodskoye, Ukr. 73/J3
Novhorod-Sivers'kyy, Ukr. 73/G2
Novhorodka, Ukr. 72/G3
Novi, Mi, US 167/E7
Novi Bečej, Yugo. 50/E3
Novi di Modena, It. 63/D4
Novi Iskŭr, Bul. 51/F4
Novi Pazar, Yugo. 50/E4
Novi Pazar, Bul. 51/H4
Novi Sad, Yugo. 50/D3
Novi Sanzhary, Ukr. 73/H3
Novi Vinodolski, Cro. 45/L4
Novice, Tx, US 153/G4
Novice, Tx, US 150/E2
Novikovo, Rus. 79/N2
Novillars, Fr. 60/C3
Novinger, Mo, US 155/H3
Nóvita, Col. 180/B3
Novo (riv.), Braz. 187/N6
Novo Alexeyevka (int'l arpt.), Geo. 71/H4
Novo Aripuanã, Braz. 185/F2
Novo Hamburgo, Braz. 189/G4
Novo Horizonte, Braz. 189/G2
Novo Mesto, Slov. 50/B3
Novo Miloševo, Yugo. 50/E3
Novo Oriente, Braz. 183/F4
Novo-Titarovskaya, Rus. 73/K5
Novoalekseyevka, Kaz. 71/K2
Novoaltaysk, Rus. 74/J4
Novoanninskiy, Rus. 73/M2
Novoazovs'k, Ukr. 73/K4
Novobelokatay, Rus. 69/N5
Novobogatinskoye, Kaz. 71/J3
Novocheboksarsk, Rus. 69/K4
Novocherkassk, Rus. 73/L4
Novodevich'ye, Rus. 71/J1
Novodruzhes'k, Ukr. 73/K3
Novodugino, Rus. 68/G5
Novogrudok, Bela. 41/L5
Novohrad-Volyns'kyy, Ukr. 72/D2
Novohradské Hory (mts.), Czh. 59/H5
Novohrodivka, Ukr. 73/J3
Novoizborsk, Rus. 41/M3
Novokhopërskiy, Rus. 73/L2
Novokubansk, Rus. 73/L5
Novokuybyshevsk, Rus. 71/J1
Novokuznetsk, Rus. 74/J4
Novolazarevskaya, Rus., Ant. 192/A
Novolukoml', Bela. 41/N4
Novominskaya, Rus. 73/K4
Novomoskovsk, Rus. 70/F1
Novomoskovs'k, Ukr. 73/H3
Novomykolayivka, Ukr. 73/H4
Novomyrhorod, Ukr. 72/F3
Novonikolayevskiy, Rus. 73/M2
Novonukutskiy, Rus. 78/E1
Novooleksiyivka, Ukr. 73/H4
Novopokrovka, Ukr. 73/H3
Novopokrovskaya, Rus. 73/L5
Novorontsovka, Ukr. 73/G4
Novorossiysk, Rus. 73/J5
Novorossiyskoye, Kaz. 71/L2
Novorzhev, Rus. 41/N3
Novoselivs'ke, Ukr. 73/G5
Novoselytsya, Ukr. 72/D3
Novosergiyevka, Rus. 71/K1
Novoshakhtinsk, Rus. 73/K4
Novosibirsk, Rus. 74/J4
Novosibirskaya Oblast, Rus. 74/J4
Novosil', Rus. 70/F1
Novosil'skoye, Rus. 73/K2
Novosineglazovskiy, Rus. 69/P5
Novosokol'niki, Rus. 41/P3
Novostroyevo, Rus. 41/J4
Novotroitsk, Rus. 71/L2
Novotroyits'ke, Ukr. 73/H4
Novoukrayinka, Ukr. 72/F3
Novoul'yanovsk, Rus. 71/J1
Novouzensk, Rus. 71/J2
Novovolyns'k, Ukr. 72/C2
Novovoronezhskiy, Rus. 73/K2
Novovyatsk, Rus. 69/L4
Novoyamskoye, Rus. 70/E1
Novozybkov, Rus. 70/D1
Novska, Cro. 50/C3
Novy (int'l arpt.), Rus. 79/M2
Nový Jičín, Czh. 43/K4
Novyy Buh, Ukr. 73/G4
Novyy Oskol, Rus. 73/J2
Novyy Port, Rus. 74/H3
Novyy Rozdol, Ukr. 72/C3
Novyy Svit, Ukr. 73/H5
Novyy Urengoy, Rus. 74/H3
Nowa Dęba, Pol. 43/L3
Nowa Nowa, Austl. 133/D3
Nowa Ruda, Pol. 43/J3
Nowa Sarzyna, Pol. 43/M3
Nowa Sól, Pol. 43/H3
Nowata, Ok, US 153/G2
Nowe, Pol. 43/K2
Nowe Miasto Lubawskie, Pol. 43/K2
Nowen (peak), Ire. 32/A6
Nowendoc, Austl. 132/D1
Nowgong, India 96/B3
Nowgong (Nagaon), India 86/B3
Nowitna (riv.), Ak, US 171/G3
Nowogard, Pol. 40/F5
Nowood (riv.), Wy, US 147/K2
Nowra, Austl. 133/E2
Nowrangapur, India 95/D2
Nowshera, Pak. 98/A2
Nowy Dwór Gdański, Pol. 41/H4
Nowy Sącz, Pol. 43/L4
Nowy Staw, Pol. 41/H4
Nowy Targ, Pol. 43/L4
Nowy Tomyśl, Pol. 43/J2
Noxapater, Ms, US 162/C4
Noxon, Mt, US 144/G4
Noxubee NWR, Ms, US 162/C4
Noya, Sp. 46/A1
Noyabr'sk, Rus. 74/H3
Noyal-Pontivy, Fr. 56/C4
Noyal-sur-Vilaine, Fr. 56/D4
Noyant, Fr. 57/F5
Noye (riv.), Fr. 54/B4
Noyen-sur-Sarthe, Fr. 57/E5
Noyers-sur-Cher, Fr. 57/G6
Noyil (riv.), India 95/C4
Noyon, Fr. 54/C4
Nozay, Fr. 56/D5
Nsah, Congo 120/C3
Nsak, Gabon 120/C2
Nsanje, Malw. 123/G3
Nsawam, Gha. 115/E5
Nsoc, EqG. 120/B2
Nsondia, D.R. Congo 120/D3
Nsopzup, Myan. 86/C3
Nsukka, Nga. 115/G5
Nsumbu NP, Zam. 121/G5
Nsuta, Gha. 115/E5
Ntem (riv.), Camr. 120/B2
Nterguent, Mrta. 114/B2
Ntoroko, Ugan. 121/G2
Ntoum, Gabon 120/B2
Ntui, Camr. 120/B1
Ntulume, D.R. Congo 121/E4
Ntungamo, Ugan. 121/G3
Ntusi, Ugan. 121/G2
Ntwetwe Pan (salt pan), Bots. 122/E4
Nu (riv.), China 93/G2
Nu (mts.), China 86/C3
Nu (Salween) (riv.), China 78/D5
Nuang (peak), Malay. 89/C2
Nuangola, Pa, US 168/C1
Nuanshui, China 87/H2
Nūbah, Egypt 113/C4
Nūbārīya (canal), Egypt 113/B3
Nubian (des.), Sudan 107/F2
Nucet, Rom. 50/F2
Nucla, Co, US 149/H1
Nucourt, Fr. 30/H4
Nudaybah, Egypt 113/B3
Nüdlingen, Ger. 58/D2
Nueces (riv.), Tx, US 172/B2
Nueltin (lake), Nun, Can. 140/G2
Nuenen, Neth. 52/C6
Nueva Alejandría, Peru 184/C2
Nueva Asunción (dept.), Par. 188/D2
Nueva Ciudad Guerrero, Mex. 151/E4
Nueva Concepción, Guat. 176/D3
Nueva Constitución, Arg. 190/D2
Nueva Esparta (state), Ven. 181/E2
Nueva Esperanza, Arg. 188/D3
Nueva Florida, Ven. 180/D2
Nueva Germania, Par. 189/E2
Nueva Gerona, Cuba 177/F1
Nueva Helvecia, Uru. 191/K11
Nueva Imperial, Chile 190/B3
Nueva Italia de Ruiz, Mex. 174/E5
Nueva Loja, Ecu. 180/B4
Nueva Lubecka, Arg. 190/C5
Nueva Ocotepéque, Hon. 176/D3
Nueva Palmira, Uru. 191/J10
Nueva Patria, Mex. 175/N8
Nueva Rosita, Mex. 151/D4
Nueva Villa de Padilla, Mex. 175/F3
Nueve de Julio, Arg. 190/E2
Nuevitas, Cuba 177/G1
Nuevo, Ca, US 166/C3
Nuevo (gulf), Arg. 190/D4
Nuevo Andoas, Peru 184/B1
Nuevo Balsas, Mex. 175/F5
Nuevo Berlín, Uru. 191/J10
Nuevo Casas Grandes, Mex. 174/D2
Nuevo Chagres, Pan. 177/F4
Nuevo Ideal, Mex. 174/D3
Nuevo Ixcatlán, Mex. 176/C2
Nuevo Laredo, Mex. 151/E4
Nuevo Leon (state), Mex. 172/A2
Nuevo León, Mex. 148/E4
Nuevo Mundo, Bol. 185/E3
Nuevo Progreso, Mex. 151/F4
Nuevo Rocafuerte, Ecu. 180/C5
Nufenen, Swi. 61/F4
Nufenenpass (pass), Swi. 61/E5
Nugaaleed (valley), Som. 118/D3
Nugent, Tx, US 151/E1
Nugget (pt.), NZ 135/B4
Nuguria (isls.), PNG 136/E5
Nuhne (riv.), Ger. 53/F6
Nui (isl.), Tuv. 136/G5
Nuiqsut, Ak, US 171/H1
Nuits-Saint-Georges, Fr. 60/A3
Nukata, Japan 83/M6
Nuklunek (mt.), Ak, US 171/F4
Nuku Hiva (isl.), FrPol. 137/L5
Nuku'alofa (cap.), Tonga 137/H7
Nukufetau (isl.), Tuv. 136/G5
Nukulaelae (isl.), Tuv. 136/H5
Nukumanu Atoll (atoll), PNG 136/E5
Nukunonu (isl.), Tok. 137/H5
Nukuoro (isl.), Micr. 136/E4
Nukus, Uzb. 74/F5
Nukutavake (isl.), FrPol. 137/M6
Nulato, Ak, US 171/G3
Nules, Sp. 47/E3
Nullagine, Austl. 130/D2
Nullarbor, Austl. 131/F4
Nullarbor (plain), Austl. 127/B4
Nullarbor NP, Austl. 131/F4
Numan, Nga. 116/B3
Numana, It. 63/G6
Numansdorp, Neth. 52/B5
Numata, Japan 85/F2
Numatinna (riv.), Sudan 117/E4
Numazu, Japan 85/F3
Numbi, D.R. Congo 121/G3
Nümbrecht, Ger. 55/G2
Numbulwar, Austl. 129/D3
Numfoor (isl.), Indo. 91/H4
Nummela, Fin. 39/E4
Nummi, Fin. 41/K1
Numurkah, Austl. 133/B3
Nunapitchuk, Ak, US 171/F3
Nunawading (nbrhd.), Austl. 132/G5
Nunchía, Col. 180/C3
Nunda, NY, US 161/H3
Nundle, Austl. 132/D1
Nuneaton, Eng, UK 37/E1
Nŭng-ni, NKor. 81/D3
Nungarin, Austl. 130/C4
Nungatta NP, Austl. 133/D3
Nungo, Moz. 123/H2
Nungwe, Tanz. 121/H3
Nunivak (isl.), Ak, US 171/E4
Nunley, Ar, US 153/G3
Nunnelly, Tn, US 162/D3
Nunningen, Swi. 60/D3
Nuñoa, Peru 184/D4
Nunspeet, Neth. 52/C4
Nunthorpe, Eng, UK 35/G2
Nunukan, Indo. 88/B4
Nuomin (riv.), China 79/J1
Nuon (riv.), Libr. 114/C5
Nuoro, It. 48/A2
Nupurböle (Nupurila), Fin. 39/E4
Nupurila (Nupurböle), Fin. 39/E4
Nuqūb, Yem. 118/C2
Nuquí, Col. 180/B3
Nur (mts.), Turk. 104/E1
Nur, China 99/D4
Nura (riv.), Kaz. 99/B2
Nūrābād, Iran 103/G4
Nurata, Uzb. 74/G5
Nürburgring, Ger. 55/F3
Nure (riv.), It. 62/C3
Nuremberg, Pa, US 168/B2
Nurhak, Turk. 102/D2
Nuri (ruin), Sudan 109/F5
Nuria (peak), It. 65/C3
Nuriootpa, Austl. 131/H5
Nūrla, India 98/D2
Nurlat, Rus. 69/L5
Nūrmahal, India 98/C4
Nurmijärvi, Fin. 41/L1
Nürnberg (int'l arpt.), Ger. 58/E3
Nürnberg, Ger. 58/E4
Nūrpur, Pak. 98/B3
Nurri (mt.), Austl. 132/C1
Nursery, Tx, US 151/F3
Nürtingen, Ger. 58/C5
Nus, It. 64/D1
Nusa Tenggara Timur (prov.), Indo. 128/A2
Nūsah, Yem. 118/C2
Nūshābād, Iran 103/G3
Nushagak (riv.), Ak, US 171/G4
Nushki, Pak. 101/J3
Nutberry (hill), Sc, UK 33/C5
Nuth, Neth. 55/E2
Nuthe-Graben (riv.), Ger. 42/Q7
Nutley, NJ, US 169/J8
Nuttby (mtn.), NS, Can. 158/F3
Nutwood Downs, Austl. 128/D3
Nuuk (Godthåb), Grld. 139/M3
Nuuksion NP, Fin. 39/E4
Nuupere (pt.), FrPol. 137/X15
Nuvolento, It. 62/D2
Nuwākot, Nepal 96/D1
Nuwara Eliya, SrL. 95/D5
Nuwaybi', Egypt 109/G2
Nuy (riv.), SAfr. 124/L10
Nuza (mt.), Zim. 123/G3
Nüziders, Aus. 61/F3
Nūzvīd, India 95/D2
Nxai Pan (salt pan), Bots. 122/E3
Nxai Pan NP, Bots. 122/E3
Nxaunxau, Bots. 122/D3
Nya-Ghezi, D.R. Congo 121/G3
Nyaake, Libr. 114/D5
Nyabing, Austl. 130/C5
Nyabisindu, Rwa. 121/G3
Nyack, NY, US 169/K7
Nyah, Austl. 132/B2
Nyah West, Austl. 132/B2
Nyahua, Tanz. 119/A3
Nyahururu Falls, Kenya 119/B1
Nyainqêntanglha (peak), China 99/F5
Nyainqêntanglha (mts.), China 86/B2
Nyainrong, China 86/B1
Nyakabindi, Tanz. 119/A2
Nyakanyasi, Tanz. 121/G3
Nyaki NP, Malw. 119/A4
Nyaki NPP, Malw. 123/G1
Nyakrom, Gha. 115/E5
Nyaksimvol', Rus. 69/P3
Nyakulenga, Zam. 122/D2
Nyala, Sudan 117/E2
Nyalam, China 97/E1
Nyalikungu, Tanz. 119/A2
Nyamandhlovu, Zim. 123/F3
Nyamapande, Zim. 123/G3
Nyambiti, Tanz. 119/A2
Nyamina, Mali 114/D3
Nyamlell, Sudan 117/E3
Nyamtumbo, Tanz. 119/B4
Nyandoma, Rus. 68/J3
Nyanga (riv.), Gabon 120/B3
Nyanga (prov.), Gabon 120/B3
Nyanga, Gabon 120/B3
Nyanga NP, Zim. 123/G3
Nyanga-Nord, Rsv. de la, Gabon,Congo 120/B3
Nyangui (peak), Zim. 123/G3
Nyanyadzi, Zim. 123/G3
Nyanza (prov.), Kenya 119/A2
Nyanza-Lac, Buru. 121/G4
Nyanzwa, Tanz. 119/B3
Nyaruonga, Tanz. 121/G3
Nyasa (lake), Malw. 107/F6
Nyaunglebin, Myan. 94/B2
Nyazepetrovsk, Rus. 69/N4
Nyazura, Zim. 123/G3
Nybergsund, Nor. 40/E1
Nybro, Swe. 40/F3
Nyêmo, China 97/H1
Nyenasi, Gha. 115/E5
Nyeri, Kenya 119/B2
Nyerol, Sudan 117/G3
Nyikog (riv.), China 78/E5
Nyima, China 99/E5
Nyimba, Zam. 123/F2
Nyírábrány, Hun. 50/F2
Nyíradony, Hun. 43/L5
Nyírbátor, Hun. 43/M5
Nyíregyháza, Hun. 43/L5
Nyírmada, Hun. 43/M4
Nyiru (mt.), Kenya 119/B1
Nykirke, Nor. 38/S9
Nykøbing, Den. 40/D4
Nykøbing, Den. 40/C3
Nykøbing S, Den. 39/H7
Nyköping, Swe. 40/G2
Nykvarn, Swe. 39/A1
Nylrivier (riv.), SAfr. 123/F5
Nylstroom, SAfr. 123/F5
Nymagee, Austl. 132/C2
Nynäshamn, Swe. 40/G2
Nyngan, Austl. 132/C1
Nyoman (riv.), Bela. 68/E5
Nyon, Swi. 60/C5
Nyong (riv.), Camr. 116/A5
Nyons, Fr. 64/B4
Nýřany, Czh. 59/G3
Nyrob, Rus. 69/N3
Nýrsko (res.), Czh. 59/G4
Nýrsko, Czh. 59/G4
Nysa, Pol. 43/J3
Nysätra, Swe. 39/A1
Nyssa, Or, US 146/E2
Nysted, Den. 40/D4
Nyūdo-zaki (pt.), Japan 82/A4
Nyuk (lake), Rus. 68/F2
Nyukhcha, Rus. 69/K3
Nyuksenitsa, Rus. 69/K3
Nyúl, Hun. 50/C2
Nyunzu, D.R. Congo 121/G4
Nyurba, Rus. 75/M3
Nyuvchim, Rus. 69/L3
Nyūzen, Japan 85/E2
Nzega, Tanz. 119/A3
Nzérékoré (pol. reg.), Gui. 114/C4
Nzérékoré, Gui. 114/C5
Nzeret, D.R. Congo 116/D4
N'Zeto, Ang. 120/C4
Nzi (riv.), C.d'Iv. 114/D5

O

O'Ciese Ind. Res., Ab, Can. 144/G1
O'The Pines (lake), Tx, US 151/G1
O' The Pines (lake), Tx, US 153/G4
O'Fallon (cr.), Mt, US 156/B4
O'Hares (cr.), Austl. 134/G8
O'Higgins (lake), Chile 191/B6
O'Sullivan (lake), On, Can. 157/L2
Ō-shima (isl.), Japan 82/A3
O. T. Downs, Austl. 129/D4
O.C. Fisher (lake), Tx, US 151/D2
Oa, Mull of (pt.), Sc, UK 31/Q9
Oadby, Eng, UK 37/E1
Oahe (lake), ND,SD, US 142/F2
Oahe (dam), SD, US 154/D1
Oahu (isl.), Hi, US 142/V11
Oak Bluffs, Ma, US 158/B5
Oak Creek, Co, US 147/K3
Oak Creek, Wi, US 160/C3
Oak Forest, Il, US 167/Q16
Oak Grove, La, US 153/J4
Oak Grove, Ar, US 153/H2
Oak Grove, Co, US 149/J1
Oak Grove, Tn, US 162/D2
Oak Grove, Ky, US 162/D2
Oak Harbor, Oh, US 160/E4
Oak Harbor, Wa, US 144/C3
Oak Hill, Mi, US 160/C2
Oak Hill, Fl, US 165/H3
Oak Hill, Tn, US 162/D2
Oak Hill, Oh, US 163/F1
Oak Hill, WV, US 163/G2
Oak Hill, Ga, US 163/M7
Oak Lake, Mb, Can. 156/D3
Oak Lawn, Il, US 160/C4
Oak Park, Il, US 167/Q16
Oak Park, Mi, US 167/F7
Oak Park, Ga, US 163/F4
Oak Ridge, Tn, US 162/E2
Oak Ridge, NJ, US 168/D1
Oak Ridges, On, Can. 160/U8
Oak River, Mb, Can. 156/D2
Oak View, Ca, US 166/A2
Oakbank, Mb, Can. 156/F3
Oakburn, Mb, Can. 156/D2
Oakdale, La, US 164/B2
Oakdale, Ca, US 148/B2
Oakdale, Austl. 133/E2
Oakes, ND, US 156/E4
Oakesdale, Wa, US 144/F4
Oakey, Austl. 134/C4
Oakham, Eng, UK 37/F1
Oakhurst, Ok, US 153/F2
Oakhurst, Ca, US 148/C2
Oakland, Fl, US 164/M6
Oakland, Il, US 160/B5
Oakland, Md, US 161/G5
Oakland, NJ, US 169/J7
Oakland (lake), Mi, US 167/F6
Oakland (co.), Mi, US 167/E6
Oakland, Or, US 146/B2
Oakland, Ne, US 155/F3
Oakland, Md, US 168/B5
Oakland (bay), Wa, US 167/A3
Oakland City, In, US 162/D1
Oakland Park, Fl, US 164/P10
Oaklands, Austl. 133/C2
Oakley, Ca, US 167/L10
Oakley, Ut, US 147/H3
Oakley, Id, US 147/G2
Oakley, Ks, US 154/D4
Oakley, Ms, US 162/B4
Oakley, Eng, UK 37/F2
Oakover (riv.), Austl. 127/B3
Oakridge, Or, US 146/B2
Oaktown, In, US 162/D1
Oakville, Mb, Can. 156/F3
Oakville, Mo, US 162/B1
Oakville, On, Can. 159/R9
Oakwood, Ga, US 162/F3
Oakwood, Va, US 163/F2
Oakwood, Tx, US 151/G2
Oakwood Hills, Il, US 167/P15
Oamaru, NZ 135/B4
Ōamishirasato, Japan 83/E2
Oani, Com. 125/G6
Oat (mtn.), Ca, US 166/B2
Oatlands, Austl. 132/C4
Oatman, Az, US 148/E3
Oaxaca (state), Mex. 172/B4
Oaxaca de Juárez, Mex. 176/B2
Ob' (riv.), Rus. 77/F3
Ob' (gulf), Rus. 77/G3
Ob Luang Gorge, Thai. 94/B2
Obala, Camr. 120/B1
Obama (bay), Japan 83/J4
Obama, Japan 83/J5
Oban, Sc, UK 31/R8
Oban (hills), Nga. 115/H5
Oban, NZ 135/B4
Obanazawa, Japan 82/B4
Obando, Col. 183/K8
Obara, Japan 83/M5
Obata, Japan 83/L7
Obaya, D.R. Congo 121/F3
Obbnäs (Upinniemi), Fin. 39/E4
Obed, Ab, Can. 144/F1
Obeliai, Lith. 41/L4
Obelisk (peak), NZ 135/B4
Ober Ramstadt, Ger. 58/B3
Ober-Olm, Ger. 58/B3
Oberá, Arg. 189/F3
Oberalppass (pass), Swi. 61/E4
Oberalpstock (peak), Swi. 61/E4
Oberammergau, Ger. 61/H2
Oberasbach, Ger. 58/D4
Oberau, Ger. 61/H2
Oberburg, Swi. 60/D3
Oberderdingen, Ger. 58/B4
Oberdiessbach, Swi. 60/D4
Oberding, Ger. 59/E6
Oberdorf, Swi. 60/D3
Oberdorla, Ger. 53/H6
Oberelsbach, Ger. 58/D2
Oberentfelden, Swi. 60/E3
Oberglatt, Swi. 61/E3
Obergünzburg, Ger. 61/G2
Oberhaching, Ger. 59/E6
Oberhausen, Ger. 52/D6
Oberkirch, Ger. 60/E1
Oberkochen, Ger. 58/D5
Oberkotzau, Ger. 59/E2
Oberlausitz (reg.), Ger. 43/H3
Oberlin, La, US 164/B2
Oberlin, Ks, US 154/D4
Obernai, Fr. 60/D1
Obernburg am Main, Ger. 58/C3
Oberndorf am Neckar, Ger. 61/E1
Oberndorf bei Salzburg, Aus. 59/F7
Oberneukirchen, Aus. 59/H6
Obernkirchen, Ger. 53/G4
Oberon, Austl. 133/D1
Oberösterreich (prov.), Aus. 43/G4
Oberpfälzer Wald (for.), Ger. 59/F3
Oberrieden, Swi. 61/E3
Oberriet, Swi. 61/F3
Obersaxen, Swi. 61/F4
Oberschleissheim, Ger. 59/E6
Oberschneiding, Ger. 59/F5
Obersiggenthal, Swi. 61/E3
Oberstammheim, Swi. 61/E2
Oberstaufen, Ger. 61/G2
Oberstdorf, Ger. 61/G3
Oberthal, Ger. 55/G4
Obertrum am See, Aus. 59/G7
Obertshausen, Ger. 58/B2
Oberursel, Ger. 58/B2
Oberuzwil, Swi. 61/F3
Oberviechtach, Ger. 59/F4
Oberwald, Swi. 61/E4
Oberwart, Aus. 50/C2
Oberwesel, Ger. 55/G3
Oberwiessenthal, Ger. 59/F2
Oberwil, Swi. 60/D4
Oberwölz, Aus. 45/L3
Obfelden, Swi. 61/E3
Obi (isl.), Indo. 91/G4
Obi (isls.), Indo. 91/G4
Obi (str.), Indo. 91/G4
Obiaruku, Nga. 115/G5
Óbidos, Port. 46/A3
Óbidos, Braz. 182/C3
Obihiro, Japan 82/C2
Obilić, Yugo. 50/E4
Obing, Ger. 59/F6
Obion, Tn, US 162/C2
Obion (riv.), Tn, US 162/C2
Obion, North Fork (riv.), Tn, US 162/C2
Obion, South Fork (riv.), Tn, US 162/C2
Obira, Japan 82/B1
Obitochnaya (bay), Ukr. 73/H4
Obitsu (riv.), Japan 83/D3
Oblivskaya, Rus. 73/M3
Oblong, Il, US 162/D1
Obluch'ye, Rus. 79/L2
Obninsk, Rus. 68/H5
Obo, CAfr. 117/E4
Obo, China 78/E4
Obo Liang, China 99/F4
Obock, Djib. 118/B3
Obokote, D.R. Congo 121/F3
Obolo, Nga. 115/G5
Oborniki, Pol. 43/J2
Oborniki Śląskie, Pol. 43/J3
Obouya, Congo 120/C3
Oboyan', Rus. 73/J2
Obozerskiy, Rus. 68/J3
Obra (riv.), Pol. 43/J2
Obrenovac, Yugo. 50/E3
Obrež, Yugo. 50/E4
O'Brien, Or, US 146/B2
O'Briensbridge, Ire. 32/B4
Obrigheim, Ger. 58/B3
Obrigheim, Ger. 58/C4
Observatory, Austl. 132/G5
Obsharovka, Rus. 71/J1
Obtrumer (lake), Aus. 59/F7
Ōbu, Japan 83/L6
Obuasi, Gha. 115/E5
Obubra, Nga. 115/H5
Obudu, Nga. 115/H5
Obukhiv, Ukr. 72/F2
Obura, PNG 129/G1
Obw. (canton), Swi. 61/E4
Obzor, Bul. 51/H4
Ocala, Fl, US 165/G3
Ocampo, Mex. 174/E3
Ocaña, Col. 180/C2
Ocaña, Sp. 46/D3
Occhieppo Inferiore, It. 62/B2
Occhieppo Superiore, It. 62/A1
Occhiobello, It. 63/E4
Occhito (lake), It. 65/D4
Occidental, Cordillera (mts.), SAm. 184/B2
Occimiano, It. 62/B3
Ocean (cape), Ak, US 171/L3
Ocean (co.), NJ, US 168/D4
Ocean Beach, NY, US 169/E2
Ocean City, Md, US 163/K1
Ocean City, NJ, US 168/D5
Ocean Falls, BC, Can. 140/D3
Ocean Gate, NJ, US 168/D4
Ocean Grove, NJ, US 168/D3
Ocean Grove, Austl. 133/B4
Ocean Park, Wa, US 144/B4
Ocean Pines, Md, US 163/K1
Ocean Ridge, Fl, US 164/P9
Ocean View, De, US 163/K1
Ocean View, NJ, US 168/D5
Oceana, WV, US 163/G2
Oceana Nav. Air Sta., Va, US 163/J2
Oceano, Ca, US 148/B3
Oceanographic Museum, Mona. 62/J8
Oceanside, Ca, US 166/C4
Oceanside, NY, US 169/L9
Oceanville, NJ, US 168/D5
Ocee, Ga, US 163/M6
Ochakiv, Ukr. 72/F4
Och'amch'ire, Geo. 71/G4
Ochapowace Ind. Res., Sk, Can. 156/C2
Ochelata, Ok, US 153/G2
Ochiishi-misaki (cape), Japan 82/D2
Ochil (hills), Sc, UK 33/C4
Ochlocknee, Ga, US 165/F2
Ochlockonee (riv.), Fl, US 165/F2
Ocho Rios, Jam. 177/G2
Ochobo, Nga. 115/G5
Ochopee, Fl, US 165/H5
Ochsenfurt, Ger. 58/D3
Ochsenhausen, Ger. 61/F1
Ochsenkopf (peak), Aus. 61/F3
Ochtendung, Ger. 55/G3
Ochtrup, Ger. 53/E4
Ochtum (riv.), Ger. 53/F2
Ocilla, Ga, US 165/G2
Ockelbo, Swe. 40/G1
Ockenheim, Ger. 55/G4
Ocklawaha, Fl, US 165/H3
Ocmulgee (riv.), Ga, US 162/F4
Ocmulgee Nat'l Mon., Ga, US 162/F4
Ocna Mureş, Rom. 51/F2
Ocna Sibiului, Rom. 51/G3
Ocnele Mari, Rom. 72/C5
Ocnita, Mol. 72/D3
Ocoee, Fl, US 164/M6
Ocoña, Peru 184/C5
Ocoña (riv.), Peru 184/C4
Oconee (res.), Ga, US 163/F4
Oconee (riv.), Ga, US 163/F4
Oconomowoc, Wi, US 155/K2
Oconto (riv.), Wi, US 157/K5
Oconto, Wi, US 160/C2
Oconto Falls, Wi, US 160/B2
Ocosingo, Mex. 176/C2
Ocosta, Wa, US 144/B4
Ocotal, Nic. 176/E3
Ocotlán, Mex. 174/E4
Ocotlán de Morelos, Mex. 176/B2
Ocoyoacac, Mex. 175/Q10
Ocozocoautla de Espinosa, Mex. 176/C2
Ocracoke (isl.), NC, US 163/K3
Ocracoke, NC, US 163/K3
Ocros, Peru 184/B3
Octararo (cr.), Pa, US 168/B4
Octeville, Fr. 56/D1
Octeville-sur-Mer, Fr. 57/F1
October Revolution (isl.), Rus. 77/H2
Ocumare de la Costa, Ven. 183/N7
Ocumare del Tuy, Ven. 183/P7
Ocurí, Bol. 188/C1
Oda, Gha. 115/E5
Oda (peak), Sudan 109/H4
Oda, Japan 84/C3
Ódádhahraun (lava flow), Ice. 38/P7
Ŏdaejin, NKor. 81/E2
Odaesan NP, SKor. 84/A2
Ōdai, Japan 83/K7
Ōdaigahara-san (peak), Japan 84/E3
Ödåkra, Swe. 39/J6
Odanah, Wi, US 157/J4
Ōdate, Japan 82/B3
Odawara, Japan 85/F3
Odda, Nor. 40/B1
Odder, Den. 40/D4
Oddur (Xuddur), Som. 118/B4
Odebolt, Ia, US 155/G2
Odeborn (riv.), Ger. 53/F6
Odell, Tx, US 152/E3
Odell, Il, US 155/K3
Odell, Or, US 144/D5
Odelzhausen, Ger. 58/E6
Odem, Tx, US 151/F4
Odemira, Port. 46/A4
Ödemiş, Turk. 102/A2
Odendaalsrus, SAfr. 124/D2
Odensala, Swe. 39/A1
Odense, Den. 40/D4
Odense (int'l arpt.), Den. 40/D4
Odenthal, Ger. 55/G1
Odenton, Md, US 168/B5
Odenwald (reg.), Ger. 58/B3
Oder (Odra) (riv.), Ger.,Pol. 43/H2
Oder-Spree Kanal (canal), Ger. 42/Q7
Oderen, Fr. 60/C2
Oderhaff (lag.), Ger. 43/H2
Oderzo, It. 63/F2
Odesa, Ukr. 72/F4
Odes'ka Oblast, Ukr. 70/D3
Odessa, De, US 168/C5
Odessa, Fl, US 164/K7
Odessa, Mn, US 155/F1
Odessa, NY, US 161/H3
Odessa, Tx, US 151/C2
Odessa, Wa, US 144/E4
Odessa Meteor Crater, Tx, US 151/C2
Odet (riv.), Fr. 44/B2
Odhan, India 98/C5
Odienné, C.d'Iv. 114/D4
Odin, Ks, US 153/E1
Odin, Il, US 162/C1
Odin (mt.), BC, Can. 144/E2
Odintsovo, Rus. 69/W9
Odiongan, Phil. 88/C2
Odivelas, Port. 47/P10
Odobeşti, Rom. 51/H3
Odon (riv.), Fr. 44/C2
Odon, In, US 162/D1
Odongk, Camb. 94/D4
O'Donnell, Tx, US 152/D4
O'Donnells, Nf, Can. 159/L2
Odoorn, Neth. 52/D3
Odorheiu Secuiesc, Rom. 51/G2
Odra (Oder) (riv.), Ger.,Pol. 43/H2
Odum, Ga, US 165/G2
Odžaci, Yugo. 50/D3
Odzala, PN d', Congo 120/C2
Odzi, Zim. 123/G3
Odzi (riv.), Zim. 123/G3
Odziba, Congo 120/C3
Ōe, Japan 83/H5
Ōe-yama (peak), Japan 83/H5
Oegstgeest, Neth. 52/B4
Oeiras, Braz. 183/F4
Oelde, Ger. 53/F5
Oelemari (riv.), Sur. 182/C2
Oelrichs, SD, US 154/C2
Oelsnitz, Ger. 59/F2
Oelwein, Ia, US 155/J2
Oeno (isl.), Pitc. 137/M7
Oenpelli, Austl. 128/D3
Oensingen, Swi. 60/D3
Oer-Erkenschwick, Ger. 53/E5
Oesling (mts.), Lux. 55/E4
Oesterdam (dam), Neth. 52/B6
Oestrich-Winkel, Ger. 58/B3
Oeta NP, Gre. 49/H3
Oetz, Aus. 61/G3
Oey'ŏn (isl.), SKor. 81/D3
Of, Turk. 70/G4
Ofahoma, Ms, US 162/C4
Ofaqim, Isr. 105/B6
Ofenhorn (peak), Swi. 61/E5
Ofenpass (Pass dal Fuorn) (pass), Swi. 61/G4
Offa, Nga. 115/G4
Offaly (co.), Ire. 34/A5
Offanengo, It. 62/C3
Offement, Fr. 60/C2
Offenbach, Ger. 58/B2
Offenbach an der Queich, Ger. 58/B4
Offenburg, Ger. 60/D1
Offerle, Ks, US 152/E2
Offerman, Ga, US 165/G2
Offida, It. 65/C2
Offingen, Ger. 58/D6
Offoué (riv.), Gabon 120/B3
Offoué, Rsv. Integrale de l', Gabon 120/B3
Offranville, Fr. 57/G1
Offstein, Ger. 58/B3
Offut (A.F.B.), Ne, US 155/G3
Oftersheim, Ger. 58/B4
Oftringen, Swi. 60/D3
Ōfunato, Japan 82/B4
Oga (pen.), Japan 82/A4
Oga, Japan 82/A4
Ogachi, Japan 82/B4
Ogadēn (reg.), Eth. 118/B4
Ōgaki, Japan 83/L5
Ogallala, Ne, US 154/D3
Ogano, Japan 83/C2
Ogasawara, Japan 136/D2
Ogatsu, Japan 82/B4
Ogawa, Japan 83/E1
Ogawa, Japan 83/C1
Ogawara (lake), Japan 82/B3
Ogbomosho, Nga. 115/G4
Ogden, Ar, US 153/G4
Ogden, Ut, US 147/H3
Ogden, Ks, US 155/F4
Ogden, Ia, US 155/G2
Ogdensburg, NY, US 161/J2
Ogdensburg, NJ, US 168/D1
Ogeechee (riv.), Ga, US 163/G4
Ogema, Sk, Can. 156/B3
Oggiono, It. 62/C2
Ogi, Japan 85/F2
Ogidaki (mtn.), On, Can. 141/H4
Ogies, SAfr. 124/E2
Ogilvie, Mn, US 157/H5
Ogilvie (riv.), Yk, Can. 140/C2
Ogilvie (mts.), Yk, Can. 140/C2
Oglala, SD, US 154/C2
Oglanly, Trkm. 71/K5
Oglanly, Trkm. 103/H2
Oglesby, Il, US 155/K3
Oglesby, Tx, US 175/F2
Oglethorpe, Ga, US 162/E4
Oglio (riv.), It. 45/J4
Ogmore, Austl. 134/C3
Ogmore-by-Sea, Wal, UK 36/C4
Ognon (riv.), Fr. 42/C5
Ogoamas (peak), Indo. 91/F3
Ogodzha, Rus. 79/L1
Ogoja, Nga. 115/H5
Ogooué (riv.), Gabon 107/C5
Ogooué-Ivindo (prov.), Gabon 120/C2
Ogooué-Lolo (prov.), Gabon 120/C3
Ogooue-Maritime (prov.), Gabon 120/B3
Ogorelyshi, Rus. 68/G3
Ogose, Japan 83/C2
Ogosta (riv.), Bul. 51/F4
Ogr, Sudan 117/E2
Ogre, Lat. 41/L3
Oguchi, Japan 83/L5
Ogulin, Cro. 50/B3
Ogun (riv.), Nga. 115/F5
Ogun (state), Nga. 115/F5
Ogurchinskiy (isl.), Trkm. 71/K5
Ogurugu, Nga. 115/G5
Oğuz, Turk. 102/D2
Ogwashi Uku, Nga. 115/G5
Oh Me Edge (hill), Eng, UK 33/D6
Ohafia, Nga. 115/G5
Ohai, NZ 135/A4
Ohakune, NZ 135/C2
Ohanet, Alg. 111/H3
Ōhara, Japan 83/E3
O'Hara Head (cape), Austl. 133/E2
Oharu, Japan 83/L5
Ōhata, Japan 82/B3
Ohau (lake), NZ 135/B4
Ohey, Belg. 55/E3

O'Higgi – Oster

O'Higgins (pol. reg.), Chile 190/B1
Ohio, Co, US 149/J1
Ohio (riv.), US 139/J6
Ohio (state), US 143/K3
Ohio Caverns, Oh, US 160/E4
Ōhira, Japan 83/D1
Ohlsdorf, Aus. 59/G7
Ohlstadt, Ger. 61/H2
Ohm (riv.), Ger. 58/C1
Ōho, Japan 83/E1
Ohoopee (riv.), Ga, US 163/F4
Ohopoho, Namb. 122/B3
Ohre (riv.), Ger. 42/F2
Ohře (riv.), Czh. 42/H3
Ohrid, FYROM 49/G2
Ohrid (lake), FYROM,Alb. 50/E5
Ohrigstad, SAfr. 123/F5
Ohura, NZ 135/C2
Ōi (riv.), Japan 79/M4
Oi (riv.), China 78/D6
Ōi, Japan 83/C3
Ōi, Japan 83/D2
Ōi, Japan 83/J5
Oiapoque (riv.), Braz. 182/C2
Oiapoque, Braz. 182/D2
Oich (lake), Sc, UK 33/B2
Oieras, Port. 47/P10
Oiga, China 86/B2
Oignies, Fr. 54/B3
Oignin (riv.), Fr. 60/B5
Oil Center, NM, US 150/C1
Oil City, La, US 153/H4
Oil City, Pa, US 161/G4
Oildale, Ca, US 148/C3
Oilmont, Mt, US 145/J3
Oinasjärvi, Fin. 39/E4
Oinófita, Gre. 49/H3
Oinói, Gre. 49/N8
Oir (riv.), Fr. 56/D3
Oirschot, Neth. 52/C5
Oise (riv.), Fr. 42/B4
Oise (dept.), Fr. 54/B5
Oise à l'Aisne, Canal de l' (canal), Fr. 54/C4
Oiseaux du Djoudj, PN des, Sen. 114/A2
Ōiso, Japan 83/C3
Oissel, Fr. 57/G2
Oissery, Fr. 30/L4
Oisterwijk, Neth. 52/C5
Ōita, Japan 84/B4
Ōita (pref.), Japan 84/B4
Ōita (riv.), Japan 84/B4
Oitti, Fin. 39/F4
Oiyug, China 97/G1
Ōizumi, Japan 83/A2
Ōizumi, Japan 83/C1
Ōja (isl.), Swe. 39/A2
Ojai, Ca, US 166/A2
Ojajärvi (lake), Fin. 39/E4
Ojakkala, Fin. 39/E4
Ojcowski NP, Pol. 43/K3
Öjebyn, Swe. 38/G2
Ōji, Japan 83/J6
Ojima, Japan 83/C1
Ojinaga, Mex. 151/B3
Ojiya, Japan 85/F2
Ojo Caliente, NM, US 149/J2
Ojo de Agua, Mex. 175/Q9
Ojo de Liebre (lag.), Mex. 174/B3
Ojocaliente, Mex. 174/E4
Ojos del Salado (peak), Arg.,Chile 188/B3
Ojos Negros, Sp. 46/E2
Ojuelos de Jalisco, Mex. 175/E4
Oka (riv.), Rus. 75/L4
Oka, Nga. 115/G5
Oka, Congo 120/C3
Oka, Qu, Can. 159/M7
Okaba, Indo. 129/E2
Okabe, Japan 83/C1
Okahandja, Namb. 122/C4
Okahumpka, Fl, US 164/M6
Okaihau, NZ 135/C1
Okak (isl.), Nf, Can. 141/K3
Okala, Camr. 120/B1
Okanagan (lake), BC, Can. 140/D4
Okanagan (range), BC, Can. 144/D3
Okanagan Falls, BC, Can. 144/E3
Okanda, PN de l', Gabon 120/B3
Okano (riv.), Gabon 120/B2
Okanogan (riv.), Wa, US 144/E3
Okanogan, Wa, US 144/E3
Okapa, PNG 129/G1
Okaputa, Namb. 122/C4
Okāra, Pak. 98/B4
Okarche, Ok, US 153/F3
Okarem, Trkm. 103/H2
Okatana, Namb. 122/B3
Okatibbee (res.), Ms, US 162/C4
Okato, NZ 135/C2
Okaukuejo, Namb. 122/B3
Okavango (delta), Bots. 122/D3
Okavango (riv.), Bots. 122/D3
Ōkawa, Japan 84/B4
Okawville, Il, US 162/C1
Okay, Ok, US 153/G3
Okaya, Japan 85/F2
Okayama, Japan 84/C3
Okayama (pref.), Japan 84/C3
Okazaki, Japan 83/M6
Okazize, Namb. 122/C4
Okch'ŏn, SKor. 81/D4
Oke Iho, Nga. 115/F4
Okęcie (int'l arpt.), Pol. 43/L2
Okeechobee, Fl, US 165/H4
Okeechobee (lake), Fl, US 143/K6
Okeene, Ok, US 153/E2
Okefenokee (swamp), Ga, US 165/G2
Okefenokee Heritage Center, Ga, US 165/G2
Okefenokee Nat'l Wildlife Refuge, Ga, US 165/G2
Okegawa, Japan 83/D2
Okehampton, Eng, UK 36/C5
Okemah, Ok, US 153/F3
Okement (riv.), Eng, UK 36/B5
Okemos, Mi, US 160/D3
Okene, Nga. 115/G5
Okerembete, Nga. 115/G5
Okesa, Ok, US 153/F2
Oketo, Ks, US 155/F4
Okha, Rus. 75/Q4
Okhaldhungā, Nepal 97/F2
Ókhi, Óros (peak), Gre. 49/J3
Okhotsk (sea), Rus. 77/P4
Okhotsk, Rus. 75/Q4
Okhta (riv.), Rus. 69/T6
Okhtyrka, Ukr. 73/H2
Oki (isls.), Japan 75/P6
Okidaitō (isl.), Japan 85/L8
Okiep, SAfr. 124/B3
Okinawa (isl.), Japan 77/M7
Okinawa (pref.), Japan 85/J8
Okino-shima (isl.), Japan 84/C4
Okino-Tori-Shima (Parece Vela) (isl.), Japan 77/N7
Okinoerabu (isl.), Japan 85/K7
Okitipupa, Nga. 115/G5
Okkan, Myan. 86/B5
Okku, SKor. 81/D5
Oklahoma (state), US 143/G4
Oklahoma City (cap.), Ok, US 153/F3
Oklahoma High Top (peak), Ok, US 153/G3
Oklaunion, Tx, US 152/E3
Oklawaha (riv.), Fl, US 165/H3
Okmulgee, Ok, US 153/G3
Oko, Nga. 115/G5
Okobaji (lakes), Ia, US 155/G2
Okobojo (cr.), SD, US 154/D1
Okok (riv.), Ugan. 119/A1
Okolona, Ms, US 162/C3
Okondeka, Namb. 122/B3
Okondja, Gabon 120/C3
Okoppe, Japan 82/C1
Okotoks, Ab, Can. 145/H2
Okovango (riv.), Namb. 107/E6
Okoyo, Congo 120/C3
Oksbøl, Den. 40/C4
Oksino, Rus. 69/M2
Oksjärvi (lake), Fin. 39/D4
Oksskolten (peak), Nor. 38/E2
Oktaha, Ok, US 153/G3
Oktwin, Myan. 94/B2
Oktyabr', Kaz. 71/L2
Oktyabr'sk, Rus. 71/J1
Oktyabr'skiy, Rus. 69/M5
Oktyabr'skiy, Rus. 71/G3
Oktyabr'skiy, Rus. 68/J3
Oktyabr'skiy, Rus. 75/R4
Oktyabr'skiy, Rus. 79/K1
Oktyabr'skiy, Kaz. 78/A2
Oktyabr'skoye, Rus. 71/K1
Oktyabr'skoye, Ukr. 73/H5
Ōkuchi, Japan 84/B4
Okulovka, Rus. 68/G4
Okunev Nos, Rus. 69/M2
Okushiri, Japan 82/A2
Okushiri (isl.), Japan 79/M3
Okuta, Nga. 115/F4
Okutama (lake), Japan 83/C2
Okutama, Japan 83/C2
Okwa (riv.), Bots. 122/D4
Ol Doinyo Sabuk NP, Kenya 119/B2
Ola, Rus. 75/R4
Ola, Ar, US 153/H3
Ola, Id, US 146/E1
Ola, Ga, US 163/M8
Ólafsfjördhur, Ice. 38/N6
Ólafsvík, Ice. 38/M7
Olaine, Lat. 41/K3
Olalla, Wa, US 167/B3
Olan, Pic d' (peak), Fr. 64/C3
Olancha, Ca, US 148/C2
Olancha (peak), Ca, US 148/C2
Olanchito, Hon. 176/E3
Öland (isl.), Swe. 38/F4
Ölands södra udde (pt.), Swe. 40/G3
Olary, Austl. 131/J5
Olathe, Ks, US 153/G1
Olathe, Co, US 149/J1
Olathe Nav. Air Sta., Ks, US 153/G1
Olavarría, Arg. 190/E3
Oława, Pol. 43/J3
Ölbach (riv.), Ger. 53/F5
Olberg, Az, US 149/G4
Olbia, It. 48/A2
Olching, Ger. 59/E6
Ol'chon (isl.), Rus. 78/F1
Olcott, NY, US 160/V9
Old (riv.), Ca, US 167/L11
Old Bahama (chan.), Cuba 177/G1
Old Baldy (peak), Wa, US 144/E3
Old Bar, Austl. 132/E1
Old Bedford (canal), Eng, UK 37/G2
Old Bethpage, NY, US 169/M9
Old Bridge, NJ, US 169/H10
Old Castile (reg.), Sp. 66/B2
Old City, WBnk. 105/C5
Old Crow, Yk, Can. 171/L2
Old Faithful, Wy, US 147/H1
Old Field (pt.), NY, US 169/E2
Old Forge, NY, US 161/J3
Old Forge, Pa, US 161/J4
Old Fort Niagara, NY, US 160/U9
Old Harbor, Ak, US 171/H4
Old Hickory (lake), Tn, US 162/D2
Old Lyme, Ct, US 161/K4
Old Man of Hoy, Sc, UK 31/V14
Old Mill Creek, Il, US 167/Q15
Old Nene (riv.), Eng, UK 37/F2
Old Perlican, Nf, Can. 159/L1
Old Rhine (riv.), Neth. 52/B4
Old Saybrook, Ct, US 169/F1
Old Shawneetown, Il, US 162/C2
Old Speck (mtn.), Me, US 161/L2
Old Tampa (bay), Fl, US 164/K8
Old Tappan, NJ, US 169/K8
Old Town, Fl, US 165/G3
Old Windsor, Eng, UK 30/B2
Old Wives (lake), Sk, Can. 145/L2
Oldcastle, Ire. 32/C2
Oldeani (peak), Tanz. 119/A2
Oldeani, Tanz. 119/A2
Oldebroek, Neth. 52/C4
Oldemarkt, Neth. 52/C3
Olden, Mo, US 153/J2
Olden, Tx, US 151/E1
Oldenburg, Ger. 40/D4
Oldenburg, In, US 160/D5
Oldenburg, Ger. 53/F2
Oldenzaal, Neth. 52/D4
Oldham, Eng, UK 35/F4
Oldham (co.), Eng, UK 35/F4
Oldleighlin, Ire. 32/C4
Oldman (riv.), Ab, Can. 144/G3
Oldmans (cr.), NJ, US 168/C4
Oldmeldrum, Sc, UK 33/D2
Oldoog (isl.), Ger. 53/E1
Olds, Ab, Can. 145/G2
Oldsmar, Fl, US 164/K7
Olduvai Gorge, Tanz. 119/A2
Oldwick, NJ, US 168/D2
Olean, NY, US 161/G3
O'Leary, PE, Can. 158/E2
Olecko, Pol. 41/K4
Oleggio, It. 62/B2
Oleiros, Port. 46/B3
Oleiros, Sp. 46/A1
Olekma (riv.), Rus. 75/N4
Olëkminsk, Rus. 75/N3
Oleksandrivka, Ukr. 73/G3
Oleksandriya, Ukr. 72/G3
Olele (pt.), Wa, US 167/B2
Olemari (riv.), Sur. 181/H4
Ølen, Nor. 40/A2
Olenegorsk, Rus. 68/G1
Olenëk (riv.), Rus. 77/L3
Olënek, Rus. 75/M3
Olenek (bay), Rus. 75/M2
Olenitsa, Rus. 68/G2
Olenivka, Ukr. 73/J4
Olentangy (riv.), Oh, US 160/E4
Olenty (riv.), Kaz. 99/B1
Oléron (isl.), Fr. 66/C1
Olesa de Montserrat, Sp. 47/K6
Oles'ko, Ukr. 72/C3
Oleśnica, Pol. 43/J3
Olesno, Pol. 43/K3
Olevano Romano, It. 65/C4
Olevs'k, Ukr. 72/D2
Oley, Pa, US 168/C3
Olfen, Ger. 53/E5
Olga (mt.), Austl. 131/F3
Ol'ga, Rus. 79/M3
Olginate, It. 62/C2
Ol'ginka, Rus. 70/F3
Ölgiy, Mong. 99/E2
Ølgod, Den. 40/C4
Olhão, Port. 46/B4
Olho d'Água das Flores, Braz. 187/F1
Olib (isl.), Cro. 45/L4
Oliena, It. 48/A2
Olifants (riv.), SAfr. 122/C4
Olifantshoek, SAfr. 124/P12
Olifantsrivier (riv.), SAfr. 123/F5
Olimarao (isl.), Micr. 136/D4
Olimbía (Olympia) (ruin), Gre. 49/G4
Ólimbos NP (Olympos NP), Gre. 49/H2
Ólimbos, Óros (Mount Olympus) (peak), Gre. 49/H2
Olímpia, Braz. 189/G2
Olimpos Beydağları NP, Turk. 104/B1
Olinalá, Mex. 176/B2
Olinda, Braz. 183/H5
Olinda (pt.), Moz. 123/H3
Olinda, Ca, US 146/B3
Olindina, Braz. 187/F1
Olinskiy, Rus. 71/H3
Oliva, Sp. 47/E3
Oliva, Arg. 188/D5
Oliva de la Frontera, Sp. 46/B3
Olivais, Port. 46/A3
Olivares, Cerro de (peak), Arg.,Chile 188/B4
Olive, Mt, US 145/M5
Olive Branch, Ms, US 162/C3
Olive Branch, Il, US 162/C2
Olive Hill, Ky, US 163/F1
Olivehurst, Ca, US 146/C4
Oliveira, Braz. 186/D4
Olivenza, Sp. 46/B3
Oliver, BC, Can. 144/E3
Oliver (cr.), Tx, US 150/K6
Oliver (res.), Ga, US 162/E4
Oliver, Wi, US 157/H4
Oliver Springs, Tn, US 162/E2
Oliveros, Arg. 188/D5
Olivet, Fr. 57/G5
Olivet, SD, US 154/F2
Olivia, Mn, US 155/G1
Olivone, Swi. 61/E4
Ol'khovatka, Rus. 73/K2
Olla, La, US 164/B2
Ollachea, Peru 184/D4
Ollagüe (vol.), Bol.,Chile 188/B2
Ollainville, Fr. 30/J6
Ollería, Sp. 47/E3
Olleros, Peru 184/B3
Ollie, Mt, US 156/B4
Ollioules, Fr. 64/B6
Ollon, Swi. 60/D5
Olmaliq, Uzb. 99/A3
Olmedo, Sp. 46/C2
Olmesutye, Kenya 119/A2
Olmitz, Ks, US 152/E1
Olmos, Peru 184/B2
Olmué, Chile 190/N8
Olney, Tx, US 153/E4
Olney, Il, US 162/C1
Olney, Eng, UK 37/F2
Olney, Mt, US 144/G3
Olney, Md, US 168/A5
Olofström, Swe. 40/F3
Oloitokitok, Kenya 119/B2
Olomouc, Czh. 43/J4
Olomoucký (pol. reg.), Czh. 43/J4
Olonets, Rus. 41/Q1
Olongapo, Phil. 88/C2
Olonne-sur-Mer, Fr. 44/C3
Olorgasailie Nat'l Mon., Kenya 119/B2
Oloron-Sainte-Marie, Fr. 44/C5
Olorunda, Nga. 115/F5
Olot, Sp. 47/G1
Olovyannaya, Rus. 78/H1
Oloy (range), Rus. 75/S3
Olpe, Ks, US 153/F1
Olpe, Ger. 55/G1
Olpe (riv.), Ger. 53/F6
Olsberg, Ger. 53/F6
Olsburg, Ks, US 155/F4
Ol'sha, Rus. 41/P4
Ol'shany, Ukr. 73/H2
Olst, Neth. 52/D4
Ølstykke, Den. 39/J7
Olsztyn, Pol. 41/J5
Olsztynek, Pol. 43/L2
Olt (riv.), Rom. 70/C3
Olt (prov.), Rom. 51/G3
Olta, Arg. 188/C4
Olten, Swi. 60/D3
Olteniţa, Rom. 51/H3
Oltepesi, Kenya 119/B2
Olteţ (riv.), Rom. 51/F3
Olton, Tx, US 152/C3
Oltre il Colle, It. 61/F6
Oltu (riv.), Turk. 71/G4
Oltu, Turk. 102/E1
Oluan Pi (cape), Tai. 87/J4
Oluanpi, Tai. 87/J4
Oluku, Nga. 115/G5
Olur, Turk. 71/G4
Olustee, Ok, US 152/E3
Olutanga (isl.), Phil. 88/C4
Olvera, Sp. 46/C4
Olympe (peak), Fr. 64/B5
Olympia (cap.), Wa, US 144/C4
Olympia (Olimbía) (ruin), Gre. 49/G4
Olympia Heights, Fl, US 164/P11
Olympic (mts.), Wa, US 144/C4
Olympic Dam, Austl. 131/H4
Olympic Game Farm, Wa, US 167/A1
Olympic National Forest, Wa, US 167/A2
Olympic NP, Wa, US 144/C4
Olympic Park, SKor. 81/G6
Olympus (peak), Cyp. 104/C2
Olympus (mt.), Wa, US 144/C4
Olympus NP (Ólimbos NP), Gre. 49/H2
Olympus, Mount (Óros Ólimbos) (peak), Gre. 49/H2
Olyutorskiy (bay), Rus. 75/S3
Om Hājer, Erit. 117/H2
Oma (riv.), Rus. 69/K2
Oma, Ms, US 164/C2
Ōma, Japan 82/B3
Oma, China 99/D5
Ōma-zaki (pt.), Japan 82/B3
Ōmachi, Japan 85/E2
Omae-zaki (pt.), Japan 85/F3
Ōmagari, Japan 82/B4
Omagh, NI, UK 34/A2
Omagh (dist.) 34/A2
Omaguas, Peru 184/C2
Omaha, Ar, US 153/H2
Omaha, Ga, US 162/E4
Omaha, Ne, US 155/G3
Omaha, Tx, US 153/G4
Omaha Beach, Fr. 57/E2
Omaha Ind. Res., Ne, US 155/F2
Omak, Wa, US 144/E3
Oman (gulf), Asia 77/E7
Oman (ctry.) 77/E8
Omar Torrijos Herrera (int'l arpt.), Pan. 180/B2
Omaruru, Namb. 122/B4
Omaruru (riv.), Namb. 122/B4
Omas, Peru 184/B4
Omatako (riv.), Namb. 122/C4
Omate, Peru 184/D5
Ombai (str.), ETim.,Indo. 128/B2
Ombalantu, Namb. 122/B3
Ombella-Mpoko (pref.), CAfr. 116/C4
Ombésa, Camr. 120/B1
Ombombo, Namb. 122/B3
Omboué, Gabon 120/B3
Ombrone (riv.), It. 67/F2
Ombu, China 99/E5
Ombúes de Lavalle, Uru. 191/K10
Ombúes de Oribe, Uru. 191/K10
Omdurman (Umm Durmān), Sudan 117/G2
Ōme, Japan 83/C2
Omeath, Ire. 34/B3
Omega, Ga, US 165/G2
Omeo, Austl. 133/C3
'Omer, Isr. 105/B6
Ömerli, Turk. 102/E2
Ömerli (dam), Turk. 103/N6
Ömerli (res.), Turk. 103/N7
Ometepe (isl.), Nic. 176/E4
Ometepec, Mex. 176/B2
Ōmi, Japan 83/K5
Ōmihachiman, Japan 83/K5
Omiš, Cro. 50/C4
Omitara, Namb. 122/C4
Omitlán (riv.), Mex. 176/B2
Ōmiya, Japan 85/G2
Ōmiya, Japan 83/K7
Ōmiya, Japan 83/H4
Ommaney (cape), Ak, US 171/M4
Ommen, Neth. 52/D3
Ömnögovĭ (prov.), Mong. 78/E3
Omo NP, Eth. 117/G4
Omo Wenz (riv.), Eth. 107/F4
Omodeo (lake), It. 48/A2
Omoko, Nga. 115/G5
Omolon (riv.), Rus. 77/Q3
Omono (riv.), Japan 82/B4
Ompah, On, Can. 161/H2
Omro, Wi, US 155/K1
Omsk, Rus. 74/H4
Omskaya Oblast, Rus. 74/H4
Omsukchan, Rus. 75/R3
Ōmu, Japan 82/C1
Omu Aran, Nga. 115/G4
Omugo, Ugan. 121/G2
Omul (peak), Rom. 51/G3
Omuo, Nga. 115/G5
Ōmura, Japan 84/A4
Omurtag, Bul. 51/H4
Ōmuta, Japan 84/B4
Omutninsk, Rus. 69/M4
Onadikondo, D.R. Congo 121/F3
Onaga, Ks, US 155/F4
Onagawa, Japan 82/B4
Onaka, SD, US 154/E1
Onalaska, Wi, US 155/J2
Onalaska (lake), Mn, Wi, US 155/J2
Onalaska, Tx, US 151/G2
Onalaska, Wa, US 144/C4
Onaman (lake), On, Can. 157/L3
Onamia, Mn, US 157/H4
Onancock, Va, US 163/K2
Onanole, Mb, Can. 156/D2
Onaping (lake), On, Can. 160/F1
Onarga, Il, US 160/B4
Oñate, Sp. 44/B5
Onawa, Ia, US 155/F2
Onaway, Mi, US 160/D2
Onaway, Id, US 144/F4
Oncativo, Arg. 188/D4
Onchan, IM, UK 34/D3
Oncócua, Ang. 122/B3
Onda, Sp. 47/E3
Ondangua, Namb. 122/C3
Ondava (riv.), Slvk. 43/L4
Onder, India 96/A3
Ondo, Nga. 115/G5
Ondo (state), Nga. 115/G5
Öndörhaan, Mong. 78/G2
Ondorushu (falls), Ang. 122/B3
Onè, It. 63/E2
One Tree Hill (hill), NZ 135/F6
Oneco, Fl, US 165/G4
Onefour, Ab, Can. 145/J3
Onega (bay), Rus. 68/G2
Onega (pen.), Rus. 68/H2
Onega, Rus. 68/H3
Onega (riv.), Rus. 74/D3
Onega (lake), Rus. 192/D
Onehunga (nbrhd.), NZ 135/F6
Oneida, NY, US 161/J3
Oneida (lake), NY, US 161/H3
Oneida, Tn, US 162/E2
Oneida, Pa, US 168/B2
Oneida Ind. Res., Wi, US 155/K1
O'Neill, Ne, US 154/E2
Onekama, Mi, US 160/C2
Oneonta, NY, US 161/J3
Oneonta, Al, US 162/D4
Onex, Swi. 60/C5
Ongenga, Namb. 122/B3
Ongeri, D.R. Congo 121/F4
Ongi, Mong. 78/E2
Ongiyn (riv.), Mong. 78/E2
Ongjin, NKor. 81/C4
Ongobit, Kenya 119/B2
Ongole, India 95/D3
Ongtüstik Qazaqstan, Kaz. 74/G5
Ongtüstik Qazaqstan Oblast, Kaz. 74/G5
Onhaye, Belg. 55/D3
Onhne, Myan. 86/C5
Oni, Geo. 71/G4
Onida, SD, US 154/D1
Onil, Sp. 47/E3
Onilahy (riv.), Madg. 125/G8
Onishi, Japan 83/C1
Onitsha, Nga. 115/G5
Onjŏng, NKor. 81/C3
Onjŏng, NKor. 81/C3
Onjuku, Japan 83/E3
Onkaparinga (riv.), Austl. 131/M8
Onkimaanjärvi (lake), Fin. 39/D4
Onley, Va, US 163/K2
Onnaing, Fr. 54/C3
Onny (riv.), Eng, UK 36/D2
Ono, Japan 84/D3
Ōno, Japan 84/E3
Ōno, Japan 83/L5
Onoda, Japan 84/B4
Onoke (lake), NZ 135/J9
Onokhoy, Rus. 78/F1
Onomichi, Japan 84/C3
Onon, Mong. 78/G2
Onon (riv.), Mong. 78/F2
Onon, Mong. 78/G2
Onoto, Ven. 181/E2
Onotoa (isl.), Kiri. 136/G5
Onoway, Ab, Can. 145/G1
Onrusrivier, SAfr. 124/L11
Onslow, Austl. 130/B2
Onstwedde, Neth. 52/E2
Ontake-san (peak), Japan 85/E3
Ontario, Ca, US 166/C2
Ontario, Or, US 146/E1
Ontario (lake), Can.,US 139/K5
Ontario (prov.), Can. 140/H3
Ontario International (arpt.), Ca, US 166/C2
Ontelaunee (lake), Pa, US 168/C3
Onteniente, Sp. 47/E3
Ontonagon, Mi, US 157/K4
Ontonagon Ind. Res., Mi, US 157/K4
Ontong Java (isl.), Sol. 136/E5
Onverwacht, Sur. 182/C1
Onward, Ms, US 162/B4
Onyang, SKor. 81/D4
Onyx, Ca, US 148/C3
Onzaga, Col. 180/C3
Onzain, Fr. 57/G5
Onzo (riv.), Ang. 120/C5
Oobagooma, Austl. 128/A4
Ood Weyne, Som. 118/C3
Oodnadatta, Austl. 131/G3
Oola, Ire. 32/B4
Ooldea, Austl. 131/F4
Oolitic, In, US 162/D1
Oologah (lake), Ok, US 153/G2
Oologah, Ok, US 153/G2
Ooltgensplaat, Neth. 52/B5
Oona River, BC, Can. 171/M5
Oost-Vlaanderen (prov.), Belg. 54/C2
Oost-Vlieland, Neth. 52/C2
Oostanaula (riv.), Ga, US 162/E3
Oostburg, Neth. 54/C1
Oostburg, Wi, US 160/C3
Oostelijk Flevoland (polder), Neth. 52/C3
Oostende (Ostend), Belg. 54/B1
Oosterbeek, Neth. 52/C5
Oosterend, Neth. 52/C2
Oosterhout, Neth. 52/B5
Oosterscheidedam (dam), Neth. 52/A5
Oosterschelde (riv.), Neth. 42/B3
Oosterwolde, Neth. 52/D3
Oosterzele, Belg. 54/C2
Oostkamp, Belg. 54/C1
Oostmahorn, Neth. 52/D2
Oostvaarderplassen (lake), Neth. 52/C4
Oostvorne, Neth. 52/B5
Oostzaan, Neth. 52/B4
Ootmarsum, Neth. 52/D4
Opa-Locka, Fl, US 164/P11
Opaka, Bul. 51/H4
Opal, SD, US 154/C1
Opala, D.R. Congo 121/F3
Opalenica, Pol. 43/J2
Opalton, Austl. 134/A3
Opari, Sudan 121/H2
Oparino, Rus. 69/L4
Opatija, Cro. 45/L4
Opatów, Pol. 43/L3
Opava, Czh. 43/J4
Opelika, Al, US 162/E4
Opelousas, La, US 164/B2
Opeongo (lake), On, Can. 161/G2
Opera, It. 62/C3
Öpfingen, Ger. 61/F1
Opglabbeek, Belg. 55/E1
Opheim, Mt, US 145/L3
Ophir, Ak, US 171/G3
Ophir, Co, US 149/J2
Ophir, Or, US 146/A2
Ophthalmia (range), Austl. 130/C2
Opi, Nga. 115/G5
Opin, Indo. 91/G4
Opishnya, Ukr. 73/H3
Opladen, Ger. 55/G1
Oploo, Neth. 52/C5
Opmeer, Neth. 52/B3
Opochka, Rus. 41/N3
Opoczno, Pol. 43/L3
Opole, Pol. 43/J3
Opole Lubelskie, Pol. 43/L3
Opolis, Ks, US 153/G2
Opolskie (prov.), Pol. 43/J3
Opornyy, Kaz. 71/K3
Opotiki, NZ 135/D2
Opovo, Yugo. 50/E3
Opp, Al, US 165/E2
Oppdal, Nor. 38/D3
Oppeano, It. 63/E3
Oppegård, Nor. 38/S8
Oppenau, Ger. 60/E1
Oppenheim, Ger. 58/B3
Oppland (co.), Nor. 38/D3
Oppmannasjön (lake), Swe. 39/L6
Opportunity, Wa, US 144/F4
Optima (lake), Ok, US 152/D2
Optima Nat'l Wild. Ref., Ok, US 152/D2
Opua, NZ 135/C1
Opwijk, Belg. 55/D2
Oquawka, Il, US 155/J3
Or 'Aqiva, Isr. 105/B4
Or Yehuda, Isr. 105/B4
Or, Mont d' (peak), Fr. 60/C4
Ora, Ms, US 164/D2
Ōra, Japan 83/C1
Ora (riv.), Mex. 174/D3
Ora (Auer), It. 61/H5
Oracle, Az, US 149/G4
Oradea, Rom. 50/E2
Oradell, NJ, US 169/J8
Oradell (res.), NJ, US 169/J8
Orahovac, Yugo. 50/E4
Orahovica, Cro. 50/C3
Orai, India 96/B3
Oraibi Wash (riv.), Az, US 149/G2
Orain (riv.), Fr. 60/B4
Oraison, Fr. 64/B5
Oral, Kaz. 71/J2
Oran, Mo, US 162/C2
Oran, Alg. 112/E5
Ŏrang, NKor. 81/E2
Orang (riv.), NKor. 81/E2
Orange, Austl. 133/D1
Orange (cape), Braz. 182/D1
Orange, Fr. 64/A4
Orange (riv.), SAfr. 107/D7
Orange (riv.), SAfr. 124/B3
Orange (mts.), Sur. 181/H4
Orange, Ca, US 166/G8
Orange, Ct, US 169/E1
Orange, Fl, US 165/F2
Orange (co.), Fl, US 164/M6
Orange (co.), NY, US 168/D1
Orange (co.), NY, US 169/H7
Orange, NJ, US 169/J8
Orange, Tx, US 151/H2
Orange, Va, US 163/H1
Orange Beach, Al, US 164/E2
Orange City, Fl, US 165/H3
Orange City, Ia, US 155/F2
Orange Cove, Ca, US 148/C2
Orange Grove, Ms, US 164/D2
Orange Park, Fl, US 165/H2
Orange Springs, Fl, US 165/H3
Orange Walk, Belz. 176/D2
Orangeburg, NY, US 169/K7
Orangeburg, SC, US 163/G4
Orangevale, Ca, US 146/C4
Orangeville, On, Can. 160/S8
Orangeville, Pa, US 168/B1
Orango (isl.), GBis. 114/A4
Oranienburg, Ger. 42/Q6
Oranjekanaal (riv.), Neth. 52/D3
Oranjemund, Namb. 124/B3
Oranjestad, NAnt. 180/D1
Oranmore, Ire. 32/B3
Oransbari, Indo. 91/H4
Orapa, Bots. 122/E4
Oras, Phil. 88/D2
Orăştie, Rom. 51/F3
Oraville, Il, US 162/C2
Oraviţa, Rom. 50/E3
Orb (riv.), Fr. 44/E5
Orba (riv.), It. 62/B3
Orbassano, It. 64/D2
Orbe (riv.), Swi. 60/C4
Orbe, Swi. 60/C4
Orbec, Fr. 57/F2
Orbey, Fr. 60/D1
Órbigo (riv.), Sp. 46/C1
Orbiquet (riv.), Fr. 57/F2
Orbost, Austl. 133/D3
Örbyhus, Swe. 40/G1
Orcas (isl.), Wa, US 144/C3
Orcemont, Fr. 30/H6
Orcera, Sp. 46/D3
Orchamps, Fr. 60/B3
Orchamps-Vennes, Fr. 60/C3
Orchard (lake), Mi, US 167/F6
Orchard City, Co, US 149/J1
Orchard Homes, Mt, US 145/G4
Orchard Lake Village, Mi, US 167/F6
Orchard Mesa, Co, US 147/J4
Orchard Valley, Wy, US 154/B3
Orchards, Wa, US 144/C5
Orchies, Fr. 54/C3
Orchy (riv.), Sc, UK 33/B4
Orciano di Pesaro, It. 63/F6
Orcières, Fr. 64/C3
Orco (riv.), It. 45/G4
Orcopampa, Peru 184/C4
Orcotuna, Peru 184/C3
Ord, Ne, US 154/E3
Ord (mt.), Austl. 128/B4
Ord (riv.), Austl. 128/C3
Ord River, Austl. 128/C4
Ordaz (int'l arpt.), Mex. 174/D4
Orderville, Ut, US 149/F2
Ordes, Sp. 46/A1
Ordesa y Monte Perdido, PN, Sp. 47/F1
Ordos (Mu Us Shamo) (des.), China 78/F4
Ordu, Turk. 70/F4
Ordu (prov.), Turk. 70/F4
Ordubad, Azer. 103/F2
Ordway, Co, US 152/C1
Ordzhonikidze, Azer. 71/H4
Ordzhonikidze, Kaz. 71/M1
Ordzhonikidze, Ukr. 73/H5
Ordzhonikidze, Ukr. 73/H4
Ore, Nga. 115/G5
Ore City, Tx, US 153/G4
Orealla, Guy. 181/G3
Oreana, Nv, US 146/D3
Oreana (peak), Nv, US 146/D4
Örebro (prov.), Swe. 38/E4
Örebro, Swe. 40/F2
Orebro (int'l arpt.), Swe. 40/F2
Oregon, Oh, US 160/E4
Oregon (state), US 142/B3
Oregon, Il, US 155/K2
Oregon, Mo, US 155/G4
Oregon (inlet), NC, US 163/K3
Oregon Caves Nat'l Mon., Or, US 146/B2
Oregon City, Or, US 146/B1
Oregon Dunes National Recreation Area, Or, US 146/A2
Oregon Trail Ruts, Wy, US 154/B2
Öregrund, Swe. 40/H1
Orekhovo-Zuyevo, Rus. 68/H5
Orekhovsk, Bela. 41/P4
Orël, Rus. 70/F1
Orellana, Peru 184/C2
Orellana la Vieja, Sp. 46/C3
Orem, Ut, US 147/H3
Orenberg (int'l arpt.), Rus. 71/K2
Orenburg, Rus. 71/K2
Orenburgskaya Oblast, Rus. 71/K1
Orense, Sp. 46/B1
Orestiás, Gre. 51/H5
Øresund (sound), Swe. 40/E4
Oreti (riv.), NZ 135/B4
Oretta, La, US 164/B2
Orewa, NZ 135/F6
Orford, NH, US 161/K3
Orford, Austl. 132/C4
Orford (pt.), Eng, UK 37/H2
Orford, Eng, UK 37/H2
Organ (mts.), NM, US 152/A4
Organ, NM, US 149/J4
Organ Pipe Cactus National Monument, Az, US 174/B1
Organabo, FrG. 182/C1
Órgãos (mts.), Braz. 187/N7
Orgaz, Sp. 46/D3
Orgelet, Fr. 60/B4
Orgères-en-Beauce, Fr. 57/G4
Orgeurs, Fr. 30/H5
Orgeval, Fr. 30/H5
Orgon, Fr. 64/B5
Orgosolo, It. 48/A2
Orhaneli, Turk. 70/D5
Orhangazi, Turk. 51/J5
Orhei, Mol. 72/E4
Orhon (riv.), Mong. 78/E2
Orhy, Pic d' (peak), Fr. 44/C5
Oria, Sp. 46/D4
Orick, Ca, US 146/A3
Oriel (mt.), Ire. 32/D2
Orient, Ia, US 155/G3
Orient (pt.), NY, US 169/F1
Oriental, Mex. 175/M7
Oriental, NC, US 163/J3
Oriental, Cordillera (mts.), SAm. 184/B2
Orientale, (pol. reg.), D.R. Congo 121/F2
Oriente, Arg. 190/E3
Origny-Sainte-Benoîte, Fr. 54/C4
Orihuela, Sp. 47/E3
Orikhiv, Ukr. 73/H4
Orillia, On, Can. 161/G2
Orimattila, Fin. 41/L1
Orin, Wy, US 154/B2
Orinda, Ca, US 167/J11
Orinoca, Bol. 188/C1
Orinoco (riv.), Col.,Ven. 179/C2
Orinoco (delta), Ven. 179/C2
Orio al Serio (int'l arpt.), It. 62/C2
Oriolo, It. 48/E2
Oriolo Romano, It. 65/B3
Orion (lake), Mi, US 167/F6
Orion, Il, US 155/J3
Orion, Phil. 88/C2
Orissa (state), India 92/D3
Orissa Coast (canal), India 97/F5
Orissaare, Est. 41/K2
Oristano, It. 48/A3
Oristano (gulf), It. 66/F3
Orituco (riv.), Ven. 183/P8
Oriva, Wy, US 154/B1
Orivesi, Fin. 41/L1
Oriximiná, Braz. 182/C3
Orizaba, Mex. 175/M8
Orizona, Braz. 186/C3
Orjen (peak), Yugo. 50/D4
Órjiva, Sp. 46/D4
Orke (riv.), Ger. 53/F6
Örkelljunga, Swe. 40/E3
Orkhomenós, Gre. 49/H3
Orkney (isls.), UK 192/G
Orkney, SAfr. 124/D2
Orkney, Sk, Can. 145/L3
Orla, Tx, US 151/C2
Orland Park, Il, US 167/Q16
Orlândia, Braz. 189/H2
Orlando, Fl, US 164/N6
Orlando (int'l arpt.), Fl, US 164/N7
Orlando, WV, US 163/G1
Orlando, Capo d' (cape), It. 48/D3
Orleães, Braz. 189/G4
Orléanais (reg.), Fr. 44/D2
Orléans, Fr. 57/G5
Orleans, Ca, US 146/B3
Orleans, Ne, US 154/E3
Örlenbach, Ger. 58/D2
Orlik (res.), Czh. 59/H3
Orlová, Czh. 43/K4
Orlovista, Fl, US 164/N6
Orlovskaya Oblast, Rus. 70/E1
Orlovskiy, Rus. 73/M4
Orlu, Nga. 115/G5
Orly, Fr. 30/K5
Orly (int'l arpt.), Fr. 30/K5
Orman (dam), SD, US 154/C1
Ormanlı, Turk. 51/K5
Ormāra, Pak. 101/H3
Ormea, It. 62/A4
Ormes (riv.), Fr. 57/F4
Ormília, Gre. 49/H2
Ormiston, Sc, UK 33/D5
Ormiston, Sk, Can. 145/M3
Ormäjärvi (lake), Fin. 39/E3
Ormoc, Phil. 88/D3
Ormond Beach, Fl, US 165/H3
Ormond-by-the-Sea, Fl, US 165/H3
Ormskirk, Eng, UK 35/F4
Ornain (riv.), Fr. 44/F2
Ornans, Fr. 60/C3
Ornavasso, It. 61/E6
Orne (dept.), Fr. 57/F3
Orne (riv.), Fr. 42/C4
Ørnes, Nor. 38/E2
Orneta, Pol. 41/J4
Ornö (isl.), Swe. 39/B1
Ornö, Swe. 39/B1
Örnsköldsvik, Swe. 38/F3
Oro, NKor. 81/D2
Orø (isl.), Den. 39/H7
Oro Grande, Ca, US 166/C1
Oro Ingenio, Bol. 188/C2
Oro Valley, Az, US 149/G4
Oro, Monte d' (peak), Fr. 48/A1
Orobayaya, Bol. 185/F4
Orocó, Braz. 183/G5
Orocué, Col. 180/D3
Orodara, Burk. 114/D4
Orofino, Id, US 144/F4
Orogrande, Id, US 146/F1
Orohena (peak), FrPol. 137/X15
Orolo (riv.), It. 63/E1
Oroluk (isl.), Micr. 136/E4
Oromocto, NB, Can. 158/D3
Oron (riv.), Fr. 64/A2
Oron, Nga. 120/B1
Oron-la-Ville, Swi. 60/C4
Orona (Hull) (isl.), Kiri. 137/H5
Orongorongo (riv.), NZ 135/H9
Oronoque (riv.), Guy. 182/B2
Orontes (riv.), Syria 104/E2
Oropesa, Sp. 46/C3
Oropoi, Kenya 117/G5
Oroqen Zizhiqi, China 79/J1
Oroquieta, Phil. 88/C3
Orós, Braz. 183/G4
Orosei, It. 48/A2
Orosei (gulf), It. 66/F2
Orosháza, Hun. 50/E2
Oroszlány, Hun. 50/D2
Orotukan, Rus. 75/R3
Orovada, Nv, US 146/E3
Oroville (lake), Ca, US 146/C4
Oroville, Ca, US 146/C4
Oroville, Wa, US 144/E3
Orphin, Fr. 30/H6
Orpington (nbrhd.), Eng, UK 30/D2
Orpund, Swi. 60/D3
Orr, Mn, US 157/H3
Orrefors, Swe. 40/F3
Orrell, Eng, UK 35/F4
Orrick, Mo, US 155/G4
Orrin (res.), Sc, UK 33/B2
Orrin (riv.), Sc, UK 33/B2
Orroli, It. 48/A3
Orroroo, Austl. 131/H5
Orrtanna, Pa, US 168/A4
Orrville, Oh, US 160/F4
Orrville, Al, US 162/D4
Orry-la-Ville, Fr. 30/K4
Orsa, Swe. 40/F1
Orsago, It. 63/F2
Orsay, Fr. 30/J5
Örsbaken (bay), Swe. 39/A2
Orsett, Eng, UK 30/E2
Orsha, Bela. 41/P4
Orsiera (peak), It. 64/D2
Orsk, Rus. 71/L2
Orslandet (isl.), Fin. 39/D5
Orso, Capo d' (cape), It. 66/D6
Orsogna, It. 65/D3
Orsonnens, Swi. 60/C4
Orşova, Rom. 50/F3
Ørsta, Nor. 38/C3
Örsundsbro, Swe. 40/G2
Orta, Turk. 70/E4
Orta (lake), It. 45/H4
Orta Nova, It. 48/D2
Ortaca, Turk. 102/B2
Ortaköy, Turk. 102/C2
Ortaköy, Turk. 102/C1
Orte, It. 65/B3
Orte (riv.), It. 65/C3
Orte Scalo, It. 65/B3
Ortega, Col. 180/C4
Ortegal (cape), Sp. 66/B2
Ortenberg, Ger. 58/C2
Orth an der Donau, Aus. 51/P7
Orthez, Fr. 44/C5
Ortigara (peak), It. 61/H5
Ortigueira, Sp. 66/B2
Orting, Wa, US 167/C3
Ortiz, Co, US 149/J2
Ortiz, Ven. 183/N8
Ortiz, Mex. 174/C2
Ortles (peak), It. 61/G4
Ortles (mts.), It. 45/J3
Orto-Tokoy, Kyr. 99/C3
Ortón (riv.), Bol. 185/E3
Ortona, Fl, US 165/H4
Ortona, It. 65/D3
Ortonville, Mi, US 167/F6
Ortonville, Mn, US 155/F1
Ortucchio, It. 65/C4
Örtze (riv.), Ger. 53/H3
Orūmīyeh, Iran 103/F2
Orurillo, Peru 184/D4
Oruro (dept.), Bol. 188/C1
Oruro, Bol. 188/C1
Orust (isl.), Swe. 40/D2
Orvault, Fr. 56/D6
Orvieto, It. 65/B2
Orvilliers, Fr. 30/G5
Orwell, Oh, US 160/F4
Orwell, Vt, US 161/K3
Orwell (riv.), Eng, UK 37/H2
Orwigsburg, Pa, US 168/B2
Orxon (riv.), China 79/H2
Oryakhovo, Bul. 51/F4
Orzhytsya, Ukr. 72/G3
Orzinuovi, It. 62/C3
Orzysz, Pol. 41/J5
Os, Nor. 40/A1
Osa, Rus. 69/M4
Osa (pen.), CR 177/F4
Osage, Mn, US 157/G4
Osage, Sk, Can. 156/C3
Osage, Ia, US 155/H2
Osage (riv.), Mo, US 155/G5
Osage, Tx, US 150/F2
Osage, Wy, US 154/B2
Osage Beach, Mo, US 153/H1
Osage City, Ks, US 153/G1
Ōsaka (pref.), Japan 84/D3
Ōsaka (int'l arpt.), Japan 83/H6
Ōsaka, Japan 83/J6
Ōsaka Castle, Japan 83/H6
Osakis, Mn, US 157/G5
Osakis (lake), Mn, US 155/G1
Osan, SKor. 81/D4
Osasco, Braz. 187/K8
Ōsato, Japan 83/C1
Osawatomie, Ks, US 155/G4
Osborn (mt.), Ak, US 171/E3
Osborne, Ks, US 154/E4
Osburg, Ger. 55/F4
Osburn, Id, US 144/G4
Osby, Swe. 40/E3
Oscar, Ok, US 153/F4
Oscar, FrG. 182/C2
Osceola (co.), Fl, US 164/N7
Osceola, Ar, US 162/C3
Osceola, Ia, US 155/H3
Osceola, Mo, US 153/H1
Osceola, Ne, US 154/F3
Oschersleben, Ger. 42/F2
Oschiri, It. 48/A2
Oscura (mts.), NM, US 152/A4
Osdorf, Ger. 53/G1
Osento (riv.), It. 65/D3
Osgood, In, US 162/E1
Osh, Kyr. 99/B3
Oshakati, Namb. 122/B3
Oshamambe, Japan 82/B2
Oshawa, On, Can. 160/V8
Oshika (pen.), Japan 82/B4
Oshikango, Namb. 122/B3
Oshima (pen.), Japan 79/M3
Oshino, Japan 83/B3
Oshivelo, Namb. 122/C3
Oshkosh, Wi, US 155/K1
Oshkosh, Ne, US 154/C3
Oshmyany, Bela. 41/L4
Oshnovīyeh, Iran 103/F2
Oshogbo, Nga. 115/G5
Oshwe, D.R. Congo 120/D3
Osijek, Cro. 50/D3
Osio Sotto, It. 62/C2
Osipaonica, Yugo. 50/E3
Osire, Namb. 122/C4
Oskaloosa, Ks, US 155/G4
Oskaloosa, Ia, US 155/H3
Oskar-Fredriksborg, Swe. 39/B1
Oskarshamn, Swe. 40/G3
Oskarström, Swe. 40/E3
Öskemen, Kaz. 99/D2
Oskol (riv.), Ukr.,Rus. 70/F2
Oslo, Mn, US 156/F3
Oslo (co.), Nor. 38/S8
Oslo (cap.), Nor. 40/D2
Oslofjorden (fjord), Nor. 38/S9
Osmancık, Turk. 70/E4
Osmaneli, Turk. 51/K5
Osmaniye, Turk. 104/E1
Os'mino, Rus. 41/N2
Ösmo, Swe. 39/A2
Osnabrock, ND, US 156/E3
Osnabruck, On, Can. 161/J2
Osnabrück, Ger. 53/F4
Osnaburgh (lake), On, Can. 157/J2
Osnaburgh House, On, Can. 157/J2
Osnago, It. 62/C2
Osny, Fr. 30/J4
Oso (mt.), Ca, US 167/M12
Oso (riv.), D.R. Congo 121/G3
Oso, Wa, US 144/D3
Osogna, Swi. 61/E5
Osona, Namb. 122/C4
Osório, Braz. 189/G4
Osorno, Sp. 46/C1
Osorno, Chile 190/B4
Osoyoos, BC, Can. 144/E3
Osoyoos Ind. Res., BC, Can. 144/E3
Ospedaletti, It. 62/A5
Ospedaletto Euganeo, It. 63/E3
Ospitaletto, It. 62/D2
Osprey (reef), Austl. 127/D2
Oss, Neth. 52/C5
Ossa (mt.), Austl. 132/C4
Ossa (mts.), Port. 46/B3
Ossabaw (isl.), Ga, US 165/H2
Ossabaw (sound), Ga, US 163/G5
Ossabaw Island Heritage Preserve, Ga, US 165/H2
Osse (riv.), Nga. 115/G5
Össeby-Garn, Swe. 39/B1
Osséja, Fr. 44/D5
Osseo, Wi, US 155/J1
Ossett, Eng, UK 35/G4
Ossi, It. 48/A2
Ossian, In, US 160/D4
Ossineke, Mi, US 160/E2
Ossining, NY, US 169/K7
Ossining, NY, US 169/K7
Ossipee, NH, US 161/L3
Ossora, Rus. 75/S4
Ostashkov, Rus. 68/G4
Ostbevern, Ger. 53/E4
Osted, Den. 39/H7
Osteen, Fl, US 165/H3
Ostellato, It. 63/E4
Osten, Ger. 53/G1
Ostend (Oostende), Belg. 54/B1
Oster, Rus. 68/G5

Oster, Ukr. 72/F2
Öster Ringsjön (lake), Swe. 39/K7
Osterburg, Ger. 42/F2
Osterburken, Ger. 58/C4
Österbybruk, Swe. 40/G1
Österbymo, Swe. 40/F3
Ostercappeln, Ger. 53/F4
Osterdalälven (riv.), Swe. 40/F1
Osterems (chan.), Ger. 52/D1
Östergötland (co.), Swe. 38/E4
Osterhofen, Ger. 59/G5
Osterholz-Scharmbeck, Ger. 53/F2
Osteria Grande, It. 63/E5
Ostermiething, Aus. 59/F6
Osterode am Harz, Ger. 53/H5
Östersund, Swe. 38/E3
Österunda, Swe. 39/A1
Östervåla, Swe. 40/G1
Osterwiek, Ger. 53/H5
Ostfildern, Ger. 58/C5
Østfold (co.), Nor. 38/D4
Ostfriesland (reg.), Ger. 53/E2
Östhammar, Swe. 40/H1
Ostheim vor der Rhön, Ger. 58/D2
Osthofen, Ger. 58/B3
Ostia Antica, It. 65/B4
Ostia Antica (ruin), It. 65/B4
Ostiano, It. 62/D3
Ostiglia, It. 63/E3
Ostional Nat'l Wild. Ref., CR 176/E4
Østmarka (reg.), Nor. 38/S8
Ostøya (isl.), Nor. 38/S8
Ostra, It. 63/G6
Östra Silen (lake), Swe. 40/E2
Ostra Vetere, It. 63/G6
Ostrach (riv.), Ger. 58/C6
Ostrava, Czh. 43/K4
Ostravský (pol. reg.), Slvk. 43/J4
Ostrhauderfehn, Ger. 53/E2
Oštri Rt (cape), Yugo. 50/D4
Ostricourt, Fr. 54/C3
Ostróda, Pol. 41/H5
Ostrogozhsk, Rus. 73/K2
Ostroh, Ukr. 72/D2
Ostrołęka, Pol. 43/L2
Ostrolenka, Rus. 69/N5
Ostroshitskiy Gorodok, Bela. 41/M4
Ostrov, Rus. 41/N3
Ostrov, Czh. 59/F2
Ostrovets, Bela. 41/L4
Ostrovskoye, Rus. 68/J4
Ostrów Mazowiecka, Pol. 43/L2
Ostrów Wielkopolski, Pol. 43/J3
Ostrowiec Świętokrzyski, Pol. 43/L3
Ostryna, Bela. 41/L5
Ostrzeszów, Pol. 43/J3
Ostseebad Binz, Ger. 40/E4
Ostseebad Göhren, Ger. 40/E4
Ostseebad Prerow, Ger. 40/E4
Oststeinbek, Ger. 53/H1
Östuna, Swe. 39/A1
Ostuni, It. 49/E2
Ostwald, Fr. 58/A5
O'Sullivan (dam), Wa, US 144/E4
Osŭm (riv.), Bul. 49/J1
Osŭm (riv.), Slvk. 51/G4
Ōsumi (pen.), Japan 84/B5
Ōsumi (isls.), Japan 136/C1
Ōsumi (str.), Japan 79/L5
Osun (state), Nga. 115/G5
Osuna, Sp. 46/C4
Osupugo (peak), Kenya 119/A2
Osvaldo Cruz, Braz. 189/G2
Oswaldkirk, Eng, UK 35/G3
Oswaldtwistle, Eng, UK 35/F4
Oswegatchie, NY, US 161/J2
Oswegatchie (riv.), NY, US 161/J2
Oswego, Ks, US 153/G2
Oswego, NY, US 161/H3
Oswego (riv.), NY, US 161/H3
Oswego, Il, US 167/P16
Oswestry, Eng, UK 35/E6
Oświęcim (Auschwitz), Pol. 43/K3
Osyka, Ms, US 164/C2
Osypenko, Ukr. 73/J4
Ōta, Japan 85/F2
Ōta (riv.), Japan 84/C3
Otahuhu, NZ 135/F6
Ōtake, Japan 84/C3
Ōtaki, Japan 85/G3
Otaki, NZ 135/C3
Ōtaki, Japan 83/B2
Ōtakine-yama (peak), Japan 85/G2
Otanche, Col. 183/L7
Otaru, Japan 82/B2
Otasawiam (riv.), On, Can. 157/M3
Otautau, NZ 135/B4
Otavalo, Ecu. 180/B4
Otavi, Namb. 122/C3
Ōtawara, Japan 85/G2
Otay, Ca, US 166/C5
Otchinjau, Ang. 122/B3
Otego, NY, US 161/J3
Oţelu Roşu, Rom. 50/F3
Otematata, NZ 135/B4
Otepa, FrPol. 137/L6
Otepää, Est. 41/M2
Otero de Rey, Sp. 46/B1
Oteros (riv.), Mex. 174/C3
Otgon Tenger (peak), Mong. 78/D2
Othello, Wa, US 144/E4
Othis, Fr. 30/L4
Othonoí (isl.), Gre. 49/F3
Oti (riv.), Gha. 115/F4
Otinhungwa, Namb. 122/B3
Otira, NZ 135/B3
Otis, Ks, US 152/E1
Otis, La, US 164/B2
Otis, NM, US 150/B1
Otis Air National Guard Base, Ma, US 158/B5
Otjihajavara, Namb. 122/C4
Otjikango, Namb. 122/C4
Otjikondo, Namb. 122/B3
Otjimbingue, Namb. 122/C4
Otjinene, Namb. 122/C4
Otjiwarongo, Namb. 122/C4
Otjohorongo, Namb. 122/B4
Otjokavare, Namb. 122/B3
Otjosondjou (riv.), Namb. 122/C4
Otjosondu, Namb. 122/C4
Otley, Eng, UK 35/G4
Otočac, Cro. 50/B3
Otofuke, Japan 82/C2
Otog Qi, China 78/F4
Otog Qianqi, China 78/F4
Otok, Cro. 50/D3
Ōtone, Japan 83/D1
Otopeni (int'l arpt.), Rom. 51/H3
Otorohanga, NZ 135/C2
Otoskwin (riv.), On, Can. 157/J2
Otowa, Japan 83/M6
Otra (riv.), Nor. 74/A4
Otradnaya, Rus. 73/L5
Otradnoye, Rus. 69/T7
Otradnyy, Rus. 71/J1
Otranto (str.), Eur. 67/H2
Otrokovice, Czh. 43/J4
Otse, Bots. 124/D2
Otsego, Mi, US 160/D3
Ōtsu, Japan 83/J5
Ōtsuchi, Japan 82/B4
Ōtsuki, Japan 83/B2
Otta, Nga. 115/F5
Ottaviano, It. 65/D6
Ottawa, Ks, US 153/G1
Ottawa (cap.), Can. 161/J2
Ottawa (int'l arpt.), On, Can. 161/J2
Ottawa, Oh, US 160/D4
Ottawa (riv.), Can. 139/K5
Ottawa (isls.), Can. 139/J4
Ottawa, Il, US 155/K3
Ottawa (Outaouais) (riv.), Can. 161/G1
Ottawa Hills, Oh, US 160/E4
Ottawa NWR, Oh, US 160/E4
Ottensheim, Aus. 59/H6
Otter (riv.), Eng, UK 36/C5
Otter (cr.), Vt, US 161/K3
Otter, Mt, US 154/A1
Otter Creek (res.), Ut, US 147/H4
Otter Tail (lake), Mn, US 157/G4
Otter Tail (riv.), Mn, US 156/F4
Otterbach, Ger. 55/G5
Otterberg, Ger. 55/G4
Otterburn, Eng, UK 33/D6
Otterburne, Mb, Can. 156/F3
Otterlo, Neth. 52/C4
Otterndorf, Ger. 53/F1
Ottersberg, Ger. 53/G2
Ottershaw, Eng, UK 30/B2
Ottertail, Mn, US 157/G4
Ottery Saint Mary, Eng, UK 36/C5
Otthon, Sk, Can. 156/C2
Ottignies-Louvain-la-Neuve, Belg. 55/D2
Öttingen im Bayern, Ger. 58/D5
Ottmarsheim, Fr. 60/D2
Ottnang am Hausruck, Aus. 59/G6
Ottobeuren, Ger. 61/G2
Ottobrunn, Ger. 59/E6
Ottone, It. 62/C4
Ottosdal, SAfr. 124/D2
Ottsville, Pa, US 168/C3
Ottumwa, Ia, US 155/H3
Ottweiler, Ger. 55/G5
Otukpa, Nga. 115/G5
Otumba de Gómez Farías, Mex. 175/L7
Oturkpo, Nga. 115/H5
Otuzco, Peru 184/B2
Otway (rocks), Chile 191/B7
Otway (bay), Chile 191/C7
Otway NP, Austl. 132/B3
Otwell, In, US 162/D1
Otwock, Pol. 43/L2
Otyniya, Ukr. 72/C3
Ötztal Alps (mts.), Aus. 45/J3
Ötztaler Ache (riv.), Aus. 61/G3
Ou (mts.), Japan 82/B4
Ou (riv.), Laos 86/D4
Ouachita (lake), Ar, US 153/H3
Ouachita (riv.), Ar,La, US 143/H5
Ouachita (mts.), Ok, US 143/G5
Ouâd Nâga, Mrta. 114/B2
Ouadane, Mrta. 110/C5
Ouadda, CAfr. 116/D3
Ouaddaï (reg.), Chad 116/C2
Ouaddaï (pref.), Chad 116/D2
Ouagadougou (int'l arpt.), Burk. 115/E3
Ouagadougou (cap.), Burk. 115/E3
Ouahazeïne (well), Chad 116/C1
Ouahigouya, Burk. 115/E3
Ouaka (riv.), CAfr. 116/D4
Ouaka (pref.), CAfr. 116/D4
Oualâta, Mrta. 114/D2
Oualia, Mali 114/C3
Oualidia, Mor. 110/C2
Ouallam, Niger 115/F3
Ouanary, FrG. 182/D1
Ouanda Djalle, CAfr. 116/D3
Ouandago, CAfr. 116/C4
Ouandja, CAfr. 116/D3
Ouandja-Vakaga, Rsv. de Faune de la, CAfr. 116/D3
Ouango, CAfr. 116/D4
Ouanne (riv.), Fr. 44/E3
Ouaqui (riv.), FrG. 182/C2
Ouaqui, FrG. 182/C2
Ouara (riv.), CAfr. 117/E4
Ouarane (reg.), Mrta. 110/C5
Ouareau (riv.), Qu, Can. 161/H1
Ouargaye, Burk. 115/F4
Ouargla, Alg. 111/G3
Ouargla (wilaya), Alg. 111/G3
Ouarkziz, Jebel (mts.), Mor. 110/C3
Ouarzazate (int'l arpt.), Mor. 110/D3
Ouarzazate, Mor. 110/D3
Ouatagouna, Mali 115/F3
Oubangui (riv.), Congo 116/C5
Oubritenga (prov.), Burk. 115/E3
Ouche (riv.), Fr. 60/B3
Oucques, Fr. 57/G5
Oud-Beijerland, Neth. 52/B5
Oud-Turnhout, Belg. 52/B6
Ōuda, Japan 83/J7
Oudalan (prov.), Burk. 115/E3
Ouddorp, Neth. 52/A5
Oude IJssel (riv.), Neth. 52/D5
Oude Pekela, Neth. 52/E2
Oude Westereems (chan.), Neth. 52/D1
Oude-Tonge, Neth. 52/B5
Oudenaarde, Belg. 54/C2
Oudenbosch, Neth. 52/B5
Oudenburg, Belg. 54/C1
Oudeschild, Neth. 52/B2
Oudewater, Neth. 52/B4
Oudon (riv.), Fr. 44/C3
Oudong, China 87/F3
Oudtshoorn, SAfr. 124/C4
Oued el Hadjar (well), Mali 114/E2
Oued Zem, Mor. 110/D2
Ouéléssébougou, Mali 114/D4
Ouémé (riv.), Ben. 115/F4
Ouéme (prov.), Ben. 115/F5
Ouen (isl.), NCal. 137/V13
Ouenza, Alg. 112/L7
Ouerrha (riv.), Mor. 112/B2
Ouessé, Ben. 115/F4
Ouesso, Congo 120/D2
Ouesso (int'l arpt.), Congo 120/D2
Ouest (prov.), Camr. 115/H5
Ouest (pt.), Haiti 177/H1
Ouest (pt.), Haiti 177/H2
Ouezzane, Mor. 112/B2
Oughterard, Ire. 32/A3
Ouham (riv.), CAfr. 116/C4
Ouham (pref.), CAfr. 116/C4
Ouham-Pendé (pref.), CAfr. 116/C4
Ouidah, Ben. 115/F5
Ouistreham, Fr. 57/E2
Oujaf, Mrta. 114/D2
Oujda, Mor. 112/D2
Oujda (prov.), Mor. 112/C2
Oujda (Angads) (int'l arpt.), Mor. 112/D2
Oujeft, Mrta. 114/B1
Oulad Teïma, Mor. 110/C3
Oulad-Rezzag, Mor. 112/C3
Oulangan NP, Fin. 68/F2
Ould Birni (well), Alg. 111/E4
Ould Yenjé, Mrta. 114/C3
Oule (riv.), Fr. 64/B4
Ouled Djellal, Alg. 66/E4
Ouljet es Soltane, Mor. 112/B3
Oullins, Fr. 64/A1
Oulnina (peak), Austl. 131/H5
Oulu, Fin. 68/E2
Oulu (prov.), Fin. 38/H2
Oulujärvi (lake), Fin. 38/H2
Oulx, It. 64/C2
Oum Chalouba, Chad 116/D2
Oum El Bouaghi, Alg. 112/K7
Oum er Rbia, Oued (riv.), Mor. 110/D2
Oum Hadjer, Chad 116/C2
Oumé, C.d'Iv. 114/D5
Ounara, Mor. 110/C3
Ounasjoki (riv.), Fin. 38/H2
Oundle, Eng, UK 37/F2
Oungre, Sk, Can. 156/C3
Ounianga Sérir, Chad 108/D5
Ounianga-Kébir, Chad 108/D5
Ouogo, CAfr. 116/C4
Oupeye, Belg. 55/E2
Our (riv.), Eur. 55/E4
Ouray, Co, US 149/J1
Ouray (peak), Co, US 149/J1
Ouray, Ut, US 147/J3
Ouray NWR, Ut, US 147/J3
Ource (riv.), Fr. 42/C5
Ourcq (riv.), Fr. 42/B4
Ourcq, Canal de l' (canal), Fr. 30/K5
Øure Anarjokka NP Nor. 38/H1
Øure Dividal NP, Nor. 38/F1
Ourém, Braz. 183/E3
Ouri, Chad 108/C4
Ouricuri, Braz. 183/F4
Ourimbah, Austl. 133/E1
Ourinhos, Braz. 189/G2
Ourique, Port. 46/A4
Ouro Branco, Braz. 183/G5
Ouro Fino, Braz. 187/K7
Ouro Modi, Mali 114/D3
Ouro Preto, Braz. 187/E4
Ourofon, Niger 115/H3
Ouroux-sur-Saône, Fr. 60/A4
Ourthe Occidentale (riv.), Belg. 55/E3
Ourthe Orientale (riv.), Belg. 55/E3
Ourtzarh, Mor. 112/B2
Ouse (riv.), Eng, UK 35/H4
Ouse, Austl. 132/C4
Ousley, Ga, US 165/G2
Oussouye, Sen. 114/A3
Oust (riv.), Fr. 44/B3
Outão, Port. 47/Q11
Outaouais (Ottawa) (riv.), Qu, Can. 161/G1
Outarville, Fr. 57/H4
Outeïd Arkas (well), Mali 114/D2
Outer Hebrides (isls.), Sc, UK 31/P8
Outer Santa Barbara Passage (chan.), Ca, US 148/C4
Outes, Sp. 46/A1
Outjo, Namb. 122/C4
Outlook, Mt, US 156/B3
Outlook, Sk, Can. 145/L2
Outreau, Fr. 54/A2
Outremont, Qu, Can. 159/N6
Ouvéa (isl.), NCal. 137/V12
Ouvéze (riv.), Fr. 44/F4
Ouyen, Austl. 132/B2
Ouyou Bézédinga (well), Niger 116/B1
Ouzinkie, Ak, US 171/H4
Ouzouer-le-Marché, Fr. 57/G5
Ovacık, Turk. 102/D2
Ovacık, Turk. 70/E4
Ovada, It. 62/B4
Ovalau (isl.), Fiji 137/Y18
Ovalle, Chile 188/B4
Ovan, Gabon 120/C2
Ovana (peak), Ven. 181/E3
Ovando, Mt, US 145/H4
Ovar, Port. 46/A2
Ovejaria (peak), Arg. 188/C3
Ovens (riv.), Austl. 133/C3
Overath, Ger. 55/G2
Overbrook, Ks, US 153/G1
Overbrook, Ok, US 153/F3
Överenhörna, Swe. 39/A1
Overflakkee (isl.), Neth. 52/B5
Overflow NWR, Ar, US 162/B4
Overgaard, Az, US 149/G3
Overhalla, Nor. 38/D2
Overijse, Belg. 55/D2
Overijssel (prov.), Neth. 52/D3
Overijssels (riv.), Neth. 52/D4
Överkalix, Swe. 38/G2
Overland Park, Ks, US 153/G1
Overlea, Md, US 168/B5
Overloon, Neth. 52/C5
Overo (peak), Arg. 190/C5
Overpelt, Belg. 52/C6
Overseal, Eng, UK 37/E1
Överselö, Swe. 39/A1
Overstrand, Eng, UK 37/H1
Overton, Eng, UK 37/E4
Overton, Wal, UK 35/F6
Overton, Nv, US 148/E2
Overton, Tx, US 151/G1
Övertorneå, Swe. 68/D2
Överum, Swe. 40/G3
Ovett, Ms, US 164/D2
Ovid, NY, US 161/H3
Ovidiopol', Ukr. 72/F4
Oviedo, Sp. 46/C1
Oviši, Lat. 41/J3
Ovoca, Ire. 34/B6
Ovoot, Mong. 78/G2
Övörhangay (prov.), Mong. 78/E2
Øvre Årdal, Nor. 40/B1
Övre Fryken (lake), Swe. 40/E1
Øvre Pasvik NP, Nor. 38/J1
Øvre Sirdal, Nor. 40/B2
Ovriá, Gre. 49/G3
Ovruch, Ukr. 72/E2
Owaka, NZ 135/B4
Owama, D.R. Congo 121/E3
Owando, Congo 120/C3
Ōwani, Japan 82/B3
Owariasahi, Japan 83/M5
Owase, Japan 84/E3
Owassa, Al, US 164/E2
Owassa (lake), NJ, US 168/D1
Owasso, Ok, US 153/G2
Owatonna, Mn, US 155/H1
Owego, NY, US 161/H3
Owel (lake), Ire. 32/C2
Owen (mt.), NZ 135/C3
Owen, Ger. 58/C5
Owen, Wi, US 155/J1
Owen, Austl. 131/H5
Owen Falls (dam), Ugan. 121/H2
Owen Roberts (int'l arpt.), UK 177/F2
Owen Sound, On, Can. 160/F2
Owen Stanley (range), PNG 129/G1
Owendo, Gabon 120/B2
Owenga, NZ 135/E4
Oweniny (riv.), Ire. 32/A1
Owenkillew (riv.) 34/A2
Owens, Tx, US 152/D4
Owens (peak), Ca, US 148/D3
Owens (riv.), Ca, US 148/C2
Owens (lake), Ca, US 148/D2
Owens Cross Roads, Al, US 162/D3
Owensboro, Ky, US 162/D2
Owensburg, In, US 162/D1
Owensville, Mo, US 153/J1
Owensville, In, US 162/D1
Owenton, Ky, US 162/E1
Owerri, Nga. 115/G5
Owingen, Ger. 61/F2
Owings, Md, US 168/B6
Owings Mills, Md, US 168/B5
Owingsville, Ky, US 162/F1
Owl Creek (mts.), Wy, US 147/J2
Owo, Nga. 115/G5
Owosso, Mi, US 160/D3
Owrāmān, Iran 103/F3
Owutu, Nga. 115/G5
Owyhee (mts.), Id, US 146/E2
Owyhee, Nv, US 146/E3
Owyhee (riv.), Id, US 142/C3
Owyhee (dam), Or, US 146/E2
Owyhee, South Fork (riv.), Id,Nv, US 146/E2
Ox (Slieve Gamph) (mts.), Ire. 32/A1
Oxapampa, Peru 184/C3
Oxbow, Sk, Can. 156/C3
Oxbow (lake), Mi, US 167/F6
Oxelösund, Swe. 40/G2
Oxford, NS, Can. 158/F3
Oxford (canal), Eng, UK 37/E3
Oxford, Eng, UK 37/E3
Oxford, NZ 135/C3
Oxford, Al, US 162/E4
Oxford, Ar, US 153/J2
Oxford, In, US 160/C4
Oxford, Me, US 161/L2
Oxford, Mi, US 167/F6
Oxford, Ms, US 162/C3
Oxford, NC, US 163/H2
Oxford, Ne, US 154/E3
Oxford, NY, US 161/J3
Oxford, Oh, US 160/D5
Oxford, Pa, US 168/C4
Oxfordshire (co.), Eng, UK 37/E3
Oxhey, Eng, UK 30/B2
Oxie, Swe. 40/E4
Oxkutzcab, Mex. 176/D1
Oxley (cr.), Austl. 134/E7
Oxley, Austl. 133/B2
Oxnard (arpt.), Ca, US 166/A2
Oxnard, Ca, US 166/A2
Oxnard Beach, Ca, US 166/A2
Oxon Hill (farm), Md, US 168/A6
Oxon Hill-Glassmanor, Md, US 168/B6
Oxshott, Eng, UK 30/B3
Oxted, Eng, UK 30/D3
Oxton, Sc, UK 33/D5
Oy-Tal, Kyr. 99/B3
Oya, Malay. 90/D3
Oyabe, Japan 85/E2
Oyama, Japan 85/F2
Oyama, Japan 83/B3
Oyama, BC, Can. 144/E2
Ōyamada, Japan 83/K6
Ōyamazaki, Japan 83/J6
Oyapock (riv.), FrG.,Braz 179/D2
Oyé Yeska (well), Chad 108/C5
Oye-Plage, Fr. 54/B2
Oyem, Gabon 120/B2
Oyen, Ab, Can. 145/J2
Øyer, Nor. 40/D1
Øyeren (lake), Nor. 38/T8
Oykell (riv.), Sc, UK 31/R8
Oylen, Mn, US 157/G4
Oymyakon, Rus. 75/Q3
Oyo, Nga. 115/F5
Oyo (state), Nga. 115/F4
Oyo, Congo 120/C3
Ōyodo (riv.), Japan 84/B5
Ōyodo, Japan 83/J7
Oyón, Peru 184/B3
Oyonnax, Fr. 60/B5
Oyster (cr.), Tx, US 151/G3
Oyster Bay, NY, US 169/L8
Oyster Bay (har.), NY, US 169/L8
Oyster Bay Cove, NY, US 169/L8
Oyster Bay Nat'l Wild. Ref., NY, US 169/L8
Oyten, Ger. 53/G2
Oyugis, Kenya 119/A2
Ozamiz, Phil. 88/C3
Ozanne (riv.), Fr. 44/D2
Ozarichi, Bela. 70/D1
Ozark, Al, US 165/F2
Ozark (mts.), Ar,Mo, US 143/H4
Ozark, Ar, US 153/H3
Ozark, Mo, US 153/H2
Ozark (plat.), Mo, US 155/H4
Ozark Nat'l Scenic Riverways, Mo, US 162/B2
Ozarks (lake), Mo, US 143/H4
Ożarów, Pol. 72/A2
Ozawkie, Ks, US 155/G4
Ózd, Hun. 43/L4
Ozello, Fl, US 164/K6
Ozernovskiy, Rus. 75/R4
Ozernoy (cape), Rus. 75/S4
Ozernoye, Rus. 71/J2
Ozërnyy, Rus. 71/M2
Ozero Sasyk (lake), Ukr. 51/J3
Ozero Yalpuh (lake), Urk. 72/E5
Ozerskiy, Rus. 79/N2
Ozëry, Bela. 41/L5
Ozette (lake), Wa, US 144/B3
Ozette Ind. Res., Wa, US 144/B3
Ozherel'ye, Rus. 68/H5
Ozieri, It. 48/A2
Ozimek, Pol. 43/K3
Özkonak, Turk. 102/C2
Ozoir-la-Ferrière, Fr. 30/L5
Ozona, Fl, US 164/K7
Ozona, Tx, US 150/D2
Ozondjacheberg (peak), Namb. 122/C4
Ozone, Ar, US 153/H3
Ozone Park (nbrhd.), NY, US 169/K9
Ozora, Hun. 50/D2
Ozorków, Pol. 43/K3
Ozouer-le-Voulgis, Fr. 30/L6
Ōzu, Japan 84/C4
Ozuluama de Mascareñas, Mex. 176/B1
Ozurget'i, Geo. 71/G4
Ozzano dell'Emilia, It. 63/E5

P

P'abal-li, NKor. 81/E2
P'aju, SKor. 81/F6
P'aro-ho (lake), SKor. 81/D3
P'yŏngan-bukto (prov.), NKor. 81/C2
P. K. Le Rouxdam (res.), SAfr. 124/D3
Pa Sak (riv.), Thai. 93/H4
Pääjärvi (lake), Fin. 39/F3
Pa-an, Myan. 94/B2
Paar (riv.), Ger. 42/F4
Paarl, SAfr. 124/L10
Påarp, Swe. 39/J6
Pabbi, Pak. 98/A2
Pabean, Indo. 89/F4
Pabellón de Arteaga, Mex. 174/E4
Pabianice, Pol. 43/K3
Pablo Nat'l Wild. Ref., Mt, US 145/G4
Pābna (pol. reg.), Bang. 97/G3
Pābna, Bang. 97/G3
Pabradė, Lith. 41/L4
Pabu, Fr. 56/B3
Pacaás Novos, PN dos, Braz. 185/F3
Pacaás Novos, Serra dos (mts.), Braz. 185/E3
Pacajá (riv.), Braz. 182/D3
Pacajus, Braz. 183/G4
Pacaltsdorp, SAfr. 124/C4
Pacaraimã, Sierra (mts.), SAm. 182/A2
Pacasmayo, Peru 184/B2
Pacatuba, Braz. 183/G3
Pacaya Samiria, Res. Nacional, Peru 184/C2
Paccha, Peru 184/C3
Pacé, Fr. 56/D4
Pace, Fl, US 164/E2
Paceco, It. 48/C4
Pachacamac (ruin), Peru 184/B4
Pachaconas, Peru 184/C4
Pachamarca (riv.), Peru 184/C4
Pacheco (pass), Ca, US 148/B2
Pachelma, Rus. 71/G1
Pachino, It. 48/D4
Pachitea (riv.), Peru 184/C3
Pachiza, Peru 184/B2
Pachmarhī, India 96/B4
Pacho, Col. 183/L7
Pachuca, Mex. 175/L6
Pachwa, Ugan. 121/G2
Pacific (range), BC, Can. 144/B2
Pacific, Wa, US 167/C3
Pacific Beach, Wa, US 144/B4
Pacific City, Or, US 146/B1
Pacific Palisades (nbrhd.), Ca, US 166/E7
Pacific Rim NP, BC, Can. 144/B3
Pacifico (mtn.), Ca, US 166/B2
Pacinan (cape), Indo. 89/F4
Pacitan, Indo. 89/E5
Paço de Arcos, Port. 47/P10
Pacolet (riv.), SC, US 163/G3
Pácora, Col. 183/K7
Pacoval, Braz. 182/C3
Pacy-sur-Eure, Fr. 57/G2
Pad Īdan, Pak. 101/J3
Padada, Phil. 88/D4
Padam, India 98/D3
Padampur, India 95/D1
Padang (isl.), Indo. 89/C2
Padang, Indo. 89/C3
Padang Endau, Malay. 89/C2
Padangcermin, Indo. 89/D4
Padangpanjang, Indo. 89/C3
Padangsidempuan, Indo. 89/B2
Padangtigi, Indo. 89/A1
Padany, Rus. 68/G3
Padas (riv.), Malay. 88/A4
Padaung, Myan. 86/B5
Padcaya, Bol. 188/C2
Paddington (nbrhd.), Eng, UK 30/C2
Paddock Lake, Wi, US 167/P14
Paddock Wood, Eng, UK 30/E3
Paden City, WV, US 160/F5
Paderborn (arpt.), Ger. 53/F5
Paderborn, Ger. 53/F5
Paderno, It. 63/F2
Pāderu, India 95/D2
Padibe, Ugan. 117/G5
Padiham, Eng, UK 35/F4
Padilla, Bol. 188/C1
Padina, Yugo. 50/E3
Padjelanta NP (nat'l park), Nor. 68/B2
Padova, It. 63/E3
Padova (prov.), It. 63/E2
Padrauna, India 96/D2
Padre (isl.), Tx, US 143/G6
Padre Bernardo, Braz. 186/C2
Padre Island National Seashore, Tx, US 175/F3
Padrón, Sp. 46/A1
Pādru, India 92/B2
Padstow, Eng, UK 36/B5
Paducah, Tx, US 152/D3
Paducah, Ky, US 162/C2
Padul, Sp. 46/D4
Padula, It. 48/D2
Paduli, It. 65/D5
Paech'ŏn, NKor. 81/D4
Paegam, NKor. 81/E2
Paekakariki, NZ 135/H8
Paeksan-ni, NKor. 81/D2
Paektŏk-san (peak), SKor. 81/E4
Paektu-san (peak), NKor. 81/E2
Paengnyŏng (isl.), NKor. 79/J4
Paeroa, NZ 135/C2
Paese, It. 63/F2
Páez, Col. 180/C3
Páez, Col. 180/C4
Pafúri, Moz. 123/F4
Pag, Cro. 50/B3
Pag (isl.), Cro. 67/G1
Pagadian, Phil. 88/C4
Pagai Selatan (isl.), Indo. 90/B4
Pagai Utara (isl.), Indo. 90/B4
Pagan (isl.), NMar. 136/D3
Pagan, Myan. 86/B4
Pagancillo, Arg. 188/B4
Pagani, It. 65/D6
Paganica, It. 65/C3
Pagaralam, Indo. 89/C4
Pagatan, Indo. 90/D4
Pagawyun, Myan. 94/B3
Page, ND, US 156/F4
Page, Ok, US 153/G3
Page, Az, US 149/G2
Pagėgiai, Lith. 41/J4
Pageland, SC, US 163/G3
Pager (riv.), Ugan. 117/G5
Pagerdewa, Indo. 89/D3
Pāgla, Bang. 97/H3
Paglieta, It. 65/D3
Pagny-sur-Moselle, Fr. 55/F6
Pago Pago (cap.), ASam. 137/T10
Pago Pago (int'l arpt.), ASam. 137/T10
Pagoda (peak), Co, US 147/K3
Pagosa Springs, Co, US 149/J2
Pagri, China 97/G2
Paguate, NM, US 149/J3
Pagwa River, On, Can. 157/M2
Pagwachuan (riv.), On, Can. 157/M3
Pah-Rum (peak), Nv, US 146/D3
Pahala, Hi, US 142/U11
Pahang (state), Malay. 89/C2
Pahang (riv.), Malay. 90/B3
Páhara (lag.), Nic. 177/F3
Pahāri Buzurg, India 96/C3
Pahārpur, Pak. 98/A3
Pahāsu, India 96/B1
Pahiatua, NZ 135/C3
Pahlgām, India 98/C2
Pahokee, Fl, US 165/H4
Pahranagat Nat'l Wild. Ref., Nv, US 148/E2
Pahrump, Nv, US 148/E2
Pahuatlán, Mex. 175/L6
Pahute (mesa), Nv, US 148/D2
Pai (lake), China 80/C5
Paiania (arpt.), Gre. 49/N9
Paicines, Ca, US 148/B2
Paide, Est. 41/L2
Paignton, Eng, UK 36/C6
Paiján, Peru 184/B2
Päijänne (lake), Fin. 38/H3
Paikü (lake), China 97/E1
Pailemán, Arg. 190/D4
Pailin, Camb. 94/C3
Paimbœuf, Fr. 56/C6
Paime, Col. 183/L7
Paimio, Fin. 41/K1
Painan, Indo. 89/C3
Paine (peak), Chile 191/B6
Paine, Chile 190/N8
Painesville, Oh, US 160/F4
Painio (lake), Fin. 39/D4
Painscastle, Wal, UK 36/C2
Paint (riv.), Mi, US 157/K4
Paint Bank, Va, US 163/G2
Paint Rock, Tx, US 150/E2
Painted (des.), Az, US 142/D4
Painted Rock (res.), Az, US 149/F4
Painted Rocks (dam), Az, US 149/F4
Paintsville, Ky, US 163/F2
Paipa, Col. 180/C3
Paisley, Sc, UK 33/B5
Paisley, On, Can. 160/F2
Paisley, Or, US 146/C2
Paita, Peru 184/A2
Paithan, India 95/B2
Pajala, Swe. 38/G2
Paján, Ecu. 180/A5
Pajas Blancas (Córdoba) (int'l arpt.), Arg. 188/C4
Pajęczno, Pol. 43/K3
Pak Ban, Laos 94/C1
Pak Beng, Laos 94/C2
Pak Chong, Thai. 94/C3
Pak Thong Chai, Thai. 94/C3
Pakanbaru, Indo. 89/C2
Pakawau, NZ 135/C3
Pakch'ŏn, NKor. 81/C3
Pakenham (cape), Chile 191/B6
Pakenham, Austl. 132/G6
Pákhnes (peak), Gre. 49/J5
Pakhra (riv.), Rus. 69/W9
Pakistan (ctry.) 77/F7
Paklenica NP (nat'l park), Cro. 45/L4
Pakokku, Myan. 86/B4
Pakowki (lake), Ab, Can. 145/J3
Pākpattan, Pak. 98/B4
Pakrac, Cro. 50/C3
Pakruojis, Lith. 41/K4
Paks, Hun. 50/D2
Paksey, Bang. 97/G3
Pakue, Indo. 91/F4
Pakwach, Ugan. 121/G2
Pakxe, Laos 94/D3
Pala, Ca, US 166/C4
Pala, Chad 116/B3
Pala Ind. Res., Ca, US 166/C4
Palace, Mona. 62/J8
Palacios, Tx, US 151/F3
Paladru (lake), Fr. 64/B2
Palafrugell, Sp. 47/G2
Palagonia, It. 48/D4
Palagruža (isls.), Cro. 67/H2
Pálairos, Gre. 49/G3
Palais (riv.), Fr. 57/E4
Palaiseau, Fr. 30/J5
Pālakollu, India 95/D2
Palalarivier (riv.), SAfr. 123/F4
Palamás, Gre. 49/H3
Palamós, Sp. 47/G2
Palana, Rus. 75/R4
Palana, Austl. 133/C4
Palanan, Phil. 88/C1
Palanan (pt.), Phil. 88/C1
Palanas, Phil. 88/C2
Palanga, Lith. 41/J4
Palangkaraya, Indo. 90/D4
Pālanpur, India 101/K4
Palapye, Bots. 123/E4
Palar (riv.), India 92/C5
Palas de Rey, Sp. 46/B1
Palasa, Indo. 91/F3
Palāsa, India 95/E2
Palāsbāri, India 97/H2
Palata, It. 65/D4
Palatine, Il, US 167/P15
Palatka, Rus. 75/R3
Palatka, Fl, US 165/H3
Palattsy, Kaz. 99/D2
Palau, Mex. 151/D4
Palau (ctry.) 136/C4
Palau We (isl.), Indo. 93/G6
Palauk, Myan. 94/B3
Palaw, Myan. 94/B3
Palawan (isl.), Phil. 77/L9
Palawan Passage (chan.), Phil. 91/E2
Palaya, Bol. 188/B1
Palayan, Phil. 88/C2
Palazzo dei Penitenzieri, It. 65/G7
Palazzo del Sant'Uffizio, VatC. 65/G7
Palazzo Salviati, It. 65/G8
Palazzo Torlonia, It. 65/G7
Palazzolo Acreide, It. 48/D4
Palazzolo dello Stella, It. 63/G2
Palazzolo sull'Oglio, It. 62/C2
Palca, Bol. 184/E5
Palcenham, Austl. 133/B4
Palco, Ks, US 154/E4
Paldiski, Est. 41/L2
Pale, Bosn. 50/D4
Paleleh, Indo. 91/F3
Palembang, Indo. 89/D3
Palen (lake), Ca, US 148/E4
Palena, It. 65/D4
Palena, Chile 190/C4
Palena (riv.), Chile 190/B4
Palencia, Sp. 46/C1
Palenque, Mex. 176/D2
Palenque, PN, Mex. 176/C2
Palermo, It. 48/C3
Palermo, Ca, US 146/C4
Palermo, ND, US 156/C3
Palermo, On, Can. 160/T9
Palermo, NJ, US 168/D5
Palese (int'l arpt.), It. 48/E2
Palestina, Col. 183/K7
Palestina, Chile 188/B2
Palestine, Ar, US 162/B3
Palestine, Il, US 162/D1
Palestine, Tx, US 150/G2
Palestine (lake), Tx, US 151/G1
Palestrina, It. 65/B4
Palestro, It. 62/B3
Pālghar, India 101/K5
Pālghāt, India 95/C4
P'algong-san (peak), SKor. 81/D5
P'algong-san (peak), SKor. 84/A2
Palgrave (pt.), Namb. 122/B4
Palgrave (mt.), Austl. 130/B2
Palhāna, India 96/C3
Palhano, Braz. 183/G4
Palhoça, Braz. 189/G3
Pāli, India 96/D4
Pāli, India 92/B2
Pali-Aike, PN, Chile 191/C7
Paliā Kalān, India 96/C1
Paliano, It. 65/C4
Palić, Yugo. 50/D2
Palidoro, It. 65/B4
Palikir (cap.), Micr. 136/E4
Palima, Indo. 91/F4
Palioúrion (cape), Gre. 49/H3
Palisade, Mn, US 157/H4
Palisades, NY, US 169/K8
Palisades (cliff), NJ,NY 169/K8
Palisades, Id, US 147/H2
Palisades (dam), Id, US 147/H2
Palisades Interstate Park, NJ, US 168/D1
Palisades Park, NJ, US 169/K8
Paliseul, Belg. 55/E4
Pālitāna, India 101/K4
Palivere, Est. 41/K2
Palizada, Mex. 172/C4
Paljenik (peak), Bosn. 50/C3
Palk (str.), India, SrL. 92/C6
Pālkonda, India 95/D2
Pallamallawa, Austl. 132/D1
Pallano (peak), It. 65/D3
Pallarenda, Austl. 134/B2
Pallas Grean, Ire. 32/B4
Pallas-Ounastunturin NP, Fin. 38/H1
Pallasca, Peru 184/B3
Pallaskenry, Ire. 32/B4
Pallasovka, Rus. 71/H2
Pallastunturi (peak), Fin. 38/H1
Pallisa, Ugan. 119/A1
Palliser (cape), NZ 135/C3
Pallu, India 98/C5
Palm (isls.), Austl. 129/G4
Palm Bay, Fl, US 165/H3
Palm Beach (nbrhd.), Austl. 134/H8
Palm Beach, Fl, US 164/P9
Palm Beach (int'l arpt.), Fl, US 164/P9
Palm Beach (co.), Fl, US 164/P9
Palm Beach Gardens, Fl, US 164/P9
Palm Beach Shores, Fl, US 164/P9
Palm City, Ca, US 166/C5
Palm City, Fl, US 165/H4
Palm Desert, Ca, US 148/D4
Palm Harbor, Fl, US 164/K7
Palm Island Aboriginal Settlement, Austl. 134/B2
Palm River-Clair Mel, Fl, US 164/L8
Palm Springs, Ca, US 148/D4
Palma, Moz. 119/C4
Palma, Sp. 47/G3
Palma (riv.), Braz. 186/D2
Palma Campania, It. 65/D6
Palma del Río, Sp. 46/C4
Palma di Montechiaro, It. 48/C4
Palma Mallorca (int'l arpt.), Sp. 47/G3
Palma Soriano, Cuba 177/H1
Palmácia, Braz. 183/G4
Palmanova, It. 63/G2
Palmar (riv.), Ven. 177/H4
Palmares, Braz. 183/H5
Palmarito, Ven. 180/D3
Palmarito, Bol. 185/F5
Palmas (cape), Libr. 114/D5
Palmas, Braz. 189/G3
Palmas, Braz. 186/C1
Palmdale, Ca, US 166/B1
Palmeira, CpV. 107/K10
Palmeira, Braz. 189/G3
Palmeira das Missões, Braz. 189/F3
Palmeira dos Índios, Braz. 183/G5
Palmeirais, Braz. 183/F4
Palmeiras (riv.), Braz. 186/D2
Palmeiras de Goiás, Braz. 186/C3
Palmeirina, Braz. 183/G5
Palmela, Port. 47/Q10
Palmer, Sk, Can. 145/L3
Palmer, US, Ant. 192/V
Palmer, Ak, US 171/J3
Palmer, Ma, US 161/K3
Palmer, Tx, US 150/L7
Palmer, Wa, US 167/D3
Palmer Lake, Co, US 152/B1
Palmer Land (phys. reg.), Ant. 192/V
Palmer Rapids, On, Can. 161/H2
Palmerston, On, Can. 160/F3
Palmerston, NZ 135/B4
Palmerston (cape), Austl. 134/C3
Palmerston Atoll (atoll), CookIs. 137/J6
Palmerston North, NZ 135/C3
Palmerston NP, Austl. 134/B2
Palmerton, Pa, US 168/C2
Palmerville, Austl. 134/B1
Palmetto, Fl, US 165/G4
Palmetto, Ga, US 163/L7
Palmetto Bend (dam), Tx, US 151/F3
Palmi, It. 48/D3
Palmilla, Chile 190/C2
Palmillas (pt.), Cuba 177/F1
Palmira, Col. 180/B4
Palmital, Braz. 189/G2
Palmitas, Uru. 191/K10
Palmitos, Braz. 189/F3
Palmyra, Mi, US 160/E4
Palmyra (isl.), PacUS 137/J4
Palmyra, In, US 162/D1
Palmyra, Mo, US 155/J4
Palmyra, Pa, US 168/B3
Palmyra, Va, US 163/H2
Palmyra, Wi, US 155/K2
Palmyra (Tadmur) (ruin), Syria 102/D3
Palmyras (pt.), India 92/E3
Palnackie, Sc, UK 34/E2
Palo, Phil. 88/D3
Palo Alto, Pa, US 168/B2
Palo Alto Battlefield Nat'l Hist. Site, Tx, US 151/F4
Palo Duro (cr.), Tx, US 152/C3
Palo Pinto, Tx, US 151/E1
Palo Santo, Arg. 188/E3
Palo Verde, Ca, US 148/E4
Palo Verde, PN, CR 172/D5
Paloemeu (riv.), Sur. 182/C2
Paloh, Indo. 90/C3
Paloich, Sudan 117/G3
Palombara Sabina, It. 65/B3
Palometas, Bol. 188/D1
Palomeu (riv.), Sur. 181/H4
Palon (peak), It. 63/E2
Pāloncha, India 95/D2
Paloncillo (mts.), NM, US 149/H5
Palos (cape), Sp. 47/E4
Palos Blancos, Bol. 188/D2
Palos de la Frontera, Sp. 46/B4
Palos Hills, Il, US 167/Q16
Palos Verdes (pt.), Ca, US 166/F8
Palos Verdes (hills), Ca, US 166/F8
Palos Verdes Estates, Ca, US 166/F8
Palosco, It. 62/C2
Palouse (riv.), Wa, US 144/F4
Palouse, Wa, US 144/F4
Palpa, Peru 184/C4
Palpalá, Arg. 188/C3
Palpetu (cape), Indo. 91/G4
Paltamo, Fin. 68/E2
Paltang, SKor. 81/G6
Palu, Indo. 91/E4
Palu (isl.), Indo. 128/A2
Palu, Turk. 102/D2
Paluan, Phil. 88/C2
Palwal, India 96/A1
Pama, Burk. 115/F4
Pama, Chile 188/B4
Pamangkat, Indo. 90/C3
Pamanukan (cape), Indo. 89/D4
Pamar, Col. 180/D5
Pambeguwa, Nga. 115/H4
Pambula, Austl. 133/D3
Pamekasan, Indo. 89/F4
Pameungpeuk, Indo. 89/D4
Pāmgarh, India 96/D5
Pamiers, Fr. 44/D5
Pamir (reg.), Taj.,China 74/H6
Pamir (riv.), Afg.,Taj. 74/H6
Pamlico (riv.), NC, US 163/J3
Pamlico (sound), NC, US 163/J3
Pamoni, Ven. 181/E4
Pampa, Tx, US 152/D3
Pampa de Agnia, Arg. 190/C4
Pampa de los Guanacos, Arg. 188/D3
Pampa de los Salinas, Arg. 188/C4
Pampa del Indio, Arg. 188/E3
Pampa del Sacramento (plain), Peru 184/C2
Pampa del Tamarugal (plain), Chile 188/B1
Pampa Grande, Bol. 188/C1
Pampa Húmeda (plain), Arg. 190/E2
Pampa Pelada (plain), Arg. 190/C5
Pampa Seca (plain), Arg. 190/D3
Pampachiri, Peru 184/C4
Pampacolca, Peru 184/C4
Pampas (plain), Arg. 179/C6
Pampas (riv.), Peru 184/C4
Pampas, Peru 184/C4
Pampas, Peru 184/B3
Pampilhosa da Serra, Port. 46/B2
Pamplico, SC, US 163/H4
Pamplona, Col. 180/C3
Pamplona, Sp. 44/C5
Pampulha (int'l arpt.), Braz. 186/E3
Pāmpur, India 98/C2
Pamukova, Turk. 51/K5
Pamunkey Ind. Res., Va, US 163/J2
Pan de Azúcar, Bol. 188/C2
Pan de Azúcar, PN, Chile 188/B3
Pana, Gabon 120/C3
Pana, Il, US 155/K4
Panaba, Mex. 176/D1
Panabo, Phil. 88/D4
Panaca, Nv, US 148/E2
Panacachi, Bol. 188/C1
Panacea, Fl, US 165/F2
Panadura, SrL. 95/C5
Pānāgar, India 96/B4
Panagyurishte, Bul. 51/G4
Panaitan (isl.), Indo. 90/B5
Panaji, India 95/B3
Panamá (bay), Pan. 177/G4
Panama (ctry.) 139/J9
Panama (canal), Pan. 139/K9
Panamá (cap.), Pan. 180/B2
Panama (isth.), Pan. 173/F5
Panama (gulf), Pan. 139/K9
Panama City, Fl, US 165/F2
Panama, Ok, US 153/G3
Panamá Viejo (ruin), Pan. 180/B2
Panambi, Braz. 189/F4
Panamint (range), Ca, US 148/D2
Panao, Peru 184/B3
Panaon (isl.), Phil. 88/D3
Panaro (riv.), It. 45/J4
Panarukan, Indo. 89/F4
Panasoffkee (lake), Fl, US 164/L6
Panay (isl.), Phil. 77/M8
Panay (gulf), Phil. 88/C3
Pancake (range), Nv, US 146/E4
Pančevo, Yugo. 50/E3
Panchagarh, Bang. 97/G2
Panchor, Malay. 89/D2
Pančicev vrh (peak), Yugo. 50/E4
Pancilet (res.), India 97/F4
Panciu, Rom. 51/H3
Panda, D.R. Congo 121/F5
Panda, Moz. 123/G5
Pandale, Tx, US 151/D2
Pandamatenga, Bots. 122/E3
Pandan, Phil. 88/D2
Pandan, Phil. 88/C3
Pandan (str.), Sing. 89/H7
Pandaria, India 96/C4
Pandeglang, Indo. 89/D4
Pandėlys, Lith. 41/L3
Pāndhurna, India 95/C1
Pandie Pandie, Austl. 131/H3
Pandino, It. 62/C3
Pando, Uru. 191/L11
Pando (state), Bol. 185/E3
Pāndoh, India 98/D4
Pandora (passage), PNG 129/G2
Pandrup, Den. 40/C3
Pandua, India 97/G4
Panduro, Bol. 185/E5

Panela – Penge

Panelas, Braz. 183/G5
Panevėžys, Lith. 41/L4
Panfilov, Kaz. 99/D3
Panfilovo, Rus. 73/M2
Pang (riv.), Myan. 86/C4
Pang Kalom, Laos 86/D4
Pang Long, Myan. 86/C4
Pangai, Tonga 137/H6
Pangaíon (peak), Gre. 49/J2
Pangala, Congo 120/C3
Pangandaran, Indo. 89/E4
Pangani (riv.), Tanz. 119/B2
Pangani, Tanz. 119/B3
Pangbourne, Eng, UK 37/E4
Pangburn, Ar, US 153/J3
Pangi, D.R. Congo 121/F3
Pangia, PNG 129/G1
Pangjiabu, China 80/G6
Pangkajene, Indo. 91/E4
Pangkalanberandan, Indo. 89/B1
Pangkalanpembuang, Indo. 90/D4
Pangkalansusu, Indo. 89/B1
Pangkalaseang (cape), Indo. 91/F4
Pangkalpinang, Indo. 89/D3
Pangnirtung, Nun, Can. 141/K2
Pangsau (pass), India 86/C3
Panguipulli, Chile 190/B3
Panguitch, Ut, US 149/F2
Panguma, SLeo. 114/C4
Pangururan, Indo. 89/B2
Pangutaran, Phil. 88/C4
Pangutaran (isl.), Phil. 88/C4
Pangutaran Group (isls.), Malay. 88/B4
P'an'gyo, NKor. 81/D3
Panhandle, Tx, US 152/D3
Pania-Mutombo, D.R. Congo 121/E4
Paniai (lake), Indo. 91/J4
Panicale, It. 65/B1
Panié (peak), NCal. 137/U12
Pānihāti, India 97/G4
Pānīpat, India 98/D5
Panitan, Phil. 88/C3
Panj (riv.), Afg.,Taj. 74/G6
Panj (riv.), Afg. 101/K1
Panj (Pyandzh) (riv.), Afg.,Taj. 99/B4
Panjakent, Taj. 74/G6
Panjang, Indo. 89/D4
Panjgraon, India 98/D4
Panjgūr, Pak. 101/H3
Panjwīn, Iraq 103/F3
Panke (riv.), Ger. 42/Q6
Pankow, Ger. 42/Q6
Pankshin, Nga. 115/H4
P'anmun-ŭp, NKor. 81/D4
P'anmunjŏm, NKor. 81/D4
Panna, India 96/C3
Pannawonica, Austl. 130/C2
Pannikin (isl.), Austl. 134/F7
Pano Lefkara, Cyp. 104/C2
Pano Panayia, Cyp. 104/C2
Pano Platres, Cyp. 104/C2
Panora, Ia, US 155/G3
Panorama, Braz. 189/G2
Panshan, China 81/B2
Panshi, China 79/K3
Panshizhen, China 87/F2
Pānskura, India 97/F4
Pant, Eng, UK 36/C1
Pantai Remis, Malay. 89/C1
Pantanal (reg.), Braz. 189/E1
Pantanal (reg.), Braz. 186/A3
Pantanal Matogrossense PN, Braz. 188/E1
Pantano Wash (riv.), Az, US 149/G4
Pantar (isl.), Indo. 128/A2
Pante Makasar, ETim. 128/B2
Pantego, NC, US 163/J3
Pantego, Tx, US 150/K7
Pantelleria, It. 48/B4
Pantelleria (isl.), It. 29/F5
Pantha, Myan. 93/F3
Panther Swamp NWR, Ms, US 162/B4
Panthersville, Ga, US 163/M7
Panti, Indo. 89/C2
Pantigliate, It. 62/C3
Pantijan Abor. Land, Austl. 128/B4
Pantin, Fr. 30/K5
Pantoja, Peru 180/C5
Pantón, Sp. 46/B1
Pantukan, Phil. 88/D4
Panu, D.R. Congo 120/D3
Pánuco (riv.), Mex. 172/B3
Pánuco, Mex. 176/B1
Panwol, SKor. 81/F7
Panyabungan, Indo. 89/B2
Panyam, Nga. 115/H4
Panzhihua, China 86/D3
Panzós, Guat. 176/D3
Pao (riv.), Ven. 183/M8
Pão de Açúcar, Braz. 187/F1
Paola, It. 48/E3
Paola, Ks, US 153/G1
Paola, Fl, US 164/N6
Paola, Malta 48/M7
Paoli, In, US 162/D1
Paoli, Ok, US 153/F3
Paoli, Pa, US 168/C3
Paonia, Co, US 149/J1
Paonta Sahib, India 98/D4
Paoua, CAfr. 116/C4
Paoy Pet, Camb. 94/C3
Paozi, China 81/B1
Paoziyan, China 81/C2
Pap, Uzb. 99/B3
Pápa, Hun. 50/C2
Papa Westray (isl.), Sc, UK 31/V14
Papagayo (gulf), CR 172/D5
Papago Ind. Res., Az, US 149/F4
Papakura, NZ 135/F7
Papantla, Mex. 175/M6
Papaplaya, Peru 184/C2
Papar, Malay. 88/A4
Papara, FrPol. 137/X15
Papatoetoe, NZ 135/F6
Papeete (cap.), FrPol. 137/X15
Papeete (Faaa) (int'l arpt.), FrPol. 137/X15
Papenburg, Ger. 53/E2
Papendrecht, Neth. 52/B5
Papenoo, FrPol. 137/X15
Papetoai, FrPol. 137/X15
Paphos, Cyp. 104/C2
Paphos (dist.), Cyp. 104/C2
Papilė, Lith. 41/K3
Papillion, Ne, US 155/F3
Papineauville, Qu, Can. 161/J2
Papingut (peak), Alb. 49/G2
Papiu, Sudan 117/F4
Paposo, Chile 188/B3
Pāppadāhāndi, India 95/D2
Pappenheim, Ger. 58/D5
Papua (gulf), PNG 129/G2
Papua New Guinea (ctry.) 136/D5
Papudo, Chile 190/C2
Papun, Myan. 94/B2
Papunya, Austl. 131/F2
Paquera, CR 177/E4
Pará (state), Braz. 181/G5
Pará (riv.), Braz. 186/D3
Para (riv.), Braz. 182/D3
Pará (falls), Ven. 181/E3
Para (dist.), Sur. 181/H3
Pará de Minas, Braz. 186/D3
Para de Oeste (riv.), Braz. 181/H4
Para Wirra NP, Austl. 131/M8
Para, South (riv.), Austl. 131/M8
Paraburdoo, Austl. 130/C2
Paracale, Phil. 88/C2
Paracambi, Braz. 187/N7
Paracas (pen.), Peru 184/B4
Paracas, Res. Nacional, Peru 184/B4
Paracatu, Braz. 186/D3
Paracatu (riv.), Braz. 186/D3
Paracel (isls.), Asia 86/F5
Parachilna, Austl. 131/H4
Paracho de Verduzco, Mex. 174/E5
Parachute, Co, US 147/J4
Paraćin, Yugo. 50/E4
Paracuru, Braz. 183/G3
Paradhísion (int'l arpt.), Gre. 102/B2
Paradip, India 92/E3
Paradise, Nf, Can. 159/L2
Paradise, Guy. 182/B1
Paradise, Ca, US 146/C4
Paradise, Ks, US 154/E4
Paradise, Mi, US 160/D1
Paradise, Mt, US 144/G4
Paradise, Nv, US 148/E2
Paradise, Pa, US 168/B4
Paradise, Tx, US 150/K6
Paradise Hills, NM, US 149/J3
Paradise Valley, Az, US 149/G4
Paradise Valley, Ab, Can. 145/J1
Paradox, Co, US 149/H1
Parafield (arpt.), Austl. 131/M8
Parafiyivka, Ukr. 73/G1
Paragominas, Braz. 183/E3
Paragonah, Ut, US 149/F2
Paragould, Ar, US 162/B2
Paragua (riv.), Ven. 181/F3
Paraguá (riv.), Bol. 185/F4
Paraguaçu (riv.), Braz. 179/E4
Paraguaçu, Braz. 187/L6
Paraguaçu Paulista, Braz. 189/G2
Paraguai (riv.), SAm. 179/D5
Paraguaipoa, Ven. 180/D2
Paraguaná (pen.), Ven. 173/G5
Paraguarí (dept.), Par. 189/E3
Paraguarí, Par. 189/E3
Paraguay (ctry.) 179/C5
Paraguay (riv.), Par. 186/A4
Paraiba (riv.), Braz. 189/J2
Paraiba (state), Braz. 183/G4
Paraíba do Sul (riv.), Braz. 179/E5
Paraíba do Sul, Braz. 187/N7
Paraibano, Braz. 183/F4
Paraibuna (riv.), Braz. 187/L8
Paraim (riv.), Braz. 186/D1
Parainen (Pargas), Fin. 41/K1
Paraíso, CR 177/F4
Paraíso, Mex. 176/C2
Paraíso do Norte, Braz. 189/F2
Paraíso do Tocantins, Braz. 186/C1
Paraisópolis, Braz. 187/L7
Parakou, Ben. 115/F4
Parama (isl.), PNG 129/F2
Paramakkudi, India 95/C4
Paramaribo (dist.), Sur. 181/H3
Paramaribo (cap.), Sur. 182/C1
Parambu, Braz. 183/F4
Paramillo (peak), Col. 180/C3
Paramillo, PN, Col. 173/F6
Paramirim (riv.), Braz. 187/E2
Paramirim, Braz. 187/E2
Paramithía, Gre. 49/G3
Paramoti, Braz. 183/G4
Paramount, Ca, US 166/F8
Paramus, NJ, US 169/J8
Paramushir (isl.), Rus. 77/Q5
Paraná (riv.), SAm. 179/D5
Paranã (riv.), Braz. 186/D2
Paraná (state), Braz. 186/C4
Paraná, Arg. 188/D4
Paranã, Braz. 186/D2
Paraná Ibicuy (riv.), Arg. 191/J10
Paraná Madeirinha (riv.), Braz. 182/B4
Paraná Urariá (riv.), Braz. 181/G5
Paranaguá (bay), Braz. 189/G3
Paranaguá, Braz. 189/G3
Paranaíba, Braz. 189/G1
Paranaíba (riv.), Braz. 186/D3
Paranapanema (riv.), Braz. 189/G2
Paranapiacaba, Serra do (mts.), Braz. 186/C5
Parañaque, Phil. 88/E6
Paranatinga (riv.), Braz. 179/D4
Paranavaí, Braz. 189/F2
Parang, Phil. 88/C4
Paraopeba, Braz. 186/D3
Paraopeba (riv.), Braz. 186/D3
Parapara, Ven. 183/N8
Paraparaumu (arpt.), NZ 135/H8
Paraparaumu, NZ 135/J8
Parapetí (riv.), Bol. 188/D1
Parás, Mex. 151/E4
Parāsi, Nepal 96/D2
Parati, Braz. 187/M8
Paratico, It. 62/C2
Paratinga (riv.), Braz. 187/L8
Paratinga, Braz. 187/E2
Paraúna, Braz. 186/C3
Paravūr, India 95/C4
Paray-Vieille-Poste, Fr. 30/K5
Paràzinho, Braz. 183/H4
Pārbati (riv.), India 101/L4
Pārbatipur, Bang. 97/G3
Parçay-Meslay, Fr. 57/F6
Parcé-sur-Sarthe, Fr. 57/E5
Parchim, Ger. 42/F2
Parczew, Pol. 43/M3
Pardes Hanna-Karkur, Isr. 105/B4
Pārdi, India 101/K4
Parding, China 99/E5
Pardo (riv.), Braz. 189/H2
Pardo (riv.), Braz. 186/B4
Pardone (cape), SAfr. 124/D4
Pardoo, Austl. 130/C2
Pardubice, Czh. 43/H3
Pardubický (pol. reg.), Czh. 43/J4
Pare, Indo. 89/F4
Pare (mts.), Tanz. 119/B2
Parece Vela (Okino-Tori-Shima) (isl.), Japan 77/N7
Parecis (mts.), Braz. 179/C4
Parede, Port. 47/P10
Paredes de Nava, Sp. 46/C1
Paredón, Mex. 151/D5
Paredón, Mex. 176/C2
Paredones, Chile 190/C2
Parelhas, Braz. 183/G4
Parempuyre, Fr. 44/C4
Parenda, India 95/B2
Parentis-en-Born, Fr. 44/C4
Parepare, Indo. 91/E4
Parera, Arg. 190/D2
Parets del Valles, Sp. 47/L6
Pargas (Parainen), Fin. 41/K1
Pargny-sur-Saulx, Fr. 55/D6
Pargolovo, Rus. 69/T6
Paria (pen.), Ven. 173/J5
Paria (gulf) 179/C1
Paria (riv.), Ut, US 149/G2
Paria, Bol. 188/C1
Pariacoto, Peru 184/B3
Pariaguán, Ven. 181/E2
Pariaman, Indo. 89/C3
Parichi, Bela. 70/D1
Parigi, Indo. 91/F4
Parigné-L'Évêque, Fr. 57/F5
Parikkala, Fin. 38/J3
Parima (mts.), Braz. 181/E4
Parima (riv.), Braz. 181/F4
Parinacota (peak), Bol. 184/D5
Parinacota (peak), Bol.,Chile 188/B1
Parinari, Peru 184/C2
Pariñas (pt.), Peru 184/A2
Paringa, Austl. 132/B2
Parîngu Mare (peak), Rom. 51/F3
Parintins, Braz. 182/B3
Paris, Tx, US 153/G4
Paris, Ar, US 153/H3
Paris (dept.), Fr. 54/B6
Paris, On, Can. 160/F3
Paris, Me, US 161/L2
Paris, Il, US 160/C5
Paris (cap.), Fr. 30/K5
Paris, Id, US 147/H2
Paris, Tn, US 162/C2
Paris, Ky, US 162/E1
Paris, Ms, US 162/C3
Paris, Mo, US 155/H4
Paris (Le Bourget) (arpt.), Fr. 30/K5
Parishville, NY, US 161/J2
Parita (bay), Pan. 177/F4
Park (riv.), ND, US 156/F3
Park (range), Co, US 147/K3
Park (pt.), Eng, UK 36/A5
Park City, Ks, US 153/F2
Park City, Il, US 167/Q15
Park City, Ky, US 162/D2
Park Falls, Wi, US 157/J5
Park Forest, Il, US 160/C4
Park Hill, Ok, US 153/G3
Park Rapids, Mn, US 157/G4
Park Ridge, Il, US 167/Q16
Park Ridge, NJ, US 169/J7
Park River, ND, US 156/F3
Park Valley, Ut, US 147/G3
Park View, Ia, US 155/J3
Parkano, Fin. 38/G3
Parkbeg, Sk, Can. 145/L2
Parkchester (nbrhd.), NY, US 169/K8
Parkdale, Ar, US 153/J4
Parkdale, Or, US 146/C1
Parker, Ks, US 153/G1
Parker, Pa, US 161/G4
Parker (lake), Fl, US 164/M7
Parker, Az, US 148/E3
Parker, SD, US 155/F2
Parker, Co, US 154/B4
Parker (peak), SD, US 154/C2
Parker (pt.), Austl. 129/E4
Parker (co.), Tx, US 150/K7
Parker, Tx, US 151/F1
Parker Dam, Az, Ca, US 149/E3
Parker River Nat'l Wild. Ref., Ma, US 161/L3
Parker's Cove, Nf, Can. 159/K2
Parkers Prairie, Mn, US 157/G4
Parkersburg, Ia, US 155/H2
Parkersburg, WV, US 163/G1
Parkersburg, Il, US 162/C1
Parkes, Austl. 133/D1
Parkesburg, Pa, US 168/C4
Parkeston, Eng, UK 37/H3
Parkgate, NI, UK 34/B2
Parkhill, On, Can. 160/F3
Parkhurst, Eng, UK 37/E5
Parkin, Ar, US 162/B3
Parkland, Wa, US 144/C4
Parkman, Sk, Can. 156/D3
Parks, Ar, US 153/H3
Parkside, Sk, Can. 145/L1
Parkside, Pa, US 168/C4
Parksley, Va, US 163/K2
Parkstetten, Ger. 59/F5
Parkston, SD, US 154/F2
Parksville, SC, US 163/F4
Parksville, BC, Can. 144/B3
Parkton, Md, US 168/B4
Parkton, NC, US 163/H3
Parkville, Md, US 168/B5
Parkville, Pa, US 168/B4
Parkway-Sacramento, Ca, US 167/L9
Parkwood, NC, US 163/H3
Parla, Sp. 47/N9
Parliament Buildings, NZ 135/H9
Parlier, Ca, US 148/C2
Parlin, Co, US 149/J1
Parma, Oh, US 160/F4
Parma (prov.), It. 62/C3
Parma, It. 62/D4
Parma (riv.), It. 62/D3
Parma, Id, US 146/E2
Parma, Mo, US 162/C2
Parmain, Fr. 30/J4
Parmelee, SD, US 154/D2
Parnaguá, Braz. 186/D1
Parnaíba (riv.), Braz. 179/E3
Parnaíba, Braz. 183/F3
Parnamirim, Braz. 183/G5
Parnarama, Braz. 183/F4
Parnassós (peak), Gre. 49/H3
Parnassós NP, Gre. 49/H3
Parnassus, NZ 135/C3
Parndana, Austl. 131/H5
Parnell, Tx, US 152/D3
Parnell (nbrhd.), NZ 135/F6
Párnis (peak), Gre. 49/N8
Párnis Óros NP, Gre. 49/N8
Párnon (mts.), Gre. 49/H4
Pärnu, Est. 41/L2
Pärnu (bay), Est. 41/L2
Pärnu-Jaagupi, Est. 41/L2
Paro, Bhu. 97/G2
Paron, Fr. 44/E2
Parona di Valpolicella, It. 63/D3
Paroo (riv.), Austl. 127/D3
Páros, Gre. 49/J4
Páros (isl.), Gre. 67/K3
Parow, SAfr. 124/L10
Parowan, Ut, US 149/F2
Parpan, Swi. 61/F4
Parrachée (mtn.), Fr. 64/C2
Parral, Chile 190/C3
Parramatta (nbrhd.), Austl. 134/H8
Parramore (isl.), Md, US 163/K2
Parras de la Fuente, Mex. 174/E3
Parrett (riv.), Eng, UK 36/D4
Parris Island, SC, US 163/G4
Parris Island Marine Base, SC, US 163/G4
Parrish, Fl, US 164/L8
Parrish, Al, US 162/D4
Parrita, CR 177/E4
Parrot Jungle, Fl, US 164/P11
Parrott, Ga, US 165/F2
Parr's Halt, Bots. 123/E4
Parrsboro, NS, Can. 158/E3
Parry (chan.), Can. 139/F2
Parry (isls.), Can. 139/F2
Parry (bay), Nun, Can. 141/H2
Parry Sound, On, Can. 160/F2
Parsberg, Ger. 59/E4
Parseierspitze (peak), Aus. 61/G3
Parshall, ND, US 156/C4
Parsippany-Troy Hills, NJ, US 169/H8
Parson, BC, Can. 144/F2
Parsons, Ks, US 153/G2
Parsons (mtn.), SC, US 163/F3
Parsons, Tn, US 162/C3
Parsons (mt.), Austl. 129/D3
Parsons (range), Austl. 129/D3
Parsons, WV, US 163/H1
Partago, Ben. 115/F4
Pårtefjället (peak), Swe. 38/F2
Partenstein, Ger. 58/C2
Parthenay, Fr. 44/C3
Partille, Swe. 40/E3
Partinico, It. 48/C3
Partizansk, Rus. 79/L3
Partizánske, Slvk. 43/K4
Partridge, Ks, US 153/E2
Partry (mts.), Ire. 32/A2
Partūr, India 92/C4
Paru (riv.), Braz. 181/H4
Paru de Oeste (riv.), Braz. 179/D2
Paruro, Peru 184/D4
Pārvathīpuram, India 95/D2
Parwich, Eng, UK 35/G5
Paryang, China 99/D5
Parys, SAfr. 124/D2
Pas de Morgins (pass), Fr. 60/C5
Pas-de-Calais (dept.), Fr. 54/A3
Pasadena, Nf, Can. 159/J1
Pasadena (lake), Fl, US 164/L7
Pasadena, Ca, US 166/F7
Pasadena, Tx, US 151/M9
Pasadena, Md, US 168/B5
Pasado (cape), Ecu. 180/A5
Pasaje, Ecu. 184/B1
Pasaman (peak), Indo. 89/C2
Pasān, India 96/D4
Pasanauri, Geo. 71/H4
Pasarbantal, Indo. 89/C3
Pasarkuok, Indo. 89/C3
Pasarsorkam, Indo. 89/B2
Pasarwajo, Indo. 128/A1
Pasawng, Myan. 94/B2
Pasay, Phil. 88/F6
Pascagoula (riv.), Ms, US 164/D2
Pascagoula, Ms, US 164/D2
Paşcani, Rom. 72/D4
Pasching, Aus. 59/H6
Pasco (co.), Fl, US 164/L7
Pasco, Fl, US 164/L7
Pasco (dept.), Peru 184/C3
Pasco, Wa, US 144/E4
Pascua (riv.), Chile 191/B6
Pascua, Isla de (Easter) (isl.), Chile 137/Q7
Pascuales, Ecu. 184/B1
Pasewalk, Ger. 40/E5
Pashkovo, Rus. 71/G1
Pashkovskiy, Rus. 73/K5
Pasian di Prato, It. 63/G1
Pasiano, It. 63/F2
Pasig, Phil. 88/F6
Pāsighāt, India 86/B2
Pasinler, Turk. 102/E2
Pasión, Río de la (riv.), Guat. 176/D2
Pasir Mas, Malay. 89/C1
Pasir Puteh, Malay. 89/C1
Pasłęk, Pol. 41/H4
Pasłęka (riv.), Pol. 43/L2
Pasley (cape), Austl. 130/D5
Pašman (isl.), Cro. 45/L5
Pasni, Pak. 101/H3
Paso de Indios, Arg. 190/C4
Paso de la Patria, Arg. 188/E3
Paso de los Libres, Arg. 189/E4
Paso de los Toros, Uru. 191/K10
Paso de Ovejas, Mex. 175/N7
Paso de Patria, Par. 188/E3
Paso del Cerro, Uru. 189/F4
Paso del Macho, Mex. 175/N8
Paso del Planchón (peak), Chile 190/C2
Paso Flores, Arg. 190/C4
Paso Real, Ven. 183/P8
Paso Robles (El Paso de Robles), Ca, US 148/B3
Paspébiac, Qu, Can. 158/E1
Pasrūr, Pak. 98/C3
Pass Christian, Ms, US 164/D2
Pass Peak (mt.), Yk, Can. 171/M3
Passa Quatro, Braz. 187/M7
Passage East, Ire. 32/D5
Passage Key Nat'l Wild. Ref., Fl, US 165/G4
Passage West, Ire. 32/B6
Passagem Franca, Braz. 183/F4
Passaic, NJ, US 169/J8
Passaic (riv.), NJ, US 168/D2
Passais, Fr. 57/E3
Passau, Ger. 59/G5
Passero (pt.), It. 48/D4
Passi, Phil. 88/C3
Passignano sul Trasimeno, It. 65/B1
Passo Corese, It. 65/B3
Passo Fundo, Braz. 189/F4
Passo Fundo, Barragem do (res.), Braz. 189/F3
Passons, It. 63/G1
Passoré (prov.), Burk. 115/E3
Passos, Braz. 189/H2
Passwang (peak), Swi. 60/D3
Passy, Fr. 60/C6
Pastavy, Bela. 41/M4
Pastaza (riv.), Peru 180/B5
Pastaza (dept.), Ecu. 180/B5
Pastaza (riv.), Ecu.,Peru 179/B3
Pastek (riv.), Pol. 41/J5
Pasto, Col. 180/B4
Pastol (bay), Ak, US 171/F3
Pastoriza, Sp. 46/B1
Pastos Bons, Braz. 183/E4
Pastura (peak), Az, US 149/H2
Pasuquin, Phil. 88/C1
Pasuruan, Indo. 89/F4
Pasvalys, Lith. 41/L3
Pásztó, Hun. 43/K5
Pata, CAfr. 116/D3
Pata, Bol. 184/D4
Patacamaya, Bol. 188/C1
Patag NP, Phil. 88/C3
Patagonia (phys. reg.), Arg. 179/B8
Patagonia, Az, US 149/G5
Patah (peak), Indo. 90/B4
Patamdesar, India 98/C5
Pātan, India 96/B4
Pātan, India 101/K4
Pāṭan (Lalitpur), Nepal 97/E2
Pataná (peak), Braz. 189/G3
Patani, Nga. 115/G5
Patani, Indo. 91/G3
Patapédia (riv.), Qu, Can. 158/D1
Patapsco, Md, US 168/B4
Patapsco (riv.), Md, US 168/A5
Pataudi, India 98/D5
Patay, Fr. 57/G4
Pataz, Peru 184/B2
Patchewollock, Austl. 132/B2
Patchogue, NY, US 169/E2
Patchway, Eng, UK 36/D3
Pate (isl.), Kenya 119/C2
Patea, NZ 135/C2
Pategi, Nga. 115/G4
Pateley Bridge, Eng, UK 35/G3
Patenga, Bang. 97/H4
Paterna, Sp. 47/E3
Paternion, Aus. 45/K3
Paternò, It. 48/D4
Paterno, It. 65/C3
Pateros, Wa, US 144/E3
Paterson, NJ, US 169/J8
Paterson, Austl. 133/E1
Paterson (cape), Austl. 133/B4
Pathalgaon, India 96/D4
Pathanāmthitta, India 95/C4
Pathānkot, India 98/C3
Pātharghāta, Bang. 97/G4
Patharkot, Nepal 97/E2
Pathein (Bassein), Myan. 86/B5
Pathfinder (dam), Wy, US 147/K2
Pathfinder (res.), Wy, US 147/K2
Pathfinder NWR, Wy, US 147/K2
Pathiu, Thai. 94/B4
Pathlow, Sk, Can. 145/M1
Pati, Indo. 89/E4
Pati, Indo. 128/B2
Patía (riv.), Col. 180/B4
Patía, Col. 180/B4
Patiāla, India 98/D4
Patikul, Phil. 88/C4
Pātiram, India 97/G3
Patiya, Bang. 97/H4
Patkaglik, China 99/E4
Patna, Sc, UK 33/B6
Patna, India 97/E3
Patnāgarh, India 95/D1
Patnanongan (isl.), Phil. 88/C2
Patnongon, Phil. 88/C3
Patnos, Turk. 103/E2
Pato Branco, Braz. 189/F3
Patoka, In, US 162/D1
Patoka (riv.), In, US 162/D1
Patoka (lake), In, US 162/D1
Patos, Alb. 49/F2
Patos, Braz. 183/G4
Patos de Minas, Braz. 186/D3
Patos, dos (lake), Braz. 189/G4
Patoutville, La, US 164/C3
Patquía, Arg. 188/C4
Pátrai, Gre. 49/G3
Patrai (gulf), Gre. 49/G3
Pātrasāer, India 97/F4
Patrātu, India 97/E4
Patricia (mt.), Austl. 131/F2
Patricia, Ab, Can. 145/J2
Patricia, Tx, US 151/C1
Patricio Lynch (isl.), Chile 191/A6
Patrick (A.F.B.), Fl, US 165/H3
Patrick Springs, Va, US 163/G2
Patrington, Eng, UK 35/H4
Patrocínio, Braz. 186/D3
Patroon, Tx, US 151/H2
Patsaliga (cr.), Al, US 165/E2
Patscherkofel (peak), Aus. 61/H3
Pattani, Thai. 94/C5
Pattensen, Ger. 53/G4
Patterson, Ar, US 153/J3
Patterson, Ga, US 165/G2
Patterson, La, US 164/C3
Patterson, Mo, US 162/B2
Patti, It. 48/D3
Patti, India 98/C4
Pattingham, Eng, UK 36/D1
Pattison, Ms, US 164/C2
Pattoki, Pak. 98/B4
Patton, Pa, US 161/G4
Pattonsburg, Mo, US 155/G3
Pattukkottai, India 95/C4
Pattullo (mt.), BC, Can. 171/N4
Patu, Braz. 183/G4
Patuākhāli, Bang. 97/H4
Patuākhāli (pol. reg.), Bang. 97/G4
Patuca (riv.), Hon. 172/D5
Patuca (pt.), Hon. 177/E3
Patuca (mts.), Hon. 176/E3
Patuha (peak), Indo. 89/D4
Pătulele, Rom. 50/F3
Patuxent (riv.), Md, US 168/B5
Patuxent NWR, Md, US 168/B5
Patuxent River State Park, Md, US 168/B5
Páty, Hun. 51/Q9
Pátzcuaro, Mex. 175/E5
Pau, Fr. 44/C5
Pau dos Ferros, Braz. 183/G4
Paucarbamba, Peru 184/C4
Paucartambo, Peru 184/D4
Paucartambo, Peru 184/C3
Pauillac, Fr. 44/C4
Pauini (riv.), Braz. 185/E2
Pauini, Braz. 185/E2
Pauksa (peak), Myan. 86/B5
Pauktaw, Myan. 94/B2
Paul B. Wurtsmith (A.F.B.), Mi, US 160/E2
Paul Isnard, FrG. 182/C1
Paul Smiths, NY, US 161/J2
Paulaya (riv.), Hon. 176/E3
Paulden, Az, US 149/F3
Paulding, Oh, US 160/D4
Paulding, Ms, US 164/D1
Paulding (co.), Ga, US 163/L7
Paulina, Or, US 146/D1
Pauline, Ks, US 153/G1
Pauline (mt.), BC, Can. 144/E1
Paulínia, Braz. 187/J7
Paulins Kill (riv.), NJ, US 168/D2
Paulista, Braz. 183/H4
Paulistana, Braz. 183/F5
Paullina, Ia, US 155/G2
Paullo, It. 62/C3
Paulo Afonso, Braz. 183/G5
Paulo Afonso, PN de, Braz. 183/G5
Paulo Ramos, Braz. 183/E4
Paulpietersburg, SAfr. 125/E2
Pauls Valley, Ok, US 153/F3
Paulsboro, NJ, US 168/C4
Paulton, Eng, UK 36/D4
Pauma Valley, Ca, US 166/D4
Pauna, Col. 183/M7
Paungde, Myan. 86/B5
Pauri, India 99/C5
Pausa, Ger. 59/E1
Pavant (range), Ut, US 147/G4
Pavão, Braz. 187/E3
Pāveh, Iran 103/F3
Pavel Banya, Bul. 49/J1
Pavia, It. 62/C3
Pavia (prov.), It. 62/C2
Pavie, Fr. 44/D5
Pavilion, BC, Can. 144/D2
Pavillion, Wy, US 147/J2
Pavilly, Fr. 57/F1
Pāvilosta, Lat. 41/J3
Pavino, Rus. 69/K4
Pavlikeni, Bul. 51/G4
Pavlodar, Kaz. 99/C1
Pavlodar Oblast, Kaz. 99/B1
Pavlof (vol.), Ak, US 171/F4
Pavlohrad, Ukr. 73/H3
Pavlovo, Rus. 68/J5
Pavlovsk, Rus. 69/T7
Pavlovsk, Rus. 73/L2
Pavlovskaya, Rus. 73/K4
Pavlovskiy, Kaz. 69/P5
Pavlysh, Ukr. 73/G3
Pavo, Ga, US 165/G2
Pavón, Col. 180/C4
Pavone Canavese, It. 62/A2
Pavone del Mella, It. 62/D3
Pavullo nel Frignano, It. 63/D5
Pavy, Rus. 41/N2
Paw Paw, Mi, US 160/D3
Paw Paw Lake, Mi, US 160/C3
Pawa, D.R. Congo 121/F2
Pawan (riv.), Indo. 90/D4
Pawāyan, India 96/C1
Pawé (peak), Camr. 116/A4
Pawhuska, Ok, US 153/F2
Pawia, Gha. 115/E4
Pawn (riv.), Myan. 86/C4
Pawnee, Ok, US 153/F2
Pawnee (riv.), Ks, US 154/E4
Pawnee, Il, US 155/K4
Pawnee Buttes (butte), Co, US 154/C3
Pawnee City, Ne, US 155/F3
Pawnee Indian Village, Ks, US 154/F4
Pawnee Rock, Ks, US 152/E1
Pawtucket, RI, US 161/L4
Paxoí (isl.), Gre. 67/H3
Paxoí (Yáios), Gre. 49/G3
Paxson, Ak, US 171/J3
Paxton, Tx, US 151/G2
Paxton, Il, US 160/B4
Paxton, Austl. 133/E1
Pay, Rus. 68/G3
Pay-Khoy (mts.), Rus. 74/G3
Payagyi, Myan. 94/B2
Payaheislam, Indo. 91/G3
Payakumbuh, Indo. 89/C3
Payerne, Swi. 60/C4
Payette, Id, US 146/E1
Payette (riv.), Id, US 146/E2
Payette, North Fork (riv.), Id, US 146/E1
Payette, South Fork (riv.), Id, US 146/E1
Payne (cr.), Fl, US 164/M8
Payne (lake), Qu, Can. 141/J3
Paynes Find, Austl. 130/C4
Paynesville, Mn, US 157/G5
Paynesville, Austl. 133/C3
Paynton, Sk, Can. 145/K1
Pays de Caux (reg.), Fr. 44/D2
Pays de France (reg.), Fr. 30/K4
Pays de la Loire (pol. reg.), Fr. 56/D5
Pays de la Loire (reg.), Fr. 44/C3
Paysandú, Uru. 191/J10
Paysandú (dept.), Uru. 189/E5
Payson, Ut, US 147/H3
Payson, Az, US 149/G3
Payson, Il, US 155/J4
Payún (peak), Arg. 190/C3
Payyannūr, India 95/B3
Paz (riv.), Guat. 176/D3
Paz de Ariporo, Col. 180/D3
Paz de Río, Col. 180/C3
Pāzanān, Iran 103/G4
Pazar, Turk. 102/D1
Pazar, Turk. 71/G4
Pazarcık, Turk. 102/D2
Pazardzhik, Bul. 49/J1
Pazaryeri, Turk. 70/D5
Pazin, Cro. 45/K4
Pe Ell, Wa, US 144/C4
Pea (riv.), Al, US 165/F2
Pea Ridge, Ar, US 153/G2
Peabiru, Braz. 189/F2
Peabody, Ks, US 153/F1
Peabody, Ma, US 161/L3
Peace (riv.), BC, Can. 140/D3
Peace (riv.), Can. 139/F4
Peace Memorial Park, Japan 84/C3
Peace River, Ab, Can. 140/E3
Peace Valley, Mo, US 153/J2
Peach Springs, Az, US 149/F3
Peachland, BC, Can. 144/E3
Peachtree (cr.), Ga, US 163/M7
Peachtree City, Ga, US 162/E4
Peak Charles NP, Austl. 130/D5
Peak District NP, Eng, UK 35/G5
Peak Hill, Austl. 130/C3
Peak Hill, Austl. 133/D1
Peakeen (mtn.), Ire. 32/A6
Peal de Becerro, Sp. 46/D4
Peale (mt.), Ut, US 149/H1
Peapack-Gladstone, NJ, US 168/D2
Pearblossom, Ca, US 166/C1
Pearce (pt.), Austl. 128/C3
Pearisburg, Va, US 163/G2
Pearl (riv.), La,Ms, US 143/J5
Pearl, Ms, US 162/B4
Pearl, Tx, US 150/E2
Pearl and Hermes (reef), Hi, US 137/H2
Pearl Beach, Mi, US 167/G6
Pearl City, Il, US 155/K2
Pearl River, NY, US 169/J7
Pearl River (est.), China 87/G4
Pearland, Ca, US 166/B1
Pearland, Tx, US 151/M9
Pearsall, Tx, US 151/E3
Pearson, Ga, US 165/G2
Pearson (int'l arpt.), On, Can. 160/T8
Pearston, SAfr. 124/D4
Peary (chan.), Nun, Can. 141/R7
Pease (riv.), Tx, US 152/E3
Pease, Mn, US 157/H5
Peaugres, Fr. 64/A2
Péaule, Fr. 56/C5
Pebane, Moz. 123/H3
Pebas, Peru 184/D1
Pebble (isl.), Mald. 191/E6
Pebworth, Eng, UK 37/E2
Peć, Yugo. 50/E4
Pecan Bayou (bayou), Tx, US 151/E2
Pecan Island, La, US 164/B3
Peccia, Swi. 61/E5
Peccioli, It. 63/D6
Pécel, Hun. 51/R10
Pech de Guillaument (peak), Fr. 44/E5
Pechanga Ind. Res., Ca, US 166/C4
Pechanga Ind. Res., Ca, US 148/D4
Pechea, Rom. 51/H3
Pechenga, Rus. 68/F1
Pechengi (res.), Ukr. 73/J3
Pechora, Rus. 69/N2
Pechora (bay), Rus. 69/M1
Pechora (riv.), Rus. 77/C3
Pechory, Rus. 41/M3
Pecica, Rom. 50/E2
Peckham, Ok, US 153/F2
Pecks Pond (pond), Pa, US 168/C1
Peclet, Aiguille de (peak), Fr. 64/C2
Peconic (riv.), NY, US 169/F2
Pecos (riv.), US 139/G6
Pecos, Tx, US 151/C2
Pecos Nat'l Hist. Park, NM, US 152/B3
Pecq, Belg. 54/C2
Pecquencourt, Fr. 54/C3
Pécs, Hun. 50/D2
Pecy, Fr. 30/M6
Pedasí, Pan. 180/A3
Pedaso, It. 65/C1
Peddāpuram, India 95/D2
Pedder (lake), Austl. 127/D5
Peddie, SAfr. 124/D4
Pedemonte, It. 63/D3
Pedernales, Ven. 181/F2
Pedernales (riv.), Tx, US 175/F2
Pédernec, Fr. 56/B3
Pederneiras, Braz. 189/G2
Pedirka, Austl. 131/G3
Pedley, Ca, US 166/C3
Pedley, Ab, Can. 144/F1
Pedra Azul, Braz. 187/E3
Pedra do Feitiço, Ang. 120/C4
Pedra Lume, CpV. 107/K10
Pedralva, Braz. 187/L7
Pedregal, Ven. 180/D2
Pedreguer, Sp. 47/F3
Pedreira, Braz. 187/K7
Pedreiras, Braz. 183/E4
Pedricktown, NJ, US 168/C4
Pedro (pt.), SrL. 95/D4
Pedro, SD, US 154/C1
Pedro Afonso, Braz. 182/D5
Pedro Avelino, Braz. 183/G4
Pedro Bay, Ak, US 171/H4
Pedro Betancourt, Cuba 177/F1
Pedro Carbo, Ecu. 180/A5
Pedro Cays (isl.), Jam. 173/F4
Pedro Chico, Col. 180/D4
Pedro Gomes, Braz. 189/F1
Pedro II Braz. 183/F4
Pedro IV (isl.), Braz. 181/E4
Pedro Juan Caballero, Par. 189/F2
Pedro Leopoldo, Braz. 186/D3
Pedro Luro, Arg. 190/E3
Pedro Montt, Chile 188/B3
Pedro Osório, Braz. 189/F4
Pedro R. Fernández, Arg. 188/E4
Peduyim, Isr. 105/B6
Pee Dee (riv.), NC, US 163/G3
Pee Dee NWR, NC, US 163/G3
Peebles, Sc, UK 33/C5
Peebles, Oh, US 163/F1
Peedamulla Abor. Land, Austl. 130/B2
Peekskill, NY, US 168/E1
Peel (isl.), Austl. 134/F6
Peel (inlet), Austl. 130/B5
Peel (sound), Nun, Can. 140/G1
Peel (co.), On, Can. 160/T8
Peel (riv.), Yk, Can. 140/C2
Peel, IM, UK 34/D3
Peel Fell (peak), Eng, UK 33/D6
Peeltown, Tx, US 150/L7
Peene (riv.), Ger. 40/E5
Peer, Belg. 55/E1
Peerless, Mt, US 145/M3
Peers, Ab, Can. 144/F1
Peetz, Co, US 154/C3
Pegarah, Austl. 133/B4
Pegasus (bay), NZ 135/C3
Pegli, It. 62/B5
Peglia (peak), It. 65/B2
Pegnitz (riv.), Ger. 42/F4
Pegnitz, Ger. 59/E3
Pego, Sp. 47/E3
Pego do Altar (res.), Port. 46/A3
Pegognaga, It. 63/D4
Pégomas, Fr. 64/C5
Pegswood, Eng, UK 35/G1
Pegu (Bago), Myan. 86/C5
Peguis Ind. Res., Mb, Can. 156/F2
Pegwell (bay), Eng, UK 37/H4
Pehlivanköy, Turk. 51/H5
Péhonko, Ben. 115/F4
Pehowa, India 98/D5
Pehuajó, Arg. 190/E2
Pehuenche (pass), Chile 190/C2
Pei Xian, China 80/D4
Peigan Ind. Res., Ab, Can. 145/H3
Peijiachuankou, China 80/B3
Peikang, Tai. 87/J4
Peillac, Fr. 56/C5
Peine, Chile 188/B2
Peine, Ger. 53/H4
Peipus (lake), Est.,Rus. 74/C4
Peitawu (peak), Tai. 87/J4
Peiting, Ger. 61/G2
Peixe, Braz. 186/C2
Peixe, Rio do (riv.), Braz. 186/C2
Peixoto (res.), Braz. 186/D4
Pejantan (isl.), Indo. 89/D2
Pejerreyes, Chile 188/B4
Pekalongan, Indo. 89/E4
Pekan, Malay. 89/C2
Pekan Nanas, Malay. 90/B3
Pekhora (riv.), Rus. 69/W9
Pekin, Il, US 155/K3
Pekin (New Pekin), In, US 162/D1
Pelabuhanratu, Indo. 89/D4
Pelabuhanratu (bay), Indo. 89/D4
Pelado (vol.), Mex. 175/Q10
Pelagie (isls.), It. 67/G4
Pelahatchie, Ms, US 162/C4
Pelaihari, Indo. 90/D4
Pelalawan, Indo. 89/C2
Pelat (peak), Fr. 64/C4
Peleaga (peak), Rom. 50/F3
Peleduy, Rus. 75/M4
Pelee (pt.), On, Can. 160/E4
Pelee (isl.), On, Can. 160/E4
Pelée (peak), Fr. 173/N9
Pelequén, Chile 190/N9
Pelham, Austl. 134/A2
Pelham, Al, US 162/D4
Pelham, Ga, US 165/F2
Pelham, NY, US 169/K8
Pelham, On, Can. 160/U9
Pelham Bay Park, NY, US 169/K8
Pelham Manor, NY, US 169/K8
Pelhřimov, Czh. 43/H4
Pelican (pt.), Namb. 122/B4
Pelican, Ak, US 171/L4
Pelican (lake), Mn, US 157/N6
Pelican (isl.), Tx, US 151/N9
Pelican Island Nat'l Wild. Ref., Fl, US 165/H4
Pelican Rapids, Mn, US 156/F4
Pélissanne, Fr. 64/B5
Pelister (peak), FYROM 49/G2
Pelister NP, FYROM 49/G2
Peljekaise NP, Swe. 38/F2
Pelješac (pen.), Cro. 49/E1
Pelkie, Mi, US 157/K4
Pell City, Al, US 162/D4
Pell Lake, Wi, US 167/P14
Péllа, Gre. 49/H2
Pélla (ruin), Gre. 49/H2
Pella, Ia, US 155/H3
Pellegrini, Arg. 190/E3
Pellestrina, It. 63/F3
Péllice (riv.), It. 64/D3
Pello, Fin. 68/E2
Pellston, Mi, US 160/D2
Pelly (bay), Nun, Can. 140/H2
Pelly (riv.), Yk, Can. 140/C2
Pelly Crossing, Yk, Can. 171/L3
Peloponnesus (reg.), Gre. 67/J3
Peloritani (mts.), It. 48/D4
Pelotas (riv.), Braz. 189/G3
Pelotas, Braz. 189/F4
Pelplin, Pol. 41/H5
Pelsor, Ar, US 153/H3
Pelto (lake), La, US 164/C3
Pélussin, Fr. 64/A2
Pelvoux (peak), Fr. 64/C3
Pelvoux, Fr. 64/C3
Pemalang, Indo. 89/E4
Pemali (cape), Indo. 91/F4
Pematangsiantar, Indo. 89/B2
Pemba, Moz. 123/J2
Pemba (prov.), Tanz. 119/B3
Pemba (isl.), Tanz. 119/B3
Pemba, Zam. 123/E3
Pemba (isl.), Afr. 107/G5
Pemberton, Austl. 130/C5
Pemberton, BC, Can. 144/C2
Pemberton, NJ, US 168/D4
Pembina, ND, US 156/F3
Pembina (hills), Mb, Can. 156/E3
Pembina (riv.), Can.,US 156/E3
Pembina Historical Site, ND, US 156/F3
Pembine, Wi, US 157/L5
Pembroke, Wal, UK 36/B3
Pembroke, Fl, US 164/M8
Pembroke, Ga, US 163/G4
Pembroke, Ky, US 162/D2
Pembroke, Ma, US 161/L3
Pembroke, NC, US 163/H3
Pembroke, NH, US 161/L3
Pembroke, On, Can. 161/H2
Pembroke, Va, US 163/G2
Pembroke Dock, Wal, UK 36/B3
Pembroke Pines, Fl, US 164/P11
Pembrokeshire (co.), Wal, UK 36/A3
Pembrokeshire Coast NP, Wal, UK 36/A3
Pembury, Eng, UK 37/G4
Pemebonwon (dam), Mi, US 157/L5
Pemenee (falls), Wi, US 157/L5
Pemuco, Chile 190/B3
Pen Argyl, Pa, US 168/C2
Pen y Gurnos (peak), Wal, UK 36/C2
Pen-y-Cae, Wal, UK 35/E6
Pen-y-Ghent (peak), Eng, UK 35/F3
Pen-y-Gogarth (pt.), Wal, UK 34/E5
Peña Blanca (mtn.), Pan. 177/F4
Peña de Cerredo (mtn.), Sp. 46/C1
Pena Forte, Braz. 183/G4
Penafiel, Port. 46/A2
Peñafiel, Sp. 46/C2
Peñaflor, Chile 190/N8
Peñalara (peak), Sp. 66/C2
Penalva, Braz. 183/E3
Penamacor, Port. 46/B2
Penambulai (isl.), Indo. 129/D1
Penampang, Malay. 88/B4
Penang (int'l arpt.), Malay. 89/C1
Penápolis, Braz. 189/G2
Peñaranda de Bracamonte, Sp. 46/C2
Peñarroya (peak), Sp. 47/E2
Peñarroya-Pueblonuevo, Sp. 46/C3
Penarth, Wal, UK 36/C4
Penas (gulf), Arg. 190/B5
Peñas (cape), Arg. 191/D7
Peñas, Bol. 184/D5
Peñas (cape), Sp. 46/C1
Peñasco (riv.), NM, US 151/B1
Pencahue, Chile 190/C2
Pench (riv.), India 96/B5
Penchard, Fr. 30/L5
Penco, Chile 190/B3
Peñd (res.), Col. 183/K6
Pend Oreille (mt.), Id, US 144/F3
Pend Oreille (lake), Id, US 144/F3
Pend Orielle (riv.), Wa, US 144/F3
Pendé (riv.), CAfr. 116/C4
Pendelikón (peak), Gre. 49/N8
Pendembu, SLeo. 114/C4
Pendências, Braz. 183/G4
Pender, Ne, US 155/F2
Pender (bay), Austl. 128/A4
Pender Bay Abor. Land, Austl. 128/A4
Pendik (nbrhd.), Turk. 103/N7
Pendjar (riv.), Burk. 115/F4
Pendjari, PN de la, Ben. 115/F4
Pendle (hill), Eng, UK 35/F4
Pendleton, In, US 160/D5
Pendleton, Or, US 146/D1
Pendleton Mil. Res., Va, US 163/K2
Pendolo, Indo. 91/F4
Pendopo, Indo. 89/C3
Pendroy, Mt, US 145/H3
Pene-Mende, D.R. Congo 121/G4
Peneda-Gerês, PN, Port. 46/A2
Penedo, Braz. 187/F1
Penegoes, Wal, UK 36/C1
Penetanguishene, On, Can. 160/G2
Penfield, Pa, US 161/G4
Peng Xian, China 86/D2
Penganga (riv.), India 92/C4
Penge (nbrhd.), Eng, UK 30/C2
Penge, SAfr. 123/F5
Penge, D.R. Congo 121/F4

Penggo – Pino Ha

Penggong, China 80/K9
Penghu (isls.), Tai. 87/H4
Penghu, China 87/H3
Penghu (Pescadores) (isls.), China 87/H4
Penglai, China 80/E3
Penglaizhen, China 86/E2
Penguin, Austl. 132/C4
Penha, Braz. 189/G3
Penhalonga, Zim. 123/G3
Penhir (pt.), Fr. 56/A4
Penhold, Ab, Can. 145/H1
Penibético (mts.), Sp. 46/D4
Penice (peak), It. 62/C4
Peniche, Port. 46/A3
Penicuik, Sc, UK 33/C5
Peninsula (pt.), NY, US 161/H3
Península de Paria, PN, Ven. 181/F2
Peñíscola, Sp. 47/F2
Peñita, Chile 188/B4
Penitente, Serra do (mts.), Braz. 183/E5
Penkridge, Eng, UK 36/D1
Penmaenmawr, Wal, UK 34/E5
Penmarc'h (pt.), Fr. 56/A5
Penmarch, Fr. 56/A5
Penn, ND, US 156/E3
Penn Forest (res.), Pa, US 168/C2
Penn Hills, Pa, US 161/G4
Penn Yan, NY, US 161/H3
Penna (peak), It. 65/B1
Penna, Punta della (cape), It. 65/D3
Pennant (pt.), NS, Can. 158/F3
Pennant, Sk, Can. 145/K2
Pennask (mt.), BC, Can. 144/D3
Penne (pt.), It. 49/E2
Penne, It. 65/C3
Pennell (mt.), Ut, US 149/G2
Penner (riv.), India 92/C5
Penney Farms, Fl, US 165/H3
Penniac, NB, Can. 158/D2
Pennine Alps (mts.), Swi. 45/G4
Pennine Chain (mts.), Eng, UK 35/F2
Pennington, NJ, US 168/D3
Pennington Gap, Va, US 163/F2
Pennino (peak), It. 65/B1
Penns (cr.), Pa, US 168/A2
Penns Creek (mtn.), Pa, US 168/A2
Penns Grove, NJ, US 168/C4
Penns Park, Pa, US 168/D3
Pennsauken, NJ, US 168/C4
Pennsboro, WV, US 160/F5
Pennsburg, Pa, US 168/C3
Pennsville, NJ, US 168/C4
Pennsylvania (hill), NY, US 161/H3
Pennsylvania (state), US 143/L3
Penny (str.), Nun, Can. 141/S7
Pennypack (cr.), Pa, US 168/C3
Penobscot (bay), Me, US 158/C3
Penobscot (riv.), Me, US 158/C3
Peñol, Col. 183/K6
Penola, Austl. 132/B3
Peñón Blanco, Mex. 174/D3
Penon de Al Hoceima (isl.), Sp. 112/C2
Penong, Austl. 131/G4
Penonomé, Pan. 180/A2
Penpont, Sc, UK 34/E1
Penrhyn (Tongareva) (isl.), Cookls. 137/J5
Penrhyn Mawr (pt.), IM, UK 34/D5
Penrhyn Mawr (pt.), Wal, UK 34/D6
Penrith, Eng, UK 35/F2
Penrith (nbrhd.), Austl. 134/G8
Penrose, Co, US 152/B1
Penryn, Eng, UK 36/A6
Pensacola (mts.), Ant. 192/X
Pensacola, Fl, US 164/E2
Pensacola (bay), Fl, US 164/E2
Pensacola (dam), Ok, US 153/G2
Pense, Sk, Can. 156/B2
Penshurst, Eng, UK 30/D3
Penshurst, Austl. 132/B3
Pensiangan, Malay. 88/B4
Pensilva, Eng, UK 36/B5
Pensilvania, Col. 183/K7
Pentagon Fed. Govt. Res., Va, US 168/A6
Pentecost (isl.), Van. 136/F6
Pentecoste, Braz. 183/G3
Penteleu (peak), Rom. 51/H3
Penthalaz, Swi. 60/C4
Penticton, BC, Can. 144/E3
Penticton Ind. Res., BC, Can. 144/E3
Pentire (pt.), Eng, UK 36/B5
Pentland (hills), Sc, UK 33/C5
Pentland, Austl. 134/B3
Pentland Firth (inlet), Sc, UK 31/V14
Pentwater, Mi, US 160/C3
Pentyrch, Wal, UK 36/C3
Peñuelas, PN, Chile 190/N8
Penvénan, Fr. 56/B3
Pènwègon, Myan. 94/B2
Penwell, Tx, US 151/C2
Penwith (pen.), Eng, UK 36/A6
Penza, Rus. 71/H1
Penzenskaya Oblast, Rus. 71/G1
Penzance, Eng, UK 36/A6
Penzance, Sk, Can. 145/M2
Penzberg, Ger. 61/H2
Penzé (riv.), Fr. 56/B3
Penzhina (riv.), Rus. 75/S3
Penzhina (bay), Rus. 75/S3
Penzing, Ger. 61/G1
Penzlin, Ger. 42/G2
Peoria, Az, US 149/F4
Peoria, Il, US 155/K3
Pepe (cape), Cuba 177/F1
Pepel, SLeo. 114/B4
Pepin (lake), Mn,Wi, US 155/H1
Pepinster, Belg. 55/E2
Peqin, Alb. 49/F2
Pequaming, Mi, US 157/K4
Pequannock, NJ, US 169/H8
Pequea (cr.), Pa, US 168/B4
Pequeña Isla del Maíz (isl.), Nic. 177/F3
Pequest (riv.), NJ, US 168/D2
Pequot Lakes, Mn, US 157/G4
Perabumulih, Indo. 89/D3
Perai-Tepuí, Ven. 181/F3
Perak (riv.), Malay. 89/C1
Perak (state), Malay. 89/C1
Perales (riv.), Sp. 47/M9
Peralta, Sp. 46/E1
Peralta, Uru. 191/K10
Peralta, NM, US 149/J3
Pérama, Gre. 49/J5
Pérama, Gre. 49/N9
Peranāmbattu, India 95/C3
Percé, Qu, Can. 158/E1
Percée (peak), Fr. 60/C6
Percha (dam), NM, US 149/J4
Perche, Collines du (hills), Fr. 44/D2
Perchtoldsdorf, Aus. 51/N7
Percilla, Tx, US 151/G2
Percival, Sk, Can. 156/C2
Percival (lakes), Austl. 130/E2
Percy, Fr. 57/D3
Percy, Il, US 162/C1
Percy (isls.), Austl. 127/E3
Percy Isles (chan.), Austl. 134/C3
Perdekop, SAfr. 125/E2
Pérdhika, Gre. 49/G3
Perdido, Al, US 164/E2
Perdido (mtn.), Sp. 44/D5
Perdões, Braz. 186/D4
Perdue, Sk, Can. 145/L1
Perechyn, Ukr. 43/M4
Peregian Beach, Austl. 134/D4
Perehins'ke, Ukr. 72/C3
Pereira, Col. 183/K8
Pereira Barreto, Braz. 189/G2
Pereiro, Braz. 183/G4
Perelló, Sp. 47/F2
Peremëtnoye, Kaz. 71/J2
Peremyshl', Rus. 68/H5
Peremyshlyany, Ukr. 72/C3
Perenjori, Austl. 130/C4
Peresechnaya, Ukr. 73/H2
Pereshchepyne, Ukr. 73/H3
Pereslavl'-Zalesskiy, Rus. 68/H4
Peretola (int'l arpt.), It. 63/E6
Perevolotskiy, Rus. 71/K2
Pereyaslav-Khmel'nyts'kyy, Ukr. 72/F2
Pereyaslavka, Rus. 79/M2
Perg, Aus. 59/H6
Pergamino, Arg. 190/E2
Pergamum (ruin), Turk. 70/C5
Pergine Valsugana, It. 61/H5
Perham, Mn, US 157/G4
Peri-Mirim, Braz. 183/E3
Periam, Rom. 50/E2
Péribonca (riv.), Qu, Can. 158/B1
Perico, Cuba 177/F1
Perico, Arg. 188/C3
Pericos, Mex. 174/D3
Pericos, Mex. 174/D4
Peridot, Az, US 149/G4
Périers, Fr. 56/D2
Périgueux, Fr. 44/D4
Perijá (mts.), Ven. 177/H4
Peringat, Malay. 89/C1
Perisher Village, Austl. 133/D3
Peristéra (isl.), Gre. 49/H3
Peristéri, Gre. 49/N8
Perito Moreno, Arg. 190/C5
Perito Moreno, PN, Arg. 191/B5
Periyakulam, India 95/C4
Perkasie, Pa, US 168/C3
Perkins, Ok, US 153/F3
Perkins, Mi, US 160/C2
Perkins, Ga, US 163/G4
Perkinston, Ms, US 164/D2
Perkiomen (cr.), Pa, US 168/C3
Perl, Ger. 55/F5
Perlas (lag.), Nic. 172/E5
Perlas, (pt.), Nic. 177/F3
Perleberg, Ger. 42/F2
Perlez, Yugo. 50/E3
Perlis (state), Malay. 94/B5
Perm', Rus. 69/N4
Përmet, Alb. 49/G2
Permian Basin Petroleum Museum, Tx, US 151/C2
Permskaya Oblast, Rus. 69/N4
Pernambuco (state), Braz. 183/G5
Pernate, It. 62/B3
Pernell, Ok, US 153/F3
Pernes-les-Fontaines, Fr. 64/B4
Pernik, Bul. 50/F4
Perniö, Fin. 41/K1
Peron (pen.), Austl. 130/B3
Peron, North (isl.), Austl. 128/C3
Péronne, Fr. 54/B4
Perosa Argentina, It. 64/D3
Perote, Al, US 165/F2
Perote, Mex. 175/M7
Pérouges, Fr. 60/B6
Perovo (nbrhd.), Rus. 69/W9
Perranporth, Eng, UK 36/A6
Perray (riv.), Fr. 30/H6
Perriers-sur-Andelle, Fr. 57/G2
Perrigny, Fr. 60/B4
Perrin, Tx, US 153/E4
Perrine, Fl, US 164/P11
Perris (res.), Ca, US 166/C3
Perris, Ca, US 166/C3
Perris St. Rec. Area, Ca, US 166/C3
Perro (lag.), NM, US 152/B3
Perron des Encombres (peak), Fr. 64/C2
Perros-Guirec, Fr. 56/B3
Perry (riv.), Nun, Can. 140/F2
Perry, Fl, US 165/G2
Perry (lake), Ks, US 155/G4
Perry, Ga, US 162/F4
Perry, Ia, US 155/G3
Perry, Mo, US 155/J4
Perry, Ok, US 153/F2
Perry (co.), Pa, US 168/A3
Perry Hall, Md, US 168/B5
Perryman, Md, US 168/B5
Perrysburg, Oh, US 160/E4
Perryton, Tx, US 152/D2
Perrytown, Ar, US 153/H4
Perryville, Ak, US 171/G4
Perryville, Ar, US 153/H3
Perryville, Ky, US 162/E2
Perryville, Md, US 168/B4
Perryville, Mo, US 162/C2
Perryville, Tn, US 162/C3
Persan, Fr. 30/J4
Persepolis (ruin), Iran 103/H4
Perseverancia, Bol. 185/F4
Pershagen, Swe. 39/A1
Pershore, Eng, UK 36/D2
Pershotravens'k, Ukr. 72/D2
Pershotravnevoye, Ukr. 73/J4
Pershotravnevoye, Ukr. 72/D2
Persian (gulf), Asia 77/D7
Perstorp, Swe. 40/E3
Pertandangan (cape), Indo. 89/C2
Perth, Austl. 132/C4
Perth, Austl. 130/K6
Perth (int'l arpt.), Austl. 130/K6
Perth, On, Can. 161/H2
Perth, Sc, UK 33/C4
Perth Amboy, NJ, US 169/H9
Perth and Kinross (co.), Sc, UK 33/C4
Perth Zoo, Austl. 130/K6
Perth-Andover, NB, Can. 158/D2
Perthville, Austl. 133/D1
Pertokar, Erit. 117/H1
Pertuis, Fr. 64/B5
Pertuis Breton (inlet), Fr. 44/C3
Pertusato (cape), Fr. 48/A2
Peru (ctry.) 179/B3
Peru, Ks, US 153/F2
Peru, In, US 160/C4
Peru, Ne, US 155/G3
Peru, Il, US 155/K3
Perućačko (lake), Bosn. 50/D4
Perugia, It. 65/B1
Perugia (prov.), It. 65/B1
Peruíbe, Braz. 187/K9
Perushtitsa, Bul. 49/J1
Péruwelz, Belg. 54/C2
Pervari, Turk. 102/E2
Pervomaysk, Rus. 69/J5
Pervomays'k, Ukr. 72/F3
Pervomays'ke, Ukr. 73/G5
Pervomayskiy, Rus. 71/G1
Pervomayskiy, Rus. 71/J2
Pervomayskiy, Rus. 78/H1
Pervomayskoye, Rus. 71/H2
Pervomayskoye, Rus. 73/L3
Pervomays'kyy, Ukr. 73/J3
Pervoural'sk, Rus. 69/N4
Perwez, Belg. 55/D2
Péry, Swi. 60/D3
Pesa (riv.), It. 63/E5
Pesagi (peak), Indo. 89/D4
Pesaro, It. 63/F6
Pesaro E Urbino (prov.), It. 63/F5
Pescadero (pt.), Ca, US 148/A2
Pescadero, Ca, US 148/A2
Pescadore (chan.), Tai. 87/H4
Pescadores (Penghu) (isls.), China 87/H4
Pescantina, It. 63/D3
Pescara (riv.), It. 65/D3
Pescara (prov.), It. 65/C3
Pescara, It. 65/D3
Pescasseroli, It. 65/C4
Peschanokopskoye, Rus. 73/L4
Peschanyy (cape), Kaz. 71/J4
Peschici, It. 48/E2
Pescia, It. 63/D6
Pescina, It. 65/C3
Pescocostanzo, It. 65/D4
Peseux, Swi. 60/C4
Pesha (riv.), Rus. 69/L2
Peshawar (int'l arpt.), Pak. 98/A2
Peshāwar, Pak. 98/A2
Peshkopi, Alb. 49/G2
Peshtera, Bul. 49/J1
Peshtigo (riv.), Wi, US 157/L5
Peshtigo, Wi, US 160/C2
Peski, Rus. 68/H5
Peskovka, Rus. 69/M4
Pesmes, Fr. 60/B3
Peso da Régua, Port. 46/B2
Pesochnyy, Rus. 69/T6
Pesqueira, Braz. 183/G5
Pesquería (riv.), Mex. 151/D5
Pessac, Fr. 44/C4
Pest (co.), Hun. 43/K5
Pest (prov.), Hun. 50/D2
Pestovkoye (lake), Rus. 69/W8
Pestovo, Rus. 68/G4
Petacciato, It. 65/D4
Petah Tiqwa, Isr. 105/B4
Petal, Ms, US 164/D2
Petalión (gulf), Gre. 67/K3
Petaluma (riv.), Ca, US 167/J10
Petaluma, Ca, US 146/B4
Pétange, Lux. 55/E4
Petārbār, India 97/E4
Petare, Ven. 183/P7
Pétas, Gre. 49/G3
Petatlán, Mex. 175/E5
Petatlán (riv.), Mex. 174/D3
Petauke, Zam. 123/F2
Petawawa, On, Can. 161/H2
Petawawa (riv.), On, Can. 161/G2
Peten Itzá (lake), Guat. 176/D2
Petenwell (dam), Wi, US 155/J1
Peter (isl.), Nor. 192/U
Peter (pond), Sk, Can. 140/F3
Peterborough, Austl. 131/H5
Peterborough, On, Can. 161/G2
Peterborough, Eng, UK 37/F1
Peterborough (co.), Eng, UK 37/F1
Peterculter, Sc, UK 33/D2
Peterhead, Sc, UK 33/E1
Peterlee, Eng, UK 35/G2
Peterman, Al, US 164/E2
Petermann Aboriginal Land, Austl. 131/F3
Peteroa (vol.), Chile 190/C2
Petersaurach, Ger. 58/D4
Petersberg, Ger. 58/C1
Petersburg, Ak, US 171/M4
Petersburg, In, US 162/D1
Petersburg, Il, US 155/K3
Petersburg, ND, US 156/E3
Petersburg, Tx, US 152/D4
Petersburg, Va, US 163/J2
Petersburg, WV, US 163/H1
Petersburg Nat'l Bfld., Va, US 163/J2
Petersfield, Mb, Can. 156/F2
Petersfield, Eng, UK 37/F4
Petershagen, Ger. 53/F4
Petershagen, Ger. 42/Q6
Petershausen, Ger. 59/E6
Peterson (A.F.B.), Co, US 152/B1
Pétervására, Hun. 43/L4
Peterview, Nf, Can. 159/K1
Petilia Policastro, It. 48/E3
Pétionville, Haiti 177/H2
Petit Buëch (riv.), Fr. 64/B4
Petit Goâve, Haiti 177/H2
Petit Loango, PN du, Gabon 120/B3
Petit Mont Blanc (peak), Fr. 64/C2
Petit Rosne (riv.), Fr. 30/J4
Petit-Cap, Qu, Can. 158/E1
Petit-Couronne, Fr. 57/G2
Petit-de-Grat, NS, Can. 159/G3
Petit-Matane, Qu, Can. 158/D1
Petit-Noir, Fr. 60/B4
Petit-Saguenay, Qu, Can. 158/B1
Petitcodiac, NB, Can. 158/E3
Petite Miquelon (isl.), Nf, Can. 159/J2
Petite Nation (riv.), Qu, Can. 161/J1
Petite Rivière de l'Artibonite, Haiti 177/H2
Petite Rivière Noire (peak), Mrts. 125/T15
Petite-Rosselle, Fr. 55/F5
Petkeljärven NP, Fin. 68/F3
Petlād, India 101/K4
Petlalcingo, Mex. 176/B2
Peto, Mex. 176/D1
Petorca, Chile 190/C2
Petoskey, Mi, US 160/D2
Petra (isls.), Rus. 75/M2
Petre (pt.), On, Can. 161/H3
Petrel, Sp. 47/E3
Petrella (peak), It. 65/C5
Petrella Tifernina, It. 65/D4
Petretsovo, Rus. 69/N3
Petrey, Al, US 165/E2
Petrich, Bul. 49/H2
Petrified Forest NP, Az, US 149/H3
Petrikov, Bela. 70/D1
Petrila, Rom. 51/F3
Petritoli, It. 65/C1
Petrivka, Ukr. 72/F4
Petrodvorets, Rus. 69/S7
Petrograd (nbrhd.), Rus. 69/T7
Petrokhanski Prokhod (pass), Bul. 51/F4
Petrokrepost' (bay), Rus. 69/U7
Petrokrepost', Rus. 69/U7
Petrolândia, Braz. 183/G5
Petrolia, Tx, US 153/E3
Petrolia, On, Can. 160/E3
Petrolina, Braz. 183/F5
Petropavl, Kaz. 74/G4
Petropavlivka, Ukr. 73/J3
Petropavlovsk-Kamchatskiy, Rus. 75/R4
Petropavlovskoye, Rus. 71/H3
Petrópolis, Braz. 187/N7
Petros, Tn, US 162/E2
Petroşani, Rom. 51/F3
Petroso (peak), It. 65/C4
Petrovaradin, Yugo. 50/D3
Petrovsk, Rus. 71/H1
Petrovsk-Zabaykal'skiy, Rus. 78/F1
Petrovskaya, Rus. 73/J5
Petrovs'ke, Ukr. 73/K3
Petrovskiy Yam, Rus. 68/G3
Petrovskoye, Rus. 71/L1
Petrozavodsk, Rus. 68/G3
Petrus Steyn, SAfr. 124/E2
Petrusburg, SAfr. 124/D3
Petrusville, SAfr. 124/D3
Petrykivka, Ukr. 73/H3
Pettenbach, Aus. 59/H7
Petteril (riv.), Eng, UK 35/F2
Pettibone, ND, US 156/E4
Pettigrew, Ar, US 153/H3
Pettus, Tx, US 150/F3
Petushki, Rus. 68/H5
Petworth, Eng, UK 37/F5
Petzeck (peak), Aus. 45/K3
Peuerbach, Aus. 59/G6
Peulik (mt.), Ak, US 171/G4
Peumo, Chile 190/N9
Peureulak, Indo. 89/B1
Pevek, Rus. 75/T3
Pevely, Mo, US 162/B1
Pevensey, Eng, UK 37/G5
Pewaukee, Wi, US 167/P13
Pewaukee (lake), Wi, US 167/X13
Pewsey, Eng, UK 37/E4
Peyia, Cyp. 104/C2
Peyk, Iran 103/G3
Peymeinade, Fr. 64/C5
Peyrehorade, Fr. 44/C5
Peyrins, Fr. 64/B2
Peyrolles-en-Provence, Fr. 64/B5
Peyruis, Fr. 64/B4
Peza (riv.), Rus. 69/K2
Pézenas, Fr. 44/E5
Pezu, Pak. 98/A3
Pfaffenhausen, Ger. 61/G1
Pfaffenhofen an der Ilm, Ger. 58/D6
Pfaffenhofen an der Ilm, Ger. 59/E5
Pfaffenhoffen, Fr. 55/G6
Pfäffikon, Swi. 61/E3
Pfaffing, Ger. 59/F6
Pfaffnau, Swi. 60/D3
Pfahl (ridge), Ger. 59/F4
Pfälzer Wald (mts.), Ger. 55/G5
Pfälzerwald (mts.), Ger. 58/A4
Pfalzgrafenweiler, Ger. 58/B5
Pfarrhof Esternberg, Aus. 59/G5
Pfarrkirchen, Ger. 59/F6
Pfatter, Ger. 59/F5
Pfeffenhausen, Ger. 59/E5
Pfettrach (riv.), Ger. 59/E5
Pfieffe (riv.), Ger. 53/G6
Pfinztal, Ger. 58/B5
Pflugerville, Tx, US 151/F2
Pforzheim, Ger. 58/B5
Pfreimd (riv.), Ger. 59/F3
Pfreimd, Ger. 59/F3
Pfronstetten, Ger. 61/F1
Pfronten, Ger. 61/G2
Pfroslkopf (peak), Aus. 61/G4
Pfullendorf, Ger. 61/F2
Pfunds, Aus. 61/G4
Pfungstadt, Ger. 58/B3
Phagwāra, India 98/C4
Phalaborwa, SAfr. 123/F4
Phalauda, India 98/D5
Phalempin, Fr. 54/C2
Phālia, Pak. 98/B3
Phalodi, India 101/K3
Phalombe, Malw. 123/G2
Phalsbourg, Fr. 55/G6
Phaltan, India 95/B2
Phan, Thai. 94/B2
Phan Rang Viet. 94/E4
Phan Thiet, Viet. 94/E4
Phanat Nikhom, Thai. 94/C3
Phang Hoei (range), Thai. 94/C3
Phangan (isl.), Thai. 93/H6
Phangnga, Thai. 94/B4
Phanom, Thai. 94/B4
Phanom Dongrak (mts.), Thai. 93/H5
Phāphlu, Nepal 97/F2
Pharr, Tx, US 151/E4
Phat Diem, Viet. 87/E4
Phatthalung, Thai. 94/C5
Phaya Fo (peak), Thai. 94/C2
Phayao, Thai. 94/B2
Pheasant (hills), Sk, Can. 156/C2
Phelan, Ca, US 166/C2
Phelps, Wi, US 157/K4
Phelps (lake), NC, US 163/J3
Phenix City, Al, US 162/E4
Phepane (riv.), SAfr. 122/D5
Phet Buri, Thai. 94/B3
Phetchabun, Thai. 94/C2
Phiafai, Laos 94/D3
Phibun Mangsahan, Thai. 94/D3
Phichai, Thai. 94/C2
Phichit, Thai. 94/C2
Phidim, Nepal 97/F2
Phil Campbell, Al, US 162/D3
Philadelphia, NY, US 161/J2
Philadelphia, Ms, US 162/C4
Philadelphia (int'l arpt.), Pa, US 168/C4
Philadelphia, Pa, US 168/C4
Philip, SD, US 154/D1
Philip S.W. Goldson (int'l arpt.), Belz. 176/D2
Philipp, Ms, US 162/B4
Philippeville, Belg. 55/D3
Philippi, WV, US 163/G1
Philippine (sea), Asia 77/M8
Philippines (ctry.) 77/M8
Philippsburg, Ger. 58/B4
Philipsburg, Pa, US 161/G4
Philipsburg, Neth. 173/J4
Philipsburg, Mt, US 145/H4
Philipsdam (dam), Neth. 52/B5
Philipstown, Ire. 32/C3
Philipstown, SAfr. 124/D3
Phillaur, India 98/C4
Phillip (isl.), Austl. 133/B4
Phillips, Wi, US 157/J5
Phillips, Me, US 161/L2
Phillips Arm, BC, Can. 144/B2
Phillipsburg, Mo, US 153/H2
Phillipsburg, Ga, US 165/G2
Phillipsburg, Ks, US 154/E4
Phillipsburg, NJ, US 168/C2
Philo, Ca, US 146/B4
Philomath, Or, US 146/B1
Philoteris (ruin), Egypt 113/B6
Philpot, Ky, US 162/D2
Phimai, Thai. 94/C3
Phimai (ruin), Thai. 94/C3
Phipps (mtn.), Austl. 133/C3
Phitsanulok, Thai. 94/C2
Phnom Penh (Phnum Pénh) (cap.), Camb. 94/D4
Phnum Penh (int'l arpt.), Camb. 94/D4
Phnum Pénh (Phnom Penh) (cap.), Camb. 94/D4
Phnum Tbeng Meanchey, Camb. 94/D3
Pho (pt.), Thai. 94/C5
Phoenix (isls.), Kiri. 137/H5
Phoenix (cap.), Az, US 149/F4
Phoenix (mtn.), NC, US 163/G2
Phoenix, Or, US 146/B2
Phoenix (Rawaki) (isl.), Kiri. 137/H5
Phoenix Park, Ire. 34/B5
Phoenix Sky Harbor (int'l arpt.), Az, US 149/F4
Phoenixville, Pa, US 168/C3
Phon, Thai. 94/C3
Phon Phisai, Thai. 94/C2
Phon Thong, Thai. 94/C2
Phongsali, Laos 86/D4
Phou Bia (peak), Laos 94/C2
Phou Huatt (peak), Viet. 86/E5
Phou Khoun, Laos 94/C2
Phou Loi (peak), Laos 86/D4
Phou Xai Lai Leng (peak), Laos 94/D2
Phra Nakhon Si Ayutthaya, Thai. 94/C3
Phra Phutthabat, Thai. 94/C3
Phra Thong (isl.), Thai. 94/B4
Phrae, Thai. 94/C2
Phsar Ream, Camb. 94/C4
Phu Hin Rong Kla NP, Thai. 94/C2
Phu Hoi, Viet. 94/E4
Phu Kradung, Thai. 94/C2
Phu Kradung NP, Thai. 94/C2
Phu Loc, Viet. 94/D2
Phu Luong, Viet. 94/D1
Phu Luong (peak), Viet. 86/E4
Phu Ly, Viet. 94/D1
Phu My, Viet. 94/E3
Phu Nhon, Viet. 94/E3
Phu Phan NP, Thai. 94/D2
Phu Quoc (isl.), Camb. 93/H5
Phu Quoc (isl.), Viet. 94/C4
Phu Quoc, Viet. 94/C4
Phu Rieng Sron, Viet. 94/D4
Phu Rua NP, Thai. 94/C2
Phu Tho, Viet. 86/E4
Phu Vang, Viet. 94/D2
Phuc Loi, Viet. 94/D2
Phuc Yen, Viet. 86/E4
Phuket (isl.), Thai. 93/G6
Phuket, Thai. 94/B5
Phulabāni, India 95/E1
Phularwan, Pak. 98/B3
Phulbāri, Bang. 97/G3
Phulbāri, India 97/H3
Phuldungsei, India 86/B4
Phūlpur, India 96/D3
Phultala, Bang. 97/G4
Phumi Banam, Camb. 94/D4
Phumi Chhlong, Camb. 94/D3
Phumi Choan, Camb. 94/C4
Phumi Chuuk, Camb. 94/D4
Phumi Kampong Putrea Chas, Camb. 94/D3
Phumi Kampong Trabek, Camb. 94/D3
Phumi Kouk Kduoch, Camb. 94/C3
Phumi Krek, Camb. 94/D4
Phumi Labang Siek, Camb. 94/D3
Phumi Mlu Prey, Camb. 94/D3
Phumi O Pou, Camb. 94/D3
Phumi Phang, Camb. 94/C3
Phumi Phsa Romeas, Camb. 94/D3
Phumi Phsar, Camb. 94/D3
Phumi Prek Kak, Camb. 94/D3
Phumi Prek Preah, Camb. 94/D3
Phumi Samraong, Camb. 94/C3
Phumi Spoe Tbong, Camb. 94/D3
Phumi Sre Ta Chan, Camb. 94/D3
Phumi Ta Krei, Camb. 94/C3
Phumi Thma Pok, Camb. 94/C3
Phumi Toek Sok, Camb. 94/C3
Phumi Veal Renh, Camb. 94/C4
Phuntsholing, Bhu. 97/G2
Phutthaisong, Thai. 94/C3
Pi (riv.), China 78/H5
Pi Xian, China 86/D2
Pia, D.R. Congo 121/F2
Piaçabuçu, Braz. 187/F1
Piacenza, It. 62/C3
Piacenza (prov.), It. 62/C3
Piacoa, Ven. 181/F2
Piadena, It. 62/D3
Piaggine, It. 48/D2
Pian di Serra (peak), It. 63/F7
Pian-Upe Game Rsv., Ugan. 119/A1
Piancastagnaio, It. 48/B1
Pianella, It. 65/D3
Pianello val Tidone, It. 62/C4
Pianezza, It. 62/A2
Piangipane, It. 63/F5
Pianling, China 81/B2
Piano di Sorrento, It. 65/D6
Pianoro, It. 63/E5
Pianosa (isl.), It. 48/A1
Piaoli, China 87/F3
Piapot Ind. Res., Sk, Can. 156/B2
Piarco (int'l arpt.), Trin. 181/F2
Piasco, It. 64/D3
Piaseczno, Pol. 43/L2
Piatra Neamţ, Rom. 72/D4
Piauí (riv.), Braz. 183/F5
Piauí (state), Braz. 183/F4
Piave (riv.), It. 45/K3
Piazza, It. 62/D2
Piazza, It. 62/D2
Piazza al Serchio, It. 62/D5
Piazza Armerina, It. 48/D4
Piazza Brembana, It. 61/F6
Piazzola sul Brenta, It. 63/E2
Pibor (riv.), Sudan 117/G4
Pibor Post, Sudan 117/G4
Pic (isl.), On, Can. 157/L3
Pic (riv.), On, Can. 157/L3
Pica, Chile 188/B2
Picacho, Az, US 149/G4
Picacho del Centinela (peak), Mex. 151/C3
Picahos, Cerro Dos (peak), Mex. 174/B2
Picardie (pol. reg.), Fr. 44/E2
Picardy (reg.), Fr. 54/B4
Picatinny Arsenal, NJ, US 168/D2
Picauville, Fr. 56/D2
Picayune, Ms, US 164/D2
Piccaninny (cr.), Austl. 133/B3
Piccolo (lag.), It. 49/E2
Picentino (riv.), It. 65/D6
Pichacani, Peru 184/D5
Pichanal, Arg. 188/C2
Picher, Ok, US 153/G2
Pichidangui, Chile 190/C2
Pichidegua, Chile 190/N9
Pichilemu, Chile 190/B2
Pichincha (dept.), Ecu. 180/B4
Pichincha, Ecu. 180/B5
Pichkiryayevo, Rus. 71/G1
Pichl bei Wels, Aus. 59/G6
Pichor, India 96/B3
Pichucalco, Mex. 176/C2
Pickens, Ok, US 153/G3
Pickens, SC, US 163/F3
Pickens, Ms, US 162/C4
Pickering, Eng, UK 35/H3
Pickering, On, Can. 160/U8
Pickford, Mi, US 160/D1
Pickle Lake, On, Can. 157/J2
Pickton, Tx, US 153/G4
Pickwick (dam), Tn, US 162/C3
Pickwick (lake), Al,Ms, US 162/C3
Pickwick Dam, Tn, US 162/C3
Picnic Bay, Austl. 134/B2
Pico (isl.), Azor., Port. 47/S12
Pico da Neblina, PN do, Braz. 181/E4
Pico de Orizaba, PN, Mex. 175/M7
Pico de Salamanca, Arg. 190/D5
Pico Rivera, Ca, US 166/F8
Pico Truncado, Arg. 190/D5
Picos, Braz. 183/F4
Picota, Peru 184/B2
Picsi, Peru 184/B2
Picton, On, Can. 161/H3
Picton, NZ 135/C3
Picton, Austl. 133/E2
Pictou (isl.), NS, Can. 159/F3
Pictou, NS, Can. 159/F3
Picture Butte, Ab, Can. 145/H3
Picture Gorge (gorge), Or, US 146/D1
Picture Rock (pass), Or, US 146/C2
Picture Rocks, Pa, US 168/B1
Pictured Rocks Nat'l Lakeshore, Mi, US 157/L4
Picuí, Braz. 183/G4
Picuris Ind. Res., NM, US 149/K2
Pidcoke, Tx, US 150/F2
Piddle (riv.), Eng, UK 36/D5
Pidhorodne, Ukr. 73/H3
Pidi, D.R. Congo 121/F4
Pidurutagala (peak), SrL. 95/D5
Pidvolochys'k, Ukr. 72/D3
Pie (isl.), On, Can. 157/K3
Pie Town, NM, US 149/H3
Piedade, Port. 47/P10
Piedade do Rio Grande, Braz. 187/M6
Piedecuesta, Col. 180/C3
Piediluco (lake), It. 65/B2
Piedimulera, It. 61/E5
Piedmont, Al, US 162/E4
Piedmont, Ca, US 167/K11
Piedmont, Mo, US 162/B2
Piedmont, Ok, US 153/F3
Piedmont, SD, US 154/C1
Piedmont, SC, US 163/F3
Piedmont (upland), SC, US 163/G3
Piedmont NWR, Ga, US 162/F4
Piedra, Ca, US 148/C2
Piedra Grande, Ven. 180/D2
Piedra Sola, Uru. 189/E5
Piedrabuena, Sp. 46/C3
Piedrahita, Sp. 46/C2
Piedras (pt.), Arg. 191/K11
Piedras, Col. 183/L8
Piedras Coloradas, Uru. 191/K10
Piedras Negras, Mex. 175/N8
Piedras, Río de las (riv.), Peru 184/D3
Piedritas, Arg. 190/E2
Piekary Śląskie, Pol. 43/K3
Piekenierskloof (pass), SAfr. 124/L10
Pieksämäki, Fin. 68/E3
Pielinen (lake), Fin. 38/J3
Piemonte (pol.reg.), It. 45/G4
Pieniński NP, Pol. 43/L4
Piennes, Fr. 55/E5
Pieńsk, Pol. 43/H3
Piera, Sp. 47/K6
Pierce, Co, US 154/B3
Pierce (lake), Fl, US 164/M8
Pierce, Fl, US 164/M8
Pierce, Id, US 144/G4
Pierce, Ne, US 154/F2
Pierce (co.), Wi, US 157/Q7
Pierce City, Mo, US 153/G2
Pierceville, Ks, US 152/D2
Pieris, It. 63/G2
Piermont, NY, US 169/K7
Pierowall, Sc, UK 31/V14
Pierre (cap.), SD, US 154/D1
Pierre Menue (peak), It. 64/C2
Pierre Part, La, US 164/C3
Pierre Plate (peak), Fr. 64/D5
Pierre-de-Bresse, Fr. 60/B4
Pierre-Levée, Fr. 30/M5
Pierrefeu-du-Var, Fr. 64/C6
Pierrefitte-sur-Seine, Fr. 30/K5
Pierrefonds, Qu, Can. 159/N7
Pierrefontaine-les-Varans, Fr. 60/C3
Pierrelatte, Fr. 64/A4
Pierrelaye, Fr. 30/J4
Pierres, Fr. 57/G3
Pierrevert, Fr. 64/B5
Pierry, Fr. 54/C5
Pierson, Fl, US 165/H3
Piešťany, Slvk. 43/J4
Piesting (riv.), Aus. 51/P7
Piet Retief, SAfr. 125/E2
Pietarsaari (Jakobstad), Fin. 68/D3
Pieterlen, Swi. 60/D3
Pietermaritzburg, SAfr. 125/E3
Pietersburg, SAfr. 123/F4
Pietra Ligure, It. 62/B5
Pietracatella, It. 65/D4
Pietralunga, It. 63/F7
Pietramelara, It. 65/D5
Pietrasanta, It. 62/D6
Pietravairano, It. 65/D5
Pietravecchia (peak), It. 62/A5
Pietrosul (peak), Rom. 51/G2
Pieve del Cairo, It. 62/B3
Pieve di Cento, It. 63/E4
Pieve di Soligo, It. 63/F2
Pieve di Teco, It. 62/A4
Pieve Emanuele, It. 62/C3
Pieve Ligure, It. 62/C5
Pieve Porto Morone, It. 62/C3
Pieve Santo Stefano, It. 63/F6
Pieve Vergonte, It. 61/E6
Pievepelago, It. 62/D5
Pigum (isl.), SKor. 81/C5
Pigeon (riv.), Can.,US 157/J3
Pigeon, Mi, US 160/E3
Pigeon (riv.), On, Can. 140/G4
Pigeon (lake), Ab, Can. 145/H1
Pigeon House (mtn.), Austl. 133/E2
Piggott, Ar, US 162/B2
Piggs Peak, Swaz. 125/E2
Piglio, It. 65/C4
Pigna, It. 64/D5
Pignataro Maggiore, It. 65/D5
Pigs (bay), Cuba 172/E3
Pigu, Gha. 115/E4
Pigüé, Arg. 190/E3
Pihāni, India 96/C2
Pijáo, Col. 183/K8
Pijijiapan, Mex. 176/C3
Pijnacker, Neth. 52/B4
Pijol (peak), Hon. 176/E3
Pike (co.), Pa, US 168/C1
Pikelot (isl.), Micr. 136/D4
Pikes (peak), Co, US 152/B1
Pikes Creek (res.), Pa, US 168/B1
Pikesville, Md, US 168/B5
Piketberg, SAfr. 124/L10
Piketon, Oh, US 163/F1
Pikeville, Ky, US 163/F2
Pikeville, Tn, US 162/E3
Pikit, Phil. 88/D4
Pikou, China 81/B3
Piła, Pol. 43/J2
Pila, Arg. 191/J12
Pilane, Bots. 122/E5
Pilanesberg (range), SAfr. 124/P12
Pilani, India 98/C5
Pilão Arcado, Braz. 187/E1
Pilar, Arg. 190/E1
Pilar, Arg. 188/D4
Pilar, Braz. 187/G1
Pilar, Par. 188/E3
Pilar, Phil. 91/F1
Pilatus (peak), Swi. 61/E4
Pilaya (riv.), Bol. 188/C2
Pilchuck (riv.), Wa, US 167/D1
Pilcomayo (riv.), SAm. 179/C5
Pilgrims Hatch, Eng, UK 30/D2
Pili, Phil. 88/C2
Pīlībhīt, India 96/B1
Pilica (riv.), Pol. 70/B2
Pílion (peak), Gre. 49/H3
Pilis (mts.), Hun. 51/R9
Pilis (peak), Hun. 51/Q9
Pilis, Hun. 50/D2
Piliscsaba, Hun. 51/Q9
Pilisvörösvár, Hun. 51/Q9
Pilkhua, India 98/D5
Pillar (cape), Austl. 132/C4
Pillar (peak), Eng, UK 35/E3
Pillar (pt.), Ca, US 167/J12
Pillar (pt.), Wa, US 144/B3
Pilliga, Austl. 132/D1
Pillow, Pa, US 168/B2
Pilões, Serra dos (mtn.), Braz. 189/H1
Pilon du Roi (peak), Fr. 64/B6
Pílos, Gre. 49/G4
Pilot (peak), Id, US 144/G5
Pilot (peak), Nv, US 146/E4
Pilot (mtn.), Tn, US 162/E2
Pilot (peak), Tn, US 162/E2
Pilot Butte, Sk, Can. 156/B2
Pilot Grove, Mo, US 153/H1
Pilot Grove (cr.), Tx, US 150/L6
Pilot Knob, Mo, US 162/B2
Pilot Mound, Mb, Can. 156/E3
Pilot Mountain, NC, US 163/G2
Pilot Point, Ak, US 171/G4
Pilot Point, Tx, US 153/F4
Pilot Rock, Or, US 146/D1
Pilot Station, Ak, US 171/F3
Pilottown, La, US 164/D3
Pilsting, Ger. 59/F5
Piltene, Lat. 41/J3
Piltown, Ire. 32/C5
Pilyugino, Rus. 71/K1
Pima, Az, US 149/H4
Pimamga-Moke, D.R. Congo 120/D3
Pimenta Bueno, Braz. 185/F3
Pimpi, Indo. 91/F3
Pimpri-Chinchwad, India 95/B2
Piña (pt.), Pan. 177/G5
Pinacate, Cerro (peak), Mex. 149/F5
Pináculo (peak), Arg. 191/B6
Pinaleno (mts.), Az, US 149/G4
Pinamalayan, Phil. 88/C2
Pinamar, Arg. 191/F3
Pinang (isl.), Malay. 90/A2
Pinang (cape), Malay. 89/B1
Pinangah, Malay. 88/B4
Pinar del Río, Cuba 177/F1
Pınarbaşı, Turk. 102/D2
Pınarhisar, Turk. 51/H5
Piñas, Ecu. 184/B1
Pinatubo (mt.), Phil. 88/C2
Pinawa, Mb, Can. 156/G2
Pinchbeck, Eng, UK 35/H6
Pincher Creek, Ab, Can. 145/H3
Pinckney, Mi, US 160/E3
Pinckneyville, Il, US 162/C1
Pinconning, Mi, US 160/E3
Pîncota, Rom. 50/E2
Pincourt, Qu, Can. 159/N7
Pińczów, Pol. 43/L3
Pind Dādan Khān, Pak. 98/B3
Pinda, Ang. 120/C5
Pindall, Ar, US 153/H2
Pindamonhangaba, Braz. 187/L7
Pindaré (riv.), Braz. 183/E4
Pindaré-Mirim, Braz. 183/E3
Píndhos NP, Gre. 49/G3
Pindi Bhattiān, Pak. 98/B4
Pindi Gheb, Pak. 98/B3
Pindiu, PNG 129/G1
Pindobaçu, Braz. 187/E1
Pindobal, Braz. 182/D3
Pindus (mts.), Gre. 67/J2
Pindwāra, India 92/B3
Pine (cape), Nf, Can. 159/L2
Pine, Az, US 149/G3
Pine, Co, US 152/B1
Pine (isl.), Fl, US 165/G4
Pine (pt.), Fl, US 165/G3
Pine, Id, US 147/F2
Pine (riv.), Mi, US 160/D3
Pine (hills), Ms, US 164/C2
Pine (ridge), Ne, US 154/C2
Pine (cr.), Pa, US 168/A1
Pine, Tx, US 153/G4
Pine Apple, Al, US 164/E2
Pine Barrens (phys. reg.), NJ, US 168/D4
Pine Bluff, Ar, US 153/H3
Pine Bluff Arsenal, Ar, US 153/H3
Pine Bluffs, Wy, US 154/B3
Pine Bush, NY, US 161/J4
Pine Castle, Fl, US 164/N7
Pine City, Mn, US 157/H5
Pine Creek (lake), Ok, US 153/G3
Pine Creek, Austl. 128/C3
Pine Creek (pt.), Ct, US 169/E1
Pine Dock, Mb, Can. 156/F2
Pine Falls, Mb, Can. 156/F2
Pine Flat (res.), Ca, US 148/C2
Pine Grove, La, US 164/C2
Pine Grove, Pa, US 168/B2
Pine Hill, Al, US 164/E2
Pine Hill, NJ, US 168/D4
Pine Island, Fl, US 164/K6
Pine Island, Mn, US 155/H1
Pine Island Bay (flat), Ant. 192/S
Pine Island Nat'l Wild. Ref., Fl, US 165/G4
Pine Knot, Ky, US 162/E2
Pine Level, Al, US 165/E1
Pine Mills, Tx, US 151/G1
Pine Point, NW, Can. 140/E2
Pine Prairie, La, US 164/B2
Pine Ridge, SD, US 154/C2
Pine Ridge Ind. Res., SD, US 154/C2
Pine River, Mn, US 157/G4
Pine River, Mb, Can. 156/D2
Pine Springs, Tx, US 150/B2
Pine Stump Junction, Mi, US 160/D1
Pine Valley, Ut, US 149/F2
Pine Valley, Ca, US 148/D4
Pine, South Branch (riv.), Mi, US 167/G6
Pinebluff, NC, US 163/H3
Pinecliff (lake), NJ, US 169/H7
Pinecreek, Mn, US 156/G3
Pinedale, Wy, US 147/J2
Pinedale, Ca, US 148/C2
Pinedale, Az, US 149/G3
Pinega (riv.), Rus. 74/E3
Pinega, Rus. 68/J2
Pinehurst, Ga, US 162/F4
Pinehurst, Id, US 144/F4
Pinehurst, NC, US 163/H3
Pinehurst, Tx, US 151/G2
Pineland, Fl, US 165/G4
Pineland, SC, US 163/G4
Pineland, Tx, US 151/H2
Pinelands, SAfr. 124/L10
Pinellas (co.), Fl, US 164/K8
Pinellas (pt.), Fl, US 164/K8
Pinellas Park, Fl, US 164/K8
Pineola, Fl, US 164/L6
Piñera, Uru. 191/K10
Pinerolo, It. 64/D3
Pinesdale, Mt, US 145/G4
Pineto, It. 65/D2
Pinetop-Lakeside, Az, US 149/H3
Pinetops, NC, US 163/J3
Pinetown, SAfr. 125/E3
Pinetta, Fl, US 165/G2
Pineuilh, Fr. 44/D4
Pineview, Ga, US 165/G1
Pineville, Ky, US 162/F2
Pineville, La, US 164/B2
Pineville, Mo, US 153/G2
Pineville, SC, US 163/G4
Pineville, WV, US 163/G2
Piney, Ar, US 153/H3
Piney (isl.), Fl, US 165/F2
Piney Green, NC, US 163/J3
Piney Point, Fl, US 164/K8
Piney Point, Md, US 163/J1
Piney Point Village, Tx, US 151/M9
Piney River, Va, US 163/H2
Ping (riv.), Thai. 93/G4
Ping (riv.), Myan. 94/B2
Ping Chau (isl.), China 87/M6
Pingbian Miaozu Zizhixian, China 86/D4
Pingchang, China 87/E2
Pingchao, China 87/J1
Pingding, China 80/C3
Pingdingshan, China 80/C4
Pingdu, China 80/D3
Pingelap (isl.), Micr. 136/F4
Pingelly, Austl. 130/C5
Ping'erguan, China 94/D1
Pingfa, China 87/E3
Pinggu, China 80/H6
Pingguo, China 93/J3
Pinghai, China 87/H3
Pinghai, China 87/G4
Pinghu, China 80/L9
Pingjing (pass), China 80/C5
Pingjinpu, China 87/E2
Pingle, China 87/F3
Pinglu, China 80/C3
Pinglu, China 80/B4
Pingquan, China 80/D2
Pingree, Id, US 147/G2
Pingsha, China 87/G4
Pingshan, China 80/C3
Pingshi, China 87/G3
Pingshun, China 80/C3
Pingtang, China 93/J2
Pingtou, China 78/F5
P'ingtung, Tai. 87/J4
Pingwang, China 80/L9
Pingxiang, China 87/E4
Pingxiang, China 87/G3
Pingxiang, China 80/C3
Pingxing Guan (pass), China 80/C3
Pingyang, China 79/J4
Pingyao, China 80/C3
Pingyi, China 80/D4
Pingyin, China 94/E1
Pingyin, China 80/D3
Pingyong, China 87/F3
Pingyu, China 80/C4
Pingyuan, China 80/D3
Pinhal, Braz. 187/K7
Pinhal Novo, Port. 47/Q10
Pinheiro, Braz. 183/E3
Pinheiro Machado, Braz. 189/F4
Pinheiros, Braz. 187/E3
Pinhel, Port. 46/B2
Pinhook (swamp), Fl, US 165/G2
Pinhuã (riv.), Braz. 185/E2
Pini (isl.), Indo. 89/B2
Pinjar (lake), Austl. 130/K6
Pinjarra, Austl. 130/B5
Pink Hill, NC, US 163/J3
Pink Mountain, BC, Can. 142/AA13
Pinkafeld, Aus. 50/C2
Pinkawillinie Consv. Park, Austl. 131/G5
Pinkegat (chan.), Neth. 52/C2
Pinlebu, Myan. 93/G3
Pinnacles Nat'l Mon., Ca, US 148/B2
Pinnån (riv.), Swe. 39/K6
Pinnaroo, Austl. 131/J5
Pinnau (riv.), Ger. 53/G1
Pinneberg, Ger. 53/G1
Pino Hachado, (pass), Arg. 190/C3

Map Section
260
261

Rhyl, Wal, UK 34/E5
Rhynie, Sc, UK 33/D2
Rhyolite, Nv, US 148/D2
Riaba, EqG. 120/B2
Riachão, Braz. 183/E4
Riachão das Neves, Braz. 186/D1
Riachão do Jacuípe, Braz. 187/F1
Riacho de Santana, Braz. 187/E2
Riacho Monte Lindo (riv.), Arg. 188/E3
Riacho Pilagá (riv.), Arg. 188/E3
Riachuelo, Uru. 191/K11
Riachuelo, Braz. 183/H4
Riaillé, Fr. 56/D5
Riala, Swe. 39/B1
Rialto, Ca, US 166/C2
Riangnom, Sudan 117/F3
Rianjo, Sp. 46/A1
Riano, It. 65/B3
Riaño, Sp. 46/C1
Rians, Fr. 64/B5
Riāsi, India 98/C3
Riau (isls.), Indo. 90/B3
Riau (prov.), Indo. 89/C2
Riaza, Sp. 46/D2
Rib (mtn.), Wi, US 155/K1
Rib Lake, Wi, US 157/J5
Ribadeo, Sp. 46/B1
Ribadesella, Sp. 46/C1
Riban'i Manamby (mts.), Madg. 125/H9
Ribas do Rio Pardo, Braz. 189/F2
Ribauè, Moz. 123/H2
Ribble (riv.), Eng, UK 35/F4
Ribblesdale (valley), Eng, UK 35/F3
Ribe, Den. 40/C4
Ribe (co.), Den. 40/C4
Ribeauvillé, Fr. 60/D1
Ribécourt-Dreslincourt, Fr. 54/B4
Ribeira (riv.), Braz. 189/G3
Ribeira Brava, Port. 110/A2
Ribeira Brava, CpV. 107/J10
Ribeira de Pena, Port. 46/B2
Ribeira do Pombal, Braz. 187/F1
Ribeira Grande, CpV. 107/J9
Ribeira Grande, Azor., Port. 47/T13
Ribeirão, Braz. 183/H5
Ribeirão Preto, Braz. 189/H2
Ribeiro Gonçalves, Braz. 183/E4
Ribera, It. 48/C4
Ribera, NM, US 152/B3
Riberalta, Bol. 185/E3
Ribiers, Fr. 64/B4
Rîbniţa, Mol. 72/E4
Ribnitz-Damgarten, Ger. 40/E4
Ribstone, Ab, Can. 145/J1
Ribstone (cr.), Ab, Can. 145/J1
Říčany u Prahy, Czh. 59/H3
Ricaurte, Col. 180/B4
Riccia, It. 65/D5
Riccione, It. 63/F6
Ricco'del Golfo, It. 62/C5
Rice, Mn, US 157/G5
Rice (lake), On, Can. 161/G2
Rice, Ca, US 148/E3
Rice, Wa, US 144/E3
Rice, Tx, US 151/F1
Rice Lake, Wi, US 157/J5
Rice Lake NWR, Mn, US 157/H4
Riceboro, Ga, US 165/H2
Riceville, Ia, US 155/H2
Rich (mtn.), Ar, US 153/G3
Rich, Mor. 110/D2
Rich Hill, Mo, US 153/G1
Rich Square, NC, US 163/J2
Richard B. Russell (dam), SC, US 163/F3
Richard Toll, Sen. 114/B2
Richards, Mo, US 153/G2
Richards (isl.), NW, Can. 140/C2
Richard's Bay, SAfr. 125/F3
Richards Landing, On, Can. 160/D1
Richardson, Tx, US 150/L7
Richardson Lakes (lakes), NH, US 158/B3
Richardton, ND, US 156/C4
Richboro, Pa, US 168/C3
Riche (cape), Austl. 130/C5
Richebourg, Fr. 30/G5
Richel (isl.), Neth. 52/C2
Richelieu (riv.), Qu, Can. 161/K2
Richelieu, Qu, Can. 159/P7
Richey, Mt, US 156/B4
Richfield, Ut, US 149/F1
Richfield, Id, US 147/F2
Richfield, Mn, US 157/P7
Richfield, Pa, US 168/A2
Richford, Vt, US 161/K2
Richhill, NI, UK 34/B3
Richibucto, NB, Can. 158/E2
Richland, Mo, US 153/H2
Richland, Ga, US 165/F1
Richland, Ms, US 162/B4
Richland, Tx, US 151/F2
Richland, Wa, US 144/E4
Richland, Pa, US 168/B3
Richland, NJ, US 168/D5
Richland Balsam (peak), NC, US 163/F3
Richland Center, Wi, US 155/J2
Richland Creek (res.), Tx, US 151/F2
Richland Hills, Tx, US 150/K7
Richland Springs, Tx, US 151/E2
Richlands, Va, US 163/G2
Richlands, NC, US 163/J3
Richlandtown, Pa, US 168/C3
Richmond, Austl. 134/A3
Richmond, BC, Can. 144/C3
Richmond, Qu, Can. 161/K2
Richmond, NZ 135/C3
Richmond, SAfr. 124/C3
Richmond, SAfr. 125/E3
Richmond, Eng, UK 35/G3
Richmond, Ar, US 153/G4
Richmond, Ks, US 153/F1
Richmond, Mn, US 157/G5
Richmond, In, US 160/D5
Richmond, Mi, US 160/E3
Richmond, Il, US 167/P15
Richmond, Ut, US 147/H3
Richmond, Ky, US 162/E2
Richmond, Mo, US 155/H4
Richmond, Tx, US 151/M9
Richmond (cap.), Va, US 163/J2
Richmond (co.), NY, US 168/D2
Richmond Beach-Innis Arden, Wa, US 167/B2
Richmond Dale, Oh, US 163/F1
Richmond Heights, Fl, US 164/P11
Richmond Hill, On, Can. 160/U8
Richmond Nat'l Bfld. Park, Va, US 163/J2
Richmond Park (bor.), Eng, UK 30/C2
Richmond Town (nbrhd.), NY, US 169/J9
Richmond Upon Thames (bor.), Eng, UK 30/B2
Richmond-Windsor, Austl. 134/G8
Richmondville, NY, US 161/J3
Richmound, Sk, Can. 145/K2
Richtersveld NP, SAfr. 124/B3
Richterswil, Swi. 61/E3
Richthofen (mt.), Co, US 154/B3
Richton, Ms, US 164/D2
Richville, NY, US 161/J2
Richwiller, Fr. 60/D2
Richwood, Tx, US 150/G3
Richwood, La, US 153/H4
Richwood, Oh, US 160/E4
Richwood, WV, US 163/G1
Richwoods, Mo, US 162/B1
Rickenbach, Ger. 60/D2
Ricketts Glen St. Park, Pa, US 168/B1
Rickman, Tn, US 162/E2
Rickmansworth, Eng, UK 30/B2
Ricla, Sp. 46/E2
Rico, Ga, US 163/L7
Ricse, Hun. 43/L4
Ridā', Yem. 118/C2
Riddells Creek, Austl. 133/B3
Ridderkerk, Neth. 52/B5
Riddle, Id, US 146/E2
Riddle, Or, US 146/B2
Rideau (riv.), On, Can. 161/J2
Rideau (lake), On, Can. 161/H2
Ridge, Mt, US 154/B1
Ridge Farm, Il, US 160/C5
Ridge Manor, Fl, US 164/L6
Ridge Spring, SC, US 163/G4
Ridgecrest, La, US 164/C2
Ridgecrest, Ca, US 148/D3
Ridgefield, NJ, US 169/K8
Ridgefield, Ct, US 169/E1
Ridgefield NWR, Or, US 144/C5
Ridgefield Park, NJ, US 169/J8
Ridgeland, Ms, US 162/B4
Ridgeland, SC, US 163/G4
Ridgely, Tn, US 162/C2
Ridgely, Md, US 168/C6
Ridgetown, On, Can. 160/F3
Ridgeville, SC, US 163/G4
Ridgeway, Mo, US 155/H3
Ridgeway, Va, US 163/H2
Ridgewood (nbrhd.), NY, US 169/K9
Ridgewood, NJ, US 169/J8
Ridgewood State Park, NJ, US 168/D2
Ridgway, Pa, US 161/G4
Ridgway, Co, US 149/J1
Riding Mill, Eng, UK 35/G2
Riding Mountain NP, Mb, Can. 156/D2
Riding Mtn. (mtn.), Mb, Can. 156/D2
Ridlees Cairn (hill), Eng, UK 33/D6
Ridley (cr.), Pa, US 168/C4
Riec-sur-Belon, Fr. 56/B5
Riecito (riv.), Col. 180/D3
Ried im Innkreis, Aus. 59/G6
Ried im Traunkreis, Aus. 59/H6
Riede, Ger. 53/F3
Riedenburg, Ger. 59/E5
Riedisheim, Fr. 60/D2
Riedlingen, Ger. 61/F1
Riegelsberg, Ger. 55/F5
Riegelsville, Pa, US 168/C2
Riegsee (lake), Ger. 61/H2
Riehen, Swi. 60/D2
Riemst, Belg. 55/E2
Rieneck, Ger. 58/C2
Rienzi, Ms, US 162/C3
Riesa, Ger. 43/G3
Rieschweiler-Mühlbach, Ger. 55/G5
Riesco (isl.), Chile 191/B7
Riese Pio X, It. 63/E2
Riet (riv.), SAfr. 124/D3
Rietavas, Lith. 41/J4
Rietberg, Ger. 53/F5
Rietbron, SAfr. 124/C4
Rietfontein, Namb. 122/D4
Rietfontein (riv.), Namb. 122/D4
Rieti, It. 65/B3
Rieti (prov.), It. 65/B3
Rievaulx, Eng, UK 35/G3
Riez, Fr. 64/C5
Riffe (lake), Wa, US 144/C4
Rifle, Co, US 147/K4
Rifsnes (pt.), Ice. 38/N6
Rift Valley (prov.), Kenya 119/A1
Rig-Rig, Chad 116/B2
Riga (gulf), Eur. 74/C4
Riga (Rīga) (cap.), Lat. 41/L3
Rigacikun, Nga. 115/G4
Rigby, Id, US 147/H2
Rīgestān (pol. reg.), Afg. 101/H2
Riggins, Id, US 146/E1
Rigi (peak), Swi. 61/E3
Rignano Flaminio, It. 65/B3
Rignano sull'Arno, It. 63/E6
Rigolet, Nf, Can. 141/L3
Rigside, Sc, UK 33/C5
Riguldi, Est. 41/K2
Riḩāb, Jor. 105/E4
Rihand (riv.), India 96/D3
Rihand (dam), India 96/D3
Rihand Sāgar (res.), India 92/D3
Riihimäki, Fin. 41/L1
Riiser-Larsen (pen.), Ant. 192/C
Riiser-Larsen Ice Shelf, Ant. 192/Y
Riisitunturin NP, Fin. 68/F2
Rijeka, Cro. 45/L4
Rijen, Neth. 52/B5
Rijksmuseum Kröller Müller, Neth. 52/C4
Rijnsburg, Neth. 52/B4
Rijsbergen, Neth. 52/B5
Rijssen, Neth. 52/D4
Rijswijk, Neth. 52/B4
Rikers (isl.), NY, US 169/K8
Rikitea, FrPol. 137/M7
Rikuchū-Kaigan NP, Japan 82/C4
Rikuzentakata, Japan 82/B4
Rila, Bul. 49/H1
Rila (mts.), Bul. 49/H1
Riley, Or, US 146/D2
Riley, Ks, US 155/F4
Riley Brook, NB, Can. 158/D2
Rillieux-la-Pape, Fr. 60/A6
Rillito, Az, US 149/G4
Rilski Manastir, Bul. 49/H1
Rīmah (wadi), SAr. 100/D3
Rimatara (isl.), FrPol. 137/K7
Rimavská Sobota, Slvk. 43/L4
Rimbach, Ger. 58/B3
Rimbey, Ab, Can. 145/G1
Rimbo, Swe. 39/B1
Rimé (riv.), Chad 116/C2
Rimersburg, Pa, US 161/G4
Rimforsa, Swe. 40/F2
Rimini, It. 63/F5
Rîmnicu Sărat, Rom. 51/H3
Rîmnicu Vîlcea, Rom. 51/G3
Rimogne, Fr. 55/D4
Rimouski, Qu, Can. 158/C1
Rimouski (riv.), Qu, Can. 158/C1
Rimouski-Est, Qu, Can. 158/C1
Rimpar, Ger. 58/C3
Rimpfischhorn (peak), Swi. 60/D5
Rimsting, Ger. 59/F7
Rimutaka (range), NZ 135/H9
Rimutaka Forrest Park, NZ 135/H9
Rinas (int'l arpt.), Alb. 49/F2
Rinbung, China 97/G1
Rinchnach, Ger. 59/F5
Rincon (peak), Az, US 149/G4
Rincón, Uru. 191/G2
Rincon, NM, US 149/J4
Rincón (peak), Arg.,Chile 188/C3
Rincon, Ga, US 163/G4
Rincón de la Vieja, PN, CR 172/D5
Rincón de Romos, Mex. 174/E4
Rinconada, Arg. 188/C2
Rindge, NH, US 161/K3
Ringarooma, Austl. 132/C4
Ringaskiddy, Ire. 32/B6
Ringboy (pt.), NI, UK 34/C3
Ringebu, Nor. 40/D1
Ringelspitz (peak), Swi. 61/F4
Ringgold, La, US 153/H4
Ringgold, Ga, US 162/E3
Ringim, Nga. 115/H3
Ringkøbing, Den. 40/C3
Ringkøbing (co.), Den. 40/C3
Ringkøbing (fjord), Den. 40/B3
Ringling, Ok, US 153/F3
Ringling, Mt, US 145/J4
Ringling Museum of Art, Fl, US 165/G4
Ringmer, Eng, UK 37/G5
Ringoes, NJ, US 168/D3
Ringold, Ok, US 153/G3
Ringsend, NI, UK 34/B1
Ringsön (isl.), Swe. 39/A2
Ringsted, Den. 40/D4
Ringtown, Pa, US 168/B2
Ringvaart (riv.), Neth. 52/B4
Ringvassøy (isl.), Nor. 38/F1
Ringway (Manchester) (int'l arpt.), Eng, UK 35/F5
Ringwood, NJ, US 169/H7
Ringwood, Austl. 131/G2
Ringwood (nbrhd.), Austl. 132/G5
Ringwood, Eng, UK 37/E5
Ringwood State Park, NJ, US 168/D1
Rinia (isl.), Gre. 49/J4
Riñihue, Chile 190/B3
Rinteln, Ger. 53/G4
Rinxent, Fr. 54/A2
Rio, La, US 164/D2
Río Abiseo, PN, Peru 184/B2
Rio Azul, Braz. 189/G3
Rio Blanco, Co, US 147/K4
Río Blanco, Chile 190/N8
Río Blanco, Bol. 184/D5
Río Blanco, Mex. 175/M8
Rio Bonito, Braz. 187/P7
Rio Branco, Braz. 184/E3
Rio Branco, Uru. 189/F5
Rio Branco do Sul, Braz. 189/G3
Río Bravo, Mex. 151/E5
Rio Brilhante, Braz. 189/F2
Río Bueno, Chile 190/B4
Río Cauto, Cuba 177/G1
Río Ceballos, Arg. 188/C4
Río Chico, Arg. 191/C6
Río Clarillo, PN, Chile 190/N8
Rio Claro, Trin. 181/F2
Rio Claro, Braz. 187/M7
Rio Claro, Braz. 189/H2
Río Colorado, Arg. 190/D3
Río Cuarto, Arg. 190/D2
Río de Bavispe (riv.), Mex. 174/C2
Rio de Contas, Braz. 187/E2
Rio de Janeiro (int'l arpt.), Braz. 187/N7
Rio de Janeiro, Braz. 187/N7
Rio de Janeiro (state), Braz. 187/E4
Rio Dell, Ca, US 146/A3
Rio do Sul, Braz. 189/G3
Rio Frio, Port. 47/Q10
Río Gallegos, Arg. 191/C6
Rio Grande (riv.), Mex. 151/B3
Rio Grande (canal), Co, US 152/A2
Rio Grande (riv.), US 172/A2
Rio Grande (plain), Tx, US 172/B2
Rio Grande, Oh, US 163/F1
Río Grande, Arg. 191/D7
Rio Grande, Braz. 189/F5
Rio Grande, NJ, US 168/D5
Rio Grande City, Tx, US 151/E4
Rio Grande da Serra, Braz. 187/K8
Río Grande de Matagalpa (riv.), Nic. 172/D5
Río Grande de Santiago (riv.), Mex. 174/D4
Rio Grande do Norte (state), Braz. 183/G4
Rio Grande do Piauí, Braz. 183/F4
Rio Grande do Sul (state), Braz. 189/F4
Rio Grande Valley (int'l arpt.), Tx, US 151/F4
Rio Hondo, Tx, US 150/F4
Rio Jaú, PN do, Braz. 181/F5
Río Lagartos, Mex. 176/D1
Rio Largo, Braz. 183/H5
Rio Maior, Port. 46/A3
Río Mayo, Arg. 190/C5
Rio Muni (pol. reg.), EqG. 120/B2
Rio Negrinho, Braz. 189/G3
Río Negro, Chile 190/B4
Río Negro (prov.), Arg. 190/E3
Río Negro, Chile 190/B4
Río Negro (res.), Uru. 189/F5
Rio Negro, Braz. 189/F1
Rio Negro (dept.), Uru. 189/F5
Rio Pardo, Braz. 189/F4
Rio Rancho, NM, US 149/J3
Rio Real, Braz. 187/F1
Rio Saliceto, It. 63/D4
Río Segundo, Arg. 188/D4
Río Simpson, PN, Chile 190/B5
Río Tala, Arg. 191/J10
Río Tercero, Arg. 188/C5
Río Tigre, Ecu. 180/B5
Rio Tinto, Braz. 183/H4
Río Verde, Chile 191/C7
Rio Verde, Braz. 186/C3
Río Verde, Mex. 175/F4
Rio Verde de Mato Grosso, Braz. 189/F1
Rio Vista, Ca, US 167/L10
Rio Vista, Tx, US 151/F1
Riobamba, Ecu. 180/B5
Ríohacha, Col. 180/C2
Rioja, Peru 184/B2
Riolo Terme, It. 63/E5
Riom, Fr. 44/E4
Riom-ès-Montagne, Fr. 44/E4
Riomaggiore, It. 62/C5
Rion-des-Landes, Fr. 44/C5
Riondel, BC, Can. 144/F3
Ríonegro, Col. 180/C3
Ríonegro, Col. 183/K6
Rionero in Vulture, It. 48/D2
Rionero Sannitico, It. 65/D4
Riorges, Fr. 44/F3
Ríos, Sp. 46/B2
Ríos (lake), Chile 190/B5
Ríosucio, Col. 180/B3
Ríosucio, Col. 183/K7
Rioz, Fr. 60/C3
Riozinho (riv.), Braz. 185/E2
Ripa Sottile (lake), It. 65/B3
Ripalimosano, It. 65/D4
Ripalti, Punta dei (pt.), It. 48/B1
Ripanj, Yugo. 50/E3
Riparbella, It. 62/D7
Ripatransone, It. 65/C2
Ripky, Ukr. 72/F2
Ripley, Eng, UK 35/G5
Ripley, Eng, UK 30/B3
Ripley, Ca, US 148/E4
Ripley, Ms, US 162/C3
Ripley, Ok, US 153/F2
Ripley, WV, US 163/G1
Ripley, Tn, US 162/C3
Ripley, Oh, US 162/F1
Ripoll, Sp. 47/G1
Ripoll (riv.), Sp. 47/L6
Ripollet, Sp. 47/L6
Ripon, Eng, UK 35/G3
Ripon, Qu, Can. 161/J2
Ripon, Ca, US 148/B2
Ripon, Wi, US 155/K2
Riposto, It. 48/D4
Ripples, NB, Can. 158/D2
Rippon, WV, US 161/H5
Ripponden, Eng, UK 35/G4
Rippowam (riv.), Ct, US 169/L7
Riri Bāzār, Nepal 96/D2
Ris-Orangis, Fr. 30/K6
Risaralda (dept.), Col. 180/A4
Risaralda, Col. 183/K7
Risasi, D.R. Congo 121/F3
Rîşcani, Mol. 72/D4
Rishiri, Japan 82/B1
Rishiri (isl.), Japan 79/N2
Rishiri-Rebun-Sarobetsu NP, Japan 82/B1
Rishon Leziyyon, Isr. 105/B5
Rishrāsh (wadi), Egypt 113/C6
Rising Star, Tx, US 151/E1
Rising Sun, In, US 162/E1
Rising Sun, Md, US 168/B4
Rising Sun-Lebanon, De, US 168/C5
Riske Creek, BC, Can. 144/C2
Risle (riv.), Fr. 44/D2
Risley (Estell Manor), NJ, US 168/D5
Risnjak (peak), Cro. 45/L4
Risnjak NP, Cro. 50/B3
Rîşnov, Rom. 51/G3
Rison, Ar, US 153/H4
Risør, Nor. 40/C2
Risoul, Fr. 64/C3
Riss (riv.), Ger. 61/F1
Risse (riv.), Fr. 60/C5
Rişşū (peak), Egypt 113/B5
Risti, Est. 41/L2
Ristiina, Fin. 41/M1
Rita Blanca (cr.), Tx, US 152/C2
Ritacuba (peak), Col. 180/C3
Ritaiō (isl.), Japan 136/D2
Rito (cr.), NM, US 149/H3
Ritoio (peak), It. 63/E6
Ritterhude, Ger. 53/F2
Rittman, Oh, US 160/F4
Rittō, Japan 83/J5
Ritzville, Wa, US 144/E4
Riva, It. 61/G6
Riva Ligure, It. 62/A5
Riva Presso Chieri, It. 62/A3
Riva San Vitale, Swi. 61/E6
Rivadavia, Arg. 190/E2
Rivadavia, Arg. 188/D3
Rivadavia, Arg. 188/B4
Rival (riv.), Fr. 64/B2
Rivalta, It. 62/D3
Rivalta di Torino, It. 62/A2
Rivanazzano, It. 62/C4
Rivanna (riv.), Va, US 163/H2
Rivara, It. 64/D2
Rivarolo Canavese, It. 62/A2
Rivarolo Mantovano, It. 62/D3
Rivas, Nic. 176/E4
Rīvash, Iran 101/G1
Rive-de-Gier, Fr. 64/A1
River Bourgeois, NS, Can. 159/G3
River Cess, Libr. 114/C5
River Denys, NS, Can. 159/G3
River Edge, NJ, US 169/J8
River Falls, Al, US 164/E2
River Falls, Wi, US 157/Q7
River Hébert, NS, Can. 158/E3
River John, NS, Can. 158/F3
River Kwai Bridge, Thai. 94/B3
River Oaks, Tx, US 150/K7
River Rouge, Mi, US 167/F7
River Vale, NJ, US 169/J8
Rivera, Swi. 61/E5
Rivera (isl.), Chile 190/B5
Rivera, Arg. 190/E3
Rivera (dept.), Uru. 189/F4
Rivera, Uru. 189/F4
Riverdale, ND, US 156/D4
Riverdale, NJ, US 169/H8
Riverdale (nbrhd.), NY, US 169/K8
Riverdale, Ca, US 148/C2
Riverdale, Ga, US 163/M7
Rivergaro, It. 62/C4
Riverhead, NY, US 169/F2
Riverhurst, Sk, Can. 145/L2
Riverport, NS, Can. 158/E3
Rivers, Mb, Can. 156/D2
Rivers (state), Nga. 115/G5
Riversdale, SAfr. 124/C4
Riverside, Tx, US 151/G2
Riverside (co.), Ca, US 166/C3
Riverside, Ca, US 166/C3
Riverside, Or, US 146/D2
Riverside (canal), Co, US 154/B3
Riverside, Pa, US 168/B2
Riverside, NJ, US 168/D3
Riverside-Albert, NB, Can. 158/E3
Riverstone (nbrhd.), Austl. 134/G8
Riverstown, Ire. 32/B6
Riverstown, Ire. 32/B1
Riverton, Mb, Can. 156/F2
Riverton, NS, Can. 159/F3
Riverton, Austl. 131/H5
Riverton, NZ 135/B4
Riverton, Wy, US 147/J2
Riverton, Ut, US 147/H3
Riverview, NB, Can. 158/E2
Riverview, Mi, US 160/E3
Riverview, Fl, US 164/L8
Riverwoods, Il, US 167/Q15
Rîves, Fr. 64/B2
Riviera, Az, US 148/E3
Riviera, Tx, US 151/F4
Riviera Beach, Fl, US 164/P9
Riviera Beach, Md, US 168/B5
Rivière-à-Pierre, Qu, Can. 158/A2
Rivière-au-Renard, Qu, Can. 158/E1
Rivière-Bleue, Qu, Can. 158/C2
Rivière-du-Loup, Qu, Can. 158/C2
Rivière-Éternité, Qu, Can. 158/B1
Riviersonderendreeks (mts.), SAfr. 124/L11
Rivignano, It. 63/G2
Rivne, Ukr. 72/D2
Rivnens'ka Oblast, Ukr. 70/C2
Rivoli, It. 64/D2
Rivolta d'Adda, It. 62/C3
Rixensart, Belg. 55/D2
Rixheim, Fr. 60/D2
Riyadh (Ar Riyāḑ) (cap.), SAr. 100/E4
Rīyāq, Leb. 105/D1
Rizal, Phil. 88/C2
Rizal (prov.), Phil. 88/F6
Rize, Turk. 71/G4
Rizhao, China 80/D4
Rizokarpasso, Cyp. 104/D2
Rizzuto (cape), It. 49/E3
Rjukan, Nor. 40/C2
Rkîz, Mrta. 114/B2
Rkîz (lake), Mrta. 114/B2
Rö, Swe. 39/B1
Roa, Nor. 40/D1
Roa, Sp. 46/D2
Road Town (cap.), BVI 173/M8
Roade, Eng, UK 37/F2
Roadside, Sc, UK 33/D3
Roan (plat.), Ut, US 147/J4
Roan Fell (hill), Sc, UK 35/F1
Roan High (peak), NC, US 163/F2
Roanne (riv.), Fr. 64/B3
Roanne, Fr. 44/F3
Roanoke, Al, US 162/E4
Roanoke, Tx, US 150/K6
Roanoke (riv.), Va, US 163/H2
Roanoke (pt.), NY, US 169/F2
Roanoke, Va, US 163/H2
Roanoke Rapids, NC, US 163/J2
Roans Prairie, Tx, US 151/G2
Roaring (cr.), Pa, US 168/B2
Roaring Fk. (riv.), Co, US 147/K4
Roaring Springs, Tx, US 152/D4
Roatán (isl.), Hon. 172/D4
Roatán, Hon. 176/E2
Robards, Ky, US 162/D2
Robassomero, It. 64/D2
Robāţ Karīm, Iran 103/G3
Robāţ-e Khān, Iran 103/J3
Robāţ-e Sang, Iran 101/G1
Robb, Ab, Can. 144/F1
Robbiate, It. 62/C2
Robbins (isl.), Austl. 132/C4
Robbins, NC, US 163/H3
Robbinsville, NC, US 162/F3
Robbio, It. 62/B3
Robe (riv.), Ire. 32/A2
Robē, Eth. 118/A4
Robe (mt.), Austl. 132/B1
Robe, Austl. 132/A3
Robecchetto con Induno, It. 62/B2
Röbel, Ger. 40/E4
Röbel, Ger. 42/G2
Robersonville, NC, US 163/J3
Robert (peak), Fr. 60/B5
Robert Lee, Tx, US 150/D2
Roberta, Ga, US 162/E4
Roberts (mt.), Ak, US 171/E4
Roberts, Id, US 147/G2
Roberts, Il, US 160/B4
Roberts, Mt, US 147/J1
Roberts (Monrovia) (int'l arpt.), Libr. 114/C5
Roberts Creek (mtn.), Nv, US 146/E4
Roberts Creek, BC, Can. 144/C3
Robertsbridge, Eng, UK 37/G5
Robertsfors, Swe. 38/G2
Robertsganj, India 96/D3
Robertson, SAfr. 124/L10
Robertson, Wy, US 147/H3
Robertsport, Libr. 114/C5
Robertstown, Ire. 32/D3
Roberval, Qu, Can. 158/A1
Robesonia, Pa, US 168/B3
Robilante, It. 64/D4
Robin Hood's Bay, Eng, UK 35/H3
Robins (A.F.B.), Ga, US 163/F4
Robinson, Il, US 162/D1
Robinson, Tx, US 151/F2
Robinson (mtn.), Mt, US 144/G3
Robinson (range), Austl. 127/A3
Robinson Crusoe (isl.), Chile 179/B6
Robinson Gorge NP, Austl. 134/C4
Robinson River, Austl. 129/E4
Robinson River, PNG 129/H2
Robinson River Abor. Land, Austl. 129/E4
Robinson Springs, Al, US 162/D4
Robinvale, Austl. 132/B2
Robion, Fr. 64/B5
Robledo (mtn.), NM, US 149/J4
Roblin, Mb, Can. 156/D2
Roboré, Bol. 188/E1
Robsart, Sk, Can. 145/K3
Robson (mt.), BC, Can. 144/E1
Robstown, Tx, US 151/F4
Roby, Mo, US 153/H2
Roby, Tx, US 151/D1
Roc (pt.), Fr. 56/D3
Roc de France (peak), Fr. 47/G1
Roc du Haut du Faite (peak), Fr. 60/D1
Roca Partida (isl.), Mex. 174/B5
Roca Partida, Punta (pt.), Mex. 176/C2
Roca, Cabo da (cape), Port. 47/P10
Rocafuerte, Ecu. 180/A5
Rocanville, Sk, Can. 156/D2
Rocas (isl.), Braz. 183/H3
Rocca di Mezzo, It. 65/C3
Rocca di Papa, It. 65/B4
Rocca San Casciano, It. 63/E5
Roccabianca, It. 62/D3
Roccagorga, It. 65/C4
Roccamandolfi, It. 65/D5
Roccamonfina, It. 65/C5
Roccarainola, It. 65/D6
Roccasecca, It. 65/C4
Roccastrada, It. 48/B1
Roccavione, It. 64/D4
Rocciamelone (peak), It. 64/D2
Rocha, Uru. 191/G2
Rocha (dept.), Uru. 191/G2
Rochambeau (int'l arpt.), FrG. 182/C1
Rochdale, Eng, UK 35/F4
Rochdale (co.), Eng, UK 35/F4
Roche, Swi. 60/C5
Roche, Eng, UK 36/B6
Roche Bernaude (peak), Fr. 64/C2
Roche de la Muzelle (peak), Fr. 64/C3
Roche du Sapin Sec (peak), Fr. 60/C1
Roche Faurio (peak), Fr. 64/C3
Roche-lez-Beaupré, Fr. 60/C3
Rochebrune, Pic de (peak), Fr. 64/C3
Rochefort, Belg. 55/E3
Rochefort, Fr. 44/C4
Rochefort-en-Terre, Fr. 56/C5
Rochefort-sur-Loire, Fr. 57/E6
Rochelaire, Pic de (peak), Fr. 64/C3
Rochelle, Ga, US 165/G2
Rochelle, Il, US 155/K3
Rochelle, Tx, US 151/E2
Rochelle Park, NJ, US 169/J8
Rochemaure, Fr. 64/A3
Rochers de la Tude (peak), Fr. 47/G1
Rochers du Bourbet (peak), Fr. 60/C3
Roches Blanches (peak), Fr. 64/C6
Rochester, Austl. 133/B3
Rochester, Eng, UK 37/G4
Rochester, NY, US 161/H3
Rochester, In, US 160/C4
Rochester, NH, US 161/L3
Rochester, Vt, US 161/K3
Rochester, Wi, US 167/P14
Rochester, Mi, US 167/F6
Rochester, Mn, US 155/H1
Rochester, Ky, US 162/D2
Rochester, Il, US 155/K4
Rochester Hills, Mi, US 160/E3
Rochford, Eng, UK 30/F2
Rochfortbridge, Ire. 32/C3
Rock (lake), ND, US 156/E3
Rock, Mi, US 157/L4
Rock (riv.), Il, US 143/J3
Rock (cr.), Mt, US 147/J1
Rock (riv.), Ia,Mn, US 155/F2
Rock Bluff, Fl, US 165/F2
Rock Cave, WV, US 163/G1
Rock Creek, Yk, Can. 171/L3
Rock Falls, Wi, US 155/J1
Rock Falls, Il, US 155/K3
Rock Forest, Qu, Can. 161/L2
Rock Glen, Pa, US 168/B2
Rock Hall, Md, US 168/B5
Rock Hill, SC, US 163/G3
Rock Island, Il, US 155/J3
Rock Island, Tx, US 150/F3
Rock Mills, Al, US 162/E4
Rock Port, Mo, US 155/G3
Rock Rapids, Ia, US 155/F2
Rock River, Wy, US 154/B3
Rock Springs, Wy, US 147/J3
Rock Springs, Mt, US 145/L4
Rock Valley, Ia, US 155/F2
Rockall (isl.), UK 29/C3
Rockaway (pt.), NY, US 169/K9
Rockaway (inlet), NY, US 169/K9
Rockaway (riv.), NJ, US 168/D2
Rockaway, NJ, US 168/D2
Rockaway (Rockaway Beach), Or, US 144/C5
Rockaway Beach (Rockaway), Or, US 144/C5
Rockaway Park (nbrhd.), NY, US 169/K9
Rockcorry, Ire. 32/C1
Rockdale, Il, US 167/P17
Rockdale (nbrhd.), Austl. 134/H8
Rockdale (co.), Ga, US 163/M7
Rockdale, Tx, US 151/F2
Rockefeller (plat.), Ant. 192/R
Rockenhausen, Ger. 55/G4
Rockett, Tx, US 150/L7
Rockfield, Ky, US 162/D2
Rockford, Oh, US 160/D4
Rockford, Il, US 155/K2
Rockford, Al, US 162/D4
Rockford, Wa, US 144/F4
Rockglen, Sk, Can. 145/M3
Rockhampton, Austl. 134/C3
Rockhampton Downs, Austl. 129/D4
Rockhill, Tx, US 150/L6
Rockingham, Vt, US 161/K3
Rockingham, Austl. 130/K7
Rockingham, NC, US 163/H3
Rockland, Tx, US 151/G2
Rockland, On, Can. 161/J2
Rockland, Id, US 147/G2
Rockland (co.), NY, US 168/D1
Rockland Lake, NY, US 169/K7
Rocklands (res.), Austl. 132/B3
Rockledge, Fl, US 165/H3
Rockledge, Pa, US 168/C3
Rocklin, Ca, US 146/C4
Rockmart, Ga, US 162/E3
Rockport, Ar, US 153/H3
Rockport, Ms, US 164/C2
Rockport, Ca, US 146/B4
Rockport, Ky, US 162/D2
Rockport, In, US 162/D2
Rockport, Wa, US 144/D3
Rockport, Tx, US 150/F3
Rocks (pt.), NZ 135/C3
Rocks, Md, US 168/B4
Rocksprings, Tx, US 151/D2
Rockstone, Guy. 181/G3
Rockton, Il, US 160/B3
Rockvale, Co, US 152/B1
Rockville, NS, Can. 158/D4
Rockville, In, US 160/C5
Rockville, Ut, US 149/F2
Rockville, Md, US 163/J1
Rockville Centre, NY, US 169/L9
Rockwall, Tx, US 150/L7
Rockwall (co.), Tx, US 150/L7
Rockwell, Ia, US 155/H2
Rockwell City, Ia, US 155/G2
Rockwood, Me, US 161/M2
Rockwood, Tn, US 162/E3
Rockwood, On, Can. 160/S8
Rockwood, Tx, US 150/E2
Rocky (pt.), Austl. 128/C2
Rocky (mts.), Can.,US 139/E4
Rocky (pt.), Namb. 122/B3
Rocky (mtn.), Ky, US 162/F2
Rocky (pt.), NY, US 169/F1
Rocky (riv.), NC, US 163/G3
Rocky, Ok, US 152/E3
Rocky Boys Ind. Res., Mt, US 145/K3
Rocky Cape NP, Austl. 132/C4
Rocky Ford, Co, US 152/C1
Rocky Ford, Ga, US 163/G4
Rocky Fork (lake), Oh, US 160/E5
Rocky Island (lake), On, Can. 160/E1
Rocky Mount, Mo, US 153/H1
Rocky Mount, NC, US 163/J3
Rocky Mount, Va, US 163/H2
Rocky Mountain Arsenal, Co, US 152/B1
Rocky Mountain House, Ab, Can. 144/G1
Rocky Mountain NP, Co, US 154/A3
Rocky Point, NC, US 163/J3
Rocky Reach (dam), Wa, US 144/D4
Rockyford, Ab, Can. 145/H2
Rockypoint, Wy, US 154/B1
Rocroi, Fr. 55/D4
Roda, Sp. 66/C3
Rodach (riv.), Ger. 59/E2
Rodach bei Coburg, Ger. 58/D2
Rodalben, Ger. 55/G5
Rodanthe, NC, US 163/K3
Rødberg, Nor. 40/C1
Rødbyhavn, Den. 40/D4
Rødbyvatn (lake), Nor. 38/S9
Rødding, Den. 40/C4
Roden (riv.), Eng, UK 35/F6
Rodenbach, Ger. 58/C2
Rodeo, Ca, US 167/K10
Rodeo, NM, US 149/H5
Rodeo, Mex. 174/D3
Roderfield, WV, US 163/G2
Rödermark, Ger. 58/B3
Rodessa, La, US 153/H4
Rodewisch, Ger. 59/F1
Rodez, Fr. 44/E4
Rodholívos, Gre. 49/H2
Ródhos (ruin), Gre. 102/B2
Ródhos (Rhodes), Gre. 102/B2
Rodigo, It. 62/D3
Roding (riv.), Eng, UK 30/D2
Roding, Ger. 59/F4
Rodinga (mt.), Austl. 131/G3
Rödinghausen, Ger. 53/F4
Rodney (cape), NZ 135/C2
Rodoč, Bosn. 50/C4
Rodolfo Sánchez Toboada, Mex. 174/A2
Rødovre, Den. 39/J7
Rodrigues, Braz. 184/C2
Rodríguez, Uru. 191/K11
Rødvig, Den. 39/J7
Rodyns'ke, Ukr. 73/J3
Roe (riv.), NI, UK 34/B2
Roebourne, Austl. 130/C2
Roebuck (bay), Austl. 127/B2
Roebuck, SC, US 163/G3
Roebuck Plains, Austl. 128/A4
Roedtan, SAfr. 123/F5
Roen (peak), It. 61/H5
Roer (riv.), Neth. 52/D6
Roermond, Neth. 52/C6
Roes Welcome Sound (str.), Nun, Can. 141/H2
Roeselare, Belg. 54/C2
Roesiger (lake), Wa, US 167/D2
Roff, Ok, US 153/F3
Rogač, Cro. 50/C4
Rogachev, Bela. 70/D1
Rogachëvka, Rus. 73/K2
Rogagua (lake), Bol. 185/E4
Rogaland (co.), Nor. 38/C4
Rogaška Slatina, Slov. 45/L3
Rogatica, Bosn. 50/D4
Rogers, ND, US 156/E4
Rogers, Ar, US 153/G2
Rogers (mt.), Va, US 163/G2
Rogers, BC, Can. 144/F2
Rogers, Tx, US 150/F2
Rogers City, Mi, US 160/E2
Rogersville, NB, Can. 158/E2
Rogersville, Mo, US 153/H2
Rogersville, Tn, US 163/F2
Rogersville, Al, US 162/D3
Roggwil, Swi. 60/D3
Rogliano, Fr. 48/A1
Roglio (riv.), It. 63/D5
Rognac, Fr. 64/B6
Rognes, Fr. 64/B5
Rognon (riv.), Fr. 44/F2
Rognonas, Fr. 64/A5
Rogo, Nga. 115/G4
Rogoaguado (lake), Bol. 185/E4
Rogoźno, Pol. 43/J2
Rogue (riv.), Or, US 146/A2
Rogue River, Or, US 146/B2
Rohatyn, Ukr. 72/C3
Rohl (riv.), Sudan 117/F4
Rohnert Park, Ca, US 146/B4
Rohr, Ger. 59/E5
Rohrbach bei Mattersburg, Aus. 50/C2
Rohrbach in Oberösterreich, Aus. 59/G5
Rohrbach-lès-Bitche, Fr. 55/G5
Rohri, Pak. 101/J3
Röhrmoos, Ger. 59/E6
Rohtak, India 98/D5
Rohtās, India 96/D3
Rohwer, Ar, US 153/J4
Roi Et, Thai. 94/C2
Roia (riv.), It. 64/D5
Roiffieux, Fr. 64/A2
Roine (lake), Fin. 41/L1
Roissy, Fr. 30/K5
Roissy-en-France, Fr. 30/K4
Roja, Lat. 41/K3
Rojas, Arg. 190/E2
Rojo (cape), PR 173/M8
Rojo, Cabo (cape), Mex. 176/B1
Roka, Kenya 119/B2
Rokan, Indo. 89/C2
Rokan (river), Indo. 89/C2
Rokan (riv.), Indo. 90/B3
Rokeby Croll Creek NP, Austl. 134/A1
Rokel (riv.), SLeo. 114/C4
Rokiškis, Lith. 41/L4
Rokkasho, Japan 82/B3
Rokkō-san (peak), Japan 83/H6
Rokot (cape), Indo. 89/B3
Rokugō, Japan 83/A3
Rokycany, Czh. 59/G3
Rokytka (riv.), Czh. 59/H2
Rokytne, Ukr. 72/D2
Rokytne, Ukr. 72/F3
Rolampont, Fr. 60/B2
Roland, Mb, Can. 156/F3
Roland, Ia, US 155/H2
Rolândia, Braz. 186/C4
Rolava (riv.), Czh. 59/F2
Røldal, Nor. 40/B2
Rolde, Neth. 52/D3
Rolette, ND, US 156/E3
Rolfe, Ia, US 155/G2
Rolim de Moura, Braz. 185/F3
Roll, Az, US 149/F4
Rolla, ND, US 156/E3
Rolla, Mo, US 153/J2
Rolle, Swi. 60/C5
Rolle, SAfr. 123/F5
Rolling Fork, Ms, US 162/B4
Rolling Hills, Ab, Can. 145/J2
Rolling Hills Estates, Ca, US 166/F8
Rolling Meadows, Il, US 167/P15
Rolling Prairies (plain), Tx, US 152/D4
Rollingbay, Wa, US 167/B2
Rolo, It. 63/D4
Rom (peak), Ugan. 117/G5
Roma, Swe. 40/H3
Roma (prov.), It. 65/B4
Roma, Austl. 134/C4
Roma, Tx, US 151/E4
Roma (Rome) (cap.), It. 65/B4
Romagna (reg.), It. 67/F1
Romagnano Sesia, It. 62/B2
Romagnat, Fr. 44/E4
Romain (cape), SC, US 163/H4
Romaine (riv.), Fr. 60/B2
Romaine (riv.), Qu, Can. 141/K3
Roman, Rom. 72/D4
Roman, Bul. 51/F4
Roman Kosh (peak), Ukr. 73/H5
Romanche (riv.), Fr. 64/C2
Romang (str.), Indo. 128/B1
Romang (isl.), Indo. 128/B1
Romania (ctry.) 29/G4
Romano (cape), Fl, US 165/H5
Romano Canavese, It. 62/A2
Romano d'Ezzelino, It. 63/E2
Romano di Lombardia, It. 62/C2
Romanovka, Rus. 71/H2
Romanovka, Rus. 78/G1
Romans d'Isonzo, It. 63/G2
Romans-sur-Isère, Fr. 64/B2
Romanshorn, Swi. 61/F2
Romanzof (cape), Ak, US 171/E3
Romashki, Rus. 71/H2
Rombas, Fr. 55/F5
Romblon, Phil. 88/C2
Rome (Roma) (cap.), It. 65/B4
Rome, NY, US 161/J3
Rome, Pa, US 161/H4
Rome, Wi, US 167/N14
Rome, Or, US 146/E2
Rome, Il, US 155/K3
Rome, Ga, US 162/E3
Romenay, Fr. 60/B4
Romeo, Mi, US 160/E3
Romeo, Co, US 149/K2
Romeoville, Il, US 167/P16
Romford (nbrhd.), Eng, UK 30/D2
Römhild, Ger. 58/D2
Romillé, Fr. 56/D4
Romilly-sur-Andelle, Fr. 57/G2
Rommani, Mor. 110/D2
Rommerskirchen, Ger. 55/F1
Romney, WV, US 161/G5
Romney Marsh (phys. reg.), Eng, UK 37/G4
Romny, Ukr. 73/G2
Rømø (isl.), Den. 42/E1
Romodan, Ukr. 73/G3
Romodanovo, Rus. 71/H1
Romoland, Ca, US 166/C3
Romont, Swi. 60/C4
Romorantin-Lanthenay, Fr. 57/G6
Romsey, Eng, UK 37/E5
Romsey, Austl. 133/B3
Rømskog, Nor. 40/D2
Romulus, Mi, US 160/E3
Ron, Viet. 94/D2
Ron (cape), Viet. 87/E5
Ron Phibun, Thai. 94/B4
Ronaldsway (Isle of Man) (arpt.), IM, UK 34/D3
Ronan, Mt, US 145/G4
Roncade, It. 63/F2
Roncador, Braz. 189/F3
Roncador Cay (isl.), Col. 173/F5
Roncador, Serra do (mts.), Braz. 186/B2
Ronceverte, WV, US 163/G2
Ronchamp, Fr. 60/C2
Ronchi dei Legionari (int'l arpt.), It. 63/G2
Ronchi dei Legionari, It. 63/G2
Ronciglione, It. 65/B3
Ronco (riv.), It. 63/F5
Ronco All'Adige, It. 63/E3
Ronco Scrivia, It. 62/B4
Roncoferraro, It. 63/D3
Roncq, Fr. 54/C2
Ronda, Sp. 46/C4
Rondane NP, Nor. 38/D3
Rondo, Ar, US 162/B3
Rondônia (state), Braz. 182/A5
Rondonópolis, Braz. 186/B3
Rondu, Pak. 98/C2
Rong (riv.), China 93/J2
Rong Kwang, Thai. 94/C2
Rong Xian, China 93/K3
Rong'an, China 87/F3
Rongchang, China 86/E2
Rongcheng, China 81/B4
Rongcheng, China 80/G7
Ronge (lake), Sk, Can. 140/F3
Rongelap (isl.), Mrsh. 136/F3
Rongerik (isl.), Mrsh. 136/F3
Rongjiang, China 87/F3
Rongjiawan, China 87/G2
Rongkou, China 87/H2
Rongshui Miaozu Zizhixian, China 93/J2
Rõngu, Est. 41/M2
Roniu (peak), FrPol. 137/X15
Ronkonkoma, NY, US 169/E2
Rønne, Den. 40/F4
Rönne (riv.), Swe. 39/K6
Ronne Ice Shelf, Ant. 192/W
Ronneby, Swe. 40/F3
Rønnede, Den. 39/J7
Ronnenberg, Ger. 53/G4
Rönninge, Swe. 39/A1
Ronquerolles, Fr. 30/J4
Ronsard (cape), Austl. 130/B3
Ronsberg, Ger. 61/G2
Ronse, Belg. 54/C2
Ronuro (plat.), Braz. 185/H4
Roodeport, SAfr. 124/P13
Roodhouse, Il, US 155/J4
Rooiberg (peak), Namb. 124/B2
Roosendaal, Neth. 52/B5
Roosevelt (isl.), Ant. 192/N
Roosevelt (riv.), Braz. 179/C4
Roosevelt (mt.), BC, Can. 140/D3
Roosevelt, Ok, US 152/E3
Roosevelt, NY, US 169/L9
Roosevelt (isl.), NY, US 169/K8
Roosevelt, Az, US 149/G4
Roosevelt, Ut, US 147/J3
Roosevelt, NJ, US 168/D3
Roosville, BC, Can. 144/G3
Root (mt.), Ak, US 171/L4
Root (riv.), Wi, US 167/P14
Root, West Branch (riv.), Wi, US 167/P14
Roper (riv.), Austl. 128/D3
Roper, NC, US 163/J3
Roper Valley, Austl. 128/D3
Ropesville, Tx, US 152/C4
Roque Pérez, Arg. 191/J11
Roquebillière, Fr. 64/D4
Roquebrune-Cap-Martin, Fr. 64/D5
Roquebrune-sur-Argens, Fr. 64/C6
Roquefort-la-Bédoule, Fr. 64/B6
Roquemaure, Fr. 64/A4
Roquesteron, Fr. 64/D5
Roquetas de Mar, Sp. 46/D4
Roquevaire, Fr. 64/B6
Roraima (peak), Ven. 181/F3
Roraima (state), Braz. 181/F4
Rørby, Den. 39/H7
Rori, India 98/C5

Rorke's – Saint A
Map Section
266
267

Rorke's Drift, SAfr. 125/E3
Rorke's Drift Battlesite, SAfr. 125/E3
Rorketon, Mb, Can. 156/E2
Røros, Nor. 38/D3
Rorschach, Swi. 61/F3
Rosa, La, US 164/B2
Rosà, It. 63/E2
Rosa (lake), Bahm. 177/H1
Rosa (cape), Alg. 112/L6
Rosa Punta (pt.), Mex. 174/C3
Rosa Zárate, Ecu. 180/B4
Rosablanche (peak), Swi. 60/D5
Rosal, Sp. 46/A2
Rosales, Mex. 151/B3
Rosalia, Ks, US 153/F2
Rosalia, Wa, US 144/F4
Rosalie (lake), Fl, US 164/N8
Rosalina, Par. 189/F2
Rosamond, Ca, US 148/C3
Rosamorada, Mex. 174/D4
Rosanna (riv.), Aus. 61/G3
Rosans, Fr. 64/B4
Rosario, Arg. 190/E2
Rosario, Phil. 88/C1
Rosario, Uru. 191/K11
Rosario, Phil. 88/E7
Rosario (riv.), Arg. 188/C3
Rosario, Par. 189/E3
Rosario, Bol. 185/E4
Rosário, Braz. 183/E3
Rosario, Mex. 174/D4
Rosario, Mex. 174/C3
Rosario de la Frontera, Arg. 188/C3
Rosario de Lerma, Arg. 188/C3
Rosario del Tala, Arg. 191/J10
Rosário do Sul, Braz. 189/F4
Rosário Oeste, Braz. 185/G4
Rosarno, It. 48/D3
Rosas, Col. 180/B4
Rosas (gulf), Sp. 47/G1
Rosate, It. 62/C3
Rosay, Fr. 30/G5
Rosbach vor der Höhe, Ger. 58/B2
Rosche, Ger. 53/H3
Roscoe, Mo, US 153/H2
Roscoe, Il, US 155/K2
Roscoe, Tx, US 151/D1
Roscoff, Fr. 56/B3
Roscommon, Ire. 32/B2
Roscommon (co.), Ire. 32/B2
Roscommon, Mi, US 160/D2
Roscrea, Ire. 32/C4
Rosdorf, Ger. 53/G5
Rose (isl.), ASam. 137/J6
Rose (peak), Az, US 149/H4
Rose Belle, Mrts. 125/T15
Rose Bud, Ar, US 153/H3
Rose City, Mi, US 160/D2
Rose Hill, Ks, US 153/F2
Rose Hill, Ms, US 162/C4
Rose Hill, Va, US 163/F2
Rose Lodge, Or, US 146/B1
Rose Valley, Sk, Can. 156/C1
Roseau, Mn, US 156/G3
Roseau (riv.), Mn, US 156/F3
Roseau (cap.), Dom. 173/N9
Roseau River, Mb, Can. 156/F3
Roseaux, Haiti 177/H2
Rosebery, Austl. 132/C4
Roseboro, NC, US 163/H3
Rosebud, Ga, US 163/N7
Rosebud, Tx, US 151/F2
Rosebud (riv.), Ab, Can. 145/H2
Rosebud, Mt, US 145/L4
Rosebud (cr.), Mt, US 145/L4
Rosebud Ind. Res., SD, US 154/D2
Roseburg, Or, US 146/B2
Rosedale, Ca, US 148/C3
Rosedale, Ms, US 162/B4
Rosedale, Va, US 163/G2
Rosedale, Austl. 133/C4
Rosedale, Md, US 168/B5
Roseglen, ND, US 156/D4
Rosehearty, Sc, UK 33/D1
Roseira, Braz. 187/L7
Roseires (dam), Sudan 117/G3
Roseisle, Mb, Can. 156/E3
Roseland, La, US 164/C2
Roseland, NJ, US 169/H8
Roselette, Aiguille de (peak), Fr. 60/C6
Roselle, NJ, US 169/H9
Roselle, Il, US 167/P16
Roselle Park, NJ, US 169/H9
Rosemark, Tn, US 162/C3
Rosemead, Ca, US 166/F7
Rosemère, Qu, Can. 159/N6
Rosemount, Oh, US 163/F1
Rosemount, Mn, US 157/P7
Rosenberg, Tx, US 151/G3
Rosenberg, Ger. 58/D4
Rosenfeld, Ger. 61/E1
Rosenhayn, NJ, US 168/C5
Rosenhof, Sk, Can. 145/L2
Rosenort, Mb, Can. 156/F3
Rosepine, La, US 164/B2
Roses, Sp. 47/G1
Roseto, Pa, US 168/C2
Roseto degli Abruzzi, It. 65/D2
Rosetown, Sk, Can. 145/L2
Rosetta, Ms, US 164/C2
Rosetta (Massabb Rashīd) (mouth), Egypt 113/B1
Rosetta Branch (riv.), Egypt 104/B4
Roseville, Oh, US 160/E5
Roseville, Mi, US 167/G6
Roseville, Ca, US 146/C4
Roseville, Il, US 155/J3
Roseville, Mn, US 157/P6
Rosevine, Tx, US 151/H2
Rosewood, Austl. 128/C4
Rosh Ha'ayin, Isr. 105/B4
Rosh Hakarmel (pt.), Isr. 105/B3
Rosh Haniqra (pt.), Isr. 105/C2
Rosh Pina (arpt.), Isr. 105/D3
Rosh Pinah, Namb. 124/B2
Rosh Pinna, Isr. 105/D3
Rosharon, Tx, US 151/M9
Rosheim, Fr. 60/D1
Roshkhvār, Iran 101/G2
Rosholt, SD, US 156/F5
Rosholt, Wi, US 155/K1
Rosiclare, Il, US 162/C2
Rosières-en-Santerre, Fr. 54/B4
Rosignano Marittimo, It. 62/D7
Rosignano Solvay, It. 62/D7
Rosignol, Guy. 182/B1
Roşiori de Vede, Rom. 51/G3
Rositsa, Bul. 51/H4
Roskilde, Den. 40/E4
Roskilde (co.), Den. 40/D4
Roskilde (inlet), Den. 39/H7
Roslags-Bro, Swe. 39/B1
Roslags-Kulla, Swe. 39/B1
Roslags-Näsby, Swe. 39/B1
Roslavl', Rus. 70/E1
Roslev, Den. 40/C3
Roslyakova, Rus. 68/G1
Roslyatino, Rus. 69/K4
Roslyn, Wa, US 144/D4
Rosmalen, Neth. 52/C5
Rosmaninhal, Port. 46/B3
Rosneath, Sc, UK 33/B4
Rosny-sous-Bois, Fr. 30/K5
Rosny-sur-Seine, Fr. 57/G2
Rosolina, It. 63/F3
Rosolini, It. 48/D4
Rosporden, Fr. 56/B5
Rösrath, Ger. 55/G2
Ross (dist.), Sc, UK 33/C1
Ross (isl.), Ant. 192/M
Ross (sea), Ant. 192/P
Ross, Austl. 132/C4
Ross (mt.), NZ 135/C3
Ross, NZ 135/B3
Ross (pt.), On, Can. 160/V8
Ross, Tx, US 151/F2
Ross (lake), Wa, US 144/D3
Ross Barnett (res.), Ms, US 162/C4
Ross Carbery, Ire. 32/A6
Ross Ice Shelf, Ant. 192/N
Ross Lake NRA, Wa, US 144/D3
Ross River, Yk, Can. 171/M3
Ross-on-Wye, Eng, UK 36/D3
Rossa, Swi. 61/F5
Rossa (peak), It. 45/K3
Rossall (pt.), Eng, UK 35/E4
Rossano Stazione, It. 48/E3
Rossano Veneto, It. 63/E2
Rossbach, Ger. 59/F5
Rossberg (peak), Fr. 60/D2
Rossburn, Mb, Can. 156/D2
Rossdorf, Ger. 58/B3
Rossel (isl.), PNG 136/E6
Rosselange, Fr. 55/F5
Rosser, Mb, Can. 156/F3
Rosser, Tx, US 150/L7
Rosshaupten, Ger. 61/G2
Rossie, NY, US 161/J2
Rossiglione, It. 62/B4
Rossignol (lake), NS, Can. 158/E3
Rössing, Namb. 122/B4
Rössjöholmsån (riv.), Swe. 39/J6
Rosskeeragh (pt.), Ire. 31/P9
Rossland, BC, Can. 144/F3
Rosslare (bay), Ire. 32/D5
Rosslare (pt.), Ire. 32/D5
Rosslare, Ire. 32/D5
Rosslea, NI, UK 32/C1
Rosslyn Village, On, Can. 157/K3
Rosso, Mrta. 114/B2
Rossosh', Rus. 73/K2
Rossport, On, Can. 157/L3
Rossstock (peak), Swi. 61/E4
Rosstal, Ger. 58/D4
Rosston, Ar, US 153/H4
Rossville, Il, US 160/C4
Røst, Nor. 38/E2
Rostāq, Iran 103/H5
Rostāq, Afg. 99/A4
Rostellan, Ire. 32/B6
Rosthern, Sk, Can. 145/L1
Rostock, Ger. 40/E4
Rostov, Rus. 68/H4
Rostov (int'l arpt.), Rus. 73/K4
Rostov, Rus. 73/K4
Rostovskaya Oblast, Rus. 71/G2
Rostrenen, Fr. 56/B4
Rostrevor, NI, UK 34/B3
Roswell, NM, US 152/B4
Roswell, Ga, US 163/M6
Rot (riv.), Ger. 42/E4
Rota (isl.), NMar. 136/D3
Rota, Sp. 46/B4
Rotan, Tx, US 152/D4
Rote Wand (peak), Aus. 61/F3
Rotebro, Swe. 39/A1
Rotenburg, Ger. 53/G2
Rotenburg an der Fulda, Ger. 53/G7
Roter Main (riv.), Ger. 42/F3
Rötgen, Ger. 55/F2
Roth (riv.), Ger. 61/G1
Roth bei Nürnberg, Ger. 58/E4
Rothaargebirge (mts.), Ger. 53/F6
Rothau, Fr. 60/D1
Rothbury, Eng, UK 33/E6
Röthenbach an der Pegnitz, Ger. 58/E4
Rothenberg, Ger. 58/B3
Rothenburg, Swi. 61/E3
Rothenburg ob der Tauber, Ger. 58/D4
Rothera, UK, Ant. 192/V
Rotherham, Eng, UK 35/G5
Rotherham (co.), Eng, UK 35/G5
Rothes, Sc, UK 33/C1
Rothesay, Sc, UK 33/A5
Rotheux-Rimière, Belg. 55/E2
Rothsay, Mn, US 156/F4
Rothschild, Wi, US 155/K1
Rothwell, Eng, UK 35/G4
Rothwell, Eng, UK 37/F2
Roti (isl.), Indo. 91/F6
Rotifunk, SLeo. 114/B4
Roto, Austl. 133/B1
Rotonda, Fl, US 165/G4
Rotondo (peak), It. 65/C2
Rotorua, NZ 135/D2
Rotselaar, Belg. 55/D2
Rott (riv.), Ger. 42/G4
Rott am Inn, Ger. 59/F7
Rottach-Egern, Ger. 42/F5
Rotte (riv.), Fr. 55/F6
Rotten (riv.), Swi. 60/E5
Rottenacker, Ger. 61/F1
Röttenbach, Ger. 58/E4
Rottenberg, Ger. 58/C2
Rottenburg am Neckar, Ger. 58/B6
Rottenburg an der Laaber, Ger. 59/F5
Rotterdam, Neth. 52/B5
Rotterdam (int'l arpt.), Neth. 52/B5
Rottershausen, Ger. 58/D2
Rotthalmünster, Ger. 59/G6
Rottingdean, Eng, UK 37/F5
Röttingen, Ger. 58/C3
Rottne, Swe. 40/F3
Rottnest (isl.), Austl. 130/B5
Rottofreno, It. 62/C3
Rottum (riv.), Ger. 61/F1
Rottumeroog (isl.), Neth. 52/D1
Rottumerplaat (isl.), Neth. 52/D1
Rottweil, Ger. 61/E1
Rotuma (isl.), Fiji 136/G6
Rötz, Ger. 59/F4
Roubaix, Fr. 54/C2
Roubion (riv.), Fr. 44/F4
Roudnice nad Labem, Czh. 59/H2
Rouen, Fr. 57/G2
Rouffach, Fr. 60/D2
Rougé, Fr. 56/D5
Rouge (riv.), Qu, Can. 141/J4
Rouge, Middle (riv.), Mi, US 167/F7
Rougemont, Fr. 60/C3
Rougemont-le-Château, Fr. 60/C2
Rough (riv.), Ky, US 162/D2
Rough River (lake), Ky, US 162/D2
Rouleau, Sk, Can. 156/B2
Roullet-Saint-Estèphe, Fr. 44/D4
Round (hill), Oh, US 160/F4
Round (hill), In, US 162/E1
Round (hill), Ky, US 162/E2
Round (hill), Pa, US 168/B3
Round Butte (dam), Or, US 146/C1
Round Hill (pt.), Austl. 134/C4
Round Lake, Il, US 167/P15
Round Lake Beach, Il, US 167/P15
Round Lake Park, Il, US 167/P15
Round Mountain, Nv, US 146/E4
Round Mountain, Tx, US 150/E2
Round Rock, Tx, US 151/F2
Round Spring, Mo, US 153/J2
Round Top, Tx, US 151/F2
Round Valley (res.), NJ, US 168/D2
Round Valley Ind. Res., Ca, US 146/B4
Roundup, Mt, US 145/K4
Roundway (hill), Eng, UK 36/E4
Rounthwaite, Mb, Can. 156/E3
Roura, FrG. 182/C1
Rousay (isl.), Sc, UK 31/V14
Rouse Hill (nbrhd.), Austl. 134/G8
Rouses Point, NY, US 161/K2
Rouseville, Pa, US 161/G4
Rousies, Fr. 54/D3
Rousínov, Czh. 43/J4
Rousset, Fr. 64/B6
Roussillon, Fr. 64/B5
Roussillon, Fr. 64/A2
Routhierville, Qu, Can. 158/D1
Rouvre (riv.), Fr. 57/E3
Rouvres, Fr. 30/M4
Rouvroy, Belg. 55/E4
Rouxmesnil-Bouteilles, Fr. 57/G1
Rouxville, SAfr. 124/D3
Rouyn-Noranda, Qu, Can. 141/J4
Rovaniemi (int'l arpt.), Fin. 68/E2
Rovaniemi, Fin. 68/E2
Rovasenda, It. 62/B2
Rovato, It. 62/C2
Roven'ki, Rus. 73/K3
Roven'ky, Ukr. 73/K3
Rover, Mo, US 153/J2
Rover, Ar, US 153/H3
Roverbella, It. 63/D3
Rovereto, It. 61/H6
Rovereto, It. 63/D4
Roviano, It. 65/C3
Rovieng Tbong, Camb. 94/D3
Rovigo, It. 63/E3
Rovigo (prov.), It. 63/E2
Rovinj, Cro. 63/G3
Rovira, Col. 183/K8
Rovnoye, Rus. 71/H2
Rovuma (riv.), Moz. 119/A4
Rowell, Ar, US 153/H4
Rowena, Austl. 132/D1
Rowena, Tx, US 151/D2
Rowland, NC, US 163/H3
Rowledge, Eng, UK 30/A3
Rowlett (cr.), Tx, US 150/L6
Rowlett, Tx, US 150/L7
Rowley (isl.), Nun, Can. 141/J2
Rowley Shoals (isl.) 127/A2
Rowta, India 97/J2
Roxa (isl.), GBis. 114/B4
Roxas, Phil. 88/C3
Roxas, Phil. 88/C1
Roxas, Phil. 88/B3
Roxboro, NC, US 163/H2
Roxborough, Trin. 181/F2
Roxburgh, NZ 135/B4
Roxbury, Ks, US 153/F1
Roxbury, NY, US 161/J3
Roxen (lake), Swe. 40/F2
Roxie, Ms, US 164/C2
Roxo (cape), Sen. 114/A3
Roxton, Tx, US 153/G4
Roxwell, Eng, UK 30/E1
Roy, NM, US 152/B3
Roy, Wa, US 167/B3
Roy, Ut, US 147/G3
Roy, Mt, US 145/K4
Roy Hill, Austl. 130/C2
Roya (riv.), Fr. 45/G5
Royal (canal), Ire. 35/B3
Royal Botanical Garden, On, Can. 160/T9
Royal Center, In, US 160/C4
Royal Chitwan NP, Nepal 97/E2
Royal City, Wa, US 144/E4
Royal (gorge), Co, US 152/B1
Royal Natal NP, SAfr. 124/E3
Royal NP, Austl. 132/D2
Royal Oak, Mi, US 167/F7
Royal Paekje Tombs, SKor. 81/D4
Royal Palm Beach, Fl, US 164/P9
Royal Pines, NC, US 163/F3
Royal Tombs, Viet. 94/D2
Royal Tunbridge Wells, Eng, UK 37/G4
Royalton, Mn, US 157/G5
Royalton, Vt, US 161/K3
Royalton, Pa, US 168/B3
Royalty, Tx, US 151/C2
Royan, Fr. 44/C4
Roydon, Eng, UK 30/D1
Roye, Fr. 60/C2
Roye, Fr. 54/B4
Royersford, Pa, US 168/C3
Røyken, Nor. 40/D2
Royse City, Tx, US 150/L7
Royston, Eng, UK 35/G4
Royston, Ga, US 163/F3
Royston, Eng, UK 37/F2
Royston, BC, Can. 144/B3
Royton, Eng, UK 35/F4
Rožaj, Yugo. 50/E4
Rozay-en-Brie, Fr. 54/B6
Rozdil'na, Ukr. 72/F4
Rozdol'ne, Ukr. 73/G5
Rozel, Chl, UK 56/C2
Rozellville, Wi, US 155/J1
Rozenburg, Neth. 52/B5
Rozendo, Moz. 123/H3
Rozhaya (riv.), Rus. 69/W9
Rozhyshche, Ukr. 72/C2
Rozivka, Ukr. 73/J4
Rožmberk (lake), Czh. 59/H4
Rožmital pod Třemšínem, Czh. 59/G3
Rožňava, Slvk. 43/L4
Roztoczański PN, Pol. 72/B2
Roztoky, Czh. 59/H2
Rozzano, It. 62/C3
Rrëshen, Alb. 49/F2
Rrogozhinë, Alb. 49/F2
Rtishchevo, Rus. 71/G1
Ru (cape), Malay. 89/C2
Ruabon, Wal, UK 35/E6
Ruacana (falls), Ang. 122/B3
Ruacana, Namb. 122/B3
Ruaha NP, Tanz. 119/A3
Ruamahanga (riv.), NZ 135/J9
Ruapuke (isl.), NZ 135/B4
Ruatapu, NZ 135/B3
Ruawai, NZ 135/C2
Rub' al Khali (des.), SAr. 77/D7
Rubeho (mts.), Tanz. 119/B3
Rubelles, Fr. 30/L6
Rubeshibe, Japan 82/C2
Rubi (riv.), D.R. Congo 121/F2
Rubi, D.R. Congo 121/F2
Rubí, Sp. 47/L7
Rubiataba, Braz. 186/C2
Rubidoux, Ca, US 166/C3
Rubiera, It. 63/D4
Rubigen, Swi. 60/D4
Rubim, Braz. 187/E3
Rubizhne, Ukr. 73/K3
Rubondo NP, Tanz. 121/G3
Rubonia, Fl, US 164/K8
Rubottom, Ok, US 153/F4
Rubřina (riv.), Czh. 59/G4
Rubtsovsk, Rus. 99/D1
Rubuga, Tanz. 119/A3
Ruby, Ak, US 171/G3
Ruby, La, US 164/B2
Ruby (lake), Nv, US 146/F3
Ruby (mts.), Nv, US 146/F3
Ruby (riv.), Mt, US 147/G1
Ruby Lake NWR, Nv, US 146/F3
Ruby Valley, Nv, US 146/F3
Rubyvale, Austl. 134/B3
Rucava, Lat. 41/J3
Ruch'i, Rus. 68/J2
Rucphen, Neth. 52/B5
Ruda Woda (lake), Pol. 43/K2
Rudall River NP, Austl. 130/D2
Rūdarpur, India 96/D2
Rudauli, India 96/C2
Ruddell, Sk, Can. 145/L1
Ruddington, Eng, UK 35/G6
Rudensk, Bela. 41/M5
Rüdersdorf, Ger. 42/Q7
Rüdesheim, Ger. 55/G4
Rüdesheim, Ger. 55/G4
Rudewa, Tanz. 119/A4
Rudi, Tanz. 119/B3
Rudiano, It. 62/C3
Rūdiškės, Lith. 41/L4
Rudkøbing, Den. 40/D4
Rudky, Ukr. 72/B3
Rudnaya Pristan', Rus. 79/M3
Rudnik, Pol. 43/M3
Rudnya, Rus. 41/P4
Rudnytsya, Ukr. 72/E3
Rūdnyy, Kaz. 69/P5
Rudolf (isl.), Rus. 74/F1
Rudolf (Turkana) (lake), Kenya 107/F4
Rudolph, Wi, US 155/K1
Rudong, China 80/E4
Rudozem, Bul. 49/J2
Ruds-Vedby, Den. 39/H7
Rūdsar, Iran 103/G2
Rudston, Eng, UK 35/H3
Rudyard, Mi, US 160/D1
Rudyard, Mt, US 145/J3
Rue, Swi. 60/C4
Rue (pt.), NI, UK 34/B1
Rue, Fr. 54/A3
Rueda, Sp. 46/C2
Rueil-Malmaison, Fr. 30/J5
Ruell (riv.), Sc, UK 33/A4
Ruelle-sur-Touvre, Fr. 44/D4
Ruen (peak), Bul. 50/F4
Ruenya (riv.), Zim. 123/G3
Ruetzbach (riv.), Aus. 61/H3
Rufā'ah, Sudan 117/G2
Rufe, Ok, US 153/G3
Ruffano, It. 49/F3
Ruffec, Fr. 44/D3
Ruffin, SC, US 163/G4
Rufiji (riv.), Tanz. 107/F5
Rufina, It. 63/E6
Rufino, Arg. 190/E2
Rufisque, Sen. 114/A3
Rufunsa, Zam. 123/F2
Rufus Woods (lake), Wa, US 144/E3
Rugāji, Lat. 41/M3
Rugao, China 80/E4
Rugby, ND, US 156/E3
Rugby, Eng, UK 37/E2
Rugeley, Eng, UK 37/E1
Rügen (isl.), Ger. 40/E4
Ruggell, Lcht. 61/F3
Rugles, Fr. 57/F3
Ruḩama, Isr. 105/B5
Ruhmannsfelden, Ger. 59/F5
Ruhnu saar (isl.), Lat. 41/K3
Ruhr (reg.), Ger. 42/E3
Ruhr (riv.), Ger. 42/D3
Ruhrgebiet (phys. reg.), Ger. 52/D6
Ruhstorf an der Rott, Ger. 59/F5
Ruicheng, China 80/B4
Ruidosa, Tx, US 151/B3
Ruidoso, NM, US 152/B4
Ruihong, China 87/H2
Ruinen, Neth. 52/D3
Ruins of Cahabra, Al, US 162/D4
Ruipa, Tanz. 119/B4
Ruiru, Kenya 119/B2
Ruiselede, Belg. 54/C1
Ruislip (nbrhd.), Eng, UK 30/B2
Ruiz, Mex. 174/D4
Rujen (peak), FYROM 49/H1
Rūjiena, Lat. 41/L3
Ruki (riv.), D.R. Congo 107/D5
Rukua, Indo. 128/B1
Rukumkot, Nepal 96/D1
Rukuru, South (riv.), Tanz. 123/G1
Rukwa (prov.), Tanz. 119/A3
Rukwa (lake), Tanz. 107/F5
Rule, Tx, US 152/E4
Ruleville, Ms, US 162/B4
Rulhieres (cape), Austl. 128/B3
Rulles (riv.), Belg. 55/E4
Rülzheim, Ger. 58/B4
Rum, Aus. 61/H3
Rum (riv.), Mn, US 157/H5
Rum Cay (isl.), Bahm. 173/G3
Rum Jungle, Austl. 128/C3
Ruma, Yugo. 50/D3
Ruma Bāzār, Bang. 86/B4
Ruma NP, Kenya 119/A2
Rumāḩ, SAr. 100/E3
Rumán, Ven. 181/F3
Rumaylah, Sudan 117/G2
Rumaysh, Leb. 105/C2
Rumbalara, Austl. 131/G3
Rumbek, Sudan 117/F4
Rumeli Hisar, Turk. 103/N6
Rumelifeneri, Turk. 103/N6
Rumes, Belg. 54/C2
Rumia, Pol. 40/H4
Rumilly, Fr. 60/B6
Rümlang, Swi. 61/E3
Rumley, Tx, US 151/E2
Rumney, NH, US 161/L3
Rumney, Wal, UK 36/C3
Rumoi, Japan 82/B2
Rumphi, Malw. 119/A4
Rumson, NJ, US 168/E3
Rumst, Belg. 55/D1
Rumuruti, Kenya 119/B1
Run (riv.), Mn, US 155/H1
Runabay (pt.), NI, UK 34/B1
Runan, China 80/C4
Runanga, NZ 135/B3
Runaway (cape), NZ 135/D2
Runcorn, Eng, UK 35/F5
Rundēni, Lat. 41/M3
Runding, Ger. 59/F4
Rundu, Namb. 122/C3
Runere, Tanz. 119/A2
Runge, Tx, US 151/F3
Rungsted, Den. 39/J7
Rungu, D.R. Congo 121/F2
Rungwa (riv.), Tanz. 119/A3
Rungwa, Tanz. 119/A3
Rungwa, Tanz. 121/G4
Rungwa Game Reserve, Tanz. 119/A3
Rungwe (peak), Tanz. 119/A4
Runio (riv.), Fr. 56/C5
Runkel, Ger. 58/B2
Runmarö (isl.), Swe. 39/B1
Runn (lake), Swe. 40/F1
Runnelstown, Ms, US 164/D2
Runnemede, NJ, US 168/C4
Running (cr.), Co, US 152/B1
Running Springs, Ca, US 166/C2
Running Water Draw (riv.), Tx,NM, US 152/C3
Runwell, Eng, UK 30/E2
Ruo (riv.), China 75/K5
Ruokolahti, Fin. 41/N1
Ruoqiang, China 99/E4
Rupat (isl.), Indo. 90/B3
Rupea, Rom. 51/G2
Rupel (riv.), Belg. 55/D1
Rupert, Id, US 147/G2
Rupert (riv.), Qu, Can. 141/J3
Rupert, Ga, US 162/E4
Rupert, WV, US 163/G2
Rupert House (Waskaganish), Qu, Can. 141/J3
Rūpnagar, India 98/D4
Ruppichteroth, Ger. 55/G2
Rupt-sur-Moselle, Fr. 60/C2
Rupununi (riv.), Guy. 181/G4
Rur (riv.), Ger. 42/D3
Rur-Strasse (lake), Ger. 55/F2
Rural Hall, NC, US 163/G2
Rural Retreat, Va, US 163/G2
Rurrenabaque, Bol. 185/E4
Rurutu (isl.), FrPol. 137/K7
Rusagonis, NB, Can. 158/D3
Rusape, Zim. 123/G3
Rüschegg, Swi. 60/D4
Rüschlikon, Swi. 61/E3
Ruscom (riv.), On, Can. 167/G7
Ruse (pol. reg.), Bul. 49/K1
Ruse, Bul. 51/G4
Rusera, India 97/F3
Rush, Co, US 152/B1
Rush, Ire. 34/B4
Rush (cr.), Co, US 154/C4
Rush City, Mn, US 157/H5
Rush Springs, Ok, US 153/F3
Rushall, Eng, UK 37/E4
Rushan, China 80/E3
Rushden, Eng, UK 37/F2
Rushford, Mn, US 155/J2
Rushoon, Nf, Can. 159/K2
Rushville, In, US 160/D5
Rushville, Il, US 155/J3
Rushville, Ne, US 154/C2
Rushworth, Austl. 133/B3
Rusk, Tx, US 150/G2
Ruskin, Fl, US 164/L8
Ruskington, Eng, UK 35/H5
Ruskovce, Slvk. 50/C1
Rusnė, Lith. 41/J4
Russ, Fr. 60/D1
Russas, Braz. 183/G4
Russbach (riv.), Aus. 51/N7
Russell, Ks, US 152/E1
Russell, Mb, Can. 156/D2
Russell, On, Can. 161/J2
Russell, NY, US 161/J2
Russell, NZ 135/C1
Russell (isls.), Austl. 134/F7
Russell (isl.), Nun, Can. 141/R7
Russell (res.), SC, US 163/F3
Russell Cave Nat'l Mon., Al, US 162/E3
Russell Springs, Ky, US 162/E2
Russells Point, Oh, US 160/E4
Russellville, Mo, US 153/H1
Russellville, Ar, US 153/H3
Russellville, Ky, US 162/D2
Russellville, Tn, US 163/F2
Russellville, Al, US 162/D3
Rüsselsheim, Ger. 58/B3
Russi, It. 63/F5
Russia (ctry.) 74/H3
Russian (riv.), Ca, US 146/B4
Russian Mission, Ak, US 171/F3
Russkaya, Rus., Ant. 192/Q
Russkiy Brod, Rus. 70/F1
Rust'avi, Geo. 71/H4
Rustburg, Va, US 163/H2
Rustenburg, SAfr. 123/E5
Ruston, La, US 153/H4
Ruston, Wa, US 167/C3
Rusutjärvi, Fin. 39/E4
Rutana, Buru. 121/G3
Rute, Sp. 46/C4
Rutenga, Zim. 123/F4
Ruth, Ms, US 164/C2
Ruth, Nv, US 147/F4
Rüthen, Ger. 53/F6
Rutherford, NJ, US 169/J8
Rutherford, Tn, US 162/C2
Rutherford, Al, US 162/E4
Rutherfordton, NC, US 163/G3
Rutherglen, Sc, UK 33/B5
Rutherglen, On, Can. 161/G1
Rutherglen, Austl. 133/C3
Rutheron, NM, US 149/J2
Rüthi, Swi. 61/F3
Ruthin, Wal, UK 35/E5
Ruthven, On, Can. 167/G7
Rüti, Swi. 61/F4
Rüti, Swi. 61/E3
Rutland, ND, US 156/F4
Rutland, Vt, US 161/K3
Rutland, Oh, US 163/F1
Rutland Plains, Austl. 134/A1
Rutland Water (res.), Eng, UK 37/F1
Rutledge, Mn, US 157/H4
Rutledge, Tn, US 163/F2
Rutog, China 99/C5
Rutshuru (riv.), D.R. Congo 121/G3
Rutshuru, D.R. Congo 121/G3
Rutten, Neth. 52/C3
Ruukki, Fin. 68/E2
Ruurlo, Neth. 52/D4
Ruvo di Puglia, It. 48/E2
Ruvu (riv.), Tanz. 119/B3
Ruvu, Tanz. 119/B3
Ruvu, Tanz. 119/B3
Ruvubu (riv.), Buru. 121/G3
Ruvuma (prov.), Tanz. 119/B4
Ruvuma (riv.), Tanz. 107/F6
Ruwa, Zim. 123/F3
Ruwāndūz, Iraq 103/F2
Ruwenzori (range), Ugan. 121/G2
Ruwī, Oman 101/G4
Ruxton, Co, US 152/C2
Ruy, Fr. 64/B1
Ruya (riv.), Zim. 123/F3
Ruyang, China 80/C4
Ruyigi, Buru. 121/G3
Ruyuan Yaozu Zizhixian, China 87/G3
Ruzayevka, Rus. 71/H1
Ruzhany, Bela. 43/N2
Ruzhyn, Ukr. 72/E3
Ruzizi (riv.), D.R. Congo 121/G3
Ružomberok, Slvk. 43/K4
Ruzyně (int'l arpt.), Czh. 59/H2
Ruzzah (peak), Egypt 113/B4
Rwanda (ctry.) 107/F5
Rwenjaza, Ugan. 121/G2
Rwenzori NP, Ugan. 121/G3
Ryabobskiy, Rus. 73/L2
Ryan, Ok, US 153/F3
Ryan (inlet), Sc, UK 34/C2
Ryan (mt.), Austl. 134/A1
Ryan (mt.), Austl. 133/D1
Ryazan', Rus. 68/H5
Ryazanskaya Oblast, Rus. 68/H5
Ryazhsk, Rus. 70/G1
Rybachiy (pen.), Rus. 38/K1
Rybinsk, Rus. 68/H4
Rybinsk (res.), Rus. 29/J2
Rybnik, Pol. 43/K3
Rybnoye, Rus. 68/H5
Ryd, Swe. 40/F3
Rydaholm, Swe. 40/F3
Ryde, Ca, US 167/L10
Ryde (nbrhd.), Austl. 134/H8
Ryde, Eng, UK 37/E5
Rydebäck, Swe. 39/J7
Rydet, Swe. 40/D3
Rye, Co, US 152/B2
Rye, Tx, US 151/G2
Rye, Ar, US 153/J4
Rye (riv.), Eng, UK 35/H3
Rye, NY, US 169/L8
Rye (bay), Eng, UK 37/G5
Rye, Eng, UK 37/G5
Rye Brook, NY, US 169/L7
Rye Patch (dam), Nv, US 146/D3
Rye Patch (res.), Nv, US 146/D3
Ryegate, Mt, US 145/K4
Rygge, Nor. 40/D2
Ryki, Pol. 43/L3
Ryley, Ab, Can. 145/H1
Ryl'sk, Rus. 73/H2
Rylstone, Austl. 133/D1
Ryn-Peski (plain), Kaz. 71/J2
Ryōkami, Japan 83/B2
Ryökkä, Fin. 39/E4
Ryōtsu, Japan 85/F1
Ryōzen-yama (peak), Japan 83/K5
Rypin, Pol. 43/K2
Rysy (peak), Pol. 43/L4
Ryton, Eng, UK 35/G2
Ryton-on-Dunsmore, Eng, UK 37/E2
Rytterknægten (peak), Den. 40/F4
Ryttylä, Fin. 39/E4
Ryūgasaki, Japan 85/G3
Ryukyu (isls.), Japan 77/M7
Ryūō, Japan 83/K5
Ryūō, Japan 83/B2
Rzeszów, Pol. 43/M3
Rzhev, Rus. 68/G4
Rzhyshchiv, Ukr. 72/F3

S

's-Graveland, Neth. 52/C4
's Gravendeel, Neth. 52/B5
's-Gravenhage (The Hague) (cap.), Neth. 52/B4
's Heerenberg, Neth. 52/D5
's Hertogenbosch, Neth. 52/C5
S'ør-Trøndelag (co.), Nor. 38/D3
Sa, Thai. 94/C2
Şā al Ḩajar (ruin), Egypt 113/B3
Sa Dec, Viet. 94/D4
Sa Pa, Viet. 94/C1
Saab (int'l arpt.), Swe. 40/F2
Sa'ad, Isr. 105/B6
Sääksjärvi (lake), Fin. 41/K1
Saal an der Donau, Ger. 59/E5
Saalbach (riv.), Ger. 58/B4
Saaldorf, Ger. 59/E2
Saale (riv.), Ger. 42/F3
Saalfelden am Steinernen Meer, Aus. 45/K3
Saâne (riv.), Fr. 57/F1
Saane (riv.), Swi. 60/D5
Saanen, Swi. 60/D5
Saanta (peak), Kenya 119/B1
Saar (riv.), Ger. 55/F5
Saarbrücken, Ger. 55/F5
Saarbrücken (Ensheim) (arpt.), Ger. 55/G5
Saarburg, Ger. 55/F4
Sääre, Est. 41/K3
Saaremaa (isl.), Est. 68/D4
Saarland (state), Ger. 45/G2
Saarlouis, Ger. 55/F5
Saas, Swi. 61/F4
Saas Fee, Swi. 60/D5
Saastal (valley), Swi. 60/D5
Sa'ata, Sudan 117/F2
Saatlı, Azer. 103/G2
Saatta, Erit. 117/H1
Sab (riv.), Camb. 94/D3
Saba (isl.), NAm. 173/J4
Saba (isl.), NAnt. 173/N8
Šabac, Yugo. 50/D3
Sabadell, Sp. 47/L6
Sabae, Japan 84/E3
Sabah (reg.), Malay. 77/L9
Sabalgarh, India 96/A2
Sabana, Cuba 177/H1
Sabana (arch.), Bang. 177/F1
Sabana de Uchire, Ven. 181/E2
Sabanalarga, Col. 180/C2
Sabanalarga, Col. 180/C3
Sabancuy, Mex. 176/D2
Sabaneta, Ven. 180/D2
Sabang, Indo. 89/A1
Sabanita, Pan. 177/G4
Sabará, Braz. 186/E3
Sabaragamuwa (prov.), SrL. 95/D5
Sabasţīyah, WBnk. 105/C4
Sabat (riv.), Sudan 107/F4
Sabato (riv.), It. 65/D5
Sabaudia, It. 65/C5
Sabaudia (lake), It. 65/C5
Sabaya, Bol. 188/B1
Sabbio Chiese, It. 62/D2
Sabbioneta, It. 62/D4
Sabdê, China 86/D2
Sabetha, Ks, US 155/G4
Sabhā, Libya 108/B3
Sabie (riv.), Moz. 125/F2
Sabierivier (riv.), SAfr. 123/F5
Sabile, Lat. 41/K3
Sabin, Mn, US 156/F4
Sabinal (riv.), Tx, US 151/E3
Sabinal, Tx, US 151/E3
Sabiñánigo, Sp. 47/E1
Sabinas, Mex. 151/D4
Sabinas (riv.), Mex. 172/A2
Sabinas Hidalgo, Mex. 151/D4
Sabine (lake), La, US 151/H3
Sabine (riv.), La, US 172/C1
Sabine NWR, La, US 151/H3
Sabine Pass, Tx, US 151/H3
Sabini, Monti (mts.), It. 48/C1
Sabirabad, Azer. 103/G1
Sabkhat al Bardawīl (lag.), Egypt 104/C4
Sabkhat al Hayshah (swamp), Libya 108/B2
Sabkhat al Kabīyah (swamp), Tun. 48/A5
Sabkhat al Milḩ (swamp), Libya 108/C2
Sabkhat ash Shuwayrib (swamp), Libya 108/C2
Sabkhat Ghuzayyil (swamp), Libya 108/C2
Sabkhat Shunayn (swamp), Libya 108/D2
Sablayan, Phil. 88/C2
Sable (cape), NS, Can. 158/E4
Sable (cape), Fl, US 172/E2
Sable (isl.), NS, Can. 141/L4
Sable (isl.), Can. 139/M5
Sablé-sur-Sarthe, Fr. 57/E5
Sables (riv.), Qu, Can. 158/B1
Saboeiro, Braz. 183/G4
Sabon Gida, Nga. 115/H5
Sabongidda, Nga. 115/G5
Sabor (riv.), Port. 46/B2
Sabou, Burk. 115/E3
Saboyá, Col. 183/M7
Sabra (cape), Indo. 91/H4
Şabrātah, Libya 67/G4
Sabratha (ruin), Libya 67/G4
Sabrina (coast), Ant. 192/J
Sabrūm, India 97/H4
Sabual, India 86/B4
Sabugal, Port. 46/B2
Sabula, Ia, US 155/J2
Sabulubek, Indo. 89/B3
Şabyā, SAr. 100/D5
Sabzevār, Iran 103/J2
Sac City, Ia, US 155/G2
Sacaca, Bol. 188/C1
Sacajawea (peak), Or, US 146/E1
Sacajawea (lake), Wa, US 144/E4
Sácama, Col. 180/C3
Sacandica, Ang. 120/C4
Sacanta, Arg. 188/D4
Sacarnoochee (riv.), Ms, US 162/C4
Sacaton, Az, US 149/G4
Sacavém, Port. 47/P10
Saccarel (peak), Fr. 64/D4
Saccarello (peak), It. 62/A4
Sacco (riv.), It. 48/C2
Sacedón, Sp. 46/D2
Săcele, Rom. 51/G3
Sachanga, Ang. 122/C2
Sachigo (riv.), On, Can. 140/G3
Sachojere, Bol. 185/E4
Sachs Harbour, NW, Can. 140/D1
Sachse, Tx, US 150/L7
Sachseln, Swi. 61/E4
Sachsen (state), Ger. 42/G3
Sachsen-Anhalt (state), Ger. 42/F3
Sachsenbrunn, Ger. 58/D2
Sachsenhagen, Ger. 53/G4
Sacile, It. 63/F2
Säckingen, Ger. 60/D2
Sackville, NB, Can. 158/E3
Saclay, Fr. 30/J5
Saco, Me, US 161/L3
Saco, Al, US 165/F2
Saco (bay), Me, US 158/B4
Saco (riv.), Me, US 161/L3
Saco, Mt, US 145/L3
Saco do Giraul, Ang. 122/B2
Sacra di San Michele, It. 64/D2
Sacramento, Mex. 151/D4
Sacramento (co.), Ca, US 167/M10
Sacramento (riv.), Ca, US 142/B4
Sacramento (mts.), NM, US 142/E5
Sacramento (cap.), Ca, US 146/C4
Sacramento, Ky, US 162/D2
Sacramento Metropolitan (arpt.), Ca, US 167/L9
Sacramento NWR, Ca, US 146/B4
Sacramento River Deep Water Ship Canal, Ca, US 167/L10
Sacratif (cape), Sp. 46/D4
Sacriston, Eng, UK 35/G2
Sacro (peak), It. 48/E2
Sacro Monte, It. 62/B2
Sada, May. 125/H6
Sada, SAfr. 124/D4
Sádaba, Sp. 46/E1
Sadābād, India 96/B2
Sa'dah, Yem. 100/D5
Sadani, Tanz. 119/B3
Sadasar, India 92/B2
Sādāt Maḩalleh, Iran 103/G2
Sadd al Qir'awn (dam), Leb. 105/D1
Saddam (int'l arpt.), Iraq 103/F3
Saddle (mtn.), Az, US 149/G2
Saddle (riv.), NJ, US 169/J8
Saddle (mtn.), Or, US 144/C5
Saddle Brook, NJ, US 169/J8
Saddle Mtn. NWR, Wa, US 144/E4
Saddle River, NJ, US 169/J7
Saddle Rock, NY, US 169/K8
Saddleback (mesa), NM, US 152/C3
Saddlestring, Wy, US 147/K1
Saddleworth, Eng, UK 35/G4
Saddleworth, Austl. 131/H5
Sadêng, China 86/B2
Sādhaura, India 98/D4
Sadi, Eth. 117/G3
Sadīch, Iran 101/G3
Sadiola, Mali 114/C3
Sadiya, India 86/B3
Sadjoavato, Madg. 125/J6
Sadler, Tx, US 153/F4
Sado (riv.), Port. 46/A3
Sado (isl.), Japan 79/M4
Sadovo, Bul. 51/G4
Sadovoye, Rus. 71/H3
Sadowara, Japan 84/B4
Sādri, India 92/B2
Sadripante (mt.), Phil. 88/D3
Sādullāpur, Bang. 97/G3
Sadulshahar, India 98/C5
Saerbeck, Ger. 53/E4
Saeul, Lux. 55/E4
Safané, Burk. 114/E3
Safāpur, India 98/C2
Safāqis (gov.), Tun. 111/H2
Safed Koh (range), Pak. 98/A3
Safety Harbor, Fl, US 164/K8
Saffig, Ger. 55/G3
Säffle, Swe. 40/E2
Safford, Az, US 149/H4
Saffron Walden, Eng, UK 37/G2
Safi, Mor. 110/C2
Safi (cape), Mor. 110/C2
Safīd (riv.), Afg. 101/J1
Safid Khers (mts.), Afg. 101/K1
Safid Kūh (mts.), Afg. 101/H2
Safidon, India 98/D5
Safien, Swi. 61/F4
Safīpur, India 96/C2
Şāfītā, Syria 104/E2
Safonovo, Rus. 68/G5
Safranbolu, Turk. 70/E4
Şafţ al 'Inab, Egypt 113/B3
Şafţ al Mulūk, Egypt 113/B3
Şafţ Turāb, Egypt 113/C3
Sag Harbor, NY, US 169/F2
Saga, China 97/E1
Saga, Japan 84/B4
Saga (pref.), Japan 84/A4
Sagaba, Ang. 122/D1
Sagae, Japan 82/B4
Sagaing (state), Myan. 93/F3
Sagaing, Myan. 86/B4
Sagami (sea), Japan 85/F3
Sagami (riv.), Japan 83/C2
Sagami (lake), Japan 83/C2
Sagami (bay), Japan 83/C3
Sagamihara, Japan 85/F3
Sagamiko, Japan 83/C2
Sagamore Hill Nat'l Hist. Site, NY, US 169/M8
Sagan, Indo. 91/H4
Sagana, Kenya 119/B2
Saganaga (lake), Can.,US 157/J3
Sāgar, India 96/B4
Sāgar, India 95/B3
Sagard, Ger. 40/E4
Sagarejo, Geo. 71/H4
Sagarmatha (zone), Nepal 97/F2
Sagarmatha (Everest) (mtn.), China, Nepal 97/F2
Sagarmatha NP, Nepal 97/F2
Sagata, Sen. 114/A3
Sagauli, India 97/E2
Sagavanirktok (riv.), Ak, US 171/J2
Sagay, Phil. 88/C3
Sagay, Phil. 88/D3
Sage, Ar, US 153/J2
Sage (cr.), Mt, US 145/J3
Sagemace (bay), Mb, Can. 156/D1
Saggart, Ire. 34/B5
Şaghīr (canal), Egypt 113/C2
Saginaw, Mi, US 160/E3
Saginaw (bay), Mi, US 160/E3
Saginaw, Or, US 146/B2
Saginaw, Tx, US 150/K7
Sagittario (riv.), It. 65/C4
Sagiz, Kaz. 71/K2
Sagle, Id, US 144/F3
Saglek (bay), Nf, Can. 141/K3
Sagola, Mi, US 157/K4
Sagone (gulf), Fr. 48/A1
Sagsay (riv.), Mong. 99/E2
Sagter Ems (riv.), Ger. 53/E2
Sagu, Indo. 128/A2
Sagua de Tánamo, Cuba 177/H1
Sagua la Grande, Cuba 177/F1
Saguache, Co, US 149/J1
Saguache (cr.), Co, US 149/J1
Saguaro NP, Az, US 149/G4
Saguia el Hamra (riv.), WSah. 110/C4
Sagunto, Sp. 47/E3
Sagy, Fr. 30/H4
Sa'gya, China 97/G1
Sagyz (riv.), Kaz. 71/K2
Saḩāb, Jor. 105/D5
Sahaba, Sudan 109/F5
Sahagún, Col. 180/C2
Sahagún, Sp. 46/C1
Sahagún, Mex. 175/L7
Saḩam, Jor. 105/D3
Sahand (mtn.), Iran 103/F2
Sahara (des.), Afr. 107/B2
Sahāranpur, India 98/D5
Saharsa, India 97/F3
Sahaspur, India 96/B1
Sahaswān, India 96/B1
Sahavato, Madg. 125/J8
Sahāwar, India 96/B2
Sahel (riv.), Alg. 112/H4
Sāhibganj, India 97/F3
Şahin, Turk. 51/H5
Şahinli, Turk. 51/H5
Sāhīwāl, Pak. 98/B4
Sahiwal, Pak. 98/B4
Şaḩneh, Iran 103/F3
Sahoué, Gabon 120/B2
Şahrajat al Kubrá, Egypt 113/C3
Sahrho, Jebel (mts.), Mor. 110/D3
Sahu, Indo. 91/G3
Sahuaripa, Mex. 174/C2
Sahuarita, Az, US 149/G5
Sahuayo de Morelos, Mex. 174/E4
Šahy, Slvk. 43/K4
Sai (riv.), India 96/C2
Sai (chan.), India 92/D2
Sai (riv.), Japan 84/E2
Sai Buri, Thai. 94/C5
Sai Kung, China 87/M7
Sai Yok, Thai. 94/B3
Sai Yok NP, Thai. 94/B3
Saibai (isl.), Austl. 129/F2
Sa'id Bundas, Sudan 117/E3
Saïda, Alg. 112/F5
Saïdia, Mor. 112/C2
Saidor, PNG 129/G1
Saidpur, India 96/D3
Saidpur, Bang. 97/G3
Saidu, Pak. 98/B2
Saignelégier, Swi. 60/D3
Saignon, Fr. 64/B5
Saigō, Japan 84/C2
Saigon, Viet. 94/D4
Saijō, Japan 84/C4
Saikai NP, Japan 84/A4
Saiki, Japan 84/B4
Saillans, Fr. 64/B3
Sailly, Fr. 30/H4
Sailly-sur-la-Lys, Fr. 54/B2
Sailolof, Indo. 91/H4
Sailu, India 92/C4
Saima, China 81/C2
Saimaa (lake), Fin. 38/J3
Sain Alto, Mex. 174/E4
Şā'īn Dezh, Iran 103/F2
Sainghin-en-Weppes, Fr. 54/B2
Sains-du-Nord, Fr. 54/D3
Saint (swamp), Fl, US 165/H3
Saint Mary's (riv.), NS, Can. 159/F3
Saint Abb's (pt.), Sc, UK 33/D5
Saint Abbs, Sc, UK 33/D5
Saint Adolphe, Mb, Can. 156/F3
Saint Agnes (pt.), Eng, UK 36/A6
Saint Agnes, Eng, UK 36/A6
Saint Alban's, Nf, Can. 159/K2
Saint Albans, Eng, UK 30/C1
Saint Albans, Vt, US 161/K2
Saint Albans, WV, US 163/G1
Saint Albert, Ab, Can. 145/H1
Saint Ambroise, Mb, Can. 156/E2
Saint Andrews (bay), Sc, UK 33/D4
Saint Andrews, NB, Can. 158/D3
Saint Andrews, Sc, UK 33/D4

San Mar – Santo D

San Martino Buon Albergo, It. 63/E3
San Martino di Lupari, It. 63/E2
San Martino di Venezze, It. 63/E3
San Martino in Passiria (Sankt Martin in Passieir), It. 61/H4
San Martino in Pensilis, It. 65/E4
San Martino in Rio, It. 63/D4
San Martino in Strada, It. 62/C3
San Martino Siccomario, It. 62/C3
San Martino-di-Lota, Fr. 48/A1
San Mateo, Phil. 88/F6
San Mateo, Peru 184/B3
San Mateo, Sp. 47/F2
San Mateo, Ven. 183/N7
San Mateo, Fl, US 165/H3
San Mateo (cr.), Ca, US 166/C4
San Mateo (co.), Ca, US 167/K12
San Mateo, Ven. 181/E2
San Mateo, NM, US 149/J3
San Mateo (mts.), NM, US 149/J3
San Mateo Atarasquillo, Mex. 175/Q10
San Mateo Xoloc, Mex. 175/Q9
San Matías (gulf), Arg. 179/C7
San Matías, Bol. 185/G5
San Mauricio, Ven. 181/E2
San Maurizio d'Opaglio, It. 62/B2
San Mauro Pascoli, It. 63/F5
San Mauro Torinese, It. 62/A2
San Michele al Tagliamento, It. 63/F2
San Miguel, Arg. 188/E4
San Miguel, Bol. 185/E4
San Miguel, Bol. 185/F5
San Miguel (riv.), Bol. 188/D1
San Miguel (riv.), Bol. 185/F4
San Miguel (riv.), Col. 180/B4
San Miguel, ESal. 176/D3
San Miguel, Mex. 151/C3
San Miguel (gulf), Pan. 177/G4
San Miguel, Pan. 180/B2
San Miguel, Peru 184/C4
San Miguel, Peru 184/B2
San Miguel (bay), Phil. 88/C2
San Miguel (isl.), Ca, US 148/B3
San Miguel (riv.), Co, US 149/H1
San Miguel, NM, US 149/J4
San Miguel (cr.), Tx, US 151/E3
San Miguel Coatlinchan, Mex. 175/R10
San Miguel de Allende, Mex. 175/E4
San Miguel de Huachi, Bol. 185/E4
San Miguel de los Bancos, Ecu. 180/B4
San Miguel de Tucumán, Arg. 188/C3
San Miguel del Monte, Arg. 191/J11
San Miguel Tlaixpan, Mex. 175/R9
San Miguel Totolapan, Mex. 172/A4
San Miguelito, Bol. 184/D3
San Miguelito, Bol. 185/F5
San Miniato, It. 63/D6
San Nicola la Strada, It. 65/D5
San Nicolas (isl.), Ca, US 148/C4
San Nicolás de los Arroyos, Arg. 190/E2
San Nicolás Hidalgo, Mex. 151/D5
San Nicolò, It. 62/C3
San Nicolò a Tordino, It. 65/C2
San Onofre, Col. 180/C2
San Onofre, Ca, US 166/C4
San Onofre (mtn.), Ca, US 166/C4
San Pablo, Bol. 184/D5
San Pablo, Bol. 185/F4
San Pablo, Chile 190/B4
San Pablo, Col. 180/B4
San Pablo, Peru 184/B2
San Pablo, Phil. 88/C2
San Pablo (int'l arpt.), Sp. 46/C4
San Pablo, Ven. 181/E2
San Pablo (res.), Ca, US 167/K11
San Pablo, Ca, US 167/K11
San Pablo (bay), Ca, US 146/B4
San Pablo, Co, US 152/B2
San Pablo Bay NWR, Ca, US 167/K10
San Pablo de Borbur, Col. 183/L7
San Pablo de las Salinas, Mex. 175/Q9
San Pablo de Lipez, Bol. 188/C2
San Pablo Huixtepec, Mex. 176/B2
San Paolo, It. 62/D3
San Pascual, Phil. 88/E3
San Pawl il-Baħar, Malta 48/L7
San Pédro, C.d'Iv. 114/D5
San Pedro, Arg. 191/J10
San Pedro, Arg. 188/C3
San Pedro, Belz. 176/E2
San Pedro, Bol. 188/C1
San Pedro, Bol. 185/E4
San Pedro, Bol. 185/E3
San Pedro, Bol. 185/F5
San Pedro, Bol. 184/E3
San Pedro, Chile 188/B2
San Pedro (pt.), Chile 188/B3
San Pedro, Chile 190/N8
San Pedro (vol.), Chile 188/B2
San Pedro, Col. 183/K6
San Pedro (riv.), Guat. 176/D2
San Pedro (riv.), Mex.,US 149/G4
San Pedro (dept.), Par. 186/A4
San Pedro, Par. 189/E3
San Pedro (mts.), Sp. 46/B3
San Pedro (riv.), Az, US 174/C1
San Pedro (nbrhd.), Ca, US 166/F8
San Pedro (chan.), Ca, US 148/C4
San Pedro Arriba, Mex. 175/Q10
San Pedro Carchá, Guat. 176/D3
San Pedro de Arimena, Col. 180/D3
San Pedro de Cajas, Peru 184/C3
San Pedro de Cururu, Bol. 185/F4
San Pedro de la Cueva, Mex. 174/C2
San Pedro de Las Bocas, Ven. 181/F3
San Pedro de las Colonias, Mex. 151/C5
San Pedro de Lloc, Peru 184/B2
San Pedro de Lóvago, Nic. 177/E3
San Pedro de Macorís, DRep. 173/H4
San Pedro del Paraná, Par. 189/E3
San Pedro del Pinatar, Sp. 47/E4
San Pedro Huamelula, Mex. 176/C2
San Pedro Pochutla, Mex. 176/B3
San Pedro Sula, Hon. 176/D3
San Pedro Tapanatepec, Mex. 176/C2
San Pedro Totoltepec, Mex. 175/Q10
San Pellegrino Terme, It. 62/C2
San Perlita, Tx, US 151/F4
San Piero a Sieve, It. 63/E6
San Piero in Bagno, It. 63/E6
San Pierre, In, US 160/C4
San Pietro (isl.), It. 66/E3
San Pietro in Casale, It. 63/E4
San Pietro in Gù, It. 63/E2
San Pietro in Vincoli, It. 63/F5
San Pietro in Volta, It. 63/E3
San Pitch (riv.), Ut, US 147/H4
San Polo d'Enza, It. 62/D4
San Polo di Piave, It. 63/F2
San Possidonio, It. 63/D4
San Prisco, It. 65/D5
San Quentin, Ca, US 167/K11
San Quintín, Mex. 174/B2
San Quintín (cape), Mex. 174/B2
San Rafael, Arg. 190/C2
San Rafael, Bol. 184/D4
San Rafael, Bol. 185/F5
San Rafael, Chile 190/C2
San Rafael, Col. 183/K6
San Rafael, Mex. 175/N6
San Rafael, Peru 184/B3
San Rafael, Peru 184/B2
San Rafael (mts.), Ca, US 148/C3
San Rafael (hills), Ca, US 166/F7
San Rafael (riv.), Ut, US 147/H4
San Rafael, Ca, US 146/B5
San Rafael (des.), Ut, US 147/H4
San Rafael, NM, US 149/J3
San Rafael de Orituco, Ven. 183/P8
San Rafael del Moján, Ven. 180/D2
San Rafael Swell (upland), Ut, US 147/H4
San Ramón, Bol. 185/E4
San Ramón, Bol. 185/F4
San Ramón, CR 177/E4
San Ramón, Peru 184/C3
San Ramón, Uru. 191/L11
San Ramon, Ca, US 167/L11
San Ramón de la Nueva Orán, Arg. 188/C2
San Remo, It. 62/A5
San Rocco al Porto, It. 62/C3
San Romano, It. 63/D6
San Roque, Sp. 46/C4
San Roque, Col. 183/K6
San Rosendo, Chile 190/B3
San Saba (riv.), Tx, US 175/F2
San Saba, Tx, US 151/E2
San Salvador (cap.), ESal. 176/D3
San Salvador (riv.), Uru. 191/J10
San Salvador (isl.), Ecu. 184/J7
San Salvador, Arg. 188/E4
San Salvador (Watling) (isl.), Bahm. 173/G3
San Salvador de Jujuy, Arg. 188/C3
San Salvador el Seco, Mex. 175/M7
San Salvador, Isla (isl.), Bahm. 173/G3
San Salvatore Monferrato, It. 62/B4
San Salvo, It. 65/D3
San Sebastián, Sp. 44/C5
San Sebastián, Arg. 191/C7
San Sebastián, Ven. 183/N8
San Sebastián de los Reyes, Sp. 47/N8
San Sebastián de Yalí, Nic. 176/E3
San Sebastiano, It. 62/D2
San Secondo Parmense, It. 62/D4
San Severino Marche, It. 65/C1
San Severo, It. 48/D2
San Simeon, Ca, US 148/B3
San Simon (riv.), Az, US 149/H4
San Simón, Bol. 185/E4
San Simon Wash (riv.), Az, US 149/F4
San Telmo, (pt.), Mex. 174/E5
San Timoteo, Ven. 180/D2
San Tomé, Ven. 181/E2
San Valentín (peak), Chile 190/B5
San Valentino, It. 63/G2
San Vicente, Arg. 188/D4
San Vicente, Chile 190/C2
San Vicente, Chile 190/N9
San Vicente, ESal. 176/D3
San Vicente, Mex. 174/A2
San Vicente (res.), Ca, US 166/D5
San Vicente, Ven. 180/E3
San Vicente de Alcántara, Sp. 46/B3
San Vicente de Cañete, Peru 184/B4
San Vicente del Caguán, Col. 180/C4
San Vicente del Raspeig, Sp. 47/E3
San Vincenzo, It. 45/J5
San Vito (cape), It. 48/C3
San Vito, CR 177/F4
San Vito al Tagliamento, It. 63/F2
San Vito Chietino, It. 65/D3
San Vito Romano, It. 65/B4
San Xavier Ind. Res., Az, US 149/G4
San Ygnacio, Tx, US 151/E4
San Ysidro, Ca, US 166/C5
San Ysidro, NM, US 149/J3
Sana (riv.), Bosn. 50/C3
Sanā', Yem. 118/D1
Saña, Peru 184/B2
Şan'ā (Sanaa) (cap.), Yem. 118/C2
Sanaa (int'l arpt.), Yem. 118/C2
Sanaa (Şan'ā) (cap.), Yem. 118/C2
Sanae IV, SAfr., Ant. 192/Z
Sanafā, Egypt 113/C3
Sanaga (riv.), Camr. 107/C4
Sanajärvi (lake), Fin. 39/F4
Sanak (isl.), Ak, US 171/F5
Sanām, SAr. 100/D4
Sanana (isl.), Indo. 91/G4
Sanandaj, Iran 103/F3
Sanandita, Bol. 188/D2
Sananduva, Braz. 189/G3
Sanankoroba, Mali 114/D3
Sanary-sur-Mer, Fr. 64/B6
Sanatorium, Ms, US 164/D2
Sanaur, India 98/D4
Sanāw, Yem. 100/F5
Sānāwad, India 92/C3
Sanborn, ND, US 156/E4
Sanborn, Mn, US 155/G1
Sanborn, NY, US 160/V9
Sanbu, China 78/E4
Sancha, China 87/F3
Sancha, China 78/E5
Sancha (riv.), China 86/E3
Sanchahe, China 81/B2
Sánchez Grande, Uru. 191/K10
Sanch'ŏng, SKor. 81/D5
Sanco, Tx, US 150/D1
Sancti Spíritu, Arg. 190/E2
Sancti Spíritus, Cuba 177/G1
Sand, Nor. 40/B2
Sand (hills), Ne, US 142/F3
Sand (cr.), SD, US 154/E1
Sand (pt.), Eng, UK 36/D4
Sand (riv.), SAfr. 124/D3
Sand am Main, Ger. 58/D3
Sand Arroyo (riv.), Ks,Co, US 152/D2
Sand Coulee, Mt, US 145/J4
Sand Draw (riv.), Ne,Co, US 154/D3
Sand Key (isl.), Fl, US 164/K8
Sand Lake, Tx, US 150/L7
Sand Lake NWR, SD, US 156/E5
Sand Lake NWR, SD, US 154/E1
Sand Patch (pt.), Austl. 133/D3
Sand Point, Ak, US 171/F4
Sandspit, BC, Can. 171/M5
Sand Springs, Mt, US 145/L4
Sanda (isl.), Sc, UK 34/C1
Sanda, Japan 83/H6
Sandakan, Malay. 88/B4
Sandan, Camb. 94/D3
Sandane, Nor. 38/C3
Sandanski, Bul. 75/H2
Sandaré, Mali 114/C3
Sandarne, Swe. 40/G1
Sanday (isl.), Sc, UK 31/V14
Sandbach, Eng, UK 35/F5
Sandberg, Ger. 58/C2
Sandborn, In, US 162/D1
Sande, Nor. 38/R9
Sande, Ger. 53/F1
Sandebukta (bay), Nor. 38/R9
Sandefjord, Nor. 40/D2
Sanderson, Tx, US 151/C2
Sandersville, Ms, US 164/D2
Sandersville, Ga, US 163/F4
Sandgate (nbrhd.), Austl. 134/F6
Sandhamn, Swe. 39/B1
Sandhead, Sc, UK 34/D2
Sandhill, On, Can. 160/T8
Sandhurst, Eng, UK 37/F4
Sandia, Peru 184/D4
Sandia Mil. Res., NM, US 149/J3
Sandia Park, NM, US 149/J3
Sandia Peak Tramway, NM, US 149/J3
Sandia Pueblo Ind. Res., NM, US 149/J3
Sandıklı, Turk. 102/B2
Sandīla, India 96/C2
Sandillon, Fr. 57/H5
Sanding (isl.), Indo. 89/C3
Sandino, Cuba 172/E3
Sandnes, Nor. 40/A2
Sandoa, D.R. Congo 121/E5
Sandomierz, Pol. 43/L3
Sandoná, Col. 180/B4
Sándorfalva, Hun. 50/E2
Sandougou (riv.), Sen. 114/B3
Sandoval, Il, US 162/C1
Sandover (riv.), Austl. 131/G2
Sandoway, Myan. 86/B5
Sandown, Eng, UK 37/E5
Sandpoint, Id, US 144/F3
Sandrakatsy, Madg. 125/J7
Sandrigo, It. 63/E2
Sandringham (nbrhd.), Austl. 132/G5
Sandrivier (riv.), SAfr. 123/F4
Sandrohy, Madg. 125/H8
Sands, Mi, US 157/L4
Sands (pt.), NY, US 169/L8
Sands Point, NY, US 169/L8
Sandstedt, Ger. 53/F2
Sandstone, Austl. 130/C3
Sandstone Nat'l Wild. Ref., Mn, US 157/H4
Sandu, China 87/G2
Sandu Shuizu Zizhixian, China 87/E3
Sandungen (lake), Nor. 38/S9
Sandusky, Mi, US 160/E3
Sandusky, Oh, US 160/E4
Sandusky (riv.), Oh, US 160/E4
Sandvika, Nor. 40/D2
Sandviken, Swe. 40/G1
Sandweiler, Lux. 55/F4
Sandwell (co.), Eng, UK 36/D2
Sandwich, Ma, US 161/L4
Sandwich, NH, US 161/L3
Sandwich (cape), Austl. 134/B2
Sandwich, Il, US 155/K3
Sandwich, Eng, UK 37/H4
Sandwīp (isl.), Bang. 97/H4
Sandy (lake), Nf., Can. 159/J1
Sandy (cape), Austl. 134/D4
Sandy, Ut, US 147/H3
Sandy (lake), On, Can. 140/G3
Sandy, Eng, UK 37/F2
Sandy (pt.), SC, US 163/G4
Sandy (pt.), RI, US 169/G1
Sandy Creek, NY, US 161/H3
Sandy Hook (isl.) 169/J10
Sandy Hook, Ky, US 163/F1
Sandy Hook (bay), NJ, US 168/D3
Sandy Hook Lighthouse, NJ, US 169/J10
Sandy Lake, Mb, Can. 156/D2
Sandy Point, NS, Can. 158/E4
Sandy Springs, Ga, US 163/M7
Sandykachi, Trkm. 101/H1
Sandyville, WV, US 163/G1
Sanem, Lux. 55/E4
Sånfjällets NP, Swe. 38/E3
Sanford, Mb, Can. 156/F3
Sanford (mt.), Ak, US 171/K3
Sanford, Co, US 149/K2
Sanford, Fl, US 165/H3
Sanford, Me, US 161/L3
Sanford, Ms, US 164/D2
Sanford, NC, US 163/H3
Sanfront, It. 64/D3
Sanga, D.R. Congo 121/G4
Sanga, Ang. 122/B1
Sangachaly, Azer. 103/G1
Sangamon (riv.), Il, US 155/J3
Sangān (mtn.), Afg. 101/H2
Sangano, It. 64/D2
Sangar, Rus. 75/N3
Sangar Sarāy, Afg. 98/A2
Sangardo, Gui. 114/C4
Sangareddi, India 95/C2
Sangaréya, Gui. 114/B4
Sangaria, India 98/C5
Sangatte, Fr. 54/A2
Sangay (vol.), Ecu. 180/B5
Sangbé, Camr. 116/B4
Sangde, D.R. Congo 121/G3
Sangejing, China 78/F3
Sangenjo, Sp. 46/A1
Sanger, Tx, US 153/F4
Sanger, Ca, US 148/C2
Sanggan (riv.), China 80/C2
Sanggarmai, China 86/D1
Sanggau, Indo. 90/D3
Sanggou (bay), China 81/B4
Sangha (pol. ref), Congo 120/C2
Sangha (pref.), CAfr. 116/B5
Sangha (riv.), D.R. Congo 116/C5
Sangha (riv.), CAfr. 107/D4
Sanghar, Pak. 101/J3
Sangihe (isl.), Phil. 77/M9
Sangihe (isl.), Indo. 91/G3
Sangiyn Dalay (lake), Mong. 78/D2
Sangiyn Dalay, Mong. 78/E2
Sangju, SKor. 81/E4
Sangkha, Thai. 94/C3
Sangkhla, Thai. 94/B3
Sangkulirang, Indo. 91/E3
Sāngla, Pak. 98/B4
Sangley Point Nav. Air Sta., Phil. 88/E7
Sangmélima, Camr. 120/C2
Sangō, Japan 83/J6
Sangpang (mts.), Myan. 86/B3
Sangre de Cristo (mts.), Co, US 154/B4
Sangre Grande, Trin. 181/F2
Sangri, China 97/J1
Sangro (riv.), It. 48/D2
Sangrūr, India 98/C4
Sangsang, China 97/F1
Sangster (int'l arpt.), Jam. 177/G2
Sangue, Rio do (riv.), Braz. 185/G3
Sangüesa, Sp. 44/C5
Sanguie (prov.), Burk. 115/E4
Sanguinetto, It. 63/E3
Sangwŏn, NKor. 81/D3
Sanhe (pref), Afr. 120/C2
Sanhe, China 80/H7
Sanhuang, China 87/F3
Sanhūr, Egypt 113/B6
Sani (pass), Les. 124/E3
Sāni Bheri (riv.), Nepal 96/D1
Sanibel (isl.), Fl, US 165/G4
San'in Kaigin NP, Japan 84/D3
Saniquellie, Libr. 114/C5
Sanito, Phil. 88/C4
Sanjahā, Egypt 113/C3
Sanje, Zam. 123/E2
Sanjia, China 87/F4
Sanjiang, China 87/E2
Sanjō, Japan 85/F2
Sankanbiriwa (peak), SLeo. 114/C4
Sankeyushu, China 81/C2
Sankh (riv.), India 97/E4
Sānko, India 98/C2
Sankoroni (riv.), Gui. 114/C4
Sankosh (riv.), India 97/G2
Sānkra, India 101/K3
Sankt Aegyd am Neuwalde, Aus. 45/L3
Sankt Agatha, Aus. 59/G6
Sankt Andrä-Wördern, Aus. 51/N7
Sankt Andreasberg, Ger. 53/H5
Sankt Anton am Arlberg, Aus. 61/G3
Sankt Augustin, Ger. 55/G2
Sankt Blasien, Ger. 60/E2
Sankt Florian am Inn, Aus. 59/G6
Sankt Gallen, Swi. 61/F3
Sankt Gallenkirch, Aus. 61/F3
Sankt Georgen bei Salzburg, Aus. 59/F7
Sankt Georgen im Attergau, Aus. 59/G7
Sankt Georgen im Schwarzwald, Ger. 61/E1
Sankt Goar, Ger. 55/G3
Sankt Goarshausen, Ger. 55/G3
Sankt Ingbert, Ger. 55/G5
Sankt Jakob (San Giacomo), It. 61/H4
Sankt Johann am Walde, Aus. 59/G6
Sankt Johann im Pongau, Aus. 45/K3
Sankt Johann in Tirol, Aus. 45/K3
Sankt Leonhard im Pitztal, Aus. 61/G3
Sankt Leonhard in Passeier (San Leonardo in Passiria), It. 61/H4
Sankt Marien, Aus. 59/H6
Sankt Martin im Mühlkreis, Aus. 59/H6
Sankt Martin in Passeier (San Martino in Passiria), It. 61/H4
Sankt Michael in Obersteiermark, Aus. 45/L3
Sankt Moritz, Swi. 61/F5
Sankt Moritz (Saint Moritz), Swi. 45/H3
Sankt Oswald bei Freistadt, Aus. 59/H5
Sankt Pantaleon, Aus. 59/F6
Sankt Pauli, Ger. 53/G1
Sankt Peter am Hart, Aus. 59/G6
Sankt Peter in der Au, Aus. 59/H6
Sankt Peter-Ording, Ger. 40/C4
Sankt Pölten, Aus. 43/H4
Sankt Stephan, Swi. 60/D4
Sankt Ulrich bei Steyr, Aus. 59/H6
Sankt Valentin, Aus. 59/H6
Sankt Veit, Aus. 50/B1
Sankt Veit an der Glan, Aus. 45/L3
Sankt Wendel, Ger. 55/G5
Sankt Wolfgang, Ger. 59/F6
Sankuru (riv.), D.R. Congo 121/E4
Sanlong, China 79/J5
Sanlúcar de Barrameda, Sp. 46/B4
Sanmatenga (prov.), Burk. 115/E3
Sanmenxia, China 80/B4
Sanming, China 87/H3
Sannan, Japan 83/H5
Sannār, Sudan 116/G2
Sannazzaro de'Burgondi, It. 62/B3
Sannicandro Garganico, It. 48/D2
Sannikova (str.), Rus. 75/P2
Sannio (mts.), It. 65/D5
San'nohe, Japan 82/B3
Sannois, Fr. 30/J5
Sannūr (wadi), Egypt 113/C6
Sano, Japan 85/F2
Sañogasta, Arg. 188/C4
Sanok, Pol. 43/M4
Sanostee, NM, US 149/H2
Sanpoil (riv.), Wa, US 144/E3
Sanqiao, China 80/K9
Sanquhar, Sc, UK 33/C6
Sanquianga, PN, Col. 180/B4
Sans Bois (mts.), Ok, US 153/G3
Sansalé, Gui. 114/B4
Sansepolcro, It. 63/F6
Sansha, China 87/J3
Sanshilipu, China 78/F4
Sansui, China 87/F3
Sant Adrià de Besòs, Sp. 47/L7
Sant 'Antioco (isl.), It. 66/E3
Sant Boi de Llobregat, Sp. 47/L7
Sant Carles de la Ràpita, Sp. 47/F2
Sant Celoni, Sp. 47/L6
Sant Cugat del Vallès, Sp. 47/L7
Sant Eufemia (gulf), It. 48/D3
Sant Feliu de Guíxols, Sp. 47/G2
Sant Feliu de Llobregat, Sp. 47/L7
Sant Julià, And. 44/D5
Sant Pere de Ribes, Sp. 47/K7
Sant Sadurní d'Anoia, Sp. 47/K7
Sant Vicenç de Castellet, Sp. 47/K6
Sant Vicenç dels Horts, Sp. 47/L7
Santa (riv.), Peru 184/B3
Santa, Peru 184/B3
Santa, Id, US 144/F4
Santa Ana, Bol. 188/E1
Santa Ana, Bol. 185/F5
Santa Ana, Bol. 188/C2
Santa Ana, Col. 180/D4
Santa Ana, Ecu. 184/A1
Santa Ana, ESal. 176/D3
Santa Ana (vol.), ESal. 176/D3
Santa Ana, Hon. 176/E3
Santa Ana, Mex. 174/C2
Santa Ana (riv.), Ca, US 166/C3
Santa Ana (riv.), Ca, US 166/C3
Santa Ana (mts.), Ca, US 166/C3
Santa Ana, Ca, US 166/G8
Santa Ana (mts.), Ca, US 148/D4
Santa Ana, Ven. 180/C3
Santa Ana, Ven. 180/D2
Santa Ana, Ven. 182/A1
Santa Ana del Alto Beni, Bol. 185/E4
Santa Ana Ind. Res., NM, US 152/A3
Santa Ana Ind. Res., NM, US 149/J3
Santa Ana Nat'l Wild. Ref., Tx, US 151/E4
Santa Anna, Tx, US 150/E2
Santa Bárbara, Braz. 187/E3
Santa Bárbara, Chile 190/B3
Santa Bárbara, Col. 183/K7
Santa Bárbara, Hon. 176/D3
Santa Bárbara, Mex. 174/D3
Santa Barbara, Phil. 88/C1
Santa Barbara, Ca, US 166/A2
Santa Barbara (chan.), Ca, US 148/B3
Santa Barbara (isl.), Ca, US 148/C4
Santa Barbara (co.), Ca, US 166/A1
Santa Bárbara, Ven. 181/E4
Santa Bárbara, Ven. 180/D2
Santa Bárbara, Ven. 180/D3
Santa Bárbara d'Oeste, Braz. 189/H2
Santa Barbara Mountains NRA, Ca, US 166/E7
Santa Catalina, Ven. 180/D3
Santa Catalina, Pan. 177/F4
Santa Catalina (isl.), CA, US 142/B5
Santa Catalina (gulf), Ca, US 148/D4
Santa Catalina, Phil. 88/C3
Santa Catarina (isl.), Braz. 189/G3
Santa Catarina (state), Braz. 189/G3
Santa Catarina, Mex. 175/E3
Santa Clara, Cuba 177/G1
Santa Clara, Mex. 174/E3
Santa Clara (res.), Port. 46/A4
Santa Clara (riv.), Ca, US 166/B2
Santa Clara, Ca, US 167/L12
Santa Clara (co.), Ca, US 167/L12
Santa Clara, Ca, US 148/B2
Santa Clara, Ut, US 149/F2
Santa Clara, Ven. 181/E2
Santa Clara de Olimar, Uru. 191/G2
Santa Clarita, Ca, US 166/B2
Santa Claus, In, US 162/D1
Santa Clotilde, Peru 180/C5
Santa Coloma de Farners, Sp. 47/G2
Santa Coloma de Gramanet, Sp. 47/L7
Santa Comba, Sp. 46/A1
Santa Croce (peak), It. 65/C5
Santa Croce di Magliano, It. 65/D4
Santa Croce sull'Arno, It. 63/D6
Santa Cruz, Arg. 120/D4
Santa Cruz (prov.), Arg. 190/C5
Santa Cruz (riv.), Arg. 179/B8
Santa Cruz (riv.), Bol. 185/F5
Santa Cruz, Braz. 183/G4
Santa Cruz, Chile 190/C2
Santa Cruz, CR 176/E4
Santa Cruz (isl.), Ecu. 184/J7
Santa Cruz (mts.), Guat. 176/D3
Santa Cruz, Mex. 149/G5
Santa Cruz (riv.), Mex.,US 149/G5
Santa Cruz, Peru 184/C2
Santa Cruz, Phil. 88/D4
Santa Cruz, Phil. 88/B2
Santa Cruz, Phil. 88/C1
Santa Cruz, Phil. 88/C2
Santa Cruz, SaoT. 120/A2
Santa Cruz (isls.), Sol. 136/F6
Santa Cruz (isl.), Ca, US 148/C4
Santa Cruz da Graciosa, Azor., Port. 47/S12
Santa Cruz das Flores, Azor., Port. 47/R12
Santa Cruz de Bucaral, Ven. 180/D2
Santa Cruz de El Seibo, DRep. 173/H4
Santa Cruz de la Palma, Sp. 110/A3
Santa Cruz de la Sierra, Bol. 188/D1
Santa Cruz de la Zarza, Sp. 46/D3
Santa Cruz de Mudela, Sp. 46/D3
Santa Cruz de Orinoco, Ven. 181/E2
Santa Cruz de Tenerife, Sp. 110/A3
Santa Cruz del Quiché, Guat. 176/D3
Santa Cruz del Sur, Cuba 177/G1
Santa Cruz do Capibaribe, Braz. 183/G4
Santa Cruz do Cuando, Ang. 122/D3
Santa Cruz do Piauí, Braz. 183/F4
Santa Cruz do Rio Pardo, Braz. 189/G2
Santa Cruz do Sul, Braz. 189/F4
Santa Elena, Arg. 188/D4
Santa Elena, Arg. 188/E4
Santa Elena, Bol. 185/E4
Santa Elena, Hon. 176/E2
Santa Elena (bay), CR 176/E4
Santa Elena, Ecu. 180/A5
Santa Elena (cape), CR 176/E4
Santa Elena (peak), Arg. 190/D5
Santa Elena, Peru 184/C2
Santa Elena de Turuchipa, Bol. 188/C1
Santa Elena de Uairén, Ven. 181/F3
Santa Eugenia de Ribeira, Sp. 46/A1
Santa Eulalia del Río, Sp. 47/F3
Santa Fe, Arg. 188/D4
Santa Fe (prov.), Arg. 188/D4
Santa Fe, Bol. 185/E3
Santa Fe, Cuba 177/F1
Santa Fé, Sp. 46/D4
Santa Fe (riv.), Fl, US 165/G3
Santa Fe (lake), Fl, US 165/G3
Santa Fe (cap.), NM, US 149/K3
Santa Fe (mts.), NM, US 152/B3
Santa Fe, Tx, US 151/M9
Santa Fé do Sul, Braz. 189/G2
Santa Fe Springs, Ca, US 166/F8
Santa Felicia (dam), Ca, US 166/B2
Santa Filomena, Braz. 183/E5
Santa Giustina (lake), It. 61/H5
Santa Helena, Braz. 183/E3
Santa Helena, Braz. 189/F3
Santa Helena de Goiás, Braz. 186/C3
Santa Inés (isl.), Chile 191/B7
Santa Inês, Braz. 187/F2
Santa Inês, Braz. 183/E3
Santa Isabel, Arg. 190/E2
Santa Isabel, Arg. 190/D3
Santa Isabel, Braz. 187/K8
Santa Isabel, Bol. 188/C2
Santa Isabel, Col. 177/F3
Santa Isabel, Ecu. 184/B1
Santa Isabel (riv.), Guat. 176/D2
Santa Isabel (isl.), Sol. 136/E5
Santa Isabel, Ven. 181/E4
Santa Isabel de Sihuas, Peru 184/C5
Santa Isabel do Ivaí, Braz. 189/F2
Santa Isabel do Pará, Braz. 182/D3
Santa Isabel, Pico de (peak), EqG. 120/B2
Santa Juliana, Braz. 186/D3
Santa Lucía, Arg. 188/E4
Santa Lucía (riv.), Arg. 189/E4
Santa Lucía, Ecu. 180/B5
Santa Lucía, Peru 184/D4
Santa Lucía, Uru. 191/K11
Santa Lucía, Sp. 110/B4
Santa Lucía, Ven. 183/P7
Santa Lucia (range), Ca, US 148/B2
Santa Lucía, Ven. 180/D2
Santa Lucia di Piave, It. 63/F2
Santa Luz, Braz. 187/F1
Santa Luzia (isl.), CpV. 107/J10
Santa Luzia, Braz. 183/G4
Santa Luzia, Braz. 183/E3
Santa Magdalena, Arg. 190/E2
Santa Magdalena (isl.), Mex. 174/B3
Santa Margarita (isl.), Mex. 174/B3
Santa Margarita (riv.), Ca, US 166/C4
Santa Margarita (riv.), Ca, US 148/D4
Santa Margherita Ligure, It. 62/C5
Santa María, Arg. 188/C3
Santa María, Bol. 188/D1
Santa María, Bol. 185/F4
Santa María, Chile 190/N8
Santa María, Ecu. 184/J7
Santa María (isl.), Ecu. 184/J7
Santa Mariá, Mex. 175/L7
Santa María (riv.), Mex. 174/D2
Santa María (bay), Mex. 174/C3
Santa Maria (cape), Port. 46/B4
Santa María, Ven. 181/E3
Santa Maria, Braz. 189/F4
Santa Maria (riv.), Braz. 189/F4
Santa Maria (isl.), Chile 190/B3
Santa Maria, CpV. 107/K10
Santa Maria, Phil. 88/D4
Santa Maria, Phil. 88/C1
Santa Maria, Phil. 88/E6
Santa Maria (isl.), Azor., Port. 47/T13
Santa Maria, Ca, US 148/B3
Santa Maria a Monte, It. 63/D6
Santa Maria a Vico, It. 65/D5
Santa Maria Capua Vetere, It. 65/D5
Santa Maria da Boa Vista, Braz. 183/G5
Santa Maria da Vitória, Braz. 186/D2
Santa María de Cayón, Sp. 46/D1
Santa María de Erebató, Ven. 181/E3
Santa María de Ipire, Ven. 181/E2
Santa María de Nanay, Peru 184/C1
Santa Maria degli Angeli, It. 65/B1
Santa María del Oro, Mex. 174/D3
Santa Maria della Versa, It. 62/C4
Santa Maria di Leuca (cape), It. 67/H3
Santa Maria di Leuca, Capo (cape), It. 75/F3
Santa Maria do Pará, Braz. 183/E3
Santa Maria do Suaçuí, Braz. 187/E3
Santa Maria la Carità, It. 65/D6
Santa Maria la Fossa, It. 65/D5
Santa Maria Maddalena, It. 63/E4
Santa Maria Maggiore, It. 61/E5
Santa Maria Nuova, It. 63/G7
Santa María Xadani, Mex. 172/B4
Santa Maria, Cabo de (cape), Moz. 125/F2
Santa Marta, Col. 180/C2
Santa Marta Grande, Cabo de (cape), Braz. 189/G4
Santa Marta, Sierra Nevada de (mts.), Col. 180/C2
Santa Monica (bay), Ca, US 166/B3
Santa Monica (mts.), Ca, US 166/B2
Santa Monica, Ca, US 166/F7
Santa Monica Mountains NRA, Ca, US 166/B2
Santa Olalla del Cala, Sp. 46/B4
Santa Paula (peak), Ca, US 166/A2
Santa Paula, Ca, US 166/A2
Santa Pola, Sp. 47/E3
Santa Pola, Cabo de (cape), Sp. 47/E3
Santa Quitéria, Braz. 183/F4
Santa Quitéria do Maranhão, Braz. 183/F3
Santa Rita, Braz. 183/H4
Santa Rita, Braz. 183/E3
Santa Rita, NM, US 149/H4
Santa Rita, Ven. 181/E2
Santa Rita, Ven. 180/D2
Santa Rita de Cássia, Braz. 186/D1
Santa Rita do Sapucaí, Braz. 187/L7
Santa Rosa, Arg. 188/C5
Santa Rosa, Arg. 188/C2
Santa Rosa, Arg. 190/D3
Santa Rosa, Braz. 189/F3
Santa Rosa, Bol. 185/E4
Santa Rosa, CR 176/E4
Santa Rosa, Uru. 191/K11
Santa Rosa, Bol. 185/E3
Santa Rosa, Bol. 188/C1
Santa Rosa, Braz. 182/C4
Santa Rosa, Par. 189/E3
Santa Rosa, Ecu. 184/B1
Santa Rosa, Peru 184/D4
Santa Rosa, Ca, US 146/B4
Santa Rosa (range), Nv, US 146/E3
Santa Rosa (isl.), Ca, US 148/C4
Santa Rosa, NM, US 152/B3
Santa Rosa (mts.), Nv, US 142/C3
Santa Rosa, Ven. 180/D3
Santa Rosa, Ven. 180/D2
Santa Rosa, Ven. 180/E3
Santa Rosa and San Jacinto Mountains NM, Ca, US 148/D4
Santa Rosa de Aguán, Hon. 176/E3
Santa Rosa de Amanadona, Ven. 181/E4
Santa Rosa de Cabal, Col. 183/K8
Santa Rosa de Calamuchita, Arg. 188/C5
Santa Rosa de Copán, Hon. 176/D3
Santa Rosa de la Roca, Bol. 185/F5
Santa Rosa de Osos, Col. 180/C3
Santa Rosa de Viterbo, Braz. 189/H2
Santa Rosa del Palmar, Bol. 185/F5
Santa Rosa del Sara, Bol. 188/D1
Santa Rosa Wash (riv.), Az, US 149/F4
Santa Rosa, PN, CR 172/C5
Santa Rosalía (pt.), Mex. 174/B2
Santa Rosalía, Mex. 174/B3
Santa Rosalía, Ven. 180/D2
Santa Rosalía, Ven. 181/E3
Santa Sofia, It. 63/E6
Santa Susana (mts.), Ca, US 166/B2
Santa Teresa, Austl. 131/G3
Santa Teresa, Braz. 187/E5
Santa Teresa (riv.), Braz. 186/C2
Santa Teresa, Braz. 186/C2
Santa Teresa, Ven. 183/P7
Santa Teresa Abor. Land, Austl. 131/G2
Santa Teresa, PN, Uru. 191/G2
Santa Teresinha, Braz. 186/C1
Santa Teresita, Arg. 191/F3
Santa Victoria, Arg. 188/D2
Santa Vitória, Braz. 186/C3
Santa Vitória do Palmar, Braz. 191/G2
Santa Ynez (mts.), Ca, US 166/A2
Santa Ynez (riv.), Ca, US 148/C3
Santa Ynez Ind. Res., Ca, US 148/B3
Santa Ysabel Ind. Res., Ca, US 148/D4
Santaella, Sp. 46/C4
Sant'Agata Bolognese, It. 63/E4
Sant'Agata di Militello, It. 48/D3
Sant'Agata Feltria, It. 63/F6
Sant'Agnello, It. 65/D6
Sant'Agostino, It. 63/E4
Sāntāhār, Bang. 97/G3
Sant'Alberto, It. 63/F4
Santana, Braz. 186/D2
Santana (isl.), Braz. 183/F3
Santana, Port. 110/A2
Santana, Port. 47/P11
Santana da Boa Vista, Braz. 189/F4
Santana do Acaraú, Braz. 183/F3
Santana do Cariri, Braz. 183/G4
Santana do Ipanema, Braz. 183/G5
Santana do Livramento, Braz. 189/F4
Sant'Anastasia, It. 65/D6
Santander (dept.), Col. 177/H5
Santander, Sp. 46/D1
Santander, Phil. 88/C3
Santander de Quilichao, Col. 180/B4
Santander Jiménez, Mex. 175/F3
Sant'Andrea del Pizzone, It. 65/D5
Sant'Angelo in Formis, It. 65/D5
Sant'Angelo in Vado, It. 63/F6
Sant'Angelo Lodigiano, It. 62/C3
Sant'Antioco, It. 66/F3
Sant'Antioco (isl.), It. 48/A3
Sant'Antonino di Susa, It. 64/D2
Sant'Antonio, It. 63/D3
Sant'Antonio Abate, It. 65/D6
Santañy, Sp. 47/G3
Sant'Apollinare in Classe, It. 63/F5
Santaquin, Ut, US 147/H4
Santarcángelo, It. 63/F5
Santarém (dist.), Port. 46/A3
Santarém, Port. 46/A3
Santarém, Braz. 182/C3
Santarém Novo, Braz. 183/E3
Sant'Arsenio, It. 48/D2
Santee, Ca, US 166/D5
Santee (pt.), SC, US 163/H4
Santee (dam), SC, US 163/G4
Santee (riv.), SC, US 163/H4
Santee Ind. Res., Ne, US 154/F2
Santee Nat'l Wild. Ref., SC, US 163/G4
Sant'Egidio alla Vibrata, It. 65/C2
Sant'Elia a Pianisi, It. 65/D4
Sant'Elia Fiumerapido, It. 65/C4
Sant'Elpidio a Mare, It. 65/C1
Santena, It. 62/A3
Santerno (riv.), It. 45/J4
Santeuil, Fr. 30/H4
Santhia, It. 62/B3
Santiago, Bol. 188/D1
Santiago, Braz. 189/F4
Santiago (cape), Chile 191/B6
Santiago (cap.), Chile 190/N8
Santiago (riv.), Ecu. 184/B1
Santiago (pt.), EqG. 120/B2
Santiago (mtn.), Pan. 177/F4
Santiago, Pan. 180/A2
Santiago, Par. 189/E3
Santiago (riv.), Peru 180/B5
Santiago, Peru 184/C4
Santiago, Phil. 88/C1
Santiago (int'l arpt.), Sp. 46/A1
Santiago (peak), Ca, US 166/C3
Santiago (res.), Ca, US 166/C3
Santiago (mts.), Tx, US 142/F5
Santiago (peak), Tx, US 151/C3
Santiago (Arturo Merino Benitez) (int'l arpt.), Chile 190/N8
Santiago Cuautlalpan, Mex. 175/Q9
Santiago Cuautlalpan, Mex. 175/R10
Santiago de Cao, Peru 184/B2
Santiago de Chocorvos, Peru 184/C4
Santiago de Chuco, Peru 184/B3
Santiago de Compostela, Sp. 46/A1
Santiago de Cuba, Cuba 177/H1
Santiago de los Caballeros, DRep. 173/G4
Santiago de Machaca, Bol. 184/D5
Santiago de Pacaguaras, Bol. 184/D4
Santiago del Estero (prov.), Arg. 188/D3
Santiago del Estero, Arg. 188/C3
Santiago do Cacém, Port. 46/A3
Santiago Ixcuintla, Mex. 174/D4
Santiago Jamiltepec, Mex. 176/B2
Santiago Juxtlahuaca, Mex. 176/B2
Santiago Miahuatlán, Mex. 175/M6
Santiago Papasquiaro, Mex. 174/D3
Santiago Pinotepa Nacional, Mex. 176/B2
Santiago Tilapa, Mex. 175/Q10
Santiago Tolman, Mex. 175/R9
Santiago Vázquez, Uru. 191/K11
Santiago Zacatepec, Mex. 176/C2
Santiam, North (riv.), Or, US 146/B1
Santiam, South (riv.), Or, US 146/B1
Santigi, Indo. 91/F3
Sant'Ilario d'Enza, It. 62/D4
Sāntipur, India 97/G4
Säntis (peak), Swi. 61/F3
Santisteban del Puerto, Sp. 46/D3
Santō, Japan 83/K5
Santō, Japan 83/G5
Santo, Tx, US 151/E1
Santo Amara (isl.), Braz. 187/K8
Santo Amaro (isl.), Braz. 187/K8
Santo Amaro, Braz. 187/F2
Santo Amaro das Brotas, Braz. 187/F1
Santo Anastácio, Braz. 189/G2
Santo André, Braz. 187/K8
Santo Ângelo, Braz. 189/F3
Santo Antão (isl.), CpV. 107/J9
Santo Antônio, SaoT. 120/A2
Santo Antônio do Içá, Braz. 180/E5
Santo Antônio do Leverger, Braz. 186/A2
Santo Antônio do Sudoeste, Braz. 189/F3
Santo Antônio dos Lopes, Braz. 183/E4
Santo Augusto, Braz. 189/F3
Santo Corazón, Bol. 188/E1
Santo Domingo, Bol. 185/E3
Santo Domingo, Cuba 177/F1
Santo Domingo, Chile 190/N8
Santo Domingo (cap.), DRep. 173/H4
Santo Domingo (pt.), Mex. 174/B3
Santo Domingo, Mex. 175/E4

Santo D – Seabro

Santo Domingo de la Calzada, Sp. 44/B5
Santo Domingo de los Colorados, Ecu. 180/B5
Santo Domingo Petapa, Mex. 176/C2
Santo Domingo Pueblo, NM, US 149/J3
Santo Domingo Tehuantepec, Mex. 176/C2
Santo Domingo Zanatepec, Mex. 176/C2
Santo Stefano (isl.), It. 65/C6
Santo Stefano Belbo, It. 62/B4
Santo Stefano d'Aveto, It. 62/C4
Santo Stefano di Magra, It. 62/C5
Santo Stino di Livenza, It. 63/F2
Santo Tomás (vol.), Ecu. 184/J7
Santo Tomas (mt.), Phil. 88/C1
Santo Tomás, Peru 184/B2
Santo Tomás, Peru 184/C4
Santo Tomás, Mex. 174/A2
Santo Tomás, (pt.), Mex. 174/A2
Santo Tomé, Arg. 189/E4
Santo Tomé, Arg. 188/D4
Santoña, Sp. 44/B5
Sant'Onofrio, It. 65/G8
Sant'Oreste, It. 65/B3
Santorso, It. 63/E2
Santos, Braz. 187/K8
Santos Dumont (int'l arpt.), Braz. 187/N7
Santos Dumont, Braz. 187/N6
Santos Mercado, Bol. 185/E3
Santos Reyes Nopala, Mex. 176/B2
Santuario, Col. 183/K7
Santuario, Col. 183/K6
Santuario di Crea, It. 62/B3
Santuario di Monte Vergine, It. 65/D6
Santuario di Oropa, It. 62/A1
Santunying, China 80/J6
Şanūr, WBnk. 105/C4
Sanwa, Japan 83/D1
Sanxing, China 80/L8
Sanya, China 87/F5
Sanyang, China 87/H2
Sanyati (riv.), Zim. 123/F3
Sanyuanba, China 87/E1
Sanyuanpu, China 81/C1
Sanza Pombo, Ang. 120/C4
São Bartolomeu (riv.), Braz. 186/D3
São Benedito, Braz. 183/F4
São Benedito do Rio Prêto, Braz. 183/F3
São Bento, Braz. 183/G4
São Bento, Braz. 183/E3
São Bento do Sapucaí, Braz. 187/L7
São Bento do Sul, Braz. 189/G3
São Bento do Una, Braz. 183/G5
São Bernardo do Campo, Braz. 187/K8
São Borja, Braz. 189/F4
São Braz, Cabo de (cape), Ang. 120/C5
São Carlos, Braz. 189/H2
São Cristóvão, Braz. 187/F1
São Desidério, Braz. 186/D2
São Domingos, Braz. 186/D2
São Domingos (riv.), Braz. 186/D2
São Domingos, GBis. 114/A3
São Domingos do Capim, Braz. 182/E3
São Domingos do Maranhão, Braz. 183/E4
São Félix do Araguaia, Braz. 186/C1
São Félix do Piauí, Braz. 183/F4
São Félix do Xingu, Braz. 182/D4
São Fidélis, Braz. 187/E4
São Filipe, CpV. 107/J11
São Francisco (riv.), Braz. 179/F3
São Francisco (isl.), Braz. 189/G3
São Francisco, Braz. 186/D2
São Francisco do Sul, Braz. 189/G3
São Fransisco de Assis, Braz. 189/F4
São Fransisco de Paula, Braz. 189/G4
São Gabriel, Braz. 189/F4
São Gabriel da Palha, Braz. 187/E3
São Gonçalo, Braz. 187/N7
São Gonçalo do Sapuçaí, Braz. 187/L6
São Gotardo, Braz. 189/H1
Sao Hill, Tanz. 119/A4
São Joachim da Barra, Braz. 189/H2
São João Batista, Braz. 183/E3
São João Batista, Braz. 189/G3
São João da Aliança, Braz. 186/D2
São João da Boa Vista, Braz. 187/K6
São João da Madeira, Port. 46/A2
São João da Pesqueira, Port. 46/B2
São João da Ponte, Braz. 186/D2
São João das Lampas, Port. 47/P10
São João de Meriti, Braz. 187/N7
São João del Rei, Braz. 186/D4
São João do Araguaia, Braz. 182/D4
São João do Jaguaribe, Braz. 183/G4
São João do Paraíso, Braz. 187/E2
São João do Piauí, Braz. 183/F5
São João dos Patos, Braz. 183/F4
São João Evangelista, Braz. 187/E3
São João Nepomuceno, Braz. 187/N6
São João, Serra de (mts.), Braz. 185/F3
São Joaquim, Braz. 189/G4
São Joaquim, PN de, Braz. 189/G4
São Jorge (isl.), Azor., Port. 47/S12
São José, Braz. 189/G3
São José da Laje, Braz. 183/G5
São José de Mipibu, Braz. 183/H4
São José de Ribamar, Braz. 183/E3
São José do Belmonte, Braz. 183/G4
São José do Campestre, Braz. 183/H4
São José do Egito, Braz. 183/G4
São José do Gurupi, Braz. 183/E3
São José do Norte, Braz. 189/F5
São José do Peixe, Braz. 183/F4
São José do Rio Pardo, Braz. 187/K6
São José do Rio Prêto, Braz. 189/G2
São José dos Campos, Braz. 187/L8
São José dos Pinhais, Braz. 189/G3
São Julião, Braz. 183/F4
São Lourenço, Port. 47/P11
São Lourenço, Braz. 187/L7
São Lourenço (riv.), Braz. 185/G5
São Lourenço da Mata, Braz. 183/H5
São Lourenço do Sul, Braz. 189/G4
São Lourenço d'Oeste, Braz. 189/F3
São Lucas, Ang. 120/D5
São Luís, Braz. 183/E3
São Luís de Montes Belos, Braz. 186/C3
São Luís do Curu, Braz. 183/G3
São Luís do Quitunde, Braz. 183/H5
São Luís Gonzaga, Braz. 189/F4
São Mamede, Braz. 183/G4
São Marcos (bay), Braz. 179/E3
São Marcos (riv.), Braz. 186/D3
São Martinho do Porto, Port. 46/A3
São Mateus, Braz. 187/F3
São Mateus (riv.), Braz. 187/E3
São Mateus do Maranhão, Braz. 183/E4
São Mateus do Sul, Braz. 189/G3
São Miguel (isl.), Azor., Port. 47/T13
São Miguel, Braz. 183/G4
São Miguel do Araguaia, Braz. 186/C2
São Miguel do Guamá, Braz. 183/E3
São Miguel do Tapuio, Braz. 183/F4
São Miguel d'Oeste, Braz. 189/F3
São Miguel dos Campos, Braz. 187/F1
São Nicolau (isl.), CpV. 107/J10
São Paulo, Braz. 187/K8
São Paulo (state), Braz. 186/C4
São Paulo de Olivença, Braz. 184/D1
São Paulo do Potengi, Braz. 183/H4
São Pedro do Piauí, Braz. 183/F4
São Pedro do Sul, Port. 46/A2
São Pedro do Sul, Braz. 189/F4
São Rafael, Braz. 183/G4
São Raimundo das Mangabeiras, Braz. 183/E4
São Raimundo Nonato, Braz. 183/F5
São Romão, Braz. 186/D3
São Roque (cape), Braz. 183/H4
São Roque do Pico, Azor., Port. 47/S12
São Sebastião (pt.), Moz. 123/G4
São Sebastião, Braz. 187/L8
São Sebastião (isl.), Braz. 186/D4
São Sebastião da Boa Vista, Braz. 182/D3
São Sebastião do Paraíso, Braz. 189/H2
São Sebastião do Tocantins, Braz. 182/D4
São Sebastião do Umbuzeiro, Braz. 183/G5
São Simão (riv.), Braz. 185/F4
São Simão (res.), Braz. 186/C3
São Simão, Braz. 186/C3
São Teotónio, Port. 46/A4
São Tiago (isl.), CpV. 107/K10
São Tomé (int'l arpt.), SaoT. 120/A2
São Tomé (isl.), SaoT. 120/A2
São Tomé (cap.), SaoT. 120/A2
São Tomé and Príncipe (ctry.) 107/C4
São Tomé, Cabo de (cape), Braz. 187/E4
São Vicente (cape), Port. 46/A4
São Vicente, Braz. 187/K8
São Vicente (isl.), CpV. 107/J10
São Vicente Ferrer, Braz. 183/E3
Saône (riv.), Fr. 66/E1
Saône-et-Loire (dept.), Fr. 60/B4
Saori, Japan 83/L5
Saouru, Oued (riv.), Alg. 111/E3
Sapāhār, Bang. 97/G3
Sápai, Gre. 75/J2
Sapallanga, Peru 184/C4
Sapanca, Turk. 51/K5
Saparua, Indo. 91/G4
Sapatgrām, India 97/H2
Sapawe, On, Can. 157/J3
Sapé, Braz. 183/H4
Sapele, Nga. 115/G5
Sapelo (isl.), Ga, US 165/H2
Şaphane, Turk. 70/D5
Sapiéndza (isl.), Gre. 75/G4
Sapkyo, SKor. 81/D4
Sapo (mts.), Pan. 177/G5
Sapo NP, Libr. 114/C5
Sapo-Sapo, D.R. Congo 121/E4
Saponé, Burk. 115/E3
Saposoa, Peru 184/B2
Sapozhok, Rus. 71/G1
Sappa (cr.), Ks, US 154/D4
Sappa, Middle Fork (cr.), Ks, US 152/D1
Sappa, South Fork (cr.), Ks, US 152/D1
Sappemeer, Neth. 52/D2
Sapphire, Austl. 134/B3
Sapporo, Japan 82/B2
Sapri, It. 48/D2
Sapsi (isl.), SKor. 81/D3
Sapt Kosi (riv.), Nepal 97/F2
Sapucaí (riv.), Braz. 187/L7
Sapucaí (riv.), Braz. 189/H2
Sapucaia, Braz. 187/P6
Sapudi (isl.), Indo. 89/F4
Sapulpa, Ok, US 153/F3
Sapulut, Malay. 88/B4
Sāqiyat Sīdī Yūsuf, Tun. 112/L6
Saqqez, Iran 103/F2
Saquena, Peru 184/C2
Saquisilí, Ecu. 180/B5
Şar (mts.), Yugo 75/G1
Şar (mts.), Yugo. 50/E4
Sar Dasht, Iran 103/F2
Sara, Phil. 88/C3
Sara Buri, Thai. 94/C3
Sarāb, Iran 103/F2
Sarābiyūm, Egypt 113/D3
Saraceno (peak), It. 65/D5
Saraf Doungous, Chad 116/C2
Sarafjagān, Iran 103/G3
Saragosa, Tx, US 151/C2
Saragossa (Zaragoza), Sp. 47/E2
Saraguro, Ecu. 184/B1
Sarāi Alamgir, Pak. 98/B3
Sarāi Sidhu, Pak. 98/A4
Saraikela, India 97/E4
Sarāil, Bang. 97/H3
Saraipāli, India 95/D1
Sarajevo (cap.), Bosn. 50/D4
Saraktash, Rus. 71/L2
Saraland, Al, US 164/D2
Saramabila, D.R. Congo 121/H4
Saramacca (dist.), Sur. 181/H3
Saramati (peak), India 86/B3
Sarampiuni, Bol. 184/D4
Saran, Fr. 57/G5
Saran (peak), Indo. 90/D4
Saran', Kaz. 99/B2
Saranac Lake, NY, US 161/J2
Saranda, Tanz. 119/A3
Sarandapótamos (riv.), Gre. 75/N8
Sarandë, Alb. 75/G3
Sarandi, Braz. 189/F3
Sarandí de Navarro, Uru. 191/K10
Sarandí del Yi, Uru. 191/G2
Sarandí Grande, Uru. 191/K10
Sārangagada, India 95/E1
Sarangani (isls.), Phil. 91/G2
Sarangani (isls.), Phil. 88/D4
Sārangarh, India 95/D1
Sārangpur, India 92/C3
Saranley, Som. 119/C1
Saransk, Rus. 71/H1
Sarapul, Rus. 69/M4
Sarare (riv.), Ven. 180/D3
Sāraskheri, India 96/A3
Sarasota, Fl, US 165/G4
Sarata, Ukr. 51/J2
Saratoga, Ca, US 167/K12
Saratoga, Wy, US 147/K3
Saratoga Nat'l Hist. Park, NY, US 161/K3
Saratoga Springs, NY, US 161/K3
Saratok, Malay. 90/D3
Saratov (res.), Rus. 71/J1
Saratov, Rus. 71/H2
Saratovskaya Oblast, Rus. 71/H2
Saravan, Laos 94/D3
Sarawaget (range), PNG 129/G1
Sarawak (reg.), Malay. 77/L9
Saray, Turk. 51/H5
Saraya, Sen. 114/C3
Sarayacu, Ecu. 180/B5
Sarāyan (riv.), India 96/C2
Sarayköy, Turk. 102/B2
Sarayönü, Turk. 102/C2
Sarbāz, Iran 103/H3
Sarbhāng, Bhu. 97/H2
Sárbogárd, Hun. 50/D2
Sarcari, Bol. 188/C2
Sarcelles, Fr. 30/K5
Sarco, Chile 188/B4
Sarcoxie, Mo, US 153/G2
Sārda (riv.), India 96/C1
Sārda (canal), India 96/C2
Sarda (riv.), India 92/D2
Sardara, It. 48/A3
Sardārpura, India 98/B5
Sardārshahar, India 98/C5
Sardegna (prov.), It. 48/A2
Sardhana, India 98/D5
Sardinata, Col. 180/C2
Sardinia (isl.), It. 48/A2
Sardinia, Oh, US 162/F1
Sardis (dam), Ms, US 162/C3
Sardis, Ms, US 162/C3
Sardis, Tx, US 150/L7
Sardis, Ga, US 163/G4
Sardis (lake), Ms, US 162/C3
Sareks NP, Swe. 38/F2
Sarektjåkko (peak), Swe. 38/F2
Sarempaka (peak), Indo. 91/E4
Sārenga, India 97/F4
Sarentino, It. 61/H4
Sarepta, La, US 153/H4
Sarezzo, It. 62/D2
Sargans, Swi. 61/F3
Sargents, Co, US 149/J1
Sargodha, Pak. 98/B3
Sarh, Chad 116/C3
Sārī, Iran 103/H2
Sari (cape), Malay. 89/C2
Sari-Solenzara, Fr. 48/A2
Saria, India 98/C3
Saribi (cape), Indo. 91/J4
Sarigan (isl.), NMar. 136/D3
Sarıgazi (arpt.), Turk. 103/N7
Sarıgöl, Turk. 102/B2
Sarıkamış, Turk. 102/E1
Sarıkaya (prov.), Turk. 70/E5
Sarıkaya, Turk. 70/E5
Sarikei, Malay. 90/D3
Sarina, Austl. 134/C3
Sarine (riv.), Swi. 45/G3
Sariñena, Sp. 47/E2
Sarīr Kalanshiyū (des.), Libya 134/D3
Sarīr Kalanshiyū ar Ramlī al Kabīr (des.), Libya 134/D2
Sarīr Tibasti (des.), Libya 134/C4
Sarita, Tx, US 151/F4
Sariwŏn, NKor. 81/C3
Sarju (riv.), India 96/C1
Sark (isl.), Fr. 56/C2
Sark (isl.), Chl, UK 44/B2
Sarkad, Hun. 50/E2
Sarkant, Kaz. 74/H5
Särkijärvi (lake), Fin. 39/D4
Şarkîkaraağaç, Turk. 102/B2
Şarkışla, Turk. 102/D2
Şarköy, Turk. 51/H5
Sarlat-la-Canéda, Fr. 44/D4
Sarleinsbach, Aus. 59/G5
Sarmato, It. 62/C3
Sarmeola, It. 63/E3
Sarmi, Indo. 91/J4
Sarmiento, Arg. 190/C5
Sarmiento (peak), Chile 191/C7
Särna, Swe. 40/E1
Sarnano, It. 65/C1
Sarnen, Swi. 61/E4
Sarnia, On, Can. 160/E3
Sarnico, It. 62/C2
Sarno, It. 65/D6
Sarny, Ukr. 72/D2
Saroako, Indo. 91/F4
Sarolangun, Indo. 89/C3
Saroma (lake), Japan 82/C1
Saronic (gulf), Gre. 67/J3
Saronno, It. 62/C2
Saros (gulf), Turk. 70/C4
Sárospatak, Hun. 43/L4
Sarpsborg, Nor. 40/D2
Sarralbe, Fr. 55/G6
Sarras, Fr. 64/A2
Sarratt, Eng, UK 30/B1
Sarre (riv.), Fr. 54/F6
Sarre-Union, Fr. 55/G6
Sarrebourg, Fr. 55/G6
Sarreguemines, Fr. 55/G5
Sarria, Sp. 46/B1
Sarrians, Fr. 64/A4
Sarroch, It. 48/A3
Sarry, Fr. 55/D6
Sarsāwa, India 98/D4
Sarsina, It. 63/F6
Särsö (isl.), Swe. 39/B1
Sarstedt, Ger. 53/G4
Sarstún (riv.), Guat. 176/D3
Sartang (riv.), Rus. 75/P3
Sarteano, It. 48/B1
Sartell, Mn, US 157/G5
Sartène, Fr. 48/A2
Sarthe (dept.), Fr. 57/F4
Sarthe (riv.), Fr. 44/C3
Sarthon (riv.), Fr. 57/E4
Sartilly, Fr. 56/D3
Sartrouville, Fr. 30/J5
Sarufutsu, Japan 82/C1
Saruhanlı, Turk. 70/C5
Şarur, Azer. 103/F2
Sárvár, Hun. 50/C2
Sarvestān, Iran 103/H4
Sárvíz (riv.), Hun. 50/D2
Sary Ishikotrau (des.), Kaz. 99/C2
Saryagach, Kaz. 99/A3
Sarybasat, Kaz. 71/M3
Sarych (cape), Ukr. 73/G5
Saryg-Sep, Rus. 99/G1
Sarygamysh Köli (lake), Trkm. 71/L4
Saryshaghan, Kaz. 99/B2
Sarysu (riv.), Kaz. 74/G5
Sarzana, It. 62/C5
Sarzeau, Fr. 56/C5
Sas Van Gent, Neth. 54/C1
Sa'sa', Syria 105/E2
Sasabe, Az, US 149/G5
Sasaginnigack (lake), Mb, Can. 157/G2
Sasak, Indo. 89/B2
Sasarām, India 97/E3
Sasayama, Japan 83/H5
Sasayama (riv.), Japan 83/H5
Sásd, Hun. 50/D2
Sasebo, Japan 84/A4
Sashima, Japan 83/D1
Saskatchewan (riv.), Can. 139/G4
Saskatchewan (prov.), Can. 140/F3
Saskatoon, Sk, Can. 145/L1
Saslaya (mtn.), Nic. 176/E3
Saslaya, PN, Nic. 176/E3
Sāsni, India 96/B2
Sasolburg, SAfr. 124/D2
Sasoma, India 98/D2
Sasovo, Rus. 71/G1
Sassafras (peak), Tn, US 162/E3
Sassafras (mtn.), SC, US 163/F3
Sassafras, Md, US 168/C5
Sassafras (riv.), Md, US 168/B5
Sassandra, C.d'Iv. 114/D5
Sassandra (riv.), C.d'Iv. 114/D5
Sassari, It. 48/A2
Sasse (riv.), Fr. 64/C4
Sassello, It. 62/B5
Sassenage, Fr. 64/B2
Sassenberg, Ger. 53/F4
Sassenheim, Neth. 52/B4
Sasser, Ga, US 165/F2
Sassnitz, Ger. 40/E4
Sasso Marconi, It. 63/E5
Sassocorvaro, It. 63/F6
Sassoferrato, It. 63/F7
Sassoumbouroum, Niger 115/H3
Sasstown, Libr. 114/C5
Sassuolo, It. 63/D4
Sástago, Sp. 47/E2
Sastre, Arg. 188/D4
Sasykkol (lake), Kaz. 99/D2
Sata-misaki (cape), Japan 84/B5
Satadougou Tintiba, Mali 114/C3
Satara, SAfr. 123/F5
Satawan (isl.), Micr. 136/E4
Satellite Beach, Fl, US 165/H3
Satema, CAfr. 116/D4
Säter, Swe. 40/F1
Saticoy, Ca, US 166/A2
Satilla (riv.), Ga, US 165/G2
Satillieu, Fr. 64/A2
Satipo, Peru 184/C3
Satis, Rus. 69/J5
Sātkānia, Bang. 97/J4
Sātkhira, Bang. 97/G4
Satley, Eng, UK 35/G2
Satna, India 96/C3
Satolas (Lyon) (int'l arpt.), Fr. 60/B6
Sátoraljaújhely, Hun. 43/L4
Satpayev, Kaz. 99/A2
Satpura (range), India 92/C3
Sætre, Nor. 38/S8
Satsuma, Al, US 164/D2
Satsuma, Tx, US 151/M9
Sattahip, Thai. 94/C3
Satte, Japan 83/D1
Satteins, Aus. 61/F3
Satteldorf, Ger. 58/D4
Sattelberg, PNG 129/G1
Sättra, Swe. 39/A1
Satu Mare, Rom. 43/M5
Satu Mare (co.), Rom. 43/M5
Satuk, Thai. 94/C3
Satun, Thai. 94/C5
Satupaitea, Sam. 137/R9
Saturna, BC, Can. 144/C3
Sauce, Arg. 188/E4
Sauce, Peru 184/B2
Sauce de Luna, Arg. 188/E4
Sauce Grande (riv.), Arg. 190/E3
Saucedo, Uru. 188/E4
Saucier, Ms, US 164/D2
Saucillo, Mex. 151/B3
Sauda, Nor. 40/B2
Saudhárkrókur, Ice. 38/N6
Saudi Arabia (ctry.) 77/B7
Sauer (riv.), Ger. 53/F5
Sauerlach, Ger. 61/H2
Sauerland (reg.), Ger. 42/D3
Sauêruiná (riv.), Braz. 185/G4
Saugatuck, Mi, US 160/C3
Saugatuck (riv.), Ct, US 169/E1
Saugeen (riv.), On, Can. 160/F2
Saugeen Ind. Res., On, Can. 160/F2
Saugerties, NY, US 161/K3
Sauiá, Braz. 182/B3
Saujon, Fr. 44/C4
Sauk (riv.), Mn, US 155/G1
Sauk Centre, Mn, US 157/G5
Sauk City, Wi, US 155/K2
Sauk Rapids, Mn, US 157/G5
Saukkola, Fin. 39/D4
Saül, FrG. 182/C2
Sauland, Nor. 40/C2
Saulce-sur-Rhône, Fr. 64/A3
Sauldre (riv.), Fr. 44/D3
Saulgau, Ger. 61/F1
Saulheim, Ger. 58/B3
Saulieu, Fr. 44/F3
Saulkrasti, Lat. 41/L3
Saulnierville, NS, Can. 158/D3
Sault, Fr. 64/B4
Sault aux Cochons (riv.), Qu, Can. 158/C1
Sault Sainte Marie, On, Can. 160/D1
Sault Sainte Marie, Mi, US 160/D1
Sault-lès-Rethel, Fr. 55/D5
Saulx, Fr. 60/C2
Saulx (riv.), Fr. 42/C4
Saulxures-sur-Moselotte, Fr. 60/C2
Saumlaki, Indo. 128/C1
Saumur, Fr. 57/E6
Saunders (cape), NZ 135/B4
Saunders (peak), Austl. 130/E3
Saundersfoot, Wal, UK 36/B3
Saura (riv.), India 97/F3
Saurimo, Ang. 121/E5
Sausalito, Ca, US 167/J11
Sausseron (riv.), Fr. 30/J4
Sausset-les-Pins, Fr. 64/B6
Sausu, Indo. 91/F4
Saut-Tigre, FrG. 182/C1
Sautatá, Col. 180/B3
Sautet (lake), Fr. 64/B3
Sauteurs, Gren. 181/F1
Sautron, Fr. 56/D6
Sauzon, Fr. 56/B6
Sava, It. 75/E2
Sava (riv.), Eur. 67/J1
Savá, Hon. 176/E3
Savage, Mt, US 156/B4
Savage (mtn.), Md, US 161/G5
Savage (dam), Ca, US 166/D5
Savage, Mn, US 157/P7
Savage River, Austl. 132/C4
Savai'i (isl.), Sam. 137/H6
Savalou, Ben. 115/F5
Savanna, Ok, US 153/G3
Savanna, Il, US 155/J2
Savanna-la-Mar, Jam. 177/G2
Savannah (riv.), US 139/J6
Savannah, Mo, US 155/G4
Savannah, Tn, US 162/C3
Savannah (brook), Austl. 130/L6
Savannah, Ga, US 163/G4
Savannah NWR, Ga, US 165/H1
Savannah River Plant, SC, US 163/G4
Savannakhet, Laos 94/D2
Savant (lake), On, Can. 157/J2
Savant Lake, On, Can. 157/J2
Sävar, Swe. 38/G3
Savaştepe, Turk. 70/C5
Savate, Ang. 122/C3
Savé, Ben. 115/F4
Save (riv.), Moz. 107/F7
Save (riv.), Zim. 123/G4
Sāveh, Iran 103/G3
Savena (riv.), It. 63/E4
Savenay, Fr. 56/D6
Săveni, Rom. 72/D4
Saverdun, Fr. 44/D5
Saverne, Fr. 55/G6
Savièse, Swi. 60/D5
Savigliano, It. 64/D3
Savignano sul Panaro, It. 63/E5
Savignano sul Rubicone, It. 63/F5
Savigné-L'Évêque, Fr. 57/F4
Savigny-le-Temple, Fr. 30/K6
Savigny-sur-Braye, Fr. 57/F5
Savigny-sur-Orge, Fr. 30/K5
Savines-le-Lac, Fr. 64/C3
Saviniemi, Fin. 39/E3
Sävja, Swe. 40/G2
Savognin, Swi. 61/F4
Savoie (dept.), Fr. 60/C6
Savona, It. 62/B5
Savona (prov.), It. 62/B4
Savona, BC, Can. 144/D2
Savonburg, Ks, US 153/G2
Savoonga, Ak, US 171/D3
Savoy, Tx, US 153/F4
Savoy, Il, US 160/B4
Savoy (reg.), Fr. 66/E1
Savoy, SD, US 154/C1
Savoy, Mt, US 145/K3
Savoy Alps (mts.), Fr. 60/C6
Saxman, Ak, US 171/M4
Şavşat, Turk. 71/G4
Sävsjö, Swe. 40/F3
Savu (sea), Phil. 77/M10
Savusavu, Fiji 137/Z17
Sawahlunto, Indo. 89/C3
Sawākin, Sudan 109/H5
Sawang Daeh Din, Thai. 94/C2
Sawankhalok, Thai. 94/B2
Sawara, Japan 85/G3
Sawasaki-bana (pt.), Japan 85/F2
Sawatch (range), Co, US 154/A4
Sawbridgeworth, Eng, UK 37/G3
Sawdā', Jabal (peak), SAr. 100/D5
Sawdirī, Sudan 116/F2
Saweba (cape), Indo. 91/H4
Sawel (mtn.), NI, UK 34/A2
Sawena, Eth. 118/B4
Sāwi, India 93/F6
Sawkanah, Libya 134/B2
Sawmills, Zim. 123/F3
Sawpit, Co, US 149/H2
Sawston, Eng, UK 37/G2
Sawtell, Austl. 132/E1
Sawtooth (range), Id, US 147/F1
Sawtooth (mtn.), Mt, US 145/K3
Sawtooth Nat'l Rec. Area, Id, US 147/F1
Sawu, Indo. 128/A2
Sawu (isl.), Indo. 128/A2
Sawu (isls.), Indo. 91/F6
Sawyer, ND, US 156/D3
Sawyer, Ks, US 153/E2
Sawyers Bar, Ca, US 146/B3
Sax, Sp. 47/E3
Saxån (riv.), Swe. 39/K7
Saxarfjärden (sound), Swe. 39/B1
Saxilby, Eng, UK 35/H5
Saxis, Va, US 163/K2
Saxmundham, Eng, UK 37/H2
Saxon, Swi. 60/D5
Say, Niger 115/F3
Say-Utes, Kaz. 71/K3
Saya, Japan 83/L5
Saya, Bol. 188/C1
Sayabec, Qu, Can. 158/D1
Sayak, Kaz. 74/H5
Sayama, Japan 85/F3
Sayama, Japan 83/J6
Sayán, Peru 184/B3
Sayansk, Rus. 78/E1
Şaydā (Sidon), Leb. 105/C1
Şaydnāyā, Syria 105/E1
Sayhūt, Yem. 118/D2
Sayil (ruin), Mex. 176/D1
Sayingpan, China 86/D3
Saykhin, Kaz. 71/H2
Saylah, Egypt 113/B6
Saynbach (riv.), Ger. 55/G2
Sayner, Wi, US 157/K5
Sayram (lake), China 99/D3
Sayre, Ok, US 152/E3
Sayre, Pa, US 161/H4
Sayreville, NJ, US 169/H10
Saysu, China 99/F3
Sayula, Mex. 174/E5
Sayville, NY, US 169/E2
Saywūn, Yem. 118/D2
Sazan (isl.), Alb. 75/F2
Sazan (isl.), Gre. 50/D5
Sazdy, Kaz. 71/J3
Sazīn, Pak. 98/B2
Sazli Dere (riv.), Turk. 103/M6
Sbaa, Alg. 111/E3
Scaër, Fr. 56/B4
Scafati, It. 65/D6
Scafell Pikes (peak), Eng, UK 35/E3
Scalasaig, Sc, UK 31/Q8
Scalby, Eng, UK 35/H3
Scald Law (peak), Sc, UK 33/C5
Scalea, It. 48/D3
Scalino (peak), It. 61/F5
Scalloway, Sc, UK 31/W13
Scammon Bay, Ak, US 171/E3
Scandia, Ab, Can. 145/H2
Scandia, Ks, US 154/F4
Scandia, Mn, US 157/Q6
Scandia, Wa, US 167/B2
Scandiano, It. 63/D4
Scandicci, It. 63/E6
Scanlon, Mn, US 157/H4
Scanno, It. 65/C4
Scapa Flow (chan.), Sc, UK 31/V14
Scar Water (riv.), Sc, UK 34/E1
Scarborough, Eng, UK 35/H3
Scarborough, Trin. 181/F2
Scarborough (nbrhd.), Austl. 130/K6
Scarborough (co.), On, Can. 160/U8
Scarborough Shoal (isl.), Phil. 88/B2
Scardovari, It. 63/F4
Scarinish, Sc, UK 31/Q8
Scarpe (riv.), Fr. 42/B3
Scarperia, It. 63/E6
Scarriff, Ire. 32/B4
Scarsdale, NY, US 169/K7
Scatarie (isl.), Ns., Can. 159/H3
Scattery (isl.), Ire. 32/A4
Scauri, It. 65/C5
Sceaux, Fr. 30/J5
Scerni, It. 65/D3
Scey-sur-Saône-et-St-Albin, Fr. 60/B2
Schaefferstown, Pa, US 168/B3
Schaerbeek, Belg. 55/D2
Schaffer, Mi, US 157/L5
Schaffhausen, Swi. 61/E2
Schaffhausen (canton), Swi. 61/E2
Schäftlarn, Ger. 61/H2
Schagen, Neth. 52/B3
Schaijk, Neth. 52/C5
Schalchen, Aus. 59/G6
Schalkau, Ger. 58/E2
Schalksmühle, Ger. 53/E6
Schaller, Ia, US 155/G2
Schanck (cape), Austl. 133/B4
Schangnau, Swi. 60/D4
Scharans, Swi. 61/F4
Schardenberg, Aus. 59/G5
Schärding, Aus. 59/G6
Scharfreiter (peak), Aus. 61/H3
Scharhorn (isl.), Ger. 53/F1
Scharnebeck, Ger. 53/H2
Scharnhorst (pt.), PNG 129/G1
Scharnitz (pass), Ger. 61/H3
Scharnstein, Aus. 59/G7
Schashagen, Ger. 42/F1
Schattdorf, Swi. 61/E4
Schauenstein, Ger. 59/E2
Schaumburg, Il, US 167/P15
Scheemda, Neth. 52/D2
Scheer, Ger. 61/F1
Scheessel, Ger. 53/G2
Schefferville, Qu, Can. 167/K3
Scheibbs, Aus. 43/H4
Scheidegg, Ger. 61/F2
Scheinfeld, Ger. 58/D3
Schelde (riv.), Belg. 54/C2
Scheldt (riv.), Belg. 44/E1
Schelklingen, Ger. 58/C6
Schell City, Mo, US 153/G1
Schell Creek (range), Nv, US 147/F4
Schellerten, Ger. 53/H4
Schellville, Ca, US 167/K10
Schenectady, NY, US 161/K3
Schenefeld, Ger. 53/G1
Schererville, In, US 160/C4
Schermbeck, Ger. 52/D5
Scherpenzeel, Neth. 52/C3
Schertz, Tx, US 151/E3
Schesaplana (peak), Aus. 61/F3
Schesslitz, Ger. 58/E3
Scheveningen, Neth. 52/B4
Scheyern, Ger. 59/E5
Schiedam, Neth. 52/B5
Schieder-Schwalenberg, Ger. 53/G5
Schiehallion (peak), Sc, UK 33/B3
Schier Monnikoog (isl.), Neth. 42/D2
Schierling, Ger. 59/F5
Schiermonnikoog (isl.), Neth. 52/D1
Schiermonnikoog, Neth. 52/D2
Schiers, Swi. 61/F4
Schifferstadt, Ger. 58/B4
Schiffweiler, Ger. 55/G5
Schijndel, Neth. 52/C5
Schilde, Belg. 52/B6
Schildmeer (lake), Neth. 52/D2
Schillighörn (cape), Ger. 53/F1
Schillingfürst, Ger. 58/D4
Schiltach, Ger. 61/E1
Schiltigheim, Fr. 60/D1
Schinnen, Neth. 55/E2
Schinznach-Dorf, Swi. 60/E3
Schio, It. 63/E2
Schipbeek (riv.), Neth. 52/D4
Schiphol, Neth. 52/B4
Schipol (Amsterdam) (int'l arpt.), Neth. 52/B4
Schirmeck, Fr. 60/D1
Schkumbin (riv.), Alb. 75/G2
Schladen, Ger. 53/H4
Schladming, Aus. 45/K3
Schlanders (Silandro), It. 61/G4
Schlangen, Ger. 53/F5
Schlangenbad, Ger. 58/B2
Schlater, Ms, US 162/B4
Schleiden, Ger. 55/F2
Schleitheim, Swi. 61/E2
Schleiz, Ger. 59/E1
Schlema, Ger. 59/F1
Schleswig, Ger. 40/C4
Schleswig, Ia, US 155/G2
Schleswig-Holstein (state), Ger. 40/B4
Schleswig-Holsteinisches Wattenmeer NP, Ger. 40/C4
Schleuse (riv.), Ger. 58/D2
Schleusingen, Ger. 58/D1
Schliengen, Ger. 60/D2
Schlierbach, Aus. 59/H7
Schlieren, Swi. 61/E3
Schloss Herrenchiemsee, Ger. 59/F7
Schloss Holte-Stukenbrock, Ger. 53/F5
Schloss Sansoucci, Ger. 42/Q7
Schloss Wilhelmstein, Ger. 53/G4
Schlotheim, Ger. 53/H6
Schluchsee, Ger. 60/E2
Schlüchtern, Ger. 58/C2
Schluderns (Sluderno), It. 61/G4
Schlüsselfeld, Ger. 58/D3
Schlüsslberg, Aus. 59/G6
Schmallenberg, Ger. 53/F6
Schmeich (riv.), Ger. 58/C6
Schmelz, Ger. 55/F5
Schmiech (riv.), Ger. 61/F1
Schmitten, Swi. 60/D4
Schmitten, Ger. 58/B2
Schmutter (riv.), Ger. 58/D5
Schnaitsee, Ger. 59/F6
Schnaittach, Ger. 59/E3
Schnaittenbach, Ger. 59/F3
Schnarrtanne, Ger. 59/F1
Schnecksville, Pa, US 168/C2
Schneeberg (peak), Ger. 59/E2
Schneeberg, Ger. 59/F1
Schneeberg, Ger. 58/C3
Schneifel (upland), Ger. 42/D3
Schneverdingen, Ger. 53/G2
Schoenchen, Ks, US 152/E1
Schofield, Wi, US 155/K1
Schoharie, NY, US 161/J3
Scholle, NM, US 149/J3
Schollene, Ger. 42/G2
Schöllkrippen, Ger. 58/C2
Schömberg, Ger. 61/E1
Schömberg, Ger. 58/B5
Schönaich, Ger. 58/C5
Schönau im Schwarzwald, Ger. 60/D2
Schönberg, Ger. 40/D4
Schönberg, Ger. 59/G5
Schönbrunn, Ger. 58/D1
Schondorf am Ammersee, Ger. 61/H1
Schondra (riv.), Ger. 58/C2
Schönebeck, Ger. 42/F2
Schöneck, Ger. 58/B2
Schöneck, Ger. 59/F2
Schönecken, Ger. 55/F3
Schönefeld (int'l arpt.), Ger. 42/Q7
Schöneiche, Ger. 42/Q7
Schongau, Ger. 61/G2
Schöningen, Ger. 42/F2
Schönow, Ger. 42/Q6
Schönsee, Ger. 59/F3
Schonungen, Ger. 58/D2
Schönwald, Ger. 59/E2
Schoolcraft, Mi, US 160/D3
Schoonebeek, Neth. 52/D3
Schoonhoven, Neth. 52/B5
Schoorl, Neth. 52/B3
Schopfheim, Ger. 60/D2
Schopfheim, Ger. 55/G4
Schopfloch, Ger. 58/D4
Schöppenstedt, Ger. 53/H4
Schörfling, Aus. 59/G7
Schorndorf, Ger. 58/C5
Schortens, Ger. 53/E1
Schoten, Belg. 52/B6
Schotten, Ger. 58/C1
Schouten (isls.), Indo. 136/C5
Schouten (isl.), Austl. 132/D4
Schouwen (isl.), Neth. 52/A5
Schramberg, Ger. 61/E1
Schrankogel (peak), Aus. 61/H3
Schreckhorn (peak), Swi. 60/E4
Schreiber, On, Can. 157/L3
Schriesheim, Ger. 58/B4
Schriever, La, US 164/C3
Schrobenhausen, Ger. 58/E5
Schroeder, Mn, US 157/J4
Schroffenstein (peak), Namb. 124/B2
Schrozberg, Ger. 58/C4
Schruns, Aus. 61/F3
Schübelbach, Swi. 61/E3
Schuby, Ger. 40/C4
Schulenburg, Tx, US 151/F3
Schuler, Ab, Can. 145/J2
Schulter, Ok, US 153/G3
Schulzendorf, Ger. 42/Q7
Schunter (riv.), Ger. 53/H4
Schüpfheim, Swi. 60/E4
Schurz, Nv, US 146/D4
Schussen (riv.), Ger. 61/F2
Schussenried, Ger. 61/F1
Schutter (riv.), Ger. 58/A6
Schutterwald, Ger. 60/D1
Schüttorf, Ger. 53/E4
Schuyler, Ne, US 155/F3
Schuylkill (riv.), Pa, US 168/C3
Schuylkill (co.), Pa, US 168/B2
Schuylkill Haven, Pa, US 168/B2
Schwabach, Ger. 58/D4
Schwabhausen bei Dachau, Ger. 59/E6
Schwäbisch Gmünd, Ger. 58/C5
Schwäbisch Hall, Ger. 58/C4
Schwäbische Alb (range), Ger. 42/E4
Schwabmünchen, Ger. 61/G1
Schwaig bei Nürnberg, Ger. 58/E4
Schwaigern, Ger. 58/C4
Schwalbach, Ger. 55/F5
Schwalbach am Taunus, Ger. 58/B2
Schwalm (riv.), Ger. 42/E3
Schwalmtal, Ger. 52/D6
Schwanden, Swi. 61/F4
Schwandorf im Bayern, Ger. 59/F4
Schwanebeck, Ger. 42/Q6
Schwanenstadt, Aus. 59/G6
Schwaner (mts.), Indo. 90/D4
Schwanewede, Ger. 53/F2
Schwanfeld, Ger. 58/D3
Schwangau, Ger. 61/G2
Schwarmstedt, Ger. 53/G3
Schwartz Elster (riv.), Ger. 43/G3
Schwartzerberg (peak), Namb. 124/B2
Schwarza (riv.), Ger. 58/E1
Schwarzach, Ger. 59/F5
Schwarzach, Ger. 59/E4
Schwarzach im Pongau, Aus. 45/K3
Schwarze Laber (riv.), Ger. 59/E4
Schwarzenbach am Wald, Ger. 59/E2
Schwarzenbek, Ger. 53/H1
Schwarzenberg, Ger. 59/F1
Schwarzenbruck, Ger. 58/E4
Schwarzenburg, Swi. 60/D4
Schwarzenfeld, Ger. 59/F4
Schwarzer Mann (peak), Ger. 55/F3
Schwarzhorn (peak), Aus. 61/H3
Schwarzrand (mts.), Namb. 122/C5
Schwarzwald (Black Forest) (for.), Ger. 58/B6
Schwaz, Aus. 45/J3
Schwebheim, Ger. 58/D3
Schwechat, Aus. 51/N7
Schwechat (int'l arpt.), Aus. 51/P7
Schwedt, Ger. 43/H2
Schwegenheim, Ger. 58/B4
Schweich, Ger. 55/F4
Schweighouse-sur-Moder, Fr. 55/G6
Schweinfurt, Ger. 58/D2
Schweitenkirchen, Ger. 59/E5
Schweizer-Reneke, SAfr. 124/D2
Schwelm, Ger. 53/E6
Schwendi, Ger. 61/F1
Schwenksville, Pa, US 168/C3
Schwerin, Ger. 40/D5
Schweriner (lake), Ger. 42/F2
Schwertberg, Aus. 59/H6
Schwerte, Ger. 53/E6
Schwetzingen, Ger. 58/B4
Schwinge (riv.), Ger. 53/G1
Schwörstadt, Ger. 60/D2
Schwülme (riv.), Ger. 53/G5
Schwülper, Ger. 53/H4
Schwyz (canton), Swi. 61/E3
Schwyz, Swi. 61/E3
Sciacca, It. 48/C4
Scicli, It. 48/D4
Science Hill, Ky, US 162/E2
Science Museum of Minnesota, Mn, US 157/P7
Scilly (isls.), Eng, UK 31/Q11
Ścinawa, Pol. 43/J3
Scio, Or, US 146/B1
Scionzier, Fr. 60/C5
Sciota, Pa, US 168/C2
Scioto (riv.), Oh, US 163/F1
Sclater, Mb, Can. 156/D2
Scobey, Mt, US 145/M3
Scofield (res.), Ut, US 147/H4
Scolt (pt.), Eng, UK 37/G1
Scone, Austl. 132/D2
Scooba, Ms, US 162/C4
Scopello, It. 62/B2
Scordia, It. 48/D4
Scorff (riv.), Fr. 56/B5
Scorzè, It. 63/F2
Scotch Corner, Eng, UK 35/G3
Scotch Creek, BC, Can. 144/E2
Scotch Plains, NJ, US 169/H9
Scotchman (peak), Id, US 144/F3
Scotia (sea) 192/W
Scotia, Ca, US 146/A3
Scotland, Tx, US 153/E4
Scotland, UK 34/D1
Scotland Neck, NC, US 163/J2
Scots Bay, NS, Can. 158/E3
Scotstown, Ire. 32/C1
Scott (cape), Austl. 128/C3
Scott (cape), BC, Can. 140/D3
Scott (cape), NW, Can. 167/R7
Scott (lake), NW, Can. 140/F2
Scott, Sk, Can. 145/K1
Scott, NZ, Ant. 192/M
Scott (riv.), Ca, US 146/B3
Scott (A.F.B.), Il, US 155/K4
Scott (co.), Mn, US 157/N7
Scott (mt.), Ok, US 153/E3
Scott City, Ks, US 152/D1
Scott City, Mo, US 162/C2
Scott NP, Austl. 130/B5
Scott (reef), Austl. 128/A3
Scottburgh, SAfr. 125/E3
Scottdale, Pa, US 161/G4
Scottdale, Ga, US 163/M7
Scottish Borders (co.), Sc, UK 33/C5
Scotts (cr.), Austl. 131/M9
Scotts Bluff Nat'l Mon., Ne, US 154/C3
Scotts Hill, Tn, US 162/C3
Scotts Peak (dam), Austl. 132/C4
Scottsbluff, Ne, US 154/C3
Scottsboro, Al, US 162/D3
Scottsburg, In, US 162/E1
Scottsdale, Austl. 132/C4
Scottsdale, Az, US 149/G4
Scottsmoor, Fl, US 165/H3
Scottsville, Ky, US 162/D2
Scottville, Mi, US 160/C3
Scotty's Castle, Ca, US 148/D2
Scoudouc, NB, Can. 158/E2
Scourie, Sc, UK 31/R7
Scranton, ND, US 156/C4
Scranton, Pa, US 161/J4
Scranton, SC, US 163/H4
Scraper, Ok, US 153/G2
Screven, Ga, US 165/G2
Scribner, Ne, US 155/F3
Scripps Aquarium/Museum, Ca, US 166/C5
Scrivia (riv.), It. 62/B3
Scunthorpe, Eng, UK 35/H4
Scuol, Swi. 61/G4
Scuppernong (riv.), Wi, US 167/N14
Scurdie Ness (pt.), Sc, UK 33/D3
Scurry, Tx, US 150/L7
Scutari (lake), Yugo. 75/F1
Scye (riv.), Fr. 56/D2
Sea (isls.), Ga, US 143/K5
Sea (isls.), Ga, SC, US 163/G5
Sea Cliff, Ca, US 166/A2
Sea Cliff, NY, US 169/L8
Sea Girt, NJ, US 168/D3
Sea Isle City, NJ, US 168/D5
Sea Lake, Austl. 132/B2
Sea Pines, SC, US 163/G4
Sea Ranch Lakes, Fl, US 164/P10
Sea World of Florida, Fl, US 164/N7
Sea-Tac, Wa, US 167/C3
Seabeck, Wa, US 167/B2
Seaboard, NC, US 163/J2
Seabold, Wa, US 167/B2
Seabra, Braz. 187/E2
Seabrook, NH, US 161/L3
Seabrook, NJ, US 168/C5
Seabrook, SC, US 163/G4
Seabrook, Tx, US 151/M9

Map Section
270
271

Seadrift, Tx, US 150/F3
Seaford, Eng, UK 37/G5
Seaford, NY, US 169/M9
Seaford, De, US 163/K1
Seaforde, NI, UK 34/C3
Seaforth, On, Can. 160/F3
Seaforth, Austl. 134/C3
Seagoville, Tx, US 150/L7
Seagraves, Tx, US 152/C4
Seaham, Eng, UK 35/G2
Seahorse (pt.), Nun, Can. 167/J2
Seahurst, Wa, US 167/C3
Seal (isl.), Me, US 158/C4
Seal, Eng, UK 30/D3
Seal (riv.), MB, Can. 140/G3
Seal (pt.), Chile 190/B5
Seal (cape), SAfr. 124/C4
Seal Beach, Ca, US 166/F8
Seal Beach NWR, Ca, US 166/F8
Seal Cove, NS, Can. 158/D3
Seal Cove, Nf, Can. 159/J2
Seale, Eng, UK 30/A3
Seale, Al, US 162/E4
Sealy, Tx, US 150/F3
Seaman, Oh, US 162/F1
Seamer, Eng, UK 35/H3
Seano, It. 63/E6
Searchlight, Nv, US 148/E3
Searchmont, On, Can. 160/D1
Searcy, Ar, US 153/J3
Seascale, Eng, UK 34/E3
Seaside, Ca, US 148/B2
Seaside, Or, US 144/C5
Seaside Heights, NJ, US 168/D4
Seaside Park, NJ, US 168/D4
Seaton, Eng, UK 36/C5
Seaton (riv.), Eng, UK 36/B6
Seaton Carew, Eng, UK 35/G2
Seattle, Wa, US 144/C4
Seattle Art Museum, Wa, US 167/C2
Seattle Center, Wa, US 167/C2
Seattle-Tacoma (int'l arpt.), Wa, US 144/C4
Seatuck Nat'l Wild. Ref., NY, US 169/E2
Seba, Indo. 128/A2
Sébaco, Nic. 176/E3
Sebago (lake), Me, US 161/L3
Sebaou (riv.), Alg. 112/H4
Sebastian, Fl, US 165/H4
Sebastian, Tx, US 151/F4
Sebastián Vizcaíno (bay), Mex. 174/B2
Sebastopol, Austl. 133/A3
Sebastopol, Ca, US 146/B4
Sebastopol, Ms, US 162/C4
Sebastopol, Tx, US 151/G2
Sebatik (isl.), Malay. 88/B4
Sebayan (peak), Indo. 90/D4
Sebderat, Erit. 116/H2
Sebdou, Alg. 112/D2
Sébé (riv.), Gabon 120/C3
Sebec (lake), Me, US 158/C3
Sebeka, Mn, US 157/G4
Sébékoro, Mali 114/C3
Seben, Turk. 51/K5
Sebeş, Rom. 51/F3
Sebeta, Eth. 118/A3
Sebewaing, Mi, US 160/E3
Sebezh, Rus. 41/N3
Sebina, Bots. 123/E4
Şebinkarahisar, Turk. 102/D1
Sebiş, Rom. 50/F2
Sebkhet al Kalīyah (drylake), Alg. 112/M7
Seblat, Indo. 89/C3
Sebnitz, Ger. 43/H3
Seboruco, Ven. 180/C2
Seboto (pt.), Phil. 88/C4
Sebou (riv.), Mor. 112/E2
Sebou, Oued (riv.), Mor. 110/D2
Seboyeta, NM, US 149/J3
Sebree, Ky, US 162/D2
Sebring, Fl, US 165/H4
Sebuku (isl.), Indo. 91/E4
Sebuku (bay), Indo. 88/B5
Secaucus, NJ, US 169/J8
Secchia (riv.), It. 45/J4
Sechelt, BC, Can. 144/C3
Sechura, Peru 184/A2
Sechura (bay), Peru 184/A2
Sechura, Desierto de (des.), Peru 184/A2
Seclin, Fr. 54/C2
Seco (cr.), Tx, US 151/E3
Seco (riv.), Mex.,US 149/G5
Seco (riv.), Arg. 191/D6
Seco (riv.), Mex. 175/C2
Second Cataract (falls), Sudan 109/F4
Second Mesa, Az, US 149/G3
Second Mountain (mtn.), Pa, US 168/B3
Second San Diego Aqueduct (riv.), Ca, US 166/C4
Second Watchung (mtn.), NJ, US 169/H9
Section, Al, US 162/E3
Secunda, SAfr. 124/E2
Secure (riv.), Bol. 185/E4
Security-Widefield, Co, US 152/B1
Seda, Lith. 41/K3
Sedalia, Mo, US 153/H1
Sedalia, Ab, Can. 145/J2
Sedan, Ks, US 153/F2
Sedan, NM, US 152/C2
Sedan, Fr. 55/D4
Sedano, Sp. 46/D1
Sedaung (mtn.), Myan. 93/B3
Sedayu, Indo. 89/F4
Sedbergh, Eng, UK 35/F3
Seddenga Temple (ruin), Sudan 109/F4
Seddon, NZ 135/C3
Seddonville, NZ 135/B3
Seddülbahir, Turk. 75/K2
Sedeh, Iran 101/G2
Sederot, Isr. 105/B5
Sedgefield, Eng, UK 35/G2
Sedgewick, Ab, Can. 145/J1
Sedgwick (mt.), Yk, Can. 171/L2
Sedgwick, Ks, US 153/F2
Sedhiou, Sen. 114/B3
Sedlčany, Czh. 59/H3
Sedlo (peak), Czh. 59/H1
Sedona, Az, US 149/G3
Sedot Yam, Isr. 105/B4
Sedrata, Alg. 112/K6
Sedro-Woolley, Wa, US 144/C3
Šeduva, Lith. 41/K4
Sędziszów, Pol. 43/L3
Sędziszów Małopolski, Pol. 72/A2
Sée (riv.), Fr. 44/C2
Seeb (int'l arpt.), Oman 101/G4
Seebe, Ab, Can. 144/G2
Seeboden, Aus. 45/K3
Seedskadee NWR, Wy, US 147/J3
Seefeld in Tirol, Aus. 61/H3
Seefin (peak), Ire. 32/A6
Seefin (peak), Ire. 32/C5
Seeg, Ger. 61/G2
Seehausen, Ger. 42/F2
Seeheim, Namb. 124/B2
Seeheim-Jugenheim, Ger. 58/B3
Seeis, Namb. 122/C4
Seekirchen Markt, Aus. 59/G7
Seekooi (riv.), SAfr. 124/D3
Seeley, Ca, US 148/E4
Seeley Lake, Mt, US 145/H4
Seelow, Ger. 43/H2
Seeon-Seebruck, Ger. 59/F7
Seer Green, Eng, UK 30/B2
Sées, Fr. 53/G7
Seesen, Ger. 53/H5
Seeshaupt, Ger. 61/H2
Seeve (riv.), Ger. 53/G2
Seewalchen, Aus. 59/G7
Seewis im Prättigau, Swi. 61/F4
Séez, Fr. 64/C1
Şefaatli, Turk. 102/C2
Seffner, Fl, US 164/L8
Sefhare, Bots. 123/E4
Sefīd Rūd (riv.), Iran 103/G2
Sefrou, Mor. 112/B3
Sefton (mt.), NZ 135/B3
Sefton (co.), Eng, UK 35/E4
Segag, Eth. 118/B4
Segama (riv.), Malay. 88/B4
Segamat, Malay. 89/C2
Segarcea, Rom. 51/F3
Ségbana, Ben. 115/F4
Ségélo-Koro, C.d'Iv. 114/D4
Segelstad Bru, Nor. 40/D1
Segen Wenz (riv.), Eth. 116/H4
Seget, Indo. 91/H4
Segezha, Rus. 68/G3
Segni, It. 65/C4
Segorbe, Sp. 47/E3
Ségou, Mali 114/D3
Ségou (pol. reg.), Mali 114/D3
Segovia, Col. 180/C3
Segovia, Sp. 46/C2
Segovia, Tx, US 151/E2
Segozero (lake), Rus. 68/G3
Segrate, It. 62/C3
Segré, Fr. 57/E5
Segre (riv.), Sp. 47/F2
Seguam (isl.), Ak, US 171/D5
Seguam Pass (Str.), Ak, US 171/D5
Séguédine, Niger 134/B4
Séguéla, C.d'Iv. 114/D5
Séguénéga, Burk. 115/E3
Seguin, Tx, US 151/E3
Segundo (riv.), Arg. 188/D4
Segura (riv.), Sp. 66/C3
Segusino, It. 63/E2
Sehithwa, Bots. 122/D4
Sehnde, Ger. 53/G4
Sehonghong, Les. 124/E3
Sehore, India 92/C3
Sehwān, Pak. 101/J3
Seibersbach, Ger. 55/G4
Seiche (riv.), Fr. 56/D5
Seiches-sur-le-Loir, Fr. 57/E5
Seiersberg, Aus. 50/B2
Seika, Japan 83/J6
Seiling, Ok, US 152/E2
Seille (riv.), Fr. 42/C5
Seinäjoki, Fin. 68/D3
Seine (riv.), On, Can. 157/J3
Seine (bay), Fr. 44/C2
Seine (riv.), On, Can. 161/J3
Seine (riv.), Fr. 29/E4
Seine-et-Marne (dept.), Fr. 54/B5
Seine-Maritime (dept.), Fr. 54/A4
Seine-St-Denis (dept.), Fr. 54/B6
Seitenstetten, Aus. 59/H6
Seiwa, Japan 83/K7
Seix, Fr. 44/D5
Seixal, Port. 47/P10
Seixas (pt.), Braz. 183/H4
Sejaka, Indo. 91/E4
Sejerø (isl.), Den. 40/D4
Sejero (flat), Den. 39/H7
Sejny, Pol. 41/K4
Sekayu, Indo. 89/C3
Seke, Tanz. 119/A2
Seke-Banza, D.R. Congo 120/C4
Sekenke, Tanz. 119/A3
Seki (riv.), Turk. 104/A1
Seki, Japan 83/L5
Seki, Japan 82/D3
Sekigahara, Japan 83/K5
Sekiyado, Japan 83/D1
Sekoma, Bots. 122/D5
Sekondi, Gha. 115/E5
Sek'ot'a, Eth. 118/A2
Sel, Nor. 38/D3
Selah, Wa, US 144/D4
Selama, Malay. 89/C1
Selangor (state), Malay. 89/C2
Selaön (isl.), Swe. 39/A1
Selaphum, Thai. 94/C2
Selargius, It. 48/A3
Selaru (isl.), Indo. 91/H5
Selatan (cape), Indo. 90/D4
Selawik, Ak, US 171/F2
Selawik (lake), Ak, US 171/F2
Selayar (isl.), Indo. 91/F5
Selb, Ger. 59/F2
Selbitz, Ger. 59/E2
Selbitz (riv.), Ger. 59/E2
Selbu, Nor. 38/D3
Selby, SD, US 156/D5
Selby, Eng, UK 35/G4
Selby-On-The-Bay, Md, US 168/B6
Selci, It. 63/F6
Selçuk, Turk. 102/A2
Selden, Ks, US 154/D4
Selden, NY, US 169/E2
Seldovia, Ak, US 171/H4
Sele (riv.), It. 48/D2
Selebi-Phikwe, Bots. 123/E4
Seleka, Bots. 123/E4
Selela (pt.), Moz. 123/J2
Seleli (hill), Tanz. 121/H5
Selemdzha (riv.), Rus. 75/N4
Selenča, Yugo. 50/D3
Selenduma, Rus. 78/F1
Selenga (riv.), Rus. 78/F1
Selenge (prov.), Mong. 78/F2
Selenge (riv.), Mong. 78/F2
Selenginsk, Rus. 78/F1
Selenicë, Alb. 75/F2
Sélestat, Fr. 60/D1
Seletar (res.), Sing. 89/J6
Selety (riv.), Kaz. 99/B1
Seletyteniz (lake), Kaz. 99/B1
Seleznëvo, Rus. 41/N1
Selfoss, Ice. 38/N7
Selfridge, ND, US 156/D4
Sélia (well), Chad 116/C2
Sélibabi, Mrta. 114/B3
Seligenstadt, Ger. 58/B2
Seliger (lake), Rus. 68/G4
Seligman, Mo, US 153/H2
Seligman, Az, US 149/F3
Selim River, Malay. 89/C2
Selimbau, Indo. 90/D3
Selimiye, Turk. 102/A2
Selinsgrove, Pa, US 168/B2
Seljord, Nor. 40/C2
Selkan (tun.), Japan 82/B3
Selkirk, Sc, UK 33/D5
Selkirk, Mb, Can. 140/G3
Selkirk (mts.), BC, Can. 144/E2
Selleck, Wa, US 167/D3
Sellers, Al, US 165/E1
Sellersville, Pa, US 168/C3
Selles-sur-Cher, Fr. 57/G6
Sellières, Fr. 60/B4
Sells, Az, US 149/G5
Selly Oak, Eng, UK 36/E2
Sellye, Hun. 50/C3
Selm, Ger. 53/E5
Selma, Al, US 162/D4
Selma, Ar, US 153/J4
Selma, Ca, US 148/C2
Selma, NC, US 163/H3
Selman, Ok, US 152/E2
Selmer, Tn, US 162/C3
Selommes, Fr. 57/G5
Selongey, Fr. 60/B2
Selouma, Gui. 114/C4
Selous (mt.), Yk, Can. 171/M3
Selous, Zim. 123/F3
Selous Game Reserve, Tanz. 119/B4
Selsey, Eng, UK 37/F5
Selsey Bill (pt.), Eng, UK 37/F5
Selsingen, Ger. 53/G2
Sel'tso, Rus. 70/E1
Seltz, Fr. 58/B5
Selu (isl.), Indo. 128/C1
Sélune (riv.), Fr. 44/C2
Selvas (for.), Braz. 179/C3
Selvik, Nor. 38/R9
Selway (riv.), Id, US 147/F1
Selway (falls), Id, US 144/G4
Selwyn, Austl. 134/A3
Selwyn (range), Austl. 129/F5
Selydove, Ukr. 73/J3
Selz (riv.), Ger. 45/H2
Semara, WSah. 110/C4
Semarang, Indo. 89/E4
Semarsot, India 96/D4
Semau (isl.), Indo. 128/A2
Sembakung (riv.), Indo. 88/B4
Sembawang (nbrhd.), Sing. 89/J6
Sembé, Congo 120/C2
Semehun, SLeo. 114/B5
Sembera (riv.), Czh. 59/H2
Semberong (riv.), Malay. 89/C2
Semdinli, Turk. 103/F2
Séméac, Fr. 44/D5
Semelle (riv.), Fr. 57/F4
Semendua, D.R. Congo 120/D3
Semenivka, Ukr. 72/G1
Semenivka, Ukr. 73/G3
Semenov, Rus. 69/K4
Semeru (peak), Indo. 89/F5
Semey, Kaz. 99/D1
Semidi (isls.), Ak, US 171/G4
Semikarakorsk, Rus. 73/L4
Semilovo, Rus. 68/J5
Semiluki, Rus. 73/K2
Seminole, Fl, US 164/K8
Seminole (lake), Ga, US 165/F2
Seminole, Ok, US 153/F3
Seminole, Tx, US 151/C1
Seminoe (dam), Wy, US 147/K2
Seminoe (res.), Wy, US 147/K2
Seminole Draw (riv.), Tx, US 151/C1
Seminole Ind. Res., Fl, US 165/H4
Semipalatinsk (int'l arpt.), Kaz. 99/D1
Semirara (isl.), Phil. 88/C3
Semīrom, Iran 103/G4
Semisopochnoi (isl.), Ak, US 171/B5
Semitau, Indo. 90/D4
Semliki (riv.), D.R. Congo 121/G2
Semnān, Iran 103/H3
Semnān (gov.), Iran 103/H3
Semnon (riv.), Fr. 44/C3
Semois (riv.), Belg. 44/F2
Semouse (riv.), Fr. 60/C2
Semoy, Fr. 57/G5
Semoy (riv.), Fr. 55/D4
Sempach, Swi. 60/E3
Sempacher (lake), Swi. 60/D3
Semporna, Malay. 88/B4
Semprevisa (peak), It. 65/C4
Semsales, Swi. 60/C4
Semskefjellet (peak), Nor. 38/E2
Sen (riv.), Camb. 93/H5
Sen-san (peak), Japan 83/G7
Sena, Thai. 94/C3
Sena, Bol. 185/E3
Sena Madureira, Braz. 182/E5
Senador Pompeu, Braz. 183/G4
Senador Sá, Braz. 183/F3
Sen'afē, Erit. 118/A2
Senai, Malay. 89/C2
Senaja, Malay. 88/B4
Senaki, Geo. 71/G4
Senanga, Zam. 122/D3
Sénas, Fr. 64/B5
Senate, Sk, Can. 145/K3
Senath, Mo, US 162/B2
Senatobia, Ms, US 162/C3
Sence (riv.), Eng, UK 37/E1
Send, Eng, UK 30/B3
Sendafa, Eth. 118/A3
Sendai (riv.), Japan 84/D3
Sendai, Japan 85/G1
Sendai (int'l arpt.), Japan 85/G1
Sendai, Japan 84/B5
Sendai (bay), Japan 82/B4
Sendal (riv.), Japan 84/B5
Senden, Ger. 58/D6
Senden, Ger. 53/E5
Sendenhorst, Ger. 53/E5
Sendhwa, India 95/B1
Senebui, Indo. 89/C2
Senebui (cape), Indo. 89/C2
Senec, Slvk. 43/J4
Seneca, Mo, US 153/G2
Seneca (lake), NY, US 161/H3
Seneca, Or, US 146/D1
Seneca, SC, US 163/F3
Seneca, Ks, US 155/F4
Seneca Creek State Park, Md, US 168/A5
Seneca Falls, NY, US 161/H3
Seneca Rocks NRA, WV, US 163/H1
Senecaville (lake), Oh, US 160/F5
Seneffe, Belg. 55/D2
Sénégal (riv.), Afr. 114/B2
Senegal (ctry.) 107/A3
Sénégal (riv.), Sen. 107/A3
Senekal, SAfr. 124/D3
Seney, Mi, US 160/D1
Seney NWR, Mi, US 157/L4
Senezhskoye (lake), Rus. 69/W8
Senfi, Gha. 115/E5
Senftenberg, Ger. 43/H3
Senga Hill Mission, Zam. 121/G5
Sengenthal, Ger. 59/E4
Sênggê (riv.), China 99/D5
Sengilev, Rus. 71/J1
Sengor, Bhu. 97/H2
Senguer (riv.), Arg. 190/D3
Sengwe (riv.), Zim. 123/F3
Senhor do Bonfim, Braz. 187/E1
Senica, Slvk. 43/J4
Senirkent, Turk. 102/B2
Senise, It. 48/E2
Senj, Cro. 45/L4
Senja (isl.), Nor. 38/F1
Senkaku-Shotō (isl.), Japan 85/G8
Şenkaya, Turk. 102/E1
Senkevychivka, Ukr. 72/C2
Şenköy, Turk. 104/E1
Senlac, Sk, Can. 145/K1
Senlis, Fr. 54/B5
Senmonoron, Camb. 94/D3
Sennan, Japan 83/H7
Sennar (dam), Sudan 116/G2
Senne (riv.), Belg. 55/D2
Sennecy-le-Grand, Fr. 60/A4
Sennfeld, Ger. 58/D2
Senno, Bela. 41/N4
Sennoy, Rus. 71/G2
Sennoy, Rus. 71/H1
Sennwald, Swi. 61/F3
Sennybridge, Wal, UK 36/C3
Séno (prov.), Burk. 115/F3
Senonches, Fr. 57/G3
Senones, Fr. 60/C1
Senorbì, It. 48/A3
Senovo, Bul. 51/H4
Sens, Fr. 44/E2
Sens-de-Bretagne, Fr. 56/D4
Sensuntepeque, ESal. 176/D3
Senta, Yugo. 50/E3
Sentani, Indo. 91/K4
Sentery, D.R. Congo 121/F4
Sentinel, Ok, US 152/E3
Sentinel, Az, US 149/F4
Sentosa (isl.), Sing. 89/J6
Sentrum, SAfr. 123/E5
Senya Beraku, Gha. 115/E5
Senyavin (isls.), Micr. 136/E4
Senzig, Ger. 42/G7
Seohāra, India 96/B1
Seon, Swi. 60/E3
Seondha, India 96/B2
Seoni, India 96/B4
Seonī Mālwā, India 96/A4
Seoul (Sŏul) (cap.), SKor. 79/K4
Seoul Grand Park, SKor. 81/G7
Seoul Jikhalsi (prov.), SKor. 81/D4
Sepang (pt.), Malay. 89/D2
Sepanjang (isl.), Indo. 89/F4
Separ, NM, US 149/H4
Separation (pt.), NZ 135/C3
Sepatini (riv.), Braz. 185/E3
Sepetiba (bay), Braz. 187/M8
Sepik (riv.), PNG 136/D5
Sepino, It. 65/D5
Sep'o, NKor. 81/D3
Sepo, Indo. 91/G3
Sępólno Krajeńskie, Pol. 43/J2
Sepopa, Bots. 122/D3
Sept-Îles, Qu, Can. 167/K3
Septèmes-les-Vallons, Fr. 64/B6
Septemvri, Bul. 75/J1
Septeuil, Fr. 57/G3
Sepulveda (dam), Ca, US 166/F7
Sequeros, Sp. 46/B2
Sequim (bay), Wa, US 167/A1
Sequim, Wa, US 144/C3
Sequoia NP, Ca, US 148/C2
Sequoyah Nat'l Wildlife Res., Ok, US 153/G3
Sera (isl.), Indo. 128/C1
Serafimovich, Rus. 73/M3
Seraincourt, Fr. 30/H4
Seraing, Belg. 55/E2
Serambe, Sudan 117/E2
Serampore, India 97/G4
Sèran (riv.), Fr. 60/B6
Serang, Indo. 89/D4
Serangoon (nbrhd.), Sing. 89/J6
Serasan (str.), Indo.,Malay. 90/C3
Serasan, Indo. 90/C3
Seravezza, It. 62/D6
Serbeulangit (mts.), Indo. 89/B2
Serbia (reg.), Yugo. 67/J1
Serbia and Montenegro (see Yugoslavia) */*
Serbin, Tx, US 151/F2
Serchhīp, India 86/B4
Serchio (riv.), It. 62/D4
Serdang (cape), Indo. 89/D4
Serdo, Eth. 118/B3
Serdobsk, Rus. 71/H1
Serebryansk, Kaz. 74/J5
Serednikovo, Rus. 68/H5
Seredžius, Lith. 41/K4
Seregno, It. 62/C2
Serein (riv.), Fr. 42/D4
Serémange-Erzange, Fr. 55/F5
Seremban, Malay. 89/C2
Serengeti (plain), Tanz. 119/A2
Serengeti NP, Tanz. 119/A2
Serenje, Zam. 123/F2
Serere, Ugan. 119/A1
Sergach, Rus. 69/K5
Sergeantsville, NJ, US 168/D3
Sergen, Turk. 51/H5
Sergeya Kirova (isls.), Rus. 74/J2
Sergeyevka, Kaz. 69/Q5
Sergipe (state), Braz. 187/F1
Sergiyev Posad, Rus. 68/H4
Sergnano, It. 62/C3
Seria, Bru. 90/D3
Seriate, It. 62/C2
Sérifontaine, Fr. 54/A5
Sérifos, Gre. 75/J4
Sérifos (isl.), Gre. 75/J4
Sérignan, Fr. 44/E5
Serik, Turk. 104/B1
Serikbuya, China 99/C4
Seringa, Serra da (mts.), Braz. 182/D4
Serinyol, Turk. 104/E1
Serio (riv.), It. 62/C2
Serkout (peak), Alg. 111/G5
Sermaises, Fr. 57/H4
Sermaize-les-Bains, Fr. 55/D6
Sermata (isls.), Indo. 128/C2
Sermide, It. 63/E4
Sermoneta, It. 65/B4
Sernaglia della Battaglia, It. 63/F2
Sernovodsk, Rus. 71/J1
Sernur, Rus. 69/L4
Serón, Sp. 46/D4
Serós, Sp. 47/F2
Serottini (peak), It. 61/G5
Serov, Rus. 74/G4
Serowe, Bots. 123/E4
Serpa, Port. 46/B4
Serpeddi (peak), It. 48/A3
Serpent Mound, Oh, US 163/F1
Serpent's Mouth (str.), Trin.,Ven. 181/F2
Serpentine (dam), Austl. 132/C4
Serpentine Lakes, Austl. 131/F4
Serpukhov, Rus. 68/H5
Serquigny, Fr. 57/F2
Serra (peak), It. 62/D6
Serra, Braz. 187/E4
Serra Branca, Braz. 183/G4
Serra da Bocaina, PN, Braz. 189/H2
Serra da Bocaína, PN da, Braz. 186/D4
Serra da Canastra, PN, Braz. 189/H1
Serra da Canastra, PN da, Braz. 186/D4
Serra da Capivara, PN da, Braz. 187/E1
Serra da Capivara, PN da, Braz. 183/F5
Serra da Chela (mts.), Ang. 122/B3
Serra da Estrela (peak), Port. 46/B2
Serra da Estrela (mts.), Port. 46/A3
Serra do Cipó, PN da, Braz. 187/E3
Serra do Congo (mts.), Ang. 120/C4
Serra do Navio, Braz. 182/C2
Serra dos Órgãos, PN da, Braz. 187/N7
Serra Negra do Norte, Braz. 183/G4
Serra San Bruno, It. 48/E3
Serra San Quirico, It. 63/G7
Serra Talhada, Braz. 183/G4
Sérrai, Gre. 75/H2
Serralta di San Vito (peak), It. 48/E3
Serramanna, It. 48/A3
Serramazzoni, It. 63/D5
Serrana Bank (isl.), Col. 173/F5
Serranía de la Cerbatana (mts.), Ven. 181/E3
Serranía de la Neblina, PN, Ven. 181/E4
Serranías del Burro (mts.), Mex. 174/E2
Serranilla Bank (isl.), Col. 173/F4
Serrano, Arg. 190/E2
Serranópolis, Braz. 186/B3
Serrat (cape), Tun. 48/A4
Serravalle, It. 63/F4
Serravalle, SMar. 63/F6
Serravalle di Chienti, It. 65/B1
Serravalle Scrivia, It. 62/B4
Serravalle Sesia, It. 62/B2
Serre (riv.), Fr. 42/B4
Serre Chevalier (peak), Fr. 64/C3
Serre-Ponçon (lake), Fr. 64/C4
Serrenti, It. 48/A3
Serres, Fr. 64/B4
Serrières, Fr. 64/A2
Serrinha, Braz. 187/F1
Serris, Fr. 30/L5
Serrita, Braz. 183/G4
Sèrro, Braz. 189/J1
Sersale, It. 48/E3
Sertã, Port. 46/A3
Sertânia, Braz. 183/G5
Sertãozinho, Braz. 189/H2
Sertavul (pass), Turk. 104/C1
Serteng (mts.), China 78/C4
Sēru, Eth. 118/B4
Serui, Indo. 91/J4
Serule, Bots. 123/E4
Serurumi (riv.), Bots. 122/E4
Seruwai, Indo. 89/B1
Seruyan (riv.), Indo. 90/D4
Servance, Fr. 60/C2
Servel (Lannion) (arpt.), Fr. 56/B3
Servi, Turk. 102/E2
Sérvia, Gre. 75/G2
Serviceton, Austl. 132/B3
Servigliano, It. 65/C1
Serwaru, Indo. 128/B2
Sesayap (riv.), Indo. 88/B5
Sese (isls.), Ugan. 121/G3
Sesebi (ruin), Sudan 109/F4
Sesepe, Indo. 91/G4
Sesfontein, Namb. 122/B3
Sesheke, Zam. 122/E3
Sesia (riv.), It. 45/H4
Sesimbra, Port. 47/P11
Seskar (isl.), Rus. 41/N1
Sespe, Ca, US 166/B2
Sespe (cr.), Ca, US 166/A1
Sespe Condor Sanctuary, Ca, US 148/C3
Sessa Aurunca, It. 65/C5
Sesser, Il, US 162/C1
Sesslach, Ger. 58/D2
Sesto Calende, It. 62/B2
Sesto Campano, It. 65/D5
Sesto Fiorentino, It. 63/E6
Sesto San Giovanni, It. 62/C2
Sesto Ulteriano, It. 62/C3
Sestola, It. 63/D5
Sestra (riv.), Rus. 69/W8
Sestri Levante, It. 62/C5
Sestroretsk, Rus. 69/S6
Sestroretskiy (lake), Rus. 69/T6
Sestu, It. 48/A3
Sesvenna (peak), It. 61/G4
Sesvete, Cro. 50/C3
Šeta, Lith. 41/L4
Setana, Japan 82/A2
Sète, Fr. 44/E5
Sete Cidades, PN de, Braz. 183/F4
Sete Lagoas, Braz. 186/D3
Seth, WV, US 163/G1
Sethārja, Pak. 101/J3
Seti (riv.), Nepal 96/C1
Seti (zone), Nepal 96/C1
Sétif, Alg. 112/H4
Sétif (wilaya), Alg. 112/H4
Seto, Japan 83/M5
Seto-Naikai NP, Japan 84/C4
Setouchi, Japan 85/K6
Settat, Mor. 110/D2
Setté-Cama, Gabon 120/B3
Settecamini, It. 65/B4
Settepani (peak), It. 62/B5
Settimo Torinese, It. 62/A3
Settimo Vittone, It. 62/A1
Settle, Eng, UK 35/F3
Settsu, Japan 83/J6
Setúbal (dist.), Port. 46/A3
Setúbal (bay), Port. 46/A3
Setúbal, Port. 47/Q10
Seubersdorf, Ger. 59/E4
Seudre (riv.), Fr. 44/C4
Seugne (riv.), Fr. 44/C4
Seuil-D'Argonne, Fr. 55/E6
Seul (lake), On, Can. 140/G3
Seulimeum, Indo. 89/A1
Seulles (riv.), Fr. 57/E2
Seurre, Fr. 60/B4
Seuzach, Swi. 61/E2
Sevan, Arm. 103/F1
Sevan (lake), Arm. 71/H5
Sevastopol', Ukr. 73/G5
Sevelen, Swi. 61/F3
Seven (riv.), Eng, UK 35/H3
Seven (cr.), Ab, Can. 145/J3
Seven Heads (pt.), Ire. 32/B6
Seven Oaks, Tx, US 151/G2
Seven Sisters Falls, Mb, Can. 156/F2
Seven Valleys, Pa, US 168/B4
Sevenmile (hill), Ne, US 154/D2
Sevenoaks, Eng, UK 30/D3
Sevenoaks Weald, Eng, UK 30/D3
Seventy Mile House, BC, Can. 144/D2
Séveraisse (riv.), Fr. 64/C3
Severn (riv.), Wal, UK 35/F6
Severn (riv.), On, Can. 140/G3
Severn (riv.), Md, US 168/B5
Severn, Md, US 168/B5
Severna Park, Md, US 168/B5
Severnaya Osetiya-Alaniy, Resp., Rus. 75/Q6
Severnaya Sos'va (riv.), Rus. 69/N3
Severnaya Zemlya (isls.), Rus. 77/K2
Severnaya Zemlya (isls.), Rus. 192/Z
Severnyy, Rus. 69/P2
Severo-Kuril'sk, Rus. 75/R4
Severo-Yeniseyskiy, Rus. 74/K3
Severobaykal'sk, Rus. 75/L4
Severočeský (pol. reg.), Czh. 45/L1
Severodvinsk, Rus. 68/H2
Severomoravský (pol. reg.), Czh. 45/M1
Severomorsk, Rus. 68/G1
Severomuysk, Rus. 75/M4
Severoural'sk, Rus. 69/N3
Seversk, Ukr. 73/K3
Severskaya, Rus. 73/K5
Severukha, Rus. 69/P4
Severy, Ks, US 153/F2
Seveso, It. 62/C2
Sevier (lake), Ut, US 147/G4
Sevier (des.), Ut, US 147/G4
Sevier, Ut, US 149/F1
Sevier (riv.), Ut, US 142/D4
Sevier (plat.), Ut, US 149/F1
Sevier, East Fork (riv.), Ut, US 149/F2
Sevierville, Tn, US 163/F3
Sevilla, Col. 183/K8
Seville, Sp. 46/C4
Seville, Austl. 132/G5
Sevilleta Nat'l Wild. Ref., NM, US 149/J3
Sevlievo, Bul. 51/G4
Sevnica, Slov. 50/B2
Sevojno, Yugo. 50/D4
Sevran, Fr. 30/K5
Sevsk, Rus. 73/H1
Sewa (riv.), SLeo. 114/C5
Sewall, BC, Can. 171/M5
Sewanee, Tn, US 162/E3
Seward (pen.), Ak, US 171/E2
Seward, Ak, US 171/J3
Seward, Ne, US 155/F3
Sewaren, NJ, US 169/J9
Sewell, Chile 190/N9
Sewell Inlet, BC, Can. 171/M5
Sextons Creek, Ky, US 162/F2
Seyah Cheshmeh, Iran 103/F2
Seybaplaya, Mex. 176/D2
Seybouse, Oued (riv.), Alg. 112/K6
Seydhisfjördhur, Ice. 38/Q6
Seydişehir, Turk. 102/B2
Seyhan (dam), Turk. 104/D1
Seyhan (riv.), Turk. 104/D1
Seyitgazi, Turk. 102/B2
Seylac, Som. 118/B3
Seym (riv.), Rus. 70/E2
Seymour, Austl. 133/B3
Seymour, Ia, US 155/H3
Seymour, In, US 162/E1
Seymour, Mo, US 153/H2
Seymour, Tx, US 152/E4
Seymour, Wi, US 160/B2
Seymour Arm, BC, Can. 144/E2
Seymour Johnson (A.F.B.), NC, US 163/J3
Seyne, Fr. 64/C4
Seynod, Fr. 60/C6
Seyssel, Fr. 60/B6
Seyssinet-Pariset, Fr. 64/B2
Şeytan (riv.), Turk. 103/M6
Sežana, Slov. 45/K4
Sézanne, Fr. 54/C6
Sezimovo Ústí, Czh. 59/H4
Sezze, It. 65/C5
Sfîntu Gheorghe, Rom. 51/J3
Sfîntu Gheorghe, Rom. 51/G3
Sfîntu Gheorghe Branch (riv.), Rom. 51/J3
Sfizef, Alg. 112/E5
Sgurr a' Chaorachain (peak), Sc, UK 33/A2
Sgurr a' Choire Ghlais (peak), Sc, UK 33/B2
Sgurr a' Mhuilinn (peak), Sc, UK 33/B1
Sgurr Mór (peak), Sc, UK 33/A1
Sgurr na Ciche (peak), Sc, UK 33/A2
Sgurr na Lapaich (peak), Sc, UK 33/A1
Sha (riv.), China 80/C4
Sha Tau Kok, China 87/L6
Sha Tin, China 87/L7
Shaanxi (prov.), China 78/F5
Shab'ā, Leb. 105/D2
Shaba Nat'l Rsv., Kenya 119/B1
Shābah, Egypt 113/B2
Shabās ash Shuhadā', Egypt 113/B2
Shabās 'Umayr, Egypt 113/B2
Shabashah, Sudan 116/G2
Shabāzpur (riv.), Bang. 97/H4
Shabla, Bul. 51/J4
Shabo, Ukr. 72/F4
Shabqadar, Pak. 98/A2
Shabunda, D.R. Congo 121/F3
Shabwah, Yem. 118/C2
Shache, China 99/C4
Shackan Ind. Res., BC, Can. 144/D2
Shackleford, Eng, UK 30/B3
Shadaogou, China 87/F2
Shade Mtn. (mtn.), Pa, US 168/A2
Shadehill (dam), SD, US 156/C5
Shadehill, SD, US 156/C5
Shadeland, In, US 160/C4
Shadrinsk, Rus. 69/P4
Shaduzup, Myan. 86/C3
Shady Cove, Or, US 146/B2
Shady Grove, Fl, US 165/G2
Shady Spring, WV, US 163/G2
Shadyside, Oh, US 160/F5
Shafer (lake), In, US 160/C4
Shafranovo, Rus. 69/M5
Shafter, Ca, US 148/C3
Shafter, Nv, US 147/F3
Shafter, Tx, US 151/B3
Shaftesbury, Eng, UK 36/D4
Shaftsbury, Vt, US 161/K3
Shag Harbour, NS, Can. 158/E4
Shagamu, Nga. 115/F5
Shagan (riv.), Kaz. 99/C2
Shagany, China 81/B2
Shagany (lake), Ukr. 72/E5
Shagany (lake), Rom. 51/J3
Shageluk, Ak, US 171/G3
Shagonar, Rus. 78/C1
Shah Alam, Malay. 89/C2
Shāh Kot, Pak. 98/B4
Shāhābād, India 98/D4
Shāhābād, India 96/B2
Shāhābād, India 96/B1
Shāhābād, India 96/A3
Shahbā', Syria 105/F3
Shāhbandar, Pak. 101/J4
Shahdād, Iran 101/G2
Shāhdādkot, Pak. 101/J3
Shāhdādpur, Pak. 101/J3
Shāhdara, Pak. 98/C4
Shāhdasht, Iran 103/F4
Shahdol, India 96/C4
Shahekan, China 78/F5
Shāhganj, India 96/D2
Shaḩḩāt, Libya 67/J4
Shāhjahānpur, India 96/B2
Shāhpur, Pak. 98/B3
Shāhpur, India 98/D3
Shāhpur, India 96/A4
Shāhpur Chākar, Pak. 92/A2
Shāhpura, India 96/C4
Shahr Sultān, Pak. 98/A5
Shahr-e Bābak, Iran 103/H4
Shahr-e Kord, Iran 103/G3
Shahr-e Monjān, Afg. 98/A1
Shahrak, Iran 103/G3
Shāhrūd, Iran 103/G3
Shahryār, Iran 103/G3
Shāhzādpur, India 98/D4
Shāhzādpur, Bang. 97/G3
Shā'ib al Banāt (peak), Egypt 109/G3
Shaikhpura, India 97/E3
Shāistāganj, Bang. 97/H3
Shājāpur, India 92/C3
Shaji, China 78/F4
Shajian, China 87/H3
Shajianzi, China 81/C2
Shakargarh, Pak. 98/C3
Shakaskraal, SAfr. 125/E3
Shakawe, Bots. 122/D3
Shakespeare (isl.), On, Can. 157/K3
Shakhbuz, Azer. 71/H5
Shakhtars'k, Ukr. 73/K3
Shakhtërsk, Rus. 79/N2
Shakhtinsk, Kaz. 74/H5
Shakhty, Rus. 73/L4
Shakhun'ya, Rus. 69/K4
Shaki, Nga. 115/F4
Shakīso, Eth. 118/A4
Shakopee, Mn, US 157/N7
Shakotan (pen.), Japan 82/B2
Shaksha, Rus. 69/N5
Shaktoolik, Ak, US 171/F3
Shāl, Iran 103/G3
Shala (lake), Eth. 118/A4
Shalaanbood, Som. 119/D1
Shalbuzdag (peak), Rus. 71/H4
Shaldon, Eng, UK 36/C5
Shalford, Eng, UK 30/B3
Shali, Rus. 71/H4
Shaling, China 81/B2
Shallotte, NC, US 163/H4
Shallow Reach (inlet), Austl. 131/M8
Shallowater, Tx, US 152/D4
Shalqar, Kaz. 71/L3
Shal'skiy, Rus. 68/H3
Shaluli (mts.), China 78/D5
Shalyhyne, Ukr. 73/H2
Shama (riv.), Tanz. 119/A3
Shamary, Rus. 69/N4
Shamattawa (riv.), On, Can. 167/H3
Shambe, Sudan 116/F4
Shambu, Eth. 118/A3
Shambungu, D.R. Congo 120/D4
Shāmgarh, India 92/C3
Shamīl, Iran 103/J5
Shāmli, India 98/D5
Shammar, Jabal (mts.), SAr. 100/D3
Shamokin (cr.), Pa, US 168/B2
Shamokin, Pa, US 168/B2
Shamokin Dam, Pa, US 168/B2
Shāmpur, India 96/A2
Shamrock, Tx, US 152/D3
Shamrock Dome (mt.), Yk, Can. 171/L3
Shamsābād, India 96/A4
Shamsābād, India 96/B2
Shamva, Zim. 123/F3
Shan (state), Myan. 93/G3
Shan (plat.), Myan. 93/G3
Shan (pass), China 87/H3
Shan-Ngaw (range), Myan. 86/C3
Shanagolden, Ire. 32/A4
Shanchengzhen, China 81/C1
Shandī, Sudan 116/G2
Shandon, Ca, US 148/B3
Shandong (prov.), China 79/H4
Shandong (pen.), China 79/J4
Shandong (isl.), China 80/E3
Shangani, Zim. 123/E3
Shangani (riv.), Zim. 123/F3
Shangcai, China 80/C5
Shangcheng, China 80/C5
Shangchuan (isl.), China 87/G4
Shangdu, China 87/F2
Shangdu, China 78/G3
Shangfang, China 87/H2
Shanghai (prov.), China 79/J5
Shanghai, China 80/L8
Shanghe, China 81/C2
Shangjiahe, China 81/C2
Shangjiaodao, China 81/C2
Shangjing, China 87/H3
Shanglin, China 93/J3
Shangolume, D.R. Congo 121/F5
Shangombo, Zam. 122/D3
Shangping, China 87/G3
Shangqiu, China 80/C4
Shangrao, China 87/H2
Shangshui, China 80/C4
Shangsi, China 78/F5
Shangtang, China 80/C2
Shangyou (riv.), China 87/G4
Shanhua, Tai. 87/J4
Shani, Nga. 116/B3
Shanklin, Eng, UK 37/E5
Shankou, China 87/F2
Shanks, WV, US 161/G5
Shanmatang (mtn.), China 87/F3
Shanmen, China 87/G2
Shannawona (peak), Ire. 32/A3
Shannon, Qu, Can. 158/B2
Shannon (int'l arpt.), Ire. 32/B4
Shannon (riv.), Ire. 32/B4
Shannon, NZ 135/C3
Shannon, Ga, US 162/E3
Shannon, Ms, US 162/C3
Shannon (lake), Wa, US 144/C3
Shannon Hills, Ar, US 153/H3
Shannonbridge, Ire. 32/B3
Shanshan, China 78/C3
Shanshūr, Egypt 113/C4
Shantangyi, China 87/F3
Shanţānūf, Egypt 113/C4
Shantar (isl.), Rus. 77/N4
Shantar (isls.), Rus. 75/P4
Shantou, China 87/H4
Shanty Bay, On, Can. 161/G2
Shanwa, Tanz. 119/A2
Shanxi (prov.), China 78/G4
Shanyang, China 87/H3
Shanyao, China 87/H3
Shanyin, China 80/C3
Shaodong, China 87/F3
Shaoguan, China 87/G3
Shaoshan, China 87/G3
Shaoxing, China 87/J2
Shaoyang, China 87/F3
Shap, Eng, UK 35/F2
Shapa, China 87/F4
Shapki, Rus. 41/P2
Shapkina (riv.), Rus. 69/M2
Shaqiuhe, China 99/E2
Shaqlāwah, Iraq 103/F2
Shaqrā', SAr. 100/E3
Shaqrā', Yem. 118/C2
Sharafkhāneh, Iran 103/F2
Sharan, Rus. 69/M5
Sharanga, Rus. 69/K4
Sharbot Lake, On, Can. 161/H2
Sharga, Mong. 78/D2
Sharhorod, Ukr. 72/E3
Shari, Japan 82/D2
Sharingol, Mong. 78/F2
Sharjah (int'l arpt.), UAE 101/G3
Shark (bay), Austl. 127/A3
Shark River (inlet), NJ, US 168/D3
Sharkovshchina, Bela. 41/M4
Sharlyk, Rus. 71/K1
Sharm ash Shaykh, Egypt 109/G3
Sharnbrook, Eng, UK 37/F2
Sharnūb, Egypt 113/B2
Sharon, Ct, US 161/K4
Sharon, Pa, US 160/F4
Sharon, Tn, US 162/C2
Sharon, Vt, US 161/K3
Sharon Springs, Ks, US 152/D1
Sharonville, Oh, US 160/D5
Sharovka, Ukr. 73/H2
Sharpe (lake), SD, US 154/E1
Sharpes, Fl, US 165/H3
Sharpsburg, Ky, US 162/F1
Sharqpur, Pak. 98/C4
Sharqī, Jazīrat ash (isl.), Tun. 67/F4
Shar'ya, Rus. 69/K4
Shasha, Eth. 116/G4
Shashe, Bots. 123/E4
Shashe (riv.), Bots. 123/F4
Shashemenē, Eth. 118/A4
Shashi, China 87/G2
Shasta (lake), Ca, US 146/B3
Shasta (mt.), Ca, US 146/B3
Shasta (dam), Ca, US 146/B3
Shatalovo, Rus. 68/G5
Shāţi (wadi), Libya 134/B3
Shatsk, Rus. 71/G1
Shatsk, Bela. 41/M5
Shatskiy NP, Ukr. 43/M3
Shatt al Arab (riv.), Iraq 100/E2
Shattāy, Sudan 116/D2
Shattuck, Ok, US 152/E2
Shaughnessy, Ab, Can. 145/H3
Shaunavon, Sk, Can. 145/K3
Shavano Park, Tx, US 151/E3
Shave Ziyyon, Isr. 105/C3
Shaver Lake, Ca, US 148/C2
Shaw, La, US 164/C2
Shaw, Ms, US 162/B4
Shaw, Eng, UK 37/E4
Shaw (A.F.B.), SC, US 163/G4
Shawan, China 87/H3
Shawano, Wi, US 155/K1
Shawbury, Eng, UK 36/D1
Shawnee, Co, US 152/B1
Shawnee, Ks, US 160/E5
Shawnee, Ok, US 153/F3
Shawneetown, Il, US 162/C2
Shawnī, Egypt 113/B3
Shawville, Qu, Can. 161/H2
Shaxi, China 87/F3
Shay Gap, Austl. 130/D2
Shaykh Miskīn, Syria 105/E3
Shaykh Sa'd, Iraq 103/F3
Shaykh 'Uthmān, Yem. 118/C2
Shaykhān, Iraq 103/E2
Shaymak, Taj. 99/B4
Shazaoyuan, China 78/C4
Shazipo, China 87/F2
Shchara (riv.), Bela. 70/C1
Shchastya, Ukr. 73/K3
Shchedok, Rus. 71/G3
Shchekino, Rus. 70/F1
Shchelkovo, Rus. 69/W9
Shchel'yabozh, Rus. 69/N2
Shchel'yayur, Rus. 69/M2
Shcherbakty, Kaz. 74/H4
Shcherbinka, Rus. 69/W9
Shchigry, Rus. 73/J2
Shchors, Ukr. 72/F2
Shchuchin, Bela. 41/L5
Shchūchīnsk, Kaz. 99/B1
Shchuch'ye, Rus. 69/P5
She Xian, China 87/H2
Shea Stadium, NY, US 169/K9
Sheaville, Or, US 146/E2
Shebē, Eth. 116/H4
Shebekino, Rus. 73/J2
Sheberghān, Afg. 101/J1
Sheboygan, Wi, US 160/C3
Sheboygan Falls, Wi, US 160/C3
Shebunino, Rus. 79/N2
Shedd, Or, US 146/B1
Shediac, NB, Can. 158/E2
Shee (riv.), Sc, UK 33/C3
Sheelin (lake), Ire. 34/A4
Sheep (mt.), Ak, US 171/F2
Sheep (cr.), Id, US 146/F2
Sheep (mts.), Nv, US 148/E2
Sheep (riv.), Ab, Can. 144/G2
Sheep Mountain (peak), SD, US 154/C2
Sheepshead Bay (nbrhd.), NY, US 169/K9
Sheerness, Eng, UK 37/G4
Sheerness, Ab, Can. 145/J2
Sheet Harbour, NS, Can. 159/F3
Shefar'am, Isr. 105/C3
Shefayim, Isr. 105/B4
Sheffield, Austl. 132/C4
Sheffield, Eng, UK 35/G5

Sheffield (co.), Eng, UK 35/G5
Sheffield, Al, US 162/D3
Sheffield (isl.), Ct, US 169/M7
Sheffield, Ma, US 161/K3
Sheffield, Ia, US 155/H2
Sheffield, Tx, US 151/D2
Shefford, Eng, UK 37/F2
Shegangshi, China 87/G2
Shegovary, Rus. 68/J3
Shēh Husēn, Eth. 118/B4
Shehēt, Eth. 118/A2
Shehuen (riv.), Arg. 191/C6
Shehy (mts.), Ire. 32/A6
Sheikh, Som. 118/C3
Sheila, NB, Can. 158/E2
Shejiaping, China 80/B3
Shek Uk (peak), China 87/M7
Shekhūpura, Pak. 98/B4
Shelagskiy (cape), Rus. 75/S2
Shelbina, Mo, US 155/H4
Shelburne (bay), Austl. 129/F2
Shelburne, NS, Can. 158/E4
Shelburne, On, Can. 160/F2
Shelburn, In, US 160/C5
Shelburne, Vt, US 161/K2
Shelby, Ia, US 155/G3
Shelby, Mi, US 160/C3
Shelby, Ms, US 162/B4
Shelby, Mt, US 145/J3
Shelby, NC, US 163/G3
Shelby, Ne, US 154/F3
Shelby, Oh, US 160/E4
Shelbyville, Il, US 155/K4
Shelbyville (lake), Il, US 155/K4
Shelbyville, In, US 160/D5
Shelbyville, Ky, US 162/E1
Shelbyville, Mo, US 155/H4
Shelbyville, Tn, US 162/D3
Shelbyville, Tx, US 151/G2
Sheldon, Ia, US 155/G2
Sheldon, Il, US 160/C4
Sheldon, Mo, US 153/G2
Sheldon, ND, US 156/F4
Sheldon, Tx, US 151/M9
Sheldon, Vt, US 161/K2
Sheldon, Wi, US 157/J5
Sheldon Antelope Range, Nv, US 146/D3
Sheldon Point, Ak, US 171/F3
Shelekhov (gulf), Rus. 77/Q3
Shelekhov, Rus. 78/E1
Shelikof (str.), Ak, US 171/H4
Shell (cr.), Ne, US 154/F3
Shell (pt.), Eng, UK 37/G4
Shell Keys Nat'l Wild. Ref., La, US 151/J3
Shell Lake, Wi, US 157/J5
Shell Lake, Sk, Can. 145/L1
Shell Lake Nat'l Wild. Ref., ND, US 156/C3
Shell Rock, Ia, US 155/H2
Shell Rock (riv.), Ia, US 155/H2
Shellbrook, Sk, Can. 145/L1
Shelley, Id, US 147/G2
Shelley (isl.), Pa, US 168/B3
Shellharbour, Austl. 133/E2
Shellman, Ga, US 165/F2
Shelly, Mn, US 156/F4
Shelter (isl.), NY, US 169/F1
Shelter Island (sound), NY, US 169/F1
Shelton, Ct, US 169/E1
Shelton, Ne, US 154/E3
Shelton, Wa, US 144/C4
Shemgang, Bhu. 97/H2
Shemya (isl.), Ak, US 171/A5
Shen Xian, China 80/C3
Shenandoah, Ia, US 155/G3
Shenandoah (riv.), Va, US 163/H1
Shenandoah, Va, US 163/H1
Shenandoah, Pa, US 168/B2
Shenandoah NP, Va, US 163/H1
Shenandoah, South Fork (riv.), Va, US 162/C2
Shenchi, China 80/C3
Shendam, Nga. 115/H4
Shenge (pt.), SLeo. 114/B5
Shengena (peak), Tanz. 119/B3
Shengfang, China 80/H7
Shengjiaqiao, China 87/H2
Shëngjin, Alb. 75/F2
Shengjing (pass), China 86/E3
Shengli (pass), China 99/E3
Shengze, China 80/L9
Shenhu, China 87/H3
Shenkursk, Rus. 68/J3
Shennongjia, China 80/B5
Sheno, Eth. 118/A3
Shenqiu, China 80/C4
Shenstone, Eng, UK 37/E1
Shenyang, China 81/B2
Shenzao, China 79/J5
Shenzhen, China 87/G4
Sheoganj, India 92/B2
Sheopur, India 92/C2
Shepard, Ab, Can. 145/H2
Shepetivka, Ukr. 72/D2
Shepherd, Tx, US 151/G2
Shepherd (isls.), Van. 136/F6
Shepherdsville, Ky, US 162/E2
Sheppard (A.F.B.), Tx, US 153/E4
Shepparton, Austl. 133/B3
Sheppey, Isle of (isl.), Eng, UK 37/G4
Shepshed, Eng, UK 37/E1
Shepton Mallet, Eng, UK 36/D4
Sheqi, China 80/C4
Sherborne, Eng, UK 36/D5
Sherbro (isl.), SLeo. 114/B5
Sherbrooke, Qu, Can. 161/L2
Sherbrooke, NS, Can. 159/G3
Sherburn, Eng, UK 35/G2
Sherburne, NY, US 161/J3
Sherburne Nat'l Wild. Ref., Mn, US 155/H1
Shercock, Ire. 32/D2
Shere (hill), Nga. 115/H4
Shere, Eng, UK 30/B3
Sheremetyevo (int'l arpt.), Rus. 69/W9
Shergaon, India 97/J2
Sherghāti, India 97/E3
Sheridan, Ar, US 153/H3
Sheridan, Ca, US 146/C4
Sheridan, Il, US 155/K3
Sheridan, In, US 160/C4
Sheridan, Mt, US 147/G1
Sheridan, Or, US 146/B1
Sheridan, Wy, US 147/K1
Sheringham, Eng, UK 37/H1
Sherkin (isl.), Ire. 32/A7
Sherlovaya Gora, Rus. 78/H1
Sherman, Tx, US 153/F4
Sherman, Ms, US 162/C3
Sherman (dam), Ne, US 154/E3
Sherman (res.), Ne, US 154/E3
Sherman, NM, US 149/J4
Sherman, Il, US 155/K4
Sherman (cr.), Pa, US 168/A3
Sherman Oaks (nbrhd.), Ca, US 166/F7
Sherpur, Bang. 97/G3
Sherpur, Bang. 97/H3
Shertallai, India 95/C4
Sherwood, ND, US 156/D3
Sherwood, Ok, US 153/G3
Sherwood, PE, Can. 158/F2
Sherwood, Oh, US 160/D4
Sherwood, Tn, US 162/E3
Sherwood, Tx, US 151/D2
Sherwood (pt.), Ct, US 169/E1
Shetek (lake), Mn, US 155/G1
Shetianqiao, China 87/F3
Shetland (isls.), UK 192/G
Shetpe, Kaz. 71/K3
Sheung Shui-Fanling, China 87/L7
Shevchenko (int'l arpt.), Kaz. 71/J4
Shevchenkove, Ukr. 73/J3
Shewa (prov.), Eth. 116/H3
Shewa Gīmīra, Eth. 116/G4
Sheyang, China 80/E4
Sheyang (riv.), China 80/D4
Sheyenne, ND, US 156/E4
Sheyenne (riv.), ND, US 156/E4
Shḩīm, Leb. 105/C1
Shi (riv.), China 80/C4
Shi San Ling, China 80/H6
Shiawassee (riv.), Mi, US 160/D3
Shiawassee Nat'l Wild. Ref., Mi, US 160/D3
Shibakawa, Japan 83/B3
Shibām, Yem. 118/D2
Shibantan, China 87/F2
Shibata, Japan 85/F2
Shibayama, Japan 83/E2
Shibecha, Japan 82/D2
Shibetsu, Japan 82/C1
Shibetsu, Japan 82/D2
Shibganj, Bang. 97/G3
Shibīn (canal), Egypt 113/C3
Shibīn al Kaum, Egypt 113/C3
Shibīn al Qanāţir, Egypt 113/C4
Shiblanjah, Egypt 113/C4
Shibotsu (isl.), Rus. 82/E2
Shibushi (bay), Japan 84/B5
Shicheng (isl.), China 81/B3
Shicheng, China 81/C2
Shicheng, China 87/H3
Shicheng, China 87/H3
Shickshinny, Pa, US 168/B1
Shidao, China 81/B4
Shiderty (riv.), Kaz. 99/B1
Shidixi, China 87/F2
Shidler, Ok, US 153/F2
Shido, Japan 84/D3
Shield (cape), Austl. 129/E3
Shields, Mi, US 160/D3
Shields, ND, US 156/D4
Shi'erdaogou, China 81/D2
Shifnal, Eng, UK 36/D1
Shiga, Japan 83/J5
Shigaraki, Japan 83/K6
Shigony, Rus. 71/J1
Shihe, China 81/A3
Shihezi, China 99/E3
Shijak, Alb. 75/F2
Shijiaqiao, China 80/L9
Shijiazhuang, China 80/C3
Shijing, China 87/H3
Shijingshan, China 80/H7
Shijiu (lake), China 87/H2
Shijōnawate, Japan 83/J6
Shika, Nga. 115/G4
Shikabe, Japan 82/B2
Shikārpur, India 96/B1
Shikārpur, Pak. 101/J3
Shikata, Japan 83/G6
Shikatsu, Japan 83/L5
Shikishima, Japan 83/B2
Shikohābād, India 96/B2
Shikoku (isl.), Japan 77/N6
Shikoku (mts.), Japan 84/C4
Shikotan (isl.), Rus. 79/P3
Shikotsu (lake), Japan 82/B2
Shikotsu-Tōya NP, Japan 82/B2
Shikou, China 87/G3
Shilabo, Eth. 118/C4
Shilbottle, Eng, UK 33/E6
Shildon, Eng, UK 35/G2
Shilipu, China 87/G2
Shilka (riv.), Rus. 77/L4
Shilka, Rus. 78/H1
Shillelagh, Ire. 32/D4
Shillington, Pa, US 168/C3
Shillong, India 93/F2
Shiloango (riv.), Congo 120/C4
Shiloh, NJ, US 168/C5
Shiloh Nat'l Mil. Park, Tn, US 162/C3
Shilou, China 80/B3
Shilovo, Rus. 71/G1
Shimabara, Japan 84/B4
Shimagahara, Japan 83/K6
Shimamoto, Japan 83/J6
Shimane (pref.), Japan 84/C3
Shimanovsk, Rus. 79/K1
Shimasahi, Japan 83/K5
Shimba Hills Nat'l Rsvs., Kenya 119/B3
Shimbara (bay), Japan 84/B4
Shimber Berris (peak), Som. 118/C3
Shimen, China 80/H6
Shimenqiao, China 87/F2
Shimizu, Japan 85/F3
Shimizu, Japan 82/C2
Shimizu, Japan 83/B3
Shimo-koshiki (isl.), Japan 84/A5
Shimobe, Japan 83/A3
Shimoda, Japan 85/F3
Shimodate, Japan 85/F2
Shimofusa, Japan 83/E2
Shimoichi, Japan 83/J7
Shimokita (pen.), Japan 82/B3
Shimonita, Japan 83/B1
Shimonoseki, Japan 84/B4
Shimotsuma, Japan 83/D1
Shimoyama, Japan 83/M5
Shimsk, Rus. 41/P2
Shimukappu, Japan 82/C2
Shin (lake), Sc, UK 31/R7
Shin, Japan 83/C1
Shinan, China 94/E1
Shinano (riv.), Japan 79/M4
Shināş, Oman 101/G4
Shinch'ŏrwon, SKor. 81/D3
Shindo, SKor. 81/F6
Shiner, Tx, US 151/F3
Shingbwiyang, Myan. 86/C3
Shingleton, Mi, US 160/C1
Shingū, Japan 84/D4
Shingwidzi, SAfr. 123/F4
Shinhyŏn, SKor. 84/A3
Shinji (lake), Japan 84/C3
Shinjō, Japan 82/B4
Shinjō, Japan 83/J7
Shinkawa, Japan 83/L5
Shinminato, Japan 85/E2
Shinnecock (bay), NY, US 169/F2
Shinnecock Ind. Res., NY, US 169/F2
Shinnston, WV, US 160/F5
Shinrone, Ire. 32/C4
Shinsei, Japan 83/L5
Shintoku, Japan 82/C2
Shintone, Japan 83/E2
Shinyanga, Tanz. 119/A2
Shinyanga (prov.), Tanz. 119/A2
Shio-no-misaki (cape), Japan 84/D4
Shiogama, Japan 85/G1
Shioya-saki (pt.), Japan 85/G2
Ship (isl.), Ms, US 164/D2
Ship Bottom, NJ, US 168/D4
Shipai, China 87/H3
Shipbourne, Eng, UK 30/D3
Shiping, China 87/F3
Shipka, Bul. 51/G4
Shipley, Eng, UK 35/G4
Shipman, Va, US 163/H2
Shippan (pt.), Ct, US 169/L7
Shippegan, NB, Can. 158/E2
Shippegan (isl.), NB, Can. 158/E2
Shippensburg, Pa, US 161/H4
Shippo, Japan 83/L5
Shiprock, NM, US 149/H2
Shipston on Stour, Eng, UK 37/E2
Shipuqi (pass), China 99/C5
Shiqiao, China 87/H3
Shiqiao, China 87/E2
Shiqijie, China 79/K3
Shīr (mtn.), Iran 103/H4
Shirakami-misaki (cape), Japan 82/B3
Shirakawa, Japan 85/G2
Shirakawa, Japan 83/M4
Shirakawa-tōge (pass), Japan 84/E3
Shirako, Japan 83/E3
Shirane, Japan 83/A2
Shirane-san (peak), Japan 85/F2
Shirane-san (peak), Japan 85/F3
Shiranuka, Japan 82/D2
Shiraoi, Japan 82/B2
Shiraoka, Japan 83/D1
Shirati, Tanz. 119/A2
Shiraz (int'l arpt.), Iran 103/H4
Shīrāz, Iran 103/H4
Shirbīn, Egypt 113/C2
Shire (riv.), Malw. 123/G3
Shireet, Mong. 78/G2
Shiremoor, Eng, UK 35/G1
Shiren, China 81/D2
Shiretoko NP, Japan 82/D1
Shiretoko-misaki (cape), Japan 82/D1
Shiriya-zaki (pt.), Japan 82/B3
Shirjiu (lake), China 80/D5
Shirley, Ar, US 153/H3
Shirley, NY, US 169/F2
Shiro, Tx, US 151/G2
Shiroi, Japan 83/E2
Shiroishi, Japan 85/G1
Shirone, Japan 85/F2
Shiroyama, Japan 83/C2
Shīrvān, Iran 103/J2
Shishaldin (vol.), Ak, US 171/F5
Shishan, China 87/H3
Shishang, China 87/H3
Shīshgarh, India 96/B1
Shishhid (riv.), Mong.,Rus. 78/D1
Shishmaref, Ak, US 171/E2
Shishou, China 87/G2
Shisht al An'ām, Egypt 113/B3
Shisui, Japan 83/E2
Shitang, China 87/J2
Shitang, China 87/G3
Shithātha, Iraq 103/E3
Shiting (riv.), China 86/E2
Shituan, China 86/E2
Shivachevo, Bul. 51/H4
Shivalaya, Bang. 97/G4
Shiven (riv.), Ire. 32/B3
Shivers, Ms, US 164/D2
Shivpurī, India 96/A3
Shivpuri NP, India 96/A3
Shivwits (plat.), Az, Nv, US 149/F2
Shixing, China 93/K3
Shiyan, China 80/B4
Shizigoukou, China 78/F5
Shizipu, China 87/H2
Shizong, China 86/D3
Shizugawa, Japan 82/B4
Shizuishan, China 78/F4
Shizukuishi, Japan 82/B4
Shizunai, Japan 82/C2
Shizuoka, Japan 85/F3
Shizuoka (pref.), Japan 85/E3
Shklov, Bela. 41/P4
Shkodër, Alb. 75/F1
Shkumbin (riv.), Alb. 50/E5
Shoal (cr.), Il, US 155/K4
Shoal (pt.), Austl. 130/B4
Shoal Harbour, Nf, Can. 159/L1
Shoal Lake, Mb, Can. 156/D2
Shoalhaven Heads, Austl. 133/E2
Shoals, In, US 162/D1
Shoalwater Ind. Res., Wa, US 144/B4
Shōbara, Japan 84/C3
Shōbu, Japan 83/D1
Shōdo (isl.), Japan 84/D3
Shoe (mtn.), Ok, US 153/G3
Shoeburyness, Eng, UK 37/G3
Shoemakersville, Pa, US 168/C3
Shokanbetsu-dake (peak), Japan 82/B2
Sholāpur, India 95/B2
Sholl (peak), Arg. 191/D6
Shomron (ruin), WBnk. 105/C4
Shon (canal), Fl, US 164/N7
Shōnan, Japan 83/E2
Shonto, Az, US 149/G2
Shoreacres, BC, Can. 144/F3
Shoreham, Mn, US 156/G4
Shoreham, Mi, US 160/C3
Shoreham, Vt, US 161/K3
Shoreham-by-Sea, Eng, UK 37/F5
Shoreview, Mn, US 157/P6
Shorewood, Il, US 167/P16
Shorewood, Wi, US 167/Q13
Shorkot, Pak. 98/B4
Shorkot Road, Pak. 98/B4
Shorncliffe (nbrhd.), Austl. 134/F6
Shorne, Eng, UK 30/E2
Short (mtn.), Tn, US 162/E3
Shorter, Al, US 162/E4
Shorterville, Al, US 165/F2
Shortland (isls.), Sol. 136/E5
Shorwell, Eng, UK 37/E5
Shoshone (lake), Wy, US 147/H1
Shoshone, Ca, US 148/D3
Shoshone (mts.), Nv, US 146/E4
Shoshone (riv.), Wy, US 147/J1
Shoshone, Id, US 147/F2
Shoshone (falls), Id, US 147/F2
Shoshong, Bots. 123/E4
Shoshoni, Wy, US 147/J2
Shostka, Ukr. 73/G2
Shotley, Eng, UK 37/H3
Shotton, Eng, UK 35/G2
Shotts, Sc, UK 33/C5
Shou Xian, China 80/D4
Shouguang, China 80/D3
Shouyang, China 80/C3
Shoval, Isr. 105/B6
Show Low, Az, US 149/G3
Shōwa, Japan 83/B2
Shōwa, Japan 83/D2
Shoyna, Rus. 69/K2
Shozhma, Rus. 68/J3
Shpakovskoye, Rus. 73/M5
Shpanberga (chan.), Rus. 82/E2
Shpola, Ukr. 72/F3
Shreve, Oh, US 160/E4
Shreveport, La, US 150/H1
Shrewsbury, Eng, UK 36/D1
Shrewsbury, Pa, US 168/B4
Shriner Mtn. (mtn.), Pa, US 168/A2
Shropshire (co.), Eng, UK 35/E6
Shropshire Union (canal), Eng, UK 35/F6
Shrule, Ire. 32/A2
Shū (riv.), Kaz. 75/H5
Shū, Kaz. 74/H5
Shu (riv.), China 80/D5
Shu`bah (wadi), Libya 134/D2
Shuangbai, China 86/D3
Shuangcheng, China 75/N5
Shuangfeng, China 80/L8
Shuanghechang, China 87/E2
Shuangliao, China 80/E2
Shuangpai, China 93/K2
Shuangpaishan, China 87/G3
Shuangxi, China 87/H3
Shuangyang, China 79/K3
Shuangyashan, China 79/L2
Shubarkuduk, Kaz. 71/L2
Shubarshi, Kaz. 71/K2
Shubenacadie, NS, Can. 158/F3
Shubert, Ne, US 155/G3
Shubrā al Khaymah, Egypt 113/C4
Shubrā Khīt, Egypt 113/B2
Shubuta, Ms, US 164/D2
Shucheng, China 80/D5
Shu'fāţ, WBnk. 105/C5
Shuganu, India 86/B3
Shugurovo, Rus. 69/M5
Shuibatang, China 87/E2
Shuibei, China 87/H3
Shuiche, China 87/H3
Shuiji, China 87/H3
Shuijiang, China 87/E2
Shuikou, China 87/H3
Shuikou, China 87/G4
Shuikou, China 87/G3
Shuikouguan, China 94/D1
Shuiluo (riv.), China 86/D2
Shuimenzi, China 81/B3
Shuinan, China 87/H3
Shuiping, China 78/F5
Shuiyang (riv.), China 80/D5
Shuizhan, China 78/C4
Shujāābād, Pak. 98/A5
Shuksan (mt.), Wa, US 144/D3
Shulan, China 79/K3
Shule (riv.), China 74/K6
Shulehe, China 78/D3
Shulerville, SC, US 163/H4
Shumagin (isls.), Ak, US 171/G4
Shumanay, Uzb. 71/L4
Shumen, Bul. 51/H4
Shumerlya, Rus. 69/K5
Shumikha, Rus. 69/P5
Shumilinskaya, Rus. 73/L3
Shums'k, Ukr. 72/D2
Shuna (isl.), Sc, UK 33/A3
Shūnah (wadi), Egypt 113/C5
Shunak (peak), Kaz. 99/B2
Shūnat Nimrīn, Jor. 105/D5
Shun'ga, Rus. 68/G3
Shungnak, Ak, US 171/G2
Shunyi, China 80/H6
Shuo Xian, China 80/C3
Shuoliang, China 87/E4
Shuolong, China 94/D1
Shupīyan, India 98/C3
Shuqualak, Ms, US 162/C4
Shūr (riv.), Iran 101/G2
Shūr Āb, Iran 103/G3
Shurayk, Sudan 116/G2
Shurugwi, Zim. 123/F3
Shūsh, Iran 103/G3
Shushenskoye, Rus. 99/F1
Shūshtar, Iran 103/G3
Shuswap (lake), BC, Can. 144/E2
Shuswap (riv.), BC, Can. 144/E2
Shuwak, Sudan 116/G2
Shuwaykah, WBnk. 105/C4
Shuya, Rus. 68/J4
Shuyang, China 80/D4
Shuyeretskoye, Rus. 68/G2
Shwebandaw, Myan. 86/B5
Shwebo, Myan. 86/B4
Shwedaung, Myan. 86/B5
Shwegun, Myan. 86/C5
Shwegyin, Myan. 86/C5
Shweli (riv.), Myan. 86/C4
Shwemawdaw Pagoda, Myan. 86/C5
Shwethalyaung (Reclining Buddha), Myan. 86/C5
Shyghys Qazaqstan Oblast, Kaz. 74/J5
Shymkent, Kaz. 99/A3
Shyok (riv.), India 99/C5
Shyroke, Ukr. 73/G4
Shyshaky, Ukr. 73/H3
Si Chiang Mai, Thai. 94/C2
Si Chon, Thai. 94/B4
Si Khiu, Thai. 94/C3
Si Piso-Piso (falls), Indo. 89/B2
Si Racha, Thai. 94/C3
Si Satchanalai (ruin), Thai. 94/B2
Si Satchanalai, Thai. 94/B2
Si Xian, China 80/D4
Siagne (riv.), Fr. 64/C5
Siāh Kūh (mts.), Afg. 101/H2
Siak (riv.), Indo. 90/B3
Siaksriinderapura, Indo. 89/C2
Siālkot, Pak. 98/C3
Sialum, PNG 129/G1
Siana, India 92/B2
Siano, It. 65/D6
Sianów, Pol. 40/G4
Sianton (isl.), Indo. 89/D2
Siapa (riv.), Ven. 181/E4
Siargao (isl.), Phil. 88/D3
Siasconset, Ma, US 158/C5
Siasi, Phil. 88/C4
Siasikabole, Zam. 123/E3
Siassi, PNG 129/G1
Siaton, Phil. 88/C3
Siaton (pt.), Phil. 88/C3
Siau (isl.), Indo. 91/G3
Šiauliai, Lith. 41/K4
Siavonga, Zam. 123/F3
Sibalom, Phil. 88/C3
Sibanyati, Zam. 123/E3
Sibasa, SAfr. 123/F4
Sibay, Rus. 71/L1
Sibbhultań (riv.), Swe. 39/L6
Sibbo (Sipoo), Fin. 41/L1
Šibenik, Cro. 50/B4
Siberia (reg.), Rus. 77/H3
Siberut (isl.), Indo. 77/J10
Sibi, Pak. 101/J3
Sibidiri, PNG 129/F2
Sibigo, Indo. 89/A2
Sibiloi NP, Kenya 116/H4
Sibirtsevo, Rus. 79/L3
Sibiti, Congo 120/C3
Sibiu (prov.), Rom. 51/G2
Sibiu, Rom. 51/G3
Sible Hedingham, Eng, UK 37/G3
Sibley, Ms, US 164/C2
Sibley, Ia, US 155/G2
Sibolga, Indo. 89/B2
Siboluton, Indo. 91/F3
Sibong, India 86/B3
Siborongborong, Indo. 89/B2
Sibsāgar, India 86/B3
Sibsoo, Bhu. 97/G2
Sibu, Malay. 90/D3
Sibuatan (mtn.), Indo. 89/B2
Sibuco, Phil. 88/C4
Sibuguey (bay), Phil. 88/C4
Sibuhuan, Indo. 89/B2
Sibut, CAfr. 116/C4
Sibutu Passage (chan.), Malay,Phil. 88/B4
Sibuyan (sea), Phil. 91/F1
Sibuyan (isl.), Phil. 91/F1
Siby, Burk. 114/E4
Sicamous, BC, Can. 144/E2
Sicapoo (mt.), Phil. 88/C1
Sichifulo (riv.), Zam. 122/E3
Sichuan (prov.), China 78/E5
Sicié (cape), Fr. 64/B6
Sicilia (pol. reg.), It. 48/C4
Sicily (str.), It. 67/F3
Sicily (isl.), It. 29/F5
Sicily Island, La, US 164/C2
Sicily Island (mtn.), La, US 164/C2
Sico (riv.), Hon. 172/D4
Sicuani, Peru 184/D4
Šid, Yugo. 50/D3
Sīdamo (prov.), Eth. 116/H4
Sidaogou, China 81/D2
Sidcup (nbrhd.), Eng, UK 30/D2
Sidéradougou, Burk. 114/D4
Siderno Marina, It. 48/E3
Sideròpolis, Braz. 189/G4
Sidewinder (mtn.), Ca, US 166/C1
Sidhaulī, India 96/C2
Sidhi, India 96/C3
Sidhirókastron, Gre. 75/H2
Sidhpur, India 101/K4
Sidi Aïssa, Alg. 112/G5
Sidi Allal el Bahraoui, Mor. 112/A2
Sīdī Barrānī, Egypt 109/E2
Sidi Bel-Abbes, Alg. 112/E5
Sidi Bennour, Mor. 110/C2
Sīdī Bū Zayd (gov.), Tun. 48/A5
Sīdī Ghāzī, Egypt 113/C2
Sidi Ifni, Mor. 110/C3
Sidi Kacem, Mor. 112/B2
Sidi Kacem (prov.), Mor. 112/B2
Sīdī Nājī, Tun. 112/M6
Sīdī Şāliḩ (well), Libya 134/C2
Sīdī Sālim, Egypt 113/B2
Sidi Slimane, Mor. 112/B2
Sīdī 'Umar Bū Ḩajalah, Tun. 48/B5
Sidi Yahya du Rharb, Mor. 112/A2
Sidikalang, Indo. 89/B2
Sidlaw (hills), Sc, UK 33/C3
Sidmouth (cape), Austl. 129/F3
Sidmouth, Eng, UK 36/C5
Sīdmūkh, India 98/C5
Sidnaw, Mi, US 157/K4
Sidney, BC, Can. 144/C3
Sidney, Mb, Can. 156/E3
Sidney, Ar, US 153/J2
Sidney, Ia, US 155/G3
Sidney, Mt, US 156/B4
Sidney, Ne, US 154/C3
Sidney, NY, US 161/J3
Sidney, Oh, US 160/D4
Sidney Draw (riv.), Co, Ne, US 154/C3
Sidney Lanier (res.), Ga, US 162/E3
Sidon (Şaydā), Leb. 105/C1
Sidra (gulf), Libya 107/D1
Sidrolândia, Braz. 189/F2
Sidvokodvo, Swaz. 125/E2
Sieci, It. 63/E6
Siedlce, Pol. 43/M2
Sieg (riv.), Ger. 45/G1
Siegburg, Ger. 55/G2
Siegel (mtn.), Mt, US 144/G4
Siegen, Ger. 55/H2
Siegenburg, Ger. 59/E5
Siegendorf im Burgenland, Aus. 50/C2
Sielo, Libr. 114/C4
Siemianówka (lake), Pol. 43/M2
Siemiatycze, Pol. 43/M2
Siempang, Camb. 94/D3
Siemreab, Camb. 94/C3
Siena (prov.), It. 63/E6
Siena, It. 45/J5
Sienne (riv.), Fr. 44/C2
Sieradz, Pol. 43/K3
Sieraków, Pol. 43/J2
Sierning, Aus. 59/H6
Sierpc, Pol. 43/K2
Sierra (peak), Ca, US 166/C3
Sierra Army Depot, Ca, US 146/C3
Sierra Blanca, Tx, US 151/B2
Sierra Chilengue (mts.), Ang. 122/B2
Sierra City, Ca, US 146/C4
Sierra Colorada, Arg. 190/D4
Sierra de Amambay (mts.), Par.,Braz. 189/F2
Sierra de Calalaste (mts.), Arg. 188/C3
Sierra de Juarez (mts.), Mex. 148/E4
Sierra de Misiones (mts.), Arg. 189/F3
Sierra de Olte (hills), Arg. 190/C4
Sierra de S. Luis (mts.), Arg. 190/D2
Sierra de San Jonquín (mts.), Par. 189/F3
Sierra de la Giganta (mts.), Mex. 174/C3
Sierra de la Macarena, PN, Col. 180/C4
Sierra de Perijá (mts.), Col. 173/G6
Sierra de San Pedro Mártir, Mex. 174/B2
Sierra de Serpe de Coba (peak), Sp. 46/B1
Sierra del Carmen, Mex. 151/C3
Sierra del Nevado (mts.), Arg. 190/C3
Sierra Gorda, Chile 188/B2
Sierra Grande, Arg. 190/D4
Sierra Leone (cape), SLeo. 114/B4
Sierra Leone (ctry.) 107/A4
Sierra Madre, Ca, US 166/F7
Sierra Madre (mts.), Phil. 88/C1
Sierra Madre (mts.), Ca., US 148/C3
Sierra Madre del Sur (mts.), Mex. 172/A4
Sierra Madre Occidental (mts.), Mex. 139/G7
Sierra Madre Oriental (mts.), Mex. 139/G7
Sierra Maestra (mts.), Cuba 177/G2
Sierra Nacimiento (mts.), NM, US 152/A2
Sierra Nevada (mts.), Sp. 46/D4
Sierra Nevada (mts.), US 139/E6
Sierra Nevada de Santa Marta, Col. 177/H4
Sierra Nevada de Santa Marta, PN, Col. 173/G5
Sierra Nevada, PN, Ven. 173/G6
Sierra San Pedro Martir (mts.), Mex. 174/B2
Sierra Vieja (mts.), Mex. 151/B2
Sierra Vista, Az, US 149/G5
Sierra Vizcaíno (mts.), Mex. 174/B3
Sierras Bayas, Arg. 190/E3
Sierras de Córdoba (mts.), Arg. 188/C4
Sierre, Swi. 60/D5
Siesta Key (isl.), Fl, US 165/G4
Siete Picos (peak), Sp. 47/M8
Siete Tazas, PN, Chile 190/C2
Sieve (riv.), It. 63/E5
Sif Fatima, Alg. 111/H3
Sīfenī, Eth. 118/B2
Siffray, Gui. 114/C4
Sifié, C.d'Iv. 114/D5
Sífnos (isl.), Gre. 75/J4
Sig, Alg. 112/E5
Siga (hills), Tanz. 119/A2
Sigean, Fr. 44/E5
Sigep, Indo. 89/B3
Sigep (cape), Indo. 89/B3
Siggerud, Nor. 38/S8
Siġġiewi, Malta 48/L7
Sighetu Marmaţiei, Rom. 72/B4
Sighişoara, Rom. 51/G2
Sighty Crag (hill), Eng, UK 35/F1
Sigillo, It. 63/F7
Sigli, Indo. 89/A1
Sigli (cape), Alg. 112/H4
Siglufjördhur, Ice. 38/N6
Sigmaringen, Ger. 61/F1
Sigmarszell, Ger. 61/F2
Signa, It. 63/E6
Signakhi, Geo. 71/H4
Signal (hill), SD, US 154/C2
Signal de la Mère Boitier (peak), Fr. 44/F3
Signal de Saint-Andre (peak), Fr. 64/A1
Signal de Toussaines (peak), Fr. 56/B4
Signal d'Écouves (peak), Fr. 57/F3
Signal Hill, Ca, US 166/F8
Signau, Swi. 60/D4
Signes, Fr. 64/B6
Signy-L'Abbaye, Fr. 55/D4
Signy-le-Petit, Fr. 55/D4
Signy-Signets, Fr. 30/M5
Sigourney, Ia, US 155/H3
Sigriswil, Swi. 60/D4
Sigtuna, Swe. 40/G2
Siguatepeque, Hon. 176/E3
Sigüe, Ecu. 180/B4
Sigüenza, Sp. 46/D2
Siguiri, Gui. 114/C4
Sigulda, Lat. 41/L3
Sigura Gura (falls), Indo. 89/B2
Sigurd, Ut, US 149/G1
Sihl (riv.), Swi. 61/E3
Sihlsee (lake), Swi. 61/E3
Sihochac, Mex. 176/D2
Sihong, China 80/D4
Sihorā, India 96/C4
Sihuas, Peru 184/B3
Siilinjärvi, Fin. 68/E3
Si'īr, WBnk. 105/C5
Siirt, Turk. 102/E2
Siirt (prov.), Turk. 102/E2
Sijung, NKor. 81/D2
Sikandarābād, India 96/A1
Sikandarpur, India 97/E2
Sikandra Rao, India 96/B2
Sikanni Chief (riv.), BC, Can. 140/D3
Sikasso, Mali 114/D4
Sikasso (pol. reg.), Mali 114/D4
Sikaw, Myan. 86/C4
Sikeston, Mo, US 162/C2
Sikhote-Alin' (mts.), Rus. 75/P5
Síkinos, Gre. 75/J4
Síkinos (isl.), Gre. 75/J4
Sikinssa, C.d'Iv. 114/D5
Sikkim (state), India 92/E2
Siklós, Hun. 50/D3
Sikoúrion, Gre. 75/H3
Siktyakh, Rus. 75/N3
Sikuati, Malay. 88/B4
Sikwane, Bots. 122/E5
Silai (riv.), India 97/F4
Šilalė, Lith. 41/K4
Silandro (Schlanders), It. 61/G4
Silao, India 97/E3
Silao, Mex. 175/E4
Sīlat Az Zahr, WBnk. 105/C4
Silay, Phil. 88/C3
Silchar, India 86/B3
Sildā, India 97/F4
Şile, Turk. 51/J5
Silea, It. 63/F2
Sileby, Eng, UK 37/E1
Silel (riv.), Som. 118/B3
Silenen, Swi. 61/E4
Siler City, NC, US 163/H3
Silesia (reg.), Pol. 43/H3
Silet, Alg. 111/G5
Siletz (riv.), Or, US 146/B1
Siletz, Or, US 146/B1
Silgadhī, Nepal 96/C1
Silifke, Turk. 104/C1
Silīguri, India 97/G2
Siling (lake), China 99/E5
Silisili (mt.), Sam. 137/R9
Silistra, Bul. 51/H3
Silivri, Turk. 51/J5
Siljan (lake), Swe. 40/F1
Siljansnäs, Swe. 40/F1
Silkeborg, Den. 40/C3
Silksworth, Eng, UK 35/G2
Sill (riv.), Aus. 61/H3
Silla, Sp. 47/E3
Silla Tombs, SKor. 84/A3
Sillajguay (peak), Chile 188/B1
Sillajhuay (peak), Bol. 188/B1
Sillamäe, Est. 41/M2
Sillānwāli, Pak. 98/B4
Sillaro (riv.), It. 63/E4
Sillé-le-Guillame, Fr. 57/E4
Silleda, Sp. 46/A1
Sillen (lake), Swe. 39/A2
Sillian, Aus. 45/K3
Sillil, Som. 118/B3
Silloth, Eng, UK 35/E2
Sillustani (ruin), Peru 184/D4
Silly-le-Long, Fr. 30/L4
Silo, Ok, US 153/F3
Siloam Springs, Ar, US 153/G2
Silopi, Turk. 102/E2
Silsbee, Tx, US 151/G2
Silsden, Eng, UK 35/G4
Silsersee (lake), Swi. 61/F5
Siltcoos (lake), Or, US 146/A2
Silton, Sk, Can. 156/B2
Siltou (well), Chad 116/B1
Siluas, Indo. 90/C3
Siluko, Nga. 115/G5
Šilutė, Lith. 41/J4
Silva, Mo, US 162/B2
Silvan (dam), Turk. 102/E2
Silvāni, India 96/B4
Silvania, Col. 183/L8
Silvânia, Braz. 186/C3
Silvaplana, Swi. 61/F5
Silver (mtn.), Ca, US 166/C1
Silver (cr.), Ia, US 155/G3
Silver (riv.), Il, US 155/K4
Silver (cr.), Or, US 146/D2
Silver (lake), Or, US 146/C2
Silver, Tx, US 150/D1
Silver Bay, Mn, US 157/J4
Silver Bell, Az, US 149/G4
Silver City, NM, US 149/H4
Silver City, SD, US 154/C1
Silver Cliff, Co, US 152/B1
Silver Creek, Yk, Can. 171/L3
Silver Creek, NY, US 161/G3
Silver Lake, Mn, US 155/G1
Silver Lake, Or, US 146/C2
Silver Lake, Wi, US 167/P14
Silver Lake NWR, ND, US 156/E3
Silver Lake-Fircrest, Wa, US 167/C2
Silver Meadow (lake), NJ, US 168/C5
Silver Run, Md, US 168/A4
Silver Spring, Md, US 168/A6
Silver Springs, Fl, US 165/G3
Silver Springs, Nv, US 146/D4
Silver Star, Mt, US 147/G1
Silver Water, On, Can. 160/E2
Silverado, Ca, US 166/C3
Silverdale, Eng, UK 35/F3
Silverdale, Wa, US 144/C4
Silverdale, Austl. 133/E1
Silverstone, Eng, UK 37/E2
Silverton, Austl. 132/B1
Silverton, Eng, UK 36/C5
Silverton, Co, US 149/J2
Silverton, NJ, US 168/D3
Silverton, Or, US 146/B1
Silverton, Tx, US 152/D3
Silverton, Wa, US 144/D3
Silverwood (lake), Ca, US 166/C2
Silves, Port. 46/A4
Silves, Braz. 182/B3
Silvi, It. 65/D2
Silvia, Col. 180/B4
Silvies (riv.), Or, US 146/D2
Silvio Pettirossi (Asunción) (int'l arpt.), Par. 188/E3
Silvretta (mts.), Aus. 61/G4
Silyānah (gov.), Tun. 48/A4
Silyānah, Tun. 112/L6
Silz, Aus. 61/G3
Sim (cape), Mor. 110/C3
Sima, Com. 125/H6
Sima, Congo 120/C3
Simao, China 86/D4
Simão Dias, Braz. 187/F1
Şimareh (riv.), Iran 103/F3
Simav, Turk. 102/B2
Simba, D.R. Congo 121/E2
Simbach am Inn, Ger. 59/G6
Simbai, PNG 129/G1
Simbo, Tanz. 121/G4
Simbruini (mts.), It. 65/B3
Simcoe (lake), On, Can. 161/G2
Simcoe, On, Can. 160/F3
Simcoe (lake), Qu, Can. 167/J4
Simdega, India 97/E4
Simen (mts.), Eth. 116/H2
Simen Mountains NP, Eth. 116/H2
Simeria, Rom. 50/F3
Simeto (riv.), It. 67/G3
Simeulue (isl.), Indo. 77/J9
Simeyiz, Ukr. 73/H5
Simferopol (int'l arpt.), Ukr. 73/G5
Simferopol', Ukr. 73/H5
Simga, India 95/D1
Sími, Gre. 102/A2
Simi (hills), Ca, US 166/B2
Simi Valley, Ca, US 166/B2
Simijaca, Col. 183/M7
Simikot, Nepal 99/D6
Similaun (peak), Aus., It. 61/G4
Similkameen (riv.), BC, Can. 144/D3
Simití, Col. 180/C3
Simitli, Bul. 75/H2
Simiyu (riv.), Tanz. 119/A2
Simla, India 98/D4
Şimleu Silvaniei, Rom. 51/F2
Simme (riv.), Swi. 45/G3
Simmelsdorf, Ger. 59/E3
Simmerath, Ger. 55/F2
Simmerbach (riv.), Ger. 55/G4
Simmern, Ger. 55/G4
Simmertal, Ger. 55/G4
Simmesport, La, US 164/C2
Simmons, Mo, US 153/H2
Simmszand (isl.), Neth. 52/D2
Simnas, Lith. 41/K4
Simni (isl.), NKor. 81/C3
Simo, Fin. 68/E2
Simões, Braz. 183/F4
Simões Filho, Braz. 187/F2
Simojovel de Allende, Mex. 176/C2
Simón Bolívar (int'l arpt.), Ecu. 180/B5
Simón Bolívar (int'l arpt.), Ven. 183/P7
Simoncello (peak), It. 63/F6
Simonds, NB, Can. 158/D2
Simonstown, SAfr. 124/L11
Simonton, Tx, US 151/G3
Simpang, Indo. 89/D3
Simpang Tiga (int'l arpt.), Indo. 89/C2
Simpang-kiri (riv.), Indo. 90/A3
Simpangulim, Indo. 89/B1
Simpelveld, Neth. 55/E2
Simplício Mendes, Braz. 183/F4
Simplon, Swi. 60/E5
Simplonpass (pass), Swi. 60/E5
Simpson (isl.), On, Can. 157/L3
Simpson, La, US 164/B2
Simpson (riv.), Nun, Can. 140/G2
Simpson (pen.), Nun, Can. 140/G2
Simpson, Sk, Can. 145/M2
Simpson, Mt, US 145/J3
Simpson (des.), Austl. 127/C3
Simpson Desert Consv. Park, Austl. 131/H3
Simpson Desert NP, Austl. 131/H3
Simpsons Gap NP, Austl. 131/G2
Simrishamn, Swe. 40/F4
Sims, Ar, US 153/H3
Sims Bayou (riv.), Tx, US 151/M9
Simunul, Phil. 88/B4
Simupu (isl.), Indo. 128/A1
Sin-le-Noble, Fr. 54/C3
Sinabang, Indo. 89/B2
Sinadhago, Som. 118/C4
Sinai (pen.), Egypt 109/G2
Sinaia, Rom. 51/G3
Sinait, Phil. 88/C1
Sinaloa (state), Mex. 174/D3
Sinaloa de Leyva, Mex. 174/C3
Sinalunga, It. 45/J5
Sinarca (riv.), It. 65/D4
Sīnāwin, Libya 111/H3
Sinazongwe, Zam. 123/E3
Sincé, Col. 180/C2
Sincelejo, Col. 180/C2
Sinceny, Fr. 54/C4
Sinch'ang, NKor. 81/E2
Sinch'ŏn, NKor. 81/C3
Sinclair, Wy, US 147/K3
Sinclair (pt.), Austl. 131/G5
Sinclair (res.), Ga, US 163/F4
Sind (riv.), India 92/C2
Sindal, Den. 40/D3
Sindañgan, Phil. 88/C3
Sindangbarang, Indo. 89/D4
Sindelfingen, Ger. 58/C5
Sindh (prov.), Pak. 92/A2
Sindhulimādi, Nepal 97/E2
Sindi, Est. 41/L2
Sindī (wadi), Sudan 117/E2
Sındırgı, Turk. 70/D5
Sindou, Burk. 114/D4
Sinegorskiy, Rus. 73/L3
Sinekçi, Turk. 51/H5
Sinello (riv.), It. 65/D3
Sinendé, Ben. 115/F4
Sines (cape), Port. 46/A4
Sines, Port. 46/A4
Sinfra, C.d'Iv. 114/D5
Sing Buri, Thai. 94/C3
Singapore (ctry.) 77/K9
Singapore (str.), Indo., Sing. 89/H7
Singapore City (nbrhd.), Sing. 89/J6
Singar, India 92/B2
Singaraja, Indo. 89/F5
Singen, Ger. 61/E2
Sîngeorz-Băi, Rom. 72/C4
Singerei, Mol. 72/E4
Singida (prov.), Tanz. 119/A3
Singida, Tanz. 119/A3
Singim, China 99/E3
Singitic (gulf), Gre. 67/K2
Singkaling Hkamti, Myan. 86/B3
Singkang, Indo. 91/F4
Singkawang, Indo. 90/C3
Singkep (isl.), Indo. 90/B4
Singkil, Indo. 89/B2
Singkuang, Indo. 89/B2
Singleton (mt.), Austl. 131/F2
Singleton (mt.), Austl. 130/C4
Singleton, Austl. 133/E1
Singou, Rés. Tot. de Faune Du Burk. 115/F4
Singra, Bang. 97/G3
Singu, Myan. 86/C4
Singuédeze (riv.), Moz. 123/F4
Sin'gye, NKor. 81/D3
Singou, Res Tot. de Faune du, Burk. 115/F4
Sinhŭng, NKor. 81/D2
Sinincay, Ecu. 180/B5
Siniscola, It. 48/A2
Siniye Lipyagi, Rus. 73/K2
Sinjah, Sudan 116/G2
Sinjār, Iraq 102/E2
Sinjil, WBnk. 105/C4
Sinkāt, Sudan 109/H5
Sinking (riv.), Ire. 32/B2
Sinlumkaba, Myan. 93/G3
Sinmak, NKor. 81/D3
Sinn (riv.), Ger. 42/E3
Sinnam-dok-san (peak), NKor. 81/D2
Sinnamary, FrG. 182/C1
Sinnamary (riv.), FrG. 182/C1
Sinnar, India 92/B4
Sînnicolau Mare, Rom. 50/E2
Sinnūris, Egypt 113/B6
Sinnyŏng, SKor. 81/E4
Sino (co.), Libr. 114/C5
Sinoe (lake), Rom. 67/L1
Sinop, Braz. 186/B1
Sinop (prov.), Turk. 70/E4
Sinop (pt.), Turk. 70/E4
Sinop, Turk. 70/E4
Sinos, Rio dos (riv.), Braz. 189/G4
Sinp'a-ŭp, NKor. 81/D2
Sinp'o, NKor. 81/E2
Sinp'yŏng, NKor. 81/D3
Sinsheim, Ger. 58/B4
Sint Annaland, Neth. 52/B5
Sint Hubert, Neth. 52/C5
Sint Jacobiparochie, Neth. 52/C2
Sint Maartensdijk, Neth. 52/B5
Sint-Genesius-Rode, Belg. 55/D2
Sint-Gillis-Waas, Belg. 52/B6
Sint-Katelijne-Waver, Belg. 55/D1
Sint-Laureins, Belg. 54/C1
Sint-Martens-Voeren, Belg. 55/E2
Sint-Michielsgestel, Neth. 52/C5
Sint-Niklaas, Belg. 52/B6
Sint-Oedenrode, Neth. 52/C5
Sint-Pieters-Leeuw, Belg. 55/D2
Sint-Truiden, Belg. 55/E2
Sint'ae-ri, NKor. 81/E2
Sint'aein, SKor. 81/D5
Sintang, Indo. 90/D3
Sinton, Tx, US 151/F3
Sintra (range), Port. 47/P10
Sintra, Port. 47/P10
Sinú (riv.), Col. 173/F6
Sinŭiju, NKor. 81/C2
Sinujif, Som. 118/D3
Sinwŏn, NKor. 81/C3
Sinyang, NKor. 81/D3
Sinyavino, Rus. 69/U7
Sinzheim, Ger. 58/B5

Sinzig – Sospir

Sinzig, Ger. 55/G2
Sió (riv.), Hun. 50/D2
Sio, Kenya 119/A1
Siocon, Phil. 88/C4
Siófok, Hun. 50/D2
Sioma Ngwezi NP, Zam. 122/D3
Sion, Swi. 60/D5
Sion Mills, NI, UK 31/Q9
Sion-les-Mines, Fr. 56/D5
Sioule (riv.), Fr. 44/E4
Sioux Center, Ia, US 155/F2
Sioux City, Ia, US 155/F2
Sioux Falls, SD, US 155/F2
Sioux Lookout, On, Can. 157/J2
Sioux Narrows, On, Can. 157/G3
Sioux Rapids, Ia, US 155/G2
Sipalay, Phil. 88/C3
Sipaliwini (riv.), Sur. 181/G4
Sipaliwini (dist.), Sur. 181/H4
Siparia, Trin. 181/F2
Sipí, Col. 180/B3
Siping, China 80/F2
Sipitang, Malay. 88/A4
Sipiwesk (lake), Mb, Can. 140/G3
Siple (isl.), Ant. 192/R
Sipocot, Phil. 88/C2
Siponto (ruin), It. 48/D2
Sipoo (Sibbo), Fin. 41/L1
Sipoonselkä (bay), Fin. 39/F4
Sipsey (riv.), Al, US 162/D4
Sipura (isl.), Indo. 90/A4
Sipura (str.), Indo. 89/B3
Siqueira Campos, Braz. 189/G2
Siquia (riv.), Nic. 172/E5
Siquijar (isl.), Phil. 88/C3
Siquisique, Ven. 180/D2
Sir Edward Pellew Group (isls.), Austl. 129/E3
Sir James Macbrien (mt.), NW, Can. 140/D2
Sir James Mitchell NP, Austl. 130/C5
Sir John (cape), Austl. 133/C5
Sir Muttra, India 96/A2
Sir Sandford (mt.), BC, Can. 144/F2
Sir Seewoosagur Ramgoolam (int'l arpt.), Mrts. 125/T15
Sir Seretse Khama (Gaborone) (int'l arpt.), Bots. 122/E5
Sir Thomas (mt.), Austl. 131/F3
Sira (riv.), Nor. 38/C4
Sīra, India 95/C3
Sirac (peak), Fr. 64/C3
Siracusa (Syracuse), It. 48/D4
Sirājganj, Bang. 97/G3
Şiran, Turk. 102/D1
Sīrē, Eth. 118/A3
Siren, Wi, US 157/H5
Sirente (peak), It. 65/C3
Siret (riv.), Rom. 70/C3
Siret, Rom. 72/D4
Sirha, Nepal 97/F2
Sirhind, India 98/D4
Sīrīk, Iran 103/J5
Sirik (cape), Malay. 90/D3
Sirikit (res.), Thai. 86/D5
Sirinhaém, Braz. 183/H5
Sīrīs, WBnk. 105/C4
Sirit (res.), Thai. 93/H4
Sirius Point (cape), Ak, US 171/B5
Sīrjān, Iran 103/H4
Sirmione, It. 62/D3
Sirnach, Swi. 61/F3
Şırnak, Turk. 102/E2
Sirohi, India 92/B3
Sirolo, It. 63/G6
Sirombu, Indo. 89/B2
Sironj, India 96/A3
Síros (isl.), Gre. 75/J4
Sirotinskaya, Rus. 73/M3
Siroua (peak), Mor. 110/D3
Sırpsındığı, Turk. 51/H5
Sirs al Layyānah, Egypt 113/B4
Sirsa, India 98/C5
Sirsāganj, India 96/B2
Sirsi, India 96/B1
Sirtica (reg.), Libya 134/C2
Siruma, Phil. 88/C2
Sīrvān (riv.), Iran 103/F3
Širvintos, Lith. 41/L4
Sisak, Cro. 50/C3
Sisaket, Thai. 94/D3
Sishen, SAfr. 124/C2
Sishui, China 80/D4
Sisian, Arm. 103/F2
Sisib (lake), Mb, Can. 156/E1
Sisikon, Swi. 61/E4
Siskiyou (mts.), Or, US 146/B2
Sisophon, Camb. 94/C3
Sissach, Swi. 60/D3
Sisséla, Gui. 114/C4
Sisseton, SD, US 156/F5
Sisseton-Wahpeton Ind. Res., SD, US 155/F1
Sissili (prov.), Burk. 115/E4
Sissonne, Fr. 54/C4
Sissonville, WV, US 163/G1
Sister Bay, Wi, US 160/C2
Sister Grove (cr.), Tx, US 150/L6
Sisteron, Fr. 64/B4
Sistersville, WV, US 160/F5
Sistina, It. 63/G2
Sistine Chapel, VatC. 65/G7
Sisto (riv.), It. 65/C5
Siswā Bāzār, India 96/D2
Sitacocha, Peru 184/B2
Sītākunda, Bang. 93/F3
Sitalike, Tanz. 121/G4
Sītāmarhi, India 97/E2
Sītāpur, India 96/C2
Sitārganj, India 96/B1
Siteki, Swaz. 125/E2
Sitges, Sp. 47/K7
Sithoniá (pen.), Gre. 70/C5
Sitía, Gre. 67/K4
Sitian, China 78/C3
Sitidgi (lake), NW, Can. 171/M2
Siting, China 87/E3
Sítio d'Badia, Braz. 186/D2
Sítio Novo do Grajaú, Braz. 183/E4
Sitka, Ak, US 171/L4
Sitno (peak), Slvk. 50/D1
Sito Ganno, India 98/C4
Sitoti, Zam. 122/D3
Sittard, Neth. 55/E2
Sittensen, Ger. 53/G2
Sitter (riv.), Swi. 61/F3
Sittingbourne, Eng, UK 37/G4
Sitton (peak), Ca, US 166/C3
Sittwe (Akyab), Myan. 93/F3
Situbondo, Indo. 89/F4
Siuntio (Sjundeå), Fin. 39/E4
Siuslaw (riv.), Or, US 146/B2
Sivac, Yugo. 50/D3
Sivakāsi, India 95/C4
Sivaki, Rus. 79/K1
Sīvand, Iran 103/H4
Sivas, Turk. 102/D2
Sivas (prov.), Turk. 70/F5
Sivash (sound), Ukr. 73/H4
Sivé, Mrta. 114/B3
Siverek, Turk. 102/D2
Siverskiy, Rus. 41/P2
Siviriez, Swi. 60/C4
Sivomaskinskiy, Rus. 69/P2
Sivrihisar, Turk. 102/B2
Sivry-Courtry, Fr. 30/L6
Siwa, Indo. 91/F4
Siwa Oasis (oasis), Egypt 109/E2
Sīwah, Egypt 109/E2
Siwālik (range), India,Nepal 92/D2
Siwān, India 97/E2
Siwāni, India 98/C5
Six Flags Great Adventure, NJ, US 168/D3
Six Flags Great America, Il, US 167/Q15
Six Flags Magic Mountain, Ca, US 166/B2
Six Flags Over Georgia, Ga, US 163/L7
Six Flags Over Texas, Tx, US 150/K7
Six-Fours-la-Plage, Fr. 64/B6
Sixes, Or, US 146/A2
Sixmile (lake), La, US 164/C3
Sixmilebridge, Ire. 32/B4
Sixmilecross, NI, UK 34/A2
Sixth Cataract (falls), Sudan 116/G1
Sixtymile, Yk, Can. 171/K3
Siyabuswa, SAfr. 123/F5
Siyāna, India 96/B1
Siyang, China 80/D4
Siyäzän, Azer. 71/J4
Siyichang, China 86/E2
Siyitang, China 78/F3
Sizhoutou, China 87/J2
Siziano, It. 62/C3
Sizun, Fr. 56/A4
Sizyahsk, Rus. 69/M2
Sjælland (isl.), Den. 38/D5
Sjællands (pen.), Den. 39/H7
Sjenica, Yugo. 50/D4
Sjöberg, Swe. 39/A1
Sjöbo, Swe. 40/E4
Sjónfridh (peak), Ice. 38/M6
Sjösa, Swe. 39/A2
Sjundeå (Siuntio), Fin. 39/E4
Sjuntorp, Swe. 40/E2
Skadovs'k, Ukr. 72/G4
Skaftafell NP, Ice. 38/P7
Skagen, Den. 40/D3
Skagens (The Skaw) (cape), Den. 40/D3
Skagern (lake), Swe. 40/F2
Skagerrak (str.), Nor.,Den. 29/E3
Skaget (peak), Nor. 40/C1
Skagit (riv.), Wa, US 144/D3
Skagway, Ak, US 171/L3
Skaidi, Nor. 38/H1
Skaistkalne, Lat. 41/L3
Skála, Gre. 75/H4
Skälderviken (bay), Swe. 40/E3
Skálfandafljót (riv.), Ice. 38/P7
Skalica, Slvk. 43/J4
Skalice (riv.), Czh. 45/K2
Skalka (res.), Czh. 59/F2
Skælskør, Den. 40/D4
Skanderborg, Den. 40/C3
Skåne (reg.), Swe. 40/E4
Skaneateles, NY, US 161/H3
Skanes (int'l arpt.), Tun. 48/B5
Skånland, Nor. 38/F1
Skänninge, Swe. 40/F2
Skanör, Swe. 40/E4
Skantzoura (isl.), Gre. 75/J3
Skara, Swe. 40/E2
Skaraborg (co.), Swe. 38/E4
Skärblacka, Swe. 40/F2
Skārdu, Pak. 98/C2
Skåre, Swe. 40/E2
Skärholmen, Swe. 39/A1
Skarszewy, Pol. 40/H4
Skarven (lake), Swe. 39/A1
Skarżysko-Kamienna, Pol. 43/L3
Skateraw, Sc, UK 33/D5
Skattkärr, Swe. 40/E2
Skaudvilė, Lith. 41/K4
Skavaböle (Hyrylä), Fin. 39/F4
Skævinge, Den. 39/J7
Skaw, The (Skagens) (cape), Den. 40/D3
Skawina, Pol. 43/K4
Skederid, Swe. 39/B1
Skedviken (lake), Swe. 39/B1
Skeena (mts.), BC, Can. 140/D3
Skeena (riv.), BC, Can. 142/AA13
Skegemog (lake), Mi, US 160/D2
Skegness, Eng, UK 35/J5
Skeleton Coast Park, Namb. 122/B3
Skellefteå, Swe. 38/G2
Skellefteälven (riv.), Swe. 68/C2
Skelleftehamn, Swe. 38/G2
Skellytown, Tx, US 152/D3
Skelmanthorpe, Eng, UK 35/G4
Skelmersdale, Eng, UK 35/F4
Skelmorlie, Sc, UK 33/B5
Skelton, Eng, UK 35/H2
Skerne (riv.), Eng, UK 35/G2
Skerries, Ire. 34/B4
Skhimatárion, Gre. 75/H3
Skhirat, Mor. 112/A3
Skhirat Temara (prov.), Mor. 112/A3
Skhiza (isl.), Gre. 75/G4
Skhodnya (riv.), Rus. 69/W9
Ski, Nor. 40/D2
Skíathos, Gre. 75/H3
Skiatook, Ok, US 153/F2
Skibbereen, Ire. 32/A6
Skibby, Den. 39/H7
Skidaway Island, Ga, US 165/H2
Skidegate, BC, Can. 171/M5
Skidel', Bela. 41/L5
Skídhra, Gre. 75/H2
Skidmore, Mo, US 155/G3
Skidmore, Tx, US 150/F3
Skidway Lake, Mi, US 160/D2
Skien, Nor. 40/C2
Skierniewice (prov.), Pol. 43/K3
Skierniewice, Pol. 43/L3
Skiff, Ab, Can. 145/J3
Skikda, Alg. 112/K6
Skillet Fork (riv.), Il, US 162/C1
Skinári (cape), Gre. 75/G4
Skinnskatteberg, Swe. 40/F2
Skipness, Sc, UK 33/A5
Skipperville, Al, US 165/F2
Skipsea, Eng, UK 35/H4
Skipton, Eng, UK 35/F4
Skiptvet, Nor. 38/T9
Skirfare (riv.), Eng, UK 35/F3
Skíros, Gre. 75/J3
Skivarpsån (riv.), Swe. 39/K7
Skive, Den. 40/C3
Skjærhollen, Nor. 40/D2
Skjeberg, Nor. 40/D2
Skjelåtinden (peak), Nor. 38/E2
Skjern, Den. 40/C4
Skjern (riv.), Den. 40/C4
Škofja Loka, Slov. 45/L3
Skoger, Nor. 38/R8
Skoghall, Swe. 40/E2
Skogstorp, Swe. 40/G2
Skokholm (isl.), Wal, UK 36/A3
Skokie, Il, US 160/C3
Skokie (riv.), Il, US 167/Q15
Skokloster, Swe. 40/G2
Skokomish Ind. Res., Wa, US 144/C4
Sköldvik, Fin. 39/F4
Skole, Ukr. 72/B3
Sköllersta, Swe. 40/F2
Skolniki Park, Rus. 69/W9
Skomer (isl.), Wal, UK 36/A3
Skon, Camb. 94/D3
Skookumchuck, BC, Can. 144/G3
Skópelos, Gre. 75/H3
Skópelos (isl.), Gre. 75/H3
Skopin, Rus. 70/F1
Skopje (cap.), FYROM 75/G1
Skopje (int'l. arpt.), FYROM 67/J2
Skorodnoye, Bela. 72/E2
Skorodnoye, Rus. 73/J2
Skotterud, Nor. 40/E2
Skoútari, Gre. 75/H2
Skövde, Swe. 40/E2
Skovorodino, Rus. 79/J1
Skownan, Mb, Can. 156/E2
Skrīveri, Lat. 41/L3
Skrudaliena, Lat. 41/M4
Skrunda, Lat. 41/K3
Skukum (mt.), Yk, Can. 171/L3
Skukuza, SAfr. 123/F5
Skull, Ire. 32/A6
Skull (valley), Ut, US 147/G3
Skull Valley, Az, US 149/F3
Skull Valley Ind. Res., Ut, US 147/G3
Skultorp, Swe. 40/E2
Skultuna, Swe. 40/G2
Skunk (riv.), Ia, US 155/J3
Skuodas, Lith. 41/J3
Skurup, Swe. 43/G1
Skutskär, Swe. 40/G1
Skvyra, Ukr. 72/E3
Skwentna, Ak, US 171/H3
Skwierzyna, Pol. 43/H2
Skye (isl.), Sc, UK 31/Q8
Skykomish (riv.), Wa, US 144/D4
Skykomish, Wa, US 144/D4
Skyring (sound), Chile 191/B7
Skytop, Pa, US 168/C1
Slade NWR, ND, US 156/E4
Sladkovskoye, Rus. 69/Q4
Sladt (pt.), Austl. 129/F2
Slagelse, Den. 40/D4
Slagle, La, US 164/B2
Slaidburn, Eng, UK 35/F4
Slakovský Les (for.), Czh. 59/F2
Slamannan, Sc, UK 33/C5
Slamet (peak), Indo. 89/E4
Slaná (riv.), Slvk. 43/L4
Slana, Ak, US 171/K3
Slane, Ire. 34/B4
Slangerup, Den. 39/J7
Slănic, Rom. 51/G3
Slănic-Moldova, Rom. 51/H2
Slantsy, Rus. 41/N2
Slaný, Czh. 59/H2
Slapy (res.), Czh. 59/H3
Śląskie (prov.), Pol. 43/K3
Slate (isls.), On, Can. 157/L3
Slatedale, Pa, US 168/C2
Slater, Mo, US 155/H4
Slater, Ia, US 155/H3
Slatina, Rom. 51/G3
Slatington, Pa, US 168/C2
Slaton, Tx, US 152/D4
Slattum, Nor. 40/D1
Slaughter, La, US 164/C2
Slaughter Beach, De, US 168/C6
Slaughterville, Ok, US 153/F3
Slave (coast), Afr. 115/F5
Slave (riv.), NW, Can. 140/E2
Slave (riv.), Can. 139/F3
Slave Lake, Ab, Can. 140/E3
Slavgorod, Rus. 99/C1
Slavkov u Brna, Czh. 45/M2
Slavonia (reg.), Cro. 50/C3
Slavonska Požega, Cro. 50/C3
Slavonski Brod, Cro. 50/D3
Slavuta, Ukr. 72/D2
Slavyanka, Rus. 79/L3
Slavyanovo, Bul. 51/G4
Slavyansk-na-Kubani, Rus. 73/K5
Sławno, Pol. 40/G4
Slayton, Mn, US 155/G2
Sleaford, Eng, UK 35/H6
Sleen, Neth. 52/D3
Sleeper (isls.), On, Can. 167/H3
Sleeping Bear Dunes Nat'l Lakeshore, Mi, US 160/C2
Sleepy Eye, Mn, US 155/G1
Sleepy Hollow, Il, US 167/P15
Sleepy Hollow, NY, US 169/K7
Sleetmute, Ak, US 171/G3
Slemp, Ky, US 163/F2
Sliabh na Caillighe (peak), Ire. 32/C2
Slide (mtn.), NY, US 161/J4
Slidell, La, US 164/D2
Slidre, Nor. 40/C1
Sliedrecht, Neth. 52/B5
Sliema, Malta 48/M7
Slieve Anierin (peak), Ire. 32/C1
Slieve Aughty (mts.), Ire. 32/B3
Slieve Bernagh (peak), Ire. 32/B4
Slieve Binnian (peak), NI, UK 34/C3
Slieve Bloom (mts.), Ire. 32/C4
Slieve Car (peak), Ire. 32/A1
Slieve Croob (peak), NI, UK 34/C3
Slieve Donard (peak), NI, UK 34/C3
Slieve Elva (peak), Ire. 32/A3
Slieve Fyagh (peak), Ire. 32/A1
Slieve Gamph (mts.), Ire. 32/A1
Slieve Gamph (Ox) (mts.), Ire. 32/A1
Slieve Gullion (peak), NI, UK 34/B3
Slieve Martin (peak), UK 32/D1
Slieve Snaght (peak), Ire. 34/A1
Slievecallan (peak), Ire. 32/A4
Slievecarran (peak), Ire. 32/A3
Slievefelim (mts.), Ire. 32/B4
Slievekimalta (peak), Ire. 32/B4
Slievenamon (hill), Ire. 32/C5
Slieverve, Ire. 32/C5
Sligo, Ire. 32/B1
Sligo (bay), Ire. 32/B1
Sligo (arpt.), Ire. 32/B1
Sligo (co.), Ire. 32/B1
Slioch (peak), Sc, UK 33/A1
Slite, Swe. 41/H3
Sliven, Bul. 51/H4
Slivnitsa, Bul. 50/F4
Sloan, Nv, US 148/E3
Sloan, Ia, US 155/F2
Sloan, NY, US 160/V10
Sloatsburg, NY, US 169/J7
Slobidka, Ukr. 72/E4
Slobodskoy, Rus. 69/L4
Slobozia, Rom. 51/H3
Slobozia, Mol. 72/E4
Slocan (lake), BC, Can. 144/F3
Slocan, BC, Can. 144/F3
Slocan Park, BC, Can. 144/F3
Slochteren, Neth. 52/D2
Slocomb, Al, US 165/F2
Slocum, Tx, US 150/G2
Sloten, Neth. 52/C3
Sloterdijk, Neth. 52/C4
Slotermeer (lake), Neth. 52/C3
Slottskogen, Swe. 39/A1
Slough, Eng, UK 30/B2
Slough (co.), Eng, UK 30/B2
Slovakia (ctry.) 29/F4
Slovechne, Ukr. 72/E2
Slovenia (ctry.) 29/F4
Slovenj Gradec, Slov. 50/B2
Slovenska Bistrica, Slov. 50/B2
Slovenska Ľupča, Slvk. 43/K4
Slovenske Konjice, Slov. 50/B2
Slovenské Rudohorie (mts.), Slvk. 43/L4
Slov'yans'k, Ukr. 73/J3
Słowiński PN, Pol. 40/G4
Słubice, Pol. 43/H2
Sluch' (riv.), Ukr. 70/C2
Sluderno (Schluderns), It. 61/G4
Sluis, Neth. 54/C1
Słupca, Pol. 43/J2
Słupia (riv.), Pol. 40/G4
Słupsk, Pol. 40/G4
Slutsk, Bela. 70/C1
Slyne Head (pt.), Ire. 30/F10
Slyudyanka, Rus. 78/E1
Smackover, Ar, US 153/H4
Smålandsstenar, Swe. 40/E3
Small, Id, US 147/G1
Smallfield, Eng, UK 30/C3
Smallwood (res.), Can. 139/L4
Smarden, Eng, UK 30/F3
Smaylovskiy, Kaz. 71/M1
Smearlagh (riv.), Ire. 32/A5
Smederevo, Yugo. 50/E3
Smederevska Palanka, Yugo. 50/E3
Smedjebacken, Swe. 40/F1
Smendou (riv.), Alg. 112/J4
Smethport, Pa, US 161/G4
Smidovich, Rus. 79/L2
Śmigiel, Pol. 43/J2
Smila, Ukr. 72/F3
Smilax, Ky, US 163/F2
Smilde, Neth. 52/D3
Smiley, Tx, US 151/F3
Smiley, Sk, Can. 145/K2
Smiltene, Lat. 41/L3
Smirnykh, Rus. 79/N2
Smith (isl.), Qu, Can. 167/J2
Smith, Nv, US 146/D4
Smith (pt.), Tx, US 151/N9
Smith (isl.) 163/J1
Smith (riv.), Va, US 162/G2
Smith Center, Ks, US 154/E4
Smith Mountain (dam), Va, US 163/H2
Smith Mtn. (lake), Va, US 163/H2
Smith River, Ca, US 146/A3
Smithburg, NJ, US 168/D3
Smithdale, Ms, US 164/C2
Smithers, BC, Can. 140/D3
Smithers (lake), Tx, US 151/M9
Smithfield, Ut, US 147/H3
Smithfield, NC, US 163/H3
Smithland, Ky, US 162/C2
Smiths, Al, US 162/E4
Smiths Creek, Mi, US 167/G6
Smiths Falls, On, Can. 161/H2
Smiths Grove, Ky, US 162/D2
Smithton, Mo, US 153/H1
Smithton, Austl. 132/C4
Smithtown, NY, US 169/E2
Smithtown (bay), NY, US 169/E2
Smithville, On, Can. 160/T9
Smithville, In, US 160/C5
Smithville, Ga, US 165/F2
Smithville, Mo, US 155/G4
Smithville (lake), Mo, US 155/G4
Smithville, Ok, US 153/G3
Smithville, Tn, US 162/E3
Smithville, Tx, US 150/F2
Smoke Creek (des.), Nv, US 146/D3
Smoky (cape), Austl. 132/E1
Smoky (riv.), Ab, Can. 140/E3
Smoky (riv.), Ab, Can. 144/E1
Smoky (hills), Ks, US 154/E4
Smoky Bay, Austl. 131/G5
Smoky Hill (riv.), Ks, US 142/F4
Smoky Hill, North Fork (riv.), Co, Ks, US 152/C1
Smoky Hill, North Fork (riv.), Co, Ks, US 154/C4
Smøla (isl.), Nor. 38/C3
Smolan, Ks, US 153/F1
Smolensk, Rus. 68/G5
Smolenskaya Oblast, Rus. 68/F5
Smolevichi, Bela. 41/N4
Smólikas (peak), Gre. 75/G2
Smolnaya (arpt.), Rus. 69/T7
Smolyan, Bul. 75/J2
Smoot, Wy, US 147/H2
Smorgon', Bela. 41/M4
Smrčina (peak), Czh. 59/G5
Smutná (riv.), Czh. 59/H4
Smuts, Sk, Can. 145/L1
Smyadovo, Bul. 51/H4
Smyrna, Tn, US 162/D3
Smyrna, Ga, US 163/L7
Smyrna (riv.), De, US 168/C5
Smyrna, De, US 168/C5
Snaefell (peak), IM, UK 34/D3
Snake (isl.), Austl. 133/C4
Snake (riv.), US 139/F5
Snake (cr.), SD, US 154/E1
Snake Indian (riv.), Ab, Can. 144/E1
Snake River (plain), Id, US 147/G2
Snake River Birds Of Prey Natural Area, Id, US 146/E2
Snares (isls.), NZ 135/A5
Snåsa, Nor. 38/E2
Sneads, Fl, US 165/F2
Sneads Ferry, NC, US 163/J3
Snedsted, Den. 40/C3
Sneedville, Tn, US 163/F2
Sneek, Neth. 52/C2
Sneekermeer (lake), Neth. 52/C2
Sneeuberg (peak), SAfr. 124/B4
Sneeuberg (mts.), SAfr. 124/D3
Sneeuwkop (peak), SAfr. 124/L11
Sneffels (mt.), Co, US 149/J1
Snejbjerg, Den. 40/C3
Snelgrove, On, Can. 160/T8
Snellville, Ga, US 163/M7
Snettisham, Eng, UK 37/G1
Snezhnogorsk, Rus. 74/J3
Sněžka (peak), Czh. 43/H3
Snežnik (peak), Slov. 45/L4
Śniardwy (lake), Pol. 43/L2
Snihurivka, Ukr. 73/G4
Snilow (int'l arpt.), Ukr. 72/B3
Snina, Slvk. 72/B3
Snizhne, Ukr. 73/K3
Snodland, Eng, UK 37/G4
Snøhetta (peak), Nor. 38/D3
Snohomish (riv.), Wa, US 167/C2
Snohomish (co.), Wa, US 167/C2
Snohomish, Wa, US 167/C2
Snook, Tx, US 150/F2
Snoqualmie, Wa, US 167/D2
Snoqualmie (riv.), Wa, US 167/D2
Snoqualmie (falls), Wa, US 167/D2
Snoqualmie Falls, Wa, US 167/D2
Snoqualmie, Middle Fk. (riv.), Wa, US 167/D2
Snoqualmie, North Fork (riv.), Wa, US 167/D2
Snoqualmie, South Fork (riv.), Wa, US 167/D3
Snøtind (peak), Nor. 38/E2
Snow, Ok, US 153/G3
Snow (mtn.), Me, US 161/L2
Snow (peak), Wa, US 144/E3
Snow Hill, NC, US 163/J3
Snow Hill, Md, US 163/K1
Snowcrest (mtn.), BC, Can. 144/F3
Snowdon (peak), IM, UK 34/D5
Snowdonia NP, Wal, UK 34/D6
Snowdoun, Al, US 162/D4
Snowflake, Mb, Can. 156/E3
Snowflake, Az, US 149/G3
Snowtown, Austl. 131/H5
Snowville, Ut, US 147/G3
Snowy (mtn.), NY, US 161/J3
Snowy Peak (mt.), Ak, US 171/K2
Snyatyn, Ukr. 72/C3
Snyder, Ar, US 153/J4
Snyder, Ok, US 152/E3
Snyder, Tx, US 151/D1
Snyder (co.), Pa, US 168/A2
Snydertown, Pa, US 168/B2
Soacha, Col. 183/L8
Soalala, Madg. 125/H7
Soalara, Madg. 125/G8
Soamanonga, Madg. 125/H8
Soana (riv.), It. 64/D1
Soanierana-Ivongo, Madg. 125/J7
Soanindrariny, Madg. 125/H7
Soar (riv.), Eng, UK 35/G6
Soavina, Madg. 125/H8
Soavina, Madg. 125/J8
Soavinandriana, Madg. 125/H7
Soba, Nga. 115/H4
Sobaek (mts.), SKor. 81/D5
Soberanía, Bol. 185/E4
Sobernheim, Ger. 55/G4
Soběslav, Czh. 59/H4
Sobger (riv.), Indo. 91/K4
Sobhādero, Pak. 101/J3
Sobradinho (res.), Braz. 179/E3
Sobradinho, Braz. 186/D2
Sobral, Braz. 183/F3
Sobrance, Slvk. 72/B3
Sobretta (peak), It. 61/G5
Sobue, Japan 83/L5
Soc Trang, Viet. 94/D4
Socabaya, Peru 184/D5
Socastee, SC, US 163/H4
Sochaczew, Pol. 43/L2
Sochi, Rus. 70/F4
Sŏch'ŏn, SKor. 81/D4
Söchtenau, Ger. 59/F7
Soci, It. 63/E6
Social Circle, Ga, US 162/F4
Society (isls.), FrPol. 137/K6
Society Hill, SC, US 163/H3
Socompa (vol.), Arg.,Chile 188/B3
Socorro, Braz. 187/K7
Socorro, Col. 180/C3
Socorro, NM, US 149/J3
Socorro, Tx, US 151/A2
Socorro (isl.), NM, Mex. 174/C5
Socotá, Col. 180/C3
Socota, Peru 184/B2
Socotra (isl.), Yem. 77/E8
Socrum, Fl, US 164/L7
Socuéllamos, Sp. 46/D3
Soda (lake), Ca, US 148/D3
Soda Creek, BC, Can. 144/C1
Soda Springs, Id, US 147/H2
Sodankylä, Fin. 68/E2
Soddy-Daisy, Tn, US 162/E3
Sodegaura, Japan 83/D3
Söderbärke, Swe. 40/F1
Söderby-Karl, Swe. 39/B1
Söderfors, Swe. 40/G1
Söderhamn, Swe. 40/G1
Söderköping, Swe. 40/G2
Södermanland (co.), Swe. 38/E4
Söderöra (isl.), Swe. 39/C1
Södersvik, Swe. 39/B1
Södertälje, Swe. 40/G2
Sodo, Eth. 116/H4
Södra Sandby, Swe. 39/K7
Sŏdu (riv.), NKor. 81/E2
Sodus Point, NY, US 161/H3
Sodwana Bay NP, SAfr. 125/F2
Soe, Indo. 128/B2
Soekmekaar, SAfr. 123/F4
Soest, Ger. 53/F5
Soest, Neth. 52/C4
Soeste (riv.), Ger. 42/D2
Soesterberg, Neth. 52/C4
Soeurs, Passage des (chan.), Fr. 56/C6
Sofádhes, Gre. 75/H3
Sofala (prov.), Moz. 123/G3
Sofia (int'l arpt.), Bul. 51/F4
Sofia (riv.), Madg. 125/J6
Sofiya (prov.), Bul. 75/H1
Sofiya (cap.), Bul. 51/F4
Sofiyivka, Ukr. 73/G3
Sofiysk, Rus. 79/L1
Sofporog, Rus. 68/F2
Sogakofe, Gha. 115/F5
Sogamoso (riv.), Col. 180/C3
Sogamoso, Col. 180/C3
Sögel, Ger. 53/E3
Sogeri, PNG 129/F1
Şoghād, Iran 103/H4
Sogn Og Fjordane (co.), Nor. 38/C3
Sognafjorden (inlet), Nor. 38/C3
Sogndal, Nor. 40/B1
Søgne, Nor. 40/B2
Sogod, Phil. 88/D3
Soğuksu NP, Turk. 70/E4
Söğüt, Turk. 102/B1
Söğütlü, Turk. 51/K5
Sogwass (peak), Ugan. 116/G5
Sŏgwip'o, SKor. 79/K5
Soh, Iran 103/G3
Sohāgī, India 96/C3
Sohāgpur, India 96/B4
Soham, Eng, UK 37/G2
Sohren, Ger. 55/G4
Sŏhŭng, NKor. 81/D3
Soignies, Belg. 55/D2
Soignolles-en-Brie, Fr. 30/L6
Soila, China 86/C2
Soings-en-Sologne, Fr. 57/G6
Soissons, Fr. 54/C5
Sōja, Japan 84/C3
Sojat, India 92/B2
Sŏjosŏn (bay), NKor. 81/C3
Sok (riv.), Rus. 71/J1
Sok (pt.), Thai. 94/C3
Sōka, Japan 83/D2
Sokal', Ukr. 72/C2
Sokch'o, SKor. 81/E3
Söke, Turk. 102/A2
Sokh, Uzb. 99/B4
Sokhor (peak), Rus. 78/F1
Sokhós, Gre. 75/H2
Sokhumi, Geo. 71/G4
Sokna, Nor. 40/C1
Soko (isls.), China 87/K8
Soko Banja, Yugo. 50/E4
Sokodé, Togo 115/F4
Sokol, Rus. 68/J4
Sokol (peak), Czh. 59/G4
Sokółka, Pol. 43/M2
Sokolo, Mali 114/D3
Sokolov, Czh. 59/F2
Sokolovo-Kundryuchenskoye, Rus. 73/K4
Sokołów Podlaski, Pol. 43/M2
Sokoto (state), Nga. 115/G3
Sokoto (riv.), Nga. 115/G3
Sokoto (plain), Nga. 115/G4
Sokoto, Nga. 115/G3
Sokyryany, Ukr. 72/D3
Sol'-Iletsk, Rus. 71/K2
Sola, Nor. 40/A2
Sola (int'l arpt.), Nor. 40/A2
Solana, Phil. 88/C1
Solana Beach, Ca, US 166/C5
Solânea, Braz. 183/H4
Solano, Ven. 181/E4
Solano (pt.), Col. 180/B3
Solano, Phil. 88/C1
Solano (co.), Ca, US 167/L10
Solarolo, It. 63/E5
Solca, Rom. 72/C4
Sölden, Aus. 61/H4
Soldier (riv.), Ia, US 155/G3
Soldiers Grove, Wi, US 155/J2
Soldotna, Ak, US 171/H3
Solec Kujawksi, Pol. 43/K2
Soledad, Col. 180/C2
Soledad, Ca, US 148/B2
Soledad, Ven. 181/F2
Soledad Canyon (canyon), Ca, US 166/B2
Soledad de Doblado, Mex. 175/N7
Soledad de Graciano, Mex. 175/E4
Soledade, Braz. 183/G4
Soledade, Braz. 189/F4
Soleduck (riv.), Wa, US 144/B3
Solen, ND, US 156/D4
Solenzo, Burk. 114/D3
Solesino, It. 63/E3
Solesmes, Fr. 57/E5
Solesmes, Fr. 54/C3
Soleuvre (peak), Lux. 55/E4
Solferino, It. 62/D3
Solhan, Turk. 102/E2
Soliera, It. 63/D4
Soligalich, Rus. 68/J4
Soligo, It. 63/F2
Solihull, Eng, UK 37/E2
Solihull (co.), Eng, UK 37/E2
Solikamsk, Rus. 69/N4
Solimões (riv.), Braz. 181/E5
Solingen, Ger. 52/E6
Solitaire, Namb. 122/C4
Sollefteå, Swe. 38/F3
Sollentuna, Swe. 40/G2
Sóller, Sp. 47/G3
Søllerød, Den. 39/J7
Sollerön, Swe. 40/F1
Solliès-Pont, Fr. 64/C6
Solling (mts.), Ger. 42/E3
Sollum (gulf), Libya 109/E2
Sollum (gulf), Egypt 67/K5
Solmsbach (riv.), Ger. 58/B2
Søln (peak), Nor. 38/D3
Solna, Swe. 39/B1
Solnan (riv.), Fr. 44/F3
Solnechnogorsk, Rus. 69/W8
Solntsevo, Rus. 69/W9
Solntsevo, Rus. 73/J2
Solo (riv.), Indo. 90/D5
Solofra, It. 65/D6
Solok, Indo. 89/C3
Solokh-Aul, Rus. 70/F4
Sololá, Guat. 176/D3
Solomon (sea), PNG,Sol. 136/D5
Solomon, Ak, US 171/F3
Solomon, Az, US 149/H4
Solomon, Ks, US 153/F1
Solomon (riv.), Ks, US 154/E4
Solomon Islands (ctry.) 136/E6
Solomon, North Fork (riv.), US 152/D1
Solomon, North Fork (riv.), Ks, US 154/D4
Solomon, South Fork (riv.), Ks, US 152/E1
Solomon, South Fork (riv.), Ks, US 154/D4
Solon, China 79/J2
Solonchak Goklenkui (swamp), Trkm. 71/L4
Solonópole, Braz. 183/G4
Solopaca, It. 65/D5
Solor (isl.), Indo. 128/A2
Solor (isls.), Indo. 128/A2
Solothurn, Swi. 60/D3
Solothurn (canton), Swi. 60/D3
Solotvyna, Ukr. 72/B4
Solovetskiy (isls.), Rus. 68/G2
Solov'yevsk, Rus. 79/J1
Solre-le-Château, Fr. 55/D3
Solsona, Sp. 47/F2
Solt, Hun. 50/D2
Šolta (isl.), Cro. 48/E1
Solţānābād, Iran 103/J2
Soltau, Ger. 53/G3
Sol'tsy, Rus. 41/P2
Soltustik Qazaqstan Oblast, Kaz. 74/G4
Soltvadkert, Hun. 50/D2
Solunska (peak), FYROM 75/G2
Solva (riv.), Wal, UK 36/A3
Solvang, Ca, US 148/B3
Sölvesborg, Swe. 40/F3
Solway Firth (inlet), Eng.,Sc, UK 34/E2
Solwezi, Zam. 123/E2
Solymár, Hun. 51/Q9
Som Det, Thai. 94/C2
Soma, Turk. 70/C5
Sōma, Japan 85/G2
Somabhula, Zim. 123/F3
Somain, Fr. 54/C3
Somalia (ctry.) 107/G4
Sombor, Yugo. 50/D3
Sombra, On, Can. 167/H6
Sombreffe, Belg. 55/D2
Sombrerete, Mex. 174/E4
Sombrio, Braz. 189/G4
Somercotes, Eng, UK 35/G5
Someren, Neth. 52/C6
Somero, Fin. 41/K1
Somers, Wi, US 167/Q14
Somers, Mt, US 145/G3
Somers, Austl. 133/B4
Somers Point, NJ, US 168/D5
Somerset (isl.), Can. 139/H2
Somerset, Mb, Can. 156/E3
Somerset (isl.), Nun, Can. 140/G1
Somerset (co.), Eng, UK 36/D4
Somerset, La, US 164/C1
Somerset, Ma, US 161/L4
Somerset, Pa, US 161/G4
Somerset, Ky, US 162/E2
Somerset, NY, US 160/V9
Somerset (co.), NJ, US 168/D2
Somerset, NJ, US 168/D3
Somerset, Oh, US 160/E5
Somerset, Wi, US 157/Q6
Somerset East, SAfr. 124/D4
Somerset West, SAfr. 124/L11
Somersham, Eng, UK 37/G2
Somersworth, NH, US 161/L3
Somerton, Az, US 148/E4
Somerton, Eng, UK 36/D4
Somerville, Austl. 133/B4
Somerville, NJ, US 168/D2
Somerville (lake), Tx, US 151/F2
Somerville, Tn, US 162/C3
Somerville, Tx, US 150/F2
Someş (riv.), Rom. 70/B3
Someşul Mare (riv.), Yugo. 51/G2
Someswar (range), India 97/E2
Somis, Ca, US 166/B2
Sŏmjin (riv.), SKor. 81/D5
Somma Lombardo, It. 62/B2
Sommacampagna, It. 63/D3
Sommam (riv.), Alg. 112/H4
Sommariva del Bosco, It. 62/A3
Somme (riv.), Fr. 42/B3
Somme (dept.), Fr. 54/B4
Somme (bay), Fr. 44/D1
Somme, Canal de la (canal), Fr. 54/B4
Somme-Leuze, Belg. 55/E3
Somme-Soude (riv.), Fr. 55/D6
Sommedieue, Fr. 55/E5
Sommeiller (peak), Fr. 64/C2
Sommelsdijk, Neth. 52/B5
Sommen (lake), Swe. 40/F2
Sommet de Finiels (peak), Fr. 44/E4
Sommet des Bains (peak), Fr. 64/C3
Sommet du Caduc (peak), Fr. 64/C4
Sommevoire, Fr. 60/A1
Somogy (prov.), Hun. 50/C2
Somonauk, Il, US 160/B4
Somoto, Nic. 176/E3
Somovo, Rus. 73/K2
Son, Nor. 38/S9
Son (riv.), India 92/D3
Son, Neth. 52/C5
Son Ha, Viet. 94/E3
Son La, Viet. 86/D4
Son Servera, Sp. 47/G3
Son Tay, Viet. 86/E4
Sona, It. 63/D3
Sona-Bata, D.R. Congo 120/C4
Sonāmarg, India 98/C2
Sonāmukhi, India 97/F4
Sonāmukhi, Bang. 97/G3
Sonāmura, India 97/H4
Sonār (riv.), India 96/B4
Sonātala, Bang. 97/G3
Sonbarsa, India 97/E2
Sonchamp, Fr. 30/H6
Sŏnch'ŏn, NKor. 81/C3
Soncino, It. 62/C3
Sondalo, It. 61/G5
Sondby, Fin. 39/F4
Sønder Nissum, Den. 40/C3
Sønderborg, Den. 40/C4
Sonderborg (int'l arpt.), Den. 40/C4
Sonderend (riv.), SAfr. 124/L11
Sønderjylland (co.), Den. 40/C4
Sondica (int'l arpt.), Sp. 44/B5
Søndre Strømfjord, Den. 167/L2
Sondrio, It. 61/F5
Sondrio (dept.), It. 61/F5
Sone Ka Gurja, India 96/A2
Song (peak), China 80/C4
Song Cau, Viet. 94/E3
Song Dinh, Viet. 94/D4
Song Ma, Viet. 86/D4
Song Phi Nong, Thai. 94/C3
Song Xian, China 80/C4
Song-Kel' (lake), Kyr. 99/C3
Sŏngch'ŏn, NKor. 81/D3
Songcun, China 87/H2
Songea, Tanz. 119/A4
Songeons, Fr. 54/A4
Songhua (riv.), China 77/M5
Songhwa, NKor. 81/C3
Sŏnghwan, SKor. 81/D4
Songi (isl.), SKor. 81/C5
Songino, Mong. 78/D2
Songjiang, China 80/L8
Songjianghe, China 81/D1
Songjŏng, SKor. 81/D5
Sŏngju, SKor. 81/E5
Songkhla, Thai. 94/C5
Songkhram (riv.), Thai. 93/H4
Songling, China 79/J2
Songmen, China 87/J2
Songming, China 86/D3
Sŏngnam, SKor. 81/G7
Songnim, NKor. 81/C3
Songo, Ang. 120/C4
Songo, Moz. 123/G2
Songololo, D.R. Congo 120/C4
Songsak, India 97/H3
Songshan, China 87/F4
Songshu, China 81/B3
Songshuzhen, China 81/D1
Songt'an, SKor. 81/D4
Songtao, China 87/F5
Songtao Miaozu Zizhixian, China 87/F2
Songwŏn, NKor. 81/C2
Songxi, China 87/H3
Songxia, China 87/H3
Songyan, China 87/E3
Songzi (pass), China 80/C5
Songzi, China 87/F2
Songzi Hudu (riv.), China 87/G2
Sonhāt, India 96/D4
Soni, Japan 83/K6
Sonīpat, India 98/D5
Sonmiāni, Pak. 101/J3
Sonneberg, Ger. 58/E2
Sonnefeld, Ger. 58/E2
Sonning, Eng, UK 37/F4
Sonnino, It. 65/C5
Sonnjoch (peak), Aus. 61/H3
Sonntagshorn (peak), Ger. 45/K3
Sonobe, Japan 83/H5
Sonoita, Az, US 149/G5
Sonoma (cr.), Ca, US 167/J10
Sonoma (mts.), Ca, US 167/J10
Sonoma (co.), Ca, US 167/J10
Sonoma, Ca, US 146/B4
Sonoma (lake), Ca, US 146/B4
Sonora (state), Mex. 174/C2
Sonora (riv.), Mex. 174/C2
Sonora (pass), Ca, US 146/D4
Sonora, Tx, US 151/D2
Sonoran Desert Nat'l Mon., Az, US 149/F4
Sonoyta, Mex. 149/F5
Sonoyta (riv.), Mex. 174/B2
Sonpur, India 97/E3
Sonqor, Iran 103/F3
Sŏnsan, SKor. 81/E4
Sonsbeck, Ger. 52/D5
Sonseca, Sp. 46/D3
Sonsón, Col. 183/K7
Sonsonate, ESal. 176/D3
Sonsorol (isls.), Palau 136/C4
Sonta, Yugo. 50/D3
Sontag, Ms, US 164/C2
Sontheim, Ger. 61/G2
Sontheim an der Brenz, Ger. 58/D5
Sonthofen, Ger. 61/G2
Sontra, Ger. 53/G6
Sonvico, Swi. 61/E5
Sook, Malay. 88/B4
Sooner (lake), Ok, US 153/F2
Sooyaac, Som. 119/C1
Sop Hao, Laos 94/D1
Sop Kai, Laos 94/C1
Sop Nhom, Laos 94/C1
Sop Prap, Thai. 94/B2
Soper, Ok, US 153/G3
Soperton, Ga, US 163/F4
Sopetrán, Col. 180/C3
Sophie, FrG. 182/C2
Sopi (cape), Indo. 91/G3
Sopka, Laos 94/C1
Sopo (riv.), Sudan 117/E3
Sopó, Col. 183/M8
Sopor, India 98/C2
Sopot, Pol. 40/H4
Sopot, Bul. 51/G4
Sopron, Hun. 50/C2
Soquel, Ca, US 148/B2
Sôr (riv.), Wal, UK 36/D3
Sor Karatuley (salt pan), Kaz. 71/K3
Sor Kaydak (swamp), Kaz. 71/K3
Sor Mertvyy Kultuk (swamp), Kaz. 71/K3
Sør-Varanger, Nor. 38/J1
Sora, It. 65/C4
Sorae, SKor. 81/F7
Soragna, It. 62/D4
Sŏrak-san (peak), SKor. 81/E3
Sŏraksan Nat'l Pk., SKor. 81/E3
Sŏraksan NP, SKor. 84/A1
Sorata, Bol. 184/D4
Sorbas, Sp. 46/D4
Sorbolo, It. 62/D4
Sorcy-Saint-Martin, Fr. 55/E6
Sorel (pt.), Chl, UK 56/C2
Sorel, Qu, Can. 161/K1
Sorell-Midway Point, Austl. 132/C4
Soresina, It. 62/C3
Sörforsa, Swe. 40/G1
Sorfta, Eth. 118/A4
Sorgues, Fr. 64/A5
Sorgun, Turk. 102/C2
Sori, It. 62/C5
Soria, Sp. 46/D2
Soriano (dept.), Uru. 190/G3
Soriano, Uru. 191/J10
Soriano nel Cimino, It. 65/B3
Sorigny, Fr. 57/F6
Sorikmerapi (peak), Indo. 89/B2
Soritor, Peru 184/B2
Sørmarka (reg.), Nor. 38/S8
Sormonne (riv.), Fr. 55/D4
Sorø, Den. 40/D4
Soro, Rio do (riv.), Braz. 186/D1
Soroca, Mol. 72/E3
Sorocaba, Braz. 189/H2
Sorochinsk, Rus. 71/K1
Sorol (isl.), Micr. 136/D4
Soron, India 96/B2
Sorong, Indo. 91/H4
Sororieng (mtn.), Guy. 182/B1
Soroti, Ugan. 119/A1
Sørøya (isl.), Nor. 38/G1
Sørøysundet (chan.), Nor. 38/G1
Sorpestausee (lake), Ger. 53/E6
Sorraia (riv.), Port. 46/A3
Sorrento, It. 65/D6
Sorrento, La, US 164/C2
Sorrento, Fl, US 164/M6
Sorrento, BC, Can. 144/E2
Sorris-Sorris, Namb. 122/B4
Sorsele, Swe. 38/F2
Sorso, It. 48/A2
Sorsogon, Phil. 88/C2
Sort, Sp. 47/F1
Sorunda, Swe. 39/A1
Sõrve (pt.), Est. 41/K3
Sos del Rey Católico, Sp. 46/E1
Sosa, Ger. 59/F1
Sŏsan, SKor. 81/D4
Sŏsan Haean NP, SKor. 81/C4
Sösdala, Swe. 40/E3
Söse (riv.), Ger. 53/H5
Sosenskiy, Rus. 70/E1
Soshanguve, SAfr. 123/F5
Soskovo, Rus. 70/E1
Sosna (riv.), Rus. 70/F1
Sosneado (peak), Arg. 190/C2
Sosnivka, Ukr. 72/C2
Sosnogorsk, Rus. 69/M3
Sosnovets, Rus. 68/G2
Sosnovka, Rus. 71/G1
Sosnovka, Rus. 69/L4
Sosnovka, Rus. 68/J2
Sosnovo, Rus. 41/P1
Sosnovo-Ozerskoye, Rus. 78/G1
Sosnovskoye, Rus. 68/J5
Sosnovyy Bor, Rus. 41/N2
Sosnowiec, Pol. 43/K3
Sosnytsya, Ukr. 73/G1
Soso, Ms, US 164/D2
Soso, CAfr. 120/C2
Sosonpal, India 95/D2
Sospel, Fr. 64/D5
Sospiro, It. 62/D3

Sosúa – Stockh

Sosúa, DRep. 173/G4
Sos'va (riv.), Rus. 74/G3
Sot (riv.), India 96/B1
Sotik, Kenya 119/A2
Sotkajärvi (lake), Fin. 39/E4
Soto del Real, Sp. 47/N8
Soto la Marina, Mex. 175/F4
Sotouboua, Togo 115/F4
Sotteville-lès-Rouen, Fr. 57/G2
Sottrum, Ger. 53/G2
Sotuta, Mex. 176/D1
Souanké, Congo 120/C2
Soubre, C.d'Iv. 114/D5
Soudan, Fr. 56/D5
Soudan, Mn, US 157/H4
Soudan, Ar, US 162/B3
Soudan, Austl. 129/E5
Soude (riv.), Fr. 55/D6
Souderton, Pa, US 168/C3
Soúdha, Gre. 75/J5
Souellaba (pt.), Camr. 120/B2
Souesmes, Fr. 57/H6
Souffelweyersheim, Fr. 55/G6
Soufflenheim, Fr. 55/G6
Souffles, Pic des (peak), Fr. 64/C3
Souflíon, Gre. 51/H5
Soufrière (peak), StV. 173/N9
Soufrière (peak), Guad. 173/N8
Sougéta, Gui. 114/B4
Souillac, Mrts. 125/T15
Souillac, Fr. 44/D4
Souk Ahras (wilaya), Alg. 112/K6
Souk Ahras, Alg. 112/K6
Souk el Arba du Rharb, Mor. 112/A2
Sŏul (Seoul) (cap.), SKor. 79/K4
Soulanges (co.), Qu, Can. 159/M7
Soulijärvi (lake), Fin. 39/E4
Soulles (riv.), Fr. 56/D2
Soultz-Haut-Rhin, Fr. 60/D2
Soultz-sous-Forêts, Fr. 58/A5
Soum (prov.), Burk. 115/E3
Soumagne, Belg. 55/E2
Sound of Bute (sound), Sc, UK 33/A5
Sound, The (chan.), Den. 38/E5
Sounding (lake), Ab, Can. 145/J1
Sounding (cr.), Ab, Can. 145/J2
Souppes-sur-Loing, Fr. 44/E2
Sour El Ghozlane, Alg. 112/G4
Sour Lake, Tx, US 151/G2
Sourbaral (peak), Chad 116/D2
Sources, Mont aux (peak), Les. 124/E3
Sourdeval, Fr. 57/E3
Sourdough (peak), Id, US 146/F1
Soure, Port. 46/A2
Soure, Braz. 182/D3
Souris, ND, US 156/D3
Souris (riv.), ND, US 156/D3
Souris, Mb, Can. 156/D3
Souris, PE, Can. 159/F2
Souris (riv.), Can.,US 140/F4
Souris (riv.), Sk, Can. 145/N3
Sourou (prov.), Burk. 114/E3
Sours, Fr. 57/G4
Sous, Oued (riv.), Mor. 110/C3
Sousa, Braz. 183/G4
Sout (riv.), SAfr. 124/C3
South (cr.), Austl. 134/G8
South (mts.), NS, Can. 158/E3
South (bay), Nun, Can. 167/H2
South (sound), Ire. 32/A4
South (isl.), NZ 127/H7
South (cape), NZ 135/A4
South (pt.), La, US 164/C3
South (riv.), NC, US 163/H3
South (mtn.), Pa, US 168/A3
South Africa (ctry.) 107/E7
South Alligator (riv.), Austl. 128/D3
South Amboy, NJ, US 169/H10
South America (cont.) 202/*
South Anna (riv.), Va, US 163/H2
South Augusta, Ga, US 163/F4
South Australia (state), Austl. 127/C3
South Ayrshire (co.), Sc, UK 33/B6
South Bay, Fl, US 165/H4
South Baymouth, On, Can. 160/E2
South Beloit, Il, US 155/K2
South Bend, Tx, US 153/E4
South Bend, In, US 160/C4
South Bend, Wa, US 144/C4
South Benfleet, Eng, UK 37/G3
South Berwick, Me, US 161/L3
South Boston, Va, US 163/H2
South Branch, Nf, Can. 159/H2
South Brent, Eng, UK 36/C6
South Brook, Nf, Can. 159/J1
South Burlington, Vt, US 161/K2
South Caicos (isl.), UK 177/J1
South Carolina (state), US 143/K5
South Charleston, WV, US 163/G1
South China (sea), Asia 77/L8
South Cle Elum, Wa, US 144/D4
South Coffeyville, Ok, US 153/G2
South Colby, Wa, US 167/B2
South Colton, NY, US 161/J2
South Dakota (state), US 142/F3
South Dorset Downs (uplands), Eng, UK 36/D5
South Dos Palos, Ca, US 148/B2
South Downs (hills), Eng, UK 37/F5
South Dum Dum, India 97/G4
South East (pt.), Austl. 133/C4
South East (cape), Austl. 127/D5
South Elgin, Il, US 167/P16
South Elmsall, Eng, UK 35/G4
South Entrance (inlet), PNG 129/F2
South Esk (riv.), Sc, UK 33/C3
South Fallsburg, NY, US 161/J4
South Farmingdale, NY, US 169/M9
South Foreland (pt.), UK 54/A1
South Fork, Co, US 149/J2
South Fork Ind. Res., Nv, US 146/F3
South Fork Koyukuk (riv.), Ak, US 171/H2
South Fork Kuskokwim (riv.), Ak, US 171/H3
South Fox (isl.), Mi, US 157/M5
South Fulton, Tn, US 162/C2
South Gate, Ca, US 166/F8
South Gate, Md, US 168/B5
South Georgia (isl.), UK 26/H8
South Glamorgan (co.), Wal, UK 36/C4
South Gloucestershire (co.), Eng, UK 36/D3
South Grand (riv.), Mo, US 153/G1
South Grand (riv.), Mo, US 155/G4
South Hams (plain), Eng, UK 36/C6
South Haven, Mi, US 160/C3
South Heart, ND, US 156/C4
South Hill, Va, US 163/H2
South Holland, Il, US 167/Q16
South Holmwood, Eng, UK 30/C3
South Horr, Kenya 119/B1
South Houston, Tx, US 151/M9
South Hutchinson, Ks, US 153/F1
South Island NP, Kenya 119/B1
South Kinangop, Kenya 119/B2
South Kirkby, Eng, UK 35/G4
South Kitui Nat'l Rsv., Kenya 119/B2
South Koel (riv.), India 97/E4
South Korea (ctry.) 77/M6
South Lake Tahoe, Ca, US 146/D4
South Lanarkshire (co.), Sc, UK 33/C5
South Llano (riv.), Tx, US 151/D2
South Loup (riv.), Ne, US 154/E3
South Luangwa NP, Zam. 123/F2
South Lyon, Mi, US 167/E7
South Magnetic Pole, Ant. 192/K
South Manitou (isl.), Mi, US 160/C2
South Miami, Fl, US 164/P11
South Mills, NC, US 163/J2
South Milwaukee, Wi, US 160/C3
South Molton, Eng, UK 36/C4
South Monroe, Mi, US 160/E4
South Naknek, Ak, US 171/G4
South Nation (riv.), On, Can. 161/J2
South New River (canal), Fl, US 164/P10
South Normanton, Eng, UK 35/G5
South Nyack, NY, US 169/K7
South Ockenden, Eng, UK 30/D2
South Ogden, Ut, US 147/H3
South Ohio, NS, Can. 158/D4
South Orange, NJ, US 169/H9
South Orkney (isls.), UK 192/X
South Ossetia (reg.), Geo. 71/G4
South Oxhey, Eng, UK 30/B2
South Oyster (bay), NY, US 169/M9
South Pacific (ocean) 26/B7
South Padre Island, Tx, US 150/F4
South Palm Beach, Fl, US 164/P9
South Para (res.), Austl. 131/M8
South Paris, Me, US 161/L2
South Pasadena, Fl, US 164/K8
South Pasadena, Ca, US 166/F7
South Pekin, Il, US 155/K3
South Perth (nbrhd.), Austl. 130/K6
South Petherton, Eng, UK 36/D5
South Pine (riv.), Austl. 134/E6
South Plainfield, NJ, US 169/H9
South Plains, Tx, US 152/D3
South Platte (riv.), Co, Ne, US 154/C3
South Platte (riv.), Co, US 154/B4
South Platte, Middle Fork (riv.), Co, US 152/A1
South Polar (plat.), Ant. 192/Y
South Pole, Ant. 192/A
South Portland, Me, US 161/L3
South Prairie, Wa, US 167/C3
South Prong South Alafia (riv.), Fl, US 164/L8
South Pugwash, NS, Can. 158/F3
South Range Refuge, Ut, US 147/G4
South River, On, Can. 161/G2
South River, NJ, US 169/H10
South Rockwood, Mi, US 167/F7
South Ronaldsay (isl.), Sc, UK 31/V14
South Saint Paul, Mn, US 157/P7
South San Francisco, Ca, US 167/K11
South Sandwich (isls.), UK 26/H8
South Saskatchewan (riv.), Sk, Can. 140/E3
South Seaville, NJ, US 168/D5
South Shetland (isls.), UK 192/W
South Shields, Eng, UK 35/G2
South Shore, SD, US 155/F1
South Shore, Ky, US 163/F1
South Sioux City, Ne, US 155/F2
South Sister (peak), Or, US 146/C1
South Skunk (riv.), Ia, US 155/H2
South Sulphur (riv.), Tx, US 151/G1
South Sulphur (riv.), Tx, US 153/G4
South Taranaki Bight (bay), NZ 135/C2
South Tucson, Az, US 149/G4
South Tyne (riv.), Eng, UK 35/F2
South Ubian, Phil. 88/C4
South Uist (isl.), Sc, UK 31/Q8
South Umpqua (riv.), Or, US 146/B2
South Valley Stream, NY, US 169/L9
South West (cape), Austl. 132/C4
South West (cape), NZ 135/A4
South West City, Mo, US 153/G2
South West NP, Austl. 132/C4
South West Port Mouton, NS, Can. 158/E4
South West Rocks, Austl. 132/E1
South Whittier, Ca, US 166/F8
South Wichita (riv.), Tx, US 152/D4
South Williamsport, Pa, US 168/B1
South Woodham Ferrers, Eng, UK 30/E2
South Yorkshire (co.), Eng, UK 35/G5
South Zanesville, Oh, US 160/E5
Southall (nbrhd.), Eng, UK 30/B2
Southam, Eng, UK 37/E2
Southampton, On, Can. 160/F2
Southampton (isl.), Nun, Can. 167/H2
Southampton (cape), Nun, Can. 167/H2
Southampton (isl.), Can. 139/J3
Southampton, Eng, UK 37/E5
Southampton (co.), Eng, UK 37/E5
Southampton, NY, US 169/F2
Southampton Water (inlet), Eng, UK 37/E5
Southaven, Ms, US 162/B3
Southborough, Eng, UK 37/G4
Southbourne, Eng, UK 37/F5
Southbridge, Ma, US 161/K3
Southbridge, NZ 135/C3
Southbury, Ct, US 161/K4
Southeast (pt.), Bahm. 177/H1
Southeast (dist.), Bots. 122/E5
Southeast (pt.), Jam. 177/G2
Southeast (cape), Ak, US 171/E3
Southend, Sc, UK 34/C1
Southend (int'l arpt.), Eng, UK 37/G3
Southend-on-Sea, Eng, UK 37/G3
Southend-on-Sea (co.), Eng, UK 37/G3
Southern (riv.), Austl. 130/K7
Southern (dist.), Bots. 122/E5
Southern (dist.), Isr. 104/D4
Southern, Malw. 123/G2
Southern (mts.), NZ 127/G7
Southern (prov.), SLeo. 114/B5
Southern (prov.), SrL. 95/D5
Southern (prov.), Zam. 123/E3
Southern Cook (isls.), Cookls. 137/J6
Southern Cross, Austl. 130/C4
Southern Harbour, Nf, Can. 159/L2
Southern Highlands (prov.), PNG 129/F1
Southern Indian (lake), Mb, Can. 140/G3
Southern NP, Sudan 116/F4
Southern Pines, NC, US 163/H3
Southern Shores, NC, US 163/K2
Southern Uplands (hills), Sc, UK 35/D1
Southern Ural (mts.), Rus. 69/N5
Southern Ute Ind. Res., Co, US 149/H2
Southery, Eng, UK 37/G1
Southesk Tablelands (plat.), Austl. 127/B2
Southey, Sk, Can. 156/B2
Southfield, Mi, US 160/E3
Southgate, Mi, US 160/E3
Southgate (nbrhd.), Eng, UK 30/C2
Southgate (riv.), BC, Can. 144/B2
Southlake, Tx, US 150/K7
Southland, Tx, US 152/D4
Southminster, Eng, UK 37/G3
Southold, NY, US 169/F1
Southport, Eng, UK 35/E4
Southport, Fl, US 165/F2
Southport, NY, US 161/H3
Southport, NC, US 163/H4
Southside, Al, US 162/D4
Southside, Tn, US 162/D2
Southside Place, Tx, US 151/M9
South Tyneside (co.), Eng, UK 35/G2
Southwark (bor.), Eng, UK 30/A1
Southwell, Eng, UK 35/H5
Southwold, Eng, UK 37/H2
Southwood NP, Austl. 134/C4
Southworth, Wa, US 167/C3
Soutpansberg (mts.), SAfr. 123/F4
Sovata, Rom. 51/G2
Soverato Marina, It. 48/E3
Sovere, It. 62/D2
Sovetsk, Rus. 69/L4
Sovetsk, Rus. 41/J4
Sovetskaya, Rus. 73/L5
Sovetskaya Gavan', Rus. 79/N2
Sovetskiy, Rus. 69/L4
Sovetskoye, Rus. 71/H3
Sovets'kyy, Ukr. 73/H5
Sōwa, Japan 83/D1
Sowa Pan (salt pan), Bots. 122/E4
Sowerby Bridge, Eng, UK 35/G4
Soweto, SAfr. 124/D2
Sōya-misaki (cape), Japan 82/B1
Soyana (riv.), Rus. 68/J2
Soyang (lake), SKor. 84/A2
Soyaux, Fr. 44/D4
Soyen, Ger. 59/F6
Soyhières, Swi. 60/D3
Soyo, Ang. 120/C4
Sozh (riv.), Bela. 70/D1
Sozopol, Bul. 51/H4
Spa, Belg. 55/E3
Spaceport USA, Fl, US 165/H3
Spada (lake), Wa, US 167/D2
Spaichingen, Ger. 61/E1
Spain (ctry.) 29/D4
Spakenburg, Neth. 52/C4
Spalding, Eng, UK 35/H6
Spalding, Mi, US 160/C2
Spalding, Austl. 131/H5
Spalding, Sk, Can. 145/M1
Spallumcheen, BC, Can. 144/E2
Spalt, Ger. 58/D4
Spanaway, Wa, US 144/C4
Spangenberg, Ger. 53/G6
Spangle, Wa, US 144/F4
Spangler, Pa, US 161/G4
Spanish (pt.), Ire. 32/A4
Spanish Fork, Ut, US 147/H3
Spanish Fort, Al, US 164/E2
Spanish River Ind. Res., On, Can. 160/E1
Spanish Town, Jam. 177/G2
Spannort (peak), Swi. 61/E4
Spar City, Co, US 149/J2
Sparanise, It. 65/D5
Sparkman, Ar, US 153/H4
Sparks, Ga, US 165/G2
Sparks, Nv, US 146/D4
Sparks, Tx, US 150/F2
Sparlingville, Mi, US 167/G6
Sparreholm, Swe. 40/G2
Sparta, Ga, US 163/F4
Sparta, Mo, US 153/H2
Sparta, Mi, US 160/D3
Sparta, NC, US 163/G2
Sparta, Tn, US 162/E3
Sparta, Il, US 162/C1
Sparta, Wi, US 155/J2
Sparta, NJ, US 168/D1
Sparta (Spárti), Gre. 75/H4
Spartanburg, SC, US 163/G3
Spartel (cape), Mor. 112/B2
Spárti (Sparta), Gre. 75/H4
Spartivento (cape), It. 48/E4
Sparwood, BC, Can. 144/G3
Spas-Demensk, Rus. 68/G5
Spassk-Dal'niy, Rus. 79/L3
Spasskaya Guba, Rus. 68/G3
Spáta, Gre. 75/N9
Spátha (cape), Gre. 75/H5
Spavinaw, Ok, US 153/G2
Spay, Ger. 55/G3
Spean (riv.), Sc, UK 33/B3
Spean Bridge, Sc, UK 33/B3
Spearfish, SD, US 154/C1
Spearman, Tx, US 152/D2
Spearville, Ks, US 152/E2
Speculator, NY, US 161/J3
Speedway, In, US 160/C5
Speer (peak), Swi. 61/F3
Speers, Sk, Can. 145/L1
Speicher, Swi. 61/F3
Speicher, Ger. 55/F4
Speichersdorf, Ger. 59/E3
Speke, Eng, UK 35/F5
Speke (int'l arpt.), Eng, UK 35/F5
Speke (gulf), Tanz. 119/A2
Spelle, Ger. 53/E4
Spello, It. 65/B2
Spence Bay, Nun, Can. 140/G2
Spencer (cape), Austl. 131/H5
Spencer (gulf), Austl. 127/C4
Spencer (cape), Ak, US 171/E2
Spencer, In, US 160/C5
Spencer, Ia, US 155/G2
Spencer, NC, US 163/G3
Spencer, Tn, US 162/E3
Spencer, Wi, US 155/J1
Spencer, WV, US 163/G1
Spencerville, Ok, US 153/G3
Spencerville, Oh, US 160/D4
Spences Bridge, BC, Can. 144/D2
Spenge, Ger. 53/F4
Spennymoor, Eng, UK 35/G2
Spentrup, Den. 40/D3
Sperkhiás, Gre. 75/H3
Sperkhiós (riv.), Gre. 75/H3
Sperlonga, It. 65/C5
Sperrin (mts.) 34/A2
Spessart (range), Ger. 58/C3
Spétsai, Gre. 75/H4
Spey (bay), Sc, UK 33/C1
Spey (riv.), Sc, UK 33/B2
Speyer, Ger. 58/B4
Speyerbsch (riv.), Ger. 58/B4
Speyside, On, Can. 160/T8
Spezzano Albanese, It. 48/E3
Špičák (peak), Czh. 59/F2
Spicer (isls.), Nun, Can. 167/H2
Spicer, Mn, US 155/G1
Spicewood, Tx, US 150/E2
Spickard, Mo, US 155/H3
Spiddle, Ire. 32/A3
Spiekeroog (isl.), Ger. 53/E1
Spiez, Swi. 60/D4
Spigno Monferrato, It. 62/B4
Spijkenisse, Neth. 52/B5
Spike (mt.), Ak, US 171/K2
Spilamberto, It. 63/E4
Spílion, Gre. 75/J5
Spillersboda, Swe. 39/B1
Spillimacheen (riv.), BC, Can. 144/F2
Spillimacheen, BC, Can. 144/F2
Spilsby, Eng, UK 35/J5
Spilve (int'l arpt.), Lat. 41/L3
Spina (peak), It. 48/A2
Spinea, It. 63/F3
Spinetta Marengo, It. 62/B4
Spino d'Adda, It. 62/C3
Spirano, It. 62/C2
Spirit, Wi, US 157/J5
Spirit (lake), Ia, US 155/G2
Spirit Lake, Ia, US 155/G2
Spirit Lake, Id, US 144/F4
Spirit, North (lake), On, Can. 157/H1
Spiritwood, Sk, Can. 145/L1
Spiro, Ok, US 153/G3
Spišská Nová Ves, Slvk. 43/L4
Spitak, Arm. 71/H4
Spiti (riv.), India 98/D3
Spitsbergen (isl.), Nor. 74/B2
Spitsbergen (isl.), Sval. 192/E
Spittal an der Drau, Aus. 45/K3
Spivey, Ks, US 153/E2
Spivey (lake), Ga, US 163/M7
Splendora, Tx, US 151/G2
Split, Cro. 50/C4
Split (int'l arpt.), Cro. 50/C4
Split (lake), Mb, Can. 140/G3
Split (mtn.), Ca, US 148/C2
Splitrock (res.), NJ, US 169/H8
Spluga, Passo dello (pass), Swi. 61/F5
Splügen, Swi. 61/F4
Špoģi, Lat. 41/M3
Spokane, Mo, US 153/H2
Spokane, Wa, US 144/F4
Spokane Ind. Res., Wa, US 144/E4
Spokoynaya, Rus. 73/L5
Spöl (riv.), It. 61/G5
Spoleto, It. 65/B2
Spoltore, It. 65/D3
Spook Cave, Ia, US 155/J2
Spoon (riv.), Il, US 155/K3
Spooner, Wi, US 157/J5
Spotorno, It. 62/B5
Spotswood, NJ, US 169/H10
Spotsylvania Courthouse, Va, US 163/J1
Sprague, Mb, Can. 157/G3
Sprague (riv.), Or, US 146/C2
Sprague, Wa, US 144/F4
Sprang, Neth. 52/C5
Spranger (mt.), BC, Can. 144/D1
Spratly (isls.) 90/D2
Spray, Or, US 146/D1
Spree (riv.), Ger. 43/H2
Sprendlingen, Ger. 55/G4
Spresiano, It. 63/F2
Sprimont, Belg. 55/E3
Spring (lake), Ca, US 148/D3
Spring (cr.), Nv, US 146/E3
Spring (cr.), Ne, US 154/D3
Spring (mts.), Nv, US 148/E2
Spring, Tx, US 151/M8
Spring (riv.), Ar, US 162/B2
Spring City, Pa, US 168/C3
Spring City, Tn, US 162/E3
Spring City, Ut, US 147/H4
Spring Grove, Il, US 167/P15
Spring Grove, Mn, US 155/J2
Spring Grove, Pa, US 168/B4
Spring Hill, Ar, US 153/H4
Spring Hill, Fl, US 164/K7
Spring Hill, Ks, US 153/G1
Spring Hill, Tn, US 162/D3
Spring Lake, Fl, US 164/L7
Spring Lake, NJ, US 168/D3
Spring Lake, NC, US 163/H3
Spring Valley, Ca, US 166/D5
Spring Valley, NY, US 169/J7
Spring Valley, Mn, US 155/H2
Spring Valley, Tx, US 151/M9
Springbok, SAfr. 124/B3
Springbokvlatke (valley), SAfr. 123/F5
Springboro, Oh, US 160/D5
Springdale, Ar, US 153/G2
Springdale, Ut, US 149/F2
Springdale, Wa, US 144/F3
Springdale, SC, US 163/G3
Springe, Ger. 53/G4
Springer, Ok, US 153/F3
Springer, NM, US 152/B2
Springerville, Az, US 149/H3
Springfield, Co, US 152/C2
Springfield, Fl, US 165/F2
Springfield, Ga, US 163/G4
Springfield, Ky, US 162/E2
Springfield, Ma, US 161/K3
Springfield, Mi, US 160/D3
Springfield, Mo, US 153/H2
Springfield, Oh, US 160/E5
Springfield, NJ, US 169/H9
Springfield, Or, US 146/B1
Springfield, SD, US 154/F2
Springfield, Mn, US 155/G1
Springfield (cap.), Il, US 155/K4
Springfield, Tn, US 162/D2
Springfield, Va, US 168/A6
Springfield, Vt, US 161/K3
Springfontein, SAfr. 124/D3
Springhill, La, US 153/H4
Springhill, NS, Can. 158/E3
Springs, SAfr. 124/E2
Springs, NY, US 169/F1
Springside, Sk, Can. 156/C2
Springsure, Austl. 134/C4
Springtown, Tx, US 150/K7
Springvale, Me, US 161/L3
Springvale (nbrhd.), Austl. 132/G5
Springview, Ne, US 154/E2
Springville, NY, US 161/G3
Springville, Ut, US 147/H3
Springville, Al, US 162/D4
Springville, Ia, US 155/J2
Springwater, NY, US 161/H3
Springwater, Sk, Can. 145/K2
Springwater Nat'l Wild. Ref., ND, US 156/D4
Sprockhövel, Ger. 53/E6
Sprowston, Eng, UK 37/H1
Spruce (mtn.), Nv, US 147/F3
Spruce (peak), WV, US 163/H1
Spruce Knob NRA, WV, US 163/H1
Spruce Lake, Sk, Can. 145/K1
Spruce Pine, NC, US 163/F3
Spruce Run (res.), NJ, US 168/C2
Sprucewoods, Mb, Can. 156/E3
Spui (riv.), Neth. 52/B5
Spur, Tx, US 152/D4
Spurn (pt.), Eng, UK 35/J4
Spuzzum, BC, Can. 144/D3
Spydeberg, Nor. 38/T9
Spydeberg (peak), Nor. 38/S9
Squa Pan (lake), Me, US 158/C2
Squamish (riv.), BC, Can. 144/C3
Squamish, BC, Can. 144/C3
Square Butte, Mt, US 145/J4
Squaw Creek Nat'l Wild. Ref., Mo, US 155/G3
Squaw Harbor, Ak, US 171/F4
Squaw Lake, Mn, US 157/G4
Squaw Valley, Ca, US 148/C2
Squaxin Island Ind. Res., Wa, US 167/A3
Squinzano, It. 75/F2
Squire, WV, US 163/G2
Squires, Mo, US 153/H2
Squires (mt.), Austl. 131/E3
Srbobran, Yugo. 50/D3
Sre Ambel, Camb. 94/C4
Sre Khtum, Camb. 94/D3
Sre Noy, Camb. 94/D3
Srebrenica, Bosn. 50/D3
Sredna (mts.), Bul. 75/J1
Srednebelaya, Rus. 79/K1
Srednekolymsk, Rus. 75/R3
Sredniy Ikorets, Rus. 73/K2
Srednogorie, Bul. 51/G4
Srednyaya Akhtuba, Rus. 71/H2
Śrem, Pol. 43/J2
Sremčica, Yugo. 50/E3
Sremska Mitrovica, Yugo. 50/D3
Sreng (riv.), Camb. 94/C3
Srepok (riv.), Camb. 94/D3
Sretensk, Rus. 79/H1
Sri Dungargarh, India 101/K3
Sri Gangānagar, India 98/B5
Sri Jayawardanapura (Kotte), SrL. 95/C5
Sri Kshetra (ruin), Myan. 86/B5
Sri Lanka (ctry.) 77/H9
Srikākulam, India 95/D2
Srimangal, Bang. 97/H3
Srīnagar, India 98/C2
Srīrampur, India 95/B2
Srīvardhan, India 95/B2
Środa Śląska, Pol. 43/J3
Środa Wielkopolska, Pol. 43/J2
St-Floris, PN de, CAfr. 116/D3
Staaten (riv.), Austl. 129/F4
Staaten River NP, Austl. 129/F4
Stabbursdalen NP, Nor. 38/H1
Staberhuk (pt.), Ger. 40/D4
Stabroek, Belg. 52/B6
Stacyville, Ia, US 155/H2
Stadbroke, North (isl.), Austl. 127/E3
Stade, Ger. 53/G1
Staden, Belg. 54/C2
Stadl-Paura, Aus. 59/G6
Stadskanaal, Neth. 52/D3
Stadtbergen, Ger. 58/D6
Stadthagen, Ger. 53/G4
Stadtlauringen, Ger. 58/D2
Stadtlohn, Ger. 52/D5
Stadtoldendorf, Ger. 53/G5
Stadtsteinach, Ger. 59/E2
Stäfa, Swi. 61/E3
Staffanstorp, Swe. 40/E4
Staffelberg (peak), Ger. 58/E2
Staffelegg (pass), Swi. 60/E3
Staffelsee (lake), Ger. 61/H2
Staffelstein, Ger. 58/D2
Staffhorst, Ger. 53/F3
Staffora (riv.), It. 62/C3
Stafford, Eng, UK 35/F6
Stafford, Ct, US 161/K4
Stafford, Tx, US 151/M9
Stafford, Va, US 163/J1
Stagno, It. 62/D6
Stagnone, Isole della (isl.), It. 48/B4
Stahnsdorf, Ger. 42/Q7
Staicele, Lat. 41/L3
Staindrop, Eng, UK 35/G2
Staines, Eng, UK 30/B2
Stains, Fr. 30/K5
Stakes (mt.), Ca, US 167/M12
Stäket, Swe. 39/A1
Stakhanov, Ukr. 73/K3
Stalbridge, Eng, UK 36/D5
Stalden, Swi. 60/D5
Stalham, Eng, UK 37/H1
Stallarholmen, Swe. 39/A1
Stallworthy (cape), Nun, Can. 167/S6
Stalowa Wola, Pol. 43/M3
Stalwart, Sk, Can. 145/M2
Stalybridge, Eng, UK 35/F5
Stambaugh, Mi, US 157/K4
Stamboliyski, Bul. 75/J1
Stamford, Tx, US 152/E4
Stamford (lake), Tx, US 151/E1
Stamford, NY, US 161/J3
Stamford, Ct, US 169/L7
Stamford, Austl. 134/A3
Stamford, Eng, UK 37/F1
Stamford Bridge, Eng, UK 35/H4
Stampa, Swi. 61/F5
Stampede (res.), Ca, US 146/C4
Stampriet, Namb. 122/C5
Stamps, Ar, US 153/H4
Stamullen, Ire. 34/B4
Stanardsville, Va, US 163/H1
Stanberry, Mo, US 155/G3
Stanchfield, Mn, US 157/H5
Standard, Ab, Can. 145/H2
Standerton, SAfr. 124/E2
Standing Indian (peak), NC, US 163/F3
Standing Rock, Al, US 162/E4
Standing Rock Ind. Res., SD, US 154/D1
Standish, Mi, US 160/E3
Standish, Me, US 161/L3
Standish-with-Langtree, Eng, UK 35/F4
Stanfield, Az, US 149/G4
Stanfield, Or, US 144/E5
Stanford, Ky, US 162/E2
Stanford, Mt, US 145/J4
Stanford Rivers, Eng, UK 30/D1
Stanford-le-Hope, Eng, UK 37/G3
Stange, Nor. 40/D1
Stangelville, Wi, US 160/C2
Stanger, SAfr. 125/E3
Stanghella, It. 63/E3
Stanhope, Eng, UK 35/F2
Stanhope, NJ, US 168/D2
Stanišić, Yugo. 50/D3
Stanislaus (co.), Ca, US 167/M12
Stanislaus (riv.), Ca, US 146/C4
Stanke Dimitrov, Bul. 75/H1
Stanley, NB, Can. 158/D2
Stanley, ND, US 156/C3
Stanley, Sc, UK 33/C4
Stanley, Eng, UK 35/G2
Stanley, Austl. 132/C4
Stanley, NM, US 149/K3
Stanley, Wi, US 155/J1
Stanley (mt.), Austl. 131/F2
Stanley (res.), India 92/C5
Stanley (cap.), Falk. 191/F6
Stanley, China 87/L8
Stanley (mt.), Austl. 133/B5
Stanleytown, Va, US 163/H2
Stanleyville, NC, US 163/G2
Stanovo, Yugo. 50/E4
Stanovoy (range), Rus. 77/M4
Stans, Swi. 61/E4
Stanstead Plain, Qu, Can. 161/K2
Stansted, Eng, UK 30/D3
Stansted (int'l arpt.), Eng, UK 37/G3
Stansted Mountfitchet, Eng, UK 37/G3
Stanthorpe, Austl. 134/C5
Stanton, Eng, UK 37/G2
Stanton, Al, US 162/D4
Stanton, Ca, US 166/G8
Stanton, De, US 168/C4
Stanton, Ky, US 162/F2
Stanton, Ia, US 155/G3
Stanton, Mi, US 160/D3
Stanton, ND, US 156/D4
Stanton, Ne, US 155/F3
Stanton, NJ, US 168/D2
Stanton, Tn, US 162/C3
Stanton, Tx, US 151/D1
Stanwell, Eng, UK 30/B2
Stanwood, Wa, US 144/C3
Stanychno-Luhans'ke, Ukr. 73/K3
Staphorst, Neth. 52/D3
Stapleford, Eng, UK 37/E4
Stapleford Abbotts, Eng, UK 30/D2
Staplehurst, Ne, US 155/F3
Staplehurst, Eng, UK 37/G4
Staples, Mn, US 157/G4
Staples, On, Can. 167/G7
Stapleton, Al, US 164/E2
Stapleton, Ga, US 163/F4
Stapleton, Ne, US 154/D3
Stąporków, Pol. 43/L3
Star', Rus. 70/E1
Star, Tx, US 151/E2
Star City, Ar, US 153/J4
Star City, Sk, Can. 145/M1
Star Lake, NY, US 161/J2
Stara Pazova, Yugo. 50/E3
Stara Planina (mts.), Yugo. 50/F3
Stara Vyzhivka, Ukr. 72/C2
Stara Zagora, Bul. 51/G4
Starachowice, Pol. 43/L3
Staranzano, It. 63/G2
Staraya Racheyka, Rus. 71/J1
Staraya Russa, Rus. 41/P2
Starbuck, Mb, Can. 156/F3
Starbuck, Mn, US 157/G5
Starbuck (isl.), Kiri. 137/K5
Starcke NP, Austl. 134/B1
Stargard Szczeciński, Pol. 40/F5
Stari Grad, Cro. 50/C4
Stark, Ks, US 153/G2
Starke, Fl, US 165/G3
Starkey, Or, US 146/D1
Starkville, Ms, US 162/C4
Starkweather, ND, US 156/E3
Starnberg, Ger. 59/E6
Starnbergersee (lake), Ger. 61/H2
Starobil's'k, Ukr. 73/K3
Staroderevyankovskaya, Rus. 73/K4
Starodub, Rus. 70/E1
Starogard Gdański, Pol. 40/H5
Starokostyantyniv, Ukr. 72/D3
Starominskaya, Rus. 73/K4
Staronizhestebliyevskaya, Rus. 73/K5
Staroshcherbinovskaya, Rus. 73/K4
Starotitarovskaya, Rus. 73/J5
Starovelichkovskaya, Rus. 73/K5
Start, La, US 153/J4
Start (pt.), Sc, UK 31/V14
Start (bay), Eng, UK 36/C6
Start (pt.), Eng, UK 36/C6
Startup, Wa, US 167/D2
Staryy Kistruss, Rus. 68/J5
Staryy Krym, Ukr. 73/H5
Staryy Oskol', Rus. 73/J2
Staryy Studenets, Rus. 69/L5
Staryye Dorogi, Bela. 70/D1
Staszów, Pol. 43/L3
State College, Pa, US 161/H4
State Fair Park (Cotton Bowl), Tx, US 150/L7
State Fairgrounds, De, US 168/C6
State Line, Ms, US 164/D2
Staten (isl.), NY, US 168/D2
Statenville, Ga, US 165/G2
States (int'l arpt.), Chl, UK 56/C2
Statesboro, Ga, US 163/G4
Statesville, NC, US 163/G3
Statham, Ga, US 162/F4
Statts Mills, WV, US 163/G1
Statue of Liberty Nat'l Mon., NY, US 169/J9
Staufen im Breisgau, Ger. 60/D2
Staufenberg, Ger. 42/E3
Staunton, Il, US 155/K4
Staunton, Eng, UK 36/D3
Staunton, Va, US 163/H1
Staunton on Wye, Eng, UK 36/D2
Stavanger, Nor. 40/A2
Staveley, Eng, UK 35/F3
Staveley, Eng, UK 35/G5
Stavelot, Belg. 55/E3
Stavely, Ab, Can. 145/H2
Staveren, Neth. 52/C3
Stavern, Nor. 40/D2
Stavropol', Rus. 73/M5
Stavropol'skiy Kray, Rus. 74/E5
Stavrós, Gre. 75/H2
Stavsnäs, Swe. 39/B1
Stavyshche, Ukr. 72/F3
Stawell, Austl. 132/B3
Stayner, On, Can. 160/F2
Stayton, Or, US 146/B1
Steamboat Slough (riv.), Ca, US 167/L10
Steamboat Springs, Co, US 147/K3
Stearns, Ky, US 162/E2
Stebbins, Ak, US 171/F3
Stebnyk, Ukr. 72/B3
Steckborn, Swi. 61/E2
Stederau (riv.), Ger. 53/H3
Steeg, Aus. 61/G3
Steel (mtn.), Id, US 147/F2
Steele, ND, US 156/E4
Steele, Mo, US 162/C2
Steele (cr.), Austl. 132/F5
Steele's Knowe (hill), Sc, UK 33/C4
Steeleville, Il, US 162/C1
Steelpoortrivier (riv.), SAfr. 125/E2
Steelton, Pa, US 168/B3
Steelville, Mo, US 153/J2
Steenbergen, Neth. 52/B5
Steenkool, Indo. 91/H4
Steens Mtn. Recreation Lands, Or, US 146/D2
Steensby (inlet), Nun, Can. 167/J1
Steenvoorde, Fr. 54/B2
Steenwijk, Neth. 52/D3
Steep (pt.), Austl. 130/B3
Steep Holm (isl.), Eng, UK 36/C4
Steep Rock, Mb, Can. 156/E2
Steeping (riv.), Eng, UK 35/J5
Ştefăneşti, Rom. 72/D4
Stefansson (isl.), Nun, Can. 140/F1
Steffen (peak), Chile 190/C5
Steffisburg, Swi. 60/D4
Steg, Swi. 60/D5
Stege, Den. 40/E4
Steglitz, Ger. 42/Q7
Steiermark (prov.), Aus. 43/H5
Steigerwald (for.), Ger. 45/J2
Steilacoom, Wa, US 167/B3
Steilloopbrug, SAfr. 123/F4
Steimbke, Ger. 53/G3
Stein, Neth. 55/E2
Stein (riv.), BC, Can. 144/D2
Stein am Rhein, Swi. 61/E2
Stein bei Nünnberg, Ger. 58/E4
Steina (riv.), Ger. 61/E2
Steinach, Ger. 58/E2
Steinach (riv.), Ger. 58/E2
Steinach, Ger. 59/F5
Steinach am Brenner, Aus. 61/H3
Steinau an der Strasse, Ger. 58/C2
Steinbach, Mb, Can. 156/F3
Steinbach an der Steyr, Aus. 59/H7
Steinbourg, Fr. 55/G6
Steinen, Ger. 60/D2
Steinen (riv.), Braz. 185/H4
Steinerkirchen an der Traun, Aus. 59/G6
Steinfeld, Ger. 58/B4
Steinfeld, Ger. 58/C3
Steinfeld, Ger. 53/F3
Steinfort, Lux. 55/E4
Steingaden, Ger. 61/G2
Steinhagen, Ger. 53/F4
Steinhatchee, Fl, US 165/G3
Steinhausen, Swi. 61/E3
Steinhausen, Namb. 122/C4
Steinhausen an der Rottum, Ger. 61/F1
Steinheid, Ger. 58/D2
Steinheim, Ger. 53/G5
Steinheim am Albuch, Ger. 58/D5
Steinheim an der Murr, Ger. 58/C5
Steinhorst, Ger. 53/H3
Steinhuder (lake), Ger. 53/G4
Steinkjer, Nor. 38/D2
Steinsland, Nor. 40/A1
Steinstücken, Ger. 42/Q7
Steinweiler, Ger. 58/B4
Stekene, Belg. 52/B6
Steklyanka, Rus. 68/J4
Stella (peak), It. 61/F5
Stella, Ne, US 155/G3
Stella, SAfr. 124/D2
Stellarton, NS, Can. 159/F3
Stelle, Ger. 53/H2
Stellenbosch, SAfr. 124/L10
Stello (peak), Fr. 48/A1
Stelvio, Passo di (pass), It. 61/G4
Stelvio, PN dello (nat'l park), It. 45/J3
Stenay, Fr. 55/E5
Stendal, Ger. 42/F2
Stende, Lat. 41/K3
Steneto NP, Bul. 51/G4
Stenhamra, Swe. 39/A1
Stenhousemuir, Sc, UK 33/C4
Stenlille, Den. 39/H7
Stenløse, Den. 39/J7
Stensån (riv.), Swe. 39/K6
Stenungsund, Swe. 40/D2
Step'anavan, Arm. 71/H4
Stepaside, Ire. 34/B5
Stephan, SD, US 154/E1
Stephansposching, Ger. 59/F5
Stephens, Ar, US 153/H4
Stephens City, Va, US 163/H1
Stephens Creek, Austl. 132/B1
Stephensburg, Ky, US 162/D2
Stephenson, Mi, US 160/C2
Stephenville, Nf, Can. 159/H1
Stephenville, Tx, US 151/E1
Stephenville Crossing, Nf, Can. 159/H1
Stepnoy, Rus. 69/P5
Stepnoye, Rus. 71/H3
Stepnoye, Rus. 71/H2
Steptoe (valley), Nv, US 147/F4
Steptoe, Wa, US 144/F4
Sterkspruit, SAfr. 124/D3
Sterkstroom, SAfr. 124/D3
Sterling, Ak, US 171/H3
Sterling, Co, US 154/C3
Sterling, Ga, US 165/H2
Sterling, Il, US 155/K3
Sterling, Ks, US 153/E1
Sterling, Mi, US 160/D2
Sterling City, Tx, US 151/D2
Sterling Heights, Mi, US 160/E3
Sterlington, La, US 153/H4
Sterlitamak, Rus. 71/K1
Sternstein (peak), Aus. 59/H5
Sterzing (Vipiteno), It. 61/H4
Stęszew, Pol. 43/J2
Štěti, Czh. 59/H2
Stetsonville, Wi, US 155/J1
Stettler, Ab, Can. 145/H1
Steubenville, Oh, US 160/F4
Stevenage, Eng, UK 37/F3
Stevens Point, Wi, US 155/K1
Stevens Village, Ak, US 171/J2
Stevenson (cr.), Austl. 131/G3
Stevenson, Al, US 162/E3
Stevenson, Wa, US 144/D5
Stevenson Entrance (Str.), Ak, US 171/H4
Stevenston, Sc, UK 33/B5
Stevensville, Mi, US 160/C3
Stevensville, Mt, US 145/G4
Stevensville, Md, US 168/B6
Stevinsluizen (dam), Neth. 52/C3
Stewardson, Il, US 162/C1
Stewart (mt.), Ab, Can. 144/F1
Stewart, BC, Can. 171/N4
Stewart (riv.), Yk, Can. 140/C2
Stewart (isl.), NZ 127/G7
Stewart, Al, US 162/D4
Stewart, Ms, US 162/C4
Stewart Crossing, Yk, Can. 171/L3
Stewart Lake Nat'l Wild. Ref., ND, US 156/C4
Stewart River, Yk, Can. 171/L3
Stewart Valley, Sk, Can. 145/L2
Stewarton, Sc, UK 33/B5
Stewartstown, NI, UK 34/B2
Stewartstown, Pa, US 168/B4
Stewartville, Mn, US 155/H2
Stewiacke, NS, Can. 158/F3
Steyning, Eng, UK 37/F5
Steynrus, SAfr. 124/D2
Steynsburg, SAfr. 124/D3
Steyr (riv.), Aus. 43/H5
Steyr, Aus. 59/H6
Steyregg, Aus. 59/H6
Steytlerville, SAfr. 124/D4
Stia, It. 63/E6
Stiava, It. 62/D6
Stickney (mt.), Wa, US 167/D2
Stiens, Neth. 52/C2
Stigler, Ok, US 153/G3
Stigtomta, Swe. 40/G2
Stikine, BC, Can. 171/M4
Stikine (riv.), BC, Can. 171/M4
Stilbaai, SAfr. 124/C4
Stiles, Wi, US 160/B2
Stiles, Tx, US 151/D2
Stilfontein, SAfr. 124/D2
Stilís, Gre. 75/H3
Still Creek (res.), Pa, US 168/C2
Still Pond, Md, US 168/B5
Stilling, Den. 40/D3
Stillmore, Ga, US 163/F4
Stillwater, Ok, US 153/F2
Stillwater (res.), NY, US 161/J3
Stillwater (riv.), Mt, US 147/J1
Stillwater (range), Nv, US 146/D4
Stillwater, Mn, US 157/Q6
Stillwater (lake), Pa, US 168/C1
Stillwater, Pa, US 168/B1
Stillwater NWR, Nv, US 146/D4
Stilo (cape), It. 48/E3
Stilwell, Ok, US 153/G3
Štimlje, Yugo. 50/E4
Stimpfach, Ger. 58/D4
Stimson (mt.), Mt, US 145/H3
Stinchar (riv.), Sc, UK 34/D1
Stinking Water (cr.), Ne, US 154/D3
Stinnett, Tx, US 152/D3
Štip, FYROM 75/H2
Stiring-Wendel, Fr. 55/F5
Stírka (peak), Czh. 59/G4
Stirling, Austl. 131/G2
Stirling (mt.), Austl. 130/C4
Stirling (nbrhd.), Austl. 131/M9
Stirling (nbrhd.), Austl. 130/K6
Stirling, Ab, Can. 145/H3
Stirling, On, Can. 161/H2
Stirling, Sc, UK 33/C4
Stirling (co.), Sc, UK 33/B4
Stirling Range NP, Austl. 130/C5
Stirone (riv.), It. 62/C3
Stites, Id, US 144/G4
Stjørdal, Nor. 38/D3
Stob a' Choin (peak), Sc, UK 33/B4
Stob Choire Claurigh (peak), Sc, UK 33/B3
Stochov, Czh. 59/G2
Stock (lake), Fr. 55/F6
Stock, Eng, UK 30/E2
Stockach, Ger. 61/F2
Stockbridge, Mi, US 160/D3
Stockbridge, Ma, US 161/K3
Stockbridge, Ga, US 163/M7
Stockbridge, Eng, UK 37/E4
Stockbridge Ind. Res., Wi, US 155/K1
Stockbury, Eng, UK 30/E3
Stockdale, Tx, US 151/F3
Stockerau, Aus. 51/N7
Stockertown, Pa, US 168/C2
Stockett, Mt, US 145/J4
Stockheim, Ger. 58/E2
Stockholm, Sk, Can. 156/C2

Map Section 274 275

Swansea, Austl. 132/D4
Swansea, Wal, UK 36/C3
Swansea (co.), Wal, UK 36/B3
Swansea (bay), Eng, UK 36/C3
Swanson (res.), Ne, US 154/D3
Swanton, Oh, US 160/E4
Swanton, Vt, US 161/K2
Swanville, Mn, US 157/G5
Swart Kei (riv.), SAfr. 124/D3
Swarthmore, Pa, US 168/C4
Swartruggens, SAfr. 123/E5
Swartswood (lake), NJ, US 168/D1
Swartz (cr.), Mi, US 167/E6
Swartz Creek, Mi, US 160/E3
Swarzędz, Pol. 43/J2
Swarzenbach an der Sächsischen Saale, Ger. 59/E2
Swarzrand (mts.), Namb. 124/B2
Swāt (riv.), Pak. 98/B2
Swatara, Mn, US 157/H4
Swatara (cr.), Pa, US 168/B3
Swatragh, NI, UK 34/B2
Swauk (pass), Wa, US 144/D4
Sway, Eng, UK 37/E5
Swayambhunath, Nepal 97/E2
Swaziland (ctry.) 107/F7
Sweden (ctry.) 29/F2
Swedesboro, NJ, US 168/C4
Swedru, Gha. 115/E5
Sweeden, Ky, US 162/D2
Sweeny, Tx, US 150/G3
Sweers (isl.), Austl. 129/E4
Sweet Grass Ind. Res., Sk, Can. 145/K1
Sweet Home, Or, US 146/B1
Sweet Home, Tx, US 151/F3
Sweet Springs, Mo, US 155/H4
Sweet Water, Al, US 164/E1
Sweetwater, Ok, US 152/E3
Sweetwater (lake), ND, US 156/E3
Sweetwater (res.), Ca, US 166/D5
Sweetwater (riv.), Wy, US 147/J2
Sweetwater, Tn, US 162/E3
Sweetwater, Fl, US 164/P11
Sweetwater, Tx, US 151/D1
Swellendam, SAfr. 124/C4
Świdnica, Pol. 43/J3
Świdnik, Pol. 43/M3
Świdwin, Pol. 40/F5
Świebodzice, Pol. 43/J3
Świebozin, Pol. 43/H2
Świecie, Pol. 43/K2
Świętokrzyskie (prov.), Pol. 43/K3
Świętokrzysky NP, Pol. 43/L3
Swift (riv.), BC, Can. 144/C1
Swift Current, Sk, Can. 145/L2
Swifterbant, Neth. 52/C3
Swifton, Ar, US 162/B3
Swiftown, Ms, US 162/B4
Swifts Creek, Austl. 133/C3
Swilly, Lough (inlet), Ire. 31/Q9
Swimming River (res.), NJ, US 168/D3
Swindmish Ind. Res., Wa, US 144/C3
Swindon, Eng, UK 37/E3
Swindon (co.), Eng, UK 37/E3
Swineford, Ire. 32/B2
Swineshead, Eng, UK 35/H6
Świnoujście, Pol. 40/F5
Swinton, Eng, UK 35/G5
Swisshome, Or, US 146/B1
Swist Bach (riv.), Ger. 55/F2
Switzerland (ctry.) 29/E4
Sword Beach, Fr. 57/E2
Swords, Ire. 34/B5
Swoyersville, Pa, US 168/C1
Syābru, Nepal 97/E1
Syamozero (lake), Rus. 68/G3
Syas'stroy, Rus. 41/Q1
Syava, Rus. 69/K4
Sycamore, Ga, US 165/G2
Sycamore, Il, US 155/K3
Sycamore, Al, US 162/D4
Sycan (riv.), Or, US 146/C2
Syców, Pol. 43/J3
Sydney, ND, US 156/E4
Sydney, NS, Can. 159/G2
Sydney, Fl, US 164/L8
Sydney, Austl. 134/H8
Sydney (Manra) (isl.), Kiri. 137/H5
Sydney-Kingsford Smith (int'l arpt.), Austl. 134/H8
Syeverodonets'k, Ukr. 73/K3
Sykäri (lake), Fin. 39/F4
Syke, Ger. 53/F3
Sykeston, ND, US 156/E4
Sykesville, Md, US 168/B5
Sykkylven, Nor. 38/C3
Syktyvkar, Rus. 69/L3
Sylacauga, Al, US 162/D4
Sylarna (peak), Swe. 38/E3
Sylhet (pol. reg.), Bang. 97/H3
Sylhet, Bang. 93/F3
Sylling, Nor. 38/R8
Sylva (riv.), Rus. 69/N4
Sylva, NC, US 163/F3
Sylvan Grove, Ks, US 153/E1
Sylvan Lake, Mi, US 167/F6
Sylvan Lake, Ab, Can. 145/G1
Sylvania, Oh, US 160/E4
Sylvania, Al, US 162/E3
Sylvania, Sk, Can. 145/M1
Sylvania, Ga, US 163/G4
Sylvenstein-Stausee (lake), Ger. 61/H2
Sylvester, Ga, US 165/G2
Sylvester (lake), Austl. 129/E4
Sylvester, Tx, US 151/D1
Sylvia, Ks, US 153/E2
Synel'nykove, Ukr. 73/H3
Synnott (range), Austl. 128/B4
Syntagma, Gre. 75/N8
Synya, Rus. 69/N2
Syosset, NY, US 169/L8
Syowa, Japan, Ant. 192/C
Syracuse, In, US 160/D4
Syracuse, Ks, US 152/D2
Syracuse, Ne, US 155/F3
Syracuse, NY, US 161/H3
Syracuse (Siracusa), It. 48/D4
Syracuse Hancock (int'l arpt.), NY, US 161/H3
Syrdarīya (riv.), Kaz. 77/F5
Syria (ctry.) 77/B6
Syriam, Myan. 93/G4
Syrian (des.), Jor. 100/C2
Syrskiy, Rus. 70/F1
Sysmä, Fin. 41/L1
Sysola (riv.), Rus. 69/L3
Syston, Eng, UK 37/E1
Sytkivtsi, Ukr. 72/E3
Syzran', Rus. 71/J1
Szabolcs-Szatmár-Bereg (co.), Hun. 43/L4
Szamotuły, Pol. 43/J2
Szarvas, Hun. 50/E2
Százhalombatta, Hun. 51/Q10
Szczebrzeszyn, Pol. 43/M3
Szczecin, Pol. 40/F5
Szczecinek, Pol. 40/G5
Szczytna, Pol. 43/J3
Szczytno, Pol. 43/L2
Szeged, Hun. 50/E2
Szeghalom, Hun. 50/E2
Székesfehérvár, Hun. 50/D2
Szekszárd, Hun. 50/D2
Szendro, Hun. 50/E1
Szent László-Vize (riv.), Hun. 51/Q10
Szentendre, Hun. 51/R9
Szentes, Hun. 50/E2
Szentlorinc, Hun. 50/C2
Szerencs, Hun. 43/L4
Szeskie (peak), Pol. 41/K4
Sziget-Szentmiklós, Hun. 51/R10
Szigetvár, Hun. 50/C2
Szirák, Hun. 43/K5
Szolnok, Hun. 50/E2
Szombathely, Hun. 50/C2
Szprotawa, Pol. 43/H3
Sztum, Pol. 41/H5
Szubin, Pol. 43/J2
Szydłowiec, Pol. 43/L3

T

T'aipei (cap.), Tai. 87/J3
Ta Fou San, Laos 94/C1
Ta Khmau, Camb. 94/D4
Ta Phraya, Thai. 94/C3
Ta Seng, Camb. 94/D3
Ta Waewae (bay), NZ 135/A4
Tabaco, Phil. 88/C2
Tabanan, Indo. 89/F5
Tabango, Phil. 88/D3
Tabaquite, Trin. 181/F2
Ţabarqah, Tun. 112/L6
Ţabas, Iran 103/J3
Tabasará (mts.), Pan. 177/F4
Tabasco (state), Mex. 172/C4
Tabatinga, Serra da (mts.), Braz. 186/D1
Tabayama, Japan 83/B2
Tabbs (bay), Tx, US 151/M9
Tabda, Som. 119/C1
Tabelbala, Alg. 110/E3
Tabelbalet (well), Alg. 111/G4
Taber, Ab, Can. 145/H3
Tabernes de Valldigna, Sp. 47/E3
Tabiang, Kiri. 136/F5
Tabibuga, PNG 129/G1
Tabing (int'l arpt.), Indo. 89/C3
Tabio, Col. 183/L8
Tabira, Braz. 183/G4
Tabiteuea (isl.), Kiri. 136/G5
Tabitta, Austl. 133/B2
Tablas (isl.), Phil. 91/F1
Tablas (str.), Phil. 88/C2
Tablas de Daimiel, PN, Sp. 46/D3
Table (mtn.), Ire. 32/D3
Table (mtn.), SAfr. 124/L10
Table (cape), NZ 135/D2
Table (mtn.), Wa, US 144/D4
Table (bay), SAfr. 124/B4
Table Rock (dam), Mo, US 153/H2
Table Rock (lake), Mo, US 153/G2
Tableland Station, Austl. 128/B4
Tabletop (mt.), PNG 129/G1
Tabligbo, Togo 115/F5
Tábor, Czh. 59/H4
Tabor City, NC, US 163/H3
Tabora, Tanz. 121/H4
Tabora, Tanz. 119/B4
Tabora (prov.), Tanz. 119/A3
Tabory, Rus. 69/P4
Tabou, C.d'Iv. 114/D5
Tabrīz, Iran 103/F2
Tabuaeran (Fanning) (isl.), Kiri. 137/K4
Tabubil, PNG 91/K5
Tabūk, SAr. 109/H2
Tabuk, Phil. 88/C1
Tabuleiro do Norte, Braz. 183/G4
Ţaburbah, Tun. 48/A4
Taburno (peak), It. 65/D5
Tabursuq, Tun. 112/L6
Tabuyung, Indo. 89/B2
Tabwemasana (peak), Van. 136/F6
Täby, Swe. 39/B1
Tacabamba, Peru 184/B2
Tacámbaro de Codallos, Mex. 175/E5
Tacaná (vol.), Mex. 176/C3
Tacaratu, Braz. 183/G5
Tacarcuna (mtn.), Pan. 180/B2
Tacheng, China 99/D2
Tachia (riv.), Tai. 87/J3
Tachibana (bay), Japan 84/A4
Tachikawa, Japan 85/F3
Tachinger (lake), Ger. 59/F7
Tachira (state), Ven. 177/H5
Tachoshui, Tai. 87/J3
Tachov, Czh. 59/F3
Tacipi, Indo. 91/F4
Tacloban, Phil. 88/D3
Tacna, Az, US 149/F4
Tacna, Peru 188/B1
Tacna (dept.), Peru 184/D5
Tacobamba, Bol. 188/C1
Tacoma, Wa, US 144/C4
Tacopaya, Bol. 188/C1
Tacora (vol.), Chile 188/B1
Tacotalpa, Mex. 176/C2
Tacuarembó (dept.), Uru. 191/G2
Tacuarembó, Uru. 189/F4
Tacuarembo (dept.), Uru. 189/F5
Tacurong, Phil. 88/D4
Tacutu (riv.), Braz. 181/F4
Tadaoka, Japan 83/H7
Tadcaster, Eng, UK 35/G4
Ta'Delimara (pt.), Malta 48/M7
Tādepallegūdem, India 95/D2
Tadine, NCal. 137/V12
Tadjoura, Djib. 118/B3
Tadley, Eng, UK 37/E4
Tadmur, Syria 102/D3
Tadmur (Palmyra) (ruin), Syria 102/D3
Tadó, Col. 180/B3
Tado, Japan 83/L5
Tadohae Hasang NP, SKor. 81/C5
Tadotsu, Japan 84/C3
Tadoussac, Qu, Can. 158/C1
Tādpatri, India 95/C3
Tadrart (mts.), Alg. ,Libya 108/H4
Taduno, Indo. 91/F4
Tadworth, Eng, UK 30/C3
Tadzewu, Gha. 115/F5
T'aean, SKor. 81/D4
T'aebaek, SKor. 81/E4
T'aebaek (mts.), NKor.,SKor. 79/K4
Taebudo (isl.), SKor. 81/F7
Taech'ŏng (isl.), SKor. 81/C4
Taech'ŏn, SKor. 81/D4
T'aech'ŏn, NKor. 81/C3
Taedŏk, SKor. 81/D5
Taedong (riv.), NKor. 81/D3
Taedong, NKor. 81/C3
Taegang-got (pt.), NKor. 81/D3
Taegu, SKor. 81/E5
Taegu-jikhalsi (prov.), SKor. 84/A3
Taegwan, NKor. 81/C2
Taehŭksan (isl.), SKor. 81/C5
Taehŭng, NKor. 81/D2
Taehwa (isl.), NKor. 81/C3
T'aein, SKor. 81/D5
Taejŏn, SKor. 81/D4
Taejŏn-jikhalsi (prov.), SKor. 81/D4
Taeryŏng (riv.), NKor. 81/C2
T'aet'an, NKor. 81/C3
Tafalla, Sp. 44/C5
Ţafas, Syria 105/E3
Tafassasset, Oued (riv.), Alg. 111/H4
Taff (riv.), Wal, UK 36/C3
Tafí Viejo, Arg. 188/C3
Tafiré, C.d'Iv. 114/D4
Tafraout, Mor. 110/C3
Tafresh, Iran 103/G3
Taft, Iran 103/H4
Taft, Ok, US 153/G3
Taft, Fl, US 164/N7
Taft, Ca, US 148/C3
Taft, Phil. 88/D3
Taft, Tx, US 151/F4
Taftān (mtn.), Iran 101/H3
Taga, Japan 83/K5
Taga Dzong, Bhu. 97/G2
Taganrog, Rus. 73/K4
Tagant (pol. reg.), Mrta. 114/C2
Tagarav (peak), Trkm. 103/J2
Tagawa, Japan 84/B4
Tagbilaran, Phil. 88/C3
Taggia, It. 62/A5
Taghit, Alg. 111/E3
Taghmon, Ire. 32/D5
Tagish, Yk, Can. 171/M3
Tagliacozzo, It. 65/C3
Tagliamento (riv.), It. 45/K3
Taglio di Po, It. 63/F4
Tagolo (pt.), Phil. 88/C3
Tagoloan, Phil. 88/D3
Tagounit, Mor. 110/D3
Taguasco, Cuba 177/G1
Taguatinga, Braz. 186/D2
Taguatinga, Braz. 186/C2
Tagudin, Phil. 88/C1
Taguig, Phil. 88/F6
Tagula (isl.), PNG 136/E6
Tagum, Phil. 88/D4
Tagun (riv.), Rus. 69/P4
Tagus (riv.), Port.,Sp. 66/B3
Tagus (riv.), Sp. 29/D5
Tagus (Tajo) (riv.), Sp. 46/C3
Tagus Rio Tejo (lake), Port. 47/P10
Tahakopa, NZ 135/B4
Tahan (peak), Malay. 89/C1
Tahanea (isl.), FrPol. 137/L6
Tahanroz'ka (gulf), Ukr.,Rus. 70/F3
Tahar-Souk, Mor. 112/B3
Tahara, Japan 83/M6
Tahat (peak), Alg. 111/G5
Tahat, Oued et (riv.), Alg. 112/F5
Tahe, China 79/J1
Tahilt, Mong. 78/D2
Tahir (pass), Turk. 102/E2
Tahiti (isl.), FrPol. 137/L6
Tahkuna (pt.), Est. 41/K2
Tahlequah, Ok, US 153/G3
Tahmoor, Austl. 133/E2
Tahnaout, Mor. 110/D3
Tahoe (lake), Ca,Nv, US 140/D5
Tahoka, Tx, US 152/D4
Taholah, Wa, US 144/B4
Tahoua, Niger 115/G3
Tahoua (dept.), Niger 115/G3
Tahquamenon (falls), Mi, US 160/D1
Taḩtā, Egypt 109/F3
Tahua, Bol. 184/E4
Tahuamanu (riv.), Peru 184/D3
Tahuamanú, Peru 184/D3
Tahuata (isl.), FrPol. 137/L6
Tahulandang (isl.), Indo. 91/G3
Tahuna, Indo. 91/G3
Tahuya (riv.), Wa, US 167/B3
Tahuya, Wa, US 167/A3
Ţahwāy, Egypt 113/B4
Taï, C.d'Iv. 114/D5
Tai (lake), China 79/J5
Tai Long Wan (bay), China 87/M7
Tai Mo Shan (peak), China 87/L7
Tai O, China 87/K8
Tai Po, China 87/L7
Tai Xian, China 80/E4
Taï, PN de, C.d'Iv. 114/D5
Taiama, SLeo. 114/B4
Tai'an, China 81/B2
Tai'an, China 80/D3
Tai'angang, China 80/L8
Taiarapu (pen.), FrPol. 137/X15
Taiaret (well), Mor. 110/B5
Taibai (peak), China 78/F5
Taibus, China 78/H3
Taicang, China 80/L8
T'aichung, Tai. 87/J3
Taiei, Japan 83/E2
Taigu, China 80/C3
Taihang (mts.), China 80/C3
Taihape, NZ 135/C2
Taihe, China 80/C4
Taihsi, Tai. 87/J4
Taihu, China 87/H2
Taikang, China 80/C4
Taiki, Japan 82/C2
Tailai, China 79/J2
Taileleo, Indo. 89/B3
Tailem Bend, Austl. 131/H5
Tailfingen, Ger. 58/B5
Taima, Japan 83/J6
Tain, Sc, UK 33/B1
Tain-L'Hermitage, Fr. 64/A2
T'ainan, Tai. 87/J4
Taínaron (cape), Gre. 75/H4
Taingainony, Madg. 125/H8
Taino, It. 62/B2
Taió, Braz. 189/G3
Taiobeiras, Braz. 187/E2
Taiohae, FrPol. 137/L5
Taiping, China 94/D1
Taiping, Malay. 89/C1
Taiping, China 87/F4
Taiping, China 87/H2
Taiping, China 87/G1
Taiping (peak), China 79/J2
Taipinggou, China 79/L2
Taipingshao, China 81/C2
Taipu, Braz. 183/H4
Tais, Indo. 89/C4
Taisha, Japan 84/C3
Taishan, China 87/G4
Taishi, Japan 83/J6
Taishun, China 87/H3
Taiskirchen im Innkreis, Aus. 59/G6
Taissy, Fr. 55/D5
Taitao (pen.), Chile 179/B7
Taiti (peak), Kenya 119/A1
T'aitung, Tai. 87/J4
Taiwan (ctry.) 87/J3
Taiwan (str.), China,Tai 87/H3
Taixing, China 80/E4
Taíyetos (mts.), Gre. 75/H4
Taiyuan, China 80/C3
Taizhao, China 86/B2
Taizhou, China 80/D4
Taizi (riv.), China 80/F2
Ta'izz, Yem. 118/C2
Tāj Mahal, India 96/B2
Tajarhī, Libya 134/B3
Tajikistan (ctry.) 77/G6
Tajima, Japan 85/F2
Tajimi, Japan 83/M5
Tajique, NM, US 149/J3
Tajiri, Japan 83/H7
Tājirwīn, Tun. 112/L7
Tajo (Tagus) (riv.), Sp. 46/C3
Tājpur, India 96/B1
Tajrīsh, Iran 103/G3
Tajumulco (vol.), Guat. 176/D3
Tajuña (riv.), Sp. 46/D2
Tājūrā, Libya 67/G4
Tak, Thai. 94/B2
Takāb, Iran 103/F2
Takahagi, Japan 85/G2
Takahama, Japan 83/J5
Takahama, Japan 83/L6
Takahashi (riv.), Japan 84/C3
Takahashi, Japan 84/C3
Takahata, Japan 85/G1
Takaishi, Japan 83/H6
Takajärvi (lake), Fin. 39/E3
Takaka, NZ 135/C3
Takama, Guy. 182/B1
Takamatsu, Japan 84/D3
Takami-yama (peak), Japan 83/K7
Takanabe, Japan 84/B4
Takane, Japan 83/A2
Takanosu, Japan 82/B3
Takanosu-yama (peak), Japan 83/C2
Takaoka, Japan 85/E2
Takapau, NZ 135/D3
Takapuna, NZ 135/F6
Takarazuka, Japan 83/H6
Takaroa (isl.), FrPol. 137/L6
Takasaki, Japan 85/F2
Takashima, Japan 83/K5
Takatomi, Japan 83/L5
Takatori, Japan 83/J7
Takatsuki, Japan 83/K5
Takatsuki, Japan 83/J6
Takaungu, Kenya 119/B2
Takayama, Japan 85/E2
Takefu, Japan 84/E3
Takehara, Japan 84/C3
Tākestān, Iran 103/G2
Taketa, Japan 84/B4
Taketoyo, Japan 83/L6
Takev, Camb. 94/D4
Takh, India 98/D3
Takhatgarh, India 92/B2
Takhatpur, India 96/C4
Takhli, Thai. 94/C3
Takht-i-Bhāi, Pak. 98/A2
Takhta, Rus. 73/M5
Takhta-Bazar, Trkm. 74/G6
Takhtamygda, Rus. 79/J1
Taki, Japan 83/L7
Takiéta, Niger 115/H3
Takijuq (lake), Nun, Can. 140/E2
Takikawa, Japan 82/B2
Takingeun, Indo. 89/B1
Takino, Japan 83/G6
Takla Makan (des.), China 77/H6
Tāknis, Libya 67/J4
Tako, Japan 83/E2
Takoradi, Gha. 115/E5
Takouch (cape), Alg. 112/K6
Takoukout, Niger 115/H3
Taksimo, Rus. 75/M4
Taksony, Hun. 51/R10
Takum, Nga. 115/H5
Takundi, D.R. Congo 120/D4
Tala, Kenya 119/B2
Talā, Egypt 113/B3
Tala, Uru. 191/L11
Tala, Mex. 174/E4
Tala Mugongo, Ang. 120/D5
Talacasto, Arg. 188/B4
Talacre, Wal, UK 35/E5
Talagang, Pak. 98/B3
Talagante, Chile 190/N8
Tālah, Tun. 112/L7
Talaimannar, SrL. 95/C4
Talāja, India 101/K4
Talak (phys. reg.), Niger 115/G2
Talala, Ok, US 153/G2
Talalayivka, Ukr. 73/G2
Talamanca (mts.), CR 177/F4
Talamba, Pak. 98/B4
Talamona, It. 61/F5
Talang (peak), Indo. 89/C3
Talanga, Hon. 176/E3
Talangbatu, Indo. 89/D4
Talangbetutu, Indo. 89/D3
Talange, Fr. 55/F5
Talant, Fr. 60/A3
Talara, Peru 184/A2
Talas, Turk. 102/C2
Talas (riv.), Kaz. 99/B3
Talas, Kyr. 99/B3
Talata Ampano, Madg. 125/H8
Talata Mafara, Nga. 115/G3
Talaud (isl.), Phil. 77/M9
Talavera de la Reina, Sp. 46/C3
Talawakele, SrL. 95/D5
Talawdī, Sudan 116/F3
Talawgyi, Myan. 86/C3
Talayuela, Sp. 46/C3
Talbingo (dam), Austl. 133/D2
Talbingo (res.), Austl. 133/D2
Talbingo, Austl. 133/D2
Talbot (mt.), Austl. 130/E3
Talbot, Ab, Can. 145/J1
Talbot (co.), Md, US 168/B6
Talbotton, Ga, US 162/E4
Talca, Chile 190/C2
Talcahuano, Chile 190/B3
Tālcher, India 95/E1
Talcho, Niger 115/F3
Talco, Tx, US 153/G4
Talcott, WV, US 163/G2
Taldan, Rus. 79/J1
Taldykuduk, Kaz. 71/J2
Taldyqorghan, Kaz. 99/C3
Taleex, Som. 118/D3
Talence, Fr. 44/C4
Talent (riv.), Swi. 60/C4
Talent, Or, US 146/B2
Tālesh, Iran 103/G2
Talfer (Talvera) (riv.), It. 61/H4
Talgar, Kaz. 74/H5
Tali Post, Sudan 116/F4
Taliabu (isl.), Indo. 91/F4
Tālibwāla, Pak. 98/B4
Talihina, Ok, US 153/G3
T'alin, Arm. 103/E1
Talinay, PN, Chile 188/B4
Taliouine, Mor. 110/D3
Talipaw, Phil. 88/C4
Talisayan, Indo. 91/E3
Talisayan, Phil. 88/D3
Talitsa, Rus. 69/P4
Taliwang, Indo. 91/E5
Tal'ka, Bela. 41/N5
Talkeetna, Ak, US 171/H3
Ţalkhā, Egypt 113/C2
Tall 'Afar, Iraq 102/E2
Tall al Muqayyar (ruin), Iraq 100/E2
Tall ar Rub' (ruin), Egypt 113/C3
Tall 'Āsūr (peak), WBnk. 105/C5
Tall Kayf, Iraq 103/E2
Tall Kūjik, Syria 102/E2
Tall Rāk, Egypt 113/C3
Tall Timay (ruin), Egypt 113/C3
Talladega, Al, US 162/D4
Tallaght, Ire. 34/B5
Tallahala (cr.), Ms, US 164/D1
Tallahassee (cap.), Fl, US 165/F2
Tallahatchie (riv.), Ms, US 162/B3
Tallangatta, Austl. 133/C3
Tallanstown, Ire. 34/B4
Tallapoosa (riv.), Al, US 162/E4
Tallapoosa, Ga, US 162/E4
Tallard, Fr. 64/C4
Tallassee, Al, US 162/E4
Tallering (peak), Austl. 130/B4
Talleyville, De, US 168/C4
Tallgrass Prairie Nat'l Prsv., Ks, US 155/F4
Tallinn (cap.), Est. 41/L2
Tallmadge, Oh, US 160/F4
Tallman Mountain State Park, NY, US 169/K7
Talloires, Fr. 60/C6
Tallow, Ire. 32/B5
Tallowa (dam), Austl. 133/E2
Talmage, Ut, US 147/H3
Talmassons, It. 63/G2
Talmoon, Mn, US 157/H4
Tal'ne, Ukr. 72/F3
Talo (peak), Eth. 116/H3
Taloda, India 95/B1
Taloga, Ok, US 152/E2
Tāloqān, Afg. 101/J1
Talovaya, Rus. 73/L2
Talpa, Tx, US 150/E2
Talpa de Allende, Mex. 174/D4
Talshand, Mong. 78/D2
Talsi, Lat. 41/K3
Talsperre Pöhl (res.), Ger. 59/F1
Taltal, Chile 188/B3
Taltson (riv.), NW, Can. 140/E2
Talty, Tx, US 150/L7
Taluk, Indo. 89/C3
Talukbayur, Indo. 91/E3
Talumphuk (pt.), Thai. 94/C4
Talut (pt.), Fr. 56/B5
Talvera (Talfer) (riv.), It. 61/H4
Talwandi Bhāi, India 98/C4
Talwandi Sābo, India 98/C5
Talwāra, India 98/C4
Taly, Rus. 73/L3
Ţalyā, Egypt 113/C4
Tam Ky, Viet. 94/E3
Tam Le, Viet. 94/D2
Tam Quan, Viet. 94/E3
Tama (riv.), Japan 83/D2
Tama, Japan 83/C2
Tama Abu (range), Malay. 88/A5
Tamagawa, Japan 83/C2
Tamaha, Ok, US 153/G3
Tamaho, Japan 83/B2
Tamaki (str.), NZ 135/F6
Tamaki, Japan 83/L7
Tamalameque, Col. 180/C2
Ţamalāy, Egypt 113/B3
Tamale, Gha. 115/E4
Tamamura, Japan 83/C1
Taman', Rus. 73/J5
Taman (bay), Rus. 73/J5
Taman, Indo. 90/D5
Taman Negara NP, Malay. 89/C1
Taman-Rasset, Oued (riv.), Alg. 111/F5
Tamaná (peak), Col. 180/B3
Tamana (isl.), Kiri. 136/G5
Tamanaco (riv.), Ven. 183/P8
Tamanar, Mor. 110/C3
Tamanghasset (pol. reg.), Alg. 115/F1
Tamanghasset, Oued (riv.), Alg. 111/F5
Tamanhint, Libya 134/B3
Tamanrasset, Alg. 111/G5
Tamanrasset (wilaya), Alg. 111/F4
Tamanthi, Myan. 86/B3
Tamaqua, Pa, US 168/C2
Tamar (riv.), Eng, UK 36/B5
Tamara (isl.), Japan 85/H8
Tamarac, Fl, US 164/P10
Tamarack, Mn, US 157/H4
Tamarak NWR, Mn, US 157/G4
Tamari, Japan 83/E1
Tamarike, Indo. 129/F2
Tamarindo Nat'l Wild. Ref., CR 176/E4
Tamarite de Litera, Sp. 47/F2
Tamaro (peak), Swi. 61/E5
Tamási, Hun. 50/D2
Tamassoumît, Mrta. 114/B2
Tamatama, Ven. 181/E4
Tamatsukuri, Japan 83/E1
Tamaulipas (state), Mex. 172/B3
Tamazula de Gordiano, Mex. 174/E5
Tamazunchale, Mex. 176/B1
Tamba, Japan 83/H5
Tamba (uplands), Japan 83/H5
Tambach, Kenya 119/A1
Tambacounda (pol. reg.), Sen. 114/B3
Tambacounda, Sen. 114/B3
Tambakara, Mali 114/C3
Tambaoura, Falaise de (cliff), Mali 114/C3
Tambar Springs, Austl. 132/D1
Tambara, Moz. 123/G3
Tambawel, Nga. 115/G3
Tambea, Indo. 91/F4
Tambelan (isls.), Indo. 90/C3
Tambellup, Austl. 130/C5
Tambey, Rus. 74/H2
Tambisan, Malay. 88/B4
Tambo (peak), Swi. 61/F5
Tambo, Austl. 134/B4
Tambo (riv.), Peru 184/C3
Tambo (riv.), Austl. 133/C3
Tambo Colorado (ruin), Peru 184/C4
Tambo de Mora, Peru 184/B4
Tambo Grande, Peru 184/A2
Tambobamba, Peru 184/C4
Tambohorano, Madg. 125/G7
Tambopata (riv.), Peru 184/D4
Tambora (peak), Indo. 91/E5
Tambores, Uru. 189/E4
Tamboril, Braz. 183/F4
Tamboritha (mt.), Austl. 133/C3
Tambov, Rus. 71/G1
Tambovskaya Oblast, Rus. 71/G1
Tambre (riv.), Sp. 46/A1
Tambu, Indo. 91/E4
Tambul, PNG 129/F1
Tambunan, Malay. 88/B4
Tambura, Sudan 117/E4
Tamchaket, Mrta. 114/C2
Tame, Col. 180/D3
Tame (riv.), Eng, UK 37/E1
Tameside (co.), Eng, UK 35/F5
Tâmega (riv.), Port. 46/B2
Tamel Aike, Arg. 191/C6
Tamentit, Alg. 111/E4
Támesis, Col. 183/K7
Tamgak (peak), Niger 115/H2
Tamghas, Nepal 96/D1
Tamiahua, Mex. 176/B1
Tamiahua (lag.), Mex. 176/B1
Tamiami (canal), Fl, US 165/H5
Tamiami, Fl, US 164/P11
Tamiang (pt.), Indo. 89/B1
Tamil Nādu (state), India 92/C5
Taminango, Col. 180/B4
Tamines, Belg. 55/D3
Ţāmiyah, Egypt 113/B6
Tamkuhi, India 97/E2
Tamlūk, India 97/F4
Tāmma, India 86/B3
Tammany (mt.), NJ, US 168/C2
Tammaro (riv.), It. 65/D5
Tammela, Fin. 41/K1
Tammisaari (Ekenäs), Fin. 41/K2
Ţammūn, WBnk. 105/C4
Tamo, Ar, US 153/J3
Tampa, Ks, US 153/F1
Tampa, Fl, US 164/L8
Tampa (bay), Fl, US 164/K8
Tampa (int'l arpt.), Fl, US 164/K8
Tampalakamam, SrL. 95/D4
Tampang, Indo. 89/D4
Tampere, Fin. 41/K1
Tampere-Pirkkala (int'l arpt.), Fin. 41/K1
Tampico, Mex. 176/B1
Tampin, Malay. 89/C2
Tampines (nbrhd.), Sing. 89/J6
Tampoc (riv.), FrG. 181/H4
Tampon Ambohitra (peak), Madg. 125/J6
Tampulonanjing (peak), Indo. 89/B2
Tamra, Isr. 105/C3
Tamrah, SAr. 100/E4
Tamsalu, Est. 41/M2
Tamshiyacu, Peru 184/C2
Tamuín, Mex. 176/B1
Tamuín (riv.), Mex. 176/B1
Tāmulpur, India 97/H2
Tamur (riv.), Nepal 97/F2
Tamworth, Austl. 132/D1
Tamworth, Eng, UK 37/E1
Tamyang, SKor. 81/D5
Tan (riv.), China 93/K3
Tan An, Viet. 94/D4
Tan-Tan, Mor. 110/C3
Tana (riv.), Fin. 74/C3
Tana (riv.), Nor. 38/H1
Tana, Nor. 38/J1
Tana (lake), Eth. 107/F3
Tana (riv.), Kenya 107/G5
Tana River Primate Nat'l Rsv., Kenya 119/C2
Tanabe, Japan 84/D4
Tanabe, Japan 83/J6
Tanabi, Braz. 189/G2
Tanacross, Ak, US 171/K3
Tanafjorden (estu.), Nor. 38/J1
Tanaga (isl.), Ak, US 171/C6
Tanaga (mt.), Ak, US 171/C6
Tanagura, Japan 85/G2
Tanahbala (isl.), Indo. 90/A4
Tanahmasa (isl.), Indo. 89/B3
Tanahmerah, Indo. 129/F1
Tanahputih, Indo. 89/C2
Tanakpur, India 96/C1
Tanambe, Madg. 125/J7
Tanami, Austl. 128/C4
Tanami (des.), Austl. 127/C2
Tanami Desert Wildlife Sanctuary, Austl. 128/C5
Tanana, Ak, US 171/H2
Tanana (riv.), Ak, US 171/J3
Tanandava, Madg. 125/G8
Tanangozi, Tanz. 119/A3
Tanaro (riv.), It. 45/G4
Tancacha, Arg. 188/D5
Tancarville, Fr. 57/F2
Tancheng, China 80/D4
Tanch'ŏn, NKor. 81/E2
Tancítaro, Pico de (peak), Mex. 174/E5
Tancitaro, PN de, Mex. 172/A4
Tandā, India 96/D2
Tanda, C.d'Iv. 114/E5
Tanda (lake), Mali 114/D3
Tānda, India 96/B1
Tandag, Phil. 88/D3
Tandaltī, Sudan 116/F2
Ţăndărei, Rom. 51/H3
Tāndi, India 98/D3
Tandian, China 81/C2
Tandil, Arg. 190/F3
Tandjilé (pref.), Chad 116/C3
Tandjoaré, Togo 115/F4
Tāndliānwāla, Pak. 98/B4
Tando Ādam, Pak. 101/J3
Tando Allāhyār, Pak. 101/J3
Tando Muhammad Khān, Pak. 101/J3
Tandou (lake), Austl. 127/D4
Tandragee, NI, UK 34/B3
Tandrano, Madg. 125/H8
Taneatua, NZ 135/D2
Tanega (isl.), Japan 79/L5
Tanem (range), Myan.,Thai. 93/G4
Taneytown, Md, US 161/H5
Taneyville, Mo, US 153/H2
Tanezrouft (des.), Alg. 107/B2
Tanezrouft-n-Ahenet (des), Alg. 111/F5
Tang (riv.), China 80/C4
Tanga (prov.), Tanz. 119/B3
Tanga, Tanz. 119/B3
Tangail, Bang. 97/G3
Tangail (pol. reg.), Bang. 97/G3
Tangalī, Iran 103/H2
Tangali, Gui. 114/C4
Tangang, China 87/G2
Tanganyika (lake), D.R. Congo 107/F5
Tangará da Serra, Braz. 185/G4
Tangdan, China 86/D3
Tangent (pt.), Ak, US 171/G1
Tanger, Mor. 112/B2
Tanger (prov.), Mor. 112/A2
Tangerang, Indo. 89/D4
Tangerhütte, Ger. 42/F2
Tangerine, Fl, US 164/M6
Tangermünde, Ger. 42/F2
Tangfang, China 80/J7
Tanggula (pass), China 99/F5
Tanggula (mts.), China 99/E5
Tanghe, China 80/C4
Tangi, Pak. 98/A2
Tangier, Va, US 163/K2
Tangier (sound), Md, US 163/J1
Tangier (Boukhalf) (int'l arpt.), Mor. 112/B2
Tangipahoa (riv.), Ms, US 164/C2
Tangipahoa, La, US 164/C2
Tangjin, SKor. 81/D4
Tangkak, Malay. 89/C2
Tanglewilde-Thompson Place, Wa, US 167/B3
Tangmai, China 86/B2
Tango, Ang. 120/C5
Tangqi, China 80/L9
Tangra (lake), China 99/E5
Tangshan, China 80/J7
Tangtou, China 87/F3
Tangub, Phil. 88/C3
Tanguiéta, Ben. 115/F4
Tangwan, China 87/F3
Tangxi, China 87/H2
Tangyan (riv.), China 87/F2
Tangyin, China 80/C4
Tangyuan, China 79/K2
Tanhaçu, Braz. 187/E2
Taniantaweng (mts.), China 86/C2
Tanigumi, Japan 83/L4
Tanimbar (isl.), Indo. 77/N10
Taninges, Fr. 60/C5
Tanintharyi (state), Myan. 93/G5
Tanis (ruin), Egypt 113/C3
Taniwel, Indo. 91/G4
Tanjay, Phil. 88/C3
Tanjiachang, China 87/F2
Tanjong Malim, Malay. 89/C2
Tanjung, Indo. 90/E4
Tanjung Sedano (pt.), Indo. 89/F4
Tanjungbalai, Indo. 89/B2
Tanjungbatu, Indo. 89/C2
Tanjungenim, Indo. 89/C3
Tanjungkarang-Telukbetung, Indo. 89/D4
Tanjungpandan, Indo. 90/C4
Tanjungpinang, Indo. 89/D2
Tanjungpura, Indo. 89/B2
Tanjunguban, Indo. 89/D2
Tānk, Pak. 98/A3
Tankersley, Tx, US 151/D2
Tankwa Karoo NP, SAfr. 124/B4
Tann, Ger. 59/F6
Tanna (isl.), Van. 136/F6
Tanna, Ger. 59/E1
Tannan, Japan 83/H5
Tannersville, Pa, US 168/C1
Tannheim, Aus. 61/G3
Tannu-Ola (mts.), Rus. 78/C1
Tano (riv.), Gha. 115/E5
Tânout, Niger 115/H3
Tanqiu, China 87/G3
Tanque Verde, Az, US 149/G4
Tanquián de Escobedo, Mex. 176/B1
Tansen, Nepal 96/D2
Tānsing, Nepal 96/D2
Ţanţā, Egypt 113/B3
Tantabin, Myan. 86/C5
Tantallon, Sk, Can. 156/D2
Tantallon, Md, US 168/A6
Tantangara (dam), Austl. 133/D2
Tantō, Japan 83/G5
Tantou, China 87/H2
Tantoyuca, Mex. 176/B1
Tantu, China 79/J2
Tanuku, India 95/D2
Tanumshede, Swe. 40/D2
Tanunda, Austl. 132/A2
Tanxu, China 94/E1
Tanyang, SKor. 81/E4
Tanza, Phil. 88/E7
Tanzania (ctry.) 107/F5
Tanzawa-yama (peak), Japan 83/C3
Tanzishan, China 87/G3
Tao (isl.), Myan. 94/B4
Tao (riv.), China 78/E5
Taochuan, China 87/F3
Tao'er (riv.), China 79/J2
Taolañaro, Madg. 125/H9
Taole, China 78/F4
Taolin, China 87/G3
Taonan, China 79/J2
Taormina, It. 48/D4
Tāoru, India 98/D5
Taos, NM, US 152/B2
Taos, Mo, US 153/H1
Taoudenni, Mali 110/E5
Taounate, Mor. 112/B2
Taounate (town), Mor. 112/B2
Taourirt, Alg. 111/F4
Taourirt, Mor. 112/C2
Taoxi, China 87/H2
Taoyuan, China 93/K2
T'aoyüan, Tai. 87/J3
Tap Mun Chau (isl.), China 87/M7
Tap O'Noth (hill), Sc, UK 33/D2
Tapa, Est. 41/L2
Tapacarí, Bol. 188/C1
Tapachula, Mex. 176/C3
Tapah, Malay. 89/C1
Tapajós (riv.), Braz. 179/D3
Tapajós (Amazônia), PN de, Braz. 185/G2
Tapaktuan, Indo. 89/B2
Tapan, Indo. 89/C3
Tapanahoni (riv.), Sur. 181/H4
Tapanti Nat'l Wild. Ref., CR 177/F4
Tapanui, NZ 135/B4
Tapará, Serra da (mts.), Braz. 182/C3
Tapauá (riv.), Braz. 185/E2
Tapauá, Braz. 185/E2
Tapaz, Phil. 88/C3
Tapenagá (riv.), Arg. 188/E3
Taperoá, Braz. 183/G4
Tapeta, Libr. 114/C5
Taphan Hin, Thai. 94/C2
Tapi Aike, Arg. 191/C6
Tapia de Casariego, Sp. 46/B1
Tapiche (riv.), Peru 184/C2
Tapili, D.R. Congo 121/F2
Tapilula, Mex. 176/C2
Taping (riv.), Myan. 86/C3
Tapini, PNG 129/G2
Tapis (peak), Malay. 89/C1
Tāplejun, Nepal 97/F2
Tapo, Peru 184/C3
Tapoa (prov.), Burk. 115/F3
Tapolca, Hun. 50/C2
Tappahannock, Va, US 163/J2
Tappan (lake), Oh, US 160/F4
Tappan, NY, US 169/K7
Tappan Zee (riv.), NY, US 169/K7
Tappan Zee (lake), NY, US 169/E1
Tappanahoni (riv.), Sur. 182/C2
Tappen, ND, US 156/E4
Tappi-zaki (pt.), Japan 82/B3
Tappino (riv.), It. 65/D4
Tapps (lake), Wa, US 167/C3
Tāpti (riv.), India 92/B3
Tapul Group (isls.), Phil. 88/C4
Tapun, India 86/C3
Taqab, Sudan 109/F5
Taqātu' Hayyā, Sudan 100/C5
Taqian, China 87/H2
Taquari, Braz. 189/G4
Taquari (riv.), Braz. 186/A3
Taquari (riv.), Braz. 189/F1
Taquaritinga, Braz. 189/G2
Taquarituba, Braz. 189/G2
Taquaruçu (res.), Braz. 186/B4
Taquil, Ecu. 184/B1
Tar (riv.), Ire. 32/B5
Tar (riv.), Kyr. 99/B3
Tar (riv.), NC, US 163/J3
Tara, Rus. 74/H4
Tara (riv.), Yugo. 50/D4
Tara, Zam. 123/E3
Tara, Austl. 134/C4
Taraba (state), Nga. 115/H5
Taraba (riv.), Nga. 115/H4
Tarabuco, Bol. 188/C1
Ţarābulus, Leb. 104/D2
Ţarābulus (Tripoli) (cap.), Libya 67/G4
Taraclia, Mol. 51/J3
Taradale, NZ 135/D2
Tarairí, Bol. 188/D2
Tarakan (int'l arpt.), Indo. 91/E3
Tarakan, Indo. 91/E3
Tarakit (peak), Kenya 119/A1
Taraklı, Turk. 51/K5
Tārākot, Nepal 96/D1
Taraku (isl.), Rus. 82/E2
Taralga, Austl. 133/D2
Taramana, Indo. 128/B2
Taranagar, India 98/C5
Tarancón, Sp. 46/D2
Tarangire NP, Tanz. 119/A2
Taranna, Austl. 132/C4
Taranto, It. 75/E2
Taranto (gulf), It. 67/H2
Tarapacá, Col. 180/D5
Tarapacá (pol. reg.), Chile 188/B1
Tarapoa, Ecu. 180/B5
Tarapoto, Peru 184/B2
Tarare, Fr. 44/F4
Tarariras, Uru. 191/K11
Tararua (range), NZ 135/J9
Tarascon, Fr. 64/A5
Tarascon-sur-Ariège, Fr. 44/D5
Tarashcha, Ukr. 72/F3
Tarata, Bol. 188/C1
Tarata, Peru 188/B1
Tarauacá, Braz. 184/D3
Tarauacá (riv.), Braz. 184/D2
Taravai (isl.), FrPol. 137/M7
Tarawa (isl.), Kiri. 136/G4
Tarawa (cap.), Kiri. 136/G4
Tarawera (vol.), NZ 135/D2
Tarazona, Sp. 46/E2
Tarazona, Sp. 46/E3
Tarbagatay (mts.), Kaz. 99/D2
Tarbaj, Kenya 119/C1
Tarbat Ness (pt.), Sc, UK 33/C1
Tarbela (res.), Pak. 98/B2
Tarbela (dam), Pak. 98/B2
Tarbela (res.), India 99/B5
Tarbert, Sc, UK 31/Q8
Tarbert, Ire. 32/A4
Tarbes, Fr. 44/D5
Tarbolton, Sc, UK 33/B5
Tarboro, Ga, US 165/H2
Tarboro, NC, US 163/J3
Tarbûl Abu Khashîrât (peak), Egypt 113/C6
Tarcento, It. 45/K3
Tarcoola, Austl. 131/G4
Tarcutta, Austl. 133/C2
Tardes (riv.), Fr. 44/E3
Tardienta, Sp. 47/E2
Tardoire (riv.), Fr. 44/D4
Tardoki-Jani (peak), Rus. 79/M2
Taree, Austl. 132/E1
Tarf Water (riv.), Sc, UK 34/D2
Ţarfā' (wadi), Egypt 109/F2
Tarfaya, Mor. 110/B4
Target Rock Nat'l Wild. Ref., NY, US 169/M8
Targuist, Mor. 112/B2
Tarhūnah, Libya 67/G4
Tari, PNG 129/F1
Tariana, Col. 180/D4
Tarīf, UAE 100/F4
Tarifa, Sp. 46/C4
Tarifa, Ecu. 184/B1
Tarija (dept.), Bol. 188/C2
Tarija (int'l arpt.), Bol. 188/C2
Tarija, Bol. 188/C2
Tariku (riv.), Indo. 91/J4
Tariku-Taritatu (plain), Indo. 91/J4
Tarim (riv.), China 74/J5
Tarim (basin), China 74/J6
Tarīm, Yem. 118/D1
Tarim Liuchang, China 99/E3
Tarime, Tanz. 119/A2
Tarin (riv.), Afg. 101/J2
Tarin (Torino), It. 45/G4
Taring, Indo. 89/B2
Taritatu (riv.), Indo. 91/J4
Tarkastad, SAfr. 124/D4
Tarkhankut (cape), Ukr. 73/G5
Tarkio, Mo, US 155/G3
Tarkio (cr.), Mo, Ia, US 155/G3
Tarko-Sale, Rus. 74/H3
Tarkwa, Gha. 115/E5
Tarlac, Phil. 88/C2
Tarland, Sc, UK 33/D2
Tarlton Downs, Austl. 131/H2
Tarma, Peru 184/C3
Tarmstedt, Ger. 53/G2
Tarn (riv.), Fr. 67/D2
Tarn Tāran, India 98/C4
Tarna (riv.), Mong. 78/E2
Tarnak (riv.), Afg. 101/J2
Tårnby, Den. 39/J7
Tarnobrzeg, Pol. 43/L3
Tarnogskiy Gorodok, Rus. 69/J3
Tarnów, Pol. 43/L3
Tärnsjö, Swe. 40/G1
Tärnskär (isl.), Swe. 39/B1
Taro (riv.), It. 45/J4
Taro (lake), China 99/D5
Tarō, Japan 82/B4
Taroko NP, Tai. 87/J3
Ţārom, Iran 103/H4
Taroms'ke, Ukr. 73/H3
Taroom, Austl. 134/C4
Tarouca, Port. 46/B2
Taroudannt, Mor. 110/C3
Tarp, Ger. 40/C4
Tarpa, Hun. 50/F1
Tarpon (lake), Fl, US 165/G3
Tarpon Springs, Fl, US 164/K7
Tarporley, Eng, UK 35/F5

Tarqui – Thoiry

Tarqui, Peru 180/C5
Tarquinia, It. 48/B1
Tarqūmiyah, WBnk. 105/C5
Tarrafal, CpV. 107/K10
Tarragona, Sp. 47/F2
Tarraleah, Austl. 132/C4
Tarrant, Al, US 162/D4
Tarrant (co.), Tx, US 150/K7
Tàrrega, Sp. 47/F2
Tarrenz, Aus. 61/G3
Tarryall (mts.), Co, US 152/B1
Tarrytown, Fl, US 164/L6
Tarrytown, NY, US 169/K7
Tarshīhā, Isr. 105/C2
Tarsus, Turk. 104/D1
Tarsus (riv.), Turk. 104/D1
Tartagal, Arg. 188/E4
Tartagal, Arg. 188/D2
Tärtär, Azer. 103/F1
Tartaro (riv.), It. 63/E2
Tartas, Fr. 44/C5
Tartu, Est. 41/M2
Ţarţūs, Syria 104/D2
Ţarţus (dist.), Syria 104/D2
Tarui, Japan 83/L5
Tarumizu, Japan 84/B5
Tarusa, Rus. 68/H5
Ţārūţ, Egypt 113/C3
Tarutao NP, Thai. 94/B5
Tarutung, Indo. 89/B2
Tarutyne, Ukr. 51/J2
Tarvagatay (mts.), Mong. 78/D2
Tarvin, Eng, UK 35/F5
Tarzan, Tx, US 151/D1
Tarzana (nbrhd.), Ca, US 166/E7
Taşağıl, Turk. 104/B1
Tasawāh, Libya 134/B3
Täsch, Swi. 60/D5
Taşçı, Turk. 102/C2
Taseko (mtn.), BC, Can. 144/C2
Taseko (riv.), BC, Can. 144/C2
Tash-Kömür, Kyr. 99/B3
Tashanta, Rus. 99/E2
Tashi Gang, Bhu. 97/H2
Ţashk (lake), Iran 103/H4
Tashkent (cap.), Uzb. 99/A3
Tashkent (int'l arpt.), Uzb. 99/A3
Tashkepri, Trkm. 101/H1
Tashtagol, Rus. 99/E1
Tasikmalaya, Indo. 89/E4
Taşkent, Turk. 102/C2
Taşköprü, Turk. 70/E4
Taşlıçay, Turk. 103/E2
Tasman (bay), NZ 127/H7
Tasman (cape), Austl. 132/C4
Tasman (pt.), Austl. 129/E3
Tasman (pen.), Austl. 127/D5
Tasman (sea) 136/E8
Tasman NP, NZ 135/C3
Tasmania (state), Austl. 127/D5
Tăşnad, Rom. 50/F2
Taşova, Turk. 70/F4
Tasquillo, Mex. 175/K6
Tassara, Niger 115/G2
Tassili Oua-n Ahaggar (mts.), Alg. 111/G5
Tassili-n-Ajjer (mts.), Alg. 111/G4
Tastrup, Den. 39/J7
Tastuba, Rus. 69/N5
Taşucu, Turk. 104/C1
Tasu, BC, Can. 171/M5
Tasudi, Myan. 94/B2
Tata, Mor. 110/D3
Tata, Hun. 50/D2
Tata, D.R. Congo 116/F5
Tata Mailau (peak), ETim. 128/B2
Tataba, Indo. 91/F4
Tatabánya, Hun. 50/D2
Tatakoto (isl.), FrPol. 137/L6
Tatalin (riv.), China 78/D4
Tatamy, Pa, US 168/C2
Tatar (str.), Rus. 77/P5
Tatarbunary, Ukr. 51/J3
Tatarlar, Turk. 51/H5
Tatarsk, Rus. 74/H4
Tatarstan, Resp., Rus. 74/E4
Tatau, Malay. 90/D3
Tataurovo, Rus. 69/L4
Tatāwīn (gov.), Tun. 111/H2
Tatāwīn, Tun. 66/F4
Tate, Ga, US 162/E3
Tate-yama (peak), Japan 85/E2
Tatebayashi, Japan 83/D1
Tatéma, Gui. 114/B4
Tateshina, Japan 83/A1
Tateville, Ky, US 162/E2
Tateyama, Japan 85/F3
Tathlina (lake), NW, Can. 140/E2
Tathlīth, SAr. 100/D5
Tathra, Austl. 133/D3
Tatilt (well), Mrta. 114/B2
Tatitlek, Ak, US 171/J3
Tatkon, Myan. 94/B1
Tatlayoko Lake, BC, Can. 144/B2
Tatlikbulak, China 99/E4
Tatnam (cape), Mb, Can. 140/G3
Tatomi, Japan 83/B2
Tatranský NP, Slvk. 43/K4
Tatsfield, Eng, UK 30/D3
Tatsinskiy, Rus. 73/L3
Tatsuno, Japan 85/E3
Tatsuta, Japan 83/L5
Tattershall, Eng, UK 35/H5
Tatuí, Braz. 189/H2
Tatum, Tx, US 151/G1
Tatura, Austl. 133/B3
Tatvan, Turk. 102/E2
Tauá, Braz. 183/F4
Taubaté, Braz. 187/L8
Tauber (riv.), Ger. 42/E4
Tauberbischofsheim, Ger. 58/C3
Tauca, Peru 184/B3
Tauchik, Kaz. 71/J3
Taufkirchen, Ger. 59/F6
Taufkirchen an der Pram, Aus. 59/G6
Taufstein (peak), Ger. 58/C1
Tauherenikau (riv.), NZ 135/J9
Taulignan, Fr. 64/A4
Taulihawa, Nepal 96/D2
Taum Sauk (mtn.), Mo, US 162/B2
Taumarunui, NZ 135/C2
Taung, SAfr. 124/D2
Taungdwingyi, Myan. 86/B4
Taunggyi, Myan. 86/C4
Taungthonlon (peak), Myan. 86/B3
Taungup (pass), Myan. 86/B5
Taungup, Myan. 86/B5
Taungzun, Myan. 94/B3
Taunsa, Pak. 98/A4
Taunton, Ma, US 161/L4
Taunton, Eng, UK 36/C4
Taunton, On, Can. 160/V8
Taunus (range), Ger. 58/A2
Taunusstein, Ger. 58/B2
Taupo (lake), NZ 127/H6
Taupo, NZ 135/D2
Tauragė, Lith. 41/K4
Tauranga, NZ 135/D2
Taurion (riv.), Fr. 44/D3
Taurisano, It. 75/F3
Tauroa (pt.), NZ 135/C1
Taurus (mts.), Turk. 102/C2
Tauste, Sp. 46/E2
Tauta, PNG 129/G1
Taute (riv.), Fr. 44/C2
Tautira, FrPol. 137/X15
Tauu (isls.), PNG 136/E5
Tavanbulag, Mong. 78/E2
Tavannes, Swi. 60/D3
Tavänti (lake), Fin. 39/F3
Tavares, Fl, US 164/M6
Tavarnelle, It. 63/E6
Tavarnuzze, It. 63/E6
Tavas, Turk. 102/B2
Tavaux, Fr. 60/B3
Tavazzano, It. 62/C3
Tavda (riv.), Rus. 74/G4
Tavda, Rus. 69/Q4
Tavel, Fr. 64/A4
Taverham, Eng, UK 37/H1
Tavernerio, It. 62/C2
Tavernes, Fr. 64/C5
Taverny, Fr. 30/J4
Taveta, Kenya 119/B2
Taveuni (isl.), Fiji 137/Y18
Taviano, It. 75/F3
Tavin, Mong. 78/F2
Tavira, Port. 46/B4
Tavistock, Eng, UK 36/B5
Tavo (riv.), It. 65/D3
Tavoy (pt.), Myan. 94/B3
Tavoy (Dawei), Myan. 94/B3
Tavrichanka, Rus. 79/L3
Tavşanlı, Turk. 102/B2
Tavy (riv.), Eng, UK 36/B6
Taw (riv.), Eng, UK 36/C5
Tawa, NZ 135/H9
Tawaeli, Indo. 91/E4
Tawakoni (lake), Tx, US 151/F1
Tawaramoto, Japan 83/J6
Tawas City, Mi, US 160/E2
Tawau, Malay. 88/B4
Tawau (int'l arpt.), Malay. 88/B4
Tawe (riv.), Wal, UK 36/C3
Tawern, Ger. 55/F4
Tāwi (riv.), India 98/C3
Tawi, Tanz. 119/B4
Tawi-tawi (isl.), Phil. 88/B4
Tawo, China 87/F2
Ţāwūq, Iraq 103/F3
Tāwurghā', Libya 67/G4
Tāwurghā, Sabkhat (swamp), Libya 67/G4
Tawzar (gov.), Tun. 111/G2
Tawzar, Tun. 66/F4
Taxco, Mex. 175/K8
Taxila, Pak. 98/B3
Taxila (ruin), Pak. 98/B3
Taxkorgan Tajik Zizhixian, China 99/C4
Tay (riv.), Sc, UK 33/C3
Tay (lake), Sc, UK 33/B3
Tay Ninh, Viet. 94/D4
Tayabamba, Peru 184/B3
Tayandu (isls.), Indo. 128/C1
Taybola, Rus. 68/G1
Tayeegle, Som. 118/C4
Taylor, Ar, US 153/H4
Taylor, Pa, US 161/J4
Taylor, Al, US 165/F2
Taylor, Mi, US 167/F7
Taylor (riv.), Co, US 147/K4
Taylor, Az, US 149/G3
Taylor (mt.), NM, US 149/J3
Taylor, Ne, US 154/E3
Taylor, Tx, US 151/F2
Taylor Town, Tx, US 153/G4
Taylors, SC, US 163/F3
Taylorsville, Ms, US 164/D2
Taylorsville, In, US 160/D5
Taylorsville, Ca, US 146/C3
Taylorsville, Ky, US 162/E1
Taylorsville, NC, US 163/G3
Taylorsville-Bennion, Ut, US 147/H3
Taylortown, La, US 153/H4
Taylorville, Il, US 155/K4
Taymā', SAr. 102/D5
Taymouth, NB, Can. 158/D2
Taymyr (pen.), Rus. 77/H2
Taymyr (isl.), Rus. 75/L2
Taymyr (riv.), Rus. 74/K2
Taymyrskiy Aut. Okrug, Rus. 74/J2
Tayoltita, Mex. 174/D3
Tayport, Sc, UK 33/D4
Tayrona, PN, Col. 180/C2
Tayshet, Rus. 75/K4
Taytay, Phil. 88/B3
Taytay, Phil. 88/F6
Tayu, Indo. 89/E4
Taz (riv.), Rus. 77/H3
Taza (prov.), Mor. 112/C2
Taza, Mor. 112/B2
Tazawako, Japan 82/B4
Tazekka (peak), Mor. 112/B2
Tazenakht, Mor. 110/D3
Tazewell, Va, US 163/G2
Tazewell, Tn, US 163/F2
Tazicheng, China 79/J2
Tāzirbū (oasis), Libya 134/D3
Tazovskiy, Rus. 74/H3
Tazrouk, Alg. 111/G5
Tāzughrān, Tun. 48/B4
Tazumal (ruin), ESal. 176/D3
T'bilisi (cap.), Geo. 71/H4
Tbilisskaya, Rus. 73/L5
Tchamba, Camr. 116/B3
Tchamba, Togo 115/F4
Tchaourou, Ben. 115/F4
Tchetti, Ben. 115/F5
Tchibanga, Gabon 120/B3
Tchikala-Tcholohanga, Ang. 122/C2
Tchin Tabaradene, Niger 115/G3
Tchindjenje, Ang. 122/B2
Tchollíré, Camr. 116/B3
Tchula, Ms, US 162/B4
Tczew, Pol. 41/H4
Te Anau, NZ 135/A4
Te Anu (lake), NZ 135/A4
Te Araroa, NZ 135/D2
Te Aroha, NZ 135/C2
Te Awamutu, NZ 135/C2
Te Kao, NZ 135/C1
Te Karaka, NZ 135/D2
Te Kauwhata, NZ 135/C2
Te Kopuru, NZ 135/C2
Te Kuiti, NZ 135/C2
Te Teko, NZ 135/D2
Tea (riv.), Braz. 181/E5
Teacapán, Mex. 174/D4
Teague, Tx, US 151/F2
Tealby, Eng, UK 35/H5
Teaneck, NJ, US 169/J8
Teano, It. 65/D5
Teapa, Mex. 176/C2
Teapot Dome Nav. Petroleum Rsv., Wy, US 154/A2
Teapot Dome Naval Res., Wy, US 147/K2
Tearce, FYROM 75/G1
Teasdale, Ut, US 149/G1
Tebak (peak), Indo. 89/D4
Teberda, Rus. 71/G4
Tébessa (wilaya), Alg. 111/G2
Tebessa (mts.), Alg. 112/L7
Tébessa, Alg. 112/L7
Tebesselamane (well), Mali 115/F2
Tebicuary (riv.), Par. 188/E3
Tebingtinggi, Indo. 89/C3
Tebingtinggi, Indo. 89/B2
Tebingtinggi (isl.), Indo. 89/C2
Tebtunis (ruin), Egypt 113/B6
Tebulos-Mta (peak), Rus. 71/H4
Tecalitlán, Mex. 174/E5
Tecamac, Mex. 175/R9
Tecamachalco, Mex. 175/M8
Tech (riv.), Fr. 47/G1
Techirghiol, Rom. 51/J3
Tecirli, Turk. 102/D2
Tecka, Arg. 190/C4
Tecka (riv.), Arg. 190/C4
Teckla, Wy, US 154/B2
Tecklenberg, Ger. 53/E4
Teckomatorp, Swe. 39/K7
Tecolutla, Mex. 175/M6
Tecomán, Mex. 174/E5
Tecopa, Ca, US 148/D3
Tecozautla, Mex. 175/K6
Tecpan de Galeana, Mex. 175/E5
Tecuala, Mex. 174/D4
Tecuci, Rom. 51/H3
Tecumseh, Ok, US 153/F3
Tecumseh, Mi, US 160/E3
Tecumseh, On, Can. 167/G7
Tecumseh, Ne, US 155/F3
Ted Ceidaar Dabole, Som. 118/B4
Tedjert (well), Alg. 111/H1
Tedodita Sakan, Myan. 86/C5
Tedzhen (riv.), Trkm. 74/G6
Tees (bay), Eng, Uk 35/G2
Tees (riv.), Eng, UK 35/G3
Teesside (int'l arpt.), Eng, UK 35/G3
Tefé (riv.), Braz. 185/E2
Tefé, Braz. 185/E1
Tefé (int'l arpt.), Braz. 185/E1
Tefé (lake), Braz. 185/E1
Teferič, Yugo. 50/E4
Tega (lake), Japan 83/E2
Tega Cay, SC, US 163/G3
Tegal, Indo. 89/E4
Tegel (int'l arpt.), Ger. 42/Q6
Tegelen, Neth. 52/D6
Tegeler (lake), Ger. 42/Q6
Tegheri (well), Libya 111/H4
Teghra, India 97/E3
Tegina, Nga. 115/G4
Tegineneng, Indo. 89/D4
Teglio, It. 61/G5
Tégouma (riv.), Niger 115/H3
Tegouma (riv.), Niger 116/A2
Tegsh, Mong. 78/D2
Tegualda, Chile 190/B4
Tegucigalpa (cap.), Hon. 176/E3
Tehachapi, Ca, US 148/C3
Tehachapi (mts.), Ca, US 148/C3
Tehamiyam, Sudan 100/C5
Tehek (lake), Nun, Can. 140/G2
Tehoru, Indo. 91/G4
Tehrān (cap.), Iran 103/G3
Tehrān (gov.), Iran 103/G2
Tehri, India 99/C5
Tehuacán, Mex. 175/M8
Tehuacana, Tx, US 151/F2
Tehuantepec (riv.), Mex. 176/C2
Tehuantepec (gulf), Mex. 139/H8
Tehuantepec (isth.), Mex. 175/G5
Teide, Pico de (peak), Sp. 110/A3
Teifi (riv.), Wal, UK 36/B2
Teifiside (valley), Wal, UK 36/B2
Teiga (plat.), Sudan 117/E2
Teign (riv.), Eng, UK 36/C5
Teignmouth, Eng, UK 36/C5
Teignousse (str.), Fr. 56/B6
Teisendorf, Ger. 59/F7
Teith (riv.), Sc, UK 33/B4
Teixeira Pinto, GBis. 114/A3
Tejakula, Indo. 89/F5
Tejen, Trkm. 101/H1
Tejn, Den. 40/F4
Tejupilco de Hidalgo, Mex. 175/E5
Tekamah, Ne, US 155/F3
Tékane, Mrta. 114/B2
Tekapo (lake), NZ 135/B3
Tekāri, India 97/E3
Tekax de Álvaro Obregón, Mex. 176/D1
Teke, Turk. 51/J5
Tekeli, Kaz. 99/C3
Tekes (riv.), China 74/J5
Tekezē Wenz (riv.), Eth. 100/C6
Tekiliktag (peak), China 99/D4
Tekirdağ (prov.), Turk. 51/H5
Tekirdağ, Turk. 51/H5
Tekit, Mex. 176/D1
Tekkali, India 95/E2
Tekke, Turk. 102/D1
Tekkeköy, Turk. 70/F4
Tekman, Turk. 102/E2
Tekoa, Wa, US 144/F4
Teksneslia, Nor. 38/S9
Teku, Indo. 91/F4
Tel 'Akko (ruin), Isr. 105/C3
Tel Aviv (dist.), Isr. 104/D3
Tel Aviv-Yafo, Isr. 105/B4
Tel Hazor NP, Isr. 105/D2
Tel Megiddo (ruin), Isr. 105/C3
Tela, Hon. 176/E3
Télagh, Alg. 112/D2
Télataï, Mali 115/F2
T'elavi, Geo. 71/H4
Telde, Sp. 110/B3
Télé (lake), Mali 114/D2
Telefomin, PNG 91/K5
Telegraph, Tx, US 151/E2
Telegraph Creek, BC, Can. 171/M4
Telekhany, Bela. 70/C1
Telêmaco Borba, Braz. 189/G3
Telemark (co.), Nor. 38/D4
Telen (riv.), Indo. 91/E3
Teleorman (prov.), Rom. 51/G4
Telephone, Tx, US 153/F4
Telertheba (peak), Alg. 111/G4
Teles Pires (riv.), Braz. 179/D3
Telescope (peak), Ca, US 148/D2
Telese, It. 65/D5
Telford, Pa, US 168/C3
Telford Dawley, Eng, UK 36/D1
Telfs, Aus. 61/H3
Telgate, It. 62/C2
Telgruc-sur-Mer, Fr. 56/A4
Telgte, Ger. 53/E5
Telica, Nic. 176/E3
Télig (well), Mali 110/E5
Télimélé, Gui. 114/B4
Telipok, Malay. 88/B4
Teljo (peak), Sudan 117/E2
Tell, Tx, US 152/D3
Tell Atlas (mts.), Alg. 66/D3
Tell City, In, US 162/D2
Teller, Ak, US 171/E2
Telli (lake), Mrta. 110/C4
Tellico (lake), Tn, US 162/E3
Tellico Plains, Tn, US 162/E3
Tellier, Arg. 191/D5
Tellin, Belg. 55/E3
Telluride, Co, US 149/J2
Telmen (lake), Mong. 78/D2
Telok Anson, Malay. 89/C1
Teloloapan, Mex. 175/F5
Telotskoye (lake), Rus. 99/E1
Telsen, Arg. 190/D4
Telšiai, Lith. 41/K4
Teltow (reg.), Ger. 43/G2
Teltow, Ger. 42/Q7
Teluk Punggur (pt.), Indo. 89/C3
Telukbayur, Indo. 89/C3
Telukdalem, Indo. 89/B2
Telukmelano, Indo. 90/C4
Telukmerbau, Indo. 89/C2
Tema, Gha. 115/E5
Temacine, Alg. 111/G2
Temagami (lake), On, Can. 160/F1
Temanggung, Indo. 89/E4
Temax, Mex. 176/D1
Tembagapura, Indo. 91/J4
Tembesi (riv.), Indo. 89/C3
Tembilahan, Indo. 89/C3
Tembisa, SAfr. 124/E2
Temblador, Ven. 181/F2
Tembo, D.R. Congo 120/D4
Tembo Aluma, Ang. 120/D4
Tembue, Moz. 123/G2
Teme (riv.), Eng, UK 36/C2
Temecula, Ca, US 166/C4
Temelkovo, Bul. 51/F4
Temerin, Yugo. 50/D3
Temerloh, Malay. 90/B3
Teminabuan, Indo. 91/H4
Temir, Kaz. 71/L2
Temirtaū, Kaz. 99/B1
Témiscaming, Qu, Can. 161/G1
Temma, Austl. 132/C4
Temnik (riv.), Rus. 78/E1
Temoaya, Mex. 175/Q10
Temoe (isl.), FrPol. 137/M7
Temora, Austl. 133/C2
Tempe, Az, US 149/G4
Tempe Downs, Austl. 131/G3
Tempelhof (arpt.), Ger. 42/Q7
Tempelhof, Ger. 42/Q7
Temperance, Mi, US 160/E4
Temperanceville, Va, US 163/K2
Tempio Pausania, It. 48/A2
Temple, Ok, US 153/E3
Temple, La, US 164/B2
Temple (bay), Austl. 129/F3
Temple (mt.), Ab., Can. 144/F2
Temple, Tx, US 150/F2
Temple, Pa, US 168/C3
Temple City, Ca, US 166/F7
Temple of Lady Chua Xu, Viet. 94/D4
Temple Terrace, Fl, US 164/L7
Templemore, Ire. 32/C4
Templepatrick, NI, UK 34/B2
Templestowe (nbrhd.), Austl. 132/G5
Templetouhy, Ire. 32/C4
Templeuve, Fr. 54/C2
Templeville, Md, US 168/C5
Templin, Ger. 43/G2
Templiner (lake), Ger. 42/Q7
Tempoal de Sánchez, Mex. 176/B1
Têmpung, China 78/D4
Temryuk, Rus. 73/J5
Temryuk (gulf), Rus. 73/J5
Temse, Belg. 55/D1
Temuco, Chile 190/B3
Temuka, NZ 135/B4
Temyasovo, Rus. 71/L1
Ten Boer, Neth. 52/D2
Ten Mile, Tn, US 162/E3
Ten Sleep, Wy, US 147/K1
Ten Thousand (isls.), Fl, US 165/H5
Tena, Ecu. 180/B5
Tenabo, Mex. 176/D1
Ténado, Burk. 115/E3
Tenafly, NJ, US 169/K8
Tenaha, Tx, US 151/G2
Tenakee Springs, Ak, US 171/L4
Tenāli, India 95/D2
Tenancingo, Mex. 175/K8
Tenango, Mex. 175/R10
Tenango de Arista, Mex. 175/Q10
Tenasserim (range), Myan. 94/B3
Tenasserim, Myan. 94/B3
Tenay, Fr. 60/B6
Tenbury, Eng, UK 36/D2
Tenby, Wal, UK 36/B3
Tencarola, It. 63/E3
Tendaho, Eth. 118/B3
Tende, Fr. 64/D4
Tenderovsk (bay), Ukr. 51/K2
Tenderovsk Spit (isl.), Mol. 51/K2
Tendō, Japan 82/B4
Tendoy, Id, US 147/G1
Tendrara, Mor. 111/E2
Tendre (peak), Swi. 60/C4
Ténenkou, Mali 114/D3
Tenente Portela, Braz. 189/F3
Ténéré (des.), Niger 115/H1
Ténéré du Tafassasset (des.), Niger 111/H5
Tenerife, Col. 180/C2
Tenerife (isl.), Sp. 107/A2
Tenes (riv.), Sp. 47/L6
Ténès, Alg. 112/F4
Teng (riv.), Myan. 93/G3
Teng Xian, China 80/D4
Teng'aopu, China 81/B2
Tengchong, China 86/C3
Tenggarong, Indo. 91/E4
Tengger (des.), China 78/E4
Tengiz (lake), Kaz. 74/G4
Tengqiao, China 94/E2
Tenguel, Ecu. 180/B5
Tenibre (peak), Fr. 64/C4
Tenibres (peak), It. 64/C4
Teniente Enciso, PN, Par. 188/D2
Tenigerbad, Swi. 61/E4
Teningen, Ger. 60/D1
Tenino, Wa, US 144/C4
Tenja, Cro. 50/D3
Tenjo, Col. 183/L8
Tenkāsi, India 95/C4
Tenke, D.R. Congo 121/F5
Tenkiller (lake), Ok, US 153/G3
Tenkodogo, Burk. 115/E4
Tenmile (cr.), Tx, US 150/L7
Tenmile Wash (riv.), Az, US 149/F4
Tenna (riv.), It. 65/C1
Tennant Creek, Austl. 128/D4
Tennessee (state), US 143/J4
Tennessee (riv.), US 143/J5
Tennessee Ridge, Tn, US 162/D2
Tennessee-Tombigbee Waterway (canal), Ms, US 162/C3
Tenneville, Belg. 55/E3
Tennille, Al, US 165/F2
Tennille, Ga, US 163/F4
Tennuaca (well), Mor. 110/B5
Teno, Chile 190/C2
Tenojoki (riv.), Fin. 38/H1
Tenom, Malay. 88/A4
Tenosique de Pino Suárez, Mex. 176/D2
Tenri, Japan 83/J6
Tenryū, Japan 85/E3
Tenryū (riv.), Japan 85/E3
Tensas (basin), La, US 151/J2
Tensas (riv.), La, US 153/J5
Tensas River NWR, La, US 151/J1
Tensift (pol. reg.), Mor. 110/C3
Tensift, Oued (riv.), Mor. 110/C3
Tenstrike, Mn, US 157/G4
Tenta, Eth. 118/A3
Tentena, Indo. 91/F4
Tenterden, Eng, UK 37/G4
Tenterfield, Austl. 132/E1
Tentolomatinan (peak), Indo. 91/F3
Tenus (peak), Kenya 119/A1
Teo, Sp. 46/A1
Teocaltiche, Mex. 172/A3
Teocelo, Mex. 175/N7
Teodelina, Arg. 190/E2
Teodoro Sampaio, Braz. 189/F2
Teófilo Otoni, Braz. 187/E3
Teopisca, Mex. 176/C2
Teotihuacán (ruin), Mex. 175/R9
Teotihuacán, Mex. 175/R9
Teotitlán del Camino, Mex. 176/B2
Tepa, Indo. 128/C1
Tepache, Mex. 174/C2
Tepalcatepec, Mex. 174/E5
Tepalcingo, Mex. 175/L8
Tepatitlán de Morelos, Mex. 172/A3
Tepatlaxco, Mex. 175/M7
Tepeapulco, Mex. 175/L7
Tepebaşı, Turk. 104/C1
Tepee (mtn.), Ok, US 152/E3
Tepehuaje, Mex. 175/F4
Tepehuanes, Mex. 174/D3
Tepeji del Río de Ocampo, Mex. 175/K7
Tepelenë, Alb. 75/G2
Tepelská Plošina (mts.), Czh. 59/F2
Tepetlaoxtoc, Mex. 175/R9
Tepexi, Mex. 175/M8
Tepexpan, Mex. 175/R9
Tēpī, Eth. 116/G4
Tepic, Mex. 174/D4
Teplá (riv.), Czh. 42/G3
Teplá Vltava (riv.), Czh. 59/G5
Teplice, Czh. 43/G3
Tepoca (cape), Mex. 174/B2
Tepoca, Cabo (cape), Mex. 174/B2
Tepoto (isl.), FrPol. 137/L6
Tepotzotlán, Mex. 175/Q9
Tepoztlán, Mex. 175/K8
Tequila, Mex. 174/E4
Tequisquiapan, Mex. 175/F4
Tequixquiac, Mex. 175/K7
Ter (riv.), Sp. 47/G1
Ter Aar, Neth. 52/B4
Ter Apel, Neth. 53/E3
Téra, Niger 115/F3
Tera (riv.), Sp. 46/B1
Teraina (Washington) (isl.), Kiri. 137/J4
Terakeka, Sudan 116/F4
Teramo, It. 65/C2
Teramo (prov.), It. 65/C2
Terang, Austl. 132/B3
Terborg, Neth. 52/D5
Terbuny, Rus. 70/F1
Tercan, Turk. 102/E2
Terceira (isl.), Azor., Port. 47/S12
Tercero (riv.), Arg. 188/D5
Terebovlya, Ukr. 72/C3
Terek (riv.), Rus. 71/H4
Terek, Rus. 71/H4
Terekhovka, Bela. 72/F1
Terekli-Mekteb, Rus. 71/H3
Terempa, Indo. 89/D2
Terengganu (riv.), Malay. 89/C1
Terengganu (state), Malay. 89/C1
Terenuthis (ruin), Egypt 113/B4
Terenzano, It. 63/G2
Terepaima, PN, Ven. 180/D2
Teresina, Braz. 183/F4
Teresópolis, Braz. 187/P7
Terespol, Pol. 43/M2
Terevinto, Bol. 188/D1
Tergnier, Fr. 54/C4
Tergun Daba (mts.), China 78/D4
Terhathum, Nepal 97/F2
Terheijden, Neth. 52/B5
Teriberka, Rus. 68/G1
Teriberskiy (pt.), Rus. 68/G1
Terkaplesterpoelen (lake), Neth. 52/C2
Terlan (Terlano), It. 61/H4
Terlano (Terlan), It. 61/H4
Terlingua, Tx, US 150/C3
Termas del Arapey, Uru. 188/E4
Termeno (Tramin), It. 61/H5
Termessos (Güllükdağı) NP, Turk. 102/B2
Termini Imerese, It. 48/C4
Terminiers, Fr. 57/G4
Terminillo (peak), It. 65/B3
Terminio (peak), It. 65/D6
Términos (lag.), Mex. 176/D2
Terminus (dam), Ca, US 148/C2
Termit-Kaoboul, Niger 116/A2
Termiz, Uzb. 101/J1
Termo, Ca, US 146/C3
Termoli, It. 65/D4
Termonfeckin, Ire. 34/B4
Termunten, Neth. 52/E2
Ternate, Indo. 91/G3
Ternay, Fr. 64/A1
Ternberg, Aus. 59/H7
Terneuzen, Neth. 52/A6
Terney, Rus. 79/M2
Terni (prov.), It. 65/B2
Terni, It. 65/B2
Ternin (riv.), Fr. 44/F3
Ternivka, Ukr. 73/J3
Ternoise (riv.), Fr. 54/B3
Ternopil', Ukr. 72/C3
Ternopil's'ka Oblast, Ukr. 70/C2
Ternovka, Rus. 73/L2
Terowie, Austl. 132/C2
Terpeniya (bay), Rus. 75/Q5
Terpeniya (cape), Rus. 79/N2
Terpní, Gre. 75/H2
Terra Ceia, Fl, US 164/K8
Terra Cotta, On, Can. 160/T8
Terra del Sole, It. 63/E5
Terra Nova, Braz. 183/G5
Terra Nova NP, Nf, Can. 159/K1
Terra Rica, Braz. 189/F2
Terrabonne (bay), La, US 164/C3
Terrace, BC, Can. 140/D3
Terrace Bay, On, Can. 157/L3
Terrace Heights, Wa, US 144/D4
Terracina, It. 65/C5
Terråk, Nor. 38/E2
Terral, Ok, US 153/F4
Terralba, It. 48/A3
Terranuova Bracciolini, It. 63/E6
Terrassa, Sp. 47/L6
Terrasson-la-Villedieu, Fr. 44/D4
Terre Haute, In, US 160/C5
Terre Hill, Pa, US 168/B3
Terrebonne (co.), Qu, Can. 159/N6
Terrebonne, Qu, Can. 159/N6
Terrell, Tx, US 151/F1
Terrenceville, Nf, Can. 159/K2
Terreton, Id, US 147/G2
Terrey Hills (nbrhd.), Austl. 134/H8
Terri (peak), Swi. 61/F4
Terrigal, Austl. 133/E1
Terrington Saint Clement, Eng, UK 37/G1
Terry, Mt, US 145/M4
Tersakan, Trkm. 103/H2
Tersakkan (riv.), Kaz. 99/A1
Terschelling (isl.), Neth. 52/C2
Tertenia, It. 48/A3
Teruel, Sp. 47/E2
Terutao (isl.), Thai. 93/G6
Tervakoski, Fin. 39/E4
Tervel, Bul. 51/H4
Terza Grande (peak), It. 45/K3
Terzo d'Aquileia, It. 63/G2
Tes-Khem (riv.), Rus. 78/C1
Tešanj, Bosn. 50/C3
Tescott, Ks, US 153/F1
Tescou (riv.), Fr. 44/D5
Teseney (Tessenie), Erit. 116/H2
Tesero, It. 61/H5
Teshekpuk (lake), Ak, US 171/G1
Teshi, Gha. 115/E5
Teshikaga, Japan 82/D2
Teshio, Japan 82/B1
Teshio (riv.), Japan 82/C1
Teshio-dake (peak), Japan 82/C2
Tesiyn (riv.), Mong. 78/D2
Teslić, Bosn. 50/C3
Teslin (riv.), Yk, Can. 140/C2
Teslin (lake), BC, Can. 140/C3
Teslin, Yk, Can. 171/M3
Tësovo-Netyl'skiy, Rus. 41/P2
Tessalit, Mali 115/F1
Tessaoua, Niger 115/G3
Tessé-la-Madeleine, Fr. 57/E3
Tessenderlo, Belg. 55/E1
Tessenie (Teseney), Erit. 116/H2
Tessy-sur-Vire, Fr. 57/D3
Test (riv.), Eng, UK 37/E4
Testa del Gargano (pt.), It. 48/E2
Testa del Rutor (peak), It. 64/D1
Tét, Hun. 50/C2
Têt (riv.), Fr. 47/G1
Tetas (pt.), Chile 188/B2
Tete, Moz. 123/G3
Tete (prov.), Moz. 123/G2
Tête d'Alpe (peak), Fr. 64/D5
Tête de Faux (peak), Fr. 60/D1
Tête de l'Enchastraye (peak), Fr. 64/C4
Tête de l'Estrop (peak), Fr. 64/C4
Tête de Moïse (peak), Fr. 64/C4
Tête de Siguret (peak), Fr. 64/C4
Tête de Soulaure (peak), Fr. 64/C3
Tête du Torraz (peak), Fr. 60/C6
Tête Jaune Cache, BC, Can. 144/E1
Tête Nord des Fours (peak), Fr. 64/C1
Tête Ronde (peak), Swi. 60/D5
Tetela, Mex. 175/M7
Teterow, Ger. 40/E5
Teteven, Bul. 51/G4
Tetford, Eng, UK 35/H5
Tetiaroa (isl.), FrPol. 137/L6
Tetiyiv, Ukr. 72/E3
Tëtkino, Rus. 73/H2
Tetlin, Ak, US 171/K3
Teton (riv.), Id, US 147/H2
Teton (range), Wy, US 147/H2
Teton, Id, US 147/H2
Tetonia, Id, US 147/H2
Tétouan, Mor. 112/B2
Tétouan (prov.), Mor. 112/B2
Tetovo, FYROM 75/G1
T'et'ritsqaro, Geo. 71/H4
Tettnang, Ger. 61/F2
Tetulia, Bang. 97/G2
Tetulia (riv.), Bang. 97/H4
Teublitz, Ger. 59/F4
Teuchezhsk, Rus. 73/K5
Teuco (riv.), Arg. 188/D3
Teufen, Swi. 61/F3
Teúl de González Ortega, Mex. 174/E4
Teulada (cape), It. 48/A3
Teulon, Mb, Can. 156/F2
Teupasenti, Hon. 176/E3
Teuri (isl.), Japan 82/B1
Teuschnitz, Ger. 59/E2
Teutoburger Wald (for.), Ger. 53/F4
Teutopolis, Il, US 162/C1
Tevere (Tiber) (riv.), It. 45/K5
Teverya, Isr. 105/D3
Teviot (riv.), Sc, UK 33/D6
Teviotdale (valley), Sc, UK 33/D6
Tevli, Bela. 43/N2
Tewantin-Noosa, Austl. 134/D4
Tewaukon Nat'l Wild. Ref., ND, US 156/F5
Tewkesbury, Eng, UK 36/D3
Texada (isl.), BC, Can. 144/B3
Texana (lake), Tx, US 151/F3
Texarkana, Ar, US 153/G4
Texarkana, Tx, US 153/G4
Texas, Austl. 132/D1
Texas (state), US 142/F5
Texas City, Tx, US 151/N9
Texas Point NWR, La, US 151/H3
Texas Safari Wildlife Park, Tx, US 151/F2
Texas Stadium, Tx, US 150/L7
Texcoco, Mex. 175/R9
Texel (isl.), Neth. 42/C2
Texhoma, Ok, US 152/D2
Texmelucan, Mex. 175/L7
Texoma (lake), Ok, US 143/G5
Teyateyaneng, Les. 124/D3
Teykovo, Rus. 68/J4
Tezio (peak), It. 65/B1
Teziutlán, Mex. 175/M7
Tezonapa, Mex. 175/N8
Tezontepec, Mex. 175/L7
Tezontepec de Aldama, Mex. 175/K6
Tezoyuca, Mex. 175/R9
Tezpur, India 86/B3
Tezu, India 86/C3
Tezze, It. 63/E2
Tha (riv.), Laos 86/D4
Tha Chin (riv.), Thai. 94/B3
Tha Mai, Thai. 94/C3
Tha Rua, Thai. 94/C3
Tha Sala, Thai. 94/B4
Tha Tum, Thai. 94/C3
Tha Wang Pha, Thai. 94/C2
Tha-Anne (riv.), Nun, Can. 140/G2
Thaba Nchu, SAfr. 124/D3
Thabana-Ntlenyana (peak), Les. 124/E3
Thabankulu (peak), SAfr. 125/E2
Thabazimbi, SAfr. 123/E5
Thabor (peak), Fr. 64/C2
Thādiq, SAr. 100/E3
Thaen (pt.), Thai. 94/B4
Thagaya, Myan. 94/B2
Thai Binh, Viet. 87/E4
Thai Nguyen, Viet. 86/E4
Thailand (ctry.) 77/K8
Thailand (gulf), Asia 77/K8
Thākurdwāra, India 96/B1
Thākurgaon, Bang. 97/G2
Thākurmunda, India 95/E1
Thal, Pak. 98/A3
Thal (des.), Pak. 98/A4
Tha'l (mtn.), Sudan 116/E2
Thal (des.), India 99/B5
Thalang, Thai. 94/B4
Thaleban NP, Thai. 94/C5
Thaleischweiler-Fröschen, Ger. 55/G5
Thalerhof (int'l arpt.), Aus. 50/B2
Thalgau, Aus. 59/G7
Thalheim bei Wels, Aus. 59/H6
Thalmann, Ga, US 165/H2
Thalmässing, Ger. 58/E4
Thalwil, Swi. 61/E3
Thame (riv.), Eng, UK 37/F3
Thame, Eng, UK 37/F3
Thames (riv.), Eng., UK 37/G4
Thames (riv.), On, Can. 160/F3
Thames, NZ 135/C2
Thames Barrier, Eng, UK 30/D2
Thāna, India 95/B2
Thāna Bhawan, India 98/D5
Thāna Kasbā, India 96/A3
Thanatpin, Myan. 86/C5
Thanbyuzayat, Myan. 94/B3
Thānesar, India 98/D5
Thāneswar, Bang. 97/H3
Thang Duc, Viet. 94/D3
Thanggu, India 97/G2
Thangool, Austl. 134/C4
Thanh Hoa, Viet. 86/E5
Thanh Lang Xa, Viet. 93/J4
Thanh Phu, Viet. 94/D4
Thanh Tri, Viet. 94/D4
Thānkot, Nepal 97/E2
Thann, Fr. 60/D2
Thannhausen, Ger. 61/G1
Thanya Buri, Thai. 94/C3
Thaoge (riv.), Bots. 122/D3
Thaon-les-Vosges, Fr. 60/C1
Thap Put, Thai. 94/B4
Thap Sakae, Thai. 94/B4
Thar (riv.), Fr. 56/D3
Thar (des.), Pak. 98/A5
Tharād, India 101/K4
Thargomindah, Austl. 134/A5
Tharrawaddy, Myan. 86/B5
Thásos, Gre. 75/J2
Thásos (isl.), Gre. 70/C4
That Khe, Viet. 87/E4
That Phanom, Thai. 94/D2
Thatcham, Eng, UK 37/E4
Thatcher, Id, US 147/H2
Thatcher, Az, US 149/H4
Thaton, Myan. 94/B2
Thaungdut, Myan. 86/B3
Thaur, Aus. 61/H3
Thaxted, Eng, UK 37/G3
Thaxton, Ms, US 162/C3
Thaya (riv.), Aus. 43/H4
Thayer, Mo, US 153/J2
Thayer, Ks, US 153/G2
Thayetmyo, Myan. 86/B5
Thayngen, Swi. 61/E2
Thazi, Myan. 86/C4
The Alamo, Tx, US 151/E3
The Atomium, Belg. 55/D2
The Ballpark, Tx, US 150/K7
The Bourne (riv.), Eng, UK 30/B3
The Broads NP, Eng, UK 37/H1
The Buck (peak), Sc, UK 33/D2
The Burren (reg.), Ire. 32/A3
The Calf (peak), Eng, UK 35/F3
The Caprock (cliff), NM, US 152/C3
The Cheviot (peak), Eng, UK 33/D6
The Colony, Tx, US 150/L6
The Curragh, Ire. 32/D3
The Dalles (dam), Or, US 146/C1
The Dalles, Or, US 146/C1
The English Companys (isls.), Austl. 129/E2
The Entrance, Austl. 133/E1
The Everglades (swamp), Fl, US 165/H5
The Fens (phys. reg.), Eng, UK 35/H6
The Fens (phys. reg.), Eng, UK 37/G1
The Flat Tops (mts.), Co, US 147/K4
The Gap (pass), Ire. 32/C5
The Gap, Austl. 132/B1
The Grampians (range), Austl. 132/B3
The Granites (peak), Austl. 131/F2
The Hague ('s-Gravenhage) (cap.), Neth. 52/B4
The Hermitage, NZ 135/B3
The Key Ind. Res., Sk, Can. 156/C2
The Lakes NP, Austl. 133/C3
The Lizard (pen.), Eng, UK 36/A6
The Loup, NI, UK 34/B2
The Machars (pen.), Sc, UK 34/D2
The Malpais (lava flow), NM, US 149/H3
The Malpais (lava flow), NM, US 149/J4
The Naze (pt.), Eng, UK 37/H3
The Oaks, Ca, US 166/B1
The Oaks, Austl. 133/E2
The Paps (peak), Ire. 32/A5
The Pas, Mb, Can. 140/F3
The Peak (peak), NC, US 163/G2
The Pilot (mtn.), Austl. 133/D3
The Pine (hills), Mt, US 145/M4
The Pinnacles (peak), BC, Can. 144/E2
The Plains, Oh, US 160/E5
The Quantocks (hills), Eng, UK 36/C4
The Range, Zim. 123/F3
The Raven (pt.), Ire. 32/D5
The Rhinns (pt.), Sc, UK 34/C2
The Rock, Austl. 133/C2
The Royal NP, Austl. 134/H9
The Saddle (peak), Sc, UK 33/A2
The Seven Hogs (isl.), Ire. 30/N10
The Sisters (isl.), NZ 135/E3
The Solent (chan.), Eng, UK 37/E5
The Storr (peak), Sc, UK 31/Q8
The Swale (riv.), Eng, Ire. 37/G4
The Twins (peak), Ab, Can. 144/F1
The Valley (cap.), Angu. 173/N8
The Woodlands, Tx, US 151/G2
The Wrekin (co.), Eng, UK 36/D1
The Wrekin (hill), Eng, UK 36/D1
The Yellow (mtn.), Austl. 133/C1
Theale, Eng, UK 37/E4
Thebes (ruin), Egypt 109/G3
Thedaw, Myan. 94/B1
Thedford, Ne, US 154/D3
Theilheim, Ger. 58/D3
Thelepte, Tun. 66/F4
Thelon (riv.), NW,Nun, Can. 140/F2
Thelon (riv.), Can. 139/G3
Themar, Ger. 58/D1
Thémericourt, Fr. 30/H4
Theo (mt.), Austl. 131/F2
Theodore, Sk, Can. 156/C2
Theodore, Al, US 164/D2
Theodore, Austl. 134/C4
Theodore Roosevelt (dam), Az, US 149/G4
Theodore Roosevelt (lake), Az, US 149/G4
Theodore Roosevelt NP, ND, US 156/C4
Theodosia, Mo, US 153/H2
Théoule-sur-Mer, Fr. 64/C6
Thérain (riv.), Fr. 44/D2
Thermaic (gulf), Gre. 70/B4
Thermal, Ca, US 148/D4
Thermalito, Ca, US 146/C4
Thérmi, Gre. 75/H2
Thermopílai (Thermopylae) (pass), Gre. 75/H3
Thermopolis, Wy, US 147/J2
Thermopylae (Thermopílai) (pass), Gre. 75/H3
Thérouanne (riv.), Fr. 30/L4
Thésée, Fr. 57/G6
Thesprotikón, Gre. 75/G3
Thessalon, On, Can. 160/E1
Thessaloníki, Gre. 75/H2
Thessaly (reg.), Gre. 67/J3
Thet (riv.), Eng, UK 37/G2
Thetford, Eng, UK 37/G2
Thetford Mines, Qu, Can. 158/B2
Thetkala, Myan. 86/C5
Theunissen, SAfr. 124/D3
Theux, Belg. 55/E2
Thève (riv.), Fr. 30/K4
Theydon Bois, Eng, UK 30/D2
Thiais, Fr. 30/K5
Thíamis (riv.), Gre. 75/G3
Thiant, Fr. 54/C3
Thiaucourt-Regniéville, Fr. 55/E6
Thiberville, Fr. 57/F2
Thibodaux, La, US 164/C3
Thick (mtn.), Pa, US 161/H4
Thickwood (hills), Sk, Can. 145/L1
Thief River Falls, Mn, US 156/F3
Thielle (riv.), Swi. 60/C4
Thielsen (mt.), Or, US 146/B2
Thien Ngon, Viet. 94/D4
Thiene, It. 63/E2
Thiérache (reg.), Fr. 54/C4
Thierhaupten, Ger. 58/D5
Thiers, Fr. 44/E4
Thiers-sur-Thève, Fr. 30/K4
Thierville-sur-Meuse, Fr. 55/E5
Thiès, Sen. 114/A3
Thiès (pol. reg.), Sen. 114/A3
Thiet Tra, Viet. 86/E4
Thika, Kenya 119/B2
Thimād al Khuwaymah (well), Libya 134/C2
Thimphu (cap.), Bhu. 97/G2
Thingvellir NP, Ice. 38/N7
Thio, NCal. 137/V12
Thionville, Fr. 55/F5
Thiou, Burk. 115/E3
Thíra, Gre. 75/J4
Thíra (isl.), Gre. 67/K3
Third Cataract (falls), Sudan 109/F5
Third Lake, Il, US 167/Q15
Thirlmere (lake), Eng, UK 35/E2
Thirlmere, Austl. 133/E2
Thiron Gardais, Fr. 57/G4
Thironne (riv.), Fr. 57/G4
Thirsk, Eng, UK 35/G3
Thirsty (mt.), Austl. 130/D5
Thirtymile (pt.), NY, US 160/W9
Thiruvananthapuram, India 95/C4
Thise, Fr. 60/C3
Thisted, Den. 40/C3
Thistilfjördhur (estu.), Ice. 38/P6
Thistle (isl.), Austl. 131/H5
Thistle (mt.), Yk, Can. 171/L3
Thithia (isl.), Fiji 137/Y18
Thívai, Gre. 75/H3
Thiverval-Grignon, Fr. 30/H5
Thjósa (riv.), Ice. 38/N7
Thlanship, India 86/B3
Thlewiaza (riv.), Nun, Can. 140/G2
Thoen, Thai. 94/B2
Thoeng, Thai. 94/C2
Thohoyandou, SAfr. 123/F4
Thoi Binh, Viet. 94/D4
Thoiry, Fr. 30/H5

Tholen – Torii-t

Tholen (isl.), Neth. 52/B5
Tholen, Neth. 52/B5
Tholey, Ger. 55/G5
Thomas, Ok, US 153/E3
Thomas, WV, US 163/H1
Thomasboro, Il, US 160/B4
Thomaston, Al, US 162/D4
Thomaston, Ga, US 162/E4
Thomastown, Ire. 32/C4
Thomastown, Ms, US 162/C4
Thomasville, Mo, US 153/J2
Thomasville, Al, US 164/E2
Thomasville, Ga, US 165/G2
Thomasville, NC, US 163/G3
Thomasville, Pa, US 168/B4
Thomes (cr.), Ca, US 146/B4
Thompson (peak), NM, US 152/B3
Thompson, ND, US 156/F4
Thompson, Mi, US 160/C2
Thompson, Ct, US 161/L4
Thompson, Ut, US 149/H1
Thompson, Mb, Can. 140/G3
Thompson (peak), Ca, US 146/B3
Thompson (riv.), Ia,Mo, US 155/G3
Thompson (lake), Austl. 130/K7
Thompson (riv.), BC, Can. 144/D2
Thompson Falls, Mt, US 144/G4
Thompsonville, Mi, US 160/D2
Thompsonville, Il, US 162/C2
Thomsen (riv.), NW, Can. 140/E1
Thomson, Ga, US 163/F4
Thomson, Il, US 155/J3
Thomson (riv.), Austl. 127/D3
Thon Lac Nghiep, Viet. 94/E4
Thon Song Pha, Viet. 94/E4
Thongwa, Myan. 94/B2
Thonnance-lès-Joinville, Fr. 60/B1
Thonon-les-Bains, Fr. 60/C5
Thonotosassa, Fl, US 164/L7
Thonotosassa (lake), Fl, US 164/L7
Thoreau, NM, US 149/H3
Thorens-Glières, Fr. 60/C6
Thorigny-sur-Marne, Fr. 30/L5
Thorlákshöfn, Ice. 38/N7
Thorn (cr.), Il, US 167/Q16
Thornaby-on-Tees, Eng, UK 35/G2
Thornbury, On, Can. 160/F2
Thornbury, Eng, UK 36/D3
Thorndale, Tx, US 151/F2
Thorndale, Pa, US 168/C4
Thorne, Eng, UK 35/H4
Thorne, On, Can. 161/G1
Thorne Bay, Ak, US 171/M4
Thornfield, Mo, US 153/H2
Thornhill, Sc, UK 34/E1
Thornhill, Sc, UK 33/B4
Thornhurst, Pa, US 168/C1
Thornley, Eng, UK 35/G2
Thornthwaite, Eng, UK 35/G3
Thornton, Ar, US 153/H4
Thornton, Ca, US 167/M10
Thornton, Co, US 154/B4
Thornton, Tx, US 151/F2
Thornton Cleveleys, Eng, UK 35/E4
Thornton Dale, Eng, UK 35/H3
Thorntonville, Tx, US 151/C2
Thorntown, In, US 160/C4
Thornwood Common, Eng, UK 30/D1
Thorold, On, Can. 160/U9
Thorold South, On, Can. 160/U9
Thorp, Wi, US 155/J1
Thorp, Wa, US 144/D4
Thorpe, Eng, UK 30/B2
Thorpe Thewles, Eng, UK 35/G2
Thorpe-le-Soken, Eng, UK 37/H3
Thorsby, Al, US 162/D4
Thorsby, Ab, Can. 145/G1
Thórshöfn, Ice. 38/P6
Thouarcé, Fr. 57/E6
Thouaré-sur-Loire, Fr. 56/D6
Thoubāl, India 86/B3
Thouet (riv.), Fr. 44/C3
Thourotte, Fr. 54/B5
Thousand (isl.), On, Can. 161/H2
Thousand Oaks, Ca, US 166/B2
Thousand Springs (cr.), Nv, US 147/F3
Thowa (riv.), Kenya 119/B2
Thrace (reg.), Bul.,Gre. 67/K2
Thracian (sea), Gre. 70/C4
Thread (cr.), Mi, US 167/E6
Thredbo Village, Austl. 133/D3
Three Bridges, NJ, US 168/D2
Three Creek, Id, US 147/F2
Three Forks, Mt, US 145/J5
Three Guardsmen (mt.), Yk, Can. 171/L3
Three Hills, Ab, Can. 145/H2
Three Kings (isls.), NZ 135/B1
Three Lakes, Wi, US 157/K5
Three Mile (isl.), Pa, US 168/B3
Three Mile Plains, NS, Can. 158/E3
Three Notch, Al, US 165/F1
Three Oaks, Mi, US 160/C4
Three Pagodas (pass), Myan. 94/B3
Three Points (cape), Gha. 115/E5
Three Rivers, Mi, US 160/D4
Three Rivers, NM, US 149/J4
Three Rivers, Austl. 130/C3
Three Springs, Austl. 130/B4
Three Valley, BC, Can. 144/E2
Threehills (cr.), Ab, Can. 145/H2
Thrifty, Tx, US 150/E2
Throckmorton, Tx, US 152/E4
Throssel (lake), Austl. 127/B3
Thrums, BC, Can. 144/F3
Thrumster, Sc, UK 31/S7
Thrushel (riv.), Eng, UK 36/B5
Thu Dau Mot, Viet. 94/D4
Thu Duc, Viet. 94/D4
Thud (pt.), Austl. 129/F3
Thuin, Belg. 55/D3
Thuir, Fr. 44/E5
Thulba (riv.), Ger. 58/C2
Thule Air Base, Den. 167/X7
Thun, Swi. 60/D4
Thunder (mtn.), Wi, US 157/K5
Thunder (bay), On, Can. 157/K3
Thunder Bay, On, Can. 157/K3
Thunder Butte (cr.), SD, US 154/C1
Thundersley, Eng, UK 30/E2
Thuner (lake), Swi. 45/G3
Thung Chang, Thai. 94/C2
Thung Salaeng Luang NP, Thai. 94/C2
Thung Song, Thai. 94/B4
Thüngersheim, Ger. 58/C3
Thunkar, Bhu. 97/H2
Thur (riv.), Swi. 45/H3
Thurgau (canton), Swi. 61/E2
Thüringen, Aus. 61/F3
Thüringen (state), Ger. 45/J1
Thüringer Schiefergebirge (mts.), Ger. 58/E2
Thüringer Wald (for.), Ger. 42/F3
Thurlaston, Eng, UK 37/E2
Thurles, Ire. 32/C4
Thurloo Downs, Austl. 132/B1
Thurlow, Mt, US 145/L4
Thurmont, Md, US 161/H5
Thurnau, Ger. 59/E2
Thurø By, Den. 40/D4
Thurrock (co.), Eng, UK 37/G3
Thursday Island, Austl. 129/F2
Thursley, Eng, UK 30/A3
Thurso, Qu, Can. 161/J2
Thurso, Sc, UK 31/V14
Thurston (co.), Wa, US 167/A3
Thurston (isl.), Ant. 192/T
Thury-en-Valois, Fr. 30/M4
Thury-Harcourt, Fr. 57/E3
Thusis, Swi. 61/F4
Thyez, Fr. 60/C5
Thyolo, Malw. 123/G3
Ti-m-Merhsoï (riv.), Niger 115/G2
Ti-n-Essako, Mali 115/F2
Ti-n-Jedane, Oued (riv.), Alg. 111/G4
Ti-n-Toumma (reg.), Niger 116/A1
Ti-n-Zaouâtene, Mali 115/F2
Ti-Tree Abor. Land, Austl. 131/G2
Tia, Austl. 132/D1
Tiahuanco (ruin), Bol. 188/B1
Tian Shan (mts.), China 77/H5
Tianbao, China 87/H3
Tiancang, China 78/D3
Tianchang, China 80/D4
Tiandeng, China 87/E4
Tian'e, China 93/J2
Tianguá, Braz. 183/F3
Tianguistenco, Mex. 175/Q10
Tianhua, China 87/G3
Tianjin (prov.), China 79/H4
Tianjin, China 80/H7
Tianlin, China 93/J3
Tianmen, China 87/G2
Tianmu (mts.), China 80/K9
Tianping, China 87/F3
Tianqiao, China 87/F2
Tianshifu, China 81/C2
Tianshui, China 78/F5
Tianshuihai, China 99/C4
Tianzhen, China 80/C2
Tianzhu, China 87/F3
Tianzhuangtai, China 81/B2
Tiaret, Alg. 112/F5
Tiassalé, C.d'Iv. 114/D5
Tiatucurá, Uru. 191/K10
Tiavea, Sam. 137/S9
Tibagi (riv.), Braz. 186/C4
Tibagi, Braz. 189/G3
Tibaná, Col. 180/C3
Tibati, Camr. 116/B4
Tibba, Pak. 98/A5
Tibbee (cr.), Ms, US 162/C4
Tibberton, Eng, UK 36/D1
Tibbie, Al, US 164/D2
Tibble, Swe. 39/A1
Tibé, Pic de (peak), Gui. 114/C4
Tiber (riv.), It. 67/G2
Tiber (dam), Mt, US 145/J3
Tiber (Tevere) (riv.), It. 45/K5
Tiberias (lake), Isr. 104/D3
Tiberias, Isr. 105/D3
Tibert (peak), It. 64/D4
Tibesti (mts.), Chad 107/D3
Tibet (reg.), China 77/H6
Tibet (Xizang) (aut. reg.), China 78/C5
Tibiri, Niger 115/G3
Tibnīn, Leb. 105/C2
Tibooburra, Austl. 131/J4
Tibro, Swe. 40/F2
Tibshelf, Eng, UK 35/G5
Tiburon (cape), Haiti 173/G4
Tiburon, Ca, US 167/K11
Tiburón, Isla (isl.), Mex. 174/B2
Ticaco, Peru 184/D5
Ticehurst, Eng, UK 37/G4
Tichigan (lake), Wi, US 167/P14
Tîchît, Mrta. 114/C2
Tichla, Mor. 110/B5
Tichnor, Ar, US 153/J3
T'īcho, Eth. 118/A4
Ticino (canton), Swi. 61/E5
Ticino (riv.), Swi. 61/E6
Tickfaw, La, US 164/C2
Ţicleni, Rom. 51/F3
Ticllos, Peru 184/B3
Ticonderoga, NY, US 161/K3
Ticul, Mex. 176/D1
Tīdah, Egypt 113/B2
Tidaholm, Swe. 40/E2
Tiddim, Myan. 86/B4
Tideswell, Eng, UK 35/G5
Tidikelt (plain), Alg. 111/F4
Tidioute, Pa, US 161/G4
Tidjikdja, Mrta. 114/C2
Tidone (riv.), It. 62/C3
Tidore (isl.), Indo. 91/G3
Tidsit (lake), WSah. 110/B5
Tie Plant, Ms, US 162/C4
Tiébélé Corabie, Burk. 115/E4
Tiébissou, C.d'Iv. 114/D5
Tiéboro, Chad 134/C4
Tiechang, China 81/D2
Tiede, PN del, Sp. 110/A3
Tiefencastel, Swi. 61/F4
Tiefensee, Ger. 42/Q6
Tiéfinzo, C.d'Iv. 114/D4
Tiège, Belg. 55/E2
Tiel, Neth. 52/C5
Tieli, China 79/K2
Tieling, China 80/E2
Tielt, Belg. 54/C2
Tielt-Winge, Belg. 55/D2
Tiemba (riv.), C.d'Iv. 114/D4
Tiemen (pass), China 99/E3
Tien Yen, Viet. 94/D1
Tien Yen, Viet. 94/D2
Tienen, Belg. 55/D2
Tiénigbe, C.d'Iv. 114/D4
Tieniu (pass), China 87/H3
Tiercé, Fr. 57/E5
Tieri, Austl. 134/C3
Tieroko (peak), Chad 134/C4
Tierp, Swe. 40/G1
Tierra Amarilla, NM, US 149/J2
Tierra Amarilla, Chile 188/B3
Tierra Blanca (cr.), Tx,NM, US 152/C3
Tierra Blanca, Mex. 175/N8
Tierra Colorada, Mex. 175/F5
Tierra del Fuego (isl.), Arg. 179/C8
Tierra del Fuego, Antártida e Islas del Atlántico Sur, Arg. 191/C7
Tierra del Fuego, PN, Chile 191/C7
Tierradentro, Col. 180/B4
Tierranueva, Mex. 175/E4
Tiétar (riv.), Sp. 46/C2
Tietê (riv.), Braz. 179/D5
Tieton, Wa, US 144/D4
Tieton (peak), Wa, US 144/D4
Tieyon, Austl. 131/G3
Tifariti, WSah. 110/C4
Tiffany, Co, US 149/J2
Tiffany (mtn.), Wa, US 144/E3
Tiffin (riv.), Oh, US 160/D4
Tiffin, Oh, US 160/E4
Tiflet, Mor. 112/A3
Tifton, Ga, US 165/G2
Tigapuluh (mts.), Indo. 89/C3
Tigeaux, Fr. 30/L5
Tiger (hills), Mb, Can. 156/D3
Tiger (lake), Fl, US 164/N8
Tigerton, Wi, US 155/K1
Tighina (Bendery), Mol. 72/E4
Tighvein (hill), Sc, UK 33/A6
Tigil', Rus. 75/R4
Tignall, Ga, US 163/F4
Tignère, Camr. 116/B4
Tignieu-Jameyzieu, Fr. 60/B6
Tignish, PE, Can. 158/E2
Tigray (prov.), Eth. 116/H2
Tigre (riv.), Ven. 173/J6
Tigre (riv.), Ven. 181/F2
Tigre, Arg. 191/J11
Tigres (bay), Ang. 122/A3
Tigris (riv.), Iraq 77/C6
Tiguent, Mrta. 114/A2
Tigui (well), Chad 134/C5
Tiguidit, Falaise de (cliff), Niger 115/G2
Tigy, Fr. 57/H5
Tigzirt, Alg. 112/H4
Tihamat al Yaman (valley), Yem. 118/B1
Tihosuco, Mex. 176/D1
Tihuatlán, Mex. 176/B1
Tiilikkajärven NP, Fin. 68/F3
Tijāra, India 96/A2
Tijger (falls), Sur. 182/B2
Tījī, Libya 134/A1
Tijuana, Mex. 166/C5
Tijuca, PN da, Braz. 187/N7
Tijucas, Braz. 189/G3
Tijuco (riv.), Braz. 186/C3
Tikal (ruin), Guat. 176/D2
Tikal, Guat. 175/H5
Tīkamgarh, India 96/B3
Tikanlik, China 99/E3
Tikarapāra, India 95/D1
Tikaré, Burk. 115/E3
Tikchik Lakes, Ak, US 171/G3
Tikehau (isl.), FrPol. 137/L6
Tikhoretsk, Rus. 73/L5
Tikhvin, Rus. 68/G4
Tiko, Camr. 120/B1
Tikrīt, Iraq 103/E3
Tiksi, Rus. 75/N2
Tikveš (lake), FYROM 75/H2
Tila, Mex. 176/C2
Tiläänjärvi (lake), Fin. 39/F4
Tilburg, Neth. 52/C5
Tilbury, On, Can. 160/E3
Tilbury, Eng, UK 30/E2
Tilcha, Austl. 131/J4
Tilden, Il, US 162/C1
Tilden, Tx, US 151/E3
Tilford, Eng, UK 30/A3
Tilford, SD, US 154/C1
Tilghman, Md, US 168/B6
Tilghman (isl.), Md, US 168/B6
Tilhar, India 96/B2
Tilin, Myan. 86/B4
Tilisarao, Arg. 190/D2
Till (riv.), Eng, UK 33/D5
Tillabéry, Niger 115/F3
Tillamook (bay), Or, US 146/A1
Tillamook, Or, US 144/C5
Tillar, Ar, US 153/J4
Tille (riv.), Fr. 42/C5
Tillery (lake), NC, US 163/G3
Tilley, Sk, Can. 145/J2
Tillicoultry, Sc, UK 33/C4
Tillières-sur-Avre, Fr. 57/G3
Tillmans Corner, Al, US 164/D2
Tillsonburg, On, Can. 160/F3
Tilly-sur-Seulles, Fr. 57/E2
Tilomar, ETim. 128/B2
Tilomonte, Chile 188/B2
Tilopozo, Chile 188/B2
Tilpa, Austl. 132/C1
Tilst, Den. 40/D3
Tilston, Mb, Can. 156/D3
Tilt (riv.), Sc, UK 33/C3
Tiltagara, Austl. 132/C1
Tiltil, Chile 190/N8
Tilton, Il, US 160/C4
Tim, Den. 40/C3
Tim, Rus. 73/J2
Ţimā, Egypt 102/B5
Timan (ridge), Rus. 74/F3
Timaná, Col. 180/C4
Timane (riv.), Par. 188/D2
Timanfaya, PN de, Sp. 110/B3
Timaru, NZ 135/B4
Timashevo, Rus. 71/J1
Timashevsk, Rus. 73/K5
Timbákion, Gre. 75/J5
Timbalier (bay), La, US 164/C3
Timbaúba, Braz. 183/H4
Timbédra, Mrta. 114/C2
Timber (mtn.), Tx, US 151/C2
Timber Lake, SD, US 156/D5
Timberlake, Va, US 163/H2
Timberville, Va, US 163/H1
Timbiquí, Col. 180/B4
Timbiras, Braz. 183/F4
Timbo, Gui. 114/C4
Timbó, Braz. 189/G3
Timboon, Austl. 132/B3
Timbué (pt.), Moz. 123/H3
Timbuni (riv.), Indo. 91/H4
Timehri (int'l arpt.), Guy. 181/G3
Timelkam, Aus. 59/G6
Timenocalin (well), Libya 134/A3
Timetrine, Mali 115/E2
Timetrout (peak), Mor. 66/B4
Timfristós (peak), Gre. 75/G3
Timgad (ruin), Alg. 66/E4
Tîmia, Niger 115/H2
Timimoun, Alg. 111/F3
Timiris (cape), Mrta. 114/A2
Timiş (riv.), Rom. 70/B3
Timiş (prov.), Rom. 50/E3
Timişoara (int'l arpt.), Rom. 50/E3
Timişoara, Rom. 50/E3
Timmins, On, Can. 167/H4
Timmonsville, SC, US 163/H3
Timms (hill), Wi, US 157/J5
Timoleague, Ire. 32/B6
Timon, Braz. 183/F4
Timonium, Md, US 168/B5
Timor (isl.), Indo. 77/M10
Timor (sea), Asia,Austl. 77/M11
Timor Timur (prov.), Indo. 128/A2
Timóteo, Braz. 187/E3
Timpas, Co, US 152/C2
Timpson, Tx, US 151/G2
Timpton (riv.), Rus. 75/N4
Tims Ford (dam), Tn, US 162/D3
Tims Ford (lake), Tn, US 162/D3
Timsāḩ (lake), Egypt 113/D3
Timsher, Rus. 69/M3
Timucuan Nat'l Prsv., Fl, US 165/H2
Timurnī, India 96/A4
Tin Can Bay, Austl. 134/D4
Tin Shui Wai, China 87/K7
Tina (riv.), SAfr. 124/B1
Tinaca (pt.), Phil. 88/D4
Tinaco, Ven. 180/D2
Tinahely, Ire. 32/D4
Tinca, Rom. 50/E2
Tinchebray, Fr. 57/E3
Tincup, Co, US 149/J1
Tinderry (mtn.), Austl. 133/D2
Tindivanam, India 95/C3
Tindouf (wilaya), Alg. 110/D3
Tindouf, Alg. 110/C4
Tiné, Oued (riv.), Chad 116/D2
Tinée (riv.), Fr. 64/C4
Tineo, Sp. 46/B1
Ting (riv.), China 87/H3
Tinga (peak), CAfr. 116/D3
Tingalpa (res.), Austl. 134/F7
Tingaringy NP, Austl. 132/D3
Tingha, Austl. 132/D1
Tingi (mts.), SLeo. 114/C4
Tingjegaon, Nepal 96/D1
Tinglin, China 80/L9
Tingmerkpuk (mt.), Ak, US 171/F2
Tingo María, Peru 184/C3
Tingping, China 87/F3
Tingréla, C.d'Iv. 114/D4
Tingri, China 97/F1
Tingsryd, Swe. 40/F3
Tinguiririca (vol.), Chile 190/C2
Tinh Gia, Viet. 94/D2
Tinharé (isl.), Braz. 187/F2
Tinian (isl.), NMar. 136/D3
Tinicum Nat'l Consv. Area, Pa, US 168/C4
Tinker (A.F.B.), Ok, US 153/F3
Tinkisso (riv.), Gui. 114/C4
Tinley Park, Il, US 167/Q16
Tinogasta, Arg. 188/C4
Tínos, Gre. 75/J4
Tínos (isl.), Gre. 67/K3
Tinqueux, Fr. 54/C5
Tinrhir, Mor. 110/D3
Tinsman, Ar, US 153/H4
Tinsukia, India 86/B3
Tinta, Peru 184/D4
Tintagel (pt.), Eng, UK 36/B5
Tintagel, Eng, UK 36/B5
Tîntâne, Mrta. 114/C2
Tinténiac, Fr. 56/D4
Tintern Abbey, Eng, UK 36/D3
Tintigny, Belg. 55/E4
Tintina, Arg. 188/D3
Tintinara, Austl. 132/B2
Tinto (peak), Sc, UK 33/C5
Tinto (riv.), Sp. 46/B4
Tinton Falls (New Shrewsbury), NJ, US 168/D3
Tintwistle, Eng, UK 35/G5
Tinui, NZ 135/D3
Tinyahuarco, Peru 184/B3
T'i'o, Erit. 118/B2
Tioga, Tx, US 153/F4
Tioga, ND, US 156/C3
Tioga (peak), Ca, US 148/C2
Tioga, WV, US 163/G1
Tiom, Indo. 91/J4
Tioman (isl.), Malay. 90/B3
Tione di Trento, It. 61/G5
Tionesta, Pa, US 161/G4
Tip Top (mt.), On, Can. 157/L3
Tipac (hill), Braz. 182/D2
Tipasa, Alg. 112/G4
Tipasa (wilaya), Alg. 112/F4
Tipp City, Oh, US 160/D5
Tipperary, Ire. 32/B5
Tipperary (co.), Ire. 32/C4
Tippettville, Ga, US 165/G1
Tipton, Ok, US 152/E3
Tipton, Mo, US 153/H1
Tipton, Pa, US 161/G4
Tipton, In, US 160/C4
Tipton, Ks, US 154/E4
Tipton, Ia, US 155/J3
Tiptonville, Tn, US 162/C2
Tiptree, Eng, UK 37/G3
Tiptūr, India 95/C3
Tiputa, FrPol. 137/L6
Tir Rhiwiog (peak), Wal, UK 36/C1
Tira, Tx, US 153/G4
Tīra Sujānpur, India 98/D4
Tiracambu, Serra do (mts.), Braz. 183/E4
Tiran (isl.), SAr. 109/G3
Tiran (str.), Egypt, SAr. 109/G3
Tiran Sinafir (isl.), SAr. 102/C5
Tiranë (cap.), Alb. 75/F2
Tirano, It. 61/G5
Tiraque, Bol. 188/C1
T'irarē Shet' (riv.), Eth. 118/A2
Tirari (des.), Austl. 131/H4
Tiraspol, Mol. 72/E4
Tirat Karmel, Isr. 105/B3
Tirat Ẕevi, Isr. 105/D4
Tire, Turk. 102/A2
Tirebolu, Turk. 70/F4
Tiree (isl.), Sc, UK 31/Q8
Tirest (well), Mali 115/F1
Tirgol, Eth. 116/G4
Tîrgovişte, Rom. 51/G3
Tîrgu Bujor, Rom. 51/H3
Tîrgu Cărbuneşti, Rom. 51/F3
Tîrgu Frumos, Rom. 72/D4
Tîrgu Jiu, Rom. 51/F3
Tîrgu Lăpuş, Rom. 51/F2
Tîrgu Mureş, Rom. 51/G2
Tîrgu Neamţ, Rom. 72/D4
Tîrgu Ocna, Rom. 51/H2
Tîrgu Secuiesc, Rom. 51/H2
Tiris (reg.), WSah. 110/B5
Tiris Zemmour (pol. reg.), Mrta. 110/C4
Tiritiri Matangi (isl.), NZ 135/F6
Tirlyanskiy, Rus. 69/N5
Tîrnava Mare (riv.), Rom. 51/G2
Tîrnava Mică (riv.), Rom. 51/F2
Tîrnăveni, Rom. 51/G2
Tírnavos, Gre. 75/H3
Tiro, Gui. 114/C4
Tirol (prov.), Aus. 42/F5
Tirrenia, It. 62/D6
Tirschenreuth, Ger. 59/F3
Tirso (riv.), It. 66/F2
Tirstup (int'l arpt.), Den. 40/D3
Tirúa, Chile 190/B3
Tiruchendūr, India 95/C4
Tiruntán, Peru 184/C2
Tirupati (int'l arpt.), India 95/C3
Tirūr, India 95/B4
Tiruttani, India 92/C3
Tiruvalla, India 95/C4
Tiruvannāmalai, India 95/C3
Tisa (riv.), Yugo. 67/K1
Tisbury, Eng, UK 36/D4
Tisdale, Sk, Can. 145/M1
Tishkovo, Rus. 71/J3
Tishomingo, Ok, US 153/F3
Tishomingo, Ms, US 162/C3
Tishomingo Nat'l Wildlife Res., Ok, US 153/F3
Ţīsīyah, Syria 105/E4
Tissa, Mor. 112/B2
Tissemsilt, Alg. 112/F5
Tissemsilt (wilaya), Alg. 112/F5
Tissø (lake), Den. 39/H7
Tista (riv.), Bang. 97/G2
Tisvilde, Den. 39/J6
Tisza (riv.), Hun. 70/B3
Tiszaföldvár, Hun. 50/E2
Tiszafüred, Hun. 50/E2
Tiszakécske, Hun. 50/E2
Tiszalök, Hun. 50/E1
Tiszavasvári, Hun. 43/L5
Tit, Alg. 111/F4
Titano (peak), SMar. 63/F6
Titao, Burk. 115/E3
Titay, Phil. 88/C4
Titel, Yugo. 50/E3
Titerno (riv.), It. 65/D5
Titi, Congo 120/C3
Titicaca (lake), Bol.,Peru 179/B4
Titisee-Neustadt, Ger. 60/E2
Titlagarh, India 95/D1
Titlis (peak), Swi. 61/E4
Tito, It. 48/D2
Titov Veles, FYROM 75/G2
Titov vrh (peak), FYROM 75/G2
Titsey, Eng, UK 30/D3
Titting, Ger. 58/E5
Tittmoning, Ger. 59/F6
Titu, Rom. 51/G3
Titule, D.R. Congo 121/F2
Titusville, Pa, US 161/G4
Titusville, Fl, US 165/H3
Titusville, NJ, US 168/D3
Tiuni, India 98/D4
Tiva (riv.), Kenya 119/B2
Tivaouane, Sen. 114/A3
Tivat, Yugo. 50/D4
Tiverton, On, Can. 160/F2
Tiverton, Eng, UK 36/C5
Tivoli, It. 65/B4
Tivoli, Tx, US 151/F3
Tiwanacu, Bol. 188/B1
Ţīwī, Oman 101/G4
Tixán, Ecu. 184/B1
Tixtla de Guerrero, Mex. 175/F5
Tizayuca, Mex. 175/L7
Tizi Ouzou (wilaya), Alg. 112/H4
Tizi Ouzou, Alg. 112/H4
Tizimín, Mex. 176/D1
Tizmant ash Sharqīyah, Egypt 113/C6
Tiznados (riv.), Ven. 183/N8
Tiznap (riv.), China 101/L1
Tiznit, Mor. 110/C3
Tjæreborg, Den. 40/C4
Tjeldstø, Nor. 40/A1
Tjeukemeer (lake), Neth. 52/C3
Tjøme, Nor. 40/D2
Tjorn (isl.), Den. 40/D3
Tkhab (peak), Rus. 73/K5
Tkibuli, Geo. 71/G4
Tlachichuca, Mex. 175/M7
Tlacolula de Matamoros, Mex. 176/B2
Tlacotalpan, Mex. 175/P8
Tlacotepec, Mex. 175/F5
Tlalixcoyan, Mex. 175/N8
Tlalmanalco, Mex. 175/Q10
Tlalnepantla, Mex. 175/Q9
Tláloc (vol.), Mex. 175/Q10
Tlalpan (nbrhd.), Mex. 175/Q10
Tlaltenango de Sánchez Román, Mex. 174/E4
Tlaltizapan, Mex. 175/K8
Tlapa de Comonfort, Mex. 176/B2
Tlapacoya (ruin), Mex. 175/Q10
Tlapacoyan, Mex. 175/M7
Tlapehuala, Mex. 175/E5
Tlaquepaque, Mex. 174/E4
Tlaquiltenango, Mex. 175/K8
Tlatlauquitepec, Mex. 175/M7
Tlaxcala (state), Mex. 172/A5
Tlaxcala, Mex. 175/L7
Tlaxco, Mex. 175/L7
Tlaxcoapan, Mex. 175/K6
Tlell, BC, Can. 171/M5
Tlemcen, Alg. 112/D2
Tlokweng, Bots. 122/E5
Tmassah, Libya 134/B3
To-grenda, Nor. 38/S8
Toa Payoh (nbrhd.), Sing. 89/J6
Toabré, Pan. 180/A2
Toaca (peak), Rom. 51/G2
Toachi (riv.), Ecu. 180/B4
Toadlena, NM, US 149/H2
Toamasina, Madg. 125/J7
Toamasina (prov.), Madg. 125/J7
Toandos (pen.), Wa, US 167/B2
Toasi, Gha. 115/E5
Toast, NC, US 163/G2
Toau (isl.), FrPol. 137/L6
Toay, Arg. 190/D3
Toba (lake), Indo. 90/A3
Toba, China 78/D5
Toba, Japan 83/L7
Toba (inlet), BC, Can. 144/B2
Toba (riv.), BC, Can. 144/B2
Toba Kākar (range), Pak. 101/J2
Toba Tek Singh, Pak. 98/B4
Tobago (isl.), Trin. 173/J5
Tobarra, Sp. 46/E3
Tobbio (peak), It. 62/B4
Tobeatic Game Sanct., NS, Can. 158/E3
Tobercurry, Ire. 32/B1
Tobermore, NI, UK 34/B2
Tobermorey, Austl. 131/H2
Tobermory, On, Can. 160/F2
Tōbetsu, Japan 82/B2
Tobias, Ang. 120/C5
Tobias Barreto, Braz. 187/F1
Tobin (lake), Austl. 127/B3
Tobique (riv.), NB, Can. 158/D2
Tobishima, Japan 83/L5
Toblol (riv.), Kaz.,Rus. 77/F4
Toboali, Indo. 89/D3
Tobol (riv.), Rus. 69/Q5
Tobol, Kaz. 71/M1
Tobruk (Ţubruq), Libya 67/J4
Tobseda, Rus. 69/M1
Tobu, Japan 83/A1
Toburdanovo, Rus. 69/K5
Tobyhanna (lake), Pa, US 168/C1
Tobyhanna (riv.), Pa, US 168/C1
Tobyhanna, Pa, US 168/C1
Tobyhanna St. Park, Pa, US 168/C1
Tobyl (riv.), Rus.,Kaz. 74/G4
Tobysh (riv.), Rus. 69/L2
Tocache, Peru 184/B3
Tocaima, Col. 183/L8
Tocantínia, Braz. 182/D5
Tocantinópolis, Braz. 183/E4
Tocantins (riv.), Braz. 179/E4
Tocantins (state), Braz. 182/D5
Tocco da Casauria, It. 65/C3
Toccoa, Ga, US 163/F3
Toccoa (riv.), Ga, US 162/E3
Toce (riv.), It. 45/H3
Tochigi (pref.), Japan 85/F2
Tochigi, Japan 85/F2
Tochimilco, Mex. 175/L8
Tochio, Japan 85/F2
Tocina, Sp. 46/C4
Töcksfors, Swe. 40/D2
Toco, Tx, US 153/G4
Toco, Trin. 181/F2
Tocomechi, Bol. 188/D1
Tocopilla, Chile 188/B2
Tocumen, Pan. 180/B2
Tocumwal, Austl. 133/B2
Tocuyito, Ven. 180/D2
Tocuyo (riv.), Ven. 173/H5
Toda, Japan 83/D2
Toda Bhīm, India 92/C2
Toddington, Eng, UK 37/F3
Todenyang, Kenya 116/G4
Tödi (peak), Swi. 61/E4
Todi, It. 65/B2
Todmorden, Eng, UK 35/F4
Todos os Santos (bay), Braz. 187/F2
Todos Santos, Bol. 188/B1
Todos Santos, Bol. 185/E4
Todos Santos, Bol. 188/C1
Todos Santos, Mex. 174/C4
Todt Hill (nbrhd.), NY, US 169/J9
Todtmoos, Ger. 60/E2
Todtnau, Ger. 60/D2
Toe (pt.), Ire. 32/A7
T'oejo, NKor. 81/D3
Toffal (hill), Mrta. 110/C5
Toffo, Ben. 115/F5
Tofield, Ab, Can. 145/H1
Tofte, Nor. 38/S9
Tofua (isl.), Tonga 137/H6
Tōgane, Japan 83/E2
Togatax, China 99/D4
Togba (well), Mrta. 114/C2
Toggenburg (valley), Swi. 61/F3
Togher, Ire. 34/B5
Togiak, Ak, US 171/F4
Töging am Inn, Ger. 59/F6
Togo, Sk, Can. 156/D2
Tōgō, Japan 83/M5
Togo (ctry.) 107/C4
Tögrög, Mong. 78/C2
Togtoh, China 80/B2
Tōgyu-san NP, SKor. 81/D5
Togyz, Kaz. 71/M3
Tohāna, India 98/C5
Tohatchi, NM, US 149/H3
Tohickon (cr.), Pa, US 168/C3
Tohivea (peak), FrPol. 137/X15
Tōhoku (prov.), Japan 85/F1
Tohom, China 78/F3
Tohopekaliga (lake), Fl, US 165/H3
Tohopekaliga, East (lake), Fl, US 164/N7
Tohor (cape), Malay. 89/C2
Tohoun, Togo 115/F5
Toi, Japan 85/F3
Toibalawe, India 93/F5
Toijala, Fin. 39/D3
Tōin, Japan 83/L5
Toiyabe (range), Nv, US 146/E4
Tojō, Japan 84/C3
Tōjō, Japan 83/H6
Tok, Ak, US 171/K3
Tokachi (riv.), Japan 82/C2
Tōkai, Japan 83/L5
Tokaj, Hun. 43/L4
Tōkamachi, Japan 85/F2
Tokanui, NZ 135/B4
Tokar, Sudan 109/H5
Tokar Game Reserve, Sudan 109/H5
Tokar Nat'l Rsv., Sudan 109/F4
Tokara (isls.), Japan 136/B1
Tokarevka, Rus. 71/G2
Tokat, Turk. 102/D1
Tokat (prov.), Turk. 70/F4
Tŏkchŏk (arch.), NKor. 81/C4
Tŏkchŏk (isl.), NKor. 81/C4
Tŏkch'ŏn, NKor. 81/D3
Tokeen, Ak, US 171/M4
Tokeland, Wa, US 144/C4
Tokelau (terr.), NZ 137/H5
Toki (riv.), Japan 83/M5
Toki, Japan 83/M5
Tokigawa, Japan 83/C2
Tokio, ND, US 156/E4
Tokkya Chaung, Myan. 94/B3
Tokmak, Ukr. 73/H4
Tokmok, Kyr. 74/H5
Tokomaru Bay, NZ 135/D2
Tokoname, Japan 83/L6
Tokonou, Gui. 114/C4
Tokoro, Japan 82/D1
Tokoro (riv.), Japan 82/C2
Tokoroa, NZ 135/C2
Tokorozawa, Japan 85/F3
Tŏksŏng, NKor. 79/K3
Toksook Bay, Ak, US 171/E3
Toksovo, Rus. 69/T6
Toksun, China 99/E3
Toktogul (res.), Kyr. 99/B3
Toktogul, Kyr. 99/B3
Tokuno (isl.), Japan 85/K7
Tokunoshima, Japan 85/K7
Tokur, Rus. 79/L1
Tokushima, Japan 84/D3
Tokushima (pref.), Japan 84/C4
Tokuyama, Japan 84/B3
Tokwe (riv.), Zim. 123/F3
Tōkyō (pref.), Japan 85/F3
Tōkyō (cap.), Japan 85/F3
Tōkyō (bay), Japan 83/D2
Tōkyō Disneyland, Japan 83/D2
Tola, Nic. 176/E4
Tolaga Bay, NZ 135/D2
Tolar, Tx, US 151/F1
Tolar Grande, Arg. 188/C3
Tolbazy, Rus. 69/M5
Tolbo, Mong. 78/C2
Toledo, Oh, US 160/E4
Toledo, Col. 180/C3
Toledo, Sp. 46/C3
Toledo, Or, US 146/B1
Toledo, Il, US 162/C1
Toledo, Ia, US 155/H3
Toledo, Phil. 88/C3
Toledo, Uru. 191/K11
Toledo, Braz. 189/F3
Toledo, Bol. 188/C1
Toledo, Wa, US 144/C4
Toledo Bend (dam), Tx, US 164/B2
Toledo Bend (res.), Tx, US 172/C1
Toledo, Montes de (mts.), Sp. 46/C3
Tolentino, It. 65/C1
Tolfa, It. 65/A3
Tolfaccia (peak), It. 65/A3
Tolhuaca, PN, Chile 190/C3
Toli, China 99/D2
Toliara, Madg. 125/G8
Toliara (prov.), Madg. 125/G8
Tolima, Col. 180/C5
Tolima (dept.), Col. 180/C4
Tolitoli, Indo. 91/F3
Tolka (riv.), Ire. 34/B5
Tolkis (Tolkkinen), Fin. 39/F4
Tolkkinen (Tolkis), Fin. 39/F4
Tolland, Ab, Can. 145/J1
Tollarp, Swe. 39/K7
Tollette, Ar, US 153/H4
Tolley, ND, US 156/D3
Tollo, It. 65/D3
Tølløse, Den. 39/H7
Tolmezzo, It. 45/K3
Tolna, ND, US 156/E4
Tolna (prov.), Hun. 50/D2
Tolna, Hun. 50/D2
Tolo, D.R. Congo 120/D3
Tolo (gulf), Indo. 91/F4
Tolo (chan.), China 87/L7
Tolochin, Bela. 41/N4
Tolokiwa (isl.), PNG 129/G1
Tolongoina, Madg. 125/H8
Tolono, Il, US 160/B5
Tolosa, Sp. 44/B5
Tolsan (isl.), SKor. 81/D5
Tolstoy, SD, US 154/E1
Tolt (riv.), Wa, US 167/D2
Tolt (res.), Wa, US 167/D2
Tolt, North Fork (riv.), Wa, US 167/D2
Tolt, South Fork (riv.), Wa, US 167/D2
Toltén, Chile 190/B3
Toltén (riv.), Chile 190/B3
Tolú, Col. 180/C2
Toluca, Il, US 155/K3
Toluca, Mex. 175/Q10
Tolúviejo, Col. 180/C2
Tol'yatti, Rus. 71/J1
Tolybay, Kaz. 71/M2
Tom' (riv.), Rus. 74/J4
Tom, Ok, US 153/G4
Tom Price, Austl. 130/C2
Tom White (mt.), Ak, US 171/K3
Toma, Burk. 114/E3
Toma, PNG 129/G2
Tomah, Wi, US 155/J2
Tomahawk, Wi, US 157/K5
Tomahawk, Ab, Can. 144/G1
Tomakin, Austl. 133/E2
Tomakivka, Ukr. 73/H4
Tomakomai, Japan 82/B2
Tomamae, Japan 82/B1
Tomanao, Phil. 88/D4
Tomanivi (peak), Fiji 137/Y18
Tomar, Port. 46/A3
Tomari, Rus. 79/N2
Tómaros (peak), Gre. 75/G3
Tomarpaån (riv.), Swe. 39/L7
Tomarza, Turk. 102/C2
Tomás, Peru 184/C4
Tomás Barrón, Bol. 188/C1
Tomás de Berlanga, Ecu. 184/J7
Tomashëvka, Bela. 43/M3
Tomaszów Lubelski, Pol. 43/M3
Tomaszów Mazowiecki, Pol. 43/L3
Tomat, Sudan 117/E3
Tomatin, Sc, UK 33/C2
Tomatlán, Mex. 174/D5
Tomave, Bol. 188/C2
Tomb of Qinshihuang, China 80/B4
Tombador, Serra do (mts.), Braz. 185/G3
Tomball, Tx, US 151/M8
Tombe, Sudan 116/F4
Tombigbee (riv.), Al, Ms, US 143/J5
Tomboco, Ang. 120/C4
Tombolo, It. 63/E2
Tombouctou (pol. reg.), Mali 110/D5
Tombouctou, Mali 114/E2
Tombstone, Az, US 149/G5
Tombua, Ang. 122/A2
Tomé (isl.), Fr. 44/B2
Tomé, Chile 190/B3
Tome, NM, US 149/J3
Tomé-Açu, Braz. 182/D3
Tomea (isl.), Indo. 128/A1
Tomelilla, Swe. 40/E4
Tomelloso, Sp. 46/D3
Tomika, Japan 83/L5
Tomina, Bol. 188/C1
Tomingley, Austl. 133/D1
Tomini (gulf), Indo. 77/M10
Tominian, Mali 114/D3
Tomiño, Sp. 46/A2
Tomintoul, Sc, UK 33/C2
Tomioka, Japan 83/B1
Tomisato, Japan 83/E2
Tomiura, Japan 83/D3
Tomiyama, Japan 85/F3
Tomizawa, Japan 83/A3
Tommot, Rus. 75/N4
Tomo (riv.), Col. 180/D3
Tomorlog, China 99/F4
Tompa, Hun. 50/D2
Tompe, Indo. 91/E4
Tompkins, Sk, Can. 145/K2
Tompkinsville, Ky, US 162/E2
Tompo, Indo. 91/F3
Toms (riv.), NJ, US 168/D3
Toms River, NJ, US 168/D4
Tomsk, Rus. 74/J4
Tomskaya Oblast, Rus. 74/J4
Tömük, Turk. 104/D1
Tonalá, Mex. 176/C2
Tonale, Passo del (pass), It. 61/G5
Tonalea, Az, US 149/G2
Tonasket, Wa, US 144/E3
Tonate, FrG. 182/C1
Tonawanda (cr.), NY, US 160/V9
Tonawanda (res.), NY, US 160/V9
Tonawanda, NY, US 160/V9
Tonbridge, Eng, UK 30/D3
Tonckens (falls), Sur. 182/B1
Toncontín (int'l arpt.), Hon. 176/E3
Tondabayashi, Japan 83/J7
Tondano, Indo. 91/F3
Tondi Kiwindi, Niger 115/F3
Tondo, D.R. Congo 120/D3
Tondon, Gui. 114/B4
Tondoro, Namb. 122/C3
Tondu (peak), Fr. 60/C6
Tone (riv.), Japan 85/G3
Tone, Japan 83/E2
Tone (riv.), Eng, UK 36/C5
Tonekābon, Iran 103/G2
Tonelagee (peak), Ire. 34/B5
Tong (riv.), China 78/F5
Tong Fuk, China 87/K8
Tong Xian, China 80/H7
Tonga, Sudan 116/F3
Tonga (ctry.) 137/H7
Tongaat, SAfr. 125/E3
Tongala, Austl. 133/B3
Tong'an, China 87/H3
Tongareva (Penrhyn) (isl.), CookIs. 137/J5
Tongariro (vol.), NZ 135/C2
Tongariro NP, NZ 135/C2
Tongatapu (isl.), Tonga 137/H7
Tongbai, China 80/C4
Tongbei, China 79/K2
Tongbu, SKor. 81/G6
Tongbu (nbrhd.), SKor. 81/G6
Tongch'ang, NKor. 81/C2
Tongcheng, China 80/D5
Tongcheng, China 87/G2
T'ongch'ŏn, NKor. 81/D3
Tongchuan, China 80/B4
Tongdaemun (nbrhd.), SKor. 81/G6
Tongdao Dongzu Zizhixian, China 87/F3
Tongduch'on, SKor. 81/G6
Tongeren, Belg. 55/E2
Tonggou, China 81/C2
Tonggu, China 93/K2
Tonggu (peak), China 87/H3
Tonghae, SKor. 81/E4
Tongham, Eng, UK 30/A3
Tonghua, China 81/C2
Tonghua, China 81/C2
Tongjiadian, China 79/J3
Tongliao, China 80/E2
Tongling, China 87/H2
Tongmu, China 87/G3
Tongnae, SKor. 81/E5
Tongnan, China 86/E2
Tongnim, NKor. 81/C3
Tongno (riv.), NKor. 81/D2
Tongo, Austl. 132/B1
Tongo (peak), Indo. 91/E5
Tongobory, Madg. 125/H8
Tongren, China 87/F3
Tongsa (riv.), Bhu. 97/H2
Tongsa Dzong, Bhu. 97/H2
Tongshan, China 87/G2
Tongsin, NKor. 81/D2
Tongtian (riv.), China 78/D5
Tongue, Sc, UK 31/R7
Tongue (riv.), Mt, US 142/E2
Tongxu, China 80/C4
Tongyu, China 79/J3
Tongyuan, China 87/H2
Tongyuanpu, China 81/B2
Tonino-Anivskiy (pen.), Rus. 82/C1
Tönisvorst, Ger. 52/D6
Tonj (riv.), Sudan 116/F4
Tonj, Sudan 116/F4
Tonk, India 92/C2
Tonkawa, Ok, US 153/F2
Tonkin (gulf), China,Viet. 77/K7
Tonkoui (peak), C.d'Iv. 114/D5
Tonle Sap (lake), Camb. 93/H5
Tonneins, Fr. 44/D4
Tonnerre, Fr. 44/E3
Tönning, Ger. 40/C4
Tōno, Japan 82/B4
Tonopah, Az, US 149/F4
Tonoshō, Japan 84/D3
Tonosí, Pan. 180/A3
Tonota, Bots. 123/E4
Tons (riv.), India 96/C3
Tønsberg, Nor. 40/D2
Tonstad, Nor. 40/B2
Tonsina, Ak, US 171/J3
Tonto Nat'l Mon., Az, US 149/G4
Tontouta (Noumea) (int'l arpt.), NCal. 137/V13
Tonya, Turk. 70/F4
Toodyay, Austl. 130/C4
Tooele, Ut, US 147/G3
Tooele Army Dep., Ut, US 147/G3
Tooke (lake), Fl, US 164/K6
Tool, Tx, US 151/F1
Tooleybuc, Austl. 132/B2
Toomsboro, Ga, US 163/F4
Toomuc (cr.), Austl. 132/G6
Toomyvara, Ire. 32/B4
Tooradin, Austl. 132/C3
Tooraweenah, Austl. 132/D1
Tooromt, Mong. 78/C1
Toosey Ind. Res., BC, Can. 144/C2
Toot Hill, Eng, UK 30/D1
Tootsi, Est. 41/L2
Toowoomba, Austl. 134/C4
Top (mt.), Austl. 131/G2
Top of the World (peak), Wy, US 154/B2
Top Springs, Austl. 128/C4
Topaipí, Col. 183/L7
Topanaga State Park, Ca, US 166/B2
Topanga, Ca, US 166/B2
Topanga Beach, Ca, US 166/E7
Topawa, Az, US 149/G5
Tope de Coroa (mtn.), CpV. 107/J10
Topeka, In, US 160/D4
Topeka (cap.), Ks, US 155/G4
Topia, Mex. 174/D3
Topkapi Palace, Turk. 103/M6
Topliţa, Rom. 72/C4
Topock, Az, US 148/E3
Topohoco, Bol. 184/D5
Topol'čany, Slvk. 43/K4
Topol'níky, Slvk. 50/C2
Topolobampo, Mex. 174/C3
Topoloveni, Rom. 51/G3
Topolovgrad, Bul. 51/H4
Topozero (lake), Rus. 38/J2
Toppenish, Wa, US 144/D4
Toppenish (cr.), Wa, US 144/D4
Toprakkale, Turk. 104/E1
Topsham, Eng, UK 36/C5
Topton, Pa, US 168/C3
Toquepala, Peru 184/D5
Toquerville, Ut, US 149/F2
Toquima (range), Nv, US 146/E4
Tor, Eth. 116/G4
Tor (bay), Eng, UK 36/C6
Tor Lupara, It. 65/B4
Tora, D.R. Congo 121/G2
Torahime, Japan 83/K5
Torata, Peru 184/D5
Torawitan (cape), Indo. 91/G3
Torbalı, Turk. 102/A2
Torbat-e Ḩeydarīyeh, Iran 101/G1
Torbay, Nf, Can. 159/L2
Torbay (co.), Eng, UK 36/C6
Torbeck, Haiti 177/H2
Torbert (mt.), Ak, US 171/H3
Torbeyevo, Rus. 71/G1
Torch (lake), Mi, US 160/D2
Torcy, Fr. 30/K5
Tordera (riv.), Sp. 47/L6
Tordesillas, Sp. 46/C2
Tordino (riv.), It. 65/C2
Töreboda, Swe. 40/F2
Torekov, Swe. 39/J6
Torelló, Sp. 47/G1
Torez, Ukr. 73/K3
Torfaen (co.), Wal, UK 36/C3
Torgelow, Ger. 40/E5
Torghay, Kaz. 74/G4
Torghay, Kaz. 74/G5
Torhamnsudde (pt.), Swe. 40/F3
Torhout, Belg. 54/C1
Tori, India 97/E4
Tori-shima (isl.), Japan 136/D1
Toride, Japan 83/E2
Torigni-sur-Vire, Fr. 57/E2
Torii-tōge (pass), Japan 85/E3

Map Section
278
279

Tunda C – Useles

Tunda Chissococua, Ang. 122/C1
Tundazi (hill), Zim. 123/F3
Tundla, India 96/B2
Tunduma, Tanz. 121/H5
Tunduru, Tanz. 119/B4
Tundyk (riv.), Kaz. 99/C1
Tundzha (riv.), Bul. 67/K2
Tune, Den. 39/J7
Tung Chung, China 87/K7
Tung Lung (riv.), China 87/M8
Tungabhadra (riv.), India 92/C4
Tungabhadra (res.), India 92/C4
Tungamah, Austl. 132/C3
Tungaru, Sudan 116/F3
Tungawan, Phil. 88/C4
Tungelsta, Swe. 39/B1
Tungku, Malay. 88/B4
Tŭngsan-got (pt.), NKor. 81/C4
Tungshih, Tai. 87/J3
Tungsten, NW, Can. 140/D2
Tungurahua (prov.), Ecu. 180/B5
Tünhel, Mong. 78/F2
Tuni, India 95/D2
Tunica, La, US 164/C2
Tunica, Ms, US 162/B3
Tūnis (cap.), Tun. 48/B4
Tūnis (gov.), Tun. 48/B4
Tunisia (ctry.) 107/C1
Tunjá, Col. 180/C3
Tunkhannock, Pa, US 161/J4
Tunku Abdul Rahman NP, Malay. 88/B4
Tunliu, China 80/C3
Tunnel Creek NP, Austl. 128/B4
Tunnels of Vinh Moc, Viet. 94/D2
Tuntum, Braz. 183/E4
Tuntutuliak, Ak, US 171/F3
Tunungayualuk (isl.), Nf, Can. 167/K3
Tunuyán (riv.), Arg. 190/C2
Tunuyán, Arg. 190/C2
Tuo (riv.), China 78/E5
Tuokou, China 87/F3
Tuolu, China 87/E4
Tuolumne (riv.), Ca, US 146/D5
Tuolumne Grove, Ca, US 148/C2
Tuong Duong, Viet. 94/D2
Tuoniang (riv.), China 93/J3
Tuoro sul Trasimeno, It. 65/B1
Tuotuo (riv.), China 99/F5
Tuotuoheyan, China 78/C5
Tūp Āghāj, Iran 103/F2
Tupã, Braz. 189/G2
Tupaciguara, Braz. 189/G1
Tupai (isl.), FrPol. 137/K6
Tupambaé, Uru. 191/G2
Tupanatinga, Braz. 183/G5
Tupanciretã, Braz. 189/F4
Tuparro (riv.), Col. 180/D3
Tupelo, Ok, US 153/F3
Tupelo, Ms, US 162/C3
Tupelo Nat'l Bfld., Ms, US 162/C3
Tupi Paulista, Braz. 189/G2
Tupik, Rus. 68/G5
Tupinambarana (isl.), Braz. 182/B3
Tupiza, Bol. 188/C2
Tupman, Ca, US 148/C3
Tupper Lake, NY, US 161/J2
Tupungato, Arg. 190/C2
Tupungato (peak), Arg. 190/P8
Tuquan, China 79/J2
Tura (riv.), Rus. 74/G4
Tura, Rus. 75/L3
Tura, India 97/H3
Tura, China 99/E4
Ţurá, Egypt 113/C5
Turabah, SAr. 100/D4
Turakina, NZ 135/C3
Turan, Rus. 78/C1
Tur'ān, Isr. 105/C3
Turan Lowland (plain), Uzb. 74/G5
Turana (mts.), Rus. 79/L1
Turanganui (riv.), NZ 135/J9
Turangi, NZ 135/C2
Turano (riv.), It. 65/B3
Ţurayf, SAr. 102/D4
Turbaco, Col. 180/C2
Turbat, Pak. 101/H3
Turbenthal, Swi. 61/E3
Turbeville, SC, US 163/G4
Turbo, Col. 180/B2
Turbotville, Pa, US 168/B1
Turckheim, Fr. 60/D1
Turda, Rom. 51/F2
Tureia (isl.), FrPol. 137/M7
Turek, Pol. 43/K2
Turenki, Fin. 39/E4
Tŭrgovishte, Bul. 51/H4
Turgutlu, Turk. 102/A2
Turhal, Turk. 102/D1
Türi, Est. 41/L2
Turiaçu (bay), Braz. 183/E3
Turiaçu, Braz. 183/E3
Turiamo, Ven. 183/N7
Turin (Torino), It. 62/A2
Turiys'k, Ukr. 72/C2
Turka, Ukr. 43/M4
Turka, Rus. 78/F1
Turkana (Rudolf) (lake), Kenya 107/F4
Turkana Nat'l Rsv., Kenya 119/A1
Türkeli, Turk. 70/E4
Túrkeve, Hun. 50/E2
Turkey (ctry.) 77/B5
Turkey (cr.), Tx, US 151/E3
Turkey (riv.), Ia, US 155/J2
Turkey Creek (lake), La, US 164/C2
Turkey Creek, Austl. 128/C4
Türkheim, Ger. 61/G1
Turki, Rus. 73/M2
Türkistan, Kaz. 99/A3
Türkmenabat, Trkm. 74/G6
Turkmen-Kala, Trkm. 101/H1
Turkmenistan (ctry.) 77/E6
Türkoğlu, Turk. 102/D2
Turks (isls.), Haiti 173/G3
Turks and Caicos (isls.), UK 139/K7
Turks Island Passage (chan.), UK 177/J1
Turku (int'l arpt.), Fin. 41/K1
Turku (Åbo), Fin. 41/K1
Turku Ja Pori (prov.), Fin. 38/G3
Turkwel (riv.), Kenya 119/A1
Turley, Ok, US 153/G2
Turlingua (cr.), Tx, US 151/C3
Turlock, Ca, US 148/B2
Turmalina, Braz. 187/E3
Turmantas, Lith. 41/M4
Turmero, Ven. 183/N7
Turnagain (cape), NZ 135/D3
Turnberry, Sc, UK 33/B6
Turnbull (dry lake), Or, US 146/E2
Turnbull (mt.), Az, US 149/G4
Turnbull NWR, Wa, US 144/F4
Turneffe (isls.), Belz. 172/D4
Turner, Me, US 161/L2
Turner (mt.), Austl. 130/C2
Turner, Mt, US 145/K3
Turner Valley, Ab, Can. 144/G2
Turnersville, Tx, US 150/F2
Turnersville, NJ, US 168/C4
Turnhouse (int'l arpt.), Sc, UK 33/C5
Turnhout, Belg. 52/B6
Turnov, Czh. 43/H3
Turnu Măgurele, Rom. 51/G4
Turon, Ks, US 153/E2
Turon (riv.), Austl. 133/D1
Tuross Head, Austl. 133/E3
Turov, Bela. 72/D1
Turpan, China 99/E3
Turquino (peak), Cuba 177/G2
Turrell, Ar, US 162/B3
Turretot, Fr. 57/F1
Turriaco, It. 63/G2
Turriers, Fr. 64/C4
Turriff, Sc, UK 33/D1
Tursunzoda, Taj. 74/G6
Turt, Mong. 78/E1
Turtle (riv.), ND, US 156/F3
Turtle (isls.), SLeo. 114/B5
Turtle (cr.), SD, US 154/E1
Turtle (pt.), Austl. 128/C3
Turtle Lake, ND, US 156/D4
Turtle Mountain Ind. Res., ND, US 156/E3
Turtle River, Mn, US 157/G4
Turtleford, Sk, Can. 145/K1
Turton, Eng, UK 35/F4
Turton, SD, US 154/E1
Turukhansk, Rus. 74/J3
Turvo (riv.), Braz. 186/C4
Tuscaloosa, Al, US 162/D4
Tuscaloosa (lake), Al, US 162/D4
Tuscano (arch.), Fr. 48/B1
Tuscano (arch.), It. 66/F2
Tuscany (reg.), It. 67/F2
Tuscarawas (riv.), Oh, US 160/F4
Tuscarora, Nv, US 146/E3
Tuscarora Mtn. (mtn.), Pa, US 168/A3
Tuscola, Il, US 160/B5
Tuscola, Tx, US 151/E1
Tuscumbia, Mo, US 153/H1
Tuscumbia, Al, US 162/D3
Tushar (mts.), Ut, US 149/F1
Tushino (nbrhd.), Rus. 69/W9
Tushka, Ok, US 153/F3
Tuskahoma, Ok, US 153/G3
Tuskegee, Al, US 162/E4
Tuskegee Institute Nat'l Hist. Site, Al, US 162/E4
Tusket, NS, Can. 158/E4
Tussy, Ok, US 153/F3
Tustin, Ca, US 166/G8
Tuszyn, Pol. 43/K3
Tutak, Turk. 103/E2
Tutayev, Rus. 68/H4
Tutbury, Eng, UK 35/G6
Tutin, Yugo. 50/E4
Tutóia, Braz. 183/F3
Tutong, Bru. 88/A4
Tutrakan, Bul. 51/H3
Tuttle, ND, US 156/E4
Tuttle, Ok, US 153/F3
Tuttle Creek (res.), Ks, US 153/F1
Tuttlingen, Ger. 61/E2
Tutuala, ETim. 128/B2
Tutubu, Tanz. 121/H4
Tutuila (isl.), ASam. 137/T10
Tuţūn, Egypt 113/B6
Tutupaca (vol.), Peru 184/D5
Tututalak (mt.), Ak, US 171/F2
Tutwiler, Ms, US 162/B3
Tutzing, Ger. 61/H2
Tuul (riv.), Mong. 78/F2
Tuulos, Fin. 39/E3
Tuusula, Fin. 41/L1
Tuusulajärvi (lake), Fin. 39/E4
Tuvalu (ctry.) 136/G5
Ţuwayq, Jabal (mts.), SAr. 100/E3
Tuxford, Eng, UK 35/H5
Tuxford, Sk, Can. 145/M2
Tuxpan, Mex. 174/D4
Tuxpan, Mex. 174/E5
Tuxpan de Rodríguez Cano, Mex. 176/B1
Tuxtla Gutiérrez, Mex. 176/C2
Túy, Sp. 46/A1
Tuy (riv.), Ven. 183/P7
Tuy An, Viet. 94/E3
Tuy Hoa, Viet. 94/E3
Tuyen Hoa, Viet. 94/D2
Tuyen Quang, Viet. 94/D1
Tuymazy, Rus. 69/M5
Tūysarkān, Iran 103/G3
Tuyuk, Kaz. 99/C3
Tuz (lake), Turk. 102/C2
Ţūz Khurmātū, Iraq 103/F3
Tuzha, Rus. 69/K4
Tuzigoot Nat'l Mon., Az, US 149/F3
Tuzla, Turk. 104/D1
Tuzla, Bosn. 50/D3
Tuzla, Turk. 103/N7
Tuzluca, Turk. 103/E1
Tuzlukçu, Turk. 102/B2
Tuzly, Ukr. 51/K3
Tuzule, D.R. Congo 121/E4
Tvååker, Swe. 40/E3
Tvedestrand, Nor. 40/C2
Tver', Rus. 68/G4
Tverskaya Oblast, Rus. 41/P3
Tvertsa (riv.), Rus. 68/G4
Tvŭrditsa, Bul. 51/G4
Twapia, Zam. 123/F2
Twardogóra, Pol. 43/J3
Tway, Sk, Can. 145/M1
Tweed (riv.), Sc, UK 33/C5
Tweed, On, Can. 161/H2
Tweed Heads, Austl. 134/D5
Tweed-New Haven (arpt.), Ct, US 169/F1
Tweedmouth, Eng, UK 33/D5
Tweedsmuir, Sc, UK 33/C5
Twello, Neth. 52/D4
Twente (pol. reg.), Neth. 52/D4
Twente (canal), Neth. 52/D4
Twenty Mile (cr.), On, Can. 160/T9
Twentynine Palms, Ca, US 148/D3
Twentynine Palms Marine Corps Base, Ca, US 148/D3
Twig, Mn, US 157/H4
Twin (falls), Id, US 147/F2
Twin Bridges, Mt, US 147/G1
Twin Buttes (res.), Tx, US 151/D2
Twin City, Ga, US 163/F4
Twin Falls, Id, US 147/F2
Twin Hills, Ak, US 171/F4
Twin Lake, Mi, US 160/C3
Twin Lakes, Wi, US 167/P14
Twin Rivers, NJ, US 168/D3
Twin Rocks, Or, US 144/C5
Twin Valley, Mn, US 156/F4
Twin, North (lake), Wi, US 157/K4
Twingi, Zam. 123/F1
Twist, Ger. 52/E3
Twiste (riv.), Ger. 53/G6
Twistringen, Ger. 53/F3
Twitchell (res.), Ca, US 148/B3
Two Butte (cr.), Co, US 152/C2
Two Harbors, Mn, US 157/J4
Two Hills, Ab, Can. 145/J1
Two Medicine (riv.), Mt, US 145/H3
Two Rivers (res.), NM, US 152/B4
Two Rivers, Wi, US 160/C2
Twodot, Mt, US 145/J4
Twycross, Eng, UK 37/E1
Twyfelfontein Rock Engravings, Namb. 122/B4
Twyford, Eng, UK 37/F4
Twymyn (riv.), Wal, UK 36/C1
Twynholm, Sc, UK 34/D2
Tyachiv, Ukr. 72/B3
Tyao (riv.), India 86/B4
Tyatya (vol.), Rus. 82/E1
Tybee Nat'l Wild. Ref., Ga, US 165/H1
Tychy, Pol. 43/K3
Tydd Saint Giles, Eng, UK 37/G1
Tye, Tx, US 151/E1
Tyémé, C.d'Iv. 114/D4
Tyendinaga, On, Can. 161/H2
Tygart (lake), WV, US 163/H1
Tygda, Rus. 79/K1
Tyger (riv.), SC, US 163/G3
Tygh Valley, Or, US 146/C1
Tyi Grounto (plat.), Niger 134/B4
Tyldesley, Eng, UK 35/F4
Tyler, Mn, US 155/F1
Tyler, Tx, US 151/G1
Tylers Green, Eng, UK 30/A2
Tylersville, Pa, US 168/A2
Tylertown, Ms, US 164/C2
Tymovskoye, Rus. 79/N1
Týn, Czh. 43/H4
Tynagh, Ire. 32/B3
Tynan, Tx, US 150/F3
Tynda, Rus. 75/N4
Tyndall, Mb, Can. 156/F2
Tyndall (A.F.B.), Fl, US 165/F2
Tyndall, SD, US 154/F2
Tyndrum, Sc, UK 33/B4
Tyne (riv.), Sc, UK 33/D5
Tyne and Wear (co.), Eng, UK 35/G2
Tyne Valley, PE, Can. 158/F2
Tynemouth, Eng, UK 35/G1
Tyner, Ky, US 162/F2
Tynset, Nor. 38/D3
Tyonek, Ak, US 171/H3
Tyre (Şūr), Leb. 105/C2
Tyresö, Swe. 39/B1
Tyrifjorden (lake), Nor. 40/C1
Tyringe, Swe. 40/E3
Tyrma (riv.), Rus. 79/L2
Tyrnyauz, Rus. 71/G4
Tyro, Ks, US 153/G2
Tyrone, Ok, US 152/D2
Tyrone, Pa, US 161/G4
Tyrone, NM, US 149/H4
Tyrone, Ga, US 163/L8
Tyronza, Ar, US 162/B3
Tyrrell (cr.), Austl. 132/B2
Tyrrellspass, Ire. 32/C3
Tyrrhenian (sea), It. 29/F4
Tyshkivka, Ukr. 72/F3
Tysnes, Nor. 40/A1
Tysnesøy (isl.), Nor. 40/A2
Tysons Corner, Va, US 168/A6
Tysse, Nor. 40/A1
Tystberga, Swe. 40/G2
Tytuvėnai, Lith. 41/K4
Tyub-Karagan (pt.), Kaz. 71/J3
Tyulen'i (isls.), Rus. 71/J3
Tyuleniy (isl.), Rus. 71/H3
Tyumenskaya Oblast, Rus. 69/Q4
Tyumen', Rus. 69/Q4
Tyumen (int'l arpt.), Rus. 69/Q4
Tyup, Kyr. 99/C3
Tyva Resp., Rus. 74/K4
Tywi (riv.), Wal, UK 36/B3
Tywyn, Wal, UK 36/B1
Tzaneen, SAfr. 123/F4
Tzucacab, Mex. 176/D1

U

U S Army Ammunition Plant, Ok, US 153/F3
U. S. Naval Weapons Station, Ca, US 166/F8
U.C.-Irvine, Ca, US 166/G8
U.K. Sovereign Base Area (gov.), Cyp. 104/C2
U.S.S. Alabama Battleship Park, Al, US 164/E2
Ua Huka (isl.), FrPol. 137/M5
Ua Pou (isl.), FrPol. 137/L5
Uad Assag (riv.), WSah. 110/B4
Uad Atui (riv.), WSah. 110/B5
Uad el Jat (riv.), WSah. 110/B4
Uad Tenuaiur (riv.), WSah. 110/A5
Uadi Uadaimo (wadi), Som. 118/D3
Uamba (riv.), D.R. Congo 120/D4
Uamh Bheag (peak), Sc, UK 33/B4
Uanda, Austl. 134/B3
Uato-Lari, ETim. 128/B2
Uatuma (riv.), Braz. 182/B3
Uatumã (riv.), Braz. 181/G5
Uauá, Braz. 187/F1
Uaupés (riv.), Braz. 180/D4
Uaxactún (ruin), Guat. 176/D2
Ub, Yugo. 50/E3
Uba, Nga. 116/B3
Ubá, Braz. 187/E4
Ubach over Worms, Neth. 55/F2
Übach-Palenberg, Ger. 55/F2
Ubagan (riv.), Kaz. 69/Q5
Ubaitaba, Braz. 187/F2
Ubajara, Braz. 183/F3
Ubajara, PN de, Braz. 183/F3
Ubangi (riv.), D.R. Congo 107/D4
Ubatã, Braz. 187/F2
Ubaté, Col. 183/M7
Ubatuba, Braz. 187/L8
Ubay, Phil. 88/D3
Ubaye (riv.), Fr. 45/G4
Ubbergen, Neth. 52/C5
Ube, Japan 84/B4
Úbeda, Sp. 46/D3
Uberaba, Braz. 189/H1
Uberaba (lake), Braz. 185/G5
Überherrn, Ger. 55/F5
Uberlândia, Braz. 186/C3
Überlingen, Ger. 61/F2
Überlingersee (lake), Ger. 61/E2
Ubia (peak), Indo. 91/J4
Ubiaja, Nga. 115/G5
Ubina, Bol. 188/C2
Ubinas, Peru 184/D5
Ubly, Mi, US 160/E3
Ubombo, SAfr. 125/F2
Ubon Ratchathani, Thai. 94/D3
Ubrique, Sp. 46/C4
Ubundu, D.R. Congo 121/F3
Ubute, D.R. Congo 121/F3
Ucar, Azer. 103/F1
Ucayali (riv.), Peru 179/B3
Ucayali (dept.), Peru 184/C3
Uccle, Belg. 55/D2
Uch, Pak. 98/A5
Uch-Adzhi, Trkm. 101/H1
Uch-Aral, Kaz. 74/J5
Ucha (riv.), Rus. 69/W8
Uchab, Namb. 122/C3
Uchaly, Rus. 69/N5
Uchāna, India 98/D5
Ucharonidge, Austl. 128/D4
Uchinskoye (res.), Rus. 69/W8
Uchiura (bay), Japan 79/N3
Uchiza, Peru 184/B3
Uchkeken, Rus. 73/M6
Uchquduq, Uzb. 74/G5
Uchte (riv.), Ger. 42/F2
Uchte, Ger. 53/F3
Uchumarca, Peru 184/B2
Uchumayo, Peru 184/D5
Uchur (riv.), Rus. 75/P4
Ücker (riv.), Ger. 40/E5
Uckermark (reg.), Ger. 43/G2
Uckfield, Eng, UK 37/G5
Ucluelet, BC, Can. 144/B3
Ucon, Id, US 147/H2
Üçpınar, Turk. 104/C1
Ucross, Wy, US 147/K1
Ucua, Ang. 120/C5
Ucumasi, Bol. 188/C1
Uda (riv.), Rus. 75/M4
Udaipur, India 92/B3
Udaipur Garhi, Nepal 97/F2
Udaipura, India 96/B4
Udamalpet, India 95/C4
Udara, Nga. 115/G4
Uddevalla, Swe. 40/D2
Uddingston, Sc, UK 33/B5
Uddjaure (lake), Swe. 38/F2
Üdem, Ger. 52/D5
Uden, Neth. 52/C5
Udenhout, Neth. 52/C5
Uder, Ger. 53/H6
Udgīr, India 95/C2
Udhampur, India 98/C3
Udi, Nga. 115/G5
Udimskiy, Rus. 69/K3
Udine (prov.), It. 63/G1
Udine, It. 45/K3
Udmurtiya Resp., Rus. 74/F4
Udomlya, Rus. 68/G4
Udon (riv.), Fr. 57/E3
Udon Thani, Thai. 94/C2
Ueckermünde, Ger. 40/F5
Ueda, Japan 85/F2
Uele (riv.), D.R. Congo 107/E4
Uelen, Rus. 142/W12
Uelsen, Ger. 52/D3
Uelzen, Ger. 53/H3
Ueno, Japan 83/K6
Ueno, Japan 83/B1
Uenohara, Japan 85/F3
Uere (riv.), D.R. Congo 117/E4
Uetendorf, Swi. 60/D4
Uetersen, Ger. 53/G1
Uetze, Ger. 53/H4
Ufa, Rus. 69/M5
Ufa (riv.), Rus. 69/N5
Uffenheim, Ger. 58/D3
Uffing, Ger. 61/H2
Uffington, Eng, UK 37/E3
Ufra, Trkm. 103/H2
Ugab (riv.), Namb. 122/B4
Ugāle, Lat. 41/K3
Ugalla (riv.), Tanz. 121/G4
Ugalla, Tanz. 121/G4
Ugalla River Game Rsv., Tanz. 121/G4
Uganda (ctry.) 107/F4
Ugbobo Ani, Nga. 115/G5
Ugento, It. 75/F3
Ugep, Nga. 115/H5
Ughelli, Nga. 115/G5
Ugie (riv.), Sc, UK 33/E1
Ugine, Fr. 60/C6
Uglegorsk, Ukr. 73/K3
Uglegorsk, Rus. 79/N2
Ugleural'skiy, Rus. 69/N4
Uglich, Rus. 68/H4
Ugljan (isl.), Cro. 45/L4
Uglovoye, Rus. 79/L3
Ugod, Hun. 50/C2
Ugol'nyye Kopi, Rus. 75/T3
Ugra (riv.), Rus. 68/G5
Ugŭrchin, Bul. 51/G4
Ugweno, Tanz. 119/B2
Uherské Hradiště, Czh. 43/J4
Uhingen, Ger. 58/C5
Uhland, Tx, US 150/F3
Úhlava (riv.), Czh. 43/G4
Úhlavka (riv.), Czh. 59/F3
Uhrichsville, Oh, US 160/F4
Uia di Ciamarella (peak), It. 64/D2
Uiangombe, Ang. 120/C5
Uig, Sc, UK 31/Q7
Uig, Sc, UK 31/Q8
Uíge (prov.), Ang. 120/C4
Uíge, Ang. 120/C4
Ŭihŭng, SKor. 81/E4
Ŭijŏngbu, SKor. 81/G6
Ŭiju, NKor. 81/C2
Uil, Kaz. 71/K2
Uil (riv.), Kaz. 71/K2
Uilkraal (riv.), SAfr. 124/L11
Uilpata (Gora Peak), Rus. 71/G4
Uinta (basin), Ut, US 147/H3
Uinta (mts.), Ut, US 147/H3
Uinta and Ouray Ind. Res., Ut, US 147/H3
Uiraúna, Braz. 183/G4
Ŭiryŏng, SKor. 81/E5
Ŭisŏng, SKor. 84/A2
Uitenhage, SAfr. 124/D4
Uitgeest, Neth. 52/B3
Uithoorn, Neth. 52/B4
Uithuizen, Neth. 52/D2
Uiwang, SKor. 81/F7
Ujae (isl.), Mrsh. 136/F4
Ujelang (isl.), Mrsh. 136/F4
Újfehértó, Hun. 43/L5
Ujhāni, India 96/B1
Uji (riv.), Japan 84/D3
Uji, Japan 83/J6
Ujiji, Tanz. 121/G4
Ujitawara, Japan 83/J6
Ujjain, India 92/C3
Ujohbilang, Indo. 90/E3
Ujung Pandang, Indo. 91/E5
Ujunggading, Indo. 89/B2
Ujunggenteng, Indo. 89/D4
Ukara (isl.), Tanz. 119/A2
Ukata, Nga. 115/G4
Ukerewe (isl.), Tanz. 119/A2
Ukhiya, Bang. 93/F3
Ukhta, Rus. 69/M3
Ukiah, Ca, US 146/B4
Ukiah, Or, US 146/D1
Uklāna, India 98/C5
Ukmergė, Lith. 41/L4
Ukraine (ctry.) 29/G4
Ukwama, Tanz. 119/A4
Ukwatutu, D.R. Congo 117/E4
Ul Bend NWR, Mt, US 145/L4
Ula, Turk. 67/L3
Ulaan-Uul, Mong. 78/G3
Ulaanbaatar (cap.), Mong. 78/F2
Ulaanbaatar (int'l arpt.), Mong. 78/F2
Ulaandel, Mong. 78/G2
Ulaangom, Mong. 99/F2
Ulaanjirem, Mong. 78/F2
Ulan Erge, Rus. 71/H3
Ulan Ul (lake), China 99/F5
Ulan-Burgasy (mts.), Rus. 78/F1
Ulan-Kholl, Rus. 71/H3
Ulan-Ude, Rus. 78/F1
Ulangati, D.R. Congo 121/F3
Ulanhot, China 79/J2
Ulatis (cr.), Ca, US 167/L10
Ulaya, Tanz. 119/B3
Ulchin, SKor. 84/A2
Ulcinj, Yugo. 75/F2
Ulcumayo, Peru 184/C3
Uldz (riv.), Mong. 78/G2
Ulefoss, Nor. 40/C2
Ulemiste (int'l arpt.), Est. 41/L2
Ulen, Mn, US 156/F4
Ulgain (riv.), China 79/H2
Ulhāsnagar, India 95/B2
Uliastay, Mong. 78/D2
Ulindi (riv.), D.R. Congo 121/F3
Ulithi (isl.), Micr. 136/C3
Uljma, Yugo. 50/E3
Ulla, Bela. 41/N4
Ulla (riv.), Sp. 46/A1
Ulla Ulla, Bol. 184/D4
Ulla Ulla, Res. Nacional, Bol. 184/D4
Ulladulla, Austl. 133/E2
Ullāpāra, Bang. 97/G3
Ullapool, Sc, UK 31/R8
Ullared, Swe. 40/E3
Ulldecona, Sp. 47/F2
Ullensvang, Nor. 40/B1
Ullerslev, Den. 39/G7
Üllő, Hun. 51/R10
Ulloma, Bol. 188/B1
Ullsfjorden (estu.), Nor. 38/F1
Ullswater (lake), Eng, UK 35/F2
Ullŭng (isl.), SKor. 79/L4
Ŭllyul, NKor. 81/C3
Ulm, Ar, US 153/J3
Ulm, Ger. 58/C6
Ulman, Mo, US 153/H1
Ulmarra, Austl. 132/E1
Ulmen, Ger. 55/F3
Ulonguè, Moz. 123/G2
Ulricehamn, Swe. 40/E3
Ulrichen, Swi. 61/E5
Ulrichsberg, Aus. 59/G5
Ulrichstein, Ger. 58/C1
Ulrum, Neth. 52/D2
Ulsan, SKor. 84/A3
Ulstein, Nor. 38/C3
Ulster (reg.), Ire. 34/A3
Ulster, Pa, US 161/H4
Ulster (riv.), Ger. 58/C1
Ulster American Folk Park, NI, UK 34/A2
Ulu, Sudan 116/G3
Ulu, Indo. 91/G3
Ulúa (riv.), Hon. 172/D4
Ulua (riv.), Hon. 176/E3
Uluçınar, Turk. 104/D1
Uludağ (peak), Turk. 102/B1
Uludoruk (peak), Turk. 103/F2
Uluguru (mts.), Tanz. 119/B3
Ulukışla, Turk. 102/C2
Ulundi, SAfr. 125/E3
Ulungur (riv.), China 78/B2
Ulungur (lake), China 78/B2
Uluru (Ayers Rock) (peak), Austl. 131/F3
Uluru NP, Austl. 131/F3
Ulutau (peak), Kaz. 99/A2
Ulverston, Eng, UK 35/E3
Ulverstone, Austl. 132/C4
Ulvik, Nor. 40/B1
Ulvila, Fin. 41/J1
Ul'yanovka, Rus. 41/P2
Ul'yanovka, Ukr. 72/F3
Ul'yanovo, Rus. 70/E1
Ul'yanovsk, Rus. 69/L5
Ul'yanovskaya Oblast, Rus. 71/H1
Ulysses, Ks, US 152/D2
Ulysses, Pa, US 161/H4
Ulysses, Ne, US 155/F3
Um Dafuq, Sudan 116/D3
Umala, Bol. 188/C1
Uman', Ukr. 72/F3
Umán, Mex. 176/D1
Umanum (pt.), Phil. 88/D3
Umari, Braz. 183/G4
Umarizal, Braz. 183/G4
Umarkot, India 95/D2
Umāsi La (pass), India 98/D3
Umatilla, Fl, US 165/H3
Umatilla (riv.), Or, US 146/D1
Umatilla, Or, US 144/E5
Umatilla Ind. Res., Or, US 146/D1
Umatilla NWR, Or, US 146/D1
Umba, Rus. 68/G2
Umbakumba, Austl. 129/E3
Umbeara, Austl. 131/G3
Umberto I, Arg. 188/D4
Umbogintwini, SAfr. 125/E3
Umboi (isl.), PNG 136/D5
Umbrail (peak), Swi. 61/G4
Umbrailpass (pass), Swi. 61/G4
Umbria (pol. reg.), It. 63/F6
Umbria (prov.), It. 45/K5
Umbuluze (riv.), Afr. 123/F5
Ume (riv.), Swe. 74/B3
Ume (riv.), Zim. 123/F3
Umeå, Swe. 38/G3
Umeälven (riv.), Swe. 38/F2
Umedpur, Bang. 97/G4
Umët, Rus. 71/G1
Umfolozi (riv.), SAfr. 125/E3
Umfreville (lake), On, Can. 157/G2
Umfuli (riv.), Zim. 123/F3
Umgeni (riv.), SAfr. 125/E3
Umhausen, Aus. 61/G3
Umiat, Ak, US 171/H2
Umkirch, Ger. 60/D1
Umkomaas, SAfr. 125/E3
Umm al Abīd, Libya 134/B3
Umm al Arānib, Libya 134/B3
Umm al Birak, SAr. 100/C4
Umm al Ghirbāl (well), Libya 134/B2
Umm al Khashab, SAr. 100/D5
Umm al Qaywayn, UAE 101/G3
Umm Buru, Sudan 116/D2
Umm Dam, Sudan 116/F2
Umm Dhibbān, Sudan 116/G2
Umm Dhibbān, Sudan 116/F2
Umm Durmān (Omdurman), Sudan 116/G2
Umm el Faḥm, Isr. 105/C3
Umm Inderaba, Sudan 116/F2
Umm Jawzah, Jor. 105/D4
Umm Kaddādah, Sudan 117/E2
Umm Lajj, SAr. 109/H3
Umm Qaşr, Iraq 103/F4
Umm Qawzayn, Sudan 117/E2
Umm Qays (Gedara) (ruin), Jor. 105/D3
Umm Ruwābah, Sudan 116/F2
Umm Sayyālah, Sudan 116/F2
Ummendorf, Ger. 61/F1
Umnak (isl.), Ak, US 171/E5
Umnak Pass (str.), Ak, US 171/E5
Umniati, Zim. 123/F3
Umniati (riv.), Zim. 123/F3
Umphang, Thai. 94/B2
Umpqua (riv.), Or, US 142/B3
Umpqua, Or, US 146/B2
Umpulo, Ang. 122/C2
Umraniye, Turk. 102/B2
Umred, India 95/C1
Ŭmsŏng, SKor. 81/D4
Umtata, SAfr. 124/E3
Umu Duru, Nga. 115/G5
Umuahia, Nga. 115/G5
Umuarama, Braz. 189/F2
Umuda (isl.), PNG 129/F2
Umunede, Nga. 115/G5
Umurbey, Turk. 75/K2
Umzimvubu (riv.), SAfr. 124/E3
Umzingwani (riv.), Zim. 123/F4
Umzinto, SAfr. 125/E3
Una, India 98/D4
Una (riv.), Bosn.,Cro. 67/H1
Una (mt.), NZ 135/C3
Una (riv.), Cro.,Bosn. 45/L4
Una, Braz. 187/F2
Unadilla, NY, US 161/J3
Unadilla, Ga, US 162/F4
Unaí, Braz. 186/D3
Unaka (mts.), Tn, US 163/F2
Unalakleet, Ak, US 171/F3
Unalaska, Ak, US 171/E5
Unalaska (isl.), Ak, US 171/E5
Unas (isl.), Fin. 39/F4
'Unayzah, SAr. 100/D3
Uncastillo, Sp. 47/E1
Unchahra, India 96/C3
Uncompaghre (riv.), Co, US 147/K4
Uncompaghre (plat.), Co, US 147/J4
Uncompahgre (peak), Co, US 149/J1
Undaunda, Zam. 123/F2
Unden (lake), Swe. 40/F2
Undenheim, Ger. 58/B3
Underberg, SAfr. 124/E3
Underbool, Austl. 132/B2
Underwood, ND, US 156/D4
Underwood-Petersville, Al, US 162/D3
UNDOF Zone, Syria 105/D2
Undu (pt.), Fiji 137/Z17
Unduavi, Bol. 184/E5
Une, Col. 183/L8
Unecha, Rus. 70/E1
Unga (isl.), Ak, US 171/F4
Ungama (bay), Kenya 119/C2
Ungarie, Austl. 133/C1
Ungava (pen.), Qu, Can. 167/J2
Ungava (pen.), Can. 139/K3
Ungava (bay), Can. 139/L4
Unggi, NKor. 79/L3
Ungheni, Mol. 72/D4
Ungwariba (pt.), Austl. 129/E3
Unhošt, Czh. 59/H2
Unhŭng, NKor. 81/E2
União, Braz. 183/F4
União da Vitória, Braz. 189/G3
União dos Palmares, Braz. 183/G5
Unimak (isl.), Ak, US 171/E5
Unimak (str.), Ak, US 171/E5
Unini (riv.), Braz. 181/F5
Unini, Peru 184/C3
Union (canal), Sc, UK 33/C5
Union, Oh, US 160/D5
Union, NJ, US 169/H9
Union, Or, US 146/E1
Union (mt.), Az, US 149/F3
Unión, Arg. 190/D2
Union, Al, US 162/D4
Union, Ms, US 162/C4
Union, Mo, US 162/B1
Union, WV, US 163/G2
Unión, Par. 189/E3
Union, SC, US 163/G3
Union (lake), NJ, US 168/C5
Union Beach, NJ, US 169/J10
Union Bridge, Md, US 168/A4
Union Center, SD, US 154/C1
Union City, Ok, US 153/F3
Union City, In, US 160/D4
Union City, Pa, US 161/G4
Union City, Mi, US 160/D3
Union City, Ca, US 167/K11
Union City, NJ, US 169/J8
Union City, Tn, US 162/C2
Union City, Ga, US 163/L7
Union Creek, Or, US 146/B2
Unión de Reyes, Cuba 177/F1
Unión de Tula, Mex. 174/D5
Union Flat (cr.), Wa, US 144/F4
Union Grove, Wi, US 160/B3
Unión Hidalgo, Mex. 176/C2
Union Mills, Md, US 168/A4
Union Park, Fl, US 164/N6
Union Pier, Mi, US 160/C4
Union Point, Ga, US 163/F4
Union Springs, NY, US 161/H3
Union Springs, Al, US 162/E4
Uniondale, NY, US 169/L9
Uniondale, SAfr. 124/C4
Unionhall, Ire. 32/A6
Uniontown, Ar, US 153/G3
Uniontown, Pa, US 161/G5
Uniontown, Ky, US 162/D2
Uniontown, Al, US 162/D4
Uniontown, Md, US 168/A4
Unionville, Mi, US 160/E3
Unionville, In, US 160/C5
Unionville, Ga, US 165/G2
Unionville, Nv, US 146/D3
Unionville, Mo, US 155/H3
Unionville, On, Can. 160/U8
Unionville, Va, US 163/J1
Unita (riv.), Ut, US 147/J3
United Arab Emirates (ctry.) 77/C7
United Kingdom (ctry.) 29/D3
United Nations, NY, US 169/K9
United Nations Mem. Cemetery, SKor. 84/A3
United States (ctry.) 139/G5
United States (range), Nun, Can. 167/T6
United States Coast Guard Receiving Center, NJ, US 168/D6
United States Department of Energy, Md, US 168/A5
United States Naval Academy, Md, US 168/B6
United States Naval Reservation Mil. Res., PR 173/M8
Unitsa, Rus. 68/G3
Unity, Or, US 146/D1
Unity, Wi, US 155/J1
Unity, Sk, Can. 145/K1
Unity Pd. (pond), Me, US 158/C3
Universal City, Tx, US 150/E3
Universal Studios Florida, Fl, US 164/M7
University of Minnesota Landscape Arboretum, Mn, US 157/N7
University Park, NM, US 149/J4
University Park, Tx, US 150/L7
University Place, Wa, US 167/B3
Unjha, India 101/K4
Unjŏn, NKor. 81/C3
Unkel, Ger. 55/G2
Unkurda, Rus. 69/N5
Unley (nbrhd.), Austl. 131/M8
Unna, Ger. 53/E5
Unnāo, India 96/C2
Ŭnp'a, NKor. 81/C3
Unsan, NKor. 81/C2
Ŭnsan-ŭp, NKor. 81/D3
Unshin (riv.), Ire. 32/B1
Unst (isl.), Sc, UK 31/W13
Unsu-Nodongjagu, NKor. 81/D2
Unter Pleichfeld, Ger. 58/D3
Unterägeri, Swi. 61/E3
Unterargen (riv.), Ger. 61/F2
Untergriesbach, Ger. 59/G5
Unterhaching, Ger. 59/E6
Unteriberg, Swi. 61/E3
Unterkulm, Swi. 60/E3
Unterlüss, Ger. 53/H3
Unterschleissheim, Ger. 59/E6
Untersee (lake), Swi. 61/E2
Unterseen, Swi. 60/D4
Untersiggenthal, Swi. 61/E3
Unterthingau, Ger. 61/G2
Untervaz, Swi. 61/F4
Unterweissenbach, Aus. 59/H6
Unuli Horog, China 99/F4
Unverre, Fr. 57/G4
Ünye, Turk. 70/F4
Unzen-Amakusa NP, Japan 84/A4
Unzen-dake (peak), Japan 84/B4
Unzha (riv.), Rus. 74/E4
Unzimkulu, SAfr. 125/E3
Uonquén, Ven. 181/F3
Uozu, Japan 85/E2
Upala, CR 177/E4
Upalco, Ut, US 147/H3
Upanema, Braz. 183/G4
Upata, Ven. 181/F2
Upemba (lake), D.R. Congo 121/F5
Upemba, PN de l', D.R. Congo 121/F5
Uphall, Sc, UK 33/C5
Upi, Phil. 88/D4
Upington, SAfr. 124/C3
Upinniemi (Obbnäs), Fin. 39/E4
Upiriwombe, Zam. 119/A4
Upland, In, US 160/D4
Upland, Pa, US 168/C4
Upleta, India 101/K4
Upminster (nbrhd.), Eng, UK 30/D2
Upolu (isl.), Sam. 137/S9
Upolu (pt.), Hi, US 142/S9
Upper (falls), Wy, US 147/H1
Upper (pen.), Mi, US 143/J2
Upper (lake), Ca, US 146/C3
Upper (bay), NY, US 168/D2
Upper Arlington, Oh, US 160/E4
Upper Arrow (lake), BC, Can. 144/F2
Upper Blackville, NB, Can. 158/E2
Upper Darby, Pa, US 168/C4
Upper Demerara-Berbice (pol. reg.), Guy. 181/G3
Upper Dicker, Eng, UK 37/G5
Upper East (pol. reg.), Gha. 115/E4
Upper Engadine (valley), Swi. 61/F5
Upper Fairmount, Md, US 163/K1
Upper Falls, Md, US 168/B5
Upper Ganges (canal), India 96/A1
Upper Hale, Eng, UK 30/A3
Upper Hutt, NZ 135/J9
Upper Iowa (riv.), Ia, US 155/J2
Upper Klamath (lake), Or, US 146/B2
Upper Klamath NWR, Or, US 146/C2
Upper Lake, Ca, US 146/B4
Upper Lough Erne (lake), NI, UK 31/Q9
Upper Marlboro (Marlboro), Md, US 168/B6
Upper Mesa (falls), Id, US 147/H1
Upper Missouri River Breaks Nat'l Mon., Mt, US 145/K4
Upper Ouachita NWR, La, US 151/H1
Upper Peoria (lake), Il, US 155/K3
Upper Red (lake), Mn, US 157/G3
Upper Rouge (riv.), Mi, US 167/F7
Upper Saddle River, NJ, US 169/J7
Upper Sandusky, Oh, US 160/E4
Upper Sioux Ind. Res., Mn, US 155/G1
Upper Souris NWR, ND, US 156/D3
Upper Takutu-Upper Essequibo (pol. reg.), Guy. 181/G4
Upper Thames (valley), Eng, UK 37/E3
Upper Trajan's Wall (wall), Mol. 70/D3
Upper Vaughan, NS, Can. 158/E3
Upper West (pol. reg.), Gha. 115/E4
Upper Yarra (res.), Austl. 133/B3
Upperglade, WV, US 163/G1
Upperlands, NI, UK 34/B2
Uppingham, Eng, UK 37/F1
Upplands-Bro, Swe. 39/A1
Upplands-Väsby, Swe. 40/G2
Uppsala (co.), Swe. 38/F3
Uppsala, Swe. 40/G2
Upsala, On, Can. 157/J3
Upshi, India 98/D3
Upson, Wi, US 157/J4
Upstart (cape), Austl. 134/B2
Upstart (bay), Austl. 129/G4
Upton, Wy, US 154/B1
Upton, Ky, US 162/E2
Upton upon Severn, Eng, UK 36/D2
Urabá (gulf), Col. 177/G4
Uracoa, Ven. 181/F2
Urad Qianqi, China 80/B2
Uraga (chan.), Japan 83/D3
Urahoro, Japan 82/C2
Urajärvi (lake), Fin. 39/F3
Urakawa, Japan 82/C2
Ural (riv.), Kaz. 71/J2
Ural (mts.), Rus. 29/L2
Ural (Zhāyya) (riv.), Rus. 74/F5
Uralla, Austl. 132/D1
Ural'skiy, Rus. 71/J2
Ural'skoye, Rus. 71/L1
Urambo, Tanz. 121/H4
Urana (lake), Austl. 133/C2
Urana, Austl. 133/C2
Urangeline (cr.), Austl. 133/C2
Urania, La, US 164/B2
Uranium City, Sk, Can. 140/F3
Uranquinty, Austl. 133/C2
Urapunga, Austl. 128/D3
Uraras, Namb. 122/B4
Uraricoera (riv.), Braz. 181/F4
Uraricoera, Braz. 181/F4
Urasoe, Japan 85/J7
Uravan, Co, US 149/H1
Urawa, Japan 85/F3
Uray, Rus. 74/G3
Urayasu, Japan 83/D2
Urazovka, Rus. 69/K5
Urazovo, Rus. 73/K2
Urbach, Ger. 58/C5
Urbana, Mo, US 153/H2
Urbana, Il, US 160/B4
Urbana, Oh, US 160/E4
Urbana, Md, US 168/A5
Urbandale, Ia, US 155/H3
Urbania, It. 63/F6
Urbano Santos, Braz. 183/F3
Urbenville, Austl. 134/D5
Urbino, It. 63/F6
Urcos, Peru 184/D4
Urda, Kaz. 71/H2
Urda, Sp. 46/D3
Urdinarrain, Arg. 191/J10
Urdorf, Swi. 61/E3
Urdzhar, Kaz. 99/D2
Ure (riv.), Eng, UK 35/G3
Urein, Egypt 113/B3
Ureki, Geo. 71/G4
Urengoy, Rus. 74/H3
Ures, Mex. 174/C2
Ureshino, Japan 83/K6
Ureterp, Neth. 52/D2
Urewera NP, NZ 135/D2
Urfa, Turk. 102/D2
Urfa (prov.), Turk. 102/D2
Urft (lake), Ger. 55/F2
Urft (riv.), Ger. 53/G6
Urgal, Rus. 79/L1
Urganch, Uzb. 74/G5
Urgnano, It. 62/C2
Urho Kekkosen NP, Fin. 38/H1
Uri, India 98/C2
Uri-Rotstock (peak), Swi. 61/E4
Uriah, Al, US 164/E2
Uriangato, Mex. 175/E4
Uribante (riv.), Ven. 180/D3
Uribia, Col. 180/C2
Uricani, Rom. 72/B5
Urich, Mo, US 153/G1
Urie (riv.), Sc, UK 33/D2
Urim, Isr. 105/B6
Urimán, Ven. 181/F3
Uriménil, Fr. 60/C1
Uriondo, Bol. 188/C2
Urique (riv.), Mex. 174/D3
Uriranteriña, Ven. 181/F3
Uritskiy, Kaz. 74/G4
Urjala, Fin. 41/K1
Urk, Neth. 52/C3
Urla, Turk. 70/C5
Urlaţi, Rom. 51/H3
Urlingford, Ire. 32/C4
Urman, Rus. 69/N5
Urmar, India 98/C4
Urmi (riv.), Rus. 78/L2
Urmia (lake), Iran 103/F2
Urmitz, Ger. 55/G3
Urmston, Eng, UK 35/F5
Urnäsch, Swi. 61/F3
Urnersee (lake), Swi. 61/E4
Uroševac, Yugo. 50/E4
Urr Water (riv.), Sc, UK 34/E1
Urrin (riv.), Ire. 32/D4
Ursensollen, Ger. 59/E4
Ursulo Galván, Mex. 175/N7
Urtazym, Rus. 71/L1
Uru Uru (lake), Bol. 188/C1
Uruaçu, Braz. 186/C2
Uruapan, Mex. 148/D5
Uruapan, Mex. 174/E5
Urubamba, Peru 184/C4
Urubamba (riv.), Peru 184/C3
Urubichá, Bol. 185/F4
Urubu (riv.), Braz. 181/G5
Urubuquara (hill), Braz. 182/C3
Uruburetama, Braz. 183/G3
Urucará, Braz. 182/B3
Urucu (riv.), Braz. 185/E2
Uruçuí, Braz. 183/E4
Uruçuí Preto (riv.), Braz. 183/E5
Uruçuí, Serra do (mts.), Braz. 183/E5
Urucuia (riv.), Braz. 186/D3
Urucurituba, Braz. 182/B3
Uruguai (riv.), Braz. 189/F3
Uruguaiana, Braz. 189/E4
Uruguay (ctry.) 179/D6
Uruguay (riv.), SAm. 179/D5
Urumaco, Ven. 180/D2
Ürümqi (int'l arpt.), China 99/E3
Ürümqi, China 99/E3
Urunga, Austl. 132/E1
Uruoca, Braz. 183/F3
Urup (isl.), Rus. 77/Q5
Ururi, It. 65/E4
Urus-Martan, Rus. 71/H4
Urussanga, Braz. 189/G4
Urussu, Rus. 71/K1
Uruwira, Tanz. 121/G4
Uruyén, Ven. 181/F3
Uryumkan (riv.), Rus. 79/H1
Uryupinsk, Rus. 73/M2
Urzhum, Rus. 69/L4
Urziceni, Rom. 51/H3
Us, Fr. 30/H4
Us (riv.), Rus. 78/C1
Usa (riv.), Rus. 74/F3
Usa, Japan 84/B4
USAF Academy, Co, US 154/B4
USAF Res., Tn, US 162/D3
Usagara, Tanz. 119/A2
Uşak, Turk. 102/B2
Uşak (prov.), Turk. 102/B2
Usakos, Namb. 122/B4
Usborne (mt.), UK 191/F6
Uscio, It. 62/C5
Usedom (isl.), Ger. 40/E4
Usedom, Ger. 40/E5
Useldange, Lux. 55/E4
Useless Loop, Austl. 130/B3

Map Section
280
281

Vershi – Vyazem

Vershino-Shakhtaminskiy, Rus. 79/H1
Versigny, Fr. 30/L4
Verskla (riv.), Ukr.,Rus. 74/D4
Versmold, Ger. 53/F4
Versoix, Swi. 60/C5
Vert-le-Grand, Fr. 30/K6
Vert-le-Petit, Fr. 30/K6
Vert-Saint-Denis, Fr. 30/K6
Vertana (peak), It. 61/G4
Verte (peak), Fr. 60/C6
Vertemate, It. 62/C2
Vertientes, Cuba 177/G1
Vertiyivka, Ukr. 72/F2
Vertou, Fr. 44/C3
Vertova, It. 62/C2
Vertus, Fr. 54/D6
Verviers, Belg. 55/E2
Vervins, Fr. 54/C4
Verwoerdburg, SAfr. 124/Q12
Verwood, Eng, UK 37/E5
Veryan (bay), Eng, UK 36/B6
Verzasca (riv.), Swi. 61/E5
Verzasca (Gerra), Swi. 61/E5
Verzée (riv.), Fr. 57/D5
Verzel (peak), It. 64/D2
Verzenay, Fr. 55/D5
Verzuolo, It. 64/D3
Verzy, Fr. 55/D5
Vescovato, Fr. 48/A1
Vescovato, It. 62/D3
Vesdre (riv.), Belg. 44/F1
Vesele, Ukr. 73/H4
Veselí nad Lužnicí, Czh. 59/H4
Veselynove, Ukr. 72/F4
Veselyy (res.), Rus. 71/G3
Vesgre (riv.), Fr. 54/A6
Veshenskaya, Rus. 73/L3
Veshkayma, Rus. 71/H1
Vesijärvi (lake), Fin. 41/L1
Vesle (riv.), Fr. 42/C4
Vesoul, Fr. 60/C2
Vespolate, It. 62/B3
Vest-Agder (co.), Nor. 38/C4
Vest-Sjælland (prov.), Den. 40/D4
Vest-Vlaanderen (prov.), Belg. 54/B2
Vestbjerg, Den. 40/C3
Vestby, Nor. 40/D2
Vestbygd, Nor. 40/B2
Vester Ringsjön (lake), Swe. 39/K7
Vesterålen (isls.), Nor. 38/E1
Vestfjorden (inlet), Nor. 68/B2
Vestfold (co.), Nor. 38/D4
Vestmannaeyjar, Ice. 38/N7
Vestmarka (reg.), Nor. 38/S8
Vestone, It. 62/D2
Vestvågøy, Nor. 38/E1
Vestvågøya (isl.), Nor. 38/E1
Vésubie (riv.), Fr. 64/D5
Vesuvio (Vesuvius) (vol.), It. 65/D6
Vesuvius, Va, US 163/H2
Vesuvius (Vesuvio) (vol.), It. 65/D6
Ves'yegonsk, Rus. 68/H4
Veszprém, Hun. 50/C2
Veszprém (prov.), Hun. 50/C2
Vészto, Hun. 50/E2
Vet (riv.), SAfr. 124/D3
Veteran, Ab, Can. 145/J1
Vétheuil, Fr. 30/H4
Vetka, Bela. 70/D1
Vetlanda, Swe. 40/F3
Vetluga (riv.), Rus. 74/E4
Vetluzhskiy, Rus. 69/K4
Vetralla, It. 65/B3
Vétraz, Fr. 60/C5
Vetrino, Bela. 41/N4
Větřni, Czh. 59/H5
Vettore (peak), It. 65/C2
Veude (riv.), Fr. 44/D3
Veulettes-sur-Mer, Fr. 57/F1
Veurne, Belg. 54/B1
Veuve (riv.), Fr. 57/F5
Vevay, In, US 162/E1
Vevey, Swi. 60/C5
Vex, Swi. 60/D5
Veybach (riv.), Ger. 55/F2
Veyle (riv.), Fr. 60/B5
Veynes, Fr. 64/B3
Veyo, Ut, US 149/F2
Veyrier-du-Lac, Fr. 60/C6
Vézelise, Fr. 60/C1
Vézère (riv.), Fr. 44/D4
Vezin-le-Coquet, Fr. 56/D4
Vezirköprü, Turk. 70/E4
Vezza (riv.), It. 65/B3
Vezza d'Oglio, It. 61/G5
Vezzano Ligure, It. 62/C5
Vi Thanh, Viet. 94/D4
Viacha, Bol. 188/B1
Viadana, It. 62/D4
Viale, Arg. 188/D4
Vian, Ok, US 153/G3
Viana, Ang. 120/C5
Viana, Braz. 183/E3
Viana del Bollo, Sp. 46/B1
Viana do Alentejo, Port. 46/A3
Viana do Castelo, Port. 46/A2
Viana do Castelo (dist.), Port. 46/A2
Vianden, Lux. 55/F4
Vianen, Neth. 52/C4
Viangchan (Vientiane) (cap.), Laos 94/C2
Viangphoukha, Laos 86/D4
Viar (riv.), Sp. 46/C4
Viareggio, It. 62/D6
Viarmes, Fr. 30/K4
Viaur (riv.), Fr. 44/E4
Vibank, Sk, Can. 156/C2
Vibo Valentia, It. 48/E3
Viborg, Den. 40/C3
Viborg (co.), Den. 40/C3
Viborg, SD, US 155/F2
Viburnum, Mo, US 162/B2
Viby, Swe. 39/L6
Viby, Den. 39/J7
Vic, Sp. 47/G2
Vic-en-Bigorre, Fr. 44/D5
Vic-Fezensac, Fr. 44/D5
Vicam, Mex. 174/C3
Vícar, Sp. 46/D4
Vicarello, It. 62/D6
Vicchio, It. 63/E6
Vice, Peru 184/A2
Vicente (pt.), Ca, US 166/F8
Vicente Guerrero, Mex. 148/E4
Vicente Guerrero, Mex. 174/A2
Vicente Guerrero, Mex. 174/E4
Vicente López, Arg. 191/J11
Vicenza (prov.), It. 61/H6
Vicenza, It. 63/E2
Viceroy, Sk, Can. 145/M3
Vichada (riv.), Col. 180/D3
Vichada (dept.), Col. 180/D3
Vichadero, Uru. 189/F4
Vichaya, Bol. 188/B1
Vichuga, Rus. 68/J4
Vichy, Mo, US 153/J1
Vichy, Fr. 44/E3
Vici, Ok, US 152/E2
Vick, La, US 164/B2
Vickham (cape), Austl. 133/A4
Vicksburg, Mi, US 160/D3
Vicksburg, Az, US 149/F4
Vicksburg, Ms, US 162/B4
Vicksburg Nat'l Military Park, Ms, US 153/J4
Vico, Fr. 48/A1
Vico (lake), It. 48/C1
Vico del Gargano, It. 50/B5
Vico Equense, It. 65/D6
Vicopisano, It. 62/D6
Viçosa, Braz. 183/G5
Viçosa, Braz. 187/E4
Viçosa do Ceará, Braz. 183/F3
Vicosoprano, Swi. 61/F5
Vicou Gorge NP, Gre. 75/G3
Vicovaro, It. 65/B3
Vicq, Fr. 30/H5
Victoire, Sk, Can. 145/L1
Victor, Co, US 152/B1
Victor, Ca, US 146/C4
Victor, Ia, US 155/H3
Victor Harbor, Austl. 131/H5
Víctor Rosales, Mex. 174/E4
Victoria, Ks, US 152/E1
Victoria, Gui. 114/B4
Victoria, Rom. 51/G3
Victoria (falls), Zim. 122/E3
Victoria, Gren. 181/F1
Victoria, Hon. 176/E3
Victoria (peak), Belz. 176/D2
Victoria (str.), Nun, Can. 140/F2
Victoria (isl.), Can. 139/F2
Victoria, Chile 190/B3
Victoria (isl.), NW,Nun, Can. 140/E1
Victoria, Ms, US 162/C3
Victoria, Mo, US 162/B1
Victoria, Phil. 88/C2
Victoria, Malay. 88/A4
Victoria (riv.), Austl. 128/C3
Victoria (peak), Phil. 88/B3
Victoria (mt.), Myan. 86/B4
Victoria, Col. 183/L7
Victoria, Mn, US 157/N7
Victoria, Arg. 188/D5
Victoria, On, Can. 160/T8
Victoria, Tx, US 151/F3
Victoria, Tx, US 151/F2
Victoria (cap.), BC, Can. 144/C3
Victoria (state), Austl. 127/D4
Victoria (riv.) 127/C2
Victoria (lake), Austl. 133/C3
Victoria (lake), Ugan. 107/F5
Victoria, Va, US 163/H2
Victoria (Rabat), Malta 48/L6
Victoria Beach, Mb, Can. 156/F2
Victoria de las Tunas, Cuba 177/G1
Victoria Falls (int'l arpt.), Zim. 122/E3
Victoria Falls, Zim. 122/E3
Victoria Land (pol. reg.), Ant. 192/M
Victoria Nile (riv.), Ugan. 121/G2
Victoria River Downs, Austl. 128/C4
Victoria West, SAfr. 124/C3
Victorias, Phil. 88/C3
Victoriaville, Qu, Can. 161/L1
Victorica, Arg. 190/D3
Victorino, Ven. 180/E4
Victorville, Ca, US 166/C1
Vicuña, Chile 188/B4
Vicuña Mackenna, Arg. 190/D2
Vida, Mt, US 145/M4
Vidal, Ca, US 148/E3
Vidal (cape), SAfr. 125/F3
Vidalia, La, US 164/C2
Vidalia, Ga, US 163/F4
Vidauban, Fr. 64/C6
Videira, Braz. 189/G3
Videla, Arg. 188/D4
Videle, Rom. 51/G3
Vidhošt (peak), Czh. 59/G4
Vidigueira, Port. 46/B3
Vidigulfo, It. 62/C3
Vidin, Bul. 51/F4
Vidisha, India 96/A4
Vidlitsa, Rus. 41/Q1
Vidnoye, Rus. 69/W9
Vidor, Tx, US 151/G2
Vidor, It. 63/F2
Vidöstern (lake), Swe. 40/F3
Vidourle (riv.), Fr. 44/E5
Vie (riv.), Fr. 44/D2
Viechtach, Ger. 59/F4
Viedma, Arg. 190/E4
Viedma (lake), Arg. 191/B6
Viehberg (peak), Aus. 59/H5
Vieille-Eglise-en-Yvelines, Fr. 30/H6
Vieira Grande (riv.), Braz. 182/D3
Vieja (peak), Tx, US 151/B2
Vieja Palestina, Mex. 151/D3
Viejo (peak), Peru 184/B2
Viekšniai, Lith. 41/K3
Viella, Sp. 44/D5
Vielsalm, Belg. 55/E3
Vienenburg, Ger. 53/H5
Vienna, Mo, US 153/J1
Vienna, WV, US 160/F5
Vienna, Ga, US 165/G1
Vienna, Il, US 162/C2
Vienna, Va, US 168/A6
Vienna (Wien) (cap.), Aus. 51/N7
Vienne, Fr. 64/A1
Vienne (riv.), Fr. 66/D1
Vientiane (int'l arpt.), Laos 94/C2
Vientiane (Viangchan) (cap.), Laos 94/C2
Vieques (isl.), PR 173/M8
Viére (riv.), Fr. 55/D6
Vierlingsbeek, Neth. 52/D5
Viernheim, Ger. 58/B3
Vierre (riv.), Belg. 55/E4
Viersen, Ger. 52/D6
Vierwaldstättersee (Lucerne) (lake), Swi. 61/E3
Vierzon, Fr. 57/H6
Viesca, Mex. 174/E3
Viesīte, Lat. 41/L3
Vieste, It. 48/E2
Viet Tri, Viet. 86/E4
Vietnam (ctry.) 77/K8
Vietri sul Mare, It. 65/D6
Vieux Chaillol (peak), Fr. 64/C3
Vieux Fort, StL. 173/N9
Vieux-Boucau-les-Bains, Fr. 44/C5
Vieux-Charmont, Fr. 60/C2
Vieux-Condé, Fr. 54/C3
Vieux-Thann, Fr. 60/D2
Vievis, Lith. 41/L4
Viewpark, Sc, UK 33/B5
Vieytes, Arg. 191/K11
Vieze (riv.), Swi. 60/C5
Vif, Fr. 64/B2
Vig, Den. 39/H7
Viga, Phil. 88/D2
Vigan, Phil. 88/C1
Vigarano Mainarda, It. 63/E4
Vigasio, It. 63/D3
Vigevano, It. 62/B3
Viggiù, It. 61/E6
Vigia, Braz. 182/D3
Vigie (int'l arpt.), StL. 173/N9
Vigliano Biellese, It. 62/B2
Viglio (peak), It. 65/C4
Vignacourt, Fr. 54/B3
Vignanello, It. 65/B3
Vignemale (peak), Fr. 44/C5
Vigneulles-lès-Hattonchâtel, Fr. 55/E6
Vigneux-sur-Seine, Fr. 30/K5
Vignola, It. 63/D5
Vignot, Fr. 55/E6
Vigny, Fr. 57/G4
Vigo, Sp. 46/A1
Vigodarzere, It. 63/E3
Vigone, It. 64/D3
Vigonovo, It. 63/F3
Vigonza, It. 63/E3
Vigrestad, Nor. 40/A2
Viguzzolo, It. 62/B4
Vihanti, Fin. 68/E2
Vihāri, Pak. 98/B4
Vihti, Fin. 41/L1
Vihtijärvi (lake), Fin. 39/E4
Viiala, Fin. 39/D3
Viitasaari, Fin. 68/E3
Viivikonna, Est. 41/M2
Vijayanagar, India 86/C3
Vijosë (riv.), Eur. 67/H2
Vik, Nor. 40/B1
Vík, Ice. 38/N7
Vikajärvi, Fin. 68/E2
Vikedal, Nor. 40/A2
Vikeke, ETim. 128/B2
Viken, Swe. 39/J6
Vikersund, Nor. 40/C2
Vikeså, Nor. 40/B2
Vikevåg, Nor. 40/A2
Vikhren (peak), Bul. 75/H2
Viking, Ab, Can. 145/J1
Vikmanshyttan, Swe. 40/F1
Vila Bela da Santíssima Trindade, Braz. 185/G4
Vila Bittencourt, Braz. 180/D5
Vila da Maganja, Moz. 123/H3
Vila de Porto Santo, Port. 110/A2
Vila de Sena, Moz. 123/G3
Vila do Bispo, Port. 46/A4
Vila do Conde, Port. 46/A2
Vila do Porto, Azor., Port. 47/T13
Vila Franca de Xira, Port. 47/P10
Vila Franca do Campo, Azor., Port. 47/T13
Vila Nova de Fozcoa, Port. 46/B2
Vila Nova de Gaia, Port. 46/A2
Vila Nova de Milfontes, Port. 46/A4
Vila Nova do Seles, Ang. 122/B1
Vila Pouca de Aguiar, Port. 46/B2
Vila Real, Port. 46/B2
Vila Real (dist.), Port. 46/B2
Vila Velha, Braz. 182/D2
Vila Velha Argolas, Braz. 187/E4
Vila Velha de Ródão, Port. 46/B3
Vila Verde, Port. 46/A2
Vila Viçosa, Port. 46/B3
Vila-Vila, Chile 188/B1
Vilacaya, Bol. 188/C1
Viladecans, Sp. 47/K7
Vilafranca del Penedès, Sp. 47/K7
Vilaine (riv.), Fr. 44/B3
Viļaka, Lat. 41/M3
Vilama (lake), Arg. 188/C2
Vilanandro (cape), Madg. 125/H7
Vilanculos, Moz. 123/G4
Viļāni, Lat. 41/M3
Vilanova i la Geltrù, Sp. 47/K7
Vilar Formoso, Port. 46/B2
Vilcabamba, Peru 184/B3
Vîlcea (prov.), Rom. 51/F3
Vil'cha, Ukr. 72/E2
Vilches, Sp. 46/D3
Vilcún, Chile 190/B4
Vileyka, Bela. 41/M4
Vilhelmina, Swe. 38/F2
Vilhena, Braz. 185/F4
Viliya (riv.), Bela. 68/E5
Viljandi, Est. 41/L2
Viljoenskroon, SAfr. 124/D2
Vilkaviškis, Lith. 41/K4
Vilkija, Lith. 41/K4
Vil'kitsogo (str.), Rus. 75/K2
Villa Abecia, Bol. 188/C2
Villa Aberastain, Arg. 188/B4
Villa Adriana (ruin), It. 65/B4
Villa Alemana, Chile 190/N8
Villa Alhué, Chile 190/N9
Villa Ana, Arg. 188/E4
Villa Ángela, Arg. 188/D3
Villa Aroma, Bol. 188/C1
Villa Atamisqui, Arg. 188/D4
Villa Atuel, Arg. 190/D2
Villa Bartolomea, It. 63/E3
Villa Bella, Bol. 185/E3
Villa Berthet, Arg. 188/D3
Villa Bruzual, Ven. 180/D2
Villa Cañás, Arg. 190/E2
Villa Carcina, It. 62/D2
Villa Carlos Paz, Arg. 188/C4
Villa Chañar Ladeado, Arg. 190/E2
Villa Constitución, Arg. 190/E2
Villa Corzo, Mex. 176/C2
Villa Cuauhtemoc, Mex. 175/Q10
Villa d'Almè, It. 62/C2
Villa de Arista, Mex. 175/E4
Villa de Cos, Mex. 174/E4
Villa de Costa Rica, Mex. 174/D3
Villa de Cura, Ven. 183/N7
Villa de La Paz, Mex. 175/E4
Villa de Reyes, Mex. 175/E4
Villa de Soto, Arg. 188/C4
Villa del Carbón, Mex. 175/Q9
Villa del Carmen, Uru. 191/K10
Villa del Río, Sp. 46/C4
Villa del Rosario, Arg. 188/D4
Villa di Serio, It. 62/C2
Villa Dolores, Arg. 190/D1
Villa Flores, Mex. 176/C2
Villa Florida, Par. 189/E3
Villa Gesell, Arg. 191/F3
Villa Grove, Il, US 160/B5
Villa Grove, Co, US 149/K1
Villa Guardia, It. 62/C2
Villa Guillermina, Arg. 188/E4
Villa Hayes, Par. 188/E3
Villa Hernandarias, Arg. 188/E4
Villa Hidalgo, Mex. 174/C2
Villa Hidalgo, Mex. 174/D4
Villa Huidobro, Arg. 190/D2
Villa Industrial, Chile 184/D5
Villa Iris, Arg. 190/E3
Villa Isabela, DRep. 177/J2
Villa Jaragua, DRep. 177/J2
Villa Juárez, Mex. 174/C3
Villa Juárez, Mex. 174/D3
Villa La Angostura, Arg. 190/C4
Villa Lázaro Cárdenas, Mex. 175/M6
Villa Literno, It. 65/D6
Villa López, Mex. 174/D3
Villa Mantero, Arg. 191/J10
Villa María, Arg. 188/D5
Villa María Grande, Arg. 188/E4
Villa Martín, Bol. 188/C2
Villa Mazán, Arg. 188/C4
Villa Minetti, Arg. 188/D4
Villa Minozzo, It. 62/D5
Villa Montes, Bol. 188/D2
Villa Nueva, Nic. 176/E3
Villa Nueva, Guat. 176/D3
Villa Nueva, Arg. 190/C2
Villa Ocampo, Arg. 188/E4
Villa Ojo de Agua, Arg. 188/D4
Villa Opicina, It. 63/G2
Villa Oropeza, Bol. 188/C1
Villa Park, Ca, US 166/G8
Villa Park, Il, US 167/Q16
Villa Regina, Arg. 190/D3
Villa Rica, Ga, US 162/E4
Villa Rica, Peru 184/C3
Villa Rosario, Col. 180/C3
Villa San José, Arg. 188/E5
Villa Sandino, Nic. 177/E3
Villa Santa Maria, It. 65/D4
Villa Sarmiento, Arg. 190/D2
Villa Serrano, Bol. 188/C1
Villa Talavera, Bol. 188/C1
Villa Tunari, Bol. 188/C1
Villa Unión, Mex. 151/D3
Villa Unión, Mex. 176/C2
Villa Unión, Arg. 188/B4
Villa Unión, Mex. 174/D4
Villa Valeria, Arg. 190/D2
Villa Verucchio, It. 63/F6
Villa Viscarra, Bol. 188/C1
Villaba, Sp. 44/C5
Villaba, Phil. 88/D3
Villablino, Sp. 46/B1
Villacañas, Sp. 46/D3
Villacarrillo, Sp. 46/D3
Villada, Sp. 46/C1
Villadiego, Sp. 46/C1
Villadose, It. 63/E3
Villadossola, It. 61/E5
Villafamés, Sp. 47/E2
Villafranca, Sp. 46/E1
Villafranca d'Asti, It. 62/B4
Villafranca de los Barros, Sp. 46/B3
Villafranca del Bierzo, Sp. 46/B1
Villafranca del Cid, Sp. 47/E2
Villafranca di Verona, It. 63/D3
Villafranca in Lunigiana, It. 62/C5
Villafranca Piemonte, It. 64/D3
Villagarcía, Sp. 46/A1
Village, Ar, US 153/H4
Village (cr.), Tx, US 150/K7
Village (cr.), Ar, US 162/B2
Village Mills, Tx, US 151/G2
Villagrán, Mex. 175/F3
Villaguay, Arg. 188/E4
Villahermosa, Mex. 176/C2
Villahermosa, Sp. 46/D3
Villahermosa, Col. 183/K8
Villaines-la-Juhel, Fr. 57/E4
Villajoyosa, Sp. 47/E3
Villalba, Sp. 46/B1
Villalcampo (res.), Sp. 46/B2
Villaldama, Mex. 151/D4
Villalón de Campos, Sp. 46/C1
Villalonga, Arg. 190/E3
Villalpando, Sp. 46/C2
Villamartín, Sp. 46/C4
Villandro (peak), It. 61/H4
Villanova, It. 63/F5
Villanova, It. 63/E5
Villanova d'Asti, It. 62/A3
Villanova Mondovì, It. 62/A4
Villanterio, It. 62/C3
Villanueva, Hon. 176/E3
Villanueva, Col. 180/C2
Villanueva, Mex. 174/E4
Villanueva de Arosa, Sp. 46/A1
Villanueva de Córdoba, Sp. 46/C3
Villanueva de la Serena, Sp. 46/C3
Villanueva de los Infantes, Sp. 46/D3
Villanueva de Oscos, Sp. 46/B1
Villanueva del Arzobispo, Sp. 46/D3
Villanuova sul Clisi, It. 62/D2
Villány, Hun. 50/D3
Villar, Bol. 188/C1
Villar del Arzobispo, Sp. 47/E3
Villar Perosa, It. 64/D3
Villar-Saint-Pancrace, Fr. 64/C3
Villarcayo, Sp. 44/B5
Villard, Mn, US 157/G5
Villard-Bonnot, Fr. 64/B2
Villard-de-Lans, Fr. 64/B2
Villardevós, Sp. 46/B2
Villaret (cape), Austl. 128/A4
Villarreal de los Infantes, Sp. 47/E3
Villarrica (lake), Chile 190/B3
Villarrica, Chile 190/B3
Villarrica (vol.), Chile 190/C3
Villarrica, Par. 189/E3
Villarrica, PN, Chile 190/C3
Villarrobledo, Sp. 46/D3
Villarrubia de los Ojos, Sp. 46/D3
Villars-les-Dombes, Fr. 60/B6
Villars-sur-Glâne, Swi. 60/D4
Villars-sur-Var, Fr. 64/D5
Villas, NJ, US 168/D5
Villasana de Mena, Sp. 44/B5
Villasanta, It. 62/C2
Villastellone, It. 62/A3
Villaverde (nbrhd.), Sp. 47/N9
Villaverde del Río, Sp. 46/C4
Villaverla, It. 63/E2
Villavicencio, Col. 180/C3
Villaviciosa, Sp. 46/C1
Villaviciosa de Odón, Sp. 47/N9
Villazón, Bol. 188/C2
Ville Platte, La, US 164/B2
Villebarou, Fr. 57/G5
Villecresnes, Fr. 30/K5
Villedieu-les-Poêles, Fr. 56/D3
Villefermoy (pond), Fr. 30/L6
Villefontaine, Fr. 64/B1
Villefranche-de-Rouergue, Fr. 44/E4
Villefranche-sur-Cher, Fr. 57/G6
Villefranche-sur-Mer, Fr. 64/D5
Villejuif, Fr. 30/K5
Villelaure, Fr. 64/B5
Villemur-sur-Tarn, Fr. 44/D5
Villena, Sp. 47/E3
Villeneuve, Swi. 60/C5
Villeneuve-D'Ascq, Fr. 54/C2
Villeneuve-le-Comte, Fr. 30/L5
Villeneuve-le-Roi, Fr. 30/K5
Villeneuve-lès-Avignon, Fr. 64/A5
Villeneuve-Loubet, Fr. 64/D5
Villeneuve-Saint-Denis, Fr. 30/L5
Villeneuve-Saint-Georges, Fr. 30/K5
Villeneuve-Saint-Germain, Fr. 54/C5
Villeneuve-sur-Lot, Fr. 44/D4
Villeneuve-sur-Yonne, Fr. 44/E2
Villeneuve-Tolosane, Fr. 44/D5
Villennes-sur-Seine, Fr. 30/H5
Villeparisis, Fr. 30/K5
Villepinte, Fr. 30/K5
Villepreux, Fr. 30/J5
Villeroy, Fr. 30/L4
Villers-Bocage, Fr. 57/E2
Villers-Bretonneux, Fr. 54/B4
Villers-Cotterêts, Fr. 54/C5
Villers-en-Arthies, Fr. 30/H4
Villers-le-Bouillet, Belg. 55/E2
Villers-le-Lac, Fr. 60/C3
Villers-lès-Nancy, Fr. 55/F6
Villers-Saint-Genest, Fr. 30/L4
Villers-Saint-Paul, Fr. 54/B5
Villers-Semeuse, Fr. 55/D4
Villers-sur-Mer, Fr. 57/E2
Villersexel, Fr. 60/C2
Villerupt, Fr. 55/E5
Villeta, Col. 183/L7
Villette, Fr. 30/H5
Villeurbanne, Fr. 60/A6
Villevaudé, Fr. 30/K5
Villiers, SAfr. 124/E2
Villiers-en-Lieu, Fr. 55/D6
Villiers-le-Bel, Fr. 30/K4
Villiers-Saint-Georges, Fr. 54/C6
Villiers-sur-Marne, Fr. 30/K5
Villiers-sur-Morin, Fr. 30/L5
Villiersdorp, SAfr. 124/L10
Villieu-Loyes-Mollon, Fr. 60/B6
Villingen-Schwenningen, Ger. 61/E1
Villisca, Ia, US 155/G3
Villmar, Ger. 58/B2
Villongo, It. 62/C2
Villorba, It. 63/F2
Villupuram, India 95/C4
Vilnius (int'l arpt.), Lith. 41/L4
Vilnius (cap.), Lith. 41/L4
Vilonia, Ar, US 153/H3
Vils, Aus. 61/G2
Vils (riv.), Ger. 42/F4
Vilsbiburg, Ger. 59/F6
Vilseck, Ger. 59/E3
Vil'shanka, Ukr. 72/F3
Vilshofen, Ger. 59/G5
Vilters, Swi. 61/F3
Vilvoorde, Belg. 55/D2
Vilyuy (riv.), Rus. 77/L3
Vilyuy (range), Rus. 75/M3
Vilyuysk, Rus. 75/N3
Vimercate, It. 62/C2
Vimeu (reg.), Fr. 54/A3
Vimioso, Port. 46/B2
Vimmerby, Swe. 40/F3
Vimodrone, It. 62/C3
Vimoutiers, Fr. 57/F3
Vimperk, Czh. 59/G4
Vina (riv.), Camr. 116/B4
Viña del Mar, Chile 190/N8
Vinadio, It. 64/D4
Vinaigre (peak), Fr. 64/C6
Vinanivao, Madg. 125/J6
Vinaroz, Sp. 47/F2
Vinay, Fr. 64/B2
Vincennes (lake), Fr. 30/L5
Vincennes, Fr. 30/K5
Vincennes (bay), Ant. 192/H
Vincennes, In, US 162/D1
Vincent, Ca, US 166/B1
Vincent, Al, US 162/D4
Vincent, Tx, US 151/D1
Vincentown, NJ, US 168/D4
Vinces, Ecu. 180/B5
Vincey, Fr. 60/C1
Vinchiaturo, It. 65/D5
Vinchina, Arg. 188/B4
Vinchina (riv.), Arg. 188/B4
Vinchos, Peru 184/C4
Vinci, It. 63/D6
Vindeby, Den. 40/D4
Vindeln, Swe. 38/F2
Vindhya (range), India 96/A4
Vine Grove, Ky, US 162/E2
Vineland, Mn, US 157/H4
Vineland, On, Can. 160/U9
Vineland, NJ, US 168/C5
Vineland Station, On, Can. 160/U9
Vineta, Namb. 122/B4
Vineuil, Fr. 57/G5
Vingåker, Swe. 40/F2
Vingerklip, Namb. 122/B4
Vinh, Viet. 94/D2
Vinh Long, Viet. 94/D4
Vinh Quoi, Viet. 94/D4
Vinh Thanh, Viet. 94/E3
Vinh Yen, Viet. 94/D1
Vinhais, Port. 46/B2
Vinhedo, Braz. 187/K8
Vinica, FYROM 49/H2
Vinings, Ga, US 163/M7
Vinita, Ok, US 153/G2
Vînju Mare, Rom. 50/F3
Vinkeveen, Neth. 52/B4
Vinkovci, Cro. 50/D3
Vinningen, Ger. 55/G5
Vinnyts'ka Oblast, Ukr. 70/D2
Vinnyts'ka (prov.), Bul. 51/J1
Vinnytsya, Ukr. 72/E3
Vinon-sur-Verdon, Fr. 64/B5
Vinovo, It. 64/D3
Vinslöv, Swe. 39/K6
Vinson Massif (peak), Ant. 192/U
Vinsulla, BC, Can. 144/D2
Vintar, Phil. 88/C1
Vinton, Ia, US 155/H2
Viny, Rus. 41/Q2
Viola, Ar, US 153/J2
Viola, NY, US 169/J7
Viola, Il, US 155/J3
Viola, De, US 168/C5
Violet Grove, Ab, Can. 144/G1
Violet Town, Austl. 133/B3
Violet Valley Abor. Land, Austl. 128/B4
Viosne (riv.), Fr. 54/A5
Viotá, Col. 183/L8
Vipiteno (Sterzing), It. 61/H4
Virac, Phil. 88/D2
Viracopos (int'l arpt.), Braz. 189/H2
Viranşehir, Turk. 102/D2
Virār, India 95/B2
Virbalis, Lith. 41/K4
Virden, Mb, Can. 156/D3
Virden, NM, US 149/H4
Virden, Il, US 155/K4
Vire, Fr. 57/E3
Vire (riv.), Fr. 44/C2
Virei, Ang. 122/B2
Viren (lake), Swe. 40/F2
Vireux-Wallerand, Fr. 55/D3
Virgelle, Mt, US 145/J3
Virgil, On, Can. 160/U9
Virgin (isls.), UK,US 139/L8
Virgin (riv.), Az, Ut, US 149/F2
Virgin Gorda (isl.), UK 173/M8
Virgin Gourda (int'l arpt.), UK 173/M8
Virgin Islands NP, USVI 173/M8
Virginia, Mn, US 157/H4
Virginia, Ire. 32/C2
Virginia (state), US 143/L4
Virginia, Il, US 155/J4
Virginia, SAfr. 124/D3
Virginia Beach, Va, US 163/K2
Virginia City, Nv, US 146/D4
Virginia City, Mt, US 147/H1
Virginia Dale, Co, US 154/B3
Virginia Water, Eng, UK 30/B2
Virgolândia, Braz. 187/E3
Viriat, Fr. 60/B5
Virieu-le-Grand, Fr. 60/B6
Virkkala, Fin. 39/E4
Virochey, Camb. 94/D3
Viroflay, Fr. 30/J5
Viroin (riv.), Belg. 55/D3
Viroqua, Wi, US 155/J2
Virovitica, Cro. 50/C3
Virserum, Swe. 40/F3
Virton, Belg. 55/E4
Virtsu, Est. 41/K2
Virú, Peru 184/B3
Viru Viru (int'l arpt.), Bol. 188/D1
Viru-Jaagupi, Est. 41/M2
Virudunagar, India 95/C4
Virunga, D.R. Congo 121/G3
Virunga, PN des, D.R. Congo 121/G3
Viry-Châtillon, Fr. 30/K6
Vis (isl.), Cro. 67/H2
Vis, Cro. 50/C4
Visaginas, Lith. 41/M4
Visalia, Ca, US 148/C2
Visan, Fr. 64/A4
Visandre (riv.), Fr. 30/M5
Visayan (sea), Phil. 91/F1
Visbek, Ger. 53/F3
Visby, Swe. 40/H3
Visciano, It. 65/D6
Visconde do Rio Branco, Braz. 187/E4
Viscount Melville (sound), NW,Nun, Can. 141/R7
Visé, Belg. 55/E2
Višegrad, Bosn. 50/D4
Viseu, Port. 46/B2
Viseu (dist.), Port. 46/B2
Viseu, Braz. 183/E3
Vişeu de Sus, Rom. 72/C4
Vishera (riv.), Rus. 69/L3
Vishnëvoye, Ukr. 72/F2
Vishoek, SAfr. 124/L11
Visinesti, Mol. 72/E4
Viskafors, Swe. 40/E3
Vislanda, Swe. 40/F3
Visnagar, India 101/K4
Višnjevac, Cro. 50/D3
Viso (peak), It. 64/D3
Visoko, Bosn. 50/D4
Visp, Swi. 60/D5
Visperterminen, Swi. 60/D5
Visselhövede, Ger. 53/G3
Vissenbjerg, Den. 40/D4
Vissoie, Swi. 60/D5
Vista, Ca, US 166/C4
Vistonís (lake), Gre. 49/J2
Vistula (riv.), Pol. 29/H3
Visviri, Chile 184/D5
Vit (riv.), Bul. 49/J1
Vita, Mb, Can. 156/F3
Viterbo (prov.), It. 65/B3
Viterbo, It. 65/B3
Vitez, Bosn. 50/C3
Viti Levu (isl.), Fiji 136/G6
Vitiaz (str.), PNG 129/G1
Vitichi, Bol. 188/C2
Vitigudino, Sp. 46/B2
Vitim (plat.), Rus. 75/M4
Vitim (riv.), Rus. 77/L4
Vitim, Rus. 75/M4
Vitimskiy, Rus. 75/M4
Vitinia, It. 65/B4
Vítkuv Kamen (peak), Czh. 59/H5
Vitomirica, Yugo. 50/E4
Vitor, Peru 184/D5
Vitoria, Sp. 44/B5
Vitória, Braz. 187/E4
Vitoría, Braz. 182/C3
Vitória da Conquista, Braz. 187/E2
Vitória de Santo Antão, Braz. 183/H5
Vitória do Mearim, Braz. 183/E3
Vitorino Freire, Braz. 183/E4
Vitosha NP, Bul. 51/F4
Vitré, Fr. 56/D4
Vitrey-sur-Mance, Fr. 60/B2
Vitrolles, Fr. 64/B6
Vitry-en-Artois, Fr. 54/B3
Vitry-le-François, Fr. 55/D6
Vitry-sur-Seine, Fr. 30/K5
Vitshumbi, D.R. Congo 121/G3
Vitsyebsk, Bela. 41/P4
Vitsyebskaya Voblasts, Bela. 68/E5
Vittangi, Swe. 38/G2
Vittel, Fr. 60/B1
Vittoria, It. 48/D4
Vittorio Veneto, It. 45/K4
Vitträsk (lake), Fin. 39/E4
Vittsjö, Swe. 39/K6
Vitulano, It. 65/D5
Vitulazio, It. 65/D5
Viu, It. 64/D2
Vivarais (mts.), Fr. 44/F4
Viveiro, Sp. 46/B1
Viverone (lake), It. 62/B2
Viverone, It. 62/B3
Vivian, La, US 153/H4
Viviers, Fr. 64/A4
Vivonne, Fr. 44/D3
Vizcachilla, Bol. 188/C2
Vizcaya Museum, Fl, US 164/P11
Vize, Turk. 51/H5
Vizhas (riv.), Rus. 69/K2
Vizhas, Rus. 69/K2
Vizianagaram, India 95/D2
Vizille, Fr. 64/B2
Vizinga, Rus. 69/L3
Viziru, Rom. 51/H3
Vlaardingen, Neth. 52/B5
Vlădeasa (peak), Rom. 51/F2
Vladikavkaz, Rus. 71/H4
Vladimirskaya Oblast, Rus. 68/J5
Vladimir, Rus. 68/J4
Vladivostok, Rus. 79/L3
Vlagtwedde, Neth. 53/E2
Vlăhiţa, Rom. 51/G2
Vlajna (peak), Yugo. 50/E4
Vlasenica, Bosn. 50/D3
Vlasotince, Yugo. 50/F4
Vleuten, Neth. 52/C4
Vlieland (isl.), Neth. 42/C2
Vliestroom (chan.), Neth. 52/C2
Vlijmen, Neth. 52/C5
Vlissingen, Neth. 52/A6
Vlorë, Alb. 49/F2
Vlotho, Ger. 53/F4
Vltava (riv.), Czh. 43/H4
Vnukovo (int'l arpt.), Rus. 69/W9
Vobarno, It. 62/D2
Voca, Tx, US 151/E2
Vöcklabruck, Aus. 59/G6
Vöcklamarkt, Aus. 59/G6
Vodice, Cro. 45/L4
Vodlozero (lake), Rus. 68/H3
Vodňany, Czh. 59/H4
Vodskov, Den. 40/D3
Voerde, Ger. 52/D5
Vogan, Togo 115/F5
Vogar, Mb, Can. 156/E2
Vogelsberg (mts.), Ger. 45/H1
Voghera, It. 62/C4
Vogogna, It. 61/E6
Vogorno (lake), Swi. 61/E5
Vogtareuth, Ger. 59/F7
Vogtland (reg.), Ger. 42/F3
Voh, NCal. 137/U12
Vohburg an der Donau, Ger. 59/E5
Vohenstrauss, Ger. 59/F3
Vohilava, Madg. 125/J8
Vohilava, Madg. 125/H8
Vohimena (cape), Madg. 125/H9
Vohimena, Madg. 125/J7
Vohipeno, Madg. 125/H8
Vohiposa, Madg. 125/H8
Vohitrambo, Madg. 125/H8
Võhma, Est. 41/L2
Voi, Kenya 119/B2
Void-Vacon, Fr. 55/E6
Voight (cr.), Wa, US 167/C3
Voil (lake), Sc, UK 33/B4
Voinjama, Libr. 114/C4
Voinsles, Fr. 30/M5
Voiron, Fr. 64/B2
Voise (riv.), Fr. 44/D2
Voisey (bay), Nf, Can. 141/K3
Voiteur, Fr. 60/B4
Vojakkala, Fin. 39/E4
Vojosë (riv.), Alb. 50/D5
Vojvodina (prov.), Yugo. 50/D3
Voka, Congo 120/C4
Vokhma, Rus. 69/K4
Völklingen, Ger. 55/F5
Volano, It. 61/H6
Volary, Czh. 59/G5
Volborg, Mt, US 145/M5
Volcán Barú, PN, Pan. 177/F4
Volcán Poás, PN, CR 177/E4
Volcano (isls.), Japan 136/C2
Volcans, PN des, Rwa. 121/G3
Volchiy Nos (cape), Rus. 41/Q1
Volda, Nor. 38/C3
Volendam, Neth. 52/C3
Volga, SD, US 155/F1
Volga (riv.), Rus. 29/J3
Volga-Baltic Waterway (canal), Rus. 68/H3
Volgelsheim, Fr. 60/D1
Volgodonsk, Rus. 73/M4
Volgograd (res.), Rus. 71/H2
Volgograd, Rus. 71/H2
Volgograd (int'l arpt.), Rus. 71/H2
Volgogradskaya Oblast, Rus. 71/G2
Volimbos, Gre. 67/K4
Volkach, Ger. 58/D3
Volkach (riv.), Ger. 58/D3
Volkeradam (dam), Neth. 52/B5
Völkermarkt, Aus. 45/L3
Volketswil, Swi. 61/E3
Volkhov (riv.), Rus. 68/F4
Volkhov, Rus. 41/Q2
Volkmarsen, Ger. 53/G6
Volksrust, SAfr. 125/E2
Vollenhove, Neth. 52/C3
Volnovakha, Ukr. 73/J4
Volochanka, Rus. 74/K2
Volochayevka, Rus. 79/L2
Volochys'k, Ukr. 72/D3
Volodars'ke, Ukr. 73/J4
Volodarsky (nbrhd.), Rus. 69/T7
Volodymyr-Volyns'kyy, Ukr. 72/C2
Vologda, Rus. 68/H4
Vologodskaya Oblast, Rus. 68/J3
Vologne (riv.), Fr. 42/D4
Volokolamsk, Rus. 68/G4
Volokonovka, Rus. 73/J2
Volonne, Fr. 64/C4
Vólos, Gre. 49/H3
Volos (gulf), Gre. 49/H3
Volosovo, Rus. 41/N2
Volot, Rus. 41/P3
Volovets', Ukr. 43/M4
Volovo, Rus. 70/F1
Volozhin, Bela. 41/M4
Volpago del Montello, It. 63/F2
Volpiano, It. 62/A2
Völs, Aus. 61/H3
Vols, Fin. 39/E4
Vol'sk, Rus. 71/H1
Volta (pol. reg.), Gha. 115/F5
Volta (riv.), Gha. 115/F5
Volta (lake), Gha. 107/B4
Volta Mantovana, It. 62/D3
Volta Redonda, Braz. 187/M7
Voltaire (cape), Austl. 128/B3
Voltana, It. 63/E4
Volterra, It. 63/D7
Voltlage, Ger. 53/E4
Voltri, It. 62/B5
Volturara Irpina, It. 65/D6
Volturino (peak), It. 48/D2
Volturno (riv.), It. 48/D2
Volubilis (ruin), Mor. 112/B2
Volvera, It. 64/D3
Vólvi (lake), Gre. 49/H2
Vólvi (lake), Yugo. 51/F5
Volx, Fr. 64/B5
Volyně, Czh. 59/G4
Volyňka (riv.), Czh. 59/G4
Volyno-Podol'sk Upland (upland), Ukr. 72/D3
Volyns'ka Oblast, Ukr. 70/C2
Volzhsk, Rus. 69/L5
Volzhskiy, Rus. 71/H2
Vom, Nga. 115/H4
Vomano (riv.), It. 65/C2
Vombsjön (lake), Swe. 39/K7
Vonda, Sk, Can. 145/L1
Vondrozo, Madg. 125/H8
Vonêche, Belg. 55/D3
Von Frank (mt.), Ak, US 171/H3
Vónitsa, Gre. 49/G3
Vonne (riv.), Fr. 44/D3
Võnnu, Est. 41/M2
Voorburg, Neth. 52/B4
Voorne (isl.), Neth. 52/B5
Voorschoten, Neth. 52/B4
Voorst, Neth. 52/D4
Vopnafjördhur, Ice. 38/P6
Vorab (peak), Swi. 61/F4
Vorarlberg (prov.), Aus. 42/E5
Vorbach (riv.), Ger. 58/C4
Vorchdorf, Aus. 59/G6
Vorden, Neth. 52/D4
Vorderrhein (riv.), Swi. 45/H3
Vorderweissenbach, Aus. 59/H5
Vordingborg, Den. 40/D4
Vorë, Alb. 49/F2
Voreppe, Fr. 64/B2
Vorkuta, Rus. 69/P2
Vorkuta (int'l arpt.), Rus. 69/Q2
Vormsi (isl.), Est. 41/K2
Vóroi, Gre. 49/J5
Vorokhta, Ukr. 72/C3
Vorona (riv.), Rus. 71/G1
Voronezh (riv.), Rus. 70/F1
Voronezh, Rus. 73/K2
Voronezh (int'l arpt.), Rus. 73/K2
Voronezhskaya Oblast, Rus. 71/G2
Voronovo, Bela. 41/L4
Voronovytsya, Ukr. 72/E3
Vorontsovka, Rus. 73/L2
Voron'ya (riv.), Rus. 68/G1
Voropayevo, Bela. 41/M4
Vorozhba, Ukr. 73/H2
Vorskla (riv.), Ukr. 70/E2
Vorst, Belg. 55/E1
Vorstershoop, SAfr. 124/C2
Võrts (lake), Est. 68/E4
Võru, Est. 41/M3
Vorya (riv.), Rus. 69/X8
Vorzel', Ukr. 72/F2
Vosburg, SAfr. 124/C3
Vösendorf, Aus. 51/N7
Vosges (dept.), Fr. 60/C1
Vosges (mts.), Fr. 42/D5
Voskresenka, Rus. 71/H2
Voskresensk, Rus. 68/H5
Voskresenskoye, Rus. 69/K4
Voskresenskoye, Rus. 68/H4
Voss, Nor. 40/B1
Vossburg, Ms, US 164/D2
Vostochnyy, Rus. 79/L3
Vostok (cape), Ant. 192/V
Vostok, Rus., Ant. 192/H
Vostok (isl.), Kiri. 137/K6
Votice, Czh. 59/H3
Votkinsk (res.), Rus. 69/M4
Votkinsk, Rus. 69/M4
Votorantim, Braz. 189/H2
Votuporanga, Braz. 189/G2
Vouga (riv.), Port. 46/A2
Vougba, CAfr. 116/D4
Vouglans (lake), Fr. 60/B5
Voujeaucourt, Fr. 60/C3
Voúla, Gre. 49/N9
Voulangis, Fr. 30/L5
Voutinainen, Fin. 39/E4
Vouvray, Fr. 57/F6
Vouvry, Swi. 60/C5
Voúxa (cape), Gre. 49/H5
Vouziers, Fr. 55/D5
Vouzon, Fr. 57/H5
Vovchans'k, Ukr. 73/J2
Voves, Fr. 57/G4
Vovodo (riv.), CAfr. 117/E4
Voy-Vozh, Rus. 69/M3
Voyageurs NP, Mn, US 157/H3
Voyeykov Ice Shelf, Ant. 192/J
Voytolovka (riv.), Rus. 69/T7
Vozhe (lake), Rus. 68/H3
Vozhega, Rus. 68/J3
Vozherovo, Rus. 69/K4
Voznesens'k, Ukr. 72/F4
Vrå, Den. 40/C3
Vradiyivka, Ukr. 72/F4
Vraine (riv.), Fr. 60/B1
Vramsån (riv.), Swe. 39/K6
Vrancea (prov.), Rom. 51/H3
Vrangelya (isl.), Rus. 77/T2
Vranje, Yugo. 50/E4
Vranjska Banja, Yugo. 50/E4
Vranov nad Teplou, Slvk. 43/L4
Vrapčište, FYROM 49/G2
Vratsa, Bul. 51/F4
Vrbas (riv.), Bosn. 67/H1
Vrbas, Yugo. 50/D3
Vrchy (peak), Czh. 59/H4
Vrede, SAfr. 124/E2
Vredefort, SAfr. 124/D2
Vreden, Ger. 52/D4
Vredenburg-Saldanha, SAfr. 124/K10
Vredendal, SAfr. 124/B3
Vresse-sur-Semois, Belg. 55/D4
Vrhnika, Slov. 45/L4
Vriddhāchalam, India 95/C4
Vries, Neth. 52/D2
Vriezenveen, Neth. 52/D4
Vrigstad, Swe. 40/F3
Vrin (riv.), Fr. 42/B5
Vrindāban, India 96/A2
Vrnjačka Banja, Yugo. 50/E4
Vrondádhos, Gre. 49/K3
Vroomshoop, Neth. 52/D4
Vršac, Yugo. 50/E3
Vryburg, SAfr. 124/D2
Vryheid, SAfr. 125/E2
Vsetín, Czh. 43/K4
Vsevidof (mt.), Ak, US 171/E5
Vsevolozhsk, Rus. 69/T6
Vtáčnik (peak), Slvk. 43/K4
Vu Liet, Viet. 94/D2
Vuca, Eth. 117/G4
Vučitrn, Yugo. 50/E4
Vught, Neth. 52/C5
Vukovar, Cro. 50/D3
Vulcan, Ab, Can. 145/H2
Vulcan, Rom. 51/F3
Vulcan, Mo, US 153/J2
Vulcăneşti, Mol. 51/J3
Vulcano (isl.), It. 48/D3
Vŭlchedrŭm, Bul. 51/F4
Vŭlchi Dol, Bul. 51/H4
Vulci (ruin), It. 48/B1
Vung Tau, Viet. 94/D4
Vunisea, Fiji 136/G6
Vuntut NP, Yk., Can. 171/K2
Vuoggatjålme, Swe. 38/F2
Vuohijärvi (lake), Fin. 41/M1
Vuollerim, Swe. 38/G2
Vuoska (lake), Rus. 41/N1
Vuotso, Fin. 68/E1
Vŭrbitsa, Bul. 51/H4
Vuria (peak), Kenya 119/B2
Vurnary, Rus. 69/K5
Vŭrshets, Bul. 51/F4
Vuruena, Res. Florestal do, Braz. 186/A1
Vuyyūru, India 95/D2
Vvedenka, Kaz. 69/P5
Vwawa, Tanz. 121/H5
Vyāra, India 92/B3
Vyatka (riv.), Rus. 74/E4
Vyatskiye Polyany, Rus. 69/L4
Vyatskoye, Rus. 68/J4
Vyazemskiy, Rus. 79/L2

Map Section
282
283

Vyaz'ma – Weilhe

Vyaz'ma, Rus. 68/G5
Vyazovaya, Rus. 69/N5
Vyborg (nbrhd.), Rus. 69/T7
Vyborg (bay), Rus. 41/N1
Vyborg, Rus. 41/N1
Vychegda (riv.), Rus. 74/F3
Vygozero (lake), Rus. 68/G3
Vyhorlat (peak), Slvk. 43/M4
Vyksa, Rus. 68/J5
Vylkove, Ukr. 51/J3
Vym' (riv.), Rus. 69/L3
Vynnyky, Ukr. 72/C3
Vynohradiv, Ukr. 43/M4
Vypolzovo, Rus. 68/G4
Vyritsa, Rus. 41/P2
Vyrnwy (riv.), Wal, UK 36/C1
Vyselki, Rus. 73/K5
Vyshgorodok, Rus. 41/N3
Vyshhorod, Ukr. 72/F2
Vyshniy Volochek, Rus. 68/G4
Vyshnivets', Ukr. 72/C3
Vyškov, Czh. 43/J4
Vyškovce nad Ipl'om, Slvk. 50/D1
Vysokogornyy, Rus. 79/M1
Vysokopillya, Ukr. 73/G4
Vysokovsk, Rus. 68/H4
Vysokoye, Bela. 43/M2
Vysotsk, Rus. 41/N1
Vyšší Brod, Czh. 59/H5
Vytegra, Rus. 68/H3
Vyyezdnoye, Rus. 69/J5
Vyzhnytsya, Ukr. 72/C3
Vzmor'ye, Rus. 79/N2

W

W du Benin, PN du, Ben. 115/F4
W du Burkino Faso, PN du, Burk. 115/F4
W du Niger, PN du, Niger 115/F3
W.F. George (res.), Al,Ga, US 162/E5
Wa, Gha. 115/E4
Waadi Luud (wadi), Som. 118/D3
Waajid, Som. 118/B5
Waal, Ger. 61/G2
Waal (riv.), Neth. 42/C3
Waal (riv.), Neth. 52/C5
Waalre, Neth. 52/C6
Waalwijk, Neth. 52/C5
Waany-Garawa Aboriginal Land, Austl. 129/E4
Waarschoot, Belg. 54/C1
Waasis, NB, Can. 158/D3
Wabag, PNG 129/F1
Wabamun, Ab, Can. 144/G1
Wabamun (lake), Ab, Can. 144/G1
Wabana, Nf, Can. 159/L2
Wabasca (riv.), Ab, Can. 140/E3
Wabash, In, US 160/D4
Wabash (riv.), Il, In, US 143/J4
Wabasha, Mn, US 155/H1
Wabasso, Mn, US 155/G1
Wabē Gestro Wenz (riv.), Eth. 118/B4
Wabē Shebelē Wenz (riv.), Eth. 107/G4
Wabeno, Wi, US 157/K5
Wabern, Ger. 53/G6
Wabigoon (lake), On, Can. 157/H3
Wabigoon, On, Can. 157/H3
Wąbrzeźno, Pol. 43/K2
Wabu, SKor. 81/G6
Wabu (lake), China 80/D4
Wabuda (isl.), PNG 129/F2
Waccamau (riv.), SC, US 163/H4
Waccasassa (bay), Fl, US 165/G3
Wachenheim an der Weinstrasse, Ger. 58/B4
Wachi, Japan 83/H5
Wach'īlē, Eth. 118/A4
Wachtebeke, Belg. 54/C1
Wachtendonk, Ger. 52/D6
Wächtersbach, Ger. 58/C2
Wackernheim, Ger. 58/B3
Wackersdorf, Ger. 59/F4
Waco, Tx, US 151/F2
Waconda (lake), Ks, US 154/E4
Waconia, Mn, US 157/N7
Waconia (lake), Mn, US 157/N7
Wad al Ḩaddād, Sudan 117/G2
Wad an Nail, Sudan 117/G2
Wad Bandah, Sudan 117/E2
Wad Ḩāmid, Sudan 117/G1
Wad Medanī, Sudan 117/G2
Wada, Japan 83/E3
Wadayama, Japan 83/G5
Waddān, Libya 108/C2
Waddell (dam), Az, US 149/F4
Waddenzee (sound), Neth. 42/C2
Waddington, Eng, UK 35/H5
Waddington, Eng, UK 35/F4
Waddinxveen, Neth. 52/B4
Waddy (pt.), Austl. 134/D4
Wade, Ok, US 153/F4
Wadebridge, Eng, UK 36/B5
Wadena, Sk, Can. 156/C2
Wadena, Mn, US 157/G4
Wädenswil, Swi. 61/E3
Wadern, Ger. 55/F4
Wadersloh, Ger. 53/F5
Wadesboro, NC, US 163/G3
Wadgassen, Ger. 55/F5
Wadhurst, Eng, UK 37/G4
Wādī al Layl, Tun. 112/M6
Wādī an Natrûn, Egypt 113/B4
Wādī As Sīr, Jor. 105/D5
Wādī Az Zarqā', Tun. 112/L6
Wādī Ḩalfā', Sudan 109/F4
Wādī Mūsá, Jor. 104/D4
Wading (riv.), NJ, US 168/D4
Wading River, NY, US 169/F2
Wadley, Ga, US 163/F4
Wadowice, Pol. 43/K4
Wadsworth, Tx, US 151/G3
Wadsworth, Oh, US 160/F4
Wadsworth, Il, US 167/Q15
Waegwan, SKor. 81/E5
Waelder, Tx, US 151/F3
Wafangdian, China 81/A3
Wafangdian, China 87/F1
Wafania, D.R. Congo 120/E3
Waffenrod, Ger. 58/D2
Wāgah, Pak. 98/C4
Wagait Abor. Land, Austl. 128/C3
Wagaru, Myan. 94/B3
Wagat, Ouadi (riv.), Chad 116/D2
Wagener, SC, US 163/G4
Wagenfeld-Hasslingen, Ger. 53/F3
Wageningen, Sur. 182/B1
Wageningen, Neth. 52/C5
Wager (bay), Nun, Can. 140/G2
Wagga Wagga, Austl. 133/C2
Waggrakine, Austl. 130/B4
Waghäusel, Ger. 58/B4
Wagin, Austl. 130/C5
Waging am See, Ger. 59/F7
Waginger (lake), Ger. 59/F7
Wägitaler-see (lake), Swi. 61/E3
Wagna, Aus. 50/B2
Wagner, SD, US 154/E2
Wagoner, Ok, US 153/G3
Wagontire, Or, US 146/D2
Wągrowiec, Pol. 43/J2
Wāh, Pak. 98/B3
Wah Wah (mts.), Ut, US 147/G4
Wahai, Indo. 91/G4
Wāḩāt ad Dākhilah (oasis), Egypt 109/F3
Wāḩāt al Farāfirah (oasis), Libya,Egypt 109/E3
Wahkon, Mn, US 157/H4
Wahlern, Swi. 60/D4
Wahoo, Ne, US 155/F3
Wahpeton, ND, US 156/F4
Wahrenholz, Ger. 53/H3
Wai, India 95/B2
Waialua, Hi, US 142/S9
Waiau (riv.), NZ 135/C3
Waiau, NZ 135/C3
Waibamiao, China 80/D2
Waiblingen, Ger. 58/C5
Waibstadt, Ger. 58/B4
Waidhaus, Ger. 59/F3
Waidhofen an der Thaya, Aus. 45/L2
Waidhofen an der Ybbs, Aus. 59/H7
Waigeo (isl.), Indo. 91/H3
Waigolshausen, Ger. 58/D3
Waigoumen, China 78/H3
Waiheke (isl.), NZ 135/G6
Waihou (riv.), NZ 135/C2
Waika, D.R. Congo 121/F3
Waikabubak, Indo. 91/E5
Waikanae, NZ 135/C3
Waikari, NZ 135/C3
Waikato (riv.), NZ 127/H6
Waikerie, Austl. 131/H5
Waikouaiti, NZ 135/B4
Wailuo, China 87/F4
Waimangaroa, NZ 135/B3
Waimate, NZ 135/B4
Waimes, Belg. 55/F3
Wainfleet, On, Can. 160/U10
Wainfleet All Saints, Eng, UK 35/J5
Waingangā (riv.), India 92/C3
Waingapu, Indo. 91/F5
Waini (riv.), Guy. 181/G2
Wainuiomata, NZ 135/H9
Wainuiomata (riv.), NZ 135/H9
Wainwright, Ab, Can. 145/J1
Wainwright, Ak, US 171/F1
Wainwright, Ok, US 153/G3
Waiohine (riv.), NZ 135/J8
Waipahu, Hi, US 142/S9
Waipapa (pt.), NZ 135/B4
Waipara, NZ 135/C3
Waipawa, NZ 135/D2
Waipio, Hi, US 142/S9
Waipiro, NZ 135/D2
Waipukurau, NZ 135/D2
Wairarapa (lake), NZ 135/J9
Wairau (riv.), NZ 135/C3
Wairoa (riv.), NZ 135/C1
Wairoa, NZ 135/D2
Waischenfeld, Ger. 59/E3
Waitakere, NZ 135/F6
Waitakere (range), NZ 135/F6
Waitaki (riv.), NZ 135/B4
Waitangi, NZ 135/E3
Waitara, NZ 135/C2
Waitemata (har.), NZ 135/F6
Waitotara, NZ 135/C2
Waitsburg, Wa, US 144/E4
Waiuku, NZ 135/C2
Waiyevu, Fiji 137/Z17
Waizenkirchen, Aus. 59/G6
Wajima, Japan 85/E2
Wajir, Kenya 119/C1
Waka, D.R. Congo 120/E2
Waka, Eth. 117/H4
Waka, D.R. Congo 120/E3
Waka (cape), Indo. 91/G4
Wakakusa, Japan 83/A2
Wakapitu (lake), NZ 135/B4
Wakarusa, In, US 160/C4
Wakasa, Japan 84/D3
Wakasa (bay), Japan 83/H4
Wakaw, Sk, Can. 145/M1
Wakayama, Japan 84/D3
Wakayama (pref.), Japan 84/D4
Wake (isl.), Pac., US 136/F3
Wakeeney, Ks, US 152/E1
Wakefield, Eng, UK 35/G4
Wakefield (co.), Eng, UK 35/G4
Wakefield, Ks, US 155/F4
Wakefield, Mi, US 157/K4
Wakefield, Ne, US 155/F2
Wakefield, Oh, US 163/F1
Wakema, Myan. 86/B5
Waki, Japan 84/D3
Wakita, Ok, US 153/F2
Wakkanai, Japan 82/B1
Wakool, Austl. 133/B2
Wakpala, SD, US 156/D5
Waku Kungo, Ang. 122/B1
Wakulla, Fl, US 165/F2
Wakuya, Japan 82/B4
Wal (peak), Camr. 116/B4
Wal Athiang, Sudan 117/F4
Wala (riv.), Tanz. 119/A3
Walachia (reg.), Rom. 67/K1
Walagan, China 79/J1
Walagunya Abor. Land, Austl. 130/D2
Walamba, Zam. 123/F2
Walan, Austl. 133/B3
Wałbrzych, Pol. 43/J3
Walbury (hill), Eng, UK 37/E4
Walcha, Austl. 132/D1
Walcheren (isl.), Neth. 52/A5
Walcott, ND, US 156/F4
Walcott (lake), Id, US 147/G2
Walcott, Wy, US 147/K3
Walcourt, Belg. 55/D3
Wałcz, Pol. 43/J2
Wald, Swi. 61/E3
Wald, Ger. 59/F4
Waldbillig, Lux. 55/F4
Waldbreitbach, Ger. 55/G2
Waldbröl, Ger. 55/G2
Waldbronn, Ger. 58/B5
Waldbrunn, Ger. 58/C3
Waldburg, Ger. 61/F2
Waldeck, Sk, Can. 145/L2
Walden, On, Can. 160/F1
Waldenbuch, Ger. 58/C5
Waldenburg, Swi. 60/D3
Waldenburg, Ger. 58/C4
Waldershof, Ger. 59/F3
Walderslade, Eng, UK 30/E3
Waldesch, Ger. 55/G3
Waldfischbach-Burgalben, Ger. 55/G5
Waldheim, Sk, Can. 145/L1
Waldighofen, Fr. 60/D2
Walding, Aus. 59/H6
Waldkappel, Ger. 53/G6
Waldkirch, Ger. 60/D1
Waldkraiburg, Ger. 59/F6
Waldmohr, Ger. 55/G5
Waldmünchen, Ger. 59/F4
Waldnaab (riv.), Ger. 59/F3
Waldo, Ar, US 153/H4
Waldo, Fl, US 165/G3
Waldo (lake), Or, US 146/B2
Waldorf, Md, US 163/J1
Waldport, Or, US 146/A1
Waldrach, Ger. 55/F4
Waldron, Ar, US 153/G3
Waldron, In, US 160/D5
Waldsassen, Ger. 59/F3
Waldshut-Tiengen, Ger. 61/E2
Waldstetten, Ger. 58/C5
Waldviertel (reg.), Aus. 43/H4
Waldwick, NJ, US 169/J8
Walea (str.), Indo. 91/F4
Waleabahi (isl.), Indo. 91/F4
Walensee (lake), Swi. 61/F3
Walenstadt, Swi. 61/F3
Wales (isl.), Nun, Can. 141/H2
Wales, UK 36/B3
Wales, Ak, US 171/E2
Wales, Ut, US 147/H4
Wales, Wi, US 167/P14
Walewale, Gha. 115/E4
Walferdange, Lux. 55/F4
Walgett, Austl. 132/D1
Walhalla, Ger. 59/F4
Walhalla, ND, US 156/F3
Walhalla, Mi, US 160/C3
Walhalla, SC, US 163/F3
Walhalla Historical Site, ND, US 156/F3
Walikale, D.R. Congo 121/G3
Walker (bay), SAfr. 124/L11
Walker, Mn, US 157/G4
Walker, Mo, US 153/G2
Walker, Mi, US 160/D3
Walker (lake), Nv, US 146/D4
Walker (riv.), Nv, US 146/D4
Walker Art Center, Mn, US 157/P7
Walker River Ind. Res., Nv, US 146/D4
Walker, West (riv.), Ca, Nv, US 146/D4
Walkerburn, Sc, UK 33/C5
Walkers Ferry, Malw. 123/G2
Walkerston, Austl. 134/C3
Walkersville, Md, US 161/H5
Walkerton, On, Can. 160/F2
Walkerton, In, US 160/C4
Walkertown, NC, US 163/G2
Walkill (riv.), NY, US 168/D1
Wall, SD, US 154/C2
Wall, Tx, US 151/D2
Wall Of Ghenghis Khan (wall), Mong. 78/G2
Walla Walla, Wa, US 144/E4
Walla Walla, Austl. 133/C2
Wallace, Ca, US 146/C4
Wallace, Id, US 144/G4
Wallace, Ks, US 152/D1
Wallace, Ne, US 154/D3
Wallace, NS, Can. 158/F3
Wallace Lake, Mb, Can. 157/G2
Wallaceburg, On, Can. 160/E3
Wallacia, Austl. 133/E1
Wallaga Lake NP, Austl. 133/E3
Wallal Downs, Austl. 130/D1
Wallaroo, Austl. 131/H5
Wallasey, Eng, UK 35/E5
Wallblake (int'l arpt.), UK 173/N8
Walldorf, Ger. 58/B4
Walldorf, Ger. 58/D1
Walldürn, Ger. 58/C3
Walled (lake), Mi, US 167/F6
Walled City Hist. Site, SKor. 81/G7
Walled Lake, Mi, US 167/F6
Wallendbeen, Austl. 133/D2
Wallenhorst, Ger. 53/F4
Wallenpaupack (lake), Pa, US 161/J4
Waller, Tx, US 151/G2
Wallerawang, Austl. 133/E1
Wallern im Burgenland, Aus. 50/C2
Wallers, Fr. 54/C3
Wallersdorf, Ger. 59/F5
Wallersee (lake), Aus. 59/G7
Wallerstein, Ger. 58/D5
Wallingford, Ct, US 161/K4
Wallingford, Eng, UK 37/E3
Wallington, NJ, US 169/J8
Wallis (isls.), Wall. 137/H6
Wallis and Futuna (dpcy.), Fr. 136/G6
Wallisellen, Swi. 61/E3
Wallisville, Tx, US 151/N9
Walloon Brabant (prov.), Belg. 55/D2
Wallowa (mts.), Or, US 146/E1
Wallowa (riv.), Or, US 146/E1
Walls, Sc, UK 31/W13
Wallsend, Eng, UK 35/G2
Wallula, Wa, US 144/E4
Wallumbilla, Austl. 134/C4
Walney, Isle of (isl.), Eng, UK 35/E3
Walnut (riv.), Ks, US 153/F2
Walnut, Ca, US 166/G7
Walnut (cr.), Ga, US 163/M8
Walnut, Il, US 155/K3
Walnut (cr.), Ks, US 155/E4
Walnut, Ms, US 162/C3
Walnut Canyon Nat'l Mon., Az, US 149/G3
Walnut Creek, Ca, US 167/K11
Walnut Grove, Al, US 162/D3
Walnut Grove, Ca, US 167/L10
Walnut Grove, Ga, US 162/F4
Walnut Grove, Mo, US 153/H2
Walnut Grove, Ms, US 162/C4
Walnut Park, Ca, US 166/F8
Walnut Ridge, Ar, US 162/B2
Walnut Springs, Tx, US 150/F1
Walnutport, Pa, US 168/C2
Walpole, Austl. 130/C5
Walpole, NH, US 161/K3
Walpole Island. Ind. Res., On, Can. 160/E3
Walpole-Nornalup NP, Austl. 130/C5
Walrus (isls.), Ak, US 171/F4
Walsall, Eng, UK 36/E1
Walsall (co.), Eng, UK 37/E1
Walsenburg, Co, US 152/B2
Walsh, Co, US 152/C2
Walsh, Austl. 134/A2
Walsingham (cape), Nun, Can. 141/K2
Walsingham, Eng, UK 37/G1
Walsrode, Ger. 53/G3
Walt Disney World, Fl, US 165/H3
Waltenhofen, Ger. 61/G2
Walter F. George (res.), Ga, US 165/F2
Walterboro, SC, US 163/G4
Walters, Ok, US 153/E3
Walters, La, US 164/C2
Walter's Ash, Eng, UK 30/A2
Walterville, Or, US 146/B1
Walthall, Ms, US 162/C4
Waltham Abbey, Eng, UK 30/D1
Waltham Forest (bor.), Eng, UK 30/A1
Waltham Saint Lawrence, Eng, UK 30/A2
Walthill, Ne, US 155/F2
Walthourville, Ga, US 165/H2
Waltman, Wy, US 147/K2
Walton, In, US 160/C4
Walton, Ky, US 162/E1
Walton, NY, US 161/J3
Walton, WV, US 163/G1
Walton-le-Dale, Eng, UK 35/F4
Walton-on-Thames, Eng, UK 30/B2
Walton-on-the-Naze, Eng, UK 37/H3
Waltrop, Ger. 53/E5
Walungchung Gola, Nepal 97/F2
Walvis Bay, Namb. 122/B4
Walworth, Wi, US 167/N14
Walworth (co.), Wi, US 167/N14
Walyahmoning (peak), Austl. 130/C4
Walyunga NP, Austl. 130/L6
Walzenhausen, Swi. 61/F3
Wama, Ang. 122/B2
Wamac, Il, US 162/C1
Wamaza, D.R. Congo 121/F4
Wamba, Nga. 115/H4
Wamba, D.R. Congo 121/F2
Wamba, Kenya 119/B1
Wamberal, Austl. 133/E1
Wamego, Ks, US 155/F4
Wamel, Neth. 52/C5
Wamena, Indo. 91/J4
Wami (riv.), Tanz. 119/B3
Wamic, Or, US 146/C1
Wampool (riv.), Eng, UK 35/E2
Wampsville, NY, US 161/J3
Wamsutter, Wy, US 147/K3
Wān Hsa-la, Myan. 94/B1
Wān Hwè-ün, Myan. 86/C5
Wanaaring, Austl. 132/C1
Wanaka, NZ 135/B4
Wanaka (lake), NZ 135/B4
Wanamassa, NJ, US 168/D3
Wanamingo, Mn, US 155/H1
Wanapum (dam), Wa, US 144/E4
Wanaque, NJ, US 169/H7
Wanaque (res.), NJ, US 168/D1
Wanblee, SD, US 154/D2
Wanci, Indo. 128/A1
Wanda (mts.), China 79/L2
Wandering, Austl. 130/C5
Wandi, Ugan. 121/G2
Wanding, China 86/C3
Wandlitz, Ger. 42/Q6
Wando, SKor. 81/D5
Wandoan, Austl. 134/C4
Wandong, Austl. 133/B3
Wandsbek, Ger. 53/H1
Wandsworth (bor.), Eng, UK 30/C2
Wanette, Ok, US 153/F3
Wanfried, Ger. 53/H6
Wanfu, China 81/B2
Wang (riv.), Thai. 93/G4
Wang Hip (peak), Thai. 94/B4
Wang Noi, Thai. 94/C3
Wang Saphung, Thai. 94/C2
Wanganella, Austl. 133/B2
Wanganui, NZ 135/C2
Wangaratta, Austl. 133/C3
Wangasi Turu, Gha. 115/E4
Wangcun, China 87/F2
Wangdu, China 80/C3
Wangdü Phodrang, Bhu. 97/G2
Wangen, Ger. 61/F2
Wangen an der Aare, Swi. 60/D3
Wangen bei Olten, Swi. 60/D3
Wangerooge (isl.), Ger. 53/E1
Wangerooge (arpt.), Ger. 53/E1
Wanggamet (peak), Indo. 91/F6
Wanggao, China 87/F3
Wanghai Shan (peak), China 81/A2
Wängi, Swi. 61/E3
Wangiwangi (isl.), Indo. 128/A1
Wangjiang, China 87/H2
Wangjiapu, China 81/B2
Wangkui, China 79/K2
Wangling, China 87/G3
Wangmao, China 87/F4
Wangmo Bouyeizu Miaozu Zizhixian, China 86/E3
Wangolodougou, C.d'Iv. 114/D4
Wangou, China 81/D1
Wangpan (bay), China 80/E5
Wangpang (sea), China 87/J2
Wangqing, China 79/K3
Wangqingmen, China 81/C2
Wangtan, China 87/J2
Wangting, China 80/L8
Wani (peak), Indo. 91/F4
Wanica (dist.), Sur. 181/H3
Wanie-Rukula, D.R. Congo 121/F2
Wanilla, Austl. 131/G5
Wanipitie (lake), On, Can. 160/F1
Wanjiabu, China 87/G2
Wanjialing, China 81/B3
Wank (peak), Ger. 61/H2
Wankie (Hwange) NP, Zim. 123/E3
Wanle Weyne, Som. 119/D1
Wann, Ok, US 153/G2
Wannaska, Mn, US 157/G3
Wannīn (spr.), Libya 108/B2
Wanning, China 93/K4
Wanouchi, Japan 83/L5
Wanquan (lake), China 99/D5
Wanquan, China 80/C2
Wanquan (riv.), China 87/F5
Wanrong, China 80/B4
Wansbeck (riv.), Eng, UK 35/G1
Wanshengchang, China 87/E2
Wansra, Indo. 91/H4
Wanstead (nbrhd.), Eng, UK 30/D2
Wantage, Eng, UK 37/E3
Wantagh, NY, US 169/M9
Wantan, China 87/F2
Wanwei, China 94/E1
Wanxian, China 87/F2
Wanze, Belg. 55/E2
Wao, Phil. 88/D4
Wapakoneta, Oh, US 160/D4
Wapanocca NWR, Ar, US 162/B3
Wapanucka, Ok, US 153/F3
Wapato, Wa, US 144/D4
Wapella, Sk, Can. 156/D2
Wapello, Ia, US 155/J3
Wapenamanda, PNG 129/F1
Wapinda, D.R. Congo 121/E2
Wapiti, Wy, US 147/J1
Waples, Tx, US 150/K7
Wapoga (riv.), Indo. 91/J4
Wappapello (lake), Mo, US 162/B2
Wappingers Falls, NY, US 161/K4
Wapsipinicon (riv.), Ia, US 155/H2
Wapske, NB, Can. 158/D2
Wapwallopen (cr.), Pa, US 168/B1
Wapwallopen, Pa, US 168/B1
Wāqid, Egypt 113/B3
Waqqāş, Jor. 105/D3
War, WV, US 163/G2
War Horse Nat'l Wild. Ref., Mt, US 145/K4
Warabi, Japan 83/D2
Waranga (basin), Austl. 133/B3
Waratah, Austl. 132/C4
Waratah (bay), Austl. 133/C4
Warba, Mn, US 157/H4
Warboys, Eng, UK 37/F2
Warburg, Ger. 53/G6
Warburg, Ab, Can. 144/G1
Warburton, Pak. 98/B4
Warburton, Austl. 130/E3
Warburton (cr.), Austl. 127/C3
Warburton, Austl. 133/B3
Warburton (Central Australia) Abor. Rsv., Austl. 131/E3
Warburton Range Abor. Reserve, Austl. 130/E3
Warche (riv.), Belg. 55/F3
Ward, NZ 135/C3
Ward Cove, Ak, US 171/M4
Ward Hunt (cape), PNG 129/H2
Warden (pt.), Eng, UK 37/G4
Warden, SAfr. 124/E2
Warden, Wa, US 144/E4
Wardenburg, Ger. 53/F2
Wardlow, Ab, Can. 145/J2
Wardo, Indo. 91/J4
Ward's Stone (peak), Eng, UK 35/F3
Wardsville, Mo, US 153/H1
Ware, Eng, UK 37/F3
Ware Shoals, SC, US 163/F3
Waregem, Belg. 54/C2
Wareham, Eng, UK 36/D5
Waremme, Belg. 55/E2
Waren, Ger. 40/E5
Waren, Indo. 91/J4
Warendorf, Ger. 53/E5
Waretown, NJ, US 168/D4
Warffum, Neth. 52/D2
Warfield, BC, Can. 144/F3
Wargrave, Eng, UK 37/F4
Warialda, Austl. 132/D1
Warin Chamrap, Thai. 94/D3
Waring, Tx, US 151/E3
Waringstown, NI, UK 34/B3
Wark, Eng, UK 35/F1
Warka, Pol. 43/L3
Warkworth, On, Can. 161/H2
Warkworth, NZ 135/C2
Warlingham, Eng, UK 30/C3
Warlmanpa Abor. Land, Austl. 131/G2
Warlmanpa Aboriginal Land, Austl. 128/D4
Warm Lake, Id, US 146/F1
Warm Springs, Or, US 146/C1
Warm Springs (res.), Or, US 146/D2
Warm Springs, Va, US 163/H1
Warm Springs Ind. Res., Or, US 146/C1
Warman, Sk, Can. 145/L1
Warmbad, SAfr. 123/F5
Warmbad, Namb. 124/B3
Warme Bode (riv.), Ger. 53/H5
Warmebach (riv.), Ger. 53/G6
Warmenhuizen, Neth. 52/B3
Warmeriville, Fr. 55/D5
Warmia (reg.), Pol. 43/K1
Warmińsko-Mazurskie (prov.), Pol. 43/L2
Warminster, Eng, UK 36/D4
Warminster, Pa, US 168/C3
Warnemünde, Ger. 40/E4
Warner, SD, US 156/E5
Warner, Ok, US 153/G3
Warner (mts.), Ca, US 146/C3
Warner Robins, Ga, US 162/F4
Warnes, Bol. 188/D1
Warnow (riv.), Ger. 40/D5
Warnsveld, Neth. 52/D4
Waroona, Austl. 130/B5
Waropko, Indo. 129/F1
Warrabri, Austl. 131/G2
Warrabri Abor. Land, Austl. 128/D5
Warragamba, Austl. 133/B3
Warragamba, Austl. 133/E1
Warragul, Austl. 133/B4
Warrakunta (pt.), Austl. 129/D3
Warrandirinna (lake), Austl. 131/H3
Warrandyte (nbrhd.), Austl. 132/G5
Warrego (range), Austl. 127/D3
Warrego (riv.), Austl. 127/D3
Warren, Austl. 132/C1
Warren (riv.), Austl. 130/C5
Warren, Ar, US 153/H4
Warren, Id, US 146/F1
Warren, In, US 160/D4
Warren, Mi, US 160/E3
Warren, Mn, US 156/F3
Warren (peak), Mt, US 145/H5
Warren (co.), NJ, US 168/C2
Warren, NJ, US 168/D2
Warren, Oh, US 160/F4
Warren, Or, US 144/C5
Warren, Pa, US 161/G4
Warren, RI, US 161/L4
Warrenpoint, NI, UK 34/B3
Warrens, Wi, US 155/J1
Warrensburg, Mo, US 153/H1
Warrensburg, NY, US 161/K3
Warrenton, SAfr. 124/D3
Warrenton, Ga, US 163/F4
Warrenton, Mo, US 155/J4
Warrenton, NC, US 163/H2
Warrenton, Or, US 144/C4
Warrenton, Va, US 163/J1
Warrenville, Il, US 167/P16
Warri, Nga. 115/G5
Warrina, Austl. 131/G4
Warringah, Austl. 133/E1
Warrington, Eng, UK 35/F5
Warrington (co.), Eng, UK 35/F5
Warrington, Fl, US 164/E2
Warrior, Al, US 162/D4
Warrior Reefs (reef), Austl. 129/F2
Warrnambool, Austl. 132/B3
Warroad, Mn, US 157/G3
Warrumbungle NP, Austl. 132/D1
Warsaw (Warszawa) (cap.), Pol. 43/L2
Warsaw, In, US 160/D4
Warsaw, Mo, US 153/H1
Warsaw, NY, US 161/G3
Warsaw, Ky, US 162/E1
Warsaw, Va, US 163/J2
Warsaw, NC, US 163/H3
Warscheneck (peak), Aus. 50/B2
Warshiikh, Som. 118/C5
Warslow, Eng, UK 35/G5
Warsop, Eng, UK 35/G5
Warstein, Ger. 53/F6
Warszawa (Warsaw) (cap.), Pol. 43/L2
Warta (riv.), Pol. 70/A1
Wartberg an der Krems, Aus. 59/H7
Wartberg ob der Aist, Aus. 59/H6
Wartburg, Tn, US 162/E2
Warthen, Ga, US 163/F4
Wartrace, Tn, US 162/D3
Waru, Indo. 91/H4
Warwick, Austl. 134/D5
Warwick, Eng, UK 37/E2
Warwick, Ga, US 165/G2
Warwick, Md, US 168/C5
Warwick, NY, US 168/D1
Warwick, RI, US 161/L4
Warwickshire (co.), Eng, UK 37/E2
Wasa, BC, Can. 144/G3
Wasagu, Nga. 115/G4
Wasatch (range), Ut, US 142/D4
Wasāwewāla, Pak. 98/B4
Wasbank, SAfr. 125/E3
Wasburn (riv.), Eng, UK 35/G4
Wascana (riv.), Sk, Can. 145/M2
Wasco, Ca, US 148/C3
Wascott, Wi, US 157/J4
Waseca, Mn, US 155/H1
Wash, The (bay), Eng, UK 35/J6
Washaw (bay), Mb, Can. 156/F2
Washburn, Wi, US 157/J4
Washburn, ND, US 156/D4
Washburn (lake), Nun, Can. 140/F1
Washdyke, NZ 135/B4
Washimiya, Japan 83/D1
Washingborough, Eng, UK 35/H5
Washington, Eng, UK 35/G2
Washington (state), US 142/B2
Washington (cap.), US 168/A6
Washington (int'l arpt.), DC, US 168/A6
Washington, Ga, US 163/F4
Washington, Ia, US 155/J3
Washington, Il, US 155/K3
Washington, In, US 162/D1
Washington, Ks, US 155/F4
Washington, Ky, US 162/F1
Washington, La, US 164/B2
Washington (isl.), Mi, US 160/C2
Washington (co.), Mn, US 157/Q6
Washington, Mo, US 155/J4
Washington, Ms, US 164/C2
Washington, NJ, US 168/D2
Washington, Pa, US 160/F4
Washington, Tx, US 151/F2
Washington, Ut, US 149/F2
Washington, Va, US 163/H1
Washington (lake), Wa, US 167/C2
Washington (mt.), Wa, US 144/C4
Washington, NC, US 163/J3
Washington (isl.), Wi, US 157/L5
Washington, WV, US 163/G1
Washington (Teraina) (isl.), Kiri. 137/J4
Washington Court House (Washington), Oh, US 160/E5
Washington Dulles (int'l arpt.), DC, US 163/J1
Washingtonville, Pa, US 168/B1
Washita (riv.), Ok,Tx, US 152/D3
Washita Battlefield Nat'l Hist. Site, Ok, US 152/E3
Washita Nat'l Wildlife Res., Ok, US 152/E3
Washtenaw (co.), Mi, US 167/E7
Washtucna, Wa, US 144/E4
Wasilków, Pol. 43/M2
Wasilla, Ak, US 140/B2
Wāsiṃt (gov.), Iraq 103/F3
Wasior, Indo. 91/H4
Wasiri, Indo. 128/B1
Wasjabo, Sur. 182/B1
Waskada, Mb, Can. 156/D3
Waskaganish (Rupert House), Qu, Can. 141/J3
Waskasa (bay), Japan 84/D3
Waskey (mt.), Ak, US 171/G4
Wasletan, Indo. 128/C1
Waspán, Nic. 177/F3
Wassau Nat'l Wild Ref., Ga, US 165/H2
Wasselonne, Fr. 55/G6
Wassen, Swi. 61/E4
Wassenaar, Neth. 52/B4
Wassenberg, Ger. 55/F1
Wasser, Namb. 124/B2
Wasserbillig, Lux. 55/F4
Wasserburg, Ger. 58/D6
Wasserburg am Inn, Ger. 59/F6
Wasserkuppe (peak), Ger. 58/C2
Wasserliesch, Ger. 55/F4
Wassertrüdingen, Ger. 58/D4
Wassou, Gui. 114/B4
Wassuk (range), Nv, US 142/C4
Wassy, Fr. 60/A1
Wast Water (lake), Eng, UK 35/E3
Wasu, PNG 129/G1
Wat Bot, Thai. 94/C2
Wat Mahathat, Thai. 86/C5
Wat Phra Si Ratana Mahathat, Thai. 86/D5
Wat Phu, Laos 94/D3
Wat Xieng Thong, Laos 86/D5
Wataga, Il, US 155/J3
Watampone, Indo. 91/F4
Watarai, Japan 83/L7
Watarase (riv.), Japan 85/F2
Watari, Japan 85/G1
Watauga, Tx, US 150/K7
Watauga (lake), Tn, US 163/G2
Watch Hill (pt.), RI, US 169/G1
Watchet, Eng, UK 36/C4
Watchfield, Eng, UK 37/E3
Watchung (mts.), NJ, US 169/H9
Watchung, NJ, US 169/H9
Water of Ae (riv.), Sc, UK 34/E1
Water of Girvan (riv.), Sc, UK 34/D1
Water of Girvan (riv.), Sc, UK 33/B6
Water of Ken (riv.), Sc, UK 34/D1
Water Valley, Ky, US 162/C2
Water Valley, Ms, US 162/C3
Water Valley, Ab, Can. 144/G2
Waterbeach, Eng, UK 37/G2
Waterberg, Namb. 122/C4
Waterberg Plateau Park, Namb. 122/C4
Waterberge (mts.), SAfr. 123/E5
Waterbury, Vt, US 161/K2
Waterbury, Ct, US 161/K4
Waterdown, On, Can. 160/T9
Wateree (lake), SC, US 163/G3
Waterfall, Austl. 133/E2
Waterflow, NM, US 149/H2
Waterford (arpt.), Ire. 32/C5
Waterford, Ire. 32/C5
Waterford (har.), Ire. 32/C5
Waterford (co.), Ire. 32/C5
Waterford, Mi, US 160/E3
Waterford, Wi, US 160/B3
Waterford, Ct, US 169/F1
Waterford Works, NJ, US 168/D4
Watergate (bay), Eng, UK 36/A6
Watergrasshill, Ire. 32/B5
Waterhen (lake), Mb, Can. 156/E1
Waterhouse (riv.), Austl. 128/D3
Wateringbury, Eng, UK 30/E3
Waterloo, Austl. 128/C4
Waterloo, Belg. 55/D2
Waterloo, On, Can. 160/F3
Waterloo, Qu, Can. 161/K2
Waterloo, NY, US 161/H3
Waterloo, Ia, US 155/H2
Waterloo, Il, US 162/B1
Waterloo Battlesite, Belg. 55/D2
Waterloo Village, NJ, US 168/D2
Waterlooville, Eng, UK 37/E5
Watermael-Boitsfort, Belg. 54/D2
Waterproof, La, US 164/C2
Watersmeet, Mi, US 157/K4
Waterton Lakes NP, Ab, Can. 145/G3
Waterton Lks. Nat'l Pk., Ab, Can. 140/E4
Waterton Park, Ab, Can. 145/H3
Waterton-Glacier International Peace Park, Can.,US 145/H3
Watertown, NY, US 161/J3
Watertown, Fl, US 165/G2
Watertown, Wi, US 155/K2
Watertown, SD, US 155/F1
Watertown, Mn, US 157/N7
Waterval-Boven, SAfr. 123/F5
Waterville, Ire. 30/N11
Waterville, Ks, US 155/F4
Waterville, NY, US 161/J3
Waterville, Oh, US 160/E4
Waterville, Wa, US 144/D4
Watervliet, Belg. 54/C1
Watervliet, NY, US 161/K3
Watford, On, Can. 160/F3
Watford, Eng, UK 30/B1
Watford City, ND, US 156/C4
Wa'th, Sudan 117/G3
Wath-upon-Dearne, Eng, UK 35/G4
Watheroo, Austl. 130/C4
Watheroo NP, Austl. 130/B4
Wātī Kuliyāh (wadi), Egypt 113/D4
Watkins Glen, NY, US 161/H3
Watkinsville, Ga, US 163/F4
Watling (San Salvador) (isl.), Bahm. 173/G3
Watlington, Eng, UK 37/F3
Watmuri, Indo. 128/C1
Watonga, Ok, US 153/E3
Watonwan (riv.), Mn, US 155/G1
Watowato (peak), Indo. 91/G3
Watrous, NM, US 152/B3
Watrous, Sk, Can. 145/M2
Watsa, D.R. Congo 121/G2
Watseka, Il, US 160/C4
Watson, Ar, US 153/J4
Watson, Ok, US 153/G3
Watson, Il, US 162/C1
Watson, Sk, Can. 145/M1
Watson Lake, Yt, Can. 142/AA13
Watsontown, Pa, US 168/B1
Watsonville, Ca, US 148/B2
Watten, Fr. 54/B2
Wattenheim, Ger. 58/B3
Wattens, Aus. 61/H3
Wattignies, Fr. 54/C2
Watton, Eng, UK 37/G1
Wattrelos, Fr. 54/C2
Watts Bar (dam), Tn, US 162/E3
Watts Bar (lake), Tn, US 162/E3
Wattwil, Swi. 61/F3
Wau, PNG 129/G1
Waubay, SD, US 156/F5
Waubay (lake), SD, US 154/F1
Waubay NWR SD, US 155/F1
Waubun, Mn, US 156/G4
Wauchope, Austl. 132/E1
Wauchula, Fl, US 165/H4
Wauconda, Il, US 167/P15
Waugh (mtn.), Id, US 147/F1
Waukarlycarly (lake), Austl. 127/B3
Waukegan, Il, US 160/C3
Waukesha, Wi, US 160/B3
Waukesha (co.), Wi, US 167/P14
Waukomis, Ok, US 153/F2
Waukon, Ia, US 155/J2
Waun Fâch (peak), Wal, UK 36/C3
Waun-Oer (peak), Wal, UK 36/C1
Wauna, Wa, US 167/B3
Wauneta, Ne, US 154/D3
Waupaca, Wi, US 155/K1
Waupun, Wi, US 155/K2
Waurika, Ok, US 153/F3
Waurika (lake), Ok, US 153/E3
Wausau, Wi, US 155/K1
Wausaukee, Wi, US 160/C2
Wauseon, Oh, US 160/D4
Wautoma, Wi, US 155/K1
Wauwatosa, Wi, US 160/B3
Wave Hill, Austl. 128/C4
Waveland, Ar, US 153/H3
Waveland, Ms, US 164/D2
Waveney (riv.), Eng, UK 37/H2
Waver (riv.), Eng, UK 35/E2
Waverley, Austl. 133/C4
Waverley, NS, Can. 158/F3
Waverley, NZ 135/C2
Waverley Downs, Austl. 132/B1
Waverly, Fl, US 164/M8
Waverly, Ga, US 165/H2
Waverly, Ia, US 155/H2
Waverly, Ks, US 153/G1
Waverly, La, US 153/J4
Waverly, Ne, US 155/F3
Waverly, NY, US 161/H3
Waverly, Oh, US 163/F1
Waverly, Tn, US 162/D2
Waverly (nbrhd.), Austl. 132/G5
Waverly Hall, Ga, US 162/E4
Wavre, Belg. 55/D2
Wavrin, Fr. 54/B2
Wāw, Sudan 117/E4
Wāw al Kabīr, Libya 108/C3
Wawa, On, Can. 141/H4
Wawa, Nga. 115/G4
Wawa (riv.), Nic. 177/E3
Wawanesa, Mb, Can. 156/E3
Wawasang (peak), Nic. 177/E3
Wawayanda St. Park, NJ, US 168/D1
Wawo, Indo. 91/F4
Wawoi (riv.), PNG 129/F1
Wawota, Sk, Can. 156/C3
Waxahachie, Tx, US 150/L7
Waxahachie (cr.), Tx, US 150/L7
Waxxari, China 99/E4
Wayakuba, Indo. 91/G4
Wayamli, Indo. 91/G3
Wayatinah, Austl. 132/C4
Waycross, Ga, US 165/G2
Waygay, Indo. 91/G4
Wayhaya, Indo. 91/F4
Wayland, NY, US 161/H3
Wayland, Mi, US 160/D3
Wayne, Il, US 167/P16
Wayne, Mi, US 167/F7
Wayne, Ne, US 155/F2
Wayne, NY, US 161/H3
Wayne, NJ, US 169/J8
Wayne, WV, US 163/F1
Wayne, Ok, US 153/F3
Wayne, Pa, US 168/C3
Wayne (co.), Pa, US 168/C3
Wayne City, Il, US 162/C1
Waynesboro, Ga, US 163/F4
Waynesboro, Tn, US 162/D3
Waynesboro, Va, US 163/H1
Waynesboro, Ms, US 164/D2
Waynesboro, Pa, US 161/H5
Waynesburg, Pa, US 160/F5
Waynesville, Mo, US 153/H2
Waynesville, NC, US 163/F3
Waynoka, Ok, US 152/E2
Wayside, Ms, US 162/B4
Wayuan, China 87/G3
Waza, Camr. 116/B3
Waza, PN de, Camr. 116/B3
Waziers, Fr. 54/C3
Wazīrābād, Pak. 98/C3
Wazuka, Japan 83/J6
Wda (riv.), Pol. 43/K2
Wé, NCal. 137/V12
We (isl.), Malay. 89/A1
Weald, The (grsld.), Eng, UK 37/F4
Weam, PNG 129/F2
Wear (riv.), Eng, UK 35/G2
Wear (riv.), Eng, UK 35/F2
Wear Head, Eng, UK 35/F2
Weare, NH, US 161/L3
Weatherford, Ok, US 153/E3
Weatherford (lake), Tx, US 150/K7
Weatherford, Tx, US 151/F1
Weatherly, Pa, US 168/C2
Weaubleau, Mo, US 153/H2
Weaver (lake), Mb, Can. 156/F1
Weaver (riv.), Eng, UK 35/F5
Weaverville, Ca, US 146/B3
Weaverville, NC, US 163/F3
Webb, Al, US 165/F2
Webb, Ms, US 162/B4
Webb, Sk, Can. 145/K2
Webb (A.F.B.), Tx, US 151/D1
Webb City, Mo, US 153/G2
Webber, Ks, US 154/E4
Webbers Falls, Ok, US 153/G3
Webberville, Mi, US 160/D3
Weber (mt.), Mn, US 157/J4
Weber (riv.), Ut, US 147/H3
Webi Jubba (riv.), Som. 107/G4
Webi Shabeelle (riv.), Som. 118/C4
Webster, Fl, US 164/L6
Webster, Mt, US 156/B4
Webster, Ma, US 161/L3
Webster, SD, US 156/F5
Webster, Tx, US 151/M9
Webster City, Ia, US 155/H2
Webster Groves, Mo, US 155/J4
Webster Springs (Addison), WV, US 163/G1
Webuye, Kenya 119/A1
Wedde-Warden, Ger. 53/F1
Weddell (sea) 192/X
Weddell (isl.), Mald. 191/E6
Wedderburn, Austl. 132/B3
Weddin Mountains NP, Austl. 133/C1
Weddington, NC, US 163/G3
Wedel, Ger. 53/G1
Wedemark, Ger. 53/G3
Wedge (mt.), BC, Can. 144/C2
Wedgeport, NS, Can. 158/E4
Wedmore, Eng, UK 36/D4
Wednesbury, Eng, UK 36/D1
Wednesfield, Eng, UK 36/D1
Wedowee, Al, US 162/E4
Weduar (cape), Indo. 128/D1
Wedweil, Sudan 117/E3
Wedza, Zim. 123/F3
Wee Waa, Austl. 132/D1
Weed, Ca, US 146/B3
Weedon Bec, Eng, UK 37/E2
Weedon-Centre, Qu, Can. 161/L2
Weedpatch (hill), In, US 160/C5
Weedville, Pa, US 161/G4
Weehawken, NJ, US 169/J8
Weekapaug, RI, US 169/G1
Weekes, Sk, Can. 156/C1
Weeki Wachee, Fl, US 164/K6
Weeki Wachee Springs, Fl, US 164/K6
Weeks, La, US 164/C3
Weeksbury, Ky, US 163/F2
Weeksville, NC, US 163/J2
Weenen, SAfr. 125/E3
Weeping Water, Ne, US 155/F3
Weerselo, Neth. 52/D4
Weert, Neth. 52/C6
Weesatche, Tx, US 151/F3
Weesen, Swi. 61/F3
Weesp, Neth. 52/C4
Weethalle, Austl. 133/C1
Weeze, Ger. 52/D5
Wegberg, Ger. 55/F1
Weggis, Swi. 61/E3
Węgorzewo, Pol. 41/J4
Węgrów, Pol. 43/M2
Wegscheid, Ger. 59/G5
Wehingen, Ger. 61/E1
Wehnī, Eth. 117/H2
Wehr, Ger. 60/D2
Wehra (riv.), Ger. 60/D2
Wehre (riv.), Ger. 53/G6
Wehrheim, Ger. 58/B2
Wei (riv.), China 79/H4
Wei Xian, China 80/C3
Wei Xian, China 80/C3
Weibersbrunn, Ger. 58/C3
Weichang, China 79/H3
Weiden, Ger. 59/F3
Weidenthal, Ger. 58/A4
Weidman, Mi, US 160/D3
Weifang, China 80/D3
Weihai, China 81/B4
Weihenzell, Ger. 58/D4
Weikersheim, Ger. 58/C4
Weil (riv.), Ger. 58/B2
Weil der Stadt, Ger. 58/B5
Weilburg, Ger. 58/B2
Weiler-Simmerberg, Ger. 61/F2
Weilerswist, Ger. 55/F2
Weilheim, Ger. 61/H2

Weilheim an der Teck, Ger. 58/C5
Weilmünster, Ger. 58/B2
Weimar, Ger. 42/F3
Weimar, Tx, US 150/F3
Weinan, China 80/B4
Weiner, Ar, US 162/B3
Weinfelden, Swi. 61/F2
Weingarten, Ger. 61/F2
Weingarten, Ger. 58/B4
Weinheim, Ger. 58/B3
Weinsberg, Ger. 58/C4
Weinstadt, Ger. 58/C5
Weinviertel (reg.), Aus. 45/M2
Weipa, Austl. 129/F3
Weipa Abor. Rsv., Austl. 129/F3
Weipa South, Austl. 129/F3
Weir, Ks, US 153/G2
Weir, Tx, US 151/F2
Weirsdale, Fl, US 165/H3
Weirton, WV, US 160/F4
Weischlitz, Ger. 59/F2
Weisendorf, Ger. 58/D3
Weisenheim am Berg, Ger. 58/B3
Weiser, Id, US 146/E1
Weiser (riv.), Id, US 146/E1
Weishan, China 80/D4
Weishan (lake), China 79/H5
Weishi, China 80/C4
Weiskirchen, Ger. 55/F4
Weismain, Ger. 58/E2
Weiss (dam), Al, US 162/E3
Weiss (lake), Al, US 162/E3
Weissach, Ger. 58/B5
Weisse Elster (riv.), Ger. 42/G3
Weisse Laber (riv.), Ger. 59/E4
Weissenbach am Lech, Aus. 61/G3
Weissenburg im Bayern, Ger. 58/D4
Weissenfels, Ger. 42/F3
Weissenhorn, Ger. 61/G1
Weissensee, Ger. 42/Q6
Weissenstadt, Ger. 59/E2
Weissenthurm, Ger. 55/G3
Weisser (peak), Ger. 55/F3
Weisser Main (riv.), Ger. 59/E2
Weisshorn (peak), Swi. 60/D5
Weissmies (peak), Swi. 60/D5
Weisswasser, Ger. 43/H3
Weistrach, Aus. 59/H6
Weitefeld, Ger. 55/G2
Weiterstadt, Ger. 58/B3
Weitian, China 87/H3
Weitra, Aus. 43/H4
Weixi, China 93/G2
Weiyuan, China 78/E4
Weiyuan (riv.), China 86/D4
Weiz, Aus. 50/B2
Weizhou (isl.), China 93/J3
Weizhou (isl.), Viet. 87/F4
Weiziyu, China 81/C2
Wejherowo, Pol. 40/H4
Wekame, Myan. 94/B3
Wekiva (riv.), Fl, US 164/N6
Welātām, Myan. 93/G2
Welbekend, SAfr. 124/E2
Welch, Ok, US 153/G2
Welch, WV, US 163/G2
Welch (hill), Pa, US 168/A3
Welcome, NC, US 163/G3
Welda, Ks, US 153/G1
Welden, Ger. 58/D6
Weldiya, Eth. 118/A3
Weldon, Tx, US 151/G2
Weldon (riv.), Ia, Mo, US 155/H3
Weldon, Eng, UK 37/F2
Weleetka, Ok, US 153/F3
Welega (pol. reg.), Eth. 117/G3
Welel (peak), Eth. 117/G3
Welford, Austl. 134/A4
Welford, Eng, UK 37/E4
Welham Green, Eng, UK 30/C1
Welkenraedt, Belg. 55/E2
Welk'īt'ē, Eth. 117/H3
Welkom, SAfr. 124/D3
Welland (riv.), Eng, UK 35/H6
Welland (canal), On, US 160/U10
Welland, On, Can. 160/U10
Wellandport, On, Can. 160/U9
Wellborn, Fl, US 165/G2
Wellen, Belg. 55/E2
Wellesley (isls.), Austl. 129/E4
Wellesley (isls.) 127/C2
Wellford, SC, US 163/F3
Wellin, Belg. 55/E3
Wellingborough, Eng, UK 37/F2
Wellington, Austl. 133/D1
Wellington (lake), Austl. 132/C3
Wellington, On, Can. 161/H3
Wellington (isl.), Chile 179/B7
Wellington (chan.), Nun, Can. 141/S7
Wellington, SAfr. 124/L10
Wellington (int'l arpt.), NZ 135/H9
Wellington (cap.), NZ 135/H9
Wellington, Ks, US 153/F2
Wellington, Tx, US 152/D3
Wellington, Nv, US 146/D4
Wellington, Co, US 154/B3
Wellington, Eng, UK 36/C5
Wellington, Eng, UK 36/D2
Wellington (co.), On, Can. 160/S8
Wellman, Tx, US 152/C4
Wellman, Ia, US 155/J3
Wells (lake), Austl. 127/B3
Wells, BC, Can. 144/D1
Wells, Eng, UK 36/D4
Wells, Tx, US 150/G2
Wells, NY, US 161/J3
Wells, Me, US 161/L3
Wells, Nv, US 147/F3
Wells, Mn, US 155/H2
Wells-next-the-Sea, Eng, UK 37/G1
Wellsboro, Pa, US 161/H4
Wellsburg, WV, US 160/F4
Wellsford, NZ 135/C2
Wellston, Ok, US 153/F3
Wellston, Mi, US 160/D2
Wellston, Oh, US 163/F1
Wellsville, Ks, US 153/G1
Wellsville, NY, US 161/H3
Wellsville, Ut, US 147/H3
Wellsville, Mo, US 155/J4
Wellsville, Pa, US 168/B3
Wellwood, Mb, Can. 156/E2
Welo (prov.), Eth. 118/A3
Wels, Aus. 59/H6
Welschbillig, Ger. 55/F4
Welsh, La, US 164/B2
Welshnofen (Nova Levante), It. 61/H5
Welshpool, Wal, UK 36/C1
Welty, Ok, US 153/F3
Welver, Ger. 53/E5
Welwel, Eth. 118/C4
Welwyn, Sk, Can. 156/D2
Welzheim, Ger. 58/C5
Wem, Eng, UK 35/F6
Wembere (riv.), Tanz. 119/A3
Wembley Stadium, Eng, UK 30/C2
Wemding, Ger. 58/D5
Wemindji, Qu, Can. 141/J3
Wemmel, Belg. 55/D2
Wemyss Bay, Sc, UK 33/B5
Wen Xian, China 80/C4
Wenago, Eth. 118/A4
Wen'an, China 80/H7
Wenatchee, Wa, US 144/D4
Wenatchee (mts.), Wa, US 144/D4
Wenchang, China 87/F5
Wencheng, China 87/J3
Wenchi, Gha. 115/E5
Wendeburg, Ger. 53/H4
Wendell, Mn, US 156/F4
Wenden, Ger. 55/G2
Wenden, Az, US 149/F4
Wendeng, China 81/B4
Wendi, China 87/F4
Wendji, D.R. Congo 120/D3
Wendlingen am Neckar, Ger. 58/C5
Wendo, Eth. 118/A4
Wendou Borou, Gui. 114/B4
Wendover, Nv, US 147/F3
Wendover, Eng, UK 37/F3
Wendron, Eng, UK 36/A6
Wendte, SD, US 154/D1
Wengdong, China 87/F3
Wengjiang, China 87/G2
Wengshui, China 93/G2
Wengyang, China 87/J2
Wengyuan, China 93/K3
Wenlock Edge (ridge), Eng, UK 36/D2
Wenne (riv.), Ger. 53/F6
Wennigsen, Ger. 53/G4
Wennington, Eng, UK 35/F3
Wenona, Il, US 155/K3
Wenonah, NJ, US 168/C4
Wenquan, China 87/E2
Wenquan, China 86/D2
Wenquan, China 87/F4
Wenquan, China 99/F5
Wenquanzhen, China 87/G3
Wenshan, China 93/H3
Wenshang, China 80/D4
Wenshui, China 80/C3
Wensleydale (valley), Eng, UK 35/F3
Went (riv.), Eng, UK 35/G4
Wentang, China 87/G2
Wentworth, Austl. 132/B2
Wentworth, NC, US 163/H2
Wenxi, China 80/B4
Wenzhou, China 87/J3
Weohyakapka (lake), Fl, US 164/N8
Weott, Ca, US 146/B3
Wepener, SAfr. 124/D3
Wépion, Belg. 55/D3
Wer, India 96/A2
Werda, Bots. 122/D5
Werdër, Eth. 118/C4
Werder, Ger. 42/P7
Werdohl, Ger. 53/E6
Were Īlu, Eth. 118/A3
Werinama, Indo. 91/G4
Werkendam, Neth. 52/B5
Werl, Ger. 53/E5
Werlte, Ger. 53/E3
Wermelskirchen, Ger. 55/G1
Wern (riv.), Ger. 58/C3
Wernau, Ger. 58/C5
Wernberg-Köblitz, Ger. 59/F3
Werne an der Lippe, Ger. 53/E5
Werneck, Ger. 58/D3
Werner Lake, On, Can. 157/G2
Werneuchen, Ger. 42/Q6
Wernigerode, Ger. 53/H5
Werong (mt.), Austl. 133/D2
Werota, Eth. 117/H3
Werra (riv.), Ger. 42/E3
Werre (riv.), Ger. 42/E2
Werrikimbe NP, Austl. 132/E1
Werrimull, Austl. 132/B2
Werrington, Eng, UK 35/F5
Werris Creek, Austl. 132/D1
Werse (riv.), Ger. 53/E5
Wertach (riv.), Ger. 58/D6
Wertheim, Ger. 58/C3
Wertheim Nat'l Wild. Ref., NY, US 169/F2
Werther, Ger. 53/F4
Werther, Ger. 53/H6
Wertingen, Ger. 58/D5
Wervershoof, Neth. 52/C3
Wervik, Belg. 54/C2
Weschnitz (riv.), Ger. 58/B3
Wesefgebirge (mts.), Ger. 53/F4
Wesel, Ger. 52/D5
Wesel-Datteln (canal), Ger. 53/E5
Wesely E. Seale (dam), Tx, US 151/F3
Wesenberg, Ger. 42/G2
Weser (riv.), Ger. 42/E2
Weslaco, Tx, US 151/F4
Wesley, Ia, US 155/H2
Wesley Hills, NY, US 169/J7
Wessel (cape), Austl. 129/E2
Wessel (isls.), Austl. 127/C2
Wesselburen, Ger. 40/C4
Wesseling, Ger. 55/F2
Wesselsbron, SAfr. 124/D2
Wessex (reg.), Eng, UK 36/D4
Wessington, SD, US 154/E1
Wessington Springs, SD, US 154/E1
Wesson, Ar, US 153/H4
Wesson, Ms, US 164/C2
West (isl.), Austl. 129/E3
West (pt.), Austl. 132/C4
West (cape), NZ 135/A4
West (bay), La, US 164/D3
West, Tx, US 151/F2
West (pt.), Wa, US 167/C2
West Abor. Land, Austl. 129/E3
West Allis, Wi, US 160/B3
West Arichat, NS, Can. 159/G3
West Augusta, Ga, US 163/F4
West Augusta, Va, US 163/H1
West Babylon, NY, US 169/E2
West Bank 105/C4
West Baraboo, Wi, US 155/K2
West Barns, Sc, UK 33/D5
West Bay, NS, Can. 159/G3
West Bend, Sk, Can. 156/C2
West Bend, Wi, US 160/B3
West Bend, Ia, US 155/G2
West Bengal (state), India 92/E3
West Bergholt, Eng, UK 37/G3
West Berkshire (co.), Eng, UK 37/E4
West Bijou (cr.), Co, US 154/B4
West Blocton, Al, US 162/D4
West Branch, Mi, US 160/D2
West Branch Devers (canal), Tx, US 151/N9
West Brattleboro, Vt, US 161/K3
West Bridgford, Eng, UK 35/G6
West Bromwich, Eng, UK 36/E1
West Byfleet, Eng, UK 30/B3
West Caicos (isl.), UK 177/H1
West Calder, Sc, UK 33/C5
West Caldwell, NJ, US 169/H8
West Cap Howe NP, Austl. 130/C5
West Carthage, NY, US 161/J3
West Chester, Pa, US 168/C4
West Chicago, Il, US 167/P16
West Chyulu Game Consv. Area, Kenya 119/B2
West Clandon, Eng, UK 30/B3
West Coast NP, SAfr. 124/L10
West Columbia, Tx, US 150/G3
West Columbia, SC, US 163/G4
West Cornforth, Eng, UK 35/G2
West Covina, Ca, US 166/G7
West Creek, NJ, US 168/D4
West Crossett, Ar, US 153/J4
West Des Moines, Ia, US 155/H3
West Dover, NS, Can. 158/F3
West Dunbartonshire (co.), Sc, UK 33/B4
West Elk (mts.), Co, US 147/K4
West Elmira, NY, US 161/H3
West End, Eng, UK 30/B3
West Falkland (isl.), UK 191/E6
West Fargo, ND, US 156/F4
West Farleigh, Eng, UK 30/E3
West Fayu (isl.), Micr. 136/D4
West Flamborough, On, Can. 160/S9
West Fork, Ar, US 153/G3
West Frankfort, Il, US 162/C2
West Frisian (isls.), Neth. 42/C2
West Frostproof, Fl, US 164/M8
West Glamorgan (co.), Wal, UK 36/C3
West Glen (riv.), Eng, UK 35/H6
West Green, Ga, US 165/G2
West Grove, Pa, US 168/C4
West Ham (nbrhd.), Eng, UK 30/D2
West Hanningfield, Eng, UK 30/E2
West Haven, Ct, US 169/F1
West Haverstraw, NY, US 168/E1
West Hawk Lake, Mb, Can. 157/G3
West Helena, Ar, US 162/B3
West Hempstead, NY, US 169/L9
West Hills, NY, US 169/M8
West Hollywood, Ca, US 166/F7
West Horndon, Eng, UK 30/E2
West Horseley, Eng, UK 30/B3
West Ice Shelf, Ant. 192/F
West Indies (isls.), NAm. 139/L7
West Islet (isl.), Austl. 127/E3
West Islip, NY, US 169/E2
West Jefferson, NC, US 163/G2
West Jordan, Ut, US 147/H3
West Kennebago (mtn.), Me, US 161/L2
West Kilbride, Sc, UK 33/B5
West Kingsdown, Eng, UK 30/D3
West Kirby, Eng, UK 35/E5
West Knock (peak), Sc, UK 33/D3
West Lafayette, Oh, US 160/F4
West Lafayette, In, US 160/C4
West Lake Hills, Tx, US 151/F2
West Lamma (chan.), China 87/L8
West Lebanon, In, US 160/C4
West Liberty, Oh, US 160/E4
West Liberty, Ky, US 163/F2
West Liberty, Ia, US 155/J3
West Linn, Or, US 146/B1
West Lorne, On, Can. 160/F3
West Lothian (co.), Sc, UK 33/C5
West Lunga NP, Afr. 122/E2
West Malling, Eng, UK 30/E3
West Melbourne, Fl, US 165/H3
West Memphis, Ar, US 162/B3
West Mersea, Eng, UK 37/G3
West Miami, Fl, US 164/P11
West Midlands (co.), Eng, UK 37/E1
West Milford, NJ, US 169/H7
West Milford, WV, US 163/G1
West Milton, Pa, US 168/B1
West Monroe, La, US 153/H4
West Monroe, Mi, US 160/E4
West New Britain (prov.), PNG 129/H1
West New York, NJ, US 169/J8
West Nicholson, Zim. 123/F4
West Nishnabotna (riv.), Ia, US 155/G3
West Nodaway (riv.), Ia, US 155/G3
West Nueces (riv.), Tx, US 151/E3
West Nyack, NY, US 169/K7
West Olive, Mi, US 160/C3
West Orange, Tx, US 151/H2
West Orange, NJ, US 169/J8
West Palm Beach (canal), Fl, US 164/P9
West Palm Beach, Fl, US 164/P9
West Paterson, NJ, US 169/J8
West Pensacola, Fl, US 164/E2
West Plains, Mo, US 153/J2
West Plains (Plains), Ks, US 152/D2
West Point, Ca, US 146/C4
West Point, Il, US 155/J3
West Point, Ia, US 155/J3
West Point, Ga, US 162/E4
West Point (dam), Ga, US 162/E4
West Point, Ms, US 162/C4
West Point, Ne, US 155/F3
West Point (res.), Ga, US 162/E4
West Point Mil. Acad, NY, US 161/J4
West Poplar, Sk, Can. 145/L3
West Reading, Pa, US 168/C3
West Redding, Ct, US 169/E1
West Richland, Wa, US 144/E4
West Road (riv.), BC, Can. 144/B1
West Sacramento, Ca, US 167/L9
West Saint Paul, Mn, US 157/P7
West Salem, Il, US 162/C1
West Sayville, NY, US 169/E2
West Seneca, NY, US 160/V10
West Siberian (plain), Rus. 74/H3
West Sister Island Nat'l Wild. Ref., Oh, US 160/E4
West Sussex (co.), Eng, UK 37/F4
West Tawakoni, Tx, US 153/F4
West Thurrock, Eng, UK 30/D2
West Tisbury, Ma, US 158/B5
West Union, WV, US 160/F5
West Union, Il, US 160/C5
West Union, Ia, US 155/J2
West Union, Oh, US 163/F1
West Unity, Oh, US 160/D4
West University Place, Tx, US 151/M9
West Valley City, Ut, US 147/H3
West Vancouver, BC, Can. 144/C3
West Virginia (state), US 143/K4
West Walker (riv.), Ca,Nv, US 148/C1
West Warwick, RI, US 161/L4
West Water (riv.), Sc, UK 33/D3
West Winfield, NY, US 161/J3
West Wyalong, Austl. 133/C1
West Yellowstone, Mt, US 147/H1
West York, Pa, US 168/B4
West Yorkshire (co.), Eng, UK 35/G4
West-Nieuwland, Neth. 52/A5
West-Terschelling, Neth. 52/C2
Westall (pt.), Austl. 131/G5
Westboro, Wi, US 157/J5
Westbourne, Mb, Can. 156/E2
Westbrook, Mn, US 155/G1
Westbrook, Ct, US 169/F1
Westbury, NY, US 169/L9
Westbury, Eng, UK 36/D4
Westby, Wi, US 155/J2
Westchester (co.), NY, US 169/E1
Westchester County (arpt.), NY, US 169/L7
Westcliffe, Co, US 152/B1
Westcott, Eng, UK 30/B3
Westdorpe, Neth. 54/C1
Westend, Ca, US 148/D3
Westerblokker, Neth. 52/C3
Westerbork, Neth. 52/D3
Westerburg, Ger. 55/G2
Westerham, Eng, UK 30/D3
Westerheim, Ger. 61/G1
Westerholt, Ger. 53/E1
Westerkappeln, Ger. 53/E4
Westerland, Ger. 40/C4
Westerlo, Belg. 55/D1
Westerly, RI, US 161/L4
Western (des.), Egypt 109/F3
Western (pol. reg.), Gha. 115/E5
Western (chan.), SKor. 84/A3
Western (prov.), Kenya 119/A1
Western (prov.), PNG 129/F1
Western (prov.), SrL. 95/C5
Western Area (prov.), SLeo. 114/B4
Western Australia (state), Austl. 127/B3
Western Cape (prov.), SAfr. 124/C4
Western Caprivi Game Park, Namb. 122/D3
Western Ghats (mts.), India 92/B4
Western Highlands (uplands), PNG 129/G1
Western Run (riv.), Md, US 168/B4
Western Sahara 107/A2
Western Samoa (ctry.) 137/H6
Western Sayan (mts.), Rus. 78/C1
Western Sayans (mts.), Rus. 74/J4
Western Springs (nbrhd.), NZ 135/F6
Westernport, Md, US 161/G5
Westerschelde (chan.), Belg. 52/A6
Westerstede, Ger. 53/E2
Westerville, Oh, US 160/E4
Westervoort, Neth. 52/C5
Westerwald (mts.), Ger. 42/D3
Westfield, NB, Can. 158/D3
Westfield, Ma, US 161/K3
Westfield, NY, US 161/G3
Westfield, NJ, US 169/H9
Westfield, Wi, US 155/K2
Westgat (chan.), Neth. 52/D2
Westhampton, NY, US 169/F2
Westhampton Beach, NY, US 169/F2
Westhausen, Ger. 58/D5
Westheim, Ger. 58/B4
Westhill, Sc, UK 33/D2
Westhofen, Ger. 58/B3
Westhoff, Tx, US 151/F3
Westhope, ND, US 156/D3
Westhoughton, Eng, UK 35/F4
Westkapelle, Neth. 52/A5
Westlake, La, US 164/B2
Westlake Village, Ca, US 166/B2
Westland, Mi, US 167/F7
Westland NP, NZ 135/B3
Westlock, Ab, Can. 140/E3
Westmalle, Belg. 52/B6
Westminster, Ca, US 166/F8
Westminster, SC, US 163/F3
Westminster, Co, US 154/B4
Westminster, Md, US 168/B4
Westminster, City of (bor.), Eng, UK 30/A1
Westmont, Pa, US 161/G4
Westmont, Il, US 167/P16
Westmont (Haddon), NJ, US 168/C4
Westmoreland, Ks, US 155/F4
Westmoreland, Austl. 129/E4
Westmorland (reg.), Eng, UK 35/F3
Westmorland, Ca, US 148/E4
Westmount, Qu, Can. 159/N7
Westmuir, Sc, UK 33/C3
Westoak, Ga, US 163/L7
Weston, Co, US 152/B2
Weston, Oh, US 160/E4
Weston, Ga, US 165/F2
Weston, Id, US 147/H2
Weston, WV, US 163/G1
Weston, Wi, US 155/H1
Weston, Wy, US 154/B1
Weston, Malay. 88/A4
Weston, Ct, US 169/E1
Weston Zoyland, Eng, UK 36/D4
Weston-super-Mare, Eng, UK 36/D4
Westonaria, SAfr. 124/P13
Westover, WV, US 160/G5
Westover (A.F.B.), Ma, US 161/K3
Westover, SD, US 154/D2
Westphalia, Ks, US 153/G1
Westport, NS, Can. 158/D3
Westport, Ire. 32/A2
Westport, On, Can. 161/H2
Westport, NZ 135/B3
Westport, In, US 162/E1
Westport, Wa, US 144/B4
Westport, Ct, US 169/E1
Westray (isl.), Sc, UK 31/V14
Westside, Ga, US 162/F3
Westview, Sk, Can. 156/C2
Westville, Ok, US 153/G3
Westville, Ga, US 165/F1
Westville, In, US 160/C4
Westville, Il, US 160/C4
Westville, NS, Can. 159/F3
Westville, SC, US 163/G3
Westward Ho!, Eng, UK 36/B4
Westwold, BC, Can. 144/E2
Westwood, NJ, US 169/J8
Westwood, Zam. 123/F2
Westwood, Ca, US 146/C3
Westwood, Ky, US 163/F1
Westwood Lakes, Fl, US 164/P11
Westworth Village, Tx, US 150/K7
Westzaan, Neth. 52/B4
Wet (mts.), Co, US 154/B4
Wetan (isl.), Indo. 128/C1
Wetar (isl.), Indo. 128/B1
Wetar (str.), ETim.,Indo. 128/B2
Wetaskiwin, Ab, Can. 145/H1
Wete, D.R. Congo 121/F4
Wete, Tanz. 119/B3
Wetheral, Eng, UK 35/F2
Wetherby, Eng, UK 35/G4
Wetlet, Myan. 94/A1
Wetmore, Ks, US 155/G4
Wetter (riv.), Ger. 58/B2
Wetter, Ger. 53/E6
Wetterau (reg.), Ger. 58/C2
Wetteren, Belg. 54/C2
Wetterhorn (peak), Swi. 60/E4
Wettingen, Swi. 61/E3
Wettringen, Ger. 53/E4
Wetumka, Ok, US 153/F3
Wetumpka, Al, US 162/D4
Wetuppa, Austl. 132/B2
Wetzikon, Swi. 61/E3
Wetzlar, Ger. 58/B1
Wetzstein (peak), Ger. 59/E2
Wevelgem, Belg. 54/C2
Wewahitchka, Fl, US 165/F2
Wewak, PNG 136/D5
Wewoka, Ok, US 153/F3
Wexford, Ire. 32/D5
Wexford (co.), Ire. 32/D5
Wexford (har.), Ire. 32/D5
Wey (riv.), Eng, UK 30/A3
Weyanoke, La, US 164/C2
Weyauwega, Wi, US 155/K1
Weybourne, Eng, UK 37/H1
Weybridge, Eng, UK 30/B2
Weyburn, Sk, Can. 156/C3
Weygand (ruin), Alg. 111/F4
Weyhausen, Ger. 53/H4
Weyland (pt.), Austl. 131/G5
Weymouth, NS, Can. 158/D3
Weymouth (cape), Austl. 129/F3
Weymouth, Eng, UK 36/D5
Weymouth (bay), Eng, UK 36/D5
Weymouth North, NS, Can. 158/E3
Wezep, Neth. 52/D4
Whakatane, NZ 135/D2
Whale Cove, Nun, Can. 140/G2
Whaletown, BC, Can. 144/B2
Whaley Bridge, Eng, UK 35/G5
Whalsey (isl.), Sc, UK 31/W13
Whangamata, NZ 135/C2
Whangaparaoa (head), NZ 135/F6
Whangarei, NZ 135/C1
Wharfe (riv.), Eng, UK 35/G3
Wharncliffe, WV, US 163/G2
Wharton, Tx, US 151/F3
Whataroa, NZ 135/B3
Whatatutu, NZ 135/D2
Whatley, Al, US 164/E2
Wheatland, Mo, US 153/H2
Wheatland, Wy, US 154/B2
Wheatland No. 2 (res.), Wy, US 154/B3
Wheatley, On, Can. 160/E3
Wheatley, Ar, US 162/B3
Wheatley, Eng, UK 37/E3
Wheaton, Mn, US 156/F5
Wheaton, Mo, US 153/G2
Wheaton, Il, US 160/B4
Wheaton Aston, Eng, UK 36/D1
Wheaton Village, NJ, US 168/C5
Wheaton-Glenmont, Md, US 168/A5
Wheeler (peak), NM, US 152/B2
Wheeler, Tx, US 152/D3
Wheeler (peak), Nv, US 147/F4
Wheeler, Ms, US 162/C3
Wheeler, Or, US 144/C5
Wheeler (lake), Al, US 162/D3
Wheeler NWR, Al, US 162/D3
Wheeler Springs, Ca, US 166/A1
Wheelersburg, Oh, US 163/F1
Wheeless, Ok, US 152/C2
Wheeling, WV, US 160/F4
Wheeling, Il, US 167/Q15
Wheeling, Mo, US 155/H4
Wheelock, Tx, US 151/F2
Wheelwright, Arg. 190/E2
Whelen Springs, Ar, US 153/H4
Whenuapai (arpt.), NZ 135/F6
Whernside (peak), Eng, UK 35/F3
Whickham, Eng, UK 35/G2
Whidbey (pt.), Austl. 131/G5
Whidbey (isl.), Wa, US 144/C4
Whiddy (isl.), Ire. 32/A6
Whigham, Ga, US 165/F2
Whinham (mt.), Austl. 131/F3
Whiskeytown-Shasta-Trinity Nat'l Rec. Area, Ca, US 146/B3
Whistler, BC, Can. 144/C2
Whitakers, NC, US 163/J2
Whitbourne, Nf, Can. 159/L2
Whitburn, Sc, UK 33/C5
Whitburn, Eng, UK 35/G2
Whitby, Eng, UK 35/H3
Whitby, On, Can. 160/V8
Whitchurch, Eng, UK 35/F6
Whitchurch, Eng, UK 37/E4
Whitchurch, Wal, UK 36/C3
Whitchurch, Eng, UK 37/F3
Whitchurch-Stouffville, On, Can. 161/G3
Whitcombe (mt.), NZ 135/B3
White (sea), Swe. 68/B3
White, Ar, US 153/J4
White (lake), On, Can. 157/M3
White (bay), Nf, Can. 141/L3
White (riv.), Co, US 147/J3
White (pass), Va, US 163/G2
White, Ga, US 162/E3
White, SD, US 155/F1
White (pass), Wa, US 144/D4
White (lake), Austl. 127/B3
White, Vernon Fork (riv.), In, US 162/E1
White Bear (riv.), Nf, Can. 159/J1
White Bear, Sk, Can. 145/K2
White Bear Lake, Mn, US 157/P6
White Bird, Id, US 146/E1
White Bluff, Tn, US 162/D2
White Butte, SD, US 156/C5
White Castle, La, US 164/C2
White City, Ks, US 153/F1
White City, Sk, Can. 156/B2
White City, Fl, US 165/H4
White City, Fl, US 165/F3
White Cliffs, Austl. 132/B1
White Cloud, Mi, US 160/D3
White Coomb (peak), Sc, UK 33/C6
White Deer (cr.), Pa, US 168/A1
White Earth, Mn, US 156/G4
White Earth, ND, US 156/C3
White Earth (riv.), ND, US 156/C3
White Earth Indian (res.), Mn, US 157/G4
White Esk (riv.), Sc, UK 33/C6
White Hall, Ar, US 153/H3
White Hall, Al, US 162/D4
White Hall, Md, US 168/B4
White Haven, Pa, US 168/C1
White Horse Draw (riv.), Tx, US 151/B2
White House, Tn, US 162/D2
White Lake, Wi, US 157/K5
White Lake, On, Can. 161/H2
White Lake Nat'l Wild. Ref., ND, US 156/C4
White Marsh, Md, US 168/B5
White Mills, Ky, US 162/D2
White Mountain, Ak, US 171/F3
White Mountain (peak), Ca, US 148/C2
White Nile (riv.), Sudan 107/F4
White Oak, Ga, US 165/H2
White Oak, Oh, US 162/E1
White Oak (bayou), Tx, US 151/M9
White Oak, Tx, US 151/G1
White Oak, Md, US 168/B5
White Otter (lake), On, Can. 157/J3
White Pigeon, Mi, US 160/D4
White Pine, Tn, US 163/F2
White Plains, NY, US 169/K7
White Plains, NC, US 163/G2
White Rapids (dam), Mi, US 160/C2
White River, SD, US 154/D2
White River NWR, Ar, US 162/B3
White Rock, Tx, US 153/F4
White Rock (cr.), Ks, US 155/E4
White Rock, NM, US 149/J3
White Rock (lake), Tx, US 150/L7
White Salmon, Wa, US 144/D5
White Sands (des.), NM, US 149/J4
White Sands, NM, US 149/J4
White Sands Missile Range, NM, US 149/J4
White Sands Nat'l Mon., NM, US 151/A1
White Sands Space Harbor, NM, US 149/J4
White Settlement, Tx, US 150/K7
White Shield, ND, US 156/D4
White Springs, Fl, US 165/G2
White Sulphur Springs, Mt, US 145/J4
White Sulphur Springs, WV, US 163/G2
White Swan, Wa, US 144/D4
White Volta (riv.), Gha. 107/B4
White Waltham, Eng, UK 30/A2
White Woman (cr.), Co,Ks, US 154/D4
White, East Fork (riv.), In, US 162/D1
White, West Fork (riv.), Wa, US 167/D3
Whiteadder Water (riv.), Sc, UK 33/D5
Whitecourt, Ab, Can. 140/E3
Whiteface (riv.), Mn, US 157/H4
Whiteface, Tx, US 152/C4
Whiteface (res.), Mn, US 157/H4
Whiteface (mtn.), NY, US 161/K2
Whitefield, Eng, UK 35/F4
Whitefield, NH, US 161/L2
Whitefish (lake), Mn, US 157/G4
Whitefish (pt.), Wi, US 160/C2
Whitefish (bay), Mi, US 160/D1
Whitefish, Mt, US 144/G3
Whitefish Point, Mi, US 160/D1
Whitefish Station, Yk, Can. 171/L2
Whiteford (pt.), Wal, UK 36/B3
Whiteford, Md, US 168/B4
Whitegate, Ire. 32/B6
Whitegate, Ire. 32/B4
Whitehall, NY, US 161/K3
Whitehall, Oh, US 160/E5
Whitehall, Mi, US 160/C3
Whitehall, Wi, US 155/J1
Whitehall, Mt, US 145/H5
Whitehall (Fullerton), Pa, US 168/C2
Whitehaven, Eng, UK 34/E2
Whitehead, NI, UK 34/C2
Whitehills, Sc, UK 33/D1
Whitehorse (cap.), Yk, Can. 171/L3
Whitehorse (hill), Eng, UK 37/E3
Whitehorse, SD, US 156/D5
Whitehouse, Ga, US 163/M7
Whitehouse, Oh, US 160/E4
Whitehouse, Tx, US 151/G1
Whiteland, In, US 160/C5
Whiteman (A.F.B.), Mo, US 153/H1
Whitemark, Austl. 133/D5
Whitemouth (lake), Mb, Can. 157/G3
Whitemouth, Mb, Can. 156/G3
Whitemouth (riv.), Mb, Can. 156/G3
Whitepine, Co, US 149/J1
Whiteriver, Az, US 149/H4
Whites City, NM, US 150/B1
Whites Lake, NS, Can. 158/F3
Whitesboro, Ok, US 153/G3
Whitesboro, Tx, US 153/F4
Whitesburg, Ky, US 163/F2
Whiteside (chan.), Chile 191/C7
Whitestone Hill Bfld. Hist. Site, ND, US 156/E4
Whitesunday NP, Austl. 129/H5
Whitesville, Ky, US 162/D2
Whitesville, NJ, US 168/D3
Whitesville, NY, US 161/H3
Whitetail, NM, US 152/B4
Whitetail, Mt, US 156/B3
Whitetop, Va, US 163/G2
Whiteville, Tn, US 162/C3
Whiteville, NC, US 163/H3
Whitewater, Ks, US 153/F2
Whitewater (lake), On, Can. 157/K2
Whitewater (bay), Fl, US 165/H5
Whitewater, Co, US 147/J4
Whitewater, Wi, US 155/K2
Whitewater, Mt, US 145/L3
Whitewater Baldy (peak), NM, US 149/H4
Whitewood, Sk, Can. 156/C2
Whitewright, Tx, US 153/F4
Whithorn, Sc, UK 34/D2
Whitianga, NZ 135/C2
Whiting, In, US 167/R16
Whiting, Ia, US 155/F2
Whiting, Ks, US 155/G4
Whiting, Wi, US 155/K1
Whiting Bay, Sc, UK 33/A6
Whiting Field Nav. Air Sta., Fl, US 164/E2
Whitland, Wal, UK 36/B3
Whitlash, Mt, US 145/J3
Whitley Bay, Eng, UK 35/G1
Whitley City, Ky, US 162/E2
Whitmore Lake, Mi, US 160/E3
Whitney, On, Can. 161/G2
Whitney (mt.), Ca, US 142/C4
Whitney, Tx, US 151/F2
Whitney Point, NY, US 161/J3
Whitsand (bay), Eng, UK 36/B6
Whitsett, Tx, US 151/E3
Whitstable, Eng, UK 37/H4
Whitsunday (isl.) 127/D3
Whitsunday Island NP, Austl. 134/C3
Whitt, Tx, US 153/E4
Whittaker, Mi, US 167/E7
Whittier, Ak, US 171/J3
Whittier, Ca, US 166/F8
Whittington, Eng, UK 35/F6
Whittlesea, Austl. 132/G5
Whittlesey (mt.), Wi, US 157/J4
Whittlesey, Eng, UK 37/F1
Whitton, Austl. 133/C2
Whitwell, Eng, UK 35/G5
Whitwell, Tn, US 162/E3
Whitworth, Eng, UK 35/F4
Wholdaia (lake), NW, Can. 140/F2
Why, Az, US 149/F4
Whyalla, Austl. 131/H5
Whycocomagh, NS, Can. 159/G3
Whyjonta, Austl. 132/B1
Wi (isl.), SKor. 81/D5
Wiang Kosai NP, Thai. 94/B2
Wiarton, On, Can. 160/F2
Wiawer, Ugan. 119/A1
Wiawso, Gha. 115/E5
Wibaux, Mt, US 156/B4
Wichabai, Guy. 181/G4
Wich'alē, Eth. 118/A3
Wichelen, Belg. 54/C2
Wichian Buri, Thai. 94/C3
Wichita (riv.), Tx, US 152/E4
Wichita (mts.), Ok, US 153/E3
Wichita, Ks, US 153/F2
Wichita Falls, Tx, US 153/E4
Wichita Mountains NWR, Ok, US 153/E3
Wick, Sc, UK 31/S7
Wick Hill, Eng, UK 30/A2
Wickede, Ger. 53/E6
Wickede (Dortmund) (int'l arpt.), Ger. 53/E5
Wickenburg, Az, US 149/F4
Wickepin, Austl. 130/C5
Wickes, Ar, US 153/G3
Wickford, Eng, UK 30/E2
Wickham, Austl. 130/C2
Wickham Market, Eng, UK 37/H2
Wickiup (res.), Or, US 146/B2
Wickliffe, Ky, US 162/C2
Wicklow (pt.), Ire. 34/B6
Wicklow (mts.), Ire. 32/D4
Wicklow, Ire. 34/B6
Wicklow (pass), Ire. 34/B5
Wicklow (co.), Ire. 32/D4
Wickriede (riv.), Ger. 53/F4
Wid (riv.), Eng, UK 30/E2
Widgiemooltha, Austl. 130/D4
Widnau, Swi. 61/F3
Widnes, Eng, UK 35/F5
Więcbork, Pol. 43/J2
Wied (riv.), Ger. 45/G1
Wiedau (riv.), Ger. 53/G2
Wiefelstede, Ger. 53/F2
Wiehengebirge (ridge), Ger. 53/F4
Wiehl, Ger. 55/G2
Wielenbach, Ger. 61/H2
Wieliczka, Pol. 43/L4
Wielkopolski NP, Pol. 43/J2
Wielkopolskie (prov.), Pol. 43/J2
Wielsbeke, Belg. 54/C2
Wieluń, Pol. 43/K3
Wien (prov.), Aus. 43/J4
Wien (riv.), Aus. 51/N7
Wien (Vienna) (cap.), Aus. 51/N7
Wiener Neudorf, Aus. 51/N7
Wiener Neustadt, Aus. 50/C2
Wienerwald (reg.), Aus. 51/N7
Wienwald (reg.), Aus. 45/L2
Wieprz (riv.), Pol. 70/B2
Wierden, Neth. 52/D4
Wieren, Ger. 53/H3
Wieringermeerpolder (polder), Neth. 52/B3
Wieringerwerf, Neth. 52/C3
Wierum, Neth. 52/D2
Wieruszów, Pol. 43/K3
Wiesbaden, Ger. 58/B2
Wiese (riv.), Ger. 45/G3
Wiese (isl.), Rus. 192/A
Wieseck (riv.), Ger. 58/B1
Wiesendangen, Swi. 61/E2
Wiesensteig, Ger. 58/C5
Wiesent (riv.), Ger. 58/E4
Wiesentheid, Ger. 58/D3
Wiesloch, Ger. 58/B4
Wiesmoor, Ger. 53/E2
Wietmarschen, Ger. 53/D4
Wietze (riv.), Ger. 53/G3
Wietze, Ger. 53/G3
Wietzendorf, Ger. 53/G3
Wiezyca (peak), Pol. 40/H4
Wigan, Eng, UK 35/F4
Wigan (co.), Eng, UK 35/F4
Wiggins, Ms, US 164/D2
Wight, Isle of (isl.), UK 44/C1
Wigierski NP, Pol. 43/M1
Wigmore, Eng, UK 30/E3
Wignehies, Fr. 54/D3
Wigry (lake), Pol. 41/K5
Wigston, Eng, UK 37/E1
Wigton, Eng, UK 35/E2
Wigtown, Sc, UK 34/D2
Wigtown (bay), Sc, UK 34/D2
Wijchen, Neth. 52/C5
Wijhe, Neth. 52/D4
Wijk bij Duurstede, Neth. 52/C5
Wijk en Aalburg, Neth. 52/C5
Wikieup, Az, US 149/F3
Wik'ro, Eth. 118/A2
Wikwemikong, On, Can. 160/F2
Wikwemikong Ind. Res., On, Can. 160/F2
Wil, Swi. 61/F3
Wilber, Ne, US 155/F3
Wilberforce (cape), Austl. 129/E2
Wilberforce, Austl. 134/G8
Wilberfoss, Eng, UK 35/H4
Wilbur, Wa, US 144/E4
Wilburgstetten, Ger. 58/D4
Wilburton, Ok, US 153/G3
Wilcannia, Austl. 132/B1
Wilchingen, Swi. 61/E2
Wilcox, Sk, Can. 156/B2
Wilcox, Pa, US 161/G4
Wilczek (isl.), Rus. 74/G1
Wild (coast), SAfr. 124/E4
Wild Creek (res.), Pa, US 168/C2
Wild Horse (hill), Ne, US 154/D3
Wild Rice (riv.), Mn, US 156/F4
Wild Rose, Wi, US 155/K1
Wild World, Md, US 168/B6
Wildau, Ger. 42/Q7
Wildbad im Schwarzwald, Ger. 58/B5
Wildberg, Ger. 58/B5
Wilder, Id, US 146/E2
Wildersville, Tn, US 162/C3
Wilderswil, Swi. 60/D4
Wildervank, Neth. 52/D2
Wildeshausen, Ger. 53/F3
Wildfield, On, Can. 160/T8
Wildflecken, Ger. 58/C2
Wildgrat (peak), Aus. 61/G3
Wildhaus, Swi. 61/F3
Wildhay (riv.), Ab, Can. 144/E1
Wildhorn (peak), Swi. 60/D5
Wildomar, Ca, US 166/C3
Wildrose, ND, US 156/C3
Wildspitze (peak), Aus. 61/G4
Wildstrubel (peak), Swi. 60/D5
Wildsville, La, US 164/C2
Wildwood, Mn, US 157/H4
Wildwood, Fl, US 165/G3
Wildwood, Ab, Can. 144/G1
Wildwood, NJ, US 168/D6
Wildwood Crest, NJ, US 168/D6
Wiley, Co, US 152/C1
Wilge (riv.), SAfr. 124/E2
Wilhelm (mt.), PNG 129/G1
Wilhelm II (coast), Ant. 192/F
Wilhelmina (mts.), Sur. 181/G4
Wilhelminakanaal (canal), Neth. 52/C5
Wilhelmsburg, Ger. 53/G1
Wilhelmshaven, Ger. 53/F1
Wilhelmshorst, Ger. 42/Q7
Wilhelmstal, Namb. 122/C4
Wilhering, Aus. 59/H6
Wilkes Land (phys. reg.), Ant. 192/J
Wilkes-Barre, Pa, US 168/C1
Wilkes-Barre/Scranton Int'l (arpt.), Pa, US 168/C1
Wilkesboro, NC, US 163/G2
Wilkeson, Wa, US 167/C3
Wilkie, Sk, Can. 145/K1
Wilkins (sound), Ant. 192/U
Wilkinson Heights, SC, US 163/G4
Will (mt.), BC, Can. 171/N4
Will (co.), Il, US 167/P16
Will Rogers World (int'l arpt.), Ok, US 153/F3
Willa Cather Memorial, Ne, US 154/E3
Willacoochee, Ga, US 165/G2
Willamette (riv.), Or, US 146/B1
Willandra Billabong (cr.), Austl. 133/B1
Willandra NP, Austl. 132/C2
Willandra NP, Austl. 133/B1
Willapa (bay), Wa, US 144/C4
Willapa NWR, Wa, US 144/C4
Willard, Mt, US 156/B4
Willard, Ok, US 152/E2
Willard, Mo, US 153/H2
Willard, Oh, US 160/E4
Willard, Ut, US 147/G3
Willard, NM, US 149/J3
Willaston, Eng, UK 35/F5
Willaura, Austl. 132/B3
Willcox, Az, US 149/H4
Willcox Playa (dry lake), Az, US 149/G4
Willebadessen, Ger. 53/G5
Willebroek, Belg. 55/D1
Willemstad (cap.), NAnt. 180/D1
Willemstad, Neth. 52/B5
Willernie, Mn, US 157/Q6
Willeroo, Austl. 128/C3
Willerzie, Belg. 55/D4
Willesden (nbrhd.), Eng, UK 30/C2
William (mt.), Austl. 132/B3
William Bay NP, Austl. 130/C5
William Bill Dannely (res.), Al, US 164/E1
William Creek, Austl. 131/H4
William P. Hobby (arpt.), Tx, US 151/M9
Williams, Mn, US 157/G3
Williams (A.F.B.), Az, US 149/G4
Williams, Az, US 149/F3
Williams, Austl. 130/C5
Williams, SC, US 163/G4
Williams Bay, Wi, US 155/K2
Williams Lake, BC, Can. 144/C1
Williams Lake Ind. Res., BC, Can. 144/C1
Williamsburg (nbrhd.), NY, US 169/K9
Williamsburg, Ky, US 162/E2
Williamsburg, NM, US 149/J4
Williamsburg, Ia, US 155/H3
Williamsburg, Va, US 163/J2
Williamsfield, Oh, US 160/F4
Williamson (riv.), Or, US 146/C2
Williamson, WV, US 163/F2
Williamsport, In, US 160/C4
Williamsport, Pa, US 168/A1
Williamsport-Lycoming County (arpt.), Pa, US 168/B1
Williamston, SC, US 163/F3
Williamston, NC, US 163/J3
Williamstown, NY, US 161/J3
Williamstown, WV, US 160/F5
Williamstown, Vt, US 161/K2
Williamstown, Ky, US 162/E1
Williamstown, Mo, US 155/J3
Williamstown (nbrhd.), Austl. 132/F5
Williamstown, Pa, US 168/B2
Williamstown, NJ, US 168/D4
Williamsville, Mo, US 162/B2
Williamsville, NY, US 160/V10
Willich, Ger. 52/D6
Willimantic, Ct, US 161/K4
Willingboro, NJ, US 168/D3
Willingen, Ger. 53/F6
Willington, Eng, UK 35/G2

Xinjia – Zabīd
Map Section 286 287

Xinjiang (reg.), China 77/H5
Xinjiang, China 80/B4
Xinjiang Uygur (aut. reg.), China 99/D3
Xinjie, China 94/E2
Xinjin, China 81/A3
Xinkaihe, China 81/B2
Xinle, China 80/C3
Xinlitun, China 81/B1
Xinlong, China 87/H3
Xinmiao, China 79/J2
Xinmin, China 81/B1
Xinping Xian, China 86/D3
Xinqiang, China 87/G2
Xinqiao, China 87/F4
Xinshao, China 87/F3
Xinshi, China 80/L9
Xinsi, China 78/E5
Xintai, China 80/D4
Xinxiang, China 80/C4
Xinxing, China 79/J3
Xinxu, China 93/J3
Xinyang, China 80/C4
Xinye, China 80/C4
Xinyi, China 93/K3
Xinyi, China 80/D4
Xinyu, China 87/G3
Xinyuan, China 99/D3
Xinzheng, China 80/C4
Xinzhou, China 87/F5
Xinzhou, China 87/G2
Xinzhou, China 87/F2
Xinzo de Limia, Sp. 46/B1
Xiong Xian, China 80/H7
Xiongyuecheng, China 81/B2
Xiping, China 80/C4
Xiqin, China 87/H3
Xiqing (mts.), China 78/E5
Xique-Xique, Braz. 187/E1
Xishan, China 87/G2
Xishui, China 93/J2
Xitang, China 80/L9
Xitianmu (peak), China 87/H2
Xitiao (riv.), China 80/K9
Xitole, GBis. 114/B4
Xiu (riv.), China 87/G2
Xiuning, China 87/H2
Xiuwen, China 93/J2
Xiuwu, China 80/C4
Xiuyan, China 81/B2
Xixabangma (peak), China 97/E1
Xixi (riv.), China 86/D2
Xixi, China 87/H3
Xixia, China 80/B4
Xiyang (riv.), China 93/J3
Xizang (Tibet) (aut. reg.), China 92/E2
Xize, China 87/J2
Xizhai, China 87/F2
Xochicalco (ruin), Mex. 175/K8
Xochimilco (nbrhd.), Mex. 175/Q10
Xoka, China 86/B2
Xonacatlán, Mex. 175/Q10
Xorkol, China 78/C4
Xpujil, Mex. 176/D2
Xu (riv.), China 87/H3
Xuan'en, China 87/F2
Xuanhua, China 80/G6
Xuanwei, China 86/E3
Xuchang, China 80/C4
Xudat, Azer. 71/J4
Xuddur (Oddur), Som. 118/B4
Xue (mts.), China 86/C3
Xugin Gol (riv.), China 78/D4
Xugou, China 80/L8
Xuguanzhen, China 80/L8
Xujiatun, China 81/B2
Xun (riv.), China 78/F5
Xun Xian, China 80/C4
Xungru, China 97/E1
Xunjiansi, China 87/F2
Xunke, China 79/K2
Xunyang, China 80/B4
Xupu, China 80/L8
Xur, China 78/D4
Xuru (lake), China 99/E6
Xushui, China 80/G7
Xuwen, China 87/F4
Xuyi, China 80/D4
Xuyong, China 86/E2
Xuzhou, China 80/D4

Y

Y Llethr (peak), Wal, UK 34/E6
Yaak (riv.), Mt, US 144/G3
Ya'an, China 86/D2
Yaapeet, Austl. 132/B2
Yaaq-Baraawe, Som. 119/C1
Ya'bad, WBnk. 105/C4
Yabassi, Camr. 120/B1
Yabēlo, Eth. 118/A4
Yabia, D.R. Congo 121/E2
Yablanitsa, Bul. 51/G4
Yablis, Nic. 177/F3
Yablonov, Ukr. 72/C3
Yablonovo, Rus. 78/G1
Yablonovskiy, Rus. 73/K5
Yablonovyy (range), Rus. 77/L4
Yabrīn, SAr. 100/E4
Yabrūd, WBnk. 105/C5
Yabrūd, Syria 105/F1
Yabucoa, PR 173/M8
Yabuki, Japan 85/G2
Yabuzukahon, Japan 83/C1
Yacaré Norte (riv.), Par. 188/E2
Yachats, Or, US 146/A1
Yacheng, China 94/E2
Yachi (riv.), China 87/E3
Yachiho, Japan 83/A1
Yachimata, Japan 83/E2
Yachiyo, Japan 83/G5
Yachiyo, Japan 83/E2
Yachiyo, Japan 83/D1
Yacimiento Río Turbio, Arg. 191/B6
Yaco, Bol. 188/C1
Yacolt, Wa, US 144/C5
Yacopí, Col. 183/L7
Yacuiba, Bol. 188/D2
Yacuma (riv.), Bol. 185/E4
Yacumbu, PN, Ven. 180/D2
Yad Mordekhay, Isr. 105/B5
Yad-Mordechai NP, Isr. 105/B5
Yadé (mass.), CAfr. 116/B4
Yadkin (riv.), NC, US 163/G2
Yadkinville, NC, US 163/G2
Yadong, China 97/G2
Yadrin, Rus. 69/K5
Yaeyama (isls.), Japan 85/G8
Yāfā, Isr. 105/C3
Yafren, Libya 67/G4
Yağcılar, Turk. 70/D5
Yagi, Japan 83/J5
Yagodnoye, Rus. 75/Q3
Yagorlytsk (gulf), Ukr. 51/K2
Yagoua, Camr. 116/B3
Yagradagzê (peak), China 78/D4
Yaguale (riv.), Hon. 176/E3
Yaguarón (riv.), Uru. 191/G2
Yaguarú, Bol. 185/F4
Yaguas (riv.), Peru 180/D5
Yague del Sur (riv.), DRep. 177/J2
Yagur, Isr. 105/C3
Yahagi (riv.), Japan 83/M6
Yahk, BC, Can. 144/F3
Yahongqiao, China 80/H7
Yahotyn, Ukr. 72/F2
Yahualica de Gonzalez Gallo, Mex. 174/E4
Yahyalı, Turk. 102/C2
Yáios (Paxoí), Gre. 49/G3
Yaita, Japan 85/F2
Yaizu, Japan 85/F3
Yajalón, Mex. 176/C2
Yakacık, Turk. 104/E1
Yakapınar, Turk. 104/D1
Yakeshi, China 79/J2
Yakima, Wa, US 144/D4
Yakima (riv.), Wa, US 144/D4
Yakima Firing Range, Wa, US 144/D4
Yakima Ind. Res., Wa, US 144/D4
Yakishiri (isl.), Japan 82/B1
Yako, Burk. 115/E3
Yakoma, D.R. Congo 121/E1
Yakoruda, Bul. 49/H1
Yakovlevo, Rus. 73/J2
Yaksu-nodongjagu, NKor. 81/D2
Yaku (isl.), Japan 79/L5
Yakumo, Japan 82/B2
Yakuno, Japan 83/G5
Yakutat, Ak, US 171/L4
Yakutat (bay), Ak, US 171/K4
Yakutsk, Rus. 75/N3
Yakymivka, Ukr. 73/H4
Yala, Thai. 94/C5
Yala NP, SrL. 95/D5
Yalaha, Fl, US 164/M6
Yalahua (lag.), Mex. 176/E1
Yalakom (riv.), BC, Can. 144/C2
Yalama, Azer. 71/J4
Yalangoz, Turk. 104/E1
Yalata Abor. Land, Austl. 131/F4
Yalbac (hills), Belz. 176/D2
Yalding, Eng, UK 30/E3
Yale, Ok, US 153/F2
Yale, Mi, US 160/E3
Yale, BC, Can. 144/D3
Yalgoo, Austl. 130/C4
Yalgorup NP, Austl. 130/B5
Yalinga, CAfr. 116/D4
Yallock, Austl. 132/C2
Yalnızçam, Turk. 71/G4
Yalobusha (riv.), Ms, US 162/B4
Yaloké, CAfr. 116/C4
Yalong (riv.), China 77/K6
Yalova, Turk. 51/J5
Yalova, Turk. 51/H5
Yalpuh (lake), Gre. 51/J3
Yalta, Ukr. 70/E3
Yalu (riv.), China, NKor. 75/N5
Yaluwe, D.R. Congo 121/F3
Yalvaç, Turk. 102/B2
Yamachiche, Qu, Can. 161/K1
Yamada, Japan 82/B4
Yamaga, Japan 84/B4
Yamagata, Japan 75/P6
Yamagata, Japan 85/G1
Yamagata (pref.), Japan 82/A4
Yamaguchi (pref.), Japan 84/B3
Yamaguchi, Japan 84/B3
Yamakita, Japan 83/C3
Yamal (pen.), Rus. 74/G2
Yamalo-Nenetskiy Aut. Okrug, Rus. 74/H3
Yamanaka (lake), Japan 83/B3
Yamanashi, Japan 83/B2
Yamanie (falls), Austl. 134/B2
Yamanie Falls NP, Austl. 134/B2
Yamantau (peak), Rus. 69/N5
Yamaoka, Japan 83/M5
Yamarna Abor. Reserve, Austl. 130/D4
Yamashiro, Japan 83/J6
Yamaska (riv.), Qu, Can. 158/A3
Yamato, Japan 85/F2
Yamato (riv.), Japan 83/J6
Yamato, Japan 83/E1
Yamato, Japan 83/B2
Yamato, Japan 83/C3
Yamato-Kōriyama, Japan 83/J6
Yamatotakada, Japan 83/J6
Yamazoe, Japan 83/K6
Yamba, Austl. 132/E1
Yambah, Austl. 131/G2
Yambata, D.R. Congo 121/E2
Yambéring, Gui. 114/B4
Yambio, Sudan 117/F4
Yambol, Bul. 51/H4
Yambrasbamba, Peru 184/B2
Yamdena (isl.), Indo. 91/H5
Yamethin, Myan. 86/C4
Yamin (peak), Indo. 91/K4
Yamm, Rus. 41/N2
Yamma Yamma (lake), Austl. 127/D3
Yamoto, Japan 82/B4
Yamoussoukro (cap.), C.d'Iv. 114/D5
Yampa (riv.), Co, US 147/K3
Yampil', Ukr. 72/D3
Yampil', Ukr. 72/E3
Yamuna (riv.), India 92/C2
Yamunānagar, India 98/D4
Yamzho Yumco (lake), China 93/F2
Yan, Nga. 116/B3
Yan (riv.), SrL. 92/D6
Yan (riv.), China 78/F4
Yan Yean (res.), Austl. 132/G5
Yana (riv.), Rus. 77/N3
Yanac, Austl. 132/B3
Yanagawa, Japan 84/B4
Yanahuanca, Peru 184/B3
Yanai, Japan 84/C4
Yanaizu, Japan 83/L5
Yanam, India 95/D2
Yan'an, China 80/B3
Yanaoca, Peru 184/D4
Yanaul, Rus. 69/M4
Yanbian, China 93/H2
Yanbu' al Baḩr, SAr. 109/H3
Yancannia, Austl. 132/B1
Yancey, Tx, US 151/E3
Yanceyville, NC, US 163/H2
Yancheng, China 80/C4
Yancheng, China 80/E4
Yanchep NP, Austl. 130/B4
Yanco (cr.), Austl. 133/B2
Yanco, Austl. 133/C2
Yandeearra Abor. Reserve, Austl. 130/C2
Yanderra, Austl. 133/E2
Yandev, Nga. 115/H5
Yandong, China 87/E3
Yandongi, D.R. Congo 121/E2
Yandoon, Myan. 86/B5
Yanfolila, Mali 114/C4
Yang Talat, Thai. 94/C2
Yangalia, CAfr. 116/D4
Yangambi, D.R. Congo 121/F2
Ya'ngamdo, China 86/B2
Yangamo, Camr. 116/B4
Yangbi (riv.), China 93/G2
Yangchangba, China 86/E3
Yangcheng, China 80/C4
Yangcheng (lake), China 80/L8
Yangcun, China 87/G4
Yangdang (mts.), China 87/H3
Yangdŏk, NKor. 81/D3
Yanggang-do (prov.), NKor. 81/D2
Yanggao, China 80/C2
Yanggok, SKor. 81/F6
Yanggu, SKor. 81/D3
Yanggu, China 80/C3
Yangjiang, China 87/F4
Yangjiawan, China 86/E3
Yangliuqing, China 80/H7
Yangloudong, China 87/G2
Yangma (isl.), China 81/A4
Yangmei, Tai. 87/J3
Yangming (peak), China 87/F3
Yangon (state), Myan. 93/G4
Yangon (Rangoon) (cap.), Myan. 86/C5
Yangon (Rangoon) (int'l arpt.), Myan. 86/C5
Yangp'yŏng, SKor. 81/D4
Yangqiaopan, China 78/F4
Yangqu, China 80/C3
Yangquan, China 80/C3
Yangsan, SKor. 81/E5
Yangshan, China 93/K3
Yangshuo, China 93/K3
Yangtouyan, China 86/D3
Yangtze (Chang) (riv.), China 80/D5
Yangudi Rassa NP, Eth. 118/B3
Yangxi, China 87/G3
Yangxin, China 87/G2
Yangxin, China 80/D3
Yangxu, China 87/E4
Yangyang, SKor. 81/E3
Yangyuan, China 80/C2
Yangzhong, China 80/D4
Yangzhou, China 80/D4
Yanja, D.R. Congo 120/D3
Yanji, China 79/K3
Yanji, China 79/K3
Yanjia, China 81/A2
Yanjin, China 80/C4
Yanjin, China 86/E2
Yanjing, China 86/C2
Yankara, Nga. 115/G4
Yankari NP, Nga. 116/A3
Yankee Stadium, NY, US 169/K8
Yankton, SD, US 154/F2
Yankton Ind. Res., SD, US 154/E2
Yanling, China 80/C4
Yanmen (pass), China 80/C3
Yanonge, D.R. Congo 121/F2
Yanqing, China 80/G6
Yanrey, Austl. 130/B2
Yanshan, China 93/H3
Yanshan, China 80/D3
Yanshi, China 80/C4
Yanshi, China 87/H3
Yanshiping, China 78/C5
Yanshou, China 79/K2
Yantaa (riv.), Fin. 39/E4
Yantabulla, Austl. 132/C1
Yantai, China 80/E3
Yantara, Austl. 132/B1
Yantarnyy, Rus. 41/H4
Yanting, China 86/E2
Yantis, Tx, US 153/G4
Yantley, Al, US 162/C4
Yantra (riv.), Bul. 67/K2
Yanush, Ok, US 153/G3
Yanwa, China 86/C3
Yanxi, China 87/H3
Yanyuan, China 86/D3
Yanzhou, China 80/D4
Yao, Chad 116/C2
Yao, Japan 83/J6
Yao'an, China 93/H2
Yaodian, China 80/B3
Yaogu, China 87/G4
Yaotsu, Japan 83/M5
Yaoundé (cap.), Camr. 120/B2
Yap (isls.), Micr. 136/C4
Yapacana, PN, Ven. 181/E4
Yapacani (riv.), Bol. 185/E5
Yapei, Gha. 115/E4
Yapen (isl.), Indo. 91/J4
Yapen (str.), Indo. 91/J4
Yapirga, Bol. 188/D1
Yapraklı, Turk. 70/E4
Yaqueling, China 87/F2
Yaqui (riv.), Mex. 139/G7
Yaquina (bay), Or, US 146/A1
Yara, Cuba 177/G1
Yaracuy (state), Ven. 180/D2
Yaraka, Austl. 134/B4
Yaralıgöz (peak), Turk. 70/E4
Yaransk, Rus. 69/K4
Yardımcı (pt.), Turk. 104/B1
Yardley, Pa, US 168/D3
Yardville-Groveville, NJ, US 168/D3
Yardymly, Azer. 103/G2
Yare (riv.), Eng, UK 37/H1
Yarega, Rus. 69/M3
Yaremcha, Ukr. 72/C3
Yarensk, Rus. 69/L3
Yarí (riv.), Col. 180/C4
Yari-ga-take (peak), Japan 85/E2
Yarīm, Yem. 118/C2
Yarımca, Turk. 51/J5
Yaritagua, Ven. 180/D2
Yarkant (riv.), China 74/H6
Yarkovo, Rus. 69/Q4
Yarloop, Austl. 130/B5
Yarlung Zangbo (Brahmaputra) (riv.), China 97/G1
Yarmolyntsi, Ukr. 72/D3
Yarmouth, NS, Can. 158/D4
Yarmuk (riv.), Syria,Jor. 105/D3
Yarnell, Az, US 149/F3
Yaroslavskaya Oblast, Rus. 68/H4
Yaroslavl', Rus. 68/H4
Yaroslavskiy, Rus. 79/L3
Yarpuz, Turk. 104/E1
Yarra (riv.), Austl. 132/G5
Yarra Glen, Austl. 132/G5
Yarra Junction, Austl. 133/B3
Yarragon, Austl. 133/C4
Yarram, Austl. 133/C4
Yarraman, Austl. 134/D4
Yarrawonga, Austl. 133/C3
Yarrow Point, Wa, US 167/C2
Yartsevo, Rus. 68/G5
Yartsevo, Rus. 74/K3
Yarumal, Col. 180/C3
Yarzhong, China 86/C2
Yasa, D.R. Congo 121/E3
Yasato, Japan 83/E1
Yasawa Group (isls.), Fiji 136/G6
Yasel'da (riv.), Bela. 70/C1
Yasenskaya, Rus. 73/K4
Yashalta, Rus. 73/M4
Yashbum, Yem. 118/C2
Yashi, Nga. 115/G3
Yashikera, Nga. 115/F4
Yashima, Japan 82/B4
Yashio, Japan 83/D2
Yashiro, Japan 83/G6
Yashkino, Rus. 71/K1
Yashkul', Rus. 71/H3
Yasinya, Ukr. 72/C3
Yasnogorka, Ukr. 73/J3
Yasnyy, Rus. 71/L2
Yasothon, Thai. 94/D3
Yass, Austl. 133/D2
Yasu (riv.), Japan 83/K6
Yasu, Japan 83/K5
Yasugi, Japan 84/C3
Yāsūj, Iran 103/G4
Yasun Burnu (pt.), Turk. 70/F4
Yasuni, PN, Ecu. 180/B5
Yasynuvata, Ukr. 73/J3
Yat (well), Niger 108/B4
Yata (riv.), CAfr. 116/D3
Yata (riv.), Bol. 185/E4
Yata, Bol. 185/E4
Yata-Ngaya, Rsv. de Faune de la, CAfr. 116/D3
Yatabe, Japan 85/G2
Yatağan, Turk. 102/B2
Yataity, Par. 189/E3
Yate, Eng, UK 36/D3
Yateley, Eng, UK 37/F4
Yatenga (prov.), Burk. 115/E3
Yates Center, Ks, US 153/G2
Yathkyed (lake), Nun, Can. 140/G2
Yatina, Bol. 188/C2
Yatolema, D.R. Congo 121/F2
Yatomi, Japan 83/L5
Yatsu-ga-take (peak), Japan 83/A2
Yatsuo, Japan 85/E2
Yatsushiro, Japan 84/B4
Yatsushiro, Japan 83/B2
Yatta (plat.), Kenya 119/B2
Yaţţah, WBnk. 105/C6
Yatton, Eng, UK 36/D4
Yauca, Peru 184/C4
Yauca (riv.), Peru 184/C4
Yauco, PR 173/M8
Yauli, Peru 184/B3
Yaúna Moloca, Col. 180/D5
Yaupi, Ecu. 180/B5
Yaupon Beach, NC, US 163/H4
Yaután, Peru 184/B3
Yauyos, Peru 184/C4
Yauza (riv.), Rus. 69/W9
Yavapai Ind. Res., Az, US 149/F3
Yavarí (riv.), Braz.,Peru 179/B3
Yavarí Mirim (riv.), Peru 184/C2
Yavaros, Mex. 174/C3
Yavatmāl, India 95/C1
Yavay (pen.), Rus. 74/H2
Yavita, Ven. 181/E4
Yaviza, Pan. 180/B2
Yavne, Isr. 105/B5
Yavne'el, Isr. 105/D3
Yavoriv, Ukr. 43/M4
Yavuzeli, Turk. 102/D2
Yawahara, Japan 83/E2
Yawata, Japan 83/J6
Yawatahama, Japan 84/C4
Yaxchilán (ruin), Guat. 176/D2
Yaxing, China 94/E2
Yaxley, Eng, UK 37/F1
Yaygın, Turk. 102/E2
Yayladaği, Turk. 104/E2
Yayladere, Turk. 102/E2
Yaysan, Kaz. 71/L2
Yayuan, China 81/D2
Yazd, Iran 103/H4
Yazd (gov.), Iran 103/H3
Yazhma, Rus. 69/K2
Yazhou, China 87/E3
Yazmān, Pak. 98/A5
Yazoo (riv.), Ms, US 162/B4
Yazoo City, Ms, US 162/B4
Yazykovo, Rus. 71/H1
Ybbs (riv.), Aus. 43/H4
Ybbs an der Donau, Aus. 45/L2
Ybor City, Fl, US 164/L8
Ybycuí, Par. 189/E3
Yding Skovhøj (peak), Den. 40/C3
Ye, Myan. 94/B3
Ye Xian, China 78/G5
Ye Xian, China 80/D3
Ye-ngan, Myan. 86/C4
Yea, Austl. 133/B3
Yeaddiss, Ky, US 163/F2
Yeadon, Eng, UK 35/G4
Yean, SKor. 81/E4
Yeay Sen (cape), Camb. 94/C4
Yebbi-Bou, Chad 108/C4
Yecheng, China 99/C4
Yech'ŏn, SKor. 81/E4
Yecla, Sp. 47/E3
Yécora, Mex. 174/C2
Yecuatla, Mex. 175/N7
Yedashe, Myan. 94/B2
Yedigöller NP, Turk. 70/D4
Yedikule, Turk. 103/M6
Yeditepe, Turk. 104/E2
Yeed, Som. 118/B4
Yeeda River, Austl. 128/A4
Yeelirrie, Austl. 130/D3
Yefimovskiy, Rus. 68/G4
Yéfira, Gre. 49/H2
Yefremov, Rus. 70/F1
Yegorlak (riv.), Rus. 71/G3
Yegorlykskaya, Rus. 73/L4
Yegorova (cape), Rus. 79/M3
Yehi'am's Fortress NP, Isr. 105/C3
Yehualtepec, Mex. 175/M8
Yehud, Isr. 105/B4
Yei (riv.), Sudan 117/F4
Yei, Sudan 121/G1
Yejmiadzin, Arm. 103/F1
Yekaterinburg (Sverdlovsk), Rus. 69/P4
Yekaterinoslavka, Rus. 79/K1
Yekaterinovka, Rus. 71/H1
Yekateriny (chan.), Rus. 82/E1
Yekepa, Libr. 114/C5
Yekia Sahal (well), Chad 116/C1
Yelabuga, Rus. 69/M5
Yelan', Rus. 71/G2
Yelarbon, Austl. 134/C5
Yelets, Rus. 70/F1
Yelgu, Sudan 117/G3
Yélimané, Mali 114/C3
Yelizavetinka, Rus. 71/L2
Yelizavetino, Rus. 41/N2
Yelizavetopol'skoye, Rus. 71/M1
Yelizovo, Rus. 75/R4
Yelkhovka, Rus. 71/J1
Yell (isl.), Sc, UK 31/W13
Yellamanchili, India 95/D2
Yellandu, India 95/D2
Yellel, Alg. 112/F5
Yellow (sea), Asia 77/M6
Yellow (riv.), Wi, US 155/J1
Yellow (riv.), Ga, US 163/M7
Yellow (Huang) (riv.), China 78/G4
Yellow Creek, Sk, Can. 145/M1
Yellow Dog (pt.), Mi, US 157/L4
Yellow Grass, Sk, Can. 156/B3
Yellow House Draw (stream), Tx, US 152/C4
Yellow Jacket, Co, US 149/H2
Yellow Pine, Al, US 164/D2
Yellow Pine, Id, US 146/F1
Yellowknife (riv.), NW, Can. 140/E2
Yellowknife (cap.), NW, Can. 140/E2
Yellowstone (riv.), US 139/G5
Yellowstone NP, US 147/H1
Yellowtail (dam), Mt, US 147/K1
Yellville, Ar, US 153/H2
Yelm, Wa, US 144/C4
Yel'nya, Rus. 68/G5
Yelshanka, Rus. 71/H2
Yel'sk, Bela. 72/E2
Yelverton, Eng, UK 36/B6
Yelwa, Nga. 115/G4
Yelwa, Nga. 115/H4
Yema, D.R. Congo 120/C4
Yema (riv.), China 78/D4
Yemaotai, China 81/B1
Yemassee, SC, US 163/G4
Yemen (ctry.) 77/D8
Yemetsk, Rus. 68/J3
Yemil'chyne, Ukr. 72/D2
Yen Bai, Viet. 86/E4
Yen Minh, Viet. 86/E4
Yenagoa, Nga. 115/G5
Yenakiyeve, Ukr. 73/K3
Yenangyaung, Myan. 86/B4
Yenanma, Myan. 86/B5
Yenda, Austl. 133/C2
Yende, Congo 120/D2
Yende Millimou, Gui. 114/C4
Yendi, Gha. 115/E4
Yenge (riv.), D.R. Congo 121/E3
Yengisar, China 99/C4
Yengo, Congo 120/C2
Yengo NP, Austl. 133/E1
Yengué, Gabon 120/B3
Yeniçağa, Turk. 51/L5
Yenice (riv.), Turk. 70/E4
Yenice, Turk. 104/D1
Yenice, Turk. 51/L5
Yenice, Turk. 51/H6
Yeniceoba, Turk. 102/C2
Yeniköy, Turk. 51/H5
Yeniköy, Turk. 103/M6
Yenişehir, Turk. 51/J5
Yenisey (riv.), Rus. 77/H3
Yeniseysk, Rus. 74/K4
Yenne, Fr. 64/B1
Yeno, Gabon 120/B3
Yenshui, Tai. 87/J4
Yeo (lake), Austl. 130/E3
Yeo (lake) 127/B3
Yeo Lake Nature Reserve, Austl. 130/E3
Yeoval, Austl. 133/D1
Yeovil, Eng, UK 36/D5
Yeping, China 87/H3
Yeppoon, Austl. 134/C3
Yeraifia (well), WSah. 110/B4
Yerakhtur, Rus. 71/G1
Yerakovoúni (peak), Gre. 49/H3
Yeraliyev, Kaz. 71/J4
Yerbas Buenas, Chile 190/C2
Yères (riv.), Fr. 54/A4
Yerevan (cap.), Arm. 103/F1
Yerichaña, Ven. 181/E3
Yerington, Nv, US 146/D4
Yerköy, Turk. 102/C2
Yerlisu, Turk. 51/H5
Yermak, Kaz. 99/C1
Yermekeyevo, Rus. 69/M5
Yermish', Rus. 68/J5
Yermitsa, Rus. 69/M2
Yermo, Ca, US 148/D3
Yermolayevo, Rus. 71/K1
Yerofey Pavlovich, Rus. 79/J1
YeroḩLam, Isr. 104/D4
Yerolimín, Gre. 49/H4
Yerre (riv.), Fr. 44/D2
Yerres, Fr. 30/K5
Yerseke, Neth. 52/B5
Yershov, Rus. 71/J2
Yershovka, Kaz. 69/Q5
Yertoma, Rus. 69/K3
Yerupaja (peak), Peru 184/B3
Yerushalayim (Jerusalem) (cap.), Isr. 105/C5
Yerville, Fr. 57/F1
Yesa, Bol. 188/D1
Yesagyo, Myan. 86/B4
Yesan, SKor. 81/D4
Yeşildere, Turk. 104/C1
Yeşiıhisar, Turk. 102/C2
Yeşilırmak (riv.), Turk. 70/F4
Yeşilkent, Turk. 104/E1
Yeşilova, Turk. 102/B2
Yesodot, Isr. 105/B5
Yesŏng (riv.), NKor. 81/D3
Yessentuki, Rus. 71/G3
Yessey, Rus. 75/L3
Yeste, Sp. 46/D3
Yesud Hama'ala, Isr. 105/D2
Yete I, D.R. Congo 120/E3
Yetholm, Sc, UK 33/D5
Yetminster, Eng, UK 36/D5
Yetti (reg.), Mrta. 110/D4
Yeu, Ile d' (isl.), Fr. 44/B3
Yevlax, Azer. 71/H4
Yevpatoriya, Ukr. 73/G5
Yèvre (riv.), Fr. 55/D5
Yèvres, Fr. 57/G4
Yevreyskaya (aut. obl.), Rus. 79/L2
Yevsuh, Ukr. 73/K3
Yeya (riv.), Rus. 70/G3
Yeysk, Rus. 73/K4
Yeysk (bay), Rus. 73/K4
Yffinac, Fr. 56/C4
Ygatimí, Par. 189/F3
Ygos-Saint-Saturnin, Fr. 44/C5
Yi (riv.), Uru. 191/F2
Yi Xian, China 81/A2
Yi Xian, China 80/G7
Yi'ong (riv.), China 86/B2
Yialousa, Cyp. 104/D2
Yiangkou, China 81/B2
Yiannitsá, Gre. 49/H2
Yiánnouli, Gre. 49/H3
Yíaros (isl.), Gre. 49/J4
Yibin, China 86/E2
Yichang, China 78/G5
Yichang, China 87/F2
Yicheng, China 80/C5
Yicheng, China 80/B4
Yichuan, China 80/C4
Yichun, China 79/K2
Yichun, China 87/G3
Yidun, China 86/C2
Yifeng, China 93/K2
Yiftaḩ, Isr. 105/D2
Yığılca, Turk. 51/K5
Yihuang, China 87/H3
Yilan, China 79/K2
Yıldız (peak), Turk. 102/D1
Yildiz Park, Turk. 103/N6
Yıldızeli, Turk. 102/D2
Yilehuli (mts.), China 79/J1
Yiliang, China 86/E3
Yiliping, China 78/C4
Yima, China 80/B4
Yimen, China 86/D3
Yimin (riv.), China 79/J2
Yin (mts.), China 75/L5
Yinan, China 80/D4
Yinchuan, China 78/F4
Yindarlgooda (lake), Austl. 127/B4
Ying (riv.), China 78/G5
Yingcheng, China 87/G2
Ying'emen, China 81/C1
Yinggehai, China 94/E2
Yingkou, China 81/B2
Yingpanxu, China 87/G3
Yingqian, China 87/G3
Yingshan, China 80/C5
Yingshang, China 80/D4
Yingshouyingzi, China 80/H6
Yingtan, China 87/H2
Yingui, Camr. 120/B1
Yining, China 99/D3
Yinyang, China 80/L8
Yi'ong (riv.), China 78/C5
Yirga 'Alem, Eth. 118/A4
Yirga Ch'efē, Eth. 118/A4
Yirkā, Isr. 105/C3
Yirol, Sudan 117/F4
Yirrkala, Austl. 129/E3
Yirshi, China 79/H2
Yishan, China 87/F3
Yishui, China 80/D4
Yíthion, Gre. 49/H4
Yitong (riv.), SKor. 80/C5
Yiwanquan, China 78/C3
Yiwu, China 78/C3
Yixing, China 80/K8
Yiyang, China 80/C4
Yiyang, China 87/G2
Yiyuan, China 80/D3
Yizhang, China 93/K2
Yizheng, China 80/D4
Ylakiai, Lith. 41/J3
Ylöjärvi, Fin. 41/K1
Ymir (mtn.), BC, Can. 144/F3
Ymir, BC, Can. 144/F3
Yngaren (lake), Swe. 40/G2
Yngern (lake), Swe. 39/A1
Yoakum, Tx, US 151/F3
Yobe (state), Nga. 115/H3
Yoboki, Djib. 118/B3
Yocalla, Bol. 188/C1
Yŏch'ŏn, SKor. 81/D5
Yockanookany (riv.), Ms, US 162/C4
Yocona (riv.), Ms, US 162/C3
Yoder, Ks, US 153/F2
Yoder, Wy, US 154/B3
Yodo (riv.), Japan 83/J6
Yodŏk, NKor. 81/D3
Yoduma (riv.), Rus. 75/P4
Yoff (Dakar) (int'l arpt.), Sen. 114/A3
Yog (pt.), Phil. 88/D2
Yogo, Japan 83/K4
Yoğuntaş, Turk. 51/H5
Yogyakarta, Indo. 89/E4
Yogyakarta (prov.), Indo. 89/E5
Yoho NP, BC, Can. 144/F2
Yoichi, Japan 82/B2
Yojoa (lake), Hon. 176/D3
Yŏju, SKor. 81/D4
Yokadouma, Camr. 120/C2
Yōkaichi, Japan 83/K5
Yokana, D.R. Congo 121/E2
Yokawa, Japan 83/H6
Yokena, Ms, US 164/C1
Yokkaichi, Japan 83/L6
Yoko, Camr. 116/B4
Yokohama, Japan 85/F3
Yokolo, D.R. Congo 121/E3
Yokoshiba, Japan 83/E2
Yokosuka, Japan 85/F3
Yokote, Japan 82/B4
Yokoze, Japan 83/C2
Yola, Nga. 116/B3
Yolaina (mts.), Nic. 177/E4
Yolboyu, Turk. 102/D2
Yolo (co.), Ca, US 167/L9
Yolo, Ca, US 167/L9
Yolombo, D.R. Congo 121/E3
Yom (riv.), Thai. 93/H4
Yombi, Gabon 120/B3
Yŏmju, NKor. 81/C3
Yomou, Gui. 114/C5
Yon (riv.), Fr. 44/C3
Yon (riv.), China 87/F4
Yonago, Japan 84/C3
Yonaguni (isl.), Japan 85/G8
Yonaha-dake (peak), Japan 85/K7
Yŏnan, NKor. 81/D4
Yoncalla, Or, US 146/B2
Yoneshiro (riv.), Japan 82/B3
Yonezawa, Japan 85/G2
Yong Peng, Malay. 89/C2
Yŏng-yang, SKor. 84/A2
Yŏngam, SKor. 81/D5
Yongamp'o, NKor. 81/C3
Yong'an (pass), China 87/F3
Yong'an, China 87/E2
Yong'an, China 87/H3
Yŏngbyŏn, NKor. 81/C3
Yongchang, China 78/E4
Yongcheng, China 80/D4
Yŏngch'ŏn, SKor. 84/A3
Yongde, China 93/G3
Yongding (riv.), China 75/M6
Yŏngdŏk, SKor. 84/A2
Yŏngdong, SKor. 81/D4
Yongdungp'o (nbrhd.), SKor. 81/F6
Yongfeng, China 78/F5
Yongfu, China 93/J3
Yonggang, NKor. 81/C3
Yŏnggwang, SKor. 81/D5
Yŏnghae, SKor. 81/E4
Yonghe, China 80/B3
Yŏnghŭng (riv.), NKor. 81/D3
Yŏnghŭng, NKor. 81/D3
Yongji, China 80/B4
Yŏngjong (isl.), SKor. 81/F6
Yŏngju, SKor. 84/A2
Yongle, China 87/E4
Yongling, China 81/C2
Yongmun-san (peak), SKor. 81/D4
Yongnian, China 80/C3
Yongning, China 94/E1
Yongningjian, China 81/A3
Yongo, D.R. Congo 121/E3
Yongping, China 87/H3
Yongping, China 80/B3
Yongqiang, China 87/J3
Yongqing, China 80/H7
Yongren, China 93/H2
Yŏngsan (riv.), SKor. 81/D5
Yongshan, China 86/D2
Yongsheng, China 86/D3
Yongshun, China 93/J2
Yŏngwŏl, SKor. 84/A2
Yŏngwŏn, NKor. 81/D3
Yongxin, China 93/K2
Yongzhou, China 87/F3
Yonibana, SLeo. 114/B4
Yonkers, NY, US 169/K8
Yonne (riv.), Fr. 42/B5
Yono, Japan 83/D2
Yonsa, NKor. 81/E2
Yŏnsan, NKor. 81/D3
Yopal, Col. 180/C3
Yopurga, China 99/C4
Yoqne'am 'Illit, Isr. 105/C3
Yorba Linda, Ca, US 166/G8
Yorii, Japan 83/C1
York, Austl. 130/C4
York (cape), Austl. 129/F2
York (sound), Austl. 128/B3
York, Eng, UK 35/G4
York (co.), Eng, UK 35/G4
York (co.), On, Can. 160/T8
York (riv.), Qu, Can. 158/E1
York, Al, US 162/C4
York, Ne, US 154/F3
York, Pa, US 168/B4
York (co.), Pa, US 168/B4
York, SC, US 163/G3
York (riv.), Va, US 163/J2
York Factory, Mb, Can. 140/G3
York Haven, Pa, US 168/B3
York Minster, Eng, UK 35/G4
York Sound (bay) 127/B2
York Springs, Pa, US 168/A4
Yorke (pen.), Austl. 127/C4
Yorketown, Austl. 131/H5
Yorkshire, NY, US 161/G3
Yorkshire Dales NP, Eng, UK 35/F3
Yorkshire Wolds (hills), Eng, UK 35/H3
Yorkton, Sk, Can. 156/C2
Yorktown, Ar, US 153/J3
Yorktown, In, US 160/D4
Yorktown, Tx, US 151/F3
Yorktown, Va, US 163/J2
Yorktown Heights, NY, US 169/E1
Yorkville, Il, US 160/B4
Yoro, Hon. 176/E3
Yorō, Japan 83/L5
Yōrō (riv.), Japan 83/E3
Yoroi-zaki (pt.), Japan 83/L7
Yoron (isl.), Japan 85/K7
Yorosso, Mali 114/D3
Yorton, Eng, UK 35/F6
Yos Sudarso (isl.), Indo. 91/J5
Yosemite (falls), Ca, US 148/C2
Yosemite NP, Ca, US 148/C2
Yoshida, Japan 84/C4
Yoshida, Japan 83/C1
Yoshii (riv.), Japan 84/D3
Yoshii, Japan 83/B1
Yoshikawa, Japan 83/D2
Yoshima (riv.), Japan 84/D3
Yoshimi, Japan 83/C1
Yoshino (riv.), Japan 84/C4
Yoshino, Japan 83/J7
Yoshino-Kumano NP, Japan 84/E3
Yoshkar-Ola, Rus. 69/L4
Yŏsu, SKor. 81/D5
Yotaú, Bol. 185/F5
Yōtei-san (peak), Japan 82/B2
Yotsukaidō, Japan 83/E2
You (riv.), China 86/E3
Youbou, BC, Can. 144/B3
Youdunzi, China 78/C4
Youghal, Ire. 32/C6
Youghal (bay), Ire. 32/C6
Youghiogheny (riv.), Pa, US 161/G5
Youhamba (riv.), CAfr. 116/D4
Young, Az, US 149/G3
Young, Uru. 191/K10
Young, Sk, Can. 145/M2
Young, Austl. 133/D2
Young America, Mn, US 157/N7
Young Nick's (pt.), NZ 135/D2
Youngs (lake), Wa, US 167/C3
Youngstown, Fl, US 165/F2
Youngstown, Oh, US 160/F4
Youngstown, In, US 160/C5
Youngstown, NY, US 160/U9
Youngstown, Ab, Can. 145/J2
Youngsville, La, US 164/C2
Youngsville, NM, US 149/J2
Yountville, Ca, US 167/K10
Youshui, China 87/G3
Youssoufia, Mor. 110/C2
Youxi, China 87/F3
Youxikou, China 87/H3
Youyang, China 93/J2
Youyi, China 79/L2
Yoví (peak), Ven. 181/E3
Yozgat, Turk. 102/C2
Ypané (riv.), Par. 186/A4
Ypé Jhú, Par. 189/F2
Ypsilanti, ND, US 156/E4
Ypsilanti, Mi, US 167/E7
Yr Eifl (peak), Wal, UK 34/D6
Yreka, Ca, US 146/B3
Yser (riv.), Fr. 42/B3
Ysieux (riv.), Fr. 30/K4
Ystad, Swe. 40/E4
Ystad, Swe. 39/K7
Ystalyfera, Wal, UK 36/C3
Ystrad Mynach, Wal, UK 36/C3
Ystwyth (riv.), Wal, UK 36/B2
Ysyk Köl (lake), Kyr. 74/H5
Ythan (riv.), Sc, UK 33/D2
Ytrac, Fr. 44/E4
Ytre Enebakk, Nor. 38/T8
Ytre Sula (isl.), Nor. 40/A1
Ytterby, Swe. 40/D3
Ytterbyn, Swe. 38/G2
Ytterjärna, Swe. 39/A1
Yu (riv.), China 93/J3
Yü (peak), Tai. 87/J4
Yu Xian, China 80/C3
Yu Xian, China 80/C4
Yuan (riv.), China 77/K7
Yuan (lake), China 80/C5
Yuan (Red) (riv.), China 86/D4
Yuan'an, China 80/B5
Yuanba, China 78/F5
Yuanbao (mtn.), China 87/F3
Yuanping, China 80/C3
Yuanqu, China 80/B4
Yuanshan, China 86/E2
Yuanshi, China 80/C3
Yuantan, China 87/H2
Yuantan, China 87/G4
Yuanyang, China 80/C4
Yuba, Ok, US 153/F4
Yuba (riv.), Ca, US 146/C4
Yuba City, Ca, US 146/C4
Yūbari, Japan 82/B2
Yūbetsu, Japan 82/C1
Yūbetsu (riv.), Japan 82/C2
Yucaipa, Ca, US 166/C2
Yucatán (state), Mex. 172/D3
Yucatan (pen.), Mex. 139/J7
Yucatan (chan.), NAm. 139/J7
Yucca, Az, US 149/E3
Yucca House Nat'l Mon., Co, US 149/H2
Yucca Valley, Ca, US 148/D3
Yucheng, China 80/D3
Yucheng, China 80/C4
Yuci, China 80/C3
Yudu, China 87/G3
Yuechi, China 87/E2
Yuehedian, China 87/G1
Yuelaichang, China 87/E2
Yuen Long, China 87/L7
Yuendumu, Austl. 131/F2
Yuendumu Abor. Land, Austl. 131/F2
Yueqing, China 87/J2
Yuexi, China 93/H2
Yuexi (riv.), China 86/D2
Yuexi, China 87/H2
Yueyang, China 87/G2
Yug (riv.), Rus. 74/E4
Yugawara, Japan 83/C3
Yugorskiy (pen.), Rus. 69/P1
Yuhang, China 80/L9
Yuhuan, China 87/J2
Yui, Japan 83/B3
Yujiaxi, China 87/F2
Yūki, Japan 85/F2
Yuki Kengundu, D.R. Congo 120/D3
Yukon, Mo, US 153/J2
Yukon (riv.), Can.,US 171/F3
Yukon Crossing, Yk, Can. 171/L3
Yukon Territory Can. 140/C2
Yüksekova, Turk. 103/F2
Yukuhashi, Japan 84/B4
Yulamasi, China 81/A1
Yulara, Austl. 131/F3
Yuldybayevo, Rus. 71/L1
Yuleba, Austl. 134/C4
Yulee, Fl, US 165/H2
Yuli, Nga. 115/H4
Yuli, China 99/E3
Yulin, China 80/B3
Yulin, China 87/F5
Yulin, China 87/F4
Yuling (pass), China 87/H2
Yulongxue (peak), China 86/D3
Yuma (des.), Az, US 148/E4
Yuma, Az, US 154/C3
Yuma, Co, US 154/C3
Yuma Marine Air Sta., Az, US 142/D5
Yuma Proving Ground, Az, US 148/E4
Yumbarra Consv. Park, Austl. 131/G4
Yumbe, Ugan. 121/G2
Yumbel, Chile 190/B3
Yumbi, D.R. Congo 120/D2
Yumbi, D.R. Congo 121/F3
Yumbi, D.R. Congo 120/D3
Yumbo, Col. 180/B4
Yumen, China 78/D4
Yumenzhen, China 78/D3
Yumin, China 99/D2
Yumurtalık, Turk. 104/D1
Yun (riv.), China 80/C5
Yun Xian, China 86/D3
Yun Xian, China 80/B4
Yuna, Austl. 130/B4
Yunak, Turk. 102/B2
Yuncheng, China 80/C4
Yuncheng, China 80/B4
Yundum, Gam. 114/A3
Yundum (Banjul) (int'l arpt.), Gam. 114/A3
Yungang Caves, China 80/C2
Yungas (phys. reg.), Bol. 185/E4
Yungay, Chile 190/B3
Yunguyo, Peru 184/D5
Yunhe, China 87/H2
Yunjiang, China 87/F3
Yunkai (mts.), China 87/F4
Yunkanjini Abor. Land, Austl. 131/F2
Yunlong, China 93/G2
Yunnan (prov.), China 93/H3
Yunta, Austl. 131/H5
Yuntai (peak), China 80/D4
Yunxi, China 80/B4
Yunyan (riv.), China 80/D4
Yunyanzhen, China 80/B3
Yunzhong (mtn.), China 80/C3
Yuping, China 93/J2
Yupukarri, Guy. 181/G4
Yuqiao (res.), China 80/H7
Yura, Bol. 188/C2
Yuracyacu, Peru 184/B2
Yuratishki, Bela. 41/L4
Yurga, Rus. 74/J4
Yurgamysh, Rus. 69/Q5
Yuri (isl.), Rus. 82/E2
Yurimaguas, Peru 184/B2
Yuroma, Rus. 69/K2
Yuruari (riv.), Ven. 181/F3
Yürük, Turk. 51/H5
Yurungkax (riv.), China 99/C4
Yur'ya, Rus. 69/L4
Yur'yev-Pol'skiy, Rus. 68/H4
Yur'yevets, Rus. 68/J4
Yur'yevets, Rus. 68/J4
Yur'yivka, Ukr. 73/J3
Yuryuzan', Rus. 69/N5
Yuryuzan' (riv.), Rus. 69/N5
Yuscarán, Hon. 176/E3
Yushan NP, Tai. 87/J4
Yushe, China 80/C3
Yushu, China 81/C2
Yushu, China 79/K3
Yusŏng, SKor. 81/D4
Yusufeli, Turk. 71/G4
Yutai, China 80/D4
Yutian, China 99/D4
Yutian, China 80/H7
Yuto, Arg. 188/C2
Yuty, Par. 189/E3
Yutz, Fr. 55/F5
Yuxi, China 87/H3
Yuxikou, China 87/H2
Yuyao, China 87/J2
Yuza, Japan 82/A4
Yuzawa, Japan 82/B4
Yuzhno-Kuril'sk, Rus. 82/D2
Yuzhno-Sakhalinsk, Rus. 79/N2
Yuzhno-Sakhalinsk (int'l arpt.), Rus. 79/N2
Yuzhno-Sukhokumsk, Rus. 71/H3
Yuzhnoural'sk, Rus. 69/P5
Yuzhnyy, Rus. 73/L4
Yuzhnyy, Rus. 99/D1
Yvel (riv.), Fr. 56/C4
Yvelines (dept.), Fr. 57/G3
Yverdon, Swi. 60/C4
Yvetot, Fr. 57/F1
Yvette (riv.), Fr. 54/B6
Yvoir, Belg. 55/D3
Yvonand, Swi. 60/C4
Yvron (riv.), Fr. 30/L6
Ywathit, Myan. 94/B2
Yxlan (isl.), Swe. 39/B1
Yxlö (isl.), Swe. 39/B2
Yzeron (riv.), Fr. 64/A1
Yzeure, Fr. 44/E3

Z

Za (riv.), China 78/D5
Za (riv.), Mor. 112/C2
Zaachila, Mex. 176/B2
Zaandam, Neth. 42/C2
Zaandijk, Neth. 52/B4
Zaanstad, Neth. 52/B4
Zabaykal'sk, Rus. 79/H2
Żabbar, Malta 48/M7
Zaber (riv.), Ger. 58/C4
Zabīd, Yem. 118/B2
Zabīd (wadi), Yem. 118/B2

Time Zones of the World

165° W	1 A.M.
150° W	2 A.M.
135° W	3 A.M.
120° W	4 A.M.
105° W	5 A.M.
90° W	6 A.M.
75° W	7 A.M.
60° W	8 A.M.
45° W	9 A.M.
30° W	10 A.M.
15° W	11 A.M.
0°	NOON

ARCTIC OCEAN

GREENLAND

NOON

11 A.M.

6 A.M.

7 A.M.

5 A.M.

6 A.M.

3 A.M.
ALASKA

Nuuk

Reykjavík ICELAND

Anchorage

Whitehorse

CANADA

Edmonton

Winnipeg

UNITED KINGDOM

IRELAND

Montréal

London

Seattle

1 A.M.

NEWFOUNDLAND
8:30 A.M.

ST. PIERRE
& MIQUELON
9 A.M.

Paris

FRANCE

Boise

Chicago

Detroit

Halifax

UNITED STATES

New York
Washington

PORTUGAL

SPAIN

Madrid

San Francisco

Denver

Atlanta

AZORES

Algie

Los Angeles

Phoenix

BERMUDA

ATLANTIC

MOROCCO

CANARY IS.

ALGERI

Houston

W. SAHARA

Honolulu

MEXICO

Miami

BAHAMAS

MAURITANIA

MALI

HAWAII

Mexico

CUBA

HAITI DOM.
REP.

PUERTO
RICO

CAPE-
VERDE

Dakar SENEGAL

1 A.M.

PACIFIC

BELIZE
GUATEMALA HONDURAS

JAMAICA

ANTIGUA & BARBUDA

DOMINICA

GAMBIA

GUINEA-BISSAU

BURKINA
FASO

EL SALVADOR NICARAGUA

GRENADA

BARBADOS

GUINEA

BENIN N

COSTA RICA

PANAMA

TRINIDAD & TOBAGO

SIERRA LEONE

CÔTE
D'IVOIRE

GHANA

L

1 A.M.

COLOMBIA

VENEZUELA

GUYANA

LIBERIA

TOGO

SÃO TO
&
PRINCE

OCEAN

Bogotá

SURI. FR. GUIANA

Midnight

KIRIBATI

ECUADOR

INT'L DATE LINE

GÁLAPAGOS IS.

Manaus

OCEAN

Recife

Marquesas Is.
2:30 A.M.

PERU

BRAZIL

ASCENSION

Lima

PITCAIRN IS.

EASTER I.

La Paz
BOLIVIA

Rio de Janeiro

PARAGUAY

FRENCH POLYNESIA

TRISTAN DA CUNHA

CHILE

Santiago

Buenos
Aires

URUGUAY

ARGENTINA

FALKLAND
Is.

S. GEORGIA

Time Zones of the World

Standard Time Zones	3 A.M.	4 A.M.	5 A.M.	6 A.M.
Areas Using Half Hour Deviations		5:30 P.M.		

© HAMMOND WORLD ATLAS CORPORATION   HL-A-A-A

1 A.M.	2 A.M.	3 A.M.	4 A.M.	5 A.M.	6 A.M.	7 A.M.	8 A.M.	9 A.M.	10 A.M.	11 A.M.	NOON